Baseball Prospectus

2006

Mark Armour • Andrew Baharlias • Jim Baker

James Click • Clifford J. Corcoran • Clay Davenport

John Erhardt • Gary Gillette • Steven Goldman

Thomas Gorman • Gary Huckabay • Jay Jaffe

Rany Jazayerli • Christina Kahrl • Jonah Keri

Mark McClusky • Dave Pease • Dayn Perry

Nate Silver • Keith Woolner

WORKMAN PUBLISHING • NEW YORK

Library of Congress Cataloging-in-Publication Data is available.

ISBN-13: 978-0-7611-3995-9
ISBN-10: 0-7611-3995-8

Workman books are available at special discounts when
purchased in bulk for premiums and sales promotions as well
as for fund-raising or educational use. Special editions or book
excerpts can also be created to specification. For details,
contact the Special Sales Director at the address below.

Design by Barbara Balch
Cover design by Paul Gamarello

Workman Publishing Company, Inc.
708 Broadway
New York, NY 10003-9555
www.workman.com

Printed in the U.S.A.
First printing February 2006

10 9 8 7 6 5 4 3 2 1

Contents

Foreword by *Christina Kahrl* iv

Tools

Statistical Introduction 1
by *Keith Woolner, Clay Davenport, and Nate Silver*
Rearranging PECOTA by *Nate Silver* 6

Teams

Arizona Diamondbacks 13

Atlanta Braves 31

Baltimore Orioles 48

Boston Red Sox 66

Chicago Cubs 83

Chicago White Sox 99

Cincinnati Reds 117

Cleveland Indians 133

Colorado Rockies 151

Detroit Tigers 167

Florida Marlins 182

Houston Astros 195

Kansas City Royals 209

Los Angeles Angels 226

Los Angeles Dodgers 242

Milwaukee Brewers 260

Minnesota Twins 276

New York Mets 293

New York Yankees 309

Oakland Athletics 326

Philadelphia Phillies 345

Pittsburgh Pirates 360

St. Louis Cardinals 377

San Diego Padres 391

San Francisco Giants 405

Seattle Mariners 420

Tampa Bay Devil Rays 435

Texas Rangers 451

Toronto Blue Jays 467

Washington Nationals 483

Fungoes

Where Does Statistical Analysis Fall Down? Reality and Perception
by *Gary Huckabay* 499

Adventures in Win Expectancy by *Keith Woolner* 506

Iceberg Stories: The Business of Baseball, 2005–2006 by *Andrew Bahrlias* 515

Injury Accounting by *Thomas Gorman* 523

Top 50 Prospects by *Rany Jazayerli, Dayn Perry, and Baseball Prospectus* 531

Managers: The Dress Rehearsal
by *Steven Goldman, Christina Kahrl, and Keith Woolner* 542

Team Name Key and Park Factors by *Clay Davenport* 544

Index 547

Biographies 553

Foreword

by Christina Kahrl

Welcome to the eleventh edition of *Baseball Prospectus.* Whether you're a long-time reader or picking this book up for the first time, we hope you'll enjoy what you find within. Starting from the original five of us who self-indulgently decided to write the book we wanted to read, to the organization that's been built up around that core idea, it's been a long and entertaining road in getting here.

What this book is most basically about is teams and players, what happened last year, and what should happen this year. These simple goals aren't quite so simple as all that: in doing this, we have to evaluate franchises, general managers, scouting directors, and players alike, and almost always with an eye towards individual histories that exceed the time that Prospectus has existed. That means doing our homework, not simply crunching data, but learning from it, and adding that knowledge to historical fact to get a sense of both what was and why, but what will be, and why. It is because we love baseball, as both fans and professionals, that we all invest that time, and exert the same sense of curiosity, to create this book, year after year.

Whether you're the sort who automatically rejects an argument from authority and asks "show me," or if your enjoyment of the game is more straightforward than that, either way, you're a fan of the game, and that makes you our sort of person. However, we're particularly grateful to you if you've decided to have an open-minded approach to the game. A lot of what we do here is challenge assertions about the game, truisms about how it should be played, and observations of how it is played. That does not automatically involve a disrespect towards older methods and older approaches. We've consistently advanced the idea that the best-run organizations are the ones that will add statistical analysis to their other methods of evaluating managers or GMs, players or teams. There's more than one way to win, and more than one way to build a winner. The best baseball executives, past, present, and future, will utilize a lot of the ideas we present here, but they'll be successful because these will not be the only ideas they use.

We also devote a lot of time talking about the things that happen in the baseball industry that happen away from the diamond. Although we all enjoy the action on the field first and foremost, it's important to recognize that the industry of baseball is a business. Sports coverage in this country has long since moved beyond the playing field and into the boardroom, but readers tend to be as ill-served by the media away from the field as on it. As a result, in the same way that we try to use data to parse what's really happening in games, we cover what actually happens within the game, whether in baseball's always-contentious labor negotiations, an owner's attempt to coax local politicos into giving him a stadium, or the feudalistic way in which the Washington Nationals have been managed by Major League Baseball. Whether you're a fan or a voter, it makes sense to understand what people in the industry are doing, and not just settle for listening to what they're saying.

Our most basic goal is to expand what we know about baseball, and as much fun as that is from the start, that ambition comes with a responsibility. Both we and you need to keep in mind is that, whether what we bring up here or in our daily content at www.baseballprospectus .com, neither we nor our arguments are infallible. That means recognizing when we're wrong as well as enjoying when we're right. A good part of what we do is sort out what happened and why, even when that means popping the hood and sorting out what we've done wrong.

This happens less on the analysis side of things than when we advance our own educated guesses as to what we think the numbers are telling us. Last year, we were extremely skeptical of the chances of both the Houston Astros and the Chicago White Sox, not just whether or not they'd win their divisions, but whether or not they'd be able to post winning records. In both cases, the teams proved us spectacularly wrong, and in both cases, they relied on basic building blocks as old as the game itself, quality starting pitching and power hitting, and anyone from John McGraw to Earl Weaver to Ozzie Guillen will tell you those are things you want. But both teams validated much of what we've said over the years: filling out your roster with free talent and homegrown organizational soldiers, finding relief pitching on the cheap instead of buying it with top dollar, and managing your team's pitching assets carefully. That doesn't make us right, but it should make us appreciate how much Kenny Williams and Tim Purpura were. It gives us an extra appreciation for Williams's bold moves this past winter. Individual rules for how good teams stay good might change, but Williams's radical roster reconstruction after victory comes straight from the playbooks of Branch Rickey or George Weiss.

This year's book has a few differences from those of years past. We decided to add more player comments by cutting down on some full-length player comments, and adding the shorter "Line Outs" section to the end of each chapter. We also felt that adding some commentary and data for managers was a critical addition, so this year, you'll find an initial effort on that score. But perhaps best of all, we've made space for an outstanding collection of "Fungoes," touching on every aspect of the game. Some of these deal with important issues that transcend any one season, particularly Gary Huckabay's cautions on the limits of statistical analysis and Andrew Baharlias's observations on the game's significant legal questions. But we also have a pair of excellent analytical pieces in Thomas Gorman's analysis of injuries and their impact on the National League West this past season, and Keith Woolner's further explorations of Win Expectancy and what it tells us about player performance.

In the end, this book isn't about bromides as it is about teamwork. Like any team, that means working together towards a common goal, and giving you the best baseball annual possible. The extent to which this is a shared goal between Baseball Prospectus contributors old and new alike is probably best reflected in the tireless efforts of my co-editor, Steven Goldman. In his two years with the team, no one has been more committed to producing a quality product, both here and in his unstinting efforts as editor of our book on the Red Sox victory in 2004, *Mind Game.* Fortune gave me the opportunity to edit Steven's first book, *Forging Genius,* and also served as the foundation of the friendship and camaraderie that, for me, made editing this year's annual perhaps the most entertaining of any of the eleven. His generosity of spirit, as well as that of his wife Stefanie, is something more precious to me than words permit.

The data that makes up the basic framework of this book is the product of the unstinting efforts of Keith Woolner, Clay Davenport, and Nate Silver. Working to weave together several different data streams, an interpretive model, several analytical tools, and a projection system, Keith, Clay and Nate might be the team's best acrobats within the annual exercise in monkey-juggling that putting this book together requires.

Beyond Steven and I, several other people spent considerable time laboring on this book's production, ironing out wrinkles and making the quick assembly of this book possible. Will Weiss has been a colleague of Steve's at the YES Network for years, and between his sharp eye and enthusiasm for the project, made both my life and Steven's easier in his editorial contributions. Ben Murphy has graduated from Baseball Prospectus intern to the man who makes all things possible, and where past years involved the laborious cutting and pasting of player data into team

chapters, Ben's programming skills eliminated the labor and saved us considerable time. Although everyone on the Prospectus data team deserves more credit than I've already given them, it's important to single out James Click for his quick responses to any author's data query. Most of the charts and tables in this book are the product of his mastery of data, as well as his careful re-framing of the most ill-phrased request.

I also have to give tremendous credit to the authors whose work you'll find within. From old hands and fellow founders like Rany Jazayerli or Clay Davenport to the new additions to the Prospectus team, we're fortunate to command so much loyalty and enthusiasm in a project this large. To a certain level, when it comes to writing a team chapter, there's a knack to it, and some are better at it than others. Three rookie authors in this year's edition truly stand out, which is why I'd like to thank John Erhardt, Jay Jaffe, and Cliff Corcoran specifically for their contributions.

As a matter of practical logistics, few designers could handle a project with this unique balance of size and quick turnaround times. We have been uniquely gifted to have found perhaps the only design team capable of doing it, the husband and wife team of Pen & Palette, Don and Jan Rodgers. They've been working on this project for nine of the last eleven years, and it's impossible to imagine being able to deliver a finished book without them. Beyond their unflappability in the face of impossible deadlines and commitment to delivering the best layout and design work, it's my good fortune to consider them friends.

The publishing industry provides us with further assistance, and without any of these people, we wouldn't be here. First, we should note our reliance and gratitude for the patience and guidance of our agent, Sydelle Kramer. At Workman, we're grateful to both Peter Workman and Richard Rosen for their enthusiasm for the project, year after year, and also to Katherine Camargo and her staff in Production. On the publicity side, we felt Workman had spoiled us with Stacey Alper's unstinting effort in years past, but we've been delightfully well-served by Oleg Lyubner, who has stepped into her shoes.

Finally, beyond these more directly involved people, Baseball Prospectus as an organization and as a resource would fall well short of providing you with the quality content for which we're known without the assistance, insight, contributions, or observations of innumerable people both inside and outside the industry. While we're no doubt going to forget some, we do want to offer our heartfelt thanks to Cory Schwartz, Gary Gillete, Pete Palmer, Tom Fontaine, David Smith, Ted Turocy, Neal Davis, Cleve Corner, Dr. David Tate, Ted Frank, Jim Fonseca, Neal Traven, Jay Jaffe, Nick Stone, Alex Ciepley, Wendy Wolf, Alex Belth, Jim Charlton, Keith Scherer, F. X. Flinn, Andy Andres, Kevin Goldstein, King Kaufman, Rich Lederer,

Larry Mahnken, Rob McMillin, Marc Normandin, Peter Quadrino, Peter Schworm, Dave Studenmund, Darren Viola, Lee Froehlich, Jon Weisman, Sherri and Dave Nichols, Jim Hendry, Doug White, Christian Ruzich, Brad Davies, Louie Belina, Jeff Erickson, Bernie Miklasz, Brian Kenny, Bob Ley, Fred Claire, Ed Randall, Jamey Newberg, Vicky Gillette, Brent Gambill, Dave Cokin, Alan Schwarz, John Sickels, Rob Neyer, David Leonhardt, Allen Barra, Lynn Lashbrook, Charlie White, Rob Goldman, Stu Shea, Mike Murphy (both of them), Jane Kravcik-Murphy, Annie Schulz, Bill Bavasi, David Cameron, Derek Zumsteg, Jeff Shaw, John Schuerholz, Tim Purpura, Kevin Towers, Brad Kullman, Jim Caple, Matt Oshinsky, Josh Levin, David Schoenfield, Eric Neel, Ken Rosenthal, Brad Wochomurka, Chris Schofield, Mike Rice, Jon Daniels, Mark Newman, Keith Law, J.P. Ricciardi, Tony LaCava, Michael Hindman, Brian Parker, John Lombardo, Jeff Bridich, Marc Gustafson, Chuck McMichael, Scott Boras, Billy Beane, David Forst, Sandy Alderson, Bryn Alderson, Tyler Pope, Farhan Zaidi, Wayne Krivsky, Mark Shapiro, Jeff Moorad, John Henry, Paul Mahler, Dick Craswell, John Abbamondi, Michael Solomon, Paul Dickson, Josh Lewin, George Foster, Bill Walsh, Jeff Passan, Tom Gisriel, Terry Ryan, Jim Bowden, Dan Patrick, Louie Belina, Mike Sorce, Andrew Friedman, Brian Cashman, Scott Davis, John Vohs, Blake Davis, Ted Turner, Ron Shandler, Brad Wilkerson, Jason Kubel, Chris Antonetti, Matt Tagliaferri, Peter Gammons, Jayson Stark, Tom Tippett, Rodney Fort, Steve Phillips, Fred Harner, Ken Warren, Theron Skyles, Brian Sabean, Dick Tidrow, Kim Ng, Ben Baumer, Eddie Epstein, Joe Posnanski, Bob Dutton, Chris Pittaro, Eric Kubota, Dick Dorf, Pat Gillick, Eddie Bane, Gary Hughes, Richard Chow, Jeffrey Lissack, George Schofield, Kathy Schofield, Dave Kaval, Tod Johnson, Matthew Raphaelson, Paul Miramonti, John Mayne, Dan Young, Alex Rodriguez, F.P. Santangelo, Craig Counsell, Walt Jocketty, Ben Murphy, Tony LaRussa, Gerry Hunsicker, Cliff Pennington, Bill King, Gord Ash, John Abbamondi, Joe Ritzo, Shawn Holliday, Bobby Evans, Matthew Blankenheim, John Manuel, Kevin Goldstein, Stan Conte, Dan Noffsinger, Dany Berghoff, Joe Adler, Mark Johnson, Sam Geaney, Toby Hyde, Roger Caplinger, James Andrews, Mike Reinold, Cecilia Garibay, Glenn Fleisig, Scott Nelson, Jim Matthew Leach, Dinn Mann, Tim Kremchek, Lewis Yocum, Lonnie Soloff, Stan Conte, Keith Meister, Ben Cherington, David Laurilia, Adam Fox, Brandon Magee, Jason Karegeannes, Sean Passanisi, Ben Murphy, Chris Long, and the Padres for the BP ballpark event that was simply outstanding. Thomas Gorman would like to credit both Dave Haller and Mike Groopman for the research assistance they provided him for his essay, "Injury Accounting." We'd also like to specifically thank Rob Neyer for suggesting that we junk leagues and simply list all of the teams alphabetically. We're in the age of interleague play, after all.

Christina Kahrl
Fairfax, Virginia
January 29, 2006

Statistical Introduction

by Clay Davenport, Nate Silver, and Keith Woolner

In this book, Baseball Prospectus presents the most advanced analytical view of a player available, in print or on-line. In doing so, we employ some techniques unique to Baseball Prospectus. This section will serve as an introduction to those methods for the first-time reader, as well as a heads-up on some changes introduced this year for our loyal long-time readers.

Each player is represented by their statistics from every significant stint in the majors, minors, or prominent international leagues (Japanese and Mexican) between 2003 and 2005 . Let's take the big guy in Philly, for example, in table 1.

The first line of the entry contains the player's name and some basic biographical information. This year, we've added each player's batting and throwing hand and his height and weight, as well as presenting his primary position, birthdate, and age. The next line shows the headers for the columns of data that follow, where each horizontal line represents one stint of the player's career with some team.

The first few columns of data show time and assignment data, such as what year and team. This year, instead of the minor *league,* we're presenting the minor league level: the major leagues, Triple-A, Double-A, Hi A-ball (A+), A-ball, Short-Season A-ball (A−), and Rookie ball (Rk). For each season, we also show how old the player was at the time. For "age" in individual seasons, we always use the player's effective "baseball age," his age as of July 1 of that year.

The next few columns—PA (Plate Appearances), R, 2B, 3B, HR, RBI, BB, SO, SB, and CS—show the actual statistical totals the player compiled in those categories during this playing stint. Long-time readers will note that the stat columns have been changed this year, most notably by adding runs scored and RBI.

SPEED is another new addition this year. SPEED is a composite metric that accounts for five characteristics related to a player's baseball speed: stolen base percentage, stolen base attempts as a percentage of opportunities, triples, double plays grounded into as a percentage of opportunities, and runs scored as a percentage of times on base. Calculating Speed Scores was originally the brainchild of Bill James, but we have developed our own version that takes better advantage of play-by-play data. An average SPEED score is exactly 5.0; Carl Crawford's SPEED last year was 7.6, while Mike Piazza's was 3.4.

The next three columns (BA, OBP, SLG) show the three most commonly used rate statistics in raw, unadjusted form, batting average, on-base percentage, and slugging average.

Most of Baseball Prospectus's unique statistical insight on player evaluation comes in the remaining columns. The next column is Marginal Lineup Value Rate, or MLVR. Marginal Lineup Value estimates the value of a player by computing the change in expected run scoring between an average team, and a team with eight average players, plus our "hero." If we were to swap one of the nine average players for the 2005 version of Derrek Lee, we would, naturally,

TABLE 1. HITTER STATISTICS EXAMPLE

RYAN HOWARD   **1B**   **Bats: L Throws: L**   Height: 6' 4"   Weight: 230   Born: November 19, 1979   Age: 26

YEAR	TM	LVL	AGE	PA	R	2B	3B	HR	RBI	BB	SO	SB	CS	SPEED	BA	OBP	SLG	MLVR	EQBA	EQOBP	EQSLG	EQA	VORP	DEFENSE	
2003	CLR	A+	23	553	67	32	1	23	82	50	151	0	0	3.3	.304	.374	.514	.324	.267	.325	.478	.271	17.6	114-1B	10
2004	REA	AA	24	433	73	18	1	37	102	46	129	1	2	3.5	.297	.386	.647	.410	.255	.332	.543	.287	23.8	97-1B	3
2004	SWB	AAA	24	127	21	10	0	9	29	14	37	0	0	3.6	.270	.362	.604	.286	.233	.325	.515	.279	4.4	29-1B	-1
2004	PHI	MLB	24	42	5	5	0	2	5	2	13	0	0	3.3	.282	.333	.564	.237	.282	.333	.538	.287	2.9		
2005	SWB	AAA	25	257	38	19	0	16	54	39	66	0	0	3.3	.371	.467	.690	.678	.332	.426	.611	.342	36.2	57-1B	-4
2005	PHI	MLB	25	348	52	17	2	22	63	33	100	0	1	4.6	.288	.356	.567	.265	.281	.352	.565	.299	23.5	80-1B	-3
2006	*PHI*	*MLB*	*26*	*538*	*79*	*28*	*1*	*41*	*108*	*61*	*147*	*0*	*1*	*4.0*	*.286*	*.375*	*.612*	*.311*	*.285*	*.375*	*.615*	*.314*	*46.6*	*126-1B*	*-1*

Breakout: 39%   *Improve: 63%*   *Collapse: 15%*   *Attrition: 4%*   *Comparables: Travis Hafner, Mo Vaughn, Mike Epstein*

expect his team to score more runs. Similarly, if you replaced one such player with Cristian Guzman, expected run scoring would decrease.

Batting Order	Team A	Team B	Team C
1	Joe Average	Joe Average	Joe Average
2	Joe Average	Joe Average	Joe Average
3	Joe Average	Joe Average	Joe Average
4	Joe Average	Joe Average	Joe Average
5	Joe Average	DERREK LEE	CHRISTIAN GUZMAN
6	Joe Average	Joe Average	Joe Average
7	Joe Average	Joe Average	Joe Average
8	Joe Average	Joe Average	Joe Average
9	Joe Average	Joe Average	Joe Average
Expected runs/game	4.571	5.102	4.301
Difference in runs/game versus Team A	0	+0.531	−0.270

Since the difference in expected run scoring between Team A and Team B is entirely due to having Derrek Lee in the lineup, we call this difference his Marginal Lineup Value Rate (MLV). Marginal Lineup Value (MLV) is the number of runs a player adds or subtracts over an entire season, while MLVR is his MLV divided by the number of games that the he participated in. The distinction between MLV and MLVR is simple: MLVR is a rate of production (how well the player did on a per game basis), while MLV measures total hitting contribution by including how often he played. MLV itself is not printed in this book, but it does form the basis for VORP, which is discussed below.

As you can see in the case of Cristian Guzman, contributing a negative MLVR is certainly possible, and actually quite common.

The next three columns are EQBA, EQOBP, EQSLG. These are our "translated" rate statistics. Baseball Prospectus's Davenport Translations convert a player's statistics to a common baseline, adjusting for the player's home park, the offensive environment of the league he plays in, and, perhaps most importantly, the difficulty of the competition he plays against. Slugging .647 against Eastern League competition, as Howard did in 2004, is not the same thing as slugging .647 in the majors. Similarly, good pitchers in the Eastern League will be able to post better ERAs and strikeout rates than they would in the majors. Most fans intuitively understand this concept. The translation process adjusts for the lesser quality of opposition and converts the player's performance did to an "equivalent" (hence, the EQ- prefix) major league performance. Thus, EQBA, EQOBP, and EQSLG can be used to make an apples-to-apples comparison of any two players in organized baseball.

EQA is Equivalent Average. Like MLVr, EQA is a rate statistic, and measures the player's total offensive value to his team, combining the abilities to reach base, hit for power, and steal bases. It is also a fully adjusted static: it takes into account park factors, and a league's average offense. Unlike MLVr, the EQAs we show in BP 2006 are calculated from the player's translated statistics; they represent how his performance would look from a major league standpoint. EQA is essentially runs produced per out made, although we've applied some mathematical trickery to make the result easier to understand. One problem shared by most "new" statistics is that casual fans have no intuitive feel for their scale; even if you know that a given score is above average, it takes time to learn how to distinguish "All-Star" good from "MVP" good. As a result of the mathematical trickery mentioned, EQA sidesteps that problem by masquerading as a batting average. An average player, by definition, will hit .260. You can think of an EQA as good or bad in exactly the same way you would consider a batting average to be good or bad. If .260 is average, an EQA of .300 makes you a legitimate star. Something like .350 is a typical league-leading total, as it was last year, when Alex Rodriguez led the American League with a .351 EQA and Derrek Lee led the NL with a .344. A .400 EQA is exceptionally rare, but the greatest hitters in history—Ruth, Mantle, Williams, Bonds—have pulled it off. On the other hand, if your EQA is .220, you'd better be a great defensive player, or you'll be heading back to the minors.

The second-to-last column in Howard's statistical record is VORP, which stands for Value Over Replacement Level. VORP is an estimate of total player value, which builds on MLVR and incorporates the position the player plays, how many games he played, and what "replacement level" is for his position.

Replacement level is a concept discussed in great detail in the article "Understanding and Measuring Replacement Level" by Keith Woolner, which was published in *Baseball Prospectus 2002,* so we'll only summarize the main points here. Metrics such as MLVR, which compare a player to league-average offense, are incomplete because they do not account for the value of having a player healthy and in the lineup. Losing a starting player typically results in more starts being given to a bench player who is significantly below average. By comparing a player's production to the level of a typical bench player or "Quadruple-A" journeyman (which we dub replacement level), we recognize the value of a player's durability.

The article in *BP2002* defined replacement level as "the expected level of performance a major league team can receive from one or more of the best available players who substitute for a suddenly unavailable starting player at the same position and who can be (or were) obtained with minimal expenditure of team resources." The concept of VORP is equally applicable to position players or pitchers.

VORP is available on the BP web site ([www.baseball prospectus.com](www.baseballprospectus.com)) for all players and seasons going back over 40 years, and is updated daily during the season. A couple of additional details about how VORP is presented for *minor* league players:

- VORP for minor leaguers is computed using their translated rates of production, and so should be considered to be their major-league equivalent VORP, not their VORP relative to the minor league they actually played in.

- Minor league players are rated at their most frequently played position, rather than a weighted average across all positions they appeared at (as is done with major league players). That is, if a minor league player plays 100 games at second base, and 20 at shortstop, he would be considered to be purely a second baseman in calculating his VORP. If a major league player played 100 games at second, and 20 at shortstop, we would his compute his VORP on a weighted average basis, with second base having 5x the weight of shortstop (100 G@2B / 20 G@SS = 5).

- Minor leagues have shorter seasons than the majors do, and as a result, even excellent translated rates of production may not produce as high a VORP as for a player with the benefit of a 162 game schedule.

Although VORP looks at what position a player appears at, it does not directly consider how well he fields that position. Thus we turn to the final column in the batter's lines, Defense, to show the position, number of games, and fielding rating for the player at his primary position(s). The fielding rating is denominated in runs, thus Howard's 2005 line in Philadelphia which reads "80-1B -3" means he played the equivalent of 80 full games at first base, with a defensive performance that's three runs below average for first basemen.

The 2006 year line is the PECOTA projection for the player in the upcoming season.

Note that the player is projected into the league and park context as indicated by his team abbreviation; Johnny Damon is now a Yankee, and so forth. All PECOTAs represent a player's projected major league performance.

The numbers beneath a 2006 forecast line are slightly different this year. Breakout, Improve, Collapse, and Attrition are also a part of PECOTA, and estimate the likelihood of changes in performance relative to a player's previously-established level of production. PECOTA differs from other projection systems in that it uses historical comparables data to generate a probability distribution, rather

than just a single forecast line. History might tell us, for example, that an old, slow hitter will manage just fine eighty percent of the time, but will have a disastrous, career-ending season (a "collapse") twenty percent of the time. Conversely, a young pitcher with a high walk rate might show a sudden and marked improvement (a "breakout") fifteen percent of the time, while failing to improve much at all in his other seasons. The Breakout, Collapse, Improve, and Attrition numbers are an attempt to quantify these sorts of performance changes. To be more precise about it:

- **Breakout Rate** is the percent chance that a hitter's equivalent runs produced per PA, or a pitcher's EQERA (see more on our pitcher stats below), will improve by at least 20% relative to the weighted average of his performance over his most recent seasons of 2003–2005 (with 2005 performance weighted more heavily). High breakout rates are indicative of upside risk.

- **Improve Rate** is the percent chance that a hitter's equivalent runs produced per PA, or a pitcher's EQERA, will improve *at all* relative to his baseline performance. A player who is expected to perform just the same as he has in the recent past will have an Improve Rate of 50%. Note that Breakout Rate is a subset of Improve Rate; Improve Rate is the chance that a player improves *at all;* Breakout Rate is the chance that he improves *a lot.*

- **Collapse Rate** is the percent chance that a position player's equivalent runs produced per PA, or a pitcher's EQERA, will decline by at least 25% relative to his baseline performance over his past three seasons. High collapse rates are indicative of downside risk.

- **Attrition Rate,** new to the book this year, operates on playing time rather than performance. Specifically, it measures the likelihood that a hitter's plate appearances, or a pitcher's innings pitched, will decrease by at least 50% relative to his established level. Attrition Rate captures any reason for substantial playing time decline, including catastrophic injuries, but also a player being benched, retiring in midseason, or anything similar.

Breakout Rate and Collapse Rate can sometimes be counterintuitive for players who have already experienced a radical change in their performance levels. For example, PECOTA assigns to Adrian Beltre a Collapse Rate of 25%, even though it expects him to perform better than he did in 2005. This is because PECOTA is comparing its expectation for Beltre's 2006 performance to a weighted average of the past *three* years, including his lofty 2004, which boosts Beltre's average. Also note that we now describe a pitcher's Breakout, Improve, and Collapse Rates in terms of EQERA, whereas previous editions of the book used PERA. Finally, note that these metrics do not necessarily represent a change in performance as a result of a change in underlying ability or skill, and will also capture a player regressing to the mean after having had unusually good or bad luck. For example, Jarrod Washburn's ERAs have been much lower than his PERAs (see description below) over the course of his past three seasons; this is almost always the result of favorable luck. Washburn has a substantial Collapse Rate of 28%, but this may just mean that we expect his luck to return to normal, not that he's going to lose his fastball.

The final piece of information, listed just to the right of the hitter's Attrition Rate, are his three highest scoring comparable players, as determined by PECOTA. PECOTA evaluates comparability by analyzing a number of quantifiable factors, including production metrics (batting average, isolated power), usage metrics (plate appearances, major league career length, minor league level), phenotypic attributes (handedness, height, and weight), and a player's defensive position. Although we list only a player's three best comparables here, PECOTA uses as many as a hundred comparables in producing a player's forecast, in order to provide itself with a robust enough sample. Occasionally, a player's top three comparables will not be representative of the larger sample that PECOTA uses.

Established major leaguers are compared to other major leaguers only; minor league players may be compared to major league or minor league players. All comparables represent a snapshot of how a historical player was performing at the age of the current player; a 23 year-old being compared to Sammy Sosa is much different than a 31-year-old being compared to him.

Now, let's take a look at a pitcher's entry in table 2.

The first line and the YEAR, TM, LVL, and AGE columns are the same as in the hitter's example above, and should be self-explanatory. The next set of columns—W, L,

SV, G, GS, IP, H, BB, SO, HR—are the actual, unadjusted totals compiled by the pitcher during this stint.

The next set of columns is different for 2006. First is GB%, which is the percentage of all batted balls that were hit on the ground. For 2005, we have ground/fly data for all batted balls, including both outs and base hits. Prior to 2005, however, our data sources only provided such data for outs. Because ground balls are more likely to be turned into outs than fly balls are, the average GB% measured only from outs will be higher than for all batted balls. Furthermore, measuring GB% using just outs can be skewed by having an unusually good (or bad) infield or outfield defense. Therefore, we prefer to measure GB% using all batted balls, including both outs and hits.

To make sure that 2005 GB% data matches that of previous seasons, we've gone back to older years, and estimated the likelihood that a given hit is a grounder, fly ball, line drive, or popup. For example, based on the 2005 complete data, a single may be a line drive 45% of the time, a ground ball 30% of the time, a fly ball 20% of the time, and a popup 5% of the time. We use these estimates for every hit that a pitcher gave up to create a truer picture of his groundball tendencies. Also note that traditional G/F ratios may exclude line drives and popups. The GB% reported here is groundballs as a percentage of *all* batted balls put into play, including line drives and popups, and not just ground balls and fly balls. The average GB% for a major league pitcher was about 45% in 2005.

BABIP is batting average on balls in play, a statistic popularized by Voros McCracken's discoveries about the relatively small influence a pitcher has over the outcomes of balls in play. A high BABIP is most likely due to a poor defense, or bad luck, rather than a pitcher's own performance, and may be a good indicator of a potential rebound. BABIP excludes home runs, strikeouts, walks, and times hit by pitch, since these are not considered balls hit into play. A typical league-average BABIP is about .290.

The next column is STUFF. Stuff is a shorthand rating of a pitcher's demonstrated skills, relative to his age and level; its primary use is to evaluate prospects, not

TABLE 2. PITCHER STATISTICS EXAMPLE

FELIX HERNANDEZ   Bats: R   Throws: R   Height: 6' 3"   Weight: 170   Born: April 8, 1986   Age: 20

YEAR	TM	LVL	AGE	W	L	SV	G	GS	IP	H	BB	SO	HR	GB%	BABIP	STUFF	WHIP	ERA	PERA	EQERA	EQH9	EQBB9	EQSO9	EQHR9	VORP	WXRL
2003	EVE	A-	17	7	2	0	11	7	55.0	43	24	73	2	—	.308	28	1.22	2.29	4.96	4.44	8.7	4.6	7.2	1.0	6.8	—
2003	WIS	A	17	0	0	0	2	2	14.0	9	3	18	1	—	.250	13	0.86	1.93	4.85	4.15	8.3	2.1	8.3	2.1	2.1	—
2004	SBR	A+	18	9	3	0	16	15	92.0	85	26	114	5	—	.345	40	1.21	2.74	4.20	4.10	8.8	3.1	7.3	0.9	15.0	—
2004	SAN	AA	18	5	1	0	10	10	57.3	47	21	58	3	—	.282	35	1.19	3.30	4.37	4.37	8.1	3.6	6.8	0.8	7.6	—
2005	TAC	AAA	19	9	4	0	19	14	88.0	62	48	100	3	57	.277	45	1.25	2.25	3.68	2.94	7.1	4.7	8.1	0.3	25.3	—
2005	SEA	MLB	19	4	4	0	12	12	84.3	61	23	77	5	68	.257	53	1.00	2.67	3.25	2.82	7.0	2.5	8.2	0.5	28.1	3.1
2006	*SEA*	*MLB*	*20*	*11*	*8*	*0*	*30*	*30*	*175.0*	*152*	*67*	*158*	*11*	*55%*	*.288*	*29*	*1.25*	*3.27*	*3.51*	*3.70*	*7.7*	*3.4*	*7.6*	*0.5*	*38.8*	*5.4*

Breakout: 15%   Improve: 40%   Collapse: 22%   Attrition: 6%   Comparables: Bert Blyleven, Jim Palmer, Curt Simmons

established major league pitchers. An average major league starter, or a pitcher who has show the talent to eventually become an average major league starter, will score a 10. Pitchers who score above 20 are excellent prospects; those above 30 belong the ranks of the truly elite. The largest single component of STUFF is strikeout rate, but walk rate, home run rate, hit rate, ERA, innings pitched per game, age, and age relative to league all figure into the final STUFF rating.

The WHIP and ERA columns are familiar to most fans, and fantasy owners in particular. WHIP is the number of baserunners allowed per inning [(**W**alks + **H**its)/**IP**], which makes it analogous to OBP. ERA the pitcher's earned run average. Both of these statistics are unadjusted and untranslated.

The next column is Peripheral ERA, abbreviated as PERA. PERA is the Equivalent ERA (EQERA) a pitcher would be expected to have given his Equivalent rate stats: EqH9, EqBB9, EqSO9, and EqHR9 (see below). A PERA lower than a pitcher's actual EQERA may indicate that he was somewhat unlucky, and could be expected to improve his EQERA next season even without substantial change in peripheral rates of production.

The next five columns, all starting with "EQ," are the pitcher's rates of production (hits allowed per nine innings, strikeouts per nine innings, etc.) based on his "translated" statistics. As with the hitter example above, a pitcher's raw statistics are adjusted and converted to a neutral-park major league equivalent performance. We present the translated (or equivalent) ERA (EQERA), as well as the per 9 inning rates of hits allowed (EQH9), walks issued (EQBB9), strikeouts recorded (EQSO9), and home runs surrendered (EQHR9).

VORP is again Value Over Replacement Player. Based on the translated statistics, a pitcher's VORP is the number of extra runs that a replacement level pitcher would have allowed to score if he pitched the same number of innings as this pitcher. Slightly different standards are applied for starting and relief pitchers.

The final column is WXRL, which is another new feature for 2006. It refers to "**W**ins e**X**pected above **R**eplacement and adjusted for **L**ineup faced." It is aggregated from each pitcher's actual outing, using the Win Expectation framework introduced in *BP2005*. For starting pitchers, the acronym SNLVAR (derived from BP's longtime Support Neutral Win-Loss statistics) was previously used instead of WXRL, which was previously used for relievers alone. Now, both starter and reliever value are listed under WXRL. WXRL will be present only for major league stints, and measures how many wins an average team would have been expected to win due to this pitcher's performance, as compared to a replacement level pitcher facing the same batters.

A pitcher's 2006 line represents his PECOTA projection for the upcoming season. A pitcher's PECOTA, and the Breakout Rate, Collapse Rate, Improvement Rate, and Comparables that accompany it, are determined by a parallel method to that used for hitters. This year, there are many enhancements and improvements in PECOTA, as described in Nate's article, "Rearranging PECOTA," that follows.

Rearranging PECOTA

by Nate Silver

PECOTA, as I discovered one delirious evening this December, is an anagram for (Truman) Capote. The late author, portrayed by Philip Seymour Hoffman in the 2005 movie *Capote,* attacked his subjects with a vigor so obsessive as to become debilitating. Capote did not produce a full-length work after the publication of *In Cold Blood* in 1966, and drank himself to death in 1984. Although I cracked open a bottle of Honkers Ale at the very moment that Joel Zumaya's projection had finished running, I trust that the same fate will not befall me. I can also assure you that PECOTA does not share Capote's propensity to exaggerate the truth.

In common with Capote, however, I do have an irresistible compulsion when it comes to detail. PECOTA is already the best system of its kind, and the only one that is as likely to be used by a major league GM as the guy with the armpit stains sitting next to you in your fantasy draft. But I spent several weeks this winter pouring over every detail of the system, incorporating different kinds of data, picking the brains of my colleagues at BP, and revisiting assumptions and conclusions that were out of step with my experience of watching a ballgame and watching baseball players develop. As a result, we've included a number of new features that should help PECOTA to become an even more valuable player evaluation tool.

The most obvious, but least "analytically correct," change is that we've reversed course on our established policy, and included team-dependent stats like runs, RBIs, saves, wins, and losses in this year's book. In retrospect, the change was long overdue; Christina and Steve and Keith and I made that decision about as quickly as Ozzie Guillen gets out a sentence. That notwithstanding, these categories present some challenge from a projection standpoint. For example, a projection for RBIs should ideally account for precisely where a player hits in his team's lineup, exactly how often we expect his teammates to get on base in front of him, and so forth. But we produce these forecasts in early January, long before pitchers and catchers report, or lineups are fixed. Our compromise is to look at a how a team has performed over the past couple of years, with an appropriate amount of regression to the mean built in. We'll have a better idea in March than we do in January of just how many runs the Red Sox are likely to score. It's safe to say, however, that the Red Sox are going to score more runs than the Pirates, and that is reflected in Jason Bay's RBI projection, and also Trot Nixon's. (We do update the PECOTAs throughout spring training and the early part of the regular season on our website, available for order online).

The one category that deserves some special explanation is saves. Saves are not team dependent so much as they are *opportunity* dependent. Neil Cotts could strike out 176 batters in 64 innings, but so long as he wasn't the White Sox' closer, he wouldn't rack up any saves. Moreover, the distribution of save opportunities is highly asymmetrical; in modern bullpens, pitchers either receive a large number of save opportunities, or very few.

Ordinarily, I prefer to have as little human intervention in the PECOTAs as possible, and instead endow it with the wisdom to figure a lot of things out in its own. Without that "teach a man to fish" attitude, the objectivity and credibility of the system breaks down. Fortunately, PECOTA is resourceful. I don't need to "tell" it that David Ortiz is going to have more RBI opportunities than Juan Pierre. That's common-sensical enough that even a computer can grasp it with the aid of a few simple assumptions and algorithms. But that just doesn't work in the case of saves. I have to tell PECOTA that Tom Gordon has signed with the Phillies, and that the Phillies will use him as their closer. Otherwise, it would project Gordon with two or three saves, and that's going too far in sacrificing accuracy for objectivity's sake.

That said, the system requires Gordon to earn his keep. I don't tell PECOTA to give Gordon a certain number of saves. Rather, I tell it to treat him as though he was his team's primary closer last season, the same as it treats B. J. Ryan or Mariano Rivera or Derrick Turnbow. But Gordon still needs to earn his saves by pitching well. In fact, he still needs to earn his save *opportunities.* I saw a projection the other day that had a pitcher with a 4.00 ERA but more than 40 saves. That's a patently ridiculous projection; only twice in major league history has a pitcher accumulated 40 saves with an ERA of four or higher: Antonio Alfonseca in 2000, and Lee Smith's 1993. Nine times out of ten, that pitcher will lose his job before he gets halfway to 40 saves. PECOTA, it turns out, doesn't expect a lot of saves for Gordon, but that's because it thinks that he's a decline risk, and that Ryan Madson or Cole Hamels could be finishing games by August.

My newfound enthusiasm for projecting saves aside, it's time to run through the enhancements that are a little more important from a sabermetric and valuation standpoint. There are six major changes to PECOTA's methodology this season, which I've listed in declining order of importance:

#1. "Level" Adjustment for Minor League Players

How it works: We classify the seven levels within professional baseball along a simple numeric scale, ranging from Rookie Ball (1) to the Majors (7), and assign a player a corresponding score based on the level at which he played last season. For example, a player who played half his games in the California League (High A, Level 4) and the other half in the Eastern League (Double A, Level 5), would have a level rating of 4.5.

Level has been introduced as one of the comparability factors for minor league players; we substitute it for major league career length, which is one of the comparability factors for major league players. The adjustment is relative rather than absolute; a Triple A player might be compared to a Double-A player or a Major Leaguer if he's a good match along other dimensions, but he'll almost never be compared to someone who spent his season in the Midwest League.

Why it matters: Hunter Pence is an outfielder in the Astros chain who crushed the Sally League to the tune of a .338/.438/.615 batting line last year. He was old for his league (22 last season), and played in a hitter's park, but that sort of dominance is impressive. As a result, Pence received a very favorable Davenport Translation and (initially) a very favorable PECOTA.

Table 1 shows how the "old" version of PECOTA contrasted Pence to Prince Fielder, a consensus Top 10 prospect who played in Triple-A and the majors last year.

That's what we get by comparing Pence and Fielder to players with similar DTs and similar skills sets at the

same age, without accounting above and beyond the DTs for the level at which they played. Pence not only rated as a superior prospect to Fielder, but looked as though he could be a perennial All-Star.

Now, with the level factor in place table 2 shows the results.

Pence is still an underrated prospect, And PECOTA thinks he has a good chance to have an Aaron Rowand type of career. As we now know, that's good enough to one day be in the starting lineup of a championship team. That said, any forecast that suggests he's a better prospect than Prince Fielder ought to be drawn and quartered. The level adjustment corrects for this.

In fact, the gap appears to expand with each passing year. Table 3 shows what PECOTA expects the players to do in 2010, when Pence will be 27 and Fielder only 26.

PECOTA foresees another 50–100 points worth of growth in Fielder's OPS. On the other hand, it doesn't expect Pence to grow at all. That assessment is almost eerily similar to the scouting consensus of the respective players; Pence is said to have a hitch in his swing that will prevent him from getting too much better than he is right now.

Scouts, and many performance analysts, have emphasized for years that we need to deduct credit from a player who is old for his league, and add credit to a player who is young. As a result of this relatively simple adjustment, PECOTA now sees that too. PECOTA doesn't know that Hunter Pence has a hitch in his swing (if Pence has a hitch at all), but it knows that a 22 year-old in the Sally League usually has some thing or another wrong with him, and probably won't be a major league star. In fact, while this is not necessarily something that I'd advocate, I'd trust a Top Prospects list based *purely* on the PECOTAs to hold its own against any scout-oriented list. But save for transposing a Dustin Pedroia with a Hanley Ramirez here and there, you'd be surprised at how *similar* the two lists are.

TABLE 1. PREVIOUS PECOTA, PENCE VS. FIELDER

Before 2006	BA	OBP	SLG	VORP
Pence	.290	.350	.513	32.3
Fielder	.265	.347	.478	17.8

TABLE 2. NEW PECOTA, PENCE VS. FIELDER

After 2006	BA	OBP	SLG	VORP
Pence	.267	.324	.457	17.4
Fielder	.268	.349	.489	21.0

TABLE 3. PECOTA FOR PENCE VS. FIELDER IN 2010

2010	BA	OBP	SLG	VORP
Pence	.267	.323	.469	12.3
Fielder	.281	.373	.546	31.7

#2. Starter/Reliever Adjustment

How it works: It's safe to say that pitching in relief is an easier task than starting the game. We can enumerate any number of advantages that relievers have over starters: they don't accumulate as much fatigue because they don't have to throw anything like the same number of pitches;, they don't have to figure out how to get the same hitter out several times; they don't have to retire the top of the lineup in the first inning; they aren't scouted as thoroughly; and they get the platoon advantage more often.

Certainly, there are plenty of anecdotal examples (Byung Hyun Kim, Eric Gagne, Goose Gossage) that point toward just how profound the differences between one role and the other can be. But I had never seen a comprehensive study on the subject. So, with the assistance of Keith Woolner, I pulled together a dataset of every pitcher since 1960 who pitched in both starting and relief roles with the same team in the same season. Their performances in the respective "positions" can be seen in table 4; I've weighted things by the *minimum* number of batters the pitcher faced between the two roles.

To make a long story short, a *typical starting pitcher would expect to lose a full point off his ERA if he converted to relief.* Pretty much all the peripheral statistics behave accordingly: his strikeout rate increases, his opponent's batting average goes down (both in absolute terms and on a balls-in-play basis), and he allows substantially fewer extra base hits. The lone exception is walk rate, which actually increases a little bit, but essentially that is explained by an increase in intentional walks; relievers are asked to intentionally walk hitters two or three times as often as starting pitchers. I suspect it's also the case that a reliever can throw a pitch like a splitter relatively more

often, which helps with hit prevention but is rarely thrown for strikes.

As a result of this finding, PECOTA now incorporates a starter/reliever adjustment, which operates in a similar fashion to a park adjustment. We translate the pitcher's stats to a baseline that assumes he'd pitched all of his innings as a starter, and then translate them back to relief if that's the role PECOTA expects him to assume next year.

Why it matters: I consider this to be an extremely important finding. The most essential implication is in terms of valuation. If a garden variety, "below average" 4.75 ERA starter can be converted into an "above average" 3.75 ERA setup man, that ought to call into question the way that we evaluate performance between and amongst those roles.

There are also implications that fall more directly within PECOTA's scope. For one thing, we now have the ability to "force" the system to treat a pitcher as a starter or reliever, and adjust his projection accordingly. For example, using the conversion factors above, table 5 shows what we would have expected from Pedro Martinez's and Brad Lidge's 2005 if they had exchanged roles.

Certainly, we intend to use this "force" option sparingly, but it will be very useful if another John Smoltz case comes up. More importantly, however, accounting for a pitcher's role provides us with a better understanding of his true talent level. Ryan Dempster's 2005, for example, no longer looks like such an outlier, as much of his improvement is explained by his switch in roles. PECOTA still doesn't like Dempster particularly well—Mitch Williams Part Deux = Bad—but it likes him much better than it would have without the reliever adjustment.

But the reliever adjustment has implications even for pitchers who haven't switched roles like Dempster or Smoltz. A lot of poor starting pitchers are converted to the bullpen, find the going easier, and record some nominal improvements in their rate statistics. If we weren't aware of the reliever adjustment, we might mistake it for actual improvement. In fact, this pitcher's underlying skills probably haven't improved at all, any more than a hitter's power would "improve" if he was traded to the Rockies.

TABLE 4. PITCHER PERFORMANCE COMPARISON, STARTER VS. RELIEVER

Stat	As Starter	As Reliever	Change
K	12.9%	15.0%	+16%
1B	17.1%	16.0%	-6%
2B	4.4%	3.8%	-13%
3B	0.7%	0.6%	-14%
HR	2.6%	2.1%	-19%
BB	8.9%	9.6%	+9%
IBB	0.5%	1.4%	+159%
HBP	0.6%	0.7%	+7%
RA	5.45	4.36	-20%
ERA	4.96	3.93	-21%

TABLE 5. PECOTA EFFECT IN PROJECTING SWITCHED PITCHING ROLE PERFORMANCE

	IP	H	HR	BB	K	ERA
Pedro's 2005 as a Reliever	93.7	61	7	22	103	2.23
Lidge's 2005 as a Starter	162.3	149	14	49	207	2.89

Rather, he's been demoted to the level of his maximum competence.

In other words, by understanding and accounting for the reliever adjustment, we get less noise and more signal. As a result, the standard deviation on the pitcher projections is much higher this year; PECOTA is better able to differentiate the good pitchers from the bad ones. Last year, 56% of our pitcher projections wound up with an EQERA between 4.00 and 5.00, within half a point of the league average. This year, that number is 27%. Pitching is still comparatively hard to predict, but we're coming closer to breaking the code.

#3. Enhanced Park Factors

How it works: Previous versions of the PECOTAs used a simple, two factor park adjustment. We figured a park's impact on runs and home runs and backed into everything else from there. This worked well enough, but we have a wealth of play by play data going back to 1960, and it would be a shame to not to put it to use. For this year and going forward, we've calculated the park factor for every component separately—doubles, home runs, walks, even groundball/flyball ratio—and come up with separate factors for left-handed and right-handed hitters.

This turned out to require more finesse than I initially anticipated. Breaking things down by handedness and attempting to determine explicit park factors for the more obscure statistics like triples introduces some sample size problems. As a result, I went back and built a database listing the field dimensions, physical characteristics (e.g., grass versus turf), and geographic features (altitude, average temperature) of every major league park since 1945. These characteristics were combined with multi-year averages from our play-by-play database to produce what I believe are the most accurate park factors ever created, and are certainly the most detailed.

I should make clear that *most* of the park factor is determined from the play-by-play data. But accounting for things like altitude and distance to the power alleys serves as a sanity check against sample size flukes, and materially improves our ability to understand the way that a park plays. For that matter, we also build in a small but appropriate amount of regression to the mean. Last year, U.S. Cellular Field had a home run factor of 1354 for left-handed hitters, but 1159 for right-handed hitters. That outcome is probably a fluke; The Cell hasn't played that way in the recent past, and the small difference in distance to the alleys (377 to left field, 372 to right) isn't enough to explain it. We wound up determining that U.S. Cellular's "true" home run park factor for 2005 is 1170 for right-handed hitters, and 1200 for lefties.

Keep in mind that PECOTA's mission is to understand as best as we possibly can the true talent level of a baseball player. In order to do that, we want to eliminate the effects of luck stemming from small sample sizes: we want to know how The Cell would have played if the Sox played a million games there in 2005, rather than 81. You would not necessarily want to do things this way if you were attempting to evaluate players post-facto, rather than predicting how they're going to perform in the future.

Why it matters: Sean Casey was traded from the Reds to the Pirates this winter; he is a left-handed hitter whose value is in hitting a lot of singles and doubles. It would be natural enough to assume that this change in home parks will hurt his numbers; the G.A.B. is (somewhat incorrectly) thought of as a great hitter's park, and PNC as a neutral park. But PNC happens to give up more doubles to lefties than any park in the majors, and more singles to lefties than any park but Coors Field. It is the park that Sean Casey's mother would have built for her sonny boy.

The resulting effect on Casey's PECOTA can be seen in table 6. We'll also show you how we'd expect him to perform in Minute Maid Park, a facility that favors right-handed power hitters at the expense of everyone else (consider it the park that Casey's ex-girlfriend would have built for him).

Not only do Casey's raw statistics project better in PNC, but so does his VORP. Yes, VORP is adjusted for park effects, but it is adjusted based on how a *typical* hitter can expect to perform in his home park. Casey, given his handedness and skills profile, will take more advantage of PNC than a typical hitter would, and as a result, he really is more valuable in that ballpark. Of course, that value added will evaporate as soon as Casey leaves Pittsburgh and bats on the road, but in the meantime he's nearly a full win better as a Pirate than he would be if he was an Astro.

PECOTA "forecasts" of the overall park factors for 2006 are provided for reference in table 7. We have accounted for the change in playing dimensions in San Diego and Philadelphia, though we shouldn't expect any dramatic turnaround: only a single fence is being moved in each locale, and even then, only by a few feet. There's

TABLE 6. PARK COMPARISON WITH PECOTA EFFECT

Sean Casey	BA	OBP	SLG	VORP
Great American Ball Park	.298	.357	.428	14.6
PNC Park	.308	.366	.439	19.3
Minute Maid Park	.290	.349	.410	11.1

TABLE 7. PECOTA 2006 PARK FACTOR FORECASTS

Park	RH	LH	Park	RH	LH	Park	RH	LH	Park	RH	LH	Park	RH	LH
ARI	1050	1050	CIN	1010	1010	KCA	990	970	NYN	960	980	SFN	990	970
ATL	1000	1010	CLE	990	980	LAA	990	960	OAK	1000	980	SLN	1000	1000
BAL	1000	980	COL	1160	1160	LAN	970	980	PHI	1010	1030	TBA	960	980
BOS	1040	1010	DET	970	1000	MIL	1010	1000	PIT	980	1050	TEX	1040	1060
CHA	1040	1070	FLO	970	960	MIN	990	1010	SDN	930	950	TOR	1050	1020
CHN	1020	1000	HOU	1020	940	NYA	980	990	SEA	960	1000	WAS	930	920

also a new stadium in St. Louis; we expect, based on its reported dimensions, that Busch II will increase base hits but reduce home runs, and play about neutrally overall.

#4. Kinder, Gentler Playing Time Assumptions

What it is: Let's say that Carlos Zambrano has ten comparable pitchers that we use to inform his PECOTA forecast. He actually has many more than ten comparables—PECOTA uses as many as 100 for comparables for "common" types of players—but let's assume that Zambrano has ten comps the sake of this exercise. Let's say that nine of the ten comparables stay healthy, and pitch 220 big league innings apiece. The tenth comp blows out his rotator cuff in April, and pitches only 20 innings. How should we forecast Zambrano's playing time?

Well, we could take the average (220 times nine, plus 20, divided by ten) which works out to 200 innings. That's a perfectly reasonable way to do things, and that's what we've done in the past. But you can also make a good argument for using the median, which is 220. That will give us the "right" answer nine out of ten times. The tenth time, when Zambrano gets injured, and we'll have missed by a larger margin, but the 220 number is perhaps more representative of what a "typical" season is going to look like in Zambrano's career.

That's what we're going to do from now on: we're going take the median rather than the mean when forecasting playing time. The result is that the playing time forecasts will be more "optimistic", particularly for pitchers, who have the sort of asymmetrical injury risk profiles as described in the example above.

The change is applied *only* to playing time, and the counting stats like wins and strikeouts and home runs that are incumbent on playing time. The rate stats and valuation metrics are still calculated on a weighted mean basis, as we've done in the past. Specifically, the change is *not* applied to a player's VORP forecast. The injury risk is still embedded within Zambrano's VORP number, since the pitcher who got injured will have a very small VORP. VORP is the single best metric available for assessing both the quality and the quantity of a player's performance, and we're not about to tinker with it.

Note that our new method does not let Zambrano off of the hook completely. If a substantial number of his comparables get injured for some period of time, or lose playing time for some other reason, that will eventually have an impact on the median estimate as well as the mean. I'm not about to forecast Zambrano for 240 innings or something, not unless Livan Hernandez has adopted him a pen pal. We do assume for purposes of his playing time forecast, however, that he won't suffer some *catastrophic* injury. For you purists who have some objection to this, keep in mind that we're now presenting the Attrition Rate metric, which is an attempt to quantify the risk of exactly a catastrophic loss of playing time (because of injury or some other means).

There's one other change to note, completely unrelated to this median versus mean business. Previously, we had projected playing time for *minor league* players as sort of a hybrid minor league and probable major league playing time. You'd see a lot of pitching prospects with 110 IP or something, and a lot of hitting prospects with 400 plate appearances. Frankly, this method was never particularly well thought out, and we've replaced it with the much simpler assumption of treating a professional plate appearance (major leagues or minors) as a professional plate appearance. Whether Delmon Young spends next season in Durham or Montgomery or hitting in the Trop-Dome is really more up to the Devil Rays than it is to Delmon Young, and it isn't right to punish his valuation as a result of their decision.

Why it matters: We think it's crucially important that a forecasting system does make some objective attempt to forecast playing time. Knowing that a player is relatively more likely to get injured, or that the he won't hit enough to work himself out of a platoon, is important to his valuation. However, we've determined that a different, but no less objective method presents the best balance of information about playing time.

#5. Age-Specific Baseline Weightings

What it is: PECOTA boils down to a two-step process. The *second* step is identifying a player's comparables, and using them to understand what he's going to do from here forward. That's the glitzy part, the fun part, the part that differentiates PECOTA from other systems.

But the first step is probably more important. This step, which we call the baseline forecast, is the answer to the question *how good is the player right now?* Forget what his career path is going to look like: we first have to understand the "hence" part of "henceforth". Brian Roberts was a career .264 hitter entering 2005, but hit .314 last year; the odds of that happening based on chance alone are something like 300-to-1. The truth lies somewhere in between .264 and .314, but where?

One thing you need to figure out is what emphasis to place on which seasons. Should we place more weight on Roberts's 2005 because it came more recently? It's intuitive that we should. But how *much* weight, we've discovered, depends on how old the player is. Specifically, we should tend to place more weight on recent seasons if the player is very old or very young, but spread things out more if he's in the middle of his career. If a 28-year-old hitter goes from hitting .300 to .240, that's probably a fluke; if a 38-year-old player does the same thing, he's probably done.

Why it matters: I assumed that this would have a substantial effect on players like Brandon Wood, young prospects who develop a lot within one season as they grow into their bodies. This adjustment does have some favorable effect on Wood, but it turns out to be much more important for old players, anyone past the age of 33 or so. I can guarantee you that we're the only projection system that says that Craig Biggio is going to hit as well as Mark Loretta next year, or that Sammy Sosa is going to struggle to hit ten homers. Those projections are because of the age adjustment.

This adjustment applies to position players only, by the way. We couldn't find evidence that it improves the forecasts for pitchers, probably because pitchers don't follow much of a traditional aging curve to begin with.

#6. Groundball-Flyball Data for Hitters

What it is: We have groundball-flyball data going back to 1960, and now incorporate it into our forecasts for hitters, as well as for pitchers.

Why it matters: It doesn't much. This turned out to be an anti-climax. I'd felt for a long time like PECOTA was low

TABLE 8. PECOTA EFFECT OF VARYING JUAN PIERRE'S GROUNDBALL RATE

Groundball%	BA	OBP	SLG	EQA
High (Actual)	.297	.348	.361	.253
Average	.290	.343	.379	.255
Low	.288	.342	.391	.257

on guys like Pierre and Ichiro Suzuki and Luis Castillo, lightning-fast singles hitters who hit everything on the ground, and that the adding groundball data could be the missing link.

Table 8 shows what happens to Juan Pierre's projected batting line as we tinker with his historical groundball rate, while holding everything else constant.

Pierre's high groundball rate boosts his average by ten points or so. It's easier to get a base hit on the ground than in the air, particularly if you run as well as Pierre does. But it has the opposite effect on what little there is of his extra base power. A .297/.348/.361 line is more what a year in the life of Juan Pierre looks like than .290/.343./.379, but the effect on his EQA is negligible. PECOTA *was* low on his batting average, but probably had his overall value about right. Groundball data gives us another dimension along which to compare hitters, but it doesn't matter for hitters *nearly* as much is it does for pitchers, for whom the ability to induce groundballs is a critical skill.

There may be something else that PECOTA is getting wrong with the Ichiros of the world, something that we'll track down eventually. It may also be that he's such a unique player that any empirically-based projection system is just guessing when it tries to evaluate him. Or it may be that PECOTA's been right all along, and that any hitter who puts all his eggs in the singles basket is out of place in today's game. The latter certainly seems more plausible in light of last year's performance from Ichiro and Pierre.

There are a few other cute things that we've done with the PECOTAs. We now look at doubles and triples allowed by pitchers (and what this says about the defenses behind them), and intentional versus unintentional walks. We look at stolen base and double play opportunities explicitly instead of guesstimating them. The projections for position player *defense* have been thoroughly debugged and improved.

But that's the big stuff, and I need to get back to my six pack. Thank you for your time, and enjoy.

Arizona Diamondbacks

The game the Diambondbacks played against the Pirates in Pittsburgh on September 8th contained within it the entire range of Arizona's possibilities, positive and negative, and we can use it to get a handle on the 2005 season as a whole. The 12th inning was particularly revealing: with rookie Conor Jackson on deck, leadoff hitter Troy Glaus hit a double. Jackson was promptly called back to the dugout so that Russ Ortiz could bunt Glaus to third. Ortiz successfully laid down a bunt (with two strikes against him), sending Glaus to third, but then Luis Terrero grounded weakly to third, forcing Glaus to hold. Then when Conor Jackson was finally sent up to pinch-hit for Chris Snyder, he popped foul to first base, ending the inning. In the bottom of the inning, reliever Buddy Groom allowed a single to Rob Mackowiak, who was bunted into scoring position by Freddy Sanchez. Light-hitting catcher Humberto Cota rapped a single to score Mackowiak, ending the game.

The dramatis personae of the 12th seemed to come straight out of a performance of "A Christmas Carol," with players standing in for Dickens's spectral tour guides. Troy Glaus and Russ Ortiz were the ghosts of Diamondbacks past. They were the last of the big-ticket items bought in by a directionless team aimlessly guided by indecisive General Manager Joe Garagiola Jr. Glaus, at least, had earned his salary. Contrary to expectations, he stayed healthy, and was second on the team in VORP with 45.4 (fifth in the NL among third basemen). That he was eventually stranded on third in the paradigmatic Pittsburgh game is fitting, as the D-Back offense, which ranked 10th in the NL with 696 runs scored, couldn't quite muster enough big-league bats to make a whole offense. As for Russ Ortiz, this bunt aside, he was an unmitigated disaster, an outcome surprising to no one save Garagiola.

Terrero and Groom represented the ghosts of Diamondbacks present. The Terrero groundout was indicative of the old wave of D-Back prospects who failed to make a splash in 2005, a group that included Terrero, Alex Cintron, Scott Hairston, and Koyie Hill. They're not really all that young, and for the most part, they aren't panning out. On the mound, Buddy Groom was the team's umpteenth fruitless graybeard reclamation project, necessitated by the failure of Arizona's minor league system to produce many major-league ready arms.

Conor Jackson is the ghost of Diamondbacks' future. If you're an optimist, he represents the death of their old way of doing things. Pulling him back so Ortiz could bunt was emblematic of how he was treated upon his arrival to the majors, and how the commitment to the promising young future of the franchise was being compromised. Jackson was recalled from Tucson on July 27th and saw just 99 PAs during more than two months on the roster. That he eventually popped foul with the go-ahead run on third typified the struggles of the latest wave of desert rookies. Younger than the previous group, Jackson and Chris Snyder struggled at the big league level in 2005. The difficulties of both the young and intermediate-young prospect groups leave those waiting in the wings like Jamie D'Antona, Sergio Santos, Josh Kroeger, and Jon Zeringue all looking like they might not be on the fast track to Phoenix after all.

These ghosts would not combine to produce a Scrooge-like epiphany in 2005, despite the mediocrity of the National League West, a division every bit as bad as the NL East was good. As the season wound down, the Padres had the potential to win their division with a sub-.500 record. They didn't, but it was close, and the adjusted records make the entire division look even more suspect (see table 1).

TABLE 1. INADEQUACY FINDS A HOME: THE NL WEST

Team	W	L	RS	RA	W1	L1	EQR	EQRA	W2	L2	AEQR	AEQRA	W3	L3
Padres	82	80	681	725	76.1	85.9	698	712	79.4	82.6	682	731	75.7	86.3
Dodgers	71	91	684	752	73.7	88.3	666	731	74.0	88.0	648	744	70.8	91.3
Diamondbacks	77	85	696	853	65.3	96.8	753	839	72.5	89.5	738	854	69.7	92.3
Giants	75	87	646	744	70.3	91.7	646	740	70.8	91.2	628	747	68.2	93.9
Rockies	67	95	740	862	69.0	93.0	717	876	65.6	96.5	700	881	63.5	98.6

The W, L, RS (runs scored) and RA (runs allowed) columns should be familiar enough. W1 and L1 are projected Wins and Losses, or Pythagenports, based solely on the runs the team actually scored and allowed. W2 and L2 are projected Wins and Losses based on Equivalent Runs Scored and Equivalent Runs Allowed, which are what the team *should* have scored given their underlying offensive performance, that is, based on the number of extra-base hits, hits, walks, and so on, the things which lead to baserunners and runs. The last set of projected Wins and Losses are the most telling, as they are derived from the team's Adjusted Equivalent Runs Scored and Allowed. This is computed by adjusting the EQR and EQRA numbers according to strength of schedule, and more simply, the quality of the opponents' pitching and hitting. In Arizona's case, they faced worse than average pitching, and worse than average hitting, which is no real surprise given an unbalanced schedule and a division with only one team above .500.

Arizona *should* have scored almost 60 more runs than they actually did, as their EQR total indicates. While that's little consolation as far as 2005 is concerned, it demonstrates that the gap between the fixable offense and fixable pitching isn't as large as it seems. At any rate, pitching remains the bigger problem.

The coming season should be a unique one for the D-Backs. They occupy the shifting middle ground between rebuilding and contending. They're one of the few teams who can actually attempt to do both at once, as long as there isn't a runaway favorite to win the division. In other words, modest improvements over last year's team should be enough to keep the team in the hunt without mortgaging the future. New GM Josh Byrnes, hired away from the Red Sox in October, might have been tempted to compete right away with his existing veterans, as evidenced by the decision to acquire Johnny Estrada rather than wait for Chris Snyder to develop. Arizona essentially went without offense from their 2005 backstops, and the refusal to do so again is a promising sign; though Estrada may not approach his 2004 season again, even a repeat of last year's disappointing .233 EqA/3.0 WARP would be an improvement over what the D-Backs got from the catcher position in '05. Byrnes also had the good sense to cut loose both

Royce Clayton and Shawn Estes and deal veterans like Vazquez and Glaus, to make room for younger players.

Among these sensible moves, Byrnes also showed good judgment in retaining Mike Rizzo, the vice president of scouting operations, who many felt had an inside track to the GM position himself. He also brought in former Red Sox compatriot Peter Woodfork to be the Assistant GM. In fairness to the new group, many of the weaknesses of the 2006 roster are products of the previous regime. Byrnes can't immediately solve the presence of Russ Ortiz, the Tony Clark extension, the Luis Gonzalez long-term deal, and the backloaded contracts and deferred money from their 2001 championship.

Byrnes and company have a rosy future ahead of them. The new GM has done a commendable job so far, both for what he's done to try and clean up the mess he inherited and for not making a bunch of panic moves. Rizzo deserves a great deal of credit for assembling the team that Arizona will field from 2006 onward, as the youth movement is largely a product of his scouting work since 2000. Even if some of the current wave of prospects go the Luis Terrero route, there is still plenty to like about the first winter on Byrnes's watch, with many promising young players to keep an eye on.

Philosophically, this is pretty far removed from the formula that Arizona used to win the World Series five years ago. It appears that more than a few youngsters will get a shot at playing every day; the club has already penciled in Jackson at first base, assuming Clark doesn't vulture too much playing time. An even more significant move was getting White Sox center field prospect Chris Young for Vazquez. While that makes for a smart repudiation of Terrero, the Snakes won't rush Young: until he's ready, they've signed Eric Byrnes to be an adequate short-term placeholder.

Financially, the picture will greatly improve with the passage of time. Luis Gonzalez comes off the books after this season, and the only arbitration-eligible players of note will be Brandon Webb, Cintron, Estrada, Chad Tracy, and Jose Valverde. The rest of the veterans are essentially waiver bait. Once Gonzalez heads elsewhere, Byrnes will have a bit of extra cash to acquire a pitcher or two.

No look ahead would be complete without some cynicism, however. While the farm system gets accolades from both the scouting and performance analysis communities, they come with serious caveats. For one, most of the prospects the D-Backs have developed so far all seem to be burly sluggers with marginal defensive value. The athletic Stephen Drew and Justin Upton will be welcome exceptions. Arizona has also failed to develop many reliable pitchers; their only notable pitching prospects in that department are in the low minors and boast very short resumes. At this writing, the lack of arms hasn't been addressed at any level. While trading Javier Vazquez may have been a priority, plugging in Orlando Hernandez in his place isn't a value-for-value swap. Brandon Webb makes for a nominal ace, though having defensive whiz Orlando Hudson on hand at second base will help make that promotion stick in performance as well as in name.

In the end, the divergent realities for the 2006 Diamondbacks mean that they're really not a 77-win team looking for that extra push to distinguish themselves within the weakest division in the game. They're somewhere between a 69- and 77-win team, and probably will be stuck with 90 losses. Their offense,which was much worse than expected last year, should see some natural improvement, plus some significant architectural improvements with the additions of Estrada, Hudson and Jackson. The offense will also get a boost simply by subtracting Clayton, Terrero, and last year's catchers. The problem is that this team doesn't have a stable rotation, and you generally don't conjure those up out of thin air.

Overall, though, the news is good. This team is poised to be competitive, if not in 2006, then certainly in 2007 and beyond. While recent on-field ineptitude may have given them the high draft picks to stock up their farm system, it takes a plan to put those picks to use intelligently. With Mike Rizzo wisely retained and Josh Byrnes overseeing things, a plan certainly seems to be in place.

HITTERS

PHIL AVLAS   **C**   **Bats: R Throws: R**   Height: 5' 11"   Weight: 175   Born: December 17, 1982   Age: 23

YEAR	TM	LVL	AGE	PA	R	2B	3B	HR	RBI	BB	SO	SB	CS	SPEED	BA	OBP	SLG	MLVR	EQBA	EQOBP	EQSLG	EQA	VORP	DEFENSE	
2003	SBN	A	20	152	14	7	0	1	15	16	17	4	1	4.5	.203	.283	.278	-.164	.185	.252	.272	.197	-12.4	45-C	12
2004	LNC	A+	21	418	64	22	8	13	68	29	54	5	4	5.4	.315	.359	.516	.137	.248	.290	.403	.239	1.3	102-C	11
2005	LNC	A+	22	158	29	12	1	5	24	10	25	1	1	4.8	.367	.405	.565	.277	.286	.322	.422	.255	5.3	35-C	0
2005	TEN	AA	22	134	15	5	0	2	18	18	21	5	2	4.3	.239	.343	.336	-.096	.207	.300	.313	.227	-4.5	32-C	-3
2006	ARI	MLB	23	333	35	17	2	7	34	25	57	4	2	4.4	.242	.303	.379	-.143	.239	.299	.377	.228	0.1	80-C	1

Breakout: 19%   Improve: 43%   Collapse: 35%   Attrition: 20%   Comparables: Omar Fuentes, Brian Luderer, Robbie Hammock

Let's say you play a lot of golf, and you're pretty good. When you play your local par 72 course, you come in somewhere around 75. Three over par's pretty good, right? Now, let's say your friend Phil regularly plays at a par 36 pitch-n-putt, and his low is a 62. Is he better than you? Numbers don't lie, man: 62 is lower than 75. Most warm bodies hit well at Single-A Lancaster; struggling in Double-A isn't always just "adjusting to a higher level." In other words, don't get too terribly excited about Avlas's minor league line: he began the year by struggling at Double-A Tennessee, then got demoted to Lancaster, where he "recovered" his hitting stroke. There's still time for him to become more of a prospect, but 2005 wasn't too encouraging.

JARRED BALL   **OF**   **Bats: B Throws: R**   Height: 6' 1"   Weight: 170   Born: April 18, 1983   Age: 23

YEAR	TM	LVL	AGE	PA	R	2B	3B	HR	RBI	BB	SO	SB	CS	SPEED	BA	OBP	SLG	MLVR	EQBA	EQOBP	EQSLG	EQA	VORP	DEFENSE			
2003	SBN	A	20	514	62	23	2	4	52	41	84	32	11	6.2	.281	.342	.365	.079	.261	.311	.360	.240	-3.9	91-CF	-4	23-LF	-1
2004	LNC	A+	21	523	82	26	6	15	66	45	123	17	9	6.0	.297	.359	.472	.062	.231	.287	.363	.229	-12.6	86-CF	-2	24-RF	2
2005	TEN	AA	22	480	69	19	2	7	34	74	115	39	18	5.9	.253	.377	.363	.003	.223	.331	.329	.242	-7.3	73-CF	-8	25-RF	-1
2006	ARI	MLB	23	427	50	21	3	7	38	39	102	15	6	5.0	.244	.319	.371	-.124	.241	.315	.369	.235	-4.3	102-CF	-5		

Breakout: 27%   Improve: 55%   Collapse: 32%   Attrition: 12%   Comparables: Rashad Eldridge, Chris Magruder, Marvin Seale

His power spike in 2004 turned out to be another Single-A artifact. Once in Double-A, he drew lots of walks, but not much else, as he turned back into a singles-hitting outfielder. His speed is an asset on the bases, but not in the field, as he hasn't translated that speed into range yet. He doesn't hit enough to be an adequate corner outfielder, and his defense isn't good enough for center. It's kind of like how a bag of microwave popcorn is too much for one person, but it's not really a meal, either.

BRIAN BARDEN   **3B/2B**   **Bats: R Throws: R**   Height: 5' 11"   Weight: 190   Born: April 2, 1981   Age: 25

YEAR	TM	LVL	AGE	PA	R	2B	3B	HR	RBI	BB	SO	SB	CS	SPEED	BA	OBP	SLG	MLVR	EQBA	EQOBP	EQSLG	EQA	VORP	DEFENSE			
2003	ELP	AA	22	423	50	24	5	3	57	29	78	10	4	5.6	.287	.348	.399	-.013	.245	.303	.356	.233	-2.8	100-3B	2		
2004	ELP	AA	23	212	33	10	6	3	28	10	48	1	2	6.1	.303	.335	.462	.032	.254	.284	.396	.236	0.1	42-3B	-4		
2004	TUC	AAA	23	358	50	30	5	8	50	18	83	3	1	5.7	.283	.324	.476	-.082	.229	.268	.375	.224	-7.2	60-3B	6	22-2B	1
2005	TUC	AAA	24	573	78	36	5	15	85	38	111	14	5	5.4	.307	.363	.483	.042	.255	.305	.396	.244	6.2	112-3B	6	17-2B	1
2006	*ARI*	*MLB*	*25*	*463*	*53*	*28*	*3*	*11*	*51*	*27*	*94*	*6*	*3*	*4.7*	*.257*	*.308*	*.418*	*-.073*	*.254*	*.304*	*.416*	*.240*	*3.8*	*110-3B*	*4*		

Breakout: 23%   *Improve: 55%*   *Collapse: 22%*   *Attrition: 21%*   *Comparables: Scott Hairston, Brook Jacoby, Juan Uribe*

Left exposed in the Rule 5 draft two years in a row, which nicely encapsulates how the Snakes feel about him, and no one took out a flyer either time. You're tempted to look at that Triple-A line and say "what a nice player," but, again, context turns borderline D-Back prospects into organizational soldiers because of the friendly hitting environments of Arizona's affiliates. His walk rate is still sub-optimal, so his OBP is largely driven by his average. He is a line-drive hitter, though, so it's not like he's waiting for fly balls to drop in order to reach base. May yet make a good pinch-hitter.

CHRIS CARTER   **1B/OF**   **Bats: L Throws: L**   Height: 6' 0"   Weight: 220   Born: September 16, 1982   Age: 23

YEAR	TM	LVL	AGE	PA	R	2B	3B	HR	RBI	BB	SO	SB	CS	SPEED	BA	OBP	SLG	MLVR	EQBA	EQOBP	EQSLG	EQA	VORP	DEFENSE			
2004	YAK	A-	21	305	47	15	1	15	63	46	35	2	3	3.7	.335	.436	.576	.462	.273	.352	.452	.274	14.6	24-LF	-2	13-1B	0
2005	LNC	A+	22	470	71	26	2	21	85	46	66	0	0	3.7	.296	.370	.522	.077	.225	.290	.379	.233	-15.6	67-1B	-8	23-LF	-2
2005	TEN	AA	22	151	21	4	0	10	30	19	11	0	3	3.3	.297	.397	.562	.326	.258	.347	.492	.278	6.6	22-1B	-2		
2006	*ARI*	*MLB*	*19*	*401*	*40*	*23*	*1*	*11*	*47*	*22*	*92*	*3*	*2*	*4.2*	*.232*	*.280*	*.389*	*-.176*	*.229*	*.277*	*.387*	*.219*	*-6.6*	*96-3B*	*-4*		

Breakout: 53%   *Improve: 68%*   *Collapse: 17%*   *Attrition: 18%*   *Comparables: Blake DeWitt, Brandon Wood, Hector Perozo*

One of the few prospects who didn't slump after leaving Lancaster for Tennessee, which was surprising, considering his reputation for relying on his home park more than most. He stopped DHing in 2005 and quickly proved that he couldn't handle left field. That pesky rulebook prevents the D-Backs from having four starting first basemen, and so his future is probably at DH.

ALEX CINTRON   **SS/2B**   **Bats: B Throws: R**   Height: 6' 2"   Weight: 200   Born: December 17, 1978   Age: 27

YEAR	TM	LVL	AGE	PA	R	2B	3B	HR	RBI	BB	SO	SB	CS	SPEED	BA	OBP	SLG	MLVR	EQBA	EQOBP	EQSLG	EQA	VORP	DEFENSE			
2003	ARI	MLB	24	482	70	26	6	13	51	29	33	2	3	5.4	.317	.359	.489	.154	.303	.346	.473	.277	33.4	89-SS	-9	13-3B	-1
2004	ARI	MLB	25	601	56	31	7	4	49	31	59	3	3	5.1	.262	.301	.363	-.150	.253	.293	.352	.226	-1.1	124-SS	-7	17-2B	-2
2005	ARI	MLB	26	346	36	19	2	8	48	12	33	1	2	4.5	.273	.298	.415	-.051	.265	.294	.415	.242	4.2	30-SS	-2	21-3B	0
2006	*ARI*	*MLB*	*27*	*348*	*38*	*18*	*2*	*6*	*38*	*18*	*32*	*2*	*1*	*4.7*	*.279*	*.319*	*.408*	*-.052*	*.275*	*.315*	*.406*	*.241*	*7.9*	*84-SS*	*-2*		

Breakout: 18%   *Improve: 39%*   *Collapse: 34%*   *Attrition: 22%*   *Comparables: Johnny Ray, Brent Gates, Scott Livingstone*

There's probably no use waiting around for Cintron to return to his 2003 peak, when he last looked like he'd be more than a utility infielder. Although the Snakes opted for a creative solution to their infield alignment by moving Craig Counsell at shortstop, it wasn't to let Cintron play second. Although Cintron's not as much of a liability as his detractors think—he's not a star, but he's cheap and won't sabotage an offense—the acquisition of Orlando Hudson makes him expendable.

TONY CLARK   **1B**   **Bats: B Throws: R**   Height: 6' 7"   Weight: 240   Born: June 15, 1972   Age: 34

YEAR	TM	LVL	AGE	PA	R	2B	3B	HR	RBI	BB	SO	SB	CS	SPEED	BA	OBP	SLG	MLVR	EQBA	EQOBP	EQSLG	EQA	VORP	DEFENSE	
2003	NYN	MLB	31	280	29	13	0	16	43	24	73	0	0	3.2	.232	.300	.472	-.000	.231	.299	.471	.258	3.7	57-1B	-7
2004	NYA	MLB	32	283	37	12	0	16	49	26	92	0	0	3.9	.221	.297	.458	-.071	.224	.305	.468	.261	1.1	70-1B	3
2005	ARI	MLB	33	393	47	22	2	30	87	37	88	0	0	3.6	.304	.366	.636	.384	.292	.357	.627	.316	39.0	72-1B	-5
2006	*ARI*	*MLB*	*34*	*331*	*43*	*15*	*1*	*21*	*62*	*32*	*82*	*0*	*0*	*3.6*	*.272*	*.345*	*.544*	*.167*	*.269*	*.341*	*.542*	*.286*	*15.3*	*80-1B*	*-4*

Breakout: 16%   *Improve: 31%*   *Collapse: 28%*   *Attrition: 37%*   *Comparables: Jose Canseco, Joe Adcock, Larry Parrish*

Empiricist David Hume had a wonderful method of evaluating arguments. When faced with an extraordinary claim, he considered the truth value of its opposite. If the opposite claim is even more extraordinary, he knew to reject the greater miracle. Here's an example of the Hume test in action: as a 33-year-old Clark posted the second-highest EqA in team history among players with significant playing time, a mark that was also 25 points higher than his previous best. Clark had the second-highest SLG (behind Derrek Lee, and ahead of Albert Pujols) of all NL players with more than 300 PAs. It was more than 100 points higher than his previous high in SLG. Based on that showing, Clark got a two-year deal that could block the development of younger, better first basemen. Does Clark's career year in a carefully managed role indicate he's more valuable in the short-term than the development of 23-year old minor-league stud Conor Jackson? As long as the D-Backs continue to accept the greater miracle—that Clark will maintain his '05 rates and they're better off with him in the lineup—things will not improve as quickly as they could.

ROYCE CLAYTON   **SS**   **Bats: R Throws: R**   Height: 6' 0"   Weight: 183   Born: January 2, 1970   Age: 36

YEAR	TM	LVL	AGE	PA	R	2B	3B	HR	RBI	BB	SO	SB	CS	SPEED	BA	OBP	SLG	MLVR	EQBA	EQOBP	EQSLG	EQA	VORP	DEFENSE
2003	MIL	MLB	33	539	49	16	1	11	39	49	92	5	2	4.1	.228	.301	.333	-.192	.225	.298	.335	.227	-4.1	136-SS 8
2004	COL	MLB	34	628	95	36	4	8	54	48	125	10	5	6.2	.279	.338	.397	-.084	.260	.320	.372	.243	10.1	140-SS -17
2005	ARI	MLB	35	563	59	28	4	2	44	38	105	13	3	5.9	.270	.320	.351	-.111	.262	.314	.342	.236	6.7	131-SS -5
2006	*ARI*	*MLB*	*36*	*414*	*46*	*19*	*3*	*4*	*37*	*33*	*75*	*8*	*4*	*5.1*	*.256*	*.319*	*.359*	*-.133*	*.253*	*.315*	*.357*	*.230*	*2.1*	*99-SS -6*

Breakout: 19% Improve: 48% Collapse: 31% Attrition: 30%   Comparables: Dave Concepcion, Dick Groat, Alvin Dark

Baseball is a simple game. You hit the ball, you catch the ball, you throw the ball. Clayton's ability to do all three declined once again, though the "you have to watch him play every day" camp might disagree. While his defensive reputation is still intact, and fans still point to the (increasingly) occasional highlight-reel play, most defensive metrics (Clay Davenport's numbers, Ultimate Zone Rating, Range Factor) show him as squarely middle-of-the-road, if not bottom-of-the-barrel. Cintron could have done the same job for less money. In fact, he did. Clayton wasn't offered arbitration, so in 2006 he'll join his fifth team in five years.

CRAIG COUNSELL   **SS/2B**   **Bats: L Throws: R**   Height: 6' 0"   Weight: 185   Born: August 21, 1970   Age: 35

YEAR	TM	LVL	AGE	PA	R	2B	3B	HR	RBI	BB	SO	SB	CS	SPEED	BA	OBP	SLG	MLVR	EQBA	EQOBP	EQSLG	EQA	VORP	DEFENSE		
2003	ARI	MLB	32	348	40	6	3	3	21	41	32	11	4	6.0	.234	.328	.304	-.199	.225	.320	.295	.229	-4.4	48-3B 5	19-SS	0
2004	MIL	MLB	33	540	59	19	5	2	23	59	88	17	4	6.6	.241	.330	.315	-.150	.236	.323	.309	.235	2.8	126-SS 16		
2005	ARI	MLB	34	668	85	34	4	9	42	78	69	26	7	6.6	.256	.350	.375	-.024	.248	.343	.370	.258	15.9	138-2B 14		
2006	*ARI*	*MLB*	*35*	*516*	*62*	*23*	*4*	*4*	*41*	*53*	*61*	*21*	*6*	*5.7*	*.256*	*.337*	*.353*	*-.108*	*.253*	*.333*	*.352*	*.241*	*5.4*	*122-2B 4*		

Breakout: 16% Improve: 42% Collapse: 25% Attrition: 15%   Comparables: Mark McLemore, Danny O'Connell, Walt Weiss

It's still hard to believe that he's able to hit the ball at all with his stance, and harder still to believe he can control the strike zone this well. But Counsell was his usual self in 2005, putting the bat on the ball and eking out singles, drawing a few walks, and generally avoiding outs. He fielded particularly well in 2005—Clay Davenport's fielding numbers have him winning the Gold Glove—and he'd make a fine stopgap at shortstop to begin 2006, lasting as long as it takes until this next guy is ready.

STEPHEN DREW   **SS**   **Bats: L Throws: R**   Height: 6' 0"   Weight: 185   Born: March 16, 1983   Age: 23

YEAR	TM	LVL	AGE	PA	R	2B	3B	HR	RBI	BB	SO	SB	CS	SPEED	BA	OBP	SLG	MLVR	EQBA	EQOBP	EQSLG	EQA	VORP	DEFENSE
2005	LNC	A+	22	177	33	16	3	10	39	26	25	1	1	5.5	.389	.486	.738	.674	.300	.388	.537	.308	20.7	37-SS -2
2005	TEN	AA	22	113	11	5	0	4	13	12	24	2	3	4.3	.218	.301	.386	-.115	.182	.256	.331	.204	-5.4	26-SS 1
2006	*ARI*	*MLB*	*23*	*452*	*57*	*28*	*3*	*15*	*60*	*47*	*88*	*3*	*3*	*4.5*	*.263*	*.345*	*.464*	*.052*	*.260*	*.340*	*.462*	*.266*	*20.8*	*107-SS -3*

Breakout: 28% Improve: 50% Collapse: 22% Attrition: 11%   Comparables: Jose Bautista, Rico Petrocelli, Ryan Church

In his first season with a wooden bat, he hit well enough to make Arizona management decide against bringing back Royce Clayton. He hit exceptionally well in Lancaster, then got a bit of a reality check when his OPS dropped by 527 points in Double-A. The consensus seems to be that, even considering the wealth of shortstop prospects in the Arizona system, Drew is the closest to the majors. The one knock on Drew at this point seems to be his defense, which didn't impress many in Lancaster. He's no Royce Clayton, you know.

JERRY GIL   **SS**   **Bats: R Throws: R**   Height: 6' 3"   Weight: 180   Born: October 14, 1982   Age: 23

YEAR	TM	LVL	AGE	PA	R	2B	3B	HR	RBI	BB	SO	SB	CS	SPEED	BA	OBP	SLG	MLVR	EQBA	EQOBP	EQSLG	EQA	VORP	DEFENSE
2003	SBN	A	20	447	52	16	6	4	58	10	90	19	10	7.2	.259	.275	.352	-.048	.240	.255	.346	.212	-14.6	115-SS 4
2004	TUC	AAA	21	438	53	31	8	11	58	12	94	12	1	7.2	.278	.299	.468	-.143	.224	.246	.366	.215	-13.1	111-SS -14
2005	TEN	AA	22	208	28	7	3	10	29	8	52	10	7	6.7	.256	.288	.472	.011	.226	.252	.426	.226	-0.9	50-SS 4
2006	*ARI*	*MLB*	*23*	*346*	*40*	*18*	*3*	*9*	*35*	*13*	*82*	*10*	*5*	*5.2*	*.239*	*.272*	*.397*	*-.175*	*.236*	*.269*	*.395*	*.219*	*-1.0*	*83-SS -1*

Breakout: 38% Improve: 56% Collapse: 26% Attrition: 18%   Comparables: Jeff Kunkel, Jose Nieves, Tim Olson

(continued next page)

Jerry Gil *(continued)*

Offseason knee surgery shouldn't be a factor in his development, because there wasn't much developing going on, anyway. Scouts rave about his defense and particularly his arm, but offensively, his OBP has never topped .300. With the list of hitter-friendly leagues and ballparks on his resume, that's inexcusable.

TROY GLAUS   3B   Bats: R Throws: R   Height: 6′ 5″ Weight: 240 Born: August 3, 1976   Age: 29

YEAR	TM	LVL	AGE	PA	R	2B	3B	HR	RBI	BB	SO	SB	CS	SPEED	BA	OBP	SLG	MLVR	EQBA	EQOBP	EQSLG	EQA	VORP	DEFENSE	
2003	ANA	MLB	26	367	53	17	2	16	50	46	73	7	2	5.1	.248	.343	.464	.079	.250	.351	.475	.282	21.0	83-3B	-9
2004	ANA	MLB	27	242	47	11	1	18	42	31	52	2	3	4.6	.251	.355	.575	.179	.259	.365	.595	.307	14.1	18-3B	-1
2005	ARI	MLB	28	634	78	29	1	37	97	84	145	4	2	4.4	.258	.363	.522	.186	.249	.355	.512	.291	37.5	141-3B	-9
2006	*TOR*	*MLB*	*29*	*543*	*77*	*25*	*2*	*32*	*92*	*71*	*117*	*4*	*2*	*4.3*	*.269*	*.369*	*.541*	*.207*	*.267*	*.376*	*.543*	*.299*	*36.9*	*128-3B*	*-6*

Breakout: 17%   Improve: 49%   Collapse: 14%   Attrition: 15%   Comparables: Scott Rolen, Bob Allison, Jose Canseco

A risky signing, but give the D-Backs credit: they kept him on the field, and made the first year of his deal look like it wasn't a bad move. Then, Jeff Moorad and company soured on his work habits, making it blatantly obvious that they wanted to trade him. Public questioning of a player's work ethic right before trying to unload him probably isn't the best way to get full value in return, but they did so by getting defensive stud Orlando Hudson and a passable closer, Miguel Batista, from Toronto, while unloading Glaus's salary on the suddenly spendthrift Blue Jays. Unfortunately for Glaus, with winter in Toronto lasting until May, his wife might not be able to maintain her equestrian hobby; no wonder management said "neigh" to retaining him.

LUIS GONZALEZ   LF   Bats: L Throws: R   Height: 6′ 2″ Weight: 190 Born: September 3, 1967 Age: 38

YEAR	TM	LVL	AGE	PA	R	2B	3B	HR	RBI	BB	SO	SB	CS	SPEED	BA	OBP	SLG	MLVR	EQBA	EQOBP	EQSLG	EQA	VORP	DEFENSE	
2003	ARI	MLB	35	679	92	46	4	26	104	94	67	5	3	4.4	.304	.402	.532	.265	.290	.388	.510	.304	42.8	151-LF	10
2004	ARI	MLB	36	451	69	28	5	17	48	68	58	2	2	5.1	.259	.373	.493	.146	.245	.360	.471	.283	15.9	102-LF	-7
2005	ARI	MLB	37	672	90	37	0	24	79	78	90	4	1	4.5	.271	.366	.459	.122	.262	.358	.451	.280	26.7	147-LF	1
2006	*ARI*	*MLB*	*38*	*534*	*61*	*28*	*2*	*19*	*71*	*61*	*73*	*4*	*2*	*4.5*	*.272*	*.362*	*.462*	*.085*	*.269*	*.357*	*.460*	*.275*	*14.2*	*126-LF*	*-3*

Breakout: 8%   Improve: 31%   Collapse: 30%   Attrition: 12%   Comparables: Fred Lynn, Moises Alou, George Brett

Once upon a time there was a baseball team, and that baseball team had two Semi-Famous Expensive Outfielders, Luis and Shawn. Both outfielders loved to play, loved to smile, and loved children. But there was a problem. Every time the Semi-Famous Expensive Outfielders took to the field, management was incapable of watching them play. Instead, they reminisced about all the semi-famous moments in the Semi-Famous Outfielder's pasts that made them Semi-Famous. Gonzalez isn't a bad player, but his 2006 salary is too high. Having adequate replacements available at the league minimum makes him seem even more expensive.

ANDY GREEN   INF   Bats: R Throws: R   Height: 5′ 9″ Weight: 170 Born: July 7, 1977   Age: 28

YEAR	TM	LVL	AGE	PA	R	2B	3B	HR	RBI	BB	SO	SB	CS	SPEED	BA	OBP	SLG	MLVR	EQBA	EQOBP	EQSLG	EQA	VORP	DEFENSE		DEFENSE	
2003	ELP	AA	26	544	70	38	2	2	51	38	51	17	9	5.2	.302	.366	.400	.026	.242	.297	.328	.224	-12.1	59-2B	-1	39-SS	-4
2004	TUC	AAA	27	350	56	31	3	9	45	34	45	10	4	5.9	.327	.394	.534	.165	.256	.321	.404	.254	7.7	34-3B	0	29-2B	-1
2004	ARI	MLB	27	116	13	2	1	1	4	5	17	1	1	5.7	.202	.241	.266	-.425	.200	.239	.264	.184	-10.4	13-3B	-1		
2005	TUC	AAA	28	607	125	46	13	19	80	68	82	9	6	6.3	.343	.422	.587	.320	.272	.343	.445	.270	30.1	58-2B	-1	40-LF	4
2005	ARI	MLB	28	39	5	1	0	0	2	7	3	0	0	4.2	.226	.359	.258	-.176	.194	.333	.226	.223	-0.7				
2006	*ARI*	*MLB*	*28*	*470*	*55*	*28*	*3*	*9*	*48*	*41*	*69*	*5*	*2*	*5.0*	*.258*	*.328*	*.403*	*-.058*	*.254*	*.324*	*.401*	*.245*	*5.2*	*111-2B*	*-1*		

Breakout: 23%   Improve: 42%   Collapse: 31%   Attrition: 22%   Comparables: Ron Belliard, Joe Randa, Jim Davenport

Got to enjoy his Age 27 season in Tucson, where he smacked 78 extra-base hits, the second highest total in the minor leagues. In the majors, he drew walks, but did little else. He's running out of chances, but his track record suggests he'd be a nifty backup.

SHAWN GREEN   RF   Bats: L Throws: L   Height: 6′ 4″ Weight: 200 Born: November 10, 1972 Age: 33

YEAR	TM	LVL	AGE	PA	R	2B	3B	HR	RBI	BB	SO	SB	CS	SPEED	BA	OBP	SLG	MLVR	EQBA	EQOBP	EQSLG	EQA	VORP	DEFENSE		DEFENSE	
2003	LAN	MLB	30	691	84	49	2	19	85	68	112	6	2	4.9	.280	.355	.460	.136	.284	.357	.471	.284	25.9	155-RF	12		
2004	LAN	MLB	31	671	92	28	1	28	86	71	114	5	2	4.7	.266	.352	.459	.101	.266	.351	.461	.278	24.0	103-1B	-4	48-RF	-3
2005	ARI	MLB	32	656	87	37	4	22	73	62	95	8	4	5.3	.286	.355	.477	.139	.276	.347	.471	.279	29.4	115-RF	4	35-CF	-2
2006	*ARI*	*MLB*	*33*	*580*	*72*	*32*	*3*	*19*	*79*	*58*	*89*	*5*	*3*	*4.9*	*.284*	*.359*	*.466*	*.097*	*.280*	*.355*	*.464*	*.274*	*16.8*	*136-RF*	*-3*		

Breakout: 11%   Improve: 47%   Collapse: 20%   Attrition: 10%   Comparables: Jim Northrup, Chris Chambliss, Ken Griffey

There's talk of him playing center field for Arizona in '06, helping to make room for one of their many corner outfield prospects. He saw a decent amount of time at center last year, where he rated below average, but not worse than Luis Terrero. Like many southpaws, he's vulnerable to left-handed pitching. The Dodgers are on the hook for a good chunk of his salary, which makes him less of an Expensive Problem than the team's other Semi-Famous Expensive Outfielder.

SCOTT HAIRSTON — 2B/LF — Bats: R Throws: R — Height: 6′ 0″ — Weight: 190 — Born: May 25, 1980 — Age: 26

YEAR	TM	LVL	AGE	PA	R	2B	3B	HR	RBI	BB	SO	SB	CS	SPEED	BA	OBP	SLG	MLVR	EQBA	EQOBP	EQSLG	EQA	VORP	DEFENSE			
2003	ELP	AA	23	374	53	21	7	10	47	30	80	6	2	6.3	.276	.345	.469	.064	.232	.297	.410	.244	2.4	74-2B	-5		
2004	TUC	AAA	24	128	29	8	3	5	20	11	21	0	3	6.4	.313	.375	.565	.162	.255	.320	.455	.258	4.9	18-2B	-3		
2004	ARI	MLB	24	362	39	15	6	13	29	21	88	3	3	5.6	.248	.293	.442	-.057	.237	.283	.423	.238	5.3	79-2B	-7		
2005	TUC	AAA	25	237	45	8	3	16	40	21	40	3	0	5.5	.311	.384	.608	.254	.253	.317	.480	.270	3.3	31-LF	3	16-CF	-1
2006	ARI	MLB	26	331	40	17	3	12	44	25	70	3	2	5.2	.252	.315	.451	-.021	.249	.311	.449	.251	6.4	80-2B	-3		

Breakout: 28% Improve: 46% Collapse: 34% Attrition: 30% Comparables: Jeffrey Hammonds, Pedro Garcia, Ozzie Timmons

Basically has nowhere to play. His bat is inadequate for an outfield corner, and the D-Backs have better-hitting prospects at those positions anyway. He also doesn't have the glove to play second. He finished the year on the 60-day DL with a dislocated shoulder that required labrum surgery. His prospect status has taken a hit after the missed development time, not to mention his struggles while healthy. That both Hairstons are looking at careers of utility usage is probably not funny to the Hairston family.

KOYIE HILL — C — Bats: B Throws: R — Height: 6′ 0″ — Weight: 190 — Born: March 9, 1979 — Age: 27

YEAR	TM	LVL	AGE	PA	R	2B	3B	HR	RBI	BB	SO	SB	CS	SPEED	BA	OBP	SLG	MLVR	EQBA	EQOBP	EQSLG	EQA	VORP	DEFENSE	
2003	JAX	AA	24	107	9	7	0	0	7	6	19	2	1	4.5	.228	.271	.297	-.180	.216	.253	.285	.191	-7.8	23-C	4
2003	LVG	AAA	24	330	48	18	0	3	36	15	39	5	0	5.1	.314	.345	.401	-.005	.260	.298	.339	.227	-5.1	76-C	-5
2004	LVG	AAA	25	383	57	26	0	13	54	28	69	0	1	3.6	.286	.339	.471	-.042	.223	.274	.362	.221	-9.5	80-C	6
2005	TUC	AAA	26	193	22	9	1	5	26	23	37	3	0	4.1	.244	.337	.399	-.168	.195	.277	.305	.213	-9.3	40-C	0
2005	ARI	MLB	26	91	6	5	0	0	6	11	27	0	1	4.5	.218	.308	.282	-.242	.208	.300	.260	.209	-2.7	24-C	-1
2006	ARI	MLB	27	258	22	12	1	5	25	18	52	2	1	4.2	.230	.290	.352	-.209	.227	.286	.351	.213	-4.5	64-C	-1

Breakout: 37% Improve: 52% Collapse: 33% Attrition: 35% Comparables: Chris Bando, Mike Matheny, Mike Ryan

He has yet to translate his acceptable minor league walk rate into something more like a career, and it doesn't look like he will. He put up okay numbers by admittedly pathetic D-Back catcher standards while regrouping in Triple-A after an abysmal start. If he was unable to push Chris Snyder's .202/.297/.301 line out of the everyday lineup, he's no longer a prospect.

CONOR JACKSON — 1B — Bats: R Throws: R — Height: 6′ 3″ — Weight: 205 — Born: May 7, 1982 — Age: 24

YEAR	TM	LVL	AGE	PA	R	2B	3B	HR	RBI	BB	SO	SB	CS	SPEED	BA	OBP	SLG	MLVR	EQBA	EQOBP	EQSLG	EQA	VORP	DEFENSE			
2003	YAK	A-	21	300	44	35	1	6	60	36	41	3	0	4.7	.319	.410	.533	.387	.258	.325	.437	.263	3.5	20-RF	0		
2004	LNC	A+	22	313	64	19	2	11	54	45	36	4	3	4.8	.345	.438	.562	.348	.266	.352	.422	.270	4.0	57-LF	1		
2004	ELP	AA	22	256	33	13	2	6	37	24	36	3	3	4.4	.301	.367	.456	.073	.250	.310	.390	.244	-6.2	41-LF	-1		
2005	TUC	AAA	23	409	66	38	2	8	73	69	32	3	2	4.0	.354	.457	.553	.340	.288	.390	.436	.291	19.6	71-1B	5	17-LF	0
2005	ARI	MLB	23	99	8	3	0	2	8	12	11	0	0	2.9	.200	.303	.306	-.225	.188	.293	.282	.213	-4.0	18-1B	-2		
2006	ARI	MLB	24	459	54	29	1	12	57	54	59	2	1	4.4	.269	.359	.439	.047	.265	.354	.437	.268	8.5	109-1B	0		

Breakout: 24% Improve: 48% Collapse: 28% Attrition: 17% Comparables: Nate Espy, Paul McAnulty, Paul Konerko

You'd be forgiven if you saw his stat line and pictured an out of shape guy like Drew Carey. Jackson has the dreaded Old Player Skills: he walks, he hits for power, steals three bases a year, clomps around at first, and remembers with a faint smile his days of playing third base. He routinely tallies more walks than strikeouts, even in college, which is the most reassuring aspect of his gaudy numbers. He's not your ordinary D-Back slugger, as the home runs aren't quite there yet, but he's got a great swing, has controlled the strike zone exceptionally well at all levels, and if some of those doubles turn into home runs in Phoenix, he'll be scary. The Snakes have said the job is his to lose in camp. Hopefully, they'll stand by that.

JOSH KROEGER   RF   **Bats: L Throws: L**   Height: 6′ 3″   Weight: 210   Born: August 31, 1982   Age: 23

YEAR	TM	LVL	AGE	PA	R	2B	3B	HR	RBI	BB	SO	SB	CS	SPEED	BA	OBP	SLG	MLVR	EQBA	EQOBP	EQSLG	EQA	VORP	DEFENSE			
2003	LNC	A+	20	345	50	30	6	5	55	35	58	6	6	5.3	.341	.409	.528	.274	.277	.340	.436	.265	6.0	58-RF	2	12-CF	1
2003	ELP	AA	20	222	26	9	2	3	22	10	54	3	5	4.7	.274	.315	.380	-.098	.230	.271	.337	.212	-9.4	27-CF	-1	26-RF	1
2004	ELP	AA	21	272	44	28	4	9	46	21	48	2	1	5.2	.331	.393	.588	.313	.273	.331	.486	.274	8.9	57-RF	-2		
2004	TUC	AAA	21	229	30	23	0	10	41	15	47	2	1	3.8	.332	.376	.587	.214	.255	.300	.441	.253	-1.1	43-RF	-1	11-CF	0
2004	ARI	MLB	21	55	5	3	0	0	2	1	21	0	1	4.2	.167	.182	.222	-.601	.148	.164	.204	.132	-8.0				
2005	TUC	AAA	22	516	73	28	3	14	62	36	108	17	4	6.3	.261	.316	.422	-.164	.215	.265	.344	.217	-33.9	58-RF	3	48-CF	-3
2006	PHI	MLB	23	396	47	22	2	11	48	26	84	7	4	5.1	.256	.311	.420	-.067	.255	.311	.422	.244	0.0	95-RF	0		

Breakout: 38%   Improve: 66%   Collapse: 14%   Attrition: 16%   Comparables: Lloyd Moseby, Kirk Gibson, Shawn Green

Clearly overmatched in his 2004 stint of emergency duty, he took a huge step backward in 2005, his first full season at Triple-A. He's always been considered a "tools" player, and though he made progress in his transformation from athlete to baseball player, he's got a lot more room to grow if he's going to make it. Snagged by the Phillies off of waivers this winter, where he might get that time.

MIGUEL MONTERO   C   **Bats: L Throws: R**   Height: 5′ 11″   Weight: 190   Born: July 9, 1983   Age: 22

YEAR	TM	LVL	AGE	PA	R	2B	3B	HR	RBI	BB	SO	SB	CS	SPEED	BA	OBP	SLG	MLVR	EQBA	EQOBP	EQSLG	EQA	VORP	DEFENSE			
2003	MSO	Rk	19	216	24	10	2	4	32	9	15	2	3	3.6	.301	.352	.434	.090	.253	.290	.372	.229	-3.2	47-C	1		
2004	SBN	A	20	449	47	22	2	11	59	36	74	8	2	4.6	.263	.330	.409	.080	.238	.293	.370	.233	-4.7	80-C	3	14-1B	1
2005	LNC	A+	21	397	73	24	1	24	82	26	52	1	2	4.0	.349	.403	.625	.340	.268	.314	.466	.264	16.3	59-C	1		
2005	TEN	AA	21	119	13	1	2	2	13	7	26	1	0	5.2	.250	.311	.352	-.123	.221	.272	.322	.213	-5.1	28-C	0		
2006	ARI	MLB	22	457	50	23	2	14	57	28	74	2	1	4.3	.254	.308	.418	-.076	.251	.304	.416	.239	4.9	108-C	0		

Breakout: 26%   Improve: 51%   Collapse: 26%   Attrition: 11%   Comparables: Mike Jacobs, Ryan Doumit, Phil Avlas

Montero broke out in 2005, though the usual organization-wide caveats apply, as he hit .404/.445/.718 at home and "just" .307/.371/.553 on the road. But even with the Lancaster boost, his High-A season was pretty impressive, resulting in a Cal League batting title. He had the usual/expected slump after being promoted to Double-A, so the permanence of his offensive gains are in doubt. He improved his defense in 2005, to the point where he was no longer a liability behind the plate. With neither Chris Snyder nor Koyie Hill doing much to inspire confidence, he could be on the organization's radar sooner than you think. Like, now.

KENNY PEREZ   2B/SS   **Bats: B Throws: R**   Height: 6′ 2″   Weight: 190   Born: September 28, 1981   Age: 24

YEAR	TM	LVL	AGE	PA	R	2B	3B	HR	RBI	BB	SO	SB	CS	SPEED	BA	OBP	SLG	MLVR	EQBA	EQOBP	EQSLG	EQA	VORP	DEFENSE			
2003	SAR	A+	21	251	32	17	4	2	39	15	24	11	4	7.1	.278	.319	.413	.100	.268	.304	.426	.254	9.0	58-SS	-6		
2004	PME	AA	22	431	47	31	5	5	61	23	59	12	4	6.0	.280	.323	.420	-.009	.253	.291	.381	.236	1.7	84-SS	-8	14-2B	-2
2005	PME	AA	23	274	35	9	1	4	28	18	35	7	3	5.7	.285	.328	.375	-.009	.262	.308	.349	.235	-1.5	21-2B	-6	20-SS	-1
2005	LNC	A+	23	106	25	7	1	1	10	9	15	0	0	5.4	.320	.377	.443	.000	.253	.306	.362	.233	0.5	22-SS	0		
2006	ARI	MLB	24	404	44	22	3	5	36	25	54	6	3	5.3	.264	.312	.376	-.116	.260	.308	.375	.232	3.8	96-SS	-3		

Breakout: 18%   Improve: 42%   Collapse: 28%   Attrition: 16%   Comparables: Kevin Estrada, Dionys Cesar, Ron Oester

Boston traded Perez and pitcher Kyle Bono to the D-Backs in exchange for about ten minutes of Jose Cruz, Jr. Arizona didn't have many middle infielders with any plate discipline to speak of, so Perez is a welcome addition. He doesn't generate a whole lot of oomph with his bat, and was demoted from Triple-A Pawtucket all the way down to High-A Lancaster after changing organizations. Perez moved from shortstop to second base, so watch out for budding signs of the "utility" label.

CARLOS QUENTIN   RF   **Bats: R Throws: R**   Height: 6′ 2″   Weight: 220   Born: August 28, 1982   Age: 23

YEAR	TM	LVL	AGE	PA	R	2B	3B	HR	RBI	BB	SO	SB	CS	SPEED	BA	OBP	SLG	MLVR	EQBA	EQOBP	EQSLG	EQA	VORP	DEFENSE			
2004	LNC	A+	21	297	64	14	1	15	51	25	33	5	1	5.2	.310	.428	.562	.297	.240	.328	.433	.263	0.7	53-RF	4		
2004	ELP	AA	21	246	39	19	0	6	38	18	23	0	6	2.9	.357	.443	.533	.335	.284	.353	.439	.268	6.5	54-RF	0		
2005	TUC	AAA	22	561	98	28	4	21	89	72	71	9	1	5.2	.301	.422	.520	.188	.247	.356	.415	.273	5.9	73-RF	9	48-CF	0
2006	ARI	MLB	23	480	58	26	2	15	61	48	68	4	2	4.6	.268	.359	.450	.062	.265	.354	.448	.271	11.0	113-RF	3		

Breakout: 26%   Improve: 56%   Collapse: 22%   Attrition: 12%   Comparables: Dwight Evans, Ron Swoboda, Jesse Barfield

Out of the umpteen corner infield/outfield prospects in this organization, Quentin should get first dibs on a major league gig. Both he and Luis Gonzalez are Tommy John survivors, so whoever draws the right field assignment is going to have his arm tested by runners. He handled Triple-A pitching better than expected, given the supposed inflation of his low minors performances, and has nothing left to prove in Tucson. Some believe he's athletic enough to handle center, which would alleviate the corner outfield problem some, but he doesn't run particularly well, so it's really wishful thinking. If he starts 2006 at Tucson, be sure to send any thank you notes to Tony Clark and the former D-Backs regime.

MARK REYNOLDS   SS/3B   Bats: R Throws: R   Height: 6′ 1″   Weight: 200   Born: August 3, 1983   Age: 22

YEAR	TM	LVL	AGE	PA	R	2B	3B	HR	RBI	BB	SO	SB	CS	SPEED	BA	OBP	SLG	MLVR	EQBA	EQOBP	EQSLG	EQA	VORP	DEFENSE			
2004	YAK	A-	20	274	58	19	1	12	41	25	66	5	1	6.2	.274	.372	.517	.238	.228	.290	.423	.245	7.0	44-SS	-2	15-3B	-2
2005	SBN	A	21	479	65	26	2	19	76	37	107	4	1	4.6	.253	.319	.454	.099	.231	.282	.413	.237	3.5	55-SS	-5	32-3B	-7
2006	ARI	MLB	22	484	51	27	2	14	58	32	120	4	2	4.1	.235	.293	.400	-.137	.232	.290	.398	.228	0.7	114-SS	-9		

Breakout: 28%   Improve: 46%   Collapse: 25%   Attrition: 6%   Comparables: Raul Tablado, Yurendell De Caster, Matthew Brown

Showed some good pop in a park that traditionally favors pitchers. After playing shortstop throughout college, he's seen time at second and third in his pro career. Unless he develops a more discerning eye at the plate, he's likely staring at a career of utility infielding. If the D-Backs ever need to sacrifice a Virginian to the Volcano Gods, Reynolds is their man.

SERGIO SANTOS   SS   Bats: R Throws: R   Height: 6′ 3″   Weight: 200   Born: July 4, 1983   Age: 22

YEAR	TM	LVL	AGE	PA	R	2B	3B	HR	RBI	BB	SO	SB	CS	SPEED	BA	OBP	SLG	MLVR	EQBA	EQOBP	EQSLG	EQA	VORP	DEFENSE	
2003	LNC	A+	20	389	55	13	2	8	49	41	64	5	4	4.4	.287	.368	.408	.006	.228	.299	.326	.223	-6.4	84-SS	-10
2003	ELP	AA	20	147	13	7	1	2	16	8	25	0	0	3.3	.255	.293	.365	-.165	.214	.254	.317	.204	-6.9	35-SS	-2
2004	ELP	AA	21	376	53	19	5	11	52	24	89	3	2	5.3	.282	.332	.461	.012	.233	.280	.386	.230	-1.4	83-SS	-11
2005	TUC	AAA	22	532	55	21	3	12	68	34	108	2	2	4.0	.239	.288	.367	-.307	.195	.239	.293	.191	-34.5	124-SS	-19
2006	TOR	MLB	22	400	40	19	2	10	42	25	84	2	2	4.2	.230	.283	.371	-.196	.229	.282	.370	.216	-1.3	96-SS	-9

Breakout: 51%   Improve: 68%   Collapse: 16%   Attrition: 19%   Comparables: Troy Glaus, Matt Williams, Wes Helms

With Stephen Drew and Justin Upton in the organization (not to mention other middle-infield prospects like Green, Reynolds, and Perez), Santos will never be a shortstop. Good thing, too, as he led the PCL in errors among shortstops, so look for his glove on Ebay. Offensively, he's a righty who doesn't handle lefties well, and his strike zone judgment leaves something to be desired, but scouts still have faith that he'll put his power to good use, maybe at third base. Thrown in with Glaus, it'll be up to Toronto to iron him out.

CHRIS SNYDER   C   Bats: R Throws: R   Height: 6′ 3″   Weight: 220   Born: February 12, 1981   Age: 25

YEAR	TM	LVL	AGE	PA	R	2B	3B	HR	RBI	BB	SO	SB	CS	SPEED	BA	OBP	SLG	MLVR	EQBA	EQOBP	EQSLG	EQA	VORP	DEFENSE	
2003	LNC	A+	22	290	53	16	2	10	53	35	43	0	1	4.1	.314	.414	.518	.243	.251	.338	.421	.262	9.6	56-C	0
2003	ELP	AA	22	213	21	14	0	4	26	19	29	0	0	3.0	.202	.286	.340	-.236	.157	.233	.280	.187	-18.4	47-C	4
2004	ELP	AA	23	401	66	31	0	15	57	46	57	3	1	4.2	.301	.389	.520	.189	.237	.318	.420	.255	8.9	81-C	1
2004	ARI	MLB	23	110	10	6	0	5	15	13	25	0	0	2.9	.240	.327	.458	.020	.232	.321	.442	.262	3.9	28-C	1
2005	ARI	MLB	24	370	24	14	0	6	28	40	87	0	1	3.6	.202	.297	.301	-.247	.196	.292	.298	.213	-9.5	102-C	-2
2006	ARI	MLB	25	338	34	17	1	10	41	32	63	0	1	4.3	.250	.330	.417	-.042	.247	.326	.415	.249	7.9	82-C	0

Breakout: 49%   Improve: 72%   Collapse: 13%   Attrition: 32%   Comparables: Marc Hill, Steve Swisher, A. J. Hinch

Ladies and gentlemen, your 2005 negative VORP leader for the D-Backs. It takes a mighty modest line to be considered a league average offensive catcher these days, but Snyder came nowhere near it. In his case, "Catcher of the Future" sounds more like a premise for a bad science fiction story than a career projection. That vague shape he sees in his rear view mirror is Miguel Montero, and in front of him is the brick wall erected after Arizona picked up Johnny Estrada from the Braves this winter.

KELLY STINNETT   C   Bats: R Throws: R   Height: 5′ 11″ Weight: 220   Born: February 4, 1970   Age: 36

YEAR	TM	LVL	AGE	PA	R	2B	3B	HR	RBI	BB	SO	SB	CS	SPEED	BA	OBP	SLG	MLVR	EQBA	EQOBP	EQSLG	EQA	VORP	DEFENSE	
2003	CIN	MLB	33	197	14	13	0	3	19	13	51	0	0	3.5	.229	.294	.352	-.176	.228	.289	.350	.225	-2.2	46-C	-1
2004	KCA	MLB	34	66	10	0	0	3	7	5	16	0	0	4.8	.305	.379	.458	.129	.310	.385	.466	.291	4.8	18-C	-2
2005	ARI	MLB	35	142	15	4	0	6	12	12	32	0	0	3.0	.248	.317	.419	-.030	.240	.315	.403	.248	3.7	37-C	-3
2006	NYA	MLB	36	97	8	3	0	2	10	6	22	0	0	3.4	.235	.286	.360	-.181	.237	.297	.375	.223	-0.5	27-C	-1

Breakout: 6%   Improve: 24%   Collapse: 51%   Attrition: 60%   Comparables: Phil Roof, Bill Haselman, Jerry McNertney

(continued next page)

Kelly Stinnett *(continued)*

Was their most productive catcher by most meaningful counting and rate stats, which isn't bad for a journeyman after-thought. The D-Backs could have done worse for a veteran placeholder until at least one young catcher is ready, but instead they tried to send him to Tucson. He refused the outright assignment, then hit the jackpot by signing with the Yankees as a free agent.

LUIS TERRERO CF **Bats: R Throws: R** Height: 6' 2" Weight: 205 Born: May 18, 1980 Age: 26

YEAR	TM	LVL	AGE	PA	R	2B	3B	HR	RBI	BB	SO	SB	CS	SPEED	BA	OBP	SLG	MLVR	EQBA	EQOBP	EQSLG	EQA	VORP	DEFENSE		
2003	TUC	AAA	23	510	83	20	15	3	46	31	103	23	19	7.8	.287	.345	.413	-.034	.246	.303	.364	.231	-6.3	111-CF	2	
2004	TUC	AAA	24	238	36	9	6	9	35	17	48	15	3	8.0	.313	.374	.535	.117	.255	.314	.427	.260	4.3	41-CF	2	13-RF -1
2004	ARI	MLB	24	254	21	14	0	4	14	20	78	10	2	5.4	.245	.319	.358	-.129	.231	.304	.336	.233	-0.8	55-CF	-6	
2005	ARI	MLB	25	182	23	6	1	4	20	14	40	3	2	5.2	.230	.313	.354	-.138	.228	.311	.352	.236	-2.3	47-CF	-2	
2006	*ARI*	*MLB*	*26*	*202*	*26*	*9*	*2*	*5*	*22*	*15*	*45*	*6*	*2*	*6.5*	*.261*	*.334*	*.425*	*-.016*	*.258*	*.330*	*.424*	*.254*	*5.9*	*51-CF*	*-1*	

Breakout: 39% Improve: 61% Collapse: 28% Attrition: 37%   Comparables: Brad Komminsk, Jose Gonzalez, David McCarty

At one time, he was an exciting, very raw prospect. Eight years later, he's still quite raw but the "prospect" part doesn't really apply. "Youngish player" is slightly more accurate. "Guy who wears a hat" is even better. Unfortunately, being a rare victim of the hidden ball trick will be his legacy, as he doesn't look like the center fielder of the future any longer. He's inexpensive, which may secure his role as a fourth or fifth outfielder, but he can't hit and he can't field.

CHAD TRACY 1B/3B/RF **Bats: L Throws: R** Height: 6' 2" Weight: 200 Born: May 22, 1980 Age: 26

YEAR	TM	LVL	AGE	PA	R	2B	3B	HR	RBI	BB	SO	SB	CS	SPEED	BA	OBP	SLG	MLVR	EQBA	EQOBP	EQSLG	EQA	VORP	DEFENSE		
2003	TUC	AAA	23	576	91	31	4	10	80	41	52	0	2	4.0	.324	.372	.456	.094	.275	.327	.399	.253	15.7	125-3B	12	
2004	ARI	MLB	24	531	45	29	3	8	53	45	60	2	3	3.9	.285	.343	.407	.009	.273	.331	.392	.252	6.8	120-3B	-2	
2005	ARI	MLB	25	552	73	34	4	27	72	35	78	3	1	4.8	.308	.359	.553	.268	.298	.349	.548	.297	39.6	73-1B	-2	42-RF 1
2006	*ARI*	*MLB*	*26*	*582*	*72*	*34*	*3*	*21*	*82*	*46*	*75*	*3*	*2*	*4.7*	*.289*	*.350*	*.484*	*.109*	*.286*	*.345*	*.482*	*.274*	*18.8*	*136-1B*	*1*	

Breakout: 16% Improve: 50% Collapse: 23% Attrition: 8%   Comparables: Mike Ivie, Ron Jackson, Joe Rudi

The doubles that everyone expected would turn into home runs did just that, and how often does that happen? That a line-drive, high batting-average hitter with adequate plate discipline like Tracy took a few steps forward has to be comforting for someone like Brian Barden. Arizona reportedly doesn't think Tracy is done developing, and that Conor Jackson could be made available to accommodate him. To sacrifice Jackson in order to preserve the jobs of Green or Gonzalez—both of whom play positions to which the younger, cheaper Tracy could easily relocate—would be, to put it mildly, insane.

DAN UGGLA 2B **Bats: R Throws: R** Height: 5' 11" Weight: 190 Born: March 11, 1980 Age: 26

YEAR	TM	LVL	AGE	PA	R	2B	3B	HR	RBI	BB	SO	SB	CS	SPEED	BA	OBP	SLG	MLVR	EQBA	EQOBP	EQSLG	EQA	VORP	DEFENSE		
2003	LNC	A+	23	597	104	31	7	23	90	46	105	24	9	6.9	.290	.355	.504	.115	.223	.278	.382	.231	-8.1	94-3B	10	40-2B -1
2004	LNC	A+	24	160	29	13	3	6	38	17	21	2	4	5.3	.336	.419	.600	.362	.244	.310	.413	.245	2.6	17-2B	4	
2004	ELP	AA	24	316	29	12	2	4	30	15	55	10	7	5.1	.258	.301	.353	-.200	.204	.242	.277	.189	-24.9	45-3B	-4	16-2B 1
2005	TEN	AA	25	566	88	33	3	21	87	52	103	15	8	5.5	.297	.378	.502	.220	.246	.311	.415	.250	10.7	93-2B	-11	10-SS -1
2006	*FLO*	*MLB*	*26*	*442*	*45*	*21*	*2*	*10*	*41*	*29*	*95*	*7*	*3*	*4.7*	*.237*	*.296*	*.371*	*-.168*	*.243*	*.300*	*.393*	*.232*	*0.5*	*105-2B*	*-3*	

Breakout: 32% Improve: 46% Collapse: 28% Attrition: 19%   Comparables: Dale Berra, Alex Gonzalez, Terry Shumpert

While on the surface he might look like a hustling, dirtier version of Tony Graffanino, there are a few cautions. He spent three years in Lancaster's bandbox, and only "broke out" after an extended stay at Double-A. He'll also be 26 by Opening Day. His history of "eventually getting it" made him one of Florida's Rule 5 picks. With the Marlins he has a chance to start at second. The bar is low, but considering he'll move from low minors hitter's parks in offensive leagues to a major-league pitcher's park, the results should be predictably Uggla.

MARLAND WILLIAMS CF **Bats: R Throws: R** Height: 5' 9" Weight: 170 Born: June 22, 1981 Age: 25

YEAR	TM	LVL	AGE	PA	R	2B	3B	HR	RBI	BB	SO	SB	CS	SPEED	BA	OBP	SLG	MLVR	EQBA	EQOBP	EQSLG	EQA	VORP	DEFENSE		
2003	LNC	A+	22	465	85	15	1	4	30	31	99	57	7	8.3	.287	.340	.355	-.110	.227	.274	.287	.218	-27.3	89-CF	8	
2004	ELP	AA	23	533	82	21	10	8	44	40	116	49	8	9.1	.259	.317	.392	-.120	.213	.267	.329	.221	-28.1	108-CF	-5	
2005	TEN	AA	24	424	55	13	7	7	46	37	108	38	7	8.3	.234	.297	.360	-.146	.201	.254	.314	.213	-28.8	67-CF	-4	30-LF 1
2006	*ARI*	*MLB*	*25*	*384*	*48*	*17*	*4*	*6*	*29*	*25*	*100*	*24*	*9*	*6.1*	*.225*	*.280*	*.347*	*-.235*	*.223*	*.277*	*.346*	*.215*	*-12.4*	*92-CF*	*-1*	

Breakout: 36% Improve: 62% Collapse: 18% Attrition: 16%   Comparables: Rod Lindsey, Julio Ramirez, Rick Asadoorian

Like many organizations, Arizona hasn't been good at turning players with tools into players with skills. Williams is a toolsy former football star who was rewarded with a 40-man roster spot and a repeat year at Double-A, this time with new affiliate Tennessee. He's still lightning fast, but lacks any sort of baseball-specific skill. Unless MLB adopts the Little League pinch-running rule, he's the next Wilkin Ruan.

JON ZERINGUE RF Bats: R Throws: R Height: 6' 2" Weight: 215 Born: August 29, 1983 Age: 22

YEAR	TM	LVL	AGE	PA	R	2B	3B	HR	RBI	BB	SO	SB	CS	SPEED	BA	OBP	SLG	MLVR	EQBA	EQOBP	EQSLG	EQA	VORP	DEFENSE	
2004	LNC	A+	20	246	36	14	3	10	41	14	53	9	5	5.6	.335	.374	.552	.232	.260	.294	.423	.244	-3.4	35-RF	4
2005	TEN	AA	21	467	46	18	4	6	51	19	86	11	8	5.2	.241	.283	.342	-.190	.214	.246	.315	.200	-43.1	114-RF	1
2006	*ARI*	*MLB*	*22*	*435*	*44*	*21*	*3*	*8*	*44*	*19*	*90*	*8*	*4*	*4.8*	*.242*	*.281*	*.369*	*-.196*	*.239*	*.277*	*.367*	*.213*	*-15.3*	*103-RF*	*1*

Breakout: 41%   Improve: 59%   Collapse: 23%   Attrition: 10%   Comparables: Jesse Barfield, Charles Thomas, Scott Neuberger

Is it a good idea to wean ex-college players off of the aluminum bat by dropping them into the California League? It might be good for their confidence, but one has to wonder what it does to them developmentally. Zeringue was considered close to the majors after his 2004 campaign, but any residual enthusiasm went the way of Star Wars: Episode II after his embarrassingly bad 2005 season. Zeringue has always been a guy who needs to hit the ball to get on base, and his Double-A season shows just what happens when your one skill is taken from you. As if that wasn't enough, he also led the Southern League in errors among outfielders. On the plus side, he's young and his 2005 batting average was about a hundred points lower than his career low to date. These things have a way of trying to reach equilibrium, so there's every likelihood of a decent rebound.

PITCHERS

GREG AQUINO Bats: R Throws: R Height: 6' 1" Weight: 150 Born: January 11, 1978 Age: 28

YEAR	TM	LVL	AGE	W	L	SV	G	GS	IP	H	BB	SO	HR	GB%	BABIP	STUFF	WHIP	ERA	PERA	EQERA	EQH9	EQBB9	EQSO9	EQHR9	VORP	WXRL
2003	ELP	AA	25	7	3	0	20	20	106.7	115	38	91	5	—	.324	3	1.43	3.46	4.87	4.53	9.2	4.0	5.1	0.9	12.5	—
2004	TUC	AAA	26	1	3	1	21	2	29.7	33	18	19	2	—	.304	-30	1.72	6.36	5.52	7.06	9.2	6.1	4.0	0.6	-4.8	—
2004	ARI	MLB	26	0	2	16	34	0	35.3	24	17	26	4	52%	.213	-4	1.16	3.06	5.03	3.44	7.4	4.0	6.1	1.1	7.6	1.1
2005	ARI	MLB	27	0	1	1	35	0	31.3	42	17	34	7	44%	.385	-6	1.88	7.76	5.73	7.64	10.6	4.4	8.5	1.9	-9.4	0.2
2006	*ARI*	*MLB*	*28*	*2*	*2*	*2*	*40*	*0*	*42.3*	*43*	*22*	*32*	*5*	*47%*	*.294*	*-6*	*1.52*	*4.79*	*4.95*	*5.26*	*8.8*	*4.2*	*6.3*	*1.0*	*2.6*	*0.2*

Breakout: 34%   Improve: 63%   Collapse: 14%   Attrition: 36%   Comparables: Al Corwin, Bob Chakales, Ricky Stone

A problem with pitchers who are converted position players is that they have to be placed on the 40-man roster sooner than most. With some of their minor league service time wrapped up in their fielding days, their organization needs to hurry to decide whether or not to protect them from the Rule 5 draft, even if the decision is based on a handful of innings. Aquino is still raw as a pitcher, is homer-prone, and is too generous with the free pass. Like fellow converted infielder Guillermo Mota, Aquino throws gas and has a much-improved slider as a complementary pitch. Also like Mota, he has better control and is more effective when not trying to throw the ball as hard as is humanly possible.

ADAM BASS Bats: R Throws: R Height: 6' 6" Weight: 210 Born: July 31, 1981 Age: 24

YEAR	TM	LVL	AGE	W	L	SV	G	GS	IP	H	BB	SO	HR	GB%	BABIP	STUFF	WHIP	ERA	PERA	EQERA	EQH9	EQBB9	EQSO9	EQHR9	VORP	WXRL
2003	YAK	A-	21	0	0	3	27	0	33.7	26	14	34	2	—	.263	-18	1.19	0.80	6.16	3.82	9.7	5.0	5.3	1.8	6.1	—
2004	LNC	A+	22	10	8	0	28	27	146.7	180	49	117	12	—	.357	-14	1.56	5.03	5.65	6.46	10.7	3.9	4.3	1.3	-13.9	—
2005	TEN	AA	23	5	10	0	27	27	158.0	158	40	120	14	40%	.304	-9	1.25	3.99	5.53	5.17	9.8	2.6	4.5	1.5	7.2	—
2006	*ARI*	*MLB*	*24*	*5*	*10*	*0*	*29*	*20*	*121.7*	*143*	*49*	*70*	*23*	*41%*	*.298*	*-6*	*1.58*	*6.06*	*6.13*	*6.14*	*10.3*	*3.3*	*4.8*	*1.7*	*-7.3*	*0.1*

Breakout: 7%   Improve: 39%   Collapse: 20%   Attrition: 0%   Comparables: Paul Stewart, Justin Reid, Jeremy Griffiths

The D-Backs' minor league parks all favor hitters, which means pitchers really earn their sub-four ERAs. Bass shaved almost a full walk per nine innings off his rate stats, though he lost some of his strikeouts in the process. He also kept a few more balls in the park, a requirement if he's to be taken seriously. He won't be a star, but you can be a little optimistic here.

KYLE BONO Bats: R Throws: R Height: 6′ 2″ Weight: 200 Born: June 29, 1983 Age: 23

YEAR	TM	LVL	AGE	W	L	SV	G	GS	IP	H	BB	SO	HR	GB%	BABIP	STUFF	WHIP	ERA	PERA	EQERA	EQH9	EQBB9	EQSO9	EQHR9	VORP	WXRL
2005	WIL	A+	22	2	2	0	24	0	48.7	39	32	56	5	44%	.296	-18	1.46	4.07	6.60	6.40	9.4	7.0	6.8	1.6	-4.0	—
2006	ARI	MLB	23	2	4	0	25	5	52.3	57	44	38	12	39%	.287	-19	1.93	6.98	7.30	6.78	9.4	7.5	6.4	1.8	-5.3	-0.5

Breakout: 19% Improve: 47% Collapse: 22% Attrition: 16%   Comparables: Rob Burger, Chris Saenz, Ben Howard

His control in the Red Sox system was much better, as his K/BB rate never dipped below 3.4. Bono doesn't have overpowering stuff, but he does have three pitches, he's started and relieved with success, and he keeps the ball down. In other words, with a history of good peripherals, he's one to watch, despite his 2005 hiccup.

BRIAN BRUNEY Bats: R Throws: R Height: 6′ 3″ Weight: 220 Born: February 17, 1982 Age: 24

YEAR	TM	LVL	AGE	W	L	SV	G	GS	IP	H	BB	SO	HR	GB%	BABIP	STUFF	WHIP	ERA	PERA	EQERA	EQH9	EQBB9	EQSO9	EQHR9	VORP	WXRL
2003	ELP	AA	21	0	2	14	28	0	31.3	29	13	28	1	—	.298	-2	1.34	2.59	4.35	4.94	8.1	4.4	5.8	0.6	2.3	—
2003	TUC	AAA	21	3	1	12	32	0	32.0	24	18	32	0	—	.273	12	1.31	2.81	4.06	3.48	7.0	5.5	7.8	0.3	7.3	—
2004	TUC	AAA	22	2	0	5	31	0	38.0	18	20	42	1	—	.198	15	1.00	1.18	3.75	2.25	5.5	5.2	8.0	0.2	13.4	—
2004	ARI	MLB	22	3	4	0	30	0	31.3	20	27	34	2	39%	.257	7	1.50	4.31	4.65	4.06	6.7	7.0	8.7	0.6	3.9	0.4
2005	ARI	MLB	23	1	3	12	47	0	46.0	56	35	51	6	41%	.385	-2	1.98	7.43	5.03	7.08	9.7	6.0	8.8	1.1	-10.2	-0.6
2006	ARI	MLB	24	2	3	4	34	1	43.3	40	27	43	5	42%	.297	6	1.54	4.74	4.74	5.31	8.0	5.1	8.3	0.9	3.4	0.3

Breakout: 33% Improve: 60% Collapse: 21% Attrition: 35%   Comparables: Eric Plunk, Bart Johnson, Rich Gossage

Yes, he was one of the more hit-unlucky pitchers in all of baseball last year (.385 BABIP), but his problems go deeper than that. Bruney's always been stingy with the home run, and has had no trouble striking hitters out; with success in most of the right places in the minor leagues, he's worth being patient with, but he'll never amount to anything with that walk rate.

JASON BULGER Bats: R Throws: R Height: 6′ 4″ Weight: 200 Born: December 6, 1978 Age: 27

YEAR	TM	LVL	AGE	W	L	SV	G	GS	IP	H	BB	SO	HR	GB%	BABIP	STUFF	WHIP	ERA	PERA	EQERA	EQH9	EQBB9	EQSO9	EQHR9	VORP	WXRL
2003	LNC	A+	24	2	1	0	4	4	17.3	23	5	20	3	—	.385	-16	1.62	6.76	7.56	7.56	13.0	3.8	5.9	3.2	-3.6	—
2004	LNC	A+	25	0	1	11	21	0	23.7	14	10	31	0	—	.275	-3	1.01	1.52	4.64	3.80	7.2	5.9	7.2	0.4	4.3	—
2004	ELP	AA	25	0	3	8	24	0	25.3	25	19	26	0	—	.338	-21	1.74	3.91	5.47	5.11	8.8	8.4	5.8	0.4	1.3	—
2005	TUC	AAA	26	3	6	4	56	0	56.0	50	27	55	3	52%	.320	-3	1.38	3.54	4.28	4.61	8.4	4.6	6.3	0.5	6.0	—
2005	ARI	MLB	26	1	0	0	9	0	10.0	14	5	9	1	30%	.406	-1	1.90	5.40	4.22	5.06	10.1	4.2	6.8	0.8	0.3	0.2
2006	ARI	MLB	27	2	3	1	52	1	46.7	49	29	35	6	47%	.301	-10	1.65	5.26	5.57	5.57	9.1	5.0	6.3	1.1	0.7	0.0

Breakout: 18% Improve: 39% Collapse: 37% Attrition: 23%   Comparables: Frank Reberger, Jason Isringhausen, Jerry Johnson

Like most D-Backs pitchers, Bulger has a walk problem. He's been seeing a lot of action as a closer since his High-A days, but his peripherals don't really suggest he's got that special something to get The Three Most Magicalest Outs to get that Most Wonderfullest of Stats: a save.

LANCE CORMIER Bats: R Throws: R Height: 6′ 1″ Weight: 190 Born: August 19, 1980 Age: 25

YEAR	TM	LVL	AGE	W	L	SV	G	GS	IP	H	BB	SO	HR	GB%	BABIP	STUFF	WHIP	ERA	PERA	EQERA	EQH9	EQBB9	EQSO9	EQHR9	VORP	WXRL
2003	LNC	A+	22	6	5	0	15	15	94.3	102	16	59	6	—	.300	-6	1.25	3.82	4.95	6.51	9.8	2.0	3.4	1.1	-9.4	—
2003	ELP	AA	22	2	3	0	9	8	41.3	59	22	26	3	—	.364	-19	1.96	6.10	5.70	6.75	10.8	5.5	4.0	1.1	-5.5	—
2003	TUC	AAA	22	1	1	0	5	4	27.7	26	5	11	1	—	.257	3	1.12	2.60	4.00	3.33	8.7	2.0	3.0	0.3	6.8	—
2004	ELP	AA	23	2	3	0	10	8	63.0	66	17	58	3	—	.341	16	1.32	2.29	4.29	3.43	8.9	2.9	5.4	0.7	15.2	—
2004	TUC	AAA	23	3	3	0	8	8	50.3	50	17	37	0	—	.321	17	1.33	2.68	3.75	3.22	8.4	3.2	5.0	0.2	13.3	—
2004	ARI	MLB	23	1	4	0	17	5	45.3	62	25	24	13	52%	.329	-33	1.92	8.15	7.14	6.75	11.4	4.4	4.0	2.3	-12.9	-0.7
2005	ARI	MLB	24	7	3	0	67	0	79.3	86	43	63	7	50%	.341	-1	1.63	5.11	4.54	5.20	9.2	4.4	6.4	0.8	-0.7	2.2
2006	ATL	MLB	25	3	4	1	45	3	67.3	69	31	50	7	50%	.301	-2	1.48	4.61	4.79	5.38	9.0	3.7	6.2	0.9	4.1	0.4

Breakout: 32% Improve: 53% Collapse: 13% Attrition: 13%   Comparables: Jose Paniagua, Brian Williams, Dave Giusti

It's amazing what happens when you post low ERAs in hitter's parks a few times, despite allowing too many baserunners. Cormier has pretty average stuff, but got promoted in 2004 largely because of a fairly good season between El Paso and Tucson. He doesn't strike out very many batters, so like every guy who cuts things fine, he needs to keep his walks down in order to have any success. He did just that in the first half in '05 (2.70 ERA), but he wore down after pitching 50 relief innings before the All-Star break, allowing an ugly 34 runs in 29.1 second-half innings. Dealt to Atlanta in the Estrada deal, we'll see if the post-Mazzone Braves can still work their magic with nondescript relievers.

SHAWN ESTES

Bats: R Throws: L   Height: 6′ 2″   Weight: 200   Born: February 18, 1973   Age: 33

YEAR	TM	LVL	AGE	W	L	SV	G	GS	IP	H	BB	SO	HR	GB%	BABIP	STUFF	WHIP	ERA	PERA	EQERA	EQH9	EQBB9	EQSO9	EQHR9	VORP	WXRL
2003	CHN	MLB	30	8	11	0	29	28	152.3	182	83	103	20	55%	.342	-6	1.74	5.73	5.19	6.29	10.1	4.3	5.4	1.2	-16.9	0.8
2004	COL	MLB	31	15	8	0	34	34	202.0	223	105	117	30	54%	.311	-7	1.62	5.84	5.44	5.22	9.5	4.2	4.6	1.1	4.3	1.6
2005	ARI	MLB	32	7	8	0	21	21	123.7	132	45	63	15	50%	.297	-2	1.43	4.80	5.07	4.56	9.4	3.0	4.2	1.1	8.9	1.6
2006	*ARI*	*MLB*	*33*	*6*	*9*	*0*	*27*	*21*	*122.3*	*134*	*53*	*68*	*14*	*51%*	*.296*	*-5*	*1.53*	*5.02*	*5.17*	*5.40*	*9.6*	*3.6*	*4.7*	*1.0*	*5.3*	*1.3*

Breakout: 22%   Improve: 52%   Collapse: 21%   Attrition: 8%   Comparables: *Darren Oliver, Omar Olivares, John Curtis*

Since 1998, his ERA is 4.98; only five other pitchers have a higher ERA over that span. It ain't all park effects either; Estes is just not very good. His strikeout rate hit a career low last year. This may have been due to a foot injury, but if not he may have crossed the terminus from "bad but within the limits of tolerable pain" to "Paris Hilton." Good news for potential employers: he pitched well away from home (3.00 ERA vs. 6.35 in Arizona). If you're the team that's signing him, you're probably used to looking for crumbs of hope like that one.

BUDDY GROOM

Bats: L Throws: L   Height: 6′ 2″   Weight: 208   Born: July 10, 1965   Age: 40

YEAR	TM	LVL	AGE	W	L	SV	G	GS	IP	H	BB	SO	HR	GB%	BABIP	STUFF	WHIP	ERA	PERA	EQERA	EQH9	EQBB9	EQSO9	EQHR9	VORP	WXRL
2003	BAL	MLB	38	1	3	1	60	0	45.3	58	14	34	7	51%	.347	-5	1.59	5.36	4.79	4.98	10.1	2.7	6.3	1.3	3.4	0.5
2004	BAL	MLB	39	4	1	0	60	0	52.7	67	16	32	6	46%	.341	-7	1.58	4.78	4.28	4.61	10.2	2.5	4.9	0.8	7.5	0.3
2005	NYA	MLB	40	1	0	0	24	0	25.7	32	7	13	3	45%	.326	-10	1.52	4.90	4.78	4.44	10.6	2.4	4.4	1.0	2.4	0.4
2005	ARI	MLB	40	0	1	1	23	0	15.3	19	5	7	2	52%	.315	-18	1.57	4.71	5.17	4.02	10.3	2.9	3.4	1.1	1.6	0.2
2006	*ARI*	*MLB*	*40*	*1*	*1*	*0*	*14*	*0*	*13.3*	*17*	*4*	*8*	*2*	*47%*	*.320*	*-18*	*1.56*	*5.19*	*5.52*	*6.64*	*11.1*	*2.7*	*4.9*	*1.3*	*0.8*	*0.0*

Breakout: 26%   Improve: 31%   Collapse: 43%   Attrition: 57%   Comparables: *Harry Gumbert, Terry Mulholland, Jeff Fassero*

Shaved his mustache so he could pitch for the Yankees, failed to become one of "Joe Torre's Boys," and headed West to regrow his facial hair in the prickly heat of the desert. Good for him. As more and more young hipsters grow the ironic mustache, it's nice to see someone who genuinely takes his facial hair seriously.

EDGAR GONZALEZ

Bats: R Throws: R   Height: 6′ 0″   Weight: 220   Born: February 23, 1983   Age: 23

YEAR	TM	LVL	AGE	W	L	SV	G	GS	IP	H	BB	SO	HR	GB%	BABIP	STUFF	WHIP	ERA	PERA	EQERA	EQH9	EQBB9	EQSO9	EQHR9	VORP	WXRL
2003	ELP	AA	20	2	2	0	6	6	36.0	40	11	30	1	—	.333	20	1.42	3.50	3.93	4.42	8.8	2.9	5.4	0.5	4.8	—
2003	TUC	AAA	20	8	7	0	20	19	129.7	126	28	69	4	—	.276	25	1.19	3.75	3.86	4.14	8.6	2.1	4.3	0.4	20.8	—
2004	TUC	AAA	21	5	5	0	15	15	94.0	99	25	66	15	—	.294	1	1.32	4.88	5.19	4.42	9.2	2.5	5.0	1.4	12.3	—
2004	ARI	MLB	21	0	9	0	10	10	46.3	72	18	31	15	45%	.373	-16	1.94	9.33	6.89	7.82	12.5	3.0	5.2	2.6	-18.9	-0.6
2005	TUC	AAA	22	11	6	0	28	24	167.0	185	38	116	20	46%	.319	4	1.34	4.37	4.71	4.82	9.7	2.0	4.7	1.1	14.4	—
2006	*ARI*	*MLB*	*23*	*6*	*10*	*1*	*49*	*17*	*142.0*	*158*	*44*	*85*	*21*	*46%*	*.296*	*-2*	*1.42*	*5.00*	*5.02*	*5.14*	*9.7*	*2.5*	*5.0*	*1.3*	*6.4*	*1.3*

Breakout: 24%   Improve: 76%   Collapse: 4%   Attrition: 0%   Comparables: *Rick Rhoden, Bob Friend, Joe Niekro*

He's been a prospect for a while, and has had to survive in some pretty hitter-friendly home parks, but he has yet to really blow anyone away with a performance that puts him over the top. His control is major-league ready; the rest of him is not. If he doesn't show some improvement soon, he could get passed by the other Gonzalez.

ENRIQUE GONZALEZ

Bats: R Throws: R   Height: 5′ 10″ Weight: 195   Born: July 14, 1982   Age: 23

YEAR	TM	LVL	AGE	W	L	SV	G	GS	IP	H	BB	SO	HR	GB%	BABIP	STUFF	WHIP	ERA	PERA	EQERA	EQH9	EQBB9	EQSO9	EQHR9	VORP	WXRL
2003	SBN	A	20	4	3	3	55	0	72.0	58	29	63	5	—	.257	-22	1.21	2.12	6.47	4.82	9.8	5.0	5.5	1.9	5.7	—
2004	LNC	A+	21	13	6	0	42	17	142.3	128	44	110	13	—	.278	-18	1.21	3.23	5.73	5.07	9.1	3.7	4.5	1.5	8.0	—
2005	TEN	AA	22	11	8	0	27	27	161.3	160	52	146	8	49%	.336	12	1.31	3.46	4.46	5.09	9.2	3.2	5.4	0.8	8.9	—
2006	*ARI*	*MLB*	*23*	*6*	*11*	*0*	*29*	*23*	*136.3*	*149*	*62*	*84*	*20*	*50%*	*.295*	*0*	*1.54*	*5.34*	*5.45*	*5.47*	*9.5*	*3.7*	*5.2*	*1.2*	*0.9*	*1.0*

Breakout: 4%   Improve: 35%   Collapse: 20%   Attrition: 0%   Comparables: *Pasqual Coco, Brian Bannister, Jim Magrane*

Man, that's a lot of unearned runs. That was really the only blemish on his year, as his rate stats were promising: good K/BB, K/9, and HR/9, which helped him lead the Smokies in innings and strikeouts. The closest thing to a major-league ready pitching prospect this organization has.

MIKE GOSLING
Bats: L   Throws: L   Height: 6′ 2″   Weight: 210   Born: September 23, 1980   Age: 25

YEAR	TM	LVL	AGE	W	L	SV	G	GS	IP	H	BB	SO	HR	GB%	BABIP	STUFF	WHIP	ERA	PERA	EQERA	EQH9	EQBB9	EQSO9	EQHR9	VORP	WXRL
2003	TUC	AAA	22	9	12	0	26	26	136.3	190	56	89	13	—	.356	-6	1.80	5.61	5.18	6.40	10.8	4.0	4.8	1.1	-12.5	—
2004	TUC	AAA	23	9	5	0	24	21	128.3	160	53	67	16	—	.320	-17	1.66	5.82	5.66	6.28	10.1	3.9	3.5	1.2	-9.8	—
2004	ARI	MLB	23	1	1	0	6	4	25.3	26	13	14	5	44%	.276	-11	1.54	4.62	6.48	3.96	9.7	4.3	4.3	1.8	3.1	0.3
2005	TUC	AAA	24	4	6	0	18	17	92.3	129	30	76	11	50%	.386	-3	1.72	5.95	4.83	6.44	11.1	2.8	5.2	1.1	-8.9	—
2005	ARI	MLB	24	0	3	0	13	5	32.3	40	19	14	2	37%	.325	-19	1.82	4.46	5.08	5.08	9.9	4.8	3.5	0.5	0.5	-0.2
2006	*ARI*	*MLB*	*25*	*4*	*8*	*0*	*40*	*18*	*102.7*	*123*	*47*	*55*	*17*	*46%*	*.305*	*-14*	*1.65*	*5.89*	*6.16*	*6.07*	*10.5*	*3.7*	*4.5*	*1.5*	*-4.9*	*0.1*

Breakout: 13%   Improve: 48%   Collapse: 23%   Attrition: 1%   Comparables: Bud Black, Barry Moore, Dave Fleming

Even giving him the benefit of the doubt regarding his home ballparks in the minors, there's not a whole lot to get excited about here. Mediocre peripherals are still that, no matter how smart the guy is who has them. As Stanford arms go, he's more Justin Wayne than Mike Mussina.

BRAD HALSEY
Bats: L   Throws: L   Height: 6′ 1″   Weight: 180   Born: February 14, 1981   Age: 25

YEAR	TM	LVL	AGE	W	L	SV	G	GS	IP	H	BB	SO	HR	GB%	BABIP	STUFF	WHIP	ERA	PERA	EQERA	EQH9	EQBB9	EQSO9	EQHR9	VORP	WXRL
2003	TAM	A+	22	10	4	0	14	13	84.0	96	14	56	3	—	.322	2	1.31	3.43	4.50	5.60	10.8	1.8	4.1	1.0	0.0	—
2003	TRN	AA	22	7	5	0	15	15	91.3	123	22	78	4	—	.378	19	1.59	4.93	3.98	5.40	10.2	2.4	5.6	0.7	2.1	—
2004	COH	AAA	23	11	4	0	24	23	144.0	128	37	109	8	—	.278	22	1.15	2.62	3.97	3.20	8.3	2.5	5.4	0.6	37.5	—
2004	NYA	MLB	23	1	3	0	8	7	32.0	41	14	25	4	46%	.352	2	1.72	6.47	4.81	6.42	10.2	3.5	6.1	1.1	-4.3	0.0
2005	ARI	MLB	24	8	12	0	28	26	160.0	191	39	82	20	42%	.320	0	1.44	4.61	4.80	5.02	10.1	2.0	4.1	1.1	-0.5	2.0
2006	*ARI*	*MLB*	*25*	*7*	*11*	*0*	*32*	*24*	*151.0*	*168*	*43*	*89*	*20*	*45%*	*.298*	*4*	*1.39*	*4.77*	*4.79*	*5.00*	*9.7*	*2.3*	*4.9*	*1.1*	*10.9*	*2.1*

Breakout: 18%   Improve: 55%   Collapse: 20%   Attrition: 6%   Comparables: Scott McGregor, Jerry Augustine, Allan Anderson

A control lefty with pretty uninspiring strikeout numbers, Admiral Halsey was adequate in the D-Back rotation after beating out Mike Gosling for the job. Halsey's season wasn't actually that promising, though, as he was torched by righties to the tune of .309/.357/.489, and his acceptable ERA disguises 19 unearned runs. If there's some consolation to be taken from 2005, it's that he pitched better at home than on the road. Likely staring at a 2006 of LOOGYing.

BRANDON LYON
Bats: R   Throws: R   Height: 6′ 1″   Weight: 180   Born: August 10, 1979   Age: 26

YEAR	TM	LVL	AGE	W	L	SV	G	GS	IP	H	BB	SO	HR	GB%	BABIP	STUFF	WHIP	ERA	PERA	EQERA	EQH9	EQBB9	EQSO9	EQHR9	VORP	WXRL
2003	BOS	MLB	23	4	6	9	49	0	59.0	73	19	50	6	44%	.351	9	1.56	4.12	3.94	4.38	9.5	2.8	7.2	0.9	7.7	0.1
2005	ARI	MLB	25	0	2	14	32	0	29.3	44	10	17	6	43%	.358	-23	1.84	6.45	5.81	6.68	11.6	2.6	4.6	1.7	-6.6	1.5
2006	*ARI*	*MLB*	*26*	*1*	*1*	*3*	*13*	*0*	*16.3*	*18*	*5*	*11*	*2*	*47%*	*.302*	*-3*	*1.40*	*4.34*	*4.51*	*6.06*	*9.5*	*2.7*	*5.8*	*1.0*	*2.9*	*0.2*

Breakout: 44%   Improve: 56%   Collapse: 23%   Attrition: 54%   Comparables: Donnie Moore, Will McEnaney, Jeff Brantley

Headed for Tommy John surgery after a few years of elbow trouble. Guys with high strikeout totals and high walk totals are everywhere in this system, so he's not guaranteed a job if or when he returns at full strength. "At full strength" is relative, anyway, given his injury problems.

BRANDON MEDDERS
Bats: R   Throws: R   Height: 6′ 2″   Weight: 200   Born: January 26, 1980   Age: 26

YEAR	TM	LVL	AGE	W	L	SV	G	GS	IP	H	BB	SO	HR	GB%	BABIP	STUFF	WHIP	ERA	PERA	EQERA	EQH9	EQBB9	EQSO9	EQHR9	VORP	WXRL
2003	ELP	AA	23	5	3	7	56	0	69.3	65	26	72	3	—	.313	0	1.31	4.42	4.21	5.14	8.2	4.1	6.6	0.7	3.5	—
2005	TUC	AAA	25	3	2	8	36	0	36.3	31	18	44	3	55%	.318	4	1.35	2.48	4.33	3.06	8.2	4.8	7.9	0.8	10.0	—
2005	ARI	MLB	25	4	1	0	27	0	30.3	21	11	31	2	48%	.253	22	1.05	1.78	3.30	1.80	6.9	3.0	8.4	0.6	12.6	0.7
2006	*ARI*	*MLB*	*26*	*2*	*3*	*3*	*54*	*1*	*54.3*	*50*	*24*	*49*	*6*	*44%*	*.286*	*6*	*1.36*	*4.04*	*4.10*	*4.44*	*8.0*	*3.7*	*7.5*	*0.9*	*8.0*	*0.7*

Breakout: 11%   Improve: 26%   Collapse: 54%   Attrition: 18%   Comparables: Bill Campbell, Paul Shuey, Scott Strickland

Late in the season, Medders tripped on the dugout steps and tweaked his groin. A classic short-armer, he had a nice 2005 at two levels. He'll be in the bullpen mix in 2006, but recovering from a torn labrum isn't exactly a sure thing, promising 2005 or not.

GARRETT MOCK   Bats: R   Throws: R   Height: 6' 4"   Weight: 215   Born: April 25, 1983   Age: 23

YEAR	TM	LVL	AGE	W	L	SV	G	GS	IP	H	BB	SO	HR	GB%	BABIP	STUFF	WHIP	ERA	PERA	EQERA	EQH9	EQBB9	EQSO9	EQHR9	VORP	WXRL
2004	YAK	A-	21	2	0	0	5	5	23.3	18	4	14	1	—	.243	-6	0.94	1.55	4.84	4.43	8.1	2.0	2.8	0.8	2.9	—
2004	SBN	A	21	3	2	0	8	8	54.0	49	12	37	2	—	.281	0	1.13	3.00	4.56	5.79	9.3	2.6	3.5	0.7	-1.1	—
2005	LNC	A+	22	14	7	0	28·	28	174.3	202	33	160	19	51%	.344	0	1.35	4.18	4.95	5.36	10.0	2.1	4.9	1.3	4.7	—
2006	ARI	MLB	23	7	11	0	27	26	153.0	169	44	87	21	47%	.294	6	1.39	5.10	4.89	5.21	9.7	2.4	4.8	1.2	4.9	1.6

Breakout: 15%   Improve: 59%   Collapse: 5%   Attrition: 0%   Comparables: Mike Ziegler, Brian Reith, Justin Miller

Don't let the ERA fool you: Lancaster's a tough place to pitch. He's got a good sinking fastball and a big breaking ball, and handled the Cal League well enough to lead it in strikeouts. He was also the Arizona organizational leader in that department. His hit rate is worrisome, but since it came in the offensive Cal League, reserve judgment until he hits the high minors. Worth watching.

BILL MURPHY   Bats: L   Throws: L   Height: 6' 0"   Weight: 190   Born: May 9, 1981   Age: 25

YEAR	TM	LVL	AGE	W	L	SV	G	GS	IP	H	BB	SO	HR	GB%	BABIP	STUFF	WHIP	ERA	PERA	EQERA	EQH9	EQBB9	EQSO9	EQHR9	VORP	WXRL
2003	KNC	A	22	7	4	0	14	14	92.0	61	32	87	5	—	.229	-6	1.01	2.25	5.88	5.01	8.6	4.5	5.7	1.6	5.4	—
2003	MID	AA	22	3	3	0	11	11	55.0	44	26	34	4	—	.234	-13	1.27	4.09	5.92	4.88	8.4	5.2	4.2	1.2	4.1	—
2004	CAR	AA	23	6	4	0	20	20	103.7	80	59	113	17	—	.253	-34	1.34	4.08	7.44	5.53	9.3	6.3	6.6	2.6	0.7	—
2004	ELP	AA	23	3	3	0	6	6	31.0	41	17	24	6	—	.361	-28	1.87	6.68	7.92	7.63	11.4	5.9	4.7	2.6	-6.9	—
2005	TUC	AAA	24	6	8	0	23	21	121.0	135	78	87	14	49%	.324	-16	1.76	5.65	6.07	5.70	10.0	5.9	4.7	1.2	-1.3	—
2006	ARI	MLB	25	4	9	0	30	18	102.7	115	76	69	19	43%	.298	-15	1.86	6.63	7.00	6.69	9.8	6.1	5.6	1.6	-12.3	-0.7

Breakout: 5%   Improve: 19%   Collapse: 36%   Attrition: 2%   Comparables: Brent Billingsley, Trey Poland, Jeff Wilson

His strikeout rate has been nearly cut in half since his final year at Cal State Northridge. That's especially troubling considering his walk rate, which remains just as high. Being a pitcher in the Diamondbacks minor league system is difficult enough when you have two or three weaknesses, but Murphy is having to work on just about everything. It was downright tragic that his reconstruction began with a trip to the bruising, high-offense Arizona Fall League, but he was surprisingly successful there despite the offensive environment: a 36:4 K/BB ratio in just over 27 innings. Short-term success in the AFL aside, he's in the wrong organization to work through a control problem.

DUSTIN NIPPERT   Bats: R   Throws: R   Height: 6' 7"   Weight: 200   Born: May 6, 1981   Age: 25

YEAR	TM	LVL	AGE	W	L	SV	G	GS	IP	H	BB	SO	HR	GB%	BABIP	STUFF	WHIP	ERA	PERA	EQERA	EQH9	EQBB9	EQSO9	EQHR9	VORP	WXRL
2003	SBN	A	22	6	4	0	17	17	95.7	66	32	96	4	—	.245	1	1.02	2.82	5.19	5.40	8.7	4.3	6.0	1.2	1.9	—
2004	ELP	AA	23	2	5	0	14	14	71.7	77	40	73	0	—	.350	10	1.63	3.64	4.40	5.78	8.9	5.8	6.0	0.3	-1.4	—
2005	TEN	AA	24	8	3	0	18	18	117.3	95	42	97	4	55%	.285	11	1.17	2.38	4.62	3.89	8.3	3.8	4.9	0.6	21.1	—
2005	ARI	MLB	24	1	0	0	3	3	14.7	10	13	11	1	47%	.214	-5	1.57	5.51	5.65	5.02	6.9	7.5	6.3	0.6	0.1	0.3
2006	ARI	MLB	25	6	11	0	31	22	136.0	139	74	90	15	51%	.292	0	1.56	5.28	5.15	5.53	9.0	4.4	5.5	1.0	0.9	1.0

Breakout: 5%   Improve: 27%   Collapse: 30%   Attrition: 0%   Comparables: Zach Day, Jim Hughes, Rich Gale

Came back from Tommy John surgery with some success, as his walk rate was just about average at Tennessee before his September cup of coffee, which was not so good. He throws hard, keeps the ball down, and at 6'7", is a scary-looking fellow on the mound. A rotation featuring Nippert and Brandon Webb is well on its way to being freakishly big.

RUSS ORTIZ   Bats: R   Throws: R   Height: 6' 1"   Weight: 210   Born: June 5, 1974   Age: 32

YEAR	TM	LVL	AGE	W	L	SV	G	GS	IP	H	BB	SO	HR	GB%	BABIP	STUFF	WHIP	ERA	PERA	EQERA	EQH9	EQBB9	EQSO9	EQHR9	VORP	WXRL
2003	ATL	MLB	29	21	7	0	34	34	212.3	177	102	149	17	47%	.255	13	1.31	3.82	4.46	4.37	8.3	4.0	5.8	0.7	31.7	5.1
2004	ATL	MLB	30	15	9	0	34	34	204.7	197	112	143	23	45%	.291	4	1.51	4.13	4.93	4.40	8.8	4.5	5.6	0.9	32.3	5.3
2005	ARI	MLB	31	5	11	0	22	22	115.0	147	65	46	18	38%	.319	-27	1.84	6.89	6.16	6.39	10.6	4.6	3.2	1.4	-18.3	-1.0
2006	ARI	MLB	32	5	9	0	29	18	111.0	123	54	60	16	43%	.291	-12	1.59	5.57	5.60	6.09	9.7	3.9	4.5	1.2	-1.5	0.5

Breakout: 8%   Improve: 35%   Collapse: 32%   Attrition: 12%   Comparables: Jim Slaton, Chan Ho Park, Dan Petry

If denial, as Robert Bly asserts, is the "naive person's inability to face the harsh facts of life," then the Diamondbacks were certainly in denial about Russ Ortiz, who had been offering harsh facts for a few years before signing with Arizona. Take away years of good run support, good defense, good pitchers' parks, and a "resurgence" under Leo Mazzone, and you're left with a replacement-level pitcher with a Victor Zambrano-sized walk problem that not even Rick Peterson would claim to be able to fix.

MICAH OWINGS   Bats: R Throws: R   Height: 6′ 5″   Weight: 220   Born: September 28, 1982 Age: 23

YEAR	TM	LVL	AGE	W	L	SV	G	GS	IP	H	BB	SO	HR	GB%	BABIP	STUFF	WHIP	ERA	PERA	EQERA	EQH9	EQBB9	EQSO9	EQHR9	VORP	WXRL
2005	LNC	A+	22	1	1	0	16	0	22.0	17	4	30	0	43%	.362	17	0.95	2.45	2.95	3.38	7.6	2.1	7.6	0.4	5.3	—
2006	ARI	MLB	23	2	3	1	22	4	48.3	46	17	39	6	45%	.282	10	1.29	4.07	4.08	4.21	8.3	2.9	6.8	1.0	6.8	0.8

Breakout: 12% Improve: 23% Collapse: 49% Attrition: 30%   Comparables: Jeff Taglienti, Eric Cyr, Shawn Sonnier

Small sample size or not, one has to be encouraged when a pitching prospect doesn't implode in this system. Unlike some other hard-throwing pitchers in this organization (he shows mid- to high-90's heat), Owings has a history of good control, he's shown improvement over the last few years, and he's not a project. Keep an eye on him.

RAMON PENA   Bats: R Throws: R   Height: 6′ 2″   Weight: 190   Born: January 9, 1982   Age: 24

YEAR	TM	LVL	AGE	W	L	SV	G	GS	IP	H	BB	SO	HR	GB%	BABIP	STUFF	WHIP	ERA	PERA	EQERA	EQH9	EQBB9	EQSO9	EQHR9	VORP	WXRL
2003	SBN	A	21	9	5	0	27	27	160.3	149	30	119	3	—	.287	15	1.12	2.86	4.06	6.12	9.5	2.2	4.4	0.5	-8.8	—
2004	ELP	AA	22	3	3	0	7	7	43.0	47	5	36	4	—	.333	9	1.21	5.44	4.60	5.44	9.4	1.3	5.0	1.3	0.8	—
2005	TEN	AA	23	7	13	0	25	25	148.3	165	40	95	17	42%	.314	-26	1.38	4.43	6.32	5.94	10.7	2.8	3.8	2.0	-5.4	—
2006	ARI	MLB	24	5	11	0	27	22	128.7	152	43	67	22	46%	.300	-4	1.51	5.86	5.72	6.02	10.3	2.7	4.4	1.5	-6.2	0.3

Breakout: 15% Improve: 47% Collapse: 9% Attrition: 0%   Comparables: Ismael Ramirez, Dan Perkins, Mike Lincoln

How do you get from Adriano Rosario to Ramon Pena? First answer: Practice! Second answer: By falsifying your visa and aging five years in just a few days, that's how. Scouts are excited about this guy and his high-90s fastball, but he hasn't had the success to warrant the enthusiasm. Like so many others in this system, he needs to improve his walk rate in order to be a viable prospect. Very young kids with raw stuff are forgiven since they're young; middle-aged prospects who are raw are projects, and this isn't the best place for the latter.

JOSE VALVERDE   Bats: R Throws: R   Height: 6′ 4″   Weight: 255   Born: July 24, 1979   Age: 26

YEAR	TM	LVL	AGE	W	L	SV	G	GS	IP	H	BB	SO	HR	GB%	BABIP	STUFF	WHIP	ERA	PERA	EQERA	EQH9	EQBB9	EQSO9	EQHR9	VORP	WXRL
2003	TUC	AAA	23	1	1	5	22	0	29.0	26	14	26	1	—	.291	2	1.38	3.10	3.81	3.49	7.9	5.1	7.0	0.3	6.6	—
2003	ARI	MLB	23	2	1	10	54	0	50.3	24	26	71	4	36%	.200	36	0.99	2.15	3.31	2.76	5.5	4.2	11.6	0.7	16.1	3.7
2004	ARI	MLB	24	1	2	8	29	0	29.7	23	17	38	7	39%	.254	9	1.35	4.24	5.22	4.60	7.7	4.6	10.1	1.8	2.4	0.6
2005	ARI	MLB	25	3	4	15	61	0	66.3	51	20	75	5	36%	.284	29	1.07	2.44	3.27	2.59	7.1	2.6	9.3	0.7	21.9	2.9
2006	ARI	MLB	26	3	4	20	50	0	54.7	46	24	56	6	39%	.277	15	1.27	3.52	3.61	3.56	7.3	3.5	8.5	0.9	11.3	1.4

Breakout: 17% Improve: 34% Collapse: 46% Attrition: 9%   Comparables: Bobby Howry, Tom Niedenfuer, Steve Bedrosian

He's excellent when healthy, but his violent delivery will pretty much ensure that he's rarely healthy. Diamondback fans have to hope that new pitching coach Bryan Price had nothing to do with the Mariners' well-documented history of destroying young arms.

CLAUDIO VARGAS   Bats: R Throws: R   Height: 6′ 3″   Weight: 220   Born: June 19, 1978   Age: 28

YEAR	TM	LVL	AGE	W	L	SV	G	GS	IP	H	BB	SO	HR	GB%	BABIP	STUFF	WHIP	ERA	PERA	EQERA	EQH9	EQBB9	EQSO9	EQHR9	VORP	WXRL
2003	MON	MLB	25	6	8	0	23	20	114.0	111	41	62	16	37%	.265	-7	1.33	4.34	5.22	4.58	9.4	3.0	4.5	1.2	16.9	3.0
2004	MON	MLB	26	5	5	0	45	14	118.3	120	64	89	26	36%	.280	-25	1.55	5.25	6.06	5.45	9.6	4.4	6.1	1.8	-1.3	0.6
2005	NWO	AAA	27	2	2	0	5	5	28.0	24	12	35	4	41%	.308	12	1.29	4.18	5.06	5.06	8.8	4.4	8.1	1.7	1.6	—
2005	WAS	MLB	27	0	3	0	4	4	12.7	22	7	5	4	30%	.360	-43	2.29	9.21	8.10	10.80	13.5	4.7	3.4	2.7	-7.0	-0.1
2005	ARI	MLB	27	9	6	0	21	19	119.7	124	40	90	21	37%	.290	-1	1.37	4.81	5.18	4.57	9.3	2.8	6.2	1.6	9.9	1.9
2006	ARI	MLB	28	7	11	1	38	22	146.7	152	54	101	24	39%	.283	1	1.41	4.83	4.99	5.08	9.1	3.0	5.8	1.4	10.3	2.0

Breakout: 21% Improve: 55% Collapse: 19% Attrition: 9%   Comparables: Shawn Boskie, Craig Swan, Pete Smith

After he blew up in Washington to start the year, he was snagged off waivers, mostly to fill in while Russ Ortiz hit the DL. Though improving upon the 2005 version of Ortiz isn't hard to do, Vargas did a pretty good job; his peripherals improved despite moving from an extreme pitcher's park to an extreme hitter's park. Still too erratic and homer-prone, even with the step forward in 2005.

JAVIER VAZQUEZ   Bats: R   Throws: R   Height: 6' 2"   Weight: 175   Born: July 25, 1976   Age: 29

YEAR	TM	LVL	AGE	W	L	SV	G	GS	IP	H	BB	SO	HR	GB%	BABIP	STUFF	WHIP	ERA	PERA	EQERA	EQH9	EQBB9	EQSO9	EQHR9	VORP	WXRL
2003	MON	MLB	26	13	12	0	34	34	230.7	198	57	241	28	40%	.285	32	1.11	3.24	3.63	3.55	8.0	2.0	8.5	1.1	59.7	6.3
2004	NYA	MLB	27	14	10	0	32	32	198.0	195	60	150	33	41%	.279	6	1.29	4.91	4.76	4.71	8.9	2.5	6.4	1.4	21.9	3.9
2005	ARI	MLB	28	11	15	0	33	33	215.7	223	46	192	35	44%	.308	14	1.25	4.42	4.31	4.31	9.0	1.8	7.3	1.4	22.7	4.1
2006	*CHA*	*MLB*	*29*	*14*	*10*	*0*	*32*	*32*	*213.7*	*210*	*48*	*172*	*32*	*41%*	*.283*	*22*	*1.21*	*3.96*	*3.88*	*3.96*	*8.5*	*1.9*	*7.0*	*1.3*	*41.9*	*5.8*

Breakout: 20%   Improve: 64%   Collapse: 5%   Attrition: 1%   Comparables: Don Sutton, Mike Mussina, Robin Roberts

The argument that Mel Stottlemyre was a terrible pitching coach grew a little stronger when Vazquez rebounded in the desert, of all places. It was understandable that his propensity to allow home runs would be magnified in Arizona, but the rest of his game improved, particularly his control. But it wasn't just his walk rate that came around: he hit significantly fewer batters as a D-Back than as a Yankee, and his wild pitches stayed away from double digits (some attribute that to getting away from Jorge Posada, though that's an exaggerated indictment of Posada's defense). But like he did in 2004, Vazquez performed significantly worse after the All-Star break, throwing the permanence of his improvement into doubt. The White Sox are Vazquez's third team in as many years; there he'll be pitching coach Don Cooper's latest project.

OSCAR VILLARREAL   Bats: L   Throws: R   Height: 6' 0"   Weight: 170   Born: November 22, 1981   Age: 24

YEAR	TM	LVL	AGE	W	L	SV	G	GS	IP	H	BB	SO	HR	GB%	BABIP	STUFF	WHIP	ERA	PERA	EQERA	EQH9	EQBB9	EQSO9	EQHR9	VORP	WXRL
2003	ARI	MLB	21	10	7	0	86	1	98.0	80	46	80	6	50%	.269	15	1.29	2.57	3.99	3.43	7.8	3.8	6.7	0.6	23.0	2.1
2005	TUC	AAA	23	0	3	0	12	8	17.3	19	4	8	1	68%	.321	-19	1.33	5.20	4.15	6.23	9.3	2.1	3.1	0.5	-1.2	—
2005	ARI	MLB	23	2	0	0	11	0	13.7	11	6	5	2	33%	.225	-25	1.24	5.26	6.08	4.72	8.8	4.1	3.4	1.4	0.7	0.1
2006	*ATL*	*MLB*	*24*	*3*	*3*	*1*	*41*	*2*	*53.7*	*55*	*21*	*34*	*6*	*47%*	*.289*	*-6*	*1.42*	*4.47*	*4.63*	*5.59*	*9.2*	*3.2*	*5.3*	*1.0*	*3.8*	*0.4*

Breakout: 13%   Improve: 38%   Collapse: 36%   Attrition: 29%   Comparables: Jeff Pico, Elias Sosa, Mike Fornieles

Step 1: put Oscar Villarreal in the bullpen. Step 2: Keep him healthy by _____. Step 3: Profit. Villarreal had nerve transposition surgery in his elbow, battled shoulder problems, and passed a kidney stone to boot. Like Valverde, he's effective when healthy, has a good track record that portends future success, and will be an injury risk every time he steps on the mound. That's not a good combination, but we'll see if he'll become any more durable as a Brave, now that he's been dealt with Cormier in the Johnny Estrada deal.

BRANDON WEBB   Bats: R   Throws: R   Height: 6' 2"   Weight: 230   Born: May 9, 1979   Age: 27

YEAR	TM	LVL	AGE	W	L	SV	G	GS	IP	H	BB	SO	HR	GB%	BABIP	STUFF	WHIP	ERA	PERA	EQERA	EQH9	EQBB9	EQSO9	EQHR9	VORP	WXRL
2003	ARI	MLB	24	10	9	0	29	28	180.7	140	68	172	12	67%	.269	35	1.15	2.84	3.64	3.08	7.6	3.1	7.8	0.6	52.1	6.3
2004	ARI	MLB	25	7	16	0	35	35	208.0	194	119	164	17	66%	.294	16	1.50	3.59	4.53	4.14	8.5	4.7	6.3	0.6	24.5	3.6
2005	ARI	MLB	26	14	12	0	33	33	229.0	229	59	172	21	66%	.310	22	1.26	3.54	3.90	3.55	8.7	2.1	6.2	0.8	46.2	5.3
2006	*ARI*	*MLB*	*27*	*13*	*12*	*0*	*33*	*33*	*215.7*	*209*	*74*	*157*	*14*	*61%*	*.295*	*18*	*1.31*	*3.71*	*3.78*	*3.90*	*8.5*	*2.8*	*6.1*	*0.6*	*38.4*	*5.6*

Breakout: 5%   Improve: 35%   Collapse: 9%   Attrition: 2%   Comparables: Joey Hamilton, Rick Reuschel, Mark Gubicza

Everything was in place for him to implode following a 2004 season where he flirted with disaster: high walk rate, lots of groundballs, team with bad defensive efficiency. Instead, he took a huge step forward in the control department, which was the most critical of his weaknesses (and the only thing that was fully his responsibility anyway). Most encouraging, though, is that he didn't sacrifice his strikeout rate by improving his command, doubly good news for an extreme sinkerballer. This was also the second year in a row where his BABIP hugged the league average closely enough that you can't credit luck for his success. He still struggles mightily against lefties, as the 830 versus 569 OPS split suggests.

TIM WORRELL   Bats: R   Throws: R   Height: 6' 4"   Weight: 215   Born: July 5, 1967   Age: 38

YEAR	TM	LVL	AGE	W	L	SV	G	GS	IP	H	BB	SO	HR	GB%	BABIP	STUFF	WHIP	ERA	PERA	EQERA	EQH9	EQBB9	EQSO9	EQHR9	VORP	WXRL
2003	SFN	MLB	36	4	4	38	76	0	78.3	74	28	65	5	53%	.299	10	1.30	2.87	3.69	4.27	8.7	2.9	6.7	0.6	14.1	3.9
2004	PHI	MLB	37	5	6	19	77	0	78.3	75	21	64	10	49%	.294	2	1.23	3.68	4.19	4.19	8.8	2.2	6.6	1.0	13.6	2.6
2005	PHI	MLB	38	0	1	1	19	0	17.0	29	3	17	4	38%	.446	-1	1.88	7.41	4.91	8.84	12.8	1.5	7.9	2.0	-6.4	-0.7
2005	ARI	MLB	38	1	1	0	32	0	31.7	30	9	22	4	47%	.277	-2	1.23	2.27	4.55	3.41	8.5	2.3	5.7	1.1	6.5	1.2
2006	*ARI*	*MLB*	*38*	*2*	*3*	*2*	*49*	*0*	*57.0*	*63*	*17*	*40*	*8*	*45%*	*.303*	*-6*	*1.40*	*4.73*	*4.76*	*5.02*	*9.6*	*2.5*	*5.9*	*1.2*	*3.8*	*0.3*

Breakout: 22%   Improve: 54%   Collapse: 23%   Attrition: 22%   Comparables: Ron Reed, Roberto Hernandez, Rick Aguilera

Battled personal issues for part of the season, and eventually landed on his feet in Arizona, where his veteran presence was supposed to help stabilize a very young, very erratic bullpen. It's not a good sign for your pitching development program when a free pitcher becomes one of your most valuable commodities. Whatever his issues, if he left his heart in San Francisco, he's gone back for it, signing a two-year contract with the Giants.

Line Outs

Position/Player	TM	LVL	AGE	PA	R	2B	3B	HR	RBI	BB	SO	SB-CS	SPEED	BA/OBP/SLG	MLVR	EQBA/OBP/SLG	EQA	VORP
RF C. Gonzalez	SBN	A	19	569	91	28	6	18	92	48	86	7-3	5.2	.307/.371/.489	.275	.286/.338/.460	.272	16.1
OF Q. McCracken#	ARI	MLB	34	240	23	4	3	1	13	23	35	4-0	5.9	.237/.312/.298	-.215	.231/.310/.292	.224	-5.3

Pitcher	TM	LVL	AGE	W	L	SV	IP	H	BB	SO	HR	GB%	BABIP	STUFF	WHIP	ERA	PERA	EQERA	EQH9	EQBB9	EQSO9	EQHR9	VORP
J. Cannon*	TUC	AAA	30	3	5	0	73.3	72	43	44	11	44%	.277	-35	1.57	4.17	7.11	5.94	9.7	6.2	3.7	1.8	-2.6
M. Chico*	LNC	A+	22	7	2	0	110.0	101	39	102	13	43%	.293	-7	1.27	3.76	5.69	4.75	8.8	4.0	5.2	1.5	10.0
	TEN	AA	22	1	7	0	52.7	75	15	35	8	36%	.379	-25	1.71	5.98	6.88	7.74	12.4	2.8	4.0	2.4	-12.4
R. Choate*	TUC	AAA	29	1	1	3	40.0	44	22	20	4	66%	.299	-37	1.65	3.38	6.23	5.31	9.9	5.5	3.0	1.2	1.3
J. Neighborgall	MSO	Rk	21	1	2	0	22.7	21	45	29	1	68%	.339	-116	2.91	11.10	14.00	15.50	9.5	32.0	6.0	1.0	-19.8

Carlos Gonzalez had a monster season at Low-A South Bend, and is a good bet to go all Barry Bonds on the Cal League once he hits Lancaster next year. He exhibited good strike zone control, power, and defense in his first exposure to pro ball, and is well worth keeping an eye on. **Quinton McCracken** is the subject of this sentence, so he's got that going for him.

Jon Cannon really only had one good year, and that was in 2003, when he played in Mexico. In los Estados Unidos, he's like every other D-Back pitching "prospect": moderate-to-acceptable strikeout rate, lots of walks. **Matt Chico** was demoted after a horrid debut in Double-A, salvaged some dignity in Single-A Lancaster. Organizational faith or not, the peripherals just aren't there. **Randy Choate** is a lefty, so he'll pop up somewhere, preferably with better control. His one positive is that he's quite stingy with the home run, an Arizona rarity. If Rick Vaughn bypassed the penal system and opted for a technical education instead, he'd be **Jason Neighborgall**. Arizona thought highly enough of his triple-digit heat to take him in the third round of last year's draft, but he could cut that walk rate in half and still wouldn't be a prospect. As if the walk total wasn't enough, he also launched 23 wild pitches. **Matt Torra** is still not out of the woods after a heavy college workload at UMass; threw just ten innings in short-season ball before calling it a year. Scout's reviews are mixed, though you can't help but root for someone who didn't surrender a home run his final year of college. As a starter.

Atlanta Braves

On the surface, the Atlanta Braves' 2005 season could have been mistaken for about a half-dozen others over the past 15 years. Stop us if you've heard this script before: Andruw Jones and Chipper Jones led an offense that was near the top of the league in runs scored, while John Smoltz paced a staff that, courtesy of pitching coach Leo Mazzone, had its share of successful reclamation projects. The team started slowly, but by Labor Day there was little doubt that they were en route to yet another NL East title. Manager Bobby Cox did an award-worthy job, and GM John Schuerholz made a key in-season acquisition to boost the team's chances. Finally, another early exit from the playoffs stripped some of the luster from a season worthy of the remarkable dynasty the Braves have built since 1991.

In reality, this was a Braves season unlike any other, and as the 2006 season dawns, it's clear that the team faces major questions about its ability to stay atop the NL East. But until another team steps forward and knocks the Braves out of their lofty perch, it's folly to bet against them. Like the Yankees of the 1950s, the Braves rebuild and win at the same time.

It didn't look that way at the outset of 2005. On the contrary, Schuerholz's winter maneuvers appeared addled. Smoltz's desire to to return to the rotation, where he'd thrived until an abortive comeback from Tommy John surgery in 2001 sent him to the bullpen, forced the General Manager's hand. In what looked like a panic move, Schuerholz dispatched the team's second-best pitching prospect, Jose Capellan, to Milwaukee for notional closer Danny Kolb, a groundballing, low-strikeout journeyman who'd lucked into the Brewers' closing job. Days later, Schuerholz sent the team's top pitching prospect, Dan Meyer, to Oakland in a trade for Tim Hudson whose ability to continue throwing his splitter was in question due to injury.

The most questionable facet of Schuerholz's offseason redesign was the duo he signed to play the outfield corners. He waved goodbye to J. D. Drew and traded away both halves of the surprisingly effective platoon of Eli Marrero and Charles Thomas, emerging with a starting pair for the outfield corners straight out of the Wayback Machine; in left was the fragile, 38-year-old Brian Jordan, a mainstay of the team's lineup from 1999–2001 but a shadow of his former self. In right was Raul Mondesi, the

BRAVES PROSPECTUS

2005 record: 90–72; First place, NL East; Lost to Astros in Division Series

Pythagenport record: 90–72

Runs scored per game: 4.75 (4th in NL)

Runs allowed per game: 4.16 (5th in NL)

Team EqA: .264 (6th in NL)

2005 Batters Age: 28.5 (3rd youngest in NL)

2005 Pitchers Age: 29.5 (8th oldest in NL)

Ballpark: Turner Field; Neutral park; Park Factor of 0.998

2005: Do you suppose winning the NL East ever gets boring?

2006: The team has weathered many a defection, but can it survive without Leo Mazzone? Can it survive *with* Edgar Renteria?

game's oldest 34-year-old. Mondesi was coming off a league-leading two contract terminations in 2004.

By mid-June, this dubious master plan was in tatters, leaving the Braves just a game above .500. Hudson was one of three starting pitchers on the DL, Kolb had long since lost the closer's job, Mondesi had been released, and Jordan was struggling and soon bound for the disabled list. Worse yet, Chipper Jones was sidelined by a torn ligament in his foot.

The Braves threw a handful of homegrown rookies into the breach. Outfielders Ryan Langerhans and Kelly Johnson didn't set the world on fire, but they out-hit their aged predecessors. Infielder Wilson Betemit, who'd been trying to crack the roster since 2001, caught fire while Chipper missed 50 games. Catcher Brian McCann, recalled from Double-A Mississippi when backup Eddie Perez went on the DL, took over the starting role when Johnny Estrada was sidelined. Kyle Davies proved a reasonable stopgap for a desperate rotation. John Foster, Blaine Boyer, and Macay McBride provided solid innings in a bullpen that had to be reshuffled to cover for Kolb's collapse.

Jeff Francoeur stood out from this surfeit of rookies. Noted for ample power and excellent defense, the only blemish on Francoeur's bid for major league stardom was his lack of plate discipline, underscored by his failure to draw a single walk in 77 PAs during a late-season 2004 stint with Greenville. Returning to Double-A to start the season, he drew just 16 unintentional walks in 367 PAs, but when the Braves turned to him just before the All-Star break, he responded with a home run in his debut and went on to hit over .400 with power during his first month. Although he wouldn't draw an unintentional walk until his 139th plate appearance, the hot streak quashed any concerns about his limitations. The team streaked past the surprising Nationals and into first place for good. By season's end, Francoeur had hit .300/.336/.549 with 14 homers and narrowly missed Rookie of the Year honors despite playing in only 70 games.

In 2005, the Braves got more production out of their rookies (as measured by VORP) than any team but the A's and Pirates. Their rookie hitters were 63.1 runs above replacement, second only to the Rockies' 83.1, but in about 40 % fewer plate appearances. The 2005 crop topped the production level of any batch of young Braves since 1991, not too shabby considering that Braves rookies in that time included both Joneses, Javy Lopez, Rafael Furcal, Ryan Klesko, Jason Schmidt, Jermaine Dye, Kevin Millwood, and Jason Marquis.

The team's success with young players illustrates the deep fecundity of its farm system as well as Schuerholz's discerning eye for young players. In another parallel to the Yankees of the 1950s, he is able both to use the farm to reload the major league roster while also unhesitatingly including his youngsters in trades. Yet, for somebody who trades so many prospects, Schuerholz's deals have rarely come back to haunt him. Between October 1990, when he took the helm, and the end of 2005, Schuerholz has traded 84 prospects. Of those, only six have accumulated even 10 Wins Above Replacement Player (WARP) after leaving the Atlanta system, with Schmidt and Dye by far the two biggest fish to get away.

Trades of unproven talent proved crucial to patching up the 2005 pitching staff. Just before Opening Day, the Braves sent second baseman Nick Green to Tampa Bay for Jorge Sosa. It seemed like an odd fix, because Sosa had posted a 5.14 ERA in three seasons with the Rays. After starting the year in the bullpen, Sosa was forced into the rotation, where he logged a 2.62 ERA in 20 starts. At the trading deadline, Schuerholz pulled off one of the few notable deals, sending rookie pitcher Roman Colon (who'd thrown 44.1 unspectacular innings as a Brave) and minor-league hurler Zach Miner to acquire reliever Kyle Farnsworth from the Tigers. Within a month, Farnsworth had taken the closer's baton from Chris Reitsma and pitched well down the stretch.

If Farnsworth was instrumental in getting the Braves into the playoffs, he was also on the spot for the Braves' latest October meltdown. It was just the beginning of a bad winter. Atlanta's off-season started on a down note when Mazzone accepted boyhood friend Sam Perlozzo's invitation to join him in the Baltimore Oriole dugout. Considered by many to be one of the best pitching coaches in baseball history, Mazzone leaves behind both an incredible legacy and a huge void. Multiple studies suggest Mazzone had a considerable effect on lowering his charges' ERAs, and his ability to make effective pitchers out of the likes of Sosa or Jaret Wright, to name an emblematic pair, gave the team a huge advantage. New pitching coach Roger McDowell steps into an enormous set of shoes. While Cox has called McDowell "one of the true up-and-coming teachers of the game," his recent two-year stint in the pitcher's house of horrors otherwise known as Las Vegas (2005 team ERA: 6.21), paid the Dodgers few immediate dividends.

In terms of position players, the team's biggest concern entering the winter was its ability to retain Furcal, who in his Age 27 season hit .284/.348/.429, swiped 46 bases and turned in his best year with the glove. In a weak free-agent market, Furcal appeared to be the winter's biggest prize. Before anyone opened a checkbook, Chipper Jones stepped forward and agreed to restructure his contract, hoping to help the Braves retain their shortstop. He drew praise for his team-first gesture, but the goodwill Jones engendered forestalled any attempt by the team to shift him to left (where he played in 2002–2003) or first base. This is no quibble; Jones is a clear liability at the hot corner. Playing third, he's 12 runs below average per 100 games over the course of his career, marking him as one of the least effective defenders in history.

By cementing Jones at third, the Braves also blocked Andy Marte, one of the game's top prospects. Marte hadn't fared very well in three brief stints with the Braves, but in his Age 21 year in Triple-A he hit .275/.372/.506 and played outstanding defense, suggesting the high estimations of his future remain valid. Meanwhile, the emergence of Betemit provided the team with an economical in-house solution to replace Furcal. Though not as slick with the glove or as fast on the basepaths as Furcal, Betemit has an upside, having hit .305/.359/.435 at 23. With Betemit and Marte both starting, the Braves could have gone into the future with the game's best young, dynamic left side of the infield. Furthermore, the budget-conscious Schuerholz could have then used the savings from Furcal's defection to find a replacement for Mike Hampton (out for 2006 after undergoing Tommy John surgery) as the team's number three starter.

Instead, when Furcal spurned both the Braves' four-year, $36 million offer and the Cubs' five-year, $50 million offer to sign with the Dodgers for three years and $39 million, Schuerholz responded by pulling the trigger on a deal that sent Marte to the Red Sox for Edgar Renteria and cash. Renteria had signed a four-year, $40 million deal with Boston prior to 2005, but his first season in Fenway was bad enough to sour the Red Sox on him for good. He hit just .276/.335/.385, weak numbers in a hitter-friendly environment, and his defense was pathetic. Renteria was 21 runs worse than the average shortstop; Furcal was 20 above average. The Sox sent along $8 million to cover his 2006–2008 years, which cut the Braves' financial commitment to Renteria down to $6 million a year, and Boston's also on the hook to pay the $3 million buyout of his 2009 option. That's cheaper than Furcal but still $6 million a year for a 30-year-old shortstop with some unappealing trends. Over the past two years Renteria has accumulated 7.4 wins above replacement; Furcal, two years younger, has produced 14.9 in that same time. Some bargain.

There's a thread that connects the Jones situation to the Smoltz situation of a year ago. In both cases, Schuerholz accommodated the preferences of one of the pillars of the Braves dynasty, and reacted by trading a top prospect. Marte has a far higher upside than Jose Capellan, but the return on the trade was similarly underwhelming.

The Braves look like they'll have below-average defense on the left side of their infield, they've stranded Betemit in a utility role after he just took a huge step forward, and are left hoping that Langerhans or Johnson can solve the production problems in left while Adam LaRoche does adequately at first. Granted, the team can cover some of the runs it has lost on offense and defense with the above-average offense they get from Marcus Giles, Andruw Jones, and the catching tandem of McCann and Todd Pratt.

But the Braves lineup remains one impact hitter away from being imposing.

Meanwhile, on a pitching staff no longer benefiting from Leo Mazzone's counsel, the rotation beyond Smoltz and Hudson looks shaky. John Thomson is the number three, and in the mix for the back end are Sosa, whose low ERA belied shaky peripherals, and the underwhelming Horacio Ramirez. In the wings are Davies and prospects Anthony Lerew and Chuck James, neither of whom has played more than a half-season above Double-A. As of early January, the Braves had yet to acquire a closer to replace Farnsworth, who went to the Yankees. The relievers they've netted in trades appear in need of Mazzone-caliber miracles to be effective. McDowell certainly has his work cut out for him. Joey Devine, the team's 2005 1st-round pick, is clearly the closer of the future, but having allowed three history-making home runs in less than seven innings of big league work, it seems clear that the future isn't here yet.

The Braves' off-season, then, was one of equivocation. The addition of Renteria is a low-percentage gamble that undermines the very youth that kept the team atop the division in 2005, while the freezing of Jones at third base is the kind of over-commitment to a veteran leader that teams not as smart of the Braves typically make. The result is a stalemate between where the team is and where it needs to go. The Braves might have what it takes to stay ahead for now, but if they don't make a substantial commitment to a stronger team down the road, the demise of the Braves dynasty will loom larger than ever before.

HITTERS

WILSON BETEMIT INF **Bats: B Throws: R** Height: 6' 3" Weight: 190 Born: July 28, 1980 Age: 25

YEAR	TM	LVL	AGE	PA	R	2B	3B	HR	RBI	BB	SO	SB	CS	SPEED	BA	OBP	SLG	MLVR	EQBA	EQOBP	EQSLG	EQA	VORP	DEFENSE		
2003	RIC	AAA	22	518	55	23	13	8	65	38	115	8	5	6.3	.262	.315	.414	.015	.251	.309	.406	.246	9.0	98-3B	-12	
2004	RIC	AAA	23	390	48	24	2	13	59	32	99	3	3	4.3	.278	.336	.466	.079	.260	.320	.430	.256	13.6	76-3B	-4	15-SS -2
2005	ATL	MLB	24	270	36	12	4	4	20	22	55	1	3	5.5	.305	.359	.435	.110	.300	.357	.441	.271	11.5	48-3B	-6	15-SS 0
2006	ATL	MLB	24	326	41	16	3	8	38	28	64	3	2	5.5	.275	.340	.433	.015	.275	.340	.447	.262	12.7	79-3B	-2	

Breakout: 25% Improve: 47% Collapse: 30% Attrition: 27% Comparables: Ron Oester, Bobby Smith, Eduardo Perez

Betemit's status as a top Braves prospect predates the current crop of Martes and Francoeurs by a good four or five years. His failure to deliver on the early hype is mitigated by the revelation that he was just 14 when the Braves signed him out of the Dominican Republic—a transgression that cost the team $100,000 and the right to sign a player out of the Dominican Republic for six months—but they got to keep Betemit. Five years later, after making the roster because he was out of options, he finally lived up to some of his promise, stepping into the lineup with Chipper out and hitting .325/.360/.578 in June, nicely papering over the slugger's absence. His hitting cooled off, but he contributed at shortstop as well, helping to cover for Furcal's shoulder woes. It was just his Age 23 season, so there's still plenty of room for growth, but with the infield set with three regulars, Betemit may evolve into a super-utilityman.

GREGOR BLANCO   CF   **Bats: L Throws: L**   Height: 5′ 11″   Weight: 170   Born: December 12, 1983   Age: 22

YEAR	TM	LVL	AGE	PA	R	2B	3B	HR	RBI	BB	SO	SB	CS	SPEED	BA	OBP	SLG	MLVR	EQBA	EQOBP	EQSLG	EQA	VORP	DEFENSE	
2003	MYR	A+	19	524	66	19	7	5	36	54	114	34	16	7.4	.271	.357	.375	.114	.271	.342	.396	.258	13.9	110-CF -11	11-RF 1
2004	MYR	A+	20	488	73	17	9	8	41	47	114	25	9	8.0	.269	.342	.405	.103	.257	.320	.392	.251	4.7	97-CF -12	
2005	MIS	AA	21	479	64	11	12	6	37	73	124	28	12	6.9	.252	.367	.384	.060	.240	.339	.376	.256	5.0	108-CF 0	
2006	*ATL*	*MLB*	*22*	*497*	*64*	*21*	*5*	*7*	*40*	*50*	*124*	*19*	*7*	*5.4*	*.248*	*.329*	*.370*	*-.106*	*.249*	*.329*	*.381*	*.246*	*2.2*	*117-CF -7*	

Breakout: 15%   Improve: 40%   Collapse: 30%   Attrition: 7%   Comparables: David Krynzel, Tim Raines Jr., Cesar Crespo

This Venezuelan speedster was held captive in High-A in 2003 and 2004, but when finally promoted to Double-A, he had trouble making contact and showed even less punch. Those triples, a product of his speed, inflate a rather anemic slugging percentage. The increased walk rate is nice, suggesting that he at least understands his role as a table-setter. Scouts seem to like his glove; managers called him the best defensive outfielder in the Carolina League in 2004. In a world where free-swinging Ryan Howard wins Rookie of the Year and fellow non-selectives Willy Taveras and Jeff Francoeur finish second and third in the ROY voting, he's worth keeping an eye on as a more disciplined alternative.

JOSH BURRUS   OF   **Bats: R Throws: R**   Height: 5′ 11″   Weight: 190   Born: August 20, 1983   Age: 22

YEAR	TM	LVL	AGE	PA	R	2B	3B	HR	RBI	BB	SO	SB	CS	SPEED	BA	OBP	SLG	MLVR	EQBA	EQOBP	EQSLG	EQA	VORP	DEFENSE
2003	DNV	Rk	19	211	25	11	1	1	16	15	48	10	4	5.8	.254	.318	.339	-.011	.227	.270	.305	.209	-38.0	41-LF -3
2004	ROM	A	20	549	82	30	3	11	46	33	123	30	10	6.7	.272	.330	.410	.071	.255	.296	.377	.236	-19.9	106-LF 4
2005	MYR	A+	21	335	54	20	0	11	53	28	75	25	8	7.0	.284	.349	.462	.165	.254	.305	.403	.250	-6.9	67-LF 0
2005	MIS	AA	21	196	21	6	2	5	21	22	53	9	4	6.5	.221	.311	.366	-.079	.205	.281	.348	.224	-13.5	44-LF 3
2006	*ATL*	*MLB*	*22*	*517*	*63*	*26*	*3*	*12*	*52*	*35*	*125*	*21*	*8*	*5.4*	*.244*	*.301*	*.382*	*-.141*	*.244*	*.301*	*.394*	*.235*	*-6.7*	*122-LF 0*

Breakout: 32%   Improve: 54%   Collapse: 16%   Attrition: 7%   Comparables: Andy Burress, Jackson Melian, Brandon Pernell

A local boy the Braves tapped in the 1st round in 2001, Burrus struggled in his first three years of pro ball, repeating the Appy League with rate stats Rafael Belliard wouldn't sign for, even the second time around. After a quantum leap forward in 2004 (read: a modest season at Rome), Burrus continued progressing in 2005, splitting his season between High-A and Double-A (plus a Katrina-induced taste of Triple-A), hitting a combined .263/.338/.427, primarily in two pitchers' parks. Contact is his biggest problem; that's a ton of strikeouts for a guy with only modest power. On the plus side, he did walk more once he learned to lay off the breaking stuff. While it's been a long time in coming, the Braves now have a speedy 22-year-old building on a half-season of Double-A.

ERIC CAMPBELL   3B   **Bats: R Throws: R**   Height: 6′ 0″   Weight: 195   Born: August 6, 1985   Age: 20

YEAR	TM	LVL	AGE	PA	R	2B	3B	HR	RBI	BB	SO	SB	CS	SPEED	BA	OBP	SLG	MLVR	EQBA	EQOBP	EQSLG	EQA	VORP	DEFENSE
2005	DNV	Rk	19	298	77	26	2	18	64	28	64	15	4	6.7	.313	.383	.634	.547	.257	.307	.473	.265	26.1	64-3B 0
2006	*ATL*	*MLB*	*20*	*435*	*49*	*26*	*2*	*11*	*49*	*28*	*103*	*11*	*4*	*4.6*	*.235*	*.287*	*.393*	*-.156*	*.235*	*.287*	*.405*	*.231*	*-1.7*	*103-3B -1*

Breakout: 19%   Improve: 40%   Collapse: 40%   Attrition: 10%   Comparables: Luis Maza, Kody Kirkland, Edwin Encarnacion

In the words of Homer Simpson, "I have two questions: 'How much?' and 'Give it to me.'" This 2nd round 2004 pick tore up the Appalachian League, leading the circuit in several major offensive categories. He's got a long swing—"unbridled," as one analyst puts it—and his plate discipline could use a bit of work, but at that age, whose couldn't? Shifted from shortstop prior to last season, his defense at third base is considered very good. There's a lot to recommend him as he moves upward.

MATT ESQUIVEL   OF   **Bats: R Throws: R**   Height: 6′ 2″   Weight: 220   Born: December 17, 1982   Age: 23

YEAR	TM	LVL	AGE	PA	R	2B	3B	HR	RBI	BB	SO	SB	CS	SPEED	BA	OBP	SLG	MLVR	EQBA	EQOBP	EQSLG	EQA	VORP	DEFENSE	
2003	DNV	Rk	20	250	41	10	4	11	42	20	72	7	4	6.2	.282	.352	.514	.301	.241	.288	.427	.244	1.5	53-CF -1	
2004	ROM	A	21	461	69	32	3	16	64	35	140	14	4	5.8	.285	.356	.494	.241	.263	.315	.442	.259	2.2	66-RF -3	39-CF 1
2005	MYR	A+	22	527	58	31	0	17	81	49	140	9	6	4.0	.265	.343	.440	.109	.239	.301	.393	.240	-14.2	103-RF -6	
2006	*ATL*	*MLB*	*23*	*479*	*55*	*24*	*2*	*15*	*59*	*35*	*139*	*7*	*3*	*4.5*	*.240*	*.302*	*.402*	*-.116*	*.240*	*.302*	*.414*	*.239*	*-4.3*	*113-RF -5*	

Breakout: 25%   Improve: 45%   Collapse: 30%   Attrition: 4%   Comparables: Jeff Deardorff, Angel Molina, Byron Gettis

Built like a running back, which he was—a heavily recruited Texas one, at that—Esquivel has displayed considerable power thus far. (The translations pump up his SLG because Myrtle Beach is a pitchers' park.) He's had serious trouble making contact, striking out 31.5% of the time in his pro career. His walk rate isn't bad, but could use some improvement. He's a big boy, but athletic enough to play center, which may buy him some slack.

JOHNNY ESTRADA   **C**   **Bats: B Throws: R**   Height: 5′ 11″   Weight: 200   Born: June 27, 1976   Age: 30

YEAR	TM	LVL	AGE	PA	R	2B	3B	HR	RBI	BB	SO	SB	CS	SPEED	BA	OBP	SLG	MLVR	EQBA	EQOBP	EQSLG	EQA	VORP	DEFENSE	
2003	RIC	AAA	27	402	40	29	0	10	66	30	30	0	0	3.0	.328	.393	.494	.303	.294	.357	.459	.281	27.7	81-C	0
2004	ATL	MLB	28	516	56	36	0	9	76	39	66	0	0	3.2	.314	.378	.450	.165	.307	.369	.445	.282	34.7	116-C	-5
2005	ATL	MLB	29	383	31	26	0	4	39	20	38	0	0	3.3	.261	.303	.367	-.105	.256	.299	.365	.233	3.5	93-C	9
2006	*ARI*	*MLB*	*30*	*416*	*38*	*23*	*0*	*8*	*49*	*27*	*45*	*0*	*0*	*3.6*	*.275*	*.332*	*.402*	*-.040*	*.271*	*.328*	*.400*	*.246*	*8.8*	*99-C*	*0*

Breakout: 9%   *Improve: 27%*   *Collapse: 42%*   *Attrition: 16%*   Comparables: Bill Fahey, Joe Azcue, Ben Molina

Estrada didn't do much in the Phillies organization, and perhaps no one except Schuerholz envisioned his breaking out, first at Richmond in 2003, then in Atlanta in 2004. A regression was predictable, but Estrada did fairly well before absorbing the brunt of a violent collision at the plate with Darin Erstad on June 6. Estrada suffered a mild concussion, and while he returned within a week, lingering pain hampered him the rest of the year and gave the Braves an opportunity to take a long look at Brian McCann. All told, Estrada hit .282/.328/.406 before the crash, .241/.279/.332 after. That was enough to convince Schuerholz to deal Estrada to Arizona, where he'll start, but as a 30-ish catcher with a bad back and an offensive game overly reliant on batting average, he's a risk.

JULIO FRANCO   **AARP**   **Bats: R Throws: R**   Height: 6′ 1″   Weight: 188   Born: August 23, 1958   Age: 47

YEAR	TM	LVL	AGE	PA	R	2B	3B	HR	RBI	BB	SO	SB	CS	SPEED	BA	OBP	SLG	MLVR	EQBA	EQOBP	EQSLG	EQA	VORP	DEFENSE
2003	ATL	MLB	44	223	28	12	2	5	31	25	43	0	1	4.4	.294	.372	.452	.152	.289	.368	.447	.280	9.9	46-1B -4
2004	ATL	MLB	45	360	37	18	3	6	57	36	68	4	2	4.9	.309	.378	.441	.146	.303	.372	.431	.280	17.0	71-1B -6
2005	ATL	MLB	46	264	30	12	1	9	42	27	57	4	0	4.8	.275	.348	.451	.092	.266	.342	.451	.276	10.2	48-1B -1
2006	*NYN*	*MLB*	*47*	*473*	*35*	*14*	*1*	*8*	*33*	*29*	*57*	*4*	*1*	*4.9*	*.253*	*.329*	*.400*	*-.063*	*.257*	*.333*	*.424*	*.257*	*5.0*	*73-1B 0*

Breakout: N/A   *Improve: N/A*   *Collapse: N/A*   *Attrition: N/A*   Comparables: Methuselah, Dick Clark, Minnie Minoso

What's not to love? Including his time in the Japanese, Mexican, and minor leagues, Franco can claim over 3,700 hits in pro ball. Amid all of the Braves' rookies, he was the ultimate in veteran presence, a man old enough to have fathered many of his teammates. He's humble, affable, and more importantly, still able to turn on a fastball. He got off to a slow start, but from June 10, he hit .310/.384/.528. Signed by the Mets for a two-year gig in a pinch-hitting role, it's quite conceivable he could be helping a major-league team when he reaches 50. PECOTA really can't generate a comparison, so you can file the projection under Random Amusements.

JEFF FRANCOEUR   **RF**   **Bats: R Throws: R**   Height: 6′ 4″   Weight: 200   Born: January 8, 1984   Age: 22

YEAR	TM	LVL	AGE	PA	R	2B	3B	HR	RBI	BB	SO	SB	CS	SPEED	BA	OBP	SLG	MLVR	EQBA	EQOBP	EQSLG	EQA	VORP	DEFENSE	
2003	ROM	A	19	567	78	26	9	14	68	30	68	14	6	6.3	.281	.325	.445	.181	.267	.297	.431	.248	8.9	125-CF -4	
2004	MYR	A+	20	367	56	26	0	15	52	22	70	10	6	5.2	.293	.346	.506	.273	.270	.314	.480	.267	8.0	82-RF 2	
2005	MIS	AA	21	367	40	28	2	13	62	21	76	13	4	5.5	.275	.322	.487	.149	.251	.288	.450	.252	-3.3	71-RF -2	11-CF 0
2005	ATL	MLB	21	274	41	20	1	14	45	11	58	3	2	5.1	.300	.336	.549	.230	.293	.330	.543	.285	17.4	66-RF 3	
2006	*ATL*	*MLB*	*22*	*578*	*76*	*34*	*2*	*25*	*88*	*28*	*113*	*13*	*5*	*5.2*	*.274*	*.316*	*.484*	*.043*	*.275*	*.316*	*.499*	*.266*	*14.9*	*135-RF -1*	

Breakout: 28%   *Improve: 65%*   *Collapse: 14%*   *Attrition: 4%*   Comparables: Ruben Mateo, Juan Gonzalez, Cal Ripken

Cue the theme from *The Natural*. Number 27 on our Top 50 Prospect List a year ago, scouts raved about his five-tool talents and incredible bat speed, but we viewed his lack of plate discipline with trepidation. In the Southern League to start 2005, Francoeur showed little patience before being called to The Show just before the All-Star break. He homered in his debut and just kept hitting; by August 10 he was batting .400/.407/.767 in 91 plate appearances, but had yet to draw a walk. Not until his 139th PA, on August 24, did he finally deign to accept a free pass. Even so, Francoeur gave the Braves a literal shot in the arm, with his defense in right field, making opposing third-base coaches look foolish with 13 assists in just 67 games. While his hack-n-whack approach remains problematic—when was the last time you saw an MVP candidate with anything approaching a 58/8 K/UIBB rate?—he's just 22, and there are no shortage of other reasons to be excited about him.

RAFAEL FURCAL   **SS**   **Bats: B Throws: R**   Height: 5′ 10″   Weight: 165   Born: October 24, 1977   Age: 28

YEAR	TM	LVL	AGE	PA	R	2B	3B	HR	RBI	BB	SO	SB	CS	SPEED	BA	OBP	SLG	MLVR	EQBA	EQOBP	EQSLG	EQA	VORP	DEFENSE
2003	ATL	MLB	25	731	130	35	10	15	61	60	76	25	2	8.2	.292	.352	.443	.102	.287	.347	.438	.276	49.7	150-SS -15
2004	ATL	MLB	26	627	103	24	5	14	59	58	71	29	6	7.3	.279	.344	.414	.027	.273	.339	.406	.265	31.0	127-SS 3
2005	ATL	MLB	27	684	100	31	11	12	58	62	78	46	10	7.9	.284	.348	.429	.067	.278	.344	.430	.274	42.3	147-SS 20
2006	*LAN*	*MLB*	*28*	*666*	*100*	*31*	*5*	*11*	*59*	*57*	*76*	*34*	*10*	*6.5*	*.282*	*.346*	*.408*	*-.003*	*.289*	*.352*	*.426*	*.268*	*33.8*	*155-SS 7*

Breakout: 12%   *Improve: 41%*   *Collapse: 20%*   *Attrition: 2%*   Comparables: Ray Durham, Bump Wills, Tony Fernandez

(continued next page)

Rafael Furcal *(continued)*

Furcal's exceptional walk year solidified his status as one of the game's best shortstops; only Miguel Tejada (27.3), Derek Jeter (23.4) and Julio Lugo (21.7) can claim higher WARP3s over the last three seasons. Not only did Furcal do well at the plate, he also led the majors with 20 Fielding Runs Above Average. Furcal's best offensive asset is his speed, as his 82 percent success rate in stolen bases and 11 triples will attest. January surgery to repair torn knee cartilage was expected to be minor. While his plate discipline has held steady, his OBP is still less than ideal for a leadoff hitter, and it will be interesting to see whether his new manager, Grady Little, realizes that or simply decides to bat a very fast and wealthy man atop the lineup.

MARCUS GILES　　　**2B**　　　**Bats: R Throws: R**　　Height: 5' 8"　Weight: 180　Born: May 18, 1978　　Age: 28

YEAR	TM	LVL	AGE	PA	R	2B	3B	HR	RBI	BB	SO	SB	CS	SPEED	BA	OBP	SLG	MLVR	EQBA	EQOBP	EQSLG	EQA	VORP	DEFENSE
2003	ATL	MLB	25	625	101	49	2	21	69	59	80	14	4	6.0	.316	.390	.526	.293	.311	.384	.526	.306	62.1	135-2B 14
2004	ATL	MLB	26	431	61	22	2	8	48	36	70	17	4	6.4	.311	.378	.443	.150	.305	.369	.434	.284	30.6	88-2B 8
2005	ATL	MLB	27	650	104	45	4	15	63	64	108	16	3	6.3	.291	.365	.461	.143	.284	.360	.461	.284	41.0	143-2B 9
2006	*ATL*	*MLB*	*28*	*617*	*91*	*36*	*4*	*16*	*70*	*61*	*93*	*16*	*4*	*5.5*	*.286*	*.365*	*.453*	*.091*	*.287*	*.365*	*.467*	*.281*	*35.8*	*144-2B 7*

Breakout: 9%　Improve: 34%　Collapse: 24%　Attrition: 7%　　Comparables: Chuck Knoblauch, Craig Biggio, Junior Spivey

After some ouchies that caused him to miss six of the team's first eight games, Giles was, by his own standards, the picture of health in 2005. He set a career high in games played, and if he wasn't as productive as in his breakout season of two years ago, he wasn't Nick Green, either. In a lineup that got sub-par production from three of the four corner positions—at least until Francoeur showed up—having a middle infielder with this kind of pop is key. He's got a broad range of offensive skills, his defensive numbers are very good, and there's really nothing to dislike about his game so long as he stays off the DL.

TODD HOLLANDSWORTH　　**OF**　　**Bats: L Throws: L**　　Height: 6' 2"　Weight: 215　Born: April 20, 1973　　Age: 33

YEAR	TM	LVL	AGE	PA	R	2B	3B	HR	RBI	BB	SO	SB	CS	SPEED	BA	OBP	SLG	MLVR	EQBA	EQOBP	EQSLG	EQA	VORP	DEFENSE
2003	FLO	MLB	30	252	32	23	3	3	20	22	55	2	3	6.1	.254	.317	.421	-.003	.257	.319	.426	.252	0.0	55-LF -1
2004	CHN	MLB	31	166	28	6	2	8	22	17	26	1	1	5.6	.318	.392	.547	.299	.311	.386	.541	.308	13.5	26-RF 2
2005	CHN	MLB	32	289	23	17	2	5	35	18	53	4	4	5.4	.254	.301	.388	-.088	.251	.301	.393	.237	-3.6	64-LF -3
2005	ATL	MLB	32	40	3	0	0	1	1	5	13	0	1	2.8	.171	.275	.257	-.341	.171	.275	.257	.191	-3.0	
2006	*CLE*	*MLB*	*33*	*206*	*24*	*11*	*1*	*4*	*24*	*15*	*37*	*2*	*2*	*5.3*	*.261*	*.317*	*.402*	*-.059*	*.265*	*.326*	*.424*	*.249*	*1.3*	*52-LF -2*

Breakout: 10%　Improve: 25%　Collapse: 43%　Attrition: 39%　　Comparables: George Altman, Gordy Coleman, Thomas Howard

The well-traveled fourth outfielder spent most of the year in Chicago as point man in Dusty Baker's nefarious plot to foil the development of Jason Dubois. Once that mission was accomplished, the Cubs shipped Hollandsworth to Atlanta in a waiver-wire deal that netted Dusty a cattleprod to use on Matt Murton. Coming to a team stacked with lefty-hitting outfielders, Hollandsworth was redundant, and Cox left him off of the postseason roster. A free agent, he'll find work with a club that appreciates his pinch-hitty goodness.

KELLY JOHNSON　　　**OF**　　**Bats: L Throws: R**　　Height: 6' 1"　Weight: 180　Born: February 22, 1982　Age: 24

YEAR	TM	LVL	AGE	PA	R	2B	3B	HR	RBI	BB	SO	SB	CS	SPEED	BA	OBP	SLG	MLVR	EQBA	EQOBP	EQSLG	EQA	VORP	DEFENSE	
2003	GRN	AA	21	374	46	22	5	6	45	35	81	10	3	6.4	.275	.340	.425	.099	.258	.315	.414	.254	12.0	85-SS 5	
2004	GRN	AA	22	534	70	35	3	16	50	49	102	9	9	4.9	.282	.350	.468	.139	.255	.317	.425	.253	-3.1	66-LF 2	36-CF -1
2005	RIC	AAA	23	192	35	12	3	8	22	34	22	7	1	6.7	.310	.438	.581	.414	.279	.404	.506	.313	13.9	15-LF 0	12-RF 0
2005	ATL	MLB	23	332	46	12	3	9	40	40	75	2	1	4.8	.241	.334	.397	-.029	.238	.333	.400	.256	1.4	73-LF 10	
2006	*ATL*	*MLB*	*24*	*492*	*63*	*27*	*3*	*14*	*61*	*51*	*93*	*7*	*3*	*5.3*	*.269*	*.348*	*.445*	*.039*	*.270*	*.348*	*.458*	*.270*	*12.9*	*116-LF 6*	

Breakout: 28%　Improve: 52%　Collapse: 20%　Attrition: 14%　　Comparables: Ron Swoboda, Dwight Evans, Lee Walls

Once the Braves finally noticed the giant fork sticking out of Raul Mondesi, they recalled Johnson, a 2000 supplemental 1st-round pick. His performance helped stop the team's outfield from hemorrhaging. Johnson's defense was outstanding, he showed very good patience—his 4.12 P/PA ranked 12th in the NL among those with 250 or more plate appearances—and about the same amount of pop as Langerhans; the difference between the two was about 25 points of batting average. When Francoeur showed up, Johnson initially got more playing time than Langerhans in left, but he eventually wound up on the short end, which was something of a waste. He'd have been better served by going back to Triple-A. He may be the odd man out come springtime, but long term, he has more upside than Langerhans.

ANDRUW JONES   **CF**   **Bats: R Throws: R**   Height: 6' 1"   Weight: 185   Born: April 23, 1977   Age: 29

YEAR	TM	LVL	AGE	PA	R	2B	3B	HR	RBI	BB	SO	SB	CS	SPEED	BA	OBP	SLG	MLVR	EQBA	EQOBP	EQSLG	EQA	VORP	DEFENSE	
2003	ATL	MLB	26	659	101	28	2	36	116	53	125	4	3	4.7	.277	.338	.513	.165	.274	.335	.511	.282	38.2	148-CF	19
2004	ATL	MLB	27	646	85	34	4	29	91	71	147	6	6	4.5	.261	.345	.488	.116	.257	.340	.480	.274	28.6	151-CF	13
2005	ATL	MLB	28	672	95	24	3	51	128	64	112	5	3	4.4	.263	.347	.575	.243	.258	.341	.575	.297	52.8	153-CF	5
2006	ATL	MLB	29	640	88	31	2	35	111	62	117	5	3	4.5	.276	.353	.525	.156	.276	.352	.541	.290	41.0	149-CF	2

Breakout: 16%   Improve: 50%   Collapse: 10%   Attrition: 4%   Comparables: Jesse Barfield, Jim Rice, Del Ennis

Last year in this space we wrote of the "whiff of unrealized promise" that unfairly seemed to surround Jones. Fifty-one homers and a near-miss in the MVP voting later, it's safe to say the promise has been realized, at least in the public mind. Just as Chipper went down, Andruw—seemingly surrounded by seven rookies and a rotation held together with duct tape and Leo Mazzone's best wishes—got hot, hitting .311/.423/.696 in the six weeks his namesake was sidelined. His home run pace (31 in June through August) was unsustainable, but he wound up posting monster numbers even with an OBP just a few points above his career norm. The key was a wider stance in which his head stayed lower and moved less, allowing him a better view of the ball. Note that he cut down his strikeouts and was hit by more pitches than ever before. But Jones's big year with the bat masked his decline with the glove; he was just four runs above average after averaging 16 FRAA over the previous four years. It's a minor quibble, however. He may not hit 51 dingers again, but at 29, he's still in his prime years and building a pretty good case for Cooperstown.

BRANDON JONES   **OF**   **Bats: L Throws: R**   Height: 6' 1"   Weight: 190   Born: December 10, 1983   Age: 22

YEAR	TM	LVL	AGE	PA	R	2B	3B	HR	RBI	BB	SO	SB	CS	SPEED	BA	OBP	SLG	MLVR	EQBA	EQOBP	EQSLG	EQA	VORP	DEFENSE
2004	DNV	Rk	20	235	35	6	5	3	33	23	33	4	2	5.7	.297	.366	.416	.188	.263	.310	.362	.236	-6.2	
2005	ROM	A	21	189	37	12	3	8	27	29	29	4	1	6.3	.308	.423	.577	.489	.276	.372	.495	.295	10.8	35-RF -4
2006	ATL	MLB	22	476	58	25	3	8	49	46	79	5	3	4.8	.263	.337	.395	-.050	.263	.337	.407	.252	2.5	112-RF -4

Breakout: 8%   Improve: 24%   Collapse: 43%   Attrition: 8%   Comparables: Richard Brown, Kory DeHaan, John-Ford Griffin

It's tough to keep up with the Joneses in this organization. It was especially tough to keep up with this one after he made four stops along the chain in 2005, some of them in the service of rehabbing a broken hand that cost him two months early on. Overall, Jones hit .318/.425/.525, showing power and patience, driving the ball to all fields, and displaying the athleticism that allowed him to star in three sports in high school. The Braves' top outfield prospect, he figures to start the year in High-A, but don't be surprised if he's moving up before too long.

CHIPPER JONES   **3B**   **Bats: B Throws: R**   Height: 6' 4"   Weight: 210   Born: April 24, 1972   Age: 34

YEAR	TM	LVL	AGE	PA	R	2B	3B	HR	RBI	BB	SO	SB	CS	SPEED	BA	OBP	SLG	MLVR	EQBA	EQOBP	EQSLG	EQA	VORP	DEFENSE	
2003	ATL	MLB	31	656	103	33	2	27	106	94	83	2	2	4.7	.305	.402	.517	.296	.299	.397	.512	.309	45.0	143-LF -11	
2004	ATL	MLB	32	567	69	20	1	30	96	84	96	2	0	4.2	.248	.362	.485	.130	.242	.355	.473	.285	23.5	90-3B -6	27-LF 0
2005	ATL	MLB	33	432	66	30	0	21	72	72	56	5	1	4.8	.296	.412	.556	.347	.289	.407	.557	.323	43.4	93-3B -9	
2006	ATL	MLB	34	508	70	26	1	20	75	74	72	4	1	4.6	.290	.395	.498	.198	.290	.395	.513	.303	35.1	120-3B -8	

Breakout: 12%   Improve: 39%   Collapse: 21%   Attrition: 6%   Comparables: Ken Singleton, Ryan Klesko, Bob Elliott

Despite missing seven weeks due to injury, Jones had a great year with the bat. Not only did he lead the team in OBP and finish second in slugging, a mere 19 points behind Andruw and his 51 jacks, he also led the NL in Win Expectancy Added (James Click's stat to capture clutch performance) with 5.6 wins. But for all his hitting prowess, Jones is a brutal fielder according to Clay Davenport's fielding numbers—12 runs below average per 100 games over the course of his career. Rather than move him to left (where he played in 2002–2003), or to first base, where he'd out-produce LaRoche, the Braves dealt potential third base replacement Andy Marte to get Edgar Renteria. And yet, sooner or later, Jones will have to shift to left or first.

BRIAN JORDAN   **OF**   **Bats: R Throws: R**   Height: 6' 1"   Weight: 205   Born: March 29, 1967   Age: 39

YEAR	TM	LVL	AGE	PA	R	2B	3B	HR	RBI	BB	SO	SB	CS	SPEED	BA	OBP	SLG	MLVR	EQBA	EQOBP	EQSLG	EQA	VORP	DEFENSE	
2003	LAN	MLB	36	253	28	9	0	6	28	23	30	1	1	4.1	.299	.372	.420	.132	.305	.374	.425	.279	9.4	44-LF -1	11-CF 1
2004	TEX	MLB	37	233	27	13	1	5	23	16	35	2	2	4.6	.222	.275	.363	-.279	.212	.270	.351	.219	-10.7	40-RF 2	
2005	ATL	MLB	38	251	25	8	2	3	24	14	46	2	0	5.4	.247	.295	.338	-.163	.243	.291	.335	.225	-6.1	40-LF 3	16-RF 1
2006	ATL	MLB	39	183	17	9	2	3	20	11	33	1	1	5.5	.260	.309	.383	-.116	.260	.308	.395	.235	-2.3	47-LF 1	

Breakout: 26%   Improve: 37%   Collapse: 26%   Attrition: 45%   Comparables: Tom Paciorek, Hank Bauer, Bill Robinson

(continued next page)

Brian Jordan *(continued)*

Schuerholz's signing of Jordan and Raul Mondesi to man the corner outfield slots ranked among the most harebrained schemes of any GM. "Sure, it's not 1999 now, but who knows what tomorrow will bring? Perhaps time is just a great Möbius Strip and 1999 will come again soon!" Having spent the first half proving that he was a shell of his former self, Jordan mercifully spent two months on the DL, and was limited afterwards. One great catch in the Division Series aside, he looked—to borrow a phrase from Scribbly Tate—doner than a pot roast in a burning whorehouse. All told, Jordan was a fantastic athlete who lacked the plate discipline to be an elite major-league hitter, but that's pretty good for a guy who didn't turn to the game full-time until he was 25. Hold the elegy, though: the Braves offered Jordan arbitration, so he might back.

JAMES JURRIES   **1B/OF**   **Bats: R Throws: R**   Height: 6' 0"   Weight: 190   Born: April 13, 1979   Age: 27

YEAR	TM	LVL	AGE	PA	R	2B	3B	HR	RBI	BB	SO	SB	CS	SPEED	BA	OBP	SLG	MLVR	EQBA	EQOBP	EQSLG	EQA	VORP	DEFENSE			
2003	GRN	AA	24	520	73	35	4	9	54	48	108	4	2	5.2	.284	.354	.434	.138	.259	.317	.409	.251	12.9	79-3B	4	28-1B	-2
2004	RIC	AAA	25	351	46	16	0	18	56	32	96	0	1	3.2	.267	.336	.487	.098	.241	.310	.427	.251	-1.3	62-1B	-7		
2005	RIC	AAA	26	417	53	23	3	21	72	41	107	1	1	3.3	.284	.357	.537	.209	.253	.323	.466	.269	6.4	27-RF	-2	25-1B	-1
2006	*ATL*	*MLB*	*27*	*393*	*46*	*19*	*1*	*15*	*54*	*34*	*100*	*1*	*1*	*3.9*	*.245*	*.315*	*.435*	*-.048*	*.246*	*.314*	*.448*	*.252*	*2.3*	*94-1B*	*-2*		

Breakout: 18%   Improve: 39%   Collapse: 39%   Attrition: 17%   Comparables: Earl Snyder, Roy Sievers, Matt Mieske

This highly-acclaimed Tulane product jumped from nine homers in Double-A in 2003 to 25 split between Double- and Triple-A in 2004. After starting 2005 with five homers in his first 38 at-bats, Jurries was suspended 15 games for testing positive for a performance-enhancing substance, one he admitted to taking while playing winter ball in Venezuela. Penance done, he finished with 21 homers and respectable rate stats, a lot of strikeouts, but a slightly better K/UIBB ratio than the year before. A third baseman when he entered pro ball, Jurries spent most of 2004 at first, and shuttled between first and the corner outfield positions last year. He's not loved for his fielding, but in a league where Xavier Nady gets flipped for Mike Cameron, he's useful, and he'd fit as the replacement for Franco in the platoon at first base. Entering his Age 27 season, the time is nigh.

RYAN LANGERHANS   **OF**   **Bats: L Throws: L**   Height: 6' 3"   Weight: 190   Born: February 20, 1980   Age: 26

YEAR	TM	LVL	AGE	PA	R	2B	3B	HR	RBI	BB	SO	SB	CS	SPEED	BA	OBP	SLG	MLVR	EQBA	EQOBP	EQSLG	EQA	VORP	DEFENSE			
2003	GRN	AA	23	385	42	23	2	6	38	46	85	10	10	5.0	.253	.348	.387	.046	.237	.320	.380	.243	0.2	87-CF	5		
2003	RIC	AAA	23	145	13	10	2	4	11	11	29	2	1	4.7	.280	.338	.477	.152	.272	.335	.484	.277	4.9	32-RF	1		
2004	RIC	AAA	24	534	103	34	3	20	72	70	113	5	9	5.1	.298	.397	.518	.269	.276	.373	.472	.286	38.6	70-CF	-1	28-LF	2
2005	ATL	MLB	25	371	48	22	3	8	42	37	75	0	2	4.8	.267	.348	.426	.051	.261	.341	.426	.265	7.8	43-LF	4	40-RF	0
2006	*ATL*	*MLB*	*26*	*426*	*54*	*23*	*2*	*13*	*55*	*48*	*88*	*3*	*2*	*5.0*	*.266*	*.354*	*.446*	*.048*	*.266*	*.354*	*.460*	*.272*	*11.8*	*101-RF*	*1*		

Breakout: 25%   Improve: 52%   Collapse: 25%   Attrition: 20%   Comparables: Trot Nixon, Michael Tucker, Harry Anderson

Just when it seemed that the toolsy farmhand would never break out, Langerhans put together a fine 2004 at Richmond. Out of options, the Braves kept him around to start the season, and as Mondesi and Jordan pancaked, he got his chance. Though his performance was streaky, it was still an upgrade. Langerhans showed a reasonable amount of patience, some gap power, and excellent defense. He'll duel Johnson for playing time in left field.

ADAM LaROCHE   **1B**   **Bats: L Throws: L**   Height: 6' 3"   Weight: 180   Born: November 6, 1979   Age: 26

YEAR	TM	LVL	AGE	PA	R	2B	3B	HR	RBI	BB	SO	SB	CS	SPEED	BA	OBP	SLG	MLVR	EQBA	EQOBP	EQSLG	EQA	VORP	DEFENSE	
2003	GRN	AA	23	260	42	12	1	12	37	34	53	1	2	4.2	.283	.381	.511	.273	.258	.347	.482	.281	10.6	60-1B	0
2003	RIC	AAA	23	300	33	21	0	8	35	27	58	1	2	3.3	.295	.360	.466	.184	.271	.339	.444	.269	7.3	71-1B	-2
2004	ATL	MLB	24	354	45	27	1	13	45	27	78	0	0	4.1	.278	.333	.488	.111	.272	.328	.478	.272	13.4	80-1B	-8
2005	ATL	MLB	25	500	53	28	0	20	78	39	87	0	2	3.2	.259	.320	.455	.038	.253	.315	.456	.261	7.7	114-1B	-5
2006	*ATL*	*MLB*	*26*	*504*	*60*	*27*	*1*	*19*	*74*	*47*	*90*	*0*	*1*	*3.8*	*.271*	*.344*	*.464*	*.058*	*.272*	*.343*	*.478*	*.272*	*12.8*	*119-1B*	*-3*

Breakout: 23%   Improve: 59%   Collapse: 18%   Attrition: 14%   Comparables: Tino Martinez, Todd Helton, Jason Giambi

Son of LaLob, brother of the more highly-heralded Dodger prospect Andy, LaRoche was the lefty-swinging half of the Braves' first base platoon. The duo's combined .262/.327/.456 performance didn't measure up to the league positional average of .280/.361/.482. Their defense was below average as well, giving the Braves a reasonable excuse to upgrade, either by shifting Chipper Jones across the diamond or dipping into the free-agent or trade markets. Power isn't really LaRoche's problem; his ISO was right about league average for the position. It's his plate discipline that's lacking, or rather regressing. Take away the seven intentional walks and he walked once for every 14.1 at-bats, well below his rookie campaign (once every 12.5 AB) and his minor-league rate (once every 11.3 AB). Meh.

ANDY MARTE   **3B**   **Bats: R**   **Throws: R**   Height: 6' 1"   Weight: 180   Born: October 21, 1983   Age: 22

YEAR	TM	LVL	AGE	PA	R	2B	3B	HR	RBI	BB	SO	SB	CS	SPEED	BA	OBP	SLG	MLVR	EQBA	EQOBP	EQSLG	EQA	VORP	DEFENSE
2003	MYR	A+	19	541	69	35	1	16	63	67	109	5	2	4.3	.285	.372	.469	.271	.273	.349	.473	.280	38.8	117-3B -10
2004	GRN	AA	20	450	52	28	1	23	68	58	105	1	1	3.4	.269	.364	.525	.222	.235	.322	.460	.266	18.6	102-3B 9
2005	RIC	AAA	21	460	51	26	2	20	74	64	83	0	3	3.2	.275	.372	.506	.182	.253	.349	.460	.276	26.5	108-3B 9
2005	ATL	MLB	21	66	3	2	1	0	4	7	13	0	1	4.0	.140	.227	.211	-.508	.140	.227	.211	.170	-7.3	15-3B -5
2006	*BOS*	*MLB*	*22*	*539*	*69*	*29*	*1*	*22*	*81*	*56*	*105*	*0*	*1*	*3.8*	*.261*	*.339*	*.467*	*.062*	*.259*	*.345*	*.476*	*.271*	*20.5*	*127-3B -2*

Breakout: 33%   *Improve: 46%*   *Collapse: 23%*   *Attrition: 7%*   *Comparables: Rico Petrocelli, Manny Ramirez, Ron Santo*

In a season when so many Braves rookies made an impact with the big club, Marte, #1 on our Top 50 Prospect List last year, was noticeably absent. Though he wet his feet when Chipper Jones went down, Marte didn't produce, and the Braves sensibly sent him back to Triple-A. Once again, he showed the broad range of skills that made us so high on him— power, excellent control of the strike zone, good defense—and his raw stats bear an uncanny resemblance to 2004's except that he shaved about 20 strikeouts and improved his K/UIBB rate from 1.9 to 1.3 while moving up a level. Dealt to the Red Sox for Edgar Renteria, Marte now has Mike Lowell in front of him and is likely to start the season in Pawtucket.

BRIAN McCANN   **C**   **Bats: L**   **Throws: R**   Height: 6' 3"   Weight: 190   Born: February 20, 1984   Age: 22

YEAR	TM	LVL	AGE	PA	R	2B	3B	HR	RBI	BB	SO	SB	CS	SPEED	BA	OBP	SLG	MLVR	EQBA	EQOBP	EQSLG	EQA	VORP	DEFENSE
2003	ROM	A	19	453	40	31	3	12	71	24	73	7	4	4.0	.290	.329	.462	.220	.275	.303	.446	.254	15.9	63-C 7
2004	MYR	A+	20	421	45	35	0	16	66	31	54	2	2	3.2	.278	.337	.494	.227	.251	.302	.457	.255	13.9	70-C 9
2005	MIS	AA	21	198	27	13	2	6	26	25	26	2	3	4.5	.265	.359	.476	.181	.238	.318	.423	.256	4.8	43-C 3
2005	ATL	MLB	21	200	20	7	0	5	23	18	26	1	1	4.1	.278	.345	.400	.011	.276	.347	.403	.262	7.1	50-C -3
2006	*ATL*	*MLB*	*22*	*480*	*57*	*26*	*1*	*16*	*68*	*39*	*70*	*3*	*2*	*4.4*	*.273*	*.337*	*.452*	*.033*	*.273*	*.337*	*.466*	*.266*	*21.1*	*113-C -1*

Breakout: 34%   *Improve: 60%*   *Collapse: 15%*   *Attrition: 8%*   *Comparables: Ed Kranepool, Eric Chavez, Rich Gedman*

When injuries claimed both Estrada and Perez, McCann got called up and never looked back. He homered in his second game, and made such an impression on starter John Smoltz that he soon became his personal catcher. By August he was carrying the bulk of the catching load and drawing high marks for handling a staff in flux all season and holding his own with the stick. Though he didn't flash a lot of it at the major-league level, he's got plenty of power, as anybody who tuned into the Division Series—when he homered twice—could tell you. The surprise was his plate discipline; between Mississippi and Atlanta, he drew an unintentional walk for every 9.9 at-bats, compared to once every 15.4 coming into the year. The Braves liked what they saw and dealt Estrada, so the job is McCann's to lose.

PETE ORR   **INF**   **Bats: L**   **Throws: R**   Height: 6' 1"   Weight: 170   Born: June 8, 1979   Age: 27

YEAR	TM	LVL	AGE	PA	R	2B	3B	HR	RBI	BB	SO	SB	CS	SPEED	BA	OBP	SLG	MLVR	EQBA	EQOBP	EQSLG	EQA	VORP	DEFENSE	
2003	GRN	AA	24	288	22	10	2	2	31	25	48	14	5	5.8	.226	.299	.304	-.152	.209	.270	.296	.209	-14.3	42-SS 3	16-3B -1
2004	RIC	AAA	25	484	69	16	10	1	35	20	59	24	11	7.7	.320	.349	.404	.051	.301	.331	.375	.249	12.5	89-2B 11	12-3B 3
2005	ATL	MLB	26	157	32	8	1	1	8	6	23	7	1	7.6	.300	.331	.387	-.017	.296	.331	.382	.256	4.8	18-2B 0	
2006	*ATL*	*MLB*	*27*	*200*	*26*	*8*	*2*	*1*	*17*	*11*	*27*	*6*	*2*	*6.4*	*.278*	*.323*	*.361*	*-.110*	*.278*	*.322*	*.372*	*.238*	*2.7*	*51-2B 3*	

Breakout: 23%   *Improve: 38%*   *Collapse: 35%*   *Attrition: 35%*   *Comparables: Bob Addis, Jim Gantner, Keith Miller*

Signed as an non-drafted free agent out of junior college, this Ontario native was nobody's idea of a prospect. Prior to 2004, he'd never topped a 617 OPS in any of his four minor-league seasons, including a pair of anemic performances in Double-A. But Orr earned a spot on the 40-man roster with a surprising year at Richmond and a bit of Olympic stardom (he was Baseball Canada's MVP). The spring trade of Nick Green opened up a bench role, and Cox kept him busy. Whether subbing for a banged-up Giles, pinch-hitting a team-high 54 times, or getting coffee, Orr tackled his task with enthusiasm. He also played good defense, and if his strike zone judgment was lacking, well, he wasn't Enrique Wilson either. He may vanish as quickly as he arrived, but in the meantime he's handy enough to keep around.

BRAYAN PENA   **C**   **Bats: B**   **Throws: R**   Height: 5' 11"   Weight: 210   Born: January 7, 1982   Age: 24

YEAR	TM	LVL	AGE	PA	R	2B	3B	HR	RBI	BB	SO	SB	CS	SPEED	BA	OBP	SLG	MLVR	EQBA	EQOBP	EQSLG	EQA	VORP	DEFENSE
2003	MYR	A+	21	300	24	14	1	2	27	11	28	2	5	3.3	.294	.320	.371	.070	.290	.314	.379	.237	4.8	59-C 1
2004	GRN	AA	22	295	30	10	4	2	30	15	29	3	5	4.5	.314	.349	.401	.074	.286	.318	.365	.238	3.2	71-C -13
2005	RIC	AAA	23	313	27	21	2	0	25	28	19	3	1	4.1	.326	.383	.415	.123	.300	.358	.375	.262	12.0	60-C -5
2005	ATL	MLB	23	40	2	2	0	0	4	1	7	0	0	4.0	.179	.200	.231	-.518	.179	.200	.231	.156	-3.5	
2006	*ATL*	*MLB*	*24*	*344*	*34*	*19*	*1*	*1*	*32*	*21*	*30*	*2*	*2*	*4.4*	*.274*	*.320*	*.349*	*-.133*	*.275*	*.320*	*.359*	*.230*	*1.6*	*83-C -4*

Breakout: 15%   *Improve: 35%*   *Collapse: 42%*   *Attrition: 14%*   *Comparables: Cam Carreon, Ben Molina, Michael Barrett*

(continued next page)

Brayan Pena (*continued*)

Leapfrogged by McCann when the injury bug bit, this Havana native isn't as bad as that would suggest. Though Pena's defensive reputation is a bit inflated thus far, he would seem to have all the makings for a career of backup backstopping if nothing else. Expect him to be the odd man out unless McCann struggles, and to find himself in another organization before he's 25. When undead catcher caddies like Pat Borders and John Flaherty are considered valuable commodities, this guy can help somebody.

EDDIE PEREZ   C   **Bats: R Throws: R**   Height: 6′ 1″   Weight: 185   Born: May 4, 1968   Age: 38

YEAR	TM	LVL	AGE	PA	R	2B	3B	HR	RBI	BB	SO	SB	CS	SPEED	BA	OBP	SLG	MLVR	EQBA	EQOBP	EQSLG	EQA	VORP	DEFENSE
2003	MIL	MLB	35	369	26	17	1	11	45	17	47	0	1	3.0	.271	.304	.420	-.044	.267	.301	.420	.246	6.6	92-C -13
2004	ATL	MLB	36	185	14	12	0	3	13	11	29	0	0	3.1	.229	.286	.353	-.197	.227	.280	.349	.220	-3.1	46-C 6
2005	ATL	MLB	37	39	3	2	0	2	6	1	5	0	0	2.6	.211	.231	.421	-.180	.211	.231	.421	.218	-0.3	
2006	ATL	MLB	38	121	10	5	0	3	13	7	19	0	0	2.7	.220	.267	.337	-.276	.220	.267	.348	.202	-4.0	33-C -1

Breakout: 7%   Improve: 18%   Collapse: 46%   Attrition: 56%   Comparables: Bob Scheffing, John Flaherty, Clyde McCullough

Shoulder tendonitis shelved Perez for most of the year, so he couldn't take up any of the slack left by Estrada's injury. That wasn't a bad thing; it was one less reason for the organization to keep McCann in the sticks. Approaching 38 years of age and facing free agency, Perez may have backed up his last backstop.

VAN POPE   3B   **Bats: R Throws: R**   Height: 6′ 0″   Weight: 200   Born: February 26, 1984   Age: 22

YEAR	TM	LVL	AGE	PA	R	2B	3B	HR	RBI	BB	SO	SB	CS	SPEED	BA	OBP	SLG	MLVR	EQBA	EQOBP	EQSLG	EQA	VORP	DEFENSE
2004	DNV	Rk	20	261	39	18	2	5	39	11	44	5	1	5.5	.270	.333	.429	.133	.239	.269	.367	.221	-19.2	
2005	ROM	A	21	435	48	24	7	6	60	42	70	0	1	4.5	.277	.347	.422	.139	.261	.318	.392	.247	8.0	95-3B -1
2005	MYR	A+	21	95	7	1	0	1	5	9	21	0	0	3.2	.167	.253	.214	-.419	.160	.230	.207	.167	-11.1	23-3B 1
2006	ATL	MLB	22	438	45	23	3	6	44	30	84	1	2	4.3	.242	.300	.362	-.171	.242	.299	.373	.225	-4.6	104-3B -1

Breakout: 31%   Improve: 52%   Collapse: 28%   Attrition: 9%   Comparables: Tripper Johnson, Michael Sandoval, Pete LaForest

A 5th round 2004 pick out of Meridian College, Pope is an acrobatic third baseman in a system deep with hot-cornermen. He made huge strides with his plate discipline last year, cutting his K/UIBB ratio from 4.0 to 1.7 and upping his walk rate from one every 21.2 at-bats to one every 9.2. He was overmatched in his brief taste of High-A ball, but at least he got to preview his new digs for 2006.

JAMIE ROMAK   OF   **Bats: R Throws: R**   Height: 6′ 2″   Weight: 220   Born: September 30, 1985 Age: 20

YEAR	TM	LVL	AGE	PA	R	2B	3B	HR	RBI	BB	SO	SB	CS	SPEED	BA	OBP	SLG	MLVR	EQBA	EQOBP	EQSLG	EQA	VORP	DEFENSE
2004	DNV	Rk	18	181	25	5	1	5	22	14	56	1	1	4.6	.190	.287	.329	-.139	.168	.228	.284	.186	-37.6	
2005	DNV	Rk	19	144	25	10	1	7	27	14	38	2	1	4.7	.274	.368	.540	.350	.231	.295	.425	.245	-5.5	31-RF 0
2006	ATL	MLB	20	266	28	14	1	8	31	17	75	3	2	4.6	.226	.284	.389	-.174	.227	.284	.401	.226	-8.8	65-RF -2

Breakout: 41%   Improve: 54%   Collapse: 31%   Attrition: 25%   Comparables: Jordan Pickens, Josh Gray, Jamar Hill

The Ontario talent pipeline strikes again, eh? Romak hadn't exactly impressed in his Gulf Coast and Appalachian League stints, though lower back trouble had much to do with that. Shifted from third base to right field, he repeated the Appy last year—something that raised eyebrows, though he was still one of the team's youngest hitters—and gave the Braves plenty of reasons not to give up on him. Alas, a broken bone in his hand ended his season in early August.

JARROD SALTALAMACCHIA C **Bats: B Throws: R**   Height: 6′ 4″   Weight: 195   Born: May 2, 1985   Age: 21

YEAR	TM	LVL	AGE	PA	R	2B	3B	HR	RBI	BB	SO	SB	CS	SPEED	BA	OBP	SLG	MLVR	EQBA	EQOBP	EQSLG	EQA	VORP	DEFENSE
2004	ROM	A	19	365	42	19	2	10	51	34	83	1	0	3.7	.272	.348	.437	.138	.252	.310	.392	.245	3.8	50-C -5
2005	MYR	A+	20	528	70	35	1	19	81	57	99	4	2	3.8	.314	.394	.519	.343	.287	.351	.463	.280	35.3	93-C -11
2006	ATL	MLB	21	514	57	28	1	15	66	42	104	3	1	3.8	.260	.324	.422	-.038	.261	.324	.434	.253	15.5	121-C -11

Breakout: 13%   Improve: 40%   Collapse: 38%   Attrition: 3%   Comparables: Justin Huber, J. R. House, Justin Morneau

In a system deep in young catching talent, "Salty" has the Braves licking their chops. With Francouer's graduation to the majors and Marte's trade, he now rates as the Braves' top prospect, as well as one of the top catching prospects anywhere. Tall for a catcher—leading some to speculate he'll eventually be moved—he has drawn comparisons to Joe Mauer, but switch-hitting Jason Varitek might be a more accurate comp. He's got a sweet swing, good plate discipline, and plenty of power. He has also improved defensively, despite nabbing only 26 percent of baserunners. With McCann and Pena, the Braves can afford to take their time with him.

SCOTT THORMAN   **1B**   **Bats: L Throws: R**   Height: 6' 3"   Weight: 200   Born: January 6, 1982   Age: 24

YEAR	TM	LVL	AGE	PA	R	2B	3B	HR	RBI	BB	SO	SB	CS	SPEED	BA	OBP	SLG	MLVR	EQBA	EQOBP	EQSLG	EQA	VORP	DEFENSE
2003	MYR	A+	21	495	44	26	2	12	56	42	79	0	0	3.3	.243	.311	.391	.046	.240	.297	.407	.242	-9.6	116-1B -1
2004	MYR	A+	22	176	20	11	1	4	29	12	19	1	0	4.1	.299	.358	.461	.231	.290	.340	.467	.278	6.9	43-1B 3
2004	GRN	AA	22	387	31	14	3	11	51	39	73	5	3	4.3	.252	.326	.406	-.002	.231	.297	.375	.235	-12.8	93-1B -7
2005	MIS	AA	23	383	49	21	2	15	65	28	76	2	2	4.2	.305	.360	.506	.264	.283	.330	.478	.273	14.9	90-1B -2
2005	RIC	AAA	23	224	23	10	3	6	27	9	42	0	0	4.9	.276	.312	.438	-.009	.257	.295	.406	.241	-3.6	52-1B 0
2006	*ATL*	*MLB*	*24*	*512*	*58*	*26*	*2*	*16*	*66*	*34*	*100*	*2*	*1*	*4.1*	*.258*	*.312*	*.421*	*-.061*	*.258*	*.312*	*.434*	*.247*	*0.0*	*121-1B -2*

Breakout: 22%   Improve: 52%   Collapse: 28%   Attrition: 4%   Comparables: Julio Zuleta, Ryan Garko, Dale Murphy

A 1st round pick in 2000, Thorman finally reached Triple-A late last year after spending the better parts of two seasons in Double-A. He's got some power, as the 21 homers attest, but his plate discipline is severely lacking, and he ain't no Francouer. The Braves need an upgrade at first base, but Thorman's got a ways to go before he's a viable solution.

PITCHERS

KEVIN BARRY   **Bats: R Throws: R**   Height: 6' 2"   Weight: 210   Born: August 18, 1978   Age: 27

YEAR	TM	LVL	AGE	W	L	SV	G	GS	IP	H	BB	SO	HR	GB%	BABIP	STUFF	WHIP	ERA	PERA	EQERA	EQH9	EQBB9	EQSO9	EQHR9	VORP	WXRL
2003	GRN	AA	24	4	4	5	51	0	56.3	54	32	68	1	—	.344	-3	1.53	4.96	4.31	7.12	9.3	5.8	7.1	0.3	-9.2	—
2004	GRN	AA	25	2	1	4	20	0	24.7	15	10	31	0	—	.263	5	1.01	0.73	3.97	2.38	7.5	4.8	7.1	0.4	8.1	—
2004	RIC	AAA	25	3	3	2	30	0	35.7	25	25	40	1	—	.279	0	1.40	2.52	4.24	4.50	7.1	7.4	7.9	0.3	4.2	—
2005	RIC	AAA	26	5	3	1	32	8	79.0	60	44	73	8	34%	.252	-10	1.32	2.85	5.62	3.91	8.3	6.0	6.5	1.2	13.8	—
2006	*ATL*	*MLB*	*27*	*3*	*4*	*0*	*26*	*7*	*60.0*	*58*	*46*	*49*	*8*	*39%*	*.291*	*-7*	*1.73*	*5.42*	*5.92*	*6.05*	*8.6*	*6.2*	*6.8*	*1.1*	*-0.9*	*0.1*

Breakout: 6%   Improve: 12%   Collapse: 61%   Attrition: 14%   Comparables: Bob Gibson, Jason Bere, Jaret Wright

Ping-ponging between Double- and Triple-A over the past two years, this Rider University grad has succeeded despite wildness, posting a 2.33 ERA in 146.2 innings, striking out 151 and walking 85. Seen by some as organizational fodder, he was exclusively a reliever until the second half, when he was dropped into Richmond's rotation. The early returns were impressive: in his final six starts, he allowed just four runs and 16 hits in 36 innings, whiffing 37 and walking 15. If the Braves let him build on that, and he does, he'll help.

BLAINE BOYER   **Bats: R Throws: R**   Height: 6' 3"   Weight: 190   Born: July 11, 1981   Age: 24

YEAR	TM	LVL	AGE	W	L	SV	G	GS	IP	H	BB	SO	HR	GB%	BABIP	STUFF	WHIP	ERA	PERA	EQERA	EQH9	EQBB9	EQSO9	EQHR9	VORP	WXRL
2003	ROM	A	21	12	8	0	30	26	136.7	146	58	115	5	—	.323	-7	1.49	3.69	5.21	7.13	10.3	4.7	4.5	0.9	-22.3	—
2004	MYR	A+	22	10	10	0	28	28	154.0	138	49	95	4	—	.275	5	1.21	2.98	4.57	5.38	9.0	3.6	3.8	0.5	3.6	—
2005	MIS	AA	23	2	4	0	14	8	48.3	62	18	40	4	55%	.389	-16	1.66	5.03	5.66	6.61	11.5	3.8	4.7	1.5	-5.4	—
2005	ATL	MLB	23	4	2	0	43	0	37.7	32	17	33	1	47%	.301	12	1.27	3.10	3.58	3.35	7.9	3.8	7.2	0.2	11.1	0.3
2006	*ATL*	*MLB*	*24*	*3*	*4*	*1*	*46*	*5*	*67.7*	*75*	*33*	*43*	*7*	*51%*	*.310*	*-10*	*1.61*	*5.18*	*5.61*	*5.79*	*9.9*	*4.0*	*5.2*	*1.0*	*-0.3*	*0.1*

Breakout: 22%   Improve: 49%   Collapse: 23%   Attrition: 4%   Comparables: Joe Grahe, Tom Poholsky, Bob Kelly

A Marietta product who's spent most of his six minor-league seasons as a starter, it wasn't until last summer that he broke out of the low minors. After getting knocked around at Double-A, he was transferred to relief. By mid-June he was in the Braves' bullpen and was largely effective; twice he went four weeks between allowing a run. He held righty batters to a .200/.277/.278 clip, but his control suffered against lefties. With a pair of plus pitches—his curve and his sinker—he'll probably stay in the bullpen.

JIM BROWER   **Bats: R Throws: R**   Height: 6' 2"   Weight: 205   Born: December 29, 1972   Age: 33

YEAR	TM	LVL	AGE	W	L	SV	G	GS	IP	H	BB	SO	HR	GB%	BABIP	STUFF	WHIP	ERA	PERA	EQERA	EQH9	EQBB9	EQSO9	EQHR9	VORP	WXRL
2003	SFN	MLB	30	8	5	2	51	5	100.0	90	39	65	8	59%	.284	0	1.29	3.96	4.32	4.59	8.8	3.2	5.3	0.7	14.6	3.0
2004	SFN	MLB	31	7	7	1	89	0	93.0	90	36	63	6	56%	.301	3	1.35	3.29	4.18	3.98	8.8	3.2	5.4	0.6	17.7	2.6
2005	SFN	MLB	32	2	1	1	32	0	30.3	40	15	25	5	54%	.368	-11	1.81	6.53	5.46	6.32	10.9	4.0	6.6	1.4	-3.1	-0.2
2005	ATL	MLB	32	1	2	0	37	0	30.0	33	17	28	6	38%	.325	-6	1.67	4.20	5.64	4.15	9.8	4.7	7.7	1.8	4.4	0.1
2006	*ATL*	*MLB*	*33*	*3*	*3*	*2*	*55*	*0*	*62.7*	*68*	*29*	*45*	*6*	*49%*	*.312*	*-8*	*1.54*	*4.77*	*5.09*	*5.51*	*9.6*	*3.7*	*5.9*	*0.9*	*2.4*	*0.1*

Breakout: 13%   Improve: 40%   Collapse: 33%   Attrition: 19%   Comparables: Mike Dejean, Dan Osinski, Joe Boever

(continued next page)

Jim Brower (continued)

A journeyman reliever straight out of Central Casting, Brower was ridden hard in two years as a Giant, pitching a combined 193 innings and making 89 appearances in 2004 alone. He got off to a horrible start in 2005 and the Giants jettisoned him in mid-June. The Braves immediately snapped him up and used in low-leverage situations, where he performed adequately. Where he once did a very good job of handling righties, last year he was an equal-opportunity whipping boy (.301/.405/.483 vs. right, .303/.375/.505 vs. left). That's mop-and-bucket territory. Expect to find him somewhere with a minor-league contract.

KYLE DAVIES   **Bats: R Throws: R**   Height: 6′ 2″   Weight: 210   Born: September 9, 1983   Age: 22

YEAR	TM	LVL	AGE	W	L	SV	G	GS	IP	H	BB	SO	HR	GB%	BABIP	STUFF	WHIP	ERA	PERA	EQERA	EQH9	EQBB9	EQSO9	EQHR9	VORP	WXRL
2003	ROM	A	19	8	8	0	27	27	146.3	128	53	148	9	—	.290	4	1.24	2.89	5.37	5.24	9.7	3.9	5.8	1.4	5.5	—
2004	MYR	A+	20	9	2	0	14	14	75.3	55	32	95	3	—	.301	31	1.16	2.63	4.20	4.33	8.0	4.7	8.2	0.8	10.0	—
2004	GRN	AA	20	4	0	0	11	10	62.0	40	22	73	9	—	.225	14	1.00	2.32	5.68	3.63	8.1	3.6	7.6	2.1	12.5	—
2005	RIC	AAA	21	5	2	0	13	13	73.3	66	34	62	6	42%	.299	16	1.36	3.44	4.67	3.53	8.6	4.4	6.3	0.9	16.4	—
2005	ATL	MLB	21	7	6	0	21	14	87.7	98	49	62	8	35%	.321	5	1.68	4.93	4.72	5.32	9.5	4.6	5.7	0.8	3.4	1.1
2006	ATL	MLB	22	8	9	0	33	24	139.7	136	67	108	18	41%	.284	8	1.45	4.59	4.94	4.98	8.6	3.9	6.4	1.1	10.1	1.9

Breakout: 11%   Improve: 41%   Collapse: 13%   Attrition: 0%   Comparables: Jim Clancy, Larry Christenson, Tony Cloninger

Number 47 on our Top Prospect list last year, this suburban Atlanta high-schooler inherited the mantle of the Braves' top pitching prospect after Meyer and Capellan were traded. Recalled from Richmond when Hampton first went down in mid-May, he held opponents scoreless in three of his first four starts, allowing just two runs in 23.1 innings despite 11 walks. He arrived with a reputation for command of his low-90s fastball and supporting repertoire, but those walks foreshadowed piñata time. He allowed a 6.44 ERA the rest of the way, and helped little after Cox shifted him to the bullpen. Still, it's easy to forget that he began 2004 in High-A. With a bit more experience, he should be able to contribute substantially.

JOEY DEVINE   **Bats: R Throws: R**   Height: 5′ 11″   Weight: 195   Born: September 19, 1983   Age: 22

YEAR	TM	LVL	AGE	W	L	SV	G	GS	IP	H	BB	SO	HR	GB%	BABIP	STUFF	WHIP	ERA	PERA	EQERA	EQH9	EQBB9	EQSO9	EQHR9	VORP	WXRL
2005	MIS	AA	21	1	1	5	18	0	20.0	19	12	28	2	46%	.370	0	1.55	2.70	6.63	7.11	10.4	6.2	8.5	1.9	-3.2	—
2006	ATL	MLB	22	2	3	0	28	2	44.0	49	35	35	9	43%	.305	-18	1.92	7.09	7.68	7.81	9.9	6.5	6.6	1.8	-8.5	-0.8

Breakout: 31%   Improve: 65%   Collapse: 9%   Attrition: 17%   Comparables: Rob Burger, Jeremy Lambert, Tony Pluta

The selection of Devine, a reliever from North Carolina State, marked the first time the Braves tapped a college pitcher in the 1st round since 1987. With a thin bullpen, the Braves fast-tracked him to Atlanta, promoting him after just 25 innings. Devine quickly made history by allowing grand slams in his first two major league appearances. After an injury to Boyer cleared a spot on the postseason roster, he nearly surrendered another in the Division Series opener, and then allowed the fateful Chris Burke homer that sent the Braves to their long winter's rest. Such half-baked desperation by the front office did Devine no favors; the intent may have been Huston Street, but the execution was more David Clyde. He'll get a shot at making the Braves this spring, but a bit of seasoning in Triple-A wouldn't hurt.

BRADY ENDL   **Bats: R Throws: L**   Height: 6′ 5″   Weight: 235   Born: April 14, 1982   Age: 24

YEAR	TM	LVL	AGE	W	L	SV	G	GS	IP	H	BB	SO	HR	GB%	BABIP	STUFF	WHIP	ERA	PERA	EQERA	EQH9	EQBB9	EQSO9	EQHR9	VORP	WXRL
2004	DNV	Rk	22	2	3	1	16	0	28.0	24	7	33	1	—	.315	-19	1.11	2.89	5.26	7.01	10.2	3.5	4.6	1.1	-4.0	—
2005	MYR	A+	23	6	7	0	20	20	109.0	87	61	101	8	49%	.274	-13	1.36	3.39	5.75	6.11	8.8	6.1	5.2	1.2	-5.8	—
2006	ATL	MLB	24	4	7	0	24	17	95.7	101	68	64	13	46%	.294	-9	1.76	6.15	6.28	6.79	9.3	5.7	5.5	1.2	-11.2	-0.5

Breakout: 14%   Improve: 44%   Collapse: 25%   Attrition: 0%   Comparables: Adrian Burnside, Ryan Carter, Sean Henn

The Division III Player of the Year in 2004, the Braves drafted Endl in the 10th round out of Wisconsin-Whitewater that same year. Shifted from the bullpen to the rotation to start the year, he struggled with his command, particularly with a new changeup. His translated numbers weren't so impressive, and he was old for his league, but as he hones his repertoire and adjusts to his new role, his stock could rise.

KYLE FARNSWORTH   **Bats: R**   **Throws: R**   Height: 6′ 4″   Weight: 230   Born: April 14, 1976   Age: 30

YEAR	TM	LVL	AGE	W	L	SV	G	GS	IP	H	BB	SO	HR	GB%	BABIP	STUFF	WHIP	ERA	PERA	EQERA	EQH9	EQBB9	EQSO9	EQHR9	VORP	WXRL
2003	CHN	MLB	27	3	2	0	77	0	76.3	53	36	92	6	51%	.272	25	1.17	3.30	3.35	3.70	6.8	3.8	9.8	0.7	16.8	1.8
2004	CHN	MLB	28	4	5	0	72	0	66.7	67	33	78	10	44%	.335	8	1.50	4.72	4.26	5.05	8.8	4.0	9.2	1.2	4.0	0.5
2005	DET	MLB	29	1	1	6	46	0	42.7	29	20	55	1	47%	.295	39	1.15	2.32	2.74	2.53	6.1	4.2	11.4	0.2	15.2	2.2
2005	ATL	MLB	29	0	0	10	26	0	27.3	15	7	32	4	36%	.193	26	0.80	1.98	3.81	2.08	6.6	2.1	10.0	1.4	10.7	2.1
2006	*NYA*	*MLB*	*30*	*4*	*3*	*7*	*63*	*0*	*67.7*	*55*	*27*	*79*	*7*	*43%*	*.288*	*23*	*1.21*	*3.33*	*3.46*	*3.47*	*7.1*	*3.7*	*10.1*	*0.8*	*15.2*	*1.4*

Breakout: 24%   Improve: 54%   Collapse: 11%   Attrition: 10%   Comparables: Lee Smith, Rich Gossage, Jeff Nelson

After six disappointing seasons ("Nuke Laloosh come to life but without the winning personality," wrote Bronx Banter's Alex Belth), the Cubs shipped the flamethrower to Detroit for a trio of suspects and a half-eaten frozen pizza. He flourished as a Tiger, inheriting the closer role once Percival went down and Urbina was traded. But Farnsworth rejected the Tigers' overtures for a multi-year contract, and in July drew a six-game suspension for body-slamming Royals reliever Jeremy Affeldt. Worried they'd lose him after the season anyway, the Tigers shipped Farnsworth to Atlanta for Roman Colon and Zach Miner. Farnsworth stepped in and excelled, leading the team in WXRL with 2.06; the rest of the bullpen was a combined 0.84 wins below replacement level. Alas, Farnsworth's pumpkin chariot crashed in the postseason, when he set the stage for the Braves' elimination by blowing a 6–1 lead, yielding a grand slam to Lance Berkman and a solo shot to Brad Ausmus. A Type A free agent, he's off to the bullpen in the Bronx, where he might thrive or wilt. The Braves will settle for the draft picks, thankyewverramuch.

JOHN FOSTER   **Bats: L**   **Throws: L**   Height: 6′ 0″   Weight: 200   Born: May 17, 1978   Age: 28

YEAR	TM	LVL	AGE	W	L	SV	G	GS	IP	H	BB	SO	HR	GB%	BABIP	STUFF	WHIP	ERA	PERA	EQERA	EQH9	EQBB9	EQSO9	EQHR9	VORP	WXRL
2003	IND	AAA	25	2	2	0	27	0	41.3	44	13	37	4	—	.315	-10	1.38	3.70	5.18	5.40	9.9	3.6	6.1	1.4	0.9	—
2003	MIL	MLB	25	2	0	0	23	0	21.0	30	8	16	5	52%	.373	-11	1.81	4.71	5.73	4.50	11.5	2.9	5.7	2.0	2.2	0.1
2005	ATL	MLB	27	4	2	1	62	0	34.7	27	19	32	3	42%	.261	2	1.33	4.15	4.46	4.46	7.6	4.7	7.6	0.8	4.2	-0.1
2006	*ATL*	*MLB*	*28*	*2*	*2*	*2*	*49*	*0*	*39.3*	*39*	*19*	*34*	*4*	*44%*	*.296*	*-1*	*1.45*	*4.35*	*4.74*	*5.40*	*8.7*	*3.9*	*7.1*	*1.0*	*3.6*	*0.3*

Breakout: 20%   Improve: 41%   Collapse: 38%   Attrition: 37%   Comparables: Aaron Fultz, Mike Myers, Dave Hamilton

A 1999 draftee whom the team traded along with Wes Helms to acquire Ray King in December 2002, Foster's career was derailed by vertigo and shoulder woes to the point that he was out of baseball in 2004. Discovering himself pain-free over the winter, he went to camp with the Braves. When they jettisoned Tom Martin in mid-April, he became the team's primary LOOGY. He was spotty but not horrible before elbow soreness caused him to cede the top lefty spot to McBride late in the season. It's anybody's guess as to whether he can hang on going forward.

MIKE HAMPTON   **Bats: R**   **Throws: L**   Height: 5′ 10″   Weight: 180   Born: September 9, 1972   Age: 33

YEAR	TM	LVL	AGE	W	L	SV	G	GS	IP	H	BB	SO	HR	GB%	BABIP	STUFF	WHIP	ERA	PERA	EQERA	EQH9	EQBB9	EQSO9	EQHR9	VORP	WXRL
2003	ATL	MLB	30	14	8	0	31	31	190.0	186	78	110	14	56%	.284	10	1.39	3.84	4.40	4.40	9.1	3.3	4.7	0.7	28.3	4.7
2004	ATL	MLB	31	13	9	0	29	29	172.3	198	65	87	15	54%	.315	4	1.53	4.28	4.59	4.75	9.8	3.0	4.0	0.7	24.1	4.4
2005	ATL	MLB	32	5	3	0	12	12	69.3	74	18	27	5	51%	.299	2	1.33	3.51	4.43	4.04	9.5	2.2	3.3	0.7	15.0	2.2

When healthy, Hampton pitched about as well as a guy who strikes out 3.5 per nine innings can. But he made four trips to the DL for a herniated disc and tightness in his forearm, and was limited to 14.1 innings after mid-May. An MRI revealed the forearm injury to be referred pain from a torn ulnar collateral ligament, necessitating Tommy John surgery that will sideline him for all of 2006 (given his $13.5 million salary, perhaps the most expensive TJ rehab season ever). After receiving considerable help from the Rockies and the Marlins in paying off Hampton's salary over the past few years, the Braves are on the hook for a staggering $43 million from 2006–2008; any rumors that he might retire in the face of that payday should be taken with an aquarium-grade brick of salt.

MATT HARRISON   **Bats: L**   **Throws: L**   Height: 6′ 5″   Weight: 205   Born: August 16, 1985   Age: 20

YEAR	TM	LVL	AGE	W	L	SV	G	GS	IP	H	BB	SO	HR	GB%	BABIP	STUFF	WHIP	ERA	PERA	EQERA	EQH9	EQBB9	EQSO9	EQHR9	VORP	WXRL
2004	DNV	Rk	18	4	4	0	13	12	66.0	72	10	49	3	—	.321	-2	1.24	4.09	4.78	7.45	10.5	1.8	3.1	1.0	-13.2	—
2005	ROM	A	19	12	7	0	27	27	167.0	151	30	118	17	43%	.270	-8	1.08	3.23	5.71	5.37	9.9	2.0	4.1	1.8	4.0	—
2006	*ATL*	*MLB*	*20*	*8*	*9*	*0*	*26*	*24*	*144.0*	*158*	*38*	*77*	*24*	*43%*	*.281*	*4*	*1.36*	*5.00*	*5.14*	*5.40*	*9.7*	*2.1*	*4.4*	*1.5*	*3.5*	*1.4*

Breakout: 21%   Improve: 69%   Collapse: 1%   Attrition: 1%   Comparables: Jon Connolly, Craig Anderson, Mark Turnbow

(continued next page)

Matt Harrison (*continued*)

This big southpaw upped his stock with an impressive showing in the Sally League, starting off with 16.2 scoreless innings. He's a control guy who pounds the strike zone with a low-90s fastball, changeup, and an improving curve. Harrison's shown excellent command throughout his minor league career, walking just 1.6 per nine innings. He's one of the few low-minors finesse guys who lack a true out pitch nevertheless worth keeping an eye on.

TIM HUDSON   **Bats: R Throws: R**   Height: 6′ 0″   Weight: 160   Born: July 14, 1975   Age: 30

YEAR	TM	LVL	AGE	W	L	SV	G	GS	IP	H	BB	SO	HR	GB%	BABIP	STUFF	WHIP	ERA	PERA	EQERA	EQH9	EQBB9	EQSO9	EQHR9	VORP	WXRL
2003	OAK	MLB	27	16	7	0	34	34	240.0	197	61	162	15	61%	.258	28	1.07	2.70	3.71	3.17	8.2	2.3	6.1	0.5	75.2	8.5
2004	OAK	MLB	28	12	6	0	27	27	188.7	194	44	103	8	59%	.305	23	1.29	3.53	3.71	3.86	9.2	2.0	4.6	0.3	46.2	4.8
2005	ATL	MLB	29	14	9	0	29	29	192.0	194	65	115	20	59%	.291	7	1.35	3.52	4.66	3.90	9.3	2.9	5.0	0.9	41.2	5.4
2006	ATL	MLB	30	13	9	0	30	30	195.0	198	59	113	15	57%	.288	9	1.32	3.69	4.07	4.16	9.0	2.5	4.8	0.7	32.5	4.8

Breakout: 8%   Improve: 28%   Collapse: 30%   Attrition: 1%   Comparables: Larry Jackson, Mel Stottlemyre, Joe Horlen

The Braves acquired Hudson from Oakland last winter in a deal that cost them their top pitching prospect, Dan Meyer. Hudson's declining strikeout rate, rising salary, impending free agency, and the concern that injury might curtail his use of the splitter played into Oakland's reasons for dealing him. While his performance was still solid, he missed a month with a strained oblique, his home run rate more than doubled, and his command suffered. Hudson actually threw the splitter more often than in 2004, but seldom to right-handed batters. Signed to a four-year, $47 million extension last spring, he's still a very good pitcher, but the Braves are paying him to be a great one.

CHUCK JAMES   **Bats: L Throws: L**   Height: 6′ 0″   Weight: 170   Born: November 9, 1981   Age: 24

YEAR	TM	LVL	AGE	W	L	SV	G	GS	IP	H	BB	SO	HR	GB%	BABIP	STUFF	WHIP	ERA	PERA	EQERA	EQH9	EQBB9	EQSO9	EQHR9	VORP	WXRL
2003	DNV	Rk	21	2	1	0	11	11	50.3	26	19	68	1	—	.232	6	0.89	1.25	4.67	4.87	7.3	5.5	6.3	0.6	3.6	—
2004	ROM	A	22	10	5	0	26	22	132.7	92	48	156	6	—	.272	11	1.06	2.24	4.57	4.65	8.0	4.2	6.2	0.8	13.1	—
2005	MYR	A+	23	3	3	0	7	7	41.7	20	8	59	1	35%	.226	37	0.67	1.08	3.03	3.26	6.3	2.1	8.1	0.5	10.1	—
2005	MIS	AA	23	9	1	0	16	16	86.0	62	18	104	4	29%	.286	25	0.93	2.09	3.79	4.13	8.0	2.2	7.4	0.9	13.2	—
2005	RIC	AAA	23	1	3	0	6	6	33.7	21	10	30	4	20%	.200	13	0.92	3.47	4.88	3.73	7.5	3.2	6.6	1.4	6.5	—
2006	ATL	MLB	24	8	8	1	40	18	134.0	123	53	116	18	31%	.276	11	1.32	4.32	4.43	4.67	8.2	3.2	7.1	1.2	14.3	2.2

Breakout: 11%   Improve: 32%   Collapse: 30%   Attrition: 0%   Comparables: Don Gullett, Luis Tiant, Roger Moret

James has achieved an unfortunate notoriety for his non-pitching exploits. A pre-draft roof-jumping stunt broke both wrists and caused him to slide to the 20th round, then a brawl at the Sally League All-Star Game in 2004 that cost him a mid-season promotion to High-A. Still, James deserves recognition for his pitching: including his taste of big-league action, his 2005 totals included a 2.10 ERA in 167 innings, a 194/39 K/BB ratio and just eight homers allowed, numbers in line with his previous two seasons. Undersized and reliant on a combo of a low-90s moving fastball and a great changeup—his breaking pitches are works in progress—he also features a deceptive delivery. Despite his low home run rate, James's absurdly low G/F ratio indicates he may have trouble keeping the ball in the park at the big league level. He's projected as a back-of-the-rotation starter or perhaps a reliever, but may exceed those expectations.

DAN KOLB   **Bats: R Throws: R**   Height: 6′ 4″   Weight: 210   Born: March 29, 1975   Age: 31

YEAR	TM	LVL	AGE	W	L	SV	G	GS	IP	H	BB	SO	HR	GB%	BABIP	STUFF	WHIP	ERA	PERA	EQERA	EQH9	EQBB9	EQSO9	EQHR9	VORP	WXRL
2003	IND	AAA	28	0	1	4	26	0	39.3	26	13	46	1	—	.258	13	0.99	1.37	3.65	3.41	7.1	3.9	8.0	0.5	9.0	—
2003	MIL	MLB	28	1	2	21	37	0	41.3	34	19	39	2	62%	.283	15	1.28	1.96	3.70	2.18	7.6	3.7	7.6	0.4	15.9	3.1
2004	MIL	MLB	29	0	4	39	64	0	57.3	50	15	21	3	63%	.247	-10	1.13	2.98	4.37	3.07	8.7	2.3	3.1	0.5	13.8	3.0
2005	ATL	MLB	30	3	8	11	65	0	57.7	78	29	39	5	54%	.378	-11	1.87	5.93	4.62	6.12	10.6	4.0	5.4	0.7	-4.6	-2.0
2006	MIL	MLB	31	3	3	4	53	0	56.0	63	25	33	5	54%	.311	-13	1.57	4.79	5.06	5.71	10.0	3.9	5.0	0.8	3.3	0.3

Breakout: 16%   Improve: 40%   Collapse: 39%   Attrition: 26%   Comparables: Tom Timmermann, Jay Powell, Kevin Gryboski

A mantra for aspiring general managers: closers are made, not born. Triggered by Smoltz's desire to return to the rotation, Schuerholz's most dubious move last winter involved trading Jose Capellan to Milwaukee for "Proven Closer" Kolb. Though he saved 60 games in two years with the Brew Crew, Kolb's K/9 had plummeted to absurdly low rates, and his second-half ERA in 2004 was triple that of his first half (4.88/1.62). The trade proved disastrous for the Braves, as Kolb lost his job by Memorial Day and was left off the postseason roster. Kolb's failure had a ripple effect on the bullpen: successor Reitsma couldn't hold the job either, forcing Schuerholz to rent Farnsworth. Key among Kolb's woes was a .378 BABIP, which suggests a bit of bad luck, but given that he was throwing nothing but fastballs (96 percent to lefties, 93 percent to righties), it's quite apparent he wasn't doing much to fool hitters. Perhaps out of disgust, the Braves dealt him back to the Brewers for Wes Obermueller.

ANTHONY LEREW   Bats: L Throws: R   Height: 6′ 3″ Weight: 210 Born: October 28, 1982   Age: 23

YEAR	TM	LVL	AGE	W	L	SV	G	GS	IP	H	BB	SO	HR	GB%	BABIP	STUFF	WHIP	ERA	PERA	EQERA	EQH9	EQBB9	EQSO9	EQHR9	VORP	WXRL
2003	ROM	A	20	7	6	0	25	25	143.7	112	43	127	7	—	.257	4	1.08	2.38	5.05	5.05	9.0	3.3	5.0	1.2	8.2	—
2004	MYR	A+	21	8	9	0	27	27	144.0	145	46	125	12	—	.317	-8	1.33	3.75	5.53	6.26	10.1	3.6	5.5	1.6	-10.0	—
2005	MIS	AA	22	6	2	0	14	14	75.7	70	32	64	6	47%	.299	-6	1.35	3.92	5.65	5.40	9.5	4.3	5.1	1.4	1.6	—
2005	RIC	AAA	22	4	4	0	13	13	72.3	63	23	53	9	46%	.258	3	1.19	3.49	5.09	4.43	9.0	3.1	5.5	1.3	9.0	—
2006	*ATL*	*MLB*	*23*	*6*	*8*	*0*	*32*	*17*	*112.7*	*119*	*51*	*75*	*16*	*45%*	*.292*	*-1*	*1.51*		*5.08*	*5.43*	*5.53*	*9.4*	*3.7*	*5.5*	*1.2*	*1.7*	*0.8*

Breakout: 14%   Improve: 44%   Collapse: 15%   Attrition: 0%   Comparables: *William Martinez, John Ennis, Rich Hand*

Lerew added about four miles to his fastball in 2004; it can touch 97 but generally sits in the low 90s. As he's dialed it up, he's lost some command, though he remains an aggressive pitcher with three quality offerings. Like many other prospects here, he shot through the system in 2005, splitting his year between Double- and Triple-A and even getting a September cup of coffee in Atlanta. While he didn't do a great job of preventing runs, he's still projected as a mid-rotation starter. Expect him to start the year in Triple-A.

MACAY McBRIDE   Bats: L Throws: L   Height: 5′ 11″ Weight: 180 Born: October 24, 1982   Age: 23

YEAR	TM	LVL	AGE	W	L	SV	G	GS	IP	H	BB	SO	HR	GB%	BABIP	STUFF	WHIP	ERA	PERA	EQERA	EQH9	EQBB9	EQSO9	EQHR9	VORP	WXRL
2003	MYR	A+	20	9	8	0	27	27	164.7	164	49	139	5	—	.309	23	1.29	2.95	4.09	4.87	9.3	3.0	5.5	0.6	13.0	—
2004	GRN	AA	21	1	7	0	38	12	103.3	113	46	102	9	—	.342	-8	1.54	4.44	5.08	6.06	10.1	4.4	5.8	1.2	-5.2	—
2005	MIS	AA	22	3	1	0	6	3	24.7	21	12	16	2	64%	.264	-18	1.34	3.64	6.26	5.48	9.0	5.1	3.9	1.6	0.3	—
2005	RIC	AAA	22	1	5	2	25	1	43.7	49	22	47	5	45%	.376	1	1.62	4.32	4.95	5.56	9.9	4.7	7.6	1.2	0.2	—
2005	ATL	MLB	22	1	0	1	23	0	14.0	18	7	22	0	43%	.486	15	1.79	5.79	2.40	6.60	9.0	3.6	12.0	0.0	-2.4	1.1
2006	*ATL*	*MLB*	*23*	*3*	*4*	*2*	*63*	*4*	*64.0*	*67*	*33*	*51*	*7*	*49%*	*.309*	*-3*	*1.55*		*5.06*	*5.27*	*5.76*	*9.3*	*4.1*	*6.6*	*1.0*	*0.5*	*0.1*

Breakout: 16%   Improve: 54%   Collapse: 16%   Attrition: 10%   Comparables: *Shane Rawley, Johnny Klippstein, Dick Selma*

A 2001 1st rounder out of Sylvania, Georgia, McBride struggled at Double-A in 2004 until shifted to the bullpen, where mechanical adjustments upped his velocity into the mid-90s. Summoned to Atlanta in late July, he was largely effective in the second LOOGY role: his 1.08 WXRL was second on the team, and his ERA was distorted by a bombing in an 11–3 loss and the performances of the relievers behind him (his Fair Run Average was 3.68). Mostly, he missed a lot of bats; more than half of the 42 outs he recorded came on strikeouts. Long-term, the Braves may still be thinking of him as a starter rather than a reliever, which probably means more time in the minors.

HORACIO RAMIREZ   Bats: L Throws: L   Height: 6′ 1″ Weight: 170 Born: November 24, 1979 Age: 26

YEAR	TM	LVL	AGE	W	L	SV	G	GS	IP	H	BB	SO	HR	GB%	BABIP	STUFF	WHIP	ERA	PERA	EQERA	EQH9	EQBB9	EQSO9	EQHR9	VORP	WXRL
2003	ATL	MLB	23	12	4	0	29	29	182.3	181	72	100	21	53%	.282	0	1.39	4.00	5.01	4.56	9.5	3.3	4.5	1.1	24.1	3.8
2004	ATL	MLB	24	2	4	0	10	9	60.3	51	30	31	7	59%	.234	-3	1.34	2.39	5.22	3.84	8.4	4.1	4.3	1.1	14.6	1.9
2005	ATL	MLB	25	11	9	0	33	32	202.3	214	67	80	31	50%	.282	-16	1.39	4.63	5.58	5.09	9.9	2.8	3.3	1.4	17.5	3.4
2006	*ATL*	*MLB*	*26*	*10*	*10*	*0*	*29*	*27*	*165.0*	*176*	*55*	*76*	*19*	*51%*	*.281*	*-1*	*1.40*		*4.34*	*4.74*	*4.95*	*9.5*	*2.7*	*3.8*	*1.0*	*15.3*	*2.8*

Breakout: 17%   Improve: 47%   Collapse: 15%   Attrition: 8%   Comparables: *Allan Anderson, Mike Caldwell, Mike Maroth*

As a fifth starter promoted to #3 in the wake of rotation mayhem, you can at least say that he took the ball every fifth day and ate innings. But of all Braves pitchers to throw 200-plus innings during the Mazzone era, none finished with a worse RA+ than Ramirez's 96, and only Greg Maddux in 2003 (98) joined him in being worse than the adjusted league average. His peripherals are brutal; his ERA might have been half a run higher. The one thing he's got going for him is a significant platoon split (2003–2005: .247/.309/.358 vs. lefties, .278/.346/.460 vs. righties), so if he wants to stick around on first-division clubs, he'd be better off as a LOOGY.

CHRIS REITSMA   Bats: R Throws: R   Height: 6′ 5″ Weight: 235 Born: December 31, 1977 Age: 28

YEAR	TM	LVL	AGE	W	L	SV	G	GS	IP	H	BB	SO	HR	GB%	BABIP	STUFF	WHIP	ERA	PERA	EQERA	EQH9	EQBB9	EQSO9	EQHR9	VORP	WXRL
2003	CIN	MLB	25	9	5	12	57	3	84.0	92	19	53	14	56%	.300	-12	1.32	4.29	4.93	4.07	9.6	1.8	5.1	1.5	11.8	2.4
2004	ATL	MLB	26	6	4	2	84	0	79.7	89	20	60	9	56%	.328	1	1.37	4.07	4.03	4.48	9.6	2.0	5.9	0.9	12.4	0.9
2005	ATL	MLB	27	3	6	15	76	0	73.3	79	14	42	3	54%	.310	5	1.27	3.93	3.53	4.26	9.2	1.6	4.7	0.4	12.9	0.7
2006	*ATL*	*MLB*	*28*	*4*	*4*	*8*	*60*	*0*	*66.3*	*72*	*17*	*40*	*7*	*52%*	*.302*	*-4*	*1.34*		*3.89*	*4.26*	*4.58*	*9.6*	*2.1*	*5.0*	*0.9*	*9.0*	*0.8*

Breakout: 16%   Improve: 50%   Collapse: 19%   Attrition: 16%   Comparables: *Steve Crawford, Braden Looper, Brian Meadows*

(continued next page)

Chris Reitsma *(continued)*

After an uneven start to the year as the Braves' primary setup man, Reitsma inherited the closer role from Kolb and didn't allow a run in his first month on the job. He chugged along, taking occasional lumps but converting 15 of his first 17 save opportunities, but shortly after the Farnsworth trade, Reitsma went through a rocky stretch, blowing three saves in ten days, after which he was forced to hand over the keys to the ninth inning and return to his setup role. Though his K rate dropped, his walk rate fell too, and he allowed just three homers all year. He doesn't get a lot of love from Braves fans, but he should be back in 2006. Continuing a longstanding trend, he performed much better with a day of rest between outings (2.44 ERA) than when used consecutively (4.87 ERA).

JOHN SMOLTZ   Bats: R Throws: R   Height: 6′ 3″   Weight: 220   Born: May 15, 1967   Age: 39

YEAR	TM	LVL	AGE	W	L	SV	G	GS	IP	H	BB	SO	HR	GB%	BABIP	STUFF	WHIP	ERA	PERA	EQERA	EQH9	EQBB9	EQSO9	EQHR9	VORP	WXRL
2003	ATL	MLB	36	0	2	45	62	0	64.3	48	8	73	2	48%	.287	42	0.87	1.12	2.29	1.57	7.1	1.0	9.3	0.3	31.1	5.3
2004	ATL	MLB	37	0	1	44	73	0	81.7	75	13	85	8	50%	.315	25	1.08	2.75	3.10	2.88	8.2	1.3	8.3	0.8	26.7	7.0
2005	ATL	MLB	38	14	7	0	33	33	229.7	210	53	169	18	49%	.284	25	1.15	3.06	3.72	3.48	8.4	1.9	6.1	0.7	60.1	6.8
2006	ATL	MLB	39	13	9	1	37	27	190.0	185	41	138	19	46%	.287	13	1.19	3.49	3.71	3.88	8.6	1.8	6.0	0.9	36.8	5.1

Breakout: 0%   Improve: 7%   Collapse: 39%   Attrition: 2%   Comparables: Gaylord Perry, Bob Gibson, Don Sutton

A starter for the first time since his abortive return from Tommy John surgery in June 2001, Smoltz turned in a vintage season that could be mistaken for his missing 2000 campaign. He was the rock of the rotation, holding up far better than anyone could have imagined, particularly as other Braves starters were dropping like flies. But the cost of his 229.2 innings—his most since '97 and the seventh-highest total in the majors—was a sore shoulder that pushed him back to a Game Two start in the Division Series, would have kept him from starting Game Five, and kept him sitting as the Braves were eliminated in the 18-inning Game Four. He's still a fine pitcher, but his workload warrants close monitoring. There's no guarantee the injury gods will smile on him again.

JORGE SOSA   Bats: B Throws: R   Height: 6′ 2″   Weight: 170   Born: April 28, 1977   Age: 29

YEAR	TM	LVL	AGE	W	L	SV	G	GS	IP	H	BB	SO	HR	GB%	BABIP	STUFF	WHIP	ERA	PERA	EQERA	EQH9	EQBB9	EQSO9	EQHR9	VORP	WXRL
2003	TBA	MLB	26	5	12	0	29	19	128.7	137	60	72	14	41%	.302	-3	1.53	4.62	4.99	4.85	9.7	4.1	4.9	0.9	15.7	2.2
2004	TBA	MLB	27	4	7	1	43	8	99.3	100	54	94	17	38%	.302	-3	1.55	5.53	4.84	5.56	9.0	4.5	7.9	1.3	1.0	2.0
2005	ATL	MLB	28	13	3	0	44	20	134.0	122	64	85	12	37%	.269	1	1.39	2.55	4.68	3.05	8.5	4.1	5.3	0.8	41.3	5.0
2006	ATL	MLB	29	5	6	1	38	12	97.0	98	43	66	13	40%	.285	-4	1.45	4.61	4.98	5.20	9.0	3.6	5.6	1.1	7.3	1.1

Breakout: 9%   Improve: 28%   Collapse: 39%   Attrition: 9%   Comparables: Charles Hudson, Steve Arlin, Sheldon Jones

The hands-down winner of the 2005 Jaret Wright Award for Unforeseen Improvement Under Leo Mazzone is this flamethrower, acquired from the D-Rays on March 31 for reserve infielder Nick Green. Sosa arrived sporting a career ERA of 5.14 after three seasons in Piniella Hell. In his defense, he converted to pitching after toiling in the outfield for six years in the Rockies system, and hit Tampa with only 67 minor league innings of work. Despite the long, strange trip, Sosa was a godsend for the Braves, propping up a shaky bullpen and then stepping into a decimated rotation. But despite the polish acquired in the Mazzone Finishing School, his peripherals look more like those of a pitcher with an ERA twice his 2.55. His strikeout rate fell off heavily after a one-season spike of 8.5 per 9 IP, and his K/BB declined as well, though eight intentional walks distort the degree. His most promising gain was in cutting his homer rate in half, and a drop in BABIP didn't hurt, though that's probably unsustainable. In short, bet heavily on a regression in 2006, but hope that working with a real pitching coach taught him a thing or two.

JAKE STEVENS   Bats: L Throws: L   Height: 6′ 1″   Weight: 205   Born: March 15, 1985   Age: 21

YEAR	TM	LVL	AGE	W	L	SV	G	GS	IP	H	BB	SO	HR	GB%	BABIP	STUFF	WHIP	ERA	PERA	EQERA	EQH9	EQBB9	EQSO9	EQHR9	VORP	WXRL
2004	ROM	A	19	9	5	2	27	19	135.0	100	39	140	7	—	.266	21	1.03	2.27	4.35	4.14	8.0	3.2	5.8	0.8	20.8	—
2005	MYR	A+	20	10	9	0	28	28	148.0	167	62	102	13	42%	.332	-11	1.55	4.93	5.65	6.58	10.6	4.1	4.0	1.2	-15.8	—
2006	ATL	MLB	21	6	8	0	25	22	124.0	131	56	75	20	41%	.282	0	1.51	5.21	5.59	5.67	9.4	3.7	5.0	1.4	0.7	0.9

Breakout: 18%   Improve: 54%   Collapse: 15%   Attrition: 0%   Comparables: Mike Connolly, Dennis Ulacia, Jan Granado

Folks were high on this 2003 3rd rounder after he dominated the Sally League in 2004, but he got roughed up following the promotion to High-A in 2005. His ERA more than doubled, his hit rate spiked by 50 percent, and his K/BB ratio got sawed in half, all despite the pitcher-friendly Myrtle Beach environs. Poor conditioning was reportedly a factor. Scouts may love his big, projectable body and a repertoire that includes a power curve, fastball, and changeup, but he'll have to put up better numbers to feel the love here.

JOHN THOMSON Bats: R Throws: R Height: 6′ 3″ Weight: 175 Born: October 1, 1973 Age: 32

YEAR	TM	LVL	AGE	W	L	SV	G	GS	IP	H	BB	SO	HR	GB%	BABIP	STUFF	WHIP	ERA	PERA	EQERA	EQH9	EQBB9	EQSO9	EQHR9	VORP	WXRL
2003	TEX	MLB	29	13	14	0	35	35	217.0	234	49	136	27	49%	.302	11	1.30	4.85	4.29	4.25	9.0	2.0	5.4	1.0	25.1	3.3
2004	ATL	MLB	30	14	8	0	33	33	198.3	210	52	133	20	51%	.312	14	1.32	3.72	4.17	4.40	9.3	2.1	5.4	0.9	33.8	5.0
2005	ATL	MLB	31	4	6	0	17	17	98.7	111	28	61	6	48%	.324	17	1.41	4.47	3.95	4.93	9.5	2.3	5.0	0.5	9.7	1.6
2006	ATL	MLB	32	9	8	0	29	24	149.3	157	40	92	17	48%	.290	5	1.32	4.15	4.41	4.68	9.3	2.2	5.1	1.0	17.2	2.8

Breakout: 13% Improve: 50% Collapse: 15% Attrition: 6% Comparables: Pat Dobson, Dick Ruthven, Bob Shaw

After toiling for most of his career in two parks that have broken pitchers' hearts—Coors Field and the Ballpark at Arlington—Thomson was rescued by the Braves, and turned in a very solid season in 2004. He was off to a good start in 2005 before he strained the flexor tendon in his right middle finger. Sidelined for three months, he struggled on returning, posting a 5.55 ERA, compared to 3.42 before. Nonetheless, the Braves picked up his $4.75 million option for 2006, and he should return to being a rotation regular.

Line Outs

Position/Player	TM	LVL	AGE	PA	R	2B	3B	HR	RBI	BB	SO	SB-CS	SPEED	BA/OBP/SLG	MLVR	EQBA/OBP/SLG	EQA	VORP
SS Y. Escobar	ROM	A	22	212	30	13	3	4	19	14	30	0-2	4.6	.313/.358/.470	.258	.291/.328/.432	.258	11.4
SS L. Hernandez#	MIS	AA	21	463	47	12	5	2	32	41	56	5-5	5.0	.243/.315/.311	-.133	.230/.291/.302	.213	-15.3
SS T. Pena	RIC	AAA	24	520	49	25	4	5	40	21	113	17-15	6.1	.249/.285/.347	-.206	.231/.268/.319	.208	-18.9
C M. Ramirez	DNV	Rk	20	278	45	19	0	8	47	31	41	1-2	3.5	.347/.424/.527	.495	.294/.351/.420	.267	28.7
2B J. Schuerholz#	MIS	AA	25	334	38	12	2	4	21	27	51	8-1	5.3	.278/.347/.371	.028	.248/.301/.330	.225	-6.9
	RIC	AAA	25	161	10	2	1	0	12	16	29	1-2	4.4	.175/.255/.203	-.492	.163/.240/.191	.168	-18.8
3B W. Timmons	MIS	AA	25	513	73	31	2	7	34	62	46	4-7	4.1	.272/.388/.403	.133	.242/.332/.360	.245	5.1

Picher	TM	LVL	AGE	W	L	SV	IP	H	BB	SO	HR	GB%	BABIP	STUFF	WHIP	ERA	PERA	EQERA	EQH9	EQBB9	EQSO9	EQHR9	VORP
F. Brooks*	RIC	AAA	26	3	4	0	56.0	46	24	49	4	29%	.273	-8	1.25	2.73	4.75	4.92	8.5	4.6	6.1	0.8	4.0
P. Bush	MYR	A+	25	1	3	4	42.7	36	13	40	3	39%	.292	-14	1.15	2.32	5.18	5.40	9.2	3.6	4.9	1.1	0.9
	MIS	AA	25	2	0	1	52.7	29	22	52	2	40%	.214	-4	0.97	2.39	4.91	4.72	7.2	4.7	5.9	0.8	4.7
M. Childers	RIC	AAA	26	4	2	2	73.3	69	21	62	4	46%	.305	0	1.23	3.93	4.18	5.07	9.1	3.0	5.7	0.6	4.2

Yunel Escobar hit well, but at 22, the Cuban was old for his league, and older than Hernandez by 20 months. **Luis Hernandez** may draw raves as the organization's best defensive infielder and he may have more than doubled his walk rate by moving up a level, but like Pena ahead of him, he is a vortex of suck with the bat. **Tony Pena Jr.** will ever be able to hit enough to be Neifi Lite. **Max Ramirez** converted from third to catcher, has great arm strength, but is otherwise raw. His power and good approach at the plate earned half of the Appy's Player of the Year award with Campbell. At 25, **Jon Schuerholz** finally made it into the high minors, but he doesn't really belong there; consider it field research for the front-office job that awaits him. **Wes Timmons** has great strike-zone judgment but little power, and in a system that doesn't exactly lack for third basemen.

Frank Brooks has been in eight organizations (including the Pirates twice) in less than three years; trades, waivers, Rule 5s, conditional deals. Ah, the life of an itinerant LOOGY. **Paul Bush** is a potential sleeper, but he was lit up in the AFL for 11 homers in 25.2 innings. **Matt Childers** is the younger half of a brother act that's seen Beloit, Mudville, Huntsville, Indianapolis and now Richmond together, like some endless vacation spent in the back of their parents' wood-paneled station wagon.

Baltimore Orioles

I t was the Year of the In-Season Turnaround. Previously only eight times had a major league team managed to be both 14 games over and 14 games under .500 in the same season. Last year, three teams did it. The Houston and Oakland reversal of fortunes were widely discussed last fall; they had both been 15 games under but finished strongly, with the Astros riding their resurrection all the way to the World Series. The third team to do it last year, however, was the cause of considerably less celebration. That was the Orioles, and, characteristically for the way this franchise has been run for the last decade, they did it backwards. They became just the fourth team to ride from high to low. The other three were:

- The 1890 Philadelphia Athletics. The A's were 41–21 just after the Fourth of July when they ran out of money. They started dumping salary, but it wasn't enough. By the time September rolled around they announced that they wouldn't be able to make payroll, so all the players left. The team was reduced to scrounging up local players at road games in order to avoid forfeits. Not surprisingly, they lost their last 22 games by an average score of 13–3, finishing the season with a record of 54–78.

- The 1927 White Sox. They never had a chance, matched up against the '27 Yankees, but you wouldn't have known that at the time. On June 6 the Sox were 31–17, just a game behind New York. The next day they arrived at Yankee Stadium to start a four-game series. They were swept, and from there on it was all downhill. They reached their low point after a 12-game losing streak in September that included another sweep at Yankee Stadium, this time for five games.

- The 1978 Oakland A's. One of the most disorganized teams of all time, worse even than the 2005 Orioles. Winners of three straight World Series just four years earlier, owner Charley Finley was unable and unwilling to adjust to the free agent revolution. He dumped everybody in an effort to save money, including his entire front office, eventually running the team himself with the help of a teenage kid who would later become

ORIOLES PROSPECTUS

2005 record: 74–88; Fourth place, AL East

Pythagenport record: 73–89

Runs scored per game: 4.50 (10th in AL)

Runs allowed per game: 4.94 (10th in AL)

Team EqA: .263 (6th in AL)

2005 Batters Age: 31.9 (3rd oldest in AL)

2005 Pitchers Age: 28.5 (7th youngest in AL)

Ballpark: Oriole Park; Slight pitcher's park; Park Factor of 0.981

2005: A hot start from a mediocre ballclub can be hazardous to a manager's career. Just ask Lee Mazzilli.

2006: If destiny is defined by action, welcome to the team that signed Kevin Millar.

MC Hammer. Though all that was left was a hollow shell, the club still somehow managed to jump out to a 19–5 start. Shortly thereafter manager Bobby Winkles simply walked off the job; he was replaced by the man he had replaced the previous year, Jack McKeon. As late as August 7 the A's were still a respectable 60–54, but without any support from above the players ultimately gave up, going just 9–39 the rest of the way.

The Orioles story will show that they jumped out of the gate thanks to the brilliant performance of their middle infield. That Miguel Tejada, former MVP, could get red-hot and carry a team to victory after victory is no surprise—he got that MVP award for carrying the 2002 A's through a 20-game winning streak and to a division title. That Brian Roberts was every bit Tejada's equal through the first two months of the season was a shock. Roberts had hit 12 home runs in a four-year career entering 2005; he had 8 by the end of April. By the end of June he was hitting .365—he'd never before hit .350 for even one month, let alone three. Melvin Mora continued his recent success, giving the Orioles a powerful 1-2-3 punch.

The pitching wasn't as strong overall, but it had its moments. Eric Bedard emerged as the early staff ace. Two years after Tommy John surgery, Bedard looked like a Cy Young candidate, going 5–1 with a dazzling 2.08 ERA in his first nine games. Closer B. J. Ryan was unhittable, but it came to be that he was the only pitcher to maintain his performance all season.

The wheels started to come off in mid-May as injuries hit. Sammy Sosa's foot problems were inconsequential—he wasn't hitting anyway—but Luis Matos hurt his hand and Bedard went down with a strained knee. The team reported that Bedard had no more than a strain and would be out for two weeks as a precaution; he was gone for six weeks, and when returned the magic was gone. Melvin Mora pulled his hamstring; he lingered, unable to play, for 12 days before the team finally put him on the DL, and like Bedard, when he came back things weren't the same. When Javy Lopez broke his hand and Geronimo Gil sprained his thumb, the starting catcher was suddenly Sal Fasano, veteran of a thousand budget hotels in minor league cities across the nation.

An offense that had generated nearly six runs per game in April could not manage even four runs per through July and August. A large part of the problem was the designated hitters, who acted as if the letters "DH" stand for "Don't Hit." In every year beginning with a "2", two things have been true. First, the Orioles have used a "whoever's available" approach to the DH slot: no player in the last six years has DH'd more than 61 games in a season. Second, they've unerringly picked players who couldn't do the job. The best aggregate DH performance by a Baltimore team this millennium is the weak .250/.329/.398 posted by the 2001 squad. Since then, they've actually declined every year (see table 1).

Especially frustrating for Baltimore is that these are not bad players. The same hitters who hit for a .233 EQA in the DH slot last year hit a collective .282 when they played in the field (see table 2).

Had this group managed to hit for a .282 EQA when at DH, they would have generated 36 more runs for the team. Had they even managed a league-average .260 EQA, they would have generated 20 more runs. Their futility at the plate—presumably precipitated while sitting on the bench and staring into space while their teammates shagged grounders and flies—cost the O's between two and four games in the standings. The signing of Ramon Hernandez suggests that we will see a lot more of Javy Lopez in the DH slot. Given Javy's numbers last season that is not necessarily a solution.

As the losing became endemic, a clubhouse which had barely held together through the early winning came apart completely apart. One of baseball's dirty little secrets is that most teams tend to split into English- and Spanish-speaking cliques. The Orioles were no exception. Miguel Tejada was the only player with the reputation and personality that might have been ablenecessary to bridge the divide, but in Baltimore it didn't happen, in part because he couldn't even deliver the Spanish bloc within the team. Sosa in particular was annoyed with Tejada's rah-rah style, but he wasn't even dealing with the vintage Tejada, who appeared to wear down and get less chipper as the

TABLE 2. BUT I DON'T *LIKE* DHing, 2005

Player DH	Games	EQA@ DH	EQA@ NonDH	Difference
Jay Gibbons	40	.251	.306	−55
Sammy Sosa	35	.238	.248	−10
Javy Lopez	28	.244	.289	−45
Rafael Palmeiro	15	.199	.295	−96
Bernie Castro	9	.237	.291	−54
Alex Freire	9	.214	.264	−50
B. J. Surhoff	7	.141	.241	−100
Chris Gomez	6	.288	.261	+27
David Newhan	5	.000	.233	−233
Walter Young	3	.348	.282	+66
Sal Fasano	3	.345	.276	+69
Miguel Tejada	2	.087	.306	−219
Total	**153**	**.233**	**.282**	**−49**

TABLE 1. ORIOLES DHs DON'T HIT

Year	BA	OBA	SLG	EQA	Most Frequent DH	(DH Games)
2000	.261	.334	.389	.252	Baines	(61)
2001	.250	.329	.398	.260	Batista	(33)
2002	.247	.314	.387	.248	Cordova	(56)
2003	.240	.314	.370	.243	Segui	(52)
2004	.243	.300	.349	.231	Newhan	(32)
2005	.210	.277	.362	.233	Gibbons	(40)

season wore on. He was, of course, bearing the weight of a secret. He knew that Palmeiro had tested positive for steroids long before the public did; he also knew that his B-12 injections were going to be part of the story. Meanwhile, the alleged ace of the staff (the best-paid one, at any rate), Sidney Ponson, was arrested in midsummer for drunken driving. Already in management's dog house for the poor example he set for younger pitchers like Bedard, as well as for an off-season stint in an Aruban jail, he was fired. The Orioles told him to hit the road and, oh, by the way, we're voiding the remainder of your contract.

In early August the Palmeiro story hit and it took Oriole players about an hour to grow sick and tired of being asked questions about steroids. The cold shoulder they gave Raffy on his return from a ten-day suspension was a big part of why in early September he was sent home for the duration—the second player that the O's were ultimately happy just to have removed from the clubhouse, regardless of the availability of a replacement.

Manager Lee Mazzilli earned his share of his criticism. Many players, especially the bullpen pitchers, had zero confidence in him. (Of course, their pitching did nothing to earn his confidence in them.) The front office also caused dissension: the decision to call up Jeff Fiorentino from A-ball—one of the most baffling choices made by any management team last year—was seen as a slap in the face to veteran backups. The front office had long been divided by a contentious power-sharing arrangement between co-GMs Mike Flanagan and Jim Beattie, and the relationship was further strained when a dispute between them developed over the use of psychological testing for team-building. Ownership was distracted by an ongoing battle with the Commissioner's office about how to divvy up a new television contract with their equally new neighbors, the Nationals. When nothing significant happened at the July trading deadline, the players felt they had been abandoned, and pretty much gave up.

Mazzilli was fired and replaced by bench coach Sam Perlozzo, but nothing changed. The O's played out the string, nothing more; they couldn't wait for the season to end, and it showed. Usually, when a team plays under an interim manager like they just don't care, that manager doesn't get to remove the "interim" preceding his title. Perlozzo was no ordinary interim manager, though, and he had an ace up his sleeve; or, to be more precise, an ace-maker.

It just so happens that Perlozzo's best friend is Leo Mazzone, pitching coach extraordinaire of the Atlanta Braves. They grew up together in Cumberland, a small town in the hills of western Maryland, where they played against each other in Legion ball. When Mazzone got married, Perlozzo was his best man. They had often talked about how cool it would be to work together in the majors. Now they will get their chance. Mazzone worked for the Braves under a series of one-year contracts, and friendship proved a stronger lure than the large amount of Yankee gold dangled in front of him.

It seems fair, then, to think of the Orioles as having a duumvirate in the dugout this year, with Mazzone having carte blanche over pitching decisions. Some hold out great hope that the Mazzone Magic will turn the Oriole pitching staff around; others note that outgoing coach Ray Miller had a pretty good reputation as a pitching coach himself. At the very least, it will rapidly become clear just how much of the Braves' success was Mazzone's and how much might belong to Bobby Cox. Next year the Baltimore front office should be more streamlined, as Flanagan emerged from the season's wreckage as the sole GM. Unfortunately, since his boardroom victory, he's done nothing of consequence to help the O's roster in the off-season. Tejada had some angry words at winter ball that generated a lot of trade rumors, but the Orioles can't get fair value back for him, and have resisted any rash moves.

A rational assessment of the Orioles and the rest of the AL East says that the Birds have a much better chance of finishing last than first. They have a few legitimate stars in the infield, but that can't make up for a woefully inadequate outfield, a bad rotation, and a bad bullpen that just lost its only real star. They can hope that a new pitching coach will make an enormous difference, but Mazzone will need to take 160 runs off of the pitching side of the ledger if he's to continue his streak of coaching staffs that finish first or second in runs allowed. That's a huge total, and yet it still wouldn't have been enough to raise the Orioles into the 2005 playoffs. Expecting Mazzone to vault the team out of its eight-year doldrums is to believe that the coach can perform miracles. Mazzone is very good, but as yet no one has observed him walking on water.

HITTERS

ERIC BYRNES OF Bats: R Throws: R Height: 6' 2" Weight: 200 Born: February 16, 1976 Age: 30

YEAR	TM	LVL	AGE	PA	R	2B	3B	HR	RBI	BB	SO	SB	CS	SPEED	BA	OBP	SLG	MLVR	EQBA	EQOBP	EQSLG	EQA	VORP	DEFENSE			
2003	OAK	MLB	27	460	64	27	9	12	51	42	71	10	2	7.2	.263	.333	.459	.064	.262	.338	.460	.274	18.8	76-CF	-1	32-LF	1
2004	OAK	MLB	28	632	91	39	3	20	73	46	111	17	1	5.9	.283	.347	.467	.072	.283	.349	.472	.284	23.0	96-LF	4	24-CF	4
2005	OAK	MLB	29	214	30	15	2	7	24	14	27	2	2	6.1	.266	.336	.474	.077	.274	.350	.500	.282	6.9	43-LF	7		
2005	COL	MLB	29	60	2	2	0	0	5	7	11	2	0	4.5	.189	.283	.226	-.371	.173	.271	.212	.193	-3.8				
2005	BAL	MLB	29	179	17	7	1	3	11	11	33	3	0	4.9	.192	.246	.299	-.365	.194	.261	.303	.206	-11.8	43-LF	-1		
2006	*ARI*	*MLB*	*30*	*465*	*61*	*27*	*5*	*14*	*56*	*40*	*77*	*9*	*3*	*6.0*	*.265*	*.337*	*.450*	*.023*	*.262*	*.333*	*.448*	*.262*	*8.3*	*110-LF*	*3*		

Breakout: 20%   Improve: 48%   Collapse: 18%   Attrition: 15%   Comparables: Leon Roberts, Jeffrey Hammonds, Glenallen Hill

There's nothing wrong with being a rah-rah, full-tilt type, except that it can lead to slamming into walls—something Byrnes did about two weeks before he was traded to Colorado, an incident that suspiciously coincided with the point when his offense disappeared. Byrnes has a large platoon split (right-handers eat him up), so he's a marginal choice as a starting left fielder. With the Snakes, he's a placeholder in center until Chris Young is ready.

BERNIE CASTRO 2B Bats: B Throws: R Height: 5' 10" Weight: 160 Born: July 14, 1979 Age: 26

YEAR	TM	LVL	AGE	PA	R	2B	3B	HR	RBI	BB	SO	SB	CS	SPEED	BA	OBP	SLG	MLVR	EQBA	EQOBP	EQSLG	EQA	VORP	DEFENSE	
2003	POR	AAA	23	453	57	17	5	2	24	25	43	49	13	7.5	.311	.349	.388	.066	.301	.341	.376	.259	13.6	94-2B	-5
2004	POR	AAA	24	332	38	8	1	0	20	22	30	17	9	6.1	.263	.310	.295	-.282	.242	.288	.265	.205	-17.0	61-2B	-8
2005	OTT	AAA	25	550	81	21	5	1	36	42	50	41	6	7.7	.315	.364	.382	.028	.289	.340	.349	.255	9.2	117-2B	-6
2005	BAL	MLB	25	89	14	3	1	0	7	9	10	6	2	8.1	.287	.360	.350	-.023	.304	.382	.367	.271	2.6	11-2B	-1
2006	*WAS*	*MLB*	*26*	*497*	*63*	*18*	*4*	*0*	*32*	*34*	*51*	*26*	*8*	*6.0*	*.268*	*.321*	*.324*	*-.169*	*.281*	*.330*	*.349*	*.240*	*4.7*	*117-2B*	*-3*

Breakout: 17%   Improve: 53%   Collapse: 21%   Attrition: 16%   Comparables: Wally Backman, Sandy Alomar Sr., Ramon Vazquez

Your basic speed demon with no power, Castro would be a fit in the lineup if John McGraw managed the O's. He's got no arm at all, effectively limiting him to second base and making it hard to carry him as pinch-runner. Picked up by the Nationals, he should get reasonable playing time backing up the always-fragile Jose Vidro. His lack of power will hardly be noticed in RFK.

BRANDON FAHEY SS Bats: L Throws: R Height: 6' 2" Weight: 183 Born: January 18, 1981 Age: 25

YEAR	TM	LVL	AGE	PA	R	2B	3B	HR	RBI	BB	SO	SB	CS	SPEED	BA	OBP	SLG	MLVR	EQBA	EQOBP	EQSLG	EQA	VORP	DEFENSE	
2003	FRD	A+	22	391	41	11	3	1	22	22	56	4	2	5.4	.233	.279	.288	-.195	.214	.253	.278	.193	-26.9	106-SS	4
2004	FRD	A+	23	206	20	7	0	3	19	22	20	3	3	3.5	.271	.354	.359	.003	.226	.297	.313	.220	-5.0	55-SS	-2
2004	BOW	AA	23	225	20	7	1	1	15	17	27	3	1	4.4	.236	.293	.293	-.206	.232	.283	.289	.208	-9.3	63-SS	11
2005	BOW	AA	24	556	63	21	4	3	47	44	71	17	8	5.8	.291	.349	.367	.064	.280	.333	.350	.245	10.8	139-SS	13
2006	*BAL*	*MLB*	*25*	*450*	*45*	*15*	*2*	*3*	*34*	*27*	*60*	*8*	*3*	*4.8*	*.245*	*.294*	*.311*	*-.225*	*.249*	*.303*	*.326*	*.214*	*-1.9*	*107-SS*	*5*

Breakout: 18%   Improve: 40%   Collapse: 28%   Attrition: 13%   Comparables: Matt Demarco, John Donaldson, Jeff Terrell

If Fahey can continue hitting as he did in '05, he would be a nice utility player. His glove is major-league caliber; the problem is that he's had to gain 25 pounds since being drafted just to be called "thin." Consequently, he puts no drive on the ball. He went to the AFL to play second base, but there his hitting dipped to the .215 EqAs of previous years.

SAL FASANO C Bats: R Throws: R Height: 6' 2" Weight: 230 Born: August 10, 1971 Age: 34

YEAR	TM	LVL	AGE	PA	R	2B	3B	HR	RBI	BB	SO	SB	CS	SPEED	BA	OBP	SLG	MLVR	EQBA	EQOBP	EQSLG	EQA	VORP	DEFENSE	
2004	COH	AAA	32	255	21	15	1	10	33	10	46	0	0	3.0	.233	.278	.432	-.110	.189	.227	.334	.196	-16.8	71-C	2
2005	BAL	MLB	33	174	25	3	0	11	20	9	41	0	0	3.5	.250	.310	.475	.031	.258	.326	.509	.278	8.1	47-C	-9
2006	*PHI*	*MLB*	*34*	*147*	*15*	*6*	*0*	*7*	*23*	*8*	*39*	*0*	*0*	*3.7*	*.232*	*.283*	*.447*	*-.094*	*.231*	*.283*	*.449*	*.239*	*3.3*	*39-C*	*-2*

Breakout: 29%   Improve: 40%   Collapse: 36%   Attrition: 59%   Comparables: Jeff Newman, Mark Parent, Del Wilber

Had an astonishingly good run, stepping up when injuries made him the starting catcher, popping homers at an unprecedented rate. He also gave up stolen bases at an unprecedented rate, gutting his fielding rating. Signed with the Phillies, where he's not exactly the perfect reserve behind Mike Lieberthal, but he'll do.

JEFF FIORENTINO　　　　**OF**　　　　**Bats: L Throws: R**　　　Height: 6' 1"　Weight: 185　Born: April 14, 1983　　　Age: 23

YEAR	TM	LVL	AGE	PA	R	2B	3B	HR	RBI	BB	SO	SB	CS	SPEED	BA	OBP	SLG	MLVR	EQBA	EQOBP	EQSLG	EQA	VORP	DEFENSE		
2004	DEL	A	21	203	40	15	2	10	36	20	50	2	2	5.4	.296	.374	.570	.335	.251	.314	.462	.262	6.6	40-CF	-1	
2005	FRD	A+	22	451	70	18	4	22	66	34	90	12	6	6.1	.286	.346	.508	.169	.249	.296	.435	.248	5.4	70-CF	-4	18-LF 0
2005	BAL	MLB	22	47	7	2	0	1	5	2	10	1	0	6.5	.250	.277	.364	-.182	.256	.298	.372	.240	-0.4	11-CF	1	
2006	*BAL*	*MLB*	*23*	*477*	*57*	*24*	*3*	*16*	*61*	*30*	*99*	*7*	*4*	*4.9*	*.252*	*.303*	*.426*	*-.057*	*.256*	*.312*	*.447*	*.250*	*6.8*	*113-CF*	*-1*	

Breakout: 15%　Improve: 46%　Collapse: 25%　Attrition: 9%　　　Comparables: Eric Valent, Curtis Granderson, Cody Ross

It was shocking that the Orioles reached all the way down to Fiorentino when injuries hit. He started out well enough, but when he cooled off he was sent all the way back to Frederick, where he continued slumping for a good two more months. Fiorentino is not a natural center fielder and isn't likely to play there in the majors, making the decision to plug him into the position more odd still.

MARK FLEISHER　　　　**1B**　　　　**Bats: R Throws: R**　　　Height: 6' 4"　Weight: 235　Born: September 18, 1983 Age: 22

YEAR	TM	LVL	AGE	PA	R	2B	3B	HR	RBI	BB	SO	SB	CS	SPEED	BA	OBP	SLG	MLVR	EQBA	EQOBP	EQSLG	EQA	VORP	DEFENSE	
2005	ABE	A-	21	267	34	12	0	7	32	25	55	0	2	2.9	.277	.356	.420	.148	.228	.284	.346	.222	-24.7	38-1B	3
2006	*BAL*	*MLB*	*22*	*425*	*39*	*17*	*1*	*11*	*48*	*28*	*95*	*0*	*1*	*3.1*	*.222*	*.278*	*.354*	*-.211*	*.226*	*.287*	*.371*	*.217*	*-13.6*	*101-1B*	*6*

Breakout: 40%　Improve: 56%　Collapse: 30%　Attrition: 9%　　　Comparables: Kelly Hunt, Nathan Gold, Tyler Vonschell

A former 14th round pick, Fleisher had a nice debut, demonstrating enough power to suggest a 25–30 HR season in the majors sometime in the future, although without much batting average he'd have to hit 25 HR to be an acceptable first baseman. Twenty-two year-olds in short-season ball are notoriously unpredictable; they often rate well because they are more experienced, not because they are more talented.

ALEJANDRO FREIRE　　　　**1B**　　　　**Bats: R Throws: R**　　　Height: 6' 2"　Weight: 185　Born: August 23, 1974　　　Age: 31

YEAR	TM	LVL	AGE	PA	R	2B	3B	HR	RBI	BB	SO	SB	CS	SPEED	BA	OBP	SLG	MLVR	EQBA	EQOBP	EQSLG	EQA	VORP	DEFENSE	
2003	NRW	AA	28	564	71	31	1	18	80	48	87	1	0	3.7	.311	.383	.486	.264	.244	.295	.368	.232	-19.5	87-1B	-10
2005	OTT	AAA	30	442	57	24	1	19	69	40	57	1	0	3.6	.299	.376	.512	.212	.251	.318	.410	.252	-1.7	60-1B	-4
2005	BAL	MLB	30	72	7	3	0	1	4	6	17	0	0	3.4	.246	.319	.338	-.135	.250	.333	.344	.242	-1.0	12-1B	0
2006	*BAL*	*MLB*	*31*	*312*	*29*	*13*	*1*	*7*	*35*	*19*	*56*	*0*	*0*	*3.6*	*.246*	*.297*	*.370*	*-.143*	*.250*	*.306*	*.388*	*.231*	*-4.9*	*76-1B*	*-3*

Breakout: 19%　Improve: 37%　Collapse: 38%　Attrition: 30%　　　Comparables: Marty Cordova, Shane Spencer, Terry Harper

A good example of what happens by starting the season hot, as opposed to getting hot for some other 80 at-bat stretch. Freire was hitting .380 in Ottawa at the start of May, and even though his average fell off from there, the idea that he was tearing it up had taken hold. He wasn't doing anything he hadn't done in his ten previous non-prospect years, and if you switched his April with his June, he probably wouldn't have gotten The Call.

JAY GIBBONS　　　　**RF/1B**　　　　**Bats: L Throws: L**　　　Height: 6' 0"　Weight: 200　Born: March 2, 1977　　　Age: 29

YEAR	TM	LVL	AGE	PA	R	2B	3B	HR	RBI	BB	SO	SB	CS	SPEED	BA	OBP	SLG	MLVR	EQBA	EQOBP	EQSLG	EQA	VORP	DEFENSE		
2003	BAL	MLB	26	682	80	39	2	23	100	49	89	0	1	3.9	.277	.330	.456	.061	.278	.336	.462	.272	15.9	143-RF	-7	11-1B 0
2004	BAL	MLB	27	379	36	14	1	10	47	29	64	1	1	3.7	.246	.303	.379	-.174	.243	.306	.375	.238	-7.5	62-RF	-2	13-1B 1
2005	BAL	MLB	28	518	72	33	3	26	79	28	56	0	0	4.3	.277	.317	.516	.121	.284	.335	.541	.289	24.4	63-RF	2	19-1B 0
2006	*BAL*	*MLB*	*29*	*448*	*52*	*22*	*1*	*16*	*66*	*32*	*57*	*0*	*1*	*4.3*	*.267*	*.322*	*.449*	*.015*	*.272*	*.331*	*.471*	*.263*	*10.0*	*106-RF*	*0*	

Breakout: 16%　Improve: 44%　Collapse: 31%　Attrition: 15%　　　Comparables: Troy O'Leary, Mel Hall, Dick Kryhoski

Despite our fears that his 2004 injuries would prove to be a lingering drag on his hitting, Gibbons bounced back to have the best season of his career. He did have a couple of back spasms during the year, and he was benched against lefties more frequently than he had been in the past, which explains a little bit of his EQA. At 29, he's getting into the phase of a career when being someone with an old player's skills at the plate combined with arbitration eligibility make him a bit of a risk, financially as well as in the lineup.

CHRIS GOMEZ   **INF**   **Bats: R Throws: R**   Height: 6' 1"   Weight: 195   Born: June 16, 1971   Age: 35

YEAR	TM	LVL	AGE	PA	R	2B	3B	HR	RBI	BB	SO	SB	CS	SPEED	BA	OBP	SLG	MLVR	EQBA	EQOBP	EQSLG	EQA	VORP	DEFENSE			
2003	MIN	MLB	32	183	14	9	3	1	15	7	13	2	1	4.6	.251	.279	.354	-.207	.249	.284	.353	.224	-2.0	18-2B	0	16-3B	2
2004	TOR	MLB	33	374	41	11	1	3	37	28	41	3	2	5.1	.282	.337	.346	-.136	.275	.336	.338	.242	2.5	72-SS	-8	13-1B	1
2005	BAL	MLB	34	248	27	11	0	1	18	27	17	2	1	3.8	.279	.359	.342	-.057	.287	.378	.356	.266	2.1	27-1B	1	14-2B	1
2006	*BAL*	*MLB*	*35*	*186*	*20*	*8*	*1*	*1*	*17*	*15*	*15*	*1*	*1*	*4.7*	*.265*	*.330*	*.338*	*-.116*	*.270*	*.340*	*.354*	*.238*	*0.9*	*47-1B*	*-1*		

Breakout: 28%   *Improve: 51%*   *Collapse: 34%*   *Attrition: 46%*   *Comparables: Carney Lansford, Glenn Beckert, Jeff Cirillo*

Having Tejada enables the Orioles to continue the tradition, established with Cal Ripken, of dispensing with the need to carry a backup shortstop. Instead, they used Gomez as the short half of a platoon at first base, generally putting him in against lefties. Players with career EqAs of .246 are stuck holding backup middle infield jobs because their offense doesn't justify them as starters even there; playing one at first base the basic failure to stock the roster with the easiest to find players, those at the left end of the defensive spectrum. The O's renewed Gomez's contract for 2006.

TRIPPER JOHNSON   **3B**   **Bats: R Throws: R**   Height: 6' 1"   Weight: 200   Born: April 28, 1982   Age: 24

YEAR	TM	LVL	AGE	PA	R	2B	3B	HR	RBI	BB	SO	SB	CS	SPEED	BA	OBP	SLG	MLVR	EQBA	EQOBP	EQSLG	EQA	VORP	DEFENSE	
2003	FRD	A+	21	474	43	25	3	5	50	46	92	7	8	4.2	.273	.359	.384	.074	.253	.325	.376	.243	7.1	116-3B	8
2004	FRD	A+	22	525	62	19	2	21	74	51	93	14	5	5.1	.269	.343	.454	.108	.236	.301	.407	.246	5.3	120-3B	-8
2005	BOW	AA	23	557	62	29	4	11	59	41	108	7	5	5.3	.249	.309	.387	-.006	.244	.302	.380	.238	0.9	123-3B	-2
2006	*BAL*	*MLB*	*24*	*461*	*51*	*21*	*2*	*12*	*53*	*33*	*87*	*6*	*3*	*4.7*	*.245*	*.303*	*.389*	*-.108*	*.250*	*.313*	*.408*	*.240*	*2.7*	*109-3B*	*-1*

Breakout: 24%   *Improve: 47%*   *Collapse: 20%*   *Attrition: 9%*   *Comparables: Scott Hodges, Ron Jackson, Andy Phillips*

In the first halves of his last three seasons, Tripper Johnson has had projected major league EqAs of .294, .283, and .278, which are not simply above average, they're almost All-Star caliber. But in the second halves, his projected EqAs have been .247, .238, and .232, which are on the wrong side of borderline major league. There is no obvious reason why he has consistently fallen so dramatically from one half to the next-perhaps something about Maryland in summer seems to disagree with the Washington state native.

JAVY LOPEZ   **C**   **Bats: R Throws: R**   Height: 6' 3"   Weight: 200   Born: November 5, 1970   Age: 35

YEAR	TM	LVL	AGE	PA	R	2B	3B	HR	RBI	BB	SO	SB	CS	SPEED	BA	OBP	SLG	MLVR	EQBA	EQOBP	EQSLG	EQA	VORP	DEFENSE	
2003	ATL	MLB	32	495	89	29	3	43	109	33	90	0	1	4.1	.328	.378	.687	.519	.324	.374	.685	.333	72.3	110-C	4
2004	BAL	MLB	33	638	83	33	3	23	86	47	97	0	0	4.0	.316	.370	.503	.177	.318	.375	.509	.299	48.2	122-C	-4
2005	BAL	MLB	34	423	47	24	1	15	49	19	68	0	1	3.8	.278	.322	.458	.052	.286	.337	.483	.276	19.7	71-C	-5
2006	*BAL*	*MLB*	*35*	*461*	*53*	*23*	*2*	*17*	*69*	*25*	*75*	*0*	*1*	*4.1*	*.285*	*.329*	*.465*	*.061*	*.290*	*.339*	*.487*	*.270*	*23.4*	*109-C*	*-3*

Breakout: 1%   *Improve: 14%*   *Collapse: 43%*   *Attrition: 15%*   *Comparables: Terry Steinbach, Carlton Fisk, Bob Watson*

It was a given that Lopez wouldn't match his 2003 season in Baltimore. Besides losing the motivation of a free-agent year, he was a 32-year-old catcher with more than 1100 games on his knees. His production declined again last year: his rate stats were down across the board, and a broken hand cost him two months. On the plus side, 2006 is the final year of his three-year deal, and with the addition of Ramon Hernandez, he'll be DHing. If anything were to bring his hitting back up, it would be that-unless he sulks over the "demotion."

VAL MAJEWSKI   **OF**   **Bats: L Throws: L**   Height: 6' 2"   Weight: 200   Born: June 19, 1981   Age: 25

YEAR	TM	LVL	AGE	PA	R	2B	3B	HR	RBI	BB	SO	SB	CS	SPEED	BA	OBP	SLG	MLVR	EQBA	EQOBP	EQSLG	EQA	VORP	DEFENSE			
2003	DEL	A	22	240	38	15	8	7	48	28	20	10	1	7.3	.303	.383	.553	.401	.268	.329	.488	.278	7.8	36-RF	-2	21-CF	-1
2003	FRD	A+	22	168	15	18	1	5	20	7	23	0	0	3.3	.289	.321	.509	.203	.262	.292	.482	.258	5.7	27-CF	-2		
2004	BOW	AA	23	476	71	24	5	15	80	33	68	14	4	6.2	.307	.359	.490	.237	.298	.344	.471	.279	17.5	51-LF	-2	41-CF	-1
2006	*BAL*	*MLB*	*25*	*243*	*31*	*12*	*1*	*9*	*33*	*16*	*32*	*3*	*1*	*5.4*	*.277*	*.327*	*.460*	*.045*	*.282*	*.337*	*.482*	*.270*	*10.6*	*60-CF*	*-1*		

Breakout: 17%   *Improve: 34%*   *Collapse: 33%*   *Attrition: 13%*   *Comparables: Mike Colangelo, Alex Johnson, Ivan Calderon*

Going into '05, Majewski was the Orioles' first or second-best position prospect. Going into ought-six, he's a big question mark. He tore his labrum at the tail end of 2004, and last winter's rehab program did not fix it. That meant surgery instead of spring training, and no season until the Arizona Fall League, where he struggled to outhit Brandon Fahey. Whether that is rust or a permanent degradation can't be known until spring training. If the Orioles send him to Ottawa as planned, he'll be pretty long in the tooth before he loses his rookie status.

NICK MARKAKIS RF Bats: L Throws: L Height: 6′ 1″ Weight: 175 Born: November 17, 1983 Age: 22

YEAR	TM	LVL	AGE	PA	R	2B	3B	HR	RBI	BB	SO	SB	CS	SPEED	BA	OBP	SLG	MLVR	EQBA	EQOBP	EQSLG	EQA	VORP	DEFENSE			
2003	ABE	A-	19	239	22	14	3	1	28	30	33	13	5	5.6	.283	.372	.395	.186	.275	.346	.402	.263	3.4	44-RF	-1	11-CF	0
2004	DEL	A	20	404	57	22	3	11	64	42	66	12	3	5.5	.299	.371	.470	.199	.263	.324	.404	.255	-2.3	62-RF	1		
2005	FRD	A+	21	401	59	25	1	12	62	43	65	2	1	4.7	.300	.379	.480	.193	.259	.325	.411	.255	-1.3	86-RF	-2		
2005	BOW	AA	21	143	19	16	2	3	30	18	30	0	1	4.2	.339	.420	.573	.493	.334	.411	.564	.323	20.2	19-CF	2	15-RF	-1
2006	BAL	MLB	22	539	61	30	2	11	61	44	95	4	2	4.5	.263	.326	.403	-.041	.267	.336	.422	.254	5.8	127-RF	-2		

Breakout: 9%   Improve: 28%   Collapse: 36%   Attrition: 8%   Comparables: Laynce Nix, Richard Brown, Jody Gerut

Scouts have always been high on Markakis, and it's easy to understand why: He's got a sweet swing, a cannon of an arm, and decent speed. Until busting out at Bowie last year, though, his production hadn't matched the hype. He has been an extremely prolific doubles hitter so far, averaging 45 per 600 at-bats where an average player would only hit 31, so the power potential is there. He's still on schedule for a late September cameo, but to stick, those doubles will have to presage some home runs.

ELI MARRERO OF Bats: R Throws: R Height: 6′ 1″ Weight: 180 Born: November 17, 1973 Age: 32

YEAR	TM	LVL	AGE	PA	R	2B	3B	HR	RBI	BB	SO	SB	CS	SPEED	BA	OBP	SLG	MLVR	EQBA	EQOBP	EQSLG	EQA	VORP	DEFENSE			
2003	SLN	MLB	29	116	10	4	2	2	20	7	18	0	1	5.6	.224	.267	.355	-.206	.224	.267	.355	.216	-4.6	13-RF	0		
2004	ATL	MLB	30	278	37	18	1	10	40	23	50	4	1	5.4	.320	.374	.520	.260	.312	.367	.504	.296	19.1	42-LF	4	19-RF	2
2005	KCA	MLB	31	99	11	4	0	4	9	7	18	1	0	4.7	.159	.222	.341	-.373	.161	.232	.368	.215	-6.8				
2005	BAL	MLB	31	56	8	3	2	3	10	4	20	0	0	5.3	.220	.268	.540	.021	.224	.286	.551	.275	1.4				
2006	BAL	MLB	32	196	23	9	1	7	26	14	41	1	1	5.0	.245	.303	.427	-.060	.249	.313	.447	.251	1.3	50-LF	0		

Breakout: 14%   Improve: 36%   Collapse: 40%   Attrition: 38%   Comparables: Lee Lacy, Rip Repulski, Jackie Brandt

Marrero acquired a reputation for versatility several years ago, based on his ability to both catch and play the outfield. However, he hasn't caught a game in two years, and had all of 36 innings in 2003. He hasn't played anything except outfield and first base lately, and even then, it's usually when there's a left-handed pitcher on the mound. That isn't versatility, that's a niche.

LUIS MATOS CF Bats: R Throws: R Height: 6′ 0″ Weight: 208 Born: October 30, 1978 Age: 27

YEAR	TM	LVL	AGE	PA	R	2B	3B	HR	RBI	BB	SO	SB	CS	SPEED	BA	OBP	SLG	MLVR	EQBA	EQOBP	EQSLG	EQA	VORP	DEFENSE			
2003	OTT	AAA	24	193	28	16	4	1	25	13	34	6	1	7.3	.303	.347	.457	.141	.294	.342	.454	.277	5.7	23-RF	-1	21-CF	1
2003	BAL	MLB	24	476	70	23	3	13	45	28	90	15	7	6.0	.303	.353	.458	.116	.307	.361	.467	.281	26.9	103-CF	6		
2004	BAL	MLB	25	356	36	18	0	6	28	19	60	12	4	5.7	.224	.275	.333	-.295	.223	.277	.333	.220	-12.6	87-CF	0		
2005	BAL	MLB	26	430	53	20	2	4	32	27	58	17	9	6.2	.280	.340	.373	-.037	.294	.360	.397	.265	7.8	112-CF	7		
2006	BAL	MLB	27	372	48	18	2	7	40	22	55	12	5	6.1	.273	.327	.402	-.033	.278	.337	.422	.256	9.9	89-CF	1		

Breakout: 28%   Improve: 52%   Collapse: 27%   Attrition: 23%   Comparables: Gabe Kapler, Marlon Byrd, Jermaine Allensworth

It was another disappointing season for Matos. He missed more time to injury, undergoing surgery to repair a stress fracture to his shin, incurred while making a catch at Fenway. Hey, they don't call it the Green Monster for nothing. In Matos's absence Markakis, Majewski, and Fiorentino all showed signs that they are close to making the jump to the majors, and all three have played center. More ominous still, the Orioles picked up Corey Patterson from the Cubs. Matos's grip on the job is insecure, to say the least.

MELVIN MORA 3B Bats: R Throws: R Height: 5′ 11″ Weight: 198 Born: February 2, 1972 Age: 34

YEAR	TM	LVL	AGE	PA	R	2B	3B	HR	RBI	BB	SO	SB	CS	SPEED	BA	OBP	SLG	MLVR	EQBA	EQOBP	EQSLG	EQA	VORP	DEFENSE			
2003	BAL	MLB	31	407	68	17	1	15	48	49	71	6	3	5.6	.317	.418	.503	.300	.324	.426	.516	.319	35.8	53-LF	6	12-RF	-1
2004	BAL	MLB	32	630	111	41	0	27	104	66	95	11	6	5.1	.340	.419	.562	.359	.343	.425	.572	.330	64.3	135-3B	-14		
2005	BAL	MLB	33	656	86	30	1	27	88	50	112	7	4	4.7	.283	.348	.474	.115	.293	.366	.497	.291	32.6	146-3B	-8		
2006	BAL	MLB	34	613	83	30	2	23	90	58	101	7	3	4.8	.284	.360	.475	.123	.289	.371	.498	.287	37.8	143-3B	-6		

Breakout: 2%   Improve: 24%   Collapse: 40%   Attrition: 2%   Comparables: Ray Boone, Jeff Kent, Doug Decinces

For four months of last season—April, May, June, and September—Mora's hitting was right in line with his previous two years. Those four months projected to his 593 at-bats: .298 average, .302 EqA, 35 doubles, 33 homers, 100 runs, 108 RBI. However, he pulled his hamstring on June 21st, and for the next two months he was a completely different hitter, projecting to a .253 average, .242 EqA, with 21 doubles, 15 homers, 59 runs, and 50 RBI in the same number of ABs. The Orioles were 42–28 and in first by two games when Mora came up lame, and then went 20–42 while he was hobbled or missing. They gave up first place for good on June 24th. Mora has already had a surprising career, and at 34, it's hard to say whether he can continue to be an MVP-caliber hitter in '06.

DAVID NEWHAN   **UT**   **Bats: L Throws: R**   Height: 5' 10" Weight: 180 Born: September 7, 1973 Age: 32

YEAR	TM	LVL	AGE	PA	R	2B	3B	HR	RBI	BB	SO	SB	CS	SPEED	BA	OBP	SLG	MLVR	EQBA	EQOBP	EQSLG	EQA	VORP	DEFENSE		
2003	CSP	AAA	29	263	43	17	2	3	28	16	36	6	4	5.4	.348	.392	.471	.185	.280	.321	.373	.242	3.8	32-2B	-4	16-1B -2
2004	OKL	AAA	30	292	57	21	6	9	38	26	55	10	0	7.9	.328	.387	.557	.319	.272	.325	.424	.263	9.5	36-2B	0	
2004	BAL	MLB	30	407	66	15	7	8	54	27	72	11	1	7.6	.311	.361	.453	.079	.312	.365	.462	.288	18.0	21-RF	-1	18-LF 1
2005	BAL	MLB	31	244	31	9	0	5	21	22	45	9	2	6.8	.202	.279	.312	-.287	.209	.295	.321	.228	-9.9	27-CF	0	13-RF -1
2006	*BAL*	*MLB*	*32*	*240*	*29*	*10*	*1*	*4*	*22*	*16*	*44*	*5*	*2*	*5.7*	*.253*	*.308*	*.365*	*-.126*	*.257*	*.317*	*.383*	*.237*	*-1.0*	*60-CF*	*-3*	

Breakout: 8%   *Improve: 26%*   *Collapse: 47%*   *Attrition: 35%*   *Comparables: Frank Baumholtz, Wayne Kirby, Marvin Benard*

The Orioles rewarded Newhan's hot month in 2004 with a nearly guaranteed roster spot for 2005. He did just about all he could to make them regret it. Newhan was one of the few Orioles who did not start the season hot-and he never got hot, ever-hitting .220 in his best month. That's not a reasonable level for a utility infielder; that he was almost entirely playing in the outfield exacerbated matters.

RAFAEL PALMEIRO   **Suspect Bats: L Throws: L**   Height: 6' 0" Weight: 190 Born: September 24, 1964 Age: 41

YEAR	TM	LVL	AGE	PA	R	2B	3B	HR	RBI	BB	SO	SB	CS	SPEED	BA	OBP	SLG	MLVR	EQBA	EQOBP	EQSLG	EQA	VORP	DEFENSE	
2003	TEX	MLB	38	654	92	21	2	38	112	84	77	2	0	4.7	.260	.359	.508	.118	.251	.356	.498	.289	29.5	52-1B	4
2004	BAL	MLB	39	651	68	29	0	23	88	86	61	2	1	3.3	.258	.359	.436	.019	.259	.364	.440	.281	15.8	127-1B	7
2005	BAL	MLB	40	422	47	13	0	18	60	43	43	2	0	3.9	.266	.339	.447	.055	.272	.354	.464	.283	12.6	85-1B	2
2006	*BAL*	*MLB*	*41*	*411*	*43*	*15*	*0*	*15*	*58*	*46*	*47*	*3*	*1*	*4.0*	*.265*	*.349*	*.433*	*.037*	*.269*	*.359*	*.454*	*.274*	*13.3*	*98-1B*	*1*

Breakout: 14%   *Improve: 31%*   *Collapse: 45%*   *Attrition: 12%*   *Comparables: Carl Yastrzemski, Stan Musial, Graig Nettles*

Aeschylus, Sophocles, or Euripides would have relished the chance to write Palmeiro's story, not just because of the fall from power, but because of the hubris displayed in the unnecessarily vehement denial of steroid use that accompanied it. Right now, the boos that greeted Palmeiro's abortive post-suspension return (he went just 2-for-26) are carrying a lot more weight with the Hall of Fame voters than his 3,020 hits and 569 home runs, and that's not likely to change before 2010. Unless Bonds fails a test, Palmeiro will be the symbol for the unrepentant user. That is the truth as the world sees it. The real truth-if he took it, and if so how often, and if he didn't then how did he test positive-no longer matters. Physically, he might be able to play another year. Mentally, maybe not. Retirement after this season was already at least a 50-50 shot, even before his "B-12" experience.

NOLAN REIMOLD   **OF**   **Bats: R Throws: R**   Height: 6' 4" Weight: 207 Born: October 12, 1983 Age: 22

YEAR	TM	LVL	AGE	PA	R	2B	3B	HR	RBI	BB	SO	SB	CS	SPEED	BA	OBP	SLG	MLVR	EQBA	EQOBP	EQSLG	EQA	VORP	DEFENSE	
2005	ABE	A-	21	212	33	15	2	9	30	29	44	2	0	5.1	.294	.392	.550	.381	.246	.320	.452	.264	2.8	29-RF	1	15-CF -1
2005	FRD	A+	21	97	17	6	0	6	11	12	27	3	0	5.5	.265	.371	.554	.246	.218	.309	.444	.260	1.5	13-CF	-1
2006	*BAL*	*MLB*	*22*	*473*	*55*	*26*	*2*	*15*	*59*	*41*	*118*	*5*	*2*	*4.5*	*.231*	*.303*	*.410*	*-.092*	*.235*	*.312*	*.429*	*.246*	*0.8*	*112-RF*	*-1*

Breakout: 15%   *Improve: 33%*   *Collapse: 32%*   *Attrition: 5%*   *Comparables: Jim Kavourias, Ryan Ludwick, Ty Meadows*

Reimold is a polished college player, so you can't get too excited about his performance at Aberdeen. College guys frequently pound the short-season leagues, which have a lot of players straight out of high school. However, his performance at Frederick is an impressive additional endorsement. Reimold has big-time power, having finished second in slugging at NCAA Division I last year. He's fast enough, at least for now, to play center. There's some concern, however, that he'll add more weight and slow down. If he does bulk up, he has the arm for right.

BRIAN ROBERTS   **2B**   **Bats: B Throws: R**   Height: 5' 9" Weight: 172 Born: October 9, 1977 Age: 28

YEAR	TM	LVL	AGE	PA	R	2B	3B	HR	RBI	BB	SO	SB	CS	SPEED	BA	OBP	SLG	MLVR	EQBA	EQOBP	EQSLG	EQA	VORP	DEFENSE	
2003	OTT	AAA	25	207	36	13	1	0	15	27	12	19	6	7.4	.315	.401	.399	.157	.286	.372	.358	.269	7.5	36-2B	0
2003	BAL	MLB	25	508	65	22	4	5	41	46	58	23	6	6.5	.270	.337	.367	-.059	.272	.344	.377	.259	14.1	104-2B	3
2004	BAL	MLB	26	719	107	50	2	4	53	71	95	29	12	6.9	.273	.344	.376	-.094	.272	.347	.380	.259	13.4	147-2B	-3
2005	BAL	MLB	27	635	92	45	7	18	73	67	83	27	10	6.9	.314	.387	.515	.265	.326	.408	.546	.317	61.9	137-2B	6
2006	*BAL*	*MLB*	*28*	*667*	*98*	*36*	*5*	*12*	*64*	*66*	*78*	*25*	*7*	*5.8*	*.282*	*.356*	*.418*	*.042*	*.287*	*.367*	*.438*	*.275*	*35.6*	*155-2B*	*2*

Breakout: 4%   *Improve: 28%*   *Collapse: 28%*   *Attrition: 1%*   *Comparables: Ray Durham, Bill Doran, Jim Gilliam*

(continued next page)

Brian Roberts *(continued)*

Roberts was the biggest reason the Orioles jumped out to an early lead. While he cooled off significantly in the second half (.335 EQA before the All-Star break, .280 after), his "after" performance would still have marked the best season of his career. You can't talk about building on the season, though, because of the September 21st collision with Bubba Crosby that just about tore his left arm off. The surgery to repair his elbow went well, and he is expected to be ready for spring. The severity of the injury was such that we won't know if his abilities have been compromised in any way until we've seen him play.

BRANDON SNYDER   C   Bats: R Throws: R   Height: 6′ 2″   Weight: 205   Born: November 23, 1986   Age: 19

YEAR	TM	LVL	AGE	PA	R	2B	3B	HR	RBI	BB	SO	SB	CS	SPEED	BA	OBP	SLG	MLVR	EQBA	EQOBP	EQSLG	EQA	VORP	DEFENSE	
2005	BLU	Rk	18	179	26	8	0	8	35	28	36	7	2	4.7	.271	.380	.493	.196	.194	.282	.323	.224	-15.3	19-C	3
2006	BAL	MLB	19	428	43	18	1	10	47	34	84	7	3	4.8	.229	.291	.357	-.180	.233	.300	.374	.228	0.0	102-C	1

Breakout: 43%   Improve: 61%   Collapse: 23%   Attrition: 14%   Comparables: Corey Smith, John Buck, Enrique Cruz

The Orioles' #1 draft pick last year, Snyder's catching skills were surprisingly good, given that he's fresh out of high school and wasn't even a full-time catcher there. Snyder showed excellent patience and reasonably good power in his short time at Bluefield, but he's a long way from Baltimore.

SAMMY SOSA   RF   Bats: R Throws: R   Height: 6′ 0″   Weight: 210   Born: November 12, 1968   Age: 37

YEAR	TM	LVL	AGE	PA	R	2B	3B	HR	RBI	BB	SO	SB	CS	SPEED	BA	OBP	SLG	MLVR	EQBA	EQOBP	EQSLG	EQA	VORP	DEFENSE	
2003	CHN	MLB	34	589	99	22	0	40	103	62	143	0	1	3.9	.279	.358	.553	.246	.273	.351	.549	.297	35.6	131-RF	-3
2004	CHN	MLB	35	539	69	21	0	35	80	56	133	0	0	3.4	.253	.332	.517	.107	.245	.325	.505	.277	19.8	121-RF	7
2005	BAL	MLB	36	424	39	15	1	14	45	39	84	1	1	3.4	.221	.295	.376	-.150	.227	.311	.397	.246	-7.4	66-RF	-1
2006	BAL	MLB	37	311	31	12	1	12	44	28	63	0	0	3.8	.242	.312	.418	-.058	.246	.322	.438	.252	1.8	76-RF	-2

Breakout: 8%   Improve: 20%   Collapse: 39%   Attrition: 35%   Comparables: Deron Johnson, Dale Murphy, Lee May

Sosa's podiatrist had a bigger year than he did. An abscess and infection on Sosa's left foot wiped out most of May, and a growth under a big toenail wiped out his September. Before the injuries, he was basically matching what he had done in Chicago in 2004, putting up a .275 EqA, but afterwards he managed only .233. He got passive at the plate, trying to work walks since he couldn't jack homers any longer. Simultaneously, he got active in the clubhouse: he had a big role in the breakdown of discipline under Mazzilli, and feuded with Tejada. There's no reason to think that with healthy feet in 2006, he couldn't bounce back to a .270-.280 EqA, but neither we nor the Orioles recommend spending any money to test the idea.

NATE SPEARS   2B   Bats: L Throws: R   Height: 5′ 11″   Weight: 155   Born: May 3, 1985   Age: 21

YEAR	TM	LVL	AGE	PA	R	2B	3B	HR	RBI	BB	SO	SB	CS	SPEED	BA	OBP	SLG	MLVR	EQBA	EQOBP	EQSLG	EQA	VORP	DEFENSE			
2004	DEL	A	19	424	50	12	11	5	38	47	63	7	6	5.6	.275	.358	.407	.075	.246	.313	.361	.237	-0.4	74-2B	9	13-SS	1
2005	FRD	A+	20	484	63	30	6	6	41	36	82	8	4	6.4	.294	.349	.429	.073	.260	.304	.374	.237	1.0	103-2B	13		
2006	BAL	MLB	21	492	52	24	4	6	44	30	80	6	4	5.1	.245	.294	.357	-.166	.249	.303	.374	.227	0.7	116-2B	7		

Breakout: 15%   Improve: 38%   Collapse: 31%   Attrition: 7%   Comparables: Teuris Olivares, Travis Dawkins, Jason Bourgeois

Spears's viability as a prospect rests on being a first-rate defensive second baseman, with just enough bat to make the total package worthwhile. He profiles as the classic #2 hitter: good bat control, sprays the ball around, hits behind runners, bunts well-he led the Carolina League in sacrifices-all the little-ball stuff. He's very similar to Brandon Fahey in a lot of ways, though he's been a better hitter thus far. He gets rave reviews for his attitude, so expect him to push his limitations.

B. J. SURHOFF   1B/OF   Bats: L Throws: R   Height: 6′ 1″   Weight: 200   Born: August 4, 1964   Age: 41

YEAR	TM	LVL	AGE	PA	R	2B	3B	HR	RBI	BB	SO	SB	CS	SPEED	BA	OBP	SLG	MLVR	EQBA	EQOBP	EQSLG	EQA	VORP	DEFENSE			
2003	BAL	MLB	38	351	32	20	0	5	41	29	29	2	2	4.2	.295	.353	.404	.048	.297	.362	.415	.270	8.6	24-LF	-1	19-1B	-1
2004	BAL	MLB	39	375	49	12	1	8	50	30	46	2	0	4.6	.309	.365	.420	.042	.308	.368	.417	.276	10.8	34-RF	-1	30-LF	1
2005	BAL	MLB	40	319	30	11	2	5	34	11	32	0	0	4.3	.257	.282	.356	-.181	.264	.300	.375	.236	-8.3	42-LF	-1	13-1B	1
2006	BAL	MLB	41	168	15	6	1	2	19	9	16	1	0	4.8	.261	.302	.348	-.154	.266	.311	.365	.227	-4.4	43-LF	0		

Breakout: 12%   Improve: 27%   Collapse: 46%   Attrition: 61%   Comparables: Bob Boone, Willie Stargell, Harold Baines

Surhoff finished the year as part of an unlikely first-base platoon with Chris Gomez—and no, it didn't work out too well. He still wants to play, but he's realistic enough to know that 41-year-old reserves are not hot commodities on the free agent market. If somebody wants him, great, but retirement is certainly possible. Eighteen years, 2,326 hits, 1,062 runs and 1,153 RBIs makes for a pretty good career.

MIGUEL TEJADA   SS   **Bats: R Throws: R**   Height: 5' 9"   Weight: 192   Born: May 25, 1976   Age: 30

YEAR	TM	LVL	AGE	PA	R	2B	3B	HR	RBI	BB	SO	SB	CS	SPEED	BA	OBP	SLG	MLVR	EQBA	EQOBP	EQSLG	EQA	VORP	DEFENSE
2003	OAK	MLB	27	703	98	42	0	27	106	53	65	10	0	5.7	.278	.336	.472	.101	.277	.340	.475	.280	50.4	159-SS -15
2004	BAL	MLB	28	725	107	40	2	34	150	48	73	4	1	4.5	.311	.360	.534	.202	.313	.364	.541	.303	65.1	158-SS 15
2005	BAL	MLB	29	704	89	50	5	26	98	40	83	5	1	4.6	.304	.349	.515	.201	.313	.366	.543	.303	62.9	158-SS -3
2006	BAL	MLB	30	664	85	38	3	25	104	42	72	5	1	4.9	.298	.346	.490	.133	.303	.357	.514	.285	52.4	155-SS 1

Breakout: 11%   Improve: 37%   Collapse: 26%   Attrition: 2%   Comparables: Brooks Robinson, Buddy Bell, Carney Lansford

Tejada was part of the Orioles' quick-start gang, setting a blistering RBI pace-31 in April-but cooled with the rest of the team in the mid-summer, so much so that he failed to reach 100 RBI. Tejada was in the middle of several controversies last year, one involving Sosa, one with Palmeiro. His 2005 was extremely similar to his 2004, especially in translation, with the biggest differences by far coming from RBI and runs scored-the products of having 20% fewer at-bats with runners in scoring position.

WALTER YOUNG   1B   **Bats: L Throws: R**   Height: 6' 5"   Weight: 290   Born: February 18, 1980   Age: 26

YEAR	TM	LVL	AGE	PA	R	2B	3B	HR	RBI	BB	SO	SB	CS	SPEED	BA	OBP	SLG	MLVR	EQBA	EQOBP	EQSLG	EQA	VORP	DEFENSE
2003	LYN	A+	23	480	76	15	2	20	87	35	88	2	4	4.5	.278	.348	.462	.161	.247	.303	.428	.247	-2.8	75-1B -2
2004	BOW	AA	24	548	88	28	1	33	98	47	145	2	3	4.0	.272	.341	.537	.239	.248	.309	.478	.263	9.4	64-1B 3
2005	OTT	AAA	25	506	48	29	1	13	81	30	91	1	1	3.6	.288	.334	.438	.032	.260	.306	.397	.243	-6.7	59-1B -8
2005	BAL	MLB	25	37	2	1	0	1	3	4	7	0	0	2.6	.303	.378	.424	.115	.303	.395	.424	.288	1.6	
2006	BAL	MLB	26	418	43	17	1	14	56	25	92	0	1	4.0	.245	.294	.401	-.108	.249	.303	.420	.238	-3.5	100-1B -1

Breakout: 21%   Improve: 34%   Collapse: 42%   Attrition: 10%   Comparables: Juan Diaz, Frank Howard, Bucky Jacobsen

Young hit his weight through last May in Ottawa, no mean feat when your weight is somewhere north of 300 pounds. In fact, his listed weight of 322 is higher than that of any player in major league history; somewhere, Cecil Fielder is smiling. He never got his power stroke going, though, hitting just 14 home runs. Outrighted over the winter, he's not likely to do much to make a name for himself for any reason but his bulk.

PITCHERS

JAMES BALDWIN   **Bats: R Throws: R**   Height: 6' 3"   Weight: 230   Born: July 15, 1971   Age: 34

YEAR	TM	LVL	AGE	W	L	SV	G	GS	IP	H	BB	SO	HR	GB%	BABIP	STUFF	WHIP	ERA	PERA	EQERA	EQH9	EQBB9	EQSO9	EQHR9	VORP	WXRL
2003	OMA	AAA	31	3	2	0	8	8	46.3	48	13	24	3	—	.281	-10	1.32	4.08	5.32	6.55	10.2	3.5	3.5	1.0	-4.6	—
2003	ROC	AAA	31	0	2	0	5	5	29.7	25	3	18	2	—	.244	3	0.94	2.42	4.50	4.50	8.7	1.3	3.9	1.0	3.4	—
2004	TOL	AAA	32	5	7	1	18	16	115.7	110	20	61	12	—	.268	-11	1.12	3.73	5.22	4.89	9.5	2.0	3.3	1.3	8.7	—
2004	NOR	AAA	32	3	2	0	5	5	31.0	34	5	24	3	—	.320	5	1.26	2.90	4.80	4.50	10.5	1.8	4.8	1.2	3.7	—
2005	OTT	AAA	33	3	2	0	8	8	47.0	52	4	25	6	46%	.287	-10	1.19	4.60	5.36	6.15	10.7	1.0	3.2	1.6	-2.8	—
2005	TEX	MLB	33	0	2	1	8	0	17.3	18	7	9	3	40%	.278	-14	1.44	5.20	5.71	4.67	9.3	3.6	4.7	1.6	1.4	-0.1
2005	BAL	MLB	33	0	0	0	20	0	39.3	36	9	20	5	31%	.254	-6	1.14	3.21	4.89	3.72	8.8	2.1	4.7	1.2	7.1	0.0
2006	BAL	MLB	34	3	4	1	37	5	71.7	85	18	33	12	40%	.293	-17	1.44	5.24	5.45	6.32	10.5	2.2	4.1	1.5	1.6	0.2

Breakout: 18%   Improve: 43%   Collapse: 30%   Attrition: 28%   Comparables: Jim Barr, Eddie Fisher, Stan Bahnsen

Baldwin-type players are like disposable batteries: you store them in your Triple-A closet in the event of emergency, and you don't get too bummed if you have to dispose of them after only a few uses. Baldwin went through that twice last year: starting out with Ottawa, getting called up to Baltimore, claimed by Texas when the O's tried to send him back, and reclaimed by Baltimore when the Rangers tried to do the same thing.

RICK BAUER   Bats: R Throws: R   Height: 6' 6"   Weight: 218   Born: January 10, 1977   Age: 29

YEAR	TM	LVL	AGE	W	L	SV	G	GS	IP	H	BB	SO	HR	GB%	BABIP	STUFF	WHIP	ERA	PERA	EQERA	EQH9	EQBB9	EQSO9	EQHR9	VORP	WXRL
2003	OTT	AAA	26	3	1	0	7	7	36.7	31	13	21	1	—	.252	-1	1.20	2.45	4.98	3.67	8.7	4.2	3.9	0.5	7.4	—
2003	BAL	MLB	26	0	0	0	35	0	61.3	58	24	43	5	47%	.296	1	1.34	4.55	4.26	4.99	8.5	3.5	6.2	0.7	4.9	0.4
2004	OTT	AAA	27	3	5	0	11	11	63.0	69	19	42	3	—	.325	7	1.40	4.00	4.48	4.33	9.5	3.2	4.5	0.6	8.8	—
2004	BAL	MLB	27	2	1	0	23	2	53.7	49	20	37	4	60%	.273	4	1.29	4.69	4.19	4.70	8.4	3.2	5.9	0.7	7.0	1.1
2005	OTT	AAA	28	3	8	1	30	10	74.3	84	35	43	12	50%	.312	-40	1.60	4.00	6.81	5.30	10.7	5.0	3.9	1.9	2.4	—
2006	*TEX*	*MLB*	*29*	*3*	*4*	*0*	*40*	*6*	*70.3*	*84*	*32*	*35*	*10*	*49%*	*.305*	*-18*	*1.65*	*5.86*	*5.73*	*6.04*	*10.2*	*4.1*	*4.5*	*1.2*	*-1.4*	*0.0*

Breakout: 12%   Improve: 36%   Collapse: 35%   Attrition: 8%   Comparables: Steven Connelly, Tim Pugh, Bob Milacki

Bauer was the odd man out when the team decided to bring up a third catcher, and though he popped off a bit more than he should have at the news he was going down again, he did have a point. He's been a reliable, if unspectacular, member of the Oriole pen for four years, wanting but never getting a chance to start. After this latest demotion he knew that he and the Orioles were pretty much done. He'll take his chances with the Rangers in 2006.

ERIK BEDARD   Bats: L Throws: L   Height: 6' 1"   Weight: 191   Born: March 6, 1979   Age: 27

YEAR	TM	LVL	AGE	W	L	SV	G	GS	IP	H	BB	SO	HR	GB%	BABIP	STUFF	WHIP	ERA	PERA	EQERA	EQH9	EQBB9	EQSO9	EQHR9	VORP	WXRL
2004	BAL	MLB	25	6	10	0	27	26	137.3	149	71	121	13	41%	.326	17	1.60	4.59	4.26	4.96	9.0	4.2	7.2	0.8	13.0	2.2
2005	BAL	MLB	26	6	8	0	24	24	141.7	139	57	125	10	41%	.323	31	1.38	4.00	3.80	3.99	8.4	3.6	7.7	0.6	24.7	3.7
2006	*BAL*	*MLB*	*27*	*9*	*10*	*0*	*30*	*26*	*161.0*	*161*	*63*	*128*	*18*	*43%*	*.297*	*17*	*1.39*	*4.25*	*4.51*	*4.53*	*8.9*	*3.4*	*7.1*	*1.0*	*20.2*	*3.2*

Breakout: 14%   Improve: 47%   Collapse: 14%   Attrition: 2%   Comparables: Grant Jackson, Jim Rooker, Bob Kuzava

Bedard was on his way to a spectacular season when he sprained his knee in May. What was supposed to be a minimal 15-day stay on the DL dragged on for eight weeks. Somewhere in there, Bedard lost his release point and never recovered it. Following his return, his walk rate more than doubled, his hit rate jumped, and things just kept getting worse the longer the season went on. His stuff is undeniably good, but his control and his inability to stay healthy have held him back.

CHRIS BRITTON   Bats: R Throws: R   Height: 6' 3"   Weight: 220   Born: December 16, 1982   Age: 23

YEAR	TM	LVL	AGE	W	L	SV	G	GS	IP	H	BB	SO	HR	GB%	BABIP	STUFF	WHIP	ERA	PERA	EQERA	EQH9	EQBB9	EQSO9	EQHR9	VORP	WXRL
2004	DEL	A	21	9	4	1	27	8	84.0	76	31	80	11	—	.286	-27	1.27	3.75	6.61	5.56	10.3	4.3	5.2	2.2	0.3	—
2005	FRD	A+	22	6	0	6	46	0	78.7	47	23	110	5	50%	.264	15	0.89	1.60	3.93	3.19	7.2	3.1	8.1	1.0	19.6	—
2006	*BAL*	*MLB*	*23*	*3*	*3*	*1*	*25*	*5*	*54.7*	*56*	*24*	*39*	*10*	*43%*	*.278*	*-1*	*1.45*	*4.83*	*5.32*	*5.02*	*9.0*	*3.8*	*6.4*	*1.5*	*3.4*	*0.5*

Breakout: 5%   Improve: 25%   Collapse: 33%   Attrition: 18%   Comparables: Pat Neshek, Heath Bell, Doug Sessions

Britton was the Orioles' minor league Pitcher of the Year, a rare honor for a non-closing reliever. He's been around for several seasons, had some adventures-like having a metal plate inserted in his forehead after he failed to catch a come-backer-and missed all of 2003 with injury. He has generally pitched well, using a mid-90s fastball and slider, without getting any attention. That changed after this year; it's amazing how striking out twelve batters per game and holding opponents to a .172 average will do that.

TIM BYRDAK   Bats: L Throws: L   Height: 5' 11" Weight: 160   Born: October 31, 1973   Age: 32

YEAR	TM	LVL	AGE	W	L	SV	G	GS	IP	H	BB	SO	HR	GB%	BABIP	STUFF	WHIP	ERA	PERA	EQERA	EQH9	EQBB9	EQSO9	EQHR9	VORP	WXRL
2004	OTT	AAA	30	2	1	2	33	1	34.3	46	12	43	4	—	.429	-1	1.69	4.20	4.67	5.71	11.2	3.6	7.8	1.3	-0.4	—
2004	POR	AAA	30	3	0	0	20	2	38.0	48	17	25	3	—	.349	-26	1.71	5.45	5.54	7.23	10.8	4.8	4.1	1.0	-6.8	—
2005	OTT	AAA	31	3	2	11	37	0	38.7	23	15	44	4	42%	.218	-3	0.98	2.09	5.09	4.08	7.4	4.6	7.6	1.3	6.0	—
2005	BAL	MLB	31	0	1	1	41	0	26.7	27	21	31	1	51%	.351	12	1.80	4.04	3.90	4.55	8.1	6.8	10.1	0.3	2.9	0.7
2006	*BAL*	*MLB*	*32*	*2*	*2*	*2*	*56*	*0*	*41.7*	*43*	*25*	*35*	*5*	*45%*	*.306*	*-6*	*1.61*	*5.13*	*5.42*	*6.68*	*9.1*	*5.1*	*7.6*	*1.0*	*1.4*	*0.0*

Breakout: 23%   Improve: 37%   Collapse: 37%   Attrition: 37%   Comparables: Scott Eyre, Valerio De Los Santos, Dave Hamilton

Two years after he last pitched in the major leagues, Tim Byrdak found himself completely outside of organized ball, working in the Northern League. Even though he didn't pitch that well, the raw numbers were enough to get him noticed by the majors again, and he began his slow climb back. He's been surprisingly effective for the Birds. Working in the tightly-confined space of the situational lefty fits his tightly-confined talents.

DANIEL CABRERA   Bats: R   Throws: R   Height: 6′ 7″   Weight: 220   Born: May 28, 1981   Age: 25

YEAR	TM	LVL	AGE	W	L	SV	G	GS	IP	H	BB	SO	HR	GB%	BABIP	STUFF	WHIP	ERA	PERA	EQERA	EQH9	EQBB9	EQSO9	EQHR9	VORP	WXRL
2003	DEL	A	22	5	9	0	26	26	125.3	105	78	120	6	—	.279	-21	1.46	4.24	6.34	7.20	9.4	7.3	5.2	1.3	-20.4	—
2004	BOW	AA	23	0	1	0	5	5	27.3	11	12	35	1	—	.169	25	0.84	2.64	3.55	4.26	5.7	4.6	8.5	0.4	3.8	—
2004	BAL	MLB	23	12	8	1	28	27	147.7	145	89	76	14	45%	.279	-3	1.58	5.00	5.22	4.67	8.9	5.0	4.4	0.8	18.0	2.9
2005	BAL	MLB	24	10	13	0	29	29	161.3	144	87	157	14	52%	.294	26	1.43	4.52	4.15	4.87	8.0	4.9	8.6	0.7	11.4	2.9
2006	BAL	MLB	25	9	11	0	32	28	169.3	162	89	137	17	47%	.290	14	1.48	4.64	4.72	5.17	8.5	4.6	7.2	0.9	12.2	2.5

Breakout: 21%   Improve: 52%   Collapse: 19%   Attrition: 6%   Comparables: Jim Clancy, Rich Gale, J. R. Richard

Cabrera came to camp last winter looking a lot bigger than before. He attributed it to eating meat every day for the first time in his life, something he couldn't afford to do before reaching the majors. He's become a great big guy, with power pitches that would be a lot more effective if he had any idea of where they were going. He and Bedard are the two players that have Oriole fans hoping that Leo Mazzone's magic works as well in Maryland as it did in Georgia.

BRUCE CHEN   Bats: L   Throws: L   Height: 6′ 1″   Weight: 210   Born: June 19, 1977   Age: 29

YEAR	TM	LVL	AGE	W	L	SV	G	GS	IP	H	BB	SO	HR	GB%	BABIP	STUFF	WHIP	ERA	PERA	EQERA	EQH9	EQBB9	EQSO9	EQHR9	VORP	WXRL
2003	PAW	AAA	26	5	5	1	16	15	85.0	80	15	73	12	—	.272	-12	1.12	4.24	5.71	5.60	9.9	2.0	5.9	2.1	0.0	—
2004	OTT	AAA	27	4	3	0	22	17	95.0	85	30	108	12	—	.297	6	1.21	3.22	4.71	4.42	8.6	3.3	7.7	1.5	12.0	—
2004	BAL	MLB	27	2	1	0	8	7	47.7	39	16	32	7	42%	.232	10	1.15	3.02	4.63	3.28	8.1	2.9	5.8	1.2	14.3	1.4
2005	BAL	MLB	28	13	10	0	34	32	197.3	187	63	133	33	39%	.262	1	1.27	3.83	5.10	4.04	8.9	2.9	6.1	1.5	32.4	4.4
2006	BAL	MLB	29	11	11	0	31	30	189.0	191	59	126	27	41%	.280	12	1.32	4.24	4.54	4.47	9.0	2.7	6.0	1.2	24.4	3.9

Breakout: 11%   Improve: 42%   Collapse: 15%   Attrition: 2%   Comparables: Alex Kellner, Denny Lemaster, Pete Schourek

Where the Mazzone signing might get really interesting is with Chen. He clashed with Mazzone when he first came up with the Braves, primarily (according to reports) because he wasn't open to being as aggressive as Leo's first-pitch-strike philosophy dictated. Chen spent the next six years butting heads with pretty much every pitching coach he met, so that's hardly a knock on Leo. Chen has finally become the pitcher Leo would have made him: he rarely throws the same speed twice in a row, works away-away-away, and throws strikes a lot more often than he did as a young Brave. He's now been with Baltimore longer than any organization since leaving the Braves, so perhaps he's finally ready to settle in.

ERIC DuBOSE   Bats: L   Throws: L   Height: 6′ 3″   Weight: 223   Born: May 15, 1976   Age: 30

YEAR	TM	LVL	AGE	W	L	SV	G	GS	IP	H	BB	SO	HR	GB%	BABIP	STUFF	WHIP	ERA	PERA	EQERA	EQH9	EQBB9	EQSO9	EQHR9	VORP	WXRL
2003	OTT	AAA	27	9	5	0	19	19	114.0	112	34	107	7	—	.309	13	1.28	3.39	4.43	4.92	9.4	3.4	6.3	0.9	8.3	—
2003	BAL	MLB	27	3	6	0	17	10	73.7	60	25	44	6	56%	.245	8	1.15	3.79	4.38	3.88	8.0	3.1	5.4	0.8	16.5	2.4
2004	BAL	MLB	28	4	6	0	14	14	74.7	76	44	48	12	46%	.279	-9	1.61	6.39	5.62	5.97	9.2	4.9	5.4	1.3	-2.1	0.6
2005	BOW	AA	29	8	10	0	21	20	122.0	113	29	114	10	46%	.308	-9	1.16	3.25	5.40	6.19	10.1	3.2	5.0	1.4	-7.4	—
2005	BAL	MLB	29	2	3	0	15	3	29.3	28	19	17	4	40%	.255	-20	1.60	5.53	5.83	5.83	8.9	5.8	5.2	1.2	-2.3	0.6
2006	BAL	MLB	30	5	8	0	36	20	112.7	122	48	66	16	45%	.289	-7	1.50	5.13	5.35	5.47	9.6	3.7	5.2	1.2	2.5	0.9

Breakout: 19%   Improve: 63%   Collapse: 11%   Attrition: 0%   Comparables: Brian Bohanon, Darren Oliver, Paul Splittorff

DuBose had a nice half-season in Baltimore, but that was three years and an elbow surgery ago. He hasn't pitched effectively since the bone chips became a problem, and he had the distinction of being the first, but not last, Oriole in 2005 to get arrested for DUI. That spring training gaffe prevented the Orioles from sending him to Ottawa.

BRANDON ERBE   Bats: R   Throws: R   Height: 6′ 4″   Weight: 180   Born: December 25, 1987   Age: 18

YEAR	TM	LVL	AGE	W	L	SV	G	GS	IP	H	BB	SO	HR	GB%	BABIP	STUFF	WHIP	ERA	PERA	EQERA	EQH9	EQBB9	EQSO9	EQHR9	VORP	WXRL
2005	BLU	Rk	17	1	1	1	11	3	23.3	8	10	48	1	33%	.241	20	0.77	3.09	4.87	5.75	6.6	6.2	9.3	0.9	-0.3	—
2006	BAL	MLB	18	3	4	0	16	8	56.0	46	30	61	6	42%	.279	27	1.35	4.90	4.38	5.41	7.2	4.6	9.8	1.0	2.2	0.5

Breakout: 41%   Improve: 99%   Collapse: 0%   Attrition: 38%   Comparables: Francisco Rodriguez, Felix Hernandez, Jacob McGee

Yes, it was a great start to a career, and the strikeouts were especially eye-popping. It's still just the Appalachian League, and it was only 23 innings, and he's only a 17-year-old kid, albeit one with a 97-mph fastball. With that kind of arm, you only worry about whether he can stay healthy and whether he can maintain control, which can often amount to the same thing: good mechanics means better control and less arm strain, while control also means fewer pitches and less chance of overuse-related injuries.

DAVID HAEHNEL   Bats: L Throws: L   Height: 6′ 4″ Weight: 180 Born: July 21, 1982   Age: 23

YEAR	TM	LVL	AGE	W	L	SV	G	GS	IP	H	BB	SO	HR	GB%	BABIP	STUFF	WHIP	ERA	PERA	EQERA	EQH9	EQBB9	EQSO9	EQHR9	VORP	WXRL
2004	ABE	A-	21	3	1	16	28	0	36.3	23	11	58	1	—	.293	7	0.94	1.24	4.36	4.64	8.2	4.4	7.6	0.8	3.5	—
2005	DEL	A	22	1	1	16	28	0	34.0	20	10	34	1	41%	.232	-2	0.88	0.79	4.26	2.84	6.8	3.4	5.4	0.6	9.7	—
2005	FRD	A+	22	3	1	2	23	0	34.3	27	10	37	1	45%	.302	2	1.08	3.41	4.09	5.18	8.2	3.0	6.0	0.5	1.5	—
2006	*BAL*	*MLB*	*23*	*2*	*3*	*1*	*26*	*4*	*49.7*	*52*	*22*	*31*	*8*	*39%*	*.280*	*-7*	*1.49*	*5.19*	*5.40*	*5.44*	*9.3*	*3.9*	*5.6*	*1.4*	*1.1*	*0.2*

Breakout: 5%   Improve: 19%   Collapse: 47%   Attrition: 25%   Comparables: *Pete Zamora, Shea Douglas, Brian Passini*

Haehnel has been able to beat hitters with one pitch: a fastball with crazy movement, abetted by a deceptive delivery. He's started each of the past two years with long scoreless streaks (19.2 innings last year, 23 the year before) and racked up save after save. There is some desire to move him to the rotation, but until and unless he improves his breaking pitches, that isn't likely to happen.

J. J. JOHNSON   Bats: R Throws: R   Height: 6′ 5″ Weight: 213 Born: June 27, 1983   Age: 23

YEAR	TM	LVL	AGE	W	L	SV	G	GS	IP	H	BB	SO	HR	GB%	BABIP	STUFF	WHIP	ERA	PERA	EQERA	EQH9	EQBB9	EQSO9	EQHR9	VORP	WXRL
2003	BLU	Rk	20	3	2	0	11	11	51.3	62	18	46	2	—	.357	-11	1.56	3.68	5.62	6.52	11.2	4.5	4.0	1.1	-5.1	—
2004	DEL	A	21	8	7	0	20	17	106.7	97	30	93	9	—	.291	-7	1.19	3.29	5.54	5.27	9.9	3.2	4.6	1.4	3.7	—
2005	FRD	A+	22	12	9	1	28	27	159.7	139	64	168	11	52%	.303	6	1.27	3.49	5.08	5.44	9.2	4.2	6.0	1.0	2.7	—
2006	*BAL*	*MLB*	*23*	*7*	*10*	*0*	*25*	*25*	*142.7*	*154*	*65*	*87*	*18*	*48%*	*.295*	*5*	*1.53*	*5.19*	*5.31*	*5.52*	*9.6*	*4.0*	*5.4*	*1.1*	*1.4*	*1.2*

Breakout: 11%   Improve: 52%   Collapse: 11%   Attrition: 0%   Comparables: *Anthony Lerew, Jason Hammel, Zach Day*

Johnson had a breakthrough year, pitching his way onto the Orioles' 40-man roster by leading the Carolina League in innings and strikeouts. A 2001 5th round pick, Johnson has made incremental progress each season, showing more improvement than the standard aging curve would allow for. He has a basic fastball/curveball arsenal, but uses them aggressively, as evidenced by his 20 HBPs, third-most in the minors.

JORGE JULIO   Bats: R Throws: R   Height: 6′ 1″ Weight: 190 Born: March 3, 1979   Age: 27

YEAR	TM	LVL	AGE	W	L	SV	G	GS	IP	H	BB	SO	HR	GB%	BABIP	STUFF	WHIP	ERA	PERA	EQERA	EQH9	EQBB9	EQSO9	EQHR9	VORP	WXRL
2003	BAL	MLB	24	0	7	36	64	0	61.7	60	34	52	10	47%	.291	-8	1.52	4.38	5.08	4.94	8.6	4.8	7.3	1.3	4.9	1.5
2004	BAL	MLB	25	2	5	22	65	0	69.0	59	39	70	11	42%	.270	2	1.42	4.57	4.80	4.15	7.9	4.7	8.6	1.3	14.0	2.1
2005	BAL	MLB	26	3	5	0	67	0	71.7	76	24	58	14	40%	.294	-10	1.41	5.90	4.98	5.85	9.3	3.0	7.2	1.6	-4.5	-0.6
2006	*NYN*	*MLB*	*27*	*3*	*3*	*2*	*50*	*0*	*56.7*	*51*	*22*	*47*	*7*	*43%*	*.275*	*4*	*1.30*	*3.81*	*4.12*	*4.54*	*8.1*	*3.3*	*7.0*	*1.0*	*7.6*	*0.6*

Breakout: 44%   Improve: 67%   Collapse: 17%   Attrition: 15%   Comparables: *Dan Miceli, Steve Foucault, Jim Ray*

Julio was a constant drag on the team, entering close games and leaving them with the outcome no longer in doubt. He was torched for a 9.64 ERA over the final two months, earning himself a spot near the bottom of the league in WXRL. His problem seems to be stamina, as he's only good for about 20 pitches. A team that takes pitches and makes him work, even a little, reaps a huge reward. Whether or not Mazzone can fix him is an open question, but the Orioles have dangled him all winter, perhaps hoping not to find out.

RYAN KEEFER   Bats: L Throws: R   Height: 6′ 3″ Weight: 202 Born: August 10, 1981   Age: 24

YEAR	TM	LVL	AGE	W	L	SV	G	GS	IP	H	BB	SO	HR	GB%	BABIP	STUFF	WHIP	ERA	PERA	EQERA	EQH9	EQBB9	EQSO9	EQHR9	VORP	WXRL
2003	DEL	A	21	7	12	0	26	26	148.7	162	34	94	11	—	.300	-22	1.32	4.36	6.11	6.30	11.2	2.5	3.4	1.8	-11.0	—
2004	FRD	A+	22	4	4	4	63	0	87.3	89	26	73	10	—	.307	-31	1.32	3.09	6.40	4.55	10.3	3.4	5.1	2.2	9.7	—
2005	BOW	AA	23	7	3	1	54	1	84.3	64	32	92	7	44%	.279	-5	1.14	3.20	4.92	4.81	8.6	4.2	6.9	1.1	6.9	—
2006	*BAL*	*MLB*	*24*	*2*	*4*	*1*	*31*	*4*	*57.3*	*67*	*25*	*33*	*10*	*45%*	*.299*	*-12*	*1.59*	*5.67*	*6.13*	*5.95*	*10.3*	*3.8*	*5.2*	*1.5*	*-2.1*	*-0.1*

Breakout: 11%   Improve: 32%   Collapse: 27%   Attrition: 12%   Comparables: *Matt Parker, Mike McNutt, Kevin Olore*

Keefer's projections have always shown him to be right on the edge of making the majors, with projected ERAs in the upper fours—below average perhaps, but still above replacement level. He's done a little better since converting to relief full-time. Not having to hold back has put an extra four or five miles on his fastball, pushing it from a little below average to a little above. The Orioles were impressed enough to put him on the 40-man roster.

STEVE KLINE Bats: B Throws: L   Height: 6′ 1″   Weight: 210   Born: August 22, 1972   Age: 33

YEAR	TM	LVL	AGE	W	L	SV	G	GS	IP	H	BB	SO	HR	GB%	BABIP	STUFF	WHIP	ERA	PERA	EQERA	EQH9	EQBB9	EQSO9	EQHR9	VORP	WXRL
2003	SLN	MLB	30	5	5	3	78	0	63.7	56	30	31	5	52%	.255	-15	1.35	3.81	4.91	4.33	8.8	3.9	4.0	0.7	9.5	0.9
2004	SLN	MLB	31	2	2	3	67	0	50.3	37	17	35	3	57%	.245	4	1.07	1.79	4.10	2.42	8.0	2.8	5.8	0.6	19.7	1.5
2005	BAL	MLB	32	2	4	0	67	0	61.0	59	30	36	11	57%	.262	-23	1.44	4.28	5.79	4.75	9.0	4.5	5.3	1.6	4.8	-0.8
2006	*SFN*	*MLB*	*33*	*2*	*3*	*2*	*59*	*0*	*53.0*	*55*	*22*	*33*	*5*	*53%*	*.292*	*-11*	*1.45*	*4.42*	*4.76*	*5.22*	*9.2*	*3.4*	*5.2*	*0.9*	*3.3*	*0.2*

Breakout: 8%   Improve: 33%   Collapse: 47%   Attrition: 23%   Comparables: Joe Gibbon, Mark Guthrie, Buddy Groom

By WXRL, Kline was the worst reliever on the Orioles, and fifth-worst in the league. As the only lefty in the pen, other than the closer, B. J. Ryan, for a good chunk of the year, Kline was repeatedly brought into games in key situations to retire a left-handed batter. Unfortunately, after an outstanding .186 EqA against left-handers in 2004, he had a .299 EqA against them in 2005. His performance against right-handed hitters was pretty much unchanged; the lefties did it all. He'll be back this year, albeit with the Giants since his trade for LaTroy Hawkins.

RADHAMES LIZ Bats: R Throws: R   Height: 6′ 2″   Weight: 170   Born: June 10, 1983   Age: 23

YEAR	TM	LVL	AGE	W	L	SV	G	GS	IP	H	BB	SO	HR	GB%	BABIP	STUFF	WHIP	ERA	PERA	EQERA	EQH9	EQBB9	EQSO9	EQHR9	VORP	WXRL
2005	ABE	A-	22	5	4	0	11	11	56.0	36	19	82	1	45%	.324	16	0.98	1.77	4.21	5.08	7.9	4.6	6.8	0.5	3.0	—
2005	DEL	A	22	2	3	0	10	10	38.3	33	23	55	2	36%	.360	0	1.46	4.46	5.20	6.69	8.7	6.9	7.7	1.0	-4.4	—
2006	*BAL*	*MLB*	*23*	*5*	*9*	*0*	*26*	*19*	*112.0*	*108*	*79*	*92*	*14*	*41%*	*.288*	*4*	*1.66*	*5.66*	*5.61*	*6.01*	*8.5*	*6.2*	*7.3*	*1.1*	*-4.2*	*0.3*

Breakout: 10%   Improve: 38%   Collapse: 20%   Attrition: 2%   Comparables: Junior Guerrero, Travis Harper, Tim Redding

Liz joins Erbe and Olson as the system's young pitchers making early splashes. He's actually been with the organization for a couple of years in the Dominican Summer League. Liz started last year at Delmarva, and was sent down to Aberdeen when the short-season league got started. As a result, he had more professional experience than the average NY-P player, even if he wasn't much older, and it showed in the way he dominated the league. He has a very good fastball, striking out 15 of 19 batters faced in one game.

ADAM LOEWEN Bats: L Throws: L   Height: 6′ 6″   Weight: 220   Born: April 9, 1984   Age: 22

YEAR	TM	LVL	AGE	W	L	SV	G	GS	IP	H	BB	SO	HR	GB%	BABIP	STUFF	WHIP	ERA	PERA	EQERA	EQH9	EQBB9	EQSO9	EQHR9	VORP	WXRL
2003	ABE	A-	19	0	2	0	7	7	23.3	13	9	25	0	—	.225	11	0.94	2.70	4.57	4.57	7.5	4.6	5.8	0.4	2.5	—
2004	DEL	A	20	4	5	0	20	19	85.3	77	58	82	3	—	.323	-1	1.58	4.11	5.58	6.14	9.1	7.6	5.2	0.6	-4.8	—
2005	FRD	A+	21	10	8	0	28	27	142.0	130	86	146	8	62%	.324	4	1.52	4.12	5.32	5.78	9.2	6.1	5.9	0.8	-2.7	—
2006	*BAL*	*MLB*	*22*	*5*	*10*	*0*	*25*	*23*	*123.0*	*127*	*96*	*83*	*10*	*56%*	*.303*	*-1*	*1.80*	*5.59*	*5.84*	*6.07*	*9.1*	*6.8*	*6.0*	*0.7*	*-5.7*	*0.3*

Breakout: 12%   Improve: 43%   Collapse: 14%   Attrition: 1%   Comparables: Corwin Malone, Adam Harben, Preston Larrison

Loewen was diagnosed with a partial labrum tear late in '04, and so far has resisted surgery. In 2005 he was alternately brilliant and horrible, where "horrible" usually meant being totally incapable of throwing a strike. The brilliant Loewen showed up in the AFL; he posted a league-leading 1.67 ERA in a serious hitter's league. The shortcoming that keeps Loewen from being a dominant pitcher is an inaptitude for repetition, a failure to keep his mechanics consistent from one pitch to the next, one batter to the next, or one game to the next.

RODRIGO LOPEZ Bats: R Throws: R   Height: 6′ 1″   Weight: 187   Born: December 14, 1975   Age: 30

YEAR	TM	LVL	AGE	W	L	SV	G	GS	IP	H	BB	SO	HR	GB%	BABIP	STUFF	WHIP	ERA	PERA	EQERA	EQH9	EQBB9	EQSO9	EQHR9	VORP	WXRL
2003	BAL	MLB	27	7	10	0	26	26	147.0	188	43	103	24	46%	.347	0	1.57	5.82	4.91	5.80	10.3	2.5	5.9	1.4	-4.9	2.0
2004	BAL	MLB	28	14	9	0	37	23	170.7	164	54	121	21	49%	.281	10	1.28	3.59	4.32	3.47	8.6	2.6	6.0	1.0	49.0	6.4
2005	BAL	MLB	29	15	12	0	35	35	209.3	232	63	118	28	44%	.294	1	1.41	4.90	4.84	4.97	9.7	2.7	5.0	1.1	8.0	3.8
2006	*BAL*	*MLB*	*30*	*10*	*11*	*0*	*32*	*29*	*180.7*	*195*	*54*	*108*	*24*	*45%*	*.291*	*7*	*1.37*	*4.45*	*4.74*	*4.69*	*9.6*	*2.6*	*5.3*	*1.1*	*18.6*	*3.2*

Breakout: 20%   Improve: 59%   Collapse: 12%   Attrition: 2%   Comparables: Greg Harris, Rick Langford, Jim Colborn

Although on the one hand it looks like Lopez has followed an up-down pattern for the last four years, his peripheral ERAs over that time have all been between 4.30 and 4.90. Fundamentally, he's an average pitcher, reliant on off-speed stuff and heavily dependent on location. That isn't all bad, of course. Often it's quite handy.

JOHN MAINE   **Bats: R Throws: R**   Height: 6′ 4″ Weight: 190 Born: May 8, 1981   Age: 25

YEAR	TM	LVL	AGE	W	L	SV	G	GS	IP	H	BB	SO	HR	GB%	BABIP	STUFF	WHIP	ERA	PERA	EQERA	EQH9	EQBB9	EQSO9	EQHR9	VORP	WXRL
2003	DEL	A	22	7	3	0	14	14	76.3	43	18	108	1	—	.258	35	0.80	1.53	3.18	4.20	7.1	2.7	7.6	0.4	11.0	—
2003	FRD	A+	22	6	1	0	12	12	70.3	48	20	77	5	—	.243	12	0.97	3.07	4.85	4.85	8.2	3.0	7.2	1.5	5.4	—
2004	BOW	AA	23	4	0	0	5	5	28.0	16	7	34	1	—	.227	26	0.82	2.25	3.08	3.76	6.8	2.7	8.2	0.3	5.4	—
2004	OTT	AAA	23	5	7	0	22	22	119.7	123	52	105	12	—	.316	6	1.46	3.91	4.93	4.47	9.1	4.2	6.2	1.1	14.9	—
2005	OTT	AAA	24	6	11	0	23	23	128.3	128	42	111	13	41%	.307	5	1.33	4.56	4.74	5.39	9.3	3.3	6.0	1.1	2.9	—
2005	BAL	MLB	24	2	3	0	10	8	40.0	39	24	24	8	45%	.248	-19	1.57	6.30	6.35	6.35	9.3	5.4	5.4	1.8	-4.4	0.1
2006	*NYN*	*MLB*	*25*	*7*	*9*	*0*	*35*	*23*	*133.0*	*127*	*54*	*97*	*15*	*42%*	*.279*	*5*	*1.36*	*4.52*	*4.71*	*5.21*	*8.6*	*3.4*	*6.1*	*1.0*	*7.3*	*1.6*

Breakout: 15% Improve: 55% Collapse: 17% Attrition: 0%   Comparables: Shawn Hillegas, Barry Latman, Kelvim Escobar

Maine is similar to Lopez, in the sense of being an extremely location-dependent pitcher. He doesn't have the gas to challenge everybody who comes up, and in his brief calls to the majors he's tried to cut it too fine. When you nibble and miss, you have to come in and take your lumps. He was far more overpowering in the low minors, and if he can adapt in the same way that Josh Towers has, he'll be useful at the back end of a big league rotation.

GARRETT OLSON   **Bats: R Throws: L**   Height: 6′ 1″ Weight: 200 Born: October 18, 1983   Age: 22

YEAR	TM	LVL	AGE	W	L	SV	G	GS	IP	H	BB	SO	HR	GB%	BABIP	STUFF	WHIP	ERA	PERA	EQERA	EQH9	EQBB9	EQSO9	EQHR9	VORP	WXRL
2005	ABE	A-	21	2	1	1	11	6	40.0	22	13	40	1	61%	.226	-1	0.88	1.57	4.95	4.21	7.2	4.2	5.0	0.7	5.6	—
2006	*BAL*	*MLB*	*22*	*5*	*8*	*0*	*26*	*18*	*107.7*	*108*	*61*	*66*	*11*	*53%*	*.284*	*-1*	*1.56*	*5.09*	*5.16*	*5.50*	*8.9*	*4.9*	*5.5*	*0.9*	*1.7*	*0.9*

Breakout: 2% Improve: 12% Collapse: 50% Attrition: 3%   Comparables: Clint Brannon, Kurt Isenberg, Nate Bump

Like Brandon Erbe, Olson had a big year in the ultra-low minors, but there the comparison ends. Olson is a collegian, a supplemental 1st round pick out of Cal Poly. He made a name for himself in the Alaska League in the summer of '04, and followed it up with a dazzling college season. He has an outstanding curveball that invites comparisons to Barry Zito's. College pitcher, great curve, and his name's G. Olson? That should sound familiar to Oriole fans.

JOHN PARRISH   **Bats: L Throws: L**   Height: 5′ 11″ Weight: 176 Born: November 26, 1977   Age: 28

YEAR	TM	LVL	AGE	W	L	SV	G	GS	IP	H	BB	SO	HR	GB%	BABIP	STUFF	WHIP	ERA	PERA	EQERA	EQH9	EQBB9	EQSO9	EQHR9	VORP	WXRL
2003	BOW	AA	25	3	3	6	49	0	76.3	58	33	85	5	—	.269	-5	1.19	2.01	5.12	4.22	8.6	5.1	7.5	1.3	10.8	—
2003	BAL	MLB	25	0	1	0	14	0	23.7	17	8	15	2	52%	.227	1	1.06	1.90	4.30	2.74	7.4	3.1	5.9	0.8	8.8	0.3
2004	BAL	MLB	26	6	3	1	56	1	78.0	68	55	71	4	57%	.303	10	1.58	3.46	4.22	4.10	7.7	5.8	7.6	0.5	16.1	1.1
2005	BAL	MLB	27	1	0	0	14	0	17.3	19	17	25	1	51%	.429	18	2.08	3.12	3.93	2.95	7.9	8.3	12.3	0.5	5.0	-0.2
2006	*BAL*	*MLB*	*28*	*2*	*2*	*2*	*43*	*0*	*44.3*	*41*	*29*	*41*	*3*	*50%*	*.302*	*3*	*1.59*	*4.41*	*4.79*	*5.13*	*8.3*	*5.8*	*8.2*	*0.7*	*4.5*	*0.4*

Breakout: 14% Improve: 25% Collapse: 54% Attrition: 31%   Comparables: Tippy Martinez, Rod Scurry, Don Ferrarese

Parrish took over as the pen's long man after Bauer was sent down. The pitchers were still doing well enough that there just wasn't any work. When he did pitch he was extremely wild, even by his own lax standards for control. He was eventually diagnosed with a strained elbow ligament, which turned into a tear. He'll be out at least part of 2006, recovering from his July TJ operation.

HAYDEN PENN   **Bats: R Throws: R**   Height: 6′ 3″ Weight: 185 Born: October 13, 1984   Age: 21

YEAR	TM	LVL	AGE	W	L	SV	G	GS	IP	H	BB	SO	HR	GB%	BABIP	STUFF	WHIP	ERA	PERA	EQERA	EQH9	EQBB9	EQSO9	EQHR9	VORP	WXRL
2003	BLU	Rk	18	1	4	0	12	11	52.3	58	19	38	4	—	.312	-20	1.47	4.30	7.30	6.57	11.5	4.7	3.5	2.2	-5.3	—
2004	DEL	A	19	4	1	1	13	6	43.3	30	19	41	4	—	.234	-1	1.13	3.33	6.07	4.95	8.6	4.9	5.4	1.6	2.9	—
2004	FRD	A+	19	6	5	0	13	13	73.3	59	20	61	7	—	.260	7	1.08	3.81	5.48	4.83	8.7	3.0	5.5	1.7	5.9	—
2004	BOW	AA	19	3	0	0	4	4	20.3	22	9	20	0	—	.379	20	1.53	4.88	3.92	5.66	9.1	3.9	6.5	0.4	-0.1	—
2005	BOW	AA	20	7	6	0	20	19	110.3	101	37	120	11	48%	.326	16	1.25	3.83	4.67	5.09	9.3	3.5	7.1	1.3	6.0	—
2005	BAL	MLB	20	3	2	0	8	8	38.3	46	21	18	6	44%	.303	-11	1.75	6.34	6.00	6.46	10.2	4.8	4.2	1.4	-5.4	0.1
2006	*BAL*	*MLB*	*21*	*7*	*10*	*0*	*35*	*27*	*146.0*	*153*	*63*	*94*	*21*	*46%*	*.286*	*3*	*1.48*	*4.94*	*5.22*	*5.18*	*9.3*	*3.8*	*5.8*	*1.2*	*6.6*	*1.6*

Breakout: 27% Improve: 64% Collapse: 6% Attrition: 0%   Comparables: Rick Wise, Jon Garland, Paxton Crawford

Penn was rushed to the majors after nine strong starts in Bowie, and after getting one quality start in eight major league tries he was appropriately sent back. Primarily a basketball player in high school, Penn's best pitch is his changeup, followed by a fastball and curve. His name was mentioned in numerous trade rumors last summer, at a time when the Orioles could still think they were in contention, but there was nothing personal about it; he was just the highest-ranked prospect on the team that they were willing to trade.

SIDNEY PONSON Bats: R Throws: R   Height: 6′ 1″ Weight: 220 Born: November 2, 1976 Age: 29

YEAR	TM	LVL	AGE	W	L	SV	G	GS	IP	H	BB	SO	HR	GB%	BABIP	STUFF	WHIP	ERA	PERA	EQERA	EQH9	EQBB9	EQSO9	EQHR9	VORP	WXRL
2003	BAL	MLB	26	14	6	0	21	21	148.0	147	43	100	10	53%	.298	24	1.28	3.77	3.81	3.81	8.6	2.5	5.9	0.5	33.7	4.1
2003	SFN	MLB	26	3	6	0	10	10	68.0	64	18	34	6	56%	.275	6	1.21	3.71	4.36	4.23	9.3	2.2	4.2	0.8	15.2	1.8
2004	BAL	MLB	27	11	15	0	33	33	215.7	265	69	115	23	54%	.332	4	1.55	5.30	4.58	5.07	10.1	2.6	4.4	0.9	16.8	2.9
2005	BAL	MLB	28	7	11	0	23	23	130.3	177	48	68	16	54%	.358	-3	1.73	6.22	4.89	6.07	10.8	3.2	4.5	1.0	-13.8	0.3
2006	*SLN*	*MLB*	*29*	*8*	*8*	*0*	*28*	*22*	*136.7*	*148*	*46*	*78*	*14*	*53%*	*.299*	*2*	*1.42*	*4.43*	*4.75*	*5.17*	*9.6*	*2.8*	*4.7*	*0.9*	*11.2*	*2.0*

Breakout: 19% Improve: 57% Collapse: 23% Attrition: 6%   Comparables: Jack Fisher, Richard Dotson, Stan Bahnsen

Ponson's pitching was bad enough, but the alcohol-related incidents—a fight with a judge on a Curacao beach last off-season, and a mid-season DUI—were intolerable. He was thrown off the team, and Angelos and Co. were looking for ways to void the final year of his contract. Forget about baseball for the moment. These are symptoms of someone who needs help Tony LaRussa and Dave Duncan once helped a troubled Bob Welch get his career back in order, and if they can work any similar magic with Ponson, it'll be a good deed for all concerned.

AARON RAKERS Bats: R Throws: R   Height: 6′ 3″ Weight: 205 Born: January 22, 1977 Age: 29

YEAR	TM	LVL	AGE	W	L	SV	G	GS	IP	H	BB	SO	HR	GB%	BABIP	STUFF	WHIP	ERA	PERA	EQERA	EQH9	EQBB9	EQSO9	EQHR9	VORP	WXRL
2003	BOW	AA	26	5	0	8	31	0	39.3	27	19	42	7	—	.209	-34	1.17	2.75	8.82	4.54	10.2	6.1	7.5	3.7	4.0	—
2003	OTT	AAA	26	2	4	1	21	0	26.3	19	11	26	1	—	.254	-6	1.14	5.13	4.74	6.93	7.7	4.7	6.9	0.7	-3.7	—
2004	OTT	AAA	27	4	5	1	54	1	78.7	65	25	80	8	—	.277	0	1.14	2.74	4.66	3.70	8.2	3.3	6.9	1.2	15.9	—
2005	OTT	AAA	28	6	5	7	57	0	77.0	69	21	92	9	44%	.311	3	1.17	2.57	4.38	3.89	8.9	2.9	7.9	1.3	14.1	—
2005	BAL	MLB	28	1	0	0	10	0	13.7	11	3	11	3	33%	.222	5	1.02	3.28	5.40	3.38	8.1	2.0	7.4	2.0	3.7	0.8
2006	*BAL*	*MLB*	*29*	*3*	*3*	*3*	*61*	*2*	*56.0*	*55*	*21*	*42*	*8*	*40%*	*.280*	*0*	*1.35*	*4.22*	*4.55*	*4.57*	*8.7*	*3.2*	*6.8*	*1.2*	*7.5*	*0.7*

Breakout: 24% Improve: 42% Collapse: 28% Attrition: 18%   Comparables: Alejandro Pena, Cris Carpenter, Steve Bedrosian

After another fine season in the minors, Rakers (pronounced "rockers") got a chance to pitch in Baltimore, and once again was mostly okay. We say "mostly" only because three home runs in 13 innings is actually pretty bad. That's a direct result of his stuff, which overall isn't good. His split-fingered fastball is generally excellent, but every once in a while it doesn't sink. That's when the hitter gets to take a slow jog around the bases.

CHRIS RAY Bats: R Throws: R   Height: 6′ 3″ Weight: 200 Born: January 12, 1982 Age: 24

YEAR	TM	LVL	AGE	W	L	SV	G	GS	IP	H	BB	SO	HR	GB%	BABIP	STUFF	WHIP	ERA	PERA	EQERA	EQH9	EQBB9	EQSO9	EQHR9	VORP	WXRL
2003	ABE	A-	21	2	0	0	9	8	38.3	32	10	44	0	—	.311	12	1.10	2.82	3.72	5.70	8.9	3.2	5.7	0.2	-0.4	—
2004	DEL	A	22	2	3	0	10	9	50.0	43	17	46	3	—	.286	-3	1.20	3.42	5.17	5.55	9.6	4.0	4.8	1.0	0.3	—
2004	FRD	A+	22	6	3	0	14	14	73.3	82	20	74	6	—	.362	2	1.39	3.81	5.15	5.02	10.2	3.0	6.0	1.5	4.6	—
2005	BOW	AA	23	1	2	18	31	0	37.3	17	7	40	3	51%	.179	7	0.64	0.97	4.28	2.67	7.0	2.1	7.0	1.1	11.0	—
2005	BAL	MLB	23	1	3	0	41	0	40.7	34	18	43	5	35%	.276	17	1.28	2.65	3.98	3.32	7.5	4.0	9.5	1.1	10.9	-0.3
2006	*BAL*	*MLB*	*24*	*2*	*3*	*3*	*54*	*0*	*53.0*	*52*	*21*	*43*	*6*	*44%*	*.289*	*5*	*1.37*	*4.12*	*4.46*	*4.63*	*8.6*	*3.4*	*7.3*	*1.0*	*7.2*	*0.6*

Breakout: 20% Improve: 43% Collapse: 27% Attrition: 27%   Comparables: Jorge Julio, Travis Phelps, Elias Sosa

Ray has made the transition to relief and shot all the way through the system. His fastball can reach the upper 90s, and he complements it with a very good slider and a developing changeup. He's got future closer written all over him, though the Orioles don't want to make this year the future if they don't have to.

SENDY RLEAL Bats: R Throws: R   Height: 6′ 1″ Weight: 165 Born: June 21, 1980 Age: 26

YEAR	TM	LVL	AGE	W	L	SV	G	GS	IP	H	BB	SO	HR	GB%	BABIP	STUFF	WHIP	ERA	PERA	EQERA	EQH9	EQBB9	EQSO9	EQHR9	VORP	WXRL
2003	FRD	A+	23	3	5	11	44	0	57.0	35	23	59	8	—	.194	-32	1.02	3.16	7.92	4.68	9.2	4.7	7.0	3.4	5.1	—
2004	BOW	AA	24	4	0	3	39	0	47.3	41	12	60	7	—	.304	-1	1.12	2.66	5.20	4.20	9.4	2.6	8.2	2.0	7.0	—
2005	BOW	AA	25	4	4	16	56	0	70.7	46	18	75	4	45%	.251	0	0.91	2.04	4.13	4.13	7.9	3.0	6.3	0.8	10.7	—
2006	*BAL*	*MLB*	*26*	*2*	*3*	*1*	*25*	*3*	*49.7*	*50*	*18*	*36*	*10*	*39%*	*.270*	*-2*	*1.36*	*4.79*	*5.17*	*5.13*	*9.0*	*3.1*	*6.4*	*1.7*	*3.8*	*0.4*

Breakout: 10% Improve: 30% Collapse: 40% Attrition: 22%   Comparables: Jim Farrell, Jose Acevedo, Rafael Betancourt

Rleal has a funky name and an even funkier delivery. He sort of rocks on the rubber and then jumps towards the plate. It's strange, but it works for him. He uses a fastball/changeup combo, and he substantially cut down the home runs allowed this past year. He could probably work out of the Oriole pen next year, giving big league broadcasters fits. (Hint: say his name the way the Quebecois say the last half of "Montreal.")

B. J. RYAN   **Bats: L Throws: L**   Height: 6′ 6″   Weight: 230   Born: December 28, 1975   Age: 30

YEAR	TM	LVL	AGE	W	L	SV	G	GS	IP	H	BB	SO	HR	GB%	BABIP	STUFF	WHIP	ERA	PERA	EQERA	EQH9	EQBB9	EQSO9	EQHR9	VORP	WXRL
2003	BAL	MLB	27	4	1	0	76	0	50.3	42	27	63	1	54%	.339	33	1.37	3.40	2.98	3.33	7.0	4.6	10.7	0.2	14.7	1.3
2004	BAL	MLB	28	4	6	3	76	0	87.0	64	35	122	4	47%	.309	50	1.14	2.28	2.56	2.35	6.4	3.3	11.7	0.4	37.5	5.0
2005	BAL	MLB	29	1	4	36	69	0	70.3	54	26	100	4	46%	.321	50	1.14	2.43	2.52	2.52	6.6	3.3	12.4	0.5	24.9	3.4
2006	TOR	MLB	30	5	5	44	80	0	72.3	54	27	100	5	46%	.304	39	1.12	2.61	2.62	2.78	6.5	3.4	12.1	0.6	23.9	3.6

Breakout: 23%   Improve: 37%   Collapse: 21%   Attrition: 9%   Comparables: Jeff Nelson, Jim Kern, Rich Gossage

Ryan will be a much richer man in 2006 thanks to a season that vaulted him directly into the top rank of closers. Though it was his first full season in that role, the peripheral numbers were so dominating that he was assured to be treated as a front-line closer in salary negotiations. A season like Ryan's 2005 was worth about $8 million, objectively, to an average team. The Blue Jays' contract of $47 million over five years only makes sense if Ryan continues to perform at this level for the duration of the deal, and the average salaries continue to increase the way they have over the last 15 years—at 8% inflation, it comes to $8 million per year in current value. Expecting a 29-year-old to repeat his best-ever season five more times, however, is not a good strategy.

JOHN STEPHENS   **Bats: R Throws: R**   Height: 6′ 1″   Weight: 212   Born: November 15, 1979   Age: 26

YEAR	TM	LVL	AGE	W	L	SV	G	GS	IP	H	BB	SO	HR	GB%	BABIP	STUFF	WHIP	ERA	PERA	EQERA	EQH9	EQBB9	EQSO9	EQHR9	VORP	WXRL
2003	OTT	AAA	23	6	7	0	27	27	158.7	155	39	132	15	—	.289	5	1.22	3.97	4.83	4.95	9.5	2.7	6.0	1.3	11.0	—
2004	PAW	AAA	24	9	6	0	24	21	143.0	148	32	101	23	—	.289	-11	1.26	4.47	5.58	5.06	10.0	2.3	5.0	1.8	8.3	—
2005	CHR	AAA	25	0	2	0	10	3	29.3	34	8	14	2	41%	.323	-14	1.43	3.99	4.97	5.28	10.2	2.8	3.1	0.6	1.0	—
2005	OTT	AAA	25	4	2	0	12	9	51.0	52	8	41	6	45%	.313	2	1.18	4.41	4.71	4.89	9.8	1.6	5.4	1.3	3.9	—
2006	BAL	MLB	26	4	6	0	29	11	85.0	99	24	45	14	41%	.295	-6	1.43	5.15	5.39	5.44	10.3	2.4	4.8	1.4	2.4	0.6

Breakout: 18%   Improve: 40%   Collapse: 26%   Attrition: 3%   Comparables: Bryan Rekar, Frank Pastore, Nelson Briles

Stephens has settled in to the high minors as a pitcher who would be a bit below average in the majors. Still, he's just 26, and could pop up somewhere and have a year like Jeff Ballard's 1989, John Doherty's 1993, or Kirk Rueter's any-year. Sometimes, control artists make it, if for just a day, but ah, what a day.

TODD WILLIAMS   **Bats: R Throws: R**   Height: 6′ 3″   Weight: 210   Born: February 13, 1971   Age: 35

YEAR	TM	LVL	AGE	W	L	SV	G	GS	IP	H	BB	SO	HR	GB%	BABIP	STUFF	WHIP	ERA	PERA	EQERA	EQH9	EQBB9	EQSO9	EQHR9	VORP	WXRL
2003	DUR	AAA	32	3	2	4	56	0	69.7	55	14	36	2	—	.234	-10	0.99	1.55	4.18	3.48	8.5	2.6	3.3	0.4	15.2	—
2004	OTT	AAA	33	1	1	2	14	0	20.7	19	3	11	0	—	.279	-12	1.06	3.04	4.05	4.05	8.6	1.8	3.2	0.4	3.4	—
2004	OKL	AAA	33	2	2	9	27	0	29.7	37	7	11	2	—	.321	-33	1.48	3.03	5.22	6.75	10.7	2.8	2.1	0.9	-3.7	—
2004	BAL	MLB	33	2	0	0	29	0	31.3	26	9	13	2	68%	.247	-9	1.12	2.88	4.70	2.64	8.5	2.3	3.5	0.6	12.2	0.8
2005	BAL	MLB	34	5	5	1	72	0	76.3	72	26	38	5	66%	.276	-4	1.28	3.30	4.38	3.67	8.8	3.1	4.5	0.6	14.6	1.7
2006	BAL	MLB	35	2	2	1	47	0	50.7	57	18	23	4	59%	.304	-15	1.47	4.50	4.53	5.41	9.9	3.0	4.1	0.6	3.8	0.3

Breakout: 5%   Improve: 18%   Collapse: 51%   Attrition: 25%   Comparables: Jim Corsi, Bob Locker, Mike Munoz

Fooling us, Todd Williams did it again. He was the only Oriole reliever besides Ryan to post a WXRL above 1.0. He started out well down in the bullpen hierarchy and was close to losing his job after a rough patch in May/June, but righted himself and started moving up the totem pole as Reed, Kline, and Julio all flamed out ahead of him. Williams is still a soft-tossing reliever, however, and not a good bet to continue having real ERAs a run under his PERA.

Line Outs

Position/Player	TM	LVL	AGE	PA	R	2B	3B	HR	RBI	BB	SO	SB-CS	SPEED	BA/OBP/SLG	MLVR	EQBA/OBP/SLG	EQA	VORP
OF P. Bergeron*	BOW	AA	27	387	54	14	2	5	33	34	82	13-6	6.4	.296/.357/.391	.114	.262/.313/.340	.234	-5.4
OF W. Cliffords*	BOW	AA	24	371	36	19	1	1	31	51	68	8-7	4.9	.241/.345/.317	-.039	.231/.327/.302	.231	-19.2
C G. Gil	BAL	MLB	29	132	7	3	0	4	17	5	23	0-0	2.5	.192/.220/.312	-.401	.195/.235/.333	.201	-7.4
C E. Whiteside	OTT	AAA	25	343	28	22	1	4	27	21	65	1-3	3.2	.233/.283/.347	-.224	.211/.260/.313	.203	-18.6

Pitcher	TM	LVL	AGE	W	L	SV	IP	H	BB	SO	HR	GB%	BABIP	STUFF	WHIP	ERA	PERA	EQERA	EQH9	EQBB9	EQSO9	EQHR9	VORP
J. Grimsley	BAL	MLB	37	1	2	0	22.0	24	9	10	5	63%	.279	-29	1.50	5.73	6.55	5.73	9.8	3.7	4.1	2.0	-1.0
L. Ramirez	DEL	A	23	9	7	0	162.3	131	54	155	7	39%	.286	5	1.14	2.55	4.78	4.61	8.2	4.0	5.0	0.8	17.0
S. Reed	BAL	MLB	40	1	2	0	32.7	41	11	15	5	42%	.319	-21	1.59	6.61	5.67	5.94	10.8	3.0	4.1	1.4	-3.1
E. Rodriguez	OTT	AAA	23	2	3	3	62.0	57	36	51	2	35%	.311	-3	1.50	3.77	4.45	4.60	8.5	5.6	5.8	0.3	6.7

Peter Bergeron hopped from the Cubs to a spot with the Atlantic League's Nashua Pride, and then to the Orioles. Whatever reputation he once had as a prospect is long gone. **Woody Cliffords** looked promising in the low minors, but nothing's been the same for him since a 2004 foot injury sapped his speed and hobbled his stance. **Geronimo Gil** will exist until, sooner or later, the Orioles will realize that they don't have to accept zero production from their backup catcher, especially since they want to rest their starting catcher more often. **Eli Whiteside** got his first taste of the majors last year; his bat's always been on the low side of acceptable, and with Ramon Hernandez in front of him, he may never see the majors again.

Jason Grimsley was awful from the day the Orioles got him, although he is to be commended for an amazingly fast recovery from Tommy John surgery. Like all old men, he's gone to Arizona. **Luis Ramirez** made a big splash a year ago by striking out a record 12 batters in a row. Not everyone who sets a record is a hot prospect, and Ramirez certainly isn't one; he's old for his league, and doesn't come close to being overpowering with any of his pitches. **Steve Reed's** turn to the dark side happened around August 1 of 2004; his stats for the last two months of 2004 and all of 2005 form a pair. Age appears to have run him down; when the Orioles cut him in July, no one called. **Eddy Rodriguez,** the forgotten reliever, buried since mid-August of 2004. He was pretty bad to start the year, running his ERA up to 5.60 by mid-May. But a 14-game scoreless streak helped get it back down into the 3.00's by the end of the summer.

Boston Red Sox

As this is written, the Boston Red Sox do not have a shortstop, a center fielder, or a first baseman. They have three third basemen, seven starting pitchers, and two general managers. Their best hitter and one of their top starters have asked to be traded, and the team is trying to accommodate both players. Presumably some of this will be worked out, but it is hard to say when. It would be easy to blame all of this uncertainty on the unscheduled departure of general manager Theo Epstein, but in truth the Sox continue to be affected by the huge number of changes the club had to make after the 2004 championship. The 2004 team won it all as impending free agency meant that particular collection of talent's time together was due to expire, and champions or not, the Red Sox were forced to begin a rebuilding phase that has not yet ended.

Coming off a World Series title that made a fair bit of news, the Red Sox won just three fewer regular season games last season, but at times it seemed more like 30, considering the emaciated state of the pitching staff. The overriding problem was the health of Curt Schilling and Keith Foulke; the '04 team's most valuable pitchers were injured and/or ineffective the entire season. Overall, the team allowed 4.97 runs per game, about .21 runs worse than the league. In comparison, the 2004 team allowed 4.74, which was .27 runs *better* than the league, a regression of half a run per game.

The problem areas were Schilling, Foulke, and the rest of the bullpen. Table 1 summarizes these problems.

Instead of having two star pitchers combine for 310 excellent innings, the Red Sox got 140 bad innings from them. Foulke's collapse threw the rest of the bullpen into a jumble which was never properly sorted out. Though Red Sox starters other than Schilling performed just as well as they had the year before, the effective replacement

RED SOX PROSPECTUS

2005 record: 95–67; Second place, AL East; Lost to White Sox in Division Series

Pythagenport record: 90–72

Runs scored per game: 5.62 (1st in AL)

Runs allowed per game: 4.97 (11th in AL)

Team EqA: .276 (2nd in AL)

2005 Batters Age: 32.0 (2nd oldest in AL)

2005 Pitchers Age: 34.1 (2nd oldest in AL)

Ballpark: Fenway Park; Moderate hitter's park; Park Factor of 1.028

2005: The offensive juggernaut kept cranking, but pitching and defense took two steps back.

2006: Front office shenanigans and a vulnerable rotation will keep Red Sox Nation on tenterhooks.

of stars with replacement-level doppelgangers was a blow that few teams would have been able to withstand.

The twin failures of Schilling and Foulke were an unhappy reminder of the biggest story last off-season, the failure to re-sign Pedro Martinez. One of the optimistic scenarios advanced at the time was that, while they might not replace Pedro per se, the team could replace the combination of Pedro (who had an off year in 2004) and Derek Lowe (who had a horrible regular season) with the signings of David Wells, Matt Clement, and, for insurance, Wade Miller. This proved to be wishful thinking. Meanwhile, of the three relievers responsible for setting up Foulke—Mike Timlin, Alan Embree, and Matt Mantei—only Timlin was effective. As a result, the team had to give in-season tryouts to the likes of Scott Cassidy, Mike Remlinger, Chad Harville, Matt Perisho, Mike Stanton, and both Jessica and Ashlee Simpson. Blaine Neal made the Opening Day roster and threw eight bad innings, which is actually more work than any of the pitchers in the previous sentence managed. Late in the summer, the team called up Manny Delcarmen and Jonathan Papelbon to help right the ship, though only the latter contributed. By September, when he had to pull a starter, manager Terry Francona could only rely on Timlin and Papelbon to get batters out.

TABLE 1. RUNS PER GAME, 2005 VS. 2004

Year	Schilling	Other Starters	Foulke	Other Relievers
2004	3.26	4.62	2.17	4.27
2005	5.69	4.46	5.91	5.05

The offense remained the best in the league in 2005, although the production was concentrated in an increasingly small group of players. By September, Manny Ramirez and David Ortiz were getting little help. While the 2003 club included six players who hit 25 or more home runs, only three players managed to hit 15 last season. The 2003 starting infield managed 85 round-trippers, while the "slugger" among last year's inner quartet was Bill Mueller, with only ten. That the offense still managed to outscore the rest of the league is a testament to the strength of four star players: Ramirez and Ortiz, who combined for 92 home runs and 293 runs batted in, and Jason Varitek and Johnny Damon, who served as reliable accomplices.

On October 31, after a season in which so much had gone amiss, Theo Epstein chose not to continue as the Red Sox' general manager. Epstein's three-year stewardship had resulted in three playoff appearances, a world title, and a secure place as the most popular Red Sox executive in team history. The Red Sox have employed a lot of talent in their organization, including former and future GMs, thereby allowing Red Sox Nation and the Olde Towne scribes to credit or blame whomever they wish when something goes right or wrong. If you believe that Epstein was the irreplaceable genius of the operation, his departure was a disaster that will lead to a slow but inevitable deterioration of all the progress the organization has made in recent years. On the other hand, if you saw Epstein as an important cog in a smooth-running collection of hard-working baseball intellectuals, the team only needs to find another cog or two and keep rolling.

At this writing the latter seems to be the correct evaluation. There is as yet no evidence to suggest that the direction or philosophy of the team is going to change. Even without a general manager at the December winter meetings, the team took a measured, rational approach to meeting its needs, acquiring a starting second baseman, Mark Loretta for their backup catcher, Doug Mirabelli, and dealing their starting shortstop, the disappointing Edgar Renteria, for third baseman Andy Marte, who instantly became the team's best prospect since Nomar Garciaparra. As for the pitching staff, adding Beckett to the holdovers and slotting in Papelbon at some point should improve the rotation. By Christmas, the team added Rudy Seanez and Guillermo Mota to the pen. While both are risky propositions, they're still better bets than the likes of Embree and Mantei. The organization also has a few options in the system on the brink of promotion.

When Epstein was hired, he famously suggested that he wanted to build a "100 million dollar development machine." The farm system he inherited three years ago was widely considered among the most depleted in base-

ball, and it is vastly improved. Late summer saw the arrival of Papelbon, the most promising home-grown pitcher to reach the Red Sox in a decade. When the Marlins were looking to deal Josh Beckett, only the Red Sox had both the prospects and the ability to take on Mike Lowell's salary. If the BoSox continue to both to seed the major league team and to acquire players from other organizations, their revenue advantages will allow them to contend for titles yearly no matter who the general manager is. Adherence to the policy is more important than the specific individual administrating it.

For the second consecutive year, the Red Sox entered the off-season with perhaps the most coveted free agent on the market (first Pedro Martinez, then Johnny Damon), and each time they allowed a team from New York to outbid them. In late December, Damon signed with the Yankees, perhaps creating an eight game shift in the AL East's standings all by himself. The Red Sox wisely considered age and risk before stepping out of the bidding, and in both cases made the unpopular decision not to go beyond their salary line. Epstein is gone, but the practical approach lives on.

Looking ahead, things are still blurry. Last season's most-used starting infield (Kevin Millar, Mark Bellhorn, Bill Mueller, and Edgar Renteria) is scattered to the four winds, Kevin Youkilis seems likely to be as good as Mueller, although he'll get most of his playing time at first base. J. T. Snow will serve as insurance. Mark Loretta will play second, moving Tony Graffanino into a reserve role, and Mike Lowell will start at third. Marte would likely hit as well as any of their starting infielders, but he doesn't have a place to play above Pawtucket at the moment. The loss of Damon has caused the Red Sox to redouble their efforts to convince Manny Ramirez to stay, which is more likely to happen now that Miguel Tejada has decided to stay with the Orioles. Regardless, the team needs a center fielder and someone to platoon with Trot Nixon in right field. Even with Manny and Ortiz in the fold, the 2006 team is likely to decline on offense, so improvements in pitching and defense represent the club's most likely path to the playoffs. That makes the acquisition of a shortstop, still unresolved at this writing, key.

The 2006 Red Sox are still loaded with talent, and if they can find a way to fill a few holes before they get into the thick of the season, they should contend in what's become a very difficult division. The organization needs to leverage its strengths—a large revenue base, intelligent use of its resources, and increasing depth in the farm system—to combat the continuing turnover you can expect from a fairly old team.

HITTERS

ALEX CORA   **2B/SS   Bats: L Throws: R**   Height: 6' 0"   Weight: 180   Born: October 18, 1975   Age: 30

YEAR	TM	LVL	AGE	PA	R	2B	3B	HR	RBI	BB	SO	SB	CS	SPEED	BA	OBP	SLG	MLVR	EQBA	EQOBP	EQSLG	EQA	VORP	DEFENSE			
2003	LAN	MLB	27	505	39	24	3	4	34	16	59	4	2	5.0	.249	.287	.338	-.181	.258	.293	.353	.227	-7.1	123-2B	5		
2004	LAN	MLB	28	472	47	9	4	10	47	47	41	3	4	4.7	.264	.364	.380	.003	.270	.365	.390	.265	13.4	122-2B	3		
2005	CLE	MLB	29	156	11	5	2	1	8	5	18	6	0	6.4	.205	.250	.288	-.357	.221	.269	.303	.216	-5.7	22-SS	4	13-2B	3
2005	BOS	MLB	29	113	14	3	2	2	16	6	12	1	2	6.0	.269	.310	.394	-.094	.275	.327	.402	.249	0.1	24-2B	-2		
2006	BOS	MLB	30	279	33	12	2	4	26	14	30	5	2	5.1	.260	.307	.368	-.119	.258	.312	.375	.232	2.7	68-2B	1		

Breakout: 19%   Improve: 34%   Collapse: 38%   Attrition: 33%   Comparables: Bernie Allen, Denny Doyle, Marlon Anderson

The Indians gave Cora a two-year deal last year to play short, but the emergence of Jhonny Peralta sent him to the bench and then to the Red Sox, who could afford such a luxury on the second team. As a utility man, Cora's as good as you are going to find, but if he hits like he did in 2004, he's a borderline candidate to start, and with the departure of Renteria that just might happen. After last year, the Red Sox might be looking for defense first at the position, so Cora's bat might not be a hindrance.

JOHNNY DAMON   **CF   Bats: L Throws: L**   Height: 6' 2"   Weight: 190   Born: November 5, 1973   Age: 32

YEAR	TM	LVL	AGE	PA	R	2B	3B	HR	RBI	BB	SO	SB	CS	SPEED	BA	OBP	SLG	MLVR	EQBA	EQOBP	EQSLG	EQA	VORP	DEFENSE	
2003	BOS	MLB	29	684	103	32	6	12	67	68	74	30	6	7.3	.273	.345	.405	-.024	.269	.347	.401	.268	20.0	140-CF	5
2004	BOS	MLB	30	702	123	35	6	20	94	76	71	19	8	6.8	.304	.380	.477	.140	.298	.380	.474	.293	42.7	140-CF	8
2005	BOS	MLB	31	688	117	35	6	10	75	53	69	18	1	7.4	.316	.366	.439	.115	.317	.377	.451	.292	40.9	139-CF	-4
2006	NYA	MLB	32	651	93	29	5	13	69	56	67	15	4	6.2	.290	.352	.423	.049	.293	.365	.441	.274	29.4	152-CF	1

Breakout: 4%   Improve: 30%   Collapse: 20%   Attrition: 2%   Comparables: Ken Griffey Sr., Steve Finley, Kenny Lofton

As the season ended, the team's biggest quandary was how much money to offer Damon. Arguably Boston's best all-around player in 2004 and for the first half of 2005 (.343/.386/.473 at the All-Star break) his late season drop-off complicated any potential offer. A left shoulder injury sapped much of his power and was clearly bothering him by September. He needs to stay in center field to be a star. Signed to a four-year deal by the Yankees, Damon might get Mayor Bloomberg to go shaggy in years one and two, but hizzoner will be back to the business cut in years three and four.

CHRIS DURBIN   **OF   Bats: R Throws: R**   Height: 6' 0"   Weight: 180   Born: September 8, 1981   Age: 24

YEAR	TM	LVL	AGE	PA	R	2B	3B	HR	RBI	BB	SO	SB	CS	SPEED	BA	OBP	SLG	MLVR	EQBA	EQOBP	EQSLG	EQA	VORP	DEFENSE			
2004	SAR	A+	22	518	75	32	6	7	44	39	79	8	10	5.5	.279	.344	.417	.107	.260	.313	.403	.245	5.6	75-CF	-1	37-RF	1
2005	PME	AA	23	439	55	31	1	12	57	35	67	3	4	3.8	.282	.344	.457	.120	.257	.316	.423	.254	-2.8	82-LF	1		
2006	BOS	MLB	24	421	49	26	1	10	52	25	69	2	2	4.2	.261	.309	.412	-.058	.259	.314	.420	.243	0.8	100-LF	0		

Breakout: 21%   Improve: 44%   Collapse: 26%   Attrition: 21%   Comparables: Adam Johnson, Chris Aguila, Damon Hollins

Durbin is one of the outfield candidates for Pawtucket along with Murphy, Moss, and Stern, and has the advantage of being the only right-handed hitter in the group. A fine center fielder at Rice, he has moved to the corners so the organization could look at others in center. He is still considered a good defensive centerfielder, but he is going to have to hit better to make the big club. This is an organization-wide problem-a surplus of middle-of-the-diamond players who have not yet shown they can hit enough to be better than bench players in the major leagues.

JACOBY ELLSBURY   **CF   Bats: L Throws: L**   Height: 6' 1"   Weight: 185   Born: September 11, 1983   Age: 22

YEAR	TM	LVL	AGE	PA	R	2B	3B	HR	RBI	BB	SO	SB	CS	SPEED	BA	OBP	SLG	MLVR	EQBA	EQOBP	EQSLG	EQA	VORP	DEFENSE	
2005	LOW	A-	21	165	28	3	5	1	19	24	20	23	3	8.2	.317	.418	.432	.241	.254	.332	.339	.252	-1.6	26-CF	-1
2006	BOS	MLB	22	430	56	12	5	0	24	34	65	29	8	5.5	.258	.318	.319	-.165	.256	.323	.325	.230	-1.6	102-CF	-2

Breakout: 14%   Improve: 33%   Collapse: 40%   Attrition: 10%   Comparables: Kennard Jones, Endy Chavez, Richard Thompson

With their first pick (23rd overall) in the 2005 draft, the Red Sox took Ellsbury, who led Oregon State to its first College World Series appearance since 1952. Inevitably, the speedy centerfielder drew comparisons to Damon. Like Damon, he has fine on-base skills, good speed and gap power to go along with good defensive range and a below-average arm. Expect a rapid advancement through the lower minors, but how far he goes beyond that depends on his bat.

TONY GRAFFANINO   **INF**   **Bats: R Throws: R**   Height: 6′ 1″   Weight: 195   Born: June 6, 1972   Age: 34

YEAR	TM	LVL	AGE	PA	R	2B	3B	HR	RBI	BB	SO	SB	CS	SPEED	BA	OBP	SLG	MLVR	EQBA	EQOBP	EQSLG	EQA	VORP	DEFENSE			
2003	CHA	MLB	31	278	51	15	3	7	23	24	37	8	0	7.4	.260	.331	.428	-.008	.255	.330	.433	.268	12.9	26-SS	1	23-2B	2
2004	KCA	MLB	32	310	37	11	0	3	26	27	38	10	2	5.8	.263	.332	.335	-.137	.259	.332	.328	.244	4.1	72-2B	13		
2005	KCA	MLB	33	215	29	5	2	3	18	22	28	3	1	5.4	.298	.377	.393	.060	.307	.394	.418	.287	8.5	19-2B	-2	15-1B	0
2005	BOS	MLB	33	200	39	12	1	4	20	9	23	4	1	5.7	.319	.355	.457	.124	.319	.365	.476	.288	12.1	48-2B	-3		
2006	BOS	MLB	34	341	45	16	2	5	34	28	44	6	2	5.6	.279	.343	.394	-.013	.277	.348	.401	.256	9.7	82-2B	0		

Breakout: 18%   Improve: 39%   Collapse: 35%   Attrition: 24%   Comparables: Johnny Temple, Bill Pecota, Ed Charles

A fine utility infielder. Like Denny Doyle in 1975, Graffanino came to the Red Sox in mid-season, won the second base job, and played well for a playoff-bound team. In Doyle's case, it took the Red Sox two more years to realize his half-season had been a fluke. Though he's a much better player than Doyle, Graffy won't get the same courtesy. Though re-signed to a one-year deal, he's now behind Mark Loretta on the depth charts.

GABE KAPLER   **OF**   **Bats: R Throws: R**   Height: 6′ 2″   Weight: 210   Born: July 31, 1975   Age: 30

YEAR	TM	LVL	AGE	PA	R	2B	3B	HR	RBI	BB	SO	SB	CS	SPEED	BA	OBP	SLG	MLVR	EQBA	EQOBP	EQSLG	EQA	VORP	DEFENSE			
2003	COL	MLB	27	75	10	2	0	0	4	8	18	2	0	4.7	.224	.307	.254	-.307	.197	.284	.227	.199	-3.9				
2003	BOS	MLB	27	172	29	11	1	4	23	14	23	4	2	5.7	.291	.349	.449	.073	.288	.351	.442	.272	5.0	25-RF	-2	12-LF	-1
2004	BOS	MLB	28	309	51	14	1	6	33	15	49	5	4	6.1	.272	.311	.390	-.130	.267	.310	.382	.240	-3.7	66-RF	1	10-CF	0
2005	BOS	MLB	29	103	15	7	0	1	9	3	15	1	0	6.0	.247	.282	.351	-.210	.250	.298	.344	.230	-2.6	16-RF	2		
2006	BOS	MLB	30	218	26	11	1	4	22	14	35	3	2	6.0	.256	.308	.386	-.097	.254	.313	.394	.237	-1.8	55-RF	0		

Breakout: 35%   Improve: 56%   Collapse: 26%   Attrition: 35%   Comparables: Mark Smith, Jolbert Cabrera, Tom Paciorek

After playing an important role for the 2004 champions, Kapler took a job in Japan for more money and more playing time. He played horribly and not often, and was back with the Red Sox on August 1. An Achilles injury ended his season early and will keep him out until May or June. Trot Nixon's inability to hit lefties combined with the fragility and age of the team's three starting outfielders opens up a potential role for a fourth outfielder who can handle southpaws, but the Red Sox won't wait for Kapler, who was released in November. The women of Red Sox Nation will again weep over the absence of "Gabe the Babe."

JED LOWRIE   **2B/SS**   **Bats: B Throws: R**   Height: 6′ 0″   Weight: 180   Born: April 17, 1984   Age: 22

YEAR	TM	LVL	AGE	PA	R	2B	3B	HR	RBI	BB	SO	SB	CS	SPEED	BA	OBP	SLG	MLVR	EQBA	EQOBP	EQSLG	EQA	VORP	DEFENSE			
2005	LOW	A-	21	238	36	12	0	4	32	34	30	7	5	5.0	.328	.429	.448	.285	.258	.338	.361	.248	9.6	40-SS	-4	11-2B	0
2006	BOS	MLB	22	465	54	20	1	7	42	38	70	6	4	4.4	.245	.311	.348	-.146	.243	.316	.355	.228	4.3	110-SS	-5		

Breakout: 12%   Improve: 28%   Collapse: 44%   Attrition: 10%   Comparables: Dominic Rich, Mike Edwards, Samuel Taylor

Lowrie was the Pac-10 player of the year for Stanford in 2004, but an off season allowed the Red Sox to take him with the 33rd pick in the draft. Though he was a second baseman in college, the Red Sox like to challenge their prospects defensively and moved Lowrie to short. The organization liked what it saw and will leave him there for now. The switch-hitter excelled on offense, leading the NY-Penn League in on-base-percentage. Lowrie is an advanced player, so expect him to move quickly through the system.

ALEJANDRO MACHADO   **2B**   **Bats: B Throws: R**   Height: 6′ 0″   Weight: 160   Born: April 26, 1982   Age: 24

YEAR	TM	LVL	AGE	PA	R	2B	3B	HR	RBI	BB	SO	SB	CS	SPEED	BA	OBP	SLG	MLVR	EQBA	EQOBP	EQSLG	EQA	VORP	DEFENSE			
2003	WIC	AA	21	329	59	13	5	1	31	34	45	19	9	7.8	.287	.368	.377	.072	.272	.344	.372	.256	8.2	75-2B	7		
2003	HUN	AA	21	172	14	4	1	0	13	15	24	11	1	6.2	.226	.302	.265	-.194	.208	.272	.245	.202	-13.1	38-2B	2		
2004	BRV	A+	22	210	34	10	2	1	19	22	27	11	6	6.2	.355	.424	.446	.341	.330	.392	.414	.283	21.1	38-SS	-5		
2004	HAR	AA	22	395	54	5	4	4	26	41	39	19	9	6.3	.280	.365	.353	-.011	.258	.334	.324	.240	-0.7	77-2B	9	11-SS	2
2005	PAW	AAA	23	423	60	17	2	3	43	32	47	21	4	6.6	.300	.359	.379	.004	.279	.337	.353	.252	5.9	63-2B	4	39-SS	4
2006	BOS	MLB	24	461	61	21	3	3	37	33	56	16	5	5.9	.274	.331	.360	-.079	.272	.336	.367	.244	8.1	109-2B	4		

Breakout: 19%   Improve: 38%   Collapse: 21%   Attrition: 12%   Comparables: Luis Rivas, Rob Andrews, Toby Harrah

The Venezuelan was originally signed by the Braves, but has also spent time in the Royals, Brewers, and Expos farm systems. His versatility and baserunning got him to Boston at the end of the season and earned him a spot on the post-season roster. His ability to play both the infield and outfield makes him an asset in the days of bloated bullpens. Red Sox fans who still haven't quite recovered from watching Cesar Crespo are appropriately cautious.

KEVIN MILLAR   **1B/OF**   **Bats: R Throws: R**   Height: 6' 0"   Weight: 210   Born: September 24, 1971   Age: 34

YEAR	TM	LVL	AGE	PA	R	2B	3B	HR	RBI	BB	SO	SB	CS	SPEED	BA	OBP	SLG	MLVR	EQBA	EQOBP	EQSLG	EQA	VORP	DEFENSE			
2003	BOS	MLB	31	618	83	30	1	25	96	60	108	3	2	4.2	.276	.348	.472	.082	.271	.349	.470	.280	19.0	94-1B	7	16-LF	0
2004	BOS	MLB	32	588	74	36	0	18	74	57	91	1	1	3.6	.297	.383	.474	.136	.293	.379	.473	.293	28.5	57-1B	-3	48-RF	-1
2005	BOS	MLB	33	519	57	28	1	9	50	54	74	0	1	3.4	.272	.355	.399	.005	.272	.363	.408	.273	7.1	90-1B	11	14-LF	-2
2006	*BAL*	*MLB*	*34*	*442*	*51*	*20*	*1*	*13*	*59*	*47*	*65*	*1*	*1*	*4.1*	*.265*	*.348*	*.426*	*.027*	*.269*	*.359*	*.447*	*.271*	*10.0*	*105-1B*	*2*		

Breakout: 15%   Improve: 40%   Collapse: 27%   Attrition: 20%   Comparables: Ray Boone, Jeff Conine, Pedro Guerrero

No player was blamed more than Millar for the team's failure to repeat. The poster child for the fun-loving clubhouses of 2003 ("Cowboy Up") and 2004 ("The Idiots"), the fans grew less enamored of his hijinks once his slugging percentage dropped below .400. Terry Francona was accused of catering to Millar's veteran status, perhaps to keep his friend Manny Ramirez happy, or maybe because Millar had some incriminating photos of Francona in a leisure suit. It's hard to fault Millar for that, but he's a mediocre first baseman who hits like a shortstop. Red Sox fans are fickle, but when the dust settles, Millar's feats with the 2003 and 2004 teams will be fondly remembered. Signed to a one-year contract by the Orioles, he'll blend seamlessly into their cadre of "We know you do something but we're not sure what it is" players.

DOUG MIRABELLI   **C**   **Bats: R Throws: R**   Height: 6' 1"   Weight: 215   Born: October 18, 1970   Age: 35

YEAR	TM	LVL	AGE	PA	R	2B	3B	HR	RBI	BB	SO	SB	CS	SPEED	BA	OBP	SLG	MLVR	EQBA	EQOBP	EQSLG	EQA	VORP	DEFENSE	
2003	BOS	MLB	32	176	23	13	0	6	18	11	36	0	0	4.2	.258	.307	.448	-.042	.255	.309	.441	.255	4.2	43-C	-4
2004	BOS	MLB	33	182	27	12	0	9	32	19	46	0	0	3.1	.281	.368	.525	.165	.274	.363	.522	.296	13.4	42-C	-12
2005	BOS	MLB	34	152	16	7	0	6	18	14	48	2	0	4.5	.228	.309	.412	-.088	.224	.316	.418	.255	3.1	35-C	2
2006	*SDN*	*MLB*	*35*	*146*	*15*	*7*	*0*	*5*	*19*	*16*	*45*	*2*	*0*	*4.1*	*.228*	*.319*	*.404*	*-.093*	*.237*	*.327*	*.435*	*.256*	*3.7*	*38-C*	*-2*

Breakout: 16%   Improve: 27%   Collapse: 50%   Attrition: 49%   Comparables: Bob Brenly, Phil Roof, Todd Pratt

The backup catcher goes by the nickname "The Stud Who Hits Bombs" on the popular Sons of Sam Horn message board. Last season he hit fewer bombs, and also lost a few weeks to a wrist injury. Despite being Wakefield's designated catcher, he didn't lead the league in passed balls for the first time since 2002. He's a fine reserve who would hit better if he was used in a strict platoon against lefties. He'll get the chance to start in San Diego, but he might find Petco Park less to his liking than Fenway.

BRANDON MOSS   **RF**   **Bats: L Throws: R**   Height: 6' 0"   Weight: 180   Born: September 16, 1983   Age: 22

YEAR	TM	LVL	AGE	PA	R	2B	3B	HR	RBI	BB	SO	SB	CS	SPEED	BA	OBP	SLG	MLVR	EQBA	EQOBP	EQSLG	EQA	VORP	DEFENSE			
2003	LOW	A-	19	252	29	15	4	7	34	15	53	7	5	5.8	.237	.290	.430	.046	.204	.246	.389	.219	-30.5	59-RF	2		
2004	AUG	A	20	490	66	25	6	13	101	46	75	19	8	5.6	.339	.402	.515	.349	.302	.354	.448	.277	17.4	92-RF	4	12-LF	0
2005	PME	AA	21	567	87	31	4	16	61	53	129	6	3	5.7	.268	.337	.441	.079	.247	.314	.410	.252	-6.6	126-RF	-1		
2006	*BOS*	*MLB*	*22*	*544*	*67*	*32*	*3*	*15*	*67*	*39*	*105*	*7*	*3*	*5.2*	*.266*	*.322*	*.431*	*-.008*	*.264*	*.327*	*.440*	*.255*	*4.7*	*128-RF*	*1*		

Breakout: 22%   Improve: 46%   Collapse: 26%   Attrition: 6%   Comparables: Laynce Nix, Cody Ross, Jody Gerut

A great season with Augusta in 2004 moved Moss high on the team's prospect list, but he found Double-A to be much more challenging. Still, he led the team in hits, runs and total bases, and also had 14 assists in right field. The Red Sox have a lot of candidates for the Pawtucket outfield, so Moss will likely begin the year back in Portland. A disappointing showing in the Arizona Fall League did not help his cause. He needs a big year to get back on track.

BILL MUELLER   **3B**   **Bats: B Throws: R**   Height: 5' 10"   Weight: 180   Born: March 17, 1971   Age: 35

YEAR	TM	LVL	AGE	PA	R	2B	3B	HR	RBI	BB	SO	SB	CS	SPEED	BA	OBP	SLG	MLVR	EQBA	EQOBP	EQSLG	EQA	VORP	DEFENSE			
2003	BOS	MLB	32	596	85	45	5	19	85	59	77	1	4	4.2	.326	.398	.540	.294	.324	.399	.541	.313	57.8	124-3B	4		
2004	BOS	MLB	33	460	75	27	1	12	57	51	56	2	2	4.7	.283	.365	.446	.056	.277	.363	.441	.279	15.3	92-3B	6	13-2B	-2
2005	BOS	MLB	34	590	69	34	3	10	62	59	74	0	0	3.8	.295	.369	.430	.089	.296	.379	.437	.286	24.8	137-3B	6		
2006	*LAN*	*MLB*	*35*	*431*	*52*	*22*	*1*	*10*	*52*	*49*	*56*	*1*	*1*	*4.4*	*.278*	*.365*	*.429*	*.053*	*.285*	*.371*	*.448*	*.277*	*20.1*	*102-3B*	*1*		

Breakout: 12%   Improve: 32%   Collapse: 40%   Attrition: 18%   Comparables: Bill Doran, Bill Madlock, Ray Boone

Despite nagging injuries, Mueller played the second highest number of games in the field in his career, and had a 6.5 WARP3, second only to his great 2003 season. Although his professional style doesn't garner a lot of attention, he's been one of the best players on the Red Sox every year, and they've never paid him more than $2.5 million. The combination of his age and the acquisition of the younger Mike Lowell made Mueller expendable. Signed to a two-year deal with the Dodgers, where he'll spend his golden years with fellow former Giant Ned Colletti.

DAVID MURPHY CF Bats: L Throws: L Height: 6′ 4″ Weight: 192 Born: October 18, 1981 Age: 24

YEAR	TM	LVL	AGE	PA	R	2B	3B	HR	RBI	BB	SO	SB	CS	SPEED	BA	OBP	SLG	MLVR	EQBA	EQOBP	EQSLG	EQA	VORP	DEFENSE
2003	SAR	A+	21	173	18	5	1	1	18	20	33	6	2	5.4	.242	.329	.307	-.044	.230	.306	.320	.227	-6.1	40-CF -1
2004	SAR	A+	22	297	35	11	0	4	38	25	46	3	5	4.0	.261	.323	.346	-.030	.233	.288	.324	.215	-12.3	56-CF -2
2005	PME	AA	23	534	71	25	4	14	75	46	83	13	6	5.8	.275	.337	.430	.069	.254	.317	.400	.249	5.4	129-CF -15
2006	BOS	MLB	24	472	53	23	2	7	46	32	75	8	4	4.8	.252	.304	.362	-.137	.250	.309	.369	.229	-2.6	112-CF -5

Breakout: 22% Improve: 41% Collapse: 28% Attrition: 12% Comparables: Woody Cliffords, Doug Clark, Jake Weber

The Red Sox' first pick in the 2003 draft, Murphy has trudged through the minor leagues. His offense picked up considerably in May after a rough start. Coupled with his impressive showing in the Arizona Fall League (.319/.354/.527), Murphy will undoubtedly get a full-time gig in Pawtucket, with hopes of a role with the big club in 2007. The team believes the power potential is there: he's strong enough and hits the ball a long way, he just needs to center the bat on the ball more often. He already plays major league quality defense in center field. A good year at the plate would help him shed the fourth outfielder label.

TROT NIXON OF Bats: L Throws: L Height: 6′ 2″ Weight: 196 Born: April 11, 1974 Age: 32

YEAR	TM	LVL	AGE	PA	R	2B	3B	HR	RBI	BB	SO	SB	CS	SPEED	BA	OBP	SLG	MLVR	EQBA	EQOBP	EQSLG	EQA	VORP	DEFENSE
2003	BOS	MLB	29	512	81	24	6	28	87	65	96	4	2	5.7	.306	.396	.578	.326	.302	.398	.576	.321	42.2	119-RF -3
2004	BOS	MLB	30	167	24	9	1	6	23	15	24	0	0	4.6	.315	.377	.510	.193	.308	.376	.500	.298	10.6	34-RF -1
2005	BOS	MLB	31	470	64	29	1	13	67	53	59	2	1	4.8	.275	.357	.446	.073	.275	.367	.455	.285	15.2	106-RF 8
2006	BOS	MLB	32	413	56	22	2	15	59	48	60	2	1	4.9	.284	.369	.482	.146	.282	.375	.491	.288	18.3	98-RF 0

Breakout: 5% Improve: 21% Collapse: 39% Attrition: 17% Comparables: Roger Maris, David Justice, Cliff Floyd

Nixon had a terrible September, but Boston's lack of a reliable backup put him in the lineup against left-handers, who all might as well be Lefty Grove to Trot. The question with Nixon is whether his off-year was symptomatic of his injuries or represented an actual decline in his skills. For many people in New England, he is the symbol of the gritty guy with the dirty uniform, in contrast to Manny Ramirez, team space case. But Nixon is similarly prone to the occasional baserunning or defensive gaffe, and he spends part of ever year on the DL. If Nixon can get healthy, he may have another 2003 in him. If it isn't this year, he likely won't be in Boston in 2007.

JOHN OLERUD 1B Bats: L Throws: L Height: 6′ 5″ Weight: 220 Born: August 5, 1968 Age: 37

YEAR	TM	LVL	AGE	PA	R	2B	3B	HR	RBI	BB	SO	SB	CS	SPEED	BA	OBP	SLG	MLVR	EQBA	EQOBP	EQSLG	EQA	VORP	DEFENSE
2003	SEA	MLB	34	632	64	35	0	10	83	84	67	0	1	3.1	.269	.372	.390	.032	.276	.383	.400	.278	13.0	145-1B 11
2004	SEA	MLB	35	311	29	13	1	5	22	40	41	0	0	3.7	.245	.354	.360	-.069	.251	.361	.378	.266	1.2	72-1B 7
2004	NYA	MLB	35	188	16	7	0	4	26	21	20	0	0	2.9	.280	.367	.396	-.022	.284	.374	.407	.276	2.7	45-1B 0
2005	BOS	MLB	36	192	18	7	0	7	37	16	20	0	0	3.1	.289	.344	.451	.072	.288	.354	.459	.280	5.9	49-1B 5
2006	BOS	MLB	37	148	15	7	0	3	19	14	17	0	0	3.8	.271	.342	.406	-.004	.269	.347	.414	.258	1.7	39-1B 1

Breakout: 13% Improve: 31% Collapse: 37% Attrition: 57% Comparables: Wally Joyner, Chris Chambliss, Tino Martinez

Olerud was signed as insurance after Roberto Petagine got hurt in the spring, then spent much of the season out-hitting Millar. By the end of the season, Francona had finally seen the obvious, at which point Olerud stopped hitting. Now retired, Olerud finishes with a fine career line of .295/.398/.465 and 2239 career hits. There are first basemen in the Hall of Fame with lesser credentials than Olerud, including modern players like Orlando Cepeda and Tony Perez. In his prime, he hit for a high average with mid-range power and lots of walks, a devastating combination, but would have had a better reputation if his offensive skills were concentrated in just one area, like Tony Gwynn. Still, not bad for a player Cito Gaston said wouldn't make it.

DAVID ORTIZ DH Bats: L Throws: L Height: 6′ 4″ Weight: 230 Born: November 18, 1975 Age: 30

YEAR	TM	LVL	AGE	PA	R	2B	3B	HR	RBI	BB	SO	SB	CS	SPEED	BA	OBP	SLG	MLVR	EQBA	EQOBP	EQSLG	EQA	VORP	DEFENSE
2003	BOS	MLB	27	509	79	39	2	31	101	58	83	0	0	4.2	.288	.369	.592	.284	.283	.372	.592	.314	40.7	42-1B -1
2004	BOS	MLB	28	669	94	47	3	41	139	75	133	0	0	4.0	.301	.380	.603	.305	.296	.378	.602	.320	60.8	29-1B -2
2005	BOS	MLB	29	713	119	40	1	47	148	102	124	1	0	3.9	.300	.397	.604	.366	.302	.409	.623	.336	75.6	
2006	BOS	MLB	30	695	107	39	1	43	130	88	122	0	0	3.8	.292	.384	.578	.296	.290	.390	.589	.314	61.0	162-DH

Breakout: 4% Improve: 24% Collapse: 44% Attrition: 0% Comparables: Fred McGriff, Carlos Delgado, Willie McCovey

(continued next page)

David Ortiz *(continued)*

Big Papi has reached Orr/Bird/Brady status in Boston with his great statistics and numerous game-ending homers over the past few seasons. Having such a great player as your DH comes with a cost—the ability to rest some of your older, banged-up, veterans over the course of the season by keeping them off the field. Ramirez's DH appearances the past four seasons: 50, 26, 18, and two. It's a small price to pay.

DUSTIN PEDROIA 2B **Bats: R Throws: R** Height: 5' 9" Weight: 180 Born: August 17, 1983 Age: 22

YEAR	TM	LVL	AGE	PA	R	2B	3B	HR	RBI	BB	SO	SB	CS	SPEED	BA	OBP	SLG	MLVR	EQBA	EQOBP	EQSLG	EQA	VORP	DEFENSE	
2004	SAR	A+	20	127	23	8	3	2	14	13	4	0	2	5.5	.336	.417	.523	.398	.318	.381	.518	.302	15.2	30-SS	-1
2005	PME	AA	21	296	39	19	2	8	40	34	26	7	3	4.9	.324	.409	.508	.318	.302	.381	.480	.295	26.9	56-2B	-1
2005	PAW	AAA	21	239	39	9	1	5	24	24	17	1	0	5.0	.255	.356	.382	-.029	.237	.326	.359	.245	0.8	38-2B	6
2006	BOS	MLB	22	551	75	36	3	12	68	47	45	5	2	4.9	.299	.365	.458	.122	.297	.370	.467	.280	33.6	129-2B	3

Breakout: 19%   Improve: 45%   Collapse: 21%   Attrition: 10%   Comparables: Gary Sheffield, Ron Hunt, Marcus Giles

The team's first pick in the 2004 draft, Pedroia sped through four levels to get to the doorstop of the major leagues. He played shortstop at Arizona State, but the team moved him to second base last year, pairing him with Hanley Ramirez in Portland. His only above-average tool is his bat, but he continues to impress with it. His hitting slowed down at bit in Pawtucket when he was hit by a pitch in the left wrist. Pedroia was due to compete for the second base job before the Mark Loretta acquisition. He might see time back at shortstop, but more likely will spend a full year at Pawtucket.

ROBERTO PETAGINE 1B **Bats: L Throws: L** Height: 6' 1" Weight: 215 Born: June 2, 1971 Age: 35

YEAR	TM	LVL	AGE	PA	R	2B	3B	HR	RBI	BB	SO	SB	CS	SPEED	BA	OBP	SLG	MLVR	EQBA	EQOBP	EQSLG	EQA	VORP	DEFENSE	
2003	YOM	JPL	32	408	81	17	0	34	72	77	5	1	70	4.1	.323	.451	.683	.598	.305	.395	.502	.305	39.5		
2004	YOM	JPL	33	463	70	17	0	29	84	75	76	2	0	4.3	.290	.413	.561	.352	.276	.369	.418	.275	19.4		
2005	PAW	AAA	34	336	54	18	2	20	69	63	46	0	1	3.7	.327	.452	.635	.518	.245	.351	.424	.270	5.3	59-1B	5
2005	BOS	MLB	34	36	4	2	0	1	9	4	5	0	0	2.7	.281	.361	.438	.074	.290	.389	.452	.292	1.2		
2006	BOS	MLB	35	247	29	11	1	8	33	30	44	0	0	4.1	.262	.354	.432	.043	.261	.360	.440	.269	5.0	61-1B	1

Breakout: 14%   Improve: 39%   Collapse: 39%   Attrition: 40%   Comparables: J. T. Snow, Phil Cavarretta, Johnny Grubb

Signed by the Red Sox in February, a knee injury in March could not have come at a worse time, as it led to the club signing John Olerud. That meant Petagine was stuck in Pawtucket for most of the season. Millar's general ineptitude cried out for a replacement, but Francona did not see fit to give a role to Petagine no matter how well he hit in Triple-A. Analysts have long championed Petagine as a player never given the shot he deserved, but that battle has long since been lost and it's time to find a new cause.

ANDREW PINCKNEY 3B **Bats: B Throws: R** Height: 6' 1" Weight: 195 Born: April 7, 1982 Age: 24

YEAR	TM	LVL	AGE	PA	R	2B	3B	HR	RBI	BB	SO	SB	CS	SPEED	BA	OBP	SLG	MLVR	EQBA	EQOBP	EQSLG	EQA	VORP	DEFENSE			
2004	LOW	A-	22	271	24	9	1	3	25	22	75	2	8	3.1	.275	.339	.357	.020	.221	.272	.290	.200	-39.2	27-1B	2	16-3B	-2
2005	GRN	A	23	556	91	33	9	21	98	36	78	6	0	6.2	.311	.362	.535	.266	.254	.292	.426	.246	9.2	91-3B	-1		
2006	BOS	MLB	24	453	47	25	2	8	50	20	91	3	2	4.4	.244	.282	.373	-.167	.242	.286	.380	.219	-6.6	107-3B	-2		

Breakout: 20%   Improve: 44%   Collapse: 31%   Attrition: 8%   Comparables: Jeff Phelps, Antoin Gray, Trevor Mote

A late-round pick in 2003, his great 2005 season in is tempered by the fact that he was old for the Sally League. In an organization with few impact bats, Pinckney will have every opportunity to advance. A so-so third baseman (he's led his league in errors the last two years), the Red Sox have considered trying him at catcher, but he might end up playing first.

HANLEY RAMIREZ SS **Bats: B Throws: R** Height: 6' 1" Weight: 170 Born: December 23, 1983 Age: 22

YEAR	TM	LVL	AGE	PA	R	2B	3B	HR	RBI	BB	SO	SB	CS	SPEED	BA	OBP	SLG	MLVR	EQBA	EQOBP	EQSLG	EQA	VORP	DEFENSE	
2003	AUG	A	19	459	69	24	3	8	50	32	73	36	13	7.4	.275	.327	.403	.091	.254	.293	.386	.238	3.7	102-SS	-9
2004	SAR	A+	20	261	33	8	4	1	24	17	39	12	7	6.4	.310	.364	.389	.123	.285	.328	.372	.247	7.2	60-SS	-8
2004	PME	AA	20	139	26	7	2	5	15	10	26	12	3	8.4	.310	.360	.512	.199	.278	.326	.459	.269	8.1	32-SS	0
2005	PME	AA	21	514	66	21	7	6	52	39	62	26	13	6.5	.271	.335	.385	.005	.252	.313	.361	.240	3.9	109-SS	3
2006	FLO	MLB	22	499	62	24	4	6	44	33	75	20	8	5.8	.258	.313	.367	-.132	.264	.317	.389	.241	10.7	118-SS	-3

Breakout: 25%   Improve: 47%   Collapse: 25%   Attrition: 4%   Comparables: Kenny Perez, Felipe Lopez, Jason Bourgeois

Ramirez was the consensus best positional prospect in the system for a few years, and he is still young (22 this year). That said, he has yet to have a big year at the plate, was passed by no-tools Pedroia, and the team's signing of Renteria to a four-year contract last winter was not exactly a show of confidence. He still has the physical skills to be a fine defensive shortstop, particularly a great arm. We still don't know what he's going to become. There's no indication that he is ready for the major leagues, but the Marlins are apparently going to let him a try.

MANNY RAMIREZ **LF** **Bats: R Throws: R** Height: 6' 0" Weight: 200 Born: May 30, 1972 Age: 34

YEAR	TM	LVL	AGE	PA	R	2B	3B	HR	RBI	BB	SO	SB	CS	SPEED	BA	OBP	SLG	MLVR	EQBA	EQOBP	EQSLG	EQA	VORP	DEFENSE
2003	BOS	MLB	31	679	117	36	1	37	104	97	94	3	1	3.6	.325	.427	.587	.404	.321	.428	.584	.337	67.8	119-LF -8
2004	BOS	MLB	32	663	108	44	0	43	130	82	124	2	4	3.3	.308	.397	.613	.352	.305	.398	.612	.326	57.7	121-LF -9
2005	BOS	MLB	33	650	112	30	1	45	144	80	119	1	0	4.0	.292	.388	.594	.333	.296	.399	.614	.330	59.9	139-LF -13
2006	BOS	MLB	34	635	95	32	1	39	118	76	110	1	1	3.6	.296	.386	.570	.292	.293	.392	.581	.314	49.7	148-LF -11

Breakout: 4%   Improve: 21%   Collapse: 31%   Attrition: 2%   Comparables: Sammy Sosa, Frank Robinson, Kevin Mitchell

Yawn. The usual mid-season soap opera marred Ramirez's typical Hall of Fame offensive season. Ramirez started slowly, but his problems were almost solely due to his uncharacteristic inability to hit left-handed pitchers. He was hitting just .163/.290/.314 in 86 at bats at the All-Star break against southpaws, before rebounding to hit .316/.433/.759 against them in the second half (for the season he was .236/.358/.527). He has been passed by David Ortiz in the hearts of Red Sox Nation, but Ramirez remains unsurpassed among AL hitters.

EDGAR RENTERIA **SS** **Bats: R Throws: R** Height: 6' 1" Weight: 160 Born: August 7, 1975 Age: 30

YEAR	TM	LVL	AGE	PA	R	2B	3B	HR	RBI	BB	SO	SB	CS	SPEED	BA	OBP	SLG	MLVR	EQBA	EQOBP	EQSLG	EQA	VORP	DEFENSE
2003	SLN	MLB	27	660	96	47	1	13	100	65	54	34	7	6.2	.330	.394	.480	.260	.328	.392	.482	.304	68.3	151-SS 1
2004	SLN	MLB	28	636	84	37	0	10	72	39	78	17	11	5.6	.287	.327	.401	-.005	.287	.328	.401	.253	20.2	146-SS -9
2005	BOS	MLB	29	686	100	36	4	8	70	55	100	9	4	5.8	.276	.335	.385	-.048	.278	.347	.392	.260	19.6	147-SS -21
2006	ATL	MLB	30	636	84	33	3	10	64	54	79	14	5	5.5	.284	.347	.405	-.005	.284	.347	.417	.261	27.2	148-SS -8

Breakout: 15%   Improve: 39%   Collapse: 21%   Attrition: 5%   Comparables: Dave Concepcion, Paul Molitor, Steve Sax

Well, that didn't really work out, now did it? Inked to a four-year, $40 million deal last winter, the Red Sox hoped that his 2002–2003 gains were real, but he has now had consecutive mediocre seasons at the plate. He also had a dreadful year in the field, leading the majors with 30 errors while showing little range. The Red Sox gave up seven wins just at this single position. The Braves are hoping that he can return to his old form. The Red Sox figured it was not going to happen in Boston and wisely cut bait.

KELLY SHOPPACH **C** **Bats: R Throws: R** Height: 5' 11" Weight: 210 Born: April 29, 1980 Age: 26

YEAR	TM	LVL	AGE	PA	R	2B	3B	HR	RBI	BB	SO	SB	CS	SPEED	BA	OBP	SLG	MLVR	EQBA	EQOBP	EQSLG	EQA	VORP	DEFENSE
2003	PME	AA	23	385	45	30	2	12	60	35	83	0	0	3.7	.282	.353	.488	.137	.247	.312	.445	.259	11.7	82-C 11
2004	PAW	AAA	24	453	62	25	0	22	64	46	138	0	0	3.6	.233	.320	.461	.002	.210	.295	.416	.244	1.3	97-C 0
2005	PAW	AAA	25	432	60	16	0	26	75	46	116	0	0	3.5	.253	.352	.507	.125	.226	.317	.444	.260	11.1	83-C 10
2006	BOS	MLB	26	375	42	18	1	16	53	32	101	0	0	3.5	.233	.307	.436	-.051	.232	.311	.445	.250	7.7	90-C 2

Breakout: 28%   Improve: 48%   Collapse: 25%   Attrition: 18%   Comparables: Dave Ross, Pete LaForest, Bob Tillman

Shoppach is a top-shelf defensive catcher, drawing rave reviews for his game calling. Offensively, he has major league power and takes a lot of walks. He doesn't really have much more to prove in Triple-A. The flaw in his game, and it's a big one, is that he averages a strikeout per game, leaving little room for error in his other at-bats. He improved a bit in this area in 2005. With Mirabelli gone, he's in line to be the No. 2 catcher, but he might have more value to a team that wants to give him a chance to compete for the starting job.

CHAD SPANN **3B** **Bats: R Throws: R** Height: 6' 1" Weight: 190 Born: October 25, 1983 Age: 22

YEAR	TM	LVL	AGE	PA	R	2B	3B	HR	RBI	BB	SO	SB	CS	SPEED	BA	OBP	SLG	MLVR	EQBA	EQOBP	EQSLG	EQA	VORP	DEFENSE
2003	AUG	A	19	467	55	21	3	5	63	40	64	9	5	4.6	.312	.379	.413	.203	.285	.337	.386	.254	15.5	100-3B 8
2004	SAR	A+	20	227	26	9	0	4	22	9	53	6	2	5.2	.252	.291	.350	-.079	.224	.257	.321	.207	-11.7	51-3B 0
2005	WIL	A+	21	454	55	23	4	13	48	39	106	1	4	3.6	.247	.322	.422	.005	.221	.277	.372	.226	-8.7	71-3B 5
2006	BOS	MLB	22	462	51	25	2	12	53	27	105	3	2	4.1	.239	.290	.387	-.138	.238	.294	.394	.229	-2.8	109-3B 1

Breakout: 41%   Improve: 57%   Collapse: 21%   Attrition: 9%   Comparables: Corey Myers, Chris Bass, Rolando Segura

(continued next page)

Chad Spann *(continued)*

A terrific 2003 season propelled him up the system's prospect lists, but he has not returned to that level since. He's still young and showed some power last season, exemplified by his two-out, walk-off grand slam in Portland's 5–3 win over Trenton in the first game of the Eastern League playoffs. The Red Sox might move Pinckney past Spann on the third base depth chart this season.

ADAM STERN OF **Bats: L Throws: R** Height: 5′ 11″ Weight: 180 Born: February 12, 1980 Age: 26

YEAR	TM	LVL	AGE	PA	R	2B	3B	HR	RBI	BB	SO	SB	CS	SPEED	BA	OBP	SLG	MLVR	EQBA	EQOBP	EQSLG	EQA	VORP	DEFENSE			
2003	MYR	A+	23	117	11	2	0	0	6	13	21	7	3	5.5	.194	.282	.214	-.263	.184	.258	.203	.186	-16.4	13-RF	2	13-CF	0
2004	GRN	AA	24	434	64	26	6	8	47	35	58	27	10	7.3	.322	.378	.480	.232	.289	.336	.430	.267	17.4	91-CF	-1		
2005	PAW	AAA	25	91	16	8	0	2	14	8	10	3	1	5.9	.321	.385	.494	.224	.276	.345	.414	.268	2.9	15-CF	-1		
2006	BOS	MLB	26	137	19	7	1	2	14	9	20	5	1	6.2	.271	.324	.402	-.038	.269	.329	.410	.253	3.6	36-CF	0		

Breakout: 28% Improve: 50% Collapse: 33% Attrition: 39% Comparables: Ty Cline, Max Venable, Gene Locklear

Selected in the 2004 Rule 5 draft, the Red Sox kept Stern on the roster most of the season, save for assorted (apparently legitimate) injury rehab games in Triple-A. The Red Sox played short-handed a number of times rather than risk losing Stern to the Braves, testifying to their continuing belief in him. A good defensive centerfielder with on-base skills, Stern should be sent to Triple-A, where he could use a few hundred at-bats.

JASON VARITEK C **Bats: B Throws: R** Height: 6′ 2″ Weight: 210 Born: April 11, 1972 Age: 34

YEAR	TM	LVL	AGE	PA	R	2B	3B	HR	RBI	BB	SO	SB	CS	SPEED	BA	OBP	SLG	MLVR	EQBA	EQOBP	EQSLG	EQA	VORP	DEFENSE	
2003	BOS	MLB	31	516	63	31	1	25	85	51	106	3	2	4.2	.273	.351	.512	.130	.270	.353	.512	.290	32.5	119-C	1
2004	BOS	MLB	32	536	67	30	1	18	73	62	126	10	3	4.5	.296	.390	.482	.155	.291	.388	.476	.298	39.5	119-C	4
2005	BOS	MLB	33	538	70	30	1	22	70	62	117	2	0	4.6	.281	.366	.489	.151	.281	.376	.502	.298	39.8	124-C	0
2006	BOS	MLB	34	484	62	25	1	20	71	56	106	5	1	4.3	.271	.361	.477	.116	.269	.366	.486	.284	28.9	114-C	-2

Breakout: 5% Improve: 18% Collapse: 37% Attrition: 10% Comparables: Bob Brenly, Aaron Robinson, Stan Lopata

After signing a seemingly ill-considered four-year, $40 million dollar contract, Varitek went out and easily justified the first year of the deal. Of course, it was never the first year, nor the second, that was going to be the problem; it's still probable that the Sox felt that the only way to secure two good years of Varitek was to also pay for the two bad ones that were likely to come after. Now sporting an NHL-style "C" on his uniform, Jason is four months younger than Ivan Rodriguez and eight months younger than Jorge Posada, but he's played hundreds fewer major league games than both, thanks in large part to Scott Boras's tough negotiating tactics. Those tactics may have cost Varitek money at the time, but could add some length to his career.

KEVIN YOUKILIS 3B **Bats: R Throws: R** Height: 6′ 1″ Weight: 220 Born: March 15, 1979 Age: 27

YEAR	TM	LVL	AGE	PA	R	2B	3B	HR	RBI	BB	SO	SB	CS	SPEED	BA	OBP	SLG	MLVR	EQBA	EQOBP	EQSLG	EQA	VORP	DEFENSE			
2003	PME	AA	24	417	74	23	1	6	37	86	40	7	0	5.3	.327	.487	.465	.339	.277	.420	.407	.301	32.3	92-3B	9		
2003	PAW	AAA	24	132	9	3	0	2	15	18	21	0	1	2.8	.165	.295	.248	-.285	.150	.277	.223	.193	-10.9	29-3B	-1		
2004	PAW	AAA	25	177	25	12	0	3	18	19	28	2	0	4.7	.266	.350	.403	.004	.235	.315	.358	.242	-0.3	35-3B	3		
2004	BOS	MLB	25	248	38	11	0	7	35	33	45	0	1	4.1	.260	.367	.413	-.002	.255	.365	.407	.272	4.3	57-3B	5		
2005	PAW	AAA	26	194	30	15	1	8	27	35	29	1	2	4.7	.322	.459	.592	.466	.286	.412	.516	.313	20.8	22-3B	-3	16-1B	2
2005	BOS	MLB	26	95	11	7	0	1	9	14	19	0	1	4.7	.278	.400	.405	.096	.282	.411	.397	.287	3.5	16-3B	1		
2006	BOS	MLB	27	404	50	21	1	11	48	55	68	2	1	4.6	.258	.368	.421	.049	.256	.374	.429	.274	13.6	96-3B	3		

Breakout: 14% Improve: 34% Collapse: 38% Attrition: 19% Comparables: Steve Boros, Craig Kusick, Jim Essian

Francona does not like to use his bench except in rigid patterns, like a platoon in right field or Mirabelli catching Wakefield. Having Youkilis around to spell Mueller once a week, play some first base, pinch hit for the middle infielders-that was not a role that seemed to interest Francona. As a result, Youkilis spent much of the season in Pawtucket, where he mashed, but he also hit well in his Boston stints. Mueller has moved on, but the team acquired two more third basemen—Lowell and Andy Marte. Youkilis is penciled in as the Sox' starting first baseman, pending the inevitable counterproductive job challenge from J. T. Snow.

PITCHERS

ABE ALVAREZ

Bats: L **Throws: L** **Height: 6′ 2″** **Weight: 190** **Born: October 17, 1982** **Age: 23**

YEAR	TM	LVL	AGE	W	L	SV	G	GS	IP	H	BB	SO	HR	GB%	BABIP	STUFF	WHIP	ERA	PERA	EQERA	EQH9	EQBB9	EQSO9	EQHR9	VORP	WXRL
2004	PME	AA	21	10	9	0	26	26	135.3	132	32	108	13	—	.292	8	1.21	3.59	4.59	4.25	9.1	2.2	5.3	1.1	20.0	—
2005	PAW	AAA	22	11	6	0	26	26	144.7	143	31	109	17	40%	.290	5	1.20	4.85	4.56	5.20	9.1	2.0	5.5	1.2	6.3	—
2006	BOS	MLB	23	8	8	0	35	20	133.3	149	35	81	20	41%	.297	4	1.38	4.94	4.85	4.97	9.7	2.3	5.4	1.2	9.6	1.7

Breakout: 22% Improve: 54% Collapse: 8% Attrition: 1% Comparables: George Stone, Dave Fleming, Joe Kennedy

A 2nd round pick in 2003, Alvarez has been fast-tracked through the system due to his maturity and good control of all his pitches. He's a classic finesse lefty, who with a fastball topping out at 85–88 mph requires deception and command of multiple pitches. The organization loves his approach, and he has been rewarded with brief call-ups each of the past two seasons. The Red Sox believe Alvarez is still growing into his body, and will give him every opportunity to remain a starter while he does. But a move to the bullpen is possible, depending on the team's needs.

BRONSON ARROYO

Bats: R **Throws: R** **Height: 6′ 5″** **Weight: 190** **Born: February 24, 1977** **Age: 29**

YEAR	TM	LVL	AGE	W	L	SV	G	GS	IP	H	BB	SO	HR	GB%	BABIP	STUFF	WHIP	ERA	PERA	EQERA	EQH9	EQBB9	EQSO9	EQHR9	VORP	WXRL
2003	PAW	AAA	26	12	6	0	24	24	149.7	148	23	155	9	—	.321	24	1.14	3.43	3.77	4.94	9.3	1.7	7.0	0.9	10.7	—
2004	BOS	MLB	27	10	9	0	32	29	178.7	171	47	142	17	45%	.291	23	1.22	4.03	3.92	4.37	8.7	2.2	6.7	0.8	27.7	3.8
2005	BOS	MLB	28	14	10	0	35	32	205.3	213	54	100	22	40%	.281	4	1.30	4.52	4.64	4.51	9.2	2.4	4.3	0.9	18.7	2.9
2006	BOS	MLB	29	12	11	0	34	31	201.0	216	49	121	25	42%	.292	10	1.32	4.47	4.45	4.47	9.3	2.2	5.3	1.0	23.6	3.9

Breakout: 14% Improve: 56% Collapse: 9% Attrition: 2% Comparables: Dick Ruthven, Esteban Loaiza, Danny Darwin

After having a breakout season in 2004, last year Arroyo was a league-average innings eater. His problem was losing 30% of his K-rate, finishing 86th among 93 ERA qualifiers in strikeouts per nine. League-average 200 inning pitchers are commanding four years at big money, but the Red Sox seemed interested in finding a more expensive version of Arroyo as the off-season began. If he comes back, he might consider curtailing the night life and the rock band activity until he firms up a spot in the rotation.

RANDY BEAM

Bats: L **Throws: L** **Height: 6′ 3″** **Weight: 205** **Born: May 21, 1982** **Age: 24**

YEAR	TM	LVL	AGE	W	L	SV	G	GS	IP	H	BB	SO	HR	GB%	BABIP	STUFF	WHIP	ERA	PERA	EQERA	EQH9	EQBB9	EQSO9	EQHR9	VORP	WXRL
2004	LOW	A-	22	1	2	2	9	0	16.7	10	3	19	1	—	.220	-7	0.78	1.62	5.40	4.20	8.4	2.4	5.4	1.8	2.3	—
2004	AUG	A	22	2	1	10	18	0	23.3	10	4	27	0	—	.189	9	0.60	0.00	3.32	2.49	5.8	2.1	6.2	0.4	7.5	—
2005	WIL	A+	23	2	3	5	19	0	28.0	19	11	28	2	43%	.227	-9	1.07	2.25	4.91	3.86	8.4	4.2	5.6	1.1	5.0	—
2005	PME	AA	23	2	3	2	34	0	46.3	35	20	49	3	37%	.281	-3	1.19	2.53	4.78	4.36	8.3	4.8	6.6	0.8	6.0	—
2006	BOS	MLB	24	2	3	1	26	4	48.3	53	22	32	9	38%	.288	-8	1.54	5.53	5.66	5.59	9.4	4.0	5.9	1.5	0.8	0.1

Breakout: 3% Improve: 12% Collapse: 55% Attrition: 30% Comparables: Brian Passini, Eric Cyr, Danny Borrell

An 18th round selection out of Florida Atlantic in 2004, Beam has put up consecutive seasons of highly effective relief. The tall left-hander throws a fastball in the high 80s, a changeup, and a big, slow curveball that breaks in to right handed hitters. After a great stint in the 2005 Arizona Fall League, he's in line to be the primary left-handed reliever in Pawtucket this season.

CHAD BRADFORD

Bats: R **Throws: R** **Height: 6′ 5″** **Weight: 205** **Born: September 14, 1974** **Age: 31**

YEAR	TM	LVL	AGE	W	L	SV	G	GS	IP	H	BB	SO	HR	GB%	BABIP	STUFF	WHIP	ERA	PERA	EQERA	EQH9	EQBB9	EQSO9	EQHR9	VORP	WXRL
2003	OAK	MLB	28	7	4	2	72	0	77.0	67	30	62	7	67%	.279	8	1.26	3.04	4.28	3.21	8.4	3.6	7.1	0.8	23.2	2.7
2004	OAK	MLB	29	5	7	1	68	0	59.0	51	24	34	5	63%	.257	-8	1.27	4.42	4.66	4.66	8.5	3.4	5.0	0.8	9.6	0.8
2005	BOS	MLB	30	2	1	0	31	0	23.3	29	4	10	1	69%	.341	-6	1.41	3.86	4.07	3.33	10.0	1.5	3.7	0.4	5.1	0.3
2006	NYN	MLB	31	2	2	1	43	0	44.3	47	14	24	2	64%	.299	-8	1.36	3.74	4.01	5.01	9.5	2.6	4.5	0.5	5.0	0.4

Breakout: 13% Improve: 28% Collapse: 39% Attrition: 27% Comparables: Bob Locker, Dennis Lamp, Tim Crabtree

One half of the Red Sox submarine-throwing pair of situational bookends, Bradford continues to handle right-handed hitters (.282/.316/.310) while getting creamed by lefties (.409/.480/.545), typical of pitchers with this style. This skill set is difficult to manage, because if the opposing manager calls for a lefty pinch-hitter, Bradford is transformed from an asset into a liability. An extreme groundball pitcher, he gives up a lot of hits per ball in play, while keeping walks and extra base hits to a minimum. Back surgery derailed his effectiveness in '05; the Mets signed him to a one-year deal banking on a rebound season.

CLAY BUCHHOLZ   **Bats: L Throws: R**   Height: 6′ 3″   Weight: 190   Born: August 14, 1984   Age: 21

YEAR	TM	LVL	AGE	W	L	SV	G	GS	IP	H	BB	SO	HR	GB%	BABIP	STUFF	WHIP	ERA	PERA	EQERA	EQH9	EQBB9	EQSO9	EQHR9	VORP	WXRL
2005	LOW	A-	20	0	1	0	15	15	41.3	34	9	45	2	51%	.296	-1	1.04	2.62	4.89	5.35	9.3	2.8	5.4	1.2	1.1	—
2006	BOS	MLB	21	6	7	0	27	17	106.3	120	37	65	15	49%	.301	2	1.48	5.47	5.24	5.51	9.8	3.1	5.4	1.2	0.3	0.7

Breakout: 8%   Improve: 48%   Collapse: 12%   Attrition: 3%   Comparables: Kevin Deaton, Neal Frendling, Brian Slocum

A shortstop at McNeese State, Bucholz transferred to Angelina (Texas) Community College last spring and became a pitcher/outfielder. After a 12–1, 0.95 season, with 1.5 strikeouts per inning, the Red Sox nabbed him with the 42nd pick in the 2005 draft. A power pitcher with a 95 mph fastball, hard slider, circle change, and curveball, Buchholz had a fine debut at Lowell, including a 1.16 ERA and 32 strikeouts in his final 23 innings. It's early, but he's worth keeping an eye on.

MATT CLEMENT   **Bats: R Throws: R**   Height: 6′ 3″   Weight: 190   Born: August 12, 1974   Age: 31

YEAR	TM	LVL	AGE	W	L	SV	G	GS	IP	H	BB	SO	HR	GB%	BABIP	STUFF	WHIP	ERA	PERA	EQERA	EQH9	EQBB9	EQSO9	EQHR9	VORP	WXRL
2003	CHN	MLB	28	14	12	0	32	32	201.7	169	79	171	22	56%	.266	17	1.23	4.11	4.40	4.36	8.3	3.2	6.9	1.0	27.0	4.8
2004	CHN	MLB	29	9	13	0	30	30	181.0	155	77	190	23	52%	.284	25	1.28	3.68	4.22	3.91	8.2	3.5	8.4	1.1	38.4	4.5
2005	BOS	MLB	30	13	6	0	32	32	191.0	192	68	146	18	47%	.303	21	1.36	4.57	4.21	4.39	8.6	3.2	6.7	0.8	23.7	4.2
2006	BOS	MLB	31	12	9	0	30	30	190.3	187	67	143	18	48%	.292	17	1.33	4.11	4.12	4.19	8.5	3.1	6.6	0.8	29.5	4.5

Breakout: 15%   Improve: 54%   Collapse: 8%   Attrition: 5%   Comparables: Mike Krukow, Todd Stottlemyre, Bob Lemon

Clement got a lot of flak in Boston because he was stepping into Pedro Martinez's slot in the rotation, and he was no Pedro. His 10 first half wins earned him an All-Star nod, but he struggled in the second half, perhaps due to being struck in the head by a Carl Crawford line drive on July 26. Most troublingly, he had his lowest K rate since his rookie year (6.88), with numbers of 7.46 in the first half and 5.96 after the break. Even when healthy he's miscast as a No. 1 starter, but he can be an asset in the right situation.

MANNY DELCARMEN   **Bats: R Throws: R**   Height: 6′ 2″   Weight: 190   Born: February 16, 1982   Age: 24

YEAR	TM	LVL	AGE	W	L	SV	G	GS	IP	H	BB	SO	HR	GB%	BABIP	STUFF	WHIP	ERA	PERA	EQERA	EQH9	EQBB9	EQSO9	EQHR9	VORP	WXRL
2004	SAR	A+	22	3	6	0	19	18	73.0	84	20	76	10	—	.356	-25	1.42	4.68	6.91	6.78	12.0	3.0	6.3	2.9	-9.0	—
2005	PME	AA	23	4	4	3	31	0	39.0	31	20	49	3	58%	.298	-4	1.31	3.23	4.66	6.14	8.3	5.6	7.9	1.0	-2.2	—
2005	PAW	AAA	23	3	1	2	15	0	21.0	17	13	23	0	35%	.309	7	1.43	1.29	4.43	1.77	8.0	6.2	8.0	0.4	8.6	—
2006	BOS	MLB	24	3	3	1	31	2	51.7	56	29	41	7	48%	.312	-2	1.65	5.32	5.69	5.41	9.4	5.0	6.9	1.1	1.5	0.2

Breakout: 19%   Improve: 52%   Collapse: 23%   Attrition: 16%   Comparables: Tom Shearn, Gary Majewski, Grant Balfour

Delcarmen, a 2nd round pick in 2000, was on the fast track to Boston before undergoing Tommy John surgery in mid-2003, which cost him a year. The Boston native has a mid-90s fastball, a big 12-to-6 curveball, and a nice change, but he's had control problems since being converted to relief in the 2004 Arizona Fall League. Still, it was puzzling that the team gave tryouts to a succession of bad relief pitchers rather than offer a regular role to Delcarmen, who was marginally effective pitching only one inning a week. The organization claims to really like him, so he should get a better gig in 2006.

LENNY DiNARDO   **Bats: L Throws: L**   Height: 6′ 4″   Weight: 190   Born: September 19, 1979   Age: 26

YEAR	TM	LVL	AGE	W	L	SV	G	GS	IP	H	BB	SO	HR	GB%	BABIP	STUFF	WHIP	ERA	PERA	EQERA	EQH9	EQBB9	EQSO9	EQHR9	VORP	WXRL
2003	SLU	A+	23	3	8	1	19	13	85.0	64	14	93	1	—	.280	27	0.92	2.01	3.15	4.95	8.3	1.8	6.6	0.3	5.8	—
2003	BIN	AA	23	1	3	0	7	7	40.0	35	13	36	3	—	.276	8	1.20	3.60	4.97	5.21	9.0	3.6	6.4	1.2	1.6	—
2004	BOS	MLB	24	0	0	0	22	0	27.7	34	12	21	1	62%	.359	2	1.66	4.22	3.72	4.66	9.6	3.4	6.2	0.3	3.0	-0.2
2005	PAW	AAA	25	6	3	0	23	22	108.7	109	35	93	7	67%	.328	12	1.32	3.15	4.29	4.71	9.2	3.3	5.8	0.7	10.6	—
2005	BOS	MLB	25	0	1	0	8	1	14.7	13	5	15	1	68%	.308	15	1.23	1.84	3.00	3.60	7.2	3.0	9.0	0.6	3.6	-0.0
2006	BOS	MLB	26	6	7	1	47	13	106.7	120	38	70	9	57%	.318	1	1.47	4.78	4.74	4.93	9.7	3.1	5.8	0.7	8.2	1.3

Breakout: 16%   Improve: 48%   Collapse: 26%   Attrition: 9%   Comparables: Steve Barber, Mike Krukow, John Butcher

After spending most of 2004 with the big club as a Rule 5 guy, DiNardo pitched well in Pawtucket and in a few brief Boston outings. An extreme groundball pitcher, he's dependent on good infield defense, which he didn't have in Pawtucket last year. His 87 mph fastball keeps him off most prospect lists, but with the degree of movement on his pitches, the Red Sox believe he can be a mid-rotation major league starting pitcher. There is nothing in his record to indicate they are wrong.

KEITH FOULKE Bats: R Throws: R   Height: 6' 0" Weight: 195 Born: October 19, 1972   Age: 33

YEAR	TM	LVL	AGE	W	L	SV	G	GS	IP	H	BB	SO	HR	GB%	BABIP	STUFF	WHIP	ERA	PERA	EQERA	EQH9	EQBB9	EQSO9	EQHR9	VORP	WXRL
2003	OAK	MLB	30	9	1	43	72	0	86.7	57	20	88	10	32%	.223	24	0.89	2.08	3.56	2.27	7.1	2.2	9.2	1.0	37.0	6.8
2004	BOS	MLB	31	5	3	32	72	0	83.0	63	15	79	8	38%	.251	24	0.94	2.17	3.31	2.20	7.5	1.5	8.2	0.8	36.7	4.4
2005	BOS	MLB	32	5	5	15	43	0	45.7	53	18	34	8	27%	.317	-8	1.55	5.91	5.17	5.36	9.8	3.4	6.5	1.3	-0.1	-1.0
2006	*BOS*	*MLB*	*33*	*3*	*3*	*9*	*44*	*0*	*51.0*	*51*	*15*	*39*	*8*	*33%*	*.283*	*2*	*1.29*	*4.30*	*4.35*	*4.51*	*8.7*	*2.6*	*6.8*	*1.2*	*7.1*	*0.8*

Breakout: 6% Improve: 26% Collapse: 49% Attrition: 20%   Comparables: Jeff Reardon, Enrique Romo, Scott Sullivan

After being a key cog on the 2004 championship team, things got as bad as they could get for Foulke last season. After three months of dreadful pitching mixed with misguided off-field comments and controversy, he had surgery on his left knee. He returned in September, pitched no better, and then had surgery on his right knee. No one knows what to expect, but it would go a long way toward straightening out the pitching staff if he returns to form as one of the game's elite closers.

JEREMI GONZALEZ Bats: R Throws: R   Height: 6' 0" Weight: 220 Born: January 8, 1975   Age: 31

YEAR	TM	LVL	AGE	W	L	SV	G	GS	IP	H	BB	SO	HR	GB%	BABIP	STUFF	WHIP	ERA	PERA	EQERA	EQH9	EQBB9	EQSO9	EQHR9	VORP	WXRL
2003	TBA	MLB	28	6	11	0	25	25	156.3	131	69	97	18	37%	.246	5	1.28	3.92	5.00	4.04	8.6	4.0	5.6	1.0	34.5	4.7
2004	TBA	MLB	29	0	5	0	11	8	50.3	72	20	22	9	40%	.356	-19	1.83	6.98	5.68	6.71	11.7	3.3	3.6	1.4	-7.3	0.0
2004	DUR	AAA	29	4	2	1	19	8	57.7	50	19	44	7	—	.259	-14	1.20	3.90	5.63	4.97	8.9	3.6	5.1	1.5	3.8	—
2005	PAW	AAA	30	5	2	0	11	11	69.0	63	14	62	8	36%	.294	7	1.12	2.61	4.91	3.68	9.3	2.3	5.9	1.4	14.1	—
2005	BOS	MLB	30	2	1	0	28	3	56.0	64	16	28	7	39%	.305	-12	1.43	6.11	4.87	5.49	9.6	2.5	4.4	1.1	-2.7	0.1
2006	*BOS*	*MLB*	*31*	*5*	*6*	*1*	*42*	*11*	*92.7*	*107*	*32*	*54*	*16*	*39%*	*.298*	*-10*	*1.50*	*5.58*	*5.56*	*5.65*	*10.0*	*3.1*	*5.2*	*1.4*	*0.4*	*0.4*

Breakout: 7% Improve: 30% Collapse: 35% Attrition: 2%   Comparables: Paul Foytack, Tim Worrell, Andy Hawkins

About all you need to know about the Red Sox pitching struggles last season is that Gonzalez not only got into 28 games, but made the post-season roster. On the bright side, he looks to be healthy and pitched very well in Pawtucket. Now 31 years old, Gonzalez is a known quantity, which is to say that he will be of little help. He has been released but will likely get a chance somewhere else.

CRAIG HANSEN Bats: R Throws: R   Height: 6' 6" Weight: 210 Born: November 15, 1983 Age: 22

YEAR	TM	LVL	AGE	W	L	SV	G	GS	IP	H	BB	SO	HR	GB%	BABIP	STUFF	WHIP	ERA	PERA	EQERA	EQH9	EQBB9	EQSO9	EQHR9	VORP	WXRL
2006	*BOS*	*MLB*	*22*	*3*	*2*	*1*	*23*	*3*	*43.7*	*50*	*10*	*33*	*5*	*50%*	*.324*	*10*	*1.37*	*4.09*	*4.57*	*4.16*	*10.0*	*2.0*	*6.6*	*0.9*	*7.1*	*0.7*

Breakout: 26% Improve: 63% Collapse: 5% Attrition: 35%   Comparables: Julian Tavarez, Don Schulze, Rick Jones

One of the more heralded players in the 2005 draft, the Red Sox nabbed Hansen with the 28th pick after he fell due to signability concerns (read: Scott Boras). Boston gave him the major league contract he demanded, then called the 6-foot-5-inch righty up after 12 scoreless appearances in the minors. Arm fatigue caused the team to use him cautiously and eventually shut him down. He has a fastball that tops out in the high 90s and throws a sinking fastball or a hard slider as his second pitch (depending on what is working). Hansen will have every opportunity to claim a regular bullpen role in the spring.

CHAD HARVILLE Bats: R Throws: R   Height: 5' 9" Weight: 180 Born: September 16, 1976 Age: 29

YEAR	TM	LVL	AGE	W	L	SV	G	GS	IP	H	BB	SO	HR	GB%	BABIP	STUFF	WHIP	ERA	PERA	EQERA	EQH9	EQBB9	EQSO9	EQHR9	VORP	WXRL
2003	SAC	AAA	26	3	5	18	48	0	57.0	42	21	57	5	—	.245	-1	1.11	2.05	4.89	3.71	7.9	4.2	7.4	1.4	11.2	—
2003	OAK	MLB	26	1	0	1	21	0	21.7	25	17	18	3	45%	.344	-13	1.94	5.81	5.73	5.73	9.8	7.0	7.0	1.2	-0.7	0.4
2004	HOU	MLB	27	3	2	0	56	0	53.0	54	26	46	8	58%	.299	-7	1.51	4.75	4.89	5.74	9.1	4.1	6.9	1.2	-1.6	-1.3
2005	HOU	MLB	28	0	2	0	37	0	38.3	36	24	33	7	48%	.284	-12	1.57	4.46	5.92	4.97	9.2	5.2	7.1	1.7	2.6	-0.5
2006	*TBA*	*MLB*	*29*	*2*	*2*	*1*	*40*	*0*	*44.7*	*44*	*23*	*34*	*6*	*47%*	*.286*	*-7*	*1.50*	*4.60*	*5.13*	*5.93*	*8.7*	*4.6*	*6.5*	*1.1*	*3.2*	*0.2*

Breakout: 31% Improve: 54% Collapse: 26% Attrition: 40%   Comparables: Richie Lewis, Greg Harris, Julio Santana

Keeps getting chances because he throws hard, but he hasn't pitched well yet. Harville was the last man in the Houston pen until the Red Sox claimed him off waivers in late August, He turned out to be another one of the many bullpen flyers the team took that did not work. Released and signed by Tampa Bay.

JON LESTER

Bats: L Throws: L   Height: 6′ 3″   Weight: 200   Born: January 7, 1984   Age: 22

YEAR	TM	LVL	AGE	W	L	SV	G	GS	IP	H	BB	SO	HR	GB%	BABIP	STUFF	WHIP	ERA	PERA	EQERA	EQH9	EQBB9	EQSO9	EQHR9	VORP	WXRL
2003	AUG	A	19	6	9	0	24	21	106.0	102	44	71	7	—	.278	-17	1.38	3.65	6.24	5.88	9.9	4.4	3.8	1.5	-3.1	—
2004	SAR	A+	20	7	6	0	21	20	90.3	82	37	97	2	—	.329	23	1.32	4.29	4.00	5.85	8.7	4.2	6.6	0.4	-2.4	—
2005	PME	AA	21	11	6	0	26	26	148.3	114	57	163	10	48%	.291	23	1.15	2.61	4.41	3.90	8.2	4.1	7.1	0.9	26.6	—
2006	*BOS*	*MLB*	*22*	*7*	*9*	*0*	*27*	*23*	*135.7*	*142*	*64*	*103*	*16*	*45%*	*.304*	*11*	*1.52*	*5.17*	*5.08*	*5.18*	*9.1*	*4.2*	*6.7*	*1.0*	*5.4*	*1.5*

Breakout: 5%   Improve: 40%   Collapse: 22%   Attrition: 0%   Comparables: Kurt Ainsworth, Noah Lowry, Ryan Ketchner

The best pitcher in the Eastern League last year. He led the circuit in ERA and strikeouts and is one of the best pitching prospects in the game. A 2nd round selection out of high school in 2002, Lester throws two fastballs in the low 90s, a big curve, and a changeup. A great organizational success story, he has improved at each level, adding speed on his fastball and a new cutter while maintaining his control. Had the Manny-for-A-Rod deal gone through, Lester would have headed to the Rangers. The Red Sox hope that some day he is part of the calculus when evaluating the non-deal. Will start the year in Pawtucket but might not need a full season there.

MATT MANTEI

Bats: R Throws: R   Height: 6′ 1″   Weight: 200   Born: July 7, 1973   Age: 32

YEAR	TM	LVL	AGE	W	L	SV	G	GS	IP	H	BB	SO	HR	GB%	BABIP	STUFF	WHIP	ERA	PERA	EQERA	EQH9	EQBB9	EQSO9	EQHR9	VORP	WXRL
2003	ARI	MLB	30	5	4	29	50	0	55.0	37	18	68	6	40%	.258	28	1.00	2.62	3.33	2.67	6.8	2.7	10.2	1.0	18.1	3.9
2005	BOS	MLB	32	1	0	0	34	0	26.3	23	24	22	1	38%	.301	-10	1.78	6.50	5.06	6.08	8.1	8.1	7.4	0.3	-2.9	-0.3
2006	*DET*	*MLB*	*32*	*1*	*1*	*1*	*21*	*0*	*23.3*	*23*	*16*	*20*	*3*	*37%*	*.292*	*-8*	*1.65*	*5.54*	*5.70*	*7.09*	*8.7*	*5.9*	*7.7*	*1.2*	*-0.3*	*-0.1*

Breakout: 11%   Improve: 32%   Collapse: 43%   Attrition: 46%   Comparables: John Hudek, Dwayne Henry, Alan Mills

An interesting, low-risk gamble by the Red Sox last winter, Mantei pitched poorly before being shut down with a sprained ankle. His K rate was by far the worst of his career, and he walked nearly a batter an inning, so there may have been some arm issues as well. In the unlikely event that he ever puts together six healthy months again, he might have some value. A mass breakout of world peace is more likely: according to the *Baseball Encyclopedia,* Mantei has spent 948 days, or roughly six full seasons, on the shelf, making him the second most-idle player in history since the DL came into regular use in the late 1940s. He's a non-roster invite with the Tigers this spring.

EDGAR MARTINEZ

Bats: R Throws: R   Height: 6′ 0″   Weight: 160   Born: October 23, 1981   Age: 24

YEAR	TM	LVL	AGE	W	L	SV	G	GS	IP	H	BB	SO	HR	GB%	BABIP	STUFF	WHIP	ERA	PERA	EQERA	EQH9	EQBB9	EQSO9	EQHR9	VORP	WXRL
2005	WIL	A+	23	1	1	7	28	0	34.3	20	12	46	3	46%	.239	0	0.93	2.10	5.17	4.31	7.8	4.0	7.8	1.4	4.5	—
2005	PME	AA	23	0	0	1	15	0	18.0	12	8	13	0	37%	.240	-11	1.11	1.50	3.78	2.70	7.6	4.9	4.9	0.0	5.4	—
2006	*BOS*	*MLB*	*24*	*3*	*3*	*0*	*27*	*5*	*55.7*	*61*	*30*	*37*	*9*	*39%*	*.295*	*-9*	*1.64*	*5.60*	*5.95*	*5.66*	*9.4*	*4.8*	*5.8*	*1.3*	*0.3*	*0.2*

Breakout: 1%   Improve: 5%   Collapse: 69%   Attrition: 16%   Comparables: Allan Simpson, Jose Capellan, Francisco Rosario

Signed by the Red Sox in 1999, the Venezuelan was converted from catching to the mound in August 2004. He was impressive at two levels, throwing a mid-90s fastball with late life as well as a changeup and slider. The Red Sox were impressed enough to add him to the 40-man roster in October. Still shaped like a catcher at six feet and 225 pounds, he may need to change his body type to have a chance at any kind of sustained career.

CLA MEREDITH

Bats: R Throws: R   Height: 6′ 1″   Weight: 190   Born: June 4, 1983   Age: 23

YEAR	TM	LVL	AGE	W	L	SV	G	GS	IP	H	BB	SO	HR	GB%	BABIP	STUFF	WHIP	ERA	PERA	EQERA	EQH9	EQBB9	EQSO9	EQHR9	VORP	WXRL
2004	AUG	A	21	1	0	6	13	0	15.3	8	3	18	0	—	.222	11	0.72	0.00	3.14	1.88	6.9	2.5	6.3	0.0	5.9	—
2004	SAR	A+	21	0	2	12	16	0	16.3	15	3	16	0	—	.333	7	1.10	2.21	2.81	3.94	9.0	1.7	5.6	0.0	3.0	—
2005	PME	AA	22	1	0	9	12	0	15.0	5	3	12	0	75%	.143	6	0.53	0.00	3.29	1.32	5.3	2.0	5.3	0.0	6.5	—
2005	PAW	AAA	22	2	5	10	40	0	48.3	63	12	42	6	56%	.370	-3	1.55	5.59	4.56	5.47	10.6	2.4	6.0	1.3	0.7	—
2006	*BOS*	*MLB*	*23*	*3*	*3*	*1*	*28*	*3*	*50.3*	*59*	*16*	*30*	*5*	*56%*	*.317*	*-3*	*1.48*	*5.12*	*4.88*	*5.34*	*10.1*	*2.8*	*5.3*	*0.9*	*1.6*	*0.2*

Breakout: 24%   Improve: 66%   Collapse: 12%   Attrition: 26%   Comparables: Bill Castro, Ed Farmer, Jamie Vermilyea

Boston's 6th round selection in the 2004 draft, Cla (pronounced "clay") Meredith made brief appearances at five minor league levels before making his major league debut on May 8. His stay in Boston was brief and ineffective and his so-so performance in Pawtucket has tempered the hype somewhat. A submariner with a sinking fastball, slider and changeup, he might also have been let down by the mediocre Pawtucket defense. The Red Sox have been grooming him as a closer, but he had difficulty with left-handers last year. Will likely share end-of-game duties with Beam in Pawtucket, but he might be challenged by Martinez soon.

WADE MILLER
Bats: R Throws: R Height: 6′ 2″ Weight: 200 Born: September 13, 1976 Age: 29

YEAR	TM	LVL	AGE	W	L	SV	G	GS	IP	H	BB	SO	HR	GB%	BABIP	STUFF	WHIP	ERA	PERA	EQERA	EQH9	EQBB9	EQSO9	EQHR9	VORP	WXRL
2003	HOU	MLB	26	14	13	0	33	33	187.3	168	77	161	17	48%	.292	20	1.31	4.13	4.09	4.62	8.6	3.4	7.0	0.8	24.2	4.6
2004	HOU	MLB	27	7	7	0	15	15	88.7	76	44	74	11	40%	.262	13	1.35	3.35	4.60	3.48	8.1	4.1	6.8	1.0	21.8	2.9
2005	BOS	MLB	28	4	4	0	16	16	91.0	96	47	64	8	46%	.307	11	1.57	4.95	4.53	4.72	8.8	4.6	6.2	0.7	6.9	0.8
2006	*BOS*	*MLB*	*29*	*7*	*8*	*0*	*29*	*21*	*123.3*	*127*	*57*	*87*	*16*	*43%*	*.293*	*4*	*1.49*	*4.85*	*4.97*	*5.07*	*8.9*	*4.1*	*6.2*	*1.0*	*9.8*	*1.8*

Breakout: 8%   Improve: 36%   Collapse: 31%   Attrition: 8%   Comparables: Bobby Witt, Juan Guzman, Don Larsen

Miller was signed last winter with the hope that he'd be available by mid-summer. He was ready by early May, but never put together a run of good starts. He had labrum surgery at the end of the season, making him a long shot to be much better than he was in 2005. Still unsigned in mid-January, he might get another chance with Boston in the spring, but the team has a lot of candidates for the rotation.

MIKE MYERS
Bats: L Throws: L Height: 6′ 4″ Weight: 214 Born: June 26, 1969 Age: 37

YEAR	TM	LVL	AGE	W	L	SV	G	GS	IP	H	BB	SO	HR	GB%	BABIP	STUFF	WHIP	ERA	PERA	EQERA	EQH9	EQBB9	EQSO9	EQHR9	VORP	WXRL
2003	ARI	MLB	34	0	1	0	64	0	36.3	38	21	21	4	58%	.283	-20	1.62	5.70	5.65	5.15	9.6	4.7	4.7	1.0	0.7	-0.2
2004	SEA	MLB	35	4	1	0	50	0	27.7	29	17	23	3	47%	.333	-6	1.66	4.87	5.08	4.76	9.2	5.1	7.0	1.0	4.0	0.4
2004	BOS	MLB	35	1	0	0	25	0	15.0	16	6	9	2	60%	.286	-12	1.47	4.20	5.40	3.60	9.6	3.6	4.8	1.2	3.7	-0.0
2005	BOS	MLB	36	3	1	0	65	0	37.3	30	13	21	3	55%	.245	-5	1.15	3.14	4.42	3.19	7.9	3.2	5.2	0.7	10.1	1.2
2006	*NYA*	*MLB*	*37*	*2*	*1*	*1*	*38*	*0*	*31.7*	*34*	*12*	*18*	*4*	*52%*	*.293*	*-15*	*1.44*	*4.43*	*4.79*	*5.77*	*9.4*	*3.6*	*5.1*	*0.9*	*3.4*	*0.2*

Breakout: 24%   Improve: 36%   Collapse: 43%   Attrition: 42%   Comparables: Joe Gibbon, Hank Aguirre, Mike Fetters

The most extreme LOOGY in the game today, Myers shut down lefties (.158/.198/.211) while turning every right-handed hitter into Rogers Hornsby (.385/.510/.641). Although valuable against the best left-handed hitters in the league, he cannot not be brought in if the other team is likely to pinch hit. When Giambi, Sheffield, and Matsui are coming up, you can't ask Myers to face all three-his split is too extreme to allow him to do anything with Sheffield other than intentionally walk him. Roughly a third of the batters Myers pitched to were righties, which demonstrates the risks inherent in relying on this kind of pitcher. Signed by the Yankees to a two-year deal; we'll see if Joe Torre was paying attention.

JON PAPELBON
Bats: R Throws: R Height: 6′ 4″ Weight: 230 Born: November 23, 1980 Age: 25

YEAR	TM	LVL	AGE	W	L	SV	G	GS	IP	H	BB	SO	HR	GB%	BABIP	STUFF	WHIP	ERA	PERA	EQERA	EQH9	EQBB9	EQSO9	EQHR9	VORP	WXRL
2003	LOW	A-	22	1	2	0	13	6	32.7	43	9	36	2	—	.398	-20	1.59	6.33	6.32	8.62	13.2	3.4	5.5	2.0	-10.5	—
2004	SAR	A+	23	12	7	0	24	24	129.7	97	43	153	6	—	.287	13	1.08	2.64	4.55	4.77	8.6	3.8	6.9	1.0	11.1	—
2005	PME	AA	24	5	2	0	14	14	87.0	59	23	83	9	45%	.234	2	0.94	2.48	5.18	4.05	8.3	3.0	6.0	1.5	13.8	—
2005	PAW	AAA	24	1	2	1	7	4	27.7	21	3	27	2	45%	.264	21	0.87	2.92	3.38	3.38	7.8	1.0	6.8	0.7	6.6	—
2005	BOS	MLB	24	3	1	0	17	3	34.0	33	17	34	4	35%	.326	15	1.47	2.65	4.41	2.86	8.3	4.4	8.8	1.0	11.0	1.1
2006	*BOS*	*MLB*	*25*	*6*	*6*	*1*	*42*	*15*	*101.0*	*108*	*36*	*74*	*15*	*41%*	*.300*	*3*	*1.43*	*4.91*	*4.97*	*4.96*	*9.3*	*3.2*	*6.5*	*1.2*	*8.4*	*1.2*

Breakout: 8%   Improve: 26%   Collapse: 36%   Attrition: 3%   Comparables: Art Mahaffey, Kelvim Escobar, Barry Latman

By playoff time, Papelbon was the best pitcher on the team, which was not altogether a good thing. Called up twice to make three emergency starts, he pitched well enough to stay in the bullpen for the pennant race and was very effective. Papelbon was used like a 1970s fireman, a multi-inning late game relief ace in front of Mike Timlin. This was not so much Francona thinking outside the box, but that that he lost faith in everyone else in the bullpen. Papelbon pitches from a three-quarter arm angle, possesses a mid-90s fastball, slider, curve and changeup, though he used just the fastball and slider out of the pen. Despite his success in the relief role, if there's no spot in the rotation for him he'll start the season in Triple-A.

DAVID PAULEY
Bats: R Throws: R Height: 6′ 2″ Weight: 170 Born: June 17, 1983 Age: 23

YEAR	TM	LVL	AGE	W	L	SV	G	GS	IP	H	BB	SO	HR	GB%	BABIP	STUFF	WHIP	ERA	PERA	EQERA	EQH9	EQBB9	EQSO9	EQHR9	VORP	WXRL
2003	FTW	A	20	7	7	1	22	21	117.7	109	38	117	9	—	.298	-12	1.25	3.29	6.28	5.70	10.5	3.8	6.1	2.1	-1.2	—
2004	LEL	A+	21	7	12	0	27	26	153.3	155	60	128	8	—	.319	0	1.40	4.17	5.20	6.12	9.7	4.6	4.8	0.9	-8.5	—
2005	PME	AA	22	9	7	0	27	27	156.0	169	34	104	18	54%	.306	-10	1.30	3.81	5.36	5.60	10.4	2.3	4.2	1.5	0.0	—
2006	*BOS*	*MLB*	*23*	*7*	*9*	*0*	*28*	*23*	*135.3*	*161*	*49*	*70*	*19*	*49%*	*.308*	*-2*	*1.55*	*5.71*	*5.59*	*5.75*	*10.3*	*3.2*	*4.6*	*1.2*	*-3.3*	*0.6*

Breakout: 16%   Improve: 62%   Collapse: 13%   Attrition: 0%   Comparables: Tim Stauffer, Ed Kofler, Mike Wood

(continued next page)

David Pauley (*continued*)

Part of the return for Dave Roberts last winter, Pauley put in a solid season in his first look at Double-A. He throws a high 80s fastball and changeup, but often relies on a big curve as his out pitch. He looks like a back-of-the-rotation guy. He will likely spend the season in Pawtucket getting ready, but there are a lot of starters ahead of him in the system.

ANIBAL SANCHEZ **Bats: R Throws: R** Height: 6' 0" Weight: 180 Born: February 27, 1984 Age: 22

YEAR	TM	LVL	AGE	W	L	SV	G	GS	IP	H	BB	SO	HR	GB%	BABIP	STUFF	WHIP	ERA	PERA	EQERA	EQH9	EQBB9	EQSO9	EQHR9	VORP	WXRL
2004	LOW	A-	20	4	4	0	15	15	76.3	43	29	101	3	—	.230	11	0.94	1.77	5.29	4.90	7.8	5.3	6.6	1.1	5.3	—
2005	WIL	A+	21	6	1	0	14	14	78.7	53	24	95	7	48%	.253	17	0.98	2.40	4.68	4.07	8.3	3.2	7.3	1.4	12.4	—
2005	PME	AA	21	3	5	0	11	11	57.3	53	16	63	5	46%	.322	17	1.20	3.46	4.55	5.04	9.3	2.9	7.0	1.1	3.4	—
2006	FLO	MLB	22	8	9	0	28	22	139.7	128	60	121	16	43%	.282	15	1.34	4.23	4.55	4.62	8.3	3.5	6.8	1.0	13.0	2.3

Breakout: 11%   Improve: 49%   Collapse: 9%   Attrition: 0%   Comparables: Chin-Hui Tsao, Seung Song, Mike Meyers

Dominated the Carolina League for two months, then moved up to Portland and continued to pitch well. After allowing just three earned runs in his first five outings in Double-A, he tired in August and was limited to 60 pitches per outing. Armed with a lively 95 mph fastball and a plus curveball, his best pitch is a nasty changeup that he hides well with consistent arm speed. He had ligament surgery on his pitching arm in 2003, but has completely recovered. Although Hanley Ramirez was the big-name prospect in the Beckett deal, Sanchez was the guy the team hated to give up. He would likely have gotten to Boston in 2006.

CURT SCHILLING **Bats: R Throws: R** Height: 6' 5" Weight: 235 Born: November 14, 1966 Age: 39

YEAR	TM	LVL	AGE	W	L	SV	G	GS	IP	H	BB	SO	HR	GB%	BABIP	STUFF	WHIP	ERA	PERA	EQERA	EQH9	EQBB9	EQSO9	EQHR9	VORP	WXRL
2003	ARI	MLB	36	8	9	0	24	24	168.0	144	32	194	17	45%	.306	44	1.05	2.95	3.07	2.96	7.7	1.6	9.4	0.9	50.5	5.6
2004	BOS	MLB	37	21	6	0	32	32	226.7	206	35	203	23	43%	.288	35	1.06	3.26	3.34	2.98	8.2	1.3	7.6	0.8	76.2	7.8
2005	BOS	MLB	38	8	8	9	32	11	93.3	121	22	87	12	36%	.381	16	1.53	5.69	3.73	5.18	9.7	2.0	7.8	1.0	2.1	0.0
2006	BOS	MLB	39	6	7	6	35	13	99.7	104	22	81	12	41%	.305	10	1.26	4.17	4.13	4.54	9.0	1.9	7.1	1.0	17.5	2.1

Breakout: 8%   Improve: 24%   Collapse: 39%   Attrition: 14%   Comparables: Gaylord Perry, Jerry Koosman, Bert Blyleven

Although Red Sox Nation expects Schilling to be the ace of the rotation once again, there is plenty of reason to think that his ankle is never going to allow him to be the power pitcher he used to be. He's a smart man and could probably gut through a couple of above-average seasons on finesse and guile. Although he remains a controversial figure wherever he goes, the story of his 2004 post-season becomes even more amazing as the extent of his injury becomes more apparent. It is said that an athlete should leave it "all" on the field. Schilling did just that.

MIKE STANTON **Bats: L Throws: L** Height: 6' 1" Weight: 210 Born: June 2, 1967 Age: 39

YEAR	TM	LVL	AGE	W	L	SV	G	GS	IP	H	BB	SO	HR	GB%	BABIP	STUFF	WHIP	ERA	PERA	EQERA	EQH9	EQBB9	EQSO9	EQHR9	VORP	WXRL
2003	NYN	MLB	36	2	7	5	50	0	45.3	37	19	34	6	41%	.240	-7	1.24	4.57	4.87	5.08	8.1	3.5	6.3	1.2	3.3	0.5
2004	NYN	MLB	37	2	6	0	83	0	77.0	70	33	58	6	48%	.277	2	1.34	3.16	4.26	3.79	8.5	3.6	6.0	0.7	16.5	1.2
2005	NYA	MLB	38	1	2	0	28	0	14.0	17	6	12	1	38%	.364	0	1.64	7.07	3.68	6.75	9.2	3.7	7.4	0.6	-2.1	-0.3
2005	WAS	MLB	38	2	1	0	30	0	27.7	31	9	14	2	45%	.322	-11	1.45	3.57	4.18	4.50	9.6	2.6	4.2	0.6	3.4	1.1
2006	WAS	MLB	39	2	2	1	44	0	40.7	42	16	26	5	45%	.288	-15	1.42	4.54	5.01	5.84	9.6	3.3	5.1	1.0	1.0	0.0

Breakout: 13%   Improve: 32%   Collapse: 40%   Attrition: 30%   Comparables: Grant Jackson, Jose Mesa, Chris Hammond

The Red Sox acquired Stanton prior to the season-ending series with the Yankees, giving Francona a second LOOGY to play with. He pitched a single garbage-time inning. Now seventh on the all-time list of games pitched (1027), he's left-handed and "just" 38, so he has a few more years of chances coming. He'll get them with the Nationals.

MIKE TIMLIN **Bats: R Throws: R** Height: 6' 4" Weight: 210 Born: March 10, 1966 Age: 40

YEAR	TM	LVL	AGE	W	L	SV	G	GS	IP	H	BB	SO	HR	GB%	BABIP	STUFF	WHIP	ERA	PERA	EQERA	EQH9	EQBB9	EQSO9	EQHR9	VORP	WXRL
2003	BOS	MLB	37	6	4	2	72	0	83.7	77	9	65	11	54%	.268	9	1.03	3.55	3.78	3.56	8.3	1.0	6.8	1.1	20.4	2.8
2004	BOS	MLB	38	5	4	1	76	0	76.3	75	19	56	8	52%	.294	5	1.23	4.13	4.01	3.66	8.8	2.1	6.2	0.8	19.1	2.7
2005	BOS	MLB	39	7	3	13	81	0	80.3	86	20	59	2	46%	.336	22	1.32	2.24	3.14	2.39	8.6	2.2	6.4	0.2	28.9	2.3
2006	BOS	MLB	40	4	3	7	60	0	65.3	69	14	47	7	48%	.302	0	1.28	3.98	4.05	4.64	9.2	2.0	6.3	0.9	11.0	1.0

Breakout: 9%   Improve: 27%   Collapse: 66%   Attrition: 24%   Comparables: Ron Reed, Steve Reed, Doug Jones

There was a lot of hand-wringing in Boston when the team had to turn to Timlin to close games, since he supposedly did not have the "closer's mentality." Predictably, he pitched as well in the 9th inning as he previously had pitched in the 8th. Timlin has never been a great pitcher, but he has been one of the more dependable hurlers in the game for 14 years. Had he been used differently he might have saved 300 or more games, which would have landed him on a few All-Star teams without making him any more valuable than he already is. His 893 games are 17th on the all-time list, and he's going to pass several more pitchers this year.

TIM WAKEFIELD Bats: R Throws: R Height: 6' 2" Weight: 206 Born: August 2, 1966 Age: 39

YEAR	TM	LVL	AGE	W	L	SV	G	GS	IP	H	BB	SO	HR	GB%	BABIP	STUFF	WHIP	ERA	PERA	EQERA	EQH9	EQBB9	EQSO9	EQHR9	VORP	WXRL
2003	BOS	MLB	36	11	7	1	35	33	202.3	193	71	169	23	45%	.288	20	1.30	4.09	4.16	4.20	8.4	3.1	7.3	0.9	33.2	3.8
2004	BOS	MLB	37	12	10	0	32	30	188.3	197	63	116	29	49%	.280	0	1.38	4.88	5.06	5.01	9.5	2.8	5.2	1.2	13.3	2.2
2005	BOS	MLB	38	16	12	0	33	33	225.3	210	68	151	35	44%	.261	5	1.23	4.15	4.87	4.11	8.5	2.8	6.0	1.3	34.5	4.5
2006	BOS	MLB	39	12	12	0	37	31	203.7	212	66	132	26	43%	.289	6	1.36	4.65	4.58	4.74	9.0	2.8	5.7	1.0	20.1	3.5

Breakout: 13% Improve: 41% Collapse: 21% Attrition: 0% Comparables: Tom Seaver, Joe Niekro, Charlie Hough

Wakefield was Boston's best starter in 2005, which says more about the staff than it does about Wakefield, who had a fairly typical season, albeit with the better control than usual. He's got a throwback contract that essentially gives the team a yearly option for as long as they want it. Wakefield remains very valuable pitcher and should have at least another decent year or two ahead of him. Hoyt Wilhelm posted a 2.16 ERA from age 39 through his retirement at age 48, but that's not the norm; knuckleballers decline rapidly with age, just like everyone else.

DAVID WELLS Bats: L Throws: L Height: 6' 4" Weight: 225 Born: May 20, 1963 Age: 43

YEAR	TM	LVL	AGE	W	L	SV	G	GS	IP	H	BB	SO	HR	GB%	BABIP	STUFF	WHIP	ERA	PERA	EQERA	EQH9	EQBB9	EQSO9	EQHR9	VORP	WXRL
2003	NYA	MLB	40	15	7	0	31	30	213.0	242	20	101	24	47%	.302	9	1.23	4.14	4.22	3.76	9.6	0.8	4.1	1.0	41.6	4.8
2004	SDN	MLB	41	12	8	0	31	31	195.7	203	20	101	23	52%	.281	6	1.14	3.73	4.26	4.16	9.5	0.8	4.2	1.0	37.0	5.6
2005	BOS	MLB	42	15	7	0	30	30	184.0	220	21	107	21	50%	.324	14	1.31	4.45	4.07	4.12	9.8	1.0	5.0	0.9	25.1	3.6
2006	BOS	MLB	43	9	9	1	40	22	151.7	189	20	73	19	48%	.317	-5	1.37	4.80	4.82	5.12	10.8	1.1	4.2	1.0	11.7	2.1

Breakout: 17% Improve: 26% Collapse: 45% Attrition: 15% Comparables: Warren Spahn, Gaylord Perry, Danny Darwin

Like the entire rotation, Wells was a league-average pitcher who usually kept the team in games. With this offense, it's a great recipe for success if you have a good bullpen—which the Red Sox did not. At his request, he was ticketed to move on again this winter, but at press time he was still lodged in Beantown. Maybe the Red Sox balked at paying for over-size shipping.

CHARLIE ZINK Bats: R Throws: R Height: 6' 1" Weight: 190 Born: August 26, 1979 Age: 26

YEAR	TM	LVL	AGE	W	L	SV	G	GS	IP	H	BB	SO	HR	GB%	BABIP	STUFF	WHIP	ERA	PERA	EQERA	EQH9	EQBB9	EQSO9	EQHR9	VORP	WXRL
2003	SAR	A+	23	7	9	0	24	19	136.0	123	64	94	10	—	.265	-40	1.38	3.90	7.20	6.62	10.6	5.5	4.4	2.2	-14.0	—
2003	PME	AA	23	3	2	0	6	6	39.3	21	14	18	1	—	.167	-2	0.89	3.44	5.30	4.54	7.3	4.0	3.3	0.5	4.2	—
2004	PME	AA	24	1	8	0	18	18	93.3	101	72	50	3	—	.315	-16	1.85	5.79	5.97	6.55	9.5	7.8	3.3	0.4	-9.7	—
2005	PME	AA	25	8	5	0	29	15	105.3	102	53	70	12	42%	.291	-40	1.47	4.87	6.89	6.61	10.2	6.0	3.9	1.7	-11.0	—
2006	BOS	MLB	26	3	6	0	28	12	75.3	97	64	36	15	41%	.313	-34	2.13	8.05	8.35	8.13	11.2	7.5	4.3	1.7	-20.7	-1.6

Breakout: 7% Improve: 27% Collapse: 43% Attrition: 5% Comparables: Johnny Hunter, Paul O'Malley, Eddie Candelario

After a year and a half of mediocre pitching, the organization apparently put some pressure on Zink to work a little harder on his five-day routine. Late in the season he tried a new grip on his knuckleball and pitched several good innings. The Red Sox sent him to the Arizona Fall League to see if he was legit, and he pitched poorly. He needs a good year in Triple-A to get back on track; right now his status as a rare knuckleballer is more of a novelty than anything else.

Line Outs

Position/Player	TM	LVL	AGE	PA	R	2B	3B	HR	RBI	BB	SO	SB-CS	SPEED	BA/OBP/SLG	MLVR	EQBA/OBP/SLG	EQA	VORP
1B I. Bladergroen*	WIL	A+	22	306	25	6	3	4	31	30	77	0-1	3.9	.240/.337/.331	-.096	.216/.290/.295	.212	-21.0
C A. Concepcion	PME	AA	24	373	42	19	1	6	45	33	86	3-3	4.7	.249/.316/.368	-.061	.224/.287/.332	.223	-11.1

Pitcher	TM	LVL	AGE	W	L	SV	IP	H	BB	SO	HR	GB%	BABIP	STUFF	WHIP	ERA	PERA	EQERA	EQH9	EQBB9	EQSO9	EQHR9	VORP
T. Bausher	PAW	AAA	26	3	2	5	71.3	66	36	65	9	45%	.295	-18	1.43	3.41	5.80	5.00	9.1	5.3	6.2	1.4	4.6
J. Delgado	GRN	A	21	7	3	2	72.0	57	39	69	3	61%	.280	-10	1.33	3.50	5.32	5.32	8.2	6.3	5.3	0.8	2.1
H. Garcia	GRN	A	21	3	5	6	44.7	49	18	54	3	53%	.380	-5	1.50	2.01	5.36	5.15	10.5	4.5	6.4	1.2	2.2
M. Perisho*	FLO	MLB	30	2	0	0	14.0	12	11	10	1	31%	.289	-13	1.71	1.93	5.14	2.57	8.4	6.4	5.8	0.6	5.4
M. Remlinger*	CHN	MLB	39	0	3	0	33.0	31	12	30	5	43%	.292	1	1.30	4.91	4.68	4.96	8.8	3.0	7.4	1.4	1.3

Ian Bladergroen was acquired from the Mets in the Mientkiewicz deal; he spent most of the season recovering from 2004 wrist surgery. Still possibly worth keeping an eye on. **Alberto Concepcion's** chances of making it are predicated on his being able to catch—he also plays 3B, but won't hit enough to stay there.

Tim Bausher was claimed off waivers last winter. He had a decent season in the Pawtucket bullpen and might show up in Boston this season. **Michael Bowden** was the 47th selection in the 2005 draft, and a high-ceiling high-schooler with a 95 mph fastball and great secondary pitches. **Jesus Delgado**, hard-throwing Venezuelan, earned a spot on the 40-man roster with his performance in the Sally League; dealt to Florida as part of the Beckett trade. A fringe prospect, **Harvey Garcia** had a nice year at Greenville and was included in the Beckett deal; relies almost totally on his fastball. **Matt Perisho** spent two weeks with the Red Sox in September, throwing three pitches, the third of which was crushed for a double by Brian Roberts; he's a Met this spring. **Mike Remlinger** was the worst of all the attempts to fix the bullpen last season. He was a good pitcher as recently as 2004, so it's probably not over.

Chicago Cubs

Any team that has a starting pitching trinity like Mark Prior, Kerry Wood, and Carlos Zambrano should be able to boast of a playoff-worthy rotation. Yet in the four seasons since Prior reached the major leagues, the Cubs have been to the playoffs only once and have yet to win 90 games. We're entering Year Four of the Dusty Era, a time when the organization has promised repeatedly that it's really very serious about winning, yet in Year Three, they not only failed to contend, they didn't even manage a winning record. If there is a strategic vision for victory, it seems as far from fruition as it was after the 2002 season.

Whatever hopes the Cubs harbor seem to depend on the potential greatness of their starting rotation. Building up a vaunted rotation over time is no easy feat. It requires the wisdom to manage your starting pitchers well, the patience to grow some of that talent, and the initiative and aggressiveness to take advantage of the opportunities that exist in the free agent market. The great rotations of recent history, such as the mid-'80s Mets and the '90s Braves, didn't just rely on homegrown talent; they were reinforced through trades and free agency. Finally, in today's game, building a great rotation requires a balance of methods old and new: good scouting, statistical analysis of pitcher performance, careful management of workloads, and the best medical support and training staff a team can afford.

Jim Hendry's Cubs have done some, but not all, of these things. That isn't a criticism; some teams don't get any of it right. What is certain is that through the draft, his Cubs have assembled the best collection of starting pitchers the team has had in more than 30 years (see table 1).

SNLVAR is Support-Neutral Value Added Against Replacement Level, which basically levels the competition to give us a sense of how well a pitcher's performance would rate if he was facing the same hitters in the same conditions, and without any consideration for the run support his teammates generate for him. So what does that tell us? We'll get to the contemporary Cubs in a moment. On the fun side, it reminds us of how good Rick Reuschel was in his heyday, and that even Jaime Navarro had his moments—that's what earned him his ill-fated monster contract with the White Sox, after all. But what's missing is more telling: Greg Maddux's 1989 and the front four of the '84 Cubs, not even NL Cy Young Award winner Rick Sutcliffe. (Add in what Sutcliffe did with the Indians that

CUBS PROSPECTUS

2005 record: 79–83; Fourth place, NL Central

Pythagenport record: 79–83

Runs scored per game: 4.34 (9th in NL)

Runs allowed per game: 4.41 (7th in NL)

Team EqA: .261 (7th in NL)

2005 Batters Age: 30.3 (7th oldest in NL)

2005 Pitchers Age: 28.7 (4th youngest in NL)

Ballpark: Wrigley Field; Neutral park; Park Factor of 1.009

2005: Famous names, famous failures, and another early start to the off-season.

2006: A winter spent on making the wrong moves won't help Prior and Wood stay healthy or bring joy to Wrigleyville.

year, and his season total was 4.2, good enough for a four-way tie for 40th place on the Cubs' list covering 1972 to the present.) When the Cubs have won in the recent past, it was the result of depth and balance, not a star-studded rotation.

In fact, the Cubs have had very few great seasons from their starting pitchers. From 1972 through 2005, there were nearly 500 pitcher seasons where a starter logged a SNLVAR of 6.0 or higher; the Cubs have had nine, or slightly more than half as many as you'd expect to find on one of the 24

TABLE 1. WASTED GREATNESS: CUBS TOP TEN SNLVAR, 1972–2005

Rank	Player	Year	SNLVAR
1.	Greg Maddux	1992	8.8
2.	Rick Reuschel	1977	8.6
3.	Mark Prior	2003	7.6
4.	Kerry Wood	2003	7.4
5.	Carlos Zambrano	2004	6.9
6.	Carlos Zambrano	2005	6.8
7.	Carlos Zambrano	2003	6.5
8.	Mike Morgan	1992	6.4
9.	Rick Reuschel	1973	6.2
10.	Jaime Navarro	1995	5.9

teams that have been in existence over that entire period. Again, the data's park- and period-adjusted, so the only bias here is in who the Cubs have employed and for how long and how well. That makes Zambrano's success that much more remarkable: in his three full seasons in a major league rotation, he's given the Cubs three of their seven best starter seasons of the last 34 years. If you want to tab somebody as the greatest Cubs starter in the era of divisional play, think Zambrano, not Maddux.

That brings us to the other two "aces" in the Cubs' crop of golden-armed wunderkinds. For all the talk of his perfect mechanics, Prior has yet to pitch a full season. Wood hasn't managed it in either of the last two; he's only made it through a complete campaign only twice in his eight major league seasons. While we can dicker over whether Prior's going to be fine from here on out or not, or argue about Wood's elbow and whether the original sin against it was in high school or during the '98 stretch drive, it doesn't matter; when it comes to assessing what the future holds, the Cubs would be irresponsible if they built around an assumption that they'll ever get 90-plus starts from Prior, Wood, and Zambrano in a season. These are clearly fragile assets.

The opportunity and risk that Prior and Wood (if he can continue to start) represent make it that much more important for the Cubs to make sure that if they do get anything close to full seasons from them again, they leverage that into winning a playoff slot. Last season, the three best rotations in baseball (by SNLVAR) were the Cardinals, Braves, and Astros. What they might lack in homegrown virtue, all three have made up for in talent, and all three rotations were built with some element of risk. But even if the Cubs have the good fortune to field their full rotation and go into an October series with delusions of grandeur, they're going to need more than those three arms to advance to the World Series.

The challenge for Jim Hendry and Dusty Baker is to remember that when you're not a perennially great ballclub, you have to take your chances to make the best of the shots you might get. The Cubs of 2003–2005 have never ranked higher than 6th in the league in runs scored, and never higher than 7th for team Equivalent Average. Mediocrity in the lineup has been the most-frequently overlooked facet of a Cubs team that, despite the injuries to its famous pitchers, has seen them provide some of the best pitching in franchise history.

Unfortunately, the Cubs are no better positioned now than they were in years past when it comes to providing their starters with the runs they need to turn mere excellence into wins. Hendry has made a point of letting the older mercenaries depart, waving good-bye to Jeromy Burnitz and the Garciaparra Experiment. Instead, the Cubs made a point of trading for Juan Pierre, an ostensible lead-off man, a gesture that, at best, acknowledges the team's on-base problems but doesn't solve them. Pierre might enjoy hitting in Wrigley Field more than in Miami, but if he doesn't hit over .300 he won't post an OBP high enough to be an effective leadoff hitter. The offensive capabilities of the projected starting shortstop, Ronny Cedeno, are dubious, likely leading to another dose of too much Neifi Perez. The "big" free agent pickup this winter has been Jacque Jones, another one of the former Twins who have seemed so often favored on the watch of team president (and former Twins honcho) Andy MacPhail. A weak-hitting regular, in 2005 Jones finished 36th out of 50 in VORP among big league corner outfielders with 400+ PA. This was an improvement over 2004, when he finished 51st out of 52. If that's one of your core sluggers, you have the fundamental problem of not being able to identify what a slugger is.

Instead of fixing the lineup, Hendry and Baker have instead gone down ex-Phillies GM Ed Wade's road to perdition, finding hope and faith in their massive investments in a bullpen for 2006 and beyond. Investing $38.5 million over the next three years to retain Ryan Dempster and acquiring retreads Bobby Howry and Scott Eyre are classic examples of paying too high a price for people not too far removed from being pitchers you'd find dumpster-diving. Worse yet, the Cubs have been down this road before, having invested too much money in Mike Remlinger and Joe Borowski in 2003, and not learning anything from that mishap. Added to a pen that already has Scott Williamson and Mike Wuertz, and which might also wind up with Kerry Wood if his arm will only allow him that much, and you've got a massive concentration of the team's talent and discretionary money buried in an area of the team that cannot carry the rest of it to a playoff berth.

If playoff baseball is going to be more than just a South Side activity in Chicago, the Cubs are going to have to score runs. How then can the Cubs possibly field a lineup to take advantage of what they have to hope will be healthy seasons from their star pitchers? History provides a clue. It seems strange to have to turn Gene Michael or Don Zimmer for a clue, but it wouldn't kill the Cubs to build a platoon now and again. Michael got good work out of a left field platoon of Jerry Mumphrey and Brian Dayett in 1987, and Zim got a good year from Dwight Smith and Lloyd McClendon in '89. The Cubs don't have Andre Dawson or Sammy Sosa, but with Derrek Lee and Aramis Ramirez carrying the offense, they don't need to. For instance, while Jones has been an awful everyday player, he could be valuable in platoon role: he slugged .466 against RHPs in '05, and .464 against them in '04. If the Cubs focus on what Jones can do instead of on what they're paying him ($16 million over the next three years), they'll be the better for it.

Could Hendry and Baker make Jones half of an effective platoon? Only if they take a chance that a lefty masher like Mike Restovich, who will be in camp, can be the other half. To help themselves score enough runs to win, Baker is going to have to have the flexibility to manage this team and use everybody, instead of simply letting Pierre run and Lee mash, and hope for the best. While he has never extensively platooned, Baker did manage to get a few good years out of get Marvin Benard as a platoon outfielder with the Giants. Similarly, Baker is going to have to have patience with young players like Cedeno and Matt Murton; breaking in young players is another thing you generally don't find in his track record. Failing that sort of creativity, it's going to be another frustrating season in Wrigleyville, whether the three aces are all healthy or not.

HITTERS

MICHAEL BARRETT   **C**   **Bats: R Throws: R**   Height: 6′ 2″   Weight: 200   Born: October 22, 1976   Age: 29

YEAR	TM	LVL	AGE	PA	R	2B	3B	HR	RBI	BB	SO	SB	CS	SPEED	BA	OBP	SLG	MLVR	EQBA	EQOBP	EQSLG	EQA	VORP	DEFENSE
2003	MON	MLB	26	250	33	9	2	10	30	21	37	0	0	4.9	.208	.280	.398	-.189	.199	.272	.385	.227	-3.8	63-C -3
2004	CHN	MLB	27	502	55	32	6	16	65	33	64	1	4	4.5	.287	.337	.489	.102	.280	.328	.479	.270	24.8	120-C -3
2005	CHN	MLB	28	475	48	32	3	16	61	40	61	0	3	3.7	.276	.345	.479	.122	.271	.342	.483	.277	28.1	115-C -12
2006	CHN	MLB	29	422	46	23	2	13	53	33	58	0	1	4.1	.272	.336	.443	.017	.273	.336	.450	.262	16.0	100-C -3

Breakout: 12%   *Improve: 41%*   *Collapse: 26%*   *Attrition: 14%*   *Comparables: Del Crandall, Dan Wilson, Terry Steinbach*

Since Ron Santo's day, Cubs fans have fetishized their concern over third base. But their catching hasn't been too solid either, not since Randy Hundley was Santo's teammate. An underrated player, Barrett became the first Cubs starting catcher to post back-to-back good seasons since Jody Davis nearly 20 years ago. He should make it three in a row this year. Concerns about his weakness against the running game are overstated; the Cubs feature a lot of slow-delivery power pitchers and it would take a small howitzer to compensate.

HENRY BLANCO   **C**   **Bats: R Throws: R**   Height: 5′ 11″ Weight: 220   Born: August 29, 1971   Age: 34

YEAR	TM	LVL	AGE	PA	R	2B	3B	HR	RBI	BB	SO	SB	CS	SPEED	BA	OBP	SLG	MLVR	EQBA	EQOBP	EQSLG	EQA	VORP	DEFENSE
2003	ATL	MLB	31	163	11	8	0	1	13	10	21	0	0	3.5	.199	.252	.272	-.371	.197	.250	.283	.193	-9.3	43-C 0
2004	MIN	MLB	32	342	36	19	1	10	37	21	56	0	3	3.9	.206	.260	.368	-.318	.202	.259	.369	.217	-14.1	96-C 14
2005	CHN	MLB	33	174	16	6	0	6	25	11	24	0	0	3.3	.242	.287	.391	-.127	.235	.284	.389	.233	0.7	48-C 11
2006	CHN	MLB	34	168	15	7	0	5	20	11	26	0	0	3.7	.232	.288	.381	-.174	.233	.288	.387	.225	-0.3	43-C 4

Breakout: 35%   *Improve: 54%*   *Collapse: 36%*   *Attrition: 49%*   *Comparables: Joe Oliver, Danny Sheaffer, Brian Dorsett*

Blanco makes a nice catch-and-throw backup for a more offensive-minded starting catcher. While the Cubs overpaid for the privilege (he'll make $1.5 million in '06), he did play about as well as advertised, throwing out almost half of attempted base thieves. Offensively, he fits right in as a member of one of the most punchless benches in baseball.

JEROMY BURNITZ   **RF**   **Bats: L Throws: R**   Height: 6′ 0″   Weight: 210   Born: April 14, 1969   Age: 37

YEAR	TM	LVL	AGE	PA	R	2B	3B	HR	RBI	BB	SO	SB	CS	SPEED	BA	OBP	SLG	MLVR	EQBA	EQOBP	EQSLG	EQA	VORP	DEFENSE		
2003	NYN	MLB	34	259	38	18	0	18	45	21	55	1	4	3.8	.274	.344	.581	.257	.277	.344	.596	.296	16.3	37-RF -2	18-CF 1
2003	LAN	MLB	34	246	25	4	0	13	32	14	57	4	0	5.5	.204	.252	.391	-.190	.208	.255	.394	.225	-8.8	46-LF 0	10-CF -1
2004	COL	MLB	35	606	94	30	4	37	110	58	124	5	6	5.1	.283	.356	.559	.179	.263	.337	.521	.282	31.7	60-RF 2	58-CF -5
2005	CHN	MLB	36	670	84	31	2	24	87	57	109	5	4	4.7	.258	.322	.435	.013	.254	.319	.436	.258	8.3	153-RF 9	
2006	PIT	MLB	37	544	66	29	1	21	82	50	92	5	4	4.9	.269	.340	.469	.057	.267	.339	.480	.270	12.8	128-RF 0	

Breakout: 30%   *Improve: 56%*   *Collapse: 14%*   *Attrition: 13%*   *Comparables: Fred Lynn, Dave Parker, Tino Martinez*

Reggie Sanders "settled down" and played for the Cardinals in consecutive seasons, so Burnitz is currently the game's great wandering slugger; the Pirates will be his sixth team in the last six years. The last time Burnitz didn't bop 30 home runs was also the last time he was expected to star on a putative contender, the 2002 Mets. Now that he's 37, it's unlikely that he'll do either again—mash thirty or star—but he's had an excellent career for someone who didn't really get going until he was on the wrong side of 27.

RONNY CEDENO   **SS**   **Bats: R Throws: R**   Height: 6′ 0″   Weight: 180   Born: February 2, 1983   Age: 23

YEAR	TM	LVL	AGE	PA	R	2B	3B	HR	RBI	BB	SO	SB	CS	SPEED	BA	OBP	SLG	MLVR	EQBA	EQOBP	EQSLG	EQA	VORP	DEFENSE	
2003	DAY	A+	20	408	43	18	1	4	36	21	82	19	6	6.6	.211	.257	.295	-.193	.194	.231	.296	.195	-30.3	77-SS 2	28-2B -1
2004	WTN	AA	21	424	39	19	5	6	48	24	74	10	10	5.1	.279	.328	.401	.032	.261	.301	.376	.236	4.0	115-SS 5	
2005	IOW	AAA	22	268	42	14	1	8	36	20	31	11	3	5.7	.355	.403	.518	.288	.318	.361	.460	.282	23.4	64-SS 4	
2005	CHN	MLB	22	87	13	3	0	1	6	5	11	1	0	4.7	.300	.356	.375	.012	.296	.352	.370	.258	3.6	18-SS -1	
2006	*CHN*	*MLB*	*23*	*473*	*57*	*23*	*2*	*7*	*44*	*26*	*69*	*12*	*5*	*5.1*	*.274*	*.320*	*.387*	*-.082*	*.275*	*.320*	*.394*	*.243*	*13.4*	*112-SS 2*	

Breakout: 25%   Improve: 46%   Collapse: 30%   Attrition: 15%   Comparables: Luis Rivas, Tom Veryzer, Rennie Stennett

As a shortstop, there's little he can't do: his tremendous arm conjures up memories of Shawon Dunston, but Cedeno has softer hands and better range. Whether or not he'll become a better hitter is the question. He has a nice, even swing, but he's easily overpowered, and has no notion of working the count. Promoted aggressively throughout his career, he could struggle for a year or two before settling in as a genuinely useful hitter in the big leagues. He's penciled in as the Opening Day shortstop, but it remains to be seen if the Cubs can show some patience and let him grow up in the big leagues, or if they'll get frustrated and turn to Neifi Perez.

BRIAN DOPIRAK   **1B**   **Bats: R Throws: R**   Height: 6′ 4″   Weight: 230   Born: December 20, 1983   Age: 22

YEAR	TM	LVL	AGE	PA	R	2B	3B	HR	RBI	BB	SO	SB	CS	SPEED	BA	OBP	SLG	MLVR	EQBA	EQOBP	EQSLG	EQA	VORP	DEFENSE
2003	BOI	A-	19	218	25	4	0	13	37	24	58	0	2	2.5	.240	.330	.464	.105	.197	.265	.382	.221	-22.3	41-1B 5
2003	LNS	A	19	82	8	3	0	2	10	2	22	0	0	2.8	.269	.305	.385	.034	.241	.269	.380	.222	-3.7	13-1B -1
2004	LNS	A	20	597	94	38	0	39	120	48	123	4	3	3.7	.307	.363	.593	.400	.264	.313	.506	.272	20.3	114-1B -15
2005	DAY	A+	21	553	53	26	0	16	76	37	107	1	4	2.5	.235	.289	.381	-.086	.203	.253	.341	.208	-44.1	116-1B -11
2006	*CHN*	*MLB*	*22*	*466*	*47*	*21*	*1*	*17*	*62*	*32*	*100*	*0*	*1*	*3.4*	*.236*	*.292*	*.408*	*-.127*	*.237*	*.293*	*.415*	*.234*	*-7.3*	*110-1B -7*

Breakout: 34%   Improve: 61%   Collapse: 21%   Attrition: 4%   Comparables: Scott Thorman, Jason Hart, Leo Daigle

The ill-starred point man in the Cubs' hugely overrated tandem of Dunedin High School sluggers—Ryan Harvey's the other—Dopirak's Double-A debut was an unmitigated disaster. Happily, he's still very young, so he'll almost certainly repeat the level and see if he learned anything about commanding the strike zone. His glove doesn't get good marks, so if Harvey's a Rob Deer wannabe, maybe Dopirak is like the legendary Joey Meyer, claimant to the title of longest home run ever hit.

MIKE FONTENOT   **2B**   **Bats: L Throws: R**   Height: 5′ 8″   Weight: 160   Born: June 9, 1980   Age: 26

YEAR	TM	LVL	AGE	PA	R	2B	3B	HR	RBI	BB	SO	SB	CS	SPEED	BA	OBP	SLG	MLVR	EQBA	EQOBP	EQSLG	EQA	VORP	DEFENSE	
2003	BOW	AA	23	511	63	24	5	12	66	50	89	16	5	5.8	.325	.399	.481	.303	.307	.372	.469	.289	44.4	112-2B 14	
2004	OTT	AAA	24	586	73	30	10	8	49	48	111	14	7	6.5	.279	.346	.420	.012	.256	.323	.383	.248	8.4	135-2B -13	
2005	IOW	AAA	25	446	60	22	10	6	39	59	77	3	2	5.8	.272	.377	.430	.032	.237	.330	.360	.245	2.7	58-2B 1	35-3B -4
2006	*CHN*	*MLB*	*26*	*402*	*47*	*19*	*3*	*7*	*36*	*37*	*73*	*5*	*2*	*4.7*	*.254*	*.332*	*.385*	*-.078*	*.255*	*.333*	*.391*	*.247*	*6.9*	*96-2B 0*	

Breakout: 11%   Improve: 37%   Collapse: 32%   Attrition: 24%   Comparables: Don Wert, Marco Scutaro, Damion Easley

One of the first 20 players picked in the '01 draft, he's now a washout as prospects go. Fontenot would still make a better placeholder for an open second base job than a number of veterans, but it's going to take someone really desperate. Nobody thinks he's anything more than adequate afield, and scouts deride his long, slow, overly segmented hitting stroke. He did smack RHPs for a .275/.377/.466 clip in the PCL.

NOMAR GARCIAPARRA   **DL**   **Bats: R Throws: R**   Height: 6′ 0″   Weight: 167   Born: July 23, 1973   Age: 32

YEAR	TM	LVL	AGE	PA	R	2B	3B	HR	RBI	BB	SO	SB	CS	SPEED	BA	OBP	SLG	MLVR	EQBA	EQOBP	EQSLG	EQA	VORP	DEFENSE	
2003	BOS	MLB	29	718	120	37	13	28	105	39	61	19	5	7.4	.301	.345	.524	.170	.297	.346	.526	.292	59.7	151-SS -9	
2004	BOS	MLB	30	169	24	7	3	5	21	8	16	2	0	5.3	.321	.367	.500	.158	.320	.367	.497	.295	13.7	35-SS -5	
2004	CHN	MLB	30	184	28	14	0	4	20	16	14	2	1	4.7	.297	.364	.455	.096	.291	.359	.436	.275	10.6	40-SS -2	
2005	CHN	MLB	31	247	28	12	0	9	30	12	24	0	0	4.1	.283	.320	.452	.050	.275	.315	.445	.260	8.9	33-3B -5	23-SS -1
2006	*LAN*	*MLB*	*32*	*321*	*37*	*16*	*1*	*9*	*40*	*20*	*31*	*2*	*1*	*5.0*	*.273*	*.324*	*.427*	*-.022*	*.279*	*.330*	*.445*	*.259*	*14.4*	*78-SS -3*	

Breakout: 8%   Improve: 28%   Collapse: 38%   Attrition: 21%   Comparables: Shawon Dunston, George Kell, Jeff Cirillo

Paul Molitor had three seasons with more than a 100 days spent on the DL, on the way to logging a career total of 556 DL days. Nomar's got two 100-plus seasons so far (2001 and 2005) and his career total is now 367. Molitor may not have had the benefits of advances in sports medicine, but that cuts both ways; Garciaparra can be rebuilt again and again, but like a GM car, after a few too many recalls and repairsyou have to wonder if it isn't time for a new set of wheels. Ned Colletti took a page from Jim Hendry's playbook, bringing Garciaparra to the Dodgers in a one-year deal for $6 million, plus $4 million more in playing time incentives. Colletti may want to read up on lemon laws: Nomar's speed is shot, and his power has gone into a steep dive since he left Fenway; in the last three years, away from the Fens, he's hit .281/.325/.448. That isn't star material, especially not at first base, where Nomar is supposed to play in the hope he'll avoid injury and snap back to form at a less demanding defensive position.

ADAM GREENBERG OF **Bats: L Throws: L** Height: 5′ 9″ Weight: 180 Born: February 21, 1981 Age: 25

YEAR	TM	LVL	AGE	PA	R	2B	3B	HR	RBI	BB	SO	SB	CS	SPEED	BA	OBP	SLG	MLVR	EQBA	EQOBP	EQSLG	EQA	VORP	DEFENSE				
2003	DAY	A+	22	313	42	11	5	3	27	38	46	26	9	7.6	.299	.387	.410	.181	.273	.348	.399	.266	2.3	43-RF	1	19-LF	-1
2004	DAY	A+	23	375	52	10	12	3	28	42	65	16	8	7.2	.291	.381	.424	.152	.256	.331	.383	.252	-6.2	40-LF	0	29-RF	1
2004	WTN	AA	23	132	22	7	2	3	10	14	30	3	0	6.6	.274	.364	.451	.150	.253	.328	.408	.261	-1.0	12-LF	0		
2005	WTN	AA	24	368	51	12	9	4	33	56	68	15	4	7.5	.269	.386	.407	.106	.240	.340	.370	.255	-5.4	70-RF	-2	13-CF	0
2006	*CHN*	*MLB*	*25*	*405*	*52*	*18*	*4*	*6*	*33*	*39*	*77*	*11*	*4*	*6.1*	*.254*	*.334*	*.380*	*-.082*	*.255*	*.334*	*.386*	*.249*	*-0.3*	*97-RF*	*1*		

Breakout: 10% Improve: 33% Collapse: 34% Attrition: 17%   *Comparables: Jason Conti, Dave Martinez, McKay Christensen*

A good organizational soldier, Greenberg's big opportunity, to be Doug Dascenzo to Corey Patterson's reprise of the Jerome Walton blue-chip disaster role, was literally swatted down when his bean was creased by a fastball in his first big league at-bat. He's back in action this winter but might get stuck in a career track similar to Dascenzo's as a speed-'n-defense reserve. As is, he's too young to strike Dusty Baker's fancy and probably doomed to a season spent amidst the tall corn of Iowa.

JERRY HAIRSTON 2B/CF **Bats: R Throws: R** Height: 5′ 10″ Weight: 185 Born: May 29, 1976 Age: 30

YEAR	TM	LVL	AGE	PA	R	2B	3B	HR	RBI	BB	SO	SB	CS	SPEED	BA	OBP	SLG	MLVR	EQBA	EQOBP	EQSLG	EQA	VORP	DEFENSE				
2003	BAL	MLB	27	249	25	12	2	2	21	23	25	14	5	5.3	.271	.353	.372	-.048	.275	.360	.376	.265	6.8	47-2B	-1		
2004	BAL	MLB	28	328	43	19	1	2	24	29	29	13	8	6.3	.303	.378	.397	.027	.306	.382	.401	.275	9.3	23-RF	1	14-CF	0
2005	CHN	MLB	29	423	51	25	2	4	30	31	46	8	9	5.4	.261	.336	.368	-.058	.260	.335	.375	.244	0.5	43-CF	0	37-2B	-2
2006	*CHN*	*MLB*	*30*	*414*	*54*	*21*	*2*	*5*	*36*	*34*	*42*	*12*	*5*	*5.3*	*.266*	*.341*	*.379*	*-.062*	*.267*	*.342*	*.385*	*.251*	*6.3*	*99-2B*	*-1*		

Breakout: 19% Improve: 44% Collapse: 23% Attrition: 20%   *Comparables: Alan Bannister, Mike Hershberger, Charlie Moore*

Although not really suited for everyday play in center, Hairston has at least given himself a career by moving to the outfield. He can spot for Todd Walker against the league's tougher lefties at second, fill in as an outfielder, and he gives the Cubs' bench somebody who could actually get on base now and again. His repeated injuries seem to have ruined him as a runner, but he's an adequate reserve.

RYAN HARVEY RF **Bats: R Throws: R** Height: 6′ 5″ Weight: 220 Born: August 30, 1984 Age: 21

YEAR	TM	LVL	AGE	PA	R	2B	3B	HR	RBI	BB	SO	SB	CS	SPEED	BA	OBP	SLG	MLVR	EQBA	EQOBP	EQSLG	EQA	VORP	DEFENSE	
2004	BOI	A-	19	257	42	8	0	14	43	20	77	2	2	4.4	.268	.331	.485	.096	.212	.258	.377	.219	-29.0	37-RF	3
2005	PEO	A	20	506	71	30	2	24	100	24	137	8	4	5.5	.257	.302	.484	.074	.221	.254	.419	.228	-22.4	94-RF	-6
2006	*CHN*	*MLB*	*21*	*442*	*47*	*22*	*1*	*17*	*55*	*20*	*123*	*4*	*3*	*4.5*	*.231*	*.272*	*.412*	*-.160*	*.232*	*.273*	*.419*	*.225*	*-10.2*	*105-RF*	*-3*

Breakout: 42% Improve: 60% Collapse: 20% Attrition: 8%   *Comparables: Luis Lopez, Wily Pena, Thomas Collaro*

The ath-a-lete's athlete, Harvey is the organization's other Dunedin High 1st round pick with a blue chip rep and tools. Fast, with a tremendous throwing arm and raw power, he could be a great right fielder. After a slow start, he heated up in the second half, finishing as the Midwest League's home run leader, but failed to dispel concerns about his approach at the plate. Harvey's got a long swing, he can be overpowered, he hasn't learned to lay off of breaking stuff out of the zone, and he doesn't change his approach with two strikes. Those are the sorts of weaknesses that could make him easy meat in the higher levels if he doesn't start improving. If you have all of Rob Deer's skills but not his patience, you don't get to grow up to be Rob Deer.

DERREK LEE 1B **Bats: L Throws: L** Height: 6' 4" Weight: 185 Born: September 6, 1975 Age: 30

YEAR	TM	LVL	AGE	PA	R	2B	3B	HR	RBI	BB	SO	SB	CS	SPEED	BA	OBP	SLG	MLVR	EQBA	EQOBP	EQSLG	EQA	VORP	DEFENSE
2003	FLO	MLB	27	643	91	31	2	31	92	88	131	21	8	5.7	.271	.379	.508	.226	.274	.380	.524	.303	41.0	152-1B 15
2004	CHN	MLB	28	686	90	39	1	32	98	68	128	12	5	5.0	.278	.356	.504	.148	.271	.348	.494	.284	32.1	158-1B 15
2005	CHN	MLB	29	691	120	50	3	46	107	85	109	15	3	5.8	.335	.418	.662	.534	.327	.412	.658	.344	95.6	156-1B 13
2006	CHN	MLB	30	663	101	38	2	38	112	76	116	12	4	5.3	.298	.383	.570	.281	.299	.384	.579	.312	51.0	154-1B 8

Breakout: 12% Improve: 36% Collapse: 21% Attrition: 3% Comparables: Dave Winfield, Cliff Floyd, Eric Karros

Whether you prefer Equivalent Average or VORP, raw stats or interpretive data, Lee was the best hitter in the National League. That he didn't win the MVP, while Andre Dawson did—but shouldn't have—in 1987, is more evidence that unfairness is as constant as death and taxes, and that voting results are only as credible as the voters. The important question is whether or not Lee can keep it up. There's no reason to see why he can't: he never gets nicked up, and he hasn't had a bad year since establishing himself six years ago. As far as his aging gracefully, he's the most athletic slugger at first base since a young Eddie Murray.

RICHARD LEWIS 2B **Bats: R Throws: R** Height: 6' 1" Weight: 190 Born: June 29, 1980 Age: 26

YEAR	TM	LVL	AGE	PA	R	2B	3B	HR	RBI	BB	SO	SB	CS	SPEED	BA	OBP	SLG	MLVR	EQBA	EQOBP	EQSLG	EQA	VORP	DEFENSE
2003	GRN	AA	23	512	59	23	3	6	47	44	101	19	9	6.1	.239	.305	.341	-.087	.224	.281	.336	.221	-16.9	116-2B -8
2004	WTN	AA	24	425	68	27	10	10	59	37	94	7	6	6.5	.329	.391	.532	.347	.299	.351	.479	.281	34.4	96-2B 3
2004	IOW	AAA	24	125	14	8	1	3	11	4	21	4	0	6.0	.246	.280	.407	-.216	.219	.250	.349	.214	-5.4	28-2B 3
2005	IOW	AAA	25	285	28	10	3	2	23	18	64	4	2	5.1	.217	.277	.300	-.382	.193	.245	.266	.186	-23.9	67-2B -1
2005	WTN	AA	25	83	8	1	1	1	7	13	18	2	1	5.0	.246	.373	.333	-.023	.216	.322	.302	.227	-1.9	16-2B 3
2006	CHN	MLB	26	236	25	11	2	4	20	15	51	3	2	5.0	.238	.294	.356	-.191	.239	.295	.362	.221	-1.3	59-2B 0

Breakout: 24% Improve: 45% Collapse: 32% Attrition: 36% Comparables: Mariano Duncan, Bobby Smith, Tim Hulett

Still notionally a prospect, Lewis did not recover quickly from the time lost to the broken leg of '04, and after a slow start at Iowa he had to be demoted to Double-A. At one point, the Cubs were joking about the Braves' hitting instruction, or lack thereof, confidently thinking that they'd turned Lewis around and found ways to exploit his quick bat. That's pretty bold talk from the outfit that has seen its share of highly-regarded hitting prospects—Corey Patterson, Dave Kelton, Brian Dopirak, to name a few—stall out. At this point, Lewis is too old to be considered a prospect, and he was removed from the 40-man this winter.

JOSE MACIAS UT **Bats: B Throws: R** Height: 5' 10" Weight: 173 Born: January 25, 1972 Age: 34

YEAR	TM	LVL	AGE	PA	R	2B	3B	HR	RBI	BB	SO	SB	CS	SPEED	BA	OBP	SLG	MLVR	EQBA	EQOBP	EQSLG	EQA	VORP	DEFENSE		
2003	MON	MLB	31	286	31	15	2	4	22	11	45	4	3	5.8	.239	.273	.353	-.249	.232	.268	.342	.213	-12.8	28-LF 1	18-3B 0	
2004	CHN	MLB	32	202	23	6	3	3	22	5	38	4	1	6.7	.268	.292	.376	-.135	.262	.286	.369	.230	-1.6			
2005	CHN	MLB	33	186	15	8	0	1	13	6	24	4	3	4.7	.254	.274	.316	-.243	.253	.275	.320	.212	-7.1	11-3B -3	13-2B 0	
2006	CHN	MLB	34	87	10	4	1	1	8	3	13	1	1	5.2	.259	.291	.364	-.173	.260	.292	.371	.221	-0.7	25-3B 0		

Breakout: 28% Improve: 51% Collapse: 34% Attrition: 56% Comparables: Nelson Liriano, Quinton McCracken, Mike Mordecai

If putrescence is a disease of the batting order, Macias is one of its symptoms. Macias owes his career to his ability to play six positions, a virtue when you start off with the assumption you need seven relievers in your pen. If you stick with six, you've got room for two baseball players instead of one Macias and one infrequently used reliever.

SCOTT MOORE 3B **Bats: L Throws: R** Height: 6' 2" Weight: 180 Born: November 17, 1983 Age: 22

YEAR	TM	LVL	AGE	PA	R	2B	3B	HR	RBI	BB	SO	SB	CS	SPEED	BA	OBP	SLG	MLVR	EQBA	EQOBP	EQSLG	EQA	VORP	DEFENSE
2003	WMI	A	19	421	40	16	6	6	45	41	110	2	4	4.4	.239	.325	.363	.030	.224	.292	.358	.226	-6.9	95-3B -10
2004	LAK	A+	20	453	52	13	4	14	56	49	125	2	4	4.2	.223	.322	.384	-.016	.197	.280	.348	.221	-15.3	114-3B -15
2005	DAY	A+	21	536	77	31	2	20	82	55	134	22	7	5.8	.281	.358	.485	.186	.246	.316	.431	.259	16.5	116-3B -18
2006	CHN	MLB	22	511	60	26	2	17	59	45	139	10	4	4.5	.235	.308	.408	-.103	.236	.308	.415	.242	2.5	120-3B -11

Breakout: 30% Improve: 57% Collapse: 19% Attrition: 6% Comparables: Pete Paciorek, Scott Kirby, Carlos Pena

Touted as the next Eric Chavez by the Tigers when they picked him, Moore resembled Chavez only in that he hit lefty and was also a high school shortstop bound for the hot corner. Moore was a much more rough-edged stone, and the Tigers didn't seem to polish him in any phase of the game. Dumped on the Cubs in the Farnsworth trade, Moore did, at least, arrive with an upbeat attitude and a good work ethic, qualities that helped him finally establish himself as a prospect. He's still not considered to be very smooth at third, but if the Cubs learned their lesson after jerking Dave Kelton all over the diamond they will just leave Moore alone.

MATT MURTON   **OF**   **Bats: R Throws: R**   Height: 6' 1"   Weight: 215   Born: October 3, 1981   Age: 24

YEAR	TM	LVL	AGE	PA	R	2B	3B	HR	RBI	BB	SO	SB	CS	SPEED	BA	OBP	SLG	MLVR	EQBA	EQOBP	EQSLG	EQA	VORP	DEFENSE			
2003	LOW	A-	21	227	30	11	2	2	29	27	39	9	3	5.6	.286	.374	.397	.147	.248	.316	.359	.243	-14.0	47-LF	-2		
2004	SAR	A+	22	425	60	16	4	11	55	42	61	5	4	5.0	.301	.372	.452	.211	.277	.338	.434	.265	6.0	96-LF	5		
2004	DAY	A+	22	89	13	1	1	2	8	8	10	2	0	5.8	.253	.326	.367	-.027	.224	.291	.336	.226	-6.1	19-LF	-1		
2005	WTN	AA	23	347	46	17	4	8	46	29	42	18	5	5.9	.342	.403	.498	.323	.312	.366	.469	.287	17.4	61-LF	4	14-RF	-1
2005	CHN	MLB	23	158	19	3	2	7	14	16	22	2	1	5.3	.321	.386	.521	.280	.314	.384	.536	.308	12.5	37-LF	-1		
2006	*CHN*	*MLB*	*24*	*542*	*66*	*26*	*3*	*12*	*59*	*43*	*83*	*9*	*3*	*5.0*	*.281*	*.343*	*.418*	*.004*	*.283*	*.343*	*.425*	*.260*	*8.5*	*127-LF*	*0*		

Breakout: 7%   *Improve: 26%*   *Collapse: 32%*   *Attrition: 9%*   *Comparables: Lee Walls, Rondell White, Rick Reichardt*

Perhaps aided by Von Joshua, his hitting coach at West Tenn, Murton has shortened his stroke as a pro, giving him tremendous plate coverage and power to all fields. Joshua compares Murton's stroke and power on contact to one of his past disciples, Magglio Ordonez. Murton also has the speed to become a quality glove in either outfield corner, but with the Jacque Jones signing, he'll wind up in left. Murton should be the Cubs' best hitting outfielder, but a slow start could give John Mabry more at-bats than would be good for the Cubs' immediate or long-term future. One of the few real carrot-tops in baseball, and there are never enough of those to go around

COREY PATTERSON   **CF**   **Bats: L Throws: R**   Height: 5' 10"   Weight: 180   Born: August 13, 1979   Age: 26

YEAR	TM	LVL	AGE	PA	R	2B	3B	HR	RBI	BB	SO	SB	CS	SPEED	BA	OBP	SLG	MLVR	EQBA	EQOBP	EQSLG	EQA	VORP	DEFENSE	
2003	CHN	MLB	23	347	49	17	7	13	55	15	77	16	5	8.0	.298	.329	.511	.163	.293	.326	.506	.279	22.7	79-CF	-3
2004	CHN	MLB	24	682	91	33	6	24	72	45	168	32	9	7.4	.266	.320	.452	.006	.261	.315	.440	.260	19.4	151-CF	2
2005	CHN	MLB	25	476	47	15	3	13	34	23	118	15	5	6.8	.215	.254	.348	-.254	.212	.255	.350	.214	-17.0	111-CF	2
2005	IOW	AAA	25	101	16	4	0	5	12	8	19	6	1	6.6	.297	.366	.505	.143	.258	.319	.425	.259	2.2	23-CF	5
2006	*BAL*	*MLB*	*26*	*564*	*80*	*26*	*4*	*19*	*67*	*31*	*112*	*26*	*9*	*6.5*	*.260*	*.305*	*.434*	*-.038*	*.265*	*.314*	*.455*	*.256*	*13.7*	*132-CF*	*1*

Breakout: 31%   *Improve: 70%*   *Collapse: 12%*   *Attrition: 12%*   *Comparables: Dave Martinez, Marty Keough, Oddibe McDowell*

It's now fashionable to say that Patterson was rushed, but was he? He had over 1400 minor league PAs before he was called up to stay, and he'd played full seasons in A-ball and Double-A, and more than half of a season in the PCL. This wasn't a case like Jon Nunnally or Jose Guillen, going straight from A-ball to the majors and having to learn to swim in the deep end. Instead, it looks more like Patterson was ruined, not rushed, and that happened in the major leagues. Maybe more time in the minors would have helped make him more patient, but that isn't guaranteed, and what is it that major league hitting coaches are for, if they can't help a hitter assess and address his most glaring weaknesses? It remains to be seen if Patterson can reclaim his promise, but if he does, it will be as an Oriole.

ERIC PATTERSON   **2B**   **Bats: L Throws: R**   Height: 5' 11"   Weight: 170   Born: April 8, 1983   Age: 23

YEAR	TM	LVL	AGE	PA	R	2B	3B	HR	RBI	BB	SO	SB	CS	SPEED	BA	OBP	SLG	MLVR	EQBA	EQOBP	EQSLG	EQA	VORP	DEFENSE	
2005	PEO	A	22	496	90	26	11	13	71	53	94	40	11	7.9	.333	.405	.535	.359	.285	.345	.451	.276	29.0	103-2B	9
2005	WTN	AA	22	37	5	2	0	0	2	6	7	3	2	5.1	.200	.324	.267	-.219	.186	.293	.252	.216	-2.8		
2006	*CHN*	*MLB*	*23*	*522*	*71*	*30*	*6*	*11*	*52*	*42*	*117*	*20*	*8*	*5.7*	*.261*	*.324*	*.419*	*-.041*	*.262*	*.325*	*.426*	*.254*	*14.9*	*123-2B*	*6*

Breakout: 7%   *Improve: 26%*   *Collapse: 32%*   *Attrition: 4%*   *Comparables: Scott Pratt, Brooks Conrad, Jermaine Clark*

Showed much more power than what was expected when the Cubs picked him out of Georgia Tech in the 8th round of the '04 draft. A star from a top college program is supposed to be able to bitchslap the Midwest League, but the Cubs' confidence in Patterson's prospectdom is perhaps better reflected in his promotion to West Tenn for the Southern League playoffs. He still has a few finer points to pick up in his play at second, but he might well be the one Cubs hitting prospect without a significant weakness.

NEIFI PEREZ   **2B/SS**   **Bats: B Throws: L**   Height: 6' 0"   Weight: 175   Born: June 2, 1973   Age: 33

YEAR	TM	LVL	AGE	PA	R	2B	3B	HR	RBI	BB	SO	SB	CS	SPEED	BA	OBP	SLG	MLVR	EQBA	EQOBP	EQSLG	EQA	VORP	DEFENSE			
2003	SFN	MLB	30	344	27	19	4	1	31	14	23	3	2	5.2	.256	.285	.348	-.194	.256	.287	.349	.223	-4.8	42-2B	5	35-SS	7
2004	SFN	MLB	31	344	28	12	1	2	33	21	35	0	1	3.9	.232	.276	.295	-.314	.230	.276	.292	.205	-14.4	49-SS	2	32-2B	3
2004	CHN	MLB	31	65	12	5	0	2	6	3	6	1	0	5.0	.371	.400	.548	.385	.365	.394	.524	.311	8.6	13-SS	1		
2005	CHN	MLB	32	597	59	33	1	9	54	18	47	8	4	4.6	.274	.298	.383	-.094	.271	.296	.385	.236	6.6	120-SS	17	18-2B	-2
2006	*CHN*	*MLB*	*33*	*407*	*42*	*21*	*1*	*4*	*37*	*16*	*38*	*3*	*2*	*4.3*	*.263*	*.295*	*.358*	*-.170*	*.264*	*.296*	*.365*	*.221*	*1.7*	*97-SS*	*6*		

Breakout: 21%   *Improve: 42%*   *Collapse: 23%*   *Attrition: 20%*   *Comparables: Tito Fuentes, Rafael Ramirez, Deivi Cruz*

(continued next page)

Neifi Perez *(continued)*

What's more important for pondering future performance, a .368/.403/.559 April, or the previous three years, or five, or heck, his entire career? He's supposed to be back only as insurance against Cedeno's faltering, but as Perez proved while "backing up" Nomar, some insurance policies only work if you never have to use them. The league's leading "manage me or I'll hurt you" hitter, Perez finished fourth in the NL among non-pitchers for sac bunts and third in GIDPs. Re-signed to a two-year deal, but then, the Cubs are the only people who value him.

FELIX PIE   **CF**   **Bats: L Throws: L**   Height: 6′ 2″   Weight: 170   Born: February 8, 1985   Age: 21

YEAR	TM	LVL	AGE	PA	R	2B	3B	HR	RBI	BB	SO	SB	CS	SPEED	BA	OBP	SLG	MLVR	EQBA	EQOBP	EQSLG	EQA	VORP	DEFENSE
2003	LNS	A	18	552	72	22	9	4	47	41	98	19	13	6.5	.285	.346	.388	.106	.263	.313	.380	.240	1.2	120-CF 5
2004	DAY	A+	19	460	79	17	9	8	47	38	113	31	16	8.4	.299	.361	.442	.152	.265	.319	.406	.253	8.3	98-CF 6
2005	WTN	AA	20	261	41	17	5	11	25	16	53	13	9	7.5	.304	.349	.554	.286	.269	.306	.491	.264	11.5	55-CF -2
2006	*CHN*	*MLB*	*21*	*471*	*62*	*26*	*3*	*15*	*53*	*30*	*104*	*17*	*7*	*6.3*	*.266*	*.316*	*.447*	*-.014*	*.267*	*.316*	*.455*	*.256*	*12.4*	*111-CF 2*

Breakout: 23%   *Improve: 52%*   *Collapse: 26%*   *Attrition: 11%*   Comparables: *Corey Patterson, Dick Kokos, Gregor Blanco*

Creepy, as far as his top comp, isn't it? Pie is all raw potential. Although he has tremendous speed, he has no real instinct for basestealing, and he's still learning the best routes to take in center. He could have excellent power, but he's still learning how to use his hands. The results hint that he's a quick study, but any talk of having him start '06 in Wrigley was far too ambitious. He needs all the time he can get in the minors after a bone bruise on his ankle abruptly ended his '05 campaign. Happily, he'll get that time now that Juan Pierre is a Cub, but like lunch in Twin Peaks, the future belongs to Pie.

ARAMIS RAMIREZ   **3B**   **Bats: R Throws: R**   Height: 6′ 1″   Weight: 219   Born: June 25, 1978   Age: 28

YEAR	TM	LVL	AGE	PA	R	2B	3B	HR	RBI	BB	SO	SB	CS	SPEED	BA	OBP	SLG	MLVR	EQBA	EQOBP	EQSLG	EQA	VORP	DEFENSE
2003	PIT	MLB	25	415	44	25	1	12	67	25	68	1	1	3.3	.280	.330	.448	.060	.275	.325	.444	.265	17.5	95-3B -6
2003	CHN	MLB	25	255	31	7	1	15	39	17	31	1	1	4.4	.259	.314	.491	.070	.254	.306	.487	.266	11.5	61-3B -4
2004	CHN	MLB	26	606	99	32	1	36	103	49	62	0	2	2.9	.318	.373	.578	.316	.310	.364	.565	.306	50.8	138-3B -15
2005	CHN	MLB	27	506	72	30	0	31	92	35	60	0	1	3.4	.302	.358	.568	.288	.297	.354	.569	.302	42.3	115-3B -14
2006	*CHN*	*MLB*	*28*	*591*	*81*	*32*	*1*	*32*	*101*	*48*	*75*	*1*	*1*	*3.7*	*.293*	*.356*	*.540*	*.198*	*.295*	*.357*	*.549*	*.294*	*42.0*	*138-3B -8*

Breakout: 18%   *Improve: 51%*   *Collapse: 19%*   *Attrition: 5%*   Comparables: *Tony Perez, Larry Parrish, Tim Wallach*

Life in a major market and exposure on a super station have done wonders for Ramirez's defensive rep just as he's begun to lose his defensive value. He used to start a good number of DPs from third, but whether it's a matter of getting older or having Todd Walker on the pivot, that isn't the case these days. Although he's apparently never going to become a particularly patient hitter—Ramirez has drawn more than 40 unintentional walks once in his career—he's still putting runs on the board, and should continue to be one for the next two or three years, or, almost to the end of his Cubs contract.

BRANDON SING   **1B/OF**   **Bats: R Throws: R**   Height: 6′ 5″   Weight: 210   Born: March 13, 1981   Age: 25

YEAR	TM	LVL	AGE	PA	R	2B	3B	HR	RBI	BB	SO	SB	CS	SPEED	BA	OBP	SLG	MLVR	EQBA	EQOBP	EQSLG	EQA	VORP	DEFENSE	
2003	DAY	A+	22	154	20	6	0	4	23	17	29	0	3	3.6	.235	.318	.368	-.003	.207	.278	.344	.216	-10.7	31-LF -3	
2003	WTN	AA	22	156	15	7	0	5	23	10	39	2	1	4.2	.209	.256	.367	-.130	.193	.238	.355	.210	-12.5	36-1B 2	
2004	DAY	A+	23	504	86	27	0	32	94	84	101	1	3	3.4	.270	.399	.571	.339	.221	.333	.470	.272	11.3	110-1B -8	
2005	WTN	AA	24	508	74	29	0	26	71	91	110	2	5	3.2	.276	.404	.538	.310	.230	.344	.446	.271	9.4	75-1B 2	31-RF -1
2006	*CHN*	*MLB*	*25*	*479*	*56*	*22*	*1*	*20*	*63*	*58*	*116*	*1*	*1*	*3.6*	*.236*	*.334*	*.440*	*-.016*	*.237*	*.335*	*.447*	*.261*	*2.7*	*113-1B -2*	

Breakout: 26%   *Improve: 59%*   *Collapse: 21%*   *Attrition: 9%*   Comparables: *Ken Harrelson, Eric Munson, Jeff Bailey*

Like a good eiswein, Sing seems to simply get better the later he's been left to grow. After spending much of the previous three years at Daytona, Sing finally passed the Double-A test, and at 25 he's not too old to have a career. He just can't afford a misstep from this point on. Perhaps predictably for someone who hasn't had a settled position, Sing needs reps at first before he'll be an asset there, but that and a good year at the plate in Iowa would make him nice trade bait.

GEOVANY SOTO   **C**   **Bats: R Throws: R**   Height: 6′ 1″   Weight: 230   Born: January 20, 1983   Age: 23

YEAR	TM	LVL	AGE	PA	R	2B	3B	HR	RBI	BB	SO	SB	CS	SPEED	BA	OBP	SLG	MLVR	EQBA	EQOBP	EQSLG	EQA	VORP	DEFENSE
2003	DAY	A+	20	336	26	12	2	2	38	31	58	0	0	3.6	.242	.312	.316	-.070	.224	.283	.320	.217	-12.9	76-C 0
2004	WTN	AA	21	380	47	16	0	9	48	40	71	1	2	3.5	.271	.355	.401	.069	.244	.318	.363	.241	0.6	100-C 4
2005	IOW	AAA	22	342	30	14	0	4	39	48	77	0	1	2.9	.253	.357	.342	-.140	.215	.311	.281	.219	-13.1	86-C 4
2006	*CHN*	*MLB*	*23*	*291*	*28*	*12*	*1*	*5*	*27*	*27*	*60*	*0*	*1*	*4.0*	*.234*	*.309*	*.347*	*-.180*	*.234*	*.310*	*.352*	*.225*	*-1.2*	*71-C 1*

Breakout: 35%   *Improve: 57%*   *Collapse: 32%*   *Attrition: 22%*   Comparables: *Steve Swisher, Carlos Maldonado, Jean Boscan*

A nimble backstop with a strong arm, Soto might be ready to replace Henry Blanco right now, not that that's much of a standard. The question is whether Soto's quick bat and decent patience at the plate will be good enough to make him more than a career reserve. He also has some experience at the infield and outfield spots, a quirky (or Quirk-y) virtue for a backup catcher.

RYAN THERIOT   **INF**   **Bats: R Throws: R**   Height: 5' 11"   Weight: 170   Born: December 7, 1979   Age: 26

YEAR	TM	LVL	AGE	PA	R	2B	3B	HR	RBI	BB	SO	SB	CS	SPEED	BA	OBP	SLG	MLVR	EQBA	EQOBP	EQSLG	EQA	VORP	DEFENSE		
2003	LNS	A	23	252	29	8	1	1	17	31	34	21	5	6.4	.259	.353	.318	.011	.221	.293	.279	.217	-12.8	51-2B	3	
2003	WTN	AA	23	211	20	3	0	1	9	29	21	9	8	4.7	.236	.351	.270	-.089	.222	.323	.265	.220	-6.1	48-SS	2	
2004	DAY	A+	24	384	47	14	3	1	34	48	43	13	11	5.4	.273	.367	.342	.016	.230	.308	.292	.221	-14.4	64-2B 10	37-SS	-4
2005	WTN	AA	25	499	52	28	4	1	53	45	38	24	10	5.9	.304	.365	.391	.078	.264	.315	.342	.236	-2.0	82-2B 5	31-SS	-3
2006	*CHN*	*MLB*	*26*	*402*	*44*	*16*	*2*	*0*	*25*	*33*	*49*	*12*	*4*	*4.8*	*.241*	*.307*	*.300*	*-.240*	*.242*	*.308*	*.306*	*.215*	*-4.7*	*96-2B*	*1*	

Breakout: 16%   Improve: 44%   Collapse: 32%   Attrition: 16%   Comparables: Brooks Badeaux, Bud Harrelson, Jay Pecci

The former LSU star finally made it to The Show, but it took a rash of September injuries for it to happen. (Even his debut wasn't without disappointment, as Theriot was picked off after his first big league hit.) It wasn't all Theriot's fault that he took so long; in part, his assignments within the organization were determined by Luis Montanez's ultimately pointless struggles to become the shortstop of the future, as well as being leapfrogged by Ronny Cedeno. A hitter without platoon issues, Theriot might yet become a serviceable infield reserve.

TODD WALKER   **2B**   **Bats: L Throws: R**   Height: 6' 0"   Weight: 181   Born: May 25, 1973   Age: 33

YEAR	TM	LVL	AGE	PA	R	2B	3B	HR	RBI	BB	SO	SB	CS	SPEED	BA	OBP	SLG	MLVR	EQBA	EQOBP	EQSLG	EQA	VORP	DEFENSE
2003	BOS	MLB	30	646	92	38	4	13	85	48	54	1	1	4.3	.283	.333	.428	-.004	.277	.333	.426	.263	20.7	131-2B -20
2004	CHN	MLB	31	423	60	19	4	15	50	43	52	0	3	4.9	.274	.352	.468	.091	.266	.344	.457	.272	19.8	83-2B -5
2005	CHN	MLB	32	431	50	25	3	12	40	31	40	1	1	4.8	.305	.355	.474	.155	.297	.351	.469	.279	25.9	90-2B -8
2006	*CHN*	*MLB*	*33*	*411*	*47*	*22*	*2*	*9*	*47*	*33*	*43*	*1*	*1*	*4.5*	*.279*	*.341*	*.424*	*.007*	*.280*	*.341*	*.432*	*.260*	*15.0*	*98-2B -5*

Breakout: 9%   Improve: 33%   Collapse: 38%   Attrition: 16%   Comparables: B. J. Surhoff, Billy Goodman, Jeff Cirillo

Walker seems to have settled into a nice niche as the semi-dangerous non-star, sort of the Jean-Claude Van Damme of second base. Like the Belgian menace, Walker's a bit stiff, but having finally hit lefties pretty hard this past season (.352/.398/.582, including five of his dozen bombs), Walker might at least escape the typecasting of a full-fledged platoon role.

PITCHERS

DAVID AARDSMA   **Bats: R Throws: R**   Height: 6' 5"   Weight: 200   Born: December 27, 1981   Age: 24

YEAR	TM	LVL	AGE	W	L	SV	G	GS	IP	H	BB	SO	HR	GB%	BABIP	STUFF	WHIP	ERA	PERA	EQERA	EQH9	EQBB9	EQSO9	EQHR9	VORP	WXRL
2004	FRE	AAA	22	6	4	11	44	0	55.3	46	30	53	2	—	.284	5	1.37	3.09	4.14	3.64	7.6	5.3	6.8	0.3	11.8	—
2005	NRW	AA	23	6	2	0	9	8	46.0	44	13	30	2	51%	.300	0	1.24	2.93	4.47	4.47	9.1	3.0	4.1	0.6	5.6	—
2005	WTN	AA	23	4	1	2	33	3	50.7	48	32	43	3	55%	.324	-24	1.58	3.91	6.23	5.29	9.6	6.6	5.1	1.1	1.6	—
2006	*CHN*	*MLB*	*24*	*3*	*5*	*1*	*38*	*9*	*71.0*	*76*	*41*	*46*	*9*	*49%*	*.295*	*-12*	*1.64*	*5.28*	*5.83*	*5.74*	*9.5*	*4.8*	*5.3*	*1.2*	*-0.5*	*0.3*

Breakout: 3%   Improve: 20%   Collapse: 41%   Attrition: 3%   Comparables: Jason Sekany, Mark Johnson, Jon McDonald

Part of the package received from the Giants in the fit of pique that rid the Cubs of LaTroy Hawkins, Aardsma might not fit in. His control issues seem chronic and the organization is already crowded with pitching talent. Dusty's not known for his patience, but maybe Hendry's hoping that the Alphabet King can harness his mid-90s heat and become the next Joe Nathan.

RYAN DEMPSTER   **Bats: R Throws: R**   Height: 6' 3"   Weight: 215   Born: May 3, 1977   Age: 29

YEAR	TM	LVL	AGE	W	L	SV	G	GS	IP	H	BB	SO	HR	GB%	BABIP	STUFF	WHIP	ERA	PERA	EQERA	EQH9	EQBB9	EQSO9	EQHR9	VORP	WXRL
2003	CIN	MLB	26	3	7	0	22	20	115.7	134	70	84	14	46%	.334	-3	1.76	6.53	5.23	6.45	9.9	4.8	5.8	1.1	-14.3	0.0
2004	CHN	MLB	27	1	1	2	23	0	20.7	16	13	18	1	53%	.259	0	1.40	3.91	4.43	3.98	8.0	5.3	7.1	0.4	4.3	1.0
2005	CHN	MLB	28	5	3	33	63	6	92.0	83	49	89	4	59%	.316	21	1.43	3.13	3.69	3.50	8.2	4.5	7.9	0.4	21.8	5.5
2006	*CHN*	*MLB*	*29*	*3*	*4*	*19*	*49*	*0*	*54.0*	*51*	*28*	*48*	*4*	*54%*	*.301*	*3*	*1.45*	*3.97*	*4.27*	*4.95*	*8.3*	*4.3*	*7.3*	*0.7*	*7.0*	*0.9*

Breakout: 37%   Improve: 63%   Collapse: 26%   Attrition: 16%   Comparables: Gregg Olson, Hal Reniff, Jim Gott

(continued next page)

Ryan Dempster *(continued)*

If you remember the Transformers toy craze of the '80s, you might also remember that most of the transformations were pretty lame. If you've got a killer, attack missile-equipped giant cyborg, what possible advantage do you gain from disguising it as a giant robotic space puppy? The element of surprise? Baker's exercise in vanity—trying to transform Dempster into a starter again—was the equivalent of taking a great weapon and folding it into a useless shape. After six starts and a 5.35 ERA, Dempster went back to the pen, where he cranked out one of the best Cub relief seasons ever. Intriguingly, it wasn't his strikeout rate that improved but his GB/FB ratio, which he basically doubled to better than 3-1 in relief. The Cubs let his success go to their heads; it isn't the money ($15.5 million) that's as troubling as the length. Do they really expect Dempster to pitch three full seasons?

SEAN GALLAGHER Bats: R Throws: R Height: 6' 1" Weight: 210 Born: December 30, 1985 Age: 20

YEAR	TM	LVL	AGE	W	L	SV	G	GS	IP	H	BB	SO	HR	GB%	BABIP	STUFF	WHIP	ERA	PERA	EQERA	EQH9	EQBB9	EQSO9	EQHR9	VORP	WXRL
2005	PEO	A	19	14	5	0	26	26	146.0	107	55	139	10	49%	.262	14	1.11	2.71	5.22	4.24	8.3	3.8	6.1	1.2	20.9	—
2006	CHN	MLB	20	8	9	0	26	24	144.0	133	63	109	19	45%	.270	13	1.36	4.28	4.61	4.63	8.2	3.6	6.2	1.2	16.2	2.7

Breakout: 5%   Improve: 33%   Collapse: 21%   Attrition: 0%   Comparables: Travis Foley, Gil Meche, Wes Anderson

He wasn't expected to come this far this fast, but a rash of injuries at Peoria created an opportunity, and he ran with it, throwing 36.1 innings without an earned run to start the season, and allowing only two home runs in his first 93 innings. However, concerns that he's not in the best shape were haunting him as he ran out of steam at season's end. He also doesn't have the best stuff out there, weaving in merely decent fastballs and change-ups to set up his plus curveball.

RICH HILL Bats: L Throws: L Height: 6' 5" Weight: 190 Born: March 11, 1980 Age: 26

YEAR	TM	LVL	AGE	W	L	SV	G	GS	IP	H	BB	SO	HR	GB%	BABIP	STUFF	WHIP	ERA	PERA	EQERA	EQH9	EQBB9	EQSO9	EQHR9	VORP	WXRL
2003	BOI	A-	23	1	6	0	14	14	68.3	57	32	99	5	—	.329	-20	1.30	4.35	7.23	7.38	10.9	6.0	7.2	2.4	-12.1	—
2003	LNS	A	23	0	1	0	15	4	29.3	14	36	50	0	—	.270	-22	1.71	2.76	7.30	6.20	6.6	17.1	10.6	0.4	-1.6	—
2004	DAY	A+	24	7	6	0	28	19	109.3	88	72	136	9	—	.296	-30	1.46	4.03	7.26	6.98	9.9	8.1	7.4	1.8	-15.0	—
2005	WTN	AA	25	4	3	0	10	10	57.7	42	21	90	9	43%	.297	-1	1.09	3.28	6.79	5.05	9.8	4.2	9.4	3.1	3.2	—
2005	IOW	AAA	25	6	1	0	11	10	65.0	53	14	92	11	44%	.300	22	1.03	3.60	4.62	4.33	8.5	2.0	9.2	1.9	8.8	—
2005	CHN	MLB	25	0	2	0	10	4	23.7	25	17	21	3	39%	.306	-10	1.77	9.11	5.25	8.62	9.4	6.0	7.1	1.1	-9.1	-0.4
2006	CHN	MLB	26	5	7	1	36	17	102.3	94	61	93	15	43%	.281	3	1.51	5.04	5.21	5.53	8.2	4.9	7.5	1.3	2.7	0.8

Breakout: 40%   Improve: 78%   Collapse: 3%   Attrition: 5%   Comparables: Dick Stigman, Rod Scurry, Bobby Bolin

The Cubs' system is rightly praised for the amount of pitching talent it cultivates, but Hill's skill set probably perplexes even their pitching gurus. Although Hill finished first in the minor leagues in K/9 and third overall in total strikeouts, his velocity fluctuates from the high 80s into the low 90s, which is a huge difference if he's going to make it as a starter. What he does exceptionally well is fool people with his curveball. The hope is that the addition of a cut fastball this past season will keep him from being sent over to the bullpen, but Hendry's willing to wait and watch before slotting him one role or the other. That patience may be necessary, but Hill's six months older than Mark Prior, so he really isn't a young gun.

JON LEICESTER Bats: R Throws: R Height: 6' 2" Weight: 220 Born: February 7, 1979 Age: 27

YEAR	TM	LVL	AGE	W	L	SV	G	GS	IP	H	BB	SO	HR	GB%	BABIP	STUFF	WHIP	ERA	PERA	EQERA	EQH9	EQBB9	EQSO9	EQHR9	VORP	WXRL
2003	WTN	AA	24	6	7	6	45	9	106.3	89	53	106	7	—	.278	-20	1.34	3.89	5.65	6.01	8.9	5.2	6.0	1.3	-4.6	—
2004	IOW	AAA	25	6	2	0	12	12	65.7	61	36	60	3	—	.309	8	1.48	3.70	4.50	4.78	8.4	5.6	6.0	0.4	5.8	—
2004	CHN	MLB	25	5	1	0	32	0	41.7	40	15	35	7	53%	.289	-1	1.32	3.88	4.57	4.35	8.9	3.0	6.8	1.3	6.8	0.6
2005	IOW	AAA	26	3	8	1	24	16	98.0	115	42	73	17	50%	.326	-32	1.60	5.51	6.33	6.05	10.5	4.1	4.7	2.0	-4.8	—
2006	TEX	MLB	27	4	6	0	40	10	82.0	95	39	48	13	47%	.303	-12	1.63	5.83	5.72	5.85	9.9	4.3	5.3	1.3	-1.5	0.2

Breakout: 21%   Improve: 51%   Collapse: 17%   Attrition: 4%   Comparables: Galen Cisco, Ken Clay, Dan Murray

Leicester's always had a nice moving fastball that he occasionally dials up into the mid-90s, but he's 27 now, and still hasn't figured out the other stuff that might make him a good starting pitcher. He can't consistently get a breaking pitch over for a swing-and-miss strike; minor league guru John Sickels has noted that he might be tipping his curve. Relief arms being comparatively easy to find, the Cubs decided they didn't have room for Leicester, dealing him to Texas. He could become very useful.

GREG MADDUX
Bats: R **Throws: R** Height: 6' 0" Weight: 175 Born: April 14, 1966 Age: 40

YEAR	TM	LVL	AGE	W	L	SV	G	GS	IP	H	BB	SO	HR	GB%	BABIP	STUFF	WHIP	ERA	PERA	EQERA	EQH9	EQBB9	EQSO9	EQHR9	VORP	WXRL
2003	ATL	MLB	37	16	11	0	36	36	218.3	225	33	124	24	55%	.290	9	1.18	3.96	4.27	4.69	9.6	1.3	4.7	1.0	25.1	4.8
2004	CHN	MLB	38	16	11	0	33	33	212.7	218	33	151	35	55%	.294	6	1.18	4.02	4.54	4.33	9.4	1.3	5.7	1.4	34.8	4.5
2005	CHN	MLB	39	13	15	0	35	35	225.0	239	36	136	29	54%	.299	7	1.22	4.24	4.43	4.43	9.7	1.4	5.0	1.2	28.6	4.1
2006	CHN	MLB	40	12	11	0	34	30	202.7	211	37	115	22	52%	.286	6	1.22	3.77	3.98	4.30	9.2	1.5	4.7	0.9	32.2	4.8

Breakout: 32% Improve: 62% Collapse: 5% Attrition: 5% Comparables: Dennis Martinez, Warren Spahn, Tom Seaver

Back in the uniform he never should have had to take off in the first place, he's now as out of place as Jimmy Buffett touring with the Sex Pistols. The pitcher formerly famous as Greg Maddux provided durable mediocrity on a staff not known for either. Parked in a more Don Sutton-like stage, he'll give you at least 33 starts, and if you field an adequate lineup to support him with, he'll win games for you. The Cubs aren't very gifted on that score, making it likely that he'll spend the last year of his deal watching the playoffs on TV. Notoriously close-mouthed about the art of pitching, Maddux might well make as good a pitching coach as his brother Mike, if he has any interest. That's still years off; people who take their turns with Maddox's regularity don't grow on trees.

CARLOS MARMOL
Bats: R **Throws: R** Height: 6' 2" Weight: 190 Born: October 14, 1982 Age: 23

YEAR	TM	LVL	AGE	W	L	SV	G	GS	IP	H	BB	SO	HR	GB%	BABIP	STUFF	WHIP	ERA	PERA	EQERA	EQH9	EQBB9	EQSO9	EQHR9	VORP	WXRL
2004	LNS	A	21	14	8	0	26	24	154.7	131	53	154	15	—	.286	-19	1.19	3.20	6.57	5.74	10.2	4.3	5.3	2.0	-2.2	—
2005	DAY	A+	22	6	2	0	13	13	72.3	60	37	71	7	42%	.285	-12	1.34	2.99	6.58	4.97	9.0	6.2	5.8	1.7	4.7	—
2005	WTN	AA	22	3	4	0	14	14	81.3	70	40	70	10	47%	.282	-19	1.35	3.65	7.11	4.94	10.0	5.2	5.4	2.2	5.5	—
2006	CHN	MLB	23	5	9	0	26	22	121.3	128	76	82	21	44%	.286	-6	1.68	5.77	6.34	6.20	9.4	5.2	5.5	1.5	-6.4	0.2

Breakout: 2% Improve: 20% Collapse: 35% Attrition: 0% Comparables: Carlos Chantres, Ryan Cameron, Alex Santos

Sometimes pitching prospects come from top college programs, sometimes they come from academies in Latin America, sometimes they come from a Texas high school, and sometimes, like Marmol, they come out of nowhere. A Dominican who spent his first four years as a pro in the outfield, the Cubs made him a pitcher in '03. He throws a nice moving fastball, but also has surprising command of a changeup and some interesting breaking stuff. That assortment, coupled with his speedy ascent and success at Double-A has ended talk of a future in the bullpen. Despite being a little rough around the edges, he's come very far very fast. In a system loaded with highly-touted young pitchers, he's the sleeper.

SEAN MARSHALL
Bats: L **Throws: L** Height: 6' 5" Weight: 190 Born: August 30, 1982 Age: 23

YEAR	TM	LVL	AGE	W	L	SV	G	GS	IP	H	BB	SO	HR	GB%	BABIP	STUFF	WHIP	ERA	PERA	EQERA	EQH9	EQBB9	EQSO9	EQHR9	VORP	WXRL
2003	BOI	A-	20	5	6	0	14	14	73.7	66	23	88	1	—	.328	24	1.21	2.56	3.93	5.20	9.1	3.4	6.0	0.4	3.2	—
2004	LNS	A	21	2	0	0	7	7	48.7	29	4	51	1	—	.235	27	0.68	1.11	3.18	3.57	7.3	1.0	5.4	0.4	10.2	—
2004	WTN	AA	21	2	2	0	6	6	29.0	36	12	23	2	—	.362	-5	1.66	5.90	5.34	7.22	11.0	4.1	4.7	0.9	-5.2	—
2005	DAY	A+	22	4	4	0	12	12	69.0	63	26	61	7	60%	.298	-10	1.29	2.74	6.23	4.43	9.4	4.4	5.1	1.8	8.4	—
2005	WTN	AA	22	0	1	0	4	4	25.0	16	5	24	1	47%	.234	20	0.84	2.52	3.86	3.86	7.3	1.9	6.2	0.8	4.5	—
2006	CHN	MLB	23	7	9	0	27	23	136.7	141	57	85	17	52%	.285	3	1.44	4.83	4.97	5.29	9.1	3.5	5.1	1.1	5.7	1.5

Breakout: 5% Improve: 28% Collapse: 30% Attrition: 0% Comparables: Adam Walker, Billy Traber, Charlie Manning

One of the many talented young pitchers in the system blighted with injury problems, Marshall missed time in '04 with a finger injury and was shelved by shoulder trouble this past season. When able to pitch, he has advanced quickly due to his ability to mix curves and sinkers for strikes. The Cubs are particularly excited for his future—they'll be even more excited if he shows the ability to pitch a complete season.

SERGIO MITRE
Bats: R **Throws: R** Height: 6' 4" Weight: 210 Born: February 16, 1981 Age: 25

YEAR	TM	LVL	AGE	W	L	SV	G	GS	IP	H	BB	SO	HR	GB%	BABIP	STUFF	WHIP	ERA	PERA	EQERA	EQH9	EQBB9	EQSO9	EQHR9	VORP	WXRL
2003	WTN	AA	22	7	9	0	25	24	145.7	162	41	128	6	—	.335	13	1.39	3.34	4.35	5.72	10.0	2.7	5.3	0.7	-1.9	—
2004	IOW	AAA	23	6	4	1	18	15	102.7	97	39	95	9	—	.314	15	1.32	2.98	4.56	3.75	8.7	3.8	6.3	0.9	20.7	—
2004	CHN	MLB	23	2	4	0	12	9	51.7	71	20	37	6	59%	.374	1	1.76	6.62	4.70	6.37	11.1	3.0	5.5	1.0	-4.6	0.5
2005	IOW	AAA	24	5	6	0	13	13	70.7	72	22	55	5	63%	.313	8	1.33	4.33	4.37	4.50	9.0	2.8	5.1	0.8	8.6	—
2005	CHN	MLB	24	2	5	0	21	7	60.3	62	23	37	11	69%	.268	-16	1.41	5.37	5.58	5.43	9.8	3.2	5.1	1.7	0.5	0.4
2006	FLO	MLB	25	6	8	1	38	19	123.7	128	48	82	10	57%	.301	0	1.42	4.43	4.80	5.09	9.4	3.2	5.2	0.8	6.9	1.4

Breakout: 26% Improve: 65% Collapse: 8% Attrition: 3% Comparables: Bob Anderson, Andy Hassler, Kevin Brown

(continued next page)

Sergio Mitre *(continued)*

Not really a top prospect, Mitre lives and dies with his high-80s sinker. Put in front of a great infield, he might be able to survive his spotty command of breaking stuff. Dropped on the Marlins in the Pierre trade, he'll go into their rotation, but don't expect much. Part of the Vatican All-Stars, along with Justin Pope, Royce Ring, Max Bishop, and Cardinal Fang.

RICKY NOLASCO · Bats: R Throws: R · Height: 6' 2" · Weight: 220 · Born: December 13, 1982 · Age: 23

YEAR	TM	LVL	AGE	W	L	SV	G	GS	IP	H	BB	SO	HR	GB%	BABIP	STUFF	WHIP	ERA	PERA	EQERA	EQH9	EQBB9	EQSO9	EQHR9	VORP	WXRL
2003	DAY	A+	20	11	5	0	26	26	149.0	129	48	136	7	—	.282	10	1.19	2.96	4.91	4.79	9.3	3.4	5.9	1.2	12.7	—
2004	WTN	AA	21	6	4	0	19	19	107.0	104	37	115	13	—	.317	-1	1.32	3.70	5.49	5.31	10.1	3.5	6.6	1.7	3.3	—
2004	IOW	AAA	21	2	3	0	9	9	40.7	68	16	28	7	—	.409	-12	2.06	9.29	5.86	8.58	12.6	3.6	4.6	1.5	-14.2	—
2005	WTN	AA	22	14	3	0	27	27	161.7	151	46	173	13	46%	.320	8	1.22	2.89	4.98	4.57	9.7	2.9	6.6	1.4	17.6	—
2006	*FLO*	*MLB*	*23*	*7*	*10*	*0*	*29*	*23*	*142.0*	*148*	*56*	*106*	*19*	*45%*	*.297*	*7*	*1.44*	*4.81*	*5.36*	*5.23*	*9.5*	*3.3*	*5.9*	*1.2*	*3.6*	*1.4*

Breakout: 15%   Improve: 48%   Collapse: 11%   Attrition: 0%   Comparables: Kyle Farnsworth, John Hudgins, Jin Cho

Nolasco gets high marks for his poise. He can throw three pitches for strikes and he's succeeded at the upper levels despite his relative youth. The 2005 Southern League Pitcher of the Year he started hot and finished well, capping an excellent season with eight shutout innings against Carolina in the Southern League playoffs. He can get a bit fine with lefties, losing them by nibbling, but he might iron that out in time. He's now the one who's gotten away, or the pitching prospect with the track record for health that gave the Marlins the good sense to ask for him in the Pierre deal. He'll be up before season's end.

ROBERTO NOVOA · Bats: R Throws: R · Height: 6' 5" · Weight: 200 · Born: August 15, 1979 · Age: 26

YEAR	TM	LVL	AGE	W	L	SV	G	GS	IP	H	BB	SO	HR	GB%	BABIP	STUFF	WHIP	ERA	PERA	EQERA	EQH9	EQBB9	EQSO9	EQHR9	VORP	WXRL
2003	LAK	A+	23	4	5	0	19	15	99.0	93	25	71	8	—	.273	-31	1.19	3.73	6.63	5.85	10.3	2.8	4.4	2.3	-2.6	—
2004	ERI	AA	24	7	0	4	41	0	79.0	63	18	59	7	—	.240	-11	1.03	2.96	4.82	4.70	8.7	2.4	4.8	1.2	7.5	—
2004	DET	MLB	24	1	1	0	16	0	21.0	25	6	15	4	44%	.350	-7	1.55	5.57	5.48	5.91	10.1	2.5	5.9	1.7	-1.2	-0.1
2005	IOW	AAA	25	2	2	4	19	0	27.3	20	11	18	1	60%	.260	-11	1.14	3.30	4.50	4.15	8.0	3.8	4.5	0.3	4.2	—
2005	CHN	MLB	25	4	5	0	49	0	44.7	47	25	47	4	38%	.339	9	1.61	4.43	3.94	4.34	8.9	4.5	8.5	0.8	5.4	-0.2
2006	*CHN*	*MLB*	*26*	*2*	*2*	*2*	*41*	*0*	*43.0*	*41*	*17*	*32*	*5*	*45%*	*.279*	*-3*	*1.36*	*4.16*	*4.42*	*5.23*	*8.6*	*3.3*	*6.1*	*1.1*	*4.9*	*0.4*

Breakout: 31%   Improve: 56%   Collapse: 25%   Attrition: 35%   Comparables: Amaury Telemaco, Rick Bauer, Wayne Rosenthal

Is Novoa a speed gun junkie? When he tries to get into the mid-90s his fastball flattens out, but when he settles down into the low 90s it acquires a bit of movement and becomes a better pitcher. Since his slider isn't particularly crisp, he might be better off attacking hitters instead of scoreboard speed meters. Almost certain to be crowded out of the pen this spring if everyone's healthy.

WILL OHMAN · Bats: L Throws: L · Height: 6' 2" · Weight: 195 · Born: August 13, 1977 · Age: 28

YEAR	TM	LVL	AGE	W	L	SV	G	GS	IP	H	BB	SO	HR	GB%	BABIP	STUFF	WHIP	ERA	PERA	EQERA	EQH9	EQBB9	EQSO9	EQHR9	VORP	WXRL
2004	IOW	AAA	26	3	3	0	45	1	52.3	53	29	75	6	—	.379	2	1.57	4.30	4.91	5.26	9.3	5.8	9.3	1.2	1.9	—
2005	CHN	MLB	27	2	2	0	69	0	43.3	32	24	45	6	52%	.241	6	1.29	2.91	4.68	2.98	7.7	4.7	8.7	1.3	12.6	0.1
2006	*CHN*	*MLB*	*28*	*2*	*2*	*3*	*56*	*0*	*45.3*	*40*	*24*	*43*	*4*	*49%*	*.289*	*4*	*1.42*	*3.88*	*4.34*	*4.74*	*7.9*	*4.4*	*7.8*	*0.9*	*6.5*	*0.6*

Breakout: 14%   Improve: 26%   Collapse: 41%   Attrition: 28%   Comparables: Paul Spoljaric, Paul Assenmacher, Mark Guthrie

No matter how many times Ohman's elbow has gone under the knife, he can still throw 90, and he's still snapping off a plus slider. He wasn't perfect in the LOOGY role, though: despite holding lefties overall to .173/.272/.321, he allowed four home runs to the guys he's supposed to get out, such as Hideki Matsui, Luis Gonzalez, Jim Edmonds. Sure, they're every-day hitters, but platoon lefty Adam LaRoche did it as well. If he cuts those mistakes, Ohman can be excellent in the role.

CARMEN PIGNATIELLO · Bats: R Throws: L · Height: 6' 0" · Weight: 180 · Born: September 12, 1982 · Age: 23

YEAR	TM	LVL	AGE	W	L	SV	G	GS	IP	H	BB	SO	HR	GB%	BABIP	STUFF	WHIP	ERA	PERA	EQERA	EQH9	EQBB9	EQSO9	EQHR9	VORP	WXRL
2003	DAY	A+	20	8	11	0	26	26	156.3	144	55	140	13	—	.285	-14	1.27	4.38	6.49	6.24	10.4	3.8	5.9	2.2	-10.4	—
2004	WTN	AA	21	9	7	0	27	27	148.0	167	39	137	16	—	.341	-2	1.39	4.56	5.20	6.52	10.8	2.6	5.5	1.5	-14.7	—
2005	WTN	AA	22	5	4	0	16	10	80.7	67	28	77	3	58%	.299	14	1.18	2.68	4.11	4.34	8.6	3.5	5.9	0.6	10.7	—
2005	IOW	AAA	22	1	5	0	22	5	47.3	52	20	43	6	49%	.326	-6	1.52	5.52	5.13	6.08	9.7	3.8	6.1	1.3	-2.5	—
2006	*CHN*	*MLB*	*23*	*5*	*7*	*0*	*29*	*14*	*94.3*	*100*	*41*	*65*	*13*	*50%*	*.296*	*-1*	*1.49*	*4.99*	*5.27*	*5.46*	*9.4*	*3.6*	*5.7*	*1.2*	*2.5*	*0.8*

Breakout: 25%   Improve: 70%   Collapse: 7%   Attrition: 0%   Comparables: J. D. Durbin, Jason Brester, Charlie Manning

Not one to impress the speed gun, Pignatiello's a hurler from a nearby Hammond high school who hasn't gotten much in the way of props others in the system have. Such is life as a soft-tossing lefty, but he has yet to fail, and if he's now ticketed for a relief role, he has the command to be something more than just a situational reliever. Lefty long relievers are a pretty rare breed, though, and it's particularly strange for someone to be slotted for LOOGY-dom before his 23rd birthday when he's averaged eight K's per nine his entire career.

RENYEL PINTO   Bats: L Throws: L   Height: 6' 4" Weight: 190 Born: July 8, 1982   Age: 23

YEAR	TM	LVL	AGE	W	L	SV	G	GS	IP	H	BB	SO	HR	GB%	BABIP	STUFF	WHIP	ERA	PERA	EQERA	EQH9	EQBB9	EQSO9	EQHR9	VORP	WXRL
2003	DAY	A+	20	3	8	0	20	19	114.7	91	45	104	4	—	.266	14	1.19	3.22	4.83	5.00	8.8	4.2	5.9	0.9	7.2	—
2004	WTN	AA	21	11	8	0	25	25	141.7	107	72	179	10	—	.301	19	1.26	2.92	4.79	4.32	8.4	5.2	7.7	1.0	19.0	—
2005	WTN	AA	22	10	3	0	22	21	129.7	101	58	123	3	52%	.300	21	1.23	2.71	4.33	4.40	8.2	4.5	5.9	0.4	16.4	—
2005	IOW	AAA	22	1	2	0	6	6	22.7	31	24	24	3	46%	.452	-21	2.42	9.52	6.46	10.65	11.0	8.7	6.8	1.1	-13.3	—
2006	FLO	MLB	23	6	9	0	28	22	128.3	124	79	104	12	49%	.296	5	1.58	4.88	5.44	5.39	8.8	5.1	6.4	0.9	1.4	1.0

Breakout: 9%   Improve: 39%   Collapse: 21%   Attrition: 1%   Comparables: Doug Davis, Luis Martinez, Dustin Nippert

The system's pitcher of the year in '04 didn't really add to his luster as a prospect by sailing through a repeat engagement at Double-A. More of a pitcher than a flamethrower, Pinto's sound delivery consistently cranks out a moving fastball that gets into the low 90s, as well as a good change. His slider still hasn't come around, and that might contribute to his struggles against lefty hitters, who just aren't being fooled by his just changing speeds. He struggled in Triple-A for similar reasons. Now that he's with the Marlins he'll be under more pressure to break through, but he has the talent to be a quality starter.

MARK PRIOR   Bats: R Throws: R   Height: 6' 5" Weight: 220 Born: September 7, 1980 Age: 25

YEAR	TM	LVL	AGE	W	L	SV	G	GS	IP	H	BB	SO	HR	GB%	BABIP	STUFF	WHIP	ERA	PERA	EQERA	EQH9	EQBB9	EQSO9	EQHR9	VORP	WXRL
2003	CHN	MLB	22	18	6	0	30	30	211.3	183	50	245	15	45%	.315	51	1.10	2.43	2.94	2.90	7.8	1.9	9.3	0.6	66.9	7.6
2004	CHN	MLB	23	6	4	0	21	21	118.7	112	48	139	14	40%	.333	33	1.35	4.02	3.76	3.99	8.3	3.2	9.3	1.0	25.6	3.6
2005	CHN	MLB	24	11	7	0	27	27	166.7	143	59	188	25	38%	.283	25	1.21	3.67	4.08	3.92	8.1	3.0	9.3	1.4	31.8	4.2
2006	CHN	MLB	25	13	9	0	30	30	196.3	164	60	200	21	42%	.276	33	1.14	3.28	3.37	3.61	7.4	2.5	8.4	0.9	41.5	6.0

Breakout: 24% Improve: 51% Collapse: 11% Attrition: 7%   Comparables: Don Wilson, Erik Hanson, Fergie Jenkins

Artists can be a flaky lot, with some given to destroying the works they feel fall beneath their level. When you're talking about an artist as great as Prior can be, what's to be done when he's still short of the greatness of which we've seen flashes? Happily, life doesn't always imitate art, so there's no need to get self-destructive. It's not the end of the world if Prior merely settles into becoming a very good starter instead of a great one. Once he shrugged off early Achilles and elbow issues and came off of the DL to stay at the end of June, he took his regular turn, making 13 quality starts out of 18. While 16 home runs allowed in those 108.1 IP aren't signs of domination, the 126 strikeouts are a pretty solid indicator that he's not too far gone.

GLENDON RUSCH   Bats: L Throws: L   Height: 6' 1" Weight: 225 Born: November 7, 1974 Age: 31

YEAR	TM	LVL	AGE	W	L	SV	G	GS	IP	H	BB	SO	HR	GB%	BABIP	STUFF	WHIP	ERA	PERA	EQERA	EQH9	EQBB9	EQSO9	EQHR9	VORP	WXRL
2003	MIL	MLB	28	1	12	1	32	19	123.3	171	45	93	11	45%	.387	7	1.75	6.42	4.14	6.28	10.6	2.8	5.8	0.8	-15.1	0.5
2004	CHN	MLB	29	6	2	2	32	16	129.7	127	33	90	10	45%	.295	16	1.23	3.47	3.85	3.78	8.9	2.1	5.6	0.6	28.7	3.3
2005	CHN	MLB	30	9	8	0	46	19	145.3	175	53	111	14	40%	.355	7	1.57	4.52	4.17	4.77	10.0	3.0	6.2	0.8	11.5	2.4
2006	CHN	MLB	31	5	7	1	43	12	104.3	112	34	72	13	44%	.298	-3	1.40	4.56	4.79	5.37	9.5	2.7	5.6	1.1	9.0	1.2

Breakout: 17% Improve: 51% Collapse: 25% Attrition: 13%   Comparables: Joe Nuxhall, Alex Kellner, Mike Flanagan

Rusch was the polar opposite of Dempster. He's lefty instead of righty and should start instead of relieve. Dusty apparently used a sextant charting out which was which. Rusch can't overpower lefty hitters and can't cut it in a situational role in the bullpen, but he can throw strikes and take the mound every fifth day. Returned to a role in which he could do some good, he was fine as a fifth starter. He won't hold the job forever, but as staff filler you could do worse.

JAE-KUK RYU Bats: R Throws: R Height: 6′ 3″ Weight: 210 Born: May 30, 1983 Age: 23

YEAR	TM	LVL	AGE	W	L	SV	G	GS	IP	H	BB	SO	HR	GB%	BABIP	STUFF	WHIP	ERA	PERA	EQERA	EQH9	EQBB9	EQSO9	EQHR9	VORP	WXRL
2003	LNS	A	20	6	1	0	11	11	72.0	59	19	57	2	—	.264	14	1.08	1.75	4.66	4.26	8.9	3.1	4.8	0.8	10.1	—
2003	WTN	AA	20	2	5	0	11	11	58.0	63	25	45	3	—	.317	3	1.52	5.43	5.15	6.55	9.8	3.9	4.8	0.9	-6.1	—
2004	WTN	AA	21	1	0	0	14	0	18.3	22	10	19	0	—	.379	-5	1.75	2.95	4.91	4.91	10.3	5.4	5.9	0.5	1.4	—
2005	WTN	AA	22	11	8	0	27	27	169.7	154	49	133	12	47%	.295	0	1.20	3.34	5.10	5.04	9.4	2.9	4.8	1.2	10.0	—
2006	CHN	MLB	23	7	10	0	26	24	140.3	147	59	88	19	45%	.288	4	1.47	5.03	5.19	5.46	9.3	3.5	5.2	1.2	3.2	1.4

Breakout: 8%   Improve: 52%   Collapse: 16%   Attrition: 0%   Comparables: Paxton Crawford, Dewon Brazelton, Anthony Lerew

Another product of the Cubs' random prospect mining in the Orient (courtesy of scout Leon Lee), Ryu took a big step forward, dispelling concerns about his elbow, showing off mid-90s velocity and a wicked curve he can pump across for strikes. The elbow will remain a trouble spot as long as his mechanics remain a mess, but the crowded big league rotation will give him time to work on that in Iowa in '06.

RAUL VALDES Bats: L Throws: L Height: 5′ 11″ Weight: 190 Born: November 27, 1977 Age: 28

YEAR	TM	LVL	AGE	W	L	SV	G	GS	IP	H	BB	SO	HR	GB%	BABIP	STUFF	WHIP	ERA	PERA	EQERA	EQH9	EQBB9	EQSO9	EQHR9	VORP	WXRL
2005	WTN	AA	27	2	0	0	5	5	23.0	28	3	18	1	51%	.397	-5	1.35	5.09	4.43	7.66	11.3	1.6	4.0	0.8	-5.1	—
2005	IOW	AAA	27	6	7	1	25	17	98.7	135	39	73	7	48%	.389	-6	1.76	5.93	4.81	6.59	10.9	3.7	4.5	0.8	-11.1	—
2006	CHN	MLB	28	3	6	0	27	11	77.7	93	33	43	11	48%	.311	-13	1.62	5.70	5.95	6.41	10.6	3.5	4.5	1.2	-4.8	0.0

Breakout: 31%   Improve: 63%   Collapse: 12%   Attrition: 5%   Comparables: Jeffrey Williams, Jeriome Robertson, Jamie Walker

A Cubano import; it's a bit hard to get a clean read on him. This was his first professional season, and although he missed a month in the spring with a broken thumb, the Cubs were aggressive about pushing him up the ladder. He's got a good mix of heat and breaking stuff and throws both the curve and slider for strikes, but the results on the diamond weren't impressive.

JERMAINE VAN BUREN Bats: R Throws: R Height: 6′ 1″ Weight: 220 Born: July 2, 1980 Age: 25

YEAR	TM	LVL	AGE	W	L	SV	G	GS	IP	H	BB	SO	HR	GB%	BABIP	STUFF	WHIP	ERA	PERA	EQERA	EQH9	EQBB9	EQSO9	EQHR9	VORP	WXRL
2004	WTN	AA	24	3	2	21	51	0	53.0	23	24	64	2	—	.194	4	0.89	1.87	4.12	3.38	6.2	5.1	7.3	0.6	11.8	—
2005	IOW	AAA	25	2	3	25	52	0	54.7	33	22	65	5	46%	.250	8	1.01	1.97	4.35	2.79	7.0	3.8	8.2	1.0	16.1	—
2006	BOS	MLB	25	3	3	2	32	2	55.0	51	32	47	7	41%	.283	2	1.51	4.69	4.85	5.06	8.0	5.1	7.5	1.0	5.6	0.5

Breakout: 3%   Improve: 9%   Collapse: 73%   Attrition: 19%   Comparables: Scott Williamson, Paul Giel, Mike Jackson

Van Buren's success is a credit to the Cubs' willingness to comb the indy leagues, like Joe Borowski was before him. His velocity dropped this year, forcing Van Buren to rely more heavily on a power slider to finish people, but he's still dialing it up around 90 and might get his missing MPH back and become a relief stalwart. Dealt to Boston as part of the Cubs' drive to avoid losing talent in the Rule 5 draft. The last famous Van Buren was Martin, the president, nicknamed "O.K." (short for "Old Kinderhook"). Our generation has do better than that for this Van Buren, although a pitcher officially nicknamed "O.K." would probably get seven large in arbitration.

TODD WELLEMEYER Bats: R Throws: R Height: 6′ 3″ Weight: 200 Born: August 30, 1978 Age: 27

YEAR	TM	LVL	AGE	W	L	SV	G	GS	IP	H	BB	SO	HR	GB%	BABIP	STUFF	WHIP	ERA	PERA	EQERA	EQH9	EQBB9	EQSO9	EQHR9	VORP	WXRL
2003	IOW	AAA	24	5	5	0	13	12	66.0	68	33	56	7	—	.300	-7	1.53	5.18	5.62	5.91	9.6	5.3	6.3	1.4	-2.2	—
2003	CHN	MLB	24	1	1	1	15	0	27.7	25	19	30	5	40%	.299	-1	1.59	6.50	5.20	6.83	8.5	5.5	8.8	1.6	-5.0	-0.3
2004	IOW	AAA	25	1	1	0	14	4	23.0	24	12	23	2	—	.333	-7	1.57	3.91	5.24	4.84	9.7	5.2	6.4	0.8	1.9	—
2004	CHN	MLB	25	2	1	0	20	0	24.3	27	20	30	1	35%	.413	10	1.93	5.93	3.86	5.61	8.8	6.3	9.1	0.4	-0.3	0.5
2005	IOW	AAA	26	3	2	0	12	12	53.7	47	25	48	2	37%	.300	8	1.34	3.02	4.13	4.13	8.3	4.5	5.7	0.3	8.5	—
2005	CHN	MLB	26	2	1	1	22	0	32.3	32	22	32	7	48%	.305	-10	1.67	6.13	5.85	6.12	9.2	5.6	8.1	1.9	-3.1	0.4
2006	CHN	MLB	27	3	5	1	37	6	69.3	70	42	58	10	41%	.297	-5	1.62	5.38	5.68	6.00	9.0	5.1	6.8	1.2	-0.8	0.1

Breakout: 18%   Improve: 42%   Collapse: 21%   Attrition: 8%   Comparables: Jason Isringhausen, Jason Bere, Calvin Schiraldi

When your manager is as fickle as a tabloid starlet with a sweet tooth for experienced men, it isn't easy to be a semi-wild young fireballer. Still, while the Cubs cut bait on others, they held onto Wellemeyer. Until he solves his control issues he won't justify that confidence, but the Cubs put him into Iowa's rotation last summer to give him the reps to try. The pen is already crowded, so he'll have to wait for the veterans to start getting hurt before he really gets to demonstrate if it did any good.

JEROME WILLIAMS Bats: R Throws: R   Height: 6' 3" Weight: 180 Born: December 4, 1981 Age: 24

YEAR	TM	LVL	AGE	W	L	SV	G	GS	IP	H	BB	SO	HR	GB%	BABIP	STUFF	WHIP	ERA	PERA	EQERA	EQH9	EQBB9	EQSO9	EQHR9	VORP	WXRL
2003	FRE	AAA	21	4	2	0	10	10	57.0	52	16	40	3	—	.272	19	1.19	2.68	4.18	3.21	8.4	2.7	5.5	0.6	14.9	—
2003	SFN	MLB	21	7	5	0	21	21	131.0	116	49	88	10	50%	.277	20	1.26	3.30	4.29	4.01	8.8	3.1	5.6	0.7	29.3	4.1
2004	SFN	MLB	22	10	7	0	22	22	129.3	123	44	80	14	54%	.279	9	1.29	4.25	4.82	4.61	9.2	2.8	5.0	0.9	14.8	2.4
2005	SFN	MLB	23	0	2	0	4	3	16.7	21	4	11	2	48%	.352	2	1.50	6.47	4.76	6.35	10.6	2.1	5.3	1.1	-1.7	0.0
2005	CHN	MLB	23	6	8	0	18	17	106.0	98	45	59	12	45%	.272	0	1.35	3.91	5.19	4.24	9.2	3.6	4.7	1.0	16.4	2.4
2006	*CHN*	*MLB*	*24*	*8*	*10*	*0*	*30*	*27*	*158.0*	*164*	*61*	*98*	*20*	*49%*	*.287*	*4*	*1.43*	*4.71*	*4.91*	*5.17*	*9.2*	*3.2*	*5.1*	*1.1*	*9.1*	*2.1*

Breakout: 4%   Improve: 28%   Collapse: 28%   Attrition: 1%   Comparables: Jay Tibbs, Frank Rodriguez, John Denny

The Cubs lucked out. After early problems with his velocity while coming back from the elbow surgery shut him down in August '04 first got him demoted to Fresno and then made him available. Jim Hendry was happy to take advantage of the Giants' overreaction. Back in full working order, he finished particularly strong, logging seven quality starts in his last nine. His power fastball-slider combo is more than good enough to make him a top starter; the question is whether or not he can handle a full season in the rotation, and whether Baker's the manager to help him do it.

SCOTT WILLIAMSON Bats: R Throws: R   Height: 6' 0" Weight: 185 Born: February 17, 1976 Age: 30

YEAR	TM	LVL	AGE	W	L	SV	G	GS	IP	H	BB	SO	HR	GB%	BABIP	STUFF	WHIP	ERA	PERA	EQERA	EQH9	EQBB9	EQSO9	EQHR9	VORP	WXRL
2003	CIN	MLB	27	5	3	21	42	0	42.3	34	25	53	6	39%	.280	16	1.39	3.19	4.46	3.19	7.7	4.7	10.0	1.3	11.6	1.8
2003	BOS	MLB	27	0	1	0	24	0	20.3	20	9	21	1	54%	.333	12	1.43	6.21	3.43	6.00	7.7	3.9	8.6	0.4	-1.2	-0.2
2004	BOS	MLB	28	0	1	1	28	0	28.7	11	18	28	0	47%	.162	16	1.01	1.25	3.95	1.65	5.3	5.6	8.6	0.3	14.2	1.3
2005	CHN	MLB	29	0	0	0	17	0	14.3	15	6	23	3	38%	.414	14	1.47	5.66	4.30	5.52	9.2	3.7	12.9	1.8	-0.1	-0.1
2006	*CHN*	*MLB*	*30*	*3*	*2*	*3*	*46*	*0*	*48.0*	*38*	*24*	*57*	*5*	*44%*	*.285*	*18*	*1.29*	*3.43*	*3.69*	*4.07*	*7.1*	*4.2*	*9.7*	*0.9*	*9.3*	*0.8*

Breakout: 24%   Improve: 59%   Collapse: 12%   Attrition: 14%   Comparables: Greg Harris, Don Elston, Billy Wagner

A couple of years and a Tommy John procedure separate Williamson from his last good season, but the Cubs have picked up his option for '06 in anticipation of getting a follow-up season not unlike what Dempster gave them in '05 after rehabbing in '04. His velocity's not what it was, but it's still in the low 90s, and he commands the slider as well as he did of old. If he's back and on, the Cubs pen could be stacked, even without allowing for the additions of Howry and Eyre.

KERRY WOOD Bats: R Throws: R   Height: 6' 5" Weight: 225 Born: June 16, 1977 Age: 29

YEAR	TM	LVL	AGE	W	L	SV	G	GS	IP	H	BB	SO	HR	GB%	BABIP	STUFF	WHIP	ERA	PERA	EQERA	EQH9	EQBB9	EQSO9	EQHR9	VORP	WXRL
2003	CHN	MLB	26	14	11	0	32	32	211.0	152	100	266	24	44%	.279	37	1.19	3.20	3.84	3.33	7.3	3.9	10.3	1.0	55.9	7.4
2004	CHN	MLB	27	8	9	0	22	22	140.3	127	51	144	16	49%	.307	28	1.27	3.72	4.00	3.93	8.4	3.0	8.2	1.0	28.8	3.7
2005	CHN	MLB	28	3	4	0	21	10	66.0	52	26	77	14	36%	.252	11	1.18	4.23	4.87	4.31	7.9	3.3	9.7	1.9	9.2	1.0
2006	*CHN*	*MLB*	*29*	*6*	*5*	*1*	*26*	*15*	*100.0*	*81*	*40*	*101*	*12*	*43%*	*.267*	*20*	*1.21*	*3.52*	*3.70*	*3.92*	*7.2*	*3.3*	*8.3*	*1.0*	*22.4*	*2.6*

Breakout: 15%   Improve: 43%   Collapse: 17%   Attrition: 18%   Comparables: Rick Sutcliffe, Jose DeLeon, Len Barker

Finally shut down because his shoulder hurt and he couldn't go longer than 50 pitches, the Cubs are publicly spinning his latest repair for a fraying rotator cuff as no big thing and suggest he'll be ready to pitch before the team heads north. But what if he doesn't come back that all well? At 29, it seems a shame to talk about whether he could he handle a Ted Lyons/David Cone–style Sunday pitcher role. Could the Cubs let themselves settle for it? It's really a terrible shame, in that Woody's a player who genuinely likes the game as well as having tremendous talent for playing it.

MIKE WUERTZ Bats: R Throws: R   Height: 6' 3" Weight: 200 Born: December 15, 1978 Age: 27

YEAR	TM	LVL	AGE	W	L	SV	G	GS	IP	H	BB	SO	HR	GB%	BABIP	STUFF	WHIP	ERA	PERA	EQERA	EQH9	EQBB9	EQSO9	EQHR9	VORP	WXRL
2003	IOW	AAA	24	3	9	1	43	16	124.0	140	35	92	16	—	.307	-21	1.41	4.57	5.49	5.71	10.3	3.0	5.6	1.7	-1.5	—
2004	IOW	AAA	25	1	1	19	37	0	44.7	30	15	59	4	—	.260	14	1.01	2.42	4.01	3.38	7.0	3.6	8.9	1.1	10.5	—
2004	CHN	MLB	25	1	0	1	31	0	29.0	22	17	30	4	32%	.269	3	1.34	4.34	4.71	4.40	7.5	4.7	8.5	1.3	4.6	0.3
2005	CHN	MLB	26	6	2	0	75	0	75.7	60	40	89	6	43%	.302	21	1.32	3.80	3.57	4.28	7.4	4.4	9.6	0.7	10.4	1.2
2006	*CHN*	*MLB*	*27*	*3*	*3*	*3*	*58*	*1*	*64.3*	*59*	*29*	*62*	*8*	*42%*	*.288*	*7*	*1.36*	*4.10*	*4.31*	*4.76*	*8.1*	*3.7*	*7.9*	*1.1*	*8.3*	*0.7*

Breakout: 27%   Improve: 55%   Collapse: 26%   Attrition: 14%   Comparables: Charlie Hough, Larry Sherry, Brad Lidge

Amidst so much chaos in the Cubs' pen in '05, the only pitcher not named Dempster to add any real value was Wuertz. He throws hard and has better command of his breaking stuff than most relievers, but the addition of veteran imports Bobby Howry and Scott Eyre should relegate him to the middle innings.

CARLOS ZAMBRANO **Bats: B Throws: R** Height: 6′ 5″ Weight: 250 Born: June 1, 1981 Age: 25

YEAR	TM	LVL	AGE	W	L	SV	G	GS	IP	H	BB	SO	HR	GB%	BABIP	STUFF	WHIP	ERA	PERA	EQERA	EQH9	EQBB9	EQSO9	EQHR9	VORP	WXRL
2003	CHN	MLB	22	13	11	0	32	32	214.0	188	94	168	9	59%	.294	30	1.32	3.11	3.80	3.63	8.2	3.6	6.4	0.4	47.6	6.5
2004	CHN	MLB	23	16	8	0	31	31	209.7	174	81	188	14	53%	.280	32	1.22	2.75	3.88	3.18	8.1	3.2	7.2	0.6	62.8	6.9
2005	CHN	MLB	24	14	6	0	33	33	223.3	170	86	202	21	52%	.258	26	1.15	3.26	4.00	3.55	7.7	3.3	7.6	0.9	51.2	6.8
2006	*CHN*	*MLB*	*25*	*15*	*10*	*0*	*33*	*33*	*224.0*	*192*	*84*	*191*	*18*	*52%*	*.276*	*23*	*1.23*	*3.29*	*3.53*	*3.65*	*7.6*	*3.1*	*7.0*	*0.7*	*49.3*	*6.7*

Breakout: 12%   Improve: 35%   Collapse: 15%   Attrition: 0%   Comparables: Dean Chance, Mark Gubicza, Stan Williams

As noted in the essay, Zambrano really has been this good for this long, and his three-year arc is the best of any Cubs starter over more than 30 years. Nevertheless, worries about his elbow haven't gone away, but when he's the one reliable commodity among the big three, and with Prior and Wood-watches becoming Wrigleyville's Kremlinology, Cubs Nation is justifiably nervous for Zambrano's well-being. The big Venezuelan is a genuine pleasure to watch as he grinds his opponents to powder, keeping his infielders busy and overpowering hitters, and rarely hiding how he feels about it when he's on.

Line Outs

Position/Player	TM	LVL	AGE	PA	R	2B	3B	HR	RBI	BB	SO	SB-CS	SPEED	BA/OBP/SLG	MLVR	EQBA/OBP/SLG	EQA	VORP
UT B. Coats*	WTN	AA	23	483	47	32	6	1	49	38	80	17-5	6.0	.282/.340/.390	.019	.262/.309/.367	.240	4.8
CF S. Fuld*	PEO	A	23	504	82	32	6	5	37	50	44	18-11	5.9	.300/.377/.433	.152	.255/.313/.369	.239	-2.0
OF B. Grieve*	IOW	AAA	29	342	44	19	1	14	51	48	59	0-0	3.6	.266/.371/.481	.088	.213/.302/.358	.232	-16.5
1/3 S. McClain	IOW	AAA	33	481	75	27	2	30	93	45	84	1-1	3.4	.291/.358/.577	.224	.217/.269/.384	.226	-9.3
CF C. Walker	DAY	A+	25	587	97	21	14	6	57	41	111	60-21	8.8	.284/.344/.409	.068	.242/.293/.352	.231	-14.9

Pitcher	TM	LVL	AGE	W	L	SV	IP	H	BB	SO	HR	GB%	BABIP	STUFF	WHIP	ERA	PERA	EQERA	EQH9	EQBB9	EQSO9	EQHR9	VORP
J. Koronka*	IOW	AAA	25	9	11	0	136.0	135	48	96	12	46%	.307	2	1.35	4.24	4.85	4.51	9.1	3.3	4.6	0.9	16.2
J. Mateo	DAY	A+	22	10	5	2	109.3	99	27	123	9	40%	.321	-2	1.15	3.21	4.92	5.09	9.2	2.9	6.5	1.5	5.9
R. Wells	DAY	A+	22	10	2	2	98.7	93	22	106	5	47%	.328	6	1.17	2.74	4.14	4.33	9.0	2.5	6.0	0.8	13.5

Just as some pitchers are notable simply because they survive, so it is with some hitters. Picked in the 18th round of the 2000 draft out of a Georgia high school, **Buck Coats** hit well in his first year at Double-A. He might grow up into a McEwing-style supersub type. **Sam Fuld** had a fine first season as a pro, showing great command of the zone and a baseball rat's sensibilities on and off the field. **Ben Grieve** is trying to adapt to a reserve role by speeding up his swing. Memories of his greatness should remind everyone of the danger of getting too high on young players with an old player's skills. **Scott McClain** lost years to the wrong organizations and a Japanese sojourn, but got a September cameo after Ramirez's quad injury. A good player who deserved better. **Chris Walker** is an example of how much the Cubs love speed; draft speed, promote speed, and get left wondering why all that speed seems to go nowhere, year after year. The Cubs are pumped about Walker stealing 60 bags in each of the last two years, but he was a college player about to turn 26, and not yet out of A-ball. If you got excited about Esix Snead, here's your new distraction.

Angel Guzman is always touted and almost never pitching, this year losing time to forearm and elbow problems, but he was healthy enough to show off his 96 mph fastball and nasty curve in the AFL. It's impossible to predict when or if he'll ever pitch a full season. **John Koronka** was smartly snagged in a minor deal in '03; the soft-tosser is stretched as a fifth starter, but might make it as a situational lefty. **Juan Mateo** comes out of the Cubs' unheralded Dominican program, and is slowly maturing. Watch him. **Randy Wells** is converted catcher in only his second full season on the mound, he might be fast-tracked in a relief role.

Chicago White Sox

You wouldn't believe how lucky the Spartans got in the Peloponnesian War. Athens had a two-to-one advantage in hoplites, five-to-one in chariots, and their hostage-taking skills were second to none. Okay, so maybe Pericles isn't the general he used to be, and the plague thing clearly didn't help. But do you really think that an army of helots is going to capture that city more than one time in ten?

The preceding passage does not appear in any translation of Thucydides. Nor are you likely to see anything similar in a history of the French Revolution, or the invention of the printing press, or the 1968 Democratic National Convention. Each of those events is sufficiently unique as to defy easy characterization.

Baseball is different. The game is certainly complex—if Scott Podsednik flaps his wings on first base, does David Riske hang that slider?—but it follows a set of rules that are more or less the same from Beijing to the Bronx, and that have been more or less unchanged for the past 150 years. We might not have seen *this game* before, but we have seen a dozen, a thousand, very much like it.

It is in that context that we bring up the L-word. A great number of people, from stat geeks to shock jocks, have made the claim that the Chicago White Sox were lucky to win the World Series. Oh, they might not come right out and say it, instead disguising it the euphemistic phrasing of their choosing ("they outperformed their Pythagorean projection"/"they got hot at just the right time"), but it's a near universal undercurrent in the coverage of the Sox and their championship, in a way that it wasn't for teams like the 2000 Yankees or the 2003 Marlins.

On its face, the argument is almost certainly true. There are 30 teams today, many of them closely bunched together in ability level. A World Series champion must win three short series against tough competition in games that are often decided by a single bounce of the baseball or a single blown call. It's unlikely that *any* team enters the season with better than a 15 or a 20 percent chance of winning it all; the White Sox defied those odds, but so did the Red Sox in 2004, or the Diamondbacks in 2001.

But that's not what people mean when they say that the White Sox got lucky. Rather, they mean that the White Sox outperformed their expectations. The question arises: were those expectations set too low?

It would be useful to come up with some working definition of what we mean by "luck." Luck (and the related concept of randomness) are in fact notoriously

WHITE SOX PROSPECTUS

2005 record: 99–63; First place, AL Central; Beat Astros in World Series, 4–0

Pythagenport record: 91–71

Runs scored per game: 4.57 (9th in AL)

Runs allowed per game: 3.98 (3rd in AL)

Team EqA: .253 (10th in AL)

2005 Batters Age: 29.7 (5th oldest in AL)

2005 Pitchers Age: 29.3 (6th oldest in AL)

Ballpark: U.S. Cellular Field; Slight hitter's park; Park Factor of 1.023

2005: The secret ingredient wasn't little ball but starting pitching as the Sox took the title of Iron Chef.

2006: Most of the roster returns, and several positions have been upgraded. They'll be right back in the thick of it.

hard concepts to pin down; a fuller discussion would take us to topics like quantum mechanics and determinism, which are better left for a freshman philosophy seminar. What *we* mean when we use the L-word is as follows:

Luck, in baseball, is the degree of divergence between an actual outcome, and the probability of that outcome based on persistent, measurable underlying abilities.

The key word in that definition is "persistent." Scott Podsednik ended Game 2 with a walk-off homer against Brad Lidge. Perhaps we would have predicted before the at bat that Podsednik's chances of hitting a home run were 1-in-500. But you can't hit one one-hundred-fiftieth of a home run. You either hit a home run or you don't, and in that particular circumstance, Podsednik did. Maybe it was the pitch that Lidge threw, the time of the day, what Podsednik ate for lunch, what the guy in Row 15 Seat 4 was wearing, or some combination of all of those things. If you could replicate *all* of those conditions *exactly*, then Podsednik would hit that home run every time. Podsednik's ability to hit that home run isn't *persistent* because if you changed any of those conditions very slightly—if Lidge threw a slider instead of a fastball, if Podsednik's reflexes were a hair slower because he had an extra helping of pasta—then a home run would likely not have resulted. We know that because Podsednik hit zero home runs against Brad Lidge or anybody else during the regular season. Persistent abilities are those that can be repeated across different (but related) situations and across different periods of time (e.g. different baseball games). Brad Lidge can throw a baseball 97 miles per hour; that's a persistent ability. Scott Podsednik hitting that fastball for a home run is not a persistent ability.

Our definition of luck also requires that the ability be "measurable." That is a little bit different than "predictable" in that we get to take advantage of hindsight. In fact, that's the subject of this article. Before the season, our PECOTA system predicted that the White Sox would win 82 regular season games. This projection was similar to that put forward by any other number of pundits, as well as the Vegas over-under line. In fact, they won 99 games. How much of that difference was because of luck? How much was because the Sox were better all along than we gave them credit for? What *should* we have predicted if we knew then what we know now?

Pretty much every type of "luck" that takes place during a baseball season can be placed into one of three categories:

- **Type I Luck** consists of differences between persistent, measurable abilities and the outcomes of discrete plate appearances during a baseball game. By outcomes, we mean doubles, strikeouts, sacrifice flies, things like that: what we sometimes call peripheral statistics. We know that Chipper Jones hit a certain number of doubles last season. Is this number more or less than he "should" have hit, based on his actual skill?

- **Type II Luck** consists of differences between the number of runs that a team scores or allows, and the number of runs that they'd usually score or allow based on their peripheral statistics. This type of luck is encapsulated in the statistic PERA (the pitcher's ERA estimated from his peripheral statistics). Sometimes a pitcher will have a great strikeout rate, a great walk rate, a decent enough home run rate, but he'll have a high ERA because he happened to give up the wrong hits at the wrong times. That's Type II Luck. Note that we don't count something as Type II Luck if we can explain it as a result of some other persistent ability. Hideo Nomo always had ERAs higher than his PERAs because his fancy wind-up didn't take well to pitching out of the stretch, so he gave

up a lot more hits with runners on base. That wasn't luck, that was Hideo Nomo.

- **Type III Luck** consists of differences between the number of games that a team wins, and the number of games that they'd usually win based on their runs scored and allowed. Basically, this is a team's Pythagenport W–L record (our modified version of Bill James's Pythagorean Theorem). However, we should also consider any other persistent abilities affecting the way that runs are distributed across different games. For example, if teams with good bullpens consistently outperform their Pythagorean record, we should account for that.

By classifying a team's luck according to this scheme, we are able to draw a chain of events from a team's underlying ability level to the actual number of games that they won during the regular season. Think of it as PECOTA in reverse. It's easiest to do this if we work backward through the process, using the White Sox' 99–63 record as our starting point.

Type III Luck

The White Sox scored 741 runs and allowed 645 during the regular season, which results in a Pythagenport record of 91–71. Their 99–63 record was eight games ahead of that pace, a direct result of their extremely strong (35–19) record in one-run games. However, the White Sox also played some very impressive baseball during the postseason, scoring 67 runs and allowing just 34 against superior competition. These are "real" games, even if they aren't part of the regular season. We can apply these runs to their regular season total, which bumps their Pythagenport record up by two games to 93–69.

We also need to consider whether there was anything systematic about the White Sox that caused them to outperform their Pythagenport. A 1999 study by Keith Woolner and Rany Jazayerli found that teams with great bullpens do in fact outperform their Pythagenport record by an average of 1.3 wins. The White Sox did indeed have a great bullpen; their relievers combined for 75 Adjusted Runs Prevented on the season, which placed them second in the American League behind Cleveland (104). We'll therefore apply a one-win correction to their Type III Luck tally, keeping the extra 0.3 wins as pocket change.

White Sox fans would also cite the influence of Ozzie Guillen; perhaps there's something The Oz is doing, either strategically or motivationally, that is leading his team to perform especially well in close games. While this *could* be true, every study on the subject has concluded that a manager has no *persistent* impact on his team's tendency to outperform its Pythagorean record. If Ozzie Guillen is

TABLE 1. EFFECTS OF TYPE III LUCK ON 2005 WHITE SOX

Adjustment based on regular season RS/RA	−8 Wins
Adjustment based on post-season RS/RA	+2 Wins
Adjustment based on bullpen	+1 Wins
Total Type III Luck	**−5 Wins**

great at motivating his athletes, or managing his bullpen, most of that should show up in his team's runs scored and runs allowed totals.

Similarly, we aren't aware of any studies suggesting that a team that plays "small ball" tends to outperform their Pythagorean record—if a team that scored 43 percent of its runs on the long ball can be classified as a small ball outfit anyway. In fact, the available evidence on the subject, particularly work by BP's James Click, suggests that things like sacrifice bunts tend to take away from a team's win expectation more often than not.

A summary of the effects of Type III Luck on the White Sox record is seen in table 1.

Type II Luck

Type II Luck operates at the runs level. We run a report on our website—the Adjusted Standings Report—that is designed to account for Type II Luck by comparing a team's actual runs scored and allowed to that predicted by their Equivalent Runs (EqR) scored and allowed. Remember that EqR boils down to a very fancy formula that accounts for almost all of a team's key peripheral statistics.

According to the Adjusted Standings Report, White Sox hitters produced 741 EqR—exactly the figure that they scored in real life. On the other hand, the White Sox' pitchers do require a correction. A number of White Sox pitchers (especially in the bullpen) outperformed their PERAs. While the staff "should" have allowed 685 runs based on their peripheral statistics; they actually surrendered just 645. The difference is equal to 40 runs, or about four wins.

However, unlike the case of position players, pitchers do show some persistent tendency to overperform or underperform their PERAs. Some pitchers like Nomo perform consistently worse with runners on base, whereas others like Tom Glavine and Mark Buehrle have a knack for changing their pitching approach to manage the game situation (see the Buehrle player comment in this chapter for more). Specifically, our studies for PECOTA have found that about one-quarter of the difference between PERA and ERA is carried over from season to season. Thus, we'll give the White Sox pitchers back one of the four wins that we just took away from them.

A couple of additional adjustments are worth considering. One element that EqR *doesn't* account for is station-to-station baserunning, apart from the effects of stolen bases and times caught stealing. Conceivably, the Go-Go Sox could score more often from first base on a double than the usual team does, or advance from first to third more often on a single. Fortunately, we have a separate measure to track this ability. Equivalent Baserunning Runs (EqBR), introduced by James Click in *Baseball Prospectus 2005,* looks at baserunner advancement while controlling for things like park effects and the quality of the outfield defense. The White Sox scored only three extra runs last season as a result of their station-to-station baserunning, which for our purposes is not enough to bother with. Keep in mind that while Willie Harris and Scott Podsednik run well, the White Sox also had Paul Konerko and A. J. Pierzynski in their everyday lineup. Moreover, *aggressive* baserunning is not the same thing as *good* baserunning.

A final area to consider is double plays, which are also not reflected in the EqR formulas. We track this statistic on our website as well, looking at GIDP and GIDP allowed as a percentage of double play opportunities. While the White Sox hitters grounded into an almost exactly average number of double plays, the pitchers induced 18 more GIDP than we would have expected. This is almost certainly a function of the White Sox's good defense and the pitching staff's groundball tendencies, which are persistent abilities. Inducing 18 extra double plays is roughly equal to saving seven runs, which is enough to credit the pitchers with another win.

In total, we find that the White Sox won two extra games as a result of Type II Luck, as seen in table 2.

Type I Luck

Type I Luck—the difference between a team's underlying ability level and its raw statistics—is the trickiest kind to identify, but perhaps the most important in terms of a

TABLE 2. EFFECTS OF TYPE II LUCK IN THE 2005 WHITE SOX

Adjustments based on offense	
EqR produced	No Adjustment
Station-to-station baserunning	No Adjustment
Grounded into Double Play	No Adjustment
Adjustments based on defense	
EqR allowed	−4 Wins
Pitching skill correction	+1 Wins
GIDP Induced	+1 Wins
Total Type II Luck	**−2 Wins**

team's strategic planning. If a team does not have a good understanding of a player's true ability level, they will make mistakes when signing free agents, completing trades, and the like. Projection systems like PECOTA are designed in large part to evaluate Type I luck. If a player hits .320, but has never hit better than .280 in the past, strikes out frequently, and doesn't run to first base well, then PECOTA will figure that the .320 average not reflective of his true ability, and will ding his projection accordingly.

In fact, a player's 2006 PECOTA forecast should provide a very good sense of what the player's true talent level was in 2005. We could describe PECOTA (or any other good forecasting system) forecast by these terms:

2006 Forecast = 2005 True Ability Level + Age Adjustment

or

2005 True Ability Level = 2006 Forecast − Age Adjustment

In other words, all we need to do to get a good estimate of a player's true ability level in 2005 is to take a player's 2006 PECOTA, and subtract out any adjustment the system made due to his age. Table 3 presents the results of that exercise for the White Sox starting lineup, using OPS (normalized to a neutral park and league) as our benchmark.

Jermaine Dye and Paul Konerko outperformed their true ability level somewhat, while Juan Uribe and Aaron Rowand should have done a little better, but on balance, the 741-run performance of the 2005 White Sox lineup was a very good representation of their underlying talent level, and there is no evidence of Type I Luck at work for the offense.

This gets slightly trickier for the pitchers. We do not want to use a measure like ERA to track Type I luck. ERA is a function of a pitcher's peripheral statistics *plus* a lot of "noise" (Type II Luck). Instead, we want a purer measure

TABLE 4. 2005 PERFORMANCE VERSUS TRUE ABILITY LEVEL, WHITE SOX PITCHERS

Pitcher	2005 STUFF	True Ability Level (PECOTA)
Starting		
Buehrle	22	15
Contreras	17	17
Garland	7	7
Garcia	13	15
Hernandez	3	4
McCarthy	19	18
Average	**14**	**13**
Bullpen		
Hermanson	1	−5
Cotts	26	7
Jenks	16	11
Marte	13	10
Politte	14	5
Vizcaino	−7	−6
Average	**11**	**4**

of a pitcher's underlying ability level. A good choice is STUFF, which is formulated primarily from a pitcher's most persistent underlying abilities—his strikeouts, walks, and home runs allowed. Table 4 shows the STUFF numbers for the White Sox' starting rotation and bullpen, respectively.

The good news is that this really is a very talented group of starting pitchers, especially with Javier Vazquez set to replace Orlando Hernandez. The relievers are another story. Almost to a man, White Sox relievers pitched over its head last season, outperforming their true ability level by an average of seven STUFF points. Roughly speaking, a difference of one point in STUFF is equal to six points (0.06) worth of ERA. Thus, the bullpen outperformed its ability level by 0.42 in ERA, which amounts to about 21 runs or two wins on the season, given the number of innings that the bullpen pitched.

We'll deduct this amount from the White Sox' victory total as Type I Luck. Note that this correction is separate and distinct from the Type II adjustment we made earlier. Not only did the bullpen allow fewer runs then they should have based on their peripherals (Type II Luck), but those peripherals themselves were inflated in the cases of pitchers like Neil Cotts and Cliff Politte (Type I Luck).

Ideally, the effects of injuries should also be accounted for as Type I Luck, but it is difficult to distinguish an injury that resulted from "bad luck," from a chronic condition, or that might have been preventable.

TABLE 3. 2005 PERFORMANCE VERSUS TRUE ABILITY LEVEL, WHITE SOX HITTERS

Player	2005 OPS	True Ability Level (PECOTA)
Crede	.778	.766
Dye	.880	.813
Everett	.772	.806
Iguchi	.807	.777
Konerko	.939	.881
Pierzynski	.753	.750
Podsednik	.731	.725
Rowand	.759	.787
Uribe	.739	.762
Average	**.795**	**.785**

TABLE 5. EFFECTS OF TYPE I LUCK ON 2005 WHITE SOX

W–L Record, Less Type II and III Luck	92–70
Adjustments based on underlying skill	
Offense	No Adjustment
Starting pitching	No Adjustment
Bullpen	−2 Wins
Total Type I Luck	**−2 Wins**

TABLE 6. 2005 WHITE SOX TRUE ABILITY LEVEL

Regular Season W–L	99–63
Total Type III Luck	−5 Wins
Total Type II Luck	−2 Wins
Total Type I Luck	−2 Wins
Persistent Underlying Team Ability	**90–72**

Should we credit the White Sox for being without the services of Frank Thomas for most of the season, when his foot problems have been bothering him for years? Should we punish them for having an unusually healthy pitching staff—or is that a testament to the good works of Don Cooper and Herm Schneider? We'll leave these as questions for future research. In the meantime, the effects of Type I Luck on the White Sox' record can be seen in table 5.

The effects of the three different types of luck can be combined into something that we'll call Persistent Underlying Team Ability (or PUTA, an acronym that might entertain Ozzie Guillen). PUTA is our estimate of the White Sox true talent level for the 2005 season. If you simulated the 2005 season a million times (using slightly different initial conditions), this is the average number of wins that the White Sox would end up with (see table 6).

The White Sox were lucky by any reasonable definition of the term; their PUTA record of 90–72 is nine wins below their actual record of 99–61. Just as certainly, however, they were a far better team than anyone gave them credit for. In particular, the maturation of Jon Garland and Jose Contreras, and the across-the-board improvement in their position defense, were factors that we failed to account for prior to the season. These should continue to pay dividends going forward.

It should also be remembered that 90-win talent is nothing to sneeze at; a 90-win team will make the playoffs just over half the time, and what happens from there forward is *always* going to be mostly a matter of luck. In other words, the White Sox were nothing out of the ordinary. A subjective but informed look at the last 25 World Series champions suggests that the 2005 White Sox were at least as strong as the 1982 Cardinals, the 1985 Royals, the 1987 Twins, the 1988 Dodgers, the 1990 Reds, the 1996 and 2000 Yankees, and the 1997 and 2003 Marlins.

More important, the White Sox front office, from Kenny Williams on downward, are humble enough to understand that they *aren't* a 99-win club. A recent analysis by Nate Silver[1] demonstrated that teams that project to have 87–92 win talent should adopt a "strong buy" strategy; these teams stand to gain the most, financially and competitively, from adding additional talent. With their acquisitions of Jim Thome and Javier Vazquez, the White Sox have taken exactly this approach. Although there is room for debate on the particulars—why not deal Podsednik instead of Rowand, or Brian Anderson instead of Chris Young?—the Sox have demonstrated none of the complacency that distinguishes the One-Hit Wonders from the perennial contenders.

HITTERS

BRIAN ANDERSON   CF   **Bats: R Throws: R**   Height: 6′ 2″   Weight: 205   Born: March 11, 1982   Age: 24

YEAR	TM	LVL	AGE	PA	R	2B	3B	HR	RBI	BB	SO	SB	CS	SPEED	BA	OBP	SLG	MLVR	EQBA	EQOBP	EQSLG	EQA	VORP	DEFENSE	
2004	WNS	A+	22	287	43	22	4	8	46	29	44	10	1	6.8	.319	.394	.531	.304	.275	.342	.469	.278	15.9	63-CF	0
2004	BIR	AA	22	208	26	9	3	4	27	19	30	3	2	5.4	.270	.346	.416	.081	.253	.320	.386	.247	1.3	40-CF	-2
2005	CHR	AAA	23	500	71	24	3	16	57	44	115	4	2	4.7	.295	.360	.469	.125	.272	.337	.430	.265	17.4	111-CF	-2
2006	CHA	MLB	24	469	60	24	3	18	63	36	100	5	2	4.7	.269	.329	.468	.054	.267	.334	.464	.265	14.2	111-CF	-1

Breakout: 26%   *Improve: 50%*   *Collapse: 26%*   *Attrition: 18%*   *Comparables: Ron Swoboda, Roy Sievers, Dwight Evans*

Anderson has at least an even-money chance of being better than Aaron Rowand. He won't match Rowand's range in center, but he has the speed to handle the position, and certainly has the arm, having moonlighted as a reliever in college while at Arizona. Right now he looks something like Bobby Kielty, both statistically and phenotypically, although

(continued next page)

---

1. http://www.baseballprospectus.com/article.php?articleid=4618

Brian Anderson (continued)

without the Carrot Top-on-meth look. But Anderson has room to add more weight to his frame, and PECOTA thinks he could wind up with more power than you'd think. Hitting two home runs off King Felix in a game last August is a good start.

GEOFF BLUM   **INF**   **Bats: B Throws: R**   Height: 6' 3"   Weight: 193   Born: April 26, 1973   Age: 33

YEAR	TM	LVL	AGE	PA	R	2B	3B	HR	RBI	BB	SO	SB	CS	SPEED	BA	OBP	SLG	MLVR	EQBA	EQOBP	EQSLG	EQA	VORP	DEFENSE				
2003	HOU	MLB	30	447	51	19	0	10	52	20	50	0	0	4.0	.262	.295	.379	-.124	.255	.290	.375	.232	0.3	69-3B	7	18-2B	-3
2004	TBA	MLB	31	365	38	21	0	8	35	24	58	2	3	4.4	.215	.266	.348	-.285	.215	.270	.355	.217	-15.3	43-3B	-2	41-2B	0
2005	SDN	MLB	32	252	26	13	1	5	22	24	28	3	2	4.7	.241	.321	.375	-.057	.251	.329	.396	.252	1.9	26-3B	5	18-2B	0
2005	CHA	MLB	32	99	6	2	1	1	3	4	15	0	1	4.6	.200	.232	.274	-.425	.202	.242	.277	.183	-8.3				
2006	*SDN*	*MLB*	*33*	*264*	*27*	*11*	*1*	*4*	*28*	*18*	*36*	*1*	*1*	*4.5*	*.240*	*.297*	*.353*	*-.189*	*.249*	*.305*	*.380*	*.229*	*-0.4*	*65-3B*	*1*		

Breakout: 24%   Improve: 52%   Collapse: 26%   Attrition: 41%   Comparables: Tim Bogar, Billy Gardner, Scott Leius

With one swing of the bat, Blum went from "Why is FOX showing so many pictures of the batboy?" to World Series Hero. It's been three years since he's hit anything, so Blum ought to hold on tight to that memory and the full World Series share it earned him. San Diego brought him back, hoping to cater to the *Point Break* demographic.

JOE BORCHARD   **OF**   **Bats: B Throws: R**   Height: 6' 5"   Weight: 220   Born: November 25, 1978   Age: 27

YEAR	TM	LVL	AGE	PA	R	2B	3B	HR	RBI	BB	SO	SB	CS	SPEED	BA	OBP	SLG	MLVR	EQBA	EQOBP	EQSLG	EQA	VORP	DEFENSE				
2003	CHR	AAA	24	472	62	20	2	13	53	27	103	2	4	4.4	.253	.307	.398	-.032	.239	.296	.386	.235	-4.5	108-CF	-1		
2004	CHR	AAA	25	336	44	21	0	16	48	30	68	4	3	4.2	.266	.333	.495	.091	.234	.301	.432	.249	-4.3	67-RF	-2	12-CF	1
2004	CHA	MLB	25	221	26	4	1	9	20	19	57	1	0	4.5	.174	.249	.338	-.453	.167	.247	.333	.205	-18.3	52-RF	0		
2005	CHR	AAA	26	549	69	20	0	29	67	50	143	6	4	3.8	.263	.335	.480	.071	.234	.303	.419	.247	-9.0	109-RF	-8	13-CF	-1
2006	*CHA*	*MLB*	*27*	*341*	*38*	*13*	*1*	*13*	*45*	*25*	*86*	*2*	*2*	*4.0*	*.243*	*.303*	*.418*	*-.074*	*.242*	*.307*	*.415*	*.239*	*-1.8*	*82-RF*	*-3*		

Breakout: 31%   Improve: 53%   Collapse: 27%   Attrition: 24%   Comparables: Jeff Liefer, John Herrnstein, Jason Jones

Depending on who you talk to, Borchard's problem is either that he doesn't care enough about the game, or that he cares too much to relax at the big-league level. Those are the sort of mixed messages you get when a prospect disappoints this many people. Borchard's out of options, and while he probably has the bat to stick as a fourth outfielder, he might not get the chance since he's become too clunky to handle center field. Likely scenarios include his becoming a Ham Fighter, or opening up an ice cream parlor with Dermal Brown and George Lombard.

JOE CREDE   **3B**   **Bats: R Throws: R**   Height: 6' 3"   Weight: 195   Born: April 26, 1978   Age: 28

YEAR	TM	LVL	AGE	PA	R	2B	3B	HR	RBI	BB	SO	SB	CS	SPEED	BA	OBP	SLG	MLVR	EQBA	EQOBP	EQSLG	EQA	VORP	DEFENSE	
2003	CHA	MLB	25	578	68	31	2	19	75	32	75	1	1	3.9	.261	.308	.433	-.039	.257	.309	.430	.253	15.5	148-3B	0
2004	CHA	MLB	26	539	67	25	0	21	69	34	81	1	2	3.8	.239	.299	.418	-.135	.236	.298	.419	.245	-6.8	140-3B	-8
2005	CHA	MLB	27	469	54	21	0	22	62	25	66	1	1	3.3	.252	.303	.454	-.022	.254	.313	.465	.263	7.8	123-3B	9
2006	*CHA*	*MLB*	*28*	*508*	*58*	*25*	*1*	*20*	*70*	*30*	*71*	*1*	*1*	*3.9*	*.259*	*.311*	*.447*	*-.011*	*.258*	*.316*	*.443*	*.251*	*9.0*	*120-3B*	*2*

Breakout: 28%   Improve: 54%   Collapse: 21%   Attrition: 15%   Comparables: Jeff King, Dale Berra, Kevin Elster

If you're wondering whether or not Joe Crede's breakout was for real, you're not alone: if he doesn't add 15 points to that EQA, upgrading at third base will go onto the team's laundry list, and Crede will join Ray Knight and Marty Castillo in the ranks of briefly famous third base postseason stars. We've liked his defense for years, so it was good to see him show it off in the playoffs.

JERMAINE DYE   **RF**   **Bats: R Throws: R**   Height: 6' 5"   Weight: 220   Born: January 28, 1974   Age: 32

YEAR	TM	LVL	AGE	PA	R	2B	3B	HR	RBI	BB	SO	SB	CS	SPEED	BA	OBP	SLG	MLVR	EQBA	EQOBP	EQSLG	EQA	VORP	DEFENSE	
2003	OAK	MLB	29	253	28	6	0	4	20	25	42	1	0	3.8	.172	.261	.253	-.402	.169	.262	.256	.196	-21.0	56-RF	3
2004	OAK	MLB	30	590	87	29	4	23	80	49	128	4	2	5.0	.265	.329	.464	.004	.263	.330	.468	.271	12.0	130-RF	2
2005	CHA	MLB	31	579	74	29	2	31	86	39	99	11	4	4.9	.274	.333	.512	.128	.278	.346	.534	.291	27.7	136-RF	2
2006	*CHA*	*MLB*	*32*	*495*	*62*	*22*	*2*	*22*	*72*	*38*	*92*	*6*	*3*	*4.7*	*.264*	*.327*	*.467*	*.045*	*.263*	*.332*	*.463*	*.263*	*7.8*	*117-RF*	*0*

Breakout: 13%   Improve: 53%   Collapse: 27%   Attrition: 15%   Comparables: Larry Parrish, Jim Lemon, Tom Brunansky

Dye stayed healthy, rounded out Chicago's terrific outfield defense, and ranked behind only Vlad, Sheffield, and Ichiro in VORP among AL right fielders. PECOTA expects some age-related decline, but with just one guaranteed year left on his contract that isn't the concern that it otherwise might be.

CARL EVERETT   **DH**   **Bats: B Throws: R**   Height: 6′ 0″   Weight: 190   Born: June 3, 1971   Age: 35

YEAR	TM	LVL	AGE	PA	R	2B	3B	HR	RBI	BB	SO	SB	CS	SPEED	BA	OBP	SLG	MLVR	EQBA	EQOBP	EQSLG	EQA	VORP	DEFENSE			
2003	TEX	MLB	32	309	53	13	3	18	51	31	48	4	1	6.1	.274	.356	.544	.164	.264	.351	.536	.295	16.3	29-LF	-2	27-RF	2
2003	CHA	MLB	32	289	40	14	0	10	41	22	36	4	3	4.3	.301	.377	.473	.166	.299	.376	.469	.287	18.5	55-CF	-3		
2004	MON	MLB	33	141	8	10	0	2	14	8	19	0	0	2.5	.252	.319	.378	-.063	.244	.307	.378	.239	-1.1	17-LF	-1	13-RF	2
2004	CHA	MLB	33	169	21	7	1	5	21	8	26	1	0	5.0	.266	.320	.422	-.080	.263	.317	.414	.254	1.3				
2005	CHA	MLB	34	547	58	17	2	23	87	42	99	4	5	4.3	.251	.311	.435	-.033	.253	.322	.450	.263	6.3	13-LF	0		
2006	*SEA*	*MLB*	*35*	*407*	*45*	*18*	*2*	*13*	*57*	*30*	*72*	*3*	*2*	*4.8*	*.262*	*.322*	*.424*	*-.021*	*.267*	*.333*	*.447*	*.259*	*9.5*	*97-DH*			

Breakout: 21%   Improve: 46%   Collapse: 25%   Attrition: 20%   Comparables: Dave Philley, Jeffrey Leonard, Al Cowens

In the parallel universe where the Indians play well in late September, the decision to stick with Carl Everett in the DH slot would take on tragic proportions. Sure, Kenny Williams had his heart set on Ken Griffey and was left at the altar by Carl Lindner, but any Matt Stairs type could have substantially upgraded the Sox attack at little price. What's more, after an unusually quiet season, Everett finally blew up at his manager in the press after he was demoted from the #3 slot in the order. For all the talk about the White Sox's probable regression to the mean in 2006, we should remember at least this one case of addition by subtraction. This year's Ari Fleischer Award goes to the Mariners' Bill Bavasi, who, when pressed about Everett's moodiness, said he would "break up any monotony or boredom."

JOSHUA FIELDS   **3B**   **Bats: R Throws: R**   Height: 6′ 2″   Weight: 210   Born: December 14, 1982   Age: 23

YEAR	TM	LVL	AGE	PA	R	2B	3B	HR	RBI	BB	SO	SB	CS	SPEED	BA	OBP	SLG	MLVR	EQBA	EQOBP	EQSLG	EQA	VORP	DEFENSE	
2004	WNS	A+	21	279	36	12	4	7	39	18	74	0	0	5.1	.285	.333	.445	.078	.243	.285	.389	.233	-1.1	57-3B	-2
2005	BIR	AA	22	551	76	27	0	16	79	55	142	7	6	5.0	.252	.341	.409	.027	.223	.299	.375	.236	-3.2	127-3B	-10
2006	*CHA*	*MLB*	*23*	*482*	*55*	*22*	*2*	*16*	*57*	*34*	*121*	*4*	*3*	*4.6*	*.236*	*.298*	*.408*	*-.099*	*.235*	*.302*	*.405*	*.235*	*-1.2*	*114-3B*	*-7*

Breakout: 38%   Improve: 50%   Collapse: 23%   Attrition: 7%   Comparables: Ryan Owens, Drew Henson, Corey Smith

It's no accident that PECOTA compares him to Drew Henson. This will be a big year for Fields, who has hit for just enough power to keep people interested but otherwise looks like the former quarterback that he is. While Fields's walk rate has improved materially, his contact hitting needs to develop, as does his footwork at third; he barely played the position in college. There is some upside here, but it is more in the mold of a Shea Hillenbrand-type career than a legitimate star-in-the-making.

ROSS GLOAD   **1B**   **Bats: L Throws: L**   Height: 6′ 0″   Weight: 180   Born: April 5, 1976   Age: 30

YEAR	TM	LVL	AGE	PA	R	2B	3B	HR	RBI	BB	SO	SB	CS	SPEED	BA	OBP	SLG	MLVR	EQBA	EQOBP	EQSLG	EQA	VORP	DEFENSE			
2003	CHR	AAA	27	544	72	40	6	18	70	29	60	6	3	5.2	.315	.349	.524	.258	.284	.323	.471	.269	16.8	102-1B	6	13-LF	0
2004	CHA	MLB	28	259	28	16	0	7	44	20	37	0	3	2.5	.321	.375	.479	.141	.319	.376	.485	.290	11.8	25-1B	-2	16-RF	1
2005	CHR	AAA	29	262	45	22	1	15	45	22	37	0	1	4.4	.364	.416	.657	.550	.307	.358	.527	.295	19.3	37-1B	5		
2006	*CHA*	*MLB*	*30*	*312*	*36*	*16*	*1*	*12*	*45*	*19*	*52*	*0*	*1*	*4.1*	*.271*	*.318*	*.456*	*.021*	*.269*	*.322*	*.452*	*.256*	*4.0*	*76-1B*	*0*		

Breakout: 6%   Improve: 25%   Collapse: 46%   Attrition: 28%   Comparables: Wes Covington, Jerry Lynch, Dick Kryhoski

It had to kill Gload to see Carl Everett's oh-fers while he was crushing the ball in Charlotte, but this is the sort of thing a guy that wears the Quad-A label grows accustomed to. Gload might stick in Chicago with the decisions to non-tender Willie Harris and Timo Perez, but his value is limited by the Sox's offensive balance: there are no All-Stars in the everyday lineup, but also nobody that you clearly need to pinch hit for.

WILLIE HARRIS   **2B/CF**   **Bats: L Throws: R**   Height: 5′ 9″   Weight: 170   Born: June 22, 1978   Age: 28

YEAR	TM	LVL	AGE	PA	R	2B	3B	HR	RBI	BB	SO	SB	CS	SPEED	BA	OBP	SLG	MLVR	EQBA	EQOBP	EQSLG	EQA	VORP	DEFENSE			
2003	CHR	AAA	25	117	22	6	1	6	13	17	20	9	3	6.6	.380	.470	.640	.648	.354	.443	.602	.343	22.0	17-2B	2		
2003	CHA	MLB	25	147	19	3	1	0	5	10	28	12	2	8.1	.204	.259	.241	-.435	.200	.260	.237	.202	-8.4	29-CF	0		
2004	CHA	MLB	26	464	68	15	2	2	27	51	79	19	7	6.7	.262	.343	.323	-.194	.257	.344	.317	.245	-2.5	76-2B	1	25-CF	-1
2005	CHR	AAA	27	125	21	11	1	1	10	16	27	10	2	8.2	.266	.360	.413	.027	.235	.321	.362	.249	0.2	27-2B	1		
2005	CHA	MLB	27	135	17	2	1	1	8	13	25	10	3	7.5	.256	.333	.314	-.167	.261	.348	.319	.250	0.0	27-2B	-3		
2006	*CHA*	*MLB*	*28*	*256*	*34*	*10*	*2*	*3*	*19*	*25*	*44*	*10*	*3*	*6.5*	*.262*	*.339*	*.360*	*-.073*	*.260*	*.344*	*.357*	*.245*	*3.5*	*63-2B*	*0*		

Breakout: 19%   Improve: 36%   Collapse: 44%   Attrition: 32%   Comparables: Alex Cole, Steve Hovley, Dell Alston

(continued next page)

Willie Harris *(continued)*

Harris has long been described as a Tony Phillips clone, which not only vastly underrates Phillips, but also understates how rare it is to see a player take on anything approaching the super-utility role in the modern game. That said, Harris is deserving of a roster spot. He's perhaps the only player in baseball who can be a defensive asset at both second base and center field, and manages to steal bases at a decent clip in spite of being only a slightly less obvious pinch running ringer than Herb Washington. It's not clear that Rob Mackowiak is an upgrade.

FRANCISCO HERNANDEZ   **C**   **Bats: B Throws: R**   Height: 5′ 9″   Weight: 160   Born: February 4, 1986   Age: 20

YEAR	TM	LVL	AGE	PA	R	2B	3B	HR	RBI	BB	SO	SB	CS	SPEED	BA	OBP	SLG	MLVR	EQBA	EQOBP	EQSLG	EQA	VORP	DEFENSE	
2004	BRI	Rk	18	199	32	13	1	5	30	13	32	0	0	3.9	.326	.372	.492	.306	.281	.311	.418	.251	11.8	44-C	6
2005	GRF	Rk	19	237	37	19	0	6	34	19	25	0	1	3.2	.349	.405	.524	.365	.274	.314	.405	.249	9.3	37-C	8
2005	KAN	A	19	171	15	5	0	3	18	13	29	0	0	3.0	.222	.292	.314	-.183	.191	.241	.268	.186	-15.3	39-C	5
2006	*CHA*	*MLB*	*20*	*368*	*36*	*17*	*1*	*9*	*40*	*20*	*56*	*0*	*0*	*3.6*	*.244*	*.289*	*.373*	*-.154*	*.243*	*.293*	*.370*	*.220*	*-1.2*	*88-C*	*9*

Breakout: 27%   *Improve: 42%*   *Collapse: 36%*   *Attrition: 13%*   *Comparables: Daniel Tosca, Jeffrey Mathis, Miguel Montero*

On the plus side, Hernandez was just 19, and both the scouts and our numbers suggest that he could be a premium defensive catcher. On the negative side, he's very small, very slow, and hit an empty .222 against Sally League pitching. Did we mention that he was just 19?

TADAHITO IGUCHI   **2B**   **Bats: R Throws: R**   Height: 5′ 10″   Weight: 185   Born: December 4, 1974   Age: 31

YEAR	TM	LVL	AGE	PA	R	2B	3B	HR	RBI	BB	SO	SB	CS	SPEED	BA	OBP	SLG	MLVR	EQBA	EQOBP	EQSLG	EQA	VORP	DEFENSE
2003	FKU	JPL	28	596	109	37	1	27	81	81	14	42	112	6.2	.340	.430	.573	.446	.327	.414	.461	.305	53.8	
2004	FKU	JPL	29	566	96	34	2	24	89	47	90	18	0	6.2	.333	.399	.549	.354	.321	.379	.457	.289	41.9	
2005	CHA	MLB	30	570	74	25	6	15	71	47	114	15	5	5.8	.278	.342	.438	.034	.281	.353	.454	.279	23.8	129-2B -16
2006	*CHA*	*MLB*	*31*	*578*	*78*	*26*	*4*	*14*	*61*	*47*	*100*	*14*	*4*	*5.3*	*.277*	*.341*	*.424*	*.022*	*.275*	*.346*	*.420*	*.261*	*20.2*	*136-2B -9*

Breakout: 2%   *Improve: 14%*   *Collapse: 50%*   *Attrition: 7%*   *Comparables: Ken Hamlin, Ed Charles, Bobby Avila*

Iguchi's defense is an interesting case. He won a Gold Glove on the other side of the Pacific, where it's apparently considered ungentlemanly for an opposing runner to come in hard on the double play. Iguchi went through phases at the start of the year where he was maladroit around the deuce, either standing right in the baseline and risking his manhood, or overcompensating and standing too far away. Between that concern and a bat that's just average, there's the sense that while Iguchi provided excellent bang for the buck, he could be the victim of an upgrade at the trade deadline.

PAUL KONERKO   **1B**   **Bats: R Throws: R**   Height: 6′ 3″   Weight: 210   Born: March 5, 1976   Age: 30

YEAR	TM	LVL	AGE	PA	R	2B	3B	HR	RBI	BB	SO	SB	CS	SPEED	BA	OBP	SLG	MLVR	EQBA	EQOBP	EQSLG	EQA	VORP	DEFENSE
2003	CHA	MLB	27	495	49	19	0	18	65	43	50	0	0	2.5	.234	.305	.399	-.107	.231	.307	.397	.245	-5.0	106-1B 3
2004	CHA	MLB	28	643	84	22	0	41	117	69	107	1	0	2.9	.277	.359	.535	.166	.274	.360	.531	.297	38.0	133-1B -6
2005	CHA	MLB	29	664	98	24	0	40	100	81	109	0	0	3.1	.283	.375	.534	.232	.287	.387	.552	.313	46.1	140-1B 9
2006	*CHA*	*MLB*	*30*	*623*	*80*	*26*	*0*	*32*	*101*	*67*	*96*	*0*	*0*	*3.5*	*.280*	*.362*	*.505*	*.160*	*.278*	*.367*	*.501*	*.286*	*26.7*	*146-1B 3*

Breakout: 7%   *Improve: 44%*   *Collapse: 11%*   *Attrition: 3%*   *Comparables: Eric Karros, Cecil Fielder, Nick Esasky*

Any valuation of his shiny new $60 million deal needs to account for the fact that Paul E. is the most popular athlete in the country's third largest city at a time when the White Sox are determined to leverage their championship into long-term credibility. Konerko would be overpaid for any club but the Comiskeymen. While PECOTA expects his offense to hold up reasonably well, there's the chance that Konkero's defense lapses into DH territory before the Sox's commitment to Jim Thome has expired. Another concern is injury; any slow first baseman entering his thirties is an injury candidate, and there are widespread (and unrefuted) rumors that Konerko has an arthritic hip. The White Sox are probably more aware of these risks than you'd think, just as the Red Sox were when they re-upped Jason Varitek last winter.

JERRY OWENS   **OF**   **Bats: L Throws: L**   Height: 6′ 3″   Weight: 195   Born: February 16, 1981   Age: 25

YEAR	TM	LVL	AGE	PA	R	2B	3B	HR	RBI	BB	SO	SB	CS	SPEED	BA	OBP	SLG	MLVR	EQBA	EQOBP	EQSLG	EQA	VORP	DEFENSE	
2004	SAV	A	23	469	69	17	2	1	37	46	59	30	13	6.3	.292	.365	.349	.034	.253	.307	.298	.222	-30.1	46-LF -4	17-CF -2
2005	BIR	AA	24	578	99	21	6	2	52	52	72	38	20	7.0	.331	.393	.406	.168	.295	.347	.366	.252	-2.8	116-LF 10	
2006	*CHA*	*MLB*	*25*	*479*	*53*	*18*	*4*	*1*	*32*	*27*	*74*	*17*	*7*	*5.5*	*.262*	*.306*	*.327*	*-.173*	*.260*	*.310*	*.324*	*.218*	*-12.6*	*113-LF 1*	

Breakout: 11%   *Improve: 31%*   *Collapse: 42%*   *Attrition: 12%*   *Comparables: Richard Thompson, Kerry Robinson, Osmany Santana*

Owens will be talked about as competition for Brian Anderson in the spring papers, but that's in the spirit of Saddam Hussein's competition in B'aath Party primaries, or being a non-Daley in the Chicago mayoral race. Although Owens could stick on the roster this spring, the moons have to align perfectly for players with this little power to develop into anything other than fifth outfielders. You can ignore that Owens played left in Birmingham last year; he plays the best defensive center field in the organization, but the White Sox understandably gave priority to Chris Young.

PABLO OZUNA   **INF**   **Bats: R Throws: R**   Height: 5' 10"   Weight: 185   Born: August 25, 1974   Age: 31

YEAR	TM	LVL	AGE	PA	R	2B	3B	HR	RBI	BB	SO	SB	CS	SPEED	BA	OBP	SLG	MLVR	EQBA	EQOBP	EQSLG	EQA	VORP	DEFENSE			
2003	CSP	AAA	28	230	30	13	7	1	17	9	23	12	6	8.2	.269	.300	.406	-.116	.224	.257	.340	.211	-9.9	17-2B	0	17-CF	-1
2004	SWB	AAA	29	505	77	27	3	6	76	22	43	31	12	7.4	.307	.343	.415	.032	.268	.302	.353	.235	-2.9	56-2B	1	56-SS	5
2005	CHA	MLB	30	214	27	7	2	0	11	7	26	14	7	7.3	.276	.313	.330	-.162	.285	.329	.340	.238	-2.8	29-3B	2	11-SS	2
2006	*CHA*	*MLB*	*31*	*234*	*28*	*8*	*2*	*1*	*16*	*7*	*27*	*10*	*3*	*5.9*	*.254*	*.283*	*.312*	*-.239*	*.252*	*.287*	*.309*	*.204*	*-6.8*	*58-3B*	*1*		

Breakout: 10%   Improve: 24%   Collapse: 56%   Attrition: 37%   Comparables: Homer Bush, Hank Schenz, Jerry Terrell

The White Sox bench combined for −8.6 VORP last year, the fifth-worst figure in baseball. Ozuna was no small part of the problem. Much of his playing time came at third base, and Ozzie Guillen often saw fit to stick him in the leadoff spot. In spite of his performance, Ozuna was signed to a guaranteed contract for 2006. The White Sox have committed worse sins, but they're dangerously thin on position player talent and aren't guaranteed to be as fortunate with the injury bug this time around.

TIMO PEREZ   **OF**   **Bats: L Throws: L**   Height: 5' 9"   Weight: 170   Born: April 8, 1975   Age: 31

YEAR	TM	LVL	AGE	PA	R	2B	3B	HR	RBI	BB	SO	SB	CS	SPEED	BA	OBP	SLG	MLVR	EQBA	EQOBP	EQSLG	EQA	VORP	DEFENSE			
2003	NYN	MLB	28	375	32	21	0	4	42	18	29	5	6	4.8	.269	.301	.364	-.125	.272	.304	.370	.235	-8.6	39-LF	-3	38-CF	3
2004	CHA	MLB	29	312	38	12	0	5	40	15	29	3	1	4.8	.246	.285	.338	-.277	.242	.287	.329	.221	-13.1	43-RF	2	20-CF	0
2005	CHA	MLB	30	192	13	8	0	2	15	12	25	2	2	4.3	.218	.266	.296	-.330	.216	.276	.301	.207	-12.2	19-LF	1	17-RF	1
2006	*CHA*	*MLB*	*31*	*147*	*15*	*6*	*0*	*2*	*14*	*8*	*17*	*1*	*1*	*4.6*	*.253*	*.297*	*.350*	*-.164*	*.251*	*.302*	*.347*	*.218*	*-4.3*	*39-LF*	*0*		

Breakout: 39%   Improve: 55%   Collapse: 35%   Attrition: 49%   Comparables: Bob Boyd, Bill Bean, Terry Francona

Perez hit .348/.385/.512 in 2000, mostly as a member of the Norfolk Tides, but more famously as a New York Met who came up with a couple of big post-season hits after Derek Bell went down. He's hit .275/.317/.391 for the rest of his career; including his untranslated minor league numbers and an unimpressive tenure in Japan to start his career. For all practical intents, you might as well be playing Jeffrey Maier. Non-tendered.

A. J. PIERZYNSKI   **C**   **Bats: L Throws: R**   Height: 6' 3"   Weight: 220   Born: December 30, 1976   Age: 29

YEAR	TM	LVL	AGE	PA	R	2B	3B	HR	RBI	BB	SO	SB	CS	SPEED	BA	OBP	SLG	MLVR	EQBA	EQOBP	EQSLG	EQA	VORP	DEFENSE	
2003	MIN	MLB	26	531	63	35	3	11	74	24	55	3	1	4.9	.312	.360	.464	.130	.311	.360	.468	.284	35.1	129-C	10
2004	SFN	MLB	27	508	45	28	2	11	77	19	27	0	1	3.2	.272	.319	.410	-.042	.268	.313	.404	.247	9.1	114-C	-1
2005	CHA	MLB	28	496	61	21	0	18	56	23	68	0	2	3.7	.257	.308	.420	-.055	.258	.317	.436	.256	12.1	123-C	3
2006	*CHA*	*MLB*	*29*	*482*	*49*	*24*	*1*	*14*	*63*	*20*	*56*	*0*	*1*	*4.2*	*.274*	*.315*	*.429*	*-.017*	*.273*	*.319*	*.425*	*.247*	*12.3*	*114-C*	*0*

Breakout: 15%   Improve: 41%   Collapse: 26%   Attrition: 8%   Comparables: Terry Kennedy, Sandy Alomar, Russ Nixon

How many other players would have bothered to run on that dropped third strike? Eliminate the 30 percent who are too lazy, the 40 percent who are too bashful, and the 29 percent who are too mature to try a stunt like that, and you're left with . . . A. J. Pierzysnki, Orlando Hudson, and Milton Bradley by our count. Pierzysnki's career perfectly illustrates the point that clubhouse chemistry is a distillation of winning, and not the other way around. Performance-wise, he's a risk, but he seldom strikes out so he should get that batting average up a few points. His contract extension ($3 million for five years) drew some criticism, but league average catchers don't grow on trees.

SCOTT PODSEDNIK   **LF/CF**   **Bats: L Throws: L**   Height: 6' 0"   Weight: 170   Born: March 18, 1976   Age: 30

YEAR	TM	LVL	AGE	PA	R	2B	3B	HR	RBI	BB	SO	SB	CS	SPEED	BA	OBP	SLG	MLVR	EQBA	EQOBP	EQSLG	EQA	VORP	DEFENSE			
2003	MIL	MLB	27	620	100	29	8	9	58	56	91	43	10	7.7	.314	.379	.443	.146	.308	.374	.442	.287	41.1	122-CF	-5	10-RF	1
2004	MIL	MLB	28	706	85	27	7	12	39	58	105	70	13	7.7	.244	.313	.364	-.106	.238	.308	.354	.246	10.4	152-CF	-10		
2005	CHA	MLB	29	562	80	28	1	0	25	47	75	59	23	7.2	.290	.351	.349	-.058	.299	.368	.363	.265	5.8	117-LF	11		
2006	*CHA*	*MLB*	*30*	*564*	*88*	*23*	*4*	*6*	*44*	*45*	*79*	*43*	*14*	*6.2*	*.274*	*.336*	*.374*	*-.053*	*.272*	*.341*	*.371*	*.250*	*2.6*	*132-LF*	*-1*		

Breakout: 3%   Improve: 30%   Collapse: 33%   Attrition: 10%   Comparables: Pat Kelly, Darryl Hamilton, Marvin Benard

(continued next page)

Scott Podsednik *(continued)*

Podsednik almost never swings at a bad pitch, and sees almost four pitches a plate appearance; the middling walk rates are mostly a consequence of pitchers having no incentive to throw him anything outside of the strike zone. On defense, he gets great jumps on the ball, the result of good instincts and hustle rather than physical tools. He was caught stealing a lot last year, but almost all of that came in the second half, when he had a strained groin and Guillen wouldn't stop running him; exclude that post-ASB performance and he's stolen at an 83% clip on his major league career. His overall baserunning was a little bit off last season, but is usually going to be worth an extra couple of runs. All of those things add value. The problem is that if Podsednik hits *any* worse than he did last year he goes from being an unorthodox corner outfield solution to an unplayable one. At this point, the Sox's defense of Podsednik's abilities has become a cause unto itself, and it has probably become politically impossible to bench him for any length of time. So long as Brian Anderson and Chris Young were both in the system, there was the hope that one of them would force the issue, but with Young gone Podsednik will now get an almost infinite amount of slack. If Podsednik's performance reverts back to 2004 standards, there is an active trade market at the deadline, and the White Sox find themselves just a hairsbreadth behind the Twins or the Indians, that could be the ultimate litmus test for Kenny Williams and Ozzie Guillen.

CASEY ROGOWSKI **1B** **Bats: L Throws: L** Height: 6′ 3″ Weight: 230 Born: May 1, 1981 Age: 25

YEAR	TM	LVL	AGE	PA	R	2B	3B	HR	RBI	BB	SO	SB	CS	SPEED	BA	OBP	SLG	MLVR	EQBA	EQOBP	EQSLG	EQA	VORP	DEFENSE		
2003	WNS	A+	22	421	46	20	1	7	38	53	73	18	4	5.4	.246	.354	.367	.023	.224	.317	.358	.244	-13.3	101-1B	13	
2004	WNS	A+	23	566	88	28	2	18	90	91	94	16	9	5.3	.286	.401	.471	.207	.237	.338	.396	.258	-1.0	108-1B	8	14-LF 0
2005	BIR	AA	24	580	83	37	6	9	78	58	111	20	12	5.5	.293	.374	.444	.159	.262	.329	.404	.255	1.0	129-1B	8	
2006	*CHA*	*MLB*	*25*	*489*	*59*	*24*	*2*	*15*	*57*	*45*	*103*	*8*	*4*	*5.0*	*.251*	*.326*	*.415*	*-.034*	*.249*	*.331*	*.411*	*.250*	*-0.7*	*116-1B*	*5*	

Breakout: 19%   Improve: 47%   Collapse: 27%   Attrition: 9%   Comparables: Kevin Burns, Travis Lee, Brett Roneberg

Statheads of all stripes praise the "doubles power" and "underrated plate discipline" of this "rugged" and "surprisingly athletic" Birmingham Baron, and note that he "cooked up a good season" at a ballpark that "makes Dodger Stadium looks like Coors Field", but skeptics warn that he was "old for his league", and that his "downcut swing" could make him "the second coming of Travis Lee"; N.B. avoid the crème brulee.

AARON ROWAND **CF** **Bats: R Throws: R** Height: 6′ 1″ Weight: 210 Born: August 29, 1977 Age: 28

YEAR	TM	LVL	AGE	PA	R	2B	3B	HR	RBI	BB	SO	SB	CS	SPEED	BA	OBP	SLG	MLVR	EQBA	EQOBP	EQSLG	EQA	VORP	DEFENSE		
2003	CHR	AAA	25	133	15	9	0	3	13	11	12	0	0	3.6	.242	.316	.392	-.034	.216	.292	.364	.230	-3.3	21-CF	0	11-RF 0
2003	CHA	MLB	25	168	22	8	0	6	24	7	21	0	0	4.6	.287	.327	.452	.042	.284	.325	.458	.266	6.4	43-CF	-1	
2004	CHA	MLB	26	529	94	38	2	24	69	30	91	17	5	6.7	.310	.361	.544	.196	.307	.360	.543	.299	42.0	115-CF	3	
2005	CHA	MLB	27	635	77	30	5	13	69	32	116	16	5	6.0	.270	.329	.407	-.031	.273	.339	.420	.265	14.7	150-CF	10	
2006	*PHI*	*MLB*	*28*	*561*	*73*	*30*	*3*	*16*	*72*	*33*	*91*	*11*	*4*	*5.5*	*.280*	*.333*	*.444*	*.021*	*.279*	*.334*	*.446*	*.262*	*17.8*	*132-CF*	*1*	

Breakout: 10%   Improve: 42%   Collapse: 26%   Attrition: 4%   Comparables: Larry Herndon, Roberto Kelly, Marty Cordova

Any assessment of the Jim Thome deal largely depends on what can be expected of Rowand's offense going forward. The White Sox evidently think that it will look more like 2005 than 2004, an assessment with which PECOTA wholeheartedly agrees. Let's see...big season fueled by an uncharacteristically high batting average? Check. Age 26/27 peak elapsed? Check. Marty Cordova on your comparables list? Check. All of that said, Rowand is a fine pickup for the Phillies. He might benefit from a few additional off days; Rowand is asked to do a lot out there, and looked tired in the second half of the season, going through long stretches in August and September where he failed to drive the ball at all.

MICAH SCHNURSTEIN **3B** **Bats: R Throws: R** Height: 6′ 1″ Weight: 200 Born: July 18, 1984 Age: 21

YEAR	TM	LVL	AGE	PA	R	2B	3B	HR	RBI	BB	SO	SB	CS	SPEED	BA	OBP	SLG	MLVR	EQBA	EQOBP	EQSLG	EQA	VORP	DEFENSE		
2003	GRF	Rk	18	208	35	9	1	1	16	11	39	0	1	4.2	.264	.312	.337	-.127	.224	.261	.287	.195	-22.1	49-3B	5	
2004	KAN	A	19	531	53	33	0	6	59	27	104	15	4	4.7	.278	.322	.381	-.018	.236	.270	.330	.213	-19.7	125-3B	-21	
2005	WNS	A+	20	537	78	21	3	15	68	40	98	12	8	5.2	.268	.331	.416	-.026	.227	.275	.350	.219	-14.4	115-3B	-18	10-2B -1
2006	*CHA*	*MLB*	*21*	*488*	*51*	*20*	*2*	*12*	*51*	*23*	*93*	*7*	*4*	*4.8*	*.237*	*.276*	*.367*	*-.188*	*.235*	*.280*	*.364*	*.213*	*-9.5*	*115-3B*	*-10*	

Breakout: 44%   Improve: 65%   Collapse: 22%   Attrition: 6%   Comparables: Angel Chavez, Scott Hodges, Alex Ahumada

Schnurstein has an underdeveloped approach at the plate, but if it's any consolation, all of his skills—power, contact hitting, plate discipline—are equally underdeveloped, and none are so poor as to inhibit improvement from a guy who will be playing in Double-A as a 21-year-old next year. He'll need to show growth in at least two of those three areas to be taken seriously a prospect. Clay Davenport's defensive system thinks his defense might be the bigger problem, but that assessment reflects an erratic arm rather than a lack of range. The Warthogs experimented with him as a second baseman last season, a position that might better suit his skills.

CHRIS STEWART   C   **Bats: R Throws: R**   Height: 6' 4"   Weight: 200   Born: February 19, 1982   Age: 24

YEAR	TM	LVL	AGE	PA	R	2B	3B	HR	RBI	BB	SO	SB	CS	SPEED	BA	OBP	SLG	MLVR	EQBA	EQOBP	EQSLG	EQA	VORP	DEFENSE
2003	WNS	A+	21	245	18	8	2	2	27	27	29	1	0	4.1	.207	.294	.290	-.184	.191	.266	.286	.202	-17.4	76-C 19
2004	BIR	AA	22	288	26	11	2	1	17	22	59	2	4	4.2	.231	.299	.300	-.176	.218	.278	.285	.205	-15.8	75-C 1
2005	BIR	AA	23	340	39	21	0	11	51	24	37	3	3	3.9	.286	.341	.460	.126	.252	.299	.420	.246	5.3	84-C 11
2006	CHA	MLB	24	348	35	14	1	7	36	21	51	2	1	4.1	.237	.288	.359	-.178	.235	.293	.355	.217	-4.0	84-C 5

Breakout: 24%   Improve: 41%   Collapse: 34%   Attrition: 18%   Comparables: Jason Phillips, David Parrish, Ryan Jorgensen

Be skeptical of the modest power breakout at Birmingham; it came from a guy who got a lot of days off, and whose bat was regarded as a joke by most observers coming into the season. Still, for someone who projects at a .217 EqA, Stewart's likely to have a big league career, as he has one of the four or five best catching arms in baseball.

RYAN SWEENEY   RF   **Bats: L Throws: L**   Height: 6' 4"   Weight: 200   Born: February 20, 1985   Age: 21

YEAR	TM	LVL	AGE	PA	R	2B	3B	HR	RBI	BB	SO	SB	CS	SPEED	BA	OBP	SLG	MLVR	EQBA	EQOBP	EQSLG	EQA	VORP	DEFENSE
2003	BRI	Rk	18	75	11	3	0	2	5	7	10	3	0	4.7	.313	.387	.448	.280	.271	.321	.389	.252	-2.0	11-RF 0
2004	WNS	A+	19	564	71	22	3	7	66	40	65	8	6	4.9	.283	.342	.379	.001	.245	.296	.342	.225	-27.7	126-RF 6
2005	BIR	AA	20	476	64	22	3	1	47	35	53	6	6	5.4	.298	.357	.371	.035	.273	.322	.342	.236	-13.7	107-RF 0
2006	CHA	MLB	21	501	51	24	2	4	43	27	65	4	3	5.1	.264	.308	.354	-.133	.263	.313	.351	.223	-12.7	118-RF 1

Breakout: 22%   Improve: 45%   Collapse: 23%   Attrition: 5%   Comparables: Alex Fernandez, Trent Oeltjen, Carl Crawford

There was a lot of talk about White Sox's tremendous organizational outfield depth over the course of the season, but if people were lumping Sweeney in with Brian Anderson and Chris Young, they weren't paying attention. Although power is generally the last skill to develop, there are serious questions about how much a guy whose slugging ability falls below the Sean Burroughs Threshold can expect to grow. PECOTA has trouble finding comparables for Sweeney who eventually developed worthwhile major league bats. Sweeney is not unathletic, hence the Crawford comp, but Crawford had significant advantages in the defense and baserunning departments.

FRANK THOMAS   DH   **Bats: R Throws: R**   Height: 6' 5"   Weight: 257   Born: May 27, 1968   Age: 38

YEAR	TM	LVL	AGE	PA	R	2B	3B	HR	RBI	BB	SO	SB	CS	SPEED	BA	OBP	SLG	MLVR	EQBA	EQOBP	EQSLG	EQA	VORP	DEFENSE
2003	CHA	MLB	35	662	87	35	0	42	105	100	115	0	0	2.7	.267	.390	.562	.278	.265	.391	.564	.316	55.7	24-1B -1
2004	CHA	MLB	36	311	53	16	0	18	49	64	57	0	2	3.9	.271	.434	.562	.309	.269	.436	.564	.332	29.1	
2005	CHA	MLB	37	124	19	3	0	12	26	16	31	0	0	2.9	.219	.315	.590	.148	.223	.331	.612	.302	7.4	
2006	CHA	MLB	38	355	44	12	0	25	64	46	82	0	0	3.7	.245	.349	.531	.142	.244	.354	.526	.286	17.3	85-DH

Breakout: 6%   Improve: 19%   Collapse: 47%   Attrition: 31%   Comparables: Cliff Johnson, Harmon Killebrew, Joe Adcock

Thomas wasn't an active participant, but we hope that his graciousness and enthusiasm during the championship run will take one argument away from those who would deny him a place in the Hall of Fame. In the meantime, he's having trouble convincing suitors that he's over his foot and ankle problems. How many other free agents could post a 950 OPS for little more than pocket change?

JUAN URIBE   SS   **Bats: R Throws: R**   Height: 5' 11"   Weight: 175   Born: July 22, 1979   Age: 26

YEAR	TM	LVL	AGE	PA	R	2B	3B	HR	RBI	BB	SO	SB	CS	SPEED	BA	OBP	SLG	MLVR	EQBA	EQOBP	EQSLG	EQA	VORP	DEFENSE
2003	COL	MLB	23	337	45	19	3	10	33	17	60	7	2	6.5	.253	.297	.427	-.092	.235	.278	.403	.235	5.6	68-SS 7 10-2B 1
2004	CHA	MLB	24	542	82	31	6	23	74	32	96	9	11	5.6	.283	.327	.506	.064	.279	.326	.506	.273	25.0	71-2B 1 33-SS 5
2005	CHA	MLB	25	529	58	23	3	16	71	34	77	4	6	4.7	.252	.301	.412	-.093	.254	.311	.428	.252	7.5	142-SS 9
2006	CHA	MLB	26	554	69	26	3	20	69	33	85	6	4	5.0	.267	.315	.448	.004	.265	.320	.444	.253	17.7	130-SS 7

Breakout: 26%   Improve: 56%   Collapse: 17%   Attrition: 4%   Comparables: Gary Gaetti, Dale Berra, Don Money

Uribe can be a valuable player even in a down year at the plate. People associate good shortstop defense with an Omar Vizquel type of offensive profile—a contact hitter who steals a lot of bases—so players like Uribe and his predecessor Jose Valentin often wind up underrated. His 4.5 WARP (Wins Above Replacement Player) last season compared favorably to the more famous (and more liberally compensated) Orlando Cabrera and Edgar Renteria.

ROB VALIDO   SS   **Bats: R Throws: R**   Height: 6' 2"   Weight: 180   Born: May 16, 1985   Age: 21

YEAR	TM	LVL	AGE	PA	R	2B	3B	HR	RBI	BB	SO	SB	CS	SPEED	BA	OBP	SLG	MLVR	EQBA	EQOBP	EQSLG	EQA	VORP	DEFENSE	
2003	BRI	Rk	18	242	39	15	2	6	31	17	28	17	6	6.7	.307	.364	.479	.286	.266	.304	.411	.250	13.9	58-SS	2
2004	KAN	A	19	502	66	25	0	4	44	36	59	28	13	6.1	.251	.313	.332	-.119	.210	.259	.275	.199	-31.7	111-SS	-1
2005	WNS	A+	20	541	86	28	7	8	59	21	64	52	5	8.3	.288	.320	.417	-.028	.243	.266	.349	.227	-12.6	117-SS	16
2006	CHA	MLB	21	506	63	21	3	7	42	17	62	33	10	6.1	.249	.278	.354	-.194	.248	.283	.351	.219	-0.1	119-SS	7

Breakout: 32%   Improve: 59%   Collapse: 22%   Attrition: 4%   Comparables: William Bergolla, Joaquin Arias, Luis Rivas

On the other hand, there's Valido, who fits the shortstop stereotype to a tee. Vizquel and Rey Ordonez provide some reasonable goalposts for where his career could end up. As Vizquel showed, this skills set is far more valuable when coupled with enough walks for a .350 OBP. Valido was suspended for using performance-enhancing drugs in May, and his bat regressed slightly after the suspension. In spite of that, his organization is high on him, and he'll move up quickly.

CHRIS WIDGER   C   **Bats: R Throws: R**   Height: 6' 2"   Weight: 210   Born: May 21, 1971   Age: 35

YEAR	TM	LVL	AGE	PA	R	2B	3B	HR	RBI	BB	SO	SB	CS	SPEED	BA	OBP	SLG	MLVR	EQBA	EQOBP	EQSLG	EQA	VORP	DEFENSE	
2003	SLN	MLB	32	111	9	9	0	0	14	6	20	0	0	2.9	.235	.279	.324	-.222	.235	.279	.314	.214	-2.4	31-C	0
2005	CHA	MLB	34	152	18	8	0	4	11	10	22	0	2	3.5	.241	.296	.383	-.141	.245	.309	.396	.240	-0.3	38-C	-5
2006	CHA	MLB	35	245	22	11	0	6	27	16	40	0	1	3.7	.241	.293	.375	-.146	.239	.298	.371	.222	-1.4	61-C	-2

Breakout: 22%   Improve: 44%   Collapse: 36%   Attrition: 36%   Comparables: Brian Dorsett, Ray Murray, Mike Matheny

It's easy to misread his surname as "Widget," as in a generic product from the Backup Catcher Assembly Plant in Bangalore or Guadalajara. He certainly isn't a guy that you'd want starting every day if A. J. Pierznyski runs into a first baseman or a backstop or a stripper's pole or something. Chris Stewart already has the superior defensive reputation, and could have his job by July.

CHRIS YOUNG   CF   **Bats: R Throws: R**   Height: 6' 2"   Weight: 170   Born: September 5, 1983   Age: 22

YEAR	TM	LVL	AGE	PA	R	2B	3B	HR	RBI	BB	SO	SB	CS	SPEED	BA	OBP	SLG	MLVR	EQBA	EQOBP	EQSLG	EQA	VORP	DEFENSE	
2003	BRI	Rk	19	269	47	18	3	7	28	23	40	21	7	7.5	.290	.357	.479	.261	.249	.298	.410	.246	1.9	60-CF	-3
2004	KAN	A	20	548	83	31	5	24	56	67	146	31	9	6.7	.261	.365	.503	.199	.225	.307	.418	.253	3.2	133-CF	7
2005	BIR	AA	21	546	100	41	3	26	77	70	129	32	6	7.1	.277	.377	.545	.286	.243	.332	.485	.279	26.1	121-CF	-1
2006	ARI	MLB	22	568	82	36	3	24	76	56	132	23	8	5.6	.263	.343	.495	.090	.259	.338	.493	.275	24.5	133-CF	1

Breakout: 38%   Improve: 55%   Collapse: 13%   Attrition: 4%   Comparables: Bob Coluccio, Chin-Feng Chen, Jonny Gomes

How'd they get rid of *that* guy? While Javier Vazquez makes a more worthwhile acquisition target than Larry Andersen, Young could wind up being the Pale Hose answer to the Jeff Bagwell All-Time Trivia Question, "Name a great prospect your organization burned for little or no return." Young is the perfect prospect for the post-*Moneyball* world in that his statistics are every bit as interesting as his tools, especially considering that he was playing in one of the toughest hitting environments in minor league baseball. The lone chink in his armor is his ability to hit for contact, but he's smart enough to work for a fastball he can mash instead of looking foolish on a slider that he can't. Besides, if a guy's *downside* is Mike Cameron, what's not to like? PECOTA absolutely loves him, expecting both a big breakout in 2006 and good growth on top of it.

PITCHERS

JEFF BAJENARU   **Bats: R Throws: R**   Height: 6' 1"   Weight: 190   Born: March 21, 1978   Age: 28

YEAR	TM	LVL	AGE	W	L	SV	G	GS	IP	H	BB	SO	HR	GB%	BABIP	STUFF	WHIP	ERA	PERA	EQERA	EQH9	EQBB9	EQSO9	EQHR9	VORP	WXRL
2003	BIR	AA	25	4	2	14	50	0	64.7	53	28	62	2	—	.279	-10	1.25	3.20	4.55	5.72	8.4	4.7	5.6	0.6	-0.8	—
2004	BIR	AA	26	2	0	12	32	0	33.7	19	11	51	3	—	.239	1	0.89	1.34	4.75	4.45	7.7	3.9	8.3	1.5	3.9	—
2004	CHR	AAA	26	1	2	10	16	0	20.0	12	3	16	2	—	.182	1	0.75	1.80	3.93	3.44	7.4	1.5	5.9	1.0	4.4	—
2005	CHR	AAA	27	4	6	19	61	0	70.3	45	29	83	4	35%	.263	12	1.05	1.41	3.93	2.71	6.9	4.5	8.1	0.7	21.3	—
2006	CHA	MLB	28	3	3	3	51	2	50.3	48	23	43	8	37%	.279	1	1.41	4.67	4.47	4.87	8.2	4.0	7.4	1.3	5.8	0.6

Breakout: 20%   Improve: 48%   Collapse: 21%   Attrition: 25%   Comparables: Shawn Hillegas, John Wyatt, Alan Mills

Bajenaru's minor league ERAs have been impressive, but there are reasons for skepticism. His out pitch is the knuckle-curve, a creature that tends to fool minor league hitters that see him only once a game, resulting in a lot of strikeouts and fly balls to the warning track, but which major league hitters would be inclined to lay off in anticipation of his merely average fastball. Give him credit for chutzpah: the website jeffbajenaru.com lists him as "JEFF BAJENARU–CLOSER."

LANCE BROADWAY Bats: R Throws: R Height: 6' 4" Weight: 190 Born: August 20, 1983 Age: 22

YEAR	TM	LVL	AGE	W	L	SV	G	GS	IP	H	BB	SO	HR	GB%	BABIP	STUFF	WHIP	ERA	PERA	EQERA	EQH9	EQBB9	EQSO9	EQHR9	VORP	WXRL
2005	WNS	A+	21	1	3	0	11	11	55.0	68	20	58	4	53%	.400	7	1.60	4.58	4.88	5.86	10.7	3.6	5.9	1.0	-1.6	—
2006	CHA	MLB	22	6	9	0	26	22	125.3	143	56	82	16	52%	.312	4	1.58	5.49	5.30	5.60	9.9	3.9	5.7	1.1	1.9	1.1

Breakout: 24% Improve: 63% Collapse: 8% Attrition: 0% Comparables: Zach Day, Manny Parra, Denny Bautista

In contrast to Bajenaru, Broadway deserves some extra credit relative to his statistics. For one thing, he generates a large number of groundballs, a critical skill when you're planning on moving up to Charlotte and, eventually, Chicago. For another, he played professional ball after already having logged 117 innings at TCU, and the White Sox didn't have him throw his breaking stuff very often. Perhaps as a result of the fatigue, his fastball velocity was erratic; we have reports of his hitting as high as 94 mph, but he wasn't there consistently. Broadway is a sleeper, especially in an organization that can afford to treat him carefully over the next year or two.

MARK BUEHRLE Bats: L Throws: L Height: 6' 2" Weight: 195 Born: March 23, 1979 Age: 27

YEAR	TM	LVL	AGE	W	L	SV	G	GS	IP	H	BB	SO	HR	GB%	BABIP	STUFF	WHIP	ERA	PERA	EQERA	EQH9	EQBB9	EQSO9	EQHR9	VORP	WXRL
2003	CHA	MLB	24	14	14	0	35	35	230.3	250	61	119	22	49%	.301	8	1.35	4.14	4.32	4.63	9.7	2.4	4.6	0.8	30.8	4.2
2004	CHA	MLB	25	16	10	0	35	35	245.3	257	51	165	33	51%	.299	12	1.26	3.89	4.24	4.06	9.3	1.8	5.7	1.1	55.3	5.9
2005	CHA	MLB	26	16	8	0	33	33	236.7	240	40	149	20	48%	.295	22	1.18	3.12	3.73	3.88	9.2	1.6	5.6	0.7	54.8	5.7
2006	CHA	MLB	27	14	11	0	33	33	222.7	237	48	136	28	48%	.291	13	1.28	4.02	4.01	4.09	9.2	1.9	5.3	1.0	41.4	5.8

Breakout: 17% Improve: 54% Collapse: 9% Attrition: 0% Comparables: Ken Holtzman, Jim Abbott, Tom Glavine

Smart pitchers have the capacity to vary their approach depending on the game situation. Tom Glavine, for example, has a philosophy of challenging hitters with the bases empty, but nibbling with runners on. Its a canny strategy; Glavine allows a lower OBP when the bases are empty and the offense's first order of business is getting someone on, and a lower SLG when men are on and opposition's priority is on getting the runners home. As a result, Glavine has a history of ERAs lower than his peripherals would imply; he gives up his share of hits, walks and home runs to hitters, but he tends to give them up at the right times. Buehrle is doing something along these lines. Over the past three seasons he has allowed 2.3 BB/9 on the road, but just 1.5 BB/9 at home. This goes a long way toward helping him avoid big innings. Perhaps it's a lefty thing, or maybe Buehrle is taking a copy of *Baseball Prospectus* on his "fishing expeditions" to the Ozarks. Either way, he's a great pitcher, and has one of the only arms that PECOTA feels safe banking on 220+ innings from.

JOSE CONTRERAS Bats: R Throws: R Height: 6' 4" Weight: 225 Born: December 6, 1971 Age: 34

YEAR	TM	LVL	AGE	W	L	SV	G	GS	IP	H	BB	SO	HR	GB%	BABIP	STUFF	WHIP	ERA	PERA	EQERA	EQH9	EQBB9	EQSO9	EQHR9	VORP	WXRL
2003	NYA	MLB	31	7	2	0	18	9	71.0	52	30	72	4	52%	.265	32	1.15	3.30	3.45	3.33	6.9	3.7	9.0	0.5	20.8	2.3
2004	NYA	MLB	32	8	5	0	18	18	95.7	93	42	82	22	42%	.265	-7	1.41	5.64	5.62	5.62	8.9	3.7	7.2	1.9	0.0	1.5
2004	CHA	MLB	32	5	4	0	13	13	74.7	73	42	68	9	50%	.332	14	1.67	5.30	4.52	5.23	8.6	4.6	7.6	1.0	-0.5	0.6
2005	CHA	MLB	33	15	7	0	32	32	204.7	177	75	154	23	45%	.263	17	1.23	3.61	4.38	3.93	8.5	3.4	6.8	1.0	42.1	5.0
2006	CHA	MLB	34	11	9	0	30	27	172.7	164	62	136	23	45%	.279	15	1.31	4.29	4.08	4.41	8.2	3.2	6.8	1.1	26.5	3.9

Breakout: 23% Improve: 55% Collapse: 15% Attrition: 4% Comparables: Orlando Hernandez, Connie Johnson, Sonny Siebert

The mechanical flaw involving Jose Contreras's release point was well known in baseball and scouting circles at the time the White Sox acquired him in last year's challenge trade for Esteban Loaiza. Kudos to Contreras, pitching coach Don Cooper, and Contreras's countryman Orlando Hernandez for digging up old video of his time in Cuba and reminding him of how he used to get things done. Correcting his delivery substantially improved the command on Contreras's fastball, which in turn made his splitter one of the best weapons in baseball. Contreras doesn't throw the splitter for strikes, and never did, but batters can no longer spot the pitch as easily, nor can they afford to lay off it when they're behind in the count. One of the downsides of no longer sucking is that Contreras will be asked to pitch deeper into games, and that coupled with his having thrown innumerable pitches in Cuba makes him an injury risk.

NEAL COTTS Bats: L Throws: L Height: 6' 2" Weight: 200 Born: March 25, 1980 Age: 26

YEAR	TM	LVL	AGE	W	L	SV	G	GS	IP	H	BB	SO	HR	GB%	BABIP	STUFF	WHIP	ERA	PERA	EQERA	EQH9	EQBB9	EQSO9	EQHR9	VORP	WXRL
2003	BIR	AA	23	9	7	0	21	21	108.3	67	56	133	2	—	.253	27	1.14	2.16	3.97	4.15	7.1	5.3	7.6	0.4	16.4	—
2003	CHA	MLB	23	1	1	0	4	4	13.3	15	17	10	1	42%	.350	-26	2.40	8.12	6.59	7.24	9.2	11.2	6.6	0.7	-2.8	-0.1
2004	CHA	MLB	24	4	4	0	56	1	65.3	61	30	58	13	47%	.273	-8	1.39	5.65	5.23	5.51	8.7	3.9	7.4	1.7	2.2	-0.5
2005	CHA	MLB	25	4	0	0	69	0	60.3	38	29	58	1	47%	.242	26	1.11	1.94	3.22	2.30	6.8	4.4	8.7	0.2	23.8	2.0
2006	CHA	MLB	26	3	3	3	62	0	56.3	52	27	52	7	45%	.285	6	1.40	4.30	4.13	4.80	8.0	4.2	8.0	1.0	8.5	0.7

Breakout: 21% Improve: 44% Collapse: 36% Attrition: 21% Comparables: Pedro A. Martinez, Kevin Walker, B. J. Ryan

(continued next page)

Neal Cotts *(continued)*

With his facial scruff and longish hair, he has considerably more upside as a South Side sex symbol than Scott Podsednik. That's assuming Cotts doesn't regress to pitching like Kyle Farnsworth in a day game, and PECOTA is not so certain about that. Note that Cotts's strikeout, walk, and groundball numbers were virtually unchanged between 2004 and 2005, but his VORP jumped from 2.2 to 23.8 on account of a reduced BABIP and home run rate. This led to an ERA that was far out of line with his peripheral numbers. With two or three statistical red flags, there's virtually no chance that Cotts duplicates his 2005. Moreover, while Cotts's mechanics are less of a concern than they once were, they're still on the busy side, and make his command an uphill battle. That's the "other" Pedro Martinez, the Padre lefty, among his comparables.

FELIX DIAZ   **Bats: R Throws: R**   Height: 6′ 1″   Weight: 180   Born: July 27, 1980   Age: 25

YEAR	TM	LVL	AGE	W	L	SV	G	GS	IP	H	BB	SO	HR	GB%	BABIP	STUFF	WHIP	ERA	PERA	EQERA	EQH9	EQBB9	EQSO9	EQHR9	VORP	WXRL
2003	CHR	AAA	22	5	7	0	27	18	115.7	122	33	83	12	—	.294	-7	1.34	3.97	5.13	5.21	9.9	3.0	5.3	1.4	4.9	—
2004	CHR	AAA	23	10	2	0	19	17	115.0	95	24	96	14	—	.257	10	1.03	2.97	4.53	3.70	8.6	2.1	6.2	1.3	23.1	—
2004	CHA	MLB	23	2	5	0	18	7	49.3	62	16	33	13	38%	.318	-15	1.58	6.75	6.08	6.26	10.7	2.7	5.5	2.1	-2.0	-0.3
2005	CHR	AAA	24	6	8	0	21	21	122.3	149	33	108	15	44%	.371	3	1.49	5.00	4.82	5.55	10.4	2.6	6.0	1.3	0.7	—
2006	*CHA*	*MLB*	*25*	*7*	*9*	*1*	*55*	*16*	*136.7*	*153*	*41*	*91*	*26*	*41%*	*.295*	*-2*	*1.42*	*5.26*	*5.10*	*5.27*	*9.7*	*2.6*	*5.7*	*1.6*	*7.6*	*1.3*

Breakout: 19%   *Improve: 49%*   *Collapse: 11%*   *Attrition: 0%*   *Comparables: Mark Brownson, Ray Crone, Joe Decker*

There's a pretty clear distinction between the haves and the have-nots in the White Sox system, but Diaz straddles the line. He wasn't going to get a chance in this organization after being hit very hard in the Cell two summers ago, but his strikeout-to-walk numbers are reasonable, and his high ERA was mostly a product of the tough hitting environment in Charlotte. Released outright when the Sox purged their 40-man roster in November, he could be coming to a bullpen near you.

FREDDY GARCIA   **Bats: R Throws: R**   Height: 6′ 4″   Weight: 235   Born: June 10, 1976   Age: 30

YEAR	TM	LVL	AGE	W	L	SV	G	GS	IP	H	BB	SO	HR	GB%	BABIP	STUFF	WHIP	ERA	PERA	EQERA	EQH9	EQBB9	EQSO9	EQHR9	VORP	WXRL
2003	SEA	MLB	27	12	14	0	33	33	201.3	196	71	144	31	45%	.277	3	1.33	4.52	4.98	5.16	9.5	3.2	6.4	1.4	26.6	4.2
2004	SEA	MLB	28	4	7	0	15	15	107.0	96	32	82	8	45%	.278	28	1.20	3.20	3.64	3.30	8.3	2.5	6.5	0.6	33.9	3.6
2004	CHA	MLB	28	9	4	0	16	16	103.0	96	32	102	14	48%	.300	26	1.24	4.46	3.92	4.18	8.4	2.6	8.4	1.0	20.4	2.3
2005	CHA	MLB	29	14	8	0	33	33	228.0	225	60	146	26	50%	.285	13	1.25	3.87	4.25	4.05	9.2	2.4	5.8	1.0	45.7	5.1
2006	*CHA*	*MLB*	*30*	*12*	*10*	*0*	*31*	*31*	*201.7*	*208*	*59*	*139*	*27*	*46%*	*.288*	*13*	*1.32*	*4.24*	*4.23*	*4.25*	*8.9*	*2.6*	*6.0*	*1.1*	*32.8*	*4.8*

Breakout: 9%   *Improve: 51%*   *Collapse: 7%*   *Attrition: 1%*   *Comparables: Pete Vuckovich, Mike Moore, Kevin Millwood*

It's hard to know where Garcia picked up a reputation for inconsistency. Apart from a career year in Seattle in 2001, his ERAs have hovered between 3.81 and 4.51 in each of his other six big league seasons. Garcia's strikeout rate is a particular source of concern after declining by almost 25% from the year previous. It's not that Garcia can't be an effective pitcher in his present form, but a downward shift in strikeout rate can be a leading indicator for an arm problem, especially for a pitcher who had Lou Piniella as his first big league manager. We have no real gripe with the White Sox's pitch count philosophy, which involves lots of starts in the 100–115 pitch range, but we'd advocate keeping Garcia toward the lower end of that spectrum, particularly in the first half of the season.

JON GARLAND   **Bats: R Throws: R**   Height: 6′ 6″   Weight: 205   Born: September 27, 1979   Age: 26

YEAR	TM	LVL	AGE	W	L	SV	G	GS	IP	H	BB	SO	HR	GB%	BABIP	STUFF	WHIP	ERA	PERA	EQERA	EQH9	EQBB9	EQSO9	EQHR9	VORP	WXRL
2003	CHA	MLB	23	12	13	0	32	32	191.7	188	74	108	28	49%	.273	-1	1.37	4.51	5.17	4.55	9.3	3.5	5.0	1.2	26.8	3.9
2004	CHA	MLB	24	12	11	0	34	33	217.0	223	76	113	34	48%	.280	-5	1.40	4.89	5.17	4.79	9.5	3.0	4.4	1.2	23.4	2.9
2005	CHA	MLB	25	18	10	0	32	32	221.0	212	47	115	26	48%	.270	7	1.17	3.50	4.55	3.93	9.3	2.0	4.7	1.0	50.7	6.0
2006	*CHA*	*MLB*	*26*	*12*	*11*	*0*	*32*	*32*	*200.0*	*217*	*57*	*108*	*29*	*47%*	*.285*	*6*	*1.37*	*4.53*	*4.54*	*4.59*	*9.4*	*2.5*	*4.7*	*1.2*	*25.3*	*4.1*

Breakout: 6%   *Improve: 42%*   *Collapse: 18%*   *Attrition: 2%*   *Comparables: Jeff Weaver, Dan Petry, Jaime Navarro*

I'm convinced that Garland's improvement is the result of his recognizing that, while he has good "stuff," it isn't the kind of stuff that misses bats. His two-seamer particularly doesn't have the late downward break of someone like Brandon Webb's, and he's never found it particularly natural to throw it down in the zone. Instead, Garland adopted a neo-classical approach to pitching, using his curve as a strikeout pitch, changing location with the two-seamer, and mixing in an improved changeup to keep hitters off-balance. He's the White Sox starter least likely to duplicate his 2005 performance, but even so, 200 innings of league average ball would be an acceptable return for the extension they've given him.

GIO GONZALEZ   Bats: R   Throws: L   Height: 5' 11"   Weight: 180   Born: September 19, 1985   Age: 20

YEAR	TM	LVL	AGE	W	L	SV	G	GS	IP	H	BB	SO	HR	GB%	BABIP	STUFF	WHIP	ERA	PERA	EQERA	EQH9	EQBB9	EQSO9	EQHR9	VORP	WXRL
2004	BRI	Rk	18	1	2	0	7	6	24.0	17	8	36	0	—	.327	19	1.04	2.25	4.09	5.73	8.6	4.5	6.5	0.4	-0.3	—
2004	KAN	A	18	1	2	0	8	8	40.7	39	20	34	1	—	.297	12	1.45	3.76	4.58	5.26	9.2	5.0	4.6	0.5	1.5	—
2005	KAN	A	19	5	3	0	11	10	57.7	36	22	84	3	49%	.277	38	1.01	1.87	4.05	4.05	7.8	4.2	8.6	0.8	9.2	—
2005	WNS	A+	19	8	3	0	13	13	73.3	61	25	79	5	40%	.304	25	1.17	3.56	4.31	4.69	8.2	3.3	6.5	0.9	7.2	—
2006	*PHI*	*MLB*	*20*	*8*	*8*	*0*	*29*	*22*	*139.3*	*126*	*67*	*113*	*16*	*44%*	*.275*	*15*	*1.39*	*4.41*	*4.47*	*4.70*	*8.0*	*4.0*	*6.9*	*1.0*	*13.9*	*2.4*

Breakout: 22%   *Improve: 62%*   *Collapse: 21%*   *Attrition: 0%*   Comparables: *Clayton Andrews, Ryan Ketchner, Scott Kazmir*

All else being equal, you'd probably rather have a 23-year-old pitching prospect than a guy who can't buy a six pack yet. The former, by the fact of his survival alone, would have demonstrated an insusceptibility to injury in a way the latter hadn't had the chance to yet. That's the only caveat with Gonzalez, who looked like a man among boys at Kannapolis and Winston-Salem. His STUFF number was among the best in the minors, propelled by a curveball that instantly becomes the best in the Phillies system. He's regarded as a self-confident guy, but don't be surprised to hear some less-complimentary synonyms for self-confidence used if he runs into a road bump.

CHARLIE HAEGER   Bats: R   Throws: R   Height: 6' 1"   Weight: 200   Born: September 19, 1983   Age: 22

YEAR	TM	LVL	AGE	W	L	SV	G	GS	IP	H	BB	SO	HR	GB%	BABIP	STUFF	WHIP	ERA	PERA	EQERA	EQH9	EQBB9	EQSO9	EQHR9	VORP	WXRL
2004	BRI	Rk	20	1	6	0	10	10	57.3	70	22	23	6	—	.315	-43	1.61	5.03	8.61	7.76	12.8	5.2	1.7	2.5	-12.8	—
2004	KAN	A	20	1	3	0	5	5	31.3	31	12	21	0	—	.307	0	1.37	2.01	4.75	5.93	9.5	4.2	3.6	0.3	-1.1	—
2005	WNS	A+	21	8	2	0	14	13	81.7	82	40	64	3	53%	.329	7	1.49	3.19	4.82	4.59	9.1	4.8	4.5	0.4	9.0	—
2005	BIR	AA	21	6	3	0	13	13	85.7	84	45	48	1	51%	.307	4	1.51	3.78	4.84	5.81	8.9	5.1	3.4	0.2	-2.0	—
2006	*CHA*	*MLB*	*22*	*5*	*9*	*0*	*28*	*21*	*121.3*	*140*	*71*	*64*	*18*	*50%*	*.301*	*-12*	*1.74*	*6.30*	*6.18*	*6.68*	*10.1*	*4.7*	*4.3*	*1.3*	*-11.8*	*-0.4*

Breakout: 3%   *Improve: 29%*   *Collapse: 31%*   *Attrition: 1%*   Comparables: *Don Graves, Mike Esposito, Jason Standridge*

Haeger retired from baseball at 20, only to figure out that trying to make it as a knuckleballer would be a far more interesting career choice than anything on the curriculum at Madonna College of Livonia, MI. He benefited from the buzz effect surrounding the very good rotation in Winston-Salem, and his organization takes him seriously, adding him to the 40-man roster this winter in lieu of more traditional prospects. Unlike other knuckleballers, he's shown the ability to keep the ball down, but otherwise his presence here rests more on backstory than stats.

DANIEL HAIGWOOD   Bats: R   Throws: L   Height: 6' 2"   Weight: 197   Born: November 19, 1983   Age: 22

YEAR	TM	LVL	AGE	W	L	SV	G	GS	IP	H	BB	SO	HR	GB%	BABIP	STUFF	WHIP	ERA	PERA	EQERA	EQH9	EQBB9	EQSO9	EQHR9	VORP	WXRL
2004	KAN	A	20	10	4	0	22	22	116.3	102	59	101	10	—	.285	-13	1.38	4.88	6.28	6.28	9.7	5.7	4.8	1.4	-8.2	—
2005	WNS	A+	21	8	2	0	15	15	76.3	79	33	84	8	46%	.345	0	1.47	3.77	5.54	5.42	9.9	4.3	6.3	1.4	1.5	—
2005	BIR	AA	21	6	1	0	11	11	67.3	39	31	76	0	48%	.253	32	1.04	1.74	3.86	3.14	6.7	4.6	7.1	0.3	17.2	—
2006	*PHI*	*MLB*	*22*	*7*	*9*	*0*	*25*	*23*	*130.0*	*130*	*73*	*96*	*17*	*44%*	*.289*	*6*	*1.56*	*5.15*	*5.39*	*5.41*	*8.8*	*4.7*	*6.2*	*1.1*	*2.3*	*1.2*

Breakout: 6%   *Improve: 44%*   *Collapse: 20%*   *Attrition: 0%*   Comparables: *Noah Lowry, Tom Gorzelanny, Clayton Andrews*

Haigwood neither lights up the radar gun nor has especially good control, and was considered a second-tier prospect until he strung together an impressive series of outings in Birmingham. The problem is that Birmingham is a pitcher's park in a pitcher's league, and has been the site of many a "breakout" performance among ghosts of White Sox prospects past, from Corwin Malone to Scott Ruffcorn to Jon Rauch. Any good major league front office should pin a chart of minor league run factors right next to their big magnetic board. There's more that distinguishes Birmingham from Albuquerque than the quality of the soul food.

DUSTIN HERMANSON   Bats: R   Throws: R   Height: 6' 2"   Weight: 200   Born: December 21, 1972   Age: 33

YEAR	TM	LVL	AGE	W	L	SV	G	GS	IP	H	BB	SO	HR	GB%	BABIP	STUFF	WHIP	ERA	PERA	EQERA	EQH9	EQBB9	EQSO9	EQHR9	VORP	WXRL
2003	SLN	MLB	30	1	2	1	23	0	29.7	35	14	12	4	49%	.326	-28	1.65	5.45	5.70	5.70	10.5	3.9	3.3	1.2	0.3	0.3
2003	SFN	MLB	30	2	1	0	9	6	39.0	35	10	27	5	45%	.261	8	1.15	3.00	4.50	3.55	9.0	2.1	5.7	1.2	10.8	1.0
2004	SFN	MLB	31	6	9	17	47	18	131.0	132	46	102	15	45%	.302	4	1.36	4.53	4.33	4.74	9.0	2.9	6.2	1.0	14.3	2.6
2005	CHA	MLB	32	2	4	34	57	0	57.3	46	17	33	4	39%	.247	1	1.10	2.04	4.04	2.75	8.2	2.7	5.3	0.6	19.9	3.9
2006	*CHA*	*MLB*	*33*	*2*	*2*	*2*	*45*	*0*	*49.7*	*53*	*17*	*33*	*7*	*41%*	*.292*	*-7*	*1.41*	*4.58*	*4.49*	*4.80*	*9.3*	*3.0*	*5.7*	*1.2*	*5.6*	*0.5*

Breakout: 12%   *Improve: 41%*   *Collapse: 32%*   *Attrition: 23%*   Comparables: *Juan Acevedo, Don Aase, Dick Drago*

(continued next page)

Dustin Hermanson (continued)

Look beyond the saves and the ERA, and Hermanson was what he always has always been: a very ordinary pitcher with a walk rate just on the happy side of par. As with Cotts, the odds of his matching his ERA of a year ago are probably 25-to-1 against. Hermanson also has a long history of back problems, and as many of you sitting at home will know, that's not something that gets better when you hit your mid-thirties. As contrarian as this sounds, the White Sox might have thought about picking up some bullpen help this winter.

ORLANDO HERNANDEZ　　Bats: R　Throws: R　　Height: 6' 2"　Weight: 220　Born: October 11, 1965　Age: 40

YEAR	TM	LVL	AGE	W	L	SV	G	GS	IP	H	BB	SO	HR	GB%	BABIP	STUFF	WHIP	ERA	PERA	EQERA	EQH9	EQBB9	EQSO9	EQHR9	VORP	WXRL
2004	NYA	MLB	38	8	2	0	15	15	84.7	73	36	84	9	40%	.286	29	1.29	3.29	3.92	3.18	7.8	3.5	8.4	0.8	27.6	3.2
2005	CHA	MLB	39	9	9	1	24	22	128.3	137	50	91	18	40%	.306	3	1.46	5.12	4.97	5.25	9.8	3.6	6.3	1.2	6.9	1.4
2006	ARI	MLB	40	5	8	1	26	18	109.0	113	51	81	15	41%	.294	-1	1.51	5.02	5.14	5.35	9.1	3.8	6.2	1.2	5.7	1.2

Breakout: 9%　Improve: 38%　Collapse: 31%　Attrition: 27%　Comparables: Joe Niekro, Sal Maglie, Tom Candiotti

Perhaps there's a sort of reverse discrimination against someone who throws multiple pitches, or perhaps it's something that Hernandez just won't do-que, but it's odd that he hasn't been tried as a relief pitcher. It's one thing to sacrifice a 200 inning pitcher for the sake of a good set-up man, but another when the guy hasn't topped 22 starts in five years. Can't see him fooling Delmon Young with an eighth inning eephus pitch as a Las Vegas Marlin ten years from now? It could happen if he's given the Satchel Paige career path.

BOBBY JENKS　　Bats: R　Throws: R　　Height: 6' 3"　Weight: 240　Born: March 14, 1981　Age: 25

YEAR	TM	LVL	AGE	W	L	SV	G	GS	IP	H	BB	SO	HR	GB%	BABIP	STUFF	WHIP	ERA	PERA	EQERA	EQH9	EQBB9	EQSO9	EQHR9	VORP	WXRL
2003	ARK	AA	22	7	2	0	16	16	83.0	56	51	103	2	—	.270	26	1.29	2.17	4.40	3.48	7.3	6.8	8.5	0.5	18.3	—
2005	BIR	AA	24	1	2	19	35	0	41.0	34	20	48	1	61%	.320	-2	1.32	2.85	4.38	5.31	8.5	5.1	6.9	0.5	1.3	—
2005	CHA	MLB	24	1	1	6	32	0	39.3	34	15	50	3	47%	.316	35	1.25	2.75	2.95	3.18	7.5	3.4	11.1	0.7	10.4	1.4
2006	CHA	MLB	25	3	4	17	54	0	50.7	47	29	50	5	50%	.304	10	1.48	4.25	4.18	4.81	8.0	4.9	8.6	0.7	7.3	0.9

Breakout: 20%　Improve: 46%　Collapse: 24%　Attrition: 27%　Comparables: Mark Wohlers, Sammy Stewart, Ken Ryan

The curious case of Bobby Jenks can be as simple or as complicated as you want to be. Forget the checkered personal history, the postseason heroics, the beer gut, the at-bat that might be responsible for Jeff Bagwell's retirement. The bottom line is this: if Jenks can keep his walk rate below four walks per nine, he'll succeed, and if he can't, he won't. He was just above that threshold in Birmingham last year, and just below it in Chicago. A purely statistical projection isn't of much help here. To the extent that ballplayers have personal issues, 90 percent of them boil down to self-confidence, and it's hard to imagine a bigger confidence boost than getting the last out of the World Series. Ozzie Guillen is also a big piece of the puzzle. When Scott Podsednik hit his walk-off to win Game 2 against the Astros, Guillen's first instinct was not to congratulate Pods, but to find Jenks in the crowd and to make sure that he was doing okay after blowing the save earlier. Almost inevitably, there will be moments that require the same finesse and compassion next season, and Guillen, who makes no pretension of being a perfect man, is the right manager to provide it.

RAY LIOTTA　　Bats: L　Throws: L　　Height: 6' 3"　Weight: 220　Born: April 3, 1983　Age: 23

YEAR	TM	LVL	AGE	W	L	SV	G	GS	IP	H	BB	SO	HR	GB%	BABIP	STUFF	WHIP	ERA	PERA	EQERA	EQH9	EQBB9	EQSO9	EQHR9	VORP	WXRL
2004	GRF	Rk	21	5	1	0	14	11	63.7	59	28	65	1	—	.331	0	1.37	2.54	4.57	6.20	9.1	4.9	4.3	0.3	-4.1	—
2005	KAN	A	22	8	3	0	20	20	115.3	108	35	107	5	56%	.326	8	1.24	2.26	4.61	4.94	9.6	3.5	5.0	0.8	8.0	—
2005	WNS	A+	22	6	2	0	8	8	49.7	46	16	37	1	60%	.315	10	1.25	1.45	4.25	3.33	8.5	3.3	4.1	0.4	12.3	—
2006	CHA	MLB	23	8	10	0	26	26	146.3	161	68	79	17	52%	.296	0	1.56	5.35	5.04	5.48	9.5	4.1	4.6	1.0	3.7	1.5

Breakout: 6%　Improve: 28%　Collapse: 26%　Attrition: 0%　Comparables: Neal Musser, Matt Coenen, Greg Kubes

Liotta's main skill is the ability to induce groundballs. That would be niftier if he'd pitched at a more advanced level, although he took well to the Carolina League upon his promotion. You can see a Brandon Webb parallel if you squint hard enough, but Webb had his sinker, whereas Liotta's fastball tends to drift on him if he cranks it up above 90. Still, Liotta could be in Paul Maholm's shoes a year from now. The scene in "Hannibal" where he eats his own brain still gives me the creeps.

DAMASO MARTE

Bats: L Throws: L Height: 6' 0" Weight: 170 Born: February 14, 1975 Age: 31

YEAR	TM	LVL	AGE	W	L	SV	G	GS	IP	H	BB	SO	HR	GB%	BABIP	STUFF	WHIP	ERA	PERA	EQERA	EQH9	EQBB9	EQSO9	EQHR9	VORP	WXRL
2003	CHA	MLB	28	4	2	11	71	0	79.7	50	34	87	3	41%	.260	36	1.05	1.58	3.01	1.85	6.4	3.8	9.7	0.3	37.9	4.4
2004	CHA	MLB	29	6	5	6	74	0	73.7	56	34	68	10	41%	.257	6	1.23	3.42	4.48	3.11	7.6	4.0	8.0	1.1	24.0	2.4
2005	CHA	MLB	30	3	4	4	66	0	45.3	45	33	54	5	40%	.342	13	1.72	3.77	4.47	3.88	8.5	6.4	10.3	1.0	8.2	1.1
2006	*PIT*	*MLB*	*31*	*3*	*3*	*5*	*59*	*0*	*53.0*	*47*	*27*	*52*	*6*	*42%*	*.288*	*7*	*1.39*	*3.83*	*4.24*	*4.30*	*7.8*	*4.2*	*8.2*	*0.9*	*8.4*	*0.7*

Breakout: 10% Improve: 17% Collapse: 56% Attrition: 18% Comparables: Jim Brewer, Ricardo Rincon, Mike Stanton

The notion of the "dangerously wild" pitcher may be a myth. Marte has always relied heavily on his slider, but now that he's been around the league a few times, hitters have come to recognize that the pitch usually darts right on out of the strike zone. Although the takeaway (Rob Mackowiak) wasn't great, the Sox were right to cut their losses.

BRANDON McCARTHY

Bats: R Throws: R Height: 6' 7" Weight: 180 Born: July 7, 1983 Age: 22

YEAR	TM	LVL	AGE	W	L	SV	G	GS	IP	H	BB	SO	HR	GB%	BABIP	STUFF	WHIP	ERA	PERA	EQERA	EQH9	EQBB9	EQSO9	EQHR9	VORP	WXRL
2003	GRF	Rk	19	9	4	0	16	15	101.0	105	15	125	7	—	.355	8	1.19	3.65	4.94	6.13	10.2	1.9	5.7	1.6	-5.8	—
2004	KAN	A	21	8	5	0	15	15	94.0	80	21	113	10	—	.312	9	1.07	3.64	5.20	5.09	9.7	2.4	6.5	1.7	5.0	—
2004	WNS	A+	21	6	0	0	8	8	52.0	31	3	60	3	—	.230	39	0.65	2.08	3.54	3.35	7.3	0.6	7.6	1.1	12.1	—
2004	BIR	AA	21	3	1	0	4	4	26.0	23	6	29	2	—	.309	24	1.12	3.46	4.38	4.38	9.1	2.2	6.9	1.1	3.3	—
2005	CHR	AAA	22	7	7	0	20	19	119.3	104	32	130	16	41%	.292	23	1.14	3.92	4.32	4.09	8.3	2.5	8.0	1.4	19.6	—
2005	CHA	MLB	22	3	2	0	12	10	67.0	62	17	48	13	38%	.251	11	1.18	4.03	4.93	3.97	9.2	2.3	6.6	1.6	13.6	1.6
2006	*CHA*	*MLB*	*22*	*10*	*9*	*0*	*34*	*28*	*159.7*	*161*	*42*	*125*	*28*	*40%*	*.281*	*16*	*1.27*	*4.43*	*4.33*	*4.41*	*8.7*	*2.3*	*6.8*	*1.4*	*23.1*	*3.4*

Breakout: 15% Improve: 52% Collapse: 6% Attrition: 1% Comparables: Ralph Terry, Don Sutton, Britt Burns

It's a wonder that McCarthy's curveball didn't get more praise as he was rocketing through the Sox's system. It's a scary enough pitch on its own, but all the more so when it comes from guy who stands 6'7" and throws straight overhand. With his overall combination of repertoire and command, he sometimes resembles a mad scientist version of Roy Oswalt, with a few Kurt Rambis genes mixed in. Don't worry about where he starts on the depth chart next year; he's going to have a long and successful career.

CLIFF POLITTE

Bats: R Throws: R Height: 5' 11" Weight: 180 Born: February 27, 1974 Age: 32

YEAR	TM	LVL	AGE	W	L	SV	G	GS	IP	H	BB	SO	HR	GB%	BABIP	STUFF	WHIP	ERA	PERA	EQERA	EQH9	EQBB9	EQSO9	EQHR9	VORP	WXRL
2003	TOR	MLB	29	1	5	12	54	0	49.3	52	17	40	11	36%	.289	-9	1.40	5.66	5.26	5.26	9.1	3.1	7.1	1.8	2.2	-0.5
2004	CHA	MLB	30	0	3	1	54	0	51.3	52	22	48	6	43%	.317	7	1.44	4.39	3.98	4.15	8.8	3.5	7.8	0.9	10.6	0.6
2005	CHA	MLB	31	7	1	1	68	0	67.3	42	21	57	7	33%	.208	14	0.94	2.01	4.04	2.09	7.1	2.9	7.8	1.0	28.3	3.8
2006	*CHA*	*MLB*	*32*	*3*	*3*	*3*	*50*	*0*	*55.3*	*54*	*18*	*45*	*10*	*36%*	*.273*	*2*	*1.28*	*4.18*	*4.16*	*4.34*	*8.4*	*2.8*	*7.0*	*1.4*	*9.3*	*0.8*

Breakout: 14% Improve: 28% Collapse: 43% Attrition: 17% Comparables: Jeff Brantley, Enrique Romo, Scott Bankhead

It's hard to remember three guys in the same bullpen who got more out of average peripherals than Politte, Neal Cotts, and Dustin Hermanson. Opponents hit just .154/.244/.292 against Politte with men on base last season, which explains the low ERA. Those three pitchers made a collective $3.3 million last season, so we should give Don Cooper and Kenny Williams their due. The lesson that any number of viable middle relievers meet the test for "freely-available talent" is something the GM on the other side of town would do well to understand.

LUIS VIZCAINO

Bats: R Throws: R Height: 6' 1" Weight: 170 Born: August 6, 1974 Age: 31

YEAR	TM	LVL	AGE	W	L	SV	G	GS	IP	H	BB	SO	HR	GB%	BABIP	STUFF	WHIP	ERA	PERA	EQERA	EQH9	EQBB9	EQSO9	EQHR9	VORP	WXRL
2003	MIL	MLB	28	4	3	0	75	0	62.0	64	25	61	16	36%	.289	-16	1.44	6.39	5.78	6.21	9.2	3.2	7.9	2.3	-5.7	-1.3
2004	MIL	MLB	29	4	4	1	73	0	72.0	61	24	63	12	37%	.255	-2	1.18	3.75	4.61	4.09	8.3	2.8	7.2	1.4	10.0	2.8
2005	CHA	MLB	30	6	5	0	65	0	70.0	74	29	43	8	45%	.303	-7	1.47	3.73	4.89	3.86	9.6	3.7	5.5	1.0	15.2	0.3
2006	*ARI*	*MLB*	*31*	*2*	*3*	*2*	*47*	*0*	*53.0*	*55*	*21*	*36*	*7*	*42%*	*.287*	*-8*	*1.43*	*4.57*	*4.73*	*5.07*	*9.1*	*3.2*	*5.7*	*1.2*	*5.0*	*0.3*

Breakout: 25% Improve: 50% Collapse: 28% Attrition: 22% Comparables: Billy Loes, Shigetoshi Hasegawa, Dick Drago

His numbers bloodied by a disastrous six-run session in his second outing of the year against Cleveland, Vizcaino struggled to climb back up the depth chart after pitchers like Politte and Bobby Jenks surpassed him. A good rule of thumb is that if you can't trust a reliever in high-leverage situations, he might not belong on your roster at all. Vizcaino's ERA ended up in acceptable territory, but his strikeouts were way down and his flyball tendencies won't play any better in 'Zona than they did in Chicago.

Line Outs

Position/Player	TM	LVL	AGE	PA	R	2B	3B	HR	RBI	BB	SO	SB-CS	SPEED	BA/OBP/SLG	MLVR	EQBA/OBP/SLG	EQA	VORP
C J. Burke	CHR	AAA	33	411	50	22	1	10	53	36	53	1-3	3.8	.265/.350/.416	.014	.211/.276/.310	.210	-18.3
1B/3B L. Daigle	WNS	A+	25	473	85	33	1	29	112	50	72	10-4	5.2	.341/.414/.637	.454	.254/.313/.448	.260	4.0
C B. Davis#	CHA	MLB	29	138	13	6	0	4	16	8	26	0-0	3.9	.237/.280/.377	-.170	.235/.284/.373	.217	-1.2
SS P. Lopez	BIR	AA	21	258	26	7	1	3	24	13	29	0-2	3.7	.238/.287/.314	-.202	.220/.260/.306	.202	-12.3
	CHR	AAA	21	199	14	6	0	3	17	7	24	1-1	4.0	.202/.236/.282	-.417	.182/.217/.251	.175	-19.0

Pitcher	TM	LVL	AGE	W	L	SV	IP	H	BB	SO	HR	GB%	BABIP	STUFF	WHIP	ERA	PERA	EQERA	EQH9	EQBB9	EQSO9	EQHR9	VORP
J. Adkins	CHR	AAA	27	4	9	0	127.3	148	43	92	20	45%	.329	-22	1.50	5.37	5.98	6.26	10.4	3.5	4.8	1.8	-9.2
K. Honel	BIR	AA	22	5	7	0	93.3	101	64	70	10	42%	.322	-37	1.77	5.88	7.28	7.79	10.7	6.9	4.6	1.8	-21.7
C. Malone*	BIR	AA	25	5	5	1	97.3	100	55	81	6	52%	.336	-23	1.59	4.53	5.90	6.68	9.9	6.0	4.8	1.1	-11.2
A. Munoz*	CHR	AAA	23	8	14	1	132.7	150	60	109	16	45%	.337	-10	1.58	4.27	5.30	5.51	9.9	4.4	5.7	1.2	1.3
S. Tracey	BIR	AA	24	14	6	0	163.7	154	76	106	13	48%	.293	-24	1.41	4.07	6.47	6.06	9.8	5.0	3.8	1.5	-7.8

Jamie Burke is nothing if not determined to lengthen his entry at The Baseball Cube, having taken up third base at Charlotte last year. **Leo Daigle** won the Carolina League Triple Crown and got picked up by the Orioles; we considered writing him up, then saw his .229/.278/.381 PECOTA. **Ben Davis** completes the circle by being slow, strikeout prone, and powerless, but his best PECOTA comp is Mike Matheny, so there's always hope; after losing most of '05 to injury, that line is his '06 projection. **Pedro Lopez** has a generic middle infielder's name and a generic middle infielder's skill set; his defense is considered good.

Jon Adkins is not young anymore, and has failed to impress as either a starter or a reliever. **Kris Honel** was shut down in 2004 after his mechanics had devolved into a complete mess; he was never supposed to be a power arm, so the high walk rates are a discouraging sign. **Corwin Malone** is even further down the charts, but at least he has the excuse of Tommy John surgery; he has one more season to right himself, probably as a reliever. **Arnie Munoz** might have a better chance at a big career than the lot, but needs either improved command or a secondary pitch to complement his plus curveball. **Sean Tracey** is the only other pitcher on the 40-man roster, but his stock has regressed as he's failed to convert a power arm into real, live strikeouts.

Cincinnati Reds

Normally, a 73–89 record and a fifth-place finish, 27 games off the divisional pace, would hardly seem disastrous. But the 2005 Reds were a total catastrophe. At the center of the storm was sophomore general manager Dan O'Brien, who has done so much damage in his brief tenure that he has most citizens of the Queen City seeing red—blood red. O'Brien has been on the job for two years and has done nothing to improve the club, and the Reds are really no better off than they were in July 2003, when GM Jim Bowden and manager Bob Boone finally got the boots that they had so richly deserved. Far worse, the Reds have now squandered the once-in-a-generation opportunity to significantly increase revenue and attendance that presented itself when Cincinnati's new ballpark opened in 2003.

Given his record, O'Brien is a good candidate to become the contemporary poster boy for spectacularly incompetent management. In his first two years, the typical GM steers his team to an improvement of seven games, but O'Brien has presided over a mere four-game uptick. It itself, the weak recovery is not necessarily damning—GMs like Theo Epstein, who took over a contending club and then won the World Series in his second year, and Kevin Towers, who won the NL pennant in his third season, saw weak recoveries in their first two seasons. Other GMs— Mark Shapiro and J. P. Ricciardi, for example—sacrificed fast improvement in favor of sound long-term rebuilding plans which included dumping and trading expensive veterans and stockpiling prospects. In O'Brien's case, though, the numbers mask the depth of the problem.

O'Brien has botched nearly every major decision and transaction he has made in Cincinnati, at least until he dealt Sean Casey. O'Brien finally got a clue in December, when he sent the popular but overvalued non-slugger to the Pirates. However, Casey was likely dumped due to the club's impending sale, not a recent epiphany by O'Brien, who had already picked up the *tres cher* option year on Casey's contract after 2004. A smart GM would have dumped Casey then, when his trade value would have been at its highest. Casey was never going to really be worth $6 million plus per year, and O'Brien luckily rolled boxcars when the even more desperate Bucs took the overpriced first baseman off their hands without Cincy having to eat half of his contract.

REDS PROSPECTUS

2005 record: 73–89; Fifth place, NL Central

Pythagenport record: 74–88

Runs scored per game: 5.06 (1st in NL)

Runs allowed per game: 5.49 (16th in NL)

Team EqA: .273 (1st in NL)

2005 Batters Age: 29.1 (6th youngest in NL)

2005 Pitchers Age: 29.0 (6th youngest in NL)

Ballpark: Great American Ballpark; Slight pitcher's park; Park Factor of 0.988

2005: The hitters were exploding, and the pitchers . . . were exploding too.

2006: A change of ownership came too late to help this year.

That's the positive note. To date, the lowlights of the O'Brien regime include:

- Giving manager Dave Miley a contract extension in December 2004, only to fire him in June 2005. It was obvious that Miley was set up to be O'Brien's fall guy. The team wasn't winning with the "outstanding" talent that the GM put together, so the skipper had to go.

- Re-signing D'Angelo Jimenez over the objections of the manager and other players after Jimenez got into a fistfight at the 2004 postseason team picnic. O'Brien then insisted that Jimenez play instead of Ryan Freel, just as he would also insist that Rich Aurilia play over Felipe Lopez at the start of 2005.

- Taking two years to resolve the overcrowded outfield situation. As a square peg won't fit in a round hole, four starting outfielders don't fit into three lineup slots. No matter how the manager tries to work it, at least one player is going to be upset at not starting and, sooner or later, things will boil over and become an issue in the clubhouse. This was only finally resolved with the decision to trade Casey and move Adam Dunn to first base.

• Indulging in an insane infatuation with middle-aged free agent infielder Rich Aurilia, who was re-signed for 2006 (with a mutual option for 2007). The Reds have now recreated their outfield problem in the infield, with Aurilia, the "Team MVP," taking time away from Freel, Lopez, and Edwin Encarnacion. They can't all play at the same time, and while Lopez and Encarnacion might be regulars on the next good Reds teamFreel might even be around as a spare part—Aurilia will not. Aurilia took advantage of the Great American Ballpark's friendly dimensions to post a good season in 2005, but it was his first moderately productive year with the bat since 2001. It's likely not a sign of a late-career renaissance.

What was good about the Reds in 2005 was their league-leading offense. The Reds' lineup wasn't merely good because of the GAP's charity as a home field. Cincinnati finished first in the league in runs and home runs, and they *also* led in Equivalent Average, which is park-adjusted. The starting eight at the end of 2005 were all Bowden's players: LaRue, Dunn, Freel, Lopez, Encarnacion, Griffey, Pena, and Kearns. O'Brien deserves none of the credit for the team's powerhouse attack.

The Reds boasted only two good starting pitchers, in Aaron Harang and Brandon Claussen, and both came over in salary-dump deadline deal—Harang from the Athletics for Jose Guillen, Claussen from the Yankees for Aaron Boone—shortly after Bowden was fired and months before O'Brien was hired.

In horrifying contrast, O'Brien has signed five "name" pitchers on his own initiative: Eric Milton, Ramon Ortiz, Ben Weber, David Weathers, and Kent Mercker. He also re-signed Paul Wilson to a two-year deal after 2004, even though the Reds reportedly knew that his shoulder would soon go to pulp. Weathers and Mercker were solid as the Reds' two most reliable relievers in 2005, but the other moves were killers. O'Brien has had two years to make his mark, to give the fans some reasonable hope that things are getting better, two years to sign even merely mediocre pitchers. As Milton and Ortiz took their every-fifth-day drubbings, the extent of his failure was obvious. Despite his efforts, the Reds' record has remained relatively constant because the hitters O'Brien inherited have improved, offsetting the damage his pitchers have wrought since being brought aboard. Even with their league-leading 820 runs scored (15 more than the Cardinals), the Reds managed to allow 889, giving them the dubious (and rare) distinction of dominating the 2005 NL in opposite ways (see table 1). But however disappointing they were to their fans, from a statistical point of view, they weren't especially unlucky, finishing less than two games under their projected record, even given their promiscuous pitching staff. If the Reds had fielded a merely league-average pitching staff, they would have won about 90 games, and could well have beaten out the Astros for the wild card.

CEO John Allen has said that O'Brien had the club headed in the right direction, emphasizing that he was turning around the farm system. It is hard to see the evidence for this. The club is touting Homer Bailey and Jay

TABLE 1. WEARING OUT THE SCOREBOARD OPERATOR

Year	League	Team	Runs	Runs Allowed	Record	Finish
2005	NL	Cincinnati	820	889	73–89	5th of 6
2001	NL	Colorado	923	906	73–89	5th of 5
1997	NL	Colorado	923	908	83–79	3rd of 5
1996	NL	Colorado	961	964	83–79	3rd of 4
1995	NL	Colorado	785	783	77–67	2nd of 4
1991	AL	Texas	829	814	85–77	3rd of 7
1986	AL	Cleveland	831	841	84–78	5th of 7
1973	NL	Atlanta	799	774	88–74	3rd of 6
1970	NL	San Francisco	831	826	86–76	3rd of 6
1968	NL	Cincinnati	690	673	83–79	4th of 10
1959	NL	Cincinnati	764	738	74–80	5th of 8
1940	NL	Pittsburgh	809	783	78–76	4th of 8
1932	NL	Philadelphia	844	796	78–76	4th of 8
1929	AL	Detroit	926	928	70–84	6th of 8

Bruce as future stars, just as it did David Espinosa, Dane Sardinha, and Ty Howington in the past. You can't even Mapquest how far most of these guys are from contributing in the majors, if they ever make it. The Cincinnati player development system is worthy of the term "farm" only in the sense that the Stalinist collectives of the 1930s Ukraine were a farm system—they caused millions to starve to death. While the Reds system is unlikely to cause widespread famine, the club will have to subsist on a truly thin diet in the next few years: the organization is almost completely bereft of blue chip talent.

It's axiomatic that bad management makes bad decisions, which begets desperation after years of losing—which in turn begets the desperately worse decisions made when general managers are trying to save their jobs by doing something. Player agents just *love* it when GMs are flailing around in such circumstances. With the team's ownership perceived as being too cheap, and having precious little credibility of his own, O'Brien didn't clear payroll so he could afford good pitching. Instead, he squandered the team's limited treasury on players like Milton and Ortiz because no one would have faith in him if he waited for better opportunities to spend the team's money.

Despite the genuine anguish, there is some hope for a quick turnaround in Cincy. It won't happen in the typical way, with a crop of talented prospects maturing at the same time, catapulting a miserable team into contention.

No, if the Reds come around, the transformation will resemble that of the 1991 Twins, a veteran team that had a magnificent last hurrah. Of course, those Twins had the good sense to sign gunslinger Jack Morris to a one-year contract to bolster a weak starting staff, while Mr. O'Brien had the bad judgment to hire Eric Milton for what will assuredly be three expensive gory years if the Reds keep running their left-handed meat puppet out there every fifth day.

The world champion Twins of '91 had nothing like the potential murderers' row that the Reds could feature in 2006 and 2007. The Reds have three legitimate franchise sluggers—Griffey, Dunn, and Kearns—any one of whom could become the paladin who would lead the Reds back to glory. First, though, the team is going to have to deal more realistically with its lack of pitching. In 1995, Bowden's Reds won the NL Central with a starting rotation consisting of Pete Schourek, John Smiley, and whatever sandlotters could be coaxed out to the ballpark that day. That they won with this group was a glorious, never-to-be-repeated accident. Since then, the Reds have been trying to duplicate the 1995 "formula." They won't win again until they try taking the novel route of their divisional rivals in Chicago, St. Louis, and Houston, and simply build a strong rotation. Unless O'Brien can do that, his regime will only be notable remembered for its failures.

HITTERS

RICH AURILIA   2B/SS   Bats: R Throws: R   Height: 6' 1"   Weight: 185   Born: September 2, 1971   Age: 34

YEAR	TM	LVL	AGE	PA	R	2B	3B	HR	RBI	BB	SO	SB	CS	SPEED	BA	OBP	SLG	MLVR	EQBA	EQOBP	EQSLG	EQA	VORP	DEFENSE		
2003	SFN	MLB	31	545	65	26	1	13	58	36	82	2	2	3.9	.277	.325	.410	-.002	.275	.324	.414	.254	19.0	119-SS	-4	
2004	SEA	MLB	32	286	27	13	0	4	28	22	43	1	0	3.5	.241	.304	.337	-.206	.247	.315	.351	.237	-0.8	70-SS	-3	
2004	SDN	MLB	32	157	22	8	2	2	16	15	28	0	0	5.5	.254	.331	.384	-.038	.257	.333	.386	.254	1.4	26-3B	-3	
2005	CIN	MLB	33	467	61	23	2	14	68	37	67	2	0	4.8	.282	.338	.444	.074	.278	.337	.442	.269	20.6	62-2B	3	27-SS -1
2006	CIN	MLB	34	389	45	20	1	9	46	31	59	2	1	4.5	.265	.327	.409	-.047	.266	.329	.415	.251	10.4	93-SS	-1	

Breakout: 22%   Improve: 47%   Collapse: 27%   Attrition: 26%   Comparables: Joe Randa, Ray Knight, Scott Brosius

A second-half surge (.315/.377/.481) earned Aurilia a new contract with the Reds even though everyone else had the sense to stay away from the brittle infielder. The Reds have now created a problem with as much logic and forethought as teenagers in the thrall of their raging hormones use when making dating decisions. Aurilia can't play short any more and is subpar at second. He's lost some bat speed, but he could serve a useful role as a right-handed bat on the bench and as a reserve at second and third, but on O'Brien's watch, regrettably, there's more than that to come.

WILLIAM BERGOLLA   2B/SS   Bats: R Throws: R   Height: 6' 0"   Weight: 175   Born: February 4, 1983   Age: 23

YEAR	TM	LVL	AGE	PA	R	2B	3B	HR	RBI	BB	SO	SB	CS	SPEED	BA	OBP	SLG	MLVR	EQBA	EQOBP	EQSLG	EQA	VORP	DEFENSE		
2003	POT	A+	20	557	77	25	3	2	31	29	59	52	18	7.8	.272	.309	.342	-.067	.246	.280	.325	.221	-19.6	127-2B	6	
2004	CHT	AA	21	511	79	26	1	4	38	40	63	36	6	7.3	.283	.342	.369	-.010	.252	.305	.332	.235	-7.9	90-2B	-4	21-SS 1
2005	LOU	AAA	22	422	59	23	5	2	38	19	39	16	3	6.8	.292	.325	.390	-.052	.270	.305	.359	.237	-0.6	77-2B	4	17-SS -5
2005	CIN	MLB	22	38	3	0	0	0	1	0	10	0	0	5.2	.132	.132	.132	-.796	.132	.132	.132	.101	-6.1			
2006	CIN	MLB	23	448	51	21	2	2	32	23	49	16	4	5.6	.260	.302	.337	-.190	.261	.303	.342	.223	-0.1	106-2B	1	

Breakout: 22%   Improve: 47%   Collapse: 26%   Attrition: 14%   Comparables: Luis Rivas, Damion Easley, Willie Bloomquist

(continued next page)

William Bergolla *(continued)*

Bergolla is the kind of utility player that used to have a dedicated roster spot, but who now is typically doomed to the Triple-A shuttle. At second, he has outstanding range, he's capable of playing short as well, and he's a good percentage basestealer. If the Reds come to their senses and release Womack or Aurilia during the season, Bergolla might get a chance to show what he can do with the bat, but he's more likely to be picking splinters out of his butt in Cincy when he's not in Louisville.

SEAN CASEY   **1B**   **Bats: L Throws: R**   Height: 6' 4"   Weight: 220   Born: July 2, 1974   Age: 31

YEAR	TM	LVL	AGE	PA	R	2B	3B	HR	RBI	BB	SO	SB	CS	SPEED	BA	OBP	SLG	MLVR	EQBA	EQOBP	EQSLG	EQA	VORP	DEFENSE
2003	CIN	MLB	29	629	71	19	3	14	80	51	58	4	0	4.9	.291	.350	.408	.045	.287	.346	.407	.264	13.0	140-1B -10
2004	CIN	MLB	30	633	101	44	2	24	99	46	36	2	0	4.7	.324	.381	.534	.326	.317	.372	.524	.302	55.9	140-1B -11
2005	CIN	MLB	31	587	75	32	0	9	58	48	48	2	0	4.3	.312	.371	.423	.126	.307	.367	.420	.277	22.6	130-1B 10
2006	PIT	MLB	31	579	69	33	2	11	69	46	48	3	1	4.7	.308	.366	.439	.092	.306	.365	.450	.275	19.3	136-1B 0

Breakout: 6%   Improve: 41%   Collapse: 24%   Attrition: 9%   Comparables: Hal Morris, Ed Kranepool, Chris Chambliss

A top candidate for the "First Baseman Who Made the Most Money in His Career with the Least Justification" award. In a stroke of good fortune, the Reds were able to deal Casey to Pittsburgh in the kind of deal that Vanna White would spell "ST——PID" if no one asked for an O. Casey has gained at least 22 pounds in the past four years; if that weight translated into solid power, it would be an acceptable tradeoff for his diminished range afield. However, his home run stroke, never constant, deserted him again last year, and he led the majors in grounding into double plays with 27—the only lefty hitter in the top five in GIDPs. At this point, he would lose a footrace to a two-toed sloth with a pulled hamstring.

JACOB CRUZ   **OF**   **Bats: L Throws: L**   Height: 6' 0"   Weight: 210   Born: January 28, 1973   Age: 33

YEAR	TM	LVL	AGE	PA	R	2B	3B	HR	RBI	BB	SO	SB	CS	SPEED	BA	OBP	SLG	MLVR	EQBA	EQOBP	EQSLG	EQA	VORP	DEFENSE
2003	LOU	AAA	30	149	25	8	0	7	29	14	22	3	0	4.8	.348	.409	.568	.412	.289	.352	.463	.282	5.5	25-RF -2
2004	CIN	MLB	31	167	22	8	0	3	28	16	43	0	0	4.0	.224	.317	.340	-.128	.224	.313	.347	.234	-1.8	18-RF -1
2005	CIN	MLB	32	145	12	10	0	4	18	16	46	0	0	4.4	.236	.324	.409	-.030	.228	.322	.402	.252	2.3	
2006	CIN	MLB	33	104	12	5	0	3	13	11	26	0	0	4.6	.254	.338	.425	-.016	.255	.339	.431	.260	1.3	29-RF -2

Breakout: 22%   Improve: 46%   Collapse: 35%   Attrition: 51%   Comparables: Dave Clark, John Vander Wal, Brian Daubach

What would be the reason to retain a lefty-hitting reserve with a .226/.319/.368 line against right-handed pitchers in the past two seasons? Cruz is really a Triple-A player worthy of only occasional trips to the downtown Cincy Starbucks, but he sticks with the Reds because he's cheap and doesn't complain. In the Reds view, that's apparently worth carrying a guy who can only hit mistake fastballs for power, has minus range in the outfield, and is a terrible baserunner. Signed to a minor league deal with the Reds in the offseason, he's already ticketed for a roster slot in Cincinnati.

CHRIS DENORFIA   **OF**   **Bats: R Throws: R**   Height: 6' 1"   Weight: 185   Born: July 15, 1980   Age: 25

YEAR	TM	LVL	AGE	PA	R	2B	3B	HR	RBI	BB	SO	SB	CS	SPEED	BA	OBP	SLG	MLVR	EQBA	EQOBP	EQSLG	EQA	VORP	DEFENSE			
2003	POT	A+	22	530	60	10	5	4	39	54	106	20	7	6.5	.236	.317	.304	-.123	.212	.283	.291	.212	-32.4	126-CF 8			
2004	POT	A+	23	320	52	18	4	11	51	48	66	10	6	6.3	.312	.416	.532	.349	.266	.356	.454	.278	17.2	72-CF 6			
2004	CHT	AA	23	253	30	10	2	6	27	30	42	5	2	5.2	.249	.340	.394	-.005	.222	.305	.352	.235	-5.2	63-CF 4			
2005	CHT	AA	24	207	40	17	3	7	26	17	38	4	3	6.2	.330	.391	.564	.340	.281	.331	.491	.274	12.4	28-CF 1	17-RF	1
2005	LOU	AAA	24	371	50	12	6	13	61	41	54	8	3	5.9	.310	.391	.505	.231	.281	.360	.450	.280	20.7	69-CF -4	11-RF	0
2005	CIN	MLB	24	44	8	3	0	1	2	6	9	1	0	5.5	.263	.364	.421	.074	.263	.364	.421	.278	1.9				
2006	CIN	MLB	25	516	64	24	3	13	57	48	96	9	4	5.6	.262	.335	.413	-.030	.263	.336	.419	.256	10.2	121-CF 2			

Breakout: 20%   Improve: 48%   Collapse: 28%   Attrition: 14%   Comparables: Jermaine Allensworth, Lee Walls, Wayne Comer

With the kind of broad-based skills that statheads love and teams like the Reds don't really appreciate, Denorfia has real promise should he get the opportunity. However, unless the Reds move one of their big three outfielders, Denorfia will probably spend the year languishing in a reserve role—assuming that the club doesn't do something as stupid as playing Womack over Denorfia. An aggressive, heads-up player, his line-drive power might translate well at the GABP.

ADAM DUNN **1B/OF** **Bats: L Throws: R** Height: 6' 5" Weight: 240 Born: November 9, 1979 Age: 26

YEAR	TM	LVL	AGE	PA	R	2B	3B	HR	RBI	BB	SO	SB	CS	SPEED	BA	OBP	SLG	MLVR	EQBA	EQOBP	EQSLG	EQA	VORP	DEFENSE	
2003	CIN	MLB	23	469	70	12	1	27	57	74	126	8	2	5.4	.215	.354	.465	.069	.212	.348	.466	.281	10.1	93-LF -6	
2004	CIN	MLB	24	681	105	34	0	46	102	108	195	6	1	4.6	.266	.388	.569	.320	.259	.381	.553	.310	53.4	149-LF -17	
2005	CIN	MLB	25	671	107	35	2	40	101	114	168	4	2	5.1	.247	.387	.540	.245	.242	.383	.541	.307	45.0	124-LF -10	29-1B 1
2006	CIN	MLB	26	645	94	30	1	41	108	104	148	6	2	5.2	.263	.393	.558	.246	.264	.395	.566	.313	46.6	150-LF -7	

Breakout: 24% Improve: 67% Collapse: 10% Attrition: 0% Comparables: Troy Glaus, Boog Powell, Hee Seop Choi

PECOTA was extremely close in predicting Dunn's 2005 slugging and OBP, but the Reds, their fans, and the rabble-rousing sports media in Cincy nevertheless wouldn't get off of Dunn's back. The Brobdingnagian slugger can't carry the team to a pennant if every angry peasant in the Ohio Valley is poking him in the ankles with their pitchforks because they think he strikes out too much. He has a 149-point home/road split in OPS in favor of the Great American Ball Park since it opened. Though he was never as bad a left fielder as his reputation would suggest, Dunn will play first base now that Casey is gone.

EDWIN ENCARNACION **3B** **Bats: R Throws: R** Height: 6' 1" Weight: 195 Born: January 7, 1983 Age: 23

YEAR	TM	LVL	AGE	PA	R	2B	3B	HR	RBI	BB	SO	SB	CS	SPEED	BA	OBP	SLG	MLVR	EQBA	EQOBP	EQSLG	EQA	VORP	DEFENSE
2003	POT	A+	20	243	40	15	1	6	29	24	32	7	1	5.8	.321	.387	.484	.265	.290	.350	.470	.281	18.4	56-3B -8
2003	CHT	AA	20	284	40	13	1	5	36	22	44	8	3	5.7	.272	.331	.390	.030	.253	.305	.390	.244	2.5	62-3B -1
2004	CHT	AA	21	525	73	35	1	13	76	53	79	17	3	6.0	.281	.352	.443	.101	.248	.313	.396	.250	7.5	115-3B -6
2005	LOU	AAA	22	330	44	23	0	15	54	33	53	7	2	4.7	.314	.388	.548	.290	.281	.354	.497	.288	26.2	75-3B 4
2005	CIN	MLB	22	234	25	16	0	9	31	20	60	3	0	4.0	.232	.308	.436	-.019	.227	.303	.441	.255	3.8	54-3B 3
2006	CIN	MLB	23	534	70	30	1	22	75	47	97	8	3	5.1	.275	.344	.485	.089	.276	.345	.492	.277	26.2	125-3B 0

Breakout: 43% Improve: 63% Collapse: 13% Attrition: 8% Comparables: Eric Chavez, Dwight Evans, Larry Parrish

Starring at Louisville in his first year at Triple-A, Encarnacion got a chance to play regularly with the Reds after they traded Joe Randa. Offensively, Encarnacion has a quick bat with line-drive power that could easily translate into over-the-fence power when he matures. He has good speed and steals bases at a good clip. Defensively, he has plus range and all the tools to be an asset at the hot corner, though he makes too many errors for the old-school guys to tolerate, especially throwing errors. With manager Jerry Narron prattling on during the offseason about how he likes young players to earn their positions, Encarnacion could well be demoted if he accidentally conks a few season ticket-holders in the front row boxes behind first base early on.

RYAN FREEL **2B/OF** **Bats: R Throws: R** Height: 5' 10" Weight: 180 Born: March 8, 1976 Age: 30

YEAR	TM	LVL	AGE	PA	R	2B	3B	HR	RBI	BB	SO	SB	CS	SPEED	BA	OBP	SLG	MLVR	EQBA	EQOBP	EQSLG	EQA	VORP	DEFENSE	
2003	LOU	AAA	27	238	38	11	1	3	12	21	32	25	6	7.8	.274	.336	.377	-.017	.243	.305	.336	.239	-3.7	36-2B 6	
2003	CIN	MLB	27	151	23	6	1	4	12	9	13	9	4	6.7	.285	.344	.431	.051	.283	.338	.428	.263	5.6	18-CF 0	
2004	CIN	MLB	28	584	74	21	8	3	28	67	88	37	10	7.4	.277	.375	.368	.038	.275	.371	.365	.268	19.1	44-3B 2	30-RF 1
2005	CIN	MLB	29	428	69	19	3	4	21	51	59	36	10	7.1	.271	.371	.371	.021	.270	.370	.377	.272	15.2	44-2B 2	19-LF 1
2006	CIN	MLB	30	445	65	19	3	4	32	44	62	29	8	5.8	.259	.344	.351	-.098	.260	.345	.356	.251	6.1	106-2B 2	

Breakout: 5% Improve: 24% Collapse: 34% Attrition: 18% Comparables: Keith Miller, Bobby Adams, Alan Bannister

After hustling his way into regular status in 2004, Freel was jobbed twice in the offseason. First, the Reds inexplicably traded for Tony Womack, then they re-signed the obstreperous Rich Aurilia. With good range and hands in the outfield and the ability to play center as well as second and third, Freel will likely be the Reds supersub until they come to their senses. A good runner who makes the most of his speed, Freel is too aggressive on the basepaths. In stealing bases, he'd be better off picking his spots a little less frequently.

KEN GRIFFEY JR. **CF** **Bats: L Throws: L** Height: 6' 3" Weight: 205 Born: November 21, 1969 Age: 36

YEAR	TM	LVL	AGE	PA	R	2B	3B	HR	RBI	BB	SO	SB	CS	SPEED	BA	OBP	SLG	MLVR	EQBA	EQOBP	EQSLG	EQA	VORP	DEFENSE
2003	CIN	MLB	33	200	34	12	1	13	26	27	44	1	0	4.9	.247	.370	.566	.248	.240	.360	.551	.301	16.3	40-CF -4
2004	CIN	MLB	34	348	49	18	0	20	60	44	67	1	0	4.1	.253	.351	.513	.181	.247	.345	.500	.285	22.1	74-CF -3
2005	CIN	MLB	35	555	85	30	0	35	92	54	93	0	1	3.6	.301	.369	.576	.319	.296	.365	.580	.309	52.3	121-CF -18
2006	CIN	MLB	36	503	67	25	1	29	88	58	90	1	1	4.2	.281	.367	.541	.204	.282	.369	.549	.299	34.7	119-CF -12

Breakout: 15% Improve: 38% Collapse: 19% Attrition: 10% Comparables: Larry Walker, Fred Lynn, Sammy Sosa

(continued next page)

Ken Griffey Jr. *(continued)*

An excellent and long overdue comeback season, good enough for the Comeback Player of the Year Award. While his overall stats were good but not great, they look a helluva lot better if one subtracts his dreadful April when he hit only one homer in 82 at-bats because he hadn't fully recovered from his hamstring surgery of the previous August. Even so, Junior only avoided hitting the DL for the fifth season in a row by suffering his latest injury in September, after rosters had expanded. He missed the last 26 games after spraining his right foot rounding second; it's the kind of injury one expects of little leaguers, not major leaguers. Defensively, he looked at times like the Griffey of old, but the team really needs to move him to left where he has a good chance of being average or better, range-wise.

RYAN HANIGAN C **Bats: R Throws: R** Height: 6' 1" Weight: 185 Born: August 16, 1980 Age: 25

YEAR	TM	LVL	AGE	PA	R	2B	3B	HR	RBI	BB	SO	SB	CS	SPEED	BA	OBP	SLG	MLVR	EQBA	EQOBP	EQSLG	EQA	VORP	DEFENSE	
2003	DYT	A	22	358	43	12	0	1	31	40	44	3	4	3.5	.277	.363	.325	.016	.225	.297	.279	.210	-16.6	82-C -3	
2004	POT	A+	23	493	58	21	0	5	56	49	51	6	5	4.0	.296	.369	.380	.072	.243	.307	.317	.226	-10.8	65-C 5	
2005	CHT	AA	24	388	45	14	1	4	29	50	41	4	1	4.4	.321	.418	.405	.155	.271	.355	.350	.253	-1.4	44-1B -1	44-C -5
2006	CIN	MLB	25	319	30	13	1	4	28	28	44	2	1	4.5	.244	.317	.332	-.179	.245	.318	.337	.225	-4.5	77-C 0	

Breakout: 26% Improve: 38% Collapse: 39% Attrition: 21% Comparables: Bruce Benedict, Ellie Rodriguez, Alex Trevino

Hanigan improved offensively in his first action in Double-A last year, making himself into a marginal prospect. That's faint praise considering that the Reds' stockpile of catching prospects is something like the nuclear arsenal of Belarus—impressive on paper but functionally unusable.

KEVIN HOWARD 2B **Bats: L Throws: R** Height: 6' 2" Weight: 180 Born: June 25, 1981 Age: 25

YEAR	TM	LVL	AGE	PA	R	2B	3B	HR	RBI	BB	SO	SB	CS	SPEED	BA	OBP	SLG	MLVR	EQBA	EQOBP	EQSLG	EQA	VORP	DEFENSE
2003	DYT	A	22	572	80	26	3	9	75	50	67	12	5	5.3	.285	.355	.401	.105	.243	.299	.363	.233	-4.9	123-2B 11
2004	POT	A+	23	536	68	24	0	11	79	58	70	8	7	4.1	.284	.364	.406	.090	.240	.309	.359	.235	-2.7	116-2B -2
2005	CHT	AA	24	520	63	23	2	12	70	33	64	13	8	5.0	.296	.346	.428	.058	.252	.292	.374	.232	-3.1	116-2B -3
2006	NYA	MLB	25	429	45	17	1	7	43	24	65	5	3	4.4	.249	.295	.356	-.162	.252	.306	.371	.227	0.6	102-2B 0

Breakout: 23% Improve: 47% Collapse: 31% Attrition: 16% Comparables: Josh Klimek, Dave Meliah, Joe Thurston

As a 5th rounder from the 2002 draft, Howard was one of the few overachieving position players in the the Reds farm system. He's a line-drive hitter with moderate power and some plate discipline, but he doesn't excel in any one area. After a decent year in Double-A, Howard followed up with a boffo fall campaign in Arizona (.409/.475/.557 in 25 games). As a reward, he was dealt to the Yankees in December in the Womack trade. With the Yankees, he'll end up as nothing more than an organizational player; a future in the majors as a utility infielder is unlikely because his arm isn't really strong enough to play on the left side of the infield.

D'ANGELO JIMENEZ 2B **Bats: B Throws: R** Height: 6' 0" Weight: 190 Born: December 21, 1977 Age: 28

YEAR	TM	LVL	AGE	PA	R	2B	3B	HR	RBI	BB	SO	SB	CS	SPEED	BA	OBP	SLG	MLVR	EQBA	EQOBP	EQSLG	EQA	VORP	DEFENSE
2003	CHA	MLB	25	304	35	11	5	7	26	32	46	4	3	5.9	.255	.332	.410	-.035	.251	.334	.416	.258	7.8	66-2B -5
2003	CIN	MLB	25	329	34	13	2	7	31	34	43	7	4	5.2	.290	.365	.421	.087	.286	.361	.424	.273	16.0	72-2B 7
2004	CIN	MLB	26	649	76	28	3	12	67	82	99	13	7	5.0	.270	.364	.394	.053	.266	.360	.388	.264	27.4	142-2B 0
2005	CIN	MLB	27	119	14	7	0	0	5	14	23	2	1	5.2	.229	.319	.295	-.190	.229	.319	.286	.223	-2.3	24-2B 1
2005	CHT	AA	27	399	55	20	0	9	45	69	34	16	4	5.6	.278	.401	.422	.120	.202	.300	.296	.221	-13.0	69-SS 8
2006	TEX	MLB	28	379	46	16	2	7	36	39	52	6	3	5.0	.255	.335	.383	-.056	.251	.339	.381	.247	7.7	91-2B 1

Breakout: 29% Improve: 44% Collapse: 25% Attrition: 18% Comparables: Luis Alicea, Tom Herr, Frank Menechino

Jimenez's career prospects as a big-league regular are on the razor's edge now after he played/brawled his way out of Cincinnati. He was outrighted in late May after a disastrous start to the 2005 season and spent the rest of the year in Double-A, making the Reds the fourth organization to give up on him. Signed by Texas in December to a minor league contract, he'll get a shot at the keystone as veteran insurance for Ian Kinsler.

AUSTIN KEARNS		OF			**Bats: R Throws: R**				Height: 6′ 3″	Weight: 220	Born: May 20, 1980						Age: 26	
YEAR	TM	LVL	AGE	PA	R	2B	3B	HR	RBI	BB	SO	SB	CS	SPEED	BA	OBP	SLG	MLVR	EQBA	EQOBP	EQSLG	EQA	VORP	DEFENSE

2003 CIN MLB 23 338 39 11 0 15 58 41 68 5 2 4.6 .264 .364 .455 .105 .260 .359 .455 .280 12.8 41-RF -1 36-CF 0
2004 LOU AAA 24 104 19 7 1 2 15 19 16 3 1 5.7 .337 .471 .518 .386 .310 .440 .481 .320 9.5 22-RF 1
2004 CIN MLB 24 246 28 10 2 9 32 28 71 2 1 4.6 .230 .321 .419 -.009 .226 .317 .415 .252 2.5 57-RF -5
2005 LOU AAA 25 123 24 15 1 7 21 11 30 0 0 4.0 .342 .407 .685 .538 .303 .366 .596 .313 12.2 26-RF 0
2005 CIN MLB 25 448 62 26 1 18 67 48 107 0 0 4.4 .240 .333 .452 .042 .238 .330 .455 .269 9.1 101-RF 2
2006 CIN MLB 26 459 62 27 2 21 69 53 100 3 1 4.9 .275 .367 .510 .156 .276 .368 .517 .292 22.4 109-RF 0

Breakout: 33% Improve: 66% Collapse: 9% Attrition: 19% Comparables: Pat Burrell, Dale Murphy, Ron Swoboda

It takes a really boneheaded organization to not appreciate the synchronicity of having a pair of gifted, powerful young outfielders to build a franchise around, but the Reds have been equal to the task of sabotaging at least one career between Dunn and Kearns. Although Kearns earned a spanking by reporting to camp overweight and out-of-shape last year, he should have spent the spring listening to the Reds talk about how their two titans were going to lead the club back to glory. Instead, he spent the spring hearing trade rumors and competing with Wily Mo Pena for a job because Dan O'Brien hadn't yet figured out that dividing five players among four positions does neither the club nor the players any good. Kearns's 38 days of banishment in Louisville will have the convenient effect of delaying his free-agency by a year (till after 2008), assuming he spends all of the next two years in the majors.

JASON LaRUE C **Bats: R Throws: R** Height: 5′ 11″ Weight: 200 Born: March 19, 1974 Age: 32

2003 CIN MLB 29 436 52 23 1 16 50 33 111 3 3 4.3 .230 .321 .422 -.032 .228 .314 .427 .253 8.6 107-C -5
2004 CIN MLB 30 443 46 24 2 14 55 26 108 0 2 3.7 .251 .334 .431 .037 .249 .327 .431 .259 15.7 104-C -5
2005 CIN MLB 31 417 38 27 0 14 60 41 101 0 0 3.2 .260 .355 .452 .088 .258 .350 .458 .277 22.7 104-C -1
2006 CIN MLB 32 333 33 17 1 12 42 28 77 1 1 3.6 .245 .326 .430 -.035 .246 .328 .437 .256 9.0 80-C -2

Breakout: 16% Improve: 40% Collapse: 30% Attrition: 24% Comparables: Mike Macfarlane, Hal Smith, Ozzie Virgil

LaRue has settled comfortably into a useful role, and even improved in 2005, posting modest career highs in BA, SLG, and OBP. Platooning with Javier Valentin helped, but LaRue's increased walk rate was mostly negated by his big drop in getting on base by taking one (or several) for the team. LaRue's power comes on mistake fastballs; his long swing and average bat speed make him vulnerable to breaking and off-speed stuff. Defensively, LaRue's accurate arm remains his primary asset, gunning 33% of base bandits.

FELIPE LOPEZ SS **Bats: B Throws: R** Height: 6′ 1″ Weight: 185 Born: May 12, 1980 Age: 26

2003 LOU AAA 23 156 22 11 0 2 18 12 38 2 5 4.7 .280 .333 .399 .011 .246 .307 .359 .229 0.4 25-SS -3
2003 CIN MLB 23 227 28 7 2 2 13 28 59 8 5 6.9 .213 .313 .299 -.223 .212 .311 .298 .223 -4.3 45-SS -8
2004 LOU AAA 24 325 50 11 3 9 43 25 71 2 2 5.3 .273 .329 .423 -.028 .246 .303 .374 .237 2.0 61-SS -8
2004 CIN MLB 24 293 35 18 2 7 31 25 81 1 1 5.4 .242 .314 .405 -.049 .238 .307 .396 .243 4.3 44-SS 2 23-3B -1
2005 CIN MLB 25 645 97 34 5 23 85 57 111 15 7 6.4 .291 .352 .486 .159 .287 .349 .487 .282 45.8 134-SS -11
2006 CIN MLB 26 546 71 26 3 15 61 51 106 10 5 5.6 .265 .337 .427 -.007 .266 .338 .433 .260 21.7 128-SS -7

Breakout: 24% Improve: 46% Collapse: 21% Attrition: 10% Comparables: Ron Oester, Tony Phillips, Kurt Stillwell

Lopez had the breakout season we predicted last year, and, at 26, should be headed for even better numbers if the hammerheads in the organization stop focusing on his strikeouts and instead focus on ways to help him improve his hitting from the starboard side of the plate. Lopez has decent bat speed, but his swing is a bit long and he can get pull-happy. In 2005, he had a huge home/road split in favor of the GABP. That was due to the park favoring left-handed power in 2005, as Lopez managed to loft a lot of fly balls just over the right-field fence. Whether he can continue to do that as pitchers adjust is a good question. Having an excellent arm and other plus defensive tools has not yet translated into being a good all-around defender in Lopez's case, as he has shown minus range; better positioning and experience should help in that regard.

JAVON MORAN OF Bats: R Throws: R Height: 5' 11" Weight: 175 Born: September 30, 1982 Age: 23

YEAR	TM	LVL	AGE	PA	R	2B	3B	HR	RBI	BB	SO	SB	CS	SPEED	BA	OBP	SLG	MLVR	EQBA	EQOBP	EQSLG	EQA	VORP	DEFENSE			
2003	BAT	A-	20	267	33	9	3	1	12	16	32	27	11	7.1	.284	.326	.356	.050	.261	.296	.344	.229	-11.1	46-CF	2	13-LF	0
2004	DYT	A	21	105	11	2	0	0	7	10	15	11	3	5.3	.383	.448	.404	.280	.323	.376	.344	.266	3.6	21-CF	-1		
2004	LWD	A	21	459	73	18	9	2	38	24	78	41	17	8.4	.285	.340	.385	.060	.268	.306	.357	.236	-4.5	81-CF	-1	18-RF	-1
2005	SAR	A+	22	230	35	4	2	2	23	14	32	13	7	6.4	.329	.378	.395	.160	.298	.342	.365	.251	4.6	25-CF	-2	24-LF	2
2005	CHT	AA	22	88	14	5	1	0	2	5	21	7	4	7.5	.301	.341	.386	-.006	.266	.300	.351	.227	-1.4	17-CF	4		
2006	CIN	MLB	23	423	46	17	3	2	28	21	75	17	5	5.6	.258	.299	.327	-.210	.259	.300	.332	.219	-7.2	101-CF	2		

Breakout: 5% Improve: 23% Collapse: 51% Attrition: 12% Comparables: Wilkin Ruan, Onil Joseph, Todd Hogan

Moran's first-half performance in the FSL earned him a ticket to Chattanooga, where he impressed as much as a speedster with no power and no strike-zone judgment can. Moran's the ultimate "but" prospect: he has speed, but he doesn't steal at a high rate; he has defensive value as a center fielder, but he's not outstanding; he can hit for average, but he has zero power; he could bat leadoff, but he doesn't walk nearly enough. But with the Reds, the "but" prospects are pretty much all you've got.

RAINER OLMEDO SS/2B Bats: B Throws: R Height: 5' 11" Weight: 155 Born: May 31, 1981 Age: 25

YEAR	TM	LVL	AGE	PA	R	2B	3B	HR	RBI	BB	SO	SB	CS	SPEED	BA	OBP	SLG	MLVR	EQBA	EQOBP	EQSLG	EQA	VORP	DEFENSE			
2003	CHT	AA	22	175	23	11	0	2	15	14	29	3	3	4.5	.294	.349	.400	.084	.260	.309	.376	.238	2.3	43-SS	-1		
2003	CIN	MLB	22	243	24	6	1	0	17	13	46	1	1	5.1	.239	.280	.274	-.306	.236	.279	.266	.199	-9.4	43-SS	-8	13-2B	1
2004	LOU	AAA	23	319	33	13	7	2	26	23	40	2	3	5.1	.286	.342	.398	-.031	.262	.318	.365	.239	2.0	59-2B	8	23-SS	-3
2005	CIN	MLB	24	85	10	4	1	1	4	6	22	4	0	7.6	.221	.282	.338	-.223	.218	.287	.333	.232	-1.1	16-2B	0		
2006	CIN	MLB	25	242	29	10	1	2	20	15	40	6	2	5.5	.260	.312	.351	-.153	.261	.313	.356	.230	3.1	60-2B	0		

Breakout: 35% Improve: 49% Collapse: 28% Attrition: 28% Comparables: Tommy Hinzo, Larry Milbourne, Curtis Wilkerson

Despite his good-glove reputation and scouting reports that give him plus range, arm, and hands, Olmedo has not shown above-average range at either middle infield position in his brief major league career. This could partly be due to his 2004 elbow injury; he didn't come off the DL till mid-June last year after recuperating from Tommy John surgery. He's not likely to improve much offensively, so Olmedo will end up fighting it out with William Bergolla and non-roster invite Frank Menechino for a reserve slot.

WILY MO PENA RF Bats: R Throws: R Height: 6' 3" Weight: 215 Born: January 23, 1982 Age: 24

YEAR	TM	LVL	AGE	PA	R	2B	3B	HR	RBI	BB	SO	SB	CS	SPEED	BA	OBP	SLG	MLVR	EQBA	EQOBP	EQSLG	EQA	VORP	DEFENSE			
2003	CIN	MLB	21	180	20	6	1	5	16	12	53	3	2	5.8	.218	.283	.358	-.187	.217	.278	.355	.221	-5.0	23-CF	-1	11-RF	-2
2004	CIN	MLB	22	364	45	10	1	26	66	22	108	5	2	4.6	.259	.316	.527	.145	.256	.311	.521	.274	18.8	38-RF	-5	43-CF	5
2005	CIN	MLB	23	335	42	17	0	19	51	20	116	2	1	4.3	.254	.304	.492	.062	.251	.301	.502	.266	9.5	46-RF	-2	22-CF	-3
2006	CIN	MLB	24	382	53	20	1	25	65	29	107	4	2	4.9	.282	.345	.558	.194	.283	.346	.566	.292	24.1	91-RF	-3		

Breakout: 54% Improve: 70% Collapse: 11% Attrition: 27% Comparables: Jesse Barfield, Willie Stargell, Pete Incaviglia

Pena managed to tread water in 2005. That's not fatal for a 24-year-old with Pena's power potential, but playing in only 428 games (combined majors and minors) in 2002–05 because the Reds wouldn't solve their outfield logjam could substantially retard his development, and Pena still makes the kinds of fundamental mistakes that he should have left behind in Double-A. It's also hindered him from improving against RHPs, who can often get him to chase outside breaking pitches. After adding 30 pounds of muscle in the past two years, Pena appears to have lost some of his range in the outfield, but he'll need to keep himself toned up; in 2005, Pena was on the DL for a more than month after straining his left quad. A full season in the 2006 lineup with 600-plus plate appearances should show the world what Pena really can do.

JAVIER VALENTIN C Bats: B Throws: R Height: 5' 10" Weight: 190 Born: September 19, 1975 Age: 30

YEAR	TM	LVL	AGE	PA	R	2B	3B	HR	RBI	BB	SO	SB	CS	SPEED	BA	OBP	SLG	MLVR	EQBA	EQOBP	EQSLG	EQA	VORP	DEFENSE	
2003	TBA	MLB	27	142	13	7	1	3	15	5	31	0	0	3.3	.222	.254	.356	-.267	.224	.261	.358	.215	-4.0	35-C	0
2004	CIN	MLB	28	222	18	10	1	6	20	17	36	0	0	3.8	.233	.293	.381	-.116	.228	.288	.376	.231	0.3	46-C	2
2005	CIN	MLB	29	254	36	11	0	14	50	30	37	0	0	3.6	.281	.362	.520	.213	.273	.357	.514	.293	20.8	58-C	-3
2006	CIN	MLB	30	231	24	11	0	9	31	21	39	0	0	3.9	.253	.324	.441	-.019	.254	.325	.448	.257	8.0	57-C	-2

Breakout: 18% Improve: 40% Collapse: 38% Attrition: 30% Comparables: Jason Varitek, Mark Salas, Don Pavletich

In one of those surprises that makes the game so fascinating—and makes BP look good when it says "has enough pop to pull a 15-homer season at some point"—Valentin had his career year in 2005. Mediocre pitchers probably aren't going to challenge him with fastballs again in 2006, which will hurt his power numbers. He's adequate behind the plate, though the roly-poly "switch hitter" couldn't hit Jennifer Lopez's backside with a bat right-handed from three feet away.

JOEY VOTTO   **1B**   **Bats: L Throws: R**   Height: 6' 3"   Weight: 200   Born: September 10, 1983   Age: 22

YEAR	TM	LVL	AGE	PA	R	2B	3B	HR	RBI	BB	SO	SB	CS	SPEED	BA	OBP	SLG	MLVR	EQBA	EQOBP	EQSLG	EQA	VORP		DEFENSE
2003	BIL	Rk	19	301	47	17	3	6	38	56	80	4	0	4.9	.317	.452	.487	.365	.264	.375	.394	.275	12.0		61-1B -6
2003	DYT	A	19	233	19	8	0	1	20	34	64	2	5	2.7	.231	.348	.287	-.074	.193	.293	.253	.203	-20.7		48-1B 1
2004	DYT	A	20	473	60	26	2	14	73	79	110	9	2	4.6	.302	.419	.486	.277	.252	.355	.406	.269	6.7		87-1B -1
2004	POT	A+	20	96	11	7	0	5	20	11	21	1	1	3.0	.298	.385	.560	.332	.256	.335	.494	.276	3.7		19-1B 0
2005	SAR	A+	21	528	64	23	2	17	83	52	122	4	5	4.1	.256	.330	.425	.068	.232	.300	.388	.240	-14.7		105-1B -1
2006	*CIN*	*MLB*	*22*	*483*	*54*	*24*	*1*	*15*	*56*	*49*	*124*	*4*	*2*	*4.0*	*.237*	*.318*	*.398*	*-.095*	*.238*	*.320*	*.404*	*.244*	*-3.3*		*114-1B -1*

Breakout: 21%   Improve: 50%   Collapse: 28%   Attrition: 2%   *Comparables: A. J. Zapp, Pete Paciorek, Joe Dusan*

Another marginal prospect who gets more attention than he deserves because he's among the best of the sorry lot in the Reds organization. Votto has ball-crushing power, but, it's of the classic long swing/slow bat variety that will get nullified by pitching in the high minors if he can't adjust. At 22, he's spent two and a half years in A-ball and needs to make his move in 2006. If you want an ominous sign, he failed to impress the AFL last year.

PITCHERS

HOMER BAILEY   **Bats: R Throws: R**   Height: 6' 4"   Weight: 185   Born: May 3, 1986   Age: 20

YEAR	TM	LVL	AGE	W	L	SV	G	GS	IP	H	BB	SO	HR	GB%	BABIP	STUFF	WHIP	ERA	PERA	EQERA	EQH9	EQBB9	EQSO9	EQHR9	VORP	WXRL
2005	DYT	A	19	8	4	0	28	21	103.7	89	62	125	5	49%	.332	19	1.46	4.43	4.77	6.12	8.6	6.0	7.5	0.8	-5.8	—
2006	*CIN*	*MLB*	*20*	*5*	*8*	*0*	*26*	*18*	*108.3*	*98*	*76*	*101*	*11*	*46%*	*.292*	*11*	*1.61*	*5.02*	*5.30*	*5.26*	*8.1*	*5.8*	*7.7*	*0.9*	*2.4*	*0.9*

Breakout: 45%   Improve: 78%   Collapse: 7%   Attrition: 0%   *Comparables: Rich Harden, Francisco Rodriguez, Justin Jones*

The classic scout's dream, a high school pitcher with a plus fastball and a drop-dead curve who's only 20. Bailey had a good-looking season in the Midwest League if you look at only the unadjusted numbers, and a credible season after adjustments for a top prospect still in his teens. The Reds are treating him with kid gloves because of their recent high-profile disasters with their top high school pitchers, but he's still at least two years (assuming he can skip a level) and two parsecs away from pitching in Cincy.

BOBBY BASHAM   **Bats: R Throws: R**   Height: 6' 3"   Weight: 205   Born: March 7, 1980   Age: 26

YEAR	TM	LVL	AGE	W	L	SV	G	GS	IP	H	BB	SO	HR	GB%	BABIP	STUFF	WHIP	ERA	PERA	EQERA	EQH9	EQBB9	EQSO9	EQHR9	VORP	WXRL
2003	CHT	AA	23	5	10	0	17	17	94.0	133	24	56	16	—	.341	-56	1.67	5.17	7.80	7.70	13.0	2.5	3.5	3.2	-21.5	—
2005	SAR	A+	25	5	2	0	10	10	50.3	60	6	42	3	59%	.385	-1	1.31	3.76	4.53	5.62	10.7	1.4	4.2	1.1	-0.1	—
2005	CHT	AA	25	5	3	0	10	10	51.3	52	9	46	5	55%	.341	-4	1.19	2.98	5.73	4.99	10.4	1.8	5.2	1.8	3.3	—
2006	*CIN*	*MLB*	*26*	*4*	*8*	*0*	*29*	*16*	*103.0*	*128*	*25*	*51*	*19*	*50%*	*.308*	*-9*	*1.49*	*5.73*	*6.03*	*6.01*	*11.0*	*2.0*	*4.1*	*1.6*	*-5.9*	*0.0*

Breakout: 26%   Improve: 61%   Collapse: 10%   Attrition: 1%   *Comparables: Nate Bump, Heath Totten, Nic Ungs*

Basham pitched with an undiagnosed injury in 2003 and then missed all of 2004 after surgery in May to repair his torn labrum. Now the right-hander needs to bring his fastball back to average or his slider back to a plus out pitch if he's going to succeed in Triple-A. He'll need to do both to craft a future in the majors.

MATT BELISLE   **Bats: B Throws: R**   Height: 6' 3"   Weight: 190   Born: June 6, 1980   Age: 26

YEAR	TM	LVL	AGE	W	L	SV	G	GS	IP	H	BB	SO	HR	GB%	BABIP	STUFF	WHIP	ERA	PERA	EQERA	EQH9	EQBB9	EQSO9	EQHR9	VORP	WXRL
2003	GRN	AA	23	6	8	0	21	21	125.3	128	42	94	5	—	.304	4	1.36	3.52	4.67	5.64	9.9	3.3	4.5	0.7	-0.5	—
2004	LOU	AAA	24	9	11	0	28	28	162.7	192	51	106	16	—	.331	-2	1.49	5.26	4.99	5.77	10.2	3.1	4.5	1.0	-3.1	—
2005	CIN	MLB	25	4	8	1	60	5	85.7	101	26	59	11	54%	.330	-6	1.48	4.41	4.70	4.91	9.7	2.5	5.5	1.1	3.5	0.6
2006	*CIN*	*MLB*	*26*	*3*	*4*	*2*	*48*	*3*	*70.7*	*77*	*25*	*45*	*8*	*53%*	*.304*	*-5*	*1.43*	*4.57*	*4.77*	*4.99*	*9.6*	*2.9*	*5.3*	*0.9*	*4.5*	*0.5*

Breakout: 33%   Improve: 60%   Collapse: 10%   Attrition: 15%   *Comparables: Hipolito Pichardo, Mark Fidrych, Mike Garman*

(continued next page)

Matt Belisle *(continued)*

Belisle's top prospect label was removed after a serious back injury in 2001. Now he's yet another spear-carrier in the Reds phalanx of hard-working, blue-collar former high school pitchers with middling stuff (fastball, slider, change). His 2006 role is unsettled, as he could end up in middle relief or be inserted into the rotation, but he'll end up in Louisville quickly if he doesn't learn how to mix up his pitches to left-handed hitters.

CHRIS BOOKER — Bats: R Throws: R — Height: 6' 3" — Weight: 230 — Born: December 9, 1976 — Age: 29

YEAR	TM	LVL	AGE	W	L	SV	G	GS	IP	H	BB	SO	HR	GB%	BABIP	STUFF	WHIP	ERA	PERA	EQERA	EQH9	EQBB9	EQSO9	EQHR9	VORP	WXRL
2004	CHT	AA	27	2	0	5	28	0	39.0	26	25	57	0	—	.302	-2	1.31	1.38	4.63	3.60	8.0	8.0	8.0	0.3	7.8	—
2005	LOU	AAA	28	8	4	20	59	0	65.0	45	28	91	2	34%	.312	22	1.12	2.49	3.32	3.61	6.9	4.6	9.2	0.3	13.8	—
2006	PHI	MLB	29	2	3	1	29	2	49.0	48	36	48	10	33%	.284	-5	1.71	5.84	6.58	6.25	8.6	6.1	8.3	1.8	-1.6	-0.2

Breakout: 28%   Improve: 48%   Collapse: 21%   Attrition: 19%   Comparables: Mike Armstrong, Bill Laxton, Brian Boehringer

Booker dominated in relief in Louisville after pitching ten years in the bushes. He'd never harnessed his stuff until last season, his third after missing 2002 due to shoulder surgery, but Booker throws a very heavy fastball with plus velocity, allowing only 29 long balls in 531 minor league IP. Now with the Phillies, he's capable of pitching middle relief in the majors.

TRAVIS CHICK — Bats: R Throws: R — Height: 6' 3" — Weight: 220 — Born: June 10, 1984 — Age: 22

YEAR	TM	LVL	AGE	W	L	SV	G	GS	IP	H	BB	SO	HR	GB%	BABIP	STUFF	WHIP	ERA	PERA	EQERA	EQH9	EQBB9	EQSO9	EQHR9	VORP	WXRL
2003	JAM	A-	19	1	2	0	13	10	52.0	63	26	48	3	—	.357	-15	1.71	5.71	6.53	7.76	10.9	5.6	4.8	1.8	-12.2	—
2004	FTW	A	20	5	0	0	7	7	42.3	32	9	55	4	—	.283	18	0.97	2.13	5.31	4.38	9.2	2.5	6.9	1.8	5.3	—
2004	GRB	A	20	6	4	0	28	11	91.3	79	27	112	11	—	.298	-6	1.16	4.04	5.61	5.71	9.4	3.2	6.6	1.9	-1.1	—
2005	CHT	AA	21	2	2	0	8	8	46.3	47	27	21	5	40%	.284	-26	1.60	4.86	7.11	5.68	9.9	5.7	2.8	1.8	-0.4	—
2005	MOB	AA	21	2	9	0	19	19	97.3	107	40	92	12	39%	.339	-17	1.51	5.27	6.20	6.77	10.5	4.0	5.8	2.0	-12.3	—
2006	CIN	MLB	22	5	10	0	24	22	121.7	132	59	84	24	38%	.286	-1	1.57	5.78	6.17	5.87	9.6	4.0	5.7	1.7	-5.7	0.3

Breakout: 25%   Improve: 66%   Collapse: 5%   Attrition: 0%   Comparables: Matt Yeatman, Doug Waechter, Matt Peterson

Chick jumped the express train to The Show, instead choosing to take the local in 2005 by pitching poorly at Double-A in both the San Diego and Cincy systems. Like a lot of hard-throwing youngsters, he had to take something off of his fastball in order to avoid walking the bases loaded against more experienced hitters who didn't swing at every pitch in same ZIP code as the ballpark. He's got lots of time to improve his decent slider and minus change, and he'll probably need it.

BRANDON CLAUSSEN — Bats: L Throws: L — Height: 6' 2" — Weight: 200 — Born: May 1, 1979 — Age: 27

YEAR	TM	LVL	AGE	W	L	SV	G	GS	IP	H	BB	SO	HR	GB%	BABIP	STUFF	WHIP	ERA	PERA	EQERA	EQH9	EQBB9	EQSO9	EQHR9	VORP	WXRL
2003	COH	AAA	24	2	1	0	11	11	68.7	53	18	39	4	—	.227	1	1.03	2.75	4.62	4.48	8.3	2.9	4.2	0.8	8.0	—
2004	LOU	AAA	25	8	6	0	18	18	100.3	98	47	111	10	—	.325	10	1.45	4.67	4.78	5.23	9.0	4.8	7.6	1.1	4.0	—
2004	CIN	MLB	25	2	8	0	14	14	66.0	80	35	45	9	42%	.332	-6	1.74	6.14	5.19	6.25	10.1	4.3	5.3	1.1	-8.9	0.5
2005	CIN	MLB	26	10	11	0	29	29	166.7	178	57	121	24	36%	.303	3	1.41	4.21	4.85	4.63	9.2	2.8	5.9	1.3	14.9	3.3
2006	CIN	MLB	27	9	11	0	29	27	163.0	171	57	117	24	40%	.292	9	1.40	4.69	5.04	4.82	9.3	2.9	5.9	1.3	11.2	2.3

Breakout: 19%   Improve: 55%   Collapse: 10%   Attrition: 1%   Comparables: Mike Mason, Bob Ojeda, Alex Kellner

Claussen has only an average fastball, but he can cut it, sink it, or run it in on lefties. He also throws an average change and uses a late-breaking slider as an out pitch. Like a lot of southpaws with mediocre stuff, he depends on a deceptive delivery. However, unlike those southpaws, he's not a groundball pitcher, which accounts for his unfavorable home statistics. Claussen will start 2005 in the Reds rotation, but he needs to keep his slider down and use his sinker to great effect at the GABP. His upside is still that of a decent #3 starter, but it won't be easy getting there.

TODD COFFEY — Bats: R Throws: R — Height: 6' 5" — Weight: 230 — Born: September 9, 1980 — Age: 25

YEAR	TM	LVL	AGE	W	L	SV	G	GS	IP	H	BB	SO	HR	GB%	BABIP	STUFF	WHIP	ERA	PERA	EQERA	EQH9	EQBB9	EQSO9	EQHR9	VORP	WXRL
2003	DYT	A	22	3	3	9	39	0	56.0	61	14	53	1	—	.343	-2	1.34	2.25	4.09	5.40	10.0	2.9	5.2	0.5	1.2	—
2004	CHT	AA	23	4	1	20	40	0	45.3	36	4	53	3	—	.284	10	0.88	2.38	3.59	4.01	8.6	0.8	6.8	1.1	7.5	—
2005	CIN	MLB	24	4	1	1	57	0	58.0	84	11	26	5	54%	.371	-10	1.64	4.50	4.40	4.70	11.0	1.5	3.5	0.7	2.4	0.6
2006	CIN	MLB	25	3	4	4	70	0	76.0	82	18	44	7	51%	.298	-4	1.32	3.97	4.21	4.34	9.6	2.0	4.8	0.8	11.7	0.8

Breakout: 35%   Improve: 54%   Collapse: 12%   Attrition: 12%   Comparables: Braden Looper, T. J. Tucker, Jose Santiago

Coffey started 2005 in Louisville after seven years in the Reds system, including stops with six different clubs and the obligatory sabbatical after Tommy John surgery. Problem is, the Reds rushed him too quickly. Yes, rushed is the correct word despite his long sojourn, as Coffey had only 40 IP in Double-A and 22 IP in Triple-A before facing big-league hitters. Organizations like the Reds, with their fetish for prep pitchers, have to show that greater patience, making a seven-year horizon completely normal. Coffey found out that a mid-90s fastball and a sharp slider don't guarantee success in the bigs. He'll supposedly revive his split-finger fastball in 2006; if he manages to add that to his repertoire, he may yet become an effective reliever.

PHILLIP DUMATRAIT Bats: R Throws: L Height: 6' 2" Weight: 170 Born: July 12, 1981 Age: 24

YEAR	TM	LVL	AGE	W	L	SV	G	GS	IP	H	BB	SO	HR	GB%	BABIP	STUFF	WHIP	ERA	PERA	EQERA	EQH9	EQBB9	EQSO9	EQHR9	VORP	WXRL
2003	POT	A+	21	4	1	0	7	7	37.7	36	14	32	2	—	.295	5	1.33	3.34	4.95	5.20	9.4	3.7	5.4	1.0	1.6	—
2003	SAR	A+	21	7	5	1	21	20	104.3	74	59	74	4	—	.227	-11	1.28	3.02	6.02	5.27	8.5	6.2	4.6	1.1	3.5	—
2005	CHT	AA	23	4	12	0	24	24	127.7	115	70	101	4	54%	.305	1	1.45	3.17	4.99	5.21	8.6	5.6	4.7	0.5	5.3	—
2006	*CIN*	*MLB*	*24*	*5*	*9*	*0*	*26*	*20*	*111.3*	*118*	*76*	*73*	*13*	*50%*	*.299*	*-7*	*1.74*	*5.80*	*6.04*	*6.06*	*9.4*	*5.7*	*5.4*	*1.0*	*-8.0*	*-0.1*

Breakout: 6%   Improve: 31%   Collapse: 35%   Attrition: 1%   Comparables: *Charlie Manning, Chuck Crowder, Brian O'Connor*

One of the two prospects the Reds obtained in the controversial Williamson trade in 2003, Dumatrait missed the 2004 season after Tommy John surgery. Despite his 4–14 record, the slender southpaw pitched pretty well in his first year back. Dumatrait is ticketed for Louisville in 2006, but could be called up to Cincinnati in the second half if he continues to keep the ball down while the Reds' other starters don't.

JUSTIN GERMANO Bats: R Throws: R Height: 6' 2" Weight: 190 Born: August 6, 1982 Age: 23

YEAR	TM	LVL	AGE	W	L	SV	G	GS	IP	H	BB	SO	HR	GB%	BABIP	STUFF	WHIP	ERA	PERA	EQERA	EQH9	EQBB9	EQSO9	EQHR9	VORP	WXRL
2004	MOB	AA	21	2	1	0	5	5	32.3	31	7	20	3	—	.286	1	1.18	2.51	4.99	4.40	10.0	2.3	3.8	1.2	4.1	—
2004	POR	AAA	21	9	5	0	20	20	122.7	113	25	98	12	—	.277	19	1.12	3.37	4.22	3.77	8.8	2.0	5.7	1.0	24.3	—
2004	SDN	MLB	21	1	2	0	7	5	21.3	31	14	16	2	53%	.397	-11	2.11	8.87	4.76	10.32	11.1	5.2	5.6	0.8	-9.0	-0.3
2005	POR	AAA	22	7	6	0	19	19	112.0	111	32	100	13	45%	.311	10	1.28	3.70	4.66	4.66	9.2	2.5	6.1	1.2	11.5	—
2005	LOU	AAA	22	3	2	0	8	8	49.3	62	5	38	7	46%	.359	11	1.36	4.02	4.65	4.83	10.5	0.9	5.4	1.4	4.3	—
2006	*CIN*	*MLB*	*23*	*7*	*10*	*0*	*29*	*22*	*139.7*	*153*	*41*	*92*	*20*	*46%*	*.299*	*7*	*1.38*	*4.81*	*5.00*	*4.94*	*9.7*	*2.4*	*5.5*	*1.2*	*6.8*	*1.6*

Breakout: 21%   Improve: 68%   Collapse: 1%   Attrition: 0%   Comparables: *Rick Wise, Adam Eaton, Tom Morgan*

The other part of the booty from the Randa deal (along with Chick), Germano is a righty with a minus fastball whose bread-and-butter pitch is his curve. Without average velocity, he'll need to improve his change-up and have surgical command to survive for long in the bigs. At 24, he's got a couple of years yet, but his ceiling is as a #5 starter.

CARLOS GUEVARA Bats: R Throws: R Height: 6' 0" Weight: 175 Born: March 18, 1982 Age: 24

YEAR	TM	LVL	AGE	W	L	SV	G	GS	IP	H	BB	SO	HR	GB%	BABIP	STUFF	WHIP	ERA	PERA	EQERA	EQH9	EQBB9	EQSO9	EQHR9	VORP	WXRL
2003	DYT	A	21	0	1	0	12	3	39.3	37	14	39	4	—	.295	-15	1.30	3.44	7.25	5.75	11.0	4.2	6.0	2.8	-0.6	—
2004	DYT	A	22	3	4	9	44	0	56.7	47	24	90	6	—	.339	-13	1.25	2.86	6.31	5.26	10.0	5.4	8.2	2.3	1.9	—
2005	SAR	A+	23	4	3	14	44	0	51.3	39	14	65	2	48%	.296	5	1.03	2.46	4.10	4.66	8.2	3.4	7.1	0.7	5.0	—
2006	*CIN*	*MLB*	*24*	*2*	*3*	*1*	*27*	*4*	*51.7*	*55*	*25*	*41*	*10*	*43%*	*.292*	*-4*	*1.54*	*5.30*	*5.99*	*5.35*	*9.4*	*4.0*	*6.5*	*1.7*	*-0.1*	*0.1*

Breakout: 11%   Improve: 44%   Collapse: 21%   Attrition: 18%   Comparables: *Mike Natale, David Cash, Kevin Olore*

A Division II college pitcher, Guevara pitched well in 2005, but then he should be ahead of Class-A hitters at age 23. With a minus fastball, his ticket to The Show will have to be punched by his screwball—a pitch that is very rarely thrown nowadays. To make it, Guevara will have to combat the prejudice against short righties, right-handers with sub-par fastballs, and disciples of Dr. Mike Marshall.

JOSH HALL Bats: R Throws: R Height: 6' 2" Weight: 1 90 Born: December 16, 1980 Age: 25

YEAR	TM	LVL	AGE	W	L	SV	G	GS	IP	H	BB	SO	HR	GB%	BABIP	STUFF	WHIP	ERA	PERA	EQERA	EQH9	EQBB9	EQSO9	EQHR9	VORP	WXRL
2003	CHT	AA	22	8	10	0	26	25	153.0	152	53	114	9	—	.293	-1	1.34	3.47	5.07	5.32	9.4	3.4	4.6	1.1	4.6	—
2003	CIN	MLB	22	0	2	0	6	5	24.7	33	15	18	4	46%	.349	-8	1.95	6.56	5.61	7.36	10.9	4.9	5.6	1.4	-6.6	0.2
2005	SAR	A+	24	0	3	0	7	7	29.0	46	14	21	5	62%	.394	-49	2.07	6.83	8.58	10.16	14.0	5.7	3.8	3.2	-14.3	—
2005	CHT	AA	24	5	6	0	18	18	112.3	115	35	92	7	54%	.329	-1	1.34	3.53	4.98	5.23	9.6	3.2	4.7	1.1	4.5	—
2006	*CIN*	*MLB*	*25*	*5*	*9*	*0*	*26*	*19*	*114.7*	*133*	*50*	*64*	*16*	*51%*	*.305*	*-7*	*1.60*	*5.74*	*5.95*	*6.02*	*10.3*	*3.6*	*4.6*	*1.2*	*-7.6*	*0.0*

Breakout: 26%   Improve: 62%   Collapse: 5%   Attrition: 0%   Comparables: *Clay Hensley, Matt Achilles, Mark Johnson*

(continued next page)

Josh Hall *(continued)*

Hall made his major league debut at 22 in August 2003, at which point his career went off the tracks. Shoulder surgeries at the end of both 2003 and 2004 kept his career stalled, but Hall finally made it back for the first act of his comeback. He pitched well enough to revive hopes, but he needs at least a year before being ready to test himself against big-league lumber—at least, if he's to have a fighting chance. Of course, with the Reds, he might instead be just more cannon fodder.

AARON HARANG Bats: R Throws: R Height: 6′ 7″ Weight: 240 Born: May 9, 1978 Age: 28

YEAR	TM	LVL	AGE	W	L	SV	G	GS	IP	H	BB	SO	HR	GB%	BABIP	STUFF	WHIP	ERA	PERA	EQERA	EQH9	EQBB9	EQSO9	EQHR9	VORP	WXRL
2003	SAC	AAA	25	8	2	0	12	12	69.7	62	17	60	5	—	.277	14	1.13	2.71	4.46	4.18	8.9	2.7	6.3	1.1	10.5	—
2003	OAK	MLB	25	1	3	0	7	6	30.3	41	9	16	5	37%	.350	-7	1.65	5.35	5.23	5.52	11.3	2.6	4.6	1.5	1.0	0.5
2003	CIN	MLB	25	4	3	0	9	9	46.0	48	10	26	6	48%	.290	1	1.26	5.28	4.73	4.93	9.5	1.8	4.5	1.2	1.0	0.8
2004	CIN	MLB	26	10	9	0	28	28	161.0	177	53	125	26	45%	.313	4	1.43	4.86	4.77	4.71	9.5	2.7	6.2	1.3	9.1	2.8
2005	CIN	MLB	27	11	13	0	32	32	211.7	217	51	163	22	40%	.311	20	1.27	3.83	4.03	3.82	8.8	2.0	6.3	0.9	38.9	4.9
2006	*CIN*	*MLB*	*28*	*11*	*11*	*0*	*31*	*31*	*196.3*	*201*	*55*	*142*	*24*	*43%*	*.292*	*15*	*1.30*	*4.19*	*4.48*	*4.28*	*9.1*	*2.3*	*6.0*	*1.1*	*23.4*	*3.9*

Breakout: 13% Improve: 57% Collapse: 10% Attrition: 2% Comparables: *Doc Medich, Ed Halicki, Freddy Garcia*

Harang survived the nine-car pile-up that was the Reds rotation in 2005 quite nicely, blossoming into a solid starter despite his average stuff across the board (two-seamer, four-seamer, cutter, slider, split). His ERA and record were much better in the second half, but that seems flukish, as his other stats were worse. Better command of his sinker resulted in more dead worms and fewer gopher balls. While he's not going to get any better, Harang should be a solid third man in a big league rotation for years to come.

LUKE HUDSON Bats: R Throws: R Height: 6′ 3″ Weight: 190 Born: May 2, 1977 Age: 29

YEAR	TM	LVL	AGE	W	L	SV	G	GS	IP	H	BB	SO	HR	GB%	BABIP	STUFF	WHIP	ERA	PERA	EQERA	EQH9	EQBB9	EQSO9	EQHR9	VORP	WXRL
2004	CHT	AA	27	7	7	0	16	16	86.7	71	25	91	9	—	.284	-13	1.11	3.32	6.09	5.74	9.9	3.6	5.6	1.8	-1.2	—
2004	CIN	MLB	27	4	2	0	9	9	48.3	36	25	38	3	36%	.250	15	1.26	2.42	4.37	3.04	7.4	4.4	6.5	0.6	14.4	2.2
2005	CIN	MLB	28	6	9	0	19	16	84.7	83	50	53	14	39%	.284	-19	1.57	6.38	6.17	6.27	9.2	5.0	5.2	1.5	-9.8	-0.1
2006	*CIN*	*MLB*	*29*	*4*	*7*	*0*	*30*	*13*	*89.3*	*94*	*43*	*60*	*14*	*40%*	*.287*	*-8*	*1.54*	*5.42*	*5.74*	*6.01*	*9.4*	*4.0*	*5.6*	*1.4*	*-1.3*	*0.3*

Breakout: 16% Improve: 44% Collapse: 27% Attrition: 18% Comparables: *Turk Lown, Ken Schrom, Dennis Stark*

Hudson spent the first half of 2005 on the DL with shoulder inflammation, a troubling sign for a pitcher who missed all of 2003 after surgery on his labrum. He can throw the speedball in the mid-90s, but his command isn't usually good unless he takes something off of it, but that means taking risks when hitters set it on "dead red." With a minus change-up, Hudson needs to harness his sharp breaking ball and learn better control if he is going to fulfill his potential.

BEN KOZLOWSKI Bats: L Throws: L Height: 6′ 6″ Weight: 220 Born: August 16, 1980 Age: 25

YEAR	TM	LVL	AGE	W	L	SV	G	GS	IP	H	BB	SO	HR	GB%	BABIP	STUFF	WHIP	ERA	PERA	EQERA	EQH9	EQBB9	EQSO9	EQHR9	VORP	WXRL
2003	FRI	AA	22	3	2	0	11	10	54.7	71	27	29	4	—	.332	-23	1.79	5.43	6.33	7.00	11.3	5.2	3.5	1.3	-8.4	—
2004	STO	A+	23	4	2	0	10	8	47.0	40	19	32	1	—	.275	-10	1.26	3.83	5.11	6.14	8.8	5.1	3.9	0.4	-2.6	—
2004	FRI	AA	23	3	2	1	8	7	38.7	38	20	23	5	—	.277	-30	1.50	4.88	7.25	7.00	10.5	5.8	3.8	2.0	-5.6	—
2005	CHT	AA	24	4	4	0	20	20	111.3	129	31	82	10	52%	.337	-17	1.44	4.04	5.75	5.92	10.8	2.9	4.2	1.6	-3.8	—
2005	LOU	AAA	24	2	3	0	8	8	44.7	52	18	30	3	43%	.340	0	1.57	4.63	4.60	5.80	9.8	4.0	4.6	0.6	-1.0	—
2006	*CIN*	*MLB*	*25*	*5*	*9*	*0*	*30*	*18*	*110.3*	*134*	*52*	*58*	*18*	*48%*	*.308*	*-13*	*1.68*	*6.05*	*6.52*	*6.28*	*10.8*	*3.9*	*4.3*	*1.5*	*-10.4*	*-0.3*

Breakout: 15% Improve: 49% Collapse: 17% Attrition: 1% Comparables: *Jeff Andra, Nate Teut, Lance Caraccioli*

After 2003 Tommy John surgery and October 2004 arthroscopic surgery on his elbow, Kozlowski has yet to regain either the velocity on his fastball or command of his curveball. His eight starts in Louisville at the end of 2005 were promising, but they were his first exposure in Triple-A and he'll need at least another season before he's ready to be tested in the big tent.

KENT MERCKER   Bats: L Throws: L   Height: 6' 2"   Weight: 190   Born: February 1, 1968   Age: 38

YEAR	TM	LVL	AGE	W	L	SV	G	GS	IP	H	BB	SO	HR	GB%	BABIP	STUFF	WHIP	ERA	PERA	EQERA	EQH9	EQBB9	EQSO9	EQHR9	VORP	WXRL
2003	ATL	MLB	35	0	0	1	18	0	17.0	15	7	7	1	37%	.246	-13	1.29	1.06	4.32	1.62	8.6	3.2	3.2	0.5	7.6	0.2
2003	CIN	MLB	35	0	2	0	49	0	38.3	31	25	41	5	45%	.283	5	1.46	2.35	4.70	3.05	7.7	5.2	8.7	1.2	10.9	-0.2
2004	CHN	MLB	36	3	1	0	71	0	53.0	39	27	51	4	41%	.259	11	1.25	2.55	4.15	2.60	7.4	4.3	7.8	0.7	18.8	1.3
2005	CIN	MLB	37	3	1	4	78	0	61.7	64	19	45	8	44%	.304	-4	1.35	3.65	4.62	3.90	9.0	2.6	5.9	1.2	10.8	1.1
2006	*CIN*	*MLB*	*38*	*2*	*2*	*2*	*39*	*0*	*36.3*	*38*	*14*	*27*	*5*	*44%*	*.294*	*-7*	*1.42*	*4.41*	*4.85*	*4.66*	*9.3*	*3.2*	*6.2*	*1.2*	*3.7*	*0.3*

Breakout: 10%   Improve: 19%   Collapse: 61%   Attrition: 28%   Comparables: Mike Stanton, Dennis Cook, Tug McGraw

Mercker's average two-seamer is complemented by a good change-up which he turns over to lefties so it fades down and away. However, his minus curve and slider leave him with no out pitch against right-handers, meaning he's now just a designated lefty. Now that the Reds have added Chris Hammond, a pitcher better against both righties and lefties than Mercker, the question as to why the club needed to spend $2.6 million over two years for Mercker's limited functionality deserves to be asked.

ERIC MILTON   Bats: L Throws: L   Height: 6' 3"   Weight: 220   Born: August 4, 1975   Age: 30

YEAR	TM	LVL	AGE	W	L	SV	G	GS	IP	H	BB	SO	HR	GB%	BABIP	STUFF	WHIP	ERA	PERA	EQERA	EQH9	EQBB9	EQSO9	EQHR9	VORP	WXRL
2003	MIN	MLB	27	1	0	0	3	3	17.0	15	1	7	2	37%	.236	7	0.94	2.65	4.41	2.76	8.8	0.6	3.9	1.1	6.3	0.5
2004	PHI	MLB	28	14	6	0	34	34	201.0	196	75	161	43	33%	.271	-6	1.35	4.75	5.41	4.91	9.2	3.1	6.5	1.8	19.4	3.0
2005	CIN	MLB	29	8	15	0	34	34	186.3	237	52	123	40	34%	.317	-17	1.55	6.47	5.60	6.40	10.5	2.3	5.3	1.9	-24.3	-0.0
2006	*CIN*	*MLB*	*30*	*9*	*12*	*0*	*32*	*28*	*171.3*	*184*	*50*	*111*	*29*	*37%*	*.285*	*4*	*1.36*	*4.83*	*5.11*	*4.97*	*9.5*	*2.4*	*5.3*	*1.5*	*9.5*	*2.2*

Breakout: 44%   Improve: 78%   Collapse: 7%   Attrition: 5%   Comparables: Mike McCormick, Pete Schourek, Greg Swindell

In the long and sometimes sad history of the Reds, no one had managed to post a full-season 6.47 ERA before Eric Milton did last year, nor allow 40 home runs in a season. Nor has any Reds GM made as illogical a mistake on as important a free-agent signing. It wasn't as if Milton was an unknown quantity, nor was he coming off a career year. His flyball/gopher ball tendencies were not a secret. Milton lives and (mostly) dies with a four-seam fastball. With his velocity down to average at best, and with mediocre off-speed stuff, he's dead meat when he makes a mistake over the plate. A published scouting report on Milton after 2004 said he had a "lot of 'quality intangibles.'" What it didn't say is that major league hitters feast on pitchers with "plus intangibles" and mediocre stuff.

BUBBA NELSON   Bats: R Throws: R   Height: 6' 2"   Weight: 200   Born: August 26, 1981   Age: 24

YEAR	TM	LVL	AGE	W	L	SV	G	GS	IP	H	BB	SO	HR	GB%	BABIP	STUFF	WHIP	ERA	PERA	EQERA	EQH9	EQBB9	EQSO9	EQHR9	VORP	WXRL
2003	GRN	AA	21	8	10	0	23	20	119.0	106	45	77	7	—	.261	-5	1.27	3.18	5.34	4.78	9.3	3.7	4.1	1.1	10.3	—
2004	CHT	AA	22	1	2	0	10	9	53.0	61	12	35	5	—	.320	-8	1.38	4.08	5.26	6.84	10.9	2.3	3.9	1.4	-7.1	—
2004	LOU	AAA	22	1	10	0	12	12	59.7	74	26	45	12	—	.332	-16	1.68	7.09	6.34	7.84	10.9	4.1	5.4	2.0	-14.9	—
2005	CHT	AA	23	2	4	12	42	0	68.3	67	27	70	5	38%	.332	-12	1.38	4.61	5.37	5.92	9.8	4.0	6.1	1.2	-2.3	—
2006	*CIN*	*MLB*	*24*	*2*	*4*	*1*	*28*	*4*	*52.3*	*62*	*26*	*34*	*11*	*39%*	*.301*	*-16*	*1.68*	*6.35*	*6.91*	*6.51*	*10.6*	*4.1*	*5.3*	*1.9*	*-5.9*	*-0.5*

Breakout: 12%   Improve: 44%   Collapse: 22%   Attrition: 11%   Comparables: Jim Abbott, Brian Sanches, Adam Johnson

The Reds system is chock full of ex-Braves prospects, especially former prep pitchers, most of whom the Braves had given up on. Nelson was converted to relief in 2005, pitched tolerably well in Double-A despite minor injuries, then was trashed in nine appearances in the AFL in the fall.

RAMON ORTIZ   Bats: R Throws: R   Height: 6' 0"   Weight: 150   Born: May 23, 1973   Age: 33

YEAR	TM	LVL	AGE	W	L	SV	G	GS	IP	H	BB	SO	HR	GB%	BABIP	STUFF	WHIP	ERA	PERA	EQERA	EQH9	EQBB9	EQSO9	EQHR9	VORP	WXRL
2003	ANA	MLB	30	16	13	0	32	32	180.0	209	63	94	28	42%	.298	-10	1.51	5.20	5.39	5.89	10.4	3.1	4.6	1.3	-3.3	1.2
2004	ANA	MLB	31	5	7	0	34	14	128.0	139	38	82	18	41%	.306	0	1.38	4.43	4.72	4.30	9.4	2.4	5.3	1.2	25.0	1.3
2005	CIN	MLB	32	9	11	0	30	30	171.3	206	51	96	34	45%	.312	-17	1.50	5.36	5.68	5.42	10.2	2.5	4.5	1.8	-3.4	1.4
2006	*WAS*	*MLB*	*33*	*7*	*10*	*0*	*33*	*21*	*143.7*	*150*	*46*	*82*	*20*	*43%*	*.280*	*-5*	*1.37*	*4.48*	*5.21*	*5.40*	*9.7*	*2.6*	*4.5*	*1.3*	*6.4*	*1.5*

Breakout: 26%   Improve: 59%   Collapse: 20%   Attrition: 134%   Comparables: Willie Blair, Jose Lima, John Montefusco

Another of Dan O'Brien's panic moves, Ortiz started out the season with a strained groin and ended with his head posted on a pike on Pete Rose Way. Although Ortiz wasn't good on the road, he was basically pitching batting practice in Cincinnati, compiling a 5.63 ERA as enemy batters hit .332 off him. Unlike in 2003–04, it wasn't just left-handers; everyone was jumping out of their shoes to crush his offerings. At his best, Ortiz throws an average fastball, sinker, and slider and a plus change, but he needs to have good location to succeed. Signed by Washington, look for him to make a "comeback" in 2006 because of RFK's faraway fences and heavy air.

ELIZARDO RAMIREZ Bats: R Throws: R   Height: 6′ 0″   Weight: 140   Born: January 28, 1983   Age: 23

YEAR	TM	LVL	AGE	W	L	SV	G	GS	IP	H	BB	SO	HR	GB%	BABIP	STUFF	WHIP	ERA	PERA	EQERA	EQH9	EQBB9	EQSO9	EQHR9	VORP	WXRL
2003	CLR	A+	20	13	9	0	27	25	157.3	181	33	101	4	—	.323	10	1.36	3.78	4.22	6.71	10.3	2.1	4.0	0.6	-19.2	—
2004	CLR	A+	21	5	1	0	9	9	59.0	55	8	33	3	—	.278	3	1.07	2.44	4.63	4.31	9.6	1.4	3.4	1.0	8.1	—
2004	REA	AA	21	2	5	0	8	8	33.7	51	14	20	4	—	.367	-19	1.93	6.68	5.66	9.26	12.1	3.9	3.9	1.3	-14.2	—
2004	CHT	AA	21	1	0	0	5	5	31.0	35	4	23	6	—	.305	0	1.26	3.19	6.75	4.30	11.7	1.2	4.6	2.8	4.2	—
2005	LOU	AAA	22	7	7	0	21	21	131.3	150	18	82	14	53%	.319	8	1.28	3.77	4.43	4.16	9.7	1.3	4.4	1.1	21.1	—
2005	CIN	MLB	22	0	3	0	6	4	22.3	33	10	9	5	41%	.341	-25	1.93	8.48	6.56	8.10	12.0	3.5	3.1	1.9	-7.7	-0.5
2006	*CIN*	*MLB*	*23*	*7*	*10*	*0*	*38*	*25*	*141.0*	*168*	*36*	*74*	*23*	*48%*	*.304*	*-4*	*1.45*	*5.26*	*5.56*	*5.41*	*10.6*	*2.1*	*4.3*	*1.4*	*-0.5*	*0.8*

Breakout: 20%   Improve: 64%   Collapse: 2%   Attrition: 0%   Comparables: Joe Niekro, Mark Lemongello, Bob Friend

The thin righty made four emergency starts for the Reds in 2005, but he's not as close as that might seem to being ready for primetime. He lacks a plus pitch and, while he posted a good ERA in Louisville, his peripheral numbers were headed in the wrong direction.

BRIAN SHACKELFORD Bats: L Throws: L   Height: 6′ 1″   Weight: 190   Born: August 30, 1976   Age: 29

YEAR	TM	LVL	AGE	W	L	SV	G	GS	IP	H	BB	SO	HR	GB%	BABIP	STUFF	WHIP	ERA	PERA	EQERA	EQH9	EQBB9	EQSO9	EQHR9	VORP	WXRL
2004	LOU	AAA	27	8	1	0	59	0	73.0	58	42	63	6	—	.263	-14	1.37	3.58	5.35	4.30	8.1	6.3	6.0	0.9	10.0	—
2005	LOU	AAA	28	1	6	1	31	0	32.7	35	10	21	1	57%	.333	-13	1.38	5.23	4.18	5.57	9.2	3.3	4.2	0.3	0.1	—
2005	CIN	MLB	28	1	0	0	37	0	29.7	21	9	17	2	45%	.226	-3	1.01	2.42	4.40	2.83	7.8	2.5	5.0	0.6	9.1	0.4
2006	*CIN*	*MLB*	*29*	*1*	*2*	*1*	*46*	*0*	*36.0*	*39*	*17*	*22*	*5*	*48%*	*.296*	*-15*	*1.55*	*5.02*	*5.51*	*5.86*	*9.7*	*3.8*	*5.1*	*1.2*	*0.7*	*0.0*

Breakout: 13%   Improve: 27%   Collapse: 49%   Attrition: 41%   Comparables: Dennis Powell, Rich Rodriguez, Mike Munoz

Converted from the outfield to pitching in mid-2002, Shackelford became a prospect in 2004. He pitched credibly in limited exposure in Cincy in the second half, replacing Keisler in the borderline superfluous/second lefty middle relief role. Shackelford is a sinker-cutter pitcher who, given his limited pitching pedigree, could well develop enough command with experience to graduate to a more important bullpen role. He was effective against right-handed hitters as well, a very good omen.

ALLAN SIMPSON Bats: R Throws: R   Height: 6′ 4″   Weight: 180   Born: August 26, 1977   Age: 28

YEAR	TM	LVL	AGE	W	L	SV	G	GS	IP	H	BB	SO	HR	GB%	BABIP	STUFF	WHIP	ERA	PERA	EQERA	EQH9	EQBB9	EQSO9	EQHR9	VORP	WXRL
2003	TAC	AAA	25	2	5	1	43	0	62.7	60	42	69	7	—	.308	-16	1.63	4.16	6.37	5.31	9.6	7.4	8.2	1.7	1.9	—
2004	CSP	AAA	26	2	1	4	27	0	35.3	30	10	43	1	—	.333	16	1.13	2.80	3.67	3.93	8.4	2.9	7.9	0.3	6.4	—
2004	COL	MLB	26	2	1	0	32	0	39.0	44	20	46	4	40%	.392	14	1.64	5.08	3.76	5.31	9.1	4.0	9.1	0.7	1.2	0.0
2005	LOU	AAA	27	4	4	1	50	0	64.3	51	38	89	5	33%	.315	6	1.38	4.06	4.67	4.82	8.0	6.3	9.3	0.9	5.3	—
2006	*CIN*	*MLB*	*28*	*2*	*3*	*1*	*46*	*2*	*47.7*	*47*	*33*	*46*	*7*	*39%*	*.302*	*-3*	*1.67*	*5.51*	*5.93*	*5.95*	*8.7*	*5.7*	*8.0*	*1.3*	*-1.2*	*-0.1*

Breakout: 26%   Improve: 50%   Collapse: 23%   Attrition: 22%   Comparables: John D'Acquisto, Doug Bair, Eric Plunk

The hard-throwing right-hander with perpetual control problems started the season in Colorado, then was traded to the Reds for Jose Acevedo, and finished out the minor league season in Louisville before being given a shot of espresso in the Queen City. He pitched extremely well in the high-profile AFL, which puts a bullet next to his name on the roster of a team like the Reds with a pitching staff in flux. A true coach's project.

JASON STANDRIDGE Bats: R Throws: R   Height: 6′ 4″   Weight: 230   Born: November 9, 1978   Age: 27

YEAR	TM	LVL	AGE	W	L	SV	G	GS	IP	H	BB	SO	HR	GB%	BABIP	STUFF	WHIP	ERA	PERA	EQERA	EQH9	EQBB9	EQSO9	EQHR9	VORP	WXRL
2003	DUR	AAA	24	2	4	1	12	10	60.0	62	28	37	5	—	.285	-14	1.50	4.50	5.65	5.65	9.9	5.2	4.4	1.1	-0.3	—
2003	TBA	MLB	24	0	5	0	8	7	35.3	38	16	20	7	47%	.279	-14	1.53	6.37	6.17	6.17	10.0	4.1	4.9	1.8	-1.4	0.5
2004	DUR	AAA	25	8	4	0	20	20	119.3	120	44	76	7	—	.301	6	1.37	3.85	4.63	4.71	9.1	3.8	4.4	0.6	11.5	—
2005	OKL	AAA	26	5	3	0	15	10	76.0	83	36	47	3	58%	.336	-2	1.57	4.50	4.76	5.47	9.3	4.5	3.9	0.5	1.1	—
2005	CIN	MLB	26	2	2	0	32	0	31.0	38	16	17	3	52%	.347	-16	1.74	4.06	5.06	3.94	9.8	4.2	4.5	0.8	4.9	0.2
2006	*CIN*	*MLB*	*27*	*3*	*5*	*1*	*40*	*6*	*70.3*	*82*	*36*	*42*	*9*	*52%*	*.311*	*-14*	*1.66*	*5.62*	*6.02*	*5.87*	*10.3*	*4.2*	*4.9*	*1.1*	*-4.0*	*-0.2*

Breakout: 16%   Improve: 47%   Collapse: 34%   Attrition: 8%   Comparables: Steve Comer, Dallas Green, Ken Clay

A 1997 1st rounder for Tampa Bay, Standridge spent eight years harnessing his control while losing his fastball along the way. The Reds signed him in July after he had refused an outright assignment by Texas, and converted him to relief, where he continued to be pounded. A favorite of GM Dan O'Brien, he fits the profile: a former prep standout who's toiled for a long time in the minors without great success. He has no future in the majors.

PAUL WILSON Bats: R Throws: R   Height: 6' 5" Weight: 235 Born: March 28, 1973   Age: 33

YEAR	TM	LVL	AGE	W	L	SV	G	GS	IP	H	BB	SO	HR	GB%	BABIP	STUFF	WHIP	ERA	PERA	EQERA	EQH9	EQBB9	EQSO9	EQHR9	VORP	WXRL
2003	CIN	MLB	30	8	10	0	28	28	166.7	190	50	93	24	46%	.302	-3	1.44	4.64	4.99	4.83	10.0	2.4	4.5	1.2	9.0	2.6
2004	CIN	MLB	31	11	6	0	29	29	183.7	192	63	117	26	45%	.293	2	1.39	4.36	4.91	4.27	9.4	2.8	5.1	1.2	21.2	4.1
2005	CIN	MLB	32	1	5	0	9	9	46.3	68	17	30	10	42%	.367	-13	1.83	7.78	5.92	7.40	11.5	3.0	5.2	1.8	-12.1	-0.5
2006	CIN	MLB	33	5	8	0	30	17	112.7	128	37	67	18	43%	.297	-6	1.46	5.23	5.50	5.67	10.1	2.8	4.9	1.4	0.6	0.7

Breakout: 13%   Improve: 42%   Collapse: 26%   Attrition: 9%   Comparables: Mike Smithson, Jim Lonborg, Aaron Sele

When healthy, Wilson has dead-average stuff, mixing two-seamers, four-seamers, curves, and change-ups effectively, and pitching to spots. The 2004 season was Wilson's sixth in The Show, and it was his first with a winning record, as well as his first allowing fewer hits than IP, though his Adjusted ERA was still a bit below league average. During his career year, he made his fourth trip to the DL as well, albeit a brief stint for a sore lower back. The rose-colored glasses were donned, and the club signed the popular and competitive hurler to a two-year, $8 million deal despite reports that his shoulder was not 100%. In 2005, he missed two thirds of the season with a rotator cuff and frayed labrum. Further deponent sayeth not.

RYAN WAGNER Bats: R Throws: R   Height: 6' 4" Weight: 210 Born: July 15, 1982   Age: 23

YEAR	TM	LVL	AGE	W	L	SV	G	GS	IP	H	BB	SO	HR	GB%	BABIP	STUFF	WHIP	ERA	PERA	EQERA	EQH9	EQBB9	EQSO9	EQHR9	VORP	WXRL
2003	CIN	MLB	20	2	0	0	17	0	21.7	13	12	25	2	53%	.229	21	1.15	1.66	3.80	1.69	6.3	4.6	9.3	0.8	9.5	1.1
2004	CIN	MLB	21	3	2	0	49	0	51.7	59	27	37	7	55%	.317	-8	1.66	4.70	4.96	5.13	9.7	4.3	5.6	1.0	0.5	-0.3
2005	CIN	MLB	22	3	2	0	42	0	45.7	56	17	39	4	64%	.366	3	1.60	6.11	4.15	6.23	9.6	3.0	6.8	0.8	-4.7	-0.5
2006	CIN	MLB	23	2	3	2	40	1	49.7	51	22	40	4	55%	.311	4	1.45	4.24	4.53	4.82	9.0	3.6	6.7	0.7	5.0	0.4

Breakout: 34%   Improve: 60%   Collapse: 10%   Attrition: 31%   Comparables: Terry Adams, Eric King, Elias Sosa

Wagner was disabled on July 8 and missed the rest of 2005 with an inflamed shoulder. He pitched well the first two months before his shoulder acted up and he started getting bombed. One of Wagner's big problems is that there isn't enough difference in speed between his tight, plus slider and his two-seam fastball. Unless he regains some velocity when his shoulder heals, he will need a better change-up or a split to upset hitters' timing. Given his youth and lack of experience (128 pro IP in less than two and a half seasons), Wagner still has a chance to develop into a good reliever.

DAVE WEATHERS Bats: R Throws: R   Height: 6' 3" Weight: 231 Born: September 25, 1969 Age: 36

YEAR	TM	LVL	AGE	W	L	SV	G	GS	IP	H	BB	SO	HR	GB%	BABIP	STUFF	WHIP	ERA	PERA	EQERA	EQH9	EQBB9	EQSO9	EQHR9	VORP	WXRL
2003	NYN	MLB	33	1	6	7	77	0	87.7	87	40	75	6	52%	.325	10	1.45	3.08	4.06	3.55	8.8	3.7	6.8	0.6	21.6	2.8
2004	NYN	MLB	34	5	3	0	32	0	33.7	41	15	25	5	51%	.343	-10	1.66	4.27	5.24	4.98	10.5	3.7	5.8	1.3	2.1	-0.4
2004	HOU	MLB	34	1	4	0	26	0	32.0	31	13	26	5	50%	.295	-5	1.38	4.78	5.34	5.34	9.0	3.4	6.5	1.4	0.2	-0.4
2005	CIN	MLB	35	7	4	15	73	0	77.7	71	29	61	7	52%	.283	3	1.29	3.94	4.15	4.04	8.1	3.1	6.5	0.8	11.6	2.6
2006	CIN	MLB	36	3	4	7	57	0	64.7	66	25	47	7	50%	.295	-7	1.41	4.34	4.68	4.98	9.1	3.2	5.9	1.0	5.8	0.5

Breakout: 19%   Improve: 37%   Collapse: 36%   Attrition: 20%   Comparables: Jose Mesa, Todd Jones, Tim Worrell

Weathers has a limited bag of tricks—four-seamer, sinker, and slider—all slightly above average. He depends on good command and keeping the ball on the ground while outsmarting the hitters. He was able to do that very well outside of the Great American Big Fly Ballpark in 2005, but opposing hitters tattooed his number onto the right field wall in Cincy. Weathers was the club's closer in the second half, racking up double-digit saves for the first time in his career. Cincinnati would be a lot better off if Todd Coffey can mature into a closer and leave Weathers to pitch the seventh and eighth innings, but they may not have the luxury of that choice.

Line Outs

Position/Player	TM	LVL	AGE	PA	R	2B	3B	HR	RBI	BB	SO	SB-CS	SPEED	BA/OBP/SLG	MLVR	EQBA/OBP/SLG	EQA	VORP
OF C. Dickerson*	SAR	A+	23	498	68	17	7	11	43	53	124	19-3	7.2	.236/.325/.383	-.006	.210/.287/.344	.228	-19.3
C M. Perez	SAR	A+	21	311	36	11	0	4	33	16	63	7-1	5.5	.268/.305/.347	-.064	.238/.275/.313	.213	-14.4
	LOU	AAA	21	80	5	3	0	1	5	5	19	0-0	2.8	.208/.275/.292	-.330	.184/.244/.254	.184	-6.9
OF J. Romano	LOU	AAA	26	241	34	17	2	4	32	14	36	5-1	5.9	.308/.349/.455	.094	.278/.321/.414	.256	5.4
C D. Sardinha	LOU	AAA	26	327	36	10	0	10	36	22	72	1-0	3.7	.224/.284/.358	-.216	.195/.251/.305	.200	-20.8
OF B. J. Szymanski#	DYT	A	22	214	32	8	1	10	26	21	57	7-1	4.9	.262/.332/.471	.095	.223/.282/.406	.238	-2.6

Pitcher	TM	LVL	AGE	W	L	SV	IP	H	BB	SO	HR	GB%	BABIP	STUFF	WHIP	ERA	PERA	EQERA	EQH9	EQBB9	EQSO9	EQHR9	VORP
R. Gardner	CHT	AA	23	3	6	0	66.0	80	24	47	6	61%	.359	-18	1.58	5.73	5.85	7.24	10.9	3.6	4.2	1.5	-11.8
J. Hancock	LOU	AAA	27	1	2	0	44.0	59	17	38	5	56%	.394	-8	1.73	5.93	5.24	6.85	10.9	3.8	5.4	1.2	-6.2
R. Keisler*	LOU	AAA	29	5	2	2	56.3	54	13	46	6	41%	.293	1	1.19	2.88	4.77	3.79	9.1	2.5	5.3	1.3	11.0
	CIN	MLB	29	2	1	0	56.0	64	28	43	10	39%	.303	-15	1.64	6.27	5.49	6.91	9.6	4.1	6.1	1.6	-10.4
C. Medlock	SAR	A+	22	6	3	0	108.7	95	22	98	6	38%	.295	4	1.08	3.06	4.43	4.77	8.9	2.3	5.2	1.0	9.6
J. Valentine	LOU	AAA	25	0	7	3	53.7	56	39	44	4	40%	.329	-24	1.77	5.70	5.81	6.15	9.2	7.3	5.6	0.9	-3.2

Chris Dickerson advanced to the rear in 2005, his first year in fast competition. Although he's athletic and projectible, he's got to turn it around in 2006 if he is to have a meaningful future. **Miguel Perez** is the prototype of a poor prospect touted by an organization because their larder is bare. A catch-and-throw backup receiver in the majors at best. **Jason Romano** became a free agent when the Reds tried to outright him in July, and signed with the Marlins before missing the rest of the season with a bum knee. If healthy, he could help as a fifth outfielder. **Dane Sardinha** turned in his worst pro season in terms of EQA; his campaign was ended in early August by a sprained MCL. In talking about **B. J. Szymanski,** you have a right to be skeptical when the first thing you read about a baseball player is how good of a football player he was in college. Szymanski will be almost 24 before he gets his 300th pro AB.

Jung Bong spent the year on the DL. He started out recuperating from 2004 shoulder surgery, then had his left hand broken by a hard ground ball in his first rehab game. **Rich Gardner** was the Reds' Minor League Player of the Year in 2004; they might as well have painted a big, fat target on his back, because he went down in May trying to pitch through biceps tendinitis, then came back to find he needed shoulder surgery. It'll be a miracle if he returns to anything like his 2004 form before 2007. **Josh Hancock** spent much of 2005 struggling with injuries, and most of the rest getting pasted. Designated for assignment in January when the Reds signed Grant "Declaration" Balfour. **Randy Keisler** fell flat on his keister in the most extended audition in the majors of his eight-year pro career. The soft-tossing lefty didn't neutralize lefties with his big curve or keep right-handed hitters at bay with his change-up. A low-ceiling, low-round college draftee in 2002, **Calvin Medlock** has the kind of stuff that can get hitters out in the low minors but usually fails in the higher levels. The Reds non-tendered **Joe Valentine** in December, allowing him to sign with Houston, an organization that has a lot better idea of what to do with young pitchers. Valentine still has mid- to high-90s velocity, but he has failed completely to develop a usable second pitch. Good coaching and a fresh start might yet make him a successful pitcher.

Cleveland Indians

In April 2005, Cleveland Indians general manager Mark Shapiro signed two of his young stars to long-term contracts, extended the contract of a third, and got to enjoy watching his team thrust itself back into the AL Central race for the first time since 2001. In many ways, Shapiro's actions, in conjunction with his team's on-field improvement, were reminiscent of the dawn of the great Indians teams of the '90s, when his predecessor, John Hart, executed a strategy of buying out the arbitration years of his young stars to control costs and sustain his team's success. While the similar approach is more than mere coincidence—Shapiro joined Hart's front office just six months into the latter's tenure as GM and learned by watching—the financial realities of Cleveland baseball are very different. A half-decade into the new millennium suggest that Shapiro will have to attempt to replicate Hart's successes with a fraction of the budget, especially relative to the league.

Watching Shapiro face the challenge of winning big in a small market brings to mind something Bill James wrote in his 1992 *Baseball Book.* Around the same time that baseball's first small-market casualty, the Pittsburgh Pirates, lost four-time All-Star Bobby Bonilla to the New York Mets, James theorized that after 15 years of free-agency, the spending potential of the smaller market teams had finally been maxed out, and the immediate result would be the reversal of a century's worth of increasing on-field parity. To James, the leading indicator of the health of the game's economic structure would be the future success, or lack thereof, of a particular small-market team that couldn't even compete when the playing field was level. "The Cleveland Indians," James wrote of baseball's worst team during its most balanced decade, "are the canary in baseball's coalmine."

James concluded his essay with the words "the canary just dropped off the perch," but the Indians began to move toward the other end of the competitive spectrum that very fall. In September 1991, owner Dick Jacobs promoted Hart, who had spent the previous two seasons as the Indians' director of baseball operations, to general manager, assigning him the task of taking a franchise that had come within eleven games of first place just twice since 1960 and turning it into a winner by the time the Indians would move into their new ballpark in 1994.

INDIANS PROSPECTUS

2005 record: 93–69; Second place, AL Central

Pythagenport record: 96–66

Runs scored per game: 4.88 (4th in AL)

Runs allowed per game: 3.96 (1st in AL)

Team EqA: .273 (3rd in AL)

2005 Batters Age: 28.0 (Youngest in AL)

2005 Pitchers Age: 28.9 (7th oldest in AL)

Ballpark: Jacobs Field; Moderate pitcher's park; Park Factor of 0.962

2005: Came on like gangbusters, but a closing slump kept them just out of the playoffs.

2006: With outstanding depth and young talent, they'll pressure the champs from wire to wire.

The promotion of Hart was stage two of what Jacobs called his "Blueprint for Success," which began with the acquisition of young talent via the draft and high-profile trades under Hart's predecessor Hank Peters. Thanks to Peters and his staff, the organization Hart inherited already possessed Albert Belle, Carlos Baerga, Sandy Alomar, Jr., Charles Nagy, Jim Thome, and Brian Giles, and they had just drafted a young Manny Ramirez. This was nothing new—the Indians cultivated talent before, most notably in the mid-80s. Where Hart's Indians diverged from previous clubs was Hart's ability to turn that talent into a competitive team. He complemented those homegrown players with young players, such as Kenny Lofton, Paul Sorrento, Jose Mesa, and Omar Vizquel, acquired cheaply from other organizations, plus a few veterans whose salary had declined with age, like Eddie Murray and Orel Hershiser. Having taken over a team that lost 105 games in 1991, Hart made the Indians a contender in just his third season as GM, and in his fourth built a playoff team, Cleveland's first in more than 40 years.

Hart's rapid success was striking, but even more impressive was the manner in which he anticipated the ability of an up-and-coming young team to price itself out of existence through rising salaries. Following his first full season as GM, Hart began signing his young stars to multi-year contracts—Baerga, Lofton, Belle, and Sorrento that winter, Thome and Alomar the next year, Ramirez and Omar Vizquel prior to the 1996 season—locking them into reasonable salaries through their arbitration years. Sometimes he'd trade them in advance of their free agency, receiving valuable puzzle pieces such as David Justice, Bob Wickman, and Jeff Kent, who became a trading chip himself. Other times, he'd hold onto them until their free agency arrived, then replace them with the fruits of his farm system.

The result was not just winning, but sustained winning. Hart's Indians won their division in six of the seven years following the 1994 strike, and reached the World Series twice. Hart's team-building skills allowed the Cleveland canary to spread its wings, but what allowed it to not only survive but soar alongside the superstation-powered Braves and megamarket Yankees was the combination of Hart's sound financial strategy coincident with winning and moving into a new ballpark. Having delivered a winner in conjunction with the opening of Jacobs Field, Hart benefited from the increased revenue flow of a new ballpark that sold out a record 455 consecutive games. The result was a ballclub that could afford one of the seven highest payrolls in baseball each year from 1996–2001 and the means to fill holes with high-priced All-Stars such as Justice, Matt Williams, Travis Fryman, Roberto Alomar, Chuck Finley, Ellis Burks, and Juan Gonzalez.

Still, even with Hart's careful financial planning, the bill eventually came due as high payrolls, an aging roster, and declining revenue all combined to hobble the Indians by 2002. When Hart left at the end of the 2001 season, his 34-year-old assistant, Mark Shapiro, inherited the fourth-highest payroll in baseball and an aging team that was losing its footing in an increasingly competitive AL Central. In a way, the Indians, who would suffer their first losing season since 1993 the following year, were back where they started when Hart hired Shapiro as a Baseball Operations Assistant in February 1992, just two years after his graduation from Princeton.

As Director of Minor League Operations beginning in 1994, and later as Assistant General Manager, Shapiro kept the Indians' farm system stocked with talented players such as Victor Martinez, C. C. Sabathia, Jhonny Peralta, Fernando Cabrera, and Fausto Carmona. Upon his promotion to General Manager in November 2001, Shapiro began to repeat the process that built the dominant Indians team of the previous decade while sowing the seeds he had planted under Hart. With a strong minor league system in hand, Shapiro's first order of business was to buy out Sabathia's arbitration years for an average salary of $2.375 million. At the 2002 trading deadline, Shapiro dealt Finley to St. Louis for Coco Crisp, a rare Cardinals prospect.

Previously, he had sent pending free agent ace Bartolo Colon to the Expos for minor leaguers Brandon Phillips, Cliff Lee, and Grady Sizemore. That winter, Shapiro let Jim Thome sign with Philadelphia and used the compensation pick to draft Brad Snyder, one pick in a spectacular draft that also yielded top prospects Michael Aubrey and Adam Miller, and sluggers Ryan Garko and Ryan Mulhern. In the freely available talent department, he added a few undesirables. Rafael Betancourt, for example, was a 27-year-old converted infielder with a metal rod in his pitching elbow; his only big league action came in Japan. Travis Hafner was also an easy get—the Rangers were eager to unload the defensively challenged first base prospect in advance of Mark Teixeira's arrival.

As he waited for that core to develop into a winning ballclub, Shapiro let Vizquel, the last vestige of Hart's Indians, depart via free agency, rounding out his major league club on the cheap with make-good offers to injured players such as Bobby Howry, Aaron Boone, Scott Sauerbeck, Juan Gonzalez, and Kevin Millwood. After his rebuilt Indians threatened the three-time division champion Twins in late 2004, Shapiro wasted little time locking up key components. In April 2005, Shapiro extended Sabathia's contract through 2008—albeit at a dramatically increased salary—and inked Hafner and Martinez to three- and five-year deals, respectively, with average salaries in the $2–3 million range.

Despite stumbling out of the gate with a 9–14 record in April, Shapiro's Tribe rewarded his commitment, catapulting themselves into the AL playoff picture by playing .604 baseball the rest of the way. On September 24, with just seven games left in the season, the Indians found themselves alone in the wild card slot, a game ahead of both the Yankees and Red Sox, and just a game and a half behind the White Sox in the Central. But, just as the Indians' 2004 season appeared to go up in smoke after a single blown lead against the Twins on August 15, their 2005 season ran out of gas when the Tribe blew a 3–0 sixth-inning lead in Kansas City on September 25, resulting in the first of six losses in those final seven games, a run that won the wild card—for Boston.

Five of those six losses came in one-run games, a microcosm of the entire season. How significant were the defeats? In terms of winning percentage, the Indians finished with the fourth-largest discrepancy between their record in one-run games and non-one-run games in Major League history (see table 1).

Bill James's Plexiglass Principle, that teams are most likely to snap back toward .500 (otherwise known as regression to the mean), is especially relevant with regards to a team's record in one-run games. This bodes well for the Indians' chances in 2006, as does the fact that the three

TABLE 1. ONE-RUN WINNING PERCENTAGE DIFFERENTIALS, ALL-TIME

Year	Team	1-Run%	>1%	Diff
1935	NYA	.341	.705	.364
1948	CLE	.333	.696	.363
1963	MIN	.333	.639	.306
2005	CLE	.379	.683	.304

teams ahead of them on the above list all had World Series appearances on their horizons.

There are other positive indicators for the Indians of 2006 and beyond. Excluding the rebuilding seasons of 2003 and 2004, the 2005 team was Cleveland's youngest since 1993. That club finished only 76–86 but was on the verge of embarking on eight winning seasons and a pair of World Series appearances. More significantly, three of the Indians' four best hitters today play three of the four key skill positions: Sizemore in center, Peralta at short, and Martinez behind the plate. That sort of strength up the middle brings to mind the Torre Yankees, with Bernie Williams, Derek Jeter, and Jorge Posada in those same positions.

Given a core of talent which includes two players who will be just 23 on Opening Day and a third, Martinez, entering his peak Age 27 season, and the tremendous production of Hafner, Shapiro has had the luxury of fleshing out his lineup with inexpensive, league-average players while he waits for his farm system to bear more fruit. The result is the B-Squad: Ron Belliard, Ben Broussard, Aaron Boone, and Casey Blake. None of these men are long-term solutions; they are role players whose primary jobs are to keep their positions warm for the moment and avoid negating the production of the Big Four for a while. Meanwhile, Shapiro has expertly balanced risk and cost by hoarding draft picks, focusing on position-player prospects in trades instead of pitchers, who tend to be more volatile (remember: TINSTAAPP, There Is No Such Thing As A Pitching Prospect), and buying low on players such as Millwood, Howry, and Bettancourt.

Shapiro's search for the undervalued has led him to his two major acquisitions for 2006, Paul Byrd and Jason Johnson, who will replace Millwood and Scott Elarton in the rotation. Both Byrd and Johnson throw strikes. Building upon the strides made by Shapiro when he headed the farm system, former Indians hurler and current Director of Player Development John Farrell has introduced organization-wide strike-throwing incentives, where pitchers are rewarded for decreasing their walk rates, increasing their strikeout rates, throwing first-pitch strikes and strikes on 1-1 counts. Last year, under the guidance of pitching coach Carl Willis, four of the five pitchers in the Indians' major league starting rotation posted career-low walk rates, with Millwood posting the second best mark of his career. Howry, Betancourt, David Riske, and Matt Miller posted career-low walk rates out of the major league pen, while Sauerbeck posted his second best.

Farrell's strike-throwing program is an extension of the Indians' increased focus on their farm system, which is ready to produce several key players. Broussard and Blake failed to provide league-average production in 2005, so look for Ryan Garko and Brad Snyder to replace them at some point in 2006. Similarly, while Howry's emergence as an elite setup man led to his reaping big free agent rewards in Wrigley, Francisco Cabrera has emerged as a more than capable replacement. And should anyone in the rotation falter, Fausto Carmona, and perhaps 2004 draftee Jeremy Sowers, will be ready to produce for the big club.

The Indians have improved by at least a dozen games in each of last two seasons. If they simply hold steady in 2006 while working in some or all of those players, they could be one or two key free agents away from ending in 2007 what, in the wake of the mismatched Sox World Series victories of the last two years, is now the second-longest championship drought in baseball.

The only question that remains is if Shapiro, with less financial flexibility than Hart had, will be able to suppress costs while continuing to improve the team. The launch of the team's new television network will give him some extra room to maneuver, but exactly how much remains to be seen. On a certain level, Hart's Indians were a big-spending franchise that needed the revenue generated by those hundreds of consecutive sellouts to finance and feed their success—hardly James's canary, but rather a bird of prey. Until Shapiro's teams purchase that same loyalty from Cleveland consumers, he will not have the same ability to buy his way out of trouble that Hart had in the '90s. Call it Cortez-style team-building: win, or die.

HITTERS

MIKE AUBREY   1B   Bats: L Throws: L   Height: 6′ 0″   Weight: 195   Born: April 15, 1982   Age: 24

YEAR	TM	LVL	AGE	PA	R	2B	3B	HR	RBI	BB	SO	SB	CS	SPEED	BA	OBP	SLG	MLVR	EQBA	EQOBP	EQSLG	EQA	VORP	DEFENSE	
2003	LKC	A	21	154	22	13	0	5	19	14	22	0	0	3.1	.348	.409	.551	.464	.303	.352	.488	.284	8.9	37-1B	5
2004	KIN	A+	22	258	34	14	1	10	60	27	26	3	1	4.0	.339	.438	.550	.461	.310	.388	.521	.306	22.5	49-1B	-2
2004	AKR	AA	22	156	13	7	0	5	22	15	18	0	0	2.5	.261	.340	.425	.012	.225	.295	.366	.235	-5.7	25-1B	1
2005	AKR	AA	23	119	17	5	1	4	20	7	18	1	0	4.0	.283	.336	.462	.103	.263	.312	.441	.261	0.9	24-1B	2
2006	*CLE*	*MLB*	*24*	*332*	*38*	*17*	*1*	*11*	*45*	*21*	*49*	*1*	*1*	*4.1*	*.266*	*.320*	*.435*	*-.007*	*.270*	*.329*	*.460*	*.261*	*6.2*	*80-1B*	*3*

Breakout: 14%   Improve: 43%   Collapse: 34%   Attrition: 20%   Comparables: Milt May, Clay Dalrymple, James Jurries

Some shine came off Aubrey's star in 2004 when Double-A cooled his bat and hamstring problems ended his season. Last year, things got even worse; he again started the season with a cold bat, and an awkward slide into second aggravated an old back injury, ending his season in early June. The injury resulted in lingering pain which repeatedly interrupted his attempts to rehab during the season. After finally giving his back proper rest over the winter, Aubrey is expected to take a third crack at Double-A in the spring.

JOSH BARD   C   Bats: B Throws: R   Height: 6′ 3″   Weight: 210   Born: March 30, 1978   Age: 28

YEAR	TM	LVL	AGE	PA	R	2B	3B	HR	RBI	BB	SO	SB	CS	SPEED	BA	OBP	SLG	MLVR	EQBA	EQOBP	EQSLG	EQA	VORP	DEFENSE
2003	BUF	AAA	25	130	14	7	0	5	21	14	17	1	2	3.1	.330	.408	.522	.355	.308	.388	.508	.298	14.2	29-C 3
2003	CLE	MLB	25	328	25	13	1	8	36	22	53	0	2	2.9	.244	.293	.373	-.143	.247	.302	.387	.238	-0.4	79-C 7
2004	BUF	AAA	26	168	25	10	0	4	18	11	23	0	0	4.4	.263	.310	.404	-.071	.230	.279	.346	.220	-4.6	33-C -1
2005	CLE	MLB	27	94	6	4	0	1	9	9	11	0	0	3.6	.193	.266	.277	-.345	.207	.287	.293	.215	-3.9	25-C 1
2006	*CLE*	*MLB*	*28*	*229*	*21*	*10*	*0*	*5*	*25*	*19*	*33*	*0*	*0*	*4.1*	*.239*	*.305*	*.358*	*-.148*	*.243*	*.314*	*.378*	*.233*	*1.0*	*57-C 0*

Breakout: 34%   Improve: 52%   Collapse: 28%   Attrition: 39%   Comparables: Chris Bando, Alan Ashby, Raul Casanova

Appropriately enough, nobody is claiming to be the author of this Bard's work. A backup catcher straight out of central casting, Bard has a better defensive rep than Victor Martinez, but hasn't shown any ability to hit from either side of the plate. His value in a trade as a plausible starting catcher for somebody else has just about been used up.

BRIAN BARTON   OF   Bats: R Throws: R   Height: 6′ 3″   Weight: 205   Born: April 25, 1982   Age: 24

YEAR	TM	LVL	AGE	PA	R	2B	3B	HR	RBI	BB	SO	SB	CS	SPEED	BA	OBP	SLG	MLVR	EQBA	EQOBP	EQSLG	EQA	VORP	DEFENSE			
2005	LKC	A	23	160	31	14	1	4	32	18	21	7	2	5.4	.414	.506	.624	.711	.347	.413	.510	.316	15.4	25-RF	1		
2005	KIN	A+	23	272	42	15	6	3	32	34	57	13	8	7.0	.274	.404	.435	.175	.242	.340	.381	.254	3.3	32-CF	2	23-LF	1
2006	*CLE*	*MLB*	*24*	*490*	*64*	*29*	*5*	*7*	*48*	*38*	*105*	*13*	*6*	*5.4*	*.276*	*.343*	*.414*	*.012*	*.281*	*.353*	*.437*	*.265*	*13.7*	*116-CF*	*1*		

Breakout: 8%   Improve: 39%   Collapse: 32%   Attrition: 8%   Comparables: Kory DeHaan, Richard Gomez, Jeff Duncan

A non-drafted free agent out of the University of Miami, Barton has excellent patience and decent pop, but acquired a poor defensive reputation in right field despite having decent foot speed. Even worse, his bat cooled significantly after a late-June promotion to Kinston, bad news for a player who will turn 24 in April.

RON BELLIARD   2B   Bats: R Throws: R   Height: 5′ 8″   Weight: 190   Born: April 7, 1975   Age: 31

YEAR	TM	LVL	AGE	PA	R	2B	3B	HR	RBI	BB	SO	SB	CS	SPEED	BA	OBP	SLG	MLVR	EQBA	EQOBP	EQSLG	EQA	VORP	DEFENSE
2003	COL	MLB	28	499	73	31	2	8	50	49	71	7	2	5.8	.277	.351	.409	-.000	.257	.333	.384	.253	15.3	104-2B -7
2004	CLE	MLB	29	663	78	48	1	12	70	60	98	3	2	3.9	.282	.348	.426	.037	.287	.358	.439	.275	29.9	146-2B -5
2005	CLE	MLB	30	579	71	36	1	17	78	35	72	2	2	4.4	.284	.325	.450	.052	.297	.347	.479	.280	24.0	139-2B 11
2006	*CLE*	*MLB*	*31*	*508*	*57*	*28*	*1*	*10*	*58*	*38*	*67*	*2*	*1*	*4.4*	*.267*	*.323*	*.399*	*-.047*	*.271*	*.333*	*.421*	*.252*	*14.8*	*120-2B 0*

Breakout: 13%   Improve: 32%   Collapse: 36%   Attrition: 16%   Comparables: Mike Lansing, Joe Randa, Damion Easley

Belliard has seen his power increase over the past three seasons, but his walk rate has gone the opposite direction, a troubling combination that will result in a severe drop in production when his still-modest power dries up. Meanwhile, Belliard saw a curious spike in his Fielding Rate in 2005, which was either a random fluctuation he's unlikely to repeat, or a result of playing beside Jhonny Peralta. The Indians have picked up his option for 2006, but will have to look elsewhere for a long-term solution at second base.

CASEY BLAKE OF/3B **Bats: R Throws: R** Height: 6' 2" Weight: 195 Born: August 23, 1973 Age: 32

YEAR	TM	LVL	AGE	PA	R	2B	3B	HR	RBI	BB	SO	SB	CS	SPEED	BA	OBP	SLG	MLVR	EQBA	EQOBP	EQSLG	EQA	VORP	DEFENSE		
2003	CLE	MLB	29	613	80	35	0	17	67	38	109	7	9	4.5	.257	.312	.411	-.056	.262	.320	.424	.253	9.7	131-3B	-2	16-1B 0
2004	CLE	MLB	30	667	93	36	3	28	88	68	139	5	8	4.1	.271	.354	.486	.120	.277	.361	.500	.287	27.8	149-3B	-11	
2005	CLE	MLB	31	581	72	32	1	23	58	43	116	4	5	4.3	.241	.308	.438	-.023	.254	.329	.473	.269	4.3	133-RF	2	
2006	CLE	MLB	32	491	57	25	1	17	66	40	98	3	3	4.3	.254	.322	.432	-.016	.258	.332	.456	.260	8.3	116-RF	-2	

Breakout: 10%   Improve: 43%   Collapse: 33%   Attrition: 11%   Comparables: Sam Chapman, Jeff Conine, Jim Lemon

After five years as a waiver-wire hot potato, Blake had his career year in 2004 at the age 30, while playing a brutal third base. Shifted to right field to make room for Aaron Boone, Blake went back to being a spud. Despite leading the AL in pitches per plate appearance in 2005, Blake's bat is light for an infield or outfield corner, which are the only spots he's "capable" of playing (he was second among AL right fielders in errors last year). The Indians inked him to a two-year, $5.4 million deal after his 2004 season, one of Mark Shapiro's few mistakes.

AARON BOONE 3B **Bats: R Throws: R** Height: 6' 2" Weight: 200 Born: March 9, 1973 Age: 33

YEAR	TM	LVL	AGE	PA	R	2B	3B	HR	RBI	BB	SO	SB	CS	SPEED	BA	OBP	SLG	MLVR	EQBA	EQOBP	EQSLG	EQA	VORP	DEFENSE		
2003	CIN	MLB	30	443	61	19	3	18	65	35	74	15	3	6.5	.273	.339	.469	.085	.267	.333	.468	.274	24.8	80-3B	11	18-2B 4
2003	NYA	MLB	30	205	31	13	0	6	31	11	30	8	0	6.1	.254	.302	.418	-.071	.255	.307	.415	.258	6.3	52-3B	5	
2005	CLE	MLB	32	561	61	19	1	16	60	35	92	9	3	4.8	.243	.299	.378	-.121	.256	.320	.407	.254	-2.7	139-3B	0	
2006	CLE	MLB	33	477	56	22	2	14	57	30	76	7	3	5.2	.256	.310	.409	-.065	.260	.319	.431	.249	7.1	113-3B	3	

Breakout: 22%   Improve: 50%   Collapse: 26%   Attrition: 21%   Comparables: Scott Brosius, Chris Sabo, Gary Gaetti

It took Boone two months to get back up to speed after missing all of 2004 with the ACL Tear Heard 'Round the World, but from June 4 on he hit .284/.342/.435, comfortably above average for an AL third baseman. That, combined with the fact that Boone's career numbers are an exact match for average at his position, was enough for the Indians to exercise his 2006 option and add a mutual option for 2007, making him a part of their B-Squad for at least another year.

BEN BROUSSARD 1B **Bats: L Throws: L** Height: 6' 2" Weight: 220 Born: September 24, 1976 Age: 29

YEAR	TM	LVL	AGE	PA	R	2B	3B	HR	RBI	BB	SO	SB	CS	SPEED	BA	OBP	SLG	MLVR	EQBA	EQOBP	EQSLG	EQA	VORP	DEFENSE	
2003	CLE	MLB	26	426	53	21	3	16	55	32	75	5	2	5.1	.249	.312	.443	-.017	.250	.319	.451	.263	4.7	103-1B	-6
2004	CLE	MLB	27	484	57	28	5	17	82	52	95	4	2	5.2	.275	.370	.488	.138	.282	.376	.501	.297	24.2	113-1B	0
2005	CLE	MLB	28	505	59	30	5	19	68	32	98	2	2	5.4	.255	.307	.464	.023	.268	.328	.497	.275	9.2	117-1B	-5
2006	CLE	MLB	29	462	58	24	3	18	65	40	86	3	2	5.3	.261	.330	.461	.039	.265	.340	.486	.271	13.4	109-1B	-1

Breakout: 16%   Improve: 44%   Collapse: 28%   Attrition: 12%   Comparables: Greg Walker, Dave Revering, Gordy Coleman

Broussard has been keeping first base warm for Michael Aubrey for the past three seasons, but with Aubrey indefinitely delayed, Broussard has turned into the guest that wouldn't leave. Broussard's strong finish in 2004 suggested the Tribe might have an embarrassment of riches at first base in 2005 and beyond, but with Aubrey's injury, Broussard's post-age-27 decline and Travis Hafner's entrenchment at DH, Cleveland may soon be forced to turn to Plan D.

JASON COOPER LF **Bats: L Throws: L** Height: 6' 2" Weight: 220 Born: December 6, 1980 Age: 25

YEAR	TM	LVL	AGE	PA	R	2B	3B	HR	RBI	BB	SO	SB	CS	SPEED	BA	OBP	SLG	MLVR	EQBA	EQOBP	EQSLG	EQA	VORP	DEFENSE	
2003	LKC	A	22	301	50	17	7	12	36	32	52	3	2	5.9	.297	.385	.551	.384	.256	.324	.470	.268	4.7	57-LF	3
2003	KIN	A+	22	250	36	17	2	9	36	25	46	3	0	5.3	.307	.380	.528	.348	.288	.353	.517	.293	14.6	36-LF	1
2004	AKR	AA	23	477	54	24	6	14	69	47	106	2	2	4.6	.239	.321	.424	-.037	.213	.287	.374	.230	-23.3	91-LF	-4
2005	AKR	AA	24	245	41	9	2	11	42	30	67	3	2	5.2	.254	.359	.478	.135	.222	.315	.415	.254	-4.1	50-LF	4
2005	BUF	AAA	24	284	43	12	3	14	58	23	76	1	4	4.9	.257	.317	.494	.051	.233	.294	.444	.248	-4.1	69-LF	-3
2006	CLE	MLB	25	480	55	22	2	17	62	41	112	3	2	4.5	.235	.305	.413	-.082	.238	.314	.436	.248	0.4	113-LF	-1

Breakout: 21%   Improve: 51%   Collapse: 21%   Attrition: 10%   Comparables: John-Ford Griffin, Eric Valent, Dave Henderson

A shoulder injury in his sophomore year at Stanford forced Cooper to spend his final two college seasons at DH. He's since gotten back up to speed in the outfield thanks to an excellent work ethic and good speed for a corner outfielder (though the latter hasn't manifested itself on the bases). He hasn't been too much the blue chipper since A-ball, but he has shown increasing power and an inability to hit his fellow lefties. Not a lot of teams scout for reverse platoon players, though.

COCO CRISP　　OF　　Bats: B Throws: R　Height: 6′ 0″　Weight: 180　Born: November 1, 1979　Age: 26

YEAR	TM	LVL	AGE	PA	R	2B	3B	HR	RBI	BB	SO	SB	CS	SPEED	BA	OBP	SLG	MLVR	EQBA	EQOBP	EQSLG	EQA	VORP	DEFENSE			
2003	BUF	AAA	23	258	42	19	6	1	24	26	24	20	8	8.0	.360	.434	.511	.409	.347	.420	.504	.314	32.1	51-CF	4		
2003	CLE	MLB	23	440	55	15	6	3	27	23	51	15	9	7.0	.266	.302	.353	-.147	.270	.313	.365	.237	-7.6	51-CF	-2	39-LF	3
2004	CLE	MLB	24	529	78	24	2	15	71	36	69	20	13	6.2	.297	.344	.446	.057	.305	.355	.459	.275	17.2	89-CF	-9	32-LF	5
2005	CLE	MLB	25	643	86	42	4	16	69	44	81	15	6	6.3	.300	.345	.465	.119	.316	.370	.499	.293	30.2	134-LF	6		
2006	*CLE*	*MLB*	*26*	*662*	*94*	*36*	*5*	*15*	*76*	*47*	*76*	*19*	*7*	*6.3*	*.295*	*.347*	*.445*	*.073*	*.299*	*.357*	*.470*	*.276*	*27.5*	*154-LF*	*2*		

Breakout: 17%　Improve: 53%　Collapse: 15%　Attrition: 1%　　Comparables: Wally Moon, Shannon Stewart, Mark Kotsay

One could argue that Covelli Loyce Crisp was rushed to the majors after being acquired from the Cardinals in the Chuck Finley deal, resulting in some harsh treatment in these pages. Crisp seems to have finally caught up to the league with his peak seasons still ahead of him. A career .299 hitter in the minors, Crisp has hit exactly that in the majors over the past two seasons. In 2005 he added twenty points of slugging, largely via doubles (he tied teammate Travis Hafner for fifth in the AL), and pushed his success rate on the bases past 70 percent. A better defender in left than he was in center, the Tribe can get away with Crisp hitting like a centerfielder in left if Grady Sizemore can hit like a corner outfielder while starting in center.

JASON DuBOIS　　OF　　Bats: R Throws: R　Height: 6′ 5″　Weight: 220　Born: March 26, 1979　Age: 27

YEAR	TM	LVL	AGE	PA	R	2B	3B	HR	RBI	BB	SO	SB	CS	SPEED	BA	OBP	SLG	MLVR	EQBA	EQOBP	EQSLG	EQA	VORP	DEFENSE			
2003	WTN	AA	24	521	57	31	4	15	73	57	118	2	4	3.9	.269	.367	.458	.195	.245	.326	.427	.259	0.2	104-RF	-4	13-1B	-1
2004	IOW	AAA	25	436	75	26	1	31	99	41	97	2	0	4.3	.314	.388	.629	.379	.268	.336	.513	.284	17.4	60-LF	2	19-1B	-1
2005	CHN	MLB	26	152	15	12	0	7	22	7	49	0	1	3.0	.239	.289	.472	.000	.232	.283	.465	.247	1.3	32-LF	-1		
2005	BUF	AAA	26	57	7	3	0	4	10	3	14	1	1	4.1	.283	.333	.566	.201	.238	.293	.450	.247	-0.5	11-RF	-1		
2005	CLE	MLB	26	50	6	0	0	2	2	5	25	0	0	3.2	.222	.300	.356	-.149	.222	.314	.356	.236	-0.8				
2006	*CLE*	*MLB*	*27*	*308*	*37*	*15*	*1*	*14*	*47*	*24*	*81*	*0*	*1*	*4.0*	*.259*	*.325*	*.475*	*.047*	*.263*	*.335*	*.501*	*.272*	*11.2*	*75-LF*	*-2*		

Breakout: 21%　Improve: 51%　Collapse: 19%　Attrition: 28%　　Comparables: Bubba Trammell, Jay Buhner, Josh Phelps

Acquired from the Cubs in a low-profile challenge trade for former Rookie of the Year candidate Jody Gerut, Dubois (pronounced doo-BOYCE) is a fourth outfielder with pop who deserves a chance to beat out Casey Blake for the right field job should the Indians fail to acquire a better option. He must forego the all or nothing approach he's adopted in the majors and rediscover the patience that made his power so valuable in the minors, lest he become the next Jeff Liefer.

RYAN GARKO　　1B/C　　Bats: R Throws: R　Height: 6′ 2″　Weight: 225　Born: January 2, 1981　Age: 25

YEAR	TM	LVL	AGE	PA	R	2B	3B	HR	RBI	BB	SO	SB	CS	SPEED	BA	OBP	SLG	MLVR	EQBA	EQOBP	EQSLG	EQA	VORP	DEFENSE			
2003	MHV	A-	22	181	23	8	1	4	16	12	19	1	1	3.9	.273	.337	.406	.098	.223	.267	.348	.213	-12.2	35-C	-7		
2004	KIN	A+	23	280	44	17	1	16	58	26	34	4	1	4.5	.328	.425	.609	.510	.285	.360	.531	.296	19.8	26-1B	0	21-C	2
2004	AKR	AA	23	194	29	15	0	6	38	14	28	1	0	3.9	.331	.397	.523	.289	.287	.344	.461	.276	11.7	21-C	2	16-1B	2
2005	BUF	AAA	24	518	75	25	3	19	77	44	92	1	3	4.1	.303	.384	.498	.209	.279	.354	.457	.277	19.1	63-1B	-4	55-C	-8
2006	*CLE*	*MLB*	*25*	*489*	*57*	*25*	*1*	*17*	*67*	*33*	*81*	*1*	*1*	*4.2*	*.271*	*.331*	*.447*	*.031*	*.275*	*.341*	*.472*	*.268*	*17.3*	*115-1B*	*-2*		

Breakout: 17%　Improve: 42%　Collapse: 27%　Attrition: 15%　　Comparables: John Ellis, Gus Triandos, Sandy Alomar

Never much of a catcher, Garko has always been able to hit, steamrolling through the Indians' system while hitting like a demon at every level. With first base currently an organizational hole, the Indians had Garko play there in more than half of his games in Triple-A and then full-time in the Arizona Fall League. Garko is expected to start 2006 in Triple-A to continue adapting to his new position, but at least initially he'd make a good platoon partner for Broussard. Regardless, Garko should become the Indians' full-time first baseman before the season is out.

JUAN GONZALEZ　　DH　　Bats: R Throws: R　Height: 6′ 3″　Weight: 220　Born: October 16, 1969　Age: 36

YEAR	TM	LVL	AGE	PA	R	2B	3B	HR	RBI	BB	SO	SB	CS	SPEED	BA	OBP	SLG	MLVR	EQBA	EQOBP	EQSLG	EQA	VORP	DEFENSE
2003	TEX	MLB	33	346	49	17	1	24	70	14	73	1	1	3.9	.294	.329	.572	.187	.287	.327	.564	.290	19.0	53-RF	4
2004	KCA	MLB	34	138	17	4	1	5	17	9	19	0	1	4.3	.276	.326	.441	-.005	.272	.328	.440	.261	2.2	27-RF	-3
2006	*CLE*	*MLB*	*36*	*137*	*14*	*5*	*0*	*4*	*18*	*5*	*24*	*0*	*0*	*3.8*	*.255*	*.285*	*.399*	*-.120*	*.259*	*.293*	*.421*	*.233*	*-0.2*	*36-DH*

Breakout: 4%　Improve: 11%　Collapse: 63%　Attrition: 53%　　Comparables: Frank Thomas, Gary Ward, George Hendrick

Gonzalez hasn't had a healthy season since his first tour with the Indians in 2001. His second stint with the Tribe lasted all of three pitches; after starting the season on the DL with a strained hamstring, in his first game back he re-aggravated the injury grounding out in the top of the first. It would be a shame to have that as Juan Gone's final moment on a major league diamond, but one couldn't blame him for calling it a career at this point, or potential employers preferring to bet on a player with more durability.

FRANKLIN GUTIERREZ   CF   Bats: R Throws: R   Height: 6' 2"   Weight: 175   Born: February 21, 1983   Age: 23

YEAR	TM	LVL	AGE	PA	R	2B	3B	HR	RBI	BB	SO	SB	CS	SPEED	BA	OBP	SLG	MLVR	EQBA	EQOBP	EQSLG	EQA	VORP	DEFENSE	
2003	VRO	A+	20	470	65	28	5	20	68	39	111	17	5	6.5	.282	.345	.513	.230	.246	.301	.476	.263	15.4	102-CF	4
2004	AKR	AA	21	298	38	24	2	5	35	23	77	6	3	5.1	.302	.372	.466	.148	.273	.334	.426	.264	9.5	45-CF	-3
2005	AKR	AA	22	425	70	25	2	11	42	30	77	14	4	6.4	.261	.322	.423	.015	.240	.298	.396	.244	-1.8	82-CF	3
2005	BUF	AAA	22	75	10	6	2	0	7	6	13	2	2	6.9	.254	.320	.403	-.069	.231	.299	.365	.232	-1.3	16-CF	3
2006	*CLE*	*MLB*	*23*	*469*	*58*	*27*	*3*	*14*	*57*	*32*	*98*	*11*	*4*	*5.4*	*.254*	*.312*	*.426*	*-.041*	*.258*	*.321*	*.450*	*.256*	*11.2*	*111-CF*	*0*

Breakout: 27%   Improve: 51%   Collapse: 18%   Attrition: 8%   Comparables: Louis Francisco, Corey Hart, Jesse Barfield

Despite a brief appearance as a pinch-runner with the big club in September, most of Gutierrez's playing time since coming over in the Milton Bradley trade has been at Double-A Akron. An outstanding defender with good speed, Gutierrez could be roaming center in Cleveland as soon as 2007 if the Indians decide to move Grady Sizemore to one of the corners. The only question is his bat, which has been fairly quiet since he left Vero Beach. It'll make the difference between his being a good starter or just a fifth outfielder.

TRAVIS HAFNER   DH   Bats: L Throws: R   Height: 6' 3"   Weight: 240   Born: June 3, 1977   Age: 29

YEAR	TM	LVL	AGE	PA	R	2B	3B	HR	RBI	BB	SO	SB	CS	SPEED	BA	OBP	SLG	MLVR	EQBA	EQOBP	EQSLG	EQA	VORP	DEFENSE	
2003	CLE	MLB	26	324	35	19	3	14	40	22	81	2	1	4.4	.254	.327	.485	.083	.259	.333	.497	.278	11.8	37-1B	-1
2004	CLE	MLB	27	573	96	41	3	28	109	68	111	3	2	4.7	.311	.410	.583	.373	.322	.420	.607	.337	61.8		
2005	CLE	MLB	28	578	94	42	0	33	108	79	123	0	0	4.1	.305	.408	.595	.410	.322	.431	.643	.349	68.7		
2006	*CLE*	*MLB*	*29*	*609*	*86*	*34*	*2*	*33*	*103*	*81*	*124*	*2*	*1*	*4.4*	*.286*	*.389*	*.553*	*.267*	*.291*	*.401*	*.584*	*.317*	*54.9*	*143-DH*	

Breakout: 5%   Improve: 36%   Collapse: 31%   Attrition: 8%   Comparables: Jim Gentile, Mike Epstein, David Ortiz

There are two hulking, late-blooming, cheaply acquired, left-handed designated hitters who have dominated American League pitchers over the past two seasons. One, David Ortiz, was the top American League All-Star vote-getter in 2005 and the subject of a fervent MVP campaign. The other, Travis Hafner, didn't even make the All-Star team, but the argument could be made that Hafner is the superior hitter. In their Age 27 breakout seasons, Hafner posted a .338 EQA to Ortiz's .315. In their superior Age 28 follow-up seasons, Hafner again led, .348 to .321. Ortiz continued to improve last year at 29. There's no reason to expect less from Hafner, who could finally get his due as one of the game's true superstars should the Indians make the postseason.

JOSE HERNANDEZ   UT   Bats: R Throws: R   Height: 6' 1"   Weight: 180   Born: July 14, 1969   Age: 36

YEAR	TM	LVL	AGE	PA	R	2B	3B	HR	RBI	BB	SO	SB	CS	SPEED	BA	OBP	SLG	MLVR	EQBA	EQOBP	EQSLG	EQA	VORP	DEFENSE			
2003	COL	MLB	33	286	33	6	1	8	27	27	95	1	1	4.3	.237	.308	.362	-.157	.221	.294	.344	.226	-0.4	67-SS	-1		
2003	PIT	MLB	33	213	19	9	1	3	21	16	56	1	0	3.7	.223	.282	.326	-.223	.219	.277	.323	.217	-4.5	50-3B	4		
2004	LAN	MLB	34	238	32	12	1	13	29	26	61	3	1	5.0	.289	.370	.540	.256	.288	.368	.533	.300	21.3	38-2B	1		
2005	CLE	MLB	35	253	28	7	0	6	31	14	60	1	3	3.6	.231	.277	.338	-.224	.246	.302	.358	.229	-10.4	38-1B	-2	18-3B	0
2006	*CLE*	*MLB*	*36*	*158*	*17*	*6*	*0*	*5*	*19*	*12*	*38*	*1*	*1*	*4.5*	*.242*	*.302*	*.393*	*-.108*	*.246*	*.311*	*.415*	*.240*	*0.9*	*41-1B*	*0*		

Breakout: 16%   Improve: 42%   Collapse: 34%   Attrition: 53%   Comparables: Gary Ward, Bob Kennedy, Kurt Bevacqua

The short end of a part-time first base platoon, Hernandez made his stellar 2004 campaign look like the fluke it was by providing only a modest improvement over Ben Broussard's numbers against lefties. Hernandez's ability to fill in everywhere but catcher and knock the occasional pitch out of the park will keep him employed, but having already gone through six teams in the last six seasons, he'll run out of takers before long.

JOE INGLETT   UT   Bats: L Throws: R   Height: 5' 10"   Weight: 170   Born: June 29, 1978   Age: 28

YEAR	TM	LVL	AGE	PA	R	2B	3B	HR	RBI	BB	SO	SB	CS	SPEED	BA	OBP	SLG	MLVR	EQBA	EQOBP	EQSLG	EQA	VORP	DEFENSE			
2003	KIN	A+	25	108	21	10	1	0	15	20	14	1	0	5.8	.329	.454	.471	.386	.287	.392	.411	.288	7.6	17-2B	3		
2003	AKR	AA	25	321	41	16	1	4	25	37	36	1	2	3.8	.283	.377	.391	.063	.238	.318	.336	.234	-2.9	66-2B	-3		
2004	AKR	AA	26	298	49	19	7	1	20	31	28	3	5	6.0	.320	.393	.455	.181	.265	.329	.367	.241	4.0	51-2B	-4		
2005	BUF	AAA	27	356	57	20	9	2	40	17	41	13	6	7.2	.330	.376	.465	.177	.296	.338	.412	.261	14.5	54-2B	-1	20-CF	2
2006	*CLE*	*MLB*	*28*	*362*	*41*	*19*	*3*	*3*	*32*	*26*	*46*	*5*	*3*	*5.2*	*.268*	*.325*	*.374*	*-.075*	*.272*	*.335*	*.395*	*.247*	*8.3*	*87-2B*	*-1*		

Breakout: 19%   Improve: 41%   Collapse: 42%   Attrition: 21%   Comparables: Todd Walker, Bill Spiers, Mickey Morandini

(continued next page)

Joe Inglett *(continued)*

Inglett has progressed steadily over his past four minor league seasons. In 2005, he forced his way into the lineup at Triple-A Buffalo, finishing the season with a stellar .330/.376/.465 line. A small, bat-control type, Inglett hits for high average with doubles power and a very low strikeout rate. He's also willing to take a walk. With nothing better than Ramon Vazquez at the major league level, the Indians plan to play Inglett at several positions in Triple-A in the hopes of promoting him to fill a utility role.

KEVIN KOUZMANOFF   3B   Bats: R Throws: R   Height: 6′ 1″   Weight: 200   Born: July 25, 1981   Age: 24

YEAR	TM	LVL	AGE	PA	R	2B	3B	HR	RBI	BB	SO	SB	CS	SPEED	BA	OBP	SLG	MLVR	EQBA	EQOBP	EQSLG	EQA	VORP	DEFENSE	
2003	MHV	A-	21	234	31	8	1	8	33	21	36	2	1	4.1	.272	.342	.437	.141	.229	.283	.385	.232	-4.1	51-3B	11
2004	LKC	A	22	531	74	35	5	16	87	44	75	5	4	4.3	.330	.394	.526	.337	.285	.333	.444	.265	27.3	114-3B	0
2005	KIN	A+	23	287	47	20	4	12	58	24	51	3	1	5.7	.339	.401	.591	.444	.295	.342	.500	.284	23.0	55-3B	5
2006	*CLE*	*MLB*	*24*	*433*	*50*	*23*	*2*	*12*	*54*	*25*	*83*	*2*	*1*	*4.4*	*.261*	*.308*	*.415*	*-.055*	*.265*	*.318*	*.438*	*.250*	*8.9*	*103-3B*	*3*

Breakout: 8%   Improve: 28%   Collapse: 39%   Attrition: 11%   Comparables: Andy Phillips, James Jurries, Greg Dobbs

After injuring his back when he chased a foul ball into a dugout in the Arizona Fall League in 2004, Kouzmanoff, who sniffed Double-A that year, found himself back in the Carolina League to start 2005. He then missed two months due to lingering back pain, dashing his hopes of a promotion. Kouzmanoff continues to rake, but with Aaron Boone re-upped at the major league level, just seven games of experience above A-ball at age 24 and now a problematic back, he is unlikely to be heard from.

VICTOR MARTINEZ   C   Bats: B Throws: R   Height: 6′ 2″   Weight: 170   Born: December 23, 1978   Age: 27

YEAR	TM	LVL	AGE	PA	R	2B	3B	HR	RBI	BB	SO	SB	CS	SPEED	BA	OBP	SLG	MLVR	EQBA	EQOBP	EQSLG	EQA	VORP	DEFENSE			
2003	BUF	AAA	24	314	42	19	0	7	45	26	32	3	5	3.8	.328	.395	.474	.271	.303	.371	.455	.283	23.8	56-C	-9	13-1B	-1
2003	CLE	MLB	24	174	15	4	0	1	16	13	21	1	1	3.4	.289	.345	.333	-.073	.291	.351	.329	.244	2.7	38-C	0		
2004	CLE	MLB	25	591	77	38	1	23	108	60	69	0	1	3.3	.283	.359	.492	.141	.288	.367	.510	.296	39.8	122-C	-8		
2005	CLE	MLB	26	622	73	33	0	20	80	63	78	0	1	3.4	.305	.378	.475	.204	.322	.401	.515	.312	53.2	138-C	-3		
2006	*CLE*	*MLB*	*27*	*586*	*66*	*30*	*1*	*17*	*79*	*57*	*71*	*0*	*1*	*3.6*	*.277*	*.351*	*.437*	*.056*	*.281*	*.362*	*.462*	*.275*	*30.8*	*137-C*	*-1*		

Breakout: 4%   Improve: 23%   Collapse: 42%   Attrition: 1%   Comparables: Earl Battey, Johnny Romano, Terry Steinbach

The switch-hitting Martinez may be the best offensive catcher the game has seen since Mike Piazza was in his prime. Equally dangerous from both sides of the plate, Martinez led major league backstops in VORP and EQA in 2005, his VORP total being nearly 15 runs higher than that of second-place Jason Varitek, and almost twice that of NL leader Michael Barrett. This despite Martinez's stumbling out of the gate—Victor hit .192/.264/.274 through May 27, then flipped the switch and hit .347/.418/.549 over his final 401 at-bats.

RYAN MULHERN   1B   Bats: R Throws: R   Height: 6′ 2″   Weight: 195   Born: November 29, 1980   Age: 25

YEAR	TM	LVL	AGE	PA	R	2B	3B	HR	RBI	BB	SO	SB	CS	SPEED	BA	OBP	SLG	MLVR	EQBA	EQOBP	EQSLG	EQA	VORP	DEFENSE	
2003	MHV	A-	22	253	32	25	1	5	30	19	68	6	2	5.1	.279	.340	.463	.177	.223	.269	.381	.225	-22.4	47-1B	-6
2004	LKC	A	23	414	48	28	1	7	43	32	87	3	2	3.9	.255	.319	.392	-.025	.210	.257	.317	.205	-33.0	95-1B	9
2005	KIN	A+	24	185	32	11	0	17	48	19	50	2	2	3.9	.321	.395	.711	.580	.254	.312	.522	.276	6.8	34-1B	-3
2005	AKR	AA	24	277	40	18	3	15	46	28	64	4	2	4.1	.311	.386	.594	.370	.271	.343	.508	.286	13.9	46-1B	2
2006	*CLE*	*MLB*	*25*	*470*	*51*	*24*	*1*	*15*	*60*	*32*	*128*	*3*	*1*	*3.9*	*.228*	*.286*	*.395*	*-.141*	*.232*	*.294*	*.417*	*.235*	*-6.8*	*111-1B*	*1*

Breakout: 12%   Improve: 36%   Collapse: 31%   Attrition: 14%   Comparables: Earl Snyder, T. R. Marcinczyk, Danny Peoples

Mulhern didn't really factor into the Indians' plans until Aubrey went down with his second season-ending injury in as many years. Meanwhile, Mulhern not only leveled the Carolina League, but continued to crush the ball with Akron after a late-June promotion, finishing fourth in the minor leagues with a combined .640 slugging percentage. If Mulhern can follow up on his breakout minor league season, Ryan Garko might want to watch his back.

JHONNY PERALTA SS Bats: R Throws: R Height: 6' 1" Weight: 180 Born: May 28, 1982 Age: 24

YEAR	TM	LVL	AGE	PA	R	2B	3B	HR	RBI	BB	SO	SB	CS	SPEED	BA	OBP	SLG	MLVR	EQBA	EQOBP	EQSLG	EQA	VORP	DEFENSE			
2003	BUF	AAA	21	255	25	12	1	1	21	15	45	1	3	3.9	.257	.310	.329	-.115	.246	.302	.317	.218	-4.2	60-SS	13		
2003	CLE	MLB	21	268	24	10	1	4	21	20	65	1	3	4.2	.227	.295	.326	-.220	.232	.302	.344	.226	-3.8	69-SS	3		
2004	BUF	AAA	22	623	109	44	2	15	86	54	126	8	4	5.5	.326	.384	.493	.236	.303	.362	.455	.283	47.9	77-SS	-2	59-3B	0
2005	CLE	MLB	23	569	82	35	4	24	78	58	128	0	2	4.3	.292	.366	.520	.231	.307	.390	.559	.314	52.1	137-SS	15		
2006	CLE	MLB	24	552	70	31	3	19	73	51	114	3	2	4.7	.274	.345	.462	.075	.279	.355	.488	.277	34.1	130-SS	7		

Breakout: 15% Improve: 51% Collapse: 24% Attrition: 13% Comparables: Don Money, Wil Cordero, Ron Hansen

If one discounts 2003, when Peralta was forced into the Indians' starting shortstop job well ahead of schedule due to an Omar Vizquel injury, one can see that his outstanding 2005 campaign simply continued the progress he has made at the plate since hitting Double-A in 2002. Handed the shortstop job in spring training, Peralta had nothing less than one of the 20 best seasons ever by a shortstop under the age of 24. In what should have been his rookie season, Peralta was a legitimate Gold Glove and MVP candidate who was overlooked for the former and shut out of the voting for the latter. He should be a cornerstone of this franchise for a long time.

BRANDON PHILLIPS SS Bats: R Throws: R Height: 5' 11" Weight: 190 Born: June 28, 1981 Age: 25

YEAR	TM	LVL	AGE	PA	R	2B	3B	HR	RBI	BB	SO	SB	CS	SPEED	BA	OBP	SLG	MLVR	EQBA	EQOBP	EQSLG	EQA	VORP	DEFENSE			
2003	BUF	AAA	22	170	14	7	0	3	13	12	22	7	3	5.5	.175	.247	.279	-.334	.157	.230	.260	.186	-16.8	42-2B	2		
2003	CLE	MLB	22	388	36	18	1	6	33	14	77	4	5	4.3	.208	.242	.311	-.356	.212	.250	.321	.200	-20.9	103-2B	8		
2004	BUF	AAA	23	579	83	34	4	8	50	44	56	14	11	5.6	.303	.363	.430	.092	.285	.343	.400	.259	20.7	69-2B	1	65-SS	-9
2005	BUF	AAA	24	516	79	24	1	15	46	39	90	7	5	5.2	.256	.326	.409	-.050	.233	.299	.369	.234	-0.1	109-SS	6		
2006	CLE	MLB	25	424	48	21	1	7	41	27	68	6	3	4.6	.252	.306	.371	-.123	.256	.315	.391	.237	6.5	101-SS	2		

Breakout: 38% Improve: 64% Collapse: 17% Attrition: 23% Comparables: Glenn Hoffman, Jerry Hairston, Jay Bell

In an attempt to provide insurance for an unproven Jhonny Peralta as the season began, the Indians moved Phillips back to shortstop in Triple-A. That they didn't move him back to second after Peralta proved he could handle the major league job suggests that Plan B was to try to trade Phillips, who is now out of options. Showcased in the majors just before the trading deadline, he made just two starts before returning to Buffalo, proof of a league-wide lack of interest at the price Shapiro wanted for him. Phillips had his worst minor league season since first reaching Triple-A as member of the Expos' system in 2002. He is now firmly ensconced in the "Promising Prospects Mysteriously Gone Bad" category.

GRADY SIZEMORE CF Bats: L Throws: L Height: 6' 2" Weight: 200 Born: August 2, 1982 Age: 23

YEAR	TM	LVL	AGE	PA	R	2B	3B	HR	RBI	BB	SO	SB	CS	SPEED	BA	OBP	SLG	MLVR	EQBA	EQOBP	EQSLG	EQA	VORP	DEFENSE			
2003	AKR	AA	20	558	96	26	11	13	78	46	73	10	9	6.8	.304	.373	.480	.192	.273	.334	.445	.265	22.2	111-CF	-13	11-LF	1
2004	BUF	AAA	21	472	73	23	8	8	51	42	72	15	10	6.9	.287	.360	.438	.085	.268	.338	.403	.258	11.2	103-CF	-4		
2004	CLE	MLB	21	159	15	6	2	4	24	14	34	2	0	5.6	.246	.333	.406	-.118	.255	.342	.416	.267	0.9	39-CF	-1		
2005	CLE	MLB	22	701	111	37	11	22	81	52	132	22	10	6.8	.289	.348	.484	.149	.306	.373	.523	.298	44.2	153-CF	-4		
2006	CLE	MLB	23	641	89	34	6	19	82	53	106	15	7	6.4	.286	.350	.466	.098	.291	.360	.492	.281	36.5	150-CF	-2		

Breakout: 24% Improve: 56% Collapse: 16% Attrition: 1% Comparables: Todd Hollandsworth, Rondell White, Ellis Burks

The Indians' 2005 starting outfield was supposed to be Casey Blake, Coco Crisp and Juan Gonzalez. That lasted all of three days, as Gonzalez's pulled hamstring forced the Indians to turn to Sizemore sooner than planned. Turns out he was right on time. Despite doing little against lefties (.245/.296/.364) and walking at a rate well below his minor league average (13.58 BB/AB vs. 9.11 BB/AB), Sizemore finished the 2005 season third among major league centerfielders in VORP, behind Andruw Jones and Ken Griffey Jr. He has the speed and mobility for center, although he's still more than a little rough-edged at the position. At 23, there's still plenty of time for him to improve, but if center doesn't work out, a merely adequate arm might push him to left field rather than right.

BRAD SNYDER   **OF**   **Bats: L Throws: L**   Height: 6′ 3″   Weight: 200   Born: May 25, 1982   Age: 24

YEAR	TM	LVL	AGE	PA	R	2B	3B	HR	RBI	BB	SO	SB	CS	SPEED	BA	OBP	SLG	MLVR	EQBA	EQOBP	EQSLG	EQA	VORP	DEFENSE		
2003	MHV	A-	21	270	52	11	6	6	31	41	82	14	5	7.6	.284	.393	.467	.248	.235	.325	.394	.253	4.2	64-CF	-4	
2004	LKC	A	22	361	52	15	5	10	54	48	78	11	4	5.9	.280	.382	.461	.184	.239	.322	.378	.247	0.5	55-CF	2	16-LF 0
2004	KIN	A+	22	125	20	7	1	6	21	13	28	4	2	5.4	.355	.424	.600	.530	.323	.387	.560	.314	16.0	24-CF	-1	
2005	KIN	A+	23	241	36	10	2	6	28	24	64	12	1	7.1	.278	.365	.431	.109	.248	.313	.380	.248	-0.2	47-CF	0	
2005	AKR	AA	23	336	56	21	5	16	54	25	94	5	3	6.3	.280	.345	.539	.213	.253	.315	.489	.269	6.8	37-RF	5	17-LF 0
2006	*CLE*	*MLB*	*24*	*506*	*64*	*24*	*3*	*16*	*60*	*42*	*133*	*10*	*4*	*5.7*	*.251*	*.318*	*.422*	*-.037*	*.255*	*.328*	*.446*	*.257*	*9.5*	*119-CF*	*1*	

Breakout: 19%   Improve: 44%   Collapse: 36%   Attrition: 10%   Comparables: George Lombard, Mel Hall, Vic Wertz

Drafted behind Aubrey in the first round of 2003, Snyder pulled ahead of his injured draft-mate in 2005, tearing through Double-A after a June promotion and continuing his hot hitting in the Arizona Fall League. Snyder has a rifle arm, enough speed to play center, enough power to play the corners, and takes his share of walks. He could be the solution to the Indians' right field problems, perhaps as soon as the second half of this season.

EIDER TORRES   **2B**   **Bats: B Throws: R**   Height: 5′ 8″   Weight: 160   Born: January 16, 1983   Age: 23

YEAR	TM	LVL	AGE	PA	R	2B	3B	HR	RBI	BB	SO	SB	CS	SPEED	BA	OBP	SLG	MLVR	EQBA	EQOBP	EQSLG	EQA	VORP	DEFENSE		
2003	KIN	A+	20	491	63	13	0	1	39	39	73	43	14	6.9	.248	.314	.284	-.116	.227	.282	.266	.210	-30.1	79-2B	9	38-SS 1
2004	KIN	A+	21	469	68	24	3	3	46	22	46	48	6	8.2	.302	.337	.391	.068	.279	.309	.374	.249	4.1	109-2B	1	
2005	AKR	AA	22	484	73	27	5	6	57	16	66	33	9	7.8	.285	.322	.407	.012	.260	.294	.373	.239	-1.7	101-2B	-5	
2006	*CLE*	*MLB*	*23*	*522*	*64*	*25*	*3*	*4*	*39*	*21*	*68*	*29*	*8*	*5.7*	*.260*	*.296*	*.349*	*-.164*	*.264*	*.304*	*.368*	*.233*	*4.6*	*123-2B*	*0*	

Breakout: 25%   Improve: 54%   Collapse: 23%   Attrition: 7%   Comparables: Jason Bourgeois, Maicer Izturis, Ramon Nivar

Despite serving a 15-game steroid suspension in April, Torres actually saw his power increase slightly in his first year of Double-A. Of course, everything's relative: Torres had no power to begin with. Nor does he have any patience at the plate. Torres is a small, bunt-and-run type and an excellent base stealer, but at best he projects as a utility man in the majors. Even with those modest ambitions, he'll have to learn to walk to be of any use.

RAMON VAZQUEZ   **INF**   **Bats: L Throws: R**   Height: 5′ 11″ Weight: 170   Born: August 21, 1976   Age: 29

YEAR	TM	LVL	AGE	PA	R	2B	3B	HR	RBI	BB	SO	SB	CS	SPEED	BA	OBP	SLG	MLVR	EQBA	EQOBP	EQSLG	EQA	VORP	DEFENSE	
2003	SDN	MLB	26	479	56	17	4	3	30	52	88	10	3	6.3	.261	.342	.341	-.063	.269	.349	.357	.255	11.7	102-SS	-12
2004	SDN	MLB	27	128	12	3	2	1	13	11	24	1	1	5.7	.235	.297	.322	-.203	.246	.305	.331	.228	-2.7	15-SS	-1
2004	POR	AAA	27	219	36	21	1	8	34	33	28	2	0	4.7	.299	.402	.554	.311	.251	.345	.443	.274	10.1	43-2B	-3
2005	BOS	MLB	28	64	6	2	0	0	4	3	14	0	0	5.3	.197	.234	.230	-.497	.183	.234	.217	.171	-5.5		
2005	BUF	AAA	28	91	13	3	1	0	4	7	16	1	1	6.0	.214	.275	.274	-.349	.185	.239	.232	.176	-8.4	16-SS	3
2006	*CLE*	*MLB*	*29*	*147*	*16*	*7*	*1*	*2*	*12*	*12*	*26*	*2*	*1*	*5.0*	*.239*	*.305*	*.342*	*-.169*	*.242*	*.314*	*.361*	*.230*	*1.0*	*39-SS*	*-1*

Breakout: 34%   Improve: 45%   Collapse: 37%   Attrition: 48%   Comparables: Tim Jones, Rob Wilfong, Craig Counsell

Acquired straight-up for Alex Cora in early July, Vazquez appeared in just 12 games for the Indians. A poor defensive shortstop and a hitter without much power, Vazquez's value lies in his willingness to take ball four. Absent other useful skills, that's small consolation. With other things on their minds, the Indians re-signed Vazquez to a one-year contract to be their futility man for 2006.

PITCHERS

BEAR BAY   **Bats: R Throws: R**   Height: 6′ 2″   Weight: 160   Born: August 7, 1983   Age: 22

YEAR	TM	LVL	AGE	W	L	SV	G	GS	IP	H	BB	SO	HR	GB%	BABIP	STUFF	WHIP	ERA	PERA	EQERA	EQH9	EQBB9	EQSO9	EQHR9	VORP	WXRL
2004	LNS	A	20	11	9	0	28	28	168.3	166	30	139	7	—	.310	11	1.16	3.10	4.33	5.89	9.8	2.1	4.3	0.8	-5.2	—
2005	KIN	A+	21	6	5	0	15	15	85.3	82	15	85	14	43%	.304	-9	1.14	3.38	6.05	5.04	10.5	1.8	5.9	2.5	5.0	—
2005	AKR	AA	21	3	3	0	8	8	45.3	45	13	40	5	50%	.320	6	1.28	4.77	5.15	5.36	9.9	3.1	5.6	1.4	1.2	—
2006	*CLE*	*MLB*	*22*	*8*	*9*	*0*	*29*	*23*	*141.7*	*155*	*42*	*85*	*22*	*44%*	*.291*	*5*	*1.39*	*4.93*	*5.09*	*5.29*	*9.7*	*2.6*	*5.2*	*1.3*	*6.6*	*1.6*

Breakout: 21%   Improve: 64%   Collapse: 10%   Attrition: 0%   Comparables: Sun-Woo Kim, Ricardo Aramboles, Eric Ireland

A 2003 draft-and-follow obtained from the Cubs for Cliff Bartosh, the ironically nicknamed Ronald Perry Bay is a scrawny 6′3″, 155 pounds . He's so skinny, in fact, that he's had trouble maintaining the velocity of his occasionally mid-90s heater and has suffered late-season fatigue in both of his minor league seasons. A July promotion to Double-A surely didn't help matters in 2005. Perhaps the Indians should put Bay on the C. C. Sabathia meal plan.

RAFAEL BETANCOURT   Bats: R   Throws: R   Height: 6' 2"   Weight: 170   Born: April 29, 1975   Age: 31

YEAR	TM	LVL	AGE	W	L	SV	G	GS	IP	H	BB	SO	HR	GB%	BABIP	STUFF	WHIP	ERA	PERA	EQERA	EQH9	EQBB9	EQSO9	EQHR9	VORP	WXRL
2003	AKR	AA	28	0	0	16	31	0	45.3	33	13	75	0	—	.351	26	1.02	1.39	2.76	4.25	7.9	3.6	9.8	0.2	6.3	—
2003	CLE	MLB	28	2	2	1	33	0	38.0	27	13	36	5	26%	.227	14	1.05	2.13	4.17	2.70	7.4	3.2	8.6	1.2	14.5	1.6
2004	CLE	MLB	29	5	6	4	68	0	66.7	71	18	76	7	41%	.352	24	1.33	3.91	3.13	4.04	8.5	2.2	9.3	0.8	14.5	1.4
2005	CLE	MLB	30	4	3	1	54	0	67.7	57	17	73	5	35%	.295	32	1.09	2.79	2.93	3.19	7.6	2.3	9.6	0.7	19.9	1.1
2006	*CLE*	*MLB*	*31*	*3*	*3*	*4*	*54*	*0*	*61.0*	*57*	*18*	*55*	*8*	*37%*	*.282*	*10*	*1.22*	*3.56*	*3.87*	*4.16*	*8.2*	*2.5*	*7.8*	*1.1*	*13.0*	*1.1*

Breakout: 23% Improve: 38% Collapse: 26% Attrition: 11% Comparables: Alejandro Pena, Matt Mantei, Odell Jones

One of two members of the Indians organization to serve a suspension for violating the league's steroid policy in 2005, there's a certain irony in a pitcher with a titanium plate in his throwing elbow being suspended for putting unnatural substances in his body. Betancourt at least had the courtesy to get suspended while on the DL for shoulder soreness. Other than that rough spot, Betancourt rebounded from his mediocre sophomore season to be an essential part of the best bullpen in baseball and yet another Indians pitcher who posted a career-low walk rate in 2005. Not bad for a guy who was signed just shy of his 28th birthday after a tryout.

ANDREW BROWN   Bats: R   Throws: R   Height: 6' 6"   Weight: 230   Born: February 17, 1981   Age: 25

YEAR	TM	LVL	AGE	W	L	SV	G	GS	IP	H	BB	SO	HR	GB%	BABIP	STUFF	WHIP	ERA	PERA	EQERA	EQH9	EQBB9	EQSO9	EQHR9	VORP	WXRL
2004	AKR	AA	23	3	6	0	17	17	77.3	66	36	67	7	—	.262	-5	1.32	4.66	5.21	5.45	8.6	4.7	5.7	1.1	1.2	—
2004	JAX	AA	23	1	3	0	8	8	40.3	36	14	58	5	—	.326	10	1.24	4.02	5.45	6.63	9.7	3.8	8.3	1.9	-4.3	—
2005	BUF	AAA	24	4	2	4	49	0	69.7	52	19	81	7	38%	.269	11	1.02	3.36	4.03	4.03	7.7	2.8	8.2	1.1	11.7	—
2006	*CLE*	*MLB*	*25*	*3*	*3*	*1*	*22*	*4*	*47.7*	*44*	*20*	*41*	*7*	*37%*	*.275*	*8*	*1.33*	*4.30*	*4.47*	*4.81*	*8.2*	*3.6*	*7.4*	*1.2*	*5.7*	*0.7*

Breakout: 27% Improve: 52% Collapse: 14% Attrition: 28% Comparables: Tommy Greene, Shawn Sonnier, Danys Baez

The PTBNL in the Milton Bradley deal, Brown has twice missed an entire season due to an elbow injury (most recently in 2003), and has never thrown more than 127 innings in a professional season. The resulting durability questions prompted the Indians to convert him to relief last year. It worked like a charm. After walking four men per nine innings in his career as a minor league starter, Brown shaved that down to 2.5, while his strikeout rate shot up, resulting in a spectacular 4-1 K/BB ratio. Twice called up to the majors in 2005, Brown never made it into a game with the Indians. Expect that to change in 2006.

FERNANDO CABRERA   Bats: R   Throws: R   Height: 6' 4"   Weight: 170   Born: November 16, 1981   Age: 24

YEAR	TM	LVL	AGE	W	L	SV	G	GS	IP	H	BB	SO	HR	GB%	BABIP	STUFF	WHIP	ERA	PERA	EQERA	EQH9	EQBB9	EQSO9	EQHR9	VORP	WXRL
2003	AKR	AA	21	9	4	5	36	15	109.0	96	40	115	8	—	.293	11	1.25	2.97	4.54	4.20	8.7	3.8	7.6	1.2	16.3	—
2004	BUF	AAA	22	4	3	5	45	0	76.0	57	43	93	9	—	.268	7	1.32	3.79	4.79	4.54	7.6	5.5	9.1	1.2	8.6	—
2005	BUF	AAA	23	6	1	3	30	0	51.3	36	11	68	3	35%	.292	34	0.92	1.23	2.90	1.99	6.9	2.2	9.4	0.5	19.9	—
2005	CLE	MLB	23	2	1	0	15	0	30.7	24	11	29	1	38%	.277	26	1.14	1.47	2.97	2.37	7.4	3.3	8.6	0.3	12.4	0.6
2006	*CLE*	*MLB*	*24*	*3*	*3*	*3*	*53*	*1*	*57.0*	*52*	*24*	*56*	*7*	*39%*	*.288*	*12*	*1.33*	*3.93*	*4.31*	*4.25*	*8.1*	*3.6*	*8.4*	*1.1*	*9.1*	*0.9*

Breakout: 13% Improve: 32% Collapse: 48% Attrition: 22% Comparables: Ugueth Urbina, Jim Ray, Antonio Osuna

Cabrera dominated pitching out of the Buffalo pen in 2005, posting a 1.23 ERA and a nifty 6.2 K/9. He also posted a 1.47 ERA in 30.2 innings across two major league call-ups. A tall, skinny righty with an elbows-and-knees delivery and a blazing fastball, Cabrera is considered a candidate for the Indians' closer job down the road. For the moment he'll have to settle for being a dominating set-up man.

FAUSTO CARMONA   Bats: R   Throws: R   Height: 6' 4"   Weight: 180   Born: December 7, 1983   Age: 22

YEAR	TM	LVL	AGE	W	L	SV	G	GS	IP	H	BB	SO	HR	GB%	BABIP	STUFF	WHIP	ERA	PERA	EQERA	EQH9	EQBB9	EQSO9	EQHR9	VORP	WXRL
2003	LKC	A	19	17	4	0	24	24	148.3	117	14	83	10	—	.228	-7	0.88	2.06	5.31	5.51	9.7	1.1	3.3	1.6	1.4	—
2004	KIN	A+	20	5	2	0	13	13	70.0	68	20	57	6	—	.292	1	1.26	2.83	5.29	5.16	10.0	3.1	5.3	1.5	3.2	—
2004	AKR	AA	20	4	8	0	15	15	87.0	114	21	63	3	—	.369	23	1.55	4.76	3.69	4.98	10.3	2.1	4.7	0.4	6.2	—
2005	AKR	AA	21	6	5	0	14	14	90.7	100	20	57	7	57%	.312	3	1.32	4.07	4.77	5.38	10.5	2.2	4.0	0.9	2.2	—
2005	BUF	AAA	21	7	4	0	13	12	83.0	76	15	49	10	54%	.261	6	1.10	3.25	4.80	3.57	8.8	1.7	4.4	1.2	18.2	—
2006	*CLE*	*MLB*	*22*	*9*	*10*	*0*	*29*	*26*	*160.7*	*181*	*40*	*77*	*20*	*51%*	*.294*	*4*	*1.37*	*4.68*	*4.81*	*5.07*	*10.0*	*2.2*	*4.1*	*1.0*	*10.7*	*2.2*

Breakout: 4% Improve: 48% Collapse: 12% Attrition: 0% Comparables: Justin Germano, Dustin Moseley, Derrin Ebert

(continued next page)

Fausto Carmona (continued)

Carmona is a classic sinker/slider groundball pitcher with fantastic control (1.6 BB/9 in 565.1 minor league innings to go with a 3.5 K/BB ratio and a 1.6 groundball/flyball ratio). He only got better after a late-June promotion to Triple-A as his velocity continued to increase, though there were some concerns about the continued downward trend in his strike-out rate. Like Andrew Brown, Carmona has yet to make his big-league debut, despite twice being called up to the big club. The Indians are hoping he'll do that by earning a spot in the rotation this spring.

JASON DAVIS				Bats: R		Throws: R					Height: 6' 6"		Weight: 190		Born: May 8, 1980			Age: 26	
YEAR	TM	LVL	AGE	W	L	SV	G	GS	IP	H	BB	SO	HR	GB%	BABIP	STUFF	WHIP	ERA	PERA	EQERA	EQH9	EQBB9	EQSO9	EQHR9	VORP	WXRL
2003	CLE	MLB	23	8	11	0	27	27	165.3	172	47	85	25	50%	.282	-4	1.32	4.68	5.13	5.30	9.8	2.5	4.6	1.3	8.2	2.4
2004	BUF	AAA	24	3	2	0	9	9	54.0	53	18	39	4	—	.301	6	1.31	3.00	4.58	4.75	9.0	3.4	5.1	0.8	5.0	—
2004	CLE	MLB	24	2	7	0	26	19	114.3	148	51	72	13	54%	.348	-1	1.74	5.51	4.74	5.79	10.2	3.6	5.1	0.9	-2.6	0.7
2005	BUF	AAA	25	8	5	0	16	16	95.7	106	27	77	9	58%	.336	4	1.39	4.61	4.64	6.25	9.7	2.8	5.4	1.0	-6.9	—
2005	CLE	MLB	25	4	2	0	11	4	40.3	44	20	32	4	52%	.333	6	1.59	4.69	4.61	5.05	9.4	4.4	7.0	0.9	3.8	0.0
2006	CLE	MLB	26	6	8	0	34	20	119.7	135	45	70	14	51%	.305	-3	1.50	5.08	5.24	5.56	10.0	3.3	5.1	1.0	2.3	0.9
Breakout: 20%	Improve: 48%	Collapse: 14%	Attrition: 1%			Comparables: Sean Bergman, Jay Tibbs, Bob Anderson																			

Rushed into the Indians' starting rotation out of Double-A at age 23, the fireballing Davis had one solid season and then developed shoulder problems. Then came the control problems and the staying-in-the-majors problems that finally landed him in Triple-A after 282 big league innings. Moved to the bullpen, he failed to replicate his successful showing the previous September, though he wasn't given much of an opportunity to do so. He returned to the starting rotation upon his demotion and appeared to right himself, though the results of two more spot starts for the big club were mixed.

DAN DENHAM				Bats: R		Throws: R					Height: 6' 2"		Weight: 190		Born: December 24, 1982			Age: 23	
YEAR	TM	LVL	AGE	W	L	SV	G	GS	IP	H	BB	SO	HR	GB%	BABIP	STUFF	WHIP	ERA	PERA	EQERA	EQH9	EQBB9	EQSO9	EQHR9	VORP	WXRL
2003	LKC	A	20	5	2	0	14	14	73.0	75	22	63	4	—	.313	0	1.33	3.08	5.35	5.74	10.8	3.3	4.8	1.3	-1.1	—
2003	KIN	A+	20	5	5	0	14	14	72.0	82	27	39	2	—	.311	0	1.51	4.50	4.84	6.88	10.4	3.7	3.6	0.5	-10.1	—
2004	KIN	A+	21	7	4	0	13	13	71.0	73	29	62	6	—	.332	-6	1.44	4.18	6.01	6.01	10.6	4.5	5.5	1.6	-3.1	—
2004	AKR	AA	21	5	3	0	14	13	76.0	84	30	50	12	—	.296	-16	1.50	4.74	6.51	5.91	10.5	3.7	4.3	1.9	-2.6	—
2005	AKR	AA	22	9	7	0	21	21	140.0	115	30	108	6	49%	.270	19	1.04	3.15	4.06	4.47	8.8	2.3	4.9	0.5	16.7	—
2006	CLE	MLB	23	7	9	0	28	24	138.3	157	54	77	20	45%	.298	-1	1.53	5.41	5.64	5.76	10.1	3.4	4.8	1.3	-1.7	0.8
Breakout: 11%	Improve: 47%	Collapse: 11%	Attrition: 0%			Comparables: Nick Regilio, Beau Hale, William Martinez																			

Armed with a new cut fastball and an improved changeup-the latter taught to him by Steve Ontiveros-the Indians' 1st round pick of 2001 rebounded from a dismal Double-A debut and disastrous Arizona Fall League stint in '04 to post what was easily his best professional season. Things ended on a sour note, however, as Denham tanked in three Triple-A starts after an August promotion.

KYLE DENNEY				Bats: R		Throws: R					Height: 6' 2"		Weight: 190		Born: July 27, 1977			Age: 28	
YEAR	TM	LVL	AGE	W	L	SV	G	GS	IP	H	BB	SO	HR	GB%	BABIP	STUFF	WHIP	ERA	PERA	EQERA	EQH9	EQBB9	EQSO9	EQHR9	VORP	WXRL
2003	AKR	AA	25	7	3	0	18	18	104.0	97	24	87	7	—	.286	4	1.16	2.42	4.73	4.36	9.4	2.6	5.5	1.2	13.6	—
2003	BUF	AAA	25	2	1	0	6	6	30.7	35	10	26	4	—	.319	-5	1.47	5.28	5.76	6.07	10.6	3.0	5.8	1.8	-1.6	—
2004	BUF	AAA	26	10	5	0	24	24	134.7	134	39	113	17	—	.286	-3	1.28	4.41	5.23	5.44	9.4	3.0	5.7	1.4	2.3	—
2005	BUF	AAA	27	1	1	0	9	9	38.7	52	10	22	9	39%	.323	-27	1.60	5.12	7.04	5.63	12.0	2.6	3.8	2.6	-0.1	—
2006	CLE	MLB	28	4	5	0	25	9	72.0	83	25	42	11	45%	.302	-8	1.50	5.15	5.63	6.14	10.2	3.1	5.0	1.3	2.0	0.5
Breakout: 25%	Improve: 55%	Collapse: 27%	Attrition: 26%			Comparables: Paul Mitchell, Allen Ripley, Jim Brower																			

Denney's story would be funny if it wasn't so tragic. After undergoing Tommy John surgery in his second full season as a pro, Denny was hit in the calf by a stray bullet while riding the team bus in 2004, but he avoided serious injury thanks to the knee-high cheerleader boots he was wearing as part of a rookie hazing ritual. Back in Triple-A for 2005, he missed the start of the season after being hit in the knee by a thrown bat and later spent a month on the DL with neuritis in his pitching elbow. Things would get worse: in late June, a line drive hit Denney behind his right ear, causing a fractured skull, brain contusion, and a punctured ear drum, ending his season. He pitched in winter ball, and his command of three pitches should help him make it, assuming adversity doesn't come a' callin' again.

JAKE DITTLER
Bats: R Throws: R   Height: 6′ 4″   Weight: 220   Born: November 24, 1982   Age: 23

YEAR	TM	LVL	AGE	W	L	SV	G	GS	IP	H	BB	SO	HR	GB%	BABIP	STUFF	WHIP	ERA	PERA	EQERA	EQH9	EQBB9	EQSO9	EQHR9	VORP	WXRL
2003	LKC	A	20	6	4	0	17	17	89.0	86	20	82	4	—	.307	7	1.19	2.63	4.59	6.30	10.2	2.5	5.1	1.1	-6.6	—
2003	KIN	A+	20	5	1	0	8	8	48.7	47	11	32	2	—	.283	10	1.19	2.40	4.44	4.82	9.4	2.3	4.4	0.8	4.0	—
2004	AKR	AA	21	5	12	0	21	20	107.7	119	40	85	7	—	.323	9	1.48	5.01	4.58	5.92	9.7	3.4	5.2	0.8	-3.8	—
2005	AKR	AA	22	10	9	0	28	27	173.0	187	61	107	12	65%	.305	-3	1.43	3.64	5.15	5.80	10.3	3.8	3.9	0.9	-3.7	—
2006	*CLE*	*MLB*	*23*	*8*	*10*	*0*	*28*	*25*	*147.7*	*165*	*60*	*75*	*15*	*57%*	*.301*	*-1*	*1.53*	*5.08*	*5.23*	*5.56*	*9.9*	*3.6*	*4.4*	*0.9*	*1.7*	*1.2*

Breakout: 14%   Improve: 66%   Collapse: 3%   Attrition: 0%   Comparables: Sergio Mitre, Jake Westbrook, Scott Randall

The Indians' 2nd round pick in 2001, Dittler had a rough Double-A debut in 2004, due in part to soreness in his scapula and lower back. Healthy again in 2005, Dittler saw his ERA drop by almost a run and a half despite a lack of overall improvement in his peripheral stats and a sharp decline in his strikeout rate. The secret to his success was the extreme sink on his fastball, resulting in a 2.7 groundball-to-flyball ratio.

SCOTT ELARTON
Bats: R Throws: R   Height: 6′ 8″   Weight: 240   Born: February 23, 1976   Age: 30

YEAR	TM	LVL	AGE	W	L	SV	G	GS	IP	H	BB	SO	HR	GB%	BABIP	STUFF	WHIP	ERA	PERA	EQERA	EQH9	EQBB9	EQSO9	EQHR9	VORP	WXRL
2003	CSP	AAA	27	6	8	0	20	20	118.7	146	39	92	15	—	.332	-14	1.56	5.31	5.83	6.21	10.7	3.6	5.4	1.7	-8.0	—
2003	COL	MLB	27	4	4	0	11	10	51.7	73	20	20	13	42%	.317	-31	1.80	6.27	6.58	7.09	11.6	3.0	3.0	2.0	-10.6	-0.8
2004	COL	MLB	28	0	6	0	8	8	41.3	57	20	23	8	40%	.343	-18	1.86	9.81	5.61	8.52	10.8	3.7	4.2	1.5	-13.8	-1.2
2004	CLE	MLB	28	3	5	0	21	21	117.3	107	42	80	25	35%	.241	-10	1.27	4.53	5.60	4.44	8.8	3.0	5.8	1.8	19.0	2.4
2005	CLE	MLB	29	11	9	0	31	31	181.7	189	48	103	32	34%	.274	-7	1.30	4.61	5.25	5.15	9.9	2.5	5.1	1.5	14.6	2.7
2006	*KCA*	*MLB*	*30*	*6*	*11*	*0*	*30*	*22*	*137.7*	*162*	*42*	*76*	*22*	*38%*	*.301*	*-2*	*1.48*	*5.44*	*5.65*	*5.55*	*10.3*	*2.7*	*5.0*	*1.4*	*-0.9*	*0.8*

Breakout: 18%   Improve: 54%   Collapse: 13%   Attrition: 4%   Comparables: Dennis Rasmussen, Andy Hawkins, Cal Eldred

Despite becoming the fourth member of the Indians' rotation to post a career-best walk rate in 2005 (the lone exception was Kevin Millwood, who posted his second-best career mark), Elarton made no other meaningful improvements. Due to a league-leading flyball rate, he still gives up homers in bunches-at one point he allowed a homer in ten straight starts—while his strikeout rate continues its career-long downward trend. Were he to pitch in a big ballpark with a stellar outfield defense, he could show superficial improvement for a year or two, but his tastes seem to run towards the apocalyptic, having signed a two-year deal with the Royals.

JEREMY GUTHRIE
Bats: B Throws: R   Height: 6′ 1″   Weight: 200   Born: April 8, 1979   Age: 27

YEAR	TM	LVL	AGE	W	L	SV	G	GS	IP	H	BB	SO	HR	GB%	BABIP	STUFF	WHIP	ERA	PERA	EQERA	EQH9	EQBB9	EQSO9	EQHR9	VORP	WXRL
2003	AKR	AA	24	6	2	0	10	9	62.7	44	14	35	0	—	.223	13	0.93	1.44	3.84	2.91	7.5	2.5	3.8	0.3	17.5	—
2003	BUF	AAA	24	4	9	0	18	18	96.7	129	30	62	15	—	.333	-35	1.64	6.51	6.63	7.67	11.9	3.3	4.5	2.2	-21.9	—
2004	AKR	AA	25	8	8	0	23	21	130.3	145	42	94	16	—	.309	-19	1.44	4.21	6.11	5.76	10.7	3.4	4.4	1.6	-2.3	—
2005	BUF	AAA	26	12	10	0	25	25	136.3	152	49	100	15	44%	.329	-8	1.47	5.08	5.36	6.10	10.0	3.7	4.9	1.2	-7.5	—
2006	*CLE*	*MLB*	*27*	*5*	*7*	*0*	*26*	*16*	*112.0*	*130*	*45*	*61*	*17*	*45%*	*.300*	*-7*	*1.56*	*5.63*	*5.84*	*6.09*	*10.3*	*3.5*	*4.7*	*1.3*	*-4.3*	*0.2*

Breakout: 18%   Improve: 49%   Collapse: 16%   Attrition: 0%   Comparables: Dan Smith, Ken Clay, Jason Middlebrook

In 2003, the Indians promoted Guthrie to Triple-A just nine starts into his professional career. It was too much too soon. Guthrie struggled mightily at Buffalo and his control vanished altogether in 2004, prompting an even quicker demotion to Double-A. At that point, the Indians thought the problem was mechanical. They bumped him to Buffalo in 2005, where he continued to struggle, giving reason to believe that either self-doubt is an issue, or he's another Stanford washout. Guthrie would not be the first pitcher picked out of the Pac 10 powerhouse to flop since Mike Mussina made it to the show.

BOBBY HOWRY
Bats: L Throws: R   Height: 6′ 5″   Weight: 220   Born: August 4, 1973   Age: 32

YEAR	TM	LVL	AGE	W	L	SV	G	GS	IP	H	BB	SO	HR	GB%	BABIP	STUFF	WHIP	ERA	PERA	EQERA	EQH9	EQBB9	EQSO9	EQHR9	VORP	WXRL
2004	BUF	AAA	30	1	1	0	18	0	26.0	22	6	24	3	—	.264	-7	1.08	5.19	5.11	5.84	8.8	2.6	6.2	1.5	-0.7	—
2004	CLE	MLB	30	4	2	0	37	0	42.7	37	12	39	5	38%	.271	13	1.15	2.74	4.01	2.95	8.0	2.3	7.8	1.1	15.6	0.2
2005	CLE	MLB	31	7	4	3	79	0	73.0	49	16	48	4	40%	.221	12	0.89	2.47	3.45	3.07	7.3	2.0	6.1	0.5	23.3	3.1
2006	*CHN*	*MLB*	*32*	*2*	*2*	*3*	*46*	*0*	*47.7*	*47*	*15*	*36*	*6*	*42%*	*.281*	*-2*	*1.29*	*3.98*	*4.14*	*4.45*	*8.7*	*2.6*	*6.1*	*1.1*	*6.7*	*0.5*

Breakout: 9%   Improve: 27%   Collapse: 46%   Attrition: 20%   Comparables: Jim Brosnan, Rick White, Dave Weathers

(continued next page)

Bobby Howry *(continued)*

The Tribe's most dominating set-up man in 2005, Howry held righties to a .208 EqA and lefties to .198. Down the stretch he was almost unhittable, walking a mere five batters and allowing just one home run over his final 35.2 innings-strong evidence that he was not aversely affected by posting career highs in games and innings pitched. Having signed a three-year deal with the Cubs, Howry will spend 2006 as the primary set-up man and closer-in-waiting behind Ryan Dempster. Howry moves to Wrigley Field as a flyball pitcher with a low strikeout rate, so there is reason to doubt the quality of his encore.

CLIFF LEE Bats: L Throws: L Height: 6′ 3″ Weight: 190 Born: August 30, 1978 Age: 27

YEAR	TM	LVL	AGE	W	L	SV	G	GS	IP	H	BB	SO	HR	GB%	BABIP	STUFF	WHIP	ERA	PERA	EQERA	EQH9	EQBB9	EQSO9	EQHR9	VORP	WXRL
2003	BUF	AAA	24	6	1	0	11	11	63.3	62	31	61	4	—	.310	9	1.47	3.27	4.87	4.28	9.1	5.3	6.8	0.9	8.9	—
2003	CLE	MLB	24	3	3	0	9	9	52.3	41	20	44	7	41%	.252	16	1.17	3.61	4.59	4.59	7.9	3.5	7.6	1.2	6.8	1.0
2004	CLE	MLB	25	14	8	0	33	33	179.0	188	81	161	30	38%	.314	6	1.53	5.43	4.88	5.27	9.1	3.7	7.4	1.4	7.4	2.7
2005	CLE	MLB	26	18	5	0	32	32	202.0	194	52	143	22	36%	.282	17	1.22	3.79	4.12	4.25	8.9	2.4	6.4	1.0	37.2	4.6
2006	*CLE*	*MLB*	*27*	*11*	*9*	*0*	*29*	*29*	*176.7*	*176*	*59*	*127*	*24*	*38%*	*.282*	*13*	*1.33*	*4.26*	*4.56*	*4.62*	*8.8*	*2.9*	*6.2*	*1.1*	*21.7*	*3.6*

Breakout: 17% Improve: 57% Collapse: 11% Attrition: 5%   Comparables: Denny Lemaster, Joe Price, Jarrod Washburn

Now officially the second-best part of the Bartolo Colon deal (after Sizemore), Lee found his control in 2005, dropping his walk rate by almost two walks per nine and reducing his hit batsmen from eleven to zero. Despite a corresponding drop in his strikeout rate, the rest of Lee's peripheral stats took strong steps in the right direction. He benefited from the third-best run support in the American League and placed second in wins, generating a number of typically misplaced Cy Young votes. His extreme flyball rate remains troubling.

THOMAS MASTNY Bats: R Throws: R Height: 6′ 6″ Weight: 220 Born: February 4, 1981 Age: 25

YEAR	TM	LVL	AGE	W	L	SV	G	GS	IP	H	BB	SO	HR	GB%	BABIP	STUFF	WHIP	ERA	PERA	EQERA	EQH9	EQBB9	EQSO9	EQHR9	VORP	WXRL
2003	AUB	A-	22	8	0	0	14	14	63.7	56	12	68	1	—	.309	10	1.07	2.26	3.92	5.88	9.7	2.4	5.3	0.6	-1.9	—
2004	CWV	A	23	10	3	0	27	27	149.0	123	41	143	4	—	.292	14	1.10	2.17	4.09	4.73	8.7	3.3	4.8	0.4	13.6	—
2005	KIN	A+	24	7	3	2	29	11	88.0	78	26	94	4	57%	.320	3	1.18	2.35	4.30	4.73	9.3	3.2	5.8	0.8	8.1	—
2005	AKR	AA	24	1	1	0	5	3	20.7	18	5	18	0	32%	.290	6	1.11	2.17	4.12	4.12	9.2	2.7	5.0	0.5	3.2	—
2006	*CLE*	*MLB*	*25*	*5*	*6*	*0*	*29*	*12*	*89.3*	*97*	*34*	*54*	*10*	*49%*	*.299*	*-2*	*1.46*	*4.96*	*5.03*	*5.43*	*9.6*	*3.3*	*5.2*	*1.0*	*2.9*	*0.7*

Breakout: 5% Improve: 32% Collapse: 27% Attrition: 1%   Comparables: Kyle Snyder, Travis Thompson, Eric Schmitt

A big fella who throws downhill, Mastny doesn't have great stuff, but does have a reputation as a guy who, to invoke standard scoutspeak, "knows how to pitch," "hits his spots" (a 3.8 K/BB ratio in 321.1 professional innings), and "keeps hitters off balance" with a deceptive delivery. Acquired from the Blue Jays in exchange for John McDonald, Mastny excelled as a swingman last year and will start 2005 with Buffalo with the possibility of filling that role for the Indians.

ADAM MILLER Bats: R Throws: R Height: 6′ 4″ Weight: 175 Born: November 26, 1984 Age: 21

YEAR	TM	LVL	AGE	W	L	SV	G	GS	IP	H	BB	SO	HR	GB%	BABIP	STUFF	WHIP	ERA	PERA	EQERA	EQH9	EQBB9	EQSO9	EQHR9	VORP	WXRL
2004	LKC	A	19	7	4	0	19	19	91.0	79	28	106	7	—	.320	15	1.18	3.36	4.86	5.07	9.1	3.3	6.4	1.2	5.1	—
2004	KIN	A+	19	3	2	0	8	8	43.3	29	12	46	1	—	.252	34	0.95	2.08	3.54	4.87	7.5	2.9	7.1	0.4	3.3	—
2005	KIN	A+	20	2	4	0	12	12	59.7	76	17	45	5	48%	.376	-3	1.56	4.82	5.28	7.69	11.3	2.7	4.2	1.2	-13.9	—
2006	*CLE*	*MLB*	*21*	*6*	*8*	*0*	*24*	*21*	*122.7*	*137*	*45*	*68*	*19*	*46%*	*.292*	*0*	*1.48*	*5.37*	*5.49*	*5.75*	*9.9*	*3.2*	*4.8*	*1.3*	*-1.0*	*0.8*

Breakout: 28% Improve: 68% Collapse: 3% Attrition: 0%   Comparables: Marcos Castillo, Joe Foote, J. D. Martin

Generally considered to be best pitching prospect in baseball not named Felix Hernandez, Miller missed the first half of 2005 with a sprained ligament in his pitching elbow. He managed to avoid Tommy John surgery for now but according to the Indians, struggled upon his return due to a closed-off delivery that they're working to correct. When healthy, Miller combines determination and intelligence with a blazing fastball and a wicked slider that's a good ten miles per hour slower than the heater. He has also added a second, slower changeup to his repertoire. Nonetheless, he didn't really come around until the very end of the Arizona Fall League season.

KEVIN MILLWOOD   **Bats: R Throws: R**   Height: 6' 4"   Weight: 220   Born: December 24, 1974   Age: 31

YEAR	TM	LVL	AGE	W	L	SV	G	GS	IP	H	BB	SO	HR	GB%	BABIP	STUFF	WHIP	ERA	PERA	EQERA	EQH9	EQBB9	EQSO9	EQHR9	VORP	WXRL
2003	PHI	MLB	28	14	12	0	35	35	222.0	210	68	169	19	43%	.292	20	1.25	4.01	3.93	4.34	8.8	2.5	6.2	0.8	36.3	5.6
2004	PHI	MLB	29	9	6	0	25	25	141.0	155	51	125	14	46%	.337	20	1.46	4.85	4.04	5.17	9.5	2.9	7.0	0.8	9.6	1.5
2005	CLE	MLB	30	9	11	0	30	30	192.0	182	52	146	20	47%	.286	22	1.22	2.86	4.01	3.58	8.8	2.5	6.8	0.9	50.4	5.7
2006	*TEX*	*MLB*	*31*	*11*	*10*	*0*	*31*	*31*	*191.7*	*202*	*55*	*133*	*24*	*46%*	*.296*	*14*	*1.34*	*4.38*	*4.29*	*4.42*	*9.0*	*2.6*	*6.2*	*1.0*	*26.8*	*4.2*

Breakout: 12%   *Improve: 47%*   *Collapse: 18%*   *Attrition: 3%*   *Comparables: Chris Bosio, Jim Lonborg, Steve Trachsel*

Millwood's discounted one-year deal with Cleveland would have been further discounted had his elbow acted up again. Fortunately for both parties, his sole, brief DL stint in 2005 resulted from a groin pull. A textbook example of the uselessness of pitching won/lost records, Millwood went 9–11 despite his leading the AL in ERA for a 93-win ballclub. The reason: the third-worst run support in the AL. That said, his 2.86 ERA benefited from a league-best .194 opponents' average with runners in scoring position-a feat unlikely to be repeated in 2006 pitching in the hitters' haven of Arlington. In his six seasons prior to joining the Tribe, Millwood twice followed a strong year with an average or injury-shortened one. Don't be surprised if it happens again.

ED MUJICA   **Bats: R Throws: R**   Height: 6' 2"   Weight: 180   Born: May 10, 1984   Age: 22

YEAR	TM	LVL	AGE	W	L	SV	G	GS	IP	H	BB	SO	HR	GB%	BABIP	STUFF	WHIP	ERA	PERA	EQERA	EQH9	EQBB9	EQSO9	EQHR9	VORP	WXRL
2003	BNC	Rk	19	2	6	0	14	10	55.7	57	20	41	3	—	.300	-22	1.38	4.36	6.58	7.27	10.6	4.7	3.5	1.7	-9.6	—
2004	LKC	A	20	7	7	2	26	19	124.0	130	32	89	18	—	.293	-33	1.31	4.65	6.83	6.83	10.9	2.8	3.9	2.4	-16.2	—
2005	KIN	A+	21	1	0	14	25	0	26.0	17	2	32	3	40%	.241	13	0.73	2.08	4.50	3.38	8.2	0.8	7.5	1.9	5.9	—
2005	AKR	AA	21	2	1	10	27	0	34.3	36	5	33	2	45%	.351	9	1.20	2.89	3.74	3.74	9.6	1.6	6.1	0.8	7.0	—
2006	*CLE*	*MLB*	*22*	*2*	*3*	*1*	*23*	*3*	*44.3*	*50*	*15*	*28*	*8*	*39%*	*.292*	*-7*	*1.46*	*5.44*	*5.73*	*6.02*	*10.1*	*2.9*	*5.4*	*1.6*	*-0.1*	*0.0*

Breakout: 23%   *Improve: 55%*   *Collapse: 17%*   *Attrition: 34%*   *Comparables: Kyle Jackson, Manny Ulloa, Erik Thompson*

Moved to the bullpen at the end of 2004, the hard-throwing Mujica was untouchable as Kinston's closer and merely dominant as the closer for Akron after a late-June promotion. The Indians added him to their 40-man roster in November to protect him from the Rule 5 draft, suggesting he's on the fast track to the major league pen.

RAFAEL PEREZ   **Bats: L Throws: L**   Height: 6' 3"   Weight: 170   Born: May 15, 1982   Age: 24

YEAR	TM	LVL	AGE	W	L	SV	G	GS	IP	H	BB	SO	HR	GB%	BABIP	STUFF	WHIP	ERA	PERA	EQERA	EQH9	EQBB9	EQSO9	EQHR9	VORP	WXRL
2003	BNC	Rk	21	9	3	0	13	12	69.0	56	16	63	1	—	.276	4	1.04	1.70	4.31	5.98	8.8	3.2	4.0	0.4	-2.7	—
2004	LKC	A	22	7	6	0	23	22	115.0	121	47	99	9	—	.326	-18	1.46	4.85	5.86	7.32	10.2	4.6	4.4	1.3	-21.2	—
2005	KIN	A+	23	8	5	0	14	14	77.7	54	32	48	6	66%	.213	-17	1.11	3.36	5.96	5.58	8.5	4.6	3.5	1.3	0.2	—
2005	AKR	AA	23	4	3	1	15	8	66.7	53	12	46	5	61%	.245	0	0.97	1.75	4.62	4.19	8.8	2.0	4.3	1.0	9.8	—
2006	*CLE*	*MLB*	*24*	*6*	*8*	*0*	*31*	*18*	*116.3*	*130*	*52*	*55*	*14*	*57%*	*.294*	*-10*	*1.56*	*5.38*	*5.46*	*5.94*	*9.9*	*3.9*	*4.1*	*1.0*	*-2.9*	*0.4*

Breakout: 18%   *Improve: 56%*   *Collapse: 9%*   *Attrition: 0%*   *Comparables: C. J. Wilson, Derek Thompson, Buddy Blair*

Despite striking out a season-high nine batters in his first Double-A start at Akron, Perez was eventually moved to the bullpen. He, like Mujica, was added to the 40-man roster in November after posting a 1.75 ERA and a 3.8 K/BB ratio.

ARTHUR RHODES   **Bats: L Throws: L**   Height: 6' 2"   Weight: 205   Born: October 24, 1969   Age: 36

YEAR	TM	LVL	AGE	W	L	SV	G	GS	IP	H	BB	SO	HR	GB%	BABIP	STUFF	WHIP	ERA	PERA	EQERA	EQH9	EQBB9	EQSO9	EQHR9	VORP	WXRL
2003	SEA	MLB	33	3	3	3	67	0	54.0	53	18	48	4	46%	.316	12	1.31	4.17	3.67	4.50	8.8	3.0	7.8	0.7	11.1	1.8
2004	OAK	MLB	34	3	3	9	37	0	38.7	46	21	34	9	42%	.330	-10	1.75	5.12	5.67	4.99	10.0	4.5	7.3	1.8	4.4	0.4
2005	CLE	MLB	35	3	1	0	47	0	43.3	33	12	43	2	44%	.270	27	1.04	2.08	2.93	2.93	7.3	2.5	9.0	0.4	14.5	1.6
2006	*CLE*	*MLB*	*36*	*2*	*1*	*2*	*35*	*0*	*34.0*	*33*	*11*	*29*	*4*	*45%*	*.290*	*4*	*1.28*	*3.66*	*4.00*	*4.35*	*8.5*	*2.9*	*7.3*	*0.9*	*6.6*	*0.5*

Breakout: 24%   *Improve: 45%*   *Collapse: 22%*   *Attrition: 37%*   *Comparables: Mark Guthrie, Tug McGraw, Gary Lavelle*

Despite a knee injury and family issues, Rhodes's season more closely resembled his dominant 2001 and 2002 than his 2004 in Oakland, when he sucker-punched sabermetric arguments against the concept of a "proven closer." Rhodes, though, is a special case: just watch him against the Yankees, a team he hasn't held scoreless in any of his last eight outings over the past three seasons. The lesson is that when Rhodes is in your bullpen, you need to understand his limitations; the individual Yankees change, but the pitcher's reaction to them remains the same Despite Rhodes's reputation as one of the top lefties in the game, he's had a reverse split since 2002.

DAVID RISKE **Bats: R Throws: R** Height: 6' 2" Weight: 170 Born: October 23, 1976 Age: 29

YEAR	TM	LVL	AGE	W	L	SV	G	GS	IP	H	BB	SO	HR	GB%	BABIP	STUFF	WHIP	ERA	PERA	EQERA	EQH9	EQBB9	EQSO9	EQHR9	VORP	WXRL
2003	CLE	MLB	26	2	2	8	68	0	74.7	52	20	82	9	41%	.247	26	0.96	2.29	3.59	2.60	7.1	2.5	9.8	1.1	28.9	3.9
2004	CLE	MLB	27	7	3	5	72	0	77.3	69	41	78	11	37%	.291	6	1.42	3.73	4.50	3.58	8.0	4.4	8.4	1.2	21.9	1.2
2005	CLE	MLB	28	3	4	1	58	0	72.7	55	15	48	11	42%	.214	-3	0.96	3.09	4.63	3.73	8.2	1.9	6.2	1.4	17.9	0.2
2006	CLE	MLB	29	3	2	3	47	0	54.3	50	17	41	7	41%	.269	3	1.23	3.57	3.94	4.01	8.2	2.7	6.6	1.1	11.3	0.9

Breakout: 11% Improve: 35% Collapse: 41% Attrition: 24% Comparables: Stan Belinda, Cris Carpenter, Nelson Cruz

David Riske is one of the most aptly named pitchers in baseball history. His rate stats fluctuate wildly from month to month and year to year. The only detectible trends in Riske's numbers: his strikeout rate has steadily declined over the past three seasons, while his home run rate has headed in the other direction. As he exits his peak years, David will become even Riske-er.

C. C. SABATHIA **Bats: L Throws: L** Height: 6' 7" Weight: 235 Born: July 21, 1980 Age: 25

YEAR	TM	LVL	AGE	W	L	SV	G	GS	IP	H	BB	SO	HR	GB%	BABIP	STUFF	WHIP	ERA	PERA	EQERA	EQH9	EQBB9	EQSO9	EQHR9	VORP	WXRL
2003	CLE	MLB	22	13	9	0	30	30	197.7	190	66	141	19	46%	.292	21	1.30	3.60	4.18	3.81	8.8	3.0	6.3	0.8	45.9	4.9
2004	CLE	MLB	23	11	10	0	30	30	188.0	176	72	139	20	42%	.289	17	1.32	4.12	4.29	4.05	8.4	3.2	6.2	0.9	39.7	4.7
2005	CLE	MLB	24	15	10	0	31	31	196.7	185	62	161	19	50%	.294	24	1.26	4.03	3.99	4.35	8.7	2.9	7.3	0.9	32.8	4.5
2006	CLE	MLB	25	13	10	0	33	31	201.0	197	63	154	20	47%	.292	20	1.29	3.85	4.09	4.20	8.7	2.8	6.6	0.9	33.5	4.9

Breakout: 16% Improve: 48% Collapse: 14% Attrition: 2% Comparables: Britt Burns, Jerry Reuss, Andy Pettitte

It's hard to believe that Sabathia is only 25, but it's good to see that the Indians are aware of it, carefully keeping his innings pitched below 200 in each of the past three seasons. Despite annual concerns about his weight and workload, the strained oblique Sabathia suffered warming up for his first spring training start resulted in his lone career trip to the DL . What's more, save for a spike in his groundball rate in 2005, Ol' Crooked Cap's performance has been alarmingly consistent over the past five seasons, with two encouraging exceptions: his walk rate has been trending downward while his strikeout rate has increased in each of the last three seasons. If his control continues to improve as he enters his peak seasons, Sabathia should prove himself worthy of the $17.75 million extension he signed last April.

SCOTT SAUERBECK **Bats: R Throws: L** Height: 6' 3" Weight: 190 Born: November 9, 1971 Age: 34

YEAR	TM	LVL	AGE	W	L	SV	G	GS	IP	H	BB	SO	HR	GB%	BABIP	STUFF	WHIP	ERA	PERA	EQERA	EQH9	EQBB9	EQSO9	EQHR9	VORP	WXRL
2003	PIT	MLB	31	3	4	0	53	0	40.0	30	25	32	5	55%	.231	-9	1.38	4.05	5.31	4.38	7.8	5.3	6.7	1.2	4.0	0.4
2003	BOS	MLB	31	0	1	0	26	0	16.7	17	18	18	1	62%	.356	-8	2.10	6.47	5.71	6.75	8.8	9.3	8.8	0.5	-2.5	-0.3
2005	CLE	MLB	33	1	0	0	58	0	35.7	35	16	35	4	52%	.323	8	1.43	4.03	4.25	4.75	9.0	4.0	8.8	1.0	4.3	0.2
2006	CLE	MLB	34	1	1	1	32	0	27.7	26	15	24	2	52%	.302	0	1.48	4.30	4.54	5.13	8.5	4.6	7.5	0.7	3.1	0.2

Breakout: 30% Improve: 56% Collapse: 20% Attrition: 31% Comparables: Joe Gibbon, Tippy Martinez, John Wyatt

After missing 2004 due to shoulder surgery, Sauerbeck continued his LOOGY ways with the Indians, averaging less than two-thirds of an inning per game and holding lefties to a .162/.284/.324 line. The problem is that righties drilled him, hitting.377/.441/.508. This, of course, is the problem with situational lefties: There's no guarantee they're actually going to get to face the batter they're brought in to face, and when there's a righty in the box, the advantage swings decidedly in the other direction. Unperturbed by this reality, the Indians re-upped Sauerbeck, who held the first batters he faced to a .163 average in 2005, for 2006 with a club option for 2007.

JEREMY SOWERS **Bats: L Throws: L** Height: 6' 1" Weight: 165 Born: May 17, 1983 Age: 23

YEAR	TM	LVL	AGE	W	L	SV	G	GS	IP	H	BB	SO	HR	GB%	BABIP	STUFF	WHIP	ERA	PERA	EQERA	EQH9	EQBB9	EQSO9	EQHR9	VORP	WXRL
2005	KIN	A+	22	8	3	0	13	13	71.3	60	19	75	5	55%	.291	11	1.11	2.78	4.52	4.66	9.0	2.8	6.0	1.1	7.1	—
2005	AKR	AA	22	5	1	0	13	13	82.3	74	9	70	8	49%	.288	12	1.01	2.08	4.37	3.68	9.4	1.1	5.4	1.3	16.7	—
2006	CLE	MLB	23	10	9	0	30	25	158.0	167	38	101	20	47%	.290	11	1.30	4.24	4.46	4.57	9.3	2.1	5.5	1.1	19.5	3.1

Breakout: 6% Improve: 28% Collapse: 23% Attrition: 0% Comparables: Abe Alvarez, Casey Fossum, Mike Hinckley

Sowers is one of six 2004 first-rounders, all college pitchers, to get as far as Triple-A in 2005. Of those, only two excelled at every level they reached: American League Rookie of the Year Huston Street, and Sowers. Of course, Sowers made just one start at Triple-A (in September), but he earned the promotion after pitching well. Like Mastny, Sowers has unexceptional stuff but an outstanding sense of how to use it. Thanks to his great control—1.6 BB/9 and a five-to-one K/BB ratio across three levels in 2005—he'll start 2006 in Buffalo. He should join the major league rotation no later than 2007.

BRIAN TALLET **Bats: L Throws: L**   Height: 6′ 7″ Weight: 200 Born: September 21, 1977 Age: 28

YEAR	TM	LVL	AGE	W	L	SV	G	GS	IP	H	BB	SO	HR	GB%	BABIP	STUFF	WHIP	ERA	PERA	EQERA	EQH9	EQBB9	EQSO9	EQHR9	VORP	WXRL
2003	BUF	AAA	25	4	4	0	15	15	84.0	89	34	67	10	—	.299	-16	1.46	5.14	6.07	6.19	10.4	4.6	5.5	1.7	-5.2	—
2003	CLE	MLB	25	0	2	0	5	3	19.0	23	8	9	2	49%	.323	-13	1.63	4.74	5.12	6.52	10.2	3.7	4.2	0.9	-1.2	-0.1
2005	BUF	AAA	27	6	5	0	22	17	97.7	98	25	61	17	41%	.271	-29	1.26	4.05	6.15	5.19	9.9	2.8	4.2	2.0	4.3	—
2006	CLE	MLB	28	4	6	0	34	11	85.7	97	36	45	13	44%	.294	-14	1.55	5.51	5.78	5.97	10.1	3.6	4.6	1.3	-1.9	0.2

Breakout: 21% Improve: 62% Collapse: 18% Attrition: 5%   Comparables: Steve Avery, Randy Keisler, Trever Miller

Tallet underwent Tommy John Surgery in late 2003, returned to action in late 2004, and spent 2005 regaining his strength with Buffalo. Given his age and the number of younger, more exciting starting pitching prospects queued up in the Indians' system, it would seem his best remaining hope with the Tribe is to find work in long relief or as a swing man. Dealt to Toronto, where he might help out in that role or as a fifth starter.

JAKE WESTBROOK **Bats: R Throws: R**   Height: 6′ 3″ Weight: 200 Born: September 29, 1977 Age: 28

YEAR	TM	LVL	AGE	W	L	SV	G	GS	IP	H	BB	SO	HR	GB%	BABIP	STUFF	WHIP	ERA	PERA	EQERA	EQH9	EQBB9	EQSO9	EQHR9	VORP	WXRL
2003	CLE	MLB	25	7	10	0	34	22	133.0	142	56	58	9	62%	.304	-1	1.49	4.33	4.83	4.62	9.8	3.7	3.9	0.6	17.5	2.6
2004	CLE	MLB	26	14	9	0	33	30	215.7	208	61	116	19	63%	.277	12	1.25	3.38	4.30	3.68	8.7	2.4	4.6	0.8	53.5	5.6
2005	CLE	MLB	27	15	15	0	34	34	210.7	218	56	119	19	62%	.291	10	1.30	4.49	4.32	5.39	9.5	2.4	5.0	0.8	12.2	3.1
2006	CLE	MLB	28	13	10	0	33	31	199.3	209	57	109	15	58%	.294	9	1.33	3.97	4.15	4.40	9.3	2.5	4.7	0.7	28.4	4.4

Breakout: 22% Improve: 71% Collapse: 8% Attrition: 2%   Comparables: Kevin Brown, Dennis Lamp, Mike Moore

Westbrook's 2004 season, in which he was third in the AL in ERA, was indeed too good to be true. His 2005 campaign was not without its positive signs, though. Both his strikeout and walk rates improved for the second straight year, and better yet, he posted the second best groundball-to-flyball ratio in the majors among qualified pitchers and was fourth in double-plays induced, suggesting that while Westbrook may not be the top-of-the-rotation guy he posed as in '04, he just might have a career as a solid innings eater somewhere in the middle.

BOB WICKMAN **Bats: R Throws: R**   Height: 6′ 1″ Weight: 240 Born: February 6, 1969   Age: 37

YEAR	TM	LVL	AGE	W	L	SV	G	GS	IP	H	BB	SO	HR	GB%	BABIP	STUFF	WHIP	ERA	PERA	EQERA	EQH9	EQBB9	EQSO9	EQHR9	VORP	WXRL
2004	CLE	MLB	35	0	2	13	30	0	29.7	33	10	26	4	58%	.341	4	1.50	4.24	4.45	4.15	9.2	2.7	7.1	1.2	5.8	1.9
2005	CLE	MLB	36	0	4	45	64	0	62.0	57	21	41	9	52%	.265	-5	1.26	2.47	4.87	2.66	9.0	3.1	6.0	1.3	22.4	4.7
2006	CLE	MLB	37	3	4	20	41	0	45.0	48	15	31	4	52%	.305	-5	1.41	3.88	4.51	4.54	9.5	3.0	5.9	0.8	7.4	1.0

Breakout: 17% Improve: 31% Collapse: 51% Attrition: 23%   Comparables: Todd Jones, Jose Mesa, Ted Power

Absent a better, more affordable closer option, the Indians re-signed the aging and expanding Wickman following his late-season comeback from Tommy John surgery in 2004. Despite some shaky peripherals, he turned in a strong season thanks to a league-best .149 opponents' average with runners on base. Odds are that won't happen again, but after a heavy flirtation with Trevor Hoffman didn't pan out, the Indians re-signed the Big Guy. He was, generously speaking, their sixth-best reliever in 2005.

Line Outs

Position/Player	TM	LVL	AGE	PA	R	2B	3B	HR	RBI	BB	SO	SB-CS	SPEED	BA/OBP/SLG	MLVR	EQBA/OBP/SLG	EQA	VORP
DH J. Liefer*	BUF	AAA	30	361	59	27	2	19	68	35	62	2-1	4.4	.321/.388/.595	.365	.264/.326/.459	.266	7.8
OF R. Ludwick	BUF	AAA	26	213	27	10	2	4	16	17	48	0-1	4.7	.191/.272/.330	-.291	.167/.240/.284	.191	-18.4
SS I. Ochoa	AKR	AA	22	467	46	13	6	2	30	30	81	16-12	5.9	.265/.330/.339	-.077	.241/.300/.309	.220	-9.7

Pitcher	TM	LVL	AGE	W	L	SV	IP	H	BB	SO	HR	GB%	BABIP	STUFF	WHIP	ERA	PERA	EQERA	EQH9	EQBB9	EQSO9	EQHR9	VORP
M. Miller	CLE	MLB	33	1	0	1	29.7	22	10	23	1	62%	.263	14	1.08	1.82	3.41	2.17	7.8	3.1	7.1	0.3	12.9
N. Pesco	KIN	A+	21	11	10	0	153.3	168	39	101	15	47%	.317	-11	1.35	3.82	5.46	5.95	10.7	2.5	3.8	1.4	-5.8
T. Sipp*	LKC	A	21	4	1	0	69.0	47	19	71	5	43%	.256	6	0.96	2.22	4.83	4.41	8.4	3.3	5.8	1.3	8.4
	KIN	A+	21	2	2	2	47.3	34	23	59	4	39%	.291	1	1.21	2.66	5.08	4.87	8.3	5.1	7.3	1.2	3.6
B. Slocum	AKR	AA	24	7	5	0	102.3	98	36	95	9	48%	.317	-5	1.31	4.40	5.20	5.66	9.8	4.0	5.7	1.2	-0.6
J. Stanford*	AKR	AA	28	2	0	0	14.7	15	4	13	1	55%	.341	-15	1.29	2.45	5.93	5.27	11.2	3.3	4.6	1.3	0.5
K. Tadano	BUF	AAA	25	5	5	5	96.3	105	22	86	16	35%	.321	-16	1.32	4.39	5.23	5.42	9.9	2.3	6.1	1.8	1.9
B. Traber*	AKR	AA	25	3	2	0	34.0	25	5	27	2	48%	.235	9	0.88	2.65	4.26	4.26	8.5	1.7	4.8	0.9	4.7
	BUF	AAA	25	3	7	0	76.7	96	30	55	7	52%	.346	-10	1.64	5.75	5.00	6.98	10.4	3.8	4.8	0.9	-11.9
J. Young	CSP	AAA	25	9	8	0	105.7	127	44	92	16	51%	.362	-15	1.62	6.39	5.84	6.09	10.2	3.9	5.5	1.6	-5.8
	BUF	AAA	25	2	0	0	23.0	26	9	21	4	50%	.328	-2	1.52	5.87	5.96	6.75	10.3	4.0	6.4	2.0	-2.9

When Travis Hafner went down with concussion-like symptoms following a mid-May beaning, the Indians installed **Jeff Liefer** at DH, thus becoming the fifth team in four years to marvel at the fact that he's unable to make the adjustments necessary to carry his impressive Triple-A hitting to the majors. After three surgeries in three years (hip, knee, knee), **Ryan Ludwick's** 2005 season came to an end when he broke his wrist; he was hitting .191 at the time, but he'll try to come back with the Tigers. **Ivan Ochoa** can pick it at short, but lacks the average or power to make his modest patience of any real use. Worse, his base stealing became a liability in his first season in Double-A.

A sidearmer, **Matt Miller** got off to a great start in 2005, only to be shut down in mid-July with a strained elbow. He's handy if healthy. **Nick Pesco** is considered a top prospect, and relies on a fantastic changeup, but he cooled off after a hot start with Kinston in the Carolina League and may find himself back there to start 2006. The hard-throwing **Tony Sipp** was moved into the bullpen after promotion to the Carolina League, posting a 1.65 ERA with 11 Ks per nine innings. He's expected to advance quickly. After two years in the Carolina League, during which he posted a combined 4.40 ERA, **Brian Slocum** moved up to Akron, where he did the same. His three appearances out of the Aeros' bullpen must have gone well because he continued to work out of the pen in the Arizona Fall League, posting a 3.15 ERA (despite walking 18 in 20 innings), after which he was added to Cleveland's 40-man roster. **Jason Stanford** began working his back from Tommy John surgery in July of last year, something he'll continue to do in Triple-A in 2006. After a bulging disc ended his 2004 season, **Kazuhito Tadano** spent most of 2005 in Buffalo pitching adequately, but not well enough to earn more than a single relief appearance with the big club. **Billy Traber,** like Tallet, underwent Tommy John Surgery in late 2003 and missed all of 2004. A six-year minor league free agent, he signed with the Nationals in November. **Jason Young** was claimed off of waivers from the Rockies in August. He hasn't pitched particularly well since mid-2002 and saw little improvement in his performance despite finally getting out of Colorado.

Colorado Rockies

*Let there be freedom from perturbation with respect
to the things which come from external causes.*

— MARCUS AURELIUS

There have been more theories proposed about how to win at altitude than have been offered up to solve global warming: contact hitters, changeup pitchers, speed and defense, walks and home runs, humidors, a pressurized dome, or an extra roster spot, to name a few. The assumption behind all of these ideas is that Colorado is unique among places to play baseball.

It is not. Colorado's altitude is like the wind in Wrigley or the heat in Arlington, phenomena that result from the collision of nature and the decision to locate ballclubs in such climes in the first place. No one proposes wacky tricks to combat those forces of nature, like countervailing wind mills on Sheffield and Waveland behind the Wrigley bleachers, or freon-infused caps for Rangers players, because the effects caused by these environments are regarded as falling within an arbitrary range of acceptable distortions. Rather than simply being seen as an outlier among a range of disparate baseball habitats, Colorado is viewed as an aberration, a place and park that must be defeated through outlandish means rather than simply tolerated and adapted to.

Despite trying many of these faddish solutions, the Rockies have remained mired at a level of performance that may best be described as "perpetual beige," not quite terrible and yet never in contention. About the only thing they haven't tried is the one thing sure to work: the ancient Greek philosophy of stoicism, which holds that if one has inward calm and clarity of purpose, they need not be manipulated by external, illusory forces.

Stoicism was founded by Zeno of Citium rather than Zeno the Baseball Fan, but external, illusory forces could easily be a reference to the affects of elevation upon the flight of the baseball. As the "Stanford Encyclopedia of Philosophy" explains,

> The passions or *pathê* are literally "things which one undergoes" and are to be contrasted with actions or things that one does. Thus, the view that one should be "apathetic," in its original Hellenistic sense, is not the view that you shouldn't care about anything, but rather

ROCKIES PROSPECTUS

2005 record: 67–95; Fifth place, NL West

Pythagenport record: 69–93

Runs scored per game: 4.57 (5th in NL)

Runs allowed per game: 5.32 (15th in NL)

Team EqA: .250 (15th in NL)

2005 Batters Age: 27.7 (Youngest in NL)

2005 Pitchers Age: 27.6 (Youngest in NL)

Ballpark: Coors Field; Severe hitter's park; Park Factor of 1.122

2005: By mid-season, even Rockies lifer Todd Helton threw up his hands.

2006: If there's a plan for how to turn this franchise around, it's hiding from them in an undisclosed location.

the view that you should not be psychologically subject to anything—manipulated and moved by *it,* rather than yourself being actively and positively in command of your reactions and responses to things as they occur or are in prospect.

The goal of the stoic is to accept his ballpark as part of the order of things. In the words of Will Durant, "The wise man will study science only sufficiently to find the law of Nature, and will then adapt his life to that Law. *Zen kata physim,* to live according to Nature—this is the purpose and sole excuse of science and philosophy."

Thin mountain air is a natural fact, and to live according to Nature is to craft a good ballclub, one that adheres to solid principles of team construction, and therefore can win anywhere, without reference to the environment. As Epictetus the Stoic said, "Wherever I go it will be well with me, for it was well with me here, not on account of the place, but of my judgments which I shall carry away with me, for no one can deprive me of these; on the contrary, they alone are my property, and cannot be taken away, and to possess them suffices me wherever I am or whatever I do." In other words, when you feel confident that you've built a good team, you won't sweat over where your ballpark is.

As plans go, this is not a particularly radical prescription, but it does have the virtue of never having been tried by the Rockies. In addition to their ballpark, another immutable fact that the Rockies have to accept is the need to outscore one's opponents by a decent margin in order to win ballgames more often than losing them. Pete Palmer and Jim Thorne's seminal book *The Hidden Game of Baseball* espoused the theory that teams in extreme environments—particularly hitting environments—face a considerably more difficulty path to the playoffs than teams that play in more neutral confines.

Further research showed that teams should build their teams to contrast their park: teams in hitting parks should focus on pitching and vice versa, as a way to protect themselves against the statistical distortions caused by their environment. The Rockies are a case in point: their focus is always on the terrible things the park does to their pitching, but in fact the pitching has been downright competent at times. It is the offense that has let the team down time and again, though this has been obscured by the gaudy numbers put up in their park. Only once in the team's history has the offense been even fractionally above average, as measured by EQA, .260 being average (see table 1).

Conversely, the pitching staff has been quite credible at times. For example, the 2000 staff, led by starters Pedro Astacio and Brian Bohanon and relievers Gabe White, Jose Jimenez, and Gabe White, posted a translated ERA of 3.68. Despite a season from Todd Helton that would have looked good in any park, the offense was dragged down by bad hitters like Tom Goodwin, Brian Hunter, Mike Lansing, Neifi Perez, and Brent Mayne, whose bats couldn't produce even if Coors were atop Mt. Everest. Only in 2000 did the Rockies outscore their opponents by more than a few runs, but the margin still only propelled the team to an 82–80 finish.

One obvious remedy for the team's offensive woes would be the adoption of an Oakland-style emphasis on walks. With the exception of 2003, the team has usually ranked low in free passes, finishing towards the bottom of the league in six of eight seasons since 1998. In their history, the Rockies have had eight player seasons of 90 or more walks, six of them from Todd Helton. If Nature dictates that a lot of home runs are going to be hit in your building, then Nature would also politely suggest that you should maximize the number of runners on base when those home runs are hit. There are two ways the Rockies can go about doing this: find eight guys who can hit like Ty Cobb in his prime at sea level and bring them to Denver, or they can adopt an organization-wide emphasis on selectivity.

Until they achieve the stoic ideal, the Rockies will continue to grapple with the distorted perceptions caused by their park. There's a larger, equally philosophical question in play here: does player performance simply *seem* distorted, or does actual ability change over time spent in the Mile High kingdom? One interesting effect that has been observed is that the Rockies' performance declines as a road trip progresses, and increases the longer they stay at Coors, but it is unknown if this effect also grows stronger with the passing of the seasons. It's possible that the more seasons players spend at Coors, the more they alter their style of play to take advantage of the unique aspects of altitude. If that is indeed the case, then their general performance elsewhere should decline. The performance of Rockies' hitters at home and on the road can be compared, much in the same manner that park factors are computed (but excluding the opposition in this case). In figure 1, the results are displayed broken down by the number of prior seasons the players played in Colorado where "Experience" is measured by previous seasons in Colorado. The difference between home and road performance increases the longer a player plays in Colorado.

TABLE 1. ROCKIES TEAM EQAS, 1993–2005

YEAR	EQA	YEAR	EQA	YEAR	EQA
1993	.245	1998	.252	2003	.258
1994	.250	1999	.246	2004	.260
1995	.254	2000	.249	2005	.250
1996	.260	2001	.262		
1997	.260	2002	.249		

FIGURE 1. COLORADO PARK FACTORS BY SEASONS OF EXPERIENCE

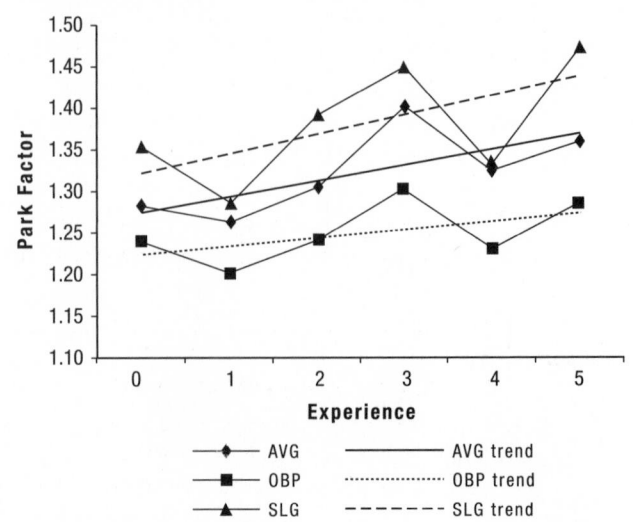

What this means for the Rockies, primarily, is that the longer they keep their players, the more overvalued they are likely to become. As players increasingly adjust to Coors Field, their ability to perform at lower altitudes degrades, and teams acquiring players from Colorado are likely to see a decline in performance. Additionally, the more experienced the team that the Rockies field, the harder it's going to be for them to win on the road.

However, this effect may not be unique to Coors Field. It's possible that players from all parks alter their games the more seasons they play in a single environment. In figure 2, the same data set is displayed, but for all parks except Coors. The data is consistently between 1.02 and 1.04, indicating that all players play better at home, but because the slope is near zero, players don't show any consistent ability to learn to play to their environments the longer they play there. Other extreme parks like San Diego, San Francisco, Texas, and Los Angeles also show no consistent trend one way or the other.

These numbers strongly suggest that players *do* continually change their approach when Coors is their home park. The same trend doesn't seem to exist in other extreme environments, suggesting something truly unique about Coors. What contributes to this adaptation trend—altitude, or the fact that Colorado's park factor is such an outlier, or Rockies hitters becoming so conditioned by the results of what they do at home that they keep pursuing the rewards of a contact-driven approach at the plate is difficult to determine. But it does support the idea that players who spend long stretches with the Rockies are less likely to succeed—or at least take more time than most players to adjust—once they leave the altitude. It remains to be seen if selectivity—a quality the Rockies largely have not had—would suffer from the same effect.

FIGURE 2. NON-COORS PARK FACTORS BY EXPERIENCE

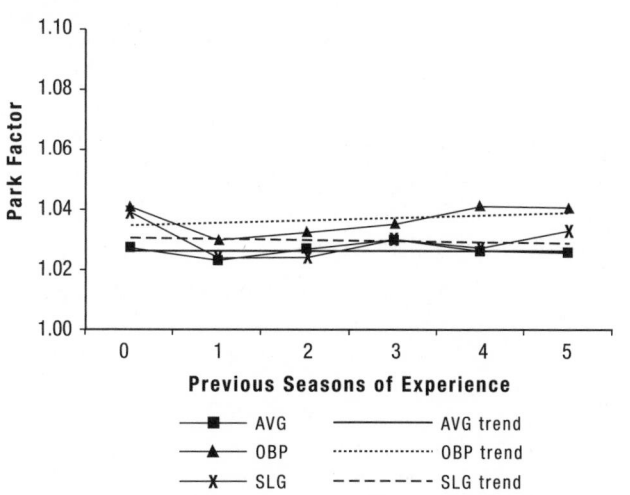

Regardless, during the 2005–2006 offseason the Rockies had an opportunity to make a clean break with the past, and instead, they punted. Finally out from under the massive contracts mistakenly doled out to Mike Hampton, Denny Neagle, Charles Johnson, and Preston Wilson, the Rockies were free to spend wisely on players that could help them rather than on people they were paying to stay away. Instead, the Rockies have added Ray King, Jose Mesa, and Yorvit Torrealba, and they went out of their way to re-sign Mike DeJean. The Rockies correctly identified their bullpen as a top priority for the offseason—they only managed 3.7 WXRL in 2005, good for 26th in the majors—but players like King and Mesa aren't going to be a noticeable improvement over the options the Rockies already have in-house, and they cost significantly more. Despite the presence of Jeff Francis and his reverse platoon split, the rotation still doesn't boast much talent.

Todd Helton is getting to the age when players with his skill set start to decline precipitously, and as much as he has meant to the Rockies, it would be best to try to move him while he can still return good value. Owed at least $16.6 million per season through 2012, Helton is preventing a small payroll team from addressing issues elsewhere on the roster. That wasn't so bad when he was contributing 12 wins per season, but his 9.6 WARP in 2005 and first trip to the DL is only a small taste of things to come. Another rough season will likely dry up the market for Helton, and in two years, they'll be lucky to trade him for fifty cents on the dollar.

That's a tough move to make given the recent purge of big contracts and the need to prove to fans that the team isn't just pulling a Florida Marlins, but beyond Helton and Matt Holliday, the Rockies didn't have a positional regular with a VORP over 21.0 or WARP over 3.1. There are a few prospects gaining on a major league job—Ian Stewart at third, Chris Iannetta behind the plate, 2005 1st round pick Troy Tulowitzki at short, and outfielders Matt Miller and Joe Koshansky, but none of them has logged a full season above high A-ball. Everything would have to break just right for the Rockies to field even half of those hitters in their major league lineup before 2008.

Rather than worrying about beating Nature, the Rockies need to acquire quality players, continue to sell high on their hitters, buy low on their pitchers, and remember that signing players to eight- and ten-year contracts makes about as much sense as the lyrics to *Bobby McGee*. The fact that batters who spend extended periods of time in Coors start to suffer in other parks should only serve to reinforce the fact that short contracts are better and batters need to be traded to take advantage of the general lack of understanding of park factors.

With the bad contracts of the past finally coming off of the books, and the pathetic state of the NL West, the

Rockies may be able to move into contention sooner than it initially appears. The last time they tried to buy their way into relevance with the contractapalooza of the early 2000s, they torpedoed the franchise for half a decade. This time they will have to build with patience and practical-ity. As the noted Stoic philosopher/emperor Marcus Aure-lius wrote, "If you are distressed by any external thing, it is not this thing which disturbs you, but your own judg-ment about it. And it is in your power to wipe out that judgment now."

HITTERS

DANNY ARDOIN   C   Bats: R Throws: R   Height: 6' 0" Weight: 220 Born: July 8, 1974   Age: 31

YEAR	TM	LVL	AGE	PA	R	2B	3B	HR	RBI	BB	SO	SB	CS	SPEED	BA	OBP	SLG	MLVR	EQBA	EQOBP	EQSLG	EQA	VORP	DEFENSE
2003	OKL	AAA	29	264	35	11	2	7	35	21	58	0	2	4.1	.243	.311	.393	-.050	.219	.281	.344	.219	-7.8	51-C 5
2004	OKL	AAA	30	289	50	12	0	10	44	41	66	1	1	3.9	.308	.422	.485	.252	.257	.355	.376	.260	7.5	67-C 5
2005	CSP	AAA	31	169	27	12	2	6	24	20	38	3	1	4.4	.338	.438	.577	.380	.269	.350	.434	.272	8.1	39-C 7
2005	COL	MLB	31	241	28	10	0	6	22	20	69	1	1	3.9	.229	.320	.362	-.144	.217	.306	.349	.233	-0.3	68-C 16
2006	COL	MLB	31	247	25	12	1	7	27	23	61	2	1	3.8	.250	.331	.416	-.042	.231	.313	.392	.239	2.5	61-C 5

Breakout: 31% Improve: 53% Collapse: 27% Attrition: 42%   Comparables: Doug Mirabelli, Bob Tillman, Kelly Stinnett

A career minor leaguer signed by the Rockies before the 2005 season, Ardoin took well to Colorado Springs, home of the Fountain of Offense, and earned a June call-up. He again proved that major league pitching is better than Triple-A pitch-ing, but behind the plate he nailed just under 50% of all base stealers and posted excellent overall defensive numbers. Ardoin is the dictionary definition backup catcher, and with Yorvit Torrealba brought in to start, that's the role he'll be in.

GARRETT ATKINS   3B   Bats: R Throws: R   Height: 6' 3" Weight: 210 Born: December 12, 1979 Age: 26

YEAR	TM	LVL	AGE	PA	R	2B	3B	HR	RBI	BB	SO	SB	CS	SPEED	BA	OBP	SLG	MLVR	EQBA	EQOBP	EQSLG	EQA	VORP	DEFENSE
2003	CSP	AAA	23	492	80	30	1	13	67	45	52	2	4	3.9	.319	.382	.481	.156	.270	.335	.422	.260	19.7	110-3B -4
2004	CSP	AAA	24	516	88	43	3	15	94	57	45	0	0	4.0	.366	.434	.578	.371	.306	.375	.469	.292	43.0	104-3B 0
2005	COL	MLB	25	573	62	31	1	13	89	45	72	0	2	3.4	.287	.347	.426	.040	.270	.333	.404	.256	13.6	133-3B -12
2006	COL	MLB	26	589	70	35	2	14	71	52	70	1	1	4.0	.298	.364	.454	.101	.276	.344	.428	.262	15.7	138-3B -6

Breakout: 17% Improve: 49% Collapse: 19% Attrition: 6%   Comparables: Kevin Orie, Ed Sprague, Joe Crede

For the rest of this chapter, let's just assume that everyone hit significantly better at home than on the road. That will save everyone a lot of time and the printer a lot of ink if we don't have to keep saying things like "Atkins looked okay, but only managed .238/.301/.347 on the road." They all do that. It's not their fault, it's just in their nature, like snakes. A snake found on the road will bite. A Rockie found on the road will bite too, just not in the same way. Atkins missed most of April with a hamstring injury, but the Rockies kept the hot corner warm for him and he got the rest of the year to prove what we already knew: he's a defensive liability and nothing special with the bat. There are plenty of alterna-tives behind him, and Atkins hasn't shown any knack for another position.

JEFF BAKER   3B   Bats: R Throws: R   Height: 6' 2" Weight: 210 Born: June 21, 1981   Age: 25

YEAR	TM	LVL	AGE	PA	R	2B	3B	HR	RBI	BB	SO	SB	CS	SPEED	BA	OBP	SLG	MLVR	EQBA	EQOBP	EQSLG	EQA	VORP	DEFENSE
2003	ASH	A	22	305	44	17	0	11	44	30	79	4	2	4.0	.289	.377	.479	.183	.224	.289	.384	.235	-2.2	61-3B -4
2004	VIS	A+	23	321	60	23	1	11	64	47	70	1	0	4.1	.330	.439	.547	.379	.264	.358	.431	.275	16.4	68-3B 0
2005	CSP	AAA	24	247	40	16	1	10	41	16	44	3	1	4.4	.303	.348	.513	.104	.260	.301	.431	.250	5.9	57-3B -5
2005	COL	MLB	24	43	6	4	0	1	4	5	12	0	0	4.7	.211	.302	.395	-.145	.184	.279	.342	.219	-0.7	
2006	COL	MLB	25	380	47	22	2	14	51	30	80	2	1	4.3	.277	.340	.478	.075	.257	.321	.451	.257	9.2	91-3B 0

Breakout: 28% Improve: 60% Collapse: 24% Attrition: 24%   Comparables: Tony Perez, Ron Jackson, Ryan Gripp

Pitchers are normally the ones stamped with large "if healthy" warning labels. Baker has had chronic wrist problems, and when he finally seemed over them, he went off and lost time to a bruised thumb and strained quad. He's a solid hit-ter, and he's progressed very quickly since an impressive college career at Clemson, but at some point injuries become more than bad luck. He's sandwiched between Garrett Atkins and Ian Stewart at third. Though likely a better player than Atkins, his path to job security probably depends on his ability to play another position.

CLINT BARMES   **SS**   **Bats: R Throws: R**   Height: 6' 0"   Weight: 175   Born: March 6, 1979   Age: 27

YEAR	TM	LVL	AGE	PA	R	2B	3B	HR	RBI	BB	SO	SB	CS	SPEED	BA	OBP	SLG	MLVR	EQBA	EQOBP	EQSLG	EQA	VORP	DEFENSE	
2003	CSP	AAA	24	529	63	35	1	7	54	22	63	12	7	5.1	.276	.316	.394	-.103	.233	.275	.340	.217	-12.6	122-SS	-5
2004	CSP	AAA	25	580	104	42	2	16	51	28	61	20	8	6.2	.328	.376	.505	.125	.271	.315	.406	.250	16.7	117-SS	8
2004	COL	MLB	25	75	14	3	1	2	10	3	10	0	1	5.1	.282	.320	.437	-.043	.268	.307	.423	.244	1.2		
2005	COL	MLB	26	373	55	19	1	10	46	16	36	6	4	5.4	.289	.330	.434	.013	.273	.317	.420	.251	13.4	78-SS	-5
2006	*COL*	*MLB*	*27*	*562*	*67*	*31*	*3*	*13*	*65*	*25*	*63*	*9*	*4*	*5.1*	*.288*	*.328*	*.433*	*.004*	*.267*	*.309*	*.408*	*.241*	*12.3*	*132-SS*	*-2*

Breakout: 27%   Improve: 52%   Collapse: 22%   Attrition: 13%   Comparables: Pat Meares, Johnny Logan, Jim Davenport

There are a few simple tricks baseball players can pull to cement themselves a special place in the public's heart. Step one: Get off to a hot start. That way, even if you end the year with the same production as a slow-starting player, you'll largely be perceived as the better hitter. Two: Do something that faintly reeks of baseball immortality. Hitting .400 for a few weeks is a dependable headline-grabber. Three: If you're going to get hurt, have a good story. Chop off your fingertip while hedging bushes, get jumped by your truck while washing it, or best of all, break your collarbone while carrying deer meat up a flight of stairs. If you follow these simple tips, everyone will focus on your .329/.371/.516 line before you got hurt rather than your .209/.252/.252 September, or that you're a 26-year old rookie, or your mediocre defense.

LARRY BIGBIE   **OF**   **Bats: L Throws: L**   Height: 6' 4"   Weight: 215   Born: November 4, 1977   Age: 28

YEAR	TM	LVL	AGE	PA	R	2B	3B	HR	RBI	BB	SO	SB	CS	SPEED	BA	OBP	SLG	MLVR	EQBA	EQOBP	EQSLG	EQA	VORP	DEFENSE			
2003	BAL	MLB	25	318	43	15	1	9	31	29	60	7	1	6.1	.303	.365	.456	.141	.306	.374	.468	.292	14.7	73-LF	4		
2004	BAL	MLB	26	528	76	23	1	15	68	45	113	8	3	5.8	.280	.341	.427	-.012	.280	.345	.429	.269	6.4	102-LF	1	27-CF	1
2005	BAL	MLB	27	229	22	9	1	5	21	21	49	3	3	5.1	.248	.314	.374	-.109	.256	.332	.399	.253	-2.8	55-LF	-2		
2005	COL	MLB	27	70	5	1	1	0	2	3	18	2	0	6.4	.212	.257	.258	-.394	.200	.246	.246	.187	-4.5	10-CF	0		
2006	*SLN*	*MLB*	*28*	*328*	*44*	*16*	*2*	*8*	*38*	*31*	*71*	*5*	*2*	*5.7*	*.272*	*.342*	*.426*	*.006*	*.273*	*.343*	*.441*	*.264*	*7.0*	*79-LF*	*-2*		

Breakout: 22%   Improve: 42%   Collapse: 32%   Attrition: 25%   Comparables: Gary Rajsich, Todd Hollandsworth, Len Gabrielson

For such an unremarkable player, Bigbie caused quite a stir last summer. The Rockies flipped Eric Byrnes to Baltimore for Bigbie in anticipation of a deal with the Red Sox that would include Kelly Shoppach. The Sox reneged, resulting in their entire front office pointing fingers at each other like it was the end of "Reservoir Dogs." The Rockies claimed they never would have done the deal for Bigbie if they weren't going to get Shoppach. Since we're operating in a game where oversight from the commissioner's office only seems to come into play where major headlines are concerned, the Red Sox were embarrassed but the Rockies were screwed. Subsequently, they settled for moving him to St. Louis to get Ray King this winter.

J. D. CLOSSER   **C**   **Bats: B Throws: R**   Height: 5' 10"   Weight: 175   Born: January 15, 1980   Age: 26

YEAR	TM	LVL	AGE	PA	R	2B	3B	HR	RBI	BB	SO	SB	CS	SPEED	BA	OBP	SLG	MLVR	EQBA	EQOBP	EQSLG	EQA	VORP	DEFENSE	
2003	TUL	AA	23	463	62	28	5	13	54	47	79	3	2	4.6	.283	.359	.471	.179	.261	.333	.447	.267	21.3	94-C	5
2004	CSP	AAA	24	344	53	19	1	7	54	41	47	0	2	3.6	.299	.384	.440	.019	.248	.331	.356	.243	2.2	76-C	-2
2004	COL	MLB	24	121	5	6	0	1	10	6	22	0	0	2.9	.319	.364	.398	.005	.301	.347	.363	.251	3.8	29-C	2
2005	COL	MLB	25	271	31	12	2	7	27	32	48	1	0	4.4	.219	.314	.376	-.134	.204	.304	.353	.234	0.9	65-C	-12
2006	*COL*	*MLB*	*26*	*316*	*36*	*17*	*2*	*8*	*38*	*34*	*52*	*1*	*1*	*4.5*	*.267*	*.351*	*.430*	*.022*	*.248*	*.331*	*.406*	*.250*	*6.5*	*77-C*	*-3*

Breakout: 35%   Improve: 57%   Collapse: 25%   Attrition: 33%   Comparables: Javier Valentin, Alan Ashby, Jorge Posada

Here's the reason the Rockies wanted Kelly Shoppach so badly. Two years ago, Closser looked like the long-term solution at catcher for the Rockies, flashing good power and good plate discipline. But since reaching the majors, his power has disappeared, and his defense has been atrocious (only 11-for-64 throwing out base thieves). The Rockies have said they still think he can turn it around and that they're going to be patient, but they also like Ardoin and traded for Torrealba. Patience with Closser may involve waiting for him to get back on track in Colorado Springs.

J. J. DAVIS   **OF**   **Bats: R Throws: R**   Height: 6' 5"   Weight: 240   Born: October 25, 1978   Age: 27

YEAR	TM	LVL	AGE	PA	R	2B	3B	HR	RBI	BB	SO	SB	CS	SPEED	BA	OBP	SLG	MLVR	EQBA	EQOBP	EQSLG	EQA	VORP	DEFENSE	
2003	NAS	AAA	24	468	68	29	4	26	67	35	85	23	6	6.7	.284	.342	.554	.295	.273	.330	.529	.286	23.0	105-RF	-3
2005	NWO	AAA	26	195	34	10	0	12	31	18	53	3	4	4.7	.282	.359	.546	.259	.255	.321	.468	.263	3.1	30-RF	1
2005	CSP	AAA	26	78	12	3	0	3	15	7	20	1	1	4.3	.224	.295	.403	-.217	.179	.246	.298	.202	-7.5	16-RF	-2
2006	*COL*	*MLB*	*27*	*297*	*39*	*15*	*1*	*13*	*42*	*22*	*73*	*7*	*2*	*4.7*	*.261*	*.321*	*.469*	*.019*	*.242*	*.303*	*.443*	*.249*	*-1.0*	*72-RF*	*-1*

Breakout: 20%   Improve: 45%   Collapse: 30%   Attrition: 27%   Comparables: Scott Morgan, Bucky Jacobsen, Dante Bichette

(continued next page)

J. J. Davis *(continued)*

A 1st round pick of the Pirates way back in 1997, Davis came over from the Nats in the Preston Wilson trade. Davis has showed that he's not a bad Triple-A hitter when he's not complaining about wanting to pitch, something he hasn't done since high school. The prom was a long time ago; it's time to let go, J. J. Davis has never been given regular playing time at the major league level, but this minor league free agent's power could be useful to a team.

JOE GAETTI OF Bats: R Throws: R Height: 5′ 11″ Weight: 205 Born: October 16, 1981 Age: 24

YEAR	TM	LVL	AGE	PA	R	2B	3B	HR	RBI	BB	SO	SB	CS	SPEED	BA	OBP	SLG	MLVR	EQBA	EQOBP	EQSLG	EQA	VORP	DEFENSE			
2004	ASH	A	22	441	62	24	1	16	55	55	107	16	6	5.1	.257	.370	.457	.058	.194	.283	.339	.223	-28.1	43-RF	1	32-CF	2
2005	MOD	A+	23	459	90	29	8	21	87	52	114	5	7	6.3	.332	.418	.605	.419	.268	.340	.452	.269	20.0	75-CF	-4	21-LF	-2
2006	COL	MLB	24	483	62	27	4	17	61	44	138	6	3	4.7	.259	.333	.461	.026	.240	.314	.435	.250	3.0	114-CF	-3		

Breakout: 28% Improve: 53% Collapse: 25% Attrition: 10% Comparables: Kirk Asche, Justin Sherrod, Michael Coleman

Finally healthy after back problems in 2004, Gaetti did everything you could want a prospect to do in High-A Modesto. His strikeouts are a little high and he was old for the level, but he had 58 extra-base hits and his OBP and SLG started with the numbers "4" and "6", respectively. His Double-A performance will tell us whether he has a future.

BRAD HAWPE 1B/OF Bats: L Throws: L Height: 6′ 3″ Weight: 200 Born: June 22, 1979 Age: 27

YEAR	TM	LVL	AGE	PA	R	2B	3B	HR	RBI	BB	SO	SB	CS	SPEED	BA	OBP	SLG	MLVR	EQBA	EQOBP	EQSLG	EQA	VORP	DEFENSE			
2003	TUL	AA	24	379	52	27	0	17	68	31	84	1	3	3.0	.277	.338	.503	.187	.239	.296	.443	.248	-3.9	48-RF	0	17-1B	-2
2004	CSP	AAA	25	385	62	19	1	31	86	36	91	3	2	4.0	.322	.384	.652	.344	.260	.322	.504	.275	11.8	76-RF	7	10-LF	1
2004	COL	MLB	25	118	12	3	2	3	9	11	34	1	1	5.1	.248	.322	.400	-.098	.231	.308	.385	.241	-1.4	26-RF	2		
2005	COL	MLB	26	351	38	10	3	9	47	43	70	2	2	5.1	.262	.350	.403	-.004	.247	.340	.387	.256	3.0	79-RF	2		
2006	COL	MLB	27	394	51	20	2	17	58	40	84	2	2	4.6	.282	.358	.500	.137	.262	.338	.472	.269	8.9	94-RF	0		

Breakout: 34% Improve: 61% Collapse: 20% Attrition: 23% Comparables: Eric Anthony, Joe Hague, George Altman

Handed the right field job after his big 2004 in Colorado Springs, Hawpe's season was a disappointment. The Rockies strictly platooned him (he had only 32 PAs against southpaws), but he managed only a .262/.350/.403 line after a hot start, and missed two months with a hamstring injury. The good news is that Hawpe has been very successful in his transition to the outfield, posting above average numbers as a defender. If he can get a little bit of that lost power back, Hawpe should be a cheap, productive outfielder, and will get to sound his barbaric Hawpe yawp over the roofs of Denver for the next few years.

TODD HELTON 1B Bats: L Throws: L Height: 6′ 2″ Weight: 206 Born: August 20, 1973 Age: 32

YEAR	TM	LVL	AGE	PA	R	2B	3B	HR	RBI	BB	SO	SB	CS	SPEED	BA	OBP	SLG	MLVR	EQBA	EQOBP	EQSLG	EQA	VORP	DEFENSE	
2003	COL	MLB	29	703	135	49	5	33	117	111	72	0	4	4.0	.358	.458	.630	.523	.332	.435	.591	.339	88.5	156-1B	24
2004	COL	MLB	30	683	115	49	2	32	96	127	72	3	0	4.8	.347	.469	.620	.477	.318	.443	.573	.342	83.8	149-1B	24
2005	COL	MLB	31	625	92	45	2	20	79	106	80	3	0	4.7	.320	.445	.534	.355	.297	.426	.505	.321	57.9	140-1B	19
2006	COL	MLB	32	622	87	39	2	25	96	101	74	3	1	4.5	.319	.433	.551	.350	.296	.409	.520	.313	41.1	145-1B	13

Breakout: 2% Improve: 31% Collapse: 24% Attrition: 4% Comparables: Ryan Klesko, David Justice, John Olerud

Branch Rickey used to say that it was better to trade a player a year too early than a year too late. Helton, a 32-year old first baseman with a career .337/.433/.607 line, is a case in point. He's been a great hitter in Colorado and on the road, and is one of the best defensive first basemen in the majors. The problem is that the Rockies owe him a minimum of $106.7 million through 2011. While a 12-win player is worth that kind of money, Helton seems headed down to the seven-eight win range. As great as Helton has been, now is the time to move him. He's still one of the ten most valuable players in the NL, but everyone was having a great time on the Titanic up until 11:40 P.M. or so, too. Of course, given the size of his contract, getting fair value for him, or even significant financial relief, is easier wished for than done.

MATT HOLLIDAY LF Bats: R Throws: R Height: 6′ 4″ Weight: 230 Born: January 15, 1980 Age: 26

YEAR	TM	LVL	AGE	PA	R	2B	3B	HR	RBI	BB	SO	SB	CS	SPEED	BA	OBP	SLG	MLVR	EQBA	EQOBP	EQSLG	EQA	VORP	DEFENSE	
2003	TUL	AA	23	578	65	28	5	12	72	43	74	15	9	5.4	.253	.313	.395	-.021	.234	.291	.376	.233	-24.8	121-LF	-1
2004	COL	MLB	24	438	65	31	3	14	57	31	86	3	3	5.0	.290	.349	.487	.078	.271	.331	.456	.266	8.0	104-LF	0
2005	COL	MLB	25	526	68	24	7	19	87	36	79	14	3	6.5	.307	.361	.505	.180	.288	.345	.485	.283	30.3	120-LF	-1
2006	COL	MLB	26	572	81	33	4	20	80	45	86	13	5	5.5	.299	.359	.499	.154	.277	.339	.471	.271	14.4	134-LF	-2

Breakout: 31% Improve: 56% Collapse: 14% Attrition: 8% Comparables: Bob Allison, Charlie Spikes, Carlos Lee

There's a lot of Coors Field in him, but Holliday is performing well above the expected levels his performance indicated up until 2004. After struggling in consecutive years at Double-A in 2002 and 2003, Holliday played himself into the Rockies' outfield picture with a hot AFL, a good spring training, and an injury to Preston Wilson. Holliday's road numbers are bad, and he doesn't draw enough walks to make anyone comfortable, but the Rockies are getting so much more than what they could have expected. Whatever changed in 2004—the Rockies say it was a combination of physical growth and increased confidence—it seems to have stuck.

CHRIS IANNETTA C **Bats: R Throws: R** Height: 5' 11" Weight: 195 Born: April 8, 1983 Age: 23

YEAR	TM	LVL	AGE	PA	R	2B	3B	HR	RBI	BB	SO	SB	CS	SPEED	BA	OBP	SLG	MLVR	EQBA	EQOBP	EQSLG	EQA	VORP	DEFENSE	
2004	ASH	A	21	152	23	5	1	5	17	27	29	0	1	3.4	.314	.454	.496	.270	.253	.373	.403	.272	7.1	32-C	7
2005	MOD	A+	22	312	51	17	3	11	58	45	61	1	2	4.2	.276	.381	.490	.124	.228	.320	.385	.248	2.4	68-C	0
2005	TUL	AA	22	70	7	3	1	2	11	8	15	0	0	3.6	.233	.329	.417	-.027	.218	.305	.401	.246	0.3	14-C	1
2006	COL	MLB	23	366	43	20	3	10	43	41	79	1	1	4.0	.255	.344	.430	.001	.236	.325	.406	.247	5.8	88-C	1

Breakout: 27%   Improve: 50%   Collapse: 34%   Attrition: 16%   Comparables: Jason Dewey, Kelly Shoppach, Steve Lomasney

Iannetta's glovework initially got all the attention, but since it's an inviolable law of the universe that a catcher cannot be praised simultaneously for both his defense and offense, his surprising bat has led to increased talk that he's only an average defensive backstop. He's a catcher who's mastered High-A ball at 22, won't have to move from behind the plate as he moves up, and hits for power with patience. Everything else is just commentary.

JOSEPH KOSHANSKY 1B **Bats: L Throws: L** Height: 6' 4" Weight: 225 Born: May 26, 1982 Age: 24

YEAR	TM	LVL	AGE	PA	R	2B	3B	HR	RBI	BB	SO	SB	CS	SPEED	BA	OBP	SLG	MLVR	EQBA	EQOBP	EQSLG	EQA	VORP	DEFENSE	
2004	TRI	A-	22	276	41	18	0	12	43	31	84	1	0	4.2	.234	.330	.460	.124	.182	.248	.337	.207	-34.8		
2005	ASH	A	23	525	92	31	1	36	103	53	122	6	6	3.9	.291	.373	.603	.273	.208	.271	.414	.234	-18.4	115-1B	11
2006	COL	MLB	24	464	48	23	1	17	60	34	139	2	1	3.5	.228	.290	.409	-.136	.212	.274	.386	.218	-16.8	110-1B	5

Breakout: 28%   Improve: 48%   Collapse: 27%   Attrition: 10%   Comparables: Derek Michaelis, Bryon Gainey, Tim Flaherty

Koshansky was second in the minors in total home runs, which provides a lesson in park factors and how they're applied. The right field wall in Asheville is closer to the plate than this book is to you right now. Okay, so it's not quite that close, but it is just 300 feet from the plate, and Koshansky took advantage, batting .355/.432/.763 with 25 home runs in 228 at bats. He hit just .227/.311/.440 with 11 home runs in 225 at bats on the road, but the Rockies insist his dingers would have been home runs anywhere and that he has the best pure power in the system. Koshansky plays surprisingly good defense and is still largely under the radar, and if he handles Double-A well, he'll start showing up on prospect lists.

AARON MILES 2B **Bats: B Throws: R** Height: 5' 8" Weight: 170 Born: December 15, 1976 Age: 29

YEAR	TM	LVL	AGE	PA	R	2B	3B	HR	RBI	BB	SO	SB	CS	SPEED	BA	OBP	SLG	MLVR	EQBA	EQOBP	EQSLG	EQA	VORP	DEFENSE	
2003	CHR	AAA	26	590	80	34	5	11	50	40	52	8	9	5.0	.304	.351	.445	.142	.281	.332	.417	.257	23.0	120-2B	4
2004	COL	MLB	27	559	75	15	3	6	47	29	53	12	7	5.6	.293	.329	.368	-.117	.274	.311	.347	.233	1.0	116-2B	-4
2005	COL	MLB	28	337	37	12	3	2	28	8	38	4	2	5.7	.281	.306	.355	-.146	.268	.295	.338	.224	-3.3	69-2B	6
2006	SLN	MLB	29	375	42	15	2	3	30	18	39	5	2	4.7	.261	.302	.343	-.181	.263	.303	.356	.222	-0.8	90-2B	0

Breakout: 22%   Improve: 49%   Collapse: 28%   Attrition: 25%   Comparables: Horace Clarke, Nelson Liriano, Larry Milbourne

Acquired two years ago in expectation that he'd be the second baseman of the present, Miles was reduced to splitting time with Luis Gonzalez. He managed only a .292/.317/.365 line against righties, and his glove isn't good enough to keep him in the lineup. He's 30, and wasn't likely to survive the next Rockies Biannual Youth Movement. Dan O'Dowd got a head start on that by packaging him with Bigbie to get Ray King.

MATTHEW MILLER OF **Bats: R Throws: R** Height: 6' 2" Weight: 210 Born: December 26, 1982 Age: 23

YEAR	TM	LVL	AGE	PA	R	2B	3B	HR	RBI	BB	SO	SB	CS	SPEED	BA	OBP	SLG	MLVR	EQBA	EQOBP	EQSLG	EQA	VORP	DEFENSE				
2004	TRI	A-	21	184	17	8	0	8	25	13	18	0	0	2.7	.269	.337	.461	.168	.232	.274	.385	.226	-9.5				
2005	ASH	A	22	549	79	34	0	30	100	26	71	9	8	4.3	.331	.375	.575	.279	.249	.282	.432	.241	-12.1	87-LF	3	33-CF	0
2006	COL	MLB	23	483	52	25	1	14	61	20	72	4	2	3.8	.265	.302	.418	-.077	.246	.285	.394	.225	-8.0	114-LF	0		

Breakout: 20%   Improve: 45%   Collapse: 34%   Attrition: 8%   Comparables: Joseph Gomes, Richard Correll, Cliff Wren

(continued next page)

Matthew Miller *(continued)*

As opposed to the left-handed Koshansky, Miller's power isn't a result of the short distance to right field in Asheville, but he still showed the same extreme home/road splits on his way to being named the Sally League MVP. A 13th round pick, Miller's performance was a big surprise; if he can consolidate that in Double-A, the Rockies may finally have a legitimate outfield prospect on their hands. With a "dirty uniform" style that the Rockies like and the paucity of talent in front of him, Miller could move quickly.

TONY MILLER   **OF**   **Bats: R Throws: R**   Height: 5′ 9″   Weight: 180   Born: August 18, 1980   Age: 25

YEAR	TM	LVL	AGE	PA	R	2B	3B	HR	RBI	BB	SO	SB	CS	SPEED	BA	OBP	SLG	MLVR	EQBA	EQOBP	EQSLG	EQA	VORP	DEFENSE			
2003	VIS	A+	22	312	47	14	5	4	31	40	58	11	7	6.6	.248	.349	.383	-.032	.210	.298	.323	.223	-11.5	63-CF	4		
2004	TUL	AA	23	491	61	17	2	11	36	68	99	20	12	5.1	.273	.385	.403	.094	.247	.344	.367	.253	5.2	83-CF	3	21-LF	2
2005	TUL	AA	24	553	102	17	6	18	58	87	116	26	14	6.9	.280	.400	.461	.183	.242	.351	.389	.262	11.9	77-CF	4	37-LF	2
2006	COL	MLB	25	469	62	23	4	11	49	51	100	12	6	5.5	.267	.353	.422	.016	.248	.334	.398	.250	3.3	111-CF	2		

Breakout: 19%   Improve: 50%   Collapse: 24%   Attrition: 14%   Comparables: Kurt Airoso, Mike Cameron, Marco Cunningham

Miller usually gets forgiven for his apparent lack of progress because he also played football at Toledo; it's felt that he needs time to learn to play baseball. That may be true, but Miller's walk rate shows that he already knows how to take care of the strike zone. He's most likely ticketed for a backup role in the majors, but thin air and opportunity can make all sorts of people rich and famous.

DUSTAN MOHR   **OF**   **Bats: R Throws: R**   Height: 6′ 2″   Weight: 210   Born: June 19, 1976   Age: 30

YEAR	TM	LVL	AGE	PA	R	2B	3B	HR	RBI	BB	SO	SB	CS	SPEED	BA	OBP	SLG	MLVR	EQBA	EQOBP	EQSLG	EQA	VORP	DEFENSE			
2003	MIN	MLB	27	385	50	22	0	10	36	33	106	5	2	4.5	.250	.314	.399	-.090	.247	.318	.395	.249	-3.6	64-RF	2	24-LF	-1
2004	SFN	MLB	28	320	52	20	1	7	28	46	64	0	3	4.5	.274	.394	.437	.110	.268	.386	.423	.283	9.6	42-RF	-1	24-LF	2
2005	COL	MLB	29	293	34	10	3	17	38	23	94	1	2	5.1	.214	.280	.466	-.076	.202	.271	.449	.241	-2.2	44-RF	2	14-LF	1
2006	COL	MLB	30	240	31	13	2	11	35	24	62	1	1	4.7	.264	.343	.493	.088	.245	.324	.466	.261	3.3	59-RF	1		

Breakout: 30%   Improve: 53%   Collapse: 30%   Attrition: 40%   Comparables: Ken Hunt, Dave Henderson, Jim Hickman

The pre-season favorite for the right field job, Mohr tanked, a startling development considering his change in home parks. He's still only 30, kills southpaws, and his defense is decent, so he'll land a job somewhere, probably rebound a bit, and get named the player most likely to be the next Greg Colbrunn by the Greg Colbrunn Fan Club.

JAYSON NIX   **2B**   **Bats: R Throws: R**   Height: 5′ 11″   Weight: 180   Born: August 26, 1982   Age: 23

YEAR	TM	LVL	AGE	PA	R	2B	3B	HR	RBI	BB	SO	SB	CS	SPEED	BA	OBP	SLG	MLVR	EQBA	EQOBP	EQSLG	EQA	VORP	DEFENSE	
2003	VIS	A+	20	632	107	46	0	21	86	54	131	24	8	5.9	.281	.351	.475	.121	.226	.288	.384	.236	-5.7	135-2B	21
2004	TUL	AA	21	510	58	17	1	14	58	40	101	14	3	5.4	.213	.292	.346	-.183	.191	.256	.315	.207	-30.2	118-2B	10
2005	TUL	AA	22	547	68	27	0	11	47	29	92	10	6	5.2	.236	.289	.355	-.175	.204	.255	.314	.204	-31.4	130-2B	-3
2006	COL	MLB	23	445	50	23	2	10	45	29	81	7	4	4.6	.246	.304	.390	-.124	.228	.287	.368	.220	-4.0	106-2B	2

Breakout: 52%   Improve: 68%   Collapse: 17%   Attrition: 11%   Comparables: Carlos Casimiro, Dave Hilton, Dan Uggla

In the words of Harlan Ellison, "Fool me once, shame on you. Fool me twice and I'm a pervert." Nix has been embarrassed twice at Tulsa, and while the first time around some of it could be blamed on not making contact often enough, everything else got worse last year. The Rockies love his defense, and are being patient with him. They think they can work on his swing, correcting his tendency to fly open trying to pull the ball. He's still on the young side and could return to being the hitter who used to spray the ball to all fields, but then again, some guys just can't get past Double-A.

JORGE PIEDRA   **OF**   **Bats: L Throws: L**   Height: 6′ 0″   Weight: 190   Born: April 17, 1979   Age: 27

YEAR	TM	LVL	AGE	PA	R	2B	3B	HR	RBI	BB	SO	SB	CS	SPEED	BA	OBP	SLG	MLVR	EQBA	EQOBP	EQSLG	EQA	VORP	DEFENSE			
2003	TUL	AA	24	401	56	17	7	18	52	31	50	5	2	5.5	.275	.342	.513	.203	.245	.305	.460	.260	1.0	62-RF	3	14-LF	1
2004	CSP	AAA	25	409	71	29	5	15	55	23	56	4	3	5.4	.334	.372	.557	.201	.278	.315	.448	.260	3.0	70-LF	3	20-RF	1
2004	COL	MLB	25	97	15	8	0	3	10	5	19	0	1	4.9	.297	.340	.484	.061	.278	.323	.444	.257	2.2	12-CF	1		
2005	CSP	AAA	26	207	35	20	1	6	45	18	23	4	2	5.0	.312	.372	.527	.174	.259	.313	.430	.254	-0.4	27-RF	-2	15-LF	-2
2005	COL	MLB	26	124	19	8	1	6	16	10	15	2	1	5.2	.312	.371	.562	.284	.291	.352	.536	.295	10.3	14-RF	-1		
2006	COL	MLB	27	356	46	21	3	12	50	26	47	5	2	4.8	.290	.347	.485	.107	.268	.328	.457	.263	7.3	86-LF	0		

Breakout: 22%   Improve: 48%   Collapse: 30%   Attrition: 21%   Comparables: Ray Webster, Henry Rodriguez, Ross Gload

Piedra was all set to become an above-average player without anybody noticing—up until Jose Canseco decided to write a book. Piedra tested positive for steroids, and suddenly he's the bad guy. This subject's about as exhausted as Paris Hilton's publicist, and we're not here to pass moral judgment or repeatedly point out that there's no study quantifying the effects of steroids on baseball performance, so let's just note that Piedra played well when they let him. As long as the Rockies are struggling to find outfielders, Piedra will make for a nice little player.

OMAR QUINTANILLA   2B/SS   Bats: L Throws: R   Height: 5′ 9″   Weight: 190   Born: October 24, 1981   Age: 24

YEAR	TM	LVL	AGE	PA	R	2B	3B	HR	RBI	BB	SO	SB	CS	SPEED	BA	OBP	SLG	MLVR	EQBA	EQOBP	EQSLG	EQA	VORP	DEFENSE	
2004	MOD	A+	22	497	75	32	5	11	72	37	54	1	3	4.0	.315	.370	.481	.197	.274	.321	.416	.253	17.7	103-SS	1
2004	MID	AA	22	105	20	10	0	2	20	10	9	2	0	4.8	.351	.419	.521	.365	.302	.371	.465	.288	9.1	23-SS	4
2005	MID	AA	23	320	46	14	2	4	25	23	40	2	3	4.8	.293	.347	.395	.026	.264	.317	.357	.237	3.3	70-SS	0
2005	COL	MLB	23	137	16	1	1	0	7	9	15	2	1	5.9	.219	.270	.242	-.394	.209	.266	.233	.189	-8.5	31-SS	-3
2006	*COL*	*MLB*	*24*	*453*	*55*	*23*	*4*	*8*	*47*	*32*	*58*	*4*	*3*	*5.2*	*.289*	*.342*	*.421*	*.013*	*.268*	*.323*	*.397*	*.244*	*10.5*	*107-SS*	*1*

Breakout: 19%   Improve: 45%   Collapse: 24%   Attrition: 13%   Comparables: Joe Thurston, Ken Boswell, Tom Sergio

Quintanilla came to Colorado in the Kennedy-Witasick-Byrnes deal. The Rockies rushed him to the majors to help replace the injured Clint Barmes. He's a line-drive hitter and the kind of player who's not going to take advantage of the thin air, but might be helped by the expansive outfield and wide power alleys of Coors. He obviously still needs some time in the minors before he's really ready to contribute at the major league level. The Rockies don't have star talent in the middle infield, and they think he has the tools to stick at short, but Barmes might push him to second.

JEFF SALAZAR   OF   Bats: L Throws: L   Height: 6′ 0″   Weight: 180   Born: November 24, 1980   Age: 25

YEAR	TM	LVL	AGE	PA	R	2B	3B	HR	RBI	BB	SO	SB	CS	SPEED	BA	OBP	SLG	MLVR	EQBA	EQOBP	EQSLG	EQA	VORP	DEFENSE			
2003	ASH	A	22	574	109	23	4	29	98	77	74	28	14	6.4	.284	.387	.527	.247	.221	.305	.414	.248	1.4	126-CF	17		
2004	VIS	A+	23	356	79	18	9	13	44	38	33	17	2	8.1	.347	.419	.586	.424	.279	.342	.448	.274	16.0	71-CF	5		
2004	TUL	AA	23	263	39	13	2	1	17	35	31	10	3	6.5	.223	.331	.312	-.152	.204	.297	.283	.219	-14.4	46-CF	2	16-LF	1
2005	TUL	AA	24	315	47	13	2	6	35	44	49	12	8	5.8	.278	.381	.410	.085	.242	.337	.351	.247	-0.1	50-CF	4	17-LF	2
2005	CSP	AAA	24	269	42	17	3	6	26	32	58	5	2	5.8	.263	.349	.436	-.039	.227	.306	.369	.238	-3.4	51-CF	3		
2006	*COL*	*MLB*	*25*	*487*	*61*	*26*	*3*	*12*	*52*	*49*	*80*	*9*	*4*	*5.2*	*.263*	*.342*	*.422*	*-.007*	*.244*	*.323*	*.398*	*.245*	*2.6*	*115-CF*	*5*		

Breakout: 23%   Improve: 49%   Collapse: 24%   Attrition: 9%   Comparables: Bobby Higginson, Mike Jorgensen, Ed Kirkpatrick

After his huge '03 season in Asheville, Salazar has struggled to regain his power stroke. He's always been just a little too old for his levels, and his Asheville numbers were helped by the park's unique dimensions, but he does have exceptional plate discipline. He may make a career of playing good defense in center, drawing his walks, and popping a few doubles in the wide-open outfields of the NL West.

RYAN SHEALY   1B   Bats: R Throws: R   Height: 6′ 5″   Weight: 240   Born: August 29, 1979   Age: 26

YEAR	TM	LVL	AGE	PA	R	2B	3B	HR	RBI	BB	SO	SB	CS	SPEED	BA	OBP	SLG	MLVR	EQBA	EQOBP	EQSLG	EQA	VORP	DEFENSE	
2003	VIS	A+	23	404	70	31	1	14	73	42	72	0	0	3.9	.299	.391	.519	.259	.238	.312	.413	.251	-3.3	76-1B	-1
2004	TUL	AA	24	550	88	32	3	29	99	61	123	1	1	3.8	.318	.411	.584	.418	.277	.355	.500	.288	30.4	125-1B	-3
2005	CSP	AAA	25	466	85	30	2	26	88	41	81	4	0	4.9	.328	.393	.601	.333	.276	.333	.485	.278	17.2	101-1B	8
2005	COL	MLB	25	104	14	7	0	2	16	13	22	1	0	3.3	.330	.413	.473	.239	.303	.392	.461	.297	7.4	17-1B	1
2006	*COL*	*MLB*	*26*	*487*	*64*	*28*	*2*	*22*	*76*	*44*	*98*	*3*	*1*	*4.4*	*.288*	*.360*	*.516*	*.167*	*.267*	*.339*	*.487*	*.275*	*14.2*	*115-1B*	*1*

Breakout: 18%   Improve: 45%   Collapse: 27%   Attrition: 12%   Comparables: Derrek Lee, Deron Johnson, Butch Huskey

Shealy hasn't looked back after his senior season at Florida State, and he's done everything a power-hitting prospect should do. Unfortunately, he's a first baseman blocked by some guy named Helton. The Rockies are attempting to teach him to play the outfield. He's reportedly losing weight and taking well to his new position, so he should be in the mix to platoon with Brad Hawpe this year, There isn't a worse park than Coors in which to convert a slow first baseman into an outfielder.

SETH SMITH   OF   Bats: L Throws: L   Height: 6′ 3″   Weight: 215   Born: September 30, 1982   Age: 23

YEAR	TM	LVL	AGE	PA	R	2B	3B	HR	RBI	BB	SO	SB	CS	SPEED	BA	OBP	SLG	MLVR	EQBA	EQOBP	EQSLG	EQA	VORP	DEFENSE			
2004	CAS	Rk	21	260	46	21	3	9	61	25	47	9	1	5.7	.369	.427	.601	.451	.278	.314	.425	.256	0.5	40-RF	-2		
2005	MOD	A+	22	581	87	45	6	9	72	44	115	5	3	5.2	.300	.353	.458	.047	.252	.297	.368	.232	-20.7	106-RF	1	17-CF	-3
2006	*COL*	*MLB*	*23*	*453*	*49*	*28*	*3*	*9*	*52*	*28*	*95*	*4*	*2*	*4.6*	*.270*	*.317*	*.417*	*-.050*	*.250*	*.299*	*.393*	*.231*	*-6.8*	*107-RF*	*-3*		

Breakout: 17%   Improve: 46%   Collapse: 28%   Attrition: 8%   Comparables: Rich Lane, Thomas Brice, Robert Malek

(continued next page)

Seth Smith *(continued)*

A 2nd round pick out of Mississippi in 2004, Smith had an insane debut but reverted back into a doubles machine in the California League last year. Another college football player whom the Rockies expect to develop as he learns the game, Smith has a healthy XBH rate, but he'll need to control the strike zone better as he moves up the ladder. He had LASIK surgery in the off-season, and the Rockies expect it to help his middling outfield defense, and perhaps also some of that missing plate discipline.

IAN STEWART 3B Bats: L Throws: R Height: 6′ 3″ Weight: 205 Born: April 5, 1985 Age: 21

YEAR	TM	LVL	AGE	PA	R	2B	3B	HR	RBI	BB	SO	SB	CS	SPEED	BA	OBP	SLG	MLVR	EQBA	EQOBP	EQSLG	EQA	VORP	DEFENSE	
2003	CAS	Rk	18	257	40	14	5	10	43	29	54	4	1	5.4	.317	.401	.558	.322	.244	.315	.418	.252	10.6	51-3B	-2
2004	ASH	A	19	580	92	31	9	30	101	66	112	19	9	6.0	.319	.398	.594	.320	.251	.321	.459	.265	25.2	115-3B	20
2005	MOD	A+	20	499	83	32	7	17	86	52	113	2	2	5.3	.274	.353	.497	.077	.225	.292	.385	.236	-2.6	106-3B	5
2006	*COL*	*MLB*	*21*	*487*	*58*	*27*	*3*	*16*	*63*	*44*	*103*	*5*	*3*	*4.9*	*.268*	*.337*	*.454*	*.031*	*.248*	*.318*	*.429*	*.250*	*6.9*	*115-3B*	*3*

Breakout: 24% Improve: 56% Collapse: 23% Attrition: 8% Comparables: Kelly Johnson, Corey Smith, Adrian Gonzalez

Stewart's 2004 established him as one of the game's elite prospects, but in 2005 his progress was slowed by a hamstring injury, although he finished strongly. He'll be a 21-year old in Double-A, and he's established that he's going to stay at third all the way to the majors, so he's on track for the Rockies' third base job in 2008, if not sooner. He injured his wrist sliding in the AFL, but it was only a bone bruise and shouldn't cause any problems down the road.

CORY SULLIVAN CF Bats: L Throws: L Height: 6′ 0″ Weight: 180 Born: August 20, 1979 Age: 26

YEAR	TM	LVL	AGE	PA	R	2B	3B	HR	RBI	BB	SO	SB	CS	SPEED	BA	OBP	SLG	MLVR	EQBA	EQOBP	EQSLG	EQA	VORP	DEFENSE			
2003	TUL	AA	23	605	81	34	8	5	61	39	83	17	13	5.9	.300	.347	.417	.101	.283	.328	.407	.254	15.2	132-CF	4		
2005	COL	MLB	25	414	64	15	4	4	30	28	83	12	3	6.9	.294	.343	.386	-.027	.276	.328	.366	.249	7.6	71-CF	-2	17-LF	0
2006	*COL*	*MLB*	*26*	*349*	*46*	*17*	*3*	*5*	*33*	*25*	*59*	*9*	*3*	*5.7*	*.290*	*.346*	*.415*	*.012*	*.269*	*.327*	*.391*	*.246*	*3.5*	*84-CF*	*0*		

Breakout: 22% Improve: 47% Collapse: 25% Attrition: 26% Comparables: Bob Addis, Russ Snyder, Charles Thomas

Sullivan missed the 2004 season with a torn labrum, but earned a spot on the major league roster with a strong spring training, meaning he's skipped both High-A and Triple-A in his career. When Preston Wilson was traded, Sullivan took over in center; his defense was acceptable but his offense was not. Of course, he's never hit for power and hitting even this well in the majors after an entire year off is impressive, until you remember his home park. A platoon of Sullivan and Jeff Salazar would make some sense if only both of them weren't left-handed.

PITCHERS

JOSE ACEVEDO Bats: R Throws: R Height: 6′ 0″ Weight: 185 Born: December 18, 1977 Age: 28

YEAR	TM	LVL	AGE	W	L	SV	G	GS	IP	H	BB	SO	HR	GB%	BABIP	STUFF	WHIP	ERA	PERA	EQERA	EQH9	EQBB9	EQSO9	EQHR9	VORP	WXRL
2003	LOU	AAA	25	6	2	0	29	3	60.3	56	20	57	5	—	.292	-3	1.26	3.43	4.81	4.66	8.8	3.7	6.5	1.2	6.1	—
2003	CIN	MLB	25	2	0	0	5	4	27.0	17	6	23	3	39%	.209	24	0.85	2.67	3.86	2.81	7.0	1.8	7.4	1.1	9.0	1.0
2004	CIN	MLB	26	5	12	0	39	27	157.7	188	45	117	30	40%	.318	-9	1.48	5.94	5.06	5.68	10.1	2.3	5.8	1.6	-11.9	0.9
2005	COL	MLB	27	2	4	1	36	5	64.0	86	16	31	13	35%	.326	-26	1.59	6.47	5.56	5.83	10.7	2.0	3.8	1.6	-5.5	0.1
2006	*COL*	*MLB*	*28*	*3*	*5*	*1*	*40*	*7*	*74.0*	*88*	*21*	*43*	*13*	*40%*	*.305*	*-7*	*1.48*	*5.50*	*5.08*	*5.60*	*9.8*	*2.3*	*5.1*	*1.4*	*4.7*	*0.6*

Breakout: 30% Improve: 55% Collapse: 23% Attrition: 22% Comparables: Willie Blair, Bob Priddy, Scott Bankhead

Last year we pointed out that Acevedo had a 6.65 ERA as a starter and 0.00 as a reliever. In 2005, it was 8.87 as a starter, 4.87 in relief, and while those numbers continue the trend, 4.87 isn't a number that brings gentlemen callers to anyone's doorstep. Acevedo still has his odd combination of command and gopheritis, and with his strikeout numbers dropping, he'll have to fight to hang on as the designated long reliever and spot starter.

MARCOS CARVAJAL Bats: R Throws: R Height: 6′ 4″ Weight: 175 Born: August 19, 1984 Age: 21

YEAR	TM	LVL	AGE	W	L	SV	G	GS	IP	H	BB	SO	HR	GB%	BABIP	STUFF	WHIP	ERA	PERA	EQERA	EQH9	EQBB9	EQSO9	EQHR9	VORP	WXRL
2003	OGD	Rk	18	2	1	2	23	0	38.0	32	22	50	1	—	.326	5	1.42	3.08	5.30	5.05	8.3	7.6	6.6	0.5	2.2	—
2004	CGA	A	19	4	2	1	36	0	72.0	50	35	72	2	—	.264	9	1.18	1.88	4.52	3.72	7.8	5.3	5.6	0.4	14.1	—
2005	COL	MLB	20	0	2	0	39	0	53.0	52	21	47	8	51%	.301	9	1.38	5.09	4.70	4.53	8.6	3.4	7.2	1.3	4.1	-0.2
2006	*SEA*	*MLB*	*21*	*2*	*2*	*1*	*28*	*1*	*40.3*	*41*	*21*	*33*	*5*	*46%*	*.304*	*1*	*1.53*	*4.76*	*5.18*	*5.41*	*9.1*	*4.6*	*6.9*	*1.0*	*2.9*	*0.2*

Breakout: 18% Improve: 29% Collapse: 38% Attrition: 36% Comparables: Tommie Sisk, Eduardo Rodriguez, Rich Gossage

Taken by the Brewers in the 2004 Rule 5 draft, the Rockies bought Carvajal for $75,000 and stuck the kid with all of three innings above A-ball in their pen. Surprisingly, he wasn't that bad. Carvajal works with a mid-90s fastball that sometimes gets up to 98, and while his breaking pitches need work, he was a surprising steal and a credit to the Rockies scouting staff. Dealt to Seattle, where his prospects, like any ex-Rockie pitcher's, improve.

AARON COOK Bats: R Throws: R   Height: 6′ 3″ Weight: 170 Born: February 8, 1979   Age: 27

YEAR	TM	LVL	AGE	W	L	SV	G	GS	IP	H	BB	SO	HR	GB%	BABIP	STUFF	WHIP	ERA	PERA	EQERA	EQH9	EQBB9	EQSO9	EQHR9	VORP	WXRL
2003	COL	MLB	24	4	6	0	43	16	124.0	160	57	43	8	60%	.336	-12	1.75	6.02	4.90	5.67	10.4	3.6	2.7	0.5	-7.1	0.6
2004	COL	MLB	25	6	4	0	16	16	96.7	112	39	40	7	57%	.314	4	1.56	4.28	4.74	3.92	9.7	3.3	3.3	0.5	18.3	2.2
2005	COL	MLB	26	7	2	0	13	13	83.3	101	16	24	8	61%	.307	-2	1.40	3.67	4.76	3.49	10.0	1.6	2.3	0.8	15.7	2.5
2006	COL	MLB	27	5	8	0	29	18	108.0	138	34	44	11	59%	.324	-8	1.59	5.35	4.94	5.29	10.5	2.5	3.6	0.8	6.5	1.3

Breakout: 7%   Improve: 33%   Collapse: 37%   Attrition: 9%   Comparables: Chris Holt, John Doherty, Bill Swift

The shining example of someone succeeding at altitude with a low strikeout rate and a heavy sinker, Cook missed the start of the season because of surgery to remove a rib that was causing blood clots in his lungs. It's silly to predict a decline because of that strikeout rate when Cook has obviously figured out how to keep the ball in the park, but everyone would be a lot more comfortable if he would get a few outs on his own from time to time.

DAVID CORTES Bats: R Throws: R   Height: 5′ 11″ Weight: 190 Born: October 15, 1973   Age: 32

YEAR	TM	LVL	AGE	W	L	SV	G	GS	IP	H	BB	SO	HR	GB%	BABIP	STUFF	WHIP	ERA	PERA	EQERA	EQH9	EQBB9	EQSO9	EQHR9	VORP	WXRL
2003	DOS	MEX	29	4	3	18	48	0	53.3	58	18	39	3	—	.313	4	1.43	2.70	3.98	3.64	8.6	2.8	6.6	0.8	11.8	—
2005	COL	MLB	31	2	0	2	50	0	52.7	50	10	36	9	33%	.266	-5	1.14	4.10	4.82	3.61	8.6	1.5	5.7	1.5	9.4	0.3
2006	COL	MLB	32	2	2	2	39	0	40.7	46	13	27	7	38%	.301	-6	1.45	5.12	4.69	5.04	9.3	2.6	5.8	1.3	3.5	0.3

Breakout: 21%   Improve: 38%   Collapse: 35%   Attrition: 36%   Comparables: Donne Wall, Jose Cabrera, Eric Gunderson

Another reliever of the type the Rockies seem to wind up with, Cortes had all of 6.2 major league innings before 2005 but he had posted excellent strikeout and walk rates in the minors. He excelled against righties (.229/.267/.413) but was no slouch against lefties (.278/.313/.456), and while it's tough to see him keeping up that performance in Coors after the league figures him out, he's an example of why it's silly to overpay for middle relief help.

ZACH DAY Bats: R Throws: R   Height: 6′ 4″ Weight: 210 Born: June 15, 1978   Age: 28

YEAR	TM	LVL	AGE	W	L	SV	G	GS	IP	H	BB	SO	HR	GB%	BABIP	STUFF	WHIP	ERA	PERA	EQERA	EQH9	EQBB9	EQSO9	EQHR9	VORP	WXRL
2003	MON	MLB	25	9	8	0	23	23	131.3	132	59	61	8	64%	.285	5	1.45	4.18	4.75	4.34	9.4	3.7	3.8	0.6	23.9	3.2
2004	MON	MLB	26	5	10	0	19	19	116.7	117	45	61	13	55%	.283	1	1.39	3.93	4.92	4.06	9.4	3.2	4.2	0.9	20.1	2.9
2005	WAS	MLB	27	1	2	0	12	5	36.0	41	25	16	4	51%	.303	-29	1.83	6.75	5.94	7.43	10.2	5.7	3.7	1.0	-7.3	0.3
2005	CSP	AAA	27	2	3	0	7	7	36.7	46	15	17	4	47%	.323	-20	1.66	5.89	6.08	6.32	10.2	3.9	2.9	1.2	-3.0	—
2005	COL	MLB	27	0	1	0	5	3	11.3	20	7	7	2	42%	.419	-23	2.38	7.17	5.68	7.82	12.1	5.0	4.3	1.4	-3.1	-0.1
2006	COL	MLB	28	3	6	0	30	11	76.7	94	33	39	9	53%	.320	-11	1.66	5.63	5.18	6.08	10.1	3.5	4.5	0.9	2.6	0.5

Breakout: 16%   Improve: 44%   Collapse: 31%   Attrition: 25%   Comparables: Dallas Green, Gary Waslewski, Don August

Day may have been safer training with the Taliban than pitching last year, as he was hit by comebackers twice. The first broke his wrist and sidelined him for three months, the second broke his thumb, ending his season. He pitches like Aaron Cook, striking out very few batters, keeping the ball in the park, and letting the defense pick him up. It's a tough act to maintain at altitude, but he'll get a shot at the fifth spot in the rotation.

MIKE DeJEAN Bats: R Throws: R   Height: 6′ 2″ Weight: 212 Born: September 28, 1970 Age: 35

YEAR	TM	LVL	AGE	W	L	SV	G	GS	IP	H	BB	SO	HR	GB%	BABIP	STUFF	WHIP	ERA	PERA	EQERA	EQH9	EQBB9	EQSO9	EQHR9	VORP	WXRL
2003	MIL	MLB	32	4	7	18	58	0	64.7	69	27	58	12	55%	.308	-8	1.48	4.87	5.10	5.10	9.2	3.3	7.2	1.7	2.9	-0.1
2004	BAL	MLB	33	0	5	0	37	0	39.7	49	28	36	2	50%	.388	0	1.94	6.12	4.50	6.00	9.9	5.6	7.3	0.4	-0.6	-1.7
2004	NYN	MLB	33	0	0	0	17	0	21.3	21	5	24	0	61%	.362	21	1.22	1.69	2.53	2.11	8.9	2.1	8.9	0.0	8.5	0.6
2005	NYN	MLB	34	3	1	0	28	0	25.7	36	18	17	3	60%	.367	-23	2.10	6.30	5.67	6.67	11.3	5.7	5.3	1.0	-3.5	-0.1
2005	COL	MLB	34	2	3	0	38	0	36.7	26	12	35	0	48%	.265	20	1.04	3.19	3.22	3.22	6.7	2.7	7.9	0.2	8.9	0.9
2006	COL	MLB	35	2	3	2	52	0	58.7	64	27	45	6	52%	.321	-1	1.56	4.96	4.44	5.17	9.0	3.7	6.8	0.8	5.3	0.4

Breakout: 22%   Improve: 48%   Collapse: 24%   Attrition: 13%   Comparables: Jim Gott, Dave Weathers, Bill Campbell

(continued next page)

Mike DeJean *(continued)*

If the bullpen is supposed to be a priority for 2006, why are the Rockies wasting $1.15 million on Mike DeJean? Beyond the 21 innings he threw for the Mets in 2004, he's been an utterly forgettable pitcher the last three years, he's 35, and he still lets lefties crank instant souvenirs. The other arms the Rockies have assembled to audition for the 2006 pen aren't exactly a who's-who list of great relievers, but at least they're cheap.

SCOTT DOHMANN								Bats: R		Throws: R				Height: 6' 1"		Weight: 180		Born: February 13, 1978			Age: 28
YEAR	TM	LVL	AGE	W	L	SV	G	GS	IP	H	BB	SO	HR	GB%	BABIP	STUFF	WHIP	ERA	PERA	EQERA	EQH9	EQBB9	EQSO9	EQHR9	VORP	WXRL
2003	TUL	AA	25	9	4	4	50	4	93.7	94	29	102	11	—	.317	-30	1.31	4.13	6.26	5.95	10.6	3.7	6.9	2.3	-3.4	—
2004	COL	MLB	26	0	3	0	41	0	46.0	41	19	49	8	38%	.282	8	1.30	4.11	4.30	3.91	8.0	3.3	8.4	1.4	9.3	-0.4
2005	CSP	AAA	27	2	1	1	34	0	39.0	41	16	53	5	41%	.375	2	1.46	4.38	4.89	4.66	9.5	4.0	8.4	1.4	4.0	—
2005	COL	MLB	27	2	1	0	32	0	31.0	33	19	35	6	34%	.325	0	1.68	6.10	5.34	5.34	8.7	5.1	9.0	1.7	-0.9	-0.2
2006	*COL*	*MLB*	*28*	*2*	*2*	*1*	*35*	*1*	*37.7*	*39*	*19*	*34*	*6*	*38%*	*.302*	*2*	*1.54*	*5.28*	*4.98*	*6.04*	*8.5*	*4.1*	*7.9*	*1.3*	*3.3*	*0.2*

Breakout: 24%   Improve: 43%   Collapse: 36%   Attrition: 44%   Comparables: Al Reyes, Dave Tobik, Claude Raymond

Originally a starter, the Rockies moved him to the bullpen, hoping that he would add 3–5 mph on his fastball and benefit from working short stints rather than conserving himself for a full game. The results have been great so far, as Dohmann has struck out 270 and walked 90 in 231.2 innings since the conversion. He's a flyball pitcher—not something that plays well in Colorado—but the Rockies will give him a shot to make the bullpen because they recognize that the peril of pitching in Coors Field is one of the classic blunders, ranking only behind a land war in Asia, and going against a Sicilian when death is on the line.

JEFF FRANCIS								Bats: L		Throws: L				Height: 6' 5"		Weight: 200		Born: January 8, 1981			Age: 25
YEAR	TM	LVL	AGE	W	L	SV	G	GS	IP	H	BB	SO	HR	GB%	BABIP	STUFF	WHIP	ERA	PERA	EQERA	EQH9	EQBB9	EQSO9	EQHR9	VORP	WXRL
2003	VIS	A+	22	12	9	0	27	27	160.7	135	45	153	8	—	.278	8	1.12	3.47	4.72	5.25	8.6	3.4	5.4	0.9	5.9	—
2004	TUL	AA	23	13	1	0	17	17	113.7	73	22	147	9	—	.253	25	0.84	1.98	4.03	3.43	8.0	2.1	8.3	1.3	25.3	—
2004	CSP	AAA	23	3	2	0	7	7	41.0	35	7	49	3	—	.320	35	1.02	2.85	3.35	3.57	8.0	1.6	8.3	0.7	9.1	—
2004	COL	MLB	23	3	2	0	7	7	36.7	42	13	32	8	45%	.318	8	1.50	5.15	5.06	4.82	9.6	2.9	6.8	1.7	2.4	0.6
2005	COL	MLB	24	14	12	0	33	33	183.7	228	70	128	26	39%	.349	1	1.62	5.68	4.90	5.09	9.9	3.1	5.5	1.2	0.1	1.0
2006	*COL*	*MLB*	*25*	*9*	*12*	*0*	*30*	*30*	*176.7*	*197*	*61*	*126*	*24*	*43%*	*.309*	*15*	*1.46*	*4.98*	*4.64*	*4.63*	*9.2*	*2.8*	*6.2*	*1.1*	*18.5*	*3.2*

Breakout: 23%   Improve: 61%   Collapse: 10%   Attrition: 0%   Comparables: Dennis Bennett, John Smiley, Chris Nabholz

One of the best pitching prospects in the game before the season, Francis's smooth mechanics and impeccable command were all the rage, but like all before him, he bowed down before the thin air of Colorado. Or did he? Francis has a career 4.61 ERA at Coors, against an ugly 6.38 on the road with equally nasty peripherals to boot; he wasn't unlucky, he just wasn't as good away from Colorado. His major league BABIP is a healthy .347 in Coors and .341 on the road; combine that with the natural improvement that's expected from a young pitcher, and Francis should be better in 2006.

BRIAN FUENTES								Bats: L		Throws: L				Height: 6' 4"		Weight: 220		Born: August 9, 1975			Age: 30
YEAR	TM	LVL	AGE	W	L	SV	G	GS	IP	H	BB	SO	HR	GB%	BABIP	STUFF	WHIP	ERA	PERA	EQERA	EQH9	EQBB9	EQSO9	EQHR9	VORP	WXRL
2003	COL	MLB	27	3	3	4	75	0	75.3	64	34	82	7	41%	.303	19	1.30	2.75	3.81	2.62	7.7	3.7	8.7	0.7	24.3	2.0
2004	COL	MLB	28	2	4	0	47	0	44.7	46	19	48	5	36%	.347	10	1.46	5.64	3.94	5.32	8.7	3.4	8.3	0.8	0.6	1.4
2005	COL	MLB	29	2	5	31	78	0	74.3	59	34	91	6	40%	.305	27	1.25	2.91	3.60	2.76	7.3	3.8	10.0	0.7	21.8	5.4
2006	*COL*	*MLB*	*30*	*3*	*5*	*24*	*67*	*0*	*63.3*	*59*	*28*	*66*	*8*	*42%*	*.302*	*16*	*1.37*	*4.19*	*3.83*	*3.98*	*7.7*	*3.5*	*9.2*	*1.0*	*11.3*	*1.4*

Breakout: 11%   Improve: 26%   Collapse: 36%   Attrition: 9%   Comparables: Paul Assenmacher, Roberto Hernandez, Rick Aguilera

One of the few pitchers who appears to have figured out how to pitch in Coors, Fuentes now owns a 3.71 ERA at altitude. Finally made the closer, he started to get a little of the recognition he deserves for one of the more amazing feats of pitching in the last decade. The Rockies are talking about locking him into a multi-year deal, which sounds like a good idea until you remember that relievers are often interchangeable.

JASON JENNINGS
Bats: L Throws: R Height: 6′ 2″ Weight: 230 Born: July 17, 1978 Age: 27

YEAR	TM	LVL	AGE	W	L	SV	G	GS	IP	H	BB	SO	HR	GB%	BABIP	STUFF	WHIP	ERA	PERA	EQERA	EQH9	EQBB9	EQSO9	EQHR9	VORP	WXRL
2003	COL	MLB	24	12	13	0	32	32	181.3	212	88	119	20	50%	.336	3	1.65	5.11	4.82	5.06	9.6	3.8	5.2	0.9	4.2	1.6
2004	COL	MLB	25	11	12	0	33	33	201.0	241	101	133	27	50%	.332	0	1.70	5.51	5.08	4.95	9.8	4.0	5.1	1.0	12.8	2.4
2005	COL	MLB	26	6	9	0	20	20	122.0	130	62	75	11	50%	.306	5	1.57	5.02	4.84	4.69	9.0	4.2	5.0	0.8	6.4	1.3
2006	COL	MLB	27	8	11	0	31	26	157.3	181	70	102	18	50%	.317	6	1.60	5.31	4.93	5.03	9.5	3.6	5.7	1.0	10.3	2.2

Breakout: 13%   Improve: 46%   Collapse: 13%   Attrition: 4%   Comparables: Joey Jay, Walt Terrell, Storm Davis

In a case of extremely fortunate timing—for him—Jennings missed his first significant time in four years with a broken middle finger just after signing a two-year, $6.9 million contract to avoid arbitration. He's been remarkably consistent, and when you consider that he's pitching in the game's highest run-scoring environment, he's an undervalued talent. Jennings will be ready for the spring and, more importantly, he's exactly the kind of pitcher the Rockies should consider signing to a longer term deal since they'll be able to point to his raw stats and get him potentially under market value.

UBALDO JIMENEZ
Bats: R Throws: R Height: 6′ 2″ Weight: 165 Born: January 22, 1984 Age: 22

YEAR	TM	LVL	AGE	W	L	SV	G	GS	IP	H	BB	SO	HR	GB%	BABIP	STUFF	WHIP	ERA	PERA	EQERA	EQH9	EQBB9	EQSO9	EQHR9	VORP	WXRL
2003	ASH	A	19	10	6	0	27	27	153.7	129	67	138	11	—	.268	-3	1.28	3.45	6.10	5.35	9.6	4.7	5.2	1.6	4.0	—
2004	VIS	A+	20	4	1	0	9	9	44.3	29	12	61	1	—	.289	36	0.93	2.23	3.40	4.25	7.0	3.2	8.1	0.4	6.3	—
2005	MOD	A+	21	5	3	0	14	14	72.3	61	40	78	5	39%	.311	4	1.40	3.98	5.32	5.06	8.3	6.1	6.2	0.9	4.2	—
2005	TUL	AA	21	2	5	0	12	11	63.0	58	31	53	12	31%	.264	-18	1.41	5.43	7.56	6.33	10.2	5.6	6.0	2.6	-4.7	—
2006	COL	MLB	22	5	9	0	26	21	115.0	125	71	88	21	37%	.299	4	1.70	6.14	5.71	5.62	8.9	4.9	6.7	1.5	0.1	0.8

Breakout: 9%   Improve: 53%   Collapse: 20%   Attrition: 0%   Comparables: Brad Baker, Aaron Myette, Francisco Cruceta

After missing most of 2004 with a broken shoulder blade, the main concern for Jimenez in 2005 was proving that he was completely over the injury. He lost the feel for his big-breaking curveball early in the season, but was throwing well later. His low-90s fastball is a solid pitch, and he still strikes out more than his fair share of batters, but his walk rate is a source of concern. He needs to take a significant step forward in 2006.

BYUNG-HYUN KIM
Bats: R Throws: R Height: 5′ 11″ Weight: 180 Born: January 21, 1979 Age: 27

YEAR	TM	LVL	AGE	W	L	SV	G	GS	IP	H	BB	SO	HR	GB%	BABIP	STUFF	WHIP	ERA	PERA	EQERA	EQH9	EQBB9	EQSO9	EQHR9	VORP	WXRL
2003	ARI	MLB	24	1	5	0	7	7	43.0	34	15	33	6	55%	.233	13	1.14	3.56	4.97	3.24	8.2	3.0	6.5	1.3	11.0	1.2
2003	BOS	MLB	24	8	5	16	49	5	79.3	70	18	69	6	50%	.278	20	1.11	3.18	3.52	3.86	7.9	2.0	7.6	0.7	16.2	3.0
2004	PAW	AAA	25	2	6	0	22	19	60.7	71	12	39	6	—	.319	-11	1.37	5.34	4.77	6.86	10.4	1.9	4.3	1.0	-8.4	—
2005	COL	MLB	26	5	12	0	40	22	148.0	156	71	115	17	43%	.320	4	1.54	4.86	4.82	4.40	9.0	3.9	6.2	1.0	13.3	0.9
2006	COL	MLB	27	7	10	1	37	20	135.3	150	51	93	18	45%	.306	5	1.48	5.01	4.60	4.74	9.1	3.0	6.0	1.1	13.7	2.2

Breakout: 11%   Improve: 44%   Collapse: 22%   Attrition: 5%   Comparables: Ned Garver, Jim Slaton, Mike Norris

Initially thought of as a bullpen option, Kim was gradually moved into the rotation where he was significantly better, posting a 4.37 ERA starting compared to 8.06 out of the pen. Some wonder if the headaches caused by figuring what he can do for you aren't worth the ones he distributes to opposing batters with his funky delivery. Still, his sporadic history of impressive performance that will land him another chance to get jerked between the pen and the rotation.

SUN-WOO KIM
Bats: R Throws: R Height: 6′ 1″ Weight: 180 Born: September 4, 1977 Age: 28

YEAR	TM	LVL	AGE	W	L	SV	G	GS	IP	H	BB	SO	HR	GB%	BABIP	STUFF	WHIP	ERA	PERA	EQERA	EQH9	EQBB9	EQSO9	EQHR9	VORP	WXRL
2003	EDM	AAA	25	10	8	0	22	22	132.3	147	53	83	18	—	.291	-28	1.51	5.03	6.38	6.38	10.2	4.3	4.6	1.9	-11.1	—
2004	MON	MLB	26	4	6	0	43	17	135.7	145	55	87	17	52%	.303	-5	1.47	4.58	5.05	5.12	9.8	3.3	5.1	1.1	4.4	2.0
2005	NWO	AAA	27	4	2	0	9	9	49.0	46	15	38	4	50%	.294	2	1.24	2.76	4.75	4.94	9.1	3.0	4.9	1.0	3.5	—
2005	WAS	MLB	27	1	2	0	12	2	29.3	41	8	17	3	53%	.373	-8	1.67	6.14	4.45	6.53	11.3	2.1	4.7	0.9	-2.4	0.4
2005	COL	MLB	27	5	1	0	12	8	53.3	56	13	38	7	40%	.299	8	1.29	4.22	4.33	3.83	8.8	2.0	5.8	1.2	8.2	0.6
2006	COL	MLB	28	4	7	1	35	13	98.7	118	36	60	14	48%	.316	-3	1.56	5.56	5.08	5.38	9.8	2.9	5.4	1.2	4.5	0.8

Breakout: 19%   Improve: 52%   Collapse: 16%   Attrition: 13%   Comparables: Bubba Church, Russ Kemmerer, Art Ditmar

Claimed off of waivers from the Nats and thrust into the rotation, Kim pitched well for the Rockies, a fact that many would attribute to small sample size given a generally terrible career up until that point. He'll battle Zach Day and Jose Acevedo for a job.

DAN MICELI   **Bats: R Throws: R**   Height: 6′ 0″   Weight: 225   Born: September 9, 1970   Age: 35

YEAR	TM	LVL	AGE	W	L	SV	G	GS	IP	H	BB	SO	HR	GB%	BABIP	STUFF	WHIP	ERA	PERA	EQERA	EQH9	EQBB9	EQSO9	EQHR9	VORP	WXRL
2004	HOU	MLB	33	6	6	2	74	0	77.7	74	27	83	10	49%	.311	13	1.30	3.59	3.92	3.81	8.4	2.8	8.4	1.0	15.0	1.7
2005	COL	MLB	34	1	2	0	19	0	18.3	19	13	19	1	39%	.360	3	1.75	5.90	4.26	5.21	8.5	5.7	8.1	0.5	-0.2	-0.1
2006	TBA	MLB	35	2	2	2	40	0	44.3	43	18	37	5	42%	.287	0	1.36	4.31	4.51	5.04	8.6	3.6	7.2	1.0	4.7	0.4

Breakout: 19% Improve: 33% Collapse: 34% Attrition: 27% Comparables: Juan Berenguer, Ray Moore, Stan Bahnsen

Just when you thought it was all over for Miceli, the Rockies reeled him back in just long enough to throw 18 innings of forgettable relief before multiple stress fractures in his foot ended his season in August. It looked like he was finally done this time last year, but obviously anything can happen when there are teams with bullpens like the Rockies'.

FRANKLIN MORALES   **Bats: L Throws: L**   Height: 6′ 0″   Weight: 170   Born: January 24, 1986   Age: 20

YEAR	TM	LVL	AGE	W	L	SV	G	GS	IP	H	BB	SO	HR	GB%	BABIP	STUFF	WHIP	ERA	PERA	EQERA	EQH9	EQBB9	EQSO9	EQHR9	VORP	WXRL
2004	CAS	Rk	18	6	4	0	15	15	65.0	92	39	82	8	—	.447	-13	2.02	7.62	7.02	7.97	11.7	5.8	5.4	2.2	-17.6	—
2005	ASH	A	19	8	4	1	21	15	96.3	73	48	108	6	55%	.295	14	1.26	3.08	5.22	4.63	8.2	5.5	6.5	1.0	9.8	—
2006	COL	MLB	20	5	9	0	26	20	111.7	122	71	81	14	52%	.311	4	1.73	5.87	5.39	5.57	9.0	5.1	6.4	1.0	1.8	0.9

Breakout: 25% Improve: 65% Collapse: 8% Attrition: 1% Comparables: Darwin Peguero, Justin Jones, Roger Luque

The Rockies love Morales and his mid-90s heat, biting curveball, and changeup. It's hard to argue with 190 strikeouts in 161.1 career minor league innings, and he followed that up with a solid winter campaign to boot. On the other hand, he's also a 20-year old pitcher and still in the low minors, so let's not break out the $150 autographed player jerseys at team stores just yet. His name will start popping up a lot if he improves his command and posts another solid season.

JUAN MORILLO   **Bats: R Throws: R**   Height: 6′ 1″   Weight: 160   Born: November 5, 1983   Age: 22

YEAR	TM	LVL	AGE	W	L	SV	G	GS	IP	H	BB	SO	HR	GB%	BABIP	STUFF	WHIP	ERA	PERA	EQERA	EQH9	EQBB9	EQSO9	EQHR9	VORP	WXRL
2003	CAS	Rk	19	1	6	0	15	15	64.0	85	40	44	6	—	.348	-42	1.95	5.91	8.32	9.49	11.7	8.3	3.2	2.0	-26.7	—
2004	TRI	A-	20	3	2	0	14	14	66.3	56	41	73	0	—	.315	4	1.46	2.99	5.08	6.53	9.0	7.3	5.7	0.3	-6.4	—
2005	ASH	A	21	1	3	0	7	7	33.7	40	13	43	2	56%	.409	7	1.57	4.54	4.86	7.02	10.5	4.3	6.8	1.1	-5.3	—
2005	MOD	A+	21	6	5	0	20	20	112.3	107	65	101	10	53%	.319	-9	1.53	4.41	6.00	6.08	9.1	6.3	5.2	1.2	-5.8	—
2006	COL	MLB	22	4	9	0	26	20	104.0	126	82	70	17	50%	.326	-9	2.00	7.34	6.74	6.97	10.0	6.3	5.9	1.3	-12.6	-0.7

Breakout: 22% Improve: 61% Collapse: 17% Attrition: 1% Comparables: Delvis Lantigua, D. J. Mattox, Dan Reichert

He's still wild, but once he stops trying to be cute and realizes that it's hard to hit a ball going nearly 100, those numbers will drop. He had a good season in winter ball, adding a slider and ironing out his arm speed when throwing his changeup, so he could make a big step forward in 2006. He's still a long way away and the usual injury caveats apply, but Morillo has a lot of talent and he's learning to harness it.

SANDY NIN   **Bats: R Throws: R**   Height: 6′ 0″   Weight: 170   Born: August 13, 1980   Age: 25

YEAR	TM	LVL	AGE	W	L	SV	G	GS	IP	H	BB	SO	HR	GB%	BABIP	STUFF	WHIP	ERA	PERA	EQERA	EQH9	EQBB9	EQSO9	EQHR9	VORP	WXRL
2003	CWV	A	22	7	8	0	23	23	131.0	124	19	87	4	—	.282	4	1.09	2.89	4.31	5.82	9.6	1.7	3.5	0.7	-3.1	—
2005	MOD	A+	24	4	1	0	7	7	35.3	30	7	34	3	32%	.293	2	1.05	2.55	5.08	4.28	8.8	2.4	5.1	1.3	4.9	—
2005	TUL	AA	24	10	6	0	20	20	129.7	109	16	80	15	40%	.242	-12	0.96	3.19	5.31	4.94	9.3	1.5	4.1	1.6	8.8	—
2006	COL	MLB	25	6	10	0	27	21	126.0	156	32	65	24	40%	.306	-1	1.49	5.91	5.33	5.45	10.2	2.0	4.5	1.6	2.4	1.1

Breakout: 8% Improve: 36% Collapse: 16% Attrition: 0% Comparables: Jamie Brown, Jin Cho, Bob Wolcott

Acquired from the Blue Jays, Nin had missed all of 2004 with a fractured elbow, an injury that sounds almost as painful as a dislocated urethra. He picked up where he left off, continuing to post mediocre strikeout rates but also extremely low walk and home run rates. There's nothing to distinguish Nin from any other control prospect who's too old for his level.

RAMON RAMIREZ   **Bats: R Throws: R**   Height: 5′ 11″ Weight: 170   Born: August 31, 1981   Age: 24

YEAR	TM	LVL	AGE	W	L	SV	G	GS	IP	H	BB	SO	HR	GB%	BABIP	STUFF	WHIP	ERA	PERA	EQERA	EQH9	EQBB9	EQSO9	EQHR9	VORP	WXRL
2003	TAM	A+	21	2	8	0	14	14	74.3	88	20	70	7	—	.346	-16	1.45	5.21	6.50	7.39	12.1	2.8	6.0	2.5	-14.1	—
2004	TRN	AA	22	4	6	0	18	18	114.0	115	32	128	11	—	.333	17	1.29	4.66	4.34	5.13	8.9	2.7	7.2	1.2	6.0	—
2005	TRN	AA	23	6	5	0	15	15	89.0	79	35	82	10	44%	.284	-7	1.28	3.84	5.68	5.46	9.2	4.4	5.8	1.6	1.3	—
2005	COH	AAA	23	1	3	0	6	6	27.0	32	9	26	3	48%	.382	8	1.52	5.33	4.28	5.60	9.9	3.3	6.6	1.0	0.0	—
2005	TUL	AA	23	2	1	0	9	3	25.3	27	8	23	6	41%	.300	-18	1.38	5.34	7.99	6.85	11.4	3.8	6.1	3.4	-3.3	—
2006	COL	MLB	24	4	8	0	28	16	102.3	121	47	72	20	42%	.312	0	1.65	6.33	5.76	5.86	9.7	3.7	6.2	1.6	-2.5	0.4

Breakout: 20% Improve: 56% Collapse: 10% Attrition: 0% Comparables: Francisco Rosario, Mike Johnson, Mike Nannini

Originally an outfielder in the Rangers system, Ramirez disappeared long enough to take up pitching in Japan, at which point the Yanks brought him back stateside. Sent to the Rockies in the Shawn Chacon deal, Ramirez struggled as a starter in Columbus, but has posted otherwise good numbers all the way. He'll be in the mix for a middle relief job.

EDWARDO SIERRA   Bats: R   Throws: R   Height: 6′ 3″   Weight: 185   Born: April 15, 1982   Age: 24

YEAR	TM	LVL	AGE	W	L	SV	G	GS	IP	H	BB	SO	HR	GB%	BABIP	STUFF	WHIP	ERA	PERA	EQERA	EQH9	EQBB9	EQSO9	EQHR9	VORP	WXRL
2003	KNC	A	21	3	5	17	51	0	60.3	46	24	52	2	—	.254	-13	1.16	2.09	5.53	5.53	8.9	4.9	5.2	1.0	0.4	—
2004	TAM	A+	22	2	3	28	45	0	48.7	44	45	57	2	—	.341	-23	1.83	3.33	6.35	5.76	9.3	10.3	7.1	0.8	-0.8	—
2005	TRN	AA	23	3	1	2	33	0	57.7	37	38	50	4	56%	.229	-22	1.30	3.28	6.15	5.13	7.7	7.5	5.6	1.0	2.8	—
2005	TUL	AA	23	0	3	0	13	0	15.0	23	13	7	3	47%	.392	-67	2.40	10.20	9.20	11.05	13.5	9.8	3.1	2.5	-8.9	—
2006	COL	MLB	24	2	3	0	27	4	49.0	58	51	34	7	51%	.325	-22	2.22	7.66	7.22	7.24	9.7	8.4	6.2	1.2	-7.0	-0.7

Breakout: 8%   Improve: 28%   Collapse: 40%   Attrition: 14%   Comparables: Jon Berry, Jeff Schultz, Hal Garrett

When it's said that a player was traded for "a warm body," Sierra is what they mean. Acquired from the Yankees with Ramon Ramirez for Shawn Chacon, Sierra had been the closer for the A's Low-A club in 2003 and the Yanks' FSL team in 2004, but moved to middle relief in Double-A. He's got heat, but also significant command issues, and unless he learns some control, he's going to have a hard time progressing up the ladder, even in the Colorado system.

RYAN SPEIER   Bats: R   Throws: R   Height: 6′ 7″   Weight: 200   Born: July 24, 1979   Age: 26

YEAR	TM	LVL	AGE	W	L	SV	G	GS	IP	H	BB	SO	HR	GB%	BABIP	STUFF	WHIP	ERA	PERA	EQERA	EQH9	EQBB9	EQSO9	EQHR9	VORP	WXRL
2003	VIS	A+	23	4	2	18	56	0	58.7	50	17	73	2	—	.318	3	1.14	1.53	4.20	4.04	8.9	3.6	6.8	0.6	9.7	—
2004	TUL	AA	24	3	1	37	61	0	61.7	33	25	70	3	—	.210	0	0.94	2.04	4.50	3.54	7.2	4.7	7.2	0.8	12.8	—
2005	CSP	AAA	25	2	2	6	45	0	52.3	70	18	45	2	53%	.407	-1	1.68	4.99	4.14	4.97	10.3	3.1	5.3	0.3	3.8	—
2005	COL	MLB	25	2	1	0	22	0	24.7	26	13	10	0	48%	.310	-19	1.58	3.64	4.68	3.96	9.0	4.3	3.2	0.4	2.8	-0.4
2006	COL	MLB	26	2	3	1	48	1	46.0	55	24	30	6	50%	.324	-10	1.71	5.75	5.38	5.49	9.8	4.2	5.7	1.0	0.9	0.1

Breakout: 9%   Improve: 19%   Collapse: 53%   Attrition: 14%   Comparables: Aaron Small, Rick Bauer, Bob Scanlan

One more reason not to pay for somebody like Mike DeJean. Speier's tall frame and the movement on his fastball make him tough to hit, but his sidearm delivery is borderline unfair. He's pitched well at every level through the minors and should make for a cheap, respectable middle reliever.

CHIN-HUI TSAO   Bats: R   Throws: R   Height: 6′ 2″   Weight: 175   Born: June 2, 1981   Age: 25

YEAR	TM	LVL	AGE	W	L	SV	G	GS	IP	H	BB	SO	HR	GB%	BABIP	STUFF	WHIP	ERA	PERA	EQERA	EQH9	EQBB9	EQSO9	EQHR9	VORP	WXRL
2003	TUL	AA	22	11	4	0	18	18	113.3	88	26	125	7	—	.274	23	1.01	2.46	4.11	3.86	8.3	2.5	7.5	1.1	20.7	—
2003	COL	MLB	22	3	3	0	9	8	43.3	48	20	29	11	44%	.287	-9	1.57	6.03	6.39	5.56	9.9	3.7	5.4	2.1	-0.3	0.2
2005	COL	MLB	24	1	0	3	10	0	11.0	16	5	4	3	30%	.317	-34	1.91	6.55	7.15	5.56	11.9	4.0	3.2	2.4	-1.0	-0.5
2006	COL	MLB	25	1	2	3	26	0	34.0	39	12	23	5	42%	.306	-3	1.48	5.47	4.87	5.66	9.3	2.8	6.0	1.3	2.1	0.1

Breakout: 18%   Improve: 42%   Collapse: 38%   Attrition: 49%   Comparables: Steve Kealey, Urbano Lugo, Bill Dillman

After missing nearly all of 2005 with shoulder surgery, Tsao is on track on his rehab but won't be ready to handle a full spring training workload in March. He'll spend 2006 working on his fastball and changeup, with the breaking pitches to come later, though if he remains in the bullpen as planned, he may be able to get by with just the first two. That 2003 season in Tulsa is getting smaller and smaller in the rearview mirror, and after the injuries, it's impossible to know if Tsao will burn out or become a bullpen sleeper by July.

JAMEY WRIGHT   Bats: R   Throws: R   Height: 6′ 5″   Weight: 230   Born: December 24, 1974   Age: 31

YEAR	TM	LVL	AGE	W	L	SV	G	GS	IP	H	BB	SO	HR	GB%	BABIP	STUFF	WHIP	ERA	PERA	EQERA	EQH9	EQBB9	EQSO9	EQHR9	VORP	WXRL
2004	OMA	AAA	29	8	6	0	18	18	104.7	111	35	70	13	—	.296	-15	1.39	4.21	5.90	5.72	10.1	3.7	4.3	1.4	-1.3	—
2004	COL	MLB	29	2	3	0	14	14	78.7	82	45	41	8	53%	.286	-2	1.61	4.12	5.31	3.95	9.2	4.6	4.1	0.8	14.4	2.1
2005	COL	MLB	30	8	16	0	34	27	171.3	201	81	101	22	54%	.322	-6	1.65	5.46	5.26	5.46	9.8	3.9	4.7	1.1	-7.1	0.7
2006	SFN	MLB	31	8	10	0	37	23	152.3	156	68	94	14	53%	.291	-2	1.47	4.60	4.99	5.41	9.1	3.6	5.2	0.8	7.2	1.7

Breakout: 17%   Improve: 54%   Collapse: 17%   Attrition: 10%   Comparables: Pat Rapp, Dan Petry, Don Larsen

While most teams wouldn't sign players cut by the Royals for fear of all the nasty talk behind their backs between classes or after school, the Rockies happily picked up their former prospect in the middle of 2004 and stuck with him through 250 innings of what you'd expect from a player cut by the Royals. To be fair, Wright didn't pitch that badly in 2004, and he's been in hitters' parks his entire career, but then again, taking your local garage band out of the neighborhood to a gig at Red Rocks isn't going to turn them into the Rolling Stones.

Line Outs

Position/Player	TM	LVL	AGE	PA	R	2B	3B	HR	RBI	BB	SO	SB-CS	SPEED	BA/OBP/SLG	MLVR	EQBA/OBP/SLG	EQA	VORP
OF C. Freeman	CSP	AAA	25	389	46	10	6	10	59	29	78	4-3	4.9	.280/.334/.427	-.067	.239/.286/.355	.225	-10.1
INF E. Garabito#	CSP	AAA	28	290	56	16	3	8	39	29	34	8-4	5.9	.306/.379/.484	.120	.249/.310/.371	.239	2.7
	COL	MLB	28	99	15	5	0	1	8	8	12	3-2	5.4	.307/.384/.398	.056	.292/.370/.371	.263	3.7
SS C. Nelson	ASH	A	19	349	51	13	3	3	38	25	88	7-4	6.1	.241/.304/.330	-.204	.192/.242/.268	.188	-26.6
OF R. Spilborghs	TUL	AA	25	301	52	23	3	6	54	42	49	10-3	5.7	.341/.435/.525	.378	.293/.378/.446	.288	12.7
	CSP	AAA	25	252	49	23	5	5	30	22	53	7-3	6.8	.339/.405/.551	.292	.291/.350/.460	.277	8.8
SS T. Tulowitzki	MOD	A+	20	105	17	6	0	4	14	9	18	1-0	4.6	.266/.343/.457	-.006	.211/.274/.341	.218	-2.9

Pitcher	TM	LVL	AGE	W	L	SV	IP	H	BB	SO	HR	GB%	BABIP	STUFF	WHIP	ERA	PERA	EQERA	EQH9	EQBB9	EQSO9	EQHR9	VORP
M. Esposito	CSP	AAA	23	8	9	0	155.7	197	41	94	20	51%	.335	-7	1.53	5.49	5.14	5.42	10.2	2.3	3.9	1.2	3.2
S. Lindsay	TRI	A-	20	6	1	0	66.7	37	34	107	1	39%	.303	22	1.06	1.89	4.76	5.68	7.8	7.2	7.8	0.5	-0.5
J. Miller	MOD	A+	23	1	3	25	47.7	39	17	68	3	40%	.321	2	1.17	3.77	4.17	5.36	8.3	4.2	7.7	0.8	1.2
R. Williams*	CSP	AAA	29	2	2	4	28.3	18	10	36	1	55%	.270	9	0.99	3.50	3.67	5.00	6.7	3.7	8.0	0.3	1.8
	COL	MLB	29	2	1	0	22.0	26	9	19	4	44%	.328	-5	1.59	5.73	5.16	5.56	9.5	3.2	6.8	1.6	-0.8

Choo Freeman: Trying to make a major league roster by hitting .278 with a .149 ISO in three seasons at the best hitters' park in Triple-A is like trying to pick up girls by flashing your SAT scores. **Eddy Garabito:** After parts of six seasons in Triple-A, Garabito finally made it to the majors, which means he won't have his ghost resurrected as a metaphor for the path not taken in any upcoming baseball movies. **Chris Nelson:** He's all tools and still very young, but a hamstring injury killed his season, and likely dropped him behind Troy Tulowitzki on the organizational depth chart. **Ryan Spilborghs:** Jumped from A-ball to the majors at the age of 25, but if you think that jump in slugging is anything more than park factors, there's an African prince who needs your credit card number to save his country. **Troy Tulowitzki:** The seventh pick in last June's draft, he was playing well in Modesto before a quad tear cut his season short. He's got everything a 1st rounder should have, his quad is fully healed, and the Rockies expect him to move quickly if everything goes as planned.

Mike Esposito is a bit of junkballing staff filler picked out of Arizona State in 2002, one likely to turn up in The Show when the back of the rotation falls to pieces. **Shane Lindsay:** Signed as a free agent from Australia, Lindsay can obviously strike guys out with his mid-90s fastball; if he can keep things up at higher levels, he could start climbing some prospect lists very soon. **Jim Miller's** struck out 152 batters in 99.2 innings while walking only 36. The Rockies sent him to the AFL to work on his change and slider to complements to his mid-90s heat. He won't initially be in the mix for the pen, but he'll be up before the season's done. **Randy Williams:** Claimed off of waivers from the Padres and stuck in the bullpen, where he actually didn't pitch all that badly. He may be back, but so may hula-hoops and beehives.

Detroit Tigers

Two years ago, the Tigers hit bottom, and not just any ordinary bottom, but a bottom so low that only giant squid can survive the crushing pressure of those depths. An impressive 29-game turnaround in 2004 lifted their hopes, and the additions of Magglio Ordonez and Troy Percival in the offseason further raised expectations for 2005. But not for long.

The Tigers hovered around .500 for the better part of four months. For the first 100 games of the season, they were never more than six games under or two games over the break-even point. Their typical pattern was to drop to four or five games under, and then just when it seemed safe to write them off, win four out of five to get back to even. Of course, with the White Sox leaping out to a 27–9 start and expanding that to 65–35 at the century mark, the Tigers were out of contention early. Their chances of making the playoffs dropped below 20% for good in mid-May, and was under 10% by the end of June.

Still, at the 100-game mark, Detroit's record stood at a respectable 50-50. It was at this point that the team's rapid decline commenced, though not due to lack of runs. The emergence of Curtis Granderson and Chris Shelton, the relative health of Magglio Ordonez, and the trade for Placido Polanco combined to propel the offense for the duration of the season. It was the pitching staff, especially the bullpen, that did in the Tigers. A lot of blame could be directed at GM Dave Dombrowski, since he traded two of the team's best relievers of the first half—Kyle Farnsworth and Ugueth Urbina. New closer Fernando Rodney did passably well after their departure, but other key pitchers—Franklyn German, Roman Colon, and Jamie Walker—were consistently shelled.

The Tigers won just ten of their last 39 games, a finish that cost manager Alan Trammell his job, or at least provided a convenient time to show him the door. Trammell's main qualification to manage the Tigers was that he was a beloved former star player who had been part of the organization since 1976. He had no managerial experience before taking the Tigers' reins, and time revealed a number of shortcomings that made his firing all but inevitable. Trammell was too much of a former player; it isn't clear that he either commanded or received any respect in the clubhouse, leading to the perception that players—especially veterans like Ivan Rodriguez and Dmitri Young—

TIGERS PROSPECTUS

2005 record: 71–91; Fourth place, AL Central

Pythagenport record: 74–88

Runs scored per game: 4.46 (11th in AL)

Runs allowed per game: 4.86 (8th in AL)

Team EqA: .261 (7th in AL)

2005 Batters Age: 29.0 (4th youngest in AL)

2005 Pitchers Age: 28.1 (4th youngest in AL)

Ballpark: Comerica Park; Moderate pitcher's park; Park Factor of 0.967

2005: Expensive imports lead the way to more Motor City mediocrity.

2006: Another batch of free-agent pickups won't be enough for Detroit to challenge the division's balance of power.

were able to walk all over him. He was also lost in another time—no American League team over the past three years attempted to bunt as often as Trammell's Tigers, and no team in the majors had more sacrifices from its position players. His bullpen management was derided, and the bullpen has in fact gotten worse in the second half of every season that Trammell has managed.

Factors such as these contributed to the fact that the Trammell-era Tigers underachieved. They didn't score as many runs as expected from their statistics, and even with the runs they have scored and allowed, they didn't win as many games as expected. Only the Mariners, who fired manager Bob Melvin after 2004, have underperformed their predicted (Pythagenport) wins as badly as the Tigers did during Trammell's tenure.

That's not to say that Trammell or Dombrowski deserve to shoulder the bulk of the blame for Detroit's disappointments. The Tigers endured their 12th consecutive losing season in 2005, and many problems long predate the current collection of talent at the big league level. The minor league system has been moribund almost since the moment that Lou Whitaker won Rookie of the Year in 1978. Whitaker, Trammell, Lance Parrish, Jack Morris, and Kirk Gibson emerged between 1977 and 1979, and the farm, as if exhausted from such a prolific parturition, gave out. Since then there have been only a few position players of note—Bobby Higginson, Travis Fryman, Tony Clark, and Brandon Inge—and even fewer pitchers.

Two years ago, *Baseball America* rated the Tigers organization 29th in the majors. Happily, there was considerable improvement last year. Granderson and Shelton both made the leap to the majors in style. The biggest disappointments of 2004, Brent Clevlen and Kody Kirkland, came back with MVP-caliber seasons in their respective leagues. While these players don't rate as prospective big-league stars, they appear to be on track to become major league regulars. This is, at least, a decent number of prospects to have, and that's without counting the addition of heralded 2005 1st round pick Cameron Maybin, an extremely athletic outfielder and one of the most sought-after players in last year's draft.

Most encouragingly, two of the system's recently minted pitching prospects stepped up. Justin Verlander, the organization's 1st round pick in 2004, made his professional debut in April and shot through the system, making his major league debut on the Fourth of July. Additionally, Joel Zumaya struck out 199 batters and held opponents to a .189 average—both marks were second best in the entire minor leagues last year. Both pitchers throw in the upper 90s and can touch 100 if the radar gun is just a little bit out of adjustment. Few organizations have even one pitcher as highly rated as either Verlander or Zumaya. No one else has two. Having two pitching prospects of this quality, TINSTAAPP aside, gives a minor league system instant credibility.

If the Tigers are going to win anything in the next four years, the pitchers must become stars; the current position players cannot carry the load. Magglio Ordonez is the best bet to sustain his offensive performance, but Ivan Rodriguez is already in a state of decay, and the rest of the offense, barring a landmark free agent acquisition, lacks star power. This year is probably a lost cause. The talent gap between the Tigers and the White Sox, or between the Tigers and Indians, is enormous. The focus should be on preserving the future—keeping their powder dry for the day they'll actually be on the cusp of a winning situation.

The man Dombroski chose to mind the store until then is an old friend, manager Jim Leyland. Back in 1997, Dombrowski, as GM of the Marlins, lured Leyland away from the Pirates and together they won the World Series that same year. There is little doubt that Leyland will be a better manager than Trammell, but there is some question as to whether he is really the right man for this particular job. Leyland quit his last gig with the Rockies when the team didn't mature with the same rapidity, a move that left him looking a bit like a spoiled child. The Tigers' front office contends that the time off has "rekindled" Leyland's passion for the game, but comebacks are often better as

fantasy than reality. It is a natural human tendency to remember either the good times or the bad times, but not a balanced assessment of both; Leyland's renewed enthusiasm may not be up to the carping and backbiting that will follow another sluggish start with another flawed club. Time can be cruel to managers who have been away from the dugout. After six years' idleness, Leyland may find that his instincts aren't quite as sharp as they once were.

During his years at the helm of the Pirates, Marlins, and Rockies, Leyland did consistently demonstrate a talent for assembling a bullpen. Some managers are able to continually assemble good or great bullpens out of the parts that other teams or previous managers have left lying around, as Ozzie Guillen did in Chicago, or as Bobby Cox always seems to do in Atlanta. Their facility in distinguishing potentially useful pitchers from among so many mediocre alternatives makes it easy to believe that a whole lot of pitchers have the ability to handle a major league relief role. Indeed, you can find a dozen guys every year in the minors who "added five miles to their fastball when they switched to relief," but these redeemed pitchers nevertheless have to be handled correctly. It takes real managerial talent to develop relievers within roles defined for their skill sets, to know when to tell them to start warming up, and when to bring them in. Trammell did not have that skill; Leyland did.

Despite that, the Jim Leyland who managed in the late '90s often seemed to lose faith in his bullpens, working his starters a lot harder than the average for his day—not exactly the profile of a manager you want in charge of developing this organization's capital asset, its collection of talented young hurlers. In the Baseball Prospectus annuals from Leyland's last active seasons, this predilection provoked the following comments:

> He became intoxicated with his best starters as the year went on, leaving them in to run up dangerous pitch counts; Marlin starters led baseball with an average of 101 pitches per start.
>
> — 1998

> [Livan Hernandez and Jesus Sanchez] threw over 140 pitches in a start last season, something only one other NL pitcher can claim—Curt Schilling, about ten years their senior.
>
> — 1999

> Pedro Astacio took the brunt of the abuse, throwing 130 or more pitches five times, including the major-league of high of 153 on June 6.
>
> — 2000

This was a constant theme during Leyland's last years, and it should be a source of concern for the shoulders and elbows of Leyland's new charges. Livan Hernandez turned out to be one of those rare pitchers for whom pitch counts do seem to be completely irrelevant, as his career has continued without interruption through the present day. Others among Leyland's charges, such as Jesus Sanchez and Alex Fernandez, were pushed past their breaking points.

On this count, it appears Leyland failed to appreciate just how fast the game was changing around him. The trend towards lower pitch counts was already well under way when he last managed and has continued unabated since his retirement. When Leyland broke in as a manager in the mid-1980s, the average starting pitcher threw 130 or more pitches about once every 20 games. By the mid-90s, that figure had dropped to about one in 40, to one in 60 by 2000, and last year was only about one in 300. In Florida and Colorado, Leyland was still following the one in 20 rule of his early managerial days. Whether or not he recognizes that those changes have continued, and that protecting his young pitching is a critical portion of his mandate, will be one of his first managerial tests in the Motor City.

HITTERS

VINCENT BLUE   CF   Bats: L Throws: R   Height: 6' 2"   Weight: 180   Born: February 8, 1983   Age: 23

YEAR	TM	LVL	AGE	PA	R	2B	3B	HR	RBI	BB	SO	SB	CS	SPEED	BA	OBP	SLG	MLVR	EQBA	EQOBP	EQSLG	EQA	VORP	DEFENSE	
2003	ONE	A-	20	273	47	7	8	2	26	38	56	13	3	7.6	.288	.388	.412	.178	.255	.339	.385	.257	8.3	69-CF	6
2004	WMI	A	21	552	66	19	4	2	43	49	97	19	11	5.7	.260	.328	.326	-.040	.237	.294	.298	.215	-25.4	124-CF	1
2005	LAK	A+	22	550	67	17	3	0	50	47	84	40	29	6.3	.297	.356	.343	.020	.265	.319	.313	.228	-11.9	121-CF	7
2006	DET	MLB	23	440	49	15	4	2	28	30	78	18	9	5.3	.250	.303	.318	-.196	.254	.313	.335	.223	-6.2	104-CF	2

Breakout: 25%   Improve: 49%   Collapse: 27%   Attrition: 18%   Comparables: Kennard Jones, Richard Thompson, Jared Schumaker

A 2001 10th round pick out of Lamar High School in Houston, Blue is the best defensive outfielder the Tigers have. But he is typical of speedy center fielders in that he's a burner with no power. Guys like Blue need to carry a .370+ OBP to be valuable, which leaves him, given even the most optimistic projections, a good forty points short.

BRENT CLEVLEN   RF   Bats: R Throws: R   Height: 6' 2"   Weight: 190   Born: October 27, 1983   Age: 22

YEAR	TM	LVL	AGE	PA	R	2B	3B	HR	RBI	BB	SO	SB	CS	SPEED	BA	OBP	SLG	MLVR	EQBA	EQOBP	EQSLG	EQA	VORP	DEFENSE	
2003	WMI	A	19	560	67	22	7	12	63	72	111	6	3	5.2	.260	.359	.410	.150	.239	.321	.392	.249	-9.7	132-RF	5
2004	LAK	A+	20	474	49	23	6	6	50	44	127	2	1	5.0	.223	.300	.349	-.093	.205	.270	.334	.214	-38.1	116-RF	-13
2005	LAK	A+	21	566	77	28	4	18	102	65	118	14	5	4.7	.302	.387	.484	.253	.272	.348	.445	.274	14.5	128-RF	12
2006	DET	MLB	22	541	61	25	3	14	60	45	124	6	2	4.4	.246	.311	.393	-.090	.249	.322	.413	.246	-2.1	127-RF	1

Breakout: 21%   Improve: 46%   Collapse: 22%   Attrition: 6%   Comparables: Garrett Long, Kevin West, Rodney Clifton

Clevlen repeated the FSL, won the MVP, and reestablished himself as a prospect. Last year was a virtual copy of his 2003 campaign, with both his offense and defense both returning to "above-average" status. He'll need to step it up again to be an All-Star, but at least he projects as a solid major league right fielder—quite a novelty for a team whose longest-lived outfielders of the last ten years have been Bobby Higginson, Juan Encarnacion, and Craig Monroe.

BRENT DLUGACH   SS   Bats: R Throws: R   Height: 6' 4"   Weight: 200   Born: March 3, 1983   Age: 23

YEAR	TM	LVL	AGE	PA	R	2B	3B	HR	RBI	BB	SO	SB	CS	SPEED	BA	OBP	SLG	MLVR	EQBA	EQOBP	EQSLG	EQA	VORP	DEFENSE	
2004	ONE	A-	21	195	17	7	2	1	12	8	59	5	4	5.3	.213	.256	.290	-.228	.176	.209	.241	.168	-40.5	47-SS	6
2005	WMI	A	22	518	54	26	5	5	61	19	121	13	5	5.3	.283	.317	.387	.005	.252	.274	.344	.217	-10.2	119-SS	23
2006	DET	MLB	23	419	40	19	3	4	34	11	110	7	4	4.4	.230	.254	.325	-.285	.234	.263	.342	.198	-8.3	100-SS	9

Breakout: 34%   Improve: 57%   Collapse: 26%   Attrition: 17%   Comparables: David Detienne, Ruben Castillo, Mark Schleicher

Tall and thin, Dlugach is the shortstop version of Vincent Blue: an outstanding defender who doesn't hit enough to make the total package worthwhile, not unless he develops at a better-than-average rate. His problem is plate discipline: a translated 9:1 K/BB ratio will be his undoing. That, or he could be devoured by a kraken while touring the Norwegian fjords. That could be his undoing as well; we're just baseball analysts, not the three fates, and the lack of walks seem a more likely downfall.

DAVID ESPINOSA   OF   **Bats: B Throws: R**   Height: 6′ 2″   Weight: 190   Born: December 16, 1981   Age: 24

YEAR	TM	LVL	AGE	PA	R	2B	3B	HR	RBI	BB	SO	SB	CS	SPEED	BA	OBP	SLG	MLVR	EQBA	EQOBP	EQSLG	EQA	VORP	DEFENSE			
2003	LAK	A+	21	407	57	18	7	4	46	50	78	13	10	6.7	.271	.359	.397	.119	.254	.330	.399	.254	7.2	57-CF	-2	34-RF	-4
2004	ERI	AA	22	596	89	23	5	19	52	80	134	20	7	6.2	.264	.366	.440	.071	.234	.328	.388	.253	-9.0	127-RF	2		
2005	ERI	AA	23	505	66	21	8	9	40	66	109	11	6	6.6	.262	.362	.411	.059	.237	.333	.373	.251	-8.8	84-RF	-7	23-LF	-3
2006	*DET*	*MLB*	*24*	*502*	*63*	*21*	*5*	*11*	*48*	*51*	*104*	*11*	*5*	*5.8*	*.252*	*.332*	*.401*	*-.040*	*.256*	*.343*	*.421*	*.258*	*4.4*	*118-RF*	*-3*		

Breakout: 33%   Improve: 55%   Collapse: 20%   Attrition: 9%   Comparables: Chip Ambres, Cesar Crespo, Marvin Seale

Espinosa has never developed; his translated EQAs have remained almost exactly the same year after year, without any of the growth you expect from a player in his early 20s. We talk about players peaking at ages 27 to 28, but that's an average; some guys are as good at 20 as they're ever going to be. While his hitting has stagnated, he's been moving down the defensive spectrum, from short to second to the outfield, shedding value all the way. If he can still play the infield at all, he could swing a Damian Jackson-type career.

JEFF FRAZIER   LF   **Bats: R Throws: R**   Height: 6′ 4″   Weight: 215   Born: August 10, 1982   Age: 23

YEAR	TM	LVL	AGE	PA	R	2B	3B	HR	RBI	BB	SO	SB	CS	SPEED	BA	OBP	SLG	MLVR	EQBA	EQOBP	EQSLG	EQA	VORP	DEFENSE	
2004	ONE	A-	21	93	15	5	1	1	13	9	11	2	1	5.2	.304	.387	.430	.188	.258	.318	.382	.246	-3.7	15-LF	2
2005	WMI	A	22	601	79	45	4	12	81	46	86	16	3	5.3	.287	.349	.453	.150	.255	.303	.405	.246	-12.3	126-LF	-2
2006	*DET*	*MLB*	*23*	*495*	*53*	*29*	*4*	*9*	*52*	*27*	*82*	*6*	*3*	*4.6*	*.255*	*.300*	*.395*	*-.100*	*.258*	*.310*	*.415*	*.241*	*-1.4*	*117-LF*	*-2*

Breakout: 24%   Improve: 55%   Collapse: 25%   Attrition: 6%   Comparables: Richard Correll, Chris Durbin, Josh Loggins

Older brother Charles was an outfielder who couldn't hit, and little brother Tom was a Little League World Series star; this family takes their baseball seriously. Jeff starred at Rutgers, where he set the school's home run record despite his first season being cut short by an arm-breaking HBP. Frazier has average on-base skills with above-average power and speed, which could make him a solid starting outfielder down the road.

TONY GIARRATANO   SS   **Bats: B Throws: R**   Height: 6′ 0″   Weight: 180   Born: November 29, 1982   Age: 23

YEAR	TM	LVL	AGE	PA	R	2B	3B	HR	RBI	BB	SO	SB	CS	SPEED	BA	OBP	SLG	MLVR	EQBA	EQOBP	EQSLG	EQA	VORP	DEFENSE	
2003	ONE	A-	20	206	31	11	4	3	27	12	22	9	4	6.3	.328	.369	.476	.266	.290	.325	.447	.265	21.7	44-SS	2
2004	WMI	A	21	193	20	6	1	1	13	25	22	11	3	5.3	.285	.383	.352	.097	.261	.344	.326	.247	2.5	42-SS	5
2004	LAK	A+	21	222	30	11	0	5	25	16	38	14	8	5.3	.376	.423	.505	.411	.329	.369	.451	.282	22.2	52-SS	4
2005	ERI	AA	22	386	40	22	3	3	32	32	75	12	5	5.5	.266	.334	.373	-.031	.241	.306	.339	.232	-2.4	87-SS	3
2005	DET	MLB	22	47	4	0	0	1	4	5	7	1	0	4.7	.143	.234	.214	-.519	.143	.250	.214	.183	-3.6	12-SS	-1
2006	*DET*	*MLB*	*23*	*435*	*51*	*20*	*3*	*6*	*38*	*29*	*71*	*11*	*4*	*4.8*	*.256*	*.310*	*.367*	*-.117*	*.260*	*.321*	*.386*	*.240*	*9.4*	*103-SS*	*2*

Breakout: 18%   Improve: 37%   Collapse: 31%   Attrition: 13%   Comparables: Jorge Sequea, Kenny Perez, Marco Pernalete

Giarratano was highly regarded coming into 2005, but a poor year at Erie and a lousy premature debut in Detroit has changed that. When healthy, he's a very good defensive shortstop who can hit for average and steal a base. The operative words here are "when healthy"; a shoulder injury ended his 2004 season and required surgery, and he missed time with a groin injury last year. Chalk last year up to the lingering effects of the shoulder surgery, and expect much more from him in 2006.

CURTIS GRANDERSON   CF   **Bats: L Throws: R**   Height: 6′ 1″   Weight: 180   Born: March 16, 1981   Age: 25

YEAR	TM	LVL	AGE	PA	R	2B	3B	HR	RBI	BB	SO	SB	CS	SPEED	BA	OBP	SLG	MLVR	EQBA	EQOBP	EQSLG	EQA	VORP	DEFENSE			
2003	LAK	A+	22	540	71	29	10	11	51	49	91	10	7	6.1	.286	.365	.458	.213	.263	.328	.451	.265	21.6	75-CF	2	51-LF	0
2004	ERI	AA	23	550	89	19	8	21	94	80	95	14	8	6.1	.301	.405	.513	.255	.265	.363	.445	.279	28.4	121-CF	13		
2005	TOL	AAA	24	501	79	29	13	15	65	48	129	22	6	7.5	.290	.359	.515	.225	.276	.344	.481	.282	29.2	105-CF	13		
2005	DET	MLB	24	172	18	6	3	8	20	10	43	1	1	5.4	.272	.314	.494	.083	.281	.335	.525	.284	7.7	36-CF	6		
2006	*DET*	*MLB*	*25*	*534*	*73*	*25*	*6*	*19*	*69*	*48*	*108*	*12*	*5*	*5.7*	*.271*	*.341*	*.470*	*.076*	*.275*	*.352*	*.494*	*.279*	*26.8*	*126-CF*	*8*		

Breakout: 20%   Improve: 51%   Collapse: 17%   Attrition: 11%   Comparables: Gary Geiger, Willie Kirkland, Luis Gonzalez

Once the Tigers decided to go with Granderson in center field instead of Nook Logan, they didn't look back, nor should they. Granderson has been a good hitter since his college days at Illinois-Chicago, regularly contending for batting crowns, but in the last two years he's stepped up his defense as well. He gets high marks for his intelligence and work ethic, so when he says he wants to work on building strength and improving his power, expect it to happen. The increase in strikeouts last year is the only down note. Chet Lemon's last season in center field was 1987; 19 years later the Tigers finally have a replacement.

CARLOS GUILLEN SS Bats: B Throws: R Height: 6' 1" Weight: 200 Born: September 30, 1975 Age: 30

YEAR	TM	LVL	AGE	PA	R	2B	3B	HR	RBI	BB	SO	SB	CS	SPEED	BA	OBP	SLG	MLVR	EQBA	EQOBP	EQSLG	EQA	VORP	DEFENSE			
2003	SEA	MLB	27	446	63	19	3	7	52	52	64	4	4	4.8	.276	.359	.394	.019	.282	.371	.409	.273	19.0	70-SS	0	32-3B	-1
2004	DET	MLB	28	580	97	37	10	20	97	52	87	12	5	6.7	.318	.379	.542	.278	.326	.391	.562	.315	63.9	130-SS	14		
2005	DET	MLB	29	361	48	15	4	5	23	24	45	2	3	5.1	.320	.368	.434	.140	.335	.391	.459	.291	24.8	71-SS	1		
2006	*DET*	*MLB*	*30*	*453*	*59*	*23*	*4*	*10*	*53*	*38*	*58*	*5*	*2*	*5.3*	*.291*	*.353*	*.438*	*.069*	*.295*	*.364*	*.461*	*.276*	*26.8*	*107-SS*	*3*		

Breakout: 7% Improve: 28% Collapse: 35% Attrition: 12% Comparables: Jose Vidro, Ken Caminiti, Jack Daughtery

This was a painful year for Guillen. What started out as another great season—he was hitting .361 at the end of May—was lost as the injuries piled up. His right knee, surgically repaired in the off-season, was a problem all year. To that he added an HBP to the head—which left him dizzy for a week—hamstring woes, a pulled quadriceps, and to finish off the season, a bout of the flu. He still managed to raise his batting average for the sixth straight year, the seventh player ever to do that; only Bill Hallman from the 19th century extended it past six, making it to eight.

JACK HANNAHAN 3B Bats: L Throws: R Height: 6' 2" Weight: 200 Born: March 4, 1980 Age: 26

YEAR	TM	LVL	AGE	PA	R	2B	3B	HR	RBI	BB	SO	SB	CS	SPEED	BA	OBP	SLG	MLVR	EQBA	EQOBP	EQSLG	EQA	VORP	DEFENSE	
2003	ERI	AA	23	524	64	18	0	9	45	48	78	2	0	4.2	.257	.328	.352	-.101	.217	.284	.312	.214	-20.6	132-3B	15
2004	ERI	AA	24	430	48	21	1	8	39	53	60	7	3	4.4	.273	.365	.398	.023	.235	.318	.340	.236	-2.8	98-3B	22
2005	TOL	AAA	25	269	31	15	0	4	28	25	58	6	3	5.1	.269	.342	.382	-.007	.247	.317	.347	.238	-0.7	51-3B	6
2006	*DET*	*MLB*	*26*	*247*	*24*	*9*	*1*	*4*	*21*	*18*	*48*	*2*	*1*	*4.4*	*.230*	*.292*	*.328*	*-.214*	*.234*	*.302*	*.345*	*.218*	*-5.4*	*61-3B*	*4*

Breakout: 22% Improve: 41% Collapse: 32% Attrition: 34% Comparables: Bobby Smith, Justin Gemoll, Mike Sharperson

Hannahan's bat is weak, but his defense profiles so well that he still rates a mention. Scouts and stats agree that if promoted, Hannahan would be an instant Gold Glove contender. He's got a nice backstory, too, having beaten serious drug and alcohol problems as a teen. The sad fact, however, is that he can't hit, and until he does, he's not going to get The Call.

BOBBY HIGGINSON OF Bats: L Throws: R Height: 5' 11" Weight: 195 Born: August 18, 1970 Age: 35

YEAR	TM	LVL	AGE	PA	R	2B	3B	HR	RBI	BB	SO	SB	CS	SPEED	BA	OBP	SLG	MLVR	EQBA	EQOBP	EQSLG	EQA	VORP	DEFENSE	
2003	DET	MLB	32	537	61	13	4	14	52	59	73	8	8	4.9	.235	.320	.369	-.108	.240	.330	.382	.248	-10.6	112-RF	1
2004	DET	MLB	33	529	63	24	2	12	64	70	84	5	2	4.7	.246	.353	.388	-.026	.251	.361	.400	.270	8.0	110-RF	3
2005	DET	MLB	34	27	1	0	0	0	1	1	5	0	0	5.0	.077	.111	.077	-.953	.077	.111	.077	.083	-5.6		
2006	*DET*	*MLB*	*35*	*203*	*19*	*7*	*1*	*4*	*21*	*20*	*34*	*1*	*1*	*5.0*	*.221*	*.302*	*.335*	*-.192*	*.224*	*.312*	*.352*	*.226*	*-5.5*	*51-RF*	*-2*

Breakout: 17% Improve: 38% Collapse: 42% Attrition: 46% Comparables: Mike Lum, Barney McCosky, Darryl Strawberry

Imagine a pitcher throwing two-hit ball for eight innings. That was what Bobby Higginson hit in 2005: Two hits, 24 outs. A bone spur in his elbow kept him from swinging properly. When it broke off, his season was over. That explains 2005, but his post-2000 freefall remains a mystery. Higginson could be a surprise comeback player in '06, but given that he's hit .258/.345/.402 over his past 500-plus games, a return to even a .270 EQA would be eye-popping. Of course, you could say the same about Ty Cobb, and his comeback isn't any more likely—or any less.

OMAR INFANTE SS/2B Bats: R Throws: R Height: 6' 0" Weight: 170 Born: December 26, 1981 Age: 24

YEAR	TM	LVL	AGE	PA	R	2B	3B	HR	RBI	BB	SO	SB	CS	SPEED	BA	OBP	SLG	MLVR	EQBA	EQOBP	EQSLG	EQA	VORP	DEFENSE			
2003	TOL	AAA	21	251	28	10	0	2	18	22	32	22	4	7.1	.223	.299	.295	-.196	.202	.280	.269	.217	-13.8	62-SS	-6		
2003	DET	MLB	21	241	24	6	1	0	8	18	37	6	3	6.2	.222	.278	.258	-.352	.228	.290	.260	.206	-9.9	59-SS	5		
2004	DET	MLB	22	549	69	27	9	16	55	40	112	13	7	6.6	.264	.317	.449	-.024	.269	.325	.460	.267	18.2	98-2B	-1	21-SS	1
2005	DET	MLB	23	426	36	28	2	9	43	16	73	8	0	5.6	.222	.254	.367	-.242	.229	.272	.392	.233	-7.7	67-2B	-2	44-SS	3
2006	*DET*	*MLB*	*24*	*438*	*53*	*21*	*3*	*10*	*44*	*26*	*69*	*11*	*4*	*5.5*	*.248*	*.298*	*.391*	*-.112*	*.252*	*.308*	*.411*	*.242*	*7.8*	*104-2B*	*1*		

Breakout: 36% Improve: 61% Collapse: 16% Attrition: 14% Comparables: Juan Uribe, Dick Schofield, Rafael Ramirez

Too many people wrote Infante off after an awful rookie season, and too many people praised him too highly after his sophomore year. Last year was closer to what should have been expected of him, although he did retain some of his unexpected power from 2004. The Tigers have to decide whether he's more valuable as trade bait or as a reserve. Jim Leyland has talked about rotating Polanco, Guillen, Inge, and Infante through the three infield spots, but such talk will only last until one of them is hitting .225 and gets benched. You know who the best suspect to do that is.

BRANDON INGE   **3B**   **Bats: R Throws: R**   Height: 5' 11"   Weight: 190   Born: May 19, 1977   Age: 29

YEAR	TM	LVL	AGE	PA	R	2B	3B	HR	RBI	BB	SO	SB	CS	SPEED	BA	OBP	SLG	MLVR	EQBA	EQOBP	EQSLG	EQA	VORP	DEFENSE		
2003	TOL	AAA	26	153	15	9	0	5	15	11	23	3	1	4.1	.275	.327	.444	.081	.250	.304	.419	.247	2.7	35-C 10		
2003	DET	MLB	26	362	32	15	3	8	30	24	79	4	4	4.6	.203	.265	.339	-.273	.207	.273	.353	.219	-11.7	98-C 7		
2004	DET	MLB	27	450	43	15	7	13	64	32	72	5	4	5.6	.287	.340	.453	.037	.292	.348	.465	.276	15.0	59-3B 1	35-C 6	
2005	DET	MLB	28	688	75	31	9	16	72	63	140	7	6	4.9	.261	.330	.419	-.004	.273	.350	.447	.272	13.3	158-3B 13		
2006	*DET*	*MLB*	*29*	*611*	*74*	*27*	*5*	*17*	*70*	*50*	*111*	*6*	*4*	*4.8*	*.257*	*.322*	*.416*	*-.035*	*.261*	*.333*	*.437*	*.257*	*14.5*	*143-3B 6*		

Breakout: 18%   Improve: 52%   Collapse: 21%   Attrition: 6%   Comparables: *Max Alvis, Vance Law, Brook Jacoby*

Getting out from behind the plate would seem to have helped his hitting, an idea we statheads often bandy about. But we rarely have a chance to see it demonstrated so vividly, because none of the dozen conversions from regular catcher to some other position done at the major league level in the last 50 years involved a hitter who was remotely as bad as Inge. After two seasons of almost identical value, it seems safe to say that Inge has transcended his early impotence at the plate, and will remain at this level for the time being.

DON KELLY   **SS/3B**   **Bats: L Throws: R**   Height: 6' 4"   Weight: 190   Born: February 15, 1980   Age: 26

YEAR	TM	LVL	AGE	PA	R	2B	3B	HR	RBI	BB	SO	SB	CS	SPEED	BA	OBP	SLG	MLVR	EQBA	EQOBP	EQSLG	EQA	VORP	DEFENSE		
2003	LAK	A+	23	354	48	17	4	1	38	45	25	15	2	6.5	.317	.401	.409	.221	.291	.364	.400	.274	19.6	32-3B 2	19-SS 2	
2003	ERI	AA	23	98	14	5	1	1	13	15	9	0	0	4.7	.265	.378	.386	.028	.237	.340	.358	.249	1.8	20-SS -2		
2004	ERI	AA	24	118	17	6	2	0	9	15	13	3	1	6.6	.228	.331	.327	-.154	.191	.286	.260	.207	-6.2	26-SS -2		
2005	ERI	AA	25	371	54	22	3	9	54	36	43	10	2	5.9	.340	.402	.508	.303	.294	.353	.437	.277	22.2	56-3B 0	24-SS -1	
2005	TOL	AAA	25	173	22	8	0	1	13	13	15	8	2	6.3	.250	.306	.319	-.175	.229	.287	.279	.212	-7.2	32-SS -1		
2006	*DET*	*MLB*	*26*	*473*	*56*	*21*	*4*	*5*	*40*	*39*	*55*	*9*	*3*	*5.3*	*.263*	*.327*	*.370*	*-.082*	*.267*	*.337*	*.389*	*.248*	*10.1*	*112-SS -1*		

Breakout: 22%   Improve: 52%   Collapse: 22%   Attrition: 10%   Comparables: *Bill Spiers, Mickey Morandini, Rob Wilfong*

Kelly is a borderline candidate for a major league utility job. The problem is that the Tigers aren't the team for him; they have an already-crowded infield, and other infield prospects like Tony Giarratano and Ryan Raburn rate ahead of him. He proved he had recovered from a shoulder injury that wiped out his 2004 season by having a big first half at Erie, but struggled when promoted to Triple-A Toledo.

KODY KIRKLAND   **3B**   **Bats: R Throws: R**   Height: 6' 4"   Weight: 200   Born: June 9, 1983   Age: 23

YEAR	TM	LVL	AGE	PA	R	2B	3B	HR	RBI	BB	SO	SB	CS	SPEED	BA	OBP	SLG	MLVR	EQBA	EQOBP	EQSLG	EQA	VORP	DEFENSE
2003	ONE	A-	20	295	46	15	11	4	49	25	60	14	5	7.3	.303	.390	.496	.293	.266	.330	.452	.268	26.0	64-3B -3
2004	WMI	A	21	525	50	30	11	10	61	15	149	6	8	5.4	.236	.276	.401	-.038	.211	.241	.354	.205	-25.0	121-3B -3
2005	LAK	A+	22	497	78	24	9	16	65	36	102	12	3	6.8	.266	.342	.470	.140	.241	.303	.433	.253	11.1	120-3B 9
2006	*DET*	*MLB*	*23*	*489*	*56*	*25*	*5*	*13*	*53*	*27*	*110*	*7*	*3*	*5.2*	*.242*	*.292*	*.404*	*-.111*	*.246*	*.302*	*.424*	*.240*	*2.1*	*115-3B 1*

Breakout: 27%   Improve: 50%   Collapse: 14%   Attrition: 6%   Comparables: *Nic Jackson, Marshall McDougall, Jamar Hill*

Originally a Pirate, Kirkland was a PTBNL when the Tigers traded Randall Simon. Yet another Tiger infielder with an excellent glove and a weak bat, Kirkland made great strides at the plate last year, especially recognizing and laying off of off-speed pitches. He's still a dead-red hitter, but at least he wasn't completely helpless against crooked pitches the way he had been in '04. The big test of Kirkland's newfound selectivity will come this year in his first exposure to Double-A.

NOOK LOGAN   **CF**   **Bats: B Throws: R**   Height: 6' 2"   Weight: 180   Born: November 28, 1979   Age: 26

YEAR	TM	LVL	AGE	PA	R	2B	3B	HR	RBI	BB	SO	SB	CS	SPEED	BA	OBP	SLG	MLVR	EQBA	EQOBP	EQSLG	EQA	VORP	DEFENSE
2003	ERI	AA	23	572	71	16	7	4	38	51	103	37	13	7.7	.251	.316	.333	-.150	.219	.280	.300	.217	-31.6	128-CF 19
2004	TOL	AAA	24	455	67	14	9	2	27	23	95	38	11	9.2	.263	.303	.352	-.139	.254	.295	.336	.232	-12.2	103-CF -1
2004	DET	MLB	24	147	12	5	2	0	10	13	24	8	2	6.2	.278	.340	.346	-.195	.280	.347	.348	.257	-1.2	41-CF 0
2005	DET	MLB	25	344	47	12	5	1	17	21	52	23	6	8.1	.258	.305	.335	-.181	.270	.328	.352	.248	-2.2	99-CF 8
2006	*DET*	*MLB*	*26*	*379*	*51*	*12*	*6*	*2*	*28*	*22*	*59*	*22*	*8*	*7.3*	*.260*	*.307*	*.350*	*-.143*	*.264*	*.317*	*.367*	*.238*	*1.1*	*91-CF 3*

Breakout: 41%   Improve: 63%   Collapse: 24%   Attrition: 26%   Comparables: *Randy Winn, Jesus Tavarez, Cecil Espy*

The Tigers spent the better part of 2005 trying to convince themselves that Logan was a good player, but he was never anything more than a placeholder to give Granderson a little extra seasoning. Logan is a legitimately great center fielder, and the team played up how very important that is in spacious Comerica Park, but the Tiger doth protest too much. Leyland has shown some early fascination with that speed, which could bode ill for Granderson. At best, Logan's a good fourth outfielder and pinch-runner, perhaps worth spot starts when an extreme flyball pitcher is on the mound.

CRAIG MONROE   OF   Bats: R Throws: R   Height: 6' 1"   Weight: 210   Born: February 27, 1977   Age: 29

YEAR	TM	LVL	AGE	PA	R	2B	3B	HR	RBI	BB	SO	SB	CS	SPEED	BA	OBP	SLG	MLVR	EQBA	EQOBP	EQSLG	EQA	VORP	DEFENSE			
2003	DET	MLB	26	457	51	18	1	23	70	27	89	4	2	4.6	.240	.287	.449	-.063	.244	.297	.464	.256	-2.4	68-LF	0	32-RF	0
2004	DET	MLB	27	481	65	27	3	18	72	29	79	3	4	5.1	.293	.337	.488	.114	.299	.347	.500	.282	19.5	50-LF	-5	43-RF	4
2005	DET	MLB	28	622	69	30	3	20	89	40	95	8	3	5.0	.277	.322	.446	.036	.287	.340	.472	.278	17.1	71-RF	-4	57-LF	0
2006	*DET*	*MLB*	*29*	*566*	*69*	*28*	*3*	*21*	*79*	*36*	*92*	*6*	*3*	*4.7*	*.278*	*.326*	*.464*	*.051*	*.282*	*.337*	*.488*	*.271*	*18.5*	*133-RF*	*-4*		

Breakout: 19%   Improve: 48%   Collapse: 23%   Attrition: 7%   Comparables: *Marty Cordova, Rip Repulski, Torii Hunter*

As nice a find as Monroe has been the last two years, it is worth remembering that the average EQA for a corner out-fielder is .271. Monroe isn't much better than that, and this is the peak of his career. Another year or three where he hits like this seems to be the best you can hope for, but once he loses even a little bat speed, he'll fall fast. Monroe isn't the kind of player who leads a team to a title; he's a talented understudy waiting to be replaced by a star.

MAGGLIO ORDONEZ   RF   Bats: R Throws: R   Height: 5' 11"   Weight: 170   Born: January 28, 1974   Age: 32

YEAR	TM	LVL	AGE	PA	R	2B	3B	HR	RBI	BB	SO	SB	CS	SPEED	BA	OBP	SLG	MLVR	EQBA	EQOBP	EQSLG	EQA	VORP	DEFENSE	
2003	CHA	MLB	29	674	95	46	3	29	99	57	73	9	5	4.3	.317	.380	.546	.291	.315	.383	.551	.309	52.9	150-RF	11
2004	CHA	MLB	30	222	32	8	2	9	37	16	22	0	2	4.8	.292	.351	.485	.092	.288	.349	.480	.278	8.3	41-RF	2
2005	DET	MLB	31	343	38	17	0	8	46	30	35	0	0	3.9	.302	.359	.436	.109	.311	.376	.460	.291	14.4	76-RF	-3
2006	*DET*	*MLB*	*32*	*377*	*45*	*18*	*1*	*10*	*48*	*31*	*41*	*1*	*1*	*4.4*	*.288*	*.349*	*.439*	*.063*	*.292*	*.361*	*.462*	*.275*	*12.8*	*90-RF*	*-2*

Breakout: 4%   Improve: 22%   Collapse: 39%   Attrition: 21%   Comparables: *Chet Lemon, Greg Colbrunn, Carl Furillo*

After signing the five-year, $75 million deal lavished on a player with a bizarre and unprecedented knee injury, Ordonez's deal was the talk of baseball. Good news for all: the knee was not a problem. The bad news: everything else was. Ordonez suffered from diverticulitis in the spring and then a hernia that needed surgery, which kept him out until July. When he did play, he was close to the same old Ordonez—but both of those could be the lingering effects of surgeries and illnesses sapping his strength. He'll have to show he's back at full mobility to avoid being remanded to DH.

CARLOS PENA   1B   Bats: L Throws: L   Height: 6' 2"   Weight: 210   Born: May 17, 1978   Age: 28

YEAR	TM	LVL	AGE	PA	R	2B	3B	HR	RBI	BB	SO	SB	CS	SPEED	BA	OBP	SLG	MLVR	EQBA	EQOBP	EQSLG	EQA	VORP	DEFENSE	
2003	DET	MLB	25	515	51	21	6	18	50	53	123	4	5	5.1	.248	.332	.440	.015	.253	.341	.458	.271	7.6	123-1B	-12
2004	DET	MLB	26	559	89	22	4	27	82	70	146	7	1	5.9	.241	.338	.472	.046	.246	.347	.484	.284	18.6	131-1B	-8
2005	TOL	AAA	27	309	43	17	1	12	45	45	65	3	4	4.1	.311	.424	.525	.365	.285	.386	.463	.291	17.3	63-1B	-7
2005	DET	MLB	27	295	37	9	0	18	44	31	95	0	1	3.1	.235	.325	.477	.051	.244	.343	.508	.283	8.0	48-1B	-2
2006	*DET*	*MLB*	*28*	*514*	*64*	*22*	*2*	*25*	*74*	*61*	*127*	*3*	*2*	*4.5*	*.255*	*.349*	*.482*	*.091*	*.259*	*.361*	*.506*	*.284*	*20.6*	*121-1B*	*-4*

Breakout: 20%   Improve: 50%   Collapse: 21%   Attrition: 9%   Comparables: *Dan Pasqua, Joe Hague, Ryan Klesko*

Pena was demoted to Toledo in May with a .235 EqA; after he came back in August, his EqA was .326. It may look like the demotion helped, but looks are deceiving; his strikeouts were way up and walks way down. He took a more aggressive approach, and pitchers were slow to update the book on him that said he was passive at the plate. Strikeouts are the biggest reason why he has never lived up to the numbers he originally produced as a Texas prospect. Last year's demotion did nothing to help that.

PLACIDO POLANCO   INF   Bats: R Throws: R   Height: 5' 10"   Weight: 168   Born: October 10, 1975   Age: 30

YEAR	TM	LVL	AGE	PA	R	2B	3B	HR	RBI	BB	SO	SB	CS	SPEED	BA	OBP	SLG	MLVR	EQBA	EQOBP	EQSLG	EQA	VORP	DEFENSE			
2003	PHI	MLB	27	546	87	30	3	14	63	42	38	14	2	6.2	.289	.352	.447	.104	.287	.348	.450	.278	32.0	98-2B	8	20-3B	1
2004	PHI	MLB	28	548	74	21	0	17	55	27	39	7	4	4.9	.298	.345	.441	.077	.294	.339	.440	.267	24.7	105-2B	17	11-3B	2
2005	PHI	MLB	29	173	26	7	0	3	20	12	9	0	0	4.6	.316	.376	.418	.127	.310	.370	.418	.275	8.8	26-2B	2		
2005	DET	MLB	29	376	58	20	2	6	36	21	16	4	3	4.8	.338	.386	.461	.214	.355	.409	.487	.306	30.0	81-2B	3		
2006	*DET*	*MLB*	*30*	*567*	*71*	*27*	*3*	*9*	*61*	*33*	*35*	*5*	*2*	*5.1*	*.304*	*.352*	*.420*	*.056*	*.308*	*.364*	*.441*	*.271*	*29.1*	*133-2B*	*6*		

Breakout: 13%   Improve: 33%   Collapse: 33%   Attrition: 11%   Comparables: *Bobby Avila, George Kell, Julio Franco*

Polanco had the second-best batting average in the majors last year—Derrek Lee's .335 was the only one to beat his .331—but he didn't have enough at-bats in either league to officially qualify, an absurd situation considering the 18 games of interleague play nowadays. Polanco hits for average and some power while providing excellent defense at second or third base. Despite that, he lost playing time as a Phillie to David Bell and Chase Utley, and now the Tigers are talking about doing something similar. The only benefit might be that it keeps Polanco fresh. Regardless, he won't hit over .330 again.

RYAN RABURN   **2B**   **Bats: R Throws: R**   Height: 6' 0"   Weight: 180   Born: April 17, 1981   Age: 25

YEAR	TM	LVL	AGE	PA	R	2B	3B	HR	RBI	BB	SO	SB	CS	SPEED	BA	OBP	SLG	MLVR	EQBA	EQOBP	EQSLG	EQA	VORP	DEFENSE
2003	LAK	A+	22	382	52	14	3	12	56	45	89	2	1	5.0	.222	.332	.394	.048	.200	.290	.380	.233	-5.2	82-3B 3
2004	ERI	AA	23	421	66	29	4	16	63	47	96	3	0	5.3	.301	.390	.533	.256	.269	.350	.477	.282	27.4	95-2B -5
2005	TOL	AAA	24	523	62	22	4	19	64	45	109	8	3	5.2	.253	.323	.437	.022	.241	.309	.409	.248	7.3	96-2B -6
2006	*DET*	*MLB*	*25*	*417*	*50*	*19*	*2*	*12*	*48*	*32*	*88*	*5*	*2*	*4.5*	*.252*	*.317*	*.415*	*-.048*	*.256*	*.327*	*.436*	*.255*	*12.1*	*99-2B -2*

Breakout: 18%   *Improve: 48%*   *Collapse: 22%*   *Attrition: 23%*   *Comparables: Ted Lepcio, Jack Lohrke, Alex Gonzalez*

The Tigers had high hopes for Raburn after a big 2004 season, but they were dashed. Since 2002, at all stops other than Erie, Raburn's batting average when not striking out is .326. It wasn't more than 10 points away from that when he was at Western Michigan, or Lakeland, or Toledo. At Erie in 2004, it was .407. That's got "outlier" written all over it. While Raburn's got some power, his hitting for any kind of average is always going to be a problem, and his glove doesn't provide any help to push him ahead of the infielders already in Detroit.

WILKIN RAMIREZ   **3B**   **Bats: R Throws: R**   Height: 6' 2"   Weight: 190   Born: October 25, 1985   Age: 20

YEAR	TM	LVL	AGE	PA	R	2B	3B	HR	RBI	BB	SO	SB	CS	SPEED	BA	OBP	SLG	MLVR	EQBA	EQOBP	EQSLG	EQA	VORP	DEFENSE
2005	WMI	A	19	540	69	21	2	16	65	35	143	21	8	5.6	.262	.317	.410	.020	.237	.280	.374	.228	-7.3	55-3B -7
2006	*DET*	*MLB*	*20*	*479*	*51*	*20*	*3*	*11*	*49*	*22*	*119*	*11*	*6*	*4.7*	*.228*	*.268*	*.359*	*-.217*	*.232*	*.277*	*.378*	*.216*	*-7.8*	*113-3B -9*

Breakout: 27%   *Improve: 49%*   *Collapse: 31%*   *Attrition: 11%*   *Comparables: Shawn Bowman, Dave Kelton, Neil Jenkins*

Ramirez has a quick bat, making him a favorite among scouts who react to "bat speed" in the same way that statheads do the Tex Avery howling wolf thing for "OBP." Ramirez also has strength, so he does project to be someone with 30-homer plus potential. In fact, he has all kinds of potential: the hole in his swing gives him 160-strikeout potential, and lousy footwork at third gives him 40-error potential. The good thing about strikeouts is that they're a very visible problem, attracting a lot of attention from coaches. A minor improvement can have a big effect, so if Ramirez can cut the strikeouts by 25% and keep everything else intact, his batting average should jump 30 points and his slugging average 50. Thus, instead of projecting as an average hitter he'd project as a star.

IVAN RODRIGUEZ   **C**   **Bats: R Throws: R**   Height: 5' 9"   Weight: 200   Born: November 30, 1971   Age: 34

YEAR	TM	LVL	AGE	PA	R	2B	3B	HR	RBI	BB	SO	SB	CS	SPEED	BA	OBP	SLG	MLVR	EQBA	EQOBP	EQSLG	EQA	VORP	DEFENSE
2003	FLO	MLB	31	577	90	36	3	16	85	55	92	10	6	5.6	.297	.369	.474	.189	.301	.371	.487	.291	42.2	127-C 6
2004	DET	MLB	32	575	72	32	2	19	86	41	91	7	4	4.6	.334	.383	.510	.260	.340	.391	.526	.308	55.9	118-C -2
2005	DET	MLB	33	524	71	33	5	14	50	11	93	7	3	5.9	.276	.290	.444	-.021	.285	.309	.467	.263	18.5	117-C 9
2006	*DET*	*MLB*	*34*	*479*	*58*	*25*	*3*	*14*	*62*	*22*	*80*	*7*	*3*	*5.2*	*.281*	*.318*	*.446*	*.017*	*.285*	*.329*	*.469*	*.263*	*21.0*	*113-C 1*

Breakout: 4%   *Improve: 32%*   *Collapse: 39%*   *Attrition: 15%*   *Comparables: Steve Garvey, Terry Steinbach, Elston Howard*

It was his worst offensive year since 1995, but how do you break up that decline into its component parts? Was it random bad luck, normal aging, the wear and tear of 1800 games behind the plate, or the mental stress of having a 15-year marriage fall apart? The last one isn't something that fits into PECOTA, but putting speculation about personal matters aside, Rodriguez caught 1,812 games through his Age 33 season, more than anyone else in history. Of the rest of the top ten, only two produced as many wins in the rest of their careers as they had in their Age 32 and Age 33 seasons combined, and only one—Al Lopez—had what you might call a really good season left in him, and that was during World War II. Bench, Simmons, Carter, and Freehan all fell very fast after 33, and Ivan's contract runs through 2008, when he'll be 36.

CHRIS SHELTON   **1B**   **Bats: R Throws: R**   Height: 6' 0"   Weight: 220   Born: June 26, 1980   Age: 26

YEAR	TM	LVL	AGE	PA	R	2B	3B	HR	RBI	BB	SO	SB	CS	SPEED	BA	OBP	SLG	MLVR	EQBA	EQOBP	EQSLG	EQA	VORP	DEFENSE		
2003	LYN	A+	23	389	71	24	1	21	69	68	67	1	4	3.5	.359	.478	.641	.623	.310	.416	.571	.325	49.9	39-1B 0		28-C 1
2003	ALT	AA	23	133	17	10	1	0	14	8	23	0	1	4.5	.279	.331	.377	.010	.259	.302	.349	.227	-4.6	20-1B 3		10-C 0
2004	DET	MLB	24	56	6	1	0	1	3	9	14	0	0	2.8	.196	.321	.283	-.240	.200	.327	.289	.232	-1.6			
2005	TOL	AAA	25	211	34	19	0	8	39	25	33	0	2	3.7	.331	.417	.569	.437	.300	.384	.515	.301	16.4	31-1B -2		
2005	DET	MLB	25	431	61	22	3	18	59	34	87	0	0	3.9	.299	.360	.510	.210	.309	.376	.543	.307	28.1	83-1B 0		
2006	*DET*	*MLB*	*26*	*554*	*72*	*27*	*2*	*24*	*82*	*58*	*103*	*0*	*1*	*4.1*	*.280*	*.361*	*.493*	*.143*	*.284*	*.373*	*.518*	*.292*	*27.9*	*130-1B 0*		

Breakout: 14%   *Improve: 46%*   *Collapse: 23%*   *Attrition: 11%*   *Comparables: Joe Charboneau, Kevin Mitchell, Carmelo Martinez*

The Rule 5 layoff is supposed to be a big drag on a player's development, but Shelton didn't get the memo. Scouts run him down for not being athletic, but there's a certain level of hitting ability where that stops making a difference and Shelton is way over that line. He's not a great defensive first baseman, but doesn't show up as being bad. Comerica Park's roomy dimensions also didn't phase him; he batted .316/.367/.541 in Detroit, .279/.351/.475 on the road. Shelton's future is bright enough for shades.

JUAN TEJEDA   **1B**   **Bats: R Throws: R**   Height: 6′ 2″   Weight: 190   Born: January 26, 1982   Age: 24

YEAR	TM	LVL	AGE	PA	R	2B	3B	HR	RBI	BB	SO	SB	CS	SPEED	BA	OBP	SLG	MLVR	EQBA	EQOBP	EQSLG	EQA	VORP	DEFENSE
2003	LAK	A+	21	528	63	28	4	10	76	56	68	6	3	4.9	.280	.360	.423	.158	.259	.327	.422	.259	4.0	109-1B -2
2004	ERI	AA	22	520	71	29	3	23	92	51	102	0	0	3.8	.289	.362	.516	.183	.256	.323	.456	.266	8.7	117-1B -8
2005	ERI	AA	23	523	64	27	2	14	82	41	86	2	4	4.1	.291	.354	.447	.112	.265	.324	.413	.254	1.7	103-1B -10
2006	DET	MLB	24	495	58	24	2	16	61	36	83	2	1	4.2	.253	.312	.422	-.046	.257	.322	.444	.254	2.6	117-1B -4

Breakout: 18%   Improve: 45%   Collapse: 28%   Attrition: 9%   Comparables: Joe Crede, Luis Garcia, Kevin West

Juan Tejeda, two Tejeda, three Tejeda, four... Chris Shelton's success is not good news for Tejeda, since he's basically a reduced-scale statistical clone of Shelton. Everything is distributed the same way, but there's a little less average, a little less power, and not quite as many walks. Plus he's not as good a defensive first baseman and, unlike Shelton, can't be used at catcher in an emergency. He might be able to play his way in as a DH if the big club doesn't need to save that spot for I-Rod or Ordonez.

MARCUS THAMES   **OF**   **Bats: R Throws: R**   Height: 6′ 2″   Weight: 205   Born: March 6, 1977   Age: 29

YEAR	TM	LVL	AGE	PA	R	2B	3B	HR	RBI	BB	SO	SB	CS	SPEED	BA	OBP	SLG	MLVR	EQBA	EQOBP	EQSLG	EQA	VORP	DEFENSE	
2003	COH	AAA	26	217	26	15	2	2	28	17	48	3	4	5.1	.278	.332	.407	.035	.259	.316	.382	.243	0.7	39-CF 0	11-RF 0
2003	TEX	MLB	26	84	12	2	0	1	4	8	18	0	1	3.9	.205	.298	.274	-.328	.194	.298	.264	.208	-6.1	18-RF 0	
2004	TOL	AAA	27	273	57	21	1	24	59	33	40	4	1	5.3	.329	.410	.735	.639	.285	.365	.614	.315	27.4	60-RF -6	
2004	DET	MLB	27	184	24	12	0	10	33	16	42	0	1	3.7	.255	.326	.509	.088	.258	.333	.515	.281	5.7	34-LF 1	
2005	TOL	AAA	28	314	53	18	3	22	56	41	59	4	1	4.9	.340	.427	.679	.613	.301	.383	.564	.314	27.7	31-LF 0	23-RF -3
2005	DET	MLB	28	118	11	2	0	7	16	9	38	0	0	3.6	.196	.263	.411	-.176	.198	.277	.415	.237	-2.9	17-LF -1	
2006	DET	MLB	29	435	55	19	2	21	64	44	93	2	1	4.1	.251	.331	.473	.048	.255	.342	.497	.275	13.6	103-LF -4	

Breakout: 9%   Improve: 30%   Collapse: 39%   Attrition: 14%   Comparables: Dwight Evans, Nick Esasky, Gary Roenicke

A veteran minor league outfielder, Thames has reached the point where not only is he not learning anything new at Triple-A, he's taking advantage of the pitchers who still do have things to learn. What that means is that his minor league translations are liable to run well ahead of any major league performance he gets from now on.

RONDELL WHITE   **LF**   **Bats: R Throws: R**   Height: 6′ 0″   Weight: 210   Born: February 23, 1972   Age: 34

YEAR	TM	LVL	AGE	PA	R	2B	3B	HR	RBI	BB	SO	SB	CS	SPEED	BA	OBP	SLG	MLVR	EQBA	EQOBP	EQSLG	EQA	VORP	DEFENSE
2003	SDN	MLB	31	449	49	17	3	18	66	25	71	1	4	4.1	.278	.330	.465	.112	.285	.334	.483	.273	10.8	95-LF -2
2003	KCA	MLB	31	85	13	6	1	4	21	6	8	0	0	4.8	.347	.400	.613	.396	.338	.400	.608	.331	8.7	15-LF 1
2004	DET	MLB	32	498	76	21	2	19	67	39	77	1	2	4.5	.270	.337	.453	.037	.275	.343	.464	.274	10.9	69-LF -6
2005	DET	MLB	33	400	49	24	3	12	53	17	48	1	0	5.0	.313	.347	.489	.173	.323	.366	.518	.298	24.3	60-LF -1
2006	MIN	MLB	34	402	48	21	2	13	58	23	57	1	1	4.7	.292	.338	.463	.080	.293	.347	.478	.272	15.7	96-LF -3

Breakout: 5%   Improve: 28%   Collapse: 40%   Attrition: 24%   Comparables: Lou Piniella, Glenallen Hill, Bob Watson

Since he first established himself as a regular, White has averaged 65 EQR per season. Last year, he was up to 64 in mid-August when he dived for a ball in the outfield. For any other player, this wouldn't have been a big deal, but as White had already reached his run limit, his warranty was up. He separated his shoulder on the dive, tearing the rotator cuff, and missed the last six weeks. It was his non-throwing shoulder, so White should be fine in 2006. The Tigers initially said they wanted him back, but failed to offer him arbitration. The division-rival Twins signed him to a one-year deal with a vested option for '07.

VANCE WILSON   **C**   **Bats: R Throws: R**   Height: 5′ 11″   Weight: 190   Born: March 17, 1973   Age: 33

YEAR	TM	LVL	AGE	PA	R	2B	3B	HR	RBI	BB	SO	SB	CS	SPEED	BA	OBP	SLG	MLVR	EQBA	EQOBP	EQSLG	EQA	VORP	DEFENSE
2003	NYN	MLB	30	290	28	9	1	8	39	15	56	1	2	4.3	.243	.293	.373	-.132	.244	.295	.385	.234	-1.3	74-C 5
2004	NYN	MLB	31	176	18	10	1	4	21	11	24	1	0	4.3	.274	.335	.427	.025	.272	.330	.424	.263	6.6	43-C 1
2005	DET	MLB	32	171	18	4	0	3	19	11	26	0	0	3.7	.197	.275	.283	-.328	.205	.287	.305	.216	-6.6	46-C -1
2006	DET	MLB	33	164	14	6	1	3	17	10	26	0	0	3.9	.238	.299	.350	-.170	.241	.309	.368	.228	0.1	43-C 0

Breakout: 17%   Improve: 38%   Collapse: 36%   Attrition: 38%   Comparables: Brook Fordyce, Matt Batts, Jerry McNertney

Wilson's caught-stealing percentage dropped for the third straight year in 2005. Bad enough for anybody, but especially for a defense-first catcher whose already poor hitting dropped another notch. If he has hit the wall, the Tigers are going to have to go shopping; he could drop another 10 to 15 runs and still be better than any of the catchers at Toledo or Erie.

DMITRI YOUNG   DH   Bats: B Throws: R   Height: 6' 2"   Weight: 235   Born: October 11, 1973   Age: 32

YEAR	TM	LVL	AGE	PA	R	2B	3B	HR	RBI	BB	SO	SB	CS	SPEED	BA	OBP	SLG	MLVR	EQBA	EQOBP	EQSLG	EQA	VORP	DEFENSE		
2003	DET	MLB	29	635	78	34	7	29	85	58	130	2	1	4.6	.297	.372	.537	.262	.304	.381	.555	.311	50.6	58-LF	0	15-3B -1
2004	DET	MLB	30	432	72	23	2	18	60	33	71	0	1	4.6	.272	.336	.481	.072	.278	.344	.494	.282	16.6	24-1B -2		
2005	DET	MLB	31	508	61	25	3	21	72	29	100	1	0	4.4	.271	.325	.471	.069	.281	.342	.500	.283	18.9	29-1B -1		16-LF 1
2006	*DET*	*MLB*	*32*	*539*	*63*	*25*	*3*	*21*	*78*	*36*	*103*	*1*	*1*	*4.3*	*.277*	*.333*	*.468*	*.066*	*.281*	*.344*	*.492*	*.274*	*21.1*	*127-DH*		

Breakout: 3%   Improve: 23%   Collapse: 27%   Attrition: 13%   Comparables: Andres Galarraga, Donn Clendenon, Johnny Lindell

Primarily a DH since he broke his leg in April '04, Young's probably going to be stuck there for the rest of his career. 'S alright; defense has never been his strong suit anyway. The bad news is that Young is already off to a bad start with new manager Leyland, who is unhappy with his conditioning. Normally you'd combine that with the depth the Tigers have and conclude that he's going to be traded. But he's got an $8M contract for '06 and that's a lot to swallow given his performance level.

PITCHERS

JEREMY BONDERMAN   Bats: R Throws: R   Height: 6' 2"   Weight: 210   Born: October 28, 1982   Age: 23

YEAR	TM	LVL	AGE	W	L	SV	G	GS	IP	H	BB	SO	HR	GB%	BABIP	STUFF	WHIP	ERA	PERA	EQERA	EQH9	EQBB9	EQSO9	EQHR9	VORP	WXRL
2003	DET	MLB	20	6	19	0	33	28	162.0	193	58	108	23	48%	.324	6	1.55	5.56	4.84	5.93	9.9	3.1	5.7	1.2	-11.1	0.2
2004	DET	MLB	21	11	13	0	33	32	184.0	168	73	168	24	50%	.286	23	1.31	4.89	4.29	4.63	8.3	3.3	7.7	1.1	26.3	4.2
2005	DET	MLB	22	14	13	0	29	29	189.0	199	57	145	21	48%	.313	20	1.35	4.57	4.09	4.74	9.1	2.7	6.8	0.9	19.8	3.9
2006	*DET*	*MLB*	*23*	*11*	*11*	*0*	*30*	*30*	*194.7*	*195*	*61*	*147*	*21*	*48%*	*.294*	*21*	*1.31*	*4.05*	*4.29*	*4.35*	*8.8*	*2.8*	*6.8*	*0.9*	*28.1*	*4.3*

Breakout: 38%   Improve: 76%   Collapse: 2%   Attrition: 1%   Comparables: Joe Coleman, Ryan Dempster, Richard Dotson

Bonderman was having a very good season through about July, but then he tried to pitch through a sore elbow and was awful for the last two months of the season. Assuming the tendinitis clears up—although it frequently recurs, so that is not a safe assumption—he was a better pitcher than his overall stat line indicates, so he should be better than the projections that are built from it.

ROMAN COLON   Bats: R Throws: R   Height: 6' 3"   Weight: 170   Born: August 13, 1979   Age: 26

YEAR	TM	LVL	AGE	W	L	SV	G	GS	IP	H	BB	SO	HR	GB%	BABIP	STUFF	WHIP	ERA	PERA	EQERA	EQH9	EQBB9	EQSO9	EQHR9	VORP	WXRL
2003	GRN	AA	23	11	3	2	39	12	107.0	104	33	58	9	—	.265	-33	1.28	3.36	6.08	5.54	10.3	3.2	3.4	1.6	0.7	—
2004	RIC	AAA	24	4	1	0	51	0	74.0	72	22	64	4	—	.318	5	1.27	3.65	3.96	4.58	8.9	3.0	6.1	0.6	8.2	—
2004	ATL	MLB	24	2	1	0	18	0	19.0	18	8	15	0	50%	.321	2	1.37	3.32	3.32	4.26	8.5	3.3	6.2	0.0	3.0	0.2
2005	ATL	MLB	25	1	5	0	23	4	44.3	47	14	30	10	48%	.278	-17	1.38	5.28	5.73	5.73	9.8	2.7	5.7	2.0	-0.9	0.2
2005	DET	MLB	25	1	1	0	12	3	25.0	35	7	17	7	54%	.337	-13	1.68	6.12	6.23	5.88	11.4	2.4	5.9	2.4	-1.2	0.0
2006	*DET*	*MLB*	*26*	*4*	*5*	*1*	*39*	*9*	*79.3*	*86*	*26*	*46*	*10*	*48%*	*.294*	*-5*	*1.41*	*4.67*	*4.87*	*5.30*	*9.6*	*2.9*	*5.2*	*1.0*	*6.4*	*0.8*

Breakout: 25%   Improve: 56%   Collapse: 20%   Attrition: 16%   Comparables: Xavier Hernandez, Bud Podbielan, John Gelnar

Answer to the question, "What did Caesar digest his food with?" and also "What does it sound like when you order your twenty-third rum and cola?" Colon was meant to be the reward for trading Kyle Farnsworth to the Braves, but the Tigers weren't happy with the early returns. A non-prospect for years, Colon's development coincided with a turn to full-time relief, which added about 5 mph to his fastball. The Tigers, like the Braves, have thought about moving him back to starting. The Tigers say he'll be competing for the fifth starter's spot in the spring, and will quickly discover that he should stay in relief.

NATE CORNEJO   Bats: R Throws: R   Height: 6' 5"   Weight: 200   Born: September 24, 1979   Age: 26

YEAR	TM	LVL	AGE	W	L	SV	G	GS	IP	H	BB	SO	HR	GB%	BABIP	STUFF	WHIP	ERA	PERA	EQERA	EQH9	EQBB9	EQSO9	EQHR9	VORP	WXRL
2003	DET	MLB	23	6	17	0	32	32	194.7	236	58	46	18	52%	.310	-7	1.51	4.67	5.04	4.45	10.4	2.7	2.1	0.8	17.3	3.9
2004	DET	MLB	24	1	3	0	5	5	25.7	42	11	12	4	51%	.396	-15	2.06	8.40	5.53	7.81	12.0	3.3	3.6	1.3	-7.6	-0.5
2005	ERI	AA	25	4	12	0	19	19	102.0	126	17	48	15	50%	.320	-36	1.40	4.59	6.23	6.14	11.4	1.9	2.7	2.0	-6.0	—
2006	*DET*	*MLB*	*26*	*6*	*12*	*0*	*27*	*27*	*150.0*	*196*	*41*	*47*	*24*	*49%*	*.309*	*-12*	*1.57*	*5.86*	*6.12*	*6.28*	*11.5*	*2.4*	*2.8*	*1.3*	*-10.5*	*0.0*

Breakout: 4%   Improve: 26%   Collapse: 35%   Attrition: 0%   Comparables: Cam Reimers, Henry Bonilla, Elliot Brown

Cornejo underwent surgery for a frayed labrum in July of 2004. The injury was responsible for his poor pitching in 2004, though his low strikeout rates have always been troublesome. For 2006 the hope is that his shoulder is healed, but like Kenny Baugh, the likelihood of a full recovery is slight.

CRAIG DINGMAN

Bats: R **Throws: R** Height: 6' 4" Weight: 210 Born: March 12, 1974 Age: 32

YEAR	TM	LVL	AGE	W	L	SV	G	GS	IP	H	BB	SO	HR	GB%	BABIP	STUFF	WHIP	ERA	PERA	EQERA	EQH9	EQBB9	EQSO9	EQHR9	VORP	WXRL
2004	TOL	AAA	30	1	2	0	21	0	25.7	26	11	31	5	—	.318	-12	1.44	4.55	6.66	5.92	10.0	4.8	7.8	2.6	-0.9	—
2004	DET	MLB	30	2	2	0	24	0	29.3	33	22	16	3	41%	.323	-25	1.88	6.76	6.00	6.30	9.9	6.3	4.5	0.9	-1.3	-0.0
2005	TOL	AAA	31	2	1	4	35	0	48.0	42	13	67	3	46%	.345	16	1.15	2.81	3.72	4.70	9.0	3.1	8.8	0.8	4.6	—
2005	DET	MLB	31	2	3	4	34	0	32.0	30	9	24	5	35%	.287	0	1.22	3.66	4.83	3.98	8.8	2.6	6.8	1.4	6.2	0.6
2006	*DET*	*MLB*	*32*	*2*	*3*	*3*	*49*	*0*	*46.3*	*50*	*19*	*35*	*7*	*41%*	*.300*	*-5*	*1.47*	*4.91*	*5.23*	*5.80*	*9.5*	*3.5*	*6.7*	*1.2*	*2.2*	*0.2*

Breakout: 25%   Improve: 46%   Collapse: 27%   Attrition: 31%   Comparables: Doug Henry, Ben Wade, Mike Hartley

Pitchers don't talk about a new stance the way hitters do, but Dingman is on record as saying that different positioning on the rubber was responsible for his success. That may be true in the Bull Durham "If you believe you're playing well because you're wearing women's underwear, then you ARE" sense, but a look at the PERA column says there wasn't anything different about Dingman's performance in 2005. He did strand 75% of the men who reached base on him last year, as opposed to his 67% average since 2000. But that's luck, and it's worth a run of ERA in his case. Respect the streak, but don't place bets.

SEAN DOUGLASS

Bats: R **Throws: R** Height: 6' 6" Weight: 218 Born: April 28, 1979 Age: 27

YEAR	TM	LVL	AGE	W	L	SV	G	GS	IP	H	BB	SO	HR	GB%	BABIP	STUFF	WHIP	ERA	PERA	EQERA	EQH9	EQBB9	EQSO9	EQHR9	VORP	WXRL
2003	OTT	AAA	24	10	8	0	27	27	143.0	142	58	118	6	—	.304	12	1.40	3.40	4.41	5.00	9.2	4.4	5.8	0.6	9.2	—
2004	SYR	AAA	25	5	6	0	18	18	89.0	92	37	74	7	—	.322	3	1.45	4.75	4.72	5.44	9.2	4.2	5.6	0.8	1.6	—
2004	TOR	MLB	25	0	2	0	14	3	38.7	37	28	36	6	45%	.295	-1	1.68	6.28	5.26	5.49	8.5	5.9	7.8	1.1	0.6	-0.2
2005	TOL	AAA	26	9	1	0	14	14	81.7	61	27	76	5	38%	.258	18	1.08	2.86	4.19	3.84	7.9	3.5	6.4	0.7	15.1	—
2005	DET	MLB	26	5	5	0	18	16	87.3	92	33	55	13	44%	.298	-5	1.43	5.57	5.13	5.75	9.4	3.4	5.6	1.3	-1.2	0.8
2006	*DET*	*MLB*	*27*	*6*	*9*	*0*	*31*	*20*	*119.3*	*126*	*51*	*82*	*16*	*43%*	*.296*	*2*	*1.49*	*5.11*	*5.20*	*5.62*	*9.4*	*3.8*	*6.1*	*1.1*	*2.7*	*1.0*

Breakout: 17%   Improve: 46%   Collapse: 22%   Attrition: 11%   Comparables: Rich Gale, Dave Sisler, Wayne Twitchell

Douglass always seemed to post good numbers while in the Orioles' system, but that never translated to the majors. Last season it seemed as if it was all coming together, but then it turned. Douglass went from a 3.32 ERA in his first seven starts to a 7.52 in the rest of the season. He denies any injury, so perhaps advance scouting caught up to him. Waived by the Tigers and claimed by the Indians, the Hiroshima Carp of the Japanese Central League hooked him for $500,000.

FRANKLYN GERMAN

Bats: R **Throws: R** Height: 6' 4" Weight: 260 Born: January 20, 1980 Age: 26

YEAR	TM	LVL	AGE	W	L	SV	G	GS	IP	H	BB	SO	HR	GB%	BABIP	STUFF	WHIP	ERA	PERA	EQERA	EQH9	EQBB9	EQSO9	EQHR9	VORP	WXRL
2003	TOL	AAA	23	1	4	4	24	0	29.3	21	9	32	2	—	.254	10	1.02	2.46	4.55	3.58	8.1	3.3	8.1	1.0	6.2	—
2003	DET	MLB	23	2	4	5	45	0	44.7	47	45	41	5	50%	.333	-14	2.06	6.04	5.91	6.11	8.9	8.7	7.9	1.0	-2.6	0.5
2004	TOL	AAA	24	3	5	27	49	0	49.0	46	25	60	6	—	.320	0	1.45	4.59	4.88	4.88	8.8	5.1	8.6	1.3	3.8	—
2005	DET	MLB	25	4	0	1	58	0	59.0	63	34	38	7	51%	.316	-12	1.64	3.66	5.43	3.92	9.7	5.1	5.7	1.1	11.5	0.6
2006	*DET*	*MLB*	*26*	*2*	*2*	*1*	*35*	*0*	*38.3*	*39*	*21*	*29*	*5*	*45%*	*.297*	*-6*	*1.58*	*4.92*	*5.30*	*5.90*	*9.0*	*4.9*	*6.8*	*1.0*	*1.8*	*0.1*

Breakout: 25%   Improve: 44%   Collapse: 30%   Attrition: 43%   Comparables: Barry Jones, Jeff Jones, Bill Simas

Ever had a door slip out of your hand and slam shut? That's what happened to German when he tried to cross that threshold between pitching and closing in 2003. German's lack of control simply makes him too dangerous to use in save situations, last year's ERA notwithstanding. He'll get an occasional crumb, but needs injuries or meltdowns, first by Todd Jones and then Fernando Rodney, to get another extended shot.

JASON JOHNSON

Bats: R **Throws: R** Height: 6' 6" Weight: 210 Born: October 27, 1973 Age: 32

YEAR	TM	LVL	AGE	W	L	SV	G	GS	IP	H	BB	SO	HR	GB%	BABIP	STUFF	WHIP	ERA	PERA	EQERA	EQH9	EQBB9	EQSO9	EQHR9	VORP	WXRL
2003	BAL	MLB	29	10	10	0	32	32	189.7	216	80	118	22	48%	.311	5	1.56	4.18	4.85	4.52	9.6	3.7	5.4	1.0	25.9	4.0
2004	DET	MLB	30	8	15	0	33	33	196.7	222	60	125	22	51%	.314	9	1.43	5.12	4.35	5.11	9.5	2.5	5.3	0.9	13.9	2.6
2005	DET	MLB	31	8	13	0	33	33	210.0	233	49	93	23	54%	.300	1	1.34	4.54	4.63	5.02	9.9	2.1	4.0	0.9	16.7	3.1
2006	*CLE*	*MLB*	*32*	*11*	*11*	*0*	*32*	*29*	*185.0*	*205*	*51*	*95*	*21*	*49%*	*.296*	*2*	*1.39*	*4.51*	*4.72*	*4.97*	*9.8*	*2.4*	*4.4*	*1.0*	*16.2*	*3.0*

Breakout: 14%   Improve: 53%   Collapse: 14%   Attrition: 2%   Comparables: Doc Medich, Dock Ellis, Aaron Sele

Johnson's translated strikeout rate has fallen three straight years. So far, he has compensated by cutting his walk rate down, but that strategy doesn't have much more room to work. If he'd signed with a team with a bad defense that plays in a hitter-friendly park like Kansas City or Texas, the results would have been ugly, but he had the sense to ink a deal with the Indians, where he'll get generous run support at the very least.

JAIR JURRJENS   Bats: R Throws: R   Height: 6′ 1″   Weight: 160   Born: January 29, 1986   Age: 20

YEAR	TM	LVL	AGE	W	L	SV	G	GS	IP	H	BB	SO	HR	GB%	BABIP	STUFF	WHIP	ERA	PERA	EQERA	EQH9	EQBB9	EQSO9	EQHR9	VORP	WXRL
2004	ONE	A-	18	1	5	0	7	7	39.0	50	10	31	0	—	.382	9	1.54	5.31	4.12	7.32	10.8	3.0	3.7	0.2	-7.5	—
2005	WMI	A	19	12	6	0	26	26	142.7	132	36	108	5	57%	.300	20	1.18	3.41	4.18	5.16	9.3	2.5	4.7	0.6	6.7	—
2006	*DET*	*MLB*	*20*	*7*	*10*	*0*	*27*	*24*	*145.3*	*161*	*45*	*80*	*16*	*49%*	*.300*	*8*	*1.42*	*4.81*	*4.86*	*5.14*	*9.8*	*2.8*	*4.9*	*0.9*	*7.0*	*1.8*

Breakout: 23%   Improve: 64%   Collapse: 2%   Attrition: 1%   Comparables: Angel Guzman, Brandon League, Junior Herndon

Jurrjens's assets are that he can throw three pitches with excellent command, a quality not frequently encountered in the Midwest League. His liabilities are that none of his pitches are considered to be very good on their own, although there is some hope for him to fill out and gain velocity. Most pitchers with this kind of command at this age don't progress too well. Progress, for most pitchers, comes from learning to harness their talents; Jurrjens's talents are already hitched up.

WIL LEDEZMA   Bats: L Throws: L   Height: 6′ 3″   Weight: 150   Born: January 21, 1981   Age: 25

YEAR	TM	LVL	AGE	W	L	SV	G	GS	IP	H	BB	SO	HR	GB%	BABIP	STUFF	WHIP	ERA	PERA	EQERA	EQH9	EQBB9	EQSO9	EQHR9	VORP	WXRL
2003	DET	MLB	22	3	7	0	34	8	84.0	99	35	49	12	36%	.320	-11	1.60	5.79	5.17	5.38	10.0	3.7	5.1	1.2	0.0	-0.0
2004	ERI	AA	23	10	3	0	17	16	111.7	95	24	98	8	—	.276	17	1.07	2.42	4.19	3.77	8.7	2.2	5.7	0.9	21.8	—
2004	DET	MLB	23	4	3	0	15	8	53.3	55	18	29	3	47%	.306	3	1.37	4.39	4.17	4.33	9.0	2.8	4.5	0.5	9.1	1.0
2005	TOL	AAA	24	5	3	0	11	10	51.0	52	27	44	3	47%	.320	0	1.55	5.29	4.86	5.94	9.2	5.2	5.9	0.7	-1.9	—
2005	DET	MLB	24	2	4	0	10	10	49.7	61	24	30	10	44%	.317	-17	1.71	7.06	6.04	7.99	10.5	4.3	5.3	1.8	-14.4	-0.8
2006	*DET*	*MLB*	*25*	*4*	*6*	*1*	*31*	*11*	*78.7*	*88*	*34*	*51*	*11*	*42%*	*.304*	*-5*	*1.54*	*5.39*	*5.58*	*6.52*	*9.9*	*3.8*	*5.8*	*1.2*	*-0.5*	*0.3*

Breakout: 26%   Improve: 46%   Collapse: 28%   Attrition: 16%   Comparables: Ross Baumgarten, Steve Blass, Chris Haney

Ledezma came into the season as the Tigers' fifth starter, and was a favorite sleeper candidate for many analysts, including BP. Left-handed, mid-90s fastball, good control, what was not to like? Then his control deserted him, and with it went his home run rate, and finally his health; he was on the shelf with a sore elbow through August. That elbow has been a problem before, and there's little doubt that it wasn't right last year. Ledezma ties Cla Meredith of the Red Sox as "Player Whose Name is Most Likely to be Mistaken For a Typo, 2006."

MIKE MAROTH   Bats: L Throws: L   Height: 6′ 0″   Weight: 180   Born: August 17, 1977   Age: 28

YEAR	TM	LVL	AGE	W	L	SV	G	GS	IP	H	BB	SO	HR	GB%	BABIP	STUFF	WHIP	ERA	PERA	EQERA	EQH9	EQBB9	EQSO9	EQHR9	VORP	WXRL
2003	DET	MLB	25	9	21	0	33	33	193.3	231	50	87	34	48%	.302	-14	1.45	5.73	5.46	5.46	10.4	2.3	3.9	1.5	-1.0	2.1
2004	DET	MLB	26	11	13	0	33	33	217.0	244	59	108	25	48%	.307	3	1.40	4.31	4.63	4.26	9.7	2.3	4.2	0.9	39.3	5.2
2005	DET	MLB	27	14	14	0	34	34	209.0	235	51	115	30	48%	.306	0	1.37	4.74	4.86	5.25	9.9	2.2	4.9	1.2	10.0	2.0
2006	*DET*	*MLB*	*28*	*11*	*12*	*0*	*33*	*30*	*192.7*	*214*	*48*	*100*	*22*	*47%*	*.296*	*6*	*1.36*	*4.41*	*4.68*	*4.72*	*9.8*	*2.2*	*4.6*	*1.0*	*19.4*	*3.4*

Breakout: 26%   Improve: 64%   Collapse: 10%   Attrition: 0%   Comparables: Greg Hibbard, Kirk Rueter, Dave Koslo

Apparently Maroth, along with Bonderman, Robertson, and free-agent signee Kenny Rogers give the Tigers four solid starters for their rotation in 2006. Why Maroth is considered solid is unclear; he's a soft-tossing lefty who gives up too many home runs. He's proven to be durable, which is good in an old Volkswagen Beetle kind of way. The one thing still eluding the Tigers along their comeback trail is the homegrown ace who forces out this kind of pitcher.

TROY PERCIVAL   Bats: R Throws: R   Height: 6′ 3″   Weight: 230   Born: August 9, 1969   Age: 36

YEAR	TM	LVL	AGE	W	L	SV	G	GS	IP	H	BB	SO	HR	GB%	BABIP	STUFF	WHIP	ERA	PERA	EQERA	EQH9	EQBB9	EQSO9	EQHR9	VORP	WXRL
2003	ANA	MLB	33	0	5	33	52	0	49.3	33	23	48	7	28%	.210	7	1.14	3.47	4.72	3.97	7.2	4.3	8.9	1.3	10.6	1.7
2004	ANA	MLB	34	2	3	33	52	0	49.7	43	19	33	7	36%	.245	-6	1.25	2.90	4.78	3.31	8.4	3.3	5.7	1.1	15.0	2.3
2005	DET	MLB	35	1	3	8	26	0	25.0	19	11	20	7	28%	.185	-12	1.20	5.76	6.75	5.62	8.2	4.1	7.5	2.6	-0.2	-0.7
2006	*DET*	*MLB*	*36*	*1*	*2*	*5*	*26*	*0*	*29.7*	*29*	*11*	*23*	*5*	*33%*	*.267*	*-4*	*1.33*	*4.34*	*4.74*	*5.45*	*8.5*	*3.3*	*6.8*	*1.5*	*4.1*	*0.3*

Breakout: 21%   Improve: 44%   Collapse: 37%   Attrition: 38%   Comparables: Ray Moore, Aurelio Lopez, Moe Drabowsky

He's going out kicking and screaming, but the torn forearm muscle that ended his season may have also ended his career. His skills were already deeply eroded from his glory days in Anaheim; even if he manages to come back, the odds are strongly against him being effective. With 611.2 IP and 605 games, Percival epitomizes the modern, one-inning closer. Jose Mesa is likely to take his place among the top-ten career saves leaders early this season, which says all you need to know about save totals as an indicator of value.

NATE ROBERTSON   Bats: R Throws: L   Height: 6' 2" Weight: 210 Born: September 3, 1977 Age: 28

YEAR	TM	LVL	AGE	W	L	SV	G	GS	IP	H	BB	SO	HR	GB%	BABIP	STUFF	WHIP	ERA	PERA	EQERA	EQH9	EQBB9	EQSO9	EQHR9	VORP	WXRL
2003	TOL	AAA	25	9	7	0	24	23	155.0	145	47	102	14	—	.265	-7	1.24	3.14	5.47	4.61	9.5	3.5	4.6	1.4	16.1	—
2003	DET	MLB	25	1	2	0	8	8	44.7	55	23	33	6	50%	.348	3	1.75	5.44	5.09	5.09	10.0	4.5	6.3	1.2	2.1	0.9
2004	DET	MLB	26	12	10	1	34	32	196.7	210	66	155	30	51%	.302	8	1.39	4.90	4.60	4.91	9.2	2.8	6.6	1.3	21.4	3.7
2005	DET	MLB	27	7	16	0	32	32	196.7	202	65	122	28	53%	.285	1	1.36	4.48	4.93	5.12	9.4	3.0	5.5	1.2	13.3	3.3
2006	*DET*	*MLB*	*28*	*10*	*11*	*0*	*30*	*30*	*184.7*	*194*	*58*	*116*	*19*	*49%*	*.295*	*11*	*1.36*	*4.35*	*4.52*	*4.70*	*9.3*	*2.8*	*5.6*	*0.9*	*18.9*	*3.4*

Breakout: 26%   Improve: 63%   Collapse: 6%   Attrition: 2%   Comparables: Woodie Fryman, Paul Splittorff, Alex Kellner

Robertson was one of last year's unluckiest pitchers. His bullpen support, as measured by how many more runs scored than expected from the runners he left behind, was the fourth worst in the majors, costing him a quarter run of ERA. His won/lost record was 6.5 games worse than expected, also fourth worst in the majors, so he's a little bit better, but not a lot better, than the numbers indicate, which makes for an average pitcher with plus points for durability. He did complain of a sore shoulder towards the end of '05; it appears to have been just a dead arm, but he gets that dead arm every July. His career ERA before the All-Star break is 3.74, and 5.90 after it.

FERNANDO RODNEY   Bats: R Throws: R   Height: 5' 11" Weight: 200 Born: March 18, 1977 Age: 29

YEAR	TM	LVL	AGE	W	L	SV	G	GS	IP	H	BB	SO	HR	GB%	BABIP	STUFF	WHIP	ERA	PERA	EQERA	EQH9	EQBB9	EQSO9	EQHR9	VORP	WXRL
2003	TOL	AAA	26	1	1	23	38	0	40.7	22	13	58	0	—	.256	29	0.86	1.33	3.11	2.39	6.5	3.8	10.0	0.2	13.4	—
2003	DET	MLB	26	1	3	3	27	0	29.7	35	17	33	2	41%	.393	12	1.75	6.06	3.77	5.81	9.0	4.9	9.3	0.6	-0.2	-0.5
2005	DET	MLB	28	2	3	9	39	0	44.0	39	17	42	5	40%	.291	14	1.27	2.86	4.09	2.86	8.2	3.5	8.6	1.0	13.9	0.7
2006	*DET*	*MLB*	*29*	*3*	*3*	*7*	*47*	*0*	*50.0*	*47*	*20*	*44*	*6*	*43%*	*.288*	*7*	*1.34*	*3.81*	*4.25*	*4.38*	*8.3*	*3.6*	*7.8*	*1.0*	*8.7*	*0.8*

Breakout: 17%   Improve: 34%   Collapse: 36%   Attrition: 24%   Comparables: Cliff Politte, John Wyatt, Curt Leskanic

Rodney's season didn't get started until June. Already fragile due to TJ surgery in 2004, he came down with shoulder inflammation in spring training. In the long run, the inflammation probably helped his elbow get more rest, because once finally back on the field he was as good as ever. The only problems were that his slider still hurt his arm, and he needed more time to warm up than the typical bullpen pitcher. Those limitations factored into the decision to make him the closer once Farnsworth was traded, but he was also the most consistent guy in the pen. Although he performed well enough to enter '06 as the closer, he'll instead have to set up Todd Jones.

KYLE SLEETH   Bats: R Throws: R   Height: 6' 5" Weight: 205 Born: December 20, 1981 Age: 24

YEAR	TM	LVL	AGE	W	L	SV	G	GS	IP	H	BB	SO	HR	GB%	BABIP	STUFF	WHIP	ERA	PERA	EQERA	EQH9	EQBB9	EQSO9	EQHR9	VORP	WXRL
2004	LAK	A+	22	3	4	0	9	9	54.0	47	15	55	3	—	.295	9	1.15	3.67	4.76	5.82	9.4	3.0	6.2	1.2	-1.2	—
2004	ERI	AA	22	4	4	0	13	13	80.0	93	34	57	14	—	.319	-23	1.59	6.30	6.55	6.89	11.0	4.1	4.7	2.1	-11.2	—
2006	*DET*	*MLB*	*24*	*3*	*5*	*0*	*26*	*8*	*64.0*	*77*	*29*	*37*	*12*	*45%*	*.306*	*-13*	*1.65*	*6.23*	*6.58*	*6.61*	*10.6*	*4.0*	*5.1*	*1.6*	*-6.7*	*-0.4*

Breakout: 16%   Improve: 54%   Collapse: 13%   Attrition: 13%   Comparables: Ryan Baerlocher, Elvis Perez, Brian Falkenborg

The Tigers' 1st round pick—second overall—in 2003, a lot has been expected of Sleeth. The Tigers have done a lot of fidgeting with his delivery to try and stop him from throwing across his body. In addition to this, or perhaps because of it, he's been inconsistent as a pro, the Tigers have nevertheless pushed him aggressively into the high minors. His 2005 never got started; he had elbow soreness in the spring. The soreness did not go away with rest, and he finally had Tommy John surgery in July. That's going to keep him out of action until sometime in mid-season, so he shouldn't be counted on in any way until 2007.

CHRIS SPURLING   Bats: R Throws: R   Height: 6' 6" Weight: 240 Born: June 28, 1977 Age: 29

YEAR	TM	LVL	AGE	W	L	SV	G	GS	IP	H	BB	SO	HR	GB%	BABIP	STUFF	WHIP	ERA	PERA	EQERA	EQH9	EQBB9	EQSO9	EQHR9	VORP	WXRL
2003	DET	MLB	26	1	3	3	66	0	77.0	78	22	38	9	45%	.280	-12	1.30	4.68	4.83	4.48	9.3	2.6	4.4	1.1	9.2	-0.3
2005	DET	MLB	28	3	4	0	56	0	70.7	58	22	26	8	48%	.229	-18	1.13	3.44	5.14	3.82	8.6	2.9	3.4	1.1	14.8	1.3
2006	*DET*	*MLB*	*29*	*2*	*3*	*1*	*54*	*0*	*59.7*	*64*	*18*	*28*	*8*	*45%*	*.279*	*-15*	*1.38*	*4.59*	*4.76*	*5.42*	*9.5*	*2.7*	*4.2*	*1.1*	*4.4*	*0.3*

Breakout: 11%   Improve: 32%   Collapse: 40%   Attrition: 28%   Comparables: Tom Buskey, Guillermo Mota, Doug Brocail

Spurling did a remarkable job last year with inherited runners, saving nine runs above average—sixth best in the majors. While it was a solid comeback from the TJ surgery that cost him all of 2004, his success was probably fleeting. There is nothing about his overall performance or his stuff that suggests he can continue to keep runners from scoring.

JUSTIN VERLANDER   Bats: R   Throws: R   Height: 6′ 5″   Weight: 200   Born: February 20, 1983   Age: 23

YEAR	TM	LVL	AGE	W	L	SV	G	GS	IP	H	BB	SO	HR	GB%	BABIP	STUFF	WHIP	ERA	PERA	EQERA	EQH9	EQBB9	EQSO9	EQHR9	VORP	WXRL
2005	LAK	A+	22	9	2	0	13	13	86.0	70	19	104	3	46%	.338	30	1.03	1.67	3.78	3.78	9.0	2.7	7.0	0.7	16.4	—
2005	ERI	AA	22	2	0	0	7	7	32.7	11	7	32	1	43%	.135	25	0.55	0.28	3.34	1.52	5.2	2.4	6.4	0.3	13.5	—
2005	DET	MLB	22	0	2	0	2	2	11.3	15	5	7	1	49%	.350	1	1.76	7.17	4.63	6.94	10.8	3.9	5.4	0.8	-2.0	-0.1
2006	*DET*	*MLB*	*23*	*9*	*10*	*1*	*35*	*22*	*153.0*	*151*	*50*	*112*	*17*	*44%*	*.287*	*14*	*1.31*	*4.20*	*4.34*	*4.45*	*8.7*	*2.9*	*6.5*	*1.0*	*19.4*	*2.9*

Breakout: 8%   Improve: 21%   Collapse: 28%   Attrition: 0%   Comparables: Seung Song, Dennis Tankersley, John Maine

Like Sleeth the year before, the Tigers made Verlander the second overall pick in the 2004 draft. Protracted negotiations kept him from pitching that year; he started his pro career at Lakeland in 2005. A hard thrower with an excellent curve, Verlander impressed early, earning a couple of starts in Detroit. He hit the wall in August, complaining of a tired arm, but he was able to pitch in the fall instructional league without any problems. He'll compete with Colon and Zumaya for a spot in next year's rotation, and is probably the favorite to win.

JAMIE WALKER   Bats: L   Throws: L   Height: 6′ 2″   Weight: 190   Born: July 1, 1971   Age: 35

YEAR	TM	LVL	AGE	W	L	SV	G	GS	IP	H	BB	SO	HR	GB%	BABIP	STUFF	WHIP	ERA	PERA	EQERA	EQH9	EQBB9	EQSO9	EQHR9	VORP	WXRL
2003	DET	MLB	32	4	3	3	78	0	65.0	61	17	45	9	37%	.269	-3	1.20	3.32	4.62	3.92	8.7	2.4	6.2	1.3	13.2	0.6
2004	DET	MLB	33	3	4	1	70	0	64.7	69	12	53	8	37%	.307	8	1.27	3.20	3.70	3.70	9.0	1.5	6.9	1.0	16.5	-0.1
2005	DET	MLB	34	4	3	0	66	0	48.7	49	13	30	5	43%	.282	-3	1.27	3.70	4.44	4.07	9.1	2.4	5.5	0.9	8.9	1.1
2006	*DET*	*MLB*	*34*	*2*	*2*	*2*	*49*	*0*	*44.7*	*48*	*12*	*28*	*6*	*39%*	*.290*	*-8*	*1.34*	*4.69*	*4.69*	*5.74*	*9.5*	*2.4*	*5.7*	*1.2*	*2.9*	*0.2*

Breakout: 9%   Improve: 19%   Collapse: 54%   Attrition: 37%   Comparables: Pedro Borbon, Alan Embree, Morrie Martin

Walker has very quietly turned into a reliable and effective lefty reliever, as long as you let him start his own innings. His record with inherited runners was one of the worst in the majors; charge him for the extra runs he allowed, and his ERA would jump about 75 points. While quite annoying, it was probably just bad timing, as it hasn't been a problem in the past.

KEVIN WHELAN   Bats: R   Throws: R   Height: 6′ 0″   Weight: 200   Born: January 8, 1984   Age: 22

YEAR	TM	LVL	AGE	W	L	SV	G	GS	IP	H	BB	SO	HR	GB%	BABIP	STUFF	WHIP	ERA	PERA	EQERA	EQH9	EQBB9	EQSO9	EQHR9	VORP	WXRL
2005	ONE	A-	21	1	1	4	11	0	12.0	2	6	19	1	50%	.053	-4	0.67	2.25	8.10	5.40	6.3	7.2	8.1	2.7	0.2	—
2005	WMI	A	21	0	0	11	14	0	12.3	4	2	22	0	53%	.211	11	0.49	0.73	1.59	2.38	5.6	1.6	11.1	0.0	4.0	—
2006	*DET*	*MLB*	*22*	*3*	*3*	*2*	*22*	*5*	*50.7*	*39*	*24*	*48*	*5*	*45%*	*.251*	*17*	*1.24*	*3.67*	*3.58*	*4.04*	*6.7*	*4.3*	*8.4*	*0.8*	*8.8*	*1.1*

Breakout: 12%   Improve: 42%   Collapse: 21%   Attrition: 34%   Comparables: Orber Moreno, Josh Beckett, Mike Meyers

Whelan started his college career as a catcher. As a sophomore at Texas A&M, he pitched a few games, but was still mostly a catcher. The next summer he somehow wound up as a reliever in the Cape Cod League, was sensational, and suddenly he's a prospect. Whelan had as near perfect a pro debut as you could ask for. He's likely to move up quickly, thanks to a 95–96 mph fastball and a good splitter.

JOEL ZUMAYA   Bats: R   Throws: R   Height: 6′ 3″   Weight: 210   Born: November 9, 1984   Age: 21

YEAR	TM	LVL	AGE	W	L	SV	G	GS	IP	H	BB	SO	HR	GB%	BABIP	STUFF	WHIP	ERA	PERA	EQERA	EQH9	EQBB9	EQSO9	EQHR9	VORP	WXRL
2003	WMI	A	18	7	5	0	19	19	90.3	69	38	126	3	—	.313	42	1.18	2.79	4.11	5.17	8.3	4.7	8.8	0.8	4.1	—
2004	LAK	A+	19	6	4	0	16	16	94.0	65	43	92	8	—	.245	5	1.15	3.54	5.92	5.09	8.5	4.9	6.4	1.7	4.9	—
2005	ERI	AA	20	8	3	0	18	18	107.3	71	52	143	8	41%	.276	35	1.15	2.77	4.25	3.90	7.3	5.0	8.8	0.9	19.2	—
2005	TOL	AAA	20	1	2	0	8	8	44.0	30	24	56	2	38%	.289	42	1.23	2.66	3.59	2.95	7.2	5.1	9.7	0.4	12.6	—
2006	*DET*	*MLB*	*21*	*8*	*9*	*0*	*30*	*23*	*143.3*	*126*	*80*	*140*	*18*	*38%*	*.281*	*21*	*1.44*	*4.58*	*4.71*	*4.98*	*7.8*	*4.9*	*8.7*	*1.1*	*12.5*	*2.2*

Breakout: 15%   Improve: 40%   Collapse: 26%   Attrition: 4%   Comparables: Dick Drott, Dave Morehead, Dave Boswell

Sing it: Zumaya, my Lord, Zumaya . . . Last year he was statistically almost as good as Verlander, with a bonus for playing a level above him for most of the year. Scouts see a wider gap in their talent, however, and they're probably right. While Zumaya can hit the upper 90s with his fastball, his delivery is taxing and may not be sustainable in the long term. While he was healthy this year, he did suffer back problems in 2004. There is always talk among scouts about converting him to closer, where he might hit triple figures on the gun, but Tigers management is still committed to having him start. He'll have a shot at the fifth starter's spot this spring.

Line Outs

Posistion/Player	TM	LVL	AGE	PA	R	2B	3B	HR	RBI	BB	SO	SB-CS	SPEED	BA/OBP/SLG	MLVR	EQBA/OBP/SLG	EQA	VORP
OF A. Gomez*	TOL	AAA	26	457	51	28	6	7	55	27	91	21-7	6.6	.307/.348/.450	.132	.289/.329/.415	.260	3.2
1/3 M. Hessman	TOL	AAA	27	544	69	19	1	28	74	58	154	5-4	4.0	.214/.312/.436	-.030	.192/.280/.378	.229	-10.7
SS J. McDonald	TOR	MLB	30	103	8	3	0	0	12	6	12	5-0	5.0	.290/.340/.323	-.128	.286/.343/.319	.255	2.4
	DET	MLB	30	78	10	3	1	0	4	5	12	1-1	5.5	.260/.308/.329	-.160	.278/.333/.347	.240	-0.3
C D. Sanchez	LAK	A+	24	399	58	18	0	22	68	38	52	0-1	3.6	.284/.361/.524	.253	.237/.301/.432	.250	7.3

Pitcher	TM	LVL	AGE	W	L	SV	IP	H	BB	SO	HR	GB%	BABIP	STUFF	WHIP	ERA	PERA	EQERA	EQH9	EQBB9	EQSO9	EQHR9	VORP
K. Baugh	TOL	AAA	26	12	8	0	165.3	159	60	107	13	48%	.287	-1	1.32	3.38	5.05	4.93	9.4	3.9	4.4	0.9	11.8
D. Creek*	TOL	AAA	36	2	2	0	27.3	28	14	32	2	39%	.366	-15	1.54	4.62	5.61	6.31	10.2	6.3	7.0	1.1	-2.0
	DET	MLB	36	0	0	0	22.3	27	7	18	7	32%	.299	-12	1.52	6.86	6.35	7.15	10.3	2.8	7.1	2.8	-4.0
E. de la Cruz	LAK	A+	21	4	3	5	95.7	66	36	97	5	58%	.250	-1	1.07	3.39	4.83	5.85	8.3	4.5	6.2	0.9	-2.4
M. Ginter	TOL	AAA	27	4	3	0	68.7	72	10	49	9	50%	.300	-9	1.19	4.32	5.02	5.70	10.2	1.5	4.7	1.5	-0.7
	DET	MLB	27	0	1	0	35.0	49	9	15	6	43%	.350	-19	1.66	6.17	5.45	6.44	11.4	2.2	3.7	1.5	-3.1
A. Good	TOL	AAA	25	9	5	0	134.3	129	42	89	18	46%	.276	-14	1.27	3.69	5.70	5.06	9.7	3.3	4.6	1.5	7.7
J. Grilli	TOL	AAA	28	12	9	0	167.3	170	58	120	21	52%	.294	-14	1.36	4.09	5.74	5.91	10.0	3.8	4.8	1.5	-5.5

Alexis Gomez is old and doesn't do anything very well, but he somehow fascinates Tiger management. **Mike Hessman** has power, but with a batting average lower than an SUV's gas mileage, he's an all-or-nothing hitter, swinging from his heels and hoping something good will happen, like getting out of Triple-A. It's going to work, but not in the way he thinks. The Tigers got **John McDonald** from Toronto for a PTBNL, which turned out to be McDonald himself. The Tigers were in an injury crunch at the time, and the Jays made a loan of him. **Danilo Sanchez** was old for his league, but he's a strong defensive catcher who's added some unexpected power.

It's been three years since **Kenny Baugh** went down with a torn labrum. The pitcher that reached Double-A two months after being drafted in 2001 is gone, but the one that's left may be able to help; dealt to the Padres. **Doug Creek** was waived by the Tigers; it's been five years since an organization kept him over the off-season. **Eulogio de la Cruz** is a Dominican flamethrower, but has nothing with wiggle yet; he'll need it. **Matt Ginter** was even farther back in the bullpen than Creek; he had the fourth-lowest Leverage score (a measure of how much impact his innings had on the outcome of the game) in the major leagues. In other words, he only pitched when the game was already over. **Andrew Good** was still recovering from elbow surgery in 2005. He should be around #8 or #9 on the team's starter depth chart. **Jason Grilli** pitched fifteen good innings in Detroit last year, and 474 bad innings since TJ surgery in 2002. Which number are you going to believe?

Florida Marlins

We'll get to the baseball in a bit, but first let's start with something of a civics lesson. Proponents of building private stadia on the public's dime would have you believe that their every rationale has not been thoroughly debunked, but not unlike global warming deniers, they are engaged in a self-serving effort to cloud what has become settled science—not to mention the basic tenets of capitalism, in which you assume the risk in order to receive the reward.

As such, it's hardly worth analyzing Marlins president David Samson's petulant decision (presumably undertaken at the urging of owner Jeff Loria) to gut the payroll and embark on a cross-country location-scouting tour, trolling for suckers after the state of Florida failed to deliver a ballpark financing program that sank to the normal level of munificent corporate welfare to which so many baseball teams have become accustomed. If Samson can be taken at his word that the Marlins lose money, and baseball is unhappy with the amount of revenue sharing that heads to south Florida, that's his problem, and baseball's, Not Florida's. Given the limited revenue that teams and stadia contribute to their local economies, the success or failure of the Marlins is not a priority for government action in the way that, say, the failure of an airline would be. The collapse of a major air carrier would have ramifications for the national economy far beyond the number of lost jobs, whereas with a sports franchise, it's not an economic question but an old Zen riddle: If a ballclub falls in the forest, who really cares? You build a Costco over its corpse and life goes on as before.

As too many Americans have discovered in the last few years, when a business's expenses get out of hand and it retrenches, payroll's the first thing to get chopped. The Marlins' diaspora of last winter would be a sensible reaction to such circumstances if matters were that simple for baseball teams. However, unlike the automobile industry, where customers will continue to buy cars they like regardless of how many employees put them together, or who those employees are, baseball is an entertainment, and fans come out to the ballpark in proportion to their expectations of being entertained. Even for teams with lucrative local broadcast deals, like the Yankees, attendance remains a major, if not the major, component of revenue. Holding a fire sale and blaming it on the failure of the fans and the

MARLINS PROSPECTUS

2005 record: 83–79; Third place, NL East

Pythagenport record: 79–83

Runs scored per game: 4.43 (8th in NL)

Runs allowed per game: 4.52 (10th in NL)

Team EqA: .269 (2nd in NL)

2005 Batters Age: 30.0 (8th oldest in NL)

2005 Pitchers Age: 29.2 (8th youngest in NL)

Ballpark: Pro Player Stadium; Severe pitcher's park; Park Factor of 0.948

2005: The Marlins stayed in the thick of the wild-card race through late August.

2006: The carpetbaggers waited a little longer following the franchise's second World Series win to dump talent and payroll.

politicos to support the team by providing a free ballpark is ultimately self-defeating.

Even when they were winning, the Marlins weren't a great draw; the 1994–1995 labor difficulties and initial purge following their 1997 championship season prevented them from building up a tradition of good attendance. In their inaugural season of 1993, the Fish drew a very healthy 3 million fans, good for fifth in the National League. They were doing well in 1994 when the work stoppage hit, but when play resumed in '95, their per-game attendance was down by nearly 9,000, and dropped by roughly another 2,500 in 1996. That winter, then-owner Wayne Huizenga went on a shopping spree, adding Bobby Bonilla, Alex Fernandez, Moises Alou, and Cliff Floyd to a roster that already boasted Gary Sheffield, Al Leiter, Kevin Brown, and Robb Nen. This star-studded collection went on to win the World Series and reignite fan interest. The 1997 Marlins drew 2.4 million fans to Joe Robbie Stadium, again good for fifth in the NL.

This was the last time that 2 million fans spun the Marlins' turnstiles. Having bought his World Series, Huizenga turned in his chips and bleached the roster of high-priced vets, violatiing the social contract between ballclub and fan that says a team might not always win, but it at least has to try. The Marlins dropped from 92–70 to

TABLE 1. SO CROWDED NO ONE GOES THERE ANYMORE

Year	Marlins Attendance	Mlb Rank	Per Game
2005	1,823,388	28/30	22,792
2004	1,723,105	26/30	22,091
2003	1,303,215	28/30	16,290
2002	813,118	29/30	10,038
2001	1,261,226	29/30	15,765

54–108, and the fans stayed away in droves. Despite a second championship in 2003, they've never come back. Though Marlins attendance has risen in three consecutive seasons, concurrent with the first three years of Loria's ownership, it's been stagnant relative to baseball as a whole (see table 1).

The key question, which may never be resolved: Is Miami a bad market, or did Huizenga permanently poison the well?

It remains to be seen what effect this winter's purge will have on the incremental rebuilding of Marlins attendance. In the worst case scenario, the benefit gained from slashing payroll and the losses caused by declining attendance will cross, and the Marlins won't be materially better off than they were before. In the short term, the reduction in payroll will cushion the blow; as Nate Silver has written, even if fans answer spite with spite and stay away, dropping attendance to just 1 million, that represents a loss of about $13 million in ticket revenues, while the Marlins will save as much as $77 million over the next four years just by unloading Carlos Delgado and Mike Lowell.

Still, this doesn't make the Marlins healthy; it just makes them less sick. Obviously, it would be better for the franchise if the fans don't punish the Marlins at the gate. The X-factor is how well the now no-name team performs on the field. Winning begets attendance, so even a mildly successful season will blunt fan anger and keep up demand.

GM Larry Beinfest conducted his trades with "two guidelines: Best player available and skewed toward pitching." Indeed, the trades of Josh Beckett, Carlos Delgado, Paul Lo Duca, Luis Castillo, and Juan Pierre brought in ten pitchers and three position players. At the very least, the Marlins now have an army of candidates to join holdovers Dontrelle Willis, Jason Vargas, and Scuffy Moehler in their starting rotation. Homegrown prospects Scott Olsen and Josh Johnson have been joined by Sergio Mitre, Yusmeiro Petit, and Anibal Sanchez, with more intriguing candidates coming up close behind them. If they Marlins choose wisely and have a little luck, the 2006 Marlins could have a solid rotation right off the bat.

Ironically, all the trades of veteran position players were defensible in pure baseball terms. Delgado isn't a DH in the making, he is a DH, whether the Mets know it or not. His lack of mobility would have been an increasing problem in the coming years. Pierre, Lo Duca, and Castillo rank among the most overrated players in baseball, each *doing* a great many things but putting comparatively few runs on the scoreboard. Lowell, foisted on the Red Sox in the Beckett deal, had an abysmal season and is not guaranteed to rebound.

The true difficulty posed by the trades is that they happened all at once and didn't bring enough position players in return to satisfy the team's needs. New manager Joe Girardi must show that he can quickly identify the right combination of pitchers out of this plethora of prospects, because Beinfest will likely need to use some of the excess for trades to fill out the rest of the lineup. Although the winter's action brought in catcher Miguel Olivo, catcher/first baseman Mike Jacobs, and shortstop Hanley Ramirez, none is a sure bet to stick as a big league starter this year. At second base, the Opening Day starter will be selected through a spring training battle royale between Pokey Reese and Dan Uggla. This is a fight that that will have no winners; Reese has a terrific defensive reputation at second base but his bat long ago filed for divorce, while Uggla is a 25-year-old Double-A repeater who lacks on-base skills. The outfield has the potential to be a total loss. Jeremy Hermida is one of the top prospects in baseball, and his performance last fall suggests he's ready to play in the bigs, but he's not a sure thing, either. The left field and center field candidates, Chris Aguila and Eric Reed, are replacement level types. The Marlins may be forced to abort their planned move of Miguel Cabrera to his "natural" position of third base and start Wes Helms at the hot corner, which would push that position towards replacement level as well. And with little depth behind the starters, particularly in the outfield, any injury could be devastating.

An aura of uncertainty hovers over the Marlins. Their reconstruction of the roster made financial sense, but Samson only hurt the Loria family's standing in Miami by ascribing the wrong motives to it in public. Similarly, the rebuilding made tactical sense, but again, it wasn't properly explained to the fan base. Nor were the trades resolved in such a way that the team upgraded its position player depth, a greater need than its pitching, where the Marlins already had a good stockpile of quality arms. What Girardi and Beinfest do with this accumulation of arms will determine where the Marlins go in the standings and at the gate over the next couple of years. Where the franchise itself goes physically remains to be seen.

HITTERS

CHRIS AGUILA   OF   Bats: R Throws: R   Height: 5′ 11″ Weight: 180   Born: February 23, 1979   Age: 27

YEAR	TM	LVL	AGE	PA	R	2B	3B	HR	RBI	BB	SO	SB	CS	SPEED	BA	OBP	SLG	MLVR	EQBA	EQOBP	EQSLG	EQA	VORP	DEFENSE			
2003	CAR	AA	24	380	58	21	3	11	55	36	67	6	2	5.5	.320	.384	.499	.304	.293	.347	.470	.280	13.9	43-LF	2	25-RF	2
2004	ABQ	AAA	25	374	61	23	2	11	56	37	82	8	3	5.6	.312	.380	.494	.059	.248	.313	.383	.246	0.1	45-CF	1	25-RF	2
2005	ABQ	AAA	26	153	27	13	2	7	25	14	21	8	2	6.5	.355	.412	.630	.369	.284	.337	.489	.279	9.1	32-CF	3		
2005	FLO	MLB	26	81	11	3	0	0	4	3	19	0	1	5.8	.244	.272	.282	-.275	.244	.272	.282	.194	-4.5				
2006	FLO	MLB	27	251	30	13	1	7	29	20	52	3	1	5.2	.255	.318	.410	-.067	.262	.323	.434	.252	3.6	62-CF	1		

Breakout: 20% Improve: 30% Collapse: 42% Attrition: 32%   Comparables: Steve Brye, Ron Davis, George Thomas

There are three things a ballplayer can do at the plate to help his team win: hit with patience, hit with power, or hit for average. The best players can do all three. "The Eagle" doesn't really do any of them terribly well. A million years ago, Aguila tied the national single-season record for home runs by a high-schooler. You have to figure the park was no bigger than Don Zimmer's pants, because the power just hasn't been there in the pros.

ROBERT ANDINO   SS   Bats: R Throws: R   Height: 6′ 0″ Weight: 170   Born: April 25, 1984   Age: 22

YEAR	TM	LVL	AGE	PA	R	2B	3B	HR	RBI	BB	SO	SB	CS	SPEED	BA	OBP	SLG	MLVR	EQBA	EQOBP	EQSLG	EQA	VORP	DEFENSE	
2003	GRB	A	19	467	45	17	2	2	27	46	128	6	5	4.6	.188	.266	.252	-.245	.173	.235	.241	.179	-46.8	119-SS	-2
2004	GRB	A	20	318	27	10	1	8	46	18	83	9	2	4.3	.281	.321	.403	.003	.249	.280	.357	.226	-4.0	76-SS	4
2004	JUP	A+	20	204	18	7	2	0	15	7	43	6	2	5.5	.281	.304	.337	-.038	.264	.284	.314	.215	-5.3	45-SS	3
2005	CAR	AA	21	562	63	30	0	5	48	37	111	22	7	5.6	.269	.324	.357	-.055	.236	.282	.325	.219	-15.3	124-SS	-4
2005	FLO	MLB	21	49	4	4	0	0	1	5	8	1	0	4.4	.159	.245	.250	-.409	.156	.240	.244	.185	-2.8	14-SS	-3
2006	FLO	MLB	22	470	49	21	2	6	39	28	106	10	4	4.6	.232	.283	.334	-.244	.238	.286	.353	.216	-2.2	111-SS	-3

Breakout: 53% Improve: 71% Collapse: 18% Attrition: 8%   Comparables: Ed Brinkman, Jack Heidemann, Ronny Cedeno

He just can't hit. Whatever the virtues of his glove, and they are not undisputed, he's such a bad hitter that most lineups would be stretched to carry his bat, Rey Ordonez style. Andino didn't hit in the AFL, didn't hustle, and the Marlins noticed. Robbie, bubelah, they've traded everyone but you. You could have made the team just because you're under contract. Instead, you make everyone think you're a schmagegi. Was that wise?

MIGUEL CABRERA   3B/OF   Bats: R Throws: R   Height: 6′ 2″ Weight: 185   Born: April 18, 1983   Age: 23

YEAR	TM	LVL	AGE	PA	R	2B	3B	HR	RBI	BB	SO	SB	CS	SPEED	BA	OBP	SLG	MLVR	EQBA	EQOBP	EQSLG	EQA	VORP	DEFENSE			
2003	CAR	AA	20	303	46	29	3	10	59	31	49	9	4	5.7	.365	.429	.609	.555	.337	.396	.578	.321	45.9	64-3B	12		
2003	FLO	MLB	20	342	39	21	3	12	62	25	84	0	2	3.7	.268	.325	.468	.073	.270	.329	.478	.270	8.9	54-LF	-1	31-3B	-2
2004	FLO	MLB	21	685	101	31	1	33	112	68	148	5	2	4.5	.294	.366	.512	.231	.295	.367	.514	.297	43.5	96-RF	-10	57-LF	3
2005	FLO	MLB	22	685	106	43	2	33	116	64	125	1	0	4.3	.323	.385	.561	.372	.325	.389	.578	.320	68.2	124-LF	-5	27-3B	1
2006	FLO	MLB	23	665	93	40	2	34	114	67	118	4	2	4.7	.305	.377	.553	.258	.313	.382	.585	.311	57.7	155-LF	-1		

Breakout: 25% Improve: 56% Collapse: 15% Attrition: 0%   Comparables: Frank Robinson, Albert Pujols, Greg Luzinski

A knight without teammates in a savage land. The move to third base will increase his value to the team, assuming he can hold up his end defensively; the NL East is crawling with good third basemen, and Cabrera's bat will take him right to the head of the class. One of those aforementioned third basemen is Mets wunderkind David Wright. Cabrera is almost four months younger and hasn't even scratched the upper limits of his talents.

LUIS CASTILLO   2B   Bats: B Throws: R   Height: 5′ 11″ Weight: 175   Born: September 12, 1975 Age: 30

YEAR	TM	LVL	AGE	PA	R	2B	3B	HR	RBI	BB	SO	SB	CS	SPEED	BA	OBP	SLG	MLVR	EQBA	EQOBP	EQSLG	EQA	VORP	DEFENSE	
2003	FLO	MLB	27	661	99	19	6	6	39	63	60	21	19	6.5	.314	.381	.397	.103	.320	.387	.408	.273	30.8	147-2B	4
2004	FLO	MLB	28	644	91	12	7	2	47	75	68	21	4	6.8	.291	.373	.348	.011	.293	.374	.349	.267	25.4	144-2B	6
2005	FLO	MLB	29	506	72	12	4	4	30	65	32	10	7	5.7	.301	.391	.374	.081	.308	.399	.386	.278	21.4	114-2B	12
2006	MIN	MLB	30	590	76	20	5	1	44	61	48	12	5	5.8	.299	.374	.364	.015	.300	.384	.376	.265	24.1	138-2B	2

Breakout: 11% Improve: 43% Collapse: 12% Attrition: 2%   Comparables: Steve Sax, Jose Offerman, Bip Roberts

He quietly had his best year since 2000, in large part because he scorched lefties to the tune of .423/.467/.649. Castillo has always had a better stroke from the right side, and the difference is great enough that even at his age it might be worth seeing what would happen if he just chucked the whole switch-hitting act and batted righty full-time. Right-handed batters don't have the same vision issues facing righty pitchers that left-handed hitters do against lefty pitchers. Though leg problems have robbed Castillo of some of his baserunning élan, Castillo's glove and selectivity will still be a revelation to the Twins after five years of Luis Rivas.

JEFF CONINE   1B/OF   Bats: R Throws: R   Height: 6′ 1″   Weight: 220   Born: June 27, 1966   Age: 40

YEAR	TM	LVL	AGE	PA	R	2B	3B	HR	RBI	BB	SO	SB	CS	SPEED	BA	OBP	SLG	MLVR	EQBA	EQOBP	EQSLG	EQA	VORP	DEFENSE		
2003	BAL	MLB	37	547	75	33	3	15	80	37	60	5	0	5.1	.290	.338	.460	.094	.292	.344	.468	.280	21.3	117-1B	5	
2003	FLO	MLB	37	98	13	3	0	5	15	13	10	0	0	3.7	.238	.337	.452	.050	.235	.333	.435	.266	1.3	23-LF	1	
2004	FLO	MLB	38	577	55	35	1	14	83	48	78	5	5	4.0	.280	.340	.432	.062	.284	.343	.438	.267	10.3	80-LF 10	55-1B	5
2005	FLO	MLB	39	382	42	20	2	3	33	38	58	2	0	4.7	.304	.374	.403	.115	.311	.380	.420	.284	15.5	26-1B -2	29-LF	0
2006	*BAL*	*MLB*	*40*	*296*	*34*	*15*	*1*	*7*	*37*	*24*	*43*	*2*	*1*	*4.9*	*.278*	*.337*	*.419*	*.010*	*.282*	*.348*	*.439*	*.263*	*5.9*	*72-1B*	*2*	

Breakout: 5%   Improve: 32%   Collapse: 34%   Attrition: 29%   Comparables: B. J. Surhoff, Hal McRae, Ellis Burks

For a guy drafted in the 57th round (1987) and left open to an expansion draft because Hal McRae didn't think he was good enough to help the mighty Royals, it's been a pretty good career: nearly 1,800 games, .288/.350/.449 averages, two rings—many a former 1st round pick would be happy to claim that record. Now with the Orioles, he may get a chance to start for them in left field. O's left fielders batted .239/.281/.381 last season, so as long as Conine doesn't collapse completely, he'd be a very minor improvement.

CARLOS DELGADO   1B   Bats: L Throws: R   Height: 6′ 3″   Weight: 225   Born: June 25, 1972   Age: 34

YEAR	TM	LVL	AGE	PA	R	2B	3B	HR	RBI	BB	SO	SB	CS	SPEED	BA	OBP	SLG	MLVR	EQBA	EQOBP	EQSLG	EQA	VORP	DEFENSE
2003	TOR	MLB	31	705	117	38	1	42	145	109	137	0	0	4.0	.302	.426	.593	.384	.298	.425	.588	.336	71.9	144-1B -10
2004	TOR	MLB	32	551	74	26	0	32	99	69	115	0	1	3.1	.269	.372	.535	.167	.265	.370	.535	.303	32.1	118-1B 11
2005	FLO	MLB	33	616	81	41	3	33	115	72	121	0	0	3.6	.301	.399	.582	.396	.305	.401	.600	.328	62.2	136-1B -15
2006	*NYN*	*MLB*	*34*	*594*	*75*	*30*	*1*	*31*	*100*	*74*	*114*	*0*	*0*	*3.7*	*.279*	*.378*	*.525*	*.198*	*.283*	*.383*	*.556*	*.306*	*37.0*	*139-1B -6*

Breakout: 1%   Improve: 17%   Collapse: 37%   Attrition: 9%   Comparables: Boog Powell, Greg Luzinski, Willie McCovey

Shea Stadium isn't going to hurt him anymore than Dolphins Stadium did, and that wasn't much. There is no doubt that in the short term he will be the best first baseman the Mets have had since John Olerud left town. We can speculate on two potential problems: First, Delgado's defense is scary bad and it's not likely to get any better. Second, he's signed through 2008, with a club option for 2009. Many of his PECOTA comps are guys like Luzinski and Powell, players whose careers didn't have big second acts or soft landings. It could be that the Mets will be back in the first base hunt sooner than they think.

DAMION EASLEY   INF   Bats: R Throws: R   Height: 5′ 11″ Weight: 185   Born: November 11, 1969   Age: 36

YEAR	TM	LVL	AGE	PA	R	2B	3B	HR	RBI	BB	SO	SB	CS	SPEED	BA	OBP	SLG	MLVR	EQBA	EQOBP	EQSLG	EQA	VORP	DEFENSE		
2003	TBA	MLB	33	109	8	3	1	1	7	2	18	0	0	4.6	.187	.202	.262	-.517	.189	.211	.264	.170	-9.6	21-3B	0	
2004	FLO	MLB	34	257	26	20	1	9	43	24	36	4	1	4.8	.238	.331	.457	.050	.240	.329	.467	.272	9.5	18-2B 0	16-1B	0
2005	FLO	MLB	35	301	37	19	1	9	30	26	47	4	1	4.9	.240	.312	.419	-.017	.244	.315	.441	.261	7.6	36-2B 1	24-SS	-1
2006	*ARI*	*MLB*	*36*	*233*	*28*	*13*	*1*	*7*	*31*	*20*	*35*	*3*	*1*	*5.0*	*.262*	*.334*	*.445*	*.010*	*.259*	*.330*	*.443*	*.258*	*8.2*	*58-2B*	*-2*	

Breakout: 31% Improve: 47%   Collapse: 26%   Attrition: 45%   Comparables: Mike Bordick, Don Hoak, Phil Garner

He's made a nice second career for himself with his versatility. What there was of his offense last year came off of lefties; after struggling against them for a few years, he battered them for .333/.390/.725 averages. Signed by the Diamondbacks, who have so many infielders lying around that it's hard to fathom what they wanted him for.

JUAN ENCARNACION   OF   Bats: R Throws: R   Height: 6′ 3″   Weight: 187   Born: March 8, 1976   Age: 30

YEAR	TM	LVL	AGE	PA	R	2B	3B	HR	RBI	BB	SO	SB	CS	SPEED	BA	OBP	SLG	MLVR	EQBA	EQOBP	EQSLG	EQA	VORP	DEFENSE
2003	FLO	MLB	27	648	80	37	6	19	94	37	82	19	8	6.4	.270	.313	.446	.030	.272	.315	.457	.263	7.8	152-RF -1
2004	LAN	MLB	28	350	42	18	1	13	43	21	53	3	3	4.7	.235	.289	.417	-.095	.237	.289	.425	.240	-4.8	75-RF -2
2004	FLO	MLB	28	181	21	12	1	3	19	17	33	2	1	5.3	.237	.320	.381	-.070	.241	.322	.383	.248	-0.8	45-RF -2
2005	FLO	MLB	29	559	59	27	3	16	76	41	104	6	5	5.0	.287	.349	.447	.120	.293	.354	.467	.279	20.7	125-RF -10
2006	*SLN*	*MLB*	*30*	*514*	*65*	*27*	*3*	*15*	*67*	*35*	*81*	*7*	*4*	*5.3*	*.273*	*.329*	*.439*	*.003*	*.274*	*.331*	*.455*	*.261*	*8.0*	*121-RF -4*

Breakout: 14%   Improve: 47%   Collapse: 25%   Attrition: 9%   Comparables: Derek Bell, Barry Bonnell, Torii Hunter

(continued next page)

Juan Encarnacion *(continued)*

He had his career year at age 29. The odds of his repeating that are about the same as our having left a check for $50,000, made out to you, between pages 137 and 138 of this book. Even at the top of his game last year, Encarnacion swung a very light bat for a right fielder. Signed to a three-year, $15 million deal by the Cardinals, who will rapidly discover that Larry Walker, even playing with the baseball equivalent of systemic organ failure, was a much better player.

ALEX GONZALEZ   **SS**   **Bats: R Throws: R**   Height: 6′ 0″   Weight: 170   Born: February 15, 1977   Age: 29

YEAR	TM	LVL	AGE	PA	R	2B	3B	HR	RBI	BB	SO	SB	CS	SPEED	BA	OBP	SLG	MLVR	EQBA	EQOBP	EQSLG	EQA	VORP	DEFENSE	
2003	FLO	MLB	26	579	52	33	6	18	77	33	106	0	4	4.1	.256	.313	.443	.015	.259	.313	.456	.259	21.3	148-SS	4
2004	FLO	MLB	27	596	67	30	3	23	79	27	126	3	1	4.5	.232	.270	.419	-.115	.234	.272	.425	.236	5.5	152-SS	-2
2005	FLO	MLB	28	474	45	30	0	5	45	31	81	5	3	4.6	.264	.319	.368	-.058	.271	.325	.383	.247	9.5	122-SS	-1
2006	*FLO*	*MLB*	*29*	*479*	*51*	*26*	*2*	*13*	*58*	*30*	*85*	*3*	*2*	*4.3*	*.253*	*.306*	*.411*	*-.088*	*.260*	*.310*	*.435*	*.246*	*13.7*	*113-SS*	*-2*

Breakout: 23%   Improve: 55%   Collapse: 19%   Attrition: 16%   Comparables: Ken Reitz, Charlie Hayes, Pat Meares

It took the Marlins nearly 900 games of Alex Gonzalez to get him to leave, and while he had a fewstretches of adequacy, with his peak coinciding with the Marlins' championship year in 2003. When that's someone's ceiling, it's not a bad thing to just go. If Hanley Ramirez posts a .250 EQA and does an average job with the glove, he'll be an improvement on Gonzalez's occasional power.

KRIS HARVEY   **OF**   **Bats: R Throws: R**   Height: 6′ 2″   Weight: 195   Born: January 5, 1984   Age: 22

YEAR	TM	LVL	AGE	PA	R	2B	3B	HR	RBI	BB	SO	SB	CS	SPEED	BA	OBP	SLG	MLVR	EQBA	EQOBP	EQSLG	EQA	VORP	DEFENSE			
2005	JAM	A-	21	275	34	14	3	9	38	9	60	4	0	5.6	.300	.320	.479	.121	.236	.251	.387	.219	-12.5	25-3B	-5	23-RF	0

A pitcher and outfielder at Clemson, Harvey went to the Marlins in the 2nd round of the 2005 draft and became a full-time position player. The Fish tried him at third base, but with Cabrera on the bag now, it's unclear that he'll stay there. Harvey has real power but his plate judgment needs more refinement than a barrel of Iraqi crude. Harvey is the son of fragile Marlins closer Bryan Harvey, so this will be our first chance to see if durability—or lack thereof—is in the genes.

JEREMY HERMIDA   **RF**   **Bats: L Throws: R**   Height: 6′ 4″   Weight: 200   Born: January 30, 1984   Age: 22

YEAR	TM	LVL	AGE	PA	R	2B	3B	HR	RBI	BB	SO	SB	CS	SPEED	BA	OBP	SLG	MLVR	EQBA	EQOBP	EQSLG	EQA	VORP	DEFENSE	
2003	GRB	A	19	556	73	23	5	6	49	80	100	28	2	6.5	.284	.387	.393	.159	.260	.345	.374	.261	-4.0	123-RF	-11
2004	JUP	A+	20	393	53	17	1	10	50	42	73	10	3	5.2	.297	.377	.441	.227	.278	.345	.428	.270	7.3	76-RF	-6
2005	CAR	AA	21	506	77	29	2	18	63	111	89	23	2	5.4	.293	.457	.518	.381	.258	.406	.457	.306	29.0	113-RF	7
2005	FLO	MLB	21	47	9	2	0	4	11	6	12	2	0	5.1	.293	.383	.634	.435	.293	.383	.634	.330	6.1		
2006	*FLO*	*MLB*	*22*	*577*	*77*	*27*	*2*	*19*	*68*	*76*	*112*	*17*	*4*	*4.9*	*.257*	*.361*	*.439*	*.043*	*.264*	*.365*	*.465*	*.282*	*17.7*	*135-RF*	*0*

Breakout: 15%   Improve: 39%   Collapse: 31%   Attrition: 5%   Comparables: Jack Cust, Clint Hurdle, Tom Brunansky

You can argue that this guy deserves to be the #1 prospect in the book based on his plate judgment, blossoming power, and sizzling September cup of coffee. All the questions about Hermida involve his youth and his precocious selectivity. It's impossible to predict where you'll go if you've already arrived, which is to say that Hermida already has the plate judgment of a much older player and his home run power checked in for the first time in 2005. He may already be as refined as he can be. If he stops where he is he's going to be a fine player, but if he develops along the normal curve he could be Bondsian. There are reasons not to be satisfied with Hermida's sorry-looking collection of PECOTA comparables—he's more selective than Tom Brunansky, has better bat control than Jack Cust, and Clint Hurdle got hurt at 22 and never recovered.

PAUL LO DUCA   **C**   **Bats: R Throws: R**   Height: 5′ 10″   Weight: 185   Born: April 12, 1972   Age: 34

YEAR	TM	LVL	AGE	PA	R	2B	3B	HR	RBI	BB	SO	SB	CS	SPEED	BA	OBP	SLG	MLVR	EQBA	EQOBP	EQSLG	EQA	VORP	DEFENSE			
2003	LAN	MLB	31	623	64	34	2	7	52	44	54	0	2	3.6	.273	.335	.377	-.021	.280	.340	.387	.253	12.2	120-C	13	18-1B	-2
2004	LAN	MLB	32	379	41	18	1	10	49	22	27	2	4	3.5	.301	.351	.444	.101	.304	.353	.452	.272	17.3	77-C	-1		
2004	FLO	MLB	32	207	27	11	1	3	31	14	22	2	1	5.1	.258	.314	.376	-.088	.263	.318	.379	.247	1.9	47-C	-1		
2005	FLO	MLB	33	491	45	23	1	6	57	34	31	4	3	4.3	.283	.334	.380	-.001	.290	.339	.396	.258	15.9	116-C	-4		
2006	*NYN*	*MLB*	*34*	*437*	*42*	*21*	*1*	*6*	*44*	*27*	*35*	*3*	*2*	*4.2*	*.273*	*.327*	*.373*	*-.089*	*.277*	*.331*	*.395*	*.246*	*8.9*	*104-C*	*-1*		

Breakout: 12%   Improve: 37%   Collapse: 40%   Attrition: 19%   Comparables: Jerry Grote, Manny Sanguillen, Bo Diaz

Here's a Frank Loesser/Hoagy Carmichael tune going out to all of the L.A. writers from the gang at BP: "Heart and soul, I fell in love with you . . . Heart and soul, the way a fool would do, madly, because you held me tight . . . and stole a kiss in the night . . ." The erstwhile heart, soul, and solar plexus of the Dodgers, for whom sun coast scribes still nurse giant, unfulfilled man-crushes, turns out to be a run-of-the-mill ballplayer when it comes to doing the things like hitting and fielding, only the main parts of a ballplayer's job. Leadership doesn't compensate for shortcomings in those departments, no matter how much willfully naive romantics would like to believe otherwise. Traded to the Mets, he'll be the scrappy, popular esophagus of the club, and he may even pick up a home run or two he lost to Dolphins Stadium, but not many more than that. Signed through 2007; he won't be a Met past that point.

MIKE LOWELL　　　3B　　**Bats: R Throws: R**　　Height: 6′ 4″　Weight: 205　Born: February 24, 1974　Age: 32

YEAR	TM	LVL	AGE	PA	R	2B	3B	HR	RBI	BB	SO	SB	CS	SPEED	BA	OBP	SLG	MLVR	EQBA	EQOBP	EQSLG	EQA	VORP	DEFENSE	
2003	FLO	MLB	29	557	76	27	1	32	105	56	78	3	1	3.9	.276	.350	.530	.214	.279	.352	.543	.297	44.8	124-3B	2
2004	FLO	MLB	30	671	87	44	1	27	85	64	77	5	1	4.5	.293	.365	.505	.217	.294	.366	.510	.296	43.9	149-3B	10
2005	FLO	MLB	31	557	56	36	1	8	58	46	58	4	0	4.4	.236	.298	.360	-.119	.241	.304	.375	.241	-4.8	127-3B	14
2006	BOS	MLB	32	529	65	32	1	18	76	43	65	4	1	4.4	.270	.332	.457	.045	.268	.337	.466	.267	17.8	125-3B	3

Breakout: 14%　Improve: 45%　Collapse: 36%　Attrition: 13%　　Comparables: Tim Wallach, Ken McMullen, John Valentin

Now with the Red Sox, the big question is if last year's season-long slump was, as Lowell contends, a crisis of confidence, or a sign of deteriorating reflexes. While most players as good as Lowell don't just suddenly pack it in at age 31, it has been known to happen—Kevin McReynolds had his last good year at 30, Dale Murphy at 31. One good sign was that whatever weakness Lowell had with the stick, his glove was still handy. Should he snap back to form, the Red Sox will get a player whose production is quite similar to what they got from Bill Mueller, with an increase in home runs compensating for the losses in walks and average.

BRAD McCANN　　　1B　　**Bats: R Throws: R**　　Height: 6′ 3″　Weight: 210　Born: December 9, 1982　Age: 23

YEAR	TM	LVL	AGE	PA	R	2B	3B	HR	RBI	BB	SO	SB	CS	SPEED	BA	OBP	SLG	MLVR	EQBA	EQOBP	EQSLG	EQA	VORP	DEFENSE	
2004	JAM	A-	21	122	16	6	2	3	13	7	16	0	1	4.4	.277	.328	.446	.089	.220	.264	.362	.215	-6.8	24-3B	-3
2005	GRB	A	22	527	67	35	2	28	106	37	97	1	1	3.2	.295	.355	.552	.261	.240	.286	.437	.244	-6.5	103-1B	-5
2006	FLO	MLB	23	463	45	24	1	12	57	27	101	0	1	3.3	.232	.284	.376	-.187	.238	.287	.398	.225	-10.4	110-1B	-4

Breakout: 19%　Improve: 45%　Collapse: 34%　Attrition: 7%　　Comparables: Charley Carter, Jeremy West, Danny Matienzo

The Marlins' Organizational Player of the Year for 2005, McCann is the older brother of Braves catcher Brian. A 6th round pick in 2004, he wasn't a highly regarded prospect until his Sally League breakout. Initially a third baseman, he seems moored to the bag at first for now. Although he's showing nice power, his lack of selectivity may make his bat a little light for the position. Speed is not his forte; by the time he reaches the majors the grounds crew may have to come out between innings and shoo the pigeons off his shoulders.

JUAN PIERRE　　　CF　　**Bats: L Throws: L**　　Height: 6′ 0″　Weight: 170　Born: August 14, 1977　Age: 28

YEAR	TM	LVL	AGE	PA	R	2B	3B	HR	RBI	BB	SO	SB	CS	SPEED	BA	OBP	SLG	MLVR	EQBA	EQOBP	EQSLG	EQA	VORP	DEFENSE	
2003	FLO	MLB	25	731	100	28	7	1	41	55	35	65	20	7.6	.305	.361	.373	.030	.311	.366	.378	.270	29.0	161-CF	-15
2004	FLO	MLB	26	733	100	22	12	3	49	45	35	45	24	7.6	.326	.374	.407	.114	.333	.380	.414	.273	35.1	162-CF	-12
2005	FLO	MLB	27	708	96	19	13	2	47	41	45	57	17	8.2	.276	.326	.354	-.061	.286	.337	.371	.255	12.1	155-CF	-11
2006	CHN	MLB	28	664	103	25	7	0	43	43	39	49	16	6.6	.297	.348	.361	-.053	.298	.349	.367	.253	13.0	155-CF	-6

Breakout: 13%　Improve: 35%　Collapse: 17%　Attrition: 2%　　Comparables: Lance Johnson, Luis Polonia, Darin Erstad

Pierre is not a great player, and last season he was not even a good player. As a leadoff hitter, Pierrre ranks 89th among active players in OBP. Nor is he a good outfielder; another fundamental law of the universe that teams have been slow to grasp is that there is no logical reason, no matter how fast a player is, to give him more than 10% of the team's total offensive playing time—when he will never hit a home run or get on base at an average rate. Now with the Cubs, he'll be an upgrade from that team's sorry 2005 collection of center fielders, but that's not saying much.

ERIC REED   CF   **Bats: L Throws: L**   Height: 5' 11"   Weight: 170   Born: December 2, 1980   Age: 25

YEAR	TM	LVL	AGE	PA	R	2B	3B	HR	RBI	BB	SO	SB	CS	SPEED	BA	OBP	SLG	MLVR	EQBA	EQOBP	EQSLG	EQA	VORP	DEFENSE
2003	JUP	A+	22	569	86	15	8	0	25	52	83	53	18	8.1	.300	.367	.360	.135	.289	.347	.364	.256	11.6	125-CF 17
2004	CAR	AA	23	238	32	9	6	3	14	14	55	24	5	8.9	.306	.345	.441	.136	.287	.320	.412	.262	5.8	47-CF -4
2005	CAR	AA	24	295	35	9	0	1	15	17	62	23	8	6.9	.255	.305	.299	-.178	.223	.263	.267	.201	-23.5	63-CF 6
2005	ABQ	AAA	24	179	19	5	4	1	20	3	31	17	7	7.3	.310	.335	.404	-.126	.255	.275	.334	.219	-6.4	37-CF 6
2006	*FLO*	*MLB*	*25*	*361*	*44*	*13*	*4*	*3*	*25*	*18*	*78*	*21*	*7*	*6.2*	*.246*	*.290*	*.335*	*-.222*	*.252*	*.293*	*.355*	*.225*	*-3.4*	*87-CF 4*

Breakout: 22%   Improve: 40%   Collapse: 34%   Attrition: 21%   Comparables: Richard Thompson, Alex Sanchez, Endy Chavez

Good sprinter, but not much of a baseball player. Reed is a better hitter than Esix Snead, and consequently should rise above that speed merchant's fifth outfielder/Triple-A starter career outlook, all the way to fourth outfielder/Triple-A starter. He has neither the pop nor the patience to be a quality regular, and at his age he's not going to develop them.

J. T. RESTKO   OF   **Bats: R Throws: R**   Height: 6' 5"   Weight: 190   Born: December 15, 1984   Age: 21

YEAR	TM	LVL	AGE	PA	R	2B	3B	HR	RBI	BB	SO	SB	CS	SPEED	BA	OBP	SLG	MLVR	EQBA	EQOBP	EQSLG	EQA	VORP	DEFENSE
2004	JAM	A-	19	312	40	11	1	6	46	16	74	0	2	3.8	.238	.285	.345	-.119	.195	.235	.294	.188	-59.9	66-1B -11
2005	GRB	A	20	476	69	22	3	15	70	53	91	3	0	4.7	.313	.414	.494	.282	.269	.348	.429	.270	6.9	60-LF -5
2006	*FLO*	*MLB*	*21*	*480*	*50*	*23*	*2*	*11*	*52*	*38*	*108*	*2*	*2*	*4.3*	*.238*	*.307*	*.376*	*-.143*	*.244*	*.311*	*.398*	*.237*	*-5.1*	*113-LF -9*

Breakout: 27%   Improve: 51%   Collapse: 31%   Attrition: 9%   Comparables: Jake Blalock, Jamal Harrison, Chris Duncan

Restko had a breakthrough season at Greensboro, but the Grasshoppers got a new ballpark this year, so this may just be another gift from Ishturf, the God of Park Factors. Ishturf giveth and Ishturf taketh away, and to make matters worse, he has a close collaboration going with vengeful Asthwart, Goddess of Levels. In short, when Restko moves up to high A-ball and a more neutral ballpark, he'll either regress in a hurry, or make the proper burnt offerings and everything will work out okay. He's also a big man without a position, which is a whole other theology that we'll cover in the 200-level course.

JASON STOKES   1B   **Bats: R Throws: R**   Height: 6' 4"   Weight: 220   Born: January 23, 1982   Age: 24

YEAR	TM	LVL	AGE	PA	R	2B	3B	HR	RBI	BB	SO	SB	CS	SPEED	BA	OBP	SLG	MLVR	EQBA	EQOBP	EQSLG	EQA	VORP	DEFENSE
2003	JUP	A+	21	509	67	31	3	17	89	36	135	6	4	5.2	.258	.312	.448	.147	.243	.288	.451	.249	-2.7	100-1B 1
2004	CAR	AA	22	440	66	26	0	23	78	42	121	5	0	5.0	.272	.345	.513	.202	.243	.310	.458	.261	3.9	103-1B 7
2005	ABQ	AAA	23	50	12	1	1	5	15	3	16	2	0	7.4	.283	.340	.674	.235	.242	.289	.575	.281	2.1	11-1B -1
2006	*FLO*	*MLB*	*24*	*353*	*47*	*17*	*2*	*19*	*54*	*28*	*108*	*13*	*2*	*5.1*	*.250*	*.316*	*.490*	*.029*	*.256*	*.320*	*.518*	*.275*	*11.6*	*85-1B 0*

Breakout: 44%   Improve: 60%   Collapse: 23%   Attrition: 20%   Comparables: Jesse Barfield, Willie Stargell, Albert Belle

Like Danny Glover in the "Lethal Weapon" movies, Stokes is starting to get too old for this stuff. The lad has real power—check out his comps—but injuries have hindered his development. Wrist problems held him back in the past, while last year his "hypermobile" trick thumb shelved him for all but 13 games. Stokes's plate judgment is a work in progress and he strikes out quite a bit. Until he gets some sustained playing time, it won't be certain if he can work through these issues. With the Marlins' roster being wide open, Stokes can be a dark horse for the first base job, thereby complicating the lives of Mike Jacobs, Miguel Olivo, and Josh Willingham, but at 24, the expiration of his prospect status is approaching.

JOSH WILLINGHAM   C/1B/OF   **Bats: R Throws: R**   Height: 6' 1"   Weight: 200   Born: February 17, 1979   Age: 27

YEAR	TM	LVL	AGE	PA	R	2B	3B	HR	RBI	BB	SO	SB	CS	SPEED	BA	OBP	SLG	MLVR	EQBA	EQOBP	EQSLG	EQA	VORP	DEFENSE	
2003	JUP	A+	24	251	46	17	1	12	34	46	42	9	2	5.9	.264	.422	.549	.412	.222	.351	.474	.284	14.4	35-C -4	
2004	CAR	AA	25	454	81	24	0	24	76	91	87	6	3	4.5	.281	.449	.565	.420	.231	.374	.442	.286	25.5	78-C 2	17-1B 2
2005	ABQ	AAA	26	279	56	14	3	19	54	47	54	5	1	5.5	.324	.455	.676	.453	.252	.377	.502	.299	21.9	58-C -11	
2005	FLO	MLB	26	27	3	1	0	0	4	2	5	0	0	2.9	.304	.407	.348	.082	.292	.393	.333	.267	1.4		
2006	*FLO*	*MLB*	*27*	*388*	*48*	*18*	*2*	*15*	*51*	*58*	*88*	*3*	*1*	*4.9*	*.247*	*.373*	*.456*	*.076*	*.253*	*.378*	*.483*	*.288*	*24.0*	*93-C -5*	

Breakout: 16%   Improve: 50%   Collapse: 28%   Attrition: 15%   Comparables: Tom Haller, Jim Pagliaroni, Dwight Evans

Like a character in an Agatha Christie novel, Willingham watched the bad guys kill off all the other possible catchers until he was the only one left. Then they went out and acquired Jacobs and Olivo, and now he's probably wishing that they would kill him off, too. Willingham is a bit old as prospects go, due to injuries and his indeterminate position. When and if he finally gets to play, he won't set the world on fire with his batting average, but will give the Marlins solid power and patience. Defense is another matter; if the Fish used Willingham at all three of his positions (C/1B/LF) they would make a virtue out of his shortcomings.

JOSH WILSON   SS/2B   Bats: R Throws: R   Height: 6' 1"   Weight: 160   Born: March 26, 1981   Age: 25

YEAR	TM	LVL	AGE	PA	R	2B	3B	HR	RBI	BB	SO	SB	CS	SPEED	BA	OBP	SLG	MLVR	EQBA	EQOBP	EQSLG	EQA	VORP	DEFENSE
2003	CAR	AA	22	473	53	30	6	3	58	27	70	6	5	5.6	.253	.294	.371	-.049	.247	.280	.381	.230	-1.4	110-SS -10
2004	CAR	AA	23	356	63	21	1	10	41	42	50	8	4	5.5	.315	.396	.486	.279	.289	.364	.445	.279	27.3	73-SS 1
2004	ABQ	AAA	23	261	32	12	2	5	23	19	51	6	1	5.5	.279	.337	.408	-.164	.224	.280	.323	.216	-7.4	56-SS 3
2005	ABQ	AAA	24	595	88	31	6	17	82	48	114	17	7	6.0	.257	.323	.435	-.145	.207	.267	.341	.218	-18.1	133-SS 14
2006	COL	MLB	25	446	56	27	4	11	49	30	75	8	4	4.8	.265	.320	.434	-.025	.246	.302	.410	.239	7.3	106-SS 4

Breakout: 37%   Improve: 70%   Collapse: 15%   Attrition: 21%   Comparables: Juan Uribe, Dale Berra, Kevin Elster

Utility infield candidate with a little bit of pop, a little bit of patience, but not so much of either that you'd want to make a regular out of him. Traded to the Rockies for a PTBNL, Wilson will serve as insurance in case Clint Barmes loses another battle to venison, prime rib, Kobe beef, or a particularly angry pot roast.

PITCHERS

ANTONIO ALFONSECA   Bats: R   Throws: R   Height: 6' 5"   Weight: 250   Born: April 16, 1972   Age: 34

YEAR	TM	LVL	AGE	W	L	SV	G	GS	IP	H	BB	SO	HR	GB%	BABIP	STUFF	WHIP	ERA	PERA	EQERA	EQH9	EQBB9	EQSO9	EQHR9	VORP	WXRL
2003	CHN	MLB	31	3	1	0	60	0	66.3	76	27	51	7	60%	.338	-3	1.55	5.84	4.39	5.45	9.7	3.2	6.1	0.9	-1.8	0.6
2004	ATL	MLB	32	6	4	0	79	0	73.7	71	28	45	5	62%	.289	-1	1.34	2.56	4.30	3.19	8.7	3.2	4.9	0.6	22.6	1.8
2005	FLO	MLB	33	1	1	0	33	0	27.3	29	14	16	2	63%	.342	-14	1.54	4.95	4.88	4.88	9.1	4.2	4.9	0.7	1.1	-0.0
2006	FLO	MLB	34	2	2	1	32	0	35.3	39	15	24	3	56%	.315	-11	1.51	4.59	5.05	6.01	10.0	3.4	5.4	0.8	1.2	0.1

Breakout: 9%   Improve: 28%   Collapse: 37%   Attrition: 33%   Comparables: Fred Gladding, Ben Weber, Mike Fetters

After a good season for the Braves in 2004, Alfonseca came crashing back to earth. A stress fracture in his elbow had something to do with that. A free agent at this writing, Alfonseca has never been decisively better than a league average pitcher, despite having one more finger. If healthy, he's functional, but not someone for whom you pay a premium.

JEFFREY ALLISON   Bats: R   Throws: R   Height: 6' 2"   Weight: 195   Born: November 27, 1984   Age: 21

YEAR	TM	LVL	AGE	W	L	SV	G	GS	IP	H	BB	SO	HR	GB%	BABIP	STUFF	WHIP	ERA	PERA	EQERA	EQH9	EQBB9	EQSO9	EQHR9	VORP	WXRL
2005	GRB	A	20	5	4	0	17	17	94.7	86	40	83	13	42%	.282	-24	1.33	4.18	7.06	5.73	10.2	4.8	5.1	2.4	-1.3	—
2006	FLO	MLB	21	5	9	0	24	21	118.0	124	65	79	23	41%	.280	-5	1.60	5.62	6.52	6.10	9.6	4.5	5.3	1.7	-6.6	0.1

Breakout: 9%   Improve: 46%   Collapse: 20%   Attrition: 0%   Comparables: Jimmy Barrett, Eric Thompson, Matt Butler

Sing along with Elvis Costello: "Allllllison . . . I know this world is killing you . . ." Actually, Allison came damned close to killing himself, overdosing on heroin in July, 2004. He's also had trouble with marijuana and OxyContin, the breakfast of champions, and was closely involved with another Marlins prospect who died of a methadone overdose. His return was long in coming because he resisted going into rehab. Perhaps he was finally pushed into returning by a December, 2004 *Sports Illustrated* article that seemed to boil his scouting report down to "low-to-mid 90s fastball, good curve, no brain." Upon his return, his location was understandably off. Best of luck to Allison, who has a tough road ahead—while other pitchers have to survive intense competition, injuries, and the limitations of their own talent, Allison is just trying to survive, period.

JOSH BECKETT   Bats: R   Throws: R   Height: 6' 4"   Weight: 190   Born: May 15, 1980   Age: 26

YEAR	TM	LVL	AGE	W	L	SV	G	GS	IP	H	BB	SO	HR	GB%	BABIP	STUFF	WHIP	ERA	PERA	EQERA	EQH9	EQBB9	EQSO9	EQHR9	VORP	WXRL
2003	FLO	MLB	23	9	8	0	24	23	142.0	132	56	152	9	49%	.327	40	1.32	3.04	3.32	3.63	8.1	3.1	8.5	0.6	33.8	4.5
2004	FLO	MLB	24	9	9	0	26	26	156.7	137	54	152	16	47%	.292	27	1.22	3.79	3.84	4.31	8.3	2.9	7.8	0.9	26.2	3.8
2005	FLO	MLB	25	15	8	0	29	29	178.7	153	58	166	14	43%	.294	31	1.18	3.37	3.63	3.94	7.8	2.7	7.7	0.7	34.0	5.3
2006	BOS	MLB	26	12	8	0	29	29	184.3	177	56	153	19	44%	.291	25	1.26	3.87	3.85	3.90	8.3	2.7	7.3	0.9	33.1	4.9

Breakout: 22%   Improve: 56%   Collapse: 8%   Attrition: 8%   Comparables: Tom Bradley, Bob Rush, Steve Busby

In selecting Beckett's comparables, PECOTA had injuries on its mind; Bradley and Busby were young pitchers who were pushed extremely hard by their managers and burned out in just a few years. Their misfortune was that they had the strength to endure the heavy workload, at least in the short term, whereas Beckett has hit the DL nine times in the last four seasons, buying his arm a respite. That's looking at the glass as half full. The contrary POV would be that Beckett, who has never pitched 200 innings in a season, lacks the durability to lead the Red Sox's staff or endure the more grueling games in the DH league. If Beckett survives and prospers, it will be because of his improving control—he's cut his walk rate in every season of his career—and Terry Francona realizing that he has another Pedro Martinez-style hothouse flower, a pitcher who might do great work for you if you treat him gently.

ADAM BOSTICK   Bats: L Throws: L   Height: 6' 1" Weight: 220 Born: March 17, 1983   Age: 23

YEAR	TM	LVL	AGE	W	L	SV	G	GS	IP	H	BB	SO	HR	GB%	BABIP	STUFF	WHIP	ERA	PERA	EQERA	EQH9	EQBB9	EQSO9	EQHR9	VORP	WXRL
2004	GRB	A	21	2	8	0	23	22	114.0	100	58	163	10	—	.349	1	1.39	3.79	5.52	5.60	9.3	5.8	7.6	1.4	0.0	—
2005	JUP	A+	22	4	5	0	17	17	91.3	95	36	94	7	38%	.351	-5	1.43	3.84	5.44	5.95	10.1	4.6	5.9	1.3	-3.4	—
2005	CAR	AA	22	4	3	0	9	9	44.3	42	25	39	3	47%	.310	-8	1.51	4.67	5.79	6.43	9.6	5.8	5.4	1.1	-3.9	—
2006	FLO	MLB	23	4	8	0	26	18	103.0	110	70	77	18	39%	.294	-9	1.74	6.12	6.94	6.62	9.7	5.6	5.9	1.6	-12.1	-0.6

Breakout: 10%   Improve: 46%   Collapse: 28%   Attrition: 0%   Comparables: Mike Gonzalez, Cedrick Bowers, Matt Riley

Adam Bostick doesn't throw hard, but mixes his pitches well. This led to some obscene strikeout totals in the low minors, but the results at Jupiter suggest he'll need to make some refinements, particularly in the command department, to succeed against better competition. He's still a very intriguing prospect, however. A trained martial artist can kill someone with Adam's last name.

A. J. BURNETT   Bats: R Throws: R   Height: 6' 5" Weight: 205 Born: January 3, 1977   Age: 29

YEAR	TM	LVL	AGE	W	L	SV	G	GS	IP	H	BB	SO	HR	GB%	BABIP	STUFF	WHIP	ERA	PERA	EQERA	EQH9	EQBB9	EQSO9	EQHR9	VORP	WXRL
2003	FLO	MLB	26	0	2	0	4	4	23.0	18	18	21	2	50%	.267	8	1.57	4.70	5.09	5.09	7.8	6.3	7.4	0.8	1.0	0.1
2004	FLO	MLB	27	7	6	0	20	19	120.0	102	38	113	9	52%	.291	32	1.17	3.67	3.57	3.95	8.1	2.6	7.6	0.7	25.1	3.6
2005	FLO	MLB	28	12	12	0	32	32	209.0	184	79	198	12	60%	.304	34	1.26	3.44	3.51	4.32	7.8	3.1	7.7	0.5	30.5	4.6
2006	TOR	MLB	29	13	9	0	31	31	201.3	189	72	170	17	53%	.294	23	1.29	3.76	3.71	3.95	8.1	3.2	7.3	0.7	39.6	5.5

Breakout: 25%   Improve: 70%   Collapse: 3%   Attrition: 2%   Comparables: Jim Beattie, Matt Clement, Bob Rush

One of the most sought-after free agents in a weak class, Burnett got the big wampum from the Blue Jays, signing for five years and $55 million, also known as "Dreifort Money." But for being briefly sidelined by some elbow inflammation, Burnett stayed healthy for a change and had one of his strongest campaigns. Other than his history of ill health, Burnett's fall clashes with management after a rough month were troubling—time has proved Burnett right about the Marlins being mismanaged, but management wasn't the cause of his 5.93 ERA in September. Finally, as with all pitchers exiting the DH-free league and a friendly ballpark, at least half a run of ERA will be lost in translation.

JOSHUA JOHNSON   Bats: L Throws: R   Height: 6' 7" Weight: 220 Born: January 31, 1984   Age: 22

YEAR	TM	LVL	AGE	W	L	SV	G	GS	IP	H	BB	SO	HR	GB%	BABIP	STUFF	WHIP	ERA	PERA	EQERA	EQH9	EQBB9	EQSO9	EQHR9	VORP	WXRL
2003	GRB	A	19	4	7	0	17	17	82.3	69	29	59	5	—	.254	-7	1.19	3.61	6.01	6.25	9.8	3.9	4.1	1.4	-5.5	—
2004	JUP	A+	20	5	12	0	23	22	114.3	124	47	103	4	—	.345	11	1.50	3.39	4.63	6.23	9.8	4.2	5.4	0.7	-7.9	—
2005	CAR	AA	21	12	4	0	26	26	139.7	139	50	113	4	53%	.325	15	1.35	3.87	4.17	5.49	9.3	3.4	5.0	0.5	1.7	—
2005	FLO	MLB	21	0	0	0	4	1	12.3	11	10	10	0	39%	.333	3	1.70	3.66	4.38	3.65	8.0	6.6	6.6	0.0	2.5	0.3
2006	FLO	MLB	22	6	9	0	32	20	126.7	131	65	87	12	51%	.301	0	1.55	4.98	5.35	5.53	9.4	4.2	5.4	0.8	-0.6	0.7

Breakout: 22%   Improve: 60%   Collapse: 13%   Attrition: 0%   Comparables: Roy Halladay, Kenny Pumphrey, Jason Hammel

The Organizational Pitcher of the Year, Johnson is so tall that the Marlins have replaced the button on his cap with a winking red beacon lest low-flying aircraft run into him. The former prep pick throws in the low to-mid-90s, and though he walked 10 in 12 innings during his call-up, control is actually one of his strengths. He'll be in the mix for a spot in the Marlins rotation. Johnson is such a fan of shoulder tendinitis that he's tried it twice, and there's a pretty good chance give it another go in the future.

TODD JONES   Bats: R Throws: R   Height: 6' 3" Weight: 230 Born: April 24, 1968   Age: 38

YEAR	TM	LVL	AGE	W	L	SV	G	GS	IP	H	BB	SO	HR	GB%	BABIP	STUFF	WHIP	ERA	PERA	EQERA	EQH9	EQBB9	EQSO9	EQHR9	VORP	WXRL
2003	COL	MLB	35	1	4	0	33	1	39.3	61	18	28	8	50%	.398	-21	2.01	8.24	5.36	7.71	11.6	3.4	5.4	1.5	-12.2	-1.6
2003	BOS	MLB	35	2	1	0	26	0	29.3	32	13	31	2	50%	.349	15	1.53	5.53	3.56	5.34	8.3	3.9	8.9	0.6	1.1	0.5
2004	CIN	MLB	36	8	2	1	51	0	57.0	49	25	37	4	45%	.280	-3	1.30	3.79	4.31	3.67	8.1	3.7	5.3	0.6	9.9	3.1
2004	PHI	MLB	36	3	3	1	27	0	25.3	35	8	22	3	50%	.395	1	1.70	4.98	4.44	5.13	11.3	2.4	6.5	1.0	2.0	0.3
2005	FLO	MLB	37	1	5	40	68	0	73.0	61	14	62	2	54%	.294	25	1.03	2.10	2.97	2.60	7.6	1.6	7.1	0.2	24.9	4.9
2006	DET	MLB	38	3	5	19	52	0	59.3	65	20	40	7	49%	.307	-5	1.42	4.39	4.73	4.74	9.6	2.9	6.0	0.9	5.8	0.7

Breakout: 27%   Improve: 38%   Collapse: 36%   Attrition: 13%   Comparables: Dennis Lamp, Roberto Hernandez, Tim Worrell

There is something hypnotic about save statisitics—GMs react to a "40" in the saves column like they're looking at a centerfold. Jones is a great example; the Tigers dumped him in 2001 when he had an "11" in that column, but now that he's had another 40-save season he's desirable again. Jones did have a terrific year, finishing third in the NL in WXRL. His control was better than it had been at any other time in his career, with a walk rate that was by far a career low. Given his age, he's a very shaky bet to repeat.

LOGAN KENSING   Bats: R   Throws: R   Height: 6' 1"   Weight: 185   Born: July 3, 1982   Age: 23

YEAR	TM	LVL	AGE	W	L	SV	G	GS	IP	H	BB	SO	HR	GB%	BABIP	STUFF	WHIP	ERA	PERA	EQERA	EQH9	EQBB9	EQSO9	EQHR9	VORP	WXRL
2004	JUP	A+	22	6	7	0	23	23	127.7	120	35	100	5	—	.302	9	1.21	2.96	4.62	5.21	9.3	2.9	4.7	0.8	5.3	—
2005	CAR	AA	23	4	1	0	7	7	39.7	35	14	33	4	50%	.267	-2	1.23	3.17	6.14	4.91	10.1	3.7	5.2	1.7	2.8	—
2006	FLO	MLB	23	4	6	0	35	10	86.3	103	37	50	14	49%	.309	-14	1.62	5.97	6.56	6.57	10.8	3.6	4.6	1.5	-10.7	-0.6

Breakout: 16%   Improve: 50%   Collapse: 19%   Attrition: 0%   Comparables: Dan Perkins, Spike Lundberg, Carl Scheib

For the second year in a row, Kensing reached the majors without benefit of extended time in the minors, and for the second time he was whomped. He also lost time to elbow soreness. He's expected to be healthy this spring, but with the flood of pitching possibilities the Marlins acquired over the winter, his ultimate destination may now be the bullpen.

RANDY MESSENGER   Bats: R   Throws: R   Height: 6' 0"   Weight: 220   Born: August 13, 1981   Age: 24

YEAR	TM	LVL	AGE	W	L	SV	G	GS	IP	H	BB	SO	HR	GB%	BABIP	STUFF	WHIP	ERA	PERA	EQERA	EQH9	EQBB9	EQSO9	EQHR9	VORP	WXRL
2003	CAR	AA	21	5	7	0	29	23	113.7	137	51	78	7	—	.331	-16	1.65	5.46	5.46	8.12	11.0	4.3	4.3	1.1	-31.4	—
2004	CAR	AA	22	6	3	21	58	0	69.7	67	29	71	4	—	.330	-3	1.38	2.58	4.54	4.01	9.2	4.3	5.9	0.8	11.9	—
2005	ABQ	AAA	23	4	2	7	39	0	48.7	46	17	35	5	57%	.287	-11	1.29	3.88	4.75	4.56	8.9	3.2	4.9	1.0	5.5	—
2005	FLO	MLB	23	0	0	0	29	0	37.0	39	30	29	5	49%	.312	-17	1.86	5.35	5.68	5.45	9.0	6.6	6.4	1.2	0.3	-0.4
2006	FLO	MLB	24	2	2	1	41	0	41.7	42	22	31	4	48%	.297	-8	1.53	4.63	5.17	6.42	9.2	4.3	5.9	0.9	1.6	0.1

Breakout: 35%   Improve: 61%   Collapse: 22%   Attrition: 41%   Comparables: Randy Moffitt, Dave Giusti, Phil Hennigan

Another behemoth of a Marlins pitcher, Messenger was an 11th round pick in 1999. He throws hard and that's about it, but it worked for him when he converted from starting to relief two years ago. He battled wildness upon reaching the bigs. If he gets over that, he might settle in as a middle reliever. The Marlins may audition him for the closer's role, but if he makes, it don't look for much more than Billy Koch-style flash in the pan success.

BRIAN MOEHLER   Bats: R   Throws: R   Height: 6' 3"   Weight: 235   Born: December 31, 1971   Age: 34

YEAR	TM	LVL	AGE	W	L	SV	G	GS	IP	H	BB	SO	HR	GB%	BABIP	STUFF	WHIP	ERA	PERA	EQERA	EQH9	EQBB9	EQSO9	EQHR9	VORP	WXRL
2004	GRN	AA	32	3	9	0	20	20	108.0	113	27	57	8	—	.289	-26	1.30	4.17	5.77	7.11	10.4	3.1	2.6	1.3	-17.0	—
2005	FLO	MLB	33	6	12	0	37	25	158.3	198	42	95	16	45%	.349	3	1.52	4.55	4.41	4.57	10.1	2.1	4.8	0.9	13.4	2.7
2006	FLO	MLB	34	6	8	1	35	15	111.3	131	30	60	14	46%	.307	-10	1.44	4.88	5.43	5.61	10.7	2.2	4.2	1.2	1.9	0.7

Breakout: 11%   Improve: 48%   Collapse: 21%   Attrition: 12%   Comparables: Walt Terrell, Johnny Sain, Jack Billingham

After a year off recovering from TJ surgery, Scuffy was roughly what he had been, a hittable pitcher with good control. The Marlins brought him back on a one-year contract, but with the plethora of pitching prospects clamoring for auditions, Moehler should be dealt as soon as he puts together consecutive quality starts—assuming he puts together consecutive quality starts.

GUILLERMO MOTA   Bats: R   Throws: R   Height: 6' 4"   Weight: 200   Born: July 25, 1973   Age: 32

YEAR	TM	LVL	AGE	W	L	SV	G	GS	IP	H	BB	SO	HR	GB%	BABIP	STUFF	WHIP	ERA	PERA	EQERA	EQH9	EQBB9	EQSO9	EQHR9	VORP	WXRL
2003	LAN	MLB	29	6	3	1	76	0	105.0	78	26	99	7	51%	.260	26	0.99	1.97	3.28	2.30	7.6	2.0	7.9	0.6	40.2	4.1
2004	LAN	MLB	30	8	4	1	52	0	63.0	51	27	52	4	51%	.280	10	1.24	2.14	3.96	2.49	8.1	3.7	6.8	0.6	24.8	2.9
2004	FLO	MLB	30	1	4	3	26	0	33.7	24	10	33	4	46%	.241	10	1.01	4.81	4.18	5.01	7.5	2.5	8.1	1.1	2.8	0.9
2005	FLO	MLB	31	2	2	2	56	0	67.0	65	32	60	5	42%	.314	6	1.45	4.70	3.97	5.16	8.3	4.0	7.3	0.7	1.8	1.4
2006	BOS	MLB	32	3	3	3	57	0	68.0	71	25	52	8	44%	.301	0	1.42	4.54	4.57	4.62	9.1	3.3	6.7	1.0	7.6	0.6

Breakout: 11%   Improve: 25%   Collapse: 46%   Attrition: 9%   Comparables: Dave Weathers, Andy Mcgaffigan, Dave Veres

Injuries and inconsistency cost Mota the closer's job in the early going, which is why Mota has a one-year contract from the Red Sox and Todd Jones got two from the Tigers. Mota's season was even worse than it looked; his Fair RA was 5.56. It's unlikely that he will ever again approach the Superman numbers of his Dodgers years, but if health permits he might do some league-average relief work.

SCOTT OLSEN Bats: L Throws: L   Height: 6′ 4″ Weight: 170 Born: January 12, 1984   Age: 22

YEAR	TM	LVL	AGE	W	L	SV	G	GS	IP	H	BB	SO	HR	GB%	BABIP	STUFF	WHIP	ERA	PERA	EQERA	EQH9	EQBB9	EQSO9	EQHR9	VORP	WXRL
2003	GRB	A	19	7	9	0	25	24	128.3	101	59	129	4	—	.275	18	1.25	2.81	4.86	5.16	8.8	4.9	5.8	0.7	5.9	—
2004	JUP	A+	20	7	6	0	25	25	136.3	127	54	158	8	—	.335	16	1.33	2.97	4.74	5.15	9.3	4.1	7.1	1.2	6.5	—
2005	CAR	AA	21	6	4	0	14	14	80.3	75	27	94	7	52%	.343	13	1.27	3.92	4.81	5.40	9.6	3.3	7.3	1.4	1.7	—
2005	FLO	MLB	21	1	1	0	5	4	20.3	21	10	21	5	40%	.291	14	1.52	3.99	5.66	5.66	9.1	3.9	8.3	2.2	-0.9	0.5
2006	*FLO*	*MLB*	*22*	*7*	*9*	*1*	*32*	*20*	*128.3*	*122*	*64*	*118*	*13*	*45%*	*.299*	*13*	*1.44*	*4.55*	*4.94*	*4.99*	*8.6*	*4.1*	*7.3*	*0.9*	*7.0*	*1.5*

Breakout: 24% Improve: 71% Collapse: 8% Attrition: 0% Comparables: Chuck Stobbs, Ken Holtzman, Pete Falcone

The only thing not to like here is that Olsen finished the year on the DL with elbow inflammation. Otherwise, you have a young, hard-throwing, fastball-slider-change lefty with a great on-mound demeanor who has already been major-league tested—not bad for a 6th round high school pick. He should outlast the intense competition and win a spot in the Marlins' rotation this spring.

PAUL QUANTRILL Bats: L Throws: R   Height: 6′ 1″ Weight: 180 Born: November 3, 1968   Age: 37

YEAR	TM	LVL	AGE	W	L	SV	G	GS	IP	H	BB	SO	HR	GB%	BABIP	STUFF	WHIP	ERA	PERA	EQERA	EQH9	EQBB9	EQSO9	EQHR9	VORP	WXRL
2003	LAN	MLB	34	2	5	1	89	0	77.3	61	15	44	2	54%	.265	11	0.98	1.75	3.39	2.42	8.2	1.7	4.8	0.2	29.8	3.1
2004	NYA	MLB	35	7	3	1	86	0	95.3	124	20	37	5	49%	.339	-2	1.51	4.72	4.09	4.36	10.4	1.7	3.2	0.5	12.1	1.6
2005	NYA	MLB	36	1	0	0	22	0	32.0	48	7	11	5	41%	.368	-24	1.72	6.75	5.35	6.15	11.8	1.9	2.9	1.3	-3.6	-0.0
2005	SDN	MLB	36	1	1	0	22	0	31.7	37	2	24	2	48%	.350	13	1.23	3.41	3.06	3.62	9.5	0.6	6.1	0.6	5.9	0.2
2006	*FLO*	*MLB*	*37*	*3*	*3*	*1*	*46*	*0*	*58.0*	*71*	*13*	*29*	*6*	*47%*	*.318*	*-17*	*1.44*	*4.64*	*5.11*	*6.58*	*11.1*	*1.9*	*4.0*	*0.9*	*2.0*	*0.1*

Breakout: 15% Improve: 34% Collapse: 47% Attrition: 28% Comparables: Gerry Staley, Dan Quisenberry, Mike Maddux

But for a brief spell with the Padres, Quantrill was abused by all comers during his three-team tour of 2005. A free agent as of this writing, Quantrill may have conducted his last raid; certainly it will take a leap of faith for a club to entrust him with more than a mop-up role. And this was a guy who always insisted he had to pitch a lot to be effective.

CHRIS RESOP Bats: R Throws: R   Height: 6′ 3″ Weight: 200 Born: November 4, 1982   Age: 23

YEAR	TM	LVL	AGE	W	L	SV	G	GS	IP	H	BB	SO	HR	GB%	BABIP	STUFF	WHIP	ERA	PERA	EQERA	EQH9	EQBB9	EQSO9	EQHR9	VORP	WXRL
2004	GRB	A	21	3	1	13	42	0	42.7	28	8	71	1	—	.318	27	0.84	2.11	2.88	3.98	7.5	2.0	8.6	0.4	7.3	—
2005	CAR	AA	22	3	2	24	43	0	49.0	47	16	56	2	51%	.331	6	1.29	2.57	3.97	4.15	9.3	3.2	6.8	0.8	7.7	—
2005	FLO	MLB	22	2	0	0	15	0	17.0	22	9	15	1	28%	.404	-3	1.82	8.47	4.00	8.50	10.0	4.0	7.0	0.5	-6.0	-0.0
2006	*FLO*	*MLB*	*23*	*2*	*3*	*3*	*52*	*1*	*49.3*	*51*	*22*	*40*	*6*	*42%*	*.298*	*-3*	*1.46*	*4.80*	*5.30*	*5.23*	*9.3*	*3.7*	*6.4*	*1.2*	*1.1*	*0.1*

Breakout: 35% Improve: 72% Collapse: 9% Attrition: 14% Comparables: Jorge Julio, Esteban Yan, Neil Allen

Chris Resop hit .193 in 269 pro at-bats, became a pitcher, and made the majors in less than three years. Discovering you possess an upper 90s fastball can wreak some dramatic changes in one's life. His unceremonious thrashing at the major league level hints that he might need to do more than throw hard to succeed, like use his curve more effectively to keep hitters from sitting on the hard stuff. If he can do this, he might close some day.

JASON VARGAS Bats: L Throws: L   Height: 6′ 0″ Weight: 215 Born: February 2, 1983   Age: 23

YEAR	TM	LVL	AGE	W	L	SV	G	GS	IP	H	BB	SO	HR	GB%	BABIP	STUFF	WHIP	ERA	PERA	EQERA	EQH9	EQBB9	EQSO9	EQHR9	VORP	WXRL
2005	GRB	A	22	4	1	0	5	5	33.7	16	10	33	1	35%	.188	15	0.77	0.80	4.11	2.93	6.5	3.5	5.6	0.6	9.1	—
2005	JUP	A+	22	2	3	0	9	9	55.3	47	14	60	6	37%	.287	2	1.10	3.42	5.57	5.40	9.4	3.0	6.3	1.9	1.1	—
2005	CAR	AA	22	1	0	0	3	3	19.0	13	7	25	3	42%	.256	17	1.05	2.84	6.23	4.15	8.8	3.6	8.3	2.6	2.8	—
2005	FLO	MLB	22	5	5	0	17	13	73.7	71	31	59	4	31%	.302	20	1.38	4.03	3.86	4.22	8.4	3.5	6.5	0.5	10.8	1.8
2006	*FLO*	*MLB*	*23*	*8*	*10*	*0*	*33*	*27*	*152.7*	*146*	*58*	*116*	*20*	*36%*	*.278*	*9*	*1.34*	*4.37*	*4.74*	*4.74*	*8.7*	*3.1*	*6.0*	*1.2*	*12.3*	*2.3*

Breakout: 10% Improve: 40% Collapse: 22% Attrition: 1% Comparables: Larry Jaster, Jimmy Gobble, Ed Yarnall

The Marlins drafted Vargas in the 2nd round of the 2004 draft—with Randy Velarde hanging on his family tree, they just knew he had to be good. In Florida's book, Triple-A is for wimps, so like Kensing and Olsen, Vargas skipped right from Carolina to the bigs. For a naif, Vargas did well, showing no obvious weaknesses with his fastball-slider-change combo. Vargas is among the reasons that Marlins fans—be they in Miami, Portland, or Vegas—can still be excited to go to the park.

RON VILLONE Bats: L Throws: L Height: 6' 3" Weight: 230 Born: January 16, 1970 Age: 36

YEAR	TM	LVL	AGE	W	L	SV	G	GS	IP	H	BB	SO	HR	GB%	BABIP	STUFF	WHIP	ERA	PERA	EQERA	EQH9	EQBB9	EQSO9	EQHR9	VORP	WXRL
2003	HOU	MLB	33	6	6	0	19	19	106.7	91	48	91	16	41%	.265	6	1.30	4.13	4.83	4.31	8.6	3.7	7.1	1.3	17.7	3.1
2004	SEA	MLB	34	8	6	0	56	10	117.0	102	64	86	12	42%	.264	-1	1.42	4.08	4.89	4.73	8.5	4.7	6.3	0.9	15.5	2.2
2005	SEA	MLB	35	2	3	1	52	0	40.3	33	23	41	2	47%	.301	16	1.39	2.46	3.79	3.12	7.6	5.1	9.1	0.4	11.4	-0.2
2005	FLO	MLB	35	3	2	0	27	0	23.7	24	12	29	2	40%	.367	12	1.52	6.84	3.70	7.77	8.5	4.1	9.6	0.7	-6.0	-0.0
2006	*NYA*	*MLB*	*36*	*3*	*3*	*2*	*57*	*1*	*60.0*	*58*	*29*	*49*	*7*	*42%*	*.289*	*-4*	*1.45*	*4.52*	*4.80*	*5.32*	*8.5*	*4.5*	*7.1*	*1.0*	*5.5*	*0.5*

Breakout: 25% Improve: 46% Collapse: 27% Attrition: 18% Comparables: Don McMahon, Norm Charlton, Tim Worrell

Traded to the Yankees in exchange for Ben Julianel, Villone is precisely the kind of expensive veteran that teams which are insecure about their own player evaluations sign for "insurance" despite having a couple of pitchers who are likely to do just as well for less dough. Villone pitched over his head with the M's, then pitched poorly with the Marlins. Villone can be tough on both lefties and righties, but his weak control makes using him in high-leverage situations a risky proposition.

DONTRELLE WILLIS Bats: L Throws: L Height: 6' 4" Weight: 200 Born: January 12, 1982 Age: 24

YEAR	TM	LVL	AGE	W	L	SV	G	GS	IP	H	BB	SO	HR	GB%	BABIP	STUFF	WHIP	ERA	PERA	EQERA	EQH9	EQBB9	EQSO9	EQHR9	VORP	WXRL
2003	CAR	AA	21	4	0	0	6	6	36.3	24	9	32	2	—	.222	18	0.91	1.49	4.28	2.94	8.0	2.4	5.9	1.1	10.0	—
2003	FLO	MLB	21	14	6	0	27	27	160.7	148	58	142	13	44%	.301	31	1.28	3.30	3.81	3.64	8.3	2.9	7.1	0.7	39.3	5.5
2004	FLO	MLB	22	10	11	0	32	32	197.0	210	61	139	20	48%	.312	15	1.38	4.02	4.29	4.66	9.5	2.6	5.6	0.9	24.1	4.2
2005	FLO	MLB	23	22	10	0	34	34	236.3	213	55	170	11	46%	.290	31	1.13	2.63	3.47	3.13	8.1	1.9	5.9	0.4	65.2	8.6
2006	*FLO*	*MLB*	*24*	*13*	*10*	*0*	*32*	*32*	*209.7*	*201*	*60*	*157*	*19*	*46%*	*.287*	*18*	*1.24*	*3.57*	*4.00*	*3.91*	*8.7*	*2.3*	*5.9*	*0.8*	*36.0*	*5.2*

Breakout: 12% Improve: 41% Collapse: 19% Attrition: 0% Comparables: Steve Avery, Mark Buehrle, Jim Abbott

PECOTA is trying to drop a hint with Willis's comparables. Two of the tree, Avery and Abbott, were young lefties who got pushed hard and died young. Let's hope PECOTA is wrong, because Willis is too much fun to have on the shelf. Still, the warning signs are there, like a strikeout rate that was slightly below average last year. Willis was excellent, finishing fourth in the NL in VORP, a fraction of a point behind Cy Young winner Chris Carpenter. Willis handled everyone and everything: lefties, righties, at home or away. With the team being razed around him, he likely won't get the offensive or defensive assistance he needs to win 20 again, but the quality should still be there. The potential of injury aside, there are no hidden vulnerabilities waiting to jump out of the closet—this is who he is.

Line Outs

Position/Player	TM	LVL	AGE	PA	R	2B	3B	HR	RBI	BB	SO	SB-CS	SPEED	BA/OBP/SLG	MLVR	EQBA/OBP/SLG	EQA	VORP
OF A. de Aza*	JUP	A+	21	543	75	24	9	3	37	58	87	34-17	6.7	.286/.370/.394	.142	.275/.347/.385	.260	13.5
PH L. Harris*	FLO	MLB	40	78	5	4	0	1	13	7	11	0-1	2.9	.314/.385/.414	.142	.324/.392/.423	.281	4.4
1/3 G. Sanchez	JAM	A-	21	257	34	16	0	5	42	16	24	11-5	4.8	.355/.401/.487	.281	.266/.300/.379	.237	2.2
C M. Treanor	FLO	MLB	29	153	10	8	0	0	13	16	28	0-0	3.3	.201/.301/.261	-.266	.206/.303/.265	.210	-4.4

Pitcher	TM	LVL	AGE	W	L	SV	IP	H	BB	SO	HR	GB%	BABIP	STUFF	WHIP	ERA	PERA	EQERA	EQH9	EQBB9	EQSO9	VORP
N. Bump	FLO	MLB	28	0	3	0	38.0	43	12	18	5	61%	.302	-17	1.45	4.03	5.17	4.23	9.9	2.6	4.0	1.2	4.6
V. de los Santos*	FLO	MLB	32	1	2	0	22.0	25	12	16	4	49%	.304	-18	1.68	6.14	6.04	6.04	10.1	4.4	6.0	1.6	-2.0
J. Mecir	FLO	MLB	35	1	4	0	43.3	39	17	34	2	44%	.306	6	1.29	3.12	3.95	3.74	8.3	3.3	6.4	0.4	7.7
J. Riedling	FLO	MLB	29	4	1	0	27.7	34	13	16	3	54%	.326	-20	1.70	7.15	5.02	7.22	10.0	3.8	4.7	0.9	-6.9
T. Smith	ABQ	AAA	32	7	8	0	103.7	107	31	73	12	51%	.303	-13	1.33	4.08	5.53	5.62	10.0	3.2	4.2	1.4	-0.2
I. Valdez	FLO	MLB	31	2	2	0	50.7	64	22	27	6	34%	.339	-11	1.70	5.33	5.33	5.50	10.5	3.6	4.3	1.0	-1.2

Alejandro de Aza was Rule 5'd over from Dodgers in the minor league phase of the 2004 draft. He's fast and showed hints of blossoming plate judgment last year. The undead **Lenny Harris** was brought back on a minor league contract. The first test of Joe Girardi's independence and baseball acumen: Can he finally shake loose the 25th man who came to dinner? **Gaby Sanchez** was the DH from the University of Miami nabbed in the 4th round of the 2005 draft; moved to first base and rewarded the Marlins with a great debut. Miami had suspended Sanchez from playing for undisclosed reasons, so the Marlins drafted him on faith. **Matt Treanor,** is not completely averse to talking a walk, but then as an eighth place hitter in the NL you don't have a lot of choice about that.

Nate Bump tore his labrum in July. Since he wasn't very good in the first place, the odds of a comeback are rather low. **Valerio De Los Santos** is a journeyman lefty. He's younger than dead, so he'll get more chances. Despite a number of physical problems over the years, screwballer **Jim Mecir** had a consistency that few relievers can claim, but the injuries have convinced him to hang it up. **John Riedling** is a replacement-level reliever who got some extended time with the Reds because they aren't exactly discriminating over there. Ineffectiveness disillusioned the Marlins, but the Cardinals have signed him to a minor league contract. Journeyman swingman **Travis Smith** has been kicking around the minors since 1995, getting occasional big league work. He has decent control but not indecent stuff; the Braves signed him to a minor league deal. Boy, **Ismael Valdez** looked good back in 1994. If this book has somehow fallen through a time portal and arrived in 1993, we advise you to sign him for your fantasy team before your friends get wise. That, and freshman year, your roommate is going to sleep with your girlfriend.

Houston Astros

The second week of the 2005 season began with the Houston Astros feeling pretty good about themselves. They'd just come off a three-game sweep of the Cincinnati Reds, with those games' outcomes nicely indicative of the team's plan for the year: Roger Clemens, Brad Lidge, and Roy Oswalt started and won, holding the Reds to a combined seven runs in the series. The Friday night game of the Cincy sweep was Roger Clemens's 329th career win, in front of a near-capacity crowd. By the end of the series, the Astros would be 4–1, and the expected horse race with the Cardinals for the NL Central crown was on.

Over the next 54 days—from April 10th through May 24th—the Astros would win precisely 11 games.

The strange thing is that the Astros didn't collapse because everything fell apart. During their miserable April-May span, the Astros went 11–29, a .275 winning percentage. They played badly during that stretch, but not quite *that* badly. They scored 143 runs and allowed 191; you'd expect about four more wins during a patch like that given the runs scored and allowed. The Astros just didn't get any breaks, which left them past the quarter mark of the season with an ugly 15–30 record.

It didn't just rain on the Astros during this bad patch, the sky fell on them. On May 10th, about a month into the club's descent, Jeff Bagwell was placed on the 15-day DL with chronic shoulder problems. Bagwell, an Astros icon, had been losing power for some time, and it was apparent that rest alone was not having sufficient therapeutic effect to revive it. In June, he underwent shoulder surgery that would remove him from the lineup for the balance of the year.

Perhaps coincidentally, for the production anticipated from Bagwell was not wholly replaced, the Astros started turning things around from there. A hundred days into the season they'd climbed back to .500 and respectability. Buoyed by the return of Lance Berkman from knee surgery, as well as a schedule thick with series against the hapless Royals, Rockies, Reds, and the lesser lights of the NL West and AL East, the Astros had climbed to 43–43 just before the All-Star break. Then, straight out of the gate in the second half, the Cardinals swept the Astros, making it look like they weren't a going concern after all. However, the Garnermen responded by winning 13 of their

ASTROS PROSPECTUS

2005 record: 89–73; Second place, NL Central; Lost to White Sox in World Series

Pythagenport record: 90–72

Runs scored per game: 4.28 (11th in NL)

Runs allowed per game: 3.76 (1st in NL)

Team EqA: .255 (12th in NL)

2005 Batters Age: 30.8 (5th oldest in NL)

2005 Pitchers Age: 31.0 (2nd oldest in NL)

Ballpark: Minute Maid Park; Neutral park; Park Factor of 1.008

2005: Rode three of baseball's five best starters all the way to the World Series.

2006: The last sting of the Killer B's was last year, especially if the Rocket's really retired.

next 14 games, putting themselves ten games over .500 and smack in the middle of the wild card race. For this, they could quietly thank several different deities for one of the weakest NL Wests in anyone's memory.

Down the stretch, the Astros were just good enough. They weren't going to catch the Cardinals, but they plugged away, riding their three horses in the rotation and a short stack of talented bullpen arms to an 89–73 record and their second straight wild card. When so many had written the Astros off at 15–30, they had responded by battling through the balance of the season at a 74–43 clip, better even than the Cardinals' 71–46 mark during their stretch run.

This was a spectacularly unlikely resurrection. There have been only eleven teams in baseball history that were both 14 games over .500 and 14 games under .500 in the same season. Three of them played in 2005: Houston, Oakland, and Baltimore. Of the eleven teams, four started high and finished low, and the other seven started low and finished high. But Houston reached +/−15 games in the same season, which is even more rare. Roughly eight teams out of the approximately 2,500 teams in history, or about 1 in 300, have had that dramatic a turnaround.

To put a finer point on it, the only other team that went .350 or worse through the first 45 games and then played .600 or better the rest of the way was the 1940 Cardinals. If

TABLE 1. TEAMS WITH A .350 OR BELOW WINNING PERCENTAGE THROUGH THEIR FIRST 45 GAMES

PCT at Game 45	Teams	Percent
<.200	1	0.7%
.200–.250	3	2.2%
.251–.300	12	8.7%
.301–.350	30	21.7%
.351–.400	28	20.3%
.401–.450	33	23.9%
.451–.500	16	11.6%
.501–.550	9	6.5%
.550+	6	4.3%

the threshold is increased to a .400 start, you get three more teams: the 1914 Braves, the 1975 Orioles, and the 1989 Blue Jays.

Of the teams in history that started the season with a winning percentage of .350 or lower, all but a fraction had shown their hand by playing that badly. Unlike the Astros, they weren't going to come back from a .350 start; their record reflected their talent (see table 1).

Given that track record, one way to interpret the Astros' season is that there was a 66% chance that they would play between .301–.450 the rest of the way, and an 89% likelihood that they were going to have a losing record over the remainder of the season.

But that sort of history got made by other people, and the Astros instead not simply recovered, they won the National League pennant. This was in no small part because of their amazing rotation, which led baseball in runs prevented during the 2005 season, edging out the White Sox, their opponent in the World Series. But the two teams' rotations, though similar in the value of their performance, were really very different beasts. This highlights one of the problems with aggregate information. Richard Nixon and Jimmy Carter had similar polling numbers at the ends of their respective administrations, but the 45% of respondents who rated Carter as "poor" were expressing their exasperation with an ineffectual president, whereas the 43% who rated Nixon the same way were expressing their displeasure with a misanthropic felon. Similar datascapes, different realities.

While the five men in the White Sox rotation provided depth and quality without being individually spectacular, the Astros rotation was fronted by three of the game's five best starting pitchers. That trio at the top—Clemens, Pettitte, and Oswalt—gave the Astros an excellent chance to win all three starts because of their ability to completely shut down the opposition. But behind these three were three pitchers (Brandon Backe, Wandy Rodriguez, and Ezequiel Astacio) who basically set the ball on a tee and prayed that the Astros offense would score six or seven runs. As a result, the rotation didn't have a single average performer. Last year, the National League ERA was 4.23. Astros pitchers neatly fell around it; no Houston pitcher with a significant number of innings posted an ERA between 3.29 and 4.46. Earning a World Series berth and leading the league in starting pitching with that kind of handicap is no small feat, and it's more remarkable still given the start the Astros had.

Grappling with that handicap may be something the Astros have to make a priority. As of January, Roger Clemens had not yet decided if he wanted to continue his career. Clemens has nothing left to prove in MLB; he's got a rich life outside of baseball, but he also seems to understand that there's nothing in the mundanity of life outside the game that will ever satisfy as completely as the competition of baseball. Hedging his bets, Clemens is willing to wait until May 1, the earliest date that players not offered arbitration can return to their teams, to make his 2006 debut. From the Astros' perspective, this is both unsurprising and annoying. Clemens is a player of tremendous impact, both in terms of his on-field performance and his salary. The nature of the team changes dramatically depending on whether or not Phil Garner can pencil in Roger Clemens's name onto the lineup card every fifth day. That kind of uncertainty can create circumstances where very bad decisions are made; GM Tim Purpura and his team must decide to fish or cut bait on their best pitcher very soon.

Whether they sign the 43-year-old Clemens or not, the Astros are already a very old team. Craig Biggio is 40. Jeff Bagwell, 38, will play the 2006 season with a shoulder that most 50 year-olds would claim as a disability. The farm system has one or two interesting prospects but no future stars. Hunter Pence, probably the best prospect in the system, is described by scouts in terms usually reserved for hobbled horses and Labradors with severe kidney failure. The players who are going to be part of the next Astros World Series team are either in very low levels in the minor league system, or still chasing women and flyballs on the fields of high schools and colleges around the world.

As if those prospects weren't daunting enough, most frightening of all is the apparent decision-making process in the Houston front office. One example is the two-year deal recently proffered to Brad Ausmus, which locks him up in his Age 37 and 38 seasons for $7.5 million. For a club that has publicly stated that it wants to improve its offense, signing Ausmus is a move that flies completely in the face of that claim. It's like hiring R. Kelly to chaperone your daughter's sleepover. A club with limited resources and a bad offense would be better off hiring Danny Bonaduce as a spiritual advisor than signing, and presumably playing, Brad Ausmus for two more years. A truly and thoroughly bad hitter, he's been ineffective for his entire career, with only the most transitory blips to make you wonder if he's achieved adequacy. His 2005 stands out as a fluke, and there's very little to suggest that he'll be an effective offensive player in 2006. His defense, while solid, doesn't approach the level necessary to make up for his anemic bat.

Ausmus's signing should not inspire any confidence in what decisions might next come out of the Astros front office. It's a common trap for successful clubs to overestimate the expected performance of the guys who were on their roster. Success makes it surprisingly easy for clubs to avoid taking a cold, hard look at themselves and objectively determine their strengths and weaknesses, especially coming off a successful season. The Astros desperately need to do exactly that, and Ausmus is one of the very first places the club should have cut costs and probable poor performance.

All clubs rebuild. It has to be done. Players age and decline, new players develop and ascend. These are unalterable facts of life in baseball, facts that govern optimal roster design, even when so many of us would prefer our favorites and heroes to remain in their primes forever. Front offices get to choose when to rebuild, but they don't get to make that choice in a vacuum. The immutable truth is that teams that don't rebuild when they're on top end up doing it when they're at the bottom. That's when people get fired, columnists and casual fans make the team a target for derision, and the publicity of being pathetic means lower ticket sales and a franchise slathered in malaise.

If the Astros want to avoid that, they need to rebuild right now. The temptation to try wringing one more year out of Roger Clemens must be strong, and with the twin franchise icons Bagwell and Biggio deep into the twilight of their careers, the pressure of trying to make it back to the playoffs with the familiar cast of characters will be intense. But a fair assessment of the Astros does not lead one to believe that their chance at another World Series is great. Like many pennant winners, the Astros got to the World Series because of some remarkable, outlier seasons from some great players. Clemens, Oswalt, and Pettitte are not likely to repeat their 2005 performances, either individually or as a group. Also, in 2005, the Astros qualified for the postseason with only 89 wins; in most seasons, that's a total that leaves you watching games in October, not playing them.

This year is an opportunity for the Astros to take some chances, make some investments, and start building the next great Astros team. That team probably doesn't include Bagwell, Biggio, or Clemens, and it certainly won't include Brad Ausmus. It's very difficult to convince the public that a World Series team needs to rebuild now without referencing unwelcome comparisons to past and present iterations of the Florida Marlins. But if you think that's hard, it is even more difficult to go through a long stretch of bad teams while trying to get back to respectability. The Astros' passivity is markedly different from how White Sox GM Kenny Williams approached the winter after winning the whole enchilada. Rather than invite everyone back for the equivalent of a victory lap, Williams made major changes to his ballclub with the intention of extending Chicago's time at the top. The Astros have failed to understand that this same necessity applies to them, and with even greater urgency.

HITTERS

JOSH ANDERSON   CF   **Bats: L Throws: R**   Height: 6' 2"   Weight: 195   Born: August 10, 1982   Age: 23

YEAR	TM	LVL	AGE	PA	R	2B	3B	HR	RBI	BB	SO	SB	CS	SPEED	BA	OBP	SLG	MLVR	EQBA	EQOBP	EQSLG	EQA	VORP	DEFENSE	
2003	TCV	A-	20	327	44	11	4	3	30	16	53	26	9	7.0	.286	.339	.380	.097	.258	.294	.359	.232	-10.5	71-CF	1
2004	LEX	A	21	340	69	12	3	4	31	33	47	48	9	8.3	.326	.403	.426	.174	.278	.340	.358	.259	3.6	72-CF	-5
2004	SLM	A+	21	299	45	13	6	2	21	13	53	31	4	9.6	.268	.314	.379	-.002	.254	.291	.377	.242	-3.9	66-CF	4
2005	CCH	AA	22	563	67	17	9	1	26	29	80	50	19	7.7	.282	.329	.355	-.055	.261	.305	.328	.232	-13.1	125-CF	2
2006	HOU	MLB	23	494	62	18	5	1	32	23	82	38	11	6.0	.255	.297	.323	-.219	.259	.301	.333	.225	-5.7	117-CF	1

Breakout: 11%   Improve: 40%   Collapse: 31%   Attrition: 12%   Comparables: Richard Thompson, Curtis Goodwin, Alex Sanchez

Because the folks behind rotisserie baseball pick stats that have the least to do with scoring runs on which to base their game, some people might think Josh Anderson and his ilk are borderline prospects. They're not. Anderson has little to offer other than speed, and is utterly incapable of driving the ball. He is not a prospect now, and won't ever be one.

JONNY ASH   **2B**   **Bats: L Throws: R**   Height: 5′ 9″   Weight: 180   Born: September 11, 1982   Age: 23

YEAR	TM	LVL	AGE	PA	R	2B	3B	HR	RBI	BB	SO	SB	CS	SPEED	BA	OBP	SLG	MLVR	EQBA	EQOBP	EQSLG	EQA	VORP	DEFENSE			
2004	TCV	A-	21	276	50	7	3	2	25	25	16	5	4	5.4	.297	.388	.377	.135	.248	.316	.317	.228	-6.9	37-3B	-2	14-2B	2
2005	LEX	A	22	296	44	11	2	8	38	25	20	3	7	4.4	.320	.395	.473	.232	.266	.322	.390	.246	5.4	51-2B	-5		
2005	SLM	A+	22	244	32	19	2	1	25	14	15	3	5	5.3	.320	.365	.436	.176	.299	.332	.405	.253	9.2	56-2B	-6		
2006	*HOU*	*MLB*	*23*	*491*	*49*	*23*	*3*	*3*	*42*	*27*	*41*	*3*	*3*	*4.7*	*.261*	*.309*	*.342*	*-.169*	*.265*	*.314*	*.352*	*.225*	*0.4*	*116-2B*	*-5*		

Breakout: 12%   *Improve: 27%*   *Collapse: 42%*   *Attrition: 6%*   Comparables: *Mike Lamb, Ismael Gallo, Tom Sergio*

In most systems, a good year at A-ball might put you on the organization's radar; in the Astros' chain, it's a rare distinction. Ash was a third baseman at Stanford, but his little man's offensive game plays better at second, encouraging the Astros to push him across the diamond. System-wide, Astros player development needs to be much more aggressive about promotions, in that they seem prone to stranding college hitters in the lower rungs of their system. Ash needs a bump to Double-A this summer if he's going to have a career, and he's promising enough to merit the consideration.

BRAD AUSMUS   **C**   **Bats: R Throws: R**   Height: 5′ 11″   Weight: 195   Born: April 14, 1969   Age: 37

YEAR	TM	LVL	AGE	PA	R	2B	3B	HR	RBI	BB	SO	SB	CS	SPEED	BA	OBP	SLG	MLVR	EQBA	EQOBP	EQSLG	EQA	VORP	DEFENSE	
2003	HOU	MLB	34	505	43	12	2	4	47	46	66	5	3	4.8	.229	.303	.291	-.247	.224	.298	.287	.215	-14.5	129-C	14
2004	HOU	MLB	35	441	38	14	1	5	31	33	56	2	2	4.0	.248	.306	.325	-.188	.244	.304	.319	.223	-6.9	114-C	0
2005	HOU	MLB	36	444	35	19	0	3	47	51	48	5	3	4.0	.258	.351	.331	-.075	.258	.352	.335	.248	7.1	120-C	8
2006	*HOU*	*MLB*	*37*	*287*	*26*	*12*	*1*	*2*	*25*	*27*	*33*	*3*	*2*	*4.0*	*.251*	*.329*	*.330*	*-.156*	*.255*	*.333*	*.340*	*.233*	*1.0*	*70-C*	*1*

Breakout: 23%   *Improve: 52%*   *Collapse: 26%*   *Attrition: 38%*   Comparables: *Joe Girardi, Birdie Tebbetts, Buddy Rosar*

There are few players in the history of baseball who have been as consistently bad and consistently on the field as Ausmus. His offensive production has been a significant problem for every team he's ever been on. Sherri Nichols long ago coined the "Nichols Law of Catcher Defense," which states that a catcher's defensive reputation will be inversely proportional to his offensive contribution. This is certainly true in Ausmus's case, as is the unstated corollary that one's clubhouse rep will also behave in said fashion. Though Ausmus's Gold Glove is worthy of its luster, it can't begin to make up for the runs forgone. Apparently ravenous for players likely to post an OPS within 40 points of 625, the Astros have re-upped Ausmus for two more out-encrusted years.

JEFF BAGWELL   **1B**   **Bats: R Throws: R**   Height: 6′ 0″   Weight: 195   Born: May 27, 1968   Age: 38

YEAR	TM	LVL	AGE	PA	R	2B	3B	HR	RBI	BB	SO	SB	CS	SPEED	BA	OBP	SLG	MLVR	EQBA	EQOBP	EQSLG	EQA	VORP	DEFENSE	
2003	HOU	MLB	35	702	109	28	2	39	100	88	119	11	4	4.9	.278	.373	.524	.211	.269	.364	.516	.295	40.7	154-1B	-4
2004	HOU	MLB	36	679	104	29	2	27	89	96	131	6	4	5.0	.266	.377	.465	.143	.259	.371	.455	.284	29.9	149-1B	-12
2005	HOU	MLB	37	123	11	4	0	3	19	18	21	0	0	3.6	.250	.358	.380	.005	.250	.355	.370	.266	1.4	23-1B	-1
2006	*HOU*	*MLB*	*38*	*296*	*33*	*12*	*1*	*10*	*36*	*38*	*55*	*1*	*1*	*4.2*	*.245*	*.346*	*.416*	*-.020*	*.249*	*.351*	*.428*	*.265*	*3.5*	*72-1B*	*-3*

Breakout: 9%   *Improve: 22%*   *Collapse: 37%*   *Attrition: 28%*   Comparables: *Harmon Killebrew, Todd Zeile, Wally Joyner*

Before the 2002 season, Bagwell and the Astros agreed on a five-year contract that averaged $17 million a year. The result was unsurprising; his production declined, due in part to an injury that first sapped Bagwell's power and then robbed him of his ability to take the field. Long-term contracts for players already in their 30s aren't a good idea for clubs, regardless of the popularity of the player in question. First, players have this unfortunate tendency to age. Second, clubs still overestimate the importance of star players. When the Astros finally did make the World Series, they did so in spite of Bagwell's contract, not because of it.

LANCE BERKMAN   **OF/1B**   **Bats: B Throws: L**   Height: 6′ 1″   Weight: 205   Born: February 10, 1976   Age: 30

YEAR	TM	LVL	AGE	PA	R	2B	3B	HR	RBI	BB	SO	SB	CS	SPEED	BA	OBP	SLG	MLVR	EQBA	EQOBP	EQSLG	EQA	VORP	DEFENSE			
2003	HOU	MLB	27	657	110	35	6	25	93	107	108	5	3	5.6	.288	.412	.515	.267	.279	.403	.505	.309	41.3	151-LF	5		
2004	HOU	MLB	28	687	104	40	3	30	106	127	101	9	7	4.8	.316	.450	.566	.433	.308	.440	.552	.332	72.8	88-RF	5	68-LF	-8
2005	HOU	MLB	29	565	76	34	1	24	82	91	72	4	1	4.3	.293	.411	.524	.305	.288	.407	.522	.316	46.9	83-1B	-4	32-LF	-2
2006	*HOU*	*MLB*	*30*	*629*	*93*	*34*	*2*	*27*	*96*	*102*	*91*	*5*	*2*	*4.7*	*.297*	*.415*	*.532*	*.278*	*.302*	*.421*	*.548*	*.321*	*49.1*	*147-LF*	*-1*		

Breakout: 8%   *Improve: 28%*   *Collapse: 28%*   *Attrition: 7%*   Comparables: *Eddie Murray, Jason Giambi, Reggie Smith*

Berkman is one of the most consistent hitters in baseball, and he'll need to be through 2010 for the Astros to get value out of his contract, which averages just over $14 million annually. He struggled through the first half of the 2005 campaign while recovering from a knee injury sustained while playing flag football, but his power stroke returned in the second half. He's pretty much run out of value defensively, but he's a nice guy to stick in the middle of the lineup and depend on for legitimate #3 hitter production. Probably a first baseman from here on out, now that the Astros have signed Preston Wilson.

CRAIG BIGGIO 2B Bats: R Throws: R Height: 5' 11" Weight: 180 Born: December 14, 1965 Age: 40

YEAR	TM	LVL	AGE	PA	R	2B	3B	HR	RBI	BB	SO	SB	CS	SPEED	BA	OBP	SLG	MLVR	EQBA	EQOBP	EQSLG	EQA	VORP	DEFENSE			
2003	HOU	MLB	37	714	102	44	2	15	62	57	116	8	4	5.5	.264	.350	.412	.017	.260	.342	.410	.262	18.1	147-CF	0		
2004	HOU	MLB	38	691	100	47	0	24	63	40	94	7	2	5.2	.281	.337	.469	.089	.275	.329	.458	.268	22.7	74-LF	-8	64-CF	-2
2005	HOU	MLB	39	647	94	40	1	26	69	37	90	11	1	6.0	.264	.325	.468	.070	.263	.322	.471	.271	29.5	132-2B	-5		
2006	*HOU*	*MLB*	*40*	*508*	*62*	*27*	*2*	*17*	*69*	*35*	*73*	*11*	*3*	*5.3*	*.265*	*.321*	*.445*	*-.009*	*.270*	*.326*	*.458*	*.262*	*15.3*	*120-2B*	*-5*		

Breakout: 18% Improve: 50% Collapse: 37% Attrition: 10% Comparables: Steve Finley, Gary Gaetti, Minnie Minoso

He's aged gracefully, especially considering he's been whacked by baseballs more often than any player in modern history, and he managed to set a career high in home runs last year. Unlike many aging players, he hasn't become more patient: drawing walks is no longer a part of Biggio's offensive arsenal. Defensively, his return to second base worked about as well as anyone could have expected, considering his age and poor performances at the position going back to 2001. He wasn't good, but he wasn't Alfonso Soriano either. He'll be back for his Age 40 season in 2006, which promises to be yet another hematoma-tastic campaign. He's one of the few players to play 460 games over their Age 37–39 seasons. A total of three second basemen have played 100 or more games in a seasonat age 40 or older: Rabbit Maranville (twice), Nap Lajoie (twice), and Joe Morgan (once). Joe had a .283 EQA that year, his last (1984). Biggio won't top it.

ERIC BRUNTLETT UT Bats: R Throws: R Height: 6' 0" Weight: 200 Born: March 29, 1978 Age: 28

YEAR	TM	LVL	AGE	PA	R	2B	3B	HR	RBI	BB	SO	SB	CS	SPEED	BA	OBP	SLG	MLVR	EQBA	EQOBP	EQSLG	EQA	VORP	DEFENSE			
2003	NWO	AAA	25	367	48	10	0	2	27	35	51	9	4	5.0	.259	.332	.309	-.079	.251	.320	.294	.226	-5.2	47-SS	-1	26-2B	2
2004	NWO	AAA	26	378	50	12	4	6	37	35	72	14	4	6.5	.250	.331	.364	-.106	.236	.307	.330	.231	-3.7	64-SS	1	18-CF	-1
2005	HOU	MLB	27	120	19	5	2	4	14	10	25	7	2	7.5	.220	.292	.413	-.092	.218	.295	.436	.251	1.3	11-CF	3		
2006	*HOU*	*MLB*	*28*	*177*	*23*	*8*	*1*	*4*	*18*	*15*	*32*	*5*	*2*	*5.7*	*.254*	*.326*	*.398*	*-.072*	*.258*	*.330*	*.410*	*.252*	*5.7*	*45-SS*	*1*		

Breakout: 42% Improve: 63% Collapse: 22% Attrition: 40% Comparables: Dave Anderson, Phil Linz, Terry Harmon

Just like every fine TV cop drama needs an S. Epatha Merkerson to serve as the guide wire to allow the rest of the cast to bloom into a fragrant Orbach, every club needs some version of an Eric Bruntlett to smooth over the rough patches on a team's bench. Bruntlett's got a little bit of pop in his bat, with enough of a platoon split (he hits lefties hard) that he's useful off the bench. Plus, he plays pretty much any infield position reasonably well, enough so that the club doesn't need to sweat minor injuries to the regulars. He's at his best right now, and should be able to wring out four or five more years as a useful role player.

CHRIS BURKE 2B/OF Bats: R Throws: R Height: 5' 11" Weight: 180 Born: March 11, 1980 Age: 26

YEAR	TM	LVL	AGE	PA	R	2B	3B	HR	RBI	BB	SO	SB	CS	SPEED	BA	OBP	SLG	MLVR	EQBA	EQOBP	EQSLG	EQA	VORP	DEFENSE			
2003	ROU	AA	23	622	88	23	8	3	41	57	57	34	10	6.9	.301	.379	.388	.111	.280	.350	.370	.259	17.7	93-2B	9	42-SS	-5
2004	NWO	AAA	24	556	93	33	6	16	52	55	76	37	14	7.3	.315	.396	.507	.301	.300	.373	.459	.287	42.7	121-2B	-2		
2005	ROU	AAA	25	100	15	6	2	2	11	8	13	9	0	7.3	.311	.380	.489	.197	.281	.341	.427	.277	4.4	17-2B	1		
2005	HOU	MLB	25	350	49	19	2	5	26	23	62	11	6	6.3	.248	.309	.368	-.113	.252	.312	.379	.242	-5.2	72-LF	-2		
2006	*HOU*	*MLB*	*26*	*458*	*63*	*23*	*3*	*9*	*46*	*35*	*64*	*17*	*6*	*5.9*	*.266*	*.334*	*.403*	*-.042*	*.271*	*.338*	*.415*	*.258*	*8.8*	*108-LF*	*1*		

Breakout: 14% Improve: 43% Collapse: 33% Attrition: 20% Comparables: Jackie Brandt, Juan Beniquez, Randy Ready

A member of the water bug class: runs quickly, but hasn't managed to translate that raw talent into value on a ball field. The only offensive capabilities he's ever shown were during his 2004 stint in New Orleans, and in less than 100 ABs in Round Rock during the 2005 season. He's young enough that he could develop into one of those slightly-better-than-a-slap-hitter guys who's useful for 350 PAs a year, perhaps having a lucky year or two that gives him a long career, a la Mark McLemore. If everything breaks right, he could get 3,500 major league at bats, but he's not going to push a championship team as a regular.

RAUL CHAVEZ   **C**   **Bats: R Throws: R**   Height: 5' 11"   Weight: 210   Born: March 18, 1973   Age: 33

YEAR	TM	LVL	AGE	PA	R	2B	3B	HR	RBI	BB	SO	SB	CS	SPEED	BA	OBP	SLG	MLVR	EQBA	EQOBP	EQSLG	EQA	VORP	DEFENSE			
2003	NWO	AAA	30	384	47	28	1	6	47	13	43	0	2	3.5	.273	.315	.408	.046	.249	.286	.366	.227	-4.9	55-C	2	38-3B	3
2003	HOU	MLB	30	38	5	1	1	1	4	1	6	0	0	4.8	.270	.289	.432	-.052	.270	.289	.432	.243	0.7				
2004	HOU	MLB	31	172	9	8	0	0	23	10	38	0	1	3.1	.210	.256	.259	-.391	.207	.253	.250	.183	-11.4	48-C	3		
2005	ROU	AAA	32	127	9	8	0	0	14	5	24	0	0	3.4	.252	.299	.319	-.261	.197	.230	.231	.169	-12.7	32-C	4		
2005	HOU	MLB	32	105	6	3	0	2	6	4	18	1	0	3.1	.172	.210	.263	-.463	.172	.217	.253	.175	-7.7	29-C	8		
2006	HOU	MLB	33	108	7	4	0	1	9	5	21	0	0	3.5	.216	.260	.296	-.344	.220	.264	.305	.186	-5.2	30-C	2		

Breakout: 37%   Improve: 51%   Collapse: 38%   Attrition: 60%   Comparables: Russ Gibson, Ken Huckaby, Mike DiFelice

There's absolutely nothing to recommend Chavez for a major league roster over literally dozens of guys bouncing around the minors—well, almost nothing. Roy Oswalt likes throwing to him, which means he draws an MLB paycheck and pension rather than selling insurance. Not that there's anything wrong with selling insurance, other than that there's no such thing as an "Insurance Annie."

KOBY CLEMENS   **3B**   **Bats: R Throws: R**   Height: 5' 11"   Weight: 193   Born: December 4, 1986   Age: 19

YEAR	TM	LVL	AGE	PA	R	2B	3B	HR	RBI	BB	SO	SB	CS	SPEED	BA	OBP	SLG	MLVR	EQBA	EQOBP	EQSLG	EQA	VORP	DEFENSE	
2005	GRV	Rk	18	133	14	8	0	4	17	18	26	4	0	3.8	.297	.398	.477	.282	.231	.311	.345	.239	-2.6	27-3B	0
2006	HOU	MLB	19	426	48	20	3	9	45	38	80	10	3	5.0	.228	.301	.364	-.176	.231	.305	.375	.233	-1.9	101-3B	-2

Breakout: 50%   Improve: 65%   Collapse: 20%   Attrition: 11%   Comparables: Corey Smith, David Wright, Jayson Nix

For a guy written off as an irrelevant pick, Clemens played pretty well in the Appalachian League. He impressed a few scouts, drew a few walks, and showed some raw talent on defense. He's unlikely to play with his dad in the bigs unless it's part of some sort of publicity stunt, but he's certainly earned the chance to play professionally.

BROOKS CONRAD   **2B**   **Bats: B Throws: R**   Height: 5' 11"   Weight: 190   Born: January 16, 1980   Age: 26

YEAR	TM	LVL	AGE	PA	R	2B	3B	HR	RBI	BB	SO	SB	CS	SPEED	BA	OBP	SLG	MLVR	EQBA	EQOBP	EQSLG	EQA	VORP	DEFENSE	
2003	LEX	A	23	160	20	5	2	3	11	17	25	7	1	6.7	.186	.287	.314	-.150	.157	.226	.267	.185	-16.2	38-2B	2
2003	SLM	A+	23	396	50	24	3	11	61	42	60	4	2	4.8	.284	.369	.467	.227	.259	.329	.439	.263	16.4	95-2B	4
2004	ROU	AA	24	556	84	39	6	13	83	63	105	8	7	5.4	.290	.365	.477	.187	.256	.324	.417	.257	15.4	124-2B	3
2005	CCH	AA	25	94	13	6	1	2	11	16	15	8	0	6.3	.234	.372	.416	.068	.206	.327	.373	.258	0.4	21-2B	1
2005	ROU	AAA	25	478	84	22	3	21	57	52	104	12	3	6.2	.263	.347	.481	.078	.235	.310	.411	.251	6.6	107-2B	9
2006	HOU	MLB	26	461	54	24	3	12	51	44	100	7	3	4.8	.242	.318	.403	-.085	.246	.323	.416	.249	8.6	109-2B	2

Breakout: 23%   Improve: 53%   Collapse: 25%   Attrition: 22%   Comparables: Matt Kata, Billy Smith, Kurt Stillwell

One of the Astros' more annoying habits is the snail-like pace with which they promote advanced college hitters. Conrad starred at Arizona State, but he's had to spend two full seasons below Double-A. At that pace, some guys would be better off skipping affiliation and just signing with the indy leagues, because at least there they might attract attention instead of watching their careers slowly wither on the vine. Conrad's a better right-handed hitter, but between some speed and power and underrated defensive skills, he'd make a decent temp for a team in need of a second baseman. Having seen his career stagnate with this organization, he'd be lucky to get the opportunity.

MORGAN ENSBERG   **3B**   **Bats: R Throws: R**   Height: 6' 2"   Weight: 210   Born: August 26, 1975   Age: 30

YEAR	TM	LVL	AGE	PA	R	2B	3B	HR	RBI	BB	SO	SB	CS	SPEED	BA	OBP	SLG	MLVR	EQBA	EQOBP	EQSLG	EQA	VORP	DEFENSE	
2003	HOU	MLB	27	440	69	15	1	25	60	48	60	7	2	5.0	.291	.377	.530	.235	.281	.367	.517	.297	37.7	91-3B	8
2004	HOU	MLB	28	451	51	20	3	10	66	36	46	6	4	4.7	.275	.330	.411	-.005	.269	.325	.403	.252	4.8	103-3B	-11
2005	HOU	MLB	29	624	86	30	3	36	101	85	119	6	7	4.3	.283	.388	.557	.305	.281	.385	.565	.310	53.5	145-3B	8
2006	HOU	MLB	30	552	75	27	2	25	84	64	90	5	3	4.5	.276	.365	.497	.139	.281	.370	.512	.291	33.7	130-3B	1

Breakout: 14%   Improve: 51%   Collapse: 24%   Attrition: 9%   Comparables: Doug DeCinces, Scott Brosius, Ray Boone

A hand injury cost Ensberg some playing time down the stretch, as well as a bit of power. But despite severe pain and changing his grip on the bat, Ensberg still managed a .400 OBP with significant power in August and September. He finished fourth in the MVP voting and goes into the 2006 season with a healthy paw. If he can hang onto his dramatic increase in walks, there's no reason that he can't cement his place among the NL's best players. Ensberg is an underrated defender as well; he may not look as graceful as Eric Chavez or Scott Rolen, but he's not far out of their class.

ADAM EVERETT   SS   **Bats: R Throws: R**   Height: 6' 0"   Weight: 160   Born: February 5, 1977   Age: 29

YEAR	TM	LVL	AGE	PA	R	2B	3B	HR	RBI	BB	SO	SB	CS	SPEED	BA	OBP	SLG	MLVR	EQBA	EQOBP	EQSLG	EQA	VORP	DEFENSE	
2003	HOU	MLB	26	425	51	18	3	8	51	28	66	8	1	6.1	.256	.320	.380	-.095	.250	.312	.380	.245	8.1	112-SS	1
2004	HOU	MLB	27	413	66	15	2	8	31	17	56	13	2	7.2	.273	.317	.385	-.088	.268	.310	.377	.245	9.1	95-SS	7
2005	HOU	MLB	28	587	58	27	2	11	54	26	103	21	7	6.5	.248	.290	.364	-.145	.248	.290	.373	.234	2.2	146-SS	6
2006	HOU	MLB	29	500	63	23	3	9	46	28	76	14	5	5.2	.254	.304	.376	-.137	.258	.308	.388	.237	7.2	118-SS	3

Breakout: 21%   Improve: 55%   Collapse: 19%   Attrition: 16%   Comparables: Pokey Reese, Melvin Mora, Jose Pagan

Shortstop is a wasteland in the NL right now, and Everett's 2005 season was sort of a microcosm of that situation. He caught a nasty virus, collided with Charles Gipson, and fought a general malaise at the plate all year. Everett's infant daughter Peyton underwent surgery, and pretty much the whole season just went badly, from soup to nuts. It happens in baseball, too. Everett should be healthy to begin the 2006 season, and should perform pretty well versus his peer group. The BP Staff wishes Everett and his family a happy and healthy new year.

HECTOR GIMENEZ   C   **Bats: B Throws: R**   Height: 5' 10"   Weight: 180   Born: September 28, 1982   Age: 23

YEAR	TM	LVL	AGE	PA	R	2B	3B	HR	RBI	BB	SO	SB	CS	SPEED	BA	OBP	SLG	MLVR	EQBA	EQOBP	EQSLG	EQA	VORP	DEFENSE			
2003	SLM	A+	20	418	41	17	1	7	54	29	75	2	0	4.1	.247	.304	.352	-.045	.235	.283	.359	.225	-8.9	99-C	15		
2004	ROU	AA	21	356	38	16	3	6	46	18	64	2	0	4.7	.245	.284	.366	-.142	.225	.260	.337	.211	-15.1	88-C	5		
2005	CCH	AA	22	491	47	19	1	12	58	32	88	2	3	3.7	.273	.322	.399	-.013	.250	.298	.370	.233	-2.6	86-C	13	15-1B	-1
2006	HOU	MLB	23	394	37	18	2	7	40	23	81	2	1	3.9	.229	.277	.345	-.241	.232	.281	.356	.212	-7.3	94-C	5		

Breakout: 20%   Improve: 44%   Collapse: 35%   Attrition: 11%   Comparables: Todd Hundley, Kelly Ramos, Brian Luderer

Repeating the Texas League did wonders for the young backstop. He refreshed his hitting credentials and continued to display the plus defensive skills that will get him at least a backup job in the big leagues. But when the parent club's backup catcher is the caddy for one of the best pitchers on the planet and the other apparently is some kind of Faust incarnation, what can you do?

MIKE LAMB   1B/3B   **Bats: L Throws: R**   Height: 6' 1"   Weight: 190   Born: August 9, 1975   Age: 30

YEAR	TM	LVL	AGE	PA	R	2B	3B	HR	RBI	BB	SO	SB	CS	SPEED	BA	OBP	SLG	MLVR	EQBA	EQOBP	EQSLG	EQA	VORP	DEFENSE			
2003	OKL	AAA	27	321	45	19	4	9	46	42	45	1	1	4.6	.288	.383	.485	.240	.266	.353	.447	.275	18.4	65-3B	-5		
2004	HOU	MLB	28	312	38	14	3	14	58	31	63	1	1	4.9	.288	.356	.511	.191	.278	.347	.498	.285	18.4	51-3B	-4		
2005	HOU	MLB	29	349	41	13	5	12	53	22	65	1	1	5.1	.236	.284	.419	-.081	.234	.283	.424	.241	-2.9	48-1B	-4	12-3B	2
2006	HOU	MLB	30	319	37	14	3	10	41	28	60	1	1	4.8	.254	.321	.427	-.041	.258	.326	.440	.255	4.5	77-1B	-2		

Breakout: 11%   Improve: 30%   Collapse: 38%   Attrition: 28%   Comparables: Rich Reese, Pat Putnam, Mike Lum

A capable corner guy; Lamb can do a decent job at any of those four spots, but not enough to help a championship club by starting anywhere full-time. Unfortunately, with Bagwell shelved, he spent entirely too much time as a first baseman, a problem Garner compounded by batting him in the power spots—primarily fifth—where he hit .203/.234/.399. Signed to a $1.7 million contract for 2006, and likely to bounce back to somewhere between his 2004 and 2005 seasons.

JASON LANE   OF   **Bats: R Throws: L**   Height: 6' 2"   Weight: 210   Born: December 22, 1976   Age: 29

YEAR	TM	LVL	AGE	PA	R	2B	3B	HR	RBI	BB	SO	SB	CS	SPEED	BA	OBP	SLG	MLVR	EQBA	EQOBP	EQSLG	EQA	VORP	DEFENSE			
2003	NWO	AAA	26	286	37	17	0	7	39	30	26	2	1	3.8	.298	.374	.452	.235	.281	.353	.421	.271	5.5	27-RF	-2	15-CF	0
2004	HOU	MLB	27	155	21	10	2	4	19	16	33	1	0	5.9	.272	.348	.463	.096	.265	.342	.456	.275	6.4	11-LF	0	16-RF	1
2005	HOU	MLB	28	561	65	34	4	26	78	32	105	6	2	5.3	.267	.316	.499	.102	.263	.313	.501	.272	20.5	126-RF	-2		
2006	HOU	MLB	29	560	74	30	3	24	84	46	95	6	3	4.9	.274	.340	.491	.090	.279	.344	.506	.279	20.6	131-RF	-4		

Breakout: 33%   Improve: 56%   Collapse: 11%   Attrition: 9%   Comparables: Ivan Calderon, Leon Roberts, Shane Spencer

Lane finally demonstrated some of the power that the stathead community has waited for, but he's capable of more, perhaps even reaching 40 home runs at some point in the next couple of years. His plate discipline took a bit of a slide, which isn't terribly unusual in a hitter's first full season. Lane's defense in the outfield is better than publicly perceived. He commits the sin of not looking particularly graceful when tracking down flies, but covers a fair amount of ground and can play in any of the three slots without hurting the club—particularly if the mound is occupied by a bunch of hard-throwing strikeout artists.

ORLANDO PALMEIRO   **OF**   **Bats: L Throws: R**   Height: 5′ 11″   Weight: 175   Born: January 19, 1969   Age: 37

YEAR	TM	LVL	AGE	PA	R	2B	3B	HR	RBI	BB	SO	SB	CS	SPEED	BA	OBP	SLG	MLVR	EQBA	EQOBP	EQSLG	EQA	VORP	DEFENSE			
2003	SLN	MLB	34	357	37	13	1	3	33	32	31	3	3	5.2	.271	.336	.347	-.077	.272	.337	.347	.245	-3.7	35-RF	2	23-LF	0
2004	HOU	MLB	35	154	19	5	0	3	12	18	19	2	1	4.9	.241	.344	.346	-.094	.239	.338	.336	.243	-0.4				
2005	HOU	MLB	36	226	22	17	2	3	20	15	23	3	1	5.3	.284	.341	.431	.057	.282	.336	.442	.269	7.3	21-LF	-2	17-RF	1
2006	*HOU*	*MLB*	*37*	*98*	*11*	*5*	*0*	*1*	*11*	*8*	*11*	*1*	*1*	*5.4*	*.266*	*.335*	*.389*	*-.058*	*.270*	*.340*	*.401*	*.253*	*0.5*	*28-LF*	*0*		

Breakout: 22%   Improve: 37%   Collapse: 34%   Attrition: 63%   Comparables: Bud Stewart, Frank Baumholtz, Taffy Wright

Serves either as an object lesson on the fine distinctions between fourth and fifth outfielders, or as a totem for the dozens of guys in the minors with effectively the same set of skills. He'll be around for two more years after signing a new contract.

HUNTER PENCE   **OF**   **Bats: R Throws: R**   Height: 6′ 4″   Weight: 210   Born: April 13, 1983   Age: 23

YEAR	TM	LVL	AGE	PA	R	2B	3B	HR	RBI	BB	SO	SB	CS	SPEED	BA	OBP	SLG	MLVR	EQBA	EQOBP	EQSLG	EQA	VORP	DEFENSE			
2004	TCV	A-	21	225	36	18	1	8	37	23	30	3	5	4.4	.296	.369	.518	.285	.236	.296	.410	.240	-0.3	45-CF	4		
2005	LEX	A	22	341	59	14	3	25	60	38	53	8	3	5.8	.338	.413	.652	.513	.277	.339	.518	.285	25.0	42-CF	-1	27-LF	1
2005	SLM	A+	22	171	24	8	1	6	30	18	37	1	2	3.6	.305	.374	.490	.253	.282	.339	.441	.268	7.6	28-CF	0		
2006	*HOU*	*MLB*	*23*	*512*	*66*	*26*	*3*	*19*	*73*	*43*	*103*	*5*	*3*	*4.8*	*.267*	*.330*	*.459*	*.026*	*.271*	*.335*	*.473*	*.266*	*17.2*	*121-CF*	*1*		

Breakout: 26%   Improve: 52%   Collapse: 16%   Attrition: 4%   Comparables: Ty Meadows, Brian Anderson, Xavier Nady

Pence is the only real prospect in the organization, but he's got some strikes against him. First, he's had some recurring leg problems. Second, his gaudy numbers have come in the Sally League against your Aunt Ethel. Third, he reportedly has "a long swing that won't work at upper levels." All those things may be true, but all Pence has done is produce when given a shot. If he continues that trend at Double-A this year, he'll rise to the top of a lot of prospect lists. It shouldn't be hard to keep an eye on him in this system—he'll be the one guy in double digits in the home runs column.

HUMBERTO QUINTERO   **C**   **Bats: R Throws: R**   Height: 6′ 1″   Weight: 190   Born: August 2, 1979   Age: 26

YEAR	TM	LVL	AGE	PA	R	2B	3B	HR	RBI	BB	SO	SB	CS	SPEED	BA	OBP	SLG	MLVR	EQBA	EQOBP	EQSLG	EQA	VORP	DEFENSE	
2003	MOB	AA	23	417	37	26	0	3	52	19	41	0	0	3.2	.298	.343	.389	.070	.266	.303	.370	.235	0.2	106-C	18
2004	POR	AAA	24	273	36	25	0	5	30	8	18	0	0	3.6	.317	.348	.471	.110	.273	.302	.396	.240	3.1	65-C	14
2004	SDN	MLB	24	78	7	3	0	2	10	5	16	0	2	3.2	.250	.295	.375	-.110	.264	.308	.389	.234	-0.9	19-C	0
2005	ROU	AAA	25	205	23	13	0	8	31	10	30	2	1	4.2	.288	.327	.482	.067	.252	.283	.406	.237	0.3	46-C	8
2005	HOU	MLB	25	55	6	1	0	1	8	1	10	0	0	4.7	.185	.200	.259	-.486	.182	.196	.255	.163	-4.7	14-C	-2
2006	*HOU*	*MLB*	*26*	*236*	*21*	*10*	*0*	*5*	*27*	*9*	*33*	*1*	*1*	*3.9*	*.249*	*.284*	*.374*	*-.179*	*.253*	*.288*	*.385*	*.222*	*-0.5*	*59-C*	*4*

Breakout: 28%   Improve: 40%   Collapse: 40%   Attrition: 37%   Comparables: Carlos Hernandez, Johnny Pramesa, Joe Azcue

Quintero has a tremendous throwing arm and had some moderate success with the bat in the minors, though not enough to knock anyone's socks off. If he's going to have a major league career, he needs to either find the right golfing buddy, a la Raul Chavez, or get about 10% better with the bat. He's already got the defensive skills to fall into the eight-year backup catcher role somewhere if he's lucky.

LUKE SCOTT   **OF**   **Bats: L Throws: R**   Height: 6′ 0″   Weight: 210   Born: June 25, 1978   Age: 28

YEAR	TM	LVL	AGE	PA	R	2B	3B	HR	RBI	BB	SO	SB	CS	SPEED	BA	OBP	SLG	MLVR	EQBA	EQOBP	EQSLG	EQA	VORP	DEFENSE			
2003	KIN	A+	25	272	37	12	1	13	44	27	62	6	3	4.8	.278	.360	.498	.255	.238	.301	.429	.248	-3.8	18-RF	1	16-LF	0
2003	AKR	AA	25	199	21	13	1	7	37	11	37	0	1	3.4	.273	.317	.470	.067	.228	.265	.392	.224	-10.1	17-LF	1		
2004	SLM	A+	26	287	45	20	1	8	35	41	58	6	1	5.5	.278	.376	.469	.221	.219	.297	.357	.233	-13.8	39-RF	0	25-CF	0
2004	ROU	AA	26	252	45	17	0	19	62	33	43	0	2	3.1	.298	.401	.654	.488	.228	.313	.465	.263	1.1	22-RF	1	21-LF	-2
2005	ROU	AAA	27	449	69	25	4	31	87	43	96	2	2	4.7	.286	.363	.603	.308	.246	.311	.485	.265	5.3	86-LF	9	11-RF	1
2005	HOU	MLB	27	89	6	4	2	0	4	9	23	1	1	6.6	.188	.270	.287	-.310	.188	.270	.287	.201	-5.7	17-LF	-1		
2006	*HOU*	*MLB*	*28*	*391*	*45*	*19*	*2*	*15*	*52*	*33*	*99*	*2*	*1*	*4.3*	*.234*	*.305*	*.427*	*-.083*	*.237*	*.309*	*.440*	*.248*	*-0.1*	*93-LF*	*1*		

Breakout: 27%   Improve: 45%   Collapse: 25%   Attrition: 18%   Comparables: Phil Plantier, Chris Wakeland, Eric Anthony

Scott had about a month to etch himself into the memory of Tim Purpura and the rest of baseball's current executives, and he failed. Too old to be a real prospect, he's more likely to see a lot of Triple-A time over the next several years, hoping for another shot. He did hit the mascarpone out of the ball at Round Rock, and if he keeps that up, he'll earn that shot; there are dozens of veterans less deserving of million dollar contracts than Scott.

WILLY TAVERAS   CF   Bats: R Throws: R   Height: 6' 0"   Weight: 160   Born: December 25, 1981   Age: 24

YEAR	TM	LVL	AGE	PA	R	2B	3B	HR	RBI	BB	SO	SB	CS	SPEED	BA	OBP	SLG	MLVR	EQBA	EQOBP	EQSLG	EQA	VORP	DEFENSE		
2003	KIN	A+	21	462	64	9	6	2	35	52	68	57	12	8.4	.282	.381	.350	.095	.266	.348	.341	.258	2.9	104-CF	3	
2004	ROU	AA	22	458	76	13	1	2	27	38	76	55	11	7.4	.335	.402	.386	.159	.308	.365	.357	.268	13.2	88-CF	0	11-LF -1
2005	HOU	MLB	23	628	82	13	4	3	29	25	103	34	11	7.5	.291	.325	.341	-.085	.291	.326	.346	.243	4.6	142-CF	16	
2006	*HOU*	*MLB*	*24*	*580*	*80*	*18*	*5*	*3*	*41*	*37*	*92*	*34*	*9*	*6.4*	*.272*	*.325*	*.343*	*-.134*	*.276*	*.329*	*.354*	*.241*	*3.8*	*136-CF*	*6*	

Breakout: 15%   Improve: 34%   Collapse: 32%   Attrition: 3%   Comparables: Jerome Walton, Jim Wohlford, Ty Cline

A better player than most think, Taveras didn't exactly light up the scoreboard in his first full season in the majors, but his defense was astonishing, to the tune of 31 runs saved over a replacement center fielder. He showed some significant plate discipline and even a little power in the minors. If he can avoid the minor hamstring and hand injuries that hampered him at times last year, he might be able to combine all the skills he's shown and have a reasonably valuable career.

JOSE VIZCAINO   INF   Bats: B Throws: R   Height: 6' 1"   Weight: 180   Born: March 26, 1968   Age: 38

YEAR	TM	LVL	AGE	PA	R	2B	3B	HR	RBI	BB	SO	SB	CS	SPEED	BA	OBP	SLG	MLVR	EQBA	EQOBP	EQSLG	EQA	VORP	DEFENSE			
2003	HOU	MLB	35	199	14	7	3	3	26	8	22	0	1	4.5	.249	.281	.365	-.186	.242	.275	.358	.219	-2.5	19-SS -1		14-2B 0	
2004	HOU	MLB	36	380	34	21	3	3	33	20	39	1	1	4.6	.274	.311	.374	-.094	.267	.304	.368	.234	3.2	51-SS 3		20-2B 2	
2005	HOU	MLB	37	204	15	10	2	1	23	15	40	2	0	5.5	.246	.299	.337	-.161	.246	.302	.337	.230	-2.1	12-2B 1		11-SS 0	
2006	*SFN*	*MLB*	*38*	*108*	*10*	*6*	*1*	*1*	*11*	*7*	*19*	*1*	*1*	*5.3*	*.257*	*.304*	*.358*	*-.160*	*.258*	*.307*	*.374*	*.229*	*0.5*	*30-SS 0*			

Breakout: 29%   Improve: 41%   Collapse: 32%   Attrition: 54%   Comparables: Dave Philley, Red Schoendienst, Devon White

A few years ago, Vizcaino's defense and borderline-acceptable offense made him at least a defensible choice for a roster spot, and perhaps 350–500 PAs for a club without a long-term solution in the middle infield. In 2005, his defense visibly slipped, to the point where he's indistinguishable from a Jeff Kent-caliber glove, and his offense, never his strong point, was more theoretical than actual. Being of A Certain Age [tm], he's signed with the San Francisco Giants, where he'll have an opportunity to participate in many of that club's 71 wins, provided Barry Bonds is healthy.

TOM WHITEMAN   SS   Bats: R Throws: R   Height: 6' 3"   Weight: 180   Born: July 14, 1979   Age: 26

YEAR	TM	LVL	AGE	PA	R	2B	3B	HR	RBI	BB	SO	SB	CS	SPEED	BA	OBP	SLG	MLVR	EQBA	EQOBP	EQSLG	EQA	VORP	DEFENSE			
2003	ROU	AA	23	577	65	18	2	13	70	35	102	3	8	3.3	.261	.310	.376	-.047	.241	.287	.360	.224	-5.0	98-SS -12		33-3B 2	
2004	ROU	AA	24	302	39	14	0	8	45	20	45	5	3	4.0	.336	.381	.473	.251	.293	.333	.410	.258	13.8	68-SS 8			
2004	NWO	AAA	24	107	11	6	0	0	9	8	21	2	2	4.2	.276	.336	.337	-.116	.259	.315	.300	.221	-1.4	24-SS -3			
2005	CCH	AA	25	171	13	9	0	1	15	18	40	3	4	3.9	.250	.333	.329	-.103	.210	.285	.269	.201	-8.6	21-SS 1		19-3B 1	
2005	ROU	AAA	25	268	23	5	0	5	27	27	69	0	0	3.2	.203	.284	.287	-.369	.181	.251	.245	.186	-20.9	66-SS -1			
2006	*HOU*	*MLB*	*26*	*273*	*25*	*9*	*1*	*4*	*24*	*18*	*64*	*1*	*1*	*3.8*	*.229*	*.284*	*.326*	*-.254*	*.233*	*.288*	*.336*	*.208*	*-4.0*	*67-SS -1*			

Breakout: 27%   Improve: 47%   Collapse: 33%   Attrition: 33%   Comparables: Brandon Jackson, Eddie Leon, Kent Anderson

Sometimes, timing can kill. Whiteman is a fringe prospect whose momentum was stalled by a broken thumb in July of 2004. His hitting stroke still hasn't recovered, and his star, which was never blazing to begin with, has all but fallen. He'll need to hit early and often this year to have any shot at a career. In an organization with more talent than Houston, he'd be done.

PITCHERS

EZEQUIEL ASTACIO   Bats: R Throws: R   Height: 6' 3"   Weight: 150   Born: November 4, 1979   Age: 26

YEAR	TM	LVL	AGE	W	L	SV	G	GS	IP	H	BB	SO	HR	GB%	BABIP	STUFF	WHIP	ERA	PERA	EQERA	EQH9	EQBB9	EQSO9	EQHR9	VORP	WXRL
2003	CLR	A+	23	15	5	0	25	22	147.7	140	29	83	9	—	.267	-22	1.14	3.29	5.95	5.88	10.5	2.2	3.5	1.8	-4.3	—
2004	ROU	AA	24	13	10	0	28	28	176.0	155	56	185	12	—	.307	6	1.20	3.89	4.79	5.92	9.0	3.5	6.4	1.1	-5.9	—
2005	ROU	AAA	25	4	4	1	13	12	65.7	53	12	57	6	42%	.264	11	0.99	3.01	4.35	4.35	8.7	1.7	5.8	1.0	8.6	—
2005	HOU	MLB	25	3	6	0	22	14	81.0	100	25	66	23	38%	.317	-24	1.54	5.67	6.20	6.31	11.0	2.5	6.6	2.5	-5.7	0.4
2006	*HOU*	*MLB*	*26*	*6*	*7*	*1*	*33*	*16*	*108.3*	*111*	*32*	*75*	*16*	*43%*	*.284*	*2*	*1.32*	*4.49*	*4.78*	*5.12*	*9.2*	*2.5*	*5.7*	*1.3*	*9.1*	*1.4*

Breakout: 39%   Improve: 75%   Collapse: 6%   Attrition: 10%   Comparables: Jose Melendez, Mariano Rivera, Scott Lewis

The structure of MLB is rough on swingmen. Astacio came over in a deal for one of the best closers ever, and his role is to fill in for studs when they get hurt. "Zeke—Roger Clemens can't go. Warm up, babe." Astacio has a reputation for having a rubber arm. He'll need it, because he'll be battling for a roster spot for most of his career.

BRANDON BACKE   Bats: R   Throws: R   Height: 6′ 0″   Weight: 180   Born: April 5, 1978   Age: 28

YEAR	TM	LVL	AGE	W	L	SV	G	GS	IP	H	BB	SO	HR	GB%	BABIP	STUFF	WHIP	ERA	PERA	EQERA	EQH9	EQBB9	EQSO9	EQHR9	VORP	WXRL
2003	TBA	MLB	25	1	1	0	28	0	44.7	40	25	36	6	39%	.283	-5	1.46	5.44	5.11	5.32	8.6	5.1	7.2	1.2	2.2	0.9
2004	NWO	AAA	26	6	5	0	19	9	64.3	57	26	74	7	—	.309	4	1.29	2.80	4.82	4.52	8.8	4.2	7.6	1.3	7.4	—
2004	HOU	MLB	26	5	3	0	33	9	67.0	75	27	54	10	43%	.333	-2	1.52	4.30	4.76	4.24	9.5	3.3	6.4	1.2	9.6	1.6
2005	HOU	MLB	27	10	8	0	26	25	149.3	151	67	97	19	42%	.288	-1	1.46	4.76	5.05	5.11	9.5	3.8	5.4	1.2	10.4	2.6
2006	*HOU*	*MLB*	*28*	*7*	*8*	*0*	*32*	*19*	*123.7*	*124*	*52*	*86*	*17*	*43%*	*.280*	*0*	*1.42*	*4.64*	*5.03*	*5.24*	*9.0*	*3.5*	*5.7*	*1.2*	*7.4*	*1.5*

Breakout: 15%   *Improve: 44%*   *Collapse: 22%*   *Attrition: 5%*   *Comparables: Diego Segui, Steve Blass, Bobby Castillo*

Pretty much a vanilla #5 starter, Backe's missing a great pitch and has a pretty generic repertoire. No one expects him to develop into anything more than Kyle Lohse, but with a bat comparable to Brad Ausmus. Think we jest? Backe's a career .246/.303/.393 hitter with an ERA a shade under 5.00. Ausmus is a .255/.332/.353 hitter, and he doesn't even pitch.

JIMMY BARTHMAIER   Bats: R   Throws: R   Height: 6′ 4″   Weight: 210   Born: January 6, 1984   Age: 22

YEAR	TM	LVL	AGE	W	L	SV	G	GS	IP	H	BB	SO	HR	GB%	BABIP	STUFF	WHIP	ERA	PERA	EQERA	EQH9	EQBB9	EQSO9	EQHR9	VORP	WXRL
2004	GRV	Rk	20	4	3	0	13	13	69.0	70	22	65	3	—	.322	-9	1.33	3.78	5.43	7.38	10.4	4.3	3.8	1.0	-12.8	—
2005	LEX	A	21	11	6	0	25	25	134.7	108	55	142	3	57%	.304	21	1.21	2.27	4.32	4.54	8.5	4.7	5.9	0.4	15.0	—
2006	*HOU*	*MLB*	*22*	*7*	*9*	*0*	*25*	*23*	*133.7*	*136*	*73*	*90*	*13*	*54%*	*.294*	*4*	*1.56*	*5.08*	*5.29*	*5.68*	*9.1*	*4.6*	*5.5*	*0.9*	*-0.9*	*0.9*

Breakout: 10%   *Improve: 38%*   *Collapse: 15%*   *Attrition: 0%*   *Comparables: Preston Larrison, Landon Jacobsen, Josh Teekel*

Barthmaier throws hard, reaching 94–95 flat out, and supplements the gas with a nasty curveball. The problem: he can't throw the hook for strikes. A high school draftee, he is extremely athletic, but has a lot to learn. Two years from now, he could be anywhere from a washout, a stud prospect, a longshot with a puncher's chance, or a converted outfielder.

TAYLOR BUCHHOLZ   Bats: R   Throws: R   Height: 6′ 4″   Weight: 220   Born: October 13, 1981   Age: 24

YEAR	TM	LVL	AGE	W	L	SV	G	GS	IP	H	BB	SO	HR	GB%	BABIP	STUFF	WHIP	ERA	PERA	EQERA	EQH9	EQBB9	EQSO9	EQHR9	VORP	WXRL
2003	REA	AA	21	9	11	0	25	24	144.7	136	33	114	14	—	.276	2	1.17	3.55	5.14	4.55	9.5	2.3	5.7	1.6	16.1	—
2004	NWO	AAA	22	6	7	0	20	17	98.0	107	29	74	16	—	.294	-11	1.39	5.23	5.51	5.70	10.0	2.9	5.3	1.7	-1.1	—
2005	ROU	AAA	23	6	0	0	20	14	76.7	79	27	45	14	48%	.285	-27	1.38	4.81	6.35	5.38	10.3	3.3	4.0	2.0	1.8	—
2006	*HOU*	*MLB*	*24*	*4*	*6*	*0*	*26*	*12*	*84.3*	*92*	*31*	*50*	*14*	*46%*	*.286*	*-7*	*1.45*	*5.24*	*5.62*	*5.77*	*9.8*	*3.1*	*4.8*	*1.5*	*-1.2*	*0.3*

Breakout: 8%   *Improve: 38%*   *Collapse: 28%*   *Attrition: 2%*   *Comparables: Bryan Bullington, Ryan Baerlocher, Luis De los santos*

Now that Brandon Duckworth is a bad memory and Astacio has "made it," the Astros have to hope that Buchholz does something extra to help salvage the Wagner deal with the Phillies. He might not be up to it: he's had his elbow cut, and after a hot start, recurring shoulder woes shut him down for two months. He came back at season's end and pitched well in the AFL.

MIKE BURNS   Bats: R   Throws: R   Height: 6′ 1″   Weight: 190   Born: July 14, 1978   Age: 27

YEAR	TM	LVL	AGE	W	L	SV	G	GS	IP	H	BB	SO	HR	GB%	BABIP	STUFF	WHIP	ERA	PERA	EQERA	EQH9	EQBB9	EQSO9	EQHR9	VORP	WXRL
2003	ROU	AA	24	2	13	0	38	14	105.7	129	30	89	15	—	.333	-49	1.50	6.13	6.93	7.19	11.4	3.2	5.3	2.6	-18.1	—
2004	ROU	AA	25	11	3	9	56	0	80.7	63	15	94	1	—	.304	20	0.97	1.67	3.14	3.84	7.9	2.1	6.9	0.2	15.1	—
2005	ROU	AAA	26	2	1	13	25	0	30.0	22	4	34	4	43%	.250	9	0.87	2.10	4.13	3.18	8.3	1.3	7.6	1.6	7.6	—
2005	HOU	MLB	26	0	0	0	27	0	31.0	29	8	20	6	50%	.240	-12	1.19	4.94	5.70	5.40	9.9	2.1	5.4	1.8	1.0	0.5
2006	*CIN*	*MLB*	*27*	*2*	*3*	*3*	*47*	*1*	*49.3*	*49*	*14*	*35*	*7*	*43%*	*.278*	*-2*	*1.27*	*4.20*	*4.45*	*4.78*	*8.9*	*2.3*	*5.9*	*1.3*	*5.2*	*0.5*

Breakout: 48%   *Improve: 71%*   *Collapse: 17%*   *Attrition: 39%*   *Comparables: Ron Taylor, Dave Tobik, Mike Trombley*

An organizational soldier called up to pitch in a pinch during the summer, Mr. Burns didn't embarrass himself, although he couldn't handle the short left-field porch in Your Fruity Beverage Company's Name Here Ballpark. The Reds picked him up off of waivers, and although the environment isn't any more friendly, he'll get every opportunity to make the team in a ROOGY role.

ROGER CLEMENS   Bats: R Throws: R   Height: 6' 4" Weight: 230 Born: August 4, 1962   Age: 43

YEAR	TM	LVL	AGE	W	L	SV	G	GS	IP	H	BB	SO	HR	GB%	BABIP	STUFF	WHIP	ERA	PERA	EQERA	EQH9	EQBB9	EQSO9	EQHR9	VORP	WXRL
2003	NYA	MLB	40	17	9	0	33	33	211.7	199	58	190	24	47%	.296	27	1.21	3.91	3.80	4.01	8.1	2.4	7.8	1.0	41.6	5.8
2004	HOU	MLB	41	18	4	0	33	33	214.3	169	79	218	15	52%	.283	38	1.16	2.98	3.48	3.18	7.4	3.1	8.2	0.6	61.1	7.5
2005	HOU	MLB	42	13	8	0	32	32	211.3	151	62	185	11	50%	.248	39	1.01	1.87	3.34	2.41	7.3	2.5	7.4	0.5	80.2	9.4
2006	*HOU*	*MLB*	*43*	*11*	*7*	*0*	*31*	*24*	*161.3*	*137*	*53*	*144*	*13*	*48%*	*.275*	*19*	*1.17*	*3.04*	*3.39*	*3.25*	*7.6*	*2.7*	*7.3*	*0.7*	*39.0*	*5.0*

Breakout: 11% Improve: 31% Collapse: 28% Attrition: 11%   Comparables: Nolan Ryan, Phil Niekro, Gaylord Perry

The only question left about Clemens is whether or not he's the best pitcher ever to walk the planet. The Astros faced some strategic constraints that resulted from having Clemens as part of the club—do you commit the money you would have paid him while he Hamlets about all winter? What if we don't spend the money and he retires?—and they decided that living without him allowed them to live in a more orderly universe. Clemens is in something of a unique position. It's pretty rare that there's a guy floating around in the free agency ether who's a legitimate #1 starter. Considering that he's got hardware and accomplished most everything a player can accomplish, one can certainly understand Roger's desire to stay home. But a player of his caliber can be the difference between contender and champion, and World Series rings have a certain compulsive magic about them.

MIKE GALLO   Bats: L Throws: L   Height: 6' 0" Weight: 175 Born: April 2, 1977   Age: 29

YEAR	TM	LVL	AGE	W	L	SV	G	GS	IP	H	BB	SO	HR	GB%	BABIP	STUFF	WHIP	ERA	PERA	EQERA	EQH9	EQBB9	EQSO9	EQHR9	VORP	WXRL
2003	HOU	MLB	26	1	0	0	32	0	30.0	28	10	16	3	46%	.291	-10	1.27	3.00	4.60	3.38	9.2	2.8	4.3	0.9	8.8	0.7
2004	HOU	MLB	27	2	0	0	69	0	49.3	55	20	34	12	52%	.291	-22	1.52	4.75	6.20	4.74	10.2	3.3	5.5	2.0	4.2	0.0
2005	ROU	AAA	28	4	2	0	37	1	54.3	56	20	33	2	59%	.314	-16	1.40	3.65	4.58	6.11	9.5	3.7	3.7	0.5	-3.0	—
2005	HOU	MLB	28	0	1	0	36	0	20.3	18	10	12	1	48%	.288	-9	1.38	2.66	4.50	2.70	9.0	4.1	4.9	0.4	6.4	0.1
2006	*HOU*	*MLB*	*29*	*2*	*2*	*1*	*51*	*0*	*40.3*	*43*	*17*	*23*	*6*	*49%*	*.286*	*-16*	*1.48*	*4.54*	*5.23*	*5.13*	*9.7*	*3.5*	*4.6*	*1.2*	*2.5*	*0.2*

Breakout: 14% Improve: 28% Collapse: 41% Attrition: 27%   Comparables: Felix Heredia, Tom Burgmeier, Rich Rodriguez

Lefty specialist, part of the grand conspiracy to make baseball unwatchable by increasing the number of pitching changes and by throwing as many pitches down and away as there are stars in the sky, praying the umpire will get bored and start calling them strikes. He was so unimpressive in spring training that the Astros started the year without a lefty in the pen, calling him up after giving up on knuckleballer Jared Fernandez. Gallo could very well turn into an effective LOOGY, but so could 4,328 other lefties.

JASON HIRSH   Bats: R Throws: R   Height: 6' 8" Weight: 250 Born: February 20, 1982   Age: 24

YEAR	TM	LVL	AGE	W	L	SV	G	GS	IP	H	BB	SO	HR	GB%	BABIP	STUFF	WHIP	ERA	PERA	EQERA	EQH9	EQBB9	EQSO9	EQHR9	VORP	WXRL
2004	SLM	A+	22	11	7	0	26	23	130.3	128	57	96	8	—	.305	-13	1.42	4.01	5.73	6.10	9.6	4.9	4.5	1.2	-6.9	—
2005	CCH	AA	23	13	8	0	29	29	172.3	137	42	165	12	45%	.277	16	1.04	2.87	4.42	4.42	8.8	2.9	6.5	1.0	21.1	—
2006	*HOU*	*MLB*	*24*	*8*	*9*	*0*	*28*	*23*	*140.0*	*139*	*58*	*99*	*17*	*46%*	*.284*	*7*	*1.40*	*4.64*	*4.92*	*5.06*	*8.9*	*3.4*	*5.8*	*1.1*	*7.6*	*1.7*

Breakout: 20% Improve: 49% Collapse: 11% Attrition: 0%   Comparables: John Sneed, Matt Bruback, Aaron Harang

A 2nd round pick in 2003, Hirsh's weak strikeout and walk rates in 2004 were good enough to knock him way down on most prospect lists. Then he dominated the Texas League, which in this system makes him one of the few living, breathing prospects. A tall righty who works the angles, Hirsh doesn't have overwhelming velocity. His command is solid for his size and experience, and scouts like his makeup. In a system this bereft of minor league talent, Hirsh is worth watching.

BRAD LIDGE   Bats: R Throws: R   Height: 6' 5" Weight: 200 Born: December 23, 1976   Age: 29

YEAR	TM	LVL	AGE	W	L	SV	G	GS	IP	H	BB	SO	HR	GB%	BABIP	STUFF	WHIP	ERA	PERA	EQERA	EQH9	EQBB9	EQSO9	EQHR9	VORP	WXRL
2003	HOU	MLB	26	6	3	1	78	0	85.0	60	42	97	6	40%	.278	23	1.20	3.60	3.67	3.78	7.2	4.1	9.4	0.6	17.8	3.7
2004	HOU	MLB	27	6	5	29	80	0	94.7	57	30	157	8	38%	.301	56	0.92	1.90	2.40	2.11	6.0	2.6	13.3	0.7	38.8	8.1
2005	HOU	MLB	28	4	4	42	70	0	70.7	58	23	103	5	48%	.349	45	1.15	2.29	2.66	2.79	7.4	2.7	11.9	0.6	22.1	4.6
2006	*HOU*	*MLB*	*29*	*5*	*5*	*39*	*62*	*0*	*69.0*	*49*	*26*	*92*	*6*	*41%*	*.279*	*33*	*1.08*	*2.48*	*2.80*	*2.83*	*6.4*	*3.1*	*11.0*	*0.8*	*20.0*	*3.4*

Breakout: 37% Improve: 65% Collapse: 25% Attrition: 10%   Comparables: Bryan Harvey, Tom Henke, John Wetteland

Lidge is being pilloried for his postseason failures more than he should be because Albert Pujols is just that good. He has tremendous power and control, a healthy shoulder, a slider that righties lose sleep over, and there's no team in baseball that wouldn't love to have him. Don't believe the backlash: Lidge is a complete and utter badass and could put up numbers in 2006 that would make Goose Gossage proud.

FERNANDO NIEVE   Bats: R   Throws: R   Height: 6' 0"   Weight: 195   Born: July 15, 1982   Age: 23

YEAR	TM	LVL	AGE	W	L	SV	G	GS	IP	H	BB	SO	HR	GB%	BABIP	STUFF	WHIP	ERA	PERA	EQERA	EQH9	EQBB9	EQSO9	EQHR9	VORP	WXRL
2003	LEX	A	20	14	9	0	28	28	150.3	133	65	144	10	—	.286	-8	1.32	3.65	5.83	5.89	10.0	4.8	5.4	1.6	-4.5	—
2004	SLM	A+	21	10	6	0	24	24	149.0	136	40	117	9	—	.286	5	1.18	2.96	4.87	4.68	9.0	3.0	4.9	1.1	14.5	—
2005	CCH	AA	22	4	3	0	14	14	85.0	62	29	96	7	42%	.276	21	1.07	2.65	4.56	3.87	8.2	3.9	7.9	1.1	15.2	—
2005	ROU	AAA	22	4	4	0	13	13	82.0	92	33	75	10	42%	.339	6	1.52	4.83	4.96	5.29	10.1	3.5	6.2	1.2	2.8	—
2006	*HOU*	*MLB*	*23*	*8*	*9*	*0*	*28*	*23*	*139.3*	*138*	*59*	*104*	*20*	*42%*	*.282*	*8*	*1.41*	*4.64*	*5.09*	*5.05*	*8.9*	*3.5*	*6.1*	*1.3*	*8.6*	*1.8*

Breakout: 12%   Improve: 43%   Collapse: 16%   Attrition: 0%   Comparables: Mike Meyers, Dennis Tankersley, Ian Snell

One of the few things the Astros can point to with pride as far as their player development program is their comprehensive scouting of Venezuela. For that, credit Andres Reiner. Nieve is the current star pupil, a hurler with mid-90s velocity and a good slider. He needs to work on his other stuff and acquire the moxie to mix speeds if he's going to stay in the rotation. If he can't, there's room in the pen for him to become a Dotel-like setup man.

ROY OSWALT   Bats: R   Throws: R   Height: 6' 0"   Weight: 175   Born: August 29, 1977   Age: 28

YEAR	TM	LVL	AGE	W	L	SV	G	GS	IP	H	BB	SO	HR	GB%	BABIP	STUFF	WHIP	ERA	PERA	EQERA	EQH9	EQBB9	EQSO9	EQHR9	VORP	WXRL
2003	HOU	MLB	25	10	5	0	21	21	127.3	116	29	108	15	50%	.289	23	1.14	2.97	3.89	3.53	8.8	1.9	7.0	1.0	33.3	4.3
2004	HOU	MLB	26	20	10	0	36	35	237.0	233	62	206	17	48%	.321	32	1.24	3.49	3.55	3.71	8.6	2.1	6.9	0.6	51.1	6.2
2005	HOU	MLB	27	20	12	0	35	35	241.7	243	48	184	18	51%	.310	28	1.20	2.94	3.59	3.44	9.1	1.7	6.3	0.7	65.1	7.7
2006	*HOU*	*MLB*	*28*	*15*	*9*	*0*	*32*	*32*	*214.7*	*206*	*46*	*161*	*21*	*48%*	*.286*	*20*	*1.18*	*3.32*	*3.70*	*3.65*	*8.6*	*1.8*	*6.2*	*0.9*	*44.7*	*6.2*

Breakout: 12%   Improve: 47%   Collapse: 15%   Attrition: 4%   Comparables: Steve Rogers, Mike Mussina, Larry Jackson

Great control, an above average strikeout rate, a slow curve that makes hitters wish they were facing Johan Santana, and he's tough to steal on? That adds up to one of the game's best, but on the 2005 Astros, that makes you a #3 starter. Oswalt has some headroom to improve, specifically in his ability to induce groundballs, and there's some reason to expect him to have a better 2006; he allowed a high number of hits in 2005 relative to his career line, so don't be shocked if he devours the league in 2006. A few things break his way, and he's vintage Pedro.

TROY PATTON   Bats: B   Throws: L   Height: 6' 1"   Weight: 185   Born: September 3, 1985   Age: 20

YEAR	TM	LVL	AGE	W	L	SV	G	GS	IP	H	BB	SO	HR	GB%	BABIP	STUFF	WHIP	ERA	PERA	EQERA	EQH9	EQBB9	EQSO9	EQHR9	VORP	WXRL
2004	GRV	Rk	18	2	2	0	6	6	28.0	23	5	32	1	—	.293	15	1.00	1.93	4.10	5.47	9.2	2.4	4.8	0.7	0.4	—
2005	LEX	A	19	5	2	0	15	15	78.7	59	20	94	3	55%	.306	34	1.00	1.94	3.74	4.22	8.3	2.8	6.9	0.6	11.5	—
2005	SLM	A+	19	1	4	0	10	9	41.0	34	8	38	2	44%	.291	20	1.02	2.63	3.89	3.89	8.7	1.8	5.5	0.7	7.5	—
2006	*HOU*	*MLB*	*20*	*8*	*8*	*0*	*28*	*22*	*140.3*	*133*	*48*	*103*	*17*	*47%*	*.276*	*14*	*1.28*	*4.04*	*4.31*	*4.47*	*8.5*	*2.8*	*6.0*	*1.1*	*17.3*	*2.7*

Breakout: 14%   Improve: 42%   Collapse: 20%   Attrition: 1%   Comparables: Clayton Andrews, Andy Pratt, Derrick Van Dusen

A lefty flying into the injury nexus with slight shoulder soreness, Patton possesses a plus fastball and a curve he's learning to throw for strikes. He might be the best prospect in the organization, depending on what you think of Hunter Pence, and whether you're a fan of damning folks with faint praise. He dominated in low A-ball, but not enough to evoke bells and whistles. If he strikes out 9-plus per inning this season, fanfare will then be appropriate.

ANDY PETTITTE   Bats: L   Throws: L   Height: 6' 5"   Weight: 220   Born: June 15, 1972   Age: 34

YEAR	TM	LVL	AGE	W	L	SV	G	GS	IP	H	BB	SO	HR	GB%	BABIP	STUFF	WHIP	ERA	PERA	EQERA	EQH9	EQBB9	EQSO9	EQHR9	VORP	WXRL
2003	NYA	MLB	31	21	8	0	33	33	208.3	227	50	180	21	55%	.325	28	1.33	4.02	3.62	4.38	8.8	2.1	7.4	0.8	29.3	4.6
2004	HOU	MLB	32	6	4	0	15	15	83.0	71	31	79	8	56%	.278	25	1.23	3.90	3.70	3.92	7.8	3.0	7.6	0.8	16.0	2.1
2005	HOU	MLB	33	17	9	0	33	33	222.3	188	41	171	17	51%	.272	29	1.03	2.39	3.53	2.94	8.3	1.6	6.5	0.7	72.1	8.5
2006	*HOU*	*MLB*	*34*	*13*	*9*	*0*	*30*	*30*	*197.0*	*183*	*51*	*156*	*19*	*51%*	*.283*	*19*	*1.18*	*3.43*	*3.69*	*3.82*	*8.3*	*2.1*	*6.5*	*0.9*	*38.0*	*5.4*

Breakout: 7%   Improve: 28%   Collapse: 18%   Attrition: 5%   Comparables: Bruce Hurst, Chuck Finley, Jerry Reuss

Maybe there's something to this "learn to pitch from Roger Clemens" thing. Pettitte was moderately overrated as a Yankee, the beneficiary of huge sums of money spent on offensive and bullpen stars, and the nation's continuing, exasperating infatuation with Pitcher Wins. In his first full season with the Astros, Pettitte was everything they could have hoped for, throwing 200 plus innings with an ERA south of 2.50. He struck people out, froze potential basestealers, had the lowest walk rate of his career, and kept the infielders on their toes with a steady diet of groundballs. He's likely to give back a little of the improvement, but 33 starts with an ERA near 3.00 would make the Astros pretty happy.

CHAD QUALLS   **Bats: R Throws: R**   Height: 6' 5"   Weight: 220   Born: August 17, 1978   Age: 27

YEAR	TM	LVL	AGE	W	L	SV	G	GS	IP	H	BB	SO	HR	GB%	BABIP	STUFF	WHIP	ERA	PERA	EQERA	EQH9	EQBB9	EQSO9	EQHR9	VORP	WXRL
2003	ROU	AA	24	8	11	0	28	28	175.3	174	61	132	12	—	.291	-7	1.34	3.85	5.55	5.12	9.4	3.9	4.7	1.3	9.0	—
2004	NWO	AAA	25	3	6	1	32	14	106.7	134	30	72	8	—	.348	-5	1.54	5.57	4.71	6.22	10.6	2.9	4.4	0.8	-7.4	—
2004	HOU	MLB	25	4	0	1	25	0	33.0	34	8	24	3	58%	.307	3	1.27	3.55	4.09	3.55	9.3	1.9	5.7	0.8	7.8	1.4
2005	HOU	MLB	26	6	4	0	77	0	79.7	73	23	60	7	60%	.292	5	1.21	3.27	4.02	3.91	8.8	2.4	6.3	0.8	15.5	1.9
2006	*HOU*	*MLB*	*27*	*3*	*3*	*2*	*60*	*0*	*64.7*	*64*	*24*	*43*	*6*	*56%*	*.290*	*-4*	*1.36*	*3.81*	*4.26*	*4.68*	*8.9*	*3.1*	*5.5*	*0.8*	*8.7*	*0.7*

Breakout: 28%   Improve: 62%   Collapse: 18%   Attrition: 18%   Comparables: Barry Jones, Steve Crawford, Jim Winn

One of the class of pitchers that throws approximately one pitch—something that sinks—at three different velocities. This, in turn, causes hitters to beat the ball into the turf for dozens of 6-3 putouts, even after repeating to themselves the mantra "Make this bastard bring the ball up" 40 times during the walk from the on-deck circle to the batters' box. Qualls throws hard enough that even the occasional mistake isn't a complete cookie. He's likely to have a solid career as a setup guy, with the occasional year where three or four extra balls leave the yard when he throws a spinner.

WANDY RODRIGUEZ   **Bats: B Throws: L**   Height: 5' 11" Weight: 160   Born: January 18, 1979   Age: 27

YEAR	TM	LVL	AGE	W	L	SV	G	GS	IP	H	BB	SO	HR	GB%	BABIP	STUFF	WHIP	ERA	PERA	EQERA	EQH9	EQBB9	EQSO9	EQHR9	VORP	WXRL
2003	SLM	A+	24	8	7	0	20	20	111.0	102	41	72	9	—	.263	-33	1.29	3.49	6.68	5.98	10.2	4.2	4.0	1.9	-4.3	—
2004	ROU	AA	25	11	6	0	26	25	142.7	159	57	115	15	—	.326	-26	1.51	4.48	6.34	6.40	10.8	4.6	4.8	1.8	-12.1	—
2005	ROU	AAA	26	4	2	0	8	8	46.3	43	16	48	7	41%	.300	4	1.27	3.69	5.73	4.70	9.6	3.5	6.8	1.8	4.4	—
2005	HOU	MLB	26	10	10	0	25	22	128.7	135	53	80	19	46%	.294	-9	1.46	5.52	5.36	5.85	9.9	3.5	5.1	1.3	-1.8	1.3
2006	*HOU*	*MLB*	*27*	*5*	*7*	*0*	*31*	*16*	*99.3*	*110*	*43*	*64*	*16*	*45%*	*.297*	*-8*	*1.53*	*5.41*	*5.81*	*6.87*	*9.9*	*3.6*	*5.3*	*1.4*	*-3.0*	*0.2*

Breakout: 24%   Improve: 50%   Collapse: 24%   Attrition: 19%   Comparables: Mike Kekich, Brandon Backe, Barry Moore

He wasn't ready to be pushed into the starting rotation, so while he had a couple of decent runs during the season, Rodriguez got whacked around for most of the year. He lacks the stuff to get by without nibbling, and doesn't really miss enough bats. He's left-handed, though, which means he'll have several years to figure out how to pitch. Rodriguez could end up either as a journeyman starter waiting to have the one Willie Blair year that gets you set for life, or he could try to pass as John Franco by buying a latex mask.

RUSS SPRINGER   **Bats: R Throws: R**   Height: 6' 4"   Weight: 215   Born: November 7, 1968   Age: 37

YEAR	TM	LVL	AGE	W	L	SV	G	GS	IP	H	BB	SO	HR	GB%	BABIP	STUFF	WHIP	ERA	PERA	EQERA	EQH9	EQBB9	EQSO9	EQHR9	VORP	WXRL
2004	NWO	AAA	35	1	2	0	6	26	31.0	31	14	33	3	—	.337	-18	1.45	3.48	5.59	5.59	9.9	5.6	6.2	1.2	0.0	—
2004	HOU	MLB	35	0	1	0	16	0	13.7	15	6	9	1	31%	.318	-5	1.54	2.63	4.50	2.57	9.6	3.2	5.1	0.6	4.6	0.1
2005	HOU	MLB	36	4	4	0	62	0	59.0	49	21	54	9	40%	.253	0	1.19	4.73	4.68	5.31	8.4	3.1	7.6	1.4	1.9	0.8
2006	*HOU*	*MLB*	*37*	*2*	*2*	*1*	*39*	*1*	*45.0*	*46*	*17*	*34*	*8*	*38%*	*.284*	*-8*	*1.40*	*4.72*	*5.20*	*5.41*	*9.2*	*3.1*	*6.3*	*1.5*	*2.2*	*0.2*

Breakout: 38%   Improve: 56%   Collapse: 21%   Attrition: 33%   Comparables: Cal Eldred, Aurelio Lopez, Doug Henry

Maddening. There are those rare days—now likely past—where he looks flat out unhittable, but his tendency to suddenly perform field research on the viability of the thigh-high batting practice fastball as a planetary escape vehicle leaves him with stat lines containing numbers like "9" under HR. That's okay if you're a starter and it's late in the season, but when you're throwing 60 innings for the year, not so much. Not many pitchers get to have a 13-year career with an ERA north of 5.00. He's signed on for another year; must be a heck of a guy to have around the clubhouse.

DAN WHEELER   **Bats: R Throws: R**   Height: 6' 3"   Weight: 220   Born: December 10, 1977   Age: 28

YEAR	TM	LVL	AGE	W	L	SV	G	GS	IP	H	BB	SO	HR	GB%	BABIP	STUFF	WHIP	ERA	PERA	EQERA	EQH9	EQBB9	EQSO9	EQHR9	VORP	WXRL
2003	NYN	MLB	25	1	3	2	35	0	51.0	49	17	35	6	48%	.281	-4	1.29	3.71	4.62	4.09	8.9	2.7	5.5	1.1	8.8	-0.1
2004	NYN	MLB	26	3	1	0	32	1	50.7	65	17	46	9	40%	.357	0	1.62	4.79	4.50	5.02	10.6	2.6	7.1	1.4	3.2	0.2
2004	HOU	MLB	26	0	0	0	14	0	14.3	11	3	9	1	49%	.244	1	0.98	2.52	3.86	2.57	7.7	1.9	5.1	0.6	5.1	0.3
2005	HOU	MLB	27	2	3	3	71	0	73.3	53	19	69	7	37%	.250	18	0.98	2.21	3.68	2.41	7.6	2.3	8.0	0.9	26.7	3.4
2006	*HOU*	*MLB*	*28*	*4*	*3*	*4*	*59*	*1*	*68.7*	*64*	*22*	*60*	*8*	*40%*	*.284*	*7*	*1.25*	*3.70*	*4.05*	*4.38*	*8.4*	*2.7*	*7.2*	*1.1*	*11.6*	*1.0*

Breakout: 20%   Improve: 34%   Collapse: 43%   Attrition: 14%   Comparables: Scott Sullivan, Todd Worrell, Bobby Howry

Shaking the home run bug made Wheeler an outstanding setup man. However, there's nothing in his statistical record that predicted the dramatic drop in his hit rate, so some rebound is likely. His splits are fairly even, both on the lefty/righty and home/road axes. According to one scout, "He's learned to change speeds without tipping his pitches, so he's just going to get better." Could well be.

Line Outs

Position/Player	TM	LVL	AGE	PA	R	2B	3B	HR	RBI	BB	SO	SB-CS	SPEED	BA/OBP/SLG	MLVR	EQBA/OBP/SLG	EQA	VORP
OF F. Caraballo	LEX	A	21	449	63	23	2	23	69	30	119	8-7	4.3	.279/.339/.513	.168	.233/.279/.421	.237	-12.7
OF M. Einertson	LEX	A	19	422	52	19	1	7	45	52	99	5-4	4.2	.234/.353/.352	-.049	.198/.292/.303	.216	-31.2
UT R. Huffman	ROU	AAA	28	455	57	32	2	7	45	55	54	8-3	5.0	.284/.374/.430	.072	.244/.320/.350	.240	-11.8
PH B. Kieschnick*	ROU	AAA	33	54	6	2	0	3	10	8	13	0-0	3.2	.304/.407/.543	.315	.237/.312/.389	.243	-0.3
SS D. Klassen	ROU	AAA	29	376	61	23	3	15	53	27	80	7-1	5.4	.319/.375/.535	.266	.275/.319/.432	.259	15.6
SS B. Zobrist#	LEX	A	24	306	45	17	2	2	32	47	35	16-5	6.3	.304/.415/.413	.170	.236/.322/.307	.236	-3.2
	SLM	A+	24	179	25	12	1	3	13	37	17	2-1	4.3	.333/.475/.496	.437	.293/.408/.418	.292	16.0

Pitcher	TM	LVL	AGE	W	L	SV	IP	H	BB	SO	HR	GB%	BABIP	STUFF	WHIP	ERA	PERA	EQERA	EQH9	EQBB9	EQSO9	EQHR9	VORP
M. Albers	SLM	A+	22	8	12	0	148.7	161	62	146	15	55%	.349	-12	1.50	4.66	5.73	6.55	10.8	4.3	5.5	1.5	-15.1
J. Gutierrez	LEX	A	21	9	5	0	120.7	106	43	100	10	46%	.287	-12	1.23	3.21	5.83	5.83	9.8	4.2	4.6	1.4	-2.9
B. Kieschnick	ROU	AAA	33	2	4	1	56.7	77	26	34	13	47%	.342	-65	1.82	5.71	8.50	8.67	13.0	5.0	3.5	3.0	-18.4
M. McLemore*	CCH	AA	24	5	6	0	73.7	59	34	65	5	38%	.273	-4	1.26	2.81	5.45	5.32	8.8	5.6	6.0	1.1	2.1
F. Paulino	TCV	A-	21	2	2	1	30.7	21	11	34	2	47%	.253	-15	1.04	3.81	6.59	6.59	9.2	4.9	5.6	2.0	-3.0
	LEX	A	21	1	1	0	24.3	21	6	30	2	48%	.328	9	1.11	1.85	5.09	4.70	9.4	2.7	6.7	1.6	2.3
A. Williams	SLM	A+	24	0	1	17	34.7	19	10	35	2	50%	.205	-7	0.84	2.33	4.60	4.31	7.5	3.4	5.7	0.9	4.5
	CCH	AA	24	2	1	0	30.7	27	15	19	2	52%	.275	-26	1.37	2.64	6.11	4.18	9.6	6.1	4.2	1.0	4.4

Francisco Caraballo is proof that somebody, somewhere in the chain hit for actual power, and yes, he's from Venezuela. If he continues to slug, he'll show up on prospect lists; if he starts taking walks, he'll belong on them. **Mitch Eintertson** was the guy we got a little too enthusiastic about on last year's prospect list. He's still young enough to recover from an awful first full season as a pro. **Royce Huffman** is a utility infielder experimenting with the tools of ignorance. If he's lucky, he could become the next Tom Wilson. **Danny Klassen** is still hitting better than your average utility infielder, Klassen re-upped with the Astros and might get a shot. **Ben Zobrist** is a big, rangy shortstop with excellent on-base skills, but an '04 pick and way too old for his leagues to get a good read on his future. Having torn up his knee at season's end, we now may never know.

Matt Albers is a chunky local with a heavy sinker, he didn't dominate, but he did survive; added to the 40-man, a survivor's privilege. **Juan Gutierrez** is a live-armed Venezuelan with good heat and a decent curve, he'll need to polish up his mechanics to survive. **Brooks Kieschnick** still deserves a roster spot, but what really needs to be noted is our repeated call for GMs to seriously examine the merits of having a two-way guy as the 25th man on the roster, particularly if he pitches left-handed and can occasionally hit the ball over the fence. **Mark McLemore** is not the former utility man taking a Kieschnickian turn, but a lefty from Oregon State with pretty good stuff. Persistent shoulder woes are holding him up. **Felipe Paulino** is a triple-digit flamethrower from, yes, you guessed it, Venezuela, and finally ready for a full-season debut. Could move up fast in a relief role. **Aaron Williams** is a former Twins farmhand who washed out of their pitching crowd, Williams put in a good season in the independent Frontier League, which along with a recommendation from the Twins, got him a contract with Houston. Not a prospect, but stranger guys than this have had careers.

Kansas City Royals

The Kansas City Royals have now entered the lowest level of the baseball underclass, a netherworld previously inhabited by teams whose names have become synonymous with losing, like the St. Louis Browns or the *Major League*–era Cleveland Indians. Any team can lose 100 games, but in 2005 the Royals continued a remarkable progression of futility. They have tied or broken their franchise record for losses five times in the past seven years, and reached triple digits in the loss column for the third time in four seasons. The Royals have had more 100-loss seasons in the last four years than the Chicago Cubs do in their 130-year history. The last non-expansion team to lose 100 games three times in four years was the 1952–53–54 Pirates, in an era before struggling clubs had access to the restorative powers of free agency and the amateur draft. Few teams in history have been as consistently bad, with as few extenuating circumstances, as the 21st-century Royals.

If you're feeling charitable, you might consider the Royals' incredible talent for losing games by one run to be a mitigating factor. The Royals were 18-30 in one-run games last year, better than their record in 2002 (14-27), or 2001 (11-24), or 1996 (14-26), or especially 1999 (11-32, the fourth-worst tally of all time). From 1996 through 2005, the team's record in one-run games is 158-251, a .386 winning percentage.

That's the worst record over a ten-year span in baseball history. Only one team even comes close as seen in table 1.

Things have been even worse on the road. The Royals' 4-14 record in one-run games away from home last season actually improved the team's winning percentage in one-

ROYALS PROSPECTUS

2005 record: 56–106; Fifth place, AL Central

Pythagenport record: 59–103

Runs scored per game: 4.33 (12th in AL)

Runs allowed per game: 5.77 (13th in AL)

Team EqA: .251 (12th in AL)

2005 Batters Age: 28.6 (6th youngest in AL)

2005 Pitchers Age: 26.2 (Youngest in AL)

Ballpark: Royals Stadium; Moderate hitter's park; Park Factor of 1.032

2005: Probably would have taken a Triple-A All-Star team behind the woodshed. Probably.

2006: A passel of low-wattage signings isn't the way to reach escape velocity from the Planet of 100 Losses.

run games over the six prior years. Since 1999, the Royals are an unfathomable 32-117 (.215) in one-run road games. The previous record-holder over a seven-year span, the 1924-30 Phillies, were 38-119 (.242). The Royals smashed the record by nearly 30 points.

One-run games are essentially coin flips; even the worst teams can win more than half their one-run games by sheer luck. The 2003 Tigers, the losingest AL team of all time, were 19-18 in one-run affairs. The Royals' perennial ineptitude in this category defies description.

There was no specific, Barry-Bonds-left-for-free-agency moment that sent the Royals hurtling towards sadsackdom. You don't play this badly for this long for any one reason. The Royals stand—hunched over—as a monument to the power of the accumulated erosion wrought by years of chronic mismanagement. Success in baseball boils down to three things. Payroll size, while hardly the determining factor that the owners would have you believe during every CBA negotiation, is certainly important. The second key is the amount of talent a franchise has on hand from players that have yet to reach free agency, and therefore by definition are paid below market value. Third is a team's ability to make effective use of its discretionary dollars, the portion of its payroll being used to pay market value for free-agent talent.

TABLE 1. WORST ONE-RUN RECORDS FOR TEN-YEAR SPAN

Team	Years	One-Run Record
Kansas City	1996–2005	158-251 (.386)
Brooklyn	1904–1913	195-309 (.387)
Boston (AL)	1925–1934	194-293 (.398)
Philadelphia (NL)	1922–1931	172-255 (.403)
Philadelphia (NL)	1936–1945	195-285 (.406)

A team only needs to nail two out of the three to find consistent success, which is why the A's have thrived with small payrolls and the Braves have won umpteen straight division titles despite only rare forays into the free-agent market. The team that runs the board on all three ends up like the 1998 Yankees, dominating the game. The Royals flunk all three tasks. Their payroll was the lowest in baseball last year, a fact celebrated by team apologists and those who would like to use baseball incompetence as an excuse to rein in labor costs. Last year, Cleveland won 93 games with a payroll not even $5 million more than the Royals'. Yet, the Royals were equally, and more unforgivably, atrocious at their other two responsibilities. Payroll is almost entirely irrelevant in determining how much talent a franchise is able to develop on its own. The blame for a weak pipeline of talent lies with scouting and development, not with ownership.

Consider the talent the Royals developed between 1993 and 2001 shown in table 2.

Over a nine-year span, the Royals managed to draft just three players who would have a meaningful career with the Royals: Beltran, Rosado, and DeJesus. The other players on this list were discarded by the Royals before they accomplished anything. Rusch was traded to the Mets for someone named Dan Murray; Carter was released; Giambi was gifted to Oakland for Brett Laxton; the Royals considered Mark Ellis a throw-in when they traded for Angel Berroa, but Ellis has been the superior player despite Berroa's Rookie of the Year nod in 2003. That leaves back-of-the-roster guys like Fasano and Santiago, and those are the *successes*. And the Royals didn't just make a mess of their draft picks. The only international players signed by the Royals in the 1990s who had meaningful major league careers were Carlos Febles and Runelvys Hernandez.

To be fair, the Royals current leadership is largely blameless for this stretch of incompetence. David Glass purchased the team in April 2000, and Allard Baird was named GM a month later, just days before the draft. The 2001 draft is on him, though, and that was the worst of the bunch. To date, not a single player signed from that draft has reached the majors. If it holds, this would be only the fifth team draft ever to be a complete loss.

Thanks to a long-overdue change in focus away from raw tools players, the Royals have fared much better in their last four drafts. In 2002, they selected Zack Greinke. Their first pick in 2003, Chris Lubanski, is a legitimate outfield prospect who had a fine year in the California League at age 20. Billy Butler, the first pick in 2004, is one of the best hitting prospects in the game, and J. P. Howell, selected in the supplemental first round that year, was in the Royals' rotation a year later. The Royals have seen some improvement on the international front as well; Latin signees Ambiorix Burgos and Andres Blanco both played for the Royals last season as 21 year-olds.

With Alex Gordon, the second overall pick in 2005, and whoever is selected with the first overall pick this June, the Royals have two potential franchise players to add to their stable of young talent. Drafting at the very top of the first round may not be the most elegant way to acquire talent, since it involves owning one of the worst records in baseball year after year, but it can work. The Devil Rays used consecutive Top Two selections on B. J. Upton and Delmon Young, who are now two of the most valuable commodities in the game.

The Royals are starting to develop young talent again, and the inherent value of young talent is that it's cheap. A low-payroll team simply doesn't have enough money to win if it's forced to pay market value for its talent, which is why it is so vital to have players whose compensation is determined by an arbiter (or, for pre-arbitration players, by the team itself) instead of by the New York Yankees. To put it bluntly, when you're a low-payroll team, service time is your enemy. The closer a player is to free agency, the smaller the gap between his value and his

TABLE 2. ROYALS' TALENT DEVELOPMENT 1993–2001

Year	Pick #	First Draft Pick	Career WARP	Other Signed Players with 6+ WARP
1993	5	Jeff Granger	- 0.3	Glendon Rusch (24.5), Sal Fasano (7.1)
1994	16	Matt Smith	DNP	Jose Rosado (22.0), Jose Santiago (10.5), Lance Carter (10.4)
1995	19	Juan LeBron	DNP	Carlos Beltran (41.2)
1996	14	Dee Brown	- 0.9	Jeremy Giambi (9.6)
1997	7	Dan Reichert	8.0	Jeremy Affeldt (10.2)
1998	4	Jeff Austin	0.1	None
1999	7	Kyle Snyder	2.0	Mark Ellis (12.6), Mike MacDougal (8.7)
2000	4	Mike Stodolka	DNP	David DeJesus (7.1)
2001	9	Colt Griffin	DNP	None

cost. Small-market teams must be certain their players are ready for major league competition before they turn on their service clock.

But the Royals see rushing players to the majors not as a mistake, but as a necessity. As *Kansas City Star* columnist Joe Posnanski wrote, "The Royals' plan is to take their best young players, rush them to the big leagues and hope those kids are good enough and tough enough to survive." Burgos, who was transitioning to the bullpen, started the year in Double-A and was summoned to Kansas City after a grand total of eight innings. Leo Nunez started the season in A-ball, earned a promotion to Double-A after just 13 innings (and a 9.00 ERA), then was whisked to Kauffman Stadium after all of five innings in Wichita. Howell was put on the "slow" track, actually getting eight starts in the California League before a promotion to Double-A; he was starting for the Royals three weeks later. Outfielder Shane Costa was promoted to Kansas City after just six weeks in Double-A, and he wasn't even hitting well at the time. Not surprisingly, all four players ended up returning to the minors.

Compare this approach to that of the Athletics, where almost all of their young players, from Nick Swisher and Dan Johnson to Joe Blanton to Bobby Crosby, spent a full year in Triple-A. (The only exception, Huston Street, was probably ready for the majors as a college sophomore.) Not only did the A's save themselves service time of their best prospects, but when their prospects were promoted, they were ready to produce right away, maximizing the value of that service time. In August and September the Royals used 12 pitchers who were 27 or younger; nine of them had never played a game in Triple-A. The only one who had significant Triple-A experience was Mike Wood, who—surprise!—was in the A's farm system at the time.

The Royals' failure to find talent and develop it properly is matched by the team's inability to use free agency to supplement the roster. The Royals spent $7 millon last season on two veteran pitchers, Brian Anderson and Jose Lima. They combined to go 6-18 with an astounding 6.94 ERA in 199 innings. The Indians spent the same amount of money on Kevin Millwood and were rewarded with the league's best ERA. This continues a disturbing trend for the Royals. Since Baird became GM, the Royals have paid $1.5 million or more to a free agent from another team six times. Those six players—Juan Gonzalez, Chuck Knoblauch, Lima, Albie Lopez, Benito Santiago, and Scott Sullivan—combined for 1.6 WARP in a Royals uniform, at a combined cost of $18.1 million. That doesn't include Eli Marrero ($3.2 million, −0.2 WARP), whose salary the Braves were so eager to dump that they traded him for a minor league reliever.

With this kind of track record, the proper reaction to Glass's vow to increase payroll to $50 million for 2006 was to anticipate disaster. Of all the reasons to spend millions of dollars on a free agent, the worst is "because we can."

The 2005–2006 off-season held special risk in this regard because the talent was so thin. Glass had $22 million to spend. Enter Scott Elarton, Doug Mientkiewicz, Mark Grudzielanek, Paul Bako, Reggie Sanders, and Joe Mays. Throw in Mark Redman—acquired for a pair of minor league relievers in a salary dump—and that's $21 million spent on six players, not one of whom has better than a 50-50 shot at being an above-average player in 2006.

Mientkiewicz and Grudzielanek, at least, should significantly improve the team's defense, which was the worst aspect of the team last year. Adjusted for park and league, the Royals' Defensive Efficiency was 4.48 standard deviations below average last year. That's the fifth-worst defensive showing of any team since 1972. Reggie Sanders is 38 and as fragile as stunt glass, but he does hit when he plays. As for the hurlers, Redman has posted ERAs of 4.71 and 4.90 the last two years, Elarton had a 4.61 ERA last season (his best mark since 1999), and Joe Mays's last three ERAs are 5.38, 6.30, and 5.65. At the cost of about $10 million, the Royals brought in three starting pitchers who are unlikely to perform better than Jeremy Affeldt and Mike Wood, who will either be exiled to the bullpen or given away for pennies on the dollar.

The irony is that importing veterans as short-term place-holders would have made sense last year, though not at these prices. But after a year in which the Royals rushed young players to the majors before they were ready, now they appear determined to bury them in Triple-A, if not get rid of them entirely. The Royals had to designate half a dozen players for assignment to make room for the veterans, and there was enough demand for those players that the Royals were able to trade two of them, one to the Braves. That player, Matt Diaz, hit .371 at Triple-A last season.

One last story sums up the Royals. Last summer, the team chose not to release Jose Lima , enduring one of the worst seasons by a starting pitcher in baseball history, at mid-season even though keeping Lima earned him $1.25 million in bonuses. Meanwhile, the Royals drafted a 1st round talent named Justin Bristow, who dropped to the 22nd round because he was considered a tough sign. The Royals made lukewarm overtures to Bristow. Had they been aggressive, he probably would have signed for the $1.25 million instead of going to college.

In the long term, things should get better for the Royals. They're finally starting to amass talent in the minor leagues, and they'll be adding to that with picks from the very top of the first round for the foreseeable future. In the short term, this is still an organization that would rather keep the worst starter in baseball around for three more months than sign an 18-year-old player who has a small but realistic hope of becoming a superstar one day. That's an organization worthy of its reputation as the most poorly-run franchise in the game.

HITTERS

CHIP AMBRES   OF   Bats: R Throws: R   Height: 6' 1"   Weight: 190   Born: December 19, 1979   Age: 26

YEAR	TM	LVL	AGE	PA	R	2B	3B	HR	RBI	BB	SO	SB	CS	SPEED	BA	OBP	SLG	MLVR	EQBA	EQOBP	EQSLG	EQA	VORP	DEFENSE			
2003	CAR	AA	23	457	75	23	8	10	55	72	81	9	6	6.6	.258	.376	.439	.164	.239	.345	.422	.267	13.9	106-CF	-1		
2004	CAR	AA	24	542	81	28	3	20	62	76	117	26	9	6.6	.241	.352	.449	.105	.214	.310	.391	.249	-2.7	75-CF	-5	42-RF	1
2005	PAW	AAA	25	332	47	20	3	10	50	47	64	19	5	6.0	.294	.401	.495	.225	.265	.366	.439	.283	16.2	42-CF	-7	24-LF	-1
2005	KCA	MLB	25	164	25	8	0	4	9	16	32	3	2	4.3	.241	.323	.379	-.093	.252	.341	.399	.257	-0.2	18-CF	-1	20-LF	-3
2006	*KCA*	*MLB*	*26*	*464*	*59*	*24*	*3*	*12*	*52*	*48*	*87*	*14*	*5*	*5.3*	*.249*	*.332*	*.414*	*-.026*	*.251*	*.341*	*.436*	*.263*	*9.7*	*110-CF*	*-4*		

Breakout: 21%   Improve: 46%   Collapse: 22%   Attrition: 18%   Comparables: Jose Cruz, Jim Hickman, Trot Nixon

Ambres was a shrewd acquisition, but in classic Royals fashion, the team then announced that Juan Cedeno, a lefty reliever with a 5.49 ERA in A-ball, was the key to the Graffanino trade. Ambres has the tools you'd expect from a former 1st round pick, but also has good command of the strike zone. His OBP and slugging average were both higher than Terrence Long's, but Ambres was confined to the bench until DeJesus injured his shoulder in August. He projects as a fourth outfielder, but one with definite upside.

MIKE AVILES   SS   Bats: R Throws: R   Height: 5' 11"   Weight: 193   Born: March 13, 1981   Age: 25

YEAR	TM	LVL	AGE	PA	R	2B	3B	HR	RBI	BB	SO	SB	CS	SPEED	BA	OBP	SLG	MLVR	EQBA	EQOBP	EQSLG	EQA	VORP	DEFENSE			
2004	WIL	A+	23	509	66	40	4	6	68	39	57	2	5	4.2	.300	.352	.443	.158	.272	.316	.410	.249	17.0	120-SS	9		
2005	WIC	AA	24	557	79	33	6	14	80	30	64	11	6	5.7	.280	.318	.447	.049	.250	.289	.393	.235	4.0	99-SS	-10	19-3B	3
2006	*KCA*	*MLB*	*25*	*470*	*52*	*28*	*3*	*9*	*52*	*23*	*62*	*4*	*3*	*4.6*	*.263*	*.302*	*.404*	*-.079*	*.265*	*.310*	*.426*	*.243*	*11.4*	*111-SS*	*-2*		

Breakout: 24%   Improve: 60%   Collapse: 22%   Attrition: 16%   Comparables: Kevin Elster, Jason Alfaro, Nate Grindell

The Royals have drafted a plethora of college seniors in the middle rounds of recent drafts in order to save a few bucks. Aviles, the Division II Player of the Year in 2003, is the only one to have developed into a prospect. His bat may play in the middle infield, but his glove won't. He could have Rich Aurilia's career, but barring a tectonic shift in major league philosophies to value bats over gloves among backup infielders, a lengthy career seems unlikely.

ANGEL BERROA   SS   Bats: R Throws: R   Height: 6' 0"   Weight: 170   Born: January 27, 1978   Age: 28

YEAR	TM	LVL	AGE	PA	R	2B	3B	HR	RBI	BB	SO	SB	CS	SPEED	BA	OBP	SLG	MLVR	EQBA	EQOBP	EQSLG	EQA	VORP	DEFENSE	
2003	KCA	MLB	25	622	92	28	7	17	73	29	100	21	5	6.6	.287	.338	.451	.010	.280	.332	.444	.269	32.3	156-SS	-1
2004	KCA	MLB	26	549	72	27	6	8	43	23	87	14	8	6.5	.262	.308	.385	-.107	.261	.308	.389	.241	10.2	130-SS	-13
2005	KCA	MLB	27	642	68	21	5	11	55	18	108	7	5	5.2	.270	.305	.375	-.113	.277	.320	.394	.247	8.1	156-SS	-9
2006	*KCA*	*MLB*	*28*	*558*	*62*	*24*	*4*	*9*	*54*	*20*	*86*	*9*	*4*	*5.1*	*.262*	*.299*	*.379*	*-.117*	*.264*	*.308*	*.399*	*.236*	*10.4*	*131-SS*	*-5*

Breakout: 16%   Improve: 50%   Collapse: 27%   Attrition: 6%   Comparables: Pat Meares, Mark Grudzielanek, Carlos Garcia

The Royals consider Berroa to be the anchor of their defense, which is true on a purely literal level. He has been 14 runs below average at shortstop each of the last two years, and an integral member of the majors' worst defense. He's also been a replacement-level hitter in both seasons. The four-year contract the Royals gave him after his one good year will haunt them for, well, the next four years. Yeah, he was once Rookie of the Year; so was Bob Hamelin.

ANDRES BLANCO   SS/2B   Bats: B Throws: R   Height: 5' 10"   Weight: 150   Born: April 11, 1984   Age: 22

YEAR	TM	LVL	AGE	PA	R	2B	3B	HR	RBI	BB	SO	SB	CS	SPEED	BA	OBP	SLG	MLVR	EQBA	EQOBP	EQSLG	EQA	VORP	DEFENSE	
2003	WIL	A+	19	448	61	11	3	0	25	44	50	13	7	6.1	.244	.330	.287	-.094	.229	.303	.285	.218	-13.8	106-SS	-4
2004	WIC	AA	20	351	34	10	2	0	21	18	44	7	6	4.7	.247	.299	.290	-.222	.225	.268	.265	.196	-20.6	88-SS	8
2004	KCA	MLB	20	66	9	2	2	0	5	5	6	1	2	6.6	.317	.379	.417	.091	.322	.385	.424	.274	3.6	19-SS	0
2005	OMA	AAA	21	127	13	4	2	1	9	10	23	2	0	4.8	.254	.331	.351	-.156	.235	.296	.313	.222	-2.8	34-SS	6
2005	KCA	MLB	21	82	6	0	1	0	5	5	0	5	1	5.1	.215	.220	.241	-.506	.218	.232	.244	.179	-8.3	21-2B	2
2006	*KCA*	*MLB*	*22*	*330*	*32*	*12*	*2*	*1*	*23*	*16*	*39*	*5*	*3*	*5.1*	*.244*	*.286*	*.309*	*-.241*	*.246*	*.294*	*.325*	*.209*	*-4.3*	*80-SS*	*3*

Breakout: 45%   Improve: 63%   Collapse: 24%   Attrition: 17%   Comparables: Nelson Norman, Guillermo Reyes, Kurt Stillwell

Blanco isn't much of a hitter. He isn't even a quark of a hitter; his career slugging average in the minor leagues is .303. But he's the kind of shortstop that scouts believe could contend for multiple Gold Gloves during in his career. So what do you do with a young shortstop who's all glove and no bat? If you're the Royals, you move him to second base during a September call-up, where his defensive skills are less valuable and his offensive inadequacies are more glaring. The signing of Grudzielanek allows Blanco to stay in the minors, and at shortstop, which is the silver lining on an otherwise very cloudy transaction.

EMIL BROWN   OF   Bats: R Throws: R   Height: 6' 2"   Weight: 200   Born: December 29, 1974   Age: 31

YEAR	TM	LVL	AGE	PA	R	2B	3B	HR	RBI	BB	SO	SB	CS	SPEED	BA	OBP	SLG	MLVR	EQBA	EQOBP	EQSLG	EQA	VORP	DEFENSE
2003	LOU	AAA	28	408	58	20	3	12	63	27	76	18	3	6.7	.295	.343	.463	.125	.256	.307	.400	.251	2.1	91-CF -7
2004	NWO	AAA	29	101	12	10	1	2	17	4	20	4	2	5.7	.337	.386	.533	.353	.301	.334	.444	.265	2.3	22-RF -1
2005	KCA	MLB	30	608	75	31	5	17	86	48	108	10	1	5.6	.286	.349	.455	.092	.293	.363	.479	.290	25.9	126-RF -16
2006	KCA	MLB	31	510	61	26	4	13	59	33	92	9	3	5.2	.268	.321	.427	-.014	.270	.330	.449	.260	7.2	120-RF -8

Breakout: 14%   Improve: 38%   Collapse: 37%   Attrition: 14%   Comparables: Don Lund, Mike Devereaux, Gary Ward

After Brown and Raul Ibanez, Allard Baird deserves the benefit of the doubt when he sees something in a journeyman outfielder and gives him an everyday role over the protestations of scouts and analysts alike. While he may have won the battle, Baird lost the war. Brown can hit—he batted .301/.360/.468 from May 1st on—but his defense is so bad (14 runs below average) that he still ranks as a below-average right fielder. The Royals have no better alternative than to see if Brown has a run of decent, cheap years in him.

JOHN BUCK   C   Bats: R Throws: R   Height: 6' 3"   Weight: 210   Born: July 7, 1980   Age: 25

YEAR	TM	LVL	AGE	PA	R	2B	3B	HR	RBI	BB	SO	SB	CS	SPEED	BA	OBP	SLG	MLVR	EQBA	EQOBP	EQSLG	EQA	VORP	DEFENSE
2003	NWO	AAA	22	292	32	18	2	2	39	14	53	1	0	4.5	.255	.301	.358	-.070	.261	.307	.367	.235	0.1	68-C -4
2004	NWO	AAA	24	253	31	11	0	12	35	21	39	0	1	2.9	.300	.368	.507	.231	.283	.345	.452	.272	14.4	55-C -4
2004	KCA	MLB	24	254	36	9	0	12	30	15	79	1	1	4.5	.235	.280	.424	-.100	.230	.278	.413	.235	3.4	66-C -5
2005	KCA	MLB	25	429	40	21	1	12	47	23	94	2	2	3.9	.242	.287	.389	-.139	.247	.302	.407	.243	2.4	112-C -3
2006	KCA	MLB	25	398	40	21	2	12	51	21	81	2	1	4.3	.258	.303	.420	-.060	.260	.311	.443	.248	10.6	95-C -1

Breakout: 31%   Improve: 50%   Collapse: 20%   Attrition: 25%   Comparables: Joe Oliver, George Mitterwald, Bill Nahorodny

He's got pop, and he threw out 34% of opposing base stealers last year, but he's also got a lifetime OBP of .284. It's possible to make up for a .284 OBP in other ways, but it generally requires acts described in books of Scripture. The Royals point to his .321/.341/.568 line from September 1st on as proof that he's ready to turn the corner. There are some similarities between Buck and Brandon Inge, whose career-high in OBP stood at .266 after three seasons and didn't break out until he was 27. This is one instance where the Royals' lack of talent may be a blessing; they've got nothing to lose by giving Buck another season as the full-time catcher.

BILLY BUTLER   Hitter   Bats: R Throws: R   Height: 6' 2"   Weight: 225   Born: April 18, 1986   Age: 20

YEAR	TM	LVL	AGE	PA	R	2B	3B	HR	RBI	BB	SO	SB	CS	SPEED	BA	OBP	SLG	MLVR	EQBA	EQOBP	EQSLG	EQA	VORP	DEFENSE
2004	IDA	Rk	18	323	74	22	3	10	68	57	63	5	0	5.6	.373	.486	.596	.481	.276	.365	.420	.276	31.3	47-3B 4
2005	HDS	A+	19	430	70	30	2	25	91	42	80	0	0	3.6	.348	.419	.636	.362	.264	.328	.465	.269	20.6	40-3B -6 34-LF -2
2005	WIC	AA	19	119	14	9	0	5	19	7	18	0	0	3.6	.312	.353	.527	.249	.275	.318	.466	.264	1.9	25-LF -5
2006	KCA	MLB	20	492	53	28	2	14	65	36	92	0	1	4.1	.266	.323	.431	-.008	.268	.332	.453	.259	12.1	116-LF -8

Breakout: 19%   Improve: 42%   Collapse: 33%   Attrition: 5%   Comparables: Julian Benavidez, Mike Cuddyer, Delmon Young

The best teenage hitter in a Royals uniform since Clint Hurdle, Butler's numbers are not a park illusion; he actually hit better on the road than at High Desert. Defensively, Butler may one day owe more career earnings to the invention of the DH slot than any other player. His fielding percentage at third base last season was .842, so he moved to left field at midseason. One scout said Butler was the worst defensive outfielder he'd ever seen. The Royals have enough players at the wrong end of the defensive spectrum already, but Butler is the guy you move everyone else to accommodate. In a different organization, he'd be a front-runner for Rookie of the Year honors in 2007. In Kansas City, he'll probably be in the starting lineup by May.

SHANE COSTA   OF   Bats: L Throws: R   Height: 6' 0"   Weight: 200   Born: December 12, 1981   Age: 24

YEAR	TM	LVL	AGE	PA	R	2B	3B	HR	RBI	BB	SO	SB	CS	SPEED	BA	OBP	SLG	MLVR	EQBA	EQOBP	EQSLG	EQA	VORP	DEFENSE
2004	WIL	A+	22	500	70	20	4	7	60	32	43	9	4	5.5	.308	.364	.417	.147	.282	.328	.394	.252	-3.2	61-LF -1 40-CF 0
2005	WIC	AA	23	315	37	18	2	8	43	24	23	5	1	4.5	.282	.349	.448	.103	.258	.321	.413	.257	-2.3	59-LF -7 12-RF 0
2005	KCA	MLB	23	87	13	2	0	2	7	5	11	0	0	4.4	.235	.287	.333	-.228	.237	.299	.338	.225	-3.2	19-LF -3
2006	KCA	MLB	24	433	45	23	2	7	48	25	45	3	2	4.8	.266	.315	.386	-.077	.268	.324	.407	.245	1.1	103-LF -4

Breakout: 24%   Improve: 46%   Collapse: 28%   Attrition: 12%   Comparables: Ed Kranepool, Derrick May, John Barnes

A decent prospect but no phenom, Costa was nevertheless promoted to Kansas City after 45 games in Double-A as part of the team's "Bring a Prospect to Work" promotion. Predictably, he wasn't ready. The question for Costa is whether he'll ever hit for power; even with a bump in his slugging average last year, at this point he's only got 12–15 homer power. Badly needs a full year at Triple-A.

DAVID DeJESUS   **CF**   **Bats: L Throws: L**   Height: 6' 0"   Weight: 170   Born: December 20, 1979   Age: 26

YEAR	TM	LVL	AGE	PA	R	2B	3B	HR	RBI	BB	SO	SB	CS	SPEED	BA	OBP	SLG	MLVR	EQBA	EQOBP	EQSLG	EQA	VORP	DEFENSE	
2003	WIC	AA	23	83	14	4	0	2	10	9	8	1	3	3.9	.338	.422	.479	.338	.315	.387	.484	.292	7.6	17-CF	0
2003	OMA	AAA	23	260	49	16	3	5	23	34	30	8	4	6.2	.298	.412	.470	.262	.282	.386	.452	.291	17.2	50-CF	-2
2004	OMA	AAA	24	225	38	14	4	6	16	21	30	7	6	6.4	.315	.400	.518	.270	.288	.367	.458	.279	14.0	49-CF	-2
2004	KCA	MLB	24	405	58	15	3	7	39	33	53	8	11	5.6	.287	.360	.402	.023	.288	.363	.402	.261	9.6	84-CF	0
2005	KCA	MLB	25	518	69	31	6	9	56	42	76	5	5	5.6	.293	.359	.445	.097	.303	.375	.469	.288	25.2	115-CF	-5
2006	KCA	MLB	26	591	74	31	4	12	66	51	78	8	5	5.6	.286	.356	.430	.062	.288	.366	.453	.275	27.8	138-CF	0

Breakout: 12%   Improve: 47%   Collapse: 24%   Attrition: 3%   Comparables: Wally Moon, Ken Griffey Sr., Johnny Grubb

The Royals have youngsters who can't hit and hitters who aren't young. DeJesus is the only Royal who doesn't belong in either category. He's also a decent center fielder in an outfield where everyone else covers ground like they were extras from "March of the Penguins." Fragility is always an issue (he missed the last five weeks with a sprained shoulder), but when he plays, he plays well. The Royals finally seem to be getting the message that he's a good base-runner but not a good base stealer—his attempts dropped from 19 to 10 last year. Stolen bases or no, he's still a prototypical leadoff hitter in a game surprisingly short of them.

MATT DIAZ   **OF**   **Bats: R Throws: R**   Height: 6' 1"   Weight: 200   Born: March 3, 1978   Age: 28

YEAR	TM	LVL	AGE	PA	R	2B	3B	HR	RBI	BB	SO	SB	CS	SPEED	BA	OBP	SLG	MLVR	EQBA	EQOBP	EQSLG	EQA	VORP	DEFENSE			
2003	ORL	AA	25	257	32	21	0	5	41	19	24	9	5	4.6	.383	.444	.542	.501	.326	.377	.468	.290	16.2	57-RF	5		
2003	DUR	AAA	25	280	35	18	3	8	45	16	45	6	2	5.4	.328	.382	.518	.278	.296	.351	.479	.283	12.3	53-RF	5	14-LF	2
2004	DUR	AAA	26	547	81	47	5	21	93	26	96	15	4	6.2	.332	.377	.571	.304	.292	.335	.493	.280	22.7	122-RF	9		
2005	OMA	AAA	27	277	48	22	4	14	56	12	49	10	3	5.6	.371	.408	.649	.554	.323	.352	.529	.294	18.9	58-LF	0		
2005	KCA	MLB	27	96	7	4	2	1	9	4	15	0	1	5.1	.281	.323	.404	-.030	.284	.333	.409	.255	0.6	16-LF	-2		
2006	ATL	MLB	28	402	49	23	2	12	54	22	74	6	2	4.7	.280	.328	.449	.020	.280	.328	.463	.263	9.8	96-LF	2		

Breakout: 5%   Improve: 22%   Collapse: 40%   Attrition: 13%   Comparables: Aaron Rowand, Elston Howard, Wil Cordero

The Good Allard Baird: he signed Diaz, who had hit .354 and .332 with good power in the high minors the previous two years. The Bad Allard Baird: he let Buddy Bell confine Diaz to the bench in his September call-up after Diaz had hit .371 with even more power in Omaha. Sure, he doesn't take a walk, but a guy whose average over the past three years is .348 has earned a chance to prove he's better than Terrence Long. Instead, the Royals sent Diaz to the instructional league to work on—we're not making this up—becoming a catcher. Traded to the Braves for pitcher Rico Rodriguez, the Braves will give him a shot to be a fourth outfielder or even a platoon starter.

ADAM DONACHIE   **C**   **Bats: R Throws: R**   Height: 6' 1"   Weight: 191   Born: March 3, 1984   Age: 22

YEAR	TM	LVL	AGE	PA	R	2B	3B	HR	RBI	BB	SO	SB	CS	SPEED	BA	OBP	SLG	MLVR	EQBA	EQOBP	EQSLG	EQA	VORP	DEFENSE	
2004	BUR	A	20	253	17	7	0	1	21	21	41	5	2	4.0	.189	.261	.232	-.299	.172	.232	.219	.174	-29.5	66-C	6
2005	HDS	A+	21	392	64	24	0	12	48	43	78	1	0	3.9	.294	.375	.467	-.005	.214	.287	.328	.219	-12.3	92-C	15
2006	KCA	MLB	22	324	28	13	1	5	28	22	63	1	1	3.7	.214	.271	.311	-.282	.215	.279	.328	.201	-8.0	78-C	6

Breakout: 44%   Improve: 61%   Collapse: 25%   Attrition: 20%   Comparables: Dan Conway, Cesar King, Rene Pinto

You wouldn't ordinarily call a fractured skull a blessing, but it might have been for Donachie. A 2nd round pick in 2002, he hit .203 with a single homer in his first two pro seasons, while being dogged by accusations that he wasn't serious about his career. Then his 2004 season ended when a teammate's BP swing caught him flush in the noggin. He returned last season a new player. We'll have to see how he hits outside of High Desert, but a young catcher with plate discipline and power is the very definition of a sleeper prospect.

ALEX GORDON   **3B**   **Bats: L Throws: R**   Height: 6' 1"   Weight: 215   Born: February 10, 1984   Age: 22

The Royals' highest pick ever, Gordon was universally considered a better prospect than the guy taken two picks later, Ryan Zimmerman, who hit .397 with Gold Glove defense for the Nationals two months after signing. Doing the math, that means Gordon is very, very good. He signed in September and made his pro debut in the Arizona Fall League, where he hit .260/.403/.460. He's already the most disciplined hitter in the organization—no Royal has drawn 90 walks in a season since 1989. Gordon has the defensive mettle to play third base in the majors, but with the Royals committed to Teahen there for now, Gordon's eventual destination may be right field. Mark Teixeira is a fairly good approximation of his best-case scenario.

RUBEN GOTAY   **2B**   **Bats: B Throws: R**   Height: 5' 11"   Weight: 160   Born: December 25, 1982   Age: 23

YEAR	TM	LVL	AGE	PA	R	2B	3B	HR	RBI	BB	SO	SB	CS	SPEED	BA	OBP	SLG	MLVR	EQBA	EQOBP	EQSLG	EQA	VORP	DEFENSE	
2003	WIL	A+	20	578	68	31	2	9	72	60	97	8	1	5.1	.261	.343	.384	.061	.246	.317	.387	.248	6.4	123-2B	3
2004	WIC	AA	21	467	71	22	6	9	68	51	60	9	10	5.5	.289	.373	.440	.142	.265	.337	.402	.256	14.6	105-2B	-7
2004	KCA	MLB	21	165	17	7	3	1	16	9	36	0	1	4.5	.270	.315	.375	-.085	.267	.317	.373	.241	2.5	42-2B	0
2005	KCA	MLB	22	313	32	14	2	5	29	22	51	2	2	5.4	.227	.288	.344	-.214	.234	.300	.363	.234	-7.2	76-2B	-1
2005	WIC	AA	22	122	22	8	0	3	15	12	13	0	2	4.9	.245	.320	.400	-.040	.209	.282	.338	.216	-4.0	25-2B	0
2006	*KCA*	*MLB*	*23*	*407*	*46*	*21*	*2*	*9*	*44*	*34*	*59*	*3*	*2*	*5.1*	*.260*	*.327*	*.404*	*-.040*	*.262*	*.336*	*.425*	*.255*	*13.0*	*97-2B*	*-1*

Breakout: 45%   Improve: 68%   Collapse: 18%   Attrition: 23%   Comparables: Roy Smalley Jr., Kurt Stillwell, Dale Sveum

It's hard to argue that Gotay was rushed. After all, he hit well in an extended trial in 2004, and as late as June 20th he was hitting a perfectly respectable .262/.321/.422. He then went into a 15-for-95 tailspin that only ended when he was shipped back to Double-A. The Royals publicly admitted that Gotay's confidence was completely shot. Gotay's defense isn't very good, but it's also not nearly as bad as the Royals would have you believe. He will probably spend the year in Omaha, which may be the best thing for him at this point. Many in the organization compare him to Todd Walker, and the funny thing is that they mean it as an insult.

AARON GUIEL   **OF**   **Bats: L Throws: R**   Height: 5' 10"   Weight: 200   Born: October 5, 1972   Age: 33

YEAR	TM	LVL	AGE	PA	R	2B	3B	HR	RBI	BB	SO	SB	CS	SPEED	BA	OBP	SLG	MLVR	EQBA	EQOBP	EQSLG	EQA	VORP	DEFENSE			
2003	OMA	AAA	30	233	38	9	2	8	30	33	43	3	0	5.2	.279	.408	.474	.244	.239	.345	.383	.260	-1.6	47-RF	5		
2003	KCA	MLB	30	399	63	30	0	15	52	27	63	3	5	4.6	.277	.346	.489	.069	.271	.342	.483	.276	8.5	84-RF	7		
2004	OMA	AAA	31	144	29	6	0	10	30	21	33	0	2	3.5	.310	.438	.621	.474	.244	.348	.433	.268	1.4	25-LF	1		
2004	KCA	MLB	31	156	15	4	0	5	13	17	42	1	1	4.1	.156	.263	.296	-.387	.150	.260	.286	.201	-13.0	35-LF	1		
2005	OMA	AAA	32	582	94	32	4	30	95	64	103	6	3	4.7	.276	.371	.538	.206	.216	.287	.377	.232	-24.6	86-RF	9	35-LF	1
2005	KCA	MLB	32	121	18	5	0	4	7	6	21	1	0	3.5	.294	.355	.450	.101	.306	.372	.481	.293	6.4	21-CF	-2		
2006	*KCA*	*MLB*	*33*	*332*	*33*	*15*	*1*	*10*	*39*	*25*	*73*	*2*	*1*	*4.4*	*.231*	*.297*	*.383*	*-.135*	*.232*	*.306*	*.404*	*.237*	*-4.1*	*80-RF*	*1*		

Breakout: 16%   Improve: 42%   Collapse: 35%   Attrition: 31%   Comparables: Jeromy Burnitz, Johnny Callison, Walt Moryn

The organizational soldier proved that he had completely overcome the vision problems that torpedoed his 2004 season. To get back, he accepted a minor league assignment, anchored Omaha's lineup with 30 homers, then returned to Kansas City in August and hit about as well as he did in his breakout season in 2003. Like a lot of guys in the organization, he makes a hell of a fourth outfielder. He's also 33 and has likely seen his best days. At-bat for at-bat, he's the same hitter as Matt Stairs, only with better wheels and a better glove. The Royals re-signed Stairs anyway, forcing Guiel to fight for a roster spot again this spring.

KEN HARVEY   **DH**   **Bats: R Throws: R**   Height: 6' 2"   Weight: 240   Born: March 1, 1978   Age: 28

YEAR	TM	LVL	AGE	PA	R	2B	3B	HR	RBI	BB	SO	SB	CS	SPEED	BA	OBP	SLG	MLVR	EQBA	EQOBP	EQSLG	EQA	VORP	DEFENSE	
2003	KCA	MLB	25	521	50	30	0	13	64	29	94	2	3	3.7	.266	.313	.408	-.097	.258	.310	.405	.245	-5.0	92-1B	8
2004	KCA	MLB	26	494	47	20	1	13	55	28	89	1	1	3.8	.287	.338	.421	.018	.285	.338	.421	.262	12.4	72-1B	-1
2005	KCA	MLB	27	48	4	3	0	1	5	3	13	0	0	3.1	.222	.271	.356	-.218	.227	.292	.364	.228	-1.5		
2005	OMA	AAA	27	110	10	4	1	3	18	5	18	0	0	3.6	.346	.373	.490	.217	.307	.331	.416	.258	1.9	18-1B	-1
2006	*KCA*	*MLB*	*28*	*245*	*24*	*12*	*1*	*6*	*29*	*13*	*47*	*0*	*0*	*3.8*	*.261*	*.304*	*.396*	*-.087*	*.262*	*.312*	*.417*	*.241*	*0.4*	*61-1B*	*0*

Breakout: 18%   Improve: 41%   Collapse: 46%   Attrition: 37%   Comparables: Lyle Mouton, Ricky Jordan, Chris Brown

A strained back finally accomplished what two seasons of below-average offense could not, and kept Harvey out of the Royals' lineup. He is what he is: a slow singles hitter best utilized as a pinch-hitter against the LOOGYs of the world. More back problems leading to surgery will keep him out most of the year. Released.

JUSTIN HUBER   **1B**   **Bats: R Throws: R**   Height: 6' 5"   Weight: 190   Born: July 1, 1982   Age: 24

YEAR	TM	LVL	AGE	PA	R	2B	3B	HR	RBI	BB	SO	SB	CS	SPEED	BA	OBP	SLG	MLVR	EQBA	EQOBP	EQSLG	EQA	VORP	DEFENSE	
2003	SLU	A+	21	211	26	15	0	9	36	17	30	1	1	3.4	.284	.370	.514	.294	.250	.318	.488	.270	11.0	34-C	-4
2003	BIN	AA	21	220	16	13	0	6	36	19	54	0	2	2.1	.264	.350	.425	.055	.229	.303	.383	.238	-0.3	39-C	-2
2004	BIN	AA	22	295	44	16	1	11	33	46	57	2	2	4.0	.271	.414	.487	.237	.247	.374	.447	.283	17.5	64-C	-1
2005	WIC	AA	23	396	68	22	3	16	74	51	70	7	3	5.1	.343	.432	.570	.456	.313	.397	.519	.311	35.8	67-1B	-7
2005	OMA	AAA	23	131	19	6	1	7	23	16	33	3	0	4.9	.274	.374	.531	.198	.250	.339	.474	.278	3.9	32-1B	-2
2005	KCA	MLB	23	85	6	3	0	0	6	5	20	0	0	3.5	.218	.271	.256	-.365	.221	.282	.260	.201	-6.1	16-1B	-2
2006	*KCA*	*MLB*	*23*	*547*	*66*	*28*	*2*	*19*	*71*	*54*	*109*	*4*	*2*	*4.2*	*.262*	*.342*	*.449*	*.043*	*.264*	*.352*	*.473*	*.274*	*16.2*	*128-1B*	*-5*

Breakout: 15%   Improve: 42%   Collapse: 30%   Attrition: 11%   Comparables: Derrek Lee, Chris Shelton, Dwight Evans

(continued next page)

Justin Huber *(continued)*

A nifty acquisition at the 2004 trading deadline, Huber was named Texas League MVP and MVP of the Futures Game. His September struggles in Kansas City can be blamed on an undisclosed Achilles injury that also forced him out of the AFL. Like Mike Sweeney before him, his offense took a step forward after moving from catcher to first base, but the switch makes his bat much less valuable. Also like Sweeney, he shows no signs of mastering the nuances of his new position, which is why the Royals signed Mientkiewicz. It's a one-year deal, paving the way for Huber to start in 2007.

KILA KAAIHUE   **1B**   **Bats: L   Throws: R**   Height: 6′ 3″   Weight: 233   Born: March 29, 1984   Age: 22

YEAR	TM	LVL	AGE	PA	R	2B	3B	HR	RBI	BB	SO	SB	CS	SPEED	BA	OBP	SLG	MLVR	EQBA	EQOBP	EQSLG	EQA	VORP	DEFENSE
2003	BUR	A	19	476	53	21	1	11	63	67	87	1	3	2.9	.238	.355	.380	.091	.215	.312	.363	.239	-15.0	72-1B -1
2004	BUR	A	20	467	57	23	2	15	62	64	98	1	0	3.6	.246	.360	.431	.145	.223	.318	.389	.248	-8.4	113-1B -9
2005	HDS	A+	21	605	84	31	2	20	90	97	97	2	1	3.3	.304	.428	.497	.140	.228	.337	.355	.248	-10.5	126-1B -1
2006	*KCA*	*MLB*	*22*	*487*	*51*	*21*	*1*	*13*	*54*	*50*	*98*	*1*	*1*	*3.8*	*.229*	*.315*	*.371*	*-.122*	*.230*	*.324*	*.391*	*.242*	*-5.7*	*115-1B -3*

Breakout: 20%   *Improve: 49%*   *Collapse: 21%*   *Attrition: 5%*   *Comparables: Eric Sandberg, Joey Votto, Dernell Stenson*

The Royals have drafted a number of players out of Hawaii the past several years, but only Kaaihue has delivered the goods. Like most hitters in High Desert's lineup, the jury is out on whether his offensive breakout was real or a park illusion. There's no questioning his patience at the plate; he led the entire organization in walks. He's set career highs in doubles and homers in every pro season, has no problems against southpaws (.366/.466/.552 last season), and he should start the year in Double-A at just 22. While you can't have too much pitching, you can have too many first basemen. The sooner the Royals realize that and trade their excess, the better.

TERRENCE LONG   **Millstone**   **Bats: L   Throws: L**   Height: 6′ 1″   Weight: 190   Born: February 29, 1976   Age: 30

YEAR	TM	LVL	AGE	PA	R	2B	3B	HR	RBI	BB	SO	SB	CS	SPEED	BA	OBP	SLG	MLVR	EQBA	EQOBP	EQSLG	EQA	VORP	DEFENSE	
2003	OAK	MLB	27	522	64	22	2	14	61	31	67	4	1	5.3	.245	.293	.385	-.124	.243	.296	.389	.238	-10.1	64-LF 2	63-RF 6
2004	SDN	MLB	28	313	31	19	4	3	28	19	51	3	2	4.8	.295	.335	.420	.052	.300	.339	.428	.265	7.4	37-LF 0	22-CF 0
2005	KCA	MLB	29	489	62	21	3	6	53	30	56	3	3	4.9	.279	.321	.378	-.066	.285	.337	.392	.253	0.0	91-LF -9	15-RF -1
2006	*KCA*	*MLB*	*30*	*387*	*42*	*20*	*2*	*6*	*43*	*24*	*49*	*2*	*2*	*5.2*	*.272*	*.319*	*.396*	*-.055*	*.274*	*.328*	*.417*	*.249*	*1.8*	*93-LF -4*	

Breakout: 18%   *Improve: 50%*   *Collapse: 22%*   *Attrition: 19%*   *Comparables: Mike Greenwell, Joe Orsulak, Ted Uhlaender*

The Royals' approach to their defense last year can best be described as "delusional." The front office actually had the temerity to suggest that Long—known as "Magellan" in Oakland because of his wandering routes to fly balls—deserved consideration for a Gold Glove. Long was actually eight runs below average in the outfield, which is only Gold Glove-worthy relative to Emil Brown. The first step in vanquishing mediocrity is to recognize it.

CHRIS LUBANSKI   **CF**   **Bats: L   Throws: L**   Height: 6′ 3″   Weight: 200   Born: March 24, 1985   Age: 21

YEAR	TM	LVL	AGE	PA	R	2B	3B	HR	RBI	BB	SO	SB	CS	SPEED	BA	OBP	SLG	MLVR	EQBA	EQOBP	EQSLG	EQA	VORP	DEFENSE
2004	BUR	A	19	535	64	26	7	9	56	43	104	16	11	5.7	.275	.336	.414	.111	.255	.306	.388	.241	-0.1	117-CF -11
2005	HDS	A+	20	581	91	38	6	28	116	38	131	14	1	6.6	.301	.349	.554	.079	.226	.268	.396	.231	-12.2	121-CF -2
2006	*KCA*	*MLB*	*21*	*512*	*54*	*27*	*3*	*14*	*59*	*28*	*113*	*9*	*4*	*5.3*	*.242*	*.286*	*.398*	*-.129*	*.244*	*.294*	*.419*	*.236*	*1.2*	*121-CF -3*

Breakout: 37%   *Improve: 61%*   *Collapse: 17%*   *Attrition: 10%*   *Comparables: Cody Ross, Cory Aldridge, Luke Allen*

Lubanski's numbers last season were very impressive for a 20-year-old, but were also massively inflated by his home park: he hit .359/.415/.695 at High Desert, compared to just .245/.280/.416 on the road. His defense has not lived up to pre-draft expectations, with most scouts convinced that he will eventually have to move to an outfield corner. He stole 14 bases in 15 attempts and grounded into just one double play all year, so his speed appears to be intact. He started slowly but was torrid from June on, putting a bow on his season with a ridiculous 13-for-15 clip with 3 homers in the Cal League playoffs. Scouting opinions run all over the map. Lubanski is a completely different ballplayer from what the Royals were expecting: they drafted him to be the new Johnny Damon, but he looks more like the next Geoff Jenkins. There's no prospect with a less certain future; Lubanski might become a superstar or he might become Todd Dunwoody.

MITCH MAIER   **OF**   **Bats: L Throws: R**   Height: 6' 2"   Weight: 200   Born: June 30, 1982   Age: 24

YEAR	TM	LVL	AGE	PA	R	2B	3B	HR	RBI	BB	SO	SB	CS	SPEED	BA	OBP	SLG	MLVR	EQBA	EQOBP	EQSLG	EQA	VORP	DEFENSE	
2004	BUR	A	22	345	41	24	3	4	36	27	51	34	10	7.0	.300	.354	.432	.181	.271	.317	.390	.251	6.9	71-3B	7
2004	WIL	A+	22	193	25	9	2	3	17	15	29	10	2	6.9	.264	.326	.391	.021	.243	.296	.368	.238	-1.3	48-3B	-2
2005	HDS	A+	23	227	42	26	1	8	32	12	43	6	1	5.6	.336	.370	.583	.195	.243	.273	.403	.234	-7.7	41-RF	7
2005	WIC	AA	23	342	55	21	5	7	49	15	47	10	3	7.4	.255	.289	.416	-.063	.236	.272	.389	.230	-7.3	76-CF	-6
2006	KCA	MLB	24	469	53	28	4	9	48	22	81	10	5	5.6	.254	.292	.396	-.113	.256	.300	.417	.238	0.9	111-CF	1

Breakout: 27%   Improve: 62%   Collapse: 20%   Attrition: 10%   Comparables: Jorge Piedra, Brian Gordon, Daryl Boston

Lubanski's fellow 2003 1st rounder, Maier has moved from catcher to third to the outfield, and from relevance to irrelevance along the way. He briefly got plaudits as the new "Earl of Doublin" after smoking 26 doubles in 50 games for High Desert, but the air went out of his numbers on the way to Wichita. The erosion in his plate discipline is a major red flag. Despite publicly preaching the gospel of selectivity, the Royals either don't truly believe in it or don't know how to teach it. Maier's a classic tweener, doing a little bit of everything, but not enough of anything to man a corner outfield spot in the major leagues.

CHRISTOPHER McCONNELL   **SS**   **Bats: R Throws: R**   Height: 5' 11"   Weight: 170   Born: December 18, 1985 Age: 20

YEAR	TM	LVL	AGE	PA	R	2B	3B	HR	RBI	BB	SO	SB	CS	SPEED	BA	OBP	SLG	MLVR	EQBA	EQOBP	EQSLG	EQA	VORP	DEFENSE	
2005	IDA	Rk	19	320	56	17	8	6	39	31	34	7	6	5.5	.331	.403	.516	.241	.248	.299	.370	.236	1.7	65-SS	-4
2006	KCA	MLB	20	431	47	22	5	5	38	24	51	5	4	4.7	.260	.305	.377	-.112	.261	.314	.397	.238	9.4	102-SS	-4

Breakout: 34%   Improve: 56%   Collapse: 28%   Attrition: 11%   Comparables: Eduardo Reyes, Shawn Lagana, Shaun Boyd

As damning as the Royals' record with the 1st round draft picks has been, their failure to mine the middle rounds of the draft for future major leaguers has been nearly as damaging. Their last mid-round pick to find major-league success was Mark Ellis, who was drafted in 1999 and discarded in the Angel Berroa trade. McConnell was a 9th round pick in 2004, and at 19 was the best everyday hitter for Idaho Falls in a league stocked largely with college draftees. He's a million miles from the majors, but he's included here because the development of players like McConnell means more to the future success of the Royals than just about any other factor.

DONNIE MURPHY   **2B**   **Bats: R Throws: R**   Height: 5' 10"   Weight: 180   Born: March 10, 1983   Age: 23

YEAR	TM	LVL	AGE	PA	R	2B	3B	HR	RBI	BB	SO	SB	CS	SPEED	BA	OBP	SLG	MLVR	EQBA	EQOBP	EQSLG	EQA	VORP	DEFENSE				
2003	BUR	A	20	585	77	29	6	5	98	65	78	15	6	5.6	.313	.397	.425	.258	.294	.361	.423	.275	33.8	82-2B	8	40-SS	2
2004	WIL	A+	21	549	67	32	4	10	73	52	96	1	1	4.4	.254	.326	.398	.022	.232	.294	.375	.234	-4.7	102-2B	17	15-SS	2
2005	WIC	AA	22	232	33	13	1	10	32	13	32	1	1	4.0	.313	.362	.523	.258	.283	.332	.471	.271	13.7	29-2B	3	20-SS	1
2005	KCA	MLB	22	87	4	5	0	1	8	9	23	0	1	2.2	.156	.241	.260	-.443	.158	.253	.250	.188	-7.2	24-2B	-2		
2006	KCA	MLB	23	444	51	24	2	12	52	33	78	3	2	4.3	.257	.318	.415	-.043	.259	.326	.437	.254	14.2	105-2B	3		

Breakout: 35%   Improve: 54%   Collapse: 14%   Attrition: 12%   Comparables: Tucker Ashford, Steve Garvey, Glenn Hubbard

Murphy has neither Blanco's glove nor Gotay's offensive upside, but he can outhit the former and field better than the latter. Attrition among young second basemen is such that the Law of Young Pitchers ought to apply: the best way to develop an everyday second baseman is to start with three second base prospects. None of the three is can't-miss, but none of them is older than 23. A good organization would turn one of them into a quality regular. The additions of Grudzielanek and Esteban German spell the end of Murphy's ambition for everyday playing time. There is hope that he has the defensive flexibility to emerge as a super-utility player.

PAUL PHILLIPS   **C**   **Bats: R Throws: R**   Height: 5' 11"   Weight: 180   Born: April 15, 1977   Age: 29

YEAR	TM	LVL	AGE	PA	R	2B	3B	HR	RBI	BB	SO	SB	CS	SPEED	BA	OBP	SLG	MLVR	EQBA	EQOBP	EQSLG	EQA	VORP	DEFENSE	
2004	OMA	AAA	27	335	40	17	1	6	41	20	36	4	3	4.3	.312	.358	.431	.060	.277	.319	.366	.240	3.1	76-C	5
2005	OMA	AAA	28	360	45	21	1	7	42	21	44	1	4	3.9	.268	.317	.401	-.101	.229	.268	.327	.207	-14.6	83-C	10
2005	KCA	MLB	28	67	6	4	1	1	9	0	5	0	0	4.6	.269	.269	.403	-.130	.273	.284	.409	.235	0.6	18-C	2
2006	KCA	MLB	29	277	22	13	1	3	26	10	36	0	1	3.8	.246	.277	.340	-.217	.247	.284	.358	.211	-3.5	68-C	3

Breakout: 40%   Improve: 59%   Collapse: 28%   Attrition: 22%   Comparables: Hal Smith, Fred Kendall, Ben Molina

Healthy for the second straight season after missing almost three years with elbow problems, Phillips regressed slightly at the plate, although the downturn was almost entirely in batting average. He wasn't completely overmatched as Buck's caddy in September, throwing out 7 of 11 potential base stealers. Naturally, the Royals spent extra cash and a spot on the 40-man roster to give the backup job to Paul Bako, a demonstrably inferior player.

CALVIN PICKERING

CALVIN PICKERING DH **Bats: L Throws: L** Height: 6′ 5″ Weight: 260 Born: September 29, 1976 Age: 29

YEAR	TM	LVL	AGE	PA	R	2B	3B	HR	RBI	BB	SO	SB	CS	SPEED	BA	OBP	SLG	MLVR	EQBA	EQOBP	EQSLG	EQA	VORP	DEFENSE
2003	LOU	AAA	26	102	10	3	0	4	18	17	31	0	0	2.7	.284	.422	.469	.242	.252	.383	.422	.285	3.4	12-1B -1
2003	VAQ	MEX	26	368	64	13	0	25	63	75	84	1	0	3.9	.323	.465	.625	.394	.247	.379	.489	.297	30.4	
2004	OMA	AAA	27	379	65	12	1	35	79	70	85	0	1	3.1	.314	.451	.712	.626	.266	.389	.550	.312	31.4	51-1B -7
2004	KCA	MLB	27	142	21	8	1	7	26	18	42	0	0	4.7	.246	.338	.500	.091	.242	.340	.492	.282	6.1	
2005	KCA	MLB	28	31	4	0	0	1	3	3	14	0	0	5.8	.148	.226	.259	-.468	.148	.226	.259	.184	-2.7	
2005	OMA	AAA	28	396	56	16	0	23	67	56	130	1	0	4.0	.275	.384	.528	.212	.231	.324	.418	.257	3.8	
2006	*KCA*	*MLB*	*29*	*312*	*35*	*11*	*1*	*13*	*41*	*38*	*100*	*0*	*0*	*3.8*	*.238*	*.335*	*.431*	*-.007*	*.240*	*.344*	*.454*	*.266*	*7.4*	*76-DH*

Breakout: 13% Improve: 31% Collapse: 39% Attrition: 26%   Comparables: Sam Horn, Bob Hamelin, Erubiel Durazo

The Pickering-Harvey death match for a roster spot proved to be the most over-hyped conflict since Bacon's Rebellion, a 17th Century Virginia uprising which collapsed anticlimactically when its leader was devoured by his own body lice. The Royals did the right thing by giving the job to Pickering, then reneged on their decision after all of 27 at-bats. Pickering battled knee tendinitis upon his demotion to Omaha, and started 15-for-93 (.161) with 44 strikeouts. From that point on, he hit .318/.411/.603. A free agent as of this writing, at last check he was tearing up the Mexican winter league. There's still a brief Ken Phelps–type peak waiting to be sprung here. At that point, he'll probably be traded for Jay Buhner.

MATT STAIRS

MATT STAIRS 1B **Bats: L Throws: R** Height: 5′ 9″ Weight: 210 Born: February 27, 1968 Age: 38

YEAR	TM	LVL	AGE	PA	R	2B	3B	HR	RBI	BB	SO	SB	CS	SPEED	BA	OBP	SLG	MLVR	EQBA	EQOBP	EQSLG	EQA	VORP	DEFENSE	
2003	PIT	MLB	35	357	49	20	1	20	57	45	64	0	1	3.6	.292	.389	.561	.315	.285	.382	.557	.310	28.4	38-RF -2	24-1B -4
2004	KCA	MLB	36	496	48	21	3	18	66	49	92	1	0	3.8	.267	.345	.451	.074	.262	.345	.445	.272	18.7	51-RF -4	26-1B -3
2005	KCA	MLB	37	466	55	26	1	13	66	60	69	1	2	3.9	.275	.373	.444	.112	.284	.389	.471	.296	19.9	58-1B -2	11-RF -2
2006	*KCA*	*MLB*	*38*	*342*	*37*	*16*	*1*	*11*	*46*	*40*	*55*	*1*	*1*	*4.0*	*.261*	*.350*	*.438*	*.041*	*.262*	*.360*	*.461*	*.274*	*10.3*	*82-1B -2*	

Breakout: 4% Improve: 23% Collapse: 48% Attrition: 32%   Comparables: Gene Woodling, Norm Cash, Sid Gordon

For the second straight year, Stairs enjoyed playing on a 100-loss team so much that he re-upped before the season ended for barely a million dollars. He's the one true take-'n-rake hitter on the roster, and that has value on a team where no one else managed even 50 walks. His defensive "flexibility" consists mostly of his ability to play both first base or an outfield corner with an alarming lack of dexterity. Has no obvious role on the team that doesn't take playing time away from a young hitter, but this could still end well if the Royals trade him for prospects at the trading deadline. Since they've punted on that opportunity each of the last two years, why would they change now?

MIKE SWEENEY

MIKE SWEENEY 1B **Bats: R Throws: R** Height: 6′ 3″ Weight: 220 Born: July 22, 1973 Age: 32

YEAR	TM	LVL	AGE	PA	R	2B	3B	HR	RBI	BB	SO	SB	CS	SPEED	BA	OBP	SLG	MLVR	EQBA	EQOBP	EQSLG	EQA	VORP	DEFENSE
2003	KCA	MLB	29	463	62	18	1	16	83	64	56	3	2	4.2	.293	.391	.467	.137	.284	.389	.453	.293	22.3	42-1B 4
2004	KCA	MLB	30	452	56	23	0	22	79	33	44	3	2	4.0	.287	.347	.504	.146	.285	.349	.502	.286	25.4	54-1B -2
2005	KCA	MLB	31	513	63	39	0	21	83	33	61	3	0	4.1	.300	.347	.517	.191	.308	.362	.543	.303	34.6	48-1B -2
2006	*KCA*	*MLB*	*32*	*558*	*66*	*31*	*1*	*21*	*84*	*45*	*66*	*4*	*1*	*4.2*	*.288*	*.349*	*.478*	*.113*	*.290*	*.359*	*.503*	*.284*	*28.2*	*131-DH*

Breakout: 4% Improve: 27% Collapse: 27% Attrition: 9%   Comparables: Eric Karros, Ted Kluszewski, Orlando Cepeda

Sweeney was selected as the Marvin Miller Man of the Year in a vote by his fellow players, a fitting achievement for a man universally considered one of the nicest players in the game. It was not nearly as fulfilling a season on the field, as Sweeney missed more than 35 games for the fourth straight season. He remains an effective hitter when healthy; given the league-wide offensive downturn, Sweeney's performance actually translates to a better EqA (.292 to .291) than his 1999 season, when he hit .322/.387/.520. Both Sweeney and the Royals seem resigned to the fact that making him the full-time DH is the best way to keep him healthy and productive. If the Royals finally trade him for prospects, it will be a strong sign that they are finally placing winning above sentimentality.

MARK TEAHEN

MARK TEAHEN 3B **Bats: L Throws: R** Height: 6′ 3″ Weight: 210 Born: September 6, 1981 Age: 24

YEAR	TM	LVL	AGE	PA	R	2B	3B	HR	RBI	BB	SO	SB	CS	SPEED	BA	OBP	SLG	MLVR	EQBA	EQOBP	EQSLG	EQA	VORP	DEFENSE
2003	MOD	A+	21	530	68	27	4	3	71	66	113	4	0	4.9	.283	.377	.380	.067	.251	.333	.338	.242	1.7	115-3B 12
2004	MID	AA	22	229	31	15	4	6	36	29	44	0	0	4.5	.335	.419	.543	.378	.296	.376	.477	.293	19.6	52-3B 8
2004	SAC	AAA	22	81	9	8	0	0	10	11	22	0	1	3.3	.275	.383	.391	.010	.229	.336	.303	.230	-0.9	20-3B -1
2004	OMA	AAA	22	273	33	15	1	8	31	21	69	0	0	3.6	.280	.344	.447	.027	.254	.314	.386	.244	3.2	66-3B 4
2005	KCA	MLB	23	489	60	29	4	7	55	40	107	7	2	5.8	.246	.309	.376	-.116	.252	.324	.390	.250	-1.7	123-3B 2
2006	*KCA*	*MLB*	*24*	*464*	*53*	*24*	*3*	*10*	*51*	*44*	*95*	*4*	*3*	*5.2*	*.262*	*.336*	*.406*	*-.019*	*.264*	*.346*	*.427*	*.260*	*11.6*	*110-3B 2*

Breakout: 34% Improve: 55% Collapse: 21% Attrition: 22%   Comparables: Jim Mason, Mike Darr, Bobby Smith

The centerpiece of the Carlos Beltran trade is at a career crossroads this year. His unimpressive rookie performance hides the significant defensive improvement he made during the season—he was eight runs below average at third base midway through the season—as well as the fact that he finally started pulling the inside pitch late in the year, smacking four of his seven homers (and .303/.352/.505 overall) from September 1st on. He's a disciplined hitter, but he must continue to hit for at least modest power, or succumb to Sean Burroughs Syndrome.

PITCHERS

JEREMY AFFELDT Bats: L Throws: L Height: 6′ 4″ Weight: 210 Born: June 6, 1979 Age: 27

YEAR	TM	LVL	AGE	W	L	SV	G	GS	IP	H	BB	SO	HR	GB%	BABIP	STUFF	WHIP	ERA	PERA	EQERA	EQH9	EQBB9	EQSO9	EQHR9	VORP	WXRL
2003	KCA	MLB	24	7	6	4	36	18	126.0	126	38	98	12	46%	.306	17	1.30	3.93	3.91	3.77	8.7	2.6	6.8	0.8	29.9	3.4
2004	KCA	MLB	25	3	4	13	38	8	76.3	91	32	49	6	47%	.348	0	1.63	4.95	4.20	4.99	9.5	3.4	5.2	0.6	2.9	0.3
2005	KCA	MLB	26	0	2	0	49	0	49.7	56	29	39	3	54%	.331	-1	1.71	5.25	4.15	5.54	8.7	5.0	6.8	0.5	-3.3	1.4
2006	*KCA*	*MLB*	*27*	*2*	*3*	*2*	*56*	*1*	*59.7*	*65*	*26*	*42*	*6*	*49%*	*.312*	*-3*	*1.52*	*4.81*	*5.01*	*5.23*	*9.5*	*3.9*	*6.3*	*0.8*	*2.9*	*0.3*

Breakout: 23%   Improve: 43%   Collapse: 38%   Attrition: 22%   Comparables: Scott Radinsky, Jim Crawford, Jay Powell

He has everything it takes to be a great pitcher except the results, which is something we've written, more or less, for four straight years now. It's exasperating to watch a pitcher with so many reasons to succeed fail so consistently. Affeldt is a lefty who throws 94, has a hammer curveball, and possesses both intelligence and a work ethic. Ex-pitching coach Guy Hansen was convinced he was tipping his pitches, but clearly the problem goes deeper than that. Roving instructor Mike Mason got Affeldt to start throwing a changeup in September. He finished the season with 12 scoreless innings, allowing just five hits. Adding a third pitch makes Affeldt a newly viable candidate for the rotation, assuming the Royals don't decide a change of scenery is best for all concerned.

BRIAN ANDERSON Bats: B Throws: L Height: 6′ 1″ Weight: 190 Born: April 26, 1972 Age: 34

YEAR	TM	LVL	AGE	W	L	SV	G	GS	IP	H	BB	SO	HR	GB%	BABIP	STUFF	WHIP	ERA	PERA	EQERA	EQH9	EQBB9	EQSO9	EQHR9	VORP	WXRL
2003	CLE	MLB	31	9	10	0	25	24	148.0	162	32	72	21	47%	.293	-2	1.31	3.71	4.85	5.15	9.9	2.0	4.3	1.2	9.7	2.5
2003	KCA	MLB	31	5	1	0	7	7	49.7	50	11	15	6	46%	.270	-5	1.23	3.98	4.99	3.70	9.4	2.0	2.8	1.1	12.5	1.1
2004	KCA	MLB	32	6	12	0	35	26	166.0	217	53	70	33	40%	.322	-23	1.64	5.64	5.67	5.62	10.6	2.6	3.5	1.6	-10.7	0.8
2005	KCA	MLB	33	1	2	0	6	6	30.7	39	4	17	7	45%	.308	-3	1.40	6.74	5.40	5.68	10.2	1.1	4.8	2.0	-4.3	-0.2
2006	*TEX*	*MLB*	*34*	*5*	*7*	*0*	*29*	*16*	*99.7*	*121*	*21*	*46*	*18*	*43%*	*.299*	*-9*	*1.42*	*5.35*	*5.24*	*5.58*	*10.4*	*1.9*	*4.2*	*1.5*	*4.5*	*1.0*

Breakout: 14%   Improve: 50%   Collapse: 17%   Attrition: 14%   Comparables: Bob Knepper, Vern Law, Johnny Podres

Anderson's futility nearly matched that of Jose Lima during his time with the Royals, but he had an excuse: bone chips in his elbow as well as a torn ligament that required Tommy John surgery. Anderson should be ready to pitch by midseason. When healthy, he is what he is: a league-average innings sponge with a little upside. That's worth money on the open market, and the Rangers were wise to take a flyer on him as a non-roster invite.

DENNY BAUTISTA Bats: R Throws: R Height: 6′ 5″ Weight: 170 Born: August 23, 1980 Age: 25

YEAR	TM	LVL	AGE	W	L	SV	G	GS	IP	H	BB	SO	HR	GB%	BABIP	STUFF	WHIP	ERA	PERA	EQERA	EQH9	EQBB9	EQSO9	EQHR9	VORP	WXRL
2003	JUP	A+	22	8	4	0	14	14	84.0	68	35	77	2	—	.274	10	1.23	3.21	4.67	5.47	8.8	4.6	5.7	0.7	1.1	—
2003	CAR	AA	22	4	5	0	11	11	53.3	45	35	61	5	—	.288	-7	1.50	3.71	6.30	6.84	9.5	6.7	7.2	1.8	-6.9	—
2004	BOW	AA	23	3	5	0	14	13	62.7	58	33	72	5	—	.319	4	1.45	4.74	4.87	6.20	9.0	5.2	7.4	1.0	-4.1	—
2004	WIC	AA	23	4	3	0	12	12	81.7	68	32	73	3	—	.284	12	1.22	2.53	4.50	4.62	8.3	4.3	5.5	0.6	8.5	—
2004	KCA	MLB	23	0	4	0	5	5	27.7	38	11	18	2	47%	.383	7	1.77	6.50	4.30	5.52	10.4	3.1	5.2	0.6	-1.1	0.2
2005	KCA	MLB	24	2	2	0	7	7	35.7	36	17	23	2	65%	.298	6	1.46	5.80	4.42	5.15	8.3	4.2	5.6	0.5	-0.3	0.4
2006	*KCA*	*MLB*	*25*	*4*	*7*	*0*	*31*	*15*	*97.3*	*103*	*47*	*65*	*8*	*54%*	*.306*	*1*	*1.54*	*5.02*	*5.03*	*5.58*	*9.3*	*4.4*	*6.0*	*0.7*	*2.1*	*0.7*

Breakout: 30%   Improve: 62%   Collapse: 18%   Attrition: 12%   Comparables: Dan Reichert, Bryan Clark, Ernie McAnally

The Royals haven't had a pitcher strike out nine batters in a game since July of 2002. The Rangers have had four nine-K games in the past three years. Every other team in baseball has had at least seven. You can understand why the Royals are excited about Bautista, who throws in the upper 90s all game. He was rushed to the majors, and not surprisingly strained his shoulder. He should be healthy; he would have pitched in September if the Royals weren't absurdly deliberate in his rehab process. Bautista complements his velocity with a groundball/flyball ratio approaching three. Zack Greinke and Bautista give KC a pair of potential aces. Their ultimate success may be the one thing that can spare the Royals from being officially demoted to the Atlantic League.

JONAH BAYLISS

Bats: R Throws: R Height: 6' 2" Weight: 200 Born: August 13, 1980 Age: 25

YEAR	TM	LVL	AGE	W	L	SV	G	GS	IP	H	BB	SO	HR	GB%	BABIP	STUFF	WHIP	ERA	PERA	EQERA	EQH9	EQBB9	EQSO9	EQHR9	VORP	WXRL
2003	BUR	A	22	7	12	0	26	26	140.0	129	69	133	11	—	.291	-37	1.41	3.86	7.45	7.38	11.0	6.3	5.7	2.4	-24.9	—
2004	WIL	A+	23	6	6	0	24	24	110.3	117	44	78	11	—	.307	-37	1.46	4.90	6.95	7.48	11.3	4.7	4.3	2.0	-21.4	—
2005	WIC	AA	24	1	2	8	30	0	57.0	43	26	63	5	32%	.273	-6	1.21	2.84	5.26	4.25	8.2	5.4	7.3	1.2	8.0	—
2005	KCA	MLB	24	0	0	0	11	0	11.7	7	4	10	2	25%	.167	6	0.94	4.62	5.56	3.97	7.1	3.2	7.9	1.6	1.5	-0.0
2006	PIT	MLB	25	2	3	1	28	3	50.7	54	34	39	10	36%	.289	-13	1.73	6.12	6.72	6.57	9.3	5.5	6.4	1.7	-4.2	-0.3

Breakout: 24% Improve: 55% Collapse: 16% Attrition: 16% Comparables: Victor Moreno, Brandon Backe, Kurt Knudsen

A stringy right-hander whose performance never lived up to the team's flattering remarks, he finally blossomed after moving to the bullpen. Bayliss throws very hard and fairly straight, leading to an inordinate number of flyballs, some of which invariably end up in the bleachers. Traded to the Pirates for Mark Redman, he might grow up to be a decent middle relief option.

BILLY BUCKNER

Bats: R Throws: R Height: 6' 2" Weight: 215 Born: August 27, 1983 Age: 22

YEAR	TM	LVL	AGE	W	L	SV	G	GS	IP	H	BB	SO	HR	GB%	BABIP	STUFF	WHIP	ERA	PERA	EQERA	EQH9	EQBB9	EQSO9	EQHR9	VORP	WXRL
2004	IDA	Rk	20	2	2	0	8	5	34.3	44	8	37	4	—	.392	-8	1.52	3.94	6.09	6.35	11.6	2.4	4.5	2.1	-2.8	—
2005	BUR	A	21	3	7	0	11	11	60.3	66	17	60	9	50%	.322	-12	1.38	3.88	6.87	6.40	11.2	3.0	5.9	2.8	-5.1	—
2005	HDS	A+	21	5	6	0	17	17	94.0	105	46	92	10	58%	.357	-6	1.61	5.36	5.71	6.10	9.8	5.2	5.4	1.3	-5.2	—
2006	KCA	MLB	22	6	11	0	25	24	134.0	152	63	79	18	52%	.306	1	1.60	5.52	5.84	5.68	9.9	4.3	5.3	1.1	-4.0	0.6

Breakout: 34% Improve: 72% Collapse: 4% Attrition: 0% Comparables: Steve Green, Glenn Woolard, Matt Lorenzo

Buckner is a college right-hander who dropped to the 2nd round in 2004 after coming down with mononucleosis during his junior season. He recovered the velocity on his fastball after signing, which, along with his knuckle curve, has allowed him to strike out more than a batter an inning since turning pro. He survived High Desert as well as can be expected, surrendering 10 homers despite a G/F ratio greater than 2 to 1. There's definite breakout potential once he gets out of the Cal League.

AMBIORIX BURGOS

Bats: R Throws: R Height: 6' 0" Weight: 180 Born: April 19, 1984 Age: 22

YEAR	TM	LVL	AGE	W	L	SV	G	GS	IP	H	BB	SO	HR	GB%	BABIP	STUFF	WHIP	ERA	PERA	EQERA	EQH9	EQBB9	EQSO9	EQHR9	VORP	WXRL
2004	BUR	A	20	7	11	0	27	26	133.7	109	75	172	13	—	.309	-16	1.38	4.38	6.99	6.40	9.9	7.0	7.0	2.0	-10.8	—
2005	KCA	MLB	21	3	5	2	59	0	63.3	60	31	65	6	47%	.321	20	1.44	3.98	4.02	3.88	7.9	4.3	8.9	0.8	11.6	0.6
2006	KCA	MLB	22	2	3	2	35	1	42.7	41	26	39	5	45%	.302	5	1.57	4.78	5.23	5.47	8.4	5.5	8.3	1.0	3.1	0.2

Breakout: 23% Improve: 57% Collapse: 25% Attrition: 37% Comparables: Onan Masaoka, Scott Scudder, Don Stanhouse

He has more in common with Armando Benitez than just his initials. Burgos was moved to the bullpen in spring training last year, and it was instantly impossible to think of him as anything but a reliever. He throws two pitches: an upper-90s fastball and a fall-off-the-table splitter. Once he was encouraged to focus on those pitches, he was so dominant in Double-A that he was brought to Kansas City before the end of April. He weathered a strained shoulder and a brief return to Double-A quite well. Burgos will be challenging Bobby Jenks for the title of best young closer in the division before long. Keep in mind, he's three years younger than Jenks and not shaped like a beer barrel.

SHAWN CAMP

Bats: R Throws: R Height: 6' 1" Weight: 200 Born: November 18, 1975 Age: 30

YEAR	TM	LVL	AGE	W	L	SV	G	GS	IP	H	BB	SO	HR	GB%	BABIP	STUFF	WHIP	ERA	PERA	EQERA	EQH9	EQBB9	EQSO9	EQHR9	VORP	WXRL
2003	ALT	AA	27	0	2	0	18	0	29.0	26	11	35	2	—	.316	-6	1.28	4.34	5.40	6.41	9.8	4.7	7.8	1.4	-2.4	—
2003	NAS	AAA	27	0	1	0	33	1	43.3	50	15	36	2	—	.338	-7	1.50	4.99	4.43	6.33	10.1	3.8	5.9	0.6	-3.5	—
2004	KCA	MLB	28	2	2	2	42	0	66.7	74	16	51	10	58%	.320	1	1.33	3.91	4.48	4.35	9.4	2.0	6.3	1.2	10.7	1.2
2005	OMA	AAA	29	3	6	1	21	7	67.7	71	22	42	9	49%	.300	-25	1.37	3.86	6.06	5.65	10.1	3.3	3.9	1.7	-0.4	—
2005	KCA	MLB	29	1	4	0	29	0	49.0	69	13	28	4	57%	.369	-4	1.67	6.43	4.30	6.02	10.5	2.2	4.8	0.7	-8.8	-1.4
2006	KCA	MLB	30	3	5	1	53	3	74.7	89	24	40	9	51%	.314	-11	1.51	5.18	5.47	5.41	10.5	2.9	4.8	1.0	0.8	0.1

Breakout: 37% Improve: 59% Collapse: 21% Attrition: 5% Comparables: Jim Bouton, Jim Acker, Buddy Groom

A middle reliever who succeeds by throwing strikes and keeping the ball down, Camp's ERA ballooned more than 2.5 runs last year despite essentially the same performance as in 2004 regarding homers, strikeouts, and walks. The difference stemmed almost entirely from what happened to balls in play. If you're going to send out a historically bad defense, don't compound the problem with pitchers that pitch to contact. Camp was released. After signing with Tampa Bay, his world tour isn't turning out any better than your garage band's would.

LUIS COTA Bats: R Throws: R Height: 6' 0" Weight: 193 Born: August 19, 1985 Age: 20

YEAR	TM	LVL	AGE	W	L	SV	G	GS	IP	H	BB	SO	HR	GB%	BABIP	STUFF	WHIP	ERA	PERA	EQERA	EQH9	EQBB9	EQSO9	EQHR9	VORP	WXRL
2004	IDA	Rk	18	2	1	0	13	12	48.0	61	21	40	5	—	.366	-17	1.71	5.81	6.89	7.45	11.4	4.3	3.5	1.9	-9.9	—
2005	BUR	A	19	5	8	0	26	26	148.0	143	63	137	10	52%	.317	9	1.39	4.01	5.24	5.42	9.4	4.2	5.7	1.2	2.9	—
2006	KCA	MLB	20	6	11	0	26	25	142.0	159	62	87	18	49%	.305	6	1.56	5.34	5.59	5.47	9.8	4.0	5.5	1.1	-1.1	0.9

Breakout: 20% Improve: 59% Collapse: 4% Attrition: 0% Comparables: Hayden Penn, Colby Miller, Matt Wright

Probably the best pitching prospect in the system, but years away from making an impact. Cota was a 10th round pick in 2003 who signed for first-round money as a draft-and-follow the next spring. His fastball was voted the best in the Midwest League last year, on account of velocity and late movement. The Royals have made polish a priority over potential in their recent draft picks, so Cota's upside is a refreshing change of pace. Keeping him healthy is a sufficient goal in the short term.

CHRIS DeMARIA Bats: R Throws: R Height: 6' 3" Weight: 210 Born: September 28, 1980 Age: 25

YEAR	TM	LVL	AGE	W	L	SV	G	GS	IP	H	BB	SO	HR	GB%	BABIP	STUFF	WHIP	ERA	PERA	EQERA	EQH9	EQBB9	EQSO9	EQHR9	VORP	WXRL
2003	WPT	A-	22	6	3	3	25	1	47.0	36	10	48	3	—	.262	-22	0.98	2.68	6.97	6.10	11.1	2.8	5.4	2.6	-2.3	—
2004	HIC	A	23	8	3	10	40	0	79.7	62	20	102	5	—	.295	-1	1.03	2.94	4.48	5.09	9.0	3.0	6.5	1.1	4.2	—
2005	HDS	A+	24	4	2	19	48	0	60.7	57	10	73	8	36%	.327	-10	1.10	2.22	5.09	4.17	9.4	2.0	6.3	1.7	9.3	—
2006	MIL	MLB	25	2	3	1	30	3	53.0	56	19	41	11	41%	.282	-5	1.41	5.04	5.67	5.41	9.6	2.8	6.1	1.9	1.6	0.2

Breakout: 23% Improve: 50% Collapse: 19% Attrition: 11% Comparables: John Daniels, Keith Troutman, Heath Bell

DeMaria climbed from A-ball to the majors less than a year after he was selected in the minor league portion of the Rule 5 draft. Although his best pitch is his changeup, DeMaria was surprisingly effective at High Desert, adding another data point to the argument that the best way to pitch at altitude is to change speeds; his strikeout/walk ratio in the minors last year was 92-12. Swapped to Milwaukee in a minor deal.

JIMMY GOBBLE Bats: L Throws: L Height: 6' 3" Weight: 190 Born: July 19, 1981 Age: 24

YEAR	TM	LVL	AGE	W	L	SV	G	GS	IP	H	BB	SO	HR	GB%	BABIP	STUFF	WHIP	ERA	PERA	EQERA	EQH9	EQBB9	EQSO9	EQHR9	VORP	WXRL
2003	WIC	AA	21	12	8	0	22	22	132.7	128	40	100	11	—	.282	-1	1.27	3.19	5.31	5.10	9.6	3.2	5.2	1.4	7.1	—
2003	KCA	MLB	21	4	5	0	9	9	52.7	56	15	31	8	35%	.286	7	1.35	4.61	4.96	4.96	9.6	2.6	5.1	1.2	5.6	0.4
2004	KCA	MLB	22	9	8	0	25	24	148.0	157	43	49	24	40%	.262	-14	1.35	5.35	5.53	4.80	9.5	2.4	2.8	1.3	7.7	2.1
2005	OMA	AAA	23	2	7	0	12	12	58.3	76	21	45	8	44%	.360	-9	1.66	6.64	5.31	7.28	10.8	3.2	5.0	1.4	-11.1	—
2005	KCA	MLB	23	1	1	0	28	4	53.7	64	30	38	9	35%	.329	-12	1.75	5.70	5.62	5.14	9.5	4.8	6.1	1.4	0.3	0.9
2006	KCA	MLB	24	3	6	1	38	10	82.7	98	31	45	14	40%	.302	-11	1.55	5.77	5.98	5.88	10.3	3.4	4.9	1.4	-4.3	-0.1

Breakout: 10% Improve: 34% Collapse: 28% Attrition: 7% Comparables: Pete Schourek, Mike McCormick, Dan Serafini

His strikeout rate more than doubled from 2004, but he still gave up a homer every six innings and his walk rate jumped to more than one every other inning. Take 'n rake works for hitters. The same approach on the mound—nibble and hang?—does not. Gobble was supposed to thrive in the bullpen, but his ERA was 6.19 in relief, 4.67 in the rotation. The Royals' approach to building a pitching staff has been to load up on flyball pitchers with average velocity. Can't understand why that didn't work.

ZACK GREINKE Bats: R Throws: R Height: 6' 2" Weight: 190 Born: October 21, 1983 Age: 22

YEAR	TM	LVL	AGE	W	L	SV	G	GS	IP	H	BB	SO	HR	GB%	BABIP	STUFF	WHIP	ERA	PERA	EQERA	EQH9	EQBB9	EQSO9	EQHR9	VORP	WXRL
2003	WIL	A+	19	11	1	0	14	14	87.0	56	13	78	5	—	.218	28	0.79	1.14	4.28	3.04	8.0	1.6	6.4	1.2	22.8	—
2003	WIC	AA	19	4	3	0	9	9	53.0	58	5	34	5	—	.298	10	1.19	3.23	4.88	4.53	10.5	0.9	4.5	1.6	6.1	—
2004	OMA	AAA	20	1	1	0	6	6	28.7	25	6	23	2	—	.261	22	1.08	2.51	3.86	2.89	8.4	1.9	5.8	0.6	8.4	—
2004	KCA	MLB	20	8	11	0	24	24	145.0	143	26	100	26	38%	.264	14	1.15	3.97	4.66	3.48	8.9	1.5	5.8	1.4	34.6	4.3
2005	KCA	MLB	21	5	17	0	33	33	183.0	233	53	114	23	40%	.340	9	1.56	5.80	4.63	5.19	9.9	2.5	5.3	1.0	-7.0	1.7
2006	KCA	MLB	22	10	12	0	30	30	185.3	200	45	113	24	42%	.292	14	1.32	4.40	4.68	4.57	9.4	2.2	5.5	1.1	20.3	3.4

Breakout: 18% Improve: 47% Collapse: 16% Attrition: 5% Comparables: Larry Christenson, Roger Erickson, Ralph Terry

The Royals have now had seven pitching coaches since 1999. Some of those changes were precipitant, but Guy Hansen's work with Greinke justified his dismissal. Hansen tinkered with Greinke's delivery starting in spring training, when they fought over which side of the rubber he should stand on. Eight starts into the year, Greinke's ERA stood at 3.09. From that point on, it was 6.73, with 189 hits allowed in 136 innings. The simplest explanation for the change was that he

(continued next page)

Zack Greinke *(continued)*

was throwing his fastball with significantly more velocity than he did as a rookie, but with significantly less idea where it was going; his walk rate was nearly 80% higher than in his rookie season. Greinke also threw far fewer off-speed pitches than he did as a rookie. It was if someone had convinced him that all his success had come despite, not because of, his ability to change speeds and penchant for valuing placement over velocity. However, Greinke is not Roger Clemens, and it was stupid for him to try to pitch as if he was. The kid is still just 22 years old. There's still massive upside here, and if he only becomes Brad Radke instead of Bret Saberhagen, that wouldn't be a bad thing. For it to happen, though, the Royals need to work with him, not against him.

RUNELVYS HERNANDEZ Bats: R Throws: R   Height: 6′ 1″ Weight: 200 Born: April 27, 1978   Age: 28

YEAR	TM	LVL	AGE	W	L	SV	G	GS	IP	H	BB	SO	HR	GB%	BABIP	STUFF	WHIP	ERA	PERA	EQERA	EQH9	EQBB9	EQSO9	EQHR9	VORP	WXRL
2003	KCA	MLB	25	7	5	0	16	16	91.7	87	37	48	9	45%	.267	3	1.35	4.61	4.86	4.57	8.8	3.7	4.7	0.8	13.2	2.1
2005	KCA	MLB	27	8	14	0	29	29	159.7	172	70	88	18	38%	.298	0	1.52	5.52	5.00	4.89	9.0	3.9	4.8	0.9	2.5	1.1
2006	KCA	MLB	28	7	11	0	32	24	150.0	161	62	85	20	42%	.288	-1	1.48	5.00	5.25	5.21	9.4	3.7	5.1	1.1	5.8	1.6

Breakout: 14% Improve: 39% Collapse: 21% Attrition: 6%   Comparables: *Eli Grba, Tracy Stallard, Charlie Puleo*

Hernandez owes his reputation in Kansas City to the organizational commitment to low expectations. Ordinarily a 5.52 ERA is not considered a success, but the Royals raved about his return from Tommy John surgery and consider him one of the pillars of their rotation. Hernandez wasn't all that great before his surgery; he's never whiffed more than 5.5 batters per nine. The Royals may hang their hat on pitchers rebounding in their second year following TJ surgery, but they won't want to hang their hat on Hernandez's 9.45 ERA from last August 1st on.

J. P. HOWELL   Bats: L Throws: L   Height: 6′ 0″ Weight: 180 Born: April 25, 1983   Age: 23

YEAR	TM	LVL	AGE	W	L	SV	G	GS	IP	H	BB	SO	HR	GB%	BABIP	STUFF	WHIP	ERA	PERA	EQERA	EQH9	EQBB9	EQSO9	EQHR9	VORP	WXRL
2005	HDS	A+	22	3	1	0	8	8	46.0	33	24	48	2	69%	.274	7	1.24	1.96	4.95	3.92	7.4	6.0	6.0	0.6	8.2	—
2005	WIC	AA	22	2	0	0	3	3	18.0	12	5	23	2	63%	.256	16	0.94	2.50	4.86	3.78	7.6	3.2	8.6	1.6	3.4	—
2005	OMA	AAA	22	3	1	0	7	7	37.7	40	19	29	1	57%	.355	7	1.56	4.06	4.26	4.74	9.0	4.5	5.2	0.2	3.6	—
2005	KCA	MLB	22	3	5	0	15	15	72.7	73	39	54	9	54%	.299	3	1.54	6.19	5.21	6.05	8.6	4.8	6.5	1.1	-7.9	0.1
2006	KCA	MLB	23	7	12	0	33	28	151.3	153	77	106	14	52%	.298	7	1.52	4.98	5.00	5.21	8.9	4.6	6.3	0.8	4.0	1.5

Breakout: 17% Improve: 56% Collapse: 11% Attrition: 0%   Comparables: *John Parrish, Pete Falcone, Steve Barber*

In a normal organization, he'd be one of the top pitching prospects in the game. In this one, he's already accrued a half-season of major league experience and an early stench of failure. He struck out eight in his major league debut, then got hammered in his next seven games before the inevitable return to Triple-A. He was much better in his return, spotting his upper 80s fastball on both sides of the plate and throwing a very good curveball for strikes. Scouts describe his curveball as "very heavy," an unusual distinction for the pitch, and it may explain why he has shown strong groundball tendencies in his career. Howell isn't another George or Gobble. Scouts compare him to Greinke for his ability to throw strikes with four pitches and change speeds on all of them.

JOSE LIMA   Bats: R Throws: R   Height: 6′ 3″ Weight: 205 Born: September 30, 1972 Age: 33

YEAR	TM	LVL	AGE	W	L	SV	G	GS	IP	H	BB	SO	HR	GB%	BABIP	STUFF	WHIP	ERA	PERA	EQERA	EQH9	EQBB9	EQSO9	EQHR9	VORP	WXRL
2003	KCA	MLB	30	8	3	0	14	14	73.3	80	26	32	7	42%	.296	-1	1.45	4.91	4.76	4.40	9.7	3.2	3.8	0.7	11.6	1.6
2004	LAN	MLB	31	13	5	0	36	24	170.3	178	34	93	33	49%	.273	-15	1.24	4.07	5.27	4.67	10.1	1.7	4.5	1.7	27.0	4.2
2005	KCA	MLB	32	5	16	0	32	32	168.7	219	61	80	31	38%	.320	-19	1.66	6.99	5.73	6.24	10.4	3.2	4.1	1.5	-31.6	-1.1
2006	KCA	MLB	33	6	10	0	32	21	130.7	155	40	61	20	42%	.299	-9	1.49	5.36	5.61	5.76	10.4	2.7	4.2	1.3	0.0	0.8

Breakout: 22% Improve: 50% Collapse: 27% Attrition: 9%   Comparables: *Willie Blair, Dave Mlicki, Ron Darling*

By July 15th, Lima had made 19 starts for the Royals, going 2-8 with a much-deserved 7.16 ERA. Any rational organization would have canned him right then. Even an irrational organization would have released him rather than pay him incentive bonuses beginning with his 20th start. The Royals figured they could afford to blow the cash in anticipation of his inevitable turnaround. Lima did bounce back in the second half; he was 3-8 with a 6.75 ERA. He now holds the unenviable distinction of having the worst single-season ERA in major league history by a pitcher who made 30-plus starts. He already held the National League record (6.65), set with the Astros in 2000.

MIKE MacDOUGAL Bats: B Throws: R Height: 6' 4" Weight: 190 Born: March 5, 1977 Age: 29

YEAR	TM	LVL	AGE	W	L	SV	G	GS	IP	H	BB	SO	HR	GB%	BABIP	STUFF	WHIP	ERA	PERA	EQERA	EQH9	EQBB9	EQSO9	EQHR9	VORP	WXRL
2003	KCA	MLB	26	3	5	27	68	0	64.0	64	32	57	4	59%	.335	10	1.50	4.08	4.15	4.57	8.6	4.3	7.6	0.6	9.7	-0.7
2004	KCA	MLB	27	1	1	1	13	0	11.3	16	9	14	2	51%	.452	4	2.36	5.58	5.11	5.84	10.2	5.8	9.5	1.5	-1.5	-0.9
2005	KCA	MLB	28	5	6	21	68	0	70.3	69	24	72	6	56%	.330	21	1.34	3.33	3.47	3.72	7.8	3.0	8.8	0.7	13.0	1.2
2006	KCA	MLB	29	2	4	10	50	0	53.7	54	24	46	4	53%	.312	6	1.45	4.12	4.44	4.69	8.7	4.1	7.7	0.6	7.2	0.7

Breakout: 28% Improve: 48% Collapse: 25% Attrition: 20% Comparables: Mike Timlin, George Frazier, Todd Jones

Most pitching coaches are not inherently good or bad. Rather, some work better with certain pitchers than others. Hansen couldn't figure out Greinke, but he straightened out MacDougal's mechanics so he could throw strikes consistently and taught him a new cut fastball, giving him a third weapon. MacDougal has always been a power pitcher who induced groundballs; his control may relapse, but MacDougal wouldn't be the first wild-as-sin flamethrower to suddenly find command and keep it. Robb Nen is a recent example.

LEO NUNEZ Bats: R Throws: R Height: 6' 1" Weight: 150 Born: August 14, 1983 Age: 22

YEAR	TM	LVL	AGE	W	L	SV	G	GS	IP	H	BB	SO	HR	GB%	BABIP	STUFF	WHIP	ERA	PERA	EQERA	EQH9	EQBB9	EQSO9	EQHR9	VORP	WXRL
2003	WPT	A-	19	4	3	0	8	8	38.3	31	12	41	0	—	.296	19	1.12	3.05	3.79	5.80	9.1	3.8	5.8	0.3	-0.8	—
2003	HIC	A	19	2	1	0	13	7	48.3	59	14	37	6	—	.329	-21	1.51	5.59	7.29	8.08	12.8	3.2	4.3	2.8	-12.6	—
2004	HIC	A	20	10	4	1	27	20	144.0	121	46	140	16	—	.279	-8	1.16	3.12	5.95	4.68	9.6	3.6	5.3	1.8	13.8	—
2005	KCA	MLB	21	3	2	0	41	0	53.7	73	18	32	9	38%	.354	-12	1.70	7.54	5.24	6.35	10.5	2.9	5.1	1.4	-10.5	-0.6
2006	KCA	MLB	22	1	2	1	21	1	26.7	29	10	16	4	40%	.291	-7	1.45	5.14	5.15	6.36	9.4	3.4	5.6	1.2	0.8	0.0

Breakout: 31% Improve: 56% Collapse: 26% Attrition: 50% Comparables: Mike Johnson, Don Carrithers, Wally Ritchie

The Royals claim they won't eat any part of Mike Sweeney's contract in a trade, but they paid half of Benito Santiago's salary in 2004 in order to get Nunez from the Pirates. No player is more emblematic of the Royals' insane approach to rushing their prospects than Nunez, who had no business being in the majors last season, let alone tossing 54 innings. He has two things going for him: his age, and a hard fastball he can throw for strikes. Unfortunately, his fastball proves itself to be completely straight more often than Hugh Hefner, which leads to approximately as much scoring.

ANDY SISCO Bats: L Throws: L Height: 6' 9" Weight: 260 Born: January 13, 1983 Age: 23

YEAR	TM	LVL	AGE	W	L	SV	G	GS	IP	H	BB	SO	HR	GB%	BABIP	STUFF	WHIP	ERA	PERA	EQERA	EQH9	EQBB9	EQSO9	EQHR9	VORP	WXRL
2003	LNS	A	20	6	8	0	19	19	94.0	76	31	99	3	—	.285	16	1.14	3.54	4.48	6.01	8.9	3.9	6.4	0.8	-4.0	—
2004	DAY	A+	21	4	10	0	26	25	126.0	118	65	134	11	—	.325	-12	1.45	4.21	6.22	5.84	9.9	5.6	6.5	1.7	-3.2	—
2005	KCA	MLB	22	2	5	0	67	0	75.3	68	42	76	6	42%	.313	19	1.46	3.11	3.96	3.03	7.4	4.9	8.7	0.7	21.3	0.2
2006	KCA	MLB	23	2	3	2	49	1	55.3	53	28	49	6	40%	.299	7	1.46	4.40	4.63	5.18	8.4	4.5	8.0	0.9	6.8	0.5

Breakout: 23% Improve: 43% Collapse: 35% Attrition: 28% Comparables: Bart Johnson, Dennys Reyes, Pete Schourek

Prior to 2005, the Royals had never had a pitcher under the age of 23 strike out more than a man per inning. Last season, two pitchers, Sisco and Burgos, accomplished the feat. Unlike Burgos, the giant called Sisquatch need not be limited to relief work. Sisco throws a mid-90s fastball and a slider that threatens to take the shoetops off of right-handed hitters, and his height and repertoire bring to mind Randy Johnson. Though Sisco was wisely slotted in long relief after being picked in the Rule 5 draft, he has the stuff and body to shoulder a more demanding role. It would be a waste if the Royals didn't give him that opportunity at some point this season.

KYLE SNYDER Bats: B Throws: R Height: 6' 8" Weight: 220 Born: September 9, 1977 Age: 28

YEAR	TM	LVL	AGE	W	L	SV	G	GS	IP	H	BB	SO	HR	GB%	BABIP	STUFF	WHIP	ERA	PERA	EQERA	EQH9	EQBB9	EQSO9	EQHR9	VORP	WXRL
2003	OMA	AAA	25	3	0	0	5	5	29.0	28	6	15	3	—	.258	-3	1.17	2.79	5.60	3.95	9.9	2.3	4.0	1.6	5.0	—
2003	KCA	MLB	25	1	6	0	15	15	85.3	94	21	39	11	49%	.294	-1	1.35	5.17	4.75	4.96	9.7	2.2	4.0	1.1	8.3	1.1
2005	OMA	AAA	27	2	3	0	15	12	66.0	61	22	48	3	57%	.291	2	1.26	3.55	4.36	5.06	8.7	3.2	4.6	0.6	3.8	—
2005	KCA	MLB	27	1	3	0	13	3	36.0	55	10	19	3	47%	.388	-5	1.81	6.75	4.15	5.77	10.8	2.3	4.4	0.7	-6.1	-0.5
2006	KCA	MLB	28	3	6	0	28	12	78.7	96	24	38	10	48%	.315	-10	1.53	5.45	5.63	5.86	10.7	2.8	4.4	1.1	-1.4	0.2

Breakout: 15% Improve: 37% Collapse: 32% Attrition: 12% Comparables: Tim Pugh, Sean Bergman, Bob Scanlan

Snyder had pretty much the best-case scenario for labrum surgery in the spring of 2004: a pristine operation by shoulder specialist Dr. Craig Morgan, a 12-month rehab that proceeded without a hitch, and no recurrence of shoulder problems after his return. Even then, he lost five miles per hour on his fastball, and without the separation in velocity between his fastball and a curveball he can throw for strikes, there's not much left here but to hope he might one day be a decent swingman. Snyder is another one of the Royals' pitch-to-contact guys that suffers from the defense behind him.

DANNY TAMAYO Bats: R Throws: R   Height: 6′ 1″ Weight: 240 Born: June 3, 1979   Age: 27

YEAR	TM	LVL	AGE	W	L	SV	G	GS	IP	H	BB	SO	HR	GB%	BABIP	STUFF	WHIP	ERA	PERA	EQERA	EQH9	EQBB9	EQSO9	EQHR9	VORP	WXRL
2003	WIC	AA	24	11	14	0	27	26	154.0	159	56	95	16	—	.280	-35	1.40	4.56	6.72	6.59	10.6	4.2	4.0	2.0	-15.9	—
2004	WIC	AA	25	12	7	0	25	25	142.3	166	36	123	15	—	.351	-15	1.42	3.98	5.73	5.53	10.9	2.9	5.0	1.8	1.1	—
2005	OMA	AAA	26	9	8	0	30	27	160.3	192	50	103	27	43%	.324	-28	1.51	5.28	6.15	5.98	10.8	3.0	4.1	1.9	-6.7	—
2006	KCA	MLB	27	4	10	0	30	19	115.0	142	42	57	21	43%	.306	-11	1.60	6.03	6.41	6.13	10.9	3.3	4.5	1.5	-9.0	-0.2

Breakout: 23% Improve: 53% Collapse: 15% Attrition: 0%   Comparables: Jason Middlebrook, Dan Smith, Juan Figueroa

You couldn't design a more generic, standard-issue minor league pitcher: a former college right-hander, fastball around 90, good changeup, so-so slider, decent numbers all the way up the chain, but nothing special. Tamayo might have stepped off the journeyman path last August, when he learned a new curveball grip from Howell, his Omaha teammate. In his last seven starts he had a 3.47 ERA and a 31/6 K/BB ratio, raising his chances of a meaningful major league career all the way to "slim," up from "infinitesimal."

DENNIS TANKERSLEY Bats: R Throws: R   Height: 6′ 2″ Weight: 185 Born: February 24, 1979   Age: 27

YEAR	TM	LVL	AGE	W	L	SV	G	GS	IP	H	BB	SO	HR	GB%	BABIP	STUFF	WHIP	ERA	PERA	EQERA	EQH9	EQBB9	EQSO9	EQHR9	VORP	WXRL
2003	POR	AAA	24	8	11	0	27	27	151.0	149	67	148	15	—	.305	1	1.43	4.65	5.23	5.60	9.3	4.7	7.4	1.4	0.0	—
2004	POR	AAA	25	7	4	0	19	19	120.0	114	37	86	10	—	.287	4	1.26	3.15	4.75	4.59	9.1	3.2	4.8	0.9	13.0	—
2004	SDN	MLB	25	0	5	0	9	6	35.0	35	17	29	3	49%	.302	4	1.49	5.14	4.33	6.62	8.9	3.8	6.6	0.8	-3.7	0.3
2005	OMA	AAA	26	9	8	0	32	23	136.0	148	59	104	15	41%	.319	-13	1.52	4.24	5.52	5.32	9.9	4.2	4.8	1.2	4.2	—
2006	SLN	MLB	27	5	6	0	27	13	89.7	94	41	57	12	44%	.287	-6	1.50	5.08	5.37	5.71	9.3	3.8	5.3	1.2	0.9	0.6

Breakout: 14% Improve: 42% Collapse: 19% Attrition: 1%   Comparables: Sammy Ellis, Jorge Sosa, Manuel Aybar

Four years ago, this guy and Jake Peavy were joined at the hip. Both were Padres prospects, and they were ranked 11th and 12th on our Top 50 Prospects list. Tankersley was the guy ranked 11th, which just goes to show you that picking prospects, especially pitching prospects, is a crapshoot. Tankersley is a Quadruple-A pitcher with the standard upside that goes with any pitcher that hasn't been tried out of the bullpen yet. Signed with the Cardinals; he's almost old enough for La Russa and Duncan to work their magic on him.

MIKE WOOD Bats: R Throws: R   Height: 6′ 3″ Weight: 180 Born: April 26, 1980   Age: 26

YEAR	TM	LVL	AGE	W	L	SV	G	GS	IP	H	BB	SO	HR	GB%	BABIP	STUFF	WHIP	ERA	PERA	EQERA	EQH9	EQBB9	EQSO9	EQHR9	VORP	WXRL
2003	SAC	AAA	23	9	3	0	16	16	91.3	87	23	59	5	—	.276	12	1.20	3.06	4.26	4.16	9.0	2.6	5.0	0.7	14.2	—
2004	SAC	AAA	24	11	3	0	15	15	90.0	83	24	66	8	—	.274	8	1.19	2.80	4.60	4.30	8.5	2.7	5.0	0.9	12.7	—
2004	KCA	MLB	24	3	8	0	17	17	100.0	112	28	54	16	52%	.299	-4	1.40	5.94	5.05	5.13	9.6	2.3	4.5	1.2	0.9	0.9
2005	KCA	MLB	25	5	8	2	47	10	115.0	129	52	60	18	54%	.298	-20	1.57	4.46	5.66	4.51	9.5	4.1	4.6	1.3	8.1	0.5
2006	KCA	MLB	26	5	8	2	46	12	109.0	126	39	58	12	51%	.307	-7	1.50	4.94	5.24	5.29	10.1	3.2	4.8	0.9	4.1	0.8

Breakout: 21% Improve: 40% Collapse: 33% Attrition: 11%   Comparables: John Buzhardt, Mark Grant, Steve Blass

It's well-known that win-loss records can be deceiving, but so can ERAs. Wood's ERA dropped nearly a run and a half last season, even though opposing hitters did better (.287/.367/.484) than they did in 2004 (.286/.342/.491). The explanation is Wood's performance with runners in scoring position. In 2004, they hit .345/.392/.736; last year, it was .214/.329/.328. No Royal gets more out of his stuff than Wood, but his stuff just isn't that special. His walk rate spiked last year, which is a problem. No pitcher gets enough groundballs to get away with surrendering nearly 15 baserunners per nine innings.

Line Outs

Position/Player	TM	LVL	AGE	PA	R	2B	3B	HR	RBI	BB	SO	SB-CS	SPEED	BA/OBP/SLG	MLVR	EQBA/OBP/SLG	EQA	VORP
UT J. McEwing	KCA	MLB	32	186	16	7	0	1	6	6	35	4-4	4.9	.239/.263/.294	-.325	.249/.285/.316	.212	-11.5
2B P. Maestrales#	HDS	A+	26	275	55	18	3	7	33	47	41	6-3	5.7	.333/.447/.533	.249	.229/.325/.331	.237	-2.2
OF A. Moye	HDS	A+	22	343	68	15	4	20	64	20	97	10-6	7.0	.309/.353/.569	.115	.233/.270/.407	.231	-12.3
C P. Tupman*	WIC	AA	25	422	59	16	2	2	32	46	62	1-2	4.3	.263/.355/.334	-.052	.228/.309/.288	.219	-14.2

Pitcher	TM	LVL	AGE	W	L	SV	IP	H	BB	SO	HR	GB%	BABIP	STUFF	WHIP	ERA	PERA	EQERA	EQH9	EQBB9	EQSO9	EQHR9	VORP
B. Bass	WIC	AA	23	12	8	0	165.0	185	53	102	14	54%	.323	-9	1.44	5.24	5.36	5.97	10.0	3.6	4.0	1.2	-6.6
D. J. Carrasco	KCA	MLB	28	6	8	0	114.7	129	51	49	11	55%	.306	-3	1.57	4.79	5.19	4.42	9.4	4.0	3.7	0.8	7.2
C. Griffin	WIC	AA	22	1	1	1	56.0	45	43	36	4	49%	.256	-33	1.57	4.02	7.14	5.40	8.5	8.9	4.5	1.0	1.1

Joe McEwing forces the question, what's sadder than watching a 106-loss team trot out the second base platoon of Super Joe and Denny Hocking, as the Royals did for much of August and September? **Pete Maestrales** was acquired in the Eli Marrero trade, and re-signed as a minor league free agent, only to be lost in the Rule 5 draft because they didn't protect him on their Triple-A roster. **Alan Moye's** single largest credential is his status as owner David Glass's favorite Royals prospect. There's no accounting for taste. **Matt Tupman** is a catcher whose modest on-base ability is exacerbated by a complete lack of power. His prospects for a backup job rely on his hitting lefty.

Brian Bass is an over-hyped prospect who missed most of 2004 with shoulder problems. He has average stuff and needs to be perfect to survive. He was just that in the AFL: no walks in 30 IP. A 4.79 ERA is nothing to write home about, but it made **D. J. Carrasco** the Royals' most effective starter for most of the season. Sold to the Hawks in Japan. **Colt Griffin** is the former schoolboy wonder with the 100 mph fastball throws closer to 90 now. Destined to become a ghost story told to scare new scouts before they hit the road.

Los Angeles de Los Angeles

Things have never been better for the Angels. They've won the contentious AL West twice in a row, a first in team history. With three postseason appearances in four years, they've doubled the franchise's total while building up a rabid following, topping three million in attendance for three consecutive years. Last year's gate of 3.4 million set a franchise record even as the team attempted to claim the name of the nation's second-largest media market, thereby setting up a showdown with the city of Anaheim. With the nucleus of a winner still intact and some of the game's brightest prospects in the pipeline, the road to the division title will continue to run through Anaheim for the foreseeable future, no matter what city they pledge allegiance to.

When billboard magnate Arte Moreno bought the Angels from Disney, they were fresh off of their 2002 World Championship, the one that finally laid to rest the franchise's history of near-misses. Despite a 77–85 showing in 2003, the team drew 3 million at the gate for the first time in its 43-year history, but Moreno quickly showed an unwillingness to settle for profitable mediocrity. He began pouring money into the team for use in the free-agent market. In particular, the game's first Hispanic owner targeted Hispanic free agents such as Bartolo Colon, Kelvim Escobar, and especially Vlad Guerrero, signing contracts worth a total of $147 million prior to the 2004 season. In doing so, he brought the Angels' payroll into the top tier (see table 1).

Indeed, Moreno has shown he can pay out with the big boys; only the Yanks, Red Sox, and Mets topped the Angels in salary in 2005. That's one reason why Moreno

ANGELS PROSPECTUS

2005 record: 95–67; First place, AL West; Lost to White Sox in Championship Series

Pythagenport record: 93–69

Runs scored per game: 4.70 (7th in AL)

Runs allowed per game: 3.97 (2nd in AL)

Team EqA: .258 (8th in AL)

2005 Batters Age: 30.2 (4th oldest in AL)

2005 Pitchers Age: 29.4 (5th oldest in AL)

Ballpark: Edison International Field; Moderate pitcher's park; Park Factor of 0.960

2005: They burned on the bases, but it was their deep and productive pitching staff that brought them to the LCS.

2006: The roster is an enviable mix of prospects and vets, a combination that's going to be tough to beat.

abruptly rechristened the team "the Los Angeles Angels" as the year dawned. A court ordered the awkward qualifier "of Anaheim" appended to their moniker, per a 1996 contract between Disney and Anaheim that had provided $20 million worth of stadium fixes and leased land. Nonetheless, the move announced the team's intention to battle the Dodgers for big-city supremacy. Angels billboards even went up near Dodger Stadium. While the Angels didn't outdraw Big Blue (they ran fourth in attendance behind the Yankees, Dodgers, and Cardinals), they ran rings around their L.A. counterparts on the field and in the local media.

On the field, the 2005 Angels served as a reminder that there's more than one way to skin a cat. Sabermetric gospel may preach the importance of working the count and the value of each and every out, but the Angel offense is built upon making contact and putting the ball in play. The Angels put the ball in play more often than any team in the majors, a whopping 74.9 percent of the time, and they saw fewer pitches per plate appearance (3.66) than all but two AL teams. They led the majors in steals (161) and stolen base attempts (218), and their 43 sacrifice bunts ranked fourth in the league.

For all of its frantic activity, the offense proved mediocre. The Angels ranked seventh in the AL in scoring

TABLE 1. ANGELS PAYROLLS

Year	Payroll*	Rank	Note
2001	$47.7	22	
2002	$61.7	15	
2003	$79.0	12	Moreno's first year
2004	$100.5	3	$927K paid in luxury tax
2005	$97.7	4	DH Tim Salmon ($9.75 million) missed the season

* Opening Day Payroll in millions, as reported via USA Today's Baseball Salary Database (http://asp.usatoday.com/sports/baseball/salaries/default.aspx)

(4.7 runs per game), eighth in EqA (.256), ninth in OBP (.325) and SLG (.409), and tenth in homers (147). Four regulars had OBPs below .316, and only one player (Guerrero) hit more than 17 homers. The team's two big free-agent signings for '05 were busts; neither centerfielder Steve Finley nor shortstop Orlando Cabrera hit. Rookies Dallas McPherson and Casey Kotchman made only minor contributions.

For all of the dogmas about offense that the Angels sweep to the side, run prevention is just as important, and at that, the Angels were very good. They allowed just 3.97 runs per game, third-best in the AL. They led the league in strikeouts (6.92 per 9 innings), and were virtually tied for second in K/BB (2.54) and HR/9 (0.97). Their starters led the AL in SNLVAR (Support-Neutral Lineup-Adjusted Value Above Replacement), with 25.9. Bartolo Colon ranked second (6.7) and Jarrod Washburn and John Lackey placed in the top 10; the trio were in the top eight in ERA as well. The Angels bullpen led the league in Reliever Expected Wins Added (13.5), with Francisco Rodriguez ranking first (5.6) in his first season as closer, and Scot Shields fourth (4.0). The team was sixth in Defensive Efficiency (.702, but just a point out of fourth).

One of the team's primary pitching assets is its depth. When Kelvim Escobar's elbow shut him down, the team recalled Ervin Santana, and while he took his lumps early on (a 6.20 ERA in the first half), by the time Escobar returned in September, the rookie was clicking (3.97 ERA in the second half). The Angels shunted Escobar to the bullpen, where he joined an already-strong cast. Squeezed out of the postseason rotation, Santana rescued the Angels when Colon had to leave the deciding game of the Divisional Series with the Yankees.

With Jarrod Washburn and Paul Byrd entering free agency over the winter, GM Bill Stoneman opted to let both go. Washburn has made just 54 starts over the past two years; the Mariners will be paying his medical bills (plus $37.5 million) for the next four years. Byrd left for a two-year deal with the Indians. With Santana and Escobar taking their slots in the rotation behind Colon and Lackey, Stoneman made a rather unorthodox move to round out the rotation. He signed 36-year-old Hector Carrasco after a comeback season in the Nationals' bullpen (2.04 ERA, 7.6 K/9, .193 Opp AVG, 18.1 APR). This had been preceded by nine years of nondescript toiling and a 2004 stint in Japan. Carrasco's two-year, $6.1 million deal was inspired by five late-season starts (27.2 innings, 27 K, 2.03 ERA). If that confidence proves misplaced, Joe Saunders and later Jered Weaver should both enter the picture. Again, depth makes the difference.

The bullpen gets an upgrade that's more philosophical than tactical with the acquisition of J. C. Romero. He should be the first southpaw reliever to throw significant innings for the Angels since 2003. Scioscia has heretofore avoided contemporary tactical orthodoxy, showing no compulsion to use the organization's sixth- or seventh-best reliever simply because of handedness. The results—a bullpen in the top four of the league over the past four years—speak for themselves. Romero was available for performance as much as expense: a repeat of his ugly 4.9 UIBB/9 or poor performance with men on base might drive Scioscia back to his all-righty ways.

Scioscia did a good job of leveraging the team's depth and versatility when it came to filling out his lineup card, thanks to Chone Figgins. Figgins stole 62 bases and scored 113 runs at the top of the order while bouncing around the diamond—42 games at second while Adam Kennedy was recovering from knee surgery, 50 in center to cover for Finley, 56 at third base as part of the platoon that replaced McPherson, 23 in the outfield corners, and even four at shortstop. Where he'll play in 2006 is a question of musical chairs. Centerfield is open with Finley now a Giant; in a classic "my dung heap for your compost pile" deal, he was swapped for aging 3B Edgardo Alfonzo. The mainstream press called him an "insurance policy" for McPherson in the wake of the deal, but Alfonzo's the sort who makes insurance necessary, and on the hot corner depth chart, should rank behind McPherson, Figgins, lefty-masher Robb Quinlan, utilityman Maicer Izturis, and maybe even hitting coach Mickey Hatcher.

Finley's struggles brought a call to move Darin Erstad from first base, where his bat is a huge drag on the offense, back to center field, where he played from 2001–2003. The Angels resisted an in-season move, but they're willing to do so in the wake of the Finley deal. This will finally clear the way for Kotchman at first. Erstad's aggressive nature and history of back problems may move Figgins back to center field on a moment's notice, but that's a chance the Angels can afford to take. More likely, Figgins slots in either at third base or at his natural position of second base, making Kennedy expendable.

Beyond Erstad, the offense also suffered because of Scioscia's commitment to another popular veteran of the 2002 championship team, 34-year-old Garret Anderson. He hasn't had a very clean bill of health lately: an arthritic back condition cost him a good chunk of 2004, and while he played in 142 games in 2005, he limped home with just a .255/.282/.389 showing in the second half. His defense was equally poor, an ominous sign for a player with a guaranteed payout of $36 million over the next three years. At the very least, DHing Anderson and playing Juan Rivera in left remains an option.

One big change in the lineup is the departure of catcher Bengie Molina. Always a good defender, Molina developed into a decent hitter in time for his walk year, posting career highs in homers, batting average, OBP, and

SLG in 2005. In doing so, he priced himself out of the team's range. With brother Jose unlikely to repeat his impression of an adequate hitter, the team is looking to 23-year-old Jeff Mathis as the backstop of the future, and although Mathis poked 21 homers at Triple-A Salt Lake City, his production is unimpressive by PCL standards. A late grab of Mike Piazza to share the catching and DH duties would make a great deal of sense for the Angels.

Beyond the focus on what they'll use to win now, the team has a nice handful of prospects on the horizon. Shortstop Brandon Wood drilled 43 homers in A-ball, and added a whopping 14 in the Arizona Fall League. Second baseman Howie Kendrick spent the second half in Double-A Arkansas, and holds a career minor-league batting average of .359; while he doesn't walk much or have a ton of power, he's in the ideal system to appreciate his gifts. With Kennedy's free agency pending, Kendrick is perfectly positioned to take over in 2007. In his first year of stateside ball after defecting from Cuba, first baseman Kendry Morales hit a combined .315/.362/.534, mostly in Double-A. Finally, there's Weaver, who struck out 95 in 76 innings after ending his long holdout.

In the ideologically-shaded scrum of the AL West, the Angels don't get nearly the love that the *Moneyball* A's

command among the stathead set, mainly because they don't send a lineup chockfull of sluggers with .375 OBPs. Then again, neither do the A's. Reality is always more complicated than theoretical ideals. Stoneman and Scioscia's emphasis on pitching, defense, and flexible roster management allows the Angels to get away with playing their faux-dead ball era offense. It may not be ideal, but it's sufficient for their needs. They're able to make money, willing to spend it, and no longer afraid to let some of the overpriced veterans of 2002 drift away, especially with homegrown talent on the horizon. With Kotchman, Kendrick, Wood and McPherson, the Angels have a full infield's worth of top prospects, and while they may not turn out to be the Garvey, Lopes, Russell, and Cey of the Dodgers of the '70s, they're a promising foundation to build upon. They'll be adding that talent to a team that already has Vlad the Impaler, one of the game's natural wonders, at the center of their offense. Moreno's Angels want more than the division title—they also want to dominate the second-largest media market in baseball. Both are very much within their grasp, in 2006 and beyond.

HITTERS

ERICK AYBAR · SS · Bats: B · Throws: R · Height: 5′ 11″ · Weight: 160 · Born: January 14, 1984 · Age: 22

YEAR	TM	LVL	AGE	PA	R	2B	3B	HR	RBI	BB	SO	SB	CS	SPEED	BA	OBP	SLG	MLVR	EQBA	EQOBP	EQSLG	EQA	VORP	DEFENSE
2003	CDR	A	19	529	83	30	10	6	57	17	54	32	9	8.2	.308	.346	.446	.188	.281	.309	.432	.255	21.4	120-SS -6
2004	RCU	A+	20	617	102	25	11	14	65	26	66	51	36	7.3	.330	.370	.485	.210	.283	.315	.410	.249	20.6	132-SS 6
2005	ARK	AA	21	586	101	29	10	9	54	29	51	49	23	7.8	.303	.350	.445	.092	.270	.315	.400	.252	16.2	133-SS -4
2006	*LAA*	*MLB*	*22*	*539*	*70*	*26*	*5*	*8*	*51*	*21*	*59*	*24*	*10*	*6.0*	*.272*	*.306*	*.392*	*-.081*	*.277*	*.318*	*.412*	*.247*	*17.1*	*127-SS 2*

Breakout: 19%   Improve: 40%   Collapse: 30%   Attrition: 5%   Comparables: Jimmy Rollins, Jose Reyes, Garry Templeton

A prototypical Angels player—a free swinger with a low strikeout rate who rarely walks. He's got good speed but lacks the technique and sense of timing that distinguish the merely quick from the elite base stealers. This has been a career-long problem and it's not getting better. Aybar's speed serves a more productive use, however; it allows him to leg out doubles and triples, thus giving him a shot of "power" that his bat itself does not provide. Aybar has yet to record a sub-.300 batting average as a pro, so the upside here is that of a Jose Reyes who can hit just enough to mitigate his lack of selectivity (unlike Jose Reyes). Aybar's stock is slipping as Brandon Wood's skyrockets; a starting job in the majors might require a trade.

GARRET ANDERSON · OF · Bats: L · Throws: L · Height: 6′ 3″ · Weight: 215 · Born: June 30, 1972 · Age: 34

YEAR	TM	LVL	AGE	PA	R	2B	3B	HR	RBI	BB	SO	SB	CS	SPEED	BA	OBP	SLG	MLVR	EQBA	EQOBP	EQSLG	EQA	VORP	DEFENSE
2003	ANA	MLB	31	673	80	49	4	29	116	31	83	6	3	4.9	.315	.345	.541	.256	.320	.355	.554	.299	47.0	141-LF 12
2004	ANA	MLB	32	475	57	20	1	14	75	29	75	2	1	4.9	.301	.343	.446	.071	.304	.351	.453	.276	21.1	88-CF -7
2005	LAA	MLB	33	603	68	34	1	17	96	23	84	1	1	4.0	.283	.308	.435	.004	.293	.328	.459	.267	11.2	102-LF -7
2006	*LAA*	*MLB*	*34*	*539*	*60*	*28*	*2*	*18*	*82*	*23*	*77*	*1*	*1*	*4.9*	*.284*	*.314*	*.450*	*.018*	*.288*	*.326*	*.474*	*.262*	*15.8*	*127-LF -4*

Breakout: 8%   Improve: 26%   Collapse: 34%   Attrition: 15%   Comparables: Dave Parker, B. J. Surhoff, Al Oliver

Only five players in the AL who qualified for the batting title walked fewer times than Anderson's 23 (eight of which were intentional), and only three saw fewer pitches per plate appearance. A player can get away with this sort of thing when he slugs better than .500, as Anderson did in his best years. But when his power dropped, he became a low-wattage slugger and a problem, not a solution. Anderson is a player who's gone from underrated to overrated as fast as any in recent memory.

ORLANDO CABRERA **SS** **Bats: R Throws: R** Height: 5' 10" Weight: 175 Born: November 2, 1974 Age: 31

YEAR	TM	LVL	AGE	PA	R	2B	3B	HR	RBI	BB	SO	SB	CS	SPEED	BA	OBP	SLG	MLVR	EQBA	EQOBP	EQSLG	EQA	VORP	DEFENSE	
2003	MON	MLB	28	688	95	47	2	17	80	52	64	24	2	6.2	.297	.347	.460	.062	.286	.337	.450	.276	42.1	156-SS	3
2004	MON	MLB	29	423	41	19	2	4	31	28	31	12	3	5.5	.246	.298	.336	-.164	.238	.291	.326	.223	0.5	97-SS	-2
2004	BOS	MLB	29	247	33	19	1	6	31	11	23	4	1	5.7	.294	.320	.465	.016	.286	.314	.451	.265	12.0	55-SS	-5
2005	LAA	MLB	30	583	70	28	3	8	57	38	50	21	2	6.5	.257	.309	.365	-.115	.267	.329	.387	.257	12.8	137-SS	7
2006	*LAA*	*MLB*	*31*	*557*	*65*	*27*	*2*	*7*	*53*	*32*	*50*	*14*	*4*	*5.2*	*.262*	*.307*	*.368*	*-.118*	*.267*	*.319*	*.387*	*.241*	*13.2*	*131-SS*	*1*

Breakout: 9% Improve: 34% Collapse: 28% Attrition: 10% Comparables: Phil Rizzuto, Eric Young, Johnny Logan

In the Great Shortstop Swap of 2005, the Cardinals got the one with the best bat and an average glove. The Angels got the one with the best glove and the worst bat. And, in the parlance of "It's the Great Pumpkin, Charlie Brown," the Red Sox got a rock. For all of David Eckstein's shortcomings, he was a much better deal than Cabrera or Renteria. With Aybar and Wood on the way up, Eckstein's three-year, $10.25 million deal looks a lot more attractive at than Cabrera's four-year, $32 million contract. Talk of improved play when he's on a winner didn't seem to.

ALBERTO CALLASPO **2B** **Bats: B Throws: R** Height: 5' 10" Weight: 150 Born: April 19, 1983 Age: 23

YEAR	TM	LVL	AGE	PA	R	2B	3B	HR	RBI	BB	SO	SB	CS	SPEED	BA	OBP	SLG	MLVR	EQBA	EQOBP	EQSLG	EQA	VORP	DEFENSE	
2003	CDR	A	20	565	86	38	4	2	67	42	28	20	6	6.2	.327	.377	.428	.219	.297	.338	.409	.261	24.0	120-2B	-3
2004	ARK	AA	21	601	76	29	2	6	48	47	25	15	14	4.9	.284	.338	.376	-.041	.246	.297	.327	.222	-9.4	122-SS	-5
2005	ARK	AA	22	384	53	9	0	10	49	28	17	9	8	5.1	.297	.346	.409	.031	.258	.310	.353	.235	-1.4	87-2B	3
2005	SLC	AAA	22	226	28	21	2	1	31	10	13	2	5	4.6	.316	.345	.448	-.019	.266	.292	.373	.227	-0.8	46-2B	0
2006	*LAA*	*MLB*	*23*	*507*	*55*	*26*	*2*	*4*	*47*	*27*	*33*	*7*	*4*	*4.7*	*.273*	*.313*	*.362*	*-.108*	*.277*	*.325*	*.381*	*.238*	*9.0*	*119-2B*	*2*

Breakout: 35% Improve: 60% Collapse: 22% Attrition: 10% Comparables: Bobby Valentine, Brent Abernathy, Tim Foli

In a lot of farm systems, Callaspo is the sort of guy that people would be excited about, but the Angels' bumper crop of middle infielders could leave him out in the cold. Wood, Aybar and Kendrick are all better prospects. He did bounce back from a terrible offensive year in '04, earning a promotion to Triple-A and hitting well there. However, like so many others here, he'd rather be scourged than take four wide ones. Could end up on the major league roster before any of his peers, but his career from here has a utility infielder vibe.

ALEXIS CASILLA **2B** **Bats: B Throws: R** Height: 5' 9" Weight: 160 Born: July 20, 1984 Age: 21

YEAR	TM	LVL	AGE	PA	R	2B	3B	HR	RBI	BB	SO	SB	CS	SPEED	BA	OBP	SLG	MLVR	EQBA	EQOBP	EQSLG	EQA	VORP	DEFENSE			
2004	CDR	A	19	34	6	2	1	0	1	5	4	1	1	6.7	.310	.412	.448	.238	.278	.366	.416	.268	1.4				
2005	CDR	A	20	344	62	11	3	3	17	29	31	47	12	7.3	.325	.392	.409	.143	.279	.335	.354	.253	7.7	41-SS	1	35-2B	0
2006	*MIN*	*MLB*	*21*	*452*	*59*	*16*	*4*	*1*	*29*	*30*	*51*	*31*	*12*	*5.4*	*.267*	*.321*	*.328*	*-.143*	*.268*	*.330*	*.338*	*.235*	*5.0*	*107-2B*	*0*		

Breakout: 21% Improve: 41% Collapse: 38% Attrition: 9% Comparables: Ruddy Yan, Alejandro Machado, Rafael Furcal

Casilla has good speed and isn't completely averse to taking a walk, but lacks power. After a strong start Cedar Rapids, the Angels pushed the 20-year-old all the way up to Triple-A, with predicable results. Drowning in more rounded infield candidates, the Angels dealt Casilla for disgruntled Twin J. C. Romero.

JEFF DaVANON **OF** **Bats: B Throws: R** Height: 6' 0" Weight: 190 Born: December 8, 1973 Age: 32

YEAR	TM	LVL	AGE	PA	R	2B	3B	HR	RBI	BB	SO	SB	CS	SPEED	BA	OBP	SLG	MLVR	EQBA	EQOBP	EQSLG	EQA	VORP	DEFENSE			
2003	ANA	MLB	29	378	56	16	1	12	43	42	59	17	5	6.0	.282	.360	.445	.100	.287	.370	.459	.288	17.3	61-RF	-4	24-CF	1
2004	ANA	MLB	30	336	41	11	4	7	34	46	54	18	3	6.6	.277	.372	.418	.034	.281	.380	.434	.292	13.3	28-CF	-1	14-RF	-1
2005	LAA	MLB	31	268	42	10	1	2	15	39	44	11	6	6.0	.231	.347	.311	-.138	.247	.370	.345	.260	-3.0	15-RF	0	15-CF	0
2006	*LAA*	*MLB*	*32*	*202*	*29*	*8*	*1*	*4*	*19*	*25*	*31*	*8*	*3*	*6.2*	*.266*	*.360*	*.390*	*.002*	*.271*	*.373*	*.410*	*.273*	*6.6*	*51-DH*			

Breakout: 17% Improve: 28% Collapse: 39% Attrition: 37% Comparables: Merv Rettenmund, F. P. Santangelo, Cal Abrams

(continued next page)

Jeff DaVanon (*continued*)

Fun with small sample sizes: DaVanon hit .393/.514/.536 in 28 at-bats against lefties; in 197 ABs against righties, he was a brutal .208/.322/.279. This was a reversal from 2004, when he batted .289/.383/.441 against righties but only .136/.240/.136 against lefties (in just 25 PAs). In 2003 the numbers were again reversed: .342/.457/.579 against lefties, .274/.346/.428 against righties. Assuming that DaVanon can recover his lefty stroke, the lesson here is that he's a useful fourth outfielder, but one who may not be ideal in a strict platoon. D esignated for assignment in December, he'll turn up as a reserve at a stadium near you.

DARIN ERSTAD   **1B/CF**   **Bats: L Throws: L**   Height: 6′ 2″   Weight: 210   Born: June 4, 1974   Age: 32

YEAR	TM	LVL	AGE	PA	R	2B	3B	HR	RBI	BB	SO	SB	CS	SPEED	BA	OBP	SLG	MLVR	EQBA	EQOBP	EQSLG	EQA	VORP	DEFENSE	
2003	ANA	MLB	29	282	35	7	1	4	17	18	40	9	1	5.9	.252	.309	.333	-.160	.257	.316	.339	.240	-0.6	63-CF	1
2004	ANA	MLB	30	540	79	29	1	7	69	37	74	16	1	6.5	.295	.346	.400	-.007	.300	.354	.406	.271	14.0	119-1B	11
2005	LAA	MLB	31	659	86	33	3	7	66	47	109	10	3	5.9	.273	.325	.371	-.071	.284	.345	.390	.259	-0.7	142-1B	13
2006	*LAA*	*MLB*	*32*	*545*	*62*	*24*	*3*	*6*	*51*	*36*	*80*	*9*	*3*	*5.6*	*.264*	*.315*	*.365*	*-.108*	*.269*	*.327*	*.384*	*.241*	*-3.2*	*128-1B*	*6*

Breakout: 10%   Improve: 38%   Collapse: 31%   Attrition: 12%   Comparables: Chris Chambliss, Ted Uhlaender, Dee Fondy

Mike Scioscia is besotted with Erstad's glove. To be fair, Erstad is a very good first baseman, so it's not hard to see why his soft touch would beguile a manager. But Erstad's bat is so bad that he cannot possibly save enough runs to make up for the lack of punch the Angels get from a power position. Example: Carlos Delgado had 116 equivalent runs, and −16 fielding runs (versus the average first baseman). Net result: 100 runs. Erstad had 68 equivalent runs and saved 12 runs above the average. Net result: 80 runs. There just aren't enough difficult plays in any season for a pure glove man to make the sacrifice of offense worthwhile. This is especially true for the Angels; 153 games of .273/.325/.371 from first base just isn't acceptable in a division with Mark Teixeira, Richie Sexson, and Dan Johnson, or any other division for that matter—this isn't the Deadball Era.

CHONE FIGGINS   **Super-UT**   **Bats: B   Throws: R**   Height: 5′ 8″   Weight: 160   Born: January 22, 1978   Age: 28

YEAR	TM	LVL	AGE	PA	R	2B	3B	HR	RBI	BB	SO	SB	CS	SPEED	BA	OBP	SLG	MLVR	EQBA	EQOBP	EQSLG	EQA	VORP	DEFENSE			
2003	SLC	AAA	25	319	55	14	15	4	30	29	36	16	6	7.9	.312	.379	.509	.177	.265	.332	.429	.264	11.9	34-2B	-1	27-SS	1
2003	ANA	MLB	25	264	34	9	4	0	27	20	38	13	7	7.3	.296	.345	.367	-.031	.303	.356	.374	.259	6.1	40-CF	-1	12-2B	0
2004	ANA	MLB	26	628	83	22	17	5	60	49	94	34	13	7.8	.296	.350	.419	.022	.301	.359	.431	.275	22.6	79-3B	-4	37-CF	-3
2005	LAA	MLB	27	711	113	25	10	8	57	64	101	62	17	8.0	.290	.352	.397	.021	.305	.375	.425	.284	29.7	48-3B	1	44-CF	1
2006	*LAA*	*MLB*	*28*	*659*	*101*	*26*	*8*	*7*	*52*	*53*	*90*	*40*	*13*	*6.4*	*.273*	*.334*	*.383*	*-.045*	*.278*	*.346*	*.403*	*.259*	*17.4*	*154-3B*	*0*		

Breakout: 7%   Improve: 34%   Collapse: 33%   Attrition: 3%   Comparables: Don Buford, Bump Wills, Ray Durham

Figgins isn't the MVP candidate that John Kruk claims he is, but with his skill on the bases and ability to man every position at the Big A from centerfield to ticket taker, he is quite valuable. Scioscia can slot him anywhere there is an injury and avoid putting a replacement-level player at that position. The Angels can depend on decent, but not great, defensive play, an above-average on-base percentage, and excellent speed. No other team in the division, maybe even the league, carries a player with that kind of versatility. Consider the Rangers, who played Mark DeRosa in right field at times, the Mariners, with their half-season of Bloomquisting themselves into the dirt, or the A's, who had to give up Moneyball for Scutaro-ball. Figgins protects the Angels from having to use those kinds of players. That's something, even if his bat lacks pop.

STEVE FINLEY   **CF**   **Bats: L Throws: L**   Height: 6′ 2″   Weight: 180   Born: March 12, 1965   Age: 41

YEAR	TM	LVL	AGE	PA	R	2B	3B	HR	RBI	BB	SO	SB	CS	SPEED	BA	OBP	SLG	MLVR	EQBA	EQOBP	EQSLG	EQA	VORP	DEFENSE	
2003	ARI	MLB	38	582	82	24	10	22	70	57	94	15	8	6.8	.287	.363	.500	.150	.273	.349	.486	.282	32.6	130-CF	-6
2004	ARI	MLB	39	450	61	16	1	23	48	40	52	8	4	5.1	.275	.338	.490	.095	.263	.327	.467	.269	20.0	101-CF	-9
2004	LAN	MLB	39	247	31	12	0	13	46	21	30	1	3	3.8	.263	.324	.491	.093	.265	.325	.496	.270	9.1	54-CF	4
2005	LAA	MLB	40	439	41	20	3	12	54	26	71	8	4	5.7	.222	.271	.374	-.194	.231	.290	.400	.239	-8.1	99-CF	-2
2006	*SFN*	*MLB*	*41*	*329*	*34*	*15*	*2*	*7*	*42*	*26*	*50*	*11*	*3*	*5.4*	*.244*	*.305*	*.384*	*-.132*	*.245*	*.308*	*.401*	*.242*	*2.9*	*79-CF*	*-1*

Breakout: 9%   Improve: 38%   Collapse: 38%   Attrition: 36%   Comparables: Jose Cruz Sr., Enos Slaughter, Minnie Minoso

It's almost like Father Time checked his calendar and said to Finley, "Hey, wait a minute, dude. You're 40!" Groin and shoulder injuries limited him to 112 games, and while age and injuries generally go hand in hand, it was still somewhat of a surprise given Finley's reputation for superb conditioning. The Angels traded him to San Francisco in exchange for Edgardo Alfonzo, where he'll comprise one-third of the Giants' Jurassic outfield.

NICK GORNEAULT   **OF**   **Bats: R Throws: R**   Height: 6′ 3″   Weight: 200   Born: April 19, 1979   Age: 27

YEAR	TM	LVL	AGE	PA	R	2B	3B	HR	RBI	BB	SO	SB	CS	SPEED	BA	OBP	SLG	MLVR	EQBA	EQOBP	EQSLG	EQA	VORP	DEFENSE			
2003	RCU	A+	24	400	67	36	2	14	72	20	82	11	6	5.6	.321	.362	.540	.294	.257	.291	.417	.241	-8.6	68-LF	5	22-CF	2
2003	ARK	AA	24	119	19	6	4	2	19	8	25	2	0	6.2	.345	.395	.527	.328	.301	.349	.466	.279	4.8	28-RF	2		
2004	ARK	AA	25	549	91	28	4	21	81	45	128	7	5	5.4	.281	.341	.481	.104	.231	.282	.388	.232	-22.6	54-RF	-1	51-LF	3
2005	SLC	AAA	26	554	106	26	11	26	108	58	119	7	6	6.2	.293	.366	.551	.141	.234	.301	.422	.246	-10.5	62-LF	0	59-RF	1
2006	*LAA*	*MLB*	*27*	*380*	*43*	*17*	*2*	*12*	*49*	*23*	*91*	*3*	*2*	*5.3*	*.247*	*.296*	*.413*	*-.090*	*.251*	*.307*	*.434*	*.244*	*-0.5*	*91-LF*	*0*		

Breakout: 31%   *Improve: 47%*   *Collapse: 35%*   *Attrition: 22%*   Comparables: *Anthony Sanders, Mario Encarnacion, Glenn Braggs*

It was something of a rebound year for Gorneault, although you will note that his numbers are heavily discounted for his Salt Lake environment. Gorneault has always had some power, but the Art of the Strike Zone has eluded him. Still, an outfielder who can swat the occasional extra-base hit is not completely without value. Given Gorneault's age and skill set, his mostly likely future is as a Rockies' starter or anyone else's reserve.

VLADIMIR GUERRERO   **RF**   **Bats: R Throws: R**   Height: 6′ 3″   Weight: 220   Born: February 9, 1976   Age: 30

YEAR	TM	LVL	AGE	PA	R	2B	3B	HR	RBI	BB	SO	SB	CS	SPEED	BA	OBP	SLG	MLVR	EQBA	EQOBP	EQSLG	EQA	VORP	DEFENSE	
2003	MON	MLB	27	467	71	20	3	25	79	63	53	9	5	4.6	.330	.426	.586	.362	.317	.414	.570	.325	41.6	107-RF	-1
2004	ANA	MLB	28	680	124	39	2	39	126	52	74	15	3	5.4	.337	.391	.598	.389	.344	.399	.617	.332	77.4	138-RF	1
2005	LAA	MLB	29	594	95	29	2	32	108	61	48	13	1	5.6	.317	.394	.565	.360	.333	.415	.603	.337	63.7	115-RF	0
2006	*LAA*	*MLB*	*30*	*582*	*84*	*31*	*2*	*29*	*103*	*49*	*57*	*9*	*2*	*5.2*	*.314*	*.376*	*.546*	*.267*	*.320*	*.390*	*.575*	*.313*	*49.0*	*136-RF*	*-1*

Breakout: 2%   *Improve: 21%*   *Collapse: 35%*   *Attrition: 8%*   Comparables: *Orlando Cepeda, Dave Winfield, Andre Dawson*

It's not just that it seems like he'll swing at everything; it's that he can seemingly crush anything. If a pitcher were to roll the ball to the plate, it would be even money that Vlad could golf it into the rock garden at the Big A. With the help of a league-leading 26 intentional walks, he actually walked more times than he struck out, which is amazing, given that "plate discipline" for Guerrero means skipping a second helping at the post-game spread. He struggled with a shoulder injury for much of the year; after hurting it diving for the plate in May, he tweaked it again late in the season. If he's healthy, he's one of the top five players in the game, and maybe the most fun to watch.

MAICER IZTURIS   **INF**   **Bats: B Throws: R**   Height: 5′ 8″   Weight: 150   Born: September 12, 1980   Age: 25

YEAR	TM	LVL	AGE	PA	R	2B	3B	HR	RBI	BB	SO	SB	CS	SPEED	BA	OBP	SLG	MLVR	EQBA	EQOBP	EQSLG	EQA	VORP	DEFENSE			
2003	AKR	AA	22	245	31	11	5	1	20	24	23	14	6	7.6	.280	.351	.390	.017	.249	.315	.349	.240	-1.0	41-2B	-2		
2003	BUF	AAA	22	328	43	16	4	2	29	24	28	14	6	6.9	.262	.317	.362	-.056	.251	.310	.353	.237	1.0	66-SS	7	20-2B	4
2004	EDM	AAA	23	439	65	19	2	3	36	57	30	14	12	5.1	.338	.428	.423	.220	.316	.400	.381	.277	31.4	84-SS	-4		
2004	MON	MLB	23	119	10	5	2	1	4	10	20	4	0	6.7	.206	.286	.318	-.248	.204	.283	.315	.222	-1.8	21-SS	-1		
2005	LAA	MLB	24	209	18	8	4	1	15	17	21	9	3	6.0	.246	.306	.346	-.156	.259	.329	.365	.249	-0.4	31-3B	-1	24-SS	-1
2006	*LAA*	*MLB*	*25*	*375*	*48*	*15*	*3*	*2*	*29*	*33*	*37*	*14*	*5*	*5.2*	*.257*	*.326*	*.341*	*-.124*	*.262*	*.338*	*.358*	*.244*	*7.8*	*90-SS*	*1*		

Breakout: 7%   *Improve: 34%*   *Collapse: 31%*   *Attrition: 26%*   Comparables: *Nelson Liriano, Bryan Little, Jimmy Stewart*

Injuries to both Finley and Dallas McPherson meant two things: First, Figgins, who couldn't play two positions at once, could only take up the slack in center field. Second, it meant a lot more of Izturis than is healthy for an offense.This meant a lot more Izturis than is healthy for an offense. He'll hang around until he's displaced by the younger generation of middle infielders coming up though the Angels system who can, you know, hit.

HOWIE KENDRICK   **2B**   **Bats: R Throws: R**   Height: 5′ 10″   Weight: 180   Born: July 12, 1983   Age: 22

YEAR	TM	LVL	AGE	PA	R	2B	3B	HR	RBI	BB	SO	SB	CS	SPEED	BA	OBP	SLG	MLVR	EQBA	EQOBP	EQSLG	EQA	VORP	DEFENSE	
2003	PRO	Rk	19	267	65	20	3	3	36	24	28	8	3	6.2	.368	.434	.517	.379	.299	.353	.426	.271	25.6	60-2B	1
2004	CDR	A	20	334	66	24	6	10	49	12	41	15	6	7.4	.367	.398	.578	.447	.318	.344	.507	.286	30.5	64-2B	8
2005	RCU	A+	21	304	69	23	6	12	47	14	42	13	4	7.8	.384	.421	.638	.548	.323	.353	.510	.293	28.2	59-2B	4
2005	ARK	AA	21	204	35	20	2	7	42	6	20	12	4	6.3	.342	.382	.579	.368	.302	.339	.504	.285	16.6	46-2B	3
2006	*LAA*	*MLB*	*22*	*570*	*77*	*36*	*4*	*16*	*76*	*23*	*77*	*13*	*5*	*5.8*	*.298*	*.333*	*.471*	*.089*	*.304*	*.346*	*.496*	*.277*	*36.1*	*134-2B*	*6*

Breakout: 13%   *Improve: 34%*   *Collapse: 32%*   *Attrition: 6%*   Comparables: *Brendan Harris, Victor Diaz, David Wright*

Jack Benny had a recurring joke on his radio show involving a train station track announcement, voiced by Mel Blanc. "Train leaving on Track Five for Anaheim, Azusa, and Cucamonga," Blanc would repeat with increasing desperation. "Doesn't anyone want to go to Anaheim, Azusa, or Cucamonga?" Blanc would have found a taker in Kendrick. Cucamonga

(continued next page)

Howie Kendrick *(continued)*

is where he made his rep, Anaheim is where he'll make his millions. Cucamonga is a bandbox, so Kendrick's Rogers Hornsby numbers there shouldn't be taken at face value. Still, Hornsby at a Wal-Mart-sized discount is still quite good. Kendrick kept his production up at Double-A, then mashed in the AFL. His walk rate is rather low (in part because he makes such good contact), but that's the only flaw in his offensive game. Kendrick's defense has lagged behind his hitting, so the Angels are likely to give him some extra time to improve his leatherworking skills before rushing Adam Kennedy out the door.

ADAM KENNEDY   **2B**   **Bats: L Throws: R**   Height: 6' 1"   Weight: 180   Born: January 10, 1976   Age: 30

YEAR	TM	LVL	AGE	PA	R	2B	3B	HR	RBI	BB	SO	SB	CS	SPEED	BA	OBP	SLG	MLVR	EQBA	EQOBP	EQSLG	EQA	VORP	DEFENSE
2003	ANA	MLB	27	508	71	17	1	13	49	45	73	22	9	6.0	.269	.344	.399	.006	.275	.352	.409	.268	20.2	127-2B 17
2004	ANA	MLB	28	524	70	20	5	10	48	41	92	15	5	6.2	.278	.351	.406	-.012	.284	.357	.417	.271	20.7	137-2B -6
2005	LAA	MLB	29	455	49	23	0	2	37	29	64	19	4	6.1	.300	.354	.370	.002	.315	.376	.395	.277	17.3	123-2B 4
2006	*LAA*	*MLB*	*30*	*485*	*63*	*23*	*3*	*8*	*47*	*35*	*70*	*15*	*5*	*5.5*	*.271*	*.332*	*.388*	*-.044*	*.276*	*.344*	*.409*	*.257*	*14.1*	*115-2B 1*

Breakout: 10%   Improve: 25%   Collapse: 40%   Attrition: 21%   Comparables: Mickey Morandini, Steve Lyons, Marlon Anderson

Kennedy missed the first month of the season recovering from knee surgery, but ended up fourth on the Angels in VORP anyway. Some of that is the value of having a good hitter at second base, but it's also a reflection of the lineup's general mediocrity Kennedy had an insane June (.435/.479/.529), kept his batting average high all season, and was the only Angel to finish the year over .300. He hit more balls on the ground than ever last year, perhaps boosting his average but sacrificing what little power he had. Now 30, Kennedy is just good enough to play. With Kendrick coming up fast and Kennedy's contract up at the end of the season, Stoneman has a nifty bargaining chip to offer around. There are a lot of teams that could use a hitter as reliably useful as Kennedy is.

CASEY KOTCHMAN   **1B**   **Bats: L Throws: L**   Height: 6' 3"   Weight: 210   Born: February 22, 1983   Age: 23

YEAR	TM	LVL	AGE	PA	R	2B	3B	HR	RBI	BB	SO	SB	CS	SPEED	BA	OBP	SLG	MLVR	EQBA	EQOBP	EQSLG	EQA	VORP	DEFENSE
2003	RCU	A+	20	245	42	12	0	8	28	30	16	2	0	4.0	.350	.441	.524	.415	.299	.377	.450	.288	12.4	45-1B 4
2004	ARK	AA	21	130	19	11	0	3	18	10	7	0	0	3.2	.368	.438	.544	.423	.316	.378	.484	.295	9.1	25-1B 4
2004	SLC	AAA	21	220	32	22	0	5	38	14	25	0	0	3.4	.372	.423	.558	.305	.290	.338	.427	.265	4.5	40-1B 4
2004	ANA	MLB	21	128	7	6	0	0	15	7	11	3	0	4.5	.224	.289	.276	-.333	.224	.289	.276	.213	-6.1	30-1B 1
2005	SLC	AAA	22	417	62	23	1	10	58	43	40	0	2	3.7	.289	.372	.441	-.005	.238	.315	.357	.237	-11.3	89-1B 9
2005	ANA	MLB	22	142	16	5	0	7	22	15	18	1	1	4.1	.278	.352	.484	.133	.288	.371	.512	.296	7.0	15-1B 1
2006	*LAA*	*MLB*	*23*	*463*	*51*	*22*	*1*	*10*	*57*	*33*	*51*	*1*	*1*	*4.5*	*.271*	*.329*	*.399*	*-.036*	*.275*	*.341*	*.419*	*.255*	*4.4*	*110-1B 3*

Breakout: 20%   Improve: 43%   Collapse: 33%   Attrition: 11%   Comparables: Ed Kranepool, Tom O'Malley, Ed Herrmann

The problem with this Mighty Casey is he's never at the bat, and when he is, the turn most often comes with the Mudville Nine rather than in the bigs. With Erstad dug in deeper than a Georgia tick, opportunities have been hard to come by. Although some feel Kotchman has finally turned the corner as far as driving the ball, there are still concerns that he is not showing the power you would want in a first baseman. Nevertheless, his rate stats are still miles ahead of Erstad's and should serve as a hint and a half that he has more power than the incumbent, who has hit 37 home runs since 2000. Given the failure of Angels' designated hitters—they hit .256/.317/.382 in 2005—Kotchman should at the very least be given a chance to claim that job as preparatory work for his succeeding the undead Erstad after the latter's contract is up at the end of the season. Damn the poem! Let Mighty Casey hit!

JEFF MATHIS   **C**   **Bats: R Throws: R**   Height: 6' 0"   Weight: 180   Born: March 31, 1983   Age: 23

YEAR	TM	LVL	AGE	PA	R	2B	3B	HR	RBI	BB	SO	SB	CS	SPEED	BA	OBP	SLG	MLVR	EQBA	EQOBP	EQSLG	EQA	VORP	DEFENSE
2003	RCU	A+	20	422	73	28	3	11	54	35	74	5	3	5.1	.323	.384	.500	.269	.281	.334	.434	.264	18.8	81-C 3
2003	ARK	AA	20	110	19	11	0	2	14	12	16	1	2	4.5	.284	.364	.463	.138	.236	.316	.405	.251	1.6	23-C 0
2004	ARK	AA	21	490	57	24	3	14	55	49	102	2	1	4.2	.227	.310	.394	-.104	.197	.271	.343	.217	-19.7	102-C -2
2005	SLC	AAA	22	474	78	26	3	21	73	42	85	4	3	5.1	.276	.340	.499	.008	.228	.288	.401	.237	-1.3	94-C 3
2006	*LAA*	*MLB*	*23*	*410*	*46*	*20*	*1*	*12*	*49*	*30*	*80*	*2*	*2*	*4.4*	*.241*	*.302*	*.403*	*-.096*	*.245*	*.313*	*.424*	*.245*	*6.9*	*98-C 0*

Breakout: 41%   Improve: 60%   Collapse: 24%   Attrition: 20%   Comparables: Guillermo Quiroz, Fernando Tatis, Cole Liniak

You might think that Mathis followed up a disastrous 2004 with a solid 2005, but his offensive numbers were inflated by one of the PCL's most hitter-friendly ballparks. Still, he recovered some of his power stroke, and some think he has reestablished himself as one of the best catching prospects in the game. This says as much about the organization's lack of alternatives as it does about his upside. His defensive reputation remains strong, though not so much for throwing out runners as for athleticism and mobility behind the plate.

DALLAS McPHERSON   3B   Bats: L Throws: R   Height: 6' 4"   Weight: 230   Born: July 23, 1980   Age: 25

YEAR	TM	LVL	AGE	PA	R	2B	3B	HR	RBI	BB	SO	SB	CS	SPEED	BA	OBP	SLG	MLVR	EQBA	EQOBP	EQSLG	EQA	VORP	DEFENSE	
2003	RCU	A+	22	339	65	21	6	18	59	41	79	12	6	6.9	.308	.404	.606	.429	.257	.339	.495	.279	22.6	67-3B	6
2003	ARK	AA	22	122	22	9	1	5	27	19	25	4	0	5.7	.314	.426	.569	.390	.275	.384	.512	.306	12.3	18-3B	-1
2004	ARK	AA	23	302	53	17	6	20	69	34	74	6	5	6.1	.321	.404	.660	.480	.272	.347	.554	.295	30.1	56-3B	-5
2004	SLC	AAA	23	284	54	19	8	20	57	23	95	6	3	7.0	.313	.370	.680	.322	.254	.311	.536	.276	18.9	61-3B	-10
2005	LAA	MLB	24	220	29	14	2	8	26	14	64	3	3	5.3	.244	.295	.449	-.029	.256	.317	.478	.263	2.5	54-3B	-1
2006	*LAA*	*MLB*	*25*	*443*	*61*	*23*	*3*	*24*	*70*	*38*	*119*	*8*	*4*	*5.4*	*.261*	*.330*	*.515*	*.108*	*.266*	*.342*	*.542*	*.284*	*26.8*	*105-3B*	*0*

Breakout: 25%   Improve: 57%   Collapse: 10%   Attrition: 16%   Comparables: Nick Esasky, Dave Kingman, Jay Buhner

Year One of the McPherson era in Anaheim (Los Angeles? Santa Ana? Yorba Linda?) started with the third baseman nursing a herniated disk in his back, and ended with surgery on his left hip to remove bone spurs. In between, McPherson struggled with strikeouts, whiffing in nearly a third of his at-bats. He's still the future for Anaheim at third base, but doesn't seem like the lock he did a season ago. While defense was never considered his strong suit, one must wonder if the injuries will have a long-term effect on his mobility.

BEN MOLINA   C   Bats: R Throws: R   Height: 5' 11"   Weight: 210   Born: July 20, 1974   Age: 31

YEAR	TM	LVL	AGE	PA	R	2B	3B	HR	RBI	BB	SO	SB	CS	SPEED	BA	OBP	SLG	MLVR	EQBA	EQOBP	EQSLG	EQA	VORP	DEFENSE	
2003	ANA	MLB	28	428	37	24	0	14	71	13	31	1	1	2.8	.281	.304	.443	.006	.283	.312	.456	.260	16.0	108-C	12
2004	ANA	MLB	29	361	36	13	0	10	54	18	35	0	1	2.9	.276	.313	.404	-.083	.278	.319	.404	.250	6.0	85-C	-4
2005	LAA	MLB	30	444	45	17	0	15	69	27	41	0	2	3.0	.295	.336	.446	.072	.305	.355	.475	.282	23.6	97-C	-5
2006	*LAA*	*MLB*	*31*	*358*	*35*	*16*	*0*	*9*	*47*	*18*	*32*	*0*	*1*	*3.1*	*.270*	*.309*	*.404*	*-.062*	*.275*	*.321*	*.425*	*.248*	*8.3*	*86-C*	*0*

Breakout: 13%   Improve: 34%   Collapse: 35%   Attrition: 21%   Comparables: Ray Fosse, Javy Lopez, Sandy Alomar

Tossed in those extra 20 points of batting average and 40 points of slugging by mutilating left-handers at a 1077 OPS clip. That helped make Molina the sixth most valuable catcher in baseball as measured by VORP. That was way over his 90th percentile PECOTA forecast, timed about as nicely as possible for an imminent free agent. Not offered arbitration and still teamless, he'll no doubt make top dollar somewhere, but he's not a young player, and his glovework is more reputation than results. Let the buyer beware.

JOSE MOLINA   C   Bats: R Throws: R   Height: 6' 2"   Weight: 210   Born: June 3, 1975   Age: 31

YEAR	TM	LVL	AGE	PA	R	2B	3B	HR	RBI	BB	SO	SB	CS	SPEED	BA	OBP	SLG	MLVR	EQBA	EQOBP	EQSLG	EQA	VORP	DEFENSE	
2003	ANA	MLB	28	119	12	4	0	0	6	1	26	0	0	5.2	.184	.210	.219	-.562	.184	.210	.219	.163	-12.0	38-C	-4
2004	ANA	MLB	29	213	26	10	2	3	25	10	52	4	1	5.6	.261	.296	.374	-.176	.264	.302	.378	.238	0.0	58-C	10
2005	LAA	MLB	30	199	14	4	0	6	25	13	41	2	0	3.5	.228	.286	.348	-.207	.236	.305	.368	.238	-1.5	53-C	15
2006	*LAA*	*MLB*	*31*	*184*	*17*	*7*	*1*	*4*	*17*	*9*	*39*	*3*	*1*	*4.3*	*.227*	*.273*	*.339*	*-.237*	*.231*	*.283*	*.357*	*.214*	*-3.5*	*47-C*	*5*

Breakout: 33%   Improve: 50%   Collapse: 24%   Attrition: 42%   Comparables: Bill Haselman, Mike Matheny, Ray Katt

The most accomplished defensive catcher among the Flying Molinas (over the last two seasons, we have him pegged at 47 fielding runs above replacement despite just 111.5 adjusted games at the position), as a hitter he's the Rey Ordonez of backstops. His glove makes him a worthwhile reserve, especially if used in tandem with a starter who can hit but might not be Mickey Cochrane behind the dish.

KENDRY MORALES   1B   Bats: B Throws: R   Height: 6' 1"   Weight: 220   Born: June 20, 1983   Age: 23

YEAR	TM	LVL	AGE	PA	R	2B	3B	HR	RBI	BB	SO	SB	CS	SPEED	BA	OBP	SLG	MLVR	EQBA	EQOBP	EQSLG	EQA	VORP	DEFENSE	
2005	RCU	A+	22	100	18	3	0	5	17	6	11	0	0	3.9	.344	.400	.544	.311	.296	.337	.456	.271	3.3	15-1B	-1
2005	ARK	AA	22	301	47	12	0	17	54	17	43	2	0	4.0	.306	.349	.530	.211	.267	.311	.462	.261	5.1	60-1B	-5
2006	*LAA*	*MLB*	*23*	*481*	*58*	*25*	*1*	*17*	*71*	*30*	*75*	*0*	*1*	*4.2*	*.282*	*.332*	*.461*	*.059*	*.287*	*.344*	*.485*	*.272*	*15.9*	*114-1B*	*-5*

Breakout: 10%   Improve: 40%   Collapse: 22%   Attrition: 7%   Comparables: Mike Aubrey, John Ellis, Jay Gibbons

(continued next page)

Kendry Morales *(continued)*

Kudos to the Angels scouts, who correctly identified Morales as a player of interest. Giving a practically unknown quantity a six-year major league deal virtually sight unseen could have left heaping quantities of egg on the faces of all involved. Instead, Morales came to these shores and excelled; it looks like the classic American immigrant story, the life of Andrew Carnegie if he had made it big in baseball instead of steel—at least so far. There are still a few flaws to be corrected before Morales donates 2,800 libraries or funds an endowment for world peace. He played in offense-friendly leagues, so his numbers aren't quite as good as they look at first glance. He's not big on the whole ball four thing, though he does make good contact. Finally, he has yet to establish himself defensively; he's moved around the field but seems most comfortable at first. Assuming the Angels correctly let Erstad go after 2006, Kotchman is first in line for the first base job, but if he struggles while Morales blossoms in his second pro season, things will get interesting.

MICHAEL NAPOLI   **C**   **Bats: R Throws: R**   Height: 6' 0"   Weight: 200   Born: October 31, 1981   Age: 24

YEAR	TM	LVL	AGE	PA	R	2B	3B	HR	RBI	BB	SO	SB	CS	SPEED	BA	OBP	SLG	MLVR	EQBA	EQOBP	EQSLG	EQA	VORP	DEFENSE			
2003	RCU	A+	21	195	28	10	1	4	26	23	32	5	0	5.2	.267	.364	.412	.065	.233	.316	.366	.245	-0.1	18-C	3		
2004	RCU	A+	22	584	94	29	4	29	118	88	166	9	5	4.8	.282	.394	.539	.275	.233	.330	.429	.263	17.3	71-C	12	33-1B	-3
2005	ARK	AA	23	541	96	22	2	31	99	88	140	12	4	4.6	.237	.372	.508	.153	.202	.329	.424	.263	12.0	103-C	6		
2006	*LAA*	*MLB*	*24*	*481*	*57*	*20*	*2*	*17*	*59*	*54*	*131*	*6*	*2*	*4.1*	*.226*	*.320*	*.407*	*-.070*	*.230*	*.332*	*.428*	*.256*	*9.4*	*114-C*	*4*		

Breakout: 22%   Improve: 48%   Collapse: 28%   Attrition: 10%   Comparables: Jim Pagliaroni, Mike Schmidt, Jeff Bailey

The Angels' champion Three True Outcomes guy in the minors. He proved that 2004's power and patience surge was real (usual caveats about downgrading Angels minor league hitting numbers apply), but the batting average and strikeouts remain problematic. His translations suggest that he's going to be hard-pressed to stay above the Mendoza Line in the majors. Napoli may have a Mickey Tettleton/Gene Tenace future, but first he has to show he can hit for average at Triple-A, and second, with Mathis, a younger, more accomplished defender in front of him, he's going to have to get out of Anaheim and go to an organization not so hung up on batting average.

ROBB QUINLAN   **1B/3B**   **Bats: R Throws: R**   Height: 6' 1"   Weight: 200   Born: March 17, 1977   Age: 29

YEAR	TM	LVL	AGE	PA	R	2B	3B	HR	RBI	BB	SO	SB	CS	SPEED	BA	OBP	SLG	MLVR	EQBA	EQOBP	EQSLG	EQA	VORP	DEFENSE			
2003	SLC	AAA	26	421	55	18	4	9	68	25	59	10	3	5.6	.310	.352	.445	.047	.256	.300	.369	.235	-11.5	57-1B	2	24-LF	1
2003	ANA	MLB	26	100	13	4	2	0	4	6	16	1	2	5.3	.287	.330	.372	-.041	.290	.340	.376	.247	-0.4	21-1B	-1		
2004	ANA	MLB	27	177	23	14	0	5	23	14	26	3	1	5.0	.344	.401	.525	.315	.348	.409	.544	.321	16.9	24-3B	-1	10-1B	2
2005	LAA	MLB	28	143	17	8	0	5	14	7	26	0	1	4.1	.231	.273	.403	-.144	.241	.292	.421	.241	-2.4	27-3B	-1		
2006	*LAA*	*MLB*	*29*	*228*	*25*	*11*	*1*	*5*	*27*	*13*	*37*	*2*	*1*	*4.7*	*.265*	*.311*	*.403*	*-.065*	*.269*	*.322*	*.424*	*.248*	*3.0*	*57-3B*	*0*		

Breakout: 17%   Improve: 46%   Collapse: 35%   Attrition: 38%   Comparables: Mark DeRosa, Randy Velarde, Mike Kinkade

Started the year as McPherson insurance, but between injuries and the lack of a regular gig, never really found the stroke he showed in 2004. Quinlan would be a nice spare part on a lot of teams, particularly if his hitting settles somewhere between the extremes of '04 and '05. For right now he's one of several hundred guys in major league history who are on the verge of establishing themselves as a quality role players or borderline regulars and getting into the real money before injuries hit at exactly the wrong time—the right time is after you sign the big contract.

JUAN RIVERA   **RF**   **Bats: R Throws: R**   Height: 6' 2"   Weight: 170   Born: July 3, 1978   Age: 27

YEAR	TM	LVL	AGE	PA	R	2B	3B	HR	RBI	BB	SO	SB	CS	SPEED	BA	OBP	SLG	MLVR	EQBA	EQOBP	EQSLG	EQA	VORP	DEFENSE			
2003	COH	AAA	25	337	47	21	0	7	37	26	37	1	3	3.7	.325	.374	.461	.213	.297	.353	.437	.271	9.8	54-RF	0	24-LF	1
2003	NYA	MLB	25	184	22	14	0	7	26	10	27	0	0	3.5	.266	.304	.468	.025	.267	.314	.465	.263	2.7	32-LF	-3	14-RF	0
2004	MON	MLB	26	426	48	24	1	12	49	34	45	6	2	4.6	.307	.364	.465	.173	.297	.355	.449	.276	23.7	81-RF	5	11-CF	-1
2005	LAA	MLB	27	374	46	17	1	15	59	23	44	1	9	3.4	.271	.316	.454	.030	.285	.340	.484	.266	4.8	26-RF	-1	33-LF	0
2006	*LAA*	*MLB*	*27*	*358*	*41*	*17*	*1*	*11*	*49*	*25*	*44*	*2*	*2*	*4.0*	*.277*	*.329*	*.432*	*.012*	*.282*	*.341*	*.455*	*.263*	*9.0*	*86-RF*	*-1*		

Breakout: 18%   Improve: 39%   Collapse: 27%   Attrition: 20%   Comparables: Lou Piniella, Bob Nieman, Danny Schell

Rivera was acquired with Maicer Izturis from the Nats in exchange for Citizen Jose Guillen, a decent move given that Guillen was never again going to play in Anaheim. Stuck behind Guerrero and Anderson, Rivera struggled early, but had his two best months of the season in August and September, with regular playing time. Rivera is not dissimilar to the player he replaced; his .283/.331/.452 career averages are comparable to Guillen's own .276/.324/.448. Guillen's breakthrough season came at 27; Rivera will be 27 this year. Stay tuned.

SEAN RODRIGUEZ SS **Bats: R Throws: R** Height: 6′ 0″ Weight: 180 Born: April 26, 1985 Age: 21

YEAR	TM	LVL	AGE	PA	R	2B	3B	HR	RBI	BB	SO	SB	CS	SPEED	BA	OBP	SLG	MLVR	EQBA	EQOBP	EQSLG	EQA	VORP	DEFENSE			
2004	PRO	Rk	19	292	64	14	4	10	55	51	62	9	3	6.0	.338	.486	.569	.420	.251	.354	.399	.267	21.6	62-SS	2		
2004	CDR	A	19	222	35	8	4	4	17	18	54	14	4	8.2	.250	.333	.393	.012	.214	.278	.339	.223	-7.6	24-2B	3		
2005	CDR	A	20	537	86	29	3	14	45	78	85	27	11	5.4	.250	.371	.422	.072	.211	.313	.357	.240	-0.5	84-SS	2	11-3B	0
2006	LAA	MLB	21	496	59	23	2	11	51	44	90	15	7	5.2	.241	.315	.379	-.104	.245	.327	.398	.247	10.0	117-SS	3		

Breakout: 36% Improve: 62% Collapse: 20% Attrition: 7% Comparables: Chip Ambres, Kelly Johnson, Bronson Sardinha

While it might seem there's not a lot to get excited about in talking about a shortstop behind the Kendricks and Woods in the organizational depth chart, his season in Cedar Rapids wasn't too shabby for a 20-year-old. Rodriguez's walk rate is a bright spot in this system, and a package of patience, speed, and promising power makes him an underrated prospect.

ANDREW TOUSSAINT LF **Bats: R Throws: R** Height: 6′ 2″ Weight: 175 Born: October 24, 1982 Age: 23

YEAR	TM	LVL	AGE	PA	R	2B	3B	HR	RBI	BB	SO	SB	CS	SPEED	BA	OBP	SLG	MLVR	EQBA	EQOBP	EQSLG	EQA	VORP	DEFENSE	
2004	PRO	Rk	21	236	39	12	2	12	52	34	68	6	4	4.7	.289	.411	.557	.231	.205	.283	.369	.227	-8.1	27-3B	1
2005	CDR	A	22	446	68	25	3	21	68	45	125	11	5	5.4	.261	.345	.501	.144	.215	.281	.411	.237	-17.3	79-LF	-3
2006	LAA	MLB	23	409	44	19	2	12	47	27	125	5	3	4.2	.220	.278	.378	-.182	.224	.288	.398	.227	-9.5	97-LF	-2

Breakout: 27% Improve: 43% Collapse: 38% Attrition: 13% Comparables: Jesus Basabe, Hipolito Martinez, Michael Mallory

For a 13th round pick, Toussaint made a smooth transition to pro ball, giving the lie to questions about Southern University's schedule, which was brought up by some as a way to second-guess fellow Southern star Rickie Weeks. Toussaint is worth keeping an eye on as he moves up the ladder, especially if he can control the strike zone a little more. As a 23-year-old just going to High-A, he's going to have to figure things out in a hurry and avoid a recurrence of a the lower back problems that restricted him to only 109 games in 2005.

MARK TRUMBO 1B **Bats: R Throws: R** Height: 6′ 5″ Weight: 210 Born: January 16, 1986 Age: 20

YEAR	TM	LVL	AGE	PA	R	2B	3B	HR	RBI	BB	SO	SB	CS	SPEED	BA	OBP	SLG	MLVR	EQBA	EQOBP	EQSLG	EQA	VORP	DEFENSE	
2005	ORM	Rk	19	323	45	23	1	10	45	21	67	2	2	4.7	.274	.322	.458	.091	.224	.255	.353	.211	-37.5	70-1B	6
2006	LAA	MLB	20	374	34	20	1	7	41	13	78	2	2	4.7	.232	.260	.357	-.232	.236	.270	.376	.209	-14.2	90-1B	6

Breakout: 45% Improve: 54% Collapse: 31% Attrition: 18% Comparables: Luis Candelario, Justin Humphries, William Schmitt

Give the Angels credit for thinking outside the box. They paid $1.425 million to sign Trumbo, a dominant high school pitcher, and then moved him to first base to take advantage of his perceived power potential. Slugging .458 in Rookie ball doesn't make you look like the next Babe Ruth, but Trumbo is still quite young and there's plenty of time to see how this experiment works out with both Kotchman and Morales ahead of him.

BRANDON WOOD SS **Bats: R Throws: R** Height: 6′ 3″ Weight: 185 Born: March 2, 1985 Age: 21

YEAR	TM	LVL	AGE	PA	R	2B	3B	HR	RBI	BB	SO	SB	CS	SPEED	BA	OBP	SLG	MLVR	EQBA	EQOBP	EQSLG	EQA	VORP	DEFENSE	
2003	PRO	Rk	18	181	25	13	2	5	31	16	48	1	1	4.2	.278	.348	.475	.098	.220	.278	.371	.224	-4.1	33-SS	-3
2004	CDR	A	19	531	65	30	5	11	64	46	117	21	5	6.4	.251	.322	.404	.010	.216	.275	.350	.223	-12.8	124-SS	-15
2005	RCU	A+	20	593	109	51	4	43	115	48	128	7	3	4.9	.321	.383	.672	.445	.257	.309	.506	.271	36.7	123-SS	-5
2006	LAA	MLB	21	544	61	32	2	19	77	32	122	5	2	4.4	.246	.294	.434	-.065	.251	.305	.457	.250	17.5	128-SS	-9

Breakout: 32% Improve: 57% Collapse: 23% Attrition: 5% Comparables: Corey Smith, Franklin Gutierrez, Joe Crede

His 2004 performance in the Midwest League wasn't great, but he was also just 19. We're all a bit too quick to bandy about terms like "1st round bust" and "disappointing performance" when a teenager doesn't turn into Honus Wagner right off the bat. For a case that deserves application of those words, see Matt Bush's Midwest League line from 2005. That's what you call an unqualified disappointment. Wood was not only a year older in 2005, he was a year smarter. It showed in adjustments that resulted in 101 extra-base hits in 134 games, followed by .307/.375/.711 with a home run every eight at-bats in the AFL. The plan is for Wood to start the year at Double-A, but he could move faster.

PITCHERS

PAUL BYRD
Bats: R Throws: R   Height: 6' 1"   Weight: 180   Born: December 3, 1970   Age: 35

YEAR	TM	LVL	AGE	W	L	SV	G	GS	IP	H	BB	SO	HR	GB%	BABIP	STUFF	WHIP	ERA	PERA	EQERA	EQH9	EQBB9	EQSO9	EQHR9	VORP	WXRL
2004	ATL	MLB	33	8	7	0	19	19	114.3	123	19	79	18	40%	.293	6	1.24	3.94	4.51	4.67	9.6	1.3	5.5	1.3	15.8	2.6
2005	LAA	MLB	34	12	11	0	31	31	204.3	216	28	102	22	39%	.290	9	1.19	3.74	4.21	4.35	9.5	1.2	4.5	0.9	35.4	4.1
2006	CLE	MLB	35	10	10	0	32	26	172.0	189	30	92	25	41%	.287	3	1.27	4.34	4.58	4.72	9.8	1.5	4.6	1.2	19.5	3.3

Breakout: 15%   Improve: 45%   Collapse: 17%   Attrition: 11%   Comparables: Hal Brown, Vern Law, Kevin Tapani

Having signed with the Indians, Byrd will don his fifth uniform since 2001. Byrd will travel for work, but his arm has historically refused to accompany him. This has made him an option that teams prefer to rent rather than buy. Byrd has great control; he hasn't averaged two walks per nine since 2001. As a pitcher who allows a lot of balls in play, he made a good call by moving to a team with a solid defense. The Indians' two-year deal with a club option for a third season gives him, at 35, the best job security he's ever had. Seven million per year seems to have become the going rate for good non-aces, but Byrd is, to put it in poker terms, a decent value bet, at best.

BARTOLO COLON
Bats: R Throws: R   Height: 6' 0"   Weight: 185   Born: May 24, 1973   Age: 33

YEAR	TM	LVL	AGE	W	L	SV	G	GS	IP	H	BB	SO	HR	GB%	BABIP	STUFF	WHIP	ERA	PERA	EQERA	EQH9	EQBB9	EQSO9	EQHR9	VORP	WXRL
2003	CHA	MLB	30	15	13	0	34	34	242.0	223	67	173	30	41%	.277	15	1.20	3.87	4.28	3.79	8.7	2.5	6.4	1.1	55.9	6.4
2004	ANA	MLB	31	18	12	0	34	34	208.3	215	71	158	38	41%	.288	1	1.37	5.01	4.93	4.97	9.1	2.8	6.3	1.5	22.7	3.5
2005	LAA	MLB	32	21	8	0	33	33	222.7	215	43	157	26	42%	.285	18	1.16	3.48	4.00	3.88	8.8	1.8	6.3	1.0	49.1	6.7
2006	LAA	MLB	33	13	10	0	33	31	204.0	206	50	140	27	41%	.283	13	1.26	4.05	4.31	4.27	8.9	2.2	6.0	1.1	30.1	4.5

Breakout: 14%   Improve: 53%   Collapse: 13%   Attrition: 1%   Comparables: Don Sutton, Bob Welch, Frank Castillo

The David Wells Conspicuous Consumption Diet Plan probably didn't help his back and shoulder, but Colon bounced back from a poor '04 to win a surprising Cy Young award by trimming some walks and home runs from his menu. He had a good year, not a great one; he was fifth in the AL in VORP, leagues behind Johan Santana. He's no spring chicken at 33, and over the course of his career, you've never really known if you're going to get the filet or the tripe on any given night. He's a very good pitcher, but his deteriorating physical condition is going to eat into his durability as fast as he's eating... everything else.

DANIEL DAVIDSON
Bats: L Throws: L   Height: 6' 4"   Weight: 225   Born: January 8, 1981   Age: 25

YEAR	TM	LVL	AGE	W	L	SV	G	GS	IP	H	BB	SO	HR	GB%	BABIP	STUFF	WHIP	ERA	PERA	EQERA	EQH9	EQBB9	EQSO9	EQHR9	VORP	WXRL
2003	PRO	Rk	22	8	2	0	15	13	71.3	65	15	50	3	—	.274	-13	1.12	1.64	5.32	5.45	9.3	3.1	3.1	1.1	1.1	—
2004	RCU	A+	23	12	7	0	28	28	163.3	196	41	121	15	—	.344	-20	1.45	4.57	5.90	6.64	11.1	3.1	4.0	1.6	-18.3	—
2005	ARK	AA	24	13	5	0	28	26	154.3	179	45	110	22	39%	.322	-28	1.45	4.72	6.22	6.64	10.9	3.4	4.5	1.9	-17.2	—
2006	LAA	MLB	25	5	9	0	30	19	115.7	141	45	56	23	40%	.299	-13	1.61	6.09	6.56	6.34	10.8	3.5	4.3	1.7	-10.1	-0.3

Breakout: 22%   Improve: 62%   Collapse: 11%   Attrition: 0%   Comparables: Mike Prochaska, J. D. Arteaga, Jeff Andra

Davidson gets by on command and location, using his mid-80s fastball to set up his changeup. Don't focus on that Texas League-sized ERA, but instead check out the strikeout to walk ratio. The Angels believe Davidson is deceptive enough that the hits per nine and home runs will come down. Davidson doesn't get a lot of hype, but he's been solid in his pro career. Keep an eye on him.

BRENDAN DONNELLY
Bats: R Throws: R   Height: 6' 3"   Weight: 205   Born: July 4, 1971   Age: 34

YEAR	TM	LVL	AGE	W	L	SV	G	GS	IP	H	BB	SO	HR	GB%	BABIP	STUFF	WHIP	ERA	PERA	EQERA	EQH9	EQBB9	EQSO9	EQHR9	VORP	WXRL
2003	ANA	MLB	32	2	2	3	63	0	74.0	55	24	79	2	35%	.273	38	1.07	1.58	2.84	1.85	7.0	3.0	9.4	0.2	35.7	5.6
2004	ANA	MLB	33	5	2	0	40	0	42.0	34	15	56	5	40%	.319	32	1.17	3.00	3.40	2.98	7.2	3.0	11.1	1.1	15.4	0.8
2005	LAA	MLB	34	9	3	0	66	0	65.3	60	19	53	9	32%	.277	3	1.21	3.72	4.43	4.15	8.6	2.6	7.3	1.2	11.5	0.6
2006	LAA	MLB	34	3	2	3	49	0	54.0	49	17	48	7	35%	.278	8	1.23	3.66	3.95	4.05	8.1	2.9	7.8	1.1	9.9	0.9

Breakout: 14%   Improve: 27%   Collapse: 47%   Attrition: 19%   Comparables: Jay Howell, Trevor Hoffman, Josias Manzanillo

At one time Donnelly was a poster child for the Angels' ability to dig up relievers with good heat, nasty movement, and tricky deliveries. But now it looks like the league caught on—and up to him. Frank Robinson catching him putting an extra something extra on the ball put an exclamation point on his decline, but Donnelly had already lost ground from his tremendous '03 season the previous year.

SCOTT DUNN
Bats: R Throws: R   Height: 6′ 3″ Weight: 180 Born: May 23, 1978   Age: 28

YEAR	TM	LVL	AGE	W	L	SV	G	GS	IP	H	BB	SO	HR	GB%	BABIP	STUFF	WHIP	ERA	PERA	EQERA	EQH9	EQBB9	EQSO9	EQHR9	VORP	WXRL
2003	CHT	AA	25	3	2	8	31	0	40.3	31	16	54	3	—	.295	-6	1.17	3.80	5.02	6.21	8.6	4.3	7.9	1.4	-2.6	—
2004	SLC	AAA	26	10	4	1	46	6	89.7	72	56	84	6	—	.280	-6	1.43	3.21	5.19	3.84	7.5	6.5	6.1	0.7	17.0	—
2005	SLC	AAA	27	5	7	9	47	6	92.0	83	41	98	7	44%	.319	1	1.35	3.82	4.38	4.58	8.2	4.3	6.7	0.8	10.2	—
2006	*LAA*	*MLB*	*28*	*3*	*4*	*1*	*28*	*6*	*60.3*	*62*	*34*	*44*	*8*	*42%*	*.291*	*-6*	*1.58*	*5.19*	*5.54*	*5.61*	*9.1*	*5.1*	*6.5*	*1.2*	*0.6*	*0.2*

Breakout: 10% Improve: 28% Collapse: 35% Attrition: 15%   Comparables: Chris Seelbach, Jim Duffalo, Dave Stewart

Minor league swingmen don't generally garner a lot of attention, for good reason. But Dunn keeps showing an ability to strike people out, and the Angels have a knack for filling their bullpen with non-famous people who produce. Dunn's in the right place to finally get an opportunity, but he has to show more consistent control to establish himself in the majors.

KELVIM ESCOBAR
Bats: R Throws: R   Height: 6′ 1″ Weight: 205 Born: April 11, 1976   Age: 30

YEAR	TM	LVL	AGE	W	L	SV	G	GS	IP	H	BB	SO	HR	GB%	BABIP	STUFF	WHIP	ERA	PERA	EQERA	EQH9	EQBB9	EQSO9	EQHR9	VORP	WXRL
2003	TOR	MLB	27	13	9	4	41	26	180.3	189	78	159	15	52%	.331	22	1.48	4.29	3.95	4.29	8.6	3.8	7.5	0.7	29.1	4.4
2004	ANA	MLB	28	11	12	0	33	33	208.3	192	76	191	21	47%	.298	28	1.29	3.93	3.86	3.77	8.1	3.0	7.7	0.8	53.2	6.3
2005	LAA	MLB	29	3	2	1	16	7	59.7	45	21	63	4	46%	.273	35	1.11	3.02	3.34	3.19	7.1	3.2	9.4	0.6	17.2	2.6
2006	*LAA*	*MLB*	*30*	*7*	*6*	*2*	*33*	*15*	*105.3*	*97*	*41*	*94*	*11*	*45%*	*.289*	*14*	*1.31*	*3.79*	*4.13*	*4.26*	*8.2*	*3.5*	*7.8*	*0.9*	*19.4*	*2.4*

Breakout: 13% Improve: 41% Collapse: 28% Attrition: 15%   Comparables: Bob Turley, Ray Culp, Bob Gibson

He made his first relief appearance in two years after coming back from an elbow injury, which points out one of the things to admire about the Angels' admirable traits. For all our complaints of their stubborn refusal to improve on offense, they've shown admirable flexibility and creativity when it comes to using their pitchers. Now that Byrd and Washburn are gone, Escobar will likely shift back to the rotation for 2006.

KEVIN GREGG
Bats: R Throws: R   Height: 6′ 6″ Weight: 220 Born: June 20, 1978   Age: 28

YEAR	TM	LVL	AGE	W	L	SV	G	GS	IP	H	BB	SO	HR	GB%	BABIP	STUFF	WHIP	ERA	PERA	EQERA	EQH9	EQBB9	EQSO9	EQHR9	VORP	WXRL
2003	ARK	AA	25	4	3	0	15	11	66.3	60	19	60	2	—	.295	7	1.19	3.53	4.29	5.29	9.1	3.4	5.6	0.6	2.2	—
2003	SLC	AAA	25	7	4	0	15	15	91.7	90	18	75	10	—	.286	4	1.18	4.02	4.96	5.06	9.4	2.1	6.0	1.4	5.3	—
2003	ANA	MLB	25	2	0	0	5	3	24.7	18	8	14	3	38%	.211	4	1.05	3.28	4.94	3.42	8.0	3.0	5.3	1.1	7.5	1.1
2004	ANA	MLB	26	5	2	1	55	0	87.7	86	28	84	6	45%	.322	22	1.29	4.21	3.43	4.23	8.3	2.6	8.0	0.6	18.5	0.9
2005	SLC	AAA	27	3	1	0	7	6	34.7	36	10	36	2	46%	.362	16	1.33	3.89	3.89	4.15	8.8	2.9	6.5	0.5	5.6	—
2005	LAA	MLB	27	1	2	0	33	2	64.3	70	29	52	8	47%	.316	0	1.52	5.04	4.66	5.21	9.3	4.0	7.1	1.1	3.6	-0.3
2006	*LAA*	*MLB*	*28*	*4*	*4*	*1*	*45*	*6*	*83.0*	*86*	*29*	*61*	*10*	*44%*	*.298*	*2*	*1.38*	*4.40*	*4.66*	*4.98*	*9.2*	*3.2*	*6.4*	*1.0*	*9.6*	*0.9*

Breakout: 17% Improve: 49% Collapse: 22% Attrition: 13%   Comparables: Tom Acker, Gene Brabender, Ken Forsch

To paraphrase the old Beach Boys song, maybe it's the fantasy world of Disney girls that keep him pitching so well at home. Last season, he stymied opposing batters at Anaheim, holding them to.163/.290/.276. On the road, they solved him at a .376/.417/.541 clip. Gregg pitched better after a May demotion left him time to sort out his mechanics, but unless he can get his splitter over the plate more often, he's going to have trouble becoming a reliable bullpen asset.

GREG JONES
Bats: R Throws: R   Height: 6′ 2″ Weight: 190 Born: November 15, 1976 Age: 29

YEAR	TM	LVL	AGE	W	L	SV	G	GS	IP	H	BB	SO	HR	GB%	BABIP	STUFF	WHIP	ERA	PERA	EQERA	EQH9	EQBB9	EQSO9	EQHR9	VORP	WXRL
2003	SLC	AAA	26	2	3	4	33	0	47.0	36	9	56	4	—	.274	14	0.96	4.40	3.77	4.96	7.5	2.2	8.7	1.2	3.2	—
2003	ANA	MLB	26	0	0	0	18	0	27.7	29	14	28	3	40%	.325	9	1.55	4.87	4.50	4.82	9.0	4.5	8.7	1.0	3.4	-0.2
2004	SLC	AAA	27	1	4	3	36	0	53.3	63	19	43	11	—	.325	-30	1.54	5.74	6.28	5.94	10.2	3.7	5.1	2.0	-2.0	—
2005	SLC	AAA	28	1	2	10	23	0	25.3	20	6	25	3	38%	.262	-2	1.03	3.20	4.81	3.70	7.8	2.2	6.3	1.5	5.1	—
2006	*LAA*	*MLB*	*29*	*2*	*2*	*2*	*39*	*2*	*43.7*	*45*	*14*	*30*	*7*	*38%*	*.282*	*-6*	*1.36*	*4.62*	*5.05*	*5.54*	*9.2*	*2.9*	*6.0*	*1.4*	*3.8*	*0.4*

Breakout: 31% Improve: 50% Collapse: 21% Attrition: 38%   Comparables: Mel Queen, Bob Stoddard, Steve Reed

Jones has been in the minors since 1997, dealing with ongoing shoulder problems. Last year he was healthy for the first time in his career and had his best season to date. Now Jones believers, the Angels say he and his slider have a chance to make the team.

JOHN LACKEY
Bats: R Throws: R   Height: 6′ 6″ Weight: 200 Born: October 23, 1978   Age: 27

YEAR	TM	LVL	AGE	W	L	SV	G	GS	IP	H	BB	SO	HR	GB%	BABIP	STUFF	WHIP	ERA	PERA	EQERA	EQH9	EQBB9	EQSO9	EQHR9	VORP	WXRL
2003	ANA	MLB	24	10	16	0	33	33	204.0	223	66	151	31	45%	.310	6	1.42	4.63	4.71	5.06	9.7	2.9	6.5	1.3	17.8	3.3
2004	ANA	MLB	25	14	13	0	33	32	198.3	215	60	144	22	47%	.321	15	1.41	4.67	4.19	4.63	9.2	2.5	6.0	0.9	26.6	3.6
2005	LAA	MLB	26	14	5	0	33	33	209.0	208	71	199	13	46%	.328	39	1.33	3.44	3.42	3.71	8.4	3.0	8.3	0.5	49.1	5.5
2006	*LAA*	*MLB*	*27*	*13*	*10*	*0*	*32*	*32*	*208.0*	*206*	*64*	*171*	*21*	*45%*	*.299*	*22*	*1.30*	*3.89*	*4.20*	*4.17*	*8.8*	*2.8*	*7.2*	*0.9*	*33.6*	*5.0*

Breakout: 23%   Improve: 57%   Collapse: 7%   Attrition: 2%   Comparables: Erik Hanson, Pete Vuckovich, Gaylord Perry

Angels fans, meet your new ace. Lackey has gone from 5.7 K/9 in 2002 to 8.6 in 2005, the third-best strikeout rate among AL starters. Last year we said he needed an improved off-speed pitch. This year he has a greatly improved changeup and a new cutter in his arsenal. A sleeper Cy Young candidate, especially since his 2005 batting average on balls in play was very high. With better luck, his record could have been even stronger.

DUSTIN MOSELEY
Bats: R Throws: R   Height: 6′ 4″ Weight: 190 Born: December 26, 1981 Age: 24

YEAR	TM	LVL	AGE	W	L	SV	G	GS	IP	H	BB	SO	HR	GB%	BABIP	STUFF	WHIP	ERA	PERA	EQERA	EQH9	EQBB9	EQSO9	EQHR9	VORP	WXRL
2003	CHT	AA	21	5	6	0	18	18	112.7	116	28	73	10	—	.286	-10	1.28	3.83	5.61	5.28	10.1	2.4	4.0	1.6	3.9	—
2003	LOU	AAA	21	2	3	0	8	8	50.0	46	14	27	5	—	.250	0	1.20	2.70	5.25	3.75	9.0	3.0	4.1	1.3	9.9	—
2004	CHT	AA	22	3	2	0	8	8	47.3	33	10	40	4	—	.230	8	0.91	2.66	4.74	4.33	8.2	2.3	5.2	1.2	6.2	—
2004	LOU	AAA	22	2	4	0	12	12	71.7	78	34	48	7	—	.318	0	1.56	4.64	5.30	4.67	9.6	4.5	4.8	1.0	7.4	—
2005	SLC	AAA	23	4	6	0	17	17	82.3	102	30	38	11	49%	.327	-19	1.60	5.03	5.72	5.29	10.3	3.2	3.0	1.3	2.9	—
2006	*LAA*	*MLB*	*24*	*6*	*8*	*0*	*26*	*18*	*111.7*	*129*	*42*	*51*	*17*	*46%*	*.292*	*-9*	*1.53*	*5.49*	*5.75*	*5.84*	*10.3*	*3.4*	*4.0*	*1.3*	*-3.4*	*0.4*

Breakout: 3%   Improve: 18%   Collapse: 38%   Attrition: 0%   Comparables: Tim Drew, Dan Perkins, Mickey Callaway

If you're only packing a fastball that tops out around 90, it's imperative that you find some way to miss bats if you're going to make the O.C. Although he can throw four different pitches for strikes, Moseley saw his strikeout rate crater this year in Salt Lake, and with it went his reputation as a prospect. At this point, there's no sense in thinking that Moseley will ever be anything more than a fifth starter type in the majors, if that.

JOEL PERALTA
Bats: R Throws: R   Height: 5′ 11″ Weight: 160 Born: March 23, 1976   Age: 30

YEAR	TM	LVL	AGE	W	L	SV	G	GS	IP	H	BB	SO	HR	GB%	BABIP	STUFF	WHIP	ERA	PERA	EQERA	EQH9	EQBB9	EQSO9	EQHR9	VORP	WXRL
2003	ARK	AA	27	5	4	20	47	0	52.3	39	12	48	3	—	.248	-11	0.98	2.24	5.10	4.15	9.1	3.0	5.5	1.1	7.7	—
2004	SLC	AAA	28	4	2	1	39	0	56.0	64	18	68	6	—	.379	1	1.46	4.98	4.45	5.24	9.4	3.3	7.5	1.1	2.3	—
2005	SLC	AAA	29	4	1	10	19	0	20.0	11	6	18	0	34%	.216	0	0.85	2.70	4.34	3.38	6.8	3.4	5.8	0.5	4.6	—
2005	LAA	MLB	29	1	0	0	28	0	34.7	28	14	30	6	34%	.239	2	1.21	3.89	5.03	3.97	7.9	3.7	7.9	1.6	7.1	0.8
2006	*KCA*	*MLB*	*30*	*2*	*3*	*2*	*47*	*0*	*49.3*	*51*	*19*	*35*	*7*	*39%*	*.287*	*-4*	*1.41*	*4.51*	*4.89*	*5.28*	*9.0*	*3.5*	*6.4*	*1.2*	*4.8*	*0.4*

Breakout: 20%   Improve: 42%   Collapse: 30%   Attrition: 30%   Comparables: Luis Vizcaino, Shigetoshi Hasegawa, Richie Lewis

Seven years in the minors paid off with a solid 2005, as he finally got The Call, pitching adequately from the back end of the Angels bullpen. Unfortunately, it also meant that when the Angels tried to send him through waivers, he was claimed by Kansas City. The good news for Peralta is that he should have no trouble staying in the majors with the Royals. The bad news for Peralta is that he should have no trouble staying in the majors with the Royals. He had serious trouble against lefties, but he can still help the them in a ROOGY role even if he can't, um, "right" himself.

FRANCISCO RODRIGUEZ
Bats: R Throws: R   Height: 6′ 0″ Weight: 170 Born: January 7, 1982   Age: 24

YEAR	TM	LVL	AGE	W	L	SV	G	GS	IP	H	BB	SO	HR	GB%	BABIP	STUFF	WHIP	ERA	PERA	EQERA	EQH9	EQBB9	EQSO9	EQHR9	VORP	WXRL
2003	ANA	MLB	21	8	3	2	59	0	86.0	50	35	95	12	48%	.207	25	0.99	3.03	3.92	3.16	6.4	3.7	10.0	1.2	27.4	1.8
2004	ANA	MLB	22	4	1	12	69	0	84.0	51	33	123	2	47%	.286	60	0.99	1.82	2.25	2.25	5.6	3.3	12.3	0.2	37.1	5.1
2005	ANA	MLB	23	2	5	45	66	0	67.3	45	32	91	7	46%	.259	37	1.14	2.67	3.22	2.82	6.3	4.3	12.1	0.9	22.9	5.6
2006	*LAA*	*MLB*	*24*	*6*	*6*	*42*	*62*	*1*	*74.7*	*53*	*31*	*96*	*5*	*46%*	*.280*	*35*	*1.12*	*2.67*	*2.72*	*3.22*	*6.2*	*3.8*	*11.3*	*0.6*	*23.9*	*3.6*

Breakout: 15%   Improve: 48%   Collapse: 27%   Attrition: 9%   Comparables: Byung-Hyun Kim, Scott Williamson, Jack Meyer

Rodriguez's mechanics have eroded to the point that it's now a matter of when he will suffer a catastrophic arm injury, not if. When he's healthy, he's almost unhittable, but that health won't last much longer without an overhaul of his delivery. Rodriguez "snaps his forearm shut" when he throws his fastball, putting a ton of pressure on his elbow. So, counterintuitively, his slider actually hurts him less than the most natural pitch in baseball. By the end of the season, 80% of Rodriguez's pitches were sliders, because they caused him less stress. Unless the Angels intervene, he'll be lost.

RAFAEL RODRIGUEZ   **Bats: R Throws: R**   Height: 6' 1"   Weight: 170   Born: September 24, 1984   Age: 21

YEAR	TM	LVL	AGE	W	L	SV	G	GS	IP	H	BB	SO	HR	GB%	BABIP	STUFF	WHIP	ERA	PERA	EQERA	EQH9	EQBB9	EQSO9	EQHR9	VORP	WXRL
2003	CDR	A	18	10	11	0	26	26	144.0	129	59	100	7	—	.269	0	1.31	4.31	5.81	6.82	9.8	4.7	4.4	1.3	-18.3	—
2004	CDR	A	19	1	5	0	7	7	33.3	36	19	36	5	—	.326	-12	1.65	6.49	8.51	8.22	12.0	6.8	5.9	2.9	-8.9	—
2005	CDR	A	20	5	2	0	13	13	74.3	61	27	74	5	45%	.283	14	1.18	2.79	4.97	4.08	8.8	3.8	6.1	1.1	11.9	—
2005	RCU	A+	20	4	4	0	14	14	72.0	84	33	44	11	39%	.313	-27	1.62	6.75	6.78	7.17	10.6	4.9	3.6	1.9	-12.3	—
2006	*LAA*	*MLB*	*21*	*6*	*9*	*0*	*25*	*23*	*126.0*	*138*	*62*	*75*	*23*	*41%*	*.285*	*-3*	*1.59*	*5.69*	*6.14*	*6.02*	*9.7*	*4.5*	*5.2*	*1.5*	*-5.3*	*0.3*

Breakout: 21%   *Improve: 69%*   *Collapse: 9%*   *Attrition: 0%*   Comparables: *Jimmy Barrett, Matt Butler, Brad Baker*

What the heck would we call him? Raffy-Rod? Like his (unrelated) namesake on the major league club, his slider is his out pitch. Unfortunately, he also shares with K-Rod a delivery that makes for great James Andrews journal articles. He's got a lot of potential because he can dial it up to the high 90s. R-Rod was dominating in Low-A, but predictably the small ballparks of the California League undid those numbers. He allowed more than a hit per inning and with a WHIP of 1.63, it's easy to understand why his ERA jumped to 6.75 at Rancho Cucamonga. There is good news—and it doesn't involve saving money on car insurance—if he can stay healthy and adapt, he has the stuff to move up quickly.

ERVIN SANTANA   **Bats: R Throws: R**   Height: 6' 2"   Weight: 150   Born: January 10, 1983   Age: 23

YEAR	TM	LVL	AGE	W	L	SV	G	GS	IP	H	BB	SO	HR	GB%	BABIP	STUFF	WHIP	ERA	PERA	EQERA	EQH9	EQBB9	EQSO9	EQHR9	VORP	WXRL
2003	RCU	A+	20	10	2	0	20	20	124.7	98	36	130	9	—	.267	12	1.07	2.53	5.00	4.46	8.8	3.4	6.2	1.3	14.8	—
2003	ARK	AA	20	1	1	0	6	6	29.7	23	12	23	4	—	.223	0	1.18	3.94	7.00	5.00	9.7	4.3	5.7	2.3	1.8	—
2004	ARK	AA	21	2	1	0	8	8	43.7	41	18	48	3	—	.319	16	1.35	3.30	4.85	4.43	8.9	4.2	7.0	1.1	5.6	—
2005	ARK	AA	22	5	1	0	7	7	39.0	34	15	32	2	36%	.288	8	1.26	2.31	4.82	3.86	8.4	4.3	5.5	0.7	7.2	—
2005	SLC	AAA	22	1	0	0	3	3	19.3	19	2	17	2	33%	.315	19	1.09	4.20	3.72	4.66	8.8	0.9	6.1	0.9	2.0	—
2005	ANA	MLB	22	12	8	0	23	23	133.7	139	47	99	17	36%	.300	13	1.39	4.64	4.60	4.93	9.3	3.2	6.5	1.1	11.9	2.9
2006	*LAA*	*MLB*	*23*	*10*	*10*	*0*	*30*	*30*	*172.7*	*175*	*61*	*124*	*24*	*39%*	*.285*	*14*	*1.37*	*4.48*	*4.81*	*4.72*	*9.0*	*3.2*	*6.3*	*1.2*	*16.7*	*3.0*

Breakout: 16%   *Improve: 55%*   *Collapse: 11%*   *Attrition: 0%*   Comparables: *Jake Peavy, Gary Gentry, Dan Spillner*

With a young pitcher, it's often not a question of talent, but a matter of achieving consistency through repetition. Santana's first major league season bears that out: in his 23 starts, he gave up two or fewer runs 12 times, but a less happy five runs or more six times. When he learns how to mitigate the damage in some of those shellings, and he will, he's got the stuff to be mentioned among the American League's elite hurlers. Elbow trouble has been a problem in the past, so he'll have to be handled carefully, but the Angels have a good track record with their charges.

JOE SAUNDERS   **Bats: L Throws: L**   Height: 6' 2"   Weight: 190   Born: June 16, 1981   Age: 25

YEAR	TM	LVL	AGE	W	L	SV	G	GS	IP	H	BB	SO	HR	GB%	BABIP	STUFF	WHIP	ERA	PERA	EQERA	EQH9	EQBB9	EQSO9	EQHR9	VORP	WXRL
2004	RCU	A+	23	9	7	0	19	19	105.7	106	23	76	13	—	.291	-32	1.22	3.41	6.61	5.89	10.5	2.7	4.0	2.3	-3.2	—
2004	ARK	AA	23	4	3	0	8	8	39.0	51	14	25	5	—	.357	-19	1.67	5.77	6.52	6.28	11.6	3.7	4.0	1.9	-2.9	—
2005	ARK	AA	24	7	4	0	18	18	105.7	107	32	80	9	52%	.308	-4	1.32	3.49	5.15	5.68	9.6	3.6	4.9	1.2	-0.9	—
2005	SLC	AAA	24	3	3	0	9	9	55.0	65	21	29	3	55%	.341	-3	1.56	4.58	4.50	5.95	9.5	3.4	3.4	0.5	-2.2	—
2006	*LAA*	*MLB*	*25*	*6*	*10*	*0*	*34*	*21*	*134.3*	*158*	*53*	*68*	*21*	*48%*	*.301*	*-9*	*1.57*	*5.75*	*5.97*	*6.15*	*10.4*	*3.6*	*4.4*	*1.3*	*-8.3*	*0.0*

Breakout: 17%   *Improve: 47%*   *Collapse: 14%*   *Attrition: 0%*   Comparables: *Neal Musser, Jimmy Osting, Mike Gosling*

The potential successor to Jarrod Washburn as the Angels' only left-handed starter, Saunders dominated in Arkansas before earning a ticket to Salt Lake and a late cup of coffee in Anaheim (Topic for further discussion: given modern tastes, should "cup of coffee in Anaheim" be updated to "café latte in Anaheim?"). He's not going to blow anyone away with his stuff, so his ability to change speeds with a good changeup is the key. Adding another pitch will be crucial moving forward—he doesn't have the gas to get away with just two pitches.

STEVEN SHELL   **Bats: R Throws: R**   Height: 6' 5"   Weight: 190   Born: March 10, 1983   Age: 23

YEAR	TM	LVL	AGE	W	L	SV	G	GS	IP	H	BB	SO	HR	GB%	BABIP	STUFF	WHIP	ERA	PERA	EQERA	EQH9	EQBB9	EQSO9	EQHR9	VORP	WXRL
2003	RCU	A+	20	6	8	0	22	21	127.3	123	26	100	13	—	.281	-10	1.17	4.24	5.88	5.73	10.2	2.4	4.6	1.9	-1.7	—
2004	RCU	A+	21	12	7	0	28	28	165.3	151	40	190	19	—	.317	-3	1.16	3.59	5.78	5.38	9.9	2.9	6.6	2.0	3.8	—
2005	ARK	AA	22	10	8	0	27	27	159.7	175	58	126	18	46%	.331	-8	1.46	4.56	5.64	5.94	10.2	4.0	5.3	1.5	-5.8	—
2006	*LAA*	*MLB*	*23*	*7*	*10*	*0*	*27*	*25*	*143.3*	*158*	*56*	*88*	*23*	*45%*	*.294*	*3*	*1.50*	*5.35*	*5.63*	*5.64*	*9.8*	*3.6*	*5.4*	*1.3*	*-1.6*	*0.9*

Breakout: 14%   *Improve: 57%*   *Collapse: 7%*   *Attrition: 0%*   Comparables: *Brian Falkenborg, Mike Wuertz, Brett Evert*

(continued next page)

Steven Shell *(continued)*

Walks up, strikeouts down—that's moving the wrong way. The Texas League is no place to try and make a living as a pitcher, but Shell simply didn't show much against tougher competition. The one ray of hope was an improved second half—he went from 6.89 K/9 and 3.73 BB/9 in his first 17 starts to 7.39 K/9 and 2.60 BB/9 in his last ten; 15 of his 18 homers were given up before July 1, but only three after. Needs to turn things around quickly to stay a top prospect in the organization.

SCOT SHIELDS   Bats: R   Throws: R   Height: 6′ 1″   Weight: 170   Born: July 22, 1975   Age: 30

YEAR	TM	LVL	AGE	W	L	SV	G	GS	IP	H	BB	SO	HR	GB%	BABIP	STUFF	WHIP	ERA	PERA	EQERA	EQH9	EQBB9	EQSO9	EQHR9	VORP	WXRL
2003	ANA	MLB	27	5	6	1	44	13	148.3	138	38	111	12	52%	.289	19	1.19	2.85	3.67	3.43	8.6	2.3	6.6	0.7	42.4	3.1
2004	ANA	MLB	28	8	2	4	60	0	105.3	97	40	109	6	56%	.312	30	1.30	3.33	3.27	3.44	7.8	3.1	8.6	0.5	31.4	4.7
2005	LAA	MLB	29	10	11	7	78	0	91.7	66	37	98	5	55%	.270	32	1.12	2.75	3.16	3.26	6.8	3.7	9.6	0.5	25.3	4.5
2006	*LAA*	*MLB*	*30*	*5*	*4*	*6*	*65*	*1*	*82.0*	*75*	*30*	*72*	*7*	*50%*	*.290*	*10*	*1.28*	*3.49*	*3.79*	*3.85*	*8.1*	*3.3*	*7.7*	*0.8*	*18.0*	*1.5*

Breakout: 10%   *Improve: 37%*   *Collapse: 28%*   *Attrition: 5%*   *Comparables: Greg Harris, Jeff Montgomery, Mel Rojas*

Boing! That's the sound of Shields's rubber arm, as he sailed through another year near the top of the charts in relief appearances and innings pitched. He was ninth-best in baseball and second to teammate Frankie Rodriguez in Relievers Expected Wins Added. After years of relying on what had been a deep and talented pen, Scioscia rode Shields and K-Rod hard after Donnelly and Gregg proved less reliable; Shields can handle the load.

JARROD WASHBURN   Bats: L   Throws: L   Height: 6′ 1″   Weight: 200   Born: August 13, 1974   Age: 31

YEAR	TM	LVL	AGE	W	L	SV	G	GS	IP	H	BB	SO	HR	GB%	BABIP	STUFF	WHIP	ERA	PERA	EQERA	EQH9	EQBB9	EQSO9	EQHR9	VORP	WXRL
2003	ANA	MLB	28	10	15	0	32	32	207.3	205	54	118	34	36%	.264	-2	1.25	4.43	5.09	4.56	9.5	2.3	5.1	1.4	30.7	4.0
2004	ANA	MLB	29	11	8	0	25	25	149.3	159	40	86	20	43%	.287	3	1.33	4.64	4.61	4.61	9.3	2.2	4.8	1.1	22.6	3.4
2005	ANA	MLB	30	8	8	0	29	29	177.3	184	51	94	19	41%	.296	8	1.33	3.20	4.61	3.50	9.4	2.6	4.8	0.9	47.7	5.7
2006	*SEA*	*MLB*	*31*	*10*	*11*	*0*	*31*	*28*	*175.0*	*183*	*49*	*99*	*24*	*41%*	*.280*	*3*	*1.33*	*4.34*	*4.63*	*4.70*	*9.3*	*2.5*	*4.8*	*1.2*	*19.0*	*3.3*

Breakout: 4%   *Improve: 24%*   *Collapse: 28%*   *Attrition: 4%*   *Comparables: Terry Mulholland, Mike Flanagan, Brian Bohanon*

That ERA covers up some disturbing trends, including the same sort of walk and strikeout rates that produced much less impressive results the past few years. This is one case where his 8–8 record is a better measure of his value. He showed a continuing inability to pitch well in Anaheim. That won't help him in Seattle, where signed a four-year deal in December. Perhaps the M's didn't get the memo that Washburn's best seasons are behind him.

JERED WEAVER   Bats: R   Throws: R   Height: 6′ 7″   Weight: 205   Born: October 4, 1982   Age: 23

YEAR	TM	LVL	AGE	W	L	SV	G	GS	IP	H	BB	SO	HR	GB%	BABIP	STUFF	WHIP	ERA	PERA	EQERA	EQH9	EQBB9	EQSO9	EQHR9	VORP	WXRL
2005	RCU	A+	22	4	1	0	7	7	33.0	25	7	49	3	30%	.314	23	0.97	3.82	4.02	5.74	8.3	2.3	8.3	1.1	-0.5	—
2005	ARK	AA	22	3	3	0	8	8	43.0	43	19	46	5	31%	.314	5	1.44	3.98	5.44	5.44	9.4	4.8	7.2	1.5	0.7	—
2006	*LAA*	*MLB*	*23*	*7*	*8*	*0*	*26*	*20*	*123.0*	*123*	*52*	*99*	*21*	*32%*	*.283*	*10*	*1.43*	*5.18*	*5.26*	*5.38*	*8.9*	*3.8*	*7.0*	*1.4*	*2.4*	*1.1*

Breakout: 23%   *Improve: 60%*   *Collapse: 10%*   *Attrition: 2%*   *Comparables: Andrew Brown, John Maine, John Patterson*

Perhaps the most successful college pitcher ever, Weaver was good in both High-A and Double-A after finally ending his holdout and signing in May. He didn't rust much during his time off: even after making the jump to the Texas League, Weaver struck out over a batter an inning. But he did suffer some control problems as he tried to be a little more fine against the better hitters. Weaver's got the goods to be a major league starter soon, perhaps even this season. If there's a knock on Weaver, it's that his delivery has a lot of moving parts, including all kinds of hand action, and after his release he falls off the mound in a whirl of arms and legs. There's some fear that with so much going on in his motion, consistency will become an issue. The Angels figure the delivery problems were symptomatic of his long layoff. Thus, he'll have to refine his mechanics to become a star at the top level They might also counsel Weaver to get his pitches down—check out that groundball rate.

JAKE WOODS   Bats: L   Throws: L   Height: 6' 1"   Weight: 190   Born: September 3, 1981   Age: 24

YEAR	TM	LVL	AGE	W	L	SV	G	GS	IP	H	BB	SO	HR	GB%	BABIP	STUFF	WHIP	ERA	PERA	EQERA	EQH9	EQBB9	EQSO9	EQHR9	VORP	WXRL
2003	RCU	A+	21	12	7	0	28	28	171.3	178	54	109	9	—	.294	-4	1.35	3.99	5.28	5.99	9.9	3.7	3.6	1.0	-7.2	—
2004	ARK	AA	22	9	2	0	14	14	90.0	86	19	60	5	—	.287	9	1.17	2.70	4.41	3.59	8.9	2.2	4.2	0.8	19.6	—
2004	SLC	AAA	22	6	4	0	15	14	83.0	108	42	60	13	—	.343	-11	1.81	6.07	5.78	5.99	10.1	4.6	4.8	1.4	-3.7	—
2005	SLC	AAA	23	3	1	0	15	5	36.7	50	17	36	7	38%	.371	-11	1.83	5.89	5.92	5.92	10.9	4.0	6.2	1.9	-1.4	—
2005	LAA	MLB	23	1	1	0	28	0	27.7	30	8	20	7	38%	.274	-9	1.37	4.55	6.18	5.86	10.1	2.6	6.5	2.3	-0.5	0.1
2006	LAA	MLB	24	3	4	1	54	3	61.0	71	25	37	10	42%	.305	-12	1.56	5.61	5.99	5.97	10.3	3.7	5.4	1.4	-2.3	-0.1

Breakout: 13%   Improve: 39%   Collapse: 26%   Attrition: 17%   Comparables: Bob Kipper, Ken Dayley, Rich Yett

The curveball is a fickle mistress—mastering its looping trajectory has driven many pitchers to distraction over the years. Woods has a nice curve when he has it working, but lacks the ability to consistently throw it for strikes. One night it's filthy, the next, it's bouncing or taking a one-way tour of the bleachers. If Woods can get it nailed down, he'll be a big asset for the Mariners now that he's been dealt to them, maybe even as a starter.

ESTEBAN YAN   Bats: R   Throws: R   Height: 6' 4"   Weight: 180   Born: June 22, 1975   Age: 31

YEAR	TM	LVL	AGE	W	L	SV	G	GS	IP	H	BB	SO	HR	GB%	BABIP	STUFF	WHIP	ERA	PERA	EQERA	EQH9	EQBB9	EQSO9	EQHR9	VORP	WXRL
2003	TEX	MLB	28	0	1	0	15	0	23.3	31	7	25	5	41%	.366	9	1.63	6.95	4.74	6.20	9.9	2.6	8.8	1.8	-2.3	-0.4
2003	SLN	MLB	28	2	0	1	39	0	43.3	53	16	28	8	50%	.331	-19	1.59	6.03	5.77	6.18	10.9	2.9	5.2	1.6	-2.6	-1.3
2004	DET	MLB	29	3	6	7	69	0	87.0	92	32	69	8	54%	.324	7	1.43	3.83	3.96	4.16	8.9	3.0	6.6	0.7	17.2	1.6
2005	LAA	MLB	30	1	1	0	49	0	66.7	66	30	45	8	47%	.286	-7	1.44	4.59	4.84	4.84	8.9	4.0	6.0	1.1	6.2	0.6
2006	LAA	MLB	31	3	3	1	49	0	61.0	66	22	41	8	46%	.303	-7	1.45	4.79	5.07	5.79	9.6	3.3	6.0	1.1	3.5	0.2

Breakout: 26%   Improve: 47%   Collapse: 31%   Attrition: 20%   Comparables: Ron Kline, Jeff Robinson, Dickie Noles

Not the disaster that Halos fans might have imagined during sleepless nights after his signing, but for an organization that has had such success plugging in bullpen arms from the farm system, his signing was an odd one, especially since he was used in a mop-up role. They'll pay Yan $1.25 million in 2006 to do the job that any number of players in their system could probably do for the minimum.

Line Outs

Position/Player	TM	LVL	AGE	PA	R	2B	3B	HR	RBI	BB	SO	SB-CS	SPEED	BA/OBP/SLG	MLVR	EQBA/OBP/SLG	EQA	VORP
C J. Paul	LAA	MLB	30	39	4	1	0	2	4	2	9	0-0	4.0	.189/.231/.378	-.294	.189/.250/.378	.217	-1.2
OF T. Murphy	ARK	AA	25	555	85	24	11	17	76	43	97	26-12	6.9	.288/.346/.482	.123	.240/.293/.389	.239	-18.2

Pitcher	TM	LVL	AGE	W	L	SV	IP	H	BB	SO	HR	GB%	BABIP	STUFF	WHIP	ERA	PERA	EQERA	EQH9	EQBB9	EQSO9	EQHR9	VORP
C. Bootcheck	SLC	AAA	26	7	4	0	116.3	144	50	90	13	44%	.366	-8	1.67	5.42	5.25	5.78	10.0	4.0	4.7	1.1	-2.4
J. Christiansen	SFN	MLB	35	6	1	0	42.0	48	15	17	4	54%	.299	-22	1.50	5.36	4.89	5.74	10.0	3.0	3.4	0.9	-1.3
J. Holcomb	RCU	A+	24	10	7	0	141.7	153	50	128	16	44%	.338	-22	1.43	5.02	6.01	6.73	10.4	4.2	4.8	1.6	-17.1
B. Zimmerman	RCU	A+	23	6	8	17	59.7	50	27	62	3	49%	.307	-11	1.29	3.32	4.76	4.92	8.4	5.2	5.7	0.6	4.3

Torn ligaments in his ankle cost **Lou Merloni** most of the season. The Indians signed the medical leave specialist to a minor league deal avec spring training invite. **Tommy Murphy** can run and is an improving fielder but never showed much with the bat until he repeated Double-A last year. If he doesn't sustain the improvement at Triple-A, he's not suitable for even a utility role. **Josh Paul** could caution us all that not everybody gets to pick which 15 minutes they're famous for. It hardly matters, given that he's an demonstration of what a bad idea carrying a third catcher can be if he doesn't do anything but catch. At his mid-90s peak, **Tim Salmon** was one of the game's best, (and most under-appreciated) hitters, perhaps the best Angels player ever. He'll go to spring training as an NRI.

Chris Bootcheck proves that, at 27, there's not a lot of hope for a big improvement; after being a college pitcher picked in the 1st round in 2000, more was expected of him than three years in Utah. **Jason Christiansen** is a case on point that GMs are suckers for portsiders in their late 30s, but his days of being effective ended eight years and three teams ago. **James Holcomb** had a nice year in High-A, but when you're 24 it's one of those mixed blessings—nice to see improving peripherals, but also a case where you're a little old for the party, like the creepy guy at your college who kept showing up at keggers long after he graduated. **Bob Zimmerman's** the new Blind Boy Grunt, and kept his home run rate down in the Cal League thanks to his signature sinker. He could have some real value with improved command. Hey, Arkansas—tonight he'll be staying here with you.

Los Angeles Dodgers

In the early spring of 2005, things looked rosy for the Dodger blue. The team had just won the NL West for the first time since 1995. In Paul DePodesta they had a savvy, new-school GM who'd overcome a late start to his off-season preparations, defied naysayers by shaking up the team in midseason, and watched his controversial deals pay off. In Jim Tracy, they team had a capable manager who'd weathered turnover in both the front office and the locker room, finding a winning combination among stars and scrubs. Thanks to the drafts of Director of Amateur Scouting Logan White, their farm system was bursting at the seams with talent after years of underwhelming returns.

That optimism quickly disintegrated. After an active winter in which DePodesta committed $144 million to free agents, the Dodgers entered 2005 in good shape to repeat in the West. But the injury bug started biting in February and ultimately devoured the team, a hot start notwithstanding. DePodesta and Tracy made mistakes that compounded the team's problems, and a nasty feud within the locker room highlighted the team's dysfunctional chemistry. Even in a historically weak division, the Dodgers couldn't mount a challenge, finishing with just 71 wins, their second-worst showing since leaving Brooklyn in 1958. Tracy exercised an out clause in his contract at season's end, choosing Pittsburgh as a better place to work. Unsatisfied with DePodesta's candidates to replace Tracy, owner Frank McCourt sacked his GM shortly afterwards, in the process turning the organization into a laughingstock.

Former Giants Assistant GM Ned Colletti was hired to replace Depodesta and clean up the damage. Colletti's first move, the hiring of manager Grady Little, generated guffaws, but he followed that with a coup, signing one of the off-season's few legitimate star free agents, Braves shortstop Rafael Furcal. Colletti has gone on to reshape the team with an assortment of well-traveled veterans who might look strange in Dodger blue, but he has bought time for the farm system to bear fruit while returning the Dodgers to contention.

Thanks to *Moneyball,* DePodesta came to the Dodgers with a high profile. His hiring was hailed as a sign that McCourt, having rescued the team from Fox's corporate caprice, would be a progressive owner, able to combine big-market advantages with the shrewd, successful approach of the small-market A's. Like everybody else associated

with *Moneyball,* DePodesta was a polarizing figure. His moves were criticized and ascribed ideological motives far beyond the simple needs of filling out a roster. He instantly drew the ire of L.A.'s sports media; one reactionary hack nicknamed him "Google Boy."

No DePodesta move drew more flak from such all-knowing wags than the 2004 deadline trade of the Dodgers' "heart and soul," catcher Paul Lo Duca, to the Marlins in a package that brought them starter Brad Penny and first baseman Hee Sop Choi. Penny was shelved with a nerve injury shortly afterwards, and Tracy mothballed the promising Choi rather than integrate him into the lineup. Despite the Dodgers winning their division and Lo Duca's clockwork-like late-season collapse, the move was assailed. Over the winter, sensible maneuvers such as pulling out of a potential three-way deal with the Diamondbacks and Yankees involving Randy Johnson and Shawn Green were attacked even after time had borne out DePodesta's concerns.

As he built for 2005, DePodesta avoided getting too attached to the players he'd won with. Adrian Beltre, Alex Cora, Steve Finley, Jose Hernandez, and Jose Lima all departed as free agents. All were good bets not to repeat their 2004 performances, and as a group, they cratered.

Green rebounded slightly once traded to Arizona's band-box ballpark, but he was the exception. The loss of Beltre after an MVP-caliber career year had backfire potential, but when he didn't do any better as a Mariner than he had as a Dodger before '05. The local media pretended not to notice and went right on reviling DePodesta for letting the third baseman go.

At the same time, DePodesta's free agent signings caused a good amount of legitimate head scratching. J. D. Drew, fresh off his first healthy season of his career, was signed for five years and $55 million. Derek Lowe, coming off a 5.42 ERA nightmare in Boston, drew four years and $36 million in a free agent market where the prevailing rate for mid-rotation starters was three years and $21 million. The ever-erratic Odalis Perez was re-signed for three years, $24 million. An aging Jose Valentin was signed to man third base, a position he hadn't played regularly since 2002. Only Jeff Kent's two-year, $17 million contract made sense. Yet for all of that spending, the Dodgers opened the season with an $83 million payroll, $9.9 million less than 2004, $22.9 million less than 2003, and far short of McCourt's $100 million pledge.

Spring began inauspiciously. Eric Gagne sprained his knee in late February, then resumed throwing before he completely healed. Then he followed the first injury with a second, to his elbow. He didn't return until early May, but his compromised mechanics shelved him for the season in mid-June. Another camp injury, Jayson Werth's broken wrist, was worse than first thought; he didn't get back onto the field until late May, and he would still need surgery in November to correct previously undetected soft-tissue damage. DePodesta treated Werth's injury as a short-term situation, content to let Tracy play replacement-level fodder like Jason Repko and Mike Edwards rather than trade for a hitter. Rickey Ledee was helpful in a part-time role, but then he too succumbed to injury.

Despite it all, the team sprinted to a 12–2 start, the team's best debut since 1955, but things soon went south. The Dodgers were 17–9 when Valentin tore up his knee on May 3, and had slid to 26–24 when centerfielder Milton Bradley tore a finger ligament on May 29. Without their star center fielder, the Dodger offense imploded. Averaging 4.9 runs per game up to that point, they slid to 3.7 and went 18–29 before Bradley returned. In the interim, Drew broke his wrist. Again, DePodesta stood pat. Drew never returned, and the Repkos continued to devour outs.

In all, the Dodgers would lose 1,357 player-days to injury, the third-highest total in the majors, while leading in both dollars ($36.7 million) and percentage of payroll (45%) lost to the DL. Granted, that included the full-season absence of the always-injured Darren Dreifort, but even without counting him, the Dodgers would have placed near the top in all three categories. (For an analysis of the impact of injuries on the NL West race, see Tom Gorman's essay in the Fungoes section.)

Unfortunately, Tracy and DePodesta exacerbated those losses by inexplicably keeping a washed-up Scott Erickson (6.02 ERA) on the roster until the trading deadline. Moreover, DePodesta failed to anticipate the domino effect on the bullpen once Gagne went down. Yhency Brazoban had done a tantalizing imitation of Guillermo Mota in the second half of 2004, and he acquitted himself well as the closer in his first month on the job in Gagne's place, but he spiraled downward after blowing a few key games, dragging the team with him. The bullpen was already held together with duct tape and wishful thinking; the Dodgers needed another competent arm to sop up innings while letting the likes of Steve Schmoll wet their feet in lower-leverage situations.

Tracy, for his part, strangled the offense by keeping Cesar Izturis in the leadoff spot through a 2-for-46 slump. He continually ignored Choi. The day after a four-game, seven-homer spree in mid-June, Choi began an 0-for-21 skid, permanently losing the manager's confidence, and Tracy replaced him with career backup catcher Jason Phillips, forcing the free-swinging Choi into a pinch-hitting role for which he was particularly ill-suited. As heavy hitters dropped like flies, Tracy appeared bent on denying the young Korean slugger any opportunity to pick up the slack.

The death knell for the season and the regime came in late August. A locker-room spat between Bradley and Kent resulted in the former—already famous for his anger management issues—publicly accusing the latter of racism, even after both DePodesta and Tracy intervened and warned Bradley not to take the feud to the press, to no avail. An avalanche of bad publicity ensued. Increasingly sensitive to public opinion and the notion that the team was losing its hometown market to the Angels, McCourt resolved to clean house with "character" players. He publicly apologized for the team's haplessness. DePodesta soon followed with his own mea culpa; Tracy was conspicuously mum.

DePodesta framed the relationship with his manager as "creative conflict," but Tracy saw it as something more fundamental. As he later said, "We obviously came to a point where there was a difference of opinion between Paul and I as far as how players are evaluated . . . the process in which you go about determining how they fit in. When you get to that point, you're at an impasse. Going back into the dugout as a lame-duck manager didn't appeal to me. I know the market and the expectation level. I didn't think it was a healthy situation."

Tracy resigned the day after season's end. DePodesta spent four weeks seeking a replacement, and had apparently settled on Terry Collins, the team's Director of Player

Development, but better known for presiding over late-season collapses in Houston and Anaheim. After a much-publicized *tête-à-tête* between McCourt, Dodger apparatchik Tommy Lasorda, and would-be prodigal son Orel Hershiser (then the Rangers' pitching coach), the owner canned DePodesta, exclaiming, "We want Dodgers here." DePodesta had completed less than two years of his five-year contract. The shrill local media, already forgetting the division title of 2004, roared their approval of the demise of Google Boy.

The owner's new hire was anything but a Dodger. Colletti has spent the past 11 years as Assistant GM of the rival Giants. The move had spin-doctoring written all over it, befitting the hiring of a man whose first baseball job was in the Cubs' public relations department. As with DePodesta's February 2004 hiring, McCourt didn't give his new GM much time to unpack before getting down to business.

Colletti's hiring of Little signified an end to any stathead-minded bent within the organization. Little was run out of Boston for ignoring Theo Epstein's directive to heed Pedro Martinez's pitch counts, instead playing a hunch that cost the Red Sox the 2003 AL pennant. Score one for the old school, and another for Boston native McCourt's preoccupation with alums of the Old Towne Team.

Colletti's next move, bagging Furcal to play short by outbidding the Cubs, set the tone for the winter. Furcal soon gained a partner on the left side on the infield in Bill Mueller, a former Little charge and also an ex-Giant. He wasn't the last former Red Sock to join the fold; Nomar Garciaparra was signed to an incentive-laden one-year deal. A day later, Colletti signed Kenny Lofton (another ex-Giant) to play centerfield, vacated when Bradley was dealt to the A's for outfield prospect Andre Ethier. Colletti added yet another ex-Giant in starter Brett Tomko to replace the departing Jeff Weaver.

The Dodgers now have a lineup that bears no resemblance to 2004 winners, and shares just two starters—Drew and Kent—from the one that opened 2005. Yet for all of the discontinuity, Colletti accomplished a few major things. He avoided significant long-term entanglements; only the Furcal deal goes beyond two years. He resisted the temptation to package prize prospects for veterans, and avoided blocking the likes of outfielder-to-be Joel Guzman, third baseman Andy LaRoche, or starting pitcher Chad Billingsley. The Bradley trade, though not exactly a win for the Dodgers, brought a solid upper-level outfield prospect, necessary depth for a team that just suffered through a parade of Repkos and Chin Feng-Chens. And though the binge included two Type A free agents, it won't cost the Dodgers a first-rounder; 71 wins netted the team a protected pick in the top 15.

The deals aren't without their downsides. Izturis and the three-year deal he signed before 2005 were rendered obsolete. Garciaparra hasn't completed a healthy season since 2003, and though he hit a robust .318/.347/.531 after returning from his latest injury, he'll be learning a new position, first base, in the toughest hitting environment of his career. Lofton is 39 and Mueller 35; both seem certain to decline at the plate now that they'll be hitting in Chavez Ravine. Although Tomko's eaten an average of 198 innings every year since 2002, he's also 38 runs below average for his career.

As for the prospects, outside of reliever Jonathan Broxton none is likely to have much impact on the 2006 team, at least not at the outset. As the core of the Double-A Jacksonville squad reaches Las Vegas this year, an old issue arises. Vegas is an extreme hitter's park, even for the already hitter-friendly Pacific Coast League. Historically, the organization has demonstrated a perpetual inability to evaluate the performances of its prospects in the PCL, from Greg Brock to Joe Thurston. Meanwhile, the struggles of pitching prospect Edwin Jackson in that environment doesn't bode well for Billingsley or any other hurler who has to call Vegas home.

Happily for the Dodgers, Colletti has demonstrated a quick grasp of his new situation. He's bought his prospects time to develop, and for all the turnover, the Dodgers should be able to compete in a division where, aside from a healthy Barry Bonds, few teams have substantially improved themselves. Things have changed considerably in a year, but time is on the Dodgers' side.

HITTERS

WILLY AYBAR   **2B/3B**   **Bats: B Throws: R**   Height: 6′ 0″   Weight: 175   Born: March 9, 1983   Age: 23

YEAR	TM	LVL	AGE	PA	R	2B	3B	HR	RBI	BB	SO	SB	CS	SPEED	BA	OBP	SLG	MLVR	EQBA	EQOBP	EQSLG	EQA	VORP	DEFENSE		
2003	VRO	A+	20	494	47	29	3	11	74	41	70	9	9	4.4	.274	.336	.427	.105	.242	.295	.404	.240	3.8	108-3B	15	
2004	JAX	AA	21	537	56	27	0	15	77	50	77	8	10	3.8	.276	.346	.425	.111	.257	.320	.403	.248	11.9	122-2B	11	
2005	LVG	AAA	22	449	47	26	4	5	60	40	56	1	6	3.8	.297	.356	.419	-.062	.247	.303	.342	.226	-5.1	68-3B	10	25-2B -3
2005	LAN	MLB	22	105	12	8	0	1	10	18	11	3	1	4.9	.326	.448	.453	.316	.333	.458	.483	.330	10.0	20-3B	-2	
2006	LAN	MLB	23	481	55	25	1	10	53	42	67	4	3	4.1	.262	.330	.396	-.062	.268	.336	.413	.252	10.2	114-3B	3	

Breakout: 37%   *Improve: 60%*   *Collapse: 18%*   *Attrition: 12%*   *Comparables: Dale Sveum, Roy Smalley, Tucker Ashford*

The older brother of Angels prospect Erick, this Aybar cracked our Top Prospect list at #34 last year. Shuttling between second and third, he struggled at Las Vegas in '05, the increases in his raw rate stats disguised by the PCL's inflated offensive environment. Nevertheless, he shredded NL pitching upon being promoted in late August, displaying plate discipline that had heretofore only been hinted at. The Bill Mueller signing and the trade of Antonio Perez make Aybar a candidate for a utility job, but he'd be better served with more time in Triple-A to cement last September's gains.

PAUL BAKO   C   **Bats: L Throws: R**   Height: 6' 2"   Weight: 205   Born: June 20, 1972   Age: 34

YEAR	TM	LVL	AGE	PA	R	2B	3B	HR	RBI	BB	SO	SB	CS	SPEED	BA	OBP	SLG	MLVR	EQBA	EQOBP	EQSLG	EQA	VORP	DEFENSE	
2003	CHN	MLB	31	212	19	13	3	0	17	22	47	0	1	5.2	.229	.311	.330	-.169	.229	.311	.324	.227	-2.8	57-C	-5
2004	CHN	MLB	32	156	13	8	0	1	10	15	29	1	0	4.0	.203	.288	.283	-.305	.196	.282	.268	.205	-6.2	42-C	2
2005	LAN	MLB	33	47	1	2	0	0	4	7	12	0	0	3.9	.250	.362	.300	-.086	.250	.362	.300	.245	0.6	12-C	1
2006	KCA	MLB	34	104	9	5	1	1	8	11	21	1	0	4.5	.238	.322	.327	-.157	.240	.331	.345	.233	0.7	29-C	-1

Breakout: 35%   Improve: 53%   Collapse: 29%   Attrition: 57%   Comparables: *Steve Decker, Jeff Reed, Andy Etchebarren*

A good-field/no-hit catcher whose defensive abilities are somewhat overstated, Bako tore his ACL in a rundown in June, shelving him for the season. The injury wasn't a total loss, as it forced the team to take a long look at Navarro, with happy results. Despite being 34 and coming off of knee surgery, the Royals have signed him to provide the veteran gravitas John Buck lacks. We imagine something like Edwin Newman in a mask.

MILTON BRADLEY   OF   **Bats: B Throws: R**   Height: 6' 0"   Weight: 170   Born: April 15, 1978   Age: 28

YEAR	TM	LVL	AGE	PA	R	2B	3B	HR	RBI	BB	SO	SB	CS	SPEED	BA	OBP	SLG	MLVR	EQBA	EQOBP	EQSLG	EQA	VORP	DEFENSE			
2003	CLE	MLB	25	451	61	34	2	10	56	64	73	17	7	5.4	.321	.421	.501	.316	.329	.432	.516	.323	46.8	93-CF	0		
2004	LAN	MLB	26	594	72	24	0	19	67	71	123	15	11	4.9	.267	.362	.424	.066	.271	.364	.430	.271	17.1	88-CF	5	30-RF	0
2005	LAN	MLB	27	311	49	14	1	13	38	25	47	6	1	5.8	.290	.350	.484	.160	.290	.354	.500	.290	20.1	71-CF	7		
2006	OAK	MLB	28	490	68	25	2	15	62	49	75	13	5	5.4	.279	.355	.447	.076	.283	.366	.466	.279	23.8	116-CF	1		

Breakout: 10%   Improve: 30%   Collapse: 22%   Attrition: 15%   Comparables: *Tom Tresh, Bernie Williams, Ken Henderson*

The straw that stirred the drink? Without Bradley, the Dodgers went 33–52 while scoring 3.8 per game. They went 38–39 and scored 4.7 runs per game during his two stints of activity. On a per-game basis Bradley was one of the five most productive centerfielders in the league, but unfortunately that doesn't tell the whole story. Bradley not only has issues, he's got the lifetime subscription and the tacky duffel bag, too. His L.A. tenure was marred by ugly, self-destructive incidents involving teammates, fans, media, and, according to police reports, his spouse. The last of these (three domestic violence complaints by his pregnant wife) removed the struggle to manage his anger from the human-interest category—can this intelligent, well-spoken player outrace his demons?—and repositioned him as a ticking time bomb best made someone else's problem. Ever the contrarian, Billy Beane bet the services of outfield prospect Andre Ethier to become that someone.

HEE SEOP CHOI   1B   **Bats: L Throws: L**   Height: 6' 5"   Weight: 240   Born: March 16, 1979   Age: 27

YEAR	TM	LVL	AGE	PA	R	2B	3B	HR	RBI	BB	SO	SB	CS	SPEED	BA	OBP	SLG	MLVR	EQBA	EQOBP	EQSLG	EQA	VORP	DEFENSE	
2003	CHN	MLB	24	243	31	17	0	8	28	37	71	1	1	4.6	.218	.350	.421	.010	.216	.344	.412	.263	2.6	56-1B	0
2004	FLO	MLB	25	338	48	16	1	15	40	52	78	1	0	4.4	.270	.388	.495	.216	.271	.389	.500	.303	21.8	80-1B	4
2004	LAN	MLB	25	76	5	5	0	0	6	11	18	0	0	2.8	.161	.289	.242	-.341	.161	.289	.226	.204	-5.1	17-1B	0
2005	LAN	MLB	26	366	40	15	2	15	42	34	80	1	3	3.6	.253	.336	.453	.070	.257	.338	.471	.272	8.4	75-1B	-4
2006	LAN	MLB	27	376	48	19	1	17	57	47	82	1	1	4.6	.264	.364	.490	.117	.270	.371	.511	.291	17.6	90-1B	0

Breakout: 33%   Improve: 71%   Collapse: 11%   Attrition: 17%   Comparables: *David Ortiz, Craig Kusick, Erubiel Durazo*

Tracy's mishandling of Choi was the nadir of his tenure as manager. Mothballing Choi down the stretch in 2004 after his midseason acquisition was forgivable; Tracy had a division to win. Platooning him with lefty masher Saenz at the outset of 2005 was understandable; Choi had hit just .159 against southpaws. But turning a 26-year-old with clear upside into a pinch-hitter in order to play Saenz or, worse yet, Jason Phillips, was madness, particularly after the team had fallen out of the race. Tracy blew a golden opportunity to see if one of the team's few able-bodied sluggers could show he's a regular. Yes, Choi has got holes in his swing and occasionally looks awkward in the field. Those are the kinds of problems you pay a manager—especially one with a rep for creating roles in which limited players can succeed—to figure out, not to exacerbate. Here's hoping the next manager who handles Choi gets the message.

JOSE CRUZ OF Bats: B Throws: R Height: 6' 0" Weight: 195 Born: April 19, 1974 Age: 32

YEAR	TM	LVL	AGE	PA	R	2B	3B	HR	RBI	BB	SO	SB	CS	SPEED	BA	OBP	SLG	MLVR	EQBA	EQOBP	EQSLG	EQA	VORP	DEFENSE
2003	SFN	MLB	29	648	90	26	1	20	68	102	121	5	8	4.3	.250	.366	.414	.049	.250	.365	.417	.271	6.5	149-RF 18
2004	TBA	MLB	30	631	76	25	8	21	78	76	117	11	6	6.1	.242	.333	.433	-.027	.244	.339	.439	.269	8.8	148-RF -16
2005	ARI	MLB	31	245	23	9	0	12	28	42	54	0	1	2.7	.213	.347	.436	.017	.204	.340	.418	.263	5.3	46-CF -7
2005	LAN	MLB	31	179	23	14	2	6	22	23	43	0	1	4.3	.301	.391	.532	.305	.299	.392	.548	.311	14.3	42-RF 3
2006	*LAN*	*MLB*	*32*	*395*	*50*	*18*	*1*	*15*	*51*	*55*	*83*	*2*	*2*	*4.3*	*.251*	*.357*	*.445*	*.040*	*.257*	*.364*	*.464*	*.278*	*13.5*	*94-RF -4*

Breakout: 16% Improve: 45% Collapse: 28% Attrition: 23% Comparables: Jim Russell, Tom Tresh, Wally Judnich

Slated by the Snakes to play center field every day for the first time since 2001, Cruz quickly went on the shelf with bulging discs in his lower back. Upon returning, an initial hot streak proved unsustainable, so he was shipped to Boston at the deadline. Cruz barely had time to unpack before the Sox unloaded him on the Dodgers. He arrived in L.A. with the season already shot, but put up the kind of numbers the team had expected from Drew and earned a $3.2 million return engagement. He won't hit like Drew over a full season, but when healthy, he has his uses. Playing center field regularly is not one of them.

TRAVIS DENKER 2B Bats: R Throws: R Height: 5' 9" Weight: 170 Born: August 5, 1985 Age: 20

YEAR	TM	LVL	AGE	PA	R	2B	3B	HR	RBI	BB	SO	SB	CS	SPEED	BA	OBP	SLG	MLVR	EQBA	EQOBP	EQSLG	EQA	VORP	DEFENSE
2004	OGD	Rk	18	253	44	17	1	12	43	24	52	2	3	3.9	.311	.372	.556	.182	.224	.261	.377	.221	-11.9	47-2B 3
2005	CGA	A	19	434	65	23	1	21	68	67	78	2	5	3.4	.310	.417	.556	.401	.266	.357	.465	.280	29.3	68-2B 14
2005	VRO	A+	19	125	14	3	0	2	9	15	26	1	2	4.3	.185	.296	.269	-.252	.155	.251	.229	.181	-13.0	27-2B 5
2006	*LAN*	*MLB*	*20*	*500*	*50*	*22*	*1*	*13*	*55*	*46*	*106*	*2*	*2*	*3.7*	*.226*	*.301*	*.370*	*-.169*	*.232*	*.306*	*.386*	*.232*	*1.8*	*118-2B 8*

Breakout: 18% Improve: 45% Collapse: 33% Attrition: 3% Comparables: Jayson Nix, Ruben Gotay, Asdrubal Oropeza

Just 19, Denker destroyed Sally League pitching, out-hitting his more heralded teammate, Dewitt. A promotion to Vero Beach proved a bridge too far, at least in the short term. As impressive as his power and plate discipline are, Denker's got a couple of things going against him—his glove and his size. Often compared to Marcus Giles, he'll have to work as hard as Giles did to improve his defense or find another position. Stay tuned.

BLAKE DEWITT 3B Bats: L Throws: R Height: 5' 11" Weight: 175 Born: August 20, 1985 Age: 20

YEAR	TM	LVL	AGE	PA	R	2B	3B	HR	RBI	BB	SO	SB	CS	SPEED	BA	OBP	SLG	MLVR	EQBA	EQOBP	EQSLG	EQA	VORP	DEFENSE
2004	OGD	Rk	18	331	61	19	3	12	47	28	78	1	1	4.6	.284	.350	.488	.015	.209	.247	.337	.203	-29.8	65-3B -8
2005	CGA	A	19	522	61	31	3	11	65	34	79	0	1	3.7	.283	.333	.428	.085	.253	.294	.383	.234	0.2	110-3B -6
2006	*LAN*	*MLB*	*20*	*444*	*44*	*25*	*1*	*9*	*49*	*25*	*84*	*0*	*1*	*3.8*	*.242*	*.288*	*.376*	*-.174*	*.248*	*.293*	*.392*	*.226*	*-2.1*	*105-3B -3*

Breakout: 36% Improve: 57% Collapse: 28% Attrition: 10% Comparables: Tony Blanco, Nilson Teilon, Brian Gordon

Widely regarded as the best high-school hitter available in the 2004 draft, the Dodgers made Dewitt their 1st round pick. He didn't impress in the Sally League, but did show progress over the course of the season. His translated stats show a jump of about 50 points in batting average and OBP, along with an extra 20 points of isolated power. He's still got his work cut out for him at third base, where he's relatively raw. Given LaRoche's presence ahead of him in the chain, some think he may be better off at second base.

J. D. DREW OF Bats: L Throws: R Height: 6' 1" Weight: 190 Born: November 20, 1975 Age: 30

YEAR	TM	LVL	AGE	PA	R	2B	3B	HR	RBI	BB	SO	SB	CS	SPEED	BA	OBP	SLG	MLVR	EQBA	EQOBP	EQSLG	EQA	VORP	DEFENSE		
2003	SLN	MLB	27	326	60	13	3	15	42	36	48	2	2	5.7	.289	.374	.512	.231	.287	.372	.516	.297	20.2	43-RF 1	21-CF 0
2004	ATL	MLB	28	644	118	28	8	31	93	118	116	12	3	6.8	.305	.436	.569	.403	.297	.429	.554	.331	69.5	133-RF 11	
2005	LAN	MLB	29	311	48	12	1	15	36	51	50	1	1	4.8	.286	.412	.520	.306	.287	.411	.539	.320	26.9	43-RF 1	27-CF 1
2006	*LAN*	*MLB*	*30*	*531*	*80*	*26*	*2*	*24*	*80*	*80*	*88*	*4*	*2*	*5.6*	*.291*	*.403*	*.527*	*.249*	*.298*	*.410*	*.550*	*.316*	*41.2*	*125-RF 2*	

Breakout: 7% Improve: 46% Collapse: 20% Attrition: 10% Comparables: Johnny Briggs, Johnny Grubb, Bobby Abreu

Despite an 0-for-25 start, Drew was easily on pace to justify both his salary and his status as the lineup's centerpiece before getting hurt. But as DePodesta's critics were quick to note, Drew came with a manufacturer's warning about his fragility. His 2004 featured a career-high 145 games, 28 above his average over the previous five years. Still, the latest injury came on a hit-by-pitch; Cal Ripken would have gone on the DL with a broken wrist, too. Bashing DePo is a bit more justified regarding the contractual provision allowing Drew to either leave after 2006, or stay and soak up another $33 million of Dodger green while playing in less-than-mint condition. When healthy, he's one of the top hitters in baseball, but whether he can keep it together for 140-plus games in any one season remains the issue.

MIKE EDWARDS   UT   **Bats: R Throws: R**   Height: 6′ 1″   Weight: 185   Born: November 24, 1976   Age: 29

YEAR	TM	LVL	AGE	PA	R	2B	3B	HR	RBI	BB	SO	SB	CS	SPEED	BA	OBP	SLG	MLVR	EQBA	EQOBP	EQSLG	EQA	VORP	DEFENSE			
2003	SAC	AAA	26	506	78	23	4	14	95	60	78	5	2	5.0	.298	.387	.466	.211	.276	.358	.434	.275	11.0	65-LF	1	21-RF	-2
2004	SAC	AAA	27	643	91	41	0	13	81	76	100	11	2	5.1	.287	.384	.432	.080	.239	.326	.348	.242	0.8	85-3B	-9	36-LF	-1
2005	LAN	MLB	28	257	23	9	2	3	15	16	34	1	1	4.6	.247	.300	.339	-.151	.250	.305	.354	.231	-5.6	33-3B	-4	25-LF	0
2006	PIT	MLB	29	185	21	8	1	3	18	16	32	2	1	4.6	.251	.324	.369	-.114	.249	.323	.378	.239	-1.2	47-3B	-2		

Breakout: 29%   Improve: 45%   Collapse: 38%   Attrition: 53%   Comparables: Tommie Aaron, Randy Velarde, Scott Leius

Edwards was signed out of the A's organization, where his OBPs had endeared him to DePodesta. Injuries opened a spot for him, and Tracy became overly enamored of his ability to play both third base and the outfield. After a hot start (.294/.331/.397 before the All-Star break), it became painfully clear to everyone but the manager that Edwards was little more than roster fodder; he hit just .195/.266/.274 in the second half. Reunited with Tracy in Pittsburgh, where he'll probably stick in a utility role.

JOEL GUZMAN   SS...   **Bats: R Throws: R**   Height: 6′ 4″   Weight: 198   Born: November 24, 1984   Age: 21

YEAR	TM	LVL	AGE	PA	R	2B	3B	HR	RBI	BB	SO	SB	CS	SPEED	BA	OBP	SLG	MLVR	EQBA	EQOBP	EQSLG	EQA	VORP	DEFENSE			
2003	SGA	A	18	228	33	13	0	8	29	9	62	4	4	5.4	.235	.263	.406	-.022	.204	.223	.364	.201	-11.6	57-SS	1		
2003	VRO	A+	18	251	30	13	1	5	24	11	60	0	4	4.0	.246	.279	.371	-.060	.219	.247	.360	.206	-9.6	57-SS	-7		
2004	VRO	A+	19	354	52	22	8	14	51	21	78	8	5	6.7	.307	.347	.550	.277	.265	.301	.484	.262	20.2	86-SS	11		
2004	JAX	AA	19	200	25	11	3	9	35	13	44	1	2	4.8	.280	.325	.522	.215	.263	.302	.486	.264	11.1	42-SS	-4		
2005	JAX	AA	20	496	63	31	2	16	75	42	128	7	3	4.7	.287	.351	.475	.188	.266	.320	.449	.263	23.8	92-SS	4	18-3B	-2
2006	LAN	MLB	21	504	57	27	2	19	71	32	126	5	3	4.8	.248	.300	.437	-.068	.255	.305	.456	.250	16.3	119-SS	-2		

Breakout: 26%   Improve: 53%   Collapse: 24%   Attrition: 7%   Comparables: Corey Hart, Jeffrey Francoeur, Kelly Johnson

Number seven on our Top Prospect list in 2005, Guzman is the crown jewel of the Dodger system, a man-child with more raw power than Iggy and the Stooges circa 1973. While his numbers show a somewhat alarming drop in ISO in 2005, his translations are essentially in line with what he did in 2004. Guzman's huge physique makes a move away from shortstop likely, and though he got a taste of third base at Jacksonville before LaRoche arrived, right field is a potential home thanks to his arm strength. Comparisons to Miguel Cabrera abound, but Cabrera had a solid rookie year and post-season heroics under his belt at age 20 after spending less than half the time in Double-A that Guzman has already put in. Guzman has significant star potential, but it will happen at a slower pace.

CHIN-LUNG HU   SS   **Bats: R Throws: R**   Height: 5′ 9″   Weight: 150   Born: February 2, 1984   Age: 22

YEAR	TM	LVL	AGE	PA	R	2B	3B	HR	RBI	BB	SO	SB	CS	SPEED	BA	OBP	SLG	MLVR	EQBA	EQOBP	EQSLG	EQA	VORP	DEFENSE	
2003	OGD	Rk	19	236	34	9	5	3	23	14	33	5	4	5.6	.305	.343	.432	.034	.239	.275	.338	.215	-10.4	53-SS	6
2004	CGA	A	20	357	58	15	4	6	25	20	50	17	7	6.8	.298	.342	.422	.101	.273	.306	.387	.242	6.9	84-SS	12
2005	VRO	A+	21	498	80	29	1	8	56	19	40	23	6	6.7	.313	.347	.430	.108	.269	.301	.380	.240	6.5	114-SS	10
2006	LAN	MLB	22	451	50	21	2	5	38	19	49	10	4	5.2	.262	.298	.354	-.172	.268	.304	.369	.228	7.5	107-SS	9

Breakout: 20%   Improve: 38%   Collapse: 35%   Attrition: 6%   Comparables: Gary Cates, Nelson Samboy, Jack Wilson

Hu is another Taiwanese import, an acrobatic, pint-sized shortstop. He wins raves for his glovework, though that has more to do with his range than his arm. When it comes to his bat, opinions diverge. Scouts see a hitter with good bat speed and developing power, but the Davenport Translations don't give much cause for optimism; Hu has never topped .375 SLG (translated), and it isn't as though he brings plate discipline to the table. Even if he grows up to be Cesar Izturis, that doesn't guarantee a season the caliber of Izzy's 2004.

CESAR IZTURIS   SS/2B   **Bats: B Throws: R**   Height: 5′ 9″   Weight: 155   Born: February 10, 1980   Age: 26

YEAR	TM	LVL	AGE	PA	R	2B	3B	HR	RBI	BB	SO	SB	CS	SPEED	BA	OBP	SLG	MLVR	EQBA	EQOBP	EQSLG	EQA	VORP	DEFENSE	
2003	LAN	MLB	23	586	47	21	6	1	40	25	70	10	5	5.9	.251	.282	.315	-.219	.258	.288	.323	.218	-8.9	152-SS	7
2004	LAN	MLB	24	716	90	32	9	4	62	43	70	25	9	7.1	.288	.330	.381	-.036	.291	.332	.383	.252	21.7	155-SS	-2
2005	LAN	MLB	25	474	48	19	2	2	31	25	51	8	8	5.0	.257	.302	.322	-.162	.264	.310	.338	.226	-4.2	104-SS	10
2006	LAN	MLB	26	589	67	25	4	3	44	32	62	12	5	5.2	.262	.305	.337	-.182	.269	.311	.351	.226	5.2	138-SS	6

Breakout: 15%   Improve: 38%   Collapse: 24%   Attrition: 8%   Comparables: Omar Vizquel, Cristian Guzman, Jose Vizcaino

(continued next page)

Cesar Izturis *(continued)*

Coming off of a breakout year in which he'd shown himself to be an above-replacement level hitter, Izturis received a three-year, $9.9 million contract last winter. After a blistering start through June 1 (.345/.392/.426), his season collapsed. He hit just .167/.209/.217 thereafter. First came a 2-for-46 slump as he struggled with a strained hamstring. But Tracy doggedly kept leading him off until, struggling with back woes, Izturis was sidelined again. Finally, a sore elbow turned into Tommy John surgery. He's likely to miss the first half of the season, and with Rafael Furcal and Nomar Garciaparra now in the fold, Izturis may not have a spot waiting for him at either short or second when he returns.

MATT KEMP   **OF**   **Bats: R Throws: R**   Height: 6' 4"   Weight: 210   Born: September 23, 1984   Age: 21

YEAR	TM	LVL	AGE	PA	R	2B	3B	HR	RBI	BB	SO	SB	CS	SPEED	BA	OBP	SLG	MLVR	EQBA	EQOBP	EQSLG	EQA	VORP	DEFENSE
2004	CGA	A	19	457	67	22	8	17	66	24	100	8	7	5.8	.288	.330	.499	.183	.257	.289	.432	.243	-6.5	101-RF	3
2005	VRO	A+	20	453	76	21	4	27	90	25	92	23	6	6.3	.306	.349	.569	.290	.263	.303	.494	.268	20.2	66-CF 4 34-RF -1
2006	*LAN*	*MLB*	*21*	*507*	*63*	*24*	*2*	*20*	*71*	*28*	*112*	*14*	*5*	*5.1*	*.248*	*.293*	*.438*	*-.079*	*.254*	*.298*	*.457*	*.249*	*6.4*	*119-RF 0*

Breakout: 20%   Improve: 44%   Collapse: 28%   Attrition: 5%   Comparables: *Jeffrey Francoeur, Ruben Mateo, Franklin Gutierrez*

Kemp rates as one of the best power prospects in the system, but it's fair to wonder how much of that is simply a park illusion. His home/road splits in 2005 were extreme: .361/.405/.749 with 22 homers at home, but only .246/.287/.372 with five home runs on the road. (The Vero Beach team hit 88 HRs and slugged .485 at home this year, 36 HR and .384 on the road.) Better known as a basketball prospect in high school, Kemp is still more reliant on athleticism than a good approach at the plate, and is particularly vexed by breaking stuff. He spent 2005 playing center field with solid results, but his size makes a corner outfield position more likely.

JEFF KENT   **2B**   **Bats: R Throws: R**   Height: 6' 1"   Weight: 215   Born: March 7, 1968   Age: 38

YEAR	TM	LVL	AGE	PA	R	2B	3B	HR	RBI	BB	SO	SB	CS	SPEED	BA	OBP	SLG	MLVR	EQBA	EQOBP	EQSLG	EQA	VORP	DEFENSE
2003	HOU	MLB	35	552	77	39	1	22	93	39	85	6	2	4.9	.297	.351	.509	.180	.288	.343	.497	.283	39.2	124-2B -4
2004	HOU	MLB	36	606	96	34	8	27	107	49	96	7	3	5.5	.289	.348	.531	.208	.281	.339	.517	.287	47.7	134-2B 10
2005	LAN	MLB	37	637	100	36	0	29	105	72	85	6	2	4.3	.289	.377	.512	.246	.291	.378	.526	.303	52.8	137-2B -7
2006	*LAN*	*MLB*	*38*	*573*	*73*	*32*	*2*	*23*	*83*	*57*	*85*	*6*	*2*	*4.5*	*.270*	*.348*	*.474*	*.077*	*.277*	*.354*	*.495*	*.281*	*33.6*	*134-2B -3*

Breakout: 11%   Improve: 34%   Collapse: 33%   Attrition: 9%   Comparables: *Mike Schmidt, Jeff Conine, Gary Gaetti*

On the field, the signing of Kent was one thing that went right for the Dodgers. He reversed the slight decline of his two Astros years, becoming the centerpiece of the offense and advancing his case for a spot in Cooperstown. His fielding, long underrated, fell off a bit, though it's possible that had something to do with the turnover at the other infield positions. Off the field, Kent's role in the Milton Bradley fiasco marred his otherwise stellar season, though it's hard to know how seriously to take anything Bradley says. If, as ex-teammate Lance Berkman said, Kent "ignores Latinos, blacks and whites equally," then the most he's guilty of is self-absorption. Or perhaps he's the embodiment of pure evil. The additions of Rafael Furcal and Nomar Garciaparra suggest that either Kent or Izturis is trade bait once the latter returns from injury.

ANDY LaROCHE   **3B**   **Bats: R Throws: R**   Height: 5' 11" Weight: 185   Born: September 13, 1983 Age: 22

YEAR	TM	LVL	AGE	PA	R	2B	3B	HR	RBI	BB	SO	SB	CS	SPEED	BA	OBP	SLG	MLVR	EQBA	EQOBP	EQSLG	EQA	VORP	DEFENSE
2004	CGA	A	20	283	52	20	0	13	42	29	30	12	5	5.7	.283	.375	.525	.277	.240	.309	.437	.256	7.6	61-3B 2
2004	VRO	A+	20	241	26	13	0	10	35	17	42	2	3	3.6	.233	.290	.429	-.020	.197	.245	.373	.214	-10.3	54-3B -6
2005	VRO	A+	21	271	54	14	1	21	51	19	38	6	1	5.1	.333	.380	.651	.467	.289	.332	.574	.296	30.3	55-3B -4
2005	JAX	AA	21	264	41	12	0	9	43	32	54	2	2	3.9	.273	.367	.445	.158	.248	.330	.414	.258	7.9	58-3B -2
2006	*LAN*	*MLB*	*22*	*545*	*63*	*26*	*1*	*20*	*74*	*42*	*101*	*5*	*3*	*4.2*	*.251*	*.312*	*.430*	*-.055*	*.257*	*.318*	*.448*	*.254*	*11.8*	*128-3B -5*

Breakout: 23%   Improve: 46%   Collapse: 18%   Attrition: 5%   Comparables: *Scott Hodges, Tripper Johnson, Dave Kelton*

From the family that brought you the LaLob and the Braves' starting first baseman comes the Dodgers' Minor League Player of the Year. LaRoche drew raves for tearing through the pitcher-friendly Florida State League in the first half, but it's worth noting that he had struggled there in the second half of 2004. Like Kemp, his home/road splits were drastic: .367/.408/.825 with 16 home runs at home, .302/.355/.488 with five home runs away. Elevated to Jacksonville in mid-June, his power tailed off after an initial flurry of four homers in his first nine games. Still, 30 jacks are 30 jacks. Converted from shortstop prior to 2004, he's shown considerable improvement at third, and his best defensive asset is a strong arm. He may find himself at the hot corner in Dodger Stadium before too long, but could also move to first if Guzman is shifted to third.

RICKY LEDEE   **OF**   **Bats: L   Throws: L**   Height: 6' 1"   Weight: 160   Born: November 22, 1973   Age: 32

YEAR	TM	LVL	AGE	PA	R	2B	3B	HR	RBI	BB	SO	SB	CS	SPEED	BA	OBP	SLG	MLVR	EQBA	EQOBP	EQSLG	EQA	VORP	DEFENSE			
2003	PHI	MLB	29	290	37	15	2	13	46	34	59	0	0	4.6	.247	.334	.475	.094	.246	.333	.480	.275	11.6	35-CF	-2	20-LF	0
2004	PHI	MLB	30	145	19	7	0	7	26	22	27	2	0	4.1	.285	.393	.512	.235	.276	.386	.488	.301	10.9	11-CF	2		
2005	LAN	MLB	31	266	31	16	1	7	39	20	55	0	0	4.2	.278	.335	.443	.078	.283	.337	.456	.274	8.6	44-LF	-6	10-RF	0
2006	*LAN*	*MLB*	*32*	*155*	*17*	*7*	*1*	*5*	*20*	*15*	*32*	*0*	*0*	*4.4*	*.252*	*.330*	*.427*	*-.027*	*.259*	*.336*	*.445*	*.262*	*2.9*	*40-LF*	*-3*		

Breakout: 13%   Improve: 35%   Collapse: 43%   Attrition: 45%   Comparables: Gates Brown, Dave Clark, Gordy Coleman

Ledee has been a very useful fourth outfielder/pinch-hitter type. In an outfield beset by injuries, he played regularly for the first two months, and although he started hot, a hamstring injury cost him five weeks and limited his availability to pinch-hitting and the occasional outfield cameo the rest of the way. He'll reprise his reserve role in 2006.

JAMES LONEY   **1B**   **Bats: L   Throws: L**   Height: 6' 3"   Weight: 200   Born: May 7, 1984   Age: 22

YEAR	TM	LVL	AGE	PA	R	2B	3B	HR	RBI	BB	SO	SB	CS	SPEED	BA	OBP	SLG	MLVR	EQBA	EQOBP	EQSLG	EQA	VORP	DEFENSE	
2003	VRO	A+	19	513	64	31	3	7	46	43	80	9	4	5.3	.276	.337	.400	.073	.249	.303	.390	.240	-11.4	106-1B	3
2004	JAX	AA	20	442	39	19	2	4	35	42	75	6	5	4.4	.238	.314	.327	-.099	.228	.295	.310	.218	-27.2	101-1B	4
2005	JAX	AA	21	571	74	31	2	11	65	59	87	1	4	3.8	.284	.357	.419	.115	.267	.329	.407	.255	2.3	130-1B	11
2006	*LAN*	*MLB*	*22*	*535*	*56*	*28*	*1*	*13*	*62*	*44*	*94*	*3*	*2*	*4.8*	*.252*	*.316*	*.393*	*-.097*	*.258*	*.321*	*.410*	*.245*	*-0.8*	*126-1B*	*4*

Breakout: 32%   Improve: 67%   Collapse: 16%   Attrition: 5%   Comparables: Adrian Gonzalez, Nick Leach, Brian Schmitt

The Dodgers' #1 pick in 2002, Loney had done enough by 2004 to crack our Top 50 Prospect List at #25. He was the talk of Vero Beach that spring, winning the Mulvey Award as the top rookie in camp. The fun ended there. Elevated to Double-A, Loney endured power-sapping hand injuries. Still just 21, he repeated at Jacksonville in 2005, stayed healthy, maintained his plate discipline, played good defense, and offered hope that he'd finally develop some power. He's got his work cut out for him to reclaim blue chip status, but he's back on the right track.

RUSSELL MARTIN   **C**   **Bats: R   Throws: R**   Height: 5' 11"   Weight: 202   Born: February 15, 1983   Age: 23

YEAR	TM	LVL	AGE	PA	R	2B	3B	HR	RBI	BB	SO	SB	CS	SPEED	BA	OBP	SLG	MLVR	EQBA	EQOBP	EQSLG	EQA	VORP	DEFENSE	
2003	OGD	Rk	20	220	25	13	0	6	36	26	26	3	1	3.5	.271	.368	.436	.054	.201	.281	.319	.216	-16.7	49-C	1
2003	SGA	A	20	108	15	4	1	3	14	9	11	5	2	5.8	.286	.343	.439	.167	.263	.308	.413	.251	2.3	14-C	-5
2004	VRO	A+	21	505	74	24	1	15	64	72	54	9	5	5.0	.250	.366	.421	.091	.213	.313	.371	.243	-1.9	101-C	9
2005	JAX	AA	22	500	83	17	1	9	61	78	69	15	7	5.0	.311	.430	.423	.257	.288	.391	.398	.282	30.3	112-C	7
2006	*LAN*	*MLB*	*23*	*486*	*56*	*21*	*1*	*10*	*49*	*56*	*73*	*7*	*3*	*4.7*	*.253*	*.346*	*.376*	*-.065*	*.259*	*.352*	*.392*	*.257*	*12.9*	*115-C*	*3*

Breakout: 22%   Improve: 51%   Collapse: 26%   Attrition: 12%   Comparables: Jayson Werth, Butch Wynegar, Rusty Keith

A year older than Navarro but at least a year behind him developmentally, Martin is nonetheless the backstop with more upside. He had a strong season at Jacksonville, showing outstanding plate discipline, reasonable power, and even some speed while cementing his place as one of the Dodgers' best prospects. Converted from third base prior to 2003, he made good strides behind the plate under the tutelage of Jacksonville coach Steve Yeager. He drew praise for a strong arm, improved receiving skills, and his handling of pitchers. He'll likely spend the season in Vegas, but the Dodgers can look forward to a young, productive tandem behind the plate.

DIONER NAVARRO   **C**   **Bats: B   Throws: R**   Height: 5' 10"   Weight: 180   Born: February 9, 1984   Age: 22

YEAR	TM	LVL	AGE	PA	R	2B	3B	HR	RBI	BB	SO	SB	CS	SPEED	BA	OBP	SLG	MLVR	EQBA	EQOBP	EQSLG	EQA	VORP	DEFENSE	
2003	TAM	A+	19	220	28	16	4	3	28	17	27	1	0	5.4	.299	.364	.467	.262	.289	.338	.476	.277	15.5	50-C	2
2003	TRN	AA	19	232	28	15	0	4	37	18	26	2	3	3.5	.341	.388	.471	.256	.299	.346	.429	.268	12.6	40-C	-2
2004	TRN	AA	20	291	32	14	1	3	29	33	44	1	0	3.9	.271	.354	.369	.004	.254	.330	.343	.242	0.6	52-C	4
2004	COH	AAA	20	155	18	8	2	1	16	14	17	1	0	5.2	.250	.316	.360	-.127	.236	.304	.340	.234	-2.4	39-C	9
2005	LVG	AAA	21	284	31	12	0	6	29	38	24	2	2	3.7	.266	.366	.390	-.106	.210	.304	.299	.220	-9.6	64-C	5
2005	LAN	MLB	21	198	21	9	0	3	14	20	21	0	0	4.1	.273	.354	.375	.016	.275	.358	.376	.260	7.6	49-C	0
2006	*LAN*	*MLB*	*22*	*434*	*46*	*21*	*1*	*8*	*48*	*40*	*52*	*1*	*1*	*4.8*	*.260*	*.334*	*.380*	*-.077*	*.267*	*.340*	*.397*	*.250*	*10.4*	*103-C*	*1*

Breakout: 31%   Improve: 52%   Collapse: 27%   Attrition: 18%   Comparables: Ted Simmons, Charlie Moore, Brian Luderer

Acquired in the Shawn Green deal, Navarro's performance in his first extended taste of big-league action was a rare positive in the Dodgers' otherwise dismal season. Not only did he hit for average, he took a big leap forward in the plate discipline department, almost reaching the golden ratio of one unintentional walk for every ten PAs. It's important to

(continued next page)

Dioner Navarro (continued)

remember that all of this happened in just 199 plate appearances after an altitude-inflated half-season in Las Vegas, and to note that despite an otherwise acceptable defensive performance, he struggled to control the running game (21.4 percent kill rate). But as 22-year-old catchers go, he's a keeper, especially on a team that wasted over 400 PAs on Jason Phillips.

ANTONIO PEREZ INF **Bats: R Throws: R** Height: 5' 11" Weight: 170 Born: January 26, 1980 Age: 26

YEAR	TM	LVL	AGE	PA	R	2B	3B	HR	RBI	BB	SO	SB	CS	SPEED	BA	OBP	SLG	MLVR	EQBA	EQOBP	EQSLG	EQA	VORP	DEFENSE		
2003	TBA	MLB	23	145	19	6	1	2	12	18	34	4	1	5.8	.248	.345	.360	-.092	.250	.352	.363	.260	2.7	28-2B -6		
2004	LVG	AAA	24	551	92	24	6	22	88	61	87	23	12	6.6	.296	.379	.511	.094	.242	.323	.403	.253	14.1	71-SS -6	44-2B 2	
2005	LAN	MLB	25	286	28	13	2	3	23	21	61	11	4	6.1	.297	.360	.398	.071	.303	.365	.414	.273	12.1	31-3B -1	21-2B -3	
2006	*OAK*	*MLB*	*26*	*330*	*42*	*15*	*2*	*7*	*33*	*25*	*64*	*8*	*3*	*5.1*	*.256*	*.324*	*.398*	*-.055*	*.259*	*.334*	*.414*	*.253*	*9.2*	*80-2B -2*		

Breakout: 13% Improve: 38% Collapse: 38% Attrition: 27% Comparables: Tony Graffanino, Pat Kelly, Robby Thompson

Shifted to third from second base, Perez was slated to be Valentin's platoon partner until a hamstring injury sidelined him for six weeks. He returned to inherit the lion's share of playing time and quickly got hot, with 16 hits in an eight-game span. But by mid-July, Tracy used Perez's defensive shortcomings—particularly on pop flies—as an excuse to replace him with Robles. At-bats suddenly became as rare as hen's teeth, and predictably, he cooled off. Even though Perez was bypassed for players with lesser gifts, it was a successful season in that he proved he could hit and field in the big leagues. Billy Beane took notice and snuck him into the Milton Bradley trade. He'll begin his Oakland tenure blocked at the infield positions, but in the event of injury to the starters he'll be a significant upgrade on Marco Scutaro.

JASON PHILLIPS C/1B **Bats: R Throws: R** Height: 6' 1" Weight: 175 Born: September 27, 1976 Age: 29

YEAR	TM	LVL	AGE	PA	R	2B	3B	HR	RBI	BB	SO	SB	CS	SPEED	BA	OBP	SLG	MLVR	EQBA	EQOBP	EQSLG	EQA	VORP	DEFENSE		
2003	NYN	MLB	26	453	45	25	0	11	58	39	50	0	1	2.6	.298	.373	.442	.142	.298	.371	.448	.283	21.2	78-1B -6	26-C -4	
2004	NYN	MLB	27	410	34	18	0	7	34	35	42	0	1	3.2	.218	.298	.326	-.209	.220	.296	.327	.224	-10.8	73-C 5	29-1B -2	
2005	LAN	MLB	28	432	38	20	0	10	55	25	50	0	1	3.5	.238	.287	.363	-.146	.242	.291	.379	.233	-2.8	88-C -12	18-1B -2	
2006	*TOR*	*MLB*	*29*	*374*	*34*	*18*	*0*	*9*	*45*	*25*	*43*	*0*	*0*	*3.4*	*.263*	*.318*	*.393*	*-.066*	*.261*	*.324*	*.394*	*.242*	*3.3*	*90-C -5*		

Breakout: 22% Improve: 47% Collapse: 25% Attrition: 25% Comparables: Bob Boone, Toby Hall, Dave Valle

As a stopgap, wresting Phillips from the Mets for a sinking Kaz Ishii and figuring he could out-hit Dave Ross wasn't a bad idea. Turning over the regular catching duties to him seemed reasonable in the absence of better options. But batting Phillips in the middle of the order and playing him at first base once Navarro came up was one of Tracy's most egregious mistakes. Phillips could barely manage replacement-level production as a catcher, at the plate or behind it. With Toronto, he'll hopefully get no more than a reserve role.

ANTHONY RAGLANI OF **Bats: L Throws: L** Height: 6' 2" Weight: 215 Born: April 6, 1983 Age: 23

YEAR	TM	LVL	AGE	PA	R	2B	3B	HR	RBI	BB	SO	SB	CS	SPEED	BA	OBP	SLG	MLVR	EQBA	EQOBP	EQSLG	EQA	VORP	DEFENSE	
2005	VRO	A+	22	491	82	20	5	19	77	60	98	9	2	5.8	.289	.383	.496	.224	.250	.335	.435	.268	3.2	54-LF 4	47-RF 0
2006	*LAN*	*MLB*	*23*	*501*	*62*	*25*	*3*	*16*	*61*	*53*	*111*	*6*	*3*	*5.3*	*.250*	*.334*	*.427*	*-.023*	*.256*	*.340*	*.445*	*.263*	*6.4*	*118-LF 1*	

Breakout: 27% Improve: 55% Collapse: 21% Attrition: 2% Comparables: Brad Snyder, Ryan Langerhans, Kevin Burford

The team's 5th round pick in 2004, Raglani put himself on the prospect map with plate discipline. Only one teammate, Cory Dunlap, walked more often, and Raglani's command of the strike zone is considerably more advanced than Matt Kemp's. As with the rest of the denizens of Vero Beach, he was greatly aided by his home park, batting .332/.438/.596 at home, .252/.332/.412 away.

JASON REPKO OF **Bats: R Throws: R** Height: 5' 11" Weight: 175 Born: December 27, 1980 Age: 25

YEAR	TM	LVL	AGE	PA	R	2B	3B	HR	RBI	BB	SO	SB	CS	SPEED	BA	OBP	SLG	MLVR	EQBA	EQOBP	EQSLG	EQA	VORP	DEFENSE	
2003	JAX	AA	22	467	62	14	5	10	23	42	89	21	8	6.9	.240	.317	.370	-.003	.232	.296	.372	.237	-20.3	70-LF 5	38-CF 0
2004	JAX	AA	23	205	26	11	2	6	19	13	43	10	5	6.4	.291	.341	.466	.172	.273	.318	.430	.257	0.2	32-LF 0	
2004	LVG	AAA	23	324	55	26	4	7	41	18	57	13	5	7.1	.311	.355	.493	.041	.257	.300	.398	.242	0.3	66-CF 3	
2005	LAN	MLB	24	299	43	15	3	8	30	16	80	5	0	6.8	.221	.281	.384	-.141	.226	.285	.398	.238	-3.6	41-CF 3	24-RF 1
2006	*LAN*	*MLB*	*25*	*332*	*42*	*17*	*2*	*10*	*39*	*21*	*65*	*7*	*3*	*6.4*	*.254*	*.310*	*.423*	*-.065*	*.261*	*.316*	*.441*	*.252*	*6.2*	*80-CF 1*	

Breakout: 33% Improve: 55% Collapse: 28% Attrition: 28% Comparables: Sil Campusano, Juan Beniquez, Hal Jeffcoat

Repko illustrates the perils of letting a player win a job based on a spring training performance that flies in the face of all other evidence. Previously a rock-solid non-prospect, it only took a torrid March to beguile Tracy. The predictable end result was that the Dodgers had little to show for Repko's 301 PAs other than a lot of hard-nosed play that did nothing to overcome his offensive limitations. As a defensive caddy and pinch-runner, Repko would have his uses on a post-season roster. Short of that, there's little justification for keeping him around.

OSCAR ROBLES — INF — Bats: L Throws: R — Height: 5′ 11″ Weight: 155 Born: April 9, 1976 — Age: 30

YEAR	TM	LVL	AGE	PA	R	2B	3B	HR	RBI	BB	SO	SB	CS	SPEED	BA	OBP	SLG	MLVR	EQBA	EQOBP	EQSLG	EQA	VORP	DEFENSE			
2003	MCD	MEX	27	467	81	13	9	8	53	69	29	6	3	6.8	.309	.411	.447	.067	.242	.336	.375	.251	1.3				
2004	MCD	MEX	28	397	72	23	5	8	64	62	11	8	6	5.0	.382	.479	.552	.380	.302	.389	.457	.292	42.4				
2005	MCD	MEX	29	139	27	7	0	4	21	19	8	1	1	3.7	.390	.475	.551	.333	.296	.370	.418	.275	10.3	29-2B	2		
2005	LAN	MLB	29	398	44	18	1	5	34	31	33	0	8	3.9	.272	.332	.368	-.038	.276	.338	.377	.244	2.7	50-SS	1	33-3B	-1
2006	LAN	MLB	30	466	54	20	2	6	43	47	40	2	2	4.7	.263	.341	.369	-.077	.270	.347	.385	.250	10.5	110-SS	1		

Breakout: 12%   Improve: 28%   Collapse: 35%   Attrition: 18%   Comparables: Mike Cubbage, Tim Flannery, Spider Jorgensen

Eleven years after being drafted by the Astros, Robles found himself in camp last spring, vying for a spot on the Dodgers. They went west with Norihiro Nakamura instead and Robles returned to the Mexican League. When Nakamura washed out, Robles was asked to come back and toss his hat into the third base ring. Izturis' injuries enabled him to slide back over to shortstop, where his glove was good, if not golden, and his bat wasn't as much of a liability. In fact, it was better than Izturis's, even after the novelty wore off. He won't get the chance to keep Little Cesar's seat warm; the Furcal and Mueller signings knock him back into a utility role.

JUSTIN RUGGIANO — OF — Bats: R Throws: R — Height: 6′ 2″ Weight: 205 Born: April 12, 1982 — Age: 24

YEAR	TM	LVL	AGE	PA	R	2B	3B	HR	RBI	BB	SO	SB	CS	SPEED	BA	OBP	SLG	MLVR	EQBA	EQOBP	EQSLG	EQA	VORP	DEFENSE			
2004	OGD	Rk	22	187	26	12	0	7	36	23	38	6	1	4.0	.329	.428	.542	.271	.218	.281	.331	.221	-13.5	21-CF	1	19-RF	-1
2005	VRO	A+	23	280	47	15	4	9	37	28	65	16	5	6.6	.310	.400	.517	.292	.262	.337	.439	.269	4.2	47-RF	-4	18-CF	0
2005	JAX	AA	23	185	23	10	1	6	29	17	56	8	3	5.6	.342	.422	.528	.421	.324	.389	.521	.307	15.2	20-LF	-2	15-RF	2
2006	LAN	MLB	24	481	59	24	2	14	57	38	137	12	4	5.0	.249	.317	.415	-.068	.256	.323	.432	.253	4.1	114-RF	-3		

Breakout: 14%   Improve: 39%   Collapse: 34%   Attrition: 13%   Comparables: Ty Meadows, Chin-Feng Chen, Jason Michaels

In his second year out of Texas A&M, Ruggiano advanced quickly. He enjoyed a solid first half at Vero Beach and earned a promotion to the star-studded Jacksonville squad, where he was as hot as any Sun (sorry). He strikes out a lot and could stand to walk more, but it's conceivable he'll be helping in L.A. before too long.

OLMEDO SAENZ — 1B — Bats: R Throws: R — Height: 5′ 11″ Weight: 220 Born: October 8, 1970 — Age: 35

YEAR	TM	LVL	AGE	PA	R	2B	3B	HR	RBI	BB	SO	SB	CS	SPEED	BA	OBP	SLG	MLVR	EQBA	EQOBP	EQSLG	EQA	VORP	DEFENSE			
2004	LAN	MLB	33	128	17	1	0	8	22	12	33	0	0	2.8	.279	.352	.505	.167	.277	.349	.509	.290	7.5	14-1B	0		
2005	LAN	MLB	34	351	39	24	0	15	63	27	63	0	1	3.0	.263	.325	.480	.094	.266	.329	.497	.276	11.6	54-1B	-9	14-3B	-1
2006	LAN	MLB	35	318	35	16	0	14	50	26	61	0	0	3.4	.259	.325	.467	.021	.265	.330	.487	.268	8.3	77-1B	-7		

Breakout: 12%   Improve: 42%   Collapse: 30%   Attrition: 27%   Comparables: Bob Cerv, Walt Dropo, Joe Adcock

After a wildly successful 2004 season on Tracy's bench, Saenz found himself with an expanded role in 2005. He began the year as the lefty-mashing half of a first-base platoon with Choi, occasionally covering third base for Valentin as well. For the first two months he was one of the team's hottest hitters (.341/.400/.624), but as Choi fell out of favor, Tracy became overly enamored of Saenz, who hit just .235/.297/.427 from June onwards. He was particularly brutal in the field; there's a good reason they call guys like Saenz "professional hitters"—it's much a signifier for what it leaves out as what it says. Expect Grady Little to get the message and make more limited use of him.

JOSE VALENTIN — UT — Bats: L Throws: R — Height: 5′ 10″ Weight: 175 Born: October 12, 1969 — Age: 36

YEAR	TM	LVL	AGE	PA	R	2B	3B	HR	RBI	BB	SO	SB	CS	SPEED	BA	OBP	SLG	MLVR	EQBA	EQOBP	EQSLG	EQA	VORP	DEFENSE			
2003	CHA	MLB	33	562	79	26	2	28	74	54	114	8	3	5.4	.237	.313	.463	-.015	.233	.315	.465	.264	23.6	136-SS	6		
2004	CHA	MLB	34	498	73	20	3	30	70	43	139	8	6	5.8	.216	.287	.473	-.119	.212	.288	.470	.252	7.6	116-SS	7		
2005	LAN	MLB	35	184	17	4	2	2	14	31	38	3	1	5.7	.170	.326	.265	-.229	.176	.330	.270	.231	-6.9	25-3B	-2	18-LF	-1
2006	NYN	MLB	36	169	21	8	1	5	17	22	39	3	2	5.2	.223	.331	.387	-.097	.226	.335	.410	.254	3.8	44-SS	1		

Breakout: 24%   Improve: 60%   Collapse: 22%   Attrition: 54%   Comparables: Ray Lankford, Ron Gant, Charlie Maxwell

(continued next page)

Jose Valentin (*continued*)

Valentin was an odd choice to take over the hot corner from Adrian Beltre. He was 35 years old, switching leagues, shifting to a position he hadn't played in three years, and in severe need of a platoon buddy. He predictably struggled before tearing up his knee in early May. Upon returning three months later, he couldn't find his stroke or regain the third base job. Instead, he spent most of his time in left, where he was even more of an offensive liability. In his heyday, Valentin was a quality player whose virtues—power, range, versatility, batting eye—were underrated. At the same time, the damage done by his shortcomings—strikeouts, errors, low batting averages—were exaggerated. Signed to a one-year deal with the Mets, where he'll join Julio Franco to form the Gray Latin Fire Brigade.

JAYSON WERTH   **OF**   **Bats: R Throws: R**   Height: 6′ 5″   Weight: 210   Born: May 20, 1979   Age: 27

YEAR	TM	LVL	AGE	PA	R	2B	3B	HR	RBI	BB	SO	SB	CS	SPEED	BA	OBP	SLG	MLVR	EQBA	EQOBP	EQSLG	EQA	VORP	DEFENSE		
2003	SYR	AAA	24	256	37	19	1	9	34	15	68	11	1	7.2	.237	.285	.441	-.037	.213	.266	.409	.237	-5.6	33-CF	0	16-RF -1
2004	LAN	MLB	25	325	56	11	3	16	47	30	85	4	1	6.7	.262	.338	.486	.106	.264	.337	.497	.281	10.1	59-LF	4	
2005	LAN	MLB	26	394	46	22	2	7	43	48	114	11	2	5.7	.234	.338	.374	-.043	.238	.341	.385	.261	3.4	39-LF	1	33-RF 3
2006	LAN	MLB	27	484	68	24	2	20	64	49	128	13	4	6.3	.256	.340	.465	.042	.263	.346	.486	.277	17.0	114-LF	2	

Breakout: 28%   Improve: 53%   Collapse: 24%   Attrition: 17%   Comparables: Glenallen Hill, Larry Hisle, Don Lock

For bad omens as to how the Dodgers' season would pan out, only Gagne's February knee sprain trumped Werth's broken wrist, which came in the spring-training opener. It first seemed Werth would be able to play again in a few weeks, but he didn't return until May 25. As it turned out, the wrist never fully healed, and he had off-season surgery to repair a torn ligament. He also had a bit of knee trouble repaired, and won't be ready by the start of spring training. Despite the knee problems, he showed good speed and played strong defense, even covering center field well. Once he's healthy, bet on him to build on his 2004 and put last year's nightmare behind him.

DELWYN YOUNG   **2B**   **Bats: B Throws: R**   Height: 5′ 10″   Weight: 180   Born: June 30, 1982   Age: 24

YEAR	TM	LVL	AGE	PA	R	2B	3B	HR	RBI	BB	SO	SB	CS	SPEED	BA	OBP	SLG	MLVR	EQBA	EQOBP	EQSLG	EQA	VORP	DEFENSE	
2003	SGA	A	21	491	67	38	7	15	73	36	87	5	2	5.1	.323	.381	.542	.384	.292	.336	.497	.280	38.3	110-2B	0
2004	VRO	A+	22	538	76	36	3	22	85	57	134	11	4	5.4	.281	.364	.511	.223	.242	.314	.455	.262	19.9	114-2B	-15
2005	JAX	AA	23	405	52	25	1	16	62	27	86	1	3	3.7	.296	.346	.499	.224	.272	.313	.465	.262	18.2	88-2B	-10
2005	LVG	AAA	23	169	23	12	0	4	14	8	35	0	0	3.7	.325	.361	.475	.050	.259	.291	.375	.230	-0.8	36-2B	1
2006	LAN	MLB	24	485	56	25	1	19	67	32	113	3	1	4.2	.255	.309	.449	-.032	.261	.314	.468	.257	17.6	115-2B	-8

Breakout: 21%   Improve: 46%   Collapse: 26%   Attrition: 10%   Comparables: Roy Howell, Donny Leon, Pedro Garcia

Absolutely not to be confused with Delmon Young, who is Dmitri's younger brother and was #2 on our Top Prospect List last year. This elder Young is a switch-hitter with a ton of power for a middle infielder, but he doesn't have the defensive skills to stay there. His transition to Double-A wasn't easy: he maintained consistent power and cut down his strikeouts, but his walk rate declined precipitously. Moved up to Triple-A, he had even more trouble with the strike zone, and his power all but disappeared. Since his future is as a corner outfielder, it would behoove the Dodgers accelerate the transition for both his sake and theirs.

PITCHERS

CHAD BILLINGSLEY   **Bats: R Throws: R**   Height: 6′ 2″   Weight: 215   Born: July 29, 1984   Age: 21

YEAR	TM	LVL	AGE	W	L	SV	G	GS	IP	H	BB	SO	HR	GB%	BABIP	STUFF	WHIP	ERA	PERA	EQERA	EQH9	EQBB9	EQSO9	EQHR9	VORP	WXRL
2003	OGD	Rk	18	5	4	0	11	11	54.0	49	15	62	0	—	.329	25	1.19	2.83	3.93	4.96	8.4	3.6	5.5	0.3	3.7	—
2004	VRO	A+	19	7	4	0	18	18	92.0	68	49	111	6	—	.278	20	1.27	2.35	5.21	4.17	8.3	5.6	7.7	1.3	13.7	—
2004	JAX	AA	19	4	0	0	8	8	42.3	32	22	47	1	—	.301	28	1.28	2.98	3.98	4.43	7.7	5.1	6.9	0.2	5.3	—
2005	JAX	AA	20	13	6	0	28	26	146.0	116	50	162	12	47%	.284	14	1.14	3.51	4.78	4.85	8.8	3.3	7.1	1.4	11.4	—
2006	LAN	MLB	21	8	9	0	29	22	136.7	121	66	120	15	46%	.276	15	1.36	4.15	4.51	4.62	8.0	4.0	7.0	1.0	14.4	2.4

Breakout: 17%   Improve: 52%   Collapse: 10%   Attrition: 0%   Comparables: Kyle Davies, Pete Broberg, Steve Dunning

Two words: "potential" and "stud." After rocketing up to Jacksonville in just his second year out of high school, the Dodgers' 2003 #1 pick made our Top 50 Prospect List at #20. He didn't disappoint. Billingsley struck out more than a batter per inning while posting an excellent 3/1 K/BB ratio and drawing raves from scouts who love his stuff and makeup. He may taste the big leagues in 2006.

YHENCY BRAZOBAN   Bats: R   Throws: R   Height: 6' 1"   Weight: 170   Born: June 11, 1980   Age: 26

YEAR	TM	LVL	AGE	W	L	SV	G	GS	IP	H	BB	SO	HR	GB%	BABIP	STUFF	WHIP	ERA	PERA	EQERA	EQH9	EQBB9	EQSO9	EQHR9	VORP	WXRL
2004	JAX	AA	24	4	4	13	37	0	51.0	38	22	61	4	—	.286	-8	1.18	2.65	5.32	4.75	8.4	4.8	6.8	1.3	4.5	—
2004	LAN	MLB	24	6	2	0	31	0	32.7	25	15	27	2	36%	.271	5	1.22	2.48	3.98	2.84	7.7	4.0	6.8	0.6	11.6	0.9
2005	LAN	MLB	25	4	10	21	74	0	72.7	70	32	61	11	40%	.296	-9	1.40	5.32	5.00	5.75	9.1	3.8	7.0	1.4	-2.4	0.9
2006	LAN	MLB	26	2	3	7	46	0	50.3	50	22	42	7	44%	.288	-2	1.41	4.69	4.98	5.54	8.9	3.6	6.7	1.3	1.8	0.1

Breakout: 28%   Improve: 52%   Collapse: 22%   Attrition: 37%   Comparables: Phil Hennigan, Butch Metzger, Brandon Backe

A throw-in on the Brown-Weaver trade, Brazoban seamlessly replaced Guillermo Mota as the top setup man during 2004's NL West title run. He began 2005 by climbing into the injured Gagne's closer role without a hitch. "Ghame Over" t-shirts sprouted up, and it was easy to forget the former outfielder had taken up pitching less than three years earlier. But after Gagne broke down for good in mid-June, Brazoban was a disaster. His second stint as closer began with a blown save on June 18 and ended with a blown save on August 10, when he gave up a grand slam to Ryan Howard. During that span he threw 17.2 innings, and pitched like Wayne Franklin in the fifth circle of Hell: 17.2 innings, 22 earned runs, 11 walks, nine strikeouts, five home runs, including two Howard walk-offs. Duaner Sanchez took over the closer duties from there. Mindful of Brazoban's inexperience, at some point the Dodgers should have put him somewhere he could succeed, be that garbage time in L.A. or closing in the minors. Gagne's return and the emergence of Sanchez means Brazoban can now earn his way back into the late innings.

JONATHAN BROXTON   Bats: R   Throws: R   Height: 6' 4"   Weight: 240   Born: June 16, 1984   Age: 22

YEAR	TM	LVL	AGE	W	L	SV	G	GS	IP	H	BB	SO	HR	GB%	BABIP	STUFF	WHIP	ERA	PERA	EQERA	EQH9	EQBB9	EQSO9	EQHR9	VORP	WXRL
2003	SGA	A	19	4	2	0	9	8	37.3	27	22	30	1	—	.241	0	1.31	3.14	5.14	5.14	8.0	6.4	4.6	0.5	1.8	—
2004	VRO	A+	20	11	6	0	23	23	128.3	110	43	144	7	—	.311	21	1.19	3.23	4.49	4.56	9.0	3.5	6.9	1.0	14.1	—
2005	JAX	AA	21	5	3	5	33	13	96.7	79	31	107	4	45%	.307	17	1.14	3.16	3.82	4.60	8.5	3.1	6.9	0.7	10.2	—
2005	LAN	MLB	21	1	0	0	14	0	13.7	13	12	22	0	16%	.419	14	1.83	5.91	3.14	7.53	8.2	6.9	12.6	0.0	-3.0	-0.1
2006	LAN	MLB	22	4	6	2	46	9	81.0	74	40	73	11	40%	.279	5	1.39	4.46	4.77	4.97	8.3	4.0	7.2	1.2	5.6	0.8

Breakout: 21%   Improve: 60%   Collapse: 12%   Attrition: 10%   Comparables: Jim Maloney, Pete Broberg, Steve Dunning

Broxton Rox! This beefy Georgia righty was already a top prospect before being shifted to the bullpen in mid-June. Though timed to Gagne's demise, DePodesta claimed the move was part of a systematic attempt to expose the club's minor league starters to relief pitching, resting their arms in the process. Broxton was the only top prospect to get more than a passing look in the role. In the process his, heater jumped from 93–95 mph to as high as 99, and he posted a 36/6 K/BB ratio in 24.2 relief innings. By the end of July, he was in L.A., where he took his lumps in limited duty before returning to Jacksonville for the Southern League playoffs. With the "coup de DePo," it's unclear whether the experiment will continue.

GIOVANNI CARRARA   Bats: R   Throws: R   Height: 6' 2"   Weight: 230   Born: March 4, 1968   Age: 38

YEAR	TM	LVL	AGE	W	L	SV	G	GS	IP	H	BB	SO	HR	GB%	BABIP	STUFF	WHIP	ERA	PERA	EQERA	EQH9	EQBB9	EQSO9	EQHR9	VORP	WXRL
2003	SEA	MLB	35	2	0	0	23	0	29.0	40	14	13	6	44%	.337	-34	1.86	6.83	6.75	7.36	12.0	4.3	4.0	1.8	-2.5	-0.1
2004	LAN	MLB	36	5	2	2	42	0	53.7	46	20	48	1	40%	.294	19	1.23	2.18	3.23	2.89	8.2	3.1	7.1	0.2	18.8	1.7
2005	LAN	MLB	37	7	4	0	72	0	75.7	65	38	56	6	43%	.286	-1	1.36	3.92	4.58	4.22	8.4	4.2	6.1	0.7	10.5	1.1
2006	PIT	MLB	38	2	2	1	39	0	44.7	47	20	30	5	42%	.293	-11	1.49	4.31	4.98	5.22	9.2	3.6	5.6	1.1	5.3	0.4

Breakout: 27%   Improve: 49%   Collapse: 41%   Attrition: 28%   Comparables: Al Benton, Jose Mesa, Ted Power

A useful, durable reliever who came back to earth after an outstanding 2004. Though he set a career high in appearances, Carrara showed major declines in his rate stats, and fared poorly handling inherited runners, more than doubling his Fair Run Average from 2.26 to 4.64. He refused a minor league assignment to get him off of the 40-man roster, became a free agent, and will likely find work elsewhere.

ELMER DESSENS   Bats: R   Throws: R   Height: 6' 0"   Weight: 178   Born: January 13, 1972   Age: 34

YEAR	TM	LVL	AGE	W	L	SV	G	GS	IP	H	BB	SO	HR	GB%	BABIP	STUFF	WHIP	ERA	PERA	EQERA	EQH9	EQBB9	EQSO9	EQHR9	VORP	WXRL
2003	ARI	MLB	31	8	8	0	34	30	175.7	212	57	113	22	51%	.332	2	1.53	5.07	4.62	4.92	10.1	2.6	5.1	1.1	9.1	1.6
2004	ARI	MLB	32	1	6	2	38	9	85.3	107	23	55	11	52%	.332	-3	1.52	4.75	4.41	4.52	10.2	2.2	5.0	1.0	1.7	0.6
2004	LAN	MLB	32	1	0	0	12	1	19.7	16	8	18	4	52%	.231	3	1.22	3.20	5.21	3.32	8.5	3.3	7.6	1.9	5.3	-0.2
2005	LAN	MLB	33	1	2	0	28	7	65.7	63	19	37	6	52%	.271	-3	1.25	3.56	4.45	4.18	9.0	2.5	4.7	0.8	10.1	1.3
2006	KCA	MLB	35	3	5	1	33	6	66.0	80	19	35	8	49%	.316	-11	1.50	5.26	5.41	6.25	10.6	2.6	4.8	1.0	0.3	0.2

Breakout: 8%   Improve: 28%   Collapse: 45%   Attrition: 30%   Comparables: Ray Scarborough, Cal Mclish, Bob Porterfield

(continued next page)

Elmer Dessens *(continued)*

Swingmen have their uses, but the wisdom of putting Dessens in that role might be questioned given his tendency to burn out quickly in when he takes the mound, going deep into the count. His 2004–2005 stats show a 5.73 ERA as a starter, with a 1.4 K/BB ratio and a mere 4.5 innings per start, while out of the pen he looked a lot better, with a 2.76 ERA with a 3.4 K/BB ratio. Which would you rather have? The Royals found him irresistible on the free agent market, which is like being told that the bearded lady from the circus thinks you're sexy, but at least they seem to only want him working out of the pen.

SCOTT ELBERT Bats: L Throws: L Height: 6′ 2″ Weight: 190 Born: May 13, 1985 Age: 21

YEAR	TM	LVL	AGE	W	L	SV	G	GS	IP	H	BB	SO	HR	GB%	BABIP	STUFF	WHIP	ERA	PERA	EQERA	EQH9	EQBB9	EQSO9	EQHR9	VORP	WXRL
2004	OGD	Rk	19	2	3	0	12	12	49.7	47	30	45	5	—	.298	-20	1.55	5.25	7.31	6.38	9.4	6.4	3.9	1.9	-4.2	—
2005	CGA	A	20	8	5	0	25	24	115.0	83	57	128	8	49%	.269	2	1.22	2.66	5.57	4.47	8.3	5.7	6.4	1.3	13.4	—
2006	*LAN*	*MLB*	*21*	*5*	*9*	*0*	*25*	*20*	*114.7*	*106*	*76*	*88*	*15*	*46%*	*.271*	*1*	*1.59*	*5.08*	*5.61*	*5.71*	*8.4*	*5.5*	*6.2*	*1.2*	*0.5*	*0.7*

Breakout: 7%   Improve: 37%   Collapse: 31%   Attrition: 1%   Comparables: John Curtice, David Martinez, Gary Majewski

The Dodgers' 1st round pick in 2004 (another high-schooler), Elbert fared well in his first full season of pro ball, and wound up rated the top prospect in the Sally League. Though he struggled a bit with command, he missed enough bats with his low-90s fastball and power curve , holding opponents to a .200 batting average. Elbert closed the year by posting a 1.96 ERA over his final 12 starts. There's been talk of shifting him to the pen, but he'll settle for Vero Beach in '06.

ERIC GAGNE Bats: R Throws: R Height: 6′ 2″ Weight: 195 Born: January 7, 1976 Age: 30

YEAR	TM	LVL	AGE	W	L	SV	G	GS	IP	H	BB	SO	HR	GB%	BABIP	STUFF	WHIP	ERA	PERA	EQERA	EQH9	EQBB9	EQSO9	EQHR9	VORP	WXRL
2003	LAN	MLB	27	2	3	55	77	0	82.3	37	20	137	2	50%	.250	70	0.69	1.20	1.69	1.69	5.1	2.0	13.7	0.2	39.0	9.3
2004	LAN	MLB	28	7	3	45	70	0	82.3	53	22	114	5	47%	.276	45	0.91	2.19	2.58	2.91	6.6	2.2	11.2	0.6	27.8	8.0
2005	LAN	MLB	29	1	0	8	14	0	13.3	10	3	22	2	54%	.308	13	0.97	2.71	2.70	2.70	6.8	2.0	13.5	1.4	4.0	1.1
2006	*LAN*	*MLB*	*30*	*5*	*4*	*30*	*51*	*2*	*66.3*	*42*	*16*	*94*	*5*	*44%*	*.264*	*42*	*0.86*	*1.66*	*1.75*	*1.86*	*5.7*	*1.9*	*11.4*	*0.6*	*25.1*	*3.7*

Breakout: 45%   Improve: 59%   Collapse: 3%   Attrition: 12%   Comparables: Bryan Harvey, Tom Henke, Rich Gossage

Ever hear the old expression, "It's not the fall that kills you, it's the sudden stop?" Cascade injuries are like that. By compensating for foot, leg, or back problems, pitchers compromise their mechanics and end up hurting their arms. Such was the case with Gagne, who soldiered on despite spraining his knee in the spring and never letting it heal. The Dodgers brass didn't see it coming. For all the wrath management received from the local media and fans last year, they deserved even more criticism for not protecting Gagne from his own hypercompetitive instincts. They flushed millions of dollars down the toilet, blowing a big chunk of Gagne's $8 million salary. In addition, a healthy Gagne might have put the Dodgers in a position to make the playoffs in a weak, winnable division, which would have added millions to the club's war chest. After winding up on Dr. Frank Jobe's table for quasi-Tommy John surgery, but dodging a full TJ, Gagne should be ready to go by spring training. He may not return to his 2003 form, but he'll improve the team's chances simply by staying healthy.

JOEL HANRAHAN Bats: R Throws: R Height: 6′ 3″ Weight: 215 Born: October 6, 1981 Age: 24

YEAR	TM	LVL	AGE	W	L	SV	G	GS	IP	H	BB	SO	HR	GB%	BABIP	STUFF	WHIP	ERA	PERA	EQERA	EQH9	EQBB9	EQSO9	EQHR9	VORP	WXRL
2003	JAX	AA	21	10	4	0	23	23	133.3	117	53	130	5	—	.293	20	1.28	2.43	4.41	4.27	8.8	3.8	6.2	0.7	19.0	—
2004	LVG	AAA	22	7	7	0	25	22	119.3	128	75	97	22	—	.299	-20	1.70	5.05	6.52	5.23	9.4	6.0	5.6	1.7	4.9	—
2005	VRO	A+	23	1	0	0	5	5	21.3	25	11	25	5	34%	.357	-23	1.69	5.92	9.31	7.45	13.0	6.5	7.0	4.2	-4.0	—
2005	JAX	AA	23	9	8	0	23	21	111.7	118	55	102	17	44%	.323	-48	1.55	4.91	7.53	7.18	11.3	5.2	5.5	2.8	-18.3	—
2006	*LAN*	*MLB*	*24*	*4*	*8*	*0*	*28*	*16*	*100.3*	*107*	*60*	*71*	*18*	*43%*	*.288*	*-9*	*1.66*	*5.82*	*6.56*	*6.41*	*9.7*	*4.9*	*5.7*	*1.6*	*-8.8*	*-0.2*

Breakout: 14%   Improve: 39%   Collapse: 20%   Attrition: 0%   Comparables: Ron Chiavacci, Claudio Vargas, Travis Hughes

Promoted to Vegas after excelling at Jacksonville in 2003, Hanrahan bombed like your cousin and his card-counting "system." Not faring much better there in 2004, he fell as low as Vero Beach before getting back to Jax, struggling with his control all the way. At this point, Billingsley and Broxton have lapped him. And in this pitching-rich system, there are more coming up behind them.

D. J. HOULTON

Bats: R Throws: R Height: 6' 4" Weight: 220 Born: August 12, 1979 Age: 26

YEAR	TM	LVL	AGE	W	L	SV	G	GS	IP	H	BB	SO	HR	GB%	BABIP	STUFF	WHIP	ERA	PERA	EQERA	EQH9	EQBB9	EQSO9	EQHR9	VORP	WXRL
2003	ROU	AA	23	5	4	0	18	18	109.0	93	28	101	11	—	.266	-6	1.11	3.47	5.50	4.54	8.9	2.9	6.1	1.8	12.1	—
2003	NWO	AAA	23	3	4	0	11	11	61.7	70	19	48	12	—	.297	-17	1.44	5.40	6.86	6.86	11.3	3.2	6.1	2.7	-8.3	—
2004	ROU	AA	24	12	5	0	28	28	159.0	141	47	159	14	—	.296	-1	1.18	2.94	5.21	4.79	9.3	3.3	6.1	1.4	13.5	—
2005	LAN	MLB	25	6	9	0	35	19	129.0	145	52	90	21	37%	.317	-12	1.53	5.16	5.43	5.50	10.2	3.3	5.7	1.5	-1.1	1.3
2006	*LAN*	*MLB*	*26*	*5*	*8*	*1*	*39*	*14*	*113.3*	*115*	*43*	*80*	*18*	*40%*	*.281*	*-2*	*1.39*	*4.79*	*5.21*	*5.36*	*9.2*	*3.1*	*5.7*	*1.4*	*3.8*	*0.9*

Breakout: 18% Improve: 52% Collapse: 14% Attrition: 7%   Comparables: Craig Swan, Claudio Vargas, Rob Bell

Plucked from the Astros in the Rule 5 draft, Houlton couldn't have asked for a better shot at lasting the year on a big-league roster than with this shorthanded staff. After getting pounded in relief, he wormed his way into the rotation due to the pain and suffering of others. Though he reliably took the ball every fifth day, he was drubbed regularly; five of his eight quality starts came against the lowest-scoring teams in the majors. He pitched noticeably better at pitcher-friendly Dodger Stadium (4.13 ERA, vs. 6.37 on the road). He'll have a shot at the back end of the rotation again, but now he can be sent to the minors if the going gets rough.

EDWIN JACKSON

Bats: R Throws: R Height: 6' 3" Weight: 190 Born: September 9, 1983 Age: 22

YEAR	TM	LVL	AGE	W	L	SV	G	GS	IP	H	BB	SO	HR	GB%	BABIP	STUFF	WHIP	ERA	PERA	EQERA	EQH9	EQBB9	EQSO9	EQHR9	VORP	WXRL
2003	JAX	AA	19	7	7	0	27	27	148.3	121	53	157	9	—	.280	24	1.17	3.70	4.49	5.19	8.6	3.4	7.0	1.1	6.5	—
2003	LAN	MLB	19	2	1	0	4	3	22.0	17	11	19	2	51%	.268	21	1.27	2.45	4.22	2.95	8.0	4.2	7.2	0.8	7.8	1.1
2004	LVG	AAA	20	6	4	0	19	19	90.7	90	55	70	4	—	.310	15	1.60	5.85	4.73	5.42	8.5	5.5	5.5	0.4	1.8	—
2004	LAN	MLB	20	2	1	0	8	5	24.7	31	11	16	7	45%	.308	-11	1.70	7.29	6.93	7.66	11.3	3.6	5.1	2.6	-4.1	0.3
2005	JAX	AA	21	6	4	0	11	11	62.0	52	18	44	7	48%	.249	-10	1.13	3.48	6.28	5.65	9.6	3.0	4.6	2.0	-0.3	—
2005	LVG	AAA	21	3	7	0	12	11	55.3	76	37	33	13	38%	.339	-32	2.04	8.63	7.53	8.01	11.1	5.7	3.9	2.2	-15.3	—
2005	LAN	MLB	21	2	2	0	7	6	28.7	31	17	13	2	34%	.293	-14	1.67	6.27	5.34	6.91	9.7	5.0	3.8	0.6	-4.6	0.1
2006	*TBA*	*MLB*	*22*	*5*	*10*	*0*	*33*	*25*	*127.0*	*138*	*63*	*75*	*19*	*41%*	*.289*	*-6*	*1.58*	*5.58*	*5.86*	*5.87*	*9.7*	*4.4*	*5.1*	*1.3*	*-4.7*	*0.3*

Breakout: 27% Improve: 65% Collapse: 12% Attrition: 0%   Comparables: Bubba Nelson, Dewon Brazelton, Jerry Walker

It's not simply that Jackson hasn't delivered on the promise exhibited back in 2003, it's that he's been moving backwards, with ERAs reading like Boeing's product development line. His peripherals have been even worse. Two years removed from his big breakout, Jackson returned to Jacksonville and put up numbers that weren't cringe-inducing, but they weren't tout-worthy either. If there's a silver lining, it's that his struggles have prevented him from being overworked during his injury-nexus window. Time is still on Jackson's side, especially now that he's been dealt to the D-Rays to put Danys Baez in L.A.

HONG-CHIH KUO

Bats: L Throws: L Height: 6' 0" Weight: 200 Born: July 23, 1981 Age: 24

YEAR	TM	LVL	AGE	W	L	SV	G	GS	IP	H	BB	SO	HR	GB%	BABIP	STUFF	WHIP	ERA	PERA	EQERA	EQH9	EQBB9	EQSO9	EQHR9	VORP	WXRL
2005	VRO	A+	23	1	1	0	11	3	26.0	19	10	42	2	45%	.340	12	1.12	2.08	4.88	4.12	8.6	4.9	9.4	1.5	3.9	—
2005	JAX	AA	23	1	1	3	17	0	28.3	22	11	44	1	48%	.350	19	1.17	1.91	3.67	3.67	8.3	4.0	9.3	0.7	5.8	—
2006	*LAN*	*MLB*	*24*	*3*	*4*	*1*	*31*	*4*	*56.0*	*53*	*33*	*56*	*7*	*43%*	*.300*	*5*	*1.53*	*4.69*	*5.40*	*5.19*	*8.7*	*4.9*	*8.0*	*1.2*	*2.2*	*0.3*

Breakout: 15% Improve: 34% Collapse: 34% Attrition: 22%   Comparables: Chuck McElroy, Cloyd Boyer, Bert Snow

The first Taiwanese high-schooler ever signed to a pro contract, Kuo has been sidelined by two Tommy John surgeries thus far, and through 2004 had been limited to 42.1 pro innings spread out over four years. Finally healthy, he was shifted to the bullpen. He pitched brilliantly at both Vero Beach and Jacksonville, posting eye-popping numbers that earned him a cup of coffee in September. He can bring it as high as 99 mph—rare velocity for a southpaw—and his repertoire includes both a breaking ball and a changeup. With no journeyman lefties standing in his way, he'll compete for a spot in the big league bullpen this spring.

DEREK LOWE

Bats: R Throws: R Height: 6' 6" Weight: 170 Born: June 1, 1973 Age: 33

YEAR	TM	LVL	AGE	W	L	SV	G	GS	IP	H	BB	SO	HR	GB%	BABIP	STUFF	WHIP	ERA	PERA	EQERA	EQH9	EQBB9	EQSO9	EQHR9	VORP	WXRL
2003	BOS	MLB	30	17	7	0	33	33	203.3	216	72	110	17	66%	.298	10	1.42	4.47	4.51	4.30	9.2	3.1	4.7	0.7	26.7	3.6
2004	BOS	MLB	31	14	12	0	33	33	182.7	224	71	105	15	64%	.333	7	1.61	5.42	4.35	5.83	10.1	3.2	4.7	0.6	-8.0	1.4
2005	LAN	MLB	32	12	15	0	35	35	222.0	223	55	146	28	64%	.286	6	1.25	3.61	4.55	4.63	9.3	2.1	5.5	1.2	22.5	3.8
2006	*LAN*	*MLB*	*33*	*11*	*12*	*0*	*32*	*30*	*195.3*	*198*	*63*	*117*	*15*	*61%*	*.290*	*7*	*1.33*	*4.00*	*4.26*	*4.59*	*9.2*	*2.7*	*4.8*	*0.7*	*21.2*	*3.6*

Breakout: 28% Improve: 67% Collapse: 4% Attrition: 3%   Comparables: Mike Lacoss, Rick Rhoden, Tommy John

(continued next page)

Derek Lowe *(continued)*

Using his 2004 October heroics to offset a horrific regular season and generally downward trends, Lowe netted a four-year, $36 million contract that had even DePo's most ardent supporters scratching their heads. Removed from Fenway and shoddy Red Sox infield defense, he seemed likely to improve, but it was hardly necessary to hand out a four-year deal to a League-Average Innings-Muncher (LAIM). Considering the 24 unearned runs Lowe allowed, he was actually worse than average before we even account for Dodger Stadium. And for a groundballer, he gave up a lot of big flies. The most unsettling thing about Lowe's season was the fact that he posted a better ERA after the news of his extramarital affair with a Fox TV reporter broke (2.86 ERA/3.6 RA after, as compared to 3.99/5.1 before) in early August. One man's humiliation is another man's catharsis.

GREG MILLER					**Bats: L**		**Throws: L**				**Height: 6′ 5″**		**Weight: 190**		**Born: November 3, 1984**		**Age: 21**			
YEAR	TM	LVL	AGE	W	L	SV	G	GS	IP	H	BB	SO	HR	GB%	BABIP	STUFF	WHIP	ERA	PERA	EQERA	EQH9	EQBB9	EQSO9	EQHR9	VORP	WXRL
2003	VRO	A+	18	11	4	0	21	21	115.7	103	41	111	5	—	.293	26	1.24	2.49	4.57	4.32	9.2	3.6	6.4	1.1	15.7	—
2003	JAX	AA	18	1	1	0	4	4	26.7	15	7	40	1	—	.259	25	0.82	1.01	2.84	2.84	6.4	2.5	9.9	0.7	7.8	—
2006	*LAN*	*MLB*	*21*	*2*	*4*	*0*	*22*	*7*	*52.7*	*48*	*44*	*47*	*5*	*51%*	*.288*	*-3*	*1.74*	*4.97*	*5.84*	*5.59*	*8.2*	*6.9*	*7.2*	*0.9*	*0.3*	*0.2*

Breakout: 2%   Improve: 11%   Collapse: 74%   Attrition: 18%   Comparables: Ty Howington, Scott Olsen, Mark Phillips

Miller cracked our Top 50 Prospect List in 2004 (#33) with a combination of youth and performance so rare that PECOTA couldn't find enough comps to generate a reliable forecast. Two unusual shoulder surgeries (one to remove the bursa sac, another to shave down the tip of the shoulder blade), one missed season, and a generous amount of rehab later, he finally returned to action on June 30. Kept to a strict pitch count, he was back to mid-90s velocity, using a lower arm angle than before. Though Miller struggled with command, he climbed the ladder quickly. Shoulder soreness shut him down after just four innings in the Arizona Fall League, but the medical reports are good, and he'll be ready to go in the spring. A healthy season would be a huge step forward.

JUSTIN ORENDUFF					**Bats: R**		**Throws: R**				**Height: 6′ 4″**		**Weight: 205**		**Born: May 27, 1983**		**Age: 23**			
YEAR	TM	LVL	AGE	W	L	SV	G	GS	IP	H	BB	SO	HR	GB%	BABIP	STUFF	WHIP	ERA	PERA	EQERA	EQH9	EQBB9	EQSO9	EQHR9	VORP	WXRL
2004	OGD	Rk	21	2	3	0	13	10	43.7	46	25	57	4	—	.389	-20	1.62	4.74	6.43	6.43	10.1	6.2	5.6	1.7	-3.9	—
2005	VRO	A+	22	5	3	0	12	12	60.3	35	26	81	3	37%	.256	17	1.01	2.24	4.42	4.58	7.2	5.2	8.0	0.8	6.2	—
2005	JAX	AA	22	5	2	0	14	13	66.3	59	24	65	6	30%	.305	-3	1.25	4.07	5.49	5.78	9.5	3.8	6.1	1.6	-1.2	—
2006	*LAN*	*MLB*	*23*	*5*	*9*	*0*	*24*	*19*	*112.7*	*108*	*65*	*92*	*19*	*37%*	*.275*	*3*	*1.53*	*5.29*	*5.74*	*5.78*	*8.7*	*4.8*	*6.5*	*1.5*	*-2.4*	*0.5*

Breakout: 9%   Improve: 47%   Collapse: 21%   Attrition: 2%   Comparables: Aaron Myette, Andrew Brown, Jason Lakman

A rare Dodgers college pick, Orenduff shook off a disappointing 2004 debut to dominate at Vero Beach and then climb to Jacksonville. He's a sinkerballer who doesn't overpower hitters or have as high an upside as his fellow prospects. But based on his experience, Orenduff might be closer to big-league ready than the high-schoolers.

FRANQUELIS OSORIA					**Bats: R**		**Throws: R**				**Height: 6′ 0″**		**Weight: 165**		**Born: September 12, 1981**		**Age: 24**			
YEAR	TM	LVL	AGE	W	L	SV	G	GS	IP	H	BB	SO	HR	GB%	BABIP	STUFF	WHIP	ERA	PERA	EQERA	EQH9	EQBB9	EQSO9	EQHR9	VORP	WXRL
2003	VRO	A+	21	3	6	6	33	3	75.0	69	19	53	4	—	.274	-15	1.17	3.00	5.37	5.63	10.1	2.7	4.5	1.4	-0.2	—
2004	JAX	AA	22	8	5	5	51	0	81.0	71	18	73	2	—	.300	7	1.10	3.56	3.69	5.19	8.5	2.3	5.3	0.3	3.6	—
2005	LVG	AAA	23	6	4	9	40	0	55.0	63	13	35	3	66%	.347	-1	1.38	2.62	4.18	2.89	9.3	2.1	4.2	0.5	16.9	—
2005	LAN	MLB	23	0	2	0	24	0	29.7	28	8	15	3	60%	.278	-9	1.21	3.94	4.66	4.34	9.3	2.2	4.3	0.9	4.1	0.5
2006	*LAN*	*MLB*	*24*	*3*	*3*	*3*	*60*	*1*	*60.0*	*64*	*19*	*33*	*5*	*58%*	*.296*	*-8*	*1.38*	*4.06*	*4.55*	*4.68*	*9.7*	*2.6*	*4.4*	*0.8*	*5.7*	*0.5*

Breakout: 20%   Improve: 42%   Collapse: 26%   Attrition: 17%   Comparables: Julian Tavarez, Bill Castro, Beau Kemp

Quick, name a major-league pitcher besides Antonio Alfonseca with six fingers on his pitching hand? If you guessed Osoria, you're correct, although he's got the normal number of fingers on his left hand. A mellifluously-named string-bean, he pitched well enough in his two-month stint with the Dodgers. He doesn't have the raw stuff of Brazoban, but he's a sinkerballer who makes his living on the ground (3.2 G/F ratio), and he was hell on righties, who hit just .140/.246/.193 against him. There's always a spot in the bullpen for a guy who can do that.

BRAD PENNY
Bats: R Throws: R   Height: 6' 4" Weight: 200 Born: May 24, 1978   Age: 28

YEAR	TM	LVL	AGE	W	L	SV	G	GS	IP	H	BB	SO	HR	GB%	BABIP	STUFF	WHIP	ERA	PERA	EQERA	EQH9	EQBB9	EQSO9	EQHR9	VORP	WXRL
2003	FLO	MLB	25	14	10	0	32	32	196.3	195	56	138	21	46%	.299	12	1.28	4.13	4.23	4.51	9.0	2.3	5.7	1.0	26.6	4.9
2004	FLO	MLB	26	8	8	0	21	21	131.3	124	39	105	10	46%	.298	26	1.24	3.15	3.81	3.67	8.7	2.4	6.4	0.7	32.3	4.0
2005	LAN	MLB	27	7	9	0	29	29	175.3	185	41	122	17	48%	.307	17	1.29	3.90	4.00	4.06	9.4	2.0	5.7	0.9	29.6	4.4
2006	*LAN*	*MLB*	*28*	*11*	*10*	*0*	*29*	*29*	*182.3*	*179*	*49*	*130*	*20*	*46%*	*.284*	*14*	*1.25*	*3.76*	*4.21*	*4.23*	*8.9*	*2.2*	*5.7*	*1.0*	*27.8*	*4.2*

Breakout: 10% Improve: 46% Collapse: 11% Attrition: 4%   *Comparables: Vicente Padilla, Larry Christenson, Chris Bosio*

Much to the Dodgers' collective relief, Penny showed no ill effects from the biceps injury that curtailed his 2004 season shortly after his inclusion in the now-infamous and overly lamented Lo Duca trade. He wasn't as dominant as he'd been in his tantalizing Dodger debut, but he pitched at an above-average level and took the ball every fifth day until forearm tightness shut him down in mid-September. His numbers are moving in all kinds of contradictory directions—decreased strikeout rate, significantly decreased walk rate, increased homer rate, increased G/F ratio—but there's nothing to indicate he won't continue being an effective starter. Still, it will take a return to his pre-injury form to merit the three-year, $25 million extension that DePodesta gave him.

ODALIS PEREZ
Bats: L Throws: L   Height: 6' 0" Weight: 150 Born: June 11, 1977   Age: 29

YEAR	TM	LVL	AGE	W	L	SV	G	GS	IP	H	BB	SO	HR	GB%	BABIP	STUFF	WHIP	ERA	PERA	EQERA	EQH9	EQBB9	EQSO9	EQHR9	VORP	WXRL
2003	LAN	MLB	26	12	12	0	30	30	185.3	191	46	141	28	55%	.299	6	1.28	4.52	4.58	5.03	9.7	2.0	6.3	1.4	18.2	4.1
2004	LAN	MLB	27	7	6	0	31	31	196.3	180	44	128	26	53%	.272	8	1.14	3.26	4.49	3.88	9.1	1.9	5.4	1.2	49.4	6.3
2005	LAN	MLB	28	7	8	0	19	19	108.7	109	28	74	13	47%	.292	7	1.26	4.55	4.35	4.93	9.2	2.2	5.7	1.1	8.2	2.1
2006	*LAN*	*MLB*	*29*	*8*	*8*	*0*	*28*	*22*	*137.3*	*140*	*34*	*90*	*15*	*50%*	*.288*	*7*	*1.27*	*3.92*	*4.33*	*4.45*	*9.2*	*2.1*	*5.2*	*1.0*	*18.8*	*2.8*

Breakout: 20% Improve: 54% Collapse: 6% Attrition: 1%   *Comparables: Glendon Rusch, Doug Rau, Ken Holtzman*

Perez's 2004 postseason struggles were expected to grease the skids for his departure, but even though his services weren't especially in demand elsewhere, he emerged with a contract in Benson/Milton territory. Continuing his post-millennial trend, Perez followed a good even-numbered year with a bad odd-numbered one, adding injury to insult by missing seven weeks with shoulder tendinitis, and then another five with a strained oblique. The calendar might suggest it's time for a bounce-back, but with his peripherals steadily eroding since his 2002 breakout, and shoulder woes costing him more and more downtime, the outlook isn't quite so sunny.

DUANER SANCHEZ
Bats: R Throws: R   Height: 6' 0" Weight: 190 Born: October 14, 1979   Age: 26

YEAR	TM	LVL	AGE	W	L	SV	G	GS	IP	H	BB	SO	HR	GB%	BABIP	STUFF	WHIP	ERA	PERA	EQERA	EQH9	EQBB9	EQSO9	EQHR9	VORP	WXRL
2003	NAS	AAA	23	4	4	1	41	1	61.0	63	27	34	3	—	.287	-15	1.48	3.69	4.85	4.85	9.4	4.6	4.2	0.6	4.9	—
2004	LAN	MLB	24	3	1	0	67	0	80.0	81	27	44	9	55%	.287	-11	1.35	3.38	4.94	4.25	9.8	2.9	4.5	1.0	16.3	1.0
2005	LAN	MLB	25	4	7	8	79	0	82.0	75	36	71	8	47%	.299	4	1.35	3.73	4.30	4.08	8.6	3.7	7.2	0.9	13.6	1.7
2006	*NYN*	*MLB*	*26*	*3*	*3*	*5*	*60*	*0*	*66.7*	*65*	*26*	*46*	*6*	*48%*	*.283*	*-3*	*1.36*	*3.85*	*4.34*	*4.83*	*8.7*	*3.3*	*5.8*	*0.9*	*8.4*	*0.7*

Breakout: 29% Improve: 51% Collapse: 27% Attrition: 17%   *Comparables: John Strohmayer, Elias Sosa, Brad Clontz*

The Dodgers' top reliever in 2005, which should tell you all you need to know about their season. Actually, despite the slew of injuries which aided his rise, Sanchez made significant strides by increasing his strikeout percentage from 13 percent to 20. Don't get too hung up on the corresponding rise in his walk rate, as it's distorted by six intentional passes. By the end of the year, Tracy had installed him as the closer, a move that in retrospect might have spared the Dodgers Brazoban's meltdown. Sent to the Mets in the Jae Seo trade, where he's expected to be the primary setup man for Billy Wagner.

STEVE SCHMOLL
Bats: R Throws: R   Height: 6' 2" Weight: 200 Born: February 4, 1980   Age: 26

YEAR	TM	LVL	AGE	W	L	SV	G	GS	IP	H	BB	SO	HR	GB%	BABIP	STUFF	WHIP	ERA	PERA	EQERA	EQH9	EQBB9	EQSO9	EQHR9	VORP	WXRL
2003	OGD	Rk	23	3	1	7	24	1	36.7	27	15	53	2	—	.305	-23	1.14	3.68	6.34	7.44	9.1	6.6	6.3	1.4	-6.7	—
2004	VRO	A+	24	3	3	10	37	0	65.0	57	18	58	0	—	.305	0	1.15	1.80	4.09	4.38	9.0	3.2	5.0	0.3	8.4	—
2005	LVG	AAA	25	0	3	5	22	0	26.3	24	13	31	1	46%	.365	4	1.41	4.79	3.76	4.78	7.9	4.4	7.5	0.3	2.4	—
2005	LAN	MLB	25	2	2	3	48	0	46.7	47	22	29	4	46%	.312	-12	1.48	5.01	4.82	5.59	9.3	4.0	5.2	0.8	-0.9	0.2
2006	*NYN*	*MLB*	*26*	*2*	*2*	*2*	*34*	*1*	*36.7*	*37*	*17*	*25*	*3*	*49%*	*.295*	*-6*	*1.47*	*4.55*	*4.86*	*5.60*	*9.1*	*3.9*	*5.8*	*0.8*	*1.4*	*0.1*

Breakout: 24% Improve: 55% Collapse: 22% Attrition: 36%   *Comparables: Vinnie Chulk, Ron Willis, Aaron Small*

(continued next page)

Steve Schmoll *(continued)*

A sidearmer out of the University of Maryland, Schmoll jumped to the big club after just 20 innings of Double-A. He's entertaining to watch—his delivery is near-submarine, he attacks the strike zone, and he's as animated as a sugared-up six-year-old. He was also maddeningly erratic, as his ERAs by month attest: 3.18, 9.00, 2.08, 11.32, 1.93. He was okay against righties (.244/.343/.366), but got raked over the coals by lefties (.303/.376/.494), as is the case with most righty sidearmers. Schmoll needs to get better at inducing grounders. He'll try his hand in Norfolk, after being included in the Seo trade.

CHUCK TIFFANY
Bats: L Throws: L   Height: 6′ 1″   Weight: 195   Born: January 25, 1985   Age: 21

YEAR	TM	LVL	AGE	W	L	SV	G	GS	IP	H	BB	SO	HR	GB%	BABIP	STUFF	WHIP	ERA	PERA	EQERA	EQH9	EQBB9	EQSO9	EQHR9	VORP	WXRL
2004	CGA	A	19	5	2	0	22	22	99.7	76	40	141	11	—	.298	10	1.16	3.70	5.52	5.03	9.2	4.5	7.9	1.7	5.9	—
2005	VRO	A+	20	11	7	0	22	21	110.0	91	43	134	17	36%	.294	-15	1.22	3.93	6.68	5.26	9.8	4.5	7.6	2.6	3.8	—
2006	*TBA*	*MLB*	*21*	*6*	*10*	*0*	*27*	*22*	*129.0*	*128*	*66*	*109*	*24*	*36%*	*.282*	*10*	*1.50*	*5.16*	*5.70*	*5.35*	*8.8*	*4.6*	*7.3*	*1.6*	*3.2*	*1.2*

Breakout: 16%   Improve: 47%   Collapse: 15%   Attrition: 1%   Comparables: *Travis Blackley, Ubaldo Jimenez, Cedrick Bowers*

Tiffany sparkled in his first full year of pro ball, striking out 141 in 99.2 innings, and pitching a seven-inning perfect game two weeks after starting a no-hitter. He continued to excel in High-A, despite a propensity for gopher balls that put him just one away from the league lead. He's not overpowering, but his fastball has late movement, and his curveball and circle change also rate highly. Now that he's been dealt to Tampa Bay, we'll see if the D-Rays are as sensible as the Dodgers in not rushing him.

JEFF WEAVER
Bats: R Throws: R   Height: 6′ 5″   Weight: 200   Born: August 22, 1976   Age: 29

YEAR	TM	LVL	AGE	W	L	SV	G	GS	IP	H	BB	SO	HR	GB%	BABIP	STUFF	WHIP	ERA	PERA	EQERA	EQH9	EQBB9	EQSO9	EQHR9	VORP	WXRL
2003	NYA	MLB	26	7	9	0	32	24	159.3	211	47	93	16	45%	.355	5	1.62	5.99	4.44	5.68	10.3	2.5	4.9	0.8	-6.6	0.7
2004	LAN	MLB	27	13	13	0	34	34	220.0	219	67	153	19	45%	.299	16	1.30	4.01	4.19	4.56	9.4	2.5	5.6	0.7	35.2	5.1
2005	LAN	MLB	28	14	11	0	34	34	224.0	220	43	157	35	42%	.278	4	1.17	4.22	4.83	4.54	9.5	1.6	5.9	1.5	27.0	4.2
2006	*LAN*	*MLB*	*29*	*11*	*11*	*0*	*31*	*30*	*195.7*	*198*	*49*	*135*	*25*	*44%*	*.285*	*12*	*1.26*	*4.07*	*4.43*	*4.51*	*9.2*	*2.1*	*5.5*	*1.2*	*22.8*	*3.8*

Breakout: 23%   Improve: 66%   Collapse: 6%   Attrition: 3%   Comparables: *Esteban Loaiza, Rick Wise, Steve Trachsel*

Weaver ate innings like Mr. Creosote, even when going badly. Through his first ten starts he sported a 5.97 ERA and averaged six innings per start. But after May 29, he settled down to post a 3.60 ERA and almost seven per. In comparing his two seasons as a Dodger, note that while his strikeout rate remained virtually constant, he cut his walks by more than a third. Meanwhile, his home run rate nearly doubled. The lesson seems to be, "Don't throw too many strikes, kid, or you'll spend a lot of time yelling into your glove." He won't live up to the hype that surrounded him in his early years, but the free agent market should make him a very wealthy LAIM nonetheless.

KELLY WUNSCH
Bats: L Throws: L   Height: 6′ 5″   Weight: 220   Born: July 12, 1972   Age: 33

YEAR	TM	LVL	AGE	W	L	SV	G	GS	IP	H	BB	SO	HR	GB%	BABIP	STUFF	WHIP	ERA	PERA	EQERA	EQH9	EQBB9	EQSO9	EQHR9	VORP	WXRL
2003	CHA	MLB	30	0	0	0	43	0	36.0	17	25	33	1	57%	.182	8	1.17	2.75	4.46	3.15	6.3	6.6	8.4	0.3	11.4	-0.1
2005	LAN	MLB	32	1	1	0	45	0	23.7	20	14	22	2	36%	.281	0	1.44	4.56	4.63	4.63	8.1	5.0	7.7	0.8	2.3	0.6
2006	*LAN*	*MLB*	*33*	*2*	*2*	*2*	*49*	*0*	*41.7*	*38*	*23*	*35*	*4*	*49%*	*.286*	*-6*	*1.47*	*4.17*	*4.72*	*5.32*	*8.3*	*4.6*	*6.7*	*0.8*	*3.7*	*0.3*

Breakout: 15%   Improve: 28%   Collapse: 49%   Attrition: 28%   Comparables: *Scott Sauerbeck, Mike James, Jim Kern*

Troubled by shoulder woes for much of 2004, Wunsch made good on a minor-league contract and won the LOOGY job in spring training. While not as unhittable as he'd been in the past, his funky sidearm delivery still gives lefty batters fits. His ERA was done in by the performance of the relievers following him; his Fair Run Average was a very respectable 2.46. Alas, he sprained his ankle in early July and needed season-ending surgery, and later had minor surgery on his hip as well. He'll look for work again after refusing a minor-league assignment.

Line Outs

Position/Player	TM	LVL	AGE	PA	R	2B	3B	HR	RBI	BB	SO	SB-CS	SPEED	BA/OBP/SLG	MLVR	EQBA/OBP/SLG	EQA	VORP
OF R. Carter	CGA	A	22	235	35	13	1	14	44	8	68	4-0	5.1	.281/.315/.536	.206	.239/.262/.441	.236	-7.6
OF C. Chen	LVG	AAA	27	362	59	20	2	15	63	38	82	3-3	5.3	.278/.354/.495	.022	.218/.286/.370	.229	-16.4
1B B. Myrow*	LVG	AAA	28	481	83	28	5	22	73	74	83	4-2	5.4	.282/.403/.547	.180	.217/.323/.397	.252	-5.9
INF N. Nakamura	LVG	AAA	31	408	54	17	1	22	67	45	70	0-0	3.0	.249/.331/.487	-.052	.181/.248/.329	.205	-22.6
OF X. Paul*	VRO	A+	20	326	42	15	3	7	41	32	81	1-5	4.8	.247/.328/.392	-.017	.216/.290/.351	.224	-19.4
C M. Rose#	LVG	AAA	28	236	31	20	1	5	36	25	51	2-0	5.0	.259/.343/.439	-.088	.194/.268/.314	.210	-11.7
OF C. Ross	LVG	AAA	24	448	79	21	4	22	63	49	103	4-2	4.9	.267/.348/.509	.022	.218/.293/.404	.240	-13.2

Pitcher	TM	LVL	AGE	W	L	SV	IP	H	BB	SO	HR	GB%	BABIP	STUFF	WHIP	ERA	PERA	EQERA	EQH9	EQBB9	EQSO9	EQHR9	VORP
S. Erickson	LAN	MLB	37	1	4	0	55.3	62	25	15	12	55%	.266	-43	1.57	6.02	6.96	5.96	10.9	3.8	2.3	2.0	-3.8
E. Hull	JAX	AA	25	7	7	3	117.0	105	44	117	9	46%	.303	-14	1.27	3.38	5.55	5.71	9.8	4.1	5.8	1.5	-1.3
D. Thompson*	LAN	MLB	24	0	0	0	18.0	16	10	13	0	59%	.327	8	1.44	3.50	3.50	3.50	8.5	4.5	6.0	0.0	4.0

Ryan Carter was returning from a season lost to injury, and two things stand out on his stat line: 14 homers in 224 ABs and a 69/8 K/BB ratio. After four stagnant years in Vegas, **Chin-Feng Chen** had better hope, "Who is the first native of Taiwan to play in the major leagues?" is a question that captures Alex Trebek's fancy, because that's as good as it's going to get. **Byron Myrow** is an indy league vet long past his sell by date, but might help somebody as a PH. **Norihiro Nakamura** is proof that there is such a thing as an inferior Japanese import, he'll be Grabowski's teammate on the Buffaloes. **Xavier Paul** began the year as the organization's best outfield prospect, but his performance paled in comparison to those of VB teammates Kemp, Ragliani and Ruggiano. **Mike Rose** is still awaiting his opportunity to be the next Gregg Zaun; claimed off of waivers by the Devil Rays, then non-tendered. **Cody Ross** has got some pop (56 HR in 299 Triple-A games over the last three seasons), and upped his walk rate. Another shot at a bench role isn't out of the question.

Darren Dreifort's final tally: five years, $55 million, 637 days on the DL—roughly 3.5 seasons—with a minimum of 48 in every year and more than 100 in four out of five. He also underwent eight surgeries, at least one a year, and had more meat pulled off the bone than you'd see at a Carolina barbecue. We can't blame him if he decides to stop the violence. Keeping **Scott Erickson** on the roster until the trading deadline was an indictable offense; presumably, DePo couldn't flip him for Manny Ramirez, so he finally cut bait. **Eric Hull** doesn't get much love in this pitching-saturated system, but he had a solid season at Jacksonville and a nice look in the AFL. If he can survive Vegas, he's just a phone call away. **Derek Thompson** is a onetime Tommy John survivor who re-injured his elbow shortly after a nice debut. Out for '06.

Milwaukee Brewers

Admittedly, we haven't been kind to the Brewers in the past. With the Selig family's direct mismanagement of the franchise, their ill-considered selections for front office and on-field staff, and a decade's worth of bad drafts, there have been few teams who gave reason to be picked on more consistently than Milwaukee's best. It's never been personal, however personally it was taken.

That's why there's something deliciously ironic now that the time has come to praise the Brewers and not bury them. Teams change just as much as the times. Gone are the Seligs, decamped with their in-laws and retainers and mouthpieces and dogsbodies, to settle into various roosts within MLB's corporate offices. Gone too are general managers like Sal Bando and Dean Taylor—Bando from the game, and Taylor to participate in the mismanagement of the Reds. Gone are the players associated with those days, flawed stars like Greg Vaughn, Dave Nilsson, or John Jaha. The Brewers of 2006 are not those Brewers.

In place of that ugly past, the organization now ranks among the better-run in baseball, thanks to the hiring of GM Doug Melvin after the 2002 season. A veteran of seven years as GM of the Texas Rangers, Melvin has done a remarkable job of turning around one of the game's most moribund franchises.

The Brewers had been meaningless standings filler for ten years, marking time and fondly remembering the kamikaze charge of '92, when they came up short of upsetting the Blue Jays. In the intervening years, the Brewers couldn't even field ballclubs interesting enough to keep fannies in the seats. The Brewers were consistently near the bottom of the league in attendance from 1993–2002, the lone exception coming in 2001 with the opening of Miller Park.

Dean Taylor held the GM post for three years before Melvin arrived, and had failed to build a team that would exploit that brief rediscovered interest in baseball in Milwaukee. His 2002 outfit was hit bottom, crashing to a 56–106 finish. Compare the talent Melvin inherited after that debacle, and the Brewers who will take the field in 2006 (see table 1).

People might complain that players changing teams makes modern fandom too hard, but if there was a constituency in Milwaukee that wanted to keep the likes of

BREWERS PROSPECTUS

2005 record: 81–81; Third place, NL Central

Pythagenport record: 84–78

Runs scored per game: 4.48 (6th in NL)

Runs allowed per game: 4.30 (6th in NL)

Team EqA: .261 (7th in NL)

2005 Batters Age: 29.0 (4th youngest in NL)

2005 Pitchers Age: 28.6 (3rd youngest in NL)

Ballpark: Miller Park; Neutral park; Park Factor of 1.002

2005: The long-term plan started gelling, a harbinger of better things to come.

2006: With some strong young talent and sensible management, they're about to start making noise.

Alex Sanchez or Paul Bako around because they were familiar, it's news to us. Dean Taylor's last squad was a collection of dreck and low-ceiling veterans. There was some stuff worth keeping: Jenkins and Sheets obviously were, and perhaps regrettably Ron Belliard was not. But replacing Belliard or Sanchez, or avoiding an idea as bad as giving Jeffrey Hammonds a three-year deal, were decisions that reflected Melvin's wisdom. Not every GM recognizes that there's talent to be had for bottom dollar or a waiver claim. The genius in how the Brewers have been turned around wasn't a matter of full-blown teardown and years spent waiting for draft picks to mature. In a sense, they were already there.

Instead, Melvin discarded almost everything he inherited. Barely more than a year into the job, he'd dealt or dumped everyone but Sheets and Jenkins. But the Brewers' prospects were far from contributing, and having dispensed with the junkk, Melvin had to field a team. He turned to what we sometimes refer to as the pool of "free talent," low-end major league free agents, minor league free agents, or other sorts that you can get in small deals. Melvin kept a close eye on the waiver wire as well, which allowed him to experiment with possible short-term solutions by cycling through worthwhile placeholders (see table 2). He also had the sense and sensibility to never become overly enamored of this class of players, occasionally discarding them,

TABLE 1. CHANGING OF THE GUARD

Position	2002	2006
C	Paul Bako	Damian Miller
1B	Richie Sexson	Prince Fielder
2B	Eric Young	Rickie Weeks
3B	(vacant)	Corey Koskie
SS	Jose Hernandez	J. J. Hardy
CF	Alex Sanchez	Brady Clark
RF	Jeffrey Hammonds	Geoff Jenkins
LF	Geoff Jenkins	Carlos Lee
UT	Ron Belliard	Bill Hall
S1	Ben Sheets	Ben Sheets
S2	Glendon Rusch	Chris Capuano
S3	Ruben Quevedo	Doug Davis
S4	Nick Neugebauer	Tomo Ohka
S5	Nelson Figueroa	R. Helling/D. Bush
Closer	Mike DeJean	Derrick Turnbow

Pitching is supposed to be hard to find, but Melvin lined up four solid starters to support Ben Sheets within just two years. Chris Capuano was perhaps *the* find in the Sexson trade, but Doug Davis and Victor Santos were picked up off the scrapheap for nothing. Tomo Ohka came over from the Nationals after falling out of favor with Frank Robinson just when the Nats needed a second baseman. Melvin called up Rickie Weeks, swapped spare second-sacker Junior Spivey for Ohka, and just like that the Brewers had an adequate rotation. They finished 14th in the major leagues in Support-Neutral Value Added and Support-Neutral Value Above Replacement, well ahead of both the Yankees and Red Sox. And to think, they did it without spending top dollar on Jaret Wright.

These sorts of shell games on the major league roster are great for getting you from godawful to competitive, but when you're fielding a team in Milwaukee, you pretty much need to grow your own top-tier talent. From the start, Melvin started to fix the Brewers' player development program from the start. He brought former Rangers Director of Player Development Reid Nichols with him, and put him in charge of the farm system. Coupled with the Nichols transfer, one of Melvin's savviest moves was to retain Jack Zduriencik, now the team's scouting director. Melvin and Nichols might not have picked Prince Fielder, but they had the good sense to keep the guy who did. Zduriencik also deserves credit for spotting Weeks and, just this past summer, University of Miami slugger Ryan Braun. The Brewers are also ramping up their overseas scouting, an area too long ignored.

sometimes dealing them, but consistently trading traded up and improving the club's talent base.

The importance of the Sexson deal should be clear. As much as it might have represented a public relations hit, Melvin's decision to trade the towering first baseman in his last year before free agency would not simply gift the Brewers with three-quarters of their 2004 infield. Subsequent trades of Overbay and Spivey have given the Brewers two starting pitchers, a useful outfielder, and a particularly good young pitching prospect in Zach Jackson. Melvin has also taken waiver bait like Podsednik, seen him win Rookie of the Year, and then sensibly flipped him for a quality slugger, Carlos Lee.

The farm still has a ways to go. Top pitcher picks like Mike Jones (1st round, 2001), and Mark Rogers (1st round, 2004), haven't turned out too well yet, and recent drafts haven't yielded much organizational depth. Still,

TABLE 2. FILLING HOLES

Position/Player	Acquired Through	Year(s)	Fate	Received?
C: Eddie Perez	Free Agency	2003	Free Agency	—
1B: Lyle Overbay	Sexson Trade	2004–05	Dealt to Toronto	D. Bush, G. Gross, Z. Jackson
2B/SS: Craig Counsell	Sexson Trade	2003–04	Free Agency	—
2B: Junior Spivey	Sexson Trade	2004–05	Dealt to Washington	Tomo Ohka
3B: Wes Helms	Trade	2003–05	Free Agency	—
SS: Royce Clayton	Free Agency	2003	Free Agency	—
CF: Scott Podsednik	Waiver Claim	2003–04	Dealt to Chicago	Carlos Lee
RF: John VanderWal	Free Agency	2003	Free Agency	—
UT: Keith Ginter	Trade (by D. Taylor)	2003–04	Dealt to Oakland	N. Cruz, J. Lehr
Starter: Victor Santos	Free Agency	2004–05	Released	—
Closer: Dan Kolb	Free Agency	2003–04	Dealt to Atlanta	J. Capellan

the program has taken a major step forward from the bad old days of hopelessly flawed prospects like Nick Neugebauer and Antone Williamson. It may be enough: as the Cardinals have demonstrated, a farm system that only cranks out the odd blue chip prospect and little else can still be valuable.

What's really critical is the potential synergy that's developing between Melvin's sense of timing to take advantage of the talent that Zduriencik has picked and Nichols has groomed, moving along the respectable placeholders that he dug up in the meantime to make space for the Brewers team that isn't just going to improve, but will end up pushing past the Cardinals and Astros to take over the division in the second half of the decade. Melvin doesn't screw around: when prospects like Weeks or Hardy or Fielder were ready, the veteran temps were moved out of the way. Those decisions aren't going to be quite so easy from here on out, because the Brewers will start entering the playoff picture this year. The decision about whether or not to move a Carlos Lee or Geoff Jenkins to make room for Nelson Cruz will be particularly difficult. Whether or not Cruz hits well (and he will) might not carry as much weight when the Brewers might look at Lee and Jenkins and give them a large portion of credit for why they're in contention. Pace the choices that will have to be made in the rotation or the bullpen, or when Brady Clark starts showing his age in center.

Such is the price of higher expectations, but even those can be managed. One of the less frequently acknowl-

edged achievements of Billy Beane in Oakland has been to educate the fan base and even the local media, in that they understand or accept the logic of his more aggressive roster moves. Beane hasn't simply won a grudging acceptance of his financial limitations in managing the roster, he's trusted in a way few front office execs are when it comes to making deals. Success breeds a lot of room to maneuver, of course, even erasing Beane's mistakes from most people's minds, but Beane's gift for affability and appearing to be frank seems to defuse a lot of skepticism and criticism. Although he no doubt enjoys the sly pleasure that comes from fleecing Beane in the Ginter deal, Melvin nevertheless could copy this particular page of Beane's playbook. The Brewers' commitment cannot be to any one player, but to their own self-improvement. The challenge will be to become a team that operates not simply on the basis of "what have you done for me lately," but "what will do for me next year?"

The intitiative Melvin's shown in dealing popular players like Sexson, Podsednik, and Overbay is cause for confidence on this score. Melvin and his staff already deserve a world of credit for how quickly they turned around one of the game's worst-run franchises. It's more clever still in that they didn't waste time making any noisy denunciations or wholesale acceptance of *Moneyball* principles; Doug Melvin and company simply rolled up their sleeves and built up a good ballclub. They'll get even more props when they win the division in 2007.

HITTERS

RUSS BRANYAN 3B/OF **Bats: L Throws: R** Height: 6′ 3″ Weight: 195 Born: December 19, 1975 Age: 30

YEAR	TM	LVL	AGE	PA	R	2B	3B	HR	RBI	BB	SO	SB	CS	SPEED	BA	OBP	SLG	MLVR	EQBA	EQOBP	EQSLG	EQA	VORP	DEFENSE			
2003	CIN	MLB	27	205	22	12	0	9	26	27	69	0	0	3.8	.216	.322	.438	-.012	.210	.317	.432	.257	3.0	16-3B	5	13-LF	-1
2004	BUF	AAA	28	366	58	16	2	25	75	42	102	5	2	5.0	.288	.374	.591	.316	.247	.327	.483	.274	9.5	33-1B	5	29-3B	1
2004	MIL	MLB	28	182	21	11	1	11	27	20	68	1	0	5.0	.234	.324	.525	.127	.228	.319	.513	.278	8.1	40-3B	0		
2005	MIL	MLB	29	241	23	11	0	12	31	39	80	1	0	3.5	.257	.378	.490	.178	.252	.376	.485	.294	14.6	52-3B	-2		
2006	MIL	MLB	30	180	21	8	1	8	26	25	57	1	0	4.0	.236	.348	.463	.037	.240	.349	.475	.274	7.8	46-3B	-1		

Breakout: 14% Improve: 38% Collapse: 42% Attrition: 39% Comparables: Pete Ward, Len Matuszek, John Vander Wal

After pasting right-handed pitchers at a .249/.366/.518 clip with a home run every 15 at-bats over the last three years, Branyan could have been half of a cost-effective third-base platoon until Ryan Braun is ready to assume the major league job. Instead, they traded for Corey Koskie, which led to Branyan's being outrighted in January. Branyan remains a Three True Outcomes posterboy par excellence, ready to help any open-minded team that doesn't mind strikeouts and needs power from any of their lineup's four corner slots. If an AL club wises up and makes him their lefty-hitting DH, they wouldn't regret it.

RYAN BRAUN 3B? **Bats: R Throws: R** Height: 6′ 2″ Weight: 200 Born: July 29, 1980 Age: 25

YEAR	TM	LVL	AGE	PA	R	2B	3B	HR	RBI	BB	SO	SB	CS	SPEED	BA	OBP	SLG	MLVR	EQBA	EQOBP	EQSLG	EQA	VORP	DEFENSE	
2005	WVA	A	24	164	21	16	2	8	35	9	34	2	4	3.4	.355	.396	.645	.591	.287	.316	.478	.264	9.8	34-3B	-4
2006	MIL	MLB	22	403	47	27	2	15	61	19	94	4	2	3.6	.268	.311	.471	.012	.272	.312	.483	.259	14.0	96-3B	-5

Breakout: 7% Improve: 15% Collapse: 45% Attrition: 13% Comparables: Craig Brazell, Lance Niekro, Ian Bladergroen

A polished offensive ballplayer out of the University of Miami, the Brewers were happy to be able to take him in the 1st round of the 2005 draft. He has the bat speed and power potential to become a premium hitter, and he can run to boot.

Some fret that he's got a hitch in his swing, but hitches or even slow swings haven't killed the careers of players as varied as Rob Deer and Joe Carter. Others worry that he might not be consistent enough to handle third in the big leagues, but he has the arm and agility for the position, and the Brewers wisely seem content to leave him there until he proves he can't handle it. Winter pickup Corey Koskie is under contract through 2007, but if Braun's still playing third by then, Koskie might be relegated to the bench before his contract's up.

JEFF CIRILLO   **1B/3B**   **Bats: R Throws: R**   Height: 6′ 1″   Weight: 200   Born: September 23, 1969   Age: 36

YEAR	TM	LVL	AGE	PA	R	2B	3B	HR	RBI	BB	SO	SB	CS	SPEED	BA	OBP	SLG	MLVR	EQBA	EQOBP	EQSLG	EQA	VORP	DEFENSE
2003	SEA	MLB	33	289	24	11	0	2	23	24	32	1	1	3.7	.205	.284	.271	-.334	.214	.297	.280	.213	-12.6	76-3B -2
2005	MIL	MLB	35	212	29	15	0	4	23	23	22	4	2	5.4	.281	.373	.427	.090	.275	.366	.423	.273	8.7	41-3B -1
2006	*MIL*	*MLB*	*36*	*160*	*17*	*7*	*0*	*2*	*15*	*15*	*20*	*2*	*1*	*5.0*	*.252*	*.334*	*.356*	*-.113*	*.255*	*.335*	*.365*	*.241*	*0.0*	*42-3B -2*

Breakout: 38%   *Improve: 56%*   *Collapse: 30%*   *Attrition: 47%*   *Comparables: Don Hoak, Ryne Sandberg, Bob Kennedy*

Branyan's mirror image on the roster—he's a right-handed contact hitter, not a lefty swing-and-miss type. Credit Melvin for resurrecting Cirillo at all; Milwaukee would have had a pretty sweet third base platoon if Bill Hall hadn't made some noise and claimed so much playing time. Cirillo still makes for a handy spot-starter against tough lefties, but beyond crediting Yost for using him in a role where he could do some good—.400/.484/.636 vs. LHPs—he's not somebody you can plug into the lineup if a starter breaks down.

BRADY CLARK   **OF**   **Bats: R Throws: R**   Height: 6′ 2″   Weight: 190   Born: April 18, 1973   Age: 33

YEAR	TM	LVL	AGE	PA	R	2B	3B	HR	RBI	BB	SO	SB	CS	SPEED	BA	OBP	SLG	MLVR	EQBA	EQOBP	EQSLG	EQA	VORP	DEFENSE	
2003	MIL	MLB	30	352	33	21	1	6	40	21	40	13	2	5.4	.273	.330	.403	-.019	.269	.323	.402	.260	3.9	53-RF -2	17-LF -2
2004	MIL	MLB	31	418	41	18	1	7	46	53	48	15	8	5.0	.280	.385	.397	.094	.277	.379	.390	.273	14.5	88-RF 0	
2005	MIL	MLB	32	666	94	31	1	13	53	47	55	10	13	4.2	.306	.372	.426	.120	.305	.370	.430	.272	29.0	144-CF 7	
2006	*MIL*	*MLB*	*33*	*559*	*67*	*29*	*2*	*9*	*59*	*45*	*55*	*9*	*5*	*4.6*	*.281*	*.349*	*.402*	*-.007*	*.285*	*.350*	*.412*	*.259*	*15.1*	*131-CF -1*	

Breakout: 13%   *Improve: 37%*   *Collapse: 35%*   *Attrition: 9%*   *Comparables: Gary Ward, Brian Jordan, Keith Moreland*

It's a pity he had to waste a good portion of a potentially solid career while waiting for the Reds to notice him, but Clark has managed to salvage something with the Brewers. Useful enough as a regular, Clark is the journeyman placeholder who, unlike Overbay or Spivey or their ilk, might not have to worry about the competition. He can handle center well enough, and the organization doesn't have a premium centerfield prospect ready for prime time.

CALLIX CRABBE   **2B**   **Bats: B Throws: R**   Height: 5′ 8″   Weight: 190   Born: February 14, 1983   Age: 23

YEAR	TM	LVL	AGE	PA	R	2B	3B	HR	RBI	BB	SO	SB	CS	SPEED	BA	OBP	SLG	MLVR	EQBA	EQOBP	EQSLG	EQA	VORP	DEFENSE
2003	BLT	A	20	539	79	25	6	1	46	68	52	25	9	6.9	.260	.356	.346	.029	.235	.315	.331	.234	-7.4	112-2B 5
2004	HDS	A+	21	610	89	26	11	7	62	59	64	37	11	7.2	.291	.366	.419	-.015	.226	.292	.323	.224	-18.0	132-2B -10
2005	HUN	AA	22	455	42	15	4	1	33	65	65	18	6	5.2	.243	.354	.310	-.115	.211	.308	.272	.220	-19.9	104-2B 10
2006	*MIL*	*MLB*	*23*	*428*	*46*	*18*	*2*	*1*	*27*	*43*	*61*	*12*	*4*	*4.9*	*.237*	*.318*	*.310*	*-.208*	*.240*	*.319*	*.318*	*.224*	*-2.0*	*102-2B -3*

Breakout: 31%   *Improve: 57%*   *Collapse: 19%*   *Attrition: 13%*   *Comparables: Nick Punto, Julio Cruz, Blake Blasi*

He's not Asterix's previous sidekick, embittered by Obelix moving in on his shot at stardom, nor has he ever appeared in an episode of Flash Gordon or antagonized Harry Potter. In fact, he's never antagonized anyone, including pitchers, which is why Crabbe might be doomed to be nothing more than delightfully monikered.

ENRIQUE CRUZ   **INF**   **Bats: R Throws: R**   Height: 6′ 1″   Weight: 180   Born: November 21, 1981   Age: 24

YEAR	TM	LVL	AGE	PA	R	2B	3B	HR	RBI	BB	SO	SB	CS	SPEED	BA	OBP	SLG	MLVR	EQBA	EQOBP	EQSLG	EQA	VORP	DEFENSE
2003	MIL	MLB	21	76	6	1	0	0	2	4	30	0	0	4.0	.085	.145	.099	-.835	.085	.145	.099	.105	-12.0	
2004	HDS	A+	22	403	53	19	0	17	65	36	82	12	7	4.4	.283	.347	.478	.028	.211	.271	.351	.220	-10.1	94-SS -7
2004	HUN	AA	22	116	14	3	1	2	5	14	37	2	1	5.6	.188	.284	.297	-.243	.175	.259	.282	.201	-7.8	29-SS -1
2005	HUN	AA	23	539	68	34	3	14	60	37	107	4	4	4.5	.300	.354	.466	.132	.265	.311	.426	.250	19.1	134-SS -12
2006	*MIL*	*MLB*	*24*	*450*	*44*	*22*	*1*	*10*	*46*	*29*	*107*	*3*	*2*	*4.1*	*.234*	*.289*	*.364*	*-.192*	*.237*	*.290*	*.373*	*.220*	*0.0*	*107-SS -4*

Breakout: 30%   *Improve: 56%*   *Collapse: 23%*   *Attrition: 9%*   *Comparables: Brant Ust, Dan Uggla, Tim Olson*

The former Rule 5 pick took the step forward he needed to show that he's has recovered from a wasted 2003, when he rotted on the Brewers' bench. It doesn't look like he'll stick at short, but teams can always use a utility infielder with a little bit of pop. If not, he'll always have memories of that year spent watching the game instead of playing it. He crushed lefties to the tune of .367/.419/.582, which might help.

NELSON CRUZ   **RF**   **Bats: R Throws: R**   Height: 6′ 3″   Weight: 175   Born: July 1, 1980   Age: 26

YEAR	TM	LVL	AGE	PA	R	2B	3B	HR	RBI	BB	SO	SB	CS	SPEED	BA	OBP	SLG	MLVR	EQBA	EQOBP	EQSLG	EQA	VORP	DEFENSE			
2003	KNC	A	23	514	65	26	2	20	85	29	128	10	5	5.2	.238	.292	.430	.064	.207	.247	.384	.217	-32.7	106-RF	8	17-CF	1
2004	MOD	A+	24	290	54	27	1	11	52	24	73	8	4	5.2	.345	.407	.582	.436	.280	.334	.461	.271	6.2	47-LF	5	23-RF	1
2004	MID	AA	24	289	51	14	2	14	46	26	69	8	3	5.8	.313	.377	.542	.293	.279	.338	.484	.277	10.3	54-RF	5		
2005	HUN	AA	25	286	45	19	0	16	54	31	71	10	3	4.8	.306	.388	.577	.335	.249	.322	.468	.269	4.3	65-RF	-2		
2005	NAS	AAA	25	246	33	13	0	11	27	30	62	9	4	4.6	.269	.382	.490	.181	.245	.343	.433	.267	2.7	53-RF	6		
2006	MIL	MLB	26	479	59	24	1	20	66	42	129	9	3	4.3	.242	.316	.446	-.035	.246	.317	.457	.257	3.4	113-RF	2		

Breakout: 21%   Improve: 46%   Collapse: 23%   Attrition: 15%   Comparables: Jim Chamblee, Alex Escobar, Josh Bonifay

Cruz capped a breakout season by winning the PCL Championship Series MVP and earning his first big league call-up. He has power to all fields, but some fuss that he's too fence-minded at the plate. In the field, he won't win any Gold Gloves, but his arm is strong enough to deter baserunners. The bad news is that he's not a young prospect, but his age is what helped make him available from Oakland in the first place, so he can't really afford to wait around for either Lee or Jenkins to get out of his way.

ALCIDES ESCOBAR   **SS**   **Bats: R Throws: R**   Height: 6′ 1″   Weight: 155   Born: December 16, 1986   Age: 19

YEAR	TM	LVL	AGE	PA	R	2B	3B	HR	RBI	BB	SO	SB	CS	SPEED	BA	OBP	SLG	MLVR	EQBA	EQOBP	EQSLG	EQA	VORP	DEFENSE	
2004	HEL	Rk	17	255	38	8	0	2	24	20	44	20	9	6.3	.281	.345	.342	-.147	.223	.258	.263	.194	-29.4	65-SS	9
2005	WVA	A	18	551	80	25	8	2	36	20	90	30	13	7.7	.271	.305	.362	-.039	.251	.275	.331	.218	-14.1	120-SS	2
2006	MIL	MLB	19	517	55	24	5	2	37	18	85	22	9	5.9	.248	.279	.328	-.249	.252	.280	.337	.209	-5.3	122-SS	1

Breakout: 48%   Improve: 61%   Collapse: 23%   Attrition: 8%   Comparables: Joaquin Arias, Luis Rivas, Carlos Rodriguez

How confident are the Brewers that they've got something here? Though Escobar hasn't played above the lowest full-season level, they made him the youngest player assigned to this winter's Arizona Fall League, where he was not over-matched against far more advanced prospects. If his learning curve matches his precocity, you may well see him on our Top Prospects list next year. That said, he still needs to improve his command of the strike zone, but the Brewers aren't worried (yet), citing his improving pitch identification skills. Afield, he's got the range and arm for a shortstop.

PRINCE FIELDER   **1B**   **Bats: L Throws: R**   Height: 6′ 0″   Weight: 260   Born: May 9, 1984   Age: 22

YEAR	TM	LVL	AGE	PA	R	2B	3B	HR	RBI	BB	SO	SB	CS	SPEED	BA	OBP	SLG	MLVR	EQBA	EQOBP	EQSLG	EQA	VORP	DEFENSE	
2003	BLT	A	19	594	81	22	2	27	112	71	80	2	1	3.5	.313	.409	.526	.357	.269	.348	.475	.280	24.1	125-1B	-10
2004	HUN	AA	20	577	70	29	1	23	78	65	93	11	7	4.5	.272	.366	.473	.161	.241	.325	.424	.258	1.7	132-1B	-15
2005	NAS	AAA	21	441	68	21	0	28	86	54	93	8	5	4.0	.291	.388	.569	.326	.267	.353	.504	.287	22.8	91-1B	-8
2005	MIL	MLB	21	62	2	4	0	2	10	2	17	0	0	3.0	.288	.306	.458	.044	.271	.290	.424	.244	2.0		
2006	MIL	MLB	22	537	68	25	1	26	83	54	112	5	2	4.2	.268	.349	.489	.096	.272	.350	.501	.280	21.0	126-1B	-5

Breakout: 30%   Improve: 59%   Collapse: 21%   Attrition: 6%   Comparables: Greg Luzinski, Hee Choi, Dernell Stenson

Fielder endured a homerless month in the early going, but got back on track once he stopped trying to pull everything and returned to being an all-fields hitter. That merited a June call-up to DH during interleague games, and he didn't embarrass himself. Unlike most young players with "old player's skills," Fielder's power is as much a product of his quick wrists as from mere bulk. Now that Overbay's been shipped out, Fielder's on the short list for obvious Rookie of the Year candidates, and while his PECOTA comparables underscore some important reservations about the long-term future of His Heftiness, he's going to be roly-poly fun for the next several years.

ANTHONY GWYNN   **CF**   **Bats: L Throws: R**   Height: 6′ 0″   Weight: 185   Born: October 4, 1982   Age: 23

YEAR	TM	LVL	AGE	PA	R	2B	3B	HR	RBI	BB	SO	SB	CS	SPEED	BA	OBP	SLG	MLVR	EQBA	EQOBP	EQSLG	EQA	VORP	DEFENSE	
2003	BLT	A	20	275	35	8	0	1	33	32	31	14	2	5.6	.280	.364	.326	.026	.232	.304	.277	.223	-13.5	61-CF	6
2004	HUN	AA	21	594	74	20	5	2	37	53	95	35	16	7.0	.243	.318	.311	-.141	.223	.288	.286	.213	-34.4	134-CF	-6
2005	HUN	AA	22	592	83	21	5	1	41	76	75	34	15	6.0	.271	.370	.338	-.037	.237	.323	.299	.231	-17.0	130-CF	-4
2006	MIL	MLB	23	451	47	18	3	1	29	42	69	15	6	5.3	.235	.312	.301	-.233	.239	.313	.309	.217	-10.2	107-CF	-2

Breakout: 30%   Improve: 54%   Collapse: 25%   Attrition: 16%   Comparables: Peter Bergeron, Darrell Dent, Goefrey Tomlinson

You can take the Seligs out of the Brewers, but there's still a little bit too much fascination with breeding and bloodlines in this organization. Gwynn fields like his father did in his younger and more svelte days, but unfortunately hits more like his uncle Chris. Combined, those skills make him more like one of the Goodwins than one of the Gwynns, like some one-man blend of those crummy Wonder Twins powers that never seemed to help the Justice League all that much. The best you can say is that he hit .287/.379/.366 against RHPs while getting neutered by lefties, so if he's lucky he could have an Orlando Palmeiro sort of career.

BILL HALL   **INF**   **Bats: R Throws: R**   Height: 6′ 0″   Weight: 170   Born: December 28, 1979   Age: 26

YEAR	TM	LVL	AGE	PA	R	2B	3B	HR	RBI	BB	SO	SB	CS	SPEED	BA	OBP	SLG	MLVR	EQBA	EQOBP	EQSLG	EQA	VORP	DEFENSE			
2003	IND	AAA	23	382	57	25	2	5	32	27	79	10	11	5.8	.282	.335	.407	.032	.264	.322	.391	.244	7.4	51-2B	-2	36-SS	-2
2003	MIL	MLB	23	151	23	9	2	5	20	7	28	1	2	5.9	.261	.298	.458	-.020	.257	.294	.451	.249	3.5	17-SS	1	15-2B	0
2004	MIL	MLB	24	413	43	20	3	9	53	20	119	12	6	6.5	.238	.276	.374	-.158	.236	.274	.369	.223	-2.6	47-2B	-7	34-SS	7
2005	MIL	MLB	25	544	69	39	6	17	62	39	103	18	6	6.3	.291	.342	.495	.156	.286	.339	.498	.282	36.2	56-SS	3	49-3B	-1
2006	*MIL*	*MLB*	*26*	*521*	*67*	*29*	*3*	*15*	*60*	*37*	*103*	*15*	*6*	*5.5*	*.268*	*.324*	*.439*	*-.010*	*.272*	*.325*	*.450*	*.258*	*18.0*	*123-SS*	*1*		

Breakout: 22%   *Improve: 42%*   *Collapse: 25%*   *Attrition: 11%*   *Comparables: Pat Kelly, Ty Wigginton, Andy Carey*

Hall's now in that interesting point in a career where you have to ask what his best possible use might be. He's too good to be just a utility infielder, but he doesn't hit well enough to be a reliable regular at third base. His numbers suggest he'd be a fine fit at shortstop for most teams, but the Brewers are, appropriately, more interested in Hardy.

J. J. HARDY   **SS**   **Bats: R Throws: R**   Height: 6′ 2″   Weight: 180   Born: August 19, 1982   Age: 23

YEAR	TM	LVL	AGE	PA	R	2B	3B	HR	RBI	BB	SO	SB	CS	SPEED	BA	OBP	SLG	MLVR	EQBA	EQOBP	EQSLG	EQA	VORP	DEFENSE	
2003	HUN	AA	20	481	67	26	0	12	62	58	54	6	4	4.5	.279	.368	.428	.147	.253	.332	.411	.258	18.4	106-SS	12
2004	IND	AAA	21	112	17	10	0	4	20	9	8	0	0	4.1	.277	.330	.495	.086	.234	.292	.414	.244	1.5	23-SS	1
2005	MIL	MLB	22	419	46	22	1	9	50	44	48	0	0	4.2	.247	.327	.384	-.059	.243	.325	.389	.250	8.8	106-SS	-1
2006	*MIL*	*MLB*	*23*	*486*	*54*	*25*	*1*	*13*	*57*	*49*	*54*	*1*	*1*	*4.4*	*.264*	*.342*	*.418*	*-.011*	*.268*	*.343*	*.428*	*.260*	*19.9*	*115-SS*	*4*

Breakout: 38%   *Improve: 59%*   *Collapse: 16%*   *Attrition: 15%*   *Comparables: Chris Gomez, Tucker Ashford, Jim Anderson*

Even setting aside the '04 season he lost to a shoulder injury, Hardy surprised everyone by adapting as well as he did to the league. It took some time to chip away the rust, as his first-half .187/.293/.267 numbers attest, but the Brewers didn't lose faith and Hardy rewarded them with a sizzling .308/.363/.503 after the All-Star break. Hardy's one of those players who is fun to watch, and is consistently credited with being a smart player in the field and on the bases. You shouldn't take the comparison to Gomez as bad news; Gomez got flaky and fragile later in life, but at 23, he was a promising shortstop. Hardy has better power potential and a reputation for excellent leatherwork, so look for a few All-Star games in his future.

COREY HART   **OF/3B**   **Bats: R Throws: R**   Height: 6′ 6″   Weight: 200   Born: March 24, 1982   Age: 24

YEAR	TM	LVL	AGE	PA	R	2B	3B	HR	RBI	BB	SO	SB	CS	SPEED	BA	OBP	SLG	MLVR	EQBA	EQOBP	EQSLG	EQA	VORP	DEFENSE			
2003	HUN	AA	21	535	70	40	1	13	94	28	101	25	8	6.1	.302	.340	.467	.180	.276	.307	.449	.260	20.9	114-3B	-9		
2004	IND	AAA	22	491	68	29	8	15	67	42	92	17	7	7.0	.282	.344	.486	.101	.256	.319	.435	.260	1.2	90-RF	-2		
2005	NAS	AAA	23	486	85	29	9	17	69	48	88	31	7	7.3	.308	.377	.536	.280	.286	.347	.479	.284	19.2	71-RF	5	29-LF	1
2005	MIL	MLB	23	63	9	2	1	2	7	6	11	2	0	6.4	.193	.270	.368	-.216	.193	.270	.368	.228	-1.4	11-CF	-1		
2006	*MIL*	*MLB*	*24*	*526*	*74*	*30*	*4*	*19*	*68*	*44*	*102*	*20*	*7*	*5.9*	*.272*	*.337*	*.475*	*.061*	*.276*	*.338*	*.487*	*.274*	*16.7*	*124-RF*	*0*		

Breakout: 28%   *Improve: 56%*   *Collapse: 18%*   *Attrition: 12%*   *Comparables: Andre Dawson, Dwight Evans, Lloyd Moseby*

Hart's career has been something of a mess. Even with his offensive output, the organization doesn't seem quite sure what to do with the speedy colossus. Drafted as a first baseman, they've tried him at third for three years, then moved him to the outfield, and now they might return him to third or use him as a four corners utilityman, sort of like a younger, more athletic edition of Branyan. The key thing to keep in mind is that he's young, can hit and hit well, and he's major-league ready right now. The Brewers pondered putting him between Lee and Jenkins in center instead of pushing them; this makes all sorts of sense if he can cover the ground. Random note: Hart could join Darryl Strawberry and Dave Winfield as the third player 6′6″ or taller to steal 20 bases in the modern era. If that tidbit shows up on SportsCenter, you heard it here first.

WES HELMS **3B/1B** **Bats: R Throws: R** Height: 6′ 4″ Weight: 230 Born: May 12, 1976 Age: 30

YEAR	TM	LVL	AGE	PA	R	2B	3B	HR	RBI	BB	SO	SB	CS	SPEED	BA	OBP	SLG	MLVR	EQBA	EQOBP	EQSLG	EQA	VORP	DEFENSE		
2003	MIL	MLB	27	536	56	21	0	23	67	43	131	0	1	3.5	.261	.330	.450	.040	.256	.325	.452	.265	20.1	127-3B -11		
2004	MIL	MLB	28	305	24	13	1	4	28	24	60	0	1	2.9	.263	.331	.361	-.064	.259	.326	.358	.241	-1.2	61-3B -7		
2005	MIL	MLB	29	188	18	13	1	4	24	14	30	0	1	3.7	.298	.356	.458	.137	.292	.349	.464	.278	8.8	20-3B 1	13-1B	1
2006	FLO	MLB	30	136	15	7	0	3	17	11	28	0	0	3.8	.253	.321	.399	-.078	.260	.326	.422	.250	2.6	36-3B -1		

Breakout: 9%   Improve: 29%   Collapse: 36%   Attrition: 41%   Comparables: Mike Blowers, Eduardo Perez, Greg Colbrunn

Now with Florida, where he'll get a crack at reprising the "veteran gamer, moxie included, no batteries required" role that he performed in Milwaukee. The question is whether he'll be asked to start, thereby allowing Miguel Cabrera to return to the outfield. If the Fish decide Jeremy Hermida isn't ready, Helms will probably start off with an everyday role, but he's more suited to pinch-hitting and spot starts versus lefties.

HERNAN IRIBARREN **2B** **Bats: L Throws: R** Height: 6′ 1″ Weight: 160 Born: June 29, 1984 Age: 22

YEAR	TM	LVL	AGE	PA	R	2B	3B	HR	RBI	BB	SO	SB	CS	SPEED	BA	OBP	SLG	MLVR	EQBA	EQOBP	EQSLG	EQA	VORP	DEFENSE
2005	WVA	A	21	547	72	15	8	4	48	51	99	38	15	7.1	.290	.360	.379	.090	.267	.323	.344	.242	0.9	121-2B 3
2006	MIL	MLB	22	516	61	21	6	3	38	38	104	22	8	5.2	.260	.319	.355	-.136	.263	.320	.364	.237	6.3	121-2B 1

Breakout: 7%   Improve: 33%   Collapse: 39%   Attrition: 10%   Comparables: Freddie Bynum, Derek Mann, Ramon Santiago

Labeled a prospect because the Brewers have so few of them, but Iribarren might yet work out. In some ways he's the prototypical second baseman: scrappy, solid rep with the glove, plus a good spray-hitting stroke. He has shown signs of being able to pull the ball and he'll need to develop that pop to have a job—with Weeks on hand there won't be an opening at second base for the next five years or so.

GEOFF JENKINS **OF** **Bats: L Throws: R** Height: 6′ 1″ Weight: 210 Born: July 21, 1974 Age: 31

YEAR	TM	LVL	AGE	PA	R	2B	3B	HR	RBI	BB	SO	SB	CS	SPEED	BA	OBP	SLG	MLVR	EQBA	EQOBP	EQSLG	EQA	VORP	DEFENSE
2003	MIL	MLB	28	554	81	30	2	28	95	58	120	0	0	4.2	.296	.375	.538	.257	.290	.368	.534	.301	34.1	121-LF -4
2004	MIL	MLB	29	681	88	36	6	27	93	46	152	3	1	4.8	.264	.325	.473	.083	.258	.317	.460	.264	14.6	152-LF -4
2005	MIL	MLB	30	618	87	42	1	25	86	56	138	0	0	3.8	.292	.375	.513	.235	.287	.368	.513	.297	40.9	140-RF 3
2006	MIL	MLB	31	590	70	32	2	24	86	53	131	1	1	4.2	.272	.347	.479	.084	.276	.348	.492	.277	19.6	138-RF -3

Breakout: 6%   Improve: 30%   Collapse: 31%   Attrition: 5%   Comparables: Walt Moryn, Mike Easler, Jim Northrup

While settling into the elder statesman role quite nicely, like Paul Molitor before him, Jenkins has dispensed with his former reputation for fragility. Melvin spent the offseason fending off rumors that he was shopping Jenkins or Lee, but both are nearing that part of their careers where they'll got a lot less valuable in a hurry, and the Brewers have worthwhile alternatives in Cruz and Hart. But where Lee's in his walk year, Jenkins has at least $15 million coming to him in this season and next, and another $8.5 million if they pick up his option for 2008. That, and his uncanny resemblance to Bret Favre—we're in Wisconsin, Toto, it matters—should keep him in place for the rest of the contract.

DAVID KRYNZEL **CF** **Bats: L Throws: L** Height: 6′ 1″ Weight: 180 Born: November 7, 1981 Age: 24

YEAR	TM	LVL	AGE	PA	R	2B	3B	HR	RBI	BB	SO	SB	CS	SPEED	BA	OBP	SLG	MLVR	EQBA	EQOBP	EQSLG	EQA	VORP	DEFENSE
2003	HUN	AA	21	526	72	13	11	2	34	60	119	43	21	8.2	.267	.357	.357	.032	.252	.330	.351	.246	-1.2	115-CF 8
2004	IND	AAA	22	284	36	10	4	6	26	20	63	10	8	6.5	.271	.327	.411	-.039	.248	.304	.372	.236	-2.5	62-CF 2
2005	NAS	AAA	23	503	71	25	7	11	51	43	138	24	8	7.3	.256	.324	.416	-.049	.240	.298	.377	.239	-5.7	106-CF -7
2006	MIL	MLB	24	437	56	21	6	9	40	35	111	17	7	6.2	.245	.312	.400	-.098	.249	.314	.410	.244	3.6	104-CF 0

Breakout: 36%   Improve: 56%   Collapse: 20%   Attrition: 15%   Comparables: Dave Martinez, Daryl Boston, Tito Francona

The prospect the organization likes to keep making excuses for, this time around it's a thumb injury that that killed off his hot start. It won't be the first time he's been unlucky with injuries, having lost time to a broken foot and an Ankiel curveball to the head, and he's followed it all up with breaking a clavicle in an offseason mini-bike accident that will get him off to a late start this spring. He did hit .264/.337/.456 against RHPs, so perhaps a platoon role would get him up to stay.

CARLOS LEE   **LF**   **Bats: R Throws: R**   Height: 6′ 2″   Weight: 202   Born: June 20, 1976   Age: 30

YEAR	TM	LVL	AGE	PA	R	2B	3B	HR	RBI	BB	SO	SB	CS	SPEED	BA	OBP	SLG	MLVR	EQBA	EQOBP	EQSLG	EQA	VORP	DEFENSE	
2003	CHA	MLB	27	671	100	35	1	31	113	37	91	18	4	5.4	.291	.331	.499	.121	.287	.332	.495	.280	27.5	150-LF	-2
2004	CHA	MLB	28	658	103	37	0	31	99	54	86	11	5	4.8	.305	.366	.525	.208	.301	.366	.522	.297	38.5	145-LF	15
2005	MIL	MLB	29	688	85	41	0	32	114	57	87	13	4	5.4	.265	.324	.487	.097	.260	.321	.488	.274	24.7	158-LF	-7
2006	*MIL*	*MLB*	*30*	*640*	*87*	*37*	*2*	*29*	*100*	*55*	*86*	*11*	*4*	*5.3*	*.282*	*.347*	*.506*	*.128*	*.286*	*.348*	*.519*	*.284*	*28.7*	*149-LF*	*-2*

Breakout: 23%   *Improve: 54%*   *Collapse: 18%*   *Attrition: 7%*   *Comparables: Ivan Calderon, Kevin McReynolds, Ted Kluszewski*

For as much power as Lee provided, and how that made the Lee-Podsednik swap work out as happily in Milwaukee as it did in Chicago, it wasn't that great a year. The thing about Lee's closest comparables is the worthy caution there: all three fell off of cliffs shortly after their thirtieth birthdays. Calderon and McReynolds took terrible care of themselves, while Klu simply couldn't stay healthy. There's no way to know if contemporary conditioning might keep Lee from joining them, but he's in his walk year, and going to seed now would cost him eight large over a few years.

CHRIS MAGRUDER   **OF**   **Bats: B Throws: R**   Height: 5′ 11″   Weight: 200   Born: April 26, 1977   Age: 29

YEAR	TM	LVL	AGE	PA	R	2B	3B	HR	RBI	BB	SO	SB	CS	SPEED	BA	OBP	SLG	MLVR	EQBA	EQOBP	EQSLG	EQA	VORP	DEFENSE			
2003	BUF	AAA	26	156	20	7	2	3	15	15	27	5	1	5.8	.328	.391	.474	.266	.303	.369	.441	.285	9.9	14-CF	0	12-RF	0
2004	IND	AAA	27	338	37	17	4	6	39	21	55	7	4	5.4	.272	.337	.413	-.018	.240	.298	.355	.230	-15.2	68-LF	1		
2004	MIL	MLB	27	100	11	6	1	2	10	8	21	0	1	4.6	.236	.310	.393	-.082	.233	.307	.389	.240	-1.0				
2005	MIL	MLB	28	151	16	9	0	2	13	7	33	3	0	5.4	.203	.265	.312	-.291	.207	.268	.321	.215	-6.7	17-RF	-1		
2006	*MIL*	*MLB*	*29*	*148*	*16*	*7*	*1*	*3*	*16*	*10*	*29*	*2*	*1*	*5.4*	*.250*	*.314*	*.378*	*-.120*	*.253*	*.315*	*.388*	*.238*	*-1.1*	*39-RF*	*0*		

Breakout: 27%   *Improve: 45%*   *Collapse: 33%*   *Attrition: 45%*   *Comparables: Thomas Howard, Jim Fairey, Willie Smith*

You can take a weak bat and tweener skills only so far, and now that Gabe Gross is in town, Magruder was appropriately outrighted. When you're a thirty-ish fifth outfielder without some signature skill that might get you a geijin stint in the Japanese Leagues, it's a hint that it's time to ponder what your life's work is really supposed to be.

DAMIAN MILLER   **C**   **Bats: R Throws: R**   Height: 6′ 3″   Weight: 210   Born: October 13, 1969   Age: 36

YEAR	TM	LVL	AGE	PA	R	2B	3B	HR	RBI	BB	SO	SB	CS	SPEED	BA	OBP	SLG	MLVR	EQBA	EQOBP	EQSLG	EQA	VORP	DEFENSE	
2003	CHN	MLB	33	393	34	19	1	9	36	39	91	1	0	3.8	.233	.310	.369	-.121	.231	.310	.372	.240	0.8	103-C	11
2004	OAK	MLB	34	440	39	25	0	9	58	39	87	0	1	2.5	.272	.339	.403	-.038	.269	.341	.407	.260	12.0	106-C	11
2005	MIL	MLB	35	429	50	25	1	9	43	37	94	0	1	3.7	.273	.340	.413	.029	.270	.339	.418	.262	17.0	103-C	0
2006	*MIL*	*MLB*	*36*	*280*	*25*	*14*	*1*	*7*	*31*	*25*	*57*	*0*	*0*	*3.3*	*.250*	*.320*	*.390*	*-.095*	*.253*	*.321*	*.400*	*.242*	*3.9*	*68-C*	*1*

Breakout: 13%   *Improve: 28%*   *Collapse: 38%*   *Attrition: 43%*   *Comparables: Terry Steinbach, Ray Murray, Bill Haselman*

The Brewers like to sign Wisconsin boys when possible, on the off chance that the inspiring example of a cheesehead made good might get a busload or two of fans in from Prairie du Chien or Egg Harbor on some summer night. Miller isn't a world-beater, but he isn't killing the Brewers . . . yet. But at his age, a complete breakdown becomes a very real risk, and behind him, they've got nothing.

CHAD MOELLER   **C**   **Bats: R Throws: R**   Height: 6′ 3″   Weight: 210   Born: February 18, 1975   Age: 31

YEAR	TM	LVL	AGE	PA	R	2B	3B	HR	RBI	BB	SO	SB	CS	SPEED	BA	OBP	SLG	MLVR	EQBA	EQOBP	EQSLG	EQA	VORP	DEFENSE	
2003	ARI	MLB	28	266	29	17	1	7	29	23	59	1	2	4.1	.268	.335	.435	-.001	.256	.325	.420	.255	6.9	66-C	-5
2004	MIL	MLB	29	343	25	13	1	5	27	21	74	0	1	3.3	.208	.265	.303	-.303	.206	.261	.300	.200	-15.0	92-C	5
2005	MIL	MLB	30	214	23	9	1	7	23	13	48	0	0	4.0	.206	.257	.367	-.226	.206	.260	.377	.220	-4.2	59-C	-1
2006	*MIL*	*MLB*	*31*	*191*	*16*	*9*	*1*	*5*	*20*	*13*	*40*	*0*	*0*	*3.5*	*.225*	*.283*	*.364*	*-.209*	*.229*	*.284*	*.373*	*.218*	*-2.3*	*49-C*	*-1*

Breakout: 28%   *Improve: 54%*   *Collapse: 22%*   *Attrition: 42%*   *Comparables: Ray Katt, Phil Roof, John Boccabella*

Speaking of nothing, the nicest thing you can say about Moeller is that he's a touch of Teutonic flavor in the most fair-haired, ruddy-cheeked, blue-eyed audience in Major League Baseball. That, and he can tell his friends he was one of the six guys sent to the Brewers in the Sexson trade, if very probably the least valuable.

BRAD NELSON   OF   Bats: L Throws: R   Height: 6' 2" Weight: 220 Born: December 23, 1982 Age: 23

YEAR	TM	LVL	AGE	PA	R	2B	3B	HR	RBI	BB	SO	SB	CS	SPEED	BA	OBP	SLG	MLVR	EQBA	EQOBP	EQSLG	EQA	VORP	DEFENSE	
2003	HDS	A+	20	182	23	9	1	1	18	12	22	2	2	4.1	.311	.363	.395	-.011	.246	.293	.321	.218	-9.5	30-1B	2
2003	HUN	AA	20	157	15	12	0	1	14	11	34	2	2	4.4	.210	.274	.315	-.184	.192	.242	.302	.194	-16.8	25-LF	-1
2004	HUN	AA	21	558	61	31	1	19	77	47	146	11	10	4.5	.254	.321	.434	.029	.225	.284	.388	.232	-25.3	103-LF -2 28-RF	1
2005	HUN	AA	22	238	27	8	1	6	38	26	42	1	2	3.9	.293	.370	.428	.097	.257	.324	.387	.249	-3.9	53-LF	-2
2005	NAS	AAA	22	329	50	16	2	7	39	45	74	4	5	5.1	.253	.359	.399	-.008	.236	.328	.357	.242	-9.6	54-LF -2 13-RF	1
2006	*MIL*	*MLB*	*23*	*497*	*52*	*25*	*2*	*12*	*55*	*43*	*110*	*4*	*3*	*4.7*	*.244*	*.313*	*.389*	*-.111*	*.247*	*.314*	*.399*	*.239*	*-4.7*	*117-LF -3*	

Breakout: 43% Improve: 59% Collapse: 19% Attrition: 12%   Comparables: Ollie Brown, Charlie Spikes, Andy Thompson

Once a highly-rated prospect, Nelson's been entirely overrun by Fielder's quick climb up chain, Hart's return to the out-field, and the acquisition of Cruz. There's nothing wrong with peaking at 19, as Nelson did in a .297/.353/.520 season at Beloit, it's just sort of a nuisance if you didn't hit the jackpot while doing so. Still, Nelson can hang in against righties and lefties. If he starts generating power from his fluid stroke, he'll have a future.

LYLE OVERBAY   1B   Bats: L Throws: L   Height: 6' 2" Weight: 225 Born: January 28, 1977 Age: 29

YEAR	TM	LVL	AGE	PA	R	2B	3B	HR	RBI	BB	SO	SB	CS	SPEED	BA	OBP	SLG	MLVR	EQBA	EQOBP	EQSLG	EQA	VORP	DEFENSE	
2003	ARI	MLB	26	293	23	20	0	4	28	35	67	1	0	3.4	.276	.365	.402	.015	.262	.354	.385	.263	4.0	67-1B	11
2004	MIL	MLB	27	668	83	53	1	16	87	81	128	2	1	4.2	.301	.385	.478	.222	.293	.378	.468	.292	42.6	152-1B	9
2005	MIL	MLB	28	621	80	34	1	19	72	78	98	1	0	4.2	.276	.367	.449	.123	.271	.364	.450	.282	23.5	143-1B	14
2006	*TOR*	*MLB*	*29*	*583*	*69*	*32*	*2*	*18*	*82*	*66*	*95*	*1*	*1*	*4.5*	*.280*	*.363*	*.458*	*.102*	*.278*	*.370*	*.459*	*.279*	*17.7*	*137-1B*	*8*

Breakout: 14% Improve: 42% Collapse: 21% Attrition: 8%   Comparables: Travis Lee, Doug Mientkiewicz, Norm Siebern

Melvin's mastery of knowing when to say "let's make a deal" strikes again, and Overbay's been sent to the Blue Jays, who apparently wanted an Olerud fix so bad they were willing to settle for Olerud Lite. The problem that Toronto will have to come to terms with is that they've brought him in hoping he'll build on what he did in 2004, when he's already into the downslope of what will only be an adequate sort of career. He's a nice player, but carrying him forces you to rely on getting serious power from other places in your lineup.

RICKIE WEEKS   2B   Bats: R Throws: R   Height: 6' 0" Weight: 195 Born: September 13, 1982 Age: 23

YEAR	TM	LVL	AGE	PA	R	2B	3B	HR	RBI	BB	SO	SB	CS	SPEED	BA	OBP	SLG	MLVR	EQBA	EQOBP	EQSLG	EQA	VORP	DEFENSE
2004	HUN	AA	21	565	67	35	6	8	42	55	107	11	12	5.2	.259	.366	.407	.070	.237	.326	.371	.245	4.6	128-2B -9
2005	NAS	AAA	22	246	43	14	9	12	48	28	51	10	1	6.7	.320	.435	.655	.561	.295	.391	.579	.321	30.3	54-2B -9
2005	MIL	MLB	22	412	56	13	2	13	42	40	96	15	2	5.8	.239	.333	.394	-.036	.238	.331	.398	.260	9.9	94-2B -7
2006	*MIL*	*MLB*	*23*	*562*	*75*	*31*	*4*	*18*	*68*	*59*	*113*	*14*	*6*	*5.3*	*.267*	*.361*	*.462*	*.080*	*.271*	*.362*	*.474*	*.280*	*31.1*	*132-2B -5*

Breakout: 28% Improve: 56% Collapse: 20% Attrition: 4%   Comparables: Eddie Yost, Dwight Evans, Chris Speier

Weeks is fun to watch, right down to the Sheffield-style bat waggle. Although the concerns about his defense persist, Weeks has improved enough to not be a serious problem, and his bat definitely offers enough promise to make any defensive hit worth taking. He almost had a great rookie season: Weeks was hitting .259/.351/.453 as late as August 18, but he was awful down the stretch. After the season, it was announced that he'd played out the year with a badly injured thumb. One of the more subtle forms of racism is the way in which African-American players don't get credited for being scrappy, but when a blue chip prospect makes that sort of sacrifice, it would seem clear that he's a gamer. At any rate, setting aside the decision to play through an injury, PECOTA has every reason to be as optimistic about him as it is.

PITCHERS

MIKE ADAMS   Bats: R Throws: R   Height: 6' 5" Weight: 190 Born: July 29, 1978 Age: 27

YEAR	TM	LVL	AGE	W	L	SV	G	GS	IP	H	BB	SO	HR	GB%	BABIP	STUFF	WHIP	ERA	PERA	EQERA	EQH9	EQBB9	EQSO9	EQHR9	VORP	WXRL
2003	HUN	AA	24	3	7	14	45	2	74.3	58	33	83	6	—	.271	-17	1.22	3.15	5.77	5.24	9.2	4.7	6.8	1.7	2.7	—
2004	IND	AAA	25	2	0	0	10	2	31.0	23	4	37	3	—	.282	24	0.87	2.61	3.60	3.30	7.5	1.2	8.4	1.2	7.7	—
2004	MIL	MLB	25	2	3	0	46	0	53.0	50	14	39	5	43%	.285	3	1.21	3.40	4.13	3.44	8.8	2.2	6.0	0.9	11.9	0.8
2005	MIL	MLB	26	0	1	1	13	0	13.3	12	10	14	2	35%	.286	2	1.65	2.71	5.40	2.70	8.1	6.1	8.8	1.4	4.2	-0.2
2005	NAS	AAA	26	3	4	2	26	0	36.0	35	12	45	3	61%	.376	5	1.31	5.75	4.08	6.11	8.9	3.3	7.9	1.0	-2.0	—
2006	*MIL*	*MLB*	*27*	*2*	*2*	*2*	*44*	*1*	*46.3*	*44*	*20*	*39*	*5*	*45%*	*.289*	*1*	*1.38*	*4.23*	*4.54*	*5.11*	*8.6*	*3.4*	*6.8*	*1.1*	*4.7*	*0.4*

Breakout: 15% Improve: 36% Collapse: 39% Attrition: 31%   Comparables: Tim Burke, Xavier Hernandez, Jerrod Riggan

Every fight has a loser, whether it's Ali-Frazier, Douglas-Lincoln, or Bob Barker-Adam Sandler. The contest for the closer's role between Adams and Turnbow might have initially resembled the latter, but both are useful major league pitchers. The demotion to improve the command of his fastball ended up being for the season when his shoulder acted up, but he's supposed to fine, and if he ever got consistent with his slider, he could become a dominant reliever.

JEFF BENNETT   Bats: R   Throws: R   Height: 6' 3"   Weight: 200   Born: June 10, 1980   Age: 26

YEAR	TM	LVL	AGE	W	L	SV	G	GS	IP	H	BB	SO	HR	GB%	BABIP	STUFF	WHIP	ERA	PERA	EQERA	EQH9	EQBB9	EQSO9	EQHR9	VORP	WXRL
2003	ALT	AA	23	4	4	1	33	2	59.7	45	23	62	2	—	.269	8	1.14	2.71	3.97	4.76	7.8	4.1	7.3	0.6	5.3	—
2003	NAS	AAA	23	1	3	0	9	5	23.3	26	12	16	4	—	.290	-26	1.63	6.57	7.25	8.46	10.9	5.2	5.2	2.4	-7.1	—
2004	MIL	MLB	24	1	5	0	60	0	71.3	78	26	45	12	47%	.295	-17	1.46	4.80	5.30	5.05	9.8	3.0	5.0	1.4	1.2	0.3
2005	NAS	AAA	25	2	3	13	49	0	62.3	44	25	56	6	52%	.236	-8	1.11	3.03	5.06	4.14	7.8	4.0	6.0	1.1	9.5	—
2006	*ATL*	*MLB*	*26*	*5*	*6*	*2*	*61*	*7*	*99.7*	*102*	*48*	*70*	*13*	*47%*	*.290*	*-6*	*1.50*	*4.89*	*5.25*	*5.24*	*9.1*	*3.9*	*5.8*	*1.2*	*3.4*	*0.5*

Breakout: 18%   Improve: 48%   Collapse: 21%   Attrition: 0%   Comparables: *John Daniels, Jeff Russell, Randy Moffitt*

Another of Melvin's Rule 5 explorations, Bennett got real playing time in an '04 mop-up role, then failed to impress with a season spent in the PCL. Signed to a minor league deal with the Braves, who will give him more chances to flash his mid-90s heat after he was repeatedly passed up by the Brewers last summer.

JOSE CAPELLAN   Bats: R   Throws: R   Height: 6' 3"   Weight: 170   Born: January 13, 1981   Age: 25

YEAR	TM	LVL	AGE	W	L	SV	G	GS	IP	H	BB	SO	HR	GB%	BABIP	STUFF	WHIP	ERA	PERA	EQERA	EQH9	EQBB9	EQSO9	EQHR9	VORP	WXRL
2003	ROM	A	22	1	2	0	14	12	47.3	43	19	32	2	—	.272	-23	1.31	3.81	5.48	7.11	9.5	4.7	3.7	1.0	-7.4	—
2004	MYR	A+	23	5	1	0	8	8	46.3	27	11	62	0	—	.260	35	0.82	1.94	2.93	4.19	7.1	2.7	8.2	0.2	6.7	—
2004	GRN	AA	23	5	1	0	9	8	50.3	53	19	53	1	—	.359	17	1.43	2.50	3.83	4.01	9.5	3.8	5.8	0.4	8.7	—
2004	RIC	AAA	23	4	2	0	7	7	43.0	33	15	37	0	—	.273	23	1.12	2.51	3.48	3.27	7.6	3.5	6.3	0.2	10.7	—
2005	NAS	AAA	24	5	3	6	36	12	90.7	88	42	76	4	44%	.319	3	1.43	3.87	4.42	4.62	8.7	4.3	5.5	0.5	9.8	—
2005	MIL	MLB	24	1	1	0	17	0	15.7	17	5	14	1	34%	.372	10	1.40	2.87	3.38	3.38	9.0	2.8	7.3	0.6	3.6	-0.5
2006	*MIL*	*MLB*	*25*	*3*	*5*	*1*	*47*	*6*	*71.0*	*72*	*35*	*53*	*9*	*42%*	*.293*	*-5*	*1.51*	*5.06*	*5.28*	*5.48*	*9.2*	*3.9*	*6.0*	*1.1*	*1.1*	*0.3*

Breakout: 13%   Improve: 28%   Collapse: 31%   Attrition: 6%   Comparables: *Bill Gogolewski, Eduardo Rodriguez, Bruce Howard*

After pushing speed guns into the triple-digit range as a Braves farmhand the year before, Capellan's struggles to throw his fastball with any velocity last spring came as an unwanted surprise. He also had problems throwing his curve and changeup for strikes, so the Brewers figured the best thing to do was to move him into the pen, if only to get his arm sound. That got his velocity back up into the mid-90s, and also earned him a late promotion to Milwaukee after posting a 1.44 ERA as a reliever in Nashville (as a starter, his ERA was 5.16). The Brewers haven't entirely given up on him as a starter, but if he shows up this spring unable to throw either the slider or curve for strikes, he'll still be an extra quality reliever, which isn't the worst thing in the world to have an extra of.

CHRIS CAPUANO   Bats: L   Throws: L   Height: 6' 2"   Weight: 220   Born: August 19, 1978   Age: 27

YEAR	TM	LVL	AGE	W	L	SV	G	GS	IP	H	BB	SO	HR	GB%	BABIP	STUFF	WHIP	ERA	PERA	EQERA	EQH9	EQBB9	EQSO9	EQHR9	VORP	WXRL
2003	TUC	AAA	24	9	5	0	23	23	142.7	133	43	108	9	—	.279	14	1.23	3.34	4.47	4.34	8.7	3.2	5.7	0.8	19.5	—
2003	ARI	MLB	24	2	4	0	9	5	33.0	27	11	23	3	51%	.267	5	1.15	4.64	4.50	4.78	8.4	2.8	5.9	0.8	2.9	0.2
2004	MIL	MLB	25	6	8	0	17	17	88.3	91	37	80	18	42%	.304	-1	1.45	4.99	5.30	5.30	9.4	3.5	7.2	1.7	1.0	1.5
2005	MIL	MLB	26	18	12	0	35	35	219.0	212	91	176	31	39%	.292	7	1.38	3.99	4.92	4.30	9.1	3.5	6.7	1.3	31.5	4.0
2006	*MIL*	*MLB*	*27*	*11*	*11*	*0*	*31*	*31*	*195.0*	*189*	*74*	*146*	*26*	*42%*	*.280*	*12*	*1.35*	*4.20*	*4.60*	*4.48*	*8.7*	*3.0*	*6.0*	*1.2*	*23.3*	*3.8*

Breakout: 20%   Improve: 62%   Collapse: 8%   Attrition: 1%   Comparables: *Alex Kellner, Jim Deshaies, Jim Rooker*

The 18 wins are more a product of run support than his own talent, but Capuano does bring all sorts of goodies into play. He owns a particularly sweet pickoff move, which he used to lead the majors with a dozen pickoffs. He also finished third among pitchers in RBI with nine, behind Dontrelle Willis's 11 and Jason Marquis's 10. These aren't the exactly the little things people talk about when they say a guy "does the little things well," but they do help Capuano do just a little bit better than his raw stats suggest. He needs all the help he can get, because he isn't overpowering, relying more on guile and movement than gas.

DOUG DAVIS   **Bats: R Throws: L**   Height: 6' 4" Weight: 190 Born: September 21, 1975 Age: 30

YEAR	TM	LVL	AGE	W	L	SV	G	GS	IP	H	BB	SO	HR	GB%	BABIP	STUFF	WHIP	ERA	PERA	EQERA	EQH9	EQBB9	EQSO9	EQHR9	VORP	WXRL
2003	TOR	MLB	27	4	6	0	12	11	54.0	70	26	25	6	45%	.339	-10	1.78	5.00	5.30	4.98	10.3	4.2	3.9	1.0	3.7	1.1
2003	MIL	MLB	27	3	2	0	8	8	52.3	49	21	35	8	46%	.265	4	1.34	2.58	5.19	3.12	8.7	3.3	5.4	1.4	15.3	1.7
2004	MIL	MLB	28	12	12	0	34	34	207.3	192	79	166	14	51%	.298	26	1.31	3.39	3.88	3.49	8.5	3.1	6.4	0.6	46.3	6.5
2005	MIL	MLB	29	11	11	0	35	35	222.7	196	93	208	26	46%	.283	20	1.30	3.84	4.24	4.15	8.3	3.5	7.7	1.1	35.6	5.0
2006	*MIL*	*MLB*	*30*	*12*	*11*	*0*	*32*	*32*	*202.7*	*189*	*78*	*160*	*21*	*47%*	*.282*	*15*	*1.32*	*3.84*	*4.19*	*4.15*	*8.4*	*3.0*	*6.3*	*0.9*	*32.5*	*4.8*

Breakout: 6%   Improve: 51%   Collapse: 17%   Attrition: 1%   Comparables: Chris Short, Jack Harshman, Larry McWilliams

Nyah-ha-ha, it is he, Dishonest John, owner of the game's most dastardly facial hair (forgive us for trotting out a "Beany and Cecil" reference; we couldn't resist). After an outstanding 2004, some might have been disappointed with his 2005 season, but his strikeout rate improved, and he proved he's durable. All he needs to do to be a great #2 behind Sheets is cut his home run rate back down. If Capuano is slow, Davis is even slower, relying on slow curves and a cut fastball. If that keeps him short of stardom, it's still to Melvin's credit that he remembered Davis from the Rangers chain, promptly snagging him when the Jays lost their patience—inning eaters usually aren't this easy to find. Davis gave the Brewers 23 quality starts last year (one was blown in the 7th), and anyone who can crank out winnable games at that clip is a building block.

KANE DAVIS   **Bats: R Throws: R**   Height: 6' 3" Weight: 190 Born: June 25, 1975 Age: 31

YEAR	TM	LVL	AGE	W	L	SV	G	GS	IP	H	BB	SO	HR	GB%	BABIP	STUFF	WHIP	ERA	PERA	EQERA	EQH9	EQBB9	EQSO9	EQHR9	VORP	WXRL
2005	NAS	AAA	30	4	2	1	45	0	62.7	49	23	81	5	52%	.312	6	1.15	2.44	4.22	3.92	8.0	3.8	8.0	1.1	11.1	—
2005	MIL	MLB	30	1	1	0	15	0	16.7	10	10	11	2	43%	.170	-11	1.20	2.69	5.06	3.38	7.3	5.1	5.6	1.1	4.3	0.0
2006	*MIL*	*MLB*	*31*	*2*	*3*	*2*	*53*	*1*	*49.3*	*48*	*27*	*43*	*6*	*45%*	*.295*	*-4*	*1.52*	*4.81*	*5.08*	*5.42*	*8.7*	*4.4*	*6.9*	*1.1*	*1.9*	*0.2*

Breakout: 16%   Improve: 39%   Collapse: 30%   Attrition: 14%   Comparables: Turk Wendell, Vicente Romo, Willard Schmidt

One of the nice things about relief pitching is that you really can find good help among the undead. Case in point, Kane Davis, a reliever straight from the mind of George Romero. Getting his only real break in Colorado in 2001, elbow surgery, not even a visit to the independent leagues could kill him. He's being counted on this spring, a little bit of tenderness he's totally unused to. Let's hope it isn't the one thing that stops him.

JORGE DE LA ROSA   **Bats: L Throws: L**   Height: 6' 1" Weight: 190 Born: April 5, 1981 Age: 25

YEAR	TM	LVL	AGE	W	L	SV	G	GS	IP	H	BB	SO	HR	GB%	BABIP	STUFF	WHIP	ERA	PERA	EQERA	EQH9	EQBB9	EQSO9	EQHR9	VORP	WXRL
2003	PME	AA	22	6	3	1	22	20	99.7	87	36	102	6	—	.291	15	1.23	2.80	4.42	4.33	8.7	3.8	7.2	0.9	13.5	—
2003	PAW	AAA	22	1	2	0	5	5	24.0	27	12	17	0	—	.329	-1	1.62	3.75	4.56	5.70	9.5	5.3	4.9	0.4	-0.3	—
2004	IND	AAA	23	5	6	0	20	20	85.7	80	36	86	9	—	.305	8	1.35	4.52	4.70	4.80	8.6	4.1	7.2	1.1	7.5	—
2004	MIL	MLB	23	0	3	0	5	5	22.7	29	14	5	1	53%	.318	-28	1.90	6.34	5.40	6.94	10.8	5.0	1.5	0.4	-5.9	-0.3
2005	MIL	MLB	24	2	2	0	38	0	42.3	48	38	42	1	52%	.382	2	2.03	4.47	4.26	4.87	9.1	7.1	7.7	0.2	2.8	-0.1
2006	*MIL*	*MLB*	*25*	*2*	*3*	*1*	*40*	*2*	*50.0*	*48*	*31*	*45*	*4*	*48%*	*.307*	*1*	*1.59*	*4.60*	*5.06*	*5.44*	*8.7*	*4.9*	*7.3*	*0.8*	*2.8*	*0.3*

Breakout: 28%   Improve: 50%   Collapse: 24%   Attrition: 27%   Comparables: Neal Cotts, Chuck McElroy, Darold Knowles

He was out of options coming into 2005, which put him on the staff despite obvious questions of whether he could handle it. He didn't, as the subtleties of a situational role seemed lost on him as he failed to torch lefty hitters with his mid-90s heat. Certain truths about life on this planet involve bilateral symmetry, reproduction (sex not required), and the constant demand for lefty relief help. Mr. de la Rosa racks up enough strikeouts to keep the Brewers interested, at least until they've decided what Dana Eveland's role will be.

TIMOTHY DILLARD   **Bats: B Throws: R**   Height: 6' 4" Weight: 200 Born: July 19, 1983 Age: 22

YEAR	TM	LVL	AGE	W	L	SV	G	GS	IP	H	BB	SO	HR	GB%	BABIP	STUFF	WHIP	ERA	PERA	EQERA	EQH9	EQBB9	EQSO9	EQHR9	VORP	WXRL
2004	BLT	A	20	2	5	10	43	1	77.7	88	22	61	4	—	.323	-14	1.42	3.94	5.16	7.08	11.0	3.4	4.1	1.0	-12.3	—
2005	BRV	A+	21	12	10	0	28	28	185.3	150	31	128	9	57%	.258	9	0.98	2.48	4.56	4.82	9.0	2.0	4.1	0.9	15.1	—
2006	*MIL*	*MLB*	*22*	*8*	*10*	*0*	*27*	*25*	*150.0*	*164*	*49*	*80*	*18*	*53%*	*.295*	*2*	*1.42*	*4.95*	*5.04*	*5.38*	*9.9*	*2.6*	*4.3*	*1.0*	*2.8*	*1.4*

Breakout: 11%   Improve: 48%   Collapse: 10%   Attrition: 0%   Comparables: Sergio Mitre, Nathan Kent, Shawn Sedlacek

A draft-and-follow signed out of a Mississippi community college, where Dillard had been catching. Naturally, that makes him a bit rough on the finer points of what he's supposed to do on the mound, but he throws into the low 90s and owns a nifty sinker. Those are the things you have to have; you can learn the rest. He might project to better growth if he continues to pick up on his new trade.

DANA EVELAND   **Bats: L   Throws: L**   Height: 6' 1"   Weight: 220   Born: October 29, 1983   Age: 22

YEAR	TM	LVL	AGE	W	L	SV	G	GS	IP	H	BB	SO	HR	GB%	BABIP	STUFF	WHIP	ERA	PERA	EQERA	EQH9	EQBB9	EQSO9	EQHR9	VORP	WXRL
2004	BLT	A	20	9	6	2	22	16	117.3	108	24	119	8	—	.307	4	1.13	2.84	4.88	5.45	10.0	2.4	5.3	1.3	1.8	—
2004	HUN	AA	20	0	2	0	4	4	23.7	23	4	14	0	—	.291	11	1.14	2.28	3.91	3.91	9.4	1.6	3.5	0.4	4.3	—
2005	HUN	AA	21	10	4	0	18	18	109.0	96	38	98	4	62%	.304	21	1.23	2.72	4.25	4.16	8.3	3.4	5.5	0.6	17.0	—
2005	MIL	MLB	21	1	1	1	27	0	31.7	40	18	23	2	53%	.376	-3	1.83	5.96	4.36	5.73	10.1	4.6	5.7	0.5	-1.6	0.7
2006	*MIL*	*MLB*	*22*	*6*	*8*	*1*	*45*	*17*	*111.3*	*118*	*48*	*78*	*11*	*54%*	*.305*	*0*	*1.48*	*4.77*	*4.98*	*5.26*	*9.5*	*3.4*	*5.6*	*0.9*	*4.3*	*1.0*

Breakout: 9%   Improve: 43%   Collapse: 19%   Attrition: 0%   Comparables: Manny Parra, Jason Marquis, Macay McBride

A particular favorite of pitching coach Mike Maddux, but then who doesn't like a hard-throwing lefty? Eveland also mixes in a particularly sharp slider, so it seems a shame that the Brewers are already leaning towards making him a situational reliever. On the other hand, his chunky build could be the source of future problems; Eveland's AFL assignment ended early after he hurt his knee. Weight can make knee injuries, particularly serious for a pitcher (Chris Bosio, anyone?).

YOVANI GALLARDO   **Bats: R   Throws: R**   Height: 6' 2"   Weight: 190   Born: February 27, 1986   Age: 20

YEAR	TM	LVL	AGE	W	L	SV	G	GS	IP	H	BB	SO	HR	GB%	BABIP	STUFF	WHIP	ERA	PERA	EQERA	EQH9	EQBB9	EQSO9	EQHR9	VORP	WXRL
2005	WVA	A	19	8	3	1	26	18	121.3	100	51	110	5	53%	.297	13	1.24	2.75	4.84	4.84	8.7	4.6	5.2	0.7	9.7	—
2006	*MIL*	*MLB*	*20*	*6*	*9*	*0*	*25*	*21*	*120.0*	*119*	*66*	*86*	*15*	*51%*	*.288*	*4*	*1.54*	*5.11*	*5.35*	*5.58*	*9.0*	*4.3*	*5.7*	*1.1*	*0.7*	*0.9*

Breakout: 10%   Improve: 40%   Collapse: 21%   Attrition: 0%   Comparables: Hayden Penn, Gavin Floyd, Brandon League

Picked the round after Mark Rogers in the 2004 draft, but already looking by far the better pick. He's got good command, velocity, and five pitches he can throw for strikes. A good bet to reach Double-A in '06, his projection demonstrates how exceptionally well he already projects and compares despite his relative lack of pro experience.

RICK HELLING   **Bats: R   Throws: R**   Height: 6' 3"   Weight: 220   Born: December 15, 1970   Age: 35

YEAR	TM	LVL	AGE	W	L	SV	G	GS	IP	H	BB	SO	HR	GB%	BABIP	STUFF	WHIP	ERA	PERA	EQERA	EQH9	EQBB9	EQSO9	EQHR9	VORP	WXRL
2003	BAL	MLB	32	7	8	0	24	24	138.7	156	40	86	30	38%	.294	-13	1.41	5.71	5.62	5.49	9.9	2.5	5.4	1.8	2.6	1.8
2003	FLO	MLB	32	1	0	0	11	0	16.3	11	5	12	1	50%	.227	8	0.98	0.55	4.02	1.15	6.9	2.9	6.3	0.6	9.2	0.8
2005	NAS	AAA	34	9	3	0	21	21	130.7	128	50	105	12	43%	.303	-11	1.36	4.13	5.66	6.31	9.7	4.3	4.6	1.2	-9.8	—
2005	MIL	MLB	34	3	1	0	15	7	49.0	39	18	42	2	31%	.276	21	1.16	2.39	3.54	2.61	7.6	3.2	7.1	0.4	17.5	2.2
2006	*MIL*	*MLB*	*35*	*5*	*7*	*0*	*34*	*17*	*100.0*	*106*	*42*	*64*	*17*	*39%*	*.284*	*-10*	*1.48*	*5.15*	*5.56*	*5.58*	*9.6*	*3.3*	*5.1*	*1.5*	*1.7*	*0.7*

Breakout: 16%   Improve: 42%   Collapse: 21%   Attrition: 9%   Comparables: Pedro Astacio, Scott Sanders, Dwight Gooden

Another scrapheap discovery now counted on to give the Brewers significant innings. Having gotten over his frustrations at not catching a break in 2004, he seems like David Bush's chief challenger for the fifth slot in the rotation after rattling off five quality starts of the six he made in September '05. (In the one "non-quality" start he tossed five shutout innings.) Despite his age, he still has a bit of giddyup on his heater. If he loses out in the rotation fight, Helling still has the stuff to be a valuable setup man for Turnbow.

BEN HENDRICKSON   **Bats: R   Throws: R**   Height: 6' 4"   Weight: 190   Born: February 4, 1981   Age: 25

YEAR	TM	LVL	AGE	W	L	SV	G	GS	IP	H	BB	SO	HR	GB%	BABIP	STUFF	WHIP	ERA	PERA	EQERA	EQH9	EQBB9	EQSO9	EQHR9	VORP	WXRL
2003	HUN	AA	22	7	6	0	17	16	78.3	82	28	56	6	—	.298	-13	1.40	3.45	5.52	5.52	10.4	3.5	4.4	1.4	0.7	—
2004	IND	AAA	23	11	3	0	21	21	125.0	114	26	93	6	—	.290	26	1.12	2.02	3.66	2.71	8.2	2.0	5.3	0.5	39.5	—
2004	MIL	MLB	23	1	8	0	10	9	46.3	58	20	29	6	53%	.342	-3	1.68	6.22	5.13	5.89	10.6	3.4	4.9	1.1	-4.7	0.1
2005	NAS	AAA	24	6	12	0	28	27	155.7	176	58	122	17	51%	.343	-4	1.50	4.97	5.17	5.86	9.9	3.4	5.1	1.2	-4.5	—
2006	*MIL*	*MLB*	*25*	*6*	*9*	*1*	*45*	*16*	*127.7*	*136*	*52*	*80*	*16*	*51%*	*.293*	*-5*	*1.47*	*4.94*	*5.19*	*5.42*	*9.6*	*3.2*	*5.0*	*1.1*	*3.0*	*0.9*

Breakout: 13%   Improve: 42%   Collapse: 23%   Attrition: 0%   Comparables: Brian Williams, Dave Goltz, Johnny Kucks

Not that you ever want to be compared to Dennis Tankersley, but Hendrickson seems to have a similar case of the yips when it comes to pitching in the big leagues. He's got a beautiful, big-bending curve that arcs out of a classic overhand delivery, but he's more spotty with his fastball and change. His giant step backwards in 2005 encouraged the Brewers to pick up Bush in the Overbay deal, but if Bush and Helling both falter, he has value within the organization as a fallback.

JUSTIN LEHR **Bats: R Throws: R** Height: 6' 1" Weight: 200 Born: August 3, 1977 Age: 28

YEAR	TM	LVL	AGE	W	L	SV	G	GS	IP	H	BB	SO	HR	GB%	BABIP	STUFF	WHIP	ERA	PERA	EQERA	EQH9	EQBB9	EQSO9	EQHR9	VORP	WXRL
2003	SAC	AAA	25	3	2	4	53	0	75.0	74	27	64	3	—	.306	1	1.35	3.72	4.32	5.05	9.0	3.9	6.3	0.6	4.5	—
2004	SAC	AAA	26	4	2	13	32	0	37.3	37	10	40	1	—	.330	10	1.26	2.65	3.38	3.86	8.4	2.7	6.8	0.2	7.2	—
2004	OAK	MLB	26	1	1	0	27	0	32.7	35	14	16	3	48%	.302	-15	1.50	5.23	4.96	4.96	9.6	3.6	4.1	0.8	4.2	0.2
2005	NAS	AAA	27	7	7	1	27	11	88.0	102	32	68	8	56%	.341	-10	1.52	3.99	4.93	5.44	10.1	3.5	4.8	1.0	1.6	—
2005	MIL	MLB	27	1	1	0	23	0	34.7	32	18	23	4	49%	.267	-11	1.44	3.89	5.24	4.98	8.9	4.5	5.5	1.0	2.4	-0.5
2006	*MIL*	*MLB*	*28*	*3*	*4*	*1*	*46*	*5*	*69.7*	*75*	*30*	*44*	*8*	*50%*	*.299*	*-10*	*1.52*	*4.98*	*5.32*	*5.53*	*9.8*	*3.4*	*5.1*	*1.1*	*1.6*	*0.2*

Breakout: 20%   Improve: 43%   Collapse: 30%   Attrition: 7%   Comparables: Neil Allen, Dickie Noles, Jim Hearn

"Panzer" might not be blitzing Poland anytime soon, let alone taking Nashville by storm. The Brewers will settle for letting him take his best shot at winning either the fifth starter's job or a middle relief gig. If he's been a moderately successful conversion project for a former catcher, that's about as high as his ceiling is going to go.

WES OBERMUELLER **Bats: R Throws: R** Height: 6' 2" Weight: 190 Born: December 22, 1976 Age: 29

YEAR	TM	LVL	AGE	W	L	SV	G	GS	IP	H	BB	SO	HR	GB%	BABIP	STUFF	WHIP	ERA	PERA	EQERA	EQH9	EQBB9	EQSO9	EQHR9	VORP	WXRL
2003	OMA	AAA	26	10	5	0	17	17	106.3	108	42	62	11	—	.274	-20	1.41	4.40	6.08	6.35	10.2	4.5	4.4	1.5	-8.4	—
2003	MIL	MLB	26	2	5	0	12	11	65.7	81	25	34	10	50%	.316	-8	1.61	5.07	5.51	5.10	10.5	3.1	4.2	1.3	2.2	1.3
2004	MIL	MLB	27	6	8	0	25	20	118.0	138	42	59	15	50%	.307	-8	1.53	5.80	5.07	5.45	10.1	2.9	3.9	1.1	-7.1	0.9
2005	MIL	MLB	28	1	4	0	23	8	65.0	74	36	33	7	45%	.310	-17	1.69	5.26	5.48	5.48	10.1	4.7	4.1	1.0	-1.4	0.5
2005	NAS	AAA	28	3	1	1	9	8	42.3	39	14	39	1	50%	.336	13	1.25	2.55	3.48	3.92	8.5	3.3	5.7	0.2	7.7	—
2006	*ATL*	*MLB*	*29*	*4*	*4*	*0*	*29*	*9*	*74.3*	*82*	*31*	*41*	*9*	*48%*	*.296*	*-10*	*1.51*	*4.90*	*5.23*	*5.86*	*9.7*	*3.3*	*4.6*	*1.0*	*2.6*	*0.5*

Breakout: 21%   Improve: 50%   Collapse: 30%   Attrition: 23%   Comparables: Mike Oquist, Ron Herbel, Galen Cisco

Traded to the Braves to allow Atlanta the petty satisfaction of ridding themselves of Danny Kolb, Obermueller had the good sense to re-sign with them in a minor league deal. After all, the Braves get some use out of some pretty skeevy journeymen in the back end of their staffs, so this may be his best shot at making something of himself. Even so, Obermueller's mere athleticism and lack of any bat-missing pitch should doom him to a summer spent in Richmond.

TOMOKAZU OHKA **Bats: R Throws: R** Height: 6' 1" Weight: 179 Born: March 18, 1976 Age: 30

YEAR	TM	LVL	AGE	W	L	SV	G	GS	IP	H	BB	SO	HR	GB%	BABIP	STUFF	WHIP	ERA	PERA	EQERA	EQH9	EQBB9	EQSO9	EQHR9	VORP	WXRL
2003	MON	MLB	27	10	12	0	34	34	199.0	233	45	118	24	49%	.318	6	1.40	4.16	4.49	4.71	10.1	1.8	4.8	1.0	28.0	5.0
2004	MON	MLB	28	3	7	0	15	15	84.7	98	20	38	11	45%	.299	-2	1.39	3.40	4.78	4.25	10.2	1.9	3.6	1.1	12.6	1.8
2005	WAS	MLB	29	4	3	0	10	9	54.0	44	27	17	6	42%	.220	-17	1.31	3.33	5.71	4.15	8.7	4.3	2.8	1.0	9.9	1.2
2005	MIL	MLB	29	7	6	0	22	20	126.3	145	28	81	16	42%	.313	6	1.37	4.35	4.45	4.59	10.0	1.8	5.2	1.1	13.6	2.2
2006	*MIL*	*MLB*	*30*	*9*	*10*	*0*	*31*	*26*	*164.0*	*175*	*44*	*92*	*22*	*44%*	*.285*	*2*	*1.34*	*4.33*	*4.70*	*4.70*	*9.6*	*2.1*	*4.5*	*1.2*	*16.8*	*2.9*

Breakout: 13%   Improve: 50%   Collapse: 18%   Attrition: 4%   Comparables: Jim Colborn, Rick Langford, Lew Burdette

The Nationals might have thought banishing him to Milwaukee for turning his back on Frank Robinson was Ohka's just dessert, but he'll end up thanking them for it. He makes for a nice fourth starter behind Sheets and the two lefties. He'll crank out quality starts a little more than half of the time, which makes getting him for rent-a-2B Junior Spivey simply sweet. Ohka can throw four different flavors of junk for strikes, and can be especially maddening for lefty hitters, keeping them waiting for the cookie that never comes.

MANNY PARRA **Bats: L Throws: L** Height: 6' 3" Weight: 200 Born: October 30, 1982 Age: 23

YEAR	TM	LVL	AGE	W	L	SV	G	GS	IP	H	BB	SO	HR	GB%	BABIP	STUFF	WHIP	ERA	PERA	EQERA	EQH9	EQBB9	EQSO9	EQHR9	VORP	WXRL
2003	BLT	A	20	11	2	0	23	23	138.7	127	24	117	9	—	.283	0	1.09	2.73	5.28	4.80	9.7	2.0	5.1	1.7	11.7	—
2004	HDS	A+	21	5	2	0	13	12	67.3	76	19	64	3	—	.351	10	1.41	3.48	4.37	5.16	9.1	3.2	5.2	0.7	3.3	—
2005	HUN	AA	22	5	6	0	16	16	91.0	111	21	86	4	59%	.374	17	1.45	3.96	3.91	5.18	10.1	2.2	5.5	0.7	4.3	—
2006	*MIL*	*MLB*	*23*	*8*	*10*	*0*	*29*	*23*	*143.0*	*151*	*47*	*92*	*17*	*54%*	*.294*	*6*	*1.38*	*4.63*	*4.80*	*5.03*	*9.5*	*2.6*	*5.2*	*1.1*	*8.2*	*1.8*

Breakout: 16%   Improve: 52%   Collapse: 6%   Attrition: 1%   Comparables: Billy Traber, Steve Trout, Tony Pena

He was shut down early when he required surgery on a fraying labrum, but the Brewers seem comfortable with the idea that he'll be ready by spring training. Let's face it: lefties who throw into the low 90s are worth the high hopes invested in them. If Parra succeeds in adding a splitter to his solid curve, he might end up with the assortment that helps him stick in a big league rotation.

JULIO SANTANA   **Bats: R**   **Throws: R**   Height: 6' 0"   Weight: 220   Born: January 20, 1973   Age: 33

YEAR	TM	LVL	AGE	W	L	SV	G	GS	IP	H	BB	SO	HR	GB%	BABIP	STUFF	WHIP	ERA	PERA	EQERA	EQH9	EQBB9	EQSO9	EQHR9	VORP	WXRL
2005	MIL	MLB	32	3	5	1	41	0	42.0	34	19	49	6	34%	.283	14	1.26	4.50	4.10	4.54	7.8	3.9	9.7	1.3	4.6	0.1
2006	PHI	MLB	33	2	2	2	46	0	49.3	48	21	44	7	41%	.292	3	1.40	4.39	4.53	4.82	8.5	3.6	7.6	1.2	4.6	0.4

Breakout: 23%   Improve: 50%   Collapse: 25%   Attrition: 22%   Comparables: Aurelio Lopez, Don McMahon, John Wyatt

Two years of rehabbing his elbow and wandering to Japan and back might not have lined his pockets, but at least it put him back on big league radars. The Brewers took their chances with a lot of minor league journeymen last winter, and Santana was one of the ones who panned out, doing reasonably well in a last-chance saloon type of call-up. Signed to a minor league deal with Philly, where he'll have to fight to stick, but his recent success should help.

VICTOR SANTOS   **Bats: R**   **Throws: R**   Height: 6' 3"   Weight: 190   Born: October 2, 1976   Age: 29

YEAR	TM	LVL	AGE	W	L	SV	G	GS	IP	H	BB	SO	HR	GB%	BABIP	STUFF	WHIP	ERA	PERA	EQERA	EQH9	EQBB9	EQSO9	EQHR9	VORP	WXRL
2003	OKL	AAA	26	5	4	1	20	16	108.3	112	35	65	6	—	.290	0	1.36	3.41	4.68	5.45	9.3	3.5	4.3	0.8	1.8	—
2003	TEX	MLB	26	0	2	0	8	4	25.7	29	16	15	5	47%	.312	-20	1.75	7.00	6.58	6.23	9.7	5.5	5.2	1.7	-2.9	-0.1
2004	MIL	MLB	27	11	12	0	31	28	154.0	169	57	115	18	41%	.319	7	1.47	4.97	4.52	5.10	9.6	3.0	5.9	1.0	1.4	2.8
2005	MIL	MLB	28	4	13	0	29	24	141.7	153	60	89	20	43%	.289	-7	1.50	4.57	5.20	5.39	9.8	3.5	5.2	1.3	1.7	0.9
2006	PIT	MLB	29	6	9	0	31	19	125.7	134	46	77	15	44%	.293	0	1.43	4.68	4.91	5.17	9.4	3.0	5.1	1.0	8.3	1.6

Breakout: 24%   Improve: 62%   Collapse: 11%   Attrition: 6%   Comparables: Dave Wickersham, Mike Bielecki, Bruce Dal Canton

Basically a junkballer who spins an occasionally pretty curve, Santos lost his job once Helling was resurrected. Demand for fifth starters was up this past winter, though, as Santos was flipped from Milwaukee to K.C. to Pittsburgh during this winter's game of roster footsie, winding up a Pirate through the Rule 5 draft. He'll compete for a job, providing veteran adequacy in case the prospects don't pan out. He could always wind up being offered back to the Royals, where he'd do the same for them.

DENNIS SARFATE   **Bats: R**   **Throws: R**   Height: 6' 4"   Weight: 210   Born: April 9, 1981   Age: 25

YEAR	TM	LVL	AGE	W	L	SV	G	GS	IP	H	BB	SO	HR	GB%	BABIP	STUFF	WHIP	ERA	PERA	EQERA	EQH9	EQBB9	EQSO9	EQHR9	VORP	WXRL
2003	BLT	A	22	12	2	0	26	26	139.7	114	66	140	11	—	.270	-29	1.29	2.83	7.07	5.21	9.8	6.0	6.0	2.3	5.5	—
2004	HUN	AA	23	7	12	0	28	25	129.0	128	78	113	12	—	.316	-22	1.60	3.98	6.44	5.99	10.1	6.4	5.1	1.4	-5.3	—
2005	HUN	AA	24	9	9	0	24	24	130.0	120	59	110	13	43%	.292	-24	1.38	3.88	6.49	5.46	9.7	4.9	5.0	1.8	1.9	—
2006	MIL	MLB	25	4	8	0	28	17	101.7	110	66	69	20	40%	.287	-13	1.73	6.29	6.88	6.69	9.8	5.1	5.4	1.7	-11.2	-0.5

Breakout: 3%   Improve: 17%   Collapse: 44%   Attrition: 0%   Comparables: Luke Hudson, Ron Chiavacci, Luther Hackman

Although his control leaves a lot to be desired, Sarfate's not turning out all that badly. He can throw into the mid-90s, mixes in some good breaking stuff, and he can consistently repeat his delivery. He did well enough in Double-A, so he could wind up with a career, but PECOTA is savagely critical of his range of possibilities. Given that he throws pretty hard, a move into the pen might help.

BEN SHEETS   **Bats: R**   **Throws: R**   Height: 6' 1"   Weight: 195   Born: July 18, 1978   Age: 27

YEAR	TM	LVL	AGE	W	L	SV	G	GS	IP	H	BB	SO	HR	GB%	BABIP	STUFF	WHIP	ERA	PERA	EQERA	EQH9	EQBB9	EQSO9	EQHR9	VORP	WXRL
2003	MIL	MLB	24	11	13	0	34	34	220.7	232	43	157	29	46%	.299	11	1.25	4.44	4.28	4.64	9.2	1.6	5.7	1.1	18.5	2.8
2004	MIL	MLB	25	12	14	0	34	34	237.0	201	32	264	25	45%	.292	43	0.98	2.70	3.04	3.15	7.8	1.1	9.0	0.9	65.0	7.7
2005	MIL	MLB	26	10	9	0	22	22	156.7	142	25	141	19	38%	.281	26	1.07	3.33	3.72	3.78	8.4	1.3	7.5	1.1	32.1	4.1
2006	MIL	MLB	27	14	8	0	30	30	203.7	183	37	174	23	43%	.274	26	1.08	3.22	3.37	3.46	8.1	1.4	6.8	1.0	46.3	6.3

Breakout: 30%   Improve: 65%   Collapse: 3%   Attrition: 4%   Comparables: Javier Vazquez, Juan Marichal, Dennis Leonard

Sheets's superb curve is among the game's best acts of defiance against Newtonian physics, but last season, it was responsible for a season-ending back injury in August. He is expected to be fully recovered this spring, and his return to ace-dom is the key ingredient to any hope the Brewers might entertain for contending in 2006 instead of waiting for 2007. He can overpower people with the bender, a hard fastball, or with his recently developed mastery of a change. A little bit of run support and some belated recognition from the BBWAA, and you've got a great dark horse candidate for this year's Cy Young Award.

TY TAUBENHEIM **Bats: R Throws: R** Height: 6′ 5″ Weight: 200 Born: November 17, 1982 Age: 23

YEAR	TM	LVL	AGE	W	L	SV	G	GS	IP	H	BB	SO	HR	GB%	BABIP	STUFF	WHIP	ERA	PERA	EQERA	EQH9	EQBB9	EQSO9	EQHR9	VORP	WXRL
2003	HEL	Rk	20	6	1	1	14	0	50.3	47	3	44	3	—	.292	-3	0.99	2.15	4.99	5.18	9.6	0.7	3.9	1.5	2.3	—
2004	BLT	A	21	5	3	12	47	0	90.3	78	17	106	10	—	.300	-20	1.05	3.59	5.96	5.75	10.4	2.4	6.2	2.3	-1.4	—
2005	BRV	A+	22	10	2	0	16	16	106.0	86	26	75	7	45%	.262	-3	1.06	2.63	5.33	4.68	9.4	3.0	4.2	1.2	10.0	—
2005	HUN	AA	22	2	6	0	11	11	64.0	64	24	44	7	44%	.305	-15	1.38	4.36	6.16	5.58	9.8	3.8	4.3	1.8	0.1	—
2006	*TOR*	*MLB*	*23*	*7*	*11*	*0*	*28*	*25*	*142.7*	*172*	*47*	*73*	*29*	*43%*	*.296*	*-5*	*1.53*	*5.98*	*5.92*	*6.04*	*10.4*	*3.0*	*4.4*	*1.7*	*-5.1*	*0.5*

Breakout: 2%   Improve: 25%   Collapse: 32%   Attrition: 0%   Comparables: Peter Fisher, Daniel Curtis, Beau Hale

After being picked in the 19th round of the '03 draft, with the low expectations that engenders, Taubenheim managed to pitch his way all the way up to throw-in status, getting tacked onto the back end of the Overbay trade this winter. Toronto values its strike-throwers more than most, but Taubenheim is likely to get overlooked in their pitching-laden farm system.

DERRICK TURNBOW **Bats: R Throws: R** Height: 6′ 3″ Weight: 210 Born: January 25, 1978 Age: 28

YEAR	TM	LVL	AGE	W	L	SV	G	GS	IP	H	BB	SO	HR	GB%	BABIP	STUFF	WHIP	ERA	PERA	EQERA	EQH9	EQBB9	EQSO9	EQHR9	VORP	WXRL
2003	SLC	AAA	25	1	2	2	35	0	55.0	68	24	63	5	—	.382	0	1.67	5.73	4.53	6.14	10.0	4.5	8.1	1.1	-3.3	—
2004	SLC	AAA	26	2	6	6	46	3	74.7	75	42	56	8	—	.300	-24	1.57	5.06	5.89	5.15	8.7	5.9	4.9	1.1	3.7	—
2005	MIL	MLB	27	7	1	39	69	0	67.3	49	24	64	5	51%	.249	19	1.08	1.74	3.55	2.18	7.2	3.0	7.9	0.7	26.2	4.7
2006	*MIL*	*MLB*	*28*	*3*	*5*	*22*	*58*	*0*	*59.7*	*54*	*29*	*50*	*6*	*48%*	*.280*	*1*	*1.38*	*3.82*	*4.23*	*4.38*	*8.1*	*3.8*	*6.7*	*0.8*	*9.0*	*1.1*

Breakout: 9%   Improve: 22%   Collapse: 65%   Attrition: 15%   Comparables: Todd Jones, Luis Aloma, T. J. Mathews

For all you kids who miss the SATs, try this on for size: Kolb:Turnbow:closers:fungibility. To be fair, that doesn't give Turnbow his full due. Where Kolb had stuff and saves but not really the talent, Turnbow has the mid-90s moving fastball that fools people, and that's the skill makes saves more certain, not moxie. By WXRL, Turnbow's year rates as the fourth-best relief season by a Brewer history, behind only Tommy Murphy's 1972, Doug Jones's 1997, and Rollie Fingers's 1982. Even with Kolb's being returned to sender, the glory spot is Turnbow's for the immediate future.

CARLOS VILLANUEVA **Bats: S Throws: R** Height: 6′ 3″ Weight: 201 Born: November 28, 1983 Age: 22

YEAR	TM	LVL	AGE	W	L	SV	G	GS	IP	H	BB	SO	HR	GB%	BABIP	STUFF	WHIP	ERA	PERA	EQERA	EQH9	EQBB9	EQSO9	EQHR9	VORP	WXRL
2004	BLT	A	20	8	8	1	25	21	114.7	102	30	113	20	—	.259	-50	1.15	3.77	8.13	6.82	11.4	3.3	5.4	3.5	-14.0	—
2005	BRV	A+	21	8	1	0	21	21	112.3	78	32	124	11	42%	.252	0	0.98	2.32	5.36	3.96	8.7	3.4	6.8	1.8	18.6	—
2005	HUN	AA	21	1	3	0	4	4	20.7	21	9	14	3	30%	.277	-14	1.45	7.39	6.86	7.78	10.5	4.1	4.1	2.3	-4.8	—
2006	*MIL*	*MLB*	*22*	*6*	*9*	*0*	*26*	*21*	*124.0*	*126*	*56*	*92*	*26*	*38%*	*.273*	*2*	*1.47*	*5.27*	*5.85*	*5.51*	*9.2*	*3.5*	*5.9*	*1.8*	*1.1*	*0.9*

Breakout: 14%   Improve: 51%   Collapse: 16%   Attrition: 0%   Comparables: Brian Stirm, Felix Diaz, Cory Morris

A change-up artist who relies on a scalpel instead of a saber when dicing up the strike zone, Villanueva managed to put himself onto prospect radars by showing exceptional command. However, the strikeout rates and his reliance on low-orbit outs instead of worm-killing grounders doesn't bode well for his future. Unless he comes up with something even sneakier, what happened in Double-A last season is a portent of things to come against more advanced hitters.

MATT WISE **Bats: R Throws: R** Height: 6′ 4″ Weight: 190 Born: November 18, 1975 Age: 30

YEAR	TM	LVL	AGE	W	L	SV	G	GS	IP	H	BB	SO	HR	GB%	BABIP	STUFF	WHIP	ERA	PERA	EQERA	EQH9	EQBB9	EQSO9	EQHR9	VORP	WXRL
2004	MIL	MLB	28	1	2	0	30	3	52.7	51	15	30	3	49%	.284	0	1.25	4.44	3.98	4.15	8.8	2.4	4.7	0.5	5.4	0.9
2005	MIL	MLB	29	4	4	1	49	0	64.3	37	25	62	6	42%	.190	14	0.96	3.36	3.94	3.50	6.6	3.4	8.3	0.9	14.3	1.4
2006	*MIL*	*MLB*	*30*	*3*	*3*	*3*	*49*	*0*	*61.0*	*55*	*23*	*49*	*7*	*42%*	*.271*	*0*	*1.28*	*4.01*	*4.07*	*4.76*	*8.2*	*3.0*	*6.4*	*1.1*	*7.9*	*0.6*

Breakout: 10%   Improve: 32%   Collapse: 38%   Attrition: 11%   Comparables: George Frazier, Guillermo Mota, Jim Brosnan

Signed to a two-year deal this winter, but not for major money, Wise is yet another tribute to Melvin's packrat instinct. Picked up while recovering from Tommy John surgery, he's an understated Doug Jones wannabe, throwing all sorts of junk to set up a good changeup. He's not really an ideal high-leverage setup man, showing absolutely no knack for holding runners, and with a slow delivery. He's better off being used in roles where he's pitching complete innings instead of being brought in to strand other people's baserunners.

Line Outs

Position Player	TM	LVL	AGE	PA	R	2B	3B	HR	RBI	BB	SO	SB-CS	SPEED	BA/OBP/SLG	MLVR	EQBA/OBP/SLG	EQA	VORP
UT Trent Durrington	NAS	AAA	29	360	61	15	2	5	31	41	63	30-12	7.1	.300/.389/.409	.106	.266/.336/.339	.245	2.8
3B Adam Heether	BRV	A+	23	389	48	27	2	6	54	34	48	3-1	4.1	.305/.386/.450	.228	.277/.342/.416	.264	17.5
CF Steve Moss	BRV	A+	21	485	62	19	7	9	51	36	113	18-12	6.0	.281/.332/.416	.084	.259/.309/.392	.243	2.0
C Lou Palmisano	BRV	A+	22	474	47	16	7	5	49	34	65	3-1	4.5	.255/.314/.359	-.039	.236/.290/.340	.223	-12.0
C Mike Rivera	NAS	AAA	28	228	34	12	1	16	43	9	37	3-1	4.5	.285/.320/.575	.217	.252/.280/.479	.253	6.5
UT Vinny Rottino	HUN	AA	25	516	63	20	6	6	52	40	68	2-1	4.5	.296/.351/.403	.037	.248/.292/.342	.224	-9.3

Pitcher	TM	LVL	AGE	W	L	SV	IP	H	BB	SO	HR	GB%	BABIP	STUFF	WHIP	ERA	PERA	EQERA	EQH9	EQBB9	EQSO9	EQHR9	VORP
Ricky Bottalico	MIL	MLB	35	2	2	2	41.7	43	19	29	7	50%	.286	-14	1.51	4.53	5.44	5.01	9.8	3.9	5.9	1.5	0.3
Gary Glover	MIL	MLB	28	5	4	0	64.7	74	20	58	10	43%	.339	8	1.45	5.56	4.52	5.62	9.9	2.6	7.3	1.4	-1.0
	NAS	AAA	28	6	4	1	92.0	91	29	75	9	46%	.305	-1	1.30	3.03	4.94	4.63	9.3	3.1	5.1	1.2	9.6
Mark Rogers	WVA	A	19	2	9	1	98.7	87	70	109	11	55%	.309	-19	1.59	5.11	7.36	7.17	9.9	8.0	6.5	2.0	-16.0
Mitch Stetter*	HUN	AA	24	2	3	8	51.7	46	11	47	3	59%	.305	-4	1.10	2.61	4.56	3.83	8.8	2.2	5.3	1.1	9.7
	NAS	AAA	24	1	1	0	25.3	23	11	23	5	47%	.261	-20	1.34	4.27	6.29	5.92	9.2	4.1	6.3	2.2	-0.9

Trent Durrington is a speedy and a patient hitter, and can handle the infield and catch; he'd be handy as a last man on the bench. **Adam Heether** is too old to be a prospect, but hit well enough to garner some consideration, and he didn't look overmatched in a late promotion to Double-A. **Steve Moss** might be the best of a bad lot in a system devoid of good outfield prospects at the lower levels, but he can handle center and is young enough to possibly figure out hitting. **Lou Palmisano** is a cautionary tale about getting too worked up over Pioneer League stats, going from "prospect" after nearly slugging .600 in '03 to "he catches." **Mike Rivera's** translations suggest he wouldn't be a half-bad backup, but his poor defensive rep might keep him unlucky. **Vinny Rottino** can play the four corners of the infield and outfield, and can catch in an emergency. After winning the organization's Player of the Year Award in '04, it might add up to a career in a utility role.

Ricky Bottalico is not dead yet, although some would consider winding up in John Waters's Baltimore a worse fate. **Gary Glover** was initially plugged into the fifth slot of the rotation, but lost the job when they added Ohka. Turnabout is fair play; he'll be taking a Japanese job by signing with Yomiuri. **Mike Jones,** the 2001 1st rounder, will be trying to come back from back-to-back shoulder surgeries, about as close to the kiss of death as pitchers get without tasting its Styx-flavored Chapstick. **Mark Rogers,** the Brewers' top 2004 draft choice, gets high marks for his fastball, slider and intelligence, but with rough mechanics and worse control (he hit 15 batters and threw 16 wild pitches), he's a long way from being a prospect. He did improve his delivery in instructional league, but the jury's not in on what that means in real game action. **Mitch Stetter** says, lefty relief help comes from the strangest places, so why not a 16th rounder from Indiana State?

Minnesota Twins

They lacked industry and pleasure.
Is this virtue?
No, pure ignorance.

— VOLTAIRE

In the media's haste to conjure up the false labels of who is or is not a *Moneyball* team, certain franchises have been nominated as the best examples of these caricatures of baseball operations. Through their reliance on traditional scouting methods and homegrown talent, the Twins have been held up as one of the best examples of an organization that relies on old-fashioned baseball values in player development. More important, they've been used as a feel-good story, the story that underdogs have their days. After a three-year run atop the AL Central in 2002–04, the Twins were touted as a model for "small market" franchises throughout the industry, and "proof" that you didn't have to read that damned book or look at those damned numbers.

So what do you do when the media announces that the counter-revolution has come, and after years of being the model old school franchise, you get upstaged? Welcome to the Twins' world, because 2005 marked a season in which they became yesterday's flavor in the wake of the White Sox's victory in the division and then in the World Series. The Twins have been reduced from favorites to also-rans, and from model franchise of the anti-*Moneyball* set to a cautionary tale of the fleeting nature of achievement without progress.

Certainly, GM Terry Ryan has never been accused of having a killer instinct. Rather than try to build a team that could beat the Red Sox or Yankees and take advantage of the tremendous opportunity that getting into the playoffs represents, the Twins have been satisfied with modest moves to assure themselves victory in the generally weak AL Central, the Rust Belt division populated by none of the game's biggest spenders. Past stretch drive deals that brought in the likes of Rick Reed or Shannon Stewart weren't moves that would give the powerhouses on either coast pause, and if the Twins take credit for building a large base of homegrown talent, it also deserves criticism for failing to leverage that talent into a genuinely great ballclub.

One of the hallmarks of Twins management during the salad days of 2002–04 was adequacy. As goals go, it

TWINS PROSPECTUS

2005 record: 83–79; Third place, AL Central

Pythagenport record: 83–79

Runs scored per game: 4.25 (14th in AL)

Runs allowed per game: 4.09 (5th in AL)

Team EqA: .247 (14th in AL)

2005 Batters Age: 28.0 (Youngest in AL)

2005 Pitchers Age: 28.3 (5th youngest in AL)

Ballpark: Metrodome; Neutral park; Park Factor of 1.008

2005: The defending division champs paid for years of indecisive roster management.

2006: A strong core of talent remains, but this isn't the Twins' division to lose any more.

was one the Twins didn't have to be especially creative to achieve. Their lineups weren't terrible, finishing 12th, 8th, and 14th in the major leagues in Equivalent Average, but they were nowhere close to the Yankees or Red Sox lineups of the period and never better than any pennant winner of the last five years. The willingness to settle in the rotation was similarly notable: starters like Brad Radke, Joe Mays, and Kyle Lohse were good but not great, good enough to beat the assorted midgets of their division but not good enough to beat the really good teams in the league.

In itself, this sort of willingness to make do might not have bred success, but two moves radically changed the team's fortunes and enabled them to mount their three-year run. First, the decision to pick Johan Santana in the Rule 5 draft in December of 1999 was an investment that would eventually reward the Twins with the league's best starter. Second, trading catcher A. J. Pierzynski to make room for Joe Mauer not only cleared space to improve their lineup, it brought both Joe Nathan, a pitcher primed to become one of the league's best closers, and pitching prospect Francisco Liriano, who might become the best non-Santana in the Twins' rotation by 2007. However, these sorts of thoughtful risks were the exception rather than the rule. Onetime young, adequate players like Lohse or Mays, or Doug Mientkiewicz and Jacque Jones, were allowed to hang around and become expensive, mid-career adequate players. The rotation and the lineup might have been taken in for detailing now and again, but it was never overhauled, no matter how often the Twins came up short. In cases of major injury, like Mauer's knee injury in 2004, they'd settle for an inadequate major league veteran (in this case, Henry Blanco) to fill in.

Limited ambitions were good enough during the three years where the Indians needed to tear down to bedrock and rebuild, and the White Sox learned and re-learned what combinations weren't good enough. But 2005 was different, because after three years of coming up short, the challengers to the Twins for the division had finally mutated into the combinations that wouldn't just beat the Twins, but squash any memory of their limited victories. Not only did the White Sox lead the American League in wins (99) in '05, the Indians won enough games (93) to have finished ahead of the Twins in 2003 and 2004.

The Twins weren't just beaten on the field; they'd been out-Twinned twice over. Take a look at the direct comparison between the Central's big three in table 1. In putting significantly better ballclubs on the field, the Sox didn't significantly outspend Minnesota, and Cleveland spent significantly less. It was not that the Twins failed to spend beyond their means, but that they failed to spend

wisely. Not only did all three teams compete with "small-market" budgets, both rivals relied on some of the same strengths that had elevated the Twins to their three-peat in the division. All three teams fielded good bullpens and good defensive units. All three boasted pretty good rotations, although what's lost in a cumulative team stat like SNLVA (Support Neutral Lineup-Adjusted Value Added) is that the Twins were a team with one great starter and a gaggle of mediocrities, where the White Sox, and to a lesser extent the Indians, were teams with four genuinely good starters apiece, four pitchers who were better than anyone in the Twins' rotation not named Johan Santana. That distinction's particularly important when you play in the unbalanced schedule (see table 2). Obviously, Johan Santana can only beat a team once per start, but if you're outclassed the other four days of the week, you don't really have a competitive rotation.

Where an even larger difference between the real power duo and the Twins lays, and what really made the Twins' defense of their division titles hopeless, was the total breakdown of their offense. This wasn't just a matter of their lacking a middle infielder who can hit, or their failure to find a DH who puts runs on the board. As you can see in table 3, the Twins finished last because they were consistently lousy at just about every lineup slot. Some of this was beyond their control: at second base, Luis Rivas finally gave up the ghost where his prospect-dom was concerned, and at first base, young slugger Justin Morneau came into the season weakened by a winter of

TABLE 1. THE AL CENTRAL: THEY COULDN'T ALL BE SOMEBODY

2005	Twins	White Sox	Indians
Team Equivalent Average (rank)	.245 (30th)	.251 (24th)	.270 (4th)
Team SNLVA (rank)	6.1 (10th)	9.2 (7th)	5.7 (11th)
Team Bullpen WXRL (rank)	12.4 (6th)	12.8 (4th)	12.5 (5th)
Defensive Efficiency (rank)	.703 (7th)	.713 (2nd)	.710 (3rd)
Team Salary in millions (rank)	$56.3 (20th)	$73.1 (13th)	$40.7 (26th)
One-Run W/L	27–30	35–19	22–36
Actual record	83–79	99–63	93–69
3rd Order W/L*	84–78	87–75	98–64

* 3rd Order W/L is the number of wins and losses a team would have on the basis of how many runs a team should have allowed and scored through the values of everything they did on the field.

TABLE 2. INFIGHTING

Twins versus:	Sox 7–11	Indians 9–10	versus AL Central 40–35
Sox versus:	Twins 11–7	Indians 14–5	versus AL Central 52–22
Indians versus:	Twins 10–9	Sox 5–14	versus AL Central 40–35

TABLE 3. IT TAKES A LINEUP: TWINS POSITION RANKINGS IN THE AL BY VORP

C	5th of 30
1B	28th of 30
2B	27th of 30
3B	26th of 30
SS	29th of 30
CF	14th of 30
RF	25th of 30

illness and injury. But some of the problem very much was in Terry Ryan's control. The Twins failed to commit to Jason Bartlett at short, forcing them to rely on a totally inadequate veteran reserve in Juan Castro. Mediocre veteran hitters like Jacque Jones and Shannon Stewart were guaranteed their at-bats by virtue of their price and service time, far from the hallmark of a young or hungry team trying to claw its way up.

So how will the Twins address their complete failure to matter in 2005? Did such a thorough defeat finally shake them out of their snoozy approach to team-building? What Terry Ryan is going to have to recognize is that the competitive ecology of the AL Central is fundamentally different, and will no longer have space for the Twins' brand of indolence. Kenny Williams isn't resting on his laurels, he's playing for keeps, and seeking to cement Chicago's dominance in the division for the next year or two. Mark Shapiro is building something that will last in Cleveland, slowly weaving in young stars while cherrypicking the kinds of quality free agents that can make a difference.

Unfortunately, the Twins seem to have misunderstood this more challenging competitive environment. They're trying to catch up with the White Sox and Indians by following the most broadly-drawn caricatures of how the White Sox won. Rather than recognize that the White Sox won with an Earl Weaver–style setup, scoring their runs with home runs and keeping the other guy down with a strong rotation and bullpen, the Twins are indulging themselves in the broadly-accepted conceit that the Sox won with speed and little ball tactics. Imitation being the sincerest form of flattery, the Twins added a speedy leadoff man by acquiring second baseman Luis Castillo from the Marlins, but they also feel they've addressed their power problems by bringing hackmaster Tony Batista back from Japan and signing up a 34 year-old Rondell White. White and Batista will not really improve this lineup, and both

are more probably disasters, a pair of hitters who won't add as much power as they'll generate lots of outs. Castillo will at least give the team some stability at second, but he will not give them as much of an impact leadoff hitter as they believe they did. Groundball hitters as extreme as Castillo get hits with long infield grass if they have the speed for it; they lose those hits to turf's true hops and speedy surfaces, and Castillo's so extreme when it comes to only putting balls in play in the infield that he won't get much value from turf's tendency to turn long singles into doubles.

Veteran mediocrity seems to represent a solution of necessity, because the Twins have yet to add a premium hitter, and the farm system won't be much help. Down on the farm, outside of their hopes that Jason Kubel's bum knee might heal well enough to let him DH for them in '06, the sources of homegrown help are limited. Bartlett might finally be left alone at shortstop, but in the upper levels of the farm system, the only really promising hitting prospect is Alex Romero, and he's already been boxed out by the decision to sign White.

Nor have the Twins really adjusted to the fact that their rotation isn't good enough. While the Sox are making a point of improving their rotation by adding Javier Vazquez, the Twins are playing make-believe, and continuing to crowd the rotation with the same good-enough guys who are no longer good enough. They're hoping Brad Radke can be the pitcher he was in 2004 instead of more typically the guy he was in '03 or '05 or most of his career. They're wishcasting that Kyle Lohse might build on his 2003, instead of recognizing that was a good year from a fourth starter who grew up to be an adequate fourth starter. And in doing so, they've crowded out their pitchers with real up-side, making only a single rotation slot open to Francisco Liriano, Scott Baker, J. D. Durbin, and perhaps Boof Bonser.

The Twins are already spinning their failures in 2005 as a reminder that they're the underdogs going into 2006. But just as some might don hair shirts and call it fashion, that doesn't make it so. This a victim's mentality: the Twins aren't underdogs, they're the team that has already let opportunity pass them by. The Twins have to stop making excuses with an eye towards future failure, and do more to win with a team built around Joe Mauer and Johan Santana than they did with the past teams that relied on guys like Joe Mays and Jacque Jones. There's no silver medal in baseball, and no Jim McKay to hold your hand and make you feel better for coming up short.

HITTERS

JASON BARTLETT SS Bats: R Throws: R Height: 6' 0" Weight: 170 Born: October 30, 1979 Age: 26

YEAR	TM	LVL	AGE	PA	R	2B	3B	HR	RBI	BB	SO	SB	CS	SPEED	BA	OBP	SLG	MLVR	EQBA	EQOBP	EQSLG	EQA	VORP	DEFENSE	
2003	NBR	AA	23	632	96	31	8	8	48	58	67	41	24	7.3	.296	.380	.425	.149	.276	.347	.411	.264	31.0	139-SS	7
2004	ROC	AAA	24	311	54	15	7	3	29	33	37	7	3	6.9	.331	.415	.472	.236	.303	.383	.430	.286	24.0	65-SS	8
2005	ROC	AAA	25	269	41	10	2	5	33	29	34	2	2	5.2	.332	.405	.459	.204	.303	.374	.427	.281	19.6	60-SS	4
2005	MIN	MLB	25	250	33	10	1	3	16	21	37	4	0	5.3	.241	.316	.335	-.163	.244	.328	.339	.243	1.6	65-SS	12
2006	*MIN*	*MLB*	*26*	*454*	*57*	*21*	*4*	*7*	*42*	*38*	*61*	*9*	*3*	*5.5*	*.271*	*.340*	*.394*	*-.023*	*.272*	*.349*	*.407*	*.258*	*17.3*	*108-SS*	*9*

Breakout: 12%   Improve: 43%   Collapse: 32%   Attrition: 21%   Comparables: Jerry Hairston, Dick Schofield, Mike Lansing

Although some of Bartlett's losing hold on the shortstop job can be blamed on his equally slippery grip on a hotel TV that tore off a fingernail and forced him to the DL, it appears that the Twins simply don't like him very much. This is unfortunate, because he's an asset at a position where the club has no real alternatives. The real hangup is one of those little things: Bartlett's arm angles on tougher throws give scouts the willies, and that sort of thing cuts ice in Minnesota. Cosmetic considerations and the unavailability of Miguel Tejada aside, he's exactly who the Twins need, a useful hitter who can also give them the glovework they demand.

TONY BATISTA 3B Bats: R Throws: R Height: 6' 0" Weight: 195 Born: December 9, 1973 Age: 32

YEAR	TM	LVL	AGE	PA	R	2B	3B	HR	RBI	BB	SO	SB	CS	SPEED	BA	OBP	SLG	MLVR	EQBA	EQOBP	EQSLG	EQA	VORP	DEFENSE	
2003	BAL	MLB	29	670	76	20	1	26	99	28	102	4	3	3.9	.235	.270	.393	-.167	.236	.278	.401	.232	-3.1	153-3B	6
2004	MON	MLB	30	646	76	30	2	32	110	26	78	14	6	5.3	.241	.272	.455	-.054	.235	.266	.446	.241	0.5	149-3B	12
2005	FKU	JPL	31	582	78	29	1	27	90	23	115	3	2	0.0	.263	.292	.463	.046	.262	.301	.395	.241	-2.8		
2006	*MIN*	*MLB*	*32*	*284*	*30*	*13*	*1*	*9*	*35*	*13*	*50*	*2*	*1*	*4.2*	*.245*	*.282*	*.400*	*-.131*	*.245*	*.290*	*.413*	*.231*	*-0.4*	*69-3B*	*2*

Breakout: 22%   Improve: 37%   Collapse: 34%   Attrition: 34%   Comparables: Craig Paquette, Aurelio Rodriguez, Ed Sprague

Back from Japan, but he isn't going to handicap the Twins' bottom line; Terry Ryan signed him to a heavily incentive-laden deal. The problem, rather, is that he simply is neither a solution to the team's need for a slugger nor its hole at third base. Even if Batista somehow manages to become the first Twin since '87 to hit thirty bombs, he will not improve the offense making as many outs as he will to do even that. He is a defensive asset, but he was brought in to be a starter, not Terry Tiffee's defensive replacement.

BRET BOONE 2B Bats: R Throws: R Height: 5' 10" Weight: 180 Born: April 6, 1969 Age: 37

YEAR	TM	LVL	AGE	PA	R	2B	3B	HR	RBI	BB	SO	SB	CS	SPEED	BA	OBP	SLG	MLVR	EQBA	EQOBP	EQSLG	EQA	VORP	DEFENSE	
2003	SEA	MLB	34	704	111	35	5	35	117	68	125	16	3	6.0	.294	.366	.535	.244	.302	.378	.556	.311	67.4	155-2B	8
2004	SEA	MLB	35	656	74	30	0	24	83	56	135	10	5	4.5	.251	.317	.423	-.037	.257	.326	.435	.261	19.6	145-2B	-11
2005	SEA	MLB	36	301	30	15	3	7	34	24	52	4	2	4.8	.231	.299	.385	-.118	.240	.317	.406	.249	0.7	73-2B	-4
2005	MIN	MLB	36	58	3	0	0	0	3	4	13	0	0	2.6	.170	.241	.170	-.549	.173	.259	.173	.169	-5.8	13-2B	-1
2006	*NYN*	*MLB*	*37*	*345*	*39*	*17*	*1*	*9*	*39*	*32*	*63*	*4*	*2*	*4.8*	*.246*	*.322*	*.394*	*-.088*	*.250*	*.327*	*.417*	*.251*	*8.7*	*83-2B*	*-3*

Breakout: 5%   Improve: 21%   Collapse: 40%   Attrition: 30%   Comparables: Craig Biggio, Mike Bordick, Davey Lopes

One of many veterans who suddenly fell apart at the plate in '05, but let's face it, Boone was 36, and he'd already taken a bit of a tumble in 2004. Rumors circulated that he might wind up in Washington, basically because his dad's part of Jim Bowden's posse after their days together in Cincinnati, but having missed out on Mark Grudzielanek, the Mets signed him, believing he can challenge Kaz Matsui for the second base job.

JUAN CASTRO INF Bats: R Throws: R Height: 5' 11" Weight: 195 Born: June 20, 1972 Age: 34

YEAR	TM	LVL	AGE	PA	R	2B	3B	HR	RBI	BB	SO	SB	CS	SPEED	BA	OBP	SLG	MLVR	EQBA	EQOBP	EQSLG	EQA	VORP	DEFENSE				
2003	CIN	MLB	31	341	28	14	1	9	33	18	58	2	3	4.2	.253	.290	.388	-.123	.248	.287	.388	.232	-0.5	47-2B	6	21-3B	3	
2004	CIN	MLB	32	314	36	21	2	5	26	14	51	1	0	4.8	.244	.277	.378	-.145	.241	.274	.375	.224	-3.5	43-3B	-1	21-SS	3	
2005	MIN	MLB	33	283	27	18	1	5	33	9	39	0	1	4.0	.257	.279	.386	-.160	.258	.291	.397	.237	-0.9	63-SS	15	14-3B	-3	
2006	*MIN*	*MLB*	*34*	*219*	*22*	*11*	*1*	*4*	*24*	*9*	*32*	*0*	*1*	*4.1*	*.255*	*.287*	*.379*	*-.144*	*.255*	*.295*	*.391*	*.227*	*1.0*	*55-SS*	*3*			

Breakout: 27%   Improve: 45%   Collapse: 33%   Attrition: 42%   Comparables: Jimmy Bloodworth, Billy Ripken, Dave Berg

Some people want Castro out of Cuba, but you shouldn't blame Twins fans if they'd rather send a spare to Havana. Fairly or not, Castro is the team's symbol of Terry Ryan's readiness to simply settle for much of what he had going into 2005. Castro was his signed for glove; the Twins' problem was that they needed a *shortstop,* and after souring on Bartlett, they had Castro instead of one. But hey, did we mention he can bunt? Doug Flynn groupies should be pleased.

MIKE CUDDYER   UT   Bats: R Throws: R   Height: 6′ 2″ Weight: 220 Born: March 27, 1979   Age: 27

YEAR	TM	LVL	AGE	PA	R	2B	3B	HR	RBI	BB	SO	SB	CS	SPEED	BA	OBP	SLG	MLVR	EQBA	EQOBP	EQSLG	EQA	VORP	DEFENSE			
2003	ROC	AAA	24	218	25	17	0	3	34	25	49	5	4	4.3	.306	.381	.446	.165	.266	.348	.400	.264	1.3	26-RF	1		
2003	MIN	MLB	24	114	14	1	3	4	8	12	19	1	1	4.6	.245	.325	.431	-.028	.238	.325	.426	.256	1.0	15-RF	-1		
2004	MIN	MLB	25	380	49	22	1	12	45	37	74	5	5	4.3	.263	.339	.440	.003	.261	.341	.441	.266	8.8	36-2B	2	37-3B	-6
2005	MIN	MLB	26	469	55	25	3	12	42	41	93	3	4	3.9	.263	.330	.422	-.004	.267	.345	.440	.268	8.1	90-3B	-9	18-RF	1
2006	*MIN*	*MLB*	*27*	*483*	*57*	*23*	*2*	*15*	*61*	*45*	*96*	*5*	*3*	*4.4*	*.265*	*.339*	*.435*	*.023*	*.266*	*.348*	*.449*	*.266*	*14.8*	*114-3B*	*-2*		

Breakout: 21%   Improve: 47%   Collapse: 23%   Attrition: 14%   Comparables: Doug Rader, Craig Worthington, Steve Buechele

If ever the Twins needed Cuddyer to finally live up to the promise he'd shown in 2002 as a power source, it was this past year. Instead of replacing Corey Koskie, he gave them modest production, and it doesn't look like he's going to settle in at third. The Twins seem to have decided to shift him into a rover's role by signing Batista. He'll be useful chipping in at five positions between the infield and outfield, but he's not going to become the future star he was originally envisioned to be.

DOUG DEEDS   RF   Bats: L Throws: L   Height: 6′ 2″ Weight: 180 Born: June 2, 1981   Age: 25

YEAR	TM	LVL	AGE	PA	R	2B	3B	HR	RBI	BB	SO	SB	CS	SPEED	BA	OBP	SLG	MLVR	EQBA	EQOBP	EQSLG	EQA	VORP	DEFENSE			
2004	FTM	A+	23	490	71	28	12	5	57	43	86	11	3	7.3	.294	.363	.447	.198	.271	.328	.418	.259	1.9	54-RF	2	33-LF	1
2005	NBR	AA	24	560	77	34	2	16	82	56	119	2	4	4.0	.304	.382	.479	.252	.283	.354	.447	.275	17.3	122-RF	-7		
2006	*MIN*	*MLB*	*25*	*494*	*58*	*29*	*4*	*12*	*59*	*38*	*107*	*3*	*2*	*4.7*	*.266*	*.327*	*.427*	*-.004*	*.267*	*.336*	*.441*	*.259*	*6.5*	*117-RF*	*-1*		

Breakout: 16%   Improve: 37%   Collapse: 31%   Attrition: 12%   Comparables: Jon Hamilton, Eric Gillespie, John-Ford Griffin

He may be a dark horse for the open outfield job on the big league club, but a lefty bat that pasted righthanders at a .307/.383/.464 clip would look pretty good in baseball's worst lineup. Not that Deeds is a platoon hitter, since he slugged .525 against LHPs. Picked out of Ohio State in the 9th round of the '02 draft, Deeds effectively lost '03 to wrist surgery, but he's made up for lost time.

LEW FORD   OF   Bats: R Throws: R   Height: 6′ 0″ Weight: 190 Born: August 12, 1976   Age: 29

YEAR	TM	LVL	AGE	PA	R	2B	3B	HR	RBI	BB	SO	SB	CS	SPEED	BA	OBP	SLG	MLVR	EQBA	EQOBP	EQSLG	EQA	VORP	DEFENSE			
2003	ROC	AAA	26	230	33	18	2	3	31	10	28	4	5	5.3	.303	.357	.450	.130	.277	.330	.419	.255	6.5	27-CF	-2	10-LF	0
2004	MIN	MLB	27	656	89	31	4	15	72	67	75	20	2	6.0	.299	.381	.446	.136	.297	.382	.449	.294	36.3	75-LF	-2	37-CF	-1
2005	MIN	MLB	28	588	70	30	4	7	53	45	85	13	6	6.0	.264	.338	.377	-.048	.270	.350	.390	.262	7.7	61-CF	0	15-LF	1
2006	*MIN*	*MLB*	*29*	*559*	*72*	*30*	*4*	*10*	*58*	*43*	*75*	*11*	*4*	*5.6*	*.278*	*.343*	*.416*	*.016*	*.279*	*.352*	*.429*	*.265*	*14.6*	*131-CF*	*-2*		

Breakout: 14%   Improve: 34%   Collapse: 32%   Attrition: 12%   Comparables: Alex Ochoa, Dan Gladden, Geronimo Berroa

The danger with promoting a player late in his baseball life is that you might get caught up in what he's done for you after he's already started to leave his best seasons behind. After all, if he's cheap, and he's okay, he's someone a "small market" team wants, right? Ford's just a good fourth outfielder pressed into everyday play, and at 29, he's not going to get any better than that. The Twins cannot afford to make the same mistake with Ford that they did with Jacque Jones, holding onto him beyond the time that he gets genuinely expensive.

TORII HUNTER   CF   Bats: R Throws: R   Height: 6′ 2″ Weight: 201 Born: July 18, 1975   Age: 30

YEAR	TM	LVL	AGE	PA	R	2B	3B	HR	RBI	BB	SO	SB	CS	SPEED	BA	OBP	SLG	MLVR	EQBA	EQOBP	EQSLG	EQA	VORP	DEFENSE	
2003	MIN	MLB	27	642	83	31	4	26	102	50	106	6	7	4.9	.250	.312	.451	-.023	.247	.315	.453	.259	11.7	144-CF	-5
2004	MIN	MLB	28	569	79	37	0	23	81	40	101	21	7	5.4	.271	.330	.475	.039	.270	.331	.479	.275	23.4	121-CF	-2
2005	MIN	MLB	29	416	63	24	1	14	56	34	65	23	7	6.8	.269	.337	.452	.055	.275	.351	.469	.282	19.4	90-CF	3
2006	*MIN*	*MLB*	*30*	*492*	*69*	*25*	*2*	*18*	*67*	*35*	*80*	*20*	*7*	*5.4*	*.272*	*.330*	*.460*	*.045*	*.272*	*.339*	*.474*	*.270*	*19.2*	*116-CF*	*-2*

Breakout: 21%   Improve: 40%   Collapse: 28%   Attrition: 12%   Comparables: Derek Bell, Glenallen Hill, Mike Devereaux

Hunter is the team's unrecognized star, and as much as he isn't losing anything at the plate to age, the Twins can't endure losing him for an extended period of time in an outfield otherwise bereft of real power. His range is a plus, but the bonus feature that Hunter gives the Twins is an arm better than most in center. It's an asset not only in the Metrodome, a turf park where triples are a hazard, but in the similarly spacious stadia of division rivals such as Comerica Park and Kauffman Stadium. If he can play a full season, he's the type of player who might hit 30 bombs without all of the unfortunate side effects that come with playing someone like Batista.

GARRETT JONES **1B** **Bats: L Throws: L** Height: 6′ 4″ Weight: 220 Born: June 21, 1981 Age: 25

YEAR	TM	LVL	AGE	PA	R	2B	3B	HR	RBI	BB	SO	SB	CS	SPEED	BA	OBP	SLG	MLVR	EQBA	EQOBP	EQSLG	EQA	VORP	DEFENSE	
2003	FTM	A+	22	440	52	12	5	18	67	32	98	5	4	5.4	.220	.280	.408	.022	.207	.256	.403	.224	-22.3	108-1B	9
2004	NBR	AA	23	492	68	33	2	30	92	28	98	11	4	5.0	.311	.356	.593	.354	.286	.325	.539	.286	30.0	120-1B	-7
2005	ROC	AAA	24	526	71	22	2	24	72	36	109	5	1	5.6	.244	.297	.445	-.072	.220	.275	.396	.231	-20.0	120-1B	7
2006	MIN	MLB	25	464	55	23	2	19	66	27	102	4	2	4.7	.250	.296	.447	-.043	.250	.304	.461	.251	1.8	110-1B	2

Breakout: 39% Improve: 64% Collapse: 18% Attrition: 13% Comparables: Kevin Barker, Ted Kluszewski, Kevin Witt

It looks like 2005 was the season that told us what we really needed to know about Jones: that he is not a late-bloomer but a minor league slugger who won't make the jump. A lefty-hitting first baseman hits .253/.309/.480 against right-handers in Triple-A, is only a sign of promise if you've been waiting for Mike Laga's second coming.

JACQUE JONES **OF** **Bats: L Throws: L** Height: 5′ 10″ Weight: 176 Born: April 25, 1975 Age: 31

YEAR	TM	LVL	AGE	PA	R	2B	3B	HR	RBI	BB	SO	SB	CS	SPEED	BA	OBP	SLG	MLVR	EQBA	EQOBP	EQSLG	EQA	VORP	DEFENSE	
2003	MIN	MLB	28	547	76	33	1	16	69	21	105	13	1	6.0	.304	.333	.464	.078	.299	.334	.462	.275	18.9	84-LF	-5
2004	MIN	MLB	29	606	69	22	1	24	80	40	117	13	10	5.0	.254	.315	.427	-.058	.252	.316	.427	.252	1.8	136-RF	7
2005	MIN	MLB	30	583	74	22	4	23	73	51	120	13	4	5.7	.249	.319	.438	-.013	.252	.332	.452	.269	9.6	120-RF	13
2006	CHN	MLB	31	525	66	25	2	17	63	38	101	8	4	5.0	.268	.327	.441	-.002	.269	.328	.448	.258	6.0	123-RF	1

Breakout: 18% Improve: 39% Collapse: 28% Attrition: 9% Comparables: Dave May, Claudell Washington, Al Zarilla

Bonifay's Paradox might be a new term that we don't really need, but there ought to be some shorthand we can invent to describe what happens when moderately useful players who contribute to teams that claw their way up to mediocrity become expensive and not so useful any more. If we're coining the term in honor of the former Pirates GM and his unhappy tendency to overcommit to players who weren't going to help his team get any better, it should be applied pointedly to Terry Ryan, particularly in the case of Jones. Jones's last useful season was in 2003, when he was 29 and at the end of a normal Age 25–29 spread for a player's peak years. The Twins paid more than $12 million for him over the last three years, all to avoid arbitration, and to keep a corner outfielder without power. The "greater fool" theory found a taker, as the Cubs will pay him even more ($15 million) over the next three years; if they're expecting Duke Snider to balance out their righty-heavy lineup, let the heartbreak start now.

JASON KUBEL **DH** **Bats: L Throws: R** Height: 5′ 11″ Weight: 190 Born: May 25, 1982 Age: 24

YEAR	TM	LVL	AGE	PA	R	2B	3B	HR	RBI	BB	SO	SB	CS	SPEED	BA	OBP	SLG	MLVR	EQBA	EQOBP	EQSLG	EQA	VORP	DEFENSE			
2003	FTM	A+	21	482	56	20	4	5	82	48	54	4	6	4.4	.298	.361	.400	.177	.287	.342	.412	.263	6.0	106-RF	8		
2004	NBR	AA	22	159	25	14	4	6	29	19	19	0	2	4.8	.377	.453	.667	.665	.355	.427	.623	.338	25.8	35-RF	1		
2004	ROC	AAA	22	389	71	28	0	16	71	34	40	16	3	6.3	.343	.398	.560	.343	.304	.363	.499	.294	22.9	75-RF	6	10-LF	0
2004	MIN	MLB	22	67	10	2	0	2	7	6	9	1	1	5.0	.300	.358	.433	.246	.288	.348	.424	.267	3.9				
2006	MIN	MLB	24	51	7	3	0	2	7	4	6	1	0	5.1	.293	.351	.468	.108	.293	.361	.484	.281	4.4	17-RF	1		

Breakout: 6% Improve: 25% Collapse: 59% Attrition: 42% Comparables: Jackie Brandt, Richard Hidalgo, Pedro Munoz

If Kubel hadn't blown out his knee over the winter before the '05 season, life would be a lot easier. Unfortunately, Kubel's knee isn't coming around, which begins to make him look like the new Pedro Munoz, the former Twins prospect who, like Kubel, had tremendous line-drive power to all fields, and whose career was basically stillborn because of his knee problems. It's basically impossible to know what to expect. Kubel could fix the team's need for a DH right now and give them sixty extra-base hits in a full season, or he could have so much trouble that Ryan's left to fidget over whether or not to go out and get somebody else, or commit to someone from the farm system.

MATT LeCROY **1B/C** **Bats: R Throws: R** Height: 6′ 2″ Weight: 220 Born: December 13, 1975 Age: 30

YEAR	TM	LVL	AGE	PA	R	2B	3B	HR	RBI	BB	SO	SB	CS	SPEED	BA	OBP	SLG	MLVR	EQBA	EQOBP	EQSLG	EQA	VORP	DEFENSE			
2003	MIN	MLB	27	374	39	19	0	17	64	25	82	0	1	3.3	.287	.342	.490	.115	.284	.344	.490	.280	17.3	18-C	-3	12-1B	-1
2004	MIN	MLB	28	287	25	14	0	9	39	16	60	0	0	3.1	.269	.321	.424	-.069	.265	.320	.419	.255	3.1	16-C	-6	20-1B	-3
2005	MIN	MLB	29	350	33	5	0	17	50	41	85	0	0	2.3	.260	.354	.444	.065	.263	.366	.460	.284	12.8	20-1B	-3		
2006	MIN	MLB	30	282	32	11	0	12	42	25	65	0	0	3.1	.256	.326	.448	.012	.256	.335	.462	.264	8.2	69-DH			

Breakout: 4% Improve: 23% Collapse: 37% Attrition: 33% Comparables: Gene Oliver, Hal Breeden, Willie Aikens

LeCroy is perhaps baseball's slowest man, clogging the bases with all the native speed of a boiled crab. In their desperate quest for real meat in the lineup, the Twins couldn't really afford to bat a platoon luxury like LeCroy (.306/.404/.621 vs. LHPs) in the heart of the order against RHPs (.228/.319/.322), but they didn't have much choice. If there's a team that has the roster space for a lefty-masher to back up at first and be a team's third catcher, LeCroy's all over that.

JOE MAUER   C   Bats: L   Throws: R   Height: 6′ 4″   Weight: 220   Born: April 19, 1983   Age: 23

YEAR	TM	LVL	AGE	PA	R	2B	3B	HR	RBI	BB	SO	SB	CS	SPEED	BA	OBP	SLG	MLVR	EQBA	EQOBP	EQSLG	EQA	VORP	DEFENSE
2003	FTM	A+	20	261	25	13	1	1	44	24	24	3	0	4.2	.335	.395	.412	.266	.323	.373	.419	.280	18.9	39-C 14
2003	NBR	AA	20	310	48	17	1	4	41	25	25	0	0	4.0	.341	.400	.453	.259	.315	.369	.435	.280	22.1	58-C 7
2004	MIN	MLB	21	122	18	8	1	6	17	11	14	1	0	5.4	.308	.369	.570	.273	.305	.372	.562	.311	12.6	28-C 2
2005	MIN	MLB	22	554	61	26	2	9	55	61	64	13	1	5.7	.294	.372	.411	.080	.299	.386	.422	.289	34.7	111-C 10
2006	*MIN*	*MLB*	*23*	*577*	*71*	*32*	*3*	*14*	*71*	*49*	*62*	*9*	*3*	*5.5*	*.299*	*.361*	*.453*	*.108*	*.300*	*.370*	*.467*	*.281*	*33.1*	*135-C 8*

Breakout: 7%   Improve: 48%   Collapse: 28%   Attrition: 3%   Comparables: Joe Torre, Bill Freehan, Austin Kearns

The Twins managed his comeback from the knee injury carefully, and he responded by giving them a full season that makes it clear he's every bit the prospect he was built up to be. It's hard to know how great Mauer will become, because he's unlike almost anyone in history. He's huge for a catcher, which makes some worry about whether he'll be able to stay behind the plate. Complicating things is that he's not just a good catcher, he's a very good catcher, working well with the pitching staff to deter the running game while also being a smooth receiver. So, as a catcher, does he stay or does he go? There is the expectation that Mauer is going to become a major power source as he gets older, which is a lot to risk given a catcher's standard risks for a career-altering injury. However, the upside of having him there, given his talents and the scarcity of offense at the position, is so great that it's worth seeing if he can handle the next couple of years behind the plate.

JUSTIN MORNEAU   1B   Bats: L   Throws: R   Height: 6′ 4″   Weight: 220   Born: May 15, 1981   Age: 25

YEAR	TM	LVL	AGE	PA	R	2B	3B	HR	RBI	BB	SO	SB	CS	SPEED	BA	OBP	SLG	MLVR	EQBA	EQOBP	EQSLG	EQA	VORP	DEFENSE
2003	ROC	AAA	22	299	39	11	1	16	42	28	56	0	2	3.3	.268	.344	.498	.144	.243	.322	.462	.264	4.8	58-1B -2
2003	MIN	MLB	22	115	14	4	0	4	16	9	30	0	0	4.2	.226	.287	.377	-.188	.219	.287	.362	.226	-2.6	
2004	ROC	AAA	23	326	51	23	0	22	63	32	47	1	1	3.6	.306	.377	.615	.343	.268	.341	.540	.291	19.2	68-1B 2
2004	MIN	MLB	23	312	39	17	0	19	58	28	54	0	0	3.7	.271	.340	.536	.135	.269	.343	.542	.292	15.7	59-1B -3
2005	MIN	MLB	24	543	62	23	4	22	79	44	94	0	2	3.9	.239	.304	.437	-.047	.240	.314	.449	.259	0.2	129-1B -14
2006	*MIN*	*MLB*	*25*	*583*	*72*	*27*	*2*	*28*	*91*	*48*	*97*	*0*	*1*	*4.0*	*.270*	*.336*	*.493*	*.096*	*.271*	*.345*	*.509*	*.278*	*21.4*	*137-1B -3*

Breakout: 27%   Improve: 65%   Collapse: 13%   Attrition: 8%   Comparables: Carmelo Martinez, Richie Sexson, Paul Konerko

After finally earning his long overdue call-up in '04 and finally forcing Doug Mientkiewicz out of town, much was expected. Unfortunately, 2005 was to be Morneau's Annus Terribilis: before the season even started, he had to deal with chicken pox, pneumonia, and appendicitis. Even considering that he was understandably weak coming into the season, what he did at the plate was significantly less than what the Twins expected from their young slugger. With all that behind him now, barring a bout of bubonic plague or career-ending leprosy, he should take a major step forward this season. He's capable of being an MVP-caliber slugger.

MATT MOSES   3B   Bats: L   Throws: R   Height: 6′ 0″   Weight: 210   Born: February 20, 1985   Age: 21

YEAR	TM	LVL	AGE	PA	R	2B	3B	HR	RBI	BB	SO	SB	CS	SPEED	BA	OBP	SLG	MLVR	EQBA	EQOBP	EQSLG	EQA	VORP	DEFENSE
2004	QUD	A	19	125	16	7	0	3	14	12	25	0	0	3.6	.223	.304	.366	-.059	.191	.256	.314	.202	-7.6	13-3B -3
2005	FTM	A+	20	298	37	16	1	7	42	28	59	13	4	5.7	.306	.376	.453	.211	.279	.341	.430	.268	16.0	57-3B 3
2005	NBR	AA	20	204	25	9	1	6	30	14	51	3	2	5.2	.210	.275	.366	-.137	.198	.260	.347	.212	-8.6	47-3B 4
2006	*MIN*	*MLB*	*21*	*498*	*54*	*25*	*3*	*12*	*56*	*32*	*103*	*8*	*5*	*4.9*	*.249*	*.301*	*.393*	*-.105*	*.250*	*.309*	*.406*	*.238*	*2.0*	*117-3B 3*

Breakout: 45%   Improve: 65%   Collapse: 18%   Attrition: 9%   Comparables: Dee Brown, Nate Schierholtz, Corey Smith

Like his namesake, Moses has been wandering for a bit, having had to overcome a congenital birth defect of his heart and a back problem in the previous two seasons. However, he's finally found his way as a prospect. Keep his relative youth in mind: at 20, playing in the Florida State League, let alone Double-A, is a huge challenge, and one he rose to. He still struggles at the plate when he starts trying to pull everything; the Twins have tried to keep him focused on spreading the ball around. He's not considered an asset at third yet, but he's a former high school shortstop with the range and hands for the hot corner, if perhaps not the arm.

TREVOR PLOUFFE   SS   Bats: R   Throws: R   Height: 6′ 1″   Weight: 175   Born: June 15, 1986   Age: 20

YEAR	TM	LVL	AGE	PA	R	2B	3B	HR	RBI	BB	SO	SB	CS	SPEED	BA	OBP	SLG	MLVR	EQBA	EQOBP	EQSLG	EQA	VORP	DEFENSE
2004	ELZ	Rk	18	262	29	7	2	4	28	19	34	3	1	4.3	.283	.340	.380	.044	.239	.276	.314	.211	-18.0	51-SS 3
2005	BLT	A	19	527	58	18	0	13	60	50	78	8	4	4.3	.223	.300	.345	-.148	.188	.252	.294	.199	-31.6	123-SS -5
2006	*MIN*	*MLB*	*20*	*451*	*43*	*18*	*1*	*8*	*42*	*26*	*70*	*4*	*3*	*4.4*	*.224*	*.272*	*.331*	*-.250*	*.225*	*.280*	*.341*	*.206*	*-4.8*	*107-SS 1*

Breakout: 59%   Improve: 74%   Collapse: 17%   Attrition: 5%   Comparables: Luis DePaula, Brandon Warriax, Luis Montanez

The 20th overall pick in the '04 draft, like most high school prospects, Plouffe may not be the blue chip prospect who tears through a system overnight, but he still holds considerable promise. He has a good approach at the plate; he just lacks the power and filling out that will come with age to really take advantage of it. He's a more finished product afield, flashing good range and an excellent arm. A long, long way off from helping.

NICK PUNTO 2B/SS **Bats: B Throws: R** Height: 5' 9" Weight: 170 Born: November 8, 1977 Age: 28

YEAR	TM	LVL	AGE	PA	R	2B	3B	HR	RBI	BB	SO	SB	CS	SPEED	BA	OBP	SLG	MLVR	EQBA	EQOBP	EQSLG	EQA	VORP	DEFENSE			
2003	SWB	AAA	25	119	19	7	1	0	9	7	13	7	1	7.1	.315	.353	.396	.080	.296	.340	.377	.260	4.4	25-SS	4		
2003	PHI	MLB	25	99	14	2	0	1	4	7	22	2	1	6.1	.217	.273	.272	-.302	.217	.273	.272	.199	-3.7				
2005	MIN	MLB	27	432	45	18	4	4	26	36	86	13	8	5.8	.239	.301	.335	-.196	.243	.316	.349	.236	-7.1	63-2B	-1	27-SS	2
2006	MIN	MLB	28	493	61	21	4	6	42	41	87	15	7	5.6	.255	.319	.361	-.111	.256	.327	.373	.240	6.2	116-2B	3		

Breakout: 28% Improve: 51% Collapse: 21% Attrition: 12% Comparables: U. L. Washington, Ted Kubiak, Nelson Liriano

Less frequently flogged for his inadequacies than Castro, but every bit as much of a millstone as an everyday player. Finally given an opportunity to play, he didn't get on base the way his minor league numbers would have led you to think he could, and he stole bases in ways that made you wish he'd stop trying. Since that pretty much sums up his offensive gam, you're left with a whole lot of ssscrappiness.

MIKE REDMOND C **Bats: R Throws: R** Height: 6' 1" Weight: 185 Born: May 5, 1971 Age: 35

YEAR	TM	LVL	AGE	PA	R	2B	3B	HR	RBI	BB	SO	SB	CS	SPEED	BA	OBP	SLG	MLVR	EQBA	EQOBP	EQSLG	EQA	VORP	DEFENSE	
2003	FLO	MLB	32	139	12	7	1	0	11	7	16	0	0	4.6	.240	.302	.312	-.201	.244	.300	.315	.222	-2.3	28-C	-4
2004	FLO	MLB	33	270	19	15	0	2	25	14	28	1	0	3.6	.256	.315	.341	-.128	.260	.318	.340	.235	0.3	68-C	-4
2005	MIN	MLB	34	157	17	9	0	1	26	6	14	0	0	3.1	.311	.350	.392	.021	.315	.363	.404	.268	7.1	42-C	3
2006	MIN	MLB	35	163	14	8	0	1	15	7	17	0	0	3.8	.262	.304	.344	-.154	.263	.313	.355	.225	0.5	42-C	0

Breakout: 10% Improve: 22% Collapse: 53% Attrition: 47% Comparables: Ed Fitz Gerald, Joe Girardi, Pat Borders

He was signed as a veteran backstop who might be able to handle 90–100 starts in case Mauer broke down, and Mauer didn't break down. While legitimately good players who deserve to start get mentioned as baseball's best backup catchers, Redmond is more worthy of the title: you don't want him starting, but you're also glad to have him.

LUIS RIVAS 2B **Bats: R Throws: R** Height: 5' 11" Weight: 170 Born: August 30, 1979 Age: 26

YEAR	TM	LVL	AGE	PA	R	2B	3B	HR	RBI	BB	SO	SB	CS	SPEED	BA	OBP	SLG	MLVR	EQBA	EQOBP	EQSLG	EQA	VORP	DEFENSE	
2003	MIN	MLB	23	513	69	16	9	8	43	30	65	17	7	6.9	.259	.308	.381	-.126	.257	.311	.383	.244	3.8	127-2B	-8
2004	MIN	MLB	24	353	44	19	5	10	34	13	53	15	1	7.5	.256	.283	.432	-.126	.251	.283	.426	.249	7.4	94-2B	16
2005	MIN	MLB	25	148	21	3	1	1	12	9	17	4	0	6.6	.257	.311	.316	-.182	.261	.324	.321	.238	-0.6	40-2B	-2
2005	ROC	AAA	25	157	17	14	0	2	22	8	18	3	2	5.5	.248	.280	.386	-.176	.211	.246	.336	.209	-8.1	35-2B	1
2006	TBA	MLB	26	326	37	13	3	5	30	16	42	9	3	5.9	.251	.292	.366	-.153	.256	.304	.387	.234	3.3	79-2B	2

Breakout: 31% Improve: 54% Collapse: 25% Attrition: 21% Comparables: Frank White, Keith Miller, Mike Phillips

As a group, second base prospects generally have it pretty rough. Between dodging baserunners on the deuce and trying to remain ahead of rivals moving over from short or third because they lack the arm or bat for those positions, young second basemen have to make a very solid case for themselves in order to earn and keep their jobs. Rare indeed are opportunities like that which came to Rivas, where a team throws the door wide open and invites a player to take hold of the keystone, no questions asked, but after more than 2000 plate appearances, it's pretty clear that Rivas is like Gertrude Stein's Oakland: there is no there there. A broken wrist in winter ball pretty much bollixes up his shot at a comeback with Tampa Bay.

LUIS RODRIGUEZ 2B/3B **Bats: B Throws: R** Height: 5' 9" Weight: 180 Born: June 27, 1980 Age: 26

YEAR	TM	LVL	AGE	PA	R	2B	3B	HR	RBI	BB	SO	SB	CS	SPEED	BA	OBP	SLG	MLVR	EQBA	EQOBP	EQSLG	EQA	VORP	DEFENSE			
2003	ROC	AAA	23	570	65	35	2	1	44	46	46	6	8	4.3	.295	.354	.376	.024	.273	.336	.356	.244	8.2	112-2B	4	11-SS	-1
2004	ROC	AAA	24	547	73	33	1	5	52	53	49	3	3	4.3	.286	.353	.389	-.019	.259	.329	.354	.244	3.8	110-2B	-5		
2005	ROC	AAA	25	155	19	10	0	1	17	16	14	0	1	4.2	.304	.381	.399	.059	.265	.342	.338	.242	1.4	25-2B	3		
2005	MIN	MLB	25	197	21	10	2	2	20	18	23	2	2	5.2	.269	.335	.383	-.060	.273	.350	.390	.259	2.1	24-2B	1	22-3B	-2
2006	MIN	MLB	26	349	38	16	2	3	29	28	36	3	2	4.3	.263	.327	.354	-.102	.263	.336	.365	.240	4.7	84-2B	1		

Breakout: 17% Improve: 44% Collapse: 30% Attrition: 28% Comparables: Bryan Little, Jose Vidro, D'Angelo Jimenez

(continued next page)

Luis Rodriguez *(continued)*

The middle infield did not have to be as bad as it was; some measure of confidence in minor league performance might have encouraged the Minnesota to fill their hole at second base with Rodriguez. Patient and not entirely punchless at the plate, he can field the position, and at worst makes a better reserve than Castro. Now buried in the Twin Cities by the pickups of Batista and Luis Castillo, he should be valuable to somebody.

ALEX ROMERO   OF   Bats: B Throws: R   Height: 6' 0"   Weight: 170   Born: September 9, 1983   Age: 22

YEAR	TM	LVL	AGE	PA	R	2B	3B	HR	RBI	BB	SO	SB	CS	SPEED	BA	OBP	SLG	MLVR	EQBA	EQOBP	EQSLG	EQA	VORP	DEFENSE			
2003	QUD	A	19	471	50	16	3	4	40	43	43	11	8	4.6	.296	.359	.376	.105	.262	.316	.353	.236	-3.5	109-CF	6		
2004	FTM	A+	20	442	59	21	2	6	42	54	47	6	4	4.7	.292	.387	.405	.175	.273	.353	.394	.262	3.6	67-RF	6	13-CF	0
2005	NBR	AA	21	556	65	31	2	15	77	36	69	12	11	4.9	.301	.354	.458	.179	.287	.339	.442	.266	10.9	120-LF	7	12-CF	1
2006	*MIN*	*MLB*	*22*	*556*	*70*	*32*	*2*	*13*	*69*	*38*	*68*	*8*	*5*	*5.0*	*.287*	*.339*	*.437*	*.043*	*.288*	*.348*	*.451*	*.266*	*14.6*	*131-LF*	*4*		

Breakout: 27%   Improve: 53%   Collapse: 16%   Attrition: 8%   Comparables: Curtis Granderson, Jody Gerut, Carl Yastrzemski

Romero is currently best prospect to come out of the organization's commitment to scouting Venezuela. Originally seen as a speed guy who might make it as a fourth outfielder type, Romero has pleasantly surprised the organization with his developing power. He particularly did damage against right-handed pitching, bopping at a .485 clip against them. When someone does that in Double-A before he turns 22, he moves up everybody's prospect lists. He might not get a shot in camp, but if hitters like Stewart and Ford falter, Romero will be a homegrown long-term solution.

DENARD SPAN   CF   Bats: L Throws: L   Height: 6' 1"   Weight: 180   Born: February 27, 1984   Age: 22

YEAR	TM	LVL	AGE	PA	R	2B	3B	HR	RBI	BB	SO	SB	CS	SPEED	BA	OBP	SLG	MLVR	EQBA	EQOBP	EQSLG	EQA	VORP	DEFENSE	
2003	ELZ	Rk	19	234	34	5	1	1	18	23	34	14	5	6.1	.271	.355	.319	.012	.236	.296	.283	.213	-24.3	47-CF	5
2004	QUD	A	20	278	29	4	3	0	14	34	49	15	8	5.8	.267	.363	.308	-.012	.238	.318	.275	.222	-11.7	62-CF	-3
2005	FTM	A+	21	210	38	3	3	1	19	22	25	13	4	7.1	.339	.410	.403	.222	.306	.372	.365	.267	8.4	47-CF	-3
2005	NBR	AA	21	299	47	6	5	0	26	22	41	10	8	7.2	.285	.355	.345	.017	.272	.335	.327	.238	-1.6	65-CF	-2
2006	*MIN*	*MLB*	*22*	*516*	*57*	*15*	*4*	*0*	*29*	*36*	*76*	*17*	*7*	*5.2*	*.268*	*.324*	*.317*	*-.151*	*.269*	*.332*	*.328*	*.229*	*-1.6*	*121-CF*	*-2*

Breakout: 22%   Improve: 52%   Collapse: 29%   Attrition: 8%   Comparables: Kennard Jones, Brandon Watson, Endy Chavez

No one who hits with the same authority as old Tom Goodwin of old should get much attention, yet because steals are neat and worth so much more in fantasy baseball than on an actual diamond, players like Span achieve undeserved notoriety. Unhappily, the Twins seem to be just as unrealistic as fant-heads, since they're equally excited about Span's willingness to bunt and beat the ball into the ground. His speed elicits comparisons to Deion Sanders, but he hasn't mastered the finer points of basestealing. Now that Rickey Henderson's retired, the Twins should consider bringing him in to coach Span and Luis Castillo in spring training. He's a gifted glove in center, playing aggressively shallow and getting good reads of the ball off the bat to take advantage of his speed and cover the gaps. However, his arm's no prize. All this makes him more trade bait than the man who will push Torii Hunter to a corner.

SHANNON STEWART   LF   Bats: R Throws: R   Height: 6' 1"   Weight: 210   Born: February 25, 1974   Age: 32

YEAR	TM	LVL	AGE	PA	R	2B	3B	HR	RBI	BB	SO	SB	CS	SPEED	BA	OBP	SLG	MLVR	EQBA	EQOBP	EQSLG	EQA	VORP	DEFENSE			
2003	TOR	MLB	29	340	47	22	2	7	35	27	30	1	2	4.4	.294	.347	.449	.059	.289	.349	.453	.276	6.3	68-LF	5		
2003	MIN	MLB	29	302	43	22	0	6	38	25	36	3	4	4.8	.322	.384	.470	.191	.322	.387	.476	.292	14.6	43-LF	0	13-RF	0
2004	MIN	MLB	30	429	46	17	2	11	47	47	44	6	3	4.7	.304	.380	.447	.112	.303	.383	.446	.288	16.4	70-LF	-9		
2005	MIN	MLB	31	598	69	27	3	10	56	34	73	7	5	5.0	.274	.323	.388	-.052	.278	.336	.403	.257	1.7	123-LF	2		
2006	*MIN*	*MLB*	*32*	*511*	*60*	*25*	*2*	*10*	*57*	*36*	*59*	*4*	*3*	*4.8*	*.276*	*.330*	*.399*	*-.030*	*.276*	*.339*	*.412*	*.253*	*4.8*	*120-LF*	*-3*		

Breakout: 6%   Improve: 28%   Collapse: 35%   Attrition: 12%   Comparables: Harvey Kuenn, Ken Berry, Roberto Kelly

Lost amidst so many other failures on this team was Stewart's collapse at the plate, as he posted career-lows in slugging and OBP. What he actually hit ranked around PECOTA's projected 20th percentile for him, but it was an even less useful year than that forecast because he played a full season. Less patience and less power were bad enough, but his days as a threat on the bases are long gone. He retained some value by being able to play the outfield much more this year, but whether he's in left or DHing, the Twins cannot afford for him to hit like this in the last year of his three-year, $18 million deal.

TERRY TIFFEE **1B/3B** **Bats: B Throws: R** Height: 6′ 3″ Weight: 210 Born: April 21, 1979 Age: 27

YEAR	TM	LVL	AGE	PA	R	2B	3B	HR	RBI	BB	SO	SB	CS	SPEED	BA	OBP	SLG	MLVR	EQBA	EQOBP	EQSLG	EQA	VORP	DEFENSE	
2003	NBR	AA	24	570	77	31	3	14	93	31	49	4	1	4.8	.315	.351	.464	.178	.285	.318	.432	.257	22.7	126-3B	12
2004	ROC	AAA	25	342	42	26	3	12	68	21	26	0	0	3.8	.307	.357	.522	.188	.274	.325	.460	.266	16.9	67-3B	-10
2005	ROC	AAA	26	252	33	11	1	10	39	15	24	0	1	4.1	.266	.313	.454	-.012	.234	.283	.388	.232	-1.8	44-3B	-5
2005	MIN	MLB	26	159	9	8	1	1	15	8	15	1	0	3.5	.207	.245	.293	-.368	.209	.258	.297	.200	-10.2	20-3B	-3
2006	*MIN*	*MLB*	*27*	*285*	*28*	*14*	*1*	*6*	*33*	*14*	*31*	*1*	*1*	*4.2*	*.262*	*.303*	*.397*	*-.087*	*.263*	*.311*	*.410*	*.240*	*1.5*	*70-3B*	*-2*

Breakout: 27% Improve: 44% Collapse: 32% Attrition: 28%   Tim Bogar, Jeff Hamilton, Daryl Sconiers

His career horizon has effectively disappeared with the decision to bring in Tony Batista. At best, he can hope to get a shot at some of the DH time that went to LeCroy in previous seasons, but he'll be hard-pressed to be as useful at the plate.

KEVIN WEST **OF** **Bats: R Throws: R** Height: 6′ 2″ Weight: 210 Born: January 1, 1980 Age: 26

YEAR	TM	LVL	AGE	PA	R	2B	3B	HR	RBI	BB	SO	SB	CS	SPEED	BA	OBP	SLG	MLVR	EQBA	EQOBP	EQSLG	EQA	VORP	DEFENSE	
2003	NBR	AA	23	528	54	41	1	14	79	27	110	3	5	3.5	.279	.318	.451	.076	.250	.287	.419	.239	-11.5	133-RF	0
2004	NBR	AA	24	490	68	35	1	25	87	41	98	2	3	3.6	.293	.359	.551	.278	.258	.316	.478	.266	9.1	62-RF	1
2004	ROC	AAA	24	85	10	8	0	4	22	4	19	0	0	3.3	.278	.306	.532	.090	.236	.267	.454	.244	-0.3		
2005	ROC	AAA	25	485	60	26	1	20	64	45	94	2	2	3.7	.271	.355	.478	.092	.237	.316	.415	.252	-5.2	61-RF 6	23-LF -1
2006	*MIN*	*MLB*	*26*	*412*	*45*	*20*	*1*	*15*	*55*	*28*	*91*	*1*	*1*	*3.5*	*.241*	*.298*	*.420*	*-.080*	*.241*	*.307*	*.433*	*.245*	*-2.2*	*98-RF*	*-1*

Breakout: 19% Improve: 35% Collapse: 36% Attrition: 18%   Comparables: Andy Bevins, Ryan Thompson, Candy Maldonado

Not seen as a prospect, West could wind up being a useful outfield reserve. He wouldn't be a Mike Restovich (pre-fabricated for a platoon role) type; by hitting .276/.338/.513 vs. righties, he's not exactly an easily pigeon-holed hitter. Unfortunately, he may miss half of the season with a winter knee injury.

PITCHERS

SCOTT BAKER **Bats: R Throws: R** Height: 6′ 4″ Weight: 190 Born: September 19, 1981 Age: 24

YEAR	TM	LVL	AGE	W	L	SV	G	GS	IP	H	BB	SO	HR	GB%	BABIP	STUFF	WHIP	ERA	PERA	EQERA	EQH9	EQBB9	EQSO9	EQHR9	VORP	WXRL
2004	FTM	A+	22	4	2	0	7	7	45.0	40	6	37	1	—	.291	18	1.02	2.40	3.50	3.92	8.7	1.4	4.7	0.4	8.2	—
2004	NBR	AA	22	5	3	0	10	10	70.3	44	13	72	2	—	.225	35	0.81	2.43	3.36	3.76	7.1	1.9	6.9	0.4	13.7	—
2004	ROC	AAA	22	1	3	0	9	9	54.3	65	15	36	3	—	.339	11	1.47	4.97	4.09	5.07	10.0	2.6	4.7	0.5	3.2	—
2005	ROC	AAA	23	5	8	0	22	22	134.7	123	26	107	15	37%	.280	11	1.11	3.01	4.48	3.72	8.8	1.9	5.7	1.2	27.3	—
2005	MIN	MLB	23	3	3	0	10	9	53.7	48	14	32	5	35%	.265	13	1.16	3.35	4.08	3.57	8.5	2.4	5.4	0.8	13.5	1.7
2006	*MIN*	*MLB*	*24*	*8*	*9*	*0*	*34*	*27*	*150.0*	*160*	*36*	*98*	*22*	*38%*	*.289*	*8*	*1.30*	*4.49*	*4.57*	*4.76*	*9.3*	*2.1*	*5.5*	*1.2*	*16.8*	*2.7*

Breakout: 3% Improve: 20% Collapse: 41% Attrition: 1%   Comparables: Francisco Barrios, Rick Aguilera, Mike Mussina

Initially projected as a poor man's Radke, a guy who throws strikes and doesn't kill you at the bottom of the rotation, Baker keeps outstripping expectations and getting better. He's not simply a command guy any more, not when he's now dialing it up into the mid 90s on top of a plus slider and devastating change. It's improvement with the change that really has made the difference in finishing off hitters more quickly, making him a potentially perfect fit in a Twins rotation noted for working fast and throwing strikes. The unfortunate decision to offer Lohse arbitration will set up a Baker vs. Liriano fight for the last spot in the rotation, a choice most organizations will envy.

BOOF BONSER **Bats: R Throws: R** Height: 6′ 4″ Weight: 230 Born: October 14, 1981 Age: 24

YEAR	TM	LVL	AGE	W	L	SV	G	GS	IP	H	BB	SO	HR	GB%	BABIP	STUFF	WHIP	ERA	PERA	EQERA	EQH9	EQBB9	EQSO9	EQHR9	VORP	WXRL
2003	NRW	AA	21	7	10	0	24	24	135.0	122	67	103	11	—	.269	-6	1.40	4.00	5.57	5.98	8.8	5.1	5.6	1.3	-5.5	—
2003	FRE	AAA	21	1	2	0	4	4	23.0	17	8	28	4	—	.241	22	1.09	3.13	4.91	5.32	7.8	3.7	9.8	2.0	0.7	—
2004	NBR	AA	22	12	9	0	27	27	154.3	160	56	146	22	—	.317	-7	1.40	4.37	5.62	5.85	10.0	3.5	6.2	1.8	-4.2	—
2005	ROC	AAA	23	11	9	0	28	28	160.3	153	57	168	22	40%	.312	9	1.31	3.99	4.76	4.64	8.9	3.5	7.5	1.4	16.7	—
2006	*MIN*	*MLB*	*24*	*7*	*9*	*0*	*30*	*20*	*129.0*	*134*	*54*	*100*	*20*	*39%*	*.292*	*7*	*1.45*	*5.06*	*5.17*	*5.36*	*9.0*	*3.8*	*6.6*	*1.3*	*6.0*	*1.4*

Breakout: 16% Improve: 48% Collapse: 12% Attrition: 1%   Comparables: Todd Van Poppel, Rob Bell, Mike Judd

With Nathan closing and Liriano among baseball's best prospects, a man named Boof has to settle for being the other guy in the Pierzynski heist. He's slowly becoming a more well-rounded pitching prospect, showing better durability while improving his breaking pitches and a changeup to complement low 90s velocity. Boof's problem is whether or not there's room for him in a big league rotation that will already have both Baker and Francisco Liriano competing for the last rotation slot.

TRAVIS BOWYER
Bats: R Throws: R   Height: 6′ 3″   Weight: 220   Born: August 3, 1981   Age: 24

YEAR	TM	LVL	AGE	W	L	SV	G	GS	IP	H	BB	SO	HR	GB%	BABIP	STUFF	WHIP	ERA	PERA	EQERA	EQH9	EQBB9	EQSO9	EQHR9	VORP	WXRL
2003	FTM	A+	21	5	2	1	45	0	80.0	68	56	70	1	—	.283	-9	1.55	3.83	5.09	6.87	8.5	7.5	5.6	0.4	-10.7	—
2004	FTM	A+	22	3	0	2	17	0	29.7	18	17	32	0	—	.257	-2	1.18	0.30	4.61	3.62	6.9	6.6	6.6	0.3	6.0	—
2004	NBR	AA	22	6	3	3	31	0	61.3	42	38	65	3	—	.255	4	1.31	1.76	4.78	3.39	7.4	6.2	7.1	0.6	14.3	—
2005	ROC	AAA	23	4	2	23	59	0	74.3	51	40	96	4	46%	.290	20	1.22	2.79	3.89	3.14	6.9	5.3	9.3	0.6	19.6	—
2006	FLO	MLB	24	2	3	1	28	3	49.3	46	35	50	5	45%	.306	3	1.63	4.93	5.48	5.55	8.4	5.9	8.0	0.9	0.2	0.1

Breakout: 11%   Improve: 25%   Collapse: 53%   Attrition: 20%   Comparables: Eric Plunk, Matt Anderson, Ryan Bukvich

Keeping in mind that there's almost never such a thing as a relief pitching prospect, getting into shape changed Bowyer from a guy with a good fastball to one who throws 99. That sort of velocity makes his slider and change that much more effective, and was attractive enough in trade to make him the headliner in the Castillo trade. He'll get a shot at closing for the Marlins, and if he remains committed to his career, he could be good at it.

JESSE CRAIN
Bats: R Throws: R   Height: 6′ 1″   Weight: 200   Born: July 5, 1981   Age: 24

YEAR	TM	LVL	AGE	W	L	SV	G	GS	IP	H	BB	SO	HR	GB%	BABIP	STUFF	WHIP	ERA	PERA	EQERA	EQH9	EQBB9	EQSO9	EQHR9	VORP	WXRL
2003	NBR	AA	22	1	1	9	22	0	39.0	13	10	56	0	—	.176	36	0.59	0.69	2.48	2.23	4.7	2.7	10.7	0.2	13.6	—
2003	ROC	AAA	22	3	1	10	23	0	26.0	24	10	33	0	—	.348	26	1.31	3.12	3.12	3.81	8.0	3.8	9.0	0.3	5.2	—
2004	ROC	AAA	23	3	2	19	41	0	50.7	38	17	64	5	—	.277	21	1.08	2.49	3.83	3.65	7.3	3.3	9.3	1.1	10.7	—
2004	MIN	MLB	23	3	0	0	22	0	27.0	17	12	14	2	41%	.194	-6	1.08	2.00	4.85	2.08	6.9	3.8	4.5	0.7	11.6	0.1
2005	MIN	MLB	24	12	5	1	75	0	79.7	61	29	25	6	49%	.222	-15	1.13	2.71	5.07	3.18	8.5	3.5	2.9	0.7	23.1	3.8
2006	MIN	MLB	24	3	3	2	61	0	64.3	62	24	41	7	45%	.274	-4	1.33	4.06	4.07	4.83	8.4	3.3	5.4	0.9	9.3	0.7

Breakout: 3%   Improve: 12%   Collapse: 72%   Attrition: 20%   Comparables: Bob File, Steve Ontiveros, Bobby Thigpen

Crain's a bit of a conundrum, the sort of pitcher that neither scouts nor statheads can really sort out. His electric fastball-slider combo was expected to produce a lot more strikeouts than this. It isn't just a matter of his role with the club; along with Romero, Crain was used to clean up other people's messes and stranded runners galore. That role means pitching from the stretch a lot, which generally cuts into a pitcher's throwing at full strength. Nevertheless, even with nobody on base, Crain didn't strike people out, logging only 13 Ks in 175 PAs. He has the stuff to dominate, and if he finally starts to, it would help grease the wheels to get him into the primary setup slot someday.

J. D. DURBIN
Bats: R Throws: R   Height: 6′ 0″   Weight: 190   Born: February 24, 1982   Age: 24

YEAR	TM	LVL	AGE	W	L	SV	G	GS	IP	H	BB	SO	HR	GB%	BABIP	STUFF	WHIP	ERA	PERA	EQERA	EQH9	EQBB9	EQSO9	EQHR9	VORP	WXRL
2003	FTM	A+	21	9	2	0	14	14	87.3	73	22	69	3	—	.266	8	1.09	3.09	4.59	5.68	9.1	2.7	5.0	1.0	-0.7	—
2003	NBR	AA	21	6	3	0	14	14	94.7	102	29	70	10	—	.301	-4	1.38	3.14	5.67	4.70	10.2	3.1	5.3	1.8	9.2	—
2004	NBR	AA	22	4	1	0	13	13	64.3	62	22	53	4	—	.302	9	1.31	2.52	4.43	3.86	9.1	3.3	5.4	0.7	12.2	—
2004	ROC	AAA	22	3	2	0	7	7	35.7	49	16	38	4	—	.421	12	1.82	4.54	4.38	6.57	10.7	4.1	7.3	1.0	-4.0	—
2005	ROC	AAA	23	5	5	0	22	19	104.0	97	51	90	8	49%	.309	7	1.42	4.33	4.78	4.69	8.7	4.8	6.2	0.8	10.3	—
2006	MIN	MLB	24	6	8	0	28	18	113.0	121	51	80	14	46%	.303	3	1.52	5.00	5.24	5.37	9.4	4.1	6.0	1.1	5.4	1.2

Breakout: 10%   Improve: 38%   Collapse: 21%   Attrition: 0%   Comparables: Jason Marquis, Herm Wehmeier, Kip Wells

"Maybe" is a dirty word where young pitchers are concerned, but after another injury-riddled season, what is it that Durbin is about to become? Maybe a hell of a pitcher; anybody who throws a moving 95 mph heater and a slurve as nasty as his gets people excited. But maybe he'll just stay a "maybe," because as long as he has trouble staying on the mound or throwing strikes, it's hard to really consider him a prospect. He lost six weeks in the second half to lingering shoulder tendinitis after having his labrum repaired the year before, although he was back on the mound at season's end. There's still the question of whether he's going to master changing speeds or get his breaking stuff over for strikes often enough, especially against lefties. Throw concerns about his durability into the mix, and a move to the pen might be the best outcome for all concerned.

WILLIE EYRE
Bats: R Throws: R   Height: 6′ 2″   Weight: 200   Born: July 21, 1978   Age: 27

YEAR	TM	LVL	AGE	W	L	SV	G	GS	IP	H	BB	SO	HR	GB%	BABIP	STUFF	WHIP	ERA	PERA	EQERA	EQH9	EQBB9	EQSO9	EQHR9	VORP	WXRL
2003	NBR	AA	24	6	5	0	29	10	96.3	93	38	66	6	—	.281	-15	1.36	3.46	5.38	5.28	9.5	4.3	4.7	1.1	3.3	—
2003	ROC	AAA	24	0	2	0	6	5	24.0	30	16	23	2	—	.364	-12	1.92	6.00	6.00	7.12	10.5	7.1	6.4	1.1	-4.1	—
2004	ROC	AAA	25	6	7	4	36	21	136.0	131	53	91	13	—	.282	-9	1.35	3.64	5.19	4.37	9.1	4.0	4.6	1.0	18.0	—
2005	ROC	AAA	26	10	3	7	56	0	82.7	79	28	74	3	61%	.322	8	1.29	2.72	3.89	3.89	8.8	3.4	6.0	0.4	15.4	—
2006	MIN	MLB	27	3	3	1	27	4	51.7	55	24	33	6	51%	.301	-7	1.53	4.79	5.04	5.24	9.4	4.1	5.4	0.9	3.2	0.4

Breakout: 14%   Improve: 34%   Collapse: 37%   Attrition: 31%   Comparables: Kevin Hodges, Jerry Johnson, George Culver

Welcome to life in the Twins organization: Eyre isn't a bad prospect, but he isn't an exceptional one in a system replete with that sort. So what to do? Put him in the pen, and have a quality, homegrown reliever, naturally. He had a significant reverse platoon split in Rochester, which suggests that his breaking stuff doesn't have enough wiggle to keep right-handed hitters from sitting on his fastball. Whether or not that keeps him in the International League for another go-round will have to be seen, but for everybody else, he's worth getting as a throw-in on a deal.

MATT GARZA   Bats: R Throws: R   Height: 6′ 4″ Weight: 190 Born: November 11, 1983 Age: 22

YEAR	TM	LVL	AGE	W	L	SV	G	GS	IP	H	BB	SO	HR	GB%	BABIP	STUFF	WHIP	ERA	PERA	EQERA	EQH9	EQBB9	EQSO9	EQHR9	VORP	WXRL
2005	ELZ	Rk	21	1	1	0	4	4	19.7	14	6	25	3	50%	.262	-14	1.02	3.65	9.18	7.56	11.3	5.4	5.4	3.8	-3.6	—
2005	BLT	A	21	3	3	0	10	10	56.0	53	15	64	5	47%	.338	12	1.21	3.54	5.23	5.06	10.0	2.9	6.9	1.7	3.2	—
2006	MIN	MLB	22	7	9	0	27	23	132.7	141	55	95	23	45%	.289	6	1.47	5.08	5.43	5.37	9.3	3.7	6.1	1.5	5.7	1.5

Breakout: 23% Improve: 62% Collapse: 5% Attrition: 2%   Comparables: Juan Dominguez, Dennis Tankersley, Cory Morris

Considered something of a reach as the Twins' top pick of '05, Garza has exceptional stuff but can be inconsistent. He was the WAC Pitcher of the Year at Fresno State before being drafted, but he's not quite as polished as some college pitchers. He has a good sinking fastball and a good slider, but he's still mastering a curve and change. Whether he gets that consistent third pitch will no doubt guide his career; in the meantime, the Twins are comfortable with his developing into either a starter or a reliever.

MATT GUERRIER   Bats: R Throws: R   Height: 6′ 3″ Weight: 180 Born: August 2, 1978   Age: 27

YEAR	TM	LVL	AGE	W	L	SV	G	GS	IP	H	BB	SO	HR	GB%	BABIP	STUFF	WHIP	ERA	PERA	EQERA	EQH9	EQBB9	EQSO9	EQHR9	VORP	WXRL
2003	NAS	AAA	24	4	6	0	20	19	105.3	108	18	78	15	—	.281	-16	1.20	4.53	5.61	5.52	10.2	1.9	5.6	2.0	0.9	—
2004	ROC	AAA	25	5	10	0	24	23	144.0	135	25	97	15	—	.271	3	1.11	3.19	4.65	4.46	9.0	1.8	4.7	1.2	17.6	—
2005	MIN	MLB	26	0	3	0	43	0	71.7	71	24	46	6	48%	.293	3	1.33	3.39	4.27	3.64	9.0	3.0	5.8	0.8	18.1	0.4
2006	MIN	MLB	27	3	3	2	47	0	63.3	66	18	40	8	47%	.285	-4	1.33	4.09	4.37	4.67	9.1	2.6	5.3	1.1	8.8	0.7

Breakout: 24% Improve: 50% Collapse: 20% Attrition: 26%   Comparables: Mark Huismann, Ron Taylor, Rusty Meacham

"Garbage" is such an ugly term. Whether applied to innings or items, it conveys the idea that somehow these things aren't useful. We live in a time when euphemisms are very much in vogue, so why not plug in "re-purposed," and give Guerrier his due for taking those re-purposed innings and helping finish ballgames that superior talents were better kept out of. In today's hyper-specialized pens, there aren't a lot of out-and-out middle relievers, so it's nice to see an item from the '80s, even if it's as anachronistic as a Members Only jacket.

ADAM HARBEN   Bats: R Throws: R   Height: 6′ 5″ Weight: 210 Born: August 19, 1983   Age: 22

YEAR	TM	LVL	AGE	W	L	SV	G	GS	IP	H	BB	SO	HR	GB%	BABIP	STUFF	WHIP	ERA	PERA	EQERA	EQH9	EQBB9	EQSO9	EQHR9	VORP	WXRL
2003	QUD	A	19	5	6	0	16	15	87.3	91	35	77	5	—	.317	-1	1.44	4.33	5.92	6.99	10.3	4.5	5.4	1.5	-12.9	—
2004	QUD	A	20	9	7	0	26	26	142.7	114	68	171	5	—	.311	16	1.28	3.09	4.83	5.44	8.8	5.8	6.4	0.7	2.4	—
2005	FTM	A+	21	10	5	0	25	25	135.3	102	62	119	6	57%	.261	4	1.21	2.66	5.17	4.88	8.3	5.5	5.3	0.8	10.0	—
2006	MIN	MLB	22	6	9	0	25	22	125.7	130	76	86	14	50%	.297	2	1.64	5.40	5.47	5.83	9.0	5.5	5.9	0.9	-0.8	0.8

Breakout: 8% Improve: 44% Collapse: 19% Attrition: 1%   Comparables: John Van Benschoten, Preston Larrison, Ben Fritz

That rare righthander who works with a fastball that gets into the mid 90s, and he supplements it with a power curve. If you have visions of Bert Blyleven dancing in your head, we can indulge you. His mechanics and command are still rough, though, and he hasn't mastered a change yet, so all sorts of things could go wrong at Double-A against stronger competition. Still, he'd be the best young pitcher in most systems. The Twins aren't just lucky that way; nobody does it better when it comes to picking pitching talent in bulk.

JUSTIN JONES   Bats: L Throws: L   Height: 6′ 4″ Weight: 190 Born: September 25, 1984 Age: 21

YEAR	TM	LVL	AGE	W	L	SV	G	GS	IP	H	BB	SO	HR	GB%	BABIP	STUFF	WHIP	ERA	PERA	EQERA	EQH9	EQBB9	EQSO9	EQHR9	VORP	WXRL
2003	LNS	A	18	3	5	0	16	16	71.0	56	32	87	1	—	.304	38	1.24	2.28	4.14	5.21	8.4	5.1	7.6	0.4	2.9	—
2004	LNS	A	19	3	3	0	14	14	64.3	62	22	59	6	—	.306	-6	1.31	3.78	6.27	6.27	10.6	4.0	4.9	1.8	-4.5	—
2004	QUD	A	19	0	2	0	7	4	20.3	20	14	17	2	—	.295	-24	1.67	5.32	8.20	8.68	11.1	8.2	4.8	1.9	-6.4	—
2005	FTM	A+	20	7	3	0	13	13	77.7	78	28	54	5	53%	.315	0	1.36	3.01	5.45	4.72	9.8	4.1	4.1	1.1	7.3	—
2006	MIN	MLB	21	6	9	0	26	23	128.7	144	63	72	18	50%	.298	-3	1.61	5.41	5.69	5.78	9.8	4.4	4.8	1.2	-0.7	0.8

Breakout: 10% Improve: 45% Collapse: 18% Attrition: 0%   Comparables: Jung Bong, Jorge de la Rosa, Renyel Pinto

(continued next page)

Justin Jones *(continued)*

Jones was picked up from the Cubs in the four-team Garciaparra swap. He has yet to throw 100 innings in any season as a pro, having endured a dead arm in '03, shoulder trouble in '04, and elbow problems that kept him on the shelf until July in '05. But with good velocity, four pitches he can throw for strikes, and no career-altering surgeries yet, he bears watching.

FRANCISCO LIRIANO Bats: L Throws: L Height: 6' 2" Weight: 180 Born: October 26, 1983 Age: 22

YEAR	TM	LVL	AGE	W	L	SV	G	GS	IP	H	BB	SO	HR	GB%	BABIP	STUFF	WHIP	ERA	PERA	EQERA	EQH9	EQBB9	EQSO9	EQHR9	VORP	WXRL
2004	FTM	A+	20	6	7	0	21	21	117.0	118	43	125	6	—	.350	16	1.38	4.00	4.58	5.45	9.5	3.8	6.5	1.0	1.9	—
2004	NBR	AA	20	3	2	0	7	7	39.7	45	17	49	4	—	.369	30	1.56	3.17	4.28	3.83	9.9	3.8	8.1	1.1	7.9	—
2005	NBR	AA	21	3	5	0	13	13	76.7	70	26	92	6	60%	.335	24	1.25	3.64	4.14	4.99	9.0	3.5	7.7	1.0	5.0	—
2005	ROC	AAA	21	9	2	0	14	14	91.0	56	24	112	4	55%	.259	54	0.88	1.78	2.87	2.77	6.4	2.6	9.2	0.4	27.6	—
2005	MIN	MLB	21	1	2	0	6	4	23.7	19	7	33	4	47%	.306	23	1.10	5.70	3.42	5.32	7.2	2.7	12.2	1.5	0.3	0.2
2006	*MIN*	*MLB*	*22*	*10*	*9*	*1*	*39*	*22*	*158.0*	*147*	*57*	*150*	*14*	*48%*	*.301*	*24*	*1.29*	*3.87*	*3.84*	*4.27*	*8.1*	*3.3*	*8.1*	*0.7*	*27.1*	*3.7*

Breakout: 19% Improve: 72% Collapse: 14% Attrition: 5% Comparables: Curt Simmons, Bob Moose, Johnny Podres

Baseball's best pitching prospect and a promising candidate for Rookie of the Year if he gets a full season in '06. A former outfielder who was seen as fragile, then thrown in on the Pierzynski deal with the Giants, Liriano has overcome the shoulder soreness that made him available in the first place. His inexperience on the mound shows up in little things, but with good mechanics and command of a fastball that sometimes reaches 96, trouble with holding runners and the like isn't a deal breaker for the parent organization. Where Liriano took a major step forward was mastering not one but two changeups, using both a circle and a three-finger change. To make things really unfair, he also finishes guys off with a slider that gets into the high 80s. With all of that, he led the minor leagues with 204 Ks in 2005. The comparisons to Johan Santana make some sense. As they were with Santana, the Twins will be cautious about simply plugging him into the rotation. Even so, he should be taking his turn every fifth day by May.

KYLE LOHSE Bats: R Throws: R Height: 6' 2" Weight: 190 Born: October 4, 1978 Age: 27

YEAR	TM	LVL	AGE	W	L	SV	G	GS	IP	H	BB	SO	HR	GB%	BABIP	STUFF	WHIP	ERA	PERA	EQERA	EQH9	EQBB9	EQSO9	EQHR9	VORP	WXRL
2003	MIN	MLB	24	14	11	0	33	33	201.0	211	45	130	28	43%	.291	8	1.27	4.61	4.43	4.52	9.3	2.0	5.7	1.2	29.7	4.1
2004	MIN	MLB	25	9	13	0	35	34	194.0	240	76	111	28	46%	.327	-4	1.64	5.34	5.04	5.36	10.2	3.2	4.7	1.1	7.9	2.0
2005	MIN	MLB	26	9	13	0	31	30	178.7	211	44	86	22	46%	.316	1	1.43	4.18	4.77	4.28	10.3	2.2	4.3	1.0	30.9	3.7
2006	*MIN*	*MLB*	*27*	*9*	*10*	*0*	*33*	*26*	*162.7*	*187*	*42*	*87*	*22*	*45%*	*.301*	*1*	*1.41*	*4.67*	*4.96*	*5.03*	*10.0*	*2.4*	*4.5*	*1.1*	*14.1*	*2.5*

Breakout: 6% Improve: 40% Collapse: 16% Attrition: 2% Comparables: Stan Bahnsen, Paul Quantrill, Jim Perry

Not a stathead's sort of pitcher, but not everybody can crank out a quality start half of the time, and if that's your fourth or fifth starter, you've got something. He throws hard and can get both his slider and curve over for strikes, so it would be interesting to see if he'd ever benefit from working with someone like Dave Duncan and turn some of that stuff into results. The Twins were right to offer him arbitration this winter; if Baker and Liriano both look ready, Ryan can always shop Lohse or even Brad Radke; despite greater acclaim, Radke hasn't actually outpitched Lohse in two of the last three years.

JOE MAYS Bats: B Throws: R Height: 6' 1" Weight: 190 Born: December 10, 1975 Age: 30

YEAR	TM	LVL	AGE	W	L	SV	G	GS	IP	H	BB	SO	HR	GB%	BABIP	STUFF	WHIP	ERA	PERA	EQERA	EQH9	EQBB9	EQSO9	EQHR9	VORP	WXRL
2003	MIN	MLB	27	8	8	0	31	21	130.0	159	39	50	21	49%	.303	-21	1.52	6.30	5.50	5.91	10.6	2.7	3.4	1.4	-3.0	-0.0
2005	MIN	MLB	29	6	10	0	31	26	156.0	203	41	59	23	46%	.324	-15	1.56	5.65	5.24	6.26	11.0	2.4	3.3	1.2	-8.4	0.6
2006	*KCA*	*MLB*	*30*	*5*	*10*	*0*	*40*	*17*	*127.3*	*161*	*37*	*52*	*19*	*47%*	*.312*	*-14*	*1.56*	*5.58*	*5.93*	*5.98*	*11.1*	*2.7*	*3.7*	*1.2*	*-3.6*	*0.3*

Breakout: 30% Improve: 64% Collapse: 20% Attrition: 18% Comparables: Jim Bouton, Dick Bosman, Dustin Hermanson

Although a ghastly stretch drive erased all memory of it, Mays briefly looked like he was all the way back from Tommy John surgery. Starting in May, he strung together an odd run of six consecutive quality starts: in the first two he pitched six innings giving up three runs or less, only to be left out there to blow both in the seventh, then he notched his lone complete game shutout against the Jays, and then threw three more QSs against non-patsies (the Indians, Blue Jays again, and Yankees). After that last start on June 4, he was awful, allowing 7.6 runs per nine while the team went 3–11 in his 14 starts. That got him out of the rotation in September. The Royals remembered Mays's brief return to usefulness and signed him to a one-year deal. Though Mays has pitched well at Kauffman Stadium, at least some of his success there has to be attributed to pitching against the Royals themselves.

JASON MILLER
Bats: L Throws: L   Height: 6' 1"   Weight: 200   Born: July 20, 1982   Age: 23

YEAR	TM	LVL	AGE	W	L	SV	G	GS	IP	H	BB	SO	HR	GB%	BABIP	STUFF	WHIP	ERA	PERA	EQERA	EQH9	EQBB9	EQSO9	EQHR9	VORP	WXRL
2003	QUD	A	20	5	1	0	13	12	68.7	67	21	50	4	—	.288	-5	1.28	2.36	5.82	4.98	10.1	3.6	4.4	1.5	4.5	—
2003	FTM	A+	20	3	4	0	13	10	51.0	60	21	39	3	—	.333	-12	1.59	4.24	6.02	7.30	11.3	4.2	4.9	1.6	-9.3	—
2004	FTM	A+	21	1	0	1	19	0	29.3	16	11	40	2	—	.233	13	0.92	1.54	4.72	3.04	7.4	4.1	8.8	1.4	7.6	—
2004	NBR	AA	21	0	2	2	33	1	40.0	33	21	42	2	—	.290	3	1.35	4.28	4.62	4.85	8.1	5.1	7.2	0.7	3.2	—
2005	NBR	AA	22	1	2	4	26	0	49.7	34	22	56	5	31%	.242	-1	1.13	2.72	5.09	4.11	8.0	4.9	7.2	1.4	7.6	—
2005	ROC	AAA	22	2	0	0	13	0	26.0	28	17	27	4	34%	.333	-4	1.73	3.81	5.61	4.91	9.5	6.3	7.4	1.4	2.0	—
2006	*MIN*	*MLB*	*23*	*3*	*4*	*1*	*32*	*5*	*57.7*	*61*	*31*	*44*	*11*	*35%*	*.291*	*-7*	*1.59*	*5.55*	*5.90*	*5.82*	*9.3*	*4.8*	*6.5*	*1.5*	*-0.3*	*0.1*

Breakout: 7%   Improve: 27%   Collapse: 35%   Attrition: 18%   Comparables: Glenn Bott, Scott Linebrink, Corey Thurman

Miller is not a situational lefty in the making, not when right-handed hitters hit only .180 against him in Double-A, and not when he was striking out one of three batters, lefty, righty, switch, or appropriately frightened. He throws hard, and while he was hittable at Double-A, he was still blowing people away. He can earn a shot at replacing Romero in the pen before '06 is over.

TERRY MULHOLLAND
Bats: R Throws: L   Height: 6' 3"   Weight: 220   Born: March 9, 1963   Age: 43

YEAR	TM	LVL	AGE	W	L	SV	G	GS	IP	H	BB	SO	HR	GB%	BABIP	STUFF	WHIP	ERA	PERA	EQERA	EQH9	EQBB9	EQSO9	EQHR9	VORP	WXRL
2003	CLE	MLB	40	3	4	0	45	3	99.0	117	37	42	17	49%	.297	-29	1.56	4.91	5.84	5.29	10.7	3.4	3.7	1.5	7.1	0.1
2004	MIN	MLB	41	5	9	0	39	15	123.3	163	33	60	17	51%	.346	-10	1.59	5.18	4.78	5.06	10.6	2.2	4.0	1.1	10.6	1.3
2005	MIN	MLB	42	0	2	0	49	0	59.0	61	17	18	6	59%	.279	-21	1.32	4.27	5.09	4.63	9.9	2.6	2.8	0.9	7.6	-0.2
2006	*ARI*	*MLB*	*43*	*1*	*2*	*1*	*32*	*1*	*39.0*	*49*	*13*	*20*	*5*	*54%*	*.320*	*-23*	*1.58*	*5.65*	*5.67*	*7.87*	*11.0*	*2.7*	*4.3*	*1.2*	*-1.0*	*-0.2*

Breakout: 22%   Improve: 33%   Collapse: 36%   Attrition: 42%   Comparables: Jim Kaat, Tommy John, John Franco

If you liked Mike Morgan, you probably love Mulholland. No rocking-chair Orosco-style situational flim-flam job for him, Mulholland pitches complete innings and all those other things you associate with real pitchers, not lefty specialists. He split mop-up duties with Guerrier, which, at Mulholland's age, must have made him Senior Mop Consultant of the pen's cleaning crew. Perhaps predictably, Arizona's interested in bringing him in, just as they did with Morgan at the end of his long career.

JOE NATHAN
Bats: R Throws: R   Height: 6' 4"   Weight: 200   Born: November 22, 1974   Age: 31

YEAR	TM	LVL	AGE	W	L	SV	G	GS	IP	H	BB	SO	HR	GB%	BABIP	STUFF	WHIP	ERA	PERA	EQERA	EQH9	EQBB9	EQSO9	EQHR9	VORP	WXRL
2003	SFN	MLB	28	12	4	0	78	0	79.0	51	33	83	7	34%	.239	18	1.06	2.96	3.77	3.18	7.1	3.5	8.7	0.8	23.3	2.6
2004	MIN	MLB	29	1	2	44	73	0	72.3	48	23	89	3	38%	.273	43	0.98	1.62	2.62	1.75	6.2	2.6	10.4	0.4	37.1	7.7
2005	MIN	MLB	30	7	4	43	69	0	70.0	46	22	94	5	38%	.270	46	0.97	2.70	2.58	2.71	6.2	2.8	12.0	0.6	22.9	4.4
2006	*MIN*	*MLB*	*31*	*5*	*5*	*42*	*66*	*0*	*70.3*	*54*	*21*	*84*	*7*	*35%*	*.275*	*28*	*1.07*	*2.64*	*2.81*	*2.94*	*6.7*	*2.8*	*10.1*	*0.8*	*22.7*	*3.6*

Breakout: 30%   Improve: 35%   Collapse: 41%   Attrition: 9%   Comparables: Tom Henke, Trevor Hoffman, Skip Lockwood

Although it probably doesn't help his reputation that nine of last season's saves were against the Royals, or that he blew two more, it really says more about the Twins and Royals being about as likely to score as the president of your high school comic book club. There's something vaguely disappointing about a great closer who is simply a great closer. It's a Tom Henke sort of thing, where greatness goes unobserved due to the lack of a signature. Perhaps distracting facial hair would help; '90s style goatees aren't like Goose's Fu Manchu or Rollie Fingers's waxed mustachios, they're just lazy. Until he gets a fashion consultant, Nathan will settle for mercilessly blowing away opponents with high 90s heat and a criminally nasty power slider.

PAT NESHEK
Bats: B Throws: R   Height: 6' 2"   Weight: 200   Born: September 4, 1980   Age: 25

YEAR	TM	LVL	AGE	W	L	SV	G	GS	IP	H	BB	SO	HR	GB%	BABIP	STUFF	WHIP	ERA	PERA	EQERA	EQH9	EQBB9	EQSO9	EQHR9	VORP	WXRL
2003	QUD	A	22	3	2	14	28	0	34.3	20	11	53	0	—	.286	21	0.90	0.52	3.13	3.13	7.1	4.0	9.1	0.3	8.7	—
2003	FTM	A+	22	4	1	2	20	0	29.3	22	6	29	2	—	.253	-4	0.96	2.15	5.40	4.72	9.4	2.4	6.4	2.0	2.6	—
2004	NBR	AA	23	2	1	2	26	0	35.3	34	18	38	2	—	.327	-2	1.47	3.82	4.67	4.67	9.1	4.9	6.7	0.8	3.6	—
2005	NBR	AA	24	6	4	24	55	0	82.3	69	21	95	9	42%	.297	-6	1.09	2.19	4.89	4.07	9.2	2.9	7.0	1.5	13.1	—
2006	*MIN*	*MLB*	*25*	*3*	*3*	*1*	*27*	*4*	*54.3*	*58*	*19*	*40*	*10*	*42%*	*.288*	*-1*	*1.40*	*4.81*	*5.16*	*5.14*	*9.3*	*3.1*	*6.2*	*1.5*	*4.2*	*0.5*

Breakout: 8%   Improve: 27%   Collapse: 40%   Attrition: 16%   Comparables: Jim Farrell, Eric Schmitt, Mike Wuertz

Finally added to the 40-man roster, Neshek isn't coming up courtesy of blazing stuff; he relies more on guile and command of a decent fastball-slider combo. He has a significant platoon split, allowing six of his nine homeruns to lefties. But without the sort of stuff or a trick delivery to make people overlook that sort of thing, he's either going to have to really shine in camp or polish up a changeup in order to stick.

GLEN PERKINS

Bats: L   Throws: L   Height: 6' 0"   Weight: 200   Born: March 2, 1983   Age: 23

YEAR	TM	LVL	AGE	W	L	SV	G	GS	IP	H	BB	SO	HR	GB%	BABIP	STUFF	WHIP	ERA	PERA	EQERA	EQH9	EQBB9	EQSO9	EQHR9	VORP	WXRL
2004	QUD	A	21	2	1	0	9	9	48.3	33	12	49	2	—	.250	11	0.93	1.30	4.47	3.65	8.3	3.0	5.3	0.8	9.6	—
2005	FTM	A+	22	3	2	0	10	9	55.0	41	13	66	2	43%	.295	24	0.98	2.13	3.83	4.01	8.2	2.8	7.0	0.7	9.1	—
2005	NBR	AA	22	4	4	0	14	14	79.0	80	35	67	4	40%	.326	5	1.46	4.90	4.93	5.87	9.6	4.7	5.3	0.7	-2.3	—
2006	*MIN*	*MLB*	*23*	*7*	*9*	*0*	*28*	*23*	*136.7*	*141*	*59*	*97*	*19*	*42%*	*.291*	*7*	*1.46*	*4.90*	*5.01*	*5.18*	*9.0*	*3.9*	*6.1*	*1.1*	*8.1*	*1.8*

Breakout: 7%   Improve: 40%   Collapse: 19%   Attrition: 0%   Comparables: *Ryan Snare, Mike Connolly, Jorge de la Rosa*

For all of their scouty plaudits, the Twins don't get too hung up on archetypes when it comes to finding pitchers. Picked out of the University of Minnesota, you might think Perkins is just a favorite son, especially when he has what might be called a classically Midwestern build: stocky, bordering on doughy. But the Twins skipped over that, focusing on the fact that he throws strikes and has good mechanics. He's not overpowering, but he's not a soft-tosser, either, throwing on the inside corner to set up his slider and curve. He was promoted at the end of June, somewhat of a surprise since he started slowly with wrist trouble at the season's start.

BRAD RADKE

Bats: R   Throws: R   Height: 6' 2"   Weight: 180   Born: October 27, 1972   Age: 33

YEAR	TM	LVL	AGE	W	L	SV	G	GS	IP	H	BB	SO	HR	GB%	BABIP	STUFF	WHIP	ERA	PERA	EQERA	EQH9	EQBB9	EQSO9	EQHR9	VORP	WXRL
2003	MIN	MLB	30	14	10	0	33	33	212.3	242	28	120	32	43%	.306	4	1.27	4.49	4.51	4.43	9.9	1.2	4.9	1.3	33.1	4.1
2004	MIN	MLB	31	11	8	0	34	34	219.7	229	26	143	23	47%	.296	21	1.15	3.48	3.78	3.50	9.0	1.0	5.5	0.9	59.6	7.5
2005	MIN	MLB	32	9	12	0	31	31	200.7	214	23	117	33	44%	.284	3	1.18	4.04	4.57	4.35	9.8	1.0	5.2	1.4	31.8	3.7
2006	*MIN*	*MLB*	*33*	*11*	*10*	*0*	*32*	*28*	*184.0*	*202*	*28*	*104*	*25*	*44%*	*.290*	*8*	*1.24*	*4.17*	*4.32*	*4.49*	*9.6*	*1.4*	*4.8*	*1.1*	*26.4*	*4.0*

Breakout: 9%   Improve: 42%   Collapse: 24%   Attrition: 5%   Comparables: *Dennis Martinez, Juan Marichal, Robin Roberts*

Radke's greatest asset is his reputation for reliability, and his ranking in the top ten in baseball for being least flaky (as measured by his standard deviation between starts in Support-Neutral Value Added) would seem to support that. Unfortunately, he was reliably only as good as he was in '03. That isn't shabby, but it probably isn't what the Twins were hoping for when they signed him for $9 million per for '05 and '06. His stuff, which was never dominant to begin with, just doesn't fool lefties these days (.517 SLG against LHBs). That doesn't bode well; the Indians already have lefty power, and the White Sox are making a point of adding it. With the unbalanced schedule, things aren't going to get any easier for Radke.

JAY RAINVILLE

Bats: R   Throws: R   Height: 6' 3"   Weight: 230   Born: October 16, 1985   Age: 20

YEAR	TM	LVL	AGE	W	L	SV	G	GS	IP	H	BB	SO	HR	GB%	BABIP	STUFF	WHIP	ERA	PERA	EQERA	EQH9	EQBB9	EQSO9	EQHR9	VORP	WXRL
2005	BLT	A	19	8	2	0	16	16	88.3	83	27	77	14	29%	.276	-16	1.25	3.77	7.08	4.90	10.7	3.2	5.6	2.8	6.4	—
2005	FTM	A+	19	4	3	0	9	9	54.0	54	6	35	7	40%	.278	-1	1.11	2.67	5.96	5.08	10.7	1.2	4.0	2.1	3.0	—
2006	*MIN*	*MLB*	*20*	*8*	*10*	*0*	*27*	*27*	*153.3*	*170*	*42*	*94*	*34*	*36%*	*.280*	*6*	*1.38*	*5.02*	*5.51*	*5.12*	*9.7*	*2.5*	*5.2*	*1.8*	*9.2*	*2.1*

Breakout: 6%   Improve: 48%   Collapse: 14%   Attrition: 0%   Comparables: *Ruben Quevedo, Travis Chick, Tyler Clippard*

Rainville is probably the least polished of the team's group of 2004 first-round picks in that his offspeed and breaking stuff are still works in progress, but he's got a low-90s sinker that's kept people flailing everywhere he's pitched. A Rhode Island kid who played a bit of hockey in high school, something that might excite Tom Glavine fans, he's already got that bulldog on the mound rep.

JUAN RINCON

Bats: R   Throws: R   Height: 5' 11"   Weight: 190   Born: January 23, 1979   Age: 27

YEAR	TM	LVL	AGE	W	L	SV	G	GS	IP	H	BB	SO	HR	GB%	BABIP	STUFF	WHIP	ERA	PERA	EQERA	EQH9	EQBB9	EQSO9	EQHR9	VORP	WXRL
2003	MIN	MLB	24	5	6	0	58	0	85.7	74	38	63	5	47%	.273	9	1.31	3.68	4.02	3.81	8.0	3.9	6.5	0.5	20.4	0.4
2004	MIN	MLB	25	11	6	2	77	0	82.0	52	32	106	5	48%	.270	41	1.05	2.63	2.77	2.77	6.1	3.3	11.0	0.4	28.5	2.8
2005	MIN	MLB	26	6	6	0	75	0	77.0	63	30	84	2	49%	.313	36	1.21	2.45	2.91	2.91	7.3	3.5	9.7	0.2	23.4	3.4
2006	*MIN*	*MLB*	*27*	*4*	*3*	*4*	*66*	*0*	*72.3*	*65*	*30*	*70*	*6*	*46%*	*.295*	*13*	*1.30*	*3.54*	*3.59*	*4.13*	*7.8*	*3.7*	*8.3*	*0.7*	*15.3*	*1.3*

Breakout: 16%   Improve: 30%   Collapse: 51%   Attrition: 9%   Comparables: *Scott Williamson, Greg Harris, Eddie Watt*

Rincon earned a Performance Enhancing Drug (PED) suspension in May, giving him uncharacteristic notoriety. Pretty quietly, Rincon has become one of the best relievers in baseball. In the Twins' structured pen, he's the dedicated setup man who bridges the 8th inning gap between Crain's cleaning up the starter's mess and Nathan's 9th inning coup de grace. Off-season surgery to remove a bone spur in his elbow isn't supposed to affect him in the spring, so expect more of the same.

J. C. ROMERO   **Bats: B Throws: L**   Height: 5' 11" Weight: 193 Born: June 4, 1976   Age: 30

YEAR	TM	LVL	AGE	W	L	SV	G	GS	IP	H	BB	SO	HR	GB%	BABIP	STUFF	WHIP	ERA	PERA	EQERA	EQH9	EQBB9	EQSO9	EQHR9	VORP	WXRL
2003	MIN	MLB	27	2	0	0	73	0	63.0	66	42	50	7	53%	.317	-8	1.71	5.00	5.23	4.95	9.2	5.8	6.9	1.0	6.0	1.5
2004	MIN	MLB	28	7	4	1	74	0	74.3	61	38	69	4	57%	.290	16	1.34	3.51	3.86	3.50	7.6	4.2	7.8	0.5	19.9	2.2
2005	MIN	MLB	29	4	3	0	68	0	57.0	50	39	48	6	57%	.277	-3	1.56	3.47	5.24	3.97	8.4	6.2	7.6	1.0	9.5	0.8
2006	LAA	MLB	30	2	2 · 1		54	0	49.7	52	27	39	5	51%	.309	-4	1.57	4.66	5.05	5.43	9.2	4.9	6.9	0.8	3.0	0.2

Breakout: 11%   Improve: 22%   Collapse: 49%   Attrition: 21%   Comparables: Mike Munoz, C. J. Nitkowski, Danny McDevitt

Like Crain, Romero was most often put into situations where he had to solve other people's problems. He wasn't as effective at it, allowing hitters to reach base at a .442 clip with runners already on, which is sort of like using a Molotov cocktail to put out a grease fire. Dealt to the Angels this winter, he has a good shot at bouncing back and pitching in something more than a lefty specialist role.

JOHAN SANTANA   **Bats: L Throws: L**   Height: 6' 0" Weight: 190 Born: March 13, 1979   Age: 27

YEAR	TM	LVL	AGE	W	L	SV	G	GS	IP	H	BB	SO	HR	GB%	BABIP	STUFF	WHIP	ERA	PERA	EQERA	EQH9	EQBB9	EQSO9	EQHR9	VORP	WXRL
2003	MIN	MLB	24	12	3	0	45	18	158.3	127	47	169	17	33%	.274	32	1.10	3.07	3.44	3.10	7.3	2.6	9.4	0.9	51.1	5.2
2004	MIN	MLB	25	20	6	0	34	34	228.0	156	54	265	24	44%	.252	47	0.92	2.61	3.08	2.60	6.6	2.0	9.9	0.8	89.9	9.5
2005	MIN	MLB	26	16	7	0	33	33	231.7	180	45	238	22	40%	.265	44	0.97	2.87	3.10	2.94	7.3	1.8	9.2	0.8	73.0	7.6
2006	MIN	MLB	27	16	8	0	33	33	227.3	188	49	232	27	40%	.269	36	1.04	3.00	3.02	3.20	7.2	2.0	8.7	1.0	62.0	8.2

Breakout: 16%   Improve: 32%   Collapse: 36%   Attrition: 7%   Comparables: Tom Seaver, Pedro Martinez, Billy Pierce

Owner of the best changeup this side of Pedro, and perhaps the most justifiable sense of grievance of any pitcher in baseball. For the 24 quality starts he gave the Twins in '05, Santana realized only sixteen wins. That's courtesy of the Twins' offense, which gave Santana the 30th-in run support in the AL, yet as pathetic as it was, his run support was the best of any Twins starter. He wasn't betrayed at every turn, being the beneficiary of excellent bullpen support. August was most symptomatic of his year: he gave the Twins quality starts in all six games he started, posting a 1.39 ERA. He got three wins out of that, courtesy of a whopping 13 runs scored for him in those six games. If the Twins ever take their lineup seriously, he'd be on the short list for the Cy Young for years to come, but the BBWAA likes to vote for wins, and that isn't entirely in Santana's control.

CARLOS SILVA   **Bats: R Throws: R**   Height: 6' 4" Weight: 220 Born: April 23, 1979   Age: 27

YEAR	TM	LVL	AGE	W	L	SV	G	GS	IP	H	BB	SO	HR	GB%	BABIP	STUFF	WHIP	ERA	PERA	EQERA	EQH9	EQBB9	EQSO9	EQHR9	VORP	WXRL
2003	PHI	MLB	24	3	1	1	62	1	87.3	92	37	48	7	54%	.310	-7	1.48	4.43	4.76	4.55	9.7	3.4	4.4	0.7	10.8	0.7
2004	MIN	MLB	25	14	8	0	33	33	203.0	255	35	76	23	52%	.320	1	1.43	4.21	4.59	4.11	10.3	1.4	3.1	0.9	38.1	4.8
2005	MIN	MLB	26	9	8	0	27	27	188.3	212	9	71	25	51%	.295	0	1.17	3.44	4.48	4.15	10.2	0.4	3.4	1.1	38.4	4.0
2006	MIN	MLB	27	10	11	0	37	26	174.0	209	28	70	22	49%	.302	-3	1.36	4.47	4.74	4.88	10.5	1.4	3.4	1.1	18.2	3.0

Breakout: 3%   Improve: 27%   Collapse: 28%   Attrition: 1%   Comparables: Lary Sorensen, Jim Barr, Jon Lieber

Silva is the pitcher that John Le Carre would call "Control" after he walked batters at a clip of one unintentional walk per 27 IP. That's not simply good: as Christian Ruzich has noted on BP.com, that's the best rate in more than 120 years, going back to when it took eight balls to walk someone. The problem, for Silva and for the Twins, is that he's so dependent on his defense that he's sort of the staff amphibian, the first to be affected if something changes in his environment. If the Twins sacrificed some outfield defense to play people who can help score some runs and give the whole staff some run support, it might have an outsized effect on a pitcher who needs his defense to record 90% of his outs. Like Bob Tewksbury before him, you can't help but root for a guy this old school.

ERROL SIMONITSCH   **Bats: L Throws: L**   Height: 6' 4" Weight: 225 Born: August 24, 1982   Age: 23

YEAR	TM	LVL	AGE	W	L	SV	G	GS	IP	H	BB	SO	HR	GB%	BABIP	STUFF	WHIP	ERA	PERA	EQERA	EQH9	EQBB9	EQSO9	EQHR9	VORP	WXRL
2003	ELZ	Rk	20	5	1	0	10	8	46.0	39	6	57	1	—	.319	16	0.98	1.76	3.74	5.61	9.6	1.7	5.6	0.6	0.0	—
2004	QUD	A	21	6	2	0	20	20	109.0	100	36	107	5	—	.312	3	1.25	2.56	5.01	5.19	9.7	4.0	5.0	1.0	4.7	—
2005	FTM	A+	22	8	3	0	14	13	80.3	70	12	72	5	57%	.295	9	1.02	2.69	4.38	4.74	9.2	1.8	5.2	1.1	7.3	—
2005	NBR	AA	22	6	5	0	14	14	78.7	92	28	52	6	43%	.330	-6	1.52	4.12	5.24	6.52	10.6	3.7	4.1	1.0	-7.9	—
2006	MIN	MLB	23	7	10	0	30	23	137.0	158	47	76	21	45%	.300	-2	1.50	5.40	5.43	5.74	10.0	3.1	4.7	1.3	-0.1	0.9

Breakout: 14%   Improve: 44%   Collapse: 12%   Attrition: 0%   Comparables: Brad Thomas, Jason Brester, Neal Musser

(continued next page)

Errol Simonitsch (continued)

In the organization's swarm of young hurlers, Simonitsch might be one of the ones who gets passed by. Not a power pitcher, he occasionally reaches 90 while relying on a particularly good curveball. The Twins feel he's a workhorse in the making, but he didn't keep right-handed hitters guessing in his introduction to Double-A, which is a must if he's going to stick in a rotation anywhere.

ANTHONY SWARZAK Bats: R Throws: R Height: 6' 3" Weight: 195 Born: September 10, 1985 Age: 20

YEAR	TM	LVL	AGE	W	L	SV	G	GS	IP	H	BB	SO	HR	GB%	BABIP	STUFF	WHIP	ERA	PERA	EQERA	EQH9	EQBB9	EQSO9	EQHR9	VORP	WXRL
2005	BLT	A	19	9	5	0	18	18	91.3	81	32	101	7	49%	.318	16	1.24	4.04	4.93	5.44	9.3	3.6	6.9	1.3	1.6	—
2005	FTM	A+	19	3	4	0	10	10	59.0	72	11	55	3	45%	.379	23	1.41	3.66	3.97	5.19	10.7	2.0	5.5	0.8	2.7	—
2006	MIN	MLB	20	9	9	0	27	25	151.0	157	52	113	20	44%	.296	15	1.38	4.55	4.71	4.83	9.1	3.1	6.4	1.1	14.6	2.6

Breakout: 33% Improve: 70% Collapse: 2% Attrition: 1% Comparables: Adam Wainwright, Kyle Davies, Tony Armas

The Twins picked four pitchers in the first round of the 2004 draft. Swarzak had to settle for being a 2nd round pick in that draft, and they had to buy him away from a scholarship at LSU to convince him to sign. Swarzak throws his fastball into the low 90s but it's a bit flat, so he relies on a good changeup while trying to polish up a promising 12-6 curve. Like fellow high school draftees Rainville and Waldrop, he started the season at Beloit and joined Rainville for a late-season promotion. That's quality drafting—high school picks who don't simply have talent, but who can also adapt and progress.

Line Outs

Position/Player	TM	LVL	AGE	PA	R	2B	3B	HR	RBI	BB	SO	SB-CS	SPEED	BA/OBP/SLG	MLVR	EQBA/OBP/SLG	EQA	VORP
2B B. Abernathy	ROC	AAA	27	242	35	13	0	6	25	21	20	7-3	4.9	.326/.388/.470	.186	.276/.336/.392	.256	6.9
OF D. Burns*	BLT	A	22	594	90	36	13	12	78	50	92	13-3	7.0	.271/.345/.457	.102	.231/.288/.390	.236	-22.5
1B D. Matienzo	NBR	AA	24	586	81	36	2	23	87	40	112	1-1	4.1	.282/.338/.488	.179	.261/.312/.449	.259	6.1
C C. Miller	ROC	AAA	29	211	35	7	0	11	25	27	30	0-2	4.1	.229/.379/.465	.085	.188/.313/.369	.240	-1.7
OF M. Ryan*	ROC	AAA	28	169	16	7	1	6	26	15	34	0-3	3.5	.283/.343/.461	.061	.250/.310/.404	.244	-2.6
	MIN	MLB	28	127	7	5	0	2	13	9	22	1-2	2.7	.231/.283/.325	-.259	.235/.299/.348	.225	-6.1
OF J. Tyner*	ROC	AAA	28	578	81	18	2	1	36	48	57	18-6	6.2	.286/.351/.334	-.093	.247/.307/.283	.218	-24.0
3B D. Winfree	BLT	A	19	601	80	31	5	16	101	22	93	3-2	4.4	.294/.329/.452	.090	.256/.282/.401	.234	1.1

Pitcher	TM	LVL	AGE	W	L	SV	IP	H	BB	SO	HR	GB%	BABIP	STUFF	WHIP	ERA	PERA	EQERA	EQH9	EQBB9	EQSO9	EQHR9	VORP
D. Gassner*	ROC	AAA	26	8	8	0	116.3	138	33	64	18	37%	.320	-25	1.47	4.95	5.98	5.51	10.7	2.9	3.7	1.7	1.1
B. Kemp	ROC	AAA	24	4	5	5	80.0	74	32	68	1	52%	.304	9	1.32	3.38	3.66	4.35	8.4	4.0	5.8	0.1	10.9
J. Mijares*	BLT	A	20	6	3	2	54.3	43	40	78	6	52%	.330	0	1.53	4.31	6.57	5.51	9.2	7.8	9.1	2.0	0.5
K. Slowey	BLT	A	21	3	2	0	64.3	42	8	69	4	38%	.242	20	0.78	2.24	4.05	3.90	7.9	1.4	6.6	1.2	11.3
K. Waldrop	BLT	A	19	6	11	0	151.7	182	23	108	17	57%	.329	-9	1.35	4.98	5.62	6.22	11.4	1.5	4.3	1.9	-10.3

Brent Abernathy: Thoroughly adequate as journeymen go, you can do worse, but Abernathy got hurt just as the opportunity to claim a big league job arose. Signed by the Brewers. **Deacon Burns:** A squat 5'8" power source, Burns's quick bat reminds some of Kirby Puckett. However, he's not a center fielder, and he'll have to move up fast to be something. **Danny Matienzo:** The former catcher surprised people with his Double-A debut; slugging .532 with 10 HRs against lefties might help him rise up to a LeCroy role in the majors. **Corky Miller:** A worthwhile reserve, he's still wondering which shop steward he irked to keep him from getting his membership card in the International Brotherhood of Backup Catchers. **Mike Ryan:** A lefty who can smack a fastball, he's long been suited for a pinch-hitting reserve role, which he'll get a shot at in Atlanta in '06. **Jason Tyner:** Still trying to avenge his demotion by the D-Rays just before Jason Tyner Bobblehead Day in Tampa Bay. Sadly, even that should be beyond his grasp. **David Winfree:** A high school rival of fellow Twins farmhand Matt Moses, but not as likely to develop until he starts hitting breaking stuff and improving his plate judgment.

Dave Gassner: Journeyman who might get a shot as somebody's fifth starter someday, but when that's your up-side, substitute teaching doesn't sound so bad. **Beau Kemp:** Doesn't get much benefit of the doubt, but he held righties homerless in '05, and he's given hitters fits at every level. **Jose Mijares:** Slipped onto the 40-man this winter, he's a product of the system's Venezuelan program. Likely to move up fast because of his power fastball/slider combo. **Kevin Slowey:** A strikethrower in an organization that appreciates them, Slowey was nabbed in the 2nd round of the '05 draft and pitched his way into an early promotion to Beloit. **Kyle Waldrop:** Storky 1st rounder from the '04 cadre, he has clean mechanics and command of four pitches. The question is when he'll add velocity and stamina.

New York Mets

If the History Channel has taught us anything, it's that it is extremely difficult to fight a war on two fronts. Yet that is exactly what the New York Mets have been doing since baseball realigned itself in 1994, fighting a two-front war the likes of which no other team in the sport must undertake. In terms of geography and alignment, the Mets find themselves competing with the two greatest monoliths of the game's modern era, the Braves and the Yankees. These conflicts have repeatedly driven Mets management to extremes.

Uniquely within baseball, the Mets have to simultaneously cope with a local and a divisional rivalry. In New York, they are forever fighting the Yankees for media space and the hearts, minds, and season ticket sales of fans. Competitively, they have the great misfortune to be bracketed with the Atlanta Braves, a team that has, for 14 of the last 15 years, denied all comers who might usurp their divisional crown. These are powerful and unforgiving enemies, the fighting of which often makes for less than rational decision-making.

So far, the Mets have not met either challenge. Since the Braves were transferred to the East, the Mets have finished behind them every year, with an average deficit of 16 games. Their best relative finish came in 2000, when they ended the year one game out of first place. During that same period, the Mets have bested the Yankees' record just once (2000 again) and came within one game once (1999). As with Atlanta, the average seasonal gap has been 16 games. The head-to-head numbers are equally grim: The Mets have taken two season series from the Braves (1995 and 1997) and one from the Yankees (2004). Atlanta owns a 105–74 mark against the Mets in that time, while the Yankees lead the intra-city series 29–19.

Three times since 1991 have the Braves performed poorly enough that another team could have knocked them off. Setting aside the aborted 1994 season, the first time was in 2001, when Atlanta won all of 88 games. The Braves were there for the taking, but the Mets, a club with no outfield, overplayed their run differential to a .500 record. The second chance came last year, when the Braves won just 90 games to top a division where all five teams finished .500 or better—something they couldn't have done had they not taken 13 of 19 games from New York.

If this sounds like a plea for pity for the Metsies (as Casey Stengel used to call them) it is not. They've had a

METS PROSPECTUS

2005 record: 83–79; Third place, NL East

Pythagenport record: 89–73

Runs scored per game: 4.46 (7th in NL)

Runs allowed per game: 4.00 (3rd in NL)

Team EqA: .260 (9th in NL)

2005 Batters Age: 29.0 (4th youngest in NL)

2005 Pitchers Age: 32.6 (Oldest in NL)

Ballpark: Shea Stadium; Slight pitcher's park; Park Factor of 0.975

2005: A solidly just-missed-it sort of season, achieved at great expense. Where's Buddy Harrelson?

2006: They're banking on old pitchers, but after a busy winter, this latest rush on the Braves might work.

higher payroll than the Braves in each of the last three seasons, and since 2002 have drawn about as many fans. On the other hand, the Mets' 2004–05 payrolls were about half that of their cross-town rivals, and since 2002 have drawn about two-thirds as many fans. Payroll comparisons to the Yankees are senseless, but the Mets aren't exactly paupers, having the highest salary numbers in the National League for three years running.

In their desperation to unseat their two rivals, the Mets have taken to winter excesses that would make Santa blush. If championships were based on a team's offseason activity alone, the Mets would be in the midst of a dynasty. Perhaps their hyperactivity is the residue of the team's failure to properly court Alex Rodriguez when he was footloose during the winter of 2000–2001. The Mets lamely tried to justify that failure by insisting that Rodriguez had made outlandish demands through his agent, Scott Boras, and the subsequent agate-lashing they'd gotten at the hands of the noisy local media scared them off. Since then, the team has made or tried to make at least one significant move at every position (see table 1).

Since the winter of 2001–2002, the Mets have repeatedly tried to upgrade from the outside, but passed on two of the best free agents ever, A-Rod and then Vladimir Guerrero. Like the Yankees, the Mets are forever looking for the quick fix, while their other nemesis, the Braves, have relied more on homegrown talent.

TABLE 1. NINE POINTS OF LIGHT: METS FREE AGENT SIGNINGS, 2001–2006

Catcher:	replaced Mike Piazza with Paul Lo Duca (2005–06)
First base:	traded for Mo Vaughn (2001–02); made offer to free agent Carlos Delgado (2004–05); traded for Delgado (2005–06)
Second base:	traded for Roberto Alomar (2001–02)
Third base:	had an agreement with Japanese free agent Norihiro Nakamura on which the player reneged (2002–03)
Shortstop:	signed Kaz Matsui (2003–04)
Left field:	signed Roger Cedeno (2001–02) and Cliff Floyd (2002–03)
Center field:	signed Mike Cameron (2003–04) and Carlos Beltran (2004–05)
Right field:	traded for Jeromy Burnitz (2001–02)
Starting pitchers:	signed Tom Glavine (2002–03) and Pedro Martinez (2004–05)
Relievers:	signed Billy Wagner (2005–06)

On an individual basis, the results of those signings and trades have been mostly disappointing. On a cumulative basis, they have been especially frustrating, as the team has gone just 295–351 during this period. Over the last four seasons, the Mets have cumulatively underperformed by 19 games in Pythagenport Wins. Compared to 2002–04, though, 2005 was a great leap forward: in terms of run differential swing from the previous season, the Mets were one of the most improved teams of 2005:

+174: Blue Jays
+152: Brewers
+146: Indians
+124: Diamondbacks
+121: Mets

Naturally, a list like this is usually going to be dominated by teams that have nowhere to go but up. Still, any season in which a team vaults upward by a dozen or so games—actual or expected—has to be considered a positive.

The problem is that the turnaround could have been even greater. The team got close enough to the wild card and the division title, especially considering their runs for/against figures. It's worth recapping what kept them from getting there:

First base: While the Mets spent lavishly to add Carlos Beltran to their lineup, they gave up on first base once Carlos Delgado had chosen another destination. New York had the worst production in baseball out of their first sackers, several of whom were middle infielders masquerading

as first basemen. The late arrival of Mike Jacobs saved the position from being a complete black hole. In a bit of synchronicity, Jacobs was shipped to the Marlins for the wayward object of last off-season's affections, Delgado. Had the Mets gotten Delgado in the first place, they would have finished three or four games closer in the standings in 2005. Even then, a league-average first baseman would have earned them an additional game—three if not for Jacobs's impact in his brief exposure.

Second base: The Mets got just about nothing out of their second basemen, as Kaz Matsui and Miguel Cairo essentially zeroed out the position. The Mets couldn't even put in a call for Jeff Keppinger, as he was shelved with a shoulder problem at Triple-A. The Mets have to pay Matsui for another season, making him one of the worst-ever foreign league import investments by any team.

Center field: Carlos Beltran played in all but 11 games, but what he produced for the Mets was about as much as he would have generated in 100 games of typical 2002–04 Beltran activity. The difference? Lots and lots of outs. Had Beltran given a more typical performance, last season's 25.8 VORP would have been closer to 60, and New York would have been another three games closer to the postseason. Regardless of his performance, the Mets paid above market value for him, but at least they got a player who still has prime years left in him. There is no reason to believe he can't get back to his peak output for at least two seasons of the remainder of his contract.

Closing: The difference between the Mets' closing situation and that of the Braves was that Atlanta pulled the plug on Dan Kolb early, while the Mets endured bad closing work from Braden Looper for the duration of 2005. Five teams—the Mets, Atlanta, Washington, Tampa Bay and Toronto—accounted for more than a quarter of all the leads lost after seven innings in 2005. It is axiomatic that the worse a team's closer is, the more likely it is to overpay for a free agent replacement the following winter, since nothing frustrates management like a late blown lead.

The spare parts problem: Some of the Mets' choices for spare parts were, to put it benevolently, eccentric. The Lenny Harris brand of futility players was overrepresented at Shea Stadium in 2005, as even unlikely blasts from the past like Jose Offerman and Ice Williams put in appearances. One has to wonder why the team didn't stock its bench with more viable alternatives, players who could be counted on to contribute more from the bench than carbon dioxide.

The batting order situation: Rather than bury his weakest batters at the water cooler end of the lineup, first-year manager Willie Randolph placed them at the top, where the team and its fans could confront the table setters' aversion to setting the table. It's like something out of a Bronc Burnett novel: the little pesky guys playing the little pesky guy positions have to bat at the top. The result was a .299 OBP out of the leadoff slot and a .296 mark out of the two-hole, costing the Mets a great many runs, particularly early in the game when getting out to a quick lead is often decisive.

Despite these shortcomings, there are reasons to feel good about the future. The Mets have one of the best players their system has ever generated in David Wright. Lastings Milledge, another of their highest ranking prospects, isn't too far off from making it. Another team might build the next decade around these two, but the Mets continue to act as if the future is just one year long, as they lash out at their perpetually victorious tormentors. Signing an aging Billy Wagner was emblematic of the reactive psychology at work in Shea Stadium. The average team was 65–7 when leading after seven; the Mets were around that number, going 67–10 in those situations. Wagner will improve that record, but not dramatically. The immense resources expended on Wagner could have been put to better use elsewhere.

In the end, the two-headed Yanks-Braves beast is something of a chimera. As 2000 demonstrated, thanks to the wild card it's possible for the Mets to achieve ultimate success without having to vanquish either team. They can take their usual beatings in their two-front battle, yet still make the playoffs and perhaps even sidestep their Atlanta and New York foes in the roulette wheel spin of the postseason.

On a certain level—call it the expensive one—the Mets are simply trying too hard. Sure, it's a great way to earn credits with the fans and keep the press at happy in January. We know there is no better way to get scorched in the media than to stand pat, particularly in New York. This specifically affects the Mets, who seem obsessed with, and vulnerable to, the vagaries of talk radio more than any other team. The self-appointed cognoscenti of the air waves may applaud every Mets signing as a bold grab for market share in the city of a million and one entertainments, but winning would more surely shut them up than spending.

HITTERS

MARLON ANDERSON   **2B**   **Bats: L Throws: R**   Height: 5' 11"   Weight: 190   Born: January 6, 1974   Age: 32

YEAR	TM	LVL	AGE	PA	R	2B	3B	HR	RBI	BB	SO	SB	CS	SPEED	BA	OBP	SLG	MLVR	EQBA	EQOBP	EQSLG	EQA	VORP	DEFENSE	
2003	TBA	MLB	29	531	59	27	3	6	67	41	60	19	3	6.4	.270	.328	.376	-.079	.270	.332	.381	.256	12.3	120-2B	-9
2004	SLN	MLB	30	271	31	12	0	8	28	12	38	6	2	5.4	.237	.269	.379	-.171	.237	.268	.379	.227	-4.7	25-2B -3	18-LF 2
2005	NYN	MLB	31	256	31	9	0	7	19	18	45	6	1	5.7	.264	.316	.391	-.047	.262	.317	.388	.250	3.0	18-1B 1	16-2B 1
2006	*WAS*	*MLB*	*32*	*154*	*17*	*6*	*1*	*2*	*15*	*11*	*24*	*3*	*1*	*5.5*	*.243*	*.299*	*.347*	*-.192*	*.254*	*.308*	*.375*	*.232*	*-1.3*	*40-2B -1*	

Breakout: 11%   *Improve: 28%*   *Collapse: 44%*   *Attrition: 42%*   *Comparables: Gerald Perry, Lenny Harris, Wayne Kirby*

An as-advertised season, because his line of .264/.316/.391 nearly matched his .264/.311/.381 career rates coming into the year. Too bad this isn't NHRA Super Stock, because that's quite a dial under. A new baseball maxim: If you can't be great, be good, and if you can't be good, be versatile. Like the godfather of scrubby pinch-hitter types, Lenny Harris, Anderson is someone a team should invite to camp rather than sign to a guaranteed two-year contract six months before the season begins, but that's just what that wacky Jim Bowden did in Washington.

AAROM BALDIRIS   **1B**   **Bats: R Throws: R**   Height: 6' 2"   Weight: 190   Born: January 5, 1983   Age: 23

YEAR	TM	LVL	AGE	PA	R	2B	3B	HR	RBI	BB	SO	SB	CS	SPEED	BA	OBP	SLG	MLVR	EQBA	EQOBP	EQSLG	EQA	VORP	DEFENSE	
2004	SLU	A+	21	464	57	15	5	4	45	46	64	6	6	4.8	.305	.384	.397	.147	.275	.341	.365	.249	11.4	104-3B	13
2005	BIN	AA	22	548	69	35	1	11	63	45	81	7	1	4.9	.275	.341	.416	.047	.246	.310	.378	.242	2.1	114-2B	-4
2006	*NYN*	*MLB*	*23*	*523*	*60*	*28*	*2*	*10*	*54*	*43*	*78*	*6*	*3*	*4.9*	*.262*	*.329*	*.392*	*-.069*	*.266*	*.333*	*.415*	*.253*	*9.9*	*123-3B*	*3*

Breakout: 28%   *Improve: 55%*   *Collapse: 21%*   *Attrition: 8%*   *Comparables: Aaron Hill, Chris Bass, Tucker Ashford*

Probably not the year the Mets were hoping for from Baldiris. Although he did display a little more doubles power than in the past, the big flies weren't forthcoming. To his credit, he made the move across the diamond pretty well, away from David Wright's corner of the infield and towards the Mets' more problematic mix at second. This would be the year to break out, either at Norfolk or in time split between there and a return engagement in Binghamton.

CARLOS BELTRAN   **CF**   **Bats: B Throws: R**   Height: 6' 1"   Weight: 190   Born: April 24, 1977   Age: 29

YEAR	TM	LVL	AGE	PA	R	2B	3B	HR	RBI	BB	SO	SB	CS	SPEED	BA	OBP	SLG	MLVR	EQBA	EQOBP	EQSLG	EQA	VORP	DEFENSE	
2003	KCA	MLB	26	602	102	14	10	26	100	72	81	41	4	8.2	.307	.389	.522	.214	.298	.387	.518	.312	56.4	127-CF	3
2004	KCA	MLB	27	308	51	19	2	15	51	37	44	14	3	6.9	.278	.367	.534	.206	.276	.370	.529	.304	26.6	68-CF	2
2004	HOU	MLB	27	397	70	17	7	23	53	55	57	28	0	8.7	.258	.368	.559	.239	.249	.359	.541	.308	38.9	87-CF	2
2005	NYN	MLB	28	646	83	34	2	16	78	56	96	17	6	6.0	.266	.330	.414	.013	.265	.331	.420	.261	17.6	146-CF	8
2006	*NYN*	*MLB*	*29*	*640*	*92*	*32*	*4*	*23*	*81*	*71*	*94*	*19*	*4*	*6.5*	*.283*	*.365*	*.479*	*.122*	*.287*	*.370*	*.508*	*.293*	*41.0*	*149-CF*	*3*

Breakout: 9%   Improve: 48%   Collapse: 13%   Attrition: 3%   Comparables: Tom Tresh, Bernie Williams, Carl Everett

Metitis: The condition which occurs when a previously productive player moves to the Mets and sees a substantial decline in performance. It's urban legend, of course, a mythical disease that fans everywhere probably think could be applied to their own teams in self-pitying moments. Metitis is often a result of players moving from a good hitter's park to Shea Stadium. Beltran can't use that defense; he was equally mediocre on the road. Just about everything went wrong. Beltran had less power, less patience, and not even his traditionally superb basestealing showed up in Flushing. A player who shuns the spotlight, Beltran is no longer the lineup's featured attraction, so perhaps he'll bounce back.

MIGUEL CAIRO   **2B**   **Bats: R Throws: R**   Height: 6' 1"   Weight: 210   Born: May 4, 1974   Age: 32

YEAR	TM	LVL	AGE	PA	R	2B	3B	HR	RBI	BB	SO	SB	CS	SPEED	BA	OBP	SLG	MLVR	EQBA	EQOBP	EQSLG	EQA	VORP	DEFENSE			
2003	SLN	MLB	29	287	41	15	2	5	32	13	30	4	1	6.1	.245	.289	.375	-.132	.247	.290	.388	.240	-1.6	33-2B	-5	14-LF	-1
2004	NYA	MLB	30	396	48	17	5	6	42	18	49	11	3	6.2	.292	.346	.417	.006	.298	.350	.432	.274	17.1	96-2B	-9		
2005	NYN	MLB	31	355	31	18	0	2	19	19	31	13	3	5.6	.251	.296	.324	-.191	.252	.298	.327	.230	-6.0	74-2B	4		
2006	*NYA*	*MLB*	*32*	*309*	*35*	*13*	*1*	*3*	*28*	*12*	*33*	*7*	*3*	*5.3*	*.253*	*.287*	*.343*	*-.191*	*.255*	*.298*	*.357*	*.223*	*-1.9*	*75-2B*	*-2*		

Breakout: 14%   Improve: 27%   Collapse: 40%   Attrition: 26%   Comparables: Don Kolloway, Greg Pryor, Pat Meares

It was not the Mets intention to give Cairo this much playing time, but the ever-accelerating disappointment of Kaz Matsui opened the door. That Cairo proved to be slightly more productive is not an endorsement of his season but a further indictment of Matsui's. Not offered arbitration, Cairo signed on for his second stint with the Yankees in 2006.

MIKE CAMERON   **CF**   **Bats: R Throws: R**   Height: 6' 2"   Weight: 190   Born: January 8, 1973   Age: 33

YEAR	TM	LVL	AGE	PA	R	2B	3B	HR	RBI	BB	SO	SB	CS	SPEED	BA	OBP	SLG	MLVR	EQBA	EQOBP	EQSLG	EQA	VORP	DEFENSE	
2003	SEA	MLB	30	611	74	31	5	18	76	70	137	17	7	5.8	.253	.344	.431	.025	.259	.354	.447	.276	21.4	144-CF	19
2004	NYN	MLB	31	561	76	30	1	30	76	57	143	22	6	6.4	.231	.319	.479	.039	.230	.317	.479	.270	19.9	132-CF	4
2005	NYN	MLB	32	342	47	23	2	12	39	29	85	13	1	6.5	.273	.342	.477	.127	.272	.343	.482	.284	17.6	67-RF	-4
2006	*SDN*	*MLB*	*33*	*443*	*61*	*22*	*3*	*16*	*57*	*44*	*112*	*12*	*4*	*5.6*	*.248*	*.331*	*.444*	*-.007*	*.257*	*.339*	*.479*	*.272*	*13.7*	*105-RF*	*1*

Breakout: 7%   Improve: 30%   Collapse: 34%   Attrition: 16%   Comparables: Ron Gant, Ellis Burks, Reggie Sanders

Before the collision with Beltran, his hitting was right in line with the rest of his career, but his defense had suffered terribly as a result of the move to right. This is counterintuitive to our general understanding of the game: we assume a move from a tougher defensive position will result in an improvement, especially in the outfield. A move back to center in San Diego should see him snap back to his old form. Petco will be the third consecutive pitchers' park that he'll have called home. He's held his own so far, since his lowest EqA in the past seven seasons has been a respectable .271.

RAMON CASTRO   **C**   **Bats: R Throws: R**   Height: 6' 3"   Weight: 225   Born: March 1, 1976   Age: 30

YEAR	TM	LVL	AGE	PA	R	2B	3B	HR	RBI	BB	SO	SB	CS	SPEED	BA	OBP	SLG	MLVR	EQBA	EQOBP	EQSLG	EQA	VORP	DEFENSE	
2004	FLO	MLB	28	108	9	3	0	3	8	11	30	0	0	3.4	.135	.231	.260	-.454	.144	.239	.268	.185	-8.4	27-C	1
2005	NYN	MLB	29	237	26	16	0	8	41	25	58	1	0	3.5	.244	.321	.435	.006	.243	.321	.443	.264	8.8	65-C	2
2006	*NYN*	*MLB*	*30*	*302*	*32*	*15*	*0*	*11*	*38*	*28*	*70*	*1*	*1*	*3.8*	*.236*	*.311*	*.423*	*-.078*	*.239*	*.315*	*.448*	*.253*	*8.4*	*74-C*	*2*

Breakout: 18%   Improve: 46%   Collapse: 30%   Attrition: 28%   Comparables: Tim Laudner, Sal Fasano, Charles Johnson

If baseball awarded a Backup Catcher of the Year Award, Castro would have been a contender in 2005. The honor would probably have gone to Javier Valentin of the Reds, but Castro did a very credible job to the point that it merits debate whether the Mets did themselves any favors by bringing in Paul Lo Duca to replace Piazza.

VICTOR DIAZ   OF   Bats: R Throws: R   Height: 6′ 0″   Weight: 200   Born: December 10, 1981   Age: 24

YEAR	TM	LVL	AGE	PA	R	2B	3B	HR	RBI	BB	SO	SB	CS	SPEED	BA	OBP	SLG	MLVR	EQBA	EQOBP	EQSLG	EQA	VORP	DEFENSE		
2003	JAX	AA	21	354	42	20	2	10	55	27	60	8	10	4.8	.291	.353	.462	.212	.283	.334	.472	.270	22.3	77-2B	-10	
2003	BIN	AA	21	186	29	11	0	6	23	8	32	7	5	5.1	.354	.382	.520	.318	.310	.337	.472	.271	13.4	43-2B	-7	
2004	NOR	AAA	22	573	81	31	1	24	94	31	133	6	8	4.4	.292	.332	.491	.160	.281	.322	.465	.265	12.5	125-RF	5	
2005	NOR	AAA	23	184	30	11	0	10	34	14	47	6	2	5.2	.300	.353	.541	.287	.288	.342	.513	.285	10.4	25-1B	1	11-RF 0
2005	NYN	MLB	23	313	41	17	3	12	38	30	82	6	2	5.3	.257	.329	.468	.081	.257	.331	.475	.273	10.1	74-RF	-3	
2006	NYN	MLB	24	505	64	26	2	20	69	37	113	10	4	4.8	.271	.330	.467	.039	.275	.334	.495	.272	14.3	119-RF	-3	

Breakout: 21%   Improve: 43%   Collapse: 26%   Attrition: 17%   Comparables: Billy Conigliaro, Dan Ford, Ivan Calderon

Watching him play the outfield makes one wonder how he ever could have been paid to be a middle infielder. As an outfielder, the player to whom he is often compared is Manny Ramirez. Manny got filthy rich in spite of taking weird routes to fly balls, but Diaz isn't the same kind of hitter. Diaz has had something of a reverse platoon in his brief career. With Xavier Nady picked up in the Cameron trade, Lastings Milledge in the hopper, and the Mets making goo-goo eyes at all sorts of superstar outfielders, his destiny probably lies elsewhere.

CLIFF FLOYD   LF   Bats: L Throws: R   Height: 6′ 4″   Weight: 235   Born: December 5, 1972   Age: 33

YEAR	TM	LVL	AGE	PA	R	2B	3B	HR	RBI	BB	SO	SB	CS	SPEED	BA	OBP	SLG	MLVR	EQBA	EQOBP	EQSLG	EQA	VORP	DEFENSE
2003	NYN	MLB	30	425	57	25	2	18	68	51	66	3	0	4.9	.290	.376	.518	.238	.290	.373	.522	.303	26.6	83-LF -2
2004	NYN	MLB	31	457	55	26	0	18	63	47	103	11	4	5.1	.260	.352	.462	.097	.259	.348	.465	.278	12.2	97-LF -2
2005	NYN	MLB	32	626	85	22	2	34	98	63	98	12	2	5.9	.273	.358	.505	.190	.271	.357	.515	.294	37.4	143-LF 15
2006	NYN	MLB	33	530	69	26	1	23	77	56	92	7	3	5.1	.275	.359	.485	.113	.279	.364	.513	.289	25.9	125-LF 1

Breakout: 9%   Improve: 38%   Collapse: 25%   Attrition: 11%   Comparables: Kirk Gibson, Ryan Klesko, Dave Henderson

When a player is missing calendar-sized chunks in his career, we tend to forget why he excited us so much in the first place. Seeing Floyd in 2005 was a reminder of why his name was spoken in reverent tones at the 1994 Winter Meetings. That the Mets got a decent season out of him—probably the second best of his career, after 2001—seems like gravy. Unfortunately, there wasn't enough roast beef and potatoes for it to make a difference.

BRETT HARPER   1B   Bats: L Throws: R   Height: 6′ 4″   Weight: 180   Born: July 31, 1981   Age: 24

YEAR	TM	LVL	AGE	PA	R	2B	3B	HR	RBI	BB	SO	SB	CS	SPEED	BA	OBP	SLG	MLVR	EQBA	EQOBP	EQSLG	EQA	VORP	DEFENSE
2004	SLU	A+	22	257	32	18	1	9	55	35	53	1	1	3.4	.350	.440	.564	.479	.312	.392	.519	.307	25.7	39-1B -4
2004	BIN	AA	22	191	24	12	0	7	26	14	60	0	0	3.5	.247	.309	.437	-.014	.217	.274	.384	.227	-8.2	41-1B -1
2005	SLU	A+	23	264	35	11	1	20	60	21	64	0	1	2.7	.280	.337	.586	.296	.242	.291	.501	.262	4.4	47-1B -3
2005	BIN	AA	23	256	37	11	0	16	42	26	85	0	0	2.7	.273	.352	.533	.210	.243	.319	.475	.268	5.0	51-1B -2
2006	NYN	MLB	24	473	50	22	1	19	65	37	134	0	0	3.2	.235	.299	.426	-.094	.238	.303	.451	.248	-0.9	112-1B -4

Breakout: 9%   Improve: 34%   Collapse: 41%   Attrition: 11%   Comparables: Jeff Liefer, John Rodriguez, Adam LaRoche

It's hard not to notice 36 home runs, regardless of a player's age or the leagues in which they came. If Harper does it again this year, especially if it's at Triple-A Norfolk, the Mets may have a late bloomer on their hands, one they might be able to foist off on another team for some solid middle relief help.

ANDERSON HERNANDEZ   2B/SS   Bats: B Throws: R   Height: 5′ 9″   Weight: 160   Born: October 30, 1982   Age: 23

YEAR	TM	LVL	AGE	PA	R	2B	3B	HR	RBI	BB	SO	SB	CS	SPEED	BA	OBP	SLG	MLVR	EQBA	EQOBP	EQSLG	EQA	VORP	DEFENSE		
2003	LAK	A+	20	410	47	11	4	2	28	27	69	15	7	6.6	.229	.278	.295	-.148	.214	.256	.299	.203	-24.0	98-SS	4	
2004	LAK	A+	21	104	14	3	3	0	9	6	19	5	0	7.8	.289	.327	.381	.032	.261	.294	.343	.231	-0.9	26-SS	5	
2004	ERI	AA	21	427	65	19	3	5	29	26	89	17	6	6.8	.274	.326	.376	-.072	.245	.292	.336	.226	-6.0	99-SS	-2	
2005	BIN	AA	22	289	46	14	1	7	24	14	58	11	9	6.5	.326	.360	.462	.176	.299	.336	.430	.261	16.5	54-SS	-1	
2005	NOR	AAA	22	288	34	6	4	2	30	22	46	24	9	7.3	.303	.354	.379	.057	.302	.353	.371	.262	9.8	36-2B	1	29-SS -4
2006	NYN	MLB	23	546	62	23	3	5	39	31	96	19	8	5.4	.263	.309	.351	-.157	.266	.313	.372	.234	8.6	128-SS	1	

Breakout: 21%   Improve: 46%   Collapse: 26%   Attrition: 9%   Comparables: Ramon Santiago, Nelson Liriano, Maicer Izturis

Hernandez enjoyed something of a breakout season. He showed improving power, though the same cannot be said of his judgment on the bases. Regardless, Hernandez's reality is that he's only four months younger than Reyes, the man in front of him, and Reyes has already been in the big leagues for three seasons. Still, if you can play, they'll either find a place for you, like second base, or ship you somewhere else.

MIKE JACOBS   **1B/C**   **Bats: L Throws: R**   Height: 6′ 2″   Weight: 200   Born: October 30, 1980   Age: 25

YEAR	TM	LVL	AGE	PA	R	2B	3B	HR	RBI	BB	SO	SB	CS	SPEED	BA	OBP	SLG	MLVR	EQBA	EQOBP	EQSLG	EQA	VORP	DEFENSE	
2003	BIN	AA	22	450	56	36	1	17	81	28	87	0	3	2.9	.329	.376	.548	.321	.287	.330	.495	.276	31.4	64-C -4	
2004	NOR	AAA	23	106	8	3	0	2	6	9	30	0	0	3.1	.177	.245	.271	-.396	.169	.238	.252	.182	-10.4	16-C -1	
2005	BIN	AA	24	481	66	37	2	25	93	35	94	1	2	3.5	.321	.376	.589	.363	.281	.334	.516	.283	24.9	52-1B -2	41-C -13
2005	NYN	MLB	24	112	19	7	0	11	23	10	22	0	0	2.8	.310	.375	.710	.520	.310	.375	.730	.342	14.8	27-1B -3	
2006	*FLO*	*MLB*	*25*	*584*	*71*	*30*	*1*	*29*	*96*	*42*	*125*	*0*	*1*	*3.6*	*.265*	*.324*	*.491*	*.056*	*.271*	*.328*	*.519*	*.274*	*24.6*	*137-1B -7*	

Breakout: 26%   Improve: 55%   Collapse: 18%   Attrition: 5%   Comparables: Eric Karros, Carlos Delgado, Matt Nokes

If only one could make a career out of one at-bat. Take a perfect swing, toss away the bat, admire the result and retire to Florida. Flashing his smooth, lovely lefty stroke, Jacobs's three-run homer in that first plate appearance was that sort of perfect moment. Four homers in his first four games bode well, and just when his hot start began to look like the proverbial flash in the pan, he started teeing off again. He's no kid, but catchers are allowed to have later starts to productive ten-year careers. He won't hit enough to make Marlins fans forget Carlos Delgado if they install him at first base, but he could quickly make Paul Lo Duca a memory if he gets the catching job.

JEFF KEPPINGER   **2B**   **Bats: R Throws: R**   Height: 6′ 0″   Weight: 180   Born: April 21, 1980   Age: 26

YEAR	TM	LVL	AGE	PA	R	2B	3B	HR	RBI	BB	SO	SB	CS	SPEED	BA	OBP	SLG	MLVR	EQBA	EQOBP	EQSLG	EQA	VORP	DEFENSE
2003	LYN	A+	23	370	55	21	2	3	51	23	28	3	2	5.0	.325	.365	.424	.172	.292	.328	.399	.253	12.5	87-2B -9
2004	ALT	AA	24	344	44	17	2	1	33	27	15	10	5	5.2	.337	.387	.413	.183	.316	.361	.383	.262	16.7	74-2B 3
2004	NYN	MLB	24	123	9	2	0	3	9	6	7	2	1	3.6	.284	.317	.379	-.055	.284	.317	.379	.244	2.2	29-2B 2
2005	NOR	AAA	25	273	40	15	3	3	29	16	13	5	1	5.5	.337	.377	.455	.242	.331	.371	.437	.281	20.8	52-2B 6
2006	*NYN*	*MLB*	*26*	*385*	*43*	*18*	*2*	*3*	*33*	*23*	*23*	*5*	*2*	*4.5*	*.286*	*.334*	*.370*	*-.073*	*.290*	*.338*	*.392*	*.249*	*11.3*	*92-2B 2*

Breakout: 5%   Improve: 28%   Collapse: 46%   Attrition: 20%   Comparables: Ted Sizemore, Placido Polanco, Ron Hunt

While listed as a "knee," his September injury was actually a fractured tibial plateau—the shin bone was broken at the knee—and isn't as serious as most knee maladies, as Jermaine Dye has proven. Keppinger has gotten the Tony Gwynn not-striking-out thing down, and while not striking out is a nice parlor trick, that's all it will ever be if you don't combine it with something beyond a high batting average. Still, he can outplay the expensive import the previous GM brought in ahead of him (the Joe Morgans of the world always lavishly praise meat-and-potatoes types, but in truth, most baseball execs favor more exotic fare). Barring a free agent pickup this winter, Keppinger will finally get a shot at the job in spring training, but he'll have to beat out Matsui and fend off Bret Boone.

CHASE LAMBIN   **INF**   **Bats: B Throws: R**   Height: 6′ 1″   Weight: 180   Born: July 7, 1979   Age: 26

YEAR	TM	LVL	AGE	PA	R	2B	3B	HR	RBI	BB	SO	SB	CS	SPEED	BA	OBP	SLG	MLVR	EQBA	EQOBP	EQSLG	EQA	VORP	DEFENSE	
2003	SLU	A+	24	454	58	27	2	5	49	46	81	13	8	5.3	.289	.366	.404	.154	.264	.326	.395	.251	10.9	55-2B 2	49-SS -3
2004	BIN	AA	25	465	64	22	4	10	65	48	103	4	2	5.3	.244	.331	.390	-.041	.218	.293	.344	.225	-10.6	93-2B -13	
2005	BIN	AA	26	202	26	17	0	14	29	20	38	2	0	3.7	.331	.396	.657	.490	.272	.336	.530	.288	16.9	28-3B 2	
2005	NOR	AAA	26	234	35	16	2	10	34	20	47	2	3	5.3	.289	.350	.526	.249	.277	.337	.490	.276	17.3	20-SS -4	18-2B 1
2006	*NYN*	*MLB*	*26*	*456*	*50*	*24*	*2*	*13*	*53*	*38*	*97*	*4*	*2*	*4.5*	*.247*	*.315*	*.407*	*-.082*	*.251*	*.319*	*.432*	*.250*	*10.7*	*108-2B -3*	

Breakout: 19%   Improve: 45%   Collapse: 36%   Attrition: 12%   Comparables: Doug DeCinces, Dale Sveum, Carl Everett

A 34th rounder in the '02 draft out of the generally overlooked University of Louisiana-Lafayette, Lambin put himself on the map this year, and then some. A switch-hitter, it appears he's more dangerous swinging lefty; he mashed 22 of his 24 home runs against right-handers (with a home run every 14 at-bats), and slugged .617 against them across Double- and Triple-A. Wherever that power spike came from—and these days, if you're a minor leaguer, it's only coming from Harry Caray's proverbial extra biscuit for breakfast—if he can keep it going, he won't just be auditioning for utility infield jobs for long.

KAZUO MATSUI   **2B**   **Bats: B Throws: R**   Height: 5′ 10″   Weight: 185   Born: October 23, 1975   Age: 30

YEAR	TM	LVL	AGE	PA	R	2B	3B	HR	RBI	BB	SO	SB	CS	SPEED	BA	OBP	SLG	MLVR	EQBA	EQOBP	EQSLG	EQA	VORP	DEFENSE
2003	SEI	JPL	27	642	84	36	4	33	124	55		4	13	104	5.0	.305	.364	.549	.223	.282	.344	.418	.264	20.0	
2004	NYN	MLB	28	504	65	32	2	7	44	40	97	14	3	6.2	.272	.331	.396	-.021	.270	.331	.397	.257	18.0	105-SS -3
2005	NYN	MLB	29	290	31	9	4	3	24	14	43	6	1	6.9	.255	.300	.352	-.136	.256	.299	.363	.237	-1.0	63-2B 0
2006	*NYN*	*MLB*	*30*	*325*	*37*	*15*	*2*	*4*	*27*	*23*	*54*	*6*	*2*	*5.5*	*.257*	*.314*	*.365*	*-.133*	*.260*	*.318*	*.387*	*.240*	*5.5*	*79-2B 1*

Breakout: 9%   Improve: 32%   Collapse: 44%   Attrition: 28%   Comparables: Jose Uribe, Jose Macias, Kevin Stocker

"Worst film you ever saw? Well, my next one will be better." As it was for Ed Wood, so it went for Kaz Matsui in his rookie season in the States: the next one was even worse. Injuries cut into his already slender ability. The reason you bring someone from half a world away is because they can do things that local talent cannot; it's the whole premise of the H-1 Visa. The exercise becomes pointless if you're just importing junk.

DOUG MIENTKIEWICZ — 1B — Bats: L Throws: R — Height: 6' 2" — Weight: 193 — Born: June 19, 1974 — Age: 32

YEAR	TM	LVL	AGE	PA	R	2B	3B	HR	RBI	BB	SO	SB	CS	SPEED	BA	OBP	SLG	MLVR	EQBA	EQOBP	EQSLG	EQA	VORP	DEFENSE	
2003	MIN	MLB	29	572	67	38	1	11	65	74	55	4	1	4.3	.300	.393	.450	.154	.298	.396	.450	.297	28.9	129-1B	0
2004	MIN	MLB	30	326	34	18	0	5	25	38	38	2	2	3.6	.246	.340	.363	-.111	.244	.342	.362	.250	-2.6	73-1B	-6
2004	BOS	MLB	30	119	13	6	1	1	10	10	18	0	1	4.8	.215	.286	.318	-.305	.210	.288	.305	.212	-6.4	30-1B	-2
2005	NYN	MLB	31	311	36	13	0	11	29	32	39	0	1	3.6	.240	.322	.407	-.030	.239	.323	.417	.255	-0.2	76-1B	-5
2006	KCA	MLB	32	326	33	14	0	8	37	33	41	1	1	4.2	.254	.333	.389	-.052	.255	.343	.410	.254	0.9	79-1B	-3

Breakout: 15%   Improve: 41%   Collapse: 35%   Attrition: 29%   Comparables: Greg Brock, Lee Thomas, Wally Judnich

The Mets have been making do at first base since John Olerud departed after the 1999 season. No Met who has started more than ten games at the position has come close to Olie's .310 EQA that year, save for Mike Jacobs and his 28 games in '05. Carlos Delgado should end that streak, while Minky will try to survive another couple of years on his defensive rep. He's been condemned to baseball's purgatory on the Plains, but that's not a matter of location. As Sartre noted, hell is other people, and it would seem to be especially the ones that Royals fans have to pay to see.

LASTINGS MILLEDGE — CF — Bats: R Throws: R — Height: 6' 1" — Weight: 185 — Born: April 5, 1985 — Age: 21

YEAR	TM	LVL	AGE	PA	R	2B	3B	HR	RBI	BB	SO	SB	CS	SPEED	BA	OBP	SLG	MLVR	EQBA	EQOBP	EQSLG	EQA	VORP	DEFENSE	
2004	CMB	A	19	293	66	22	1	13	58	17	53	23	6	7.6	.340	.399	.580	.429	.292	.331	.485	.278	17.3	54-CF	-5
2005	SLU	A+	20	265	48	15	0	4	22	19	41	18	13	6.1	.302	.385	.418	.163	.260	.327	.374	.244	1.7	59-CF	-3
2005	BIN	AA	20	212	33	17	0	4	24	14	47	11	5	5.9	.337	.392	.487	.266	.294	.346	.438	.271	10.2	41-CF	-4
2006	NYN	MLB	21	502	62	27	2	12	53	32	92	19	8	5.4	.260	.316	.402	-.079	.264	.320	.426	.251	9.3	118-CF	-4

Breakout: 19%   Improve: 43%   Collapse: 36%   Attrition: 8%   Comparables: Ruben Mateo, Will Smith, Jason Pridie

The split year between St. Lucie and Binghamton did nothing to halt the bandwagon. A nice star turn in the AFL made the picture even brighter, although nothing can buck up a hitter's numbers like a trip to Arizona, regardless of the time of year. If he continues the split-season program, he'll be in the Shea outfield by the middle of 2007, possibly sooner. More power will come with physical maturity, but to really live up to the hype he'll need to polish his game in the field, on the bases, and particularly by learning the strike zone.

ANGEL PAGAN — OF — Bats: B Throws: R — Height: 6' 1" — Weight: 180 — Born: July 2, 1981 — Age: 24

YEAR	TM	LVL	AGE	PA	R	2B	3B	HR	RBI	BB	SO	SB	CS	SPEED	BA	OBP	SLG	MLVR	EQBA	EQOBP	EQSLG	EQA	VORP	DEFENSE			
2003	SLU	A+	22	479	64	15	5	1	33	35	80	35	15	7.8	.249	.307	.313	-.068	.234	.283	.312	.217	-23.8	104-CF	-3		
2004	BIN	AA	23	497	71	25	8	4	63	42	96	29	5	7.9	.288	.346	.406	.037	.267	.322	.374	.252	-10.0	56-LF	2	51-CF	4
2005	NOR	AAA	24	570	69	20	10	8	40	49	111	27	15	7.0	.271	.333	.395	.016	.268	.329	.382	.250	6.8	102-CF	16		
2006	NYN	MLB	24	443	56	21	4	5	34	33	82	18	7	6.1	.253	.312	.364	-.139	.257	.316	.386	.241	0.8	105-CF	5		

Breakout: 22%   Improve: 45%   Collapse: 24%   Attrition: 15%   Comparables: Milt Cuyler, Coco Crisp, Tim Raines Jr.

A wonderfully oxymoronic name. Pagan has not developed into the power hitter the Mets hoped they were getting when they drafted him. Instead, they have groomed him as a slap-happy leadoff man, but that isn't really taking either. He doesn't get on base enough and his stolen base clip has dropped as he's advanced. Unless we see major leaps in either OBP or power (or both) in an encore year at Norfolk, he's not going to dent anybody's roster.

MIKE PIAZZA — C — Bats: R Throws: R — Height: 6' 3" — Weight: 215 — Born: September 4, 1968 — Age: 37

YEAR	TM	LVL	AGE	PA	R	2B	3B	HR	RBI	BB	SO	SB	CS	SPEED	BA	OBP	SLG	MLVR	EQBA	EQOBP	EQSLG	EQA	VORP	DEFENSE			
2003	NYN	MLB	34	273	37	13	0	11	34	35	40	0	0	3.5	.286	.377	.483	.188	.285	.375	.481	.294	20.6	61-C	-7		
2004	NYN	MLB	35	528	47	21	0	20	54	68	78	0	0	3.1	.266	.362	.444	.098	.263	.359	.441	.277	22.2	58-1B	-6	43-C	-8
2005	NYN	MLB	36	442	41	23	0	19	62	41	67	0	0	3.6	.251	.326	.452	.050	.251	.327	.464	.268	20.0	91-C	-8		
2006	NYN	MLB	37	333	33	16	0	11	43	32	52	0	0	3.4	.253	.329	.420	-.038	.257	.334	.444	.259	10.8	80-C	-6		

Breakout: 5%   Improve: 15%   Collapse: 46%   Attrition: 26%   Comparables: Joe Adcock, Tony Perez, Gary Carter

(continued next page)

Mike Piazza (continued)

Piazza has now caught about the same number of games (1,500 and change) as Carlton Fisk had at the same age. Piazza can only hope to emulate what Fisk did thereafter—three of his best EQAs came at the ages of 40, 41, and 42. While Piazza doesn't talk like a man who wants to play into his mid-40s, the Fisk model is there for temptation's sake.

GRANT PSOMAS 3B Bats: R Throws: R Height: 6′ 3″ Weight: 195 Born: September 2, 1982 Age: 23

YEAR	TM	LVL	AGE	PA	R	2B	3B	HR	RBI	BB	SO	SB	CS	SPEED	BA	OBP	SLG	MLVR	EQBA	EQOBP	EQSLG	EQA	VORP	DEFENSE	
2004	BRO	A-	21	252	23	13	2	3	29	25	48	4	1	4.6	.233	.310	.350	-.035	.200	.262	.301	.205	-35.9		
2005	HAG	A	22	419	66	27	2	19	54	62	79	6	4	3.9	.300	.403	.551	.369	.252	.340	.444	.270	20.4	90-3B	8
2005	SLU	A+	22	133	15	10	0	1	15	15	29	1	1	3.4	.305	.383	.415	.160	.272	.344	.391	.257	4.8	34-3B	5
2006	FLO	MLB	23	504	53	27	1	11	55	48	120	4	2	3.7	.234	.310	.371	-.146	.240	.314	.393	.238	0.6	119-3B	6

Breakout: 16% Improve: 39% Collapse: 31% Attrition: 7%   Comparables: Jeff Baker, Andy Phillips, Ryan Hankins

Another hard-hitting third baseman in the pipeline who might have been stuck behind Wright, Psomas was mercifully dealt to Florida, where he should rise through the system quickly. He won the Sally League Home Run Derby in 2005, and surely that counts for something.

COREY RAGSDALE SS Bats: R Throws: R Height: 6′ 4″ Weight: 170 Born: November 10, 1982 Age: 23

YEAR	TM	LVL	AGE	PA	R	2B	3B	HR	RBI	BB	SO	SB	CS	SPEED	BA	OBP	SLG	MLVR	EQBA	EQOBP	EQSLG	EQA	VORP	DEFENSE	
2003	CMB	A	20	418	50	11	4	3	27	46	133	31	8	7.6	.180	.297	.259	-.184	.167	.252	.248	.196	-35.2	104-SS	2
2004	SLU	A+	21	478	65	19	5	7	38	42	152	24	14	7.4	.221	.305	.340	-.098	.202	.271	.322	.215	-20.1	123-SS	5
2005	SLU	A+	22	311	51	16	8	10	38	33	94	8	7	6.4	.260	.347	.487	.163	.230	.307	.430	.250	8.8	68-SS	5
2005	BIN	AA	22	243	33	5	3	9	31	21	75	4	3	5.6	.226	.305	.401	-.063	.202	.277	.362	.224	-4.8	60-SS	3
2006	NYN	MLB	23	474	52	22	3	9	40	39	139	10	6	5.1	.218	.291	.349	-.219	.221	.294	.369	.224	-1.1	112-SS	2

Breakout: 36% Improve: 56% Collapse: 24% Attrition: 11%   Comparables: Alex Gonzalez, Dave Matranga, Ryan Owens

Holy Moly, that's a lot of strikeouts! Ragsdale's 169 whiffs were the third most in pro ball, topping major league leader Adam Dunn by one—and that's in more than 100 fewer plate appearances against pitchers with much lower paychecks. Consider that none of the top ten whiffers in the bigs in '05 came close to that total while in the minors, save for Preston Wilson with 135. A big man for a shortstop, at least Ragsdale has a nice arm, and one should not easily dismiss the 50 extra-base hits.

PRENTICE REDMAN OF Bats: R Throws: R Height: 6′ 3″ Weight: 185 Born: August 23, 1979 Age: 26

YEAR	TM	LVL	AGE	PA	R	2B	3B	HR	RBI	BB	SO	SB	CS	SPEED	BA	OBP	SLG	MLVR	EQBA	EQOBP	EQSLG	EQA	VORP	DEFENSE			
2003	NOR	AAA	23	481	60	29	2	11	48	40	96	24	8	6.5	.254	.326	.406	.042	.249	.321	.407	.255	-5.8	52-LF	1	50-RF	0
2004	BIN	AA	24	278	46	29	1	13	49	28	68	9	4	5.9	.286	.367	.571	.289	.238	.310	.473	.264	2.2	50-RF	1		
2004	NOR	AAA	24	234	29	17	2	4	30	17	57	9	3	6.7	.254	.308	.408	-.036	.247	.301	.392	.244	-6.8	33-LF	-3	18-CF	0
2005	BIN	AA	25	186	30	12	1	4	29	17	37	2	3	4.0	.311	.371	.472	.193	.271	.326	.406	.255	-0.9	17-LF	-3	12-RF	-1
2005	NOR	AAA	25	284	34	25	1	5	32	23	49	9	1	6.2	.297	.352	.461	.166	.284	.338	.432	.270	3.9	43-LF	-1	12-CF	0
2006	SLN	MLB	26	394	52	23	2	11	47	32	84	10	3	5.5	.260	.325	.431	-.026	.261	.326	.447	.259	5.8	94-LF	-2		

Breakout: 26% Improve: 43% Collapse: 30% Attrition: 20%   Comparables: Jeffrey Hammonds, Larry Herndon, Ron Davis

By this age, you want to be blowing people's minds. You want to be Tom Hanks in the Big parody on SNL, bowling over the competition. You want to be a man among boys. Instead, there is this: a passable season of duty divided between the B-Mets and the Tides. There's a cup of coffee in his future, maybe even an entire coffee break or fifth outfielder's spot if things break just right.

JOSE REYES SS Bats: B Throws: R Height: 6′ 0″ Weight: 160 Born: June 11, 1983 Age: 23

YEAR	TM	LVL	AGE	PA	R	2B	3B	HR	RBI	BB	SO	SB	CS	SPEED	BA	OBP	SLG	MLVR	EQBA	EQOBP	EQSLG	EQA	VORP	DEFENSE	
2003	NYN	MLB	20	290	47	12	4	5	32	13	36	13	3	8.0	.307	.334	.434	.073	.305	.334	.444	.271	18.3	68-SS	9
2004	NYN	MLB	21	225	33	16	2	2	14	5	31	19	2	8.5	.255	.271	.373	-.171	.252	.269	.369	.234	2.4	39-2B	2
2005	NYN	MLB	22	729	99	24	17	7	58	27	78	60	15	8.7	.273	.300	.386	-.068	.274	.304	.392	.249	22.4	158-SS	-7
2006	NYN	MLB	23	644	97	31	9	7	50	31	69	57	16	7.0	.279	.317	.397	-.068	.283	.322	.421	.257	24.4	150-SS	1

Breakout: 32% Improve: 60% Collapse: 23% Attrition: 3%   Comparables: Garry Templeton, Luis Aparicio, Barry Larkin

Reyes gave the Mets one of the most prodigious displays of out-making in baseball history. Screw the Mendoza Line, Reyes busted the Moreno Line, landing in the top five all-time for outs made in a single season. A 25-point drop in average would give him a shot at the all-time record set by Moreno himself in 1980 (551), a realistic possibility given the volatility of a batting average-based offenses like Reyes's. Reyes would do less damage at the bottom of the order, as everybody except Willie Randolph seems to grasp. By batting him leadoff, Randolph put the focus on what he can't do, instead of playing up what he can. On defense, he hasn't yet lived up to his potential, but he's also had to jump back and forth between short and second while settling into the majors. He can still have a very long career, even if he never gets it completely together. Lesser talents certainly have (Shawon Dunston, for one).

CHRIS WOODWARD INF Bats: R Throws: R Height: 6' 0" Weight: 180 Born: June 27, 1976 Age: 30

YEAR	TM	LVL	AGE	PA	R	2B	3B	HR	RBI	BB	SO	SB	CS	SPEED	BA	OBP	SLG	MLVR	EQBA	EQOBP	EQSLG	EQA	VORP	DEFENSE	
2003	TOR	MLB	27	386	49	22	2	7	45	28	72	1	2	4.5	.261	.316	.395	-.094	.256	.316	.398	.248	7.2	98-SS	1
2004	TOR	MLB	28	230	21	13	4	1	24	14	46	1	2	5.3	.235	.283	.347	-.271	.229	.281	.338	.218	-5.3	58-SS	-4
2005	NYN	MLB	29	190	16	10	0	3	18	13	46	0	0	3.8	.283	.337	.393	.008	.282	.339	.391	.256	3.1	23-1B	-2
2006	NYN	MLB	30	111	12	6	1	2	11	8	23	0	0	4.4	.247	.306	.373	-.143	.251	.309	.396	.236	0.9	31-SS	-1

Breakout: 18% Improve: 44% Collapse: 35% Attrition: 59% Comparables: Randy Velarde, Pat Kelly, Mark DeRosa

He played seven positions, which looks good on the resume, and should set him up for three or four more years of utility work. After all, Joe McEwing, who is three years older, still had a job in 2005. While Woodward might seem a more substantial and useful player, he actually posted a nearly identical WARP1 in '05 while playing the same role McEwing did for the Mets in '04: 0.8 to 0.7.

DAVID WRIGHT 3B Bats: R Throws: R Height: 6' 0" Weight: 190 Born: December 20, 1982 Age: 23

YEAR	TM	LVL	AGE	PA	R	2B	3B	HR	RBI	BB	SO	SB	CS	SPEED	BA	OBP	SLG	MLVR	EQBA	EQOBP	EQSLG	EQA	VORP	DEFENSE	
2003	SLU	A+	20	548	69	39	2	15	75	72	98	19	5	5.6	.270	.369	.459	.213	.243	.328	.444	.267	23.0	130-3B	6
2004	BIN	AA	21	272	44	27	0	10	40	39	41	20	6	5.8	.363	.467	.619	.572	.320	.416	.552	.324	37.0	56-3B	-1
2004	NOR	AAA	21	134	18	8	0	8	17	16	19	2	4	3.6	.298	.388	.579	.383	.284	.371	.545	.298	14.6	31-3B	2
2004	NYN	MLB	21	283	41	17	1	14	40	14	40	6	0	5.5	.293	.332	.525	.176	.289	.326	.517	.285	17.0	68-3B	-4
2005	NYN	MLB	22	657	99	42	1	27	102	72	113	17	7	5.3	.306	.388	.523	.291	.305	.388	.532	.308	57.2	159-3B	0
2006	NYN	MLB	23	655	98	40	2	29	97	75	106	17	5	5.3	.299	.385	.530	.233	.304	.390	.561	.311	59.8	153-3B	1

Breakout: 24% Improve: 64% Collapse: 10% Attrition: 0% Comparables: Jim Ray Hart, Jim Fregosi, Dick Allen

Based on WARP3, Wright's 2005 campaign ranks as the 13th highest ever for a Met position player. The difference between him and the dozen men above him is that he was decidedly younger than they were when they enjoyed their seasonal greatness. Only Darryl Strawberry in 1987 came close in youthful glory, and he was 25; the rest were 26 or older. Wright's walk rate was a source of some concern in his rookie year, but that improved as he settled in. New York would do well to lock him down for the long term.

PITCHERS

BRIAN BANNISTER Bats: R Throws: R Height: 6' 1" Weight: 205 Born: February 28, 1981 Age: 25

YEAR	TM	LVL	AGE	W	L	SV	G	GS	IP	H	BB	SO	HR	GB%	BABIP	STUFF	WHIP	ERA	PERA	EQERA	EQH9	EQBB9	EQSO9	EQHR9	VORP	WXRL
2004	SLU	A+	23	5	7	0	20	20	110.3	111	27	106	6	—	.329	1	1.25	4.24	4.85	6.73	10.1	2.7	5.5	1.1	-13.3	—
2004	BIN	AA	23	3	3	0	8	8	44.3	45	17	28	2	—	.321	-2	1.40	4.06	4.81	5.65	9.8	3.8	4.2	0.6	-0.2	—
2005	BIN	AA	24	9	4	0	18	18	109.0	91	27	94	11	49%	.278	-1	1.08	2.56	5.23	3.92	8.8	2.8	5.2	1.4	19.3	—
2005	NOR	AAA	24	4	1	0	8	8	45.3	48	13	48	0	46%	.369	28	1.35	3.18	3.20	4.60	9.4	2.8	7.2	0.2	5.0	—
2006	NYN	MLB	25	7	9	0	30	20	128.7	132	50	86	14	47%	.291	4	1.41	4.65	4.94	5.35	9.2	3.2	5.6	1.0	4.6	1.3

Breakout: 12% Improve: 45% Collapse: 20% Attrition: 0% Comparables: Dan Murray, Don Aase, Dickie Noles

At Bannister's age, there need to be definite signs that good things are happening. Happily, there are, as he excelled at both Double- and Triple-A. Not everything's perfect: Bannister is neither overpowering, nor does he have a consistent breaking pitch. A good spring this year could get him noticed by a team without quite so much free-agent density at its highest level.

HEATH BELL

Bats: R Throws: R   Height: 6′ 3″   Weight: 230   Born: September 29, 1977   Age: 28

YEAR	TM	LVL	AGE	W	L	SV	G	GS	IP	H	BB	SO	HR	GB%	BABIP	STUFF	WHIP	ERA	PERA	EQERA	EQH9	EQBB9	EQSO9	EQHR9	VORP	WXRL
2004	NOR	AAA	26	3	1	16	45	0	55.7	42	24	69	4	—	.295	9	1.18	3.23	4.25	4.25	7.8	4.6	8.7	0.8	8.0	—
2004	NYN	MLB	26	0	2	0	17	0	24.3	22	6	27	5	48%	.309	16	1.15	3.33	4.50	3.38	8.6	1.9	9.0	1.9	6.3	0.4
2005	NOR	AAA	27	1	0	6	13	2	26.7	15	5	29	1	63%	.233	19	0.75	1.69	2.88	2.88	6.5	2.2	7.6	0.4	7.6	—
2005	NYN	MLB	27	1	3	0	42	0	46.7	56	13	43	3	46%	.373	11	1.48	5.59	3.38	5.81	9.8	2.2	7.3	0.6	-2.0	-0.0
2006	*NYN*	*MLB*	*28*	*3*	*3*	*3*	*51*	*1*	*60.0*	*58*	*18*	*50*	*6*	*47%*	*.296*	*6*	*1.27*	*3.81*	*4.07*	*4.76*	*8.7*	*2.5*	*6.9*	*0.8*	*7.6*	*0.7*

Breakout: 32%   Improve: 63%   Collapse: 15%   Attrition: 18%   Comparables: Blas Minor, Tim Burke, Steve Karsay

A disappointing season. It was hoped that Bell could take charge of the set-up role. Instead, he earned a refresher course at Norfolk. Some of it was bad luck; his BABIP was on the cusp of the worst 10% of any pitcher who appeared in 2005. While it's rational to cut a guy slack when his pitches are landing safely with such regularity, it doesn't make them stop landing there.

KRIS BENSON

Bats: R Throws: R   Height: 6′ 4″   Weight: 190   Born: November 7, 1974   Age: 31

YEAR	TM	LVL	AGE	W	L	SV	G	GS	IP	H	BB	SO	HR	GB%	BABIP	STUFF	WHIP	ERA	PERA	EQERA	EQH9	EQBB9	EQSO9	EQHR9	VORP	WXRL
2003	PIT	MLB	28	5	9	0	18	18	105.0	127	36	68	14	38%	.324	0	1.55	4.97	4.79	5.55	10.2	2.7	5.1	1.2	-1.2	1.3
2004	PIT	MLB	29	8	8	0	20	20	132.3	137	44	83	7	46%	.315	19	1.37	4.22	3.99	4.60	9.1	2.7	5.0	0.5	15.0	3.0
2004	NYN	MLB	29	4	4	0	11	11	68.0	65	17	51	8	44%	.275	14	1.21	4.50	4.30	4.84	9.0	2.0	6.0	1.1	6.6	1.4
2005	NYN	MLB	30	10	8	0	28	28	174.3	171	49	95	24	45%	.264	-2	1.26	4.13	5.00	4.63	9.4	2.4	4.6	1.3	20.9	3.4
2006	*BAL*	*MLB*	*31*	*9*	*11*	*0*	*30*	*27*	*168.7*	*178*	*45*	*92*	*22*	*43%*	*.282*	*5*	*1.32*	*4.47*	*4.53*	*4.82*	*9.4*	*2.3*	*4.9*	*1.1*	*16.8*	*2.9*

Breakout: 14%   Improve: 55%   Collapse: 12%   Attrition: 6%   Comparables: Dave Mlicki, Art Ditmar, Dick Ruthven

Maybe the Mets didn't overpay for him. Maybe this is what $7 million-plus looks like nowadays: a league-average ERA and one strikeout for every eight guys you face. Certainly, in his eagerness for the pleasure of Benson's company in 2005, Omar Minaya boosted the earnings power of every good pitcher in baseball. A year later, Minaya was just as eager to shop him around, finally placing Benson on the Orioles for reliever Jorge Julio and control artist John "Remember the" Maine, and better still, getting Baltimore to take on all of Benson's salary... Never send to know for whom the bell tolls, Omar; it tolls for thee. As for the ex-Met, Benson will have the benefit of working with Leo Mazzone, so who knows, maybe everyone wins.

TOM GLAVINE

Bats: L Throws: L   Height: 6′ 1″   Weight: 185   Born: March 25, 1966   Age: 40

YEAR	TM	LVL	AGE	W	L	SV	G	GS	IP	H	BB	SO	HR	GB%	BABIP	STUFF	WHIP	ERA	PERA	EQERA	EQH9	EQBB9	EQSO9	EQHR9	VORP	WXRL
2003	NYN	MLB	37	9	14	0	32	32	183.3	205	66	82	21	49%	.303	-5	1.48	4.52	5.04	4.60	9.9	2.9	3.6	1.0	22.1	4.3
2004	NYN	MLB	38	11	14	0	33	33	212.3	204	70	109	20	54%	.270	5	1.29	3.60	4.54	3.93	9.1	2.8	4.2	0.8	40.4	5.0
2005	NYN	MLB	39	13	13	0	33	33	211.3	227	61	105	12	49%	.308	13	1.36	3.54	4.09	3.96	9.6	2.4	4.1	0.5	42.4	5.4
2006	*NYN*	*MLB*	*40*	*11*	*11*	*0*	*36*	*29*	*193.3*	*203*	*59*	*94*	*19*	*48%*	*.284*	*-3*	*1.36*	*4.02*	*4.60*	*4.68*	*9.4*	*2.6*	*4.0*	*0.9*	*21.5*	*3.6*

Breakout: 8%   Improve: 41%   Collapse: 33%   Attrition: 3%   Comparables: Kenny Rogers, Warren Spahn, Frank Tanana

For nearly a year, Glavine did a good impression of an ex-ace pitcher. From All-Star break '04 to All-Star break '05, Glavine's line was 186.2 innings, 234 hits, 78 walks, 89 strikeouts. His ERA was 4.97. As such, his second half, in which he posted a 2.22 ERA, was New York's second-most inexplicable revival after that of Jason Giambi. Glavine finished the season with ten consecutive quality starts. Health was never an issue; Glavine shows up for work like few others, missing one start since 1989. It is this ability to stay in the rotation that is going to get him to 300 wins, regardless of how few runs the Mets score for him. Another season in the low teens for wins in the last year of his contact will cut his wins-needed for that goal in half. He'll enter 2007 as a 41-year old free agent needing one typical season to get to 300. Does a return to the Braves for that milestone sound overly romantic?

DANNY GRAVES

Bats: R Throws: R   Height: 5′ 11″   Weight: 200   Born: August 7, 1973   Age: 32

YEAR	TM	LVL	AGE	W	L	SV	G	GS	IP	H	BB	SO	HR	GB%	BABIP	STUFF	WHIP	ERA	PERA	EQERA	EQH9	EQBB9	EQSO9	EQHR9	VORP	WXRL
2003	CIN	MLB	29	4	15	2	30	26	169.0	204	41	60	30	48%	.293	-21	1.45	5.33	5.70	5.11	10.7	2.0	2.9	1.5	-0.9	1.7
2004	CIN	MLB	30	1	6	41	68	0	68.3	77	13	40	12	53%	.294	-15	1.32	3.95	5.00	4.61	9.9	1.6	4.7	1.4	2.3	1.8
2005	CIN	MLB	31	1	1	10	20	0	18.3	30	12	8	4	38%	.361	-42	2.29	7.38	6.86	8.24	12.4	5.0	3.2	1.8	-6.8	0.3
2005	NYN	MLB	31	0	0	0	20	0	20.3	29	8	12	5	53%	.348	-25	1.82	5.76	6.53	7.40	12.2	3.0	4.8	2.2	-4.5	0.1
2006	*CLE*	*MLB*	*32*	*2*	*3*	*3*	*35*	*1*	*45.3*	*54*	*15*	*20*	*7*	*47%*	*.299*	*-22*	*1.53*	*5.59*	*5.75*	*7.15*	*10.6*	*2.9*	*3.9*	*1.3*	*-1.2*	*-0.2*

Breakout: 29%   Improve: 51%   Collapse: 33%   Attrition: 40%   Comparables: Gene Nelson, Chuck Crim, Tom Murphy

Graves has had a negative STF count at every stop in his career save for his rookie year. What the Mets thought they were getting when they picked him up is puzzling, and what they were thinking when they brought him back in late September is even more puzzling. Perhaps it was to prove to themselves, once and for all, that he wasn't worth his $5 million option. Signed up by the team who originally drafted him; we'll see if the Tribe can iron out his problems.

TIM HAMULACK Bats: L Throws: L Height: 6′ 4″ Weight: 210 Born: November 14, 1976 Age: 29

YEAR	TM	LVL	AGE	W	L	SV	G	GS	IP	H	BB	SO	HR	GB%	BABIP	STUFF	WHIP	ERA	PERA	EQERA	EQH9	EQBB9	EQSO9	EQHR9	VORP	WXRL
2005	BIN	AA	28	2	2	6	21	0	28.7	20	6	27	0	67%	.250	-4	0.91	1.25	3.71	4.05	7.4	2.7	5.1	0.3	4.6	—
2005	NOR	AAA	28	3	1	6	28	0	35.3	20	9	34	1	60%	.224	10	0.82	1.02	3.31	2.48	6.9	2.8	6.6	0.3	11.3	—
2006	LAN	MLB	29	2	3	1	30	2	46.0	46	20	33	5	53%	.292	-5	1.43	4.29	4.74	5.11	9.1	3.6	5.8	0.9	3.7	0.4

Breakout: 50% Improve: 73% Collapse: 7% Attrition: 22% Comparables: Dennis Powell, William Brunson, Gene Bearden

In Eliot Asinof's great 1955 novel, *Man on Spikes,* the protagonist is a career minor-league centerfielder. When his shot at the bigs finally comes . . . well, there's no need to play spoiler here, but Tim Hamulack's 23.14 ERA should give you a clue. Ten years in the making, Hamulack's debut was disappointing but it shouldn't be the end. He throws hard and cut his walk rate dramatically; the lefty set-up job could be his if things break right in spring training. Spring training in Vero Beach with the Dodgers, that is.

AARON HEILMAN Bats: R Throws: R Height: 6′ 5″ Weight: 220 Born: November 12, 1978 Age: 27

YEAR	TM	LVL	AGE	W	L	SV	G	GS	IP	H	BB	SO	HR	GB%	BABIP	STUFF	WHIP	ERA	PERA	EQERA	EQH9	EQBB9	EQSO9	EQHR9	VORP	WXRL
2003	NOR	AAA	24	6	4	0	16	16	94.3	99	32	71	5	—	.307	9	1.39	3.24	4.58	4.58	9.4	3.7	5.3	0.8	10.5	—
2003	NYN	MLB	24	2	7	0	14	13	65.3	79	41	51	13	48%	.332	-16	1.84	6.75	6.04	7.12	10.3	5.0	6.2	1.7	-12.7	-0.2
2004	NOR	AAA	25	7	10	0	26	26	151.7	156	66	123	15	—	.307	-2	1.46	4.33	5.30	5.79	9.6	4.4	5.6	1.2	-3.1	—
2004	NYN	MLB	25	1	3	0	5	5	28.0	27	13	22	4	57%	.291	6	1.43	5.46	4.88	5.20	9.1	3.9	6.2	1.3	0.7	0.4
2005	NYN	MLB	26	5	3	5	53	7	108.0	87	37	106	6	47%	.290	27	1.15	3.17	3.38	3.54	7.8	2.9	8.2	0.5	25.9	3.3
2006	NYN	MLB	27	4	5	3	41	6	75.7	74	32	63	7	47%	.299	4	1.41	4.29	4.70	5.16	8.8	3.6	6.9	0.9	6.3	0.7

Breakout: 16% Improve: 51% Collapse: 21% Attrition: 16% Comparables: Wayne Twitchell, Ken Forsch, Gene Brabender

If the universe were a fair place, every pitcher that had as disastrous a debut as Heilman would also get to have a season like 2005 to set things right. Having said that, is this a pitcher getting his career back on track or one settling into a life of limited use? He had the third-highest K/9 rate in the National League among pitchers with 100 or more innings pitched. That, and his nice STF number—19, second only to Pedro Martinez on the team—are good signs that he's ready to succeed in any role. The decision to send Benson to Baltimore does create the opportunity for Heilman to return to the rotation, so stay tuned.

GABY HERNANDEZ Bats: R Throws: R Height: 6′ 3″ Weight: 215 Born: May 21, 1986 Age: 20

YEAR	TM	LVL	AGE	W	L	SV	G	GS	IP	H	BB	SO	HR	GB%	BABIP	STUFF	WHIP	ERA	PERA	EQERA	EQH9	EQBB9	EQSO9	EQHR9	VORP	WXRL
2005	HAG	A	19	6	1	0	18	18	92.7	59	30	99	4	48%	.243	25	0.96	2.43	4.41	4.41	8.0	3.7	6.3	0.7	11.3	—
2005	SLU	A+	19	2	5	0	10	10	42.3	48	10	32	1	40%	.367	9	1.37	5.74	4.46	6.80	10.4	2.6	4.5	0.4	-5.6	—
2006	NYN	MLB	20	8	8	0	26	22	134.7	127	53	103	14	44%	.282	15	1.33	4.13	4.48	4.70	8.4	3.3	6.4	0.9	13.9	2.3

Breakout: 28% Improve: 79% Collapse: 7% Attrition: 0% Comparables: Ricky Nolasco, Edwin Jackson, Wilfredo Rodriguez

Another shiny bit of talent sent the Marlins' way, Hernandez blew through the Sally League after being picked out of a Miami high school in the 3rd round of the '04 draft. He's what you want to see in a teen phenom: good mechanics, lively fastball, and decent command. All of the off-speed and breaking stuff is still in the lab, but as live arms go, he's the one guy the Mets dealt that they may really miss.

ROBERTO HERNANDEZ Bats: R Throws: R Height: 6′ 4″ Weight: 250 Born: November 11, 1964 Age: 41

YEAR	TM	LVL	AGE	W	L	SV	G	GS	IP	H	BB	SO	HR	GB%	BABIP	STUFF	WHIP	ERA	PERA	EQERA	EQH9	EQBB9	EQSO9	EQHR9	VORP	WXRL
2003	ATL	MLB	38	5	3	0	66	0	60.0	61	43	45	10	55%	.288	-22	1.73	4.35	6.00	5.40	9.6	5.8	6.0	1.5	1.4	-0.4
2004	PHI	MLB	39	3	5	0	63	0	56.7	66	29	44	9	53%	.337	-15	1.68	4.76	5.15	6.09	10.0	4.1	6.1	1.2	-3.1	-1.3
2005	NYN	MLB	40	8	6	4	67	0	69.7	57	28	61	5	41%	.283	12	1.22	2.58	3.80	2.75	8.0	3.4	7.3	0.7	22.3	2.6
2006	PIT	MLB	41	2	3	2	40	1	47.0	49	22	36	4	49%	.310	-8	1.51	4.59	4.82	6.39	9.2	3.8	6.4	0.8	3.0	0.2

Breakout: 7% Improve: 37% Collapse: 32% Attrition: 38% Comparables: Ron Reed, Al Benton, Virgil Trucks

(continued next page)

Roberto Hernandez *(continued)*

At first glance, one would assume his improvement was a simple case of moving from the pitching hell of Philadelphia to Shea Stadium. In actuality, he pitched almost identically in New York in '05 as he did in Philadelphia in '04. It was on the road where the big swing came, his ERA deflating by about 80%. If the home value is constant and the true road value lands somewhere between the extremes, he's a handy pitcher to have around, 41 summers or not. Signed to a one-year deal by the Pirates to set up or perhaps even close.

KAZUHISA ISHII   Bats: **L** Throws: **L**   Height: 6′ 0″   Weight: 190   Born: September 9, 1973   Age: 32

YEAR	TM	LVL	AGE	W	L	SV	G	GS	IP	H	BB	SO	HR	GB%	BABIP	STUFF	WHIP	ERA	PERA	EQERA	EQH9	EQBB9	EQSO9	EQHR9	VORP	WXRL
2003	LAN	MLB	29	9	7	0	27	27	147.0	129	101	140	16	41%	.294	11	1.56	3.86	4.87	4.62	8.6	5.6	7.8	1.0	18.7	4.0
2004	LAN	MLB	30	13	8	0	31	31	172.0	155	98	99	21	36%	.263	-8	1.47	4.71	5.42	5.37	9.1	4.8	4.7	1.1	11.9	3.5
2005	NYN	MLB	31	3	9	0	19	16	91.0	87	49	53	13	39%	.272	-15	1.49	5.14	5.62	5.92	9.3	4.6	4.9	1.3	-2.5	0.7
2006	*NYN*	*MLB*	*32*	*4*	*6*	*0*	*31*	*12*	*83.3*	*86*	*47*	*57*	*11*	*39%*	*.289*	*-12*	*1.59*	*5.36*	*5.90*	*6.84*	*9.3*	*4.7*	*5.7*	*1.2*	*-1.8*	*0.1*

Breakout: 15%   Improve: 33%   Collapse: 41%   Attrition: 20%   Comparables: Spec Shea, Bob McClure, Harry Perkowski

While it isn't fair to get mad at players for getting hurt—not unless they've done it punching a wall or playing paintball with lead paint—Mets fans have got to be steamed at Steve Trachsel. When he went on the DL, it prompted the team to trade for Kaz Ishii. Like so many of their attempts at retreads, it didn't work; neither his control nor his strikeout rate improved on the Mets' watch. Coaching isn't helping, so maybe hypnosis, or doing everything on the mound the opposite way from how he's done it in the past, Costanza-style, would do the trick. Rather than deconstruct himself, Ishii's headed back to Japan to pitch for Yakult.

MATT LINDSTROM   Bats: **R** Throws: **R**   Height: 6′ 4″   Weight: 200   Born: February 11, 1980   Age: 26

YEAR	TM	LVL	AGE	W	L	SV	G	GS	IP	H	BB	SO	HR	GB%	BABIP	STUFF	WHIP	ERA	PERA	EQERA	EQH9	EQBB9	EQSO9	EQHR9	VORP	WXRL
2004	CMB	A	24	3	2	0	12	11	56.0	47	10	64	3	—	.301	4	1.02	3.21	4.42	6.11	9.2	2.2	5.6	1.0	-3.0	—
2004	SLU	A+	24	5	5	0	14	14	79.7	83	20	50	5	—	.306	-17	1.29	3.73	5.71	6.78	10.5	3.0	3.6	1.4	-9.9	—
2005	BIN	AA	25	2	5	0	35	10	73.3	90	55	58	11	56%	.345	-58	1.98	5.40	8.10	8.10	11.3	8.7	4.6	2.1	-19.4	—
2006	*NYN*	*MLB*	*26*	*2*	*4*	*0*	*29*	*6*	*57.3*	*69*	*51*	*34*	*9*	*50%*	*.316*	*-30*	*2.07*	*7.28*	*8.15*	*8.70*	*10.7*	*7.4*	*4.9*	*1.3*	*-15.5*	*-1.3*

Breakout: 9%   Improve: 37%   Collapse: 36%   Attrition: 13%   Comparables: Steve Sparks, Juan Guzman, Ryan Mills

The dichotomy in his K:BB ratio between low-A and Double-A is pretty telling, as he went from 6:1 at Cap City in '04, pitching against significantly younger players, to about even at Binghamton in '05, again against younger players. His conversion to the pen was moderately successful—he cut his BB/9 from 9.0 to 5.6—and short work might be the best way to exploit his blazing speed.

BRADEN LOOPER   Bats: **R** Throws: **R**   Height: 6′ 5″   Weight: 225   Born: October 28, 1974   Age: 31

YEAR	TM	LVL	AGE	W	L	SV	G	GS	IP	H	BB	SO	HR	GB%	BABIP	STUFF	WHIP	ERA	PERA	EQERA	EQH9	EQBB9	EQSO9	EQHR9	VORP	WXRL
2003	FLO	MLB	28	6	4	28	74	0	80.7	82	29	56	4	56%	.311	6	1.38	3.68	3.76	3.98	8.9	2.9	5.5	0.4	15.4	3.3
2004	NYN	MLB	29	2	5	29	71	0	83.3	86	16	60	5	64%	.314	13	1.22	2.70	3.58	3.04	9.2	1.6	5.7	0.5	24.5	3.6
2005	NYN	MLB	30	4	7	28	60	0	59.3	65	22	27	7	54%	.282	-20	1.47	3.95	5.34	4.88	10.2	3.2	3.8	1.1	4.8	-0.2
2006	*SLN*	*MLB*	*31*	*3*	*4*	*13*	*51*	*0*	*58.0*	*62*	*20*	*32*	*5*	*54%*	*.298*	*-11*	*1.41*	*4.28*	*4.55*	*5.35*	*9.6*	*2.8*	*4.6*	*0.8*	*4.9*	*0.5*

Breakout: 15%   Improve: 30%   Collapse: 44%   Attrition: 21%   Comparables: Antonio Alfonseca, Jay Powell, Dave Weathers

How bad was it? Looper dropped from a top-20 WXRL finish in 2004 to a negative WXRL in 2005. Among men entrusted with at least 30 save opportunities, only Jose Mesa of Pittsburgh was worse. Looper helped the Mets become one of only five teams to lose ten games in which they led after seven innings. The Mets were smart not to exercise his 2006 option, so credit Omar Minaya with realizing that this "proven" closer was not worth the expense. Where this leaves the Cardinals for having signed him to a three-year, $13.5 million deal to serve as Izzy insurance is up to the reader's imagination.

EVAN MacLANE   Bats: L   Throws: L   Height: 6' 2"   Weight: 185   Born: November 4, 1982   Age: 23

YEAR	TM	LVL	AGE	W	L	SV	G	GS	IP	H	BB	SO	HR	GB%	BABIP	STUFF	WHIP	ERA	PERA	EQERA	EQH9	EQBB9	EQSO9	EQHR9	VORP	WXRL
2004	BRO	A-	21	5	3	0	13	13	74.0	70	6	70	8	—	.290	-22	1.03	3.16	6.95	6.68	11.8	1.2	4.5	3.1	-8.1	—
2004	CMB	A	21	5	2	0	14	10	67.7	57	10	66	9	—	.267	-6	0.99	2.39	5.97	4.26	9.7	1.7	5.3	2.3	9.4	—
2005	SLU	A+	22	8	5	0	19	19	112.3	96	15	92	14	44%	.254	-18	0.99	3.21	5.95	5.43	9.7	1.6	4.8	2.2	2.0	—
2005	BIN	AA	22	3	2	0	9	9	58.7	63	9	48	7	47%	.308	4	1.23	4.14	4.99	4.99	9.8	1.6	5.0	1.6	3.9	—
2006	NYN	MLB	23	8	10	0	28	24	150.0	161	35	84	26	44%	.277	4	1.30	4.68	5.14	5.26	9.6	1.9	4.7	1.5	6.3	1.7

Breakout: 16%   Improve: 60%   Collapse: 8%   Attrition: 0%   Comparables: Mike Bacsik, Mark Difelice, Jeriome Robertson

Like most of the left-handed universe, he tops out in the mid-80s and relies on a changeup and excellent control. He didn't miss a beat with a promotion from St. Lucie to Binghamton in 2005, but he did have a few rough outings in the AFL. Like many of his ilk, he's going to have to keep fooling people with his mix of pitches instead of raw stuff, and those HR/9 rates don't make it seem likely that he will.

PEDRO MARTINEZ   Bats: R   Throws: R   Height: 5' 11"   Weight: 170   Born: October 25, 1971   Age: 34

YEAR	TM	LVL	AGE	W	L	SV	G	GS	IP	H	BB	SO	HR	GB%	BABIP	STUFF	WHIP	ERA	PERA	EQERA	EQH9	EQBB9	EQSO9	EQHR9	VORP	WXRL
2003	BOS	MLB	31	14	4	0	29	29	186.7	147	47	206	7	47%	.297	58	1.04	2.22	2.60	2.41	6.9	2.2	9.6	0.3	74.6	8.2
2004	BOS	MLB	32	16	9	0	33	33	217.0	193	61	227	26	42%	.299	34	1.17	3.90	3.64	3.64	8.1	2.4	8.8	1.0	54.4	6.3
2005	NYN	MLB	33	15	8	0	31	31	217.0	159	47	208	19	40%	.253	36	0.95	2.82	3.37	3.07	7.4	1.9	8.1	0.8	64.8	7.6
2006	NYN	MLB	34	15	8	0	32	31	212.7	173	53	205	19	42%	.269	30	1.06	2.80	3.05	3.20	7.3	2.1	8.1	0.8	56.3	7.3

Breakout: 21%   Improve: 41%   Collapse: 19%   Attrition: 0%   Comparables: Tom Seaver, Bob Gibson, Mike Mussina

This is the sort of season a team hopes for when they sign the most highly-touted pitching free agent on the market. Martinez had the fifth-best VORP in the league while cutting almost a full run off his ERA, putting '05 more in line with his first season in Boston rather than his last. The Mets gave him a couple of extra days off here and there, in keeping with the careful usage patterns of his latter days at Fenway. The team knows that Martinez will still be pitching for them in 2008, so it only makes sense to think of each game as a component of that bigger picture. Martinez missed the last week and a half of the season with a sore toe. As of January it still hadn't healed, so 2006 might get off on the wrong (ahem) foot.

JUAN PADILLA   Bats: R   Throws: R   Height: 6' 0"   Weight: 200   Born: February 17, 1977   Age: 29

YEAR	TM	LVL	AGE	W	L	SV	G	GS	IP	H	BB	SO	HR	GB%	BABIP	STUFF	WHIP	ERA	PERA	EQERA	EQH9	EQBB9	EQSO9	EQHR9	VORP	WXRL
2004	COH	AAA	27	2	1	2	44	0	57.7	49	6	52	1	—	.289	16	0.95	2.03	2.88	3.83	8.0	1.1	6.1	0.2	11.1	—
2004	CIN	MLB	27	1	0	0	12	0	14.3	23	8	12	6	36%	.370	-29	2.16	10.70	8.40	9.60	12.6	4.2	6.6	3.6	-8.3	-0.2
2004	NYA	MLB	27	0	0	0	6	0	11.3	16	4	5	1	41%	.375	-13	1.76	3.98	4.50	3.75	10.5	3.0	3.8	0.8	3.0	-0.2
2005	NOR	AAA	28	3	2	11	37	2	63.3	45	9	59	4	51%	.248	10	0.85	1.42	3.77	3.17	8.0	1.5	6.3	0.8	16.1	—
2005	NYN	MLB	28	3	1	1	24	0	36.3	24	13	17	0	52%	.207	-3	1.02	1.49	4.15	2.08	7.5	3.1	4.2	0.3	15.1	1.5
2006	NYN	MLB	29	3	3	3	52	1	53.3	55	16	33	5	48%	.287	-6	1.32	3.80	4.43	4.38	9.2	2.5	5.1	0.9	7.3	0.6

Breakout: 20%   Improve: 37%   Collapse: 31%   Attrition: 17%   Comparables: Chuck Crim, Tom Hume, Dave Heaverlo

He's spent time in Triple-A with three different organizations over the past three seasons, and in that time posted a 179:32 strikeout to walk ratio in 212.1 innings. The Mets found him wandering the streets, and for their troubles—the pen and paper for the contract—they got the pitcher with the best VORP of anyone under 40 innings pitched. If Padilla combines an approximation of his Triple-A ratios with another BAPIP in Bob Uecker territory, he'll finally make it out of the minimum-wage phase of his career.

YUSMEIRO PETIT   Bats: R   Throws: R   Height: 6' 0"   Weight: 180   Born: November 22, 1984   Age: 21

YEAR	TM	LVL	AGE	W	L	SV	G	GS	IP	H	BB	SO	HR	GB%	BABIP	STUFF	WHIP	ERA	PERA	EQERA	EQH9	EQBB9	EQSO9	EQHR9	VORP	WXRL
2004	CMB	A	19	9	2	0	15	15	83.0	47	22	122	8	—	.234	29	0.83	2.39	4.58	4.34	7.5	2.9	8.3	1.5	10.7	—
2004	SLU	A+	19	2	3	0	9	9	44.3	27	14	62	0	—	.284	42	0.93	1.22	3.00	3.21	7.1	3.2	8.8	0.2	11.2	—
2005	BIN	AA	20	9	3	0	21	21	117.7	90	18	130	15	35%	.262	19	0.92	2.91	4.49	3.61	8.1	1.6	7.3	1.6	24.8	—
2005	NOR	AAA	20	0	3	0	3	3	14.7	24	6	14	5	33%	.422	2	2.04	9.18	7.80	10.20	13.2	3.6	6.6	3.6	-7.7	—
2006	FLO	MLB	21	10	9	0	31	24	159.0	141	47	147	21	37%	.272	22	1.18	3.85	4.02	4.18	8.0	2.4	7.3	1.2	22.3	3.4

Breakout: 27%   Improve: 59%   Collapse: 15%   Attrition: 2%   Comparables: Luke Prokopec, Gary Nolan, Bruce Chen

(continued next page)

Yusmeiro Petit *(continued)*

The late call-up to Norfolk was a disaster. While that shouldn't worry anybody, it may dash any thoughts of rushing him into The Show in '06. Before that promotion, his progress had been like a graph chart of a 1920s margin stock offering. His K:BB ratios have been Schilling-esque throughout his minor league climb, even as the quality of the competition improved. He's been pitching to older hitters the last two seasons and completely dominating them. Petit is helped by a deceptive motion, but he also has a full assortment of four pitches he can pinpoint. If the Marlins are prudent they will take their time with him, but he's not that far from being ready.

JASON SCOBIE   **Bats: R Throws: R**   Height: 6′ 1″   Weight: 190   Born: September 1, 1978   Age: 27

YEAR	TM	LVL	AGE	W	L	SV	G	GS	IP	H	BB	SO	HR	GB%	BABIP	STUFF	WHIP	ERA	PERA	EQERA	EQH9	EQBB9	EQSO9	EQHR9	VORP	WXRL
2004	BIN	AA	25	5	5	1	26	24	147.0	137	49	95	11	—	.278	-5	1.27	2.82	5.30	4.84	9.8	3.6	4.1	1.0	11.8	—
2005	NOR	AAA	26	15	7	0	27	26	167.0	163	55	96	13	51%	.290	-2	1.31	3.34	5.05	4.94	9.5	3.5	3.9	0.9	11.8	—
2006	NYN	MLB	27	6	8	0	28	19	117.3	131	47	59	13	50%	.298	-7	1.52	5.00	5.47	5.74	10.0	3.4	4.2	1.0	-1.0	0.7

Breakout: 5%   Improve: 34%   Collapse: 26%   Attrition: 0%   Comparables: Don August, Joe Mays, Bob Purkey

Repeated the Binghamton-to-Norfolk trip he took in 2003 with much better results, and not a moment too soon, since he's getting to the age where the charm of America's less-populated cities has got to be wearing thin. Major league pitchers with this sort of K:BB ratio are mostly back-end starters.

JAE SEO   **Bats: R Throws: R**   Height: 6′ 1″   Weight: 210   Born: May 24, 1977   Age: 29

YEAR	TM	LVL	AGE	W	L	SV	G	GS	IP	H	BB	SO	HR	GB%	BABIP	STUFF	WHIP	ERA	PERA	EQERA	EQH9	EQBB9	EQSO9	EQHR9	VORP	WXRL
2003	NYN	MLB	26	9	12	0	32	31	188.3	193	46	110	18	41%	.285	9	1.27	3.82	4.32	4.52	9.3	2.0	4.8	0.9	25.7	4.1
2004	NYN	MLB	27	5	10	0	24	21	117.7	133	50	54	17	42%	.310	-15	1.56	4.89	5.52	4.99	10.2	3.5	3.7	1.2	7.0	1.9
2005	NOR	AAA	28	7	4	0	19	19	121.7	126	30	111	13	46%	.327	3	1.28	4.29	4.73	5.87	9.8	2.7	6.0	1.3	-3.5	—
2005	NYN	MLB	28	8	2	0	14	14	90.3	84	16	59	9	39%	.282	18	1.11	2.59	3.96	2.84	8.8	1.5	5.5	0.9	29.8	3.5
2006	LAN	MLB	29	8	10	0	31	26	148.3	154	39	95	20	43%	.285	4	1.30	4.27	4.70	4.72	9.4	2.2	5.2	1.2	14.3	2.5

Breakout: 10%   Improve: 42%   Collapse: 21%   Attrition: 0%   Comparables: Roy Smith, Chad Ogea, Herm Wehmeier

Sent back to Norfolk to work on his control, he did just that, getting back into favor by making his walk explosion of 2004 a memory. Having improved his command and his mechanics, he was called up to replace Ishii, who'd been even more clueless about such things, and was given a good two-month run to win the fifth slot for '06. While Benson was the starting pitcher dangled in deals all winter long, Seo's performance made him the more attractive commodity. That certainly seemed to be what Ned Colletti thought when he picked him up along with Hamulack in early January.

ALAY SOLER   **Bats: R Throws: R**   Height: 6′ 4″   Weight: 240   Born: October 9, 1979   Age: 26

How much is it worth to you to look in the box? Cuban pitchers and their enigmatic possibilities cause palpitations in major league front offices far beyond their actual worth. Thirteen Cuban-born pitchers have landed in the majors since 1995, and only one, Danys Baez, has a career ERA under 4.00. This is not an indictment of Cuban nationals who come here wanting to throw baseballs for a living, but more a cautionary tale about overspending in the hopes of finding the next Luis Tiant. Is this really any different than what happens in the Rule 4 Draft, though? Yes, in that Rule 4 players don't often get long-term big league contracts right out of the gate. The Mets have yet to see Soler throw in anger, but at least he hasn't gotten hurt yet. They'll sort him out in spring training and likely assign him to St. Lucie. In Cuba, Soler was known as "El Minero" (The Miner), a name derived from his birthplace of Minas de Matahambre, in Pinar Del Rio.

SHINGO TAKATSU   **Bats: R Throws: R**   Height: 6′ 0″   Weight: 180   Born: November 25, 1968   Age: 37

YEAR	TM	LVL	AGE	W	L	SV	G	GS	IP	H	BB	SO	HR	GB%	BABIP	STUFF	WHIP	ERA	PERA	EQERA	EQH9	EQBB9	EQSO9	EQHR9	VORP	WXRL
2003	YKL	JPL	34	2	3	34	44	0	42.0	42	21	26	7	—	.259	-24	1.50	0.00	6.02	4.02	9.4	5.4	4.7	1.3	7.1	—
2004	CHA	MLB	35	6	4	19	59	0	62.3	40	21	50	6	42%	.205	10	0.98	2.31	3.90	2.40	7.1	3.0	7.1	0.8	26.5	3.9
2005	CHA	MLB	36	1	2	8	31	0	28.7	30	16	32	9	39%	.300	-1	1.60	5.96	5.97	5.65	9.4	5.0	10.0	2.5	-0.3	0.8
2006	NYN	MLB	37	2	2	4	35	0	40.0	40	17	32	5	41%	.290	-5	1.42	4.23	5.01	5.09	9.0	3.6	6.6	1.2	3.5	0.3

Breakout: 20%   Improve: 34%   Collapse: 50%   Attrition: 34%   Comparables: Aurelio Lopez, Doug Bair, Jeff Brantley

PECOTA presciently predicted his fall from grace, perhaps even underestimating how severe his drop-off would be. He's still taking the bat out of the hands of more than a batter per inning, so if his luck returns on the balls in play, he could resemble his 2004 self again. Because he is so remarkably entertaining to watch on the mound, though, perhaps he could live out his days as a live demonstration pitcher, warming up in bullpens around the majors for the amusement of fans.

STEVE TRACHSEL   **Bats: R Throws: R**   Height: 6′ 4″   Weight: 200   Born: October 31, 1970   Age: 35

YEAR	TM	LVL	AGE	W	L	SV	G	GS	IP	H	BB	SO	HR	GB%	BABIP	STUFF	WHIP	ERA	PERA	EQERA	EQH9	EQBB9	EQSO9	EQHR9	VORP	WXRL
2003	NYN	MLB	32	16	10	0	33	33	204.7	204	65	111	26	42%	.280	0	1.31	3.78	4.89	4.05	9.3	2.6	4.4	1.2	39.6	6.0
2004	NYN	MLB	33	12	13	0	33	33	202.7	203	83	117	25	45%	.282	0	1.41	4.00	4.99	4.54	9.4	3.4	4.7	1.0	24.8	4.1
2005	NYN	MLB	34	1	4	0	6	6	37.0	37	12	24	6	41%	.282	2	1.32	4.14	5.20	4.95	9.7	2.7	5.4	1.5	3.0	0.7
2006	NYN	MLB	35	7	7	0	27	21	118.7	123	38	68	16	43%	.280	-3	1.36	4.40	4.91	5.17	9.3	2.7	4.8	1.2	9.0	1.7

Breakout: 10%   Improve: 28%   Collapse: 35%   Attrition: 13%   Comparables: Bob Welch, Pat Hentgen, Doug Drabek

Closed out the season with a stunning return game on August 26, followed by a handful of pedestrian starts. In his first four years with the Mets, Trachsel was remarkably consistent—if unspectacular. At the back end of the rotation he's an asset, but cheap as Trachsel is, he's a 10-and-5 guy now, and thus more difficult to move. But with Benson out of the picture, the game's slowest moundsman will be dawdling in Flushing Meadows for the foreseeable future.

VICTOR ZAMBRANO   **Bats: R Throws: R**   Height: 6′ 0″   Weight: 200   Born: August 6, 1975   Age: 30

YEAR	TM	LVL	AGE	W	L	SV	G	GS	IP	H	BB	SO	HR	GB%	BABIP	STUFF	WHIP	ERA	PERA	EQERA	EQH9	EQBB9	EQSO9	EQHR9	VORP	WXRL
2003	TBA	MLB	27	12	10	0	34	28	188.3	165	106	132	21	50%	.265	5	1.44	4.21	5.23	4.50	8.8	5.1	6.3	1.0	30.0	5.1
2004	TBA	MLB	28	9	7	0	23	22	128.0	107	96	109	13	50%	.273	10	1.59	4.43	5.22	4.44	8.3	6.3	7.2	0.8	20.0	3.1
2004	NYN	MLB	28	2	0	0	3	3	14.0	12	6	14	0	64%	.300	14	1.29	3.86	2.57	5.79	7.7	3.2	7.7	0.0	0.0	0.5
2005	NYN	MLB	29	7	12	0	31	27	166.3	170	77	112	12	53%	.304	11	1.48	4.17	4.54	4.75	9.4	3.9	5.6	0.6	18.3	3.2
2006	NYN	MLB	30	9	9	0	32	24	151.0	144	72	107	14	50%	.284	4	1.43	4.21	4.75	4.98	8.6	4.0	5.9	0.8	13.3	2.4

Breakout: 12%   Improve: 45%   Collapse: 22%   Attrition: 6%   Comparables: Tom Candiotti, Bob Buhl, Russ Ortiz

Things that look stupid in hindsight are pretty bad, but worse are the things that look stupid the moment they happen. The Zambrano–Scott Kazmir trade manages to do both. Zambrano was out-pitched by Kazmir in 2005, while costing the Mets about $1.8 million more. The other players in the deal haven't been factors yet, but none are likely to ever swing that balance back the Mets' way. On the plus side, Zambrano got his wildness under control to some extent, enough to be a serviceable fifth starter. He had a two-month run from May 6 to July 16 in which he allowed three runs or fewer in 12 straight starts. Thereafter, he was flaky, alternating very good starts and bad. The inconsistency ultimately cost him his spot in the rotation down the stretch, but the Mets are counting on him to be able to move back into the rotation in the wake of the Benson deal.

Line Outs

Position/Player	TM	LVL	AGE	PA	R	2B	3B	HR	RBI	BB	SO	SB-CS	SPEED	BA/OBP/SLG	MLVR	EQBA/OBP/SLG	EQA	VORP
3B S. Bowman	SLU	A+	20	354	44	15	1	17	53	22	110	4-1	4.1	.221/.282/.429	-.037	.195/.250/.385	.218	-12.5
LF D. Brinkley	HAG	A	23	264	48	17	4	10	41	38	57	20-13	6.8	.364/.477/.621	.625	.301/.387/.483	.294	16.4
	SLU	A+	23	226	36	5	2	5	24	24	64	9-6	6.0	.266/.367/.391	.075	.231/.315/.343	.235	-10.0
1B M. Carp*	HAG	A	19	374	49	12	1	19	63	35	96	2-2	3.7	.249/.358/.476	.160	.220/.298/.414	.245	-7.0
OF A. Concepcion	HAG	A	21	560	68	29	5	15	61	22	136	35-15	6.9	.251/.289/.413	-.030	.223/.249/.362	.216	-26.5
1B B. Daubach*	NOR	AAA	33	411	63	29	1	16	62	62	68	1-2	4.0	.325/.426/.554	.445	.271/.355/.428	.272	10.5
G. Williams	NYN	MLB	38	31	9	2	0	1	3	1	7	2-0	7.6	.233/.258/.400	-.164	.233/.258/.400	.236	0.1

Pitcher	TM	LVL	AGE	W	L	SV	IP	H	BB	SO	HR	GB%	BABIP	STUFF	WHIP	ERA	PERA	EQERA	EQH9	EQBB9	EQSO9	EQHR9	VORP
M. Aybar	NOR	AAA	33	3	0	4	32.0	26	8	27	1	49%	.284	-3	1.06	1.41	3.90	3.90	8.7	3.0	5.4	0.3	5.7
	NYN	MLB	33	0	0	0	25.3	31	7	27	4	42%	.375	9	1.50	6.05	4.15	6.23	10.0	2.4	8.7	1.4	-1.8
P. Humber	SLU	A+	22	2	6	0	70.3	74	18	65	6	45%	.340	-5	1.31	4.99	5.48	6.42	10.6	2.9	5.3	1.5	-6.1
D. Koo*	NYN	MLB	36	0	0	0	23.0	22	13	23	2	45%	.317	5	1.52	3.91	4.24	4.63	8.5	4.6	8.1	0.8	1.9
R. Ring*	NOR	AAA	24	3	0	2	38.7	34	13	26	2	57%	.281	-9	1.21	3.26	4.38	4.62	8.8	3.4	4.9	0.5	4.0
T. Yates '04	NYN	MLB	26	2	4	0	46.7	61	25	35	6	58%	.355	-10	1.84	6.36	5.21	6.70	10.8	4.3	5.8	1.1	-6.8

Shawn Bowman's story so far involves lots of strikeouts, low batting averages, and emerging power. A converted shortstop, he has good range at third, and showing power at his age in the Florida State League is no mean feat. For **Dante Brinkley's** sake, you'd like to see time compressed; if he takes a year at each of the next levels, he won't become a major league rookie until 2008, when he's 26. **Mike Carp** showed nice pop as one of the youngest players in the Sally League. **Ambiorix Concepcion** has a strikeout to walk ratio which is probably all you really need to know; if it gets better, so will he. **Brian Daubach** had the best OBP in the International League in 2005; he'll be in Cardinals camp. Go figure; **Gerald**

Williams has a major league job. "Ice" has now outlasted the following players, also born in 1966: Albert Belle, David Justice, Bernard Gilkey, and Mark Whiten. Signed to a split contract by the Cardinals with hopes of making their bench.

As long as **Manny Aybar's** striking out a batter per inning, he's going to get a shot with somebody. **Phil Humber** had a decent showing in the Florida State League, but after a promotion to the B-Mets his elbow went to soup. Humber, Philip, meet John, Thomas. He should return to the mound by the end of the year, but not in the majors. **Dae-Sung Koo** might be worth another look if only for the strikeout rate, but as a spring invitee; declining the self-styled "Mr. Koo's" option was a no-brainer. **Royce Ring** made 15 appearances yet only got through three of them without allowing a baserunner; he needs to turn it up a notch if this is not to be the sum total of his major league career. **Tyler Yates** learned that a year isn't a long time unless you're missing the prime of your career with a 75% tear in your rotator cuff. The Mets non-tendered him in December, cutting the last tie to the long-ago David Justice trade.

New York Yankees

The Yankees finished the 2005 season with a reported record $207.2 million payroll. They spent $90.5 million more than the team with the second-highest payroll, the Red Sox. The payroll gap between the Yankees and Red Sox was in itself larger than 24 team payrolls. The Yankees spent enough money to pay for Boston's roster, plus that of the Dodgers, Cardinals, or Braves. Ninety million dollars is more than the combined payrolls of the Devil Rays, Pirates, and Rockies. It is nearly $20 million more than the payroll of the world champion Chicago White Sox.

There is really only one way to characterize Yankees' spending: grossly incompetent. The Yankees spent roughly 275% of what the White Sox did in winning a championship to wipe out in the first round of the playoffs. Of course, any team can suffer an undeserved loss in a short series, but the Yankees' expenditure-to-competitive results ratio has been askew for years. They've put up great regular-season records, getting fat in a two-team division, but as has been the case since 2001, they have neglected the finer aspects of team-building. Ironically, these aspects, which include the bench and the bullpen, are less dependent on wealth than they are on the delicate art of talent evaluation. You don't need to break the bank to build a good cadre of reserves, you just have to be smart.

Normally, what George Steinbrenner chooses to pay out in salaries would be relevant only to him and his accountant, but in recent years the profligate spending has begun to have a negative impact on the team. Many sources have reported that the Yankees have lost money in recent years. They are burdened by revenue sharing, their own payroll and the concomitant luxury tax payouts to Major League Baseball. During the 2004–2005 offseason, the Yankees declined to pursue the free agent center fielder Carlos Beltran—a player who couldn't have fit their needs more perfectly if his name had been Carljoe DiMickmantleran—because of a recent diagnosis of "sudden onset financial-limitations diabetes," which results from a diet high in sugary, empty-calorie veterans. Despite Beltran's disappointing season with the Mets, the decision to pass would prove to have fatal ramifications for the Yankees' 2005 season ultimately forcing the team to make an expensive commitment to Johnny Damon, another star center fielder, but one older and less talented than Beltran.

YANKEES PROSPECTUS

2005 record: 95–67; First place, AL East; Lost to Angels in Division Series

Pythagenport record: 89–73

Runs scored per game: 5.47 (2nd in AL)

Runs allowed per game: 4.87 (9th in AL)

Team EqA: .278 (1st in AL)

2005 Batters Age: 32.8 (Oldest in AL)

2005 Pitchers Age: 34.6 (Oldest in AL)

Ballpark: Yankee Stadium; Slight pitcher's park; Park Factor of 0.981

2005: An expensive rebuilt pitching staff flopped, but the gorillas at the plate delivered again.

2006: Steinbrenner's price-to-performance ratio keeps getting worse, but the galaxy of stars will be in the playoffs again.

The team's sweet tooth for veterans has also led it to neglect good principles of player development in the same way that the Borgias of Renaissance Italy might have neglected their morals, knowing they could buy a papal indulgence later. Robinson Cano is the first player produced by the Yankee system in years who has a realistic shot at being a major league regular for any length of time. The system hasn't produced a starting outfielder since Bernie Williams, which is why all three '06 starting outfielders will be expensive mercenaries. This problem shows no likelihood of being reversed any time soon.

The failure of the farm system is acutely apparent in the team's lack of suitable middle relievers—a breed that in other organizations multiply like rabbits, harvesting them from the always-abundant crop of busted starting pitching prospects. It has been years since the Yankees had an established homegrown reliever on the big league club; the he most recent were closer Mariano Rivera and swingman Ramiro Mendoza, both of whom came up 10 years ago. (See table 1.)

Note that Boehringer, Wickman, and Proctor hardly qualify as products of the farm system, having been developed by other organizations and acquired by the Yankees via trades. Though all three made their major league debuts

TABLE 1. APPEARANCES BY YANKEE RELIEVERS, 1996–2005

	All Relievers			Homegrown Only	
1	Mariano Rivera	638		Mariano Rivera	638
2	Mike Stanton	455		Ramiro Mendoza	221
3	Jeff Nelson	331		Randy Choate	82
4	Ramiro Mendoza	221		Brian Boehringer	71
5	Tom Gordon	159		Bob Wickman	58
6	Jason Grimsley	118		Sterling Hitchcock	57
7	Graeme Lloyd	109		Scott Proctor	55
8	Paul Quantrill	108		Dale Polley	32
9	Steve Karsay	91		Mike Buddie	26
10	Tanyon Sturtze	88		Jason Anderson	25

TABLE 2. HOMEGROWN RELIEVER'S ADJUSTED RUNS PREVENTED, 1996–2005

	TEAM	ARP			TEAM	ARP
1	ANA	485.6			(NYA: All Others	85.3)
2	NYA	387.1		16	SLN	65.3
3	MIN	355.2		17	ARI	57.2
4	HOU	309.6		18	PIT	50.0
	(NYA: Rivera	301.8)		19	SFN	43.4
5	ATL	228.9		20	PHI	27.8
6	CHA	223.4		21	SDN	24.0
7	LAN	184.6		22	TBA	-0.1
8	WAS	166.3		23	NYN	-8.0
9	CLE	152.2		24	DET	-15.9
10	TEX	152.1		25	FLO	-21.9
11	TOR	140.4		26	CHN	-22.7
12	CIN	135.6		27	MIL	-38.3
13	OAK	113.7		28	BOS	-50.6
14	SEA	113.0		29	KCA	-70.9
15	BAL	103.3		30	COL	-137.5

as Yankees, they did not spend appreciable time in the Yankees system. Other candidates, more organically Yankees, include Jay Tessmer (22 games), Dave Pavlas (16), and Darrell Einertson (11).

As measured by total adjusted runs prevented—an estimation of how many runs a reliever saved over expectations—during the Torre era the Yankees have the second-best total of runs saved by homegrown relievers in baseball. While true, but not in the sense of the Yankees having a fecund farm. Rather, one player has been so disproportionately successful that it distorts the overall total. Mariano Rivera has, by himself, saved more runs than the entire homegrown contingent of 26 teams. If Rivera is removed from the equation, the team's true dearth of homegrown relievers becomes is revealed, as seen in table 2.

Almost all of "others" can be credited to Ramiro Mendoza, who came up in 1996 and hasn't been an effective reliever for the Yankees since 2002.

During this period the Yankees have not been completely without relief pitchers who put up credible numbers at Double- and Triple-A. While none would have been mistaken for Huston Street, it was reasonable to think there were some viable pitchers in the lot, pitchers who might succeed if given the chance. Not counting prospects derailed by injuries, these included Anderson, Buddie, Tessmer, Colter Bean, Juan Padilla (who turned in a very successful 2005 with the Mets), Craig Dingman, and Matt Smith. With the exception of Smith, who was bypassed in favor of Alan Embree and Wayne Franklin in the second half of 2005, these pitchers were given only fleeting chances to establish themselves in Joe Torre's 12th man/Catch-22 role, also known as the NOOGY, for No-Out Guy. The Torre NOOGY role is a self-fulfilling prophecy in which Torre, lacking confidence in the pitcher's ability, pitches him only on leap days. Rusty and anxious, the pitcher gets bombed on those rare occasions he does get to

pitch, proving to Torre that he was justified in not using the kid. The NOOGY is forthwith sent back down to Columbus and replaced by Dan Miceli.

Minor league journeymen also need not apply in the Bronx. Other clubs have gotten valuable performances from Al Reyes, Carlos Almanzar, and Joe Borowski; the Yankees punted each one after their pinstriped cameos. The only exception has been Tanyon Sturtze, whose appeal seems to be based as much on personality as talent. Still, the Sturtze example illustrates a valuable point: the only way to make assets of journeymen pitchers, be they fringe veterans or unheralded minor leaguers, is to give them a chance to succeed.

The upside on these pitchers may have been no more than mediocre middle relief, but not overpaying that mediocre relief work that can help save a team's payroll. Competitively, this often involves little sacrifice due to the volatility of reliever performance. Consider the top 20 relievers as measured by Fair Run Average (FRA)—the reliever's RA adjusted for expected runs allowed on inherited and bequeathed base runners—from 2000–2002. Just a quick scan down the list of names in table 3 reveals how quickly relievers can go from good to mediocre. Stars three years ago, some of these pitchers couldn't get arrested now.

Note that with the decline in results came a correlating decrease in innings pitched. The group fell from an average of 74 IP to 46. That's just shy of a loss 30 innings pitched by star relievers. As it is likely that replacement level pitchers picked up those innings, the damage done by the formerly elite crop was even worse than it appears.

TABLE 3. LEADING RELIEVERS, FRA 2000–02

PITCHER	'00–'02 IP	'00–'02 FRA	FRA RANK	'03–'05 IP	'03–'05 FRA	CHANGE
Arthur Rhodes	207.0	1.78	1	136.0	3.51	−1.73
Robb Nen	217.3	2.26	2	DNP	DNP	N/A
Octavio Dotel	215.3	2.33	3	187.7	3.06	−0.73
Steve Reed	181.3	2.34	4	162.0	3.81	−1.47
Jeff Nelson	180.7	2.37	5	115.7	4.28	−1.91
Dave Weathers	239.7	2.43	6	238.7	4.06	−1.63
Keith Foulke	246.7	2.54	7	215.3	2.67	−0.13
Buddy Groom	187.3	2.55	8	139.0	4.09	−1.54
Eddie Guardado	196.0	2.58	9	167.0	3.08	−0.50
Byung-Hyun Kim	250.3	2.58	10	78.3	6.06	−3.48
Mariano Rivera	202.3	2.68	11	227.7	1.60	+1.08
Kerry Ligtenberg	178.7	2.79	12	124.0	5.57	−2.78
Steve Kline	215.7	2.81	13	175.0	3.57	−0.76
Felix Rodriguez	231.0	2.87	14	158.7	3.92	−1.05
Mike Remlinger	215.7	2.89	15	145.3	4.64	−1.75
Armando Benitez	219.7	2.90	16	172.7	2.53	+0.37
Kazuhiro Sasaki	190.0	2.93	17	33.3	4.63	−1.70
Jim Mecir	215.7	2.96	18	128.0	4.19	−1.23
Ben Weber	169.0	2.98	19	115.0	4.92	−1.94
Jeff Tam	200.7	3.00	20	44.7	5.72	−2.72
Total	**4449.0**	**2.77**		**2783.3**	**3.68**	**−0.91**

Taking a longer view, table 4 shows the top 50 relievers in Fair Run Average from 1975 through 2005 (minimum of 50 IP), and spotlights how many of them put in repeat appearances in the top 50. Unsurprisingly, there was huge turnover. For example, of the top 50 relievers in 1975, 24 of them did not appear in the top 50 in 1974. Of the 1975 top 50, 34 had not ranked there as recently as 1973, and 37 had been absent from the list in 1972.

On average, of the top 50 relievers during the period of the survey, only 12 had four consecutive appearances on the list, just 15 had three consecutive appearances, and just 20 had two consecutive appearances. In other words, in a typical season there is a 60% turnover among the top relievers in baseball.

Where then, are the new relief pitchers coming from? In any given year, a large proportion of the top firemen in the game—again, as measured by FRA—are "found relievers," pitchers who were not even in the majors as recently as a year ago. Table 5 shows the number of relievers among the top 50 who did not throw at least 10 major league innings in previous seasons.

Once again, past performance improves to be a weak predictor when signing relievers to long-term contracts. On average, 20 of a given year's top 50 relievers were not in the majors the year before. These are productive players—if

TABLE 4. RELIEVER RELIABILITY, 1975–2005

Year	Year −1	Year −2	Year −3	Year	Year −1	Year −2	Year −3
1975	26	16	13	1991	19	14	17
1976	25	18	17	1992	15	9	11
1977	27	15	14	1993	17	17	12
1978	25	24	17	1994	12	10	6
1979	18	15	15	1995	19	14	10
1980	20	11	11	1996	13	10	10
1981	23	20	10	1997	15	13	12
1982	24	16	14	1998	16	14	7
1983	21	14	12	1999	16	17	11
1984	18	17	14	2000	17	16	14
1985	21	17	15	2001	20	14	8
1986	20	18	12	2002	21	14	13
1987	22	11	10	2003	16	11	11
1988	24	20	17	2004	15	12	12
1989	23	19	14	2005	13	12	5
1990	23	19	14	**Avg**	**19.5**	**15.1**	**12.2**

TABLE 5: FROM BUS LEAGUES TO STARDOM— TOP 50 RELIEVERS WITH <10 IP THE PREVIOUS SEASON

Year	Year −1	Year −2	Year −3	Year	Year −1	Year −2	Year −3
1975	19	28	33	1991	21	24	29
1976	22	27	31	1992	23	27	32
1977	17	29	31	1993	23	27	29
1978	11	19	29	1994	26	34	37
1979	25	27	30	1995	31	24	30
1980	23	33	34	1996	28	39	32
1981	16	26	36	1997	21	34	38
1982	25	26	31	1998	22	27	35
1983	22	36	36	1999	16	26	34
1984	21	26	35	2000	17	19	29
1985	19	24	31	2001	18	25	26
1986	21	24	32	2002	17	22	28
1987	20	33	36	2003	23	30	32
1988	18	24	33	2004	21	25	30
1989	15	22	26	2005	22	26	38
1990	9	23	25				
				Avg	**20.4**	**27.0**	**31.9**

even if for just a year—making the major league minimum, and they're available to any team willing to sort through their pile of second-line arms to find them.

In 2006, the Yankees have already committed nearly $12.5 million to non-Rivera relievers. This is down from approximately $19.5 million in 2004 (nearly $5 million of which went to sore-armed Steve Karsay). For all that money, the non-Rivera results were decidedly mediocre, again. This year promises more of the same. Octavio Dotel, Tommy John survivor, will be out until at least May, and what the Yankees get from him at that point is anyone's guess. Kyle Farnsworth throws hard but lacks composure, a good candidate for a Whitson-like undressing by the Bleacher Creatures. Even if his emotions stay in check, he has a long history of being consistently inconsistent. Ron Villone has never mastered the fine art of not walking people; although he can be effective, he can also exacerbate a crisis situation. Mike Myers is limited to being a one-out guy; bring a righty pinch-hitter into the game and Myers kneels before Zod. Good bullpens are developed through a combination of perspicacity and luck. No team has ever spent itself into a good one, and the Yankees won't be the first.

HITTERS

TIM BATTLE   **CF**   **Bats: R Throws: R**   Height: 6′ 2″   Weight: 185   Born: September 10, 1985   Age: 20

YEAR	TM	LVL	AGE	PA	R	2B	3B	HR	RBI	BB	SO	SB	CS	SPEED	BA	OBP	SLG	MLVR	EQBA	EQOBP	EQSLG	EQA	VORP	DEFENSE	
2004	STA	A-	18	215	28	8	2	1	20	14	74	13	6	6.9	.246	.302	.322	-.027	.235	.281	.303	.211	-20.7	51-CF	3
2005	CSC	A	19	588	97	33	11	16	60	50	195	40	16	8.2	.259	.335	.455	.112	.230	.290	.400	.240	-5.3	132-CF	4
2006	NYA	MLB	20	479	60	23	4	13	49	28	152	20	10	6.1	.226	.277	.382	-.175	.228	.287	.399	.228	-3.8	113-CF	1

Breakout: 36%   Improve: 55%   Collapse: 23%   Attrition: 13%   Comparables: Jake Blalock, Choo Freeman, Felix Pie

Things to like about Tim Battle: he survived bone cancer, his power and walks, he's crazy fast, and he's only 20. Things not to like: his professionalism has been called into question, and he struck out in nearly 40% of his at-bats. This last item is the real problem; there's a hole in his swing that could birth a baby elephant. If he's fooled this often now, more advanced hurlers could eat him alive.

MARK BELLHORN   **INF**   **Bats: B Throws: R**   Height: 6′ 1″   Weight: 200   Born: August 23, 1974   Age: 31

YEAR	TM	LVL	AGE	PA	R	2B	3B	HR	RBI	BB	SO	SB	CS	SPEED	BA	OBP	SLG	MLVR	EQBA	EQOBP	EQSLG	EQA	VORP	DEFENSE			
2003	CHN	MLB	28	173	15	7	1	2	22	29	46	3	3	5.4	.209	.341	.317	-.140	.209	.339	.317	.242	-1.4	38-3B	-4		
2003	COL	MLB	28	133	12	3	0	0	4	21	32	2	3	4.7	.236	.368	.264	-.178	.220	.356	.248	.228	-2.8	14-2B	-1	10-3B	-1
2004	BOS	MLB	29	619	93	37	3	17	82	88	177	6	1	5.6	.264	.373	.444	.047	.258	.373	.436	.284	30.0	117-2B	-5	12-3B	2
2005	BOS	MLB	30	335	41	20	0	7	28	49	109	3	0	5.2	.216	.328	.360	-.126	.212	.337	.360	.253	1.0	81-2B	-2		
2005	NYA	MLB	30	20	2	0	0	1	2	3	3	0	0	4.6	.118	.250	.294	-.393	.118	.250	.294	.198	-1.2				
2006	SDN	MLB	31	330	41	16	1	9	36	48	97	4	2	5.0	.228	.345	.398	-.057	.236	.354	.428	.266	11.2	80-2B	-4		

Breakout: 26%   Improve: 46%   Collapse: 27%   Attrition: 35%   Comparables: Tom Tresh, Dave Hollins, Connie Ryan

Fans in Fenway proved fickle: Bellhorn opened '05 in a slump, and forgetting his postseason heroics from '04, boo-birds descended upon him in flocks. His shot at salvaging his Boston career was lost when he went on the DL with a sprained thumb, after which Team Lucchino replaced him with Tony Graffanino. The Yankees signed him when Cano was in a prolonged slump, but Cano immediately came out of it, making Bellhorn a spectator for the remainder of the season. He'll get another chance in San Diego, competing with Bobby Hill and Josh Barfield, but he's at an age where he won't get too many more.

MELKY CABRERA   OF   Bats: B Throws: L   Height: 5' 11"   Weight: 170   Born: August 11, 1984   Age: 21

YEAR	TM	LVL	AGE	PA	R	2B	3B	HR	RBI	BB	SO	SB	CS	SPEED	BA	OBP	SLG	MLVR	EQBA	EQOBP	EQSLG	EQA	VORP	DEFENSE
2003	STA	A-	18	307	34	10	2	2	31	23	36	13	5	5.4	.283	.345	.355	.121	.276	.324	.362	.244	1.9	64-CF -5
2004	BCR	A	19	188	35	16	3	0	16	15	23	7	2	7.1	.333	.383	.462	.277	.301	.346	.411	.266	7.6	41-CF 1
2004	TAM	A+	19	364	48	20	3	8	51	23	59	3	1	5.0	.288	.341	.438	.142	.270	.312	.430	.254	8.8	81-CF -1
2005	TRN	AA	20	463	57	22	3	10	60	28	72	11	2	6.0	.275	.322	.411	.047	.264	.309	.399	.248	3.5	103-CF 9
2005	COH	AAA	20	110	15	3	0	3	17	9	15	2	0	5.1	.248	.309	.366	-.121	.231	.294	.340	.228	-3.2	14-CF 0
2006	*NYA*	*MLB*	*21*	*544*	*64*	*26*	*3*	*11*	*56*	*29*	*79*	*10*	*4*	*5.0*	*.267*	*.309*	*.393*	*-.078*	*.270*	*.320*	*.410*	*.246*	*7.0*	*128-CF -2*

Breakout: 25%   Improve: 46%   Collapse: 22%   Attrition: 8%   Comparables: Tony Mota, Milton Bradley, Chet Lemon

From the vantage point of a team without a center fielder, 34 good at-bats by a 20-year-old Triple-A outfielder take on the seductive, beguiling quality of the Maltese Falcon. Cabrera had hit .267/.310/.413 at Trenton—not bad for his age—and with center field bleeding outs on both sides of the ball, the Yankees moved him up to Columbus. Cabrera enjoyed a hot week, and he was on his way to New York to rescue the Yankees from sentimental Williamsism and self-defeating Womack mission-creep. Cabrera was way over his head in the majors, swinging at everything and looking terrified in the outfield. He's young enough to improve, but for now Cabrera's stardom remains the stuff that dreams are made of.

ROBINSON CANO   2B   Bats: L Throws: R   Height: 6' 0"   Weight: 170   Born: October 22, 1982   Age: 23

YEAR	TM	LVL	AGE	PA	R	2B	3B	HR	RBI	BB	SO	SB	CS	SPEED	BA	OBP	SLG	MLVR	EQBA	EQOBP	EQSLG	EQA	VORP	DEFENSE
2003	TAM	A+	20	390	50	16	3	5	50	17	49	1	1	4.7	.276	.313	.377	.058	.264	.292	.390	.235	1.2	88-2B 0
2003	TRN	AA	20	179	21	9	1	1	13	9	16	0	0	4.0	.280	.341	.366	-.017	.256	.303	.341	.226	-2.2	43-2B -3
2004	TRN	AA	21	323	43	20	8	7	44	24	40	2	4	5.5	.301	.356	.497	.207	.283	.334	.462	.269	18.0	70-2B 0
2004	COH	AAA	21	237	22	9	2	6	30	18	27	0	1	3.4	.259	.316	.403	-.062	.247	.305	.386	.240	1.1	57-2B 3
2005	COH	AAA	22	114	19	8	3	4	24	6	13	0	0	6.1	.333	.368	.574	.352	.312	.349	.529	.292	11.0	21-2B 0
2005	NYA	MLB	22	544	78	34	4	14	62	16	68	1	3	4.9	.297	.320	.458	.054	.304	.337	.477	.273	21.2	129-2B -2
2006	*NYA*	*MLB*	*23*	*603*	*72*	*31*	*4*	*14*	*72*	*25*	*70*	*2*	*2*	*4.7*	*.283*	*.316*	*.425*	*-.013*	*.286*	*.327*	*.443*	*.255*	*21.1*	*141-2B -1*

Breakout: 22%   Improve: 48%   Collapse: 24%   Attrition: 5%   Comparables: Rennie Stennett, Rick Burleson, Ron Hunt

It took Tony Womack to get the Yankees to see Cano as an attractive option at second despite his youth; whatever his shortcomings, Tony's great for shocking people out of unproductive prejudices. Cano was a vast improvement, but not without his ambiguities. He lacked concentration, committing careless errors (17 for the season, second among AL second basemen) and was especially good at an abortive 4-6 force play that often required the intervention of Hideki Matsui to keep the ball from rolling to the left field warning track. Still, the Yankees love the way he hangs in on the double play. At the plate, Cano's ADD manifested in a tendency to swing at everything: among the 313 players who had at least 250 plate appearances, Cano ranked dead last in pitches per plate appearance (3.05), and he will not walk unless the ball rolls to the plate. Not surprisingly, he's a streaky hitter. Cano is young and could get better, but he's going to need to hit .330 to post a league-average OBP.

BUBBA CROSBY   CF   Bats: L Throws: L   Height: 5' 11"   Weight: 185   Born: August 11, 1976   Age: 29

YEAR	TM	LVL	AGE	PA	R	2B	3B	HR	RBI	BB	SO	SB	CS	SPEED	BA	OBP	SLG	MLVR	EQBA	EQOBP	EQSLG	EQA	VORP	DEFENSE	
2003	LVG	AAA	26	312	57	24	8	12	57	25	47	8	0	7.3	.361	.410	.635	.466	.306	.357	.539	.301	22.7	27-RF 2	24-LF 1
2004	COH	AAA	27	137	18	5	2	1	15	14	26	3	3	5.8	.276	.365	.379	.007	.252	.330	.346	.243	-0.5	18-CF -1	
2005	COH	AAA	28	180	18	7	1	4	22	12	28	2	1	4.9	.231	.306	.362	-.144	.207	.267	.311	.209	-10.0	20-CF -1	15-RF 0
2005	NYA	MLB	28	102	15	0	1	1	6	4	14	4	1	7.3	.276	.304	.327	-.174	.278	.320	.330	.236	-1.4	16-CF 3	11-RF 0
2006	*NYA*	*MLB*	*29*	*236*	*27*	*10*	*2*	*5*	*25*	*15*	*42*	*3*	*1*	*5.6*	*.249*	*.303*	*.382*	*-.114*	*.252*	*.314*	*.398*	*.240*	*0.1*	*59-CF -1*	

Breakout: 25%   Improve: 46%   Collapse: 34%   Attrition: 31%   Comparables: Lloyd Merriman, Dave Martinez, Mike Kingery

The less Crosby plays, the better the fans think he is. That's because he's unlike every other Yanks CF of recent vintage in that he hasn't been given the opportunity to fail. He might have been the fabled "late bloomer," but two years of indecision from the Yankees killed off that opportunity. He's a good outfielder, but he's not Tris Speaker, and having a good glove is the minimum basic requirement for the fifth outfielder's job, not a reason to make him a starter. The acquisition of Johnny Damon and the return of Bernie Williams pops the soap-bubble dream of Crosby the Star Center Fielder.

ERIC DUNCAN   **3B/1B**   **Bats: L Throws: R**   Height: 6′ 3″   Weight: 195   Born: December 7, 1984   Age: 21

YEAR	TM	LVL	AGE	PA	R	2B	3B	HR	RBI	BB	SO	SB	CS	SPEED	BA	OBP	SLG	MLVR	EQBA	EQOBP	EQSLG	EQA	VORP	DEFENSE	
2004	BCR	A	19	333	52	23	2	12	57	38	84	7	1	5.7	.260	.351	.479	.190	.227	.304	.410	.248	3.6	74-3B	1
2004	TAM	A+	19	209	24	20	2	4	26	31	47	0	2	3.9	.254	.364	.458	.171	.231	.327	.426	.258	6.7	46-3B	-5
2005	TRN	AA	20	518	60	15	3	19	61	59	136	9	3	5.1	.235	.326	.408	.022	.223	.308	.387	.245	1.8	115-3B	-17
2006	NYA	MLB	21	497	58	22	2	15	63	41	112	6	3	4.7	.248	.313	.407	-.067	.251	.324	.424	.251	8.2	117-3B	-7

Breakout: 23%   Improve: 41%   Collapse: 30%   Attrition: 11%   Comparables: Kelly Johnson, Jhonny Peralta, Clint Hurdle

The 2003 1st round pick made Double-A at a tender age and suffered a predictable discount on his .258 average of the year before. He didn't even get a shot at a late rally after an August beaning caused a concussion and headaches. Duncan's defense at third is questionable, but with A-Rod rooted there, Duncan moved over to first base at mini-camp and in the AFL. He batted .362 with eight home runs in 94 Fall League at bats (albeit with lots of strikeouts) and won the league's best player award, so he'll be starting the season on a good note.

JOHN FLAHERTY   **C**   **Bats: R Throws: R**   Height: 6′ 1″   Weight: 202   Born: October 21, 1967   Age: 38

YEAR	TM	LVL	AGE	PA	R	2B	3B	HR	RBI	BB	SO	SB	CS	SPEED	BA	OBP	SLG	MLVR	EQBA	EQOBP	EQSLG	EQA	VORP	DEFENSE	
2003	NYA	MLB	35	111	16	8	0	4	14	4	19	0	0	3.7	.267	.297	.457	-.023	.267	.304	.467	.260	3.5	32-C	-1
2004	NYA	MLB	36	133	11	9	0	6	16	5	25	0	2	2.6	.252	.286	.465	-.049	.254	.293	.476	.252	2.4	37-C	-1
2005	NYA	MLB	37	136	10	5	0	2	11	6	26	0	0	3.5	.165	.206	.252	-.520	.168	.221	.272	.182	-11.1	39-C	-2
2006	BOS	MLB	38	159	11	7	0	4	20	8	31	0	0	3.7	.210	.249	.349	-.274	.209	.253	.356	.210	-5.2	41-C	0

Breakout: 12%   Improve: 39%   Collapse: 41%   Attrition: 52%   Comparables: Charlie O'Brien, Jim Hegan, Ray Mueller

Torre prefers a purely defensive backup catcher, and boy, did he get what he asked for. With Randy Johnson insisting that only an offensive gelding of a catcher can give him the undivided attention he needs, Flaherty played more than was good for anyone. He's defected to Boston, where he might put a dent in Kelly Shoppach's career while giving the Red Sox the same sort of value fellow Yankees plant Ramiro Mendoza did.

JASON GIAMBI   **DH**   **Bats: L Throws: R**   Height: 6′ 3″   Weight: 235   Born: January 8, 1971   Age: 35

YEAR	TM	LVL	AGE	PA	R	2B	3B	HR	RBI	BB	SO	SB	CS	SPEED	BA	OBP	SLG	MLVR	EQBA	EQOBP	EQSLG	EQA	VORP	DEFENSE	
2003	NYA	MLB	32	690	97	25	0	41	107	129	140	2	1	3.6	.250	.412	.527	.265	.257	.419	.548	.325	52.5	83-1B	-4
2004	NYA	MLB	33	322	33	9	0	12	40	47	62	0	1	3.4	.208	.342	.379	-.095	.211	.345	.387	.259	-0.7	42-1B	-1
2005	NYA	MLB	34	545	74	14	0	32	87	108	109	0	0	3.5	.271	.440	.535	.332	.283	.456	.570	.346	50.6	63-1B	-8
2006	NYA	MLB	35	545	72	18	1	28	82	99	113	0	0	3.6	.251	.395	.492	.172	.253	.409	.513	.308	30.6	128-1B	-9

Breakout: 9%   Improve: 22%   Collapse: 53%   Attrition: 10%   Comparables: Jack Clark, Mickey Tettleton, Harmon Killebrew

While borderline Hall of Famers like Rafael Palmeiro were being destroyed by the steroids scandal, Giambi staged an unlikely escape from his own self-injected nightmare (plus tumor, plus parasites). Giambi did little more than walk in the first two months, as if his batting eye was all that he had left, but then something changed—there has never been a satisfying answer as to what—and the power was back. Once he turned it on, he was immensely productive, leading the AL in walks and OBP and ranking in the top ten in home runs and slugging percentage. Not that he got any faster; Giambi runs as if knee-deep in lobster bisque and at top speed can stretch a double into a close out at first base. On defense, Giambi is as mobile as a pothole, but given his habit of slumping when not in the field, making him a full-time DH is not an option. Over the last three years. he's batted .217/.384/.414 as a DH vs. .274/.427/.563 at first.

DEREK JETER   **SS**   **Bats: R Throws: R**   Height: 6′ 3″   Weight: 195   Born: June 26, 1974   Age: 32

YEAR	TM	LVL	AGE	PA	R	2B	3B	HR	RBI	BB	SO	SB	CS	SPEED	BA	OBP	SLG	MLVR	EQBA	EQOBP	EQSLG	EQA	VORP	DEFENSE	
2003	NYA	MLB	29	539	87	25	3	10	52	43	88	11	5	5.9	.324	.393	.450	.200	.329	.401	.463	.298	47.9	115-SS	-19
2004	NYA	MLB	30	705	111	44	1	23	78	46	99	23	4	6.2	.292	.352	.471	.099	.296	.357	.481	.287	52.0	151-SS	2
2005	NYA	MLB	31	745	122	25	5	19	70	77	117	14	5	6.0	.309	.389	.450	.169	.320	.408	.474	.305	59.3	153-SS	9
2006	NYA	MLB	32	702	101	30	4	15	80	60	105	14	4	5.5	.298	.365	.431	.087	.301	.378	.450	.281	49.8	162-SS	-3

Breakout: 1%   Improve: 28%   Collapse: 32%   Attrition: 0%   Comparables: Julio Franco, Steve Sax, Paul Molitor

It's been taken for granted among beat writers and broadcasters that Jeter is miscast in the leadoff role, and that the Yankees instead need a "traditional" leadoff man—someone like Vince Coleman. Let's be blunt: it's rank stupidity. Jeter ranked seventh in the American League in OBP and was the highest ranked hitter to bat leadoff, which is why he scored 122 runs in 2005 (he missed tying for the league runs lead by two). The suggestion seems to be that the Yankees would be better with a leadoff man who stole more bases but scored fewer runs. Only in professional sports journalism, where many of the writers make Judith Miller look like a paragon of evenhanded, informed reporting, could that make sense. Johnny Damon will make for a good test of these folks and Joe Torre: will reality win out, or will the batting order be based on a shared foolishness?

MATT LAWTON OF **Bats: L Throws: R** Height: 5′ 10″ Weight: 190 Born: November 3, 1971 Age: 34

YEAR	TM	LVL	AGE	PA	R	2B	3B	HR	RBI	BB	SO	SB	CS	SPEED	BA	OBP	SLG	MLVR	EQBA	EQOBP	EQSLG	EQA	VORP	DEFENSE			
2003	CLE	MLB	31	429	57	19	0	15	53	47	47	10	3	5.3	.249	.343	.420	.011	.253	.351	.433	.273	6.9	59-LF	1	12-RF	-1
2004	CLE	MLB	32	680	109	25	0	20	70	74	84	23	9	5.2	.277	.366	.421	.057	.285	.376	.438	.284	17.6	118-LF	6	19-RF	0
2005	PIT	MLB	33	445	53	28	1	10	44	58	61	16	9	5.4	.273	.380	.433	.126	.272	.378	.440	.283	17.1	95-RF	8		
2005	CHN	MLB	33	83	8	2	0	1	5	4	8	1	0	3.5	.244	.289	.308	-.231	.244	.289	.308	.215	-3.3	16-LF	0		
2005	NYA	MLB	33	57	6	0	0	2	4	7	8	1	0	4.6	.125	.263	.250	-.416	.125	.276	.250	.204	-4.2	11-RF	-1		
2006	*SEA*	*MLB*	*34*	*491*	*61*	*20*	*1*	*12*	*59*	*53*	*66*	*11*	*5*	*5.2*	*.261*	*.348*	*.399*	*-.009*	*.266*	*.360*	*.421*	*.266*	*6.4*	*116-RF*	*1*		

Breakout: 23% Improve: 49% Collapse: 23% Attrition: 16% Comparables: Gene Woodling, Al Zarilla, Bobby Higginson

Lawton's bat went cold when he was traded to the Cubs, and it never warmed up again. Worse still, by the time he got to the Yankees he looked as if he'd never played the outfield. Compared to Lawton, Melky Cabrera looked like Andruw Jones. Lawton quickly lost his job, and when he wasn't included on the playoff roster, he jumped the club. Adding a pathetic quality to the proceedings, Lawton was busted for steroid use after the season. Lawton made a shamefaced apology, and has signed a one-year, incentive-laden deal with the Mariners.

TINO MARTINEZ 1B **Bats: L Throws: R** Height: 6′ 2″ Weight: 210 Born: December 7, 1967 Age: 38

YEAR	TM	LVL	AGE	PA	R	2B	3B	HR	RBI	BB	SO	SB	CS	SPEED	BA	OBP	SLG	MLVR	EQBA	EQOBP	EQSLG	EQA	VORP	DEFENSE	
2003	SLN	MLB	35	545	66	25	2	15	69	53	71	1	1	4.3	.273	.352	.429	.071	.274	.351	.433	.273	13.0	118-1B	12
2004	TBA	MLB	36	538	63	20	1	23	76	66	72	3	1	4.0	.262	.362	.461	.086	.265	.368	.469	.288	22.7	109-1B	3
2005	NYA	MLB	37	348	43	9	0	17	49	38	54	2	0	4.2	.241	.328	.439	-.000	.247	.344	.455	.276	5.3	87-1B	-7
2006	*NYA*	*MLB*	*38*	*273*	*31*	*10*	*1*	*12*	*39*	*27*	*42*	*2*	*1*	*4.3*	*.253*	*.331*	*.447*	*.017*	*.255*	*.343*	*.466*	*.269*	*6.8*	*67-1B*	*-1*

Breakout: 8% Improve: 35% Collapse: 35% Attrition: 39% Comparables: Darrell Evans, Fred Lynn, Fred McGriff

He had one great hot streak left. From May 3–15, Martinez went 15-for-45 with ten home runs, including a home run in five consecutive games. Nagging injuries sapped his power thereafter, limiting his usefulness even in a reserve role. He's probably done.

HIDEKI MATSUI OF **Bats: L Throws: R** Height: 6′ 2″ Weight: 230 Born: June 12, 1974 Age: 32

YEAR	TM	LVL	AGE	PA	R	2B	3B	HR	RBI	BB	SO	SB	CS	SPEED	BA	OBP	SLG	MLVR	EQBA	EQOBP	EQSLG	EQA	VORP	DEFENSE			
2003	NYA	MLB	29	695	82	42	1	16	106	63	86	2	2	4.1	.287	.353	.435	.078	.290	.360	.445	.278	20.9	111-LF	-10	45-CF	-4
2004	NYA	MLB	30	680	109	34	2	31	108	88	103	3	0	5.0	.298	.390	.522	.239	.301	.396	.534	.314	44.4	156-LF	-8		
2005	NYA	MLB	31	703	108	45	3	23	116	63	78	2	2	4.8	.305	.367	.496	.198	.314	.384	.520	.305	43.9	111-LF	1	25-CF	-2
2006	*NYA*	*MLB*	*32*	*650*	*87*	*35*	*2*	*20*	*92*	*64*	*81*	*3*	*1*	*4.6*	*.289*	*.361*	*.464*	*.115*	*.292*	*.374*	*.483*	*.286*	*32.5*	*152-LF*	*-3*		

Breakout: 4% Improve: 20% Collapse: 32% Attrition: 2% Comparables: Paul O'Neill, Walt Moryn, Raul Ibanez

After the season, Matsui got a four-year, $52 million deal—a deal worthy of one of the top players in the game. Unfortunately, he isn't one; he's in the second tier, and his greatest asset isn't his bat, it's his durability. The Yankees could have cause to regret the contract's length before it's done. Matsui's skill set—some average, some power, some patience, some defense, but not an excess of any of them—is such that a small decline in any department is going to call the whole package into question. Matsui's RBI totals are the byproduct of the sheer number of runners he sees: he batted with 519 runners on base, most in the majors, and he saw the third-most runners in both 2003 and 2004.

ANDY PHILLIPS INF **Bats: R Throws: R** Height: 6′ 0″ Weight: 205 Born: April 6, 1977 Age: 29

YEAR	TM	LVL	AGE	PA	R	2B	3B	HR	RBI	BB	SO	SB	CS	SPEED	BA	OBP	SLG	MLVR	EQBA	EQOBP	EQSLG	EQA	VORP	DEFENSE			
2004	COH	AAA	27	492	82	19	6	25	84	51	61	2	1	5.1	.316	.386	.560	.325	.282	.350	.481	.282	22.8	85-1B	8		
2005	COH	AAA	28	340	60	14	1	22	54	36	61	2	0	3.8	.300	.379	.573	.327	.263	.337	.477	.277	20.0	28-3B	2	26-1B	1
2005	NYA	MLB	28	41	7	4	0	1	4	1	13	0	0	5.0	.150	.171	.325	-.494	.150	.190	.300	.172	-3.9				
2006	*NYA*	*MLB*	*29*	*358*	*43*	*15*	*2*	*14*	*51*	*28*	*67*	*1*	*1*	*4.3*	*.255*	*.317*	*.444*	*-.008*	*.258*	*.328*	*.463*	*.261*	*8.4*	*86-1B*	*0*		

Breakout: 21% Improve: 42% Collapse: 30% Attrition: 20% Comparables: Andy Carey, Matt Mieske, Jim Hickman

(continued next page)

Andy Phillips (continued)

In May, Phillips was given a chance to earn at least a part-time job. Perhaps you heard Torre sing his praises, however briefly; Phillips didn't get even a week's worth of starts. On May 2 at Tampa Bay, Phillips went 0–5 with five strikeouts. Against Scott Kazmir. In a game the Yankees won. Back to Columbus, you pathetic failure! Phillips yo-yo'd up and down after that, but he was dead to Torre. Even in September, when Ruben Sierra was going 0-for-every lefty this side of Tim Robbins, Phillips rode the pine. The Yankees are saying that Phillips will have a significant role this year. Don't believe them.

JORGE POSADA   **C**   **Bats: B Throws: R**   Height: 6' 2"   Weight: 205   Born: August 17, 1971   Age: 34

YEAR	TM	LVL	AGE	PA	R	2B	3B	HR	RBI	BB	SO	SB	CS	SPEED	BA	OBP	SLG	MLVR	EQBA	EQOBP	EQSLG	EQA	VORP	DEFENSE
2003	NYA	MLB	31	588	83	24	0	30	101	93	110	2	4	3.5	.281	.405	.518	.268	.287	.413	.538	.318	54.6	130-C 7
2004	NYA	MLB	32	547	72	31	0	21	81	88	92	1	3	3.1	.272	.400	.481	.180	.275	.406	.494	.306	41.4	124-C -2
2005	NYA	MLB	33	546	67	23	0	19	71	66	94	1	0	4.5	.262	.352	.430	.047	.267	.367	.449	.283	26.8	122-C -4
2006	*NYA*	*MLB*	*34*	*493*	*62*	*20*	*1*	*18*	*68*	*68*	*89*	*1*	*1*	*3.9*	*.266*	*.372*	*.449*	*.095*	*.268*	*.385*	*.468*	*.287*	*28.3*	*116-C -2*

Breakout: 5%   *Improve: 22%*   *Collapse: 30%*   *Attrition: 16%*   Comparables: *Mickey Tettleton, Alan Ashby, Ken Singleton*

It was his weakest season since 1999, yet he still posted a .285 EQA. Though the Yankees are correctly nervous about the tendency of catchers in his age group to suffer a sudden, rapid collapse, they underrate his combination of power and patience at their own risk as it's not easily found in a backstop. In terms of pitches seen per PA it was the least patient year of Posada's career, but as fall dawned, Posada went back to his old, selective ways, seeing over four pitchers per. Not coincidentally, September was his best month since May. He has more left in the tank; his walks and power will shore up his value even as his batting average fades.

ALEX RODRIGUEZ   **3B**   **Bats: R Throws: R**   Height: 6' 3"   Weight: 210   Born: July 27, 1975   Age: 30

YEAR	TM	LVL	AGE	PA	R	2B	3B	HR	RBI	BB	SO	SB	CS	SPEED	BA	OBP	SLG	MLVR	EQBA	EQOBP	EQSLG	EQA	VORP	DEFENSE
2003	TEX	MLB	27	715	124	30	6	47	118	87	126	17	3	6.1	.298	.396	.600	.329	.289	.391	.587	.322	88.4	155-SS 4
2004	NYA	MLB	28	698	112	24	2	36	106	80	131	28	4	6.0	.286	.375	.512	.212	.290	.381	.526	.308	53.7	153-3B 8
2005	NYA	MLB	29	715	124	29	1	48	130	91	139	21	6	5.8	.321	.421	.610	.449	.333	.439	.648	.351	91.0	157-3B -5
2006	*NYA*	*MLB*	*30*	*706*	*117*	*32*	*3*	*43*	*124*	*88*	*137*	*16*	*4*	*5.5*	*.298*	*.391*	*.576*	*.310*	*.301*	*.405*	*.600*	*.324*	*76.4*	*162-3B 0*

Breakout: 8%   *Improve: 32%*   *Collapse: 38%*   *Attrition: 0%*   Comparables: *Eddie Mathews, Dave Winfield, Frank Robinson*

The media would have you believe that he's less popular in New York than Bubba Crosby. Here's journalistic progress for you: it has been 45 years since Ted Williams hung it up, but sportswriters are still trotting out the same old character assassination routines. In truth, A-Rod surmounted a number of difficult obstacles last year, including Yankee Stadium; he became the rare right-hander to beat the park's anti-righty bias, batting .351/.448/.666 with a righty-record 26 home runs at home. As for Rodriguez's over-hyped lack of "clutch" compared to David Ortiz, even though Big Papi was more likely to hit a home run when Boston was trailing, A-Rod was more likely to homer when the game was scoreless or tied. Since Boston's record when trailing after seven was 6–53 (the Yankees posted a major league best 13–58 record when trailing after seven), it's hard to argue to they derived a significantly great benefit from their DH's late-inning heroics. The team that gets ahead first wins most of the time, and Rodriguez was best at doing that less dramatic, but essential, work.

BRONSON SARDINHA   **OF**   **Bats: L Throws: R**   Height: 6' 1"   Weight: 190   Born: April 6, 1983   Age: 23

YEAR	TM	LVL	AGE	PA	R	2B	3B	HR	RBI	BB	SO	SB	CS	SPEED	BA	OBP	SLG	MLVR	EQBA	EQOBP	EQSLG	EQA	VORP	DEFENSE
2003	BCR	A	20	318	54	16	0	8	41	40	40	5	3	4.7	.275	.374	.424	.194	.245	.326	.403	.254	-3.8	32-LF 1 16-RF -1
2003	TAM	A+	20	240	23	8	2	1	17	24	57	8	2	6.1	.193	.279	.264	-.182	.192	.261	.285	.203	-19.5	57-CF -2
2004	TAM	A+	21	283	37	12	2	2	33	29	39	9	2	5.7	.315	.389	.403	.184	.291	.354	.386	.265	12.3	61-3B -7
2004	TRN	AA	21	303	37	11	1	6	29	37	65	4	1	4.6	.267	.356	.383	.025	.253	.336	.366	.249	4.8	52-3B -14
2005	TRN	AA	22	568	63	30	2	12	68	55	115	11	5	4.9	.258	.338	.398	.044	.248	.322	.387	.249	-9.1	117-RF -10
2006	*NYA*	*MLB*	*23*	*521*	*62*	*24*	*2*	*12*	*58*	*42*	*104*	*7*	*3*	*4.9*	*.252*	*.317*	*.389*	*-.081*	*.255*	*.328*	*.405*	*.248*	*0.4*	*123-RF -7*

Breakout: 30%   *Improve: 55%*   *Collapse: 19%*   *Attrition: 5%*   Comparables: *Chin-Feng Chen, Kelly Johnson, Rickie Weeks*

After playing every position except lifeguard, Sardinha has finally found a home in right field. The bad news is that moving to a power position puts more pressure on him to hit. Sardinha has a good attitude, and everyone hopes some of his doubles turn into home runs as he matures, but so far he doesn't have the bat to justify a corner outfield spot. If his bat doesn't develop this year, it will be time for his agent to start spinning his lack of a position as "versatility."

GARY SHEFFIELD RF Bats: R Throws: R Height: 5′ 11″ Weight: 205 Born: November 18, 1968 Age: 37

YEAR	TM	LVL	AGE	PA	R	2B	3B	HR	RBI	BB	SO	SB	CS	SPEED	BA	OBP	SLG	MLVR	EQBA	EQOBP	EQSLG	EQA	VORP	DEFENSE	
2003	ATL	MLB	34	678	126	37	2	39	132	86	55	18	4	6.0	.330	.419	.604	.466	.324	.412	.601	.333	77.6	143-RF	6
2004	NYA	MLB	35	684	117	30	1	36	121	92	83	5	6	4.5	.290	.393	.534	.272	.296	.401	.550	.316	54.1	132-RF	-2
2005	NYA	MLB	36	675	104	27	0	34	123	78	76	10	2	5.3	.291	.379	.512	.225	.300	.395	.539	.314	47.5	124-RF	-3
2006	*NYA*	*MLB*	*37*	*670*	*105*	*32*	*1*	*35*	*114*	*78*	*77*	*7*	*3*	*5.2*	*.306*	*.392*	*.548*	*.284*	*.309*	*.406*	*.571*	*.318*	*56.2*	*156-RF*	*0*

Breakout: 10% Improve: 41% Collapse: 11% Attrition: 3% Comparables: Dwight Evans, Ellis Burks, Hank Aaron

Note the EqAs: Sheffield's two pinstriped seasons have been of almost identical quality. Even at his age, his bat remains one of the quickest in the game, too quick in fact; Sheffield leads the league in the informal category of "potential home runs pulled foul;" if the left field foul pole was just a few feet further left, Sheffield would average a home run a game. Even without that, Sheffield has a lot left to offer. The only thing going against him is that this is the last year of his contract. The team has an option for 2007, but historically options have made Mr. Sheffield cranky and unpleasant to be around.

RUBEN SIERRA DH Bats: B Throws: R Height: 6′ 1″ Weight: 200 Born: October 6, 1965 Age: 40

YEAR	TM	LVL	AGE	PA	R	2B	3B	HR	RBI	BB	SO	SB	CS	SPEED	BA	OBP	SLG	MLVR	EQBA	EQOBP	EQSLG	EQA	VORP	DEFENSE	
2003	TEX	MLB	37	147	14	9	0	3	12	14	27	1	1	4.2	.263	.333	.398	-.061	.254	.331	.392	.251	-0.4	16-LF	-2
2003	NYA	MLB	37	189	19	8	1	6	31	13	20	1	0	4.5	.276	.323	.437	.029	.279	.333	.453	.270	4.9		
2004	NYA	MLB	38	338	40	12	1	17	65	25	55	1	0	4.5	.244	.296	.456	-.049	.244	.301	.465	.260	4.6	18-RF	0
2005	NYA	MLB	39	181	14	12	0	4	29	9	41	0	0	4.1	.229	.265	.371	-.211	.232	.280	.375	.228	-4.8		
2006	*NYA*	*MLB*	*40*	*137*	*12*	*6*	*0*	*4*	*20*	*8*	*29*	*0*	*0*	*4.7*	*.238*	*.284*	*.397*	*-.136*	*.240*	*.294*	*.414*	*.235*	*-1.3*	*36-DH*	

Breakout: 12% Improve: 32% Collapse: 45% Attrition: 53% Comparables: Tony Perez, Dave Philley, Ernie Banks

Sierra used to be the rare switch-hitter actually worth the name, but that was many moons ago. Over the last three years he has hit .235/.281/.407 against lefties, making him a non-switch-hitting, defensively immobile reserve. That didn't stop Joe Torre from letting him try to hit all pitching and play the field. In truth, there was no right way to use Sierra, since he didn't hit righties either. Nevertheless, Sierra played virtually every day in September, while hitting .148/.188/.197. That Torre, in the heat of a pennant race, neither recognized he had a dead man hacking nor gave some of Sierra's playing time to Andy Phillips was an act of criminal negligence. The Yankees didn't offer arbitration to Sierra, so the manager will have to find another dead horse to flog until the old man is eligible to re-sign with them in May.

KEVIN THOMPSON OF Bats: R Throws: R Height: 5′ 10″ Weight: 180 Born: September 18, 1979 Age: 26

YEAR	TM	LVL	AGE	PA	R	2B	3B	HR	RBI	BB	SO	SB	CS	SPEED	BA	OBP	SLG	MLVR	EQBA	EQOBP	EQSLG	EQA	VORP	DEFENSE			
2003	TAM	A+	23	203	42	13	4	5	25	32	27	16	5	8.5	.331	.433	.552	.482	.302	.391	.525	.311	17.3	39-LF	2		
2003	TRN	AA	23	371	48	16	2	5	20	37	57	47	8	7.8	.226	.310	.332	-.149	.208	.283	.320	.230	-27.5	55-LF	-4	26-CF	-3
2004	TRN	AA	24	304	43	17	0	9	17	30	40	29	10	6.5	.281	.362	.444	.127	.250	.320	.389	.251	2.0	42-CF	-4	15-LF	-1
2005	TRN	AA	25	375	59	28	5	12	43	53	68	25	6	7.0	.329	.432	.565	.461	.295	.385	.491	.302	23.0	67-LF	1		
2005	COH	AAA	25	242	28	17	0	2	28	23	45	18	5	6.6	.249	.335	.359	-.083	.220	.300	.314	.233	-8.6	38-CF	-3	14-LF	0
2006	*NYA*	*MLB*	*26*	*536*	*82*	*28*	*3*	*15*	*58*	*47*	*92*	*30*	*9*	*6.1*	*.263*	*.333*	*.426*	*.000*	*.265*	*.345*	*.444*	*.269*	*13.6*	*126-LF*	*-2*		

Breakout: 27% Improve: 55% Collapse: 21% Attrition: 14% Comparables: Jackie Brandt, Jim Landis, Wayne Comer

He most likely blew his big chance. Thompson reached Double-A in 2003, but never put up the numbers that would get him noticed by the big league club. That changed this spring when his hot start coincided with the Angel of Death passing over all Yankees center fielders. Promoted to Columbus, the mother ship claimed Cabrera instead of him. During the brief Cabrera Era, Thompson's bat went cold, so when Melky was returned to sender the Yankees no longer considered him Plan B. His probable future involves memorizing Marlon Brando's most famous lines from *On the Waterfront*.

MARCOS VECHIONACCI 3B Bats: B Throws: R Height: 6′ 2″ Weight: 170 Born: August 7, 1986 Age: 19

YEAR	TM	LVL	AGE	PA	R	2B	3B	HR	RBI	BB	SO	SB	CS	SPEED	BA	OBP	SLG	MLVR	EQBA	EQOBP	EQSLG	EQA	VORP	DEFENSE			
2004	STA	A-	17	84	13	5	0	0	8	11	13	0	0	3.8	.292	.393	.361	.194	.277	.355	.344	.251	3.5	10-3B	-1		
2005	CSC	A	18	555	83	26	8	2	62	43	83	16	2	7.1	.252	.314	.348	-.073	.229	.278	.314	.215	-22.4	65-3B	3	61-SS	1
2006	*NYA*	*MLB*	*19*	*504*	*54*	*23*	*5*	*3*	*38*	*27*	*76*	*11*	*5*	*5.2*	*.246*	*.288*	*.332*	*-.208*	*.248*	*.299*	*.346*	*.218*	*-4.3*	*119-3B*	*3*		

Breakout: 45% Improve: 56% Collapse: 26% Attrition: 3% Comparables: Jason Romano, Carlos Rodriguez, Rob Valido

(continued next page)

Marcos Vechionacci *(continued)*

Now that the Royals have acquired Mientkiewicz and Grudzielanek, can Vechionacci be far behind? If the Royals can't play winning baseball, at least they can attract Scrabble fanatics. Another product of Venezuela, Vechionacci had his first full season in 2005, and while the season was something less than a disaster, it wasn't what was hoped for after he'd hit .310/.401/.437 in his first 118 games. The lesson, as always, is caveat indicium minimus: beware the small sample (and perhaps our Monty Python Latin). Vechionacci is still quite young, and makes good contact, but his decreased strike zone judgment removes much of what made him interesting in the first place. Stay tuned.

BERNIE WILLIAMS Ex-Famous OF Bats: B Throws: R Height: 6′ 2″ Weight: 205 Born: September 13, 1968 Age: 37

YEAR	TM	LVL	AGE	PA	R	2B	3B	HR	RBI	BB	SO	SB	CS	SPEED	BA	OBP	SLG	MLVR	EQBA	EQOBP	EQSLG	EQA	VORP	DEFENSE
2003	NYA	MLB	34	521	77	19	1	15	64	71	61	5	0	4.9	.263	.367	.411	.048	.265	.373	.417	.280	21.3	112-CF -8
2004	NYA	MLB	35	650	105	29	1	22	70	85	96	1	5	3.9	.262	.360	.435	.027	.264	.367	.441	.277	19.0	93-CF -6
2005	NYA	MLB	36	545	53	19	1	12	64	53	75	1	2	3.7	.249	.321	.367	-.101	.255	.336	.385	.254	0.8	98-CF -2
2006	*NYA*	*MLB*	*37*	*383*	*43*	*15*	*1*	*8*	*45*	*38*	*54*	*1*	*1*	*4.3*	*.261*	*.335*	*.384*	*-.050*	*.264*	*.347*	*.400*	*.253*	*7.6*	*92-CF -3*

Breakout: 6%   Improve: 28%   Collapse: 35%   Attrition: 23%   Comparables: David Segui, Todd Zeile, Wally Joyner

Yankees games were the lengthiest in the majors last year. If Williams is really a bench player next year, they'll get shorter and more compelling; nothing makes for less entertaining viewing than Williams taking a regional walking tour between pitches. To Williams, hitting requires the inner stillness of a Buddhist monk and a shark's need for motion. Somehow he satisfies these things by meandering like an ant following a pheromone trail to a half-eaten candy bar. When Williams goes walkabout, even George Steinbrenner changes the channel. The Yankees don't really need a utility outfielder who can't throw across a phone booth, but sentimentality won out the day arbitration offers were due. He was an all-time great Yankee, but that day is done.

TONY WOMACK Un-UT Bats: L Throws: R Height: 5′ 9″ Weight: 170 Born: September 25, 1969 Age: 36

YEAR	TM	LVL	AGE	PA	R	2B	3B	HR	RBI	BB	SO	SB	CS	SPEED	BA	OBP	SLG	MLVR	EQBA	EQOBP	EQSLG	EQA	VORP	DEFENSE	
2003	ARI	MLB	33	230	30	10	3	2	15	8	27	8	3	7.4	.237	.270	.338	-.263	.229	.262	.330	.212	-5.1	51-SS -7	
2004	SLN	MLB	34	598	91	22	3	5	38	36	60	26	5	7.1	.307	.349	.385	.024	.305	.347	.382	.262	26.4	124-2B -14	
2005	NYA	MLB	35	344	46	8	1	0	15	12	49	27	5	7.9	.249	.276	.280	-.313	.256	.294	.290	.225	-12.3	37-LF 0	23-2B 5
2006	*CIN*	*MLB*	*36*	*293*	*33*	*10*	*2*	*1*	*19*	*13*	*38*	*11*	*4*	*6.1*	*.247*	*.285*	*.305*	*-.270*	*.248*	*.286*	*.310*	*.205*	*-8.7*	*71-2B -1*	

Breakout: 4%   Improve: 18%   Collapse: 42%   Attrition: 31%   Comparables: Al Bumbry, Jim Gantner, Lance Johnson

Like George Leigh Mallory, the Yankees sign free agents because they are there, dispensing big contracts in a manic way that doesn't bother with basic questions like, "Can this guy actually do anything?" Dave Collins, Steve Kemp, Ed Whitson—Womack ranks with any of these among the team's top suicidal forays into the open market. Womack ranked last in the majors in VORPr (value over replacement per game) among players with 200 or more PA, and last in MLVr (marginal lineup value per game); you might not be able to kill yourself by pointing Tony Womack at your own temple and pulling the trigger, but the Yankees certainly tried. What's especially sad was that Womack '05 wasn't much worse than he had been in 2003, or any other year for that matter. Despite ten years of ineptitude as evidence of Womack's abilities, the Yankees had their heads turned by Womack's fluke 2004, a season in which he posted a pretty, empty batting average. The amazing epilogue is that the Reds were actually willing to trade for the game's fastest albatross.

PITCHERS

COLTER BEAN Bats: R Throws: R Height: 6′ 6″ Weight: 255 Born: January 16, 1977 Age: 29

YEAR	TM	LVL	AGE	W	L	SV	G	GS	IP	H	BB	SO	HR	GB%	BABIP	STUFF	WHIP	ERA	PERA	EQERA	EQH9	EQBB9	EQSO9	EQHR9	VORP	WXRL
2003	COH	AAA	26	4	2	4	50	0	69.0	53	27	70	5	—	.259	-5	1.16	2.87	4.90	5.32	8.3	4.6	7.1	1.1	2.0	—
2004	COH	AAA	27	9	3	1	53	0	82.7	61	23	109	3	—	.309	29	1.02	2.29	3.28	3.39	7.5	2.9	8.9	0.5	19.6	—
2005	COH	AAA	28	4	7	0	65	0	71.7	60	39	82	5	52%	.309	-2	1.38	3.01	4.87	5.00	8.4	5.9	7.6	0.8	4.6	—
2006	*NYA*	*MLB*	*29*	*3*	*3*	*1*	*27*	*3*	*48.3*	*48*	*24*	*40*	*5*	*45%*	*.300*	*2*	*1.47*	*4.51*	*4.76*	*5.03*	*8.7*	*4.6*	*7.2*	*0.9*	*4.6*	*0.4*

Breakout: 20%   Improve: 46%   Collapse: 27%   Attrition: 21%   Comparables: Don Robinson, Eric Plunk, Tanyon Sturtze

Bean struggled with his control last year, giving the already-skeptical Yankees yet another reason to bypass him. Given Bean's previous record of minor league success and the struggles of the Yankees bullpen this year, it is evident that the Yankees won't call Bean unless every other pitcher on the team is taken out by avian flu, and maybe not even then.

KEVIN BROWN

Bats: R Throws: R Height: 6′ 4″ Weight: 200 Born: March 14, 1965 Age: 41

YEAR	TM	LVL	AGE	W	L	SV	G	GS	IP	H	BB	SO	HR	GB%	BABIP	STUFF	WHIP	ERA	PERA	EQERA	EQH9	EQBB9	EQSO9	EQHR9	VORP	WXRL
2003	LAN	MLB	38	14	9	0	32	32	211.0	184	56	185	11	66%	.296	37	1.14	2.39	3.29	3.16	8.3	2.2	7.2	0.5	63.9	7.8
2004	NYA	MLB	39	10	6	0	22	22	132.0	132	35	83	14	49%	.290	13	1.27	4.09	4.21	4.00	8.8	2.2	5.3	0.9	26.1	3.5
2005	NYA	MLB	40	4	7	0	13	13	73.3	107	19	50	5	52%	.391	16	1.70	6.51	3.89	6.41	10.9	2.2	5.7	0.6	-9.8	-0.5
2006	*NYA*	*MLB*	*41*	*5*	*5*	*0*	*20*	*13*	*84.0*	*96*	*22*	*52*	*9*	*53%*	*.312*	*0*	*1.40*	*4.57*	*4.72*	*5.21*	*10.0*	*2.5*	*5.3*	*0.9*	*8.5*	*1.2*

Breakout: 4% Improve: 31% Collapse: 22% Attrition: 32% Comparables: Gaylord Perry, Bert Blyleven, Dennis Martinez

When Dallas Green released Tommy John in 1989, he explained that the 46-year-old had the kind of body that would allow him to pitch indefinitely, but that didn't mean the results would be any good. Kevin Brown doesn't have that kind of body; he can't even pretend to go through the motions. Unlike John, it doesn't even seem as if he's even enjoying the extra time. From 1995 through 2003, Brown had a 2.70 ERA in nearly 1800 innings, this despite pitching at a time of constantly rising offense. He'll be remembered for that, not for these poorer years with the Yankees.

SHAWN CHACON

Bats: R Throws: R Height: 6′ 3″ Weight: 210 Born: December 23, 1977 Age: 28

YEAR	TM	LVL	AGE	W	L	SV	G	GS	IP	H	BB	SO	HR	GB%	BABIP	STUFF	WHIP	ERA	PERA	EQERA	EQH9	EQBB9	EQSO9	EQHR9	VORP	WXRL
2003	COL	MLB	25	11	8	0	23	23	137.0	124	58	93	12	42%	.276	13	1.33	4.60	4.48	4.28	8.4	3.4	5.5	0.7	17.3	2.9
2004	COL	MLB	26	1	9	35	66	0	63.3	71	52	52	12	36%	.314	-25	1.94	7.11	6.20	6.47	9.5	6.5	6.3	1.5	-8.0	-1.7
2005	COL	MLB	27	1	7	0	13	12	72.7	69	36	39	7	37%	.283	0	1.44	4.09	5.33	3.59	8.8	4.2	4.5	0.9	13.7	1.3
2005	NYA	MLB	27	7	3	0	14	12	79.0	66	30	40	7	43%	.240	6	1.22	2.85	4.87	2.90	8.3	3.5	4.6	0.8	25.0	3.2
2006	*NYA*	*MLB*	*28*	*8*	*9*	*0*	*35*	*21*	*136.7*	*144*	*53*	*80*	*20*	*40%*	*.282*	*-4*	*1.44*	*4.84*	*5.13*	*5.19*	*9.2*	*3.6*	*5.1*	*1.2*	*8.0*	*1.7*

Breakout: 6% Improve: 23% Collapse: 42% Attrition: 8% Comparables: Ernie Broglio, Moe Drabowsky, Steve McCatty

As an extreme flyball pitcher, Chacon was always out of place in Colorado. Some improvement was to be expected once he got away from the Rockies, but not even the Yankees could have hoped for a 2.85 ERA. Given that they barely made the playoffs, Chacon's turnaround must be considered decisive. Nevertheless, the team is hedging on his role for 2006, and wisely so. Chacon's below-average strikeout rate and good luck on balls in play—the American League hit .298 when putting the ball in play, but against Chacon they hit .240—are a bad combination. That sort of luck won't repeat itself, and when it interacts with Chacon's pitch-to-contact repertoire, his ERA is going to rise precipitously.

TYLER CLIPPARD

Bats: R Throws: R Height: 6′ 4″ Weight: 170 Born: February 14, 1985 Age: 21

YEAR	TM	LVL	AGE	W	L	SV	G	GS	IP	H	BB	SO	HR	GB%	BABIP	STUFF	WHIP	ERA	PERA	EQERA	EQH9	EQBB9	EQSO9	EQHR9	VORP	WXRL
2004	BCR	A	19	10	10	0	26	25	149.0	153	32	145	12	—	.323	2	1.24	3.44	5.30	5.67	10.2	2.4	5.1	1.5	-1.1	—
2005	TAM	A+	20	10	9	0	26	25	147.3	118	34	169	12	39%	.296	17	1.03	3.18	4.66	4.40	8.8	2.7	6.9	1.4	18.5	—
2006	*NYA*	*MLB*	*21*	*8*	*9*	*0*	*29*	*24*	*149.7*	*158*	*45*	*106*	*26*	*39%*	*.286*	*11*	*1.36*	*4.81*	*5.05*	*4.93*	*9.3*	*2.8*	*6.2*	*1.4*	*9.7*	*2.0*

Breakout: 16% Improve: 52% Collapse: 8% Attrition: 1% Comparables: Josh Beckett, Ubaldo Jimenez, John Patterson

The Yankee Clippard has struck out nearly ten batters per nine innings in his career despite not having great stuff. He has a good assortment of offspeed pitches (changeup, curve, slider), and he spots them well. If Clippard could find another mile per hour or two on his fastball, the velocity combined with his pitching acumen could be truly devastating. If not, as he moves up the ladder, he'll need to show that he's not just fooling bumpkins by being tricky.

JORGE De PAULA

Bats: R Throws: R Height: 6′ 1″ Weight: 160 Born: November 10, 1978 Age: 27

YEAR	TM	LVL	AGE	W	L	SV	G	GS	IP	H	BB	SO	HR	GB%	BABIP	STUFF	WHIP	ERA	PERA	EQERA	EQH9	EQBB9	EQSO9	EQHR9	VORP	WXRL
2003	COH	AAA	24	10	11	0	27	27	167.7	168	57	125	22	—	.279	-19	1.34	4.35	6.04	5.54	9.9	3.8	5.4	1.9	1.1	—
2005	COH	AAA	26	4	2	0	21	20	116.0	109	41	90	22	38%	.266	-28	1.29	4.58	6.55	5.40	9.7	3.8	5.4	2.2	2.4	—
2006	*NYA*	*MLB*	*27*	*5*	*7*	*0*	*34*	*13*	*99.0*	*107*	*39*	*60*	*20*	*39%*	*.275*	*-12*	*1.47*	*5.48*	*5.99*	*5.99*	*9.6*	*3.4*	*4.9*	*1.8*	*-3.0*	*0.1*

Breakout: 14% Improve: 37% Collapse: 28% Attrition: 0% Comparables: Jorge Sosa, Ben Simon, Manuel Aybar

Spent the year working his way back from TJ surgery; there's no room in the Bronx for projects, so he'll have to rediscover his command before he gets a serious look. Even before the injury, De Paula had a generous home run rate. Now he's giving them up so frequently that Columbus bat boys have been forced to make in-game trips to the sporting goods store for more baseballs. If he can't trim that down, he's no use even as a reliever.

MATT DeSALVO   **Bats: R Throws: R**   Height: 6′ 0″   Weight: 170   Born: September 11, 1980   Age: 25

YEAR	TM	LVL	AGE	W	L	SV	G	GS	IP	H	BB	SO	HR	GB%	BABIP	STUFF	WHIP	ERA	PERA	EQERA	EQH9	EQBB9	EQSO9	EQHR9	VORP	WXRL
2004	TAM	A+	23	6	3	0	13	13	75.3	48	30	80	1	—	.241	20	1.04	1.43	4.02	4.28	7.5	4.7	6.4	0.3	10.2	—
2004	TRN	AA	23	2	2	0	5	5	27.3	27	10	24	3	—	.308	0	1.36	6.59	5.33	6.67	9.0	3.7	5.7	1.3	-3.2	—
2005	TRN	AA	24	9	5	0	25	24	149.0	106	67	151	8	54%	.268	10	1.16	3.02	4.86	4.60	7.9	5.2	6.2	0.8	15.4	—
2006	*NYA*	*MLB*	*25*	*7*	*9*	*0*	*30*	*21*	*130.0*	*132*	*66*	*89*	*14*	*49%*	*.294*	*2*	*1.53*	*5.02*	*5.10*	*5.39*	*8.9*	*4.8*	*6.0*	*0.9*	*3.3*	*1.2*

Breakout: 9%   Improve: 30%   Collapse: 30%   Attrition: 0%   Comparables: *Ernie McAnally, Blue Moon Odom, Scot Shields*

A creative pitcher, DeSalvo's like a Swiss army knife, coming at hitters with up to five pitches: fastball, curve, two different sliders, and a change. (DeSalvo has said, "I have every pitch you can possibly throw.") His fastball sits in the 90–92 mph range, so it's not like he's a soft-tosser, and he's very good at keeping the ball down. In all, batters hit just .202 against him. DeSalvo's trapezius troubled him early in the year, causing him some uncharacteristic control problems. It was the second year in a row that he had back problems, and perhaps anticipating another Kevin Brown situation, the Yankees theorized DeSalvo's mechanics were the cause. He switched to a more conventional delivery, stayed healthy, and thanks to the simplified mechanics his control improved as the year went on. Assuming continued health, Triple-A is not going to be an obstacle to him. PECOTA is too pessimistic.

TOM GORDON   **Bats: R Throws: R**   Height: 5′ 9″   Weight: 180   Born: November 18, 1967   Age: 38

YEAR	TM	LVL	AGE	W	L	SV	G	GS	IP	H	BB	SO	HR	GB%	BABIP	STUFF	WHIP	ERA	PERA	EQERA	EQH9	EQBB9	EQSO9	EQHR9	VORP	WXRL
2003	CHA	MLB	35	7	6	12	66	0	74.0	57	31	91	4	48%	.306	37	1.19	3.16	2.93	3.30	7.1	3.7	10.8	0.5	21.1	2.6
2004	NYA	MLB	36	9	4	4	80	0	89.7	56	23	96	5	48%	.242	36	0.87	2.21	2.86	2.25	6.2	2.1	9.2	0.5	38.9	6.3
2005	NYA	MLB	37	5	4	2	79	0	80.7	59	29	69	8	52%	.238	12	1.09	2.57	3.97	2.72	7.1	3.3	7.7	0.9	26.6	3.3
2006	*PHI*	*MLB*	*38*	*3*	*4*	*18*	*48*	*0*	*53.0*	*45*	*20*	*43*	*5*	*47%*	*.262*	*4*	*1.22*	*3.32*	*3.30*	*3.61*	*7.4*	*3.2*	*6.9*	*0.8*	*11.7*	*1.4*

Breakout: 18%   Improve: 37%   Collapse: 42%   Attrition: 14%   Comparables: *Stu Miller, Greg Harris, Hoyt Wilhelm*

Though he's saved only 18 games since 2001, the Phillies have signed Gordon to close. He should be okay in the short term, but signing Gordon for three years (plus an optional fourth) was downright daffy. The warning signs are already there: Gordon's strikeout rate was his lowest since 1996, when he was still starting, and his home run rate was up. Obsessing over saves to the point that you lose critical judgment never won anybody anything; Pat Gillick should know this, having had Jose Mesa with the M's in 2000. Those who forget Jose Mesa are condemned to repeat him, or the nearest reasonable facsimile. Gordon may suffice.

SEAN HENN   **Bats: R Throws: L**   Height: 6′ 5″   Weight: 200   Born: April 23, 1981   Age: 25

YEAR	TM	LVL	AGE	W	L	SV	G	GS	IP	H	BB	SO	HR	GB%	BABIP	STUFF	WHIP	ERA	PERA	EQERA	EQH9	EQBB9	EQSO9	EQHR9	VORP	WXRL
2003	TAM	A+	22	4	3	0	16	16	72.3	69	37	52	3	—	.286	-16	1.47	3.61	5.96	5.69	9.9	5.7	4.5	1.2	-0.7	—
2004	TRN	AA	23	6	8	0	27	27	163.3	173	63	118	11	—	.313	2	1.45	4.41	4.85	5.29	9.1	3.7	4.5	0.8	5.6	—
2005	TRN	AA	24	2	1	0	4	4	25.3	16	9	21	1	55%	.238	9	0.99	0.71	4.24	2.31	7.3	4.2	5.0	0.4	8.5	—
2005	COH	AAA	24	5	5	0	16	16	86.3	79	27	64	5	48%	.306	11	1.23	3.23	4.29	4.29	8.6	3.1	5.1	0.6	12.2	—
2005	NYA	MLB	24	0	3	0	3	3	11.3	18	11	3	3	43%	.341	-60	2.56	11.15	9.00	11.25	12.8	8.2	2.2	2.2	-8.8	-0.5
2006	*NYA*	*MLB*	*25*	*6*	*9*	*0*	*33*	*19*	*118.3*	*134*	*55*	*68*	*17*	*46%*	*.301*	*-9*	*1.60*	*5.77*	*5.87*	*6.11*	*10.0*	*4.4*	*5.0*	*1.2*	*-7.1*	*0.0*

Breakout: 8%   Improve: 30%   Collapse: 30%   Attrition: 0%   Comparables: *Lance Caraccioli, Alex Graman, Bill Travers*

"He's not ready to be here," a visibly annoyed Joe Torre said of Henn after his second emergency start. Henn was visibly nervous, but the Yankees' miserable defense exacerbated his anxiety in two of his three starts. Now well past TJ surgery, Henn posted some decent numbers between Trenton and Columbus, but in an organization already biased against the young, he will have to labor twice as hard to overcome Torre's damning first impression.

PHILIP HUGHES   **Bats: R Throws: R**   Height: 6′ 5″   Weight: 220   Born: June 24, 1986   Age: 20

YEAR	TM	LVL	AGE	W	L	SV	G	GS	IP	H	BB	SO	HR	GB%	BABIP	STUFF	WHIP	ERA	PERA	EQERA	EQH9	EQBB9	EQSO9	EQHR9	VORP	WXRL
2005	CSC	A	19	7	1	0	12	12	68.7	46	16	72	1	49%	.269	36	0.90	1.97	3.44	3.99	7.4	2.6	6.1	0.3	11.7	—
2005	TAM	A+	19	2	0	0	5	4	17.7	8	4	21	0	46%	.222	16	0.68	3.05	3.31	3.86	6.1	2.8	7.7	0.0	3.2	—
2006	*NYA*	*MLB*	*20*	*9*	*8*	*0*	*30*	*22*	*147.7*	*136*	*46*	*114*	*14*	*46%*	*.280*	*20*	*1.23*	*3.82*	*3.75*	*4.10*	*8.1*	*2.9*	*6.7*	*0.8*	*24.3*	*3.5*

Breakout: 13%   Improve: 53%   Collapse: 18%   Attrition: 2%   Comparables: *Jake Peavy, Jerome Williams, Chad Billingsley*

The Yankees' first pick in the 2004 draft, Hughes has put up some excellent numbers, but—you've heard this before—he needs to stay healthy. He was shut down late in the season with shoulder inflammation, and he missed time in 2004 with elbow tendinitis as well. Assuming everything stays attached, he might see Double-A before he's 20. That would be a heck of an accomplishment, particularly in this organization.

RANDY JOHNSON Bats: R Throws: L Height: 6′ 10″ Weight: 230 Born: September 10, 1963 Age: 42

YEAR	TM	LVL	AGE	W	L	SV	G	GS	IP	H	BB	SO	HR	GB%	BABIP	STUFF	WHIP	ERA	PERA	EQERA	EQH9	EQBB9	EQSO9	EQHR9	VORP	WXRL
2003	ARI	MLB	39	6	8	0	18	18	114.0	125	27	125	16	46%	.357	28	1.33	4.26	3.80	4.42	9.3	1.9	8.7	1.2	14.7	1.8
2004	ARI	MLB	40	16	14	0	35	35	245.7	177	44	290	18	46%	.269	52	0.90	2.60	2.76	2.95	6.9	1.5	9.5	0.6	71.1	7.7
2005	NYA	MLB	41	17	8	0	34	34	225.7	207	47	211	32	45%	.288	26	1.13	3.79	3.93	3.93	8.2	1.9	8.3	1.2	43.8	5.6
2006	*NYA*	*MLB*	*42*	*16*	*8*	*0*	*33*	*33*	*225.3*	*202*	*39*	*192*	*23*	*43%*	*.278*	*25*	*1.07*	*3.19*	*3.14*	*3.33*	*7.9*	*1.6*	*7.4*	*0.9*	*54.9*	*7.3*

Breakout: 25% Improve: 54% Collapse: 1% Attrition: 0% Comparables: Roger Clemens, Gaylord Perry, Nolan Ryan

Shortly after signing with the Yankees, the truculent lefty got into a scuffle with a local TV cameraman. Thereafter, the Yankees party line goes, Johnson pressed too hard to prove himself a good egg, or at least a productive one, and only in the second half did he stop trying to be one of the greatest pitchers of all time and relax; apparently greatness is a Zen thing—you have to let it come to you. For proof, they point to his improved second half performance: a 3.31 ERA after the All-Star break, and September was Johnson's best month, with a 2.17 ERA. Nonetheless, Johnson set a career high in home runs allowed, mostly getting beat on what heretofore had been his signature pitch, the slider; this was true both before and after the break. The velocity is still there, and he's still healthy, more or less (his back is a chronic problem). Johnson may need to reinvent himself to survive the decline of his best weapon. If he stays only at the level of 2005, he'll still be a valuable pitcher, just not the great one of the past.

BEN JULIANEL Bats: B Throws: L Height: 6′ 2″ Weight: 180 Born: September 4, 1979 Age: 26

YEAR	TM	LVL	AGE	W	L	SV	G	GS	IP	H	BB	SO	HR	GB%	BABIP	STUFF	WHIP	ERA	PERA	EQERA	EQH9	EQBB9	EQSO9	EQHR9	VORP	WXRL
2003	PEO	A	23	4	2	9	51	0	51.7	41	25	78	1	—	.342	4	1.28	1.04	4.15	4.53	8.7	6.2	8.5	0.6	5.7	—
2004	TAM	A+	24	5	5	10	44	0	61.3	53	24	72	2	—	.331	-4	1.26	2.50	4.40	5.49	9.3	4.6	6.8	0.8	0.7	—
2005	TRN	AA	25	5	3	1	46	2	87.7	88	50	106	7	49%	.360	-14	1.57	3.90	5.72	5.83	9.9	6.6	7.0	1.2	-2.1	—
2006	*FLO*	*MLB*	*26*	*3*	*4*	*0*	*32*	*6*	*59.7*	*64*	*46*	*49*	*7*	*46%*	*.318*	*-11*	*1.84*	*5.85*	*6.65*	*6.40*	*9.7*	*6.4*	*6.5*	*1.0*	*-6.1*	*-0.4*

Breakout: 6% Improve: 35% Collapse: 36% Attrition: 6% Comparables: Les Walrond, Brian Forystek, Pete Zamora

The Marlins will reap the benefit of having this articulate, good-natured Californian in their clubhouse next year, as the Yankees chose to bet on the predictable mediocrity of Ron Villone and dealt him away this winter. Early in the season, Julianel struggled with his confidence and lost his out pitch, the slider. It came back, but not before Julianel used its absence to further refine his changeup. In addition to now having three pitches (his fastball is in the 89–91 range), he will also occasionally drop down and throw sidearm. Given his high strikeout rates and occasional wildness, Julianel is not ideally suited to a situational LOOGY role; he'd be better off pitching middle innings, where he won't be subject to a manager's anal match-up stratagems.

AL LEITER Bats: L Throws: L Height: 6′ 3″ Weight: 220 Born: October 23, 1965 Age: 40

YEAR	TM	LVL	AGE	W	L	SV	G	GS	IP	H	BB	SO	HR	GB%	BABIP	STUFF	WHIP	ERA	PERA	EQERA	EQH9	EQBB9	EQSO9	EQHR9	VORP	WXRL
2003	NYN	MLB	37	15	9	0	30	30	180.7	176	94	139	15	42%	.308	15	1.49	3.98	4.51	4.21	8.8	4.2	6.2	0.7	31.5	5.4
2004	NYN	MLB	38	10	8	0	30	30	173.7	138	97	117	16	44%	.244	8	1.35	3.21	4.95	3.41	8.2	4.7	5.5	0.8	45.6	5.9
2005	FLO	MLB	39	3	7	0	17	16	80.0	88	60	52	9	42%	.329	-13	1.85	6.64	5.71	6.80	9.5	6.1	5.3	1.0	-14.2	0.1
2005	NYA	MLB	39	4	5	0	16	10	62.3	66	38	45	4	45%	.315	3	1.67	5.49	4.81	5.65	9.0	5.5	6.4	0.6	-1.9	0.4
2006	*NYA*	*MLB*	*40*	*7*	*8*	*0*	*35*	*19*	*125.3*	*129*	*73*	*81*	*15*	*41%*	*.289*	*-11*	*1.62*	*5.15*	*5.49*	*5.67*	*9.0*	*5.5*	*5.6*	*1.0*	*2.8*	*0.9*

Breakout: 13% Improve: 34% Collapse: 40% Attrition: 20% Comparables: Woodie Fryman, Joe Niekro, Kenny Rogers

Talking retirement, though the Yanks offered him arbitration in the hopes of convincing him to return as a LOOGY and he signed a minor league deal. It's an experiment the Yankees no longer need to indulge, given their off-season moves, and last year's relief work did not reveal reservoirs of stuff as yet untapped. Alois's major league career didn't start in earnest until he was 29; from then until he turned 38 he posted a 3.46 ERA and pitched in three postseasons. He salvaged himself. Control was always an issue for him; it was the first thing to go when he finally hit the wall, as evidenced (and exacerbated) by his league-leading ten hit batsmen with runners on base.

MIKE MUSSINA Bats: R Throws: R Height: 6′ 2″ Weight: 185 Born: December 8, 1968 Age: 37

YEAR	TM	LVL	AGE	W	L	SV	G	GS	IP	H	BB	SO	HR	GB%	BABIP	STUFF	WHIP	ERA	PERA	EQERA	EQH9	EQBB9	EQSO9	EQHR9	VORP	WXRL
2003	NYA	MLB	34	17	8	0	31	31	214.7	192	40	195	21	44%	.289	35	1.08	3.40	3.35	3.47	7.8	1.6	7.9	0.8	58.4	7.0
2004	NYA	MLB	35	12	9	0	27	27	164.7	178	40	132	22	47%	.317	17	1.32	4.59	4.08	4.51	9.1	2.0	6.7	1.1	22.1	3.2
2005	NYA	MLB	36	13	8	0	30	30	179.7	199	47	142	23	45%	.328	18	1.37	4.41	4.15	4.39	9.2	2.3	6.9	1.1	22.9	3.4
2006	*NYA*	*MLB*	*37*	*11*	*9*	*0*	*30*	*28*	*175.3*	*182*	*43*	*133*	*21*	*45%*	*.300*	*16*	*1.28*	*4.08*	*4.32*	*4.35*	*9.1*	*2.3*	*6.6*	*1.0*	*25.1*	*3.9*

Breakout: 13% Improve: 45% Collapse: 17% Attrition: 9% Comparables: Jim Bunning, John Burkett, Don Sutton

(continued next page)

Mike Mussina *(continued)*

Mussina has had elbow trouble on and off for the last two seasons, provoking eerily similar results. Mussina still misses a lot of bats, so the stuff for a bounce-back season remains, but the question is whether his elbow is healing or is drifting towards a total breakdown. What's fascinating is just how little margin for error even a normally excellent pitcher has. The elbow has affected his fine control—his walks per nine are up just a hair, and he now allows as many home runs in 180 innings as he used to in 200. Mussina stands a very good chance of becoming the first pitcher in history to win 250 or more games without winning 20 in a season.

CARL PAVANO   Bats: R Throws: R   Height: 6' 5"   Weight: 230   Born: January 8, 1976   Age: 30

YEAR	TM	LVL	AGE	W	L	SV	G	GS	IP	H	BB	SO	HR	GB%	BABIP	STUFF	WHIP	ERA	PERA	EQERA	EQH9	EQBB9	EQSO9	EQHR9	VORP	WXRL
2003	FLO	MLB	27	12	13	0	33	32	201.0	204	49	133	19	44%	.299	14	1.26	4.30	4.13	4.54	9.1	2.0	5.4	0.9	25.1	5.2
2004	FLO	MLB	28	18	8	0	31	31	222.3	212	49	139	16	51%	.287	20	1.17	3.00	3.92	3.46	9.0	1.9	5.1	0.6	60.6	7.1
2005	NYA	MLB	29	4	6	0	17	17	100.0	129	18	56	17	51%	.333	-3	1.47	4.77	4.96	5.49	10.7	1.6	4.9	1.4	-1.8	1.0
2006	*NYA*	*MLB*	*30*	*10*	*9*	*0*	*32*	*25*	*159.7*	*182*	*30*	*88*	*20*	*47%*	*.302*	*5*	*1.33*	*4.37*	*4.66*	*4.64*	*10.0*	*1.8*	*4.8*	*1.1*	*16.7*	*2.8*

Breakout: 7%   Improve: 44%   Collapse: 18%   Attrition: 5%   *Comparables: Bobby Jones, Chris Bosio, Bill Wegman*

Along with Womack and Wright, Pavano made for three major free-agent misjudgments in one winter. Seduced by the sole season of Pavano's career in which he was both healthy and good, the Yankees handed him a four-year deal, ignoring his low strikeout rates and the benefit he reaped from pitching in Dolphins Stadium. Pavano had a decent start to the season, but got progressively worse until he hit the DL with shoulder tendinitis after his June 27 start. He was only supposed to be gone briefly, but his rehab lasted into August. On the verge of returning, he called the whole thing off and headed to Birmingham to meet with Dr. James Andrews. It wasn't a social call. Though no structural problems were found, he was shut down for the rest of the season. Pavano has exemplary control: his BB/9 has declined in each of the last three seasons. Unfortunately, his K/9 did exactly the same thing. Scared of their shallow starting rotation, the Yankees resisted trade entreaties on Pavano all winter long. Given an opportunity to get out from under this contract, they should take it.

SCOTT PROCTOR   Bats: R Throws: R   Height: 6' 1"   Weight: 198   Born: January 2, 1977   Age: 29

YEAR	TM	LVL	AGE	W	L	SV	G	GS	IP	H	BB	SO	HR	GB%	BABIP	STUFF	WHIP	ERA	PERA	EQERA	EQH9	EQBB9	EQSO9	EQHR9	VORP	WXRL
2004	COH	AAA	27	2	3	4	35	0	44.0	37	18	42	4	—	.277	-4	1.25	2.86	4.71	3.86	8.4	4.3	6.6	1.1	8.1	—
2004	NYA	MLB	27	2	1	0	26	0	25.0	29	14	21	5	45%	.316	-11	1.72	5.40	5.61	5.96	9.5	4.6	7.0	1.8	-0.3	0.2
2005	COH	AAA	28	6	1	14	35	1	42.7	47	11	54	8	43%	.368	-3	1.36	4.22	5.40	4.97	10.4	2.8	8.2	2.2	2.9	—
2005	NYA	MLB	28	1	0	0	29	1	44.7	46	17	36	10	31%	.271	-9	1.41	6.04	5.60	6.00	9.2	3.4	7.2	2.0	-3.4	-0.3
2006	*NYA*	*MLB*	*29*	*3*	*3*	*3*	*52*	*1*	*53.7*	*55*	*18*	*41*	*9*	*39%*	*.284*	*-2*	*1.35*	*4.51*	*4.83*	*5.13*	*8.9*	*3.1*	*6.6*	*1.4*	*5.1*	*0.4*

Breakout: 38%   Improve: 57%   Collapse: 14%   Attrition: 31%   *Comparables: Dave Tobik, Bob Stoddard, Julio Navarro*

Throws hard and throws straight. The hitters know it, and, as the old song goes, all the cats join in—the lefty-hitting cats, at any rate. They clawed Proctor at a .315/.405/.630 clip, including a home run every six at-bats. Righties had a harder time figuring him out, batting only .217/.270/.358. If crafting such roles were really worthwhile, Proctor could hold down a generic righty trash-time job. In a generic righty trash-time world, generic righties are all around you—in your office bathroom, behind you in line at Starbucks, listening in on your phone calls—but most of them aren't quite so vulnerable to lefties. A super-extreme flyball guy, Proctor should hope for a trade to the Nats and RFK.

MARIANO RIVERA   Bats: R Throws: R   Height: 6' 4"   Weight: 168   Born: November 29, 1969   Age: 36

YEAR	TM	LVL	AGE	W	L	SV	G	GS	IP	H	BB	SO	HR	GB%	BABIP	STUFF	WHIP	ERA	PERA	EQERA	EQH9	EQBB9	EQSO9	EQHR9	VORP	WXRL
2003	NYA	MLB	33	5	2	40	64	0	70.7	61	10	63	3	59%	.299	30	1.00	1.65	2.80	2.04	7.5	1.3	7.8	0.4	32.6	5.6
2004	NYA	MLB	34	4	2	53	74	0	78.7	65	20	66	3	60%	.282	24	1.08	1.94	3.22	1.95	7.6	2.2	7.1	0.3	37.9	7.5
2005	NYA	MLB	35	7	4	43	71	0	78.3	50	18	80	2	56%	.239	40	0.87	1.38	2.56	2.09	6.3	2.1	9.2	0.2	32.2	5.2
2006	*NYA*	*MLB*	*36*	*5*	*4*	*34*	*60*	*0*	*66.3*	*56*	*16*	*58*	*5*	*54%*	*.273*	*14*	*1.08*	*2.45*	*2.79*	*2.65*	*7.4*	*2.3*	*7.6*	*0.6*	*21.9*	*3.4*

Breakout: 15%   Improve: 25%   Collapse: 63%   Attrition: 8%   *Comparables: Paul Assenmacher, Stu Miller, Steve Farr*

Are there any superlatives left with which to garland Rivera? Casey Stengel would have called him "splendid." Rivera had another splendid season in 2005, perhaps his most splendid. Rivera kept his arm when all about him were losing theirs—throughout the season, Gordon and Rivera were the team's only reliable relievers. Unlike many a closer, he wasn't just earning soft saves but was a literal stopper; he was like Fort Apache: The Lead. The Yankees had the best record in baseball when leading after seven, losing just two games. Closers make for controversial Cy Young candidates, but Rivera would have made a good one; had he been a shade less splendid, the Yankees wouldn't have made the postseason.

FELIX RODRIGUEZ   Bats: R   Throws: R   Height: 6' 1"   Weight: 180   Born: September 9, 1972   Age: 33

YEAR	TM	LVL	AGE	W	L	SV	G	GS	IP	H	BB	SO	HR	GB%	BABIP	STUFF	WHIP	ERA	PERA	EQERA	EQH9	EQBB9	EQSO9	EQHR9	VORP	WXRL
2003	SFN	MLB	30	8	2	2	68	0	61.0	59	29	46	5	38%	.305	0	1.44	3.10	4.45	3.41	9.2	3.9	6.1	0.7	17.0	2.4
2004	SFN	MLB	31	3	5	0	53	0	44.7	43	19	31	7	35%	.269	-10	1.39	3.42	5.11	3.68	9.2	3.5	5.5	1.2	10.7	0.6
2004	PHI	MLB	31	2	3	1	23	0	21.0	18	10	28	1	45%	.347	21	1.33	3.00	2.95	2.95	7.6	3.8	10.5	0.4	6.2	1.0
2005	NYA	MLB	32	0	0	0	34	0	32.3	33	20	18	2	42%	.295	-15	1.64	5.02	4.96	4.68	9.1	5.5	5.0	0.6	2.7	-0.0
2006	NYA	MLB	33	2	2	1	34	0	37.0	41	19	27	5	40%	.308	-13	1.62	5.34	5.80	6.51	9.8	4.8	6.3	1.2	0.3	0.0

Breakout: 5%   Improve: 9%   Collapse: 66%   Attrition: 34%   Comparables: Alan Mills, Don Elston, Steve Bedrosian

F-Rod (pronounced "fraud") never got started with the Yankees. After a month and change of so-so pitching, Rodriguez injured his knee stepping out of the shower. Arthroscopic surgery ensued, and Rodriguez stayed on the shelf from mid-May until mid-July. Once back, he never found his way back into Torre's good graces. Torre is consistent with pitchers: if he trusts you, he'll carry you a long way. Everyone else is in the "fool me once" category. A moderately useful reliever over the past few years, the Yankees didn't offer arbitration, but someone will give him a chance.

AARON SMALL   Bats: R   Throws: R   Height: 6' 5"   Weight: 220   Born: November 23, 1971   Age: 34

YEAR	TM	LVL	AGE	W	L	SV	G	GS	IP	H	BB	SO	HR	GB%	BABIP	STUFF	WHIP	ERA	PERA	EQERA	EQH9	EQBB9	EQSO9	EQHR9	VORP	WXRL
2004	ABQ	AAA	32	9	9	0	27	24	154.7	199	29	109	18	—	.352	-8	1.47	5.06	5.04	6.20	10.8	2.1	4.1	1.3	-10.4	—
2005	COH	AAA	33	1	4	0	11	10	49.0	62	8	21	5	54%	.328	-20	1.43	4.96	5.40	6.33	11.0	1.9	2.6	1.3	-3.9	—
2005	NYA	MLB	33	10	0	0	15	9	76.0	71	24	37	4	44%	.276	11	1.25	3.20	4.26	3.08	8.6	2.8	4.4	0.5	22.0	1.5
2006	NYA	MLB	34	5	6	0	33	12	90.7	112	25	41	14	46%	.306	-15	1.50	5.38	5.71	6.10	10.8	2.5	3.9	1.3	-0.7	0.3

Breakout: 7%   Improve: 41%   Collapse: 23%   Attrition: 20%   Comparables: Roger Craig, Mike Smithson, Jim Barr

In terms of simply not losing, Small was one of the four most successful pitchers of all time, joining Tom Zachary (12–0, 1929), Dennis Lamp (11–0, 1985), and Howie Krist (10–0, 1941) as the only pitchers to reach double-figure wins without losing a game. Predictive power of such records: zero. Before being called up, Small was being abused by minor league hitters, so it's not like he had found the corner he'd been looking to turn since being drafted in 1989. The most likely explanation is that the Yankees scored an average of eight runs when he pitched, and he had one of the best BABIP rates (.276) on the Yankees as well. Had he pitched enough innings to qualify, he would have ranked in the top 15 in this category. It—and his winning streak—is extremely unlikely to last.

JOSHUA SCHMIDT   Bats: R   Throws: R   Height: 6' 4"   Weight: 175   Born: November 14, 1982   Age: 23

YEAR	TM	LVL	AGE	W	L	SV	G	GS	IP	H	BB	SO	HR	GB%	BABIP	STUFF	WHIP	ERA	PERA	EQERA	EQH9	EQBB9	EQSO9	EQHR9	VORP	WXRL
2005	STA	A-	22	5	1	13	26	0	33.0	14	8	47	0	66%	.226	7	0.67	0.27	3.38	3.68	7.1	3.4	7.1	0.3	6.3	—
2006	NYA	MLB	23	3	3	1	25	4	53.0	51	19	37	4	57%	.285	6	1.31	3.85	3.93	4.15	8.4	3.4	6.1	0.7	7.9	0.9

Breakout: 12%   Improve: 27%   Collapse: 28%   Attrition: 25%   Comparables: Dustin Nippert, Jeff Taglienti, Richie Gardner

The Colter Bean Test, Part II: the Yankees' 15th-round draft pick in 2005, Schmidt was the closer for University of the Pacific. He had a heck of a debut; Staten Island held no mysteries for him (but really, when was the last time Staten Island was mysterious? Somewhere around 1660 is our guess). He struck out boatloads of batters in both college and the pros (13.3 per nine his senior year, 12.8 on the Island), but there is a catch: Schmidt is a sidearmer. This automatically makes his performance suspect in the eyes of the scouts. It's not an exaggeration to say that he will have to keep putting up ERAs smaller than a flea's navel to make The Show with this team.

MATT SMITH   Bats: L   Throws: L   Height: 6' 5"   Weight: 220   Born: June 15, 1979   Age: 27

YEAR	TM	LVL	AGE	W	L	SV	G	GS	IP	H	BB	SO	HR	GB%	BABIP	STUFF	WHIP	ERA	PERA	EQERA	EQH9	EQBB9	EQSO9	EQHR9	VORP	WXRL
2003	TAM	A+	24	2	3	0	6	6	32.3	20	12	25	0	—	.218	0	0.99	2.23	4.25	5.16	7.6	4.2	4.6	0.3	1.5	—
2003	TRN	AA	24	2	3	0	9	9	50.7	57	24	36	6	—	.305	-22	1.60	4.26	6.80	5.88	10.3	5.1	4.8	2.0	-1.5	—
2004	TRN	AA	25	4	4	0	14	11	61.7	67	31	56	5	—	.346	-9	1.59	4.96	5.31	5.61	9.4	5.2	5.5	1.0	-0.1	—
2005	TRN	AA	26	3	4	2	22	4	54.7	46	23	59	2	57%	.317	-3	1.26	2.80	4.35	5.57	8.5	5.1	6.1	0.5	0.2	—
2005	COH	AAA	26	2	0	1	25	0	27.7	24	13	33	3	43%	.300	1	1.34	2.60	5.06	3.71	8.8	5.1	8.1	1.4	5.6	—
2006	NYA	MLB	27	2	3	0	29	5	53.7	59	33	36	7	47%	.305	-13	1.70	5.73	6.07	6.11	9.6	5.7	5.9	1.1	-2.7	-0.1

Breakout: 11%   Improve: 42%   Collapse: 37%   Attrition: 21%   Comparables: Rob Henkel, Bob Hendley, Derrick Lewis

After five years as a mediocre starter, the Yankees moved Smith to the pen. The experiment was a great success. Overall, Smith posted a 2.80 ERA, allowing all batters a .230 average. In 54 innings pitched he walked 23 and struck out 59. Lefties batted .173 against him. It was all an academic exercise—with Mike Myers and Ron Villone now in front of him, Smith will spend his sixth season in the gulag.

TANYON STURTZE
Bats: R Throws: R Height: 6' 5" Weight: 205 Born: October 12, 1970 Age: 35

YEAR	TM	LVL	AGE	W	L	SV	G	GS	IP	H	BB	SO	HR	GB%	BABIP	STUFF	WHIP	ERA	PERA	EQERA	EQH9	EQBB9	EQSO9	EQHR9	VORP	WXRL
2003	TOR	MLB	32	7	6	0	40	8	89.3	107	43	54	14	46%	.317	-18	1.68	5.95	5.52	6.01	10.1	4.1	5.2	1.3	-4.9	-0.4
2004	NYA	MLB	33	6	2	1	28	3	77.3	75	33	56	9	43%	.289	0	1.41	5.47	4.62	5.19	8.8	3.6	6.1	0.9	4.2	0.9
2005	NYA	MLB	34	5	3	1	64	1	78.0	76	27	45	10	47%	.274	-11	1.32	4.73	5.08	4.62	9.0	3.1	5.2	1.2	6.9	0.6
2006	NYA	MLB	35	3	3	1	46	0	59.7	68	23	35	9	45%	.301	-16	1.53	5.47	5.56	6.23	10.0	3.7	5.1	1.2	-1.2	-0.2

Breakout: 13%   Improve: 31%   Collapse: 38%   Attrition: 21%   Comparables: Alan Levine, Doug Henry, Mike Fetters

It's the Circle of Sturtze, or as Eric Idle sang in "Always Look On the Bright Side of Life," "You know, you come from nothing, you're going back to nothing. What have you lost? Nothing!" The prevalent theory among Yankees camp followers was that Torre had overworked Sturtze in the first half, provoking a second half collapse (6.07 ERA). There may be something too this; prior to the All-Star break, Sturtze had walked just 1.5 batters per nine innings, but afterwards, his walk rate ballooned to 5.8. On the other hand, Sturtze's control has always been his undoing, so this might just be a case of Sturtze going back to being Sturtze after a one-year sabbatical from himself.

CHIEN-MING WANG
Bats: R Throws: R Height: 6' 3" Weight: 200 Born: March 31, 1980 Age: 26

YEAR	TM	LVL	AGE	W	L	SV	G	GS	IP	H	BB	SO	HR	GB%	BABIP	STUFF	WHIP	ERA	PERA	EQERA	EQH9	EQBB9	EQSO9	EQHR9	VORP	WXRL
2003	TRN	AA	23	7	6	0	21	21	122.0	143	32	84	7	—	.325	2	1.43	4.65	4.70	5.58	9.6	2.7	4.5	1.0	0.3	—
2004	TRN	AA	24	6	5	0	18	18	109.0	112	26	90	6	—	.320	14	1.27	4.05	4.21	4.71	8.9	2.4	5.0	0.7	10.8	—
2004	COH	AAA	24	5	1	0	6	5	40.3	31	8	35	3	—	.262	21	0.97	2.01	3.96	2.56	7.7	2.1	6.3	0.9	13.1	—
2005	COH	AAA	25	2	1	0	6	6	34.0	40	6	21	4	66%	.333	-1	1.35	4.24	4.81	4.81	10.2	1.9	4.3	1.3	3.0	—
2005	NYA	MLB	25	8	5	0	18	17	116.3	113	32	47	9	66%	.270	6	1.25	4.02	4.58	4.11	9.0	2.6	3.6	0.7	16.8	2.1
2006	NYA	MLB	26	9	9	0	36	23	151.0	170	42	74	16	56%	.299	-1	1.40	4.55	4.71	4.98	9.9	2.6	4.3	0.9	11.7	2.1

Breakout: 14%   Improve: 36%   Collapse: 31%   Attrition: 6%   Comparables: Don August, Rick Matula, Zach Day

Like a good science-fiction story, Wang compels you to suspend your disbelief. His strikeout rate is too low, especially for a player who can dial it up into the 90s. He's had too many arm problems: shoulder surgery in 2001, and recurring shoulder problems in 2003 and 2005. He's a young pitcher on the Yankees, yet he succeeds. That the Taiwanese Terror is a groundball machine goes a long way towards explaining these inconsistencies in his story; he can get by with fewer strikeouts than the average pitcher. At times he's terrifically stingy with the home run, not allowing one until his seventh major league start. His great calm and presence helped him beat Torre's bias against young players. Bouncing back from his latest shoulder injury despite rumors he might be done for the year, he pitched well in September and in his sole postseason start. The main questions are whether he can continue to get by with so few strikeouts, and when his arm will break down again. Readers who bought this kind of pitcher also purchased Ray Bradbury's *Martian Chronicles* and *The Beast That Shouted Love at the Heart of the World* by Harlan Ellison.

STEVEN WHITE
Bats: R Throws: R Height: 6' 5" Weight: 205 Born: June 15, 1981 Age: 25

YEAR	TM	LVL	AGE	W	L	SV	G	GS	IP	H	BB	SO	HR	GB%	BABIP	STUFF	WHIP	ERA	PERA	EQERA	EQH9	EQBB9	EQSO9	EQHR9	VORP	WXRL
2004	BCR	A	23	5	2	0	9	9	57.7	36	26	56	4	—	.232	-14	1.07	2.65	6.49	5.26	7.9	6.1	4.9	1.6	1.9	—
2004	TAM	A+	23	6	2	0	12	12	59.7	51	19	44	4	—	.263	-13	1.17	2.56	5.89	5.89	9.8	3.8	4.4	1.5	-1.8	—
2005	TRN	AA	24	2	7	0	11	11	50.3	61	26	54	9	42%	.364	-27	1.73	6.44	7.26	8.38	11.7	5.8	6.3	2.4	-14.9	—
2006	NYA	MLB	25	3	6	0	28	12	79.7	93	45	50	17	41%	.298	-16	1.73	6.56	7.03	6.84	10.3	5.3	5.5	1.8	-11.5	-0.7

Breakout: 13%   Improve: 41%   Collapse: 17%   Attrition: 3%   Comparables: Brett Evert, Justin Echols, Scott Sobkowiak

The line for his last two starts was 12 IP, 6 H, R, 2 BB, 22 K. He then went on to the AFL and pitched well, allowing a 3.94 ERA in 29.2 innings, though he was somewhat wild. Still, these are the things you hold onto after a season in which everything went to hell due to a rib cage pull and pancreatitis. White has very good stuff, and nothing that happened to him in 2005 should have changed that.

JARET WRIGHT
Bats: R Throws: R Height: 6' 2" Weight: 230 Born: December 29, 1975 Age: 30

YEAR	TM	LVL	AGE	W	L	SV	G	GS	IP	H	BB	SO	HR	GB%	BABIP	STUFF	WHIP	ERA	PERA	EQERA	EQH9	EQBB9	EQSO9	EQHR9	VORP	WXRL
2003	SDN	MLB	27	1	5	2	39	0	47.3	69	28	41	9	48%	.405	-20	2.05	8.37	5.58	8.46	11.5	4.5	6.7	1.6	-15.7	-0.8
2004	ATL	MLB	28	15	8	0	32	32	186.3	168	70	159	11	50%	.300	29	1.28	3.29	3.64	3.93	8.2	3.1	6.8	0.5	39.9	5.6
2005	NYA	MLB	29	5	5	0	13	13	63.7	81	32	34	8	47%	.336	-10	1.77	6.08	5.59	6.68	10.5	4.5	4.6	1.1	-10.0	0.1
2006	NYA	MLB	30	5	6	1	36	13	91.7	102	37	61	12	46%	.308	-5	1.52	5.07	5.37	5.54	9.8	3.8	5.8	1.1	2.7	0.7

Breakout: 19%   Improve: 43%   Collapse: 19%   Attrition: 7%   Comparables: Stan Bahnsen, Joey Hamilton, Pat Rapp

Giving Wright a three-year contract was like buying the world's most expensive gun and then shooting yourself in the foot with it. Wright lacks the constitution to be a big league starter, and the Yankees will be lucky to get one serviceable year out of him. The greatest service that Wright performed for the Yankees was tearing scar tissue in his shoulder and disappearing for three months, allowing Wang to get established as a big league starter. Upon returning, Wright improved from "beer league" to "replacement level," so the best hope for 2006 is he takes another mid-year vacation, thereby launching Matt DeSalvo's career.

Line Outs

Position/Player	TM	LVL	AGE	PA	R	2B	3B	HR	RBI	BB	SO	SB-CS	SPEED	BA/OBP/SLG	MLVR	EQBA/OBP/SLG	EQA	VORP
INF F. Escalona	COH	AAA	26	358	42	14	1	7	45	28	58	5-0	5.3	.274/.363/.394	.033	.254/.330/.366	.251	6.2
CF B. Gardner*	STA	A-	21	332	62	9	1	5	32	39	49	19-3	6.9	.284/.377/.376	.176	.263/.327/.352	.247	-0.9
OF K. Reese*	COH	AAA	27	618	92	38	7	14	69	63	86	16-5	6.4	.276/.359/.450	.103	.249/.326/.396	.254	-7.9
SS R. Sanchez	NYA	MLB	37	46	7	1	0	0	2	2	3	0-1	4.9	.279/.326/.302	-.185	.279/.340/.302	.228	-1.1

Pitcher	TM	LVL	AGE	W	L	SV	IP	H	BB	SO	HR	GB%	BABIP	STUFF	WHIP	ERA	PERA	EQERA	EQH9	EQBB9	EQSO9	EQHR9	VORP
J. Anderson	COH	AAA	26	4	1	10	67.7	44	18	60	4	51%	.238	4	0.92	2.66	3.96	3.53	7.1	2.8	6.2	0.7	14.7
A. Embree*	BOS	MLB	35	1	4	1	37.7	42	11	30	8	42%	.309	-8	1.41	7.64	4.89	6.98	9.3	2.6	7.0	1.6	-8.3
W. Franklin*	COH	AAA	31	2	3	1	42.3	36	11	50	4	42%	.314	1	1.11	3.62	4.24	4.91	8.7	2.9	7.6	1.1	3.1
	NYA	MLB	31	0	1	0	12.7	11	8	10	1	42%	.286	-11	1.50	6.38	4.97	7.82	7.8	5.7	7.1	0.7	-3.9
R. Mendoza	COH	AAA	33	1	0	1	12.0	4	1	15	0	52%	.160	11	0.42	0.75	2.45	3.27	5.7	0.8	8.2	0.0	2.8
H. Nomo	TBA	MLB	36	5	8	0	100.7	127	51	59	16	32%	.336	-13	1.76	7.24	5.50	6.45	10.1	4.5	5.1	1.3	-18.1
	COH	AAA	36	2	3	0	37.3	30	22	41	1	37%	.309	0	1.39	3.62	4.67	6.23	8.0	7.5	6.5	0.3	-2.4

Felix Escalona hinted at having talent in the Sally League in 2001. Exposure to the Rule 5 draft (and non-stop roster hop-scotch since) queered that. **Brett Gardner,** New York's 3rd round pick in 2005 is the rare speedy leadoff wannabe who may actually have leadoff skills. **C. J. Henry,** the team's 1st round pick of 2005, comes from Oklahoma . . . just like Mickey Mantle! Mantle was in the majors at Henry's age; so much for unfair comparisons. At this point we don't have much to go on except Henry's youth and athleticism. **Kevin Reese** could be a useful fifth outfielder if he ever escapes Purgatory, OH. **Rey Sanchez** Got hurt early and never came back, a noble sacrifice given that his veteran presence would almost certainly have been used as a reason to avoid looking at Cano. The Venezuelan Teen Wonder **Jose Tabata** outperformed hyped 2005 draftees C. J. Henry and Austin Jackson. He has speed and a good idea of the strike zone for a player who may never have kissed a girl.

Jason Anderson had another good year in the minors; Anderson's trouble is that each time he's had a major league audition his control, normally pretty good, has quit on him. Tried Xanax? You can't beat the Red Sox with pitchers the Sox themselves cut, not unless you have some insight into improving them. Lefties and righties teed off on **Alan Embree** with equal fervor, so it's safe to say the Yankees lacked that insight. **Wayne Franklin** was one of a parade of desperation lefties; Franklin isn't a major league pitcher but had some staying power because Torre inexplicably believed he was a better pitcher than the results showed. **Ramiro Mendoza** is like Rudy Seanez's sickly younger brother, with DL stints in six consecutive seasons. There's no reason to expect anything different. **Hideo Nomo** was signed by the Yankees after he washed out in Tampa Bay, Nomo was sent to Columbus but never showed enough velocity to merit a recall. With an aggregate 7.70 ERA and a 113/93 K/BB ratio in 2004–2005 (184.2 innings), it's safe to say that Hideo is no 'mo.

Oakland Athletics

They had seen this movie before. The date was August 30th, a perfect night at Angel Stadium. It was a whimsically breezy late summer evening, the kind that would send the rest of the country into shivers of suppressed melancholy in anticipation of the encroaching autumn, but one Californians get to enjoy all year long. Californians, particularly those in Alameda County, have grown accustomed to enjoying their baseball a little longer than the rest of us, too. And when Bobby Kielty took Francisco Rodriguez *deep* to right field, and Huston Street notched the save in 17 tense pitches, it seemed certain that this year would be no exception. Bobby Crosby was hurt, Rich Harden was too, the September schedule was loaded and the Wild Card winner was not going to come from the West, but fans of the East Bay Elephants had seen their boys come back from the brink too many times to be worried about details like that. Had they really been 17–32 on Memorial Day, or was that 2002? An 11-inning game completed in less than three hours? The fans wouldn't even be tired at work the next day.

Then something strange happened: the Oakland A's stopped hitting. A one-run effort against John Lackey the next day was lost in the afterglow, but getting shut out by Ervin Santana in the finale? At home, finally, the A's responded with a 12-run drubbing of the Yankees, but were then blanked on five hits against Aaron Small. It was the last time they would see first place. The A's made a poor showing the next day against Shawn Chacon before dropping two in a row to the Mariners. All told, the A's would manage two runs or fewer in 14 of their final 32 contests. Their team OBP in September was .312. Trailing the pack were the men designated to be hitters: left fielder Jay Payton went .252/.298/.327 in the month, Dan Johnson .198/.274/.323, and Scott Hatteberg .194/.279/.269. Where was Jack Cust when you needed him? He was up I-80 in Sacramento, actually, competing in the PCL playoffs. His strikeout against the Tacoma Rainiers ended the River Cats' season.

It is fair to criticize A's management for the September inertia. While some teams overreact to every 2-for-23 slump, there's a thin line between Ken Macha's studied non-interventionism and outright abdication. The decision to stick with Hatteberg, who was 35 and hadn't hit all season when semi-palatable alternatives like Cust and

ATHLETICS PROSPECTUS

2005 record: 88–74; Second place, AL West

Pythagenport record: 93–69

Runs scored per game: 4.77 (6th in AL)

Runs allowed per game: 4.06 (4th in AL)

Team EqA: .254 (9th in AL)

2005 Batters Age: 29.1 (6th oldest in AL)

2005 Pitchers Age: 26.8 (2nd youngest in AL)

Ballpark: Network Associates Coliseum; Neutral park; Park Factor of 0.994

2005: The almost-contenders lost their mojo in September, settling for second place.

2006: With reinforcements in the rotation and the outfield, they'll keep after the Angels.

Matt Watson were available is hard to reconcile with the popular notion of the A's as a team that must sweat the small stuff in order to survive. Such criticism is fair, but it misses the broader implications.

Ultimately, the A's September swoon speaks to a larger problem, one which calls into question some of the more basic tenants of the *Moneyball* paradigm. Table 1 provides the rank of the 15 American League clubs in VORP at the four positions on the left side of the defensive spectrum: left field, right field, first base, and DH.

The A's score of 23.4 ranked second from the bottom, behind only a Twins team that was last in the league in runs scored. In fact, their VORP at these positions, as well

TABLE 1. VALUE OVER REPLACEMENT PLAYER, LEFT SIDE OF DEFENSIVE SPECTRUM

Team	VORP	Team	VORP	Team	VORP
Red Sox	150.5	Devil Rays	100.2	Blue Jays	32.0
Indians	129.9	Angels	99.9	Orioles	23.5
Yankees	128.5	Rangers	84.2	A's	**23.4**
Tigers	107.4	Royals	69.4	Twins	11.6
Seattle	105.8	White Sox	61.8		

as that of the Twins and Orioles, ranked behind many *National League* clubs—this while being spotted a designated hitter. Getting even a league-average offensive contribution at the corners would have made a difference of six or seven wins, enough to close the gap between them and the Angels.

That the A's managed to win 88 games in spite of punting at these positions is a testament to their strengths, particularly a strong infield (first base aside) and a pitching staff that ranks among the best in baseball. Yet, analysts have espoused from the very origin of modern sabermetrics that it ought to be easy to come up with reasonable offensive contributions at these "defense second" positions. "True shortage of talent almost never occurs at the left end of the defensive spectrum" is one of the 15 tenets that Bill James chose for his valedictory in the 1988 *Baseball Abstract.*

A corollary to James's statement, one that dovetails with Billy Beane's reputation as an arbitrager nonpareil, is that it ought to be cheaper to acquire comparably valuable talent at the positions on the left side of the defensive spectrum. That is, you ought to do everything in your power to lock up a player like Eric Chavez or Bobby Crosby when you can do so at a tolerable price, because it should be easier to come up with a reasonable left fielder on the cheap than it would be a reasonable shortstop. The quintessential example is Matt Stairs, an outfielder/DH that the A's signed for pennies on the dollar after he'd been discarded by clubs from Nagoya to Montreal, but who contributed more than 40 VORP per season over a productive three-year run from 1997–1999.

But is that how the market for baseball talent actually plays out in the post-*Moneyball* era? We have compiled a database of more than 250 free agent contracts signed during the winters of 2004–05 and 2005–06, including every major league contract for which signing terms were publicly disclosed. For each contract, we tracked two key variables:

- **Marginal cost:** measured as guaranteed salary, including any buyout clauses on option years, minus the league minimum salary of $316,000. For multi-year contracts, salary in future seasons was discounted at a rate of 5% per year to account for the typical rate of inflation in player salaries.

- **Marginal return:** measured in terms of projected Wins Above Replacement Player (WARP), which accounts for the totality of a player's offensive and defensive contributions. The projected WARP totals are based on a weighted average of player's WARP score over his previous three seasons. We built in a simple model

TABLE 2. MARGINAL COST PER WIN FOR 2005 AND 2006 FREE AGENT CLASSES

Position	Number	Marginal Cost	WARP	$/Win
C	27	$73,250,000	63.0	$1,150,000
SS	21	$166,500,000	119.6	$1,400,000
2B	19	$36,500,000	50.4	$725,000
CF	14	$216,750,000	115.3	$1,875,000
3B	18	$154,000,000	96.3	$1,600,000
RF	16	$156,500,000	85.8	$1,825,000
LF	13	$130,500,000	82.1	$1,600,000
1B/DH	21	$174,000,000	95.2	$1,825,000
Pitcher				
Starter	51	$605,500,000	352.3	$1,725,000
Middle Relief	64	$132,500,000	156.2	$850,000
Closer*	9	$154,000,000	89.8	$1,725,000
Total	**273**	**$2,000,000,000**	**1306.0**	**$1,525,000**

* A pitcher qualifies as a closer if he saved at least 20 games in the season immediately preceding his signing the contract.

for aging, assuming that a player's WARP will decline by 5% per year as of age 29, and 10% per year as of age 32.

For each contract, then, we can come up with an estimate of the marginal cost per win. Paul Konerko's new deal, for example, cost the White Sox about $53 million in present value, for an expected return of 22.3 wins above replacement, about $2.4 million per win. Table 2 presents this price per win calculation broken down by position.

More than $2 billion have been committed to free agents over the past two winters. Teams are willing to pay a lot for a win—the going rate is about $1.5 million. However, this amount varies substantially from position to position. Both starting pitchers and closers are comparatively more expensive, which is no surprise to anyone who has read a Western Hemisphere newspaper over the past two years. Players at positions like catcher, shortstop and second base are materially *cheaper* than their counterparts at the easier defensive positions on the left side of the defensive spectrum. If you take a five-win right fielder and a five-win shortstop, for example, it will cost about 30% more to acquire the right fielder. This basic result holds even if we apply some slight variations to the methodology, such as accounting for non-linearity in the relationship between WARP and marginal salary.

Billy Beane intuitively understands this dynamic when it comes to starting pitching. Because the market tends to overvalue pitching relative to offense, that's all the more reason to develop or acquire pitching when you can do so in a cost-effective manner. However, the same principle holds true within the range of position player talent. The market *does* overvalue players at positions like right field and first base—but that's an argument for compiling talent at those positions, not giving it away.

Consider the Matt Stairs model player referred to earlier, the sleeper. He is a casualty of the sabermetric crusade. If seven, eight or 15 teams recognize the value of a player like Stairs, then his cost will quickly escalate to market price. Nowadays, the sleepers are guys like Eduardo Perez, a low-profile player who is valuable because of his large platoon splits. Perez, who for years met the very definition of "freely available talent" and has never made more than $900,000 in a season, was signed this winter by the Cleveland Indians at a price in excess of $1.8 million. The loophole has been closed.

Part of the A's left end of the spectrum dilemma results from their farm system. What of the A's vaunted player development capabilities? Where is that 5th round pick out of South Carolina State, who might not look good in a pair of jeans but is putting up a 1200 OPS at Midland?

One problem in using top prospect lists to evaluate farm systems is that it punishes teams for having developed players successfully and seeing them graduate to the major league level. The Dodgers, for example, have a highly regarded list of prospects, but virtually no worthwhile young talent in the majors. Chad Billingsley might be a good prospect, but the Dodgers would trade him in a heartbeat for Harden, Swisher, Street, Joe Blanton, or Danny Haren—none of whom is older than 25 and all but one of whom has spent his entire career in the A's system. Along the same lines, while the A's present top prospect list consists mostly of hitting talent—Dallas Braden and Jairo Garcia are the only pitchers that would crack the organization's Top 10—this is only because of the successful matriculations of the top-flight arms.

We can work around this problem by looking at a list of young talent within each organization, regardless of whether it exists in the majors or the minors. In figure 1, we plot the total 2006 VORP for players aged 25 and younger within each system as projected by PECOTA, and broken down between hitting and pitching talent. Players with a negative projected VORP are excluded from the analysis; there is no reason to punish a team for having a developing player who is not yet expected to be major league caliber.

The A's total 25-and-under VORP is 181.7, which ranks sixth among the 30 MLB clubs. However, the great majority of that value is stockpiled in pitching talent. While the A's young pitchers combine for 123.8 VORP, a total that ranks behind only the Cubs, the hitters account for just 60.7 VORP, which places them 19th in the league, behind such developmental powerhouses as the Reds and the Royals.

While hitters like Daric Barton and Kevin Melillo are legitimate and perhaps underrated prospects, more typical of the system is Brian Stavisky. Stavisky was selected in the 6th round of the heavily scrutinized 2002 draft as a senior out of Notre Dame. Traditional scouts disliked him for a perceived lack of athleticism, but he had put up good numbers as a Golden Domer, particularly in the OBP department. Although Stavisky is not without hitting talent, it took him until age 25 to reach Double-A, and he does not have a defensive position. Our projection system, PECOTA, thinks that Stavisky would hit only .264/.322/.399 as a major leaguer next season. In short, the chances of him becoming major league regular are slim

Part of Stavisky's problem is a lack of home run power; he hit just 11 home runs in the Texas League last season. Another issue is that a significant amount of Stavisky's value lies in his walk rate, and PECOTA significantly curtails its expectation of his walk rate at the major league level. Consider that as a 23-year-old in the Midwest League, Stavisky drew a walk in 15.2% of his plate appearances. Last year, in the Texas League, that figure dipped to 11.8%. PECOTA figures that in the major leagues it would regress further to 8.7%. That is not a bad walk rate, but it's not enough to support average contact hitting ability and below average power hitting ability for his position.

PECOTA, of course, is just a projection system; it has its faults and biases, and it can only predict within a certain margin of error. That PECOTA tends to consider factors that are traditionally more valued by scouts than by analysts—a player's speed, body type, and his age relative to his level of competition—and that its conclusions are often closer to the prevailing opinions of scouts than the

FIGURE 1. 2006 PROJECTED VORP FOR MAJOR LEAGUE ORGANIZATIONS, PLAYERS 25 AND YOUNGER

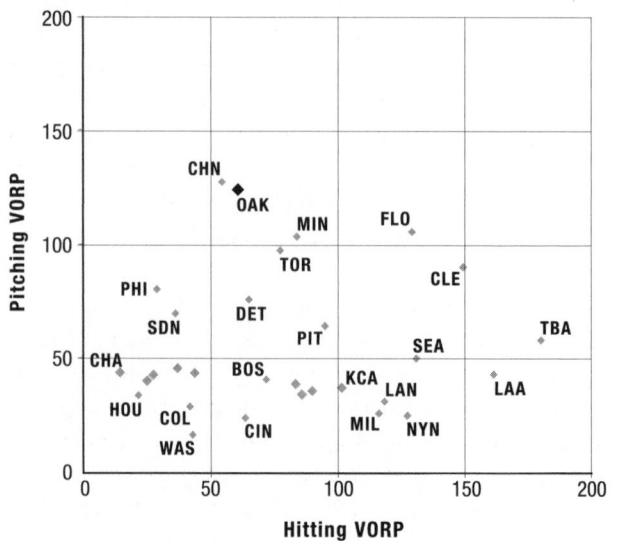

consensus of other projection systems, might or might not be a point in its favor. At the very least, it helps us to understand one important principle of "new wave" sabermetric analysis:

The qualities that are most valuable in a major league player are not necessarily the qualities that are most valuable in a prospect.

The A's did not draft Stavisky because they thought he could put up a .400 OBP in Modesto; they drafted him in the hopes that he'd one day be capable of a comparable performance at the major league level. Similarly, the Braves did not draft Jeff Francoeur because they are ignorant to the importance of walk rate or OBP, but because they thought that Francoeur's skills would develop in such a way that he'd become a valuable major league player.

Some of the confusion may stem from a conflation in the sabermetric literature of two related, but distinct concepts: walk rate, which is simply the number of bases on balls that a player draws in a given number of plate appearances, and the broader term "plate discipline." A player's walk rate, in fact, is really a function of two things: a skill component (plate discipline), and an opportunity component, namely the opposing pitcher's predilection to throw him pitches into or out of the strike zone. Plate discipline, of course, is itself made up of several interrelated skills, such as plate coverage, bat control, and pitch recognition.

It is easiest to grasp this concept at the extreme. It takes no amount of plate discipline to draw an intentional walk. More broadly, all walks run along a spectrum between purely intentional and purely unintentional. If a pitcher's sole objective was to prevent the batter from reaching on a base on balls, then he would groove 80 mph softballs down the middle of the plate. Obviously, this would not be a sound strategy. But the pitcher does have the advantage of initiating the batter-pitcher interaction, and any sufficiently skilled pitcher will seek to minimize the opposing batter's expectation by accepting a greater or lesser amount of risk in his choice of pitches. Against a hitter that has a great capacity to damage a pitch thrown in the strike zone, particularly a skilled power hitter such as Barry Bonds, issuing a walk is a more tolerable risk than it is against a weaker hitter like David Eckstein, who will seldom do worse damage than reaching first base.

One consequence of this is merely semantic. For example, Manny Ramirez is routinely cited as having superior "plate discipline", because he draws a large number of walks. In fact, pitch-by-pitch tracking reveals that Ramirez chases an above-average number of pitches outside the strike zone. Many of his walks result from pitchers fearing his power, so they don't throw him many strikes. In contrast, a hitter like Luis Castillo almost certainly has better plate discipline in the purest sense of the term.

The more important consequence is in terms of player development. If walk rate, and therefore OBP, is contingent in large part on the number of opportunities that a hitter is given to draw walks, then we need to consider how those opportunities will change as he moves up the developmental ladder. It seems probable that:

- As hitters advance through the system and face more skilled pitchers, those pitchers will be better able to differentiate the Ramirezes from the Castillos and make efficient adjustments. In more classic terms, the higher levels of competition feature more "pitchers," who will adjust their approach to suit the particular batter, and fewer "throwers," who are primarily doing battle with themselves. It is not sufficient to say, for example, that the average major league pitcher will give up 50% fewer walks to the same lineup than the average Double-A pitcher, because *who he walks* is a primary differentiator between major and minor league pitching talent.

- At the same time, a hitter's level of skill relative to other *hitters* in his league will decrease. Daric Barton was far and away the most dangerous hitter in the Stockton Ports lineup, but he would be, for the time being, only the seventh or eighth most dangerous hitter in the Oakland A's lineup. At the major league level, pitchers will be far more inclined to challenge him, saving their cute stuff for Chavez or Swisher.

Put simply, if a hitter cannot generate enough power to be "dangerous" relative to his competition, his walk rate will decrease substantially because he'll no longer see as many pitches outside of the strike zone. Maintaining his walk rate will require a more proactive strategy than simply hoping the pitcher throws four balls before he throws three strikes.

The contention that walk rate in particular is one of those qualities that does not "translate" well is not new. On the contrary, it's something that's been discussed for years by researchers like Clay Davenport and David Grabiner. However, this has come to take on more importance in recent years as the amateur and minor league talent pools have become substantially better arbitraged, with clubs like the A's and the Toronto Blue Jays viewing walk rates a large component of their arbitrage strategy. Whereas before, huge gains were to be had simply by considering a prospect's walk rate when entire organizations flatly ignored it, it is now probable that some clubs have overshot the mark. Their farm systems feature a preponderance of players with "empty" walk rates that are not adequately supported by power hitting abilityor even real plate discipline skills like pitch recognition.

This problem may be particularly acute in combinations with draft strategies that focus heavily on college hitters. The popular notion of the "Age 27 Peak" can beget the misconception that hitters improve in a more or less linear fashion until they reach age 27. In fact, a hitter's growth rate behaves as an inverse exponential function, with that growth decelerating rapidly until he reaches age 27. Most hitters are essentially done developing by the time they hit *age 24,* with only incremental gains thereafter. A college senior like Stavisky, who didn't play full-season ball until he was 23, might only have a year or two time left of highly fruitful development, whereas an 18-year-old high-schooler will have five or six years on his clock.

This has been advanced as an argument in favor of drafting college hitters—you're getting more of a finished product. But if that finished product is not good enough to be a major league regular—and college hitters drafted after the first couple of rounds usually are not—then we have a problem on our hands. You're going to wind up with a lot of fourth outfielders in the mold of Jody Gerut and John-Ford Griffin.

An 18-year-old prep, while he is much more likely to completely flame out, also has exponentially more time to grow into a major league regular. Put differently, because performances worse than major league replacement value are of no use to the major league club, *the club should tend to favor higher variance* in its choice of prospects, provided the player is not capable of a major league caliber performance already. Figure 2 presents an idealized comparison between a set of two high school draftees and a set of two college draftees. Note that while the mean performance of the two groups is the same, the "set" of high school

players is much more valuable because the one high schooler who does develop is worth much more by himself than the two college players put together. It is better to have one Delmon Young than two Jody Geruts. That the "other" high-schooler does not develop at all is of no consequence: a .200 EQA is no worse than a .220 EQA, since neither is of major league caliber.

Make no mistake: as Rany Jazayerli found this past summer in his landmark study on the amateur draft that we published on www.baseballprospectus.com, college hitters were still substantially better investments than high school hitters, at least up through 1999. Since then, however, the paradigm has shifted significantly, even within the past handful of years. In 1999, the selection of the 25th college hitter took place with the 177th overall pick of the amateur draft, toward the top of the 6th round. Last year, the selection of the 25th college hitter—University of Illinois catcher Chris Robinson—was made with the 90th overall selection, toward the top of the *3rd* round. If we merely assume that a college hitter drafted in the 2nd round today is equivalent to a college hitter drafted in the *3rd* round just ten years ago, then the advantage of the college hitter has evaporated. This is before considering that the high-school player available as an alternative will be better than he was ten years ago, because he'll have been "bumped down" by the abundance of selections from the college ranks.

The times, they are a' changin'. And they're changing in ways made possible by the sabermetric movement—all of which is great news for Billy Beane and bad news for his imitators. A skilled arbitrager does not care about whether the market is up or down; what he wants is volatility. Beane has already begun to break ranks with the old new orthodoxy and is leading the charge toward the new new orthodoxy. This past summer, the A's took high-school players with seven of their top 10 selections in the June draft, six of them pitchers. The Blue Jays, meanwhile, didn't draft a high-school player until the 11th round.

In November, Beane signed Esteban Loaiza to a three-year, $21.4 million contract. The move shocked even many of his loyalists. The A's are not supposed to spend money on players like Esteban Loaiza, especially when they have six or seven good major league starters in tow. But as a more studied analysis reveals, Beane was ahead of the curve on this one, too. Table 3 presents the expected return on investment for the seven starting pitchers signed this winter to contracts of at least $10 million, using the marginal cost method we applied above but substituting PECOTA projections over the life of the contract for a "naïve" projection based on past performance. Loaiza is the bargain of the bunch, coming in more than 30% cheaper than the group average.

FIGURE 2. IDEALIZED COMPARISON OF HIGH SCHOOL VERSUS COLLEGE DRAFTING STRATEGY

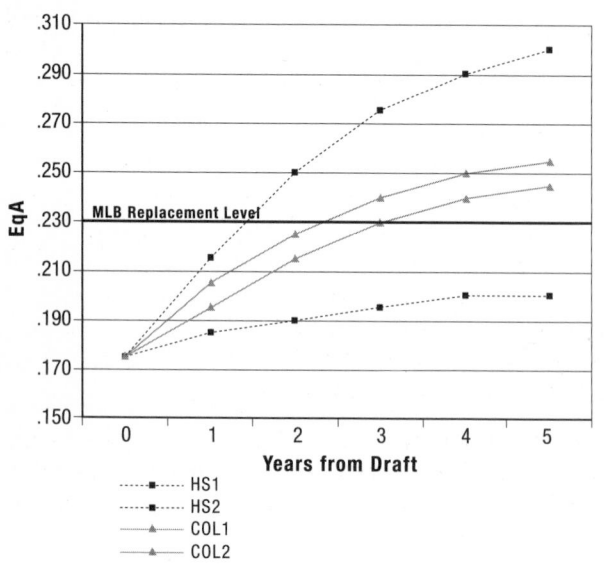

TABLE 3. COST PER WIN FOR SIGNIFICANT 2005–06 STARTING PITCHER SIGNINGS, PER PECOTA

Pitcher	Years	Marginal Cost	Wins (PECOTA)	$/Win
Esteban Loaiza, OAK	3	$19,500,000	11.1	$1,750,000
A. J. Burnett, TOR	5	$48,500,000	23.0	$2,100,000
Paul Byrd, CLE	2	$13,250,000	6.3	$2,100,000
Matt Morris, SFN	3	$24,750,000	9.5	$2,625,000
Kevin Millwood, TEX	5	$53,000,000	16.2	$3,275,000
Jarrod Washburn, SEA	4	$33,750,000	9.9	$3,400,000
Kenny Rogers, DET	2	$15,000,000	4.2	$3,575,000
Total		**$207,750,000**	**80.2**	**$2,600,000**

Five years from now, we are not going to be distinguishing organizations as "stat-oriented" or "scout-oriented" but as followers and leaders. The margins for error will be thinner, and this will take some getting used to. There is going to be some refuse from the previous, now discarded trend. (Sorry, Brian Stavisky, you're *so three years ago.*) To the untrained eye, it will seem that Billy Beane is doing some very uncharacteristic things, but if the past year is any guide, more long October nights are in the Oakland A's future.

HITTERS

DARIC BARTON 1B/C? Bats: L Throws: R Height: 6′ 0″ Weight: 205 Born: August 16, 1985 Age: 20

YEAR	TM	LVL	AGE	PA	R	2B	3B	HR	RBI	BB	SO	SB	CS	SPEED	BA	OBP	SLG	MLVR	EQBA	EQOBP	EQSLG	EQA	VORP	DEFENSE
2003	JCY	Rk	17	212	29	10	0	4	29	37	48	0	3	2.9	.294	.420	.424	.224	.238	.341	.359	.248	5.3	35-C -2
2004	PEO	A	18	393	63	23	0	13	77	69	44	4	4	3.6	.313	.445	.511	.390	.269	.382	.442	.286	26.5	51-C -1
2005	STO	A+	19	361	60	16	2	8	52	62	49	0	1	4.3	.318	.438	.469	.255	.275	.378	.388	.273	8.1	58-1B -9
2005	MID	AA	19	249	38	20	1	5	37	35	30	1	1	4.5	.316	.410	.491	.278	.285	.373	.446	.284	11.0	54-1B -6
2006	OAK	MLB	20	560	64	29	2	11	65	61	78	2	2	4.5	.268	.349	.404	.004	.271	.360	.421	.265	12.2	131-1B -6

Breakout: 13% Improve: 36% Collapse: 31% Attrition: 8% Comparables: Nick Johnson, Butch Wynegar, Michael Forbes

Barton's plate approach is remarkably mature for a 20-year-old. The ball cracks off his bat, and he'd hold his own against major league pitching right now. But is he a difference maker? That remains to be seen. Barton's power was not impressive, given the favorable hitting environments in which he played. PECOTA and the scouts share some of the same concerns here: how much improvement can be expected from a guy who is already maximizing his plate discipline, and who does not have a classic power hitter's build? Between Jason Kendall's disappointing year and the sense that Barton's offensive ceiling rates slightly lower than it did a year ago, there are rumblings that he could be moved back to catcher.

JEREMY BROWN C Bats: R Throws: R Height: 5′ 10″ Weight: 210 Born: October 25, 1979 Age: 26

YEAR	TM	LVL	AGE	PA	R	2B	3B	HR	RBI	BB	SO	SB	CS	SPEED	BA	OBP	SLG	MLVR	EQBA	EQOBP	EQSLG	EQA	VORP	DEFENSE
2003	MID	AA	23	278	37	10	1	5	37	41	38	3	0	4.3	.275	.388	.391	.083	.247	.352	.372	.259	6.4	61-C -3
2004	MID	AA	24	523	59	27	0	6	49	71	80	2	1	3.5	.256	.361	.357	-.032	.213	.305	.302	.221	-17.0	87-C 4
2005	MID	AA	25	462	65	27	1	20	72	52	88	0	0	3.1	.261	.359	.487	.146	.217	.303	.393	.242	0.0	100-C -9
2006	OAK	MLB	26	359	35	15	1	8	38	32	71	0	0	3.7	.225	.300	.355	-.170	.228	.309	.369	.228	-1.4	86-C 0

Breakout: 24% Improve: 43% Collapse: 34% Attrition: 18% Comparables: Carlos Maldonado, Jim Sundberg, Andy Dominique

Brown had far and away his best minor league campaign, though the DTs punish him a bit for getting stuck at the Double-A level. He doesn't have star potential, but catchers can develop late, and he has a better chance than you'd think of putting together a string of big league seasons. One scout we talked to confessed that Brown would be taken more seriously as a prospect if he hadn't been written up in *Moneyball.*

TRAVIS BUCK RF **Bats: L Throws: R** Height: 6′ 3″ Weight: 210 Born: November 18, 1983 Age: 22

YEAR	TM	LVL	AGE	PA	R	2B	3B	HR	RBI	BB	SO	SB	CS	SPEED	BA	OBP	SLG	MLVR	EQBA	EQOBP	EQSLG	EQA	VORP	DEFENSE	
2005	VAN	A-	21	41	7	1	0	2	9	5	8	1	1	3.3	.361	.439	.556	.562	.331	.396	.520	.303	8.2		
2005	KNC	A	21	143	17	13	0	1	22	19	19	3	1	3.6	.341	.427	.472	.283	.287	.362	.410	.271	3.0	31-RF	2
2006	OAK	MLB	22	431	48	24	1	8	48	35	74	6	3	3.8	.263	.324	.392	-.056	.267	.335	.408	.250	+2.8	102-RF	4

Breakout: 5% Improve: 27% Collapse: 45% Attrition: 11% Comparables: John Rodriguez, Richard Brown, Shayne Carnes

He had a good debut, even for a short-season player. The A's believe that he'll develop power, but he hit just six home runs in his senior season at ASU, which is what caused his stock to drop into supplemental 1st round territory. If baseball doesn't work out, his name gives him a leg up on a gay porn career, possibly in tandem with Colt Griffin. Isn't it funny how today's gay porn star is yesterday's leading man in a conventional western? Thank you, "Brokeback Mountain."

ERIC CHAVEZ 3B **Bats: L Throws: R** Height: 6′ 1″ Weight: 204 Born: December 7, 1977 Age: 28

YEAR	TM	LVL	AGE	PA	R	2B	3B	HR	RBI	BB	SO	SB	CS	SPEED	BA	OBP	SLG	MLVR	EQBA	EQOBP	EQSLG	EQA	VORP	DEFENSE	
2003	OAK	MLB	25	654	94	39	5	29	101	62	89	8	3	5.3	.282	.350	.514	.187	.281	.355	.521	.292	53.2	150-3B	17
2004	OAK	MLB	26	577	87	20	0	29	77	95	99	6	3	3.9	.276	.397	.501	.199	.275	.401	.508	.309	37.1	124-3B	8
2005	OAK	MLB	27	694	92	40	1	27	101	58	129	6	0	5.4	.269	.329	.466	.059	.273	.342	.484	.282	26.4	151-3B	7
2006	OAK	MLB	28	647	86	32	2	27	96	72	106	6	2	4.7	.271	.354	.479	.107	.274	.365	.498	.286	35.4	151-3B	6

Breakout: 7% Improve: 30% Collapse: 26% Attrition: 6% Comparables: Robin Ventura, Richie Hebner, Leon Durham

Chavez put up a .293/.358/.537 batting line from June onward, figures that would almost perfectly align with his established levels of performance. Although he's had some slow starts in the past, April and May were so out of character that it's tempting to wonder if something was bothering him. Then again, his plate discipline was off throughout the season, as Chavez not only failed to maintain his 2004 walk rate but also set a career high in strikeouts. That PECOTA looks a little low, but even if it it's not, his defense makes him one of the 10 or 15 best players in the league.

BRANT COLAMARINO 1B **Bats: L Throws: L** Height: 5′ 11″ Weight: 205 Born: December 4, 1980 Age: 25

YEAR	TM	LVL	AGE	PA	R	2B	3B	HR	RBI	BB	SO	SB	CS	SPEED	BA	OBP	SLG	MLVR	EQBA	EQOBP	EQSLG	EQA	VORP	DEFENSE	
2003	KNC	A	22	575	68	26	0	19	80	59	101	1	0	3.2	.259	.350	.426	.152	.225	.296	.387	.237	-16.6	130-1B	10
2004	MOD	A+	23	218	41	8	2	11	41	28	23	1	0	4.3	.355	.450	.601	.534	.299	.376	.492	.296	13.6	48-1B	-1
2004	MID	AA	23	338	40	22	2	8	50	27	60	0	0	3.7	.272	.331	.434	.033	.242	.297	.389	.237	-8.2	70-1B	-3
2005	MID	AA	24	207	31	13	4	10	45	18	34	0	0	5.2	.321	.377	.594	.376	.278	.332	.500	.279	9.0	46-1B	-3
2005	SAC	AAA	24	306	37	15	3	11	47	19	76	0	0	4.4	.243	.297	.436	-.099	.220	.268	.379	.224	-13.6	70-1B	2
2006	OAK	MLB	25	466	50	22	2	14	59	31	95	0	1	4.2	.242	.297	.404	-.102	.245	.307	.420	.241	-3.7	110-1B	1

Breakout: 23% Improve: 43% Collapse: 28% Attrition: 15% Comparables: Chris Richard, Aaron Rifkin, Tommy Peterman

The power is there, but Colamarino will need to develop a better batting eye in order to leverage it. Instead, his walk rate has regressed over the course of the past three seasons. He's the type of guy who could be someone's Rule 5 throwback in a couple of years.

BOBBY CROSBY SS **Bats: R Throws: R** Height: 6′ 3″ Weight: 195 Born: January 12, 1980 Age: 26

YEAR	TM	LVL	AGE	PA	R	2B	3B	HR	RBI	BB	SO	SB	CS	SPEED	BA	OBP	SLG	MLVR	EQBA	EQOBP	EQSLG	EQA	VORP	DEFENSE	
2003	SAC	AAA	23	539	86	32	6	22	90	63	110	24	4	6.8	.308	.395	.544	.340	.286	.370	.505	.298	50.3	120-SS	5
2004	OAK	MLB	24	618	70	34	1	22	64	58	141	7	3	4.4	.239	.319	.426	-.069	.238	.321	.428	.259	17.2	149-SS	0
2005	OAK	MLB	25	370	66	25	4	9	38	35	54	0	0	5.7	.276	.346	.456	.079	.280	.358	.468	.282	21.5	83-SS	7
2006	OAK	MLB	26	549	71	29	3	18	71	54	98	6	2	5.2	.269	.346	.453	.061	.273	.357	.471	.276	32.3	129-SS	4

Breakout: 24% Improve: 49% Collapse: 18% Attrition: 11% Comparables: Mike Cuddyer, Eric Soderholm, Jeff Cirillo

Crosby does virtually everything well on the baseball field. He combines a great jump with good lateral movement, starts the deuce with aplomb, and rounds out the package with a valuable and balanced offensive profile. The strikeouts were a problem in his first trip through the bigs, but he cut his K rate by 45% last season. Both of last year's injuries were random—he broke a rib on a spring training HBP, and an ankle when he ran into Sal Fasano—so you can't even criticize his durability.

JACK CUST DH Bats: L Throws: R Height: 6' 1" Weight: 200 Born: January 16, 1979 Age: 27

YEAR	TM	LVL	AGE	PA	R	2B	3B	HR	RBI	BB	SO	SB	CS	SPEED	BA	OBP	SLG	MLVR	EQBA	EQOBP	EQSLG	EQA	VORP	DEFENSE	
2003	OTT	AAA	24	415	55	18	1	9	58	80	94	5	2	4.5	.285	.422	.426	.203	.265	.400	.411	.290	13.8	74-LF	0
2003	BAL	MLB	24	84	7	7	0	4	11	10	25	0	0	3.9	.260	.357	.521	.162	.264	.369	.542	.302	4.8		
2004	OTT	AAA	25	413	55	15	1	17	55	65	127	4	0	4.8	.235	.358	.433	.018	.212	.329	.384	.253	-9.6	31-LF	-3
2005	SAC	AAA	26	600	95	28	1	19	75	115	153	2	4	3.6	.257	.402	.438	.114	.223	.352	.361	.256	-9.7	75-LF	-7
2006	*SDN*	*MLB*	*27*	*397*	*46*	*16*	*1*	*12*	*45*	*62*	*117*	*2*	*1*	*4.1*	*.224*	*.349*	*.392*	*-.060*	*.232*	*.357*	*.422*	*.266*	*4.8*	*95-LF*	*-6*

Breakout: 29%   Improve: 60%   Collapse: 23%   Attrition: 21%   Comparables: Graham Koonce, Wayne Gross, Dave Nicholson

Any credible argument on behalf of Cust jumped the shark a long time ago, and even Billy Beane has given up on him. Sure, the stathead community would have loved to see what he'd have done with 750 big league at-bats, but Cust's case for a job has never been that strong. Note how much PECOTA clips off his minor league OBPs: there's evidence that walk rate doesn't translate to the majors as well as other statistics, and it's damned hard to post a good OBP when you don't run or make contact well enough to hit .220. Couple that with a license plate that reads "BORN2DH," and the crocodile tears would have been better shed on Billy McMillon or Mumia Abu-Jamal.

ERUBIEL DURAZO DH Bats: L Throws: L Height: 6' 3" Weight: 225 Born: January 23, 1974 Age: 32

YEAR	TM	LVL	AGE	PA	R	2B	3B	HR	RBI	BB	SO	SB	CS	SPEED	BA	OBP	SLG	MLVR	EQBA	EQOBP	EQSLG	EQA	VORP	DEFENSE
2003	OAK	MLB	29	645	92	29	0	21	77	100	105	1	1	3.8	.259	.374	.430	.094	.257	.378	.430	.284	25.4	32-1B -6
2004	OAK	MLB	30	578	80	35	1	22	88	56	104	3	2	4.4	.321	.396	.523	.278	.321	.398	.526	.312	49.4	
2005	OAK	MLB	31	167	15	6	1	4	16	14	24	1	0	3.9	.237	.305	.368	-.135	.240	.317	.393	.248	-1.1	
2006	*OAK*	*MLB*	*32*	*318*	*37*	*14*	*1*	*9*	*41*	*32*	*51*	*2*	*1*	*4.3*	*.263*	*.343*	*.422*	*.013*	*.267*	*.354*	*.439*	*.268*	*11.3*	*77-DH*

Breakout: 4%   Improve: 22%   Collapse: 45%   Attrition: 25%   Comparables: Sid Bream, Gordy Coleman, Greg Brock

Durazo underwent Tommy John surgery in July and is on the same timetable that we've grown accustomed to for pitchers—a year or so required for full healing. The list of position players that have had TJ is fairly short: Luis Gonzalez came back without any problem, Rusty Greer didn't, and we don't know what will happen to Rocco Baldelli and Cesar Izturis. Even without the injury, he'd be a decline risk at his age.

MARK ELLIS 2B Bats: R Throws: R Height: 5' 11" Weight: 180 Born: June 6, 1977 Age: 29

YEAR	TM	LVL	AGE	PA	R	2B	3B	HR	RBI	BB	SO	SB	CS	SPEED	BA	OBP	SLG	MLVR	EQBA	EQOBP	EQSLG	EQA	VORP	DEFENSE
2003	OAK	MLB	26	613	78	31	5	9	52	48	94	6	2	5.9	.248	.313	.371	-.111	.246	.317	.374	.244	6.3	146-2B 7
2005	OAK	MLB	28	482	76	21	5	13	52	44	51	1	3	5.0	.316	.384	.477	.203	.324	.400	.499	.303	36.0	109-2B 9
2006	*OAK*	*MLB*	*29*	*538*	*69*	*26*	*3*	*12*	*58*	*47*	*63*	*3*	*2*	*5.0*	*.283*	*.351*	*.426*	*.045*	*.286*	*.362*	*.443*	*.270*	*25.7*	*126-2B 7*

Breakout: 6%   Improve: 28%   Collapse: 34%   Attrition: 11%   Comparables: Bobby Avila, Jeff Frye, Frank Bolling

Ellis may have discovered that half of plate discipline is swinging at a good pitch when you see one, as he hit .390 and slugged .657 when putting one of the first two pitches into play. As a happy side benefit, he cut way down on his strikeouts, which should help him avoid a slip in his batting average. With Orlando Hudson in the National League now, there's the chance that the A's join the 2002 Cardinals, 2000 Indians, and 1970s Oriole dynasty as the only squads to sweep the Gold Gloves at second, third, and short.

ANDRE ETHIER OF Bats: L Throws: L Height: 6' 3" Weight: 195 Born: April 10, 1982 Age: 24

YEAR	TM	LVL	AGE	PA	R	2B	3B	HR	RBI	BB	SO	SB	CS	SPEED	BA	OBP	SLG	MLVR	EQBA	EQOBP	EQSLG	EQA	VORP	DEFENSE	
2003	KNC	A	21	183	23	10	0	0	11	19	25	2	2	3.9	.272	.355	.333	.050	.251	.320	.329	.231	-3.0	36-CF	2
2004	MOD	A+	22	470	72	23	5	7	53	45	64	2	5	4.1	.313	.383	.442	.158	.272	.333	.379	.248	6.1	68-CF -4	17-LF 0
2005	MID	AA	23	572	104	30	3	18	80	48	93	1	4	4.4	.319	.385	.497	.252	.290	.352	.455	.276	17.3	69-LF 2	46-RF 5
2006	*LAN*	*MLB*	*24*	*541*	*60*	*29*	*2*	*10*	*60*	*41*	*95*	*2*	*2*	*4.6*	*.271*	*.332*	*.398*	*-.049*	*.278*	*.338*	*.416*	*.253*	*6.4*	*127-LF 1*	

Breakout: 16%   Improve: 40%   Collapse: 31%   Attrition: 10%   Comparables: Rowland Office, Michael Ryan, Doug Clark

The Dodgers hope that Ethier, the Arizona State product acquired for Milton Bradley, will be a late-bloomer after a power breakout in Midland last year. He runs better than his stolen base numbers indicate, but he is considered to have too weak an arm to play centerfield. His chance could come sooner rather than later, considering that Jose Cruz is the incumbent, but PECOTA thinks he'd be overmatched as a regular.

KEITH GINTER 2B/3B Bats: R Throws: R   Height: 5' 10" Weight: 190 Born: May 5, 1976   Age: 30

YEAR	TM	LVL	AGE	PA	R	2B	3B	HR	RBI	BB	SO	SB	CS	SPEED	BA	OBP	SLG	MLVR	EQBA	EQOBP	EQSLG	EQA	VORP	DEFENSE			
2003	MIL	MLB	27	415	51	15	2	14	44	37	87	1	1	3.9	.257	.352	.427	.044	.256	.346	.431	.269	15.9	50-2B	-3	34-3B	-5
2004	MIL	MLB	28	433	47	23	2	19	60	37	100	8	1	4.7	.262	.333	.479	.101	.255	.325	.469	.272	21.8	51-2B	-8	44-3B	-1
2005	OAK	MLB	29	154	12	5	0	3	25	13	25	0	0	3.0	.161	.234	.263	-.455	.163	.247	.281	.197	-12.2	23-2B	1		
2005	SAC	AAA	29	62	9	8	0	3	12	4	11	0	0	4.0	.333	.387	.632	.452	.261	.310	.457	.259	1.4				
2006	OAK	MLB	30	179	21	8	1	6	22	14	35	1	0	4.0	.241	.310	.411	-.072	.244	.320	.428	.250	3.9	46-2B	-1		

Breakout: 22% Improve: 47% Collapse: 28% Attrition: 43%   Comparables: Tim Hulett, Luis Aguayo, Steve Buechele

Ginter was destined for a backup role with the A's, and that's what he'll have next year as Mark Ellis's caddy. There's no particular reason to think he's done. He hit well in his ego rehabilitation stint in Sacto, and was understandably pressing at the plate in limited big league playing time.

SCOTT HATTEBERG 1B Bats: L Throws: R   Height: 6' 1" Weight: 195 Born: December 14, 1969 Age: 36

YEAR	TM	LVL	AGE	PA	R	2B	3B	HR	RBI	BB	SO	SB	CS	SPEED	BA	OBP	SLG	MLVR	EQBA	EQOBP	EQSLG	EQA	VORP	DEFENSE	
2003	OAK	MLB	33	619	63	34	0	12	61	66	53	0	1	3.6	.253	.342	.383	-.031	.252	.345	.388	.258	3.9	125-1B	-12
2004	OAK	MLB	34	635	87	30	0	15	82	72	48	0	0	4.2	.284	.367	.420	.048	.281	.369	.422	.279	19.1	141-1B	-14
2005	OAK	MLB	35	521	52	19	0	7	59	51	54	0	1	3.2	.256	.334	.343	-.107	.262	.349	.354	.251	-3.6	49-1B	-5
2006	OAK	MLB	36	384	37	16	0	6	42	39	39	0	1	4.1	.258	.336	.358	-.083	.261	.347	.373	.247	0.0	92-1B	-4

Breakout: 13% Improve: 35% Collapse: 45% Attrition: 30%   Comparables: J. T. Snow, John Olerud, Tino Martinez

Whether his performance level coming into the season was acceptable boiled down to a matter of taste, but it certainly didn't leave much room for error on the down side of things. To be fair to Billy Beane and Ken Macha, the worst part of Hatteberg's season came in the second half. But surely Matt Watson or *somebody* could have done more with his September at-bats. He may have done more damage to his team's pennant hopes than any player in baseball last year.

JAVIER HERRERA CF Bats: R Throws: R   Height: 5' 11" Weight: 200 Born: April 9, 1985   Age: 21

YEAR	TM	LVL	AGE	PA	R	2B	3B	HR	RBI	BB	SO	SB	CS	SPEED	BA	OBP	SLG	MLVR	EQBA	EQOBP	EQSLG	EQA	VORP	DEFENSE			
2004	VAN	A-	19	293	50	15	4	12	47	24	59	23	1	7.8	.331	.392	.555	.442	.298	.340	.482	.285	33.2	36-CF	-5	28-RF	-2
2005	KNC	A	20	422	70	18	2	13	62	47	110	26	5	6.4	.275	.374	.444	.119	.236	.316	.391	.251	1.0	88-CF	3		
2006	OAK	MLB	21	485	59	23	2	14	54	35	119	16	5	5.3	.245	.307	.404	-.083	.248	.317	.420	.249	6.2	115-CF	-1		

Breakout: 13% Improve: 36% Collapse: 44% Attrition: 12%   Comparables: Jorge Moreno, Alex Escobar, Ben Johnson

Herrera was the highest profile minor leaguer suspended for performance enhancing drugs, and because he had a notably worse year at the plate, he tended to confirm the worst fears of the sky-is-falling crowd. Herrera didn't make the book last year, but we went back and ran a PECOTA based on his 2004 batting line.

	EqBA	EqOBP	EqSLG	EQA
PECOTA Forecast	.266	.314	.444	.255
Actual 2005 DTs	.236	.316	.391	.251

PECOTA would have missed high on his batting average, but otherwise this is a good forecast; it had his OBP, EQA, and isolated power all about right. In other words, Herrera's decline was more perceived than real, and it had mostly to do with the vagaries of making rosy projections based on a batting average-driven year in short-season A-Ball. He's still a reasonable long-term prospect, and the near-term goal will be reducing the strikeouts.

DAN JOHNSON 1B Bats: L Throws: R   Height: 6' 2" Weight: 220 Born: August 10, 1979   Age: 26

YEAR	TM	LVL	AGE	PA	R	2B	3B	HR	RBI	BB	SO	SB	CS	SPEED	BA	OBP	SLG	MLVR	EQBA	EQOBP	EQSLG	EQA	VORP	DEFENSE			
2003	MID	AA	23	619	90	26	4	27	114	68	82	7	4	4.5	.290	.365	.504	.207	.257	.329	.461	.270	13.5	107-1B	6		
2004	SAC	AAA	24	640	95	29	5	29	111	89	93	0	1	3.7	.299	.403	.535	.274	.268	.366	.457	.284	24.4	95-1B	-1	15-LF	-1
2005	SAC	AAA	25	217	36	17	0	8	41	32	24	0	1	4.4	.324	.424	.549	.374	.278	.372	.451	.284	9.1	43-1B	2		
2005	OAK	MLB	25	434	54	21	0	15	58	50	52	0	1	3.2	.275	.355	.451	.089	.279	.368	.472	.289	14.5	99-1B	-8		
2006	OAK	MLB	26	577	70	29	1	21	83	62	77	1	1	4.3	.272	.353	.462	.086	.276	.364	.481	.281	20.2	135-1B	-1		

Breakout: 21% Improve: 45% Collapse: 22% Attrition: 5%   Comparables: Sid Bream, Jason Giambi, Nick Johnson

Johnson is perceived as a sort of bridge between the Giambi Years and the Barton Years—the on-again, off-again friend with benefits you call while waiting for the next big thing. However, he could turn out to be interesting on his own merits; it isn't uncommon for a player with this profile to continue to add power throughout his mid-20s. While shifting him to DH removes one immediate concern, puts pressure on him to maintain last year's performance, at the very least.

JASON KENDALL   **C**   **Bats: R Throws: R**   Height: 6′ 0″   Weight: 193   Born: June 26, 1974   Age: 32

YEAR	TM	LVL	AGE	PA	R	2B	3B	HR	RBI	BB	SO	SB	CS	SPEED	BA	OBP	SLG	MLVR	EQBA	EQOBP	EQSLG	EQA	VORP	DEFENSE
2003	PIT	MLB	29	664	84	29	3	6	58	49	40	8	7	4.9	.325	.399	.416	.168	.324	.393	.419	.284	43.3	143-C -8
2004	PIT	MLB	30	657	86	32	0	3	51	60	41	11	8	4.9	.319	.399	.390	.135	.316	.394	.387	.277	39.3	142-C 12
2005	OAK	MLB	31	676	70	28	1	0	53	50	39	8	3	4.6	.271	.345	.321	-.104	.279	.358	.336	.253	10.5	144-C -6
2006	*OAK*	*MLB*	*32*	*612*	*64*	*27*	*2*	*2*	*52*	*43*	*41*	*8*	*3*	*4.6*	*.270*	*.333*	*.338*	*-.106*	*.274*	*.343*	*.352*	*.240*	*10.5*	*143-C -1*

Breakout: 1%   Improve: 16%   Collapse: 43%   Attrition: 2%   Comparables: Brad Ausmus, Manny Sanguillen, Earl Battey

Kendall triggered a host of PECOTA's red flags entering last season. With his batting average-heavy offensive profile, declining speed, and his position, the system figured that there was about a 25% chance he'd have a year this bad or worse. Unsurprisingly, there isn't much optimism about his rebound chances. Kendall is durable at least, but one wonders if that isn't part of the problem. He'd surely be among the career leaders in Catcher Abuse Points.

BOBBY KIELTY   **OF**   **Bats: B Throws: R**   Height: 6′ 1″   Weight: 220   Born: August 5, 1976   Age: 29

YEAR	TM	LVL	AGE	PA	R	2B	3B	HR	RBI	BB	SO	SB	CS	SPEED	BA	OBP	SLG	MLVR	EQBA	EQOBP	EQSLG	EQA	VORP	DEFENSE	
2003	MIN	MLB	26	284	40	13	0	9	32	42	56	6	2	4.5	.252	.370	.420	.037	.251	.372	.417	.279	7.2	31-RF -1	
2003	TOR	MLB	26	225	31	13	1	4	25	29	36	2	1	4.4	.233	.342	.376	-.082	.226	.341	.366	.254	-2.0	47-RF -2	
2004	OAK	MLB	27	277	29	14	1	7	31	35	47	1	0	4.3	.214	.321	.370	-.153	.213	.324	.366	.246	-5.3	40-LF 1	12-RF 0
2005	OAK	MLB	28	431	55	20	0	10	57	50	67	3	2	4.2	.263	.350	.395	-.003	.269	.366	.417	.273	6.8	51-LF 4	36-RF 0
2006	*OAK*	*MLB*	*29*	*400*	*48*	*19*	*1*	*11*	*48*	*48*	*66*	*3*	*1*	*4.8*	*.255*	*.348*	*.408*	*-.002*	*.258*	*.359*	*.424*	*.266*	*7.4*	*95-LF 0*	

Breakout: 23%   Improve: 50%   Collapse: 25%   Attrition: 23%   Comparables: Dave Hollins, Turner Ward, Gary Matthews

Kielty is emblematic of a certain type of player who might fare well if evaluated on a production-per-dollar basis, but doesn't really help you win championships if he's in the lineup for more than half a year at a time. On the bright side, he's developed a significant preference for left-handed pitching, and freeing him up to be Dan Johnson's platoon partner is one of the more underrated benefits of the Milton Bradley trade.

MARK KOTSAY   **CF**   **Bats: L Throws: L**   Height: 6′ 0″   Weight: 190   Born: December 2, 1975   Age: 30

YEAR	TM	LVL	AGE	PA	R	2B	3B	HR	RBI	BB	SO	SB	CS	SPEED	BA	OBP	SLG	MLVR	EQBA	EQOBP	EQSLG	EQA	VORP	DEFENSE
2003	SDN	MLB	27	540	64	28	4	7	38	56	82	6	3	5.4	.266	.343	.384	.010	.273	.350	.398	.262	12.9	119-CF 13
2004	OAK	MLB	28	668	78	37	3	15	63	55	70	8	5	4.9	.314	.370	.459	.122	.313	.374	.462	.287	36.8	138-CF 18
2005	OAK	MLB	29	627	75	35	1	15	82	40	51	5	5	4.7	.280	.325	.421	.000	.286	.341	.436	.265	15.4	132-CF 3
2006	*OAK*	*MLB*	*30*	*622*	*75*	*34*	*3*	*13*	*72*	*46*	*61*	*5*	*3*	*4.9*	*.277*	*.332*	*.414*	*-.006*	*.280*	*.343*	*.431*	*.259*	*18.5*	*145-CF 2*

Breakout: 7%   Improve: 32%   Collapse: 24%   Attrition: 3%   Comparables: Mike Greenwell, Joe Orsulak, Tito Francona

A's fans are getting a good player here, so long as they understand that the 2004 version was a one-time thing. That said, Milton Bradley's defense rates just as well in centerfield, while Kotsay's offense looks much less acceptable if you move him to a corner. The flexibility is nice in the short term. Bradley is an excellent player for Billy Beane to trade if he gets off to a hot start.

ADAM MELHUSE   **C**   **Bats: B Throws: R**   Height: 6′ 2″   Weight: 200   Born: March 27, 1972   Age: 34

YEAR	TM	LVL	AGE	PA	R	2B	3B	HR	RBI	BB	SO	SB	CS	SPEED	BA	OBP	SLG	MLVR	EQBA	EQOBP	EQSLG	EQA	VORP	DEFENSE
2003	SAC	AAA	31	175	26	9	0	3	17	26	32	0	1	3.4	.286	.394	.408	.134	.234	.328	.329	.235	-1.2	27-C 11
2003	OAK	MLB	31	86	13	7	0	5	14	9	19	0	0	2.8	.299	.372	.584	.338	.303	.384	.605	.321	10.0	21-C 0
2004	OAK	MLB	32	230	23	11	0	11	31	16	47	0	1	3.3	.257	.309	.463	-.038	.256	.311	.464	.260	5.8	56-C -3
2005	OAK	MLB	33	102	11	7	0	2	12	5	28	0	0	5.0	.247	.284	.381	-.150	.250	.301	.406	.242	0.1	18-C 0
2006	*OAK*	*MLB*	*34*	*154*	*16*	*7*	*0*	*5*	*20*	*11*	*38*	*0*	*0*	*4.0*	*.245*	*.303*	*.413*	*-.077*	*.248*	*.313*	*.430*	*.245*	*2.4*	*40-C 0*

Breakout: 18%   Improve: 38%   Collapse: 40%   Attrition: 48%   Comparables: Bob Montgomery, Chad Kreuter, Hank Foiles

(continued next page)

Adam Melhuse *(continued)*

Melhuse has hit the age where he's no longer likely to qualify as a premium backup catcher. Ordinarily, that would be about as important as buying the name-brand paper towels, but there's a chance that Jason Kendall's offense will descend from unpleasant to unplayable this season. We'd be tempted to hedge our bets by adding a Craig Wilson or Matt LeCroy type to the roster. Actually, are there any players of that "type" *except* for Wilson and LeCroy?

KEVIN MELILLO   **2B**   **Bats: L Throws: R**   Height: 6' 0"   Weight: 190   Born: May 14, 1982   Age: 24

YEAR	TM	LVL	AGE	PA	R	2B	3B	HR	RBI	BB	SO	SB	CS	SPEED	BA	OBP	SLG	MLVR	EQBA	EQOBP	EQSLG	EQA	VORP	DEFENSE	
2004	VAN	A-	22	109	22	11	2	2	21	11	16	2	1	6.5	.340	.422	.564	.503	.281	.334	.427	.261	8.1	20-2B	2
2005	KNC	A	23	341	47	18	3	8	36	53	40	10	4	4.9	.286	.399	.457	.179	.232	.323	.369	.246	1.6	64-2B	-8
2005	STO	A+	23	104	21	7	1	9	23	12	18	2	0	4.5	.400	.471	.800	.918	.325	.385	.592	.322	14.2	21-2B	-2
2005	MID	AA	23	147	33	10	0	7	34	14	23	9	2	6.5	.282	.347	.519	.188	.248	.312	.463	.269	5.5	32-2B	-1
2006	*OAK*	*MLB*	*24*	*527*	*66*	*30*	*3*	*15*	*63*	*44*	*92*	*9*	*4*	*4.8*	*.254*	*.318*	*.421*	*-.037*	*.257*	*.328*	*.438*	*.256*	*16.1*	*124-2B*	*-7*

Breakout: 15% Improve: 41% Collapse: 21% Attrition: 5%   *Comparables: Kevin Burford, Jason Grabowski, Brooks Conrad*

The comparison that you hear a lot is Todd Walker, which works well on the offensive side and might or might not be an implicit slam against his glove. He was old for the A-ball levels, but the A's compensated by moving him quickly and he took impressively to each new environment. He's an underrated prospect and not clearly inferior to the more highly regarded Josh Barfield and Ian Kinsler. Like Kinsler and Barfield, he's more notable for having almost major league–ready skills than being someone who is likely to grow a whole lot.

JAY PAYTON   **LF**   **Bats: R Throws: R**   Height: 5' 10"   Weight: 185   Born: November 22, 1972   Age: 33

YEAR	TM	LVL	AGE	PA	R	2B	3B	HR	RBI	BB	SO	SB	CS	SPEED	BA	OBP	SLG	MLVR	EQBA	EQOBP	EQSLG	EQA	VORP	DEFENSE			
2003	COL	MLB	30	653	93	32	5	28	89	43	77	6	4	4.9	.302	.354	.512	.158	.281	.334	.483	.275	25.3	140-LF	14		
2004	SDN	MLB	31	509	57	17	4	8	55	43	56	2	0	4.9	.260	.326	.367	-.066	.266	.330	.378	.250	3.1	116-CF	12		
2005	BOS	MLB	32	144	24	7	0	5	21	10	14	0	0	4.8	.263	.312	.429	-.033	.260	.319	.435	.258	1.7	21-RF	3		
2005	OAK	MLB	32	291	38	9	1	13	42	14	33	0	1	4.4	.269	.302	.451	-.007	.273	.316	.465	.263	4.6	46-LF	4	24-CF	1
2006	*OAK*	*MLB*	*33*	*355*	*40*	*15*	*1*	*10*	*46*	*21*	*40*	*1*	*1*	*4.7*	*.267*	*.313*	*.416*	*-.042*	*.271*	*.323*	*.433*	*.250*	*5.3*	*85-LF*	*2*		

Breakout: 20% Improve: 43% Collapse: 36% Attrition: 24%   *Comparables: Ken Berry, Mike Devereaux, Billy Hatcher*

Payton is penciled into the Oakland lineup as of this writing, but like Kielty, he's not someone that a bigger budget team would stand to play every day, especially since his defense has drifted toward left-field average. The A's elected to pick up his $4 million option, a borderline call.

CLIFF PENNINGTON   **SS**   **Bats: B Throws: R**   Height: 5' 11"   Weight: 180   Born: June 15, 1984   Age: 22

YEAR	TM	LVL	AGE	PA	R	2B	3B	HR	RBI	BB	SO	SB	CS	SPEED	BA	OBP	SLG	MLVR	EQBA	EQOBP	EQSLG	EQA	VORP	DEFENSE	
2005	KNC	A	21	332	49	15	0	3	29	39	47	25	6	6.5	.276	.364	.359	-.006	.228	.304	.308	.228	-6.9	65-SS	4
2006	*OAK*	*MLB*	*22*	*400*	*46*	*17*	*2*	*5*	*32*	*30*	*60*	*16*	*7*	*5.4*	*.232*	*.294*	*.327*	*-.212*	*.235*	*.303*	*.340*	*.222*	*-0.1*	*95-SS*	*3*

Breakout: 35% Improve: 56% Collapse: 24% Attrition: 7%   *Comparables: Clint Barmes, Hector Luna, Ian Kinsler*

The A's 2005 1st round pick, Pennington runs well, and while he's not regarded as a defensive savant, he gets the job done and projects to handle the position in the majors. It's unusual—at least outside of this system—to see someone with such an advanced idea of the strike zone but who has yet to really leverage it into either power or contact hitting ability. His college numbers were not all that impressive at A&M, especially on the home run front. Kinsler and Barmes provide some sense of Pennington's upside, but this pick was a little heavy on the projection/makeup side.

DANIEL PUTNAM   **LF**   **Bats: L Throws: L**   Height: 5' 10"   Weight: 200   Born: September 17, 1982   Age: 23

YEAR	TM	LVL	AGE	PA	R	2B	3B	HR	RBI	BB	SO	SB	CS	SPEED	BA	OBP	SLG	MLVR	EQBA	EQOBP	EQSLG	EQA	VORP	DEFENSE			
2004	KNC	A	21	198	30	5	2	7	28	30	42	0	0	4.4	.220	.348	.402	.042	.189	.296	.349	.229	-11.1	49-LF	0		
2005	STO	A+	22	593	97	37	3	15	100	66	92	1	3	4.0	.307	.388	.479	.165	.263	.331	.391	.252	-5.6	102-LF	-3	25-RF	0
2006	*OAK*	*MLB*	*23*	*499*	*52*	*25*	*2*	*10*	*55*	*42*	*90*	*1*	*1*	*4.3*	*.245*	*.313*	*.377*	*-.107*	*.248*	*.323*	*.392*	*.240*	*-3.5*	*118-LF*	*-3*		

Breakout: 19% Improve: 49% Collapse: 24% Attrition: 6%   *Comparables: Jake Weber, Jesse Roman, Mike O'Keefe*

Another classic A's prospect, in that his plate discipline is well advanced over the rest of his skill set. Remember that those good-looking doubles and batting average numbers are from the California League. PECOTA doesn't like this type of profile at all, especially when it comes from someone on the right side of the defensive spectrum. It might be wrong, but given the number of analysis-oriented teams that have become heavily vested in players of this caliber, it would be worth their time to investigate this hypothesis.

RICHIE ROBNETT OF Bats: L Throws: L Height: 5' 10" Weight: 195 Born: September 17, 1983 Age: 22

YEAR	TM	LVL	AGE	PA	R	2B	3B	HR	RBI	BB	SO	SB	CS	SPEED	BA	OBP	SLG	MLVR	EQBA	EQOBP	EQSLG	EQA	VORP	DEFENSE			
2004	VAN	A-	20	195	26	14	1	4	36	28	43	1	2	4.0	.299	.395	.470	.289	.267	.345	.405	.262	10.1	35-CF	-5		
2005	STO	A+	21	518	77	30	0	20	74	56	151	8	4	5.2	.243	.324	.440	-.076	.195	.265	.335	.213	-37.6	99-RF	2	13-CF	-1
2006	OAK	MLB	22	437	47	22	2	11	47	34	122	5	3	4.4	.218	.282	.365	-.192	.221	.291	.380	.224	-11.1	104-RF	0		

Breakout: 33% Improve: 55% Collapse: 24% Attrition: 7% Comparables: Christian Snavely, Carlos Sosa, Juan Camilo

Robnett has a different type of problem—he both walks and hits for power, but strikes out so often that it undermines the rest of his game. If you believe the translations, he's unlikely to develop into a major league talent. There are rumors that he'll repeat the California League, but there's a case to be made that the only way he'll learn to cut down on his swing is if he moves to an environment where home runs aren't so easy to hit.

MARCO SCUTARO INF Bats: R Throws: R Height: 5' 10" Weight: 170 Born: October 30, 1975 Age: 30

YEAR	TM	LVL	AGE	PA	R	2B	3B	HR	RBI	BB	SO	SB	CS	SPEED	BA	OBP	SLG	MLVR	EQBA	EQOBP	EQSLG	EQA	VORP	DEFENSE			
2003	NOR	AAA	27	287	42	18	3	9	32	33	34	11	6	5.9	.311	.401	.520	.361	.290	.375	.477	.289	24.6	35-3B	0	23-2B	-3
2004	OAK	MLB	28	472	50	32	1	7	43	16	58	0	0	4.0	.273	.297	.393	-.138	.269	.299	.390	.237	3.4	107-2B	0	13-SS	0
2005	OAK	MLB	29	419	48	22	3	9	37	36	48	5	2	5.5	.247	.310	.391	-.094	.251	.325	.405	.253	6.3	74-SS	4	30-2B	2
2006	OAK	MLB	30	414	47	21	2	9	44	30	49	4	2	4.7	.256	.313	.390	-.083	.259	.323	.406	.245	9.9	99-SS	3		

Breakout: 16% Improve: 42% Collapse: 34% Attrition: 19% Comparables: Ken Aspromonte, Alex Grammas, Charlie Neal

A what-you-see-is-what-you-get guy, Scooter has some pretty clear edges over a waiver-bait middle infielder, but just as clearly was put on Earth to be a reserve.

BRIAN STAVISKY LF/DH Bats: L Throws: R Height: 6' 3" Weight: 230 Born: July 6, 1980 Age: 25

YEAR	TM	LVL	AGE	PA	R	2B	3B	HR	RBI	BB	SO	SB	CS	SPEED	BA	OBP	SLG	MLVR	EQBA	EQOBP	EQSLG	EQA	VORP	DEFENSE			
2003	KNC	A	23	402	54	20	2	6	35	62	74	4	1	4.6	.266	.396	.393	.178	.240	.343	.370	.253	-6.4	14-LF	0		
2004	MOD	A+	24	583	108	39	5	19	83	54	89	6	4	4.9	.343	.413	.550	.395	.286	.345	.442	.271	12.0	63-LF	4	32-1B	-2
2005	MID	AA	25	586	84	36	6	11	88	69	84	0	5	4.0	.316	.398	.475	.238	.280	.357	.420	.269	10.4	41-LF	-1	13-RF	-1
2006	OAK	MLB	25	504	56	27	2	10	58	44	91	1	1	4.6	.264	.332	.399	-.035	.267	.342	.415	.255	4.5	119-LF	-2		

Breakout: 11% Improve: 34% Collapse: 28% Attrition: 8% Comparables: Gary Johnson, Todd Sears, Andy Barkett

He's just young enough and strong enough that he could still add power; PECOTA expects a downward correction in his batting average but identifies a few late bloomers in the mold of Lyle Overbay further down his comparables list. Stavisky's defensive reputation is worse than his numbers, and he's been a regular DH.

KURT SUZUKI C Bats: R Throws: R Height: 5' 11" Weight: 200 Born: October 4, 1983 Age: 22

YEAR	TM	LVL	AGE	PA	R	2B	3B	HR	RBI	BB	SO	SB	CS	SPEED	BA	OBP	SLG	MLVR	EQBA	EQOBP	EQSLG	EQA	VORP	DEFENSE	
2004	VAN	A-	20	208	27	10	3	3	31	18	26	0	1	4.4	.297	.394	.440	.246	.272	.330	.397	.253	9.2	26-C	0
2005	STO	A+	21	521	85	26	5	12	65	63	61	5	3	5.1	.277	.378	.440	.060	.236	.321	.358	.242	-0.1	103-C	-3
2006	OAK	MLB	22	428	46	20	2	8	45	35	62	3	2	4.6	.241	.310	.364	-.131	.244	.320	.379	.236	3.2	102-C	-2

Breakout: 19% Improve: 42% Collapse: 31% Attrition: 7% Comparables: Phil Avlas, Brian Luderer, Russell Martin

Suzuki doesn't impress scouts very much, but unlike some of the other A's prospects, he's athletic and has other skills to round out his plate discipline. He has some upside in the mold of Ramon Hernandez, but it's a bit early to be penciling him into the 2007 lineup. In person, he looks shorter than his listed height of 6' 0". He'll get a fair shake in this organization.

NICK SWISHER 1B/OF Bats: B Throws: L Height: 6' 0" Weight: 190 Born: November 25, 1980 Age: 25

YEAR	TM	LVL	AGE	PA	R	2B	3B	HR	RBI	BB	SO	SB	CS	SPEED	BA	OBP	SLG	MLVR	EQBA	EQOBP	EQSLG	EQA	VORP	DEFENSE			
2003	MOD	A+	22	237	38	14	2	10	43	41	49	0	2	3.7	.296	.418	.550	.373	.250	.357	.455	.280	11.2	33-CF	-2		
2003	MID	AA	22	336	36	24	2	5	43	37	76	0	1	3.3	.230	.324	.380	-.064	.204	.290	.347	.227	-10.7	61-CF	-2		
2004	SAC	AAA	23	554	109	28	2	29	92	103	109	3	3	4.6	.269	.406	.537	.250	.234	.364	.440	.279	22.8	105-CF	-4	11-RF	-1
2004	OAK	MLB	23	71	11	4	0	2	8	8	11	0	0	3.9	.250	.352	.417	-.035	.254	.357	.407	.270	0.4	11-LF	0		
2005	OAK	MLB	24	522	66	32	1	21	74	55	110	0	1	3.9	.236	.322	.446	-.005	.239	.335	.461	.270	6.8	115-RF	-3	13-1B	-1
2006	OAK	MLB	25	538	66	28	1	21	75	64	105	0	1	4.0	.252	.347	.455	.053	.256	.358	.473	.276	15.7	126-RF	-3		

Breakout: 28% Improve: 56% Collapse: 21% Attrition: 14% Comparables: Lance Berkman, Art Shamsky, Jose Cruz

We'll know in the next 18 months whether he's going to reach the next level. Swisher hit .197/.244/.342 after first-pitch strikes last season but .270/.405/.561 after first-pitch balls. Those splits can often be large, especially for a guy with this type of profile, but one thing that guys like Adam Dunn and Lance Berkman learned is that it's worth jumping on the first pitch a little more often, at least enough to keep the pitchers honest. Although he is one of the best slow defensive outfielders since Dwight Evans, he is slated to move to first base.

CHARLES THOMAS OF Bats: L Throws: L Height: 6' 0" Weight: 190 Born: December 26, 1978 Age: 27

YEAR	TM	LVL	AGE	PA	R	2B	3B	HR	RBI	BB	SO	SB	CS	SPEED	BA	OBP	SLG	MLVR	EQBA	EQOBP	EQSLG	EQA	VORP	DEFENSE			
2003	MYR	A+	24	244	30	8	1	2	15	29	54	6	2	5.2	.242	.357	.319	.020	.229	.317	.317	.231	-13.2	40-LF	-1	21-RF	2
2003	GRN	AA	24	197	29	14	4	0	23	18	25	5	4	6.3	.324	.396	.449	.248	.303	.363	.443	.275	12.6	38-CF	3		
2004	RIC	AAA	25	238	31	18	4	4	32	16	40	7	5	5.9	.358	.416	.535	.388	.335	.390	.494	.299	24.8	19-CF	0	14-LF	1
2004	ATL	MLB	25	266	35	8	4	7	31	21	45	3	1	6.3	.288	.368	.445	.121	.283	.358	.439	.276	8.5	63-LF	9		
2005	OAK	MLB	26	55	4	0	0	0	1	5	8	0	1	4.9	.109	.255	.109	-.608	.109	.255	.109	.154	-7.3				
2005	SAC	AAA	26	317	43	16	3	5	33	35	56	16	4	6.7	.227	.319	.361	-.177	.201	.280	.306	.217	-16.1	65-CF	-1		
2006	OAK	MLB	27	288	34	13	2	4	27	21	51	7	3	5.6	.252	.316	.368	-.108	.255	.326	.383	.242	0.3	70-CF	1		

Breakout: 19% Improve: 28% Collapse: 34% Attrition: 24% Comparables: Larry Stahl, Frank Baker, Dave May

Thomas is a misfit in Oakland in that the A's have several guys who can play a credible centerfield, all of whom offer more at the plate. He needs to get out of town while someone still remembers his good half-year in Atlanta.

MATT WATSON OF Bats: L Throws: R Height: 5' 11" Weight: 190 Born: September 5, 1978 Age: 27

YEAR	TM	LVL	AGE	PA	R	2B	3B	HR	RBI	BB	SO	SB	CS	SPEED	BA	OBP	SLG	MLVR	EQBA	EQOBP	EQSLG	EQA	VORP	DEFENSE			
2003	NOR	AAA	24	290	40	18	1	11	55	23	23	2	2	4.2	.295	.366	.504	.271	.285	.356	.498	.288	14.0	56-LF	0		
2004	SAC	AAA	25	539	79	37	3	19	96	54	75	3	4	4.2	.305	.377	.515	.204	.270	.338	.433	.265	7.1	102-RF	-6	18-LF	-1
2005	SAC	AAA	26	498	82	27	3	17	81	67	57	12	1	6.0	.315	.404	.516	.281	.282	.361	.439	.282	14.2	96-RF	-11		
2005	OAK	MLB	26	50	4	3	0	0	5	2	4	0	0	4.5	.188	.220	.250	-.480	.191	.240	.255	.179	-4.7				
2006	OAK	MLB	27	433	53	22	1	12	54	37	58	5	2	4.8	.271	.339	.429	.020	.274	.349	.447	.267	8.9	103-RF	-3		

Breakout: 20% Improve: 40% Collapse: 25% Attrition: 17% Comparables: Dusty Baker, Lee Walls, Brady Clark

The A's re-upping of Jay Payton boiled down to a strong indictment of Watson's defense, since it's clear that even as a Triple-A threepeater, he offers more with the stick. He's about as much on the major league fringe as it gets, and his chances for a career could depend on whether he catches someone's eye in his next 50 big league plate appearances.

PITCHERS

JOE BLANTON Bats: R Throws: R Height: 6' 3" Weight: 225 Born: December 11, 1980 Age: 25

YEAR	TM	LVL	AGE	W	L	SV	G	GS	IP	H	BB	SO	HR	GB%	BABIP	STUFF	WHIP	ERA	PERA	EQERA	EQH9	EQBB9	EQSO9	EQHR9	VORP	WXRL
2003	KNC	A	22	8	7	0	21	21	133.0	110	19	144	6	—	.290	11	0.97	2.57	4.42	5.50	9.4	1.7	6.3	1.3	1.4	—
2003	MID	AA	22	3	1	1	7	5	35.7	21	7	30	1	—	.206	19	0.78	1.26	3.74	2.67	6.4	2.1	5.6	0.5	11.0	—
2004	SAC	AAA	23	11	8	0	28	26	176.3	199	34	143	13	—	.332	18	1.32	4.19	3.92	4.83	9.2	1.8	5.4	0.7	15.3	—
2005	OAK	MLB	24	12	12	0	33	33	201.3	178	67	116	23	45%	.252	7	1.22	3.53	4.71	3.94	8.9	3.1	5.3	1.0	44.4	5.7
2006	OAK	MLB	25	11	10	0	31	29	184.3	190	53	112	23	45%	.283	11	1.32	4.32	4.42	4.72	9.1	2.6	5.4	1.0	21.1	3.5

Breakout: 8% Improve: 33% Collapse: 25% Attrition: 0% Comparables: William Van Landingham, Don Aase, Bob Milacki

Blanton locates well, has the classic oversized pitcher's butt, and his mechanics are clean. He improved as the season wore on, generating more strikeouts with breaking stuff down the zone. He's not particularly exciting to watch, with a low-90s fastball and a league average slider/curve combo, and his strikeout rate does not really say "long career," but those are fairly trivial complaints.

DALLAS BRADEN Bats: L Throws: L   Height: 6' 1" Weight: 185 Born: August 13, 1983   Age: 22

YEAR	TM	LVL	AGE	W	L	SV	G	GS	IP	H	BB	SO	HR	GB%	BABIP	STUFF	WHIP	ERA	PERA	EQERA	EQH9	EQBB9	EQSO9	EQHR9	VORP	WXRL
2005	STO	A+	21	6	0	0	7	7	43.7	31	11	64	4	42%	.314	31	0.96	2.68	4.32	3.89	7.8	2.8	8.4	1.3	7.9	—
2005	MID	AA	21	9	5	0	16	16	97.0	104	32	71	5	47%	.337	14	1.40	3.90	4.41	4.69	9.2	3.5	4.9	0.7	9.7	—
2006	OAK	MLB	22	9	9	0	29	25	151.0	154	55	103	19	45%	.289	12	1.38	4.64	4.66	4.99	9.0	3.3	6.1	1.0	11.9	2.3

Breakout: 8%   Improve: 40%   Collapse: 18%   Attrition: 0%   Comparables: Abe Alvarez, Mike Hinckley, Andy Pratt

How can you not root for a screwball pitcher? Braden, a 24th round pick in 2004 who shot from rookie ball to Double-A in the span of ten months, is the sort of pitcher whom everyone could be talking about a year from now. His numbers are more impressive in the context of playing in some offense-friendly environments, and he's borrowed some of Bobby Jenks's "wrong side of the tracks" backstory. The scroogie isn't a novelty pitch, either: Braden doesn't throw much harder than 86 or 87, so it's a key part of his arsenal, complementing his slow changeup. His K rate registered a big decline after his promotion to Midland, and he admitted to having a tired arm. With an arm action that isn't pristine, that's something to watch.

KIKO CALERO Bats: R Throws: R   Height: 6' 1" Weight: 170 Born: January 9, 1975   Age: 31

YEAR	TM	LVL	AGE	W	L	SV	G	GS	IP	H	BB	SO	HR	GB%	BABIP	STUFF	WHIP	ERA	PERA	EQERA	EQH9	EQBB9	EQSO9	EQHR9	VORP	WXRL
2003	SLN	MLB	28	1	1	1	26	1	38.3	29	20	51	5	32%	.296	25	1.28	2.82	4.03	3.08	7.3	4.3	10.9	1.2	11.9	0.2
2004	SLN	MLB	29	3	1	2	41	0	45.3	27	10	47	5	44%	.218	21	0.82	2.78	3.56	2.93	6.9	1.9	8.6	1.0	14.5	2.3
2005	OAK	MLB	30	4	1	1	58	0	55.7	45	18	52	6	37%	.260	15	1.13	3.23	3.79	3.29	7.9	3.0	8.4	1.0	15.7	1.4
2006	OAK	MLB	31	3	2	3	52	0	57.0	51	19	50	8	37%	.267	8	1.22	3.69	3.93	4.39	7.9	3.0	7.8	1.2	11.5	1.0

Breakout: 18%   Improve: 30%   Collapse: 42%   Attrition: 16%   Comparables: Odell Jones, Don Elston, Enrique Romo

Calero gave up nine of his 20 earned runs over a span of three short outings in May, immediately after which he went on the DL with tendinitis. That could turn out to be both one expensive bout of Tennis Elbow for Calero, and a blessing in disguise for the A's, since it coincided with the end of Octavio Dotel's season and allowed Huston Street to emerge as the closer. Health permitting, Calero's slider should make him one of the league's better middle relievers for years to come.

JUAN CRUZ Bats: R Throws: R   Height: 6' 2" Weight: 160 Born: October 15, 1978   Age: 27

YEAR	TM	LVL	AGE	W	L	SV	G	GS	IP	H	BB	SO	HR	GB%	BABIP	STUFF	WHIP	ERA	PERA	EQERA	EQH9	EQBB9	EQSO9	EQHR9	VORP	WXRL
2003	CHN	MLB	24	2	7	0	25	6	61.0	66	28	65	7	47%	.351	11	1.54	6.05	4.33	6.21	9.4	3.6	8.4	1.0	-5.7	0.5
2003	IOW	AAA	24	4	0	0	9	9	50.7	37	11	47	1	—	.255	31	0.95	1.95	3.14	3.14	7.4	2.4	7.0	0.2	13.3	—
2004	ATL	MLB	25	6	2	0	50	0	72.0	59	30	70	7	47%	.280	14	1.24	2.75	3.80	3.17	7.9	3.4	7.9	0.8	21.6	1.1
2005	OAK	MLB	26	0	3	0	28	0	32.7	38	22	34	5	44%	.359	-4	1.84	7.43	5.35	8.55	9.9	5.9	9.1	1.3	-12.1	-0.5
2005	SAC	AAA	26	5	1	0	13	13	75.0	51	28	90	4	49%	.273	28	1.05	2.40	3.91	3.53	7.3	3.7	7.8	0.6	16.4	—
2006	OAK	MLB	27	5	5	1	37	8	82.3	82	34	65	10	44%	.294	5	1.41	4.57	4.68	5.01	8.8	3.7	7.1	1.0	7.8	1.0

Breakout: 19%   Improve: 53%   Collapse: 10%   Attrition: 7%   Comparables: Gary Bell, Ike Delock, Ramon Ortiz

Cruz pitched well as a starter in Sacramento, but ranks no higher than eighth on his organization's depth chart. He has neither a starter's frame nor a starter's notion of how to keep his pitch counts down, so there's an argument for using him in the 'pen, hoping he gets off to a good start, and punting him to the highest bidder. Trading partners are not likely to be impressed by anything he does in Triple-A, now that he's had two flameouts at the major league level.

OCTAVIO DOTEL Bats: R Throws: R   Height: 6' 0" Weight: 160 Born: November 25, 1973 Age: 32

YEAR	TM	LVL	AGE	W	L	SV	G	GS	IP	H	BB	SO	HR	GB%	BABIP	STUFF	WHIP	ERA	PERA	EQERA	EQH9	EQBB9	EQSO9	EQHR9	VORP	WXRL
2003	HOU	MLB	29	6	4	4	76	0	87.0	53	31	97	9	40%	.217	23	0.97	2.48	3.66	2.69	6.8	3.0	9.4	1.0	29.7	4.2
2004	HOU	MLB	30	0	4	14	32	0	34.7	27	15	50	4	30%	.315	31	1.21	3.11	3.37	3.89	7.0	3.6	11.4	1.0	6.9	0.5
2004	OAK	MLB	30	6	2	22	45	0	50.7	41	18	72	9	30%	.305	31	1.16	4.08	3.55	3.73	7.5	3.0	11.9	1.4	12.8	2.5
2005	OAK	MLB	31	1	2	7	15	0	15.3	10	11	16	2	26%	.222	7	1.37	3.53	4.80	3.60	6.6	6.6	9.6	1.2	3.8	0.1
2006	NYA	MLB	32	3	3	15	40	0	48.3	39	19	52	7	33%	.267	17	1.21	3.43	3.67	3.64	7.1	3.7	9.4	1.1	10.8	1.4

Breakout: 26% Improve: 44% Collapse: 29% Attrition: 27% Comparables: Troy Percival, Skip Lockwood, Don Elston

Dotel offered to come back to the A's for free, but had other ideas when the Yankees called offering $2 million. It was an odd deal; Dotel isn't expected back until midseason and it didn't include one of those Jon Lieber team option years that protect the Yankees from having to nothing to show for their investment but a year of rehab. There was probably no way to see Dotel's elbow problem coming, but the injury implications of reliever usage patterns is something that deserves more study. On account of heavy use and somewhat inefficient pitching patterns, Dotel averaged 1,424 pitches per season from 2002–2004, a total 20–25% higher than a closer like Mariano Rivera usually does.

JUSTIN DUCHSCHERER Bats: R Throws: R   Height: 6' 3" Weight: 190 Born: November 19, 1977 Age: 28

YEAR	TM	LVL	AGE	W	L	SV	G	GS	IP	H	BB	SO	HR	GB%	BABIP	STUFF	WHIP	ERA	PERA	EQERA	EQH9	EQBB9	EQSO9	EQHR9	VORP	WXRL
2003	SAC	AAA	25	14	2	0	24	23	155.0	151	18	117	12	—	.285	12	1.09	3.25	4.13	4.43	9.3	1.3	5.6	1.1	19.5	—
2003	OAK	MLB	25	1	1	0	4	3	16.3	17	3	15	1	45%	.327	16	1.22	3.31	3.31	3.86	9.4	1.7	8.3	0.6	3.9	0.4
2004	OAK	MLB	26	7	6	0	53	0	96.3	85	32	59	13	45%	.255	-6	1.21	3.27	4.87	3.34	8.7	2.9	5.3	1.1	29.4	2.1
2005	OAK	MLB	27	7	4	5	65	0	85.7	67	19	85	7	43%	.274	29	1.00	2.21	3.20	2.67	7.6	2.0	9.0	0.7	30.0	3.3
2006	OAK	MLB	28	4	3	6	59	0	71.7	66	18	56	8	44%	.277	9	1.17	3.38	3.47	3.87	8.1	2.3	7.0	0.9	16.6	1.4

Breakout: 18% Improve: 34% Collapse: 36% Attrition: 11% Comparables: John Habyan, T. J. Mathews, Darren Holmes

Speaking of questions that deserve further study, there hasn't been much work done on just what makes a pitcher better disposed to starting or relief work. Duke has been so effective in his role that it's hard to contemplate any change, especially with the A's starting pitching being what it is. But he throws three or four different pitches, had a reasonably successful minor league track record as a starter, and has a good enough feel for his craft that he ought to have no trouble retiring the same hitter several times a game. Even in this organization, his lack of a big fastball or hammer curve may limit his horizons.

RON FLORES Bats: L Throws: L   Height: 5' 11" Weight: 190 Born: August 9, 1979 Age: 26

YEAR	TM	LVL	AGE	W	L	SV	G	GS	IP	H	BB	SO	HR	GB%	BABIP	STUFF	WHIP	ERA	PERA	EQERA	EQH9	EQBB9	EQSO9	EQHR9	VORP	WXRL
2003	MID	AA	23	3	2	6	39	0	59.3	44	15	66	6	—	.254	-3	0.99	2.88	5.01	4.04	8.2	2.9	7.4	1.8	9.7	—
2004	SAC	AAA	24	4	3	1	55	0	53.0	59	18	55	4	—	.340	1	1.45	3.74	4.19	4.53	9.1	3.4	6.7	0.8	6.4	—
2005	SAC	AAA	25	5	3	3	52	0	60.3	46	30	66	5	40%	.283	0	1.26	2.39	4.66	3.41	7.8	4.8	7.1	0.9	14.1	—
2006	OAK	MLB	26	3	3	1	34	2	52.7	50	21	39	7	38%	.274	2	1.35	4.12	4.40	4.59	8.4	3.6	6.7	1.2	7.8	0.7

Breakout: 15% Improve: 28% Collapse: 42% Attrition: 21% Comparables: John Hiller, Mike Stanton, Derek Lilliquist

The A's have claimed that they don't need a lefty specialist, but given Macha's usage of Ricardo Rincon was straight out of *Three Nights in August,* Flores has a great chance to be the team's new LOOGY. He has the LOOGY weapon of choice—a slider that, like Michaelangelo's nunchucks, moves a lot and not always in the direction of his choosing. PECOTA is skeptical, but Flores's ERA will be under 4.00 if he gets a more consistent platoon advantage.

JAIRO GARCIA Bats: R Throws: R   Height: 6' 0" Weight: 165 Born: March 7, 1983 Age: 23

YEAR	TM	LVL	AGE	W	L	SV	G	GS	IP	H	BB	SO	HR	GB%	BABIP	STUFF	WHIP	ERA	PERA	EQERA	EQH9	EQBB9	EQSO9	EQHR9	VORP	WXRL
2003	KNC	A	20	0	1	0	14	9	42.3	40	19	28	0	—	.288	-7	1.39	2.55	4.69	5.13	9.4	5.1	4.0	0.2	2.1	—
2004	KNC	A	21	1	0	16	25	0	30.0	16	6	49	0	—	.291	25	0.73	0.30	3.25	2.60	7.2	2.6	8.5	0.3	9.2	—
2004	MID	AA	21	2	0	2	13	0	18.0	10	15	32	0	—	.312	17	1.39	1.50	4.24	2.65	6.4	8.5	11.6	0.5	5.6	—
2004	SAC	AAA	21	1	2	1	11	0	13.7	10	9	21	1	—	.333	13	1.39	3.94	3.95	3.95	6.6	5.9	10.5	0.7	2.5	—
2005	MID	AA	22	0	0	6	10	0	16.7	9	9	30	1	57%	.286	15	1.08	1.08	3.45	2.87	6.3	6.3	12.1	0.6	4.8	—
2005	SAC	AAA	22	3	6	20	44	0	48.3	45	20	73	6	43%	.358	18	1.35	4.47	3.94	5.62	8.6	3.6	10.1	1.3	-0.1	—
2006	OAK	MLB	23	3	3	1	24	3	48.0	43	25	44	6	38%	.275	10	1.40	4.41	4.51	5.08	7.8	4.8	8.3	1.1	5.1	0.6

Breakout: 26% Improve: 51% Collapse: 18% Attrition: 28% Comparables: Carl Erskine, Antonio Osuna, Fernando Cabrera

The A's did something smart with Garcia, giving him a head start at Midland after a 2004 in which he was promoted all the way from Kane County to the majors, his ERAs increasing in a Fibonacci sequence at each level. He rewarded them by turning in the best control numbers of his career at Sacramento. Though his ERA was slightly distorted by a very high BABIP, both his over-the-top fastball and breaking stuff are considered top shelf, so there's no concern about his ability to miss bats. His future contains an equal mix of Ugueth Urbina and Chad Harville.

RICH HARDEN **Bats: L Throws: R** Height: 6' 1" Weight: 180 Born: November 30, 1981 Age: 24

YEAR	TM	LVL	AGE	W	L	SV	G	GS	IP	H	BB	SO	HR	GB%	BABIP	STUFF	WHIP	ERA	PERA	EQERA	EQH9	EQBB9	EQSO9	EQHR9	VORP	WXRL
2003	SAC	AAA	21	9	4	0	16	14	88.7	72	35	91	6	—	.274	29	1.21	3.15	3.99	3.99	7.9	4.0	8.2	0.8	15.3	—
2003	OAK	MLB	21	5	4	0	15	13	74.7	72	40	67	5	51%	.325	27	1.50	4.46	3.98	4.34	8.6	4.7	7.8	0.6	11.2	1.9
2004	OAK	MLB	22	11	7	0	31	31	189.7	171	81	167	16	46%	.295	29	1.33	3.99	3.84	3.98	8.2	3.6	7.4	0.7	42.3	5.0
2005	OAK	MLB	23	10	5	0	22	19	128.0	93	43	121	7	43%	.257	43	1.06	2.53	3.23	3.02	7.3	3.1	8.6	0.5	40.7	5.2
2006	*OAK*	*MLB*	*24*	*12*	*8*	*0*	*31*	*27*	*174.3*	*153*	*63*	*153*	*16*	*45%*	*.279*	*27*	*1.24*	*3.53*	*3.62*	*3.92*	*7.7*	*3.3*	*7.9*	*0.8*	*35.7*	*4.9*

Breakout: 18% Improve: 40% Collapse: 21% Attrition: 5% Comparables: Josh Beckett, Andy Messersmith, Steve Busby

Since the 2004 All-Star Break, Harden has gone 18–7 with a 2.95 ERA, and 197 strikeouts against 76 walks in 226 innings pitched. There's no doubt that he has the stuff to post a line like that over a full season, but is he capable of staying healthy? The A's believe that his lat and right shoulder problems were related to a torn labrum in his *non-pitching* shoulder, on which he had corrective surgery in October (Harden should be back in plenty of time for spring training). His smooth mechanics are a point in his favor, as is the fact that the A's are vested in him in the form of a long-term contract. Still, the most likely scenario is embodied in the form of his #1 comparable, Josh Beckett, a pitcher who usually dazzles but occasionally frustrates.

DANNY HAREN **Bats: R Throws: R** Height: 6' 5" Weight: 220 Born: September 17, 1980 Age: 25

YEAR	TM	LVL	AGE	W	L	SV	G	GS	IP	H	BB	SO	HR	GB%	BABIP	STUFF	WHIP	ERA	PERA	EQERA	EQH9	EQBB9	EQSO9	EQHR9	VORP	WXRL
2003	TEN	AA	22	6	0	0	8	8	55.0	36	6	49	2	—	.227	25	0.76	0.82	3.51	2.81	7.7	1.1	5.6	0.7	15.9	—
2003	MEM	AAA	22	2	1	0	8	8	45.7	50	8	35	6	—	.301	7	1.27	4.92	5.28	5.68	10.6	1.8	6.1	1.8	-0.4	—
2003	SLN	MLB	22	3	7	0	14	14	72.7	84	22	43	9	43%	.319	1	1.46	5.08	4.81	5.67	10.2	2.5	4.8	1.1	1.7	1.4
2004	MEM	AAA	23	11	4	0	21	21	128.0	137	33	150	19	—	.351	14	1.33	4.15	4.44	4.72	9.4	2.5	7.9	1.5	12.5	—
2004	SLN	MLB	23	3	3	0	14	5	46.0	45	17	32	4	48%	.306	3	1.35	4.50	4.37	4.76	9.3	3.0	5.6	0.8	6.0	0.4
2005	OAK	MLB	24	14	12	0	34	34	217.0	212	53	163	26	47%	.290	18	1.22	3.73	4.12	4.21	9.1	2.2	6.8	1.0	39.5	5.3
2006	*OAK*	*MLB*	*25*	*12*	*10*	*0*	*32*	*29*	*191.7*	*195*	*47*	*135*	*23*	*46%*	*.290*	*18*	*1.26*	*3.93*	*4.17*	*4.30*	*9.0*	*2.3*	*6.3*	*1.0*	*31.1*	*4.6*

Breakout: 27% Improve: 60% Collapse: 9% Attrition: 2% Comparables: John Lackey, Ben McDonald, Doc Medich

Danny Haren, not Joe Blanton, is the pitcher poised to become Watson to Harden's Holmes. His slider and a two-seamer with good late movement are natural complements to one another, and he has the command to throw the latter pitch either up or down in the zone. His groundball rate was notably improved over his minor league numbers, suggesting that he's buying into the A's philosophy of taking advantage of the defense. In short, he's a breakout candidate.

JOE KENNEDY **Bats: R Throws: L** Height: 6' 4" Weight: 230 Born: May 24, 1979 Age: 27

YEAR	TM	LVL	AGE	W	L	SV	G	GS	IP	H	BB	SO	HR	GB%	BABIP	STUFF	WHIP	ERA	PERA	EQERA	EQH9	EQBB9	EQSO9	EQHR9	VORP	WXRL
2003	TBA	MLB	24	3	12	1	32	22	133.7	167	47	77	19	46%	.325	-9	1.60	6.13	5.12	6.58	10.8	3.1	5.0	1.2	-11.5	-0.5
2004	COL	MLB	25	9	7	0	27	27	162.3	163	67	117	17	51%	.304	14	1.42	3.66	4.45	3.41	8.7	3.4	5.7	0.8	41.3	4.5
2005	COL	MLB	26	4	8	0	16	16	92.0	128	44	52	12	48%	.364	-8	1.87	7.04	5.18	6.84	10.7	3.8	4.4	1.0	-20.5	-1.5
2005	OAK	MLB	26	4	5	0	19	8	60.7	64	20	45	8	41%	.299	4	1.38	4.45	4.57	4.87	9.4	3.0	6.6	1.2	6.3	0.3
2006	*OAK*	*MLB*	*27*	*9*	*9*	*1*	*40*	*22*	*152.0*	*163*	*50*	*92*	*19*	*45%*	*.293*	*2*	*1.40*	*4.50*	*4.79*	*4.99*	*9.5*	*3.0*	*5.4*	*1.1*	*14.3*	*2.4*

Breakout: 30% Improve: 71% Collapse: 12% Attrition: 6% Comparables: Dave LaPoint, Jerry Reuss, Bill Travers

Those pitching lines aren't easy on the eyes because he has been victimized by high altitude and even higher BABIPs, but there's nothing wrong with Kennedy, who most teams would be happy to have as their #4 starter. In the meantime, he'll work out of the bullpen to make room for Esteban Loaiza. While Kennedy doesn't have the big out pitch that you'd naturally associate with an ace reliever, the job could be easier on his somewhat unorthodox mechanics, and he has good splits there—a 2.73 ERA in 21 appearances—over his career.

DAN MEYER   **Bats: R Throws: L**   Height: 6' 3"   Weight: 190   Born: July 3, 1981   Age: 24

YEAR	TM	LVL	AGE	W	L	SV	G	GS	IP	H	BB	SO	HR	GB%	BABIP	STUFF	WHIP	ERA	PERA	EQERA	EQH9	EQBB9	EQSO9	EQHR9	VORP	WXRL
2003	ROM	A	22	4	4	0	15	15	81.7	76	15	95	6	—	.318	2	1.11	2.86	5.40	6.22	10.4	2.0	6.3	1.9	-5.3	—
2003	MYR	A+	22	3	6	0	13	13	78.3	69	17	63	7	—	.265	-3	1.10	2.87	5.67	4.93	9.9	2.3	5.4	2.0	5.4	—
2004	GRN	AA	23	6	3	0	14	13	65.0	50	12	86	1	—	.314	38	0.95	2.22	3.03	3.61	8.1	1.9	7.8	0.3	13.8	—
2004	RIC	AAA	23	3	3	0	12	11	61.3	62	25	60	6	—	.322	16	1.42	2.79	4.45	3.71	9.0	3.9	7.1	1.0	12.7	—
2005	SAC	AAA	24	2	8	0	19	17	89.0	101	43	63	15	39%	.313	-24	1.62	5.36	6.22	6.11	10.2	4.4	4.7	1.7	-5.0	—
2006	*OAK*	*MLB*	*24*	*6*	*7*	*0*	*28*	*17*	*106.0*	*116*	*41*	*66*	*18*	*38%*	*.288*	*-1*	*1.48*	*5.24*	*5.49*	*5.57*	*9.6*	*3.5*	*5.6*	*1.4*	*2.1*	*0.9*

Breakout: 9%   Improve: 33%   Collapse: 16%   Attrition: 0%   Comparables: Mike McCormick, Allen Watson, Chris Haney

We were worried about Meyer's 2004 numbers, which featured low home run totals that seemed to be due to the big parks of the Atlanta system rather than any ability of his to keep the ball down. Indeed, his home run rate blew up on him in 2005, but then so did a lot of things, including his shoulder. Although he's supposed to be healthy to start 2006, the sense is that his organization has already re-adjusted their expectations. One takeaway here is that you can't look at ERA projections in a vacuum when evaluating pitchers. We projected a 4.45 EqERA for Meyer last year, versus a 3.86 for Tim Hudson, a meaningful difference, but one that would be well worth accepting for the much bigger difference in their price tags. But we also projected nearly twice as many innings for Hudson, simply because he'd shown time and time again that his arm could hold up over a major league season, whereas Meyer endured comparatively light workloads in the minor leagues. That durability is a huge component of what separates a perennial All-Star from a prospect. Until a pitcher demonstrates that it's a part of his skill set, his valuation must be hedged significantly.

RICARDO RINCON   **Bats: L Throws: L**   Height: 5' 10"   Weight: 188   Born: April 13, 1970   Age: 36

YEAR	TM	LVL	AGE	W	L	SV	G	GS	IP	H	BB	SO	HR	GB%	BABIP	STUFF	WHIP	ERA	PERA	EQERA	EQH9	EQBB9	EQSO9	EQHR9	VORP	WXRL
2003	OAK	MLB	33	8	4	0	64	0	55.3	45	32	40	4	43%	.270	-1	1.39	3.25	4.67	3.33	8.2	5.3	6.5	0.7	16.0	1.0
2004	OAK	MLB	34	1	1	0	67	0	44.0	45	22	40	3	45%	.316	7	1.52	3.68	3.80	4.20	8.8	4.0	7.6	0.6	9.0	1.2
2005	OAK	MLB	35	1	1	0	67	0	37.3	34	20	27	7	42%	.260	-15	1.45	4.34	5.89	4.42	9.1	4.9	6.6	1.7	5.0	0.5
2006	*SLN*	*MLB*	*36*	*2*	*1*	*1*	*34*	*0*	*29.0*	*27*	*15*	*24*	*3*	*43%*	*.284*	*-5*	*1.44*	*4.04*	*4.49*	*5.55*	*8.3*	*4.2*	*6.9*	*0.9*	*3.9*	

Breakout: 15%   Improve: 28%   Collapse: 54%   Attrition: 40%   Comparables: John Franco, Grant Jackson, Bob McClure

Rincon has become the Sears of the left-handed relief market, competing more on the strength of a brand name that appeals to the not-quite-senile crowd than any kind of compelling product offering. Not coincidentally, he was picked up by Tony LaRussa. Rincon's command has been shot for some time now, though LaRussa could consider restricting his work to 0-2 counts.

KIRK SAARLOOS   **Bats: R Throws: R**   Height: 6' 0"   Weight: 180   Born: May 23, 1979   Age: 27

YEAR	TM	LVL	AGE	W	L	SV	G	GS	IP	H	BB	SO	HR	GB%	BABIP	STUFF	WHIP	ERA	PERA	EQERA	EQH9	EQBB9	EQSO9	EQHR9	VORP	WXRL
2003	NWO	AAA	24	5	0	0	13	7	61.3	54	11	34	4	—	.250	0	1.06	3.08	4.50	4.66	9.2	2.0	4.3	0.9	6.1	—
2003	HOU	MLB	24	2	1	0	36	4	49.3	55	17	43	4	56%	.342	7	1.46	4.93	3.78	5.58	9.7	2.7	7.0	0.7	0.2	0.1
2004	OAK	MLB	25	2	1	0	6	5	24.3	27	12	10	4	59%	.284	-18	1.60	4.44	6.29	4.44	10.4	4.1	3.3	1.5	4.1	0.5
2005	OAK	MLB	26	10	9	0	29	27	159.7	170	54	53	11	57%	.291	0	1.40	4.17	4.89	4.49	10.2	3.1	3.0	0.6	27.8	4.0
2006	*OAK*	*MLB*	*27*	*8*	*9*	*0*	*35*	*22*	*143.3*	*164*	*44*	*58*	*15*	*54%*	*.296*	*-7*	*1.45*	*4.70*	*4.90*	*5.29*	*10.1*	*2.8*	*3.6*	*0.9*	*9.7*	*1.8*

Breakout: 13%   Improve: 37%   Collapse: 28%   Attrition: 8%   Comparables: Bill Swift, Bob Shaw, Joe Horlen

You take a season like this when you can get it, Cornejo-like strikeout rate and all, but a sign of how far things have come is that pretty much nobody takes it seriously anymore, to the point that Beane couldn't churn up so much as a single Ken Rosenthal trade rumor or Buster Olney bullet point. That PECOTA ain't half bad, actually. It's a testament to how your range of options expands when you combine an extreme groundball pitcher with a great infield defense.

HUSTON STREET   **Bats: R Throws: R**   Height: 6' 0"   Weight: 190   Born: August 2, 1983   Age: 22

YEAR	TM	LVL	AGE	W	L	SV	G	GS	IP	H	BB	SO	HR	GB%	BABIP	STUFF	WHIP	ERA	PERA	EQERA	EQH9	EQBB9	EQSO9	EQHR9	VORP	WXRL
2005	OAK	MLB	21	5	1	23	67	0	78.3	53	26	72	3	44%	.253	34	1.01	1.72	3.18	2.00	7.0	3.1	8.4	0.4	33.3	4.4
2006	*OAK*	*MLB*	*22*	*5*	*4*	*25*	*61*	*0*	*67.0*	*57*	*22*	*60*	*5*	*44%*	*.273*	*17*	*1.17*	*3.03*	*3.16*	*3.63*	*7.4*	*3.0*	*8.1*	*0.7*	*16.8*	*2.4*

Breakout: 2%   Improve: 2%   Collapse: 84%   Attrition: 27%   Comparables: Oscar Villarreal, Chad Cordero, Chet Nichols

Understand, Oakland fans, that these peripherals are ordinarily associated with an ERA of about 3.00. That's why Street's Collapse rate is what it is, not because PECOTA expects him to turn into a pumpkin. Otherwise, enjoy your Rookie of the Year, who by our Adjusted Runs Prevented metric was the best relief pitcher in baseball last year. We're on thin territory when it comes to putting his future into context; it's rare for a pitcher to be born, bred, and groomed as a closer, and to achieve this kind of success at so young an age. Bruce Sutter forms a natural point of departure, but he didn't reach the majors until he was 23, and you'd have to pretend Street's heavy two-seamer was a splitter. Although Street has a very bright future, he's not in the Lidge/Rivera class just yet, and probably never will be on a consistent basis.

JAY WITASICK **Bats: R Throws: R** Height: 6′ 4″ Weight: 230 Born: August 28, 1972 Age: 33

YEAR	TM	LVL	AGE	W	L	SV	G	GS	IP	H	BB	SO	HR	GB%	BABIP	STUFF	WHIP	ERA	PERA	EQERA	EQH9	EQBB9	EQSO9	EQHR9	VORP	WXRL
2003	SDN	MLB	30	3	7	2	46	0	45.7	42	25	42	6	54%	.290	-2	1.47	4.53	4.73	4.93	8.7	4.3	7.5	1.2	3.3	0.8
2004	SDN	MLB	31	0	1	1	44	0	61.7	57	26	57	8	51%	.290	3	1.35	3.21	4.55	4.40	8.5	3.5	7.3	1.2	10.1	-0.2
2005	COL	MLB	32	0	4	0	32	0	35.7	27	12	40	2	54%	.287	27	1.09	2.52	3.28	2.52	7.1	2.8	9.1	0.5	11.4	0.9
2005	OAK	MLB	32	1	1	1	28	0	27.7	26	17	33	2	47%	.324	18	1.55	3.25	3.86	4.82	8.4	5.5	10.6	0.6	2.7	0.2
2006	*OAK*	*MLB*	*33*	*4*	*3*	*3*	*59*	*1*	*68.3*	*65*	*27*	*57*	*7*	*47%*	*.289*	*5*	*1.34*	*3.98*	*4.15*	*4.48*	*8.3*	*3.6*	*7.5*	*0.9*	*11.1*	*0.9*

Breakout: 21% Improve: 47% Collapse: 26% Attrition: 9% Comparables: Jim Gott, Dick Tidrow, Don McMahon

Witasick is the only man on the current roster whose days in green and gold overlapped with Mark McGwire's, though we have to remember him as a rookie and ignore the brief layovers in Edmonton, Kansas City, San Diego (twice), New York, Fresno, San Francisco, Lake Elsinore, Portland, Colorado Springs, and Denver. Remember to print your boarding passes early. His success at all of those levels has depended on whether he could command his fastball for 20 innings at a time. While you'd like to make the case that he learned something in Denver about the importance of avoiding gratuitous baserunners, chances are we're in for the usual bumpy ride.

KEIICHI YABU **Bats: R Throws: R** Height: 6′ 0″ Weight: 200 Born: September 28, 1968 Age: 37

YEAR	TM	LVL	AGE	W	L	SV	G	GS	IP	H	BB	SO	HR	GB%	BABIP	STUFF	WHIP	ERA	PERA	EQERA	EQH9	EQBB9	EQSO9	EQHR9	VORP	WXRL
2003	HNS	JPL	34	8	3	0	23	15	97.7	97	27	67	13	—	.271	0	1.27	0.18	4.64	4.64	9.0	2.9	5.2	1.0	10.1	—
2004	HNS	JPL	35	6	9	0	19	18	116.3	108	36	75	8	—	.267	17	1.24	3.02	4.19	3.39	8.3	3.0	4.8	0.5	27.4	—
2005	OAK	MLB	36	4	0	1	40	0	58.0	64	26	44	6	44%	.335	0	1.55	4.50	4.76	5.22	10.0	4.0	6.8	0.9	3.1	0.2
2006	*COL*	*MLB*	*37*	*2*	*2*	*1*	*33*	*0*	*43.0*	*50*	*18*	*31*	*5*	*47%*	*.327*	*-4*	*1.57*	*4.88*	*4.77*	*5.23*	*9.5*	*3.3*	*6.4*	*0.9*	*4.8*	*0.3*

Breakout: 32% Improve: 51% Collapse: 34% Attrition: 24% Comparables: Giovanni Carrara, Barney Schultz, Terry Leach

We were wondering where we might find the Japanese Giovanni Carrara. Yabu performed more or less as his Davenport Translations had advertised, intermittently fooling and appetizing hitters with his four-pitch repertoire. The hope may have been to find someone who could go Takatsu on the league for 50 innings before the scouting reports caught up to him, but that never materialized. He's signed in Denver, whose forest landscapes will remind him of his home in Mie Prefecture.

BARRY ZITO **Bats: L Throws: L** Height: 6′ 4″ Weight: 205 Born: May 13, 1978 Age: 28

YEAR	TM	LVL	AGE	W	L	SV	G	GS	IP	H	BB	SO	HR	GB%	BABIP	STUFF	WHIP	ERA	PERA	EQERA	EQH9	EQBB9	EQSO9	EQHR9	VORP	WXRL
2003	OAK	MLB	25	14	12	0	35	35	231.7	186	88	146	19	44%	.244	16	1.18	3.30	4.35	3.74	8.2	3.5	5.7	0.7	56.1	6.7
2004	OAK	MLB	26	11	11	0	34	34	213.0	216	81	163	28	40%	.299	12	1.39	4.48	4.50	4.58	9.1	3.2	6.4	1.1	32.5	4.6
2005	OAK	MLB	27	14	13	0	35	35	228.3	185	89	171	26	42%	.249	15	1.20	3.86	4.53	4.16	8.3	3.6	6.9	1.0	41.1	5.5
2006	OAK	MLB	28	13	10	0	32	32	206.3	195	77	148	24	42%	.275	15	1.32	4.07	4.22	4.43	8.3	3.4	6.4	1.0	30.8	4.7

Breakout: 11% Improve: 51% Collapse: 19% Attrition: 2% Comparables: Chuck Finley, Vinegar Bend Mizell, Wilson Alvarez

Zito was probably overrated for some period of time on the basis of a well-cultivated public image and an ERA that was a little ahead of his peripherals, but he's a very valuable pitcher. He helped his cause by adding a two-seamer toward the middle of the 2004 season, a pitch that doesn't overwhelm anyone but allows him to generate a few extra double plays, something that had been a problem in the past. For some better sense of context, that 30.8 VORP projects him to rate as the 32nd best pitcher in the majors next year, so he's just on the fringe between being a plus #2 and a true #1.

Line Outs

Position/Player	TM	LVL	AGE	PA	R	2B	3B	HR	RBI	BB	SO	SB-CS	SPEED	BA/OBP/SLG	MLVR	EQBA/OBP/SLG	EQA	VORP
UT F. Bynum*	SAC	AAA	25	421	56	16	9	2	40	38	83	23-7	7.7	.278/.347/.384	-.051	.256/.315/.344	.238	-4.8
2/S M. Rouse*	SAC	AAA	25	537	69	30	3	7	72	59	115	2-4	4.6	.269/.358/.390	-.028	.244/.322/.344	.237	2.3
CF S. Stanley*	MID	AA	25	582	87	26	4	6	46	61	62	8-8	5.1	.290/.364/.391	.049	.250/.318/.336	.233	-8.4

Pitcher	TM	LVL	AGE	W	L	SV	IP	H	BB	SO	HR	GB%	BABIP	STUFF	WHIP	ERA	PERA	EQERA	EQH9	EQBB9	EQSO9	EQHR9	VORP
S. Etherton	SAC	AAA	28	7	7	0	112.3	93	30	99	11	29%	.262	5	1.10	2.72	4.70	4.19	8.4	2.7	5.6	1.2	16.8
C. Mabeus	SAC	AAA	26	9	2	1	62.0	61	24	72	4	43%	.352	5	1.37	4.21	4.11	4.99	9.0	3.7	7.3	0.7	4.2
J. Rheinecker*	SAC	AAA	26	4	0	0	45.7	29	14	24	0	58%	.213	6	0.94	1.77	4.22	3.38	7.2	3.2	3.6	0.2	10.5

Mike Rouse and **Freddy Bynum** round out the 40-man roster as utility suspects. Of the two, Bynum can play all of the positions some of the time, and Rouse plays some of the positions all of the time, but neither is good enough to play all of the positions all of the time. **Steve Stanley's** allure has faded, even as a *Moneyball* curiosity, though the A's can probably afford to give him one last look in Sacramento.

We didn't list a lot of pitchers for the A's organization, simply because while the group of the 15 or so best arms is as good as any in baseball, the system depth behind it is clearly among the weakest. This surely played a part in Oakland going heavy on arms in the June draft. Billy Beane is a great poker player, but he can't do much when he's short-stacked. We'll start our tour with the two most promising selections from that draft, **Craig Italiano** and **Jared Lansford** (son of Carney), both of whom started in the Arizona Rookie League. Italiano is thought of as the higher upside guy and Lansford the more polished, a sentiment supported by their very limited statistical records. The player most likely to appear in the majors next year is **Chris Mabeus,** a minor league reliever who doesn't excite scouts in spite of good strikeout rates. His BABIPs are high, which could be attributed to either bad luck or a lack of finish on his pitches. Beyond that, there isn't much. **Seth Etherton** was picked up by the Padres in the Rule 5 draft; his extreme flyball rates would doom him in 29 of the 30 big league parks, but PETCO might be the exception. **John Rheinecker** lost most of his season to a torn tendon in his middle finger.

Philadelphia Phillies

Almost everything wrong with the Ed Wade regime in Philadelphia came into sharp focus shortly after the Phillies GM was fired in October. Wade's teams were mediocre and complacent, and when the opportunity was there, he was unwilling to pull the trigger on important deals. The 2005 Phillies won 88 games and weren't eliminated from wild-card contention until the last day of the season. After eight years and plenty of resources to work with in recent seasons, that's as good as it got under Wade.

The Phillies hired veteran baseball man Pat Gillick to replace Wade on November 2. Three weeks later, Gillick consummated a deal with the White Sox that addressed three major problems in one bold stroke. First, he moved Jim Thome and his huge contract to clear first base for Rookie of the Year Ryan Howard. He had to pay $22 million to the Sox to make the deal happen, but that was merely acknowledging that Wade had substantially overpaid for Thome in 2002.

Second, Gillick acquired a legitimate big-league centerfielder to solidify a problem position that had plagued the Phillies for most of the past ten years. Kenny Lofton and Jason Michaels did good jobs in center in platoon roles in 2005, but the 39-year-old Lofton has little upside, especially when compared to the 28-year-old Rowand. Granted, Rowand is no star, but considering the alternative, he's worth the risk.

Third, Gillick began the process of restocking the farm system, which has been feeble in recent years. None of the Phillies' six top farm clubs had a winning record last year, and their aggregate winning percentage of .429 was the worst in MLB. The acquisition of pitching prospects Gio Gonzalez and Daniel Haigwood are a clear indication that Gillick is committed to growing some young talent.

The centerfield mess was emblematic of Wade's inability to address the team's pressing problems—pressing, at least, if your real goal is to win instead of merely turning a nice profit. The club's actual versus projected records from 1997–2004 under Terry Francona and Larry Bowa confirm that picture (see table 1). Wade took over an overachieving team when he became GM in 1998, and his first squad overachieved again. That gave rise to a false optimism about how much potential the club actually

PHILLIES PROSPECTUS

2005 record: 88–74; Second place, NL East

Pythagenport record: 89–73

Runs scored per game: 4.98 (2nd in NL)

Runs allowed per game: 4.48 (8th in NL)

Team EqA: .267 (3rd in NL)

2005 Batters Age: 30.5 (6th oldest in NL)

2005 Pitchers Age: 29.9 (5th oldest in NL)

Ballpark: Citizen's Bank Park; Moderate hitter's park; Park Factor of 1.032

2005: The perennially-talented and perennially-disappointing Phillies failed again.

2006: Year One of Pat Gillick's unretirement finds the Phillies still sporting pronounced flaws but a dangerous team.

had, which in turn led to unnecessary panic when the club went backwards the next two years.

That panic resulted in Francona's banishment and Bowa's return, on the theory that Bowa would be better able to handle the influx of high-salaried veterans, and would kick some butt and call out the slackers. Neither assumption proved true, as Phillies prospects like Pat Burrell failed to produce and Bowa's abrasive style pushed Scott Rolen out of town. Meanwhile, Francona went on to Boston and demonstrated that his style of managing was

TABLE 1. PHILLIES ACTUAL VS. PROJECTED RECORDS

Year	Actual	Projected	Diff
1997	68–94	63–99	+5
1998	75–87	71–91	+4
1999	77–85	81–81	−4
2000	65–97	69–93	−4
2001	86–76	84–78	+2
2002	80–81	79–82	+1
2003	86–76	90–72	−4
2004	86–76	86–76	0

quite capable of coping with a fractious, veteran team loaded with big egos and even bigger salaries.

The Rowand trade's benefit to the farm system represents a halting first step to fixing what had been a festering sore on the body of the Wade administration. During his exit press conference, Wade was asked if he thought the declining farm system contributed to his dismissal. Perhaps not quite understanding the question or the extent of his player development problem, Wade answered, "Oh, I would like to think that I get a lot of credit for the farm system," he said, "vis-à-vis Chase Utley, Ryan Howard, Robinson Tejeda, Eude Brito . . . Ryan Madson, [and] the fact that on my watch, Burrell came . . . I won't take full credit for it because it's not appropriate, but our scouting staff and our development staff, even though we've been hamstrung in certain respects . . . were still able enough to have good enough players in the farm system, in the pipeline, to come up here and take us within five minutes of being in the postseason this year."

Wade apparently didn't realize how light this harvest was. In the past 10 years, the productivity of the Phillies organization has been depressing in almost every way. Table 2 shows the number of players developed by the Phillies as well as 10 selected major league organizations since 1996: the other NL East teams aside from the Marlins, the two other NL clubs who developed fewer player than the Phillies, the two other NL clubs who developed the most players, the last two World Series winners, plus the Yankees and Athletics

Players shown by organization that developed them; organization is credited with developing a major league player if they originally drafted or signed him, unless they released him before he first played in Double-A or Triple-A;

Regular season = 100 games for position players; "w/Club" totals reflect the Games/IP/Seasons played with the parent club that developed the player

Here are the Phillies organization's overall rankings in various categories among the 26 longstanding franchises (not including the four 1990s expansion franchises, who are understandably at the bottom in most categories):

- A lowly 23rd in total big league players developed.

- Last in the number of position players, player seasons, and games played; 24th in number of regular player seasons; but 9th–12th in how much those players played with the Phillies (player seasons, games, regular seasons).

- In terms of developing pitchers, the Phillies were 14th in raw numbers, 22nd in starting pitcher seasons and SP innings pitched, 25th in SP regular seasons, but 15th in SP seasons with the club, 14th in SP IP with the club, and 18th in SP regular seasons with the club.

- Only in relief pitching, the least important aspect, did the organization rise to mediocre, ranking 12th in relief seasons, 11th in relief innings pitched, and 13th in relief regular seasons.

One of the excuses the organization makes for this showing is that they have used many of their prospects in trades for veterans like Billy Wagner, and that signing free agents cost the team many high draft picks in the past five years, exacerbating their player development problem. Fair enough, but that certainly wasn't true during the whole of Wade's tenure, and it didn't produce any October

TABLE 2. MAJOR LEAGUE ORGANIZATIONAL PRODUCTIVITY, 1996–2005

Club	Players	Batters	Pitchers	Total Games	Total Regular Seasons	Games w/Club	Regular Seasons w/Club	Total Starting Pitcher Seasons	Total SP IP	SP IP w/Club	Total Relief Pitcher Seasons	Total RP IP	RP IP w/ Club
ATL	135	59	76	21001	108	9661	55	112	12954	4108	184	5974	1526
WAS	128	67	61	27121	137	9080	52	77	9579	2491	158	4728	1218
NYA	127	64	63	26185	129	6786	37	100	11406	3816	137	4602	1421
OAK	126	70	56	24241	120	8382	47	74	9511	5090	138	5551	909
LAN	125	61	64	23663	110	7289	37	130	15734	5630	173	6082	1362
NYN	122	57	65	18558	81	5248	26	84	8208	2312	160	5453	645
CHA	106	47	59	16679	78	8382	40	79	8620	4865	158	5535	1029
BOS	98	50	48	15085	75	4820	24	92	11215	1384	106	4006	662
PHI	**92**	**36**	**56**	**11716**	**61**	**6968**	**38**	**68**	**7530**	**3678**	**148**	**5546**	**1502**
CIN	87	46	41	15912	79	6626	36	43	4188	1083	138	5910	1515
MIL	79	41	38	14906	85	5411	31	67	7904	3659	80	2667	700

baseball. Right now, the higher levels of the Phillies' system are virtually devoid of talent. One scout assigned to evaluate the Philadelphia Double-A and Triple-A clubs for potential trades during 2005 found no one worth recommending to his GM aside from Gavin Floyd and Ryan Howard. The Philadelphia system is highly unlikely to provide much help in the next two years.

The Phillies are a paradigm of misguided loyalty. The hiring of an experienced outsider, Gillick, to run the team, represents a departure from the rationale behind Wade's hiring back in 1998, which was simply that he had "earned" the job—as Wade himself put it—through long service to the organization.

An integral yet often overlooked element in the Phillies' lack of success over the past 22 years has been the club's undistinguished managerial procession. After Pat Corrales gained the unusual distinction of being fired while in first place during the last-hurrah 1983 season, the Phillies employed seven managers prior to Charlie Manuel, not counting interim seat-warmers: Paul Owens (1983–84), John Felske (1985–87), Lee Elia (1987–88), Nick Leyva (1989–1991), Jim Fregosi (1991–96), Terry Francona (1997–2000), and Larry Bowa (2001–04).

Three of those seven—Owens, Felske, and Leyva—never managed in the majors before taking the Phillies' helm. A fourth, Elia, never managed anywhere *after* Philly. A fifth, Bowa, created such a tempest with his tantrums in San Diego that he didn't even last a year and a half there, and had to wait 13 years before his second chance.

Only two of these seven skipper, Fregosi and Francona, have had any success as major league skippers. Fregosi guided the Angels to their first divisional title in 1979, then caught a tiger by its tail with the macho, over-the-hill, better-living-through-booze-and-chemistry gang known as the 1993 Phillies. Fregosi's management style in that championship season was very basic: sit back, chain-smoke his way through the games, and let the mullet-wearing veterans of "Macho Row" run the clubhouse. By the time he was fired three years later, Fregosi was just going through the motions. He has held only one managerial post since Philly dismissed him—in Toronto in 1999 and 2000, where he went 167–156 and led the Blue Jays to consecutive nondescript third-place finishes. Then there is Terry Francona, who got his ring with the most unlikely team of all.

The Phillies chose undistinguished caretaker managers perhaps because they had budgeted for undistinguished teams. As salaries escalated in the late 1990s, Philadelphia acted like a cash-strapped small-market club that couldn't afford to compete. In the current decade, club ownership slowly ratcheted up its payroll to mid-market status until *finally,* with the opening of Citizens Bank Park, Philadelphia started acting like the heavyweight it really is. During Francona's last three years

TABLE 3. A PENNY SAVED IS A PENNY SAVED: PHILLIES PAYROLL RANKING

Year	Rank	% of Atlanta
Francona		
1997	23	53.5
1998	22	48.2
1999	23	38.4
2000	21	44.3
Bowa		
2001	17	59.7
2002	15	65.9
2003	10	79.5
2004	8	99.5

(1998–2000), the team's average salary was less than half of the Braves and Mets. When Francona left, the team's average salary ranked 21st in the majors. And in Bowa's four-year reign of terror in the Phillies clubhouse, it rose and eventually cracked the top ten in 2004. In 2005, Charlie Manuel had the luxury of overseeing a squad with the third-highest payroll in the game, 26 percent higher than the Braves. (See table 3.)

Philadelphia's reputation as a declining city distorts just how large the Philadelphia market still is. When one splits up the population or TV Households of the two-team markets, there are only three teams with bigger markets than the Phillies: the Yankees and Mets (21.2 million people and 6.9 million TV Households to divvy up), and the Dodgers (12.0 million Angelenos, *not* including the 4.4 million suburbanites in Angels territory in Orange and Riverside Counties). If you ever wondered why Arte Moreno changed his team's name, it's because he wants the Angels to carve out a bigger share of the 5.2 million TV Households in the L.A.-designated Market Area. That's it.

Mind you, market size is disproportionate to a team's fan base. The Cubs and Red Sox, housed in the third- and fifth-largest media markets (in terms of television households), respectively, boast a fan base covering several states, and play to perennially packed houses. The Braves, located in the country's ninth-largest market in Atlanta, also have a broad fan base, but have trouble selling out, even in the postseason. The Phillies, while they may not have fans dispersed through as wide a geographic area as some of their competitors, play in the fourth largest media market in the country.

That size offers the team a financial advantage over two-thirds of major league teams when it comes time to sign players. If they can't—or choose not to—compete on a level financial field with the aforementioned clubs, it is

because do not bring in additional revenue from either its own network or one of the congolomerate's subsidiaries. The reason for that: they are not owned by a media conglomerate or have a controlling interest in their own network like the Yankees, Mets, Cubs Red Sox and Braves, or like the Dodgers used to.

The Phillies' failures come back to management. Under Ed Wade, Philadelphia let a golden opportunity to overtake Atlanta slip away. Meanwhile, Boston and Chicago, cities that hadn't celebrated baseball titles since the Wilson administration, were handing out World Series rings.Perhaps Philadelphia's fortunes will change under Pat Gillick. At least the initial signs are positive.

HITTERS

BOBBY ABREU — RF — Bats: L Throws: R — Height: 6' 0" — Weight: 186 — Born: March 11, 1974 — Age: 32

YEAR	TM	LVL	AGE	PA	R	2B	3B	HR	RBI	BB	SO	SB	CS	SPEED	BA	OBP	SLG	MLVR	EQBA	EQOBP	EQSLG	EQA	VORP	DEFENSE	
2003	PHI	MLB	29	695	99	35	1	20	101	109	126	22	9	5.7	.300	.409	.468	.247	.299	.407	.472	.305	43.0	154-RF	0
2004	PHI	MLB	30	713	118	47	1	30	105	127	116	40	5	6.8	.301	.428	.544	.349	.293	.419	.531	.326	73.5	155-RF	2
2005	PHI	MLB	31	719	104	37	1	24	102	117	134	31	9	6.4	.286	.405	.474	.217	.278	.398	.469	.302	47.0	154-RF	-4
2006	PHI	MLB	32	645	103	33	3	22	84	100	113	23	7	5.8	.286	.400	.482	.184	.285	.401	.484	.301	34.3	150-RF	-1

Breakout: 3%   Improve: 32%   Collapse: 28%   Attrition: 1%   Comparables: Wally Moon, Von Hayes, Kirk Gibson

Abreu's fireworks at Comerica Park during the Home Run Derby finally gave him the national recognition he deserved. Then a relatively weak second half (.260/.376/.411) caused a lot of sniping from the press box and the cheap seats, with Abreu being blamed for the Phillies falling short again. Though still more than respectable, Abreu had his worst year with the bat since he became a Phillies regular in 1998. Only the third player (after Bonds pere and fils) to ever post seven consecutive 20-20 (HR/SB) seasons, Abreu is also the only Phillies player ever to post seven consecutive 100-walk seasons. Despite these marks, the club actively tried to move him in the offseason.

DAVID BELL — 3B — Bats: R Throws: R — Height: 5' 10" — Weight: 175 — Born: September 14, 1972 — Age: 33

YEAR	TM	LVL	AGE	PA	R	2B	3B	HR	RBI	BB	SO	SB	CS	SPEED	BA	OBP	SLG	MLVR	EQBA	EQOBP	EQSLG	EQA	VORP	DEFENSE	
2003	PHI	MLB	30	348	32	14	0	4	37	41	40	0	0	3.7	.195	.296	.283	-.257	.198	.295	.292	.218	-10.5	79-3B	6
2004	PHI	MLB	31	601	67	33	1	18	77	57	75	1	1	3.9	.291	.363	.458	.122	.285	.355	.446	.277	23.6	137-3B	6
2005	PHI	MLB	32	613	53	31	1	10	61	47	69	0	1	3.4	.248	.310	.361	-.119	.242	.306	.359	.234	-7.5	146-3B	9
2006	PHI	MLB	33	501	51	24	1	10	57	42	60	0	1	3.8	.252	.321	.377	-.107	.251	.322	.379	.238	0.8	118-3B	4

Breakout: 15%   Improve: 37%   Collapse: 36%   Attrition: 19%   Comparables: Joe Randa, Johnny Logan, John Valentin

Bell's back kept him sidelined for the first month of spring training, and it affected his performance the rest of the year. In his ten-year career, he has been above-average offensively only three times. Had an atypical and absolutely Grand Canyonesque left-right split: .400/.461/.593 vs. LHPs in 135 AB; .199/.260/.287 vs. RHP in 422 AB. Attempting to pull pitches from righties when your back is aching and your bat is slowing is not a good career move.

JAKE BLALOCK — LF — Bats: R Throws: R — Height: 6' 4" — Weight: 210 — Born: August 6, 1983 — Age: 22

YEAR	TM	LVL	AGE	PA	R	2B	3B	HR	RBI	BB	SO	SB	CS	SPEED	BA	OBP	SLG	MLVR	EQBA	EQOBP	EQSLG	EQA	VORP	DEFENSE			
2003	BAT	A-	19	297	36	23	7	5	31	30	81	9	4	6.5	.245	.323	.444	.132	.218	.282	.408	.238	-19.7	26-RF	2	27-LF	0
2004	LWD	A	20	592	81	40	2	16	90	61	126	4	3	4.1	.271	.350	.449	.153	.246	.309	.401	.246	-12.4	123-LF	2		
2005	CLR	A+	21	571	50	22	0	11	65	60	100	10	1	3.8	.279	.359	.388	.061	.242	.314	.351	.238	-23.1	124-LF	-1		
2006	PHI	MLB	22	497	55	23	1	13	56	42	104	5	2	4.1	.238	.307	.379	-.139	.238	.307	.381	.233	-8.0	117-LF	-2		

Breakout: 22%   Improve: 44%   Collapse: 26%   Attrition: 6%   Comparables: Kevin West, Garrett Long, Chris Duncan

In 2005, Blalock's performance went south. The strained comparisons between him and his brother Hank now seem downright silly. At 22, he's got the time to recover, but as a minor leaguer with neither top-notch hitting skills nor a true position—he was moved from third base to the outfield—he isn't a star in the making.

MICHAEL BOURN   **CF**   **Bats: L Throws: R**   Height: 5′ 11″   Weight: 180   Born: December 27, 1982   Age: 23

YEAR	TM	LVL	AGE	PA	R	2B	3B	HR	RBI	BB	SO	SB	CS	SPEED	BA	OBP	SLG	MLVR	EQBA	EQOBP	EQSLG	EQA	VORP	DEFENSE			
2003	BAT	A-	20	151	12	0	1	0	4	23	28	23	5	6.5	.280	.404	.296	.082	.246	.346	.261	.242	-15.4	18-LF	0	15-CF	1
2004	LWD	A	21	504	92	20	14	5	53	85	88	58	6	9.0	.315	.431	.467	.341	.292	.390	.420	.295	32.2	55-CF	0	50-RF	-3
2005	REA	AA	22	610	80	18	8	6	44	63	123	38	12	7.5	.268	.348	.364	-.008	.247	.324	.339	.242	-6.6	78-CF	9	52-RF	4
2006	PHI	MLB	23	506	65	20	6	4	35	49	97	24	7	5.8	.257	.333	.354	-.113	.256	.334	.356	.243	-2.1	119-CF	4		

Breakout: 11%   Improve: 27%   Collapse: 33%   Attrition: 10%   Comparables: Milt Cuyler, McKay Christensen, Michael Rodriguez

Bourn confronted the Rexrode Threshold in 2005 and failed to cross it, as his OBP and SLG plummeted when he moved up two levels to Double-A. Still, the organization is high on him, partly because of his outstanding speed, great range, and plus arm, but also because he hit well in the AFL and it needs to hype the potential of the limited pool of future talent it has. Because of the glut of center fielders in the higher levels of the organization, Bourn may get sent back to Reading in 2006.

PAT BURRELL   **LF**   **Bats: R Throws: R**   Height: 6′ 4″   Weight: 230   Born: October 10, 1976   Age: 29

YEAR	TM	LVL	AGE	PA	R	2B	3B	HR	RBI	BB	SO	SB	CS	SPEED	BA	OBP	SLG	MLVR	EQBA	EQOBP	EQSLG	EQA	VORP	DEFENSE	
2003	PHI	MLB	26	599	57	31	4	21	64	72	142	0	0	3.2	.209	.309	.404	-.075	.210	.309	.414	.249	-8.9	133-LF	2
2004	PHI	MLB	27	534	66	17	0	24	84	78	130	2	0	4.0	.257	.365	.455	.096	.251	.360	.445	.281	13.1	117-LF	3
2005	PHI	MLB	28	669	78	27	1	32	117	99	160	0	0	3.2	.281	.389	.504	.222	.271	.381	.495	.299	41.3	146-LF	-5
2006	PHI	MLB	29	599	79	26	2	27	87	83	134	1	0	3.8	.256	.364	.476	.093	.255	.364	.479	.282	19.7	140-LF	-5

Breakout: 18%   Improve: 36%   Collapse: 19%   Attrition: 9%   Comparables: Jay Buhner, Dwight Evans, Jeff Burroughs

Continuing his climb from the bottom of the Marianas Trench after his 2003 collapse, Burrell had the second-best season of career in 2005. He accomplished that by fattening up against southpaws (.318/.442/.552), just as he had in his career year of 2002. However, his range tumbled in left, possibly as a result of a foot problem that required offseason surgery. At 29, he should be able to post offensive totals similar to 2005 for years to come, and his range should rebound if his foot isn't bothering him.

ENDY CHAVEZ   **CF**   **Bats: L Throws: L**   Height: 6′ 0″   Weight: 170   Born: February 7, 1978   Age: 28

YEAR	TM	LVL	AGE	PA	R	2B	3B	HR	RBI	BB	SO	SB	CS	SPEED	BA	OBP	SLG	MLVR	EQBA	EQOBP	EQSLG	EQA	VORP	DEFENSE	
2003	MON	MLB	25	517	66	25	5	5	47	31	59	18	7	7.1	.251	.294	.354	-.207	.242	.287	.349	.227	-13.1	116-CF	2
2004	MON	MLB	26	535	65	20	6	5	34	30	40	32	7	7.8	.277	.318	.371	-.073	.271	.313	.364	.245	7.5	121-CF	-4
2005	PHI	MLB	27	111	17	3	3	0	10	4	13	2	1	7.7	.215	.243	.299	-.363	.218	.252	.309	.201	-7.3	13-CF	1
2006	NYN	MLB	28	127	16	5	1	1	10	8	13	4	1	6.4	.268	.316	.350	-.141	.272	.320	.371	.238	0.2	34-CF	0

Breakout: 33%   Improve: 44%   Collapse: 35%   Attrition: 42%   Comparables: Jason Tyner, Ty Cline, Jose Tartabull

Almost half of Chavez's at-bats with the Phils came as a pinch-hitter, which is a special kind of self-flagellation for a team in contention until the last day of the season. Chavez is a pathetically bad hitter whose sole value is as a defensive replacement and pinch runner. Non-tendered, he signed with the tools-happy Mets in December.

GREGORY GOLSON   **CF**   **Bats: R Throws: R**   Height: 6′ 0″   Weight: 190   Born: September 17, 1985   Age: 20

YEAR	TM	LVL	AGE	PA	R	2B	3B	HR	RBI	BB	SO	SB	CS	SPEED	BA	OBP	SLG	MLVR	EQBA	EQOBP	EQSLG	EQA	VORP	DEFENSE	
2005	LWD	A	19	407	51	19	8	4	27	26	106	25	9	7.7	.264	.322	.389	.036	.249	.294	.362	.232	-7.3	89-CF	-7
2006	PHI	MLB	20	406	49	21	5	5	35	22	102	14	7	5.8	.242	.290	.364	-.187	.241	.290	.365	.220	-6.3	97-CF	-5

Breakout: 25%   Improve: 48%   Collapse: 32%   Attrition: 16%   Comparables: Kenny Kelly, David Krynzel, Darnell McDonald

Philadelphia's 1st round pick in the 2004 draft followed a weak debut season with a flop'ola sophomore season in the Sally League. An excellent all-around athlete, Golson will keep getting chances until cold fusion is revived as the solution to the planet's energy woes. Leg injuries marred his year, but it would be nice if his performance bore the slightest resemblance to what the tools watchers say he can do.

BRAD HARMAN   **SS/2B**   **Bats: R Throws: R**   Height: 5' 10"   Weight: 170   Born: November 19, 1985   Age: 20

YEAR	TM	LVL	AGE	PA	R	2B	3B	HR	RBI	BB	SO	SB	CS	SPEED	BA	OBP	SLG	MLVR	EQBA	EQOBP	EQSLG	EQA	VORP	DEFENSE		
2005	LWD	A	19	471	63	23	1	11	58	45	89	5	11	3.9	.303	.380	.442	.234	.282	.343	.407	.256	22.3	78-SS	-4	26-2B -4
2006	PHI	MLB	20	496	55	25	2	11	54	41	94	4	4	3.9	.255	.322	.388	-.090	.254	.322	.390	.240	10.1	117-SS	-5	

Breakout: 14%   Improve: 30%   Collapse: 44%   Attrition: 4%   Comparables: Joe Jiannetti, Bronson Sardinha, Chad Spann

Philadelphia's Great White Australian Hope, Harman is considered the best Aussie prospect the organization has signed. Baseball America says that no Aussies have been given bonuses of more than $50K, "a welcome change from the Latin American market the organization believes has become overpriced." How convenient: having missed the bus, the cab, the jitney, and even the pedicab as smart organizations rushed to sign Latin talent in the past two decades, Philadelphia now has an excuse to look elsewhere.

RYAN HOWARD   **1B**   **Bats: L Throws: L**   Height: 6' 4"   Weight: 230   Born: November 19, 1979   Age: 26

YEAR	TM	LVL	AGE	PA	R	2B	3B	HR	RBI	BB	SO	SB	CS	SPEED	BA	OBP	SLG	MLVR	EQBA	EQOBP	EQSLG	EQA	VORP	DEFENSE
2003	CLR	A+	23	553	67	32	1	23	82	50	151	0	0	3.3	.304	.374	.514	.324	.267	.325	.478	.271	17.6	114-1B 10
2004	REA	AA	24	433	73	18	1	37	102	46	129	1	2	3.5	.297	.386	.647	.410	.255	.332	.543	.287	23.8	97-1B 3
2004	SWB	AAA	24	127	21	10	0	9	29	14	37	0	0	3.6	.270	.362	.604	.286	.233	.325	.515	.279	4.4	29-1B -1
2004	PHI	MLB	24	42	5	5	0	2	5	2	13	0	0	3.3	.282	.333	.564	.237	.282	.333	.538	.287	2.9	
2005	SWB	AAA	25	257	38	19	0	16	54	39	66	0	0	3.3	.371	.467	.690	.678	.332	.426	.611	.342	36.2	57-1B -4
2005	PHI	MLB	25	348	52	17	2	22	63	33	100	0	1	4.6	.288	.356	.567	.265	.281	.352	.565	.299	23.5	80-1B -3
2006	PHI	MLB	26	538	79	28	1	41	108	61	147	0	1	4.0	.286	.375	.612	.311	.285	.375	.615	.314	46.6	126-1B -1

Breakout: 39%   Improve: 63%   Collapse: 15%   Attrition: 4%   Comparables: Travis Hafner, Mo Vaughn, Mike Epstein

After a year of pummeling minor league pitching like the reigning heavyweight champion would pummel a Golden Gloves winner, Howard got his chance on July 1 when Jim Thome broke down. When recalled, Howard was leading the International League in BA, OBP, and SLG while awaiting resolution of the impasse at first base in Philly—which wasn't exactly a Gordian knot. With Thome having hit 89 homers and walked 215 times the previous two years, and with the club committed to him through 2085 at a quadrillion bucks per annum, the patently obvious solution was to deal Howard in the 2004–05 offseason for catching or pitching help—or both. However, sometimes good fortune is the residue of incompetence. The soothsayers disagree on where Howard's career is heading: while he has outstanding power, his bat speed isn't the greatest and he might end up merely as a very good mistake hitter.

JASON JARAMILLO   **C**   **Bats: B Throws: R**   Height: 6' 0"   Weight: 200   Born: October 9, 1982   Age: 23

YEAR	TM	LVL	AGE	PA	R	2B	3B	HR	RBI	BB	SO	SB	CS	SPEED	BA	OBP	SLG	MLVR	EQBA	EQOBP	EQSLG	EQA	VORP	DEFENSE
2004	BAT	A-	21	127	11	5	0	1	14	12	27	0	1	3.0	.232	.307	.304	-.086	.192	.252	.244	.184	-21.4	18-C -2
2005	LWD	A	22	495	46	28	4	8	63	44	72	2	3	3.7	.304	.368	.438	.210	.278	.329	.393	.250	12.9	102-C -5
2006	PHI	MLB	23	389	35	19	1	5	38	26	72	1	1	3.5	.235	.288	.338	-.228	.234	.289	.339	.209	-6.6	93-C -5

Breakout: 14%   Improve: 35%   Collapse: 47%   Attrition: 10%   Comparables: Bryce Terveen, Dustin Smith, Lukas McKnight

A 23-year-old catch-and-throw receiver compared to Johnny Estrada, Jaramillo's 2005 batting stats in the Sally League were encouraging. Still, he'll be lucky if he beats Estrada's career mark of playing in 100 games in a season before turning 28.

MATT KATA   **INF**   **Bats: B Throws: R**   Height: 6' 1"   Weight: 185   Born: March 14, 1978   Age: 28

YEAR	TM	LVL	AGE	PA	R	2B	3B	HR	RBI	BB	SO	SB	CS	SPEED	BA	OBP	SLG	MLVR	EQBA	EQOBP	EQSLG	EQA	VORP	DEFENSE		
2003	TUC	AAA	25	214	31	13	5	3	25	9	29	2	3	6.0	.289	.327	.448	-.016	.243	.282	.381	.227	-2.1	39-2B	-4	
2003	ARI	MLB	25	317	42	16	5	7	29	25	53	3	2	6.2	.257	.315	.420	-.063	.247	.305	.406	.246	4.4	46-2B	-1	19-3B 1
2004	ARI	MLB	26	176	17	9	2	2	13	13	29	4	1	6.3	.247	.301	.364	-.155	.236	.291	.348	.228	-0.6	36-2B	1	
2005	TUC	AAA	27	210	25	10	3	3	28	6	25	5	1	5.7	.310	.329	.435	-.083	.249	.265	.341	.214	-6.8	14-2B	-1	13-CF -1
2005	SWB	AAA	27	100	10	5	1	0	4	4	14	2	1	5.9	.312	.340	.385	-.003	.282	.311	.345	.231	-0.2	10-2B	2	
2006	PHI	MLB	28	273	31	12	2	3	25	16	41	4	2	5.2	.246	.294	.353	-.191	.245	.294	.354	.219	-3.3	67-2B	-1	

Breakout: 18%   Improve: 38%   Collapse: 37%   Attrition: 30%   Comparables: Domingo Cedeno, Mike Ramsey, Marv Breeding

Acquired in late July, Kata spent most of his time in Scranton. He may be condemned to Quad-A purgatory, though he has a good arm and can play second and third well and short credibly. If Kata tried to work the count at all, he might be able to parlay his limited batting skills and good speed into a nice career as a utility infielder. With the team committed to Tomas Perez and Abraham Nunez, he's got very little opportunity unless Philadelphia admits its Bell is cracked, and releases David.

MIKE LIEBERTHAL   **C**   **Bats: R Throws: R**   Height: 6' 0"   Weight: 186   Born: January 18, 1972   Age: 34

YEAR	TM	LVL	AGE	PA	R	2B	3B	HR	RBI	BB	SO	SB	CS	SPEED	BA	OBP	SLG	MLVR	EQBA	EQOBP	EQSLG	EQA	VORP	DEFENSE
2003	PHI	MLB	31	561	68	30	1	13	81	38	59	0	0	4.0	.313	.373	.453	.181	.313	.371	.456	.285	39.7	128-C -7
2004	PHI	MLB	32	528	58	31	1	17	61	37	69	1	1	3.1	.271	.335	.447	.047	.266	.328	.438	.263	20.5	122-C -3
2005	PHI	MLB	33	443	48	25	0	12	47	35	35	0	0	4.1	.263	.336	.418	.017	.256	.330	.419	.260	16.3	113-C -5
2006	*PHI*	*MLB*	*34*	*414*	*42*	*21*	*1*	*11*	*54*	*29*	*44*	*0*	*0*	*4.0*	*.267*	*.332*	*.416*	*-.028*	*.266*	*.332*	*.418*	*.253*	*11.6*	*99-C -3*

Breakout: 7%   Improve: 25%   Collapse: 42%   Attrition: 22%   Comparables: Terry Steinbach, Brian Harper, Bo Diaz

At the point in his career where he should play against lefties and only selected righties, Lieberthal soldiered on as the regular because Ed Wade couldn't put the pieces of the puzzle together. Since Lieberthal's throwing began deteriorating three years ago, the Phillies have needed a lefty-hitting reserve who played decent defense. Admittedly, that's not easy to find, but the comparatively clueless Reds came up with Javier Valentin. That's what GMs get paid the big bucks for: finding the right players to address their team's problems. The good news? Despite his six-figure odometer reading and his many physical problems, Lieberthal has not been put on the DL since 2001.

KENNY LOFTON   **CF**   **Bats: L Throws: L**   Height: 6' 0"   Weight: 180   Born: May 31, 1967   Age: 39

YEAR	TM	LVL	AGE	PA	R	2B	3B	HR	RBI	BB	SO	SB	CS	SPEED	BA	OBP	SLG	MLVR	EQBA	EQOBP	EQSLG	EQA	VORP	DEFENSE
2003	PIT	MLB	36	372	58	19	4	9	26	28	29	18	5	7.6	.277	.333	.437	.045	.271	.327	.437	.266	14.3	80-CF 4
2003	CHN	MLB	36	231	39	13	4	3	20	18	22	12	4	7.5	.327	.381	.471	.200	.324	.376	.467	.291	17.5	51-CF 0
2004	NYA	MLB	37	312	51	10	7	3	18	31	27	7	3	7.3	.275	.346	.395	-.040	.276	.352	.397	.265	6.2	61-CF 0
2005	PHI	MLB	38	401	67	15	5	2	36	32	41	22	3	7.9	.335	.392	.420	.158	.326	.386	.410	.286	28.2	84-CF 8
2006	*LAN*	*MLB*	*39*	*273*	*34*	*10*	*2*	*2*	*21*	*23*	*30*	*11*	*3*	*6.6*	*.281*	*.344*	*.365*	*-.065*	*.288*	*.350*	*.381*	*.255*	*7.7*	*67-CF 1*

Breakout: 0%   Improve: 18%   Collapse: 40%   Attrition: 36%   Comparables: Brett Butler, Lou Brock, Bill Bruton

After pouting his way through 2004 with the Yankees, Lofton was dealt to the Phillies so that GM Ed Wade could pat himself on the back for making another shrewd move and Joe Torre could manage in a tranquil, meditative state. Lofton made a nice comeback, a season that wasn't a function of playing at The Bank, though it was overrated because of his gaudy batting average. At 39, Lofton's limited power is completely gone. Signed by the frenetic Dodgers in January, WYSIWYG.

RAMON MARTINEZ   **INF**   **Bats: R Throws: R**   Height: 6' 1"   Weight: 170   Born: October 10, 1972   Age: 33

YEAR	TM	LVL	AGE	PA	R	2B	3B	HR	RBI	BB	SO	SB	CS	SPEED	BA	OBP	SLG	MLVR	EQBA	EQOBP	EQSLG	EQA	VORP	DEFENSE	
2003	CHN	MLB	30	327	30	16	1	3	34	24	50	0	1	3.8	.283	.333	.375	-.038	.282	.333	.374	.252	6.9	35-2B -4	24-3B -2
2004	CHN	MLB	31	291	22	15	1	3	30	26	40	1	0	3.7	.246	.313	.346	-.168	.240	.307	.336	.232	-2.0	59-SS 2	13-3B -1
2005	DET	MLB	32	60	4	1	0	0	5	3	4	0	0	3.7	.268	.300	.286	-.252	.273	.317	.291	.224	-1.4	10-SS -1	
2005	PHI	MLB	32	63	7	2	0	1	9	3	7	0	0	3.1	.286	.317	.375	-.076	.286	.312	.375	.250	-0.1		
2006	*PHI*	*MLB*	*33*	*148*	*15*	*6*	*0*	*1*	*14*	*10*	*17*	*0*	*0*	*4.1*	*.274*	*.326*	*.361*	*-.106*	*.273*	*.326*	*.362*	*.237*	*1.6*	*39-SS -1*	

Breakout: 14%   Improve: 34%   Collapse: 45%   Attrition: 48%   Comparables: Bob Johnson, Alex Arias, Luis Sojo

Now relegated to the spare parts bin under fungible utility infielders, which is where he should have been consigned two years ago. Martinez played a bit for Philadelphia after arriving in the Urbina-Polanco trade; it didn't take the Tigers long to realize that he wasn't worth the deal they gave him for 2005. Unsigned and unwanted as of mid-January.

JASON MICHAELS   **OF**   **Bats: R Throws: R**   Height: 6' 0"   Weight: 200   Born: May 4, 1976   Age: 30

YEAR	TM	LVL	AGE	PA	R	2B	3B	HR	RBI	BB	SO	SB	CS	SPEED	BA	OBP	SLG	MLVR	EQBA	EQOBP	EQSLG	EQA	VORP	DEFENSE	
2003	PHI	MLB	27	125	20	11	0	5	17	15	22	0	0	3.8	.330	.416	.569	.422	.327	.413	.564	.326	14.2		
2004	PHI	MLB	28	346	44	12	0	10	40	42	80	2	2	4.6	.274	.364	.415	.059	.268	.358	.408	.268	8.9	36-CF -1	25-LF 2
2005	PHI	MLB	29	341	54	16	2	4	31	44	45	3	3	5.5	.304	.399	.415	.144	.298	.392	.415	.284	17.5	61-CF 9	
2006	*PHI*	*MLB*	*30*	*380*	*51*	*19*	*2*	*10*	*46*	*46*	*65*	*3*	*2*	*5.2*	*.283*	*.374*	*.445*	*.091*	*.282*	*.374*	*.447*	*.279*	*16.4*	*91-CF 3*	

Breakout: 15%   Improve: 40%   Collapse: 28%   Attrition: 21%   Comparables: Benny Agbayani, Rico Carty, Merv Rettenmund

Michaels should have received more playing time in Philly over the past four years, but the team kept fooling around with players like Marlon Byrd and Endy Chavez. Odd, as Michaels is the sort of overachieving, hard-nosed, brawling personality that normally gets bonus points from the club's management and its blue-collar, white ethnic fan base. With good range and a .278/.361/.411 line versus righties in the past three years, Michaels is far better than the platoon/reserve pigeonhole the club has put him in.

TOMAS PEREZ **PH** **Bats: B Throws: R** Height: 5′ 11″ Weight: 170 Born: December 29, 1973 Age: 32

YEAR	TM	LVL	AGE	PA	R	2B	3B	HR	RBI	BB	SO	SB	CS	SPEED	BA	OBP	SLG	MLVR	EQBA	EQOBP	EQSLG	EQA	VORP	DEFENSE			
2003	PHI	MLB	29	323	39	18	1	5	33	23	54	0	1	4.4	.265	.316	.383	-.059	.267	.319	.390	.246	4.4	44-3B	3	19-2B	1
2004	PHI	MLB	30	187	22	13	2	6	21	9	44	0	0	5.5	.216	.257	.415	-.181	.215	.255	.412	.226	-3.4	11-3B	0	12-2B	1
2005	PHI	MLB	31	173	17	7	0	0	22	11	27	1	0	4.3	.233	.289	.277	-.283	.231	.291	.269	.207	-7.8	17-1B	1		
2006 PHI		MLB	32	97	10	5	0	1	10	6	16	0	0	4.5	.242	.291	.348	-.206	.242	.291	.350	.215	-3.1	27-3B	0		

Breakout: 21% Improve: 36% Collapse: 43% Attrition: 51% Comparables: Doug Strange, David Howard, Greg Pryor

As the scouts say, Perez "leaves the dugout swinging." It finally caught up to him in 2005, as he failed to hit a home run in 159 trips to the plate, slugging a feeble .277. Perez is adequate or better defensively at second, short, and third, and for whatever reason, the Phils positively love him, locking him up with a two-year contract for 2005–06 with an option for 2007. This leads to indefensible choices like starting Perez at first base 15 times last year, something which should cause a Phillies fan's ears to smoke in outrage.

TODD PRATT **C** **Bats: R Throws: R** Height: 6′ 3″ Weight: 230 Born: February 9, 1967 Age: 39

YEAR	TM	LVL	AGE	PA	R	2B	3B	HR	RBI	BB	SO	SB	CS	SPEED	BA	OBP	SLG	MLVR	EQBA	EQOBP	EQSLG	EQA	VORP	DEFENSE	
2003	PHI	MLB	36	155	16	10	1	4	20	22	38	0	0	4.1	.272	.400	.464	.193	.276	.397	.488	.305	11.1	33-C	-3
2004	PHI	MLB	37	148	16	5	0	3	16	18	38	0	0	3.4	.258	.351	.367	-.044	.250	.345	.352	.250	2.8	37-C	-5
2005	PHI	MLB	38	196	17	4	0	7	23	19	50	0	0	3.8	.251	.332	.394	-.034	.246	.330	.383	.250	4.9	49-C	3
2006 ATL		MLB	39	137	13	5	1	4	17	15	36	0	0	3.9	.246	.334	.397	-.064	.247	.334	.409	.251	2.7	36-C	1

Breakout: 22% Improve: 31% Collapse: 54% Attrition: 53% Comparables: Lance Parrish, Greg Myers, Walker Cooper

Set a career high in at-bats in 2005. Pratt's bad defensive reputation is undeserved since he's thrown out 27 percent of basestealers in his career (32 percent in 2005). On the other hand, his stick is overrated—he had a horrifying 524 road OPS last year. It was the third time in the past four years that Pratt has had enormous home biases in his hitting. Signed by the Braves in December, he'll be the veteran caddy for Brian McCann.

CHRIS ROBERSON **OF** **Bats: R Throws: R** Height: 6′ 2″ Weight: 180 Born: August 23, 1979 Age: 26

YEAR	TM	LVL	AGE	PA	R	2B	3B	HR	RBI	BB	SO	SB	CS	SPEED	BA	OBP	SLG	MLVR	EQBA	EQOBP	EQSLG	EQA	VORP	DEFENSE			
2003	LWD	A	23	540	64	19	5	2	32	57	108	59	16	7.6	.234	.331	.309	-.021	.215	.283	.284	.215	-35.4	101-CF	5	31-RF	-1
2004	CLR	A+	24	345	52	13	6	9	38	27	71	16	12	6.9	.307	.371	.473	.235	.262	.315	.405	.247	4.7	78-CF	-3		
2005	REA	AA	25	606	90	24	8	15	70	40	112	34	14	7.3	.311	.365	.465	.180	.271	.320	.400	.252	-4.4	72-RF	6	62-CF	5
2006 PHI		MLB	26	480	62	21	4	9	45	29	100	20	7	5.8	.258	.309	.383	-.117	.257	.309	.385	.238	-2.5	113-CF	4		

Breakout: 24% Improve: 53% Collapse: 31% Attrition: 13% Comparables: Darrell Nicholas, Wonderful Monds, Allen Dina

Like most prospects sired by big-time pro athletes, Roberson, whose father Will played for the Detroit Pistons, gets more attention than he merits. A breakout year in Clearwater in 2004 combined with his great range in center and his obvious tools boosted him onto last year's prospect lists. His .311 BA in Reading last year earned him Eastern League Rookie of the Year honors as well as the Phillies' award for best position player in the organization. Roberson is one of those players about whom opinions vary wildly. Some think he's the center fielder of the future in Philly, others believe his age makes him a fringe prospect.

JIMMY ROLLINS **SS** **Bats: B Throws: R** Height: 5′ 8″ Weight: 160 Born: November 27, 1978 Age: 27

YEAR	TM	LVL	AGE	PA	R	2B	3B	HR	RBI	BB	SO	SB	CS	SPEED	BA	OBP	SLG	MLVR	EQBA	EQOBP	EQSLG	EQA	VORP	DEFENSE	
2003	PHI	MLB	24	684	85	42	6	8	62	54	113	20	12	6.5	.263	.320	.387	-.043	.265	.323	.395	.249	16.8	152-SS	6
2004	PHI	MLB	25	719	119	43	12	14	73	57	73	30	9	8.0	.289	.348	.455	.090	.284	.343	.449	.272	43.1	153-SS	-7
2005	PHI	MLB	26	730	115	38	11	12	54	47	71	41	6	8.0	.290	.338	.431	.056	.281	.333	.430	.269	42.5	153-SS	-7
2006 PHI		MLB	27	690	101	37	8	13	67	51	75	30	10	6.2	.282	.339	.428	.011	.281	.339	.430	.262	31.3	160-SS	4

Breakout: 16% Improve: 45% Collapse: 21% Attrition: 1% Comparables: Rafael Furcal, Ray Durham, Luis Aparicio

Instead of building on his career-highs in BA/SLG/OBP from 2004 on his way to a Durham career (Ray, not N. C.), Rollins instead took a small step backwards. However, he did have his best year stealing bases since 2001, and his range was improved as a result of better positioning. Rollins had said privately for years that he couldn't wait to leave the Phillies as a free agent, though the departures of Bowa and Wade plus a Brinks truckload o'cash may well change that. At 27, he's headed into his walk year. It's time for him to establish himself as a top-flight player.

CARLOS RUIZ

CARLOS RUIZ   **C**   **Bats: R Throws: R**   Height: 5' 10"   Weight: 180   Born: January 22, 1979   Age: 27

YEAR	TM	LVL	AGE	PA	R	2B	3B	HR	RBI	BB	SO	SB	CS	SPEED	BA	OBP	SLG	MLVR	EQBA	EQOBP	EQSLG	EQA	VORP	DEFENSE	
2003	CLR	A+	24	56	5	0	0	2	9	2	5	2	2	3.9	.315	.339	.426	.174	.274	.300	.385	.234	0.4	10-C	1
2003	REA	AA	24	187	22	6	0	2	16	12	15	1	1	3.9	.266	.321	.337	-.112	.228	.277	.305	.209	-8.4	45-C	3
2004	REA	AA	25	382	45	15	2	17	50	22	37	8	4	4.6	.284	.338	.484	.112	.245	.287	.408	.238	1.1	86-C	9
2005	SWB	AAA	26	387	50	25	9	4	40	30	48	4	5	5.7	.300	.354	.458	.113	.273	.326	.413	.255	11.7	55-C	5
2006	*PHI*	*MLB*	*27*	*345*	*36*	*16*	*2*	*6*	*39*	*20*	*41*	*3*	*2*	*4.8*	*.265*	*.312*	*.388*	*-.100*	*.264*	*.313*	*.390*	*.236*	*4.3*	*83-C*	*4*

Breakout: 26%   *Improve: 41%*   *Collapse: 28%*   *Attrition: 18%*   *Comparables: Mike Heath, Jerry Grote, Charlie Moore*

After his 2004 breakout year in Double-A and a bravura performance in the AFL, Ruiz was on the fast track of the Reading R.R. to Philly. Act II was an even better year in Triple-A in 2005, though his newfound home run power in 2004 evaporated from 17 to only four. The Panamanian didn't sign his first pro contract until age 19, and didn't play professionally until he was 20, so there are mitigating circumstances to his late maturation. The Phillies signed Sal Fasano for 2006, and the Italian backup stallion is the odds-on favorite to go north with the big club next April, while Ruiz heads back to Scranton.

JIM THOME

JIM THOME   **1B**   **Bats: L Throws: R**   Height: 6' 4"   Weight: 230   Born: August 27, 1970   Age: 35

YEAR	TM	LVL	AGE	PA	R	2B	3B	HR	RBI	BB	SO	SB	CS	SPEED	BA	OBP	SLG	MLVR	EQBA	EQOBP	EQSLG	EQA	VORP	DEFENSE	
2003	PHI	MLB	32	698	111	30	3	47	131	111	182	0	3	4.3	.266	.385	.573	.316	.265	.383	.577	.314	54.6	153-1B	-8
2004	PHI	MLB	33	618	97	28	1	42	105	104	144	0	2	3.6	.274	.396	.581	.320	.266	.390	.563	.314	50.6	131-1B	-9
2005	PHI	MLB	34	242	26	7	0	7	30	45	59	0	0	3.8	.207	.360	.352	-.059	.203	.357	.354	.259	-1.1	49-1B	-1
2006	*CHA*	*MLB*	*35*	*341*	*43*	*13*	*1*	*18*	*50*	*56*	*77*	*0*	*1*	*4.0*	*.263*	*.385*	*.506*	*.183*	*.262*	*.391*	*.501*	*.297*	*16.3*	*82-1B*	*-5*

Breakout: 26%   *Improve: 42%*   *Collapse: 39%*   *Attrition: 38%*   *Comparables: Boog Powell, Willie McCovey, Bill Nicholson*

Two separate injuries in 2005 derailed Thome's express train to 500 four-baggers and a certain ticket to Cooperstown. A lower back strain cost him three weeks on the DL in May, then elbow tendinitis landed him on the DL for the rest of the season on July 1; he underwent elbow surgery in August. While these kinds of injuries can be anticipated in a slugger of Thome's age and mileage, there's no reason to believe he can't belt 30 homers for the White Sox in 2006. However, a slow start should be expected.

MICHAEL TUCKER

MICHAEL TUCKER   **OF**   **Bats: L Throws: R**   Height: 6' 2"   Weight: 185   Born: June 25, 1971   Age: 35

YEAR	TM	LVL	AGE	PA	R	2B	3B	HR	RBI	BB	SO	SB	CS	SPEED	BA	OBP	SLG	MLVR	EQBA	EQOBP	EQSLG	EQA	VORP	DEFENSE			
2003	KCA	MLB	32	432	61	20	5	13	55	39	88	8	10	5.9	.262	.331	.440	-.037	.257	.332	.435	.257	-0.4	40-RF	2	27-CF	-3
2004	SFN	MLB	33	541	77	21	6	13	62	70	106	5	2	6.2	.256	.353	.412	.004	.249	.346	.397	.262	8.3	93-RF	-2	19-CF	0
2005	SFN	MLB	34	284	32	16	1	5	33	28	48	4	0	5.2	.240	.317	.372	-.092	.236	.315	.376	.248	-1.1	49-RF	-3		
2005	PHI	MLB	34	21	3	0	0	0	3	3	4	0	0	4.5	.222	.333	.222	-.257	.222	.333	.222	.214	-0.5				
2006	*WAS*	*MLB*	*35*	*185*	*21*	*8*	*1*	*4*	*21*	*21*	*35*	*2*	*1*	*5.8*	*.246*	*.336*	*.394*	*-.064*	*.258*	*.346*	*.425*	*.261*	*2.5*	*47-RF*	*-1*		

Breakout: 31%   *Improve: 47%*   *Collapse: 34%*   *Attrition: 47%*   *Comparables: Walt Moryn, Bob Skinner, Dave May*

Acquired in late August as insurance for the stretch run, Tucker was left to pick his nose at the end of the Phillies bench for most of September, pinch-hitting only occasionally. He has some value since he can play all three outfield positions, but he can't hit lefties and hasn't hit righties well in years. Plus, his speed doesn't translate to a high stolen base percentage. Signed by the Nats for 2006, where he will log more playing time than he deserves if Washington can't coax Alfonso Soriano into playing the outfield.

CHASE UTLEY

CHASE UTLEY   **2B**   **Bats: L Throws: R**   Height: 6' 1"   Weight: 170   Born: December 17, 1978   Age: 27

YEAR	TM	LVL	AGE	PA	R	2B	3B	HR	RBI	BB	SO	SB	CS	SPEED	BA	OBP	SLG	MLVR	EQBA	EQOBP	EQSLG	EQA	VORP	DEFENSE			
2003	SWB	AAA	24	490	80	26	2	18	77	41	75	10	4	5.5	.323	.390	.517	.306	.300	.369	.491	.293	43.0	113-2B	8		
2003	PHI	MLB	24	152	13	10	1	2	21	11	22	2	0	4.6	.239	.322	.373	-.072	.244	.322	.378	.249	2.4	34-2B	3		
2004	SWB	AAA	25	144	23	8	1	6	25	18	29	4	2	5.7	.285	.368	.512	.188	.253	.337	.442	.269	6.2	33-2B	1		
2004	PHI	MLB	25	286	36	11	2	13	57	15	40	4	1	5.6	.266	.308	.468	.018	.262	.304	.461	.260	9.2	45-2B	4	12-1B	0
2005	PHI	MLB	26	628	93	39	6	28	105	69	109	16	3	6.3	.291	.376	.540	.260	.283	.368	.536	.304	54.9	135-2B	-3		
2006	*PHI*	*MLB*	*27*	*581*	*82*	*31*	*3*	*24*	*81*	*55*	*93*	*9*	*3*	*5.2*	*.280*	*.356*	*.493*	*.123*	*.279*	*.356*	*.495*	*.283*	*34.5*	*136-2B*	*2*		

Breakout: 16%   *Improve: 40%*   *Collapse: 26%*   *Attrition: 6%*   *Comparables: Tim Teufel, Doug DeCinces, Gil McDougald*

(continued next page)

Chase Utley (*continued*)

In his breakout season, Utley improved his hitting against lefties and swiped 16 bases in 19 tries. While his .219 BA will still cause some to write that he can't cope with southpaws, his .469 slugging percentage, seven homers, and 25 walks in 125 ABs show he's learned enough to be dangerous against them. The Phils should never have benched Utley against lefties on the presumption he couldn't hit them. The best way to ensure that a young left-handed hitter won't be an everyday player is to prevent him from getting the experience he needs to learn to hit southpaws. The team had both Placido Polanco and David Bell on the roster—Bell cost so much that they had to play him, Polanco was too good to not play, and Ed Wade was too stubborn to make a trade if he couldn't hornswoggle someone else. As a result, only 57 of Utley's 403 ABs in 2003-04 were versus left-handers.

SHANE VICTORINO — OF — Bats: R Throws: R — Height: 5′ 9″ — Weight: 160 — Born: November 30, 1980 — Age: 25

YEAR	TM	LVL	AGE	PA	R	2B	3B	HR	RBI	BB	SO	SB	CS	SPEED	BA	OBP	SLG	MLVR	EQBA	EQOBP	EQSLG	EQA	VORP	DEFENSE	
2003	SDN	MLB	22	82	8	2	0	0	4	7	17	7	2	5.5	.151	.232	.178	-.544	.162	.241	.189	.189	-8.4	13-CF	0
2003	JAX	AA	22	291	37	9	4	2	15	21	41	16	7	6.9	.282	.340	.368	.059	.276	.325	.376	.247	2.8	61-CF	2
2004	JAX	AA	23	324	70	13	7	16	43	20	65	9	7	7.6	.327	.373	.582	.416	.308	.348	.542	.293	31.7	69-CF	8
2004	LVG	AAA	23	212	28	9	1	3	20	11	37	7	2	6.3	.235	.278	.335	-.388	.194	.237	.270	.187	-19.1	50-CF	3
2005	SWB	AAA	24	554	93	25	16	18	70	51	74	17	9	7.2	.310	.377	.534	.265	.286	.351	.483	.282	36.3	120-CF	13
2006	*PHI*	*MLB*	*25*	*534*	*74*	*26*	*5*	*16*	*63*	*38*	*78*	*15*	*6*	*6.1*	*.279*	*.335*	*.453*	*.037*	*.278*	*.336*	*.456*	*.266*	*18.5*	*126-CF*	*7*

Breakout: 19%   Improve: 47%   Collapse: 19%   Attrition: 12%   Comparables: Jose Cardenal, Juan Beniquez, Jim Piersall

A two-time selection in the Rule 5 Draft—the Phillies plucked him in 2004—Victorino was named International League MVP. He is the shortest center fielder to play for Philadelphia since the gnome-like Ricky Otero played 140 games in 1996–97. Unlike Otero, Victorino can actually swing the bat as well as run, and he developed a line-drive power stroke in the past two years. In six previous seasons, he had never hit more than four homers, but he's mashing these days. Unfortunately, with Aaron Rowand and Jason Michaels in front of him, he's going nowhere fast.

PITCHERS

EUDE BRITO — Bats: L Throws: L — Height: 5′ 11″ — Weight: 160 — Born: August 19, 1978 — Age: 27

YEAR	TM	LVL	AGE	W	L	SV	G	GS	IP	H	BB	SO	HR	GB%	BABIP	STUFF	WHIP	ERA	PERA	EQERA	EQH9	EQBB9	EQSO9	EQHR9	VORP	WXRL
2003	CLR	A+	24	4	3	6	36	0	58.3	50	27	54	3	—	.280	-26	1.32	3.09	6.04	5.53	9.6	5.5	5.5	1.5	0.4	—
2004	REA	AA	25	8	6	4	43	7	97.7	95	41	84	10	—	.294	-22	1.39	4.42	5.57	6.15	9.7	4.4	5.3	1.3	-5.7	—
2005	SWB	AAA	26	6	2	0	28	15	98.3	97	39	76	13	47%	.304	-20	1.38	4.85	5.80	5.99	9.6	4.2	5.2	1.5	-4.1	—
2005	PHI	MLB	26	1	2	0	6	5	22.0	20	11	15	2	46%	.286	0	1.41	3.68	4.98	3.74	8.7	4.2	5.8	0.8	4.7	0.7
2006	*PHI*	*MLB*	*27*	*4*	*6*	*0*	*32*	*12*	*86.7*	*97*	*41*	*53*	*14*	*45%*	*.294*	*-10*	*1.59*	*5.55*	*5.93*	*5.91*	*9.8*	*3.9*	*5.2*	*1.4*	*-2.2*	*0.2*

Breakout: 16%   Improve: 37%   Collapse: 25%   Attrition: 3%   Comparables: Bob Shirley, Jamie Moyer, John Curtis

Brito's career had stalled in the high minors until he mysteriously discovered some extra giddyup on his fastball. That didn't translate to great success at Triple-A in 2005, but such is the state of the higher levels of the Philly system that Brito's 6–2 record and 4.85 ERA earned him the Red Barons' Pitcher of the Year award. The 26-year-old lefty got the call to the big club in August, where he was pounded in his last two starts, and will continue to be if major league hitters see more of him in 2006.

RHEAL CORMIER — Bats: L Throws: L — Height: 5′ 10″ — Weight: 185 — Born: April 23, 1967 — Age: 39

YEAR	TM	LVL	AGE	W	L	SV	G	GS	IP	H	BB	SO	HR	GB%	BABIP	STUFF	WHIP	ERA	PERA	EQERA	EQH9	EQBB9	EQSO9	EQHR9	VORP	WXRL
2003	PHI	MLB	36	8	0	1	65	0	84.7	54	25	67	4	58%	.221	19	0.93	1.70	3.44	2.22	7.0	2.6	6.7	0.4	34.5	5.0
2004	PHI	MLB	37	4	5	0	84	0	81.0	70	26	46	7	57%	.260	-4	1.19	3.56	4.58	3.66	8.7	2.7	4.7	0.8	19.8	2.4
2005	PHI	MLB	38	4	2	0	57	0	47.3	56	16	34	9	52%	.322	-16	1.52	5.90	5.48	6.23	10.4	2.8	5.9	1.7	-3.4	0.3
2006	*PHI*	*MLB*	*39*	*3*	*2*	*2*	*56*	*0*	*53.3*	*56*	*17*	*31*	*6*	*52%*	*.288*	*-11*	*1.37*	*4.25*	*4.40*	*4.66*	*9.2*	*2.7*	*4.9*	*0.9*	*5.2*	*0.4*

Breakout: 20%   Improve: 36%   Collapse: 38%   Attrition: 22%   Comparables: Rick Honeycutt, Tom Burgmeier, Jeff Fassero

After two surprisingly effective seasons as a lefty gunslinger who could retire all comers, Cormier's Age 38 campaign was filled with a succession of minor injuries—shoulder, hip, back, foot—although none was serious enough to land him on the DL. However, the ailments badly bruised Cormier's pride as well as his ERA muscle. He succeeded with his average stuff in 2003–04 because he hit his spots, threw strikes, and kept the ball down. That he can regain his fine command in 2006 and stay healthy at 39 is not a sound bet.

GAVIN FLOYD
Bats: R Throws: R   Height: 6' 5"   Weight: 210   Born: January 27, 1983   Age: 23

YEAR	TM	LVL	AGE	W	L	SV	G	GS	IP	H	BB	SO	HR	GB%	BABIP	STUFF	WHIP	ERA	PERA	EQERA	EQH9	EQBB9	EQSO9	EQHR9	VORP	WXRL
2003	CLR	A+	20	7	8	0	24	20	138.0	128	45	115	9	—	.285	-6	1.25	3.00	5.82	5.68	10.0	3.5	5.4	1.7	-1.2	—
2004	REA	AA	21	6	6	0	20	20	119.0	93	46	94	5	—	.255	22	1.17	2.57	4.32	3.61	8.1	3.8	5.3	0.5	25.4	—
2004	SWB	AAA	21	1	3	0	5	5	30.7	39	9	18	4	—	.333	0	1.56	4.98	5.23	5.81	11.0	2.6	4.4	1.2	-0.7	—
2004	PHI	MLB	21	2	0	0	6	4	28.3	25	16	24	1	49%	.304	19	1.45	3.50	4.18	3.54	8.7	4.8	6.8	0.3	6.9	0.7
2005	SWB	AAA	22	6	9	0	24	23	137.3	155	66	97	11	49%	.338	1	1.61	6.16	5.10	6.86	9.9	4.5	5.0	0.8	-19.3	—
2005	PHI	MLB	22	1	2	0	7	4	26.0	30	16	17	5	40%	.298	-18	1.77	10.04	6.23	10.38	10.7	5.2	5.5	1.7	-14.9	0.0
2006	PHI	MLB	23	6	9	0	34	24	131.3	143	63	87	18	47%	.298	-2	1.56	5.53	5.63	5.89	9.5	4.0	5.6	1.2	-3.6	0.5

Breakout: 19%   Improve: 60%   Collapse: 6%   Attrition: 0%   Comparables: Mike Moore, Darryl Kile, Dewon Brazelton

After getting cuffed around in Philly at the start of 2005, Floyd was sent to Scranton for the rest of the IL season. Floyd was mugged there, too, though he made two more starts in Philadelphia upon being recalled when the rosters expanded in September. None of this should have been a surprise, as Floyd started only five games in Triple-A before making his big league debut in 2004. At 23, Floyd needs to learn how to pitch to disciplined hitters, any one of whom can turn around his fastball or hit a mistake curve over buildings. If learning by experience, level by level, wasn't crucial to the development of all but the rarest talents, teams could simply jump their top prospects to the majors and let them learn with the big boys. It doesn't work that way, especially with a high school draftee who sets up his out pitch with a mediocre fastball.

AARON FULTZ
Bats: L Throws: L   Height: 6' 0"   Weight: 200   Born: September 4, 1973   Age: 32

YEAR	TM	LVL	AGE	W	L	SV	G	GS	IP	H	BB	SO	HR	GB%	BABIP	STUFF	WHIP	ERA	PERA	EQERA	EQH9	EQBB9	EQSO9	EQHR9	VORP	WXRL
2003	TEX	MLB	29	1	3	0	64	0	67.3	75	27	53	9	50%	.332	-2	1.51	5.22	4.54	4.80	9.0	3.5	6.7	1.0	4.4	1.3
2004	MIN	MLB	30	3	3	1	55	0	50.0	50	23	37	5	49%	.310	-2	1.42	5.04	4.26	4.62	8.7	3.7	6.2	0.7	9.1	-0.2
2005	PHI	MLB	31	4	0	0	62	0	72.3	47	23	54	6	40%	.212	7	0.97	2.24	4.17	2.74	7.4	2.7	6.4	0.8	23.5	0.6
2006	PHI	MLB	32	3	3	2	63	0	62.7	61	24	46	8	45%	.281	-3	1.35	4.22	4.38	4.68	8.6	3.2	6.2	1.1	6.7	0.6

Breakout: 14%   Improve: 32%   Collapse: 42%   Attrition: 19%   Comparables: Chuck McElroy, Lance Painter, Paul Lapalme

Throws an average-plus sinker, cutter, and curve, an average-minus slider, and a plus turned-over change. Fultz's repertoire should have produced far greater success than it did before 2005. Some of his struggles were due to a bruised shoulder he suffered in Texas in 2003, and it could be that his career year was simply the apotheosis of a veteran pitcher losing his sharpness for two seasons. With much improved control, Fultz allowed an astonishingly low hit rate and less than a runner per inning, retiring both lefties and righties with aplomb. While he'll regress toward the mean in 2006 as surely as South Philly cheesesteaks will clog arteries, Fultz has probably reached a level where he can contribute as a setup pitcher and not just as a situational lefty.

GEOFF GEARY
Bats: R Throws: R   Height: 6' 0"   Weight: 170   Born: August 26, 1976   Age: 29

YEAR	TM	LVL	AGE	W	L	SV	G	GS	IP	H	BB	SO	HR	GB%	BABIP	STUFF	WHIP	ERA	PERA	EQERA	EQH9	EQBB9	EQSO9	EQHR9	VORP	WXRL
2003	SWB	AAA	26	9	4	5	46	3	87.7	73	13	80	3	—	.277	16	0.98	2.16	3.54	3.64	8.4	1.7	6.2	0.5	18.3	—
2004	SWB	AAA	27	1	2	10	21	0	23.3	20	13	23	1	—	.292	-5	1.42	2.32	4.43	3.63	8.5	6.0	6.9	0.4	4.9	—
2004	PHI	MLB	27	1	0	0	33	0	44.7	52	16	30	8	42%	.314	-14	1.52	5.44	5.24	5.84	10.5	3.0	5.4	1.4	-0.7	0.5
2005	PHI	MLB	28	2	1	0	40	0	58.0	54	21	42	5	47%	.287	0	1.29	3.72	4.24	4.55	8.8	3.1	6.0	0.8	6.9	0.1
2006	PHI	MLB	29	3	3	1	45	0	53.3	57	18	35	7	45%	.294	-6	1.41	4.47	4.77	5.18	9.4	2.9	5.6	1.1	4.7	0.4

Breakout: 21%   Improve: 48%   Collapse: 22%   Attrition: 27%   Comparables: Brian Holton, Mark Williamson, Shigetoshi Hasegawa

The slender righty had a surprisingly good season in limited action in Philadelphia, punctuated by a trip to the DL due to a freak injury sustained in early July—while batting, he fouled a ball off his eye. Without plus velocity or an out pitch, Geary will be counting on his control and his wits to reprise his performance in 2006—just like hundreds of other middle relievers of modest stature and talent in the professional ranks.

COLE HAMELS

Bats: L Throws: L   Height: 6' 3"   Weight: 170   Born: December 27, 1983   Age: 22

YEAR	TM	LVL	AGE	W	L	SV	G	GS	IP	H	BB	SO	HR	GB%	BABIP	STUFF	WHIP	ERA	PERA	EQERA	EQH9	EQBB9	EQSO9	EQHR9	VORP	WXRL
2003	LWD	A	19	6	1	0	13	13	74.7	32	25	115	0	—	.227	57	0.76	0.84	3.16	2.90	6.3	3.7	9.0	0.3	20.5	—
2003	CLR	A+	19	0	2	0	5	5	26.3	29	14	32	0	—	.382	26	1.63	2.74	4.10	4.44	9.6	5.1	7.5	0.3	3.4	—
2004	CLR	A+	20	1	0	0	4	4	16.0	10	4	24	0	—	.312	15	0.88	1.12	2.40	2.40	7.2	2.4	9.6	0.0	5.3	—
2005	CLR	A+	21	2	0	0	3	3	16.0	7	7	18	0	40%	.212	14	0.88	2.25	3.68	4.30	5.5	5.5	6.8	0.0	2.1	—
2005	REA	AA	21	2	0	0	3	3	19.0	10	12	19	2	42%	.190	6	1.16	2.37	6.23	3.63	7.3	6.7	6.7	1.6	3.8	—
2006	*PHI*	*MLB*	*22*	*8*	*8*	*0*	*30*	*20*	*131.0*	*110*	*75*	*114*	*13*	*43%*	*.267*	*14*	*1.41*	*4.24*	*4.33*	*4.59*	*7.4*	*4.7*	*7.4*	*0.9*	*15.3*	*2.4*

Breakout: 0%   Improve: 9%   Collapse: 59%   Attrition: 6%   Comparables: Barry Zito, Mickey McDermott, Moe Drabowsky

The talented Mr. Hamels seems to be something of a hardball Jekyll and Hyde case. On the field, his poise and his three plus pitches draw universal raves. Off the field, the 22-year-old seems to be an accident that is not only waiting to happen but is compelled to happen by some invisible, malevolent force. After missing most of 2004 with elbow problems, he strained his back in the Fall Instructional League. Then he broke a metacarpal bone in his hand in a bar fight in February, making him hors de combat until June. It was later reported that Hamels instigated the brawl, and was not provoked, as he had spun the story. This brought up the old rumors that his famous broken arm in high school did not occur in a pickup football game, but was really the result of a fight. He was shut down in midseason after just six appearances in Clearwater and Reading. All of this has given the Phillies a migraine, but they're gritting their teeth and preparing to send Hamels to Double-A to start 2006. The hope is that he will advance quickly to Triple-A and perhaps even the big tent before the end of the season.

YOEL HERNANDEZ

Bats: R Throws: R   Height: 6' 2"   Weight: 170   Born: April 15, 1980   Age: 26

YEAR	TM	LVL	AGE	W	L	SV	G	GS	IP	H	BB	SO	HR	GB%	BABIP	STUFF	WHIP	ERA	PERA	EQERA	EQH9	EQBB9	EQSO9	EQHR9	VORP	WXRL
2003	REA	AA	23	6	3	2	43	1	74.0	100	31	46	4	—	.353	-19	1.77	4.26	5.33	5.93	11.3	4.2	4.1	0.8	-2.7	—
2004	REA	AA	24	1	2	6	20	0	31.3	24	15	33	0	—	.282	0	1.25	2.01	4.20	4.50	8.1	5.1	6.6	0.3	3.7	—
2004	SWB	AAA	24	0	0	0	14	2	30.7	38	7	18	4	—	.330	-20	1.47	6.45	5.64	7.71	11.0	2.4	4.2	1.5	-7.1	—
2005	REA	AA	25	2	0	0	9	0	13.7	12	6	15	0	42%	.324	-1	1.31	1.31	4.15	2.77	9.0	4.8	6.2	0.0	4.1	—
2005	SWB	AAA	25	6	4	3	40	0	55.7	53	24	52	5	53%	.320	-5	1.38	3.39	5.00	4.17	9.0	4.5	6.3	1.0	8.6	—
2006	*PHI*	*MLB*	*26*	*2*	*3*	*0*	*24*	*3*	*45.3*	*51*	*24*	*32*	*6*	*51%*	*.314*	*-8*	*1.65*	*5.50*	*5.88*	*6.14*	*10.0*	*4.3*	*6.0*	*1.2*	*-1.3*	*0.0*

Breakout: 15%   Improve: 36%   Collapse: 28%   Attrition: 24%   Comparables: Brian Williams, Bobby Chouinard, John Strohmayer

Relying on a live fastball and a sharp slider, Hernandez pitched himself onto the 40-man roster a year after elbow surgery. The 26-year-old has a realistic chance of a bullpen role in Philadelphia in 2006 after an excellent year in relief in Reading and Scranton, and a superb performance in winter ball.

CORY LIDLE

Bats: R Throws: R   Height: 5' 11"   Weight: 190   Born: March 22, 1972   Age: 34

YEAR	TM	LVL	AGE	W	L	SV	G	GS	IP	H	BB	SO	HR	GB%	BABIP	STUFF	WHIP	ERA	PERA	EQERA	EQH9	EQBB9	EQSO9	EQHR9	VORP	WXRL
2003	TOR	MLB	31	12	15	0	31	31	192.7	216	60	112	24	53%	.305	3	1.43	5.74	4.65	5.53	9.4	2.7	5.0	1.0	0.2	1.3
2004	CIN	MLB	32	7	10	0	24	24	149.0	170	44	93	24	52%	.308	-2	1.44	5.32	4.98	5.22	9.9	2.4	5.0	1.3	-2.1	1.8
2004	PHI	MLB	32	5	2	0	10	10	62.3	54	17	33	3	49%	.264	13	1.14	3.90	4.15	4.15	8.6	2.4	4.3	0.4	11.6	1.7
2005	PHI	MLB	33	13	11	0	31	31	184.7	210	40	121	18	50%	.327	13	1.35	4.53	4.11	5.13	9.9	1.8	5.4	0.9	11.2	2.7
2006	*PHI*	*MLB*	*34*	*10*	*10*	*0*	*33*	*27*	*173.7*	*187*	*45*	*101*	*20*	*51%*	*.294*	*5*	*1.33*	*4.39*	*4.50*	*4.74*	*9.5*	*2.1*	*4.9*	*1.0*	*16.7*	*2.9*

Breakout: 28%   Improve: 70%   Collapse: 8%   Attrition: 5%   Comparables: Gerry Staley, Rick Mahler, Kevin Tapani

Lidle did what he was signed to do: take the ball every fifth day and give the thumpers in his lineup a chance to beat the hell out of the opposition. He was filleted at home—5.79 ERA, .323 BAA—despite having a home run rate 45 percent higher in away games. Lidle has a plain vanilla sinker, slider, and splitter, but he uses his curve effectively against righties and his plus change to retire lefties.

JON LIEBER

Bats: L Throws: R   Height: 6' 2"   Weight: 230   Born: April 2, 1970   Age: 36

YEAR	TM	LVL	AGE	W	L	SV	G	GS	IP	H	BB	SO	HR	GB%	BABIP	STUFF	WHIP	ERA	PERA	EQERA	EQH9	EQBB9	EQSO9	EQHR9	VORP	WXRL
2004	NYA	MLB	34	14	8	0	27	27	176.7	216	18	102	20	52%	.329	14	1.32	4.33	3.92	4.22	9.9	0.8	4.8	0.9	26.1	3.1
2005	PHI	MLB	35	17	13	0	35	35	218.3	223	41	149	33	46%	.285	5	1.21	4.21	4.59	4.47	9.5	1.6	5.7	1.4	30.1	4.2
2006	*PHI*	*MLB*	*36*	*12*	*10*	*0*	*31*	*30*	*193.3*	*203*	*37*	*120*	*24*	*48%*	*.289*	*10*	*1.24*	*4.01*	*4.17*	*4.29*	*9.3*	*1.6*	*5.2*	*1.1*	*27.7*	*4.3*

Breakout: 22%   Improve: 54%   Collapse: 9%   Attrition: 3%   Comparables: Bryn Smith, Ken Forsch, John Burkett

Lieber has to be one of the most unlikely pitchers signed to a fat contract to be the staff ace on a big-payroll contender in recent years. Though Ed Wade overpaid by a princely sum, Lieber delivered reliably in 2005. The veteran sinker-slider control artist struggled after a quick start, then finished strong after he learned how to pitch at CBP, dramatically cutting his gopher ball rate in the second half. He's still vulnerable to lefty hitters, even though he turns over his plus change.

AQUILINO LOPEZ Bats: R Throws: R Height: 6' 3" Weight: 160 Born: April 21, 1975 Age: 31

YEAR	TM	LVL	AGE	W	L	SV	G	GS	IP	H	BB	SO	HR	GB%	BABIP	STUFF	WHIP	ERA	PERA	EQERA	EQH9	EQBB9	EQSO9	EQHR9	VORP	WXRL
2003	TOR	MLB	28	1	3	14	72	0	73.7	58	34	64	5	47%	.260	13	1.25	3.42	3.95	3.45	7.4	4.1	7.6	0.6	19.5	3.4
2004	TOR	MLB	29	1	1	0	18	0	21.0	21	13	13	5	43%	.262	-23	1.62	6.00	6.43	5.57	9.4	5.1	5.1	1.7	0.1	0.3
2004	SYR	AAA	29	1	6	5	32	0	42.7	58	10	32	8	—	.350	-29	1.59	7.17	6.12	7.59	11.8	2.5	4.9	2.1	-9.4	—
2005	LVG	AAA	30	3	4	5	27	0	36.7	40	6	32	9	36%	.298	-25	1.25	5.89	6.56	5.80	10.3	1.8	5.3	2.8	-0.8	—
2005	CSP	AAA	30	2	0	0	14	0	19.7	14	4	25	2	35%	.267	6	0.91	2.74	4.34	5.30	7.2	1.9	7.7	1.4	0.6	—
2005	PHI	MLB	30	0	1	0	10	0	12.7	13	7	16	2	30%	.355	13	1.58	2.13	4.15	2.77	9.0	4.2	10.4	1.4	3.7	-0.3
2006	PHI	MLB	31	2	2	2	47	0	46.3	46	16	36	7	40%	.281	-2	1.34	4.41	4.64	4.91	8.8	2.8	6.6	1.4	4.8	0.4

Breakout: 25% Improve: 48% Collapse: 28% Attrition: 21% Comparables: Nelson Cruz, Steve Bedrosian, Shigetoshi Hasegawa

Claimed off of waivers from Colorado in August, Lopez finished the season in fine form in ten games in Philly. He lost his closer's job in 2004 in Toronto when his velocity dropped, and he's never had good control. If given the chance, Lopez could be a fine setup pitcher with an average fastball, plus slider, and slow split/forkball.

RYAN MADSON Bats: L Throws: R Height: 6' 6" Weight: 180 Born: August 28, 1980 Age: 25

YEAR	TM	LVL	AGE	W	L	SV	G	GS	IP	H	BB	SO	HR	GB%	BABIP	STUFF	WHIP	ERA	PERA	EQERA	EQH9	EQBB9	EQSO9	EQHR9	VORP	WXRL
2003	SWB	AAA	22	12	8	0	26	26	157.0	157	42	138	9	—	.308	22	1.27	3.50	4.10	4.51	9.2	2.8	6.4	0.8	18.6	—
2004	PHI	MLB	23	9	3	1	52	1	77.0	68	19	55	6	55%	.276	10	1.13	2.34	3.94	2.87	8.6	2.0	5.9	0.7	26.0	2.8
2005	PHI	MLB	24	6	5	0	78	0	87.0	84	25	79	11	49%	.312	6	1.25	4.14	4.17	4.48	9.0	2.4	7.5	1.1	9.7	0.9
2006	PHI	MLB	25	4	3	3	56	1	68.7	65	21	56	7	50%	.288	9	1.25	3.67	3.73	4.18	8.4	2.5	6.9	0.9	13.1	1.0

Breakout: 27% Improve: 52% Collapse: 25% Attrition: 15% Comparables: Ron Davis, Adrian Devine, Rawly Eastwick

Slated to be the No. 1 setup pitcher in 2006, Madson has also been considered for the rotation, and probably will be again if things go awry. The difference between his somewhat lucky 2004 and his slightly disappointing 2005 was that left-handed hitters figured out the tall righty, but he should be able to recover if he returns to throwing his fastball inside to lefties to set up his plus change outside. He also features an average curve with a slurvy break.

SCOTT MATHIESON Bats: R Throws: R Height: 6' 3" Weight: 190 Born: February 27, 1984 Age: 22

YEAR	TM	LVL	AGE	W	L	SV	G	GS	IP	H	BB	SO	HR	GB%	BABIP	STUFF	WHIP	ERA	PERA	EQERA	EQH9	EQBB9	EQSO9	EQHR9	VORP	WXRL
2004	LWD	A	20	8	9	0	25	25	131.3	130	50	112	7	—	.306	2	1.37	4.32	5.03	6.38	9.7	4.1	4.5	0.9	-11.0	—
2005	CLR	A+	21	3	8	0	23	23	121.7	111	34	118	17	40%	.289	-22	1.19	4.14	6.55	5.45	9.9	3.3	5.8	2.4	1.9	—
2006	PHI	MLB	22	6	9	0	26	22	127.7	133	55	83	23	37%	.276	1	1.47	5.37	5.56	5.59	9.2	3.5	5.5	1.6	0.4	0.9

Breakout: 24% Improve: 60% Collapse: 8% Attrition: 0% Comparables: Bubba Nelson, Jamie Brown, Aaron Myette

Prospects from exotic countries like Canada and Australia seem to generate extra interest, maybe because too many people erroneously think those places can't produce top-notch talent. Mathieson is a project, an organizational favorite, and he has a big fastball, so he'll get plenty of chances. His performance in Clearwater in 2005 wasn't anything to write home to British Columbia about, but Baseball America did name him top pitching prospect in the AFL.

BRETT MYERS Bats: R Throws: R Height: 6' 4" Weight: 210 Born: August 17, 1980 Age: 25

YEAR	TM	LVL	AGE	W	L	SV	G	GS	IP	H	BB	SO	HR	GB%	BABIP	STUFF	WHIP	ERA	PERA	EQERA	EQH9	EQBB9	EQSO9	EQHR9	VORP	WXRL
2003	PHI	MLB	22	14	9	0	32	32	193.0	205	76	143	20	52%	.313	14	1.46	4.43	4.46	4.74	9.5	3.2	6.0	0.9	21.7	3.6
2004	PHI	MLB	23	11	11	0	32	31	176.0	196	62	116	31	50%	.299	-6	1.47	5.52	5.28	5.79	10.0	2.9	5.3	1.5	0.0	1.1
2005	PHI	MLB	24	13	8	0	34	34	215.3	193	68	208	31	47%	.282	19	1.21	3.72	4.32	3.94	8.6	2.7	8.0	1.3	41.6	4.9
2006	PHI	MLB	25	13	10	0	32	32	210.3	201	66	169	23	49%	.286	21	1.27	3.84	4.03	4.07	8.4	2.6	6.8	0.9	35.2	5.1

Breakout: 37% Improve: 75% Collapse: 3% Attrition: 1% Comparables: Jeff Weaver, Don Cardwell, Joe Coleman

Myers bounced back handily from his brutal 2004 by developing a new wrinkle. Previously, Myers threw only a two-seam fastball, his signature curve, and an occasional minus changeup. That's not enough to get by pitching to experienced, patient hitters, but adding a cutter gave him a different weapon to use against hitters who were sitting on his fastball, or to use when he couldn't get his curve over reliably for strikes. At 25, Myers seems poised for the kind of huge season that phanatic Philly phans have anticipated since he made his debut.

VICENTE PADILLA Bats: R Throws: R Height: 6' 2" Weight: 200 Born: September 27, 1977 Age: 28

YEAR	TM	LVL	AGE	W	L	SV	G	GS	IP	H	BB	SO	HR	GB%	BABIP	STUFF	WHIP	ERA	PERA	EQERA	EQH9	EQBB9	EQSO9	EQHR9	VORP	WXRL
2003	PHI	MLB	25	14	12	0	32	32	208.7	196	62	133	22	49%	.278	10	1.24	3.62	4.57	4.22	9.1	2.5	5.3	1.0	35.9	5.1
2004	PHI	MLB	26	7	7	0	20	20	115.3	119	36	82	16	46%	.297	5	1.34	4.53	4.80	4.96	9.6	2.6	5.7	1.2	10.9	1.7
2005	PHI	MLB	27	9	12	0	27	27	147.0	146	74	103	22	46%	.284	-4	1.50	4.71	5.42	4.81	9.4	4.3	5.8	1.4	13.2	2.8
2006	TEX	MLB	28	9	10	0	30	27	163.3	179	54	101	22	46%	.297	7	1.43	4.77	4.74	4.79	9.4	3.0	5.6	1.1	16.0	2.8

Breakout: 15% Improve: 53% Collapse: 16% Attrition: 4% Comparables: James Baldwin, Moe Drabowsky, Pete Smith

Padilla started 2005 on the wrong note, stranded on the DL with elbow tendinitis. The rest of the season was off-key as well. Back, neck, and rib cage strains also nagged the veteran righty, and in December he was dumped on the Rangers for Ricardo Rodriguez. When healthy, Padilla is a good but far from great pitcher, so he should fit right in with the Rangers' redesigned rotation.

ROBINSON TEJEDA Bats: R Throws: R Height: 6' 3" Weight: 180 Born: March 24, 1982 Age: 24

YEAR	TM	LVL	AGE	W	L	SV	G	GS	IP	H	BB	SO	HR	GB%	BABIP	STUFF	WHIP	ERA	PERA	EQERA	EQH9	EQBB9	EQSO9	EQHR9	VORP	WXRL
2003	CLR	A+	21	2	4	0	11	11	64.7	53	23	42	4	—	.244	-11	1.17	3.20	6.34	5.28	9.5	3.9	4.2	1.8	2.1	—
2004	REA	AA	22	8	14	0	27	26	150.3	148	59	133	29	—	.274	-25	1.38	5.15	6.62	6.00	10.1	3.9	5.9	2.4	-6.4	—
2005	SWB	AAA	23	2	0	0	5	5	28.3	21	13	28	0	33%	.300	22	1.20	2.23	3.62	2.96	7.2	4.6	7.2	0.3	8.0	—
2005	PHI	MLB	23	4	3	0	26	13	85.7	67	51	72	5	36%	.270	14	1.38	3.57	4.38	3.84	7.9	5.0	7.0	0.5	17.7	2.8
2006	PHI	MLB	24	4	6	0	30	14	87.7	90	46	68	15	37%	.288	-2	1.55	5.49	5.75	6.21	9.0	4.3	6.6	1.5	-0.5	0.4

Breakout: 8% Improve: 30% Collapse: 43% Attrition: 20% Comparables: Aaron Myette, Ken Cloude, Santo Alcala

Tejeda's debut season was impressive, especially considering that he had only 31 starts above Class-A before being called up. The 23-year-old with the sinker-curve-change repertoire hung in well the whole season, showing no weaknesses until a sore shoulder cost him two weeks in September. He'll get a shot at a rotation berth in the spring, but the signing of Ryan Franklin increases the chance that Tejeda will be relegated to the bullpen until Charlie Manuel tires of watching Franklin get hammered.

UGUETH URBINA Bats: R Throws: R Height: 6' 2" Weight: 205 Born: February 15, 1974 Age: 32

YEAR	TM	LVL	AGE	W	L	SV	G	GS	IP	H	BB	SO	HR	GB%	BABIP	STUFF	WHIP	ERA	PERA	EQERA	EQH9	EQBB9	EQSO9	EQHR9	VORP	WXRL
2003	TEX	MLB	29	0	4	26	39	0	38.7	33	18	41	6	26%	.284	11	1.32	4.19	4.15	3.92	7.4	4.2	9.2	1.2	8.0	0.8
2003	FLO	MLB	29	3	0	6	33	0	38.3	23	13	37	2	29%	.226	21	0.94	1.41	3.16	1.70	6.3	2.9	8.0	0.5	17.8	2.6
2004	DET	MLB	30	4	6	21	54	0	54.0	38	32	56	7	32%	.233	6	1.30	4.50	4.56	4.39	7.1	5.1	8.8	1.0	9.6	1.6
2005	DET	MLB	31	1	3	9	25	0	27.3	21	14	31	4	24%	.258	18	1.28	2.64	4.33	3.00	7.3	4.7	10.3	1.3	8.4	1.8
2005	PHI	MLB	31	4	3	1	56	0	52.3	35	25	66	8	28%	.237	17	1.15	4.13	4.06	4.24	6.9	4.1	10.6	1.4	7.3	1.5
2006	PHI	MLB	32	4	3	7	59	1	68.0	54	30	73	10	31%	.254	14	1.22	3.57	3.80	3.78	6.9	3.6	9.1	1.3	13.8	1.3

Breakout: 31% Improve: 53% Collapse: 22% Attrition: 16% Comparables: Troy Percival, Skip Lockwood, Aurelio Lopez

Bizarroworld intersects with Major League Baseball in the life of Uggy Urbina. After 2004's gut-wrenching wait for kidnappers to release his mother in Venezuela, Urbina pitched in a career-high 81 games between Detroit and Philly before returning to his home country as a free agent in the offseason. There, he was promptly involved in another bizarre incident and jailed on charges of attempted murder. With his trial yet to start as of this writing, his future is anyone's guess. A useful setup pitcher because he varies the speed on his average fastball, Urbina survives on a good changeup. But a good changeup and ability to change speeds only gets you so far in the Venezuelan Penal League.

BILLY WAGNER Bats: L Throws: L Height: 5' 11" Weight: 180 Born: July 25, 1971 Age: 34

YEAR	TM	LVL	AGE	W	L	SV	G	GS	IP	H	BB	SO	HR	GB%	BABIP	STUFF	WHIP	ERA	PERA	EQERA	EQH9	EQBB9	EQSO9	EQHR9	VORP	WXRL
2003	HOU	MLB	31	1	4	44	78	0	86.0	52	23	105	8	46%	.226	34	0.87	1.78	3.14	2.06	6.6	2.3	10.2	0.9	35.9	6.5
2004	PHI	MLB	32	4	0	21	45	0	48.3	31	6	59	5	45%	.243	34	0.77	2.42	2.89	3.09	6.8	1.0	10.0	1.0	14.6	3.1
2005	PHI	MLB	33	4	3	38	75	0	77.7	45	20	87	6	45%	.218	31	0.84	1.51	3.13	2.17	6.4	2.3	9.5	0.7	30.8	3.8
2006	NYN	MLB	34	4	4	31	60	0	57.7	41	16	59	5	43%	.245	19	0.98	2.26	2.43	2.68	6.4	2.3	8.5	0.7	17.7	2.7

Breakout: 20% Improve: 32% Collapse: 36% Attrition: 20% Comparables: Mike Jackson, Arthur Rhodes, Jim Brewer

Wagner was truly dominant in 2005, posting numbers comparable to his 1999 and 2003 seasons with Houston. It's bad enough that he can throw 100 mph frequently and in the high 90s consistently, but combining that with a deceptive delivery and a cross-body motion makes him unhittable. When he needs a second bullet to slay good right-handed hitters capable of handling his heat, he can place his average-plus slider in on their hands. The Mets outbid the Phils with a hefty four-year, $43 million offer in November; that's a lot of money to guarantee to any reliever unless you're starting your own regional sports network. Oh, wait . . .

RANDY WOLF							Bats: L		Throws: L				Height: 6' 0"		Weight: 190		Born: August 22, 1976				Age: 29
YEAR	TM	LVL	AGE	W	L	SV	G	GS	IP	H	BB	SO	HR	GB%	BABIP	STUFF	WHIP	ERA	PERA	EQERA	EQH9	EQBB9	EQSO9	EQHR9	VORP	WXRL
2003	PHI	MLB	26	16	10	0	33	33	200.0	176	78	177	27	44%	.271	13	1.27	4.23	4.53	4.67	8.6	3.2	7.3	1.2	22.8	4.4
2004	PHI	MLB	27	5	8	0	23	23	136.7	145	36	89	20	39%	.293	2	1.32	4.28	4.79	4.85	9.7	2.2	5.3	1.3	15.2	2.3
2005	PHI	MLB	28	6	4	0	13	13	80.0	87	26	61	14	36%	.312	3	1.41	4.39	5.18	4.50	10.0	2.7	6.3	1.6	10.1	1.4
2006	PHI	MLB	29	8	8	0	29	20	130.3	135	41	90	19	41%	.286	6	1.35	4.49	4.81	4.84	9.1	2.6	5.8	1.3	13.1	2.1

Breakout: 17%   Improve: 50%   Collapse: 17%   Attrition: 6%   Comparables: Denny Lemaster, Jarrod Washburn, Mike Flanagan

After two stints on the DL in 2004 with elbow tendinitis, Wolf was shelved in June 2005 and underwent Tommy John surgery on July 1. He's aiming for a mid- to late-season return in 2006, but he will certainly need a fair amount of time after that to regain his command.

Line Outs

Position/Player	TM	LVL	AGE	PA	R	2B	3B	HR	RBI	BB	SO	SB-CS	SPEED	BA/OBP/SLG	MLVR	EQBA/OBP/SLG	EQA	VORP
3B M Costanzo*	BAT	A-	21	323	47	17	3	11	50	35	89	0-1	4.6	.274/.356/.473	.217	.232/.293/.400	.238	1.3
1B R. Ruiz	REA	AA	27	385	59	29	0	27	89	30	87	0-2	3.4	.349/.405/.669	.544	.272/.321/.495	.273	13.3
SS D. Sandoval	SWB	AAA	26	427	53	20	0	7	48	31	49	11-11	4.7	.331/.379/.436	.152	.292/.341/.380	.252	15.9

Pitcher	TM	LVL	AGE	W	L	SV	IP	H	BB	SO	HR	GB%	BABIP	STUFF	WHIP	ERA	PERA	EQERA	EQH9	EQBB9	EQSO9	EQHR9	VORP
R. Cameron	REA	AA	27	6	5	19	88.3	70	31	99	11	53%	.276	-27	1.14	2.55	6.30	4.61	9.6	4.5	6.4	2.0	8.8
J. Fernandez	LOU	AAA	33	5	5	0	84.3	86	26	51	8	45%	.300	-12	1.33	4.38	5.56	5.67	9.6	3.7	3.7	1.2	-0.6
	SWB	AAA	33	4	2	0	40.7	40	14	30	4	45%	.293	-7	1.33	2.65	5.35	5.35	9.5	4.0	4.7	1.2	1.1
S. Lee	REA	AA	26	3	1	0	64.0	58	24	50	2	41%	.298	0	1.28	1.97	4.62	4.18	9.1	4.5	4.5	0.4	9.5
P. Liriano	SWB	AAA	24	4	9	0	99.3	90	48	79	11	59%	.284	-8	1.39	3.90	5.55	4.89	8.9	4.9	5.6	1.2	7.5
T. Minix	REA	AA	27	1	1	7	58.7	44	15	55	3	41%	.263	-6	1.01	1.84	4.47	3.98	8.4	3.3	5.3	0.8	9.8
B. Sanches	SWB	AAA	26	5	3	1	83.0	81	27	75	9	40%	.317	-8	1.30	3.69	5.02	4.69	9.4	3.3	6.1	1.2	8.2

The club's top pick in the 2005 draft (2nd round), reviews of **Mike Costanzo's** performance in the NY-Penn League scream, "We've got to say something positive even though there's not much to say." A 25-year-old DH-type whose career was going nowhere, **Randy Ruiz** started hitting in the Sally League late in 2003, continued to in 2004, then tested positive for steroids late that year before being promoted to Reading, where he earned some undeserved comparisons to Ryan Howard. Although the International League batting champion, it is only the bankruptcy of the Philadelphia system that keeps **Danny Sandoval** on the 40-man roster—and in this chapter—when they already have Tomas Perez and Matt Kata.

Ryan Cameron closed games in Reading with mediocre stuff, then killed in the AFL. A longshot to make the club in 2006 as a mop-up reliever. Knuckleballer **Jared Fernandez** has now logged a dozen years in pro ball, wandering around with a lamp looking for an honest pitching coach and manager who will understand that he's got at least as good a chance of pitching 150 innings with a league-average ERA as 150 other guys thought of as mediocre prospects. Signed by Milwaukee in November, Fernandez opened a few eyes with his performance in the Dominican Winter League. Physically imposing **Seung Hak Lee** has spent the past three years bouncing between Double-A and Triple-A in the system. Although selected for the Eastern League All-Star team, he subsequently pitched with diminished velocity in Reading and landed on the DL. Reed-thin sinkerballer **Pedro Liriano** tossed batting practice in his brief stint in Philadelphia; his subsequent performance in Scranton would have been good enough to earn him six more chances if he were left-handed, but he isn't. A Devil Rays refugee, **Travis Minix** was signed by the Phils in March 2005 and pitched well enough in relief in Reading and Scranton to snag a spring training invite. He'll have an outside chance of making the club as a middle reliever. **Brian Sanches** decently in relief for the Red Barons in his first full year in Triple-A, then got his head handed to him in the AFL. He has an outside chance of making the team in the spring as the last pitcher, but he's more likely to ride the shuttle during the season.

Pittsburgh Pirates

Christopher Nolan's 2000 film *Memento* concerns a man with a very rare condition known as anterograde amnesia, the inability to form new memories. During an attempted robbery of his home, Leonard Shelby (Guy Pearce) witnesses his wife's murder and vows to take revenge on the perpetrators, but because his condition prevents him from retaining any information that he collects in his investigation, he resorts to tattooing his important findings on his body. Creepy messages like "Don't trust your weaknesses," "Memory is treachery," and the partial name of his wife's killer ("John G.") stare back at him when he looks at himself in the mirror. Every ten minutes he forgets what he's doing, consults his tattoos and the contents of his pockets, and relearns what stage he's at in his vendetta. His world has been transformed into a menacing, unsupportive place where he must trust others to not take advantage of him, a place where he needs luck and guile to be more than a helpless victim.

Since their back-to-back-to-back division championship run ended in 1992, the Pirates have been suffering from their own version of anterograde amnesia. Consequently, their quest to compete has been compromised by the inability to remember what has and has not worked in years past. And while they've had some notable acquisitions, they've also had their moments of functioning like a farm team for the rest of the majors. Like Leonard Shelby, it might help if the Bucs wrote down some basic, easily understood rules, and posted them in easy-to-find locations. This way, at the end of each season, they can quickly take stock of the present, decide if they are competitive or not, and act accordingly. Members of the Pirates' front office are not required to tattoo the following clues onto their bodies, but it might help.

Do We Count Time Passing as Progress?

If on a yearly basis, you need more than a few lucky breaks just to compete, then as an organization, you're missing several crucial middle steps between Existence and Competence. "If Sean Casey returns to his 2004 form, *and* Jeromy Burnitz hits 30 homers in his new digs, *and* Joe Randa is more Cincinnati Red (.289/.356/.491) than San Diego Padre (.256/.303/.395), *and* Zach Duke and Paul Maholm each continue to throw 2.00 ERA ball, *and* Oliver Perez throws like he did in 2004, *and* the Cardinals and

PIRATES PROSPECTUS

2005 record: 67–95; Sixth place, NL Central

Pythagenport record: 71–91

Runs scored per game: 4.20 (14th in NL)

Runs allowed per game: 4.75 (13th in NL)

Team EqA: .254 (13th in NL)

2005 Batters Age: 27.7 (Youngest in NL)

2005 Pitchers Age: 28.7 (4th youngest in NL)

Ballpark: PNC Park; Neutral park; Park Factor of 0.995

2005: For want of a compass, the Lloyd McClendon era comes to an end.

2006: Too many never-weres on the pitching staff and never-will-bes in the lineup will keep attendance low.

Astros regress, *and* the Cubs flounder, *and* the Milwaukee rebuilding plan takes another year to get going, then *maybe* we have a shot at the Wild Card." That's not planning, it's prayer.

Not many expect the Pirates to actually compete in 2006, but if you squint hard enough, there may be something resembling a rebuilding effort above and beyond the usual Pittsburgh illusion of activity. It's not clear whether it's the right plan, or even if it will *remain* the plan the day after tomorrow, but with a new on-field coaching staff and a 25-man roster increasingly populated by homegrown talent, it's clear the organization has reached a turning point. But is that enough to make the team relevant? The lure of a new ballpark is wearing off—despite PNC's charms, Pittsburgh was last in the league in attendance last year.

Is It a Plan Because We Write It Down?

Bryan Smith at BaseballAnalysts.com reported that the Pirates have been consciously tailoring their drafts around PNC Park's unique dimensions. Starting with the left-field line, the signs read 325, 389, 410, 399, 375, and 320, with the 399 sign marking straightaway center field. Because of these dimensions, the team's draft strategy has centered on two types of player: college-trained left-handed pitchers who can induce fly balls to PNC's cavernous left field (Pittsburgh ranked fifth in the NL in LF putouts in 2005), and left-handed power hitters to take advantage of the short right-field porch.

This reveals two important things. The first is that Pittsburgh has something resembling a plan. It's not enough to just fail your way into getting high draft picks every year (see: Kansas City Royals), you also have to execute a plan that can turn those high draft picks into a viable team. The Pirates are close to doing that, as they seem to be finding some success stories outside the first few rounds. While youngsters like Neil Walker, Bryan Bullington, and Paul Maholm have gotten a lot of publicity (positive or negative) for being early-rounders, players like Zach Duke (20th round), Ian Snell (26th round), and Nate McLouth (25th round) have also surfaced as useful players.

This also suggests that the Pirates understand a major component of team building in a small market, which is that young players need to contribute as soon as they can, while they're inexpensive. While detractors may point out that McLouth is probably maxed out as a fourth outfielder, he's cheap and perfectly suited for that now, which is all the Pirates need. If you're developing the McLouths, you don't have to sign the Hollandsworths for more money later on. Ditto the starting pitcher situation: by focusing on college-trained pitchers, the Pirates are letting the NCAA develop reliable pitchers for them.

Their attachment to lefty power hitters partly explains the signing of Jeromy Burnitz. In 2005, Burnitz hit 24 homers, 15 of which were to right field. He also hit eight warning-track fly balls that would have been homers had he hit them at PNC Park—one in Miami, three in Milwaukee, and four at his home park, Wrigley Field. It's a stretch to think those "almosts" will become home runs this season, but at least there were clear reasons for signing him. That's more than you could say for Cam Bonifay's signings of Kevin Young, Mike Benjamin, Derek Bell, Pat Meares, and a whole host of other veteran acquisitions. But this isn't something that should inform every decision that Littlefield makes. Sean Casey is a left-handed hitter, but unlike Burnitz, he's not expected to take advantage of the short porch in right in the way that Burnitz is supposed to. Casey played 2005 in offense-friendly Cincinnati, and he didn't benefit from the cozy right-field fence. There's no reason to think he'll be more of a power hitter in Pittsburgh than he did in Cincy.

Whether Burnitz's warning track shots turn into home runs—and whether measuring warning-track power in the first place has any predictive value at all—may not ultimately matter, as there's too great a distance between the top and bottom of the NL Central to make "the plan" bear real fruit in 2006. This technically qualifies as a plan, but as with so much else in the Pirates' development over the last decade-plus, the results aren't quite there yet.

Jose M. Can Be Found Again

Bullpen arms are highly volatile commodities, and spending a lot of money on proven closers or reliable setup men can easily result in a Keith Foulke, version 2005. With the success of the 2002 Angels and the 2005 White Sox, teams should be realizing that they can be thrifty and still not have to pay a lot of money for a quality bullpen. Hanging onto Jose Mesa well past his expiration date, and not making a trade before the deadline, when they could have gotten something in return, was a double whammy of bad decision making.

The Pirates wisely said goodbye to Mr. Table this off-season, letting him settle in Denver. This year's Jose Mesa might be Roberto Hernandez, Terry Adams, Brandon Duckworth, or other Quad-A guys who may yet have a Todd Jones season in them. Littlefield also bought low on Damaso Marte, a useful reliever when healthy. If the Pirates are ever going to contend on a shoestring budget, the fact that Littlefield is capable of finding bargain relievers is a promising sign. The knock on Littlefield is that he tries to be too fancy—the ability to identify and then acquire above-average bench players and middle relievers at wholesale prices only pays dividends if you put them in the right roles. You still need a few above-average players in your lineup every day. Littlefield doesn't, and hasn't yet grasped the major points of being at the helm of a competitive small-market team: the spare parts play complementary roles, not major ones. With the exception of de facto star Jason Bay and the now-overlooked Craig Wilson, the Pirates don't really have any above-average offensive talent.

Don't Stalk Veterans

This is the equivalent of Leonard Shelby's "Don't Trust Your Weaknesses" tattoo. While most remnants of the Bonifay regime have been swept away, an organizational fascination with veteran placeholders who aren't actually holding a place for anyone has stubbornly persisted into the present. Take this winter's crop of free agents: The acquisition of Joe Randa is marginally defensible. There really aren't any third basemen ready to step up from within the organization and produce on the cheap. That Randa is only signed for one year is promising, and if Littlefield is finally willing to deal at the deadline, the third baseman could find himself elsewhere for the season's final three months.

The acquisitions of both Burnitz and Casey leave Craig Wilson without a full-time position. Wilson will likely be the short side of a platoon with either Burnitz or Casey—most likely Burnitz—but his new salary of $3.5 million means that he'll be an expensive part-time player, and few will be surprised to find him playing for another team come July. Blocking Wilson and prospect Brad Eldred with Casey violates the "play the kids!" mantra, and adding an extra win or two by plugging in expensive veterans won't make much difference in the standings, attendance, or revenue. If there's a silver lining, it's that Eldred, who has a career .549 minor league SLG, will have more time down on the farm to work on his plate discipline. If he were left-handed, perhaps the Pirates would be more eager to tap his prodigious power, but lack of strike zone control is a glaring fault, and there is no use rushing him now.

While the Pirate organization's collective memory may reset every ten minutes, there are a few signs that they're at least trying to put a plan into motion. The potential success of that plan is worth revisiting at the end of 2006, when perhaps they will be a bit closer to contending. In theory, this differs from the Royals of the world, the teams that are not only lost at sea, but don't seem to care if they ever find land. Whatever the payoff, it involves more waiting for Pirate fans, who presumably do not suffer from anterograde amnesia.

HITTERS

JASON BAY   OF   Bats: R Throws: R   Height: 6' 2"   Weight: 200   Born: September 20, 1978   Age: 27

YEAR	TM	LVL	AGE	PA	R	2B	3B	HR	RBI	BB	SO	SB	CS	SPEED	BA	OBP	SLG	MLVR	EQBA	EQOBP	EQSLG	EQA	VORP	DEFENSE			
2003	POR	AAA	24	373	64	11	1	20	59	55	71	23	4	6.2	.303	.410	.541	.374	.287	.387	.507	.308	33.3	47-CF	0	37-RF	-1
2003	PIT	MLB	24	97	13	6	1	3	12	18	28	3	1	6.8	.291	.423	.506	.304	.291	.423	.506	.318	7.5	20-LF	-1		
2004	PIT	MLB	25	467	61	24	4	26	82	41	129	4	6	4.9	.282	.358	.550	.249	.278	.350	.548	.291	26.6	109-LF	2		
2005	PIT	MLB	26	707	110	44	6	32	101	95	142	21	1	6.7	.306	.402	.559	.350	.300	.397	.562	.323	72.6	134-LF	9	25-CF	-2
2006	PIT	MLB	27	682	104	37	4	32	103	92	148	16	5	5.5	.287	.388	.531	.227	.285	.387	.545	.307	48.6	159-LF	0		

Breakout: 4%   Improve: 31%   Collapse: 27%   Attrition: 0%   Comparables: Tim Salmon, Jesse Barfield, Eric Davis

Meet the third-best player in the National League in 2005. In his first full big league campaign, Bay ranked in the top five in the NL for times on base, total bases, extra-base hits and doubles. Bay hits for average, has shown improved patience and power, plays capable defense at the corners and, last season, stole bases with ruthless efficiency. At 27, he's in his prime right now. Here's hoping the Pirates put it to good use.

JOSE BAUTISTA   3B   Bats: R Throws: R   Height: 6' 0"   Weight: 190   Born: October 19, 1980   Age: 25

YEAR	TM	LVL	AGE	PA	R	2B	3B	HR	RBI	BB	SO	SB	CS	SPEED	BA	OBP	SLG	MLVR	EQBA	EQOBP	EQSLG	EQA	VORP	DEFENSE	
2003	LYN	A+	22	195	28	14	2	4	20	27	48	1	5	5.2	.242	.359	.424	.102	.221	.322	.405	.245	3.6	44-3B	7
2004	KCA	MLB	23	26	1	1	0	0	1	1	12	0	0	4.1	.200	.231	.240	-.491	.200	.231	.240	.170	-2.5		
2004	PIT	MLB	23	42	1	2	0	0	0	2	18	0	0	2.9	.200	.238	.250	-.432	.200	.238	.250	.176	-3.6		
2005	ALT	AA	24	505	63	27	1	23	90	48	101	7	3	4.3	.283	.364	.503	.242	.258	.331	.454	.268	23.6	113-3B	-12
2005	IND	AAA	24	55	6	3	0	1	4	4	10	1	1	4.4	.255	.309	.373	-.129	.226	.284	.326	.214	-1.7	13-3B	-1
2005	PIT	MLB	24	31	3	1	0	0	1	3	7	1	0	5.1	.143	.226	.179	-.544	.143	.226	.179	.167	-3.1		
2006	PIT	MLB	25	486	54	25	2	12	53	41	113	4	3	4.1	.244	.315	.389	-.109	.242	.314	.399	.239	1.1	115-3B	-1

Breakout: 22%   Improve: 47%   Collapse: 21%   Attrition: 13%   Comparables: Clete Boyer, Steve Buechele, Craig Worthington

Bautista bounced back rather well after a lost year; in '04 the Rule 5 pick logged only 95 plate appearances across four different organizations. Once he settled in at Double-A in 2005, Bautista showed adequate plate discipline and knocked an extra-base hit every 8.7 at-bats, although he was a bit old for the league. He has the tools to be a good third baseman, but he's inconsistent. There's some thought he might be converted to a Mackowiak-style rover's role. With Joe Randa signed to a one-year deal, the Pirates have bought time for Bautista to spend at least the first half of the season, if not longer, at Indianapolis.

ADAM BOEVE   OF   Bats: R Throws: R   Height: 6' 1"   Weight: 205   Born: June 20, 1980   Age: 26

YEAR	TM	LVL	AGE	PA	R	2B	3B	HR	RBI	BB	SO	SB	CS	SPEED	BA	OBP	SLG	MLVR	EQBA	EQOBP	EQSLG	EQA	VORP	DEFENSE			
2003	WPT	A-	23	156	20	9	1	3	16	15	39	6	1	5.5	.250	.353	.402	.157	.212	.277	.339	.221	-18.5	15-RF	1		
2004	HIC	A	24	535	93	25	2	28	93	61	112	10	2	5.2	.290	.385	.536	.274	.224	.293	.386	.237	-20.9	80-LF	2	27-RF	2
2005	LYN	A+	25	301	60	15	1	13	47	39	66	12	0	5.7	.313	.419	.538	.387	.260	.337	.417	.267	1.6	65-RF	4		
2005	ALT	AA	25	184	24	9	1	5	23	22	54	5	2	4.8	.287	.375	.450	.192	.260	.339	.394	.260	-0.4	36-RF	-2		
2006	PIT	MLB	26	443	47	21	2	10	46	36	124	7	2	4.4	.229	.299	.367	-.174	.228	.298	.376	.228	-10.9	105-RF	0		

Breakout: 7%   Improve: 26%   Collapse: 37%   Attrition: 15%   Comparables: M. Encarnacion, N. Gorneault, J. Sherrod

Boeve flashed excellent power in the Sally League in 2004, but it was hardly a challenging loop for a college-trained hitter who was already old for the level. He maintained his power in the Carolina League last year, but after a promotion to Altoona, Boeve faltered. He also flailed in the AFL, part of the reason the Pirates left him off the 40-man roster for '06. The power potential is intriguing, but his age works against him. Still, he'd be a better use of major league roster space than, say, Yurendell DeCaster. He'd also make a better actor than Orlando Bloom, but that's neither here nor there.

JOSH BONIFAY   **1B**   **Bats: R Throws: R**   Height: 6' 0"   Weight: 190   Born: July 30, 1978   Age: 27

YEAR	TM	LVL	AGE	PA	R	2B	3B	HR	RBI	BB	SO	SB	CS	SPEED	BA	OBP	SLG	MLVR	EQBA	EQOBP	EQSLG	EQA	VORP	DEFENSE	
2003	ALT	AA	24	431	51	30	0	11	56	39	106	1	4	3.1	.285	.348	.448	.144	.252	.309	.407	.246	-7.6	92-LF	1
2004	ALT	AA	25	394	52	16	0	19	76	40	96	5	1	4.2	.277	.360	.490	.193	.245	.315	.421	.255	-1.0	70-1B	5
2005	ALT	AA	26	416	53	22	3	25	77	33	110	0	1	3.8	.282	.339	.556	.273	.242	.292	.453	.251	-1.0	85-1B	5
2006	*PIT*	*MLB*	*27*	*385*	*40*	*18*	*1*	*13*	*48*	*29*	*113*	*1*	*1*	*3.6*	*.234*	*.297*	*.410*	*-.119*	*.233*	*.296*	*.420*	*.237*	*-5.6*	*92-1B*	*3*

Breakout: 14%   *Improve: 28%*   *Collapse: 38%*   *Attrition: 15%*   *Comparables: Roy Sievers, Mike Coolbaugh, Earl Snyder*

One-time Harvard president Charles Eliot once called Ivy Leaguers "the stupid sons of rich men." While we'd never deign to call Josh Bonifay something as insultingly odious as "Ivy Leaguer," the son of Cam has revealed himself to be something of a nepotista. He flashed good power last season, and he's a career .488 slugger, but that's a product of long assignments in the farm's furthest reaches. He's 27 and been in Altoona long enough to have streets named after him.

JOSE CASTILLO   **2B**   **Bats: R Throws: R**   Height: 6' 1"   Weight: 200   Born: March 19, 1981   Age: 25

YEAR	TM	LVL	AGE	PA	R	2B	3B	HR	RBI	BB	SO	SB	CS	SPEED	BA	OBP	SLG	MLVR	EQBA	EQOBP	EQSLG	EQA	VORP	DEFENSE			
2003	ALT	AA	22	549	68	24	6	5	66	40	81	19	10	6.3	.287	.339	.390	.048	.272	.320	.376	.245	7.5	71-2B	2	52-SS	-1
2004	PIT	MLB	23	409	44	15	2	8	39	23	92	3	2	4.8	.256	.298	.368	-.128	.252	.296	.361	.229	-0.1	107-2B	2		
2005	PIT	MLB	24	397	49	16	3	11	53	23	59	2	3	4.6	.268	.307	.416	-.028	.266	.308	.420	.248	5.8	95-2B	-1		
2006	*PIT*	*MLB*	*25*	*506*	*57*	*24*	*3*	*11*	*56*	*32*	*80*	*6*	*3*	*5.0*	*.273*	*.321*	*.409*	*-.050*	*.271*	*.320*	*.419*	*.248*	*12.2*	*119-2B*	*1*		

Breakout: 22%   *Improve: 50%*   *Collapse: 21%*   *Attrition: 21%*   *Comparables: Reno Bertoia, Damion Easley, Bob Aspromonte*

A torn-up knee ended Castillo's season in August, but he's expected to be fine by spring training. He hasn't done any really serious hitting since Lynchburg in 2002, but he already has two full seasons in the majors under his belt. The occasional pop in his bat is intriguing; the Pirates think he can muscle up to 20 home runs, and that would make for a productive middle infielder. He has to continue to develop to justify the Pirates' faith.

RAJAI DAVIS   **OF**   **Bats: B Throws: R**   Height: 5' 11"   Weight: 180   Born: October 19, 1980   Age: 25

YEAR	TM	LVL	AGE	PA	R	2B	3B	HR	RBI	BB	SO	SB	CS	SPEED	BA	OBP	SLG	MLVR	EQBA	EQOBP	EQSLG	EQA	VORP	DEFENSE			
2003	HIC	A	22	541	84	21	7	6	54	55	65	40	13	7.2	.305	.383	.416	.177	.263	.323	.367	.247	1.3	102-CF	4	14-LF	1
2004	LYN	A+	23	570	91	27	7	5	38	59	60	57	15	8.2	.314	.388	.424	.195	.278	.341	.380	.259	11.8	116-CF	-2		
2005	ALT	AA	24	555	82	22	5	4	34	43	76	45	9	7.6	.281	.351	.369	.043	.264	.327	.347	.248	-1.8	115-CF	1		
2006	*PIT*	*MLB*	*25*	*480*	*63*	*24*	*4*	*4*	*37*	*36*	*64*	*25*	*8*	*6.2*	*.276*	*.336*	*.375*	*-.069*	*.274*	*.335*	*.385*	*.250*	*5.7*	*113-CF*	*0*		

Breakout: 20%   *Improve: 46%*   *Collapse: 26%*   *Attrition: 20%*   *Comparables: Randy Winn, Jerry Mumphrey, Coco Crisp*

Davis has shown solid on-base skills over the last three seasons, but not much power. His glove will play in center, but he strikes out too much for a guy who relies on speed. He'll likely settle in as a passable fourth outfielder—not too shabby for a 38th round pick.

HUMBERTO COTA   **C**   **Bats: R Throws: R**   Height: 6' 0"   Weight: 210   Born: February 7, 1979   Age: 27

YEAR	TM	LVL	AGE	PA	R	2B	3B	HR	RBI	BB	SO	SB	CS	SPEED	BA	OBP	SLG	MLVR	EQBA	EQOBP	EQSLG	EQA	VORP	DEFENSE	
2003	NAS	AAA	24	222	23	9	0	8	27	20	59	2	0	3.9	.205	.284	.370	-.137	.195	.268	.350	.218	-8.7	57-C	-1
2004	PIT	MLB	25	70	10	1	1	5	8	3	20	0	0	5.5	.227	.271	.500	-.013	.227	.271	.500	.253	1.9	15-C	-1
2005	PIT	MLB	26	319	29	20	1	7	43	17	80	0	0	3.3	.242	.285	.387	-.122	.239	.283	.387	.232	1.6	77-C	-2
2006	*PIT*	*MLB*	*27*	*306*	*29*	*15*	*1*	*10*	*37*	*20*	*74*	*1*	*0*	*3.9*	*.240*	*.295*	*.404*	*-.126*	*.238*	*.294*	*.414*	*.234*	*2.5*	*74-C*	*-2*

Breakout: 28%   *Improve: 51%*   *Collapse: 35%*   *Attrition: 34%*   *Comparables: Duffy Dyer, Chris Widger, Bob Tillman*

Has all of his fingers and toes, but miscast as a starting catcher in the wake of the Benito Santiago meltdown. He's the quintessential catch-and-throw backup unencumbered by anything resembling sustainable offensive skills. Steve Lake, your life is calling.

YURENDELL DE CASTER UT **Bats: R Throws: R** Height: 6' 1" Weight: 200 Born: September 26, 1979 Age: 26

YEAR	TM	LVL	AGE	PA	R	2B	3B	HR	RBI	BB	SO	SB	CS	SPEED	BA	OBP	SLG	MLVR	EQBA	EQOBP	EQSLG	EQA	VORP	DEFENSE				
2003	LYN	A+	23	361	50	24	1	13	56	22	86	3	2	5.1	.230	.283	.427	-.011	.197	.240	.380	.214	-15.4	55-3B	6	21-1B	0
2004	ALT	AA	24	357	53	18	1	14	40	22	78	4	2	4.9	.274	.328	.463	.103	.251	.297	.418	.244	5.6	84-3B	-4		
2005	IND	AAA	25	460	60	31	4	11	61	37	103	7	5	5.5	.280	.346	.453	.063	.254	.318	.407	.250	-4.2	48-RF	3	23-3B	-3
2006	PIT	MLB	26	431	46	23	2	12	51	27	106	4	2	4.9	.245	.299	.404	-.116	.243	.298	.414	.236	-2.6	102-3B	-1		

Breakout: 24% Improve: 41% Collapse: 35% Attrition: 16% Comparables: Ken Gerhart, Tony Armas, Charlie Spikes

Indianapolis manager Trent Jewett loves De Caster's defense and his approach at the plate, which was apparently enough for the Pirates to add him to the 40-man roster over the winter. That approach involves attacking pitches without much discretion. As George C. Scott said in the film *They Might Be Giants,* "[Don Quixote] thought that every windmill was a giant. That's insane. But, thinking that they might be, well . . . All the best minds used to think the world was flat. But what if it isn't? It might be round. And bread mold might be medicine. If we never looked at things and thought of what might be, why we'd all still be out there in the tall grass with the apes." Conversely, questioning the obvious sometimes leads to great revelations, but it can just as often be a tremendous waste of time. That's why the De Caster version of this picture, *They Might Be Hittable Pitches,* won't be showing at your local theatre. It's doubtful he'll ever be a regular or much more than an end-of-the-bench guy.

RYAN DOUMIT C/OF? **Bats: B Throws: R** Height: 6' 0" Weight: 190 Born: April 3, 1981 Age: 25

YEAR	TM	LVL	AGE	PA	R	2B	3B	HR	RBI	BB	SO	SB	CS	SPEED	BA	OBP	SLG	MLVR	EQBA	EQOBP	EQSLG	EQA	VORP	DEFENSE	
2003	LYN	A+	22	524	75	38	1	11	77	45	79	4	0	5.0	.275	.351	.434	.128	.248	.312	.420	.254	11.6	82-C	1
2004	ALT	AA	23	254	31	20	0	10	34	21	49	0	1	3.0	.262	.343	.489	.150	.237	.305	.445	.255	6.2	24-C	-5
2005	IND	AAA	24	188	41	11	0	12	35	16	36	1	3	4.6	.345	.415	.630	.482	.312	.379	.562	.306	22.3	35-C	-3
2005	PIT	MLB	24	256	25	13	1	6	35	11	48	2	1	4.7	.255	.324	.398	-.029	.256	.319	.410	.252	6.1	48-C	2
2006	PIT	MLB	25	325	37	17	1	13	46	23	57	2	1	4.4	.268	.334	.463	.038	.266	.333	.474	.267	15.4	79-C	0

Breakout: 23% Improve: 52% Collapse: 21% Attrition: 28% Comparables: Damon Berryhill, Frank House, Dann Bilardello

Since arriving in the high minors, Doumit has flashed solid gap-power numbers and made strides with his plate discipline. You'll occasionally hear his defense pilloried, but for the foreseeable future the Bucs are committed to him behind the plate. Some within the organization would like to see Doumit abandon switch-hitting and bat solely from the left side, but that's not likely to happen right away. In any event, Doumit will be the team's regular catcher in 2006, and once he adjusts to the highest level he could be could for 50 extra-base hits per season. He's an underrated performer.

CHRIS DUFFY CF **Bats: L Throws: L** Height: 5' 10" Weight: 170 Born: April 20, 1980 Age: 26

YEAR	TM	LVL	AGE	PA	R	2B	3B	HR	RBI	BB	SO	SB	CS	SPEED	BA	OBP	SLG	MLVR	EQBA	EQOBP	EQSLG	EQA	VORP	DEFENSE	
2003	ALT	AA	23	561	84	23	6	1	42	44	78	34	12	7.5	.273	.355	.350	.009	.262	.329	.344	.244	-2.1	134-CF	3
2004	ALT	AA	24	503	84	23	6	8	41	33	77	32	8	7.6	.309	.378	.439	.181	.290	.345	.407	.266	17.7	109-CF	9
2005	IND	AAA	25	338	55	13	7	7	31	16	57	17	9	7.6	.308	.358	.464	.125	.282	.326	.422	.259	9.4	71-CF	0
2005	PIT	MLB	25	135	22	4	2	1	9	7	22	2	2	6.6	.341	.385	.429	.181	.339	.387	.425	.278	8.2	28-CF	1
2006	PIT	MLB	26	444	58	21	4	6	40	27	72	16	5	6.4	.287	.340	.405	-.014	.285	.339	.415	.257	11.8	105-CF	2

Breakout: 17% Improve: 38% Collapse: 36% Attrition: 19% Comparables: Randy Winn, Miguel Dilone, Willie McGee

With career minor league rates of .298/.372/.407 coming into the season, Duffy wasn't thought of as much of a prospect. Despite his speed (133 steals and only 16 GIDPs in 2,248 minor league PAs) and tremendous glovework in center field, his low walk rate and lack of power were considered impediments to his ever being much more than a reserve. But when the Pirates finally tired of Tike Redman and Rob Mackowiak couldn't play everywhere at once, Duffy got the call and shined in his month on the job before sustaining a season-ending torn hammy. He's earned a chance to show he can do it again, but the organization would like him to cut down on his strikeouts and take better advantage of his speed. Still, it's his glove and modest on-base abilities that will carry him.

BRAD ELDRED 1B Bats: R Throws: R Height: 6′ 6″ Weight: 240 Born: July 12, 1980 Age: 25

YEAR	TM	LVL	AGE	PA	R	2B	3B	HR	RBI	BB	SO	SB	CS	SPEED	BA	OBP	SLG	MLVR	EQBA	EQOBP	EQSLG	EQA	VORP	DEFENSE	
2003	HIC	A	22	472	62	22	0	28	80	38	142	7	1	4.3	.250	.326	.502	.170	.206	.261	.418	.231	-19.8	104-1B	-4
2004	LYN	A+	23	388	54	22	1	21	77	35	97	5	2	4.2	.310	.397	.570	.399	.268	.336	.497	.280	16.6	88-1B	-2
2004	ALT	AA	23	158	24	9	0	17	60	6	51	0	0	2.7	.279	.329	.687	.421	.250	.293	.602	.285	9.3	38-1B	4
2005	ALT	AA	24	93	22	6	0	13	27	8	25	1	1	4.6	.333	.387	.869	.823	.293	.343	.740	.328	13.7	19-1B	0
2005	IND	AAA	24	214	31	13	1	15	48	14	57	4	0	5.3	.282	.336	.590	.237	.256	.310	.525	.278	7.8	37-1B	3
2005	PIT	MLB	24	208	23	9	0	12	27	13	77	1	1	3.3	.221	.279	.458	-.055	.221	.279	.463	.248	-1.2	46-1B	-7
2006	*PIT*	*MLB*	*25*	*488*	*60*	*23*	*1*	*29*	*82*	*35*	*149*	*3*	*1*	*4.0*	*.241*	*.304*	*.492*	*.005*	*.239*	*.303*	*.504*	*.262*	*7.1*	*115-1B*	*-2*

Breakout: 16%   Improve: 36%   Collapse: 36%   Attrition: 10%   Comparables: Ryan Howard, Pete Incaviglia, Rob Stratton

This particular monster mash might not play in major markets. Eldred owns a career .549 SLG in the minors, but he's a lumbering sort with major holes in his swing, dubious pitch-recognition skills, a slow bat, and no position to speak of. If he was in the DH league and had an especially capable hitting coach, he might have a future. But right now, if he plays every day, he's going to strike out 200 times. Gus Suhr's franchise record for games at first base, now 66 years old, will probably have to await the challenge of a better-rounded ballplayer. Eldred too will have to wait for an opportunity after the unfortunate decision to import Sean Casey.

J. J. FURMANIAK INF Bats: R Throws: R Height: 6′ 0″ Weight: 190 Born: July 31, 1979 Age: 26

YEAR	TM	LVL	AGE	PA	R	2B	3B	HR	RBI	BB	SO	SB	CS	SPEED	BA	OBP	SLG	MLVR	EQBA	EQOBP	EQSLG	EQA	VORP	DEFENSE			
2003	LEL	A+	23	355	65	22	8	9	54	36	55	10	4	7.1	.314	.397	.524	.327	.268	.337	.436	.266	17.7	76-SS	1		
2003	MOB	AA	23	116	10	4	1	3	11	8	27	0	0	3.8	.262	.336	.408	.060	.250	.312	.420	.252	3.4	31-SS	-2		
2004	POR	AAA	24	471	71	24	4	17	73	33	86	8	5	5.5	.292	.346	.487	.104	.267	.318	.430	.257	18.1	117-SS	1		
2005	POR	AAA	25	423	54	16	4	14	47	28	86	9	5	5.4	.266	.324	.437	-.020	.246	.294	.391	.237	0.9	55-3B	4	36-SS	-4
2005	IND	AAA	25	146	12	5	3	2	21	4	32	5	3	6.0	.288	.315	.410	-.042	.264	.293	.373	.231	0.6	29-SS	1		
2005	PIT	MLB	25	30	3	1	1	0	1	4	4	0	0	6.4	.192	.300	.308	-.220	.192	.300	.308	.220	-0.8				
2006	*PIT*	*MLB*	*26*	*464*	*53*	*22*	*3*	*12*	*50*	*31*	*95*	*6*	*3*	*4.9*	*.253*	*.310*	*.404*	*-.092*	*.251*	*.309*	*.414*	*.242*	*7.3*	*110-SS*	*0*		

Breakout: 23%   Improve: 47%   Collapse: 28%   Attrition: 13%   Comparables: Dale Berra, Randy Jackson, Alex Gonzalez

No, his last name is not a vanity plate of a fur fetishist. Acquired from the Padres in exchange for David Ross, Furmaniak hasn't shown adequate pop outside the hitter-friendly California and Pacific Coast Leagues. On the plus side, he's a capable defender at second, third and short, and the Pirates believe he has the speed and tracking instincts to handle all three outfield spots. His bat won't play every day, but positional flexibility and "scrappy" cachet have gotten plenty of guys long careers.

JODY GERUT OF Bats: L Throws: L Height: 6′ 0″ Weight: 200 Born: September 18, 1977 Age: 28

YEAR	TM	LVL	AGE	PA	R	2B	3B	HR	RBI	BB	SO	SB	CS	SPEED	BA	OBP	SLG	MLVR	EQBA	EQOBP	EQSLG	EQA	VORP	DEFENSE			
2003	CLE	MLB	25	524	66	33	2	22	75	35	70	4	5	4.3	.279	.336	.494	.127	.283	.344	.507	.282	20.1	60-RF	3	35-LF	2
2004	CLE	MLB	26	545	72	31	5	11	51	54	59	13	6	6.1	.252	.334	.405	-.053	.258	.343	.417	.265	5.0	112-RF	4	11-CF	-1
2005	CLE	MLB	27	157	12	9	1	1	12	18	14	1	1	4.4	.275	.357	.377	.010	.292	.380	.401	.276	2.7	20-RF	-1	16-LF	-1
2006	*PIT*	*MLB*	*28*	*263*	*32*	*15*	*1*	*7*	*32*	*26*	*30*	*3*	*1*	*4.8*	*.279*	*.355*	*.439*	*.050*	*.277*	*.354*	*.450*	*.271*	*8.0*	*65-RF*	*0*		

Breakout: 20%   Improve: 40%   Collapse: 27%   Attrition: 31%   Comparables: Danny Heep, Norm Larker, Art Shamsky

What do we really have here? Gerut was an adequate hitter in 2003, but he wasn't a young rookie. His bat was cold throughout 2004 and he tore up his knee that September. He didn't return from the DL until May '05. He looked rusty, and the Indians dealt him to the Cubs on July 18. There, Dusty Baker gave him 11 at-bats in roughly two weeks, then shipped him on to the Pirates for Matt Lawton at the deadline, which must have seemed like a steal to the Cubs at the time. Gerut lasted four games with Pittsburgh before a new knee injury sidelined him for the rest of the year. Not even getting his health back guarantees that he'll find his power stroke. He'll be reduced to a reserve role behind Craig Wilson and Jason Bay in the corners, which he's better suited for anyway.

JAVIER GUZMAN SS **Bats: R Throws: R** Height: 5' 11" Weight: 160 Born: May 4, 1984 Age: 22

YEAR	TM	LVL	AGE	PA	R	2B	3B	HR	RBI	BB	SO	SB	CS	SPEED	BA	OBP	SLG	MLVR	EQBA	EQOBP	EQSLG	EQA	VORP	DEFENSE	
2003	WPT	A-	19	184	19	9	2	2	24	10	26	4	3	5.0	.243	.283	.353	-.006	.230	.262	.342	.212	-11.0	40-SS	-5
2004	HIC	A	20	497	75	20	12	2	63	20	78	31	14	8.1	.306	.334	.413	.047	.266	.288	.354	.227	-2.8	124-SS	-4
2005	LYN	A+	21	278	40	13	7	5	35	20	41	13	5	6.9	.324	.374	.488	.266	.303	.341	.456	.273	19.6	68-SS	-5
2005	ALT	AA	21	275	27	9	1	3	24	10	46	8	5	5.3	.236	.262	.312	-.212	.227	.256	.303	.202	-13.7	69-SS	8
2006	*PIT*	*MLB*	*22*	*488*	*55*	*23*	*5*	*5*	*41*	*23*	*76*	*14*	*6*	*5.3*	*.259*	*.295*	*.362*	*-.169*	*.257*	*.294*	*.371*	*.225*	*3.6*	*115-SS*	*1*

Breakout: 25% Improve: 49% Collapse: 25% Attrition: 5%   Comparables: Teuris Olivares, Zoilo Versalles, Gary Cates

Guzman's numbers in the Carolina League last season look impressive at first blush, but his offensive production is all locked up in that .324 batting average and he looked lost in the second half after a promotion to Altoona. He does have the arm for shortstop, but he's not yet as reliable as you'd want him to be. It also came to light that he was actually 23 rather than his stated age of 21 last year, so consider him a non-prospect until he proves himself in the high minors.

BOBBY HILL 2B/3B **Bats: B Throws: R** Height: 5' 10" Weight: 180 Born: April 3, 1978 Age: 28

YEAR	TM	LVL	AGE	PA	R	2B	3B	HR	RBI	BB	SO	SB	CS	SPEED	BA	OBP	SLG	MLVR	EQBA	EQOBP	EQSLG	EQA	VORP	DEFENSE				
2003	IOW	AAA	25	408	53	23	4	6	40	37	65	8	7	5.1	.288	.365	.424	.099	.267	.338	.394	.254	11.7	83-2B	-10			
2004	PIT	MLB	26	266	28	7	2	2	27	20	39	0	3	3.3	.266	.353	.339	-.054	.264	.346	.336	.242	1.5	29-2B	3	18-3B	-2
2005	PIT	MLB	27	105	12	6	0	0	11	9	17	0	0	4.3	.269	.343	.333	-.069	.269	.343	.333	.244	0.5	17-3B	-1		
2005	IND	AAA	27	134	15	4	0	0	5	14	29	2	0	3.9	.241	.336	.276	-.214	.212	.300	.238	.208	-7.6	18-2B	-4	10-3B	-3
2006	*SDN*	*MLB*	*28*	*243*	*25*	*10*	*1*	*2*	*20*	*21*	*45*	*3*	*1*	*4.2*	*.233*	*.311*	*.312*	*-.222*	*.241*	*.319*	*.336*	*.226*	*-2.2*	*60-2B*	*-2*		

Breakout: 26% Improve: 40% Collapse: 38% Attrition: 34%   Comparables: Mike Gallego, Brooks Badeaux, Esteban Beltre

Once a top prospect in the Cubs' organization, Hill has been foundering for years. He's never displayed any power, and he'll be 28 by Opening Day. Let's see: doesn't hit for average, doesn't hit for power, doesn't steal bases any more (hard to believe that this is the same guy who stole 81 bases in the Atlantic League). Nurse, break out the paddles! This ballplayer's gone inert! Designated for assignment over the winter, then traded to the Padres for an amiable handshake or perhaps a knowing glance. He'll be the stalking horse in the competition between Mark Bellhorn and Josh Barfield for the second base job.

ROB MACKOWIAK UT **Bats: L Throws: R** Height: 5' 10" Weight: 190 Born: June 20, 1976 Age: 30

YEAR	TM	LVL	AGE	PA	R	2B	3B	HR	RBI	BB	SO	SB	CS	SPEED	BA	OBP	SLG	MLVR	EQBA	EQOBP	EQSLG	EQA	VORP	DEFENSE				
2003	PIT	MLB	27	193	20	4	4	6	19	15	53	6	0	6.8	.270	.342	.443	.073	.264	.333	.437	.271	9.5	15-3B	-1			
2004	PIT	MLB	28	554	65	22	6	17	75	50	114	13	4	6.5	.246	.319	.420	-.021	.242	.314	.413	.254	5.9	50-RF	-3	46-3B	1
2005	PIT	MLB	29	510	57	21	3	9	58	43	100	8	4	5.7	.272	.337	.389	-.007	.272	.338	.392	.255	8.7	50-3B	2	32-CF	-2
2006	*CHA*	*MLB*	*30*	*406*	*51*	*17*	*3*	*11*	*43*	*31*	*84*	*7*	*3*	*5.4*	*.257*	*.319*	*.411*	*-.045*	*.256*	*.324*	*.407*	*.246*	*4.2*	*97-3B*	*-1*		

Breakout: 19% Improve: 39% Collapse: 23% Attrition: 23%   Comparables: Hank Arft, Grady Hatton, Wayne Kirby

Mackowiak is stretched as a regular, but his ability to play six different positions, modest on-base chops, and gap power make him a useful part of any roster. In December, the White Sox acquired him for Damaso Marte, getting themselves a better insurance policy than previous reserves Timo Perez, Willie Harris, and Pablo Ozuna. Credit Kenny Williams with knowing that complacency is a champion's archenemy.

NATE McLOUTH RF **Bats: L Throws: R** Height: 5' 11" Weight: 170 Born: October 28, 1981 Age: 24

YEAR	TM	LVL	AGE	PA	R	2B	3B	HR	RBI	BB	SO	SB	CS	SPEED	BA	OBP	SLG	MLVR	EQBA	EQOBP	EQSLG	EQA	VORP	DEFENSE				
2003	LYN	A+	21	503	85	27	2	6	33	55	68	40	4	7.4	.300	.386	.411	.164	.277	.351	.407	.272	5.1	59-LF	0	48-CF	-2
2004	ALT	AA	22	578	93	40	4	8	73	48	62	31	7	6.9	.322	.384	.462	.235	.307	.363	.435	.281	21.3	98-RF	-9	23-CF	1
2005	IND	AAA	23	450	64	20	3	5	39	39	58	34	8	6.8	.297	.364	.401	.039	.274	.340	.368	.259	-5.1	73-LF	3	27-CF	0
2005	PIT	MLB	23	118	20	6	0	5	12	3	20	2	0	5.7	.257	.305	.450	.003	.252	.300	.459	.260	3.1	19-CF	-2		
2006	*PIT*	*MLB*	*24*	*499*	*68*	*28*	*3*	*8*	*50*	*40*	*64*	*22*	*6*	*5.9*	*.289*	*.352*	*.420*	*.028*	*.287*	*.351*	*.430*	*.268*	*15.3*	*118-LF*	*0*		

Breakout: 23% Improve: 47% Collapse: 24% Attrition: 10%   Comparables: Rick Manning, Hosken Powell, Johnny Damon

McLouth finds himself in an all-too-common developmental pickle: he lacks the glove for center and the bat for a corner. He hasn't shown adequate plate discipline since arriving in the high minors, and the power has never been there (career Isolated Slugging Percentage of only .135), or wasn't until last fall, when he hit four home runs in his last six games. Sometimes, stuff happens. He's left-handed, can steal a base, and he gets high marks for being a gamer, so he'll be around for a while as a popular outfield reserve, perhaps lucking into a Joe Orsulak sort of career.

RONNY PAULINO C **Bats: R Throws: R** Height: 6′ 3″ Weight: 210 Born: April 21, 1981 Age: 25

YEAR	TM	LVL	AGE	PA	R	2B	3B	HR	RBI	BB	SO	SB	CS	SPEED	BA	OBP	SLG	MLVR	EQBA	EQOBP	EQSLG	EQA	VORP	DEFENSE	
2003	LYN	A+	22	91	8	3	0	1	12	8	8	1	0	3.5	.235	.308	.309	-.124	.202	.269	.262	.199	-6.8	14-C	0
2003	ALT	AA	22	173	19	6	1	6	19	12	35	0	2	3.8	.226	.283	.390	-.090	.210	.264	.367	.216	-5.6	43-C	9
2004	ALT	AA	23	403	54	23	2	15	58	32	61	3	2	4.4	.285	.345	.482	.166	.269	.324	.452	.264	18.3	80-C	6
2005	ALT	AA	24	183	24	6	0	6	20	15	30	3	0	4.8	.292	.350	.435	.136	.268	.324	.398	.252	4.2	40-C	4
2005	IND	AAA	24	301	49	18	2	13	42	26	48	3	0	5.1	.315	.372	.538	.257	.290	.348	.494	.286	22.9	63-C	5
2006	*PIT*	*MLB*	*25*	*452*	*49*	*22*	*1*	*12*	*55*	*31*	*74*	*4*	*2*	*4.5*	*.265*	*.321*	*.415*	*-.049*	*.264*	*.320*	*.425*	*.249*	*10.3*	*107-C*	*7*

Breakout: 13% Improve: 41% Collapse: 33% Attrition: 14% Comparables: Geronimo Gil, Sandy Alomar, Ray Fosse

Paulino is one of the most underrated prospects in the system. The organization loves his defensive skills, and he's cultivated a good power stroke over the past two seasons. The problem, for the time being, is that Paulino is behind Ryan Doumit in the organizational catching queue. However, because of his superior glove, it may be Doumit who finds himself moved to another position. The Pirates have had to make a lot of decisions like this in recent years: Craig Wilson: animal, vegetable, or mineral? Is Tike Redman or isn't he? Who's on first? Whatever the case, they've rarely been decisive, meaning they might not commit to either Paulino or Doumit at catcher for a long time. Jim Tracy's first test will be to demonstrate more ability than Lloyd McClendon at sorting out options.

TIKE REDMAN OF **Bats: L Throws: L** Height: 5′ 11″ Weight: 170 Born: March 10, 1977 Age: 29

YEAR	TM	LVL	AGE	PA	R	2B	3B	HR	RBI	BB	SO	SB	CS	SPEED	BA	OBP	SLG	MLVR	EQBA	EQOBP	EQSLG	EQA	VORP	DEFENSE	
2003	NAS	AAA	26	398	60	12	7	4	29	36	32	42	9	8.3	.294	.357	.400	.107	.285	.345	.388	.266	10.7	87-CF	-2
2003	PIT	MLB	26	246	36	16	5	3	19	14	18	7	3	7.3	.330	.374	.483	.224	.325	.368	.476	.286	18.5	50-CF	1
2004	PIT	MLB	27	577	65	19	4	8	51	23	52	18	6	6.7	.280	.310	.374	-.076	.278	.307	.369	.239	3.6	136-CF	-1
2005	PIT	MLB	28	342	33	12	4	2	26	19	27	4	1	5.8	.251	.292	.332	-.179	.251	.296	.332	.225	-6.2	59-CF	0
2006	*NYN*	*MLB*	*29*	*273*	*33*	*11*	*2*	*2*	*22*	*16*	*24*	*7*	*2*	*6.1*	*.271*	*.316*	*.357*	*-.131*	*.275*	*.320*	*.378*	*.239*	*1.8*	*67-CF*	*-1*

Breakout: 20% Improve: 49% Collapse: 31% Attrition: 29% Comparables: Jose Tartabull, Joe Simpson, Marv Rackley

Redman's an average glove in center, and that's not enough to cover for middling power and a career .312 OBP. That splash he made in 2003 was a product of a .330 batting average in a third of a season. But that small sample belied his true ability. Redman could be a tolerable fifth outfielder, but otherwise he's stretched. Dropped from the 40-man over the winter and acquired by the Mets for cash.

FREDDY SANCHEZ INF **Bats: R Throws: R** Height: 5′ 11″ Weight: 180 Born: December 21, 1977 Age: 28

YEAR	TM	LVL	AGE	PA	R	2B	3B	HR	RBI	BB	SO	SB	CS	SPEED	BA	OBP	SLG	MLVR	EQBA	EQOBP	EQSLG	EQA	VORP	DEFENSE				
2003	PAW	AAA	25	244	46	17	0	5	25	31	36	8	0	6.0	.341	.430	.493	.364	.307	.397	.452	.300	24.2	34-SS	5	20-2B	-1	
2004	NAS	AAA	26	138	10	7	1	1	11	11	17	4	1	4.8	.264	.326	.360	-.134	.247	.307	.336	.232	-1.9	19-2B	0			
2005	PIT	MLB	27	488	54	26	4	5	35	27	36	2	2	5.2	.291	.336	.400	.016	.290	.335	.404	.256	11.7	54-3B	4	44-2B	-2	
2006	*PIT*	*MLB*	*28*	*481*	*56*	*25*	*2*	*5*	*45*	*35*	*52*	*4*	*2*	*4.9*	*.276*	*.333*	*.380*	*-.066*	*.274*	*.332*	*.390*	*.246*	*8.8*	*114-3B*	*2*			

Breakout: 14% Improve: 36% Collapse: 41% Attrition: 12% Comparables: Joe Randa, Danny O'Connell, Mike Bordick

In his first extended trial in the majors, Sanchez put together a decent season by middle-infield standards. If he continues to get on base at a .330 or so clip and slug north of .400, he's a solid everyday solution at short or second. He can pick it at third, but his bat isn't worth playing there. It behooves the Pirates to see whether Sanchez can maintain this level of production, but Jack Wilson and Castillo are blocking the middle, and Randa is plugged in at third.

CRAIG STANSBERRY 2B **Bats: R Throws: R** Height: 6′ 0″ Weight: 185 Born: March 8, 1982 Age: 24

YEAR	TM	LVL	AGE	PA	R	2B	3B	HR	RBI	BB	SO	SB	CS	SPEED	BA	OBP	SLG	MLVR	EQBA	EQOBP	EQSLG	EQA	VORP	DEFENSE	
2003	WPT	A-	21	184	19	9	3	2	21	13	25	5	3	4.9	.307	.370	.434	.264	.290	.334	.423	.261	15.6	45-3B	11
2004	HIC	A	22	451	57	14	5	9	67	52	88	20	8	5.8	.286	.377	.417	.104	.240	.312	.340	.234	-4.8	102-2B	13
2005	LYN	A+	23	107	17	7	2	3	19	11	13	7	1	6.9	.351	.430	.564	.482	.316	.376	.486	.297	10.0	23-2B	-4
2005	ALT	AA	23	478	62	22	11	18	67	44	114	14	5	6.9	.238	.314	.470	.083	.222	.295	.437	.252	6.4	114-2B	-6
2006	*PIT*	*MLB*	*24*	*530*	*67*	*27*	*5*	*14*	*57*	*43*	*109*	*13*	*5*	*5.4*	*.250*	*.317*	*.415*	*-.067*	*.248*	*.316*	*.425*	*.249*	*10.7*	*125-2B*	*-1*

Breakout: 20% Improve: 48% Collapse: 19% Attrition: 7% Comparables: Joe Jester, Marshall McDougall, Mike Young

After Stansberry starred at Rice, the Pirates picked him in the 5th round of the '03 draft. Products from elite college programs should be pushed aggressively, and the Pirates appropriately bumped him up to Double-A after he tore through

(continued next page)

Craig Stansberry (continued)

the Carolina League. At Altoona, Stansberry's batting average tumbled to .238, but he still smacked 51 extra-base hits in 421 at-bats, the sort of thing you notice in a second baseman. He's worth watching, and if he makes better contact, he'll help put enough runs on the board to be a second-base solution if Castillo or Sanchez don't pan out.

NEIL WALKER   **C**   **Bats: B Throws: R**   Height: 6′ 3″   Weight: 205   Born: September 10, 1985   Age: 20

YEAR	TM	LVL	AGE	PA	R	2B	3B	HR	RBI	BB	SO	SB	CS	SPEED	BA	OBP	SLG	MLVR	EQBA	EQOBP	EQSLG	EQA	VORP	DEFENSE	
2005	HIC	A	19	518	78	33	2	12	68	20	71	7	4	5.3	.301	.332	.452	.115	.263	.288	.396	.236	1.4	80-C	4
2005	LYN	A+	19	45	4	2	1	0	12	0	12	0	0	6.3	.262	.244	.357	-.205	.250	.233	.345	.209	-2.8		
2006	*PIT*	*MLB*	*20*	*489*	*50*	*31*	*2*	*8*	*56*	*17*	*72*	*5*	*3*	*5.2*	*.265*	*.294*	*.395*	*-.122*	*.263*	*.293*	*.404*	*.230*	*3.3*	*116-C*	*4*

Breakout: 30%   Improve: 54%   Collapse: 28%   Attrition: 7%   Comparables: Edgar Martinez, Brian McCann, Alex Fernandez

Walker is the first "local boy" in Pirates history to be drafted in the first round (11th overall in 2004), which will work in his favor. Walker's a switch hitter who boasts a smooth line-drive swing that should generate decent averages and gap power, but he has a glaring lack of patience. Behind the plate, Walker is athletic and strong-armed but unpolished. It's possible that he'll be moved to another position, perhaps third base, but they'll leave him behind the plate until he proves he can't catch. (This was the same approach they took with J. R. House, and that didn't turn out well.) If he reaches Pittsburgh, Walker will join Honus Wagner and Dick Groat on the Pirates' short list of local guys made good.

DARYLE WARD   **1B**   **Bats: L Throws: L**   Height: 6′ 2″   Weight: 240   Born: June 27, 1975   Age: 31

YEAR	TM	LVL	AGE	PA	R	2B	3B	HR	RBI	BB	SO	SB	CS	SPEED	BA	OBP	SLG	MLVR	EQBA	EQOBP	EQSLG	EQA	VORP	DEFENSE	
2003	LAN	MLB	28	114	6	1	0	0	9	3	19	0	0	3.5	.183	.211	.193	-.551	.193	.219	.202	.158	-13.7	11-1B	0
2004	PIT	MLB	29	321	39	17	2	15	57	22	45	0	0	4.3	.249	.305	.474	.022	.246	.300	.468	.259	5.6	63-1B	-6
2005	PIT	MLB	30	453	46	21	1	12	63	37	60	0	2	3.1	.260	.318	.405	-.024	.257	.317	.412	.253	0.3	101-1B	-9
2006	*PIT*	*MLB*	*31*	*367*	*36*	*18*	*1*	*11*	*48*	*25*	*55*	*0*	*1*	*3.8*	*.259*	*.312*	*.414*	*-.068*	*.258*	*.311*	*.425*	*.245*	*-1.1*	*88-1B*	*-4*

Breakout: 36%   Improve: 64%   Collapse: 18%   Attrition: 23%   Comparables: Larry Sheets, Terry Kennedy, Ed Herrmann

A brutal fielder and a streaky hitter, Ward doesn't produce consistently enough to be even the left-handed half of a DH platoon. He was just the latest in a long line of mediocre Pirates first basemen. With Sean Casey in hand, the Pirates let Ward go, hoping they've finally broken that streak. But that seems unlikely.

TY WIGGINTON   **3B**   **Bats: R Throws: R**   Height: 6′ 0″   Weight: 200   Born: October 11, 1977   Age: 28

YEAR	TM	LVL	AGE	PA	R	2B	3B	HR	RBI	BB	SO	SB	CS	SPEED	BA	OBP	SLG	MLVR	EQBA	EQOBP	EQSLG	EQA	VORP	DEFENSE				
2003	NYN	MLB	25	632	73	36	6	11	71	46	124	12	2	6.1	.255	.318	.396	-.050	.255	.317	.401	.252	14.0	151-3B	-1			
2004	NYN	MLB	26	338	46	23	2	12	42	23	48	6	1	5.6	.285	.334	.487	.125	.281	.330	.479	.275	17.0	55-3B	-4	21-2B	1
2004	PIT	MLB	26	206	17	7	0	5	24	22	34	1	0	3.6	.220	.306	.341	-.159	.214	.301	.341	.229	-4.8	50-3B	-2			
2005	IND	AAA	27	328	53	18	0	14	52	45	56	8	5	5.3	.293	.390	.507	.221	.251	.345	.427	.267	13.8	51-3B	0			
2005	PIT	MLB	27	170	20	9	1	7	25	14	30	0	1	4.5	.258	.324	.465	.060	.256	.326	.474	.267	4.7	34-3B	-5			
2006	*TBA*	*MLB*	*28*	*424*	*49*	*20*	*2*	*12*	*50*	*35*	*74*	*5*	*2*	*5.0*	*.261*	*.326*	*.420*	*-.020*	*.267*	*.339*	*.443*	*.261*	*12.5*	*101-3B*	*-3*			

Breakout: 21%   Improve: 48%   Collapse: 25%   Attrition: 12%   Comparables: Sean Berry, Benny Agbayani, Casey Blake

While Wigginton isn't is a championship-quality third baseman, he might still make a decent enough placeholder. The problem is that wasn't what the Pirates thought they had when they got him in the Kris Benson trade. Released in December, his ceiling is obviously limited. He's no more than a one-year solution for the Devil Rays.

CRAIG WILSON   **1B/OF**   **Bats: R Throws: R**   Height: 6′ 2″   Weight: 217   Born: November 30, 1976   Age: 29

YEAR	TM	LVL	AGE	PA	R	2B	3B	HR	RBI	BB	SO	SB	CS	SPEED	BA	OBP	SLG	MLVR	EQBA	EQOBP	EQSLG	EQA	VORP	DEFENSE				
2003	PIT	MLB	26	358	49	15	4	18	48	35	89	3	1	5.4	.262	.360	.511	.180	.257	.350	.511	.289	19.4	30-RF	3	26-1B	-2
2004	PIT	MLB	27	644	97	35	5	29	82	50	169	2	2	4.9	.264	.354	.499	.158	.260	.346	.497	.283	30.8	71-RF	-1	56-1B	-6
2005	PIT	MLB	28	238	23	14	1	5	22	30	69	3	0	4.5	.264	.387	.421	.118	.261	.381	.432	.287	9.9	27-RF	1	16-LF	1
2006	*PIT*	*MLB*	*29*	*427*	*56*	*22*	*3*	*17*	*60*	*46*	*105*	*5*	*2*	*4.9*	*.269*	*.366*	*.485*	*.118*	*.267*	*.365*	*.497*	*.287*	*18.1*	*101-RF*	*-2*		

Breakout: 9%   Improve: 38%   Collapse: 31%   Attrition: 16%   Comparables: Dick Gernert, Nate Colbert, Benny Agbayani

Wilson set a career high in OBP, but career lows in almost every meaningful power indicator, not something the Bucs wanted from him at first base or an outfield corner. Wilson's numbers were hindered by multiple injuries, but when healthy, he's a producer. Wilson's playing time in Pittsburgh has always been hard-won, but assuming arbitration doesn't price him out of the sub-wealthy (by baseball standards) Kid McClatchy's price range, he's ticketed for the starting job in right field.

JACK WILSON SS **Bats: R Throws: R** Height: 6' 0" Weight: 170 Born: December 29, 1977 Age: 28

YEAR	TM	LVL	AGE	PA	R	2B	3B	HR	RBI	BB	SO	SB	CS	SPEED	BA	OBP	SLG	MLVR	EQBA	EQOBP	EQSLG	EQA	VORP	DEFENSE
2003	PIT	MLB	25	604	58	21	3	9	62	36	74	5	5	4.9	.256	.303	.353	-.143	.254	.300	.356	.231	0.6	145-SS 0
2004	PIT	MLB	26	686	82	41	12	11	59	26	71	8	4	6.1	.308	.335	.459	.109	.304	.331	.454	.267	42.8	153-SS 14
2005	PIT	MLB	27	628	60	24	7	8	52	31	58	7	3	5.7	.257	.299	.363	-.126	.257	.300	.367	.234	3.3	153-SS 15
2006	PIT	MLB	28	595	68	28	4	8	57	30	61	6	3	4.9	.270	.312	.377	-.111	.268	.311	.387	.235	10.1	139-SS 7

Breakout: 13% Improve: 37% Collapse: 36% Attrition: 4% Comparables: Mark Grudzielanek, Bill Russell, Gary DiSarcina

If any one player's single season set off the fluke klaxon, it was Wilson's 2004. This past season confirmed the doubts about the supposed new level of ability he had established. Still, Wilson's level of performance on defense in recent years has risen to the level of his reputation: in 2005, he finished second among NL shortstops in FRAR and led all shortstops in pivot double plays. With glovework like that, it's a bit easier to tolerate his minimal ability with the bat, but if he expects a raise, another multi-year extension wouldn't be the best idea.

PITCHERS

BRYAN BULLINGTON **Bats: R Throws: R** Height: 6' 5" Weight: 220 Born: September 30, 1980 Age: 25

YEAR	TM	LVL	AGE	W	L	SV	G	GS	IP	H	BB	SO	HR	GB%	BABIP	STUFF	WHIP	ERA	PERA	EQERA	EQH9	EQBB9	EQSO9	EQHR9	VORP	WXRL
2003	HIC	A	22	5	1	0	8	7	45.3	25	11	46	3	—	.197	4	0.79	1.39	5.36	4.24	8.3	2.9	5.8	1.8	6.1	—
2003	LYN	A+	22	8	4	0	17	17	97.3	101	27	67	5	—	.299	0	1.32	3.05	5.09	4.80	10.1	2.9	4.4	1.1	8.3	—
2004	ALT	AA	23	12	7	0	26	26	145.0	160	47	100	18	—	.307	-16	1.43	4.10	5.81	5.74	10.7	3.3	4.5	1.6	-2.2	—
2005	IND	AAA	24	9	5	0	18	18	109.3	104	26	82	11	54%	.290	6	1.19	3.38	4.60	4.51	9.3	2.4	5.3	1.1	12.8	—
2006	PIT	MLB	25	5	8	1	35	16	115.3	131	40	66	16	48%	.301	-4	1.48	5.13	5.42	5.54	9.9	2.8	4.8	1.2	1.0	0.7

Breakout: 10% Improve: 31% Collapse: 28% Attrition: 0% Comparables: Jason Young, Sean Bergman, Shawn Sedlacek

Let us not forget that the Pirates made Mr. Bullington the top overall pick of the 2002 draft, and in doing so they passed over talents like B. J. Upton, Prince Fielder, Jeremy Hermida, Khalil Greene, Nick Swisher, Scott Kazmir, Joe Blanton, and Jeff Francoeur. Sure, we've got the benefit of hindsight, but in that crowd you could have hit a future star by playing "Pin the Tail on the Prospect." Bullington did make strides this past season, mostly thanks to improved off-speed stuff, but that's all out the window after October labrum surgery. He won't pitch again until June.

SEAN BURNETT **Bats: L Throws: L** Height: 6' 1" Weight: 170 Born: September 17, 1982 Age: 23

YEAR	TM	LVL	AGE	W	L	SV	G	GS	IP	H	BB	SO	HR	GB%	BABIP	STUFF	WHIP	ERA	PERA	EQERA	EQH9	EQBB9	EQSO9	EQHR9	VORP	WXRL
2003	ALT	AA	20	14	6	0	27	27	159.7	158	29	86	2	—	.284	26	1.17	3.21	3.56	4.60	9.0	1.8	3.9	0.2	17.4	—
2004	NAS	AAA	21	1	5	0	10	10	47.0	58	17	25	5	—	.338	-7	1.60	5.36	5.10	5.29	10.2	3.4	3.8	0.9	1.6	—
2004	PIT	MLB	21	5	5	0	13	13	71.7	86	28	30	9	57%	.312	-6	1.59	5.02	5.20	4.95	10.2	3.2	3.3	1.0	3.6	1.4
2006	PIT	MLB	23	3	4	1	26	6	59.3	68	19	31	5	53%	.309	-7	1.47	4.73	4.87	6.35	10.1	2.7	4.4	0.8	2.6	0.5

Breakout: 6% Improve: 37% Collapse: 33% Attrition: 26% Comparables: Rich Troedson, Bob Sykes, Jeff Pico

Reconstructive elbow surgery followed by a major shoulder injury? Sounds like something you never, ever want to see befall a promising young arm. When he was healthy, Burnett made hay with good control and groundball after groundball—a combination that could serve him well in the majors. However, if, as Shakespeare wrote, what's past is prologue, Burnett's injury history makes whatever future he has left, however substantial his past promise once was, something to be anticipated with grim foreboding.

MATT CAPPS   Bats: R Throws: R   Height: 6′ 3″   Weight: 220   Born: September 3, 1983   Age: 22

YEAR	TM	LVL	AGE	W	L	SV	G	GS	IP	H	BB	SO	HR	GB%	BABIP	STUFF	WHIP	ERA	PERA	EQERA	EQH9	EQBB9	EQSO9	EQHR9	VORP	WXRL
2004	WPT	A-	20	3	5	0	11	11	65.0	84	4	33	7	—	.336	-32	1.35	4.85	7.22	8.95	13.1	0.9	2.5	2.9	-23.2	—
2004	HIC	A	20	2	3	0	12	8	42.0	82	16	27	8	—	.425	-43	2.33	10.07	7.77	12.68	15.5	3.9	3.1	2.7	-34.6	—
2005	HIC	A	21	3	4	14	35	0	53.7	47	5	39	0	55%	.297	2	0.97	2.51	3.46	4.33	8.7	1.0	4.0	0.3	7.3	—
2005	ALT	AA	21	0	2	7	17	0	20.0	21	1	26	2	52%	.339	19	1.10	2.70	3.66	4.58	9.6	0.5	8.2	1.4	2.2	—
2006	*PIT*	*MLB*	*22*	*2*	*3*	*1*	*31*	*2*	*51.3*	*63*	*13*	*28*	*8*	*48%*	*.312*	*-9*	*1.48*	*5.63*	*5.71*	*6.08*	*10.8*	*2.1*	*4.6*	*1.4*	*-2.8*	*-0.2*

Breakout: 45%   Improve: 88%   Collapse: 0%   Attrition: 14%   Comparables: Alex Serrano, Chris Wright, Elio Serrano

Right now, Matt Capps is a dominating, one-pitch reliever. One-pitch relievers who dominate at the highest level, in any niche, are rare beasts not unlike Gunther's Dik-Dik, a pocket-sized antelope that Darwinian selection cursed with Jimmy Durante's nose. Capps sports a blazing fastball and does a fine job of pounding the strike zone. Switched to full-time relief, he pitched his way up through the Sally and Eastern Leagues and into the majors. In 78 aggregate innings he whiffed 68, walked only six, and gave up just two homers. He's made some progress with a cutter, but Capps needs to develop an off-speed pitch if he's going to stick.

MIKE CONNOLLY   Bats: L Throws: L   Height: 6′ 0″   Weight: 180   Born: June 2, 1982   Age: 24

YEAR	TM	LVL	AGE	W	L	SV	G	GS	IP	H	BB	SO	HR	GB%	BABIP	STUFF	WHIP	ERA	PERA	EQERA	EQH9	EQBB9	EQSO9	EQHR9	VORP	WXRL
2003	ALT	AA	21	7	8	0	25	23	127.3	123	38	90	10	—	.279	-1	1.26	3.39	5.24	5.09	9.7	3.1	5.2	1.3	6.9	—
2004	ALT	AA	22	8	6	0	20	20	110.7	118	39	102	10	—	.323	5	1.42	4.39	4.87	5.53	10.0	3.4	6.0	1.2	0.8	—
2005	ALT	AA	23	5	6	0	15	15	84.0	90	24	60	4	41%	.321	6	1.36	3.32	4.46	4.68	9.6	3.0	4.2	0.7	8.5	—
2005	IND	AAA	23	2	4	0	13	13	71.3	74	29	44	9	47%	.291	-9	1.44	4.42	5.58	5.06	9.9	4.0	4.4	1.3	4.2	—
2006	*PIT*	*MLB*	*24*	*6*	*9*	*0*	*29*	*20*	*123.3*	*137*	*50*	*74*	*19*	*41%*	*.295*	*-2*	*1.52*	*5.34*	*5.63*	*5.70*	*9.8*	*3.3*	*5.0*	*1.3*	*-1.1*	*0.7*

Breakout: 3%   Improve: 28%   Collapse: 26%   Attrition: 1%   Comparables: Steve Smyth, Ryan Snare, Dennis Ulacia

Never overpowering, Connolly finally pitched his way out of Altoona, but he's never been overpowering and looked overmatched after his promotion to Indy. He'll open the 2006 season back in the International League, but if his command doesn't improve, Connolly could find himself in the bullpen.

ZACH DUKE   Bats: L Throws: L   Height: 6′ 2″   Weight: 200   Born: April 19, 1983   Age: 23

YEAR	TM	LVL	AGE	W	L	SV	G	GS	IP	H	BB	SO	HR	GB%	BABIP	STUFF	WHIP	ERA	PERA	EQERA	EQH9	EQBB9	EQSO9	EQHR9	VORP	WXRL
2003	HIC	A	20	8	7	0	26	26	141.7	124	46	113	7	—	.273	-2	1.20	3.11	5.24	6.12	9.7	3.6	4.5	1.2	-7.6	—
2004	LYN	A+	21	10	5	0	17	17	97.0	73	20	106	3	—	.278	34	0.96	1.39	3.62	3.72	8.0	2.2	6.8	0.6	19.2	—
2004	ALT	AA	21	5	1	0	9	9	51.3	41	10	36	2	—	.262	19	0.99	1.58	3.83	2.92	8.2	1.8	4.7	0.5	14.7	—
2005	IND	AAA	22	12	3	0	16	16	108.0	108	23	66	8	53%	.302	13	1.21	2.92	4.19	3.76	9.3	2.1	4.4	0.8	21.5	—
2005	PIT	MLB	22	8	2	0	14	14	84.7	79	23	58	3	50%	.303	31	1.20	1.81	3.52	2.35	8.5	2.2	5.7	0.3	32.7	4.0
2006	*PIT*	*MLB*	*23*	*10*	*10*	*0*	*32*	*31*	*176.0*	*178*	*52*	*117*	*16*	*49%*	*.292*	*14*	*1.31*	*3.87*	*4.20*	*4.21*	*8.9*	*2.4*	*5.6*	*0.8*	*27.3*	*4.0*

Breakout: 5%   Improve: 25%   Collapse: 37%   Attrition: 0%   Comparables: Steve Trout, Dave Fleming, Marcelino Lopez

In less than half a season's worth of work, Duke logged the highest VORP of any NL rookie. Duke already boasted a plus fastball and curve, but what aided his breakthrough was the addition of a quality changeup to round out his repertoire. Throw in his ability to keep the ball in the infield and he's the sort of pitcher nobody wants to face. The organization loves his dedication to the craft and his competitive drive, and the numbers and stuff say he'll be a front-of-the-rotation hurler from here on out. Still, pitchers lead uncertain lives. For every Whitey Ford, who enjoyed a similar rookie campaign, there are two Joel Pineiros or Cal Eldreds.

JOSH FOGG   Bats: R Throws: R   Height: 6′ 0″   Weight: 200   Born: December 13, 1976   Age: 29

YEAR	TM	LVL	AGE	W	L	SV	G	GS	IP	H	BB	SO	HR	GB%	BABIP	STUFF	WHIP	ERA	PERA	EQERA	EQH9	EQBB9	EQSO9	EQHR9	VORP	WXRL
2003	NAS	AAA	26	0	1	0	2	2	10.0	12	1	7	1	—	.324	1	1.30	5.40	5.40	6.30	10.8	0.9	4.5	1.8	-0.8	—
2003	PIT	MLB	26	10	9	0	26	26	142.0	166	40	71	22	47%	.304	-11	1.45	5.26	5.31	5.50	10.4	2.3	4.0	1.4	-0.9	1.8
2004	PIT	MLB	27	11	10	0	32	32	178.3	193	66	82	17	48%	.302	0	1.45	4.64	4.84	4.84	9.6	3.0	3.7	0.8	13.8	3.7
2005	PIT	MLB	28	6	11	0	34	28	169.3	196	53	85	27	41%	.301	-15	1.47	5.05	5.42	5.69	10.4	2.7	4.1	1.4	-0.9	1.8
2006	*PIT*	*MLB*	*29*	*7*	*10*	*0*	*30*	*22*	*142.3*	*157*	*41*	*73*	*17*	*45%*	*.292*	*-1*	*1.39*	*4.62*	*4.87*	*5.10*	*9.7*	*2.3*	*4.3*	*1.1*	*10.0*	*1.9*

Breakout: 26%   Improve: 67%   Collapse: 13%   Attrition: 3%   Comparables: Jim Colborn, Wayne Garland, Luis Aquino

Fogg doesn't make batters miss, and he can't keep the ball in the park, which is why he's ill-equipped to be a starter in the bigs. Between his complete inability to handle lefty batters and problems getting out of the sixth inning of his starts, he'd be much better suited to a role in the bullpen. Non-tendered in December, he might still be in danger of being asked to start in some sad-sack rotation.

MIKE GONZALEZ Bats: R Throws: L Height: 6′ 2″ Weight: 210 Born: May 23, 1978 Age: 28

YEAR	TM	LVL	AGE	W	L	SV	G	GS	IP	H	BB	SO	HR	GB%	BABIP	STUFF	WHIP	ERA	PERA	EQERA	EQH9	EQBB9	EQSO9	EQHR9	VORP	WXRL
2004	PIT	MLB	26	3	1	1	47	0	43.3	32	6	55	2	57%	.294	42	0.88	1.25	2.30	1.67	6.7	1.0	10.0	0.4	20.3	1.1
2005	PIT	MLB	27	1	3	3	51	0	50.0	35	31	58	2	51%	.280	23	1.32	2.70	3.44	2.90	6.9	5.3	9.6	0.4	15.5	2.4
2006	*PIT*	*MLB*	*28*	*3*	*3*	*6*	*63*	*0*	*56.3*	*45*	*29*	*61*	*4*	*50%*	*.287*	*17*	*1.30*	*3.20*	*3.49*	*3.71*	*7.0*	*4.1*	*9.1*	*0.6*	*12.9*	*1.1*

Breakout: 20%   Improve: 36%   Collapse: 54%   Attrition: 13%   Comparables: Randy Myers, Rob Murphy, B. J. Ryan

Although his control fails him quite often, Gonzalez has whiffed 119 batters in 101.2 major league innings. He does a reasonable job at keeping the ball on the ground, and if he can harness his stuff a bit better, spotting his fastball more effectively against right-handers, he'll permanently graduate from the LOOGY role to keep the closer's job he snatched from Jose Mesa towards the end of the season. It might have happened sooner had a knee injury not shelved him from June 22 to August 17. He pitched well upon returning, allowing a .177 average in 22 innings.

TOM GORZELANNY Bats: B Throws: L Height: 6′ 2″ Weight: 200 Born: July 12, 1982 Age: 23

YEAR	TM	LVL	AGE	W	L	SV	G	GS	IP	H	BB	SO	HR	GB%	BABIP	STUFF	WHIP	ERA	PERA	EQERA	EQH9	EQBB9	EQSO9	EQHR9	VORP	WXRL
2004	HIC	A	21	7	2	0	16	15	93.0	63	34	106	9	—	.245	0	1.04	2.23	5.51	4.45	8.5	4.2	6.2	1.6	10.9	—
2004	LYN	A+	21	3	5	0	10	10	55.7	54	19	61	6	—	.329	2	1.31	4.85	6.02	6.19	10.3	3.8	6.9	2.1	-3.4	—
2005	ALT	AA	22	8	5	0	23	23	129.7	114	46	124	6	48%	.306	19	1.23	3.26	4.25	4.39	8.6	3.7	6.0	0.6	16.8	—
2006	*PIT*	*MLB*	*23*	*6*	*9*	*0*	*32*	*19*	*123.7*	*126*	*58*	*87*	*16*	*44%*	*.289*	*3*	*1.49*	*4.96*	*5.19*	*5.32*	*9.0*	*3.8*	*5.9*	*1.1*	*4.0*	*1.1*

Breakout: 15%   Improve: 47%   Collapse: 15%   Attrition: 0%   Comparables: Charlie Manning, Eric Cyr, Brent Billingsley

One of the most underrated minor league hurlers around, Gorzelanny enjoyed a mild breakout in 2005, thanks mostly to improved off-speed stuff to complement his low- to mid-90s fastball. His slider is one of the best breaking pitches in the Pirates' system and he has a strong changeup. His control improved, and as often happens, his strikeouts dropped as well, though not enough to worry about. Gorzelanny's brief major league debut belies his future as a good mid-rotation starter in the big leagues. He'll be crowded out in spring training, but he'll be back before rosters expand in September.

JOHN GRABOW Bats: L Throws: L Height: 6′ 2″ Weight: 190 Born: November 4, 1978 Age: 27

YEAR	TM	LVL	AGE	W	L	SV	G	GS	IP	H	BB	SO	HR	GB%	BABIP	STUFF	WHIP	ERA	PERA	EQERA	EQH9	EQBB9	EQSO9	EQHR9	VORP	WXRL
2003	ALT	AA	24	6	1	1	24	9	83.0	87	19	73	9	—	.307	-15	1.28	3.36	5.45	5.22	10.4	2.5	6.0	1.9	3.3	—
2004	PIT	MLB	25	2	5	1	68	0	61.7	81	28	64	8	54%	.408	4	1.77	5.11	4.02	5.54	10.1	3.5	7.9	1.0	-0.7	-0.1
2005	PIT	MLB	26	2	3	0	63	0	52.0	46	25	42	6	47%	.276	-5	1.37	4.85	4.73	5.26	8.6	4.0	6.7	1.1	0.7	1.0
2006	*PIT*	*MLB*	*27*	*2*	*2*	*2*	*51*	*0*	*47.0*	*48*	*19*	*38*	*5*	*48%*	*.306*	*1*	*1.43*	*4.35*	*4.64*	*5.37*	*9.0*	*3.3*	*6.9*	*0.9*	*4.1*	*0.3*

Breakout: 39%   Improve: 53%   Collapse: 21%   Attrition: 31%   Comparables: Mike Myers, Aaron Fultz, Paul Assenmacher

Grabow's had two extended looks in the majors, but his fastball isn't fooling anyone. He can't get his heater past lefties: they've batted .292/.346/.462 against him, while righties have actually had a slightly harder time at .280/.361/.406. Now that Damaso Marte has been brought in to handle LOOGY duty, Grabow's time may be up.

PAUL MAHOLM Bats: L Throws: L Height: 6′ 2″ Weight: 215 Born: June 25, 1982 Age: 24

YEAR	TM	LVL	AGE	W	L	SV	G	GS	IP	H	BB	SO	HR	GB%	BABIP	STUFF	WHIP	ERA	PERA	EQERA	EQH9	EQBB9	EQSO9	EQHR9	VORP	WXRL
2004	LYN	A+	22	1	3	0	8	8	44.0	39	15	28	2	—	.272	-2	1.23	1.84	5.01	3.92	9.1	3.9	3.9	0.9	7.7	—
2005	ALT	AA	23	6	2	0	16	16	81.7	73	26	75	5	64%	.308	8	1.21	3.19	4.48	4.60	8.8	3.4	5.6	0.8	8.7	—
2005	IND	AAA	23	1	1	0	6	6	35.7	40	12	21	2	55%	.325	1	1.46	3.53	4.33	5.35	9.9	3.3	4.1	0.5	1.0	—
2005	PIT	MLB	23	3	1	0	6	6	41.3	31	17	26	2	58%	.242	15	1.16	2.18	4.28	2.47	7.9	3.6	5.4	0.4	15.7	1.9
2006	*PIT*	*MLB*	*24*	*8*	*10*	*0*	*35*	*27*	*147.3*	*152*	*66*	*95*	*13*	*56%*	*.297*	*3*	*1.48*	*4.49*	*4.82*	*4.90*	*9.1*	*3.7*	*5.4*	*0.8*	*11.0*	*2.1*

Breakout: 4%   Improve: 22%   Collapse: 34%   Attrition: 1%   Comparables: Danny Jackson, Jimmy Anderson, Steve Trout

(continued next page)

Paul Maholm (*continued*)

Another gifted young Pirate port-sider, Maholm's stuff is very similar to Duke's, minus some of the wonder boy's giddy-up. A top college hurler at Mississippi State with good command of four pitches, the Pirates moved him up fast, jumping him up to Double-A after just three starts in the Sally League. The move made sense; Maholm lost most of '04 while recovering from getting his noggin and nose cracked by a hard-hit liner, and he would have been in Double-A earlier without that. The Pirates kept moving Maholm up, and he ended the season with five quality starts in six tries at the major league level. Since his stuff isn't eye-popping, Maholm will simply have to out-pitch Ian Snell and Victor Santos if he wants to build on his quality come April.

BRIAN MEADOWS   **Bats: R Throws: R**   Height: 6' 3"   Weight: 230   Born: November 21, 1975   Age: 30

YEAR	TM	LVL	AGE	W	L	SV	G	GS	IP	H	BB	SO	HR	GB%	BABIP	STUFF	WHIP	ERA	PERA	EQERA	EQH9	EQBB9	EQSO9	EQHR9	VORP	WXRL
2003	NAS	AAA	27	7	0	0	9	8	51.0	32	0	40	2	—	.210	25	0.63	1.41	3.26	3.26	7.3	0.6	5.9	0.6	12.2	—
2003	PIT	MLB	27	2	1	1	34	7	76.3	91	11	38	8	54%	.310	-6	1.34	4.72	4.32	5.14	10.2	1.2	4.0	0.9	2.9	0.5
2004	PIT	MLB	28	2	4	1	68	0	78.0	76	19	46	7	53%	.287	-3	1.22	3.58	4.19	4.54	8.7	2.0	4.8	0.8	8.6	0.2
2005	PIT	MLB	29	3	1	0	65	0	74.7	84	21	44	8	48%	.315	-9	1.41	4.58	4.44	5.16	9.8	2.4	4.8	1.0	3.3	0.2
2006	PIT	MLB	30	3	3	2	51	0	61.7	69	16	34	8	48%	.297	-10	1.38	4.59	4.76	5.22	9.9	2.1	4.6	1.1	4.1	0.3

Breakout: 36% Improve: 48% Collapse: 30% Attrition: 16% Comparables: Jeff Shaw, Ken Forsch, Russ Kemmerer

The appropriately-named Meadows has always been a field rich in bountiful opportunities—for hitters to fatten up their stats. In this, he's less like a pitcher than an annual harvest festival or a timeless symbol of fertility, like the Easter Bunny or Viagra. Righty middle relievers are fungible, mediocre or simply bad. The Pirates mistakenly offered Meadows arbitration last year, but wisely decided against it this time around, ensuring that he'll be another team's mistake in 2006.

JOSE MESA   **Bats: R Throws: R**   Height: 6' 3"   Weight: 225   Born: May 22, 1966   Age: 40

YEAR	TM	LVL	AGE	W	L	SV	G	GS	IP	H	BB	SO	HR	GB%	BABIP	STUFF	WHIP	ERA	PERA	EQERA	EQH9	EQBB9	EQSO9	EQHR9	VORP	WXRL
2003	PHI	MLB	37	5	7	24	61	0	58.0	71	31	45	7	48%	.340	-12	1.76	6.52	4.83	6.79	10.3	4.2	6.0	1.1	-8.9	-0.2
2004	PIT	MLB	38	5	2	43	70	0	69.3	78	20	37	6	49%	.320	-5	1.41	3.25	4.37	3.34	9.6	2.3	4.2	0.8	17.2	3.7
2005	PIT	MLB	39	2	8	27	55	0	56.7	61	26	37	7	46%	.318	-12	1.54	4.76	5.05	4.74	9.6	3.8	5.4	1.1	4.5	-1.2
2006	COL	MLB	40	1	2	1	35	0	39.7	53	17	25	7	45%	.337	-18	1.76	6.59	6.06	7.19	10.9	3.5	5.4	1.4	-1.8	-0.3

Breakout: 18% Improve: 27% Collapse: 55% Attrition: 38% Comparables: Roberto Hernandez, Dennis Lamp, Harry Gumbert

We always thought GM Dave Littlefield continued to re-up Jose Mesa in the hopes of flipping him to a contender at the deadline. However, Littlefield seemed curiously uninterested in actually trading Joe Table. As a result, two years in Pittsburgh seemed like a decade for those waiting with bated breath for Mesa to become a Yankee. Mercifully, the Pirates bought out their 2006 option on Mesa, making him a free agent. He occasionally vacillates his way into a quality season, but at age 39 those days are likely behind him. The Rockies have signed him to a one-year deal to set up Brian Fuentes, which could turn out to be the ugliest thing to hit baseball since Don Mossi.

JEFF MILLER   **Bats: R Throws: R**   Height: 6' 4"   Weight: 220   Born: February 1, 1980   Age: 26

YEAR	TM	LVL	AGE	W	L	SV	G	GS	IP	H	BB	SO	HR	GB%	BABIP	STUFF	WHIP	ERA	PERA	EQERA	EQH9	EQBB9	EQSO9	EQHR9	VORP	WXRL
2003	LYN	A+	23	5	6	0	27	7	75.7	89	25	59	4	—	.336	-15	1.51	4.87	5.11	7.30	10.8	3.5	4.7	1.1	-14.0	—
2004	ALT	AA	24	5	4	18	52	0	68.0	48	28	79	8	—	.247	-9	1.12	2.91	5.40	4.55	8.4	4.4	7.5	1.6	7.4	—
2005	IND	AAA	25	5	7	0	58	0	81.7	79	27	62	13	41%	.282	-26	1.30	3.53	6.03	4.75	9.8	3.5	5.3	1.9	7.3	—
2006	SFN	MLB	26	2	3	1	24	4	47.0	49	19	32	7	40%	.290	-4	1.45	4.90	5.29	5.49	9.3	3.3	5.8	1.2	1.0	0.2

Breakout: 29% Improve: 51% Collapse: 25% Attrition: 29% Comparables: Todd Van Poppel, Seung Lee, Dave Stevens

Miller was exceedingly lucky to post that quasi-nifty 3.53 ERA at Indy last season—13 home runs in 81.2 innings means a few too many mistakes. A fastball-slider guy, he's never shown much in the way of command since graduating from short-season ball, likely because he played the outfield in college, and has pitched all of his 352.2 innings in the pros.

OLIVER PEREZ Bats: L Throws: L Height: 6' 3" Weight: 160 Born: August 15, 1981 Age: 24

YEAR	TM	LVL	AGE	W	L	SV	G	GS	IP	H	BB	SO	HR	GB%	BABIP	STUFF	WHIP	ERA	PERA	EQERA	EQH9	EQBB9	EQSO9	EQHR9	VORP	WXRL
2003	SDN	MLB	21	4	7	0	19	19	103.7	103	65	117	20	39%	.317	8	1.62	5.38	5.25	5.85	9.0	5.0	9.0	1.7	-2.6	1.4
2003	PIT	MLB	21	0	3	0	5	5	23.0	26	12	24	2	40%	.364	22	1.65	5.87	4.18	5.70	9.5	4.2	8.4	0.8	-0.6	0.4
2004	PIT	MLB	22	12	10	0	30	30	196.0	145	81	239	22	39%	.280	41	1.15	2.98	3.62	3.30	7.2	3.4	9.8	0.9	52.8	6.6
2005	PIT	MLB	23	7	5	0	20	20	103.0	102	70	97	23	32%	.297	-14	1.67	5.85	6.29	5.85	9.3	5.7	7.8	2.0	-4.4	0.6
2006	*PIT*	*MLB*	*24*	*5*	*7*	*0*	*25*	*17*	*101.3*	*96*	*52*	*96*	*14*	*37%*	*.294*	*14*	*1.46*	*4.70*	*5.07*	*5.33*	*8.4*	*4.2*	*7.9*	*1.2*	*8.1*	*1.4*

Breakout: 23% Improve: 41% Collapse: 28% Attrition: 21%   Comparables: Juan Pizarro, Melido Perez, Pete Falcone

What could've possibly been a bigger buzzkill for Pirates fans than their putative ace's lost season, having Increase Mather show up at happy hour? Perez followed up his stellar 2004 with a disastrous 2005. Perez took last winter off, and the Pirates theorized that his indolence left him without any command by the time the games mattered. Ironically, they had previously worried about Perez doing too much winter work. This year they went for the middle ground, with Perez doing some strictly limited pitching in the Mexican Pacific League. Perez also needs to work on his maturity, as he missed more than two months with a self-inflicted broken toe, the result of kicking a laundry cart into submission. Still, as bad as things were, keep in mind that Perez is still only 24 and has 571 strikeouts in 515.2 career innings. If he has ironed out his mechanical issues and gets his power fastball/slider mix back in gear, he could add to those K totals.

MARK REDMAN Bats: L Throws: L Height: 6' 5" Weight: 220 Born: January 5, 1974 Age: 32

YEAR	TM	LVL	AGE	W	L	SV	G	GS	IP	H	BB	SO	HR	GB%	BABIP	STUFF	WHIP	ERA	PERA	EQERA	EQH9	EQBB9	EQSO9	EQHR9	VORP	WXRL
2003	FLO	MLB	29	14	9	0	29	29	190.7	172	61	151	16	43%	.282	22	1.22	3.59	3.95	4.04	8.3	2.6	6.5	0.8	37.5	5.0
2004	OAK	MLB	30	11	12	0	32	32	191.0	218	68	102	28	43%	.308	-3	1.50	4.71	5.09	4.95	10.0	3.0	4.5	1.2	23.4	3.6
2005	PIT	MLB	31	5	15	0	30	30	178.3	188	56	101	18	51%	.305	4	1.37	4.90	4.55	5.11	9.5	2.6	4.7	0.9	11.0	2.7
2006	*KCA*	*MLB*	*32*	*8*	*13*	*0*	*32*	*28*	*172.7*	*200*	*50*	*92*	*21*	*46%*	*.305*	*2*	*1.44*	*4.90*	*5.13*	*5.06*	*10.1*	*2.6*	*4.8*	*1.0*	*7.9*	*2.1*

Breakout: 9% Improve: 47% Collapse: 21% Attrition: 1%   Comparables: Paul Splittorff, Terry Mulholland, Charlie Leibrandt

Does he have anything left? Last season, Redman gave up 64 extra-base hits and posted a 7.08 ERA after the All-Star break. Considering how badly teams clamor for pitching at the deadline, the time to part ways with him was last July, but unsurprisingly, there wasn't a lot of demand. Taking advantage of the contract he signed he signed with Oakland after getting his World Series ring in Florida, Redman exercised his half of a mutual option for 2006, guaranteeing that Dave Littlefield would do anything to avoid paying it. So the Pirates exacted revenge by dealing him to the Royals for pitcher Jonah Bayless. He'll serve as the grizzled veteran presence at the front of the Royals rotation, giving the Royals that ring-wearing former world champ old dude thing that Jason Grimsley gave them for years.

JOSH SHARPLESS Bats: R Throws: R Height: 6' 5" Weight: 225 Born: January 26, 1981 Age: 25

YEAR	TM	LVL	AGE	W	L	SV	G	GS	IP	H	BB	SO	HR	GB%	BABIP	STUFF	WHIP	ERA	PERA	EQERA	EQH9	EQBB9	EQSO9	EQHR9	VORP	WXRL
2003	WPT	A-	22	1	1	5	22	0	31.3	19	17	45	2	—	.258	-19	1.15	2.59	7.86	5.47	9.9	7.5	7.9	2.7	0.4	—
2004	HIC	A	23	6	2	5	44	0	74.3	42	55	109	4	—	.271	-15	1.31	3.03	6.00	5.18	7.5	9.4	7.8	1.0	3.1	—
2005	LYN	A+	24	3	0	5	17	0	27.0	7	11	46	0	38%	.175	22	0.67	0.00	3.33	2.59	4.8	4.8	9.6	0.4	8.1	—
2006	*PIT*	*MLB*	*25*	*1*	*2*	*0*	*13*	*2*	*25.3*	*23*	*18*	*23*	*3*	*39%*	*.279*	*-3*	*1.62*	*5.26*	*5.58*	*7.16*	*8.1*	*5.9*	*7.6*	*1.2*	*0.6*	*0.0*

Breakout: 12% Improve: 21% Collapse: 54% Attrition: 55%   Comparables: Jeff Jones, Tim Birtsas, Victor Santos

Sharpless boasts a plus slider and a deceptive delivery that makes his relatively average fastball hard to pick up. He has excelled at keeping the ball in the park during his brief career, but the finer points of control have eluded him. He was shut down two months early with elbow soreness last season, but seemed to have recovered by the end of the instructional league season. He could come up quickly, health permitting, somewhat like Matt Capps did.

IAN SNELL Bats: R Throws: R Height: 5' 11" Weight: 160 Born: October 30, 1981 Age: 24

YEAR	TM	LVL	AGE	W	L	SV	G	GS	IP	H	BB	SO	HR	GB%	BABIP	STUFF	WHIP	ERA	PERA	EQERA	EQH9	EQBB9	EQSO9	EQHR9	VORP	WXRL
2003	LYN	A+	21	10	3	0	20	20	116.3	105	33	122	3	—	.310	31	1.19	3.33	3.66	4.78	8.7	2.9	6.8	0.6	10.3	—
2003	ALT	AA	21	4	0	0	6	6	36.7	36	10	23	2	—	.281	6	1.25	1.96	4.84	4.33	9.4	2.8	4.6	1.0	5.0	—
2004	ALT	AA	22	11	7	0	26	26	151.0	147	40	142	16	—	.311	8	1.24	3.16	4.79	4.17	9.6	2.6	6.2	1.3	23.3	—
2005	IND	AAA	23	11	3	0	18	18	112.0	90	23	104	14	43%	.255	13	1.01	3.70	4.39	4.39	8.4	2.0	6.8	1.4	14.3	—
2005	PIT	MLB	23	1	2	0	15	5	42.0	43	24	34	5	38%	.311	-1	1.60	5.14	4.89	5.31	9.1	4.7	6.6	1.1	0.7	0.2
2006	*PIT*	*MLB*	*24*	*6*	*8*	*1*	*35*	*20*	*121.7*	*126*	*43*	*91*	*16*	*41%*	*.295*	*7*	*1.39*	*4.61*	*4.90*	*4.98*	*9.1*	*2.9*	*6.3*	*1.2*	*9.1*	*1.6*

Breakout: 17% Improve: 47% Collapse: 19% Attrition: 2%   Comparables: Carl Erskine, Billy Loes, Gary Gentry

(continued next page)

Ian Snell (*continued*)

Snell has a highly impressive minor league dossier, but control was a problem for him in his major league innings last year. Chalk that up to nerves and figure he'll be better the second time around, because in the minors, he displayed excellent control. His consistently good heat and late-breaking curve should guarantee him a future as a reliever at the very least, but he might have problems making it as a starter. Snell tends to work high in the zone, so it would help if he refined his changeup and relied less on flyball outs. As is, he'll have to beat out Maholm and Brewers refugee Victor Santos in the fight for the fifth slot this spring.

SALOMON TORRES Bats: R Throws: R Height: 5′ 11″ Weight: 210 Born: March 11, 1972 Age: 34

YEAR	TM	LVL	AGE	W	L	SV	G	GS	IP	H	BB	SO	HR	GB%	BABIP	STUFF	WHIP	ERA	PERA	EQERA	EQH9	EQBB9	EQSO9	EQHR9	VORP	WXRL
2003	PIT	MLB	31	7	5	2	41	16	121.0	128	42	84	19	53%	.302	-9	1.40	4.76	5.15	4.70	9.6	2.8	5.7	1.4	10.9	1.7
2004	PIT	MLB	32	7	7	0	84	0	92.0	87	22	62	6	60%	.298	9	1.18	2.64	3.84	3.25	8.7	2.0	5.4	0.6	24.6	2.9
2005	PIT	MLB	33	5	5	3	78	0	94.7	76	36	55	7	51%	.246	-1	1.18	2.76	4.50	3.33	8.2	3.3	4.9	0.7	23.7	1.7
2006	*PIT*	*MLB*	*34*	*3*	*3*	*3*	*59*	*0*	*68.7*	*75*	*24*	*43*	*6*	*52%*	*.303*	*-8*	*1.43*	*4.35*	*4.62*	*4.96*	*9.5*	*2.8*	*5.2*	*0.8*	*6.2*	*0.4*

Breakout: 5% Improve: 22% Collapse: 47% Attrition: 12% Comparables: Mike Maddux, Matt Herges, Mike Williams

Consider Torres a source of inspiration for retreads everywhere, because he managed to be one of the 30 best relievers in the NL last season. In the past two seasons, working entirely in relief, he's been one of the best setup men in the game, logging 186.2 innings and recording a RA/9 of 3.2 per. That's quality and durability. He relies on changing speeds on his fastball to get by, and he isn't fooling many batters these days. Consider him a good bet to lose ground this year.

JOHN VAN BENSCHOTEN Bats: R Throws: R Height: 6′ 4″ Weight: 210 Born: April 14, 1980 Age: 26

YEAR	TM	LVL	AGE	W	L	SV	G	GS	IP	H	BB	SO	HR	GB%	BABIP	STUFF	WHIP	ERA	PERA	EQERA	EQH9	EQBB9	EQSO9	EQHR9	VORP	WXRL
2003	LYN	A+	23	6	0	0	9	9	48.7	33	18	49	1	—	.248	16	1.05	2.22	3.94	4.14	7.5	4.1	6.3	0.4	7.4	—
2003	ALT	AA	23	7	6	0	17	17	90.3	95	34	78	5	—	.318	4	1.43	3.69	4.83	5.95	9.9	4.0	6.0	0.9	-3.4	—
2004	NAS	AAA	24	4	11	0	23	23	131.7	135	49	101	16	—	.295	-6	1.40	4.72	5.44	5.37	9.3	3.8	5.2	1.3	3.3	—
2004	PIT	MLB	24	1	3	0	6	5	28.7	33	19	18	3	44%	.337	-13	1.81	6.90	5.52	7.98	9.8	5.2	4.9	0.9	-9.2	-0.5
2006	*PIT*	*MLB*	*26*	*2*	*4*	*0*	*21*	*6*	*51.3*	*56*	*25*	*35*	*6*	*46%*	*.305*	*-6*	*1.57*	*5.45*	*5.51*	*6.48*	*9.5*	*3.9*	*5.7*	*1.0*	*-1.6*	*0.0*

Breakout: 27% Improve: 50% Collapse: 21% Attrition: 31% Comparables: Vladimir Nunez, Edwin Hurtado, Craig McMurtry

One of the most glaring Pirate organizational misplays in recent years was the decision to develop Van Benschoten as a pitcher. The Bucs drafted him out of Kent State with the eighth overall pick of the 2001 draft. Despite the fact that double-duty Van Benschoten led Division I in homers his junior year, the Pirates opted to make him a full-time hurler. Worse yet, they pushed him aggressively, promoting him despite his unimpressive numbers since the first half of the 2003 campaign when he was in High-A. He missed all of the 2005 season after three arthroscopic surgeries, but is expected to be fully healthy by spring training. Considering that his fastball and late-breaking slider are his only plus offerings, a move to the bullpen might be advisable.

RYAN VOGELSONG Bats: R Throws: R Height: 6′ 3″ Weight: 210 Born: July 22, 1977 Age: 28

YEAR	TM	LVL	AGE	W	L	SV	G	GS	IP	H	BB	SO	HR	GB%	BABIP	STUFF	WHIP	ERA	PERA	EQERA	EQH9	EQBB9	EQSO9	EQHR9	VORP	WXRL
2003	NAS	AAA	25	12	8	0	26	26	149.0	142	54	146	12	—	.302	9	1.32	4.29	4.77	5.53	9.2	4.0	7.2	1.2	1.1	—
2004	PIT	MLB	26	6	13	0	31	26	133.0	148	67	92	22	38%	.311	-13	1.62	6.50	5.49	6.30	9.8	4.1	5.5	1.3	-13.0	1.5
2005	PIT	MLB	27	2	2	0	44	0	81.3	82	40	52	5	45%	.297	-1	1.50	4.43	4.63	4.85	9.3	4.1	5.3	0.6	6.4	0.1
2006	*PIT*	*MLB*	*28*	*3*	*4*	*1*	*42*	*4*	*75.3*	*77*	*32*	*54*	*9*	*42%*	*.290*	*-4*	*1.44*	*4.65*	*4.90*	*5.47*	*8.9*	*3.5*	*6.0*	*1.1*	*5.0*	*0.5*

Breakout: 43% Improve: 65% Collapse: 14% Attrition: 16% Comparables: Bruce Dal Canton, Mike Gardiner, Jim Hearn

The move to the bullpen was a good one for Vogelsong, but that's only in relative terms. He'd been awful as a starter in the majors, and improved to "narrowly sub-optimal" as a reliever. Improvement as he settles into the role might be possible, but it's clear that Vogelsong is never going to be an elite performer in any role. The Pirates were 7–37 in games in which Vogelsong appeared, which speaks volumes about the team's confidence in him. He led the majors in trash-time innings.

KIP WELLS

Bats: R Throws: R Height: 6' 3" Weight: 196 Born: April 21, 1977 Age: 29

YEAR	TM	LVL	AGE	W	L	SV	G	GS	IP	H	BB	SO	HR	GB%	BABIP	STUFF	WHIP	ERA	PERA	EQERA	EQH9	EQBB9	EQSO9	EQHR9	VORP	WXRL
2003	PIT	MLB	26	10	9	0	31	31	197.3	171	76	147	24	53%	.261	11	1.25	3.28	4.59	3.53	8.4	3.2	6.1	1.1	47.7	5.8
2004	PIT	MLB	27	5	7	0	24	24	138.3	145	66	116	14	51%	.321	15	1.53	4.56	4.43	4.55	9.0	3.8	6.6	0.8	16.0	3.4
2005	PIT	MLB	28	8	18	0	33	33	182.0	186	99	132	23	45%	.300	-1	1.57	5.09	5.23	5.68	9.4	4.5	6.0	1.1	-3.2	2.7
2006	*PIT*	*MLB*	*29*	*9*	*11*	*0*	*29*	*28*	*168.7*	*168*	*72*	*118*	*16*	*48%*	*.291*	*10*	*1.42*	*4.30*	*4.60*	*4.70*	*8.8*	*3.5*	*5.9*	*0.8*	*17.2*	*3.0*

Breakout: 21% Improve: 57% Collapse: 9% Attrition: 4% Comparables: Bill Bonham, Jason Schmidt, Russ Ortiz

Wells's history of spotty control went from unfortunate to even worse last season. In recent years, only Kaz Ishii and Victor Zambrano (among IP qualifiers) can rival the lack of control Wells showed last season. Walking one of every six lefty batters he faced in '05 is no way for a major league starter to make a living. Wells is 29, his ERA has increased substantially in each of the last two seasons, and he really hasn't been the same pitcher since battling elbow problems in 2004. He ranks among the game's biggest disappointments in 2005, and it's time to accept that we've already seen his best. If he has a hot first half, the Bucs would do well to flip him for goodies at the deadline.

RICK WHITE

Bats: R Throws: R Height: 6' 4" Weight: 230 Born: December 23, 1968 Age: 37

YEAR	TM	LVL	AGE	W	L	SV	G	GS	IP	H	BB	SO	HR	GB%	BABIP	STUFF	WHIP	ERA	PERA	EQERA	EQH9	EQBB9	EQSO9	EQHR9	VORP	WXRL
2003	CHA	MLB	34	1	2	1	34	0	47.7	56	13	37	11	45%	.317	-11	1.45	6.60	5.25	6.75	10.3	2.4	6.8	1.9	-6.9	0.1
2003	HOU	MLB	34	0	0	0	15	0	19.3	18	8	17	2	51%	.291	4	1.34	3.73	4.26	4.26	9.0	3.3	7.1	0.9	3.2	-0.0
2004	LVG	AAA	35	0	0	2	6	0	11.7	4	1	14	0	—	.167	10	0.43	0.00	2.53	2.53	5.1	0.8	6.8	0.0	3.6	—
2004	CLE	MLB	35	5	5	1	59	0	78.3	88	29	44	15	49%	.305	-24	1.51	5.29	5.56	5.45	9.8	3.1	4.7	1.6	1.9	0.5
2005	PIT	MLB	36	4	7	2	71	0	75.0	90	29	40	3	56%	.349	-3	1.59	3.72	4.11	4.81	10.1	3.2	4.3	0.4	6.7	0.7
2006	*PIT*	*MLB*	*37*	*2*	*3*	*2*	*45*	*0*	*53.7*	*63*	*18*	*31*	*6*	*52%*	*.317*	*-14*	*1.52*	*4.70*	*5.10*	*6.34*	*10.3*	*2.8*	*4.8*	*0.9*	*2.7*	*0.2*

Breakout: 39% Improve: 55% Collapse: 30% Attrition: 31% Comparables: Ted Power, Mike Maddux, Todd Jones

Being the poor man's Todd Jones—without the social indelicacies—can keep one in clover for quite a while. White's cheap seats souvenir rate took a major dive, something he'll need to sustain if he's to survive his dropping strikeout rates. Not offered arbitration by the Pirates, the wandering White will join his eighth organization since 2000.

DAVE WILLIAMS

Bats: L Throws: L Height: 6' 2" Weight: 210 Born: March 12, 1979 Age: 27

YEAR	TM	LVL	AGE	W	L	SV	G	GS	IP	H	BB	SO	HR	GB%	BABIP	STUFF	WHIP	ERA	PERA	EQERA	EQH9	EQBB9	EQSO9	EQHR9	VORP	WXRL
2003	NAS	AAA	24	7	4	0	16	16	77.3	78	30	56	7	—	.288	-7	1.40	4.19	5.57	5.93	9.8	4.1	5.4	1.3	-2.7	—
2004	NAS	AAA	25	6	2	0	21	21	116.7	113	33	103	10	—	.299	10	1.25	3.47	4.47	4.55	8.8	2.9	5.8	0.9	13.4	—
2004	PIT	MLB	25	2	3	0	10	6	38.7	31	13	33	4	56%	.255	12	1.14	4.42	4.26	4.74	7.8	2.8	6.9	0.9	2.7	0.5
2005	PIT	MLB	26	10	11	0	25	25	138.7	137	58	88	20	40%	.281	-5	1.41	4.41	5.32	4.86	9.5	3.5	5.3	1.3	12.6	2.4
2006	*CIN*	*MLB*	*27*	*7*	*10*	*0*	*31*	*23*	*140.7*	*149*	*53*	*95*	*20*	*43%*	*.291*	*3*	*1.44*	*4.83*	*5.15*	*5.04*	*9.4*	*3.1*	*5.6*	*1.3*	*7.2*	*1.7*

Breakout: 14% Improve: 48% Collapse: 16% Attrition: 2% Comparables: Mike Mason, Alex Kellner, Darren Oliver

A 4.41 ERA in a season in which the league ERA was 4.22 isn't very inspiring, and it's even less so when you consider Williams's thoroughly unpalatable peripherals. As a result, he doesn't figure to be more than an adequate starter in future seasons. Being traded to Cincinnati for Sean Casey just makes the outlook worse, as his flyball-favoring ways aren't going to go over too well considering the Great American Ballpark's great American generosity to home run hitters. Williams joins Chad Bentz, Shawn Chacon, Josh Phelps, and Curt Schilling as active major leaguers born in Alaska, an oversized contingent given that a grand total of nine Alaskans have played in the bigs.

Line Outs

Position/Player	TM	LVL	AGE	PA	R	2B	3B	HR	RBI	BB	SO	SB-CS	SPEED	BA/OBP/SLG	MLVR	EQBA/OBP/SLG	EQA	VORP
SS B. Bixler	HIC	A	22	554	74	23	2	9	50	38	134	21-10	5.8	.281/.343/.388	.029	.241/.287/.332	.221	-11.4
1B M. Carlin	HIC	A	24	354	53	21	4	16	65	29	70	6-1	5.6	.318/.398/.568	.384	.262/.317/.451	.262	5.1
CF A. McCutchen	WPT	A-	18	61	12	3	1	0	5	8	6	4-1	7.1	.346/.443/.442	.347	.307/.377/.401	.274	5.9
OF M. Restovich '06	CHN	MLB	27	160	19	8	1	6	20	14	35	1-1	5.0	.251/.320/.434	-.036	.252/.321/.441	.254	1.2

Pitcher	TM	LVL	AGE	W	L	SV	IP	H	BB	SO	HR	GB%	BABIP	STUFF	WHIP	ERA	PERA	EQERA	EQH9	EQBB9	EQSO9	EQHR9	VORP
B. Borner*	ALT	AA	26	6	1	0	90.7	77	13	90	8	43%	.294	-6	0.99	2.08	4.62	3.89	9.0	1.7	5.7	1.4	16.3
M. Johnston*	IND	AAA	26	2	1	0	57.7	43	30	52	5	50%	.253	-11	1.27	2.96	5.33	4.00	8.2	5.7	6.3	1.0	9.6
M. Peterson	ALT	AA	23	11	9	0	143.7	156	74	87	19	42%	.304	-38	1.60	5.51	7.08	7.21	10.6	5.7	3.7	1.8	-24.6
C. Stewart*	IND	AAA	25	7	10	0	132.0	144	67	77	18	36%	.308	-28	1.60	5.52	6.43	6.71	10.5	5.3	4.0	1.6	-15.7

Brian Bixler was the Pirates' 2nd round pick in the '04 draft out of Eastern Michigan after finishing second in Division I with a .453 average. Despite questions about his bat, he didn't embarrass himself in his first full season. **Mike Carlin** is proud owner of Miami of Ohio's single-season home run record (19); his name is French for "pug dog" and Jersey for "aging comic." The Pirates' 2005 1st round pick, **Andrew McCutchen,** had an auspicious pro debut, showing excellent plate discipline, a slick glove in center and a high-percentage approach on the bases. With exceptional bat speed, quick wrists through the zone and a strong build, the organization believes the home runs will come in time. **Michael Restovich,** erstwhile quasi-top Twins prospect, can tag lefties and he's a solid corner glove. As his projection indicates, he could help the Cubs.

Brady Borner finally handled the Eastern League in his third whack at it. Too old and too undistinguished to warrant much attention, but as a lefty he'll probably get his share of opportunities. Three years ago, the Pirates did the sensible thing and made Johnston into a reliever, but **Mike Johnston's** peripherals failed to improve. He's not a prospect, but he *is* a lefty. A key part of the Kris Benson swap with the Mets, **Matt Peterson** has a decent fastball and a big bender of a curve. There's still something of value here if the Pirates can sort Peterson out. **Cory Stewart** might be best remembered as the third wheel from the Giles deal; his low-90s velocity isn't working as a starter. Given the crowd in the rotation, a switch to the pen couldn't hurt.

St. Louis Cardinals

ichael Lewis might better have spent his time in St. Louis. For all the talk about the problems caused by Oakland's lack of resources, the Cardinals haven't had a significantly better they've done a much better job despite their particular challenges than have the last two ownership groups in Oakland.

St. Louis is not a large media market like a Chicago, New York, Los Angeles, or the San Francisco/San Jose megalopolis. Missouri isn't California, it's a flyover state; its jewel city boasts the Gateway arch, lots of Busch money, and, on the outskirts of Clayton, one of the nation's finest universities and teaching hospitals. And that's about it. It is not an area with a great deal of capital density, and its signature businesses are old-line (if generally well-run), focused on leveraging some of the greatest assets of the Midwest: grain and transportation. Despite these slender supports, the Cardinals have done a consistently outstanding job of investing their resources, putting a great baseball team on the field, providing an outstanding experience to their paying customers, and filling the seats.

Consider the 2005 edition. They cruised through the regular season, racking up 100 wins en route to an 11-game victory in the NL Central. They did this despite the absence of Scott Rolen, one of their megastars, who missed more than 100 games with shoulder injuries. Albert Pujols and Chris Carpenter led the club with Hall of Fame–caliber seasons, and fragile veterans like Reggie Sanders and Larry Walker had great seasons for Walt Jocketty and Tony LaRussa, who spotted them carefully.

The Cardinals are a well-run, professional machine, facing and overcoming obstacles that other clubs use as excuses, rolling on to the postseason in five of the past six seasons. The media have been quick to credit LaRussa for the organization's outsized success, and despite our occasional cavils, LaRussa does deserve credit for a great deal of it. Yet there is one factor that's rarely mentioned but has significant bearing on the Cardinals' recent history of consistent success. Unlike many clubs, and almost all clubs in comparable demographic and financial situations, the Cardinals invest enough money in their front office for it to serve its function. Rather than cut executive overhead, the Cardinals have a sizable front office staff that does its research and conducts due diligence in making baseball operations decisions.

CARDINALS PROSPECTUS

2005 record: 100–62; First place, NL Central; Lost to Astros in Championship Series

Pythagenport record: 98–64

Runs scored per game: 4.97 (3rd in NL)

Runs allowed per game: 3.91 (2nd in NL)

Team EqA: .265 (4th in NL)

2005 Batters Age: 31.3 (3rd oldest in NL)

2005 Pitchers Age: 29.8 (6th oldest in NL)

Ballpark: Busch Stadium II (New for 2006)

2005: The Jocketty-LaRussa tag team cranks out another veteran machine, chewing up the rest of the division.

2006: The Cardinals will still contend, but they're losing ground in every phase of the game.

For example, a million dollars a year can either buy you a mediocre pitcher (who can often be replaced for the league minimum), or it can buy several front office staffers who can scout, crunch numbers, forecast, and find ways to improve the on-field talent while spending less money. The Cardinals aggressively market the club, their fans and the city as key reasons that make St. Louis is a desirable destination for star players, to the point that star players can be signed at a discount. This, in turn, more than pays for the extra staff. There's a lesson for businesses outside of baseball here, too: better to have some extra capacity in your workforce than to think you're cutting costs by chopping staff. While other organizations may be penny wise and pound foolish, they risk forsaking opportunities to get better because things that might be caught by fully-staffed front offices fall through the cracks.

Both in the front office and in the field, a key element of the Cardinals' success is their belief in investment. In September, 2002, they offered Chris Carpenter three months after he underwent shoulder surgery. Though he was unlikely to pitch at all in 2003, the Cardinals recognized that this was the last moment when he'd be available at a low price. Since the Cardinals tendered that offer—and subsequently signed Carpenter to an extension—Carpenter has given them more than 400 outstanding innings and won a Cy Young award. That willingness to accept risk on a modest budget requires a depth of knowledge that only comes from research.

The Cardinals' self-investment extends beyond baseball operations. Most organizations have a point person or two to deal with community and political relationships. It's often a club president, sometimes working with outside counsel. Business development isn't a significant line item for most clubs, which results in little assistance and weak partnerships with local politicos. The Cardinals will begin the 2006 season in a new stadium, a structure achieved through extensive lobbying and years of hard work. It's neither coincidence nor accident that the Cardinals are so well integrated with the St. Louis community. Led by Bill De Witt, they employ a large, talented, well-connected staff to build, grow, and maintain relationships with businesses and thought leaders in the St. Louis area. That takes a lot of time and money to achieve and preserve; other teams have had the option to do the same thing, but they've usually acted on the cheap, often with no gain to show for their minimal efforts.

None of these skills and strategies mean anything if the club doesn't invest in the product on the field and succeed. Calvin Griffith was smart and thrifty, but few baseball fans would long for a new Griffith administration in their favorite team's front office. Fortunately for Cardinal fans, Walt Jocketty's been good about making solid investments. In a fiscal world where a 32-year-old Johnny Damon is worth $52 million over four years, having Albert Pujols locked up for the next five years at a slightly higher price looks brilliantly prescient.

The Cardinal team that played so well last year was exceptionally well-balanced. As measured by pitchers' runs prevented, their rotation was the eighth-best in the majors while the bullpen was the fifth-best in baseball. Even without Rolen, the offense ranked eighth in the majors in marginal lineup value. The 2005 Cardinals had no significant weaknesses, either in scoring or preventing runs.

Still, the Cardinals face significant challenges in 2006. First among them is their lack of depth in the minors. The Cardinals have done a solid job in drafting and development, but in recent years, they've used those skills to exchange young talent for established players, presumably to mitigate the risk of young players undermining their annual pennant runs. Last year, this strategy led to the trade of their two best prospects, Danny Haren and Daric Barton, to the Oakland Athletics for left-hander Mark Mulder. Many in the press, particularly in the Bay Area, pilloried the A's for making the deal, using it as an example of the A's penchant for squeezing every nickel until Jefferson's bust is replaced by Billy Beane's thumbprint. Instead, as many analysts warned, the deal was extremely expensive

for the Cardinals. Mulder was not demonstrably better than Haren in 2005, but he's considerably more expensive, to the tune of several million dollars more. That wasn't the only expense: Barton cemented his position as one of the best hitting prospects in baseball, and throw-in reliever Kiko Calero was one of the most valuable setup men in either league. As a thorough, professional, and somewhat conservative organization, the Cardinals sometimes overpay for a higher level of perceived security. They now need to pay the price for that conservatism and invest in rebuilding their farm system.

The stars are well aligned for the Cardinals to do exactly that. The losses of Larry Walker and Reggie Sanders will be somewhat dampened by the probable return of a healthy Scott Rolen. Matt Morris's defection to the Giants won't be loudly lamented, and one of the few bright spots of the Cardinals farm system, Anthony Reyes, can be expected to replace Morris and make a substantial contribution as a rotation starter beginning in 2006.

The Cardinals made one of the better low-cost gambles of the offseason by signing Junior Spivey to fill the hole left by Mark Grudzielanek's descent into Kansas City. Spivey has more upside than the departed Grudz, and if healthy, will likely beat out Aaron Miles for the majority of the playing time at second base. The outfield may not have the pop of the retired Walker and departed Sanders, but LaRussa is adept at spotting players like Larry Bigbie, So Taguchi and John Rodriguez to get strong production out of their limited skill sets by playing them to their individual strengths. Since Jocketty's always looking for a good deal, don't be surprised if he picks up a big-name slugging outfielder this spring or during the season; with the new ballpark opening up, there's likely to be enough money to take on a contract.

In the short term, the Cardinals can also count on a lack of competition as an asset. The Astros look like a team that's about to take a serious dive, while the Cubs have been spinning their wheels for years and don't appear to be executing a serious plan. If there's a team in the division that should scare the Cardinals, it's probably the Brewers, who appear to be doing everything right and have a lot of young talent coming up. But at the moment Milwaukee is well behind St. Louis. Jocketty's outfit has the time and resources to stave off a Brewer challenge for at least another year or so.

In the meantime, the Cardinals should be able to use some of their front-office muscle to restock their farm system over the next couple of years. LaRussa knows how to choose, develop and deploy all sorts of players, from role players that aren't happy on other teams, to veterans who need to be handled with kid gloves, to relievers narrowly suited for highly specialized roles. He knows his job as a manager, and with the support he receives from Jocketty's hard-charging front office, the Cardinals are well positioned to continue their run of recent excellence.

They may not always do it the way we would, but there would be fewer franchises in serious trouble if more teams were run like the Cardinals are. That means taking some well-researched chances, and having the courage to spend money, even when it feels like you shouldn't. Like we said, maybe Michael Lewis should have spent a year with Walt Jocketty.

HITTERS

RICK ANKIEL — OF — Bats: L Throws: L — Height: 6' 1" Weight: 215 Born: July 19, 1979 — Age: 26

YEAR	TM	LVL	AGE	PA	R	2B	3B	HR	RBI	BB	SO	SB	CS	SPEED	BA	OBP	SLG	MLVR	EQBA	EQOBP	EQSLG	EQA	VORP	DEFENSE
2005	QUD	A	25	223	33	10	1	11	45	27	37	0	0	3.9	.270	.368	.514	.238	.211	.281	.374	.230	-10.7	23-RF -1
2005	SFD	AA	25	146	18	7	0	10	30	10	29	0	0	3.5	.243	.295	.515	.076	.202	.252	.417	.225	-7.4	24-RF -1
2006	SLN	MLB	26	352	33	15	1	10	39	23	83	0	0	3.5	.209	.266	.352	-.264	.210	.267	.364	.207	-15.8	85-RF -2

Breakout: 28%   Improve: 48%   Collapse: 39%   Attrition: 20%   Comparables: Ivanon Coffie, Brian Shackelford, Justin Headley

Ankiel's second career as an outfielder is off to a pretty good start. He's shown power at the plate and fair plate discipline. His swing generates the coveted backspin-of-death, and he's shown surprising prowess with the glove. Yes, he's old for his level, but it's not out of the question that he'll develop quickly and end up in the Cardinals outfield later in the season. There's definitely an opening for him if he performs.

EINAR DIAZ — C — Bats: R Throws: R — Height: 5' 10" Weight: 160 Born: December 28, 1972 Age: 33

YEAR	TM	LVL	AGE	PA	R	2B	3B	HR	RBI	BB	SO	SB	CS	SPEED	BA	OBP	SLG	MLVR	EQBA	EQOBP	EQSLG	EQA	VORP	DEFENSE
2003	TEX	MLB	30	357	30	14	1	4	35	9	32	3	1	3.6	.257	.294	.341	-.224	.248	.288	.330	.221	-5.7	95-C 0
2004	MON	MLB	31	157	9	6	1	1	11	11	10	2	0	3.9	.223	.293	.302	-.240	.221	.287	.300	.218	-3.7	37-C -3
2005	SLN	MLB	32	137	14	6	0	1	17	5	12	0	0	3.9	.208	.248	.277	-.358	.214	.259	.298	.198	-7.0	34-C 2
2006	CLE	MLB	33	125	9	5	0	1	11	5	13	0	0	4.3	.236	.276	.307	-.267	.240	.284	.324	.202	-3.5	34-C 0

Breakout: 34%   Improve: 54%   Collapse: 31%   Attrition: 48%   Comparables: Danny Sheaffer, Gary Bennett, Pat Borders

His miracle contract finally ran out, bringing the compensation universe that much closer to equilibrium. The Cardinals picked him up to pair off with Yadier Molina, and he hit like a Hamill (Mark or Dorothy, take your pick), same as always. Diaz simply can't hit a baseball, and isn't any club's best option for a backup catcher spot. He signed with the Indians, where he'll serve primarily to make Victor Martinez look even better. Godspeed, Citizen Diaz.

CHRIS DUNCAN — 1B/OF — Bats: L Throws: R — Height: 6' 5" Weight: 210 Born: May 5, 1981 — Age: 25

YEAR	TM	LVL	AGE	PA	R	2B	3B	HR	RBI	BB	SO	SB	CS	SPEED	BA	OBP	SLG	MLVR	EQBA	EQOBP	EQSLG	EQA	VORP	DEFENSE	
2003	PMB	A+	22	475	26	20	0	2	42	44	115	4	4	3.1	.254	.322	.315	-.020	.234	.293	.312	.217	-29.0	113-1B -6	
2004	TEN	AA	23	455	57	23	0	16	65	64	94	8	4	4.4	.289	.393	.473	.205	.251	.347	.413	.265	5.6	78-1B -6	16-RF 1
2005	MEM	AAA	24	500	57	21	2	21	73	63	104	1	3	3.2	.265	.358	.469	.119	.250	.332	.422	.260	3.7	99-1B -10	17-RF -3
2006	SLN	MLB	25	441	50	20	1	14	55	42	98	2	1	3.7	.249	.325	.409	-.063	.250	.326	.424	.251	0.0	105-1B -3	

Breakout: 28%   Improve: 55%   Collapse: 26%   Attrition: 17%   Comparables: George Scott, Derrek Lee, Nick Johnson

Facing an uphill battle worthy of Sisyphus to unseat Albert Pujols at first base, Dave Duncan's kid has switched to the outfield. He's got some positives, including a bit of power and the ability to make pitchers throw strikes. He's also young enough to learn to play acceptable outfield defense. He'll start the season back in Triple-A, but if injuries bite the Cardinals outfield, he could wind up with some real playing time in St. Louis.

DAVID ECKSTEIN — 2B/SS — Bats: R Throws: R — Height: 5' 8" Weight: 168 Born: January 20, 1975 — Age: 31

YEAR	TM	LVL	AGE	PA	R	2B	3B	HR	RBI	BB	SO	SB	CS	SPEED	BA	OBP	SLG	MLVR	EQBA	EQOBP	EQSLG	EQA	VORP	DEFENSE
2003	ANA	MLB	28	507	59	22	1	3	31	36	45	16	5	5.7	.252	.325	.325	-.153	.259	.333	.339	.245	5.5	112-SS 10
2004	ANA	MLB	29	623	92	24	1	2	35	42	49	16	5	6.0	.276	.339	.332	-.157	.282	.346	.337	.248	6.9	133-SS 0
2005	SLN	MLB	30	705	90	26	7	8	61	58	44	11	8	5.4	.294	.363	.395	.058	.294	.363	.405	.268	32.4	150-SS 1
2006	SLN	MLB	31	616	72	25	3	3	47	44	45	10	4	5.0	.266	.328	.338	-.139	.267	.329	.350	.235	9.5	144-SS 2

Breakout: 7%   Improve: 26%   Collapse: 33%   Attrition: 9%   Comparables: Marty Barrett, Stan Rojek, Phil Rizzuto

(continued next page)

David Eckstein (*continued*)

Eckstein gave the Cardinals exactly what they wanted: a shortstop who got on base and made the routine plays. His upside is somewhere around a .370/.380 OBP/SLG, and his downside's around .325/.325. He's a fan favorite, but basically filler with a great narrative. He doesn't push a team towards a championship, but he doesn't drag it down, either. He might reach double figures in home runs one of these years.

JIM EDMONDS   CF   **Bats: L Throws: L**   Height: 6' 1"   Weight: 218   Born: June 27, 1970   Age: 36

YEAR	TM	LVL	AGE	PA	R	2B	3B	HR	RBI	BB	SO	SB	CS	SPEED	BA	OBP	SLG	MLVR	EQBA	EQOBP	EQSLG	EQA	VORP	DEFENSE	
2003	SLN	MLB	33	530	89	32	2	39	89	77	127	1	3	3.9	.275	.385	.617	.374	.274	.383	.621	.321	54.3	113-CF	8
2004	SLN	MLB	34	612	102	38	3	42	111	101	150	8	3	5.6	.301	.418	.643	.480	.297	.413	.639	.339	81.2	138-CF	13
2005	SLN	MLB	35	566	88	37	1	29	89	91	139	5	5	4.7	.263	.385	.533	.253	.261	.383	.538	.305	44.2	129-CF	21
2006	SLN	MLB	36	557	88	30	2	34	96	93	131	6	3	4.8	.285	.407	.582	.316	.286	.408	.603	.325	54.3	131-CF	1

Breakout: 19%   Improve: 37%   Collapse: 24%   Attrition: 12%   Comparables: Reggie Jackson, Willie Stargell, Mickey Mantle

This was the season that Jim Edmonds's defensive performance finally caught up with his defensive reputation. Edmonds has long been perceived as one of the game's very best center fielders. This season, he added an outstanding two wins compared to the average center fielder with his glove alone. Edmonds was once considered fragile, but has since veered onto the Paul Molitor career path, getting more durable and more productive with age. Two more reasonable seasons and Edmonds will have a solid Hall of Fame case. Just ten center fielders with more than 5,000 career PAs have had enough power to maintain a .500+ slugging percentage. Three of them—Edmonds, Junior Griffey, and Andruw Jones—are active. The other seven have plaques in Cooperstown.

JOHN GALL   1B/LF   **Bats: R Throws: R**   Height: 6' 0"   Weight: 195   Born: April 2, 1978   Age: 28

YEAR	TM	LVL	AGE	PA	R	2B	3B	HR	RBI	BB	SO	SB	CS	SPEED	BA	OBP	SLG	MLVR	EQBA	EQOBP	EQSLG	EQA	VORP	DEFENSE			
2003	MEM	AAA	25	503	62	24	1	16	73	39	56	5	2	4.2	.312	.368	.473	.239	.297	.352	.452	.275	20.5	115-1B	-11		
2004	MEM	AAA	26	563	77	34	0	22	84	48	68	1	1	3.6	.292	.350	.490	.140	.259	.312	.413	.251	-6.6	95-LF	-5	13-1B	-1
2005	MEM	AAA	27	426	61	22	0	13	64	45	42	9	2	5.0	.270	.345	.433	.047	.239	.304	.362	.237	-16.7	53-LF	-4	34-1B	-3
2005	SLN	MLB	27	39	5	3	0	2	10	1	8	0	0	5.0	.270	.282	.514	.085	.270	.282	.486	.258	1.5				
2006	SLN	MLB	28	339	38	16	1	9	41	27	46	3	1	4.2	.260	.321	.408	-.061	.262	.322	.423	.250	0.8	82-LF	-4		

Breakout: 28%   Improve: 44%   Collapse: 33%   Attrition: 23%   Comparables: Steve Brye, Chad Alexander, Ron Jackson

Smooth-swinged but a bit of a position gypsy, Gall has the rep of a minor league hitter, but Reggie Sanders's leg injury gave him an opportunity to pick up some PAs, and he didn't embarrass himself. He's not a premier prospect by any means, but he could wind up with a decent major league career in the mold of a Dustan Mohr. It's possible that the Cardinals will leave spring training with Gall on the roster as a reserve. His skills and strengths are somewhat complementary to So Taguchi. An added benefit to having Gall on the roster: frequent broadcast references to Alfred Kinsey, who got his start in biology by cataloguing the wasps that share the outfielder's surname.

TYLER GREENE   SS   **Bats: R Throws: R**   Height: 6' 2"   Weight: 185   Born: August 17, 1983   Age: 22

YEAR	TM	LVL	AGE	PA	R	2B	3B	HR	RBI	BB	SO	SB	CS	SPEED	BA	OBP	SLG	MLVR	EQBA	EQOBP	EQSLG	EQA	VORP	DEFENSE	
2005	NWJ	A-	21	159	28	12	0	1	18	15	37	13	1	6.6	.261	.352	.370	.059	.214	.278	.312	.220	-10.3	34-SS	1
2005	PMB	A+	21	92	17	4	0	2	5	5	28	6	0	7.0	.271	.326	.388	.047	.256	.304	.395	.250	1.6	20-SS	0
2006	SLN	MLB	22	352	37	17	2	6	31	21	101	12	4	5.0	.222	.276	.340	-.254	.223	.277	.352	.213	-2.9	85-SS	-1

Breakout: 26%   Improve: 35%   Collapse: 43%   Attrition: 20%   Comparables: Joseph Monahan, Chase Voshell, Aneudi Cuevas

Polished high draft pick with a shine on him in the eyes of the front office. Given the state of shortstop play in the National League, Greene could be up fairly quickly. Even if he's not the next Alex Rodriguez, he could perform well enough for the Cardinals to get a leg up on their competition. He could also be trade bait, if Jocketty's track record is any indication.

MARK GRUDZIELANEK   **2B**   **Bats: R Throws: R**   Height: 6′ 1″   Weight: 190   Born: June 30, 1970   Age: 36

YEAR	TM	LVL	AGE	PA	R	2B	3B	HR	RBI	BB	SO	SB	CS	SPEED	BA	OBP	SLG	MLVR	EQBA	EQOBP	EQSLG	EQA	VORP	DEFENSE	
2003	CHN	MLB	33	524	73	38	1	3	38	30	64	6	2	5.2	.314	.366	.416	.097	.311	.362	.419	.273	28.1	113-2B	0
2004	IOW	AAA	34	28	6	3	0	2	4	0	4	0	0	4.8	.250	.250	.571	-.020	.172	.172	.357	.179	-2.9		
2004	CHN	MLB	34	274	32	12	1	6	23	15	32	1	1	4.1	.307	.347	.432	.055	.302	.342	.426	.264	11.6	63-2B	2
2005	SLN	MLB	35	563	64	30	3	8	59	26	81	8	6	5.2	.294	.334	.407	.032	.294	.336	.411	.257	16.5	130-2B	0
2006	*KCA*	*MLB*	*36*	*376*	*41*	*19*	*2*	*6*	*41*	*17*	*49*	*5*	*3*	*4.9*	*.280*	*.317*	*.394*	*-.055*	*.281*	*.326*	*.415*	*.247*	*10.2*	*90-2B*	*-2*

Breakout: 7%   Improve: 30%   Collapse: 40%   Attrition: 31%   Comparables: Alvin Dark, Cookie Rojas, Enos Cabell

Grudzielanek is a complete cipher. He's an average defender for his position. As a hitter he's a moderate batting average guy who draws a few walks and has a little power. Like a fine button mushroom, he takes on the flavor and character of his surroundings. His ideal situation is to join a team on the cusp of significant success with a major hole at second, where his consistent play would serve to provide some comfort and improvement. Instead, the poor guy's signed with the Royals, where he'll be watching the twin tendrils of failure and contraction waving from the fountains at Kauffman Stadium.

CODY HAERTHER   **LF**   **Bats: L Throws: R**   Height: 6′ 0″   Weight: 190   Born: July 14, 1983   Age: 22

YEAR	TM	LVL	AGE	PA	R	2B	3B	HR	RBI	BB	SO	SB	CS	SPEED	BA	OBP	SLG	MLVR	EQBA	EQOBP	EQSLG	EQA	VORP	DEFENSE			
2003	JCY	Rk	19	249	31	12	6	3	39	22	30	2	1	5.0	.332	.390	.478	.287	.280	.324	.418	.254	0.4	41-LF	-1	10-3B	1
2004	PEO	A	20	363	48	20	2	5	45	32	59	7	3	4.8	.316	.383	.436	.213	.282	.340	.392	.256	-0.3	51-LF	-1		
2005	PMB	A+	21	192	29	8	7	8	30	17	31	8	3	6.4	.318	.380	.584	.437	.295	.352	.536	.295	12.9	16-LF	1		
2005	SFD	AA	21	219	30	10	1	10	37	9	44	0	1	4.3	.298	.333	.500	.171	.274	.307	.458	.256	1.5	30-LF	-2		
2006	*SLN*	*MLB*	*22*	*511*	*64*	*27*	*4*	*13*	*65*	*34*	*95*	*6*	*3*	*5.2*	*.275*	*.325*	*.434*	*-.009*	*.276*	*.326*	*.450*	*.257*	*7.9*	*120-LF*	*-1*		

Breakout: 14%   Improve: 43%   Collapse: 27%   Attrition: 6%   Comparables: Curtis Granderson, Laynce Nix, Alex Fernandez

The Cards' best outfield prospect, Haerther has shown a little bit of everything thus far: he's hit for average, some power, and played promising defense. His '04 season ended early with a fractured tibia, which kept him out of the outfield until late May, but he seemed to recover well enough. One scout compares him to a "young Rusty Greer," which hopefully refers to his Greer's performance and not his injury history. Haerther's power is a recent arrival; 2006 will be an important indicator of his likely career path. Right now it looks like he could be in St. Louis putting up major-league starter numbers by next year.

TRAVIS HANSON   **3B**   **Bats: L Throws: R**   Height: 6′ 2″   Weight: 195   Born: January 24, 1981   Age: 25

YEAR	TM	LVL	AGE	PA	R	2B	3B	HR	RBI	BB	SO	SB	CS	SPEED	BA	OBP	SLG	MLVR	EQBA	EQOBP	EQSLG	EQA	VORP	DEFENSE	
2003	PEO	A	22	573	70	31	5	9	78	35	104	3	4	4.4	.277	.325	.406	.103	.251	.288	.385	.232	-1.4	134-3B	7
2004	PMB	A+	23	249	26	11	0	2	35	19	38	2	3	3.8	.259	.321	.335	-.028	.233	.284	.316	.214	-9.7	48-2B	0
2005	SFD	AA	24	608	82	29	3	20	97	54	99	2	2	4.1	.284	.347	.458	.120	.254	.313	.403	.248	11.0	135-3B	-5
2006	*SLN*	*MLB*	*25*	*480*	*49*	*23*	*2*	*10*	*51*	*32*	*95*	*2*	*1*	*4.2*	*.248*	*.302*	*.373*	*-.150*	*.249*	*.303*	*.386*	*.230*	*-1.5*	*114-3B*	*-1*

Breakout: 26%   Improve: 46%   Collapse: 28%   Attrition: 14%   Comparables: Rich Lane, Josh Klimek, Dave Meliah

Missed most of the 2004 campaign with a nasty ankle injury, but rebounded pretty well in '05. He's got some pop, but there are whispers about his swing being a bit long and having a few too many holes. The time away also left him looking pretty rough in the field. He'll have to perform well in order to get a serious look for a major league job in 2007, and even then, he'll be trying to break into the Cardinal lineup as either a third or first baseman. Talk about following Carson.

HECTOR LUNA   **UT**   **Bats: R Throws: R**   Height: 6′ 1″   Weight: 170   Born: February 1, 1980   Age: 26

YEAR	TM	LVL	AGE	PA	R	2B	3B	HR	RBI	BB	SO	SB	CS	SPEED	BA	OBP	SLG	MLVR	EQBA	EQOBP	EQSLG	EQA	VORP	DEFENSE			
2003	AKR	AA	23	517	87	19	2	2	38	48	64	17	5	6.4	.297	.368	.359	.015	.264	.328	.327	.238	2.5	125-SS	-7		
2004	SLN	MLB	24	191	25	7	2	3	22	13	37	6	3	6.6	.249	.304	.364	-.128	.247	.302	.362	.235	-0.7	16-SS	0	10-2B	-1
2005	MEM	AAA	25	245	24	13	1	3	21	20	38	11	4	6.1	.224	.294	.332	-.242	.214	.269	.312	.211	-11.9	43-2B	1	11-SS	0
2005	SLN	MLB	25	151	26	10	2	1	18	9	25	10	2	8.0	.285	.344	.409	.041	.283	.342	.406	.267	6.2	16-2B	0	13-RF	1
2006	*SLN*	*MLB*	*26*	*370*	*46*	*16*	*3*	*4*	*30*	*27*	*58*	*15*	*5*	*5.8*	*.249*	*.312*	*.349*	*-.162*	*.251*	*.313*	*.362*	*.234*	*2.0*	*89-2B*	*1*		

Breakout: 35%   Improve: 63%   Collapse: 20%   Attrition: 22%   Comparables: Carlos Febles, Johnnie Lemaster, Dave Concepcion

If you think wives and girlfriends send mixed messages, you might want to talk to Hector Luna about Walt Jocketty. On December 11, the Cardinals sent Chuck McElroy-doppelganger Ray King to the Rockies for Larry Bigbie and second

(continued next page)

Hector Luna *(continued)*

baseman Aaron Miles. They also signed veteran infielder Deivi Cruz. At the same time, Jocketty said he would "like to see what Hector Luna might do as the team's starting second baseman." Then he went out and signed Junior Spivey and traded for Aaron Miles. Sounds like someone could use a little time with Dr. Phil. Realistically, a team looking at Spivey, Cruz, Miles, and Luna as their second base alternatives has no second baseman.

JOHN MABRY   OF/1B   Bats: L Throws: R   Height: 6′ 4″   Weight: 210   Born: October 17, 1970   Age: 35

YEAR	TM	LVL	AGE	PA	R	2B	3B	HR	RBI	BB	SO	SB	CS	SPEED	BA	OBP	SLG	MLVR	EQBA	EQOBP	EQSLG	EQA	VORP	DEFENSE			
2003	SEA	MLB	32	122	12	6	0	3	16	15	21	0	0	3.6	.212	.328	.356	-.133	.221	.336	.385	.254	-1.5				
2004	MEM	AAA	33	160	27	7	0	12	35	17	29	0	0	3.3	.338	.406	.654	.548	.270	.325	.462	.270	3.7	19-1B	0		
2004	SLN	MLB	33	270	32	11	0	13	40	26	63	0	1	3.5	.296	.363	.504	.191	.292	.359	.502	.290	13.9	25-LF	2	13-RF	-1
2005	SLN	MLB	34	268	26	15	1	8	32	20	63	0	0	3.9	.240	.295	.407	-.088	.238	.295	.411	.243	-1.9	28-RF	-2	13-LF	0
2006	*CHN*	*MLB*	*35*	*200*	*22*	*10*	*1*	*7*	*27*	*17*	*45*	*0*	*0*	*4.0*	*.251*	*.317*	*.429*	*-.048*	*.252*	*.317*	*.437*	*.251*	*1.1*	*50-RF*	*-2*		

Breakout: 13%   Improve: 35%   Collapse: 43%   Attrition: 44%   Comparables: *Walt Moryn, Jim Lemon, Dave Clark*

One of the least mysterious players in baseball, he's an average hitter, but with less of a platoon split than his usage would suggest: he hits with more power versus right-handers, but for a higher average on those rare occasions when he's allowed to face a lefty. Mabry's also a pretty reasonable defender at the corner positions. He's signed with the Cubs, where he'll fill the same role he did with the Cardinals.

YADIER MOLINA   C   Bats: R Throws: R   Height: 5′ 11″   Weight: 185   Born: July 13, 1982   Age: 23

YEAR	TM	LVL	AGE	PA	R	2B	3B	HR	RBI	BB	SO	SB	CS	SPEED	BA	OBP	SLG	MLVR	EQBA	EQOBP	EQSLG	EQA	VORP	DEFENSE	
2003	TEN	AA	20	397	32	13	1	2	51	25	45	0	1	3.2	.275	.327	.332	-.058	.249	.293	.315	.216	-12.1	100-C	13
2004	MEM	AAA	21	150	19	6	0	1	14	17	14	0	0	3.5	.302	.387	.372	.044	.284	.359	.339	.254	3.1	36-C	8
2004	SLN	MLB	21	149	12	6	0	2	15	13	20	0	1	3.0	.267	.329	.356	-.086	.265	.327	.360	.241	0.8	38-C	2
2005	SLN	MLB	22	413	36	15	1	8	49	23	30	2	3	4.3	.252	.295	.358	-.142	.253	.298	.363	.230	-1.1	108-C	17
2006	*SLN*	*MLB*	*23*	*368*	*38*	*16*	*1*	*5*	*38*	*25*	*37*	*1*	*2*	*4.4*	*.261*	*.315*	*.363*	*-.131*	*.262*	*.316*	*.376*	*.233*	*1.6*	*88-C*	*8*

Breakout: 32%   Improve: 53%   Collapse: 19%   Attrition: 12%   Comparables: *Ellie Rodriguez, Ray Fosse, Jack Shepard*

He's a glove guy, but has some potential with the bat. Molina's an extreme contact hitter, drawing a walk or striking out only 53 times in over 400 PA. A few extra breaks here and there, and Molina could invoke Jazayerli's .300 Catcher Corollary any minute now. He's got youth and defense on his side, so you can expect a long career, probably with a couple of performance spikes. However, those years are more likely to start in 2008 than 2006.

ABRAHAM NUNEZ   INF   Bats: B Throws: R   Height: 5′ 11″   Weight: 190   Born: March 16, 1976   Age: 30

YEAR	TM	LVL	AGE	PA	R	2B	3B	HR	RBI	BB	SO	SB	CS	SPEED	BA	OBP	SLG	MLVR	EQBA	EQOBP	EQSLG	EQA	VORP	DEFENSE			
2003	PIT	MLB	27	342	37	8	7	4	35	26	53	9	3	6.9	.248	.310	.357	-.133	.244	.306	.362	.238	0.9	59-2B	3	17-SS	-1
2004	PIT	MLB	28	193	17	9	0	2	13	10	36	1	3	4.0	.236	.275	.319	-.251	.235	.273	.322	.206	-7.2	22-2B	3		
2005	SLN	MLB	29	458	64	13	2	5	44	37	63	0	1	4.9	.285	.343	.361	-.033	.285	.345	.367	.251	5.0	81-3B	415-2B	-2	
2006	*PHI*	*MLB*	*30*	*336*	*38*	*14*	*2*	*4*	*30*	*25*	*49*	*3*	*2*	*5.0*	*.260*	*.318*	*.358*	*-.135*	*.259*	*.318*	*.359*	*.230*	*-0.6*	*81-3B*	*2*		

Breakout: 20%   Improve: 40%   Collapse: 36%   Attrition: 30%   Comparables: *Kevin Stocker, Ron Oester, Ted Kubiak*

After salvaging his career with a season in which he did passably well subbing for Scott Rolen, Nunez was rewarded with a two-year, $3.5 million deal with the Phillies to be a utility guy. It's the sort of move that makes you wonder if the Phillies front office was aware that there are actually several guys available who can play more than one position, many of them for a lot less than that. Nunez just had his career year at 29, and it isn't hard to find utility infielders who can give you average defense at third, and slightly sub-par defense at the middle infield spots. Nunez will be acceptable in his role for the next couple of years, but the Phillies could have saved some money filling that slot.

ALBERT PUJOLS   1B   Bats: R Throws: R   Height: 6′ 3″   Weight: 210   Born: January 16, 1980   Age: 26

YEAR	TM	LVL	AGE	PA	R	2B	3B	HR	RBI	BB	SO	SB	CS	SPEED	BA	OBP	SLG	MLVR	EQBA	EQOBP	EQSLG	EQA	VORP	DEFENSE			
2003	SLN	MLB	23	685	137	51	1	43	124	79	65	5	1	5.2	.359	.439	.667	.612	.355	.435	.672	.357	97.9	100-LF	-5	41-1B	4
2004	SLN	MLB	24	692	133	51	2	46	123	84	52	5	5	4.6	.331	.415	.657	.535	.327	.410	.651	.339	92.3	149-1B	3		
2005	SLN	MLB	25	700	129	38	2	41	117	97	65	16	2	5.6	.330	.430	.609	.484	.325	.426	.616	.342	88.3	152-1B	2		
2006	*SLN*	*MLB*	*26*	*693*	*117*	*41*	*2*	*41*	*130*	*95*	*67*	*13*	*3*	*5.1*	*.338*	*.433*	*.625*	*.467*	*.340*	*.434*	*.648*	*.347*	*88.3*	*161-1B*	*3*		

Breakout: 11%   Improve: 50%   Collapse: 17%   Attrition: 0%   Comparables: *Frank Robinson, Will Clark, Orlando Cepeda*

Absurdly great, and signed to a very favorable deal for the Cardinals. On the statistical anomaly front, check out Pujols's ABs for the last five years: 590, 590, 591, 592, 591. Only on a Tony LaRussa team could things be so rigidly organized. In terms of performance, only Barry Bonds compares. Pujols's line of .330/.430/.609 for the season is truly remarkable because he was suffering through plantar fasciitis for a good chunk of the season, and hitting a baseball without being able to plant your foot properly is exceptionally difficult. Even if there's truth to the old rumor that he may be two years older than his listed age, Pujols is still capable of putting up Bonds-like numbers. He's Mozart with a bat, a very smart baserunner, a plus defender at first base, and well-liked and respected in the community. For the city and the franchise, he's the perfect superstar.

COLBY RASMUS CF **Bats: L Throws: L** Height: 6′ 1″ Weight: 175 Born: August 11, 1986 Age: 19

YEAR	TM	LVL	AGE	PA	R	2B	3B	HR	RBI	BB	SO	SB	CS	SPEED	BA	OBP	SLG	MLVR	EQBA	EQOBP	EQSLG	EQA	VORP	DEFENSE		
2005	JCY	Rk	18	243	47	16	5	7	27	21	73	13	3	7.6	.296	.362	.514	.197	.222	.273	.361	.225	-18.2	58-CF	2	
2006	SLN	MLB	19	345	41	21	3	8	34	24	103	10	6	5.9	.226	.284	.392	-.171	.227	.284	.406	.229	-3.3	83-CF	3	

Breakout: 44% Improve: 64% Collapse: 21% Attrition: 20% Comparables: Mickey Hall, Andy Brown, Teodoro Encarnacion

An extremely athletic high school draftee who can dazzle the scouts, Rasmus has a haymaker swing that vaguely resembles Les Nessman facing Johan Santana, but with better results. He has adjusted well to wood bats, and he's got the physical tools to succeed if he can learn at a reasonable rate.

JOHN RODRIGUEZ OF **Bats: L Throws: L** Height: 6′ 0″ Weight: 185 Born: January 20, 1978 Age: 28

YEAR	TM	LVL	AGE	PA	R	2B	3B	HR	RBI	BB	SO	SB	CS	SPEED	BA	OBP	SLG	MLVR	EQBA	EQOBP	EQSLG	EQA	VORP	DEFENSE			
2003	COH	AAA	25	258	35	9	2	10	33	24	50	6	0	5.9	.263	.333	.448	.080	.242	.315	.423	.257	3.9	31-CF	0	28-LF	0
2004	COH	AAA	26	436	78	29	10	16	69	48	82	9	3	7.3	.300	.388	.557	.305	.267	.351	.480	.283	25.9	92-CF	-8		
2005	BUF	AAA	27	195	25	13	3	5	23	15	40	5	0	6.9	.247	.323	.447	-.010	.213	.278	.371	.233	-5.5	23-CF	1	16-RF	0
2005	MEM	AAA	27	136	24	5	0	17	47	13	28	1	1	3.7	.342	.419	.808	.827	.302	.366	.647	.320	15.9	16-RF	-1	12-CF	0
2005	SLN	MLB	27	173	15	6	0	5	24	19	45	2	0	4.9	.295	.382	.436	.148	.291	.377	.437	.287	8.8	32-LF	3		
2006	SLN	MLB	28	445	59	23	3	16	59	41	93	6	2	5.5	.265	.340	.462	.043	.266	.341	.478	.272	14.4	106-LF	-3		

Breakout: 16% Improve: 38% Collapse: 22% Attrition: 12% Comparables: Michael Tucker, Irv Noren, George Altman

Journeyman minor league outfielder who's earned a shot at a big league job after being thoughtlessly discarded by the Yankees. Rodriguez played well enough in a fill-in role with the Cardinals that he's likely to see significant playing time this year. He has some pop in his bat, but he'll rack up the strikeouts, and his defense is slightly subpar. Under the right circumstances, Rodriguez could forge a nice MLB career. He'll be in the outfield mix with Bigbie and Taguchi, with the Cards hoping somebody steps forward.

SCOTT ROLEN 3B **Bats: R Throws: R** Height: 6′ 4″ Weight: 225 Born: April 4, 1975 Age: 31

YEAR	TM	LVL	AGE	PA	R	2B	3B	HR	RBI	BB	SO	SB	CS	SPEED	BA	OBP	SLG	MLVR	EQBA	EQOBP	EQSLG	EQA	VORP	DEFENSE	
2003	SLN	MLB	28	657	98	49	1	28	104	82	104	13	3	4.9	.286	.382	.528	.264	.285	.379	.533	.307	59.9	148-3B	8
2004	SLN	MLB	29	592	109	32	4	34	124	72	92	4	3	5.1	.314	.409	.598	.425	.310	.402	.596	.326	65.0	137-3B	18
2005	SLN	MLB	30	223	28	12	1	5	28	25	28	1	2	4.5	.235	.323	.383	-.063	.235	.326	.393	.248	-0.5	55-3B	6
2006	SLN	MLB	31	407	54	22	2	16	58	46	60	4	1	4.8	.270	.358	.475	.095	.271	.359	.492	.283	21.7	97-3B	6

Breakout: 5% Improve: 25% Collapse: 42% Attrition: 19% Comparables: Cal Ripken, Eric Karros, Bobby Bonilla

An object lesson in how limited the impact of a truly great player is. The Cardinals rolled through the 2005 season with little help from Rolen, who was either absent or ineffective because of a torn labrum in his left shoulder. When healthy, he's a top-flight player, good with the bat and outstanding with the glove, but his injury history is beyond worrisome. As he enters his thirties, his main challenge will be to stay healthy and not let those nagging pains derail his career. The Cardinals would love to see him play 140–150 games for the remaining years of his contract, which runs through 2011.

BRENDAN RYAN SS **Bats: R Throws: R** Height: 6′ 2″ Weight: 195 Born: March 26, 1982 Age: 24

YEAR	TM	LVL	AGE	PA	R	2B	3B	HR	RBI	BB	SO	SB	CS	SPEED	BA	OBP	SLG	MLVR	EQBA	EQOBP	EQSLG	EQA	VORP	DEFENSE	
2003	NWJ	A-	21	212	20	14	4	0	13	14	25	11	3	6.0	.311	.363	.425	.215	.289	.328	.415	.258	18.4	30-SS	-4
2004	PEO	A	22	463	72	21	4	2	59	24	42	30	7	7.3	.322	.356	.404	.137	.280	.310	.352	.240	3.6	104-SS	-4
2005	PMB	A+	23	203	29	17	0	1	16	15	20	8	1	5.9	.303	.355	.410	.147	.267	.314	.363	.241	2.5	47-SS	5
2005	SFD	AA	23	172	28	8	1	2	9	15	19	6	0	6.6	.273	.343	.377	-.007	.255	.319	.359	.245	1.8	42-SS	-1
2006	SLN	MLB	24	445	52	22	2	2	36	25	52	11	3	5.5	.270	.315	.354	-.137	.272	.316	.367	.235	8.1	106-SS	1

Breakout: 17% Improve: 36% Collapse: 28% Attrition: 7% Comparables: Danny Sandoval, Willie Bloomquist, Hector Luna

(continued next page)

Brendan Ryan *(continued)*

A speedster once considered a serious prospect, he just hasn't produced with the bat outside of a bunch of leg singles. Defensively, he's somewhat erratic, but displays legitimate range and good hands. Ryan is still young enough to iron things out; he has the speed that the club loves, and he puts the ball in play. He'll be stretched to be a major league regular, but he'll get a shot if he can hit for average this year.

REGGIE SANDERS — OF — Bats: R Throws: R — Height: 6' 1" — Weight: 185 — Born: December 1, 1967 — Age: 38

YEAR	TM	LVL	AGE	PA	R	2B	3B	HR	RBI	BB	SO	SB	CS	SPEED	BA	OBP	SLG	MLVR	EQBA	EQOBP	EQSLG	EQA	VORP	DEFENSE			
2003	PIT	MLB	35	498	74	27	4	31	87	38	110	15	5	6.3	.285	.345	.567	.253	.280	.341	.565	.296	32.5	75-RF	2	35-LF	0
2004	SLN	MLB	36	486	64	27	3	22	67	33	118	21	5	7.1	.260	.315	.482	.067	.257	.312	.483	.269	15.5	73-RF	-1	33-LF	4
2005	SLN	MLB	37	329	49	14	2	21	54	28	75	14	1	6.2	.271	.340	.546	.205	.268	.337	.546	.296	23.1	71-LF	3		
2006	KCA	MLB	38	228	32	11	1	9	31	16	50	10	3	5.7	.267	.323	.458	.029	.268	.333	.483	.271	6.7	57-LF	-2		

Breakout: 5%   Improve: 17%   Collapse: 42%   Attrition: 41%   Comparables: Ron Gant, Kirk Gibson, Eric Davis

He's 38 years old and missed about seven weeks with a broken foot, but when he played, Sanders was productive. Any player his age is a candidate for a significant and sudden decline, but Sanders has been an underrated and consistent performer most of his career. Despite moving around, Sanders has played in the postseason in five of the last six years. Having signed a two-year deal with the Royals, he will now get to spend the rest of his career seeing how the other half lives.

SO TAGUCHI — OF — Bats: R Throws: R — Height: 5' 10" — Weight: 165 — Born: July 2, 1969 — Age: 36

YEAR	TM	LVL	AGE	PA	R	2B	3B	HR	RBI	BB	SO	SB	CS	SPEED	BA	OBP	SLG	MLVR	EQBA	EQOBP	EQSLG	EQA	VORP	DEFENSE			
2003	MEM	AAA	34	283	31	8	2	2	24	22	36	14	5	6.1	.256	.318	.326	-.109	.215	.265	.257	.196	-22.9	60-CF	-1		
2004	SLN	MLB	35	196	26	10	2	3	25	12	23	6	3	6.1	.291	.337	.419	.012	.288	.337	.413	.260	3.3	21-LF	1	20-CF	1
2005	SLN	MLB	36	422	45	21	2	8	53	20	62	11	2	5.8	.288	.322	.412	.013	.285	.322	.414	.258	9.7	36-RF	2	31-LF	2
2006	SLN	MLB	36	250	29	11	2	4	26	14	40	5	2	5.2	.260	.304	.371	-.141	.262	.305	.384	.233	-3.3	62-RF	1		

Breakout: 12%   Improve: 31%   Collapse: 38%   Attrition: 41%   Comparables: Frank Baumholtz, Manny Mota, Bill Stein

He's had basically one full season's worth of PAs during his stint with the Cardinals, and his aggregate line gives a pretty fair assessment of the kind of ballplayer he is: .289/.329/.422. That's not bad, particularly when you can run and play good outfield defense, as Taguchi can. LaRussa has plugged him in effectively, using him for spot duty, pinch-hitting, and pinch-running. In the process Taguchi's become a valuable asset to a successful team. A team that starts Taguchi isn't going to do itself any favors, but on a good team that needs to spell its starting outfielders, he's a great fit.

PITCHERS

CARMEN CALI — Bats: L Throws: L — Height: 5' 10" — Weight: 180 — Born: November 2, 1978 — Age: 27

YEAR	TM	LVL	AGE	W	L	SV	G	GS	IP	H	BB	SO	HR	GB%	BABIP	STUFF	WHIP	ERA	PERA	EQERA	EQH9	EQBB9	EQSO9	EQHR9	VORP	WXRL
2003	PMB	A+	24	2	1	3	62	0	70.3	72	32	70	2	—	.332	-19	1.48	4.99	5.10	8.33	10.1	5.2	5.8	0.8	-20.3	—
2004	TEN	AA	25	1	2	14	38	0	46.3	43	19	47	3	—	.312	-14	1.34	2.92	5.15	5.15	9.7	4.5	5.6	1.0	2.2	—
2005	MEM	AAA	26	4	5	2	50	0	58.3	74	28	45	6	46%	.356	-26	1.75	5.40	5.68	7.36	10.7	4.4	4.8	1.2	-11.5	—
2006	SLN	MLB	27	2	3	1	56	3	50.7	59	30	34	9	46%	.309	-19	1.75	6.12	6.72	7.02	10.3	4.9	5.6	1.5	-5.0	-0.5

Breakout: 40%   Improve: 71%   Collapse: 14%   Attrition: 17%   Comparables: Bobby Bevel, Jesus Pena, Jake Benz

A lefty depth guy who would have already moved on to his second career if he wasn't left-handed. He could bounce around for several years if he just spins his wheels a bit and still have a brief career in the bigs as a lefty specialist. There are hundreds of guys like this bouncing around Quadruple-A and below; most end up working in sales somewhere, but one or two end up with major league careers. You know the odds.

CHRIS CARPENTER — Bats: R Throws: R — Height: 6' 6" — Weight: 210 — Born: April 27, 1975 — Age: 31

YEAR	TM	LVL	AGE	W	L	SV	G	GS	IP	H	BB	SO	HR	GB%	BABIP	STUFF	WHIP	ERA	PERA	EQERA	EQH9	EQBB9	EQSO9	EQHR9	VORP	WXRL
2004	SLN	MLB	29	15	5	0	28	28	182.0	169	38	152	24	55%	.282	19	1.14	3.46	4.05	4.00	9.0	1.8	6.8	1.1	40.5	5.2
2005	SLN	MLB	30	21	5	0	33	33	241.7	204	51	213	18	55%	.285	34	1.06	2.83	3.34	3.38	8.1	1.8	7.4	0.7	67.8	8.6
2006	SLN	MLB	31	16	9	0	33	33	228.0	214	57	175	21	53%	.284	20	1.19	3.39	3.65	3.82	8.3	2.0	6.4	0.8	46.1	6.4

Breakout: 7%   Improve: 46%   Collapse: 12%   Attrition: 0%   Comparables: Erik Hanson, Shane Reynolds, Jon Lieber

There haven't been many pitchers to enjoy this level of success after missing a year with a shoulder injury—the labrum remains the final frontier of sports medicine. Carpenter was nothing short of magnificent all year, providing the Cardinals with the staff ace they needed to run roughshod over the NL Central. If there's something to worry about going into 2006, it's the combination of his previous ailments-biceps, elbow, back, labrum-and the 260-plus innings he pitched in 2005. If he's healthy, few pitchers in the league are likely to be better.

RANDY FLORES Bats: L Throws: L Height: 6' 0" Weight: 180 Born: July 31, 1975 Age: 30

YEAR	TM	LVL	AGE	W	L	SV	G	GS	IP	H	BB	SO	HR	GB%	BABIP	STUFF	WHIP	ERA	PERA	EQERA	EQH9	EQBB9	EQSO9	EQHR9	VORP	WXRL
2003	CSP	AAA	27	10	8	0	28	24	142.7	156	67	116	16	—	.310	-15	1.56	4.98	5.99	5.86	10.0	5.2	5.8	1.5	-4.0	—
2004	MEM	AAA	28	5	7	2	36	15	122.7	115	46	99	10	—	.294	-6	1.31	3.81	4.85	5.38	8.8	4.0	5.2	0.9	2.9	—
2005	SLN	MLB	29	3	1	1	50	0	41.7	37	13	43	5	42%	.302	12	1.20	3.45	3.92	5.01	8.5	2.6	8.5	1.1	3.3	0.7
2006	SLN	MLB	30	2	2	2	52	0	45.3	44	19	36	5	45%	.290	-1	1.39	4.21	4.47	5.05	8.5	3.5	6.6	0.9	4.6	0.4

Breakout: 36% Improve: 70% Collapse: 14% Attrition: 24% Comparables: Steve Mingori, Dave Hamilton, Vic Darensbourg

Yet another LaRussa reliever who averages less than an inning per outing. Flores got a shot to demonstrate that he's an effective situational lefty, and he took advantage of it, holding lefties to a .173 average. However, his low ERA disguises both his lack of success at stranding inherited baserunners and how successful subsequent pitchers were at stranding his leftovers. During the offseason, he underwent minor surgery to remove bone spurs from his pitching elbow, but he should be back in his familiar role in 2006, and probably for years to come.

CHRIS GISSELL Bats: R Throws: R Height: 6' 5" Weight: 210 Born: January 4, 1978 Age: 28

YEAR	TM	LVL	AGE	W	L	SV	G	GS	IP	H	BB	SO	HR	GB%	BABIP	STUFF	WHIP	ERA	PERA	EQERA	EQH9	EQBB9	EQSO9	EQHR9	VORP	WXRL
2003	CSP	AAA	25	8	4	1	38	10	109.0	96	35	82	8	—	.264	-2	1.20	3.55	4.90	4.64	8.6	3.5	5.6	0.9	11.2	—
2004	CSP	AAA	26	14	2	0	24	8	90.7	80	17	74	11	—	.260	-1	1.07	3.67	4.72	4.41	8.6	2.0	5.3	1.2	11.6	—
2005	MEM	AAA	27	8	8	0	23	23	137.3	134	36	123	16	41%	.306	0	1.24	3.54	4.93	4.86	9.3	2.6	5.7	1.4	11.0	—
2006	SLN	MLB	28	6	6	0	26	17	108.7	113	34	72	15	41%	.285	3	1.35	4.57	4.83	5.14	9.2	2.6	5.5	1.2	8.1	1.5

Breakout: 18% Improve: 57% Collapse: 13% Attrition: 3% Comparables: Shawn Boskie, Jim Coates, Roy Smith

Gissell's not going to be a star, but he's pitched well in some tough parks. He throws strikes, works quickly, fields his position well, and threw 200-plus innings with a 3-1 strikeout-walk ratio in Colorado Springs. Rather than continue taking million dollar chances on the likes of Jose Lima, a club should give Gissell the ball 15 times and see what happens. Sure, he posted an ERA north of 14.00 with the Rockies in a brief stint, but who hasn't? That's like criticizing a Kennedy for being found with alcohol and a dead hooker. Signed with Seibu.

JASON ISRINGHAUSEN Bats: R Throws: R Height: 6' 3" Weight: 230 Born: September 7, 1972 Age: 33

YEAR	TM	LVL	AGE	W	L	SV	G	GS	IP	H	BB	SO	HR	GB%	BABIP	STUFF	WHIP	ERA	PERA	EQERA	EQH9	EQBB9	EQSO9	EQHR9	VORP	WXRL
2003	SLN	MLB	30	0	1	22	40	0	42.0	31	18	41	2	52%	.259	16	1.17	2.36	3.27	3.27	7.2	3.5	8.1	0.4	12.0	2.6
2004	SLN	MLB	31	4	2	47	74	0	75.3	55	23	71	5	49%	.250	19	1.04	2.87	3.45	3.45	7.5	2.6	7.8	0.6	20.1	5.0
2005	SLN	MLB	32	1	2	39	63	0	59.0	43	27	51	4	52%	.247	11	1.19	2.14	3.92	2.35	7.5	3.9	7.4	0.6	22.0	3.7
2006	SLN	MLB	33	3	4	21	47	0	51.7	47	21	41	4	50%	.282	1	1.32	3.56	3.88	4.11	8.1	3.4	6.6	0.7	9.1	1.2

Breakout: 8% Improve: 23% Collapse: 64% Attrition: 12% Comparables: Roberto Hernandez, Jim Gott, Mike James

As exciting as Izzy can make his saves at times, he's really been consistent since coming over from Oakland, posting admirable ERAs and hit rates. He's had some nagging injuries, but by and large, he's been a very good closer for most of his career, despite the best efforts of Dallas Green to end it before it started.

KEVIN JARVIS Bats: R Throws: R Height: 6' 2" Weight: 200 Born: August 1, 1969 Age: 36

YEAR	TM	LVL	AGE	W	L	SV	G	GS	IP	H	BB	SO	HR	GB%	BABIP	STUFF	WHIP	ERA	PERA	EQERA	EQH9	EQBB9	EQSO9	EQHR9	VORP	WXRL
2003	SDN	MLB	33	4	8	0	16	16	92.0	113	32	49	15	52%	.318	-14	1.58	5.87	5.42	6.29	10.6	2.8	4.3	1.5	-8.7	0.7
2004	CSP	AAA	34	0	4	0	6	6	37.3	44	10	25	12	—	.276	-40	1.45	5.79	9.00	8.49	11.8	3.3	3.9	3.9	-11.2	—
2004	NAS	AAA	34	2	5	0	11	11	65.7	93	12	46	3	—	.393	6	1.60	4.11	4.14	5.48	11.0	2.0	3.9	0.5	0.9	—
2005	MEM	AAA	35	11	6	0	26	25	157.0	164	39	112	19	48%	.308	-19	1.29	3.38	5.76	5.22	10.1	2.8	4.0	1.7	6.3	—
2006	ARI	MLB	36	4	8	0	26	17	101.0	121	35	47	18	46%	.297	-14	1.54	5.79	5.78	5.91	10.5	2.8	3.9	1.5	-4.0	0.3

Breakout: 26% Improve: 62% Collapse: 9% Attrition: 5% Comparables: Bob Keegan, Kip Gross, Sid Hudson

(continued next page)

Kevin Jarvis *(continued)*

It might seem like a cruel joke to give him a full-length comment, but he did just put up a solid season as the unnecessary veteran starter a phone call away from patching a hole in the major league rotation. Jarvis showed that he's healthy again, earned a Triple-A All-Star berth, and got himself a minor league contract and spring training invite with Arizona. Wonders never cease.

TYLER JOHNSON Bats: B Throws: L Height: 6' 2" Weight: 180 Born: June 7, 1981 Age: 25

YEAR	TM	LVL	AGE	W	L	SV	G	GS	IP	H	BB	SO	HR	GB%	BABIP	STUFF	WHIP	ERA	PERA	EQERA	EQH9	EQBB9	EQSO9	EQHR9	VORP	WXRL
2003	PMB	A+	22	5	5	0	22	10	79.0	79	38	81	2	—	.330	3	1.48	3.08	4.72	5.07	9.6	5.2	6.2	0.7	4.5	—
2003	TEN	AA	22	1	0	0	20	0	27.3	16	15	39	1	—	.259	13	1.14	1.65	4.26	3.55	7.5	5.7	9.2	0.7	5.8	—
2004	TEN	AA	23	2	2	4	53	0	56.3	48	37	77	4	—	.333	-9	1.51	4.80	5.26	6.28	9.0	7.0	8.0	1.0	-4.0	—
2005	MEM	AAA	24	2	1	7	57	0	59.0	51	26	77	6	45%	.328	4	1.31	4.27	4.37	5.31	8.4	4.1	8.6	1.1	1.9	—
2006	SLN	MLB	25	3	3	1	29	3	49.3	48	31	45	5	45%	.302	2	1.58	4.75	5.27	5.37	8.6	5.1	7.5	0.9	2.1	0.3

Breakout: 22% Improve: 46% Collapse: 26% Attrition: 21% Comparables: Tug McGraw, Neal Cotts, Chuck McElroy

Johnson had huge strikeout numbers through the minors, but scouts simply don't like him. He lives off his breaking pitch, which keeps hitters mesmerized and allows him to work in his fastball as if it were five mph faster than it actually is. This helps Johnson make hitters look foolish on a regular basis-he's struck out at least one batter per inning at every level he's pitched. If he gets a shot, he could be an exceptional one-out guy in the bigs as early as this year.

RAY KING Bats: L Throws: L Height: 6' 1" Weight: 240 Born: January 15, 1974 Age: 32

YEAR	TM	LVL	AGE	W	L	SV	G	GS	IP	H	BB	SO	HR	GB%	BABIP	STUFF	WHIP	ERA	PERA	EQERA	EQH9	EQBB9	EQSO9	EQHR9	VORP	WXRL
2003	ATL	MLB	29	3	4	0	80	0	59.0	46	27	43	3	58%	.253	0	1.24	3.51	4.06	4.68	7.8	3.7	6.1	0.5	6.6	1.0
2004	SLN	MLB	30	5	2	0	86	0	62.0	43	24	40	1	55%	.237	6	1.08	2.61	3.79	3.03	7.6	3.3	5.3	0.2	19.9	3.1
2005	SLN	MLB	31	4	4	0	77	0	40.0	46	16	23	4	50%	.323	-13	1.55	3.38	4.91	4.24	10.3	3.3	4.7	0.9	7.3	-1.1
2006	COL	MLB	32	1	2	1	44	0	37.7	43	16	23	4	52%	.312	-10	1.55	4.88	4.62	5.31	9.3	3.4	5.4	0.9	3.9	0.3

Breakout: 15% Improve: 29% Collapse: 45% Attrition: 28% Comparables: Steve Kline, Juan Agosto, Warren Brusstar

King's had exactly one season where he averaged one inning or more per appearance, making him a classic LaRussa-style lefty specialist, although one perhaps slightly better against righties than most. He and the Cardinals had a well-publicized falling out due to King's lack of a role in the postseason, so he's been moved to the Rockies, which definitely falls in the "Be Careful What You Wish For" category. Perhaps the next time someone requests a trade, they'll be more specific.

CHRIS LAMBERT Bats: R Throws: R Height: 6' 1" Weight: 205 Born: March 8, 1983 Age: 23

YEAR	TM	LVL	AGE	W	L	SV	G	GS	IP	H	BB	SO	HR	GB%	BABIP	STUFF	WHIP	ERA	PERA	EQERA	EQH9	EQBB9	EQSO9	EQHR9	VORP	WXRL
2004	PEO	A	21	1	1	0	9	9	38.3	31	24	46	2	—	.305	-7	1.44	2.58	5.91	5.40	9.0	8.0	6.4	1.0	0.8	—
2005	PMB	A+	22	7	1	0	10	10	54.7	53	15	46	4	45%	.310	-1	1.24	2.63	5.54	4.85	10.0	3.3	4.8	1.4	4.3	—
2005	SFD	AA	22	3	8	0	18	18	85.0	97	48	69	10	42%	.343	-21	1.71	6.35	6.61	7.82	10.8	6.3	5.5	1.5	-20.2	—
2006	SLN	MLB	23	5	8	0	24	19	104.0	114	67	69	16	42%	.297	-7	1.73	6.03	6.53	6.64	9.7	5.3	5.5	1.4	-10.5	-0.3

Breakout: 17% Improve: 50% Collapse: 20% Attrition: 0% Comparables: Matt Yeatman, Ryan Price, Jose Garcia

The club's 2004 1st round pick out of Boston College didn't adjust well to Double-A. His stuff's not electric: his velocity is nothing to write home about, and his curveball's decent, but he can't consistently throw it for strikes. Lambert has time to learn, but needs to change speeds more effectively in order to succeed at higher levels.

JASON MARQUIS Bats: L Throws: R Height: 6' 1" Weight: 210 Born: August 21, 1978 Age: 27

YEAR	TM	LVL	AGE	W	L	SV	G	GS	IP	H	BB	SO	HR	GB%	BABIP	STUFF	WHIP	ERA	PERA	EQERA	EQH9	EQBB9	EQSO9	EQHR9	VORP	WXRL
2003	RIC	AAA	24	8	4	0	15	15	94.0	93	34	75	5	—	.298	10	1.35	3.35	4.53	4.63	9.0	3.9	5.6	0.8	9.8	—
2003	ATL	MLB	24	0	0	1	21	2	40.7	43	18	19	3	55%	.292	-16	1.50	5.53	4.87	5.98	9.7	3.5	3.8	0.7	-1.9	0.4
2004	SLN	MLB	25	15	7	0	32	32	201.3	215	70	138	26	57%	.305	6	1.42	3.71	4.73	4.33	9.9	2.9	5.5	1.1	36.7	4.8
2005	SLN	MLB	26	13	14	0	33	32	207.0	206	69	100	29	53%	.269	-9	1.33	4.13	5.29	5.29	9.7	2.9	4.1	1.3	18.2	4.2
2006	SLN	MLB	27	11	10	0	32	29	179.3	192	64	100	19	52%	.294	3	1.43	4.40	4.84	4.97	9.5	2.9	4.6	0.9	14.6	2.8

Breakout: 14% Improve: 51% Collapse: 11% Attrition: 2% Comparables: Stan Bahnsen, Mike Morgan, Jeff Suppan

Warning! Highly flammable! Marquis's velocity and strikeout rates have been heading south faster than a Canadian snowbird hits the Florida beaches in February. On the surface, his 2005 campaign wasn't anything to write home about, and beneath the surface, it was even scarier. His ERA of 4.13 looks acceptable, but Marquis allowed 15 unearned runs. Like most of the St. Louis rotation, he's acceptable filler and looks good if surrounded by a powerful offense and a reliable bullpen. He's rumored to be headed out of the Gateway City, possibly to Cincinnati for Austin Kearns, which should make Reds' fans . . . well, despondent. Lots of indicators for a slide in 2006.

MARK McCORMICK   Bats: R Throws: R   Height: 6′ 2″ Weight: 195 Born: October 15, 1983   Age: 22

YEAR	TM	LVL	AGE	W	L	SV	G	GS	IP	H	BB	SO	HR	GB%	BABIP	STUFF	WHIP	ERA	PERA	EQERA	EQH9	EQBB9	EQSO9	EQHR9	VORP	WXRL
2005	QUD	A	21	1	2	0	9	9	42.7	41	28	45	4	54%	.327	-10	1.62	5.48	6.97	6.75	10.4	7.2	6.5	1.8	-5.1	—
2006	SLN	MLB	22	4	7	0	25	16	92.0	90	80	77	11	50%	.298	-4	1.85	5.81	6.48	6.50	8.7	7.2	6.9	1.1	-4.7	-0.2

Breakout: 17%   Improve: 53%   Collapse: 16%   Attrition: 2%   Comparables: Matt Wright, Hansel Izquierdo, Roberto Maysonet

McCormick's grasp of the strike zone needs some work. He has fantastic velocity, along the lines of a Brad Lidge or Rich Harden, and throws a nasty curveball that acts more like a slider because he throws it so hard. But velocity is immaterial at this point: since McCormick can't throw anything consistently for strikes, hitters sit back and wait for him to take a little off in order to avoid a walk. Something needs to click for him to have a major league career. Maybe it'll happen this year, maybe 2010, maybe never.

MATT MORRIS   Bats: R Throws: R   Height: 6′ 5″ Weight: 210 Born: August 9, 1974   Age: 31

YEAR	TM	LVL	AGE	W	L	SV	G	GS	IP	H	BB	SO	HR	GB%	BABIP	STUFF	WHIP	ERA	PERA	EQERA	EQH9	EQBB9	EQSO9	EQHR9	VORP	WXRL
2003	SLN	MLB	28	11	8	0	27	27	172.3	164	39	120	20	49%	.281	13	1.18	3.76	4.24	4.24	8.9	1.9	5.7	1.1	31.7	4.4
2004	SLN	MLB	29	15	10	0	32	32	202.0	205	56	131	35	54%	.281	-4	1.29	4.72	5.11	5.47	9.8	2.3	5.3	1.5	10.7	3.1
2005	SLN	MLB	30	14	10	0	31	31	192.7	209	37	117	22	50%	.303	7	1.28	4.11	4.37	5.22	9.9	1.6	5.0	1.0	18.3	3.0
2006	SFN	MLB	31	10	11	0	30	28	180.3	187	41	110	19	52%	.290	10	1.27	4.00	4.28	4.51	9.2	1.9	5.1	0.9	21.8	3.6

Breakout: 36%   Improve: 78%   Collapse: 6%   Attrition: 5%   Comparables: Steve Trachsel, Bill Wegman, Charles Nagy

It's not commonplace for a player to get drafted, develop into a prospect, become a successful starting pitcher and mature into his prime, all with the same club. But it happened for Morris. Now in his late prime and beginning the downward side of his career, he's striking out and walking fewer batters, and letting too many hitters put the ball in play. He's signed with San Francisco, where SBC Park will mask some of his decline, but signing him to an eye-popping three-year, $27 million deal was not one of Brian Sabean's better ideas. With a large number of days with the three geezers Bonds, Finley, and Alou roaming the outfield behind him, he'd better keep the ball down.

MARK MULDER   Bats: L Throws: L   Height: 6′ 6″ Weight: 200 Born: August 5, 1977   Age: 28

YEAR	TM	LVL	AGE	W	L	SV	G	GS	IP	H	BB	SO	HR	GB%	BABIP	STUFF	WHIP	ERA	PERA	EQERA	EQH9	EQBB9	EQSO9	EQHR9	VORP	WXRL
2003	OAK	MLB	25	15	9	0	26	26	186.7	180	40	128	15	57%	.298	26	1.18	3.13	3.66	3.17	8.9	1.9	6.1	0.7	58.3	6.6
2004	OAK	MLB	26	17	8	0	33	33	225.7	223	83	140	25	57%	.290	8	1.34	4.43	4.64	4.52	9.1	3.1	5.3	0.9	40.1	4.7
2005	SLN	MLB	27	16	8	0	32	32	205.0	212	70	111	19	61%	.299	6	1.38	3.64	4.61	4.39	9.7	2.9	4.5	0.8	37.0	5.3
2006	SLN	MLB	28	12	9	0	30	30	187.3	196	60	116	15	56%	.299	10	1.37	4.01	4.39	4.57	9.3	2.6	5.1	0.7	23.0	3.8

Breakout: 7%   Improve: 37%   Collapse: 26%   Attrition: 2%   Comparables: Andy Pettitte, Jim Abbott, Bill Lee

Occasionally, having a strong affinity for the older of two players can be pricey. Mulder pitched fairly well in 2005, but there was plenty to be skeptical about when evaluating his performance. His strikeout rate continued a four-year decline, and he allowed a bunch of hits. The sole bright spot was a dramatic increase in his groundball/flyball ratio. A year in, it looks like the front office's inclination to treat the farm system like a cash machine was a mistake this time. Most clubs would be happier with Danny Haren than Mulder at this point, even before taking salary into consideration. Throw in a decent reliever and top it off with Daric Barton, one of the best hitting prospects in baseball, and that deal has to cause some Tums-worthy indigestion in St. Louis.

STU POMERANZ   Bats: R   Throws: R   Height: 6′ 7″   Weight: 220   Born: December 17, 1984   Age: 21

YEAR	TM	LVL	AGE	W	L	SV	G	GS	IP	H	BB	SO	HR	GB%	BABIP	STUFF	WHIP	ERA	PERA	EQERA	EQH9	EQBB9	EQSO9	EQHR9	VORP	WXRL
2004	PEO	A	19	12	4	0	17	17	101.3	95	25	88	10	—	.279	-9	1.18	3.55	6.08	6.75	10.5	2.9	4.8	1.9	-12.1	—
2005	PMB	A+	20	2	5	0	8	8	48.3	56	10	29	1	53%	.346	7	1.37	3.35	4.12	6.19	10.1	2.2	3.6	0.4	-3.1	—
2005	SFD	AA	20	5	6	0	18	18	98.7	110	40	66	12	47%	.308	-11	1.52	5.29	6.02	6.40	10.3	4.3	4.7	1.6	-8.5	—
2006	SLN	MLB	21	7	9	0	24	23	130.3	142	57	73	21	47%	.285	-2	1.53	5.51	5.81	6.12	9.7	3.6	4.6	1.4	-5.3	0.4

Breakout: 25%   Improve: 71%   Collapse: 6%   Attrition: 0%   Comparables: Sam Marsonek, Phil Wilson, Tony McKnight

Big, tall pitcher who uses his height to make his curveball look that much more droppy (Droppish? Droppifying?). He throws a knuckle-curve as a complement to his pedestrian fastball. Once he hit the Texas League last year, he was very streaky, performing well down the stretch in August. Overall, Pomeranz doesn't miss enough bats to suggest that he'll have a particularly bright future, but he's young enough to improve if he polishes his repertoire and learns to change speeds. The most positive thing going for him right now is his youth.

ANTHONY REYES   Bats: R   Throws: R   Height: 6′ 2″   Weight: 215   Born: October 16, 1981   Age: 24

YEAR	TM	LVL	AGE	W	L	SV	G	GS	IP	H	BB	SO	HR	GB%	BABIP	STUFF	WHIP	ERA	PERA	EQERA	EQH9	EQBB9	EQSO9	EQHR9	VORP	WXRL
2004	PMB	A+	22	2	0	0	6	6	30.7	32	7	36	3	—	.367	7	1.27	4.40	5.59	6.83	11.2	2.5	7.1	2.2	-4.0	—
2004	TEN	AA	22	6	2	0	12	12	74.3	62	13	102	3	—	.339	39	1.01	3.03	3.15	4.42	8.7	1.8	8.1	0.5	9.3	—
2005	MEM	AAA	23	7	6	0	23	23	128.7	105	34	136	13	36%	.283	18	1.08	3.64	4.11	4.33	8.1	2.5	7.2	1.1	17.6	—
2005	SLN	MLB	23	1	1	0	4	1	13.3	6	4	12	2	36%	.129	12	0.75	2.71	4.38	2.92	6.6	2.9	8.0	1.5	4.2	0.3
2006	SLN	MLB	24	9	7	1	37	18	134.0	125	39	111	17	39%	.278	14	1.22	3.89	4.02	4.35	8.3	2.4	6.9	1.1	20.1	2.7

Breakout: 19%   Improve: 51%   Collapse: 13%   Attrition: 1%   Comparables: Roger Nelson, Ramon Martinez, Don Wilson

The Cardinals hope he's ready to take the role of #2 starter. We'll have to see-despite a hot 2005, Reyes had some serious arm injuries in college. He's got solid stuff, particularly a reliably low-90s fastball, slider, and change, and he used that assortment to strike out better than one man per inning last year to finish second in the PCL in K/9. He'll have plenty of opportunities to stick this spring, because the Cardinals' rotation consists of one stud, one solid guy, and a bunch of question marks. Reyes can also expect great run support from the Cards' high-octane offense, so some gaudy win totals aren't out of the question if the elbow problems don't come back, or if the shoulder, which has troubled him from time to time as a pro, doesn't explode.

JEFF SUPPAN   Bats: R   Throws: R   Height: 6′ 2″   Weight: 210   Born: January 2, 1975   Age: 31

YEAR	TM	LVL	AGE	W	L	SV	G	GS	IP	H	BB	SO	HR	GB%	BABIP	STUFF	WHIP	ERA	PERA	EQERA	EQH9	EQBB9	EQSO9	EQHR9	VORP	WXRL
2003	PIT	MLB	28	10	7	0	21	21	141.0	147	31	78	11	53%	.296	15	1.26	3.57	4.10	3.59	9.4	1.8	4.5	0.7	32.5	3.7
2003	BOS	MLB	28	3	4	0	11	10	63.0	70	20	32	12	41%	.283	-9	1.43	5.57	5.54	4.97	9.7	2.8	4.4	1.6	2.2	0.2
2004	SLN	MLB	29	16	9	0	31	31	188.0	192	65	110	25	50%	.283	0	1.37	4.16	4.93	5.03	9.8	2.9	4.8	1.1	20.4	3.8
2005	SLN	MLB	30	16	10	0	32	32	194.3	206	63	114	24	47%	.298	1	1.38	3.57	4.86	4.72	9.9	2.8	4.9	1.1	27.5	4.3
2006	SLN	MLB	31	12	10	0	31	30	188.7	191	59	112	20	49%	.283	7	1.33	4.06	4.41	4.62	9.0	2.6	4.9	0.9	22.8	3.8

Breakout: 15%   Improve: 56%   Collapse: 13%   Attrition: 2%   Comparables: Pat Hentgen, Jaime Navarro, Dick Ruthven

A consistent innings eater, Suppan is a solid middle-of-the-rotation guy. The downside is that his statistical history doesn't suggest a sudden improvement. Any change in his performance will likely be downward. His mild groundball tendencies work in his favor for now, but if he doesn't keep the ball down, his ERA will get pretty yeasty.

JULIAN TAVAREZ   Bats: L   Throws: R   Height: 6′ 2″   Weight: 190   Born: May 22, 1973   Age: 33

YEAR	TM	LVL	AGE	W	L	SV	G	GS	IP	H	BB	SO	HR	GB%	BABIP	STUFF	WHIP	ERA	PERA	EQERA	EQH9	EQBB9	EQSO9	EQHR9	VORP	WXRL
2003	PIT	MLB	30	3	3	11	64	0	83.7	75	27	39	1	67%	.276	3	1.22	3.66	3.83	3.94	8.5	2.6	3.8	0.1	14.8	3.9
2004	SLN	MLB	31	7	4	4	77	0	64.3	57	19	48	1	53%	.295	14	1.18	2.38	3.43	3.29	8.6	2.4	6.1	0.1	19.2	1.8
2005	SLN	MLB	32	2	3	4	74	0	65.7	68	19	47	6	52%	.323	1	1.32	3.42	4.27	4.13	9.6	2.5	5.9	0.8	12.0	2.3
2006	BOS	MLB	33	3	3	3	59	0	64.3	72	19	38	6	52%	.309	-6	1.41	4.33	4.45	4.68	9.8	2.6	5.2	0.8	8.5	0.7

Breakout: 16%   Improve: 39%   Collapse: 37%   Attrition: 13%   Comparables: Paul Quantrill, Dale Murray, Mark Eichhorn

His volatility on the mound has decreased somewhat in recent years, but while Tavarez has settled in as a quality bullpen guy, he's still not the marryin' kind. He's played for six teams in seven years, leaving a trail of bewildered pitching coaches, teammates, and fans behind him. The two-year contract he signed with St. Louis worked out well for both parties: Tavarez pitched 130 innings with a sub-3.00 ERA, which can cause all sorts of Sins of Perception. His performance, and his agent, have allowed him to make a serious case for a four-year deal. His increased K rates and tendency to throw groundballs make him a reasonable risk, but he had to settle for two years with Boston.

BRAD THOMPSON Bats: R Throws: R Height: 6' 1" Weight: 190 Born: January 31, 1982 Age: 24

YEAR	TM	LVL	AGE	W	L	SV	G	GS	IP	H	BB	SO	HR	GB%	BABIP	STUFF	WHIP	ERA	PERA	EQERA	EQH9	EQBB9	EQSO9	EQHR9	VORP	WXRL
2003	PEO	A	21	5	3	0	30	4	65.0	70	10	43	2	—	.309	-8	1.23	2.91	4.57	5.71	10.6	1.9	3.9	0.9	-0.8	—
2004	TEN	AA	22	8	2	0	13	12	72.3	56	11	57	6	—	.248	7	0.93	2.37	4.81	3.61	9.0	1.6	4.8	1.2	14.9	—
2005	SLN	MLB	23	4	0	1	40	0	55.0	46	15	29	5	59%	.243	-6	1.11	2.95	4.58	4.08	8.8	2.4	4.6	0.8	11.5	1.6
2006	SLN	MLB	24	3	2	2	48	0	55.0	56	16	32	4	55%	.287	-3	1.29	3.59	3.92	4.40	9.0	2.3	4.8	0.7	8.4	0.7

Breakout: 34% Improve: 55% Collapse: 21% Attrition: 21% Comparables: Bill Castro, Ron Davis, Tom Walker

A classic sinker/slider guy who keeps the ball down with extreme prejudice. His strikeout rate isn't fantastic, but it doesn't have to be when he's getting more than twice as many groundball outs as flyball outs. He pitched well against both lefties and righties to earn LaRussa's trust before his 30th birthday, which is really saying something. He'll be a middle reliever and designated double play guy out of the Cardinal pen for the foreseeable future, and should perform well in that role.

ADAM WAINWRIGHT Bats: R Throws: R Height: 6' 6" Weight: 190 Born: August 30, 1981 Age: 24

YEAR	TM	LVL	AGE	W	L	SV	G	GS	IP	H	BB	SO	HR	GB%	BABIP	STUFF	WHIP	ERA	PERA	EQERA	EQH9	EQBB9	EQSO9	EQHR9	VORP	WXRL
2003	GRN	AA	21	10	8	0	27	27	149.7	133	37	128	9	—	.279	9	1.14	3.37	4.67	4.73	9.3	2.4	5.5	1.1	13.8	—
2004	MEM	AAA	22	4	4	0	12	12	63.7	68	28	64	12	—	.306	-2	1.51	5.37	5.71	6.71	9.7	4.1	7.0	1.9	-7.8	—
2005	MEM	AAA	23	10	10	0	29	29	182.0	204	51	147	18	47%	.333	7	1.40	4.40	4.54	5.03	9.7	2.5	5.3	1.0	11.5	—
2006	SLN	MLB	24	8	8	0	32	21	137.3	141	44	92	18	45%	.287	6	1.34	4.58	4.67	5.11	9.1	2.6	5.6	1.1	9.0	1.7

Breakout: 19% Improve: 56% Collapse: 10% Attrition: 0% Comparables: Rick Rhoden, Rick Aguilera, Ralph Terry

Is he a monster prospect? Not really, if he ever was. Wainwright has a plus curve and a reasonable fastball, but his performances in the minors leave something to be desired. An early hot streak made the Cards comfortable with the idea that he'd be better off rehabbing his elbow problems rather than going under the knife, but it wasn't a great season. He likely needs another full year in the minors to consolidate what he's learned. If all goes well he'll, miss a bunch of bats in the process.

Line Outs

Position/Player	TM	LVL	AGE	PA	R	2B	3B	HR	RBI	BB	SO	SB-CS	SPEED	BA/OBP/SLG	MLVR	EQBA/OBP/SLG	EQA	VORP
OF R. Gonzalez	MEM	AAA	31	387	62	21	3	14	50	38	47	3-5	4.5	.308/.375/.507	.253	.268/.319/.407	.249	-2.3
UT B. Hart	MEM	AAA	28	524	78	33	1	9	47	46	74	11-3	5.8	.269/.334/.402	-.022	.239/.292/.337	.227	-11.7
2B A. Herr	SFD	AA	24	452	56	20	1	21	81	15	108	2-3	3.4	.298/.336/.498	.172	.266/.301/.443	.251	12.8
CF S. Schumaker*	MEM	AAA	25	479	66	24	3	7	34	29	54	14-3	5.5	.287/.330/.402	-.014	.274/.309/.371	.240	-0.7
3B S. Seabol	MEM	AAA	30	224	34	18	2	9	33	20	40	0-0	3.6	.266/.330/.507	.127	.227/.279/.400	.233	-1.3
	SLN	MLB	30	114	11	5	0	1	10	8	23	0-0	4.6	.219/.272/.295	-.281	.219/.272/.286	.202	-5.4

Pitcher	TM	LVL	AGE	W	L	SV	IP	H	BB	SO	HR	GB%	BABIP	STUFF	WHIP	ERA	PERA	EQERA	EQH9	EQBB9	EQSO9	EQHR9	VORP
C. Doyne	SFD	AA	23	2	1	19	55.3	37	36	53	5	44%	.230	-19	1.32	1.95	6.48	3.60	7.9	7.9	6.7	1.3	11.1
J. Journell	MEM	AAA	27	1	4	1	42.3	39	38	49	5	41%	.324	-24	1.82	4.68	6.37	5.93	9.0	8.8	7.2	1.3	-1.5
M. Lincoln '06	SLN	MLB	31	3	3	1	53.0	55	19	36	6	49%	.290	-5	1.38	4.90	4.75	6.31	9.1	2.9	5.6	1.0	1.0
A. Reyes	SLN	MLB	35	4	2	3	62.7	38	20	67	5	36%	.231	25	0.93	2.15	3.43	2.39	6.9	2.8	9.1	0.7	23.2
M. Worrell	PMB	A+	22	2	3	35	56.0	38	19	53	6	46%	.229	-21	1.02	2.25	6.26	4.83	8.8	4.3	5.7	2.0	4.3

Raul Gonzalez remains a minor league slugger who's never gained any traction in the bigs, so his chances of a major league career are pretty much completely shot unless he catches Allard Baird's eye. The clock's long since struck midnight on the 2003 Cinderella story that made **Bo Hart** a gritty fan favorite. He's a utility guy, and not a particularly great one, so he's never going to be the best option for a club looking for a backup infielder. **Aaron Herr** is a 2000 1st round pick by the Braves out of Princeton who thrived once he left Braves' hitting instruction behind. Now with the Reds, he might grow up to be a utility man with power. **Skip Schumaker** has some speed, but no power, average, or plate discipline to speak of. He'll have to light it up early and often to get back on track. **Scott Seabol** is a minor league journeyman with enough skill to hold down a backup job at one of the corners, but he didn't impress in 2005, and he's not likely to see a better opportunity.

Cory Doyne is a former Astros flamethrowing farmhand that the Cards retreaded at the relatively tender age of 22. Worth watching: he struck out 16 in 11.1 A-ball IP to earn his first appearance at Double-A after six years as a pro. **Jimmy Journell** didn't recover well from his labrum repair of '04. In an attempt to start anew, he's left the organization that was the scene of so many disappointments to sign with the Reds. **Mike Lincoln** hasn't thrown a ball in anger since early 2004, and may never take the mound again, but we're giving you his projection just in case. On the last day of the season, **Al Reyes** tore a ligament in his elbow, ending what had been a terrific year. It also cost him a chance to pitch in the postseason. He'll miss the entire 2006 season, but surgical and rehab techniques have advanced to the point where there's no reason to expect Reyes to fall off a cliff when he returns in 2007. **Mark Worrell** is the latest edition, Worrell 3.0 spent his first full season since being picked out of the University of Arizona as a closer; he seems a lock to wind up in a Cardinals uniform at some point.

San Diego Padres

From the outset, it was clear that 2005 would be a valedictory year for the current assemblage of Padres. Succeed or fail, they would be dispersed at season's year, so there was no next year. If they didn't win *something* in 2005, it wouldn't happen at all. The balanced but aged squad contended for the NL West title in 2004, but ultimately fell short. Offensive stalwarts Phil Nevin and Ryan Klesko had begun to slip. Two of the team's best hitters, Giles and catcher Ramon Hernandez, would become free agents after 2005, and the Padres wouldn't be able to keep them both without expanding payroll. Free agency was also in the offing for ageless closer and fan favorite Trevor Hoffman, who seemed disinclined to accept a "hometown discount" offer from the Padres.

Despite having a large number of key players in their twilight seasons, the Padres also had some young, exciting players—ace Jake Peavy and shortstop Khalil Greene chief among them. Still, the farm system was clearly not strong enough to compensate for the impending age-related declines and free-agent defections, making the team's short-term ability to contend doubtful. Increasingly reclusive owner John Moores voiced his concern about the state of the farm system, and he put his money where his mouth was in March by hiring Grady Fuson as a special assistant to general manager Kevin Towers. Fuson, formerly the Rangers' Scouting Director and the A's Assistant GM and Scouting Director,had improved the player development areas of both organizations during his tenures.

Moores wasn't done. In April, he succeeded where many owners before him had failed, convincing MLB executive and former Oakland Athletics general manager Sandy Alderson to accept the role of team president. As a GM, Alderson presided over virtually every phase of a club's lifetime in Oakland, from helping repair a franchise left in ruin by Charles O. Finley to the salad days of the Bash Brothers to the lean mid-90s years. During Alderson's time in Oakland, the team was routinely near the bottom of the league in attendance, making him very familiar with the theory and practice of working within a limited budget. As MLB's Executive VP of Baseball Operations, Alderson built on his reputation for efficiency by hanging tough during the umpires' strike and subsequently making headway in getting umps to call the strike zone by the book. His established connections in the industry's executive suites certainly won't hurt.

PADRES PROSPECTUS

2005 record: 82–80; First place, NL West; Lost to Cardinals in Division Series

Pythagenport record: 76–86

Runs scored per game: 4.22 (13th in NL)

Runs allowed per game: 4.48 (8th in NL)

Team EqA: .265 (4th in NL)

2005 Batters Age: 31.5 (2nd oldest in NL)

2005 Pitchers Age: 30.7 (3rd oldest in NL)

Ballpark: Petco Park; Severe pitcher's park; Park Factor of 0.918

2005: The Friars rode their bullpen, bench, and a 22-win May to the top of the mild, mild West.

2006: A necessary roster re-working makes this team both interesting and competitive.

With an aging, top-heavy organization, an owner unwilling to increase big league payroll, and experienced leadership above and below him in the front office, GM Kevin Towers had to be concerned about his long-term prospects. From the season-opening heartbreaker in Colorado, where they blew a 10–8 lead in the ninth inning to the Rockies through the end of April, fears of an end to his run in San Diego appeared justified. The Dodgers sprinted out to a huge lead, and at the end of April the Padres were under .500 and mired in fourth place, 4.5 games back.

May was a different story. The Padres lost just one series—a three-gamer to "natural rival" Seattle in interleague play—and reeled off three winning streaks of at least six games to go 22–6 on the month. On June 1, the team boasted a 33–19 record. With Peavy getting adequate support from the rest of the rotation, Klesko again swinging the bat with authority, and robust performances from the bullpen and bench, the Padres were suddenly serious contenders.

May was a mirage. The team stumbled to a 49–61 record through the rest of the season. In an amazing stroke of luck, the Padres were nevertheless able to play Moe to the rest of the NL West's roster of Stooges and wind up calling the shots. Injuries, incompetence, and just plain bad luck claimed the rest of the division, and the Padres won it easily despite a record just above .500. How bad

TABLE 1. IS THIS TRIP REALLY NECESSARY? WORST DIVISIONAL WINNING PERCENTAGES VS. NON-DIVISION OPPONENTS

Year	Division	Win	Loss	WPct
2003	AL Central	180	250	.4186
1994	AL West	144	201	.4174
2002	AL Central	177	253	.4116
2005	NL West	189	255	.4257
2002	NL Central	184	247	.4269

was the NL West? When venturing outside the division to play actual teams its collective record was the fourth-worst since division play began in 1969 (see table 1).

A combination of injuries and disappointing performances plagued the Padres down the stretch, but two sources of strength helped pull them away from their feeble division rivals. They sported both an outstanding bullpen and an intimidating bench. The relief corps was probably the best in the league overall, finishing first in WXRL as well as in innings pitched. The bench featured one of the top pinch-hit lefty-righty combos in Mark Sweeney and Xavier Nady, plenty of speed, and a cast of competent two-way role players.

The assembly of these components by Towers and company underscores the importance of not scrimping on the details when filling out a team. The bullpen's figurehead was Hoffman, but setup man Scott Linebrink was one of the best pitchers in the league, completing the journey from waiver-wire claim to indispensable man. Akinori Otsuka contributed reliable, often spectacular relief work at a very reasonable price. To support this core, Towers looked for pitchers with a recent history of success who nonetheless would not have the leverage to command huge salaries. He found two, in left-hander Chris Hammond and the always-willing Rudy Seanez, who returned for his third tour of duty in San Diego. Hammond was effective until injuries took their toll, and Seanez pitched a career-high 60.1 IP. Both pitchers were signed to low-money one-year deals, the sorts of low-risk, high-yield gambles that a financially constrained team should take. Similarly, the bench was comprised of flexible, likely-to-succeed guys like Sweeney (a spring training non-roster invitee), Rob Fick (signed to a minor-league deal), Damian Jackson (another spring training NRI), Geoff Blum (one-year deal), and Nady and Ben Johnson, younger players not ready to graduate to regular status. Again, there wasn't a lot of money involved, and the players were selected on the basis of skill sets that matched the team's needs. Again, the selections the front office made generally blossomed. The Padres rode the advantages provided by the

bullpen and bench to a sterling 29–20 record in one-run games in 2005; their .592 winning percentage in one-run contests trailed only Arizona in the National League.

Luck in one-run games runs hot and cold on a year-to-year basis, and even within seasons—witness the Nationals' improbable run to the top of the NL East at midseason on a pile of one-run wins, followed by their regression to the mean in those same contests just weeks later. Even if the NL West continues to be the doormat division of major league baseball, the Padres needed to make some changes to remain a threat for the title in 2006.

They did, and how. The offseason was extraordinarily busy for a division-winning team, an indicator that management understands that standing pat with an 82-80 squad doesn't make a whole lot of sense. After the Cardinals swept the Padres out of the playoffs all signs pointed to Towers fleeing San Diego. Towers, with his experience and solid reputation, didn't figure to have a problem finding another position, and he was mentioned as a candidate for the vacant GM positions with the D-Backs, Red Sox, and Dodgers. After an interview with Arizona in late October, he surprised virtually everyone by announcing his intention to honor his contract with the Padres through 2007.

With front-office stability ensured, Towers and company rolled up their sleeves and did their best croupier imitations, slickly flipping their roster. The team kicked things off by trading Brian Lawrence to the Nationals for third baseman Vinny Castilla. Castilla's aging, and he's impatient and hacktastic at the plate. He shouldn't have been traded for, but he's a reliable glove at third base, and if his power plays as well at Petco as it did in Washington, at the very least he'll be an improvement over last year's hot corner horror show . Towers then dealt Xavier Nady to the Mets for centerfielder Mike Cameron. Towers had been visibly frustrated with manager Bruce Bochy's refusal to play Nady at third base, where his power would have done the Padres a world of good. If the manager was going to continue his resistance to Nady in 2006, moving him for a plus defensive center fielder with pop was an excellent way of resolving the impasse. Banjo hitter Sean Burroughs, another source of disappointment, was dispatched to Tampa Bay for the equally ill-starred Dewon Brazelton. Finally, the eternally promising, often-disappointing starter Adam Eaton and Otsuka were sent to the Rangers for 6′1″ righty Chris Young, outfielder Terrmel Sledge, and first-base prospect Adrian Gonzalez. Young is younger and cheaper than Eaton, and he's coming off of a better 2005. He'll be at the top of the Padres rotation in 2006.

If there's a dissonant note in this symphony of transactions, it's the trade of second baseman Mark Loretta to the Red Sox for catcher Doug Mirabelli. Loretta had an off season last year, due in part to a strained thumb that kept him out of the lineup, but in 2004 he might have been the best overall second baseman on the planet, and at $3 million, he's a reasonable risk for 2006. In contrast, there's not much to recommend Mirabelli over Miguel Olivo—Mirabelli's heralded ability to handle the knuckleball won't help in San Diego, currently a knuckleball-free zone. The stated rationale for this trade was to free up money for other moves, a plausible explanation given that the team had been moving around the margins of its payroll limit during the offseason, though at $1.5 million, Mirabelli isn't playing for free. There has also been speculation that there Loretta suffers from an undisclosed problem that that other teams knew about, and therefore Mirabelli was the best they could get in return.

With Loretta's departure, the Padres have attempted to do with second base what they did with so much success in the bullpen in 2005: identify multiple, preferably overlapping solutions who work cheap, and let their performance sort out who plays. Candidates for the position in 2006 include occasional power source Mark Bellhorn, former Cubs prospect Bobby Hill, and homegrown prospect Josh Barfield. Barfield should win the job easily after tearing up Triple-A in the second half of 2005, but a little insurance wasn't a bad idea.

In another division, last season's results would have dictated that the Pads go into full rebuilding mode, but the NL West doesn't figure to be any more competitive than it was a year ago. Question marks plague their immediate competition: How many weak-hitting infielders and bad pitchers do the Dodgers need? Can the Diamondbacks contend while trimming organizational fat? Does Barry Bonds have another 500 plate appearances in him? In this group, the Padres have the talent to mount another modest run at the title.

Towers has specifically addressed his own complaints about the roster. With Cameron manning center between Giles and Dave Roberts, the GM finally has the top-flight defensive outfield he's wanted for years. With Castilla, he's got a guy at third with a good glove who isn't content unless he smashes the ball 450 feet (in fact, he refuses to do most anything else). Mirabelli, gives him a defensive catcher with a sterling reputation. Towers believes he has tailored his roster to maximize its home field advantage, particularly the shift of the fence in right-center. If he's correct, the new-look Padres will thrive in 2006.

HITTERS

JOSH BARFIELD　　2B　　Bats: R Throws: R　　Height: 6′ 0″　Weight: 185　Born: December 17, 1982　Age: 23

YEAR	TM	LVL	AGE	PA	R	2B	3B	HR	RBI	BB	SO	SB	CS	SPEED	BA	OBP	SLG	MLVR	EQBA	EQOBP	EQSLG	EQA	VORP	DEFENSE	
2003	LEL	A+	20	614	99	46	6	16	128	50	122	16	4	6.0	.337	.389	.530	.351	.297	.345	.465	.278	39.5	130-2B	12
2004	MOB	AA	21	581	79	28	3	18	90	48	119	4	2	5.0	.248	.313	.417	-.002	.226	.284	.378	.231	-8.2	136-2B	3
2005	POR	AAA	22	576	74	25	1	15	72	52	108	20	5	5.5	.310	.370	.450	.127	.287	.340	.403	.262	21.3	135-2B	1
2006	SDN	MLB	23	530	66	26	3	14	62	42	108	10	4	5.0	.260	.322	.416	-.049	.270	.330	.448	.260	20.1	125-2B	2

Breakout: 31%　Improve: 56%　Collapse: 17%　Attrition: 5%　　Comparables: Cass Michaels, Tony Batista, Fernando Tatis

After his poor 2004, Barfield started off very slowly at Triple-A. That led some to worry that he'd fallen off the prospect track. Barfield bounced back, finishing the season by hitting .331/.400/.502 after June 15 in Portland, improving his walk-strikeout ratio in the process. He's never going to be a great defensive second baseman, but he drives the ball to all fields, making his bat a big league asset. He'll challenge for the starting second-base job in spring training.

TAGG BOZIED　　1B　　Bats: R Throws: R　　Height: 6′ 3″　Weight: 210　Born: July 24, 1979　　Age: 26

YEAR	TM	LVL	AGE	PA	R	2B	3B	HR	RBI	BB	SO	SB	CS	SPEED	BA	OBP	SLG	MLVR	EQBA	EQOBP	EQSLG	EQA	VORP	DEFENSE	
2003	POR	AAA	23	495	59	25	2	14	59	38	80	1	0	4.0	.273	.331	.431	.066	.261	.318	.415	.253	0.1	107-1B	6
2004	POR	AAA	24	238	41	17	1	16	58	18	29	0	0	3.9	.315	.374	.629	.396	.281	.336	.539	.290	14.2	52-1B	-1
2005	POR	AAA	25	62	6	4	0	2	10	3	6	0	0	3.1	.259	.323	.444	-.017	.235	.278	.402	.237	-1.1		
2006	SDN	MLB	26	34	4	2	0	1	5	2	6	0	0	3.9	.265	.322	.439	-.015	.275	.330	.473	.265	1.7	13-1B	0

Breakout: 18%　Improve: 41%　Collapse: 39%　Attrition: 48%　　Comparables: Brian Harper, Daryle Ward, Phil Clark

Bozied's comeback from last year's freak patella tendon rupture ended in July when he hit the DL with lower back and knee problems that the Padres attribute partly to compensating for his previous injury. You want your prospects dealing with these problems like you want R. Kelly to be teaching your daughter's eighth grade English class. After taking some time off, Bozied is supposed to be back at full strength in the spring. If so, his power gives him a got a shot at some quality major league playing time.

SEAN BURROUGHS 3B Bats: L Throws: R Height: 6' 1" Weight: 195 Born: September 12, 1980 Age: 25

YEAR	TM	LVL	AGE	PA	R	2B	3B	HR	RBI	BB	SO	SB	CS	SPEED	BA	OBP	SLG	MLVR	EQBA	EQOBP	EQSLG	EQA	VORP	DEFENSE	
2003	SDN	MLB	22	576	62	27	6	7	58	44	75	7	2	5.6	.286	.352	.402	.065	.294	.357	.416	.272	26.7	130-3B	3
2004	SDN	MLB	23	563	76	23	3	2	47	31	52	5	4	5.4	.298	.348	.365	.003	.306	.354	.374	.255	6.5	119-3B	-4
2005	POR	AAA	24	138	21	8	0	3	14	9	15	0	0	3.8	.290	.362	.427	.061	.262	.318	.376	.242	1.6	32-3B	2
2005	SDN	MLB	24	314	20	7	2	1	17	24	41	4	0	4.9	.250	.318	.299	-.157	.263	.331	.311	.236	-5.0	73-3B	8
2006	*TBA*	*MLB*	*25*	*411*	*43*	*17*	*3*	*4*	*35*	*24*	*46*	*4*	*2*	*4.8*	*.268*	*.320*	*.356*	*-.107*	*.274*	*.333*	*.376*	*.241*	*4.5*	*98-3B*	*3*

Breakout: 16% Improve: 41% Collapse: 26% Attrition: 21% Comparables: Ken Boswell, Jerry Lumpe, Dalton Jones

Former Padre Quilvio Veras was a tiny little middle infielder who frequently took mighty hacks at the plate that resulted in 275-foot flyballs that wafted harmlessly into waiting outfielders' gloves. He was an effective player for a few years, but his tendency to play against his skills could be infuriating to watch. Sean Burroughs is a much bigger, stronger player than Veras ever was, but his absurdly strikeout-defensive upper-body flick of a swing generates zero power. Traded to Tampa for another disappointing prospect in Dewon Brazelton, perhaps some new coaches will cure Burroughs's stubbornness and help him learn to swing with authority.

MATT BUSH SS Bats: R Throws: R Height: 5' 10" Weight: 170 Born: February 8, 1986 Age: 20

YEAR	TM	LVL	AGE	PA	R	2B	3B	HR	RBI	BB	SO	SB	CS	SPEED	BA	OBP	SLG	MLVR	EQBA	EQOBP	EQSLG	EQA	VORP	DEFENSE	
2005	FTW	A	19	494	56	13	3	2	32	33	76	8	4	5.0	.221	.279	.276	-.239	.204	.251	.255	.186	-36.8	125-SS	14
2006	*SDN*	*MLB*	*20*	*390*	*35*	*16*	*2*	*2*	*31*	*20*	*67*	*4*	*4*	*4.7*	*.222*	*.267*	*.293*	*-.332*	*.230*	*.274*	*.316*	*.193*	*-9.5*	*93-SS*	*5*

Breakout: 73% Improve: 80% Collapse: 13% Attrition: 12% Comparables: Brandon Warriax, Frank Gomez, Gil Velazquez

The Padres have a recent history of busted 1st round shortstops, and Bush is a good bet to continue the tradition. He's got a major league arm, but otherwise he hasn't shown much aptitude for the position. That's a problem, because his bat is not likely to carry him at another position. This is what happens when teams take a hard line on draft picks' bonuses, then fall back on the local kid as Plan B; having Stephen Drew and Khalil Greene on the same team is a problem the Pads would kill to have right about now.

ROBERT FICK 1B/C Bats: L Throws: R Height: 6' 1" Weight: 189 Born: March 15, 1974 Age: 32

YEAR	TM	LVL	AGE	PA	R	2B	3B	HR	RBI	BB	SO	SB	CS	SPEED	BA	OBP	SLG	MLVR	EQBA	EQOBP	EQSLG	EQA	VORP	DEFENSE			
2003	ATL	MLB	29	460	52	26	1	11	80	42	47	1	0	4.2	.269	.335	.418	.026	.265	.330	.414	.260	7.0	102-1B	-13		
2004	TBA	MLB	30	238	12	5	2	6	26	20	32	0	0	3.3	.201	.273	.327	-.307	.203	.282	.330	.218	-12.2	10-LF	0		
2005	SDN	MLB	31	259	25	10	2	3	30	26	33	0	2	4.4	.265	.340	.365	-.017	.275	.350	.386	.257	2.9	22-1B	2	21-C	-4
2006	*WAS*	*MLB*	*32*	*190*	*18*	*7*	*1*	*4*	*19*	*19*	*24*	*0*	*0*	*4.3*	*.246*	*.324*	*.372*	*-.114*	*.257*	*.333*	*.402*	*.249*	*1.1*	*48-1B*	*-3*		

Breakout: 22% Improve: 41% Collapse: 40% Attrition: 42% Comparables: Lee Thomas, Ed Kirkpatrick, Ed Herrmann

After cratering in Tampa Bay and Atlanta, Fick got some of that old magic back by hitting well off the bench. More important, he filled in capably at catcher when Hernandez was injured. Having an emergency catcher who can actually contribute elsewhere on the diamond offers significant strategic value when building a roster. Like Mark Sweeney, Fick priced himself out of the Padres' plans with his strong season, and signed with the Nationals.

BRIAN GILES RF Bats: L Throws: L Height: 5' 11" Weight: 195 Born: January 20, 1971 Age: 35

YEAR	TM	LVL	AGE	PA	R	2B	3B	HR	RBI	BB	SO	SB	CS	SPEED	BA	OBP	SLG	MLVR	EQBA	EQOBP	EQSLG	EQA	VORP	DEFENSE			
2003	PIT	MLB	32	481	70	30	4	16	70	85	48	0	3	4.2	.299	.430	.521	.325	.293	.424	.519	.320	36.4	91-LF	2	14-CF	1
2003	SDN	MLB	32	128	23	4	2	4	18	20	10	4	0	6.6	.298	.414	.490	.290	.302	.415	.519	.324	10.1	29-LF	0		
2004	SDN	MLB	33	711	97	33	7	23	94	89	80	10	3	5.9	.284	.374	.475	.186	.291	.378	.489	.297	40.2	156-RF	-10		
2005	SDN	MLB	34	674	92	38	8	15	83	119	64	13	5	5.9	.301	.423	.483	.302	.310	.431	.507	.323	55.8	136-RF	-6	15-CF	-3
2006	*SDN*	*MLB*	*35*	*643*	*93*	*34*	*5*	*17*	*81*	*101*	*71*	*12*	*4*	*5.4*	*.284*	*.400*	*.464*	*.159*	*.295*	*.410*	*.500*	*.307*	*42.5*	*150-RF*	*-3*		

Breakout: 7% Improve: 42% Collapse: 18% Attrition: 2% Comparables: Carl Yastrzemski, Gene Woodling, Larry Walker

It's understandable to look at Giles's two years in San Diego as a minor disappointment following his all-world performance in Pittsburgh. Away from Petco he hit much like he did with the Pirates, but 38 HR over two seasons (after nearly averaging 38 per season in his Pittsburgh years) isn't the power the Padres thought they'd be getting, even after adjusting for Petco's homer-quashing environment. Meanwhile, Jason Bay's become an elite player and Oliver Perez still holds plenty of promise for the Bucs. Giles remains a top-shelf hitter, if not a superstar. His on-base abilities will form the cornerstone of the San Diego offense for the next three years after he re-signed through 2008 at $10 million per season.

KHALIL GREENE SS **Bats: R Throws: R** Height: 5′ 11″ Weight: 210 Born: October 21, 1979 Age: 26

YEAR	TM	LVL	AGE	PA	R	2B	3B	HR	RBI	BB	SO	SB	CS	SPEED	BA	OBP	SLG	MLVR	EQBA	EQOBP	EQSLG	EQA	VORP	DEFENSE	
2003	MOB	AA	23	248	20	17	2	3	20	16	55	2	3	4.1	.275	.327	.406	.053	.261	.302	.404	.240	5.3	47-SS	2
2003	POR	AAA	23	355	42	19	0	10	47	20	52	5	4	4.0	.288	.346	.442	.121	.270	.325	.423	.258	14.0	76-SS	-6
2003	SDN	MLB	23	70	8	4	1	2	6	4	19	0	1	5.2	.215	.271	.400	-.134	.227	.282	.409	.231	-0.2	18-SS	-1
2004	SDN	MLB	24	553	67	31	4	15	65	53	94	4	2	5.2	.273	.349	.446	.095	.280	.354	.457	.279	31.5	134-SS	1
2005	SDN	MLB	25	473	51	30	2	15	70	25	93	5	0	5.4	.250	.296	.431	-.019	.259	.304	.458	.261	15.5	115-SS	-8
2006	SDN	MLB	26	554	65	29	3	17	70	39	103	5	2	4.7	.257	.318	.427	-.044	.267	.326	.460	.260	23.9	130-SS	-2

Breakout: 13% Improve: 35% Collapse: 21% Attrition: 7% Comparables: Ty Wigginton, Dale Berra, Gary Gaetti

The plate discipline is worrisome, the injury record even more so. In less than a year, Greene has twice broken a finger and once a toe, all on routine plays. Greene doesn't have a history of injuries, but it's possible that he is overextended playing shortstop at the major league level.

FREDDY GUZMAN CF **Bats: B Throws: R** Height: 5′ 10″ Weight: 165 Born: January 20, 1981 Age: 25

YEAR	TM	LVL	AGE	PA	R	2B	3B	HR	RBI	BB	SO	SB	CS	SPEED	BA	OBP	SLG	MLVR	EQBA	EQOBP	EQSLG	EQA	VORP	DEFENSE	
2003	LEL	A+	22	325	64	12	3	2	22	40	60	49	10	8.6	.285	.375	.370	.052	.253	.333	.328	.250	-2.9	48-CF	-1
2003	MOB	AA	22	204	30	5	2	1	11	26	34	38	7	8.1	.271	.368	.339	.025	.253	.338	.337	.259	-0.7	45-CF	1
2004	MOB	AA	23	156	21	5	2	1	7	16	28	17	5	7.8	.283	.359	.370	.034	.263	.332	.349	.252	0.0	33-CF	4
2004	POR	AAA	23	296	48	12	4	1	19	30	46	48	5	8.5	.292	.365	.379	-.021	.271	.340	.344	.265	1.1	67-CF	2
2004	SDN	MLB	23	80	8	3	0	0	5	3	13	5	2	7.0	.211	.250	.250	-.390	.221	.259	.260	.194	-5.2	16-CF	1
2006	SDN	MLB	25	23	4	1	0	0	2	2	3	3	0	7.6	.278	.352	.351	-.071	.289	.361	.378	.274	3.3	11-CF	0

Breakout: 33% Improve: 47% Collapse: 30% Attrition: 56% Comparables: Dave Nelson, Curtis Goodwin, Nook Logan

Guzman went under the knife for Tommy John procedure in April, causing him to miss the entire season. His shot at any significant major league playing time vanished with the acquisition of Mike Cameron. Guzman's got speed and patience, but it's hard to see how he'll ever hit enough to hold down anything more than a baserunning specialist job or fifth outfielder's slot at the major league level.

RAMON HERNANDEZ C **Bats: R Throws: R** Height: 6′ 0″ Weight: 203 Born: May 20, 1976 Age: 30

YEAR	TM	LVL	AGE	PA	R	2B	3B	HR	RBI	BB	SO	SB	CS	SPEED	BA	OBP	SLG	MLVR	EQBA	EQOBP	EQSLG	EQA	VORP	DEFENSE	
2003	OAK	MLB	27	534	70	24	1	21	78	33	79	0	0	3.7	.273	.331	.458	.068	.273	.335	.463	.272	27.9	132-C	7
2004	SDN	MLB	28	428	45	23	0	18	63	35	45	1	0	3.7	.276	.341	.477	.121	.282	.345	.487	.282	25.0	104-C	1
2005	SDN	MLB	29	391	36	19	2	12	58	18	40	1	0	4.0	.290	.322	.450	.080	.298	.332	.473	.274	20.7	90-C	-2
2006	BAL	MLB	30	453	53	22	1	15	62	27	52	0	0	4.0	.281	.330	.444	.032	.285	.340	.465	.276	21.4	107-C	-1

Breakout: 6% Improve: 34% Collapse: 28% Attrition: 11% Comparables: Joe Azcue, Del Crandall, Bo Diaz Hernandez

Hernandez's departure from the Padres was all but assured when he underwent arthroscopic wrist surgery in spite of some not too subtle comments from the organization about playing through the pain in late July, spurring the acquisitions of Ross and Olivo at the trading deadline. He returned ahead of schedule and hit well, and he's probably got a '96 Terry Steinbach season in him for the Orioles to enjoy. He's a longer shot to be worth the other three years, $21 million on his four-year deal, given catchers' typical aging patterns.

DAMIAN JACKSON UT **Bats: R Throws: R** Height: 5′ 10″ Weight: 160 Born: August 16, 1973 Age: 32

YEAR	TM	LVL	AGE	PA	R	2B	3B	HR	RBI	BB	SO	SB	CS	SPEED	BA	OBP	SLG	MLVR	EQBA	EQOBP	EQSLG	EQA	VORP	DEFENSE			
2003	BOS	MLB	29	170	34	7	0	1	13	8	28	16	8	6.4	.261	.294	.323	-.229	.258	.296	.327	.224	-3.8	16-2B	-3	11-CF	0
2004	IOW	AAA	30	108	18	6	5	3	13	11	20	3	1	7.1	.278	.352	.536	.141	.224	.284	.403	.236	0.3	20-SS	2		
2004	OMA	AAA	30	207	46	13	1	8	27	30	36	12	2	7.0	.308	.425	.538	.336	.256	.355	.416	.274	10.0	44-SS	-3		
2005	SDN	MLB	31	310	44	9	0	5	23	30	45	15	2	5.9	.255	.335	.342	-.068	.264	.345	.361	.259	6.1	11-LF	1	30-2B	3
2006	SDN	MLB	32	205	27	9	1	3	20	18	38	5	2	5.8	.252	.326	.372	-.106	.262	.334	.401	.251	4.9	52-2B	-1		

Breakout: 19% Improve: 36% Collapse: 35% Attrition: 47% Comparables: Tony Graffanino, Alan Bannister, Bill Pecota

Jackson did a nice job resurrecting his major league career in 2005, filling in for Mark Loretta at second in May. He quickly tapered off after a hot start, but still played solid defense in the infield and outfield corners, ran the bases well, and showed some patience at the plate. He's got a utility job in Washington lined up for 2006.

BEN JOHNSON   CF   Bats: R Throws: R   Height: 6' 1"   Weight: 200   Born: June 18, 1981   Age: 25

YEAR	TM	LVL	AGE	PA	R	2B	3B	HR	RBI	BB	SO	SB	CS	SPEED	BA	OBP	SLG	MLVR	EQBA	EQOBP	EQSLG	EQA	VORP	DEFENSE			
2003	LEL	A+	22	209	30	9	0	8	29	20	49	6	1	4.7	.266	.354	.446	.105	.228	.300	.386	.240	-6.4	26-RF	3	16-CF	1
2003	MOB	AA	22	139	8	5	0	1	7	10	36	0	1	3.0	.181	.252	.244	-.324	.168	.228	.245	.172	-19.1	29-RF	-3		
2004	MOB	AA	23	543	80	28	6	23	85	55	136	5	6	5.3	.251	.335	.480	.116	.226	.299	.429	.248	-9.3	88-RF	1	32-LF	-1
2005	POR	AAA	24	472	79	27	0	25	83	51	88	6	1	4.6	.312	.394	.558	.332	.283	.356	.494	.288	23.1	64-RF	0	42-CF	-7
2005	SDN	MLB	24	87	10	8	1	3	13	11	23	0	2	4.3	.213	.310	.467	.019	.224	.318	.500	.266	0.5				
2006	SDN	MLB	25	501	59	23	2	17	66	44	114	4	2	4.4	.243	.319	.419	-.064	.252	.327	.451	.258	7.4	118-RF	-2		

Breakout: 26%   Improve: 54%   Collapse: 19%   Attrition: 12%   Comparables: Kevin Mench, Frank Thomas, Ryan Ludwick

Johnson gave credit for his large step forward in 2005 to minor league hitting instructor Rob Deer, who advised Johnson to shorten his swing and use all fields. Johnson has all the tools to be a very good center fielder, but his routes and technique still need work. At the plate, he'll need to take an additional step forward to hold down a starting outfield spot. Improvement in either of those areas would make him a league-average major leaguer right away.

MIKE JOHNSON   1B   Bats: L Throws: R   Height: 6' 3"   Weight: 215   Born: June 25, 1980   Age: 26

YEAR	TM	LVL	AGE	PA	R	2B	3B	HR	RBI	BB	SO	SB	CS	SPEED	BA	OBP	SLG	MLVR	EQBA	EQOBP	EQSLG	EQA	VORP	DEFENSE	
2003	LEL	A+	23	198	22	17	1	5	24	17	48	0	1	3.2	.275	.343	.466	.124	.232	.291	.396	.235	-5.2	33-1B	-6
2004	LEL	A+	24	391	55	23	2	15	64	52	106	0	0	3.6	.254	.353	.471	.099	.197	.280	.342	.221	-22.7	67-1B	-5
2005	LEL	A+	25	333	59	20	5	21	76	37	89	0	3	5.1	.295	.366	.618	.303	.214	.272	.394	.229	-13.0	56-1B	-5
2006	SDN	MLB	26	337	33	16	1	10	39	30	121	1	1	3.7	.198	.271	.355	-.257	.206	.278	.382	.218	-13.0	81-1B	-5

Breakout: 26%   Improve: 42%   Collapse: 32%   Attrition: 17%   Comparables: Joe Gerber, Andy Tracy, Cory Aldridge

It was something of a bounceback season for the Clemson product, who added 160 points to his OPS while leading the Storm in homers. Then again, that's what 24-year-old high draft picks from major college programs should do in Single-A. He'll get a full season at Mobile in 2006, depending on how the first basemen above him shake out. He needs to progress quickly to have a significant big league career.

RYAN KLESKO   LF   Bats: L Throws: L   Height: 6' 3"   Weight: 220   Born: June 12, 1971   Age: 35

YEAR	TM	LVL	AGE	PA	R	2B	3B	HR	RBI	BB	SO	SB	CS	SPEED	BA	OBP	SLG	MLVR	EQBA	EQOBP	EQSLG	EQA	VORP	DEFENSE			
2003	SDN	MLB	32	474	47	18	0	21	67	65	83	2	5	3.4	.252	.354	.456	.115	.260	.359	.482	.285	14.6	103-1B	3		
2004	SDN	MLB	33	479	58	32	2	9	66	73	67	3	2	4.7	.291	.399	.448	.197	.297	.403	.458	.299	23.3	81-LF	-7	16-1B	1
2005	SDN	MLB	34	520	61	19	1	18	58	75	80	3	4	4.1	.248	.358	.418	.068	.257	.367	.440	.278	12.6	103-LF	-4		
2006	SDN	MLB	35	414	52	19	1	13	56	59	66	3	2	4.4	.262	.370	.435	.056	.272	.380	.469	.285	15.7	99-LF	-3		

Breakout: 23%   Improve: 48%   Collapse: 22%   Attrition: 23%   Comparables: Wally Joyner, Chris Chambliss, David Justice

The back and shoulder ailments are starting to threaten his career. When the Padres signed him to his extension he was a dynamic offensive player whose baserunning helped separate him from your standard-issue immobile slugger. Klesko has always been defensively limited—not a problem when he's a 30-30 threat with patience to boot, but a big pain now that he's regressed. His balky back is going to hinder him at first base, and he remains a liability in left field. He'd make a decent flyer for a team looking for 300–400 quality at-bats from a DH, but the Padres would have to get Klesko to waive his no-trade and eat a big contract in return to make that happen.

GEORGE KOTTARAS   C   Bats: L Throws: R   Height: 6' 0"   Weight: 180   Born: May 16, 1983   Age: 23

YEAR	TM	LVL	AGE	PA	R	2B	3B	HR	RBI	BB	SO	SB	CS	SPEED	BA	OBP	SLG	MLVR	EQBA	EQOBP	EQSLG	EQA	VORP	DEFENSE	
2003	IDA	Rk	20	164	27	8	1	7	24	19	36	1	1	4.1	.259	.348	.476	.055	.188	.260	.330	.207	-15.7	25-C	4
2004	FTW	A	21	325	40	18	1	7	46	51	41	0	0	3.0	.310	.415	.461	.313	.281	.372	.418	.278	19.0	48-C	-7
2005	LEL	A+	22	392	54	29	0	9	50	50	60	2	1	4.1	.303	.390	.469	.133	.241	.319	.357	.241	-0.3	81-C	-5
2005	MOB	AA	22	121	16	7	0	2	15	19	23	0	0	4.4	.287	.397	.416	.142	.256	.355	.394	.265	4.3	24-C	-4
2006	SDN	MLB	23	430	45	20	1	9	46	44	84	1	1	4.1	.236	.316	.360	-.149	.245	.324	.388	.241	5.3	102-C	-5

Breakout: 15%   Improve: 41%   Collapse: 32%   Attrition: 11%   Comparables: Nick Leach, Eric Sandberg, John Baker

The fraternity of former hot catching prospects is fraught with disappointment—ask Matt LeCroy or Toby Hall. Kottaras resembles a young Craig Biggio more than behemoths like LeCroy or Hall, though, and he looks like he's going to be a pretty fair defensive backstop. His 36 doubles and 69 walks last year point to some promising line-drive power and a good batting eye, traits that will serve him well at higher levels. With just 101 Double-A at-bats on his record, he won't be a factor in the big leagues in 2006. Look for Kottaras in 2007—Doug Mirabelli is not a long-term solution behind the plate.

MARK LORETTA 2B Bats: R Throws: R Height: 6' 0" Weight: 186 Born: August 14, 1971 Age: 34

YEAR	TM	LVL	AGE	PA	R	2B	3B	HR	RBI	BB	SO	SB	CS	SPEED	BA	OBP	SLG	MLVR	EQBA	EQOBP	EQSLG	EQA	VORP	DEFENSE	
2003	SDN	MLB	31	650	74	28	4	13	72	54	62	5	4	4.5	.314	.372	.441	.174	.322	.378	.457	.287	44.5	141-2B	3
2004	SDN	MLB	32	703	108	47	2	16	76	58	45	5	3	5.0	.335	.391	.495	.286	.342	.395	.504	.307	67.6	151-2B	19
2005	SDN	MLB	33	461	54	16	1	3	38	45	34	8	4	4.8	.280	.360	.347	-.001	.293	.370	.368	.265	11.0	101-2B	-1
2006	BOS	MLB	34	513	66	27	2	8	55	41	43	6	2	4.6	.294	.355	.415	.046	.292	.360	.423	.266	22.5	121-2B	1

Breakout: 4% Improve: 24% Collapse: 43% Attrition: 15% Comparables: Johnny Temple, Carney Lansford, Bill Madlock

Loretta started slowly prior to tearing a ligament in his left thumb, and never got untracked upon his return. His decidedly nonstandard career arc should keep you from counting him out completely, but he's an aged middle infielder; as a breed, they're notorious for hitting the wall rather decisively. Traded to Boston for Doug Mirabelli, where he'll start for the Red Sox and likely hit another wall, a big green one, and often.

PAUL McANULTY 1B Bats: L Throws: R Height: 5' 10" Weight: 220 Born: February 24, 1981 Age: 25

YEAR	TM	LVL	AGE	PA	R	2B	3B	HR	RBI	BB	SO	SB	CS	SPEED	BA	OBP	SLG	MLVR	EQBA	EQOBP	EQSLG	EQA	VORP	DEFENSE			
2003	FTW	A	22	540	48	27	0	7	73	67	82	5	3	3.2	.273	.370	.378	.138	.240	.318	.359	.241	-14.2	118-1B	-8		
2004	LEL	A+	23	591	98	36	3	23	87	88	106	3	1	4.3	.297	.404	.521	.293	.244	.335	.412	.260	-2.2	56-LF	2	26-1B	-1
2005	MOB	AA	24	341	39	17	2	10	42	34	66	5	2	5.1	.282	.364	.453	.137	.245	.314	.399	.249	-6.6	66-LF	5		
2005	POR	AAA	24	168	27	15	0	6	27	16	29	0	0	3.8	.344	.405	.563	.398	.306	.360	.488	.288	10.1	21-1B	-2		
2005	SDN	MLB	24	28	4	0	0	0	0	3	7	1	0	6.2	.208	.321	.208	-.301	.200	.310	.200	.207	-1.1				
2006	SDN	MLB	25	465	50	21	1	12	54	42	101	3	1	4.1	.235	.310	.374	-.142	.244	.318	.403	.243	-3.4	110-LF	-1		

Breakout: 17% Improve: 38% Collapse: 35% Attrition: 13% Comparables: Kevin Mench, Kevin Young, John Roskos

As Billy Beane says, nobody's in this business to sell jeans, but a Fred McGriff-type body is going to get more chances on average than the Cecil Fielder model, all other things being equal. The stocky McAnulty dropped some weight in 2005, and he looked quite a bit livelier in the field and on the bases as a result. Ryan Klesko's iffy health gives him a shot at some playing time at first base, though the acquisition of Adrian Gonzalez makes the path a little tougher. And look, guys: just because Paul posed with his back to the camera in the Padres media guide doesn't mean he's dead.

XAVIER NADY RF/1B Bats: R Throws: R Height: 6' 2" Weight: 205 Born: November 14, 1978 Age: 27

YEAR	TM	LVL	AGE	PA	R	2B	3B	HR	RBI	BB	SO	SB	CS	SPEED	BA	OBP	SLG	MLVR	EQBA	EQOBP	EQSLG	EQA	VORP	DEFENSE			
2003	POR	AAA	24	152	19	7	0	7	23	12	28	0	0	3.2	.265	.329	.471	.110	.246	.308	.437	.255	-0.7	32-RF	-2		
2003	SDN	MLB	24	402	50	17	1	9	39	24	74	6	2	5.0	.267	.321	.391	-.026	.274	.327	.404	.255	-0.2	96-RF	-6		
2004	POR	AAA	25	320	52	19	1	22	70	22	42	3	0	4.5	.333	.394	.632	.459	.296	.351	.532	.294	20.3	39-RF	-2	17-CF	0
2004	SDN	MLB	25	83	7	4	0	3	9	5	13	0	0	2.9	.247	.301	.416	-.082	.256	.310	.410	.247	-0.8	12-LF	-2		
2005	SDN	MLB	26	355	40	15	2	13	43	22	67	2	1	5.0	.261	.321	.439	.046	.269	.330	.462	.268	8.7	33-1B	0	27-CF	-6
2006	NYN	MLB	27	335	40	17	1	11	45	22	56	3	1	4.6	.274	.332	.447	.019	.278	.336	.474	.268	11.0	81-1B	-4		

Breakout: 14% Improve: 36% Collapse: 28% Attrition: 24% Comparables: Wes Chamberlain, George Thomas, Steve Brye

Bruce Bochy and staff never believed Nady could play third base, which meant a lot of punchless Sean Burroughs in 2005. Nady's wasted sitting on the bench and has nothing left to learn in the minors. He will compete for an outfield spot with the Mets. He'll never be an elite offensive player until he lays off the breaking stuff with more regularity.

MIGUEL OLIVO C Bats: R Throws: R Height: 6' 0" Weight: 180 Born: July 15, 1978 Age: 27

YEAR	TM	LVL	AGE	PA	R	2B	3B	HR	RBI	BB	SO	SB	CS	SPEED	BA	OBP	SLG	MLVR	EQBA	EQOBP	EQSLG	EQA	VORP	DEFENSE	
2003	CHA	MLB	24	342	37	19	1	6	27	19	80	6	4	5.6	.237	.287	.360	-.201	.232	.287	.360	.226	-4.5	96-C	11
2004	CHA	MLB	25	152	21	7	2	7	26	10	29	5	4	6.9	.270	.316	.496	.017	.266	.318	.489	.265	5.8	41-C	-4
2004	SEA	MLB	25	173	25	8	2	6	14	10	55	2	2	6.9	.200	.260	.388	-.217	.208	.267	.415	.230	-2.6	44-C	-3
2005	TAC	AAA	26	99	13	4	1	3	21	7	19	8	1	6.9	.233	.293	.400	-.132	.211	.265	.333	.222	-4.2	15-C	1
2005	SEA	MLB	26	157	14	4	0	5	18	4	49	1	1	5.1	.151	.172	.276	-.549	.160	.191	.300	.174	-14.6	46-C	-2
2005	SDN	MLB	26	123	16	7	1	4	16	4	31	6	1	6.3	.304	.341	.487	.196	.316	.352	.521	.297	11.0	32-C	0
2006	FLO	MLB	27	224	24	11	1	6	23	13	56	7	3	5.6	.237	.290	.395	-.149	.243	.294	.418	.236	2.1	56-C	-1

Breakout: 42% Improve: 57% Collapse: 27% Attrition: 42% Comparables: Ron Karkovice, Bobby Hughes, Phil Roof

A deft pickup at the trade deadline, Olivo looked like the player the Mariners were so happy to get in the Freddy Garcia trade down the stretch, making it all the stranger that the Padres didn't offer him a contract for 2006. He's agile behind the plate, has a whip for an arm, and he runs well for a catcher. The Marlins should have a cheap, intriguing catching combo in Olivo and Josh Willingham.

JOE RANDA   **3B**   **Bats: R Throws: R**   Height: 5' 11"   Weight: 190   Born: December 18, 1969   Age: 36

YEAR	TM	LVL	AGE	PA	R	2B	3B	HR	RBI	BB	SO	SB	CS	SPEED	BA	OBP	SLG	MLVR	EQBA	EQOBP	EQSLG	EQA	VORP	DEFENSE	
2003	KCA	MLB	33	557	80	31	1	16	72	41	61	1	0	4.3	.291	.348	.452	.037	.281	.344	.439	.271	25.4	121-3B	-1
2004	KCA	MLB	34	539	65	31	2	8	56	40	77	0	1	4.1	.287	.343	.408	.014	.284	.343	.410	.263	12.5	117-3B	8
2005	CIN	MLB	35	368	44	26	1	13	48	33	52	0	0	4.1	.289	.356	.491	.168	.283	.352	.491	.285	20.4	82-3B	3
2005	SDN	MLB	35	241	27	17	1	4	20	14	29	0	1	4.4	.256	.303	.395	-.045	.262	.311	.413	.248	0.8	55-3B	0
2006	*PIT*	*MLB*	*36*	*480*	*52*	*28*	*2*	*12*	*60*	*39*	*65*	*1*	*1*	*4.5*	*.265*	*.330*	*.418*	*-.030*	*.263*	*.329*	*.428*	*.254*	*8.8*	*114-3B*	*-1*

Breakout: 8%   *Improve: 32%*   *Collapse: 38%*   *Attrition: 24%*   *Comparables: Bill Madlock, Ken Boyer, Brooks Robinson*

Acquired in what at first appeared to be a canny deft deadline deal to fill the third base hole, Randa inexplicably left his bat in Cincinnati. He didn't end up giving the Padres much that they couldn't have gotten by sticking with Burroughs, and the club had no interest in a repeat engagement. Signed with the Pirates, where he'll be the starting third baseman on a mediocrity-swamped roster in 2006.

DAVE ROBERTS   **LF/CF**   **Bats: L Throws: L**   Height: 5' 10"   Weight: 180   Born: May 31, 1972   Age: 34

YEAR	TM	LVL	AGE	PA	R	2B	3B	HR	RBI	BB	SO	SB	CS	SPEED	BA	OBP	SLG	MLVR	EQBA	EQOBP	EQSLG	EQA	VORP	DEFENSE			
2003	LAN	MLB	31	435	56	6	5	2	16	43	39	40	14	8.1	.250	.331	.307	-.134	.260	.339	.316	.245	-0.8	97-CF	3		
2004	LAN	MLB	32	268	45	4	7	2	21	28	31	33	1	9.1	.253	.340	.356	-.071	.251	.335	.353	.270	6.7	42-LF	0	15-CF	2
2004	BOS	MLB	32	100	19	10	0	2	14	10	17	5	2	7.0	.256	.330	.442	-.039	.250	.333	.452	.273	1.5				
2005	SDN	MLB	33	469	65	19	10	8	38	53	59	23	12	7.3	.275	.356	.428	.087	.288	.369	.460	.282	19.7	100-CF	-15		
2006	*SDN*	*MLB*	*34*	*481*	*71*	*19*	*5*	*5*	*40*	*52*	*58*	*23*	*8*	*6.7*	*.268*	*.351*	*.371*	*-.053*	*.278*	*.360*	*.400*	*.265*	*12.4*	*114-CF*	*-4*		

Breakout: 15%   *Improve: 43%*   *Collapse: 22%*   *Attrition: 12%*   *Comparables: Kenny Lofton, Stan Javier, Johnny Hopp*

Roberts had as successful a season as anyone could have reasonably hoped—good defense, a solid bat against right-handed pitching, excellent baserunning, and only about a quarter of the season lost to various nicks and ouchies. With the trade for Mike Cameron and the Giles re-signing, Roberts will start in left field, though McAnulty, Johnson and company could challenge for playing time. Roberts-Cameron-Giles would be the best defensive outfield the Padres have ever played at Petco, and one of the best in baseball.

DAVE ROSS   **C**   **Bats: R Throws: R**   Height: 6' 2"   Weight: 205   Born: March 19, 1977   Age: 29

YEAR	TM	LVL	AGE	PA	R	2B	3B	HR	RBI	BB	SO	SB	CS	SPEED	BA	OBP	SLG	MLVR	EQBA	EQOBP	EQSLG	EQA	VORP	DEFENSE	
2003	LVG	AAA	26	99	12	4	0	5	16	11	27	0	2	3.2	.221	.313	.442	-.073	.181	.271	.355	.218	-3.7	24-C	5
2003	LAN	MLB	26	140	19	7	0	10	18	13	42	0	0	2.7	.258	.336	.556	.210	.264	.340	.576	.298	11.4	35-C	-2
2004	LAN	MLB	27	190	13	3	1	5	15	15	62	0	0	4.0	.170	.253	.291	-.357	.175	.251	.295	.202	-10.2	50-C	-1
2005	PIT	MLB	28	118	9	8	0	3	15	6	24	0	0	3.2	.222	.263	.380	-.183	.222	.267	.389	.230	-1.1	31-C	7
2006	*SDN*	*MLB*	*29*	*133*	*13*	*6*	*1*	*4*	*16*	*10*	*33*	*0*	*0*	*4.0*	*.225*	*.292*	*.380*	*-.173*	*.233*	*.299*	*.409*	*.236*	*0.9*	*35-C*	*1*

Breakout: 37%   *Improve: 56%*   *Collapse: 25%*   *Attrition: 48%*   *Comparables: John Orsino, Sal Fasano, Bill Plummer*

The Padres snagged Ross from the Pirates to pick up the catching slack after Ramon Hernandez went on the DL, but Robert Fick and others instead grabbed the playing time. He's got the flashy arm, and can call a major league game, but there's a lot of competition for the starting catcher slots on teams that will live with a .220 batting average in any given year, and Mike Matheny and Brad Ausmus have seniority.

MARK SWEENEY   **1B**   **Bats: L Throws: L**   Height: 6' 1"   Weight: 215   Born: October 26, 1969   Age: 36

YEAR	TM	LVL	AGE	PA	R	2B	3B	HR	RBI	BB	SO	SB	CS	SPEED	BA	OBP	SLG	MLVR	EQBA	EQOBP	EQSLG	EQA	VORP	DEFENSE	
2003	CSP	AAA	33	204	24	10	1	5	35	34	32	1	4	3.4	.297	.407	.461	.151	.222	.316	.330	.231	-9.1	23-RF	1
2003	COL	MLB	33	106	13	9	0	2	14	9	27	0	1	3.2	.258	.321	.412	-.045	.237	.302	.402	.239	0.2		
2004	COL	MLB	34	215	25	12	2	9	40	32	51	1	0	4.9	.266	.377	.508	.136	.243	.358	.480	.288	10.8	13-RF	2
2005	SDN	MLB	35	266	31	12	1	8	40	40	58	4	0	4.8	.294	.395	.466	.231	.300	.401	.486	.310	19.3	38-1B	-1
2006	*SFN*	*MLB*	*36*	*183*	*21*	*9*	*1*	*5*	*22*	*26*	*39*	*3*	*1*	*4.9*	*.261*	*.367*	*.423*	*.035*	*.263*	*.370*	*.441*	*.278*	*6.7*	*47-1B*	*0*

Breakout: 15%   *Improve: 37%*   *Collapse: 36%*   *Attrition: 43%*   *Comparables: Champ Summers, John Vander Wal, George Crowe*

Sweeney turned in his finest season in 2005, tattooing right-handers off the bench. He hits to all fields and isn't fazed by off-speed stuff, making him as close to the perfect pinch-hitting weapon as you're likely to find. He's too poor a defensive player and baserunner to be a candidate for a starting job. He'll get plenty of action with the Giants after signing a two-year deal.

ERIC YOUNG   2B/LF   Bats: R Throws: R   Height: 5' 9"   Weight: 180   Born: May 18, 1967   Age: 39

YEAR	TM	LVL	AGE	PA	R	2B	3B	HR	RBI	BB	SO	SB	CS	SPEED	BA	OBP	SLG	MLVR	EQBA	EQOBP	EQSLG	EQA	VORP	DEFENSE		
2003	MIL	MLB	36	457	71	18	1	15	31	48	34	25	7	6.5	.260	.344	.421	.021	.254	.337	.417	.266	18.6	92-2B	-8	
2003	SFN	MLB	36	82	9	2	0	0	3	9	10	3	5	4.9	.197	.293	.225	-.355	.197	.293	.225	.190	-6.5	17-2B	2	
2004	TEX	MLB	37	398	55	25	2	1	27	43	28	14	9	5.3	.288	.377	.381	-.019	.280	.372	.372	.265	6.2	37-LF -3	17-2B	-2
2005	SDN	MLB	38	160	22	9	0	2	12	18	12	7	6	5.7	.275	.356	.380	.025	.290	.372	.400	.262	2.3	19-LF 1	10-2B	0
2006	SDN	MLB	39	150	19	6	1	1	13	17	14	8	3	5.5	.253	.342	.329	-.133	.263	.350	.355	.251	3.3	39-2B	-1	

Breakout: 25%   Improve: 44%   Collapse: 35%   Attrition: 51%   Comparables: Enos Slaughter, Phil Rizzuto, Barry Larkin

A gruesome shoulder injury sustained by the hard-charging Young on Opening Day had most people thinking he was going to hang it up, making his return to the roster just under three months later a great story. He's a reliable option all over the diamond, perennially hits lefties well, and he'll be back with the Padres in the same role in 2006.

PITCHERS

PEDRO ASTACIO   Bats: R Throws: R   Height: 6' 2"   Weight: 210   Born: November 28, 1969   Age: 36

YEAR	TM	LVL	AGE	W	L	SV	G	GS	IP	H	BB	SO	HR	GB%	BABIP	STUFF	WHIP	ERA	PERA	EQERA	EQH9	EQBB9	EQSO9	EQHR9	VORP	WXRL
2003	NYN	MLB	33	3	2	0	7	7	36.7	47	18	20	8	39%	.317	-19	1.77	7.36	6.51	7.23	11.1	3.9	4.3	1.9	-7.2	-0.1
2005	TEX	MLB	35	2	8	0	12	12	67.0	79	11	45	13	45%	.310	3	1.34	6.04	4.70	5.09	9.7	1.4	5.9	1.6	-0.3	0.7
2005	SDN	MLB	35	4	2	0	12	10	59.7	54	26	33	4	40%	.275	4	1.34	3.17	4.58	3.20	8.5	3.7	4.6	0.6	14.4	2.1
2006	SDN	MLB	36	6	8	0	28	18	114.0	119	38	72	15	43%	.288	-4	1.38	4.50	5.14	5.58	9.6	2.7	5.0	1.2	5.5	1.2

Breakout: 14%   Improve: 42%   Collapse: 19%   Attrition: 16%   Comparables: Bob Welch, Scott Sanderson, Jim Perry

Cut loose by the Rangers on June 22, Astacio joined the Padres after signing a minor league deal. He oscillated wildly between effectiveness and early exits, then looked good down the stretch. He should be perfectly adequate as a bottom-of-the-order starter in 2006, though it won't be in San Diego after Astacio refused the Padres' arbitration offer.

BRAD BAKER   Bats: R Throws: R   Height: 6' 2"   Weight: 180   Born: November 6, 1980   Age: 25

YEAR	TM	LVL	AGE	W	L	SV	G	GS	IP	H	BB	SO	HR	GB%	BABIP	STUFF	WHIP	ERA	PERA	EQERA	EQH9	EQBB9	EQSO9	EQHR9	VORP	WXRL
2003	LEL	A+	22	3	0	12	27	4	44.7	31	14	69	2	—	.308	16	1.01	2.01	3.86	4.29	7.7	3.9	8.8	0.9	6.1	—
2003	MOB	AA	22	1	6	0	17	9	50.7	50	36	53	3	—	.322	-13	1.70	5.68	5.92	7.03	10.0	7.0	6.5	1.1	-7.7	—
2004	MOB	AA	23	2	1	30	55	0	57.3	37	24	68	2	—	.254	5	1.06	1.57	4.08	3.23	7.6	4.6	7.1	0.5	14.0	—
2005	POR	AAA	24	4	5	27	59	0	66.3	69	32	75	9	39%	.353	-9	1.52	4.75	5.23	5.23	9.6	4.4	7.4	1.5	2.7	—
2006	ATL	MLB	25	2	3	1	22	4	45.7	45	25	39	6	38%	.292	2	1.52	4.80	5.18	5.17	8.7	4.4	7.1	1.2	2.1	0.3

Breakout: 19%   Improve: 43%   Collapse: 27%   Attrition: 30%   Comparables: Renie Martin, Tom Griffin, Joe Valentine

Racked up the saves for Triple-A Portland, but this was a disappointing season after his banner 2004, with strikeout, walk, hit and home-run rates all declining. With the Padres bullpen full of strong performers, Baker made a wise decision to opt for minor league free agency and was signed by the Braves in November. He'll be in the mix for a bullpen job.

CRAIG BRESLOW   Bats: L Throws: L   Height: 6' 1"   Weight: 180   Born: August 8, 1980   Age: 25

YEAR	TM	LVL	AGE	W	L	SV	G	GS	IP	H	BB	SO	HR	GB%	BABIP	STUFF	WHIP	ERA	PERA	EQERA	EQH9	EQBB9	EQSO9	EQHR9	VORP	WXRL
2003	BLT	A	22	3	4	2	33	0	65.0	64	27	80	4	—	.343	-16	1.40	5.12	5.90	7.67	10.2	5.2	7.1	1.8	-14.0	—
2004	HDS	A+	23	1	3	0	23	0	41.3	54	24	41	5	—	.383	-38	1.89	7.19	7.30	7.97	11.1	6.9	5.3	2.0	-10.7	—
2005	MOB	AA	24	2	1	0	40	0	52.3	38	17	47	3	45%	.271	-11	1.05	2.75	4.99	4.25	8.0	3.5	5.4	1.1	7.3	—
2005	SDN	MLB	24	0	0	0	14	0	16.3	15	13	14	1	47%	.292	-5	1.71	2.21	4.86	3.78	8.1	6.5	7.0	0.5	3.9	0.1
2006	SDN	MLB	25	2	3	1	62	1	50.0	54	30	36	7	44%	.300	-16	1.68	5.65	6.61	6.40	9.9	4.9	5.7	1.3	-5.0	-0.5

Breakout: 12%   Improve: 35%   Collapse: 38%   Attrition: 12%   Comparables: Gwynne Pearsall, Juan Alvarez, Radhames Dykhoff

The Yalie lefty was nearly out of baseball for good after being cut by the Brewers. Signed by the Padres in an open try-out, Breslow steadily made his way from Double-A afterthought to a 2.20 ERA in limited action with the big club last year. The Padres non-tendered him after the season, which isn't surprising given his awful walk rates.

CESAR CARRILLO   Bats: R Throws: R   Height: 6′ 3″   Weight: 177   Born: April 29, 1984   Age: 22

YEAR	TM	LVL	AGE	W	L	SV	G	GS	IP	H	BB	SO	HR	GB%	BABIP	STUFF	WHIP	ERA	PERA	EQERA	EQH9	EQBB9	EQSO9	EQHR9	VORP	WXRL
2005	LEL	A+	21	1	2	0	7	7	25.7	30	9	29	3	62%	.360	0	1.52	7.00	5.33	7.46	10.7	3.9	6.4	1.4	-5.2	—
2005	MOB	AA	21	4	0	0	5	5	30.7	23	7	35	2	46%	.276	25	0.98	3.22	4.34	4.34	8.1	2.2	7.1	1.2	4.1	—
2006	SDN	MLB	22	7	8	0	27	20	127.0	121	48	102	13	50%	.290	13	1.33	4.23	4.65	4.79	8.8	3.1	6.4	0.9	9.0	1.8

Breakout: 47%   Improve: 85%   Collapse: 1%   Attrition: 2%   Comparables: Brad Penny, Chin-Hui Tsao, Jason Grilli

In the 2005 amateur draft, the Padres set their sights on getting a polished pitcher who had faced collegiate competition and could be expected to advance through the system quickly—the same strategy that led them to Tim Stauffer in 2004. Carrillo was the 18th player selected in the draft, and he signed with the Padres quickly. By season's end, he was pitching in Double-A. He's the best pitching prospect in the organization, and will likely make a token appearance with the Padres this year. Maybe more.

ADAM EATON   Bats: R Throws: R   Height: 6′ 2″   Weight: 190   Born: November 23, 1977   Age: 28

YEAR	TM	LVL	AGE	W	L	SV	G	GS	IP	H	BB	SO	HR	GB%	BABIP	STUFF	WHIP	ERA	PERA	EQERA	EQH9	EQBB9	EQSO9	EQHR9	VORP	WXRL
2003	SDN	MLB	25	9	12	0	31	31	183.0	173	68	146	20	47%	.285	13	1.32	4.08	4.36	4.66	8.8	3.0	6.5	1.0	21.3	3.6
2004	SDN	MLB	26	11	14	0	33	33	199.3	204	52	153	28	41%	.300	8	1.28	4.61	4.50	5.36	9.3	2.1	6.2	1.2	11.6	3.0
2005	SDN	MLB	27	11	5	0	24	22	128.7	140	44	100	14	41%	.319	11	1.43	4.27	4.42	4.97	9.4	2.8	6.4	1.0	8.0	2.3
2006	TEX	MLB	28	9	10	0	31	26	157.3	175	42	101	24	42%	.298	8	1.38	4.88	4.75	4.85	9.5	2.4	5.8	1.3	14.1	2.6

Breakout: 20%   Improve: 59%   Collapse: 9%   Attrition: 3%   Comparables: Reggie Cleveland, Todd Stottlemyre, Frank Castillo

Eaton looked like he'd finally blossomed into the front-of-the-rotation starter before straining his middle right finger flexor tendon on May 15. He wasn't the same pitcher when he finally came off the DL in September. Considering Eaton's pedigree and repertoire, there's a fair chance last year's start represented real progress towards consistent top-half-of-the-rotation performance. The Rangers have to hope so after giving up a good collection of talent led by Chris Young in a six-player deal for Eaton.

CHRIS HAMMOND   Bats: L Throws: L   Height: 6′ 1″   Weight: 195   Born: January 21, 1966   Age: 40

YEAR	TM	LVL	AGE	W	L	SV	G	GS	IP	H	BB	SO	HR	GB%	BABIP	STUFF	WHIP	ERA	PERA	EQERA	EQH9	EQBB9	EQSO9	EQHR9	VORP	WXRL
2003	NYA	MLB	37	3	2	1	62	0	63.0	65	11	45	5	37%	.314	10	1.21	2.86	3.68	3.11	8.6	1.6	6.2	0.7	19.2	2.0
2004	OAK	MLB	38	4	1	1	41	0	53.7	56	13	34	4	43%	.317	3	1.29	2.68	4.00	3.50	9.3	2.0	5.3	0.7	16.9	0.1
2005	SDN	MLB	39	5	1	0	55	0	58.7	51	14	34	9	47%	.233	-13	1.11	3.83	5.05	3.79	8.7	2.1	4.9	1.4	8.9	0.3
2006	CIN	MLB	40	1	2	1	32	0	34.0	39	9	20	6	42%	.296	-15	1.40	4.78	5.22	5.49	10.1	2.2	4.9	1.4	2.0	0.1

Breakout: 17%   Improve: 21%   Collapse: 70%   Attrition: 47%   Comparables: Buddy Groom, Tony Fossas, Mike Flanagan

Hammond is exactly the kind of pitcher on which a team with any budgetary constraints should be concentrating. He's been effective, but hasn't racked up the saves or done anything else that would drive his price, justifiably or not, through the ceiling. Hammond gave the Padres their first good left-hander reliever since Alan Embree left town. The Reds signed him to a one-year, $800,000 deal, but as you can see, PECOTA doesn't see that as money well spent.

CLAY HENSLEY   Bats: R Throws: R   Height: 5′ 11″ Weight: 190   Born: August 31, 1979   Age: 26

YEAR	TM	LVL	AGE	W	L	SV	G	GS	IP	H	BB	SO	HR	GB%	BABIP	STUFF	WHIP	ERA	PERA	EQERA	EQH9	EQBB9	EQSO9	EQHR9	VORP	WXRL
2003	HAG	A	23	4	3	0	12	12	68.0	56	20	74	4	—	.286	-3	1.12	3.18	5.55	5.98	10.2	3.6	5.8	1.6	-2.6	—
2003	SJO	A+	23	2	3	0	5	5	29.3	38	9	25	4	—	.351	-16	1.60	5.84	6.99	6.99	12.1	3.8	4.8	2.5	-4.4	—
2003	LEL	A+	23	3	4	0	8	8	44.3	50	14	40	0	—	.350	4	1.44	3.45	3.89	6.34	9.6	3.7	4.7	0.2	-3.6	—
2004	MOB	AA	24	11	10	0	27	27	159.0	167	48	125	14	—	.319	-11	1.35	4.30	5.42	6.38	10.5	3.3	4.5	1.3	-13.1	—
2005	POR	AAA	25	2	2	0	15	14	90.3	63	22	71	8	58%	.228	9	0.94	2.99	4.57	3.83	7.8	2.4	5.3	1.1	16.7	—
2005	SDN	MLB	25	1	1	0	24	1	47.7	33	17	28	0	57%	.234	6	1.05	1.70	3.72	2.35	7.2	3.1	5.1	0.2	16.8	2.0
2006	SDN	MLB	26	4	5	1	37	10	84.7	89	31	51	9	52%	.295	-6	1.43	4.56	5.14	5.25	9.7	3.0	4.8	0.9	2.4	0.5

Breakout: 14%   Improve: 35%   Collapse: 30%   Attrition: 4%   Comparables: Omar Olivares, Bobby Locke, Curt Leskanic

The last Padres pitcher to put up a 30+ VORP season in his first above-replacement level season was Andy Ashby, giving you an idea of how promising Hensley's 2005 was. Hensley doesn't have Ashby's raw stuff, but he's got solid control and poise to spare with men on base. The zero homers allowed in nearly 50 major league innings was a neat trick too, though it won't be repeated. The Padres like him in relief, but he could quickly force the issue with the retreads the team will have in the rotation this year.

TREVOR HOFFMAN — Bats: R Throws: R — Height: 6' 0" Weight: 215 Born: October 13, 1967 — Age: 38

YEAR	TM	LVL	AGE	W	L	SV	G	GS	IP	H	BB	SO	HR	GB%	BABIP	STUFF	WHIP	ERA	PERA	EQERA	EQH9	EQBB9	EQSO9	EQHR9	VORP	WXRL
2004	SDN	MLB	36	3	3	41	55	0	54.7	42	8	53	5	37%	.262	21	0.91	2.30	3.21	2.70	7.4	1.2	7.9	0.8	20.1	4.4
2005	SDN	MLB	37	1	6	43	60	0	57.7	52	12	54	3	38%	.299	21	1.11	2.96	2.97	3.75	8.0	1.7	7.6	0.5	11.2	3.7
2006	SDN	MLB	38	3	4	26	44	0	49.0	45	13	39	6	40%	.273	0	1.18	3.44	3.98	4.15	8.5	2.2	6.3	1.1	7.9	1.3

Breakout: 16%   Improve: 37%   Collapse: 40%   Attrition: 21%   Comparables: Rick Aguilera, Tug McGraw, Jay Howell

He's pulled a high wire act for years with a fastball he couldn't throw through a piece of bread, all the while remaining one of the game's best closers. Hoffman's a magician with the change-up and slow fastball; you've got to believe the ride's going to come to an end sometime, but that prediction's getting pretty old. Instead, let's look at Hoffman for what he is: one of the best relievers of his era, and a distinct threat to set the career saves record.

BRIAN LAWRENCE — Bats: R Throws: R — Height: 6' 0" Weight: 195 Born: May 14, 1976 — Age: 30

YEAR	TM	LVL	AGE	W	L	SV	G	GS	IP	H	BB	SO	HR	GB%	BABIP	STUFF	WHIP	ERA	PERA	EQERA	EQH9	EQBB9	EQSO9	EQHR9	VORP	WXRL
2003	SDN	MLB	27	10	15	0	33	33	210.7	206	57	116	27	52%	.273	0	1.25	4.19	4.92	4.57	9.4	2.2	4.5	1.2	23.2	4.4
2004	SDN	MLB	28	15	14	0	34	34	203.0	226	55	121	26	53%	.312	2	1.38	4.12	4.70	4.74	9.9	2.2	4.7	1.1	25.4	4.5
2005	SDN	MLB	29	7	15	0	33	33	195.7	211	57	109	18	48%	.298	6	1.37	4.83	4.53	4.71	9.6	2.4	4.6	0.9	12.3	3.7
2006	WAS	MLB	30	11	10	0	30	29	186.3	187	49	106	20	48%	.279	6	1.27	3.81	4.41	4.53	9.3	2.2	4.5	1.0	22.6	3.7

Breakout: 23%   Improve: 66%   Collapse: 11%   Attrition: 0%   Comparables: Jim Colborn, Rick Langford, Lew Burdette

His decline accelerated in 2005, as Lawrence was torched like a Parisian sedan by hitters all over the league. He's always been a trapeze artist, relying on form, control, and mechanics, and his effectiveness has depended on his ability to spot his slider to perfection. Meanwhile, his peripherals continue to decay. He'll benefit from Washington's defense and soggy, boggy RFK, but those effects will only serve to disguise a pitcher on his way out.

SCOTT LINEBRINK — Bats: R Throws: R — Height: 6' 2" Weight: 200 Born: August 4, 1976 — Age: 29

YEAR	TM	LVL	AGE	W	L	SV	G	GS	IP	H	BB	SO	HR	GB%	BABIP	STUFF	WHIP	ERA	PERA	EQERA	EQH9	EQBB9	EQSO9	EQHR9	VORP	WXRL
2003	HOU	MLB	26	1	1	0	9	6	31.7	38	14	17	4	42%	.343	-9	1.64	4.26	5.34	4.50	10.7	3.7	4.2	1.1	5.6	0.6
2003	SDN	MLB	26	2	1	0	43	0	60.7	55	22	51	5	40%	.296	8	1.27	2.82	4.03	3.58	8.5	3.0	6.9	0.7	15.0	0.0
2004	SDN	MLB	27	7	3	0	73	0	84.0	61	26	83	8	36%	.264	18	1.04	2.14	3.75	2.76	7.4	2.6	8.0	0.9	30.6	3.6
2005	SDN	MLB	28	8	1	1	73	0	73.7	55	23	70	4	39%	.270	23	1.06	1.83	3.22	2.35	7.2	2.6	7.9	0.5	27.4	3.7
2006	SDN	MLB	29	3	3	4	61	0	68.0	62	25	61	7	39%	.283	6	1.27	3.49	4.19	4.05	8.3	2.9	7.1	1.0	11.5	0.9

Breakout: 8%   Improve: 19%   Collapse: 52%   Attrition: 8%   Comparables: Alejandro Pena, Tim Scott, Jason Isringhausen

The best pitcher in a formidable Padres bullpen in 2005, Linebrink is a great example of how to build a bullpen without dangerously expensive ciphers of the Steve Karsay mold. He's got an outstanding fastball and doesn't get rattled by adversity. With Hoffman back and Aki Otsuka gone, Linebrink will remain the top setup man in the pen.

AKINORI OTSUKA — Bats: R Throws: R — Height: 6' 0" Weight: 200 Born: January 13, 1972 — Age: 34

YEAR	TM	LVL	AGE	W	L	SV	G	GS	IP	H	BB	SO	HR	GB%	BABIP	STUFF	WHIP	ERA	PERA	EQERA	EQH9	EQBB9	EQSO9	EQHR9	VORP	WXRL
2003	CHU	JPL	31	1	3	17	51	0	43.0	31	5	56	4	—	.270	34	0.84	0.00	2.59	2.38	6.9	1.3	9.7	0.6	14.9	—
2004	SDN	MLB	32	7	2	2	73	0	77.3	56	26	87	6	48%	.265	27	1.06	1.75	3.32	2.25	7.0	2.8	9.1	0.7	32.5	5.1
2005	SDN	MLB	33	2	8	1	66	0	62.7	55	34	60	3	51%	.302	12	1.42	3.59	3.86	4.29	7.9	4.6	7.9	0.4	9.2	1.5
2006	TEX	MLB	34	3	3	3	54	0	59.0	60	23	47	7	48%	.300	3	1.40	4.16	4.20	4.29	8.7	3.5	7.2	0.9	8.9	0.8

Breakout: 12%   Improve: 21%   Collapse: 49%   Attrition: 14%   Comparables: Dave Smith, Dave Veres, Jay Howell

Otsuka's second season was markedly worse than the first, giving mileage to the theory that his unorthodox delivery is more effective the first time through the league. That's about the only positive spin you can put on his move to Texas for 2006, where he'll have to rebound from a heavy workload in a much less friendly pitching environment.

CHAN HO PARK
Bats: R Throws: R   Height: 6' 2"   Weight: 200   Born: June 30, 1973   Age: 33

YEAR	TM	LVL	AGE	W	L	SV	G	GS	IP	H	BB	SO	HR	GB%	BABIP	STUFF	WHIP	ERA	PERA	EQERA	EQH9	EQBB9	EQSO9	EQHR9	VORP	WXRL
2003	TEX	MLB	30	1	3	0	7	7	29.7	34	25	16	5	43%	.322	-24	1.99	7.58	7.12	6.53	10.1	7.4	4.7	1.5	-4.5	-0.0
2004	TEX	MLB	31	4	7	0	16	16	95.7	105	33	63	22	47%	.301	-11	1.50	5.45	5.79	5.14	10.0	2.9	5.5	1.8	0.7	0.3
2005	TEX	MLB	32	8	5	0	20	20	109.7	130	54	80	8	50%	.352	16	1.68	5.66	4.32	4.94	9.3	4.3	6.2	0.5	2.3	1.3
2005	SDN	MLB	32	4	3	0	10	9	45.7	50	26	33	3	48%	.326	1	1.66	5.91	4.63	6.56	9.4	4.6	5.8	0.6	-6.3	0.2
2006	*SDN*	*MLB*	*33*	*6*	*9*	*0*	*31*	*21*	*131.3*	*135*	*65*	*93*	*14*	*47%*	*.297*	*-2*	*1.52*	*4.87*	*5.53*	*5.74*	*9.4*	*4.0*	*5.7*	*1.0*	*-0.7*	*0.8*

Breakout: 22%   Improve: 56%   Collapse: 21%   Attrition: 10%   Comparables: Dan Petry, Pat Rapp, Bob Turley

Park's cratering in Texas—with the health problems, huge contract, and a difficult ballpark—wasn't all that surprising. In San Diego, a lot of that pressure should be off, and Park isn't a bad bet to rebound. He's still got the back-breaking curve, and he's pitching in the right park to restore some confidence and resurrect the man he was with the Dodgers.

JAKE PEAVY
Bats: R Throws: R   Height: 6' 1"   Weight: 180   Born: May 31, 1981   Age: 25

YEAR	TM	LVL	AGE	W	L	SV	G	GS	IP	H	BB	SO	HR	GB%	BABIP	STUFF	WHIP	ERA	PERA	EQERA	EQH9	EQBB9	EQSO9	EQHR9	VORP	WXRL
2003	SDN	MLB	22	12	11	0	32	32	194.7	173	82	156	33	42%	.260	2	1.31	4.11	5.28	4.57	8.8	3.5	6.6	1.6	26.7	4.7
2004	SDN	MLB	23	15	6	0	27	27	166.3	146	53	173	13	47%	.307	39	1.20	2.27	3.54	2.99	8.1	2.6	8.3	0.7	56.0	6.5
2005	SDN	MLB	24	13	7	0	30	30	203.0	162	50	216	18	46%	.281	39	1.04	2.88	3.36	3.40	7.5	2.1	8.8	0.9	53.1	6.6
2006	*SDN*	*MLB*	*25*	*15*	*9*	*0*	*32*	*32*	*216.7*	*181*	*62*	*202*	*19*	*43%*	*.273*	*28*	*1.12*	*2.94*	*3.45*	*3.31*	*7.7*	*2.3*	*7.4*	*0.8*	*52.9*	*6.9*

Breakout: 34%   Improve: 63%   Collapse: 7%   Attrition: 0%   Comparables: Camilo Pascual, Kevin Appier, Pedro Martinez

The Padres' best hope for upsetting the heavily favored Cardinals in the playoffs was lost when Peavy aggravated a rib injury in Game One and turned in his worst performance of the season. That aside, there's nothing not to like here; Peavy's young, his stuff is filthy, and he's popular with fans. He's a Cy Young winner waiting to happen.

BRIAN SIKORSKI
Bats: R Throws: R   Height: 6' 1"   Weight: 190   Born: July 27, 1974   Age: 31

YEAR	TM	LVL	AGE	W	L	SV	G	GS	IP	H	BB	SO	HR	GB%	BABIP	STUFF	WHIP	ERA	PERA	EQERA	EQH9	EQBB9	EQSO9	EQHR9	VORP	WXRL
2003	CHB	JPL	28	4	6	1	47	0	82.7	80	23	71	9	—	.286	9	1.25	0.00	3.86	3.86	8.7	2.3	6.8	0.9	15.8	—
2004	YOM	JPL	29	5	3	5	62	0	77.7	76	22	83	9	—	-.545	15	1.26	2.66	3.91	2.96	8.5	2.7	7.7	0.8	22.3	—
2005	YOM	JPL	30	7	1	0	70	0	87.7	75	33	100	4	—	.303	25	1.23	3.28	3.30	3.71	7.4	3.5	8.3	0.4	18.3	—
2006	*SDN*	*MLB*	*31*	*3*	*3*	*1*	*26*	*4*	*52.0*	*48*	*19*	*46*	*5*	*43%*	*.290*	*7*	*1.29*	*3.54*	*4.22*	*4.10*	*8.5*	*3.0*	*7.0*	*0.9*	*8.1*	*0.9*

Breakout: 14%   Improve: 38%   Collapse: 34%   Attrition: 22%   Comparables: Dan Spillner, Dave Giusti, Dan Osinski

Having succeeded in their last attempt to import a strikeout reliever from Japan with Akinori Otsuka, the Padres went back to the well, returning former Texas Ranger Sikorski to the majors after five years in Japan. The similarities end there; Sikorski doesn't have the history of dominance or the fine control that Otsuka brought to the table. He'll have a place in the bullpen, but he'll have to earn his way into high-leverage situations.

RUDY SEANEZ
Bats: R Throws: R   Height: 5' 11"   Weight: 200   Born: October 20, 1968   Age: 37

YEAR	TM	LVL	AGE	W	L	SV	G	GS	IP	H	BB	SO	HR	GB%	BABIP	STUFF	WHIP	ERA	PERA	EQERA	EQH9	EQBB9	EQSO9	EQHR9	VORP	WXRL
2004	KCA	MLB	35	0	1	0	16	0	23.0	21	11	21	0	50%	.323	12	1.39	3.91	3.47	3.47	7.7	3.9	7.7	0.4	5.8	-0.6
2004	FLO	MLB	35	3	1	0	23	0	23.0	18	8	25	3	46%	.263	16	1.13	2.74	3.97	3.18	7.5	2.8	8.7	1.2	7.3	0.2
2005	SDN	MLB	36	7	1	0	57	0	60.3	49	22	84	4	37%	.338	39	1.18	2.69	2.80	3.25	7.1	3.0	11.2	0.6	17.3	1.7
2006	*BOS*	*MLB*	*37*	*3*	*3*	*2*	*52*	*0*	*57.0*	*58*	*24*	*54*	*9*	*39%*	*.306*	*5*	*1.44*	*4.54*	*4.77*	*4.75*	*8.9*	*3.7*	*8.3*	*1.2*	*6.3*	*0.5*

Breakout: 21%   Improve: 38%   Collapse: 38%   Attrition: 15%   Comparables: Steve Farr, Juan Berenguer, Diego Segui

"Traction Action" used to feature the kind of repertoire we make fun of clubs for coveting: 100-mph heat, a walk per inning, and Brad Pennington-ish results. Forget about that guy—Seanez is now one of the better relievers in the majors, though he can't be counted on too heavily due to his extensive injury history. The Red Sox are taking a risk signing him for setup-man money, but they've certainly got the resources to compensate if it doesn't work out.

TIM STAUFFER
Bats: R Throws: R   Height: 6′ 2″   Weight: 190   Born: June 2, 1982   Age: 24

YEAR	TM	LVL	AGE	W	L	SV	G	GS	IP	H	BB	SO	HR	GB%	BABIP	STUFF	WHIP	ERA	PERA	EQERA	EQH9	EQBB9	EQSO9	EQHR9	VORP	WXRL
2004	LEL	A+	22	2	0	0	6	6	35.3	28	9	30	0	—	.277	12	1.05	1.78	3.78	4.05	8.1	3.2	4.9	0.3	5.7	—
2004	MOB	AA	22	3	2	0	8	8	51.3	56	13	33	3	—	.327	1	1.35	2.63	4.71	4.53	10.1	2.5	3.8	0.9	5.9	—
2004	POR	AAA	22	6	3	0	14	14	81.3	83	26	50	15	—	.267	-15	1.34	3.54	6.09	5.29	10.0	3.1	4.4	1.8	2.7	—
2005	POR	AAA	23	3	5	0	13	13	75.3	90	17	64	5	45%	.362	15	1.42	5.14	4.03	5.80	10.2	2.0	5.6	0.7	-1.7	—
2005	SDN	MLB	23	3	6	0	15	14	81.0	92	29	49	10	41%	.312	-1	1.49	5.33	5.05	5.38	9.9	3.0	4.9	1.2	-0.2	0.7
2006	SDN	MLB	24	8	10	0	32	25	144.7	152	48	92	18	46%	.292	3	1.38	4.54	5.18	5.14	9.7	2.7	5.1	1.1	5.7	1.5

Breakout: 15%   Improve: 57%   Collapse: 8%   Attrition: 0%   Comparables: Roger Erickson, Rick Wise, Johnny Kucks

It was a frustrating season for Stauffer, who expected he'd seen his last minor league action when he was called up by the Padres after six solid starts at Triple-A to start the season. He pitched badly enough to be demoted with the acquisition of Chan Ho Park, and his continued struggles in Portland didn't warrant a return engagement. He's still a solid mid-wattage pitching prospect, and will be in the mix for a rotation spot this year.

SEAN THOMPSON
Bats: L Throws: L   Height: 5′ 11″   Weight: 160   Born: October 13, 1982   Age: 23

YEAR	TM	LVL	AGE	W	L	SV	G	GS	IP	H	BB	SO	HR	GB%	BABIP	STUFF	WHIP	ERA	PERA	EQERA	EQH9	EQBB9	EQSO9	EQHR9	VORP	WXRL
2003	EUG	A-	20	7	1	0	15	15	80.0	58	39	97	5	—	.270	-5	1.21	2.48	6.35	5.47	9.5	5.8	6.5	1.9	1.0	—
2004	FTW	A	21	9	6	0	27	27	148.0	125	57	157	15	—	.289	-22	1.23	3.10	6.63	5.37	9.8	4.8	5.6	2.1	3.5	—
2005	LEL	A+	22	4	1	0	6	6	33.3	26	13	45	4	38%	.293	12	1.17	2.16	5.46	4.88	8.6	4.6	7.8	1.7	2.5	—
2005	MOB	AA	22	4	5	0	20	20	113.7	127	55	94	10	47%	.357	-14	1.60	4.67	5.94	6.18	10.3	4.8	5.0	1.5	-7.1	—
2006	SDN	MLB	23	6	10	0	25	23	128.7	129	74	92	18	44%	.284	0	1.57	5.18	6.01	5.85	9.2	4.7	5.7	1.3	-4.7	0.4

Breakout: 11%   Improve: 49%   Collapse: 15%   Attrition: 0%   Comparables: Bill Murphy, Andy Pratt, Chris Narveson

Thompson's got youth, left-handedness, a nifty pickoff move, and a knee-bending curveball on his side. The bad news is that he didn't distinguish himself in his first run of Double-A action. He's 5′10″, and his height will materially affect his ability to secure a spot in a major league bullpen at some point. Sure, Tom Gordon's short and has a great curve too, but he also brings a 96 mph fastball to the party.

JARED WELLS
Bats: R Throws: R   Height: 6′ 4″   Weight: 200   Born: October 31, 1981   Age: 24

YEAR	TM	LVL	AGE	W	L	SV	G	GS	IP	H	BB	SO	HR	GB%	BABIP	STUFF	WHIP	ERA	PERA	EQERA	EQH9	EQBB9	EQSO9	EQHR9	VORP	WXRL
2003	EUG	A-	21	4	6	0	14	14	78.7	77	32	53	6	—	.279	-34	1.39	2.74	7.47	6.35	11.2	4.9	3.5	2.4	-6.0	—
2004	FTW	A	22	4	6	0	14	14	81.3	91	19	72	6	—	.336	-10	1.35	4.10	5.51	6.09	10.8	2.9	4.4	1.5	-4.3	—
2004	LEL	A+	22	4	6	0	13	12	71.7	81	30	38	5	—	.313	-23	1.55	4.52	6.03	6.42	10.5	5.1	3.0	1.2	-6.3	—
2005	LEL	A+	23	11	3	0	19	19	120.3	116	26	80	6	51%	.301	5	1.18	3.44	4.54	4.77	9.0	2.5	3.6	0.7	10.8	—
2005	MOB	AA	23	2	5	0	7	7	43.0	51	16	22	3	45%	.340	-16	1.56	4.40	5.74	6.17	10.4	3.8	3.0	1.3	-2.7	—
2006	SDN	MLB	24	5	10	0	27	21	121.7	138	54	58	18	47%	.292	-12	1.58	5.75	6.34	6.58	10.4	3.6	3.8	1.3	-13.9	-0.6

Breakout: 5%   Improve: 28%   Collapse: 28%   Attrition: 0%   Comparables: Nate Yeskie, Mitch Wylie, Zach McClellan

Wells enjoyed a big year for the Storm before being called up to Double-A, and was added to the 40-man roster in November. He's got a low-90s fastball with some movement and a reasonable slider. He didn't dominate in his stint at Mobile, and that'll be where he should start in 2006.

WOODY WILLIAMS
Bats: R Throws: R   Height: 6′ 0″   Weight: 190   Born: August 19, 1966   Age: 39

YEAR	TM	LVL	AGE	W	L	SV	G	GS	IP	H	BB	SO	HR	GB%	BABIP	STUFF	WHIP	ERA	PERA	EQERA	EQH9	EQBB9	EQSO9	EQHR9	VORP	WXRL
2003	SLN	MLB	36	18	9	0	34	33	220.7	220	55	153	20	43%	.291	17	1.25	3.87	4.06	4.39	9.1	2.1	5.7	0.8	37.6	5.1
2004	SLN	MLB	37	11	8	0	31	31	189.7	193	58	131	20	42%	.296	12	1.32	4.18	4.38	4.72	9.5	2.6	5.6	0.9	26.5	4.0
2005	SDN	MLB	38	9	12	0	28	28	159.7	174	51	106	24	36%	.299	-3	1.41	4.85	5.00	5.16	9.7	2.7	5.4	1.4	3.1	2.2
2006	SDN	MLB	39	8	10	0	34	22	147.3	154	46	96	19	41%	.288	-2	1.35	4.53	5.13	5.35	9.6	2.6	5.2	1.2	7.1	1.6

Breakout: 18%   Improve: 51%   Collapse: 30%   Attrition: 8%   Comparables: Tom Candiotti, Murry Dickson, Joe Niekro

Signed to the elder-statesman-of-the-pitching-staff role previously occupied by Boomer Wells, Williams's cut fastball looked slow from day one of 2005—a bad sign for an already-junkballing 38-year-old pitcher. The strained oblique he suffered in April won't be a problem in 2006, but the missing juice on the fastball will be. Somewhere along the line the Pads will need either a breakthrough performance by one of their young arms or a deal for reinforcements. The rotation has too many question marks as it stands.

Line Outs

Position/Player	TM	LVL	AGE	PA	R	2B	3B	HR	RBI	BB	SO	SB-CS	SPEED	BA/OBP/SLG	MLVR	EQBA/OBP/SLG	EQA	VORP
CF K. Jones*	MOB	AA	23	562	62	23	4	1	60	71	112	23-14	5.1	.281/.375/.351	.018	.255/.337/.322	.238	-5.2
1/O J. Knott	POR	AAA	26	577	81	34	4	25	78	55	112	1-0	4.0	.250/.333/.483	.050	.220/.290/.402	.240	-19.8
3B C. Smith	MOB	AA	23	571	64	30	2	18	73	46	144	4-3	4.4	.254/.317/.424	.003	.226/.280/.386	.231	-6.5
SS W. Valdez	SEA	MLB	27	132	9	5	1	0	8	6	25	2-2	5.9	.198/.235/.254	-.440	.208/.256/.264	.187	-9.2
	POR	AAA	27	171	14	5	3	1	15	15	27	8-0	6.2	.245/.310/.335	-.213	.225/.279/.303	.218	-6.4

Pitcher	TM	LVL	AGE	W	L	SV	IP	H	BB	SO	HR	GB%	BABIP	STUFF	WHIP	ERA	PERA	EQERA	EQH9	EQBB9	EQSO9	EQHR9	VORP
S. Cassidy	PAW	AAA	29	6	3	0	60.0	54	23	66	5	35%	.325	1	1.28	4.05	4.53	5.31	8.7	4.2	7.2	0.9	1.9
R. Meaux*	BIR	AA	26	5	2	3	67.0	77	18	64	2	51%	.377	-4	1.42	2.96	4.09	5.73	10.1	2.9	5.0	0.5	-1.0
	MOB	AA	26	2	0	0	17.0	16	2	12	2	52%	.264	-23	1.06	3.18	6.19	5.62	10.1	1.1	3.9	2.2	0.0
C. Oxspring	POR	AAA	28	12	6	0	160.7	148	42	125	15	43%	.284	1	1.18	4.03	4.72	5.25	9.0	2.6	4.9	1.1	6.0
D. Reyes*	SDN	MLB	28	3	2	0	43.7	57	32	35	3	67%	.378	-9	2.04	5.15	4.70	6.26	10.2	5.9	6.3	0.6	-3.1
M. Thompson	MOB	AA	24	6	6	0	114.7	116	27	68	6	47%	.307	-3	1.25	3.22	4.89	5.22	9.5	2.4	3.4	0.9	4.7
	POR	AAA	24	4	2	0	60.0	58	13	25	6	49%	.268	-6	1.18	3.15	4.97	3.88	9.3	2.0	2.8	1.1	11.1
R. Tucker*	MOB	AA	24	3	2	0	62.7	66	49	69	4	40%	.380	-28	1.83	5.31	6.64	7.24	10.3	8.3	6.3	1.2	-10.9

Speed guy **Kennard Jones** has gone from a highly-rated college prospect to just another fifth outfielder wannabe. Minor-league slugger **Jon Knott** was squeezed out with Bozied coming back and Johnson approaching from below, so the Padres have released him. His swing's long, but he's got pop and is capable of contending for a Triple-A home run crown or two. Former 1st rounder **Corey Smith** got brought over from Cleveland on the off chance that a change of organizations might do the trick; comparisons to Gary Sheffield seem deader than Elvis. **Wilson Valdez** went from starting in Seattle to starting in Portland when the Mariners dumped him on a Pads team looking for depth.

The Padres picked **Scott Cassidy** up in the trade that sent Adam Hyzdu to the Red Sox in August, and he got some garbage time with the team after roster expansion. He's a guy you keep around so as to not be forced to trade for Al Leiter when everything that can go wrong with your pitching staff does, but that's about it. **Ryan Meaux** was acquired for Geoff Blum in a deadline "blockbuster." Meaux was reasonably successful in a relief role in Double-A, but will be tested at Triple-A. The Padres are not strangers to selling off fringe major league starters to the Japanese leagues, having done it with Buddy Carlyle in 2000 and now **Chris Oxspring.** For an active mid-market team dancing on the edge of the payroll, every half-million counts. The hefty lefty managed to disappoint yet again, but **Dennys Reyes** will be in the Twins' camp, hoping to replace J. C. Romero. **Mike Thompson** might be an organizational soldier, but if he keeps surviving in the upper levels, he might see a cuppajoe someday. Erstwhile closer candidate **Rusty Tucker** lived up to his name in his first year back from TJ surgery, but it's hoped that he'll have his power fastball/slider combo up to speed this year.

San Francisco Giants

The 2005 Giants were as bad as a gravel and cheese sandwich. The team ranked 29th in Equivalent Average (.249) and 18th in Equivalent Runs Allowed (740). Obviously, Barry Bonds's injury and absence hurt them, but there were other season-killing problems. Take the starting rotation: Erstwhile ace Jason Schmidt struggled with injuries and didn't pitch like an ace even when healthy, and Jerome Williams and Kirk Reuter, who began the season as the #2 and #3 starters, pitched so poorly that management felt forced to trade one (Williams) and release the other (Rueter). In addition, most of the veteran arms in the bullpen filed for divorce and absconded with the chocolate lab and the keys to the liquor cabinet. Jim Brower, Matt Herges, Armando Benitez, Jason Christiansen, and Tyler Walker, all on the Opening Day roster, combined for a cumulative VORP of 1.6 in 191 innings. Finally, the team received subpar offensive contributions at catcher, first, third, shortstop, and right field.

The front office doesn't bear responsibility for all of this. Some of the team's misfortunes can simply be attributed to bad luck, while others were calculated risks gone awry. The family crisis that contributed to Jerome Williams's early problems illustrate the former, while the commitment to 38-year-old Marquis Grissom in center field exemplify the latter. A front office can't do much about bad luck beyond investing in depth—which the Giants failed to do—but bad decisions, including foolish gambles, are avoidable.

A more serious indictment of the front office is its longstanding failure to develop position players for the major league roster. The barren farm system's problems became evident when the veterans GM Brian Sabean favored for years started flailing and no capable call-ups were waiting in the wings. Somehow, the team's capable pitching prospects almost snuck this miserable squad into the playoffs. Thus, the 2005 Giants demonstrated both how a moribund farm system can kill you and how a decent player development program can sustain a team through even the worst roster-construction disasters.

It has been a long time since the Giants developed a hitting prospect. Bill Mueller, drafted in 1993, was the last one. Since then, the best position players developed by San Francisco have been Grade C types like Marvin Benard, Doug Mirabelli, and Armando Rios (see table 1). That's more than a disappointing system, it's a completely

dysfunctional one. If a team never develops star-caliber major league hitters, it then has to find them on the free agent market. Those players are few and far between, which makes them extraordinarily expensive, and that's assuming that the players can be induced to sign rather than take whatever the Yankees are offering. Additionally, free agent players, by virtue of the six years of service time they've already accrued, tend to be older and in many cases are entering the decline phase of their careers.

GIANTS PROSPECTUS

2005 record: 75–87; Third place, NL West

Pythagenport record: 70–92

Runs scored per game: 4.01 (15th in NL)

Runs allowed per game: 4.60 (11th in NL)

Team EqA: .250 (15th in NL)

2005 Batters Age: 32.9 (Oldest in NL)

2005 Pitchers Age: 30.3 (4th oldest in NL)

Ballpark: SBC Park; Neutral park; Park Factor of 0.995

2005: Treated fans to a sneak preview of "Life after Barry Bonds." Yes, it's a horror movie.

2006: The Giants proved they can't hang without Bonds; now he needs to prove that he can play 130 games.

TABLE 1. UNDERSIZED GIANTS: HITTERS WHO SIGNED AND DEBUTED WITH SAN FRANCISCO, 1996–2005

Debut Year	Name	Career VORP	Debut Year	Name	Career VORP
1996	Bill Mueller	271.3	2003	Lance Niekro	6.5
1995	Marvin Benard	105.6	2003	Jason Ellison	3.7
1996	Doug Mirabelli	52.4	1997	Dante Powell	2.7
1998	Armando Rios	43.0	2002	Tony Torcato	1.8
2000	Pedro Feliz	35.7	2002	Trey Lunsford	1.4
2001	Yorvit Torrealba	20.4	2004	Brian Dallimore	0.5
2000	Damon Minor	9.0	2001	Cody Ransom	0.2
1996	Jacob Cruz	7.8	2003	Francisco Santos	0.2

Since the Giants can't develop even average major league players, they have to buy them on the free market, too. Giants rosters of recent years have carried a cable car full of overpaid forgettables like Michael Tucker, Jeffrey Hammonds, Shawon Dunston, Glenallen Hill, and Brent Mayne. Alternatively, when such players haven't been available the Giants have had to give substantial playing time to their own inferior minor leaguers, homegrown but not quite fringe players like Damon Minor, Cody Ransom, and Edwards Guzman. The team's inability to develop even this level of player led the Giants to sign Jose Vizcaino and Mark Sweeney for over $3 million in 2006.

The financial inefficiency of such a team is obvious, but as the '05 Giants showed, such a squad is prone to attrition. Having to give almost 1,500 plate appearances to the homegrown foursome of Lance Niekro, Jason Ellison, Todd Linden, and Pedro Feliz was a big reason the Jurassic Grissom received as much playing time as he did. The young quartet combined for a batting line of .250/.298/.403. The Giants' inability to develop position players was both the underlying and proximate cause of their 2005 collapse.

The pitching development program is the polar opposite. The Giants have developed a number of useful pitchers in the last 10 years (see table 2). Noah Lowry and Jerome Williams may become solid mid-rotation starters. Matt Cain and Francisco Liriano are potential stars. Joe Nathan and Keith Foulke are, or have been, top-notch closers. The team also developed solid bullpen spare parts like Steve Reed and Scott Linebrink, and some competent back-of-the-rotation starters like Ryan Jensen, Brad Hennessey, and Kevin Correia.

As a result of their ability to grow their own, the team didn't have to pay free agent prices for a significant portion of their pitching. Further, the presence of talented

arms, combined with a GM noted for his trading acumen, helped the team regularly engineer deals to bring in significant major league talent. Long-forgotten pitching prospects were key to the team, which acquired Shawn Estes, Livan Hernandez, Robb Nen, Jason Schmidt, and others.

When problems arose on the major league staff last year, the team had a steady supply of replacement-level arms to bring up and press into the breach. While pitching less than half the innings of the bullpen greybeards, rookies Jeremy Accardo, Scott Munter, and Jack Taschner contributed 22.6 runs of VORP. Correia and Hennessey were more than capable fifth starters when the veteran rotation fell apart, and Cain put the team in a position to make a last-gasp run at the NL West division crown with his terrific stretch run.

The most interesting aspect of San Francisco's dearth of minor league hitters is that the organization might have planned it that way. Sabean, Vice President of Player Personnel, Dick Tidrow, and other members of the front office regularly toss quotes to reporters that admit a deliberate pitching-first draft strategy. From 1993—the year Sabean took over as Scouting Director—to 2001, the Giants spent 57% of their premium picks on pitchers ("premium" being defined as those picks that are in the top 100 each year). Only nine clubs who have used more of their premium picks on hurlers than the Giants have; they drafted more pitchers than the average club, but not by so much that the system should be starved of hitters.

The Giants made a decent, though perhaps abortive, attempt to restock the system with lumber from 2002 through 2004, spending six of their nine premium picks on position players. They even went so far as to give 2002 21st rounder Travis Ishikawa a then-record $955,000 signing bonus. A few of those picks spent the 2005 season putting up strong numbers at High-A San Jose and Double-A Norwich, so there is a decent chance that at least a couple of them could have major league careers.

Of course, fixing this system through the amateur draft is especially difficult when the team purposely gives away its picks through free agent compensation. Having signed Armando Benitez, Mike Matheny, and Omar Vizquel during the 2004–2005 offseason, Giants didn't pick until the 4th round last June. This was not accidental; the Giants are willing to put money into the major league roster while avoiding premium (read: expensive) talent in the amateur draft. Perhaps Sabean was scarred by his first draft as Giants GM, in 1997; the Giants were granted five first round picks and turned them into Tony Torcato, Nate Bump, Arturo McDowell, Chris Jones, and Jeff Urban. It should be telling how Sabean and his team use their protected 1st round pick this coming June—will they opt for the best talent available or go for signability?

TABLE 2. THIS WE CAN DO: HOMEGROWN PITCHING TALENT SIGNED BY AND DEBUTING WITH THE GIANTS, 1996–2005

Debut Year	Pitcher	Career VORP	Debut Year	Pitcher	Career VORP
1997	Keith Foulke	229.7	2005	Matt Cain	16.8
1998	Russ Ortiz	198.3	2005	Jack Taschner	8.9
1999	Joe Nathan	104.3	2004	Brad Hennessey	8.7
2000	Scott Linebrink	76.8	2005	Scott Munter	8.6
2003	Noah Lowry	57.3	2001	Ryan Jensen	7.0
2003	Jerome Williams	57.1	2003	Kevin Correia	6.2
2000	Aaron Fultz	52.2	2005	Jeremy Accardo	5.1
1996	Osvaldo Fernandez	24.3	2001	Kurt Ainsworth	3.5
2000	Chad Zerbe	22.1	2003	Jesse Foppert	1.3

Given these handicaps, the Giants couldn't do much this offseason, except add another overpriced veteran in mediocre starter Matt Morris. There's no reason they can't compete and succeed in the weak NL West, but if that happens, it will be because Barry Bonds performs like Barry Bonds and because the division remains weak. The Giants are not strong by any means, and even a reseeded farm system won't fix this roster in the short term. A year from now, the Giants will be one year closer to needing a major overhaul, and they look ill-equipped to cope with it.

HITTERS

EDGARDO ALFONZO   3B   Bats: R Throws: R   Height: 5' 11" Weight: 187 Born: November 8, 1973   Age: 32

YEAR	TM	LVL	AGE	PA	R	2B	3B	HR	RBI	BB	SO	SB	CS	SPEED	BA	OBP	SLG	MLVR	EQBA	EQOBP	EQSLG	EQA	VORP	DEFENSE
2003	SFN	MLB	29	583	56	25	2	13	81	58	41	5	2	4.6	.259	.334	.391	-.031	.258	.333	.394	.257	13.3	128-3B -9
2004	SFN	MLB	30	574	66	26	1	11	77	46	40	1	1	3.9	.289	.350	.407	.021	.283	.344	.399	.260	9.8	120-3B 2
2005	SFN	MLB	31	401	36	17	1	2	43	27	34	2	0	4.4	.277	.327	.345	-.087	.275	.328	.341	.240	-0.8	91-3B -7
2006	LAA	MLB	32	309	33	13	1	5	32	22	28	1	1	4.3	.262	.319	.365	-.102	.267	.331	.384	.242	3.1	75-3B -3

Breakout: 18%   Improve: 35%   Collapse: 37%   Attrition: 27%   Comparables: Charlie Hayes, Brook Jacoby, Rich Dauer

With his power completely gone, Alfonzo is just a hairsbreadth better than replacement level. With $7 million left on his deal, the Giants couldn't just punt him to get back the roster spot. Instead, they dealt him to the Angels for fellow overpriced, aging bust Steve Finley. With Los Angeles de Los Angeles, he'll back up Chone Figgins, assuming the Angels stick with their plan to move Darin Erstad back to the outfield/pretend Dallas McPherson doesn't exist.

ELIEZER ALFONZO   C   Bats: R Throws: R   Height: 6' 0" Weight: 205 Born: February 7, 1979   Age: 27

YEAR	TM	LVL	AGE	PA	R	2B	3B	HR	RBI	BB	SO	SB	CS	SPEED	BA	OBP	SLG	MLVR	EQBA	EQOBP	EQSLG	EQA	VORP	DEFENSE		
2004	JUP	A+	25	436	51	12	2	18	70	22	105	6	4	4.4	.281	.335	.456	.174	.245	.282	.395	.233	-2.2	42-C 2	38-1B 1
2005	SJO	A+	26	217	35	16	0	13	45	11	49	1	3	3.4	.357	.410	.638	.577	.271	.305	.423	.246	4.9	47-C 10	
2005	NRW	AA	26	189	30	9	0	9	31	8	39	1	0	4.3	.312	.354	.517	.272	.270	.308	.440	.255	6.1	36-C 3	
2006	SFN	MLB	27	351	37	15	1	12	45	15	97	2	1	3.7	.240	.282	.402	-.151	.242	.284	.420	.232	2.2	85-C 5	

Breakout: 18%   Improve: 37%   Collapse: 39%   Attrition: 15%   Comparables: Kevin Brown, John Lindsey, Shawn Wooten

Alfonzo is an organizational soldier who started knocking the ricotta out of the ball in 2005. The Giants were all set to tap him for the backup spot in the majors when they traded Yorvit Torrealba to Seattle, but Alfonzo was on the hook for a substance abuse violation, so Yamid Haad got the nod instead. The Giants re-signed Alfonzo at the end of the year and sent him to the instructional league to work on his receiving skills.

MOISES ALOU   LF/RF   Bats: R Throws: R   Height: 6' 3" Weight: 195 Born: July 3, 1966   Age: 39

YEAR	TM	LVL	AGE	PA	R	2B	3B	HR	RBI	BB	SO	SB	CS	SPEED	BA	OBP	SLG	MLVR	EQBA	EQOBP	EQSLG	EQA	VORP	DEFENSE	
2003	CHN	MLB	37	638	83	35	1	22	91	63	67	3	1	4.4	.280	.357	.462	.125	.276	.354	.458	.279	20.6	136-LF -6	
2004	CHN	MLB	38	675	106	36	3	39	106	68	80	3	0	4.8	.293	.361	.557	.243	.284	.353	.544	.298	40.2	148-LF -3	
2005	SFN	MLB	39	490	67	21	3	19	63	56	43	5	1	4.9	.321	.400	.518	.303	.315	.395	.521	.311	41.9	65-LF -5	46-RF -3
2006	SFN	MLB	39	452	61	24	2	16	65	52	50	6	1	4.6	.289	.374	.484	.147	.291	.377	.506	.295	23.0	107-LF -5	

Breakout: 11%   Improve: 32%   Collapse: 34%   Attrition: 19%   Comparables: Dave Winfield, Gene Woodling, Rico Carty

Though hobbled with leg problems, Alou was the most valuable Giant, according to VORP. Although Alou was intentionally walked just once all season, part of his increased OBP (the second-highest of his career) was undoubtedly due to opposing pitchers preferring to put Alou on first and take their chances facing someone like Pedro Feliz. His hugely diminished home run rate was a gift of SBC Park, which stripped away Wrigley Field's artificial sheen of high-end potency, and then took even more. Alou still has a strong bat and could easily earn his $6 million option in 2006, but could just as easily break down and vanish forever.

BARRY BONDS   LF   Bats: L Throws: L   Height: 6' 2" Weight: 210 Born: July 24, 1964   Age: 41

YEAR	TM	LVL	AGE	PA	R	2B	3B	HR	RBI	BB	SO	SB	CS	SPEED	BA	OBP	SLG	MLVR	EQBA	EQOBP	EQSLG	EQA	VORP	DEFENSE
2003	SFN	MLB	38	550	111	22	1	45	90	148	58	7	0	5.0	.341	.529	.749	.785	.335	.523	.746	.407	104.2	117-LF 7
2004	SFN	MLB	39	617	129	27	3	45	101	232	41	6	1	5.2	.362	.609	.812	.928	.349	.599	.786	.451	132.0	126-LF 0
2005	SFN	MLB	40	52	8	1	0	5	10	9	6	0	0	2.5	.286	.404	.667	.468	.286	.404	.667	.341	6.4	11-LF -1
2006	SFN	MLB	41	519	60	21	0	39	99	112	64	3	0	3.7	.312	.464	.658	.514	.315	.468	.687	.367	68.7	122-LF -2

Breakout: 0%   Improve: 14%   Collapse: 75%   Attrition: 4%   Comparables: Ted Williams, Edgar Martinez, Carlton Fisk

(continued next page)

Barry Bonds *(continued)*

Even if his numbers decline substantially in 2006, Bonds will produce a full win every 20 games; if he gets back to his 2001–2004 peak it's more like a win every 11 games. That means Bonds could play a historically awful left field with the leather, sit every day game after a night game, miss a month to injury, and he would still be worth almost 10 wins in the standings. If the knee holds up, Bonds could easily lead a poorly constructed Giants squad to the playoffs, but if he misses substantial playing time this team is toast. PECOTA has absolutely no comps with which to make a Bonds prediction. A Wisdom of Crowds–style poll of BP writers yielded an average projection of .309/.474/.667 in 390 PAs with 32 home runs. If it happens, no one will be able to say that Bonds built his Hall of Fame case with steroids.

RAY DURHAM				2B					Bats: B Throws: R				Height: 5' 8"		Weight: 170		Born: November 30, 1971		Age: 34	
YEAR	TM	LVL	AGE	PA	R	2B	3B	HR	RBI	BB	SO	SB	CS	SPEED	BA	OBP	SLG	MLVR	EQBA	EQOBP	EQSLG	EQA	VORP	DEFENSE
2003	SFN	MLB	31	465	61	30	5	8	33	50	82	7	7	5.9	.285	.366	.441	.118	.283	.363	.446	.276	24.3	97-2B 7
2004	SFN	MLB	32	538	95	28	8	17	65	57	60	10	4	6.8	.282	.364	.484	.143	.275	.357	.470	.282	33.9	110-2B -9
2005	SFN	MLB	33	559	67	33	0	12	62	48	59	6	3	4.3	.290	.356	.429	.086	.286	.353	.431	.272	25.4	128-2B -7
2006	*SFN*	*MLB*	*34*	*509*	*67*	*27*	*3*	*12*	*62*	*50*	*62*	*5*	*3*	*4.9*	*.283*	*.358*	*.435*	*.052*	*.285*	*.361*	*.454*	*.274*	*25.7*	*120-2B -4*

Breakout: 10% Improve: 36% Collapse: 34% Attrition: 15% Comparables: *Bill Mueller, Bill Doran, Ryne Sandberg*

Durham's still got the bat and the plate discipline, but between nagging hammys and various groin woes, his once-great range and baserunning have been diminished. That said, 32 VORP out of your second baseman is nothing to sneeze at. If the Giants' season bombs early, Durham could be dealt to a contender for some good loot. Otherwise, Durham will be a critical cog in an uneven Giants offense.

JASON ELLISON				CF					Bats: R Throws: R				Height: 5' 10"		Weight: 180		Born: April 4, 1978		Age: 28		
YEAR	TM	LVL	AGE	PA	R	2B	3B	HR	RBI	BB	SO	SB	CS	SPEED	BA	OBP	SLG	MLVR	EQBA	EQOBP	EQSLG	EQA	VORP	DEFENSE
2003	FRE	AAA	25	509	74	22	4	6	39	39	52	21	13	6.0	.295	.356	.399	.040	.267	.326	.363	.242	1.5	113-CF -2
2004	FRE	AAA	26	549	90	32	7	9	40	40	66	27	12	7.1	.315	.368	.459	.096	.274	.323	.381	.246	5.2	118-CF 6
2005	SFN	MLB	27	380	49	18	2	4	24	24	44	14	6	6.4	.264	.316	.361	-.100	.263	.316	.367	.240	-1.0	66-CF 1 19-RF -1
2006	*SFN*	*MLB*	*28*	*342*	*43*	*16*	*2*	*4*	*31*	*22*	*46*	*9*	*4*	*5.6*	*.264*	*.318*	*.365*	*-.121*	*.266*	*.320*	*.382*	*.239*	*1.1*	*83-CF 0*

Breakout: 24% Improve: 42% Collapse: 32% Attrition: 28% Comparables: *Gene Clines, Keith Miller, Manny Mota*

In last year's annual, we said Jason Ellison was, "fifth outfielder material at best," and then he went all Bonds on us in April (1200 OPS). The rest of the way he hit .243/.297/.322, matching those modest original expectations. With Finley's acquisition, the Giants have a more famous reserve center fielder, so Ellison is likely to return to Fresno or visit the waiver wire.

PEDRO FELIZ				3B/LF					Bats: R Throws: R				Height: 6' 1"		Weight: 180		Born: April 27, 1975		Age: 31		
YEAR	TM	LVL	AGE	PA	R	2B	3B	HR	RBI	BB	SO	SB	CS	SPEED	BA	OBP	SLG	MLVR	EQBA	EQOBP	EQSLG	EQA	VORP	DEFENSE
2003	SFN	MLB	28	248	31	9	3	16	48	10	53	2	2	5.4	.247	.278	.515	.029	.247	.278	.523	.262	6.4	33-3B 2 10-LF 0
2004	SFN	MLB	29	531	72	33	3	22	84	23	85	5	2	5.1	.276	.305	.485	.040	.269	.299	.475	.260	12.9	60-1B -1 38-3B 2
2005	SFN	MLB	30	614	69	30	4	20	81	38	102	0	2	4.1	.250	.295	.422	-.056	.245	.294	.425	.245	-1.0	66-3B 2 69-LF -6
2006	*SFN*	*MLB*	*31*	*452*	*54*	*23*	*2*	*16*	*64*	*25*	*77*	*2*	*2*	*4.3*	*.263*	*.307*	*.446*	*-.032*	*.265*	*.310*	*.466*	*.254*	*8.3*	*107-3B -3*

Breakout: 22% Improve: 50% Collapse: 33% Attrition: 22% Comparables: *Rip Repulski, Mike Shannon, Wally Post*

The Giants kept insisting that Feliz would become the full package if only he got a season's worth of plate appearances. Now they're saying that he can't handle the defensive yo-yoing from first to third to left and that's why he's yet to break out. The truth is that he can't take a walk and he struggles against right-handed pitchers. A .295 OBP is a high price to pay for 20 home runs. With Edgar Alfonzo gone to Anaheim, Feliz will become the full-time third baseman, where his glove, at least, will make him more of an asset.

KEVIN FRANDSEN				2B					Bats: R Throws: R				Height: 6' 0"		Weight: 175		Born: May 24, 1982		Age: 24		
YEAR	TM	LVL	AGE	PA	R	2B	3B	HR	RBI	BB	SO	SB	CS	SPEED	BA	OBP	SLG	MLVR	EQBA	EQOBP	EQSLG	EQA	VORP	DEFENSE
2004	SLO	A-	22	111	22	5	0	3	14	9	9	0	1	4.5	.296	.369	.439	.153	.239	.286	.360	.224	-3.3	19-2B 4
2005	SJO	A+	23	333	57	22	3	2	40	26	22	13	11	5.5	.351	.429	.467	.328	.313	.371	.397	.268	18.0	60-2B -1 14-SS -1
2005	NRW	AA	23	140	22	8	0	2	20	4	14	7	3	6.4	.287	.336	.395	.055	.269	.314	.383	.247	1.7	26-2B 1
2005	FRE	AAA	23	98	18	10	1	2	16	2	5	1	1	4.8	.351	.378	.543	.322	.333	.347	.518	.286	9.2	20-2B 1
2006	*SFN*	*MLB*	*24*	*554*	*72*	*31*	*3*	*6*	*57*	*27*	*49*	*15*	*7*	*4.7*	*.288*	*.333*	*.395*	*-.037*	*.290*	*.336*	*.413*	*.254*	*18.6*	*130-2B 1*

Breakout: 18% Improve: 46% Collapse: 23% Attrition: 5% Comparables: *Freddy Sanchez, Jose Lind, Ruben Salazar*

The Giants love Frandsen and it's not just because he's unfailingly polite and always remembers to bring enough chewing gum for everyone. He makes excellent contact, has an even line-drive stroke, and he's more than capable of playing second at higher levels. Comparisons to Robby Thompson abound, but they are not really apt. Frandsen probably won't field as well as Thompson did, and he definitely won't have the same kind of power. He can make up for some of that with a much better batting average, but he's a future starter, not a future star.

MARQUIS GRISSOM **CF** **Bats: R Throws: R** Height: 5′ 11″ Weight: 188 Born: April 17, 1967 Age: 39

YEAR	TM	LVL	AGE	PA	R	2B	3B	HR	RBI	BB	SO	SB	CS	SPEED	BA	OBP	SLG	MLVR	EQBA	EQOBP	EQSLG	EQA	VORP	DEFENSE
2003	SFN	MLB	36	615	82	33	3	20	79	20	82	11	3	5.9	.300	.322	.468	.087	.298	.320	.469	.268	27.5	139-CF -12
2004	SFN	MLB	37	604	78	26	2	22	90	37	83	3	1	4.6	.279	.323	.450	.027	.273	.317	.440	.259	16.2	136-CF -6
2005	SFN	MLB	38	145	8	4	0	2	15	7	18	1	1	3.1	.212	.248	.285	-.353	.212	.253	.277	.192	-9.5	32-CF -3
2006	CHN	MLB	39	183	16	8	1	4	21	10	27	1	0	4.5	.247	.292	.376	-.163	.248	.293	.382	.225	-2.5	47-CF -3

Breakout: 5% Improve: 29% Collapse: 49% Attrition: 49% Comparables: Felipe Alou, Hank Bauer, Ken Griffey Sr.

From 2002–2004 Marquis had a 926 OPS against LHPs; Dusty Baker noticed and threw Grissom a minor league contract. Or maybe he just can't relate to those crazy long-haired kids and wanted to have someone around who remembers what disco was like.

TRAVIS ISHIKAWA **1B** **Bats: L Throws: L** Height: 6′ 3″ Weight: 190 Born: September 24, 1983 Age: 22

YEAR	TM	LVL	AGE	PA	R	2B	3B	HR	RBI	BB	SO	SB	CS	SPEED	BA	OBP	SLG	MLVR	EQBA	EQOBP	EQSLG	EQA	VORP	DEFENSE
2003	SLO	A-	19	298	53	17	4	3	31	44	77	0	0	5.3	.254	.376	.391	.106	.223	.314	.353	.237	-17.3	66-1B 8
2003	HAG	A	19	231	20	5	0	3	22	33	69	3	4	3.1	.206	.329	.278	-.110	.181	.277	.255	.198	-23.5	57-1B 2
2004	HAG	A	20	415	59	19	2	15	54	45	110	10	5	5.0	.257	.357	.447	.103	.223	.299	.380	.237	-12.9	95-1B 9
2005	SJO	A+	21	514	87	28	7	22	79	70	129	1	4	5.0	.282	.387	.532	.270	.245	.333	.427	.261	4.5	125-1B 13
2006	SFN	MLB	22	474	55	25	3	12	54	49	132	3	2	4.5	.229	.314	.390	-.119	.231	.316	.408	.243	-4.9	112-1B 6

Breakout: 28% Improve: 56% Collapse: 27% Attrition: 3% Comparables: Pete Paciorek, A. J. Zapp, Bradley Hawpe

Ishikawa finally showed the power that the Giants were waiting for, but he also struck out in about 30% of plate his appearances. Sometimes strikeouts are a predictor of power in a player's future, and sometimes it just means you can't catch up to a fastball. Time will tell just which shade of foreshadowing Ishikawa's strikeouts represent. One good sign is his reverse platoon split; he actually hit better against lefties than righties. There's no doubt about his fielding; he's almost a Gold Glove quality defender right now. The team will give him the starting job at Double-A next year to see what he can do against tougher competition.

JUSTIN KNOEDLER **C** **Bats: R Throws: R** Height: 6′ 2″ Weight: 210 Born: July 17, 1980 Age: 25

YEAR	TM	LVL	AGE	PA	R	2B	3B	HR	RBI	BB	SO	SB	CS	SPEED	BA	OBP	SLG	MLVR	EQBA	EQOBP	EQSLG	EQA	VORP	DEFENSE
2003	SJO	A+	22	396	48	25	2	10	43	35	78	13	3	5.5	.257	.326	.424	.043	.227	.285	.371	.232	-6.5	96-C 8
2004	NRW	AA	23	454	64	28	3	9	47	32	98	5	3	5.2	.274	.335	.423	.054	.260	.313	.399	.247	7.2	102-C 3
2005	FRE	AAA	24	322	35	19	1	4	32	26	61	5	5	5.1	.272	.345	.387	-.057	.250	.313	.351	.233	-1.4	77-C 6
2006	SFN	MLB	25	271	29	14	1	5	29	18	54	4	2	5.0	.244	.304	.376	-.145	.246	.306	.393	.235	2.0	67-C 2

Breakout: 26% Improve: 42% Collapse: 34% Attrition: 28% Comparables: A. J. Hinch, Steve Swisher, Chris Turner

Knoedler is fantastic behind the plate and has a cannon for an arm, but it doesn't look like he will hit enough to be a starter in the majors. At press time it looked like the Giants would leave Knoedler in Triple-A to get at-bats, but he could easily enough be flipped with Haad and become Matheny's backup.

FRED LEWIS **CF** **Bats: L Throws: R** Height: 6′ 2″ Weight: 190 Born: December 9, 1980 Age: 25

YEAR	TM	LVL	AGE	PA	R	2B	3B	HR	RBI	BB	SO	SB	CS	SPEED	BA	OBP	SLG	MLVR	EQBA	EQOBP	EQSLG	EQA	VORP	DEFENSE	
2003	HAG	A	22	496	61	17	8	1	27	68	112	30	15	7.0	.250	.361	.336	.028	.222	.308	.300	.224	-20.3	107-CF -1	
2004	SJO	A+	23	538	88	20	11	8	57	84	109	33	14	7.3	.301	.424	.451	.276	.265	.363	.380	.266	14.7	112-CF -1	
2005	NRW	AA	24	588	79	28	7	7	47	69	124	30	13	6.7	.273	.361	.396	.087	.256	.336	.371	.253	5.6	63-CF -2	62-LF -1
2006	SFN	MLB	25	483	61	22	5	5	39	48	110	15	6	5.5	.248	.329	.357	-.123	.250	.332	.373	.244	0.9	114-CF -1	

Breakout: 14% Improve: 38% Collapse: 33% Attrition: 15% Comparables: Rich Becker, Bill Mott, Mike Darr

(continued next page)

Fred Lewis (continued)

In April and May, Lewis hit a combined .210/.289/.304. The rest of the way he went .308/.397/.447. Lewis spent so much time fixing his swing in the batting cage at Norwich that the team joked about naming it after him. Because of his 2004 breakthrough, the second half of '05 seems more like the real Lewis. One concern is that the Giants moved him from center to left so he could concentrate on getting out of his slump. In so doing, they diminished his offensive value. It doesn't help that he's already 25; he needs to move back to center to retain what prospect status he has, and doing a better job hanging in against lefties couldn't hurt. He hit .234/.331/.340 against them, versus .288/.372/.418 against righties.

TODD LINDEN RF Bats: B Throws: R Height: 6' 3" Weight: 210 Born: June 30, 1980 Age: 26

YEAR	TM	LVL	AGE	PA	R	2B	3B	HR	RBI	BB	SO	SB	CS	SPEED	BA	OBP	SLG	MLVR	EQBA	EQOBP	EQSLG	EQA	VORP	DEFENSE			
2003	FRE	AAA	23	528	75	24	3	11	56	40	105	14	4	5.7	.278	.356	.412	.045	.256	.328	.388	.252	-5.7	106-RF	-11	11-CF	0
2004	FRE	AAA	24	564	93	28	2	23	75	63	149	8	6	5.2	.260	.349	.466	.018	.226	.311	.388	.244	-13.7	105-RF	-1	14-LF	1
2005	FRE	AAA	25	414	81	25	4	30	80	62	97	6	2	4.7	.321	.437	.682	.575	.280	.384	.563	.312	34.0	86-RF	-8		
2005	SFN	MLB	25	186	20	8	0	4	13	10	54	3	0	5.0	.216	.280	.333	-.218	.215	.278	.337	.220	-6.7	36-RF	0		
2006	SFN	MLB	26	513	65	26	2	18	67	51	125	7	3	4.8	.252	.335	.436	-.009	.254	.338	.456	.265	7.4	121-RF	-4		

Breakout: 20% Improve: 48% Collapse: 19% Attrition: 10% Comparables: Joe Borchard, Melvin Nieves, Jim Hickman

Long rumored to be someone with a future, Linden had his first outstanding season since his time at Double-A Shreveport in 2002; his .682 slugging rate led all minor leaguers. He was also a true switch-hitter, slugging .623 vs. RHPs and .852 against lefties. Unfortunately, he looked totally lost during 187 plate appearances in the majors. Sometimes it takes a while to adjust to major league pitching, but Linden has now had three consecutive auditions, and none were very promising. In his third pass through the PCL, Linden's walk rate was quite strong, but his judgment collapsed after his promotion. Felipe Alou must give off some anti-walk pheromone: only five times in his 13-year managing career has one of his players—Barry Bonds aside—drawn more than 60 walks in a season. Thirty-six have done it for Bobby Cox during the same period, 34 for Tony LaRussa, 31 for Joe Torre, and even 19 did it for Dusty Baker, who feels the same way about walks as Joan Crawford did about wire hangers (again, not counting his time with Bonds).

EDDY MARTINEZ-ESTEVE LF Bats: R Throws: R Height: 6' 2" Weight: 215 Born: July 14, 1983 Age: 22

YEAR	TM	LVL	AGE	PA	R	2B	3B	HR	RBI	BB	SO	SB	CS	SPEED	BA	OBP	SLG	MLVR	EQBA	EQOBP	EQSLG	EQA	VORP	DEFENSE	
2004	HAG	A	20	56	4	1	1	1	11	8	8	1	1	4.2	.217	.339	.348	-.077	.198	.296	.326	.225	-2.5		
2004	SJO	A+	20	74	11	7	2	0	14	4	9	0	1	4.9	.420	.446	.580	.658	.379	.400	.499	.303	8.4		
2005	SJO	A+	21	579	89	44	3	17	94	89	82	4	2	4.1	.313	.427	.524	.364	.275	.372	.434	.281	16.9	25-LF	0
2006	SFN	MLB	22	552	68	32	2	11	65	58	92	3	2	4.1	.264	.345	.410	-.015	.266	.348	.429	.263	8.3	130-LF	-1

Breakout: 14% Improve: 40% Collapse: 28% Attrition: 8% Comparables: Rusty Keith, Garrett Atkins, Conor Jackson

Eddy was an extra-base hitting machine in San Jose this year, and the only thing holding him back from a promotion to Double-A was his shoulder. He had labrum surgery in his throwing arm in the off-season and wasn't capable of playing the field until the last two months of the minor league's shorter season. Even with a healthy arm, though, EME isn't considered a potential asset in left field. A trade to an AL team might be good for Martinez-Esteve but bad for the Giants, who don't have a lot of hitters of this quality in their system.

MIKE MATHENY C Bats: R Throws: R Height: 6' 3" Weight: 205 Born: September 22, 1970 Age: 35

YEAR	TM	LVL	AGE	PA	R	2B	3B	HR	RBI	BB	SO	SB	CS	SPEED	BA	OBP	SLG	MLVR	EQBA	EQOBP	EQSLG	EQA	VORP	DEFENSE	
2003	SLN	MLB	32	490	43	18	2	8	47	44	81	1	1	4.0	.252	.320	.356	-.103	.252	.321	.362	.241	2.2	121-C	2
2004	SLN	MLB	33	414	28	22	1	5	50	23	83	0	2	3.2	.247	.292	.348	-.171	.247	.293	.353	.225	-5.5	109-C	10
2005	SFN	MLB	34	482	42	34	0	13	59	29	91	0	2	2.8	.242	.295	.406	-.084	.239	.293	.412	.241	5.7	126-C	6
2006	SFN	MLB	35	294	27	15	1	7	34	17	55	0	1	3.3	.248	.297	.384	-.144	.250	.299	.401	.232	2.0	72-C	1

Breakout: 21% Improve: 44% Collapse: 30% Attrition: 36% Comparables: John Flaherty, Joe Oliver, Benito Santiago

The pathetic batting average and on-base percentage were expected, as was the outstanding defense. Matheny's power spike was surprising, though. His career ISO through 2004 was .097; last year he notched a .164 figure with 13 home runs and 34 doubles. If he keeps smacking the ball hard he could ALMOST be worth the $9.5 million the team is going to pay him the next two years. Also, peace could break out in the Middle East and the dodo and the great auk might hold a reunion tour.

LANCE NIEKRO 1B Bats: R Throws: R Height: 6' 3" Weight: 210 Born: January 29, 1979 Age: 27

YEAR	TM	LVL	AGE	PA	R	2B	3B	HR	RBI	BB	SO	SB	CS	SPEED	BA	OBP	SLG	MLVR	EQBA	EQOBP	EQSLG	EQA	VORP	DEFENSE			
2003	FRE	AAA	24	404	43	15	2	4	41	19	39	3	3	4.0	.302	.334	.383	-.014	.275	.311	.350	.232	0.2	71-3B	-4	16-1B	1
2004	FRE	AAA	25	258	42	21	4	12	47	14	32	1	1	5.2	.298	.337	.566	.182	.258	.296	.471	.256	2.6	34-1B	-1	20-3B	1
2005	SFN	MLB	26	302	32	16	3	12	46	17	53	0	2	3.9	.252	.295	.460	-.002	.249	.294	.466	.255	2.0	59-1B	6		
2006	*SFN*	*MLB*	*27*	*266*	*31*	*14*	*2*	*8*	*37*	*15*	*40*	*1*	*1*	*4.5*	*.268*	*.312*	*.441*	*-.027*	*.270*	*.315*	*.460*	*.255*	*3.8*	*65-1B*	*3*		

Breakout: 27% Improve: 49% Collapse: 33% Attrition: 33% Comparables: Ricky Jordan, Andy Kosco, Tom Paciorek

The Giants were right, Niekro does have some pop in that bat, but he slumped hard as the year went on—882 OPS before the All-Star Game, .572 after. More worrisome than that, though, was his 587 OPS against righties, which suggests he may need a platoon partner to have value. Sabean says he's looking for a free agent first baseman, so Niekro is probably a backup/pinch hitter next year. Since Will Clark left, Giants first basemen have batted .266/.344/.432, ranking 15th, 13th, and 16th in the NL those categories respectively. New reserve first baseman Mark Sweeney will help those numbers by keeping Niekro on the bench against those scary righties.

DAN ORTMEIER RF Bats: B Throws: L Height: 6' 4" Weight: 220 Born: May 11, 1981 Age: 25

YEAR	TM	LVL	AGE	PA	R	2B	3B	HR	RBI	BB	SO	SB	CS	SPEED	BA	OBP	SLG	MLVR	EQBA	EQOBP	EQSLG	EQA	VORP	DEFENSE	
2003	SJO	A+	22	460	62	32	6	8	56	39	89	13	6	5.7	.304	.378	.471	.240	.276	.337	.422	.262	5.1	71-RF	-2
2004	NRW	AA	23	439	55	23	6	10	48	47	110	18	2	7.0	.252	.353	.424	.069	.238	.326	.395	.257	-5.6	98-RF	7
2005	NRW	AA	24	575	85	23	6	20	79	48	115	35	12	7.3	.274	.360	.463	.172	.254	.328	.425	.263	1.5	124-RF	7
2005	SFN	MLB	24	26	1	0	0	0	1	3	5	1	0	3.2	.136	.269	.136	-.516	.136	.269	.136	.179	-2.5		
2006	*SFN*	*MLB*	*25*	*517*	*69*	*27*	*4*	*13*	*57*	*44*	*116*	*18*	*6*	*5.7*	*.253*	*.327*	*.412*	*-.051*	*.255*	*.330*	*.431*	*.258*	*3.7*	*122-RF*	*4*

Breakout: 21% Improve: 50% Collapse: 21% Attrition: 10% Comparables: Shawn Garrett, Jason Bay, Todd Linden

Ortmeier went 20-20, which is pretty rare in the Eastern League, though not necessarily telling—the last two guys to do it, Marlon Byrd and Todd Dunwoody, haven't exactly set the world on fire since. You could also be concerned about whether or not he'll hit right-handers at higher levels, since he only batted .255/.337/.445 against them in Double-A. Still, Ortmeier had a good year, especially when he spent half his season hitting in the expansive pasturage of Norwich's Dodd Stadium. (No truth to the rumor that the club added a submarine to its logo because the park torpedoes offense.) Like the vast majority of players in the organization, Ortmeier could stand to gain some walks, but the Giants love his work ethic, and he was having a good AFL before being shut down with a sore wrist.

MARCUS SANDERS SS Bats: R Throws: R Height: 6' 0" Weight: 160 Born: August 25, 1985 Age: 20

YEAR	TM	LVL	AGE	PA	R	2B	3B	HR	RBI	BB	SO	SB	CS	SPEED	BA	OBP	SLG	MLVR	EQBA	EQOBP	EQSLG	EQA	VORP	DEFENSE	
2005	AUG	A	19	501	86	19	4	5	40	69	90	57	9	7.9	.300	.407	.400	.173	.267	.354	.356	.265	15.4	107-SS	0
2006	*SFN*	*MLB*	*20*	*505*	*69*	*23*	*5*	*5*	*39*	*46*	*96*	*30*	*10*	*6.2*	*.246*	*.321*	*.356*	*-.138*	*.248*	*.324*	*.372*	*.244*	*10.0*	*119-SS*	*0*

Breakout: 10% Improve: 33% Collapse: 33% Attrition: 7% Comparables: Travis Dawkins, Elliot Johnson, Gregor Blanco

The system's best position prospect, Sanders has the hands and range for short, but there are concerns that high school shoulder surgery left him without enough arm strength for the position. There's also a concern that the shoulder might impinge on his developing power. After the season the docs went in again. Depending on how the surgery turns out, Sanders could stay at short, though a move to second or center is more likely. There must be something about the surname Sanders that makes one really fast; Barry, Deion—heck, Winnie the Pooh lived under the name of Sanders because when the honey bees got after him he could really hustle. Marcus is no exception. Not only does he have speed, he has discernment, posting an 86% stolen base success rate. He's also discerning at the plate, making him the rare prototypical leadoff hitter who walks like a leadoff hitter should. He's a prospect, but the shoulder keeps him out of the "strong buy" category.

NATE SCHIERHOLTZ RF Bats: L Throws: R Height: 6' 2" Weight: 215 Born: February 15, 1984 Age: 22

YEAR	TM	LVL	AGE	PA	R	2B	3B	HR	RBI	BB	SO	SB	CS	SPEED	BA	OBP	SLG	MLVR	EQBA	EQOBP	EQSLG	EQA	VORP	DEFENSE			
2003	SLO	A-	19	144	23	6	2	3	29	12	15	0	1	4.5	.306	.382	.460	.241	.270	.324	.428	.257	9.1	31-3B	-1		
2004	HAG	A	20	261	41	22	0	15	54	19	52	1	0	3.6	.298	.356	.583	.322	.245	.292	.470	.257	8.4	54-3B	1		
2004	SJO	A+	20	278	39	18	9	3	31	15	41	3	1	6.2	.295	.338	.469	.152	.268	.304	.413	.246	5.5	35-3B	1	17-RF	-1
2005	SJO	A+	21	545	83	37	8	15	86	32	132	5	7	5.4	.319	.363	.514	.244	.287	.323	.439	.259	7.1	108-RF	5		
2006	*SFN*	*MLB*	*22*	*521*	*59*	*30*	*4*	*13*	*65*	*31*	*120*	*4*	*2*	*4.8*	*.256*	*.305*	*.413*	*-.086*	*.258*	*.307*	*.431*	*.244*	*0.0*	*123-RF*	*2*		

Breakout: 12% Improve: 38% Collapse: 26% Attrition: 6% Comparables: Josh Kroeger, Jeremy Dodson, Michael Ryan

(continued next page)

Nate Schierholtz *(continued)*

It's hard to hit homers in San Jose as a pull-hitting lefty, but still, people wanted more from Schierholtz than he delivered. His plate discipline also leaves much to be desired, and while half the scouts in the league will tell you not to worry, the other half say he'll be brutally exploited by pitchers at higher levels. Our translations say he had a good year in a tough environment, but that doesn't mean the nay-saying scouts are wrong about his ultimate fate as a free-swinger. His move from third base to right field had mixed results: his arm strength helped him lead the league in outfield assists, but bad breaks and bad routes made line-drives an adventure.

J. T. SNOW 1B **Bats: B Throws: L** Height: 6' 2" Weight: 205 Born: February 26, 1968 Age: 38

YEAR	TM	LVL	AGE	PA	R	2B	3B	HR	RBI	BB	SO	SB	CS	SPEED	BA	OBP	SLG	MLVR	EQBA	EQOBP	EQSLG	EQA	VORP	DEFENSE	
2003	SFN	MLB	35	395	48	18	3	8	51	55	55	1	2	4.5	.273	.387	.418	.108	.271	.382	.425	.283	12.4	91-1B	7
2004	SFN	MLB	36	415	62	32	1	12	60	58	61	4	0	5.4	.327	.429	.529	.347	.317	.419	.513	.321	38.6	88-1B	-1
2005	SFN	MLB	37	408	40	17	2	4	40	32	61	1	0	4.9	.275	.343	.365	-.032	.272	.341	.370	.252	0.7	93-1B	7
2006	BOS	MLB	38	285	34	15	1	6	34	24	43	1	1	5.1	.270	.336	.413	-.005	.268	.341	.421	.257	1.8	70-1B	1

Breakout: 0%   Improve: 14%   Collapse: 51%   Attrition: 30%   Comparables: David Segui, Ruben Sierra, Wally Joyner

After the 2004 season, the Giants were satisfied with Snow, He batted .375/.476/.638 from the end of June on, giving him just the second truly outstanding season of his career (the other came in 1997). His career averages before 2004 were .263/.353/.426, so when the Giants had to decide on his $2 million option for 2005, they had to pick which of two things Snow's spike represented. Was it an uncharacteristic hot streak, or a sudden transformation into Lou Gehrig? Doubtless there were some heated debates in the board room, but whatever magic elixir invigorated Snow in '04 had been used up. He's 38 now, and though he's still a defensive wizard he has little power and no value against lefties. The Giants passed on retaining him for another year, and the Red Sox, desperate for filler at first base, took him on for as a defensive replacement/tutor for Kevin Youkilis.

OMAR VIZQUEL SS **Bats: B Throws: R** Height: 5' 9" Weight: 180 Born: April 24, 1967 Age: 39

YEAR	TM	LVL	AGE	PA	R	2B	3B	HR	RBI	BB	SO	SB	CS	SPEED	BA	OBP	SLG	MLVR	EQBA	EQOBP	EQSLG	EQA	VORP	DEFENSE	
2003	CLE	MLB	36	280	43	13	2	2	19	29	20	8	3	5.8	.244	.321	.336	-.149	.246	.329	.339	.241	3.1	61-SS	7
2004	CLE	MLB	37	631	82	28	3	7	59	57	62	19	6	6.2	.291	.353	.388	-.025	.297	.363	.399	.271	26.3	138-SS	0
2005	SFN	MLB	38	631	66	28	4	3	45	56	58	24	10	6.2	.271	.341	.350	-.075	.270	.341	.354	.249	12.3	145-SS	11
2006	SFN	MLB	39	477	61	21	2	4	40	41	47	12	6	5.2	.269	.334	.356	-.102	.271	.337	.372	.245	12.0	113-SS	4

Breakout: 13%   Improve: 44%   Collapse: 20%   Attrition: 7%   Comparables: Maury Wills, Pee Wee Reese, Ozzie Smith

Vizquel made a great first impression in San Francisco, and that was enough to keep Giants fans singing his praises long after his weaknesses were exposed. He was hot in April, sporting a nifty 845 OPS and stealing seven bases in seven tries, but he managed only a 663 OPS and 17 steals in 27 attempts the rest of the way. Give Giants scouts credit, though, because Vizquel is still handy with the leather. Vizquel might work for another year, but things could also fall apart in a hurry, as only six shortstops have played a full season at the position at age 39 or older, and just two of those, Honus Wagner and Ozzie Smith, retained anything like his youthful ability in the field.

RANDY WINN LF/CF **Bats: B Throws: R** Height: 6' 2" Weight: 175 Born: June 9, 1974 Age: 32

YEAR	TM	LVL	AGE	PA	R	2B	3B	HR	RBI	BB	SO	SB	CS	SPEED	BA	OBP	SLG	MLVR	EQBA	EQOBP	EQSLG	EQA	VORP	DEFENSE			
2003	SEA	MLB	29	654	103	37	4	11	75	41	108	23	5	7.1	.295	.346	.425	.051	.303	.357	.443	.279	18.1	134-LF	-5	17-CF	3
2004	SEA	MLB	30	694	84	34	6	14	81	53	98	21	7	6.3	.286	.346	.427	.035	.293	.354	.438	.276	25.0	119-CF	-1	32-LF	0
2005	SEA	MLB	31	430	46	25	1	6	37	37	53	12	6	5.6	.275	.342	.391	-.007	.290	.363	.420	.273	7.0	90-LF	6		
2005	SFN	MLB	31	243	39	22	5	14	26	11	38	7	5	6.7	.359	.391	.680	.559	.352	.386	.674	.329	37.7	55-CF	2		
2006	SFN	MLB	32	613	89	34	4	13	70	44	85	16	6	5.7	.293	.348	.439	.051	.295	.351	.459	.272	22.1	143-LF	-2		

Breakout: 12%   Improve: 37%   Collapse: 25%   Attrition: 4%   Comparables: Larry Herndon, Roberto Kelly, Brian Jordan

Give Sabean credit where it's due. He nabbed Winn at the trade deadline for Yorvit Torrealba, a very unhappy backup catcher, and Jesse Foppert, a prospect very slowly recovering from Tommy John surgery. At the time of the trade, Winn was supposed to be a .283/.343/.408 hitter with a suspect defensive reputation, but that's not what came in the mail from Seattle. We'd love to explain away his Mickey Mantle impression down the stretch as a small sample size problem or his being an unknown to NL pitchers, but his 243 PAs should have been more than enough to wash out any surprises, especially in the cavern the Giants call home. It's virtually impossible to expect Winn to replicate what he did last year. Rumor has it that the team is already negotiating a long-term deal with Winn, and knowing Sabean, Winn will have job security not only through the rest of Bush II, but through the Hillary Clinton and Jeb Bush administrations as well.

PITCHERS

JEREMY ACCARDO   Bats: R   Throws: R   Height: 6′ 2″   Weight: 190   Born: December 8, 1981   Age: 24

YEAR	TM	LVL	AGE	W	L	SV	G	GS	IP	H	BB	SO	HR	GB%	BABIP	STUFF	WHIP	ERA	PERA	EQERA	EQH9	EQBB9	EQSO9	EQHR9	VORP	WXRL
2004	SJO	A+	22	1	2	27	50	0	55.0	57	15	43	3	—	.310	-19	1.31	4.25	4.92	6.28	9.8	3.2	4.4	1.0	-4.0	—
2005	FRE	AAA	23	2	0	3	25	0	32.3	25	10	30	0	48%	.287	9	1.08	1.95	3.45	2.59	7.8	2.9	6.3	0.3	10.5	—
2005	SFN	MLB	23	1	5	0	28	0	29.7	26	9	16	2	42%	.255	-6	1.18	3.94	4.03	4.03	8.7	2.5	4.7	0.6	5.0	-0.0
2006	*SFN*	*MLB*	*24*	*2*	*3*	*2*	*54*	*1*	*51.3*	*54*	*18*	*33*	*5*	*49%*	*.300*	*-4*	*1.41*	*4.38*	*4.78*	*4.97*	*9.4*	*2.9*	*5.4*	*0.9*	*3.6*	*0.3*

Breakout: 15%   Improve: 37%   Collapse: 32%   Attrition: 17%   Comparables: Tom Walker, Elias Sosa, Rick Baldwin

Accardo finally made The Show on the basis of a mid-90s fastball, a developing slider, and a filthy cutter that some scouts compare to Mariano Rivera's bat-sawing Frisbee. An undrafted free agent in 2003, he has the potential to be the Giants' top setup man by the end of 2006. Quality bullpens are built with scouting finds like this one, not millionaire mediocrities.

CHRIS BEGG   Bats: R   Throws: R   Height: 6′ 4″   Weight: 195   Born: September 12, 1979   Age: 26

YEAR	TM	LVL	AGE	W	L	SV	G	GS	IP	H	BB	SO	HR	GB%	BABIP	STUFF	WHIP	ERA	PERA	EQERA	EQH9	EQBB9	EQSO9	EQHR9	VORP	WXRL
2003	SJO	A+	23	4	1	0	7	5	39.0	30	4	21	3	—	.220	-4	0.87	1.15	5.15	2.70	8.6	1.2	2.9	1.5	11.8	—
2003	NRW	AA	23	2	1	0	4	4	24.7	31	13	13	2	—	.322	-18	1.78	4.37	6.29	5.92	10.7	5.5	3.7	1.5	-0.9	—
2004	NRW	AA	24	9	1	0	16	14	94.0	87	11	61	3	—	.288	18	1.04	2.30	3.56	4.05	9.1	1.2	4.1	0.4	15.7	—
2004	FRE	AAA	24	2	5	0	9	9	41.3	55	18	17	10	—	.310	-41	1.77	6.97	7.46	7.02	11.6	4.4	2.9	2.4	-6.5	—
2005	NRW	AA	25	8	7	0	23	21	138.0	142	23	86	9	60%	.302	0	1.20	3.07	4.58	5.25	9.8	1.9	3.6	0.9	5.2	—
2006	*PIT*	*MLB*	*26*	*6*	*9*	*0*	*30*	*19*	*121.7*	*145*	*34*	*54*	*15*	*53%*	*.305*	*-7*	*1.47*	*5.18*	*5.34*	*5.66*	*10.5*	*2.3*	*3.7*	*1.1*	*-0.3*	*0.7*

Breakout: 8%   Improve: 27%   Collapse: 31%   Attrition: 2%   Comparables: Nate Bump, John Doherty, Heath Totten

Begg went begging after the draft, bouncing around three different independent leagues before getting his shot with the Giants. He's a four-pitch righty with mediocre stuff who needs pinpoint control to succeed. He didn't have that control in 2004, so the team sent him down to Double-A in '05 to see if that would help. He did put things back together again, but does the team really want a right-handed Kirk Rueter whose stuff is even more marginal?

ARMANDO BENITEZ   Bats: R   Throws: R   Height: 6′ 4″   Weight: 220   Born: November 3, 1972   Age: 33

YEAR	TM	LVL	AGE	W	L	SV	G	GS	IP	H	BB	SO	HR	GB%	BABIP	STUFF	WHIP	ERA	PERA	EQERA	EQH9	EQBB9	EQSO9	EQHR9	VORP	WXRL
2003	NYN	MLB	30	3	3	21	45	0	49.3	41	24	50	5	45%	.279	11	1.32	3.10	4.04	3.49	7.7	4.0	8.3	0.9	12.6	1.1
2003	SEA	MLB	30	0	0	0	15	0	14.3	10	11	15	1	31%	.243	8	1.47	3.15	4.50	3.21	7.1	7.1	9.6	0.6	4.7	-0.2
2004	FLO	MLB	31	2	2	47	64	0	69.7	36	21	62	6	32%	.178	16	0.82	1.29	3.70	1.78	6.3	2.6	7.5	0.8	32.8	6.2
2005	SFN	MLB	32	2	3	19	30	0	30.0	25	16	23	5	33%	.247	-12	1.37	4.50	5.52	4.91	8.3	4.6	6.4	1.5	1.5	0.7
2006	*SFN*	*MLB*	*33*	*2*	*4*	*14*	*37*	*0*	*42.7*	*38*	*22*	*35*	*5*	*37%*	*.268*	*-3*	*1.40*	*4.40*	*4.71*	*5.13*	*7.9*	*4.2*	*6.9*	*1.1*	*3.2*	*0.4*

Breakout: 1%   Improve: 9%   Collapse: 68%   Attrition: 23%   Comparables: Scott Sullivan, Jose DeLeon, Turk Wendell

He was throwing junk in April, and then his hammy went sproing, putting him on the DL for most of the year. The Giants' front office would love to think of this as a good signing undone by bad luck, but there's more to it than that. In limited playing time, Benitez put up the worst strikeout rate of his career, and much like the rest of us, he's getting older. Benitez will probably still be an above-average reliever in 2006, but he won't be worth his three-year, $21 million deal.

MATT CAIN   Bats: R   Throws: R   Height: 6′ 3″   Weight: 180   Born: October 1, 1984   Age: 21

YEAR	TM	LVL	AGE	W	L	SV	G	GS	IP	H	BB	SO	HR	GB%	BABIP	STUFF	WHIP	ERA	PERA	EQERA	EQH9	EQBB9	EQSO9	EQHR9	VORP	WXRL
2003	HAG	A	18	4	4	0	14	14	74.0	57	24	90	5	—	.283	24	1.09	2.55	5.16	4.63	9.7	3.4	7.3	1.6	7.3	—
2004	SJO	A+	19	7	1	0	13	13	72.7	58	17	89	5	—	.301	29	1.03	1.86	4.33	4.46	8.7	2.6	7.3	1.2	8.7	—
2004	NRW	AA	19	6	4	0	15	15	86.0	73	40	72	7	—	.264	17	1.31	3.35	4.88	5.10	8.8	4.3	5.9	1.0	4.6	—
2005	FRE	AAA	20	10	5	0	26	26	145.7	118	73	176	22	33%	.280	20	1.31	4.39	4.94	4.69	8.2	4.4	8.6	1.5	14.4	—
2005	SFN	MLB	20	2	1	0	7	7	46.3	24	19	30	4	29%	.160	20	0.93	2.33	4.53	2.47	6.6	3.7	5.8	0.8	17.0	2.1
2006	*SFN*	*MLB*	*21*	*8*	*10*	*0*	*35*	*27*	*151.0*	*134*	*71*	*137*	*20*	*36%*	*.273*	*17*	*1.35*	*4.34*	*4.61*	*4.78*	*7.9*	*3.8*	*7.6*	*1.1*	*14.4*	*2.4*

Breakout: 10%   Improve: 38%   Collapse: 28%   Attrition: 1%   Comparables: Denny McLain, Gary Nolan, Oliver Perez

The second-youngest rookie in 2005 proved that he was worth the hype. Cain features a four-seamer that reaches 96 mph, and a hard-diving curve that's 15 mph slower and throws hitters way off balance. With those two pitches alone he was quite successful. If he figures out a decent change or slider—both of which come in way too fast and flat right now

(continued next page)

Matt Cain (continued)

to be consistently useful in games—he could be outstanding. The Giants have worked with him on the changeup, and if the coaching takes, he'll do more than just survive in the major leagues in '06. It's worth noting, however, that his 2005 major-league line is based almost entirely on starts against the ghastly offenses of the NL West.

KEVIN CORREIA   Bats: R   Throws: R   Height: 6' 3"   Weight: 200   Born: August 24, 1980   Age: 25

YEAR	TM	LVL	AGE	W	L	SV	G	GS	IP	H	BB	SO	HR	GB%	BABIP	STUFF	WHIP	ERA	PERA	EQERA	EQH9	EQBB9	EQSO9	EQHR9	VORP	WXRL
2003	NRW	AA	22	6	6	0	16	14	86.3	80	30	73	3	—	.293	17	1.27	3.65	4.16	4.80	8.5	3.6	5.9	0.5	7.5	—
2003	SFN	MLB	22	3	1	0	10	7	39.3	41	18	28	6	38%	.304	0	1.50	3.66	5.31	3.92	9.9	3.7	5.8	1.4	9.0	0.9
2004	FRE	AAA	23	3	7	0	29	16	105.3	118	35	70	12	—	.310	-10	1.45	4.53	5.06	5.31	9.7	3.3	4.5	1.1	3.4	—
2005	FRE	AAA	24	3	2	7	31	3	46.0	50	23	35	6	41%	.310	-26	1.59	6.07	5.76	7.35	9.9	4.6	5.0	1.4	-8.8	—
2005	SFN	MLB	24	2	5	0	16	11	58.3	61	31	44	12	36%	.293	-12	1.58	4.63	6.02	4.63	9.7	4.5	6.2	1.9	5.2	0.8
2006	SFN	MLB	25	3	5	1	32	9	63.0	66	28	43	9	42%	.289	-6	1.49	5.01	5.45	6.16	9.3	3.7	5.7	1.2	0.8	0.3

Breakout: 17%   Improve: 39%   Collapse: 28%   Attrition: 28%   Comparables: Joe Slusarski, Renie Martin, Joe Nathan

The organization tried to convert Correia into a reliever in Fresno so that he'd have a role on the 25-man roster, but that turned into a fiasco. When the starters started dropping like flies in mid-summer, Correia was brought up to the bigs and did what he does: pitch slightly better than replacement level. That's not a bad thing to have hanging out in Triple-A for emergencies, but if you're gunning for the postseason, you have to hope the emergencies are few and far between.

JON COUTLANGUS   Bats: L   Throws: L   Height: 6' 1"   Weight: 180   Born: October 21, 1980   Age: 25

YEAR	TM	LVL	AGE	W	L	SV	G	GS	IP	H	BB	SO	HR	GB%	BABIP	STUFF	WHIP	ERA	PERA	EQERA	EQH9	EQBB9	EQSO9	EQHR9	VORP	WXRL
2005	SJO	A+	24	4	0	3	50	0	77.0	64	29	79	3	56%	.318	-6	1.21	3.04	4.58	5.08	8.7	4.6	5.6	0.6	4.2	—
2006	SFN	MLB	25	2	3	0	29	4	51.0	56	32	33	6	52%	.306	-13	1.71	5.64	6.15	6.38	9.7	5.1	5.4	1.0	-3.7	-0.3

Breakout: 4%   Improve: 21%   Collapse: 44%   Attrition: 17%   Comparables: Charlie Manning, Carl Sadler, Pete Zamora

Coutlangus is not something illegal you do to another person with your tongue, but it should be. Coutlangus was really old for his level. He's got a good excuse, though, because until the very end of 2004, he was a light-hitting outfielder. The Giants are one of just a few teams who make all their failed positional prospects try the mound for a few weeks before showing them the door. For their trouble, they've now got a decent enough left-handed relief prospect. Considering what situational lefties make in the majors these days, it's a worthwhile investment.

SCOTT EYRE   Bats: L   Throws: L   Height: 6' 1"   Weight: 200   Born: May 30, 1972   Age: 34

YEAR	TM	LVL	AGE	W	L	SV	G	GS	IP	H	BB	SO	HR	GB%	BABIP	STUFF	WHIP	ERA	PERA	EQERA	EQH9	EQBB9	EQSO9	EQHR9	VORP	WXRL
2003	SFN	MLB	31	2	1	1	74	0	57.0	60	26	35	4	51%	.303	-7	1.51	3.32	4.42	3.95	9.6	3.6	5.1	0.6	12.6	1.7
2004	SFN	MLB	32	2	2	1	83	0	52.7	43	27	49	8	42%	.252	-2	1.33	4.10	4.70	4.35	8.0	4.4	7.5	1.2	7.7	1.2
2005	SFN	MLB	33	2	2	0	86	0	68.3	48	26	65	3	38%	.262	21	1.10	2.64	3.36	2.82	7.1	3.2	7.9	0.4	20.9	3.8
2006	CHN	MLB	34	3	3	3	71	0	61.3	60	28	52	8	42%	.291	-3	1.42	4.47	4.70	4.95	8.7	3.7	6.9	1.1	5.2	0.4

Breakout: 5%   Improve: 21%   Collapse: 59%   Attrition: 12%   Comparables: Mike Remlinger, Ricardo Rincon, Chuck McElroy

Eyre was second in the majors in Adjusted Runs Prevented and also second in inherited runners stranded, so his was truly one of the best relief seasons of 2005. This was largely because he seems to be figuring out how to get righties out. Right-handed OPS against Eyre by year: 2002: 831, 2003: 804, 2004: 759, 2005: 609. He's not a LOOGY anymore. He's a former starting pitcher, so we probably shouldn't be too surprised. Still, the contract the Cubs gave him, worth as much as $11 million over three years, is quite a bit of scratch to bet on a player with just one outstanding season in his career.

JEFF FASSERO   Bats: L   Throws: L   Height: 6' 1"   Weight: 195   Born: January 5, 1963   Age: 43

YEAR	TM	LVL	AGE	W	L	SV	G	GS	IP	H	BB	SO	HR	GB%	BABIP	STUFF	WHIP	ERA	PERA	EQERA	EQH9	EQBB9	EQSO9	EQHR9	VORP	WXRL
2003	SLN	MLB	40	1	7	3	62	6	77.7	93	34	55	17	44%	.314	-28	1.64	5.68	5.97	6.09	10.6	3.6	5.6	2.0	-3.1	-0.3
2004	COL	MLB	41	3	8	0	40	12	111.0	136	44	59	9	53%	.337	-3	1.62	5.51	4.55	5.26	9.8	3.1	4.1	0.6	3.1	0.9
2005	SFN	MLB	42	4	7	0	48	6	91.0	92	31	60	7	51%	.308	2	1.35	4.05	4.15	4.65	9.0	2.9	5.4	0.7	8.0	-0.5
2006	SFN	MLB	43	3	4	1	42	3	61.7	68	22	43	7	51%	.312	-11	1.46	4.94	5.15	7.66	9.8	2.9	5.9	1.0	0.7	0.1

Breakout: 24%   Improve: 41%   Collapse: 38%   Attrition: 30%   Comparables: Dennis Martinez, John Franco, Jim Kaat

Sometimes Sabean's geezer fetish nets a useful bit of well-aged meat instead of carrion. Fassero was miscast as an emergency starter six times (6.43 ERA), which makes his full-season line a lot uglier than it would be if he'd been limited to a short relief or LOOGY role. As a reliever, his ERA was 3.00, and he held lefties to .194/.286/.204 with no home runs in 93 at-bats. Fassero didn't reach the majors until he was 28, so you can't hold his getting some extra time at the back end of his career against him. Still, considering his age and the weak performances of recent years, there's a good chance he'll never do this well again.

LaTROY HAWKINS   **Bats: R Throws: R**   Height: 6′ 5″   Weight: 202   Born: December 21, 1972   Age: 33

YEAR	TM	LVL	AGE	W	L	SV	G	GS	IP	H	BB	SO	HR	GB%	BABIP	STUFF	WHIP	ERA	PERA	EQERA	EQH9	EQBB9	EQSO9	EQHR9	VORP	WXRL
2003	MIN	MLB	30	9	3	2	74	0	77.3	69	15	75	4	43%	.310	32	1.09	1.86	2.90	2.32	7.8	1.7	8.5	0.5	32.5	5.4
2004	CHN	MLB	31	5	4	25	77	0	82.0	72	14	69	10	43%	.270	9	1.05	2.63	3.81	3.02	8.3	1.5	6.8	1.0	25.4	2.3
2005	CHN	MLB	32	1	4	4	21	0	19.0	18	7	13	4	46%	.255	-12	1.32	3.32	5.79	4.34	9.2	3.4	5.8	1.9	2.6	-0.5
2005	SFN	MLB	32	1	4	2	45	0	37.3	40	17	30	3	46%	.325	0	1.53	4.10	4.26	4.26	9.2	3.8	6.4	0.7	4.9	-0.1
2006	*BAL*	*MLB*	*33*	*3*	*3*	*4*	*56*	*0*	*61.0*	*64*	*19*	*43*	*7*	*42%*	*.295*	*-1*	*1.35*	*4.12*	*4.38*	*4.45*	*9.2*	*2.7*	*6.3*	*1.0*	*8.2*	*0.7*

Breakout: 5%   Improve: 18%   Collapse: 49%   Attrition: 13%   Comparables: Mike Henneman, Dick Tidrow, Jeff Russell

Due to all the blather about Hawkins's inability to handle the 9th inning, we are often forced to remind ourselves that this guy is still a decent reliever. His walk rate was up in '05, but it's probably nothing to get too worried about. His second-half ERA dropped to 2.70 once he had washed the taste of Chicago—and Dusty Baker—out of his mouth. Hawkins is expensive for what he is, perhaps the reason he was traded, with cash, to the Orioles for Steve Kline. He still tops the list of Baseball Prospectus's favorite Hawkins, leading Andy (Padres, Yankees), Wynn (Indians), and Jim (Treasure Island).

BRAD HENNESSEY   **Bats: R Throws: R**   Height: 6′ 2″   Weight: 185   Born: February 7, 1980   Age: 26

YEAR	TM	LVL	AGE	W	L	SV	G	GS	IP	H	BB	SO	HR	GB%	BABIP	STUFF	WHIP	ERA	PERA	EQERA	EQH9	EQBB9	EQSO9	EQHR9	VORP	WXRL
2003	HAG	A	23	3	9	0	15	15	79.3	81	27	44	6	—	.279	-38	1.36	4.20	6.97	8.71	11.8	4.1	3.0	2.0	-25.0	—
2004	NRW	AA	24	5	5	0	18	18	101.0	106	34	55	8	—	.295	-11	1.39	3.56	5.46	5.09	10.3	3.5	3.4	1.1	5.5	—
2004	FRE	AAA	24	4	1	0	5	5	35.7	26	15	16	2	—	.214	-5	1.15	2.02	4.81	2.67	7.5	4.3	3.2	0.5	11.0	—
2004	SFN	MLB	24	2	2	0	7	7	34.3	42	15	25	2	50%	.345	6	1.66	4.99	4.08	5.86	9.9	3.6	5.6	0.5	-1.7	0.1
2005	FRE	AAA	25	4	2	0	11	11	67.7	75	22	46	7	49%	.315	-4	1.43	5.18	5.29	5.56	10.2	3.1	4.3	1.2	0.3	—
2005	SFN	MLB	25	5	8	0	21	21	118.3	127	52	64	15	49%	.294	-6	1.51	4.64	5.25	4.72	9.8	3.7	4.5	1.1	10.4	2.6
2006	*SFN*	*MLB*	*26*	*6*	*9*	*0*	*33*	*19*	*120.7*	*132*	*48*	*65*	*14*	*49%*	*.293*	*-7*	*1.49*	*4.95*	*5.38*	*5.98*	*9.7*	*3.3*	*4.5*	*1.0*	*1.6*	*0.8*

Breakout: 17%   Improve: 40%   Collapse: 31%   Attrition: 15%   Comparables: Fred Talbot, Don Stanhouse, Mike Williams

With those peripherals, Hennessey looks like sixth starter material: good enough to take starts when someone else goes down, but not good enough to be penciled into the rotation. To be a successful starter you either need to keep batters off base or be able to reach back and strike them out when you're in a jam. Hennessey does neither.

MATT KINNEY   **Bats: R Throws: R**   Height: 6′ 5″   Weight: 220   Born: December 16, 1976   Age: 29

YEAR	TM	LVL	AGE	W	L	SV	G	GS	IP	H	BB	SO	HR	GB%	BABIP	STUFF	WHIP	ERA	PERA	EQERA	EQH9	EQBB9	EQSO9	EQHR9	VORP	WXRL
2003	MIL	MLB	26	10	13	0	33	31	190.7	201	80	152	27	41%	.310	4	1.47	5.19	4.76	5.41	9.2	3.4	6.4	1.2	0.9	1.0
2004	MIL	MLB	27	3	4	0	32	6	62.3	77	23	52	8	35%	.352	0	1.60	5.78	4.36	5.48	10.1	3.0	6.5	1.0	-2.6	0.1
2005	FRE	AAA	28	7	8	0	19	19	114.0	117	45	110	18	38%	.327	-15	1.42	5.21	5.89	5.97	10.0	3.9	6.1	1.9	-4.5	—
2005	SFN	MLB	28	2	0	0	5	1	12.0	18	6	3	2	41%	.381	-34	2.00	6.00	6.57	5.84	12.4	4.4	2.2	1.5	-0.4	0.0
2006	*SFN*	*MLB*	*29*	*5*	*8*	*1*	*36*	*14*	*110.7*	*118*	*47*	*76*	*15*	*41%*	*.295*	*-3*	*1.49*	*5.08*	*5.54*	*5.66*	*9.5*	*3.5*	*5.8*	*1.2*	*0.6*	*0.6*

Breakout: 22%   Improve: 52%   Collapse: 19%   Attrition: 1%   Comparables: Bobby Bolin, Nerio Rodriguez, Storm Davis

Kinney has the raw stuff to be a useful pitcher, which is to say that if he ever learned to cut down mistakes—and the walks and homers that come from them—he'd be a great swingman or middle reliever. But that's a little like saying Us Weekly would be crucial reading if articles about which celebrities wear ugly clothes brought you closer to God. Kinney is always going to throw hard enough to make teams interested in him, but "hard" does not necessarily equal "good." This is, of course, a good rule for life as well as baseball.

NOAH LOWRY
Bats: L Throws: L Height: 6′ 2″ Weight: 190 Born: October 10, 1980 Age: 25

YEAR	TM	LVL	AGE	W	L	SV	G	GS	IP	H	BB	SO	HR	GB%	BABIP	STUFF	WHIP	ERA	PERA	EQERA	EQH9	EQBB9	EQSO9	EQHR9	VORP	WXRL
2003	NRW	AA	22	9	6	0	23	23	118.3	127	47	97	7	—	.318	3	1.47	4.72	4.86	5.79	9.5	4.1	5.7	1.0	-2.5	—
2004	FRE	AAA	23	7	5	0	17	17	89.3	98	28	73	9	—	.320	5	1.41	4.13	4.52	5.42	9.3	3.0	5.5	1.0	1.8	—
2004	SFN	MLB	23	6	0	0	16	14	92.0	91	28	72	10	43%	.300	18	1.29	3.82	4.03	3.93	8.8	2.5	6.3	0.9	18.3	2.3
2005	SFN	MLB	24	13	13	0	33	33	204.7	193	76	172	21	41%	.295	20	1.31	3.78	4.19	4.01	8.7	3.1	6.9	0.9	36.5	4.9
2006	*SFN*	*MLB*	*25*	*11*	*11*	*0*	*31*	*31*	*194.0*	*187*	*69*	*149*	*21*	*44%*	*.286*	*17*	*1.32*	*4.07*	*4.39*	*4.50*	*8.6*	*2.9*	*6.5*	*0.9*	*23.4*	*3.8*

Breakout: 11% Improve: 47% Collapse: 24% Attrition: 0% Comparables: Jim O'Toole, Alex Kellner, Sterling Hitchcock

Lowry was the most valuable Giants pitcher according to VORP, but that's damning him with faint praise. By that standard, Lowry was only the 42nd-best pitcher in the majors. In 2004 he relied almost exclusively on a filthy change, so for the first few months of 2005 hitters just waited on that pitch and tattooed it. When he added a curveball he could throw for strikes, he became unhittable, posting a 0.69 ERA in August, and a cumulative 2.43 ERA in the second half. He's still inconsistent, but he has the tools to be a good #3 or maybe even a #2 starter.

PAT MISCH
Bats: R Throws: L Height: 6′ 2″ Weight: 170 Born: August 18, 1981 Age: 24

YEAR	TM	LVL	AGE	W	L	SV	G	GS	IP	H	BB	SO	HR	GB%	BABIP	STUFF	WHIP	ERA	PERA	EQERA	EQH9	EQBB9	EQSO9	EQHR9	VORP	WXRL
2003	SLO	A-	21	7	5	0	14	14	86.7	78	20	61	3	—	.274	-3	1.13	2.18	5.14	6.34	9.7	2.7	3.5	1.0	-6.8	—
2004	NRW	AA	22	7	6	0	26	26	159.0	138	35	123	13	—	.271	9	1.09	3.00	4.50	4.44	9.1	2.2	5.2	1.1	19.6	—
2005	NRW	AA	23	4	2	0	9	9	61.3	63	7	43	7	45%	.306	0	1.14	3.52	5.01	4.85	10.2	1.2	4.2	1.5	4.9	—
2005	FRE	AAA	23	3	9	0	19	19	102.0	135	40	69	18	43%	.357	-25	1.72	6.35	6.22	6.84	11.4	3.5	4.5	1.8	-14.1	—
2006	*SFN*	*MLB*	*24*	*6*	*10*	*0*	*29*	*22*	*134.7*	*153*	*45*	*74*	*19*	*46%*	*.298*	*-2*	*1.47*	*5.20*	*5.59*	*5.69*	*10.1*	*2.8*	*4.6*	*1.3*	*-1.8*	*0.7*

Breakout: 18% Improve: 46% Collapse: 9% Attrition: 0% Comparables: Eddie Priest, Mike Bacsik, Bob Owchinko

Misch's mechanics got out of whack in Triple-A and he couldn't keep his fastball down. Since his fastball only gets up into the mid-80s, and he was throwing it in the PCL, a lot of his starts turned into batting practice. Demoted to Norwich, with its deep fences, he got everything together again. Now Misch must retake the Triple-A test. To paraphrase Sir Alec Guinness, "You must face Darth Fresno [dramatic pause] again." It's Fresno: you don't find the goodness still in it, you just have to beat it and get out. Guinness should have said that, too.

SCOTT MUNTER
Bats: R Throws: R Height: 6′ 6″ Weight: 235 Born: March 7, 1980 Age: 26

YEAR	TM	LVL	AGE	W	L	SV	G	GS	IP	H	BB	SO	HR	GB%	BABIP	STUFF	WHIP	ERA	PERA	EQERA	EQH9	EQBB9	EQSO9	EQHR9	VORP	WXRL
2003	HAG	A	23	3	5	5	40	0	68.7	61	28	47	3	—	.267	-32	1.30	2.36	5.89	6.61	10.2	4.9	3.6	1.1	-7.0	—
2004	NRW	AA	24	2	4	3	42	0	65.0	63	22	30	4	—	.280	-22	1.31	2.35	5.20	4.04	9.7	3.5	2.9	0.9	10.8	—
2005	SFN	MLB	25	2	0	0	45	0	38.7	40	12	11	1	64%	.298	-16	1.34	2.56	4.23	3.52	9.4	2.6	2.3	0.2	8.7	0.8
2006	*SFN*	*MLB*	*26*	*2*	*2*	*1*	*43*	*0*	*43.3*	*50*	*18*	*18*	*3*	*61%*	*.305*	*-17*	*1.55*	*4.38*	*4.97*	*5.13*	*10.2*	*3.4*	*3.5*	*0.6*	*2.6*	*0.2*

Breakout: 10% Improve: 37% Collapse: 33% Attrition: 32% Comparables: Braden Looper, Casey Cox, Jim Acker

Munter throws a heavy split-fingered fastball that dives hard and burrows until it strikes something valuable, like oil or a woodchuck hoarding czarist rubles. This led to 2005's fifth-highest G/F ratio, and makes Munter quite good at inducing double plays. But even bowling with that splitter, you'd like to see Munter miss bats occasionally; his strikeout rate is absurdly low. Last word at press time is that Munter's scoped elbow will be fine in time for camp.

KIRK RUETER
Bats: L Throws: L Height: 6′ 2″ Weight: 210 Born: December 1, 1970 Age: 35

YEAR	TM	LVL	AGE	W	L	SV	G	GS	IP	H	BB	SO	HR	GB%	BABIP	STUFF	WHIP	ERA	PERA	EQERA	EQH9	EQBB9	EQSO9	EQHR9	VORP	WXRL
2003	SFN	MLB	32	10	5	0	27	27	147.0	170	47	41	14	51%	.301	-11	1.48	4.53	5.07	5.38	10.6	2.7	2.3	0.9	16.0	3.2
2004	SFN	MLB	33	9	12	0	33	33	190.3	225	66	56	21	54%	.299	-11	1.53	4.73	5.19	4.81	10.3	2.8	2.4	0.9	16.3	2.7
2005	SFN	MLB	34	2	7	0	20	18	107.3	131	47	25	12	45%	.303	-24	1.66	5.96	5.67	6.33	10.8	3.7	1.9	1.0	-10.4	0.1
2006	*SFN*	*MLB*	*35*	*4*	*7*	*0*	*28*	*12*	*85.7*	*107*	*33*	*28*	*11*	*49%*	*.306*	*-24*	*1.63*	*5.69*	*6.16*	*6.78*	*11.1*	*3.1*	*2.8*	*1.1*	*-7.2*	*-0.2*

Breakout: 5% Improve: 28% Collapse: 40% Attrition: 19% Comparables: Bob Forsch, Terry Mulholland, Claude Osteen

It's hard to say how much of Rueter's collapse was due to all his nagging injuries, how much was just Father Time, and how much was Uncle You Can't Fool So Few Batters and Live. As is, few pitchers have won so many games (130 so far) with so little stuff. The Giants tried to be polite about showing him the door, but egos were bruised on both sides. If no one gives him a small deal as a fifth starter next year, you've got to hope that everyone can make nice for a Poor Kirk Rueter Day at SBC.

BILLY SADLER
Bats: R   Throws: R   Height: 6' 0"   Weight: 190   Born: September 21, 1981   Age: 24

YEAR	TM	LVL	AGE	W	L	SV	G	GS	IP	H	BB	SO	HR	GB%	BABIP	STUFF	WHIP	ERA	PERA	EQERA	EQH9	EQBB9	EQSO9	EQHR9	VORP	WXRL
2003	HAG	A	21	0	0	1	12	0	15.0	15	13	10	4	—	.239	-63	1.87	4.80	16.50	6.75	16.5	11.2	4.5	7.5	-1.5	—
2004	SJO	A+	22	2	2	0	30	3	56.7	29	40	66	1	—	.220	-7	1.22	2.38	5.36	4.47	6.6	9.1	7.0	0.4	6.3	—
2004	NRW	AA	22	0	3	0	17	0	30.3	22	18	24	3	—	.226	-18	1.32	3.86	6.04	5.40	8.6	6.0	5.4	1.3	0.6	—
2005	NRW	AA	23	6	5	5	47	0	84.3	64	33	81	4	44%	.269	0	1.15	3.31	4.74	4.74	8.4	4.3	6.0	0.7	7.6	—
2006	*SFN*	*MLB*	*24*	*2*	*4*	*0*	*30*	*5*	*57.3*	*61*	*39*	*40*	*9*	*44%*	*.292*	*-14*	*1.74*	*6.00*	*6.74*	*6.60*	*9.5*	*5.6*	*5.8*	*1.4*	*-5.8*	*-0.4*

Breakout: 4%   Improve: 15%   Collapse: 54%   Attrition: 8%   Comparables: Frank Francisco, Brian Sanches, Scott Dunn

Sadler, a college closer at LSU, is a flamethrower in every sense of the word: low to mid-90s velocity, and a tendency to self-immolate. He has proven relatively rubber-armed, although he was strangely bass-ackwards, holding left-handed hitters to a .144 clip while righties hit .260 against him. If he improves at getting his curve over for strikes, he could give the Giants a homegrown middleman sometime this summer.

JONATHAN SANCHEZ
Bats: L   Throws: L   Height: 6' 2"   Weight: 165   Born: November 19, 1982   Age: 23

YEAR	TM	LVL	AGE	W	L	SV	G	GS	IP	H	BB	SO	HR	GB%	BABIP	STUFF	WHIP	ERA	PERA	EQERA	EQH9	EQBB9	EQSO9	EQHR9	VORP	WXRL
2005	AUG	A	22	5	7	0	25	25	125.7	122	39	166	8	48%	.373	8	1.28	4.08	4.61	5.88	9.7	3.6	7.0	1.1	-3.8	—
2006	*SFN*	*MLB*	*23*	*6*	*9*	*0*	*25*	*21*	*120.0*	*118*	*64*	*93*	*16*	*46%*	*.287*	*7*	*1.51*	*5.00*	*5.38*	*5.52*	*8.8*	*4.3*	*6.5*	*1.1*	*1.0*	*0.9*

Breakout: 24%   Improve: 74%   Collapse: 6%   Attrition: 1%   Comparables: Cory Stewart, Lindsay Gulin, Doug Davis

A 2004 27th rounder, Sanchez impressed everyone by taking the Sally League strikeout title in his first full season as a pro. That earned him a postseason promotion to the Cal League playoffs, helping give San Jose the title. He hides his low-90s fastball well, and it's obvious that younger hitters couldn't pick it up. The batters won't be so mismatched at higher levels; he'll need to develop better complementary pitches to succeed. It's hard to project a low-A pitcher, but Sanchez probably has a major league future—if he does some work.

JASON SCHMIDT
Bats: R   Throws: R   Height: 6' 5"   Weight: 200   Born: January 29, 1973   Age: 33

YEAR	TM	LVL	AGE	W	L	SV	G	GS	IP	H	BB	SO	HR	GB%	BABIP	STUFF	WHIP	ERA	PERA	EQERA	EQH9	EQBB9	EQSO9	EQHR9	VORP	WXRL
2003	SFN	MLB	30	17	5	0	29	29	207.7	152	46	208	14	41%	.257	43	0.95	2.34	3.13	2.73	7.5	1.8	8.3	0.6	76.0	8.2
2004	SFN	MLB	31	18	7	0	32	32	225.0	165	77	251	18	47%	.268	41	1.08	3.20	3.30	3.38	7.1	2.9	9.0	0.7	62.1	7.7
2005	SFN	MLB	32	12	7	0	29	29	172.0	160	85	165	16	40%	.306	23	1.42	4.40	4.17	4.64	8.4	4.1	7.9	0.8	17.5	3.0
2006	*SFN*	*MLB*	*33*	*12*	*9*	*0*	*30*	*29*	*191.0*	*164*	*66*	*175*	*18*	*42%*	*.275*	*25*	*1.20*	*3.34*	*3.66*	*3.67*	*7.6*	*2.8*	*7.7*	*0.8*	*37.4*	*5.4*

Breakout: 15%   Improve: 52%   Collapse: 5%   Attrition: 14%   Comparables: Jack Morris, Mike Scott, Roger Clemens

Schmidt's season went wrong in just about every possible way. Hits, walks, and homers were up, strikeouts were down, and he missed playing time with both a groin injury and shoulder weakness. The shoulder problem caused him to lose velocity on his hard four-seamer, and without that usually dominating pitch Schmidt struggled mightily. The team will pick up his $10.5 million option for 2006 less because they think he'll be all better than because they need him to be all better. That's not so unreasonable, considering the free agent market for starting pitchers. Safe, strong bets are few and far between, and the Giants have little talent to offer in trade, so the uncertain pitcher in the hand wasn't any more of a gamble than any number of them out in the bush.

SEUNG SONG
Bats: R   Throws: R   Height: 6' 1"   Weight: 190   Born: June 29, 1980   Age: 26

YEAR	TM	LVL	AGE	W	L	SV	G	GS	IP	H	BB	SO	HR	GB%	BABIP	STUFF	WHIP	ERA	PERA	EQERA	EQH9	EQBB9	EQSO9	EQHR9	VORP	WXRL
2003	HAR	AA	23	5	2	0	13	13	72.7	55	24	44	5	—	.223	-5	1.09	2.35	5.35	4.41	8.6	3.6	4.4	1.2	8.9	—
2003	EDM	AAA	23	7	2	0	13	13	73.7	69	33	40	6	—	.258	-9	1.38	3.79	5.58	4.82	8.7	4.7	4.2	1.1	6.2	—
2004	EDM	AAA	24	3	1	0	13	13	63.3	70	29	59	7	—	.326	0	1.56	4.27	5.14	5.43	9.6	4.6	6.1	1.1	1.2	—
2005	SJO	A+	25	5	2	0	9	6	37.0	27	17	47	3	46%	.279	-4	1.19	1.95	5.61	4.81	8.6	5.9	7.0	1.3	3.0	—
2005	NRW	AA	25	3	2	0	6	6	36.3	34	7	29	4	45%	.286	0	1.13	2.48	5.24	3.93	9.7	2.4	4.7	1.6	6.4	—
2005	FRE	AAA	25	2	4	0	10	10	55.0	50	36	37	6	45%	.272	-18	1.56	4.42	6.15	5.64	9.1	6.3	4.4	1.2	-0.2	—
2006	*SFN*	*MLB*	*26*	*5*	*8*	*0*	*27*	*17*	*104.0*	*111*	*56*	*65*	*17*	*42%*	*.286*	*-8*	*1.61*	*5.59*	*6.16*	*6.16*	*9.5*	*4.4*	*5.2*	*1.4*	*-5.8*	*0.1*

Breakout: 1%   Improve: 21%   Collapse: 39%   Attrition: 0%   Comparables: Kiko Calero, Luther Hackman, Joaquin Benoit

It's been a long time since Song was highly esteemed, but he's far from washed up. He's only been derailed once, when he broke his forearm in 2004. He still has a tendency to get way too fine with his pitches, and the walks create rallies. The Giants tried to convince him to pitch to contact and promoted him aggressively but the experiment sputtered in Triple-A. Still, it was a worthwhile flyer for Sabean to take, and the Giants might yet get a good pitcher for their troubles.

JACK TASCHNER
Bats: L Throws: L Height: 6′ 3″ Weight: 190 Born: April 21, 1978 Age: 28

YEAR	TM	LVL	AGE	W	L	SV	G	GS	IP	H	BB	SO	HR	GB%	BABIP	STUFF	WHIP	ERA	PERA	EQERA	EQH9	EQBB9	EQSO9	EQHR9	VORP	WXRL
2003	NRW	AA	25	0	6	0	34	12	75.7	78	45	46	7	—	.282	-46	1.62	5.71	7.23	7.35	10.3	6.8	4.1	1.8	-13.8	—
2004	NRW	AA	26	3	1	0	14	10	58.0	47	16	55	5	—	.264	0	1.09	2.48	4.97	4.31	8.9	3.1	5.8	1.3	7.8	—
2004	FRE	AAA	26	4	7	0	18	9	53.3	71	32	44	14	—	.329	-49	1.93	9.29	8.03	9.57	11.6	6.2	5.3	2.7	-23.2	—
2005	FRE	AAA	27	3	0	10	44	0	49.3	30	24	62	3	47%	.250	9	1.10	1.64	4.27	2.72	7.0	4.9	8.2	0.8	14.8	—
2005	SFN	MLB	27	2	0	0	24	0	22.7	15	13	19	0	31%	.242	6	1.24	1.59	3.68	2.05	7.0	4.9	7.0	0.0	8.8	0.6
2006	*SFN*	*MLB*	*28*	*1*	*1*	*1*	*36*	*0*	*28.0*	*27*	*17*	*22*	*4*	*39%*	*.284*	*-10*	*1.57*	*4.90*	*5.58*	*6.98*	*8.6*	*4.9*	*6.7*	*1.2*	*1.3*	*0.0*

Breakout: 21%   Improve: 36%   Collapse: 41%   Attrition: 56%   Comparables: Sid Monge, Al Osuna, Brad Havens

Taschner was a 2nd rounder in 1999 whose development was curtailed by shoulder surgery in '99, a nerve procedure in '01, and Tommy John surgery in '02. Taschner's fastball is finally back up to 95 mph, and it looks like his hard-breaking slider is good enough to strike out major leaguers. Health should be a sure thing as he's pretty much run out of things that can go wrong—with his arm, anyway.

BRETT TOMKO
Bats: R Throws: R Height: 6′ 4″ Weight: 215 Born: April 7, 1973 Age: 33

YEAR	TM	LVL	AGE	W	L	SV	G	GS	IP	H	BB	SO	HR	GB%	BABIP	STUFF	WHIP	ERA	PERA	EQERA	EQH9	EQBB9	EQSO9	EQHR9	VORP	WXRL
2003	SLN	MLB	30	13	9	0	33	32	202.7	252	57	114	35	47%	.321	-11	1.52	5.28	5.31	5.88	10.7	2.2	4.5	1.5	0.9	2.2
2004	SFN	MLB	31	11	7	0	32	31	194.0	196	64	108	19	44%	.283	6	1.34	4.04	4.49	4.40	9.2	2.7	4.5	0.8	26.5	3.8
2005	SFN	MLB	32	8	15	1	33	30	190.7	205	57	114	20	40%	.301	6	1.37	4.48	4.52	4.62	9.6	2.5	4.9	0.9	19.3	2.5
2006	*LAN*	*MLB*	*33*	*10*	*11*	*0*	*31*	*27*	*172.0*	*180*	*50*	*100*	*26*	*43%*	*.279*	*0*	*1.33*	*4.49*	*4.90*	*5.04*	*9.5*	*2.4*	*4.7*	*1.3*	*11.9*	*2.4*

Breakout: 10%   Improve: 52%   Collapse: 15%   Attrition: 1%   Comparables: Jim Lonborg, Ed Whitson, Don Robinson

Tomko's component stats almost look like a carbon-copy of his numbers from last year, but there he is with an ERA almost half a run higher because he just wasn't quite so "lucky" with how many of his total runs allowed were unearned in 2005. Sabean didn't offer arbitration, either because of Tomko's high-profile flameouts or his high-profile bad-mouthing of his manager and pitching coach. Too bad for Brett, because it took SBC's dimensions to keep his fly balls in the park. He signed a two-year deal with Dodgers, so he did have the sense to put himself in another pitchers' park.

MERKIN VALDEZ
Bats: R Throws: R Height: 6′ 3″ Weight: 170 Born: November 10, 1981 Age: 24

YEAR	TM	LVL	AGE	W	L	SV	G	GS	IP	H	BB	SO	HR	GB%	BABIP	STUFF	WHIP	ERA	PERA	EQERA	EQH9	EQBB9	EQSO9	EQHR9	VORP	WXRL
2003	HAG	A	21	9	5	0	26	26	156.0	119	49	166	11	—	.263	-3	1.08	2.25	5.63	4.61	9.9	3.6	6.1	1.7	15.5	—
2004	SJO	A+	22	3	1	0	7	7	35.7	30	5	44	4	—	.292	12	0.98	2.52	5.40	4.86	9.7	1.6	7.0	2.2	2.7	—
2004	NRW	AA	22	1	4	1	10	7	41.7	35	15	31	3	—	.258	-2	1.20	4.32	4.76	5.45	8.8	3.6	5.0	0.9	0.7	—
2005	NRW	AA	23	5	6	0	24	19	107.0	99	45	96	7	46%	.317	0	1.35	3.53	5.01	5.19	9.2	4.6	5.5	0.9	4.7	—
2006	*SFN*	*MLB*	*24*	*5*	*7*	*0*	*27*	*16*	*99.3*	*104*	*50*	*66*	*13*	*46%*	*.292*	*-3*	*1.55*	*5.25*	*5.74*	*5.78*	*9.4*	*4.1*	*5.5*	*1.2*	*-2.2*	*0.4*

Breakout: 11%   Improve: 39%   Collapse: 21%   Attrition: 0%   Comparables: Jason Ryan, Victor Santos, Todd Wellemeyer

Although he's one of the sytem's most promising arms, Valdez wasn't pitching at 100% all year and was moved to the pen in August to protect his sore elbow. Valdez's fastball didn't look as unhittable as it did in 2004, he has problems with mechanics, and both his breaking and off-speed stuff are works in progress at best, so you have to squint pretty hard to still see him as a future ace. In Neil Gaiman's Sandman graphic novels, the Merkin was the mother of spiders. You could probably get a lot of strikeouts that way, using one of your four right arms to throw your mid-90s fastball from unusual angles. Then again, it might mess up your mechanics, and this Merkin has trouble enough trouble on that score already.

TYLER WALKER
Bats: R Throws: R Height: 6′ 3″ Weight: 230 Born: May 15, 1976 Age: 30

YEAR	TM	LVL	AGE	W	L	SV	G	GS	IP	H	BB	SO	HR	GB%	BABIP	STUFF	WHIP	ERA	PERA	EQERA	EQH9	EQBB9	EQSO9	EQHR9	VORP	WXRL
2003	TOL	AAA	27	2	9	0	26	22	131.3	139	47	117	13	—	.313	-10	1.42	4.46	5.50	6.07	10.0	4.1	6.0	1.5	-6.6	—
2004	SFN	MLB	28	5	1	1	52	0	63.7	69	24	48	8	47%	.332	-3	1.46	4.24	4.50	4.22	9.4	3.1	6.0	1.0	10.1	1.2
2005	SFN	MLB	29	6	4	23	67	0	61.7	68	27	54	9	41%	.330	-3	1.54	4.23	4.74	4.45	9.6	3.6	7.0	1.3	6.8	0.4
2006	*SFN*	*MLB*	*30*	*2*	*3*	*3*	*44*	*0*	*49.7*	*50*	*21*	*39*	*5*	*46%*	*.299*	*-1*	*1.42*	*4.07*	*4.75*	*5.00*	*9.0*	*3.4*	*6.7*	*1.0*	*5.6*	*0.5*

Breakout: 27%   Improve: 56%   Collapse: 18%   Attrition: 22%   Comparables: Doug Henry, Steve Reed, Paul Reuschel

Felipe Alou saw a fastball that brushes 95 mph and a bulldog attitude, didn't have anyone else around he fit the profile, and gave Walker that holiest of holies, the title of "Closer." Although the results weren't great, nor were they disastrous, which is about what you'd expect if you've been reading *BP* for a while. Given a decent lead and empty bases, even a mediocrity like Walker can get you through 80% of your save situations.

BRIAN WILSON **Bats: R Throws: R**   Height: 6′ 1″   Weight: 205   Born: March 16, 1982   Age: 24

YEAR	TM	LVL	AGE	W	L	SV	G	GS	IP	H	BB	SO	HR	GB%	BABIP	STUFF	WHIP	ERA	PERA	EQERA	EQH9	EQBB9	EQSO9	EQHR9	VORP	WXRL
2004	HAG	A	22	2	5	3	23	3	57.3	63	22	41	7	—	.316	-36	1.48	5.34	6.91	6.75	11.0	4.4	3.6	2.0	-7.0	—
2005	AUG	A	23	5	1	13	26	0	33.0	23	7	30	0	71%	.253	-3	0.91	0.82	3.73	4.02	7.8	2.6	4.9	0.3	5.5	—
2005	NRW	AA	23	0	0	8	15	0	15.7	6	5	22	0	50%	.200	14	0.70	0.57	3.14	1.88	5.7	3.8	8.8	0.0	5.9	—
2005	FRE	AAA	23	1	1	0	9	0	11.3	8	8	13	0	29%	.276	-2	1.42	3.98	4.09	5.73	7.4	6.5	8.2	0.0	-0.2	—
2006	SFN	MLB	24	2	3	1	27	3	49.0	52	25	32	6	53%	.296	-9	1.56	5.17	5.64	5.72	9.4	4.2	5.4	1.0	-1.1	0.0

Breakout: 8%   Improve: 36%   Collapse: 27%   Attrition: 21%   Comparables: Doug Nickle, Jerome Gamble, Brandon Villafuerte

The Giants aren't afraid to be aggressive promoting their relievers, so when Wilson blew guys away in short stints at Single-A and Double-A, they pushed him on up to Triple-A, where he did finally slow down. Everyone who saw him at Augusta and Norwich swear by his 97 mph fastball, but he'll need to spot it better than he did at Fresno to get out of the sandbox and make it to The Show.

Line Outs

Position/Player	TM	LVL	AGE	PA	R	2B	3B	HR	RBI	BB	SO	SB-CS	SPEED	BA/OBP/SLG	MLVR	EQBA/OBP/SLG	EQA	VORP
1/3 M. Cervenak	FRE	AAA	28	547	68	29	3	19	103	38	61	5-0	5.1	.312/.369/.498	.191	.275/.321/.418	.256	3.0
OF B. Copeland*	SLO	A-	21	132	25	5	4	4	23	11	25	2-1	6.9	.306/.364/.512	.292	.253/.299/.417	.243	-4.4
SS A. Chavez	FRE	AAA	23	356	46	17	3	11	64	17	59	5-1	5.3	.281/.320/.449	-.002	.262/.294/.410	.242	6.4
OF D. DeVore*	TUC	AAA	27	163	25	9	1	7	32	13	34	3-1	4.8	.289/.344/.503	.021	.233/.281/.400	.234	-6.0
	FRE	AAA	27	227	34	13	1	11	35	20	51	1-1	4.2	.299/.361/.537	.221	.260/.314/.441	.257	0.7
C Y. Haad	FRE	AAA	27	229	23	13	1	10	34	8	32	2-0	4.4	.282/.310/.491	.044	.249/.269/.417	.235	-0.4
CF C. Timpner*	SJO	A+	22	589	85	22	12	4	39	34	93	34-13	7.8	.291/.334/.397	-.030	.265/.300/.341	.231	-11.6

Pitcher	TM	LVL	AGE	W	L	SV	IP	H	BB	SO	HR	GB%	BABIP	STUFF	WHIP	ERA	PERA	EQERA	EQH9	EQBB9	EQSO9	EQHR9	VORP
D. Bergman*	SLC	AAA	27	8	5	8	71.0	77	18	55	10	54%	.312	-17	1.34	3.17	5.25	3.71	9.5	2.4	4.9	1.5	14.8
B. Cooper	FRE	AAA	30	7	8	0	137.0	139	54	82	23	42%	.283	-41	1.41	4.53	6.87	5.55	10.3	4.2	3.7	2.1	0.7
D. Griffin	SLO	A-	20	3	2	0	37.7	33	12	49	1	40%	.368	11	1.19	2.39	4.63	5.40	9.5	4.4	6.2	0.8	0.8
A. Simon	NRW	AA	24	3	8	19	91.3	104	24	60	6	57%	.339	-16	1.40	5.03	4.82	6.52	10.2	2.9	3.8	0.9	-9.2
B. Villafuerte	FRE	AAA	29	6	3	3	76.0	83	32	57	5	54%	.339	-15	1.51	3.91	4.82	5.30	9.8	4.2	4.6	0.7	2.5

Mike Cervenak's stats have a frisson of offensive prowess, but they were boosted by the hitter-friendly Pacific Coast League, a California tradition older than raisins. The Giants were forced to wait till the 4th round (132nd pick) for their first selection of the 2005 draft because of the Benitez, Matheny, and Vizquel signings. **Ben Copeland** was the best player still available, and he's got plus defense, a good eye, speed, and decent pop. Keep an eye on him. **Angel Chavez** is a heartbeat away from starting at shortstop job in the same way that Dick Cheney is a heartbeat away from the presidency. Both thoughts terrify San Franciscans. **Doug DeVore** mashed for another season in the PCL, but only after first faltering with the Diamondbacks. SF is **Yamid Haad's** fourth organization and he's getting pretty long in the tooth. He has enough of a bat for Triple-A, but it's hard to imagine him succeeding in the majors. **Clay Timpner** might be the best defensive center fielder in his league, but doesn't have enough discipline or power to be more than a blip on the ol' prospect radar for now.

Dusty Bergman was part of the Jason Christiansen swag; too tall and too left-handed to not strike somebody's fancy. **Brian Cooper** had the best year of his undistinguished career, but the Giants DFA'd him. Someone will give him a couple of emergency starts. **Daniel Griffin** struck out 13.8 per 9 IP in 2005 to lead the entire NCAA in this category. His debut in pro ball makes us think sleeper! **Alfredo Simon** moved to the pen, which helped a little. The move looks permanent, though, and seriously lowered his stock. **Brandon Villafuerte** is not good enough to keep a major league job but not bad enough that we get to stop writing about him.

Seattle Mariners

The Mariners had hoped to do more in 2005. After going 63–99 in 2004, the team announced two big-ticket free-agent signings: third baseman Adrian Beltre for five years and $64 million, and first baseman Richie Sexson for four years and $50 million. Even the most diehard Mariner supporters would have stopped short of predicting a playoff run after such an awful year, but the two big additions coupled with bounceback seasons from a few holdovers figured to give the M's a shot at 75 wins, maybe even a .500 record if everything broke right.

Instead, the team learned a lot about itself, much of it ugly. Beltre was a shell of his 2004 MVP-caliber self, as his offensive game eroded badly. Bret Boone went over a cliff, and fan favorite Dan Wilson could no longer run on fumes, creating gaping holes at second and catcher. Top infield reserve Scott Spiezio went 3-for-47, earning his release. The mid-season exodus of Boone, Randy Winn and other starters cleared the way for the kids to claim starting jobs, but that didn't really improve things. Jose Lopez showed flashes of potential, but more often, he struggled. Jeremy Reed didn't live up to the hype, failing to hit the ball with any authority. Yuniesky Betancourt came up billed as a no-hit, great-glove player—and lived up to the billing. With veterans leaving, and second- and third-tier prospects called up for reserve duty, the bench became a disaster.

Yet for all the team's offensive struggles, the pitching staff may have been an even bigger disappointment. Ryan Franklin, Gil Meche, and Joel Pineiro all fell short of expectations. Management should have seen the first two coming, given Franklin's middling stuff and Meche's failure to fully recover from shoulder surgery. Pineiro became the latest in a growing line of M's pitchers derailed by injuries during the past five years. An elbow injury cost him the last two months of the 2004 season, and Pineiro returned in 2005 with lower velocity on his fastball, costing him two strikeouts per game. Unfortunately, he won't be the last of Seattle's pitching prospects to have their careers significantly altered by injury: current hopefuls Rafael Soriano, Jeff Heaverlo, Bobby Madritsch, Jorge Campillo, Travis Blackley, Clint Nageotte, and Scott Atchison have all had significant injuries in the last few years.

Against this backdrop, it's easy to forgive M's fans for their vigil, waiting and praying for the arrival of Felix Hernandez last season. The best pitching prospect since Doc

MARINERS PROSPECTUS

2005 record: 69–93; Fourth place, AL West

Pythagenport record: 75–87

Runs scored per game: 4.31 (13th in AL)

Runs allowed per game: 4.64 (7th in AL)

Team EqA: .251 (12th in AL)

2005 Batters Age: 29.1 (6th oldest in AL)

2005 Pitchers Age: 31.8 (3rd oldest in AL)

Ballpark: Safeco Field; Severe pitcher's park; Park Factor of 0.954

2005: The offense was supposed to carry the pitching, but someone may have forgotten to tell them.

2006: Going nowhere, but the Cult of King Felix will make the Mariners worth watching.

Gooden, Hernandez carried the hopes of Mariners Nation on his golden right arm last year. He did not disappoint. Called up shortly after his 19th birthday, Hernandez put up monster numbers in his dozen starts, creating the kind of buzz any pro sports team would kill for. Even as the M's shuffled through a miserable second half, Hernandez's starts became *events,* infused with fun and anticipation, tens of thousands of fans leaning forward with each pitch. Simultaneously, manager Mike Hargrove and pitching coach Bryan Price resisted the hype. They protected Hernandez's arm concurrently helping his development by letting him pitch out of jams whenever possible. This management tack builds on the organization's decision that it wouldn't let him throw a slider in the minors. If Hernandez were to ever go down with an arm injury, it wouldn't be through any fault of the Mariners' brass.

In the short term, the Mariners are more optimistic than one might think given their recent finishes, but less than you might wish for. The division with the highest cumulative winning percentage in the AL last year now looks to be even better. Texas has revamped its pitching staff and at press time was hot after Roger Clemens—the best pitcher in baseball a year ago. The A's stole Milton Bradley and Antonio Perez from the Dodgers and added Esteban Loaiza to what should be the league's best staff. The Angels mostly stood pat, but they're coming off a 95-

win campaign. They also own a passel of good hitting prospects, and hope for a full year of health from Vladimir Guerrero.

The Mariners started their off-season on the right foot, handing a three-year, $16 million deal to Japanese catcher Kenji Johjima. Across the International Date Line, Johjima put up vintage Mike Piazza numbers, but Japanese League translations suggest he'll probably hit more like late-career Jorge Posada. Not that there's anything wrong with that; Johjima projects as an above-average major league performer, and the M's won't have to deal with much of his downside, since his contract ends at the reasonable age of 32.

Several incumbents should also help the team improve in '06. When a healthy, still-young player falls as dramatically as Beltre did from 2004 to 2005, he often rebounds the following season. The lineup's pups should improve from their lackluster '05 seasons, too. Trade rumors that swirled around Reed glossed over his quality glovework, relative youth (he doesn't turn 25 until June), and his strong minor league track record; even if the power never comes, he'll improve. Lopez looks like the quintessential talented but raw hitter, rushed to the majors, but still gifted with good potential. Betancourt may never develop a bat, but if he sticks he'll be the best defensive shortstop in the game into the next decade. Coupled with Beltre's Gold Glove caliber defense at third, that's a big asset to a pitching staff, but maybe not *this* pitching staff. Although Hernandez owns one of the most dominating power/groundball combinations anywhere, the rest of the staff consists mostly of flyball pitchers who are far less likely to take advantage of the team's tight infield defense.

The signings that followed Johjima's—starting with Carl Everett—made little sense. Already owning a lefty-swinging starting designated hitter in Raul Ibanez, the Mariners threw $4 million at Everett, an aging hitter who's punchless against lefties and limited in the outfield. When the M's signed Matt Lawton a few weeks later, they acquired another past-his-prime quasi-outfielder, albeit one with more on-base ability and a cheaper price tag (due largely to his 2005 suspension for steroid use). Ibanez, Everett, and Lawton are all ill-suited to cover the cavernous left-center field at Safeco. This could cost the Mariners two or three gams in 2006, considering the downgrade from Randy Winn's solid defense.

At least Everett can be cast aside if he fails. But the club's four-year, $37.5 million deal with former Angel Jarrod Washburn has the potential to become a crippling error for years to come. The Mariners signed Washburn as he came off a superficially impressive season—he posted a 3.20 ERA, but that was largely due to luck. He stranded nearly 82 percent of the batters he put on base, miles above the league average of around 70 percent. These averages are usually subject to sizable year-to-year fluctuations, as are the performances of the relievers working behind them. Stellar relief work can keep starters' ERAs sparkling, but three-run doubles allowed on a reliever's first pitch can wreck those numbers. The split between Washburn's total body of work and his performance with runners in scoring position was even more dramatic and unlikely to be repeated. With a strikeout rate below 5 per 9 IP, which is unlikely to suddenly climb as he gets deeper into his 30s, Washburn will need to dodge four years' worth of bullets to come close to justifying his contract. Lacking an adequate left fielder to run down the innumerable flyballs Washburn allows, the deal could turn into a stinker starting in year one.

Ultimately this isn't about second-guessing, it's about a team's best-laid plans and what often becomes of them. The Mariners, the most profitable team in the majors according to a Forbes study released last spring, went into the offseason with a set of financial and on-field goals. They had a salary cap in mind, as well as a list of positions they wanted to upgrade. They saw boosting the pitching staff as their top need, figuring that's where they'd spend most of their money. They'd also seek out a new starting catcher, and try to patch the outfield with a veteran bat. By those standards, the team met all of its goals. In a published interview, Mariners President Chuck Armstrong noted that the team had reached its 2006 player payroll ceiling.

Heading into 2006, the Mariners have reason to expect significant improvement in multiple areas. Still, even a perfect off-season would have left them a longshot to contend in a loaded AL West. The team didn't unload any of its top prospects or core young talent, but one wonders what might have happened if different decisions had been made, and if one decision will end up hurting the team for years to come.

HITTERS

WLADIMIR BALENTIEN   CF   Bats: R Throws: R   Height: 6′ 1″   Weight: 202   Born: July 2, 1984   Age: 21

YEAR	TM	LVL	AGE	PA	R	2B	3B	HR	RBI	BB	SO	SB	CS	SPEED	BA	OBP	SLG	MLVR	EQBA	EQOBP	EQSLG	EQA	VORP	DEFENSE		
2004	WIS	A	20	276	39	12	3	15	46	12	77	10	2	6.4	.277	.315	.519	.193	.243	.276	.457	.248	2.5	46-CF -4	13-LF	0
2005	SBR	A+	21	538	76	38	8	25	93	33	160	9	2	5.9	.291	.338	.553	.167	.239	.280	.427	.243	-0.9	74-CF -6		
2006	SEA	MLB	21	478	52	23	2	17	59	24	143	7	2	4.4	.221	.266	.396	-.179	.225	.275	.418	.228	-4.9	113-CF -4		

Breakout: 14%   Improve: 31%   Collapse: 34%   Attrition: 7%   Comparables: Jeff Spencer, Franklin Gutierrez, Chris Young

The California League sharply inflates offense, causing hitting prospects to be overrated and pitching prospects to be underrated. Balentien may appear to be the best power prospect in the Mariner system by virtue of his 71 extra-base hits last year, but his translated lines tell you there's a lot of air in those numbers. He has raw talent—his power was evident at Wisconsin in '04—but Balentien's efforts at Double-A San Antonio and beyond will tell us how good he is likely to be.

ADRIAN BELTRE   3B   Bats: R Throws: R   Height: 5′ 11″   Weight: 165   Born: April 7, 1979   Age: 27

YEAR	TM	LVL	AGE	PA	R	2B	3B	HR	RBI	BB	SO	SB	CS	SPEED	BA	OBP	SLG	MLVR	EQBA	EQOBP	EQSLG	EQA	VORP	DEFENSE
2003	LAN	MLB	24	607	50	30	2	23	80	37	103	2	2	4.0	.240	.290	.424	-.056	.244	.293	.436	.248	9.7	150-3B -4
2004	LAN	MLB	25	657	104	32	0	48	121	53	87	7	2	4.4	.334	.388	.629	.459	.333	.387	.629	.328	79.5	149-3B 11
2005	SEA	MLB	26	650	69	36	1	19	87	38	108	3	1	4.5	.255	.303	.413	-.055	.264	.321	.435	.259	6.3	150-3B 8
2006	SEA	MLB	27	630	77	31	2	27	98	40	100	3	1	4.5	.275	.324	.474	.057	.280	.335	.500	.272	28.6	147-3B 6

Breakout: 11%   Improve: 34%   Collapse: 25%   Attrition: 4%   Comparables: Aramis Ramirez, Larry Parrish, Brooks Robinson

Baseball Prospectus's other new book hitting shelves this spring, *Baseball Between The Numbers,* examines a variety of hot-button debates, from steroids to the best player of all-time to how to build a playoff roster—and whether players perform better just before free agency. Even after adjusting for age and other factors, the answer is yes, they do. Beltre is used as a prime example, but he's actually forged an atypical career path. A typical walk-year spike might mark the culmination of several years of development, but Beltre's OPS the last five seasons was 722, 729, 714, 1017, and 717. Beltre will never hit .334 again, but he still has power in his arsenal. Look for production somewhere between the 2004 masterpiece and the dregs of '01–'03 and '05, something along the lines of .280/.340/.500 with continued great defense. Given Richie Sexson's age and lack of defensive value, when all's said and done Beltre could still be the better of the M's two '04 off-season deals

YUNIESKY BETANCOURT   SS   Bats: R Throws: R   Height: 5′ 10″   Weight: 190   Born: January 31, 1982   Age: 24

YEAR	TM	LVL	AGE	PA	R	2B	3B	HR	RBI	BB	SO	SB	CS	SPEED	BA	OBP	SLG	MLVR	EQBA	EQOBP	EQSLG	EQA	VORP	DEFENSE
2005	SAN	AA	23	239	25	10	3	5	20	9	18	12	7	6.7	.273	.301	.410	-.010	.259	.291	.388	.236	2.0	51-SS 2
2005	TAC	AAA	23	192	13	9	6	2	30	6	14	7	5	6.3	.295	.323	.443	.051	.286	.307	.413	.245	6.0	48-SS 11
2005	SEA	MLB	23	226	24	11	5	1	15	11	24	1	3	6.2	.256	.296	.370	-.135	.268	.317	.388	.241	0.2	52-SS -4
2006	SEA	MLB	24	540	66	28	5	8	55	22	57	15	8	5.6	.258	.292	.383	-.126	.263	.302	.404	.234	8.1	127-SS 5

Breakout: 34%   Improve: 56%   Collapse: 16%   Attrition: 6%   Comparables: Barry Larkin, Tim Foli, Orlando Cabrera

Check out the Fielding Runs Above Average—that's Ozzie Smith territory if Betancourt can keep it up for a full season. The question is, can he hit? David Eckstein makes for an interesting comparison. Considered a good on-base threat out of the leadoff spot, Eckstein has forged a successful career more out of good hand-eye coordination than high walk rates, with a career .282 batting average and no seasons above 45 walks until last year. The Mariners see many of the same skills in Betancourt, though his pitch recognition needs improvement before he can truly be compared to the Cards' little wonder. He'll get plenty of opportunities, with top prospects like Adam Jones being moved elsewhere to give Betancourt a clean shot.

WILLIE BLOOMQUIST   UT   Bats: R Throws: R   Height: 5′ 11″   Weight: 180   Born: November 27, 1977   Age: 28

YEAR	TM	LVL	AGE	PA	R	2B	3B	HR	RBI	BB	SO	SB	CS	SPEED	BA	OBP	SLG	MLVR	EQBA	EQOBP	EQSLG	EQA	VORP	DEFENSE		
2003	SEA	MLB	25	218	30	7	2	1	14	19	39	4	1	5.8	.250	.317	.321	-.179	.256	.329	.328	.240	-1.1	30-3B -1	14-SS	0
2004	SEA	MLB	26	198	27	10	0	2	18	10	48	13	2	7.3	.245	.283	.330	-.247	.246	.288	.332	.232	-3.4	25-3B 1	16-SS	-2
2005	SEA	MLB	27	263	27	15	2	0	22	11	38	14	1	7.0	.257	.289	.333	-.197	.268	.311	.350	.245	-0.4	29-3B 0	20-SS	-4
2006	SEA	MLB	28	247	30	11	2	2	20	14	42	10	3	6.0	.251	.296	.337	-.184	.256	.307	.355	.228	-1.1	61-2B -1		

Breakout: 19%   Improve: 42%   Collapse: 35%   Attrition: 32%   Comparables: Marv Breeding, Jerry Terrell, John Mcdonald

He is what he is: a useful defender at multiple positions, a very good base stealer, a fan favorite, and most of all, a terrible hitter handed far too much playing time. The problem isn't Bloomquist's flaws so much as the weak rosters the M's have had, creating too many opportunities for him. Bloomquist would be a handy 24th or 25th man for a slow, veteran team, but in Seattle he's an overused roster fob. Less playing time for Bloomquist would mean the Mariners have gotten better results from Reed, Betancourt and Lopez.

SEBASTIEN BOUCHER   **CF**   **Bats: L Throws: R**   Height: 6′ 0″   Weight: 180   Born: October 19, 1981   Age: 24

YEAR	TM	LVL	AGE	PA	R	2B	3B	HR	RBI	BB	SO	SB	CS	SPEED	BA	OBP	SLG	MLVR	EQBA	EQOBP	EQSLG	EQA	VORP	DEFENSE			
2005	WIS	A	23	207	37	14	2	2	31	26	34	11	1	6.5	.326	.411	.461	.277	.279	.347	.391	.264	0.3	22-LF	2	16-CF	1
2005	SBR	A+	23	254	54	14	3	2	21	36	49	15	3	7.6	.352	.453	.474	.322	.297	.382	.379	.277	10.7	33-CF	-2	16-LF	2
2006	SEA	MLB	24	485	59	23	4	4	40	41	107	18	6	5.3	.266	.333	.367	-.072	.271	.344	.387	.252	7.2	114-CF	-1		

Breakout: 8%   Improve: 27%   Collapse: 39%   Attrition: 9%   Comparables: Fred Lewis, Jeff Duncan, Adam Greenberg

A 7th-round pick out of Bethune-Cookman College in 2004, Boucher showed the requisite dominance you'd expect from a college-trained player in the low minors. He'll need to move quickly to make it to The Show. The 26-4 SB rate lends some credence to his speedy reputation as well as his baseball smarts, which he'll need to leverage to overcome the lack of power. He's Jamal Strong with a French-Canadian accent.

ASDRUBAL CABRERA   **2B**   **Bats: B Throws: R**   Height: 6′ 0″   Weight: 170   Born: November 13, 1985   Age: 20

YEAR	TM	LVL	AGE	PA	R	2B	3B	HR	RBI	BB	SO	SB	CS	SPEED	BA	OBP	SLG	MLVR	EQBA	EQOBP	EQSLG	EQA	VORP	DEFENSE			
2004	EVE	A-	18	267	44	16	3	5	41	21	43	7	5	6.5	.272	.330	.427	.026	.221	.266	.342	.216	-14.5	40-SS	0	17-2B	-2
2005	WIS	A	19	226	26	12	3	4	30	30	32	2	6	3.5	.318	.407	.474	.282	.286	.364	.426	.270	12.8	28-2B	1		
2005	SBR	A+	19	243	31	15	6	1	26	15	47	3	1	6.3	.284	.325	.418	-.072	.242	.279	.338	.218	-4.9	54-SS	-3		
2006	SEA	MLB	20	485	49	23	3	6	45	29	83	5	4	4.5	.244	.292	.351	-.178	.248	.302	.370	.224	2.7	114-SS	-2		

Breakout: 20%   Improve: 47%   Collapse: 28%   Attrition: 7%   Comparables: Felipe Lopez, Jesus Guzman, Antonio Perez

Another good-looking middle-infield prospect moving from shortstop to second base as a nod to Betancourt, Cabrera projects well as a hitter. He made it all the way to Triple-A last year at 19, though it's clear he was rushed. There's a solid skill set here, including precocious pitch recognition. We'll know more when Cabrera plays a full season in a more competitive environment than A-ball, where would-be prospects are often homesick, unable to order a cheeseburger after moving from another country to rural Montana, or just plain lousy.

SHIN-SOO CHOO   **LF**   **Bats: L Throws: L**   Height: 5′ 11″   Weight: 170   Born: July 13, 1982   Age: 23

YEAR	TM	LVL	AGE	PA	R	2B	3B	HR	RBI	BB	SO	SB	CS	SPEED	BA	OBP	SLG	MLVR	EQBA	EQOBP	EQSLG	EQA	VORP	DEFENSE			
2003	SBR	A+	20	469	62	18	13	9	55	44	84	18	10	6.7	.286	.365	.459	.177	.257	.322	.407	.252	-4.5	62-LF	-1	33-RF	1
2004	SAN	AA	21	578	89	17	7	15	84	56	97	40	8	7.3	.315	.382	.462	.260	.304	.362	.447	.284	24.1	80-RF	-2	44-LF	0
2005	TAC	AAA	22	500	73	21	5	11	54	69	97	20	10	6.2	.282	.382	.431	.131	.272	.361	.401	.267	5.5	112-LF	16		
2006	SEA	MLB	23	464	61	19	3	10	49	42	88	15	5	5.7	.272	.341	.404	-.007	.277	.353	.426	.265	10.0	110-LF	1		

Breakout: 14%   Improve: 49%   Collapse: 22%   Attrition: 11%   Comparables: Rick Manning, Gary Thomasson, Norm Miller

Choo put up another year of solid OBP, with lots of steals, and very good defense. The problem is that the Mariners are flush with players like him: lefty hitters who get on base, run, and catch the ball (or some combination of the above, if you include vets like Ibanez and Lawton). There may be a trade to be had by packaging one of the young lefty outfielders, one of the top middle infield prospects and one of the back-end pitching staff members for a legit power bat. A dash to the starting left-field job by Choo or Snelling this season would be a big lift to the team.

JEFFREY CLEMENT   **C**   **Bats: L Throws: R**   Height: 6′ 1″   Weight: 210   Born: August 21, 1983   Age: 22

YEAR	TM	LVL	AGE	PA	R	2B	3B	HR	RBI	BB	SO	SB	CS	SPEED	BA	OBP	SLG	MLVR	EQBA	EQOBP	EQSLG	EQA	VORP	DEFENSE
2005	WIS	A	21	127	17	5	0	6	20	12	25	1	2	3.1	.319	.386	.522	.320	.281	.337	.467	.272	7.3	20-C	-1
2006	SEA	MLB	22	360	39	15	1	12	47	24	77	3	2	3.9	.245	.303	.403	-.090	.250	.314	.425	.245	8.2	87-C	-4

Breakout: 11%   Improve: 28%   Collapse: 45%   Attrition: 13%   Comparables: Chris Barski, Garett Gentry, Aaron Rifkin

Clement's decision to bypass the Twins after they took him with their 12th-round pick of the 2002 draft led to a stellar career at USC, culminating in the M's selecting him third overall in the '05 draft. We shouldn't try to extrapolate too much from a 30-game sample, but the M's were happy with his progress and have him ticketed for Double-A in 2006. Clement still has some work to do with the glove, but this isn't a Daric Barton situation, where he won't hold the position. He could make Kenji Johjima attractive trade bait by the 2007–2008 offseason.

RAUL IBANEZ   LF   Bats: L Throws: R   Height: 6′ 2″   Weight: 200   Born: June 2, 1972   Age: 34

YEAR	TM	LVL	AGE	PA	R	2B	3B	HR	RBI	BB	SO	SB	CS	SPEED	BA	OBP	SLG	MLVR	EQBA	EQOBP	EQSLG	EQA	VORP	DEFENSE			
2003	KCA	MLB	31	670	95	33	5	18	90	49	81	8	4	5.8	.294	.345	.454	.040	.285	.341	.444	.270	12.5	117-LF	-5	19-1B	2
2004	SEA	MLB	32	524	67	31	1	16	62	36	72	1	2	4.0	.304	.353	.472	.150	.311	.363	.485	.288	22.5	105-LF	1		
2005	SEA	MLB	33	690	92	32	2	20	89	71	99	9	4	5.3	.280	.355	.436	.088	.292	.376	.463	.289	29.3	53-LF	1		
2006	*SEA*	*MLB*	*34*	*577*	*69*	*27*	*2*	*17*	*78*	*53*	*83*	*6*	*3*	*5.1*	*.275*	*.343*	*.433*	*.035*	*.280*	*.355*	*.457*	*.271*	*19.0*	*135-LF*	*-3*		

Breakout: 14%   Improve: 37%   Collapse: 25%   Attrition: 11%   Comparables: Wally Joyner, B. J. Surhoff, Ken Griffey

One thing the front office has done well in recent years is recognize Safeco Field's more favorable environment for left-handed hitters, tapping players like Ibanez to complement the roster's bigger bats. Ibanez put up decent if unspectacular numbers for the second year in a row, and figures to do the same in the final year of this three-year contract. He's a good on-base, moderate-power DH at this stage—no great shakes, but better for this team than the right-handed equivalent.

KENJI JOHJIMA   C   Bats: R Throws: R   Height: ?   Weight: ?   Born: June 8, 1976   Age: 30

YEAR	TM	LVL	AGE	PA	R	2B	3B	HR	RBI	BB	SO	SB	CS	SPEED	BA	OBP	SLG	MLVR	EQBA	EQOBP	EQSLG	EQA	VORP	DEFENSE	
2003	FKU	JPL	27	604	119	39	2	34	50	53	15	9	101	5.3	.330	.389	.593	.401	.318	.386	.469	.294	47.2		
2004	FKU	JPL	28	497	91	25	1	36	91	49	45	6	0	5.0	.338	.433	.655	.565	.325	.402	.501	.308	49.9		
2005	FKU	JPL	29	444	70	22	4	24	57	33	32	3	4	0.0	.309	.360	.557	.330	.306	.365	.469	.285	31.7		
2006	*SEA*	*MLB*	*30*	*406*	*49*	*21*	*2*	*9*	*51*	*31*	*37*	*2*	*1*	*4.7*	*.292*	*.354*	*.435*	*.069*	*.298*	*.367*	*.458*	*.276*	*24.3*	*97-C*	*1*

Breakout: 7%   Improve: 30%   Collapse: 44%   Attrition: 18%   Comparables: Joe Azcue, Red Wilson, John Stearns

One of the best signings of the offseason. Major league teams have generally been reluctant to make huge offers for Japanese players, largely because they have a tough time projecting their stats against North American competition. Clay's eponymous Davenport Translations tell us that Johjima's huge numbers the last three years in Japan have as much to do with his talent as his environment. He's not going to hit like vintage Piazza in Seattle, but given the sorry offense too many big league catchers put up, the M's snagged a backstop whose power and pitch recognition skills should immediately propel him to the head of the AL's catching class. Even the length of the contract was spot-on: Johjima turns 30 in June, so staying away from a huge four- or five-year deal and getting his services as he plateaus or falls off just a bit was smart.

ADAM JONES   CF   Bats: R Throws: R   Height: 6′ 2″   Weight: 180   Born: August 1, 1985   Age: 20

YEAR	TM	LVL	AGE	PA	R	2B	3B	HR	RBI	BB	SO	SB	CS	SPEED	BA	OBP	SLG	MLVR	EQBA	EQOBP	EQSLG	EQA	VORP	DEFENSE	
2004	WIS	A	18	555	76	23	7	11	72	33	124	8	4	5.8	.267	.314	.404	.029	.237	.276	.361	.223	-8.3	116-SS	-13
2005	SBR	A+	19	313	43	20	5	8	46	29	64	4	5	5.6	.295	.374	.494	.147	.249	.313	.395	.246	5.9	64-SS	-8
2005	SAN	AA	19	255	33	10	3	7	20	22	48	9	4	5.8	.298	.365	.461	.190	.283	.345	.435	.270	15.2	59-SS	1
2006	*SEA*	*MLB*	*20*	*540*	*59*	*26*	*3*	*11*	*57*	*32*	*114*	*8*	*4*	*5.0*	*.247*	*.296*	*.378*	*-.133*	*.252*	*.307*	*.398*	*.235*	*9.8*	*127-SS*	*-5*

Breakout: 16%   Improve: 42%   Collapse: 32%   Attrition: 3%   Comparables: Brandon Phillips, Jhonny Peralta, Kelly Johnson

The Mariners' top pick in the 2003 draft owns a broad base of skills that are improving as he matures. Of particular note are the on-base ability and power potential he showed at Double-A just as he reached his 20th birthday. High strikeout rates for hitters don't matter much in the majors, but they can make a big difference in projecting a prospect's future. Jones lowered his K rate from its sky-high 2004 level while hiking his walks. The next test is a shift to center field. They have time to wait for him to learn the position while his bat gets more seasoning. He's a Top-20 prospect in 2007 if both sides of his game keep progressing.

JOSE LOPEZ   2B/SS   Bats: R Throws: R   Height: 6′ 2″   Weight: 170   Born: November 24, 1983   Age: 22

YEAR	TM	LVL	AGE	PA	R	2B	3B	HR	RBI	BB	SO	SB	CS	SPEED	BA	OBP	SLG	MLVR	EQBA	EQOBP	EQSLG	EQA	VORP	DEFENSE			
2003	SAN	AA	19	581	82	35	2	13	69	27	56	18	8	6.1	.258	.303	.403	.023	.253	.293	.411	.243	9.8	88-SS	-9	34-2B	1
2004	TAC	AAA	20	301	40	19	0	13	39	16	30	6	2	4.7	.295	.342	.505	.152	.267	.311	.444	.259	12.5	42-SS	-1	20-3B	-2
2004	SEA	MLB	20	217	28	13	0	5	22	8	31	0	1	4.7	.232	.263	.367	-.240	.239	.273	.371	.221	-3.1	54-SS	-8		
2005	TAC	AAA	21	192	29	19	0	5	31	8	25	2	3	4.5	.319	.354	.505	.234	.288	.315	.448	.254	8.0	44-2B	-4		
2005	SEA	MLB	21	202	18	19	0	2	25	6	25	4	2	4.9	.247	.282	.379	-.149	.259	.300	.402	.243	-1.1	50-2B	3		
2006	*SEA*	*MLB*	*22*	*470*	*55*	*27*	*1*	*13*	*62*	*19*	*61*	*7*	*4*	*5.0*	*.270*	*.305*	*.428*	*-.036*	*.276*	*.316*	*.451*	*.253*	*17.1*	*111-2B*	*-3*		

Breakout: 39%   Improve: 66%   Collapse: 17%   Attrition: 10%   Comparables: Mike De La Hoz, Wil Cordero, Tommy Davis

Lopez struggled in his second prolonged exposure to the majors, this time while playing the ABBB (Anyone But Bret Boone) role. Some huge doubles numbers in the low minors point to significant power potential, but Lopez was rushed in 2004 and may still need more seasoning to refine his approach. His defense was a pleasant surprise. There will likely be more growing pains before he puts it all together. The hope is that the Mariners keep Lopez's age in mind and avoid making a rash decision like trading him for 75 cents on the dollar. He profiles a lot like another Lopez—Cincinnati's Felipe—who also struggled in his first big league exposure in his early 20s. It took Felipe four more years to break out; Jose has similar upside if the M's are willing to wait.

MICHAEL MORSE   SS/LF   **Bats: R Throws: R**   Height: 6' 4"   Weight: 180   Born: March 22, 1982   Age: 24

YEAR	TM	LVL	AGE	PA	R	2B	3B	HR	RBI	BB	SO	SB	CS	SPEED	BA	OBP	SLG	MLVR	EQBA	EQOBP	EQSLG	EQA	VORP	DEFENSE			
2003	WNS	A+	21	466	45	30	2	10	55	25	91	4	4	4.2	.245	.296	.394	-.028	.224	.265	.382	.221	-7.5	118-SS	-8		
2004	BIR	AA	22	226	30	9	5	11	38	15	46	0	3	4.8	.287	.336	.536	.242	.264	.309	.488	.263	13.4	49-SS	-9		
2004	SAN	AA	22	172	18	10	1	6	33	9	27	0	2	3.1	.274	.326	.465	.132	.262	.303	.446	.253	6.6	40-SS	1		
2005	TAC	AAA	23	202	20	12	2	4	23	16	36	1	0	4.1	.253	.317	.407	-.058	.243	.294	.380	.236	0.6	49-SS	0		
2005	SEA	MLB	23	258	27	10	1	3	23	18	50	3	1	3.9	.278	.349	.370	-.010	.293	.369	.397	.272	9.1	51-SS	-9		
2006	*SEA*	*MLB*	*24*	*437*	*46*	*21*	*2*	*11*	*54*	*25*	*85*	*3*	*2*	*4.2*	*.255*	*.305*	*.403*	*-.081*	*.260*	*.316*	*.425*	*.246*	*10.4*	*104-SS*	*-5*		

Breakout: 28%   Improve: 54%   Collapse: 27%   Attrition: 18%   Comparables: *Larry Parrish, Dave Roberts, Jermaine Dye*

Talk about a roller-coaster year. Morse went from minor league hopeful pining for a big league job to starting shortstop in Seattle to .400 hitter in his first few games. He then received his second steroids suspension as a pro, the first coming in the minors in 2004. This wasn't a second violation—Morse was caught in a procedural trap that saw him get punished twice for the same crime. The coup de grace came when the Mariners promoted Betancourt, leaving Morse to pick up playing time scraps as a spare outfielder. He's 6' 4" and athletic, but Morse's only extended show of hitting prowess came in 2004—209 Double-A ABs in the White Sox system—and he's not a good enough defender to play up the middle. Morse is best suited as the third element in a multi-player deal for a better player, just as he was in the Freddy Garcia trade.

OSWALDO NAVARRO   2B/SS   **Bats: B Throws: R**   Height: 6' 0"   Weight: 150   Born: October 2, 1984   Age: 21

YEAR	TM	LVL	AGE	PA	R	2B	3B	HR	RBI	BB	SO	SB	CS	SPEED	BA	OBP	SLG	MLVR	EQBA	EQOBP	EQSLG	EQA	VORP	DEFENSE			
2003	EVE	A-	18	248	42	12	1	0	23	10	39	16	3	7.7	.258	.302	.318	-.110	.216	.242	.271	.190	-33.0	60-SS	4		
2004	EVE	A-	19	293	38	27	1	1	30	21	59	17	4	6.8	.273	.331	.393	-.015	.220	.262	.314	.210	-27.1	37-2B	0	29-SS	7
2004	WIS	A	19	122	13	4	0	0	7	11	19	4	1	5.0	.211	.295	.248	-.232	.181	.249	.208	.178	-12.9	27-2B	0		
2005	WIS	A	20	505	57	29	0	9	69	39	60	11	7	4.3	.269	.329	.393	.015	.234	.283	.355	.225	-10.4	56-2B	1	53-SS	-7
2006	*SEA*	*MLB*	*21*	*446*	*44*	*20*	*1*	*7*	*42*	*23*	*70*	*8*	*4*	*4.8*	*.231*	*.276*	*.334*	*-.235*	*.236*	*.285*	*.352*	*.213*	*-3.9*	*106-SS*	*1*		

Breakout: 42%   Improve: 65%   Collapse: 18%   Attrition: 11%   Comparables: *Jorge Sequea, Felix Molina, Carlos Rodriguez*

A wisp of a player when he entered the Mariners' system as an 18 year-old, Navarro has improved his power as he's developed. His first full season saw some of the copious doubles he tallied in 2004 start to clear the fences. Scouts like his defense, but the M's would do well to pick one position instead of shuttling him between second and short. One of the Mariners' army of promising middle-infield prospects, though he's a long way from the Show.

JEREMY REED   CF   **Bats: L Throws: L**   Height: 6' 0"   Weight: 180   Born: June 15, 1981   Age: 25

YEAR	TM	LVL	AGE	PA	R	2B	3B	HR	RBI	BB	SO	SB	CS	SPEED	BA	OBP	SLG	MLVR	EQBA	EQOBP	EQSLG	EQA	VORP	DEFENSE			
2003	WNS	A+	22	269	37	18	1	4	52	41	17	27	6	6.5	.333	.431	.477	.333	.303	.394	.461	.301	17.6	44-RF	-1	21-CF	2
2003	BIR	AA	22	274	51	17	3	7	43	29	19	18	13	6.4	.409	.474	.591	.652	.385	.442	.570	.330	43.7	41-RF	2	21-CF	0
2004	CHR	AAA	23	322	44	14	1	8	37	36	34	12	7	5.6	.275	.357	.420	.040	.255	.337	.390	.257	5.4	64-CF	2		
2004	TAC	AAA	23	257	40	10	5	5	36	23	22	14	2	7.6	.305	.366	.455	.130	.289	.348	.416	.270	10.3	61-CF	1		
2004	SEA	MLB	23	66	11	4	0	0	5	7	4	3	1	5.3	.397	.470	.466	.387	.404	.485	.474	.340	7.3	14-CF	1		
2005	SEA	MLB	24	540	61	33	3	3	45	48	74	12	11	5.5	.254	.322	.352	-.108	.269	.346	.378	.251	-2.0	131-CF	-1		
2006	*SEA*	*MLB*	*25*	*542*	*70*	*27*	*3*	*9*	*58*	*51*	*63*	*16*	*6*	*5.8*	*.279*	*.350*	*.405*	*.014*	*.285*	*.362*	*.427*	*.268*	*20.1*	*127-CF*	*0*		

Breakout: 21%   Improve: 48%   Collapse: 23%   Attrition: 9%   Comparables: *Hosken Powell, David DeJesus, Steve Hovley*

Still a Mariner at press time, which may or may not be a good thing, depending on whom you ask. The M's center fielder disappointed many, though Safeco Field's pitcher-friendly environment made things look a little worse than they were. Still, Safeco plays as a neutral park for left-handed hitters, as opposed to a nasty one for righties. Right now, Reed's a more valuable commodity than a middling pitcher like Bronson Arroyo, who makes millions more. The bigger question for the M's is whether Reed will look more like Johnny Damon or Sean Burroughs two years from now, when he starts getting more expensive.

RICHIE SEXSON   1B   Bats: R Throws: R   Height: 6′ 7″   Weight: 206   Born: December 29, 1974   Age: 31

YEAR	TM	LVL	AGE	PA	R	2B	3B	HR	RBI	BB	SO	SB	CS	SPEED	BA	OBP	SLG	MLVR	EQBA	EQOBP	EQSLG	EQA	VORP	DEFENSE
2003	MIL	MLB	28	718	97	28	2	45	124	98	151	2	3	3.7	.272	.379	.548	.254	.267	.372	.545	.303	47.0	162-1B 19
2004	ARI	MLB	29	104	20	4	0	9	23	14	21	0	0	4.4	.233	.337	.578	.174	.225	.330	.562	.290	5.6	23-1B 3
2005	SEA	MLB	30	656	99	36	1	39	121	89	167	1	1	3.6	.263	.369	.541	.235	.276	.389	.578	.318	45.7	148-1B -5
2006	SEA	MLB	31	681	93	30	1	39	116	94	164	0	1	3.9	.268	.375	.528	.198	.273	.388	.557	.306	43.3	159-1B 0

Breakout: 15%   Improve: 43%   Collapse: 28%   Attrition: 3%   Comparables: Jim Thome, Boog Powell, Greg Luzinski

Sexson shook off a shoulder injury that cost him most of the 2004 season to post a VORP that tied Paul Konerko for third-best among AL first basemen, behind only Mark Teixeira and Jason Giambi. The problem is that Sexson has already reached the Mariners' most optimistic projections, while making $4.5 million in '05. Now he's about to play his Age 31, 32 and 33 seasons while making $11.5 million in '06 and $14 million in both 2007 and 2008. The Mariners need 40 homers, 90 walks and 150+ games played every season through 2008 to justify his contract, given that offense is what you're supposed to get from big money players on the left side of the defensive spectrum. The scary part is that Sexson's deal looks like the smart move when compared to the Adrian Beltre and Jarrod Washburn contracts.

CHRIS SNELLING   LF   Bats: L Throws: L   Height: 5′ 10″   Weight: 160   Born: December 3, 1981   Age: 24

YEAR	TM	LVL	AGE	PA	R	2B	3B	HR	RBI	BB	SO	SB	CS	SPEED	BA	OBP	SLG	MLVR	EQBA	EQOBP	EQSLG	EQA	VORP	DEFENSE	
2003	SAN	AA	21	202	24	12	2	3	25	8	30	1	7	3.7	.333	.371	.468	.298	.330	.364	.474	.278	11.7	15-RF 0	11-LF 1
2005	TAC	AAA	23	290	50	17	2	8	46	36	43	2	3	4.7	.370	.452	.553	.535	.358	.431	.515	.321	31.4	41-RF -3	11-LF 0
2005	SEA	MLB	23	34	4	2	0	1	1	5	2	0	2	3.9	.276	.382	.448	.122	.276	.400	.448	.274	0.5		
2006	SEA	MLB	24	506	65	29	1	16	74	49	76	3	3	4.5	.303	.376	.486	.179	.309	.389	.512	.297	30.3	119-RF 0	

Breakout: 12%   Improve: 35%   Collapse: 28%   Attrition: 12%   Comparables: Jeremy Giambi, Rusty Staub, Bruce Bochte

Some superstitious Mariners fans took to calling him by his middle name, Doyle, to avoid cursing him into another injury, but it didn't work. It was another knee injury this time, the seventh surgery of the Aussie's career, and the fifth on his left knee. You have to wonder when those injuries will curtail Snelling's speed, cutting into not only his base running but also his ability to leg out hits and to catch the ball in Safeco's spacious left field. A .370 average at Tacoma after missing an entire year showed that the guy could still play until this latest setback. If he can ever overcome the injury bug, he could be a big plus.

JAMAL STRONG   LF   Bats: R Throws: R   Height: 5′ 10″   Weight: 180   Born: August 5, 1978   Age: 27

YEAR	TM	LVL	AGE	PA	R	2B	3B	HR	RBI	BB	SO	SB	CS	SPEED	BA	OBP	SLG	MLVR	EQBA	EQOBP	EQSLG	EQA	VORP	DEFENSE
2003	TAC	AAA	24	241	38	6	1	2	19	25	38	26	11	6.9	.305	.390	.371	.122	.298	.376	.364	.268	8.5	53-CF -6
2004	TAC	AAA	25	280	46	11	2	3	24	38	29	19	6	6.7	.324	.421	.424	.210	.301	.390	.373	.277	13.2	50-CF -2
2005	TAC	AAA	26	431	57	16	5	4	36	43	67	25	6	7.0	.293	.371	.393	.064	.278	.342	.354	.252	4.2	86-CF -2
2005	SEA	MLB	26	24	6	0	1	0	2	2	6	0	0	7.3	.250	.333	.350	-.087	.250	.333	.350	.251	0.1	
2006	SEA	MLB	27	388	49	15	3	3	31	31	66	17	5	5.9	.268	.333	.353	-.089	.274	.344	.372	.250	5.4	93-CF -2

Breakout: 9%   Improve: 28%   Collapse: 44%   Attrition: 23%   Comparables: Paul Dade, Jermaine Allensworth, Gene Clines

His speed, defense, and OBPs the last three years at pitcher-friendly Tacoma suggest a viable big league backup outfielder, defensive replacement, and pinch-runner for anyone who'll give him a shot. An April steroids suspension made his long odds of success even longer, and the M's declined to tender him a contract at year's end. He'd be a good fit for the Yankees if they weren't so averse to players under 57 years old.

ICHIRO SUZUKI   RF   Bats: L Throws: R   Height: 5′ 11″   Weight: 157   Born: October 22, 1973   Age: 32

YEAR	TM	LVL	AGE	PA	R	2B	3B	HR	RBI	BB	SO	SB	CS	SPEED	BA	OBP	SLG	MLVR	EQBA	EQOBP	EQSLG	EQA	VORP	DEFENSE
2003	SEA	MLB	29	722	111	29	8	13	62	36	69	34	8	7.6	.312	.352	.436	.096	.321	.365	.454	.284	28.3	154-RF 11
2004	SEA	MLB	30	760	101	24	5	8	60	49	63	36	11	6.6	.372	.414	.455	.284	.383	.428	.471	.313	68.7	156-RF 1
2005	SEA	MLB	31	737	111	21	12	15	68	48	66	33	8	7.8	.303	.350	.436	.097	.318	.371	.464	.290	34.1	158-RF 12
2006	SEA	MLB	32	665	90	26	6	7	61	31	56	24	6	6.3	.308	.343	.406	.025	.314	.354	.428	.266	19.6	155-RF 4

Breakout: 4%   Improve: 23%   Collapse: 45%   Attrition: 1%   Comparables: Matty Alou, Lance Johnson, Mickey Rivers

The idea that a corner outfielder must be a bruising power hitter goes against every word ever written by Baseball Prospectus on roster construction. An intelligent team seeks to put the best team on the field, regardless of conventions. A shortstop may hit 40 home runs, and a corner outfielder may walk 100 times and steal 130 bases or hit .370 with a few homers, a bunch of doubles and triples, terrific range and the best throwing arm in the game. Ichiro isn't Barry Bonds, but we should afford him a full measure of respect for his contribution to the Mariners, both on the field and—in the millions in revenue he helps the Mariners generate through his overseas appeal—off of it, too. Expect further skills consolidation in 2006: Ichiro's lost some of the speed that let him leg out enough bleeders to hit .370, but he should continue to boost his extra-base hit totals. Look for a few more walks too; the 16 unintentionals he drew last year were unusually low for him.

YORVIT TORREALBA   C   Bats: R Throws: R   Height: 5′ 11″ Weight: 180   Born: July 19, 1978   Age: 27

YEAR	TM	LVL	AGE	PA	R	2B	3B	HR	RBI	BB	SO	SB	CS	SPEED	BA	OBP	SLG	MLVR	EQBA	EQOBP	EQSLG	EQA	VORP	DEFENSE
2003	SFN	MLB	24	218	22	10	2	4	29	14	39	1	0	5.3	.260	.312	.390	-.074	.257	.309	.386	.243	3.0	56-C 13
2004	SFN	MLB	25	192	19	7	3	6	23	17	31	2	0	5.3	.227	.302	.407	-.116	.224	.299	.402	.245	1.1	48-C 4
2005	SFN	MLB	26	103	18	8	0	1	7	9	25	1	0	5.6	.226	.301	.344	-.177	.223	.305	.362	.236	-0.6	24-C 3
2005	SEA	MLB	26	116	14	4	0	2	8	7	25	0	0	3.2	.241	.293	.333	-.212	.252	.316	.364	.240	-1.2	36-C 1
2006	*COL*	*MLB*	*27*	*231*	*26*	*12*	*2*	*6*	*27*	*19*	*41*	*2*	*1*	*5.0*	*.277*	*.342*	*.435*	*.022*	*.256*	*.323*	*.411*	*.248*	*4.7*	*58-C 3*

Breakout: 37%   Improve: 53%   Collapse: 30%   Attrition: 38%   Comparables: Joe Tipton, Ray Katt, Brad Ausmus

Considered a promising prospect after a solid 2002 season as a 23-year-old backup for the Giants, the M's snagged Torrealba along with Jesse Foppert for Randy Winn at the trade deadline, hoping to find the production they've lacked behind the plate for years. One hundred eight at-bats and a Kenji Johjima signing later, Torrealba was shipped to Colorado for Marcos Carvajal, a deal that could end up being the proverbial good trade for both teams.

MATT TUIASOSOPO   SS   Bats: R Throws: R   Height: 6′ 2″ Weight: 210   Born: May 10, 1986   Age: 20

YEAR	TM	LVL	AGE	PA	R	2B	3B	HR	RBI	BB	SO	SB	CS	SPEED	BA	OBP	SLG	MLVR	EQBA	EQOBP	EQSLG	EQA	VORP	DEFENSE
2004	EVE	A-	18	123	20	6	1	3	17	11	38	4	3	6.2	.255	.350	.415	.029	.207	.272	.328	.212	-12.0	
2005	WIS	A	19	463	72	21	3	6	45	44	96	8	5	5.2	.276	.359	.386	.058	.252	.317	.361	.239	4.4	76-SS -18
2006	*SEA*	*MLB*	*20*	*475*	*49*	*22*	*2*	*8*	*48*	*31*	*104*	*7*	*5*	*5.2*	*.245*	*.301*	*.359*	*-.152*	*.250*	*.311*	*.378*	*.230*	*6.6*	*112-SS -13*

Breakout: 38%   Improve: 59%   Collapse: 26%   Attrition: 5%   Comparables: Enrique Cruz, Adam Jones, Antonio Perez

The local boy picked in the 3rd round of 2004 out of Woodinville High improved on his debut campaign in Everett, but Tui's still got lots of holes to plug. Projections of power potential are based solely on his athleticism and not results, and his defense is atrocious. The M's could move him to third or the outfield, but then would his bat be able to carry the position? He doesn't turn 20 until May, but it's hard to see much there, even if you squint.

PITCHERS

SCOTT ATCHISON   Bats: R Throws: R   Height: 6′ 2″ Weight: 180   Born: March 29, 1976   Age: 30

YEAR	TM	LVL	AGE	W	L	SV	G	GS	IP	H	BB	SO	HR	GB%	BABIP	STUFF	WHIP	ERA	PERA	EQERA	EQH9	EQBB9	EQSO9	EQHR9	VORP	WXRL
2003	TAC	AAA	27	6	9	1	39	7	108.7	114	37	83	8	—	.304	-10	1.39	4.31	4.97	6.00	9.8	3.8	5.5	1.1	-4.7	—
2004	TAC	AAA	28	5	3	7	40	1	69.3	71	26	76	8	—	.333	-7	1.40	4.16	4.95	5.35	9.5	4.0	7.0	1.3	1.9	—
2004	SEA	MLB	28	2	3	0	25	0	30.7	29	14	36	4	54%	.329	20	1.40	3.52	3.77	3.48	8.1	3.8	9.9	1.2	9.2	0.2
2006	*SEA*	*MLB*	*30*	*2*	*3*	*2*	*44*	*2*	*47.3*	*51*	*19*	*38*	*6*	*45%*	*.312*	*-2*	*1.47*	*4.79*	*5.12*	*5.96*	*9.6*	*3.5*	*6.9*	*1.1*	*2.7*	*0.3*

Breakout: 21%   Improve: 44%   Collapse: 25%   Attrition: 32%   Comparables: Steve Parris, Mike Stanton, Tom Sturdivant

One of several pitchers pushing thirty who've recently cracked the majors for the first time and done well in Seattle. After a strong 2004, Atchison managed just 23.1 innings at three levels in 2005 due to a strained elbow. He's expected to be healthy in 2006, and will battle for a bullpen spot. The Mariner pen was cheap and modestly effective last year; it will remain cheap but possibly emerge as a Top 10 MLB ensemble if Atchison, Rafael Soriano, and others stay healthy.

YORMAN BAZARDO   Bats: R Throws: R   Height: 6′ 2″ Weight: 170   Born: July 11, 1984   Age: 21

YEAR	TM	LVL	AGE	W	L	SV	G	GS	IP	H	BB	SO	HR	GB%	BABIP	STUFF	WHIP	ERA	PERA	EQERA	EQH9	EQBB9	EQSO9	EQHR9	VORP	WXRL
2003	GRB	A	18	9	8	0	21	21	130.0	132	26	70	8	—	.279	-3	1.22	3.12	5.46	5.17	10.6	2.1	3.1	1.4	5.9	—
2004	JUP	A+	19	5	9	0	25	25	154.3	161	30	95	3	—	.304	21	1.24	3.27	3.96	5.61	9.5	1.9	3.8	0.4	-0.2	—
2005	CAR	AA	20	8	7	0	19	19	108.3	108	36	73	12	57%	.294	-16	1.33	3.99	6.24	5.98	10.4	3.3	4.3	1.8	-4.3	—
2005	SAN	AA	20	3	1	0	6	6	33.7	38	11	26	4	41%	.343	5	1.45	4.27	5.45	5.18	10.1	3.5	5.5	1.6	1.5	—
2006	*SEA*	*MLB*	*21*	*7*	*10*	*0*	*32*	*21*	*135.3*	*155*	*44*	*67*	*19*	*49%*	*.295*	*-4*	*1.47*	*5.27*	*5.36*	*5.78*	*10.2*	*2.9*	*4.2*	*1.2*	*-0.9*	*0.8*

Breakout: 16%   Improve: 59%   Collapse: 7%   Attrition: 0%   Comparables: Junior Herndon, Steve Green, Joel Pineiro

(continued next page)

Yorman Bazardo *(continued)*

Bazardo fell off a bit in Double-A after taking advantage of the pitcher-friendly Florida State League in '04, but made it to the bigs for a cup of coffee with the Marlins. His velocity has come down in the last few years, from as high as 97 at Greensboro in 2003 to the low 90s last season, although his strikeout rates have ticked upwards along the way. That may be a function of Bazardo getting smarter and no longer gunning his fastball down the middle of the plate. Regardless, retaining a veteran swingman like Ron Villone was a luxury the last-place Mariners didn't need; getting Bazardo for him just after his 21st birthday was a minor coup.

TRAVIS BLACKLEY   Bats: L   Throws: L   Height: 6' 3"   Weight: 190   Born: November 4, 1982   Age: 23

YEAR	TM	LVL	AGE	W	L	SV	G	GS	IP	H	BB	SO	HR	GB%	BABIP	STUFF	WHIP	ERA	PERA	EQERA	EQH9	EQBB9	EQSO9	EQHR9	VORP	WXRL
2003	SAN	AA	20	17	3	0	27	27	162.3	125	62	144	11	—	.250	12	1.15	2.61	5.10	4.45	8.6	4.1	6.3	1.2	19.4	—
2004	TAC	AAA	21	8	6	0	19	18	110.3	100	47	80	14	—	.275	0	1.33	3.83	5.38	4.21	8.7	4.1	5.2	1.3	16.5	—
2004	SEA	MLB	21	1	3	0	6	6	26.0	35	22	16	9	32%	.310	-28	2.19	10.04	8.10	9.79	11.8	7.1	5.1	2.7	-13.7	-0.5
2006	*SEA*	*MLB*	*23*	*3*	*4*	*0*	*22*	*7*	*57.3*	*60*	*27*	*42*	*9*	*38%*	*.292*	*-3*	*1.51*	*5.17*	*5.46*	*6.36*	*9.3*	*4.2*	*6.3*	*1.3*	*1.4*	*0.4*

Breakout: 25%   Improve: 53%   Collapse: 34%   Attrition: 35%   Comparables: Scott Aldred, Scott Scudder, Darryl Kile

Yet another victim of the Mariner pitching injury wheel of destruction. Blackley hurt his left shoulder in 2004, then had surgery in early '05 to repair two labrum tears. Like Ryan Anderson, Gil Meche, and so many other M's pitching prospects before him, Blackley is assured of not reaching his full potential. Meche's serviceable career as a back-end rotation guy is Blackley's upside. Given historical results of pitchers with labrum tears, a complete Anderson-like washout is a real possibility.

FRANCISCO CRUCETA   Bats: R   Throws: R   Height: 6' 2"   Weight: 180   Born: July 4, 1981   Age: 24

YEAR	TM	LVL	AGE	W	L	SV	G	GS	IP	H	BB	SO	HR	GB%	BABIP	STUFF	WHIP	ERA	PERA	EQERA	EQH9	EQBB9	EQSO9	EQHR9	VORP	WXRL
2003	AKR	AA	22	13	9	0	27	25	163.3	141	66	134	7	—	.274	18	1.27	3.09	4.40	4.58	8.4	4.1	5.9	0.7	17.8	—
2004	AKR	AA	23	4	8	0	15	15	88.7	89	33	45	11	—	.269	-19	1.38	5.28	6.07	5.65	9.7	3.7	3.3	1.6	-0.5	—
2004	BUF	AAA	23	6	5	0	14	14	83.0	78	36	62	6	—	.295	11	1.37	3.25	4.63	4.08	8.5	4.2	5.5	0.8	13.8	—
2005	BUF	AAA	24	6	4	0	30	13	102.3	123	32	92	16	37%	.350	-10	1.52	5.19	5.24	5.77	10.3	3.0	6.2	1.6	-1.9	—
2006	*SEA*	*MLB*	*24*	*4*	*7*	*0*	*29*	*13*	*93.3*	*99*	*39*	*63*	*15*	*39%*	*.289*	*-3*	*1.48*	*5.28*	*5.44*	*5.67*	*9.5*	*3.7*	*5.7*	*1.4*	*0.3*	*0.5*

Breakout: 11%   Improve: 39%   Collapse: 21%   Attrition: 1%   Comparables: Seung Song, Roger Erickson, Tomo Ohka

An intriguing waiver-wire claim from the Indians last August, Cruceta has alternated between very good and mediocre peripherals throughout his minor league career. He'll need better command of his fastball to become a viable major leaguer. The Indians cut him loose partly because of his taterrific tendencies in 2005, but Buffalo played as a particularly homer-friendly park last year, while Safeco suppresses homers. It's clear that no one wants to ever see Aaron Sele get 21 starts in Seattle again, except Messrs. Stoneman, Beane, and Daniels. Taking low-risk, low-cost gambles is a good way to avoid that fate.

JESSE FOPPERT   Bats: R   Throws: R   Height: 6' 6"   Weight: 210   Born: July 10, 1980   Age: 25

YEAR	TM	LVL	AGE	W	L	SV	G	GS	IP	H	BB	SO	HR	GB%	BABIP	STUFF	WHIP	ERA	PERA	EQERA	EQH9	EQBB9	EQSO9	EQHR9	VORP	WXRL
2003	SFN	MLB	22	8	9	0	23	21	111.0	103	69	101	16	40%	.293	3	1.55	5.03	5.14	5.71	8.9	5.1	7.4	1.3	1.9	1.5
2005	FRE	AAA	24	3	1	0	10	9	44.0	43	27	41	5	40%	.302	-7	1.59	4.50	5.65	5.44	9.2	5.7	6.1	1.3	0.8	—
2005	SFN	MLB	24	0	0	0	3	2	10.3	11	13	6	2	39%	.310	-37	2.32	5.24	7.84	6.10	10.5	10.5	5.2	1.7	-0.6	0.1
2005	TAC	AAA	24	0	1	0	6	6	14.0	10	8	13	0	37%	.270	0	1.29	2.57	4.05	3.38	8.1	5.4	6.1	0.0	3.3	—
2006	*SEA*	*MLB*	*25*	*3*	*6*	*0*	*27*	*12*	*78.3*	*79*	*58*	*59*	*13*	*37%*	*.285*	*-11*	*1.76*	*6.07*	*6.49*	*6.52*	*9.0*	*6.6*	*6.4*	*1.4*	*-6.4*	*-0.3*

Breakout: 8%   Improve: 23%   Collapse: 33%   Attrition: 8%   Comparables: Joaquin Benoit, Matt Kinney, Blake Stein

Though pitchers are making it back to live competition less than a year after Tommy John surgery, for some it can take two years or more for a full recovery. Before the surgery, Foppert was an elite pitching prospect in 2002, when he struck out 183 batters in 140 combined innings at Double-A and Triple-A. The M's will be watching for improved control and a return to the low- to mid-90s velocity he once had. The Mariners expect him to start the season back at Triple-A, but the rotation's not nearly as good as the team's claiming—Foppert could be the #3 starter by the trade deadline.

RYAN FRANKLIN   Bats: R   Throws: R   Height: 6' 3"   Weight: 165   Born: March 5, 1973   Age: 33

YEAR	TM	LVL	AGE	W	L	SV	G	GS	IP	H	BB	SO	HR	GB%	BABIP	STUFF	WHIP	ERA	PERA	EQERA	EQH9	EQBB9	EQSO9	EQHR9	VORP	WXRL
2003	SEA	MLB	30	11	13	0	32	32	212.0	199	61	99	34	37%	.250	-9	1.23	3.57	5.44	4.46	9.7	2.7	4.3	1.5	49.1	5.4
2004	SEA	MLB	31	4	16	0	32	32	200.3	224	61	104	33	38%	.294	-7	1.42	4.90	5.29	5.07	10.1	2.6	4.4	1.4	20.3	3.4
2005	SEA	MLB	32	8	15	0	32	30	190.7	212	62	93	28	42%	.289	-7	1.44	5.10	5.26	5.17	10.0	3.0	4.4	1.3	11.5	2.9
2006	*PHI*	*MLB*	*33*	*8*	*10*	*0*	*33*	*24*	*154.0*	*171*	*48*	*77*	*26*	*41%*	*.282*	*-7*	*1.42*	*5.00*	*5.31*	*5.41*	*9.8*	*2.6*	*4.3*	*1.5*	*6.6*	*1.6*

Breakout: 14%   Improve: 47%   Collapse: 26%   Attrition: 6%   Comparables: Roger Craig, Willie Blair, Dave Mlicki

Flyball pitchers with low strikeout rates face long odds in the big leagues. First they have to hope for a home park that turns flyballs into long outs instead of homers. They also need pinpoint control to prevent extra baserunners, minimizing the damage when the serve up a cookie. While they do tend to yield lower batting averages on balls in play than groundballers, with fewer knocks scooting through the infield, they need luck and good defense to mitigate all the batters who don't strike out and instead put the ball in play. In 2003, Franklin yielded a BABIP of .250, with a resulting 3.57 ERA. In 2005: .289 BABIP, 5.10 ERA. Wisely non-tendered after the '05 season, Franklin signed with the Phillies. Avert your eyes.

EDDIE GUARDADO   Bats: R   Throws: L   Height: 6' 0"   Weight: 194   Born: October 2, 1970   Age: 35

YEAR	TM	LVL	AGE	W	L	SV	G	GS	IP	H	BB	SO	HR	GB%	BABIP	STUFF	WHIP	ERA	PERA	EQERA	EQH9	EQBB9	EQSO9	EQHR9	VORP	WXRL
2003	MIN	MLB	32	3	5	41	66	0	65.3	50	14	60	7	34%	.247	18	0.98	2.89	3.52	2.95	7.3	2.0	8.2	1.0	22.3	3.4
2004	SEA	MLB	33	2	2	18	41	0	45.3	31	14	45	8	33%	.215	12	0.99	2.78	4.30	2.86	7.2	2.7	8.6	1.4	17.3	2.0
2005	SEA	MLB	34	2	3	36	58	0	56.3	52	15	48	7	35%	.276	9	1.19	2.72	3.99	3.67	8.3	2.4	7.7	1.1	12.7	2.7
2006	*SEA*	*MLB*	*35*	*3*	*4*	*23*	*47*	*0*	*45.7*	*42*	*12*	*39*	*6*	*36%*	*.271*	*6*	*1.17*	*3.57*	*3.70*	*4.03*	*8.1*	*2.3*	*7.2*	*1.2*	*8.9*	*1.3*

Breakout: 13%   Improve: 33%   Collapse: 44%   Attrition: 26%   Comparables: Alan Embree, Joe Hoerner, Jeff Reardon

November 2, 2005: With Guardado looking unlikely to pick up his option for the 2006 season ($5.5 million including incentives), the Mariners exercised the club option for one year, $6.25 million. Mariner Nation howls in protest, berating that kind of money for a 35-year-old 55–60 inning guy who's still useful, but clearly not that valuable. November 28, 2005: The Blue Jays sign B. J. Ryan to a five-year, $47 million contract. All is forgiven.

JEFF HARRIS   Bats: R   Throws: R   Height: 6' 0"   Weight: 195   Born: July 4, 1974   Age: 31

YEAR	TM	LVL	AGE	W	L	SV	G	GS	IP	H	BB	SO	HR	GB%	BABIP	STUFF	WHIP	ERA	PERA	EQERA	EQH9	EQBB9	EQSO9	EQHR9	VORP	WXRL
2004	TAC	AAA	30	5	3	1	26	8	74.7	60	26	53	6	—	.249	-12	1.15	4.34	5.27	5.40	8.5	4.0	4.6	1.0	1.6	—
2005	SAN	AA	31	5	0	0	11	2	34.3	25	8	31	4	41%	.233	-14	0.96	2.10	6.46	4.70	9.1	3.2	5.3	2.1	3.1	—
2005	TAC	AAA	31	5	2	1	16	9	68.0	50	17	56	8	44%	.236	-7	0.99	2.78	5.29	4.29	8.4	2.7	5.3	1.6	9.2	—
2005	SEA	MLB	31	2	5	0	11	8	53.7	48	20	25	9	36%	.232	-12	1.27	4.19	5.85	4.47	9.1	3.4	4.3	1.5	7.6	1.0
2006	*SEA*	*MLB*	*31*	*4*	*6*	*0*	*32*	*14*	*91.3*	*96*	*32*	*50*	*14*	*40%*	*.276*	*-10*	*1.40*	*4.94*	*5.03*	*5.41*	*9.4*	*3.1*	*4.6*	*1.3*	*4.1*	*0.8*

Breakout: 5%   Improve: 25%   Collapse: 28%   Attrition: 3%   Comparables: Paul Foytack, Monk Dubiel, Red Embree

Fill-in spot starter who did a decent job late in the year subbing for Gil Meche and anyone else who needed a breather. He was designated for assignment at season's end, not surprising for a 31-year-old finesse pitcher. No one claimed him, so the M's will again have some insurance just a 40-mile drive away at Tacoma.

FELIX HERNANDEZ   Bats: R   Throws: R   Height: 6' 3"   Weight: 170   Born: April 8, 1986   Age: 20

YEAR	TM	LVL	AGE	W	L	SV	G	GS	IP	H	BB	SO	HR	GB%	BABIP	STUFF	WHIP	ERA	PERA	EQERA	EQH9	EQBB9	EQSO9	EQHR9	VORP	WXRL
2003	EVE	A-	17	7	2	0	11	7	55.0	43	24	73	2	—	.308	28	1.22	2.29	4.96	4.44	8.7	4.6	7.2	1.0	6.8	—
2004	SBR	A+	18	9	3	0	16	15	92.0	85	26	114	5	—	.345	40	1.21	2.74	4.20	4.10	8.8	3.1	7.3	0.9	15.0	—
2004	SAN	AA	18	5	1	0	10	10	57.3	47	21	58	3	—	.282	35	1.19	3.30	4.37	4.37	8.1	3.6	6.8	0.8	7.6	—
2005	TAC	AAA	19	9	4	0	19	14	88.0	62	48	100	3	57%	.277	45	1.25	2.25	3.68	2.94	7.1	4.7	8.1	0.3	25.3	—
2005	SEA	MLB	19	4	4	0	12	12	84.3	61	23	77	5	68%	.257	53	1.00	2.67	3.25	2.82	7.0	2.5	8.2	0.5	28.1	3.1
2006	*SEA*	*MLB*	*20*	*11*	*8*	*0*	*30*	*30*	*175.0*	*152*	*67*	*158*	*11*	*55%*	*.288*	*29*	*1.25*	*3.27*	*3.51*	*3.70*	*7.7*	*3.4*	*7.6*	*0.5*	*38.8*	*5.4*

Breakout: 15%   Improve: 40%   Collapse: 22%   Attrition: 6%   Comparables: Bert Blyleven, Jim Palmer, Curt Simmons

(continued next page)

Felix Hernandez *(continued)*

Since 1972, only eight pitchers have led their league in groundball/flyball rate and finished in the top ten in strikeouts per opponents' plate appearance in the same season:

Year	Pitcher	GB/FB% Rank	K/PA% Rank	Year	Pitcher	GB/FB% Rank	K/PA% Rank
2005	Felix Hernandez	1	3	1992	Greg Maddux	1	7
2003	Brandon Webb	1	10	1987	Pascual Perez	1	3
2001	Roy Halladay	1	9	1983	Mike Boddicker	1	8
1995	Greg Maddux	1	6	1974	Bill Bonham	1	8

Maddux turned the trick twice during the peak of his career, and ranks as one of the five best right-handers of all time. Perez and Boddicker were good pitchers who managed the feat during one of the best seasons of each of their careers. Bill Bonham was an anomaly. The most instructive pitchers on this list may be Halladay and Webb. Halladay did it in his breakout season as a 24 year-old in 2001, and now ranks among the game's elite. Webb, like Hernandez, did it as a rookie, and looks poised to enter the game's top echelon. King Felix is already there. The undisputed ace of the Mariners' staff at age 19, Hernandez is equally lethal with a high-90s fastball, a bamboozling curve, and a devastating changeup that occasionally sinks so improbably you wonder if he splashed white-out all over Isaac Newton's notebook and started over. He's going to finish in the top three in Cy Young voting in 2006, and he won't reach legal drinking age until after Opening Day 2007. Basketball has LeBron James, hockey has Sidney Crosby, and football has Reggie Bush. Thank you, gods of baseball, for Felix Hernandez.

JEFF HEAVERLO Bats: R Throws: R Height: 6' 1" Weight: 210 Born: January 13, 1978 Age: 28

YEAR	TM	LVL	AGE	W	L	SV	G	GS	IP	H	BB	SO	HR	GB%	BABIP	STUFF	WHIP	ERA	PERA	EQERA	EQH9	EQBB9	EQSO9	EQHR9	VORP	WXRL
2003	TAC	AAA	25	5	12	0	24	24	123.7	150	38	75	8	—	.324	-4	1.52	5.38	4.94	6.93	10.7	3.3	4.4	0.9	-18.0	—
2005	TAC	AAA	27	6	3	4	46	0	82.0	92	44	71	3	56%	.360	-6	1.66	4.61	4.65	6.31	9.8	5.2	5.4	0.4	-6.4	—
2006	SEA	MLB	28	2	4	1	29	4	56.7	65	29	37	5	52%	.321	-10	1.66	5.36	5.66	6.17	10.2	4.5	5.5	0.8	-1.0	0.0

Breakout: 37% Improve: 63% Collapse: 12% Attrition: 23% Comparables: George Culver, Dave Weathers, Scott Randall

Injuries washed out Heaverlo's 2004 season, and he looked like he might be finished at the start of '05 when he posted a 12.67 ERA through his first 16.1 innings. From there, he turned his season around, with a 2.62 ERA in his last 65.2 IP. Heaverlo's GB/FB rate outpaced even King Felix's at Tacoma, as he scrapped his changeup to return to his slider. He also regained some velocity on his fastball. There's still the elephant in the room: a torn labrum suffered four years ago and the subsequent surgery to repair it, which makes him a longshot.

CESAR JIMENEZ Bats: L Throws: L Height: 5' 11" Weight: 180 Born: November 12, 1984 Age: 21

YEAR	TM	LVL	AGE	W	L	SV	G	GS	IP	H	BB	SO	HR	GB%	BABIP	STUFF	WHIP	ERA	PERA	EQERA	EQH9	EQBB9	EQSO9	EQHR9	VORP	WXRL
2003	WIS	A	18	8	11	0	28	20	125.7	134	46	76	7	—	.297	-10	1.43	2.94	5.86	5.86	10.2	4.0	3.7	1.4	-3.5	—
2004	SBR	A+	19	6	7	6	43	2	85.3	80	18	80	3	—	.314	16	1.15	2.32	3.87	4.09	8.6	2.4	5.5	0.5	14.0	—
2005	SAN	AA	20	3	5	4	45	1	68.7	64	24	54	3	50%	.307	6	1.28	2.62	4.18	3.65	8.6	3.6	5.5	0.5	14.5	—
2006	SEA	MLB	21	3	4	1	30	5	59.7	66	25	36	8	48%	.296	-7	1.52	5.02	5.42	5.44	9.8	3.7	5.1	1.2	1.6	0.3

Breakout: 8% Improve: 33% Collapse: 31% Attrition: 14% Comparables: John Parrish, Luis Gonzalez, Shane Wallace

Venezuelan lefty reliever who has quietly breezed through the Mariners' system faster than most, cracking the Triple-A roster at the end of his Age 20 season. Jimenez has shown good control at every stage while keeping the ball in the park. The M's have more than enough functional relief prospects to give Jimenez a full year at Tacoma, but he could be Soriano's lefty set-up man by late '07.

BOBBY LIVINGSTON Bats: L Throws: L Height: 6' 3" Weight: 190 Born: September 3, 1982 Age: 23

YEAR	TM	LVL	AGE	W	L	SV	G	GS	IP	H	BB	SO	HR	GB%	BABIP	STUFF	WHIP	ERA	PERA	EQERA	EQH9	EQBB9	EQSO9	EQHR9	VORP	WXRL
2003	WIS	A	20	15	7	0	26	26	178.0	176	28	105	10	—	.279	-7	1.15	2.73	5.44	5.44	10.1	1.8	3.5	1.5	3.0	—
2004	SBR	A+	21	12	6	0	28	27	186.7	187	30	141	15	—	.303	-2	1.16	3.57	5.07	5.47	9.5	1.9	4.3	1.4	2.6	—
2005	SAN	AA	22	8	4	0	18	18	116.3	103	27	78	7	51%	.282	9	1.12	2.86	4.43	4.59	8.6	2.6	4.5	0.8	12.5	—
2005	TAC	AAA	22	6	2	0	10	10	51.7	53	15	41	2	49%	.317	14	1.32	4.70	3.68	5.79	9.1	2.6	5.4	0.4	-1.1	—
2006	SEA	MLB	23	7	10	0	29	24	145.3	159	43	77	20	47%	.288	1	1.39	4.87	4.97	5.25	9.7	2.6	4.5	1.2	6.4	1.7

Breakout: 13% Improve: 55% Collapse: 8% Attrition: 0% Comparables: Andy Van Hekken, Jason Brester, Derrin Ebert

Who to believe, the stats or the scouts? The stats say Livingston has put up great K/BB rates throughout his minor league career, and looks on track to hit the majors soon. The scouts say he's a soft-tossing lefty who may struggle at the highest level. The numbers hint at that possibility too, as Livingston's peripherals eroded a bit at Tacoma, culminating in a play-off game debacle in which he yielded five homers. Lefty control pitchers are said to have a better chance at success than righties of the same stripe, and the Mariners have one of the archetypes in Jamie Moyer. There are enough candidates for the back of the rotation that they can take a patient approach with Livingston.

BOBBY MADRITSCH   Bats: L   Throws: L   Height: 6′ 2″   Weight: 190   Born: February 28, 1976   Age: 30

YEAR	TM	LVL	AGE	W	L	SV	G	GS	IP	H	BB	SO	HR	GB%	BABIP	STUFF	WHIP	ERA	PERA	EQERA	EQH9	EQBB9	EQSO9	EQHR9	VORP	WXRL
2003	SAN	AA	27	13	7	0	27	27	158.7	133	67	154	11	—	.275	-17	1.26	3.63	6.01	6.83	9.6	5.6	5.9	1.6	-19.6	—
2004	TAC	AAA	28	5	2	0	12	12	62.3	61	26	53	3	—	.307	5	1.40	3.76	4.62	5.52	9.1	4.5	5.5	0.6	0.5	—
2004	SEA	MLB	28	6	3	0	15	11	88.0	74	33	60	3	44%	.277	27	1.22	3.27	3.72	3.31	8.1	3.2	5.8	0.3	26.9	3.3
2006	*KCA*	*MLB*	*30*	*2*	*3*	*1*	*25*	*4*	*48.7*	*57*	*20*	*29*	*7*	*44%*	*.308*	*-11*	*1.57*	*5.55*	*5.76*	*6.52*	*10.2*	*3.7*	*5.4*	*1.2*	*-1.4*	*0.0*

Breakout: 9%   *Improve: 28%*   *Collapse: 46%*   *Attrition: 27%*   *Comparables: Mike Mohler, Paul Gibson, Dick Starr*

Mariner pitching prospect coming off a promising season suffers a serious arm injury. What else is new? What's sad is this might have been avoided if the Mariners had exercised prudence. Last year we wrote: "In meaningless games Madritsch racked up huge pitch counts. Sometimes he looked fresh, sometimes he was clearly dragging when (Manager Bob) Melvin sent him out for more punishment. For his failure to preserve his best healthy pitcher for next year, Melvin should have been fired far earlier than he was." There's no way to know exactly if those high pitch count outings led to the partial tear in the labrum of Madritsch's pitching shoulder, but there's just no reason to tempt fate when your season's ostensibly over. Claimed by the Royals, he's a long shot to make an impact ever again.

JULIO MATEO   Bats: R   Throws: R   Height: 6′ 0″   Weight: 170   Born: August 2, 1977   Age: 28

YEAR	TM	LVL	AGE	W	L	SV	G	GS	IP	H	BB	SO	HR	GB%	BABIP	STUFF	WHIP	ERA	PERA	EQERA	EQH9	EQBB9	EQSO9	EQHR9	VORP	WXRL
2003	SEA	MLB	25	4	0	1	50	0	85.7	69	13	71	14	34%	.240	6	0.96	3.15	4.26	3.72	8.4	1.4	7.5	1.4	25.8	1.1
2004	SEA	MLB	26	1	2	1	45	0	57.7	56	16	43	11	34%	.266	-7	1.25	4.68	5.05	4.58	9.3	2.4	6.3	1.6	9.3	0.2
2005	SEA	MLB	27	3	6	0	55	1	88.3	79	17	52	12	32%	.249	-3	1.09	3.06	4.67	3.32	8.9	1.8	5.4	1.2	23.9	1.2
2006	*SEA*	*MLB*	*28*	*3*	*3*	*2*	*51*	*0*	*65.3*	*66*	*13*	*41*	*10*	*35%*	*.271*	*-4*	*1.21*	*4.05*	*4.28*	*4.65*	*9.0*	*1.8*	*5.3*	*1.3*	*10.2*	*0.8*

Breakout: 14%   *Improve: 31%*   *Collapse: 49%*   *Attrition: 17%*   *Comparables: Cris Carpenter, Tom Walker, John Wasdin*

Very few major league pitchers see any kind of prolonged success with the kind of extremely low groundball/flyball rates that Mateo has posted in the last three years. Mateo's stretched the limits of that theory, posting ERAs in the low-3s in two of his three full big league season. Relief ERAs can be deceptive, but even more sophisticated stats like expected wins added over a replacement-level pitcher (WXRL) reflect well on Mateo, ranking him second on the M's and 32nd among AL relievers. The margin for error is slim: Mateo's home run rates are likely to remain high, and even a small slip in his strong walk rates could turn those solo homers into two- and three-run shots, diminishing his value to the team.

GIL MECHE   Bats: R   Throws: R   Height: 6′ 3″   Weight: 200   Born: September 8, 1978   Age: 27

YEAR	TM	LVL	AGE	W	L	SV	G	GS	IP	H	BB	SO	HR	GB%	BABIP	STUFF	WHIP	ERA	PERA	EQERA	EQH9	EQBB9	EQSO9	EQHR9	VORP	WXRL
2003	SEA	MLB	24	15	13	0	32	32	186.3	187	63	130	30	41%	.285	0	1.34	4.59	4.97	5.02	9.5	3.0	6.2	1.4	27.8	4.6
2004	TAC	AAA	25	1	3	0	10	10	57.0	55	27	45	8	—	.275	-13	1.44	5.05	6.09	6.26	9.4	4.9	5.3	1.6	-4.0	—
2004	SEA	MLB	25	7	7	0	23	23	127.7	139	47	99	21	40%	.300	3	1.45	5.00	4.81	4.95	9.6	3.1	6.5	1.3	11.8	2.2
2005	SEA	MLB	26	10	8	0	29	26	143.3	153	72	83	18	41%	.296	-7	1.57	5.09	5.30	5.67	9.5	4.6	5.2	1.1	-1.8	1.4
2006	*SEA*	*MLB*	*27*	*6*	*9*	*0*	*32*	*20*	*126.0*	*133*	*53*	*80*	*18*	*42%*	*.289*	*-2*	*1.48*	*4.88*	*5.24*	*5.37*	*9.4*	*3.7*	*5.4*	*1.2*	*6.3*	*1.4*

Breakout: 21%   *Improve: 51%*   *Collapse: 18%*   *Attrition: 10%*   *Comparables: Tracy Stallard, Charles Hudson, Steve Mura*

Once a fireballing prospect and one of the brightest lights in the Mariner system, Meche had shoulder surgery in early 2001 and hasn't been the same since. As orthopedic surgeon and TJ pioneer Dr. Frank Jobe has noted, the complexity of the shoulder means that whenever you hear a report stating something like "partial fraying of the rotator cuff," you can be pretty sure there was also damage to the labrum and other structures, as was the case with Meche. The allure of a young arm slinging 97 mph fastballs drives teams to do some loopy things, and in today's market, $4 million for a pitcher coming off of a 26-start season isn't all that loopy. But the M's are chasing a dream that's not coming true. Until sports medicine technology takes a big leap forward, Meche's 2003 (32 starts, 4.59 ERA in a pitcher's park) is as good as it's going to get for pitchers coming off major shoulder surgery.

JAMIE MOYER Bats: L Throws: L Height: 6' 0" Weight: 170 Born: November 18, 1962 Age: 43

YEAR	TM	LVL	AGE	W	L	SV	G	GS	IP	H	BB	SO	HR	GB%	BABIP	STUFF	WHIP	ERA	PERA	EQERA	EQH9	EQBB9	EQSO9	EQHR9	VORP	WXRL
2003	SEA	MLB	40	21	7	0	33	33	215.0	199	66	129	19	42%	.272	14	1.23	3.27	4.26	3.91	9.1	2.8	5.4	0.8	61.3	6.5
2004	SEA	MLB	41	7	13	0	34	33	202.0	217	63	125	44	42%	.275	-14	1.39	5.21	5.69	5.42	10.0	2.6	5.3	1.8	9.4	2.1
2005	SEA	MLB	42	13	7	0	32	32	200.0	225	52	102	23	38%	.301	4	1.39	4.28	4.63	4.45	9.9	2.4	4.5	1.0	27.8	3.7
2006	*SEA*	*MLB*	*43*	*6*	*8*	*0*	*32*	*17*	*117.0*	*133*	*32*	*68*	*17*	*42%*	*.300*	*-8*	*1.41*	*5.08*	*5.15*	*6.38*	*10.1*	*2.4*	*4.9*	*1.3*	*4.2*	*0.9*

Breakout: 13% Improve: 37% Collapse: 52% Attrition: 34% Comparables: Warren Spahn, Don Sutton, Phil Niekro

The big salaries, constrained rosters, and cramped scheduling of today's game make it tough for a team to try something as unusual as a home-road tandem starter arrangement, but that's exactly what the Mariners should do here. Moyer went 10–0 with a 2.95 in 17 starts at Safeco last year, but just 3–7 with a 6.11 ERA and 16 homers allowed in 15 starts on the road. Unable to miss bats (his strikeout rate was the second-lowest of his career), Moyer is at the whim of his defense and the park behind him. Without the safety of Safeco's distant outfield walls, he's a replacement-level pitcher, a pity given his ability to deceive batters and keep the ball in the park at home. Moyer's not likely to go undefeated at Safeco again, but easing in a young gun like Jesse Foppert in a part-time role partnering with Moyer could help the team now and—in Foppert's case—into the future. Moyer negotiated his own contract in the off-season, a one-year, $5.5 million deal with incremental IP incentives. Moyer's logged 200 or more innings the last five years, and seven of the last eight, but he'd be a bigger help now if used more judiciously.

CLINT NAGEOTTE Bats: R Throws: R Height: 6' 3" Weight: 200 Born: October 25, 1980 Age: 25

YEAR	TM	LVL	AGE	W	L	SV	G	GS	IP	H	BB	SO	HR	GB%	BABIP	STUFF	WHIP	ERA	PERA	EQERA	EQH9	EQBB9	EQSO9	EQHR9	VORP	WXRL
2003	SAN	AA	22	11	7	0	27	27	154.0	127	67	157	6	—	.284	18	1.26	3.10	4.64	5.08	8.8	4.8	6.9	0.7	8.4	—
2004	TAC	AAA	23	6	6	0	14	14	80.7	78	35	63	9	—	.290	-1	1.40	4.46	5.40	5.06	9.2	4.4	5.4	1.1	4.7	—
2004	SEA	MLB	23	1	6	0	12	5	36.7	48	27	24	3	59%	.372	-13	2.05	7.36	5.40	7.28	10.8	5.9	5.4	0.7	-6.6	-0.1
2005	TAC	AAA	24	2	1	2	19	0	34.0	21	22	35	2	62%	.232	-4	1.26	2.65	4.78	4.78	7.0	6.2	7.0	0.6	2.9	—
2006	*SEA*	*MLB*	*25*	*2*	*3*	*1*	*29*	*3*	*44.3*	*46*	*25*	*32*	*4*	*49%*	*.301*	*-7*	*1.58*	*5.00*	*5.21*	*6.26*	*9.1*	*4.9*	*6.2*	*0.9*	*1.2*	*0.2*

Breakout: 25% Improve: 56% Collapse: 24% Attrition: 34% Comparables: Preston Hanna, John Urrea, Bryan Clark

A deluxe pitching prospect after fanning an incredible 214 batters in 164.2 A-ball innings in 2002, Nageotte's regressed into another decent, B-level young arm who could help the big club in a pinch. A lingering bad back and a forearm injury cost him half of the 2005 season, and his inability to hone his changeup as a third pitch may relegate him to relief work. The M's were encouraged by his AFL All-Star selection. There's still upside here, but only if the Mariners handle Nageotte nearly perfectly.

JEFF NELSON Bats: R Throws: R Height: 6' 8" Weight: 230 Born: November 17, 1966 Age: 39

YEAR	TM	LVL	AGE	W	L	SV	G	GS	IP	H	BB	SO	HR	GB%	BABIP	STUFF	WHIP	ERA	PERA	EQERA	EQH9	EQBB9	EQSO9	EQHR9	VORP	WXRL
2004	TEX	MLB	37	1	2	1	29	0	23.7	17	19	22	3	49%	.246	-7	1.52	5.32	5.32	5.32	7.2	6.8	8.0	1.1	1.3	0.6
2005	SEA	MLB	38	1	3	1	49	0	36.7	32	22	34	3	36%	.296	5	1.47	3.92	4.42	4.17	8.1	5.4	8.3	0.7	6.1	-0.2
2006	*SLN*	*MLB*	*39*	*1*	*1*	*1*	*17*	*0*	*18.3*	*18*	*10*	*17*	*2*	*42%*	*.305*	*-2*	*1.53*	*5.13*	*5.03*	*6.06*	*8.6*	*4.7*	*7.8*	*0.9*	*-0.2*	*0.0*

Breakout: 12% Improve: 23% Collapse: 46% Attrition: 58% Comparables: Lee Smith, Ted Abernathy, Don McMahon

He of the Frisbee slider is near the end, his fastball no longer an effective complement to his bread-and-butter glissante. Lefties hit him hard, and there's not much market for ROOGYs, with or without playoff mystique on the résumé. The Cardinals signed him in January, hoping to find a little mileage left before the odometer goes tilt.

JOEL PINEIRO Bats: R Throws: R Height: 6' 1" Weight: 180 Born: September 25, 1978 Age: 27

YEAR	TM	LVL	AGE	W	L	SV	G	GS	IP	H	BB	SO	HR	GB%	BABIP	STUFF	WHIP	ERA	PERA	EQERA	EQH9	EQBB9	EQSO9	EQHR9	VORP	WXRL
2003	SEA	MLB	24	16	11	0	32	32	211.7	192	76	151	19	49%	.276	18	1.27	3.78	4.17	4.35	8.8	3.3	6.4	0.8	46.9	4.8
2004	SEA	MLB	25	6	11	0	21	21	140.7	144	43	111	21	46%	.299	11	1.33	4.67	4.47	4.72	9.2	2.6	6.6	1.2	18.7	3.0
2005	SEA	MLB	26	7	11	0	30	30	189.0	224	56	107	23	46%	.326	2	1.48	5.62	4.66	5.55	10.1	2.7	4.9	1.0	2.3	1.4
2006	*SEA*	*MLB*	*27*	*10*	*11*	*0*	*30*	*28*	*176.7*	*192*	*53*	*110*	*21*	*46%*	*.298*	*8*	*1.39*	*4.44*	*4.75*	*4.81*	*9.7*	*2.6*	*5.3*	*1.0*	*16.8*	*3.0*

Breakout: 15% Improve: 60% Collapse: 8% Attrition: 0% Comparables: Pedro Astacio, Todd Stottlemyre, Jim Slaton

An elbow injury cost Pineiro the last two months of the 2004 season, sounding alarms that he could be the latest home-grown Mariner arm to bite the dust. Sure enough, his ERA ballooned to a near career high in 2005. Pineiro's walk rate stayed about the same from '04 to '05 and his home run rate actually fell, but Pineiro's hits allowed skyrocketed. Much of that was due to a big jump in his batting average allowed on balls in play. Given that BABIPs are largely a function of luck, that should come down in 2006. The bigger concern was the massive downturn in Pineiro's strikeouts; scouts noted a drop in his velocity, leading to speculation that his injuries have lingered. No longer the potential star he appeared to be early in his career, at this point the M's will settle for a league-average innings-muncher.

J. J. PUTZ   Bats: R   Throws: R   Height: 6' 5"   Weight: 220   Born: February 22, 1977   Age: 29

YEAR	TM	LVL	AGE	W	L	SV	G	GS	IP	H	BB	SO	HR	GB%	BABIP	STUFF	WHIP	ERA	PERA	EQERA	EQH9	EQBB9	EQSO9	EQHR9	VORP	WXRL
2003	TAC	AAA	26	0	3	11	41	0	86.0	69	34	60	4	—	.247	-5	1.20	2.51	4.69	4.35	8.4	4.5	5.2	0.7	11.2	—
2004	SEA	MLB	27	0	3	9	54	0	63.0	66	24	47	10	51%	.304	-7	1.43	4.71	4.97	4.83	9.5	3.1	6.3	1.3	8.4	1.0
2005	SEA	MLB	28	6	5	1	64	0	60.0	58	23	45	8	56%	.286	-2	1.35	3.60	4.65	4.05	8.9	3.5	6.8	1.2	10.9	0.7
2006	*SEA*	*MLB*	*29*	*2*	*2*	*2*	*47*	*0*	*50.3*	*51*	*20*	*35*	*5*	*50%*	*.295*	*-5*	*1.42*	*4.34*	*4.63*	*5.18*	*9.1*	*3.5*	*6.0*	*0.9*	*5.2*	*0.4*

Breakout: 20%   *Improve: 43%*   *Collapse: 25%*   *Attrition: 28%*   *Comparables: Luis Sanchez, Mike James, Jim Hearn*

On the strength of a solid if unspectacular 2005, Putz was slated to set up Eddie Guardado to start the season,. He's a cheap bullpen option with a mid-90s fastball but only so-so command. Rafael Soriano's the better talent, so look for Putz to slide down to the 6th and 7th inning before long, with a possible return to set-up duty once Guardado's traded or his contract runs out.

AARON SELE   Bats: R   Throws: R   Height: 6' 5"   Weight: 230   Born: June 25, 1970   Age: 36

YEAR	TM	LVL	AGE	W	L	SV	G	GS	IP	H	BB	SO	HR	GB%	BABIP	STUFF	WHIP	ERA	PERA	EQERA	EQH9	EQBB9	EQSO9	EQHR9	VORP	WXRL
2003	ANA	MLB	33	7	11	0	25	25	121.7	135	58	53	17	43%	.291	-18	1.59	5.77	5.80	5.88	10.3	4.2	3.9	1.2	-3.0	1.6
2004	ANA	MLB	34	9	4	0	28	24	132.0	163	51	51	16	46%	.324	-12	1.66	5.05	5.25	5.39	10.4	3.2	3.2	1.0	5.2	1.6
2005	SEA	MLB	35	6	12	0	21	21	116.0	147	41	53	18	42%	.326	-14	1.62	5.66	5.54	5.84	10.8	3.2	4.0	1.4	-3.4	1.7
2006	*LAN*	*MLB*	*36*	*5*	*6*	*0*	*26*	*14*	*91.7*	*102*	*34*	*47*	*13*	*45%*	*.290*	*-14*	*1.49*	*5.08*	*5.58*	*6.27*	*10.1*	*3.1*	*4.1*	*1.3*	*-0.2*	*0.5*

Breakout: 28%   *Improve: 40%*   *Collapse: 25%*   *Attrition: 20%*   *Comparables: Jim Clancy, Jack Billingham, Bob Forsch*

August 1, 2005 was a dark day for physiotherapists in the Pioneer Square area. For four months, they'd gotten fat on the steady stream of whiplash cases that hobbled over from Safeco for treatment after witnessing the latest Sele debacle. At his best, Sele was a control pitcher and innings eater who benefited from good run support, a good defense behind him, or both. More often, he was a body with which to fill out the back of a rotation.

GEORGE SHERRILL   Bats: L   Throws: L   Height: 6' 0"   Weight: 210   Born: April 19, 1977   Age: 29

YEAR	TM	LVL	AGE	W	L	SV	G	GS	IP	H	BB	SO	HR	GB%	BABIP	STUFF	WHIP	ERA	PERA	EQERA	EQH9	EQBB9	EQSO9	EQHR9	VORP	WXRL
2004	TAC	AAA	27	4	2	13	36	0	50.3	42	9	62	4	—	.309	15	1.01	2.33	3.51	3.51	8.1	1.8	8.0	0.9	11.3	—
2004	SEA	MLB	27	2	1	0	21	0	23.7	24	9	16	3	40%	.284	-6	1.39	3.80	4.94	4.56	9.1	3.0	5.7	1.1	4.0	0.5
2005	TAC	AAA	28	1	3	7	22	0	23.7	19	6	38	0	53%	.358	23	1.05	2.28	2.74	3.91	8.2	2.3	9.8	0.4	4.3	—
2005	SEA	MLB	28	4	3	0	29	0	19.0	13	7	24	3	40%	.250	18	1.05	5.21	3.86	5.79	6.8	3.4	11.6	1.4	0.0	0.9
2006	*SEA*	*MLB*	*29*	*2*	*3*	*4*	*64*	*1*	*51.0*	*48*	*18*	*46*	*6*	*42%*	*.288*	*7*	*1.28*	*3.95*	*4.08*	*4.47*	*8.3*	*3.0*	*7.7*	*1.0*	*7.7*	*0.7*

Breakout: 21%   *Improve: 56%*   *Collapse: 21%*   *Attrition: 25%*   *Comparables: Ricardo Rincon, John Hiller, Paul Assenmacher*

Yes it was a small sample size, but Sherrill's .156/.170/.333 allowed versus lefties continued his solid track record. With tasty strikeout rates and a league-minimum salary, the M's seem to have struck the LOOGY jackpot. There are plenty more long-time minor league relievers capable of getting major league hitters out, if only teams would stop overpaying the Ray Kings and Steve Klines of the world and go looking for them.

RAFAEL SORIANO   Bats: R   Throws: R   Height: 6' 1"   Weight: 170   Born: December 19, 1979   Age: 26

YEAR	TM	LVL	AGE	W	L	SV	G	GS	IP	H	BB	SO	HR	GB%	BABIP	STUFF	WHIP	ERA	PERA	EQERA	EQH9	EQBB9	EQSO9	EQHR9	VORP	WXRL
2003	TAC	AAA	23	4	3	0	11	10	62.0	43	12	63	2	—	.250	36	0.89	3.19	3.19	4.40	7.3	2.0	7.9	0.5	7.9	—
2003	SEA	MLB	23	3	0	1	40	0	53.0	30	12	68	2	39%	.243	51	0.79	1.53	2.28	1.75	6.0	2.1	11.6	0.4	26.8	2.2
2006	*SEA*	*MLB*	*26*	*3*	*3*	*4*	*48*	*1*	*56.3*	*50*	*17*	*55*	*6*	*40%*	*.284*	*16*	*1.18*	*3.51*	*3.58*	*4.03*	*7.9*	*2.6*	*8.2*	*0.9*	*10.8*	*1.1*

Breakout: 15%   *Improve: 38%*   *Collapse: 36%*   *Attrition: 23%*   *Comparables: Rawly Eastwick, Dave Smith, Juan Rincon*

Soriano regained his mid-90s velocity of old, looking sharp in seven late-season outings as he put his Tommy John surgery behind him. He'll head to spring training as the co-setup man, along with Putz, in front of Eddie Guardado. That arrangement won't last if Soriano's arm holds up. He's one of the few players the M's consider close to untouchable, with both the statistical track record and the stuff to back up his rep. Rotoheads, here's an August 1 closer if the Mariners are out of the race and flip Guardado, a pretty likely scenario.

MATT THORNTON   **Bats: L   Throws: L**   Height: 6' 6"   Weight: 220   Born: September 15, 1976   Age: 29

YEAR	TM	LVL	AGE	W	L	SV	G	GS	IP	H	BB	SO	HR	GB%	BABIP	STUFF	WHIP	ERA	PERA	EQERA	EQH9	EQBB9	EQSO9	EQHR9	VORP	WXRL
2004	TAC	AAA	27	7	5	0	16	15	83.0	86	63	74	4	—	.332	-5	1.80	5.42	5.69	6.81	9.3	8.0	5.8	0.6	-10.8	—
2004	SEA	MLB	27	1	2	0	19	1	32.7	30	25	30	2	38%	.326	2	1.76	4.13	4.36	4.09	8.2	6.3	7.6	0.5	6.2	0.3
2005	SEA	MLB	28	0	4	0	55	0	57.0	54	42	57	13	45%	.277	-13	1.68	5.21	6.16	5.05	8.7	6.6	8.8	2.1	2.8	-0.4
2006	SEA	MLB	29	2	3	1	39	2	47.7	45	33	41	5	42%	.288	-8	1.62	5.15	5.39	6.83	8.4	6.1	7.2	1.0	1.0	0.1

Breakout: 26%   Improve: 40%   Collapse: 30%   Attrition: 41%   Comparables: Stephen Randolph, Armando Almanza, Karl Drews

Live fastball, nasty slider, a strikeout an inning in his first full year in the bigs—but yikes, check out the walks and homers! He's another Mariners' 1st-round pick from a zillion years ago (1998) who looked like a prospect but never panned out. Lousy control was the main culprit, but he added 2002 Tommy John surgery and 2004 shoulder pain to gain his membership badge in the Mariners' scarred-up slingers' club. It's hard to see Thornton suddenly finding the plate as he prepares to enter his 30s.

Line Outs

Position/Player	TM	LVL	AGE	PA	R	2B	3B	HR	RBI	BB	SO	SB-CS	SPEED	BA/OBP/SLG	MLVR	EQBA/OBP/SLG	EQA	VORP
OF T. J. Bohn	SAN	AA	25	479	67	30	2	12	57	35	96	27-9	6.2	.308/.365/.468	.212	.277/.328/.414	.259	1.7
UT H. Brown	TAC	AAA	25	380	53	30	1	7	53	33	71	8-4	5.2	.291/.366/.448	.134	.272/.333/.409	.258	12.5
1B G. Dobbs*	TAC	AAA	27	207	27	9	0	3	22	14	22	5-2	5.0	.321/.367/.416	.118	.300/.338/.374	.252	0.5
	SEA	MLB	27	153	8	7	1	1	20	9	25	1-0	3.9	.246/.288/.331	-.212	.257/.307/.343	.233	-3.8
C W. Gonzalez	TAC	AAA	31	195	25	10	1	5	28	16	13	0-0	3.9	.312/.374/.466	.200	.276/.321/.385	.246	3.4
C R. Rivera	SAN	AA	21	220	20	14	1	2	21	7	35	1-0	4.0	.278/.305/.382	-.040	.264/.294/.364	.229	-1.6
INF S. Spiezio#	SEA	MLB	32	51	2	1	0	1	1	4	18	0-0	2.2	.064/.137/.149	-.809	.065/.157/.152	.126	-8.6

Pitcher	TM	LVL	AGE	W	L	SV	IP	H	BB	SO	HR	GB%	BABIP	STUFF	WHIP	ERA	PERA	EQERA	EQH9	EQBB9	EQSO9	EQHR9	VORP
J. Campillo	TAC	AAA	26	4	1	0	66.3	63	18	43	5	54%	.297	2	1.22	2.71	4.50	3.94	9.1	2.7	4.2	0.8	11.8
S. Green	SAN	AA	26	0	1	14	24.3	17	8	18	1	67%	.225	-18	1.03	2.96	4.84	5.64	7.7	4.4	4.8	0.8	-0.1
	TAC	AAA	26	4	2	1	49.3	40	29	44	1	64%	.287	-6	1.40	3.65	4.56	5.13	8.2	5.7	5.7	0.2	2.5
N. Mateo	MOB	AA	24	3	4	1	52.7	57	15	39	2	42%	.331	-14	1.37	3.07	4.53	5.05	9.6	3.0	4.2	0.7	3.2

Not a prospect, **T. J. Bohn** could be a useful major league fifth outfielder. He's a good enough flycatcher to play center when needed, with the best throwing arm in the organization outside of Ichiro. **Hunter Brown** played seven positions at Triple-A, logging a .366 OBP and a double every 11 at-bats in pitcher-friendly Tacoma. A better utilityman candidate for the M's than stiffs like **Greg Dobbs.** Dobbs has no power, patience or defensive value; the second-worst bench in the majors last year will be better just by subtracting this guy. Designated for assignment and unsurprisingly unclaimed. The four-year contract **Wiki Gonzalez** got after 160 productive ABs in 2001 ranks with Einar Diaz's four-year deal that same year as shining examples of teams' desperation for catchers. Signed by the Nationals to a minor league deal, he's a long shot to contribute. It says a lot about how far the Marlins have fallen that **Pokey Reese** had a decent shot at the team's 2B job as we went to press. A listless hitter, **Rene Rivera** will see ample time in Seattle this year anyway thanks to a reputation as a good receiver, his youth, and a fluky .396 average in 48 late-season at-bats. **Scott Spiezio** posted the eighth-worst performance by all MLB non-pitchers with at least 50 plate appearances since 1972, ranked by MLVr. The worst during that period was Manny Alexander in 1996, with −1.013 in 73 PAs. Spiezio was released in August, but there's a year left on his three-year, $9.3 million contract.

Another M's pitcher under the knife, **Jorge Campillo** has blown out his elbow. He'll miss all of 2006, but could be a rotation dark horse in '07. **Sean Green** is an effective groundball pitcher who could crack the big league roster when the inevitable injuries occur—think of a younger Todd Williams. Acquired in the Olivo trade, **Nathanel Mateo** is a serviceable arm who could see big league playing time if the Mariners' pitching attrition continues.

Tampa Bay Devil Rays

It's hard to believe, but after the Marlins' red tag sale of last winter, Tampa Bay is now the Florida baseball team with dignity. This is not so much something they earned as something that has fallen to them by default, like a regimental flag picked out of the dirt after the machine gunners cut down the color guard. Whether it means anything more than that, whether the Devil Rays can capture an audience for themselves where the Marlins have failed, where they themselves have heretofore failed, remains to be seen.

While it is not certain that if the Devil Rays build "it," a winner, the fans will come, it is more certain than ever that success on the field is within their grasp. If the new administration headed by managing general partner Stuart Sternberg, Team President Matt Silverman, General Manager Andrew Friedman, Senior Vice-President of Baseball Operations Gerry Hunsicker, manager Joe Maddon, and the rest of the New Look cohort can depart from the practices of the disgraced Old Regime and formulate a coherent building plan, sort their options accurately and aggressively—and occasionally throw a few dollars into the mix—the Rays can make quick headway against the soft underbelly of the American League East.

One of the myths about the Old Regime, fronted by managing general partner Vince Naimoli and the franchise's original GM, Chuck LaMar, is that one of the ways the Devil Rays conspired to keep themselves buried in last place in the AL East—where they have finished in seven of the franchise's eight years of existence—is that they were too frequently burned by trading away vibrant young players for the wretched refuse of the majors. This is not true. While the trade of Bobby Abreu for Kevin Stocker, consummated on November 18, 1997, the very night of the expansion draft that brought the Devil Rays into existence, will always be the franchise's original sin, trades were not the Old Regime's undoing. Indeed, LaMar's crowning moment as GM, his one likely legacy, Scott Kazmir, came

DEVIL RAYS PROSPECTUS

2005 record: 67–95; Fifth place, AL East

Pythagenport record: 64–98

Runs scored per game: 4.63 (8th in AL)

Runs allowed per game: 5.78 (14th in AL)

Team EqA: .265 (4th in AL)

2005 Batters Age: 28.0 (Youngest in AL)

2005 Pitchers Age: 27.6 (3rd youngest in AL)

Ballpark: Tropicana Field; Slight pitcher's park; Park Factor of 0.982

2005: Remained mired in the sludgy sands of irrelevance, causing Lou Piniella to finally say "uncle."

2006: New management has the opportunity to bring rational decision-making to the Rays, but will they?

in a trade of an older player for a younger one. Rather, it was a thoroughgoing lack of judgment that afflicted the Rays. When the Old Regime had a chance to make an evaluation, be it the viability of a single ballplayer or the design for the team as a whole, they mostly missed, missed by such huge margins that it was sometimes difficult to discern what it was they had been aiming for in the first place.

The history of the first eight years of the Devil Rays is one of myopic fumbling. When the Old Regime took its first look at the stadium it would one day call home, it arbitrarily decided that since the Rays were to play on artificial turf, under a dome, the building would function as a sort of time portal back to Busch Stadium c. 1985. Therefore, they reasoned, they should build the team with an emphasis on speed. Thus were the Rays begun with Quinton McCracken, Mike Kelly, Randy Winn, and Kerry Robinson in their midst. As it turned out, the building was quite willing to yield up home runs. Even so, had Tropicana Field played precisely as they imagined it would, rounding up these deadball-era types still wouldn't have worked. The Devil Rays were born into one of the most explosive offensive eras in history, one that was only going to get worse. They couldn't have know that, of course, but they did have the benefit of hindsight—the Rays were joining a league in which the average team had bashed 177 home runs *and* stolen 107 bases. Stolen bases alone weren't going to cut it, and they didn't.

From there, the Devil Rays were much the same as Winston Churchill's description of Stanley Baldwin's government: decided only to be undecided, resolved to be irresolute, adamant for drift, solid for fluidity. The Rays careened from one "solution" to another, most infamously the free agent shopping spree that was intended to rectify the mistakes of the expansion draft and recast the Rays as sluggardly sluggers. Fred McGriff, Jose Canseco, Greg Vaughn, and Vinny Castilla were married to a pitching staff that was so weak—well, it might be easier to say they weren't married to a pitching staff at all. The rest of the roster was utterly neglected as well. Within a year the Rays lost 100 games for the first time. By then they had abandoned the power strategy, giving extensive playing time to Jason Tyner, the ultimate non-slugger. By 2003, the Rays were ready for their next get-fixed-quick tactic, celebrity manager Lou Piniella, a man whose volatility made him a poor fit for a job that required patience most of all.

Despite their reputation for making bad trades involving kids, most of LaMar's trades during this period involved veterans. Like the old Jewish joke about a restaurant where the food is terrible and the portions are too small, LaMar not only didn't trade well, he didn't trade often enough. When contending teams clamored for him to yield up any of his few viable vets, LaMar either demurred or asked for the moon—quickly garnering a reputation for inflexibility. When he did deal, the yield was negligible. Roberto Hernandez and Cory Lidle brought another slow slugger in Ben Grieve, whose career was to disintegrate on the Devil Rays' watch; Fred McGriff returned only fringe reliever Manny Aybar, who never did pitch for the Devil Rays, and confirmed non-prospect Jason Smith; Randy Winn was dealt for Antonio Perez, an intriguing prospect who was never tried.

Meanwhile, players came and went at a dizzying pace. It wasn't so much that the Rays didn't have good players during this period, but rather that when they had good players, or even poor players that nonetheless had the potential to succeed for a year or two, the Rays could not exploit them. This applied to both prospects and veterans. All of these players turned into something better after passing through the Tampa Bay organization: Corey Lidle, Tony Graffanino, Jose Guillen, Brendan Donnelly, Chris Reitsma, Tom Martin, Wilson Alvarez, Antonio Perez, Joe Kennedy, Tanyon Sturtze, Todd Williams, Javier Valentin, Al Reyes, Todd Jones, Jose Bautista, Brandon Backe. None of these were potential MVP or Cy Young award winners, but other organizations found a way to wring productive seasons from them. The same lack of insight that afflicted LaMar also affected the entire parade of Rays coaches and managers, none of whom could help these players reach the potential that other organizations found so easily.

The New Look front office moved deliberately in its first months. There has been no dramatic roster shake-up, but then no roster shake-up is really necessary, at least among the position players. The 2005 Devil Rays had a decent if unspectacular offense, ranking fourth in the American League with a team EQA of .263. The lineup should be more potent in 2005 with the return of Rocco Baldelli, a full season of Jonny Gomes, and a rebound season from Aubrey Huff, assuming he remains with the team. The integration of B. J. Upton and Delmon Young can't happen soon enough. New batting coach George Hendrick will also have to convince his charges to take four wide ones periodically; lack of selectivity has been a persistent problem during the team's short history. The starting rotation is more problematic. In 2005, Devil Rays starters had an ERA of 5.62, second to last in the American League—Kansas City had a very special 6.00 from their starters.

New pitching coach Mike Butcher will be challenged to make pitchers out of projects that thwarted his predecessor, Chuck Hernandez. It might be that no pitching coach can teach Seth McClung control or get Mark Hendrickson to strike out the occasional batter, but even a small, sustained breakthrough on the part of any of the team's non-Kazmir starters would make a big difference in the team's outlook. Even Kazmir is a project in the sense that he too requires refinement and careful handling lest the team burn him out at 22.

In a quiet winter that seems to have been spent in contemplative study of the roster's many possibilities, the Devil Rays signed just one major league free agent, Ty Wigginton, and made only two significant trades. While it's not much of an exaggeration to say that LaMar was resistant to any trade, both deals were the kind that he would have hesitated to make. In the first, the Rays acquired Sean Burroughs from the Padres for disgruntled pitcher Dewon Brazelton. This was a case of a project being exchanged for a project. The Padres couldn't persuade Burroughs to hit with authority and the Devil Rays could neither make a pitcher of Brazelton nor get along with him. If Hendrick can get through to Burroughs, a player of clear physical abilities, the deal would represent a break with the long line of replacement-level characters that have played the hot corner beneath the orange juice dome.

LaMar would likewise have been too inhibited to deal closer Danny Baez and former closer Lance Carter to the Dodgers for pitchers Edwin Jackson and Chuck Tiffany, a high risk, high reward trade. The Rays sold high on Baez, trading him at his apparent peak, in exchange for two pitching prospects that are more speculative than most. Jackson, though still quite young, no longer resembles the phenom who made it to the majors in 2003 at age 19. He will have to be rebuilt from the ground up, mechanically and psychically, a more complicated reclamation project than any the Rays have heretofore attempted. Tiffany is a good prospect, but he's not a hard thrower and having not pitched above the Florida State League he's miles from the bigs.

The Rays have moved with considerably less abandon when it comes to dealing with their roster congestion. Shortstop Julio Lugo has been much sought-after as he moves into his last year before free agency. The Rays have sorted their options, deliberated, but the only answer that potential trading partners have received is a Bartleby-like "We would prefer not to." Delmon Young has little left to learn in the minor leagues, but with Baldelli, Gomes, Carl Crawford, and Aubrey Huff still on hand, there's no room for him. Huff has been asked after for years, but again, the Devil Rays would prefer not to. The speedy Joey Gathright is coveted as a potential center field and leadoff solution by a number of teams, but the Devil Rays would prefer not to.

Ballplayers are not imperishable commodities. They don't become more attractive as they sit on the shelf. Similarly, the teams that desire them don't wait around; they pursue other options. With certain players there comes a time when their attractiveness to another club far outweighs any value they might have to their originating organization. Such is the case of Gathright, a player not good enough to crack Tampa's outfield. Similarly, the Braves and Red Sox ardently pursued Lugo, but when the Rays seemed reluctant to deal, the former acquired Edgar Renteria from the latter—an inferior player—while the Red Sox subsequently turned towards the free agent market. Gathright and Lugo are not star players. Gathright may not even be a viable regular, but need has inflated his value. That window will close, and his subsequent play will only expose his shortcomings.

The Devil Rays could be, at the very least, a .500 team, with the addition of another on-base threat (B. J. Upton, trapped in the minors due to the Old Regime's insistence that he can play shortstop, will do for starters) and two more reliable starters. Jason Hammel could cut that need in half by opening day, and, assuming health, Jeff Niemann could complete the picture in the second half. Simultaneously, Young could eventually give the club the MVP candidate it has never had, a top-tier offensive player they can build around. Things can change in a hurry for the Devil Rays if they can only coach their youngsters sufficiently that they don't squander whatever abilities they showed in the minors, if they bring them up at all rather than let them be displaced by inferior vets, as LaMar did. The Old Regime would have fumbled these opportunities. Will the New Look front office see their chances where the Old Regime was blind to them? Do they want to risk meeting the challenge of building a roster head on?

> "What is your answer, Bartleby?" said I, after waiting a considerable time for a reply, during which his countenance remained immovable, only there was the faintest conceivable tremor of the white attenuated mouth.
>
> "At present I prefer to give no answer," he said, and retired into his hermitage.

HITTERS

WES BANKSTON   **1B**   **Bats: R**   **Throws: R**   Height: 6' 4"   Weight: 200   Born: November 23, 1983   Age: 22

YEAR	TM	LVL	AGE	PA	R	2B	3B	HR	RBI	BB	SO	SB	CS	SPEED	BA	OBP	SLG	MLVR	EQBA	EQOBP	EQSLG	EQA	VORP	DEFENSE
2003	CSC	A	19	436	46	18	1	12	60	53	94	2	3	3.1	.256	.346	.405	.124	.236	.309	.386	.242	-11.5	88-RF -7
2004	CSC	A	20	551	82	30	3	23	101	73	104	9	0	5.2	.289	.390	.513	.292	.257	.339	.441	.270	11.0	89-1B 3
2005	MNT	AA	21	337	42	17	2	12	47	30	64	3	3	4.3	.292	.362	.482	.208	.270	.330	.456	.267	8.4	66-1B -1
2006	TBA	MLB	22	516	59	24	2	18	68	43	108	3	2	4.4	.260	.325	.434	-.006	.265	.337	.458	.263	10.2	121-1B -1

Breakout: 21%   Improve: 45%   Collapse: 26%   Attrition: 4%   Comparables: Juan Tejeda, Justin Huber, Justin Morneau

Although the minimum prerequisites for first base are not particularly intense—Wanted: Burly slugger. Need not be too mobile. Apply within—the Rays have had a hard time locating anyone who fits that description. Since Fred McGriff hit an aggregate .294/.383/.496 during the Devil Rays' first four years, the team's first base production has been wholly inadequate. Bankston should change that. He has good power and is randy for the strike zone. More athletic than your typical first baseman, he was moved from the outfield only because of the organization's surplus there. Bankston missed six weeks with a knee injury, and a wrist injury dented his 2003 numbers. Assuming he stays healthy, he'll be pressuring Travis Lee from the get-go.

ROCCO BALDELLI   **CF**   **Bats: R Throws: R**   Height: 6′ 4″   Weight: 195   Born: September 25, 1981   Age: 24

YEAR	TM	LVL	AGE	PA	R	2B	3B	HR	RBI	BB	SO	SB	CS	SPEED	BA	OBP	SLG	MLVR	EQBA	EQOBP	EQSLG	EQA	VORP	DEFENSE
2003	TBA	MLB	21	681	89	32	8	11	78	30	128	27	10	6.9	.289	.326	.416	-.009	.291	.332	.422	.262	19.7	149-CF 6
2004	TBA	MLB	22	562	79	27	3	16	74	30	88	17	4	6.2	.280	.326	.436	-.007	.283	.330	.444	.268	18.3	119-CF 0
2006	TBA	MLB	24	418	53	19	2	10	46	21	66	14	2	6.2	.273	.315	.415	-.035	.279	.328	.439	.259	13.2	99-CF 1

Breakout: 10%   Improve: 34%   Collapse: 25%   Attrition: 15%   Comparables: Mickey Stanley, Vernon Wells, Rondell White

Baldelli tore his ACL in October 2004. On the verge of returning, he blew out his throwing elbow and underwent season-ending Tommy John surgery. Before he got hurt, PECOTA's weighted mean projection for last year called for him to stay roughly where he was, but with some added power. That's all up in the air now. Historically, players who have come back after a year off have seen a significant degradation of their skills. However, most of them were older than Baldelli when they took their extended vacations, so the time off served to accelerate a slowing of the reflexes that was already taking place. Despite his youth, Baldelli may suffer the same effect. Speed and defense are central to his game, and it remains to be seen how the injuries will affect his running and throwing. The D-Rays voiced their confidence in Baldelli's ability to come back by signing him to a six-year contract in November.

REID BRIGNAC   **SS**   **Bats: L Throws: R**   Height: 6′ 3″   Weight: 170   Born: January 16, 1986   Age: 20

YEAR	TM	LVL	AGE	PA	R	2B	3B	HR	RBI	BB	SO	SB	CS	SPEED	BA	OBP	SLG	MLVR	EQBA	EQOBP	EQSLG	EQA	VORP	DEFENSE
2004	PRI	Rk	18	109	16	4	2	1	25	9	10	2	1	5.0	.361	.413	.474	.286	.286	.325	.380	.245	6.5	24-SS 1
2005	SWM	A	19	561	77	29	2	15	61	40	131	5	5	4.4	.264	.319	.416	.010	.229	.274	.366	.222	-8.7	124-SS -20
2006	TBA	MLB	20	489	50	25	2	12	54	27	106	3	3	4.4	.232	.277	.378	-.176	.237	.288	.399	.226	3.9	116-SS -4

Breakout: 32%   Improve: 53%   Collapse: 28%   Attrition: 5%   Comparables: Brandon Wood, Scott Moore, Corey Smith

The Old Regime's 2nd round draft pick in 2004, Brignac had a strong debut for a prep prospect, then put up a strong first full season in a tough hitting environment. If he can stay at short, he'll have above-average power for the position, and though his swing and pitch selection need improvement, he's starting from a good place given his age and inexperience.

JORGE CANTU   **2B/3B**   **Bats: R Throws: R**   Height: 6′ 1″   Weight: 170   Born: January 30, 1982   Age: 24

YEAR	TM	LVL	AGE	PA	R	2B	3B	HR	RBI	BB	SO	SB	CS	SPEED	BA	OBP	SLG	MLVR	EQBA	EQOBP	EQSLG	EQA	VORP	DEFENSE	
2003	ORL	AA	21	170	15	10	0	3	17	9	27	0	3	3.4	.215	.259	.335	-.174	.197	.237	.334	.199	-10.6	33-3B 0	
2003	DUR	AAA	21	216	26	16	1	4	30	8	21	2	1	4.7	.295	.319	.445	.056	.273	.303	.428	.252	7.1	49-SS -6	
2004	DUR	AAA	22	391	57	33	1	22	80	16	64	3	0	4.8	.302	.335	.576	.214	.264	.301	.507	.269	21.2	44-2B 5	37-SS -4
2004	TBA	MLB	22	185	25	20	1	2	17	9	44	0	0	4.7	.301	.341	.462	.124	.304	.348	.462	.277	11.6	31-2B 0	11-3B 0
2005	TBA	MLB	23	630	73	40	1	28	117	19	83	1	0	3.5	.286	.311	.497	.095	.294	.327	.520	.283	31.4	76-2B -5	57-3B -7
2006	TBA	MLB	24	617	71	36	2	24	90	25	90	1	1	4.1	.271	.306	.463	.011	.277	.318	.489	.263	24.6	144-2B -5	

Breakout: 19%   Improve: 47%   Collapse: 21%   Attrition: 7%   Comparables: Jim Presley, Ernie Banks, Willie Jones

Try to follow along with the Old Regime's reasoning: in 2003 your second baseman is Marlon Anderson, who does so well that he will never again hold a regular job. Meanwhile, Cantu plays 60 games at Durham and does pretty darn well. Still, the guy is quite young; he's impatient at the plate, and his glove leaves much to be desired, so you decide to sit on him for a year. You wind up with Rey Sanchez and Geoff Blum manning the keystone. They're abysmal. On July 17, 2004, Cantu comes up from the minors. Everything about him is the same—the glove, the impatience—but the guy does something none of your other second basemen do: he *hits*. Now it's winter. You cannot hope to contend in 2005. You can only hope to grow towards contending. So what do you do—give this Cantu kid a chance? No, you sign Roberto Alomar, who everyone knows is finished. Even he knows he's finished, and it's only by virtue of his last-minute retirement that you don't screw yourself again. Cantu offers a valuable lesson: never consider a player in a vacuum. Cantu has flaws, but he's infinitely valuable when the alternative is *nothing*.

FERNANDO CORTEZ   **2B**   **Bats: L Throws: R**   Height: 6′ 1″   Weight: 170   Born: August 10, 1981   Age: 24

YEAR	TM	LVL	AGE	PA	R	2B	3B	HR	RBI	BB	SO	SB	CS	SPEED	BA	OBP	SLG	MLVR	EQBA	EQOBP	EQSLG	EQA	VORP	DEFENSE	
2004	MNT	AA	22	394	51	20	5	3	30	32	60	8	7	5.7	.287	.345	.396	.075	.274	.326	.375	.245	7.0	94-2B 4	
2005	MNT	AA	23	239	39	11	4	0	23	15	42	12	3	7.1	.333	.377	.420	.181	.310	.344	.401	.265	10.9	35-2B -1	17-SS 3
2005	DUR	AAA	23	252	26	8	2	2	26	10	38	13	1	6.9	.227	.266	.303	-.327	.208	.249	.280	.200	-17.4	56-2B -4	
2006	TBA	MLB	24	406	44	16	4	3	32	22	66	12	4	5.7	.254	.298	.342	-.173	.259	.309	.361	.229	1.0	97-2B -1	

Breakout: 25%   Improve: 50%   Collapse: 27%   Attrition: 19%   Comparables: Bill Spiers, Sonny Jackson, Willie Bloomquist

Back in 1975, Neil Young had a hit song called "Cortez the Killer." This Cortez is far more benign—sort of Cortez the Harmless—because he can't hit. Given his track record, last year's showing at Montgomery is best viewed as a fluke. He's a decent fielder and he can nab a bag, but that's all. When Alex Gonzalez hit the DL in early July, the Rays shifted Cantu over to third and promoted Cortez to the majors. Cortez's stay lasted exactly three weeks, with predictably poor results; after the season he was taken off the 40-man roster. Young must have anticipated the Devil Rays with "Cortez." when he sang, "I still can't remember when or how I lost my way."

CARL CRAWFORD OF **Bats: L Throws: L** Height: 6' 2" Weight: 203 Born: August 5, 1981 Age: 24

YEAR	TM	LVL	AGE	PA	R	2B	3B	HR	RBI	BB	SO	SB	CS	SPEED	BA	OBP	SLG	MLVR	EQBA	EQOBP	EQSLG	EQA	VORP	DEFENSE			
2003	TBA	MLB	21	660	80	18	9	5	54	26	102	55	10	8.3	.281	.309	.362	-.120	.282	.317	.369	.251	-1.8	131-LF	6	12-CF	0
2004	TBA	MLB	22	668	104	26	19	11	55	35	81	59	15	8.8	.296	.331	.450	.041	.299	.339	.460	.278	24.6	115-LF	6	26-CF	0
2005	TBA	MLB	23	682	101	33	15	15	81	27	84	46	8	8.6	.301	.331	.469	.101	.312	.350	.498	.292	37.3	142-LF	-7		
2006	*TBA*	*MLB*	*24*	*680*	*103*	*32*	*10*	*13*	*65*	*30*	*86*	*45*	*11*	*7.6*	*.290*	*.324*	*.433*	*.016*	*.296*	*.337*	*.457*	*.269*	*19.9*	*158-LF*	*2*		

Breakout: 26% Improve: 47% Collapse: 18% Attrition: 1% Comparables: Willie Davis, Darin Erstad, Willie Wilson

Crawford has gotten a little bit better every year. Last year he set career highs in slugging percentage, batting average, and home runs while tying his career high in OBP. The only thing he didn't improve was his walk rate, which actually dropped from one every 19.2 plate appearances in 2004 to one every 25.4. He's miscast as a leadoff man; his OBP hasn't reached league average in any of his four seasons. That doesn't diminish his value: he's among the fastest players in the game, which allows him to play great defense and leg out extra-base hits, the latter giving him a frisson of power not provided by his bat. Just 24, he should keep doing this for years.

ELIJAH DUKES OF **Bats: B Throws: R** Height: 6' 2" Weight: 220 Born: June 26, 1984 Age: 22

YEAR	TM	LVL	AGE	PA	R	2B	3B	HR	RBI	BB	SO	SB	CS	SPEED	BA	OBP	SLG	MLVR	EQBA	EQOBP	EQSLG	EQA	VORP	DEFENSE			
2003	CSC	A	19	441	51	17	4	7	53	45	130	33	11	6.8	.245	.338	.366	.055	.232	.302	.358	.237	-19.6	101-LF	-3		
2004	CSC	A	20	185	26	12	2	2	15	18	47	14	1	7.2	.288	.368	.423	.137	.261	.320	.376	.251	-4.0	30-LF	1		
2004	BAK	A+	20	243	44	16	2	8	34	26	50	16	7	6.5	.332	.416	.540	.391	.290	.359	.462	.281	9.0	31-LF	3	24-CF	2
2005	MNT	AA	21	498	73	21	5	18	73	45	83	19	9	5.9	.287	.355	.478	.187	.263	.322	.444	.262	16.3	79-CF	-6	24-LF	-2
2006	*TBA*	*MLB*	*22*	*530*	*66*	*25*	*3*	*15*	*61*	*38*	*109*	*16*	*5*	*5.5*	*.256*	*.314*	*.412*	*-.053*	*.262*	*.327*	*.435*	*.256*	*10.3*	*125-CF*	*-4*		

Breakout: 16% Improve: 49% Collapse: 19% Attrition: 5% Comparables: Milton Bradley, Carlos Beltran, Ryan Langerhans

An anger management guy. As we've seen with Milton Bradley, the on-field production you get from players like this does not necessarily exceed the aggravation they cause. A product of Tampa's famous Hillsborough High—the same institution that gave us upright citizens such as Dwight Gooden and Carl Everett—Dukes is apparently incapable of reining in his emotions, even if it means sacrificing a career that could be worth millions of dollars. As with Bradley, Dukes has a domestic violence arrest on his record, moving him from the "player with a handicap you can root for him to overcome" category to one more sinister. Dukes could still be a star. With a bit more discernment in the basestealing department, Dukes could be a 30-30 guy in the majors, and perhaps a center fielder as well. All he has to do is stay calm.

JOEY GATHRIGHT CF **Bats: L Throws: R** Height: 5' 10" Weight: 170 Born: April 27, 1981 Age: 25

YEAR	TM	LVL	AGE	PA	R	2B	3B	HR	RBI	BB	SO	SB	CS	SPEED	BA	OBP	SLG	MLVR	EQBA	EQOBP	EQSLG	EQA	VORP	DEFENSE	
2003	BAK	A+	22	387	65	6	3	0	23	41	54	57	13	7.6	.324	.406	.359	.120	.288	.358	.317	.256	2.4	61-CF	0
2004	MNT	AA	23	138	23	5	1	0	8	11	30	10	6	6.8	.341	.399	.397	.205	.327	.381	.382	.271	7.6	22-CF	0
2004	DUR	AAA	23	258	34	9	1	0	8	19	46	33	13	6.9	.326	.384	.373	.036	.294	.353	.333	.253	2.8	58-CF	-2
2005	DUR	AAA	24	258	46	10	5	1	18	29	47	31	8	9.0	.305	.388	.407	.086	.279	.360	.368	.268	6.2	50-CF	-4
2005	TBA	MLB	24	215	29	7	3	0	13	10	39	20	5	7.8	.276	.316	.340	-.132	.289	.338	.353	.254	2.2	58-CF	-5
2006	*TBA*	*MLB*	*25*	*408*	*58*	*12*	*5*	*0*	*22*	*28*	*73*	*35*	*9*	*5.7*	*.263*	*.320*	*.321*	*-.155*	*.269*	*.332*	*.339*	*.241*	*1.9*	*97-CF*	*-4*

Breakout: 12% Improve: 35% Collapse: 38% Attrition: 14% Comparables: Richard Thompson, Randy Winn, Alex Sanchez

As part of the Old Regime's "How you gonna keep 'em down on the farm after you've kept 'em down on the farm?" program, Gathright made the team out of spring training when Alex Sanchez was caught in the steroids dragnet. He played well, but when Sanchez returned Gathright was sent down because his inaccurate throwing arm frustrated Lou Piniella. That the alternatives were handicapped by other, more severe flaws didn't bother anyone. Gathright was the best choice for the Rays in 2005, but he's not a good choice in the long term: he has no power, and isn't nearly selective enough. He's going to have to beat out an unlikely, nigh impossible number of infield hits to overcome those limitations. Think Otis Nixon.

JONNY GOMES   OF   **Bats: R Throws: R**   Height: 6′ 1″   Weight: 200   Born: November 22, 1980   Age: 25

YEAR	TM	LVL	AGE	PA	R	2B	3B	HR	RBI	BB	SO	SB	CS	SPEED	BA	OBP	SLG	MLVR	EQBA	EQOBP	EQSLG	EQA	VORP	DEFENSE
2003	ORL	AA	22	515	68	28	3	17	56	53	148	23	2	6.6	.249	.348	.441	.118	.231	.314	.425	.260	-6.6	101-LF -11
2004	DUR	AAA	23	470	73	27	1	26	78	51	136	8	5	4.9	.257	.368	.532	.163	.223	.328	.462	.270	3.0	99-LF -3
2005	DUR	AAA	24	202	34	13	0	14	46	30	44	7	1	5.0	.321	.446	.660	.520	.282	.399	.578	.324	18.0	23-LF -2 22-RF -4
2005	TBA	MLB	24	406	61	13	6	21	54	39	113	9	5	5.7	.282	.372	.534	.239	.295	.389	.575	.315	31.1	33-RF -3 13-LF 0
2006	*TBA*	*MLB*	*25*	*536*	*73*	*24*	*3*	*28*	*81*	*55*	*136*	*11*	*4*	*5.2*	*.256*	*.348*	*.502*	*.115*	*.261*	*.362*	*.531*	*.291*	*28.4*	*126-RF -3*

Breakout: 18%   Improve: 51%   Collapse: 21%   Attrition: 12%   Comparables: Greg Vaughn, Jay Buhner, Tim Salmon

He's had the kind of career they should make a movie about. No one has ever believed in Gomes. He was a walk-on in junior college, an 18th round pick in 2001, and had a *heart attack* in 2002. After two non-committal cups of coffee, he didn't make the team out of spring training in 2005, hit well when recalled, only to be benched for Damon Hollins and sent down shortly thereafter. Gomes didn't sulk, and after he hit like Babe Ruth for a month, even a group as obtuse as the Old Regime had to bring him back. He went on to lead the team in OBP and slugging, and ranked ninth in the AL in isolated power (.253). Gomes's batting average may not always be as high as it was in '05, but he is a legitimate power hitter and possesses an appealing scrappiness that helps him out-hustle his limitations. He's not a future MVP, but he can help a team win.

ALEX GONZALEZ   INF   **Bats: R Throws: R**   Height: 6′ 0″   Weight: 200   Born: April 8, 1973   Age: 33

YEAR	TM	LVL	AGE	PA	R	2B	3B	HR	RBI	BB	SO	SB	CS	SPEED	BA	OBP	SLG	MLVR	EQBA	EQOBP	EQSLG	EQA	VORP	DEFENSE
2003	CHN	MLB	30	593	71	37	0	20	59	47	123	3	3	4.0	.228	.295	.409	-.097	.226	.293	.407	.240	7.6	138-SS 16
2004	CHN	MLB	31	133	15	10	0	3	8	4	26	1	1	4.1	.217	.241	.364	-.280	.215	.239	.362	.206	-4.4	33-SS -1
2004	MON	MLB	31	142	19	7	0	4	16	8	32	1	1	5.3	.241	.289	.383	-.145	.231	.280	.381	.227	-0.1	33-SS -3
2005	TBA	MLB	32	381	47	20	1	9	38	26	74	2	1	4.1	.269	.323	.410	-.021	.278	.342	.435	.268	7.3	89-3B -6
2006	*TBA*	*MLB*	*33*	*310*	*33*	*15*	*1*	*7*	*36*	*20*	*58*	*2*	*1*	*4.4*	*.254*	*.307*	*.393*	*-.092*	*.259*	*.319*	*.415*	*.244*	*6.0*	*75-3B -1*

Breakout: 20%   Improve: 49%   Collapse: 26%   Attrition: 35%   Comparables: Charlie Hayes, Vern Stephens, Clete Boyer

Old Regime Brilliant Idea #4,973: (1) Take a player who wasn't much of a hitter as a shortstop and move him to third base, a position that will not only further expose his bat, but that he cannot field. (2) Win World Series. (3) Laugh at all those who mocked our genius. (Patent Pending.)

NICK GREEN   2B   **Bats: R Throws: R**   Height: 6′ 0″   Weight: 170   Born: September 10, 1978   Age: 27

YEAR	TM	LVL	AGE	PA	R	2B	3B	HR	RBI	BB	SO	SB	CS	SPEED	BA	OBP	SLG	MLVR	EQBA	EQOBP	EQSLG	EQA	VORP	DEFENSE
2003	RIC	AAA	24	436	40	26	1	11	51	26	79	7	5	4.3	.248	.303	.401	-.032	.232	.289	.384	.234	-3.3	105-2B -6
2004	ATL	MLB	25	282	40	15	3	3	26	12	63	1	2	6.3	.273	.312	.386	-.084	.269	.308	.381	.237	2.0	64-2B 4
2005	TBA	MLB	26	365	53	15	2	5	29	33	86	3	1	5.7	.239	.329	.346	-.129	.251	.347	.368	.257	-0.3	83-2B -4 12-3B -1
2006	*TBA*	*MLB*	*27*	*394*	*43*	*18*	*2*	*7*	*37*	*28*	*75*	*3*	*2*	*4.8*	*.249*	*.313*	*.375*	*-.107*	*.254*	*.325*	*.396*	*.244*	*7.2*	*94-2B -2*

Breakout: 20%   Improve: 44%   Collapse: 34%   Attrition: 19%   Comparables: Bobby Knoop, Steve Lombardozzi, Chris Woodward

Acquired for pitcher Jorge Sosa, Green gets in some good PAs against lefties (.320/.385/.444 over the last two seasons), but is no fun at all against normal people. As utility players go he's not terrible, but the Rays gave him far too much playing time.

TOBY HALL   C   **Bats: R Throws: R**   Height: 6′ 3″   Weight: 200   Born: October 21, 1975   Age: 30

YEAR	TM	LVL	AGE	PA	R	2B	3B	HR	RBI	BB	SO	SB	CS	SPEED	BA	OBP	SLG	MLVR	EQBA	EQOBP	EQSLG	EQA	VORP	DEFENSE
2003	TBA	MLB	27	498	50	23	0	12	47	23	40	0	1	3.1	.253	.295	.380	-.140	.253	.300	.390	.239	0.9	125-C 6
2004	TBA	MLB	28	440	35	21	0	8	60	24	41	0	2	2.2	.255	.300	.366	-.162	.257	.305	.368	.236	-0.9	115-C 0
2005	TBA	MLB	29	460	28	20	0	5	48	16	39	0	0	2.9	.287	.315	.368	-.082	.295	.331	.379	.251	9.5	121-C 3
2006	*TBA*	*MLB*	*30*	*396*	*33*	*18*	*0*	*6*	*41*	*16*	*36*	*0*	*1*	*3.1*	*.258*	*.294*	*.357*	*-.157*	*.264*	*.306*	*.377*	*.228*	*1.2*	*95-C -1*

Breakout: 20%   Improve: 37%   Collapse: 37%   Attrition: 19%   Comparables: Ben Molina, Brian Johnson, Sandy Alomar

Hall had what was likely his peak season, but due to what is now a pathological unwillingness to walk to first base, his best was still only good enough to get most players benched. While sabermetric types routinely condemn players who lack patience, this may not be fair—hat if, as is surely the case with some hitters, impatience is simply a lack of skill rather than a kind of stubbornness? That being the case, it's cruel to berate them for their incapability—it wasn't a choice, they were just made that way. In this sense, many impatient players are like those born with physical disabilities. The key difference is that the handicapped can lead useful, vibrant lives, while the impatient largely can't.

DAMON HOLLINS   CF   Bats: R Throws: L   Height: 5' 11"   Weight: 180   Born: June 12, 1974   Age: 32

YEAR	TM	LVL	AGE	PA	R	2B	3B	HR	RBI	BB	SO	SB	CS	SPEED	BA	OBP	SLG	MLVR	EQBA	EQOBP	EQSLG	EQA	VORP	DEFENSE			
2003	RIC	AAA	29	333	39	23	4	11	45	22	62	7	2	5.8	.274	.324	.482	.132	.241	.292	.420	.244	-7.0	73-RF	7	16-CF	1
2004	RIC	AAA	30	384	50	26	2	20	67	24	57	5	3	4.6	.301	.341	.553	.232	.253	.292	.435	.247	-4.7	90-RF	3	10-CF	0
2005	TBA	MLB	31	368	44	17	1	13	46	23	63	8	1	5.2	.249	.296	.418	-.072	.254	.312	.441	.260	4.8	71-CF	-9	19-RF	-2
2006	*TBA*	*MLB*	*32*	*320*	*36*	*15*	*2*	*8*	*38*	*20*	*56*	*5*	*2*	*4.6*	*.256*	*.304*	*.403*	*-.081*	*.261*	*.316*	*.426*	*.247*	*3.9*	*78-CF*	*-3*		

Breakout: 20%   Improve: 44%   Collapse: 34%   Attrition: 28%   Comparables: Mike Devereaux, Jacob Brumfield, Luis Olmo

A journeyman who got hot at the right time. In the minors since 1992, Hollins played himself into a job with a torrid May, batting .325/.368/.600. He did almost nothing thereafter, batting .236/.271/.404 in the second half. His outfield defense was beyond atrocious, making him a weak choice even for a reserve spot, despite his slight power.

AUBREY HUFF   1B/3B/RF   Bats: L Throws: R   Height: 6' 4"   Weight: 220   Born: December 20, 1976   Age: 29

YEAR	TM	LVL	AGE	PA	R	2B	3B	HR	RBI	BB	SO	SB	CS	SPEED	BA	OBP	SLG	MLVR	EQBA	EQOBP	EQSLG	EQA	VORP	DEFENSE			
2003	TBA	MLB	26	706	91	47	3	34	107	53	80	2	3	4.0	.311	.367	.555	.278	.314	.374	.570	.310	54.1	96-RF	-10	20-1B	2
2004	TBA	MLB	27	667	92	27	2	29	104	56	74	5	1	4.8	.297	.360	.493	.156	.299	.366	.500	.294	39.5	80-3B	-6	31-1B	2
2005	TBA	MLB	28	636	70	26	2	22	92	49	88	8	7	4.8	.261	.321	.428	-.005	.271	.338	.453	.269	8.7	90-RF	-7	18-1B	1
2006	*TBA*	*MLB*	*29*	*613*	*74*	*30*	*2*	*24*	*90*	*47*	*76*	*5*	*3*	*4.6*	*.286*	*.344*	*.477*	*.102*	*.293*	*.357*	*.503*	*.282*	*27.6*	*143-RF*	*-2*		

Breakout: 17%   Improve: 46%   Collapse: 23%   Attrition: 5%   Comparables: Ted Kluszewski, Larry Sheets, Chris Chambliss

Huff has been a prime trade target from the moment he established himself, but the Rays have already waited too long to pull the trigger. In what should have been one of his peak seasons, Huff turned in his worst performance since his rookie year. The Rays have done themselves, and Huff, a disservice by dragging him all over the field. While he's a poor third baseman, the parade of Jared Sandberg types the team placed in his stead cost them more runs on offense than Huff would have spent on defense. He's actually an adept first baseman, but the club could never commit to keeping him there, pushing him to DH and then the outfield so that lesser hitters could play first base. Huff is a good bet to bounce back.

JOHN JASO   C   Bats: L Throws: R   Height: 6' 2"   Weight: 205   Born: September 19, 1983 Age: 22

YEAR	TM	LVL	AGE	PA	R	2B	3B	HR	RBI	BB	SO	SB	CS	SPEED	BA	OBP	SLG	MLVR	EQBA	EQOBP	EQSLG	EQA	VORP	DEFENSE			
2003	HUD	A-	19	186	20	7	0	2	20	25	26	2	0	4.0	.227	.344	.312	.011	.210	.305	.315	.227	-10.3	34-C	-5		
2004	HUD	A-	20	225	34	17	2	2	35	22	32	1	0	4.7	.302	.378	.437	.238	.277	.337	.415	.262	17.2	24-C	3	14-1B	2
2005	SWM	A	21	386	61	25	1	14	50	42	53	3	1	3.5	.307	.383	.515	.274	.265	.330	.451	.268	17.7	27-C	4		
2006	*TBA*	*MLB*	*22*	*430*	*44*	*22*	*1*	*11*	*51*	*34*	*71*	*2*	*1*	*4.0*	*.248*	*.311*	*.398*	*-.082*	*.253*	*.323*	*.420*	*.248*	*8.6*	*102-C*	*2*		

Breakout: 16%   Improve: 38%   Collapse: 31%   Attrition: 13%   Comparables: Ross Gload, Eric Munson, Ryan Doumit

At 19, Jaso hit about as well as you would expect from a 12th round pick, but he has blossomed since. He's selective, and showed home run power for the first time last year. Ostensibly a catcher, he was limited to DH duties late in the season because of a shoulder injury. The next step is to play over 100 games in a season and see what shakes out.

ELLIOT JOHNSON   2B   Bats: B Throws: R   Height: 6' 0"   Weight: 160   Born: March 9, 1984   Age: 22

YEAR	TM	LVL	AGE	PA	R	2B	3B	HR	RBI	BB	SO	SB	CS	SPEED	BA	OBP	SLG	MLVR	EQBA	EQOBP	EQSLG	EQA	VORP	DEFENSE	
2003	CSC	A	19	189	22	4	0	0	15	38	32	8	5	4.6	.212	.370	.238	-.066	.197	.328	.222	.215	-10.0	42-2B	6
2004	CSC	A	20	564	92	22	7	6	41	54	91	43	15	7.9	.262	.339	.370	-.002	.238	.299	.332	.229	-12.0	123-2B	20
2005	VIS	A+	21	254	42	10	3	8	33	24	49	28	5	7.5	.273	.350	.449	-.027	.220	.284	.337	.233	-7.6	54-2B	-10
2005	MNT	AA	21	282	31	9	6	3	21	13	68	15	5	7.3	.261	.305	.375	-.058	.244	.279	.361	.226	-5.7	59-2B	-2
2006	*TBA*	*MLB*	*22*	*480*	*58*	*19*	*4*	*6*	*36*	*32*	*95*	*27*	*11*	*5.6*	*.241*	*.296*	*.343*	*-.183*	*.246*	*.308*	*.362*	*.231*	*-0.7*	*114-2B*	*-2*

Breakout: 39%   Improve: 68%   Collapse: 15%   Attrition: 5%   Comparables: Henry Mateo, Anderson Machado, Dionys Cesar

When sleeper prospects go bad: an undrafted free agent, Johnson has base-stealing speed and a good glove. Prior to 2005, he also had a good idea of his limitations as a hitter and tried to work the strike zone to get on base. Perhaps having his power boosted by the California League made him forget himself, as his plate judgment evaporated upon promotion to Double-A. Johnson will have to humble himself before the strike zone to get back on the golden stair.

PETE LAFOREST C Bats: L Throws: R Height: 6' 2" Weight: 200 Born: January 27, 1978 Age: 28

YEAR	TM	LVL	AGE	PA	R	2B	3B	HR	RBI	BB	SO	SB	CS	SPEED	BA	OBP	SLG	MLVR	EQBA	EQOBP	EQSLG	EQA	VORP	DEFENSE	
2003	DUR	AAA	25	241	40	14	2	14	38	36	56	2	1	5.1	.269	.382	.567	.283	.238	.347	.510	.287	16.9	45-C	-1
2004	DUR	AAA	26	311	37	19	0	7	31	35	64	1	1	3.9	.222	.309	.367	-.177	.183	.267	.300	.205	-18.9	72-C	-3
2005	DUR	AAA	27	292	41	18	1	21	52	17	98	2	0	5.0	.270	.318	.578	.171	.232	.278	.482	.254	6.7	31-C	1
2005	TBA	MLB	27	70	5	3	0	1	4	6	23	0	1	2.8	.172	.243	.266	-.419	.175	.257	.270	.189	-5.0	15-C	-1
2006	*TBA*	*MLB*	*28*	*307*	*30*	*13*	*1*	*11*	*36*	*25*	*88*	*2*	*1*	*3.9*	*.221*	*.288*	*.394*	*-.145*	*.226*	*.299*	*.416*	*.237*	*0.8*	*75-C*	*-3*

Breakout: 28% Improve: 49% Collapse: 32% Attrition: 32%   *Comparables: Dave Ross, Hank Foiles, Tim Laudner*

Laforest has power but lacks plate judgment—better than Hall, who lacks both. He came to catching late and isn't great behind the dish, which apparently precluded him from spelling Hall once or twice a week and popping a homer or two. He had a wild winter: DFA'd in November, he was claimed on waivers by the Padres, and then non-tendered. French is Laforest's first language, making him the ideal interlocutor for mound conferences with Pepe Le Pew.

FRANCISCO LEANDRO LF Bats: L Throws: L Height: 5' 10" Weight: 180 Born: July 19, 1980 Age: 25

YEAR	TM	LVL	AGE	PA	R	2B	3B	HR	RBI	BB	SO	SB	CS	SPEED	BA	OBP	SLG	MLVR	EQBA	EQOBP	EQSLG	EQA	VORP	DEFENSE			
2004	HUD	A-	23	167	20	8	1	1	18	18	26	3	2	4.5	.266	.359	.357	.083	.218	.286	.285	.209	-27.1	33-LF	3		
2004	CSC	A	23	125	29	9	1	2	18	19	11	7	1	6.8	.340	.440	.500	.396	.288	.370	.400	.274	2.4	29-LF	0		
2005	SWM	A	24	307	44	21	1	3	39	45	33	11	4	4.7	.304	.417	.431	.208	.248	.335	.353	.248	-7.7	46-LF	1	25-RF	-1
2005	VIS	A+	24	294	53	23	3	8	40	37	24	9	7	5.7	.355	.449	.569	.405	.272	.350	.406	.263	2.1	46-LF	5	14-CF	0
2006	*TBA*	*MLB*	*25*	*472*	*50*	*25*	*2*	*5*	*43*	*37*	*69*	*8*	*4*	*4.8*	*.250*	*.315*	*.358*	*-.125*	*.255*	*.328*	*.378*	*.240*	*-3.0*	*112-LF*	*0*		

Breakout: 18% Improve: 37% Collapse: 32% Attrition: 9%   *Comparables: Terrmel Sledge, Jake Weber, Mike Lockwood*

Leandro can hit, but because he wasn't drafted until a month before his 24th birthday he has been quite old for his leagues. Double-A will be a better test, but he'll need to get a move on to have a career.

TRAVIS LEE 1B Bats: L Throws: L Height: 6' 3" Weight: 210 Born: May 26, 1975 Age: 31

YEAR	TM	LVL	AGE	PA	R	2B	3B	HR	RBI	BB	SO	SB	CS	SPEED	BA	OBP	SLG	MLVR	EQBA	EQOBP	EQSLG	EQA	VORP	DEFENSE	
2003	TBA	MLB	28	612	75	37	3	19	70	64	97	6	2	4.7	.275	.348	.459	.079	.276	.355	.465	.282	20.7	140-1B	14
2005	TBA	MLB	30	441	54	22	2	12	49	35	66	7	4	5.3	.272	.331	.426	.020	.280	.349	.450	.273	8.2	105-1B	14
2006	*TBA*	*MLB*	*31*	*409*	*47*	*20*	*2*	*11*	*49*	*35*	*65*	*5*	*2*	*4.9*	*.265*	*.330*	*.420*	*-.010*	*.271*	*.343*	*.444*	*.262*	*6.8*	*98-1B*	*7*

Breakout: 15% Improve: 43% Collapse: 20% Attrition: 18%   *Comparables: Chris Chambliss, Leon Durham, Ed Kranepool*

He posted the second-best EQA of his career, for what it's worth. Lee remains a good glove but an underwhelming hitter, kind of J. T. Snow Extra-Lite. The Rays made the mistake of offering Lee arbitration, and he gratefully accepted. At worst, he'll keep first base warm for Bankston this spring, but if Huff is still with the team, the job really should be his. Players like Lee just don't help you win if they play everyday.

JULIO LUGO SS Bats: R Throws: R Height: 6' 0" Weight: 165 Born: November 16, 1975 Age: 30

YEAR	TM	LVL	AGE	PA	R	2B	3B	HR	RBI	BB	SO	SB	CS	SPEED	BA	OBP	SLG	MLVR	EQBA	EQOBP	EQSLG	EQA	VORP	DEFENSE	
2003	TBA	MLB	27	475	58	13	4	15	53	35	88	10	3	5.8	.275	.333	.427	.001	.275	.338	.434	.267	22.3	116-SS	10
2004	TBA	MLB	28	648	83	41	4	7	75	54	106	21	5	6.6	.275	.338	.396	-.047	.277	.343	.402	.265	24.5	141-SS	5
2005	TBA	MLB	29	687	89	36	6	6	57	61	72	39	11	7.0	.295	.362	.403	.059	.308	.383	.423	.286	42.8	153-SS	6
2006	*TBA*	*MLB*	*30*	*622*	*82*	*29*	*4*	*8*	*55*	*53*	*79*	*22*	*7*	*5.6*	*.277*	*.343*	*.389*	*-.019*	*.283*	*.356*	*.411*	*.264*	*28.3*	*145-SS*	*3*

Breakout: 9% Improve: 35% Collapse: 24% Attrition: 4%   *Comparables: Scott Fletcher, Dave Concepcion, Bob Dillinger*

One of the few examples of an astute pick-up by the Devil Rays. Lugo was signed after the Astros peremptorily released him in reaction to his arrest for perpetrating a misdemeanor assault on his wife. Lugo was later acquitted, and the Rays had gotten a decent player with little effort and no cost. Lugo had by far the best year of his career in 2005, but much of the improvement was fueled by Lugo's 20-point surge in batting average; his isolated power dropped to .107, a career low. Such increases by 29-year-olds rarely last. Lugo has a steady glove, and if his bat is nothing special, it doesn't hurt. In short, he's neutral—a team can easily do worse, or better.

EDUARDO PEREZ 1B **Bats: R Throws: R** Height: 6′ 4″ Weight: 215 Born: September 11, 1969 Age: 36

YEAR	TM	LVL	AGE	PA	R	2B	3B	HR	RBI	BB	SO	SB	CS	SPEED	BA	OBP	SLG	MLVR	EQBA	EQOBP	EQSLG	EQA	VORP	DEFENSE
2003	SLN	MLB	33	288	47	16	0	11	41	29	53	5	2	4.8	.285	.365	.478	.165	.282	.360	.482	.287	14.0	43-RF -1
2004	TBA	MLB	34	42	2	2	0	1	7	4	9	0	0	3.2	.211	.286	.342	-.266	.211	.286	.342	.221	-1.8	
2005	TBA	MLB	35	190	23	6	0	11	28	26	30	0	2	2.3	.255	.368	.497	.163	.262	.385	.519	.300	9.3	37-1B 1
2006	*CLE*	*MLB*	*36*	*174*	*21*	*8*	*0*	*8*	*26*	*23*	*30*	*0*	*1*	*3.4*	*.270*	*.370*	*.476*	*.128*	*.274*	*.381*	*.502*	*.291*	*10.6*	*45-1B -1*

Breakout: 17% Improve: 38% Collapse: 37% Attrition: 46% Comparables: Cliff Johnson, Todd Pratt, Frank Howard

Had a fine year by his modest standards, punishing lefties with .259/.371/.526 percentages. Perez is up to the limited description of his job, namely to play a little first base and bat against lefties, but those skills are in no way worth paying a premium for—there are many players who could fill that role if given the chance. Signed by the Indians, he'll protect Ben Broussard from those mean ol' southpaws.

JOSH PHELPS DH **Bats: R Throws: R** Height: 6′ 3″ Weight: 220 Born: May 12, 1978 Age: 28

YEAR	TM	LVL	AGE	PA	R	2B	3B	HR	RBI	BB	SO	SB	CS	SPEED	BA	OBP	SLG	MLVR	EQBA	EQOBP	EQSLG	EQA	VORP	DEFENSE
2003	TOR	MLB	25	453	57	18	1	20	66	39	115	1	2	3.6	.268	.358	.470	.088	.265	.356	.472	.281	16.5	
2004	TOR	MLB	26	321	38	13	2	12	51	18	73	0	0	4.5	.237	.296	.417	-.142	.234	.293	.412	.241	-2.9	11-1B 0
2004	CLE	MLB	26	80	13	6	0	5	10	4	20	0	0	3.0	.303	.338	.579	.322	.307	.350	.613	.310	6.8	
2005	TBA	MLB	27	177	21	10	0	5	26	12	48	0	0	3.3	.266	.328	.424	.009	.274	.343	.433	.270	4.6	
2005	DUR	AAA	27	243	35	14	3	14	33	15	53	0	1	4.5	.270	.329	.550	.150	.233	.286	.455	.248	-1.5	19-1B 0
2006	*DET*	*MLB*	*28*	*363*	*39*	*15*	*2*	*14*	*48*	*23*	*86*	*0*	*0*	*3.7*	*.246*	*.304*	*.427*	*-.057*	*.250*	*.314*	*.449*	*.251*	*5.4*	*87-DH*

Breakout: 15% Improve: 35% Collapse: 32% Attrition: 22% Comparables: Pete Incaviglia, Julio Zuleta, Wes Helms

He wasn't horrible, but he was nevertheless designated for assignment in June and accepted an assignment to Durham after no other team bothered to claim him. This lack of interest added insult to insult, as Phelps had been taken off the roster to make room for Reggie bloody Taylor. Phelps has zero defensive value but could still make a good platoon player. Signed to a minor league deal by the Tigers, Phelps will have a hard time making the roster.

SHAWN RIGGANS C **Bats: R Throws: R** Height: 6′ 2″ Weight: 190 Born: July 25, 1980 Age: 25

YEAR	TM	LVL	AGE	PA	R	2B	3B	HR	RBI	BB	SO	SB	CS	SPEED	BA	OBP	SLG	MLVR	EQBA	EQOBP	EQSLG	EQA	VORP	DEFENSE
2003	CSC	A	22	259	33	17	0	3	34	19	35	3	4	3.9	.280	.340	.392	.116	.242	.287	.347	.223	-5.7	51-C -2
2004	BAK	A+	23	144	20	11	0	5	22	15	23	0	1	2.7	.346	.417	.551	.426	.288	.348	.456	.273	8.9	28-C -2
2005	MNT	AA	24	348	40	21	0	8	53	26	69	1	2	3.3	.310	.365	.454	.190	.271	.317	.408	.251	8.5	66-C -1
2006	*TBA*	*MLB*	*25*	*327*	*29*	*15*	*1*	*8*	*38*	*18*	*67*	*1*	*1*	*3.6*	*.244*	*.290*	*.378*	*-.145*	*.249*	*.302*	*.400*	*.233*	*2.3*	*79-C -3*

Breakout: 12% Improve: 28% Collapse: 39% Attrition: 20% Comparables: Sherm Lollar, Joe Oliver, Joe Depastino

If Riggans could just stay healthy, he might provide the major league team with good defense and average offense. Unfortunately, durability is a skill Riggans lacks; he's averaged 62 games and 219 ABs per season as a pro. Among the more subtle skills conferred by nature on the professional athlete is physical resilience. Riggans is still waiting for his consignment to show up in the mail.

B. J. UPTON SS **Bats: R Throws: R** Height: 6′ 3″ Weight: 170 Born: August 21, 1984 Age: 21

YEAR	TM	LVL	AGE	PA	R	2B	3B	HR	RBI	BB	SO	SB	CS	SPEED	BA	OBP	SLG	MLVR	EQBA	EQOBP	EQSLG	EQA	VORP	DEFENSE	
2003	CSC	A	18	452	70	22	6	7	46	57	80	38	17	7.3	.302	.394	.445	.275	.283	.356	.426	.273	28.4	94-SS -15	
2003	ORL	AA	18	125	14	8	0	1	16	16	25	2	4	3.9	.276	.376	.381	.102	.251	.337	.362	.246	2.7	27-SS -5	
2004	MNT	AA	19	118	21	7	1	2	15	14	28	3	0	6.0	.327	.407	.471	.306	.315	.384	.456	.293	12.0	23-SS -1	
2004	DUR	AAA	19	309	65	17	1	12	36	42	72	17	5	7.1	.311	.411	.519	.264	.278	.378	.462	.291	26.5	66-SS -9	
2004	TBA	MLB	19	176	19	8	2	4	12	15	46	4	1	6.3	.258	.324	.409	-.040	.261	.331	.414	.261	4.4	16-SS -2	12-3B -3
2005	DUR	AAA	20	630	98	36	6	18	74	78	127	44	13	6.9	.303	.392	.490	.201	.274	.362	.437	.280	39.8	130-SS -14	
2006	*TBA*	*MLB*	*21*	*577*	*83*	*29*	*4*	*14*	*60*	*59*	*112*	*36*	*10*	*5.8*	*.270*	*.348*	*.425*	*.030*	*.276*	*.362*	*.449*	*.278*	*35.2*	*135-SS -9*	

Breakout: 21% Improve: 40% Collapse: 21% Attrition: 5% Comparables: Jimmy Wynn, Adrian Beltre, Roberto Alomar

In 1933, the Dodgers brought up 22-year-old Lonny Frey to play short. Frey had an above-average bat for the position but his error totals, which peaked in 1936 with 51 in just 117 games, were untenable. It wasn't until 1938 that Frey was moved to second base. There, Frey showed an above-average glove and still had a good bat for a middle infielder.

(continued next page)

B. J. Upton (continued)

Overnight he went from busted prospect to All-Star, and his team started winning pennants. B. J. ("Bossman Junior"— his real name is Melvin) Upton needs to follow in Frey's footsteps, moving to second or center field. He made 53 errors in 2005, 44 in 2004, 56 in 2003. That's his only problem. The bat is good to go now, preferably in the leadoff spot. Upton isn't ready to give up chasing his Derek Jeter dreams, but he and the Rays could wait forever for him to come to grips with the position and never get anywhere. Better to let him exploit his speed in center or give him a shorter throw from second base.

DELMON YOUNG   **RF**   **Bats: R Throws: R**   Height: 6′ 3″   Weight: 205   Born: September 14, 1985   Age: 20

YEAR	TM	LVL	AGE	PA	R	2B	3B	HR	RBI	BB	SO	SB	CS	SPEED	BA	OBP	SLG	MLVR	EQBA	EQOBP	EQSLG	EQA	VORP	DEFENSE
2004	CSC	A	18	578	95	26	5	25	116	53	120	21	6	6.0	.322	.388	.538	.356	.287	.340	.464	.276	18.2	116-RF 7
2005	MNT	AA	19	370	59	13	4	20	71	25	66	25	8	6.1	.336	.386	.582	.434	.310	.351	.543	.298	27.9	78-RF -7
2005	DUR	AAA	19	234	33	13	3	6	28	4	33	7	4	6.4	.285	.303	.447	-.020	.259	.279	.407	.234	-6.3	50-RF -7
2006	TBA	MLB	20	558	70	27	4	19	75	25	97	16	6	5.6	.279	.314	.453	.017	.285	.327	.478	.265	14.7	131-RF -4

Breakout: 15%   Improve: 48%   Collapse: 28%   Attrition: 8%   Comparables: Cesar Cedeno, Ken Griffey, Tony Conigliaro

No doubt you've heard of Dimitri's younger, better brother, the consensus #1 prospect in the game. The first overall draft pick of 2003 is more than ready for his close-up, Mr. DeMille. The only cause for pause was the near-extinction of his selectivity at Triple-A. As he was a mere teenager, we'll give him a pass for that, as well as for his frustration with the lack of a September call because the Old Regime didn't feel like springing for a plane ticket and hotel accommodations, or a rickshaw and a youth hostel for that matter. He's ready to be an impact right fielder right now, but at this writing the Rays have yet to make room for him.

PITCHERS

DANNY BAEZ   **Bats: R Throws: R**   Height: 6′ 4″   Weight: 225   Born: September 10, 1977   Age: 28

YEAR	TM	LVL	AGE	W	L	SV	G	GS	IP	H	BB	SO	HR	GB%	BABIP	STUFF	WHIP	ERA	PERA	EQERA	EQH9	EQBB9	EQSO9	EQHR9	VORP	WXRL
2003	CLE	MLB	25	2	9	25	73	0	75.7	65	23	66	9	46%	.268	8	1.16	3.80	4.12	4.12	8.2	2.8	7.7	1.1	13.9	-0.2
2004	TBA	MLB	26	4	4	30	62	0	68.0	60	29	52	6	44%	.277	3	1.31	3.57	4.28	3.88	8.6	3.6	6.5	0.7	15.9	3.1
2005	TBA	MLB	27	5	4	41	67	0	72.3	66	30	51	7	48%	.278	1	1.33	2.86	4.46	3.10	8.2	3.7	6.3	0.9	19.1	4.5
2006	LAN	MLB	28	4	5	24	58	0	64.7	60	26	49	7	48%	.275	-2	1.31	3.85	4.21	4.70	8.4	3.3	6.1	0.9	8.5	1.1

Breakout: 11%   Improve: 29%   Collapse: 46%   Attrition: 12%   Comparables: Todd Jones, Barry Jones, Ken Forsch

Being the best closer in Devil Rays history is like being the most enlightened ruler in the history of Albania. Not only are you a big fish in a very small pond, but the pond would be much better off if you were removed entirely and replaced by smaller fish who could presumably fill a variety of more valuable roles without draining the local economy. There was no real reason for Baez's slight improvement last year—his double play support was more than he was accustomed to, perhaps—and he's a good bet to regress in 2006. Hell on righties, he can be beaten by left-handers. Traded to the Dodgers, Baez will set up Eric Gagne and step in for him in case of injury. He should be more consistent than anyone the Dodgers had in that role last year.

JOE BOROWSKI   **Bats: R Throws: R**   Height: 6′ 2″   Weight: 225   Born: May 4, 1971   Age: 35

YEAR	TM	LVL	AGE	W	L	SV	G	GS	IP	H	BB	SO	HR	GB%	BABIP	STUFF	WHIP	ERA	PERA	EQERA	EQH9	EQBB9	EQSO9	EQHR9	VORP	WXRL
2003	CHN	MLB	32	2	2	33	68	0	68.3	53	19	66	5	45%	.259	20	1.05	2.64	3.36	3.09	7.5	2.3	7.9	0.7	19.6	4.3
2004	CHN	MLB	33	2	4	9	22	0	21.3	27	15	17	3	37%	.348	-19	1.97	8.03	5.64	7.66	10.1	5.6	6.0	1.2	-5.3	-0.2
2005	CHN	MLB	34	0	0	0	11	0	11.0	12	1	11	5	49%	.233	1	1.18	6.55	7.59	5.91	11.0	0.8	8.4	4.2	-1.3	-0.2
2005	TBA	MLB	34	1	5	0	32	0	35.3	26	11	16	3	49%	.217	-10	1.05	3.82	4.46	3.41	7.6	2.9	4.2	0.8	7.5	1.0
2006	FLO	MLB	35	1	1	1	25	0	27.7	27	11	18	3	43%	.278	-12	1.37	4.42	4.59	5.92	8.9	3.2	5.2	1.0	1.7	0.1

Breakout: 15%   Improve: 30%   Collapse: 40%   Attrition: 38%   Comparables: Tom Ferrick, Giovanni Carrara, Ray Moore

With an injury history longer than Wagner's Ring Cycle, Borowski has established himself as one of the most consistent non-pitching pitchers in the game. After a wrist injury kept him shelved through late May, he pitched poorly and was released by the Cubs. He was a new man upon signing with the Rays, pitching 21 innings before allowing a run. Thereafter, he went back to being hammered. Signed to a one-year deal by the Marlins, he'll be given a chance to win the closer's job. His strikeout rates have declined in three straight seasons, giving credence to suggestions that the injuries have diminished his fastball.

DEWON BRAZELTON   Bats: R   Throws: R   Height: 6' 4"   Weight: 210   Born: June 16, 1980   Age: 26

YEAR	TM	LVL	AGE	W	L	SV	G	GS	IP	H	BB	SO	HR	GB%	BABIP	STUFF	WHIP	ERA	PERA	EQERA	EQH9	EQBB9	EQSO9	EQHR9	VORP	WXRL
2003	BAK	A+	23	1	5	0	9	9	49.7	62	19	42	4	—	.351	-16	1.63	5.25	6.10	7.58	11.1	4.6	4.4	1.5	-10.7	—
2003	DUR	AAA	23	2	2	0	5	5	25.7	23	11	18	1	—	.271	0	1.32	4.20	4.38	5.47	8.8	4.7	5.1	0.4	0.4	—
2003	TBA	MLB	23	1	6	0	10	10	48.3	57	23	24	9	52%	.296	-21	1.66	6.89	6.33	8.75	10.8	4.3	4.3	1.7	-16.3	-0.9
2004	DUR	AAA	24	4	4	0	10	10	49.7	61	15	38	0	—	.359	10	1.53	4.71	3.58	6.44	10.0	2.9	5.2	0.2	-4.7	—
2004	TBA	MLB	24	6	8	0	22	21	120.7	121	53	64	12	40%	.280	1	1.44	4.77	5.03	4.88	9.4	3.8	4.5	0.8	11.1	2.6
2005	TBA	MLB	25	1	8	0	20	8	71.0	87	60	43	12	37%	.329	-30	2.07	7.61	6.75	7.49	10.2	7.5	5.3	1.5	-19.6	-0.5
2005	DUR	AAA	25	2	2	0	5	5	29.0	29	14	26	3	39%	.302	1	1.48	3.72	5.34	5.34	8.8	5.0	6.0	1.3	0.8	—
2006	*SDN*	*MLB*	*26*	*3*	*5*	*0*	*24*	*8*	*69.3*	*71*	*38*	*50*	*8*	*42%*	*.292*	*-8*	*1.56*	*5.18*	*5.83*	*7.47*	*9.4*	*4.5*	*5.7*	*1.1*	*-2.6*	*0.0*

Breakout: 34%   Improve: 59%   Collapse: 20%   Attrition: 30%   Comparables: Jesse Jefferson, Joaquin Benoit, Sean Douglass

Brazelton spent time on the restricted list after refusing a minor league assignment to Triple-A, was traded to the Padres over the winter, non-tendered, and re-signed. At no time in 2005 did he even give the illusion of being a major league pitcher, not that he ever had, really. As bad as he was as a starter, he was even worse when sent to the pen, but with only two pitches (fastball, slider) and difficulty repeating his delivery, that's where his future lies. Pitching in Petco will make him look superficially better, but don't expect miracles.

LANCE CARTER   Bats: R   Throws: R   Height: 6' 1"   Weight: 190   Born: December 18, 1974   Age: 31

YEAR	TM	LVL	AGE	W	L	SV	G	GS	IP	H	BB	SO	HR	GB%	BABIP	STUFF	WHIP	ERA	PERA	EQERA	EQH9	EQBB9	EQSO9	EQHR9	VORP	WXRL
2003	TBA	MLB	28	7	5	26	62	0	79.0	72	19	47	12	38%	.251	-10	1.15	4.33	4.81	4.46	9.2	2.2	5.4	1.3	14.4	1.9
2004	TBA	MLB	29	3	3	0	56	0	80.3	77	23	36	12	37%	.246	-17	1.22	3.47	5.15	3.32	9.3	2.5	3.9	1.3	25.2	0.8
2005	TBA	MLB	30	1	2	1	39	0	57.0	61	15	22	9	39%	.277	-21	1.33	4.89	5.49	4.08	9.6	2.4	3.5	1.4	5.1	-0.5
2005	DUR	AAA	30	1	5	0	8	7	35.0	40	12	30	8	43%	.320	-20	1.49	5.14	6.88	6.35	10.6	3.7	5.6	2.6	-2.8	—
2006	*LAN*	*MLB*	*31*	*3*	*3*	*1*	*37*	*3*	*57.7*	*61*	*18*	*32*	*9*	*41%*	*.276*	*-15*	*1.37*	*4.55*	*5.02*	*5.99*	*9.6*	*2.6*	*4.4*	*1.4*	*4.2*	*0.3*

Breakout: 7%   Improve: 28%   Collapse: 49%   Attrition: 28%   Comparables: Bob Priddy, Jose Bautista, Bob Wells

A flyball pitcher who doesn't have the stuff to get away with pitching up all the time, Piniella tried him as a situational lefty for awhile, even though Carter isn't left-handed. That worked about as well as should have been expected, and the former token Tampa All-Star was exiled to Durham for five weeks. Although the Rays have signed Carter for another season, not a lot should be expected from him. Traded to the Dodgers with Baez, perhaps he'll benefit from the team's traditional magic with pitchers.

JESUS COLOME   Bats: R   Throws: R   Height: 6' 2"   Weight: 170   Born: December 23, 1977   Age: 28

YEAR	TM	LVL	AGE	W	L	SV	G	GS	IP	H	BB	SO	HR	GB%	BABIP	STUFF	WHIP	ERA	PERA	EQERA	EQH9	EQBB9	EQSO9	EQHR9	VORP	WXRL
2003	TBA	MLB	25	3	7	2	54	0	74.0	69	46	69	9	36%	.299	2	1.55	4.50	4.64	4.28	8.6	5.5	8.2	1.0	13.0	-0.1
2004	DUR	AAA	26	2	1	2	18	0	30.7	27	16	17	0	—	.281	-19	1.40	3.52	4.91	4.30	8.6	5.5	4.0	0.3	4.2	—
2004	TBA	MLB	26	2	2	3	33	0	41.3	28	18	40	4	39%	.238	14	1.11	3.27	4.02	3.35	6.9	3.8	8.3	0.9	12.7	1.9
2005	TBA	MLB	27	2	3	0	36	0	45.3	54	18	28	7	40%	.301	-13	1.59	4.57	5.21	5.01	9.8	3.5	5.4	1.3	-0.5	-0.3
2006	*TBA*	*MLB*	*28*	*2*	*2*	*1*	*36*	*0*	*43.7*	*44*	*19*	*30*	*5*	*41%*	*.289*	*-7*	*1.45*	*4.61*	*4.97*	*5.51*	*9.1*	*3.9*	*5.9*	*1.0*	*3.3*	*0.2*

Breakout: 19%   Improve: 36%   Collapse: 40%   Attrition: 36%   Comparables: Brad Clontz, Bob Chakales, Manuel Aybar

The Rays have had five years to make a consistent reliever out of Colome, and they've largely failed. Now the injury termites are starting to nibble; shoulder inflammation kept Colome shelved for a good part of the season. Colome has asked to be moved, and if he's lucky the Rays will not only oblige him but will send him somewhere far away where he'll never have to face the Yankees again. Perhaps the only safe place is *to* the Yankees; against the Bombers, Colome has allowed 8.5 runs per nine innings and a home run for every three frames pitched. Against everyone else he's allowed just 4.9 runs and one home run per nine innings.

CASEY FOSSUM   Bats: B   Throws: L   Height: 6' 1"   Weight: 160   Born: January 6, 1978   Age: 28

YEAR	TM	LVL	AGE	W	L	SV	G	GS	IP	H	BB	SO	HR	GB%	BABIP	STUFF	WHIP	ERA	PERA	EQERA	EQH9	EQBB9	EQSO9	EQHR9	VORP	WXRL
2003	BOS	MLB	25	6	5	1	19	14	79.0	82	34	63	9	36%	.315	8	1.47	5.47	4.37	5.49	8.7	3.7	6.8	0.9	0.2	0.8
2004	ARI	MLB	26	4	15	0	27	27	142.0	171	63	117	31	47%	.334	-10	1.65	6.65	5.59	6.02	10.2	3.5	6.5	1.7	-19.0	0.2
2005	TBA	MLB	27	8	12	0	36	25	162.7	170	60	128	21	39%	.304	8	1.41	4.92	4.67	5.05	9.1	3.3	6.9	1.1	4.1	1.3
2006	*TBA*	*MLB*	*28*	*7*	*10*	*1*	*37*	*21*	*139.3*	*147*	*50*	*101*	*18*	*41%*	*.298*	*5*	*1.42*	*4.72*	*5.04*	*5.23*	*9.4*	*3.2*	*6.3*	*1.1*	*8.7*	*1.7*

Breakout: 32%   Improve: 62%   Collapse: 14%   Attrition: 11%   Comparables: Pete Falcone, Bud Daley, Doug Rau

(continued next page)

Casey Fossum *(continued)*

Improved his control slightly, but more importantly, he got out of Chase Field and spent his season in a far less hitter-friendly ballpark. Still, as breakthroughs go, the season wasn't an unmitigated triumph. Fossum opened the season in (very) long relief and had some strong outings, earning a move back into the rotation. The subsequent results were middling. The Rays had it right the first time: Fossum's best chance for sustained success is in the extended relief/swing role.

JASON HAMMEL
Bats: R   Throws: R   Height: 6' 6"   Weight: 200   Born: September 2, 1982   Age: 23

YEAR	TM	LVL	AGE	W	L	SV	G	GS	IP	H	BB	SO	HR	GB%	BABIP	STUFF	WHIP	ERA	PERA	EQERA	EQH9	EQBB9	EQSO9	EQHR9	VORP	WXRL
2003	CSC	A	20	6	2	0	14	12	76.7	70	27	50	2	—	.274	1	1.26	3.40	4.79	5.77	9.1	3.8	3.6	0.6	-1.4	—
2004	CSC	A	21	4	7	0	18	18	94.7	94	27	88	7	—	.309	-3	1.28	3.23	5.04	6.43	9.9	3.2	4.8	1.2	-8.4	—
2004	BAK	A+	21	6	2	0	11	11	71.3	52	20	65	4	—	.262	11	1.01	1.89	4.70	3.90	7.9	3.4	5.4	0.9	12.7	—
2005	MNT	AA	22	8	2	0	12	12	81.3	70	19	76	5	44%	.300	13	1.09	2.66	4.40	4.17	8.7	2.3	5.7	1.0	12.3	—
2005	DUR	AAA	22	3	2	0	10	10	54.7	57	27	48	8	45%	.306	0	1.54	4.11	5.60	4.94	9.1	4.6	6.3	1.5	4.0	—
2006	*TBA*	*MLB*	*23*	*6*	*10*	*0*	*27*	*23*	*135.3*	*144*	*53*	*87*	*18*	*45%*	*.294*	*5*	*1.46*	*5.00*	*5.27*	*5.28*	*9.5*	*3.5*	*5.6*	*1.1*	*3.9*	*1.3*

Breakout: 12%   Improve: 39%   Collapse: 19%   Attrition: 0%   Comparables: *Jason Young, Josh Karp, Gary Glover*

A 2002 10th round pick, Hammel has the build of a telephone pole, with all of a telephone pole's usual problems in repeating its delivery. That being said, until he reached Triple-A, Hammel had been able to keep his control in a good place. His first trip to Durham saw his walk rate more than double. Ascribe that to nerves and the need for further refinement of off-speed stuff to complement his low-to-mid 90s fastball. Given his youth, the Rays have time to let Hammel get it right. If he shows any consistency he'll be up this year.

TRAVIS HARPER
Bats: L   Throws: R   Height: 6' 4"   Weight: 190   Born: May 21, 1976   Age: 30

YEAR	TM	LVL	AGE	W	L	SV	G	GS	IP	H	BB	SO	HR	GB%	BABIP	STUFF	WHIP	ERA	PERA	EQERA	EQH9	EQBB9	EQSO9	EQHR9	VORP	WXRL
2003	TBA	MLB	27	4	8	1	61	0	93.0	86	31	64	9	52%	.287	2	1.26	3.77	4.24	4.34	8.9	3.1	6.1	0.8	17.9	1.3
2004	TBA	MLB	28	6	2	0	52	0	78.7	69	23	59	8	48%	.269	6	1.19	3.89	4.06	3.94	8.6	2.4	6.4	0.8	14.3	2.2
2005	TBA	MLB	29	4	6	0	52	0	73.3	88	24	40	14	32%	.315	-25	1.54	6.75	5.64	6.00	10.1	2.9	4.8	1.7	-11.7	-0.6
2006	*TBA*	*MLB*	*30*	*2*	*3*	*2*	*48*	*0*	*61.3*	*68*	*19*	*37*	*9*	*44%*	*.296*	*-9*	*1.41*	*4.67*	*4.99*	*5.34*	*9.9*	*2.7*	*5.2*	*1.2*	*4.3*	*0.3*

Breakout: 27%   Improve: 44%   Collapse: 30%   Attrition: 22%   Comparables: *Jeff Shaw, Rawly Eastwick, Carlos Reyes*

Harper had put together back-to-back strong seasons, so his '05 inconsistency was something of a surprise. His control was off, strikeouts were down, and his home run rate nearly doubled. Shoulder "discomfort" may have been the culprit, though Harper never did hit the DL. Piniella never lost confidence in Harper, using him in higher leverage situations than all but Baez, Borowski, and Chad Orvella. Joe Maddon might have a different take; Harper doesn't have much margin for error, even when healthy.

JAMES HOUSER
Bats: L   Throws: L   Height: 6' 4"   Weight: 185   Born: December 15, 1984   Age: 21

YEAR	TM	LVL	AGE	W	L	SV	G	GS	IP	H	BB	SO	HR	GB%	BABIP	STUFF	WHIP	ERA	PERA	EQERA	EQH9	EQBB9	EQSO9	EQHR9	VORP	WXRL
2003	PRI	Rk	18	0	4	0	10	10	41.0	43	13	44	1	—	.347	8	1.37	3.73	4.54	6.81	10.0	3.9	5.0	0.7	-5.3	—
2004	CSC	A	19	3	1	0	7	7	32.7	27	13	27	1	—	.277	8	1.22	2.20	4.88	3.73	8.6	4.3	4.6	0.6	6.5	—
2005	SWM	A	20	8	8	0	22	22	115.0	100	31	109	12	35%	.295	-4	1.14	3.76	5.77	5.10	9.9	2.8	5.9	1.9	6.0	—
2006	*TBA*	*MLB*	*21*	*6*	*10*	*0*	*27*	*23*	*134.3*	*144*	*51*	*89*	*23*	*37%*	*.286*	*5*	*1.45*	*5.08*	*5.59*	*5.24*	*9.6*	*3.4*	*5.8*	*1.5*	*4.1*	*1.4*

Breakout: 13%   Improve: 50%   Collapse: 12%   Attrition: 0%   Comparables: *Chris Narveson, Dan Meyer, Craig Anderson*

The Devil Rays were conservative with Houser after some elbow discomfort shut him down in 2004, keeping him in Low-A for all of 2005. Houser throws hard, but his work on off-speed stuff—a change and a curve or two—produced mixed results, as depicted by the 12 home runs he allowed. In his previous 73.2 career innings, he had allowed precisely two. Assuming he can stay healthy, he remains a good candidate to show up in the bigs sometime in 2007.

MARK HENDRICKSON
Bats: L   Throws: L   Height: 6' 9"   Weight: 230   Born: June 23, 1974   Age: 32

YEAR	TM	LVL	AGE	W	L	SV	G	GS	IP	H	BB	SO	HR	GB%	BABIP	STUFF	WHIP	ERA	PERA	EQERA	EQH9	EQBB9	EQSO9	EQHR9	VORP	WXRL
2003	TOR	MLB	29	9	9	0	30	30	158.3	207	40	76	24	47%	.330	-8	1.56	5.51	4.90	5.62	10.4	2.2	4.1	1.2	-2.2	1.3
2004	TBA	MLB	30	10	15	0	32	30	183.3	211	46	87	21	49%	.300	1	1.40	4.81	4.59	5.03	10.2	2.1	4.0	0.9	12.0	2.8
2005	TBA	MLB	31	11	8	0	31	31	178.3	227	49	89	24	46%	.329	-3	1.55	5.91	4.82	5.35	10.3	2.4	4.3	1.1	-12.8	0.8
2006	*TBA*	*MLB*	*32*	*8*	*11*	*0*	*30*	*25*	*157.7*	*182*	*38*	*70*	*20*	*47%*	*.297*	*-3*	*1.40*	*4.87*	*5.06*	*5.28*	*10.3*	*2.1*	*3.9*	*1.1*	*6.2*	*1.7*

Breakout: 23%   Improve: 61%   Collapse: 10%   Attrition: 3%   Comparables: *Dennis Rasmussen, John Halama, Paul Minner*

Huge guy, small pitcher. Hendrickson has good control, but his low strikeout rate leads to far too many balls in play. He'll turn 32 this year and has shown no signs of developing into a major league starter. The Rays need to admit that he's an odd thing that struck Lou Piniella's fancy, and move on.

SCOTT KAZMIR   Bats: L   Throws: L   Height: 6' 0"   Weight: 170   Born: January 24, 1984   Age: 22

YEAR	TM	LVL	AGE	W	L	SV	G	GS	IP	H	BB	SO	HR	GB%	BABIP	STUFF	WHIP	ERA	PERA	EQERA	EQH9	EQBB9	EQSO9	EQHR9	VORP	WXRL
2003	CMB	A	19	4	4	0	18	18	76.3	50	28	105	6	—	.262	15	1.02	2.36	5.30	4.91	8.7	4.0	8.1	1.8	5.3	—
2003	SLU	A+	19	1	2	0	7	7	33.0	29	16	40	0	—	.330	31	1.36	3.27	3.66	5.62	8.7	4.8	7.9	0.3	-0.1	—
2004	SLU	A+	20	1	2	0	11	11	50.0	49	22	51	3	—	.326	8	1.42	3.42	5.06	4.88	9.6	4.7	6.2	1.1	3.8	—
2004	BIN	AA	20	2	1	0	4	4	26.0	16	9	29	0	—	.276	24	0.96	1.73	3.65	2.92	7.3	3.3	7.7	0.4	7.4	—
2004	MNT	AA	20	1	2	0	4	4	25.0	14	11	24	0	—	.230	21	1.00	1.44	4.24	3.47	6.6	4.6	6.2	0.4	5.5	—
2004	TBA	MLB	20	2	3	0	8	7	33.3	33	21	41	4	42%	.345	34	1.62	5.68	4.19	5.50	8.4	5.0	10.0	1.0	1.9	0.7
2005	TBA	MLB	21	10	9	0	32	32	186.0	172	100	174	12	42%	.316	35	1.46	3.77	3.99	4.08	7.9	4.8	8.2	0.6	29.4	4.5
2006	*TBA*	*MLB*	*22*	*10*	*11*	*0*	*30*	*30*	*180.0*	*168*	*85*	*166*	*20*	*42%*	*.294*	*23*	*1.40*	*4.38*	*4.64*	*4.72*	*8.3*	*4.2*	*8.0*	*0.9*	*18.5*	*3.2*

Breakout: 10%   Improve: 37%   Collapse: 15%   Attrition: 2%   Comparables: Pete Falcone, Dave Morehead, Chuck Stobbs

Heir to Randy Johnson's rep as the guy the John Kruks of the world beg out of ballgames to avoid, as lefties batted just .174/.253/.201 last year. That's just the tip of the iceberg: Kazmir ranked sixth in the league in hits to innings pitched ratio, third in strikeout ratio, and had one of the best home runs to innings pitched ratios in baseball. Best of all, he got better as the year went on, posting a second-half ERA of 2.79. Leading the majors in walks is a negative, but not the sort of thing you get hung up on with hard-throwing young lefties, who often experience control problems. As long as the Rays don't let him pitch his arm off—and they did a decent job of keeping his pitch counts down last year—the best is yet to come.

SETH McCLUNG   Bats: R   Throws: R   Height: 6' 6"   Weight: 230   Born: February 7, 1981   Age: 25

YEAR	TM	LVL	AGE	W	L	SV	G	GS	IP	H	BB	SO	HR	GB%	BABIP	STUFF	WHIP	ERA	PERA	EQERA	EQH9	EQBB9	EQSO9	EQHR9	VORP	WXRL
2003	TBA	MLB	22	4	1	0	12	5	38.7	33	25	25	6	42%	.255	-10	1.50	5.35	6.03	5.06	8.9	6.0	5.8	1.4	3.2	0.8
2005	TBA	MLB	24	7	11	0	34	17	109.3	106	62	92	20	36%	.274	-12	1.55	6.59	5.63	6.44	8.7	5.1	7.4	1.5	-15.4	0.5
2006	*TBA*	*MLB*	*25*	*4*	*6*	*1*	*34*	*12*	*89.3*	*85*	*46*	*68*	*12*	*39%*	*.277*	*-1*	*1.47*	*4.98*	*5.11*	*6.20*	*8.5*	*4.6*	*6.6*	*1.1*	*3.7*	*0.7*

Breakout: 29%   Improve: 60%   Collapse: 16%   Attrition: 21%   Comparables: Jack Armstrong, Steve Renko, Rob Bell

Lou Piniella worked him hard, though to what end is hard to ascertain. McClung throws hard but is wilder than Al Pacino with a juicy bit of dialogue. He was tough on righties last year, holding them to .197/.318/.318, but lefties had no trouble at all, batting .294/.379/.583, and hitting a home run once every 15 at-bats—when they weren't walking to first base. McClung is so good at walking people that the pedestrian warning signs at Tampa Bay intersections now say "Stop" and "McClung." It only got worse when he was tried in the bullpen. Until he improves his command, McClung won't be a viable major league pitcher.

TREVER MILLER   Bats: R   Throws: L   Height: 6' 3"   Weight: 200   Born: May 29, 1973   Age: 33

YEAR	TM	LVL	AGE	W	L	SV	G	GS	IP	H	BB	SO	HR	GB%	BABIP	STUFF	WHIP	ERA	PERA	EQERA	EQH9	EQBB9	EQSO9	EQHR9	VORP	WXRL
2003	TOR	MLB	30	2	2	4	79	0	52.7	46	28	44	7	44%	.264	-3	1.41	4.61	4.82	4.64	8.1	4.8	7.4	1.0	6.3	0.9
2004	TBA	MLB	31	1	1	1	60	0	49.0	48	15	43	3	52%	.319	14	1.29	3.12	3.47	3.65	8.8	2.6	7.3	0.5	13.1	0.8
2005	TBA	MLB	32	2	2	0	61	0	44.3	45	29	35	4	43%	.333	-5	1.67	4.06	5.16	4.37	8.9	5.8	6.9	0.8	5.2	-0.9
2006	*HOU*	*MLB*	*33*	*2*	*2*	*2*	*45*	*0*	*39.7*	*39*	*20*	*31*	*4*	*47%*	*.296*	*-6*	*1.49*	*4.38*	*4.76*	*5.42*	*8.9*	*4.2*	*6.5*	*0.9*	*2.7*	*0.2*

Breakout: 13%   Improve: 31%   Collapse: 46%   Attrition: 28%   Comparables: Dan Osinski, Valerio De Los Santos, Chuck McElroy

"It's still the same old story, a fight for love and glory, a case of do or die..." Sorry, Bogie, but "As Time Goes By" doesn't have a verse that applies to situational lefties with control problems, because despite the fondest wishes of CYA-strategizing managers everywhere, wild southpaw relievers never do or die with the lefty batter you want them to. That's why one-batter strategies don't amount to a hill of beans. Miller more than doubled his unintentional walk rate from 2004, and was non-tendered. Here's looking at you, kid.

SHINJI MORI
Bats: L Throws: R Height: 6′ 3″ Weight: 194 Born: September 12, 1974 Age: 31

YEAR	TM	LVL	AGE	W	L	SV	G	GS	IP	H	BB	SO	HR	GB%	BABIP	STUFF	WHIP	ERA	PERA	EQERA	EQH9	EQBB9	EQSO9	EQHR9	VORP	WXRL
2003	SEI	JPL		7	3	2	61	0	70.0	55	22	92	6	—	.293	25	1.10	0.00	3.31	3.04	7.5	2.9	9.5	0.8	19.3	—
2004	SEI	JPL		0	4	4	34	0	49.0	50	38	49	5	—	-.489	-12	1.80	4.59	5.26	6.34	8.9	6.9	7.2	0.9	-4.1	—
2005	SEI	JPL		2	2	5	48	0	49.0	44	19	60	5	—	.310	8	1.29	4.22	4.15	5.10	8.3	4.2	8.9	1.1	2.6	—
2006	*TBA*	*MLB*	*31*	*2*	*3*	*1*	*25*	*4*	*49.3*	*51*	*22*	*40*	*7*	*41%*	*.299*	*-1*	*1.47*	*4.88*	*5.19*	*6.04*	*9.2*	*4.0*	*7.0*	*1.1*	*2.3*	*0.3*

Breakout: 16% Improve: 42% Collapse: 36% Attrition: 28% Comparables: Dan Osinski, Vicente Palacios, Fred Sanford

Signed away from the Seibu Lions of Japan's Pacific League, Mori is a longtime set-up man. He's maintained good strikeout rates, but his last couple of years haven't been among his most impressive. He may make some noise his first time around the league due to batters' lack of familiarity with him. He should be a step up from Lance Carter, for what that's worth.

JEFFREY NIEMANN
Bats: R Throws: R Height: 6′ 9″ Weight: 260 Born: February 28, 1983 Age: 23

YEAR	TM	LVL	AGE	W	L	SV	G	GS	IP	H	BB	SO	HR	GB%	BABIP	STUFF	WHIP	ERA	PERA	EQERA	EQH9	EQBB9	EQSO9	EQHR9	VORP	WXRL
2005	VIS	A+	22	0	1	0	5	5	20.3	12	10	28	3	39%	.220	4	1.08	3.99	6.27	5.30	7.2	5.8	8.2	1.9	0.6	—
2005	MNT	AA	22	0	1	0	6	3	10.3	7	5	14	0	46%	.292	7	1.17	4.37	2.70	7.20	7.2	4.5	8.1	0.0	-1.8	—
2006	*TBA*	*MLB*	*23*	*4*	*7*	*0*	*21*	*14*	*86.7*	*77*	*54*	*79*	*11*	*40%*	*.276*	*10*	*1.51*	*5.16*	*5.11*	*5.63*	*7.9*	*5.6*	*7.9*	*1.1*	*1.1*	*0.6*

Breakout: 24% Improve: 56% Collapse: 7% Attrition: 6% Comparables: Eric Plunk, Jesse Foppert, Ryan Bradley

Neimann is so tall that when the pitching coach wants to talk to him he has to ride a cable car from the dugout. The fourth overall pick in the 2004 draft saw his first professional action in 2005 and the best word to describe it might be "sporadic." The pitcher was sidelined by three different injuries, including three months for shoulder soreness. He underwent arthroscopic surgery after the season, but is expected to be ready for spring training. When Neimann did pitch the results were good, at least in terms of his peripheral numbers. Neimann was frequently dinged up in college too, so this will probably not be the last time you hear his name in connection with the DL.

CHAD ORVELLA
Bats: R Throws: R Height: 5′ 11″ Weight: 190 Born: October 1, 1980 Age: 25

YEAR	TM	LVL	AGE	W	L	SV	G	GS	IP	H	BB	SO	HR	GB%	BABIP	STUFF	WHIP	ERA	PERA	EQERA	EQH9	EQBB9	EQSO9	EQHR9	VORP	WXRL
2004	CSC	A	23	1	0	4	22	0	47.3	28	5	76	4	—	.273	15	0.70	1.33	3.95	3.74	8.1	1.2	8.3	1.5	8.9	—
2004	BAK	A+	23	0	1	4	15	0	17.7	13	4	24	2	—	.268	0	0.96	3.05	5.51	5.51	8.8	2.8	7.7	2.2	0.2	—
2005	MNT	AA	24	0	0	9	16	0	25.0	15	6	29	0	43%	.250	12	0.84	0.36	3.47	2.31	6.9	2.7	6.9	0.4	8.5	—
2005	TBA	MLB	24	3	3	1	37	0	50.0	47	23	43	4	35%	.299	8	1.38	3.60	4.09	4.26	8.0	4.1	7.6	0.7	6.8	0.8
2006	*TBA*	*MLB*	*25*	*2*	*3*	*4*	*51*	*0*	*55.7*	*50*	*18*	*49*	*7*	*39%*	*.276*	*9*	*1.23*	*3.78*	*3.92*	*4.46*	*8.1*	*2.9*	*7.6*	*1.0*	*9.3*	*0.8*

Breakout: 27% Improve: 46% Collapse: 26% Attrition: 23% Comparables: Steve Foucault, John Wetteland, Stan Belinda

When Chuck LaMar composed the Old Regime's epitaph—"The only thing that keeps this organization from being recognized as one of the finest in baseball is wins and losses at the major-league level"—he may have been thinking of Orvella, subject of a truly outstanding makeover in the minors. An undersized shortstop at N.C. State, the Rays hazarded a 13th round pick on Orvella, signed him for a whopping $2,500 and told him he was a pitcher. Cue the training montage, complete with Survivor playing "Eye of the Tiger." Orvella came up with a power sinker and blew the minors away. His final stats: a 1.22 ERA in 111 innings, 23 walks, 160 strikeouts. The majors proved a harder nut to crack, in part because his control was off, but once he settles down, there's no reason he can't close. With Baez in L.A. he'll get the chance.

CHRIS SEDDON
Bats: L Throws: L Height: 6′ 3″ Weight: 170 Born: October 13, 1983 Age: 22

YEAR	TM	LVL	AGE	W	L	SV	G	GS	IP	H	BB	SO	HR	GB%	BABIP	STUFF	WHIP	ERA	PERA	EQERA	EQH9	EQBB9	EQSO9	EQHR9	VORP	WXRL
2003	BAK	A+	19	9	11	0	26	26	133.3	147	54	95	12	—	.307	-15	1.51	5.00	6.18	7.22	10.3	4.5	4.2	1.6	-23.3	—
2004	BAK	A+	20	5	0	0	7	7	41.3	30	8	41	0	—	.278	30	0.92	0.65	3.40	2.50	7.5	2.3	5.7	0.2	13.7	—
2004	MNT	AA	20	9	10	0	21	21	119.0	129	44	102	19	—	.318	-19	1.45	4.39	6.45	5.83	10.7	3.6	5.3	2.2	-2.9	—
2005	MNT	AA	21	6	1	0	10	10	52.3	58	20	46	4	48%	.351	0	1.49	4.82	5.08	6.31	10.2	3.7	5.3	1.2	-4.0	—
2005	DUR	AAA	21	4	9	0	19	19	95.7	114	43	70	11	38%	.337	-1	1.64	5.45	5.34	6.17	9.9	4.1	5.2	1.1	-6.2	—
2006	*TBA*	*MLB*	*22*	*5*	*10*	*0*	*26*	*20*	*117.0*	*131*	*58*	*72*	*19*	*40%*	*.295*	*-4*	*1.61*	*5.81*	*6.13*	*6.13*	*9.9*	*4.4*	*5.4*	*1.4*	*-7.3*	*0.0*

Breakout: 18% Improve: 56% Collapse: 15% Attrition: 0% Comparables: Ben Norris, Diego Markwell, Andy Pratt

The Rays' 5th round pick of the 2001 draft, Seddon has made it to Triple-A at just 21, though he's never shown consistency in the minors. He doesn't throw hard, and he walks a few too many hitters than is justified by his stuff and his generous home run rate. Hammered by the grizzled vets at Triple-A, it remains to be seen if the organization's new caretakers will feel the Old Regime's urge to push Seddon despite his record.

JAMIE SHIELDS Bats: R Throws: R Height: 6' 3" Weight: 190 Born: December 20, 1981 Age: 24

YEAR	TM	LVL	AGE	W	L	SV	G	GS	IP	H	BB	SO	HR	GB%	BABIP	STUFF	WHIP	ERA	PERA	EQERA	EQH9	EQBB9	EQSO9	EQHR9	VORP	WXRL
2003	BAK	A+	21	10	10	1	26	24	143.7	161	38	119	19	—	.313	-30	1.38	4.45	6.85	6.59	11.2	3.1	4.8	2.5	-15.2	—
2004	BAK	A+	22	8	5	0	20	20	117.0	120	33	92	13	—	.307	-24	1.31	4.23	6.41	6.16	10.4	3.4	4.5	2.0	-6.9	—
2005	MNT	AA	23	7	5	0	17	16	109.3	95	31	104	6	51%	.318	11	1.15	2.80	4.59	4.41	8.9	2.9	5.7	1.0	13.8	—
2006	TBA	MLB	24	5	10	0	28	20	123.7	140	47	72	22	42%	.292	-3	1.51	5.51	5.93	5.74	10.1	3.4	5.1	1.5	-3.5	0.5

Breakout: 14%   Improve: 51%   Collapse: 12%   Attrition: 0%   Comparables: Victor Santos, Vinny Chulk, Jason Ryan

When pitchers click: Shields hadn't done much to establish himself as a prospect since going to the Rays in the 16th round of the 2000 draft, but things came together in the second half of 2005. He was the pitching Biscuit of the year for Montgomery, then went on to the AFL where he posted a 1.74 ERA, allowing a .207 batting average and a 29-2 strikeout-walk ratio in 31 innings. Shields doesn't have great stuff, but he's figured out how to use it.

ANDREW SONNANSTINE Bats: L Throws: R Height: 6' 3" Weight: 185 Born: March 18, 1983 Age: 23

YEAR	TM	LVL	AGE	W	L	SV	G	GS	IP	H	BB	SO	HR	GB%	BABIP	STUFF	WHIP	ERA	PERA	EQERA	EQH9	EQBB9	EQSO9	EQHR9	VORP	WXRL
2004	HUD	A-	21	3	1	1	9	2	27.0	18	3	24	0	—	.234	1	0.78	1.00	3.60	4.32	7.9	1.4	4.3	0.4	3.6	—
2004	CSC	A	21	2	0	0	8	5	30.7	18	7	42	0	—	.269	26	0.81	0.59	3.14	3.14	7.2	2.5	7.2	0.3	7.8	—
2005	SWM	A	22	10	4	0	18	18	116.7	103	11	103	10	45%	.281	0	0.98	2.54	4.84	4.92	9.8	1.1	5.3	1.6	8.3	—
2005	VIS	A+	22	4	1	0	10	10	64.0	71	7	75	5	34%	.375	22	1.22	3.80	3.76	4.59	9.5	1.1	6.3	1.0	7.3	—
2006	TBA	MLB	23	9	11	0	29	26	165.3	177	28	102	25	39%	.285	12	1.24	4.50	4.58	4.70	9.5	1.5	5.4	1.3	15.2	2.7

Breakout: 13%   Improve: 52%   Collapse: 14%   Attrition: 0%   Comparables: Josh Banks, Scott Baker, Shaun Marcum

A 13th round pick in 2004, Sonnanstine doesn't throw hard but has insanely good control; his 178-18 strikeout-walk ratio last year would turn Brad Radke green with envy. Despite pitching in some tough environments, Sonnanstine doesn't give up many hits and hasn't been overly disposed towards giving up home runs. In addition to his laser-like targeting, Sonny keeps the ball down and comes at the hitter from a variety of arm angles. If he prospers in Double-A, it will be time to put aside doubts about his stuff and rate him a solid prospect.

JON SWITZER Bats: L Throws: L Height: 6' 3" Weight: 190 Born: August 13, 1979 Age: 26

YEAR	TM	LVL	AGE	W	L	SV	G	GS	IP	H	BB	SO	HR	GB%	BABIP	STUFF	WHIP	ERA	PERA	EQERA	EQH9	EQBB9	EQSO9	EQHR9	VORP	WXRL
2003	ORL	AA	23	8	8	0	22	22	126.0	117	32	100	10	—	.278	-9	1.18	3.43	5.45	5.75	9.9	2.6	4.9	1.6	-2.0	—
2005	MNT	AA	25	3	1	0	6	6	31.3	33	5	20	2	37%	.307	-5	1.21	3.45	5.46	5.46	10.6	1.8	3.6	1.2	0.5	—
2005	DUR	AAA	25	0	5	0	17	8	44.3	64	22	28	6	41%	.379	-28	1.94	7.11	6.31	7.09	11.4	4.9	4.1	1.4	-7.6	—
2006	TBA	MLB	26	3	6	1	38	9	77.0	92	30	41	14	41%	.302	-16	1.59	6.01	6.33	6.43	10.7	3.5	4.6	1.5	-7.1	-0.3

Breakout: 17%   Improve: 45%   Collapse: 17%   Attrition: 3%   Comparables: Sam McConnell, Josh Stewart, Ryan Snare

Switzer missed all of 2004 after surgery for a torn labrum, and his 2005 comeback was not kind, in part because elbow problems cropped up. Prior to meeting his deductible, Switzer's hallmark was strong command. That wasn't the case last year, and the odds are against his putting everything back together again to have a career.

DOUG WAECHTER Bats: R Throws: R Height: 6' 4" Weight: 200 Born: January 28, 1981 Age: 25

YEAR	TM	LVL	AGE	W	L	SV	G	GS	IP	H	BB	SO	HR	GB%	BABIP	STUFF	WHIP	ERA	PERA	EQERA	EQH9	EQBB9	EQSO9	EQHR9	VORP	WXRL
2003	ORL	AA	22	5	3	0	13	12	76.3	74	19	45	6	—	.270	-10	1.22	4.13	5.45	5.57	9.9	2.5	3.7	1.5	0.2	—
2003	DUR	AAA	22	3	3	0	10	10	51.3	51	12	35	9	—	.261	-9	1.23	3.33	6.33	5.03	10.2	2.6	5.2	2.4	3.1	—
2003	TBA	MLB	22	3	2	0	6	5	35.3	29	15	29	4	36%	.260	21	1.25	3.31	4.46	3.41	8.1	3.9	7.3	1.0	10.9	1.4
2004	DUR	AAA	23	0	2	0	8	8	29.3	33	17	22	11	—	.253	-33	1.71	6.76	9.32	6.43	11.2	5.8	5.5	3.9	-2.6	—
2004	TBA	MLB	23	5	7	0	14	14	70.3	68	33	36	20	32%	.224	-30	1.44	6.02	7.08	6.29	9.8	4.1	4.5	2.4	-5.5	0.2
2005	TBA	MLB	24	5	12	0	29	25	157.0	191	38	87	29	36%	.308	-10	1.46	5.62	5.19	5.36	10.2	2.2	4.9	1.6	-9.4	0.6
2006	TBA	MLB	25	6	10	0	34	20	136.0	148	40	78	22	38%	.284	-1	1.38	4.95	5.20	5.61	9.7	2.6	5.0	1.4	5.8	1.3

Breakout: 32%   Improve: 54%   Collapse: 19%   Attrition: 14%   Comparables: Jay Hook, John Snyder, Phil Regan

(continued next page)

Doug Waechter *(continued)*

Finger tendinitis held Waechter back or the second year in a row. It was a different finger, so maybe you could call that progress. He also got his walks down, and his home run rate improved from "London Blitz" to "A Typical Saturday Night in Fallujah." Still, Waechter remains a very hittable pitcher with little strikeout ability. Just 25, he might put together a good year someday if the conditions are right, say, pitching in San Diego for Leo Mazzone with five healthy fingers. Until that situation rolls up, junk bonds are more likely to deliver.

Line Outs

Position/Player	TM	LVL	AGE	PA	R	2B	3B	HR	RBI	BB	SO	SB-CS	SPEED	BA/OBP/SLG	MLVR	EQBA/OBP/SLG	EQA	VORP
C C. Johnson	TBA	MLB	33	55	5	4	0	0	5	9	11	0-0	3.1	.196/.327/.283	-.216	.196/.339/.283	.233	-0.6
1/3 E. Munson*	DUR	AAA	27	424	67	22	0	25	71	38	81	1-1	3.6	.285/.351/.539	.186	.245/.310/.457	.259	3.5
CF F. Perez	SWM	A	22	588	93	17	13	6	48	58	80	57-17	7.7	.289/.361/.406	.080	.249/.306/.348	.238	-10.1
OF J. Pridie* '06	TBA	MLB	22	323	37	15	3	8	33	16	73	10-4	5.9	.239/.280/.388	-.155	.244/.291/.410	.234	0.8

Pitcher	TM	LVL	AGE	W	L	SV	IP	H	BB	SO	HR	GB%	BABIP	STUFF	WHIP	ERA	PERA	EQERA	EQH9	EQBB9	EQSO9	EQHR9	VORP
R. Bell	TBA	MLB	28	1	1	0	25.0	41	12	13	7	39%	.362	-28	2.12	8.28	7.09	7.76	12.5	4.1	4.4	2.4	-9.3
	DUR	AAA	28	1	3	0	44.3	64	20	26	12	43%	.351	-53	1.90	7.72	8.32	7.31	12.2	4.7	3.7	3.0	-8.4
W. Davis	HUD	A-	19	7	4	0	86.0	75	23	97	5	56%	.320	6	1.14	2.72	5.47	5.58	9.8	3.2	5.6	1.6	0.2
J. Salas	VIS	A+	26	2	1	1	38.3	30	18	47	6	45%	.279	-32	1.25	3.52	7.86	6.03	9.4	6.3	6.6	2.6	-1.6
	MNT	AA	26	1	0	0	22.0	25	12	18	2	54%	.333	-34	1.68	3.68	6.97	6.53	11.3	6.1	4.4	1.7	-2.1

Charles Johnson probably won't be back; he didn't seem all that interested in playing last year. One of the most over-hyped prospects and players of all time, his great 2000 stands out as a spectacular fluke. A busted 1st round pick, **Eric Munson** was doomed by his inability to come to grips with the strike zone. Signed to a minor league deal with the Astros, where there might be a role for him in the Bagwell Caddy Cadre. **Fernando Perez** was drafted out of Columbia University, the same institution that produced Lou Gehrig. The similarities end there, since Perez's emphasis is on his speed. He'll need to improve his batting average and plate discipline to avoid a Goodwinian career path (Tom Goodwin, Curtis Goodwin—take your pick). There are creatures living deep underground, strange beasts unknown to science to whom even the sun is less than a distant rumor, who have a better idea of the strike zone than **Jason Pridie,** who took a minute step forward in 2004, but lost much of last year to a knee injury. Selected by Twins in the Rule 5 draft, he seems unlikely to stick without aid of one of those convenient injuries that always seem to befall Rule 5 guys.

Rob Bell's weak control and low strikeout rates have always made him a fringe pitcher, but anxiety attacks prevented him from using whatever skill he had. A trip to the minors didn't help. **Wade Davis,** the team's 2004 3rd round pick, saw his fastball picked up a few MPH, leading to tremendous improvement after being hammered in rookie ball. Stay tuned. A converted third baseman turned reliever, **Juan Salas** made good progress in his first year on the mound.

Texas Rangers

For a man who was supposed to be in tune with the previous administration, new General Manager Jon Daniels seems to be intent on making wholesale changes. When John Hart suddenly stepped aside and Daniels interviewed—on 24 hours notice—and won the job, the word on the new head of the Texas Rangers was that he was an applied economics major from Cornell and quite young for his job. But that talk soon subsided as Daniels completed a series of moves to revamp a large portion of the Rangers' roster.

The first major move came during the winter meetings, held in the Rangers' backyard in early December. In a brilliantly executed trade that exchanged players with values drastically distorted by their environments, the Rangers sent Alfonso Soriano to the Nationals for Brad Wilkerson and somehow managed to convince Jim Bowden to throw in reserve outfielder Terrmel Sledge and promising young pitcher Armando Galarraga. The focus in the mainstream media was the difference between Soriano's 36 home runs and 104 RBI against Wilkerson's 11 and 57. How would the Rangers possibly replace the 25 home runs and 57 RBI they were "losing" in this trade? Hadn't they clearly lost nearly 50 runs in this deal?

Hardly. Even if you don't believe that advanced statistics like WARP or VORP are better than mainstream stats, look at the players' home and road stats (see table 1).

On neutral ground, Wilkerson outperformed Soriano in AVG and RBI, and though his HR total wasn't as high, the difference was only six dingers, instead of 25. Now, even if you still believe Soriano's bat is better using these numbers, the difference in the value of the players is easily closed by Wilkerson's significantly better defense at a key defensive position. Against that, there's Soriano's significantly higher salary and extra year of service time, which means arbitration and even more expense. Nor is Soriano aging especially well, either: since posting back-to-back 7.5 WARP seasons with the Yankees in 2002–03, he contributed a *total* of 7.4 WARP over his two years with the Rangers. Meanwhile, Wilkerson added 11.5 WARP to the Expos and Nationals over the past two seasons. Acquiring Wilkerson for Soriano straight up would have netted the Rangers about two extra wins while answering one of their key questions in the outfield. As an additional benefit, Daniels had cleared the way for a clearly better defender

RANGERS PROSPECTUS

2005 record: 79–83; Third place, AL West

Pythagenport record: 81–81

Runs scored per game: 5.34 (3rd in AL)

Runs allowed per game: 5.30 (12th in AL)

Team EqA: .265 (4th in AL)

2005 Batters Age: 28.4 (4th youngest in AL)

2005 Pitchers Age: 31.1 (4th oldest in AL)

Ballpark: Ballpark at Arlington; Severe hitter's park; Park Factor of 1.067

2005: Who knew that stagnation was a lifestyle choice?

2006: Some audacious moves shook up the status quo, but will it be enough?

at second in prospect Ian Kinsler; since Kinsler's also a decent-looking prospect with the bat, the Rangers might gain net value just replacing Soriano with him by 2007. Getting Sledge and Galarraga to boot just made the deal that much more one-sided, while making it clear that Daniels was not afraid to shake up a team that had accomplished much less than expected in the Hart era.

Having improved the defense, the Rangers set about finding pitchers to fill a perennially depleted rotation. With only Chris Young and Kameron Loe penciled in, and the prospect trio of John Danks, Thomas Diamond, and Edison Volquez variously a year or two away, the Rangers had to go shopping for options. When Josh Beckett was traded to the Red Sox, Texas quickly settled for nabbing Vicente Padilla from the Phillies for Ricardo Rodriguez, swapped out Chris Young for Adam Eaton of the Padres, and capped the overhaul by signing Kevin Millwood to a four-year deal with a vesting option for the fifth.

While there was some concern about the leaky nature of the Texas front office—every deal this side of peace in the Middle East was rumored to involve the Rangers—Daniels and company had succeeded in revamping their rotation despite missing on both Josh Beckett and Matt Morris. The Young-Eaton deal is an old-fashioned challenge trade, one in which one team trades a player for another of apparently equal value, each assuming that their projections are more

TABLE 1. HOME AND ROAD STATS FOR BRAD WILKERSON AND ALFONSO SORIANO

Year	Batter	Location	AB	G	AVG	OBP	SLG	HR	RBI
2005	Brad Wilkerson	Home	258	72	.236	.367	.395	6	25
2005	Alfonso Soriano	Home	311	78	.315	.355	.656	25	73
2005	Brad Wilkerson	Road	307	74	.257	.337	.414	5	32
2005	Alfonso Soriano	Road	326	78	.224	.265	.374	11	31

accurate than those of the other guy. Young will be 27 in 2006 while Eaton will be 28, so age is a minimal consideration; the real difference is that Young will be entering his second full season while Eaton has one season before he becomes a free agent. Their value in 2006 will likely be within a win of each other, even if their raw statistics are vastly different because of the huge discrepancy between pitching in Ameriquest Field versus Petco. But the Rangers exchanged five years of control for one while getting the dual opportunity of either getting Eaton locked up long-term, or letting him slip away after 2006 to make way for cheaper options.

These two pitchers are roughly equal in value: Eaton has averaged 2.7 SNLVAR (Support Neutral Lineup–adjusted Value Added over Replacement, and aren't you glad you asked?) over his career while Young posted a 3.6 in his rookie season in 2005. The real achievement of the trade involved making the added-on exchange of Sledge and first baseman Adrian Gonzalez for the Padres' Akinori Otsuka. Given that Sledge was a throw-in from Washington and Gonzalez wasn't going to get any playing time in Texas on Mark Teixeira's watch, the Rangers basically obtained the effective Otsuka for parts unlikely to help them win games in 2006.

The Millwood contract is something else entirely. After missing out on signing Morris or trading for Beckett or Barry Zito, the Rangers threw $60 million at Millwood out of the need to get somebody to put at the front of the rotation. Disregarding the increased difficulty of logging innings in the inflated offensive environment of Texas and the administration's control over pitcher workload, the innings totals required to vest the fifth year should serve as an effective guarantee against a total, Chan Ho Park-style debacle. Though Millwood has a longer history of consistent performance than pitchers like Carl Pavano and A. J. Burnett, even if the option doesn't vest, that still leaves four years and $48 million that the Rangers will pay.

But adding Millwood, Padilla, and Eaton to join Loe and perhaps Juan Dominguez should stabilize a rotation that featured more pitchers (14) than any other team last season except Washington (15) and the New York Yankees (14). More importantly, this should improve a staff that

ranked 26th in the majors by SNLVAR. Add in the defensive improvement from Wilkerson and whatever warm body replaces Soriano—Kinsler, if he's ready—and the Rangers' run prevention should be significantly improved.

Most importantly, addressing their pitching problems should add more wins to the Rangers than these investments might mean to almost any other team in baseball. Even adjusting for their park, and despite some obvious holes, their offense ranked third in equivalent runs. That means that each additional run they can prevent is worth more to the Rangers than nearly any team. Furthermore, the Rangers were just unlucky. Translating their runs scored and allowed into their Adjusted Equivalent Runs allowed and scored (adjusted for the quality of the opposition) reveals that the Rangers should have won 87 games in 2005, suggesting that even if they fielded the same team in 2006, they'd be likely to improve by eight games. Throw in a few major improvements like Millwood and it isn't impossible to imagine this team contending for the playoffs. That's not to say Millwood's massive contract can be totally justified, but the financial benefits of vying for the playoffs should outweigh the spike in payroll. If any team would find it fiscally worthwhile to pay that much for a non-superstar quality starting pitcher, it's Texas.

Remarkably, while making moves aimed to field a contender this year, Daniels has avoided trading any of the Rangers' best prospects. The system isn't stocked with a wealth of prospective blue chippers, but the Rangers have talent at the right positions. The aforementioned Kinsler solidified his breakout 2004 with a solid 2005, and even if he doesn't win the second base job in camp, he should be joining Michael Young by September. They also have outfielder Jason Botts, who should earn significant playing time sooner rather than later. Gerald Laird could step in at catcher right now, and Taylor Teagarden is destined to follow him a few years from now. On the pitching side of the ledger, the DVD trio—Danks, Volquez, and Diamond—provide a greater depth of pitching prospects than the team has possessed in some time. The Rangers have been extremely averse to moving any of them—a fact that may have cost them Beckett in their negotiations with the Marlins—but with Eaton and Padilla set to hit free agency after this season, there should be plenty of open spots for which all three can audition.

The Jon Daniels administration has shown itself to be a dynamic, aggressive group—super-aggressive if their own leaks of possible deals are counted. There was hardly a rumor that hit the wires in November and December that didn't involve the Rangers sending someone somewhere. The wisdom to know what to leak and when will come with experience, and it's all the more necessary in an industry where nobody keeps secrets especially well. Meanwhile, what's important is that Texas is focusing on information, creativity, and decisive movement, whether it's teaching all of their minor league pitchers to induce groundballs, commissioning studies on the wind patterns in Ameriquest Field, or exploring every possible option on the market.

As he gets established, Daniels will enjoy an extended window of stability based on the contract situations of his key infield players. Mark Teixeira is under Texas control for three more years; Michael Young is under contract through 2007 with a club option for 2008; Hank Blalock is locked up through 2008 with a club option for 2009. While the Rangers have acted quickly to push themelves into contention, this is a team with both a one- and five-year plan. Daniels is only signed to a three-year contract, which might help explain why the short-term scenario appeared to be getting more attention than the long-term picture this winter. The refusal to part with their few good prospects shows that the Rangers are still balancing their future with their present.

So far, the Rangers' new management team has spent according to the team's needs—they've made one great trade, a challenge trade, a few interesting small pickups, and they've kept their farm system intact. It seems certain that they'll be better in 2006 than 2005 as a result of their moves, their youth, and because they underperformed last year. Although it will be a few years before a full report card can be filled out on the Jon Daniels band, the Rangers sent a clear message that the AL West just got a lot tougher.

HITTERS

SANDY ALOMAR   C   **Bats: R Throws: R**   Height: 6' 5"   Weight: 230   Born: June 18, 1966   Age: 40

YEAR	TM	LVL	AGE	PA	R	2B	3B	HR	RBI	BB	SO	SB	CS	SPEED	BA	OBP	SLG	MLVR	EQBA	EQOBP	EQSLG	EQA	VORP	DEFENSE
2003	CHA	MLB	37	199	22	12	0	5	26	4	17	0	0	4.1	.268	.281	.407	-.125	.260	.281	.396	.233	1.4	58-C -1
2004	CHA	MLB	38	161	15	4	0	2	14	11	13	0	0	3.7	.240	.298	.308	-.295	.236	.300	.299	.219	-5.1	43-C 2
2005	TEX	MLB	39	134	11	7	0	0	14	5	12	0	0	3.9	.273	.306	.328	-.191	.270	.313	.317	.226	-0.7	36-C -5
2006	LAN	MLB	40	139	11	7	0	1	13	6	14	0	0	4.3	.245	.283	.310	-.269	.251	.288	.323	.203	-3.7	37-C -1

Breakout: 9%   Improve: 32%   Collapse: 44%   Attrition: 53%   Comparables: Bob Boone, Tom Paciorek, Tony Pena

It's been five years since he notched an OBP over .306, and three since he totaled more than 200 PAs, but a trophy case full of Gold Gloves and a few All-Star appearances seem to be enough to keep him around. Base stealers were 17-for-17 against him last year and he's turning 40 in a few months, but that didn't dissuade the Dodgers from signing him to be their reserve catcher.

JOAQUIN ARIAS   SS   **Bats: R Throws: R**   Height: 6' 2"   Weight: 160   Born: September 21, 1984   Age: 21

YEAR	TM	LVL	AGE	PA	R	2B	3B	HR	RBI	BB	SO	SB	CS	SPEED	BA	OBP	SLG	MLVR	EQBA	EQOBP	EQSLG	EQA	VORP	DEFENSE
2003	BCR	A	18	513	60	12	8	3	48	26	44	12	5	6.2	.266	.306	.343	-.012	.245	.278	.333	.216	-12.5	130-SS 20
2004	STO	A+	19	541	77	20	8	4	62	31	53	30	14	6.8	.300	.344	.396	.027	.265	.303	.347	.231	-0.3	112-SS -13
2005	FRI	AA	20	523	65	23	8	5	56	17	46	20	10	6.5	.315	.335	.423	.066	.287	.312	.389	.245	13.1	117-SS 1
2006	TEX	MLB	21	530	60	25	4	5	44	19	51	12	5	5.3	.273	.302	.371	-.116	.269	.306	.369	.228	5.1	125-SS 3

Breakout: 25%   Improve: 52%   Collapse: 22%   Attrition: 5%   Comparables: William Bergolla, Alberto Callaspo, Omar Infante

Still more tools than results, but Arias is making solid progress. Acquired in the A-Rod deal, he has put together two consecutive good seasons at the plate to go with his fine defensive reputation. What little power he has is improving, and 20-year-old shortstops who stick in Double-A are generally guys with futures. He'll have to hit for a good average to contribute at the major league level, and so far he's shown the ability to do just that.

ROD BARAJAS   C   Bats: R Throws: R   Height: 6' 2"   Weight: 220   Born: September 5, 1975   Age: 30

YEAR	TM	LVL	AGE	PA	R	2B	3B	HR	RBI	BB	SO	SB	CS	SPEED	BA	OBP	SLG	MLVR	EQBA	EQOBP	EQSLG	EQA	VORP	DEFENSE
2003	ARI	MLB	27	238	19	15	0	3	28	14	43	0	0	3.1	.218	.265	.327	-.285	.210	.256	.311	.204	-8.9	66-C 8
2004	TEX	MLB	28	381	50	26	1	15	58	13	63	0	1	4.7	.249	.276	.453	-.141	.239	.269	.440	.240	1.5	102-C 2
2005	TEX	MLB	29	445	53	24	0	21	60	26	70	0	0	3.5	.254	.306	.466	-.014	.251	.312	.471	.264	16.1	115-C 8
2006	TEX	MLB	30	370	38	19	1	14	48	19	59	0	1	3.7	.249	.292	.433	-.068	.245	.296	.431	.240	4.6	89-C 2

Breakout: 24%   Improve: 44%   Collapse: 32%   Attrition: 19%   Comparables: Jody Davis, Joe Oliver, Barry Foote

In his second season as a Ranger regular, Barajas improved his hitting away from Arlington, boosting it from .221/.262/.401 to .250/.318/.520. The only problem was that his hitting at home dropped to .257/.293/.414, which leaves him in much the same place that he began. The 21 home runs are nice, but Barajas's career line stands at .236/.278/.410, and he's still in Gerald Laird's way. Like a latter-day Rick Cerone circa 1980, we'll look back at Barajas's 2005 and end up using that as an explanation for every subsequent contract he signs.

HANK BLALOCK   3B   Bats: L Throws: L   Height: 6' 1"   Weight: 192   Born: November 21, 1980   Age: 25

YEAR	TM	LVL	AGE	PA	R	2B	3B	HR	RBI	BB	SO	SB	CS	SPEED	BA	OBP	SLG	MLVR	EQBA	EQOBP	EQSLG	EQA	VORP	DEFENSE
2003	TEX	MLB	22	615	89	33	3	29	90	44	97	2	3	4.1	.300	.350	.522	.156	.290	.347	.510	.285	43.0	132-3B -6
2004	TEX	MLB	23	713	107	38	3	32	110	75	149	2	2	4.3	.276	.355	.500	.097	.266	.350	.489	.284	30.1	155-3B 9
2005	TEX	MLB	24	705	80	34	0	25	92	51	132	1	0	3.9	.263	.318	.431	-.026	.260	.326	.438	.262	11.4	155-3B -5
2006	TEX	MLB	25	664	89	34	2	32	103	58	117	2	1	4.4	.282	.349	.510	.148	.277	.353	.507	.282	37.2	155-3B -1

Breakout: 32%   Improve: 66%   Collapse: 6%   Attrition: 0%   Comparables: Robin Ventura, Eric Chavez, Jason Thompson

Relative to what was expected of him, Blalock struggled. Despite hitting .282/.344/.436 against lefties in 2004, he regressed to .196/.228/.356 in '05. Even more troubling was his decline at the plate against righties, the people he's supposed to hit. After slugging nearly .600 against them in 2003, Blalock slipped to .526 in 2004, then .464 in 2005; his OBPs and walk rates slid as well. He's entering the third year of a five-year, $15.25 million deal, but the deal was heavily back-loaded-Blalock has only earned $1.3 million in the first two years combined-so he's about to start getting expensive. He's still only 25, and the odds that 2005 was just a bump in the road are good, but until Blalock improves his glovework and turns his hitting around, all those Eric Chavez comparisons should stop.

JASON BOTTS   OF   Bats: B Throws: R   Height: 6' 6"   Weight: 240   Born: July 26, 1980   Age: 25

YEAR	TM	LVL	AGE	PA	R	2B	3B	HR	RBI	BB	SO	SB	CS	SPEED	BA	OBP	SLG	MLVR	EQBA	EQOBP	EQSLG	EQA	VORP	DEFENSE	
2003	STO	A+	22	330	58	14	2	9	61	45	59	12	3	5.8	.314	.409	.473	.285	.280	.363	.423	.276	9.8	72-1B -1	
2003	FRI	AA	22	220	26	11	1	4	27	21	45	6	1	5.0	.263	.341	.392	.020	.244	.315	.383	.247	-4.9	23-RF -2	10-1B 1
2004	FRI	AA	23	572	85	25	3	24	92	77	126	7	4	4.5	.293	.399	.507	.263	.261	.354	.450	.277	17.5	126-1B -11	
2005	OKL	AAA	24	589	93	31	7	25	102	67	152	2	4	4.4	.286	.375	.522	.195	.256	.334	.449	.267	6.7	81-LF -8	
2005	TEX	MLB	24	30	4	0	0	0	3	3	13	0	0	3.9	.296	.367	.296	-.088	.296	.387	.296	.254	0.0		
2006	TEX	MLB	25	506	65	24	3	21	69	48	118	4	2	4.7	.268	.341	.475	.079	.264	.345	.472	.271	13.3	119-LF -6	

Breakout: 23%   Improve: 53%   Collapse: 14%   Attrition: 7%   Comparables: Mike Epstein, Joe Borchard, Michael Restovich

Botts consolidated his impressive leap in 2004 with an equally impressive 2005. He's a bit old and his strikeout totals are high, but the Rangers chalk that up to aggressiveness and aren't concerned. They're trying to convert him to the outfield in the hope of getting his bat into the lineup, what with Mark Teixeira and Adrian Gonzalez already crowding first base. If he keeps hitting, he's going to have to be really terrible in the field to work himself out of the outfield picture. Even then, the Rangers are the organization that made the historically execrable Kevin Reimer an outfield regular, so standards of outfield play may not be lower anywhere else.

DAVID DELLUCCI   OF   Bats: L Throws: L   Height: 5' 11"   Weight: 190   Born: October 31, 1973   Age: 32

YEAR	TM	LVL	AGE	PA	R	2B	3B	HR	RBI	BB	SO	SB	CS	SPEED	BA	OBP	SLG	MLVR	EQBA	EQOBP	EQSLG	EQA	VORP	DEFENSE
2003	ARI	MLB	29	189	18	11	3	2	19	19	45	9	0	7.4	.242	.328	.382	-.101	.232	.316	.366	.253	-0.2	35-RF -2
2003	NYA	MLB	29	57	8	1	0	1	4	4	13	3	0	6.1	.176	.263	.255	-.408	.176	.276	.255	.211	-3.9	14-RF 1
2004	TEX	MLB	30	386	59	13	1	17	61	47	88	9	4	5.5	.242	.342	.441	-.044	.231	.337	.429	.266	1.3	73-LF -1
2005	TEX	MLB	31	518	97	17	5	29	65	76	121	5	3	5.9	.251	.367	.513	.149	.251	.377	.528	.301	28.2	43-LF 0
2006	TEX	MLB	32	388	57	17	3	18	53	50	89	6	3	5.9	.261	.363	.495	.134	.257	.367	.493	.285	18.3	93-DH

Breakout: 23%   Improve: 50%   Collapse: 24%   Attrition: 27%   Comparables: Mack Jones, Ruppert Jones, Cal Abrams

Beating standard career patterns, Dellucci enjoyed a breakout season at age 31. He's always drawn his walks and hit for decent power, but injuries always had a way of keeping him from establishing himself as something more than a reserve. It would be tempting to attribute his newfound success to Arlington's friendly confines, but he hit better away from Texas (.262/.382/.545) than at home (.240/.354/.485). He'll regress, but even so, his two-year, $1.8 million contract looks like a bargain.

MARK DeROSA — UT — Bats: R Throws: R — Height: 6' 1" Weight: 195 Born: February 2, 1975 — Age: 31

YEAR	TM	LVL	AGE	PA	R	2B	3B	HR	RBI	BB	SO	SB	CS	SPEED	BA	OBP	SLG	MLVR	EQBA	EQOBP	EQSLG	EQA	VORP	DEFENSE		
2003	ATL	MLB	28	288	40	14	0	6	22	16	49	1	0	4.5	.263	.316	.383	-.054	.262	.312	.386	.243	5.2	26-2B 2	19-3B -1	
2004	ATL	MLB	29	341	33	16	0	3	31	23	53	1	3	4.0	.239	.293	.320	-.222	.239	.289	.319	.217	-13.7	62-3B -6		
2005	TEX	MLB	30	166	26	5	0	8	20	16	35	1	0	3.8	.243	.325	.439	-.015	.241	.333	.455	.270	3.7	21-RF -1		
2006	TEX	MLB	31	152	16	7	0	4	16	11	27	1	0	4.2	.253	.314	.389	-.084	.249	.318	.387	.238	-0.4	40-RF -1		

Breakout: 18% Improve: 40% Collapse: 44% Attrition: 51% Comparables: Matt Mieske, Gary Woods, Tommie Aaron

The Braves non-tendered DeRosa after he blew out his knee in late 2004, but a quick recovery got him a minor league contract from the Rangers. A career utility infielder, he eventually wound up in right field as a desperate alternative to Richard Hidalgo. He hit well while playing there, and Showalter mistakenly stuck with him far too long. After a respectable year, he's earned himself at least another few years of employment, playing on Sundays or as an injury sub. His experience in the outfield is a good sales point for a player who would see a lot more at-bats on a team without so many good infielders.

ADRIAN GONZALEZ — 1B — Bats: L Throws: L — Height: 6' 2" Weight: 190 Born: May 8, 1982 — Age: 24

YEAR	TM	LVL	AGE	PA	R	2B	3B	HR	RBI	BB	SO	SB	CS	SPEED	BA	OBP	SLG	MLVR	EQBA	EQOBP	EQSLG	EQA	VORP	DEFENSE
2003	CAR	AA	21	152	15	9	1	1	16	14	25	1	1	4.1	.307	.368	.409	.150	.293	.347	.416	.264	3.5	36-1B -1
2003	ABQ	AAA	21	154	17	5	1	1	18	14	25	1	0	4.6	.216	.286	.288	-.352	.177	.247	.243	.184	-17.8	37-1B 1
2003	FRI	AA	21	187	16	6	2	3	17	11	27	0	0	3.3	.283	.326	.393	.013	.261	.302	.377	.237	-4.4	43-1B 6
2004	OKL	AAA	22	506	61	28	3	12	88	39	73	1	1	3.9	.304	.364	.457	.099	.278	.333	.405	.257	3.6	121-1B 5
2005	OKL	AAA	23	368	61	17	1	18	65	32	44	0	0	3.6	.338	.399	.561	.354	.307	.362	.494	.290	21.9	82-1B 7
2005	TEX	MLB	23	162	17	7	1	6	17	10	37	0	0	3.7	.227	.272	.407	-.164	.224	.280	.401	.235	-2.7	
2006	SDN	MLB	24	480	53	24	1	14	63	35	84	1	1	4.3	.254	.313	.411	-.076	.264	.321	.443	.253	4.8	113-1B 3

Breakout: 22% Improve: 52% Collapse: 22% Attrition: 9% Comparables: Ed Kranepool, Mo Vaughn, Jim Spencer

Acquired at midseason 2003, when it was not yet certain that Mark Teixeira was the first baseman of the future, Gonzalez's glove was rumored to be so good that Teixeira would have to move or share the position. Once Teixeira became locked in at first (and sanctified with a Gold Glove), Gonzalez appeared redundant, especially since he hadn't yet shown that he could hit well enough to stick. A spring training appointment as the starting DH proved to be short-lived, but Gonzalez showed signs of life at the plate in the minors. Though he doesn't walk much, Gonzalez makes excellent contact and has a good power stroke. The Rangers sent him to San Diego along with Terrmel Sledge and Chris Young, in exchange for Adam Eaton, Akinori Otsuka and Billy Killian, not a good gamble for them.

RICHARD HIDALGO — RF — Bats: R Throws: R — Height: 6' 3" Weight: 190 Born: July 2, 1975 — Age: 30

YEAR	TM	LVL	AGE	PA	R	2B	3B	HR	RBI	BB	SO	SB	CS	SPEED	BA	OBP	SLG	MLVR	EQBA	EQOBP	EQSLG	EQA	VORP	DEFENSE
2003	HOU	MLB	28	585	91	43	4	28	88	58	104	9	7	5.2	.309	.385	.572	.320	.301	.375	.564	.307	43.8	134-RF 17
2004	HOU	MLB	29	220	21	15	2	4	30	17	53	1	2	4.1	.256	.309	.412	-.047	.253	.306	.404	.243	-0.6	51-RF 5
2004	NYN	MLB	29	358	46	11	1	21	52	27	76	3	2	3.9	.228	.296	.463	-.024	.228	.293	.458	.252	1.9	79-RF -2
2005	TEX	MLB	30	339	43	12	0	16	43	26	74	1	2	3.6	.221	.289	.416	-.125	.218	.296	.416	.241	-5.3	79-RF -3
2006	TEX	MLB	30	401	49	19	1	19	59	32	80	3	2	4.3	.259	.325	.479	.052	.255	.329	.477	.265	7.2	96-RF -1

Breakout: 22% Improve: 52% Collapse: 24% Attrition: 19% Comparables: Wally Post, Larry Parrish, Tom Brunansky

Hidalgo's contract was exactly the kind of deal smart teams make as a hedge against risk. The outfielder's one-year contract called for $5 million guaranteed, but with incentives based on plate appearances, none of which Hidalgo met. The Rangers can now let him go, content that they took a shot in the dark on a player who hit .309/.385/.572 as recently as 2003, missed, but weren't burned too badly. That the gamble didn't pay off doesn't make it a bad decision. It's hard to know what to expect of Hidalgo going forward; another incentive-laden one-year deal would make sense.

IAN KINSLER   2B   Bats: R Throws: R   Height: 6' 0"   Weight: 175   Born: June 22, 1982   Age: 24

YEAR	TM	LVL	AGE	PA	R	2B	3B	HR	RBI	BB	SO	SB	CS	SPEED	BA	OBP	SLG	MLVR	EQBA	EQOBP	EQSLG	EQA	VORP	DEFENSE	
2003	SPO	A-	21	216	32	10	6	1	15	20	34	11	3	7.7	.277	.352	.410	.113	.238	.289	.353	.229	-4.0	48-SS	-2
2004	CLN	A	22	258	52	30	1	11	53	26	37	16	6	6.3	.401	.465	.687	.720	.328	.384	.556	.312	36.5	57-SS	6
2004	FRI	AA	22	325	51	21	1	9	46	32	47	7	4	4.8	.300	.400	.480	.235	.264	.347	.425	.267	16.1	71-SS	-4
2005	OKL	AAA	23	595	102	28	2	23	94	53	89	19	5	5.7	.274	.348	.464	.052	.245	.309	.400	.248	6.4	126-2B	-5
2006	TEX	MLB	24	504	65	27	3	17	59	36	79	11	4	5.1	.270	.328	.451	.029	.265	.332	.448	.261	19.8	119-2B	-1

Breakout: 21%   Improve: 47%   Collapse: 19%   Attrition: 5%   Comparables: Daniel Garcia, Alfonso Soriano, Rick Schu

Kinsler moved up to Oklahoma last year, but it's difficult to say if he's made progress or not. As expected, his batting average dropped at Triple-A. While he continued hitting home runs at the same clip, the precipitous drop in his doubles is not a good sign, However, as Alfonso Soriano's defense rapidly atrophied, Kinsler became the unseen motivator of a year's worth of Soriano trade rumors. With that obstacle finally removed, Kinsler should start at second for the big club (even with D'Angelo Jimenez in camp), and while he won't provide the same power Soriano has, replacing Soriano's career .320 OBP and replacement-level fielding shouldn't be a problem.

GERALD LAIRD   C   Bats: R Throws: R   Height: 6' 2"   Weight: 190   Born: November 13, 1979   Age: 26

YEAR	TM	LVL	AGE	PA	R	2B	3B	HR	RBI	BB	SO	SB	CS	SPEED	BA	OBP	SLG	MLVR	EQBA	EQOBP	EQSLG	EQA	VORP	DEFENSE	
2003	OKL	AAA	23	384	50	20	5	9	42	37	61	9	3	5.9	.260	.344	.429	.071	.248	.328	.411	.257	9.7	89-C	6
2004	TEX	MLB	24	164	20	6	0	1	16	12	35	0	1	4.0	.224	.287	.286	-.367	.214	.282	.262	.204	-8.5	45-C	6
2005	OKL	AAA	25	316	51	12	4	17	55	28	61	12	2	6.3	.310	.380	.562	.289	.275	.335	.477	.278	17.8	72-C	12
2005	TEX	MLB	25	42	7	2	0	1	4	2	7	0	0	5.1	.225	.262	.350	-.259	.231	.286	.359	.224	-0.9	11-C	0
2006	TEX	MLB	26	330	37	15	2	10	38	22	67	5	2	5.0	.252	.308	.412	-.065	.249	.312	.410	.243	6.0	80-C	4

Breakout: 25%   Improve: 41%   Collapse: 35%   Attrition: 22%   Comparables: Harry Chiti, Dan Walters, Randy Knorr

For a player who's always been more about defense than offense, Laird had a heck of a season with the bat while watching "highlights" of Rod Barajas and Sandy Alomar Jr. doing his job in Texas. Alomar is finally out of the picture, so at the very least, Laird should be the backup backstop in 2006. Once Barajas turns back into a pumpkin, Laird will likely enjoy a reign just slightly longer, what with Taylor Teagarden waiting in the wings.

GARY MATTHEWS JR.   OF   Bats: B Throws: R   Height: 6' 3"   Weight: 200   Born: August 25, 1974   Age: 31

YEAR	TM	LVL	AGE	PA	R	2B	3B	HR	RBI	BB	SO	SB	CS	SPEED	BA	OBP	SLG	MLVR	EQBA	EQOBP	EQSLG	EQA	VORP	DEFENSE			
2003	BAL	MLB	28	172	21	12	1	2	20	9	29	0	3	4.7	.204	.250	.327	-.317	.205	.260	.329	.202	-9.8	39-CF	1		
2003	SDN	MLB	28	341	50	19	1	4	22	34	66	12	5	6.3	.271	.346	.379	.015	.278	.354	.395	.264	5.6	24-RF	-1	28-CF	1
2004	TEX	MLB	29	317	37	17	1	11	36	33	64	5	1	5.4	.275	.350	.461	.034	.264	.346	.447	.275	10.8	54-RF	3	25-CF	2
2005	TEX	MLB	30	525	72	25	5	17	55	47	90	9	2	6.1	.255	.320	.436	-.023	.251	.327	.444	.265	11.6	95-CF	-3	21-RF	0
2006	TEX	MLB	31	403	52	19	3	12	46	33	71	8	3	5.6	.267	.329	.435	.008	.263	.333	.433	.257	8.7	96-CF	-2		

Breakout: 13%   Improve: 42%   Collapse: 28%   Attrition: 17%   Comparables: Mark Whiten, Al Martin, George Altman

Matthews leveraged his career year in 2004 into a one-year, $1.1 million contract. His rate stats predictably regressed, but he did tally 17 home runs, despite losing nearly a month to a pulled hamstring. Matthews hits like a below-average corner outfielder—a plus in centerfield, but not so good if preferred CF solution Laynce Nix pushes him to left or right. He has a decent glove, and the Rangers are struggling for outfield solutions. An upgrade would do the Rangers good, but another year from Matthews like 2005 in center field wouldn't kill them.

MARSHALL McDOUGALL   UT   Bats: R Throws: R   Height: 6' 1"   Weight: 200   Born: December 19, 1978   Age: 27

YEAR	TM	LVL	AGE	PA	R	2B	3B	HR	RBI	BB	SO	SB	CS	SPEED	BA	OBP	SLG	MLVR	EQBA	EQOBP	EQSLG	EQA	VORP	DEFENSE			
2003	FRI	AA	24	467	61	16	3	13	69	43	68	18	3	6.1	.258	.328	.404	.012	.232	.296	.376	.238	0.4	90-SS	3	16-3B	0
2003	OKL	AAA	24	126	11	4	2	2	9	13	21	1	1	4.5	.270	.341	.396	.030	.255	.322	.363	.243	1.7	13-SS	1		
2004	OKL	AAA	25	390	48	24	0	19	69	35	80	2	1	3.6	.282	.349	.511	.129	.244	.306	.423	.249	7.5	77-3B	9	15-SS	0
2005	OKL	AAA	26	255	40	16	2	11	64	30	45	5	0	5.2	.341	.416	.578	.408	.299	.366	.478	.291	20.2	31-3B	2	11-LF	-1
2006	TEX	MLB	27	350	41	16	2	12	43	27	68	4	1	4.6	.257	.318	.432	-.021	.253	.322	.430	.252	7.2	84-3B	3		

Breakout: 22%   Improve: 38%   Collapse: 38%   Attrition: 23%   Comparables: Kevin Elster, Casey Blake, Chris Woodward

McDougall has mastered Triple-A, but doesn't look like anything more than a very good utility infielder. There are plenty of those jobs available, and why some guys get to hang onto them for a decade while the McDougalls have to wait around in the bush leagues is one of the great mysteries of baseball. The firm line between "major leaguers" and the rest of the baseball players in the world has been blurring as teams begin to accept the legitimacy of minor league performance as a predictor of major league ability. McDougall is exactly the kind of player who deserves to benefit.

KEVIN MENCH   **OF**   **Bats: R Throws: R**   Height: 6' 0"   Weight: 230   Born: January 7, 1978   Age: 28

YEAR	TM	LVL	AGE	PA	R	2B	3B	HR	RBI	BB	SO	SB	CS	SPEED	BA	OBP	SLG	MLVR	EQBA	EQOBP	EQSLG	EQA	VORP	DEFENSE			
2003	OKL	AAA	25	131	16	8	0	4	21	19	15	2	0	4.0	.267	.366	.457	.154	.234	.332	.394	.264	-1.4	16-RF	-1	12-LF	-1
2003	TEX	MLB	25	139	15	12	0	2	11	10	17	1	1	4.3	.320	.381	.464	.145	.309	.372	.455	.284	5.7	30-LF	-3		
2004	TEX	MLB	26	481	69	30	3	26	71	33	63	0	0	4.7	.279	.335	.539	.112	.270	.331	.529	.285	20.9	56-RF	4	41-LF	-2
2005	TEX	MLB	27	615	71	33	3	25	73	50	68	4	3	4.7	.264	.328	.469	.042	.263	.338	.477	.275	15.2	110-LF	2	35-RF	-5
2006	*TEX*	*MLB*	*28*	*556*	*70*	*31*	*2*	*22*	*80*	*45*	*66*	*3*	*1*	*4.5*	*.278*	*.341*	*.480*	*.095*	*.274*	*.345*	*.478*	*.273*	*16.5*	*131-LF*	*-3*		

Breakout: 19%   *Improve: 46%*   *Collapse: 21%*   *Attrition: 9%*   Comparables: *Carlos Lee, Kevin McReynolds, Ivan Calderon*

Mench has finally arrived and, unlike 2004, his performance wasn't the result of Arlington's generosity. Mench murdered southpaws again, hitting .296/.380/.600 against them, but he's below average against righties, which makes for an obvious problem if Mench is going to play every day. The Rangers offered Mench a three-year deal with an option for a total of $10–12 million over the summer, but talks have stalled. The Rangers are rumored to be getting lots of offers for his services, and while they're happy keeping him around, the odds are that he's peaked are good.

DREW MEYER   **2B/SS**   **Bats: L Throws: R**   Height: 5' 10"   Weight: 180   Born: August 29, 1981   Age: 24

YEAR	TM	LVL	AGE	PA	R	2B	3B	HR	RBI	BB	SO	SB	CS	SPEED	BA	OBP	SLG	MLVR	EQBA	EQOBP	EQSLG	EQA	VORP	DEFENSE			
2003	STO	A+	21	437	59	16	9	5	53	32	92	24	10	7.5	.281	.330	.405	.027	.252	.296	.358	.233	-1.1	92-SS	20		
2003	FRI	AA	21	109	14	1	1	0	6	11	23	9	1	6.5	.316	.385	.347	.070	.285	.352	.316	.250	1.9	26-SS	4		
2004	FRI	AA	22	256	35	6	2	2	13	22	43	4	2	5.5	.241	.309	.310	-.191	.216	.278	.277	.204	-12.5	52-SS	-8		
2005	FRI	AA	23	355	49	14	4	3	45	26	55	12	2	6.5	.321	.372	.417	.124	.292	.344	.383	.260	11.4	66-2B	-3	11-SS	0
2005	OKL	AAA	23	193	25	11	4	0	19	14	43	5	2	6.6	.247	.301	.354	-.221	.222	.270	.307	.208	-7.5	29-SS	2	10-CF	-1
2006	*TEX*	*MLB*	*24*	*438*	*47*	*17*	*4*	*3*	*32*	*25*	*84*	*10*	*4*	*5.5*	*.249*	*.295*	*.339*	*-.184*	*.246*	*.299*	*.338*	*.216*	*-3.4*	*104-SS*	*2*		

Breakout: 15%   *Improve: 38%*   *Collapse: 32%*   *Attrition: 12%*   Comparables: *Thomas Watkins, Danny Sandoval, Jason Bowers*

The tenth overall pick in the 2002 draft, Meyer has been a huge disappointment. The Rangers have pushed him up the ladder despite struggles at every level. His 2005 line initially looks better than 2004, but the term "empty batting average" doesn't do it justice. His walk rate dropped, and while his ISO improved, it only went from a Einar Diaz-level .069 to a Cristian Guzman-like .094. Meyer will have to work hard just to eke out a career as a utility man.

PHIL NEVIN   **1B**   **Bats: R Throws: R**   Height: 6' 2"   Weight: 230   Born: January 19, 1971   Age: 35

YEAR	TM	LVL	AGE	PA	R	2B	3B	HR	RBI	BB	SO	SB	CS	SPEED	BA	OBP	SLG	MLVR	EQBA	EQOBP	EQSLG	EQA	VORP	DEFENSE			
2003	SDN	MLB	32	248	30	8	0	13	46	21	44	2	0	3.9	.279	.339	.487	.154	.285	.344	.500	.285	11.0	30-1B	1	26-RF	-2
2004	SDN	MLB	33	623	78	31	1	26	105	66	121	0	0	3.7	.289	.368	.492	.206	.295	.371	.505	.297	36.8	136-1B	-7		
2005	SDN	MLB	34	306	31	11	1	9	47	19	67	1	0	4.9	.256	.301	.399	-.047	.266	.311	.418	.253	-0.4	68-1B	0		
2005	TEX	MLB	34	108	15	5	0	3	8	8	30	2	0	4.7	.182	.250	.323	-.342	.175	.259	.309	.207	-5.4				
2006	*TEX*	*MLB*	*35*	*409*	*49*	*19*	*2*	*16*	*58*	*30*	*81*	*3*	*1*	*4.7*	*.270*	*.326*	*.458*	*.036*	*.266*	*.330*	*.456*	*.261*	*7.2*	*98-1B*	*-2*		

Breakout: 13%   *Improve: 35%*   *Collapse: 30%*   *Attrition: 18%*   Comparables: *Donn Clendenon, George Scott, Andres Galarraga*

Now that the balance sheet is settled, it looks like the Rangers saved about $5 million by sending Chan Ho Park out west, a value almost covered by the $6 million they sent San Diego for taking him. So what did they pay $1 million for? A player who's almost better designated for assignment than designated hitting. Even if Nevin rebounds to his 2002–04 rates (.286/.354/.464), it's difficult to see him squeezing himself into the crowded first base, DH, and bad outfielder picture. If Adrian Gonzalez is traded and Dellucci crashes and burns, he could yet land himself a platoon DH job, but that's a whole lot less than what people thought he was a year ago.

LAYNCE NIX   **CF**   **Bats: L Throws: L**   Height: 6' 0"   Weight: 190   Born: October 30, 1980   Age: 25

YEAR	TM	LVL	AGE	PA	R	2B	3B	HR	RBI	BB	SO	SB	CS	SPEED	BA	OBP	SLG	MLVR	EQBA	EQOBP	EQSLG	EQA	VORP	DEFENSE			
2003	FRI	AA	22	375	52	23	0	15	63	34	68	9	2	4.8	.284	.344	.487	.171	.251	.311	.447	.261	9.3	70-CF	-1		
2003	TEX	MLB	22	194	25	10	0	8	30	9	53	3	0	5.2	.255	.289	.440	-.101	.243	.285	.431	.246	-0.6	28-RF	1	16-CF	1
2004	TEX	MLB	23	399	58	20	4	14	46	23	113	1	1	5.7	.248	.293	.437	-.131	.239	.289	.426	.243	-0.8	99-CF	-2		
2005	TEX	MLB	24	240	28	12	3	6	32	9	45	2	0	6.3	.240	.267	.397	-.180	.236	.272	.404	.233	-2.9	59-CF	-2		
2006	*TEX*	*MLB*	*25*	*327*	*41*	*16*	*2*	*13*	*43*	*20*	*66*	*3*	*2*	*5.5*	*.268*	*.315*	*.467*	*.029*	*.264*	*.319*	*.465*	*.258*	*9.7*	*79-CF*	*-2*		

Breakout: 41%   *Improve: 59%*   *Collapse: 28%*   *Attrition: 33%*   Comparables: *Jerry Lynch, Todd Dunwoody, Steve Whitaker*

(continued next page)

Laynce Nix *(continued)*

Nix's 2004 shoulder injury finally required surgery, shutting him down in late July. His performance in the majors has been terrible, but that's not necessarily a reflection of his talent. He was rushed in 2003, and while it's up for debate whether skipping levels inhibits development, hitting with a bum shoulder for over a year wasn't going to help. At this point, there's still room for optimism, but he'll have to stay healthy, recover the plate discipline he showed in the minors and demonstrate some ability to hit lefties to be a regular. It's a tall order.

JUAN SENREISO OF Bats: R Throws: R Height: 6' 1" Weight: 170 Born: August 4, 1981 Age: 24

YEAR	TM	LVL	AGE	PA	R	2B	3B	HR	RBI	BB	SO	SB	CS	SPEED	BA	OBP	SLG	MLVR	EQBA	EQOBP	EQSLG	EQA	VORP	DEFENSE			
2003	CLN	A	21	510	48	18	4	5	58	30	117	45	8	7.6	.216	.265	.302	-.181	.192	.232	.288	.197	-60.9	81-RF	-2	46-CF	1
2004	CLN	A	22	146	20	10	2	2	23	16	31	12	6	7.0	.315	.390	.472	.253	.268	.331	.400	.258	-0.4	15-RF	0	13-CF	1
2004	STO	A+	22	250	36	12	2	6	32	15	47	12	5	6.0	.296	.344	.442	.092	.259	.302	.377	.237	-1.4	50-CF	-2		
2005	FRI	AA	23	551	54	25	5	5	35	45	125	16	8	5.2	.284	.345	.384	.003	.259	.318	.354	.239	-15.7	127-RF	-4		
2006	*TEX*	*MLB*	*24*	*444*	*48*	*21*	*3*	*6*	*38*	*25*	*104*	*13*	*4*	*4.9*	*.243*	*.289*	*.354*	*-.179*	*.239*	*.293*	*.353*	*.219*	*-11.6*	*105-RF*	*0*		

Breakout: 14%   Improve: 33%   Collapse: 30%   Attrition: 11%   Comparables: Luis Terrero, Ryan Christenson, Gary Varner

Signed out of the Dominican, Senreiso is all tools. He did a nice job of improving his plate discipline and power numbers in 2004, but lost most of that improvement last year-a big step back when he needed another step forward. His defense isn't good enough to keep him in center, and unless he develops some power soon, he'll be a reserve outfielder at best.

VINCE SINISI LF Bats: L Throws: L Height: 6' 0" Weight: 195 Born: November 7, 1981 Age: 24

YEAR	TM	LVL	AGE	PA	R	2B	3B	HR	RBI	BB	SO	SB	CS	SPEED	BA	OBP	SLG	MLVR	EQBA	EQOBP	EQSLG	EQA	VORP	DEFENSE	
2004	STO	A+	22	287	39	13	3	7	40	33	45	7	3	5.0	.310	.383	.472	.215	.273	.340	.408	.262	0.9	56-LF	2
2005	BAK	A+	23	153	25	10	2	6	22	17	19	5	0	5.2	.363	.438	.600	.524	.305	.368	.467	.289	7.3	29-LF	3
2005	FRI	AA	23	270	27	9	0	4	29	15	39	4	4	4.1	.258	.300	.343	-.150	.227	.270	.309	.207	-21.3	57-LF	-4
2006	*TEX*	*MLB*	*24*	*403*	*43*	*18*	*2*	*8*	*41*	*24*	*65*	*5*	*2*	*4.5*	*.255*	*.301*	*.381*	*-.116*	*.251*	*.305*	*.379*	*.229*	*-7.2*	*96-LF*	*-1*

Breakout: 22%   Improve: 39%   Collapse: 30%   Attrition: 12%   Comparables: Richard Brown, Kelcey Mucker, Randy Rigsby

When people get mad at agents for orchestrating bonus holdouts after the amateur draft, Sinisi should serve a prime example of why they do it. Acknowledged to be a 1st round talent in 2003, Sinisi slipped to the 2nd round because of his bonus demands. He then suffered a broken arm in 2004, missing significant time. Healthy again, he tore up the California League, only to fall flat on his face in Double-A. There are serious doubts about his ability to hit for power down the road or to play anywhere other than 1B or DH, a combination that should torpedo his in Texas. At least he landed that first contract, because that will likely be the biggest one he ever signs.

ALFONSO SORIANO 2B Bats: R Throws: R Height: 6' 1" Weight: 180 Born: January 7, 1976 Age: 30

YEAR	TM	LVL	AGE	PA	R	2B	3B	HR	RBI	BB	SO	SB	CS	SPEED	BA	OBP	SLG	MLVR	EQBA	EQOBP	EQSLG	EQA	VORP	DEFENSE	
2003	NYA	MLB	27	734	114	36	5	38	91	38	130	35	8	6.8	.290	.338	.525	.182	.295	.346	.541	.295	61.2	153-2B	1
2004	TEX	MLB	28	658	77	32	4	28	91	33	121	18	5	6.0	.280	.324	.484	.023	.270	.317	.473	.269	31.5	140-2B	-8
2005	TEX	MLB	29	682	102	43	2	36	104	33	125	30	2	7.2	.268	.309	.512	.074	.267	.317	.518	.283	39.5	152-2B	-21
2006	*WAS*	*MLB*	*30*	*633*	*83*	*36*	*3*	*26*	*89*	*39*	*125*	*18*	*5*	*6.0*	*.259*	*.312*	*.466*	*-.001*	*.271*	*.321*	*.504*	*.270*	*31.5*	*148-2B*	*-7*

Breakout: 9%   Improve: 37%   Collapse: 32%   Attrition: 6%   Comparables: Kelly Gruber, Jeff Kent, Chris Sabo

The park factor in Arlington has always been one of the highest in the AL. There's no better example of that in 2005 than Soriano, who hit .315/.355/.656 at home and .224/.265/.374 on the road. As measured by MLVr, Soriano was the fourth-best hitter in baseball at home, and the third-worst on the road-essentially changing from Alex Rodriguez to Cesar Izturis. His 2004 was similar, though not as extreme. Now that Soriano has been dealt to the Nationals (for Brad Wilkerson and more), his offense will sink to the level of his defense—seeing Soriano move to his left is like watching a wagon train go west in real time—and if the Nats' plan to move him to the outfield sticks, they'll discover what Derek Jeter pointed out years ago, that Soriano has the vertical leap of a sumo wrestler. He's about to become a massive disappointment.

MARK TEIXEIRA　　1B　　**Bats: B Throws: R**　　Height: 6' 3"　Weight: 220　Born: April 11, 1980　　Age: 26

YEAR	TM	LVL	AGE	PA	R	2B	3B	HR	RBI	BB	SO	SB	CS	SPEED	BA	OBP	SLG	MLVR	EQBA	EQOBP	EQSLG	EQA	VORP	DEFENSE		
2003	TEX	MLB	23	589	66	29	5	26	84	44	120	1	2	3.9	.259	.331	.480	.034	.251	.326	.472	.269	12.6	105-1B	5	11-3B -3
2004	TEX	MLB	24	625	101	34	2	38	112	68	117	4	1	5.2	.281	.370	.560	.197	.273	.365	.549	.303	41.5	138-1B	0	
2005	TEX	MLB	25	730	112	41	3	43	144	72	124	4	0	4.8	.301	.379	.575	.300	.301	.387	.587	.320	61.9	153-1B	12	
2006	TEX	MLB	26	677	98	35	2	41	114	71	120	3	1	4.5	.289	.371	.562	.255	.285	.376	.559	.303	44.9	158-1B	7	

Breakout: 18%　Improve: 50%　Collapse: 14%　Attrition: 1%　　Comparables: Nate Colbert, Bob Robertson, Ryan Klesko

How much better can he get? Teixeira played the full 162 games, posted career highs in his three major rate stats, and took home a well-deserved Gold Glove to boot. His 9.3 WARP1 was the second highest total in the league, behind only MVP Alex Rodriguez's 10.2. He'll be 26 in April, meaning his peak seasons are only just beginning. The contract he signed after the draft has expired, and his agent, Scott Boras, is reportedly driving for either a three-year deal (to cover Teixeira through his arbitration seasons) or a ten-year deal. The Rangers are hoping for a five- or six-year deal which would lock up one of the best young players in the league through age 30 or 31, just when he would likely start to decline. Now that he's answered the questions about his defense, there are no holes in his game. He's about to start a run as one of the league's most dominant players.

ANTHONY WEBSTER　　OF　　**Bats: L Throws: R**　　Height: 6' 0"　Weight: 190　Born: April 10, 1983　　Age: 23

YEAR	TM	LVL	AGE	PA	R	2B	3B	HR	RBI	BB	SO	SB	CS	SPEED	BA	OBP	SLG	MLVR	EQBA	EQOBP	EQSLG	EQA	VORP	DEFENSE		
2003	KAN	A	20	402	68	18	1	2	33	31	58	20	12	6.3	.289	.353	.361	.089	.266	.314	.341	.232	-5.3	86-CF	-4	
2004	STO	A+	21	427	66	20	7	8	44	39	69	20	4	7.0	.287	.363	.439	.112	.254	.317	.387	.249	-8.6	41-LF	-1	39-CF -4
2005	BAK	A+	22	534	93	36	11	11	73	31	55	25	5	7.9	.301	.346	.484	.108	.259	.297	.392	.242	-14.8	90-LF	10	12-RF 0
2006	TEX	MLB	23	488	56	25	4	7	43	23	69	13	5	5.5	.264	.303	.381	-.107	.260	.307	.379	.232	-4.8	115-LF	2	

Breakout: 14%　Improve: 38%　Collapse: 28%　Attrition: 7%　　Comparables: Andy Burress, Scott Hunter, Ray Sadler

A speedy player whose lack of power throws his prospect status into question. He showed life in that department in 2004, then followed it up with a decent 2005 campaign for a 22-year-old in High-A ball. There are also questions about his defense, and he certainly doesn't draw enough walks to keep anyone happy except the opposing pitchers, but there's a lot of time for improvement. Right now he's backup outfielder material, but that could change.

MICHAEL YOUNG　　SS　　**Bats: R Throws: R**　　Height: 6' 0"　Weight: 175　Born: October 19, 1976　　Age: 29

YEAR	TM	LVL	AGE	PA	R	2B	3B	HR	RBI	BB	SO	SB	CS	SPEED	BA	OBP	SLG	MLVR	EQBA	EQOBP	EQSLG	EQA	VORP	DEFENSE
2003	TEX	MLB	26	710	106	33	9	14	72	36	103	13	2	6.6	.306	.339	.446	.039	.296	.335	.436	.268	34.0	157-2B -17
2004	TEX	MLB	27	739	114	33	9	22	99	44	89	12	3	6.2	.313	.353	.483	.103	.303	.348	.473	.281	51.9	156-SS -11
2005	TEX	MLB	28	732	114	40	5	24	91	58	91	5	2	5.0	.331	.385	.513	.257	.330	.394	.528	.310	72.4	153-SS -19
2006	TEX	MLB	29	696	95	36	6	19	84	48	86	8	2	5.3	.306	.355	.472	.130	.301	.360	.469	.277	45.4	162-SS -11

Breakout: 11%　Improve: 39%　Collapse: 24%　Attrition: 1%　　Comparables: Johnny Logan, Gil Mcdougald, Edgar Renteria

Young's AVG and OBP have gone up every year he's been in the majors, and aside from a sophomore slump in the power department, those numbers have improved steadily as well. PECOTA pegged him for a big decline in 2005, a forecast that for all we know he read and used for motivation last year. That's really why we do what we do here at BP; we want to motivate guys like Young, make them reach their full potential (third in the AL in VORP), and see them justify the four-year contracts they just signed. We do like to help. Young may move off of shortstop sometime down the road, but after the Soriano trade Kinsler's ticketed for second base, so that day is still a way off. If he keeps hitting like this, he'll make the Rangers' decision on picking up the fifth year option on his contract extremely easy.

PITCHERS

JOHN BANNISTER　　**Bats: R Throws: R**　　Height: 6' 3"　Weight: 198　Born: January 20, 1984　　Age: 22

YEAR	TM	LVL	AGE	W	L	SV	G	GS	IP	H	BB	SO	HR	GB%	BABIP	STUFF	WHIP	ERA	PERA	EQERA	EQH9	EQBB9	EQSO9	EQHR9	VORP	WXRL
2004	SPO	A-	20	2	2	0	16	7	59.0	49	28	67	3	—	.299	-1	1.31	3.51	5.40	6.05	9.2	5.6	5.7	1.0	-2.8	—
2005	CLN	A	21	8	10	0	29	28	157.3	171	58	127	13	52%	.328	-12	1.46	4.58	5.78	6.54	10.6	3.8	4.8	1.5	-15.9	—
2006	TEX	MLB	22	6	10	0	26	25	135.3	160	62	75	22	50%	.306	-2	1.64	6.16	5.86	6.14	10.1	4.1	5.0	1.3	-7.7	0.2

Breakout: 22%　Improve: 61%　Collapse: 5%　Attrition: 0%　　Comparables: Wardell Starling, Chris Flinn, Zach Miner

Bannister posted respectable peripherals for a 21-year-old in low A-ball, but he's still hiding behind rotation-mates Eric Hurley and Michael Schlact. Bannister doesn't have Schlact's control or Hurley's impressive strikeout numbers or

(continued next page)

John Bannister (*continued*)

triple-digit radar gun readings, but he could develop into a bottom-of-the-rotation starter if everything breaks right. There's a lot of talent in front of him, but it seems to take ten good arms to find one good pitcher. With luck, Bannister could be #10.

JOAQUIN BENOIT   Bats: R   Throws: R   Height: 6' 3"   Weight: 200   Born: July 26, 1977   Age: 28

YEAR	TM	LVL	AGE	W	L	SV	G	GS	IP	H	BB	SO	HR	GB%	BABIP	STUFF	WHIP	ERA	PERA	EQERA	EQH9	EQBB9	EQSO9	EQHR9	VORP	WXRL
2003	TEX	MLB	25	8	5	0	25	17	105.0	99	51	87	23	38%	.259	-10	1.43	5.49	5.57	4.89	8.4	4.3	7.2	1.8	6.8	0.8
2004	TEX	MLB	26	3	5	0	28	15	103.0	113	31	95	19	38%	.323	5	1.40	5.68	4.61	5.04	9.3	2.5	7.6	1.5	7.7	0.8
2005	TEX	MLB	27	4	4	0	32	9	87.0	69	38	78	9	31%	.251	16	1.23	3.72	4.03	3.62	7.2	3.9	8.0	0.8	18.0	1.9
2006	*TEX*	*MLB*	*28*	*4*	*5*	*1*	*34*	*8*	*79.3*	*80*	*33*	*61*	*13*	*36%*	*.282*	*2*	*1.41*	*4.92*	*4.79*	*5.50*	*8.6*	*3.7*	*6.9*	*1.3*	*8.0*	*0.9*

Breakout: 18%   Improve: 43%   Collapse: 32%   Attrition: 20%   Comparables: Steve Bedrosian, Vicente Palacios, Wes Gardner

Benoit has always had good peripherals, but his home run rate as a starter is killing him. Relieving, Benoit's ERA was 1.30, his strikeout rate jumped by more than 50%, and he cut his home run rate from nearly four per 100 PAs to less than one. Out of options, he will likely get another audition for the fifth spot in the rotation. He has done almost nothing to distinguish himself as deserving of that job compared to the rest of the middling arms vying for that last spot, but if finally left in the pen, he could become a significant asset.

DOUG BROCAIL   Bats: L   Throws: R   Height: 6' 5"   Weight: 235   Born: May 16, 1967   Age: 39

YEAR	TM	LVL	AGE	W	L	SV	G	GS	IP	H	BB	SO	HR	GB%	BABIP	STUFF	WHIP	ERA	PERA	EQERA	EQH9	EQBB9	EQSO9	EQHR9	VORP	WXRL
2004	TEX	MLB	37	4	1	1	43	0	52.3	54	20	43	2	55%	.335	11	1.44	4.13	3.69	4.36	8.7	3.2	6.7	0.3	8.3	0.5
2005	TEX	MLB	38	5	3	1	61	0	73.3	90	34	61	2	49%	.373	14	1.69	5.53	3.59	5.10	9.2	3.9	7.1	0.2	0.1	-0.3
2006	*SDN*	*MLB*	*39*	*2*	*3*	*2*	*46*	*0*	*53.7*	*58*	*26*	*42*	*5*	*52%*	*.320*	*-9*	*1.56*	*5.13*	*5.48*	*6.24*	*9.9*	*4.0*	*6.2*	*0.8*	*-2.7*	*-0.3*

Breakout: 19%   Improve: 32%   Collapse: 43%   Attrition: 27%   Comparables: Roberto Hernandez, Mike Fetters, Lee Smith

This may finally be the end. Brocail came back after missing all of 2002–2003 with elbow problems, and parlayed 52.1 innings in 2004 into a $1 million contract for 2005. His season wasn't as bad as it seems, but his Fair Runs Allowed was still a grizzly 5.19, and the jump in his walk rate bodes ill. Signed by the Padres, he'll be 39 in May.

RYAN BUKVICH   Bats: R   Throws: R   Height: 6' 2"   Weight: 250   Born: May 13, 1978   Age: 28

YEAR	TM	LVL	AGE	W	L	SV	G	GS	IP	H	BB	SO	HR	GB%	BABIP	STUFF	WHIP	ERA	PERA	EQERA	EQH9	EQBB9	EQSO9	EQHR9	VORP	WXRL
2003	OMA	AAA	25	1	2	5	34	0	36.7	39	25	44	2	—	.359	-3	1.74	4.90	4.75	6.00	9.2	7.2	8.8	0.8	-1.6	—
2004	OMA	AAA	26	3	4	7	38	0	47.3	33	30	60	4	—	.264	-2	1.33	4.38	5.48	5.28	7.7	6.9	8.5	1.0	1.6	—
2006	*TEX*	*MLB*	*28*	*2*	*3*	*0*	*32*	*2*	*41.7*	*37*	*42*	*43*	*3*	*46%*	*.304*	*-3*	*1.88*	*5.83*	*5.60*	*7.09*	*7.6*	*9.1*	*9.3*	*0.7*	*0.6*	*-0.1*

Breakout: 21%   Improve: 41%   Collapse: 34%   Attrition: 38%   Comparables: Earl Wilson, Ken Wright, Johnny Gray

Sometimes fate isn't cruel, it's just plain mean. Bukvich has a career minor league walk rate of 5.1, and a career major league walk rate of 7.9. He went down with Tommy John surgery just after the Rangers picked him up off of waivers from the Padres. So, what's the last thing to come back after TJ? That's right: command. The only people issuing more free passes than Bukvich these days are the Backstreet Boys, and no, they're not major-league quality relievers either.

FRANCISCO CORDERO   Bats: R   Throws: R   Height: 6' 2"   Weight: 200   Born: May 11, 1975   Age: 31

YEAR	TM	LVL	AGE	W	L	SV	G	GS	IP	H	BB	SO	HR	GB%	BABIP	STUFF	WHIP	ERA	PERA	EQERA	EQH9	EQBB9	EQSO9	EQHR9	VORP	WXRL
2003	TEX	MLB	28	5	8	15	73	0	82.7	70	38	90	4	55%	.313	30	1.31	2.94	3.32	3.21	7.1	4.0	9.3	0.4	24.3	2.3
2004	TEX	MLB	29	3	4	49	67	0	71.7	60	32	79	1	44%	.317	35	1.29	2.13	2.85	2.11	7.2	3.7	9.2	0.1	31.2	6.0
2005	TEX	MLB	30	3	1	37	69	0	69.0	61	30	79	5	45%	.316	28	1.32	3.39	3.44	3.31	7.4	3.8	9.9	0.6	16.8	3.5
2006	*TEX*	*MLB*	*31*	*4*	*5*	*22*	*58*	*0*	*64.3*	*61*	*29*	*61*	*6*	*45%*	*.302*	*12*	*1.38*	*3.83*	*3.99*	*4.00*	*8.1*	*4.0*	*8.6*	*0.8*	*13.0*	*1.6*

Breakout: 7%   Improve: 19%   Collapse: 52%   Attrition: 6%   Comparables: Jason Isringhausen, Jim Kern, Jim Mecir

Cordero battled a shoulder injury in spring training, but delivered on the first year of his two-year, $8 million contract. His ratios were almost an exact repeat of 2004—a remarkable feat for a reliever—with the only difference being a slightly higher home run rate. His contract has a clause that increases the value of his 2007 option year from $5 to $6 million if he's still the team's closer. Have we mentioned that modern bullpen management is archaic, arbitrary, and costs teams wins by misallocating talent and cash? Case in point: the extra million it's likely to cost the Rangers.

JOHN DANKS
Bats: L Throws: L Height: 6' 2" Weight: 190 Born: April 15, 1985 Age: 21

YEAR	TM	LVL	AGE	W	L	SV	G	GS	IP	H	BB	SO	HR	GB%	BABIP	STUFF	WHIP	ERA	PERA	EQERA	EQH9	EQBB9	EQSO9	EQHR9	VORP	WXRL
2004	CLN	A	19	3	2	0	14	8	49.7	38	14	64	4	—	.279	14	1.05	2.17	5.09	4.70	9.0	3.3	7.0	1.6	4.6	—
2004	STO	A+	19	1	4	0	13	13	55.0	62	26	48	5	—	.345	-6	1.60	5.24	6.11	6.96	10.5	5.3	5.1	1.5	-8.0	—
2005	BAK	A+	20	3	3	0	10	10	57.7	50	16	53	5	49%	.280	12	1.14	2.50	4.88	4.07	8.8	2.9	5.4	1.1	9.4	—
2005	FRI	AA	20	4	10	0	18	17	98.3	117	34	85	12	43%	.354	0	1.54	5.49	5.34	6.36	10.3	3.6	5.9	1.5	-8.3	—
2006	*TEX*	*MLB*	*21*	*7*	*9*	*0*	*28*	*23*	*137.0*	*150*	*59*	*89*	*23*	*44%*	*.292*	*4*	*1.53*	*5.36*	*5.37*	*5.30*	*9.4*	*3.9*	*5.8*	*1.4*	*5.4*	*1.5*

Breakout: 31% Improve: 70% Collapse: 4% Attrition: 0% Comparables: Chris George, Jon Lester, Mike Connolly

The first of "DVD," the Rangers' trio of top pitching prospects: Danks, Edison Volquez, and Thomas Diamond. Danks plays the part of the tall southpaw with the low-90s fastball and devastating curve. You may remember him from such films as "No Free Passes Today," and "Coach Said I Can't Throw My Curve Because I Need a Changeup." If everything breaks right for the Rangers, Danks will join Diamond and Volquez in the big league rotation sometime in 2007. Or he could go direct to video-for every blockbuster there are ten busts, so odds are that only one of them will have a fruitful major league career. Which one? There's no way to tell, not yet.

THOMAS DIAMOND
Bats: R Throws: R Height: 6' 3" Weight: 230 Born: April 6, 1983 Age: 23

YEAR	TM	LVL	AGE	W	L	SV	G	GS	IP	H	BB	SO	HR	GB%	BABIP	STUFF	WHIP	ERA	PERA	EQERA	EQH9	EQBB9	EQSO9	EQHR9	VORP	WXRL
2004	CLN	A	21	1	0	0	7	7	30.7	18	8	42	1	—	.262	20	0.85	2.05	3.81	4.13	7.6	3.2	7.0	0.6	4.6	—
2005	BAK	A+	22	8	0	0	14	14	81.3	53	31	101	3	48%	.289	26	1.03	1.99	4.14	3.67	7.6	4.4	7.1	0.5	16.3	—
2005	FRI	AA	22	5	4	0	14	14	69.0	66	38	68	8	36%	.307	-7	1.51	5.35	6.03	6.30	9.3	6.2	6.7	1.5	-5.1	—
2006	*TEX*	*MLB*	*23*	*7*	*9*	*0*	*28*	*23*	*134.7*	*138*	*73*	*105*	*20*	*41%*	*.294*	*8*	*1.57*	*5.38*	*5.30*	*5.31*	*8.8*	*4.9*	*7.0*	*1.2*	*4.9*	*1.4*

Breakout: 11% Improve: 30% Collapse: 28% Attrition: 1% Comparables: Junior Guerrero, Adam Johnson, Mike Meyers

A gigantic right-handed power pitcher, Diamond lacks the smooth control of Danks, but he makes up for it with an other-worldly strikeout rate. He attended the University of New Orleans and missed a start late in the season to check on his family after Hurricane Katrina. He's a bit older than Danks, but given the nature of pitching injuries, it's safer to take the slightly older player if you want to bet on who's going to have a major league career.

R. A. DICKEY
Bats: R Throws: R Height: 6' 3" Weight: 200 Born: October 29, 1974 Age: 31

YEAR	TM	LVL	AGE	W	L	SV	G	GS	IP	H	BB	SO	HR	GB%	BABIP	STUFF	WHIP	ERA	PERA	EQERA	EQH9	EQBB9	EQSO9	EQHR9	VORP	WXRL
2003	TEX	MLB	28	9	8	1	38	13	116.7	135	38	94	16	43%	.337	6	1.48	5.09	4.41	4.41	9.2	2.8	6.8	1.1	14.0	1.5
2004	TEX	MLB	29	6	7	1	25	15	104.3	136	33	57	17	47%	.328	-11	1.62	5.61	5.08	5.83	10.6	2.6	4.5	1.2	-0.7	0.7
2005	OKL	AAA	30	10	6	0	19	17	121.7	152	39	81	12	52%	.349	-11	1.57	5.99	5.41	7.27	10.7	3.2	3.9	1.2	-22.5	—
2005	TEX	MLB	30	1	2	0	9	4	29.7	29	17	15	4	52%	.263	-18	1.55	6.67	5.76	6.07	9.1	5.2	4.6	1.2	-3.1	-0.5
2006	*TEX*	*MLB*	*31*	*6*	*8*	*0*	*39*	*19*	*116.7*	*135*	*42*	*60*	*17*	*47%*	*.299*	*-10*	*1.51*	*5.53*	*5.22*	*5.63*	*9.9*	*3.2*	*4.6*	*1.2*	*1.8*	*0.8*

Breakout: 27% Improve: 62% Collapse: 16% Attrition: 1% Comparables: Dan Petry, Dustin Hermanson, Duane Pillette

The Rangers love Dickey because of his intangibles. How intangible? Off the charts intangible—go ahead, go find 'em. He wanted to become a knuckleball pitcher and was very aggressive about learning the pitch, meeting with Charlie Hough and going to the instructional league after the season. Early results were not encouraging, but he is learning a completely new way to pitch and hasn't been at it very long. He's still a long shot to be a useful major league pitcher, but he'll get every chance to be one with the Rangers. We almost forgot the obligatory mention of the missing ligament in his elbow; it's coming up in a few pages.

JUAN DOMINGUEZ
Bats: R Throws: R Height: 6' 2" Weight: 180 Born: May 18, 1980 Age: 26

YEAR	TM	LVL	AGE	W	L	SV	G	GS	IP	H	BB	SO	HR	GB%	BABIP	STUFF	WHIP	ERA	PERA	EQERA	EQH9	EQBB9	EQSO9	EQHR9	VORP	WXRL
2003	STO	A+	23	4	0	1	16	9	63.3	55	16	72	3	—	.306	5	1.12	2.84	4.53	5.58	9.4	3.2	6.3	0.9	0.1	—
2003	FRI	AA	23	5	0	0	9	9	55.3	35	21	54	2	—	.228	16	1.01	2.60	4.38	4.03	7.2	4.4	6.5	0.7	8.9	—
2004	OKL	AAA	24	5	1	0	9	9	54.7	41	19	41	3	—	.244	10	1.10	3.13	4.33	4.15	7.8	3.6	5.2	0.5	8.4	—
2004	TEX	MLB	24	1	2	0	4	4	23.0	25	5	14	2	45%	.315	12	1.30	3.91	4.24	3.86	9.3	1.9	5.0	0.8	5.2	0.8
2005	FRI	AA	25	2	0	2	15	2	37.7	30	9	31	4	43%	.250	-11	1.03	2.63	5.40	4.63	8.7	2.8	5.4	1.5	3.8	—
2005	OKL	AAA	25	2	1	0	7	7	36.0	38	10	24	6	55%	.281	-12	1.33	4.25	5.66	5.66	9.8	2.6	4.4	1.8	-0.2	—
2005	TEX	MLB	25	4	6	0	22	10	70.3	78	25	45	11	44%	.296	-4	1.46	4.22	5.00	4.12	9.4	3.1	5.6	1.2	8.9	0.8
2006	*TEX*	*MLB*	*26*	*4*	*6*	*1*	*44*	*11*	*83.7*	*95*	*30*	*50*	*13*	*45%*	*.301*	*-6*	*1.50*	*5.30*	*5.16*	*5.47*	*9.7*	*3.3*	*5.4*	*1.2*	*3.7*	*0.7*

Breakout: 9% Improve: 32% Collapse: 46% Attrition: 8% Comparables: Todd Burns, Bill Gogolewski, Tex Clevenger

(continued next page)

Juan Dominguez (*continued*)

Once the organization's best pitching prospect, Dominguez hasn't flashed that high strikeout rate from 2003 in a while, and the pitching prospects coming up behind him are closing in. He'll be in the fight for a rotation spot in 2006 and this year will tell us a lot about how the rest of his career is going to go. If he can't develop another pitch to go with his low to mid-90s fastball and great changeup, his future is likely in the pen.

SCOTT FELDMAN Bats: L Throws: R Height: 6' 5" Weight: 210 Born: February 7, 1983 Age: 23

YEAR	TM	LVL	AGE	W	L	SV	G	GS	IP	H	BB	SO	HR	GB%	BABIP	STUFF	WHIP	ERA	PERA	EQERA	EQH9	EQBB9	EQSO9	EQHR9	VORP	WXRL
2005	FRI	AA	22	1	2	14	46	0	61.0	43	23	41	3	63%	.237	-9	1.08	2.36	4.58	3.63	7.4	4.3	4.7	0.6	12.5	—
2006	TEX	MLB	23	2	3	1	29	2	49.3	54	19	26	5	57%	.294	-7	1.47	4.79	4.52	5.06	9.3	3.5	4.7	0.9	3.7	0.4

Breakout: 0% Improve: 4% Collapse: 87% Attrition: 31% Comparables: Tim Spooneybarger, Jim Hannan, Jamie Vermilyea

Feldman missed most of 2004 with Tommy John surgery, but picked up where he left off, pitching well enough in Double-A Fresno to earn a late season call-up. The Rangers shut him down to make sure he wasn't overworked, a good sign from an organization that's gone through pitchers like network television goes through CSI spin-offs. His ERA was nice, but middling peripherals indicate he still has progress to make. On the flip side, he's a 22-year-old who did pretty well while recovering from surgery, and he's already cracked The Show. He'll likely see some time in the bullpen in 2006 after someone gets injured, but a season of Triple-A wouldn't hurt.

KEVIN GRYBOSKI Bats: R Throws: R Height: 6' 5" Weight: 220 Born: November 15, 1973 Age: 32

YEAR	TM	LVL	AGE	W	L	SV	G	GS	IP	H	BB	SO	HR	GB%	BABIP	STUFF	WHIP	ERA	PERA	EQERA	EQH9	EQBB9	EQSO9	EQHR9	VORP	WXRL
2003	ATL	MLB	29	6	4	0	64	0	44.3	44	23	32	3	65%	.323	-5	1.51	3.86	4.47	4.47	9.1	4.3	5.9	0.6	6.4	0.0
2004	ATL	MLB	30	3	2	2	69	0	50.7	54	23	24	2	60%	.311	-12	1.52	2.84	4.41	4.24	9.4	3.7	3.7	0.4	10.1	0.8
2005	ATL	MLB	31	0	0	0	31	0	21.3	24	12	8	0	50%	.333	-24	1.69	2.96	4.98	4.57	10.0	4.6	2.9	0.4	3.0	0.0
2006	TEX	MLB	32	1	1	0	28	0	28.3	36	13	12	3	55%	.319	-25	1.72	5.62	5.56	6.56	10.8	4.3	3.7	0.8	-0.2	-0.1

Breakout: 25% Improve: 43% Collapse: 33% Attrition: 44% Comparables: Mike Barlow, Doug Sisk, Mike Mohler

Acquired in July for middling prospect Matt Lorenzo, Gryboski contributed little more than a fiery ending to a mid-August game in which he was ejected after giving up a game-losing home run. He was outrighted to Triple-A after the season, and with his career 99:103 K:BB ratio he's unlikely to contribute to a contending team ever again.

JOHN HUDGINS Bats: R Throws: R Height: 6' 2" Weight: 195 Born: August 31, 1981 Age: 24

YEAR	TM	LVL	AGE	W	L	SV	G	GS	IP	H	BB	SO	HR	GB%	BABIP	STUFF	WHIP	ERA	PERA	EQERA	EQH9	EQBB9	EQSO9	EQHR9	VORP	WXRL
2004	STO	A+	22	3	1	2	15	11	65.0	49	18	73	4	—	.268	7	1.03	2.35	4.77	4.33	8.5	3.4	6.4	1.2	8.5	—
2004	FRI	AA	22	5	3	0	12	12	69.0	57	18	64	12	—	.249	-11	1.09	3.13	6.68	4.97	9.9	2.8	6.1	2.7	4.4	—
2005	OKL	AAA	23	3	7	0	19	19	102.7	127	37	77	12	41%	.351	-5	1.60	5.87	5.09	6.56	10.3	3.2	4.9	1.2	-11.1	—
2006	TEX	MLB	24	6	9	0	30	19	119.3	138	44	70	21	43%	.297	-2	1.52	5.71	5.53	5.62	9.9	3.4	5.3	1.5	-0.2	0.7

Breakout: 18% Improve: 60% Collapse: 9% Attrition: 0% Comparables: Buster Narum, Tomokazu Ohka, Jason Ryan

A 3rd round pick out of Stanford, Hudgins is usually described as "polished" because he gets by with a great changeup and little else. He had good ratios in 2004 but struggled in 2005, although in '05 he was extremely hit-unlucky, suggesting the step back may have had more to do with untimely defense than his own shortcomings. He missed the last month of the season due to elbow surgery—bone growth/chips removal, not ligament related—so he should get another shot at Triple-A in 2006. He could eventually become a back-of-the-rotation starter.

ERIC HURLEY Bats: R Throws: R Height: 6' 4" Weight: 195 Born: September 17, 1985 Age: 20

YEAR	TM	LVL	AGE	W	L	SV	G	GS	IP	H	BB	SO	HR	GB%	BABIP	STUFF	WHIP	ERA	PERA	EQERA	EQH9	EQBB9	EQSO9	EQHR9	VORP	WXRL
2004	SPO	A-	18	0	2	0	8	6	28.3	31	6	21	6	—	.294	-17	1.31	5.41	8.89	7.18	12.3	2.4	4.1	4.1	-4.6	—
2005	CLN	A	19	12	6	0	28	28	155.3	135	59	152	11	39%	.300	13	1.25	3.77	5.01	5.07	9.1	3.9	6.1	1.2	8.8	—
2006	TEX	MLB	20	7	9	0	25	25	141.7	153	57	96	28	39%	.283	8	1.48	5.37	5.45	5.18	9.2	3.6	6.1	1.6	6.4	1.7

Breakout: 19% Improve: 55% Collapse: 8% Attrition: 1% Comparables: Kris Honel, Bubba Nelson, Travis Foley

The Rangers selected Hurley with a second 1st round pick in 2004, their compensation for losing John Thomson. Hurley walks a few too many batters and there are mechanical concerns, but he's also only 19, strikes out nearly a batter an inning, and rarely gives up the long ball. As with all 19-year-olds whose career is throwing a baseball in the low- to mid-90s, the potential for injury is the elephant in the room. So far, Hurley looks like a prospect.

CHRIS JAILE   Bats: R   Throws: R   Height: 6′ 3″   Weight: 190   Born: February 20, 1981   Age: 25

YEAR	TM	LVL	AGE	W	L	SV	G	GS	IP	H	BB	SO	HR	GB%	BABIP	STUFF	WHIP	ERA	PERA	EQERA	EQH9	EQBB9	EQSO9	EQHR9	VORP	WXRL
2005	CLN	A	24	1	1	3	17	0	45.0	49	13	42	5	48%	.326	-25	1.38	3.60	6.54	5.91	11.2	3.4	5.1	2.3	-1.5	—
2005	BAK	A+	24	2	3	0	13	13	63.3	65	35	58	4	47%	.326	-15	1.58	4.27	6.00	6.60	9.9	6.6	4.9	0.9	-6.7	—
2006	SEA	MLB	25	3	6	0	28	11	78.3	91	51	46	13	46%	.304	-19	1.81	6.42	6.96	6.99	10.4	5.7	5.0	1.4	-10.9	-0.7

Breakout: 9%   Improve: 37%   Collapse: 23%   Attrition: 2%   Comparables: Wayne Ough, Chris Rojas, Matt Lindstrom

A successful pitcher in high school, Jaile started his professional career as a catcher. He batted .212 in 328 games, at which point the Rangers astutely decided to move him back to the mound. Now Jaile has got the best of both worlds: he's old enough that many injury concerns associated with young pitchers don't apply, but he's only been pitching professionally for two seasons, which means he's still learning and could improve dramatically. Jaile signed with the Mariners as a minor league free agent.

WES LITTLETON   Bats: R   Throws: R   Height: 6′ 3″   Weight: 200   Born: September 2, 1982   Age: 23

YEAR	TM	LVL	AGE	W	L	SV	G	GS	IP	H	BB	SO	HR	GB%	BABIP	STUFF	WHIP	ERA	PERA	EQERA	EQH9	EQBB9	EQSO9	EQHR9	VORP	WXRL
2003	SPO	A-	20	6	0	0	12	8	52.0	36	8	47	2	—	.238	6	0.85	1.56	4.53	4.34	8.9	1.9	4.7	1.1	6.7	—
2004	STO	A+	21	8	10	0	30	23	141.0	139	56	72	7	—	.284	-15	1.38	4.15	5.72	6.13	9.7	4.7	3.0	0.9	-7.9	—
2005	FRI	AA	22	2	3	3	48	0	81.7	93	24	71	9	56%	.354	-12	1.43	3.97	5.27	4.82	10.1	3.1	5.7	1.5	7.0	—
2006	TEX	MLB	23	3	4	0	31	5	60.7	75	25	30	10	50%	.311	-15	1.65	6.11	6.01	6.02	10.6	3.7	4.5	1.4	-3.2	-0.1

Breakout: 7%   Improve: 35%   Collapse: 28%   Attrition: 7%   Comparables: Jeff Bennett, Dan Perkins, Christian Parker

Littleton had a solid debut in 2003 that seemed to support this college pitcher's reputation as a 4th round steal, but struggled mightily in 2004, completely losing the ability to fool hitters with his low-90s fastball or solid curve. Moved to the bullpen in '05, he finished strong and brought all his ratios back to where a prospect's should be. He's just 22 and has proven himself to some extent at Double-A, so the expectation that Littleton will reach the majors is not unrealistic.

KAMERON LOE   Bats: R   Throws: R   Height: 6′ 8″   Weight: 220   Born: September 10, 1981   Age: 24

YEAR	TM	LVL	AGE	W	L	SV	G	GS	IP	H	BB	SO	HR	GB%	BABIP	STUFF	WHIP	ERA	PERA	EQERA	EQH9	EQBB9	EQSO9	EQHR9	VORP	WXRL
2003	CLN	A	21	4	3	2	23	11	97.0	78	19	94	3	—	.276	12	1.00	1.95	4.11	5.09	8.6	2.3	5.7	0.8	5.2	—
2003	STO	A+	21	3	0	1	9	4	37.7	26	6	31	1	—	.233	11	0.85	0.95	3.82	3.31	7.9	2.0	4.8	0.5	9.0	—
2004	FRI	AA	22	7	7	0	19	19	113.3	122	29	97	5	—	.344	18	1.33	3.10	4.14	4.62	10.1	2.7	5.4	0.6	12.1	—
2004	OKL	AAA	22	5	2	0	8	8	52.3	52	13	42	6	—	.309	12	1.24	3.27	4.73	4.03	9.1	2.5	5.6	1.2	8.9	—
2005	OKL	AAA	23	2	1	0	5	5	28.3	32	10	23	5	46%	.314	-1	1.48	5.09	5.72	5.72	9.8	3.2	5.4	1.9	-0.4	—
2005	TEX	MLB	23	9	6	1	48	8	92.0	89	31	45	7	60%	.272	-1	1.30	3.42	4.47	3.59	8.5	3.1	4.4	0.7	17.4	1.4
2006	TEX	MLB	24	5	6	1	43	12	98.0	106	31	58	11	53%	.298	0	1.40	4.51	4.40	4.85	9.3	2.9	5.3	0.9	12.6	1.5

Breakout: 9%   Improve: 35%   Collapse: 28%   Attrition: 14%   Comparables: Carl Pavano, Jim Beattie, Dave Goltz

Despite talk that he profiles as a reliever, Loe's name is penciled into the 2006 rotation primarily because of one number: his groundball to flyball ratio. The Rangers believe their only hope of succeeding in their park is to keep the ball on the ground, and they've preached this at every level of their system. Loe proved an apt student, finishing the year with a 2.5 GB:FB ratio, and allowing only seven home runs in over 92 innings. He doesn't throw as hard as you'd expect from someone his size, but his high-80s sinker gets things done. It's not hard to see his career pan out like Walt Terrell or perhaps even Derek Lowe, never striking out enough batters for comfort, but getting enough groundouts to munch innings and help win a few ballgames.

ERASMO RAMIREZ   Bats: L   Throws: L   Height: 6′ 0″   Weight: 180   Born: April 29, 1976   Age: 30

YEAR	TM	LVL	AGE	W	L	SV	G	GS	IP	H	BB	SO	HR	GB%	BABIP	STUFF	WHIP	ERA	PERA	EQERA	EQH9	EQBB9	EQSO9	EQHR9	VORP	WXRL
2003	TEX	MLB	27	3	1	0	34	0	49.0	46	9	28	4	49%	.278	3	1.12	3.86	4.04	3.12	8.4	1.7	5.0	0.7	13.0	1.3
2004	TEX	MLB	28	5	3	0	34	0	35.7	34	7	21	5	52%	.266	-5	1.15	4.29	4.33	4.33	8.9	1.8	5.1	1.0	6.9	0.4
2005	TEX	MLB	29	0	0	0	16	0	23.0	24	3	6	3	46%	.266	-17	1.17	3.91	5.09	3.13	9.8	1.2	2.3	1.2	5.0	0.1
2006	TEX	MLB	30	1	1	1	28	0	27.3	33	6	11	4	48%	.295	-18	1.41	4.95	4.90	5.52	10.3	1.9	3.5	1.2	2.3	0.2

Breakout: 13%   Improve: 27%   Collapse: 52%   Attrition: 49%   Comparables: Al Aber, Larry Casian, Mike Magnante

After missing most of the first half of the season with a strained finger-feel free to insert your favorite Carlos Zambrano internet surfing injury joke here—Ramirez somehow kept his ERA under 4.00 while striking out exactly six batters in 23.0 innings. While that minuscule strikeout rate is a red flag, nothing definitive can be concluded from such a small sample of work and Ramirez has gotten guys out thus far. He'll get a shot at the pen again in 2006 based largely on his control numbers and the fact that he's a lefty.

NICK REGILIO   Bats: R Throws: R   Height: 6' 2"   Weight: 180   Born: September 4, 1978   Age: 27

YEAR	TM	LVL	AGE	W	L	SV	G	GS	IP	H	BB	SO	HR	GB%	BABIP	STUFF	WHIP	ERA	PERA	EQERA	EQH9	EQBB9	EQSO9	EQHR9	VORP	WXRL
2004	OKL	AAA	25	6	5	0	17	17	91.7	98	46	72	6	—	.336	0	1.57	4.71	4.98	5.58	9.5	5.1	5.2	0.7	0.2	—
2004	TEX	MLB	25	0	4	0	6	4	19.3	20	15	12	3	48%	.298	-19	1.81	6.06	6.41	6.41	9.2	6.4	5.0	1.4	-1.7	0.0
2005	TEX	MLB	26	1	2	0	18	0	17.7	22	7	14	2	40%	.345	0	1.64	4.58	4.34	4.34	9.6	3.4	6.8	1.0	1.6	-0.6
2006	*TEX*	*MLB*	*27*	*2*	*2*	*1*	*33*	*1*	*42.3*	*48*	*19*	*29*	*5*	*43%*	*.314*	*-7*	*1.59*	*5.30*	*5.23*	*6.15*	*9.8*	*4.1*	*6.2*	*1.1*	*1.9*	*0.1*

Breakout: 32%   Improve: 52%   Collapse: 28%   Attrition: 41%   Comparables: Jim Dickson, Felix Rodriguez, Mike Oquist

Death, taxes, and Nick Regilio injuries. Once again, the borderline pitcher missed a significant stretch of the season—this time with turf toe, a sore elbow, and flexor tendon surgery, so it's still not certain which side of the border he's on. How much more of this can he take, and how many virgin components does he have left?

RICARDO RODRIGUEZ   Bats: R Throws: R   Height: 6' 3"   Weight: 190   Born: May 21, 1978   Age: 28

YEAR	TM	LVL	AGE	W	L	SV	G	GS	IP	H	BB	SO	HR	GB%	BABIP	STUFF	WHIP	ERA	PERA	EQERA	EQH9	EQBB9	EQSO9	EQHR9	VORP	WXRL
2003	CLE	MLB	25	3	9	0	15	15	81.7	89	28	41	16	52%	.273	-17	1.43	5.73	5.80	6.02	10.2	3.1	4.5	1.7	-2.4	0.8
2004	OKL	AAA	26	2	2	0	6	6	37.0	42	12	18	5	—	.298	-17	1.46	5.11	6.00	6.50	10.5	3.5	3.2	1.5	-3.6	—
2004	TEX	MLB	26	3	1	0	5	4	26.7	28	12	15	1	51%	.297	6	1.50	2.02	4.00	3.00	9.0	3.7	4.7	0.3	8.7	0.9
2005	OKL	AAA	27	7	3	0	13	12	80.3	64	23	48	8	56%	.239	-4	1.08	2.91	5.33	4.26	8.4	2.8	3.9	1.2	11.3	—
2005	TEX	MLB	27	2	3	0	12	10	57.0	67	17	24	11	52%	.284	-16	1.49	5.53	5.59	5.12	10.1	2.6	3.7	1.6	-1.2	0.3
2006	*PHI*	*MLB*	*28*	*6*	*8*	*0*	*32*	*20*	*119.3*	*131*	*42*	*60*	*16*	*51%*	*.288*	*-8*	*1.45*	*5.04*	*5.17*	*5.42*	*9.7*	*2.9*	*4.3*	*1.2*	*3.0*	*1.0*

Breakout: 11%   Improve: 42%   Collapse: 21%   Attrition: 1%   Comparables: Al Fitzmorris, Jim McGlothlin, Don August

That should just about do it for the "Ricardo Rodriguez, Major League Starting Pitcher Marching and Chowder Society." He doesn't strike anyone out, walks too many guys, and gives up too many home runs. He came back from a broken elbow in 2004, only to be shut down with a shoulder injury after two forgettable months in 2005. Dumped on the Phillies for Vicente Padilla, he'll only see significant time in their rotation if everything goes terribly wrong for them.

KENNY ROGERS   Bats: L Throws: L   Height: 6' 1"   Weight: 205   Born: November 10, 1964   Age: 41

YEAR	TM	LVL	AGE	W	L	SV	G	GS	IP	H	BB	SO	HR	GB%	BABIP	STUFF	WHIP	ERA	PERA	EQERA	EQH9	EQBB9	EQSO9	EQHR9	VORP	WXRL
2003	MIN	MLB	38	13	8	0	33	31	195.0	227	50	116	22	45%	.320	9	1.42	4.57	4.45	4.68	9.9	2.2	5.1	1.0	25.4	3.1
2004	TEX	MLB	39	18	9	0	35	35	211.7	248	66	126	24	47%	.321	9	1.48	4.76	4.44	4.36	9.8	2.6	4.9	0.9	34.2	3.7
2005	TEX	MLB	40	14	8	0	30	30	195.3	205	53	87	15	47%	.291	11	1.32	3.46	4.36	3.31	9.1	2.5	3.9	0.6	41.4	4.0
2006	*DET*	*MLB*	*41*	*8*	*12*	*0*	*33*	*26*	*167.0*	*192*	*49*	*81*	*21*	*48%*	*.299*	*-5*	*1.44*	*4.87*	*5.08*	*5.56*	*10.2*	*2.6*	*4.3*	*1.1*	*7.1*	*1.9*

Breakout: 0%   Improve: 14%   Collapse: 55%   Attrition: 20%   Comparables: Jerry Koosman, Warren Spahn, Jamie Moyer

In Seattle they're eager for Jamie Moyer to pitch until he's fifty, tossing beer-league fastballs into a target the size of a pint glass. Rogers seems to have become the same kind of pitcher, but he doesn't get the love Moyer does. Punting big games (Rogers's post-season ERA is a deserved 8.85), punching water coolers, throwing cameras and cameramen, and not being frank about injuries can do that to a guy's rep. Now with the Tigers, Rogers should again miraculously post a decent ERA despite not striking out anyone, and probably still won't win any popularity contests. He can probably keep doing this until he's 45 or runs out of major league cities where he's welcome, whichever comes first.

JOSH RUPE   Bats: R Throws: R   Height: 6' 2"   Weight: 180   Born: August 18, 1982   Age: 23

YEAR	TM	LVL	AGE	W	L	SV	G	GS	IP	H	BB	SO	HR	GB%	BABIP	STUFF	WHIP	ERA	PERA	EQERA	EQH9	EQBB9	EQSO9	EQHR9	VORP	WXRL
2004	SPO	A-	21	2	0	0	4	3	18.0	14	3	19	1	—	.271	8	0.94	1.50	4.76	3.71	9.0	2.1	5.3	1.1	3.6	—
2004	STO	A+	21	2	0	0	4	3	18.3	12	4	14	0	—	.226	7	0.87	0.98	4.24	3.71	7.9	2.6	4.8	0.5	3.6	—
2004	FRI	AA	21	2	2	0	7	6	37.0	41	16	16	5	—	.277	-25	1.54	4.38	7.46	6.69	11.6	4.6	2.8	2.1	-4.2	—
2005	FRI	AA	22	4	3	0	11	10	65.0	64	26	55	7	63%	.311	0	1.38	3.74	5.63	4.76	9.4	4.5	5.8	1.4	5.8	—
2005	OKL	AAA	22	6	7	0	17	17	93.7	116	38	62	12	52%	.341	-11	1.64	6.24	5.59	7.11	10.4	3.5	4.5	1.3	-15.9	—
2006	*TEX*	*MLB*	*23*	*7*	*10*	*0*	*35*	*22*	*138.7*	*158*	*62*	*78*	*18*	*52%*	*.303*	*-3*	*1.58*	*5.43*	*5.34*	*5.42*	*9.7*	*4.1*	*5.1*	*1.1*	*2.7*	*1.1*

Breakout: 16%   Improve: 66%   Collapse: 5%   Attrition: 0%   Comparables: Bob Miller, Jake Westbrook, Bob Friend

Another piece of the 2003 Carl Everett deal, Rupe doesn't throw hard, but he has an otherwise complete arsenal of pitches. Although he made progress in Double-A last year, he struggled when called up to Oklahoma. He's still very young and some more seasoning in Triple-A is called for. Rupe hasn't done anything to take himself out of the Rangers' pitching picture except not throw as hard as the DVD trio.

BRIAN SHOUSE   **Bats: L   Throws: L**   Height: 5' 11"   Weight: 180   Born: September 26, 1968   Age: 37

YEAR	TM	LVL	AGE	W	L	SV	G	GS	IP	H	BB	SO	HR	GB%	BABIP	STUFF	WHIP	ERA	PERA	EQERA	EQH9	EQBB9	EQSO9	EQHR9	VORP	WXRL
2003	TEX	MLB	34	0	1	1	62	0	61.0	62	14	40	1	61%	.319	14	1.25	3.10	3.34	2.90	8.4	2.0	5.7	0.1	18.4	1.6
2004	TEX	MLB	35	2	0	0	53	0	44.3	36	18	34	3	57%	.260	7	1.17	2.23	4.09	2.25	7.6	3.5	6.5	0.6	19.5	1.5
2005	TEX	MLB	36	3	2	0	64	0	53.3	55	18	35	7	55%	.291	-8	1.37	5.23	4.80	5.30	8.9	3.0	5.8	1.2	-2.0	0.2
2006	*TEX*	*MLB*	*37*	*2*	*2*	*1*	*39*	*0*	*36.0*	*42*	*11*	*24*	*4*	*54%*	*.319*	*-6*	*1.46*	*4.45*	*4.61*	*4.91*	*9.9*	*2.8*	*5.9*	*0.9*	*4.7*	*0.4*

Breakout: 16%   Improve: 34%   Collapse: 50%   Attrition: 32%   Comparables: Rheal Cormier, Ed Vosberg, Tom Burgmeier

A pure, unrefined LOOGY, Shouse posted similar ratios to 2004 in very similar usage, but his ERA was three runs higher because of a few more home runs allowed and a few hits falling in. That's the peril of a situational lefty: high-leverage situations and limited innings mean a bad day at the office can really screw up the way your whole season looks. He was still very effective against lefties (.209/.271/.357), so he's still doing the job he was hired to do.

EDISON VOLQUEZ   **Bats: R   Throws: R**   Height: 6' 1"   Weight: 187   Born: July 3, 1983   Age: 22

YEAR	TM	LVL	AGE	W	L	SV	G	GS	IP	H	BB	SO	HR	GB%	BABIP	STUFF	WHIP	ERA	PERA	EQERA	EQH9	EQBB9	EQSO9	EQHR9	VORP	WXRL
2004	CLN	A	21	4	4	3	22	15	91.0	83	30	77	8	—	.285	-18	1.24	4.05	6.14	6.56	10.0	4.0	4.4	1.7	-9.1	—
2004	STO	A+	21	4	1	0	8	8	39.7	31	14	34	6	—	.234	-8	1.13	2.95	7.50	5.00	9.8	4.2	5.2	2.8	2.4	—
2005	BAK	A+	22	5	4	0	11	11	66.7	64	12	77	9	49%	.327	9	1.14	4.18	5.34	5.62	10.0	2.0	6.6	1.8	-0.1	—
2005	FRI	AA	22	1	5	0	10	10	58.7	58	17	49	6	47%	.306	7	1.28	4.14	4.89	5.05	9.2	3.2	5.7	1.3	3.5	—
2005	TEX	MLB	22	0	4	0	6	3	12.7	25	10	11	3	43%	.458	-20	2.76	14.17	6.91	13.81	13.2	6.3	6.9	1.9	-13.1	-0.9
2006	*TEX*	*MLB*	*22*	*6*	*10*	*0*	*34*	*20*	*131.7*	*149*	*51*	*83*	*23*	*45%*	*.298*	*0*	*1.52*	*5.73*	*5.47*	*5.65*	*9.7*	*3.5*	*5.6*	*1.4*	*-0.9*	*0.7*

Breakout: 48%   Improve: 82%   Collapse: 2%   Attrition: 0%   Comparables: Sun-Woo Kim, Joel Pineiro, Felix Diaz

Volquez used to be Julio Reyes, but international documents are checked for accuracy these days. The third pitcher of the DVD set is a 6'1" Dominican with a slight build and a low- to mid-90s fastball. He made strides with his changeup this year, posting great ratios in A-ball before struggling after the big leap to Double-A. He was rushed to the majors in late August and struggled with his control, but he's just a 22-year-old with less than 60 innings above high A-ball. He will get an outside shot at the fifth spot in the rotation, but is more likely to spend time in Double- and Triple-A, with a probable August or September call-up. Volquez's only injury was a slight oblique problem early in the year, so he's making his way through the injury nexus more gracefully than most.

JOHN WASDIN   **Bats: R   Throws: R**   Height: 6' 2"   Weight: 190   Born: August 5, 1972   Age: 33

YEAR	TM	LVL	AGE	W	L	SV	G	GS	IP	H	BB	SO	HR	GB%	BABIP	STUFF	WHIP	ERA	PERA	EQERA	EQH9	EQBB9	EQSO9	EQHR9	VORP	WXRL
2003	NAS	AAA	30	8	4	0	18	18	112.3	101	24	116	4	—	.305	30	1.11	3.05	3.57	5.15	8.6	2.5	7.1	0.6	5.4	—
2004	OKL	AAA	31	7	1	0	18	14	104.0	94	19	81	10	—	.278	1	1.09	3.46	4.61	5.24	8.9	2.1	4.8	1.2	4.0	—
2004	TEX	MLB	31	2	4	0	15	10	65.0	83	23	36	18	35%	.298	-25	1.63	6.78	6.38	6.24	10.9	3.0	4.6	2.2	-5.0	0.0
2005	OKL	AAA	32	9	2	0	13	11	73.0	84	24	57	11	39%	.323	-20	1.48	4.93	6.21	6.46	10.5	3.4	4.6	1.9	-6.8	—
2005	TEX	MLB	32	3	2	4	31	6	75.7	77	20	44	9	35%	.281	0	1.28	4.28	4.34	3.76	8.8	2.3	5.2	0.9	12.4	1.3
2006	*TEX*	*MLB*	*33*	*5*	*7*	*2*	*40*	*12*	*96.7*	*112*	*27*	*54*	*17*	*39%*	*.294*	*-9*	*1.43*	*5.35*	*5.17*	*5.67*	*9.9*	*2.5*	*5.0*	*1.4*	*4.7*	*0.8*

Breakout: 30%   Improve: 57%   Collapse: 19%   Attrition: 15%   Comparables: Willie Blair, Eric Show, Dave Mlicki

RHP, 33, seeks organization in need of injury replacement-caliber swing man. Can strike a batter out when need be, but usually just gets by with respectable walk rate. Enjoys long walks on the beach, nights in front of the fireplace, and sushi. Multiple references available upon request. Serious inquiries only.

C. J. WILSON   **Bats: L   Throws: L**   Height: 6' 2"   Weight: 190   Born: November 18, 1980   Age: 25

YEAR	TM	LVL	AGE	W	L	SV	G	GS	IP	H	BB	SO	HR	GB%	BABIP	STUFF	WHIP	ERA	PERA	EQERA	EQH9	EQBB9	EQSO9	EQHR9	VORP	WXRL
2003	FRI	AA	22	6	9	0	22	21	123.0	135	38	89	11	—	.307	-13	1.41	5.05	5.75	6.58	10.5	3.3	4.8	1.6	-13.0	—
2005	FRI	AA	24	0	4	0	12	12	44.7	51	14	43	7	55%	.349	-16	1.45	4.43	6.28	7.12	10.9	3.6	6.1	2.1	-7.3	—
2005	TEX	MLB	24	1	7	1	24	6	48.0	63	18	30	5	61%	.360	-6	1.69	6.94	4.62	6.22	10.1	3.2	5.3	0.9	-7.0	-0.2
2006	*TEX*	*MLB*	*25*	*4*	*6*	*1*	*43*	*10*	*81.0*	*99*	*32*	*47*	*13*	*52%*	*.317*	*-10*	*1.61*	*5.91*	*5.76*	*5.93*	*10.5*	*3.5*	*5.2*	*1.3*	*-2.7*	*0.0*

Breakout: 33%   Improve: 64%   Collapse: 6%   Attrition: 3%   Comparables: Bill Pulsipher, J. C. Romero, Leo Kiely

You have to wonder if the Rangers have shards of glass in their ice packs. Seemingly the only person in the organization who hasn't had Tommy John surgery is R. A. Dickey, and that's only because he doesn't possess the requisite ligament

(continued next page)

C. J. Wilson *(continued)*

to begin with. Wilson missed over a year with his own surgery, but impressed the Rangers enough that he replaced Pedro Astacio in June. That would seem like an easy job, but Wilson struggled just as badly as Astacio. With all the talent coming up behind him, he's likely to get lost in the shuffle. He never had that much upside to begin with, but he could occupy a back-end rotation spot at some point.

CHRIS YOUNG				Bats: R			Throws: R			Height: 6' 10"		Weight: 250		Born: May 25, 1979					Age: 27	
YEAR	TM	LVL	AGE	W	L	SV	G	GS	IP	H	BB	SO	HR	GB%	BABIP	STUFF	WHIP	ERA	PERA	EQERA	EQH9	EQBB9	EQSO9	EQHR9	VORP	WXRL
2003	BRV	A+	24	5	2	0	8	8	50.0	26	5	39	3	—	.172	0	0.62	1.62	5.52	3.89	8.2	1.2	4.9	2.0	8.4	—
2003	HAR	AA	24	4	4	0	15	15	83.0	83	22	64	9	—	.286	-14	1.27	4.01	5.97	5.40	10.3	3.0	5.3	2.0	1.7	—
2004	FRI	AA	25	6	5	0	18	18	88.3	94	31	75	9	—	.315	-20	1.42	4.48	6.05	6.48	10.9	4.1	5.1	1.7	-8.1	—
2004	OKL	AAA	25	3	0	0	5	5	30.3	20	9	34	2	—	.254	26	0.96	1.49	3.77	3.14	7.2	3.1	7.5	0.6	7.8	—
2004	TEX	MLB	25	3	2	0	7	7	36.3	36	10	27	7	36%	.264	8	1.27	4.71	4.95	4.46	8.9	2.2	6.2	1.5	5.6	0.6
2005	TEX	MLB	26	12	7	0	31	31	164.7	162	45	137	19	34%	.294	22	1.26	4.26	3.97	4.03	8.4	2.5	7.3	1.0	24.1	3.6
2006	*SDN*	*MLB*	*27*	*9*	*10*	*0*	*32*	*26*	*167.3*	*159*	*53*	*136*	*21*	*38%*	*.281*	*14*	*1.27*	*4.16*	*4.59*	*4.76*	*8.7*	*2.6*	*6.5*	*1.2*	*14.5*	*2.7*
Breakout: 12%		Improve: 42%		Collapse: 23%		Attrition: 7%			Comparables: Aaron Harang, Jeff Juden, Gene Conley																

Young will begin the second year of a three-year deal designed to keep him from pursuing a basketball career, a possible course of action given his two-sport stardom at Princeton. Consistent with concerns about the throwing motions of big men, the Rangers made some mechanical changes to his delivery. They loved the results, particularly the increased velocity on his fastball. However, after a hot start, Young wore out and struggled badly down the stretch. At 27, what you see now is probably all you're going to get. Should succeed in the spacious environs of Petco Park.

Line Outs

Position/Player	TM	LVL	AGE	PA	R	2B	3B	HR	RBI	BB	SO	SB-CS	SPEED	BA/OBP/SLG	MLVR	EQBA/OBP/SLG	EQA	VORP
INF E. German	OKL	AAA	27	563	103	27	6	5	68	65	74	43-6	6.8	.313/.400/.423	.124	.277/.350/.365	.262	14.4
OF K. C. Herren*	SPO	A-	19	246	22	15	3	4	27	28	63	6-4	5.2	.264/.346/.417	.066	.216/.283/.345	.223	-16.4
C M. Nickeas	FRI	AA	22	266	22	7	1	5	24	20	43	1-1	3.7	.202/.263/.302	-.304	.184/.243/.279	.191	-21.2
C T. Teagarden	SPO	A-	21	122	23	5	4	7	16	23	32	1-1	4.7	.281/.426/.635	.453	.208/.327/.440	.263	6.2

Pitcher	TM	LVL	AGE	W	L	SV	IP	H	BB	SO	HR	GB%	BABIP	STUFF	WHIP	ERA	PERA	EQERA	EQH9	EQBB9	EQSO9	EQHR9	VORP
F. Francisco '04	TEX	MLB	24	5	1	0	51.3	36	28	60	4	31%	.271	24	1.25	3.33	3.51	2.98	6.7	4.6	9.8	0.5	17.6
S. Karsay	TEX	MLB	33	0	1	0	15.7	26	5	9	2	58%	.400	-15	1.98	7.45	4.67	6.75	11.4	2.6	4.7	1.0	-3.6
J. Veras	OKL	AAA	24	3	5	24	61.7	63	33	72	4	49%	.366	3	1.56	3.79	4.38	4.38	8.9	4.8	7.6	0.7	8.4

Esteban German hits for average and draws walks at Triple-A, but with little power and bad reviews on defense, his best-case scenario is to end up playing second for K.C., which, by happy circumstance, he'll have a shot at this spring. **K. C. Herren** spent half the season in extended spring training working on his swing, with good results so far. His defense is good enough to keep him in center, but he's still a long way away. **Mike Nickeas** missed six weeks with a broken hand, which likely affected his overall performance at Double-A, but he hit well in the AFL. If healthy, he's a young catcher to keep an eye on. **Taylor Teagarden** is a 3rd round pick out of Texas known for defense more than offense, hit well in short season ball, and has been penciled very lightly into the 2008 starting lineup.

Frank Francisco missed virtually the entire season with Tommy John surgery, which should give him plenty of time to complete the 500 hours of community service he was sentenced to for the Oakland chair-throwing incident in 2004. Not too long ago, **Steve Karsay** was one of the best relievers in the game, but his fragility kept him from staying that good for any length of time. **Jose Veras** is a Dominican with a lively, mid-90s fastball and middling secondary stuff, he puts up good strikeout numbers but his command isn't good. He'll try to make the back end of the Yankees' pen.

Toronto Blue Jays

In poker, "changing gears" is a strategy in which a player suddenly changes his or her style of play in order to keep opponents off guard and decrease their ability to accurately assess the quality of a player's hand.

Suddenly, after three seasons spent clearing payroll, replenishing the farm system, nabbing the odd mid-market free agent, and operating on a modest budget, the Toronto Blue Jays have gone "all-in."

The usually reserved club, once content to bide its time and rebuild while waiting for the two juggernauts of the AL East to lose steam, has suddenly, but not inexplicably, opened its checkbook and conducted a massive free agent spending spree in an impressive gamble to return to competitive status.

Two considerations motivated the change. On one hand, the Blue Jays shifted gears because they found themselves in the unaccustomed position of having the means to do so. Team ownership, after buying out the lease on Rogers Centre and being finally convinced that General Manager J. P. Ricciardi's administration was spending wisely, approved a payroll increase of $210 million over three seasons. There were also tactical considerations at work; for the first time in almost a decade, the Yankees and Red Sox seem vulnerable, and the Jays' estimation of their position relative to the competition was that the gap between them could be closed with decisive action. Throw into the mix the weak free agent market—normally the place where high-payroll teams like the Yanks and Sox reload—and the Jays saw a chance to improve while boxing out their opponents from easily acquiring the one thing they both desperately needed: pitching.

Unfortunately, there are two key problems with their assessment. While the number of runs scored and allowed by the Jays in 2005 suggest that the 80–82 team had underachieved by nine wins and thus was only a game or two worse than the Yankees and Red Sox in "absolute" terms, this conclusion is misleading. The Jays scored more runs last year than would have been expected from their hits, walks, home runs, and so on. Based on *expected* runs, the 2005 Jays were more accurately assessed as an 80 to 82 win team—exactly their actual record. Miscalculating your position relative to the competition is a common mistake, but in this case it could mean a nine-win misstep. Instead of needing the talent to add just the six to eight

BLUE JAYS PROSPECTUS

2005 record: 80–82; Third place, AL East

Pythagenport record: 88–74

Runs scored per game: 4.78 (5th in AL)

Runs allowed per game: 4.35 (6th in AL)

Team EqA: .252 (11th in AL)

2005 Batters Age: 28.5 (5th youngest in AL)

2005 Pitchers Age: 28.3 (5th youngest in AL)

Ballpark: Skydome; Moderate hitter's park; Park Factor of 1.035

2005: After a one-season hiatus, the Blue Jays reclaimed their customary perch in third place in the AL East.

2006: Handed big bucks to Burnett, Ryan, and Glaus, but it's not going to be enough.

wins that would move them to 95 wins or so, thereby giving themselves a good shot at the playoffs and the subsequent financial windfall, the Blue Jays really needed to add somewhere closer to 14–16 wins worth of talent.

The Jays went into the winter with major questions at both corner outfield positions and an overstock of infielders and pitching talent in the high minors. As if unaware of their disposition of talent, they proceeded to acquire a front-line starter, a closer, and two corner infielders. The first two pieces, A. J. Burnett and B. J. Ryan, will cost the team $102 million for the next five years. Then they picked up Lyle Overbay and Troy Glaus in exchange for what they viewed as excess pitching talent—Dave Bush, Zach Jackson, and Miguel Batista—as well as second base defensive wiz Orlando Hudson and outfielder Gabe Gross.

While it's easy to argue that you can't have too much pitching, rarely is it said that you can't have too many middling corner infielders. What Toronto needed were impact bats. In previous years, the Jays had gotten value out of baseball's middle class. Their outfield platoon of Reed Johnson and Frank Catalanotto managed a league-average line for the season. They're not bad, they're just not that dangerous. With the exception of shortstop and right field (both of which were significantly below average), every Jays lineup position produced within a tenth of a run of the league average for their respective positions. Shea Hillenbrand's team-leading 32.5 VORP was the lowest team-leading total in the majors; only he and Chris Shelton of the Tigers (34.9) were under 40. None of the Jays' regulars were embarrassments in the field or at the plate, but the lack of any excellence—resulting in a monotonously average performance—kept Toronto from fielding a genuinely good lineup.

While the dismissal of Hudson will likely have greater impact than anticipated, given the the reliance Roy Halladay and Burnett have on getting groundball outs, the Glaus deal will help the Jays' mediocre lineup. Glaus should be the team's best hitter, and though there are durability concerns with a player of his age and injury history, his 2005 season seemed to allay them.

Overbay, on the other hand, doesn't help. Once upon a time he may have been an undervalued player. As it stands now, he's exactly the kind of low-upside, low-power, high-OBP player that the Jays have characteristically made a point of collecting. His acquisition will only make sense if the Jays can move either Hillenbrand or Eric Hinske, and if a defensive fall-off at third doesn't force Glaus across the diamond. The jury is still out on where the Overbay move fits in the Jays' master plan, but in the short term, it does nothing to solve their logjam of average offensive performers.

That logjam is the result of a crippling fear to take risks in that area of team building. The organization is completely bereft of a significant hitting prospect, while their rigid preference for collegiate pitchers has left the farm system stocked with capable but mediocre arms—plenty of mid-rotation help, but no prospective aces. Perhaps most symbolic of the problem was the decision to not offer arbitration to Carlos Delgado after 2004, despite obvious and widely publicized interest from other teams to sign the free agent first baseman to a multi-year deal. The Jays were convinced that he would instead take their offer and stay in Toronto, and deemed the possible repercussions of retaining him—10-and-5 trade status and a budget-breaking one-year contract—too catastrophic to risk. The decision not to offer Delgado arbitration denied the Jays two draft choices from the Marlins: their 1st round draft pick and a supplemental 1st round supplemental pick in 2005. Furthermore, when the Jays signed Koskie—and

avoided the risk of Hill not being ready in 2005—they forfeited their 2nd round pick. Instead of having four picks in the top 54, the Jays had the sixth overall pick and didn't pick get another turn until the 86th pick. Unlike the 2004 draft, where the team selected a high-upside player in David Purcey, and solidified the top of their draft with Zach Jackson in the supplemental round, the Jays selected Ricky Romero, a polished college pitcher, but one whom most analysts agree has little chance of becoming a dominant, frontline starter.

It is perhaps too easy to criticize Jays' management. They misspent money a year ago on Koskie, Scott Schoeneweis, and Hillenbrand. This winter, they clearly overspent on one pitcher with a spotty track record of health and performance, another who ranks among the game's most overrated, and a third baseman with positional concerns and an injury history. To be fair, though, a confining set of circumstances led to these moves. They offered a three-year, $33 million contract to Brian Giles, which would have added an impact bat in an obvious position of need, but he turned them down. Perhaps learning from their mistakes, the Jays have shown willingness to trade from their growing stash of arms for the bats they so desperately need. A player development-rat from the start, J. P. Ricciardi recognizes that the Jays can't be the kind of team with a free agent at every position and no homegrown talent.

Most importantly, the Jays acknowledged that they cannot hope to compete in the AL East on a $50 million payroll. Taking the long view, the Jays haven't done too badly the past few seasons; they've cleaned up the books, stocked the farm system with some decent pitching talent, and adopted the kind of smart financial management that locks players like Vernon Wells into deals that buy out their arbitration years. Finally, given the chance to make a run for the playoffs, they've acted to improve themselves and challenge the Yankees and Red Sox.

Regardless of the outcome, the Jays have changed their focus from making money to winning baseball games, and though you can fault the methods they've applied to do so, it's a bold stroke for a team in one of the games' most competitive divisions.

HITTERS

RUSS ADAMS SS **Bats: L Throws: R** Height: 6' 1" Weight: 180 Born: August 30, 1980 Age: 25

YEAR	TM	LVL	AGE	PA	R	2B	3B	HR	RBI	BB	SO	SB	CS	SPEED	BA	OBP	SLG	MLVR	EQBA	EQOBP	EQSLG	EQA	VORP	DEFENSE
2003	DUN	A+	22	305	50	9	5	3	16	38	27	9	2	6.9	.279	.380	.388	.132	.258	.340	.392	.261	11.0	66-SS -3
2003	NHV	AA	22	301	42	10	4	4	26	30	37	8	1	6.6	.277	.349	.387	.056	.262	.329	.376	.250	7.1	62-SS -6
2004	SYR	AAA	23	538	58	37	3	5	54	45	62	6	2	4.8	.288	.351	.408	.009	.263	.326	.370	.247	10.6	118-SS -8
2004	TOR	MLB	23	78	10	2	1	4	10	5	5	1	0	4.0	.306	.359	.528	.180	.296	.351	.521	.293	7.1	18-SS -4
2005	TOR	MLB	24	542	68	27	5	8	63	50	57	11	2	6.5	.256	.325	.383	-.082	.256	.335	.390	.259	13.3	123-SS -23
2006	*TOR*	*MLB*	*25*	*584*	*69*	*28*	*4*	*9*	*56*	*48*	*63*	*9*	*3*	*5.2*	*.267*	*.332*	*.391*	*-.041*	*.266*	*.339*	*.392*	*.250*	*16.9*	*137-SS -9*

Breakout: 16%   Improve: 49%   Collapse: 24%   Attrition: 10%   Comparables: Toby Harrah, Mike Lansing, Damion Easley

Adams would have been a good shortstop in the 1980s, when shortstops weren't expected to hit, or else he would be a decent starter today for a team with several solid bats already in place. There isn't any power explosion down the road in Toronto and Adams's below-average arm will continue to provoke questions about his defense. The Blue Jays need to realize they only have nine spots in their lineup and players like Adams can plug a hole but also take away the opportunity to play an above-average hitter. If your lineup is filled with nine of these guys you'll end up with 81 wins and a cool 15 in the GB column. After Adams's hot 2004 cup of coffee, Toronto can't be blamed for giving him a long leash, but he should be regarded with a wary eye from now on.

CHIP CANNON   **DH**   **Bats: L Throws: R**   Height: 6′ 5″   Weight: 215   Born: November 30, 1981   Age: 24

YEAR	TM	LVL	AGE	PA	R	2B	3B	HR	RBI	BB	SO	SB	CS	SPEED	BA	OBP	SLG	MLVR	EQBA	EQOBP	EQSLG	EQA	VORP	DEFENSE	
2004	AUB	A-	22	237	33	15	1	10	41	22	55	0	0	3.7	.271	.338	.495	.206	.214	.268	.382	.225	-21.1	42-1B	4
2005	LNS	A	23	191	22	9	2	11	36	20	47	0	0	3.6	.268	.351	.542	.262	.224	.289	.436	.246	-2.8	30-1B	2
2005	DUN	A+	23	129	28	4	2	14	39	16	32	0	1	4.8	.384	.465	.830	.849	.320	.391	.671	.334	19.2	15-1B	2
2005	NHP	AA	23	181	15	13	1	7	23	10	58	2	0	3.9	.247	.293	.459	.064	.240	.286	.444	.248	-1.8	29-1B	1
2006	*TOR*	*MLB*	*24*	*503*	*57*	*25*	*3*	*23*	*74*	*34*	*147*	*1*	*1*	*3.9*	*.241*	*.295*	*.454*	*-.041*	*.239*	*.301*	*.456*	*.248*	*-0.7*	*119-1B*	*3*

Breakout: 22%   *Improve: 39%*   *Collapse: 32%*   *Attrition: 4%*   *Comparables: Jeff Liefer, Derrick Lankford, Bryon Gainey*

Cannon's 32 home runs ranked him fifth in the minor leagues last year. On most teams needing a few power bats, that would mean he'd be ascending to the major league roster. Unfortunately, Cannon's two club feet will probably relegate him to DH should he get The Call. Unless he maintains his production against left-handed pitching, that's a part-time job at best (he batted .250/.319/.510 against lefties, .301/.371/.604 versus righties). There's obvious talent here; a team with a well-managed bench will figure out how to exploit it.

FRANK CATALANOTTO   **OF**   **Bats: L Throws: R**   Height: 5′ 11″   Weight: 190   Born: April 27, 1974   Age: 32

YEAR	TM	LVL	AGE	PA	R	2B	3B	HR	RBI	BB	SO	SB	CS	SPEED	BA	OBP	SLG	MLVR	EQBA	EQOBP	EQSLG	EQA	VORP	DEFENSE			
2003	TOR	MLB	29	533	83	34	6	13	59	35	62	2	2	5.5	.299	.351	.472	.100	.293	.350	.467	.278	17.4	52-LF	2	38-RF	-4
2004	TOR	MLB	30	273	27	19	1	1	26	17	33	1	0	4.2	.293	.344	.390	-.053	.287	.342	.381	.256	1.4	35-LF	0		
2005	TOR	MLB	31	471	56	29	5	8	59	37	53	0	2	4.4	.301	.367	.451	.115	.303	.378	.464	.289	19.9	85-LF	7		
2006	*TOR*	*MLB*	*32*	*350*	*40*	*19*	*2*	*7*	*41*	*25*	*39*	*1*	*1*	*4.8*	*.286*	*.343*	*.425*	*.032*	*.284*	*.349*	*.426*	*.261*	*7.4*	*84-LF*	*0*		

Breakout: 10%   *Improve: 31%*   *Collapse: 34%*   *Attrition: 26%*   *Comparables: Joe Orsulak, Lee Maye, Dale Mitchell*

The Jays gave Catalanotto a two-year, $5.4 million contract extension before the 2005 season, mixed him with Reed Johnson, and got league-average production out of their left fielders. Catalanotto isn't a bad hitter, but as a corner outfielder who requires an additional roster spot to be burned on a platoon partner, he's a player who comes with that extra little bit of cost. Catalanotto is another example of the Jays carrying around too many adequate hitters without having a real bopper to push these guys around the bases.

ROB COSBY   **3B**   **Bats: R Throws: R**   Height: 6′ 2″   Weight: 200   Born: April 2, 1981   Age: 25

YEAR	TM	LVL	AGE	PA	R	2B	3B	HR	RBI	BB	SO	SB	CS	SPEED	BA	OBP	SLG	MLVR	EQBA	EQOBP	EQSLG	EQA	VORP	DEFENSE			
2003	DUN	A+	22	528	53	34	2	4	52	46	61	3	5	3.7	.277	.343	.382	.074	.259	.315	.389	.244	8.3	122-3B	4	10-LF	-1
2005	NHP	AA	24	456	56	34	0	17	68	24	77	2	1	4.4	.308	.346	.507	.270	.285	.322	.468	.267	26.1	108-3B	-3		
2006	*TOR*	*MLB*	*25*	*512*	*63*	*29*	*2*	*20*	*76*	*28*	*79*	*2*	*1*	*4.2*	*.280*	*.323*	*.471*	*.056*	*.279*	*.329*	*.472*	*.264*	*16.5*	*121-3B*	*0*		

Breakout: 10%   *Improve: 26%*   *Collapse: 34%*   *Attrition: 12%*   *Comparables: Mike Lowell, Jorge Toca, Mike Ivie*

After making a good impression in spring training 2004, Cosby blew out his knee and missed all but five games. He came back strong in 2005, having the season he was supposed to have had before the injury. His plate discipline needs to improve, which is something the Jays and Cosby are working on. Until that produces results, he's vulnerable; if he loses 25 points of batting average a lot of his value will go with them. Fortunately, Cosby is still at least a year away from being a viably mediocre third baseman, because the Jays already have a few of those hanging around.

CARLO COTA   **2B**   **Bats: R Throws: R**   Height: 5' 10"   Weight: 180   Born: September 18, 1980   Age: 25

YEAR	TM	LVL	AGE	PA	R	2B	3B	HR	RBI	BB	SO	SB	CS	SPEED	BA	OBP	SLG	MLVR	EQBA	EQOBP	EQSLG	EQA	VORP	DEFENSE			
2003	AUB	A-	22	202	31	13	3	5	34	27	45	3	2	4.9	.320	.416	.521	.402	.270	.344	.445	.271	19.0	33-2B	5	11-3B	-1
2004	DUN	A+	23	519	81	37	1	11	63	45	101	2	1	4.7	.294	.356	.449	.148	.248	.301	.393	.241	2.9	65-2B	-2	50-3B	0
2005	DUN	A+	24	310	47	20	2	10	35	28	65	0	1	3.8	.304	.374	.500	.225	.249	.309	.405	.246	4.4	68-2B	-7		
2005	NHP	AA	24	156	21	8	2	2	17	9	45	1	0	6.1	.250	.301	.375	-.033	.243	.290	.367	.231	-1.8	33-2B	2		
2006	TOR	MLB	25	405	44	22	2	11	48	27	98	1	1	4.1	.246	.300	.408	-.089	.245	.306	.409	.238	4.5	97-2B	-3		

Breakout: 14%   Improve: 40%   Collapse: 31%   Attrition: 15%   Comparables: Jerry Buchek, Edgar Gonzalez, Jake Gautreau

If you haven't heard of Cota before, that's probably because there's really not much to say; if stealth bombers carried rubber chickens, would anyone care that they can fly under the radar? He didn't build on his 2004 in Dunedin, and then struggled after finally making the jump to Double-A New Hampshire as a 24-year old. If everything breaks right for him, he could make it as a utility infielder. Only in a system this thin on impact bats does he look even marginally interesting.

JOHN-FORD GRIFFIN   **OF**   **Bats: L Throws: L**   Height: 6' 2"   Weight: 210   Born: November 19, 1979   Age: 26

YEAR	TM	LVL	AGE	PA	R	2B	3B	HR	RBI	BB	SO	SB	CS	SPEED	BA	OBP	SLG	MLVR	EQBA	EQOBP	EQSLG	EQA	VORP	DEFENSE			
2003	NHV	AA	23	429	48	23	3	13	75	49	85	2	0	4.4	.279	.361	.461	.180	.260	.335	.436	.267	3.7	61-LF	2		
2004	NHP	AA	24	533	66	28	1	22	81	56	128	1	1	3.6	.248	.330	.454	.080	.225	.296	.401	.241	-17.3	23-LF	2	15-1B	-2
2005	SYR	AAA	25	582	80	21	1	30	103	62	140	1	2	3.9	.254	.335	.475	.047	.226	.305	.415	.247	-12.3	69-LF	2		
2006	TOR	MLB	26	459	50	21	1	17	61	39	115	1	1	3.8	.238	.306	.421	-.069	.236	.312	.422	.244	-2.5	109-LF	-2		

Breakout: 21%   Improve: 44%   Collapse: 27%   Attrition: 13%   Comparables: Eric Anthony, Eric Munson, Matt Padgett

Griffin is another example of why predicting baseball success is so difficult. After time lost to injuries and a bum wrist that basically restricted him to DH for most of 2004, Griffin finally made it to Triple-A and put up the power numbers expected of him. Still, he hasn't really made progress as a hitter. He strikes out too often, and at 26, he can't count on tomorrow being a better day. He might be worthy of a fifth outfielder/DH job on a team that needs some home-run punch off the bench.

GABE GROSS   **OF**   **Bats: L Throws: R**   Height: 6' 3"   Weight: 200   Born: October 21, 1979   Age: 26

YEAR	TM	LVL	AGE	PA	R	2B	3B	HR	RBI	BB	SO	SB	CS	SPEED	BA	OBP	SLG	MLVR	EQBA	EQOBP	EQSLG	EQA	VORP	DEFENSE			
2003	NHV	AA	23	369	52	23	3	7	51	52	53	3	2	4.7	.319	.423	.481	.336	.302	.394	.462	.297	21.8	77-RF	-4		
2003	SYR	AAA	23	216	22	16	2	5	23	31	56	1	1	4.1	.264	.380	.456	.152	.247	.359	.444	.277	5.3	42-RF	1		
2004	SYR	AAA	24	433	52	29	2	9	54	53	81	4	5	4.1	.294	.381	.454	.127	.270	.356	.418	.268	6.3	24-LF	-1	10-RF	0
2004	TOR	MLB	24	148	18	4	0	3	16	19	31	2	2	5.0	.209	.311	.310	-.277	.198	.308	.294	.220	-8.5	33-LF	3		
2005	SYR	AAA	25	447	64	29	4	6	46	52	83	14	2	6.6	.297	.380	.438	.111	.269	.349	.396	.266	1.1	58-LF	1	38-RF	3
2005	TOR	MLB	25	102	11	4	1	1	7	10	21	1	1	4.3	.250	.324	.348	-.133	.256	.337	.356	.244	-1.8	16-RF	1	11-LF	1
2006	MIL	MLB	26	422	51	22	2	10	46	48	87	5	3	5.0	.260	.348	.409	-.014	.264	.350	.420	.261	5.2	100-RF	0		

Breakout: 16%   Improve: 40%   Collapse: 31%   Attrition: 19%   Comparables: Pat Tabler, Dustan Mohr, Mike Cuddyer

Gross was headed back to Syracuse before a huge March penciled him into the Opening Day outfield mix. March greatness or no, he was still sent down early in the season and there he remained, still drawing enough walks to endear himself, but never hitting for power. He now looks like a platoon player, and on a roster with too many of those already, Gross was redundant. A creative, double-switching NL team could make good use of him, and having been moved to the Brewers in the Overbay deal, he'll get exactly such an opportunity as an outfield reserve.

JOHN HATTIG   **3B**   **Bats: B Throws: R**   Height: 6' 2"   Weight: 210   Born: February 27, 1980   Age: 26

YEAR	TM	LVL	AGE	PA	R	2B	3B	HR	RBI	BB	SO	SB	CS	SPEED	BA	OBP	SLG	MLVR	EQBA	EQOBP	EQSLG	EQA	VORP	DEFENSE	
2003	SAR	A+	23	465	51	29	2	6	70	59	70	9	7	4.5	.295	.385	.422	.210	.269	.345	.410	.263	21.4	97-3B	6
2004	NHP	AA	24	159	24	7	0	10	30	12	41	0	1	3.3	.296	.352	.556	.301	.270	.316	.494	.270	9.5	34-3B	4
2004	PME	AA	24	319	53	21	1	12	35	47	68	3	3	4.4	.295	.411	.519	.270	.253	.355	.441	.274	16.7	69-3B	3
2005	SYR	AAA	25	106	15	7	0	1	10	10	16	0	0	3.7	.316	.387	.421	.114	.278	.348	.364	.252	2.7	22-3B	-1
2006	TOR	MLB	26	266	28	14	1	7	31	21	54	1	1	4.1	.255	.319	.403	-.057	.253	.326	.404	.245	3.0	65-3B	1

Breakout: 12%   Improve: 32%   Collapse: 41%   Attrition: 31%   Comparables: Ben Davis, Russ Morman, Ed Sprague

It was a lost season for Hattig, who battled a variety of injuries after breaking out during 2004, and getting swapped by Boston for Terry Adams. The lack of a great arm generates questions about his ability to remain at third, a potentially crippling consideration in an organization that already has Troy Glaus, Shea Hillenbrand, and perhaps Aaron Hill in his way. This year will tell us if 2004 was a fluke or a real breakthrough. His chance to be the first major leaguer to hail from Guam depends on it.

AARON HILL   **INF**   **Bats: R Throws: R**   Height: 5′ 11″   Weight: 195   Born: March 21, 1982   Age: 24

YEAR	TM	LVL	AGE	PA	R	2B	3B	HR	RBI	BB	SO	SB	CS	SPEED	BA	OBP	SLG	MLVR	EQBA	EQOBP	EQSLG	EQA	VORP	DEFENSE			
2003	AUB	A-	21	148	22	4	0	4	34	16	20	1	1	3.4	.361	.446	.492	.437	.313	.376	.444	.286	22.0	30-SS	2		
2003	DUN	A+	21	134	26	7	0	0	11	11	10	1	0	5.2	.286	.343	.345	.032	.254	.304	.312	.226	-2.2	29-SS	-4		
2004	NHP	AA	22	564	78	26	2	11	80	63	61	3	2	4.3	.280	.369	.411	.112	.267	.346	.387	.260	21.4	134-SS	1		
2005	SYR	AAA	23	168	22	11	0	5	18	4	17	2	0	4.5	.301	.339	.468	.086	.270	.306	.431	.254	5.6	39-SS	3		
2005	TOR	MLB	23	404	49	25	3	3	40	34	41	2	1	5.3	.274	.342	.385	-.038	.276	.352	.397	.265	7.2	32-3B	2	20-2B	4
2006	TOR	MLB	24	536	62	27	2	11	58	40	59	3	2	4.7	.270	.331	.400	-.030	.268	.337	.401	.250	12.3	126-SS	4		

Breakout: 17%   Improve: 39%   Collapse: 24%   Attrition: 5%   Comparables: Buddy Bell, Brent Abernathy, Chris Gomez

After a torrid start to his big league career (while substituting for an injured Corey Koskie), Hill struggled badly in the second half (.221/.299/.308), and failed to display the home run power the Blue Jays expect him to develop. Hill's arm allows him to play any infield position, but there are concerns about his range at short, making it likely that he'll end up at second. There, his strike zone judgment and moderate power should be assets. Ricciardi is said to have a special place in his lineup for Hill. Amidst the team's glut of infielders, he may yet offer them the best combination of offense, defense, and expense.

SHEA HILLENBRAND   **1B/3B**   **Bats: R Throws: R**   Height: 6′ 1″   Weight: 210   Born: July 27, 1975   Age: 30

YEAR	TM	LVL	AGE	PA	R	2B	3B	HR	RBI	BB	SO	SB	CS	SPEED	BA	OBP	SLG	MLVR	EQBA	EQOBP	EQSLG	EQA	VORP	DEFENSE			
2003	BOS	MLB	27	200	20	17	0	3	38	7	26	1	0	3.6	.303	.335	.443	.035	.301	.337	.448	.271	7.0	27-3B	-1	18-1B	2
2003	ARI	MLB	27	354	40	18	1	17	59	17	44	0	0	3.8	.267	.302	.482	.017	.254	.290	.465	.255	7.0	51-1B	2	30-3B	-1
2004	ARI	MLB	28	604	68	36	3	15	80	24	49	2	0	4.6	.310	.348	.464	.116	.297	.334	.450	.269	24.5	126-1B	5	15-3B	-1
2005	TOR	MLB	29	645	91	36	2	18	82	26	79	5	1	4.8	.291	.343	.449	.070	.294	.351	.464	.279	23.3	66-1B	-2	51-3B	-1
2006	TOR	MLB	30	548	63	31	2	16	75	23	63	2	1	4.5	.287	.324	.446	.030	.285	.330	.447	.258	11.6	129-1B	0		

Breakout: 10%   Improve: 34%   Collapse: 30%   Attrition: 11%   Comparables: Lou Piniella, Vic Power, Ray Knight

Hillenbrand is the kind of player that deceives mediocre teams into thinking they're getting acceptable production from a key offensive position. In three of the past four seasons Hillenbrand started off hot only to regress to .280/.320/.430 for the rest of the season. Only the Red Sox took advantage of Hillenbrand's batting average-inflated line by trading him at the peak of his value. Now that the Jays have brought in Lyle Overbay, Hillenbrand may be dealt by the time you read this—but hopefully not to a team looking for a third baseman. Being able to stand near third base might raise Hillenbrand's value, but he's never been a slick fielder at the hot corner.

ERIC HINSKE   **1B**   **Bats: L Throws: R**   Height: 6′ 2″   Weight: 220   Born: August 5, 1977   Age: 28

YEAR	TM	LVL	AGE	PA	R	2B	3B	HR	RBI	BB	SO	SB	CS	SPEED	BA	OBP	SLG	MLVR	EQBA	EQOBP	EQSLG	EQA	VORP	DEFENSE	
2003	TOR	MLB	25	514	74	45	3	12	63	59	104	12	2	6.1	.243	.329	.437	-.025	.235	.329	.432	.266	17.6	120-3B	-16
2004	TOR	MLB	26	634	66	23	3	15	69	54	109	12	8	5.1	.246	.312	.375	-.161	.240	.310	.369	.239	-11.8	149-3B	8
2005	TOR	MLB	27	537	79	31	2	15	68	46	121	8	4	5.7	.262	.333	.430	.003	.262	.341	.441	.270	9.0	96-1B	-6
2006	TOR	MLB	28	420	51	22	2	12	51	41	82	8	4	5.5	.258	.335	.430	.005	.257	.341	.431	.260	7.4	100-1B	-1

Breakout: 27%   Improve: 50%   Collapse: 22%   Attrition: 16%   Comparables: Ben Broussard, Travis Lee, Sid Bream

The Jays signed Hinske to a five-year, $14.75 million deal after his award-winning 2002 rookie season, intending to lock up a quality young player through his arbitration years and giving the club a top talent at a premium price. This gambit worked out well with Vernon Wells, who signed a nearly identical contract, but Hinske is a reminder that even the best-laid plans can go horribly awry. At least Hinske repeated his merely disappointing 2003 rather than his abysmal 2004, but he's playing first instead of third. That kind of production from a key offensive position isn't going to make the Jays contenders any time soon. Hinske's continued inability to hit southpaws may mean his future lies as a platoon player. The acquisition of Overbay might push him back to third, to DH, or to somebody the Jays pay to take him off of their hands.

ORLANDO HUDSON   **2B**   **Bats: B Throws: R**   Height: 6′ 0″   Weight: 180   Born: December 12, 1977   Age: 28

YEAR	TM	LVL	AGE	PA	R	2B	3B	HR	RBI	BB	SO	SB	CS	SPEED	BA	OBP	SLG	MLVR	EQBA	EQOBP	EQSLG	EQA	VORP	DEFENSE	
2003	TOR	MLB	25	521	54	21	6	9	57	39	87	5	4	5.2	.268	.328	.395	-.066	.263	.329	.392	.250	9.2	130-2B	28
2004	TOR	MLB	26	548	73	32	7	12	58	51	98	7	3	6.1	.270	.341	.438	-.012	.263	.339	.434	.267	20.4	127-2B	17
2005	TOR	MLB	27	501	62	25	5	10	63	30	65	7	1	6.2	.271	.315	.412	-.043	.272	.325	.419	.261	11.4	120-2B	16
2006	ARI	MLB	28	519	65	26	5	10	54	46	74	7	3	5.2	.274	.342	.415	-.008	.270	.337	.413	.255	14.7	122-2B	9

Breakout: 22%   Improve: 46%   Collapse: 30%   Attrition: 14%   Comparables: Carlos Guillen, Tom Herr, Bret Barberie

(continued next page)

Orlando Hudson *(continued)*

Our weighted mean PECOTA projection last year almost perfectly nailed Hudson; we called for him to hit .271/.337/.416 with 23 doubles, three triples, and 11 home runs. You'll note our widest miss was in OBP, because we figured Hudson would keep some of his newfound patience from 2004 and walk roughly once every 11.4 PAs. Instead, he went to hacking. What didn't change is Hudson's defense; he remained the best defensive second baseman in the AL. As long as he keeps his offense in the vicinity of ordinary, his glove makes him someone worth playing. That is, for the Arizona Diamondbacks.

REED JOHNSON   **OF**   **Bats: R Throws: R**   Height: 5' 10"   Weight: 180   Born: December 8, 1976   Age: 29

YEAR	TM	LVL	AGE	PA	R	2B	3B	HR	RBI	BB	SO	SB	CS	SPEED	BA	OBP	SLG	MLVR	EQBA	EQOBP	EQSLG	EQA	VORP	DEFENSE			
2003	TOR	MLB	26	456	79	21	2	10	52	20	67	5	3	5.4	.294	.353	.427	.043	.291	.351	.430	.271	8.3	60-RF	-5	37-LF	3
2004	TOR	MLB	27	579	68	25	2	10	61	28	98	6	3	4.8	.270	.320	.380	-.128	.265	.315	.372	.241	-6.7	52-LF	0	43-RF	-1
2005	TOR	MLB	28	437	55	21	6	8	58	22	82	5	6	5.9	.269	.332	.412	-.019	.272	.342	.425	.261	3.6	66-LF	6	28-RF	1
2006	*TOR*	*MLB*	*29*	*352*	*39*	*16*	*3*	*6*	*38*	*16*	*57*	*4*	*2*	*4.8*	*.264*	*.312*	*.390*	*-.079*	*.262*	*.318*	*.391*	*.238*	*-1.7*	*85-LF*	*1*		

Breakout: 9%   *Improve: 33%*   *Collapse: 34%*   *Attrition: 31%*   *Comparables: Jay Payton, Ken Berry, Jim Wohlford*

Though generally considered a platoon player, Johnson hit almost exactly as well against righties (.262/.329/.408) as he did against lefties (.279/.335/.418) last year, mitigating much of the reason he's in the lineup in the first place. He still plays good defense, but with his offense short of being particularly good in any department, Johnson shouldn't have a near-everyday role on a team that thinks it's in contention.

COREY KOSKIE   **3B**   **Bats: L Throws: R**   Height: 6' 3"   Weight: 217   Born: June 28, 1973   Age: 33

YEAR	TM	LVL	AGE	PA	R	2B	3B	HR	RBI	BB	SO	SB	CS	SPEED	BA	OBP	SLG	MLVR	EQBA	EQOBP	EQSLG	EQA	VORP	DEFENSE	
2003	MIN	MLB	30	562	76	29	2	14	69	77	113	11	5	5.5	.292	.393	.452	.149	.289	.395	.454	.296	39.5	125-3B	11
2004	MIN	MLB	31	488	68	24	2	25	71	49	103	9	3	5.3	.251	.342	.495	.100	.250	.342	.500	.284	21.8	110-3B	-7
2005	SYR	AAA	32	30	1	2	0	0	2	3	6	0	0	2.8	.240	.367	.320	-.104	.177	.262	.215	.180	-3.0		
2005	TOR	MLB	32	404	49	20	0	11	36	44	90	4	1	4.2	.249	.337	.398	-.042	.247	.345	.399	.263	5.6	76-3B	3
2006	*MIL*	*MLB*	*33*	*410*	*48*	*19*	*2*	*13*	*51*	*52*	*92*	*5*	*2*	*4.7*	*.251*	*.351*	*.431*	*.011*	*.254*	*.352*	*.442*	*.269*	*13.3*	*98-3B*	*1*

Breakout: 4%   *Improve: 33%*   *Collapse: 29%*   *Attrition: 24%*   *Comparables: Doug Rader, Cliff Floyd, Dale Long*

So, why pay $17 million over three years for an aging third baseman with a long injury history when you're still a year or two away from contention, and have better, cheaper options in-house? Unable to attract a significant free agent in 2004, the Jays decided Koskie wasn't a bad guy to settle on, and his Canadian roots didn't hurt. So far, it's been the sort of mid-market shopping mistake that teams really regret. Koskie's not getting any younger or healthier, and while he should be closer to his established career levels in 2006, there's just as good a chance that the words "albatross" and "sinkhole" are going to come up a lot when talking about him.

ADAM LIND   **LF**   **Bats: L Throws: L**   Height: 6' 2"   Weight: 195   Born: July 17, 1983   Age: 22

YEAR	TM	LVL	AGE	PA	R	2B	3B	HR	RBI	BB	SO	SB	CS	SPEED	BA	OBP	SLG	MLVR	EQBA	EQOBP	EQSLG	EQA	VORP	DEFENSE	
2004	AUB	A-	20	294	43	23	0	7	50	24	36	1	0	4.0	.308	.367	.474	.249	.257	.308	.409	.248	-8.8	58-LF	0
2005	DUN	A+	21	554	80	42	4	12	84	49	77	2	1	4.6	.313	.375	.487	.218	.276	.334	.440	.266	7.3	119-LF	-8
2006	*TOR*	*MLB*	*22*	*533*	*59*	*34*	*2*	*13*	*67*	*35*	*82*	*1*	*1*	*4.3*	*.265*	*.316*	*.421*	*-.032*	*.263*	*.322*	*.422*	*.248*	*1.9*	*125-LF*	*-5*

Breakout: 16%   *Improve: 39%*   *Collapse: 27%*   *Attrition: 9%*   *Comparables: Ross Gload, Curtis Granderson, Laynce Nix*

The rare player on the organizational depth chart who might turn into that elusive "impact bat," Lind had a nice season in the Florida State League, hitting for power and showing just enough patience. The Jays think he made a significant jump last year, and he'll start the season in Double-A. There are significant defensive concerns, but even if he ends up at DH, by 2007 he might be the homegrown source of the lefty power that Koskie and Hinske have failed to provide.

FRANK MENECHINO   **INF**   **Bats: R Throws: R**   Height: 5' 8"   Weight: 190   Born: January 7, 1971   Age: 35

YEAR	TM	LVL	AGE	PA	R	2B	3B	HR	RBI	BB	SO	SB	CS	SPEED	BA	OBP	SLG	MLVR	EQBA	EQOBP	EQSLG	EQA	VORP	DEFENSE			
2003	OAK	MLB	32	107	10	0	0	2	9	19	16	0	0	3.4	.193	.364	.265	-.178	.193	.364	.265	.245	-0.6	15-2B	0	12-3B	0
2004	TOR	MLB	33	275	40	13	4	9	25	36	44	0	2	5.0	.301	.400	.504	.210	.294	.396	.498	.302	22.0	27-2B	0	12-SS	-2
2005	TOR	MLB	34	179	22	7	0	4	13	25	33	0	1	3.7	.216	.352	.345	-.105	.219	.363	.356	.258	-0.2	20-2B	4		
2006	*CIN*	*MLB*	*35*	*205*	*23*	*9*	*0*	*5*	*23*	*30*	*37*	*0*	*1*	*4.3*	*.242*	*.369*	*.381*	*-.027*	*.243*	*.371*	*.386*	*.263*	*5.6*	*52-2B*	*0*		

Breakout: 23%   *Improve: 52%*   *Collapse: 31%*   *Attrition: 36%*   *Comparables: Kurt Bevacqua, Geronimo Berroa, Lloyd McClendon*

Having already spent time in Oakland and Toronto, Menechino's consistently impressive walk rate may have already gotten him all the work he could hope for. He can still fill in at second, third, and short, but there's no power and that ugly batting average won't help him sell his services. He may yet find another job someplace. If he does, his scrappy reputation will endear him to fans and broadcasters alike.

MIGUEL NEGRON CF **Bats: L Throws: L** Height: 6' 2" Weight: 170 Born: August 22, 1982 Age: 23

YEAR	TM	LVL	AGE	PA	R	2B	3B	HR	RBI	BB	SO	SB	CS	SPEED	BA	OBP	SLG	MLVR	EQBA	EQOBP	EQSLG	EQA	VORP	DEFENSE
2003	CWV	A	20	115	13	8	1	1	11	2	16	6	2	5.8	.303	.330	.422	.141	.279	.289	.396	.238	-0.1	26-CF -1
2004	DUN	A+	21	417	46	16	5	9	48	38	81	3	1	4.9	.269	.341	.411	.058	.238	.299	.382	.238	-4.1	95-CF -6
2005	NHP	AA	22	523	69	21	3	12	46	32	100	23	12	6.5	.258	.304	.387	-.007	.255	.302	.386	.240	-1.6	111-CF -11
2006	*TOR*	*MLB*	*23*	*469*	*53*	*22*	*3*	*10*	*50*	*23*	*88*	*12*	*6*	*5.3*	*.260*	*.299*	*.391*	*-.104*	*.258*	*.305*	*.392*	*.234*	*-0.6*	*111-CF -6*

Breakout: 19% Improve: 49% Collapse: 23% Attrition: 16% Comparables: *Cory Sullivan, Nathan Panther, Alex Hernandez*

Sometimes, 1st round draft picks just don't pan out. Negron has been a tool-time type for years, earning rave reviews for his defense in centerfield, his arm, and his foot-speed, but injuries have hampered his development. Finally healthy for a full season while making the jump to Double-A, Negron was thoroughly unimpressive, showing neither power nor patience. He's still only 22, so there's a chance that he could put it all together and make it to the majors, but it'll probably involve a year spent regrouping at Double-A.

GUILLERMO QUIROZ C **Bats: R Throws: R** Height: 6' 1" Weight: 200 Born: November 29, 1981 Age: 24

YEAR	TM	LVL	AGE	PA	R	2B	3B	HR	RBI	BB	SO	SB	CS	SPEED	BA	OBP	SLG	MLVR	EQBA	EQOBP	EQSLG	EQA	VORP	DEFENSE
2003	NHV	AA	21	433	63	27	0	20	79	45	83	0	0	3.4	.282	.372	.518	.276	.256	.335	.486	.278	24.5	96-C 11
2004	SYR	AAA	22	288	32	19	1	8	32	28	54	0	0	3.7	.227	.309	.404	-.115	.205	.285	.367	.228	-6.0	70-C -3
2004	TOR	MLB	22	57	2	2	0	0	6	2	8	1	0	3.9	.212	.263	.250	-.449	.192	.246	.231	.184	-3.6	13-C -1
2005	SYR	AAA	23	94	11	3	0	6	18	9	19	0	0	2.9	.229	.309	.482	-.009	.199	.283	.406	.237	-0.8	23-C -1
2005	TOR	MLB	23	39	3	2	0	0	4	2	13	0	0	4.8	.194	.256	.250	-.417	.194	.275	.250	.194	-2.4	
2006	*TOR*	*MLB*	*24*	*260*	*26*	*11*	*1*	*10*	*34*	*19*	*54*	*0*	*0*	*3.7*	*.238*	*.303*	*.412*	*-.085*	*.236*	*.309*	*.413*	*.240*	*3.0*	*64-C 1*

Breakout: 34% Improve: 53% Collapse: 25% Attrition: 24% Comparables: *Marc Hill, Tucker Barr, Jaime Malave*

Quiroz struggled in his first exposure to Triple-A in 2004, and wasn't helped any by questions about his conditioning or a broken hand that cost him serious playing time. But things only got worse in 2005: he suffered an upper back/shoulder injury, and also had to deal with a second collapsed lung, the same ailment that afflicted him in 2003. So what was supposed to be a year in which he bounced back instead saw him limited to 177 PAs before heading off to the Arizona Fall League, where he didn't hit. He still showed good power in his limited time, and will be in the major league mix this year, assuming he can keep both lungs inflated.

ALEXIS RIOS OF **Bats: R Throws: R** Height: 6' 5" Weight: 180 Born: February 18, 1981 Age: 25

YEAR	TM	LVL	AGE	PA	R	2B	3B	HR	RBI	BB	SO	SB	CS	SPEED	BA	OBP	SLG	MLVR	EQBA	EQOBP	EQSLG	EQA	VORP	DEFENSE	
2003	NHV	AA	22	562	86	32	11	11	82	39	85	11	3	6.8	.352	.402	.521	.402	.336	.380	.514	.303	58.6	120-CF -1	
2004	SYR	AAA	23	195	14	10	1	3	23	9	30	2	1	3.8	.259	.292	.373	-.165	.237	.276	.342	.217	-7.2	30-CF 0	16-RF -1
2004	TOR	MLB	23	459	55	24	7	1	28	31	84	15	3	6.5	.286	.338	.383	-.075	.280	.337	.376	.254	4.1	107-RF -1	
2005	TOR	MLB	24	519	71	23	6	10	59	28	101	14	9	6.6	.262	.306	.397	-.088	.264	.317	.406	.249	-3.4	118-RF 10	
2006	*TOR*	*MLB*	*25*	*451*	*58*	*23*	*4*	*11*	*52*	*25*	*79*	*11*	*5*	*6.1*	*.278*	*.322*	*.433*	*.003*	*.277*	*.328*	*.434*	*.255*	*4.7*	*107-RF 1*	

Breakout: 17% Improve: 52% Collapse: 25% Attrition: 16% Comparables: *Chad Allen, Larry Herndon, Luis Matos*

Rios is a plus defender with an above average arm, perfectly well-suited for a job in center, but that belongs to Vernon Wells. He's still the same toolsy player he's always been, but it hasn't translated to the kind of production a competitive team needs from a starting right fielder. Rios is still young (and immature, as his September benching for lackadaisical play suggests), and is just reaching the age that most players can take a big step forward. But barring the kind of breakout the Jays need from him at the plate, he's more valuable to a team in need of a center fielder.

RYAN ROBERTS   **2B**   **Bats: R Throws: R**   Height: 5' 11"   Weight: 190   Born: September 19, 1980   Age: 25

YEAR	TM	LVL	AGE	PA	R	2B	3B	HR	RBI	BB	SO	SB	CS	SPEED	BA	OBP	SLG	MLVR	EQBA	EQOBP	EQSLG	EQA	VORP	DEFENSE	
2003	AUB	A-	22	289	52	10	3	8	36	35	63	7	3	5.8	.278	.374	.440	.218	.236	.307	.379	.240	1.2	59-3B	-3
2004	CWV	A	23	290	38	9	0	13	39	55	50	0	0	2.5	.284	.441	.498	.318	.231	.353	.386	.262	7.6	65-2B	-2
2004	DUN	A+	23	246	29	1	1	7	25	36	51	0	3	3.2	.239	.350	.356	-.016	.210	.305	.330	.227	-5.9	58-2B	-3
2005	DUN	A+	24	192	33	9	0	9	35	24	27	6	1	5.4	.287	.380	.506	.226	.226	.306	.389	.246	0.4	40-2B	-3
2005	NHP	AA	24	398	54	19	3	15	44	55	94	5	1	4.6	.272	.379	.479	.246	.257	.353	.442	.275	21.4	90-2B	-2
2006	*TOR*	*MLB*	*25*	*480*	*55*	*21*	*2*	*14*	*56*	*45*	*102*	*4*	*2*	*4.1*	*.248*	*.322*	*.406*	*-.053*	*.246*	*.329*	*.407*	*.248*	*9.0*	*113-2B*	*-5*

Breakout: 18%   Improve: 45%   Collapse: 22%   Attrition: 14%   Comparables: Morgan Ensberg, Craig Worthington, Hunter Brown

Roberts consolidated his progress from his impressive first full season as a pro in 2004. The Jays' 18th round pick from 2003, he doesn't lack for effort, but does for press; one more good season will change that. At 25, he needs to move quickly to be more than an interesting organizational soldier. If he can make the jump to Triple-A this year, the Jays will have another big league infielder on their hands.

CURTIS THIGPEN   **C**   **Bats: R Throws: R**   Height: 5' 11"   Weight: 190   Born: April 19, 1983   Age: 23

YEAR	TM	LVL	AGE	PA	R	2B	3B	HR	RBI	BB	SO	SB	CS	SPEED	BA	OBP	SLG	MLVR	EQBA	EQOBP	EQSLG	EQA	VORP	DEFENSE	
2004	AUB	A-	21	196	34	11	2	7	29	23	32	1	1	4.7	.301	.388	.518	.324	.249	.319	.418	.255	8.6	32-C	3
2005	LNS	A	22	350	41	18	2	5	35	54	34	5	0	4.0	.287	.397	.413	.175	.256	.347	.367	.256	7.3	58-C	8
2005	NHP	AA	22	153	18	8	0	4	15	9	19	0	0	4.4	.284	.340	.426	.124	.274	.325	.419	.256	5.1	30-C	8
2006	*TOR*	*MLB*	*23*	*466*	*51*	*24*	*2*	*10*	*53*	*39*	*67*	*2*	*1*	*4.3*	*.257*	*.322*	*.395*	*-.061*	*.255*	*.328*	*.396*	*.244*	*8.6*	*110-C*	*9*

Breakout: 14%   Improve: 42%   Collapse: 33%   Attrition: 8%   Comparables: Paul Hoover, Brian Luderer, Robbie Hammock

Primarily a first baseman in college (Taylor Teagarden was doing the catching for the Texas Longhorns), Thigpen has endeared himself to the Jays with very impressive plate discipline and the hints of power to come. He's one of the youngest hitters in the system to reach Double-A, and another solid season could put him on the road to Toronto, where just like everywhere else, it's impossible to have too many catchers who can hit.

VERNON WELLS   **CF**   **Bats: R Throws: R**   Height: 6' 1"   Weight: 210   Born: December 8, 1978   Age: 27

YEAR	TM	LVL	AGE	PA	R	2B	3B	HR	RBI	BB	SO	SB	CS	SPEED	BA	OBP	SLG	MLVR	EQBA	EQOBP	EQSLG	EQA	VORP	DEFENSE	
2003	TOR	MLB	24	735	118	49	5	33	117	42	80	4	1	5.2	.317	.359	.550	.245	.312	.359	.544	.301	61.9	160-CF	2
2004	TOR	MLB	25	590	82	34	2	23	67	51	83	9	2	5.3	.272	.337	.472	.032	.267	.337	.469	.275	23.2	129-CF	-1
2005	TOR	MLB	26	678	78	30	3	28	97	47	86	8	3	4.9	.269	.320	.463	.031	.269	.329	.471	.272	23.8	152-CF	11
2006	*TOR*	*MLB*	*27*	*639*	*85*	*34*	*3*	*28*	*98*	*48*	*81*	*8*	*3*	*5.0*	*.286*	*.343*	*.498*	*.128*	*.284*	*.349*	*.499*	*.280*	*34.3*	*149-CF*	*1*

Breakout: 26%   Improve: 59%   Collapse: 12%   Attrition: 1%   Comparables: Carlos Lee, Kevin McReynolds, Jermaine Dye

Since 2003, Wells has appeared to be on the cusp of greatness. The next Andruw Jones. The kind of player who hits 35–40 home runs a season while providing great defense in center field. You know, Willie Mays. Instead, Wells got impatient at the plate and added only two extra base hits over 2004, despite more than twenty extra games played and 88 more PAs. His ISO was basically the same across the last two seasons, but by posting his worst batting average since his 1999 cup of coffee, Wells is starting to look more and more like the kind of player who has to hit .300 to be an MVP-caliber player. He's heading into the traditional peak seasons and, after two years of being stalled as a hitter, 2003 seems more and more like a one-time event.

GREGG ZAUN   **C**   **Bats: B Throws: R**   Height: 5' 10"   Weight: 180   Born: April 14, 1971   Age: 35

YEAR	TM	LVL	AGE	PA	R	2B	3B	HR	RBI	BB	SO	SB	CS	SPEED	BA	OBP	SLG	MLVR	EQBA	EQOBP	EQSLG	EQA	VORP	DEFENSE	
2003	HOU	MLB	32	137	9	7	0	1	13	14	14	1	0	3.8	.217	.299	.300	-.250	.208	.292	.283	.215	-3.4	24-C	-4
2003	COL	MLB	32	51	6	1	0	3	8	5	7	0	1	4.6	.261	.333	.478	.061	.244	.320	.467	.258	1.6	12-C	-2
2004	SYR	AAA	33	26	4	1	0	0	2	2	5	1	0	5.4	.304	.346	.348	-.071	.257	.304	.300	.233	-1.0		
2004	TOR	MLB	33	392	46	24	0	6	36	47	61	0	2	3.5	.269	.367	.393	-.020	.263	.365	.381	.264	11.9	89-C	-4
2005	TOR	MLB	34	512	61	18	1	11	61	73	70	2	3	3.8	.251	.355	.373	-.038	.251	.365	.378	.265	14.4	122-C	-4
2006	*TOR*	*MLB*	*35*	*354*	*35*	*16*	*1*	*7*	*40*	*45*	*54*	*1*	*1*	*4.2*	*.252*	*.350*	*.382*	*-.033*	*.251*	*.357*	*.383*	*.255*	*7.8*	*85-C*	*-3*

Breakout: 17%   Improve: 33%   Collapse: 34%   Attrition: 35%   Comparables: Bob Stinson, Ron Hodges, Rick Dempsey

Zaun's starting job became secure when Quiroz came down with every injury you'd expect from someone who fell out of an airplane. Finally getting his first shot at everyday play, he responded with a season almost identical to his 2004, just more of it. Despite poor power numbers, he again posted a respectable OBP, and did the little things—like getting knocked out cold breaking up a double play—that get players labeled as gamers. In what's become a career somewhat like Alan Ashby's, Zaun is the kind of catcher that good teams use to hold a position down until something better comes along. Assuming Quiroz is ready, Zaun will return to being the practically perfect backup catcher.

PITCHERS

JOSH BANKS
Bats: R Throws: R Height: 6' 3" Weight: 195 Born: July 18, 1982 Age: 23

YEAR	TM	LVL	AGE	W	L	SV	G	GS	IP	H	BB	SO	HR	GB%	BABIP	STUFF	WHIP	ERA	PERA	EQERA	EQH9	EQBB9	EQSO9	EQHR9	VORP	WXRL
2003	AUB	A-	20	7	2	0	15	15	66.7	58	10	81	1	—	.324	25	1.02	2.43	3.43	5.43	9.4	1.9	6.3	0.6	1.2	—
2004	DUN	A+	21	7	1	0	11	11	60.0	49	8	60	4	—	.280	16	0.95	1.80	4.26	3.95	8.8	1.4	6.2	1.3	10.4	—
2004	NHP	AA	21	6	6	0	18	17	91.3	89	28	76	15	—	.278	-13	1.28	5.03	5.92	6.33	10.3	3.0	5.7	2.1	-7.0	—
2005	NHP	AA	22	8	12	0	27	27	162.3	159	11	145	18	45%	.307	6	1.05	3.83	4.47	5.22	9.6	0.7	5.6	1.5	6.6	—
2006	TOR	MLB	23	8	9	0	29	23	145.0	161	25	88	26	42%	.288	8	1.28	4.76	4.65	4.83	9.6	1.5	5.3	1.5	14.8	2.4

Breakout: 26% Improve: 73% Collapse: 3% Attrition: 0% Comparables: Jin Cho, Justin Duchscherer, John Hudgins

Forget his wins and losses—like a "99" on the radar gun, that 11 and 145 you can see right up there are the kinds of numbers that answer all questions. A polished college pitcher out of Florida International, Banks's performance in his first full season in Double-A wasn't just a matter of getting by against mediocre competition. Although his stuff isn't over-powering—a low-to-mid-90s fastball with a good assortment of breaking pitches—he gets everything out of it. He'll spend the year in Triple-A, but a spot in the rotation in 2007 should have his name on it.

MIGUEL BATISTA
Bats: R Throws: R Height: 6' 0" Weight: 160 Born: February 19, 1971 Age: 35

YEAR	TM	LVL	AGE	W	L	SV	G	GS	IP	H	BB	SO	HR	GB%	BABIP	STUFF	WHIP	ERA	PERA	EQERA	EQH9	EQBB9	EQSO9	EQHR9	VORP	WXRL
2003	ARI	MLB	32	10	9	0	36	29	193.3	197	60	142	13	56%	.316	23	1.33	3.54	3.79	3.65	8.9	2.5	5.9	0.6	39.9	4.2
2004	TOR	MLB	33	10	13	5	38	31	198.7	206	96	104	22	54%	.293	-2	1.52	4.80	5.04	4.64	9.2	4.1	4.4	0.9	27.1	4.6
2005	TOR	MLB	34	5	8	31	71	0	74.7	80	27	54	9	47%	.302	-1	1.43	4.10	4.40	4.52	9.3	3.2	6.4	1.0	9.5	0.9
2006	ARI	MLB	35	3	5	10	47	3	66.0	72	28	44	7	51%	.308	-9	1.51	4.85	4.88	5.57	9.6	3.4	5.6	0.9	3.5	0.4

Breakout: 9% Improve: 28% Collapse: 42% Attrition: 21% Comparables: Stu Miller, Mike Boddicker, Shigetoshi Hasegawa

Batista's peripherals took a nosedive in 2004, and both for want of a closer and because they thought he would perform better in the bullpen, the Jays moved him into the closer role. The hope was that he would simplify his game plan and dump his six- or seven-pitch repertoire in favor of a cutter-splitter combo. Despite racking up saves, it didn't actually work out that well. Batista was thoroughly average in the role, and with plans to move Dustin McGowan to the pen in the future, what's left of Batista's three-year $13.1 million contract is that much more expendable. So did the signing of B. J. Ryan. The Jays sent him back to the Diamondbacks in exchange for Troy Glaus.

DAVID BUSH
Bats: R Throws: R Height: 6' 2" Weight: 210 Born: November 9, 1979 Age: 26

YEAR	TM	LVL	AGE	W	L	SV	G	GS	IP	H	BB	SO	HR	GB%	BABIP	STUFF	WHIP	ERA	PERA	EQERA	EQH9	EQBB9	EQSO9	EQHR9	VORP	WXRL
2003	DUN	A+	23	7	3	0	14	14	77.0	64	9	75	6	—	.271	-5	0.95	2.81	5.76	5.50	10.4	1.4	6.1	2.3	0.8	—
2003	NHV	AA	23	7	3	0	14	14	81.0	73	19	73	4	—	.289	18	1.14	2.78	4.02	4.25	8.7	2.5	6.2	0.8	11.7	—
2004	SYR	AAA	24	6	6	0	16	16	99.7	108	20	88	7	—	.329	22	1.28	4.06	3.88	4.70	9.4	2.0	6.1	0.7	10.0	—
2004	TOR	MLB	24	5	4	0	16	16	97.7	95	25	64	11	43%	.282	15	1.23	3.68	4.33	3.87	8.8	2.1	5.5	0.9	22.1	2.3
2005	SYR	AAA	25	2	2	0	9	9	55.0	65	9	40	6	49%	.343	5	1.35	4.42	4.58	4.91	10.1	1.6	4.9	1.1	4.2	—
2005	TOR	MLB	25	5	11	0	25	24	136.3	142	29	75	20	46%	.282	0	1.25	4.49	4.90	4.76	9.7	1.9	5.0	1.3	16.2	2.6
2006	MIL	MLB	26	9	9	0	31	26	156.3	164	40	101	20	46%	.289	7	1.30	4.22	4.55	4.61	9.4	2.0	5.2	1.2	18.0	2.9

Breakout: 21% Improve: 53% Collapse: 15% Attrition: 1% Comparables: Josh Fogg, Eric Rasmussen, Chad Ogea

Bush was a closer in college, then a starter through his first two seasons in the majors, a fact that may have aided his health but clearly didn't help his home run-rate much. His ability to throw four pitches for strikes, including a low-90s fastball, is better suited to starting. Bush was dealt to Milwaukee as the front man in the Jays' package for Overbay, and he could wind up succeeding in just about any role Doug Melvin and Ned Yost want him in.

JESSE CARLSON Bats: L Throws: L Height: 6' 1" Weight: 160 Born: December 31, 1980 Age: 25

YEAR	TM	LVL	AGE	W	L	SV	G	GS	IP	H	BB	SO	HR	GB%	BABIP	STUFF	WHIP	ERA	PERA	EQERA	EQH9	EQBB9	EQSO9	EQHR9	VORP	WXRL
2003	LEX	A	22	3	0	13	53	0	63.3	37	16	84	2	—	.248	9	0.84	1.56	3.90	3.75	8.0	3.0	7.3	0.8	11.9	—
2004	ROU	AA	23	5	0	1	41	0	55.3	57	21	51	5	—	.317	-18	1.41	5.05	5.40	6.58	10.0	4.1	5.7	1.4	-5.8	—
2005	NHP	AA	24	3	2	5	39	0	39.3	28	5	42	2	43%	.277	8	0.84	1.83	3.65	3.16	8.0	1.5	6.6	0.7	10.0	—
2005	SYR	AAA	24	1	1	0	22	0	18.7	26	7	17	4	45%	.373	-16	1.76	4.81	7.11	5.21	12.3	3.8	6.2	2.4	0.8	—
2006	*TOR*	*MLB*	*25*	*2*	*3*	*1*	*26*	*4*	*47.0*	*53*	*16*	*30*	*8*	*44%*	*.296*	*-5*	*1.46*	*5.28*	*5.23*	*5.37*	*9.7*	*3.1*	*5.6*	*1.4*	*1.8*	*0.3*

Breakout: 13% Improve: 33% Collapse: 28% Attrition: 27% Comparables: Andy Hazlett, Jon Switzer, Bud Daley

Carlson is an object lesson in why ERA is a poor metric to use in evaluating relievers. In three of his last five stops, his ERA has been 1.83 or lower. The other two times it's been 4.82 or higher. What matters here is that Carlson has promising peripherals and seems to have left that nasty walk rate from Round Rock behind him. Despite playing for his third organization in four years as a pro, he could be a solid bullpen option.

GUSTAVO CHACIN Bats: L Throws: L Height: 5' 11" Weight: 190 Born: December 4, 1980 Age: 25

YEAR	TM	LVL	AGE	W	L	SV	G	GS	IP	H	BB	SO	HR	GB%	BABIP	STUFF	WHIP	ERA	PERA	EQERA	EQH9	EQBB9	EQSO9	EQHR9	VORP	WXRL
2003	NHV	AA	22	3	4	2	46	2	69.3	78	29	55	1	—	.335	0	1.54	4.16	4.00	6.20	9.3	4.1	5.4	0.3	-4.6	—
2004	NHP	AA	23	16	2	0	25	25	141.7	113	49	109	15	—	.244	-7	1.14	2.92	5.45	4.70	9.2	3.6	5.2	1.4	13.2	—
2005	TOR	MLB	24	13	9	0	34	34	203.0	213	70	121	20	40%	.304	11	1.39	3.72	4.49	4.05	9.4	3.1	5.3	0.8	39.3	5.0
2006	*TOR*	*MLB*	*25*	*10*	*10*	*0*	*28*	*28*	*168.3*	*182*	*59*	*104*	*23*	*44%*	*.293*	*8*	*1.43*	*4.69*	*4.79*	*4.85*	*9.4*	*3.2*	*5.4*	*1.1*	*17.6*	*3.0*

Breakout: 6% Improve: 31% Collapse: 28% Attrition: 3% Comparables: Alex Kellner, Jamie Moyer, Jerry Augustine

Chacin's improvement over the past two seasons is being attributed to the addition of a particularly sharp cut fastball. The most awkward looking delivery this side of late-night Comedy Central stand-up didn't hurt, either. Still, that kind of shtick doesn't usually work more than once, leading to speculation that Chacin may struggle in his sophomore season. His peripherals have always been middling at best. Expect to hear the phrase "regression to the mean" a lot, at least from us.

CHI-HUNG CHENG Bats: L Throws: L Height: 6' 1" Weight: 193 Born: June 20, 1985 Age: 21

YEAR	TM	LVL	AGE	W	L	SV	G	GS	IP	H	BB	SO	HR	GB%	BABIP	STUFF	WHIP	ERA	PERA	EQERA	EQH9	EQBB9	EQSO9	EQHR9	VORP	WXRL
2004	PUL	Rk	19	4	1	0	14	14	60.7	47	35	74	4	—	.297	-12	1.35	2.82	7.00	6.50	9.5	8.0	5.3	1.5	-5.4	—
2005	LNS	A	20	7	6	0	26	25	137.0	109	72	142	8	51%	.284	8	1.32	3.15	5.26	5.26	8.6	5.5	6.4	1.0	4.9	—
2006	*TOR*	*MLB*	*21*	*7*	*9*	*0*	*26*	*23*	*130.3*	*131*	*82*	*95*	*19*	*47%*	*.286*	*3*	*1.63*	*5.35*	*5.42*	*5.54*	*8.7*	*5.7*	*6.4*	*1.2*	*4.4*	*1.3*

Breakout: 24% Improve: 57% Collapse: 15% Attrition: 0% Comparables: Gary Majewski, John Curtice, Cedrick Bowers

Sometimes good things just fall into your lap. Cheng came west to work out for the Jays and showed enough promise that the Jays signed him—a modern parallel to the olden days when amateurs would send letters to major league managers saying, "If you would just pay my way to Philadelphia, I'm sure I could help you win the pennant." With stats like these, you'd think he has all the makings of a wild power pitcher, and he does, except for the velocity. His fastball is a bit slow, but his breaking pitches make up for it. If Cheng can improve his command, the Jays may have a real gem on their hands. Then again, he's only a hit-lucky 19-year-old in A-ball with a high walk rate, so there's quite a way to go before he reaches solid prospect status. While the Jays were in Taiwan signing Cheng they noticed another pitcher, Po-Hsuan Kengm and signed him as well, so it was a productive trip.

VINNY CHULK Bats: R Throws: R Height: 6' 2" Weight: 180 Born: December 19, 1978 Age: 27

YEAR	TM	LVL	AGE	W	L	SV	G	GS	IP	H	BB	SO	HR	GB%	BABIP	STUFF	WHIP	ERA	PERA	EQERA	EQH9	EQBB9	EQSO9	EQHR9	VORP	WXRL
2003	SYR	AAA	24	8	10	0	23	21	119.3	118	46	90	14	—	.280	-18	1.37	4.22	5.92	5.68	9.6	4.3	5.4	1.7	-1.0	—
2004	SYR	AAA	25	4	2	3	18	0	28.7	27	11	26	5	—	.272	-11	1.32	2.82	5.93	4.28	9.2	4.0	6.3	2.0	4.0	—
2004	TOR	MLB	25	1	3	2	47	0	56.0	59	27	44	6	44%	.315	0	1.54	4.66	4.42	4.26	9.0	3.9	6.5	0.8	9.9	0.2
2005	TOR	MLB	26	0	1	0	62	0	72.0	68	26	39	9	44%	.269	-11	1.31	3.88	4.79	4.04	9.0	3.3	4.9	1.0	13.7	1.9
2006	*TOR*	*MLB*	*27*	*3*	*3*	*1*	*48*	*0*	*54.7*	*57*	*22*	*35*	*8*	*44%*	*.284*	*-8*	*1.44*	*4.66*	*4.78*	*5.36*	*9.0*	*3.7*	*5.6*	*1.2*	*5.6*	*0.4*

Breakout: 21% Improve: 40% Collapse: 36% Attrition: 31% Comparables: Bob Priddy, Jerry Johnson, Paul Byrd

Chulk's ERA actually underrates him, as he squashed more than his fair share of rallies by holding hitters to .230/.289/.352 with runners on base. Nevertheless, Chulk isn't that different from any number of former starters who survive in the bullpen for a little while despite mediocre peripherals and stuff. Unless he adds something to his arsenal, 2006 will be a constant battle to keep his low strikeout rate from undermining his effectiveness.

SCOTT DOWNS Bats: L Throws: L Height: 6' 2" Weight: 190 Born: March 17, 1976 Age: 30

YEAR	TM	LVL	AGE	W	L	SV	G	GS	IP	H	BB	SO	HR	GB%	BABIP	STUFF	WHIP	ERA	PERA	EQERA	EQH9	EQBB9	EQSO9	EQHR9	VORP	WXRL
2003	EDM	AAA	27	8	9	0	21	21	121.7	119	39	54	13	—	.254	-26	1.30	4.29	6.05	5.90	9.5	3.6	3.3	1.6	-3.9	—
2004	EDM	AAA	28	10	6	0	22	22	135.3	143	26	67	16	—	.283	-13	1.25	3.53	5.39	4.84	9.7	2.0	3.1	1.4	11.1	—
2004	MON	MLB	28	3	6	0	12	12	63.0	79	23	38	9	54%	.337	-5	1.62	5.14	4.92	6.47	10.7	3.0	4.8	1.1	-7.3	1.0
2005	SYR	AAA	29	2	3	0	7	7	39.3	45	3	35	5	54%	.339	9	1.22	4.81	4.38	5.54	10.2	0.9	5.5	1.4	0.3	—
2005	TOR	MLB	29	4	3	0	26	13	94.0	93	34	75	12	54%	.289	9	1.35	4.31	4.37	4.47	8.9	3.2	7.0	1.0	12.2	1.9
2006	*TOR*	*MLB*	*30*	*6*	*7*	*1*	*38*	*16*	*112.0*	*125*	*36*	*68*	*16*	*49%*	*.298*	*-4*	*1.43*	*4.95*	*4.91*	*5.29*	*9.6*	*3.0*	*5.3*	*1.2*	*8.1*	*1.3*

Breakout: 25% Improve: 56% Collapse: 18% Attrition: 6% Comparables: Bo Belinsky, Brian Bohanon, Woodie Fryman

Perhaps the epitome of the replacement-level lefty, his prospect status couldn't survive two Tommy John surgeries, so it's a bit gutty of him to have made it back. Downs has a chance to contribute at the major league level, albeit as little more than a second lefty or emergency starter. It won't give him back the future he had as an Expos prospect, but it's a living.

JASON FRASOR Bats: R Throws: R Height: 5' 10" Weight: 170 Born: August 9, 1977 Age: 28

YEAR	TM	LVL	AGE	W	L	SV	G	GS	IP	H	BB	SO	HR	GB%	BABIP	STUFF	WHIP	ERA	PERA	EQERA	EQH9	EQBB9	EQSO9	EQHR9	VORP	WXRL
2004	TOR	MLB	26	4	6	17	63	0	68.3	64	36	54	4	45%	.305	6	1.46	4.08	4.17	3.65	8.3	4.4	6.7	0.5	17.8	2.6
2005	TOR	MLB	27	3	5	1	67	0	74.7	67	28	62	8	51%	.294	8	1.27	3.25	4.10	3.62	8.3	3.4	7.4	0.8	18.3	2.9
2006	*TOR*	*MLB*	*28*	*3*	*3*	*2*	*52*	*0*	*57.7*	*58*	*25*	*45*	*7*	*45%*	*.296*	*-1*	*1.44*	*4.49*	*4.55*	*5.02*	*8.7*	*3.9*	*6.8*	*1.0*	*6.9*	*0.5*

Breakout: 12% Improve: 23% Collapse: 49% Attrition: 18% Comparables: Marc Wilkins, Jeff Brantley, Steve Mingori

Frasor edged out Speier as the Jays' best reliever in 2005. A short flamethrower, there isn't much separating him from the rest of the pack where strikeouts are concerned. For two years now he's fanned just enough batters to get by, doing a good job getting his fellow pitchers out of trouble. He improved in his second big league season, but even if he doesn't keep making incremental gains, there's no reason he shouldn't turn in another above-average relief season. It's startling how hard it can be to find one when you really need one.

CHAD GAUDIN Bats: R Throws: R Height: 5' 10" Weight: 160 Born: March 24, 1983 Age: 23

YEAR	TM	LVL	AGE	W	L	SV	G	GS	IP	H	BB	SO	HR	GB%	BABIP	STUFF	WHIP	ERA	PERA	EQERA	EQH9	EQBB9	EQSO9	EQHR9	VORP	WXRL
2003	BAK	A+	20	5	3	0	14	14	80.3	63	23	70	2	—	.263	21	1.07	2.13	4.09	4.09	7.8	3.3	5.1	0.5	12.9	—
2003	TBA	MLB	20	2	0	0	15	3	40.0	37	16	23	4	40%	.260	2	1.32	3.60	4.85	3.92	9.0	3.7	5.1	0.9	9.1	0.8
2004	DUR	AAA	21	1	3	2	17	7	47.7	48	17	52	8	—	.325	11	1.36	4.72	4.94	4.75	9.1	3.2	8.0	1.7	4.5	—
2004	TBA	MLB	21	1	2	0	26	4	42.7	59	16	30	4	41%	.390	1	1.76	4.85	4.43	5.24	11.1	3.0	5.6	0.8	2.2	0.7
2005	SYR	AAA	22	9	8	0	23	23	150.3	140	35	113	12	46%	.296	18	1.16	3.35	4.15	3.79	8.7	2.3	5.4	0.8	29.6	—
2005	TOR	MLB	22	1	3	0	5	3	13.0	31	6	12	6	41%	.521	-12	2.85	13.15	7.80	12.00	15.6	3.6	7.2	3.6	-10.6	-0.5
2006	*OAK*	*MLB*	*23*	*9*	*8*	*2*	*72*	*14*	*154.0*	*160*	*46*	*99*	*20*	*43%*	*.287*	*2*	*1.34*	*4.29*	*4.56*	*4.64*	*9.2*	*2.7*	*5.8*	*1.1*	*19.0*	*2.3*

Breakout: 19% Improve: 62% Collapse: 5% Attrition: 0% Comparables: Larry Demery, Nelson Briles, Dicky Gonzalez

Gaudin excelled after finally getting a chance to work consistently in the high minors; the Devil Rays had decided that his best development program was to jump three levels at once. His strikeout rate was good, but even more impressive was his improved command. It's difficult to assess players who have been jerked around the way Gaudin has, but any way you look at it, the Jays turned him around. This winter's roster space crunch made him available, and he was traded to Toronto's green and gold cousins (the A's for a PTBNL).

LEE GRONKIEWICZ Bats: R Throws: R Height: 5' 11" Weight: 180 Born: August 21, 1978 Age: 27

YEAR	TM	LVL	AGE	W	L	SV	G	GS	IP	H	BB	SO	HR	GB%	BABIP	STUFF	WHIP	ERA	PERA	EQERA	EQH9	EQBB9	EQSO9	EQHR9	VORP	WXRL
2003	KIN	A+	24	2	3	37	51	0	56.0	50	14	46	4	—	.274	-22	1.14	2.41	5.54	5.19	9.9	2.9	5.2	1.7	2.4	—
2004	AKR	AA	25	1	4	20	52	0	65.3	65	21	68	5	—	.326	-3	1.32	3.03	4.52	4.24	9.5	3.4	6.4	1.0	9.6	—
2005	NHP	AA	26	2	0	24	38	0	38.3	24	10	45	2	50%	.253	2	0.89	1.41	4.08	3.57	7.4	3.3	6.9	0.8	8.0	—
2005	SYR	AAA	26	0	1	6	28	0	28.3	21	13	26	3	49%	.247	-9	1.20	2.23	5.40	3.38	7.8	5.1	6.4	1.4	6.6	—
2006	*TOR*	*MLB*	*27*	*2*	*3*	*1*	*24*	*3*	*46.0*	*48*	*19*	*31*	*7*	*44%*	*.285*	*-4*	*1.43*	*4.72*	*4.73*	*4.97*	*8.9*	*3.7*	*6.0*	*1.2*	*4.4*	*0.5*

Breakout: 10% Improve: 26% Collapse: 41% Attrition: 34% Comparables: Paul Byrd, Carlos Reyes, Cliff Politte

After going pro as an undrafted free agent, Toronto acquired Gronkiewicz in the minor league portion of the Rule 5 draft last year. Consider this the benefit of the Jays giving "short" righthanders the benefit of the doubt. The only thing he has going against him is his age, but with all the solid bullpen options floating around the system that may be enough to keep him down in Syracuse.

ROY HALLADAY — Bats: R Throws: R — Height: 6′ 6″ Weight: 205 Born: May 14, 1977 — Age: 29

YEAR	TM	LVL	AGE	W	L	SV	G	GS	IP	H	BB	SO	HR	GB%	BABIP	STUFF	WHIP	ERA	PERA	EQERA	EQH9	EQBB9	EQSO9	EQHR9	VORP	WXRL
2003	TOR	MLB	26	22	7	0	36	36	266.0	253	32	204	26	61%	.286	29	1.07	3.25	3.48	3.45	8.3	1.1	6.7	0.8	71.2	7.8
2004	TOR	MLB	27	8	8	0	21	21	133.0	140	39	95	13	59%	.313	19	1.35	4.20	4.00	4.00	9.0	2.4	5.9	0.8	28.2	3.4
2005	TOR	MLB	28	12	4	0	19	19	141.7	118	18	108	11	62%	.264	35	0.96	2.41	3.34	2.51	8.0	1.2	6.9	0.6	53.3	6.0
2006	TOR	MLB	29	13	7	0	28	28	184.0	181	31	133	16	57%	.291	23	1.15	3.31	3.29	3.45	8.5	1.5	6.3	0.7	45.3	6.0

Breakout: 15% Improve: 40% Collapse: 18% Attrition: 9% Comparables: Rick Reuschel, Shane Reynolds, Mark Gubicza

For nearly 900 innings, Doc Halladay has been one of the game's most dominant pitchers. Averaged out, that's just shy of 180 innings of 3.16 ERA for the past five seasons. While most teams would be happy to get that from any pitcher, Halladay holds the promise of much more. He's shown pitch efficiency reminiscent of Greg Maddux at his best, and as a result, can soak up innings. Heck, in barely more than half a season, Halladay was the third best pitcher in the AL, as measured by SNLVAR. We know you've heard this a million times, but if he can stay healthy he's worth ten wins over a replacement-level pitcher. He's a key player on a team that desperately needs high-end performance from its best talent.

ZACH JACKSON — Bats: L Throws: L — Height: 6′ 5″ Weight: 220 Born: May 13, 1983 — Age: 23

YEAR	TM	LVL	AGE	W	L	SV	G	GS	IP	H	BB	SO	HR	GB%	BABIP	STUFF	WHIP	ERA	PERA	EQERA	EQH9	EQBB9	EQSO9	EQHR9	VORP	WXRL
2005	DUN	A+	22	8	1	0	10	10	59.3	56	6	48	3	60%	.301	11	1.05	2.88	3.92	5.18	9.3	1.3	4.6	0.8	2.7	—
2005	NHP	AA	22	4	3	0	9	9	54.0	57	12	43	3	54%	.338	10	1.28	4.00	4.25	5.43	9.7	2.4	4.9	0.7	1.0	—
2005	SYR	AAA	22	4	4	0	8	8	47.3	61	21	33	3	48%	.379	3	1.73	5.14	4.44	6.10	10.2	4.1	4.8	0.6	-2.7	—
2006	MIL	MLB	23	7	10	0	28	24	141.0	155	54	86	18	50%	.300	2	1.48	5.17	5.26	5.63	9.9	3.0	4.9	1.1	-0.3	1.0

Breakout: 17% Improve: 58% Collapse: 8% Attrition: 0% Comparables: Brad Thomas, Kason Gabbard, Jason Brester

Jackson jumped all the way to Triple-A just a year after being a supplemental first rounder in 2004, tying for the minor league lead in wins along the way. His fastball tops out in the low 90s, very good for a lefty who's not Randy Johnson, and if the word is that he needs to work on his secondary pitches, keep in mind that he made it to Syracuse at age 22. His peripherals declined at each step along the way, but he should get plenty of time in Triple-A to work out the kinks. The Jays packaged him into the Overbay deal, instantly making him one of Milwaukee's best pitching prospects.

CASEY JANSSEN — Bats: R Throws: R — Height: 6′ 3″ Weight: 200 Born: September 17, 1981 Age: 24

YEAR	TM	LVL	AGE	W	L	SV	G	GS	IP	H	BB	SO	HR	GB%	BABIP	STUFF	WHIP	ERA	PERA	EQERA	EQH9	EQBB9	EQSO9	EQHR9	VORP	WXRL
2004	AUB	A-	22	3	1	0	10	10	50.0	46	10	43	2	—	.301	-8	1.12	3.60	5.17	6.70	9.8	2.9	3.8	1.1	-5.7	—
2005	LNS	A	23	4	0	0	7	7	46.0	27	4	38	0	59%	.231	21	0.67	1.37	3.14	3.56	7.1	1.0	4.8	0.2	9.7	—
2005	DUN	A+	23	6	1	0	10	10	59.7	46	12	51	2	54%	.275	13	0.97	2.26	4.15	3.99	8.1	2.4	4.8	0.6	10.1	—
2005	NHP	AA	23	3	3	0	9	9	43.0	49	4	47	3	55%	.383	18	1.23	2.93	3.59	5.27	10.3	1.1	6.5	0.8	1.6	—
2006	TOR	MLB	24	8	9	0	30	23	149.3	163	34	83	17	54%	.295	7	1.32	4.64	4.29	4.86	9.4	2.1	4.8	1.0	13.8	2.5

Breakout: 12% Improve: 38% Collapse: 11% Attrition: 0% Comparables: Chien-Ming Wang, Brian Lawrence, Cam Spence

A 2004 4th round pick, Janssen's low-90s fastball is good enough that he doesn't need to use his average breaking pitches that often. His control is also excellent—his K-BB ratio was third in the minors among pitchers with at least 100 IP. Janssen was a level behind draft-mate Zach Jackson the entire way up the chain, but unlike Jackson, Janssen's peripherals held up through three levels. He'll have to fight through the rest of the talent in the system, but everything looks good so far.

BRANDON LEAGUE — Bats: R Throws: R — Height: 6′ 2″ Weight: 180 Born: March 16, 1983 — Age: 23

YEAR	TM	LVL	AGE	W	L	SV	G	GS	IP	H	BB	SO	HR	GB%	BABIP	STUFF	WHIP	ERA	PERA	EQERA	EQH9	EQBB9	EQSO9	EQHR9	VORP	WXRL
2003	CWV	A	20	2	3	0	12	12	70.7	58	18	61	1	—	.274	22	1.07	1.91	3.88	3.88	8.6	2.8	4.8	0.3	12.9	—
2003	DUN	A+	20	4	3	0	13	12	66.3	76	20	34	3	—	.307	-11	1.45	4.75	5.46	7.27	11.1	3.1	3.2	1.1	-11.9	—
2004	NHP	AA	21	6	4	2	41	10	104.0	92	41	90	3	—	.302	15	1.28	3.38	4.04	4.84	9.1	3.8	5.9	0.4	8.5	—
2005	SYR	AAA	22	4	4	0	19	10	63.0	78	18	35	7	56%	.333	-12	1.52	5.71	5.09	6.08	10.5	2.7	4.0	1.1	-3.4	—
2005	TOR	MLB	22	1	0	0	20	0	35.7	42	20	17	8	57%	.298	-29	1.74	6.55	7.00	6.50	10.8	5.0	4.2	2.0	-3.7	0.1
2006	TOR	MLB	23	3	5	1	43	6	72.3	87	30	39	9	54%	.316	-11	1.61	5.53	5.49	5.79	10.4	3.7	4.7	1.0	-0.2	0.1

Breakout: 18% Improve: 52% Collapse: 17% Attrition: 7% Comparables: Al Santorini, Lindy McDaniel, Tommie Sisk

League has a repertoire most coaches dream of: a fastball in the upper 90s, a power sinker in the upper 80s, and an improving changeup. The Jays put him in the pen at the tender age of 22 and watched him struggle as he walked more batters than he struck out. In truth, for all that heat, League's strikeout numbers haven't been incredible, but his performance should improve with repetition and a more settled role. His long-term future is in the rotation, but it may be another year before a spot is projected for him.

TED LILLY
Bats: L   **Throws: L**   Height: 6' 1"   Weight: 177   Born: January 4, 1976   Age: 30

YEAR	TM	LVL	AGE	W	L	SV	G	GS	IP	H	BB	SO	HR	GB%	BABIP	STUFF	WHIP	ERA	PERA	EQERA	EQH9	EQBB9	EQSO9	EQHR9	VORP	WXRL
2003	OAK	MLB	27	12	10	0	32	31	178.3	179	58	147	24	40%	.291	15	1.33	4.34	4.26	4.47	9.1	2.9	7.3	1.1	25.8	3.9
2004	TOR	MLB	28	12	10	0	32	32	197.3	171	89	168	26	39%	.264	16	1.32	4.06	4.48	3.71	8.1	3.8	7.2	1.1	46.8	5.6
2005	TOR	MLB	29	10	11	0	25	25	126.3	135	58	96	23	39%	.296	-5	1.53	5.56	5.36	5.29	9.4	4.2	6.7	1.6	4.0	1.7
2006	TOR	MLB	30	8	9	0	33	22	137.7	143	53	105	22	40%	.291	6	1.42	4.81	4.87	5.10	9.0	3.5	6.6	1.3	13.2	2.2

Breakout: 10%   Improve: 38%   Collapse: 30%   Attrition: 9%   Comparables: Denny Lemaster, Dick Littlefield, John Tudor

Lilly's walk rate increased for the fourth year in a row; throw in higher hit and home run rates, and perhaps most fundamentally, an extended bout of bicep tendinitis, and presto, his ERA ballooned by a run and a half. He should be able to bounce back and provide 160–180 innings of league-average pitching, not a bad output from a fourth or fifth starter. Lilly is going to have to perform well to hold off the crowd of young pitching in the system; if the Jays are out of it by the end of July, he'll be in demand at the trading deadline.

SHAUN MARCUM
Bats: R   **Throws: R**   Height: 6' 0"   Weight: 180   Born: December 14, 1981   Age: 24

YEAR	TM	LVL	AGE	W	L	SV	G	GS	IP	H	BB	SO	HR	GB%	BABIP	STUFF	WHIP	ERA	PERA	EQERA	EQH9	EQBB9	EQSO9	EQHR9	VORP	WXRL
2004	CWV	A	22	7	4	0	13	13	79.0	64	16	83	7	—	.271	2	1.01	3.19	5.01	5.38	9.3	2.4	5.5	1.5	1.8	—
2004	DUN	A+	22	3	2	0	12	12	69.3	74	4	72	6	—	.343	9	1.13	3.12	4.81	5.35	10.6	0.7	6.0	1.7	1.9	—
2005	NHP	AA	23	7	1	0	9	9	53.3	44	10	40	5	44%	.265	4	1.01	2.53	5.01	3.75	8.9	2.1	4.6	1.3	10.3	—
2005	SYR	AAA	23	6	4	0	18	18	103.7	112	18	90	17	43%	.309	0	1.25	4.95	4.93	5.19	9.9	1.7	6.2	1.7	4.7	—
2006	TOR	MLB	24	8	9	1	37	20	140.0	154	31	88	23	44%	.292	5	1.32	4.70	4.67	4.78	9.5	2.0	5.5	1.3	14.7	2.2

Breakout: 13%   Improve: 46%   Collapse: 13%   Attrition: 1%   Comparables: Joe Presko, Ralph Terry, Felix Diaz

A dark horse candidate for the bullpen who's found favor with Ricciardi, Marcum has put up very solid numbers as a starting pitcher since being drafted in the third round of the 2003 draft. He mixes a fastball that tops out in the low 90s with a good, hard slider, and has a few other breaking pitches in the works. Depending on how the rest of the roster shakes out, Marcum, who is younger than most of the other available options, could find himself in a swingman role in 2006.

DUSTIN McGOWAN
Bats: R   **Throws: R**   Height: 6' 3"   Weight: 190   Born: March 24, 1982   Age: 24

YEAR	TM	LVL	AGE	W	L	SV	G	GS	IP	H	BB	SO	HR	GB%	BABIP	STUFF	WHIP	ERA	PERA	EQERA	EQH9	EQBB9	EQSO9	EQHR9	VORP	WXRL
2003	DUN	A+	21	5	6	0	14	14	75.7	62	25	66	1	—	.275	18	1.15	2.85	4.00	5.25	8.5	3.5	5.5	0.4	2.8	—
2003	NHV	AA	21	7	0	0	14	14	76.7	78	19	72	1	—	.328	34	1.26	3.17	3.29	4.34	8.7	2.5	6.6	0.2	10.7	—
2004	NHP	AA	22	2	0	0	6	6	31.0	24	15	29	4	—	.241	1	1.26	4.06	5.59	4.97	9.0	5.0	6.5	1.6	2.0	—
2005	NHP	AA	23	0	2	0	6	6	35.0	35	10	33	6	43%	.309	-2	1.29	3.34	6.55	5.18	10.4	3.3	6.0	2.5	1.5	—
2005	TOR	MLB	23	1	3	0	13	7	45.3	49	17	34	7	48%	.309	1	1.46	6.36	5.12	6.31	9.9	3.4	6.7	1.4	-4.3	0.2
2006	TOR	MLB	24	6	7	0	33	18	109.7	121	41	72	17	45%	.298	0	1.48	5.26	5.19	5.37	9.5	3.4	5.7	1.3	4.4	1.0

Breakout: 20%   Improve: 62%   Collapse: 6%   Attrition: 0%   Comparables: Herm Wehmeier, Jason Marquis, Kip Wells

McGowan has told the Jays that he'd like to move to the bullpen, and they're willing to oblige. Recent baseball history is littered with injured starters recovering from Tommy John surgery who convert to bullpen work and throw harder than ever before. McGowan got his fastball up to about 95 during his brief stints in the pen, and the Jays think he can be groomed for the closer role down the road. At the very least, McGowan could earn an audition for B. J. Ryan's setup man.

VINCE PERKINS
Bats: L   **Throws: R**   Height: 6' 5"   Weight: 220   Born: September 27, 1981   Age: 24

YEAR	TM	LVL	AGE	W	L	SV	G	GS	IP	H	BB	SO	HR	GB%	BABIP	STUFF	WHIP	ERA	PERA	EQERA	EQH9	EQBB9	EQSO9	EQHR9	VORP	WXRL
2003	CWV	A	21	3	1	0	8	8	44.3	19	22	60	1	—	.198	22	0.93	1.83	4.50	3.83	6.3	5.8	7.7	0.7	7.9	—
2003	DUN	A+	21	7	6	0	18	17	84.3	58	53	69	1	—	.237	4	1.32	2.46	5.06	5.17	7.8	6.9	5.3	0.3	3.7	—
2004	DUN	A+	22	1	4	0	13	9	54.7	53	24	47	2	—	.307	-3	1.41	3.95	4.96	5.98	9.4	4.8	5.1	0.7	-2.2	—
2005	NHP	AA	23	7	7	0	26	24	131.7	124	51	111	9	48%	.306	-1	1.33	4.03	4.99	5.56	9.3	4.2	5.2	0.9	0.6	—
2006	TOR	MLB	24	5	9	0	27	20	116.0	125	63	73	16	49%	.295	-4	1.62	5.77	5.50	5.94	9.3	4.9	5.5	1.1	-3.3	0.4

Breakout: 7%   Improve: 36%   Collapse: 28%   Attrition: 1%   Comparables: Sean Douglass, Jimmy Journell, Ryan Glynn

(continued next page)

Vince Perkins *(continued)*

After back and wrist injuries cost him significant portions of 2004, Perkins posted solid ratios in Double-A, highlighted by a minuscule home run rate. He features a lot of gas on the fastball and a handy slider, but there's quite a bit of work to be done on his command. He's going to be hard-pressed to distinguish himself from the other quality arms in the system unless he reduces those free passes.

DAVID PURCEY   **Bats: L Throws: L**   Height: 6′ 5″   Weight: 240   Born: April 22, 1982   Age: 24

YEAR	TM	LVL	AGE	W	L	SV	G	GS	IP	H	BB	SO	HR	GB%	BABIP	STUFF	WHIP	ERA	PERA	EQERA	EQH9	EQBB9	EQSO9	EQHR9	VORP	WXRL
2005	DUN	A+	23	5	4	0	21	21	94.3	80	56	116	8	50%	.319	-15	1.44	3.63	6.46	6.15	9.5	7.4	7.2	1.6	-5.3	—
2005	NHP	AA	23	4	3	0	8	8	43.0	32	25	45	2	47%	.275	4	1.33	2.93	4.91	4.69	7.8	6.5	6.5	0.7	4.1	—
2006	*TOR*	*MLB*	*24*	*5*	*8*	*0*	*26*	*19*	*107.7*	*110*	*78*	*84*	*15*	*46%*	*.296*	*-2*	*1.74*	*5.82*	*5.88*	*5.93*	*8.8*	*6.6*	*6.8*	*1.2*	*-2.4*	*0.4*

Breakout: 16%   *Improve: 48%*   *Collapse: 19%*   *Attrition: 1%*   Comparables: *Chad Hutchinson, Doug Davis, Vince Perkins*

One of the riskier college pitchers of late, Purcey is a huge southpaw who has gotten by with a low- to mid-90s fastball for most of his career. He's working on mastering an overhand curve, but more basically, he's trying to iron out some mechanical questions. There's a lot of potential here, especially if he can find a pitching coach with whom he works well. His raw power is unquestionable, but like Perkins, he would go a long way by developing some consistent command.

FRANCISCO ROSARIO   **Bats: R Throws: R**   Height: 6′ 0″   Weight: 160   Born: September 28, 1980   Age: 25

YEAR	TM	LVL	AGE	W	L	SV	G	GS	IP	H	BB	SO	HR	GB%	BABIP	STUFF	WHIP	ERA	PERA	EQERA	EQH9	EQBB9	EQSO9	EQHR9	VORP	WXRL
2004	NHP	AA	23	2	4	0	12	12	48.0	48	16	45	6	—	.316	-4	1.33	4.31	5.32	5.91	10.4	3.4	6.1	1.6	-1.6	—
2005	SYR	AAA	24	2	7	2	30	18	116.3	111	42	80	16	44%	.284	-17	1.32	3.95	5.77	4.81	9.4	3.7	4.9	1.5	9.9	—
2006	*TOR*	*MLB*	*25*	*4*	*7*	*0*	*27*	*14*	*92.7*	*106*	*39*	*54*	*18*	*41%*	*.292*	*-8*	*1.56*	*5.74*	*5.84*	*5.90*	*9.9*	*3.8*	*5.1*	*1.6*	*-0.7*	*0.4*

Breakout: 8%   *Improve: 31%*   *Collapse: 28%*   *Attrition: 1%*   Comparables: *Cliff Politte, Silvio Martinez, Manuel Aybar*

Beloved by scouts for his velocity, Rosario was climbing up the prospect lists before blowing out his elbow in late 2002. After taking all of 2003 to recover, he looked good in limited action in 2004, flashing the same mid-90s fastball, but also improving his command as the year went on. Last year, he didn't quite keep it up. While his ERA was good, he gave up a few too many souvenirs while failing to overpower experienced Triple-A hitters. The Jays are trying him out in the pen, but his best chance may be with another organization.

SCOTT SCHOENEWEIS   **Bats: L Throws: L**   Height: 6′ 0″   Weight: 186   Born: October 2, 1973   Age: 32

YEAR	TM	LVL	AGE	W	L	SV	G	GS	IP	H	BB	SO	HR	GB%	BABIP	STUFF	WHIP	ERA	PERA	EQERA	EQH9	EQBB9	EQSO9	EQHR9	VORP	WXRL
2003	ANA	MLB	29	1	1	0	39	0	38.7	37	10	29	2	58%	.299	9	1.22	3.95	3.49	4.42	8.6	2.3	6.5	0.5	6.4	-0.0
2003	CHA	MLB	29	2	1	0	20	0	26.0	26	9	27	1	52%	.338	20	1.35	4.50	3.08	5.13	8.5	3.1	8.9	0.3	1.7	-0.3
2004	CHA	MLB	30	6	9	0	20	19	112.7	129	49	69	17	48%	.314	-4	1.58	5.59	5.12	5.43	9.9	3.6	5.1	1.2	5.9	1.3
2005	TOR	MLB	31	3	4	1	80	0	57.0	54	25	43	2	60%	.297	9	1.39	3.32	3.77	3.45	8.5	3.9	6.8	0.3	12.9	0.7
2006	*TOR*	*MLB*	*32*	*3*	*3*	*2*	*56*	*1*	*53.0*	*58*	*20*	*36*	*5*	*53%*	*.310*	*-6*	*1.47*	*4.55*	*4.56*	*5.23*	*9.5*	*3.4*	*6.0*	*0.9*	*5.5*	*0.5*

Breakout: 24%   *Improve: 43%*   *Collapse: 30%*   *Attrition: 22%*   Comparables: *Ron Perranoski, Gary Lavelle, Sparky Lyle*

The least-publicized of the middle-class free agents signed by the Jays before the 2005 season, Schoeneweis cashed checks totaling $2.5 million while laboring in the coveted role of LOOGY. He held fellow southpaws to .188/.260/.241, so he did his job, but $44,000 an inning for a highly limited performer is a pretty expensive luxury item. He'll do it again next year for an extra $250,000. In some respect, this is the American dream: to make more while working less.

JUSTIN SPEIER   **Bats: R Throws: R**   Height: 6′ 4″   Weight: 200   Born: November 6, 1973   Age: 32

YEAR	TM	LVL	AGE	W	L	SV	G	GS	IP	H	BB	SO	HR	GB%	BABIP	STUFF	WHIP	ERA	PERA	EQERA	EQH9	EQBB9	EQSO9	EQHR9	VORP	WXRL
2003	COL	MLB	29	3	1	9	72	0	73.3	73	23	66	11	38%	.300	2	1.31	4.05	4.52	4.03	8.9	2.6	7.2	1.2	10.8	1.9
2004	TOR	MLB	30	3	8	7	62	0	69.0	61	25	52	8	36%	.272	2	1.25	3.91	4.33	3.67	8.4	3.0	6.4	0.9	17.1	-0.2
2005	TOR	MLB	31	3	2	0	65	0	66.7	48	15	56	10	33%	.216	9	0.94	2.56	4.04	2.64	7.5	2.1	7.8	1.3	23.0	1.0
2006	*TOR*	*MLB*	*32*	*3*	*3*	*3*	*55*	*0*	*61.7*	*61*	*16*	*47*	*10*	*36%*	*.277*	*2*	*1.25*	*4.07*	*4.09*	*4.13*	*8.5*	*2.4*	*6.7*	*1.3*	*10.6*	*0.9*

Breakout: 13%   *Improve: 25%*   *Collapse: 42%*   *Attrition: 16%*   Comparables: *Steve Reed, Rick Aguilera, Stan Belinda*

Just behind Frasor as the Jays' best reliever based on Fair Run Average. In all likelihood, Speier posted his career-best ERA thanks to a good amount of luck. He still gives up the long ball too often, but there are certainly worse relievers out there.

JOSH TOWERS
Bats: R Throws: R   Height: 6' 1" Weight: 180 Born: February 26, 1977   Age: 29

YEAR	TM	LVL	AGE	W	L	SV	G	GS	IP	H	BB	SO	HR	GB%	BABIP	STUFF	WHIP	ERA	PERA	EQERA	EQH9	EQBB9	EQSO9	EQHR9	VORP	WXRL
2003	SYR	AAA	26	5	7	0	21	20	132.7	133	20	76	10	—	.276	0	1.15	3.32	4.70	4.35	9.5	1.7	3.9	1.1	17.8	—
2003	TOR	MLB	26	8	1	1	14	8	64.3	67	7	42	15	43%	.267	-2	1.15	4.48	5.20	4.36	9.4	1.0	5.8	2.0	10.0	1.8
2004	TOR	MLB	27	9	9	0	21	21	116.3	148	26	51	16	49%	.322	-3	1.50	5.11	4.84	4.84	10.7	1.8	3.6	1.1	12.1	2.2
2005	TOR	MLB	28	13	12	0	33	33	208.7	237	29	112	24	45%	.306	10	1.27	3.71	4.22	4.39	9.9	1.2	4.8	1.0	35.2	4.2
2006	*TOR*	*MLB*	*29*	*11*	*10*	*0*	*29*	*29*	*180.3*	*205*	*32*	*91*	*25*	*46%*	*.295*	*6*	*1.31*	*4.44*	*4.48*	*4.63*	*9.8*	*1.6*	*4.4*	*1.1*	*23.4*	*3.7*

Breakout: 16% Improve: 46% Collapse: 15% Attrition: 2%   Comparables: Tomokazu Ohka, Vern Ruhle, Brian Lawrence

Towers's lone outstanding skill, the thing that keeps him in clover, is that minuscule walk rate. Every now and then a Brad Radke turns in a sub-4.00 ERA, but that kind of performance repeats about as often as "Two and a Half Men" deserves an Emmy. Pitchers like Towers don't overpower hitters, so they challenge them to put the ball in play and rely heavily on their defenses. With pitchers generally unable to exert that much control over where the ball goes, this strategy doesn't always pay off over an extended period of time. Sometimes their defenses turn in a particularly great year for them, but like the vagaries of getting run support, these things come and go, and a pitcher like Towers can't count on that kind assistance year after year.

JAMIE VERMILYEA
Bats: R Throws: R   Height: 6' 4" Weight: 195 Born: February 10, 1982   Age: 24

YEAR	TM	LVL	AGE	W	L	SV	G	GS	IP	H	BB	SO	HR	GB%	BABIP	STUFF	WHIP	ERA	PERA	EQERA	EQH9	EQBB9	EQSO9	EQHR9	VORP	WXRL
2004	DUN	A+	22	5	1	0	18	6	55.3	54	13	37	4	—	.298	-15	1.21	3.09	5.47	4.96	9.9	2.6	3.9	1.5	3.7	—
2004	NHP	AA	22	3	2	5	21	6	58.3	43	12	39	2	—	.241	4	0.94	2.47	3.93	4.42	8.3	2.1	4.6	0.5	7.2	—
2005	NHP	AA	23	3	3	1	27	4	65.7	67	16	52	5	56%	.318	-5	1.26	2.60	4.66	4.10	9.8	2.7	4.8	1.0	10.6	—
2005	SYR	AAA	23	3	0	0	16	4	35.3	49	11	24	6	56%	.364	-18	1.70	5.61	5.75	6.75	11.5	3.0	4.8	1.8	-4.6	—
2006	*BOS*	*MLB*	*24*	*4*	*5*	*0*	*30*	*9*	*80.0*	*94*	*24*	*43*	*9*	*54%*	*.311*	*-3*	*1.46*	*4.98*	*5.01*	*5.11*	*10.1*	*2.6*	*4.7*	*0.9*	*4.8*	*0.7*

Breakout: 14% Improve: 44% Collapse: 19% Attrition: 7%   Comparables: Tom Poholsky, Lindy McDaniel, Hipolito Pichardo

He's everything you want in a swingman/reliever role: lots of ground balls, a very low walk rate, and enough strikeouts not to raise any red flags. He should have been in the mix for the Jays' bullpen over the next year or two, but he was nabbed by Boston in the Rule 5 draft, so he'll have to take his chances in the back of Sox' pen instead.

PETE WALKER
Bats: R Throws: R   Height: 6' 2" Weight: 190 Born: April 8, 1969   Age: 37

YEAR	TM	LVL	AGE	W	L	SV	G	GS	IP	H	BB	SO	HR	GB%	BABIP	STUFF	WHIP	ERA	PERA	EQERA	EQH9	EQBB9	EQSO9	EQHR9	VORP	WXRL
2003	TOR	MLB	34	2	2	0	23	7	55.3	59	24	29	11	44%	.277	-21	1.50	4.88	6.02	4.55	9.6	3.9	4.6	1.6	6.8	0.7
2004	YKO	JPL	35	2	4	0	10	0	46.3	63	19	23	18	—	-.738	-36	1.77	6.80	7.49	6.50	11.2	3.9	3.5	2.6	-4.6	—
2005	TOR	MLB	36	6	6	2	41	4	84.0	81	33	43	10	49%	.267	-10	1.36	3.54	4.97	3.56	9.1	3.7	4.6	1.0	21.5	0.6
2006	*TOR*	*MLB*	*37*	*3*	*3*	*1*	*35*	*2*	*54.7*	*63*	*23*	*27*	*9*	*46%*	*.295*	*-21*	*1.56*	*5.27*	*5.52*	*6.07*	*10.0*	*3.8*	*4.4*	*1.3*	*2.3*	*0.2*

Breakout: 16% Improve: 35% Collapse: 45% Attrition: 37%   Comparables: Alan Levine, Doug Bair, Mike Maddux

Walker battled through years of injuries to get the majors and hasn't performed too badly. Now that he's here, he's a 37-year-old right-hander who has shown little ability to strike anyone out; Walker triumphed over adversity but is still a victim of thieving time. Yes, Virginia, the movie version of *The Natural* was a pernicious lie offering false hope of redemption, F. Scott Fitzgerald was right that there are no second acts in American lives, and the dying words of Tiny Bonham—"They're hitting me all over the field and I can't get them out"—applies more and more to each of us with every passing day. Think about that while chewing your morning corn flakes. The Jays let Walker go in what could be the last transaction of his career, but there are some terrible pitching staffs out there that will give him a shot at the 11th pitcher slot, a thin note of hope in a cruel universe.

Line Outs

Position/Player	TM	LVL	AGE	PA	R	2B	3B	HR	RBI	BB	SO	SB-CS	SPEED	BA/OBP/SLG	MLVR	EQBA/OBP/SLG	EQA	VORP
3B E. Arnold	DUN	A+	24	423	70	28	1	19	72	36	108	1-0	4.2	.274/.343/.504	.161	.220/.279/.405	.235	-2.3
1B K. Barker*	NHP	AA	29	217	18	11	1	6	27	28	42	1-2	3.9	.254/.350/.422	.112	.212/.287/.332	.221	-10.0
	SYR	AAA	29	397	58	24	1	23	87	38	89	1-0	4.4	.305/.373/.575	.290	.252/.317/.453	.263	4.7
C K. Huckaby	TOR	MLB	34	92	8	4	0	0	6	5	19	0-0	3.7	.207/.250/.253	-.437	.200/.253/.247	.187	-6.0
SS R. Tablado	NHP	AA	23	391	33	13	1	5	35	22	128	6-1	4.1	.201/.251/.284	-.272	.199/.248/.281	.194	-26.8

Pitcher	TM	LVL	AGE	W	L	SV	IP	H	BB	SO	HR	GB%	BABIP	STUFF	WHIP	ERA	PERA	EQERA	EQH9	EQBB9	EQSO9	EQHR9	VORP
S. Andrade	NHP	AA	27	3	2	3	50.3	23	16	71	3	54%	.204	5	0.78	1.97	4.40	4.20	6.6	4.2	8.2	1.0	7.0
J. Miller	SYR	AAA	27	3	1	2	50.3	39	14	56	3	47%	.283	13	1.05	2.33	3.91	3.54	7.8	3.0	7.4	0.7	11.1
I. Ramirez	NHP	AA	24	8	13	0	150.7	155	32	125	19	39%	.311	-16	1.24	4.12	5.55	5.74	10.3	2.4	5.0	1.8	-2.2
D. Romero*	DUN	A+	22	9	6	1	124.7	133	34	136	10	53%	.360	-3	1.34	3.46	4.86	5.53	10.2	3.1	6.2	1.3	0.9
R. Romero*	DUN	A+	20	1	0	0	30.7	36	7	22	2	47%	.330	-1	1.40	3.81	4.45	5.04	10.4	2.4	4.2	0.9	1.9

Eric Arnold: Had a nice power spike this year, but as a college hitter too old for his level, it's not indicative of great things to come. **Kevin Barker:** A standard issue Quadruple-A player, available at most corner stores with a big label that says "keep out of reach of contending teams." **Ken Huckaby:** You could save yourself a lot of time by just flipping over to John Flaherty or Eddie Perez's comment and changing the relevant names. **Raul Tablado** posted one of the ugliest lines you'll ever see, from the strikeouts to the lack of walks to the terrible everything else.

Steve Andrade: Always old for his level, Andrade's peripherals have been consistently excellent. A perfect cheap add-on to shore up a bullpen, but it will be with the Padres after being flipped around through the Rule 5 draft. **Justin Miller:** The conversion to relieving appears to have worked for Miller, but his future as a fireman is with another organization. **Ismael Ramirez:** Old for his first taste of Double-A, but it was a success. If he can stop leaving pitches up in the zone, he'll be worth a look. **Davis Romero:** Wafer-thin Panamanian lefty, the only numbers not to like are his height and weight (5′10″, 140), which will continue to inspire doubt until he proves himself at higher levels. **Ricardo Romero:** A consensus back-of-the-rotation starter taken sixth overall in 2005, there is no truth to the rumor that his nickname is "Overdraft."

Los Nationales

When is a baseball team's birthday?

The Nationals might have been born on February 12, 2002, when the Expos officially became wards of Major League Baseball. You might consider it to be September 29, 2004, since that was the day that baseball and Mayor Anthony Williams made the announcement that the Expos were coming to Washington. There's November 22, 2004, when, choosing between Williams's desire to honor the Negro League's Grays and Bud Selig's reactionary preference for the Senators, the team announced its compromise name, the Nationals. Maybe December 21, 2004 is the historic date, when Williams tentatively hammered out a stadium deal with a fractious city council. Or it might have been the next day, December 22, because that's when MLB allowed the Nationals to resume operations, and stopped threatening, if they didn't get that stadium vote, to move the franchise that hadn't even arrived yet to a parking lot to be named later.

Given the fitful, super slo-mo launch of the Nationals franchise, perhaps the best choice for Day One would be to tab November 2, 2004, the day that Jim Bowden was hired to be the ballclub's GM. Why that day? First, because it has nothing to do with the already bitter relationship between baseball and the city, and second, few men would be quite so hyperactive as Bowden, whatever his many faults, in transforming the transplanted Expos from "Ballclub: Players Included, Various Shapes and Sizes, Contents May Have Shifted in Shipping, Handle With Care" to the newborn Washington Nationals.

Bowden might have seemed an unlikely choice. In his previous GM job, he'd inherited a Reds franchise that had won the World Series in 1990, and he'd helped run it into the ground. Given Marge Schott' penury and Carl Lindner's interference, and both owner's shallow pockets, you could ask whether Bowden had been the architect or merely the handmaiden of failure. Coming to Washington, Bowden was handed the most difficult GM's job in the game. What little the organization had going for it under the Lorias had been been almost entirely frittered away during former GM Omar Minaya's three-year audition for his next job. Many baseball lifers might have taken the slow road to credibility, focusing on a message of "we're just taking this one decade at a time," but Bowden, the original transactions junkie, may well have been the per-

NATIONALS PROSPECTUS

2005 record: 81–81; Fifth place, NL East

Pythagenport record: 77–85

Runs scored per game: 3.94 (16th in NL)

Runs allowed per game: 4.15 (4th in NL)

Team EqA: .254 (13th in NL)

2005 Batters Age: 29.9 (8th youngest in NL)

2005 Pitchers Age: 29.5 (8th oldest in NL)

Ballpark: RFK Stadium; Severe pitcher's park; Park Factor of 0.941

2005: The Inaugural Nationals club started off in exciting fashion before falling to earth.

2006: High risks without high yields ended Jim Bowden's days in Cincinnati, so gear up for deja vu all over again.

fect fit: He gave the Washington metro area a taste of what baseball fans everywhere take for granted, a hot stove league warmed up by juicy rumors, consummated trades, and high-profile free agent signings.

Bowden's first major act was to buy the left side of his infield, giving veteran third baseman Vinny Castilla a two-year, $6.2 million deal, and shortstop Cristian Guzman a four-year, $16.8 million deal. Beyond the money, both players would cost the Nats their 2nd and 3rd round picks in the 2005 draft, helping to keep the cupboard bare in an already shallow farm system. Sadly, both signings reflected on Bowden's vocal rejection of past experience. Castilla was touted as a slugger who'd just come off of winning the NL RBI title . . . without any mention that it happened in Coors Field. Dial back to October 1999, when Bowden traded for aging Rockies slugger Fonzie Bichette, only to discover how quickly an altitude-inflated performance can come back down to earth. Similarly, mistaking Guzman for one of the game's premier shortstops, despite his declining performances as a Twin, seemed natural to the man who'd similarly overvalued Pokey Reese in Cincinnati. That said, there were some good ideas that were acted upon: taking a flyer on Esteban Loaiza was a reasonable risk, and while trading for noted angry man Jose Guillen cost the Nats a youngster with future Guillen-like potential in Juan Rivera, it gave them the original article to make a good first impression with.

Ever hungry for venues in which to get and give ballplayers, Bowden dove into the Rule 5 draft, and the choice of Tony Blanco from the Reds made sense. But by also dredging up failed Jays prospect Ty Godwin, he blew a 40-man roster spot for the rest of the year, and highlighted another one of Bowden's foibles in roster management. In his mania for giving used-up toolsy players second chances, he would trade young outfielder Jerry Owens for Alex Escobar; the White Sox sent a thank you note. He also discarded Anderson Machado to Boston; apparently having a homegrown shortstop who might outhit Guzman was too frightening a possibility. Escobar, Michael Coleman, Wil Cordero, Jeffrey Hammonds, Carlos Baerga, George Arias, the list of people Bowden dug up reads like a who's who of '90s washouts. None would add value to the inaugural Nats squad. Filling out the rosters of the Nats' ill-starred minor league affiliates was one thing, but turning to this lot wasn't doing anyone any favors.

Still, the busy winter had helped generate enthusiasm in a market hungry for baseball. Surprising industry insiders who'd predicted that Washington wouldn't really be an improvement on Montreal, ticket sales boomed, and after a number of understandable hiccups, RFK Stadium evolved into a stable venue for a normal ballpark experience. Coming into the season, Bowden and Frank Robinson could field a team laden with young veterans, and if the Nats weren't expected to contend, they weren't expected to be the Devil Rays either.

Then the season started, and the Nats started winning games, and particularly a lot of one-run games. Whether you want to credit that to heady enthusiasm or a pitching staff getting quality work from Livan Hernandez, John Patterson, and Esteban Loaiza in the rotation, and which could also count on a pen fronted by closer Chad Cordero to seal the deal, doesn't matter. The Nats were the sort of ballclub that could win tight ballgames in pitcher-friendly RFK, and Robinson's charges sprinted out to a 52-34 record through July 8, a direct result of their improbable 24-8 performance in one-run contests. The worm started turning, though, as the Nats lost a pair of games by a single run to the Phillies in the last weekend before the All-Star break.

Nevertheless, the Nationals were in first place, 2.5 games ahead of the Braves, but the Cinderella story was coming to an end. After the All-Star break, the Nats lost an incredible eight one-run games in July's remaining 17 games. The team would finish 30-31 in one-run games on the year; they'd achieved a normal distribution of wins and losses in one-run games, they'd gotten there in spectacularly uneven fashion. (See table 1.)

Bowden, however, could not let go. In his scramble to reacquire legitimacy as a GM by keeping the Nats in the running, he frenziedly played out his short deck. After fragile second baseman Jose Vidro broke down, Bowden sought a patch and traded from a purported source of strength, dealing starter Tomo Ohka to Milwaukee for second sacker Junior Spivey. On the same day, he claimed starting pitcher Ryan Drese, and asserted that the Nats had a net gain. This was doubly wrong-headed: while Ohka had his problems with manager Frank Robinson, Drese is not somebody you want in a major league rotation, and claiming him on waivers meant the Nats have to pay $1.8 million owed Drese for 2006. Nor was Spivey equal to Vidro's role in the lineup; Bowden might have pretended he'd gotten the player who'd been a slugger in Arizona, but doing so just betrayed his blind eye for park effects, and instead, he got a barely adequate temp. Operating with a system already short of adequate help ready to fill in on the major league roster, Bowden somehow managed to discard both Sunny Kim and Claudio Vargas, making a shorthanded team even more so. Bowden's blindness to his own mistakes reached an appropriate denouement when he traded for Rockies slugger Preston Wilson; if the failures of Bichette or Castilla meant nothing to him, why not make the same mistake thrice? The Nats would poke along to finish with a .500 record.

Fleeting delusions of grandeur aside, the franchise's biggest problem is the absence of an owner. An owner wouldn't let the team effectively sit still while the team's GM spends more time trying to wangle interviews with the Dodgers or the Red Sox. In this, Bowden's personal activities and inattention to his job before the winter meetings revealed him to be little better than a front office merc, and possibly no different from Minaya on the question of whether he served the team or the team served him. Even more important for the team's long-term future, an owner would also have to be on point in the stadium and stadium lease negotiations, building bridges with local politicians instead of offending them with petulant rhetoric that baseball either gets what it wants or it'll put the team in Pocatello by Seligian fiat.

TABLE 1. ROLLER COASTERS END WHERE THEY BEGIN: NATS MONTH-BY-MONTH RECORD IN ONE-RUN GAMES

Before ASB		After ASB	
April	3-2	July	0-8
May	8-4	August	4-8
June	9-1	September	2-5
July	4-3		
Total	24-10	Total	6-21

Bowden fitfully addressed some of the team's needs over the winter. Having lost Esteban Loaiza to free agency, the GM dealt from depth again, swapping out Vinny Castilla (expendable with the quick ascent of Ryan Zimmerman to the bigs) to acquire Brian Lawrence from the Padres. Lawrence might not replace Loaiza, but he should at least be a durable mediocrity behind Livan Hernandez and John Patterson. Rounding out the rotation with Ramon Ortiz and another go-round with oft-injured Tony Armas Jr. highlights that the rotation will be less a source of strength than merely good enough to get by in RFK's forgivingly wide-open spaces.

Determined to make a splash and add a slugger at the winter meetings, yet incapable of signing one, Bowden again turned to trading, picking up second baseman Alfonso Soriano for a package headlined by star outfielder Brad Wilkerson. Perhaps predictably, Soriano is neither of the things Bowden has claimed that he'll be, neither a true slugger nor the likely Opening Day left fielder. Soriano is yet another park-generated power source with stats fattened up by hitting in Texas. Pretending for the moment that Soriano might hit better than the man who's hit .260/.303/.465 on the road over the last three years, why deal one quality outfielder in Wilkerson and block another (Ryan Church)? Bowden managed to not solve a problem he didn't have, and create a new one in the process. Soriano angrily announced after the deal that he is not an outfielder, and will demand a trade rather than move to left. Although we're given to understating the importance of outfield defense in the corners, Soriano may be right: he's not much for leaving his feet afield, and Derek Jeter would make a point of showing that Soriano couldn't or wouldn't leap for throws. How's that going to play in the outfield, when the difference between a decision to jump or not to jump can mean the difference between an extra-base hit and an out?

If there's one thing that's definitely getting better, it's the team's player development program. In this, scouting director Dana Brown and his crew have been doing an outstanding job of finding talent to stock the organization. The first round of the last three drafts have produced the team's closer (Chad Cordero) and third baseman (Ryan Zimmerman), and Brown picks like Bill Bray, Clint Everts, Larry Broadway, and Collin Balester all have considerable promise. The club is also making a good faith effort to ramp up Ismael Cruz's Latin American scouting program, and if they failed to get an instructional league set up in the Dominican Republic over the winter, at least they're not waiting on a new owner before adding one.

These developments are by far the more critical ones, because it is the farm that will give new Nationals fans a reason to care, and not the activities of the man doomed to repeat history instead of learn from it. Bowden helped generate a honeymoon that temporarily masked the more squalid considerations involving the new stadium and the relationship between the city and the baseball industry, but honeymoons don't last. You don't find the words "Bowden" and "responsibility" in the same sentence very often, but in this his responsibility is to the organization's long-term future, and not to enhancing his legend as the inheritor of Trader Frank Lane's legacy for dealing for the deal's sake.

HITTERS

CARLOS BAERGA   PH   **Bats: B Throws: R**   Height: 5′ 11″ Weight: 215 Born: November 4, 1968   Age: 37

YEAR	TM	LVL	AGE	PA	R	2B	3B	HR	RBI	BB	SO	SB	CS	SPEED	BA	OBP	SLG	MLVR	EQBA	EQOBP	EQSLG	EQA	VORP	DEFENSE			
2003	ARI	MLB	34	230	31	13	0	4	39	18	20	1	1	4.4	.343	.396	.464	.196	.327	.380	.439	.286	15.7	13-1B	1	13-2B	0
2004	ARI	MLB	35	94	6	2	0	2	11	6	12	0	0	2.4	.235	.309	.329	-.187	.224	.290	.318	.216	-1.6				
2005	WAS	MLB	36	173	18	7	0	2	19	7	17	0	0	4.2	.253	.318	.335	-.113	.261	.320	.348	.236	-1.2	11-3B	0		
2006	*WAS*	*MLB*	*37*	*119*	*9*	*5*	*0*	*1*	*12*	*6*	*15*	*0*	*0*	*4.4*	*.254*	*.314*	*.332*	*-.179*	*.266*	*.323*	*.359*	*.231*	*-0.2*	*32-1B*	*-1*		

Breakout: 8%   Improve: 26%   Collapse: 47%   Attrition: 47%   Comparables: Jose Vizcaino, Larry Biittner, Dave Philley

One of the less fortunate gifts of the '90s to the present was the arrival of the Lenny Harris Generation on baseball's benches, of which Baerga's a proud lodge member. You know them, but you don't fear them: bench players who don't have power, can't run or play a position, and are at best amiable sorts in the clubhouse. It's a big step down from the '80s, when you'd find Rusty Staub or Darrell Evans on the pine, or at least a Dave Bergman or Greg Gross.

GARY BENNETT   C   Bats: R Throws: R   Height: 6′ 0″   Weight: 208   Born: April 17, 1972   Age: 34

YEAR	TM	LVL	AGE	PA	R	2B	3B	HR	RBI	BB	SO	SB	CS	SPEED	BA	OBP	SLG	MLVR	EQBA	EQOBP	EQSLG	EQA	VORP	DEFENSE
2003	SDN	MLB	31	335	26	15	0	2	42	24	48	3	0	4.3	.238	.296	.306	-.205	.248	.306	.322	.227	-5.3	85-C -10
2004	MIL	MLB	32	246	18	14	0	3	20	22	32	1	0	3.6	.224	.297	.329	-.190	.219	.293	.320	.222	-3.3	65-C -6
2005	WAS	MLB	33	225	11	7	0	1	21	21	37	0	1	2.8	.221	.298	.271	-.253	.229	.306	.289	.219	-6.6	58-C -4
2006	SLN	MLB	34	177	15	7	0	2	16	14	27	0	0	3.8	.240	.309	.320	-.211	.241	.310	.332	.219	-2.4	45-C -2

Breakout: 41%   Improve: 56%   Collapse: 27%   Attrition: 44%   Comparables: Danny Sheaffer, Mike Matheny, Rick Cerone

Nichols's Law of Catcher Defense observed the inverse relationship of a catcher's defensive rep and his hitting prowess. Bennett's employers have signed him in this very expectation, that someone this useless at the plate must be pretty good behind it. Sadly, the Nats learned what six teams had in the previous four years, that Bennett's a two-way exercise in futility. The Cards will make it eight in six.

TONY BLANCO   3B/OF   Bats: R Throws: R   Height: 6′ 1″   Weight: 175   Born: November 10, 1981   Age: 24

YEAR	TM	LVL	AGE	PA	R	2B	3B	HR	RBI	BB	SO	SB	CS	SPEED	BA	OBP	SLG	MLVR	EQBA	EQOBP	EQSLG	EQA	VORP	DEFENSE
2003	POT	A+	21	278	33	17	2	10	49	26	62	0	0	4.1	.266	.338	.477	.146	.237	.298	.453	.256	-0.2	15-1B -1
2004	POT	A+	22	258	42	10	0	17	47	27	66	2	0	3.9	.306	.403	.588	.399	.263	.345	.513	.288	12.8	33-1B -3
2004	CHT	AA	22	237	25	8	1	12	31	15	53	0	0	3.4	.245	.300	.455	.007	.221	.267	.411	.230	-10.4	46-LF -4
2005	NWO	AAA	23	68	7	4	0	2	14	2	13	1	0	3.1	.281	.294	.438	-.026	.269	.283	.412	.243	0.6	15-3B 1
2005	WAS	MLB	23	65	7	3	0	1	7	2	19	1	0	6.2	.177	.215	.274	-.424	.177	.215	.274	.179	-4.9	
2006	WAS	MLB	24	233	24	13	1	9	31	16	56	1	1	4.2	.244	.302	.436	-.069	.255	.311	.471	.256	4.9	58-LF -2

Breakout: 38%   Improve: 60%   Collapse: 28%   Attrition: 37%   Comparables: Dick Sharon, Dale Berra, Andres Mora

While handing out playing time to a scrubby bench, Frank Robinson managed to keep this Rule 5 pick tucked away in a dark place, using the same logic of an old Italian with his home-brewed wine: let it sit long enough and it might just become palatable. He's still young enough to have a career, but he'll be better off shaking off the cobwebs and getting 500 at-bats in Triple-A.

LARRY BROADWAY   1B   Bats: L Throws: L   Height: 6′ 4″   Weight: 230   Born: December 17, 1980   Age: 25

YEAR	TM	LVL	AGE	PA	R	2B	3B	HR	RBI	BB	SO	SB	CS	SPEED	BA	OBP	SLG	MLVR	EQBA	EQOBP	EQSLG	EQA	VORP	DEFENSE
2003	SAV	A	22	340	56	25	4	14	51	44	70	3	4	4.8	.307	.400	.566	.426	.265	.339	.486	.278	14.3	80-1B 11
2003	BRV	A+	22	98	8	7	1	1	7	18	20	0	1	3.9	.224	.367	.382	.116	.223	.348	.410	.267	0.6	20-1B 2
2003	HAR	AA	22	89	13	3	0	5	18	7	15	0	0	3.3	.321	.371	.551	.315	.284	.335	.502	.283	4.2	19-1B 2
2004	HAR	AA	23	552	69	20	0	22	71	68	102	2	3	3.2	.271	.362	.452	.109	.246	.330	.412	.257	1.1	121-1B 7
2005	HAR	AA	24	207	29	14	0	12	24	17	37	0	0	3.6	.269	.329	.538	.187	.232	.292	.463	.255	-0.2	45-1B -5
2005	NWO	AAA	24	64	4	3	0	0	5	7	17	2	0	4.5	.193	.281	.246	-.409	.178	.256	.213	.186	-8.0	15-1B -1
2006	WAS	MLB	25	396	42	17	1	14	50	38	84	1	1	4.0	.234	.312	.405	-.100	.245	.321	.437	.253	1.3	95-1B 1

Breakout: 23%   Improve: 52%   Collapse: 21%   Attrition: 12%   Comparables: Sid Bream, Kevin Barker, Mo Vaughn

The former slugging prospect lost much of the year to problems with his right knee, struggling to keep it planted through his swing. He was sent to the AFL to work on learning to trust it. If he can, he's fine insurance for Nick Johnson's next injury.

MARLON BYRD   OF   Bats: R Throws: R   Height: 6′ 0″   Weight: 220   Born: August 30, 1977   Age: 28

YEAR	TM	LVL	AGE	PA	R	2B	3B	HR	RBI	BB	SO	SB	CS	SPEED	BA	OBP	SLG	MLVR	EQBA	EQOBP	EQSLG	EQA	VORP	DEFENSE
2003	PHI	MLB	25	549	86	28	4	7	45	44	94	11	1	6.5	.303	.366	.418	.106	.303	.365	.423	.278	28.1	124-CF 0
2004	SWB	AAA	26	167	13	11	1	2	17	10	18	2	3	3.9	.263	.323	.388	-.075	.239	.293	.351	.225	-4.0	37-CF -1
2004	PHI	MLB	26	376	48	13	2	5	33	22	68	2	2	5.0	.228	.287	.321	-.239	.227	.284	.319	.213	-13.3	83-CF -4
2005	NWO	AAA	27	92	19	6	0	5	11	9	7	4	1	4.1	.407	.478	.667	.808	.374	.431	.576	.335	15.1	19-CF -1
2005	WAS	MLB	27	239	20	15	2	2	26	18	47	5	1	5.0	.264	.318	.380	-.050	.269	.324	.402	.257	1.3	43-LF 3
2006	WAS	MLB	28	280	31	14	2	5	28	21	48	4	2	5.1	.263	.324	.386	-.084	.275	.333	.417	.253	5.6	69-CF 0

Breakout: 15%   Improve: 41%   Collapse: 39%   Attrition: 31%   Comparables: Tracy Jones, Gabe Kapler, Wendell Magee

If you're starting to think that bad ballplayers appeared on the Nats' bench like so many roster mushrooms, you wouldn't be far off. But to be fair to Byrd, he's just not the prospect people thought he was after 2003. He doesn't have that much pop, and in his hack-happiness he virtually comes out of his shoes on every pitch. As a fifth outfielder he's not all bad, but, like Michael Tucker, he's also mostly harmless.

JAMEY CARROLL　　　INF　　**Bats: R Throws: R**　　Height: 5′ 10″　Weight: 170　Born: February 18, 1974　Age: 32

YEAR	TM	LVL	AGE	PA	R	2B	3B	HR	RBI	BB	SO	SB	CS	SPEED	BA	OBP	SLG	MLVR	EQBA	EQOBP	EQSLG	EQA	VORP	DEFENSE		
2003	MON	MLB	29	251	31	10	1	1	10	19	39	5	2	5.2	.260	.323	.326	-.203	.252	.315	.317	.231	-4.3	48-3B	6	
2004	MON	MLB	30	254	36	14	2	0	16	32	21	5	1	6.0	.289	.378	.372	.051	.280	.370	.353	.265	11.2	39-2B	-5	
2005	WAS	MLB	31	345	44	8	1	0	22	34	55	3	4	5.5	.251	.333	.284	-.174	.264	.344	.299	.235	-6.5	48-2B 2	27-SS	-1
2006 WAS		MLB	32	222	23	8	1	0	14	21	31	3	1	4.8	.242	.319	.299	-.219	.253	.329	.323	.228	0.6	56-2B	0	

Breakout: 16%　Improve: 31%　Collapse: 46%　Attrition: 40%　Comparables: Junior Kennedy, Stan Rojek, Bob Bailor

Carroll didn't exactly graduate to Babe Laufenberg status for being the guy that Washington fans keep waiting and wondering about. Because he had the advantage of not being Cristian Guzman, he did actually get to play quite a bit, and did about as well as could be expected. He got on base adequately, played a solid second, and basically reminded people that he makes a nice reserve that needs to remain a reserve.

VINNY CASTILLA　　　3B　　**Bats: R Throws: R**　　Height: 6′ 1″　Weight: 205　Born: July 4, 1967　Age: 38

YEAR	TM	LVL	AGE	PA	R	2B	3B	HR	RBI	BB	SO	SB	CS	SPEED	BA	OBP	SLG	MLVR	EQBA	EQOBP	EQSLG	EQA	VORP	DEFENSE	
2003	ATL	MLB	35	577	65	28	3	22	76	26	86	1	2	4.0	.277	.310	.461	.046	.273	.306	.461	.259	21.9	141-3B	-6
2004	COL	MLB	36	648	93	43	3	35	131	51	113	0	0	4.2	.271	.332	.535	.097	.250	.312	.499	.272	22.4	145-3B	10
2005	WAS	MLB	37	548	53	36	1	12	66	43	82	4	2	4.2	.253	.319	.403	-.018	.259	.326	.418	.257	6.8	130-3B	8
2006 SDN		MLB	38	369	37	19	1	9	47	27	60	2	1	4.1	.258	.318	.405	-.072	.268	.326	.437	.254	8.9	88-3B	1

Breakout: 17%　Improve: 34%　Collapse: 32%　Attrition: 22%　Comparables: Gary Gaetti, Tim Wallach, Jeff Conine

Like Willie Nelson in *Barbarosa*, Castilla's the tough hombre who's done things his way and become a legend. Against fastballs in his prime, no hitter was quicker on the trigger or more merciless. Castilla has done a superb job of retaining his value this late into his career, but the time has come where you have to ask what's left: the power's already fading, which leaves you with good citizenship and the occasionally nimble play at third. He won't have to be a key hitter for the Padres, not that he could be.

KORY CASTO　　　3B　　**Bats: L Throws: R**　　Height: 6′ 1″　Weight: 200　Born: December 8, 1981　Age: 24

YEAR	TM	LVL	AGE	PA	R	2B	3B	HR	RBI	BB	SO	SB	CS	SPEED	BA	OBP	SLG	MLVR	EQBA	EQOBP	EQSLG	EQA	VORP	DEFENSE		
2003	VER	A-	21	292	26	14	2	4	28	30	47	1	1	3.5	.239	.322	.355	.027	.217	.281	.341	.219	-35.7	41-RF -3	25-LF	-2
2004	SAV	A	22	525	67	35	4	16	88	31	70	1	2	3.7	.286	.337	.474	.157	.251	.288	.406	.237	3.3	110-3B	-15	
2005	POT	A+	23	594	86	36	4	22	90	84	98	6	3	5.3	.290	.394	.510	.251	.245	.330	.414	.259	17.3	131-3B	21	
2006 WAS		MLB	24	478	47	22	2	10	52	38	94	2	1	4.4	.226	.292	.356	-.203	.236	.300	.384	.229	-5.4	113-3B	1	

Breakout: 9%　Improve: 28%　Collapse: 37%　Attrition: 8%　Comparables: Corey Slavik, Jon Hamilton, Jess Graham

Casto's made extraordinary progress at third base, going from a rough-edged conversion in 2004 to his smooth glovework of '05. His arm was never going to be a problem, since he has a cannon, and he's put to rest any concerns that he'd lack the lateral flexibility or suffer other lasting problems from having his eye socket shattered by a ball in his third game at third in '04. The question is whether or not he'll hit well enough to stick, if he can build on the progress he made in '05, if he's going to become . . . well, somebody the Nats can trade. It isn't like Zimmerman's going anywhere, after all, and Casto won't be a young player for Double-A this year.

RYAN CHURCH　　　OF　　**Bats: L Throws: L**　　Height: 6′ 1″　Weight: 190　Born: October 14, 1978　Age: 27

YEAR	TM	LVL	AGE	PA	R	2B	3B	HR	RBI	BB	SO	SB	CS	SPEED	BA	OBP	SLG	MLVR	EQBA	EQOBP	EQSLG	EQA	VORP	DEFENSE		
2003	AKR	AA	24	409	47	17	3	13	52	32	64	4	3	4.6	.261	.325	.429	.015	.227	.282	.381	.229	-17.9	82-RF 6	16-CF	0
2004	EDM	AAA	25	407	74	29	8	17	79	51	62	0	1	5.0	.346	.430	.622	.530	.310	.390	.525	.308	33.2	74-RF	0	
2004	MON	MLB	25	70	6	1	0	1	6	7	16	0	0	3.6	.175	.257	.238	-.426	.175	.257	.238	.184	-6.4			
2005	WAS	MLB	26	300	41	15	3	9	42	24	70	3	2	5.7	.287	.353	.466	.157	.292	.355	.491	.285	15.3	37-LF 1	15-RF	1
2006 WAS		MLB	27	284	33	14	2	9	36	23	59	2	1	5.2	.260	.327	.433	-.019	.272	.337	.467	.266	8.8	70-LF	1	

Breakout: 13%　Improve: 32%　Collapse: 40%　Attrition: 34%　Comparables: Leron Lee, Ben Oglivie, Troy O'Leary

Whether it's a matter of not recognizing that Church is in his prime right now, or that he's a sweet power source, the Nats seem to be overlooking what they have here. Between the additions of Soriano and Tucker, the nonsensical touts of Brandon Watson, or the ill-considered pursuit of Sammy Sosa, it's as if nobody in this organization wants to get to Church on time. Left to his own devices, he'd be an effective and cheap solution for a cost-conscious club looking for a right fielder. Although the Nats have Guillen, there's no penalty for having a strong arm in left. If he gets 400 at-bats, he'll outhit that projection.

DEIVI CRUZ   INF   Bats: R Throws: R   Height: 6' 0"   Weight: 184   Born: November 6, 1972   Age: 33

YEAR	TM	LVL	AGE	PA	R	2B	3B	HR	RBI	BB	SO	SB	CS	SPEED	BA	OBP	SLG	MLVR	EQBA	EQOBP	EQSLG	EQA	VORP	DEFENSE		
2003	BAL	MLB	30	565	61	24	2	14	65	13	49	1	2	4.5	.250	.269	.378	-.184	.252	.277	.384	.227	-1.2	142-SS	-5	
2004	SFN	MLB	31	423	46	30	2	7	55	17	32	1	3	4.2	.292	.322	.431	.002	.287	.316	.422	.252	13.2	89-SS	3	
2005	SFN	MLB	32	219	26	10	1	5	19	10	31	0	1	4.6	.268	.301	.397	-.070	.263	.300	.402	.239	1.8	29-2B -1	14-SS	3
2005	WAS	MLB	32	53	2	1	0	0	1	1	3	0	0	3.7	.255	.283	.275	-.254	.269	.296	.288	.208	-1.7			
2006	*SLN*	*MLB*	*33*	*217*	*23*	*11*	*1*	*3*	*24*	*9*	*23*	*0*	*1*	*4.3*	*.272*	*.306*	*.383*	*-.113*	*.273*	*.307*	*.397*	*.234*	*3.6*	*54-SS*	*0*	

Breakout: 21% Improve: 42% Collapse: 41% Attrition: 40%   Comparables: Billy Ripken, Rafael Ramirez, Glenn Beckert

After flopping as a regular shortstop and getting a bit flabby, Cruz has turned himself around as a useful utility infielder. On the Cardinals, he's in a pretty good situation for a veteran reserve: he's a plausible challenger for playing time at second base, and if anything happens to David Eckstein, he'll get those at-bats.

FRANK DIAZ   CF   Bats: R Throws: R   Height: 6' 2"   Weight: 180   Born: October 6, 1983   Age: 22

YEAR	TM	LVL	AGE	PA	R	2B	3B	HR	RBI	BB	SO	SB	CS	SPEED	BA	OBP	SLG	MLVR	EQBA	EQOBP	EQSLG	EQA	VORP	DEFENSE		
2003	SAV	A	19	467	63	28	4	7	49	15	73	19	4	6.9	.270	.298	.400	.049	.254	.270	.390	.230	-20.5	118-RF	9	
2004	BRV	A+	20	459	46	17	8	8	57	31	76	16	6	6.5	.242	.303	.380	-.013	.227	.275	.365	.227	-28.0	100-RF 8	14-CF	0
2005	POT	A+	21	584	85	45	5	16	74	20	67	14	9	5.9	.312	.342	.498	.181	.275	.295	.433	.247	9.6	124-CF	12	
2006	*WAS*	*MLB*	*22*	*521*	*55*	*31*	*3*	*9*	*55*	*21*	*81*	*8*	*4*	*5.1*	*.251*	*.287*	*.385*	*-.157*	*.263*	*.295*	*.415*	*.235*	*-0.3*	*123-CF*	*5*	

Breakout: 25% Improve: 51% Collapse: 21% Attrition: 7%   Comparables: Ray Sadler, Andy Burress, Nic Jackson

Diaz has become the organization's "it" outfielder after impressing everyone with his progress in the field and with his shortened, quicker stroke at the plate. Although Diaz's sudden improvement might seem dramatic, he actually got it going at the plate in winter ball in Venezuela between the '04 and '05 seasons. However, as you can see, a good amount of his seeming improvement is due to his being a year older and having had the advantages of hitting in Potomac while repeating the level.

TY GODWIN   OF   Bats: L Throws: R   Height: 6' 0"   Weight: 200   Born: July 10, 1979   Age: 26

YEAR	TM	LVL	AGE	PA	R	2B	3B	HR	RBI	BB	SO	SB	CS	SPEED	BA	OBP	SLG	MLVR	EQBA	EQOBP	EQSLG	EQA	VORP	DEFENSE		
2003	DUN	A+	23	359	52	16	0	1	33	29	39	20	7	6.3	.273	.348	.332	.016	.234	.293	.303	.219	-16.4	94-CF	3	
2003	NHV	AA	23	128	20	6	3	1	13	3	27	6	1	8.1	.309	.328	.431	.113	.294	.313	.416	.254	0.1	27-RF	-4	
2004	NHP	AA	24	580	85	21	7	6	40	52	110	42	12	8.1	.253	.326	.355	-.057	.240	.302	.331	.232	-31.4	82-LF 4	29-RF	3
2005	NWO	AAA	25	555	83	22	6	9	48	50	77	22	12	6.2	.321	.387	.443	.197	.310	.366	.415	.271	15.3	105-LF -9	15-CF	0
2006	*WAS*	*MLB*	*26*	*455*	*53*	*19*	*3*	*4*	*35*	*33*	*79*	*15*	*5*	*5.8*	*.256*	*.315*	*.344*	*-.160*	*.269*	*.324*	*.371*	*.239*	*-2.8*	*108-LF*	*-2*	

Breakout: 11% Improve: 38% Collapse: 34% Attrition: 17%   Comparables: Paul Dade, Jason Ellison, Carlos Valderrama

The scouting world likes to play Alibi Ike for certain players, and Godwin's one of them. They'll try to fob you off with another explanation that it was a matter of his trying too hard or that he had vision problems one year, and hasten to mention how he's got more tools in his belt than Batman. But for all the empty compliments, Godwin still isn't a worthwhile use of a 40-man roster spot. Beating the bushes turns up dozens of Godwins, all angling for their shot at a fifth outfielder's job.

JOSE GUILLEN   RF   Bats: R Throws: R   Height: 5' 11"   Weight: 190   Born: May 17, 1976   Age: 30

YEAR	TM	LVL	AGE	PA	R	2B	3B	HR	RBI	BB	SO	SB	CS	SPEED	BA	OBP	SLG	MLVR	EQBA	EQOBP	EQSLG	EQA	VORP	DEFENSE		
2003	CIN	MLB	27	343	52	21	1	23	63	17	63	1	3	4.1	.337	.385	.629	.435	.330	.377	.619	.318	35.8	57-RF 0	15-LF	-2
2003	OAK	MLB	27	183	25	7	1	8	23	7	32	0	0	3.9	.265	.311	.459	.019	.266	.317	.462	.264	2.8	33-RF	-1	
2004	ANA	MLB	28	620	88	28	3	27	104	37	92	5	4	4.9	.294	.352	.497	.139	.301	.360	.515	.292	25.8	129-LF	2	
2005	WAS	MLB	29	610	81	32	2	24	76	31	102	1	1	4.4	.283	.338	.479	.140	.289	.340	.501	.284	26.6	132-RF	-2	
2006	*WAS*	*MLB*	*30*	*591*	*69*	*34*	*2*	*21*	*88*	*34*	*99*	*2*	*2*	*4.6*	*.281*	*.335*	*.470*	*.061*	*.294*	*.345*	*.508*	*.278*	*24.3*	*138-RF*	*0*	

Breakout: 9% Improve: 33% Collapse: 32% Attrition: 7%   Comparables: Dan Ford, Rondell White, Willie Horton

A pity the Angels and Nats won't get to mix it up every year. There should be an annual throwdown between them, given the sparring matches between Robinson and Scioscia, Guillen v. Scioscia, and their strikingly similar uniforms. The Angels reflected more contemporary sensibilities by pushing Guillen into anger management; the Nats just smiled and called him an assertive person.

CRISTIAN GUZMAN   **Menace Bats: B Throws: R**   Height: 6′ 0″   Weight: 150   Born: March 21, 1978   Age: 28

YEAR	TM	LVL	AGE	PA	R	2B	3B	HR	RBI	BB	SO	SB	CS	SPEED	BA	OBP	SLG	MLVR	EQBA	EQOBP	EQSLG	EQA	VORP	DEFENSE	
2003	MIN	MLB	25	573	78	15	14	3	53	30	79	18	9	7.8	.268	.311	.365	-.139	.267	.315	.365	.240	6.3	137-SS	3
2004	MIN	MLB	26	611	84	31	4	8	46	30	64	10	5	6.1	.274	.309	.384	-.131	.271	.310	.384	.242	8.6	143-SS	16
2005	WAS	MLB	27	484	39	19	6	4	31	25	76	7	4	5.9	.219	.260	.314	-.270	.228	.271	.330	.212	-14.9	129-SS	-8
2006	*WAS*	*MLB*	*28*	*492*	*51*	*18*	*5*	*3*	*35*	*27*	*63*	*9*	*4*	*5.4*	*.245*	*.290*	*.324*	*-.236*	*.257*	*.299*	*.350*	*.220*	*0.7*	*116-SS*	*1*

Breakout: 20%   Improve: 56%   Collapse: 25%   Attrition: 9%   Comparables: Garry Templeton, Roger Metzger, Alfredo Griffin

The baseball season is long, which reduces the scale of most of its tragedies. You don't get the *Hindenburg* or the *Titanic*, but six months of small disasters, like getting your hand caught in the toaster every other day, forgetting what happens when you lick frozen flagpoles, sitting on your lunch, or locking your keys in your car. Now, imagine four years of that—every day another mishap—and you've got Guzman, killing you by inches. You simply wish he wasn't, but there he is, and here he'll be.

BRENDAN HARRIS   **2B/3B**   **Bats: R Throws: R**   Height: 6′ 1″   Weight: 190   Born: August 26, 1980   Age: 25

YEAR	TM	LVL	AGE	PA	R	2B	3B	HR	RBI	BB	SO	SB	CS	SPEED	BA	OBP	SLG	MLVR	EQBA	EQOBP	EQSLG	EQA	VORP	DEFENSE			
2003	WTN	AA	22	497	56	34	7	5	52	51	72	6	7	5.1	.280	.364	.425	.158	.271	.341	.423	.263	23.0	94-3B	-6	15-2B	0
2004	IOW	AAA	23	272	48	21	1	11	35	16	40	0	2	4.1	.311	.353	.531	.173	.274	.314	.456	.258	11.5	49-2B	8		
2004	EDM	AAA	23	145	20	6	0	6	24	10	21	0	0	3.7	.269	.317	.454	-.015	.243	.290	.392	.239	0.0	34-3B	-4		
2004	MON	MLB	23	53	4	2	0	1	2	2	11	0	0	4.2	.160	.208	.260	-.486	.160	.208	.260	.169	-4.7				
2005	NWO	AAA	24	517	67	22	4	13	81	40	77	9	5	5.4	.270	.329	.417	-.003	.261	.310	.387	.243	5.4	81-2B	3	42-3B	4
2006	*WAS*	*MLB*	*25*	*408*	*42*	*21*	*2*	*7*	*41*	*26*	*66*	*5*	*2*	*4.6*	*.256*	*.310*	*.378*	*-.124*	*.268*	*.319*	*.408*	*.244*	*8.5*	*97-2B*	*1*		

Breakout: 20%   Improve: 42%   Collapse: 33%   Attrition: 21%   Comparables: Reno Bertoia, Damion Easley, Bob Johnson

Harris was briefly a local celebrity; before the decisions to sign Castilla and then draft Zimmerman, he seemed to be the team's third baseman of the present. It's not hard to understand why: he's a sound fielder the hot corner, and a line-drive power source. Now he has to hope for a career in a utility role. The Nats seems willing to oblige, playing him some at shortstop over the winter in the AFL. It might give him a shot at earning that comparison to Easley as an offense-minded infield reserve, and get him Jamey Carroll's job.

NICK JOHNSON   **1B**   **Bats: L Throws: L**   Height: 6′ 3″   Weight: 225   Born: September 19, 1978   Age: 27

YEAR	TM	LVL	AGE	PA	R	2B	3B	HR	RBI	BB	SO	SB	CS	SPEED	BA	OBP	SLG	MLVR	EQBA	EQOBP	EQSLG	EQA	VORP	DEFENSE	
2003	NYA	MLB	24	403	60	19	0	14	47	70	57	5	2	4.1	.284	.422	.472	.235	.289	.428	.488	.317	28.2	59-1B	-1
2004	MON	MLB	25	295	35	16	0	7	33	40	58	6	3	4.8	.251	.359	.398	.034	.244	.352	.384	.260	5.9	68-1B	4
2005	WAS	MLB	26	547	66	35	3	15	74	80	87	3	8	4.0	.289	.408	.479	.258	.296	.413	.502	.307	34.1	122-1B	12
2006	*WAS*	*MLB*	*27*	*521*	*63*	*26*	*1*	*15*	*64*	*81*	*87*	*5*	*3*	*4.5*	*.268*	*.389*	*.443*	*.101*	*.280*	*.400*	*.478*	*.296*	*25.0*	*123-1B*	*5*

Breakout: 12%   Improve: 43%   Collapse: 24%   Attrition: 6%   Comparables: Ed Bouchee, Dick Wakefield, Erubiel Durazo

After years of speculation and anticipation, at long last we now know what a full season from Nick Johnson looks like, and it was everything we thought it could be, and more. At the plate, Johnson delivered as advertised, and afield, he was light on his feet and mobile around the bag. It's important to remember that while Johnson looks hefty, he was never an all-or-nothing slugger, but rather a hitter with a panoply of skills at the plate. Given his medical history, anticipating getting more of the same year after year would be more than a little dicey, so the Nats should be willing to field offers if any are forthcoming.

BRIAN SCHNEIDER   **C**   **Bats: L Throws: R**   Height: 6′ 1″   Weight: 180   Born: November 26, 1976   Age: 29

YEAR	TM	LVL	AGE	PA	R	2B	3B	HR	RBI	BB	SO	SB	CS	SPEED	BA	OBP	SLG	MLVR	EQBA	EQOBP	EQSLG	EQA	VORP	DEFENSE	
2003	MON	MLB	26	376	34	26	1	9	46	37	75	0	2	3.1	.230	.309	.394	-.140	.222	.301	.386	.238	-2.5	95-C	17
2004	MON	MLB	27	483	40	20	3	12	49	42	63	0	1	3.9	.257	.325	.399	-.031	.249	.317	.389	.245	10.5	125-C	13
2005	WAS	MLB	28	406	38	20	1	10	44	29	48	1	0	3.9	.268	.330	.409	.018	.273	.336	.426	.263	15.9	103-C	11
2006	*WAS*	*MLB*	*29*	*367*	*32*	*16*	*1*	*7*	*41*	*31*	*52*	*0*	*1*	*3.8*	*.249*	*.318*	*.372*	*-.122*	*.260*	*.328*	*.402*	*.246*	*7.5*	*88-C*	*5*

Breakout: 17%   Improve: 43%   Collapse: 33%   Attrition: 15%   Comparables: Milt May, Bill Fahey, Ed Ott

Schneider might be particularly hurt by RFK's boggy grounds and heavy air—he hit .306/.354/.464 on the road last year—given his line-drive stroke, you might have expected him to be park-proof. Settle for counting him among the ranks of the good, not great. He's an outstanding receiver and plate blocker, and an offensive asset if he's hitting in the

(continued next page)

Brian Schneider *(continued)*

bottom third of a lineup. In need of a quality backup to handle the tougher lefties, the Nationals inexplicably signed Alberto Castillo and Mike DiFelice to see who can most closely resemble the departed Gary Bennett. At least Schneider won't have to worry about a rival, and he can no doubt enjoy the compensations that come with being signed to a four-year, $16 million contract in January.

TERRMEL SLEDGE OF **Bats: L Throws: L** Height: 6′ 0″ Weight: 180 Born: March 18, 1977 Age: 29

YEAR	TM	LVL	AGE	PA	R	2B	3B	HR	RBI	BB	SO	SB	CS	SPEED	BA	OBP	SLG	MLVR	EQBA	EQOBP	EQSLG	EQA	VORP	DEFENSE			
2003	EDM	AAA	26	572	95	26	9	22	92	61	93	13	5	6.3	.324	.397	.545	.378	.299	.369	.496	.294	46.9	46-CF	-2	43-LF	-2
2004	MON	MLB	27	440	45	20	6	15	62	40	66	3	3	5.6	.269	.336	.462	.082	.261	.329	.451	.264	10.8	65-LF	2	33-RF	3
2005	WAS	MLB	28	46	7	0	1	1	8	7	8	2	1	6.0	.243	.348	.378	-.005	.243	.348	.378	.265	0.6				
2006	*SDN*	*MLB*	*29*	*227*	*29*	*9*	*2*	*7*	*28*	*24*	*40*	*5*	*2*	*5.5*	*.265*	*.344*	*.431*	*.010*	*.275*	*.353*	*.464*	*.274*	*8.5*	*57-LF*	*-1*		

Breakout: 18% Improve: 40% Collapse: 38% Attrition: 33% Comparables: Dave Bergman, Jose Cruz, Irv Noren

After a season lost to a serious hamstring injury, Sledge spent the winter as a roster hot potato, bouncing from Texas in the Soriano trade to San Diego in the Eaton swap. There, he'll get a shot at splitting the primary outfield reserve duties with Eric Young, providing lefty power where Young will offer speed and OBP.

JUNIOR SPIVEY 2B **Bats: R Throws: R** Height: 6′ 0″ Weight: 200 Born: January 28, 1975 Age: 31

YEAR	TM	LVL	AGE	PA	R	2B	3B	HR	RBI	BB	SO	SB	CS	SPEED	BA	OBP	SLG	MLVR	EQBA	EQOBP	EQSLG	EQA	VORP	DEFENSE	
2003	ARI	MLB	28	408	52	22	2	13	50	33	95	4	3	4.9	.255	.326	.433	-.026	.245	.315	.419	.253	8.6	90-2B	-3
2004	MIL	MLB	29	262	33	13	0	7	28	25	48	5	3	4.5	.272	.359	.421	.068	.266	.351	.410	.265	11.9	58-2B	-2
2005	MIL	MLB	30	201	22	8	1	5	17	18	57	7	3	6.2	.236	.308	.374	-.100	.236	.312	.390	.244	0.5	46-2B	-2
2005	WAS	MLB	30	91	15	7	0	2	7	11	26	2	0	5.3	.221	.330	.390	-.042	.231	.337	.423	.269	1.9	21-2B	1
2006	*SLN*	*MLB*	*31*	*278*	*34*	*13*	*1*	*7*	*30*	*25*	*63*	*6*	*3*	*5.0*	*.247*	*.321*	*.395*	*-.088*	*.248*	*.322*	*.410*	*.248*	*5.9*	*68-2B*	*-2*

Breakout: 17% Improve: 41% Collapse: 37% Attrition: 37% Comparables: Steve Scarsone, Dave Campbell, Tim Hulett

There's nothing wrong with adequacy, but Spivey is burdened with the expectation that he has another 2001 in him, when he hit .301/.389/.476. He doesn't, of course; he needed the BOB's friendly confines to do it, and he's never been much of an offensive threat to right-handed pitching. He is exactly what the Brewers acquired him to be—a placeholder until a prospect like Rickie Weeks is ready. He will give the Cardinals that, although sadly without anyone like Weeks in the wings.

JOSE VIDRO 2B **Bats: B Throws: R** Height: 5′ 11″ Weight: 175 Born: August 27, 1974 Age: 31

YEAR	TM	LVL	AGE	PA	R	2B	3B	HR	RBI	BB	SO	SB	CS	SPEED	BA	OBP	SLG	MLVR	EQBA	EQOBP	EQSLG	EQA	VORP	DEFENSE	
2003	MON	MLB	28	590	77	36	0	15	65	69	50	3	2	4.3	.310	.397	.470	.161	.300	.386	.458	.293	39.8	131-2B	-11
2004	MON	MLB	29	463	51	24	0	14	60	49	43	3	1	4.1	.294	.367	.454	.149	.284	.359	.444	.278	31.0	98-2B	-14
2005	WAS	MLB	30	345	38	21	2	7	32	31	30	0	0	3.9	.275	.339	.424	.057	.280	.346	.437	.271	13.3	74-2B	-4
2006	*WAS*	*MLB*	*31*	*426*	*46*	*21*	*1*	*8*	*46*	*41*	*43*	*1*	*1*	*4.1*	*.273*	*.345*	*.396*	*-.028*	*.286*	*.355*	*.428*	*.265*	*18.3*	*101-2B*	*-5*

Breakout: 8% Improve: 28% Collapse: 38% Attrition: 15% Comparables: Bill Mueller, Johnny Ray, Todd Walker

Some believe Vidro's defense has improved, but that seems more a bit of wishcasting than achievement. If Soriano gets his way and remains a second baseman, Vidro's going to be dealt for pennies on the dollar, which isn't as egregious as it sounds since the team would be dealing him at least a year too late to get real value in return. His knee will again hamper him early in camp, but he's supposed to be ready before Opening Day. He'd make a much larger difference for a real contender than he will here, and it would be nice to see him get his due before his career winds down any further.

BRANDON WATSON OF **Bats: L Throws: R** Height: 6′ 1″ Weight: 170 Born: September 30, 1981 Age: 24

YEAR	TM	LVL	AGE	PA	R	2B	3B	HR	RBI	BB	SO	SB	CS	SPEED	BA	OBP	SLG	MLVR	EQBA	EQOBP	EQSLG	EQA	VORP	DEFENSE			
2003	HAR	AA	21	610	86	17	6	1	39	38	60	18	17	5.8	.319	.362	.375	.053	.285	.327	.344	.236	-0.3	138-CF	2		
2004	EDM	AAA	22	560	74	17	3	2	41	31	68	22	10	6.1	.293	.332	.348	-.126	.276	.313	.323	.228	-9.9	118-CF	-5		
2005	HAR	AA	23	155	13	1	0	0	6	7	21	7	5	5.7	.247	.290	.253	-.257	.225	.270	.232	.189	-13.3	33-CF	-2		
2005	NWO	AAA	23	403	69	15	3	1	25	28	33	31	13	7.0	.355	.400	.419	.220	.350	.388	.408	.280	28.8	68-CF	-1	15-RF	2
2005	WAS	MLB	23	44	8	1	1	1	5	4	8	0	2	8.0	.175	.250	.325	-.339	.190	.261	.333	.201	-4.3				
2006	*WAS*	*MLB*	*24*	*474*	*51*	*14*	*3*	*0*	*31*	*25*	*57*	*17*	*7*	*5.4*	*.268*	*.310*	*.313*	*-.202*	*.280*	*.319*	*.339*	*.228*	*-4.5*	*112-CF*	*-2*		

Breakout: 15% Improve: 40% Collapse: 39% Attrition: 11% Comparables: Alex Sanchez, Jason Tyner, Carlos Mendoza

Laughably compared to Ichiro, but that's probably more a case of the uncomfortable recognition among scouts that a player you'd compare to Jason Tyner isn't a prospect. The Nats are discussing him as a possible regular in their outfield, a notion the rest of division is happy to contemplate. If there's a silver lining to the decisions to sign both Michael Tucker and Marlon Anderson, it's that they should keep Watson in Triple-A.

JOSH WHITESELL 1B **Bats: L Throws: L** Height: 6′ 3″ Weight: 220 Born: April 14, 1982 Age: 24

YEAR	TM	LVL	AGE	PA	R	2B	3B	HR	RBI	BB	SO	SB	CS	SPEED	BA	OBP	SLG	MLVR	EQBA	EQOBP	EQSLG	EQA	VORP	DEFENSE	
2003	VER	A-	21	200	13	10	1	5	19	28	53	0	0	2.6	.246	.365	.407	.152	.213	.307	.368	.238	-12.9	46-1B	2
2004	SAV	A	22	443	56	29	0	16	54	58	91	0	1	2.7	.250	.352	.453	.120	.207	.291	.368	.230	-19.9	103-1B	-8
2005	POT	A+	23	473	59	32	2	18	66	74	125	1	1	4.3	.293	.416	.524	.305	.245	.346	.424	.267	6.8	86-1B	-3
2006	WAS	MLB	24	474	49	21	1	13	53	48	138	1	1	3.9	.217	.302	.368	-.175	.227	.311	.398	.237	-7.5	112-1B	-2

Breakout: 12% Improve: 28% Collapse: 33% Attrition: 13% Comparables: Brad Vericker, Kevin Burns, Shawn McCorkle

A tough luck story already, having lost a chunk of his college career to a car accident, Whitesell's facing long odds if he's going to make it as a prospect at first base. Credited with a nice approach at the plate, patience, and an all-fields stroke, his problems are time and age. He wasn't young for an A-ball player, and will have to make a clean jump to Double-A this year. If he can do that, even then, he has to hope for some luck, either in terms of bad things happening to other people, or getting dealt to the right team.

BRAD WILKERSON OF **Bats: L Throws: L** Height: 6′ 0″ Weight: 190 Born: June 1, 1977 Age: 29

YEAR	TM	LVL	AGE	PA	R	2B	3B	HR	RBI	BB	SO	SB	CS	SPEED	BA	OBP	SLG	MLVR	EQBA	EQOBP	EQSLG	EQA	VORP	DEFENSE				
2003	MON	MLB	26	600	78	34	4	19	77	89	155	13	10	5.8	.268	.380	.464	.098	.259	.371	.458	.283	16.8	79-LF	8	34-CF	-1
2004	MON	MLB	27	685	112	39	2	32	67	106	152	13	6	5.6	.255	.374	.498	.184	.247	.365	.481	.287	37.0	79-1B	6	49-LF	1
2005	WAS	MLB	28	658	76	42	7	11	57	84	147	8	10	5.1	.248	.351	.405	.036	.256	.359	.424	.268	13.2	84-CF	-2	32-LF	0
2006	TEX	MLB	29	643	88	31	6	24	82	82	129	10	5	5.2	.263	.362	.473	.107	.259	.366	.471	.279	25.1	150-CF	0		

Breakout: 19% Improve: 51% Collapse: 12% Attrition: 3% Comparables: Ray Lankford, Trot Nixon, Rick Monday

It wasn't just the ballpark; Wilkerson flat-out had a bad year. As the club became more obviously riven between Latinos and everybody else, the finicky former best player on the team didn't seem to get along with Bowden's imports, and as the season went down the tubes, so did Wilkerson's hitting. Frittered away in another Bowdenian indiscretion, Wilkerson has a date with a long-overdue dose of stardom ahead of him as a member of the Rangers, where he'll be hitting in the perennially lefty power-friendly Ameriquest Field.

PRESTON WILSON OF **Bats: R Throws: R** Height: 6′ 2″ Weight: 193 Born: July 19, 1974 Age: 31

YEAR	TM	LVL	AGE	PA	R	2B	3B	HR	RBI	BB	SO	SB	CS	SPEED	BA	OBP	SLG	MLVR	EQBA	EQOBP	EQSLG	EQA	VORP	DEFENSE				
2003	COL	MLB	28	661	94	43	1	36	141	54	139	14	7	5.0	.282	.343	.537	.159	.262	.325	.503	.276	38.6	149-CF	-15		
2004	COL	MLB	29	222	24	11	0	6	29	17	49	2	1	3.7	.248	.315	.391	-.131	.230	.297	.355	.229	-2.1	49-CF	-2		
2005	COL	MLB	30	295	39	15	1	15	47	25	77	3	2	4.8	.258	.322	.491	.049	.242	.311	.470	.263	9.5	66-CF	-6		
2005	WAS	MLB	30	280	34	14	1	10	43	20	71	3	4	4.4	.261	.329	.443	.062	.267	.333	.467	.267	8.2	54-CF	-5	10-LF	0
2006	HOU	MLB	31	401	52	19	1	18	59	33	94	6	3	4.3	.263	.329	.473	.040	.267	.334	.488	.270	16.9	96-CF	-6		

Breakout: 40% Improve: 62% Collapse: 21% Attrition: 22% Comparables: Jerry Martin, Deron Johnson, Wally Post

Statistical Luddites will no doubt gnash their teeth over those stupid numbers and how they must not mean anything, but what did you expect after hauling the guy down from Denver? The guy who put on the fireworks show in 2003? The statistics didn't lie, but apparently some never grasp the subtleties of the game's lingua franca. Credit Wilson's agent for being smart and placing his client back into another bandbox. In Houston, he will regain his park-generated reputation as a mid-lineup bopper and benefit from playing an outfield corner.

RYAN ZIMMERMAN 3B **Bats: R Throws: R** Height: 6′ 2″ Weight: 210 Born: September 28, 1984 Age: 21

YEAR	TM	LVL	AGE	PA	R	2B	3B	HR	RBI	BB	SO	SB	CS	SPEED	BA	OBP	SLG	MLVR	EQBA	EQOBP	EQSLG	EQA	VORP	DEFENSE	
2005	HAR	AA	20	251	40	20	0	9	32	15	34	1	5	4.6	.326	.371	.528	.289	.288	.332	.472	.267	15.9	53-3B	4
2005	WAS	MLB	20	62	6	10	0	0	6	3	12	0	0	3.8	.397	.419	.569	.550	.397	.419	.552	.329	9.3	12-3B	3
2006	WAS	MLB	21	495	59	37	2	13	68	29	76	3	4	4.7	.289	.334	.462	.056	.303	.344	.499	.273	28.3	117-3B	6

Breakout: 15% Improve: 37% Collapse: 32% Attrition: 7% Comparables: Albert Pujols, Justin Morneau, Joe Torre

(continued next page)

Ryan Zimmerman *(continued)*

The guy who doesn't show up on his comparables, but might make for a particularly apt comparison, is Brooks Robinson. Like Brooksie in his prime, Zimmerman has the range and ball field instincts to play short, but the Nats might just settle for Gold Glove-worthy defense at third. Also like Robinson, he has the line-drive stroke that travels well, capable of producing power in any environment, and his greatness at the plate or in the field is a product of his tremendous hand-eye coordination. All in all, he's an easy favorite for Rookie of the Year, and the kind of player who can become a signature player in a franchise's history; one last thing he'd have in common with Baltimore's all-time great at the hot corner.

PITCHERS

TONY ARMAS JR.   Bats: R Throws: R   Height: 6' 4" Weight: 175 Born: April 29, 1978   Age: 28

YEAR	TM	LVL	AGE	W	L	SV	G	GS	IP	H	BB	SO	HR	GB%	BABIP	STUFF	WHIP	ERA	PERA	EQERA	EQH9	EQBB9	EQSO9	EQHR9	VORP	WXRL
2003	MON	MLB	25	2	1	0	5	5	31.0	25	8	23	4	34%	.250	17	1.06	2.61	4.50	2.70	8.1	2.1	6.3	1.2	11.1	1.3
2004	MON	MLB	26	2	4	0	16	16	72.0	66	45	54	13	40%	.265	-10	1.54	4.88	5.83	4.94	9.0	5.2	6.1	1.5	4.2	1.8
2005	WAS	MLB	27	7	7	0	19	19	101.3	100	54	59	16	37%	.268	-17	1.51	4.98	5.94	5.40	9.5	4.5	4.9	1.5	5.2	1.7
2006	*WAS*	*MLB*	*28*	*6*	*8*	*0*	*30*	*20*	*123.0*	*119*	*54*	*80*	*17*	*40%*	*.268*	*-3*	*1.40*	*4.41*	*5.16*	*5.40*	*8.9*	*3.6*	*5.2*	*1.3*	*6.6*	*1.4*

Breakout: 15%   Improve: 47%   Collapse: 24%   Attrition: 12%   Comparables: Pat Zachry, Tracy Stallard, Matt Keough

A pitcher so brittle that, if Tennessee Williams were around, he'd have to write a play about him. Nevertheless, he's part of the equally fragile master plan for National success as one of the better options to round out their rotation. He was never really right last season, on the mound only long enough for a May to September romance before being shut down. He had his shoulder scoped in the fall, in anticipation that he'd be prepped for camp this year.

LUIS AYALA   Bats: R Throws: R   Height: 6' 2" Weight: 175 Born: January 12, 1978   Age: 28

YEAR	TM	LVL	AGE	W	L	SV	G	GS	IP	H	BB	SO	HR	GB%	BABIP	STUFF	WHIP	ERA	PERA	EQERA	EQH9	EQBB9	EQSO9	EQHR9	VORP	WXRL
2003	MON	MLB	25	10	3	5	65	0	71.0	65	13	46	8	59%	.269	0	1.10	2.92	4.28	3.37	8.8	1.6	5.3	1.0	19.3	3.2
2004	MON	MLB	26	6	12	2	81	0	90.3	92	15	63	6	58%	.314	12	1.18	2.69	3.61	3.01	9.1	1.4	5.6	0.6	26.5	0.2
2005	WAS	MLB	27	8	7	1	68	0	71.0	75	14	40	7	42%	.316	-3	1.25	2.66	4.33	3.31	9.7	1.7	4.7	0.9	18.8	2.2
2006	*WAS*	*MLB*	*28*	*3*	*3*	*3*	*54*	*0*	*60.7*	*62*	*14*	*38*	*6*	*49%*	*.289*	*-4*	*1.26*	*3.43*	*4.27*	*4.28*	*9.5*	*2.0*	*4.9*	*0.9*	*9.9*	*0.8*

Breakout: 6%   Improve: 17%   Collapse: 55%   Attrition: 14%   Comparables: Tom Hume, Pedro Borbon, Chuck Crim

The club's primary setup man gave a performance that earned him a two-year contract in January, but PECOTA is very pessimistic about his near-term future. He had surgery to remove a bone spur from his elbow, and naturally the Nats are saying he'll be fine. At his best, he's a sinker-slider guy who keeps the ball on the ground, but the problematic elbow seems to have forced his offerings up in the zone, where it took RFK's forgivingly open spaces to keep Ayala from getting toasted. The park can forgive a lot, but Ayala's a risky proposition, and the Nats would be better off flipping him while he's still notable for the right reasons.

COLLIN BALESTER   Bats: R Throws: R   Height: 6' 5" Weight: 190 Born: June 6, 1986   Age: 20

YEAR	TM	LVL	AGE	W	L	SV	G	GS	IP	H	BB	SO	HR	GB%	BABIP	STUFF	WHIP	ERA	PERA	EQERA	EQH9	EQBB9	EQSO9	EQHR9	VORP	WXRL
2005	SAV	A	19	8	6	0	24	23	125.0	105	42	95	11	43%	.257	-8	1.18	3.67	5.88	6.03	9.6	3.8	4.5	1.5	-5.6	—
2006	*WAS*	*MLB*	*20*	*6*	*9*	*0*	*22*	*22*	*125.3*	*122*	*57*	*80*	*17*	*41%*	*.271*	*4*	*1.43*	*4.73*	*5.38*	*5.52*	*9.1*	*3.7*	*5.1*	*1.2*	*1.5*	*1.1*

Breakout: 22%   Improve: 77%   Collapse: 4%   Attrition: 1%   Comparables: Jorge Julio, Gavin Floyd, Matt Peterson

A polished California high school pitcher picked in 2004, Balester's currently the Nationals' best pitching prospect. He's mostly a fastballer at this point, but improved command of his curve helped him garner his acclaim. His comparables make for interesting reading in that they reflect a group known for their heaters, their promise, and their disappointments. If he becomes consistent with his offspeed stuff, his upside isn't too far from Floyd's, but as with previous "best" pitching prospects, notably Everts and Hinckley, he needs to survive before you can consider him a can't-miss commodity. Nats fans should take a short—we won't say quick—drive south on I-95 and check him out if he's pitching in Potomac.

FRANCIS BELTRAN   **Bats: R Throws: R**   Height: 6' 6" Weight: 230 Born: November 29, 1979 Age: 26

YEAR	TM	LVL	AGE	W	L	SV	G	GS	IP	H	BB	SO	HR	GB%	BABIP	STUFF	WHIP	ERA	PERA	EQERA	EQH9	EQBB9	EQSO9	EQHR9	VORP	WXRL
2003	IOW	AAA	23	6	2	4	31	2	48.7	46	19	33	2	—	.280	-4	1.33	2.96	4.37	3.80	8.7	4.0	5.1	0.6	9.5	—
2004	CHN	MLB	24	2	2	0	34	0	35.0	27	22	40	8	50%	.244	0	1.40	4.63	5.50	4.72	7.9	5.2	9.2	1.8	3.4	0.1
2004	MON	MLB	24	0	0	1	11	0	14.3	20	5	8	3	55%	.347	-21	1.74	7.55	6.14	7.36	11.7	3.1	4.3	1.8	-2.6	0.2
2006	*WAS*	*MLB*	*26*	*2*	*2*	*1*	*32*	*1*	*41.0*	*37*	*18*	*34*	*4*	*46%*	*.274*	*0*	*1.34*	*3.91*	*4.48*	*5.11*	*8.3*	*3.7*	*6.5*	*1.0*	*4.0*	*0.4*

Breakout: 35%   Improve: 56%   Collapse: 22%   Attrition: 34%   Comparables: Jeff Nelson, Aaron Heilman, Barry Jones

The former Cubs flamethrower missed all of '05 recuperating from Tommy John surgery, but he's supposed to be completely ready to step into a bullpen role this summer. When he's on, he can dial it up into the mid-90s, mixing a hard, boring sinker with a slider or curve. In other words, it's the stuff of a potentially dominant reliever. A slow start wouldn't be a surprise, but once he's gets sharp, watch out.

JAY BERGMANN   **Bats: R Throws: R**   Height: 6' 4" Weight: 190 Born: September 25, 1981 Age: 24

YEAR	TM	LVL	AGE	W	L	SV	G	GS	IP	H	BB	SO	HR	GB%	BABIP	STUFF	WHIP	ERA	PERA	EQERA	EQH9	EQBB9	EQSO9	EQHR9	VORP	WXRL
2003	SAV	A	21	6	11	0	23	22	109.0	108	53	82	8	—	.290	-31	1.48	4.29	6.88	6.62	10.7	5.5	4.1	1.8	-11.6	—
2004	SAV	A	22	3	7	0	13	13	65.0	67	34	58	6	—	.316	-23	1.55	4.85	6.75	7.19	10.7	6.2	4.7	1.6	-10.8	—
2004	BRV	A+	22	3	2	8	24	0	31.7	20	18	28	0	—	.235	-11	1.20	1.14	4.97	3.72	7.4	6.5	5.6	0.3	6.1	—
2005	HAR	AA	23	2	0	5	21	0	37.0	27	16	37	3	35%	.255	-4	1.16	1.22	5.19	2.86	8.0	4.9	6.2	1.0	10.6	—
2005	NWO	AAA	23	3	2	2	20	0	37.0	26	13	39	5	40%	.250	2	1.05	3.16	5.14	4.11	8.0	3.3	7.5	1.5	5.8	—
2005	WAS	MLB	23	2	0	0	15	1	19.7	14	11	21	1	33%	.271	16	1.27	2.74	3.72	3.26	7.4	4.7	8.8	0.5	5.8	0.5
2006	*WAS*	*MLB*	*24*	*2*	*4*	*1*	*58*	*2*	*59.0*	*60*	*36*	*46*	*10*	*38%*	*.284*	*-13*	*1.61*	*5.43*	*6.49*	*6.35*	*9.4*	*5.0*	*6.2*	*1.6*	*-4.0*	*-0.4*

Breakout: 7%   Improve: 21%   Collapse: 40%   Attrition: 12%   Comparables: Rich Yett, Pete Redfern, Jimmy Haynes

PECOTA's appropriately skeptical, considering his control issues, but there's reason to believe that Bergmann could become a key contributor in a big league bullpen, particularly the Nats' pen. First, RFK's muddy, muggy environs will keep his flyball tendencies from hurting him too badly. Second, he's got an excellent mix of pitches: mid-90s heat, a good cutter and a solid slider, plus a three-quarter delivery that makes it hard to pick up his pitches.

BILL BRAY   **Bats: L Throws: L**   Height: 6' 3" Weight: 215 Born: June 5, 1983 Age: 23

YEAR	TM	LVL	AGE	W	L	SV	G	GS	IP	H	BB	SO	HR	GB%	BABIP	STUFF	WHIP	ERA	PERA	EQERA	EQH9	EQBB9	EQSO9	EQHR9	VORP	WXRL
2005	POT	A+	22	1	0	3	8	0	12.7	8	3	18	1	45%	.250	11	0.87	2.13	4.63	3.86	7.7	2.3	8.5	1.5	2.3	—
2005	NWO	AAA	22	1	4	2	23	0	21.3	23	9	25	3	39%	.351	0	1.50	5.07	5.48	6.75	9.7	3.8	8.0	1.7	-2.7	—
2006	*WAS*	*MLB*	*23*	*3*	*3*	*1*	*26*	*4*	*50.3*	*48*	*19*	*43*	*7*	*40%*	*.285*	*5*	*1.32*	*4.29*	*4.76*	*5.12*	*8.9*	*3.0*	*6.8*	*1.2*	*3.1*	*0.4*

Breakout: 48%   Improve: 80%   Collapse: 3%   Attrition: 17%   Comparables: Alberto Blanco, Joe Moeller, Bob Kipper

A college closer at William & Mary picked in the 1st round of the 2004 draft, Bray's pro career has started slowly, between signing late and then missing the first two months of 2005 to a back injury. But when he does get on the mound, he justifies scouts' enthusiasm for him with a fastball that gets into the mid-90s and a sharp, high-velocity slider. With Mike Stanton and Eischen on hand to fulfill the pen's left-handed needs, Bray might have to wait a few months, but he will be up before the season's out.

BRETT CAMPBELL   **Bats: R Throws: R**   Height: 6' 0" Weight: 170 Born: October 17, 1981 Age: 24

YEAR	TM	LVL	AGE	W	L	SV	G	GS	IP	H	BB	SO	HR	GB%	BABIP	STUFF	WHIP	ERA	PERA	EQERA	EQH9	EQBB9	EQSO9	EQHR9	VORP	WXRL
2004	VER	A-	22	0	1	0	11	0	22.0	24	10	25	3	—	.344	-38	1.55	4.09	9.78	7.91	13.0	7.0	5.6	4.2	-5.0	—
2005	SAV	A	23	4	2	19	36	0	48.0	28	15	50	2	52%	.218	-7	0.90	1.69	4.57	4.15	7.7	3.9	5.8	0.8	7.0	—
2005	POT	A+	23	0	2	1	12	0	15.0	21	10	13	3	55%	.375	-45	2.07	9.60	8.79	11.30	13.8	6.9	5.0	3.1	-9.1	—
2006	*WAS*	*MLB*	*24*	*2*	*4*	*0*	*28*	*4*	*51.7*	*58*	*32*	*33*	*10*	*45%*	*.294*	*-22*	*1.74*	*6.27*	*7.44*	*7.32*	*10.5*	*5.0*	*5.0*	*1.8*	*-8.8*	*-0.7*

Breakout: 8%   Improve: 39%   Collapse: 38%   Attrition: 11%   Comparables: Eric Herndon, Greg Aquino, Tim Worthington

When a guy is picked in the 34th round, he's either a draft-and-follow or it's an indication that he should be glad for the opportunity. Every so often, though, it's a guy who can pitch, and Campbell could fall into that category. In part, it might be because he's become a special project of minor league pitching coordinator Bret Strom, who's teaching Campbell a splitter to mix in with his power sinker/slider combo.

HECTOR CARRASCO   Bats: R Throws: R   Height: 6′ 2″   Weight: 220   Born: October 22, 1969   Age: 36

YEAR	TM	LVL	AGE	W	L	SV	G	GS	IP	H	BB	SO	HR	GB%	BABIP	STUFF	WHIP	ERA	PERA	EQERA	EQH9	EQBB9	EQSO9	EQHR9	VORP	WXRL
2003	BAL	MLB	33	2	6	1	40	0	38.3	40	20	27	5	50%	.302	-11	1.57	4.93	5.35	4.89	9.1	4.7	6.1	1.2	3.4	0.1
2004	OSA	JPL	34	8	8	5	53	0	76.0	74	37	70	12	—	-.500	-12	1.46	5.57	5.14	7.25	8.9	4.0	7.4	1.5	-14.1	—
2005	WAS	MLB	35	5	4	2	64	5	88.3	59	38	75	6	44%	.236	13	1.10	2.04	3.99	2.73	7.2	3.7	7.2	0.6	30.5	2.4
2006	LAA	MLB	36	4	4	2	54	3	71.0	70	29	52	9	45%	.284	-5	1.40	4.22	4.70	4.79	8.8	3.7	6.4	1.1	9.0	0.9

Breakout: 11%   Improve: 30%   Collapse: 44%   Attrition: 17%   Comparables: Don McMahon, Diego Segui, Tim Worrell

Resurrections this surprising might force even the biggest skeptic to find religion, because Carrasco's career had gone east of nowhere. He came back from Japan and not only rediscovered himself, he earned a $6.1 million, two-year deal with the Angels in the process. First thriving in the middle innings, Carrasco was pushed into the rotation to confront an emergency called "September," and didn't embarrass himself. However, he also drew five injury-weakened or simply weak lineups in those starts. Having performed his miracle, Carrasco is more likely to remind us why the resurrected were dead in the first place. Between his poor command and the Angels counting on him to step into the rotation as their fifth man, this is one comeback that's all comebacked out.

CHAD CORDERO   Bats: R Throws: R   Height: 6′ 0″   Weight: 195   Born: March 18, 1982   Age: 24

YEAR	TM	LVL	AGE	W	L	SV	G	GS	IP	H	BB	SO	HR	GB%	BABIP	STUFF	WHIP	ERA	PERA	EQERA	EQH9	EQBB9	EQSO9	EQHR9	VORP	WXRL
2003	BRV	A+	21	1	1	6	19	0	26.3	17	10	17	1	—	.205	-17	1.03	2.05	5.62	4.50	8.2	4.1	4.1	1.1	2.9	—
2003	MON	MLB	21	1	0	1	12	0	11.0	4	3	12	1	54%	.130	10	0.64	1.64	3.48	1.74	5.2	2.6	9.6	0.9	5.0	0.6
2004	MON	MLB	22	7	3	14	69	0	82.7	68	43	83	8	36%	.278	15	1.34	2.94	4.06	3.07	7.8	4.3	8.0	0.8	23.6	4.6
2005	WAS	MLB	23	2	4	47	74	0	74.3	55	17	61	9	37%	.221	7	0.97	1.82	4.14	3.27	7.8	2.0	7.0	1.1	20.7	4.6
2006	WAS	MLB	24	4	5	28	55	0	60.7	51	23	53	7	38%	.261	7	1.21	3.29	3.89	3.70	7.7	3.1	6.9	1.0	11.7	1.6

Breakout: 16%   Improve: 35%   Collapse: 43%   Attrition: 19%   Comparables: Jorge Julio, Frank Smith, Mike Jackson

We tend to be a bit dismissive of closers and their feats in these pages, but that's more a product of their tailored roles than any disrespect for their talents. When it comes to Cordero, we happily give the kid his due—he's a closer who's good at it, finishing 14th and 9th in WXRL in the majors in his two seasons. If he has a wart, it's his tendency to challenge right-handed hitters with high fastballs, only to see them occasionally catch up to them, as they did on six of his seven bombs allowed. In RFK, he can afford to take some chances, but if he learns to avoid this sort of mistake, he'll be better still.

RYAN DRESE   Bats: R Throws: R   Height: 6′ 3″   Weight: 220   Born: April 5, 1976   Age: 30

YEAR	TM	LVL	AGE	W	L	SV	G	GS	IP	H	BB	SO	HR	GB%	BABIP	STUFF	WHIP	ERA	PERA	EQERA	EQH9	EQBB9	EQSO9	EQHR9	VORP	WXRL
2003	OKL	AAA	27	8	6	0	20	20	122.0	143	39	68	8	—	.312	-5	1.49	4.65	5.18	6.15	10.3	3.5	4.0	1.0	-7.3	—
2003	TEX	MLB	27	2	4	0	11	8	46.0	61	24	26	8	50%	.331	-16	1.85	6.85	5.81	6.75	10.5	4.5	4.7	1.3	-9.0	0.2
2004	TEX	MLB	28	14	10	0	34	33	207.7	233	58	98	16	56%	.309	11	1.40	4.20	4.31	4.01	9.6	2.3	3.9	0.6	44.0	5.1
2005	TEX	MLB	29	4	6	0	12	12	69.7	96	24	20	5	58%	.347	-6	1.72	6.46	4.79	5.40	10.7	2.9	2.5	0.6	-6.0	0.1
2005	WAS	MLB	29	3	6	0	11	11	59.7	66	22	26	3	54%	.309	0	1.47	4.97	4.50	6.15	9.9	3.2	3.6	0.4	-1.4	0.8
2006	WAS	MLB	30	6	8	0	26	18	119.0	131	43	57	11	52%	.295	-7	1.45	4.55	5.20	5.72	10.2	3.0	3.8	0.8	2.9	1.0

Breakout: 12%   Improve: 42%   Collapse: 26%   Attrition: 10%   Comparables: Howie Fox, Bruce Dal Canton, John Dopson

There's no element of mystery here, certainly not for the hitters fortunate enough to have faced Drese, so whatever the man was smoking when he claimed Drese on waivers, obligating the Nats to pay $1.8 million this year, it must be strong enough to involve warnings against operating heavy machinery under its influence. The expense won't guarantee the Nats a fifth starter, not after he shredded his shoulder last summer, and not when he can't outpitch Armas or Ramon Ortiz.

JOEY EISCHEN   Bats: L Throws: L   Height: 6′ 1″   Weight: 190   Born: May 25, 1970   Age: 36

YEAR	TM	LVL	AGE	W	L	SV	G	GS	IP	H	BB	SO	HR	GB%	BABIP	STUFF	WHIP	ERA	PERA	EQERA	EQH9	EQBB9	EQSO9	EQHR9	VORP	WXRL
2003	MON	MLB	33	2	2	1	70	0	53.0	57	13	40	7	54%	.323	-1	1.32	3.06	4.42	4.42	9.5	2.0	6.1	1.2	8.0	-0.1
2004	MON	MLB	34	0	1	0	21	0	18.3	16	8	17	2	52%	.280	3	1.31	3.93	4.50	4.50	8.5	3.5	7.5	1.0	1.5	0.5
2005	WAS	MLB	35	2	1	0	57	0	36.3	34	19	30	1	48%	.317	4	1.49	3.22	4.21	3.72	8.7	4.5	6.7	0.2	7.8	0.3
2006	WAS	MLB	36	2	2	2	37	0	33.3	31	13	27	3	48%	.287	-3	1.32	3.66	4.16	5.19	8.6	3.3	6.4	0.7	4.5	0.4

Breakout: 23%   Improve: 40%   Collapse: 44%   Attrition: 31%   Comparables: Buddy Groom, Mike Myers, Tony Fossas

In a perfect world, there'd be a band named The Sidekicks, and their songs would be about the happiness you find in the background of other people's lives. And then, appropriately enough, irksome five-second splices of their best tunes would be played when Joey Eischen takes the mound. At his best, he's the low-leverage second lefty in a pen, the one you use when you don't have a lead. With Mike Stanton in front of him and Bray coming up from below, Eischen's a roster pimple waiting to be popped.

CLINT EVERTS Bats: R Throws: R Height: 6' 2" Weight: 170 Born: August 10, 1984 Age: 21

YEAR	TM	LVL	AGE	W	L	SV	G	GS	IP	H	BB	SO	HR	GB%	BABIP	STUFF	WHIP	ERA	PERA	EQERA	EQH9	EQBB9	EQSO9	EQHR9	VORP	WXRL
2003	VER	A-	18	2	4	0	10	10	54.0	49	35	50	4	—	.287	-11	1.56	4.17	8.32	5.73	10.9	7.8	5.4	2.6	-0.7	—
2003	SAV	A	18	0	3	0	5	5	26.0	23	10	21	1	—	.278	10	1.27	3.46	4.68	6.12	9.0	4.0	4.7	0.7	-1.4	—
2004	SAV	A	19	7	3	0	17	17	90.3	67	21	103	3	—	.286	34	0.97	2.49	3.77	4.08	8.2	2.5	6.3	0.5	14.5	—
2004	BRV	A+	19	2	2	0	4	4	20.0	16	10	19	2	—	.275	10	1.30	2.25	6.38	3.44	9.3	5.4	6.4	2.0	4.4	—
2005	VER	A-	20	0	1	0	8	1	19.0	21	12	21	0	59%	.362	-15	1.74	3.79	5.40	7.36	9.8	7.4	5.4	0.5	-3.6	—
2006	WAS	MLB	21	3	5	0	23	9	67.0	65	45	49	8	49%	.284	-8	1.64	5.24	6.10	6.35	9.0	5.5	5.8	1.1	-3.8	-0.1

Breakout: 3% Improve: 17% Collapse: 43% Attrition: 12% Comparables: Josh Rupe, Cedric Hebert, Matt Lorenzo

After Everts lost most of the year to Tommy John surgery, the Nats had to derive whatever satisfaction they could from his rapid comeback. In his ongoing rehab, the Nats plan on letting him work his snapping curve into game situations this year. Reacquiring his low 90s gas and the bender might propel Everts back into prospect ranks, as he already has the command of his change that would make him an effective big league starter. He should start off in Potomac, but a September cameo might not be out of the question.

ARMANDO GALARRAGA Bats: R Throws: R Height: 6' 3" Weight: 170 Born: January 15, 1982 Age: 24

YEAR	TM	LVL	AGE	W	L	SV	G	GS	IP	H	BB	SO	HR	GB%	BABIP	STUFF	WHIP	ERA	PERA	EQERA	EQH9	EQBB9	EQSO9	EQHR9	VORP	WXRL
2004	SAV	A	22	5	5	0	23	19	110.3	104	31	94	14	—	.280	-32	1.22	4.65	6.55	6.47	10.5	3.3	4.5	2.2	-10.0	—
2005	POT	A+	23	3	4	0	14	14	80.0	69	23	79	7	47%	.287	1	1.15	2.48	5.26	4.90	9.6	3.1	5.5	1.3	5.9	—
2005	HAR	AA	23	3	4	0	13	13	76.3	80	21	58	10	41%	.314	-12	1.32	5.19	5.86	6.23	10.3	3.1	4.6	1.7	-5.2	—
2006	TEX	MLB	24	5	9	0	28	20	118.7	145	46	64	26	42%	.297	-9	1.60	6.41	6.29	6.25	10.4	3.5	4.8	1.8	-8.4	-0.1

Breakout: 11% Improve: 38% Collapse: 22% Attrition: 0% Comparables: Vinny Chulk, Victor Santos, Jose Vaquedano

Dumping Wilkerson in the Soriano deal was expensive enough, but having to throw in Galarraga might prove to be the really galling aspect of the trade. He's got the power assortment and the aggressiveness in using it that everyone likes, mixing heat with a hard slider (a pitch some worry that he tips, however). Already a TJ survivor, Galarraga's mechanics are pretty clean, and if he polishes his changeup, he might turn out much better than all the Rangers' oft-touted and rarely successful homegrown talents.

JOHN HALAMA Bats: L Throws: L Height: 6' 5" Weight: 210 Born: February 22, 1972 Age: 34

YEAR	TM	LVL	AGE	W	L	SV	G	GS	IP	H	BB	SO	HR	GB%	BABIP	STUFF	WHIP	ERA	PERA	EQERA	EQH9	EQBB9	EQSO9	EQHR9	VORP	WXRL
2003	OAK	MLB	31	3	5	0	35	13	108.7	117	36	51	18	53%	.270	-21	1.41	4.22	5.48	5.40	10.1	3.0	4.2	1.4	2.8	0.8
2004	TBA	MLB	32	7	6	0	34	14	118.7	134	27	59	17	51%	.294	-8	1.35	4.70	5.01	4.70	10.2	1.9	4.2	1.2	12.6	1.4
2005	BOS	MLB	33	1	1	0	30	1	43.7	56	9	26	5	53%	.327	-5	1.49	6.18	4.53	6.11	10.4	1.8	5.1	1.0	-4.6	-0.1
2005	WAS	MLB	33	0	3	0	10	3	21.3	23	8	11	1	50%	.310	-9	1.45	4.65	4.15	4.98	9.1	2.9	4.2	0.4	1.6	0.2
2006	WAS	MLB	34	3	4	1	41	4	66.0	70	19	37	7	50%	.287	-12	1.34	4.28	4.78	5.38	9.8	2.4	4.4	1.0	3.7	0.4

Breakout: 23% Improve: 57% Collapse: 17% Attrition: 18% Comparables: Paul Lindblad, Bill Lee, Dave Roberts

Halama is a rare bird these days—the lefty swing man who actually gets used in spots in the rotation or to work the middle innings. Generally, this type of pitcher is going the way of the dodo, which is probably why he was yet another one of the in-season saviors who leapt to the team's rescue, only to plunge to the pavement. If he's your 11th pitcher, he won't kill you, but he's a free agent as of mid-January.

LIVAN HERNANDEZ Bats: R Throws: R Height: 6' 2" Weight: 225 Born: February 20, 1975 Age: 31

YEAR	TM	LVL	AGE	W	L	SV	G	GS	IP	H	BB	SO	HR	GB%	BABIP	STUFF	WHIP	ERA	PERA	EQERA	EQH9	EQBB9	EQSO9	EQHR9	VORP	WXRL
2003	MON	MLB	28	15	10	0	33	33	233.3	225	57	178	27	49%	.289	18	1.21	3.20	4.13	3.55	8.9	2.0	6.2	1.0	62.9	6.5
2004	MON	MLB	29	11	15	0	35	35	255.0	234	83	186	26	48%	.284	17	1.24	3.60	4.27	3.69	8.7	2.7	5.9	0.9	55.6	7.9
2005	WAS	MLB	30	15	10	0	35	35	246.3	268	84	147	25	42%	.315	6	1.43	3.98	4.69	4.58	9.8	2.8	4.9	0.9	33.6	5.2
2006	WAS	MLB	31	13	11	0	33	33	219.3	212	64	144	21	45%	.279	10	1.26	3.60	4.24	4.24	9.0	2.4	5.2	0.9	33.4	5.0

Breakout: 13% Improve: 41% Collapse: 15% Attrition: 0% Comparables: Jaime Navarro, Jim Clancy, Pat Hentgen

(continued next page)

Livan Hernandez *(continued)*

The game's great iron man of the mound kept rolling, and while his comparables aren't a happy lot, at this point, his remarkable durability seems to keep his workload from becoming a source of concern. He wasn't the fireballer of years past, but he pitched most of the year with a bad right knee, making it hard for him to push off in his delivery. He still managed to give his team 23 quality starts—six innings or more, three runs or less—and he'd have had 26 if three weren't blown after the sixth inning. Heck, he even slugged .366, smacking a couple of home runs. Think Iron Man McGinnity could do that these days? While the Nats should be chastised for not taking it easy on the big guy in September—six starts, 46 IP, 24 runs allowed—when it was clear he wasn't well, his knee should be fine this spring. You can reasonably expect him to be throwing harder and bounce back.

MIKE HINCKLEY　　　　**Bats: R　Throws: L**　　Height: 6′ 3″　Weight: 170　Born: October 5, 1982　Age: 23

YEAR	TM	LVL	AGE	W	L	SV	G	GS	IP	H	BB	SO	HR	GB%	BABIP	STUFF	WHIP	ERA	PERA	EQERA	EQH9	EQBB9	EQSO9	EQHR9	VORP	WXRL
2003	SAV	A	20	9	5	0	23	23	121.0	124	41	111	4	—	.323	10	1.36	3.64	4.68	5.83	10.0	3.6	5.0	0.8	-3.0	—
2004	BRV	A+	21	6	2	0	10	10	62.0	47	18	51	6	—	.238	-4	1.05	2.61	6.39	4.79	9.6	3.4	5.3	2.1	5.1	—
2004	HAR	AA	21	5	2	0	16	16	94.0	83	23	80	5	—	.292	24	1.13	2.87	4.03	3.83	8.6	2.4	5.7	0.7	18.0	—
2005	POT	A+	22	3	9	0	22	21	127.7	151	51	80	10	45%	.332	-16	1.58	4.93	5.74	7.47	10.8	4.0	3.4	1.1	-26.0	—
2006	*WAS*	*MLB*	*23*	*6*	*10*	*0*	*28*	*22*	*131.3*	*140*	*62*	*72*	*17*	*47%*	*.287*	*-7*	*1.54*	*5.20*	*5.94*	*6.16*	*9.9*	*3.9*	*4.3*	*1.2*	*-6.6*	*0.2*

Breakout: 11%　Improve: 47%　Collapse: 18%　Attrition: 0%　　Comparables: Scott Downs, Jimmy Osting, Doug Bridges

Considered one of the team's top pitching prospects coming into the season, Hinckley managed to disappoint. A strained shoulder held him back until May, and when he took the mound he seemed to overthrow everything, driving his velocity down and leaving him without command of any of his pitches. He's liked for his dedication to his craft, but between concerns about his slight frame and lack of durability and the worry that his curve and change don't project well if he isn't throwing in the 90s, he's on the cusp of becoming a non-prospect.

TRAVIS HUGHES　　　　**Bats: R　Throws: R**　　Height: 6′ 5″　Weight: 230　Born: May 25, 1978　Age: 28

YEAR	TM	LVL	AGE	W	L	SV	G	GS	IP	H	BB	SO	HR	GB%	BABIP	STUFF	WHIP	ERA	PERA	EQERA	EQH9	EQBB9	EQSO9	EQHR9	VORP	WXRL
2003	FRI	AA	25	4	8	0	24	10	74.0	81	26	58	6	—	.314	-24	1.45	4.99	5.99	7.00	10.7	4.1	4.8	1.5	-11.0	—
2003	OKL	AAA	25	1	3	0	11	11	57.7	79	27	36	4	—	.354	-11	1.84	5.46	5.55	7.10	11.1	4.9	4.5	0.9	-9.7	—
2004	FRI	AA	26	3	6	7	40	0	63.3	63	33	68	4	—	.331	-19	1.52	3.70	5.46	6.52	10.0	6.2	6.2	1.1	-6.1	—
2004	OKL	AAA	26	1	2	0	13	0	25.7	21	9	24	2	—	.268	-4	1.17	5.25	4.38	5.84	8.0	3.6	6.2	0.7	-0.7	—
2005	NWO	AAA	27	2	5	13	52	0	59.7	47	25	73	3	48%	.306	8	1.21	3.02	3.95	4.74	8.2	4.1	7.9	0.6	5.4	—
2005	WAS	MLB	27	1	1	0	14	0	13.0	18	8	8	4	54%	.333	-29	2.00	5.54	7.43	6.08	12.2	4.7	4.7	2.7	-0.4	-0.2
2006	*WAS*	*MLB*	*28*	*2*	*3*	*2*	*49*	*2*	*47.0*	*47*	*28*	*38*	*5*	*46%*	*.298*	*-8*	*1.58*	*4.69*	*5.63*	*5.65*	*9.2*	*4.9*	*6.4*	*1.0*	*0.6*	*0.0*

Breakout: 41%　Improve: 65%　Collapse: 14%　Attrition: 22%　　Comparables: Frank Reberger, J. J. Putz, Jason Isringhausen

Not every random pickup by the Nats wound up a sad story. The Rangers put Hughes on waivers, but why they did so is puzzling. He can dial it up to 95 on occasion, and mixes in a good slider and splitter to keep people guessing. The pen's already crowded with possible contributors, but Hughes can outlast them simply by remaining healthy.

ESTEBAN LOAIZA　　　　**Bats: R　Throws: R**　　Height: 6′ 3″　Weight: 210　Born: December 31, 1971　Age: 34

YEAR	TM	LVL	AGE	W	L	SV	G	GS	IP	H	BB	SO	HR	GB%	BABIP	STUFF	WHIP	ERA	PERA	EQERA	EQH9	EQBB9	EQSO9	EQHR9	VORP	WXRL
2003	CHA	MLB	31	21	9	0	34	34	226.3	196	56	207	17	51%	.289	39	1.11	2.90	3.33	2.89	8.0	2.2	8.1	0.6	78.0	8.0
2004	CHA	MLB	32	9	5	0	21	21	140.7	156	45	83	23	45%	.298	-2	1.43	4.86	5.02	4.76	9.7	2.7	5.0	1.3	18.9	1.9
2004	NYA	MLB	32	1	2	0	10	6	42.3	61	26	34	9	43%	.377	-12	2.06	8.51	5.80	8.20	11.0	4.8	6.4	1.6	-14.0	-0.5
2005	WAS	MLB	33	12	10	0	34	34	217.0	227	55	173	18	45%	.322	24	1.30	3.77	3.79	4.20	9.1	2.1	6.5	0.8	39.4	5.3
2006	*OAK*	*MLB*	*34*	*12*	*10*	*0*	*32*	*30*	*195.7*	*202*	*51*	*131*	*23*	*45%*	*.291*	*13*	*1.29*	*4.07*	*4.27*	*4.42*	*9.1*	*2.4*	*6.0*	*1.0*	*29.0*	*4.4*

Breakout: 13%　Improve: 45%　Collapse: 16%　Attrition: 3%　　Comparables: Rick Rhoden, John Burkett, Dave Stewart

Loaiza cashed in on his year with the Nats by signing up with Oakland to Benson money ($7 million per over three years). That might seem like a pretty big risk for Billy Beane, but couched in those terms, better Loaiza than Russ Ortiz. The problem with Loaiza is that the answer to the question "Who is he?" is sort of ambiguous. Is he the career mediocrity who gave the Pirates, Rangers, and Blue Jays workmanlike turn-taking? Is he the ace starter the White Sox had on their hands in 2003 when he developed his cutter? Is he the Whitson-like pineapple surprise who exploded upon becoming a Yankee? Or is he the solid starter that the Nationals had on their hands last year? The last iteration is what the A's will likely have on their hands. Loaiza's performance in 2005 wasn't too dissimilar from his performance with the White Sox before he went to the Yankees, and his strikeout and walk rates were closer to those of his breakout in '03. Just about the only thing that's shelved him recently were pinstriped panic attacks, so Oakland should have a durable third starter.

GARY MAJEWSKI Bats: R Throws: R Height: 6' 2" Weight: 200 Born: February 26, 1980 Age: 26

YEAR	TM	LVL	AGE	W	L	SV	G	GS	IP	H	BB	SO	HR	GB%	BABIP	STUFF	WHIP	ERA	PERA	EQERA	EQH9	EQBB9	EQSO9	EQHR9	VORP	WXRL
2003	CHR	AAA	23	6	4	4	42	1	72.7	62	29	72	3	—	.288	8	1.25	3.96	4.00	4.78	8.3	4.3	7.2	0.5	6.4	—
2004	CHR	AAA	24	3	3	14	35	0	42.3	30	16	41	2	—	.262	6	1.09	3.19	3.83	3.83	7.7	3.8	7.0	0.4	7.9	—
2004	EDM	AAA	24	1	2	1	15	0	16.3	18	8	17	0	—	.383	-2	1.60	3.87	3.86	4.96	9.4	5.0	6.6	0.0	1.2	—
2004	MON	MLB	24	0	1	1	16	0	21.0	28	5	12	2	49%	.361	-10	1.57	3.86	4.57	6.23	10.8	2.1	4.6	0.8	-2.1	-0.7
2005	WAS	MLB	25	4	4	1	79	0	86.0	80	37	50	2	47%	.288	5	1.36	2.93	4.10	3.68	8.7	3.7	4.8	0.2	19.7	3.1
2006	*WAS*	*MLB*	*26*	*3*	*3*	*2*	*57*	*0*	*61.7*	*59*	*26*	*42*	*5*	*48%*	*.281*	*-6*	*1.37*	*3.84*	*4.34*	*4.77*	*8.8*	*3.5*	*5.4*	*0.7*	*6.8*	*0.5*

Breakout: 10% Improve: 39% Collapse: 30% Attrition: 16% Comparables: Mike Garman, Vinnie Chulk, Horacio Pina

We live in an age of mayhem, which makes Majewski a pitcher with the most modern sensibilities. His career rate for plunking people, majors and minors together, is one victim every 49.3 batters faced. Translated to a full big league career, that would rank fifth among pitchers since 1960. Who's ahead of him? Surprisingly, mostly contemporary hurlers: Brian Fuentes (one HBP per 38.7 hitters), Byung-Hyun Kim (43.5), Rolando Arrojo (45.4), and Willis Roberts (46.6). There's not a Drysdale to be found among that lot. As Ayala started to break down, Majewski wound up taking on more of the setup role. He should be the better bet going forward, however violent his tendencies.

JOHN PATTERSON Bats: R Throws: R Height: 6' 5" Weight: 210 Born: January 30, 1978 Age: 28

YEAR	TM	LVL	AGE	W	L	SV	G	GS	IP	H	BB	SO	HR	GB%	BABIP	STUFF	WHIP	ERA	PERA	EQERA	EQH9	EQBB9	EQSO9	EQHR9	VORP	WXRL
2003	TUC	AAA	25	10	5	0	18	18	109.3	100	43	74	6	—	.270	7	1.31	2.63	4.77	4.26	8.5	4.3	5.0	0.7	15.7	—
2003	ARI	MLB	25	1	4	1	16	8	55.0	61	30	43	7	38%	.323	-3	1.65	6.05	4.98	5.79	9.5	4.3	6.3	1.1	-2.8	0.2
2004	MON	MLB	26	4	7	0	19	19	98.3	100	46	99	18	37%	.306	5	1.48	5.04	4.93	5.11	9.3	3.8	8.0	1.5	4.0	1.6
2005	WAS	MLB	27	9	7	0	31	31	198.3	172	65	185	19	31%	.287	28	1.19	3.13	3.84	3.52	8.1	2.7	7.7	0.9	50.9	6.7
2006	*WAS*	*MLB*	*28*	*11*	*10*	*0*	*29*	*29*	*185.0*	*164*	*63*	*156*	*22*	*36%*	*.270*	*18*	*1.22*	*3.66*	*4.18*	*4.30*	*8.2*	*2.8*	*6.6*	*1.1*	*26.3*	*4.2*

Breakout: 11% Improve: 58% Collapse: 15% Attrition: 3% Comparables: Craig Swan, Rick Helling, Tim Belcher

Eyeballs and PECOTA agreed when we touted Patterson as a breakout candidate last year, and he more than lived up to the billing, finishing 11th in the major leagues in Support-Neutral Value Added, ahead of both Loaiza (26th) and Livan (29th). After struggling to get his career started in the unforgiving BOB, he's now in the best possible ballpark for him. RFK is the sort of place where, even if the hitter picks up Patterson's big-bending curve, he'll have a tough time driving it out of the yard. The bender brings a different sort of penalty, as Patterson's long windup creates opportunities for baserunners to nab bags; he finished second in the league in stolen bases allowed with 26 (Greg Maddux led with 32). There isn't a lot of reason to expect him to regress; the park's still roomy, his elbow surgery is pretty far back in his past, and the time he missed in 2004 was a result of a strained groin.

DARRELL RASNER Bats: R Throws: R Height: 6' 3" Weight: 210 Born: January 13, 1981 Age: 25

YEAR	TM	LVL	AGE	W	L	SV	G	GS	IP	H	BB	SO	HR	GB%	BABIP	STUFF	WHIP	ERA	PERA	EQERA	EQH9	EQBB9	EQSO9	EQHR9	VORP	WXRL
2003	SAV	A	22	7	7	0	22	22	105.3	106	36	90	8	—	.303	-27	1.35	4.19	6.39	6.57	10.8	3.9	4.6	1.9	-10.6	—
2004	BRV	A+	23	6	5	0	22	21	119.3	133	31	88	6	—	.332	-5	1.37	3.17	5.09	5.87	10.8	2.9	4.2	1.1	-3.5	—
2004	HAR	AA	23	1	1	0	5	5	29.7	21	9	15	1	—	.233	2	1.01	1.21	4.50	2.25	7.7	3.2	3.2	0.3	10.4	—
2005	HAR	AA	24	6	7	0	27	26	150.3	150	29	96	10	53%	.297	0	1.19	3.59	4.76	5.00	9.6	2.2	3.8	0.9	9.7	—
2006	*WAS*	*MLB*	*25*	*6*	*9*	*0*	*34*	*18*	*126.3*	*136*	*43*	*64*	*16*	*48%*	*.285*	*-8*	*1.41*	*4.77*	*5.36*	*5.73*	*10.0*	*2.8*	*4.0*	*1.1*	*-0.1*	*0.7*

Breakout: 8% Improve: 40% Collapse: 26% Attrition: 0% Comparables: Tim Manwiller, Chris Begg, Doyle Alexander

Although Rasner is more of a control artist, he has an assortment that might herald more dominating performance. He mixes a good sinker with an improving curve, but polishing up his changeup would probably make the difference. When the upside is his possibly growing up to be a fifth starter in the big leagues, you can be forgiven if you're not worked up about a work in progress that might only turn out to be just another Elvis on velvet.

JON RAUCH

Bats: R Throws: R   Height: 6' 11" Weight: 260   Born: September 27, 1978 Age: 27

YEAR	TM	LVL	AGE	W	L	SV	G	GS	IP	H	BB	SO	HR	GB%	BABIP	STUFF	WHIP	ERA	PERA	EQERA	EQH9	EQBB9	EQSO9	EQHR9	VORP	WXRL
2003	CHR	AAA	24	7	1	0	24	23	124.7	121	35	94	16	—	.273	-17	1.25	4.11	5.70	5.17	9.7	3.1	5.4	1.8	5.7	—
2004	CHR	AAA	25	6	3	0	14	13	72.3	57	25	61	9	—	.245	0	1.13	3.11	5.19	3.99	8.6	3.7	6.1	1.5	12.1	—
2004	MON	MLB	25	3	0	0	9	2	23.3	14	7	18	1	46%	.213	15	0.90	1.55	3.22	1.61	6.4	2.4	6.4	0.4	10.8	1.2
2005	NWO	AAA	26	1	1	0	7	5	21.3	19	2	25	3	32%	.296	15	0.99	2.54	4.43	3.98	9.3	0.9	7.5	1.8	3.7	—
2005	WAS	MLB	26	2	4	0	15	1	30.0	24	11	23	3	25%	.250	3	1.17	3.60	4.30	3.99	8.0	3.1	6.4	0.9	6.1	0.4
2006	WAS	MLB	27	3	3	1	30	4	56.7	55	20	43	8	36%	.275	-3	1.31	4.23	4.93	5.34	9.0	2.8	5.9	1.3	4.5	0.5

Breakout: 9%   Improve: 23%   Collapse: 45%   Attrition: 30%   Comparables: Todd Worrell, Mark Acre, Bill Dawley

Despite losing chunks of each of the last three seasons to shoulder trouble, Rauch still managed to strike out a dozen hitters in his 12 September innings, suggesting that the big guy still has something left. For all the talk about how hard he is to hit because of his height and the steep angles at which his heater enters the zone, he's a perpetual mess mechanically. Scouting is short on cost-benefit analysis, and while you can understand the enthusiasm that's always surrounded Rauch's potential, don't get carried away with any high expectations for him.

Line Outs

Position/Player	TM	LVL	AGE	PA	R	2B	3B	HR	RBI	BB	SO	SB-CS	SPEED	BA/OBP/SLG	MLVR	EQBA/OBP/SLG	EQA	VORP
OF/1B Matt Cepicky*	NWO	AAA	27	389	52	23	3	14	68	43	85	1-3	3.6	.269/.347/.477	.120	.247/.313/.414	.250	-4.2
SS Ian Desmond	SAV	A	19	316	37	10	2	4	23	13	60	20-6	6.4	.247/.291/.334	-.126	.226/.257/.310	.207	-15.3
	POT	A+	19	243	37	13	3	3	15	21	53	13-6	7.2	.256/.325/.384	-.053	.225/.279/.333	.220	-6.3
C S. Manriquez	POT	A+	22	482	64	36	2	15	68	30	86	0-0	4.0	.287/.336/.479	.119	.249/.287/.410	.239	2.2
INF Rick Short	NWO	AAA	32	432	72	35	1	11	70	46	27	5-4	4.6	.383/.456/.569	.585	.325/.383/.446	.286	25.6

Pitchers	TM	LVL	AGE	W	L	SV	IP	H	BB	SO	HR	GB%	BABIP	STUFF	WHIP	ERA	PERA	EQERA	EQH9	EQBB9	EQSO9	EQHR9	VORP
G. Bunn	SAV	A	22	3	5	0	58.3	51	25	56	10	42%	.263	-32	1.30	3.86	8.65	6.40	11.2	5.4	5.5	3.5	-4.6
	POT	A+	22	2	6	0	60.3	72	45	65	8	40%	.381	-27	1.94	7.16	7.25	8.49	11.4	7.7	6.0	2.0	-18.7
J. Karp	HAR	AA	25	2	5	0	57.7	57	23	40	6	48%	.293	-19	1.39	4.68	6.46	6.13	10.3	4.6	4.1	1.5	-3.2
	NWO	AAA	25	3	1	0	36.0	37	14	29	8	42%	.293	-30	1.42	5.75	7.34	6.82	10.5	3.9	5.2	2.6	-4.6
M. O'Connor*	POT	A+	24	10	11	0	167.7	144	48	158	14	47%	.285	-4	1.14	3.54	5.14	5.59	9.2	3.2	5.1	1.3	0.2
A. Osuna '04	SDN	MLB	31	2	1	0	36.7	32	11	36	3	39%	.293	16	1.17	2.45	3.47	2.97	8.2	2.5	7.9	0.7	11.9
D. Thompson	SAV	A	19	2	3	0	53.7	46	24	48	3	47%	.293	6	1.30	3.35	5.15	5.51	9.1	5.0	5.2	0.9	0.5

Scott Cepicky is proof positive that the prettiest swing you ever saw isn't guaranteed to deliver anything more than its beauty. Maybe it's Freddy Adu envy, but the Nats can't seem to stop talking about how highly they think of **Ian Desmond**. It's all chalkboard what-ifs for now, but he's young enough that he might someday merit the hype. **Salomon Manriquez** might profile as a nice Mark Parent type—a reserve catcher with some pop—but he's got significant defensive kinks to iron out first. Likeable journeyman **Rick Short** won the minor league batting title, then managed to shred a shoulder upon his first big league call-up. He's been sold to the Japanese Leagues, where he'll earn his yen.

Although **Greg Bunn** has been overhyped as someone who will move up fast after getting picked in the 5th round of the 2004 draft, he does throw hard and mix in his offspeed stuff well. Once a 1st rounder out of UCLA, not even a move to the bullpen seems to be keeping **Josh Karp's** career prospects alive. **Michael O'Connor** is a local product out of downtown George Washington U., and a mini-Livan, tying for the Carolina League lead in IP. **Antonio Osuna's** tradition for hurting himself in the face of high expectations is a reminder that some pitchers only have to fool people once a year—at contract time. **Daryl Thompson** is a high school pitcher picked in 2003 on the strength of his fastball. Although he had to be shut down with shoulder trouble, he's expected to be okay this spring.

Where Does Statistical Analysis Fall Down? Reality and Perception

by Gary Huckabay

Overreaching gets one in trouble very quickly. When we overreach, there's usually a good reason. At the time, we may believe that we can live up to the promises that we end up regretting just a few days down the road. We may hold that belief because of excessive optimism stemming from inexperience, from too much coffee, or from just trying 3% too hard to impress someone.

The consequences of overreaching range from a little problem, like a fender bender or slightly late project, to a major accident or a ruined career. In baseball, there are many examples, most illustratively the way Toronto Blue Jays manager Tim Johnson lied about his war record to create a living parable for his players. Did he need the myth he was creating to manage his team? Almost certainly not. Johnson took an enormous risk—perpetuating a falsehood that endangered his credibility and career—for very little actual gain.

There's a lot of that going on in the world of statistical analysis—or at least some decision makers within the game think so. This essay will address the use of objective performance data and numeric manipulation to drive decisions about baseball operations, including assessment, development, contract negotiation, budgeting, on-field tactics, decisions about playing time, and all the associated activities involved with running an MLB organization on the Baseball Ops side.

More specifically, we'll talk about the limitations of statistical analysis. Most *Baseball Prospectus* readers know where BP stands on the subject of using performance data and analysis to serve as the core of making baseball decisions—we're for it. A lot of people are not, and the entire subject has caused some friction in the MLB Community. This piece is intended to shine some light on two types of problems with data-driven management in baseball—real problems, and perceived problems.

Reality

Data-Driven Management

First, throw the term "sabermetrics" out the window. It's slippery, doesn't describe anything of substance, and triv-ializes the nature of serious analysis. In the real world, decisions are made using a much wider array of available information than is available to the general public. In addition to performance data on players, there are also scouting reports, first-hand interactions with the players and their representatives, as well as the stored memory of watching the players personally, particularly at the major league level. Ultimately, the use of data and analysis of that data to make managerial decisions isn't specific to baseball, much less SABR, whose activities are not limited to number-crunching by any means.

What we're really talking about is Data-Driven Management. No one serious about baseball analysis wants less information—we want more, and we want it to be used in a responsible and effective manner. Most statistical analysts don't want to supplant scouting information; they're actually downright hungry to include scouting data in the model-building and decision-making process. The seminal issue isn't whether or not the data being used is from a scouting staff or from a Sports Information Director at a Junior College; it's how predictive or descriptive each piece of information is, and how it can best be used (or ignored) when making player personnel decisions. Data-Driven Management is not about the mere gathering of data, it's also about how well each piece of information informs a decision. It's about understanding the relationship between the information at hand and its potential impact on the team.

It's Not "Stats," It's Data

Players don't have stats. When you see a hitter's line for the year, you're not looking at his "stats," you're looking at aggregated data, usually with a few simple calculations or manipulations thrown in. At Bats are summed. Batting average is the result of simple division. Data can be manipulated in a number of different ways—which compels one to ask: If data is supposed to represent the reality of a player, and that data is malleable, what is the data, really?

The performance data that fans and front office execs use is really scouting data. It's simplistic, and set up so that even the most obtuse observer can keep a reasonable record of what they've seen on the field. Instead of evaluating the bat speed, technique, and strengths of a particular hitter, the data recorded is discrete, has clear rules that separate one level of performance from another, and require minimal training. It takes significant training to observe performance the way scouts do, whereas it takes relatively little training to score a game.

"If the hitter makes contact, no fielder messes up significantly, and the hitter reaches first base without being put out, but doesn't continue past first base, we call that a 'single.'" That's really what we're talking about when we talk about "stats"—performance data, created through the use of a set of accounting rules that tell us where to put the tally mark on the record for each game event.

Context and Data Collection

It is not possible for an aggregation of data to be of higher quality than the data itself. The data that's used today in the statistical analysis of baseball is better than it's ever been. Pitch-by-pitch data is available, and several organizations, including Baseball Prospectus, have comprehensive data review protocols to make sure that all the information that's recorded is as accurate as it can possibly be. Yet, it's far from comprehensive or perfect.

The data used for performance analysis is notoriously incomplete. When you look at a player's condensed stat line over the course of a season, it may look like table 1.

Hafner suffered a concussion on July 16th, and, magic elixir that head traumas are, Hafner returned from the disabled list on August 4th and began tearing the cover off the ball, hitting like a monster during a nine-game hitting streak which began the day he returned from the DL. Dumb anomalies aside, the point is that players are almost never 100% throughout the year, and there are assumptions implicit in any sort of aggregation of these performances, particularly in terms of trying to predict future performance. If a hitter has a nagging wrist injury all year, and doesn't drive the ball the way he would if healthy, the data record isn't necessarily going to help you very much in terms of figuring out what he's going to do next year—you'll need considerably more information to make a reasonable decision, and you won't find it in the performance data.

As an aggregate snapshot of the season, the data isn't a bad tool. But aside from the well-covered territory of park effects, league effects, and similar factors, there are important pieces of information missing in both the aggregate and granular data. In simpler terms, there is no such thing as an iconic Travis Hafner. Travis Hafner with the flu on April 8th is a very different player than Travis Hafner in perfect health on May 14th. Using seasonal data, you get an aggregation of all the Hafners that played in 2005; that's not necessarily a bad thing, but any analysis or decision-making based on that information should include contextual information, if possible. That can't be done with statistical analysis.

Data doesn't tend to get cleaner on its own. Aside from being subject to the aches and pains that players suffer throughout the year, small errors at the margin limit the utility of the data. The same ground ball in the 5-6 hole might be judged a hit by one official scorer and an error by another. Over the course of a season, these little glitches might even out on the individual level, but they also might skew the data by 3–4 hits for a hitter, or the difference between 5 runs being earned or unearned for a given pitcher. Most capable analysts know about the foibles of ERA and other illusions in the record, and that the hard record of the game, even on a pitch-by-pitch basis, isn't as objective as we'd sometimes like to think.

Delivering the Goods

One of the things that made number crunching important for us was that park adjustments were going to open our eyes to some talented guys we missed before. As a group, the statheads were no help. You didn't understand that parks change every year, and not just in little ways. Instead of understanding park effects better because we're taking all these little adjustments into account, now we know less than we did before, and we had to pay for the privilege.

— An NL Scout.

One of the great promises of serious analysis, and particularly of Baseball Prospectus, was the ability to adjust or translate performance data from one set of parks or leagues to another, and compare players from different leagues on an apples-to-apples basis. Within the professional leagues, we've done a fairly good job on this particular issue, but things have gotten more and more complicated on the park adjustment front. Why? Because there are more and more changes at ballparks at all levels around the country.

What should you use to measure a park's impact on offensive levels? Do you use physical characteristics like outfield depth, foul ground, temperature, humidity, or the

TABLE 1. SAMPLE PLAYER'S STAT LINE FOR A SEASON													
Player	G	AB	H	2B	3B	HR	BB	K	SB	CS	BA	OBP	SLG
Hafner, Travis	137	486	148	42	0	33	79	123	0	0	.305	.408	.595

albedo of the batter's eye? To date, we've used performance data for the hitters and pitchers who've come through the league, and their performances upon leaving it for other parks. The somewhat problematic issue is that of embedded assumptions—we don't generally have enough data to know the specific impact of a player's physical environment on that player's performance, so we end up using data aggregations and averages, which leaves us without a good tool to explain why a particular park has certain effects. That means that when the park changes, we don't know the impact of the changes. Add in that the effects can be very small, and when a minor league park might see very few games, we run into sample size concerns. In an academic setting, there is an understanding and acceptance of these limits on what we can discern, but in the real world the equivocation of the analysis can be very frustrating to the audience. Busy decision-makers responsible for multi-million dollar investments under significant time constraints don't like to spend a great deal of time listening to why the information they're getting is flawed.

League adjustments are tricky as well, but for different reasons. Affiliations shift, player development philosophies vary from team to team, and even the goals of the clubs aren't in alignment. As the leagues move closer to the majors, we can be more confident in the accuracy of translating performance statistics from level to level. This is in large part due to the Darwinian effect of moving up levels; in low A ball, the variance in performance from player to player is large. As players move up, the level of skill and performance as a whole increases, and the variance in the level of competition is reduced through the elimination of low performers.

Up the Academy

Once one escapes the confines of organized professional baseball and wanders onto the college campus, things get trickier and the overreaching gets more and more serious.

> The amazing thing to me is that people don't question that a college football athlete can have great statistics, win the Heisman Trophy, and still have no future in the NFL because professional football is a different beast. Then, those same people can't accept that a player can be a great collegiate baseball player, but have no chance of ever making a contribution in pro baseball. The college game of baseball is a different game than professional baseball, just as the NFL game is a different game than Major College Football.
>
> — Kevin Goldstein, *Baseball America*.

The College game is dramatically different than the MLB game. First off, and most obviously, the equipment is different. Hitters use aluminum instead of wood. Bats don't often snap in hitter's hands and the pitcher is at considerably more personal risk than if wooden bats were the weapon of choice. Second, and more important for the discussion of stats, the quality of opposition has a much greater variance than the minors, and it's generally of a much lower quality. Your typical 19-year-old high school draftee in low A ball has been totally immersed in baseball to an extent not seen at any college program. The college ranks are filled with good high school players; the pro ranks are filled with great ones. The Darwinian effect isn't in play for most collegians, either. You don't go on to a major program at Oklahoma State after you finish your four years at Chico State. All of these factors have combined to prevent the development of a reliable system of translating college performances to the major leagues—the translations that would have the highest value to clubs. The analytical tools that are available and mature focus on what can best be called "Supermajor" programs, the top baseball programs. The discovery and identification of hidden gems at small colleges remains a difficult task, further underscoring the importance of contextual information missing from the performance dataset.

Proper Metrics

Some of the old-line metrics are classic responses to classic questions facing every business. Teams strive to win games. Players strive to win games. It's not illogical to want to assign some responsibility for a team's success or failure to the individuals on the team. The statistical efforts to do so haven't necessarily been accurate, but many of them have been simple, and gained significant following among fans and among front office execs searching for ways to deal with an enormous amount of information. So pitcher wins become a reasonable analog for a pitcher's value; RBIs, truly a team metric, become a billboard for the individual slugger. Using RBIs to measure individual performance is a little like measuring McDonald's employees importance and effectiveness by how much money they take it at their register. Cindy in Helena, Montana brought in $7,114.09 during her shift, whereas CEO Charlie Bell brought in $0.00.

Everyone who's ever worked in sales understands the concept of the quota and the bonus. People learn very quickly which behaviors are rewarded, and which ones aren't. If you give a car salesman some price discretion and a bonus based on how many cars he sells, you can look forward to selling a whole bunch of cheap cars as your staff discounts everything on the lot to make their bonus. Similarly, once certain numbers become magical and recognized in baseball, people will start to manage to those numbers rather than necessarily doing what's best for the team as a whole. In fact, they tend to change their perception over time so that the numbers—say, starting pitcher wins or saves—are seen as the very definition of what's best for the team, when in reality, maximizing those individual numbers may come at an incredible cost to the team's success.

And that's all part and parcel of data-driven management; it's not about using information or not using information. It's about identifying and gathering the right information on which to base decisions.

Perception: The Interview

There are a lot of different projects going on in the various organizations of MLB in terms of implementing or integrating data-driven management. An executive from one of those clubs agreed to sit down with me for an extended conversation about the perception of quantitative analysis in front offices.

GH: Thanks for agreeing to eat a really expensive dinner on my dime.

EX: It's the least I can do. Can you please pass the wine list?

GH: So first off, is there a backlash against statistical analysis in front offices right now? And if there is, why?

EX: Well, there are some issues right off the bat. You're asking a general question, when the answer's meaningless. "Front Offices" aren't some sort of Stalinist icons, and ideology isn't in play. This is baseball, not politics.

GH: But is there not a trend or prevailing sentiment? You know what I mean here.

EX: I can only speak about those situations I'm familiar with, so how about if I stick to that? I think there's not necessarily a backlash, but a better understanding of the world of analysis, and an integration of those ideas into people's perspectives, rather than having a separate internal organization to do the analysis. I don't know of any team that doesn't have a stats guy or two, either internally or externally.

GH: What kind of influence do those guys usually have?

EX: Pretty slight, usually. But that's not because of the material.

GH: Why, then?

EX: Second hand, there are cultural issues. You and Gary Hughes did that thing at the Winter Meetings last year, about Stats versus Scouts. That's part of the problem. The experienced front office guys don't get along with the stats guys, and, honestly, the stats guys I've met aren't exactly Dale Carnegie graduates. Voros McCracken said that he wanted to

be listened to more at that event. You get people to pay attention by doing good work and being persuasive. The onus is on the stats guy to convince people to pay attention to him.

GH: Sure, but part of that is the traditional folks having an open mind to start with, right?

EX: By and large, we do.

GH: So the stats guys have simply failed to make their case?

EX: I think so. And it's because most of the stats guys that have been hired are the wrong guys. They're amateur mathematicians, really. They don't have training or experience in persuading people. What I've seen and heard, both personally and second hand, is that if their mathematical case isn't the one that ends up determining a roster spot or contract, they repeat the same information, only louder, and decry the lack of understanding of the other people in the process.

GH: But that's not a weakness of statistical analysis, is it? Doesn't that say more for bad hiring practices on the part of the clubs?

EX: Oh, definitely. And that's another part of what's going on. Probably the biggest part, actually.

GH: Meaning?

EX: What makes a great statistical guy [suitable] to work in baseball operations?

GH: Off the top of my head, a quantitative aptitude, training, experience, demonstrated ability to work with large datasets, experience in research design, significant presentation experience, and a thick skin. Probably a lot more stuff, but that's a quick brain dump.

EX: Ok, let's say I weed through the 40 resumes that hit my desk every week, and I decide I'm going to hire someone to work with [our Assistant General Manager] on baseball operations. How do I find that guy? There's no college degree in Baseball Operations, and if they're touting their math abilities, how I do I tell the difference? I had calculus for about half a year about 25 years ago. And even then, that's only one part of what I need out of the guy.

GH: You can't get a read on a candidate through a rigorous interview process?

EX: If I'm trying to find out their math skills? No chance.

GH: Ok, but *you* have a stats guy—more than one, in fact. How did you end up making the determination?

EX: In our case, we actually got help from a professor of statistics at a local university.

GH: Isn't that a good way around the problem?

EX: Not really. He didn't think any of the candidates were qualified enough to do the job.

GH: Huh?

EX: You heard me. The professor didn't think any of the guys who wanted the job were competent at statistics.

GH: And the candidates—they had degrees in the things like math, stats, business?

EX: Pretty much. And from big schools. I think the least regarded school anyone had their degree from was Georgia, which certainly isn't a bad school.

GH: Was there any explanation as to why they weren't qualified?

EX: I can't give you the technicalities of it, but the gist was that they were fanatical fans who didn't have the fundamentals of real-world analysis.

GH: But that's all the technical side, right? Persuasive ability, how well he or she's going to get along with everyone, you can screen that, right? And that seems to be the major deciding factor anyway, right?

EX: There's other factors related to culture, too. It's not just one's baseball perspective, so to speak. We found a couple of people outside of our normal process that we really liked, both people you know. Wanted to bring them both on board, but absolutely could not do it.

GH: Why not?

EX: In short, the cost of bringing in either of them was absolutely ridiculous.

GH: To me, that's a complete copout. There's no team that hasn't wasted ten times the cost of one of those guys on a bad player contract.

EX: It's not that simple, and you know it. Let's talk about one guy in particular. He's a more senior guy, solid résumé very professional, knows his numbers very well, able to operate well with others, tremendous ability to build consensus, comfortable talking at length with the clubbie or with the Commissioner. He wanted $180,000 a year.

GH: Was he worth it?

EX: Probably, but I do know I couldn't pay him that, or even half of it. Word of that kind of salary is going to get around, and you're going to have 20-year

baseball veterans that are insulted [by] someone with very little direct baseball experience getting a job at anything near that kind of money, when most of them are in the $50,000–$80,000 range. We're paying scouts $30K. We can't pay a relatively inexperienced guy that kind of money and not have serious revolt elsewhere. And the fastest way for us not to talk to you is to say "I'll take any salary!" If that's true, you're probably not the person we should bring in. I'm not arguing that the guy was worth the money; it was a pay cut for him, but there was no realistic way that we could do that.

GH: Ok. But surely, you could find a recent grad who had the statistical chops, and invest some time in the guy, right?

EX: Believe it or not, we couldn't find that person. And it took enough time that we gave up looking, and went the consulting route.

GH: So you've got a confluence of issues. Still seems a bit shaky to me, though. You want the guy to have spent the necessary time, but you also want him to have all these other skills other than numerical chops. Doesn't the time spent learning the math, developing the presentation and people skills— doesn't that time count as paying dues?

EX: To me, sure. I didn't have a problem with the salary at hand. It was a question of perception, not reality.

GH: That's a pretty skewed and slanted playing field you're asking a stats guy to come in and play on.

EX: Won't argue with you on that. But no one ever starts out on a level playing field.

GH: Are you worried about losing ground to other organizations that are investing more money and time in their analytical capabilities?

EX: Not really, no.

GH: There are clubs doing some pretty cool stuff.

EX: But they're not using it particularly well. One thing I've learned is that this isn't an area where clubs can actually generate an advantage. It's more of a place where you can lose ground if you do nothing, rather than one where you can gain something through action.

GH: You really think so?

EX: Absolutely. We subscribe to BP Premium, and have an intern pull and summarize the statistical reports, which Baseball Ops and scouting review periodically. It keeps us up to date. Net cost, $40 a year.

GH: $40?! Hey, if you've got 30 people reading, cough up for the subs!

EX: How about some press passes, game tickets, and the occasional day in the box?

GH: Sold. But is that enough analysis to actually inform decisions?

EX: I think it is. Like I said before, distinguishing between the people willing to do this job for a relatively low cost is fairly difficult. We're happy enough to just get some basics on things to look for and avoid. Just by reading you guys and a few other sites and books, we get that same information and perspective, and we get it across the organization, at a cost of basically nothing.

GH: But don't you lose ground to an org that has a dedicated person, or a top-flight consultant like an Eddie Epstein?

EX: If so, it's not a huge advantage they're getting. It's not like every team has a squad of Keith Woolners on staff with a team of analysts and programmers at his beck and call. And, the dirty little secret of your industry is its lack of opinion divergence. Hell, considering the computer departments of every club I know of, having the best analyst in the world wouldn't matter because they'd never have a working computer and spreadsheet.

GH: What do you mean by lack of opinion divergence?

EX: You guys generally don't have a dime's worth of difference between you when it comes to players. You like durable guys with high on base percentages who hit for power and play great defense. On the mound, you like guys that strike people out as often as possible, don't walk people, and keep the ball on the ground. Gee, no shit. Us dumb-ass scouts would never have thought of that. Do you think it's possible that maybe you'll be against wife beating and passing out meth to kids, too?

GH: Oh, come on. The key is being able to identify those guys who'll have those positive attributes, and making the best use of all your available resources. And not doing unbelievably stupid crap like giving a four-year contract to Cristian Guzman. We're about accountability, and yes, we've all been wrong, but it's more visible because everything's laid out on paper. We have to be right more often, because everything we do is totally transparent.

EX: Some of the guys are transparent. Some aren't.

GH: But you're basically saying that there's effectively no difference between any of the analysts or their proposals or work product. I'm sorry, and I really

don't want to say it this way, but that's just obtuse. I don't want to mention specific names beyond those we've already discussed, but do you really think that there's no difference in the value of having a Keith Woolner on staff, and some lesser analyst?

EX: No. But I can't justify the cost, the risk, and the upheaval of hiring a Keith Woolner at the salary it'd take to get him, and the other costs and commitments that invariably come with him, or one of the people we already talked to.

GH: But you can afford to throw away $40 Million on crappy player contracts that you'd now like to duck.

EX: Oh, be serious. Again, it's not that simple and you know it. And every time you mention something like that, you either imply or explicitly state that the club doesn't understand the concept of aging, or doesn't know the contract's going to be a rock around their neck down the road. In the case you're speaking of, we knew the last two years of a couple of deals were going to be bad, but we wanted those first couple of years so we could make a run at a title.

GH: Ok. A lot of what you're talking about is perception, and the real world problems with having people of differing viewpoints in the front office. What about the substance of analysis? If you had a wish list for the problems that analysis could solve, what would be on it?

EX: The biggest problem with statistical analysis is that it's always retrospective. That's the biggest difference between stats and traditional scouting, and it's an unconquerable strength of scouting. I've seen perhaps 15–20 prediction methods using statistical data; you have PECOTA and Vlad, Rotowire, perhaps a dozen systems done by individuals, and all of them basically work off the same information. None of them are particularly interesting, really, and their primary benefit is that someone else has done the tedious work of writing them all down. I'd like to see a prediction system that worked well, and had some actual knobs that can be tuned, in terms of the underlying assumptions.

GH: Can you get the level of accuracy you want from methods that are more dependent on subjectivity and heuristic-type projection, like the stuff from traditional scouting?

EX: Not really, no, but most of the scouts would disagree. Billy Beane has it right about scouting. Scouts are asked to do superhuman things.

Forecast a guy's physical, mental, and baseball development several years in advance, based on watching him in person perhaps a few times over a period of a few months. So you're supposed to travel all over creation, pop out of a car, live on bad food and little sleep, then pick up minutiae on another young kid that distinguishes him from every other kid you've seen, to a point where you can predict his future to be different from all those other kids. It's not realistic or fair, but it's the way things are.

GH: What's next for statistical analysis in front offices?

EX: Like most movements, its best ideas will be co-opted by the brightest people on the "other side." It doesn't take very long to teach the core pieces of serious baseball analysis to scouts and old-line baseball men. The reality is that there's never been that much difference between the guys that the scouts like, and the guys the statheads like. It's really just a question of degree.

GH: You're probably right, but from what I've seen thus far, there's a real danger of appearing to adopt data-driven management without actually doing it. There are a lot of guys who will pick and choose when to use the numbers, which means they're not using the numbers to make decisions at all; they're either not aware that systemic use of data means not picking and choosing, or they're attempting to create support for their decisions with a veneer of rigor.

EX: Surely you're not suggesting that rationales would be offered for no other reason but to cover one's ass.

GH: That would never happen.

EX: Seriously, though, it's much easier for an ex-player to learn what he needs in terms of analysis than it is for a true data star to learn what he needs in terms of observation, people, and management skills. Just the way it is.

GH: Thanks for taking the time to talk with me.

EX: I'm going to order a couple of other plates to take with me back to the office.

The supposed rise of data-driven management in baseball has had significant bumps, and it has been neither thorough nor rapid. It's not like this movement was born with Michael Lewis spending time just off Hegenberger Road, or with Bill James reaching a mass market with the Abstracts—Branch Rickey, Earnshaw Cook, and George Lindsey made their marks long ago. In many ways, we're still fighting some of the same battles they did. The penetration and assimilation of data-driven management into front offices has been uneven and slow, and every misstep or mistake made by its practitioners has rubbed off on the movement as a whole in the minds of those who don't see (or don't want to see) its usefulness.

The baseball analysis "community" lacks standards; people self-publish their work and feel confident that they're qualified to offer advice on multi-million dollar transactions. Many of these people don't have formal training in statistical methods or research design, nor exposure to all of the constraints facing decision-makers in front offices. They occupy a nexus between academia and fandom. There is an over-reliance on some simple, well-understood tool such as linear regression, not because it's the right tool for the job, but because someone remembers it from college, and they can do it in Excel rather than having to find and purchase a robust statistical package. There is excessive attention paid to the "academic" race, refining a model to another 1% of precision, without regard to its utility for making decisions that will actually help a ballclub, or the enormous error bars inherent in the entire exercise. All of these things work against the widespread adoption, much less embrace, of data-driven management.

Of course, there's also this final, uncomfortable truth about serious baseball analysis and using it in the real world of MLB front offices: Performing analysis at a high enough level to help a club, in some way, shape, or form, just isn't that hard to do. Investing some time in the basics of statistics, data design, and operations research is something that literally millions of people can do, and most ex-players, coaches, and even clubbies can achieve. The hard part is selling the information as the core of a decision-making process. That takes credibility, skills of persuasion, patience, confidence, opportunity, diligence, and perseverance. Even if you change the minds in a particular front office, you have to continually reinforce the rigor of the process, because ultimately one either uses the numbers all the time, in an appropriate, disciplined, and repeatable fashion, or one's not using them at all.

Adventures in Win Expectancy

by Keith Woolner

Introduction

In *Baseball Prospectus 2005,* we presented the Win Expectation framework (WX), a set of mathematical formulae for computing a team's win probability—the chances, given information at any point during the game, of a team winning. The framework uses the inning, number of outs, runners on base, run differential, and offensive strengths of each team, and computes all the permutations of possible final scores to determine the likelihood of one team outscoring the other.

Win probability had been studied before using empirical observations of winning from a given situation, but unlike those previous attempts, this new approach let us determine win probabilities for hypothetical situations that may not have occurred during an actual season, between teams that did not play each other, or with varying states of information about each team during the game.

The WX framework has proven to be enormously useful. In last year's article, we showed how it could be used to improve upon one of BP's signature statistics—Support Neutral Win Loss record. In addition, WX is useful when measuring relief pitcher value, both in quantifying higher leverage situations (the appropriately named Leverage statistic), and in the additional wins expected from their pitching in those situations (WX, and related stats such as WXRL). This year, we'll explore some other ways that the WX framework can be useful.

Win Expectation Formula Parameters

WinExp   Team's current inning,
            Team's baserunner state,
            Team's average runs per inning,
            Opponent's current inning,
            Opponent's baserunner state,
            Opponent's average runs per inning,
            Run differential (Team's score – Opponent's score)
            Home team

Batting and Win Expectation

One of the most popular questions we received in response to the original Win Expectation article was published was whether you can use WX for hitters. This can absolutely be done, and in fact there have been other approaches to directly measuring win probability for batters before. But the WX framework allows more flexibility to incorporate additional factors such as park effects, differing team strengths, and differences in information into the calculation.

To determine the WX of a batter's place appearance, we simply take the difference between the win probabilities immediately before and immediately after the pitch that ends his plate appearance. The difference is the win value created by the batter. For example, when David Ortiz came to bat in with two outs in top of the eighth inning and a runner on first in a tie game versus Toronto on September 14, the Red Sox had a 43.95% chance of winning the game. After Ortiz clubbed a two-run home run, the Red Sox had an 83.42% chance of winning the game. The 39.37% difference in win probability is credited to Ortiz as 0.3937 WX.

This approach actually credits all baserunner advancement to the batter, so a speedy baserunner who goes from first to third on a single increases the batter's WX, not his own. A more sophisticated approach would be to credit the batter for the baserunner advancement of a typical single, and credit the runner for the extra base. In the data shown in this article, however, we have credited the entire change in win expectation to the batter.

This approach to measuring batter value is slightly different than the formula for pitchers. For pitchers, we took the win probability at the start of their appearance—or the start of the game if a starting pitcher—looked at the innings pitched, the baserunner state when the pitcher exited, and runs allowed by the pitcher, and assumed average offensive support to determine the final win probability. The difference between the two was attributable to the defense.

Batters, however, do not participate in a block of consecutive plate appearances, as a pitcher does. Instead, their opportunities to contribute are isolated and scattered throughout the game. In these situations, we would look at each plate appearance individually, as a self contained unit, since the batter himself is not responsible for the context of the situation he faces. Furthermore, during a plate appearance there is no defensive effort by a batter's own team to worry about, so the extra steps we went through to ensure a pitcher's run support did not affect his win contributions are not necessary.

Adding up the WX from each plate appearance creates the batter's total batting value. This can be done over any span of time—a game, a month, a season, or a career. (See tables 1 and 2.)

TABLE 1. THE 15 HIGHEST AND LOWEST SEASONAL BATTING WX (1960–2005)

Year	Name	PA	WX
2004	Barry Bonds	617	12.07
2001	Barry Bonds	664	11.71
2002	Barry Bonds	612	10.45
1969	Willie McCovey	623	10.02
1998	Mark McGwire	681	9.65
2005	David Ortiz	713	8.76
1961	Mickey Mantle	646	8.67
2000	Todd Helton	697	8.62
2001	Jason Giambi	671	8.46
1967	Carl Yastrzemski	680	8.29
1971	Joe Torre	707	8.16
1989	Will Clark	676	7.88
1961	Norm Cash	673	7.58
1970	Willie McCovey	638	7.54
1970	Frank Howard	706	7.52
1971	Roger Metzger	585	−3.78
1968	Mark Belanger	530	−3.78
1970	Dave Campbell	635	−3.79
1992	Steve Sax	630	−3.79
1997	Scott Brosius	526	−3.81
1989	Andres Thomas	571	−3.88
1989	Cory Snyder	518	−3.90
1988	Benito Santiago	527	−3.94
1972	Marty Perez	513	−4.06
2000	Scott Brosius	519	−4.11
2003	Royce Clayton	543	−4.28
1970	Larry Bowa	577	−4.29
1968	Hal Lanier	518	−4.45
1997	Gary DiSarcina	583	−4.76
2002	Neifi Perez	585	−6.69

TABLE 2. 20 HIGHEST AND LOWEST CAREER BATTING WX (1960–2005)

Name	WX
Barry Bonds	115.71
Willie McCovey	74.11
Hank Aaron	71.15
Willie Mays	63.41
Frank Robinson	63.04
Jeff Bagwell	63.02
Gary Sheffield	62.06
Billy Williams	60.67
Carl Yastrzemski	60.48
Harmon Killebrew	59.39
Frank Thomas	58.14
Joe Morgan	58.02
Mike Schmidt	57.09
Mark McGwire	55.97
George Brett	55.59
Willie Stargell	54.47
Pete Rose	54.16
Reggie Jackson	53.46
Tony Gwynn	52.53
Dick Allen	52.11
Roger Metzger	−18.67
Brad Ausmus	−18.89
Tony Pena	−19.06
Rey Ordonez	−19.16
Don Sutton	−19.30
Greg Gagne	−19.35
Aurelio Rodriguez	−19.75
Gary Disarcina	−20.32
Don Kessinger	−20.58
Rey Sanchez	−21.25
Mark Belanger	−21.88
Neifi Perez	−22.25
Hal Lanier	−23.56
Ozzie Guillen	−23.95
Ed Brinkman	−24.10
Tim Foli	−24.61
Doug Flynn	−25.69
Royce Clayton	−27.29
Alfredo Griffin	−28.90
Larry Bowa	−31.50

WX for Hitters and Park Effects

Because the WX framework allows us to enter different run scoring environments, the win probabilities can take park effects into effect. The WX formula includes parameters for the team's and opponent's average runs per inning (RPI). To adjust for park, take their league-neutral RPI and multiply by the park factor where the game is being played.

For example, suppose the game is being played in Coors Field, with a park factor of 125 (using 100 as the base neutral park factor, the 125 means that playing in Coors inflates run scoring by 25%):

WX (Team's RPI, Opponent's RPI) in Coors Field (PF = 125)

➡ WX(Team's RPI × 1.25, Opponent's RPI × 1.25)

(all other parameters not listed are the same in both expressions)

How does a park factor affect WinExp? Consider a visiting team down by two runs to start the fifth inning against an opponent of equal offensive strength (average 4.5 runs per nine innings in a neutral park). In a neutral park, the team has a 24.41% chance of catching up and going on to win the game. By increasing the expected number of runs per inning, an offense-inflating park makes it easier to overcome the deficit, despite the fact that both teams benefit from the boost in offense. (See table 3.)

Leverage for Hitters

Leverage captures the notion that all runs are not created equal. Preventing a run from scoring in the 9th inning of a tie game has much more impact on the likelihood of winning than allowing yet another run when you're down 11–0 in the 5th. A run in the first situation has a higher leverage than a run in the second situation.

We first explored leverage with regard to relief pitcher usage. Closers, in particular, who are brought into close games to protect a slim lead, have value to a team

disproportionate to the number of innings they throw. By measuring the leverage at the start of each appearance, we could characterize the usage patterns, and the "value multiplier" that should apply to how that reliever was used.

The same concept can be applied to batters. Each plate appearance has a certain leverage depending on the inning, baserunners, and current score. If a team plays a lot of close games, the batters will, on average, have more opportunity to affect the probability of winning each time they come to the plate. Since the batter has little control over the situations he bats in, any systematic difference in leverage would skew his apparent value—batters who get to bat in high-leverage situations would produce more wins per run than batters who bat in mostly low-leverage situations.

It's important to emphasize that leverage says nothing about the hitter's actual performance. It is almost completely beyond his control. It's a measure of the circumstances he batted in, and how much game-importance those plate appearances had, on average. A hitter with high average leverage had a proportionally greater opportunity to influence the outcomes of games than a hitter with low average leverage, but the low-leverage hitter could have been significantly better. For example, Vinny Castilla batted 549 times in 2005 with an average leverage of 1.092, 19th best out of the 150 players with 500 or more plate appearances. Alex Rodriguez, on the other hand, had an average leverage of 0.929 over his 715 plate appearances, a striking 147th out of 150. Yet A-Rod was a vastly superior hitter to Castilla (and indeed to nearly every player in the AL). (See tables 4 and 5.)

Elective Strategies and Win Expectation

The WX framework can be used to evaluate elective strategies, such as stealing bases and sacrifice bunts as well. Rather than relying upon an overall average statistical profile, we can look at specific situations and gauge the impact a given tactic has on the chance of winning. We'll use the example of basestealing to illustrate these points, but the techniques discussed are equally applicable to sacrifice bunts and other strategies.

Base Stealing WX Value

The same methodology used to measure batting events can be used to measure the win value of stolen bases as well, and we'll show some of the best and worst basestealing seasons and careers in the tables below. But there are some other interesting aspects unique to an elective strategy like basestealing that WX can provide some information about as well.

For all the tables related to basestealing and breakeven probabilities in this article, we are considering attempted stolen bases by the *lead baserunner only*. In other words,

TABLE 3. PARK FACTORS AND WIN EXPECTANCY

PF	WX
0.50	0.1514
0.60	0.1746
0.70	0.1951
0.80	0.2134
0.90	0.2296
1.00	0.2441
1.10	0.2571
1.20	0.2688
1.30	0.2794
1.40	0.2890
1.50	0.2978

TABLE 4. TEN HIGHEST AND LOWEST SEASONAL BATTING LEVERAGE (1960–2005) MINIMUM 500 PA

Year	Name	PA	LEV
1985	Bob Brenly	505	1.254
2005	Joe Mauer	554	1.254
2000	Greg Vaughn	545	1.233
2005	Jacque Jones	585	1.231
2005	Shannon Stewart	599	1.231
2005	Lew Ford	590	1.221
1991	Ozzie Guillen	555	1.220
1980	Willie Montanez	548	1.219
1996	Ozzie Guillen	528	1.219
2005	Justin Morneau	543	1.211
2002	Paul Konerko	630	.893
2002	Carlos Lee	576	.891
1998	Andres Galarraga	648	.890
1999	Royce Clayton	520	.890
2003	Randy Winn	660	.887
1996	Kevin Elster	596	.882
1977	Bucky Dent	540	.872
1976	Bob Randall	531	.871
1977	Cesar Geronimo	538	.851
1962	Jose Pagan	644	.821

if there are runners on first and second, and both advance on a steal, we only consider the runner on second stealing third. And in analyzing each steal, we assume no other runners advance. So in the example above we only consider the runner going to third, and leave the runners on first there. This allows us to isolate the value of the lead steal itself, in terms of breakeven probabilities. Also, for the purposes of WX, pickoffs are not counted as steal attempts, and thus not considered a caught stealing. A side effect of this approach is that the SB and CS totals do not necessarily match a player's full-season or career totals, if they were part of a double-steal, or some similar play where they were not the lead runner advancing. (See tables 5 and 6.)

TABLE 6. 15 HIGHEST AND LOWEST CAREER BASESTEALING WX (1960–2005)

Name	SBA	SB	CS	LEV	WX
Rickey Henderson	1594	1363	231	1.039	13.31
Tim Raines	890	787	103	1.156	11.17
Joe Morgan	823	683	140	1.162	10.08
Lou Brock	1203	936	267	1.032	8.64
Bert Campaneris	819	647	172	1.085	8.53
Vince Coleman	878	730	148	1.050	8.28
Willie Wilson	765	655	110	1.088	7.59
Davey Lopes	644	551	93	1.013	6.72
Paul Molitor	587	485	102	1.083	5.40
Eric Davis	380	329	51	1.317	5.30
Cesar Cedeno	694	543	151	1.132	5.14
Ozzie Smith	683	562	121	1.110	5.02
Ron LeFlore	563	451	112	1.112	4.42
Marquis Grissom	499	406	93	1.170	4.34
Otis Nixon	748	593	155	1.176	3.90
Tony Fernandez	353	235	118	1.133	−1.95
Chet Lemon	114	55	59	1.019	−1.97
Vinny Castilla	61	28	33	1.028	−1.98
Bob Boone	70	35	35	.822	−2.00
Todd Zeile	76	45	31	1.062	−2.03
Harold Reynolds	351	243	108	1.074	−2.04
Rick Burleson	117	69	48	1.012	−2.08
Robin Ventura	40	20	20	1.062	−2.18
Jose Vizcaino	111	66	45	1.089	−2.18
Tony Phillips	240	158	82	1.082	−2.20
Tom Brunansky	110	60	50	1.030	−2.22
Duane Kuiper	114	52	62	1.020	−2.45
Chili Davis	207	132	75	1.025	−2.51
Alfredo Griffin	294	185	109	1.044	−2.79
Buddy Bell	104	54	50	.991	−2.81

TABLE 5. TEN HIGHEST AND LOWEST SEASONAL BASESTEALING WX (1960–2005)

Year	Name	SBA	SB	CS	LEV	WX
1962	Maury Wills	115	102	13	.985	2.098
1988	Rickey Henderson	99	89	10	1.116	2.044
1980	Ron LeFlore	113	97	16	1.173	2.005
1986	Vince Coleman	115	104	11	.991	1.698
1969	Bert Campaneris	69	61	8	1.389	1.648
1983	Rickey Henderson	121	108	13	.991	1.584
1987	Vince Coleman	125	107	18	1.126	1.505
1983	Tim Raines	100	90	10	1.078	1.501
1986	Tim Raines	75	67	8	1.331	1.480
1986	Eric Davis	89	79	10	1.321	1.438
1975	Dave Chalk	12	6	6	1.426	−.707
1979	Bobby Bonds	51	34	17	1.215	−.714
1997	Kenny Lofton	34	25	9	1.176	−.741
1974	Greg Gross	30	12	18	1.043	−.745
1967	Rod Carew	12	5	7	1.274	−.770
1968	Reggie Smith	36	22	14	.871	−.773
1970	Rod Carew	9	4	5	1.191	−.782
1987	Will Clark	20	5	15	.990	−.819
1989	Gerald Young	54	31	23	1.079	−.900
1976	Duane Kuiper	23	10	13	1.197	−1.016

SB Breakeven Percentages Using WX

Though the traditional sabermetric wisdom holds that stealing bases at a 67% success rate is needed to break even, the reality is more complex. Unlike plate appearances, which fall to a batter in a predictable order and cannot be avoided, the decision to attempt a steal is conscious and optional. And at any given point, the potential gain in win probability, and the cost of failure can vary. That means that each individual situation has its own breakeven probability—the chance of success that balances the gain and loss. Using the Win Expectation framework shown in figure 4, we can measure the breakeven point for every stolen base

attempt, and determine which baserunners are choosing the best situations to try to steal.

A good situation to steal is one with a low breakeven probability. Conversely, the best basestealers should think about running in high breakeven situations, where the cost of being thrown out is so much greater than the potential gain of stealing successfully.

By looking at the average WX for stolen bases and caught stealing for each season, we can estimate the effective breakeven probability for that year. One interesting confirmation from the data is that the average breakeven point for stealing in a high-offense era is noticeably higher than in a low-offense era (see table 7).

FIGURE 1. DECISION TREE FOR SB ATTEMPT

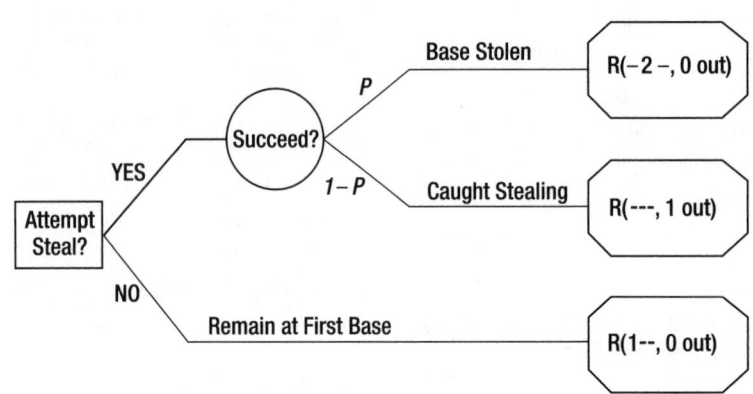

R(S,N) = expected runs in rest of inning starting from baserunner state S, and N outs

Determining Smart Times to Steal

Of course, the actual breakeven probability for a specific situation depends upon the context of the game itself, something that the WX framework is ideally suited for. The lower the breakeven probability, the better time it is to attempt a steal. In some sense, the breakeven probability can be thought of as a type of Leverage for basestealing. Higher leverage is associated with lower breakeven probabilities.

We've computed the breakeven probability for every stolen base attempt from 1960–2005. This takes into account the inning, number of outs, run differential, runners on base, league-wide offensive level and park. Not explicitly considered is the baserunner's team's offense,

the specific batters coming up while he's on base, the opposing team's offense, and current pitcher.

Using the breakeven probability as a measure of the "quality" of steal opportunity, we can quantitatively determine which basestealers (or their managers) are choosing their times to steal most effectively. A player whose steal attempts have a high average breakeven probability is picking comparatively poor times to try to advance, whereas a player with a low breakeven probability is picking "smarter" times to steal—picking situations that are more likely to benefit his team. Note that we're talking how well a runner picks his times to steal, not of whether the runner is successful in stealing or not.

For example, looking at players who attempted at least 20 steals of second base (excluding pickoffs) in 2005,

TABLE 7. STOLE BASE PERCENTAGE BREAKEVEN PERCENTAGE, 1960–2005

Year	LG	Breakeven%	LG	Breakeven%	Year	LG	Breakeven%	LG	Breakeven%
2005	AL	70.2	NL	69.9	1982	AL	69.0	NL	68.0
2004	AL	71.8	NL	70.0	1981	AL	67.6	NL	67.0
2003	AL	71.0	NL	70.3	1980	AL	69.5	NL	68.1
2002	AL	71.0	NL	69.6	1979	AL	70.5	NL	68.3
2001	AL	71.5	NL	70.8	1978	AL	68.3	NL	67.6
2000	AL	73.0	NL	71.8	1977	AL	69.2	NL	68.9
1999	AL	73.1	NL	71.5	1976	AL	67.3	NL	67.7
1998	AL	72.0	NL	70.0	1975	AL	68.5	NL	68.5
1997	AL	72.1	NL	70.3	1974	AL	67.6	NL	68.2
1996	AL	73.8	NL	71.0	1973	AL	68.3	NL	67.9
1995	AL	72.6	NL	70.8	1972	AL	64.4	NL	66.7
1994	AL	73.5	NL	70.5	1971	AL	66.8	NL	66.4
1993	AL	71.1	NL	70.2	1970	AL	67.3	NL	68.5
1992	AL	69.1	NL	66.6	1969	AL	67.1	NL	67.2
1991	AL	69.3	NL	67.8	1968	AL	65.1	NL	64.1
1990	AL	69.0	NL	68.5	1967	AL	65.6	NL	66.2
1989	AL	68.8	NL	67.3	1966	AL	66.4	NL	67.0
1988	AL	68.9	NL	67.0	1965	AL	66.5	NL	66.5
1987	AL	71.6	NL	69.9	1964	AL	66.8	NL	66.3
1986	AL	70.3	NL	68.3	1963	AL	66.9	NL	65.5
1985	AL	69.9	NL	67.5	1962	AL	68.5	NL	68.2
1984	AL	69.1	NL	67.8	1961	AL	69.2	NL	68.8
1983	AL	69.5	NL	68.0	1960	AL	68.1	NL	67.0

Brady Clark had the best breakeven percentage, with just a 68.4% rate in his 23 attempts at stealing second. The least opportune basestealer was Tadahito Iguchi, with an 80.5% breakeven percentage in his 20 attempts at swiping second. Clark picked better opportunities to attempt a steal, with a better risk/reward ratio than Iguchi did. However, he actually performed poorly in those situations, stealing with only a 43.5% success rate. Iguchi did better, stealing at a 75% success rate. But in both cases, the players hurt their team's chances of winning because they did not exceed the breakeven percentage needed for the times they chose to run—Clark failed 43.5% to 68.4%, Iguchi failed 75% to 80.5%. If Iguchi had chosen his opportuni-

ties to run as well as Clark had, his 75% success rate would have been a benefit to the team. But because he picked situations to run where getting thrown out was unusually costly to Chicago's chances of winning, even his nominally impressive 75% success rate was not a boon to his team.

Breakeven percentages tend to rise in conjunction with the offensive level. As a result, the players with the worst breakeven percentages tend to come from the past decade, where run scoring has been historically high, and thus average breakeven points also have been higher. (See tables 8 and 9.)

TABLE 8. TOP 10 HIGHEST AND LOWEST BREAKEVEN% IN A SINGLE SEASON (MINIMUM 20 ATTEMPTS)

Year	Name	SBA	SB	CS	Pick	Breakeven	Success
1996	Omar Vizquel	38	29	9	2	78.1	76.3
1995	Tony Gwynn	21	16	5	1	78.1	76.2
2000	Roberto Alomar	40	36	4	1	77.6	90.0
1999	Barry Larkin	33	25	8	0	77.5	75.8
1994	Roberto Alomar	27	19	8	1	77.4	70.4
1996	Pat Listach	30	25	5	2	77.3	83.3
1999	Roberto Alomar	38	32	6	2	77.2	84.2
1995	Stan Javier	39	34	5	0	77.2	87.2
1999	Omar Vizquel	49	40	9	2	77.2	81.6
1996	Derek Bell	30	27	3	1	77.0	90.0
1968	Bobby Bonds	23	16	7	0	61.5	69.6
1967	Horace Clarke	24	21	3	0	61.3	87.5
1972	Horace Clarke	24	18	6	0	61.3	75.0
1972	Roy White	31	23	8	2	61.2	74.2
1972	Joe Lovitto	23	12	11	1	61.1	52.2
1968	Felipe Alou	20	10	10	1	60.8	50.0
1972	Dick Allen	23	17	6	1	60.8	73.9
1988	Bill Doran	20	16	4	0	60.6	80.0
1963	Tommy Davis	25	15	10	0	59.9	60.0
1971	Bobby Murcer	20	12	8	0	59.8	60.0

TABLE 9. TEN HIGHEST AND LOWEST BREAKEVEN % IN A CAREER (1960–2005) (MINIMUM 100 ATTEMPTS)

Name	SBA	SB	CS	Pick	Breakeven	Success
Garret Anderson	109	66	43	7	74.7	60.6
Omar Vizquel	462	323	139	22	73.9	69.9
Chris Singleton	108	81	27	2	73.6	75.0
Carlos Beltran	232	203	29	6	73.5	87.5
Vladimir Guerrero	216	142	74	12	73.5	65.7
Miguel Cairo	124	93	31	2	73.4	75.0
Roberto Alomar	568	455	113	24	73.4	80.1
Cristian Guzman	162	106	56	8	73.2	65.4
Kenny Lofton	708	561	147	22	73.2	79.2
Derek Bell	209	158	51	9	73.1	75.6
Hank Aaron	265	203	62	3	65.4	76.6
Bill Robinson	115	67	48	10	65.3	58.3
Dick Allen	176	126	50	12	65.3	71.6
Felix Millan	107	67	40	1	65.2	62.6
Jose Uribe	118	73	45	6	65.2	61.9
Johnny Briggs	109	61	48	4	64.9	56.0
Felipe Alou	150	92	58	3	64.9	61.3
Jim Fregosi	114	73	41	0	64.8	64.0
Horace Clarke	205	149	56	4	64.7	72.7
Bobby Murcer	195	121	74	6	64.7	62.1

Win Values for Batting Events

We can take every instance of a single—or any event—over the course of a year and find the average WX value for a single for that year. When this is done over multiple years, a trend emerges—there is a direct relationship between the overall level of run scoring and the average win value of different events.

In high offense environments, more runs are needed on average to produce a win. Therefore, more individual batting successes—hits, walks, HBP, SB—are needed to produce a win. The individual value of any one of those events goes down. Simply put, if you need 15 hits to produce a win in one era, and 10 hits to produce a win in another, then a hit is worth $\frac{1}{15}$ of a win in the former case, and $\frac{1}{10}$ of a win in the latter.

The data bear this out—as the run environment increases, the win value of individual hits and walks decreases. Then, by running a linear regression on the average win value for an event versus the RA in a given season, we can derive a series of formulas for estimating the win value of an event in any given offensive environment.

Each formula is of the form:

Win Value (Event) = Slope × RA + Intercept

Where Slope and Intercept for a given Event are taken from table 10.

TABLE 10. WX PARAMETERS FOR BATTING EVENTS

Event	Slope	Intercept
Single	−0.00601	0.071006
Double	−0.00914	0.111553
Triple	−0.01302	0.156845
Home Run	−0.02096	0.229928
Batting Out (excl. SO)	−0.00028	−0.024190
Strikeout	−0.00044	−0.024790
Unintentional BB	−0.00334	0.043251
Intentional BB	−0.00017	0.009444
Hit By Pitch	−0.00244	0.040171
Stolen Base	−0.00538	0.045295
Caught Stealing	0.00137	−0.048210
Reached on Error	−0.00501	0.069463
Passed Ball	−0.00300	0.040320
Balk	−0.00547	0.052695
Wild Pitch	−0.00390	0.044642

We can show how the win value for each event changes with the run environment by letting RA vary over a typical range (see table 11).

TABLE 11. WX VALUES OF BATTING EVENTS IN DIFFERENT RUN ENVIRONMENTS

	Runs/9						
	3.00	3.50	4.00	4.50	5.00	5.50	6.00
Single	0.0530	0.0500	0.0469	0.0439	0.0409	0.0379	0.0349
Double	0.0841	0.0796	0.0750	0.0704	0.0658	0.0613	0.0567
Triple	0.1178	0.1113	0.1048	0.0983	0.0917	0.0852	0.0787
Home Run	0.1670	0.1566	0.1461	0.1356	0.1251	0.1146	0.1042
Batting Out (excl. SO)	−0.0250	−0.0252	−0.0253	−0.0254	−0.0256	−0.0257	−0.0259
Strikeout	−0.0261	−0.0263	−0.0266	−0.0268	−0.0270	−0.0272	−0.0274
Unintentional BB	0.0332	0.0316	0.0299	0.0282	0.0265	0.0249	0.0232
Intentional BB	0.0089	0.0088	0.0088	0.0087	0.0086	0.0085	0.0084
Hit By Pitch	0.0329	0.0316	0.0304	0.0292	0.0280	0.0268	0.0255
Stolen Base	0.0291	0.0265	0.0238	0.0211	0.0184	0.0157	0.0130
Caught Stealing	−0.0441	−0.0434	−0.0427	−0.0420	−0.0413	−0.0407	−0.0400
Reached on Error	0.0544	0.0519	0.0494	0.0469	0.0444	0.0419	0.0394
Passed Ball	0.0313	0.0298	0.0283	0.0268	0.0253	0.0238	0.0223
Balk	0.0363	0.0336	0.0308	0.0281	0.0253	0.0226	0.0199
Wild Pitch	0.0329	0.0310	0.0290	0.0271	0.0251	0.0232	0.0212

One somewhat surprising result is that the win values of outs are not affected by the run environment as much as hits or walks are. Unlike positive batting events (hits and walks), negative batting events (outs) do not vary nearly as much. The reason for this is that across different offensive eras, the same rules of baseball apply: nine innings, three outs to an inning. The number of batting outs per game remains relatively constant over time, and the number of wins and losses per game is fixed at one each, higher or lower offense implies higher or lower numbers of hits and walks, not outs. The slight variation we do see in the win value of batting outs comes from differences in the number of other kinds of outs (caught stealing, outs on base, double plays) that are linked to the offensive environment (see table 12).

Conclusions

The Win Expectation framework has proven to be useful in a variety of situations. WX has measured contextual win values for starting pitching, relief pitching, batting, and basestealing, as well as quantifying basestealing opportunity quality and situational leverage, and formed the basis for a linear weights—style system for estimating the value of game events as fractional wins dependent on the run environment. Along the way, we've been able to adjust for league offensive level, park factors, replacement level, and quality of opposition. The application of WX to other elective strategies, such as sacrifice bunts, is well within our capabilities now, too.

TABLE 12. VARIABILITY IN WX VALUE ACROSS RUN ENVIRONMENTS

Event	Percent Variation
IBB	28.0%
B3	26.6%
B4	24.8%
B1	22.8%
B2	22.6%
ERR	22.4%
UBB	21.7%
HBP	19.7%
SO	5.8%
Batting Out (excl. SO)	5.9%

Although WX is mathematically complex, it's proven to be a tool of immense robustness and wide scope. Historically, run estimation systems like Linear Weights and Runs Created were seminal in furthering context-independent sabermetric theory. The base-out expected runs matrix was similarly a critical development in describing the certain aspects of context-dependent analysis. Having an analytical framework for win expectation may be the next major technique in our toolkit for furthering our understanding of baseball.

Iceberg Stories: The Business of Baseball, 2005–2006

by Andrew Bahrlias

I n 2005, coverage of the steroids scandal overshadowed the many off-field developments in the business of baseball. These other issues, equally essential to maintaining the integrity of the sport and its bond with the fans, were left, like tips of icebergs, barely cresting above the surface of public awareness.

The Christopher House Affair, or How You Too Can Be Banned from a Ballpark

Not to be confused with either the Pierce Brosnan remake or the original Steve McQueen vehicle, this true story of bad behavior on the part of a Red Sox season ticket holder occurred on the night of April 14, 2005, when the Yankees' Gary Sheffield had a brief altercation with Mr. House during the eighth inning. After extensive review on high-definition tape, the Sox concluded that House intentionally swiped at the side of the outfielder's face with his right arm while Sheffield attempted to field a Jason Varitek hit that hugged the corner.

Security restored order and House was ejected. Usually, conflicts such as the one described above end here. Alcohol abuse is blamed and the event is forgotten; however, with the NBA's Ron Artest fan-fighting debacle of November, 2004 fresh in the minds of the public, the Red Sox chose to draw a line in the stands, as it were, against unruly behavior and suspended House's season tickets for the remainder of the 2005 season. The questions posed are: (i) can they legally do this; (ii) if it is legal, how was it effectuated; and (iii) what are the future ramifications of this incident?

The first question on legality is a slam-dunk. Yes, it's legal. Many fans believe that when they own season tickets they either have some contractual right to perpetual renewal of the tickets or even a quasi-property right, when in reality a ticket to a sporting event is a revocable license, much like a driver's or fishing license. A license is a *right or permission* granted by a competent authority (in this case, the Red Sox) to do something (in this case, attend a game at Fenway Park) which would be unlawful without

such right or permission (ever tried getting into a ballpark without a ticket?). The key to licenses are that they are fully revocable by the party granting the license. Although each jurisdiction in the United States defines a license differently, the variances are small and all follow the basic structure described above. A ticket to a Red Sox home game is merely a license to occupy a given seat in Fenway Park on a given date. A season ticket is simply 81 of these licenses.

As the Red Sox were the granting licensor and Mr. House was the licensee, the Red Sox acted within the bounds of established law when they suspended his seats for the remainder of the 2005 season. If such a case came up again for the Red Sox and the ticket holder chose to litigate, there is now established Massachusetts precedent as the court held in *Yarde Metals, Inc. v. New England Patriots Limited Partnership,* 64 Mass.App.Ct. 656 (2005), that the Patriots' decision to terminate a season ticket holder's season ticket privileges did not breach any contractual rights between the team and the holder, nor did it violate any implied covenant of good faith and fair dealing. It also affirmed that tickets to sporting events are licenses, fully revocable by the licensor at any time for any reason.

The Red Sox were able to effect an immediate suspension due primarily to the fact that Mr. House cooperated and returned his tickets (presumably for a refund of any remaining games). However, their contingency plan in the event that Mr. House did not cooperate was to automatically *invalidate his tickets.* Most professional sports franchises across the country now place bar codes on every ticket. This not only allows a team to sell home-printed tickets on the Internet, but it gives teams the opportunity to generate reports on how and where tickets are purchased, as well as provide essential stadium operations data on where people enter a stadium. This information is critical for staffing of security personnel, especially on well-attended giveaway days. Finally, teams can also keep track of usage statistics by season ticket holders and potentially suggest ways of disposing of unused tickets, whether by charitable donation or some form of ticket exchange program.

Had Mr. House failed to cooperate, the team would have invalidated his tickets with a few keystrokes and had the option to keep the seats as house seats controlled by the team, or allow the tickets to be repurchased by a different person on the open market.

The event had far-reaching ramifications, since House's behavior was largely influenced by alcohol. In May, the Red Sox intensified their policing of alcohol use in the stadium. *The Boston Globe,* noting that at least 16 new beer stands had been added since John Henry had taken over the franchise in 2001, reported that the team had doubled the number of "Compliance Supervisors" to prevent inebriated fans from purchasing more alcohol, and minors from purchasing any.

Had the Sheffield-House incident taken place in New York, House could have potentially faced more serious consequences. Inspired by the ugly trash-throwing incident during Game 6 of the 2003 ALCS between the Yankees and Red Sox (when Mayor Bloomberg was pelted by debris), a new law has recently been given sharper teeth, now penalizing rowdy fans with fines up to $25,000 and possible jail time.

As Long As We're Talking Tickets: The Rise Of the Secondary Ticket Market

Despite the complex economics associated with revenue sharing, regional television networks, luxury taxes, and stadium financing deals, the sale of tickets is at the heart of the MLB financial engine. For *all* teams, tickets are the leading source of revenue. This is true even for the Yankees. In 2005, they drew just over 4 million people at an average cost of $38 per ticket. That's more than $150 million. With an eye toward maximizing ticket revenues, it's no wonder teams are starting to pay serious attention to the Secondary Ticket Market ("STM").

Selling in the STM is defined as when a person or entity (a ticket broker) acquires tickets to an event and then resells that ticket for profit based upon the laws of supply and demand. While it is true that all ticket scalping is part of the STM, not all transactions in the STM are defined as scalping. This is because scalping is usually illegal and the STM is almost always regulated by local and state laws.

Legal transactions in the STM are generally capped at a certain percentage above the original price of the ticket (anywhere from 5% to 95% or higher), although in some jurisdictions there is no cap at all. Additionally, in order for these transactions to be legal, the broker selling the tickets must be licensed and report their income to local and state taxing authorities (so the government can get a piece of the action). While scalping is defined differently by each jurisdiction, generally speaking if only one of the above conditions is not being met, it's scalping.

While the general image of scalpers is one of bottom-feeders taking tickets out of the supply available to the general public, the emerging view is that all things not nailed down—and some things that are—are commodities to be bought and sold on eBay, and so the STM is gaining acceptance as an example of market forces working their mystical Adam Smithian magic. Indeed, the STM is a net negative only when it is used to exploit the legitimate ticket-buying public; if for example, there is collusion between the entity that is selling the tickets and the secondary ticket seller giving the secondary ticket seller an advantage over normal purchasers, or the secondary ticket seller has infiltrated a ticketing system to purchase tickets before the general public can.

Too bad the Chicago Cubs don't see it that way. In 2002, the Cubs decided to take a dip into the STM by having their parent, the Tribune Company, create a new entity by the name of Wrigley Field Premium Ticket Services, Inc. (WFPTS). Like other ticket brokers, they were charging a huge premium above the ticket face value. However, they had one distinct advantage over other brokers—their tickets came directly from the Cubs *prior* to the Cubs ever putting the tickets on the market. The Cubs made a business decision to legally sell their tickets in the STM prior to the point that the average fan had an opportunity to purchase the tickets. If the tickets didn't sell, WFPTS could sell the tickets back to the Cubs.

Cubs' fans were so outraged that they sued the team. The suit was based on the specific wording of the Illinois anti-scalping statue, which forbids the original seller from selling the tickets for more than their face value. The fans had no chance of winning the lawsuit unless the judge was willing to lift the corporate veil and acknowledge that these entities were all owned by the same company. Unfortunately for Cubs' fans, the judge refused and found their scheme to be perfectly legal. The case is heading to Appeals court.

What's most interesting about this case is how the Cubs pulled a double-steal. They not only cheated their fans, they cheated MLB as well. With respect to revenue sharing, all teams are required to contribute 34% of their Net Local Income, which is then pooled and redistributed. Ticket income is part of Net Local Income. The Cubs, however, erased a substantial profit on WFPTS business by claiming operating losses due to, among other things, rent payments to their landlord . . . the Tribune Company.

MLB, like the Cubs, decided that if you can't beat them, join them. In 2005, its Internet company, MLBAM (Major League Baseball Advanced Media), decided to get in on the action by allowing the Cubs to provide a link to WFPTS on their MLBAM controlled website. Clicking on that link takes the buyer to page declaring that, "These tickets are not being sold by the Cubs or MLB."

With one team already dipping into the STM, more will soon follow. Ticket scalping on eBay goes virtually unchecked and the number of auctions for tickets continues to rise each year. Some teams, such as the Red Sox, have actually started auctioning their own tickets to generate more ticket income and keep tickets away from the brokers.

One company, StubHub, has created an Internet meeting place for secondary ticket sellers and purchasers to do business. This is by no means a ticket broker Web site. StubHub receives a fee with each purchase, but it doesn't own any tickets, provide the shipping service or guarantee that the tickets will arrive before the event. They operate essentially as a service provider and have partnered with sports teams in the NFL, NBA and NHL, and high-profile Division I schools including the University of Southern California. StubHub has become the Internet leader in the STM and in the future, MLBAM will either have to challenge them for marketplace superiority with respect to baseball tickets, or forge a partnership and take a cut of its revenues in exchange for some form of official endorsement and click-through on all team Web sites.

The future of team auctioning of tickets could prove interesting. Teams could operate auctions to select blocks of seats to hot games and let the market dictate their worth. On the flip side, teams could attempt to boost revenue of less important games by selling tickets at *less* than face value. A ticket sold at any price is better than an unsold ticket, because an empty seat is unlikely to purchase a beer and a hot dog. Regardless, the future looks dim for the average consumer to ever get a good seat to a hot game at a reasonable price.

Whose Ball is it Anyway? Boston Red Sox v. Doug Mientkiewicz

Play by play from the 2004 World Series:

> Renteria swings and chops a weak grounder to Foulke....
> Foulke picks up the ball and tosses to Mientkiewicz,
>   who races to first....
> RED SOX WIN! RED SOX WIN! RED SOX WIN!
> Wait a minute, what's Mientkiewicz doing?
> Mientkiewicz is racing to the locker room....
> He opens a safe-deposit box and throws the ball in....
> Now he's driving away in a Brinks Armored Car....
> RED SOX SUE! RED SOX SUE!
> How about that....

It didn't quite happen this way, but when Doug Mientkiewicz caught the final out of the 2004 World Series, little did he know that his hijacking of the ball would ignite a firestorm that could burn its way as far as the labor talks for the Collective Bargaining Agreement set to expire at the end of the 2006 Season.

The Red Sox asked Mientkiewicz to return the ball several weeks after the World Series. He allowed the Red Sox to keep it "on loan" until the end of the 2005 calendar year, "unless the ultimate issue of ownership has been otherwise resolved." The issue was not, and the Red Sox filed suit in Suffolk (Massachusetts) Superior Court, seeking permanent possession of the curse-breaking sphere. Weeks later, both sides agreed to submit the dispute to arbitration through the commissioner's office. Unless settled before the grievance hearing, baseball's permanent arbitrator Shyam Das will be called upon to settle a dispute between baseball's irreconcilable opponents, the MLBPA and the LRD (the Major League Baseball Labor Relations Department, the entity formerly known as the Major League Baseball Player Relations Committee).

There are actually four parties of interest in this case: Mientkiewicz, the Red Sox, the Cardinals, and the Office of the Commissioner of Major League Baseball (MLB). To date, the Cardinals have shown no interest in acquiring memorabilia that is a symbol of their postseason futility, but the Cardinals organization could have been considered an interested party since the game took place in St. Louis and utilized equipment given to the Cardinals by MLB. Regardless, they are not a party to the lawsuit, leaving Mientkiewicz, the Red Sox and MLB.

MLB would have established a claim to the ball primarily upon the Major League Constitution, Article IX, Section 4, which states:

> The Commissioner shall have responsibility for all matters relating to the administration of the championship season and the post-season, which shall be conducted in accordance with the Major League Rules and the Major League Regulations.

Applied in context, MLB is a party of interest due to the fact that they supply all of the baseballs used in postseason games. Additionally, MLB acts as a central administrator for all postseason games, and in many instances the rules that they impose supersede any conflicting home rules by the organization hosting the postseason game. The jurisprudence comparison is Federal Law (MLB/Commissioner) trumping state law (the teams).

Major League Rules and Regulations do not address ownership of balls in play once the game has ended. Since MLB has steered clear of this dispute without even a mention of its potential ownership rights, we can now address the primary combatants. Had the case gone to court, the Red Sox were reportedly prepared to assert as their primary argument that Mientkiewicz gained possession of the ball through his employment with the Red Sox and the ball was in actuality the Red Sox's property all along. While they are correct that Mientkiewicz gained ownership through his employment with the team, the problem with this argument is that the ball was never actually the property of the Red Sox.

At the time the final out was recorded, the ball was either owned by MLB but in the custody of the Cardinals, or was the outright property of the Cardinals. Since the Cardinals had no interest in the ball after the game ended, one might conclude that ownership would either revert back to MLB or the ball would have become abandoned property to which Mientkiewicz would have the first claim. The Cardinals, had they gotten their hands on the ball, could have given it to the Red Sox as a gift, donated it to the Hall of Fame, thrown it in the trash, or in a perversely humorous twist, given it to the Yankees. The point is, it would have been their choice, but they never got that chance.

For the purposes of this essay we'll assume that MLB was the rightful owner of the ball when Mientkiewicz took it from the field because the Cardinals showed no interest in reacquiring the property after he took it. Mientkiewicz could employ the theory of abandoned property, but he would lose with that argument. As stated, MLB was the owner of the ball after the game ended. However, it was never given the opportunity to assert any direct control over the ball because Mientkiewicz took it without ever giving MLB officials or the Cardinals a chance to take it back. In Missouri, abandonment of property requires intent plus an act; a sufficient act is one that manifests a conscious purpose and intention of the owner of personal property neither to use nor to retake the property into his possession. Since neither MLB nor the Cardinals ever had the chance to dispose of the ball as they saw fit, they legally never abandoned it.

At this point a judge could consider the custom and usage in the history of baseball and professional sports in general. This would be Mientkiewicz's strongest argument. Players have a long custom and history of keeping balls of significant on-field achievements as mementos. Of course, the ball's value resided not in any personal achievement by Mientkiewicz, but in the team's historic World Series victory.

In arbitration, the game is played a little differently and the combatants are not the same. Instead of the case being Red Sox v. Mientkiewicz, it's the MLBPA and Mientkiewicz v. the Red Sox and the LRD. Adding these entities brings the rightful owner of the ball, MLB, into the mix. Arbitrator Das could conclude that the ball was the property of MLB, as discussed above, and award it to the Red Sox as an agent of MLB, since the team is a franchise operating under the rules and regulations of the Major League Constitution. It really isn't that much of a stretch. On the other hand, Das could affirm the history and custom of the game by awarding the ball to Mientkiewicz.

Whatever Das decides could have an impact on the labor negotiations since the winning side will feel temporarily more empowered, the losing one deflated. For the sake of baseball, the parties, heading toward what could be the toughest labor negotiations in the free-agency era, should figure out a way to settle this dispute before any ugliness commences. It seems like a trivial issue; after all, it's just a ball. But when two sides with as long a history of mutual antagonism cone into conflict over *any* issue, the battle is always polarizing.

Where Will Your Team Play in . . . ?

The Kansas City Royals

The Royals and the NFL Kansas City Chiefs may be the very best of tenants, cheerfully remaining in their homes as they collapse around them. The Truman Sports Complex is in critical need of repairs. The Jackson County Sports Complex Authority is so behind on mandated repairs that each team could claim its respective lease to be in default at the end of 2007. Yet, neither team has ever threatened to relocate to another venue at the conclusion of their term in 2014 or sooner.

In fact, the Royals and Chiefs signed new 25-year leases. This requires Jackson County to pump $575 million into renovation at the two stadiums. Kaufmann Stadium would receive $250 million in repairs and renovations with the Royals contributing $25 million, the state of Missouri chipping in $12.5 million in tax credits, and the Jackson County taxpayers picking up the lion's share of $212.5 million in the form of a new $3/8$ of one-cent sales tax. This sales tax should raise approximately $850 million over 25 years for the financing of the Arrowhead and Kauffman stadium projects. Jackson County voters must first approve this package in an upcoming vote on April 4, 2006.

The key to the deal for voters is the clause which states that the teams will cover any cost overruns. Jackson County residents represent only half of the attendees of Chiefs' and Royals' games, and so there is a basic question of fairness in asking them to pick up nearly 75% of the bill.

This will actually be the second time in two years that a project of this magnitude has been put to the voters. In 2004, the "Bistate II Measure," which included most of the same economic details but asked for $1.2 billion from the voters, whereas the teams were to contribute $65 million, passed in Jackson County but failed in the four other counties which needed to pass the measure in order for it to move forward. There were also proposals for a downtown stadium for the Royals, but there was so little interest in the project from the legislature and the Royals' owner that a summit to discuss the possibility planned for November, 2005, was cancelled.

Prognosis for Retaining Team: *Very Good to Excellent.* This should be a done deal in KC before you read this essay. Recent polls show that there is overwhelming support in Jackson County for keeping the teams in Kansas City. Unfortunately, when taxpayer dollars become a consideration, the overwhelming majority becomes a narrow majority. The measure is still expected to pass, though. Additionally, there are expected to be—though not yet officially announced—sweeteners for Jackson County residents, such as discounted parking or possibly discounted tickets to games or season ticket packages. Finally, the NFL has reportedly promised Kansas City that they will be awarded a Superbowl if Arrowhead Stadium is renovated with a retractable (or permanent) roof. Voters could be swayed if convinced that a Superbowl will benefit them economically.

The Los Anaheim Angels of Ventura and Orange Counties

The story here is not necessarily where the Angels will play, but the ramifications of the continuing lawsuit between the Angels and the City of Anaheim (the "City") rising from the Angels' 2005 name change to the "Los Angeles Angels of Anaheim."

When Arte Moreno purchased the Angels in 2003, he saw a franchise with tremendous potential. Despite *sharing* the geographical territory with the Los Angeles Dodgers and having only a slightly worse average-wins record during the previous 10 years—79 wins/season versus 84 wins/season for the Dodgers, not to mention a recent World Series win—the Dodgers outdrew his team by almost 10 million people. He wondered if it might have something to do with the name and the team's marketing approach.

A thorough review of his lease with the City revealed a clause in Section 11(f) that stated, "The Tenant will change the name of the Team to include the name 'Anaheim' therein, such change to be effective no later than the commencement of the 1997 Season." Moreno's attorney(s), jumping on the word "include," gave the legal OK to apply to MLB in order to change the name to Los Angeles Angels of Anaheim, because, technically, the word "Anaheim" was still included in the name of the team. MLB consented (despite the Angels having not yet approached the City) and the new name became official effective January 3, 2005.

Anaheim immediately sued to have the name changed back to Anaheim Angels and sought a preliminary injunction, which was denied. On emergency appeal later that spring, the injunction was denied a second time. The parties went back to court on January 9, 2006, in order to determine whether the City has been damaged by the name change and whether the Angels will have to compensate the City for those damages. In connection with this, it is important to note that the issue of which party ultimately should prevail was not argued during the injunc-

tion phase of the trial during the two trials of 2005. The Supreme Court of California is very clear in that, "a preliminary injunction does not create a right, but merely undertakes to protect a right from unlawful or injurious interference." Both the Angels and the City entered the game with a tie score.

The legal merits of the case will focus on the specific language of the lease and the contractual intent of the parties during contract formation. Additionally, the court will have to weigh whether the City has been deprived of a bargained for benefit by having their city turned into a hiccup at the end of the new name.

The Angels have solid legal ground to stand on. First and foremost, the lease cannot be read to mandate the team name be "Anaheim Angels," it only mandates that the team name *include* the word Anaheim. There has also been evidence presented that Disney refused to allow the contested lease clause to read, "Anaheim Angels," because they wanted to preserve flexibility for the future. Second, the lease is very specific in that the City has no control over how the team will market itself, and there are no provisions in the lease that specifically state that the City bargained for the name change as consideration for entering into the lease.

The Angels' case is not without its problems. There is a custom and usage issue to be addressed, though dual-city names are not unheard of. There has never been a team in the history of Major League Baseball that has had a dual-city name, but there are baseball teams in the minor leagues that have dual-city affiliations, and the Sacramento Kings of the NBA played as the KC-Omaha Kings from 1973 to 1975.

On the City's side, it can be asserted that when a party has a certain amount of discretion on how to perform a contract, such discretion cannot be abused to the detriment of the other party. In this case, the City will undoubtedly contend that renaming the team was an abuse of discretion, thus depriving it of the prominence for which it believes it bargained back in the lease negotiations of 1996, and that identification with a Major League Baseball team is a very valuable right to lose. Finally, testimony from the individuals who negotiated the lease will also be potentially harmful to the Angels if it is revealed that there was an unwritten promise to never include another city's name.

Prognosis: *Too early to tell, but probably good.* The victor in this case will likely determine where the Angels play in 2017. If the Angels win, they will likely stay in Anaheim and continue to generate a substantial return on the $20 million investment the City made in 1996. If the Angels lose, all signs point to an opt-out of the lease in 2016 and a move to Los Angeles in a brand new stadium.

This is a sad case in many ways. Arte Moreno has done an amazing job in turning the Angels into an extremely profitable franchise. By embracing the team's past—they were originally the Los Angeles Angels—and marketing to the greater Los Angeles area, not just the smaller Anaheim market, he has seen 3 million in attendance in each of the years he has owned the team. And Moreno was not wrong to do so. According to the Major League Constitution, the Angels and the Dodgers *share* the counties of Los Angeles, Orange and Ventura, making L.A. customers fair game. Further, the Angels recently acquired television revenue equal to that of the Dodgers. The Angels rather ludicrously billed themselves as a "small market team" during the Disney years and received welfare in the form of revenue sharing payments. Clearly the team was an unexploited asset.

The City is playing with fire in that it needs the support of the Angels as a contingency plan if it cannot attempt to lure a NFL franchise to Anaheim (rather than Los Angeles). Under the current lease, the City may construct a football stadium in the parking lot if awarded an NFL team; however, if they cannot lure an NFL expansion team, the City has said that the best use for the extra land in the parking lot is high-density housing that would likely further increase attendance at Angels games. According to the lease, high-density housing is not a permitted use and would require the consent of the Angels to build.

If Moreno prevails in the lawsuit, there is evidence to suggest—from a settlement offer made with respect to this lawsuit—that he will attempt to make things right with the City and keep the Angels where they belong. In the event that they settle prior to a decision being made, perhaps "The Los Anaheim Angels of Ventura and Orange Counties" would be an acceptable middle-ground.

The Minnesota Twins

In 1982, the Twins moved into the Hubert H. Humphrey Metrodome, a charmless facility that seemed to need replacing as soon as it opened. While there have been countless proposals over the years to build a new stadium for the Twins using both private and public funds, as in most cities and states across the nation, no one in Minnesota except select politicos seems interested in building a new stadium with taxpayer dollars.

The most recent plan, which called for a $475 million ballpark to be built in the warehouse district of downtown Minneapolis, expired on December 31, 2005. The ballpark would have been financed by a Hennepin County sales tax—0.15 percent, or 15 cents for each $100 purchased—that would have paid for 75% of the new stadium. Carl Pohlad, the Twins' 90-year-old owner, would have chipped in the rest with the team receiving 100% of the stadium revenue.

The governor and legislature need to approve any new sales tax, even a local one, but the legislature went home for the year without voting on the tax, giving Governor Tim Pawlenty an opportunity to call a special session in order to get the measure passed before the end-of-the-year deadline. Due to what appear to be political reasons—2006 is an election year—Governor Pawlenty refused to call the special session necessary and the deal died.

While the Twins are willing to go back to the drawing board, this time they're taking a more proactive approach. The Twins are essentially playing with no lease. The lease/use agreement expired at the conclusion of the 2003 season and they contend that their agreement to play in the Metrodome is a year-to-year agreement at best. To make this point crystal clear, the Twins sued the Metropolitan Sports Facilities Commission (the "Landlord"), asking the Hennepin County District Court to affirm that the team is under no long-term commitment to play in the stadium. The Landlord's rejoinder was that the Twins have a legal obligation to remain in the Metrodome until a new ballpark is built. A ruling is expected by the end of January, but an appeal is expected regardless of the decision.

Without having the 1998–2003 lease agreement between the Twins and the Landlord to review, one can only speculate on the outcome here, but from what has been reported in the news and in the legal proceedings, this looks to be an easy win for the Twins. Back in 2001, when the Twins were a prime candidate for contraction, the Landlord sued the Twins and MLB in order to force them to play in Minnesota in 2002, citing the fact that the Twins had given notice that they'd be playing in 2002 and begun accepting money for season tickets. Considering the fact that they used this agreement to keep the Twins in the Metrodome, one might conclude that they have already conceded that the Twins' lease has expired.

The Landlord's argument likely rests on the Twins being a "holdover tenant." Generally speaking, a "holdover tenant" is a tenant that has not vacated the premises and continues to act as if the lease is in full force and effect. It is important to note that the 1998–2003 use agreement was actually a three-year lease with three one-year extensions. In order for the Landlord to be successful in keeping the Twins past 2006, it would have to argue that the Twins were perpetually resetting a three-year lease each year a new use agreement was not signed. The chances of success on this argument are pretty slim.

Prognosis: *Still a strong heartbeat, but in critical condition.* The Twins want to stay in Minnesota and Minnesota wants to keep the Twins. Despite claiming large losses and his apparent willingness to go along with contraction, Pohlad has resisted efforts to sell the team to investors who would like to move the Twins to any one of numerous cities across the country, including, most recently, Reggie Jackson, who wants to take them to Las Vegas.

Where there is still a strong chance that Minnesota will get an agreement passed to fund the new stadium in 2006, because of the political climate in an election year and the difficulties they've already encountered, it's not a sure thing. At the very least, it seems unlikely that they'll return to the Metrodome in 2008.

The Twins can be successful in Minnesota. Minneapolis is a city with the resources and will to support a team. By breaking the 2 million mark in attendance in 2005 for the first time in 12 years, Minnesotans have demonstrated their passion for their Twinkies. A new stadium could provide a great boost in attendance, perhaps even to the 3 million that they drew in 1988 after winning the World Series. Despite this, if the Twins leave Minnesota behind, the chances of Minnesota ever hosting a MLB team again are nearly zero. MLB had assigned the Expos to Washington D.C. on the condition that they build a new stadium for the Nationals with 100% public money. It is extremely likely that in the event the Twins leave and Minnesota applies for a new franchise when and if baseball next expands, MLB will ask for the same deal it got from Washington. If the Twins couldn't get a new stadium after multiple tries, with private money included in the mix, it's unlikely they would succeed having abandoned the city in the interim.

With respect to the lawsuit, the Twins will prevail and get the death certificate that they're seeking. Additionally, they'll get that death certificate by the time you've finished reading this essay. Before they do, the Landlord might at least get a measure of satisfaction from asking Commissioner Selig to defend the statement he made on September 7, 2005 explaining why the A's can never move to San Jose. "We [baseball] are a social institution. We have social responsibilities. Once we move a team somewhere, the city has every right to keep that team unless circumstances force them out."

Florida, Washington, and the New Zoo Revue

The ballpark situation in Washington D.C. changes daily, making it too complicated to encapsulate in a few hundred words. Perhaps David McCullough can tell the story after he finishes his next tome discussing the oatmeal and hard cider consumption patterns of the Second Continental Congress. Suffice it to say, as this book went to print, D.C. Council Chairman Linda Cropp said she could pledge council support for the lease if the D.C. Sports and Entertainment Commission and Mayor Anthony Williams could meet ten provisions related to capping stadium costs and winning other advantages for the city from baseball. Additionally, D.C. officials have permitted the former mayor of Detroit, Dennis Archer, to mediate between the District of Columbia and Major League Baseball. The two items combined show tremendous promise and may lead to a compromise, thus staving off the arbitration that MLB has applied for under the agreement that moved the Expos to Washington.

The Marlins, on the other hand, seem closer to leaving than staying. In early 2005, a budget shortfall of $30 million on their new stadium project was never filled and by the end of the year, the estimated shortfall was closer to $100 million. One politician made a bizarre, demagogic argument that south Florida should build a stadium so it can double as a hurricane shelter (because that worked *so* well in New Orleans), an interesting bit of circumlocutional logic in that if south Florida has a need for hurricane shelters for its people, it shouldn't build a ballpark, it should build...hurricane shelters. Polls indicate that more than 80% of Florida's population has no interest in paying for any part of a stadium with taxpayer dollars. Additionally, despite having won the World Series in 2003 and being a playoff contending team in each of the two subsequent seasons, the Marlins could only draw a pathetic 3.5 million fans (about 1.77 million per year or 22,000 per game). Miami is the 5th largest urban market in the United States, at about 5.2 million people. Recognizing this, Commissioner Bud Selig authorized the Marlins to begin negotiating with other cities for their inevitable relocation.

While these games of brinksmanship between teams and legislatures are never conclusively resolved until the last moment, there is a strong chance that the Marlins will leave. There are a number of viable candidates to host the team. While Portland has long seemed a strong market, the hard line that Mayor Tom Potter has taken against public financing of a baseball stadium, combined with the hard line that MLB has taken with regards to public financing, means that Baseball may have to wait for a change of administration before it considers the city a good fit.

Las Vegas may be the next most viable candidate, though Baseball might prefer to keep it in reserve to use as leverage against local governments in the same way that it used to use Tampa Bay. But Vegas may deserve a team on its own merits. The city is booming, and it's one of the few markets where financing a new stadium won't be an issue. In addition, Vegas can boast an endless flow of tourists, a lack of proximity to other MLB franchises, and the 26th largest market in the United States, with 1.55 million people in the greater metropolitan area. Complicating the leveraging scheme, Vegas mayor, Oscar Goodman, has recently given public notice that he wants a commitment from an MLB franchise within a year. In the event that Vegas has no commitment, Goodman has warned that the valuable property in the downtown Union Park parcel which has been formally set aside for a new sports stadium will have to be given up to other developers. This by no means takes Vegas out of the picture as Goodman was also quick to remind that there are plenty of other places to put a stadium.

New Jersey has made some discreet inquiries into acquiring a major league team for the Meadowlands Sports Complex. While the Garden State could certainly support a team, such an acquisition remains impossible. Both the Mets and Yankees have veto rights because East Rutherford is in their home territory. It's one thing to lavish financial incentives in order to force a team down the throat of one owner (Peter Angelos and the Nationals); trying to put a price tag on a suitable bribe for both New York teams is another matter altogether.

Another long shot is Norfolk, Virginia. Norfolk recently reentered the relocation picture after losing out on the Expos. The City apparently has the money to build a stadium without imposing any additional tax burdens on its citizens. Currently, there is a tax on hotel rooms and rental cars, which now brings in close to $5 million annually in an escrow account. This funding was initially created to lure the NBA to Norfolk, but could easily be diverted to help build a new baseball-only stadium. Norfolk is not without its merits, either. It's only 20 miles from Virginia Beach, and constitutes the 29th largest market in the United States with approximately 1.4 million people. In addition, it's 200 miles from Washington, D.C., the next closest MLB franchise, and 90 miles from Richmond, which the Braves' Triple-A franchise may be leaving. The Marlins have also paid a visit to San Antonio, Texas, a long shot given average summer temperatures above 90° might necessitate the construction of a domed stadium.

Injury Accounting

by Thomas Gorman

A year and a half ago, Baseball Prospectus injury guru Will Carroll came to me with what seemed a fairly simple question: "How much do injuries cost their teams? Not in dollars or days, but in runs and wins?" Since I was trying to get Will to hire me, I didn't have the liberty of telling him to get lost.

The study that follows is far from perfect. Hopefully, though, it is the beginning of a framework for measuring how much the loss of a player or group of players affects a team.

But before we delve into the tangible effects of correlating injuries to wins and losses, let's look at what losing a player to injury means to a team on a superficial level. An injury severe enough to place a player on the 15- or 60-day disabled list creates numerous scenarios. The General Manager may be forced to start the service clock on a prospect to fill the void, or maybe he'll have to trade that prospect for a veteran stopgap. A manager's game card may see players put into new lineup slots or unfamiliar defensive positions. In any event, it means that a team is forced to replace the expected value of a starter with the performance of a replacement player.

Our first attempt at quantifying injuries essentially calculates and compares the values of starters and their replacements.

All of our results use baseball's primary currency, the run. The loss of 10 runs is approximately equal to a win lost, so every 10 runs lost to injury could be rephrased as a win lost.[1] For pitchers, our primary statistical measure was Runs Allowed per Nine Innings (RA/9). Most readers should be familiar with that metric.

We used Marginal Lineup Value Rate (MLVr) as the statistic that best represents the individual contribution of a position player to his team's offense, and that one probably needs more introduction. MLVr is a method of counting the effect of a batter's offensive performance on his team's run scoring. MLVr has no positional adjustment and does not account for a player's baserunning abilities.

What MLVr does is calculate how much a player's batting average, on-base percentage, and slugging rate affect the team's total batting average, on-base percentage, and slugging rate. Since those are the most critical constituent elements of a team's ability to score runs, MLVr signifies a player's contribution in runs *per game,* where the baseline of 0.000 is equal to the contribution of an average Major League hitter. A positive MLVr indicates a contribution above average, while a negative MLVr indicates a contribution below average. It is important to note that a negative MLVr does not necessarily indicate that the player was not useful. By definition, many perfectly valuable Major Leaguers have to be "below average." What is important is whether a player is better than replacement level.

A sample of 20 players and their 2005 MLVr values are displayed so that readers unfamiliar with the statistic can see its relationship to the traditional big three statistics (batting average, on-base percentage, and slugging rate). (See table 1.)

Injured Hitters

The value lost from an injured position player is the result a simple calculation: $A \times B \times C$. The A factor is the "Expected MLVr" of the injured player, a combination of BP's PECOTA system projection and the player's established rate of production. B is the approximate number of games that the player spent on the disabled list. C is an adjustment used to account for the fact that some players end up with more or less plate appearances (PAs) than one would expect. C, in essence, corrects for platoons, time-sharing arrangements and lineup characteristics that cause an uneven distribution of trips to the plate.

---

1. This 10:1 relationship gets tossed around all the time and is rarely explained. A long time ago, Bill James demonstrated that team's Win-Loss record could be very accurately estimated from a simple formula based on Runs Scored (RS) and Runs Allowed (RA). He called this the Pythagorean Formula because it sort of looked like the trigonometric function of the same name. In MLB's current run environment, that Pythagorean Formula moves up or down a single win every time about 10 runs are added or subtracted from a team's RS or RA.

TABLE 1.

Name	AVG	OBP	SLG	MLVr
Derrek Lee	0.335	0.418	0.662	0.531
Alex Rodriguez	0.321	0.421	0.610	0.446
Carlos Delgado	0.301	0.399	0.582	0.395
Jason Bay	0.306	0.402	0.559	0.348
Brian Giles	0.301	0.423	0.483	0.302
Mike Young	0.331	0.385	0.513	0.257
Bobby Abreu	0.286	0.405	0.474	0.216
Joe Randa	0.289	0.356	0.491	0.169
Jason Larue	0.260	0.351	0.452	0.089
Shea Hillenbrand	0.291	0.343	0.449	0.069
Torii Hunter	0.269	0.337	0.452	0.054
Clint Barmes	0.289	0.326	0.434	0.013
Mike Cuddyer	0.263	0.330	0.422	−0.006
Aaron Rowand	0.270	0.327	0.407	−0.031
Adrian Beltre	0.255	0.303	0.413	−0.055
Omar Vizquel	0.271	0.330	0.350	−0.076
Scott Hatteberg	0.256	0.333	0.343	−0.107
Cristian Guzman	0.219	0.256	0.314	−0.270
Tony Womack	0.249	0.271	0.280	−0.314

Expected MLVr

The A factor of the formula tries to answer a simple but critical question: What level of production would the injured starter have given his team had he not gone on the disabled list? A player that is injured early in the season will have very few appearances, leaving us a small sample size from which to extrapolate his real value. For this reason we chose to balance a player's actual rate of production with what Baseball Prospectus's PECOTA system had calculated in the offseason as his projected rate of production. The method used to balance the actual performance and the expected performance is based on the size of the sample the player established. A player with a significant number of plate appearances will have that weighted more, while a player that missed more time will rely more on his PECOTA projection. Essentially, a player that misses half the season will have an expected level that is equally weighted between performance and projection.

Critical to this balance is defining a "full season." The MLVr statistic is based on the idea that each player in the lineup is ideally apportioned one-ninth (11.1%) of his team's plate appearances per game, so we defined a full season as 11.1% of the team's plate appearances for the season. Players who fail to reach that 11.1% figure will have their actual stats adjusted to balance with their PECOTA predictions.[2]

The Expected MLVr for injured players is calculated as follows:

$$\frac{(2005 \text{ MLVr} \times 2005 \text{ PA\%}) + [\text{PECOTA MLVr} \times (.111 - 2005 \text{ PA\%})]}{.111}$$

There is no specific reason why the blending process must weigh the established MLVr and the PECOTA MLVr in linear proportion to the sample size of the in-season data. It could be argued that for players with larger sample sizes, the PECOTA data shouldn't be valued so highly, or even at all. The converse is true as well. Extremely small sample sizes may be based on too little data to be worthwhile. Our thought was that blending in exact proportion to the actual sample size was a reasonable starting point.

Two problems immediately present themselves. On the one hand, if you don't like the PECOTA projection, you're not going to like the balancing. Moises Alou's weighted mean projection from last offseason predicted a significant decline for the outfielder in 2006 (from a 2004 MLVr of .243 to a predicted 2005 MLVr of .010). The Jr. Alou didn't just stave off father time for another year; he improved his production (to an actual 2005 MLVr of 0.301). Our balancing formula for the expected performance of Alou during his DL stints is heavily influenced by the fact that PECOTA was so pessimistic.

On the other hand, sometimes the actual performance just doesn't seem right. For example, in 2005, Curt Schilling was still working through the aftermath of the ankle injury, and the effects showed up in his stats. A career 3.32 ERA pitcher, Schilling posted a miserable 5.69 ERA last year. This extremely low performance level contributed to our system arriving at a fairly low level of expected performance from Schilling.

At this point in our research, we just don't know how to do anything other than tag a player as injured (DL) or healthy (not on DL). That Schilling was on the field yet still dealing with significant health problems is undeniable, but it is not clear how to identify which part of his performance was caused by injury and which part was indicative of a new ability level.

All in all, these cases are rare and the solutions to these problems would be arbitrary and extremely difficult to implement. It'd be like saying, "In Alou's case I just don't *feel* his PECOTA and in Schilling's case I just don't *feel* his 2005 stats, so I'm going to fudge them."

Estimating Games Missed to Injury

The second major problem we face is getting reliable data on injuries. Major League Baseball clubs do not report injuries as specifically as organizations do in other major sports, making it difficult to identify the true nature of an

---

2. There wasn't a single hitter in 2005 who accumulated 11.1% of his team's plate appearances *and* spent time on the DL.

injury, or even whether an injury has occurred. It is nearly impossible to identify all the cases of players who miss a day or two or three to so called "day-to-day injuries." To limit the data collection problem, we decided that we would only count those injuries that required a player to be placed on the Disabled List.

Using MLB Disabled List transaction dates still leaves us with two significant problems. First, MLB and the traditional stat providers don't offer DL data in an easy to code format. Transactions are reported haphazardly and are often subject to change without notice. All of the DL data in this article was collected and coded by hand and is subject to both human error and error from patently incorrect information.[3]

Second, days missed and games missed aren't always equal because of travel days, rest days, and doubleheaders. The simplest solution was simply to observe that there were 182 days in the 2005 regular season and that each team plays 162 games in that period. Hence each team plays approximately 0.89 games per day. A cursory check for the accuracy of this approximation reaffirmed that it was a reasonable shortcut.

The B factor in the value lost formula is reached by multiplying the days a player spent on the DL by 0.89. This will create small inaccuracies at the periphery—like, for instance, during the final month of the season when there are very few rest days in most teams' schedules. Improving this system to actually count the number of team games missed by each player injury is saved for later work.

Adjusting for Playing Time Arrangements

Very few Major League players make every single plate appearance of every single game while they are healthy. Players have rest days, managers bench them against tough opposing pitchers, they get removed for pinch hitters or defensive substitutions, and are taken out of games in a number of other discretionary situations.

In addition, the number of plate appearances a player receives is influenced by his place in the lineup—batters at the top of the order get to the plate more often in a season than batters at the bottom. We thought it unfair to equate a player like J. T. Snow, who seldom plays against left-handed pitchers, with someone like Ray Durham, who doesn't get rested often and bats at the very top of the lineup.

This is all the more important because Keith Woolner's MLVr statistic is based on the expectation that each player gets 11.1% of each game's plate appearances. The C factor in our value formula is the adjustment to correct for abnormal playing time.

$$\frac{2005\ PA\%}{162 - \text{Games Missed to DL}} \times \frac{162}{.111}$$

The adjustment takes the form of a product of two quotients. The left quotient shows the percentage of team plate appearances a player took in ratio to the number of games he was available to play. The right one is an expression of the ideal ratio (11.1% of team PAs in 162 games). When those two ratios are multiplied, the product is a percentage where 100% would signify that the player gets as many plate appearances per game available as a player would get if he received one-ninth of his team's plate appearances.

Since a player rarely gets more that 11.1%, there are very few major leaguers who have a factor here above 100%. This is an important result that proves the significance of our adjustment. It is critical that we not give any player credit for plate appearances he wouldn't have made if healthy.

Because the adjustment counts a player as "available" on all days in which he is not on the DL, our system will have difficulty accurately counting players who try to play through injuries by taking extra rest. Since we don't have the ability to identify which players are taking days off to play through an injury and which players get days off because the manager doesn't want them in the game, there is presently no way to correct for this.

We'll also be unfairly underestimating players whose role changed mid-season. Someone who spends the first half of the season in the minors will accumulate zero plate appearances during that period; if he arrives in the majors with a bang and plays every day his seasonal numbers will still show him as little more than a part time player, even though by that point the team has come to expect more from him.

In summation, the value that would have otherwise been expected by the starter had he not been placed on the DL is equal to $A \times B \times C$, where A is Expected MLVr, B is games lost to DL, and C is an adjustment for plate appearance apportionment.

Comparing to Replacement Level

Replacement level theory is an important concept that has been more fully explained by Keith Woolner in his essay "Understanding and Measuring Replacement Level" in *Baseball Prospectus 2002*. Woolner defined replacement level as "performance that could be obtained from a readily available bench player or a fringe major-leaguer." In that article, Woolner used 105 years of MLB data to calculate the performance level of players who were not starters for their team. What he found was that replacement level was position dependent and that replacement level performance

---

3. Disabled list start dates often vary from source to source and we had to make an educated guess as to which figure was correct. Mike Groopman and David Haller deserve special recognition for doing all of this mind-numbing coding.

was 80% of average starter performance at all positions except first base (where replacement level is 75% of average), and catcher (where replacement level is 85% of average).

In our study, we compared the calculated performance expected by the injured starter to what would have been expected were that starter replaced by a replacement level player. Problematically, though, it is not always the case that a replacement player replaces a starter at the *same* position, since managers often shift a different starter into the injured player's position, using the replacement player in the newly opened defensive position. When San Diego first baseman Phil Nevin was placed on the DL in 2004, left fielder Ryan Klesko shifted to first and outfielders Terrence Long and Xavier Nady took over in left field. In terms of offensive replacement, corner outfielders were substituted for Nevin.

We have labeled this phenomenon the "defensive spectrum problem," and because of it, we chose to compare the lost starter's performance to the performance of a replacement player in the positional group of the starter. Outfielders and first basemen represented one group; second basemen, third basemen and shortstops represented a second; catchers were the only members of the third group. Defensive spectrum shifts often occur within these groupings, but almost never across them. To clarify, an injured catcher will be compared to a replacement level catcher while an injured outfielder will be compared to the average of replacement level left fielders, center fielders, right fielders, and first basemen. (See table 2.)

The comparison between our starter's expected performance lost and the performance that the team should have expected from a replacement level starter is extremely simple. If the starter's expected value lost was Starter MLVr × Games lost to DL × PA Adjustment, the theoretical replacement level player performance gained back is simply Replacement MLVr × Games starter is on DL × PA Adjustment of Starter. The second and third terms remain the same because the replacement player can only truly be said to be a "replacement" in the plate appearances that the starter would have otherwise taken.

Let's do one step by step. The balanced expected MLVr from San Diego's Ramon Hernandez is 0.013 runs per game. He missed 56 days to the DL in 2005, which we will simplify to an approximate 49.85 games missed using the 162/182 factor. Because of rest days and other time-sharing arrangements, Hernandez took only 82% of the golden one-ninth of team PAs that the MLVr statistic expects. Multiplying A × B × C indicates that Hernandez would have contributed 0.51 runs above an average player in the playing time that he missed to injury. In that same playing time a replacement level backstop would have only been good for −5.88 runs versus average. For his 2005 DL stretch, the difference between Ramon Hernandez and

a theoretical replacement catcher was 6.39 offensive runs, or almost 70% of a win.

An appendix at the end of this article lists similar calculations for all position player injuries in the NL West in 2005 that led to DL stints.

Injured Pitchers

The value lost math for pitcher injuries can be similarly summarized as A × B × C, where A represents the expected Runs Allowed per Nine Innings (RA/9) rate of the injured player, B represents the approximate number of games missed based on the length of the Disabled List stint, and C represents an adjustment for the amount a playing time a player typically received.

Expected RA/9

Our pitchers will have a balanced expectation of performance level just as our hitters did. For players with long injuries and small sample sizes we will rely heavily on their PECOTA projections. For players with short injuries and large sample sizes to work with, we will turn heavily to their established rate of production. There are a couple of wrinkles when it comes to pitchers, though.

First, Nate Silver's PECOTA system uses RA/9 at various points in its calculations but it never outputs an RA/9 projection. Instead, all projections are in ERA form. With Silver's approval we made a conversion of his projections using the ratio from five years worth of ERA and RA. More simply: since 2000 the NL's average ERA has been 4.32,

TABLE 2.

Replacement Level MLVr by Position	
p	−0.726
c	−0.144
1b	−0.066
2b	−0.147
3b	−0.071
ss	−0.169
lf	−0.024
cf	−0.104
rf	−0.067
dh	−0.088

Replacement Level MLVr by Positional Group	
1B/OF	−0.065
2B/3B/SS	−0.129
C	−0.144

while the average RA/9 has been 4.70. If you multiply Silver's projected ERA figures by (4.70/4.32) you get a decent version of what his RA/9 projection would have been.

Second, if you'll remember, we balanced actual stats versus PECOTA projections in linear proportion for hitters. A player who accumulated half of the ideal 11.1% of team plate appearances had an expected MLVr that was half based on his actual numbers and half based on his PECOTA projection. For pitchers, we did things a little differently.

As many are well aware, and as James Click analyzed in a column on the Web site this winter[4], pitcher performance is notoriously flukey from year to year. It's not uncommon for stud pitchers to lay an egg one year out of four, nor is it surprising for a nobody to catch fire for six months and torch the league. This is especially true for relievers, who face such a small number of batters each year that even a full season from a reliever represents a small sample-size.

For this reason we've set the "full-season expectation" at which we wholly trust a pitcher's stats, and leave PECOTA out of things, to 200 innings pitched. This means that a starter who misses half the season and only throws 100 innings will have half of his expected RA/9 determined by PECOTA while the other half is based on his actual pitching numbers. However, for a reliever who rarely pitches even 100 innings in an injury-free season, this means that the PECOTA projection will be super-weighted.

In essence, we're suggesting that PECOTA is a much better measure of a pitcher's true ability than a partial season that is marred by injury. The upside of this is that our heavier emphasis on projections will hedge against extreme numbers in fluke seasons. The downside is that we'll be missing the boat when a pitcher has truly turned some corner—by learning a new pitch, for example. It seems a fair trade off.[5]

To summarize: for pitchers who reach 200 innings pitched, their Expected RA/9 will simply be their 2005 RA/9. Pitchers with less playing time will have their Expected RA/9 calculated as follows:

$$\frac{(2005\ RA/9 \times 2005\ IP) + [PECOTA\ RA/9 \times (200 - 2005\ IP)]}{200}$$

Estimating Games Missed

We'll estimate games missed to the disabled list in the same way that we did for hitters, by multiplying days on DL by the ratio of games in a season to the number of days in the 2005 season (162/182).

The rub for pitchers is that starters often have their DL stints backdated to the last day they pitched so that they'll be available as soon as possible. Since no starting pitcher is likely to pitch the first couple of days after his last start, this means that we might be counting a couple of games as "missed" that our injured player wouldn't have been available for even if he had been healthy. For example, on July 7 of last year, the Yankees placed Carl Pavano on the disabled list with shoulder tendinitis, retroactive to June 28, the day after his last start. By definition, Pavano would have been eligible to return on July 13. Had he been healthy enough to return on schedule, Pavano would have missed two starts and 10 games in the official 15-day DL period.

If we wanted to do more research to find an adjustment, we could go through every starting pitcher's DL data for the last couple of years and see how many times teams manipulated the DL starting date in just this way, and also count how many games it typically encompassed each time it happened. That is saved for future work, as a difference of one or two games for each DL stint would have a minimal effect on our calculations.

Adjusting for Usage

To account for playing time, pitchers need their value lost formulas tweaked just like hitters had to have their numbers adjusted. For hitters we used team plate appearance percentage (PA%), but for pitchers we'll be able to use the simpler innings pitched statistic.

The adjustment for pitchers is a lot easier. Essentially we're just counting how many innings a pitcher pitched in the days he was available to pitch (viz. not on the Disabled List). For example, a 225-inning per year starter throws 8.7 innings a week on average; a 75-inning reliever only throws 2.9 innings every seven days. Our system has to acknowledge the fact that some pitchers get a lot more playing time than others.

$$\frac{2005\ IP}{162 - Approximate\ Number\ of\ Games\ Missed\ to\ DL}$$

The end result is a ratio that reflects how many innings the pitcher threw per day that he was available. The assumption here is that the player would have taken a similar number of innings per game if he had been healthy.

Our adjustment here will again misjudge players whose role changes significantly midseason. A starter who moves out of the rotation and into the pen before he is hurt will have accumulated so many innings as to look like more than a 3-inning a week guy to this system.

To summarize, the value lost calculation for pitchers is $A \times B \times C$, where A is the Expected RA/9 rate for the hurler, B is the approximate number of games missed, and

---

4. http://www.baseballprospectus.com/article.php?articleid=4630

5. For what it's worth, we seriously considered setting the "full-season expectation" here as high as 250 innings to hedge things even more strenuously.

C is the number of innings the pitcher could have been expected to take had he been healthy. Because RA/9 has a denominator of nine innings, and our playing time adjustment factor has a denominator of one inning, we'll also need a tiny $\times 9$ factor to balance the units.

Comparing to Replacement Level

The original Keith Woolner study on Replacement Level in *Baseball Prospectus 2002* also measured the replacement level of pitchers over time. He found that the replacement level for both relievers and starters correlated closely to some vary simple functions.

Starting Pitcher Replvl (RA/9) = 1.37 + League_RA/9 − 0.66

Relief Pitcher Replvl (RA/9) = 1.7 × League_RA/9 − 2.27

For the National League in 2005, this means that the Replacement Level RA/9 for starters was 5.28 and for relievers it was 5.50.

Which injured pitchers are replaced by replacement level starters, and which by relievers? If every one of an injured pitcher's outings were starts then he's considered a starter. If the injured pitcher accumulated at least 75 innings in 2005, he's also tagged as a starter.[6] Everyone else's lost value is compared to a replacement-level reliever.

We do the comparison between our injured pitcher and his theoretical replacement in the same way as we did it for hitters. If the value lost from the starter is Expected RA/9 × approximate number of games missed × IP/game when healthy, then the value of the replacement is Replacement Level RA/9 × games the injured player missed × IP/game the injured player took when healthy.

Let's do one out. Armando Benitez's actual RA/9 in 2005 was 5.10, while his PECOTA projected RA/9 was 3.60. Because he only took 30 innings in 2005 (and our "full-season expectation is 200 IP), his balanced Expected RA/9 is 3.82. He was on the DL for 111 days, which we assume is equivalent to approximately 98.8 games. When healthy he took 0.47 innings per game. $A \times B \times C$ (with our small $\times 9$ adjustment to convert the units) tells us that Benitez would have given up 19.91 runs had he not been on the DL. A theoretical replacement level pitcher with a replacement level RA/9 of 5.50 could have been expected to give up 28.66 runs in that period. The difference between the two, 8.74 runs, is how much Benitez's injury theoretically cost the Giants in 2005.

Moving Forward from a First Draft

Like we said at the outset, this is a first pass at a very difficult problem, and there are improvements that could be made (some of which I have already identified). It seems imprudent not to take a moment to acknowledge some of the ways we've thought to improve this effort.

- **Should we be including defense for position players?** Our best research shows that replacement level hitters tend to be average defenders, so this would probably only make a difference at the extremes, where the injured starter is either an exceptional glove man or an absolute disaster afield, *and* where the injury is long enough for minor defensive differences to produce a significant effect.

- **Should we be including the offensive contributions of injured pitchers in the NL?** The effect here is significant only for pitchers who hit well above replacement level, like Livan Hernandez, Mike Hampton, or Jason Marquis, but for that type of player it could be an effect worth calculating.

- **What is the cumulative effect of simultaneous injuries?** When teams lose one starting pitcher, they can usually survive by shifting their longman or a minor leaguer into the rotation, but what happens when they lose more than one? There is almost definitely a compounding effect when injuries occur at the same time, but we couldn't even begin to estimate its significance without taking a longitudinal look at how teams actually respond to simultaneous injuries. Tagging and identifying all that data could give us new insights into the concept of replacement level, and might also serve as a clever way to evaluate the roster construction abilities of the various GMs.

- **What is the difference between theoretical replacement level and the actual replacements?** Some GMs are pretty good about preparing for injuries by stocking a strong bench and a deep roster of Quadruple-A players at the Triple-A level. Other teams seem to prioritize their starting players at the expense of not having qualified backups ready to step in for injuries. Further studies of how teams compensate for injuries might yield interesting information about the value of backups and Triple-A players.

- **Is it fair to assume that Joe Backup replaces Frank Fragile in a 1-to-1 ratio?** A team responds to its #3 hitter hitting the DL by moving up its 4th and 5th place hitters, not by batting a bench player in the three-hole. The replacement player

---

6. There wasn't a single pitcher in 2005 who hit the DL, had at least 75 innings pitched, and didn't spend at least part of his season as a starter.

is likely going to hit at the very bottom of the lineup, which means that other starters are picking up extra plate appearances that this current system doesn't acknowledge. To quantify this effect, we would again need a longitudinal look at how teams actually respond to injuries.

Conclusion

What has this study brought us? We believe we have created a system that gives an assessment of both the actual and possible cost of injury. Results will allow us to measure the effect of injuries, or the lack thereof, on the fortunes of a team, leading to better understanding of roster construction, assessment of team medical staffs, and the effectiveness of the front office. Further work in integrating defense and better data from teams will allow more accurate measures and possibly also give us a picture of how seriously GMs view the idea of replacement level. Injuries cost wins. Now maybe we can begin to calculate how many.

TABLE 3.

Team	Batter	Pos	PA_Percent	MLVR	DL Games	PECOTA MLVr	Blended MLVr	PT_Adj Factor	Runs Lost
ARI	Jose Cruz Jr.	cf	7.00%	0.13	26.7	0.070	0.108	0.76	3.49
ARI	Kelly Stinnett	c	2.30%	−0.031	19.6	−0.141	−0.118	0.24	0.12
ARI	Luis Terrero	cf	2.90%	−0.139	21.4	−0.066	−0.085	0.3	−0.13
COL	Aaron Miles	2b	5.60%	−0.146	30.3	−0.023	−0.085	0.62	0.83
COL	Brad Hawpe	rf	5.60%	−0.004	49.0	0.197	0.096	0.72	5.69
COL	Clint Barmes	ss	6.00%	0.013	79.2	−0.061	−0.021	1.06	9.05
COL	Desi Relaford	ss	3.80%	−0.212	8.0	−0.096	−0.136	0.36	−0.02
COL	Dustan Mohr	rf	4.70%	−0.076	20.5	0.096	0.023	0.48	0.87
COL	Garrett Atkins	3b	9.20%	0.040	20.5	0.069	0.045	0.95	3.38
COL	Larry Bigbie	lf	4.90%	−0.176	15.1	0.003	−0.076	0.49	−0.08
COL	Matt Holliday	lf	8.40%	0.180	35.6	0.141	0.171	0.97	8.14
COL	Todd Greene	c	2.10%	−0.031	64.1	0.100	0.075	0.31	4.4
COL	Todd Helton	1b	10.00%	0.354	14.2	0.401	0.359	0.99	5.96
LAN	Ricky Ledee	lf	4.30%	0.077	30.3	−0.094	−0.028	0.48	0.54
LAN	Paul Bako	c	0.80%	−0.087	114.8	−0.261	−0.248	0.25	−2.96
LAN	Milton Bradley	cf	5.20%	0.159	83.7	0.05	0.101	0.97	13.48
LAN	Jose Valentin	3b	3.00%	−0.230	79.2	−0.066	−0.11	0.53	0.78
LAN	J. D. Drew	rf	5.10%	0.305	81.0	0.197	0.247	0.92	23.21
LAN	Jayson Werth	lf	6.40%	−0.044	60.5	0.019	−0.017	0.92	2.67
LAN	Jason Grabowski	lf	2.00%	−0.422	18.7	−0.087	−0.147	0.20	−0.31
LAN	Cesar Izturis	ss	7.80%	−0.162	49.8	−0.185	−0.169	1.02	−2.01
LAN	Antonio Perez	3b	4.70%	0.070	34.7	−0.084	−0.019	0.54	2.06
SDN	Ramon Hernandez	c	6.30%	0.080	49.8	−0.076	0.013	0.82	6.40
SDN	Phil Nevin	1b	6.60%	−0.124	24.9	−0.012	−0.079	0.70	−0.23
SDN	Mark Loretta	2b	7.40%	−0.001	54.3	0.014	0.004	1.00	7.24
SDN	Khalil Greene	ss	7.60%	−0.019	34.7	−0.048	−0.028	0.87	3.05
SDN	Geoff Blum	3b	5.60%	−0.163	16.9	−0.256	−0.209	0.56	−0.76
SDN	Eric Young	lf	2.60%	0.025	76.5	−0.126	−0.091	0.44	−0.86
SDN	Dave Roberts	cf	7.70%	0.087	13.4	−0.123	0.023	0.76	0.89
SFN	Moises Alou	lf	8.10%	0.301	29.4	0.010	0.222	0.89	7.53
SFN	Marquis Grissom	cf	2.40%	−0.353	53.4	−0.058	−0.122	0.32	−0.97
SFN	Edgardo Alfonzo	3b	6.60%	−0.088	35.6	−0.051	−0.073	0.76	1.52
SFN	Barry Bonds	lf	0.90%	0.468	144.2	0.656	0.641	0.74	75.11
SFN	Alex Sanchez	cf	3.10%	0.102	15.1	−0.142	−0.074	0.31	−0.04

TABLE 4.

Team	Pitcher	G	GS	IP	RA	DL Games	PECOTA RA	Balanced RA	IP/G	IP Missed	Runs Lost
ARI	Brandon Lyon	32	0	29.3	7.67	82.8	5.26	5.62	0.37	30.6	−0.39
ARI	Greg Aquino	35	0	31.3	8.33	61.4	5.03	5.55	0.31	19.1	−0.11
ARI	Jose Valverde	61	0	66.3	2.58	25.8	4.60	2.58	0.49	12.6	4.08
ARI	Oscar Villarreal	11	0	13.7	5.27	130.0	4.92	4.95	0.43	55.6	3.4
ARI	Russ Ortiz	22	22	115.0	7.20	50.7	5.47	6.46	1.03	52.4	−6.9
ARI	Shawn Estes	21	21	123.7	5.09	58.7	5.50	5.25	1.20	70.4	0.25
COL	Aaron Cook	13	13	83.3	4.10	105.0	5.75	5.06	1.46	153.6	3.68
COL	Blaine Neal	19	0	22.7	7.54	75.7	4.12	4.51	0.26	19.9	2.19
COL	Bobby Seay	17	0	11.7	7.71	43.6	4.16	4.37	0.10	4.3	0.54
COL	Chin-Hui Tsao	10	0	11.0	6.55	135.3	5.23	5.30	0.41	55.7	1.22
COL	Dan Miceli	19	0	18.3	5.89	52.5	4.38	4.52	0.17	8.8	0.96
COL	Jason Jennings	20	20	122.0	5.39	64.1	6.17	5.69	1.25	79.9	−3.66
COL	Jose Acevedo	36	5	64.0	6.61	44.5	5.50	5.86	0.54	24.2	−0.96
COL	Shawn Chacon	27	24	151.7	3.50	30.3	6.72	4.28	1.15	34.9	3.88
LAN	Wilson Alvarez	21	2	24.0	5.63	107.7	4.01	4.20	0.44	47.6	6.85
LAN	Odalis Perez	19	19	108.7	4.89	80.1	4.24	4.59	1.33	106.3	8.12
LAN	Kelly Wunsch	45	0	23.7	4.56	77.4	3.75	3.85	0.28	21.7	3.98
LAN	Eric Gagne	14	0	13.3	2.70	134.4	2.07	2.11	0.48	64.8	24.38
LAN	Elmer Dessens	28	7	65.7	4.11	50.7	4.62	4.45	0.59	30.0	3.48
LAN	Brad Penny	29	29	175.3	4.00	18.7	4.90	4.11	1.22	22.9	2.97
SDN	Woody Williams	28	28	159.7	5.19	31.2	4.37	5.02	1.22	38.0	1.08
SDN	Tim Redding	10	7	30.7	12.03	40.1	5.52	6.52	0.25	10.1	−1.15
SDN	Rudy Seanez	57	0	60.3	2.83	32.0	4.45	2.83	0.46	14.9	4.41
SDN	Pedro Astacio	24	22	126.7	4.76	20.5	6.35	5.34	0.90	18.3	−0.12
SDN	Chris Hammond	55	0	58.7	3.99	19.6	3.80	3.86	0.41	8.1	1.47
SDN	Adam Eaton	24	22	128.7	4.90	55.2	4.55	4.78	1.20	66.5	3.72
SFN	Tyler Walker	66	0	60.7	4.60	16.9	4.24	4.60	0.42	7.1	0.71
SFN	Latroy Hawkins	66	0	56.3	4.31	22.3	3.75	3.91	0.40	9.0	1.59
SFN	Kirk Rueter	20	18	107.3	6.54	14.2	5.21	5.92	0.73	10.3	−0.74
SFN	Jesse Foppert	3	2	10.3	6.10	26.7	4.67	4.75	0.08	2.0	0.17
SFN	Jason Schmidt	29	29	172.0	4.71	15.1	3.25	4.51	1.17	17.7	1.53
SFN	Armando Benitez	30	0	30.0	5.10	98.8	3.60	3.82	0.47	46.9	8.74
SFN	Al Levine	9	0	10.3	9.58	20.5	5.24	5.46	0.07	1.5	0.01

Top 50 Prospects

by Rany Jazayerli, Dayn Perry, and Baseball Prospectus

Welcome to the 2006 Top 50 Prospects list. What you'll find here are the fruits of a collaborative process that involves all Baseball Prospectus authors. Each year, there are a handful of rankings with which each of us disagrees, but we all respect the consensus. If you've read the prospect roundtables at BaseballProspectus.com, you'll know the process of hammering out this list is at times a heated and passionate one. All of us bring our own biases and closely held beliefs to the table, so there's a mix of opinions to be found here.

PECOTA projections serve as a prevailing guide (What's a player's peak going to look like? What types of prospects tend to succeed?), but it's anything but a "plug and play" endeavor. Also, while we're first and foremost quantitative analysts, we pay serious heed to scouting reports. If a player has jaw-dropping numbers but is otherwise dismissed by scouts, we'll take that into account.

The pool of eligibles comprises all prospects who have yet to exhaust their rookie status, although we reserve the right to some flexibility regarding players who have exceeded service-time limits, but have yet to exceed the 50 IP/130 PA playing-time barrier. There are no age limits, and we also consider established imports like new Mariners catcher Kenji Johjima. Because of the rookie-status qualifier, you'll find no Felix Hernandez and no B. J. Upton, so don't think that their absence from the list is a reflection of how we feel about them as players.

The debate over what kind of player makes the best prospect will always be with us. Some organizations like the Angels and Braves favor prep draftees, while others, like the A's and Blue Jays, largely eschew high-school talents. It turns out our list skews rather heavily toward the non-collegians. Here's how the top 50 breaks down when the players are divided according to role and amateur background:

Prospect Type	# (%)
High School/International hitter	24 (48.0%)
High School/International pitcher	6 (12.0%)
College hitter	12 (24.0%)
College pitcher	8 (16.0%)

Almost half the list is made up of high school or international hitters, which is a fact that might surprise those in the "college or death" crowd. This is due to the fact that the best college talents frequently fly through the minors so quickly that they don't have time to appear on prospect lists as well as our own research, which has revealed that the substantial edge that college draft picks held over high school picks in the 1980s has been largely muted in recent years. Our list is also heavy on positional talent, with only 14 of 50 spots going to pitchers. This reflects the inherent risk involved with young pitchers and the fact that the minor leagues, at this moment in time, seem a bit short on high-ceiling arms.

Now let's see how these same groups fare in terms of average rank:

Prospect Type	Average Rank
High School/International hitter	22.7
High School/International pitcher	24.0
College hitter	27.4
College pitcher	32.3

Once again, the collegians come up short. While prep/international pitchers numbered only six on the list, their average ranking topped both flavors of college draftees. Let's shift the focus a bit and see how individual organizations have been represented. Here's a list of how many prospects each club placed in the top 50 and in the honorable mentions.

Organization	Prospects on 2006 list
Diamondbacks , Dodgers	6
Angels, Marlins, Red Sox	5
Cubs, Mariners	4
Brewers, Royals	3
Indians, Padres, Phillies, Rangers, Tigers	2
A's, Astros, Braves, Cardinals, Devil Rays, Giants, Mets, Nationals, Orioles, Pirates, Rockies, Twins, White Sox, Yankees	1
Blue Jays, Reds	0

This dovetails with how we view the strength of the various systems—the Angels, Diamondbacks, and Dodgers at the top, and the Reds, Blue Jays and Yankees feeding at the bottom. And now, we proudly present the 2006 Top 50 Prospects:

1. OF Delmon Young, Tampa Bay Devil Rays, Age 20

	AVG	OBP	SLG	Defense
2004	.288	.341	.465	RF: +7
2005	.289	.323	.487	RF: −14

Let's get the sparse negatives out of the way: Young didn't hit particularly well after a promotion to Triple-A last season, his walk rates could use some improvement, and he's occasionally sub-optimal at tracking fly balls in right. Otherwise, he's the consummate ballplayer. Had Young logged enough plate appearances last season to qualify, he would have led the pitcher-friendly Southern League in slugging average as a 19-year-old. For his career, Young boasts an extra-base hit every 9.3 at bats, and he runs the bases with aplomb. The Rays are poised to give him a half season back at Triple-A Durham, which seems advisable, given his modest struggles there last season. But he'll be up for good by the All-Star break. Once he settles in at the highest level, he'll be good for 35–45 homers annually and will likely cobble together a run of 30-30 seasons.

2. OF Jeremy Hermida, Florida Marlins, Age 22

	AVG	OBP	SLG	Defense
2004	.279	.345	.428	RF: −6
2005	.262	.404	.475	RF: +7

Hermida is a great example of the silliness behind the notion of a Scouts vs. Stats debate. The two camps don't compete with each other, they complement each other. Hermida has been a top prospect with both camps for years, with scouts because of his beautiful swing and power potential, with analysts because his tremendous plate discipline at a young age gave him a great chance of reaching his power potential. The interaction between power and strike zone judgment is very strong—plate discipline allows a hitter to only swing at pitches he has a good chance of driving, and power forces opposing pitchers to work more carefully to the hitter. Both skills blossomed for Hermida in his first crack at Double-A; he slugged .518 (his career high by 77 points), and walked 111 times in 118 games. Already the answer to a trivia question as the first player in a century to hit a grand slam in his first big-league at-bat, Hermida will soon be recognized as one of the most polished young hitters in baseball.

3. 3B Ryan Zimmerman, Washington Nationals, Age 21

	AVG	OBP	SLG	Defense
2005	.315	.353	.513	3B: +9

Any discussion of Zimmerman must start with his glove; *Baseball America* sums up the general consensus of his defense by describing him as "a once-in-a-generation defender at the hot corner." Rarely has any player reached the majors preceded by such a formidable defensive reputation; rarer still has that happened to a player who does not play an up-the-middle position. (Although Zimmerman's defensive wizardry has provoked talk of moving him to shortstop.) It would be easy to lose sight of Zimmerman's offensive prowess in all this, or it would if he didn't step off the college diamond and hit .326 in Double-A, then smoke the ball for the Nats in September, batting .397 and hitting 10 doubles in 58 at-bats. No player in major-league history had ever hit ten or more doubles in a season of 75 or fewer at-bats. Two years ago we called David Wright the new Scott Rolen, which has worked out well, so we'll look into the crystal ball again and call Zimmerman the new Brooks Robinson.

4. LHP Francisco Liriano, Minnesota Twins, Age 22

	H/9	BB/9	K/9	HR/9	ERA	PERA
2004	9.6	3.8	6.9	1.1	5.20	4.50
2005	7.5	3.0	9.0	0.8	3.98	3.45

Years from now, we will likely look back at the A. J. Pierzynski trade as one of the most lopsided swaps of the current era—but it will no longer be known as the A. J. Pierzynski trade, but as the trade where the Twins acquired Francisco Liriano, along with a pretty fair prospect in Boof Bonser and a pretty fair closer in Joe Nathan, for a catcher who wore out his welcome in San Francisco in one year. Liriano has the complete Johan Santana Starter Kit, including the mid-90s fastball and disappearing change-up. He struck out 204 minor league hitters last season in just 158 innings, then whiffed 33 more (against just seven walks) in 24 innings for the Twins in September. His 237 strikeouts for the year were exceeded by just one pitcher in organized baseball, that pitcher being his buddy Johan. The pair could prove to be the best 1-2 left-handed punch in baseball as soon as, well, now.

5. 2B Howie Kendrick, Los Angeles Angels, Age 22

	AVG	OBP	SLG	Defense
2004	.319	.345	.508	2B: +8
2005	.314	.347	.508	2B: +7

Analysts rightfully pillory those hitting prospects who have too much value tied up in their batting averages—it's a stat prone to random variation, and it's not as repeatable as, say, commanding the strike zone or hitting for raw power. But there's hitting for average, and then there's HITTING FOR AVERAGE. Kendrick is doing the latter. In four minor league seasons and more than 1,000 at bats as a pro, Kendrick has maintained a .359 career average and has never hit worse than .318 at any level. He boasts a quick, line-drive stroke, hits to all fields, and has uncommon bat control. What's also encouraging is that in his last three stops, he has increased his isolated power rather dramatically. Kendrick has also made good progress with the glove, and he now figures to stick at the keystone long-term.

6. SS Brandon Wood, Los Angeles Angels, Age 21

	AVG	OBP	SLG	Defense
2004	.215	.274	.350	SS: −15
2005	.257	.308	.506	SS: −5

There are reasons for skepticism regarding Wood. He has only one exceptional season in his minor league dossier (and that one exceptional season came in the hitter-friendly Cal League), he hasn't proved himself in the high minors, and his glove may not play major league short-stop. On the other hand, that one exceptional season, in terms of power, exhausts the superlatives. In 2005, Wood slugged .672 and averaged an extra-base hit every 5.5 at bats. The only debate is what's more impressive from a prospect standpoint: his 43 homers on the season or his 53 doubles. With five triples, Wood became the first minor leaguer in over 40 years to amass 100 extra-base hits. For good measure, he then smashed the Arizona Fall League record with 14 homers in just 29 games. A board-certified endorsement should be withheld until Wood proves himself in the upper levels of the system, but there's no disputing that he had one of the greatest campaigns in the recent annals of the minor leagues.

7. 3B Andy Marte, Boston Red Sox, Age 22

	AVG	OBP	SLG	Defense
2004	.235	.323	.460	3B: +9
2005	.239	.334	.429	3B: +4

The Braves' inability to find playing time for Marte is the Red Sox' gain. Marte was our #1 overall prospect last year, and his numbers at Triple-A last season are eerily similar to his numbers in Double-A in 2004. Marte dips a little in our rankings, in small part because he did struggle in a brief major-league audition, and in large part because you have to be a little nervous about *any* player that the Braves are eager to give away. Then again, the Red Sox tend to know what they're doing. Marte should give the Sox just about everything you'd want from a third baseman other than a high batting average, and Fenway Park may give him that anyway.

8. CF Chris Young, Arizona Diamondbacks, Age 22

	AVG	OBP	SLG	Defense
2004	.225	.308	.419	CF: +7
2005	.244	.332	.485	CF: −1

Young is possibly the most underrated prospect in the game today. That's because his failings—relatively low batting averages and lofty strikeout totals—serve to obscure his more vital strong points: great raw power, strong walk rates, speed on the bases, plus defense at an up-the-middle position. Despite skipping over High-A entirely, last season Young led the Southern League in slugging while playing half his games at pitcher-friendly Birmingham. He also tallied 70 walks, 70 extra-base hits and 32 steals in 38 attempts. In terms of best-case upside, he may just let us know what Eric Davis could have done had he stayed healthy.

9. 1B Prince Fielder, Milwaukee Brewers, Age 22

	AVG	OBP	SLG	Defense
2004	.242	.325	.425	1B: −15
2005	.267	.345	.493	1B: −8

Fielder has been one of the best prospects in the minor leagues from the moment he signed with the Brewers. He is now the first player ever to rank as one of our Top 10 prospects three years in a row. It is highly unlikely Fielder will make it four—he'll be too busy making a run at NL Rookie of the Year honors. Prince has his dad's prodigious power, along with excellent plate discipline and decent agility for a big man. And unlike his dad, he won't have to wait until he's 26 for an everyday. Fielder may be a DH by the time he's 30, but he might also have 250 homers to his name by then.

10. 3B Alex Gordon, Kansas City Royals, Age 22

Gordon signed a pro contract after last season concluded, and his only pro experience to this point consists of 16 games in the AFL. He still earns this ranking because was the best college player in the nation last year; 30 out of 30 teams would have drafted him over Ryan Zimmerman, and most teams would still rather have Gordon today. The 11 previous Golden Spikes Award winners before Gordon—given to the best collegiate player—include Jason Varitek, Mark Kotsay, J. D. Drew, Pat Burrell, Mark Prior, Khalil Greene, Rickie Weeks, and Jered Weaver. Only Burrell, Prior, and Weeks were also the first college player drafted that year. Gordon hit .372/.518/.715 as a junior and stole 23 bases in 26 attempts, which gives you some idea of the breadth of his skills. He should be at least an average defensive third baseman if the presence of Mark Teahen (ahem) doesn't convince the Royals to move Gordon to right field. There's always the chance that Gordon can't make the adjustment to wood bats; otherwise, he should be an MVP candidate by 2009. Well, he would be if the Royals were any good.

11. 2B Dustin Pedroia, Boston Red Sox, Age 22

	AVG	OBP	SLG	Defense
2004	.331	.392	.512	SS: +1
2005	.274	.357	.427	2B: +5

Not long after being bumped up to Triple-A, Pedroia was stuck on the wrist. The lingering impairment dampened his numbers, but his body of work in the minors remains impressive. His career batting line of .310/.398/.473 is quite nifty by middle-infield standards, and he was one of the best players in the Eastern League last season before the promotion to Pawtucket. He's not particularly fast, but he's a smart base runner, and his defense is solid at the keystone. With Mark Loretta, Tony Graffanino and Alex Cora all on hand for 2006, Pedroia will likely be back in Pawtucket, but in 2007 he'll be Boston's starting second baseman. PECOTA sees Pedroia as having the fourth-best peak of any prospect in baseball.

12. RHP Matt Cain, San Francisco Giants, Age 21

	H/9	BB/9	K/9	HR/9	ERA	PERA
2004	8.7	3.6	6.5	1.1	4.75	4.63
2005	7.8	4.2	7.9	1.4	4.17	4.85

If Felix Hernandez is the King, then Cain may be the Crown Prince. Like the King, Cain strikes out hitters in bunches, and he was arguably more successful than Hernandez at the major league level. Hernandez aside, the only player in the majors last season who was younger than Cain was Hayden Penn. The biggest difference between the King and the Crown Prince is that while Hernandez is an extreme groundball pitcher, Cain goes the other way. Resultantly, he surrendered 22 homers in 146 Triple-A innings. If you're going to give up a lot of fly balls, San Francisco has the park to get away with it. With first-round draft picks like Cain, it makes you wonder why Brian Sabean is so eager to give them away.

13. OF Lastings Milledge, New York Mets, Age 21

	AVG	OBP	SLG	Defense
2004	.271	.319	.458	CF: −2
2005	.276	.336	.404	CF: −7

Omar Minaya has not been the slightest bit apprehensive about trading top-quality prospects (including some on this list) for major league talent that can help the Mets win now. Milledge is the one bullet left in his gun, and for good reason. The quintessential five-tool talent, Milledge is still raw—he only walked 33 times last season, and was caught stealing on 18 of 47 attempts last year—but his combination of foot speed and bat speed are as impressive as any prospect's. He hit only eight homers last season, but anyone who can hit 15 doubles in 173 at-bats in Double-A at age 20 has serious power potential. Milledge's defensive abilities make him overqualified to play right field, where the Mets have the luxury of projecting him, given Carlos Beltran's presence in center. He remains a candidate to be with another team by the trading deadline, but only if the Mets get very desperate, or very dumb.

14. SS Joel Guzman, Los Angeles Dodgers, Age 21

	AVG	OBP	SLG	Defense
2004	.265	.302	.485	SS: +7
2005	.266	.319	.448	SS: +4

Still the most expensive player ever signed from Latin America—Cuban defectors excepted—Guzman has lived up to his $2.25 million bonus so far. His numbers were down slightly in Double-A last year, but a .287/.351/.475 line for a 20-year-old shouldn't be taken lightly. He's too tall (6′ 6″) and too slow to make it at shortstop, and he'll likely reach the majors as a right fielder, a move that will only be accelerated by the Dodgers' signing of Rafael Furcal. Guzman is just one of six Dodgers prospects listed in this chapter, tied with the Diamondbacks for the most of any team.

15. RHP Justin Verlander, Detroit Tigers, Age 23

	H/9	BB/9	K/9	HR/9	ERA	PERA
2005	8.2	2.7	6.7	0.6	3.38	3.75

Matt Bush, the #1 overall pick in the 2004 draft, already looks like one of the biggest draft busts of all time. Verlander, taken with the #2 pick, is a much different story. Verlander was generally considered to have the best arm of any college pitcher that year, with a fastball that routinely hit 99 mph, but there were major concerns about his ability to throw strikes. The Tigers reworked his mechanics, he found the strike zone, and *voila*—Verlander breezed through the Florida State League and then allowed a single run in 33 Double-A innings, leading the minors with a 1.29 ERA and posting a strikeout-to-walk ratio of 136 to 26 (in 119 innings). Verlander was shut down with minor shoulder soreness in August, which is never a good sign, but was throwing better than ever in Instructional League. He has the stuff to be a #1 starter in the majors, though giving him another half-season in the minors to consolidate his progress would be wise.

16. 3B Ian Stewart, Colorado Rockies, Age 21

	AVG	OBP	SLG	Defense
2004	.252	.322	.460	3B: +20
2005	.225	.293	.385	3B: +5

The Rockies have only developed one homegrown stud hitter in their 13-year history, Todd Helton. Stewart may be the second. The team's first-round pick in 2003 had a monstrous 2004 season, earning him a place in our Top 10 last year. He missed all of April with hamstring and wrist problems, and hit .221 in his first 44 games, but from June 18th on Stewart hit .308/.383/.570. Stewart's bat will play at any position; if he continues to improve his defense at third base, he will add to the astonishing number of terrific young third baseman either on this list or already established in the majors.

17. LHP Jeremy Sowers, Cleveland Indians, Age 23

	H/9	BB/9	K/9	HR/9	ERA	PERA
2005	9.3	1.9	5.6	1.1	3.98	4.39

Since we began ranking prospects in Baseball Prospectus 1998, we've credited half a dozen prospects with being "the new Tom Glavine." None has lived up to the name. Sowers is the newest claimant to the title, and notwithstanding our track record on the subject, we think he's the safest bet yet. He was picked in the first round twice—the Reds selected Sowers out of high school but had no intention of signing him. The Indians took him #6 overall out of Vanderbilt three years later. As you might expect from a heavily-recruited pitcher who chose to play at Vanderbilt, Sowers gets high marks for his intelligence. A smart lefty who compensates for an average fastball with his ability to change speeds and throw his breaking ball for strikes . . . why, that's Tom Glavine! Sowers finished his first pro season in Triple-A, and should be in the Tribe's rotation by the All-Star Break.

18. 1B Daric Barton, Oakland Athletics, Age 20

	AVG	OBP	SLG	Defense
2004	.269	.381	.441	C: −1
2005	.279	.376	.412	1B: −15

Barton was only 19 for most of the 2005 season, yet his .410 OBP at Midland, had Barton logged enough plate appearances to quality, would have been second-best in the Texas League. For his career, Barton has a .431 OBP and has drawn 193 unintentional walks in 1,217 plate appearances. Clearly he has the plate discipline, but his power has not manifested as yet. Barton's career Isolated Slugging Percentage is only .167, and he's never posted an ISO of .200— the preferred benchmark for a corner prospect—at any level. Barton's command of the strike zone is beyond his years, but the power needs to come soon.

19. SS Stephen Drew, Arizona Diamondbacks, Age 23

	AVG	OBP	SLG	Defense
2005	.250	.333	.450	SS: −2

Like his older brother J. D., Stephen was considered the best hitter in college the year he was drafted; he was "advised" by Scott Boras and conducted a prolonged holdout, including a stint in the independent leagues, before signing; and he has had his commitment to the game questioned by scouts, in no small part because of the previous clause in this run-on sentence. His bat may or may not match up to his brother's—Drew put up some impressive numbers during his time in Lancaster, but struggled to hit for average (.218) after a late promotion to Double-A. His defensive value exceeds that of his brother. Drew and Young are the advance guard for an absolutely phenomenal collection of young talent in Arizona.

20. H Billy Butler, Kansas City Royals, Age 20

	AVG	OBP	SLG	Defense
2004	.277	.366	.421	3B: +4
2005	.267	.326	.466	LF −7

Butler's nominal position is left field, but it's clear that the only position at which he feels comfortable is the batter's box. Butler's defensive reputation is worse than any player we have ever ranked on our Top Prospects list—Jack Cust and Calvin Pickering are his only serious challengers—but as a hitter he's poetry in motion. He hit California League pitching as well as Brandon Wood last year, and Butler is a full year younger. He moved up to Double-A in August and hit .312/.353/.527, the youngest player to receive significant playing time at that level in 2005. The signing of Reggie Sanders provides some assurance that the Royals won't rush Butler to the majors as they have with so many others. The Royals were the first team to employ a career DH in Hal McRae. Butler may be the second.

21. C Kenji Johjima, Seattle Mariners, Age 29

This year's marquee import, Johjima is a highly skilled defender with a career batting line of .299/.360/.517 in the Japanese Pacific League. Here's how Clay Davenport translates his last six seasons to the U.S. major leagues:

Year	AB	HR	SB%	BA/OBP/SLG	EQA	EQR
2000	311	6	83.3	293/351/428	.272	43
2001	551	13	75.0	256/288/361	.226	50
2002	438	12	72.7	286/351/411	.265	57
2003	561	13	72.7	296/367/430	.277	80
2004	436	15	71.4	300/381/459	.289	69
2005	424	11	42.9	290/350/439	.272	59

Take the average of his last two translated seasons and you get a line of .295/.366/.449. Considering that last season the average AL backstop hit .257/.313/.393, Johjima figures to be a strong contributor for the next handful of years. Throw in his defensive chops and his reasonable contract, and he's perhaps the masterstroke of the Bavasi administration.

22. 3B Andy LaRoche, Los Angeles Dodgers, Age 22

	AVG	OBP	SLG	Defense
2004	.219	.279	.406	3B: −4
2005	.269	.331	.497	3B: −6

Adam's little brother was promoted to Double-A at midseason, teaming up with Guzman, 2B Delwyn Young, and 1B James Loney to give the Jacksonville Suns the best all-prospect infield in the minor leagues. (The infield looks even better if you include the starting battery of pitcher Chad Billingsley and catcher Russell Martin.) LaRoche's calling card is his power, with 53 homers over the past two seasons, but he also contributes with his glove and his batting eye. In any other season, LaRoche might rank as the best third-base prospect in baseball; this year, he ranks only fifth, as third base is the deepest position in the game in terms of Grade A prospects. Bill Mueller may have a two-year contract to start for the Dodgers, but it will be an upset if LaRoche isn't starting in the majors by the end of 2007.

23. C Jarrod Saltalamacchia, Atlanta Braves, Age 21

	AVG	OBP	SLG	Defense
2004	.253	.311	.393	C: −5
2005	.287	.351	.463	C: −11

You want to know an easy way to identify a top prospect before anyone else? Just jump on any high school player from the Southeast that the Braves select in the first two rounds. Recent picks meeting that description: Adam Wainwright, Macay MacBride, Jeff Francoeur, and Brian McCann. In 2003, they picked Saltalamacchia (out of West Palm Beach) with a supplemental first-rounder. The man his teammates call "Pits" (because on his jersey his surname extends from one armpit to the other) was the best offensive catcher in the minors last year. Saltalamacchia's defense trails his bat at this point, and with McCann already starting for the Braves, a position change is a distinct possibility. It would be a waste; switch-hitting catchers with this kind of bat are a decidedly rare commodity, and a savvy organization would do well to see if they could take advantage of the Braves' excess to extract Saltalamacchia in the hopes that he might turn into another Victor Martinez.

24. RHP Chad Billingsley, Los Angeles Dodgers, Age 21

	H/9	BB/9	K/9	HR/9	ERA	PERA
2004	8.1	5.5	7.4	0.9	4.32	4.82
2005	8.8	3.3	7.1	1.4	4.85	4.78

With all the upheaval in the Dodgers' front office, the one man whose job remained assured was Logan White—not even the McCourts are stupid enough to get rid of arguably the best scouting director in the game. Billingsley, the team's first-round pick in 2003, is another feather in the cap for White and his staff—he has known nothing but success since being drafted out of high school in Defiance, Ohio. He spent all of last season in Double-A, racking up nearly as many strikeouts (162) as baserunners surrendered (166). He ranks this low because his stuff, while excellent, is a tick below pitchers like Cain and Verlander, and because the Dodgers' recent record with top pitching prospects (Greg Miller, Edwin Jackson) is pretty scary.

25. RHP Anthony Reyes, St. Louis Cardinals, Age 24

	H/9	BB/9	K/9	HR/9	ERA	PERA
2004	9.4	2.0	7.8	1.0	5.11	3.86
2005	7.9	2.5	7.3	1.1	4.27	4.14

Reyes endured a litany of injuries during his college days and he's had occasional shoulder inflammation as a pro. Those are serious caveats for a young pitcher, and it's a testament to Reyes's abilities that he's ranked this high. Reyes makes hay with a plus fastball, solid slider, and a change-up that progressed nicely last season. Reyes's mechanics are a bit less than optimal. If he stays healthy and manages to curtail his fly-ball tendencies a bit, he'll be a strong

number-two starter at the highest level. Those are two sizeable ifs.

26. 1B Kendry Morales, Los Angeles Angels, Age 22

	AVG	OBP	SLG	Defense
2004	.339	.376	.508	(Cuban translation)
2005	.275	.318	.462	1B: −6

Morales hit the ground running in his first professional season in the U.S. He slugged better than .500 in the Cal and Texas Leagues and totaled 117 hits in 96 games. He then went on to have a monster showing in the Arizona Fall League. Morales flashes exceptional power from both sides of the plate and makes good contact, but his walk rates need improvement. If he develops as anticipated, he'll be good for 30 homers a year in The Show.

27. OF Carlos Quentin, Arizona Diamondbacks, Age 23

	AVG	OBP	SLG	Defense
2004	.260	.339	.436	RF: +4
2005	.247	.357	.415	RF: +9

Quentin sits comfortably in our Top 50 for the second straight year, a monument to the value of a well-rounded offensive approach. In two years as a pro he's hit .316 while averaging 21 homers and 30 doubles a year. He rarely strikes out (just 127 times in two seasons), and last year he upped his walks from 43 to 72. Add that to Quentin's one signature skill, his Ron Hunt-like ability to get hit by a pitch (29 times last year, after a minor-league record 43 plunks in 2004), and you have a guy who should reach base 100 times a season without virtue of a hit. His defense in right field was impressive enough that the Diamondbacks moved him to center last summer, and he may play there until Chris Young is ready. At either position, a string of .300/.400/.500 seasons (aided by his favorable home surroundings) may eventually be in his grasp.

28. RHP Joel Zumaya, Detroit Tigers, Age 21

	H/9	BB/9	K/9	HR/9	ERA	PERA
2004	8.8	4.8	7.1	2.0	5.69	6.11
2005	7.2	5.1	9.0	0.7	3.62	4.05

If prospects were like stocks, Zumaya would be one of the steadiest holdings in our portfolio. His value has risen consistently from day one, when he was drafted in the 11th round and then showed up in rookie camp with an unexpected additional 10 mph on his fastball. Zumaya has led the Tigers' organization in strikeouts three years in a row, including 199 Ks (second in the minors behind Francisco Liriano) in 151 innings last year. His control remains shaky, but it hasn't deteriorated as he ascended all the way to Triple-A. In the short term, the Tigers may consider breaking him in as a flame-throwing reliever; in the long term, he may team up with Verlander and Jeremy

Bonderman to give the Tigers the best trio of young starters in the game.

29. CF Felix Pie, Chicago Cubs, Age 20

	AVG	OBP	SLG	Defense
2004	.264	.318	.405	CF: +6
2005	.268	.305	.490	CF: −2

Pie boasts tremendous athleticism, and his tools have long wowed scouts. In 2005, the numbers finally followed. One of the youngest players in the Southern League, Pie authored a batting line of .304/.349/.554 before a bone bruise snuffed out his season. He also runs the bases well and shows excellent range in center. His plate discipline is lacking, but thus far he's proved himself to be a capable bad-ball hitter. Cautionary comparisons to Corey Patterson are inevitable, and perhaps even warranted. The Cubs would be well advised to go slowly with him.

30. C Jeff Clement, Seattle Mariners, Age 22

	AVG	OBP	SLG	Defense
2005	.280	.338	.456	C: −1 (125 AB)

Clement's core skill is power. He's the all-time prep home run leader, and he continued his impressive performance at USC. Some scouts don't think Clement will be able to stick at catcher, but he has a good arm and his flaws can be corrected. Clement has devastating power from the left side and his walk rates are solid. Because of the strikeouts, he doesn't profile as a high-average hitter, but the power will carry him. Clement abused the Midwest League after signing, though that's hardly a point of distinction for a player coming out of a top college program.

31. OF Brian Anderson, Chicago White Sox, Age 24

	AVG	OBP	SLG	Defense
2004	.265	.332	.433	CF: −2
2005	.267	.329	.429	CF: −2

How often do you see a World Championship team trade an incumbent everyday player to make room for a rookie? Credit goes to Anderson for inspiring Kenny Williams to make the deal. Anderson has a broad range of solid skills—gap power, good batting average, solid defense—that calls to mind the man he's replacing, Aaron Rowand. Maybe he won't be a superstar, but as Rowand just proved, you don't have to be to start in center fielder for a World Championship team.

32. OF Nick Markakis, Baltimore Orioles, Age 22

	AVG	OBP	SLG	Defense
2004	.264	.325	.404	RF: +1
2005	.280	.349	.453	OF: −1

Markakis was a two-way talent in junior college, but the O's are developing him as a position player. The 2005 sea-

son was his first full campaign in the minors, and Markakis made the most of it. Between High-A Frederick and Double-A Bowie, Markakis tallied 41 doubles, 15 homers and 61 walks. He's made progress in hitting to all fields, and his bat control is exceptional. In the outfield, he's a 'tweener who can get by in center but projects as a plus defender at the corners. Given the progress Markakis made with the bat last season, his ceiling is rising.

33. RHP Yusmeiro Petit, Florida Marlins, Age 21

	H/9	BB/9	K/9	HR/9	ERA	PERA
2004	7.5	3.1	8.6	1.0	4.01	3.94
2005	8.7	1.8	7.2	1.8	4.45	4.88

Scouts keep turning their noses up at Petit's stuff, and hitters keep turning their backs and heading back to the dugout after he strikes them out. Petit throws four pitches, on paper none of them above average. But he takes advantage of a deceptive motion to hide the ball as long as possible, making his fastball look a lot faster than the 89 that typically displays on the radar gun. His numbers look like those of a true power pitcher; he struck out six times as many hitters as he walked last season and whiffed 14 in a Triple-A playoff game. Petit is a little on the hefty side, and his extra girth seems to aid him in hiding the ball in his body. He resembles no pitcher quite so much as a right-handed Sid Fernandez, who used his extra pounds and a deceptive delivery to ride an average repertoire to 114 wins and a 3.36 career ERA.

34. 1B Justin Huber, Kansas City Royals, Age 23

	AVG	OBP	SLG	Defense
2004	.252	.367	.439	C: −3
2005	.286	.368	.471	1B: −11

Huber's fine plate work in 2005 raised his career minor league batting line to .293/.396/.493. The ex-catcher was moved off the plate by the Royals after he was pilfered from the Mets in the three-way deal involving Kris Benson, and Huber's offensive upgrade has taken some of the sting out of his loss of positional value. He strikes out a little too much for an elite prospect, but he's long on secondary skills—lots of walks and raw power. Huber is capable of a run of .275/.375/.500 seasons in the majors.

35. RHP Jered Weaver, Los Angeles Angels, Age 23

	H/9	BB/9	K/9	HR/9	ERA	PERA
2005	8.9	3.7	7.7	1.4	5.57	4.83

Weaver is a command guy with a four-pitch repertoire. He was profoundly hyped coming out of Long Beach State, where his numbers as a college junior ranked among the greatest seasons by any college pitcher ever. After a prolonged holdout he signed last May and had a strong debut in the Cal League. Weaver's control degraded after a promotion to Double-A Arkansas, and he has pronounced fly-ball tendencies. He'll strike guys out and post strong command ratios, but his ceiling will be determined by whether he can keep the ball in the park against major-league hitters.

36. RHP Jonathan Papelbon, Boston Red Sox, Age 25

	H/9	BB/9	K/9	HR/9	ERA	PERA
2004	8.6	3.8	6.9	1.0	4.85	4.55
2005	8.2	3.0	6.8	1.2	3.63	4.65

Papelbon has a plus fastball with late movement and an above-average slider. Last season, he pitched across three levels and struck out roughly a batter per inning and posted a sub-3.00 ERA at each stop. Moreover, he was critical to Boston's late-season drive to the playoffs. Papelbon needs a better third pitch, but if that doesn't happen he still has the potential to be a shutdown reliever. If the Sox trade away starting pitching to fill their holes at short and center, Papelbon will be in the Boston rotation to start the season.

37. 3B Ryan Braun, Milwaukee Brewers, Age 22

	AVG	OBP	SLG	Defense
2005	.306	.337	.528	3B: −4 (193 AB)

Braun, a University of Miami product and the #5 pick in the 2005 draft, has quick hands through the zone and a reliable power stroke. He spent most of 2005 in the Sally League, where he hit .355/.396/.645 in 152 at bats. The raw power is impressive, but he could stand to take a few more walks. The big question for Braun is whether he'll be able to stick at third. He has the arm for the position, but he may lack the quick reactions needed to man the hot corner. If not, he has the wheels to man a corner outfield spot. His bat will play anywhere. Gordon, Zimmerman, and Braun went #2-#4-#5 in the draft last year, turning third base into the deepest position in the minor leagues.

38. LHP Paul Maholm, Pittsburgh Pirates, Age 23

	H/9	BB/9	K/9	HR/9	ERA	PERA
2004	10.2	5.1	4.2	1.4	5.43	6.11
2005	8.8	3.5	5.2	0.6	4.16	4.39

Maholm has one vital merit: he keeps the ball on the ground. In 212 minor league innings, Maholm has given up only 12 homers and last season he posted a 2.55 GB/GB ratio at Altoona, a 1.76 ratio at Indy, and a 2.29 mark in six starts for the Pirates. His 2004 season was ruined by a line drive off his face that fractured some orbital bones, but he showed no ill effects upon his return last year. He won't post gaudy strikeout numbers, but if he makes even slight strides with his control Maholm will be a useful mid-rotation type for years to come. As PECOTA teaches us, limiting the power numbers of the opposition is what separates failed pitching prospects from successful ones. On this count, Maholm fares as well as any pitcher on this list.

39. 2B Ian Kinsler, Texas Rangers, Age 23

	AVG	OBP	SLG	Defense
2004	.294	.364	.485	SS: +3
2005	.244	.308	.399	2B: −5

In first half of the 2004 season, Kinsler turned heads by punishing Midwest League pitchers to the tune of .402/.465/.692 with 42 extra-base hits in 224 at bats. That limited sample of games raised expectations a bit too much, leading to disappointment in 2005. Still, Kinsler's batting line of .274/.348/.464, is strong by second-base standards, even in the inflationary PCL. He's a capable defender at the keystone, and his gap-power stroke should play very well in Arlington. He goes to spring training with a solid shot at claiming the starting job at second, and if that happens he should wind up on the AL Rookie of the Year shortlist.

40. RHP Philip Hughes, New York Yankees, Age 19

	H/9	BB/9	K/9	HR/9	ERA	PERA
2005	7.2	2.6	6.4	0.2	3.97	3.42

Hughes looks like a special talent, but there is certainly a good deal of risk here; while Hughes earns praise for his clean mechanics, he did make two trips to the DL with arm trouble and has yet to pitch above A-ball. He has exceptional command of his fastball, and the Yankees wouldn't even let him throw his plus slider last season. He makes this list in large part because PECOTA sees great things ahead for him, ranking him behind only Francisco Liriano in terms of peak value among pitching prospects. Staying healthy is obviously essential, but it helps that the Yankees are being careful with him. Keep your eye on this one.

41. SS Justin Upton, Arizona Diamondbacks, Age 18

Upton has yet to play an inning in the minors, so this is a rather conservative conjectural ranking, especially since the four players drafted immediately after him (all collegiate hitters) all rank above him on this list. But we're performance analysts here, and this is the highest we can rank him without a performance record to speak of beyond high school competition. Upton has great bat speed, command of the strike zone that belies his young age and the fastest 60-yard dash time in the history of the Perfect Game scouting service. (One exuberant scout described him as having "Alex Rodriguez's bat, and Bo Jackson's speed.") As with his brother B. J., there are questions as to whether Justin will develop the reliability to play shortstop at the major league level. There is little question that he could become a Gold Glove-caliber centerfielder if things don't work out for him in the infield. Expect him to move through the system rapidly by prep draftee standards. Like Delmon Young, who was also given a token ranking on our list immediately after he was selected #1 overall, Upton may occupy the top spot on this list in a few years.

42. 1B Mike Jacobs, Florida Marlins, Age 25

	AVG	OBP	SLG	Defense
2004	.167	.236	.250	C: −1 (96 AB)
2005	.287	.341	.556	1B: −5

At age 25, Jacobs's ceiling is somewhat limited, but he made great strides at the plate last season after missing most of 2004 with injuries. Jacobs's days behind the plate are likely behind him, but it's possible that the Marlins will give him occasional duty there. In any event, he'll go to spring training penciled in as Florida's starting first baseman. His record suggests he was hitting a bit over his head last season, but even with an anticipated regression he'll still be a useful regular.

43. RHP Fernando Cabrera, Cleveland Indians, Age 24

	H/9	BB/9	K/9	HR/9	ERA	PERA
2004	7.4	5.3	9.2	1.1	4.58	4.58
2005	7.1	2.6	9.1	0.4	2.14	2.92

The best relief prospect in baseball has the same background as most of the game's great relievers: he's a former starter. It would be unfair to call him a "failed" starter—he was a decent prospect before the Indians moved him to the bullpen halfway through the 2003 season—but he has clearly found his niche in relief. Over the past two seasons in Triple-A, he has thrown 126 innings, allowed 93 hits, walked 54 and struck out 150. The most impressive number in the previous sentence might be the first one—it's very unusual for a top reliever to spend two years in Triple-A, and Cabrera should be ready to be an impact reliever in the majors this season. Technically, Cabrera is not a rookie—he has a few too many days worth of service time—but he only has 36 innings of major league experience. (We should note that Bobby Jenks, like Cabrera, has less than 50 innings of major league experience even though he's well over the service-time threshold. We presume that a pitcher who records the final out of the season does not need the recognition that comes with being on a "prospect" list.) With a 1.75 ERA in those 36 innings, Cabrera certainly hasn't pitched like a rookie to date. Bob Wickman may have led the AL in saves last season, but Cabrera may wrest the closer's job away from him by the end of the year.

44. CF/SS Adam Jones, Seattle Mariners, Age 20

	AVG	OBP	SLG	Defense
2004	.237	.276	.361	SS: −13
2005	.264	.328	.413	SS: −7

The M's began transitioning Jones to center field in the Arizona Fall League, and he took to the position quite well. Jones has the speed, fielding instincts, and arm to be a plus defender at the position, and his bat is making progress, as well. In 2005, Jones set career bests in OBP and SLG at High-A Inland Empire, and largely kept it up after a promotion to San Antonio (the toughest park for hitters in the Texas League) despite not turning 20 until early August. If he puts up strong numbers in 2006 while getting comfortable in center, you can expect Jones to be much higher on this list next year.

45. RHP Craig Hansen, Boston Red Sox, Age 22

	H/9	BB/9	K/9	HR/9	ERA	PERA	
2005	9.9	1.4	7.1	0.7	2.13	3.55	(13 IP)

The emergence of the dominant college closer in recent years has led teams to the tremendously successful draft strategy of selecting that season's premier college closer in the first round, yielding draft picks like Chad Cordero in 2003 and Huston Street in 2004. Hansen was clearly the best reliever in the NCAA last spring as a dominant closer for St. John's, and after signing a four-year major-league contract with the Red Sox, was in the majors just weeks later. The Red Sox' creative bullpen approach may yield some very important innings to Hansen this summer.

46. OF Chris Snelling, Seattle Mariners, Age 24

	AVG	OBP	SLG	Defense
2005	.349	.427	.507	OF: −2

Yes, Chris Snelling. The same Chris Snelling who was our #19 prospect back in 2002. Snelling's indomitable ability to hit is equaled only by a penchant for injury that might lead one to believe he's secretly a Mariners *pitching* prospect. Since we first ranked him, Snelling has torn his ACL, torn his meniscus, broken his wrist and sprained his knee. Along the way he hit .326 in a brief Double-A trial in 2002; returned in 2003 after rehabbing his knee and hit .333 there; then (after missing all but 10 games in 2004) hit .370/.452/.553 in Triple-A last season. Despite all this missed time, he's just 24—barely three months older than Brian Anderson. On numbers alone, he's a top-20 prospect, but the knack for mangling himself can't be overlooked. In seven minor league seasons, Snelling is a career .327 hitter with good gap-power skills. He's a plus defender at the outfield corners, but at this point a permanent move to DH might be in the best interest of all parties.

47. LHP Rich Hill, Chicago Cubs, Age 25

	H/9	BB/9	K/9	HR/9	ERA	PERA
2004	9.9	8.1	7.4	1.8	6.98	7.26
2005	9.0	3.4	8.9	2.1	5.33	5.39

Hill has one of the best curves you'll ever see, but he's plagued by fits of extreme wildness. Last season, the Cubs saw fit to pitch him at four different levels. Hill responded by striking out a whopping 215 batters in 155 innings, mostly owing to his efforts to better locate his fastball. He's not young for a prospect, but age is not nearly the determining factor for pitchers that it is for hitters. The dramatic improvement in Hill's control last season, and his continued high strikeout rates, should be enough to overcome his vulnerability to the long ball.

48. C/1B Josh Willingham, Florida Marlins, Age 27

	AVG	OBP	SLG	Defense
2004	.229	.371	.434	C: 0
2005	.253	.372	.478	C: −13

Despite being drafted as a seasoned college hitter, Willingham has been simmering in the minors for six seasons. During that span, he's put together a career batting line of .278/.417/.515. At the plate, it's all there—patience, OBP skills, good raw power indicators. One problem is that, at age 27, he's positively antediluvian for a top-50 prospect. Another problem is that he's fairly noodle-armed behind the plate. Still, the Marlins at this writing have plans to give him a shot at regular catching duty. He figures to make up for those defensive shortcomings at the plate, but with an erstwhile catch-and-throw guy like Joe Girardi in the dugout, it's not certain how many pratfalls they'll abide. Still, Willingham deserves to be in the lineup every day at some position.

49. 2B Josh Barfield, San Diego Padres, Age 23

	AVG	OBP	SLG	Defense
2004	.226	.284	.378	2B: +3
2005	.287	.341	.404	2B: +1

After a sterling 2003 and a disappointing 2004, Barfield found a happy medium last season, hitting a solid .310/.370/.450 in Triple-A while markedly improving his defense. Barfield hit much better in the second half, hitting .343/.405/.514 from June 1st on, and has shown a broad range of offensive skills for a middle infielder. The trade of Mark Loretta to Boston gives Barfield an excellent opportunity to win the starting job in spring training. He may not have his father Jesse's power, but Josh has a good shot at having a similarly long and productive career.

50. SS Eric Aybar, Los Angeles Angels, Age 22

	AVG	OBP	SLG	Defense
2004	.283	.315	.411	SS: +6
2005	.271	.316	.401	SS: −4

Given the more world-famous middle infielders in the Angel system, it's easy to forget about Aybar. Don't. At short, Aybar is a plus defender. At the plate, he's a career .316/.362/.461 hitter with success in the high minors, and he runs the bases well. He's hit better than .300 at every stop, and has shown occasional doubles power. The walk rates aren't what you'd like, but he's proved he can hit for high averages. In essence, he does 90% of everything Howie Kendrick does at the plate, and has more defensive value. Quite soon, the Angels could boast a starting infield of Morales at first, Kendrick at second, Wood at third and Aybar at second. Nice.

Honorable Mentions

RHP Jonathan Broxton, L.A. Dodgers: Good blazing sinker, plus slider, nifty showing at Double-A Jacksonville in 2005 working primarily in relief. Broxton also racked up the Ks working out of the L.A. pen for a brief time. Unless the Dodgers get more comfortable with Broxton's third pitch, he may stay in relief. That lessens his value going forward, but his power repertoire should serve him well in that role.

SS Ronny Cedeno, Chicago Cubs: A fluke? Coming into 2005, Cedeno's career best AVG was .279, in OBP it was .328 and in SLG it was .401. But at AAA-Iowa, Cedeno busted out the lumber and hit .355/.403/.518. Compounding the "out of step with the rest of his career" concerns is the fact that his '05 batting line is particularly heavy on batting average. On the other hand, his strikeout rate dropped significantly, so maybe it's not a fluke. His glove is an asset, but it remains to be seen how well he handles major league pitching. At the very least, expect some serious fits and starts.

RHP Thomas Diamond, Texas: Tom Diamond may sound like a name culled from the netherworld of mid-budget 70s stag films, but it also makes a cool baseball moniker. Despite occasional control problems, Diamond blew away the Cal League last season (81.1 IP, 101 Ks, 3 HRs, 1.99 ERA), but he struggled with walks and, to a lesser degree, with the long ball after a promotion to Double-A Frisco. Diamond has quality stuff, but his fly-balling ways won't serve him well in Arlington.

OF Carlos Gonzalez, Arizona: Breakout alert. Despite being younger than his competitors in the Midwest League, Gonzalez hit .307/.371/.489 with an extra-base hit every 9.9 at bats. He boasts a quick, graceful left-handed swing and is a Gold Glove–caliber defender in right. Once Gonzalez fills out his frame, the power numbers should surge.

LHP Gio Gonzalez, Philadelphia: Pat Gillick deserves kudos for trading from an untenable position, turning dead weight Jim Thome into an everyday starter in Aaron Rowand. That he also got Gonzalez (and fellow lefty Daniel Haigwood) in the deal recalls some of his best work in Toronto and in Seattle. A supplemental first round pick in 2004, Gonzalez was dominant at both levels of A-ball last season at age 19, with 163 Ks against just 97 hits in 131 innings. Far be it for us to question anything Kenny Williams does of late, but this is one player he may live to regret giving up.

LHP Cole Hamels, Philadelphia: On the diamond, Hamels has injury concerns. Off the field he's a problem child. He's a lefty with command of three pitches, including a plus fastball, and the good news is that his injuries haven't involved the elbow or the structure of his shoulder. The numbers? Unassailable: 152 innings, 1.54 ERA, 208 strikeouts, two home runs allowed. If he cobbles together a healthy and effective season in 2006, then he'll vault up the list—but he must show more self-discipline and durability.

OF/3B Corey Hart, Milwaukee Brewers: Athletic and rangy, Hart can play passable defense at five different positions. At the plate he posts solid walk rates and hits for average and power. His swing is long at times, so he might not hit for high averages in the majors, but the secondary skills are solid. The Brewers may deploy him as an uber-utility player who's in the lineup five days a week, or he may settle in as the regular at third or any of the outfield positions. The former is probably the wisest tack.

1B Conor Jackson, Arizona: If OBP is life, than Jackson might single-handedly bring Social Security to its knees. Admittedly taking advantage of some fine hitter's parks along the way, Jackson has been an on-base machine at every level, including a .457 OBP in Triple-A last season. You have to admire any prospect that walks more than twice as often as he strikes out—Jackson had 69 walks against just 32 Ks for Tucson. The power has yet to come; he hit only eight homers in Triple-A, but with 38 doubles in just 333 at-bats, he's not far from adding to his home run total. The Diamondbacks like Jackson enough that they've re-signed Tony Clark, who hit .304/.366/.636 last season, to be Jackson's backup.

OF Matt Kemp, L.A. Dodgers: Kemp isn't much for taking walks, but the power stroke is imposing. He has some platoon issues, and he's vulnerable to offspeed stuff, but he's capable of 25–30 homers in the bigs. This past season, Kemp hit .306/.349/.569 at High-A Vero Beach (that SLG was tops in the FSL by a comfortable margin), and kept it up in the AFL. Think Glenallen Hill with a better glove.

C George Kottaras, San Diego: Quietly developing into one of the better-hitting catchers in the minor leagues, Kottaras has consistently posted OBPs of .390 or better, highly unusual for a backstop. His power is average at best, and he's small enough that there are concerns he may never develop much pop. Then again, a left-handed hitting catcher who can get on base doesn't need to hit for power to have a long career in the bigs. Think of Kottaras as the Greek-Canadian version of Mike LaValliere.

LHP Jon Lester, Boston: Boston's reigning minor league pitcher of the year topped the Eastern League in ERA and strikeouts in 2005. Lester pounds the zone with a low-90s fastball, and he also has command of a slider and changeup. His control could use some improvement, and his GB/FB rate is merely average. Still, dominating Double-A as he did, Lester has a promising future.

C Russell Martin, L.A. Dodgers: Martin's .430 OBP ranked second only to Jeremy Hermida in the Southern League last season. For his career, Martin boasts a .391 OBP with 205 unintentional walks in 1,486 plate appearances. Behind the plate, Martin has a strong arm and good footwork—the defense is major league quality. The question is whether he'll hit for adequate power. His career SLG is a modest .419, and his career ISO is only .139. That raises doubts about his ability to get around on major league hard stuff. Scouts like his swing and think the power will come. We'd like to see proof before getting too excited.

2B Eric Patterson, Chicago Cubs: The younger brother of Corey hit .333/.405/.535 in the Midwest League last season, claimed the batting title, and for his troubles was named the Cubs' minor league player of the year. He shows speed on the bases and has the defensive skills to stick at second. Patterson also has good pop for a middle infielder and a better concept of the strike zone than big bro.

OF Hunter Pence, Houston: Scouts hate Pence's swing and think it'll be exploited as he rises. Perhaps, but Pence did batter Sally League pitchers last season to the tune of .338/.413/.652 and swatted 31 homers across two levels. Sally League shouldn't be all that challenging for a college-trained hitter, but those numbers are not easily dismissed. Pence should see action in the high minors in 2006, and how he fares should settle some arguments.

SS Hanley Ramirez, Florida: Ramirez has been a top prospect for three years, and an enigma for nearly as long. His performance is erratic from year to year and there have been concerns from the start that he may never reach the immense potential predicted for him. In his favor is the fact that he's always been very young for his level, spending all of last season at Double-A at age 21. The Marlins thought enough of his skill to make him one of the centerpieces of the Beckett trade with Boston.

Managers: The Dress Rehearsal

by Steven Goldman, Christina Kahrl, and Keith Woolner

In this 11th edition of the Baseball Prospectus annual, we experiment with the imprecise business of profiling managers. This is much harder than it would have been had we started this series back in 1912. While John McGraw and his contemporaries were autocrats who selected their own players and decided on their own strategies, the front office has slowly usurped these prerogatives until in some organizations such tactics as the bunt have been banned by fiat. Had Ken Macha transferred his flag to Colorado, he might have been free to bunt to his heart's content, or at least as often as Clint Hurdle did: 52 times, *not* counting pitchers. In contrast, Macha bunted his position players just 18 times. Given the same opportunity, perhaps Macha would have been smarter than Hurdle and not given away so many outs in an extreme hitter's park. Perhaps Hurdle, given his druthers, would have bunted half as much.

The problem is, we don't know. All we know for sure is that a manager's initiative isn't what it used to be. There are several areas where a manager can exercise discrete influence, among them making out the day to day lineup, deciding when to bring pitchers into a game and when to take them out, when to pinch-hit, pinch-run, when to bunt, and with who. We've tried to isolate some of that here.

Most of the categories will be familiar. **G** is the number of games the manager managed. In the case of a team that used multiple managers, we have provided a line for both managers, plus a total line. **W** and **L** are the manager's won-lost record, **WINP** his winning percentage. **PYTH** is the team's Pythagorean, or expected record, **DIFF** is the difference by which the team over or underperformed that record.

Moving into the pitching categories, **AVG#P** is the average number of pitches the manager's starters threw. **>120** is the number of times the starting pitcher was allowed to throw over 120 pitches in a game. **QS** is the number of quality starts the manager received from his pitchers, defined as six innings pitched and three runs allowed (unearned and earned total) or less. **BQS** is the number of blown quality starts over which the manager presided, a number that implies how many times he tried to get too much of a good thing out of a starter who'd already given his team a good game's work. **REL** is the number of relievers used. For offensive stats, **PH**, **PH AVG**, and **PH HR** all

relate to pinch-hitters and should be self-explanatory. **PR** is the number of pinch-runners the manager used. **SB** and **CS** are stolen bases and caught stealing. **SB%** is the success rate of stolen base attempts. **SAC ATT**: the number of attempted sacrifice bunts, **SAC %** the rate of successful sacrifices. **POS SAC** is the number of times that the manager asked non-pitchers to bunt, and **SQUEEZE** is the number of squeeze plays executed. **SUBS** is the number of defensive substitutes the manager used.

Just a surface reading of the numbers reveals managers working with and against the strengths of their teams. With a deep pitching staff, **Mike Scioscia** neither pushed his starters, having just one start of over 120 pitches, yet also using fewer relievers than any manager in the game. This comes, in part, from putting less emphasis on lefty-on-lefty bullpen match-ups. Bob Melvin might have recieved a major league-leading nine pinch-hit home runs from his players, but his first primary pinch-hitter was actually self-defeating, Quinton McCracken, SLG of .292, who didn't homer once. **Bobby Cox** might surprise you for being among the game's leaders in Blown Quality Starts, but considering the absence of a quality bullpen, and you can sort of understand what pushes a veteran manager to see if a tiring starter into the seventh or eighth inning of a game. Compared to **Lee Mazzilli, Sam Perlozzo** was an activist, making more moves in 55 games than his predecessor did in 107. Fearing his bullpen **Terry Francona** pushed his starters, on a per-game basis, harder than any AL manager except **Ozzie Guillen.** Guillen was extreme in many regards, leading in pitches per start. **Ned Yost** was right behind them, and stayed out of his bullpen as much as possible. **Dusty Baker's** favorite pinch-hitter was Jose Macias; you know how well that turns out. **Jerry Narron** was slower to yank his starting pitchers than was **Dave Miley,** and got better results. Neither seemed to recognize that most Reds could not get a bunt down. **Eric Wedge** and **Alan Trammell** both displayed a grasp of their situations by being among the managers least likely to pinch-hit, in the case of the former because he had no one you would pinch-hit for, the latter because he had no one to pinch-hit with. **Phil Garner** was one of the most active managers in the NL, attempting to compensate for offensive problems by calling for more squeeze plays than anyone but **Tony LaRussa,** who led the majors with 15 despite some certified sluggers on his roster. For all that bunting, Garner had a very low success rate, while LaRussa did quite well. The main qualitative difference between **Buddy Bell** and **Tony Pena** was that Bell managed the running game better. **Jim Tracy** one of the managers most adept at leaving his starters in just long enough for them to punt a quality start. On the opposite end of negligent handling his starters was **Lloyd McClendon,** who deserved to be fired for the sheer number of good starts that he blew. **Ron Gardenhire** was something of a poor man's Ozzie Guillen, bunting lots but less, running lots but less, but getting better use out of his bench. **Joe Torre** pushes his starters but was among the least-likely to waste a quality start. Willie Randolph got more quality starts out of his pitchers than anyone except Scioscia and Garner, but got less out of them than either. Though the numbers here show Randolph to be fundamentally sound, note that his team's Pythagorean record was better than NL champ Garner's actual one. Only **John Gibbons's** Blue Jays underperformed their Pythagorean record by more among teams with full-season managers. Gibbons used more pinch-hitters than any manager in the AL and got great results—partially luck, and partially good spotting by the skipper. Charlie Manuel's team ran the bases well but couldn't get a bunt down. He was middle of the road in most other respects. He bunted less often than most managers—not asking your players to do things they can't is one hallmark of a good manager. Not asking them to do things they *shouldn't* do is another, which is why **Buck Showalter,** deep with power hitters, was baseball's manager least likely to bunt. Most of **Bruce Bochy's** attempts to pinch-hit went awry, which is why San Diego PHs batted just .209 despite top options Mark Sweeney and Robert Fick combining to go 28-for-88 (.318) in the role. Similarly, **Mike Hargrove** was among the AL managers most likely to bunt but it worked less often than for any other team. A study in extremes: thanks to having Livan Hernandez to kick around, **Frank Robinson** was the manager most likely to push his starters over 120 pitches, but lost relatively few quality starts because of it.

In the future, we hope to expand on this data as much as possible for contemporary managers. This isn't a task made any easier by the variable levels of quality across different play-by-play databases, a fact that makes in-game tactical decisions more difficult to count up, and in turn makes manager's more distant in-game achievements that much more difficult to evaluate. Nevertheless, we look forward to expanding on this sort of statistical information into the future, and hope you find this limited initial report handy in anticipating what your team's manager has done and might do in 2006. In next year's edition, we anticipate expanding this section to present a more in-depth analysis of each manager's tendencies.

Year	Tea	Mgr	G	W	L	WINP	R	RA	Pythag	DIFF	AVG#P	>120	QS	BQS	REL	PH	PH AVG	PH HR	PR	SB	CS	SB %	SAC ATT	SAC %	POS SAC	SQUEEZE	SUBS
2005	LAA	Scioscia	162	95	67	.586	761	643	.584	.003	97.2	1	93	7	377	90	.234	1	37	145	41	78%	65	66%	42	3	4
2005	ARI	Melvin	162	77	85	.475	696	856	.398	.077	96.8	3	81	18	458	310	.231	9	26	60	14	81%	104	68%	30	5	57
2005	ATL	Cox	162	90	72	.556	769	674	.566	-.010	93.9	1	75	14	483	245	.226	3	54	86	25	77%	107	70%	29	3	54
2005	BAL	Mazzilli	107	51	56	.477	499	521	.478	-.001	94.4	3	49	5	293	57	.125	1	18	50	14	78%	34	62%	20	1	38
2005	BAL	Perlozzo	55	23	32	.418	230	279	.405	.014	93.4	0	22	2	180	28	.130	0	23	22	11	67%	26	73%	19	0	35
2005	BAL	Total	162	74	88	.457	729	800	.454	.003	94.1	3	71	7	473	85	.127	1	41	72	25	74%	60	67%	39	1	73
2005	BOS	Francona	162	95	67	.586	910	805	.561	.025	94.4	3	74	7	442	108	.202	1	46	40	4	91%	24	58%	13	0	59
2005	CHA	Guillen	162	99	63	.611	741	645	.569	.042	101.9	3	89	13	410	100	.205	2	32	120	45	73%	78	68%	51	4	36
2005	CHN	Baker	162	79	83	.488	703	714	.492	-.005	97.7	10	88	4	457	240	.195	2	21	61	30	67%	93	74%	42	2	49
2005	CIN	Miley	70	27	43	.386	343	411	.411	-.025	90.9	1	22	3	203	104	.260	4	10	26	8	76%	23	57%	3	0	11
2005	CIN	Narron	93	46	46	.500	477	478	.499	.001	94.5	1	45	6	287	156	.218	4	9	35	9	80%	48	63%	13	0	26
2005	CIN	Total	163	73	89	.451	820	889	.460	-.009	92.9	2	67	9	490	260	.236	8	19	61	17	78%	71	61%	16	0	37
2005	CLE	Wedge	162	93	69	.574	790	642	.602	-.028	96.7	0	83	12	409	87	.213	0	18	57	25	70%	54	72%	38	0	33
2005	COL	Hurdle	162	67	95	.414	740	862	.424	-.011	94.2	1	63	6	459	272	.224	4	21	58	22	73%	123	72%	52	3	61
2005	DET	Trammell	162	71	91	.438	723	787	.458	-.019	93.1	0	72	9	425	74	.266	0	26	58	21	73%	61	72%	42	1	24
2005	FLO	McKeon	162	83	79	.512	717	732	.490	.023	96.3	4	82	9	448	237	.272	4	24	93	34	73%	117	70%	51	0	48
2005	HOU	Garner	163	89	73	.549	693	609	.564	-.015	96.3	5	96	7	434	250	.252	3	40	100	29	78%	122	67%	47	9	87
2005	KCA	Pena	33	8	25	.242	116	176	.303	-.060	90.6	0	12	3	88	22	.048	0	4	11	12	48%	15	80%	12	1	3
2005	KCA	Schaefer	17	5	12	.294	89	115	.375	-.081	85.3	0	4	0	46	13	.167	0	3	5	2	71%	3	100%	3	0	2
2005	KCA	Bell	112	43	69	.384	496	644	.372	.012	88.5	0	32	6	308	95	.183	1	18	29	7	81%	40	78%	29	2	15
2005	KCA	Total	162	56	106	.346	701	935	.360	-.014	88.6	0	48	9	442	130	.157	1	25	45	21	68%	58	79%	44	3	20
2005	LAN	Tracy	162	71	91	.438	685	755	.452	-.013	91.9	6	73	12	457	298	.2308	4	31	46	18	72%	81	70%	19	3	62
2005	MIL	Yost	162	81	81	.500	726	697	.520	-.020	99.5	4	87	11	395	255	.245	6	18	70	24	74%	97	68%	41	5	43
2005	MIN	Gardenhire	162	83	79	.512	688	662	.519	-.007	92.1	0	84	14	396	104	.259	2	45	89	32	74%	70	60%	40	3	35
2005	NYA	Torre	162	95	67	.586	886	789	.558	.029	95.8	4	78	5	417	94	.244	2	65	66	14	83%	43	65%	28	0	58
2005	NYN	Randolph	162	83	79	.512	722	648	.554	-.042	97.3	4	93	9	392	220	.291	5	10	134	33	80%	94	73%	39	1	65
2005	OAK	Macha	162	88	74	.543	772	658	.579	-.036	97.2	4	87	8	410	82	.157	0	17	29	13	69%	34	56%	18	0	15
2005	PHI	C. Manuel	162	88	74	.543	807	726	.553	-.010	93.1	3	80	8	441	263	.233	4	36	104	17	86%	92	67%	25	0	46
2005	PIT	McClendon	136	55	81	.404	565	649	.431	-.027	93.0	2	57	10	357	215	.212	1	8	43	18	70%	67	64%	19	2	27
2005	PIT	Mackanin	26	12	14	.462	115	120	.479	-.017	86.5	0	10	0	93	53	.133	0	1	16	1	94%	20	65%	8	0	7
2005	PIT	Total	162	67	95	.414	680	769	.439	-.025	92.0	2	67	10	450	268	.198	1	9	59	19	76%	87	64%	27	2	34
2005	SDN	Bochy	162	82	80	.506	684	726	.470	.036	94.4	2	75	7	456	274	.209	4	31	87	28	76%	97	74%	36	0	72
2005	SEA	Hargrove	162	69	93	.426	699	751	.464	-.038	96.6	1	71	10	432	121	.214	1	24	89	37	71%	69	54%	34	1	23
2005	SFN	F. Alou	162	75	87	.463	649	745	.432	.032	98.3	7	72	12	509	238	.252	3	33	59	27	69%	116	78%	52	5	72
2005	SLN	LaRussa	162	100	62	.617	805	634	.617	.000	96.6	1	92	6	436	265	.226	6	25	68	21	76%	104	74%	47	15	78
2005	TBA	Piniella	162	67	95	.414	750	936	.391	.023	93.9	9	53	10	400	118	.309	4	18	139	37	79%	59	58%	32	0	74
2005	TEX	Showalter	162	79	83	.488	865	858	.504	-.016	92.6	2	61	6	454	57	.241	3	22	59	11	84%	11	82%	9	0	19
2005	TOR	Gibbons	162	80	82	.494	775	705	.547	-.053	90.6	1	76	8	432	144	.306	3	11	60	21	74%	32	66%	20	2	59
2005	WAS	Robinson	162	81	81	.500	639	673	.474	.026	97.1	16	83	6	469	266	.199	2	48	38	27	58%	125	73%	47	2	68

Team Name Key and Park Factors

by Clay Davenport

	Name	Lge (2005)	Parent (2005)	2003	2004	2005		Name	Lge (2005)	Parent (2005)	2003	2004	2005
ABE	Aberdeen	NYP	Orioles	960	969	969	CHA	ChicagoWhiteSox	AL	WhiteSox	1021	1026	1024
ABQ	Albuquerque	PCL	Marlins	1130	1114	1110	CHB	Chiba	JPL	—	957	932	913
AGU	Aguascalientes	MEX	—	—	1081	1077	CHN	ChicagoCubs	NL	Cubs	993	1005	1010
AKR	Akron	EAS	Indians	1022	1040	1036	CHR	Charlotte	INT	WhiteSox	989	998	1006
ALT	Altoona	EAS	Pirates	954	967	974	CHT	Chattanooga	SOU	Reds	1023	1033	1048
ANA	Anaheim(LA)	AL	Angels	970	965	—	CHU	Chunichi	JCL	—	945	945	937
ARI	Arizona	NL	Diamondbacks	1054	1046	1040	CIN	Cincinnati	NL	Reds	1002	993	1002
ARK	Arkansas	TXS	Angels	1029	1025	1020	CLE	Cleveland	AL	Indians	974	959	945
ASH	Asheville	SAL	Rockies	1127	1125	1135	CLN	Clinton	MDW	Rangers	1033	1020	1008
ATL	Atlanta	NL	Braves	988	996	1011	CLR	Clearwater	FSL	Phillies	1000	1003	1019
AUB	Auburn	NYP	BlueJays	995	1005	997	CMB	CapitolCity	SAL	—	987	993	—
AUG	Augusta	SAL	Giants	990	985	984	CMP	Campeche	MEX	—	910	913	928
BAK	Bakersfield	CLF	Rangers	959	951	940	COH	Columbus OH	INT	Yankees	995	987	977
BAL	Baltimore	AL	Orioles	981	994	984	COL	Colorado	NL	Rockies	1110	1109	1104
BAT	Batavia	NYP	Phillies	1003	970	968	CSC	Charleston SC	SAL	Yankees	962	967	970
BCR	BattleCreek	MDW	—	975	977	—	CSP	ColoradoSprings	PCL	Rockies	1077	1060	1033
BIL	Billings	PIO	Reds	951	956	952	CWV	Charleston WV	SAL	—	994	999	—
BIN	Binghamton	EAS	Mets	1016	1008	1033	DAY	Daytona	FSL	Cubs	1031	1035	1019
BIR	Birmingham	SOU	WhiteSox	979	981	989	DEL	Delmarva	SAL	Orioles	964	989	1005
BLT	Beloit	MDW	Twins	1034	1032	1031	DET	Detroit	AL	Tigers	962	962	969
BLU	Bluefield	APL	Orioles	1076	1051	1025	DNV	Danville	APL	Braves	929	908	888
BNC	Burlington NC	APL	Indians	983	989	976	DOS	Dos Laredos	MEX	—	926	—	—
BOI	Boise	NWN	Cubs	1047	1056	1067	DUN	Dunedin	FSL	BlueJays	1032	1041	1052
BOS	Boston	AL	RedSox	1025	1033	1033	DUR	Durham	INT	DevilRays	1031	1034	1022
BOW	Bowie	EAS	Orioles	957	946	943	DYT	Dayton	MDW	Reds	1044	1049	1027
BRI	Bristol	APL	WhiteSox	938	943	978	EDM	Edmonton	PCL	—	946	935	—
BRO	Brooklyn	NYP	Mets	995	992	1010	ELP	El Paso	TXS	—	1102	1109	—
BRV	BrevardCounty	FSL	Brewers	956	966	978	ELZ	Elizabethton	APL	Twins	959	963	985
BUF	Buffalo	INT	Indians	988	989	1010	ERI	Erie	EAS	Tigers	1049	1046	1043
BUR	BurlingtonIA	MDW	Royals	969	955	950	EUG	Eugene	NWN	Padres	986	1003	1019
CAR	Carolina	SOU	Marlins	998	990	982	EVE	Everett	NWN	Mariners	1049	1045	1039
CAS	Casper	PIO	Rockies	1028	1012	1018	FKU	Fukuoka	JPL	—	950	953	952
CCH	CorpusChristi	TXS	Astros	—	—	976	FLO	Florida	NL	Marlins	947	942	942
CCN	Cancun	MEX	—	905	878	869	FRD	Frederick	CRL	Orioles	1015	1023	1019
CDB	Cordoba	MEX	—	1089	—	—	FRE	Fresno	PCL	Giants	995	982	959
CDR	CedarRapids	MDW	Angels	1014	1035	1041	FRI	Frisco	TXS	Rangers	985	994	993
CGA	ColumbusGA	SAL	Dodgers	—	969	981	FTM	Ft Myers	FSL	Twins	963	975	988

	Name	Lge (2005)	Parent (2005)	2003	2004	2005		Name	Lge (2005)	Parent (2005)	2003	2004	2005
FTW	Ft Wayne	MDW	Padres	961	958	959	MIS	Mississippi	SOU	Braves	—	—	954
GRB	Greensboro	SAL	Marlins	1003	1006	1029	MNT	Montgomery	SOU	DevilRays	—	965	969
GRF	GreatFalls	PIO	WhiteSox	953	952	954	MOB	Mobile	SOU	Padres	1013	1004	1002
GRN	Greenville	SAL	RedSox	1010	1018	1027	MOD	Modesto	CLF	Rockies	962	972	975
GRV	Greeneville	APL	Astros	—	947	950	MON	Montreal	NL	Expos	1034	1013	—
HAG	Hagerstown	SAL	Mets	1009	1000	979	MSO	Missoula	PIO	Diamondbacks	984	986	993
HAR	Harrisburg	EAS	Nationals	1009	1012	1022	MTR	Monterrey	MEX	—	977	975	963
HDS	High Desert	CLF	Royals	1106	1104	1104	MYR	Myrtle Beach	CRL	Braves	927	930	942
HEL	Helena	PIO	Brewers	946	948	966	NAS	Nashville	PCL	Brewers	909	924	933
HIC	Hickory	SAL	Pirates	1037	1021	1004	NBR	New Britain	EAS	Twins	983	981	978
HNS	Hanshin	JCL	—	979	981	981	NHP	New Hampshire	EAS	BlueJays	—	955	943
HOU	Houston	NL	Astros	1021	1007	995	NHV	New Haven	EAS	—	950	—	—
HRO	Hiroshima	JCL	—	1039	1049	1072	NIP	Nippon Ham	JPL	—	1029	1017	1004
HUD	Hudson Valley	NYP	DevilRays	960	963	984	NOR	Norfolk	INT	Mets	943	932	926
HUN	Huntsville	SOU	Brewers	1007	1017	1038	NRW	Norwich	EAS	Giants	967	973	978
IDA	Idaho Falls	PIO	Royals	1054	1062	1057	NWJ	New Jersey	NYP	Cardinals	989	991	979
IND	Indianapolis	INT	Pirates	1013	1013	1010	NWO	New Orleans	PCL	Nationals	886	895	907
IOW	Iowa	PCL	Cubs	975	982	1003	NYA	NY Yankees	AL	Yankees	974	979	991
JAM	Jamestown	NYP	Marlins	1067	1084	1092	NYN	NY Mets	NL	Mets	964	972	980
JAX	Jacksonville	SOU	Dodgers	962	961	955	OAK	Oakland	AL	As	1002	1004	1000
JCY	Johnson City	APL	Cardinals	1013	1032	1057	OAX	Oaxaca	MEX	—	1051	1026	1006
JUP	Jupiter	FSL	Marlins	960	954	941	OGD	Ogden	PIO	Dodgers	1043	1051	1060
KAN	Kannapolis	SAL	WhiteSox	979	990	989	OKL	Oklahoma	PCL	Rangers	941	953	973
KCA	KansasCity	AL	Royals	1055	1018	993	OMA	Omaha	PCL	Royals	954	949	968
KIN	Kinston	CRL	Indians	973	980	986	ONE	Oneonta	NYP	Tigers	1048	1050	1032
KNC	Kane County	MDW	Athletics	975	1010	1050	ORL	Orlando	SOU	—	999	—	—
KNG	Kingsport	APL	Mets	977	987	997	ORM	Orem	PIO	Angels	—	—	904
LAK	Lakeland	FSL	Tigers	1017	1008	1004	ORX	Orix BW	JPL	—	1061	1061	1052
LAA	Los Angeles	AL	Angels	—	—	964	OSA	Osaka	JPL	—	976	987	—
LAN	Los Angeles	NL	Dodgers	937	952	959	OTT	Ottawa	INT	Orioles	1004	1014	1007
LEL	Lake Elsinore	CLF	Padres	962	968	978	PAW	Pawtucket	INT	RedSox	983	988	1007
LEX	Lexington	SAL	Astros	1033	1040	1034	PEO	Peoria	MDW	Cubs	980	995	1014
LKC	Lake County	SAL	Indians	979	992	994	PHI	Philadelphia	NL	Phillies	966	993	1024
LNC	Lancaster	CLF	Diamondbacks	1091	1089	1087	PIT	Pittsburgh	NL	Pirates	998	991	993
LNS	Lansing	MDW	BlueJays	993	979	969	PMB	Palm Beach	FSL	Cardinals	968	956	950
LOU	Louisville	INT	Reds	1021	1029	1014	PME	Portland ME	EAS	RedSox	1048	1039	1016
LOW	Lowell	NYP	RedSox	1038	1033	1028	POR	Portland OR	PCL	Padres	939	946	948
LVG	Las Vegas	PCL	Dodgers	1061	1077	1089	POT	Potomac	CRL	Nationals	1038	1020	1012
LWD	Lakewood	SAL	Phillies	939	934	924	PRI	Princeton	APL	DevilRays	1056	1054	1025
LYN	Lynchburg	CRL	Pirates	1019	987	961	PRO	Provo	PIO	—	1016	1039	—
MAR	Martinsville	APL	—	983	—	—	PUE	Puebla	MEX	—	1079	1057	1037
MCD	Mexico CyDiab	MEX	—	1145	1106	1078	PUL	Pulaski	APL	BlueJays	1021	1039	1062
MCL	Monclova	MEX	—	979	978	975	QUD	Quad Cities	MDW	Cardinals	1011	991	986
MCT	Tigres-Angelopolis	MEX	—	1132	1103	1105	RAK	Rakuten	JPL	—	—	—	1003
							RCU	Rancho Cucamonga	CLF	Angels	978	981	979
MEM	Memphis	PCL	Cardinals	921	920	913	REA	Reading	EAS	Phillies	1022	1028	1025
MHV	Mahoning Valley	NYP	Indians	1045	1012	1000	REY	Reynosa	MEX	—	937	—	—
MID	Midland	TXS	As	1017	1002	995	RIC	Richmond	INT	Braves	978	983	999
MIL	Milwaukee	NL	Brewers	999	1002	1005							
MIN	Minnesota	AL	Twins	1013	1016	1014	ROC	Rochester	INT	Twins	1027	1023	1026

	Name	Lge (2005)	Parent (2005)	2003	2004	2005		Name	Lge (2005)	Parent (2005)	2003	2004	2005
ROM	Rome	SAL	Braves	939	929	917	TBA	Tampa Bay	AL	DevilRays	987	979	978
ROU	Round Rock	PCL	Astros	976	969	957	TCV	Tri-City	NYP	Astros	1011	1021	1023
SAC	Sacramento	PCL	As	963	958	957	TEN	Tennessee	SOU	Diamondbacks	1039	1034	1028
SAN	San Antonio	TXS	Mariners	908	918	944	TEX	Texas	AL	Rangers	1063	1064	1050
SAR	Sarasota	FSL	Reds	1002	992	984	TIJ	Tijuana	MEX	—	—	1066	1057
SAV	Savannah	SAL	Nationals	982	967	959	TOL	Toledo	INT	Tigers	983	965	952
SBN	South Bend	MDW	Diamondbacks	974	962	948	TOR	Toronto	AL	BlueJays	1036	1037	1034
SBR	Inland Empire	CLF	Mariners	938	952	962	TRI	Tri-City	NWN	Rockies	914	920	923
SDN	San Diego	NL	Padres	918	916	914	TRN	Trenton	EAS	Yankees	999	983	974
SEA	Seattle	AL	Mariners	950	951	959	TUC	Tucson	PCL	Diamondbacks	1101	1100	1096
SEI	Seibu	JPL	—	994	995	1008	TUL	Tulsa	TXS	Rockies	973	984	1007
SFD	Springfield	TXS	Cardinals	—	—	976	VAN	Vancouver	NWN	As	939	926	912
SFN	San Francisco	NL	Giants	979	1001	1005	VAQ	VaquerosLaguna	MEX	—	1145	1144	1151
SGA	South Georgia	SAL	—	991	—	—	VER	Vermont	NYP	Expos	982	995	1013
SJO	San Jose	CLF	Giants	929	916	903	VIS	Visalia	CLF	DevilRays	1007	1010	1014
SLC	Salt Lake	PCL	Angels	1086	1089	1081	VRC	Veracruz	MEX	—	919	925	934
SLM	Salem VA	CRL	Astros	978	968	955	VRO	Vero Beach	FSL	Dodgers	1059	1047	1044
SLN	St Louis	NL	Cardinals	971	974	990	WAS	Washington	NL	Nationals	—	—	941
SLO	Salem-Keizer	NWN	Giants	1012	997	977	WIC	Wichita	TXS	Royals	969	975	983
SLP	SanLuisPotosi	MEX	—	—	1052	1057	WIL	Wilmington	CRL	RedSox	985	984	984
SLT	Saltillo	MEX	—	1040	1050	1040	WIS	Wisconsin	MDW	Mariners	1009	999	990
SLU	St Lucie	FSL	Mets	1008	1008	1007	WMI	WMichigan	MDW	Tigers	966	972	979
SPO	Spokane	NWN	Rangers	1010	1022	1038	WNS	Winston-Salem	CRL	WhiteSox	1025	1052	1071
STA	Staten Island	NYP	Yankees	922	904	894	WPT	Williamsport	NYP	Pirates	940	967	978
STO	Stockton	CLF	As	950	954	959	WTN	WTennessee	SOU	Cubs	979	991	992
SWB	Scranton/WB	INT	Phillies	1000	1000	996	WVA	West Virginia	SAL	Brewers	960	969	944
SWM	SW Michigan	MDW	DevilRays	—	—	1017	YAK	Yakima	NWN	Diamondbacks	1005	1002	992
SYR	Syracuse	INT	BlueJays	1012	1017	1019	YKL	Yakult	JCL	—	977	1001	1016
TAB	Tabasco	MEX	—	834	840	851	YKO	Yokohama	JCL	—	1061	1068	1079
TAC	Tacoma	PCL	Mariners	923	920	907	YOM	Yomiuri	JCL	—	983	960	945
TAM	Tampa	FSL	Yankees	975	988	1004	YUC	Yucatan	MEX	—	888	894	891

Index

The following is an alphabetical index of the players in *Baseball Prospectus 2006*. Players not listed here can be found at http://www.baseballprospectus.com.

A

Aardsma, Davis 91
Abernathy, Brent 292
Abreu, Bobby 348
Accardo, Jeremy 413
Acevedo, Jose 160
Adams, Mike 268
Adams, Russ 468
Adkins, Jon 116
Affeldt, Jeremy 219
Aguila, Chris 184
Albers, Matt 208
Alfonseca, Antonio 189
Alfonzo, Edgardo 407
Alfonzo, Eliezer 407
Allison, Jeffrey 189
Alomar, Sandy 453
Alou, Moises 407
Alvarez, Abe 75
Ambres, Chip 212
Anderson, Brian (CHA) 103
Anderson, Brian (KCA) 219
Anderson, Garret 228
Anderson, Jason 325
Anderson, Josh 197
Anderson, Marlon 295
Andino, Robert 184
Andrade, Steve 482
Ankiel, Rick 379
Aquino, Greg 23
Ardoin, Danny 154
Arias, Joaquin 453
Armas, Tony Jr. 492
Arnold, Eric 482
Arroyo, Bronson 75
Ash, Jonny 198
Astacio, Ezequiel 203
Astacio, Pedro 399
Atchison, Scott 427
Atkins, Garrett 154
Aubrey, Mike 136
Aurilia, Rich 119
Ausmus, Brad 198
Aviles, Mike 212
Avlas, Phil 15
Ayala, Luis 492

Aybar, Erick 228
Aybar, Manny 307
Aybar, Willy 244

B

Backe, Brandon 204
Baerga, Carlos 485
Baez, Danny 444
Bagwell, Jeff 198
Bailey, Homer 125
Bajenaru, Jeff 110
Baker, Brad 399
Baker, Jeff 154
Baker, Scott 285
Bako, Paul 245
Baldelli, Rocco 438
Baldiris, Aarom 295
Baldwin, James 57
Balentien, Wladimir 422
Balester, Collin 492
Ball, Jarred 15
Banks, Josh 475
Bankston, Wes 437
Bannister, Brian 301
Bannister, John 459
Barajas, Rod 454
Bard, Josh 136
Barden, Brian 16
Barfield, Josh 393
Barker, Kevin 482
Barmes, Clint 155
Barrett, Michael 85
Barry, Kevin 41
Barthmaier, Jimmy 204
Bartlett, Jason 279
Barton, Brian 136
Barton, Daric 331
Basham, Bobby 125
Bass, Adam 23
Bass, Brian 225
Batista, Miguel 475
Batista, Tony 279
Battle, Tim 312
Bauer, Rick 58
Baugh, Kenny 181
Bausher, Tim 82
Bautista, Denny 219
Bautista, Jose 362
Bay, Bear 142
Bay, Jason 362
Bayliss, Jonah 220
Bazardo, Yorman 427
Beam, Randy 75
Bean, Colter 318
Beckett, Josh 189
Bedard, Erik 58

Begg, Chris 413
Belisle, Matt 125
Bell, David 348
Bell, Heath 302
Bell, Rob 450
Bellhorn, Mark 312
Belliard, Ron 136
Beltran, Carlos 296
Beltran, Francis 493
Beltre, Adrian 422
Benitez, Armando 413
Bennett, Gary 486
Bennett, Jeff 269
Benoit, Joaquin 460
Benson, Kris 302
Bergeron, Peter 65
Bergman, Dusty 419
Bergmann, Jay 493
Bergolla, William 119
Berkman, Lance 198
Berroa, Angel 212
Betancourt, Rafael 143
Betancourt, Yuniesky 422
Betemit, Wilson 33
Bigbie, Larry 155
Biggio, Craig 199
Billingsley, Chad 252
Bixler, Brian 376
Blackley, Travis 428
Bladergroen, Ian 82
Blake, Casey 137
Blalock, Hank 454
Blalock, Jake 348
Blanco, Andres 212
Blanco, Gregor 34
Blanco, Henry 85
Blanco, Tony 486
Blanton, Joe 338
Bloomquist, Willie 422
Blue, Vincent 169
Blum, Geoff 104
Boeve, Adam 362
Bohn, T. J. 434
Bonderman, Jeremy 176
Bonds, Barry 407
Bong, Jung 132
Bonifay, Josh 363
Bono, Kyle 24
Bonser, Boof 285
Booker, Chris 126
Boone, Aaron 137
Boone, Bret 279
Bootcheck, Chris 241
Borchard, Joe 104
Borner, Brady 376
Borowski, Joe 444

Bostick, Adam 190
Bottalico, Ricky 275
Botts, Jason 454
Boucher, Sebastien 423
Bourn, Michael 349
Bowden, Michael 82
Bowman, Shawn 307
Bowyer, Travis 286
Boyer, Blaine 41
Bozied, Tagg 393
Braden, Dallas 339
Bradford, Chad 75
Bradley, Milton 245
Branyan, Russ 262
Braun, Ryan 262
Bray, Bill 493
Brazelton, Dewon 445
Brazoban, Yhency 253
Breslow, Craig 399
Brignac, Reid 438
Brinkley, Dante 307
Brito, Eude 354
Britton, Chris 58
Broadway, Larry 111
Broadway, Larry 486
Brocail, Doug 460
Brooks, Frank 47
Broussard, Ben 137
Brower, Jim 41
Brown, Andrew 143
Brown, Emil 213
Brown, Hunter 434
Brown, Jeremy 331
Brown, Kevin 319
Broxton, Jonathan 253
Bruney, Brian 24
Bruntlett, Eric 199
Buchholz, Clay 76
Buchholz, Taylor 204
Buck, John 213
Buck, Travis 332
Buckner, Billy 220
Buehrle, Mark 111
Bukvich, Ryan 460
Bulger, Brian 24
Bullington, Bryan 369
Bump, Nate 193
Bunn, Greg 498
Burgos, Ambiorix 220
Burke, Chris 199
Burke, Jamie 116
Burnett, A. J. 190
Burnett, Sean 369
Burnitz, Jeromy 85
Burns, Deacon 292
Burns, Mike 204

Burrell, Pat 349
Burroughs, Sean 394
Burrus, Josh 34
Bush, David 475
Bush, Matt 394
Bush, Paul 47
Butler, Billy 213
Bynum, Freddy 344
Byrd, Marlon 486
Byrd, Paul 236
Byrdak, Tim 58
Byrnes, Eric 51

C

Cabrera, Asdrubal 423
Cabrera, Daniel 59
Cabrera, Fernando 143
Cabrera, Melky 313
Cabrera, Miguel 184
Cabrera, Orlando 229
Cain, Matt 413
Cairso, Miguel 296
Calero, Kiko 339
Cali, Carmen 384
Callaspo, Alberto 229
Cameron, Mike 296
Cameron, Ryan 359
Camp, Shawn 220
Campbell, Brett 493
Campbell, Eric 34
Campillo, Jorge 434
Cannon, Chip 469
Cannon, Jon 30
Cano, Robinson 313
Cantu, Jorge 438
Capellan, Jose 269
Capps, Matt 370
Capuano, Chris 269
Caraballo, Francisco 208
Carlin, Mike 376
Carlson, Jesse 476
Carmona, Fausto 143
Carp, Mike 307
Carpenter, Chris 384
Carrara, Giovanni 253
Carrasco, D. J. 225
Carrasco, Hector 494
Carrillo, Cesar 400
Carroll, Jamey 487
Carter, Chris 16
Carter, Lance 445
Carter, Ryan 259
Carvajal, Marcos 160
Casey, Sean 120
Casilla, Alexis 229
Cassidy, Scott 404

Castilla, Jose 363
Castilla, Vinny 487
Castillo, Luis 184
Casto, Kory 487
Castro, Bernie 51
Castro, Juan 279
Castro, Ramon 296
Catalanotto, Frank 469
Cedeno, Ronny 86
Cepicky, Matt 498
Cervenak, Mike 419
Chacin, Gustavo 476
Chacon, Shawn 319
Chavez, Angel 419
Chavez, Endy 349
Chavez, Eric 332
Chavez, Raul 200
Chen, Bruce 59
Chen, Chin-feng 259
Cheng, Chi-hung 476
Chick, Travis 126
Chico, Matt 30
Childers, Matt 47
Choate, Randy 30
Choi, Hee Seop 245
Choo, Shin-Soo 423
Christiansen, Jason 241
Chulk, Vinny 476
Church, Ryan 487
Cintron, Alex 16
Cirillo, Jeff 263
Clark, Brady 263
Clark, Tony 16
Claussen, Brandon 126
Clayton, Royce 17
Clemens, Koby 200
Clemens, Roger 205
Clement, Jeffrey 423
Clement, Matt 76
Clevlen, Brent 169
Cliffords, Woody 65
Clippard, Tyler 319
Closser, J. D. 155
Coats, Buck 98
Coffey, Todd 126
Colamarino, Brant 332
Colome, Jesus 445
Colon, Bartolo 236
Colon, Roman 176
Concepcion, Alberto 82
Concepcion, Ambiorix 307
Conine, Jeff 185
Connolly, Mike 370
Conrad, Brooks 200
Contreras, Jose 111
Cook, Aaron 161
Cooper, Brian 419
Cooper, Jason 137
Copeland, Ben 419
Cora, Alex 68
Cordero, Chad 494
Cordero, Francisco 460
Cormier, Lance 24
Cormier, Rheal 354
Cornejo, Nate 176
Correia, Kevin 414

Cortes, David 161
Cortez, Fernando 438
Cosby, Rob 469
Costa, Shane 213
Costanzo, Mike 359
Cota, Carlo 470
Cota, Humberto 363
Cota, Luis 221
Cotts, Neal 111
Counsell, Craig 17
Coutlangus, Jon 414
Crabbe, Callix 263
Crain, Jesse 286
Crawford, Carl 439
Crede, Joe 104
Creek, Doug 181
Crisp, Coco 138
Crosby, Bobby 332
Crosby, Bubba 313
Cruceta, Francisco 428
Cruz, Deivi 488
Cruz, Enrique 263
Cruz, Eugenio de la 181
Cruz, Jacob 120
Cruz, Jose 246
Cruz, Juan 339
Cruz, Nelson 264
Cuddyer, Mike 280
Cust, Jack 333

D

Daigle, Leo 116
Damon, Johnny 68
Danks, John 461
Daubach, Brian 307
DaVanon, Jeff 229
David, Kane 270
Davidson, Daniel 236
Davies, Kyle 42
Davis, Ben 116
Davis, Doug 270
Davis, J. J. 155
Davis, Jason 144
Davis, Rajai 363
Davis, Wade 450
Day, Zach 161
de Aza, Alejandro 193
De Caster, Yurendell 364
de la Rosa, Jorge 270
de los Santos, Valerio 193
De Paula, Jorge 319
Deeds, Doug 280
DeJean, Mike 161
DeJesus, David 214
Delcarmen, Manny 76
Delgado, Carlos 185
Delgado, Jesus 82
Dellucci, David 454
DeMaria, Chris 221
Dempster, Ryan 91
Denham, Dan 144
Denker, Travis 246
Denney, Kyle 144
Denorfia, Chris 120
DeRosa, Mark 455
DeSalvo, Matt 320
Desmond, Ian 498

Dessens, Elmer 253
Devine, Joey 42
DeVore, Doug 419
Dewitt, Blake 246
Diamond, Thomas 461
Diaz, Einar 379
Diaz, Felix 112
Diaz, Frank 488
Diaz, Matt 214
Diaz, Victor 297
Dickerson, Chris 132
Dickey, R. A. 461
Dillard, Timothy 270
DiNardo, Lenny 76
Dingman, Craig 177
Dittler, Jake 145
Dlugach, Brent 169
Dobbs, Greg 434
Dohmann, Scott 162
Dominguez, Juan 461
Donachie, Matt 214
Donnelly, Brendan 236
Dopirak, Brian 86
Dotel, Octavio 340
Douglass, Sean 177
Doumit, Ryan 364
Downs, Scott 477
Doyne, Cory 389
Dreifort, Darren 259
Drese, Ryan 494
Drew, J. D. 246
Drew, Stephen 17
DuBois, Jason 138
DuBose, Eric 59
Duchscherer, Justin 340
Duffy, Chris 364
Duke, Zach 370
Dukes, Elijah 439
Dumatrait, Phil 127
Duncan, Chris 379
Duncan, Eric 314
Dunn, Adam 121
Dunn, Scott 237
Durazo, Erubiel 333
Durbin, Chris 68
Durbin, J. D. 286
Durham, Ray 408
Durrington, Trent 275
Dye, Jermaine 104

E

Easley, Damion 185
Eaton, Adam 400
Eckstein, David 379
Edmonds, Jim 380
Edwards, Mike 247
Einertson, Mitch 208
Eischen, Joey 494
Elarton, Scott 145
Elbert, Scott 254
Eldred, Brad 365
Ellis, Mark 333
Ellison, Jason 408
Ellsbury, Jacoby 68
Embree, Alan 325
Encarnacion, Edwin 121
Encarnacion, Juan 185

Endl, Brady 42
Ensberg, Morgan 200
Erbe, Brandon 59
Erickson, Scott 259
Erstad, Darin 230
Escalona, Felix 325
Escobar, Alcides 264
Escobar, Kelvim 237
Escobar, Yunel 47
Espinosa, David 170
Esposito, Mike 166
Esquivel, Matt 34
Estes, Shawn 25
Estrada, Johnny 35
Etherton, Seth 344
Ethier, Andre 333
Eveland, Dana 271
Everett, Adam 201
Everett, Carl 105
Everts, Clint 495
Eyre, Scott 414
Eyre, Willie 286

F

Fahey, Brandon 51
Farnsworth, Kyle 43
Fasano, Sal 51
Fassero, Jeff 414
Feldman, Scott 462
Feliz, Pedro 408
Fernandez, Jared 359
Fick, Robert 394
Fielder, Prince 264
Fields, Josh 105
Figgins, Chone 230
Finley, Steve 230
Fiorentino, Jeff 52
Flaherty, John 314
Fleisher, Mark 52
Flores, Randy 385
Flores, Ron 340
Floyd, Cliff 297
Floyd, Gavin 355
Fogg, Josh 370
Fontenot, Mike 86
Foppert, Jesse 428
Ford, Lew 280
Fossum, Casey 445
Foster, John 43
Foulke, Keith 77
Francis, Jeff 162
Francisco, Frank 466
Franco, Julio 35
Francouer, Jeff 35
Frandsen, Kevin 408
Franklin, Ryan 429
Franklin, Wayne 325
Frasor, Jason 477
Frazier, Jeff 170
Freel, Ryan 121
Freeman, Choo 166
Freire, Alejandro 52
Fuentes, Brian 162
Fuld, Sam 98
Fultz, Aaron 355
Furcal, Rafael 35
Furmaniak, J. J. 365

G

Gaetti, Joe 156
Gagne, Eric 254
Galarraga, Armando 495
Gall, John 380
Gallagher, Sean 92
Gallardo, Yovani 271
Gallo, Mike 205
Garabito, Eddy 166
Garcia, Freddy 112
Garcia, Harvey 82
Garcia, Jairo 340
Garciaparra, Nomar 86
Gardner, Brett 325
Gardner, Rich 132
Garko, Ryan 138
Garland, Jon 112
Garza, Matt 287
Gassner, Dave 292
Gathright, Joey 439
Gaudin, Chad 477
Geary, Geoff 355
German, Esteban 466
German, Franklyn 177
Germano, Justin 127
Gerut, Jody 365
Giambi, Jason 314
Giarratano, Tony 170
Gibbons, Jay 52
Gil, Geronimo 65
Gil, Jerry 17
Giles, Brian 394
Giles, Marcus 36
Gimenez, Hector 201
Ginter, Keith 334
Ginter, Matt 181
Gissell, Chris 385
Glaus, Troy 18
Glavine, Tom 302
Gload, Ross 05
Glover, Gary 275
Gobble, Jimmy 221
Godwin, Ty 488
Golson, Gregory 349
Gomes, Jonny 440
Gomez, Alexis 181
Gomez, Chris 53
Gonzalez, Adrian 455
Gonzalez, Alex (FLO) 186
Gonzalez, Alex (TBA) 440
Gonzalez, Carlos 30
Gonzalez, Edgar 25
Gonzalez, Enrique 25
Gonzalez, Gio 113
Gonzalez, Jeremi 77
Gonzalez, Juan 138
Gonzalez, Luis (AZ) 18
Gonzalez, Mike 371
Gonzalez, Raul 389
Gonzalez, Wiki 434
Good, Andrew 181
Gordon, Alex 214
Gordon, Tom 320
Gorneault, Nick 231
Gorzelanny, Tom 371
Gosling, Mike 26
Gotay, Ruben 215

Grabow, John 371
Graffanino, Tony 69
Granderson, Curtis 170
Graves, Danny 302
Green, Andy 18
Green, Nick 440
Green, Sean 434
Green, Shawn 18
Greenberg, Adam 87
Greene, Khalil 395
Greene, Tyler 380
Gregg, Kevin 237
Greinke, Zack 221
Grieve, Ben 98
Griffey, Ken 121
Griffin, Colt 225
Griffin, Daniel 419
Griffin, John-Ford 470
Grilli, Jason 181
Grimsley, Jason 65
Grissom, Marquis 409
Gronkiewicz, Lee 477
Groom, Buddy 25
Gross, Gabe 470
Grudzielanek, Mark 381
Gryboski, Kevin 462
Guardado, Eddie 429
Guerrero, Vladimir 231
Guerrier, Matt 287
Guevara, Carlos 127
Guiel, Aaron 215
Guillen, Carlos 171
Guillen, Jose 488
Guthrie, Jeremy 145
Gutierrez, Franklin 139
Gutierrez, Juan 208
Guzman, Angel 98
Guzman, Cristian 489
Guzman, Freddy 395
Guzman, Javier 366
Guzman, Joel 247
Gwynn, Anthony 264

H

Haad, Yamid 419
Haeger, Charlie 113
Haehnel, David 60
Haerther, Cody 381
Hafner, Travis 139
Haigwood, Daniel 113
Hairston, Jerry 87
Hairston, Scott 19
Halama, John 495
Hall, Bill 265
Hall, Josh 127
Hall, Toby 440
Halladay, Roy 478
Halsey, Brad 26
Hamels, Cole 356
Hammel, Jason 446
Hammond, Chris 400
Hampton, Mike 43
Hamulack, Tim 303
Hancock, Josh 132
Hanigan, Ryan 122
Hannahan, Jack 171
Hanrahan, Joel 254

Hansen, Craig 77
Hanson, Travis 381
Harang, Aaron 128
Harben, Adam 287
Harden, Rich 341
Hardy, J. J. 265
Haren, Danny 341
Harman, Brad 350
Harper, Brett 297
Harper, Travis 446
Harris, Brendan 489
Harris, Jeff 429
Harris, Lenny 193
Harris, Willie 105
Harrison, Matt 43
Hart, Bo 389
Hart, Corey 265
Harvey, Ken 215
Harvey, Kris 186
Harvey, Ryan 87
Harville, Chad 77
Hatteberg, Scott 334
Hattig, John 470
Hawkins, LaTroy 415
Hawpe, Brad 156
Heaverlo, Jeff 430
Heether, Adam 275
Heilman, Aaron 303
Helling, Rick 271
Helms, Wes 266
Helton, Todd 156
Hendrickson, Ben 271
Hendrickson, Mark 446
Henn, Sean 320
Hennessey, Brad 415
Henry, C. J. 325
Hensley, Clay 400
Hermanson, Dustin 113
Hermida, Jeremy 186
Hernandez, Anderson 297
Hernandez, Felix 429
Hernandez, Francisco 106
Hernandez, Gaby 303
Hernandez, Jose 139
Hernandez, Livan 495
Hernandez, Luis (ATL) 47
Hernandez, Orlando 114
Hernandez, Ramon 395
Hernandez, Roberto 303
Hernandez, Runelvys 222
Hernandez, Yoel 356
Herr, Aaron 389
Herren, K. C. 466
Herrera, Javier 334
Hessman, Mike 181
Hidalgo, Richard 455
Higginson, Bobby 171
Hill, Aaron 471
Hill, Bobby 366
Hill, Koyie 19
Hill, Rich 92
Hillenbrand, Shea 471
Hinckley, Mike 496
Hinske, Eric 471
Hirsh, Jason 205
Hoffman, Trevor 401
Holcomb, James 241

Hollandsworth, Todd 36
Holliday, Matt 156
Hollins, Damon 441
Honel, Kris 116
Houlton, D. J. 255
Houser, James 446
Howard, Kevin 122
Howard, Ryan 350
Howell, J. P. 222
Howry, Bobby 145
Hu, Chin-lung 247
Huber, Justin 215
Huckaby, Ken 482
Hudgins, John 462
Hudson, Luke 128
Hudson, Orlando 471
Hudson, Tim 44
Huff, Aubrey 441
Huffman, Royce 208
Hughes, Philip 320
Hughes, Travis 496
Hull, Eric 259
Humber, Phil 307
Hunter, Torii 280
Hurley, Eric 462

I

Iannetta, Chris 157
Ibanez, Raul 424
Iguchi, Tadahito 106
Infante, Omar 171
Inge, Brandon 172
Inglett, Joe 139
Iribarren, Hernan 266
Ishii, Kazuhisa 304
Ishikawa, Travis 409
Isringhausen, Jason 385
Italiano, Craig 344
Izturis, Cesar 247
Izturis, Maicer 231

J

Jackson, Conor 19
Jackson, Damian 395
Jackson, Edwin 255
Jackson, Zach 478
Jacobs, Mike 298
Jaile, Chris 463
James, Chuck 44
Janssen, Casey 478
Jaramillo, Jason 350
Jarvis, Kevin 385
Jaso, John 441
Jenkins, Geoff 266
Jenks, Bobby 114
Jennings, Jason 163
Jeter, Derek 314
Jimenez, Cesar 430
Jimenez, D'Angelo 122
Jimenez, Ubaldo 163
Johjima, Kenji 424
Johnson, Ben 396
Johnson, Charles 450
Johnson, Dan 334
Johnson, Elliot 441
Johnson, J. J. 60
Johnson, Jason 177

Johnson, Joshua 190
Johnson, Kelly 36
Johnson, Mike 396
Johnson, Nick 489
Johnson, Randy 321
Johnson, Reed 472
Johnson, Tripper 53
Johnson, Tyler 386
Johnston, Mike 376
Jones, Adam 424
Jones, Andruw 37
Jones, Brandon 37
Jones, Chipper 37
Jones, Garrett 281
Jones, Greg 237
Jones, Jacque 281
Jones, Justin 287
Jones, Kennard 404
Jones, Mike 275
Jones, Todd 190
Jordan, Brian 37
Journell, Jimmy 389
Julianel, Ben 321
Julio, Jorge 60
Jurries, James 38
Jurrjens, Jair 178

K

Kaaihue, Kila 216
Kapler, Gabe 69
Karp, Josh 498
Karsay, Steve 466
Kata, Matt 350
Kazmir, Scott 447
Kearns, Austin 123
Keefer, Ryan 60
Keisler, Randy 132
Kelly, Don 172
Kemp, Beau 292
Kemp, Matt 248
Kendall, Jason 335
Kendrick, Howie 231
Kennedy, Adam 232
Kennedy, Joe 341
Kensing, Logan 191
Kent, Jeff 248
Keppinger, Jeff 298
Kielty, Bobby 335
Kieschnick, Brooks 208
Kim, Byung-Hyun 163
Kim, Sun-Woo 163
King, Ray 386
Kinney, Matt 415
Kinsler, Ian 456
Kirkland, Kody 172
Klassen, Danny 208
Klesko, Ryan 396
Kline, Steve 61
Knoedler, Justin 409
Knott, Jon 404
Kolb, Dan 44
Konerko, Paul 106
Koo, Dae-Sung 307
Koronka, John 98
Koshansky, Joe 157
Koskie, Corey 472
Kotchman, Casey 232

Kotsay, Mark 335
Kottaras, George 396
Kouzmanoff, Kevin 140
Kozlowski, Ben 128
Kroeger, Josh 20
Krynzel, David 266
Kubel, Jason 281
Kuo, Hong-Chih 255

L

Lackey, John 238
Laforest, Pete 442
Laird, Gerald 456
Lamb, Mike 201
Lambert, Chris 386
Lambin, Chase 298
Lane, Jason 201
Langerhans, Ryan 38
Lansford, Jared 344
LaRoche, Adam 38
LaRoche, Andy 248
LaRue, Jason 123
Lawrence, Brian 401
Lawton, Matt 315
League, Brandon 478
Leandro, Francisco 442
LeCroy, Matt 281
Ledee, Ricky 249
Ledezma, Wil 178
Lee, Carlos 267
Lee, Cliff 146
Lee, Derrek 88
Lee, Seung Hak 359
Lee, Travis 442
Lehr, Justin 272
Leicester, Jon 92
Leiter, Al 321
Lerew, Anthony 45
Lester, Jon 78
Lewis, Fred 409
Lewis, Richard 88
Lidge, Brad 205
Lidle, Cory 356
Lieber, Jon 356
Lieberthal, Mike 351
Liefer, Jeff 150
Lilly, Ted 479
Lima, Jose 222
Lincoln, Mike 389
Lind, Adam 472
Linden, Todd 410
Lindsay, Shane 166
Lindstrom, Matt 304
Linebrink, Scott 401
Liotta, Ray 114
Liriano, Francisco 288
Liriano, Pedro 359
Littleton, Wes 463
Livingston, Bobby 430
Liz, Radhames 61
Lo Duca, Paul 186
Loaiza, Esteban 496
Loe, Kameron 463
Loewen, Adam 61
Lofton, Kenny 351
Logan, Nook 172
Lohse, Kyle 288

Loney, James 249
Long, Terrence 216
Looper, Braden 304
Lopez, Aquilino 357
Lopez, Felipe 123
Lopez, Javy 53
Lopez, Jose 424
Lopez, Pedro 116
Lopez, Rodrigo 61
Loretta, Mark 397
Lowe, Derek 255
Lowell, Mike 187
Lowrie, Jed 69
Lowry, Noah 416
Lubanski, Chris 216
Ludwick, Ryan 150
Lugo, Julio 442
Luna, Hector 381
Lyon, Brandon 26

M

Mabeus, Chris 344
Mabry, John 382
MacDougal, Mike 223
Machado, Alejandro 69
Macias, Jose 88
Mackowiak, Rob 366
MacLane, Evan 305
Maddux, Greg 93
Madritsch, Bobby 431
Madson, Ryan 357
Maestrales, Pete 225
Magruder, Chris 267
Maholm, Paul 371
Maine, John 62
Majewski, Gary 497
Majewski, Val 53
Malone, Corwin 116
Manriquez, Salomon 498
Mantei, Matt 78
Marcum, Shaun 479
Markakis, Nick 54
Marmol, Carlos 93
Maroth, Mike 178
Marquis, Jason 386
Marrero, Eli 54
Marshall, Sean 93
Marte, Andy 39
Marte, Damaso 115
Martin, Russell 249
Martinez, Edgar 78
Martinez, Pedro 305
Martinez, Ramon 351
Martinez, Tino 315
Martinez, Victor 140
Martinez-Esteve, Eddy 410
Mastny, Thomas 146
Mateo, Juan 98
Mateo, Julio 431
Mateo, Nathanel 434
Matheny, Mike 410
Mathieson, Scott 357
Mathis, Jeff 232
Matienzo, Danny 292
Matos, Luis 54
Matsui, Hideki 315

Matsui, Kazuo 298
Matthews, Gary Jr. 456
Mauer, Joe 282
Mays, Joe 288
McAnulty, Paul 397
McBride, Macay 45
McCann, Brad 187
McCann, Brian 39
McCarthy, Brandon 115
McClain, Scott 98
McClung, Seth 447
McConnell, Chris 217
McCormick, Mark 387
McCracken, Quinton 30
McCutchen, Andrew 376
McDonald, John 181
McDougall, Marshall 456
McEwing, Joe 225
McGowan, Dustin 479
McLemore, Mark 208
McLouth, Nate 366
McPherson, Dallas 233
Meadows, Brian 372
Meaux, Ryan 404
Meche, Gil 431
Mecir, Jim 193
Medders, Brandon 26
Medlock, Calvin 132
Meier, Mitch 217
Melhuse, Adam 335
Melillo, Kevin 336
Mench, Kevin 457
Mendoza, Ramiro 325
Menechino, Frank 472
Mercker, Kent 129
Meredith, Cla 78
Merloni, Lou 241
Mesa, Jose 372
Messenger, Randy 191
Meyer, Danny 342
Meyer, Drew 457
Miceli, Dan 164
Michael, Jason 351
Mientkiewicz, Doug 299
Mijares, Jose 292
Miles, Aaron 157
Millar, Kevin 70
Milledge, Lastings 299
Miller, Adam 146
Miller, Corky 292
Miller, Damian 267
Miller, Greg 256
Miller, Jason 289
Miller, Jeff 372
Miller, Jim 166
Miller, Justin 482
Miller, Matt 150
Miller, Matthew 157
Miller, Tony 158
Miller, Trever 447
Miller, Wade 79
Millwood, Kevin 147
Milton, Eric 129
Minix, Travis 359
Mirabelli, Doug 70
Misch, Pat 416
Mitre, Sergio 93

Mock, Garrett 27
Moehler, Brian 191
Moeller, Chad 267
Mohr, Dustan 158
Molina, Ben 233
Molina, Jose 233
Molina, Yadier 382
Monroe, Craig 173
Montero, Miguel 20
Moore, Scott 88
Mora, Melvin 54
Morales, Franklin 164
Morales, Kendry 233
Moran, Javon 124
Mori, Shinji 448
Morillo, Juan 164
Morneau, Justin 282
Morris, Matt 387
Morse, Michael 425
Moseley, Dustin 238
Moses, Matt 282
Moss, Brandon 70
Moss, Steve 275
Mota, Guillermo 191
Moye, Alan 225
Moyer, Jamie 432
Mueller, Bill 70
Mujica, Ed 147
Mulder, Mark 387
Mulhern, Ryan 140
Mulholland, Terry 289
Munoz, Arnie 116
Munson, Eric 450
Munter, Scott 416
Murphy, Bill 27
Murphy, David 71
Murphy, Donny 217
Murphy, Tommy 241
Murton, Matt 89
Mussina, Mike 321
Myers, Brett 357
Myers, Mike 79
Myrow, Byron 259

N

Nady, Xavier 397
Nageotte, Clint 432
Nakamura, Norihiro 259
Napoli, Michael 234
Nathan, Joe 289
Navarro, Dioner 249
Navarro, Oswaldo 425
Negron, Miguel 473
Neighborgall, Jasaon 30
Nelson, Brad 268
Nelson, Bubba 129
Nelson, Chris 166
Nelson, Jeff 432
Neshek, Pat 289
Nevin, Phil 457
Newhan, David 55
Nickeas, Mike 466
Niekro, Lance 411
Niemann, Jeffrey 448
Nieve, Fernando 206
Nin, Sandy 164
Nippert, Dustin 27

Nix, Jayson 158
Nix, Laynce 457
Nixon, Trot 71
Nolasco, Ricky 94
Nomo, Hideo 325
Novoa, Roberto 94
Nunez, Abraham 382
Nunez, Leo 223

O

Obermueller, Wes 272
Ochoa, Ivan 150
O'Connor, Michael 498
Ohka, Tomokazu 272
Ohman, Will 94
Olerud, John 71
Olivo, Miguel 397
Olmedo, Rainer 124
Olsen, Scott 192
Olson, Garrett 62
Ordonez, Magglio 173
Orenduff, Justin 256
Orr, Pete 39
Ortiz, David 71
Ortiz, Ramon 129
Ortiz, Russ 27
Ortmeier, Dan 411
Orvella, Chad 448
Osoria, Franquelis 256
Osuna, Antonio 498
Oswalt, Roy 206
Otsuka, Akinori 401
Overbay, Lyle 268
Owens, Jerry 106
Owings, Micah 28
Oxspring, Chris 404
Ozuna, Pablo 107

P

Padilla, Juan 305
Padilla, Vicente 358
Pagan, Angel 299
Palmeiro, Orlando 202
Palmeiro, Rafael 55
Palmisano, Lou 275
Papelbon, Jon 79
Park, Chan Ho 402
Parra, Manny 272
Parrish, John 62
Patterson, Corey 89
Patterson, Eric 89
Patterson, John 497
Patton, Troy 206
Paul, Josh 241
Paul, Xavier 259
Pauley, David 79
Paulino, Felipe 208
Paulino, Ronny 367
Pavano, Carl 322
Payton, Jay 336
Peavy, Jake 402
Pedroia, Dustin 72
Pena, Brayan 39
Pena, Carlos 173
Pena, Ramon 28
Pena, Tony 47
Pena, Wily Mo 124

Pence, Hunter 202
Penn, Hayden 62
Pennington, Cliff 336
Penny, Brad 257
Peralta, Jhonny 141
Peralta, Joel 238
Percival, Troy 178
Perez, Antonio 250
Perez, Eddie 40
Perez, Eduardo 443
Perez, Fernando 450
Perez, Kenny 20
Perez, Miguel 132
Perez, Neifi 89
Perez, Odalis 257
Perez, Oliver 373
Perez, Rafael 147
Perez, Timo 107
Perez, Tomas 352
Perisho, Matt 82
Perkins, Glen 290
Perkins, Vince 479
Pesco, Nick 150
Petagine, Roberto 72
Peterson, Matt 376
Petit, Yusmeiro 305
Pettitte, Andy 206
Phelps, Josh 443
Phillips, Andy 315
Phillips, Brandon 141
Phillips, Jason 250
Phillips, Paul 217
Piazza, Mike 299
Pickering, Calvin 218
Pie, Felix 90
Piedra, Jorge 158
Pierre, Juan 187
Pierzynski, A. J. 107
Pignatiello, Carmen 94
Pinckney, Andrew 72
Pineiro, Joel 432
Pinto, Renyel 95
Plouffe, Trevor 282
Podsednik, Scott 107
Polanco, Placido 173
Politte, Cliff 115
Pomeranz, Stu 388
Ponson, Sidney 63
Pope, Van 40
Posada, Jorge 316
Pratt, Todd 352
Pridie, Jason 450
Prior, Mark 95
Proctor, Scott 322
Psomas, Grant 300
Pujols, Albert 382
Punto, Nick 283
Purcey, David 480
Putnam, Daniel 336
Putz, J. J. 433

Q

Qualls, Chad 207
Quantrill, Paul 192
Quentin, Carlos 20
Quinlan, Robb 234
Quintanilla, Omar 159

Quintero, Humberto 202
Quiroz, Guillermo 473

R

Raburn, Ryan 174
Radke, Brad 290
Raglani, Anthony 250
Ragsdale, Cory 300
Rainville, Jay 290
Rakers, Aaron 63
Ramirez, Aramis 90
Ramirez, Elizardo 130
Ramirez, Erasmo 463
Ramirez, Hanley 72
Ramirez, Horacio 45
Ramirez, Ismael 482
Ramirez, Luis 65
Ramirez, Manny 73
Ramirez, Max 47
Ramirez, Ramon 164
Ramirez, Wilkin 174
Randa, Joe 398
Rasmus, Colby 383
Rasner, Darrell 497
Rauch, Jon 498
Ray, Chris 63
Redman, Mark 373
Redman, Prentice 300
Redman, Tike 367
Redmond, Mike 283
Reed, Eric 188
Reed, Jeremy 425
Reed, Steve 65
Reese, Kevin 325
Regilio, Nick 464
Reimold, Nolan 55
Reitsma, Chris 45
Remlinger, Mike 82
Renteria, Edgar 73
Repko, Jason 250
Resop, Chris 192
Restko, J. T. 188
Restovich, Mike 376
Reyes, Al 389
Reyes, Anthony 388
Reyes, Dennys 404
Reyes, Jose 300
Reynolds, Mark 21
Rheinecker, John 344
Rhodes, Arthur 147
Riedling, John 193
Riggans, Shawn 443
Rincon, Juan 290
Rincon, Ricardo 342
Ring, Royce 307
Rios, Alexis 473
Riske, David 148
Rivas, Luis 283
Rivera, Juan 234
Rivera, Mariano 322
Rivera, Mike 275
Rivera, Rene 434
Rleal, Sendy 63
Roberson, Chris 352
Roberts, Brian 55
Roberts, Dave 398
Roberts, Ryan 474

Robertson, Nate 179
Robles, Oscar 251
Robnett, Richie 337
Rodney, Fernando 179
Rodriguez, Alex 316
Rodriguez, Eddy 65
Rodriguez, Felix (NYA) 323
Rodriguez, Francisco 238
Rodriguez, Ivan 174
Rodriguez, John 383
Rodriguez, Luis 283
Rodriguez, Rafael 239
Rodriguez, Ricardo 464
Rodriguez, Sean 235
Rodriguez, Wandy 207
Rogers, Kenny 464
Rogers, Mark 275
Rogowski, Casey 108
Rolen, Scott 383
Rollins, Jimmy 352
Romak, Jamie 40
Romano, Jason 132
Romero, Alex 284
Romero, Davis 482
Romero, J. C. 291
Romero, Ricardo 482
Rosario, Francisco 480
Rose, Mike 259
Ross, Cody 259
Ross, Dave 398
Rottino, Vinny 275
Rouse, Mike 344
Rowand, Aaron 108
Rueter, Kirk 416
Ruggiano, Justin 251
Ruiz, Carlos 353
Ruiz, Randy 359
Rupe, Josh 464
Rusch, Glendon 95
Ryan, B. J. 64
Ryan, Brendan 383
Ryan, Mike 292
Ryu, Jae-kuk 96

S

Saarloos, Kirk 342
Sabathia, C. C. 148
Sadler, Billy 417
Saenz, Olmedo 251
Salas, Juan 450
Salazar, Jeff 159
Salmon, Tim 241
Saltalamacchia, Jarrod 40
Sanches, Brian 359
Sanchez, Anibal 80
Sanchez, Danilo 181
Sanchez, Duaner 257
Sanchez, Freddy 367
Sanchez, Gaby 193
Sanchez, Jonathan 417
Sanchez, Rey 325
Sanders, Marcus 411
Sanders, Reggie 384
Sandoval, Danny 359
Santana, Ervin 239
Santana, Johan 291

Santana, Julio 273
Santos, Sergio 21
Santos, Victor 273
Sardinha, Bronson 316
Sardinha, Dane 132
Sarfate, Dennis 273
Sauerbeck, Scott 148
Saunders, Joe 239
Schierholtz, Nate 411
Schilling, Curt 80
Schmidt, Jason 417
Schmidt, Joshua 323
Schmoll, Steve 257
Schneider, Brian 489
Schnurstein, Micah 108
Schoeneweis, Scott 480
Schuerholz, Jon 47
Schumaker, Skip 389
Scobie, Jason 306
Scott, Luke 202
Scutaro, Marco 337
Seabol, Scott 389
Seanez, Rudy 402
Seddon, Chris 448
Sele, Aaron 433
Senreiso, Juan 458
Seo, Jae 306
Sexson, Richie 426
Shackelford, Brian 130
Sharpless, Josh 373
Shealy, Ryan 159
Sheets, Ben 273
Sheffield, Gary 317
Shell, Steven 239
Shelton, Chris 174
Sherrill, George 433
Shields, Jamie 449
Shields, Scot 240
Shoppach, Kelly 73
Short, Rick 498
Shouse, Brian 465
Sierra, Edwardo 165
Sierra, Ruben 317
Sikorski, Brian 402
Silva, Carlos 291
Simon, Alfredo 419
Simonitsch, Errol 291
Simpson, Allan 130
Sing, Brandon 90
Sinisi, Vince 458
Sipp, Tony 150
Sisco, Andy 223
Sizemore, Grady 141
Sledge, Terrmel 490
Sleeth, Kyle 179
Slocum, Brian 150
Slowey, Kyle 292
Small, Aaron 323
Smith, Corey 404
Smith, Matt 323
Smith, Seth 159
Smith, Travis 193
Smoltz, John 46
Snell, Ian 373
Snelling, Chris 426
Snow, J. T. 412
Snyder, Brad 142

Snyder, Brandon 56
Snyder, Chris 21
Snyder, Kyle 223
Soler, Alay 306
Song, Seung 417
Sonnanstine, Andrew 449
Soriano, Alfonso 458
Soriano, Rafael 433
Sosa, Jorge 46
Sosa, Sammy 56
Soto, Geovany 90
Sowers, Jeremy 148
Span, Denard 284
Spann, Chad 73
Spears, Nate 56
Speier, Justin 480
Speier, Ryan 165
Spiezio, Scott 434
Spilborghs, Ryan 166
Spivey, Junior 490
Springer, Russ 207
Spurling, Chris 179
Stairs, Matt 218
Standridge, Jason 130
Stanford, Jason 150
Stanley, Steve 344
Stansberry, Craig 367
Stanton, Mike 80
Stauffer, Tim 403
Stavisky, Brian 337
Stephens, John 64
Stern, Adam 74
Stetter, Mitch 275
Stevens, Jake 46
Stewart, Chris 109
Stewart, Cory 376
Stewart, Ian 160
Stewart, Shannon 284
Stinnett, Kelly 21
Stokes, Jason 188
Street, Huston 342
Strong, Jamal 426
Sturtze, Tanyon 324
Sullivan, Cory 160
Suppan, Jeff 388
Surhoff, B. J. 56
Suzuki, Ichiro 426
Suzuki, Kurt 337
Swarzak, Anthony 292
Sweeney, Mark 398
Sweeney, Mike 218
Sweeney, Ryan 109
Swisher, Nick 338
Switzer, Jon 449
Szymanski, B. J. 132

T

Tabata, Jose 325
Tablado, Raul 482
Tadano, Kaz 150
Taguchi, So 384
Takatsu, Shingo 306
Tallet, Brian 149
Tamayo, Danny 224
Tankersley, Dennis 224
Taschner, Jack 418
Taubenheim, Ty 274

Tavarez, Julian 388
Taveras, Willy 203
Teagarden, Taylor 466
Teahen, Mark 218
Teixeira, Mark 459
Tejada, Miguel 57
Tejeda, Juan 175
Tejeda, Robinson 358
Terrero, Luis 22
Thames, Marcus 175
Theriot, Ryan 91
Thigpen, Curtis 474
Thomas, Charles 338
Thomas, Frank 109
Thome, Jim 353
Thompson, Brad 389
Thompson, Daryl 498
Thompson, Derek 259
Thompson, Kevin 317
Thompson, Mike 404
Thompson, Sean 403
Thomson, John 47
Thorman, Scott 41
Thornton, Matt 434
Tiffany, Chuck 258
Tiffee, Terry 285
Timlin, Mike 80
Timmons, Wes 47
Timpner, Clay 419
Tomko, Brett 418
Torra, Matt 30
Torrealba, Yorvit 427
Torres, Eider 142
Torres, Salomon 374
Toussaint, Andrew 235
Towers, Josh 481
Traber, Billy 150
Tracey, Sean 116
Trachsel, Steve 307
Tracy, Chad 22
Treanor, Matt 193
Trumbo, Mark 235
Tsao, Chin-hui 165
Tucker, Michael 353
Tucker, Rusty 404
Tuiasosopo, Matt 427
Tulowitzki, Troy 166
Tupman, Matt 225
Turnbow, Derrick 274
Tyner, Jason 292

U

Ugla, Dan 22
Upton, B. J. 443
Urbina, Ugueth 358
Uribe, Juan 109
Utley, Chase 353

V

Valdes, Raul 96
Valdez, Ismael 193
Valdez, Merkin 418
Valdez, Wilson 404
Valentin, Javier 124
Valentin, Jose 251
Valentine, Joe 132
Valido, Rob 110

Valverde, Jose 28
Van Benschoten, John 374
Van Buren, Jermaine 96
Vargas, Claudio 28
Vargas, Jason 192
Varitek, Jason 74
Vazquez, Javier 29
Vazquez, Ramon 142
Vechionacci, Marcos 317
Veras, Jose 466
Verlander, Justin 180
Vermilyea, Jamie 481
Victorino, Shane 354
Vidro, Jose 490
Villafuerte, Brandon 419
Villanueva, Carlos 274
Villarreal, Oscar 29
Villone, Ron 193
Vizcaino, Jose 203
Vizcaino, Luis 115
Vizquel, Omar 412
Vogelsong, Ryan 374
Volquez, Edison 465
Votto, Joey 125

W

Waechter, Doug 449
Wagner, Billy 358
Wagner, Ryan 131

Wainwright, Adam 389
Wakefield, Tim 81
Waldrop, Kyle 292
Walker, Chris 98
Walker, Jamie 180
Walker, Neil 368
Walker, Pete 481
Walker, Todd 91
Walker, Tyler 418
Wang, Chien-ming 324
Ward, Daryle 368
Wasdin, John 465
Washburn, Jarrod 240
Watson, Brandon 490
Watson, Matt 338
Weathers, Dave 131
Weaver, Jeff 258
Weaver, Jered 240
Webb, Brandon 29
Webster, Anthony 459
Weeks, Rickie 268
Wellemeyer, Todd 96
Wells, David 81
Wells, Jared 403
Wells, Kip 375
Wells, Randy 98
Wells, Vernon 474
Werth, Jayson 252
West, Kevin 285

Westbrook, Jake 149
Wheeler, Dan 207
Whelan, Kevin 180
White, Rick 375
White, Rondell 175
White, Steven 324
Whiteman, Tom 203
Whitesell, Josh 491
Whiteside, Eli 65
Wickman, Bob 149
Widger, Chris 110
Wigginton, Ty 368
Wilkerson, Brad 491
Williams, Aaron 208
Williams, Bernie 318
Williams, Dave 375
Williams, Gerald 307
Williams, Jerome 97
Williams, Marland 22
Williams, Randy 166
Williams, Todd 64
Williams, Woody 403
Williamson, Scott 97
Willingham, Josh 188
Willis, Dontrelle 193
Wilson, Brian 419
Wilson, C. J. 465
Wilson, Craig 368
Wilson, Jack 369

Wilson, Josh 189
Wilson, Paul 131
Wilson, Preston 491
Wilson, Vance 175
Winfree, David 292
Winn, Randy 412
Wise, Matt 274
Witasick, Jay 343
Wolf, Randy 359
Womack, Tony 318
Wood, Brandon 235
Wood, Kerry 97
Wood, Mike 224
Woods, Jake 241
Woodward, Chris 301
Worrell, Mark 389
Worrell, Tim 29
Wright, David 301
Wright, Jamey 165
Wright, Jaret 324
Wuertz, Mike 97
Wunsch, Kelly 258

Y

Yabu, Keiichi 343
Yan, Esteban 241
Yates, Tyler 307
Youkilis, Kevin 74
Young, Chris (CHA) 110

Young, Chris (TEX) 466
Young, Delmon 444
Young, Delwyn 252
Young, Dmitri 176
Young, Eric 399
Young, Jason 150
Young, Michael 459
Young, Walter 57

Z

Zambrano, Carlos 98
Zambrano, Victor 307
Zaun, Gregg 474
Zeringue, Jon 23
Zimmerman, Bob 241
Zimmerman, Ryan 491
Zink, Charlie 81
Zito, Barry 343
Zumaya, Joel 180

Biographies

Mark Armour is a writer living in Oregon's Willamette Valley. He is the co-author of the award-winning *Paths to Glory,* the director of SABR's Biography Project, and a contributor to numerous baseball books and web sites. He is the Editor of *Rain Check: Baseball in the Pacific Northwest,* due in June 2006.

Andrew Baharlias served as Staff Counsel to the New York Yankees between 1997 and 2002. Since then he has primarily spent his time raising his son, Benjamin, starting his own consulting firm (BCB Sports Management), and discovering the insidious underworld of coupon clipping. Andy lives in New Jersey with his enormously talented wife, Lisa Robinson, and makes Steven Goldman buy him dessert at least three times a month.

Jim Baker has been with Baseball Prospectus since 2004 and writes the twice-weekly Prospectus Matchups column. Prior to that, he was with ESPN.com. He lives in Austin, Texas with his daughters Victoria and Olivia.

James Click has spent the past year as one of BP's regular columnists, an author on *Baseball Between the Numbers,* and a consultant for a major league team. There's no way to explain how someone of his subpar intelligence and wit managed this feat other than to blame his girlfriend, Ace, and some bastardization of the natural order of the universe. He hopes that it will be a long, long time before anyone discovers that his entire career is a sham based almost entirely on standing on shoulders of giants like the rest of the authors at BP.

Clifford J. Corcoran is the co-author of Bronx Banter, a blog about the New York Yankees on BaseballToaster.com. His previous contributions to the world of print include authoring four thrilling pages in Baseball Prospectus's *Mind Game* and editing major non-fiction works on baseball and popular music for Viking and Penguin Books. Before that he was a rock critic for *Alternative Press* and TrouserPress.com, among others, and the lead singer of the world's greatest undiscovered rock band. He lives in Northern New Jersey with his beautiful and brilliant wife-elect, her pet box turtle, and a feline tyrant named Poindexter.

Clay Davenport is a meteorologist, so you could say that he has plenty of forecasting experience—and that he's used to getting some of them wrong. He is married and lives quietly in Maryland. He urges you to support BP so that his daughter can continue going to college.

John Erhardt lives, plays guitar, and writes in Canandaigua, New York, where he runs a private restaurant for his wife, Cheryl. An inveterate reader and Simpsons junkie, his BP duties include editing the Web site, assembling The Week in Quotes, and making sure all BP authors put the right cover sheets on their TPS reports. His favorite players are Trent Durrington and Brian Moehler. Seriously.

Gary Gillette is the editor of the *ESPN Baseball Encyclopedia,* a columnist for ESPN.com's MLB Insider, co-chair of the SABR Business of Baseball Committee, and president of 24-7 Baseball, L.L.C. Aside from consulting work, his current projects include editing a new history of big-league ballparks and putting together a brand-new pro football encyclopedia. Born in rural Pennsylvania in the hometown of Deadball-era first baseman Tom Jones, Gillette played Little League ball on diamonds once trod by Christy Mathewson. He lives in Detroit with his beloved wife Vicki and their two children, Karolina and Kamil, who were signed as six-year minor league free agents in 2005.

Steven Goldman is the creator of the long-running "Pinstriped Bible" column at www.yesnetwork.com and the associated "Pinstriped Blog," the "You Could Look It Up" column for Baseball Prospectus, and is a baseball columnist for the *New York Sun.* Steven is also the author of the biography *Forging Genius: the Making of Casey Stengel,* the editor of the Baseball Prospectus book *Mind Game* and a contributor to BP's *Baseball Between the Numbers.* His work has also been seen in Yankees Magazine and on websites too numerous to mention. Steven lives in New Jersey with his wife Stefanie, daughter Sarah, and son Clemens.

Thomas Gorman was born and raised in San Francisco and attended Columbia University in the City of New York. After graduating in 2004 with a B.A. in Political Science (specializing in International Relations and Security issues) Tom returned to the City by the Bay and began his Baseball Prospectus career as a researcher for Will Carroll. He hopes that some brilliant GM hires him away from his writing career, and Tom's heeding the advice that good things happen to those that sneak burritos into section 137 on warm summer afternoons.

Gary Huckabay is the Founder of Baseball Prospectus. He lives in Clayton, California with his wife Kathy and son, Charlie. Gary earned his undergraduate and MBA degrees from the University of California, Davis. He spends a great deal of time crushing the dreams of entrepreneurs by asking for justification for the assumptions in their business plans.

Jay Jaffe is the founder of the five-year-old Futility Infielder website (www.futilityinfielder.com), one of the oldest baseball blogs. The 2005 season saw him do everything from contributing to *Mind Game* and Will Carroll's *The Juice: The Real Story of Baseball's Drug Problems,* to creating the weekly Prospectus Hit List, to debating steroids on TV with a grandstanding congressman and the son of a former president of the US, to running in the famous Milwaukee Brewers sausage race, to wedding Andra, the most supportive gal in the world. He is a graduate of Brown University and works as a graphic designer in New York City.

Rany Jazayerli has been an author for Baseball Prospectus for fully one-third of his life, and in that time has had the pleasure of watching his Royals finish with a winning record exactly once. Somehow, he hasn't burned out yet. A first-year medical student when BP 1996 was published, he is now a dermatologist in private practice in St. Charles, Illinois. He lives in nearby Naperville with his wife and two young daughters, who will be free to choose to grow up as fans of a team that actually has realistic playoff hopes.

Christina Kahrl has probably said too much already, but after spending the last five months on this book, she's just looking forward to a martini. A University of Chicago grad transplanted to the Washington, DC metro area from Chicago's South Side, she's already used to balancing her love of the game with an ambivalence about the hometown nine. Beyond her decade-old Prospectus column *Transaction Analysis*, she's written about the game for Playboy, Salon, Slate, and ESPN.com.

Jonah Keri is a stock market writer, editor and seminar speaker for a national business newspaper. He writes the Prospectus Game of the Week and Prospectus Q&A columns for the BP Web site. He recently added a gig as writer of the "Keeping Score" column for the *New York Times*. He's the editor and co-author of *Baseball Between the Numbers,* a new Baseball Prospectus publication that tackles 29 classic baseball arguments and hits bookstores right after this book does. By this time next year Jonah will have a new address, having followed his incomparable wife, the soon-to-be Dr. Angèle Fauchier, to her latest destination. Until then he's psyched to watch a Cy Young-caliber season by King Felix Hernandez with the entire Pacific Northwest sabermetric mafia.

Mark McClusky was a co-founder of all-baseball.com, a former editor and reporter at Sports Illustrated, and is currently the Products Editor at Wired magazine in San Francisco. He's waiting for Eric Chavez's breakout season, and still wondering why Jeremy Giambi didn't slide.

Ben Murphy survived the trials and tribulations of Baseball Prospectus internship, only to come back for more punishment, joining the technical staff. Ben lives in North Carolina where recently finished graduate school at UNC Chapel Hill and enjoys life with Kristen and Spud.

Dave Pease is an engineer at a wireless communications company in San Diego. If something's broken at baseballprospectus.com, he's probably to blame. Mike Cameron in sand and blue was at the top of his 2003 Christmas list; better two years late than never is what he has to say about that.

Dayn Perry is a regular contributor to Baseball Prospectus and FOXSports.com. His first book, *Winners: How Good Baseball Teams Become Great Ones,* is now available. He's also written about the game for publications like *The Miami Herald, The Washington Monthly, The Montreal Gazette* and *The New York Sun,* among others. A Mississippi native, Perry now resides in Chicago

Nate Silver is the Executive Vice President of Baseball Prospectus and the inventor of the PECOTA system. One of BP's University of Chicago graduates, he was quick to reclaim his South Side Pride during the Sox' World Series run and brashly purchased a $4.95 ALCS pennant at a Wrigleyville White Hen Pantry. PECOTA notes that Nate has just turned 28, and predicts a marked decrease in hair follicles.

Will Weiss lives on Long Island with his much more intelligent wife, Toni. Will is the senior editor of YESNetwork.com, a post he's held since its launch in March of 2002. He'd like to thank Steve Goldman, Will Carroll, Christina Kahrl, Jonah Keri and Nate Silver for their encouragement.

Keith Woolner focuses on statistical research and database development for Baseball Prospectus. He has worked in the software industry for 15 years in development, product management, and strategy. He is a graduate of the Massachusetts Institute of Technology, Stanford University, and San Fernando Beauty Academy. He is testing a new designer steroid on himself that is so undetectable, it doesn't even give the user away by adding muscle, strength, quickness, or endurance.

Author Dedications

From Steven Goldman:

To Stefanie, for her faith, support, and patience, and especially her bearing with good humor the extreme highs and lows that come with doing a project of this nature; to Sarah, for understanding that both bears and baseball book writers disappear into caves during the winter; to Clemens for thinking me his father rather than a strange creature who stalks the house at night; to Andrew Baharlias and Cliff Corcoran for their friendship, advice, and their company on sanity-restoring, high-calorie excursions; to the writers of this book, who endured their often-irascible editors with understanding; to Jonah Keri and Nate Silver for entrusting me with this task; and finally, to Christina Kahrl, my co-editor, for her friendship, bonhomie, advocacy, solidarity, and sagacity. Despite my doubts about taking on a project which by its very nature promised to be intensely difficult, the chance to work in creative partnership with her made this a party I just couldn't miss.